UNIVERSITY CASEBOOK SERIES®

ENVIRONMENTAL LAW AND POLICY

FOURTH EDITION

RICHARD L. REVESZ
Lawrence King Professor of Law and Dean Emeritus
New York University School of Law

MICHAEL A. LIVERMORE
Professor of Law
University of Virginia School of Law

CAROLINE CECOT
Assistant Professor of Law
Antonin Scalia Law School at George Mason University

JAYNI FOLEY HEIN
Natural Resources Director, Institute for Policy Integrity
Adjunct Professor of Law
New York University School of Law

FOUNDATION
PRESS

University Casebook Series is a trademark registered in the U.S. Patent and Trademark Office.

© 2008 FOUNDATION PRESS
© 2012 by THOMSON REUTERS/FOUNDATION PRESS
© 2015 LEG, Inc. d/b/a West Academic
© 2019 LEG, Inc. d/b/a West Academic
    444 Cedar Street, Suite 700
    St. Paul, MN 55101
    1-877-888-1330

Printed in the United States of America

ISBN: 978-1-64020-984-8

To my late mother, Nora Revesz,
with gratitude and love

—R.L.R.

For Lia, and all those who
labor to do good in the world

—M.A.L.

To Piotr, Henryk, and Oliwier,
and to my parents, Anna and Zbigniew

—C.C.

To William and Patrick, with love

—J.F.H.

PREFACE

Effective lawyers in the field of environmental law need a broad set of skills. They need to be at ease, for example, with complex arguments of statutory interpretation, have command of the details of how environmental benefits are valued in cost-benefit analyses, and understand the roles of the different institutions—legislatures, agencies, courts, trade associations, and advocacy groups—and the different levels of government that shape environmental law. Accordingly, the materials in this casebook are designed to provide a thorough grounding in three areas that are central to a sophisticated understanding of environmental law: the major intellectual perspectives affecting the development of environmental policy, the provisions of the major environmental statutes and regulations, and the institutional structures in which environmental regulation is carried out.

The casebook stresses how environmental goals are traded-off against other social goals, including compliance costs. Practically all environmental problems are of the non-threshold variety. Contaminants pose a risk to human life and health, and to the environment, at every concentration, though naturally these risks are smaller at lower concentrations. How stringent then should environmental regulatory standards be? Reducing the risk to zero would entail returning to a pre-industrial society, which few would want to do. Short of that, what does it mean to talk about "protecting health" or about "safety," when the choice is, for example, between a one-in-a-million and a one-in-ten-thousand probability of cancer from lifetime exposure to a contaminant? Given that there is no such thing as a "safe" level, at what level should the standard be set? To what extent should costs matter? To what extent should other consequences—environmental and non-environmental—matter?

The casebook also stresses the types of incentives—positive and negative—transmitted by environmental rules. For example, consider the case of the enactment of new environmental regulations. Since it is easier and cheaper to design new sources of pollution to meet a stringent environmental standard than to retrofit existing sources, policy-makers have a compelling reason for subjecting new sources to more stringent standards. But more stringent standards for new sources create additional incentives for existing sources to remain in operation longer than they would have in the absence of those standards. Extending the life of these dirty, inefficient sources, in turn, results in negative consequences to the environment. How should one deal with that tradeoff? How should one assess the different regulatory responses? Or, to pick another vexing choice, to what extent should voluntary audits substitute for government enforcement? What is the optimal tradeoff between the two?

This revised Fourth Edition, apart from making general updates to reflect recent changes in federal and state law, continues with trends in prior editions by expanding its treatment of climate change. Without a comprehensive statute from Congress, the work of addressing climate change and of regulating greenhouse gases is being undertaken through existing statutory frameworks. Because its causes and impacts are varied and pervasive, climate change presents a challenge to the intellectual foundations of environmental policy, the statutes and regulations implicated, and the relevant institutional structures. Chapter V, in particular, has been substantially revised and reorganized to group together materials dealing with regulation of greenhouse gases under the Clean Air Act (CAA). Attention is also given to attempts to regulate emissions of greenhouse gases and other pollutants of air pollution from power plants. This edition also focuses on the Trump Administration's efforts to weaken greenhouse gas standards adopted by the Obama Administration.

The Fourth Edition features other notable changes as well. For example, there is a substantially expanded treatment of recent efforts to use the total daily maximum load (TMDL) program under the Clean Water Act (CWA) to address the persistently difficult problem of widely diffuse "nonpoint source" water pollution. The Flint water crisis and the challenges of reducing exposure to lead in drinking water are also discussed in detail. The chapter on the National Environmental Policy Act (NEPA) also contains significant additions on how greenhouse gas emissions must be taken into account in environmental impact statements. Furthermore, there is a significantly expanded section on the management of natural resources on federal lands, with subsections on national forests, rangelands, onshore and offshore mineral resources, and protected lands. This new material can be used in an environmental law course or as a standalone resource for a natural resources or public lands course.

The casebook begins with four foundational chapters dealing with issues that are central to the design of any environmental policy. Chapter I introduces the major theoretical approaches, focusing on both economic and non-economic perspectives on environmental degradation.

Chapter II deals with the scientific predicate for environmental regulation—risk assessment—then turns its attention to the goals of such regulation—risk management. It ends by examining the distributional consequences of environmental policy and the particular concerns of the environmental justice movement. To develop these themes, the chapter uses both extended excerpts from the academic literature and cases drawn from a variety of environmental and health-and-safety statutes, including the Occupational Safety and Health Act (OSHA), the Toxic Substances Control Act (TSCA), and the Federal Insecticide, Fungicide, and Rodenticide Act (FIFRA).

Chapter III introduces and explores the choice among different regulatory tools for improving environmental quality: Should we use command-and-control regulation, marketable permit schemes, taxes, liability rules, or informational approaches, and how can each be used most effectively? The chapter contains an extended discussion of the choice between taxes and marketable permit schemes for the domestic regulation of greenhouse gases, and includes examples of programs at the state, regional, and international levels.

Chapter IV describes the rich political context in which environmental regulations are formed. It focuses on the complexities inherent in a federal system of environmental governance, accounting for both the constitutional constraints and the powerful policy arguments that together affect how decisionmaking authority is allocated among different levels of government. The chapter also examines how public-choice dynamics shape the regulatory regime.

By focusing on these foundational issues at the outset, the book gives students the skills necessary to undertake sophisticated analyses of the statutory schemes that follow. After these initial four chapters, the tone and character of the casebook changes, as the principal federal environmental statutes are examined in turn. Chapters V through IX, which deal with specific environmental problems, call for detailed statutory analysis and should be accompanied by reference to a statutory supplement.

Chapter V addresses the control of air pollution through the CAA. This chapter focuses on the recent efforts to turn the Act into an instrument for the regulation of greenhouse gases, particularly with respect to carbon dioxide. It explores the important question of whether a statute designed for the control of local and regional pollutants can provide a desirable approach for the control of global pollutants.

Chapter VI examines the control of water pollution, focusing primarily on the CWA but also exploring the Safe Drinking Water Act (SDWA). The chapter devotes attention to the different structures of the CAA and CWA, which were enacted only two years apart. These statutes differ markedly in their risk-management frameworks, in the relationship between the regulation of new sources and existing sources, and in the way in which regulatory authority is allocated between the federal government and the states.

Chapter VII deals with the control of hazardous wastes. It briefly presents the Resource Conservation and Recovery Act (RCRA) as an example of *ex ante* regulation, and then delves in depth into the *ex post* liability regime of the Comprehensive Environmental Response, Compensation, and Liability Act (CERCLA).

Chapter VIII focuses on the disclosure of environmental risks. It centers on NEPA, which governs the disclosure of environmental information for federal projects. NEPA sets forth procedural requirements, such as the preparation of environmental impact statements for major federal actions significantly affecting the environment.

Chapter IX canvasses the federal regimes designed to manage and protect the nation's natural resources, including the Endangered Species Act (ESA) and the provisions of the CWA dealing with the protection of wetlands. With the ESA in particular, attention is given to the effects of climate change on the preservation of endangered species. The chapter concludes with an examination of the statutory provisions dealing with natural resources on public lands. The chapter explores the primary federal laws governing the management of national forests, rangelands, onshore and offshore mineral leasing, and four types of protected lands: national parks, national monuments, wilderness, and wildlife refuges.

Finally, Chapter X examines the various mechanisms used to enforce environmental laws and regulations, including civil enforcement, criminal enforcement, self-enforcement by means of environmental audits, and citizen suits. It also explores the roadblocks to private enforcement posed by standing requirements.

Within each chapter, each section ends with an extensive set of notes and questions, designed to provide a deeper understanding of the cases and readings and to introduce and critique a broader set of perspectives. Among other topics, these notes and questions explore comparative perspectives (in particular, federal versus state), evaluate the leading academic perspectives on each of the environmental programs, and introduce empirical studies of particular regulatory programs. While the book does not devote a separate chapter to the field of international environmental law, the notes and questions in various chapters contain commentary on contentious international environmental law issues— such as the distributional consequences of climate change (Chapter II) and the debate concerning the desirability of a global emissions tax, as opposed to an emissions trading scheme, as the cornerstone of any global response to climate change (Chapter III).

The casebook is supported by a detailed Teacher's Manual that provides commentary on each of the notes and questions contained in the casebook, as well as some thoughts on the various ways that the materials may be approached in the classroom.

We are enormously grateful for the talents of a large group of students and recent graduates of our respective institutions, without whom preparing this and the earlier editions would not have been possible. Barnaby Chessell and Florencia Saulino, then Fellows in the Law School's Frank J. Guarini Center on Environmental and Land Use Law, were instrumental in assisting with the First Edition. In addition to Barnaby and Florencia, the law students who aided in the preparation of that edition are Brett Collings, Garrett Coyle, Amy Dona, Ryan Eney, Amanda Garcia, Amanda Goodin, Judy Harvey, Kenneth Holloway, Michael Horan, Matthew Kelly, Kevin Lynch, Katie Rosen, Ian Samuel, Stephanie Tatham, and Lauren Wishnie.

For their help in preparing the Second Edition and for taking the lead in editing the various chapters, we would like to thank the following law students: Chapters I through IV (Mark LeBel); Chapter V (Martha Roberts); Chapter VI (Adam Herling and Craig Wenner); Chapter VII (Alice Byowitz and Sheila McAnaney); Chapter VIII (Craig Wenner and Josh Zaharoff); Chapter IX (Loreal Monroe, Margot Pollans, and Craig Wenner) and Chapter X (Craig Wenner and Avi Zevin). Particular gratitude is due to Mark LeBel and Martha Roberts for taking the lead on the longest and most complex chapters. We are also grateful to Craig Wenner, a Fellow in the Law School's Guarini Center in Fall 2011, for managing the entire project with extraordinary intelligence and dedication; the whole book benefitted enormously from his skill. Lauren Nikodemos brought great organizational skills and hard work to the edition.

For the Third Edition, Clare Lakewood, an Australian lawyer, did extraordinary work on updates on all of the chapters, including the reorganization of the CAA materials to focus more attention on the regulation of greenhouse gases. We are also grateful to LeeAnn Kim for research on the last stages of the project and to Brette Weinkle for obtaining the necessary permissions with great intelligence and dedication.

The following law students at our respective institutions provided excellent research assistance for the Fourth Edition: Chapters I through III (Joseph Conrad, Kate Gaziano, Heidi Hall, and Chandra Sheppard), Chapter IV (Wade Foster), Chapter V (Natalie Jacewicz), Chapter VI (Wade Foster), Chapter VII (Isabel Carey), Chapter VIII (Zoe Palenik), Chapter IX (Zoe Palenik), and Chapter X (Alexandra St. Romain). Brette Weinkle, once again, brought her efficiency and organizational skills to obtaining the permissions.

We are very grateful to our families for the love, support, and encouragement.

RICHARD L. REVESZ
MICHAEL A. LIVERMORE
CAROLINE CECOT
JAYNI FOLEY HEIN

December 2018

SUMMARY OF CONTENTS

TABLE OF CONTENTS

TABLE OF CASES

The principal cases are in bold type.

UNIVERSITY CASEBOOK SERIES®

ENVIRONMENTAL LAW AND POLICY

FOURTH EDITION

CHAPTER I

PERSPECTIVES ON ENVIRONMENTAL LAW

1. Introduction.
2. Economic Perspective on Environmental Degradation.
3. Non-Economic Perspectives on Environmental Degradation.

1. INTRODUCTION

As an introduction to the key themes and issues of environmental law and policy in this case book, begin by considering the following hypothetical situation:

> You work for a firm asked to design an air pollution control strategy for a developing country that has made a successful transition to a market economy. Critical to this transition has been the privatization of state-owned enterprises and the promotion of private enterprise. This strategy has resulted in a considerable expansion in industrial output and in economic growth, which in turn has led to an increase in both stationary and mobile source air pollution (in other words, air pollution from sources such as power plants and vehicles, respectively).

> A particular pollutant, generated principally from stationary sources, is of greatest concern and should be the target of your air pollution control strategy. The general scientific consensus concerning the effects of the pollutant is described below:

> (a) The pollutant is a respiratory irritant associated with the onset of asthma attacks:

> Studies reveal a direct correlation between the number of hospitalizations for asthma and the amount of pollutant present in the ambient air. The pollutant is also believed to lead to the development of asthma in children.

> (b) The pollutant is a suspected human carcinogen:

> A study of the health consequences of occupational exposure to the pollutant shows that miners and steel workers exposed to high levels developed acute nonlymphocytic leukemia and other blood disorders. Additionally, changes in blood and bone marrow composition, consistent with hematotoxicity (chemical poisoning of the blood), have been recognized in humans and experimental animals at high levels.

The carcinogenic impact of the pollutant at low levels remains uncertain. Prevailing scientific consensus is that it is more probable than not that the pollutant follows a linear dose-response curve in the low-dose region.

(c)   The pollutant causes neurological damage at very high levels:

Studies in occupational settings have also revealed that workers exposed to high concentrations of the pollutant have developed problems with balance, movement, and fine motor coordination, consistent with the symptoms of Parkinson's Disease.

An international study, examining the effects of exposure to the pollutant on 10-year-old children in Bangladesh (where groundwater levels of the pollutant are relatively high), reports that children who received the highest doses of the pollutant in their drinking water had significantly lower scores on tests of intellectual function.

(d)   The pollutant is known to affect vegetation, causing injury to both trees and crops:

The pollutant is a component of ozone. Research has shown that an increase in ozone concentrations since the country began its transition toward a market economy has resulted in reductions in wood growth in forests of approximately 10 percent. There is also strong scientific evidence to suggest that current levels of ozone are reducing crop yields, particularly in sensitive species, such as soybean and cotton.

Further information is contained in the notes and questions that follow. In designing a strategy, consider specifically the ways in which competing policy responses strike different positions in the trade-off between environmental goals and other social concerns. Also, focus your attention upon the incentives your favored policy response transmits to relevant actors.

NOTES AND QUESTIONS

1. **Regulatory Standards.** What standards, or combination of standards, would you choose as the cornerstone of your policy? One approach could be to impose emissions limitations, typically expressed as a maximum quantity of pollution per unit of production, upon each stationary source of the pollutant. Alternatively, you may prefer to define ambient air quality standards, which set a maximum level of the pollutant in the ambient air. Under this system, stationary sources are precluded from contributing to a violation of the prevailing air quality standard. A third alternative may be to create a cap-and-trade system, under which an overall emissions limit would be determined and allowances would be allocated to participating

stationary sources. Finally, you may prefer to levy a tax on the producers of the pollutant or, more particularly, upon each unit of production that gives rise to emissions of the pollutant. Corrective taxes of this kind are set at a level that takes into account the damage of the pollutant upon the society. Revenue generated by the tax could be used to counteract the negative effects of the pollutant.

What do you consider to be the relative advantages of each strategy? What factors influence your choice of policy?

2. Liability Rules. A very different regime may rely primarily upon liability rules. What common law principles may form the basis of a liability regime for environmental damage? What advantages would a regime based on liability rules have over the regulatory regimes discussed above?

3. Distribution of Pollution. Assume that you are most concerned about the neurological effects of the pollutant. Would you prefer that the pollutant be evenly dispersed throughout the country or that it be concentrated at a particular location? Which of the regulatory standards described above would be best suited to achieving this objective?

Assume now that you are most concerned about the other effects of the pollutant, all of which are known (or at least believed) to occur at low dose levels. In this instance, would you prefer that the pollutant be dispersed evenly or that it be concentrated? How might you achieve your desired outcome?

In making these decisions, would you seek to maximize the aggregate social welfare—the sum of the individual welfare of each person in the community? What if the maximization of aggregate social welfare imposed disproportionate costs on certain sectors of the community? How could these distributional problems be resolved?

4. Allocation of the Pollution Reduction Burden. Consider next how you would seek to allocate the pollution control burden among stationary sources.

Would you impose more stringent requirements upon new sources, on the ground that it would be relatively more expensive for existing sources to meet new standards? What incentives would this create on the part of existing sources? What problems might this cause? How could these problems be addressed?

More generally, would you favor the minimization of aggregate costs as the preferred basis for the distribution of the pollution control burden among stationary sources? Should the pollution control burden be imposed upon those industries that can implement controls most cheaply? Alternatively, should the burden be imposed upon those industries that are most profitable? How else might the pollution control burden be allocated among stationary sources?

5. Level of Control. In designing and implementing a policy response, it is necessary to determine what constitutes a permissible level of the pollutant in the ambient air.

Consider first the human health effects of the pollutant on the general population. At very high levels, the effects of the pollutant are severe. It is known to result in neurological damage and is believed to be a carcinogen. The impacts of the pollutant at lower levels are somewhat less certain: the prevailing scientific consensus is that it most likely acts as a carcinogen (albeit of lesser potency).

If your sole objective were to ensure that the pollutant gave rise to no adverse human health effects on the community, an obvious policy response would be to categorically prohibit those processes that lead to the production of the pollutant. Assume, however, that there do not exist any cost-effective substitutes to those processes and that a categorical prohibition would cripple industry in the infancy of the nation's transition to a functioning market economy. A trade-off exists, therefore, between the costs borne by industry and the environmental harm sustained by society. Cost-benefit analysis is one method that can be used to resolve this tension. In broad terms, cost-benefit analysis involves weighing the expected costs of a proposed policy response against the expected benefits, in order to identify the policy that maximizes net social benefits (benefits minus costs). In the present scenario, however, how would you value costs and benefits? More specifically, what value would you prescribe to human life? Consider the following three policy alternatives. Policy A imposes costs of $1 billion on industry and would result in a level of control that would save 1000 lives per year. Policy B is more stringent, imposing costs of $5 billion on industry and producing a level of control that would save 1250 lives per year. Finally, Policy C is the most restrictive, imposing costs of $20 billion on industry and securing a level of control that would save 1500 lives per year. Which policy should be preferred? What techniques might be adopted to determine an appropriate value for human life? Do you believe that cost-benefit analysis is an appropriate tool for decisions of this nature? If not, how should such decisions be made?

Might a rights-based methodology be more appropriate in the present context? How would a rights-based methodology discern between each of the three policy alternatives described above?

Turn your attention to the fact that the human health effects of the pollutant are more acute on a particular sector of the population. Should your policy make particular provision for asthmatics? How would this be accounted for under cost-benefit analysis? How would this be accounted for under a rights-based methodology? If it were only a very small portion of society that suffered peculiar effects from exposure to the pollutant, would your answer differ?

6.   Non-Human Health Effects. How should the pollutant's adverse impacts upon the nation's crops and vegetation be taken into account? In addition to the costs borne by commercial farming operations, how might you account for the impact of the pollutant upon the aesthetics of the country's environment and upon the functioning of the country's ecosystems? What if the pollutant damaged crops that were of traditional cultural significance to the country?

7.   Scientific Uncertainty. As discussed above, the carcinogenic properties of the pollutant at low-dose levels are unknown, but scientific consensus suggests that the pollutant is more likely than not a carcinogen at low-dose levels. How would you account for the element of uncertainty in your policy response? What factors may influence your answer?

8.   Level of Government. Consider next what level of government you would favor in administering your preferred policy response. Assume, for the purposes of this question, that the country has a federal system of government. Would it be preferable for the regime to be administered by different jurisdictions within the country or by the federal government? How might the potential for the pollutant to travel among jurisdictions give rise to problems in the event that the policy were to be administered regionally? What incentives might exist on the part of regions to set relatively lax environmental standards? Would these problems be addressed by way of federal regulation?

9.   Role of Institutions. Consider what roles each of the legislature, the executive, and the courts would play under your regime. Of the issues you have considered above, which are best suited to resolution by way of legislative action? Which should be determined by expert agencies? What should be the role of the courts?

10. Market Failure v. Government Failure. Finally, consider the administrative and other costs associated with each type of government intervention. What kind of information do government regulators need in order to improve welfare? Does your perception of the costs associated with obtaining and using this information efficiently affect your choice of preferred strategy? Does your view of the motivations of government regulators affect your choice of preferred strategy?

2.   ECONOMIC PERSPECTIVE ON ENVIRONMENTAL DEGRADATION

Environmental perspectives can be sorted based on their main object of concern: human beings or non-human nature. These perspectives are referred to as human-centered or nature-centered. The economic perspective is the most influential human-centered perspective in U.S. environmental policy debates. The readings in this section analyze the problem of environmental degradation from an economic perspective. This perspective can be defined by reference to normative, positive, and attitudinal characteristics.

The economic perspective's normative goal is to maximize social welfare—the sum of the private welfare of each individual in a society. Pollution and other forms of environmental degradation are generally byproducts of profitable economic activity. A reduction in pollution is socially advantageous only if it increases the welfare of the victims of pollution by more than it decreases the welfare of those who cause the pollution or benefit from the economic activity. Thus, under the economic perspective, there is a socially optimal amount of pollution, and less pollution can be as undesirable as more pollution.

The positive, or descriptive, characteristic of the economic perspective is that it explains the existence of excessive pollution by reference to a divergence between the polluter's private costs and the social costs imposed by its activity. For example, a steel manufacturer's private costs consist of the inputs, such as raw materials, electricity, and labor, that it must purchase. The manufacturer may use other kinds of goods in its production process as well—the air or water to dispose of the byproducts of steel production, for example. If the manufacturer is not required to "purchase" these goods, others (either society as a whole or some subset of society, such as the plant's neighbors) will have to bear the costs of the use. The costs are therefore external to the manufacturer, or, in economic parlance, they are "externalities." An economically rational manufacturer makes its production decisions without regard to these social costs, seeking simply to maximize the difference between its private costs and the benefits that it accrues from selling its products.

Finally, the economic perspective's attitudinal characteristic is that it does not view pollution as the result of antisocial action worthy of moral opprobrium. Rather, it sees it as the natural response of rational individuals who seek to further their self-interest.

The readings differ principally in their prescriptions for the design of social mechanisms to control the undesirable aspects of environmental degradation. In particular, they have varying degrees of faith in the beneficial effects of governmental action.

Garrett Hardin's classic article analogizes the problem of pollution to that presented by an open pasture. The problem in this "commons" is that each herder has an incentive to add cattle to the pasture, though the aggregate effect is to render the land unproductive as a result of overgrazing. In a much quoted sentence, Hardin concludes that "[f]reedom in a commons brings ruin to all." A firm contemplating the discharge of pollution faces the same calculus as the herder, receiving a benefit from adding pollution to an environmental commons, such as an airshed or a river or lake. The aggregate effect of such decisions, however, is to produce an excessive amount of pollution, harming society as a whole. Hardin advocates the use of the coercive powers of government to prevent excessive exploitation of a commons.

Ronald Coase, in an essay that in part earned him the Nobel Prize in Economics, makes three important claims. First, he argues that the problem of pollution is a reciprocal one, which arises because of the simultaneous presence of two parties—for example, a factory that emits fumes and a laundry that is harmed by the presence of these fumes; the problem is not caused solely by the polluting party. Protecting the laundry by enjoining the fumes imposes harm on the factory, just as protecting the factory by not enjoining its actions imposes harm on the laundry.

Second, Coase shows that when a polluter and a pollutee, such as the factory and the laundry, can bargain costlessly, they will reach socially desirable agreements no matter the legal regime. So, if the legal regime enjoins the pollution but the harm to the factory is greater than the harm that the laundry would have suffered in the absence of such an injunction, the parties will enter into a contract under which, in return for a payment, the laundry will agree not to exercise its right to seek an injunction. Conversely, if the legal regime allows the pollution but the resulting harm to the laundry is greater than the harm that the injunction would impose on the factory, the parties will enter into a contract under which, again in return for a payment, the factory agrees not to pollute. Thus regardless of the initial legal rule, bargaining will produce two results: (1) it will lead to the same amount of pollution (the invariance claim); and (2) it will lead to the maximization of social welfare (the efficiency claim).

Finally, Coase shows that these results will not be attained if the costs of bargaining are sufficiently high. If such costs are greater than the benefit that a party can obtain from the bargain, no agreement will take place. Thus, there would be no contractual modification of a rule enjoining the fumes even if the resulting harm to the factory from the injunction were greater than the harm that the laundry would suffer in the absence of the injunction. Similarly, there would be no contractual modification of a rule allowing the fumes even if the resulting harm to the laundry were greater than the harm that the factory would suffer as a result of an injunction. When bargaining costs are high, the choice of legal rule affects both the amount of pollution and the level of social welfare.

Garrett Hardin, The Tragedy of the Commons
162 SCIENCE 1243 (1968).*

The tragedy of the commons develops in this way. Picture a pasture open to all. It is to be expected that each herdsman will try to keep as many cattle as possible on the commons. Such an arrangement may work reasonably satisfactorily for centuries because tribal wars, poaching, and disease keep the numbers of both man and beast well below the carrying capacity of the land. Finally, however, comes the day of reckoning, that is, the day when the long-desired goal of social stability becomes a reality. At this point, the inherent logic of the commons remorselessly generates tragedy.

As a rational being, each herdsman seeks to maximize his gain. Explicitly or implicitly, more or less consciously, he asks, "What is the utility *to me* of adding one more animal to my herd?" This utility has one negative and one positive component.

---

* Reprinted with the permission of the American Association for the Advancement of Science.

1. The positive component is a function of the increment of one animal. Since the herdsman receives all the proceeds from the sale of the additional animal, the positive utility is nearly + 1.

2. The negative component is a function of the additional overgrazing created by one more animal. Since, however, the effects of overgrazing are shared by all the herdsmen, the negative utility for any particular decision-making herdsman is only a fraction of − 1.

Adding together the component partial utilities, the rational herdsman concludes that the only sensible course for him to pursue is to add another animal to his herd. And another; and another. . . . But this is the conclusion reached by each and every rational herdsman sharing a commons. Therein is the tragedy. Each man is locked into a system that compels him to increase his herd without limit—in a world that is limited. Ruin is the destination toward which all men rush, each pursuing his own best interest in a society that believes in the freedom of the commons. Freedom in a commons brings ruin to all. . . .

In an approximate way, the logic of the commons has been understood for a long time, perhaps since the discovery of agriculture or the invention of private property in real estate. But it is understood mostly only in special cases which are not sufficiently generalized. Even at this late date, cattlemen leasing national land on the western ranges demonstrate no more than an ambivalent understanding, in constantly pressuring federal authorities to increase the head count to the point where overgrazing produces erosion and weed-dominance. Likewise, the oceans of the world continue to suffer from the survival of the philosophy of the commons. Maritime nations still respond automatically to the shibboleth of the "freedom of the seas." Professing to believe in the "inexhaustible resources of the oceans," they bring species after species of fish and whales closer to extinction.

The National Parks present another instance of the working out of the tragedy of the commons. At present, they are open to all, without limit. The parks themselves are limited in extent—there is only one Yosemite Valley—whereas population seems to grow without limit. The values that visitors seek in the parks are steadily eroded. Plainly, we must soon cease to treat the parks as commons or they will be of no value to anyone.

What shall we do? We have several options. We might sell them off as private property. We might keep them as public property, but allocate the right to enter them. The allocation might be on the basis of wealth, by the use of an auction system. It might be on the basis of merit, as defined by some agreed-upon standards. It might be by lottery. Or it might be on a first-come, first-served basis, administered to long queues. These, I think, are all the reasonable possibilities. They are all objectionable. But we must choose—or acquiesce in the destruction of the commons that we call our National Parks.

Pollution

In a reverse way, the tragedy of the commons reappears in problems of pollution. Here it is not a question of taking something out of the commons, but of putting something in—sewage, or chemical, radioactive, and heat wastes into water; noxious and dangerous fumes into the air; and distracting and unpleasant advertising signs into the line of sight. The calculations of utility are much the same as before. The rational man finds that his share of the cost of the wastes he discharges into the commons is less than the cost of purifying his wastes before releasing them. Since this is true for everyone, we are locked into a system of "fouling our own nest," so long as we behave only as independent, rational, free-enterprisers.

The tragedy of the commons as a food basket is averted by private property, or something formally like it. But the air and waters surrounding us cannot readily be fenced, and so the tragedy of the commons as a cesspool must be prevented by different means, by coercive laws or taxing devices that make it cheaper for the polluter to treat his pollutants than to discharge them untreated. We have not progressed as far with the solution of this problem as we have with the first. Indeed, our particular concept of private property, which deters us from exhausting the positive resources of the earth, favors pollution. The owner of a factory on the bank of a stream—whose property extends to the middle of the stream—often has difficulty seeing why it is not his natural right to muddy the waters flowing past his door. The law, always behind the times, requires elaborate stitching and fitting to adapt it to this newly perceived aspect of the commons.

The pollution problem is a consequence of population. It did not much matter how a lonely American frontiersman disposed of his waste. "Flowing water purifies itself every 10 miles," my grandfather used to say, and the myth was near enough to the truth when he was a boy, for there were not too many people. But as population became denser, the natural chemical and biological recycling processes became overloaded, calling for a redefinition of property rights.

How to Legislate Temperance?

Analysis of the pollution problem as a function of population density uncovers a not generally recognized principle of morality, namely: *the morality of an act is a function of the state of the system at the time it is performed.* Using the commons as a cesspool does not harm the general public under frontier conditions, because there is no public; the same behavior in a metropolis is unbearable. A hundred and fifty years ago a plainsman could kill an American bison, cut out only the tongue for his dinner, and discard the rest of the animal. He was not in any important sense being wasteful. Today, with only a few thousand bison left, we would be appalled at such behavior.

In passing, it is worth noting that the morality of an act cannot be determined from a photograph. One does not know whether a man killing an elephant or setting fire to the grassland is harming others until one knows the total system in which his act appears. "One picture is worth a thousand words," said an ancient Chinese; but it may take 10,000 words to validate it. It is as tempting to ecologists as it is to reformers in general to try to persuade others by way of the photographic shortcut. But the essence of an argument cannot be photographed: it must be presented rationally—in words.

That morality is system-sensitive escaped the attention of most codifiers of ethics in the past. "Thou shalt not . . ." is the form of traditional ethical directives which make no allowance for particular circumstances. The laws of our society follow the pattern of ancient ethics, and therefore are poorly suited to governing a complex, crowded, changeable world. Our epicyclic solution is to augment statutory law with administrative law. Since it is practically impossible to spell out all the conditions under which it is safe to burn trash in the back yard or to run an automobile without smog-control, by law we delegate the details to bureaus. The result is administrative law, which is rightly feared for an ancient reason—*Quis custodiet ipsos custodes?*—"Who shall watch the watchers themselves?" John Adams said that we must have "a government of laws and not men." Bureau administrators, trying to evaluate the morality of acts in the total system, are singularly liable to corruption, producing a government by men, not laws.

Prohibition is easy to legislate (though not necessarily to enforce); but how do we legislate temperance? Experience indicates that it can be accomplished best through the mediation of administrative law. We limit possibilities unnecessarily if we suppose that the sentiment of *Quis custodiet* denies us the use of administrative law. We should rather retain the phrase as a perpetual reminder of fearful dangers we cannot avoid. The great challenge facing us now is to invent the corrective feedbacks that are needed to keep custodians honest. We must find ways to legitimate the needed authority of both the custodians and the corrective feedbacks.

Ronald Coase, The Problem of Social Cost
3 J.L. & Econ. 1 (1960).[*]

The Problem to Be Examined

This paper is concerned with those actions of business firms which have harmful effects on others. The standard example is that of a factory the smoke from which has harmful effects on those occupying neighbouring properties. The economic analysis of such a situation has usually proceeded in terms of a divergence between the private and social product of the factory, in which economists have largely followed the treatment of Pigou in *The Economics of Welfare*. The conclusions to which this kind of analysis seems to have led most economists is that it would be desirable to make the owner of the factory liable for the damage caused to those injured by the smoke, or alternatively, to place a tax on the factory owner varying with the amount of smoke produced and equivalent in money terms to the damage it would cause, or finally, to exclude the factory from residential districts (and presumably from other areas in which the emission of smoke would have harmful effects on others). It is my contention that the suggested courses of action are inappropriate, in that they lead to results which are not necessarily, or even usually, desirable.

The Reciprocal Nature of the Problem

The traditional approach has tended to obscure the nature of the choice that has to be made. The question is commonly thought of as one in which A inflicts harm on B and what has to be decided is: how should we restrain A? But this is wrong. We are dealing with a problem of a reciprocal nature. To avoid the harm to B would inflict harm on A. The real question that has to be decided is: should A be allowed to harm B or should B be allowed to harm A? The problem is to avoid the more serious harm. I instanced in my previous article the case of a confectioner the noise and vibrations from whose machinery disturbed a doctor in his work. To avoid harming the doctor would inflict harm on the confectioner. The problem posed by this case was essentially whether it was worthwhile, as a result of restricting the methods of production which could be used by the confectioner, to secure more doctoring at the cost of a reduced supply of confectionery products. Another example is afforded by the problem of straying cattle which destroy crops on neighbouring land. If it is inevitable that some cattle will stray, an increase in the supply of meat can only be obtained at the expense of a decrease in the supply of crops. The nature of the choice is clear: meat or crops. What answer should be given is, of course, not clear unless we know the value of what is obtained as well as the value of what is sacrificed to obtain it. To give another example, Professor George J. Stigler instances the contamination of a stream. If we assume that the harmful effect of the pollution is that it kills the fish, the question to be decided is: is the value of the fish lost greater or less than the value of the product which the contamination of the stream makes possible. . . .

The Pricing System with Liability for Damage

I propose to start my analysis by examining a case in which most economists would presumably agree that the problem would be solved in a completely satisfactory manner: when the damaging business has to pay for all damage caused *and* the pricing system works smoothly (strictly this means that the operation of a pricing system is without cost).

A good example of the problem under discussion is afforded by the case of straying cattle which destroy crops growing on neighbouring land. Let us suppose that a farmer and a cattle-raiser are operating on neighbouring properties. Let us further suppose that, without any fencing between the properties, an increase in the size of the cattle-raiser's herd increases the total damage to the farmer's crops. . . .

To simplify the argument, I propose to use an arithmetical example. I shall assume that the annual cost of fencing the farmer's property is $9 and that the price of the crop is $1 per ton. Also, I assume that the relation between the number of cattle in the herd and the annual crop loss is as follows:

Number in Herd (Steers)	Annual Crop Loss (Tons)	Crop Loss per Additional Steer (Tons)
1	1	1
2	3	2
3	6	3
4	10	4

Given that the cattle-raiser is liable for the damage caused, the additional annual cost imposed on the cattle-raiser if he increased his herd from, say, 2 to 3 steers is $3 and in deciding on the size of the herd, he will take this into account along with his other costs. That is, he will not increase the size of the herd unless the value of the additional meat produced (assuming that the cattle-raiser slaughters the cattle), is greater than the additional costs that this will entail, including the value of the additional crops destroyed. Of course, if, by the employment of dogs, herdsmen, aeroplanes, mobile radio and other means, the amount of damage can be reduced, these means will be adopted when their cost is less than the value of the crop which they prevent being lost. Given that the annual cost of fencing is $9, the cattle-raiser who wished to have a herd with 4 steers or more would pay for fencing to be erected and maintained, assuming that other means of attaining the same end would not do so more cheaply. When the fence is erected, the marginal cost due to the liability for damage becomes zero, except to the extent that an increase in the size of the herd necessitates a stronger and therefore more expensive fence because more steers are liable to lean against it at the same time. But, of course, it may be cheaper for the cattle-raiser not to fence and to pay for the damaged crops, as in my arithmetical example, with 3 or fewer steers.

It might be thought that the fact that the cattle-raiser would pay for all crops damaged would lead the farmer to increase his planting if a cattle-raiser came to occupy the neighbouring property. But this is not so. If the crop was previously sold in conditions of perfect competition, marginal cost was equal to price for the amount of planting undertaken and any expansion would have reduced the profits of the farmer. In the new situation, the existence of crop damage would mean that the farmer would sell less on the open market but his receipts for a given production would remain the same, since the cattle-raiser would pay the market price for any crop damaged. . . .

I have said that the occupation of a neighbouring property by a cattle-raiser would not cause the amount of production, or perhaps more exactly the amount of planting, by the farmer to increase. In fact, if the cattle-raising has any effect, it will be to decrease the amount of planting. The reason for this is that, for any given tract of land, if the value of the crop damaged is so great that the receipts from the sale of the undamaged crop are less than the total costs of cultivating that tract of land, it will be profitable for the farmer and the cattle-raiser to make a bargain whereby that tract of land is left uncultivated. This can be made clear by means of an arithmetical example. Assume initially that the value of the crop obtained from cultivating a given tract of land is $12 and that the cost incurred in cultivating this tract of land is $10, the net gain from cultivating the land being $2. I assume for purposes of simplicity that the farmer owns the land. Now assume that the cattle-raiser starts operations on the neighbouring property and that the value of the crops damaged is $1. In this case $11 is obtained by the farmer from sale on the market and $1 is obtained from the cattle-raiser for damage suffered and the net gain remains $2. Now suppose that the cattle-raiser finds it profitable to increase the size of his herd, even though the amount of damage rises to $3; which means that the value of the additional meat production is greater than the additional costs, including the additional $2 payment for damage. But the total payment for damages is now $3. The net gain to the farmer from cultivating the land is still $2. The cattle-raiser would be better off if the farmer would agree not to cultivate his land for any payment less than $3. The farmer would be agreeable to not cultivating the land for any payment greater than $2. There is clearly room for a mutually satisfactory bargain which would lead to the abandonment of cultivation. . . .

I think it is clear that if the cattle-raiser is liable for damage caused and the pricing system works smoothly, the reduction in the value of production elsewhere will be taken into account in computing the additional cost involved in increasing the size of the herd. This cost will be weighed against the value of the additional meat production and, given perfect competition in the cattle industry, the allocation of resources in cattle-raising will be optimal. What needs to be emphasized is that the fall in the value of production elsewhere which would be taken into account in the costs of the cattle-raiser may well be less than the damage which the cattle would cause to the crops in the ordinary course of events. This is because it is possible, as a result of market transactions, to discontinue cultivation of the land. This is desirable in all cases in which the damage that the cattle would cause, and for which the cattle-raiser would be willing to pay, exceeds the amount which the farmer would pay for use of the land. In conditions of perfect competition the amount which the farmer would pay for the use of the land is equal to the difference between the value of the total production when the factors are employed on this land and the value of the additional product yielded in their next best use (which would be what the farmer would have to pay for the factors). If damage exceeds the amount the farmer would pay for the use of the land, the value of the additional product of the factors employed elsewhere would exceed the value of the total product in this use after damage is taken into account. It follows that it would be desirable to abandon cultivation of the land and to release the factors employed for production elsewhere. A procedure which merely provided for payment for damage to the crop caused by the cattle but which did not allow for the possibility of cultivation being discontinued would result in too small an employment of factors of production in cattle-raising and too large an employment of factors in cultivation of the crop. But given the possibility of market transactions, a situation in which damage to crops exceeded the rent of the land would not endure. Whether the cattle-raiser pays the farmer to leave the land uncultivated or himself rents the land by paying the land-owner an amount slightly greater than the farmer would pay (if the farmer was himself renting the land), the final result would be the same and would maximise the value of production. Even when the farmer is induced to plant crops which it would not be profitable to cultivate for sale on the market, this will be a purely short-term phenomenon and may be expected to lead to an agreement under which the planting will cease. The cattle-raiser will remain in that location and the marginal cost of meat production will be the same as before, thus having no long-run effect on the allocation of resources.

The Pricing System with No Liability for Damage

I now turn to the case in which, although the pricing system is assumed to work smoothly (that is, costlessly), the damaging business is not liable for any of the damage which it causes. This business does not have to make a payment to those damaged by its actions. I propose to show that the allocation of resources will be the same in this case as it was when the damaging business was liable for damage caused. As I showed in the previous case that the allocation of resources was optimal, it will not be necessary to repeat this part of the argument.

I return to the case of the farmer and the cattle-raiser. The farmer would suffer increased damage to his crop as the size of the herd increased. Suppose that the size of the cattle-raiser's herd is 3 steers (and that this is the size of the herd that would be maintained if crop damage was not taken into account). Then the farmer would be willing to pay up to $3 if the cattle-raiser would reduce his herd to 2 steers, up to $5 if the herd were reduced to 1 steer and would pay up to $6 if cattle-raising was abandoned. The cattle-raiser would therefore receive $3 from the farmer if he kept 2 steers instead of 3. This $3 foregone is therefore part of the cost incurred in keeping the third steer. Whether the $3 is a payment which the cattle-raiser has to make if he adds the third steer to his herd (which it would be if the cattle-raiser was liable to the farmer for damage caused to the crop) or whether it is a sum of money which he would have received if he did not keep a third steer (which it would be if the cattle-raiser was not liable to the farmer for damage caused to the crop) does not affect the final result. In both cases $3 is part of the cost of adding a third steer, to be included along with the other costs. If the increase in the value of production in cattle-raising through increasing the size of the herd from 2 to 3 is greater than the additional costs that have to be incurred (including the $3 damage to crops), the size of the herd will be increased. Otherwise, it will not. The size of the herd will be the same whether the cattle-raiser is liable for damage caused to the crop or not.

It may be argued that the assumed starting point—a herd of 3 steers—was arbitrary. And this is true. But the farmer would not wish to pay to avoid crop damage which the cattle-raiser would not be able to cause. For example, the maximum annual payment which the farmer could be induced to pay could not exceed $9, the annual cost of fencing. And the farmer would only be willing to pay this sum if it did not reduce his earnings to a level that would cause him to abandon cultivation of this particular tract of land. Furthermore, the farmer would only be willing to pay this amount if he believed that, in the absence of any payment by him, the size of the herd maintained by the cattle raiser would be 4 or more steers. Let us assume that this is the case. Then the farmer would be willing to pay up to $3 if the cattle raiser would reduce his herd to 3 steers, up to $6 if the herd were reduced to 2 steers, up to $8 if one steer only were kept and up to $9 if cattle-raising were abandoned. It will be noticed that the change in the starting point has not altered the amount which would accrue to the cattle-raiser if he reduced the size of his herd by any given amount. It is still true that the cattle-raiser could receive an additional $3 from the farmer if he agreed to reduce his herd from 3 steer to 2 and that the $3 represents the value of the crop that would be destroyed by adding the third steer to the herd. Although a different belief on the part of the farmer (whether justified or not) about the size of the herd that the cattle-raiser would maintain in the absence of payments from him may affect the total payment he can be induced to pay, it is not true that this different belief would have any effect on the size of the herd that the cattle-raiser will actually keep. This will be the same as it would be if the cattle-raiser had to pay for damage caused by his cattle, since a receipt foregone of a given amount is the equivalent of a payment of the same amount.

It might be thought that it would pay the cattle-raiser to increase his herd above the size that he would wish to maintain once a bargain had been made, in order to induce the farmer to make a larger total payment. And this may be true. It is similar in nature to the action of the farmer (when the cattle-raiser was liable for damage) in cultivating land on which, as a result of an agreement with the cattle-raiser, planting would subsequently be abandoned (including land which would not be cultivated at all in the absence of cattle-raising). But such manoeuvres are preliminaries to an agreement and do not affect the long-run equilibrium position, which is the same whether or not the cattle-raiser is held responsible for the crop damage brought about by his cattle.

It is necessary to know whether the damaging business is liable or not for damage caused since without the establishment of this initial delimitation of rights there can be no market transactions to transfer and recombine them. But the ultimate result (which maximises the value of production) is independent of the legal position if the pricing system is assumed to work without cost. . . .

The Cost of Market Transactions Taken into Account

The argument has proceeded up to this point on the assumption . . . that there were no costs involved in carrying out market transactions. This is, of course, a very unrealistic assumption. In order to carry out a market transaction it is necessary to discover who it is that one wishes to deal with, to inform people that one wishes to deal and on what terms, to conduct negotiations leading up to a bargain, to draw up the contract, to undertake the inspection needed to make sure that the terms of the contract are being observed, and so on. These operations are often extremely costly, sufficiently costly at any rate to prevent many transactions that would be carried out in a world in which the pricing system worked without cost.

In earlier sections, when dealing with the problem of the rearrangement of legal rights through the market, it was argued that such a rearrangement would be made through the market whenever this would lead to an increase in the value of production. But this assumed costless market transactions. Once the costs of carrying out market transactions are taken into account it is clear that such a rearrangement of rights will only be undertaken when the increase in the value of production consequent upon the rearrangement is greater than the costs which would be involved in bringing it about. When it is less, the granting of an injunction (or the knowledge that it would be granted) or the liability to pay damages may result in an activity being discontinued (or may prevent its being started) which would be undertaken if market transactions were costless. In these conditions the initial delimitation of legal rights does have an effect on the efficiency with which the economic system operates. One arrangement of rights may bring about a greater value of production than any other. But unless this is the arrangement of rights established by the legal system, the costs of reaching the same result by altering and combining rights through the market may be so great that this optimal arrangement of rights, and the greater value of production which it would bring, may never be achieved. . . .

NOTES AND QUESTIONS

1.   **Inevitability of the "Tragedy."** Why do Hardin's herders not enter into agreements to limit the number of animals that they place in the commons? What conditions would make such agreements relatively more likely? There is a vast literature about how the experience with common grazing grounds may not have been, or need not be, tragic. The major works include ROBERT C. ELLICKSON, ORDER WITHOUT LAW: HOW NEIGHBORS SETTLE DISPUTES (1991); Robert C. Ellickson, *Property in Land*, 102 YALE L.J. 1315 (1993); Carol Rose, *The Comedy of the Commons: Custom, Commerce, and Inherently Public Property*, 53 U. CHI. L. REV. 711 (1986); GLENN G. STEVENSON, COMMON PROPERTY ECONOMICS: A GENERAL THEORY AND LAND USE APPLICATIONS (1991); ELINOR OSTROM, GOVERNING THE COMMONS: THE EVOLUTION OF INSTITUTIONS FOR COLLECTIVE ACTION (1990). This literature draws a sharp distinction between "open access territories that anyone may enter and tracts that are accessible only to the members of a limited populace and their licensees." Ellickson, *Property in Land*, *supra*, at 1381. What is the relevance of this distinction?

2.   **Susceptibility to the "Tragedy."** Are certain types of resources more susceptible to the tragedy of the commons than others? What characteristics make those resources particularly prone to degradation?

3.   **Solutions to the "Tragedy."** Potential solutions to the problem of the commons include the privatization of property (each herder gets a specific plot of land), taxes levied on each animal introduced into the commons, unitization (all herders become part of a unit, contributing their gains to the unit and receiving some distribution of the surplus according to an agreed-upon formula), government efforts to encourage cooperation among the herders (such as providing means of enforcing any agreements they might reach), and numerical constraints on the total number of animals that can be introduced into the commons. In the latter case, rights can be allocated by auction, lottery, queue (first-come, first-served), or some notion of merit or need or simply to the herders that had animals in the commons prior to the introduction of the constraints. Assess the relative desirability of these approaches.

4.   **Role of Politics.** Is the political process likely to solve the problem of the commons? Assume that two candidates run for a town council. One advocates leaving the status quo of an uncontrolled commons unchanged. The other advocates controls designed to prevent overgrazing. How should a rational herder vote? Is the vote dependent on the votes of other herders?

5.   **Questions of Utility.** Is Hardin right that each person "is locked into a system that compels him to increase his herd without limit"? At what point would the rational herder decide not to add another animal? Is there overgrazing at this point?

6.   **Prisoner's Dilemma.** Hardin's "tragedy of the commons" is conceptually equivalent to the structure of the prisoner's dilemma. Under a traditional prisoner's dilemma, two prisoners, Row and Column, are to be questioned by a prosecutor. If neither confesses, they each will get convicted of a relatively minor crime, carrying a three-year sentence; if both confess,

there is sufficient evidence to convict each of a more serious crime, carrying a five-year sentence. If one of them confesses and the other does not, the defendant who confesses receives a one-year sentence (to reflect the value of his cooperation) whereas the other defendant gets a six-year sentence (to reflect her lack of cooperation).

Table I.1 presents the various payoffs (the first number in each box is Row's sentence; the second number is Column's sentence).

Table I.1.

		Column	
		No confession	Confession
Row	No confession	3,3	6,1
	Confession	1,6	5,5

If the defendants act rationally, they will both confess, even though they would both have been better off if neither had confessed. Consider what happens if Row confesses. Column is better off confessing as well, so as to get a five-year sentence rather than a six-year sentence. If, instead, Row does not confess, Column is still better off confessing, so as to get a one-year sentence rather than a three-year sentence. Thus, regardless of what Row does, Column is best off confessing (the same, of course, is true for Row): in game theory parlance, confessing is a dominant strategy.

Consider the following portrayal of the tragedy of the commons as a prisoner's dilemma from ELINOR OSTROM, GOVERNING THE COMMONS: THE EVOLUTION OF INSTITUTIONS FOR COLLECTIVE ACTION 3–5 (1990). The greatest number of animals that can graze on a meadow without destroying it is L. The cooperative strategy is for two herders to each place L/2 animals in the commons. If they do so, each will get 10 units of profit, whereas if they do not, and each person places as many animals as he pleases, they will each get zero profit. If one limits his number to L/2 whereas the other grazes as many as he wants, the former's profits are –1 units whereas the latter's are 11 units. Table I.2 presents the various payoffs (the first number in each box is Row's profits; the second number is Column's profits). Explain in detail why neither herder will limit the number of animals that he places in the commons.

Table I.2.

		Column	
		L/2	No limit
Row	L/2	10,10	−1,11
	No limit	11,−1	0,0

How might the strategy be different if the game is repeated (if, for example, the herders know that they will share meadows again in subsequent years), rather than played only once? For discussion, see ROBERT

M. AXELROD, THE EVOLUTION OF COOPERATION (1984). How does the potential for repeated dealings affect the examples discussed by Hardin?

7.   Collective Action Theory. Ostrom also explains that the tragedy of the commons is conceptually equivalent to the logic of collective action, a theory explaining why it is difficult for individuals to pursue their joint interest, which is generally traced to MANCUR OLSON, THE LOGIC OF COLLECTIVE ACTION: PUBLIC GOODS AND THE THEORY OF GROUPS (1965). *See* OSTROM, *supra*, at 5–7. Olson's central argument is that an individual who cannot be excluded from obtaining the benefits of a collective good does not have an incentive to contribute to the provision of this good. Instead, he has an incentive to "free ride" on the efforts of others. How can the tragedy of the commons be explained in free rider terms?

8.   Externalities. Restate Hardin's argument by reference to the concept of externalities.

9.   Public Goods. Economists define pure public goods as having two characteristics:

(a)   One person's enjoyment of the good doesn't diminish another person's enjoyment of the good (non-rivalry); and

(b)   One cannot exclude individuals from its enjoyment (non-excludability).

What are some typical examples of pure public goods? Why does the market not supply an appropriate amount of public goods? *See* Paul A. Samuelson, *The Pure Theory of Public Expenditure*, 36 REV. ECON. & STAT. 387 (1954). Can the tragedy of the commons be explained in public goods terms?

10.   Pure v. Impure Public Goods. Pure public goods are rare. Some goods resemble public goods but do not strictly meet the definition or meet the definition only some of the time. One form of such an "impure" public good is a non-excludable good where use by one person may diminish the enjoyment of another user. One example of this might be a free public roadway, where an additional driver can slow other drivers. Another form is a "club" or "toll" good that is non-rivalrous but where it is possible to exclude individuals from enjoyment. An example of such a good is cable television. Which kinds of these goods would not be supplied appropriately by the market? *See* James M. Buchanan, *An Economic Theory of Clubs*, 32 ECONOMICA 1 (1965). How can the tragedy of the commons be explained in these terms?

11.   Attributes of Goods. Table I.3 presents a classification of four basic types of goods that emerges when the characteristics of rivalry and excludability are dichotomized.

Table I.3.

	Excludable	Non-Excludable
Rivalrous	Private Goods *(bread, automobiles, haircuts)*	Common-Pool Resources *(fish stocks, groundwater, oil basins)*
Non-Rivalrous	Club/Toll Goods *(theaters, cable TV, toll roads)*	Public Goods *(national defense, clean air, street lights)*

This classification is adapted from Vincent Ostrom & Elinor Ostrom, *Public Goods and Public Choice*, in ALTERNATIVES FOR DELIVERING PUBLIC SERVICES: TOWARD IMPROVED PERFORMANCE 1, 12 (1977). As the Ostroms discuss, these attributes are not necessarily dichotomous. The difficulty of excluding potential beneficiaries of a good could range from low to high. Similarly, how one person's use diminishes another person's use could vary from low to high, depending on the overall level of congestion. What are examples of goods that might sometimes, but not always, display these attributes?

12. Network Effects. The concept of rivalry starts from the premise that one person's enjoyment of a good tends to diminish another person's enjoyment of the good. But one person's enjoyment of a good might instead enhance another person's enjoyment of a good, at least under certain conditions. This concept is sometimes referred to as a "network effect." *See* S.J. Liebowitz & Stephen E. Margolis, *Network Externalities: An Uncommon Tragedy*, 8 J. ECON. PERSP. 133, 133 (1994). What is an example of a good that displays network effects? *See* Michael L. Katz & Carl Shapiro, *Network Externalities, Competition, and Compatibility*, 75 AM. ECON. REV. 424, 424 (1985) (describing different kinds of network effects). Restate the concept of network effects by reference to the concept of externalities.

13. The Factory and the Laundry. A factory can produce its output by emitting between zero and five units of air pollution. Obviously, the lower the emissions, the higher the factory's pollution control costs. The emissions impose costs on a neighboring laundry, which must employ more costly production processes to achieve its desired standard of cleanliness. For the different possible levels of emissions, the factory's pollution control costs and resulting costs imposed on the laundry are set forth in Table I.4. Assume that the parties can bargain costlessly.

Table I.4.

Units of Emissions	Factory's Pollution Control Costs	Laundry's Costs from Pollution
0	25	0
1	16	4
2	9	8
3	4	12
4	1	16
5	0	20

What level of emissions maximizes social welfare? Assume, initially, that under the prevailing legal regime, the laundry is unable to enjoin the pollution. How much pollution will result if the parties can bargain without cost? What payment will the laundry make to the factory? What happens if one of the parties attempts to capture too much of the surplus from bargaining? Does it matter whether each party to the bargaining knows the costs faced by the other party?

Assume, conversely, that the legal regime gives the laundry the right to enjoin the pollution. Again, assuming costless bargaining, how much pollution will result? What payment will the factory make to the laundry? What happens if it does not have sufficient assets to make the payment? Is the resulting problem, if any, cured by the existence of credit markets?

14. The Factory and the Laundry, Continued. Assume now that, if the parties engage in bargaining, they each face transaction costs of $1.50. How much pollution will result if the factory has the right to pollute without constraints? How much pollution will result if the laundry has the right to enjoin the pollution? Redo the problem for transaction costs of $4.00 for each party. Redo the problem once again for transaction costs of $6.00 for each party. What is the highest level of transaction costs for which bargaining will lead to the socially desirable outcome?

15. The Factory and the Laundry, Continued. Assume that a Pigouvian tax (named after A.C. Pigou, whose work in the 1920s and 1930s called for "internalizing" externalities, by either taxation or compensation) is levied on the factory and that there is no bargaining. Note that such a tax would be $4.00 per unit of pollution—the cost imposed on the laundry. How much pollution will result? What happens if the taxing authority incorrectly evaluates the laundry's damages and imposes a tax of $2.00 per unit of pollution? What happens if, instead, the tax is $6.00 per unit of pollution? What happens if, instead of the tax, the factory is ordered to pay damages under the common law of nuisance? For further discussion of liability, tax, and property remedies for externalities, see Guido Calabresi & A. Douglas Melamed, *Property Rules, Liability Rules, and Inalienability: One View of the Cathedral*, 85 HARV. L. REV. 1089 (1972); Robert Cooter, *The Cost of Coase*, 11 J. LEGAL STUD. 1 (1982); Harold Demsetz, *When Does the Rule of Liability Matter?*, 1 J. LEGAL STUD. 13 (1972).

16. The Factory and the Laundry, Continued. What happens if, in the face of a Pigouvian tax of $4.00, the parties can engage in costless bargaining? The result illustrates that when bargaining is possible, Pigouvian taxes do not lead to the maximization of social welfare. This feature of the taxes led Coase to strongly criticize Pigou's prescription. In what circumstances is this problem likely to be worrisome?

17. The Factory and the Laundry, Continued. Should one be indifferent to whether the factory or the laundry is making the payment? Is Coase indifferent? Should the order in which the firms started operating matter? Does it matter if the beneficiary of the pollution reduction is a group of breathers rather than the laundry? If it is a multimillionaire who highly values clean air around the tennis court on the grounds of his country home?

18. Preferences and Wealth. In general, our preferences are determined by our level of wealth. At different wealth levels, we choose to purchase different mixes of goods and services. How might the presence of such wealth effects change Coase's analysis? Consider separately, the invariance and efficiency prongs of Coase's argument. In connection with this question, think of the victim of pollution as an individual who suffers as a result of pollution emitted by a firm. For further discussion, see Cooter, *supra*, at 15.

19. Endowment Effect. Studies show an important disparity between the willingness to pay (WTP) for an environmental amenity that one does not yet have and the willingness to accept (WTA) the loss of that amenity. Typically, the latter valuation is considerably higher. The difference between the WTP and the WTA valuations is often referred to as an endowment effect. How does this phenomenon affect Coase's analysis? For further discussion, see Cass R. Sunstein, *Endogenous Preferences, Environmental Law*, 22 J. LEGAL STUD. 217 (1993).

20. Transaction Costs. What are sources of transaction costs when there is a single polluter and a single pollutee? What are the sources of transaction costs when many pollutees must bargain with a single polluter?

21. Coase and "Coaseanism." While Coase is most often associated with his conclusions about a world with zero transaction costs, his work does not generally assume that transaction costs are low. Coase and other scholars have argued that he intended to show how people behave in the face of significant transaction costs. *See* Robert C. Ellickson, *The Case for Coase and against "Coaseanism,"* 99 YALE L.J. 611, 611–13 (1989). For example, some of Coase's earliest work argued that transaction costs explain why business organizations form instead of each individual transacting separately on the market. Ronald Coase, *The Nature of the Firm*, 4 ECONOMICA 386 (1937).

22. The Common Law and Free-Riders. Under the common law of nuisance, polluters often can be held liable for damages or enjoined from polluting. From an economic perspective, are nuisance suits likely to reduce pollution to the optimal level by forcing polluters to take into account the full costs of their activities? How do free-rider problems affect the efficacy of common law solutions to environmental problems? What legal instruments ameliorate this problem? To what extent are these instruments effective? Are there some contexts in which common law solutions are likely to work better? More generally, what difficulties exist in relying on common law remedies to address environmental problems? *See* Richard A. Epstein, *Federal Preemption, and Federal Common Law, in Nuisance Cases*, 102 NW. U. L. REV. 551, 557–58 (2008) (arguing that the need for regulation arises where transaction costs prevent adequate enforcement through private nuisance actions).

23. Moving Beyond the Common Law. Epstein has argued that environmental regulation is appropriate when high transaction costs frustrate private nuisance actions, but that it should do as little as possible to displace the substantive rules of nuisance and property law. *See* Richard A. Epstein, *Nuisance Law: Corrective Justice and Its Utilitarian Constraints*, 8 J. LEGAL STUD. 49, 101–02 (1979); *see also* Richard A. Epstein, Babbitt v. Sweet Home Chapters of Oregon: *The Law and Economics of Habitat Preservation*, 5 SUP. CT. ECON. REV. 1, 26–57 (1996) (arguing that nuisance, voluntary purchases, and the use of eminent domain are the optimal legal tools to protect endangered species and habitat). Are the doctrines of nuisance law consistent with economic efficiency? Would these doctrines be efficient in the absence of transaction costs? Even if the doctrine is theoretically efficient, are courts well-equipped to make economically efficient decisions? Are there other institutions which are better equipped to make these judgments? Has the answer to this question changed over the last hundred years?

24. Pareto Superiority and Kaldor-Hicks Superiority. Economists generally rank the relative desirability of different allocations of resources through one of two criteria. According to the criterion of Pareto superiority, a reallocation of resources is superior if at least one person is made better off and no person is made worse off. According to the criterion of Kaldor-Hicks superiority, a reallocation of resources is superior if the gainers from the reallocation could compensate the losers so that nobody is made worse off; there is no requirement, however, that such compensation actually take place. In which of these senses are Coasian solutions desirable? Which concept is more useful to evaluate environmental policy? What criticisms can be levied against the Kaldor-Hicks criterion? Epstein complains that where regulations hurt some landowners but help others, "the danger is that cohesive interest groups will seek through regulation—for which they pay nothing—benefits that would require compensation if done privately." Richard A. Epstein, *Property Rights, State of Nature Theory, and Environmental Protection*, 4 N.Y.U. J.L. & LIBERTY 1, 31 (2009). He argues that, to prevent this phenomenon, regulations which disproportionately burden certain parties should require compensation to those parties. How could we decide which regulations require compensation? How could we determine how much compensation a given party should receive? How would our decisions on compensation affect investment incentives? Can such compensation also be viewed as a fairness issue? How feasible is a broad requirement for compensation?

3. NON-ECONOMIC PERSPECTIVES ON ENVIRONMENTAL DEGRADATION

The readings in this section present non-economic perspectives on the problem of environmental degradation. These perspectives all reject the normative goal of the economic perspective—the maximization of social welfare—but they otherwise differ in important respects. The perspectives can be classified as either human-centered or nature-centered. Human-centered works derive the appropriate conditions for the treatment of the environment by reference solely to the interests of human beings. Of course, human beings might value particular animals or plants a great deal and might choose to pursue an environmental policy that is highly protective of natural objects. The fact remains, however, that under this approach nature is protected only because it is of value to human beings. The economic perspective is a special case of a human-centered theory; non-economic versions of such theories have different social goals.

In contrast, nature-centered works maintain that the human species has independent obligations toward other forms of life. Some theorists in this tradition accord rights to animals, whereas others reject the view that animals (or plants) have rights but believe, nonetheless, that nature must be protected for its own sake, not merely because it is useful to human beings. The two excerpted readings in this section reflect the wide divergence among the non-economic perspectives: Mark Sagoff's book is human-centered, whereas Paul Taylor's book is nature-centered.

Mark Sagoff's argument relies principally on two distinctions: between consumers and citizens and between pluralist and deliberative conceptions of the political process. He states that, as consumers, we concern ourselves with satisfying our personal preferences, but as citizens, we seek to promote the public interest rather than our personal interest. Second, consistent with the tradition of civic republicanism, he argues that the goal of the political process is to ascertain the public interest through a process of deliberation rather than simply to aggregate self-interested preferences.

Sagoff maintains that environmental regulation is not simply about correcting market failures by eliminating externalities. Instead, it embodies public values that our society chooses collectively; it is the product not of consumers satisfying their individual preferences but of citizens articulating a vision of a desirable society.

Sagoff considers three ways in which the costs of environmental regulation could affect regulatory standards. First, environmental laws could insist on ample margins of safety for the whole population even if strict adherence to such laws would impose ruinous costs on the economy. Second, consistent with the economic perspective, environmental laws could price the benefits of environmental quality and balance them against the resulting costs. Sagoff rejects both these solutions. He advocates a third course under which regulation allows a morally acceptable level of pollution by forcing industry to eliminate pollution up to the "knee of the curve"—a point at which the cost of controlling the next or marginal unit of pollution increases very rapidly.

Paul Taylor defines four beliefs that form the core of what he calls the biocentric outlook on nature: (1) that human beings are members of the earth's community of life on the same terms as other living things; (2) that all living species, both human and nonhuman, are interconnected; (3) that each organism is a unique individual pursuing its own good in its own way; and (4) that human beings are not inherently superior to other living things.

In light of this outlook, Taylor considers how to resolve conflicts between the interests of human beings and those of other species, and he proposes five principles for resolving such conflicts. First, the principle of self-defense asserts that it is permissible for human beings to destroy dangerous or harmful organisms that threaten human life or health. The remaining principles rely on the distinction between basic and nonbasic interests. The second principle, the principle of proportionality, asserts that nonbasic interests cannot override basic interests, even if the nonbasic interests are those of human beings and the basic interests are not. Third, the principle of minimum wrong applies in cases in which nonbasic interests of human beings will harm the basic interest of nonhumans, but where the former are regarded as so important that harming nonhumans is favored even by individuals who have adopted a respect for nature. Fourth, the principle of distributive justice applies when the basic interests of humans and nonhumans are in conflict, such as when, for example, a good that could benefit either humans or nonhumans must be allocated to one or the other; in these circumstances, each party must get an equal share of the good. Fifth, the principle of restitutive justice calls for making up wrongs caused by the principles of minimum wrong and distributive justice.

Mark Sagoff, The Economy of the Earth: Philosophy, Law, and the Environment

8–12, 28–29, 38–40, 46–52, 59–62, 205–08 (2d ed. 2008).*

The Role of Public Law in Controlling Pollution

On Earth Day in 1970, environmentalism emerged in part as a populist movement which enlisted lower-middle-class mothers concerned for the health of their children. Stories about hazardous wastes buried in urban neighborhoods, rivers that caught fire, a blowout of an oil well off the coast of Santa Barbara, accidents in chemical production facilities, and other incidents excited populist resentments that erupted in understandable moral outrage. . . . Americans agonized over cities filling

---

*   Reprinted with the permission of Cambridge University Press, copyright © 1988, 2008.

with smog, species becoming extinct, wildlife disappearing, oil spills, fish kills, detergents foaming in rivers and lakes, beach closing, and any number of horrors which led them to regard pollution as a menace gone out of control. . . .

The political response to the poisoning of neighborhoods, the destruction of wildlife, and the fouling of the water and air did not depend on a calculation of how these moral failures affected the economy. Rather, Congress acted to reduce environmental pollution and degradation in the same spirit it acted to end child labor; establish civil rights; improve unconscionable conditions in sweatshops, company towns, and mines; set a maximum workday and a minimum wage; relieve the suffering of the very poor; provide some form of public health care; combat discrimination; and establish other programs to vindicate the nation's claim to being a caring, compassionate, law-abiding community. . . .

Between 1969 and 1978, Congress enacted eight major pollution control statutes as part of a wave of environmental legislation that responded to the moral aspirations of American society. These aspirations centered on four normative issues. The first responds to popular sympathy for or empathy with the victim of pollution: the worker, neighbor, homemaker, or child who is injured or dies as a result of exposure to a toxic substance in the workplace or in the environment. The second concerns the protection of rights. Traditional forms of private law—that is, remedies for tort including nuisance—remain the first-line defense against pollution. Since it is often hard to match plaintiffs with defendants in cases of mass torts, public law has to supplement private law. A statute regulating pollution can be understood as a socially efficient way to control the kind of assault or trespass that traditionally finds its remedy in common law.

Third, Americans are concerned about pollution for cultural and patriotic reasons quite apart from the dangers that, from a scientific point of view, pollutants may pose to individuals. Americans are committed to the idea that America is and ought to remain beautiful. Smog-filled air, polluted rivers, dead lakes, and fouled land offend our cultural values and sense of national dignity and pride. Fourth, while markets may help consumers to form and to satisfy personal preferences, democratic institutions allow citizens to deliberate together to choose common goals and aspirations that they could not achieve or even conceive alone.

Society regards and should regard pollution in the typical case as a social evil to be minimized, not as a social cost to be optimized. Like any trespass, pollution has to be understood primarily as a moral failure, not as a market failure. Pollution is to be treated as an ethical problem and not primarily as an economic one. At the same time, if society were oblivious to the economic costs of pollution control, it could cause industry to cease; jobs would become scarce and inflation rampant. . . .

Even if statutory law explicitly prohibits the weighing of benefits against costs, it cannot become cost-oblivious because at some point society must recognize the law of diminishing returns. Policies undertaken to eliminate small risks, moreover, often create greater risks of other kinds. Commentators on all sides asked "how safe is safe enough?" This question implicitly inquires how we can function as a society while keeping in mind two goals—the right of individuals to be free of coercion and the need of the community to secure the advantages of overall economic growth.

How Safe is Safe Enough?

If pollution-control law were to pursue only moral and not economic objectives—if it intended purely to prohibit trespass and to protect public safety and health—agency actions could become "cost-oblivious." If regulations are oblivious to costs, they may slow or impair the growth of the economy on which social well-being or the standard of living primarily depends. Everyone will suffer on balance as a result. Accordingly, it is important to identify "resting points" or "stopping points"—levels of pollution that are acceptable given the costs of further reductions and the burden of those costs on the overall economy.

How has environmental regulation managed to keep two opposed ideas in mind at the same time, that is, both to reduce coercion and at the same time to accommodate growth? Environmental policy at its best (which may not be typical) has recognized that even if pollution is an evil to be minimized—rather than a cost to be optimized—it is to some extent a necessary evil, since economic production requires some emissions and effluents. Accordingly, society has developed a number of ethical tests and standards that it applies to set allowable levels of pollution, to determine at least for a time how safe is safe enough, clean is clean enough, and so on. These resting points . . . rely on ethical principles and moral intuitions that help society strike a balance between contradictory ideas, in this case, a principled abhorrence of pollution as coercion and an equally principled belief that economic growth is essential to social progress and welfare.

One well-known principle is the idea of de minimis risk. The law does not have to regulate risks that are so small they are hardly detectable. . . .

Another concept useful to strike a balance between pollution control and economic growth has to do with "benchmark" and "best method" standards for various industries. If the idea is to maximize through regulation the number of lives saved (or deaths or injuries avoided), moreover, then economists advise that we will do best if we equalize the marginal cost per life saved or injury avoided across programs. We need a benchmark amount—say $6 million—to test different regulations to see if they require society to spend more or less than that amount for each statistical life saved or death avoided. If there are significant cost differences, these have to be defended by some moral argument or reason, which often can be done, since some risks are more odious than others to society. A benchmark figure, a sort of average number, is needed, however, to assess regulations to make sure cost differences can be justified and explained. . . .

In many contexts, technology-forcing regulation can allow morally acceptable amounts of pollution. In many industries, initial gains to the environment are inexpensive; eventually the cost of controlling the "next" or "incremental" unit of pollution increases. At some given state of technology, one can often find an inflection point or "knee of the curve"— a point at which the cost of controlling the next or marginal unit of pollution increases very rapidly, and returns to the environment rapidly diminish per dollar spent. One morally acceptable way to allow some pollution (for example, through "cap-and-trade" markets for pollution allowances) is continually to encourage or prod industry to improve its processes and technologies to move the knee of the curve—the point at which costs may go asymptotic—ever farther out along the pollution-control axis. To the extent the government can encourage industries, through incentives and threats, to invent environment-friendly technology it can assure environmental progress while allowing at a given stage of technology the minimum amount of pollution necessary for economic growth. . . .

Values as Wants

The idea behind political deliberation and negotiation is that the process can be educational and transform confrontation into collaboration. In the context of political deliberation, in other words, positions are not construed as exogenous variables but are endogenous to the decisionmaking process. Participants, therefore, may redefine a problem or consider alternatives that permit an unexpected resolution. Because people must argue their views on the merits and from a public or intersubjective point of view in order to persuade each other, they may refine or even change their positions to make them plausible representations of the public interest or the general good. Legitimacy depends on the extent to which an outcome represents a policy all can approve after deliberation rather than the preponderance of interest or [willingness to pay] before discussion or debate.

Political deliberation can be seen as the opposite of welfare-economic valuation. Deliberation presents values as intersubjective—as legitimate because they take as their logical subject the community as a whole. Economic valuation, in contrast, takes all values to be statements of subjective interest—to express what the individual believes is good for him rather than good for us. Values enter welfare-economic calculations as exogenous variables, that is, as arbitrary preferences for which individuals are willing to pay. An analyst may therefore construe any policy as a benefit to those who approve it and as a cost to those who oppose it. . . .

Value judgments lie beyond criticism if, indeed, they are nothing but expressions of personal preference; they are incorrigible, since every person is in the best position to know what he or she wants. All valuation, according to this approach, happens *in foro interno*; debate *in foro publico*, other than an incantation in favor of efficiency or some balance of efficiency and equity, has no point. The economic approach denies the educative function of political discussion or persuasion; from its point of view, the political process is indistinguishable from an auction where policies are knocked down to the highest bidders. The reasons people give for their views (outside the journals of economic analysis, where argument is to be respected) are not to be counted; what counts is how much individuals will pay to satisfy their wants. Those willing to pay the most, for all intents and purposes, have the right view; theirs is the better judgment and the more informed opinion. . . .

Welfare economists sometimes argue that their role in guiding social policy is legitimate because they remain neutral among and thus rise above values of individuals in the client society. . . . The goal of social policy, according to this approach, is . . . to express unconditional positive regard for the preferences of all individuals, however weird. . . . Welfare economists stipulate the equivalence of "[willingness to pay]" and "value," and having postulated [willingness to pay] as the measure of value, these economists speak with scientific authority about the right and the good, since they have or are developing scientific methods for measuring it.

The Allocation and Distribution of Resources

In a course I teach on environmental ethics, I ask students to read the opinion of the Supreme Court in *Sierra Club v. Morton*. This case involves an environmentalist challenge to a decision by the U.S. Forest Service to lease the Mineral King Valley, a quasi-wilderness area in the middle of Sequoia National Park, to Walt Disney Enterprises, to develop a ski resort. . . .

I asked how many of the students had visited Mineral King or thought they would visit it as long as it remained undeveloped. There were about six hands. Why so few? Too many mosquitoes, someone said. No movies, said another. Another offered to explain in scrupulous detail the difference between chilblain and trench foot. These young people came from Boston, New York, and Philadelphia. They were not eager to subsist, for any length of time, on pemmican and rye biscuits.

Then I asked how many students would like to visit the Mineral King Valley if it were developed in the way Disney planned. A lot more hands went up. Someone wanted to know if he had to ski if he went. No; I told him if he stayed indoors, he need miss nothing. He could get snow blindness from the sour cream. He could meet Ms. Right at the après-ski sauna and at encounter sessions. The class got really excited. Two students in back of the room stood on tiptoe, bent their wrists, and leaned forward, as if to ski. I hope I have left no doubt about where the consumer interests of these young people lay.

I brought the students to order by asking if they thought the government was right in giving Disney Enterprises a lease to develop Mineral King. I asked them, in other words, whether they thought that environmental policy, at least in this instance, should be based on the principle of satisfying consumer demand. Was there a connection between what the students as individuals wanted for themselves and what they thought we should do, collectively, as a nation?

The response was nearly unanimous. The students believed that the Disney plan was loathsome and despicable, that the Forest Service had violated a public trust by approving it, and that the values for which we stand as a nation compel us to preserve the little wilderness we have for its own sake and as a heritage for future generations. On these ethical and cultural grounds, and in spite of their consumer preferences, the students opposed the Disney plan to develop Mineral King.

Consumer and Citizen Preferences

The consumer interests or preferences of my students are typical of those of Americans in general. Most Americans like a warm bed better than a pile of wet leaves at night. They would rather have their meals prepared in a kitchen than cook them over a camp stove. Disney's market analysts knew all this. They found that the resort would attract more than 14,000 tourists a day, in summer and winter alike, which is a lot more people than now hike into Mineral King. The tourists would pay to use the valley, moreover, while the backpackers just walk in. . . .

You might think that the public would have enthusiastically supported the Disney plan. Yet the public's response to the Disney project was like that of my students—overwhelming opposition. Public opinion was so unfavorable, indeed, that Congress acted to prohibit the project by making the Mineral King Valley a part of Sequoia National Park.

Were the rights of the skiers and scene makers to act freely within a market thwarted by the political action of the preservationists? Perhaps. But perhaps some of the swingers and skiers were themselves preservationists. Like my students, they may themselves condemn the likely consequences of their own consumer interests on cultural or ethical grounds.

I sympathize with my students. Like them and like members of the public generally, I, too, have divided preferences or conflicting "preference maps." Last year, I bribed a judge to fix a couple of traffic tickets, and I was glad to do so because I saved my license. Yet, at election time, I helped to vote the corrupt judge out of office. I speed on the highway; yet I want the police to enforce laws against speeding. I used to buy mixers in returnable bottles—but who can bother to return them? I buy only disposables now, but to soothe my conscience, I urge my state senator to outlaw one-way containers.

I love my car; I hate the bus. Yet I vote for candidates who promise to tax gasoline to pay for public transportation. I send my dues to the

Sierra Club to protect areas in Alaska I shall never visit. And I support the work of the American League to Abolish Capital Punishment although, personally, I have nothing to gain one way or the other. (If I hang, I will hang myself.) And of course, I applaud the Endangered Species Act, although I have no earthly use for the Colorado squawfish or the Indiana bat. The political causes I support seem to have little or no basis in my interests as a consumer, because I take different points of view when I vote and when I shop. I have an "Ecology Now" sticker on a car that drips oil everywhere it's parked. . . .

Compromise and Community

. . . The students in my class found it fairly easy to resolve the tension between their consumer interests and their public values with respect to the example of Mineral King. They recognized that private ownership, individual freedom of choice, and the profit motive . . . would undoubtedly lead to the construction of the Disney paradise. They reasoned, nevertheless, that we should act on principle to preserve this wilderness, which has an enormous cultural meaning for us, since the resort, though profitable, would not serve important social ends. The students argued that because there are a lot of places for people to party, we do not need to make a ski resort of Sequoia National Park.

But what if the stakes were reversed? What if we should have to make enormous financial sacrifices to protect an environmentally insignificant landscape? . . . Suppose industry would have to pay hundreds of millions of dollars to reduce air pollution by a small, perhaps an insignificant, amount? The students in my class answered these questions the way they answered questions about Mineral King. Just as they rejected the dogma of the perfect market, they also rejected the dogma of the perfect environment.

The students recognized that compromise is essential if we are to act as a community to accomplish any goal, however idealistic it may be. To improve air quality, for example, one needs not only a will but a way; one needs to express goals in parts per billion or, more generally, to deal with scientific uncertainties and technical constraints. The goal of environmental purity, like the goal of economic efficiency, can become a Holy Grail, in other words, suitable only as the object of an abstract religious quest. To make progress, we need to recognize that God dwells not only in the mountains but also in the details—in the minutia of testing, monitoring, and enforcement.

Although the students thought that social policy usually involves compromise, they kept faith with the ideals they held as citizens. They understood that if we are to take these ideals seriously, we must evaluate them in the context of the means available to achieve them. To will the end, in other words, one must also will the means: one must set goals in relation to the obstacles—economic, political, legal, bureaucratic, scientific, technical, and institutional—that stand in the way of carrying them out. We do not function as a political community simply by sharing public goals and by celebrating a vision of harmony between nature and society, even if ceremonies of this sort are a part of citizenship. To function as a community we must also reach the compromises necessary to move beyond incantation to political and economic implementation.

This is the reason that the Mineral King example—and the difference between citizen and consumer preferences it illustrates—may serve to introduce a course in environmental ethics, but it does not take us very far into the problems of environmental policy. The interesting problems arise when we move, in Winston Churchill's phrase, "from the wonderful cloudland of aspiration to the ugly scaffolding of attempt and achievement." Then we must chasten our goals by adjusting them to economic, legal, scientific, and political realities. How can we do this and still retain the ethical and aspirational nature of our objectives? How do we keep faith with the values of the citizen while recognizing the power of the consumer? . . .

Paul W. Taylor, Respect for Nature: A Theory of Environmental Ethics
99–102; 116–17; 119–20; 122–23; 129–32; 256; 262–306 (1986).*

The Biocentric Outlook on Nature
The Biocentric Outlook and the Attitude of Respect for Nature

The attitude we think it appropriate to take toward living things depends on how we conceive of them and of our relationship to them. What moral significance the natural world has for us depends on the way we look at the whole system of nature and our role in it. With regard to the attitude of respect for nature, the belief-system that renders it intelligible and on which it depends for its justifiability is the biocentric outlook. . . .

The beliefs that form the core of the biocentric outlook are four in number:

[1]   The belief that humans are members of the Earth's Community of Life in the same sense and on the same terms in which other living things are members of that Community.

[2]   The belief that the human species, along with all other species, are integral elements in a system of interdependence such that the survival of each living thing, as well as its chances of faring well or poorly, is determined not only by the physical conditions of its environment but also by its relations to other living things.

---

[3]   The belief that all organisms are teleological centers of life in the sense that each is a unique individual pursuing its own good in its own way.

[4]   The belief that humans are not inherently superior to other living things. . . .

Humans as Members of the Earth's Community of Life

From the perspective of the biocentric outlook on nature we see human life as *an integral part of the natural order of the Earth's biosphere.* We thus conceive of the place of humans in the system of nature in the same way we conceive of the place of other species. There is a common relationship to the Earth that we share with wild animals and plants. Full awareness of this common relationship gives us a sense of true community with them. Let us see how this sense of community develops.

The first thing we do when we accept the biocentric outlook is to take the fact of our being members of a biological species to be a fundamental feature of our existence. We do not deny the differences between ourselves and other species, any more than we deny the differences among other species themselves. Rather, we put aside these differences and focus our attention upon our nature as biological creatures. As far as our relation to the Earth's ecosystems is concerned, we see ourselves as but one species-population among many. Thus we keep in the forefront of our consciousness the characteristics we share with all forms of life on Earth. Not only is our common origin in one evolutionary process fully acknowledged, but also the common environmental circumstances that surround us all. We view ourselves as one with them, not as set apart from them. We are then ready to affirm our fellowship with them as equal members of the whole Community of Life on Earth.

Recognition of our membership in that universal Community of Life is rooted in five realities: [1] We as well as they must face certain biological and physical requirements for our survival and well-being. [2] They as well as we have a good of their own, the realization of which depends on contingencies that are not always under either our or their control. [3] Although the concepts of free will, autonomy, and social freedom apply only to humans, there is a fourth sense of freedom that holds equally of them and of us, and this kind of freedom is of great importance in any living thing's struggle to realize its good, whether human or nonhuman. [4] As a species we humans are a recent arrival on our planet, a relative newcomer to an order of life that had been established for hundreds of millions of years before we came into existence. [5] Finally, there is the fact that, while we cannot do without them, they can do without us. . . .

The Natural World as a System of Interdependence

To accept the biocentric outlook and regard ourselves and the world from its perspective is to see the whole natural domain of living things and their environment as an order of interconnected objects and events. The interactions among species-populations and between those populations and the physical environment comprise a tightly woven web. A particular change occurring in the conditions of a living population's existence or in the environmental situation will cause adjustments to be made throughout the entire structure.

As an illustration of a system of interdependence *within* the natural world we might consider some aspects of the ecology of the Everglades of Florida. In that ecosystem alligators make large depressions in marshy areas when they feed and rest. These depressions become permanent pools of water, containing a variety of forms of marine life nourished by the alligators' droppings and by bits of their food. During dry spells these pools are the only place where the marine organisms can survive. When rains come, they spread out over the Everglades, contributing to the whole grassland ecology in essential ways.

Female alligators are integral to the Everglades ecosystem in a special way. They build their nests by forming large piles of sticks and mud. These become the core of small islands of dry soil after many years, and trees begin to grow on them. The trees in turn support nesting birds which live on the fish, insects, and amphibia of the area, maintaining the balance between animal and plant life in the grasslands. Although the alligators sometimes eat nesting birds, they also protect the birds from predators.

When the alligators are trapped and killed (to supply skins to the makers of expensive shoes and handbags), the whole Everglades ecosystem suffers. The pools dry up, the marine life disappears, and the balance of life in the watery grassland is destroyed. Certain species of fish die off and, during rainy seasons, other species intrude into the area in great numbers. They had formerly been kept in check by their natural predator, the alligators. Thus the entire area undergoes deep ecological changes which, if not reversed, will spell the end of the ecosystem itself.

When one accepts the biocentric outlook, the whole realm of life is understood to exemplify a vast complex of relationships of interdependence similar to that found in each ecosystem. All the different ecosystems that make up the Earth's biosphere fit together in such a way that if one is radically changed or totally destroyed, an adjustment takes place in others and the whole structure undergoes a certain shift. . . .

Individual Organisms as Teleological Centers of Life

So far the biocentric outlook has been presented as a belief-system that sets a framework for viewing ourselves in relation to other species and for understanding how we and they alike fit into the whole natural environment of our planet. The third component of that outlook, in contrast with the first two, focuses our attention on the lives of individual organisms. The biocentric outlook includes a certain way of conceiving of each entity that has a life of its own. To accept the outlook is to sharpen and deepen our awareness of what it means to be a particular living thing.

Our knowledge of individual organisms has expanded rapidly with advances in the biological and physical sciences in the past century. Organic chemistry and microbiology have brought us close to every cell and every molecule that make up the physical structure of the bodies of organisms. We have greatly increased our understanding of how living things function as physical and chemical systems. We are acquiring ever more accurate and complete explanations of why organisms behave as they do. As we thus come to know more about their life cycles, their interactions with other organisms and with the environment, we become increasingly aware of how each of them is carrying out its life functions according to the laws of its species-specific nature. But besides this, our increasing knowledge and understanding also enable us to grasp the uniqueness of each organism as an individual. Scientists who have made careful and detailed studies of particular plants and animals have often come to know their subjects as identifiable individuals. Close observation over extended periods, whether in the laboratory or in the field, has led them to an appreciation of the unique "personalities" of their subjects. Sometimes a scientist develops a special interest in a particular animal or plant, all the while remaining strictly objective in the gathering and recording of data. . . .

Understanding individual organisms as teleological centers of life does not mean that we are falsely anthropomorphizing. It does not involve "reading into" them human characteristics. We need not, for example, consider them to have consciousness. That a particular tree is a teleological center of life does not entail that it is intentionally aiming at preserving its existence, that it is exerting efforts to avoid death, or that it even cares whether it lives or dies. . . . All organisms, whether conscious or not, are teleological centers of life in the sense that each is a unified, coherently ordered system of goal-oriented activities that has a constant tendency to protect and maintain the organism's existence.

Under this conception of individual living things, each is seen to have a single, unique point of view. This point of view is determined by the organism's particular way of responding to its environment, interacting with other individual organisms, and undergoing the regular, law-like transformations of the various stages of its species-specific life cycle. As it sustains its existence through time, it exemplifies all the functions and activities of its species in its own peculiar manner. When observed in detail, its way of existing is seen to be different from that of any other organism, including those of its species. To be aware of it not only as *a* center of life, but as *the* particular center of life that it is, is to be aware of its uniqueness and individuality. The organism is the individual it is precisely in virtue of its having its own idiosyncratic manner of carrying on its existence in the (not necessarily conscious) pursuit of its good.

This mode of understanding a particular individual is not possible with regard to inanimate objects. Although no two stones are exactly alike in their physical characteristics, stones do not have points of view. . . . The true reality of a stone's existence includes no point of view. This is not due to the fact that it lacks consciousness. . . . [P]lants and simple animal organisms also lack consciousness, but have points of view nonetheless. What makes our awareness of an individual stone fundamentally different from our awareness of a plant or animal is that the stone is not a teleological center of life, while the plant or animal is. The stone has no good of its own. We cannot benefit it by furthering its well-being or harm it by acting contrary to its well-being, since the concept of well-being simply does not apply to it. . . .

The Denial of Human Superiority

Of all the elements that make up the biocentric outlook, the fourth is the most important as far as taking the attitude of respect for nature is concerned. This fourth element consists in a total rejection of the idea that human beings are superior to other living things. Most people in our Western civilization are brought up within a belief-system according to which we humans possess a kind of value and dignity not present in "lower" forms of life. In virtue of our humanity we are held to be nobler beings than animals and plants. Our reason and free will, it is supposed, endow us with special worth because they enable us to live on a higher plane of existence than other living things are capable of. It is this belief, so deeply and pervasively ingrained in our cultural traditions, that is brought into question and finally denied outright in the fourth element of the biocentric outlook.

In what sense are human beings alleged to be superior to other animals? We are indeed different from them in having certain capacities that they lack. But why should these capacities be taken as signs of our superiority to them? From what point of view are they judged to be signs of superiority, and on what grounds? After all, many nonhuman species have capacities that humans lack. There is the flight of birds, the speed of a cheetah, the power of photosynthesis in the leaves of plants, the craftsmanship of spiders spinning their webs, the agility of a monkey in the tree tops. Why are not these to be taken as signs of their superiority over us?

One answer that comes immediately to mind is that these capacities of animals and plants are not as *valuable* as the human capacities that are claimed to make us superior. Such uniquely human characteristics as rationality, aesthetic creativity, individual autonomy, and free will, it might be held, are more valuable than any of the capacities of animals and plants. Yet we must ask: Valuable to whom and for what reason?

The human characteristics mentioned are all valuable to humans. They are of basic importance to the preservation and enrichment of human civilization. Clearly it is from the human standpoint that they are being judged as desirable and good. It is not difficult to recognize here a begging of the question. Humans are claiming superiority over nonhumans from a strictly human point of view, that is, a point of view in which the good of humans is taken as the standard of judgment. All we need to do is to look at the capacities of animals and plants from the standpoint of *their* good to find a contrary judgment of superiority. The speed of the cheetah, for example, is a sign of its superiority to humans when considered from the standpoint of a cheetah's good. If it were as slow a runner as a human it would not be able to catch its prey. And so for all the other abilities of animals and plants that further their good but are lacking in humans. In each case the judgment of human superiority would be rejected from a nonhuman standpoint. . . .

Now consider one of the most frequently repeated assertions concerning the superiority of humans over nonhumans. This is the claim that we humans are *morally* superior beings because we possess, while animals and plants lack, the capacities that give us the status of moral agents. Such capacities as free will, accountability, deliberation, and practical reason, it is said, endow us with the special nobility and dignity that belong only to morally responsible beings. Because human existence has this moral dimension it exemplifies a higher grade of being than is to be found in the amoral, irresponsible existence of animals and plants. In traditional terms, it is freedom of the will and the moral responsibility that goes with it that together raise human life above the level of the beasts.

There is a serious confusion of thought in this line of reasoning if the conclusion drawn is understood as asserting that humans are morally superior to nonhumans. One cannot validly argue that humans are morally superior beings on the ground that they possess, while others lack, the capacities of a moral agent. The reason is that, as far as moral standards are concerned, only beings that have the capacities of a moral agent can meaningfully be said to be *either* morally good *or* morally bad. Only moral agents can be judged to be morally better or worse than others, and the others in question must be moral agents themselves. Judgments of moral superiority are based on the comparative merits or deficiencies of the entities being judged, and these merits and deficiencies are all moral ones, that is, ones determined by moral standards. One entity is correctly judged morally superior to another if it is the case that, when valid moral standards are applied to both entities, the first fulfills them to a greater degree than the second. Both entities, therefore, must fall within the range of application of moral standards. This would not be the case, however, if humans were being judged superior to animals and plants, since the latter are not moral agents. . . .

Competing Claims and Priority Principles

The General Problem of Competing Claims

. . . I consider the moral dilemmas that arise when human rights and values conflict with the good of nonhumans. Such conflicts occur whenever actions and policies that further human interests or fulfill human rights are detrimental to the well-being of organisms, species populations, and life communities in the Earth's natural ecosystems. To put it another way, such conflicts occur whenever preserving and protecting the good of wild living things involves some cost in terms of human benefit. Clear examples are given in the following situations:

Cutting down a woodland to build a medical center.

Destroying a fresh water ecosystem in establishing a resort by the shore of a lake.

Replacing a stretch of cactus desert with a suburban housing development.

Filling and dredging a tidal wetland to construct a marina and yacht club.

Bulldozing a meadow full of wildflowers to make place for a shopping mall.

Removing the side of a mountain in a stripmining operation.

Plowing up a prairie to plant fields of wheat and corn. . . .

We must . . . try to find priority principles for resolving conflicts between humans and nonhumans which do not assign greater inherent worth to humans, but consider all parties as having the same worth. The principles, in other words, must be consistent with the fundamental requirement of *species-impartiality*. For only then can there be genuine fairness in the resolution of such conflicts.

Five Priority Principles for the Fair Resolution of Conflicting Claims

I shall now consider in depth five such principles, to be designated as follows:

[1]. The principle of self-defense.

[2]. The principle of proportionality.

[3]. The principle of minimum wrong.

[4]. The principle of distributive justice.

[5]. The principle of restitutive justice. . . .

[1]. *The Principle of Self-Defense.* The principle of self-defense states that it is permissible for moral agents to protect themselves against dangerous or harmful organisms by destroying them. This holds, however, only when moral agents, using reasonable care, cannot avoid being exposed to such organisms and cannot prevent them from doing serious damage to the environmental conditions that make it possible for moral agents to exist and function as moral agents. Furthermore, the principle does not allow the use of just any means of self-protection, but only those means that will do the least possible harm to the organisms consistent with the purpose of preserving the existence and functioning of moral agents. There must be no available alternative that is known to be equally effective but to cause less harm to the "attacking" organisms.

The principle of self-defense permits actions that are absolutely required for maintaining the very existence of moral agents and for enabling them to exercise the capacities of moral agency. It does not permit actions that involve the destruction of organisms when those actions simply promote the interests or values which moral agents may have as persons. Self-defense is defense against *harmful* and *dangerous* organisms, and a harmful or dangerous organism in this context is understood to be one whose activities threaten the life or basic health of those entities which need normally functioning bodies to exist as moral agents. . . .

[2]. *The Principle of Proportionality.* Before considering in detail each of the four remaining priority principles, it is well to look at the way they are interrelated. First, all four principles apply to situations where the nonhuman organisms involved are *harmless*. If left alone their activities would not endanger or threaten human life and health. Thus all four principles apply to cases of conflict between humans and nonhumans that are not covered by the principle of self-defense.

Next we must make a distinction between basic and nonbasic interests. Using this distinction, the arrangement of the four principles can be set out as follows. The principles of proportionality and minimum wrong apply to cases in which there is a conflict between the *basic* interests of animals or plants and the *nonbasic* interests of humans. The principle of distributive justice, on the other hand, covers conflicts where the interests of all parties involved are *basic*. Finally, the principle of restitutive justice applies only where, in the past, either the principle of minimum wrong or that of distributive justice has been used. Each of those principles creates situations where some form of compensation or reparation must be made to nonhuman organisms, and thus the idea of restitution becomes applicable. . . .

I might note that with reference to humans, basic interests are what rational and factually enlightened people would value as an essential part of their very existence as *persons*. They are what people need if they are going to be able to pursue those goals and purposes that make life meaningful and worthwhile. Thus for human persons their basic interests are those interests which, when morally legitimate, they have a *right* to have fulfilled. . . . [W]e do not have a right to whatever will make us happy or contribute to the realization of our value system; we do have a right to the necessary conditions for the maintenance and development of our personhood. These conditions include subsistence and security ("the right to life"), autonomy, and liberty. A violation of people's moral rights is the worst thing that can happen to them, since it deprives them of what is essential to their being able to live a meaningful and worthwhile life. And since the fundamental, necessary conditions for such a life are the same for everyone, our human rights have to do with universal values or primary goods. They are the entitlement we all have as persons to what makes us persons and preserves our existence as persons.

In contrast with these universal values or primary goods that constitute our basic interests, our nonbasic interests are the particular ends we consider worth seeking and the means we consider best for achieving them that make up our individual value systems. The nonbasic interests of humans thus vary from person to person, while their basic interests are common to all. . . .

The central idea of the principle of proportionality is that, in a conflict between human values and the good of (harmless) wild animals and plants, greater weight is to be given to basic than to nonbasic interests, no matter what species, human or other, the competing claims arise from. Within its proper range of application the principle prohibits us from allowing nonbasic interests to override basic ones, even if the nonbasic interests are those of humans and the basic are those of animals and plants.

The conditions of applicability of this principle are that the human interests concerned are nonbasic ones that are intrinsically incompatible with the attitude of respect for nature, that the competing claims arise from the basic interests of wild animals and/or plants, and that these animals and plants are harmless to humans (self-defense is not in question). . . . It should be noted that such practices as recreational fishing and hunting and buying luxury furs made from the pelts of wild creatures are actually accepted by millions of people as morally permissible. This fact merely shows the unquestioned, total anthropocentricity of their outlook on nature and their attitude toward wild creatures. It is clear, however, that from the standpoint of the life-centered system of environmental ethics defended in this book, such practices are to be condemned as being fundamentally exploitative of beings who have as much inherent worth as those who exploit them.

[3]. *The Principle of Minimum Wrong.* The principle of minimum wrong applies to situations in which (i) the basic interests of animals and plants are unavoidably in competition with nonbasic interests of humans; (ii) the human interests in question are *not* intrinsically incompatible with respect for nature; (iii) actions needed to satisfy those interests, however, are detrimental to the basic interests of animals and plants; and (iv) the human interests involved are so important that rational and factually informed people who have genuine respect for nature are not willing to relinquish the pursuit of those interests even when they take into account the undesirable consequences for wildlife.

Examples of such situations [include]: building a library or art museum where natural habitat must be destroyed; constructing an airport, railroad, harbor, or highway involving serious disturbance of a natural ecosystem; damming a river for a hydroelectric power project; replacing a wilderness forest with a timber plantation; landscaping a natural woodland to make a public park. The problem of priority in these situations is this: How can we tell when it is morally permissible for humans to pursue their nonbasic interests when doing so adversely affects the basic interests of wild animals and plants? . . .

. . . The answer lies, first, in the role such interests play in the overall view of civilized life that rational and informed people tend to adopt autonomously as part of their total world outlook. Secondly, the special value given to these interests stems from the central place they occupy in people's rational conception of their own true good. The first point concerns the cultural or social aspect of the valued interests—more specifically, the importance of their contribution to human civilization seen from a broad historical perspective. The second concerns the relation of the valued interests to an individual's view of the kind of life which, given one's circumstances and capacities, is most worth living. . . .

It is now time to make clear the content of the principle. The principle states that, when rational, informed, and autonomous persons *who have adopted the attitude of respect for nature* are nevertheless unwilling to forgo the two sorts of values mentioned above, even though they are aware that the consequences of pursuing those values will involve harm to wild animals and plants, it is permissible for them to pursue those values only so long as doing so involves fewer wrongs (violations of duties) than any alternative way of pursuing those values. . . .

[4]. *The Principle of Distributive Justice.* This fourth priority principle applies to competing claims between humans and nonhumans under two conditions. First, the nonhuman organisms are not harming us, so the principle of self-defense does not apply. Secondly, the interests that give rise to the competing claims are on the same level of comparative importance, all being *basic* interests, so the principles of proportionality and of minimum wrong do not apply. The range of application of the fourth principle covers cases that do not fall under the first three.

This principle is called the principle of distributive justice because it provides the criteria for a just distribution of interest-fulfillment among all parties to a conflict when the interests are all basic and hence of equal importance to those involved. Being of equal importance, they are counted as having the same moral weight. This equality of weight must be preserved in the conflict-resolving decision if it is to be fair to all. The principle of distributive justice requires that when the interests of the parties are all basic ones and there exists a natural source of good that can be used for the benefit of any of the parties, each party must be allotted an equal share. A fair share in those circumstances is an equal share.

When we try to put this principle of distributive justice into practice, however, we find that even the fairest methods of distribution cannot guarantee perfect equality of treatment to each individual organism. Consequently we are under the moral requirement to supplement all decisions grounded on distributive justice with a further duty imposed by the fifth priority principle, that of restitutive justice. Since we are not carrying out perfect fairness, we owe some measures of reparation or compensation to wild creatures as their due. As was true in the case of the principle of minimum wrong, recognition of wrongs being done to entities possessing inherent worth calls forth the additional obligation to do what we can to make up for these wrongs. In this way the idea of fairness will be preserved throughout the entire system of priority principles. . . .

Sometimes, however, the clash between basic human interests and the equally basic interests of nonhumans cannot be avoided. Perhaps the most obvious case arises from the necessity of humans to consume nonhumans as food. Although it may be possible for most people to eat plants rather than animals, I shall point out in a moment that this is not true of all people. And why should eating plants be ethically more desirable than eating animals?

Let us first look at situations where, due to severe environmental conditions, humans must use wild animals as a source of food. In other words, they are situations where subsistence hunting and fishing are necessary for human survival. Consider, for example, the hunting of whales and seals in the Arctic, or the killing and eating of wild goats and sheep by those living at high altitudes in mountainous regions. In these cases it is impossible to raise enough domesticated animals to supply food for a culture's populace, and geographical conditions preclude dependence on plant life as a source of nutrition. The principle of distributive justice applies to circumstances of that kind. In such circumstances the principle entails that it is morally *permissible* for humans to kill wild animals for food. This follows from the equality of worth holding between humans and animals. For if humans refrained from eating animals in those circumstances they would in effect be sacrificing their lives for the sake of animals, and no requirement to do that is imposed by respect for nature. Animals are not of *greater* worth, so there is no obligation to further their interests at the cost of the basic interests of humans. . . .

[5]. *The Principle of Restitutive Justice.* . . . As a priority principle in our present context, the principle of restitutive justice is applicable whenever the principles of minimum wrong and distributive justice have been followed. In both cases harm is done to animals and plants that are harmless, so some form of reparation or compensation is called for if our actions are to be fully consistent with the attitude of respect for nature. (In applying the minimum wrong and distributive justice principles, no harm is done to harmless *humans*, so there occurs an inequality of treatment between humans and nonhumans in these situations.) In its role as a priority principle for determining a fair way to resolve conflicts between humans and nonhumans, the principle of restitutive justice

must therefore supplement those of minimum wrong and distributive justice.

What kinds of reparation or compensation are suitable? Two factors can guide us in this area. The first is the idea that the greater the harm done, the greater the compensation required. Any practice of promoting or protecting the good of animals and plants which is to serve to restore the balance of justice between humans and nonhumans must bring about an amount of good that is comparable (as far as can be reasonably estimated) to the amount of evil to be compensated for.

The second factor is to focus our concern on the soundness and health of whole ecosystems and their biotic communities, rather than on the good of particular individuals. As a practical measure this is the most effective means for furthering the good of the greatest number of organisms. Moreover, by setting aside certain natural habitats and by maintaining certain types of physical environments in their natural condition, compensation to wild creatures can be "paid" in an appropriate way.

The general practice of wilderness preservation can now be understood as a matter of fairness to wild animals and plants in two different respects. On the one hand it is a practice falling under the principle of distributive justice, and on the other it is a way of fulfilling the requirements of restitutive justice. In its first aspect the preservation of wilderness is simply a sharing of the bounties of nature with other creatures. . . .

In a second respect the fairness of wilderness preservation derives from its suitability as a way of compensating for the injustices perpetrated on wildlife by humans. To set aside habitat areas and protect environmental conditions in those areas so that wild communities of animals and plants can realize their good is the most appropriate way to restore the balance of justice with them, for it gives full expression to our respect for nature even when we have done harm to living things in order to benefit ourselves. We can, as it were, return the favor they do us by doing something for their sake. Thus we need not bear a burden of eternal guilt because we have used them—and will continue to use them—for our own ends. There is a way to make amends.

NOTES AND QUESTIONS

1.   **Economics v. Ethics.** Assess the strength of Sagoff's distinction between ethical and economic goals. How does he define ethical goals? How does he define economic goals? Why shouldn't economic analysis apply to environmental goals? Is this view persuasive?

2.   **Outcomes of the Political Process.** What would Sagoff say if the political process, after having engaged in appropriate deliberation, picks a standard of environmental quality that is less stringent than the standard

that would maximize social welfare? Is it likely that the political process would produce such an outcome?

3. Valuing Natural Resources. Is it inconsistent with the economic perspective for Sagoff's students to oppose the Disney plan? They might value a pristine wilderness even if they never plan to go there. How could Sagoff's discussion of the Disney plan be recast in economic terms? For a critique of Sagoff's sharp distinction between the political and the economic spheres, see Daniel A. Farber, *From Plastic Trees to Arrow's Theorem*, 1986 U. ILL. L. REV. 337; Carol M. Rose, *Environmental Faust Succumbs to Temptations of Economic Mephistopheles, or, Value by Any Other Name Is Preference*, 87 MICH. L. REV. 1631 (1989). For further writings on the distinction between economic values and environmental values, see Laurence H. Tribe, *Ways Not to Think About Plastic Trees: New Foundations for Environmental Law*, 83 YALE L.J. 1315 (1974); Laurence L. Tribe, *Policy Science: Analysis or Ideology?*, 2 PHIL. & PUB. AFF. 66 (1972).

4. Substantive Standard. Does Sagoff offer a substantive standard for measuring the adequacy of environmental regulations? Does his position provide any basis for attacking a regulation on substantive grounds?

5. Procedural Standard. Does Sagoff offer a procedural standard for measuring the adequacy of environmental regulations? If such a standard is embedded in Sagoff's work, how should it be applied to evaluate the decisions of the following decision makers:

    (a) a voter?

    (b) a legislator?

    (c) the Administrator of the EPA?

6. Balancing Competing Interests. Sagoff is opposed to making "enormous financial sacrifices to protect an environmentally insignificant landscape." On what basis would he determine that the landscape is insignificant? On what basis would the economic perspective make this determination?

7. The "Knee of the Curve." Sagoff describes regulating to the "knee of the curve" while continually encouraging industry to improve its processes and technology to move the "knee" as "[o]ne morally acceptable way to allow some pollution." What are the problems with this approach to setting regulatory standards? Does this approach avoid weighing costs and benefits? *See* Michael A. Livermore & Richard L. Revesz, *Rethinking Health-Based Environmental Standards*, 89 N.Y.U. L. REV. 1184 (2014).

8. Costs and Standards. To what extent would Sagoff take costs into account in setting environmental standards? To what extent would he take costs into account in deciding on timetables for compliance with environmental standards?

9. Private v. Public Law. Sagoff argues that "remedies for tort including nuisance . . . remain the first-line defense against pollution," suggesting that "public law has to supplement private law" because "it is often hard to match plaintiffs with defendants in cases of mass torts." Consider tort doctrines of nuisance, negligence, and strict liability. If it were possible to match plaintiffs with defendants in tort cases, on what basis would a tort plaintiff receive damages that would induce a "morally acceptable amount of pollution" as described by Sagoff?

10. Private v. Public Interests. Sagoff appears to believe that when we are selfish we want less environmental quality, but when we are public-minded we want more. Is this viewpoint compelling? Consider the case of a wealthy individual who favors stringent environmental quality, but who, through a well-functioning political process, is persuaded to support the views of his fellow citizens who prefer more jobs. How would Sagoff judge the actions of this citizen?

11. Economics v. Ethics, Continued. In the concluding remarks to the book excerpted above, Sagoff distinguishes between an environmental movement based on science, economics, and rationality with one based on religion, ethics, and morality. Sagoff concludes that the environmental movement must turn away from reliance on science and turn toward its roots in religion to flourish. Are these two sources of environmental values incompatible with each other? Sagoff argues that, by reducing reliance on economic valuation of environmental amenities, the environmental movement will be more effective and environmental protection will increase. Is this view persuasive? Can you imagine circumstances in which engaging in economic valuation could inform, and even increase, the desired level of environmental protection?

12. Pioneer of Environmental Ethics. In the foreword to this edition of Taylor's book, Dale Jamieson, a professor of philosophy and environmental studies at New York University, notes that the book was an important milestone which "made environmental ethics a subject of serious academic inquiry, but also connected it to the values and lifestyles that were emerging in the environmental movement." For Jamieson, another mark of the book's distinction is that "it made no pretense of universal appeal." Jamieson argues that "Taylor was practicing philosophy as invitation rather than as coercion. His book was aimed at those who found the biocentric outlook appealing, not to those for whom this outlook had no attraction. . . . Taylor's grand achievement is not to have provided all the answers and solved all the problems, but rather to have given us a perspective and vocabulary for thinking through some profound moral challenges."

13. Biocentricity. Are each of Taylor's four beliefs necessary to a biocentric outlook on nature? What kind of outlook could be constructed on the basis of the third and fourth beliefs alone?

14. Denial of Human Superiority. Consider Taylor's belief that humans are not inherently superior to other living things. Is it consistent with Taylor's five priority principles for the fair resolution of conflicting claims? With which of these five principles is it arguably in tension?

15. Self-Defense. Consider the principle of self-defense. Under this principle, is it justifiable for a human being who climbs into a lion cage at a zoo to shoot the lion when he is attacked? Can an individual shoot a lion that has escaped from its cage as a result of the negligence of the zookeeper? Should reasonable care play a role in Taylor's theory?

16. Proportionality and Minimum Wrong. Are the principles of proportionality and minimum wrong mutually consistent? Why is it acceptable to dam a river but not to fish recreationally? What is the basis for Taylor's principle of minimum wrong? Is it consistent with his biocentric outlook? Under the principle of minimum wrong, how does one determine whether the individuals who want to destroy a natural habitat have a genuine respect for nature?

17. Basic Needs. What are the basic needs of humans? What are the basic needs of animals and plants? What types of everyday activities would be prohibited if the principle of proportionality were taken seriously?

18. Obligations to Prevent Harm: Humans and Other Living Beings. Consider the application of Taylor's theory in the following conflict between humans and other living beings:

> The bacterium *vibrio cholerae* causes cholera. Many would claim that intervention on behalf of cholera-stricken humans in distant communities is morally worthy. Yet for the biocentrist, we have morally valuable humans on the one hand and equally morally valuable, but far more numerous, *vibrio cholerae* bacteria on the other. It is morally permissible for infected humans to cure themselves [pursuant to the principle of self-defense], but in assisting them we fail to act in a way that is impartial between species.

NICHOLAS AGAR, LIFE'S INTRINSIC VALUE 80 (2001). In what way would Taylor's theory attempt to resolve this conflict?

19. Obligations to Prevent Harm: Animals and Plants. Does Taylor's theory impose an obligation on humans to prevent animals from hurting one another? Does it impose an obligation on humans to prevent animals from hurting plants?

20. Application of Taylor's Theory. What useful prescriptions for environmental policy can be derived from Taylor's theory? How would Taylor assess the permissibility of constructing a power plant that would lower the price of electricity and bring jobs to an economically depressed region but cause acid rain, thus damaging fish and plant life.

21. Modern Biocentric Approach. Nicholas Agar has more recently formulated a biocentric approach that is designed to lead to common-sense results. *See* AGAR, *supra*. Agar argues that Taylor's approach gives "inhumanly much weight to biocentric value." *Id.* at 87. In order to avoid this result, Agar formulates a method for assigning an "intrinsic value" to different living things:

> The amount of value we assign to an individual depends on the range and complexity of the goals of which an organism is capable. . . . Thus the life-representational ethic both acknowledges the preeminent place of humans on this planet and spreads value broadly enough to provide at least the raw materials for an environmental ethic.

Id. at 100. Agar justifies this view by arguing that such an ethic is a natural extension of "folk psychological" notions of the value of organisms. *Id.* at 95–97. Such a correspondence with current views makes Agar's viewpoint intuitive to a wider audience. Is something lost from the biocentric perspective by adopting this view?

22. Value of Species and Ecosystems. While Agar bases the values of species and ecosystems on the intrinsic value of individual organisms, he additionally argues that the value of a living thing can vary based on other circumstances. Agar states that "[t]he value of an individual within a species is not a function only of its own goals. Its demise affects the [other members of the species], depending on how plentiful the species is. This makes individuals belonging to endangered species more valuable than those belonging to nonendangered species." AGAR, *supra*, at 150. Similarly, "[n]ot all populations in an ecosystem will be equally important to the maintenance of overall species richness. Some could be lost with only minimal impact on other populations. The demise of others will have wider impact. . . . If a population is especially important to ecosystemic health, then its members should be viewed as more valuable." *Id.* at 152. Would a believer in the economic perspective on environmental degradation disagree with either of these statements? How is the method for the initial assignment of value to organisms different between the economic perspective and Agar's theory? Would these differences in initial method necessarily lead to greatly different prescriptions?

23. Biocentric Values and Empiricism. Unlike Taylor, Agar declines to specify a set of principles to evaluate conflicting claims:

> I may have demonstrated the genuineness of environmental intrinsic value but, beyond condemning the most obviously destructive human activities, I make little effort to describe the behavior this value entails. . . . My caution stems, in large part, from my philosophical naturalism. According to this approach, philosophy does not stand imperiously apart from science, making rules with which scientists must comply. It is therefore not for me to lay down the moral law in advance of the relevant empirical work.

AGAR, *supra*, at 172. Who do you think should do the "relevant empirical work"? Are ethical decisions ever purely scientific? Are they purely empirical?

24. The Ecological Perspective. The ecological perspective, generally traced to Aldo Leopold, is a different nature-centered approach to environmental ethics. *See* ALDO LEOPOLD, A SAND COUNTY ALMANAC (1949). Leopold states: "A thing is right when it tends to preserve the integrity, stability, and beauty of the biotic community. It is wrong when it tends otherwise." *Id.* at 224–25. More recent works within this tradition include WILLIAM OPHULS, ECOLOGY AND THE POLITICS OF SCARCITY: PROLOGUE TO A POLITICAL THEORY OF THE STEADY STATE (1977); ERIC T. FREYFOGLE, JUSTICE AND THE EARTH: IMAGES FOR OUR PLANETARY SURVIVAL (1993). Why is such equilibrium desirable? To what extent should the changing economic activities of human beings be viewed as part of the evolutionary process?

25. Taylor's Retort. Taylor criticizes this perspective:

> [S]uch a position is open to the objection that it gives no place to the good of individual organisms, other than how their pursuit of their good contributes to the well being of the system as a whole. This overlooks the fact that unless individuals have a good of their own that deserves the moral consideration of agents, no account of the organic system of nature-as-a-whole can explain why moral agents have a duty to preserve its good.

TAYLOR, *supra*, at 118. Is his criticism apt? In the last few decades, ecologists have largely rejected the equilibrium paradigm. *See* A. Dan Tarlock, *The Nonequilibrium Paradigm in Ecology and the Partial Unraveling of Environmental Law*, 27 LOY. L.A. L. REV. 1121 (1994). What are the implications of the nonequilibrium paradigm?

26. Deep Ecology. The deep ecology movement is influenced by Leopold's writings, believing, for example, that "[t]here is wisdom in the stability of natural processes unchanged by human intervention." Bill Devall, *The Deep Ecology Movement*, 20 NAT. RESOURCES J. 299, 311 (1980). However, it makes more radical prescriptions. One of the central proponents of this view writes: "Man is an integral part of nature, not over or apart from nature. Man is a 'plain citizen' of the biosphere, not its conqueror or manager. . . . Man flows with the system of nature rather than attempting to control all of the rest of nature." *Id.* at 310. The central tenets of the movement include the following:

> *Optimal human carrying capacity should be determined for the planet as a biosphere and for specific islands, valleys, and continents.* A drastic reduction of the rate of growth of population of Homo sapiens through humane birth control programs is required.

> *A new philosophical anthropology will draw on data of hunting/gathering societies for principles of healthy, ecologically viable societies.* Industrial society is not the end toward which all societies should aim or try to aim. Therefore the notion of "reinhabiting the land" with hunting gathering, and gardening as a goal and standard for postindustrial society should be seriously considered.

Id. at 311–12. The movement was inspired by Arne Naess, *The Shallow and the Deep, Long-Range Ecology Movement: A Summary*, 16 INQUIRY 95 (1973). More recent writings include BILL DEVALL, SIMPLE IN MEANS, RICH IN ENDS: PRACTICING DEEP ECOLOGY (1988); BILL DEVALL & GEORGE SESSIONS, DEEP ECOLOGY: LIVING AS IF NATURE MATTERED (1985). What arguments can be constructed in favor of deep ecology?

27. Ecofeminism. Consider the following description of ecofeminism:

> Ecofeminism argues that patriarchy, the domination of women by men, has been associated with the domination of nature. Men have justified their attempts to dominate nature by associating it with

women, objectifying both women and nature by placing them in the category of "other." Patriarchy also involves a denial of human links with the natural world and of men's feminine side. Ecofeminists regard both the despoliation of the environment and violence and militarism as rooted in the culture of domination; they argue that both have become major threats to the human race. Patriarchy, ecofeminists argue, must be replaced with an egalitarian form of social organization in which men and women have equal power, and by a social ecology in which the natural environment is treated with respect and sustained rather than manipulated and destroyed. Ecofeminists also believe that capitalism is linked to domination and must be replaced by another social order; they envision small-scale economies and local, grass-roots democracy rather than the large-scale, state-directed societies and economies of existing socialist nations.

Barbara Epstein, *Ecofeminism and Grass-Roots Environmentalism in the United States, in* TOXIC STRUGGLES: THE THEORY AND PRACTICE OF ENVIRONMENTAL JUSTICE 144 (Richard Hofrichter ed., 1993).

The classic works in ecofeminism include SUSAN GRIFFIN, WOMAN AND NATURE: THE ROARING INSIDE HER (1978); MARY DALY, GYN/ECOLOGY: THE METAETHICS OF RADICAL FEMINISM (1978). What effects do you believe that greater gender equality would have on the environment? To what extent do the precepts of ecofeminism seem consistent with those of deep ecology? Might the tenets of deep ecology interfere with the move toward greater gender equality?

28. Vegetarianism. In a portion of the book that is not excerpted, Taylor makes the following case for vegetarianism:

> [A]nyone who has respect for nature will be on the side of vegetarianism, even though plants and animals are regarded as having the same inherent worth. The point that is crucial here is the amount of arable land needed for raising grain and other plants as food for those animals that are in turn to be eaten by humans when compared with the amount of land needed for raising grain and other plants for direct human consumption. . . . [O]ne acre of cereal grains to be used for human food can produce five times more protein than one acre used for meat production; one acre of legumes (peas, lentils, and beans) can produce ten times more; and one acre of leafy vegetables fifteen times more.

TAYLOR, *supra*, at 295–96. Contrast this view with that in PETER SINGER, ANIMAL LIBERATION (2d ed. 1990). Singer argues:

> [T]he only legitimate boundary to our concern for the interests of other beings is the point at which it is no longer accurate to say that the other being has interests. To have interests, in a strict, non-metaphorical sense, a being must be capable of suffering or experiencing pleasure. If a being suffers, there can be no moral justification for disregarding that suffering, or for refusing to count it equally with the like suffering of any other being. But the

converse of this is also true. If a being is not capable of suffering, or of enjoyment, there is nothing to take into account.

SINGER, *supra*, at 171. Singer suggests two indicators of the capacity of nonhumans to suffer: "the behavior of the being, whether it writhes, utters, cries, attempts to escape from the source of pain, and so on; and the similarity of the nervous system of the being to our own." In the first edition of his book, Singer drew the line between a shrimp and a scallop, deeming it permissible to eat the latter but not the former. (In his second edition, he expresses concern that scallops and other mollusks might feel pain.)

Singer's central argument is against speciesism—a prejudice in favor of individuals of one's own species. Singer writes:

> To avoid speciesism we must allow that beings who are similar in all relevant respects have a similar right to life—and mere membership in our own biological species cannot be a morally relevant criterion for this right. Within these limits we could still hold, for instance, that it is worse to kill a normal adult human, with a capacity for self-awareness and the ability to plan for the future and have meaningful relations with others, than it is to kill a mouse, which presumably does not share all these characteristics; or we might appeal to the close family and other personal ties that humans have but mice do not have to the same degree. . . .
>
> Whatever criteria we choose, however, we will have to admit that they do not follow precisely the boundary of our own species. We may legitimately hold that there are some features of certain beings that make their lives more valuable than those of other beings; but there will surely be some nonhuman animals whose lives, by any standards, are more valuable than the lives of some humans. A chimpanzee, dog, or pig, for instance, will have a higher degree of self-awareness and a greater capacity for meaningful relations with others than a severely retarded infant or someone in a state of advanced senility.

SINGER, *supra*, at 19. How compelling is Singer's theory? Recall Taylor's priority principles for the fair resolution of competing claims. What different principles might Singer offer? For further discussion of the moral relevance of consciousness, see ROBIN ATTFIELD, THE ETHICS OF ENVIRONMENTAL CONCERN ch. 8 (2d ed. 1991).

29. Respect for Inanimate Objects. Biocentric views are based on respect for the worth of all *living* objects. Evaluate the following argument for respecting inanimate objects as well:

> If we accept life as the intrinsic or inherent good, then a foundation is laid for claims on behalf of animate Things, but claims on behalf of the inanimates are at best derivative. A river would not be morally considerate as such, but we would have duties to treat it in a certain way in order to fulfill our duties to the living things that depend on it. One might suppose that this distinction would be of little moment to an environmentalist. Life in one form or another is so ubiquitous that to protect life seems to be a handy and

plausible way to protect the entire environment. If a lake were utterly lifeless, or unconnected to the support of any life, we would have no duty to it; but it is hard to imagine such a lake. Even the Dead Sea is not quite dead.

Nonetheless, the use of life as a foundational good has drawbacks for an environmental movement. For one thing, it may be intuitively disingenuous, like pitching the case against cruelty to animals on the basis of human betterment. [Consider] the campaign to save Mono Lake from destruction as its freshwater feeder streams are increasingly diverted to meet Southern California's water demand. The lake is remote from population centers and, aside from brine shrimp and gulls, only subtly life-supporting. If there were no brine shrimp and gulls, would morality have *nothing* to say?

More importantly, a life-maximizing principle leads to odd choices. Suppose that two water plants were being weighed, each of which would supply the same amount of water at the same cost. In other words, imagine the present utility of the two projects to be identical. Further, imagine future generations to be indifferent as between which project we should choose. There would be this difference only: different amounts of life are to be affected, whether life be measured in terms of absolute biomass or diversity. The first project would destroy a grand, unique geologic formation that took shape over thousands of years but supports very little life (it is all the more rare for that). The competing water delivery plan, by requiring reconstruction of some cementencasted man-made water courses, would eliminate tons of life in the form of bacteria and algae. Does the fact that the second project would eliminate more *life* mean that the destruction of the unique formation is therefore preferred, and that all further moral conversation is cut off?

CHRISTOPHER STONE, EARTH AND OTHER ETHICS: THE CASE FOR MORAL PLURALISM 94–95 (1987). Stone had earlier written an article, which was embraced in dissent by Justice Douglas in *Sierra Club v. Morton*, 405 U.S. 727 (1972), urging the Supreme Court to confer standing on natural objects. *See* Christopher Stone, *Should Trees Have Standing?—Towards Legal Rights for Natural Objects*, 45 S. CAL. L. REV. 450 (1972). Does Stone offer a more compelling argument than Taylor?

30. Rights of Nature. In 2008, Ecuador became the first country to recognize the Rights of Nature in its Constitution. In particular, Article 71 of its Constitution provides as follows:

Nature . . . where life is reproduced and occurs, has the right to integral respect for its existence and for the maintenance and regeneration of its life cycles, structure, functions and evolutionary processes.

All persons, communities, peoples and nations can call upon public authorities to enforce the rights of nature. To enforce and interpret these rights, the principles set forth in the Constitution shall be observed, as appropriate.

The State shall give incentives to natural persons and legal entities and to communities to protect nature and to promote respect for all the elements comprising an ecosystem.

Ecuador's economy relies heavily on natural resource extraction. How should Ecuador deal with tradeoffs between economic development and environmental degradation in light of its constitutional promises? *See* Mary Elizabeth Whittemore, *The Problem of Enforcing Nature's Rights Under Ecuador's Constitution: Why the 2008 Environmental Amendments Have No Bite*, 20 PAC. RIM L. & POL'Y J. 659, 663 (2011). Between 2009 and 2016, 10 out of 13 cases in Ecuador's courts that invoked the rights of nature had succeeded. *See* Craig M. Kauffman & Pamela L. Martin, *Testing Ecuador's Rights of Nature: Why Some Lawsuits Succeed and Others Fail*, Paper Presented at the International Studies Association Annual Convention Atlanta, GA (Mar. 18, 2016). In the first successful case, the court held that the Vilcabamba River's constitutional rights had been violated by a highway construction project, and it ordered the government to restore the environment. *See* David R. Boyd, *Recognizing the Rights of Nature: Lofty Rhetoric or Legal Revolution?*, 32 NAT. RESOURCES & ENV'T 1, 13, 15 (2018).

31. Duties to Future Generations. One human-centered perspective to environmental ethics focuses on our duties to future generations. For a philosophical work in this vein, see JOHN ARTHUR PASSMORE, MAN'S RESPONSIBILITY FOR NATURE: ECOLOGICAL PROBLEMS AND WESTERN TRADITIONS (1974). How would Sagoff and Taylor deal with our obligation to future generations?

CHAPTER II

RISK ASSESSMENT, RISK MANAGEMENT, AND DISTRIBUTION OF ENVIRONMENTAL RISKS

1. RISK ASSESSMENT

Risk assessment is a "process in which information is analyzed to determine if an environmental hazard might cause harm to exposed persons and ecosystems." OFFICE OF SCI. ADVISOR, EPA, EXAMINATION OF EPA RISK MANAGEMENT PRACTICES 2 (2004). It is inherently interdisciplinary in nature—drawing on such diverse fields as biology, toxicology, ecology, engineering, geology, statistics, and the social sciences—in an attempt to create a rational framework for evaluating environmental hazards. *Id*. Risk assessment is generally recognized as the first step in the regulatory process; a regulatory agency must first analyze the magnitude of an environmental risk before it can intelligently decide on whether and how much risk should be regulated— a process known as risk management.

The first section of this chapter addresses the process of risk assessment, focusing upon three principal themes: first, the feasibility and desirability of insulating risk assessment from politics; second, the uncertainties inherent in the risk assessment process; and third, the implications of the divergence between expert and lay perceptions of risk.

The article by William Ruckelshaus primarily addresses the first of these themes, arguing that a sharp distinction should be drawn between risk assessment and risk management. Ruckelshaus was the first administrator of the Environmental Protection Agency (EPA) in the early 1970s; in the 1980s, he was drafted to lead the agency again after the leadership of Anne Gorsuch had severely impaired its credibility. He advocates keeping political considerations out of the risk assessment process—an approach that many believe EPA had not followed under Gorsuch's leadership. According to Ruckelshaus, the appropriate place for political decisions is at the risk management stage.

Ruckelshaus recognizes that risk assessment is dependent on a variety of assumptions and that these assumptions will reflect the values of the individuals responsible for the choice, whether they are scientists, civil servants, or politicians. He argues that the discretion of individual risk assessors should be constrained through generic policies governing recurring issues. Such policies were adopted in the early 1980s by EPA and a number of other federal agencies. One prescribes a no-threshold model for carcinogens, for example, so that any exposure to a carcinogen is assumed to increase the probability of cancer. Ruckelshaus argues that such policies make the process of risk assessment more uniform and less likely to be influenced by political considerations.

The next three readings address quantitative risk assessment, which as its name suggests, is a process by which human health risks attributable to environmental hazards are quantified. *Industrial Union Department, AFL-CIO v. American Petroleum Institute*, 448 U.S. 607 (1980), the *Benzene* case, is one of the Supreme Court's most important public health decisions. It involves a challenge to regulations promulgated by the Occupational Safety and Health Administration (OSHA), setting a standard for occupational exposure to benzene, a known carcinogen. The case is of great theoretical interest, illustrating the uncertainties inherent in the risk assessment of carcinogens at low doses as well as the difficulties facing courts charged with reviewing the actions of an agency "working on the frontiers of science." In addition, the case is of great practical consequence. The plurality's insistence that OSHA's regulations be struck down for failure to demonstrate the existence of a significant risk to human health prompted federal agencies to adopt the process of quantitative risk assessment in future rulemaking.

The article by Alon Rosenthal, George Gray, and John Graham describes each of the four stages of quantitative risk assessment primarily as it applies to carcinogens: hazard identification, dose-response evaluation, exposure assessment, and risk characterization.

Hazard identification—determining whether a substance is hazardous to human health—is conducted through human epidemiological studies or long-term animal bioassays. Epidemiological studies monitor the health of human populations that have been exposed to the substance (such as a community surrounding a factory from which the compound was accidentally released). In long-term animal bioassays, large doses of the substance are administered to controlled groups of animals, generally rodents, and the resulting reaction is monitored.

Dose-response evaluation involves determining the relationship between the dose of the substance to which human beings are exposed and the probability of adverse health effects. This determination is performed by extrapolating from the effects of the large doses to which rodents are exposed in animal bioassays to the far lower doses that a plausible regulatory regime is likely to regard as permissible as well as extrapolating from the effects on rodents to the likely effects on human beings.

Exposure assessment consists of determining the extent to which human populations are exposed to hazardous substances. For example, how much groundwater contaminated by a hazardous waste site do individuals in a surrounding community drink?

Finally, *risk characterization* involves providing a numerical estimate of the health risk. In the case of carcinogens, this number is often expressed as the increased probability of cancer from a lifetime exposure to the harmful substance.

The case of *Public Citizen Health Research Group v. Tyson*, 796 F.2d 1479 (D.C. Cir. 1986), serves as a counterpoint to the *Benzene* case. Like the *Benzene* case, it relates to a challenge to an OSHA rule limiting occupational exposure to a known carcinogen. Unlike in the *Benzene* case, however, EPA had conducted a quantitative risk assessment in support of its proposed rule. The differing outcomes of the two cases, decided some six years apart, demonstrate the deferential attitude courts are willing to afford to agency decisionmaking in the event that an attempt is made to quantify the relevant risks.

The excerpt from the book by Justice Stephen Breyer, which was published shortly before his appointment to the Supreme Court, focuses upon the third theme of this section: the vast disparity between lay and expert perceptions of risk. This problem was made salient by the publication of two reports by EPA, in 1987 and 1990, which showed that problems that experts regarded as most serious, such as radon contamination in homes, were regarded as relatively unimportant by the public, whereas problems that experts ranked as far less serious, such as contamination from hazardous waste sites, were perceived by the public as most significant. Other studies confirm that lay and expert perceptions of risk are significantly different.

Justice Breyer explores the reasons why the public might have different reactions to risk than experts. In particular, human beings use heuristic devices as shortcuts to characterize risk, give greater prominence to unusual events than to everyday risks, have greater feelings of moral obligation toward those who are close to them, distrust experts, are reluctant to change their minds, and have difficulty understanding the mathematical probabilities involved in assessing risk. While some commentators have argued that the solution lies in more effective communication about risk, Justice Breyer is skeptical about whether such educative approaches are likely to significantly change the cognitive processes that lead to the gap between scientific and lay perceptions of risk.

A. NATURE OF RISK ASSESSMENT

William D. Ruckelshaus, Risk, Science, and Democracy
1 ISSUES SCI. & TECH. 19 (1985).[*]

"Risk" is the key concept here. It was hardly mentioned in the early years of EPA, and it does not have an important place in the Clean Air or Clean Water Acts passed in that period. Of the events that contributed to this change, the most important were the focus of public attention on PCBs [Polychlorinated Biphenyls] and asbestos (two substances that are ubiquitous in the American environment and that are capable of causing cancer) and the realization that exposure to a very large number of unfamiliar and largely untested chemicals is universal. The discovery by cancer epidemiologists that cancer rates vary with environment suggested that pollution might play a role in causing this disease. And finally, the cancer risk was pushed to the forefront by the emergence of abandoned dumps of toxic chemicals as a consuming public issue. As a direct result of this shift in attention, the relation of EPA to its science base was altered; the problem of uncertainty was moved from the periphery to the center.

This shift occurred because the risks of effects from typical environmental exposures to toxic substances—unlike the touchable, visible, and malodorous pollution that stimulated the initial environmental revolution—are largely constructs or projections based on scientific findings. We would know nothing at all about chronic risk attributable to most toxic substances if scientists had not detected and evaluated them. Our response to such risks, therefore, must be based on a set of scientific findings. Science, however, is hardly ever unambiguous or unanimous, especially when the data on which definitive science must be founded scarcely exist. The toxic effects on health of many of the chemicals EPA considers for regulation fall into this class.

"Risk assessment" is the device that government agencies such as EPA have adopted to deal with this quandary. It is the attempt to quantify the degree of hazard that might result from human activities—for example, the risks to human health and the environment from

---

[*]   Reprinted with the permission of the National Academy of Sciences, Washington, D.C., copyright © 1985.

industrial chemicals. Essentially, it is a kind of pretense; to avoid the paralysis of protective action that would result from waiting for "definitive" data, we assume that we have greater knowledge than scientists actually possess and make decisions based on those assumptions.

Of course, not all risk assessment is on the controversial outer edge of science. We have been looking at the phenomenon of toxic risk from environmental levels of chemicals for a number of years, and as evidence has accumulated for certain chemicals, controversy has diminished and consensus among scientists has become easier to obtain. For other substances—and these are the ones that naturally figure most prominently in public debate—the data remain ambiguous.

In such cases, risk assessment is something of an intellectual orphan. Scientists are uncomfortable with it when the method must use scientific information in a way that is outside the normal constraints of science. They are encroaching on political judgments and they know it. As Alvin Weinberg has written:

> Attempts to deal with social problems through the procedures of science hang on the answers to questions that can be asked of science and yet which cannot be answered by science. I propose the term *trans-scientific* for these questions. . . . Scientists have no monopoly on wisdom where this kind of trans-science is involved; they shall have to accommodate the will of the public and its representatives.

However, the representatives of the public, in this instance policy officials in protective agencies, have their problems with risk assessment as well. The very act of quantifying risk tends to reify dreaded outcomes in the public mind and may make it more difficult to gain public acceptance for policy decision or push those decisions in unwise directions. It is hard to describe, say, one cancer case in 70 years among a population of a million as an "acceptable risk" when such a description may too easily summon up for any individual the image of some close relative on his deathbed. Also, the use of risk assessment as a policy basis inevitably provokes endless arguments about the validity of the estimates, which can seriously disrupt the regulatory timetables such officials must live by.

Despite this uneasiness, there appears to be no substitute for risk assessment, in that some sort of risk finding is what tells us that there is any basis for regulatory action in the first place. The alternative to not performing risk assessment is to adopt a policy of either reducing all *potentially* toxic emissions to the greatest degree technology allows (of which more later) or banning all substances for which there is any evidence of harmful effect, a policy that no technological society could long survive. Beyond that, risk assessment is an irreplaceable tool for setting priorities among the tens of thousands of substances that could be subjects of control actions—substances that vary enormously in their apparent potential for causing disease. In my view, therefore, we must use and improve risk assessment with full recognition of its current shortcomings.

This accommodation would be much easier from a public policy viewpoint were it possible to establish for all pollutants the environmental levels that present zero risk. This is prevented, however, by an important limitation of the current technique; the difficulty of establishing definitive no-effect levels for exposure to most carcinogens. Consequently, whenever there is any exposure to such substances, there is a calculable risk of disease. The environmentalist ethos, which is reflected in many of our environmental laws, and which requires that zero-risk levels of pollutant exposure be established, is thus shown to be an impossible goal for an industrial society, as long as we retain the no-threshold model for carcinogenesis. . . .

This situation has given rise to two conflicting viewpoints on protection. The first, usually proffered by the regulated community, argues that regulation ought not to be based on a set of unprovable assumptions but only on connections between pollutants and health effects that can be demonstrated under the canons of science in the strict sense. It points out that for the vast majority of chemical species, we have no evidence at all that suggests effects on human health from exposures at environmental levels. Because many important risk assessments are based on assumptions that are scientifically untestable, the method is too susceptible to manipulation for political ends and, the regulated community contends, it has been so manipulated by environmentalists.

The second viewpoint, which has been adopted by some environmentalists, counters that waiting for firm evidence of human health effects amounts to using the nation's people as guinea pigs, and that is morally unacceptable. It proposes that far from overestimating the risks from toxic substances, conventional risk assessments underestimate them, for there may be effects from chemicals in combination that are greater than would be expected from the sum effects of all chemicals acting independently. While approving of risk assessment as a priority-setting tool, this viewpoint rejects the idea that we can use risk assessment to distinguish between "significant" and "insignificant" risks. Any identifiable risk ought to be eliminated up to the capacity of available technology to do so.

It is impossible to evaluate the merits of these positions without first drawing a distinction between the assessment of risk and the process of deciding what to do about it, which is "risk management." The arguments in the form sketched here are really directed at both these processes, a common confusion that has long stood in the way of sensible policymaking.

Risk assessment is an exercise that combines available data on a substance's potency in causing adverse health effects with information about likely human exposure, and through the use of plausible assumptions, it generates an estimate of human health risk. Risk management is the process by which a protective agency decides what action to take in the face of such estimates. Ideally the action is based on such factors as the goals of public health and environmental protection, relevant legislation, legal precedent, and application of social, economic, and political values. *Risk Assessment in the Federal Government*, a National Research Council (NRC) document, recommends that regulatory agencies establish a strict distinction between the two processes, to allay any confusion between them. In my view Congress should do the same in all statutes seeking to deal with risk.

Returning now to the opposing viewpoints we see that both reflect the fear that risk assessment may be imbued with values repugnant to one or more of the parties involved. That is, some people in the regulated community believe that the structure of risk assessment inherently exaggerates risk, while many environmentalists believe that it will not capture all the risk that may actually exist. As we have seen, this disagreement is not resolvable in the short run through recourse to science. Risk assessment is necessarily dependent on choices made among a host of assumptions, and these choices will inevitably be affected by the values of the choosers, whether they be scientists, civil servants, or politicians.

The NRC report suggests that this problem can be substantially alleviated by the establishment of formal public rules guiding the necessary inferences and assumptions. These rules should be based on the best available information concerning the underlying scientific mechanisms. Adoption of such guidelines reduces the possibility that an EPA administrator may manipulate the findings of some risk assessment so as to avoid making the difficult, and perhaps politically unpopular, choices involved in a risk-management decision. Both industry and environmentalists fear this manipulation—from different brands of administrator, needless to say. Although we cannot remove values from risk assessment, we can and should keep those values from shifting arbitrarily with the political winds.

The explicit and open codification suggested by the NRC will also ensure that the assumptions used in risk assessment will at least be uniform among all agencies that adopt them, will be plausible scientifically, and will reflect a predictable and relatively constant policy amid this complex and chaotic hybrid discipline. It also offers the possibility that one day all the protective agencies of government will speak with one voice when they address risks, so that estimates of risk will be comparable among agencies and the public at last will be able to make a fair comparison of the individual risk-management decisions of separate agencies.

The remaining points of both positions are really about risk management and on this issue both are flawed. At its extreme, the first position—that regulation should be based solely on scientifically

provable connections between pollutants and health effects—would allow
the release of unlimited quantities of substances that cause cancer in
animals, on the assumption that there will be no analogous effect on
people and that there must be thresholds for carcinogenesis. I expect that
most Americans would reject that assumption as imprudent, given our
current knowledge about carcinogenesis (for example, the similarity of
cancer causing genes across species). At some level we have to regard the
possibility that we are controlling somewhat in excess of the true risk as
a kind of insurance, with the cost of control as its premium. The effort to
reduce apprehension, even so-called unreasonable apprehension, about
the future results of current practices is a valid social function. Risk-
management agencies such as EPA could be chartered to do precisely
that. If so, we had better make clear what we are doing, and establish
rules for doing it.

The weakness of the second viewpoint, that any identifiable risk
ought to be eliminated up to the capacity of available technology to do so,
lies in the concept of a best available technology that must invariably be
applied where risk is discovered. "Best" and "available" are terms as
infinitely debatable as the assumptions of risk assessment. There is
always a technology conceivable that is an improvement on a previous
one, and as the last increments of pollution are removed, the cost of each
successive fix goes up very steeply. Because, according to the no-
threshold assumption, even minute quantities of carcinogens can be
projected out to cause cases of disease, arguments about technology
reduce in the end to arguments about risk and cost: technology A allows
a residual risk of 10^{-5} and costs \$1 million; technology B allows a residual
risk of 10^{-6} and costs \$10 million, and so on ad infinitum. It is specious
to pretend that costs do not matter, because it is always possible to show
that at a certain level of removal, costs in fact do matter: technology Z
allows residual risks of 10^{-15} and costs \$1 trillion.

Once this is admitted, as it almost always is when we come down to
debating actual regulations, the position is reduced to arguments about
affordability. This too is treacherous ground. Firms vary in their ability
to pay, and what is affordable for one may bankrupt another. If
requirements are adjusted so as not to cripple the poorest firms, the
policy amounts to an environmental subsidy to the less efficient players
in our economy. . . .

My point is that in confronting any risk there is no way to escape the
question "Is controlling it worth it?" We must ask this question not only
in terms of the relationship of the risk reduced and the cost to the
economy but also as it applies to the resources of the agency involved.
Policy attention is the most precious commodity in government, and a
regulation that marginally protects only 20 people may take up as much
attention as a regulation that surely protects a million.

"Is it worth it?" That this question must be asked and asked carefully
is a token of how the main force of the environmental idea has been

modified by the recent focus on toxic risk to human health. In truth this question should always have been asked, but because the early goals of environmentalism were so obviously good, the requirement to ask, "Is it worth it?" was not firmly built into all our environmental laws. Who would dare to question the worth of saving Lake Erie? Environmentalism at its inception was a grand vision, one that nearly all Americans willingly shared. Somehow that vision of the essential unity of nature and of the need for bringing industrial society into harmony with it has been lost among the parts per billion, and with it we have lost the capacity to reach social consensus on environmental policy.

NOTES AND QUESTIONS

1. **Risk Assessment and Risk Management.** Why does Ruckelshaus want to distinguish between risk assessment and risk management? Why does he argue that the risk assessment process should be insulated from social policy tradeoffs? What types of experts does Ruckelshaus think should conduct risk assessments? What disciplines are most relevant?

2. **Blurring the Distinction.** Is it possible to maintain a bright-line distinction between risk assessment and risk management? Consider the risk assessment of substances suspected of being carcinogens, in which there is generally less-than-conclusive evidence of carcinogenicity. Are risk management considerations relevant to the determination of whether the substance should be labeled a carcinogen? For example, imagine that risk assessments undertaken with respect to two substances concluded that each had a 95 percent probability of carcinogenicity. Given a statutory framework requiring the banning of all substances identified as carcinogens, the consequences of labeling the first substance a carcinogen would be to impose debilitating costs on industry, whereas (given the existence of close substitutes) the consequences of labeling the second a carcinogen would be next to non-existent. Is it appropriate to factor into the risk assessment process this discrepancy in costs borne by industry? Would your answer change if the probability of carcinogenicity for each substance were 99 percent? What if it were 50 percent? If, like Ruckelshaus, you do not favor the consideration of social policy tradeoffs at the risk assessment stage, how else should these decisions be made?

For an argument that, in the face of scientific uncertainty, social policy considerations should inform the risk assessment process, see Howard A. Latin, *Good Science, Bad Regulation, and Toxic Risk Assessment*, 5 YALE J. ON REG. 89 (1988).

3. **Generic Policies.** Does Ruckelshaus's reliance upon generic cancer policies—which provide a general framework for making assumptions in the risk assessment process—serve to bolster the clear distinction he draws between risk assessment and risk management? In *Risk, Science, and Democracy*, Ruckelshaus advocates the use of generic policies in the face of uncertainty to reduce the politicization of risk assessments. How may this help resolve the tension inherent in the risk assessments of the two pollutants described above? Who does Ruckelshaus envisage setting these

policies? To what extent is the setting of these policies likely to be insulated from the political process? What problems may arise as a consequence of a reliance on general policies?

John Graham, Laura Green, and Marc Roberts are opposed to the broad adoption of generic policies, advocating instead the further tailoring of the risk assessment process to the characteristics of the chemical. JOHN D. GRAHAM ET AL., IN SEARCH OF SAFETY: CHEMICALS AND CANCER RISK (1988). They use the risk assessment of formaldehyde as a case study to highlight the policy choices that must be made in dose-response evaluation. The authors show that similar choices underlie other important components of the risk assessment process, such as the relationship between the dose administered in animal bioassays and the effective dose or dose actually reaching the target tissues. They come to two important conclusions. First, even the generic policies advocated by Ruckelshaus leave enormous room for policy judgments. Far from eliminating uncertainty, they shift it from more visible decisions, such as what model to use, to less visible ones. Second, the generic policies often lead to results inconsistent with the best scientific judgments.

Which position do you favor?

4.   Interaction Between Risk Assessors and Risk Managers. What degree of interaction do you consider appropriate between risk assessors and risk managers in the performance of their respective tasks? Should a risk manager inquire about the risk assessor's degree of confidence in making a particular finding? Conversely, is it appropriate for risk assessors to inquire about the costs of the regulation required in the event of a particular finding? Would Ruckelshaus find such interactions desirable? Is it likely that such interactions take place in federal regulatory agencies?

5.   Scientific Uncertainty. As Ruckelshaus notes, for many substances, there exists substantial scientific uncertainty concerning the relationship between exposure to the substance and the onset of adverse health effects. In the face of such uncertainty, there are two polar choices:

  (a)   not regulating until there is scientific certainty concerning this relationship; or

  (b)   regulating whenever there is at least some evidence linking the exposure to adverse health effects.

Adopting the former course of action means that, if the link is ultimately established, many individuals will have been exposed (perhaps for a period of several decades) to the risk. Conversely, following the latter course of action means that, if the substance is ultimately found to be benign, pollution control costs will have been incurred needlessly. What criteria should be used in deciding between the two courses of action? Is there an intermediate course of action that might be taken? *See* Al McGartland et al., *Estimating the Health Benefits of Environmental Regulations: Changes Needed for Complete Benefits Assessment*, 357 SCIENCE 457, 457–58 (2017). Who should make the decision about the circumstances in which regulation is appropriate?

6. Justifications for Negative Risk Assessments. Consider two possible reasons for not regulating a particular substance:

(a) the risks associated with the substance are insignificant; and

(b) the risks are significant but regulation would impose unacceptably high costs on industry.

Which reason will a decisionmaker want to give the public? Is it inevitable that the decisionmaker will seek to influence the risk assessment process so as to be able to give the first reason?

B. QUANTITATIVE RISK ASSESSMENT

Industrial Union Department, AFL-CIO v. American Petroleum Institute

448 U.S. 607 (1980).

■ JUSTICE STEVENS announced the judgment of the Court and delivered an opinion, in which THE CHIEF JUSTICE and JUSTICE STEWART joined and in Parts I, II, III-A, III-B, III-C and III-E of which JUSTICE POWELL joined:

. . . This litigation concerns a standard promulgated by the Secretary of Labor [pursuant to the Occupational Safety and Health Act] to regulate occupational exposure to benzene, a substance which has been shown to cause cancer at high exposure levels. The principal question is whether such a showing is a sufficient basis for a standard that places the most stringent limitation on exposure to benzene that is technologically and economically possible.

The Act delegates broad authority to the Secretary to promulgate different kinds of standards. The basic definition of an "occupational safety and health standard" is found in § 3(8), which provides:

"The term 'occupational safety and health standard' means a standard which requires conditions, or the adoption or use of one or more practices, means, methods, operations, or processes, reasonably necessary or appropriate to provide safe or healthful employment and places of employment." 84 Stat. 1591, 29 U.S.C. § 652(8).

Where toxic materials or harmful physical agents are concerned, a standard must also comply with § 6(b)(5), which provides:

"The Secretary, in promulgating standards dealing with toxic materials or harmful physical agents under this subsection, shall set the standard which most adequately assures, to the extent feasible, on the basis of the best available evidence, that no employee will suffer material impairment of health or functional capacity even if such employee has regular exposure to the hazard dealt with by such standard for the period of his working life. Development of standards under this subsection shall be based upon research, demonstrations, experiments, and such other information as may be appropriate. In addition to the attainment of the highest degree of health and safety protection for the employee, other considerations shall be the latest available scientific data in the field, the feasibility of the standards, and experience gained under this and other health and safety laws." 84 Stat. 1594, 29 U.S.C. § 655(b)(5).

Wherever the toxic material to be regulated is a carcinogen, the Secretary has taken the position that no safe exposure level can be determined and that § 6(b)(5) requires him to set an exposure limit at the lowest technologically feasible level that will not impair the viability of the industries regulated. In this case, after having determined that there is a causal connection between benzene and leukemia (a cancer of the white blood cells), the Secretary set an exposure limit on airborne concentrations of benzene of one part benzene per million parts of air (1 ppm). . . .

II.

. . . Any discussion of the 1 ppm exposure limit must, of course, begin with the Agency's rationale for imposing that limit. The written explanation of the standard fills 184 pages of the printed appendix. Much of it is devoted to a discussion of the voluminous evidence of the adverse effects of exposure to benzene at levels of concentration well above 10 ppm. This discussion demonstrates that there is ample justification for regulating occupational exposure to benzene and that the prior limit of 10 ppm, with a ceiling of 25 ppm (or a peak of 50 ppm) was reasonable. It does not, however, provide direct support for the Agency's conclusion that the limit should be reduced from 10 ppm to 1 ppm. . . .

. . . OSHA's rationale for lowering the permissible exposure limit to 1 ppm was based, not on any finding that leukemia has ever been caused by exposure to 10 ppm of benzene and that it will *not* be caused by exposure to 1 ppm, but rather on a series of assumptions indicating that some leukemias might result from exposure to 10 ppm and that the number of cases might be reduced by reducing the exposure level to 1 ppm. In reaching that result, the Agency first unequivocally concluded that benzene is a human carcinogen. Second, it concluded that industry had failed to prove that there is a safe threshold level of exposure to benzene below which no excess leukemia cases would occur. In reaching this conclusion OSHA rejected industry contentions that certain epidemiological studies indicating no excess risk of leukemia among workers exposed at levels below 10 ppm were sufficient to establish that the threshold level of safe exposure was at or above 10 ppm. It also rejected an industry witness' testimony that a dose-response curve could be constructed on the basis of the reported epidemiological studies and that this curve indicated that reducing the permissible exposure limit from 10 to 1 ppm would prevent at most one leukemia and one other cancer death every six years.

Third, the Agency applied its standard policy with respect to carcinogens, concluding that, in the absence of definitive proof of a safe level, it must be assumed that any level above zero presents *some* increased risk of cancer. As the federal parties point out in their brief, there are a number of scientists and public health specialists who subscribe to this view, theorizing that a susceptible person may contract cancer from the absorption of even one molecule of a carcinogen like benzene.

Fourth, the Agency reiterated its view of the Act, stating that it was required by § 6(b)(5) to set the standard either at the level that has been demonstrated to be safe or at the lowest level feasible, whichever is higher. If no safe level is established, as in this case, the Secretary's interpretation of the statute automatically leads to the selection of an exposure limit that is the lowest feasible. Because of benzene's importance to the economy, no one has ever suggested that it would be feasible to eliminate its use entirely, or to try to limit exposures to the small amounts that are omnipresent. Rather, the Agency selected 1 ppm as a workable exposure level and then determined that compliance with that level was technologically feasible and that "the economic impact of . . . [compliance] will not be such as to threaten the financial welfare of the affected firms or the general economy." 43 Fed. Reg. 5939 (1978). It therefore held that 1 ppm was the minimum feasible exposure level within the meaning of § 6(b)(5) of the Act.

Finally, although the Agency did not refer in its discussion of the pertinent legal authority to any duty to identify the anticipated benefits of the new standard, it did conclude that some benefits were likely to result from reducing the exposure limit from 10 ppm to 1 ppm. This conclusion was based, again, not on evidence, but rather on the assumption that the risk of leukemia will decrease as exposure levels decrease. Although the Agency had found it impossible to construct a dose-response curve that would predict with any accuracy the number of leukemias that could be expected to result from exposures at 10 ppm, at 1 ppm, or at any intermediate level, it nevertheless "determined that the benefits of the proposed standard are likely to be appreciable." 43 Fed. Reg. 5941 (1978). In light of the Agency's disavowal of any ability to determine the numbers of employees likely to be adversely affected by exposures of 10 ppm, the Court of Appeals held this finding to be unsupported by the record. 581 F.2d, at 503. . . .

III.

Our resolution of the issues in [this case] turns, to a large extent, on the meaning of and the relationship between § 3(8), which defines a health and safety standard as a standard that is "reasonably necessary and appropriate to provide safe or healthful employment," and § 6(b)(5), which directs the Secretary in promulgating a health and safety standard for toxic materials to "set the standard which most adequately assures, to the extent feasible, on the basis of the best available evidence, that no employee will suffer material impairment of health or functional capacity. . . ."

. . . [W]e think it is clear that § 3(8) does apply to all permanent standards promulgated under the Act and that it requires the Secretary, before issuing any standard, to determine that it is reasonably necessary and appropriate to remedy a significant risk of material health impairment. . . .

A.

Under the Government's view, § 3(8), if it has any substantive content at all, merely requires OSHA to issue standards that are reasonably calculated to produce a safer or more healthy work environment. Apart from this minimal requirement of rationality, the Government argues that § 3(8) imposes no limits on the Agency's power, and thus would not prevent it from requiring employers to do whatever would be "reasonably necessary" to eliminate all risks of any harm from their workplaces. With respect to toxic substances and harmful physical agents, the Government takes an even more extreme position. Relying on § 6(b)(5)'s direction to set a standard "which most adequately assures . . . that no employee will suffer material impairment of health or functional capacity," the Government contends that the Secretary is required to impose standards that either guarantee workplaces that are free from any risk of material health impairment, however small, or that come as close as possible to doing so without ruining entire industries.

If the purpose of the statute were to eliminate completely and with absolute certainty any risk of serious harm, we would agree that it would be proper for the Secretary to interpret §§ 3(8) and 6(b)(5) in this fashion. But we think it is clear that the statute was not designed to require employers to provide absolutely risk-free workplaces whenever it is technologically feasible to do so, so long as the cost is not great enough to destroy an entire industry. Rather, both the language and structure of the Act, as well as its legislative history, indicate that it was intended to require the elimination, as far as feasible, of significant risks of harm.

B.

By empowering the Secretary to promulgate standards that are "reasonably necessary or appropriate to provide safe or healthful employment and places of employment," the Act implies that, before promulgating any standard, the Secretary must make a finding that the workplaces in question are not safe. But "safe" is not the equivalent of "risk-free." There are many activities that we engage in every day—such as driving a car or even breathing city air—that entail some risk of accident or material health impairment; nevertheless, few people would consider these activities "unsafe." Similarly, a workplace can hardly be considered "unsafe" unless it threatens the workers with a significant risk of harm.

Therefore, before he can promulgate *any* permanent health or safety standard, the Secretary is required to make a threshold finding that a place of employment is unsafe—in the sense that significant risks are present and can be eliminated or lessened by a change in practices. This requirement applies to permanent standards promulgated pursuant to § 6(b)(5), as well as to other types of permanent standards. For there is no reason why § 3(8)'s definition of a standard should not be deemed incorporated by reference into § 6(b)(5). The standards promulgated pursuant to § 6(b)(5) are just one species of the genus of standards governed by the basic requirement. That section repeatedly uses the term "standard" without suggesting any exception from, or qualification of, the general definition; on the contrary, it directs the Secretary to select *"the* standard"—that is to say, one of various possible alternatives that satisfy the basic definition in § 3(8)—that is most protective. Moreover, requiring the Secretary to make a threshold finding of significant risk is consistent with the scope of the regulatory power granted to him by § 6(b)(5), which empowers the Secretary to promulgate standards, not for chemicals and physical agents generally, but for *"toxic* materials" and *"harmful* physical agents." . . .

In the absence of a clear mandate in the Act, it is unreasonable to assume that Congress intended to give the Secretary the unprecedented power over American industry that would result from the Government's view of §§ 3(8) and 6(b)(5), coupled with OSHA's cancer policy. Expert testimony that a substance is probably a human carcinogen—either because it has caused cancer in animals or because individuals have contracted cancer following extremely high exposures—would justify the conclusion that the substance poses some risk of serious harm no matter how minute the exposure and no matter how many experts testified that they regarded the risk as insignificant. That conclusion would in turn justify pervasive regulation limited only by the constraint of feasibility. In light of the fact that there are literally thousands of substances used in the workplace that have been identified as carcinogens or suspect carcinogens, the Government's theory would give OSHA power to impose enormous costs that might produce little, if any, discernible benefit. . . .

D.

Given the conclusion that the Act empowers the Secretary to promulgate health and safety standards only where a significant risk of harm exists, the critical issue becomes how to define and allocate the burden of proving the significance of the risk in a case such as this, where scientific knowledge is imperfect and the precise quantification of risks is therefore impossible. . . .

. . . As we read the statute, the burden was on the Agency to show, on the basis of substantial evidence, that it is at least more likely than not that long-term exposure to 10 ppm of benzene presents a significant risk of material health impairment. Ordinarily, it is the proponent of a rule or order who has the burden of proof in administrative proceedings.

In some cases involving toxic substances, Congress has shifted the burden of providing that a particular substance is safe onto the party opposing the proposed rule. The fact that Congress did not follow this course in enacting the Occupational Safety and Health Act indicates that it intended the Agency to bear the normal burden of establishing the need for a proposed standard.

In this case OSHA did not even attempt to carry its burden of proof. The closest it came to making a finding that benzene presented a significant risk of harm in the workplace was its statement that the benefits to be derived from lowering the permissible exposure level from 10 to 1 ppm were "likely" to be "appreciable." The Court of Appeals held that this finding was not supported by substantial evidence. Of greater importance, even if it were supported by substantial evidence, such a finding would not be sufficient to satisfy the Agency's obligations under the Act. . . .

Contrary to the Government's contentions, imposing a burden on the Agency of demonstrating a significant risk of harm will not strip it of its ability to regulate carcinogens, nor will it require the Agency to wait for deaths to occur before taking any action. First, the requirement that a "significant" risk be identified is not a mathematical straitjacket. It is the Agency's responsibility to determine, in the first instance, what it considers to be a "significant" risk. Some risks are plainly acceptable and others are plainly unacceptable. If, for example, the odds are one in a billion that a person will die from cancer by taking a drink of chlorinated water, the risk clearly could not be considered significant. On the other hand, if the odds are one in a thousand that regular inhalation of gasoline vapors that are 2% benzene will be fatal, a reasonable person might well consider the risk significant and take appropriate steps to decrease or eliminate it. Although the Agency has no duty to calculate the exact probability of harm, it does have an obligation to find that a significant risk is present before it can characterize a place of employment as "unsafe."

Second, OSHA is not required to support its finding that a significant risk exists with anything approaching scientific certainty. Although the Agency's findings must be supported by substantial evidence, § 6(b)(5) specifically allows the Secretary to regulate on the basis of the "best available evidence." As several Courts of Appeals have held, this provision requires a reviewing court to give OSHA some leeway where its findings must be made on the frontiers of scientific knowledge. Thus, so long as they are supported by a body of reputable scientific thought, the Agency is free to use conservative assumptions in interpreting the data with respect to carcinogens, risking error on the side of overprotection rather than underprotection. . . .

■ JUSTICE MARSHALL, with whom JUSTICE BRENNAN, JUSTICE WHITE, and JUSTICE BLACKMUN join, dissenting:

. . . In these circumstances, the Secretary's decision was reasonable and in full conformance with the statutory language requiring that he "set the standard which most adequately assures, to the extent feasible, on the basis of the best available evidence, that no employee will suffer material impairment of health or functional capacity even if such employee has regular exposure to the hazard dealt with by such standard for the period of his working life." 29 U.S.C. § 655(b)(5). On this record, the Secretary could conclude that regular exposure above the 1 ppm level would pose a definite risk resulting in material impairment to some indeterminate but possibly substantial number of employees. Studies revealed hundreds of deaths attributable to benzene exposure. Expert after expert testified that no safe level of exposure had been shown and that the extent of the risk declined with the exposure level. There was some direct evidence of incidence of leukemia, nonmalignant blood disorders, and chromosomal damage at exposure levels of 10 ppm and below. Moreover, numerous experts testified that existing evidence required an inference that an exposure level above 1 ppm was hazardous. We have stated that "well-reasoned expert testimony—based on what is known and uncontradicted by empirical evidence—may in and of itself be 'substantial evidence' when first-hand evidence on the question . . . is unavailable." *FPC v. Florida Power & Light Co.*, 404 U.S. 453, 464–465 (1972). Nothing in the Act purports to prevent the Secretary from acting when definitive information as to the quantity of a standard's benefits is unavailable. Where, as here, the deficiency in knowledge relates to the extent of the benefits rather than their existence, I see no reason to hold that the Secretary has exceeded his statutory authority.

The plurality avoids this conclusion through reasoning that may charitably be described as obscure. According to the plurality, the definition of occupational safety and health standards as those "reasonably necessary or appropriate to provide safe or healthful . . . working conditions" requires the Secretary to show that it is "more likely than not" that the risk he seeks to regulate is a "significant" one. The plurality does not show how this requirement can be plausibly derived from the "reasonably necessary or appropriate" clause. Indeed, the plurality's reasoning is refuted by the Act's language, structure, and legislative history, and it is foreclosed by every applicable guide to statutory construction. In short, the plurality's standard is a fabrication bearing no connection with the acts or intentions of Congress.

At the outset, it is important to observe that "reasonably necessary or appropriate" clauses are routinely inserted in regulatory legislation, and in the past such clauses have uniformly been interpreted as general provisos that regulatory actions must bear a reasonable relation to those statutory purposes set forth in the statute's substantive provisions. The Court has never—until today—interpreted a "reasonably necessary or appropriate" clause as having a substantive content that supersedes a specific congressional directive embodied in a provision that is focused more particularly on an agency's authority. This principle, of course, reflects the common understanding that the determination of whether regulations are "reasonably necessary" may be made only by reference to the legislative judgment reflected in the statute; it must not be based on a court's own, inevitably subjective view of what steps should be taken to promote perceived statutory goals.

The plurality suggests that under the "reasonably necessary" clause, a workplace is not "unsafe" unless the Secretary is able to convince a reviewing court that a "significant" risk is at issue. That approach is particularly embarrassing in this case, for it is contradicted by the plain language of the Act. The plurality's interpretation renders utterly superfluous the first sentence of § 655(b)(5), which, as noted above, requires the Secretary to set the standard "which most adequately assures . . . that no employee will suffer material impairment of health." Indeed, the plurality's interpretation reads that sentence out of the Act. By so doing, the plurality makes the test for standards regulating toxic substances and harmful physical agents substantially identical to the test for standards generally—plainly the opposite of what Congress intended. And it is an odd canon of construction that would insert in a vague and general definitional clause a threshold requirement that overcomes the specific language placed in a standard-setting provision. . . .

The plurality's interpretation of the "reasonably necessary or appropriate" clause is also conclusively refuted by the legislative history. While the standard-setting provision that the plurality ignores received extensive legislative attention, the definitional clause received *none at all*. An earlier version of the Act did not embody a clear feasibility constraint and was not restricted to toxic substances or to "material" impairments. The "reasonably necessary or appropriate" clause was contained in this prior version of the bill, as it was at all relevant times. In debating this version, Members of Congress repeatedly expressed concern that it would require a risk-free universe. The definitional clause was not mentioned at all, an omission that would be incomprehensible if Congress intended by that clause to require the Secretary to quantify the risk he sought to regulate in order to demonstrate that it was "significant." . . .

. . . Because the approach taken by the plurality is so plainly irreconcilable with the Court's proper institutional role, I am certain that it will not stand the test of time. In all likelihood, today's decision will come to be regarded as an extreme reaction to a regulatory scheme that, as the Members of the plurality perceived it, imposed an unduly harsh burden on regulated industries. But as the Constitution "does not enact Mr. Herbert Spencer's Social Statics," *Lochner v. New York*, 198 U.S. 45, 75 (1905) (Holmes, J., dissenting), so the responsibility to scrutinize federal administrative action does not authorize this Court to strike its own balance between the costs and benefits of occupational safety standards. I am confident that the approach taken by the plurality today, like that in *Lochner* itself, will eventually be abandoned, and that the representative branches of government will once again be allowed to determine the level of safety and health protection to be accorded to the American worker.

NOTES AND QUESTIONS

1. **Non-Delegation Doctrine.** Justice Rehnquist concurred with the judgment—albeit on different grounds—expressing the opinion that ". . . Congress, the governmental body best suited and most obligated to make the choice confronting us in this litigation, has improperly delegated that choice to the Secretary of Labor and, derivatively, to this Court." *Id.* at 671. Justice Rehnquist considered

> [t]he decision whether the law of diminishing returns should have any place in the regulation of toxic substances is quintessentially one of legislative policy. For Congress to pass that decision on to the Secretary in the manner it did violates, in my mind, John Locke's caveat . . . that legislatures are to make laws, not legislators.

Id. Do you agree with Justice Rehnquist's assessment that "[it would be] difficult to imagine a more obvious example of Congress simply avoiding a choice which was both fundamental for purposes of the statute and yet politically so divisive that the necessary decision or compromise was difficult, if not impossible, to hammer out in the legislative forge"? What could be the impact of this approach on other statutes?

Despite Justice Rehnquist's attempts to revive the non-delegation doctrine in *Benzene*, the doctrine has not been invoked by the Supreme Court as the basis for holding a statute unconstitutional since 1935. Following *Whitman v. American Trucking Associations*, 531 U.S. 457 (2001) (discussed in Chapter V), it appears that the non-delegation doctrine will not be a fruitful avenue for challenging legislation that delegates authority to federal agencies.

2. **Divided Court.** In a portion of the case not excerpted above, Justice Powell concurred in part and concurred in the judgment, but refrained from joining Part III-D of the plurality opinion (addressing whether OSHA had attempted to carry its burden of proof on the question of whether exposure to benzene at 10 ppm presents a significant risk of material health impairment). Instead, Justice Powell considered the determinative question to be whether OSHA had successfully carried its burden on the basis of record evidence. In concluding that it had not, Justice Powell found that there was insufficient information to support OSHA's determination that the available quantification techniques were too imprecise and that OSHA's finding of significant risks at current exposure levels was not supported by substantial evidence. *Id.* at 646. Given that the opinion of Justice Stevens was not supported by a majority of the Court, what is the holding of the case?

3.   Question of Interpretation. In distinguishing between the holdings of the plurality and the dissent, evaluate first what is not in dispute. Consider the steps underpinning the dissenting opinion. First, the Agency acted properly in finding that benzene is a carcinogen and that there does not exist a threshold level below which there would be no adverse human health effects. Second, for the purposes of § 6(b)(5), the standard that would "most adequately assure" that no employee would suffer material impairment from benzene would be 0 ppm. Finally, a standard promulgated at the level at which the Agency considered "feasible" for the purposes of § 6(b)(5)—1 ppm—would not result in the collapse of industry. Do the Justices in the plurality adopt a different approach to these matters?

If these matters are not in dispute, why would the dissent have upheld OSHA's regulation, whereas the plurality struck it down? The answer lies, in part, in the differing interpretations of the OSH Act. What roles do §§ 3(8) and 6(b)(5) play under the dissenting opinion? What roles do these sections play under the plurality opinion? Do you agree that § 3(8) should be considered to contain threshold requirements (in keeping with the plurality's preferred interpretation)?

In *Chevron v. NRDC*, 467 U.S. 837 (1984), decided four years after the *Benzene* case, the Supreme Court adopted a deferential attitude toward an agency's interpretation of its own statutory mandate. Do you think the *Benzene* case would have been decided differently post-*Chevron*?

4.   Toward Quantitative Risk Assessment. The plurality explicitly recognized that "[t]he Agency had found it impossible to construct a dose-response curve that would predict with any accuracy the number of leukemias that could be expected to result from exposures at 10 ppm, at 1 ppm, or at any intermediate level." Why then was the plurality unwilling to accept the Agency's conclusion that "the benefits of the proposed standard are likely to be appreciable"?

After *Benzene*, what information is necessary to pass judicial review on a subsequent challenge to a permissible exposure limit (PEL)? Consider the following passage from the plurality opinion (not excerpted above):

> OSHA's comments with respect to the insufficiency of the data were addressed primarily to the lack of data at low exposure levels. OSHA did not discuss whether it was possible to make a rough estimate, based on the more complete epidemiological and animal studies done at higher exposure levels, of the significance of the risks attributable to those levels, nor did it discuss whether it was possible to extrapolate from such estimates to derive a risk estimate for low-level exposures.

448 U.S. at 632. How should OSHA have sought to support its findings of significance?

5.   Fate of the *Benzene* Regulations. Following the *Benzene* case, OSHA did not take immediate steps in formulating substitute standards. It was not until 1984, in response to a petition filed by labor organizations (seeking that OSHA be compelled to promulgate a new standard to fill the void created in the wake of the *Benzene* case) that the second rulemaking was initiated. In

1985, OSHA set forth a proposal for a rulemaking to modify the benzene standard within 14 months. In September 1987, OSHA issued the present rule for benzene regulation. Ironically, this standard provides similar protections to those struck down by the *Benzene* Court—most notably, the PEL for occupational exposure to benzene is set at 1 ppm with a short-term exposure limit of 5 ppm. The rule has not been subject to any further judicial scrutiny. For a detailed description of the history of benzene regulation in the United States and abroad, see Ilise L. Feitshans, *Law and Regulation of Benzene*, 82 ENVTL. HEALTH PERSP. 299 (1989).

Alon Rosenthal, George M. Gray & John D. Graham, Legislating Acceptable Cancer Risk from Exposure to Toxic Chemicals
19 ECOLOGY L.Q. 269 (1992).*

EPA uses risk assessment to predict the probability of developing cancer as a result of exposure to a particular agent. As currently practiced, risk assessment of a carcinogen takes place in four steps: hazard identification, dose-response evaluation, exposure assessment, and risk characterization.

The first step, hazard identification, is the process of determining whether an "agent" (for example, an industrial chemical, a natural product in the environment, or a particular lifestyle) increases a person's risk of developing cancer. The second step, dose-response evaluation, reveals how the likelihood of cancer changes with the level of exposure. A risk assessor might estimate, for example, how the probability of lung cancer changes with the number of cigarettes smoked. The third step, exposure assessment, quantifies the amount, or dose, of the carcinogen to which people may be exposed. This may be the amount of a chemical in the air near a factory, the concentration of radon in the basement of a home, or the amounts of various foods and beverages which an individual consumes each day.

After these quantitative inputs to a risk assessment have been determined, the numbers are combined to yield an overall estimate of risk, the basic component of the final step, risk characterization. A risk characterization is usually expressed numerically as the incremental lifetime risk of cancer due to a particular agent at a particular level of exposure (also referred to as an incremental risk). This is the number that a risk manager might compare to a legislated bright line. Good risk characterizations contain not only a final risk number but also a discussion of the uncertainties in and the assumptions behind the assessment, but unfortunately this step is rarely taken. . . .

Hazard Identification

The most definitive way to determine whether a compound can cause human cancer is through the science of epidemiology. Cancer epidemiology attempts to establish associations between human exposure to a suspected cancer causing agent and the frequency of cancer in the human population. The major drawback of epidemiological studies is that they cannot measure risks before those who are exposed develop cancer, but merely identify effects which have already occurred. Risk managers want to identify human carcinogens before cancer develops, before they can be discovered by epidemiology.

Furthermore, cancer epidemiology is fraught with interpretive difficulty. Cancer is a disease with a long latency period that arises from many causes, only some of which are known. Human exposures to potential carcinogens are often complex, uncertain, and poorly documented. If exposures are mismeasured, the epidemiologist will have a difficult time detecting any association between exposure and disease, even if one exists. Moreover, epidemiological studies are often plagued by confounding factors, such as smoking, by a lack of suitable control groups, and by alternative interpretations of data. Due to practical limitations on the size of studies and the large background risk of cancer, epidemiologists usually cannot detect modest cancer risks that would still be of concern to risk managers. While some epidemiological studies of animal carcinogens have been "negative," this may simply reflect the inadequate sample sizes in these studies. When epidemiologists do detect human cancer risks, they usually do so in occupational settings where historical levels of exposure have been quite high. If findings from the workplace are to be extrapolated to environmental settings, epidemiologists must resolve uncertainties about how to extrapolate tumors observed at relatively high doses to the tumors that might occur at low levels of environmental exposure.

Credible epidemiological studies, especially several showing the same positive result, are considered adequate evidence of human carcinogenicity. Such results are difficult to obtain except when studying very potent carcinogens or carcinogens which cause an unusual type of tumor. For example, epidemiological studies identified vinyl chloride as a human carcinogen because it causes liver angiosarcoma, an extremely rare type of tumor. By contrast, there is little consensus within the scientific community on how much weight to give negative epidemiological reports, or on how to resolve controversies when there are both positive and negative epidemiological studies of a compound. As a result, fewer than sixty chemicals and mixtures have been identified as known human carcinogens.

In light of the limits of epidemiology and the need to identify hazards before they cause serious harm, scientists have resorted to animal experiments in an effort to identify agents that are potential human carcinogens. The key laboratory test used in hazard identification is the long-term rodent bioassay, which is conducted on the assumption that a rodent carcinogen may also be a human carcinogen. In addition, laboratory tests of the biological properties of chemicals provide information which can help scientists assess a chemical's potential for human carcinogenicity.

The National Toxicology Program (the NTP) of the U.S. Department of Health and Human Services has established rigorous guidelines for the conduct of rodent carcinogen bioassays. Under the NTP's guidelines, a researcher must expose fifty animals of each sex of two species (usually rats and mice) to several dose levels of the suspected carcinogen for virtually their entire lives. The dose levels selected are the maximum tolerated dose (the MTD) and fractions thereof, usually MTD/2 or MTD/4. The MTD is the highest dose that the animals can tolerate without becoming so sick that the test will not be useful in detecting tumors. High dose levels are chosen to compensate for the small number of rodents, which are expensive to house and feed. Since most bioassays are performed with only fifty animals at each dose level, the animals must be given the highest dose that they can tolerate if the researchers are to maximize their chances of seeing a statistically significant response. However, the small number of animals used greatly limits the sensitivity of the assay. For example, if a dose of a carcinogen causes an increased cancer risk of one in 100 in a rodent's lifetime, it is unlikely to be detected in a cohort of fifty rodents.

Tumors observed at the MTD are considered relevant on the theory that cancer is a disease that can be caused by a single molecule of a carcinogen interacting with the DNA in a single cell, and therefore, the response of a carcinogen at the MTD can be extrapolated to the much lower levels of exposure that humans experience. However, there is controversy within the scientific community about whether results from rodent bioassays performed at or near the MTD are applicable to the much lower level of exposure typically faced by humans.

Several hundred compounds have been shown to cause cancer in animal tests. The usefulness of these studies in predicting human carcinogenicity depends on the accuracy of certain assumptions. These include the assumption that humans respond in a similar manner to rodents; the assumption that results of exposure to high doses over the relatively short lifetimes of animals are functionally equivalent to the results of exposure to low doses over human lifetimes; and the assumption that cross-species scaling methods accurately extrapolate doses given to small test animals to reflect comparable human doses. These assumptions are hotly contested within the scientific and regulatory communities, but a frequently stated rationale is that, while they may not be accurate, they are conservative—reliance upon them will minimize the chance that a carcinogen will be falsely exonerated. On the other hand, carcinogens are unlikely to be classified as carcinogens until enough high-quality, large-sample testing has been done in a variety of rodent strains and species to reveal their carcinogenic activity. . . .

Dose-Response Evaluation

Once a carcinogenic hazard has been identified, the second step in assessing cancer risks is the determination of the relationship between the dose of the agent and the probability of developing cancer. We will discuss dose response analysis of both carcinogens and noncarcinogens, since some scientists believe that, contrary to current agency practice, a similar method should be used to assess both types of toxic responses.

Toxicologists have for many years engaged in efforts to determine what dose of a chemical is safe and what is harmful. The data they have discovered describing these dose-response relationships have been used in occupational health, environmental protection, and medicine to protect people from the toxic effects of chemicals. Central to these efforts to determine a safe level of exposure is the concept of a response threshold.

The threshold is the dose of the toxicant below which no adverse effects will occur. Above the threshold, adverse effects do occur. There are two types of thresholds: population and individual. A population threshold is the dose of a compound below which absolutely no one in the population will show a response. An individual threshold is the dose below which an individual will not have a response. Individual thresholds vary from person to person and from toxin to toxin. The population threshold can be thought of as the threshold for the most sensitive individual in the population.

The dose-response relationship for a chemical is usually determined by tests on rodents, exposing them to a variety of doses of the compound and observing any toxic responses. The lowest dose producing an adverse effect on the animals is called the lowest observable adverse effect level (LOAEL), and the next tested dose below the LOAEL is called the no observable adverse effect level (NOAEL). The threshold dose in the experiments, then, is assumed to be somewhere between the LOAEL and the NOAEL, although its actual value is unknown.

When the rodent dose-response relationship is used to establish safe human doses, the NOAEL is divided by a safety factor. This safety factor accounts for potential differences in human and rodent response, protects potentially sensitive segments of the human population, and accounts for lack of knowledge of human response when there is little or no human data. The safety factor is usually 100 or 1000, which means that toxicologists set the safe level of exposure for humans at 1/100 or 1/1000 of the animal NOAEL.

Dose-response evaluation for carcinogens differs from that used in traditional toxicology. With suspected carcinogens, the threshold concept is essentially discarded—the threshold dose below which no risk may be seen is assumed to be zero. The no-threshold model, which is prominently used in cancer risk assessment, postulates that cancer can arise from a single change to the DNA of a single cell. In other words, theoretically, a single molecule of a carcinogen has some nonzero probability of causing cancer. For this reason, assessors of cancer risk assume that any dose of a carcinogen, however small, increases the probability of tumor formation.

Further complications arise in collecting and interpreting data from rodent tests of carcinogenicity. Chemicals may exhibit carcinogenic activity in some rodent species but not in others. The same chemical may even test positive in one strain of rats while testing negative in another strain of rats. Pathologists may disagree about the classification of tumors, especially when hyperplasia (a pretumor condition), benign tumors, and malignant tumors must be distinguished. Chemicals may cause tumors in one or more sites in the rodent's body which have no obvious human counterpart.

Scientists must make judgment calls to complete a dose-response evaluation of any particular animal carcinogen. The important judgments include (a) which set of animal data (e.g. which animal species response from which bioassay) to use in the modeling process; (b) which tumor types (e.g., benign and/or malignant) and tumor sites (e.g., liver and/or Zymbal gland) in the animal to count; (c) how to extrapolate the high-dose findings from animal bioassays or occupational epidemiology to the low doses humans encounter in daily life; and (d) how to scale the doses between species, adjust for different routes of exposure (e.g., ingestion in animals versus inhalation in humans), and account for variable durations or patterns of exposure. None of these judgments can currently be resolved solely on the basis of science. In the face of this uncertainty, agency scientists make quasi-policy judgments that reflect values about how protective or conservative they should be.

Perhaps the most contentious judgment in carcinogen risk assessment is how to extend the dose-response curve from the high doses to which animals are exposed in the laboratory to the lower doses to which humans are exposed in the environment. There are several well-known statistical models for fitting the animal data and extrapolating the dose-response curve to low doses. Often each model will fit the experimental animal data quite well and have at least some plausible basis in biology. The models nonetheless may yield low-dose risk estimates for the same chemical or even from the same data set, that vary enormously, by factors of hundreds or even of thousands.

As a default position based primarily on policy considerations, EPA requires use of the linearized multistage (LMS) model in all risk assessments. Agency risk assessors can choose another model only if there is persuasive evidence to support their choice; EPA guidelines do not indicate what sort of evidence would be persuasive. EPA favors the LMS model because it is generally considered to be a conservative method of estimating low-dose risks. Among biologically plausible models, few produce higher estimates of risks than does the LMS model. Scientists derive the critical low-dose potency parameter, the so-called q_1^*, by applying LMS to the tumor incidence data in rodents. The q_1^* is the upper ninety-five percent confidence limit on the linear term of the dose-response function. This linear term is produced by the LMS model's linearization of the data: the model assumes that the dose-response relationship is linear at low doses, regardless of the shape of the dose-response curve within the range of tested doses. The q_1^*, which EPA calls the "cancer potency factor" (the CPF), is an estimate of the carcinogenic strength of a compound based on the LMS model. The cancer potency factor reflects the fact that not all carcinogenic agents are equal; CPF's differ by factors of as much as a million. . . .

Exposure Assessment

Exposure assessment is the phase of a risk assessment that determines just how much exposure to a carcinogen people actually confront. Exposure can occur through a variety of routes, including inhalation, dermal absorption, and ingestion of contaminated food or water. While some sources of pollution cause human exposure through more than one such pathway, EPA risk assessments do not always consider this possibility. More recent risk assessments, however, indicate a trend to account for as many sources and routes of exposure as possible.

Exposure assessment permits evaluation of two risk parameters: population risk (incidence) and maximum individual risk (MIR). Population risk is the traditional public health measure that reports the number of cases of disease in the population attributable to a specific source or contaminant. The person at maximum individual risk is the individual who suffers the largest incremental risk due to a particular source or contaminant. In theory, the MIR should reflect scientific information about variability in human exposure and sensitivity to chemical carcinogens.

Since little is known about which people are most sensitive to chemical carcinogens, EPA usually assumes that the person at MIR is the maximally exposed individual (the MEI). The MEI is the (usually hypothetical) person expected to receive the greatest lifetime exposure from a particular source. The MEI may be the resident living closest to a factory that emits the suspected carcinogen, or the resident who draws his or her drinking water from the well closest to a Superfund site that is leaking a suspected carcinogen.

EPA generally uses predictive models, rather than direct measurements, to calculate the exposure of the MEI. In the case of a resident at a factory fenceline, a mathematical dispersion model might estimate the air concentration of the carcinogen 200 meters from the source (EPA typically assumes in such scenarios that the fenceline, and the residence of the MEI, are 200 meters from the source). In addition, the models often assume that the MEI is outdoors breathing air at this predicted concentration twenty-four hours a day for seventy years.

Although no one spends his or her entire life outdoors at the fenceline of the factory, and although few factories produce the same products, or even exist, for seventy years, the MEI calculation is designed to be conservative. By overstating probable actual exposure, it provides a safety margin, giving an upper bound on the true lifetime exposure.

Use of the hypothetical MEI to set standards is extremely controversial. Critics of MEI-based standards argue that it is unsound to regulate, often at very great cost, on the basis of an inflated exposure scenario that never occurs. Supporters argue that highly exposed people, even if they are few in number, have a right to protection, and that the conservatism in MEI scenarios may be appropriate given the other uncertainties in risk assessment. . . .

Risk Characterization

When a risk assessor has the three important pieces of information—an identified hazard, an estimate of the dose-response relationship q_1*, and estimates of exposure (or dose)—he or she can make a numerical estimate of risk. Essentially all the assessor does is multiply the q_1* the cancer potency factor derived from the LMS procedure, by the measured or predicted exposure. The q_1* is usually expressed in units of increased lifetime probability of cancer per milligram of carcinogen per kilogram of body weight per day of exposure, and the exposure is expressed in units of milligrams of carcinogen per kilogram of body weight per day. The calculation therefore leads to an estimate of the increase in the lifetime probability of cancer from the particular level of exposure. For a properly performed risk-characterization, this number is only the beginning.

The meaning of EPA's risk estimates cannot be accurately conveyed except in light of the numerous assumptions that have been made. As two commentators have stated, risk estimates from analyses done according to EPA procedures "do not give certainty in the scientific sense, nor can they be used to establish precise numbers of persons who will be stricken with some disease." However, the number that comes from the risk characterization step is often reported and used without qualification. Advocates of risk assessment constantly call for analysts to quantify and report the full range of uncertainty in a risk assessment. In fact, because of the numerous conservative assumptions built into the EPA risk assessment process (so-called "compounded conservatism"), EPA has stated that a risk estimate produced in accord with its procedures should be regarded as a plausible upper bound on risk. That is, the actual risk will almost certainly lie somewhere between the EPA risk estimate and zero. The actual risk is very unlikely to be greater than the EPA risk estimate, is probably lower than the EPA estimate, and may even be zero.

Therefore, EPA states that, in addition to the risk number, a risk characterization should contain: (a) a discussion of the "weight of the evidence" for human carcinogenicity (e.g., the EPA carcinogen classification); (b) a summary of the various sources of uncertainty in the risk estimate, including those arising from hazard identification, dose-response evaluation, and exposure assessment; and (c) a report of the range of risk using EPA's risk estimate as the upper limit and zero as the lower limit.

NOTES AND QUESTIONS

1.   **Issues in the Risk Assessment of Potential Carcinogens.** Consider the following issues regarding the risk assessment of potential carcinogens:

   (a)   Should negative epidemiological evidence of carcinogenicity be disregarded in light of positive evidence from long-term animal bioassays?

   (b)   Should benign tumors be aggregated with malignant tumors to determine the dose-response relationship?

   (c)   What models should be used to extrapolate from high doses to low doses?

   (d)   What models should be used to extrapolate from rodents to human beings?

   (e)   How should inconsistent results in different species of rodents be treated?

There is no scientific consensus on these issues. How should a regulator reach a decision? For each issue, should a regulator always make a conservative assumption?

2.   **Manmade v. Naturally Occurring Carcinogens.** There is increasing evidence that the typical human diet naturally contains many substances that have been found to be carcinogenic in animals. In fact, some of these naturally occurring carcinogens are thought to be considerably more potent than carcinogens that are subject to regulation, at least based on animal bioassays. For example, peanut butter is a more potent rodent carcinogen than DDT (dichloro-diphenyl-trichloroethane), a pesticide that has been banned in the United States based on evidence of its carcinogenicity. *See* Bruce N. Ames et al., *Ranking Possible Carcinogenic Hazards*, 236 SCIENCE 271 (1987). Does comparing potency of manmade and naturally occurring animal carcinogens simply highlight the concern with extrapolating harms from high doses into low-dose scenarios? Or, rather, does it suggest that too little attention is devoted to understanding naturally occurring carcinogens? All else equal, should we be more concerned with manmade carcinogens over naturally occurring ones?

3.   Distinguishing Between Scientific and Policy Decisions in Dose-Response Evaluation.

Figure II.1.

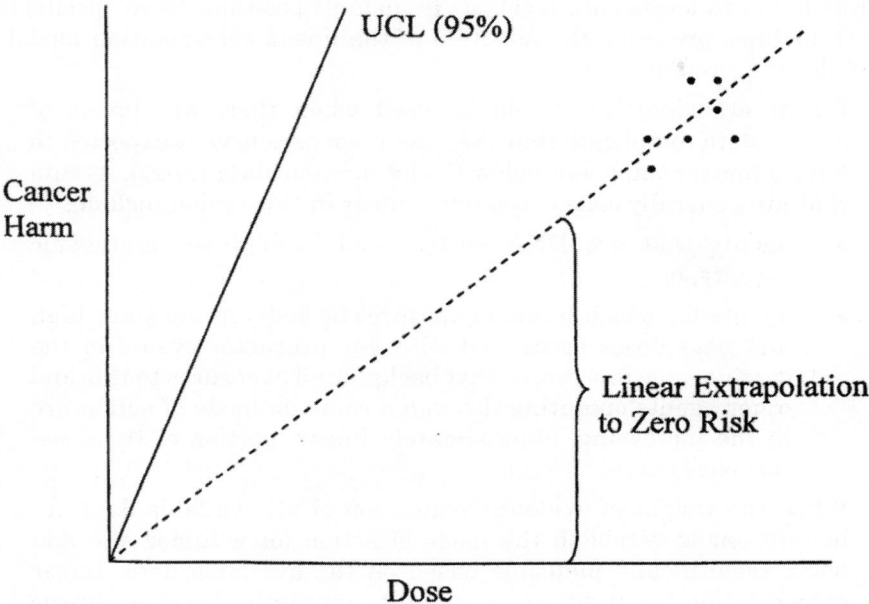

Above is a representation of a typical dose-response curve for a carcinogen. The data points in the upper-right of the graph represent observed responses from laboratory toxicological tests. In extrapolating from observed data to human responses at lower exposure levels, risk assessors must make several assumptions. First, an assumption must be made as to where to place the point at which there is no human harm: at zero (a no-threshold contaminant) or some higher dose (a threshold contaminant). Second, risk assessors must decide what type of relationship exists between the dose and the response and what curve best represents that relationship—linear, convex, or concave. Finally, they must decide the breadth of confidence they have in their extrapolation. The figure above depicts a no-threshold contaminant, a linear does-response relationship, and a 95 percent upper confidence level (UCL).

Which of these decisions are based on scientific analysis and which are based on policy determinations? What types of scientific analyses are they based on? Which are a combination of the two? Which experts are best suited to making these decisions?

4.   Default Assumptions Under EPA's Guidelines. As noted by Rosenthal, Gray, and Graham, EPA's Guidelines establish a number of default assumptions to guide risk assessments in the absence of observable data. One such assumption is that chemical carcinogens exhibit risks at any dose. *See* EPA, GUIDELINES FOR CARCINOGEN RISK ASSESSMENT (2005). This no-threshold presumption is inherently conservative. It is based on the theory that a susceptible person can contract cancer from the absorption of a single molecule of a carcinogenic substance.

In addition, EPA's Guidelines also require that the agency adopt linear extrapolation to lower dose levels as its default position. More specifically, the Guidelines prescribe the adoption of the linear extrapolation model in the following circumstances:

> *Linear extrapolation* should be used when there are [mode of action] data to indicate that the dose-response curve is expected to have a linear component below the [observable data range]. Agents that are generally considered to be linear in this region include:
>
> - agents that are DNA-reactive and have direct mutagenic activity, or
>
> - agents for which human exposures or body burdens are high and near doses associated with key precursor events in the carcinogenic process, so that background exposures to this and other agents operating through a common mode of action are in the increasing, approximately linear, portion of the dose-response curve.
>
> When the weight of evidence evaluation of all available data are insufficient to establish the mode of action for a tumor site and when scientifically plausible based on the available data, linear extrapolation is used as a default approach, because linear extrapolation generally is considered to be a health-protective approach. Nonlinear approaches generally should not be used in cases where [the relationship between the carcinogen and human health] has not been ascertained. Where alternative approaches with significant biological support are available for the same tumor response and no scientific consensus favors a single approach, an assessment may present results based on more than one approach.

Id. at 3–21. The Guidelines do not require, however, that the dose response be linear at high-dose levels in circumstances where more reliable data is available.

5. Nonparametric Dose-Response Estimation. A variety of parametric models might operate well at high doses near the range of observed outcomes, but these models sometimes produce wildly different results when extrapolated to low-dose scenarios using the same set of data. One alternative to explicitly choosing a type of dose-response relationship (such as linear) is nonparametric estimation, where a functional form for the relationship isn't specified beforehand. Generally speaking, a great deal of data is needed for reliable nonparametric estimation because the data also supplies the structure of the model. *See* Walter W. Piegorsch et al., *Nonparametric Estimation of Benchmark Doses in Environmental Risk Assessment*, 23 ENVIRONMETRICS 717 (2012). In practice, however, resource constraints or animal-welfare concerns might restrict the number of doses and the number of subjects per dose that make up the observed data. In light of such realities, how useful is nonparametric dose-response estimation in solving the extrapolation problems that stem from choosing the parametric model form? How should regulators make tradeoffs between resource constraints, ethical concerns, and model reliability?

6.   Distortions of Conservatism. Rosenthal, Gray, and Graham's article states that plausible models used to extrapolate from high doses to low doses may lead to estimates that vary by factors of hundreds or even thousands. Justice Breyer reports in his book *Breaking the Vicious Circle: Toward Effective Risk Regulation* that "[t]wo scientifically plausible models for the risk associated with aflatoxin in peanuts or grain may show risk levels differing by a factor of 40,000." STEVEN BREYER, BREAKING THE VICIOUS CIRCLE: TOWARD EFFECTIVE RISK REGULATION 47 (1993). He further reports that, according to the Office of Management and Budget (OMB), agencies "often overstate risks by factors of a thousand or even a million or more" because they pile conservative assumption upon conservative assumption. *Id.* In light of these disparities, is risk assessment at all useful? How should we address this problem?

A separate concern arises when there are differences in the degree of conservatism across different agencies and types of risk, which could distort priorities and may result in lower overall safety. To illustrate this, suppose there are two competing pesticides, A and B, and the true carcinogenic risk of A is twice that of B. But because of different degrees of conservativism in risk assessment—for example, A might be naturally occurring while B might be manmade—B's risk is estimated to be higher than A's risk. Policy makers are likely to conclude that B deserves more stringent control than A, when in fact the reverse is true. What effect would this strategy have on overall risk? For a discussion of this and other potential distortions caused by using conservative estimates in risk assessment, see Albert L. Nichols & Richard J. Zeckhauser, *The Perils of Prudence: How Conservative Risk Assessments Distort Regulation*, 10 REG. 13 (1986). Could uniform guidelines across agencies and across risks mitigate some of these concerns?

7.   Is "Conservative" Too Stringent? While regulatory agencies have frequently faced the criticism that conservative assumptions inexorably lead to regulations that are too stringent, the use of conservative assumptions for some parameters of a risk assessment do not *necessarily* lead to this result. *See* Adam M. Finkel, *Is Risk Assessment Really Too Conservative: Revising the Revisionists*, 14 COLUM. J. ENVTL. L. 427 (1989). First, choosing the most conservative of several options does not mean that the option chosen is biased upwards. *Id.* at 441–42. Second, not all choices made in a risk assessment will be conservative and different choices may have offsetting effects. *Id.* at 443–47. More generally, using conservative parameters in a risk assessment may correct for systematic defects or biases in other parts of the regulatory process. The risk assessment itself may omit pathways for human exposure or contain other flaws. *Id.* at 449–54. Regulatory steps after the risk assessment may be biased towards less stringent regulation, notably the estimation of costs. *Id.* at 457–59. In the absence of a systematic answer to all of these questions, is there independent value to risk assessments that are more accurate?

8.   Distributional Consequences of Exposure Assessment. Which measure of exposure assessment is more relevant for risk assessment:

population risk or maximum individual risk? Which measure should be used for risk management decisions? What are the possible distributional effects of ignoring maximum individual risk? Environmental justice advocates criticize risk assessment on the basis that it focuses on relatively small risks to large populations rather than on large risks to smaller sub-populations (such as minority and low-income communities). *See, e.g.,* Clifford Rechtschaffen & Eileen Guana, *Risk Assessment, in* ENVIRONMENTAL JUSTICE: LAW, POLICY & REGULATION 87–105 (2002); Carl F. Cranor, *Risk Assessment, Susceptible Subpopulations, and Environmental Justice, in* THE LAW OF ENVIRONMENTAL JUSTICE: THEORIES AND PROCEDURES TO ADDRESS DISPROPORTIONATE RISKS 307–56 (1999). *But see* W. KIP VISCUSI, PRICING LIVES: GUIDEPOSTS FOR A SAFER SOCIETY 153–59 (2018) (arguing that systematically ignoring the size of exposed populations is likely to disadvantage minorities and low-income groups that are likely to live in large population centers).

9. Issues in the Risk Assessment of Potential Carcinogens Revisited. Revisit questions 1–6 that follow the article by William Ruckelshaus, which address issues in the risk assessment process. Having read the *Benzene* decision and the article by Rosenthal, Gray, and Graham, do you consider the line between scientific determinations and policy decisions to remain as clear cut as Ruckelshaus would desire?

Public Citizen Health Research Group v. Tyson
796 F.2d 1479 (D.C. Cir. 1986).

■ Before ROBINSON, CHIEF JUDGE, WRIGHT, CIRCUIT JUDGE, and McGOWAN, SENIOR CIRCUIT JUDGE.

■ McGOWAN, SENIOR CIRCUIT JUDGE:

In these consolidated cases, we review the Occupational Safety and Health Administration's rule limiting exposure to ethylene oxide, a chemical widely used in manufacturing and in hospital instrument sterilization. . . .

. . . The final rule requires employers to ensure that their employees are not exposed to an airborne concentration of EtO [Ethylene Oxide] in excess of 1 ppm [parts per million] as an eight-hour TWA [time-weighted average]. Occupational Exposure to Ethylene Oxide, Final Standard, 49 Fed. Reg. 25,734, 25,796 (1984). Employers must monitor exposure levels regularly, depending on the concentration of EtO in the air and changes in work practices. The rule sets an "action level" of 0.5 ppm, which if detected, requires employers to engage in regular employee monitoring. . . .

OSHA models EtO's health effects by plotting a curve through known points and extrapolating into areas as yet untested. The model employs several assumptions about the relationship between EtO exposure and biological response. For example, OSHA chose to employ a linear, no-threshold model similar to that used by EPA's Carcinogen

Assessment Group. This approach assumes that EtO exposure and biological response vary proportionately, and that there is no threshold level below which EtO exposure produces no adverse health effects.

AEOU [Association of Ethylene Oxide Users—a co-petitioner] challenges OSHA's model on two grounds. First, AEOU asserts that the model unlawfully assumes that there is no threshold level of EtO exposure. This assumption, AEOU argues, contravenes the teaching of the *Benzene* case. Second, AEOU claims that the model improperly translates breathing rates for rats into equivalent human terms.

In 29 C.F.R. § 1990 (1985) *et seq.*, OSHA provides a framework for rulemaking treatment of occupational carcinogens. The regulations allow OSHA to infer a carcinogenic hazard from one or more positive human or animal studies. The regulations also provide that: "No determination will be made that a 'threshold' or 'no-effect' level of exposure can be established for a human population exposed to carcinogens in general, or to any specific substance." 29 C.F.R. § 1990.143(h) (1985).

AEOU presents a two-pronged attack on the threshold issue. First, AEOU charges that the no-threshold assumption violates the *Benzene* rule because it improperly assumes that EtO is harmful at low doses. Second, AEOU charges that OSHA improperly ignored evidence in the record that demonstrates that EtO does indeed have a threshold level. We treat these contentions in turn.

. . . AEOU asserts that OSHA's threshold position in this case is equivalent to OSHA's position on significant risk in the *Benzene* case, which the Supreme Court invalidated. In particular, AEOU argues that "[t]he Supreme Court squarely rejected OSHA standard-setting based on 'probable' or 'suspected' risks." AEOU's implied assertion is that OSHA must *unequivocally prove* the scientific validity of each and every assumption it employs.

To the extent this argument asserts that OSHA cannot make any assumptions, even if they are supported by scientific thought, Congress has clearly come to the opposite conclusion. If Congress had intended to require the agency to "prove" all of its assumptions, Congress would not have allowed the agency to rely on the "best available evidence" and the "latest available scientific information." 29 U.S.C. § 655(b)(5) (1982).

Moreover, AEOU simply misconstrues the *Benzene* opinion. In that case, the Court carefully explained that, although OSHA may not act without some record basis, the agency also must be given leeway when regulatory subject matter is not subject to strict proof one way or the other. The reason for this approach is clear: requiring strict proof would fatally cripple all of OSHA's regulatory efforts and run counter to the legislative branch's express delegation of hybrid rulemaking power to OSHA. Accordingly, in a passage critical to our inquiry here, the *Benzene* plurality stated: "[S]o long as they are supported by a body of reputable scientific thought, the Agency is free to use conservative assumptions in interpreting the data with respect to carcinogens, risking error on the side of overprotection rather than underprotection.". . .

The agency has gone to great lengths to calculate, within the bounds of available scientific data, the significance of the risk presented by EtO. The EtO proceeding thus stands in stark contrast to the agency's actions in regulating benzene exposure.

We think it clear from the above-quoted portion of the *Benzene* case that the Supreme Court intended to permit the very estimates that AEOU so vigorously attacks. Indeed, it would be anomalous for the Court to have required the agency to provide more than it has provided in regulating EtO. *See* American Textile Manufacturers Institute, Inc. v. Donovan, 452 U.S. 490, 528 n. 52 (1981) ("the agency's candor in confessing its own inability to achieve a more precise estimate should not precipitate a judicial review that nonetheless demands what the congressionally delegated 'expert' says it cannot provide"). . . .

AEOU points to one commenter who supports an EtO threshold. Dr. Thomas Darby theorized that "[w]ith ethylene oxide, like most substances, there appears to be a 'no effect dose'. . . ." . . .

AEOU argues that the Ethylene Oxide Industry Council (EOIC) supported Darby's position. EOIC stated that "no adverse health effect has been readily demonstrated in man following exposure to 10 ppm. . . ." AEOU also notes that OSHA admitted that the record contains no "direct evidence of an excess risk of cancer at chronic exposure levels below 14 ppm. . . ."

We find neither Dr. Darby's nor EOIC's comments sufficient to refute OSHA's no-threshold model. Although Dr. Darby advocated the threshold concept, his conclusion was less than forceful. Moreover, contrary to AEOU's assertion, EOIC's cited comments do not unhesitatingly support Dr. Darby. . . .

Indeed, a number of participants (including OSHA) joined EOIC in calculating the risk presented by low EtO exposures. Many participants assessed health risks down to exposure levels at 1 ppm and below. *See* 49 Fed. Reg. at 25,756–63.

. . . The exercise of a dispute in the scientific community does not allow this court to choose a particular side as the "right" one. We have no special skills to aid in the resolution of these technical questions. Rather, our role is only to demand that OSHA review all sides of the issue and reasonably resolve the matter. OSHA has the expertise we lack and it has exercised that expertise by carefully reviewing the scientific data. Unlike the *Benzene* case, OSHA here expressly found risk at the 1 ppm level based on evidence submitted by a significant portion of the scientific community. We find the no-threshold assumption to be supported by substantial evidence. . . .

Having established the basis for a quantitative risk assessment, OSHA set out to quantify the level of risk faced by workers exposed to

EtO. OSHA then analyzed that risk to determine whether it met the test of significance set out in the *Benzene* case. Applying its model to the Bushy Run database, OSHA calculated the excess risk of death to workers exposed to EtO at various levels. At 50 ppm, OSHA estimated that EtO exposure would cause 634 to 1093 excess deaths per 10,000 workers. 49 Fed. Reg. at 25,762. At 1 ppm, OSHA estimated 12–23 excess deaths per 10,000 workers exposed to EtO. *Id.* [In the Bushy Run study, researchers at the Bushy Run Research Center in Pittsburgh exposed rats to EtO at concentrations of 100, 33, and 10 ppm for 6 hours per day, 5 days per week. This study produced a number of significant results, indicating that EtO exposure was related to the development of various types of cancers.]

OSHA found that 634 to 1093 excess deaths at 50 ppm exposure levels is a significant risk within the meaning of the *Benzene* case. *Id.* at 25,764. The agency further found that reducing the PEL from 50 ppm to 1 ppm is reasonably necessary and appropriate to remedying the risk at 50 ppm. *Id.* These particular findings (significant risk and necessity) are not directly challenged on appeal.

OSHA further found that EtO exposure at 1 ppm (12–23 excess deaths estimated) poses a significant risk itself. The agency set the PEL at 1 ppm, however, not because no excess deaths would occur at that level, but because it could not show that any lower long-term limit would be feasible. *Id.* at 25,772. AEOU does not challenge OSHA's finding that the 1 ppm PEL is the lowest feasible limit.

AEOU instead charges that OSHA's estimates inflate the number of excess deaths attributable to EtO exposure. AEOU proffers two related reasons for the allegedly inflated figures. First, AEOU echoes OMB's [Office of Management and Budget's] objection that OSHA mistakenly assessed the current exposure patterns of hospital workers. . . . AEOU repeats a second OMB objection as well. OMB charges that OSHA erred in assuming that workers are exposed for eight hours per day, five days per week. A more realistic exposure pattern postulates only intermittent exposure. Had OSHA assumed the latter exposure pattern, the 1 ppm PEL would avoid only 125 cancer deaths, rather than OSHA's final estimate of 634 to 1093 detailed above. *Id.*

Assuming *arguendo* that these two challenges have merit, they do not undermine the validity of OSHA's final standard. OSHA expressly found that the 12–23 excess deaths still caused by EtO exposure at the 1 ppm PEL is a significant risk within the meaning of the *Benzene* case. That finding is unchallenged here. Assuming 12 deaths are significant, 125 deaths are *a fortiori* significant. Thus, even if AEOU correctly argues that the current standard allows only 125 excess deaths, the argument is irrelevant. We need not decide, therefore, whether OSHA erred in its risk calculation. Even if it did, the error is insufficient to affect the validity of the outcome. . . .

NOTES AND QUESTIONS

1.   *Benzene* and *Tyson*. What process did OSHA undertake in *Tyson* that it had not undertaken in the *Benzene* case? What statutory finding did the Agency make in *Tyson* that it had not made in the *Benzene* case?

Pursuant to what standard of review did the court review OSHA's EtO standard? Was this the same standard in operation in the *Benzene* case? What then accounts for the different outcomes in *Benzene* and *Tyson*?

2.   Significant Risk and *Tyson*. What was the Agency's finding of significance in the *Tyson* case? How did the Agency justify this finding? Did the Agency consider the risk posed by an EtO standard of 1 ppm to be significant? If so, on what basis did it justify setting the standard at this level?

3.   No-Threshold Assumption. In *Tyson*, industry groups challenged the assumption by OSHA that EtO should be considered a no-threshold carcinogen. Why did the court find that the general cancer policy favored by OSHA should trump the AEOU's contention that a threshold characterization would better fit the data?

4.   Limitations on the Use of EPA's Cancer Policy. When is there sufficient information to justify abandonment of an agency's cancer policy? Consider *Chlorine Chemistry Council v. EPA*, 206 F.3d 1286 (D.C. Cir. 2000), in which the D.C. Circuit held EPA's regulations of chloroform to be arbitrary and capricious and inconsistent with the Safe Drinking Water Act because EPA's default assumption of linearity and zero threshold "openly overrode the 'best available' scientific evidence, which suggested that chloroform is a threshold carcinogen." The EPA's default assumption came from its guidelines for carcinogen risk assessment. *See* EPA, GUIDELINES FOR CARCINOGEN RISK ASSESSMENT (2005). Of key importance for the D.C. Circuit was a "Notice of Data Availability" published by EPA in the Federal Register concluding that chloroform exhibited a "nonlinear mode of carcinogenic action" and a draft report which supported these conclusions. *Chlorine Chemistry Council*, 206 F.3d at 1288–89. Consider the reasons why Ruckelshaus supported the use of general policy guidelines. Would he likely support deviation in this instance?

5.   Dioxin and Linearity. EPA has been assessing the carcinogenic effects of dioxin since the mid-1980s. In 2003, EPA issued a draft risk assessment for review by the National Academy of the Sciences. EPA, DRAFT DIOXIN REASSESSMENT, NATIONAL ACADEMY OF SCIENCES (NAS) REVIEW DRAFT (2003). While the draft assessment did not contain a formal recommendation, the National Academy of Sciences report made the following comment:

> The committee unanimously agrees that the current weight of evidence on [dioxin] carcinogenicity favors the use of nonlinear methods for extrapolation [at low doses]. However, the committee recognizes that it is not scientifically possible to exclude totally a linear response at [low doses], so it recommends that EPA provide risk estimates using both approaches and describing their scientific strengths and weaknesses to inform risk managers of the

importance of choosing a linear vs. nonlinear method of extrapolation. To the extent that EPA favors using default assumptions for regulating dioxin as though it were a linear carcinogen, such a conclusion should be made as part of risk management. EPA should strictly adhere to the distinction between risk assessment, which is a scientific activity, and risk management, which takes into account other factors.

COMMITTEE ON EPA's EXPOSURE AND HUMAN HEALTH REASSESSMENT OF TCDD AND RELATED COMPOUNDS, NATIONAL RESEARCH COUNCIL, HEALTH RISKS FROM DIOXIN AND RELATED COMPOUNDS: EVALUATION OF THE EPA REASSESSMENT 135 (2006). If EPA assumed a linear dose-response relationship and a zero threshold for dioxin, would this openly override the best available scientific evidence? Does it matter that such a relationship cannot be totally ruled out? Could a court be persuaded that such an assumption was a justifiable risk management decision?

6.   Scientific Uncertainty and Judicial Review. Should one judge's opinion outweigh the accumulated expertise of an expert governmental agency? In the 1970s, as the D.C. Circuit was confronted with an increasing number of highly technical environmental disputes, Judges Bazelon and Leventhal engaged in a discussion of the proper role of the judiciary in reviewing agency decisionmaking. Part of this on-going discussion is contained in concurring opinions each judge filed in *Ethyl Corp. v. EPA*, 541 F.2d 1 (D.C. Cir. 1976), *cert. denied*, 426 U.S. 941 (1976). Judge Bazelon believed that

> in cases of great technological complexity, the best way for courts to guard against unreasonable or erroneous administrative decisions is not for the judges themselves to scrutinize the technical merits of each decision. Rather, it is to establish a decision-making process that assures a reasoned decision that can be held up to the scrutiny of the scientific community and the public. . . . The process making a de novo evaluation of the scientific evidence inevitably invites judges of opposing views to make plausible-sounding, but simplistic, judgments of the relative weight to be afforded various pieces of technical data.

Id. at 66. Judge Leventhal on the other hand advocated a more robust judicial review, premised on the theory that

> in the case of agency decision-making the courts have an additional responsibility set by Congress. . . . Our present system of review assumes judges will acquire whatever technical knowledge is necessary as background for decision of the legal questions. . . . The substantive review of administrative action is modest, but it cannot be carried out in a vacuum of understanding. Better no judicial review at all than a charade that gives the imprimatur without the substance of judicial confirmation that the agency is not acting unreasonably.

Id. at 68–69. What do you consider to be the appropriate role of the courts in reviewing agency rulemaking actions in areas where scientific expertise is required?

7. Vulnerability of Risk Assessment to Manipulation. Given the inherent uncertainty in the risk assessment process, there exists scope for political manipulation. One potential solution to such manipulation is regulatory peer review. Proposals for a peer review system that would examine the basis of regulatory decisions have garnered interest from industry and government officials alike. Would the benefits of such a check be worth the expense and time necessarily involved in such a process? J.B. Ruhl and James Salzman argue that regulatory peer review should be applied by a random sampling technique to help define the scope of the problem of agency overstatement of scientific support and to induce agencies to pay more attention to clearly articulating where science ends and policy judgment begins in the justification of their decisions. J.B. Ruhl & James Salzman, *In Defense of Regulatory Peer Review*, 84 WASH. U. L. REV. 1 (2006).

C. EXPERT V. LAY PERCEPTIONS OF RISK

Stephen Breyer, Breaking the Vicious Circle: Toward Effective Risk Regulation
33–39 (1993).*

Study after study shows that the public's evaluation of risk problems differs radically from any consensus of experts in the field. Risks associated with toxic waste dumps and nuclear power appear near the bottom of most expert lists; they appear near the top of the public's list of concerns, which more directly influences regulatory agendas. . . . To some extent, these differences may reflect that the public fears certain risks more than others with the same probability of harm. As previously pointed out, of two equal risks, one could rationally dislike or fear more the risk that is involuntarily suffered, new, unobservable, uncontrollable, catastrophic, delayed, a threat to future generations, or likely accompanied by pain or dread.

Still, these differences in the source, quality, or nature of a risk may not account for the different ranking by the public and the experts. A typical member of the public would like to minimize risks of death to himself, to his family, to his neighbors; he would normally prefer that regulation buy more safety for a given expenditure or the same amount of safety for less. Not many of us would like to shift resources to increase overall risks of death significantly in order to increase the likelihood that death will occur on a bicycle or in a fire, rather than through disease. There is a far simpler explanation for the public's aversion to toxic waste dumps than an enormous desire for supersafety, or a strong aversion to

---

the tiniest risk of harm—namely, the public does not *believe* that the risks are tiny. The public's "nonexpert" reactions reflect not different values but different understandings about the underlying risk-related facts.

My assumption that the public assigns "rational" values to risks, however, does not entail rational public reactions to risk. Psychologists have found several examples of thinking that impede rational understanding, but may have helped us survive as we lived throughout much of prehistory, in small groups of hunter-gatherers, depending upon grain, honey, and animals for sustenance. The following, rather well-documented aspects of risk perception are probably familiar.

1.   Rules of thumb. In daily life most of us do not weigh all the pros and cons of feasible alternatives. We use rules of thumb, more formally called "heuristic devices." . . . The resulting categorizations do not always accurately describe another person or circumstance, but they help us make quick decisions, most of which prove helpful. This kind of quick decision-making may help cut a swath through the modern information jungle, but it oversimplifies dramatically and thereby inhibits an understanding of risks, particularly small risks.

2.   Prominence. People react more strongly, and give greater importance, to events that stand out from the background. Unusual events are striking. We more likely notice the (low-risk) nuclear waste disposal truck driving past the school than the (much higher-risk) gasoline delivery trucks on their way to local service stations. . . .

3.   Ethics. The strength of our feelings of ethical obligation seems to diminish with distance. That is to say, feelings of obligation are stronger (or we have different, more time-consuming obligations) toward family, neighbors, friends, community, and those with whom we have direct contact, those whom we see, than toward those who live in distant places, whom we do not see but only read or hear about.

4.   Trust in experts. People cannot easily judge between experts when those experts disagree with each other. The public, since the mid-1960s, has shown increasing distrust of experts and the institutions, private, academic, or governmental, that employ them.

5.   Fixed decisions. A person who has made up his or her mind about something is very reluctant to change it.

6.   Mathematics. Most people have considerable difficulty understanding the mathematical probabilities involved in assessing risk. . . . People consistently overestimate small probabilities. What is the likelihood of death by botulism? (One in two million.) They underestimate large ones. What is the likelihood of death by diabetes? (One in fifty thousand.) People cannot detect inconsistencies in their own risk-related choices. . . .

These few, near-commonsense propositions, with strong statistical support in the technical literature, verify Oliver Wendell Holmes's own observation that "most people think dramatically, not quantitatively." They also have important consequences. . . .

When we think about nuclear power controversies, we should take account of the fact that hearing about an accident is what psychologists tell us is an heuristic "tip-off" of danger, whether or not anyone is hurt. We have "seen" Chernobyl and Three Mile Island, and we may therefore doubt nuclear power's safety, whether or not experts tell us that the reactor at Chernobyl was not properly designed, that the accident at Three Mile Island hurt no one, that military weapons, not electric power generators, are responsible for 99 percent of all nuclear waste, that nuclear power's risks are minuscule compared to the risks of coal-generated power. . . .

[This suggests] that better "risk communications," such as efforts to explain risks to the public at open meetings, may not suffice to alleviate risk regulation problems. It is not surprising that, after the EPA Administrator William Ruckelshaus spent days at such meetings in Tacoma, Washington, explaining why an ASARCO chemical plant that was leaking small amounts of arsenic could remain open, he was misunderstood, criticized, and accused of trying to drive a wedge between environmentalists and blue collar workers. . . .

There is little reason to hope for better risk communication over time. To the contrary, as science improves, scientists may more easily detect and identify ever tinier risks—the risk associated, for example, with the migration of a single molecule of plastic from a container into a soft drink; they may more easily identify geographical areas near toxic waste dumps with higher than average cancer rates. As international communications improve, the press will have an ever larger pool of unusual, and therefore more interesting, accident stories to write about. Why should we not expect an outcry from a public that reads about Love Canal, Times Beach, Alar, Chilean grapes laced with cyanide, and the leaflet of Villejuif, whether or not such examples reflect meaningful danger? (At the same time, how can one expect public reaction to potentially greater but more mundane problems, of which it is unaware?)

It is hard to make the normal human mind grapple with this inhuman type of problem. To change public reaction, one would either have to institute widespread public education in risk analysis or generate greater public trust in some particular group of experts or the institutions that employ them. The first alternative seems unlikely. The second, over the past thirty years, has not occurred. . . .

NOTES AND QUESTIONS

1. Characteristics That Affect Lay Perceptions of Risk. Justice Breyer's theoretical discussion about the discrepancy between expert and lay perceptions of risk is derived from a large academic literature on the subject. Representative works include Baruch Fischhoff, *Managing Risk Perceptions*, 2 ISSUES SCI. & TECH. 83 (1985); Roger G. Noll & James E. Krier, *Some*

Implications of Cognitive Psychology for Risk Regulation, 19 J. LEGAL STUD. 747 (1990); Paul Slovic, *Perception of Risk*, 236 SCIENCE 280 (1987); Paul Slovic et al., *Rating the Risks*, 21 ENV'T 14 (1979).

Slovic and his colleagues define eight characteristics that affect lay perceptions of risk:

1. *voluntariness of risk*: involuntary risks are perceived as more serious;

2. *immediacy of effect*: risks with delayed effects (such as cancer) are perceived as more serious;

3. *knowledge about risk*: unknown risks are perceived as more serious;

4. *control over risk*: risks that individuals cannot reduce through their own actions are perceived as more serious;

5. *newness*: new risks are perceived as more serious;

6. *chronic/catastrophic*: catastrophic risks—risks that kill large numbers of people at once—are perceived as more serious;

7. *common/dread*: dread risks—risks that people have not learned to deal with—are perceived as more serious; and

8. *severity of consequences*: fatal risks are perceived as more serious.

Given these factors, for what types of environmental risks would you expect lay perceptions to be greater than expert perceptions?

2.   *Unfinished Business.* Justice Breyer's factual views about the discrepancy between expert and lay evaluations of risk are informed to a large extent by two EPA reports: UNFINISHED BUSINESS: A COMPARATIVE ASSESSMENT OF ENVIRONMENTAL PROBLEMS, published in 1987, and REDUCING RISK: SETTING PRIORITIES AND STRATEGIES FOR ENVIRONMENTAL PROTECTION, published in 1990.

UNFINISHED BUSINESS is the report of a special taskforce of senior career managers and technical experts at EPA, commissioned by the administrator to compare the risks of different environmental problems. The group chose to focus on thirty-one problems and, for each problem, considered four types of risks: cancer risks, non-cancer health risks, ecological risks, and welfare risks (such as visibility impairment and material damage). The study reached two important conclusions:

> The [group's] rankings by risk . . . do not correspond well with EPA's current program priorities. Areas of relatively high risk but low EPA effort include: indoor radon; indoor air pollution; stratospheric ozone depletion; global warming; non-point sources; discharges to estuaries, coastal waters and oceans; other pesticide risks; accidental releases of toxics; consumer products; and worker exposures. Areas of high EPA effort but relatively low or medium risks include: [hazardous waste] sites; Superfund; underground storage tanks; and municipal non-hazardous waste sites.

EPA, UNFINISHED BUSINESS: A COMPARATIVE ASSESSMENT OF ENVIRONMENTAL PROBLEMS / OVERVIEW REPORT, at xix–xx (1987). Second, the group concluded:

> Overall, EPA's priorities appear more closely aligned with public opinion than with our estimated risks. Recent national polling data ranks areas of public concern about environmental issues as follows:
>
> *High*: chemical waste disposal, water pollution, chemical plant accidents, and air pollution;
>
> *Medium*: oil spills, worker exposure, pesticides, and drinking water;
>
> *Low*: indoor air pollution, consumer products, genetic radiation (except nuclear power), and global warming.

Id. at xx. What prescriptions for regulation should one draw from these conclusions?

UNFINISHED BUSINESS is more agnostic than Justice Breyer about whether regulatory attention should be more closely aligned with expert perceptions of risk. The report states:

> This divergence between what we found in terms of relative risks and EPA's priorities is not necessarily inappropriate. Some problems appear to be relatively low risks precisely because of the high levels of program effort that have been devoted to controlling them. And these high levels of attention may remain necessary in order to hold risks to current levels.

Id. at xix. Air pollution and water pollution control, the first two large-scale environmental programs, probably fall in this category.

Moreover, the report expressly declined to consider the economic or technological controllability of the risks. Also, in some of the areas studied by the report—particularly consumer products and worker exposure to toxic chemicals—EPA shared jurisdiction with other government agencies, and for other areas—particularly stratospheric ozone depletion and global warming—international coordination is necessary for successful response.

Is it inconsistent with the economic perspective for regulation to focus on less serious risks rather than on other more serious risks? For further discussion, see W. Kip Viscusi, *Equivalent Frames of Reference for Judging Risk Regulation Policies*, 3 N.Y.U. ENVTL. L.J. 431 (1995). What additional information would you need to determine whether EPA's priorities are appropriate?

3. ***Reducing Risk.*** The second EPA study, REDUCING RISK, was undertaken by EPA's Science Advisory Board (SAB). The SAB was asked to review the findings in UNFINISHED BUSINESS and to develop recommendations for prioritizing EPA's efforts. Most importantly, the SAB called on EPA to "target its environmental protection efforts on the basis of opportunities for the greatest risk reduction." EPA SCI. ADVISORY BD., REDUCING RISK: SETTING PRIORITIES AND STRATEGIES FOR ENVIRONMENTAL PROTECTION 6 (1990). Why is this objective desirable? Should the relative

costs of achieving different risk reductions be taken into account? Should it matter whether the risks are voluntary or involuntary? Should it matter whether the environmental problem is fully internalized, as is the case for indoor radon in owner-occupied houses?

Elsewhere in the report, the SAB formulates these recommendations in two other ways. First, it states: "We should set priorities for environmental protection based on an explicit comparison of the relative risk posed by different environmental problems, and more specifically, the opportunities for cost effective risk reduction." *Id.* at 28. Second, it states: "[T]o the extent that EPA has discretion to emphasize one environmental protection program over another, it should emphasize the program that reduces the most environmental risk at the lowest overall cost to society." *Id.* Are these three formulations consistent? Under the third formulation, is it necessarily the case that the most serious risks would be addressed first?

The process of comparing risks so as to address the most serious ones first has come to be known as comparative risk assessment or comparative risk analysis (CRA). For academic criticism of CRA, see D. Hattis & R. Goble, *Current Priority-Setting Methodology: Too Little Rationality or Too Much?*, *in* WORST THINGS FIRST?: THE DEBATE OVER RISK-BASED NATIONAL ENVIRONMENTAL PRIORITIES 107 (Adam M. Finkel & Dominic Golding eds., 1994); Donald T. Hornstein, *Reclaiming Environmental Law: A Normative Critique of Comparative Risk Analysis*, 92 COLUM. L. REV. 562 (1992); Ellen K. Silbergeld, *The Risks of Comparing Risks*, 3 N.Y.U. ENVTL. L.J. 405 (1995).

4.   **Addressing the Divide in Regulation.** If it cannot do both, should environmental regulation address risks that experts think are serious or risks that the public thinks are serious? What is the economic perspective's view on this question? What would Mark Sagoff say? The economic and non-economic perspectives on environmental degradation are discussed in Chapter I. If people are being compensated for exposure to risk, to what extent are public perceptions likely to affect the amount of compensation?

5.   **Should Lay Perceptions of Risk Count in Risk Assessments?** Is the divergence between lay and expert perceptions of risk a case of public misperception that should be solved by changing the public's perceptions? Or should the regulatory system accept the divergence and seek to adjust the decisionmaking process to accommodate the differing perceptions? In particular, should lay perceptions of risk count in risk assessments?

Paul Portney famously posed a hypothetical of a town called Happyville. In Happyville, residents were willing to pay $1000 each year for the removal of a drinking water contaminant that they believed was carcinogenic but which experts believed was safe. *See* Paul R. Portney, *Trouble in Happyville*, 11 J. POL'Y ANALYSIS & MGMT. 131 (1992). What are the annual benefits of removing the contaminant from the Happyville drinking water system?

6.   **Public Perceptions and Distortions.** Now suppose that the government has to decide which chemical waste site to clean up—one in Happyville or one in a neighboring town called Blissville. The cost of cleanup is the same. In Happyville, the site poses no real risks but the population

believes that one hundred people will die because of the waste. In Blissville, the population is unaware of the risk, but in fact one hundred cases of cancer will occur if the site is not cleaned up. Cleaning up the Happyville site will create substantial perceived benefits, whereas cleaning up the Blissville site will create real risk reduction effects that will not be valued by the residents because they do not believe that the site poses any risk. Which site should the government clean up? W. Kip Viscusi offered this spin on Portney's hypothetical to highlight his view that "[p]andering to fears of imaginary risks will not produce any actual health benefits but will squander societal resources." W. KIP VISCUSI, PRICING LIVES: GUIDEPOSTS FOR A SAFER SOCIETY 152 (2018). Would your answer change if Happyville's population believes that one hundred people will die, while fifty people in Blissville will actually die? What if only a few people will actually die in Blissville?

7. Public Perceptions and Environmental Justice. Is there a relationship between responding to public perceptions and promoting environmental justice? If so, what is the relationship? For an argument that the government should advance environmental justice by incorporating citizens' risk perceptions into its risk calculations and its regulations, see James S. Freeman & Rachel D. Godsil, *The Question of Risk: Incorporating Community Perceptions Into Environmental Risk Assessments*, 21 FORDHAM URB. L.J. 547 (1994). In empirical work, W. Kip Viscusi and James Hamilton found that, among sites with the lowest calculated actual risk levels, EPA cleaned up those sites located in areas in which constituents had more political power as measured by higher voter turnout. W. Kip Viscusi & James T. Hamilton, *Are Risk Regulators Rational? Evidence from Hazardous Waste Cleanup Decisions*, 89 AM. ECON. REV. 1010 (1999). What communities are likely to have higher political power or voter turnout? Can you articulate an argument that responding to public perceptions can actually worsen outcomes for minority and low-income communities?

8. Judicial Response to the Divide. In some areas of the law, the courts have tried to address the divergence between lay and expert perceptions of risk by, for example, prohibiting awards of damages in nuisance cases for loss of property value due to scientifically unfounded fear of contamination. Should the response of the legislative and administrative processes be different from the response of the courts?

9. Can Communication Adequately Bridge the Gap? Do you think that risk communication can significantly narrow the difference between expert and lay perceptions of risk? Have your views about risk changed as a result of the readings in this section?

2. RISK MANAGEMENT

Risk management is the process by which regulators make decisions about which risks are worth addressing and about the extent to which these risks should be controlled. As discussed in the previous section on risk assessment, risk management is generally seen as a second step in the regulatory process, following the completion of a risk assessment. At the risk management stage, regulators have an estimate of the magnitude of the environmental risks and must decide about the extent, if any, to which these risks should be controlled.

This section will begin by presenting an overview of the risk management frameworks in the major federal environmental statutes, tracing the trend—which began in the early 1980s—toward the application of cost-benefit analysis. It will then explore the practice and judicial review of cost-benefit analysis.

A. RISK MANAGEMENT FRAMEWORKS

The federal environmental statutes employ a variety of risk management frameworks, often combining several of the categories described above. For example, the National Ambient Air Quality Standards (NAAQS) under the Clean Air Act (CAA), which apply to criteria pollutants (as opposed to hazardous pollutants), must be set at the levels that, "allowing an adequate margin of safety, are requisite to protect the public health." 42 U.S.C. § 7409(b)(1). Pursuant to this standard, EPA has employed a "critical populations, critical effects" approach, seeking to protect the most sensitive members of the population against every adverse health effect. Moreover, the courts have held that the costs of pollution reduction cannot be taken into account in setting these standards. Thus, at least in theory the NAAQS are set by reference to a no-risk framework. (The practical problems with this approach are discussed in Chapter V.) Technology-based standards are also employed, but primarily as a mechanism to allocate the pollution control burden required by the NAAQS.

The CAA takes a different approach with respect to hazardous air pollutants. The pollutants are currently controlled by means of technology-based standards. Over the course of the next decade, however, EPA must promulgate more stringent standards if the technology-based standards "do not reduce lifetime excess cancer risks to the individual most exposed to emissions . . . to less than one in one million." 42 U.S.C. § 7412(f)(2)(A). These more stringent standards correspond to a negligible risk framework (a variant of a no-risk framework). The resulting standards are therefore the more stringent of those that would result from the technology-based and negligible risk frameworks, respectively.

Under the Safe Drinking Water Act (SDWA), a different two-part procedure is used. EPA first sets maximum contaminant level goals "at the level at which no known or anticipated adverse effects on the health of persons occur and which allows an adequate margin of safety." 42 U.S.C. § 300g–1(b)(4)(A). Next, EPA promulgates the national primary drinking water regulations, which constitute the enforceable standard, "as close to the maximum contaminant level goal as is feasible." The statute defines "feasible" as "feasible with the use of the best technology . . . [taking cost into consideration]." 42 U.S.C. § 300g–1(b)(4)(D). Thus, these standards are the less stringent of those that would result from the technology-based and risk threshold frameworks, respectively.

The Federal Insecticide, Fungicide, and Rodenticide Act (FIFRA) provides that pesticides can be marketed only if they "will not generally cause unreasonable adverse effects on the environment." 7 U.S.C. § 136a(c)(5)(d). Such effects, in turn, are defined as "unreasonable risk to man or the environment, taking into account the economic, social, and environmental costs and benefits." *Id.* § 136(bb). This approach has elements of both the risk-risk framework, in that it takes into account environmental costs and benefits of the pesticide, and the risk-benefit framework, in that it considers the benefits and burdens of regulation.

Since the early 1980s, the risk management frameworks of the various federal environmental statutes have been significantly affected by Executive Order 12,291, which was promulgated by President Reagan and remained in effect during the George H. W. Bush administration. Procedurally, it established a centralized process for the prepromulgation review of any major rule (defined as a rule with an annual effect on the economy of $100 million or more) by OMB. Substantively, it required that, "to the extent permitted by law," "[r]egulatory action . . . not be undertaken unless the potential benefits to society of the regulation outweigh the potential costs to society," "[r]egulatory objectives . . . be chosen to maximize the net benefits to society," and "[a]mong alternative approaches to any given regulatory objective, the alternative involving the least net cost to society . . . be chosen." Exec. Order No. 12,291, 46 Fed. Reg. 13,193 (1981). Executive Order 12,291 vested in OMB an unprecedented level of control over the administrative apparatus and established the essential architecture of central review of agency action that remains in place to this day.

President Clinton replaced this Order with Executive Order 12,866, which retains the centralized review by OMB, and provides, consistent with the approach of its predecessor, that "in choosing among alternative regulatory approaches, agencies should select those approaches that maximize net benefits . . . unless a statute requires another regulatory approach." Exec. Order No. 12,866, 58 Fed. Reg. 51,735 (1993). In response to criticisms about how agency decisions were being reviewed, the latter order imposes enhanced disclosure requirements, specifically required that agencies weigh "qualitative measures," including "distributive impacts" and "equity," when engaging in cost-benefit analysis, and set deadlines on review in an attempt to prevent the indefinite stalling of a regulation. The effect of these orders has been to push EPA in the direction of cost-benefit analysis, except in those instances, such as the promulgation of NAAQS under the CAA, where the statute prohibits the application of this framework. For a detailed description of the growth of cost-benefit analysis as the predominant risk management framework in federal environmental decisionmaking, see RICHARD L. REVESZ & MICHAEL A. LIVERMORE, RETAKING RATIONALITY:

How Cost-Benefit Analysis Can Better Protect the Environment and Our Health (2008).

In January 2007, President George W. Bush announced revisions to Executive Order 12,866, further centralizing control of administrative agencies. *See* Exec. Order No. 13,422, 72 Fed. Reg. 2763 (2007). Key revisions include a requirement that agencies identify a "market failure" before they move forward with proposed regulations and a requirement that guidance documents (in addition to actual regulations) be subject to the OMB review process. In addition, the revised order places political appointees in the agencies as Regulatory Policy Review Officers, further cementing presidential control over the bureaucracy.

President Obama revoked the Bush executive order, *see* Exec. Order No. 13,497, 74 Fed. Reg. 6,113 (2009), and issued his own order, which reaffirmed and supplemented the Clinton order in some minor but potentially important ways, *see* Exec. Order No. 13,563, 76 Fed. Reg. 3,821 (2011). This Order emphasizes public participation, agency coordination, flexible regulatory approaches, and scientific integrity. Perhaps most significantly, the Order introduces retrospective analyses of existing regulations as a routine part of an agency's mission. However, the Order does not pre-judge how a retrospective analysis would be used. It states that such review would "determine whether any such regulations should be modified, streamlined, expanded, or repealed. . . ." President Obama accompanied this Order with memoranda to agencies, directing them to make more information available on websites in a searchable form and to consider measures to reduce regulatory burdens on small businesses. So far, President Trump has reaffirmed Executive Order 12,866's goals of ensuring that regulations are net beneficial and Executive Order 13,563's endorsement of retrospective review. *See* Exec. Order No. 13,777, 82 Fed. Reg. 12,285 (2017).

Although the trend is toward increased reliance on cost-benefit analysis, several other risk management frameworks continue to play a role in environmental decisionmaking. In the following excerpt, Lester Lave provides an overview of several risk management frameworks, discussing their advantages and disadvantages.

Lester B. Lave, The Strategy of Social Regulation: Decision Frameworks for Policy
9–27 (1981).*

Six frameworks for making regulatory decisions are currently being used and two have been proposed. The frameworks range, roughly, from those requiring the least theory, data, and analysis and offering the least flexibility to those at the opposite pole; they include market regulation,

---

*   Reprinted with the permission of the Brookings Institution Press.

no-risk, technology-based standards, risk-risk (proposed), risk-benefit, cost-effectiveness, regulatory budget (proposed), and benefit-cost.

Market Regulation

Economic theory has formalized the 200-year-old insight of Adam Smith that competitive markets are efficient. In particular (under a set of stringent assumptions including complete information, no transaction costs, rational consumers and producers, no economies of scale in production, and no externalities), a competitive market produces an efficient (or Pareto optimal) equilibrium in the sense that no one can be made better off without making at least one person worse off. This efficiency principle also holds for situations involving risk, such as hazardous products or jobs, although still more stringent assumptions are needed.

Each person in such an economy presumably would decide what is best for him by looking at the array of available products and jobs. Since risk is an undesirable attribute, all risky products and jobs having no compensating attributes would be eliminated, and individuals would scrutinize those risky products and jobs that offered higher pay or some other advantage to determine which should be taken. Under the restrictive assumptions, government regulation would be unnecessary.

Clearly the U.S. economy does not satisfy the host of restrictive assumptions; both buyers and sellers can often influence price, many effects are transmitted outside the marketplace, and often buyers and sellers are woefully ignorant of the health and safety implications of a product. Market equilibrium is inefficient and a case can be made for government intervention. Some economists caution Americans to eschew perfection, arguing that they would be better off in the long run by tolerating these relatively minor evils instead of erecting a huge, self-defeating regulatory structure. Regulation requires resources, but more important, it is virtually impossible to regulate so that incentives are not distorted, and this often leads to even greater inefficiency than in the unregulated market—for example, transportation regulation, particularly of airlines and trains. Many economists argue that regulation is justified only when serious violations of the assumptions occur, and then only if the regulation can be relatively efficient. . . .

In summary, the decision to use the market to regulate risk puts faith in consumer information and judgments. It sees the costs of bureaucracy constraining private decisions as larger than costs arising from market imperfections and advises accepting current imperfections rather than creating a regulatory morass.

No-Risk

The philosophy behind the Delaney Clause of the Food, Drug, and Cosmetic Act, and food additive amendments generally, is that the public should be exposed to no additional or unnecessary risk. Carcinogens cannot be added to foods or remain as residuals in meat since this might increase the risk of cancer; according to the Clean Air Act Amendments of 1970, air pollution levels must be sufficiently low to protect the population from adverse effects, presumably even the most sensitive members.

This approach has great appeal as rhetoric. To argue that carcinogens ought to be permitted in the food supply is to argue that society must allow higher than necessary risks of cancer. Why should any unnecessary exposure be tolerated, even if the risk appears to be small?

The no-risk framework has the advantage of requiring little data and analysis and precludes agonizing about the decision to be made. According to the Delaney Clause, the only question is whether a food additive has been shown to be a carcinogen in humans or animals. Thus data (on the quality, variety, and price of food) concerning the consequences of banning may not be considered. The Delaney Clause has a simple, straightforward answer to a complicated question: ban a substance if there is evidence of carcinogenicity. Frameworks other than market regulation require answers to a set of complicated questions: What level of risks are acceptable? What benefits would serve to offset the risks? Can animal bioassays be relied on to demonstrate human carcinogenicity? Can the potency of a substance for humans be demonstrated under current exposure levels? If one requires simple answers to these questions or distrusts the complicated answers given by experts, no-risk offers an appealing solution.

Unfortunately the answers are too simple. Virtually all "natural" foods contain trace elements of carcinogens, including biological contaminants and pesticides. The Food and Drug Administration treats natural foods differently than food additives; apparently it is less troublesome to die from a cancer induced by a natural food than from one induced by a food additive. Does anyone seriously propose to ban all foods with trace levels of carcinogens? Does it make sense to treat those with trace amounts in the same way as those with large amounts of potent carcinogens? . . .

The three principal objections to this framework are the current misallocation of resources, the closing of the door to future solutions, and the inconsistency in government policy. In addition this framework cannot distinguish between a toxin that is extremely weak and to which few people are exposed and a potent carcinogen to which nearly the entire population is exposed. Insofar as there are many carcinogens and it is costly to ban at least some of them, this framework does not help to develop priorities—which substance should be treated first?—or guidelines—what level of safety ought to be sought where banning is infeasible? Instead, it sends regulators scurrying off to devote much of their attention to relatively benign substances by giving all toxins equal priority. Thus the framework is a pernicious guide to regulators confronted with complicated problems.

Although Congress has written the no-risk framework into legislation, it is a straw man unworthy of serious consideration. Even the attempt to maintain the facade is increasingly recognized by the regulatory agencies to be impossible. For example, the Food and Drug Administration has attempted to define a "negligible" risk level; any risk below a level of one in one million lifetimes would be considered to be zero for regulatory purposes. . . .

Technology-Based Standards

Recognizing the difficulty of attempting to estimate the health and safety effects of a proposed standard (much less the problem of quantifying these effects), a number of agencies have placed their reliance on engineering judgments. The best available control technology has been required extensively by the Environmental Protection Agency in regulating air and water pollution. This framework has the simplicity of requiring the estimation of neither benefits nor costs. The data and analysis required are for identifying a hazard and then for making the engineering judgment as to the best available control technology. This framework requires a second set of information for determining the best available control technology in addition to the carcinogenicity data required for the no-risk framework.

In practice, however, there is never a best technology but only successively more expensive and stringent technologies. For example, the effectiveness of an electrostatic precipitator in removing suspended particles from air is proportional to the collector plate area; effectiveness can be increased by increasing the area. In practice, engineering judgment defines best available control technology as a finite collector plate area, even though further increases in plate area would improve (minutely) the effectiveness of collection. At some point additional abatement is unwarranted because social costs exceed social benefits; but even then technology is available that would abate emissions further. In practice, best available control technology embodies implicit assumptions about the benefits and costs of further abatement.

The crucial issue in implementing this framework at present is the financial burden each industry can bear. As long as an industry is not in danger of bankruptcy, a technology that lowered emissions would be considered acceptable. Sufficient uncertainty exists about what cost level would endanger an industry that regulators rarely impose standards that come close to doing so.

In summary, the primary advantage of technology-based standards is that they require no formal evidence on costs or benefits; the only data required are those necessary for good engineering judgments. The resulting standard, however, will depend on regulators' perceptions of industry profitability. If an area is populated by an industry teetering on the brink of bankruptcy, best available control technology will be weak and few emissions will be abated. If the industry is profitable, it will require large expenditures. There is more than a theoretical possibility that the first regulation in an industry would press it to the limit of its ability to afford regulation, leaving no financial resources to handle later regulations that might be far more important. Rather than being a framework for lowering risk or even for using engineering judgments, technology-based standards is a framework for regulating economic activity through imposing costs arbitrarily among industries until all are at the same minimal level of profit.

Risk-Risk: Direct

Even if maximum protection were desired, the Delaney Clause would be a poor framework because it requires banning carcinogens. Some toxic substances, such as food additives and fungicides, prevent contamination of food, and thus it is desirable to weigh one risk against the other, as recognized by the Food and Drug Administration and the Department of Agriculture in the proposed risk-risk analysis. Balancing the toxicity of a substance against the enhanced protection it brings can be done from either of two perspectives. The narrow perspective is that of balancing the risk to the consumer of the additive against the direct health benefits. Sodium nitrite may be a carcinogen, but it protects against botulism; the risk of cancer must be balanced against that of botulism. The broad perspective takes account of both producers and consumers as shown below.

Since the risk-risk framework allows beneficial health effects to be considered along with adverse health effects, it is more flexible than no-risk. It and the remaining frameworks are qualitatively different from no-risk in that they require quantification of risk and at least partial estimation of benefits. If quantification were impossible, this framework could not be implemented because there would be no method for balancing unmatched risks (for example, chronic respiratory disease versus broken legs). Quantification is particularly difficult for the effects of toxic substances; thus this and the remaining frameworks are subject to the caution of those who contend that potency cannot be estimated from animal bioassays, or at least that potency for humans at low doses cannot be inferred reliably. . . .

While the risk-risk framework provides somewhat greater flexibility, it still precludes consideration of nonhealth effects. Conceptually it is a small step since it merely includes both the health risks and health benefits of a proposal. In practice it appears to be a major improvement over the no-risk framework—where it is applicable. Cases such as sodium nitrite[,] where the risk-risk framework is invaluable, are the exception. Few substances offer a direct health benefit to the consumer other than drugs, products for which the Food and Drug Administration already uses this framework. The framework is of limited interest because it is of such limited applicability.

Risk-Risk: Indirect

The advantage of the risk-risk framework over the no-risk framework is that it permits wider analysis of risks. One way of stating the objective is that society desires to minimize the adverse health effects associated with a given food such as bacon. Thus society would permit nitrite in bacon if the improvement in the health of consumers from botulism protection exceeded the decrement in health from the risk of cancer. Yet it is evident that the direct risk-risk framework takes only the first step of considering the health of the person consuming the food. People are also associated with the production and distribution of food; society desires to minimize the adverse health effects associated with producing as well as consuming bacon (for a fixed level of production). Workers would not countenance a regulation that offered consumers a small amount of protection at the cost of a large increase in risk to workers.

Since every human activity is risky, a regulation that requires more man-hours to produce a unit of food would increase the exposure and presumably the occupational risk of workers. The indirect risk-risk framework includes occupational risks associated with each additive or contaminant. . . .

Risk-Benefit

Unlike the risk-benefit framework, the three previous ones do not allow consideration of nonhealth effects. The folly of refusing to consider these effects is illustrated by examining one's own choices. For example, most people are willing to risk the minute chance of biological contamination rather than to be bothered with boiling drinking water. They are willing to undertake additional risks in order to get rewards such as additional income and recreational stimulation. For example, there is a risk premium in the pay of workers in hazardous occupations to attract them in the face of the higher risks. These premiums can be extremely high, as for test pilots, steeplejacks, and divers working deep in the ocean. If the effect of a regulation is to lower risk minutely at the cost of a vast increase in price, a lessening of choice or convenience, harm to the environment, or a sacrifice in social goals generally, society should not be satisfied. The frameworks previously mentioned suffer from their lack of recognition of other social goals such as the ecosystem, endangered species, and individual freedoms.

Under the risk-benefit framework, regulators would be enjoined to balance the general benefits of a proposed regulation against its general risks. This framework is intended to be somewhat vague, with all effects being enumerated, but with full quantification and valuation being left to the general wisdom of the regulators. The framework may account for cost, convenience, and even preferences in an attempt to balance benefits against risks. A vast array of frameworks can come under the risk-benefit heading, from balancing health risks against health benefits (like the risk-risk indirect framework) to consideration of all risks, costs, and benefits. The framework has an immediate appeal to congressmen and regulators since it is a general instruction to consider all social factors in arriving at a decision. While no one can oppose considering all relevant factors, no one has specified precisely how this is to be done.

The intellectual difficulty with this framework is its lack of precise definition. Are only health risks to be considered, or are risks to the present and future environment (air, water, louseworts, snail darters, and tundra) relevant? If they are not, the framework is no more complete than the previous one, and if they are, how can the risks to louseworts be added to those to the health of our great grandchildren and of current workers? Similarly, there is no guidance about how to quantify benefits: what is the value of an increase in the supply of food or electricity? . . .

Cost-Effectiveness

Many organizations, private and public, find themselves attempting to increase output even though their current budget is fixed. The intellectual contributions in defining this problem and developing rules to solve it have come from the Department of Defense. Although cost-effectiveness is often thought erroneously to refer to getting some specific project done at lowest cost, the concept is much broader, referring to accomplishing some general objective at lowest cost. President Eisenhower's secretary of defense, Charles Wilson, described the goal succinctly as an attempt to "get the most bang for the buck."

How can a goal be achieved within a fixed budget? For example, the goal of the National Cancer Institute is to lower the cancer death rate. It might achieve this goal by devoting resources to basic research, clinical trials testing new treatment techniques, public education, prevention by lowering the amounts of carcinogens in the environment, early detection of cancer, or the provision of more treatment. How should the fixed budget be allocated among these competing programs to lower both the incidence of cancer and the occurrence of death and lesser effects?

Mathematically, this is a problem of maximization under constraints; the solution is to equate the effectiveness of the last dollar spent on each activity. For this example, the National Cancer Institute ought to allocate funds among the programs (taking care that the most effective projects are done first within each program) by testing the effectiveness of each dollar. The first increment of funds should be given to the program where it would be estimated to save the most lives. The second increment of funds should be allocated by the same criterion, perhaps going to the same program. As each successive increment of funds is allocated, the number of lives it saves should fall (since the best projects were done first). When all funds have been allocated, it should be true that the last increment of funds to each program would be expected to save approximately the same number of lives. If not, then funds should be reallocated by recalling them from the program where they are least effective and giving them to the program where they are most effective. Mathematically, the ratio of lives saved to dollars expended (for the last increment of funds) should be equal across programs when all funds have been allocated. As long as the ratios are not equal, additional lives could be saved for the same budget by removing funds from the program with the lowest ratio and adding them to the program with the highest ratio. . . .

Cost-effectiveness offers a major advantage over benefit-cost analysis in that it does not require an explicit value for the social cost of premature death (or other untraded goods). Assumptions about these values are built into the goal and budget (for example, maximize lives saved for a fixed budget) but need not be stated explicitly. The flip side of this advantage, however, is that errors in stating the goal or in determining the budget can lead to bad decisions, and there is no internal mechanism for showing the errors in these decisions and the changes in goals or budget that are necessary.

Regulatory Budget

Cost-effectiveness is a good framework if the relevant costs are being measured in the analysis. Unfortunately when the only costs considered are those of the regulatory agency, the framework will misallocate resources because only one subset of the total costs of the regulation to the entire economy is being considered. The agencies have little or no reason to consider the costs that their regulations impose on others unless the costs are so high that industry bankruptcy is a relevant possibility. The agencies are instructed to protect the environment, consumers, or workers without any apparent limits on their ability to impose costs on others. That the resulting regulations are not universally perceived as desirable can be judged from the comments of the affected companies and the fact that the federal government has often exempted itself from the regulations or has been slow in implementing them.

An idea originating in the Council of Economic Advisers under Charles Schultze was to give each regulatory agency an implementation budget in the form of a limit on the total annual costs that its regulations could impose. For example, the Environmental Protection Agency might be given an implementation budget of $10 billion a year, which would mean that the costs of implementing its air, water, solid waste, radiation, and pesticide regulations could not exceed $10 billion in that year. Each agency would develop an implementation budget request, just as it currently develops its operating budget request. The administration would coordinate and impose priorities on the agencies, and then Congress would react to these requests, modifying them as necessary.

The regulatory budget is one method of implementing cost-effectiveness analysis. The goals needed for the framework are stated in the legislation for each agency, supplemented by whatever informal instructions arise from hearings, appropriations, Office of Management and Budget directives, or presidential intervention. The internal and implementation budgets would be considered and approved by Congress, based on each agency's data on effectiveness. A major advantage of the framework is that it would elicit from the agencies a clearer indication of their priorities and would enable Congress to make more intelligent decisions regarding social values.

The principal difficulties with the framework are in estimating the costs and effects of each regulation. Where a control device must be added to a smokestack, there is debate about the cost of the device and about its expected lifetime, maintenance, and reliability. For a new piece of technology, these difficulties might perhaps introduce a factor-of-two difference in estimated costs. When the regulation will require a change in process or result in banning a substance, the costs become much more uncertain. If there is a factor-of-five-or-ten difference between reasonable high and low estimates of implementation costs, the regulatory budget cannot provide a helpful constraint. . . .

Benefit-Cost

This framework is similar to the general balancing of risks against benefits; the principal difference is that it is more quantitative and formal. In addition to enumerating the various benefits of the regulation and then subjectively balancing benefits against costs, this framework would require quantification of the extent to which the benefits and costs vary with the level of regulation, and then would require each of these effects to be translated into dollars.

There are many controversial aspects to its application, including putting an explicit value on prolonging a life, quantifying other benefits, deciding the rate at which effects in the future are discounted to make them equivalent to current effects, and redistributing income. Valuing benefits, or even deciding what is a benefit, runs into the diversity of cultural backgrounds, personal goals, fears, and time horizons. . . .

Benefit-cost analysis is a sufficiently broad framework to be adapted to consider virtually any aspect of a regulation or public decision. The implications for those who gain or lose can be folded into the analysis. None of the objections to the framework have the effect of showing an inherent bias or blind spot in the analysis.

In practice, however, the picture is quite different. Benefit-cost analysis is often viewed, correctly, as a tool for defending the status quo. It is rarely used to consider who benefits or pays, and it focuses on the present, giving short shrift to even the near-term future with no importance for events more than a few decades in the future. Adjustment costs are often estimated to be higher than would be observed, reflecting a prejudice that the current situation must be the best one (when adjustment costs are not considered, the analysis is biased toward change). Finally, a number of simplifying assumptions are made that bias the analysis against change. . . .

A Comparison of Frameworks

. . . Four criteria might be used to compare frameworks:

The first is comprehensiveness. Are all the relevant issues encompassed within the framework? No-risk considers only carcinogenesis (or other health attributes); risk-risk considers all health consequences either to the consumer (direct) or more generally (indirect). Cost-effectiveness and the regulatory budget require examination of costs as well as health, but they can be considered only within the goals of the agency. Benefit-cost and risk-benefit are the most encompassing, although even they are not used in practice to address equity questions.

The second criterion is the intellectual foundation required of each framework. One can be most certain about the foundation for the simple frameworks, but drawing in additional considerations requires more knowledge, assumptions, and value judgments. The wider coverage comes at a price. In some cases there is insufficient knowledge to be able to quantify or even explore these other considerations; if so, there is no alternative to a simple framework or an ad hoc decision.

The third criterion is the resources required to implement the framework. The more complicated frameworks require exploitation of further aspects of the problem, which in turn requires more data collection and analysis. Generally the resources available to analyze alternative regulations constitute a small proportion of those available for drafting and defending the regulations, and a minuscule proportion of the cost of carrying out the regulation. If additional analysis can result in even a tiny improvement in the quality of the regulation, the reduction in implementation and other costs should more than pay for the effort.

The fourth criterion is felicitousness. The world is complicated; it changes so rapidly that an agency rarely gets to second-order priority issues. The most important issues must be treated first, and they must be raised in easily comprehended fashion. If the issues are posed in a confused or obscure manner, the decision is likely to be made on an ad hoc basis. The felicitousness of the framework is more important than its comprehensiveness.

None of these frameworks is sufficiently complete and sound to serve as an automatic way of making decisions. The current Delaney Clause framework would appear to be the most concrete; even it, however, becomes mired in controversy over proving carcinogenicity. . . .

The other frameworks have the more difficult task of quantifying risk and of attempting to quantify other aspects of the issue (for example the value of greater choice). In all cases judgment is required to examine the suitability of the quantification, the factors that could not be quantified, and the valuation of the aspects that were quantified. These issues are far too complicated for a mechanical decision-making framework to be appropriate—for example one of pursuing a project if and only the estimated benefits exceed costs.

The real question is the extent to which each of these frameworks can prove helpful in informing the decisionmaker. Must all effects be quantified accurately and all valuations be agreed upon before benefit-cost analysis is helpful? If complete quantification is not possible or if there are difficulties in estimating risk, is it better to slip back to a less demanding framework, possibly back to the no-risk framework? The answer depends on both the amount of uncertainty and the extent to which the general nature of the uncertainty is known. No analysis of health and safety regulations has managed to quantify all aspects of the issue, and it is evident that no future analysis can be expected to be complete. If this lack of completeness is deemed fatal, there is no point in considering benefit-cost analysis further.

NOTES AND QUESTIONS

1. Choosing Among Frameworks. Simplistic solutions to risk management problems are likely to be undesirable. A no-risk command might be an unattractive one if there is a competing alternative that poses only slightly greater risk but is far less costly. Similarly, setting a standard so that the probability of some important adverse consequence is lower than a given threshold (say one in a million) might lead to an undesirable outcome if an alternative standard, with a probability only slightly above this threshold, would be far less costly. Also problematic is a fixed value trade-off between cost and risk. For example, one might be willing to pay more to reduce a unit of risk when risk is high than when it is low. *See* BARUCH FISCHHOFF ET AL., ACCEPTABLE RISK 5–7 (1981). Does the rejection of the no-risk and risk threshold approaches lead inevitably in the direction of cost-benefit analysis? Are there circumstances in which the level of costs, or the cost-risk trade-off, should just not matter? Does the rejection of fixed value tradeoffs between cost and risk imply a rejection of cost-benefit analysis?

2. Market Regulation. Consider the following instances of market regulation:

    (a)   buying a more expensive house rather than one that is cheaper but closer to a hazardous waste site, to a highway, or to a mental hospital;

    (b)   buying a more expensive car that provides more protection in the event of a crash;

    (c)   paying more to avoid flying on a commuter airline; and

    (d)   receiving a higher wage to take a job with higher workplace risks.

Which, if any, of these forms of market regulation are desirable?

3. Limits to Market Regulation. There is typically a cut-off or threshold below which we will not allow market regulation. Consider the *Benzene* case in which OSHA had been directed to set a limit on workplace exposure to benzene. Why did Congress not consider it adequate that workers exposed to high levels of benzene in the workplace are usually compensated by way of higher wages? Similarly, why does Congress set minimum safety requirements for automobiles in circumstances in which consumers may prefer to pay less for less secure cars? Why is regulatory intervention warranted under these circumstances? Is it that these risks are considered unacceptable according to societal values? If the risk is borne only by the consumer, why should the government intervene in market regulation?

4.   **Range of Debate.** A standard limiting to one-in-a-million the lifetime probability of getting cancer from exposure to an environmental risk is generally considered stringent and is often advocated by environmentalist groups, whereas a one-in-ten-thousand standard is generally considered lax and is often advocated by industry groups. Why do these numbers so often frame the range for mainstream debate? For further discussion, see Alon Rosenthal et al., *Legislating Acceptable Cancer Risk from Exposure to Toxic Chemicals*, 19 ECOLOGY L.Q. 269 (1992).

5.   **Technology-Based Standards.** In general, technology-based standards under the environmental statutes are set by reference to the best available technology that has been adequately demonstrated, taking costs into account. The consideration of costs has generally been taken to mean costs that a particular industry as a whole could bear and survive, even though particular firms might not survive. Is it sensible to regulate up to the point at which the industry as a whole is about to disappear? If not, what level of profit should the industry be able to keep? How should this tension affect the assessment of technology-based standards?

6.   **Features of Technology-Based Standards.** Consider the following features of using technology-based standards as the means for determining the level of environmental protection:

(a)   more stringent standards would be imposed on more profitable industries;

(b)   more stringent standards would be imposed on industries that face less foreign competition; and

(c)   more stringent standards would be imposed on industries that manufacture products for which there are no substitutes.

Are these features desirable?

7.   **Technology-Based Standards v. Cost-Benefit Analysis.** Compare the relative environmental protection that results from technology-based standards on the one hand and from cost-benefit analysis on the other. Which should environmentalists prefer? Which should labor unions prefer? Are these answers case specific? *See* Jonathan S. Masur & Eric A. Posner, *Against Feasibility Analysis*, 77 U. CHI. L. REV. 657, 697–98 (2010). Why do environmentalists generally prefer technology-based standards?

8.   **Market Entry and Technology-Based Standards.** If technology-based standards are the sole mechanism for determining the level of environmental quality, this level will vary depending on the rate of entry of new firms. Is this desirable? Should these standards be altered when new firms enter the market (or firms exit from the market)? Frequent changes, however, could be undesirable because they would render worthless

substantial investments in pollution control technology. What is the solution?

9.   Different Applications of Technology-Based Standards. Under the various environmental statutes, technology-based standards are sometimes used to determine the level of environmental protection, as discussed by Lave, but in other instances are used as the means to allocate among various polluters the pollution control burden that is determined through the use of a different framework. For example, under the CAA, technology-based standards for automobiles, new stationary sources, and certain types of existing sources are used as the means of meeting the National Ambient Air Quality Standards, which are nominally set by reference to the no-risk framework (as is discussed at greater length in Chapter V). Is the evaluation of technology-based standards different in this latter context?

10.   Media   Quality-Based   Approaches   v.   Technology-Based Approaches. Thomas McGarity draws a distinction between media quality-based approaches on the one hand, such as ambient air quality standards, and technology-based approaches on the other. Recall that media-quality-based approaches would guarantee a particular level of quality, while technology-based approaches would result in a level of quality by reference to what is feasible. *See* Thomas O. McGarity, *Media-Quality, Technology, and Cost-Benefit Balancing Strategies for Health and Environmental Regulation*, LAW & CONTEMP. PROBS., Summer 1983, at 159. McGarity suggests that:

> [T]he general preference of Congress and especially of implementing agencies for the technology-based approach . . . is warranted by an almost universal recognition that citizens of this country have a "right" to a healthy environment and workplace, at least insofar as the societal pursuit of that right is not technologically impossible or prohibitively expensive.

Id. at 161. Is this position compelling?

11.   Risk-Risk Framework. Under a risk-risk framework should the regulatory decision be simply to minimize the aggregate risk (in the Lave example, the sum of the risk of the carcinogenic food additive and the risk of botulism)? Alternatively, should man-made risks be weighted differently from natural risks? In this connection, consider the discussion of risk perceptions in the previous section. Is this example one in which market regulation, coupled with informational requirements, would achieve the best results? For example, the food product could be classified as organic or nonorganic and the relative risks could be disclosed. For an illuminating discussion of this framework, see RISK VS. RISK: TRADEOFFS IN PROTECTING HEALTH & THE ENVIRONMENT (John D. Graham & Jonathan B. Wiener eds., 1995).

12.   Trade-offs Under Risk-Risk Analysis. Under an indirect risk-risk framework, how should the health of workers be traded-off against the health of consumers? Consider the relevance of the following factors:

(a) whether workers are receiving a higher wage to reflect the additional risk to which they are exposed;

(b) whether consumers are sufficiently informed of the risks to make informed decisions; and

(c) whether there are less risky substitutes for the product.

13. Risk-Risk Analysis and Ancillary Benefits. The literature on risk-risk analysis has been predicated on the assumption that ancillary effects are negative. Should ancillary benefits also be considered in risk-risk analysis? For example, in conducting risk-risk analysis into the use of aspirin as a treatment of headaches, should the ancillary benefit of heart attack prevention be taken into account? Are there examples of ancillary environmental benefits? For further discussion of the treatment of ancillary risks and benefits, see Samuel J. Rascoff & Richard L. Revesz, *The Biases of Risk Tradeoff Analysis: Towards Parity in Regulatory Policy*, 69 U. CHI. L. REV. 1763 (2002) (challenging the common assumption that ancillary effects are always negative). A similar issue arises regarding the scope of cost-benefit analysis—that is, whether the "co-benefits" of reducing a targeted pollutant, such as associated reductions in other pollutants, should be included in the analysis. This issue is discussed later in this section and in Chapter V.

14. Risk-Benefit Analysis. The risk-benefit framework discussed by Lave typically balances the risks that remain under different levels of regulation with the resulting costs. Therefore risk-cost, or cost-risk, might be a more appropriate term. This term would also be more parallel to cost-benefit, which is simply a special case in which the benefits of regulation are quantified. Under the risk-benefit framework, how should one decide whether it is worth spending $100 million to save thirty lives, or to restore fish to a polluted river?

15. Risk-Benefit Analysis v. Cost-Benefit Analysis. The primary difference between the risk-benefit and cost-benefit frameworks is the lack of economic quantification of environmental benefits under the risk-benefit analysis approach. How useful then is the risk-benefit analysis in practice? How would it discern between the following regulatory responses: Response A which would save 100 lives and cost $500 million, and Response B which would save 110 lives and cost $600 million? How would cost-benefit analysis evaluate these policy responses?

16. Cost-Effectiveness and Regulatory Budget Approaches. Are the cost-effectiveness and regulatory budget approaches risk management frameworks, if risk management is understood to be the process by which society chooses the risk that it wishes to bear? Under the cost-effectiveness approach, on what basis should the underlying objective be chosen? Under a regulatory budget approach, how should the budget be set?

17. Implementation of a Regulatory Budget. In a portion of his book that is not excerpted above, Lave raises some practical concerns about the implementation of a regulatory budget. What might those concerns be? Lave concludes, "While the regulatory budget is admirably matched to current

American political institutions, the result is unlikely to be an intellectually coherent framework."

On January 30, 2017, President Trump signed Executive Order 13,771, which directs each agency to repeal at least two existing regulations before issuing a new regulation (referred to as the "one-in-two-out" requirement) and imposes a regulatory budget that sets a cap on total incremental regulatory costs (set at zero for fiscal year 2017). Exec. Order No. 13,771, 82 Fed. Reg. 9,339 (2017). For fiscal year 2018, OMB set EPA's annual regulatory budget at negative $40 million, meaning that, net of its actions in 2018, EPA is expected to reduce annual costs by $40 million. *See* OMB, REGULATORY REFORM: COST CAPS FISCAL YEAR 2018. (By comparison, in fiscal year 2017, EPA was estimated to have reduced annual costs by $21.5 million.) What assumptions must be made for the Order and resulting regulatory budgets to improve welfare for society? How do you think EPA will select regulations to repeal or modify? For a critique of the Order's potential to improve welfare, see Caroline Cecot & Michael A. Livermore, *The One-In, Two-Out Executive Order Is a Zero*, 166 U. PA. L. REV. ONLINE 1 (2017).

18. Cost-Benefit Analysis and the Status Quo. Why does Lave believe that benefit-cost analysis is a tool for defending the status quo? If this criticism is valid, how could this bias be eliminated?

19. Criteria for Discerning Between Frameworks. Evaluate the four criteria advanced by Lave to make comparative decisions among the different frameworks. Are other criteria relevant as well?

Compare the various risk management frameworks using Lave's criteria. Is one framework always favored? Does one framework do poorly? For further discussion of alternative decisional frameworks, see V. Kerry Smith, *A Conceptual Overview of the Foundations of Benefit-Cost Analysis*, *in* BENEFITS ASSESSMENT: THE STATE OF THE ART (Judith D. Bentkover et al. eds., 1986).

20. Risk Management Frameworks in Federal Environmental Statutes. Consider the hybrid decisional frameworks of the federal environmental statutes, which are discussed in the introduction to this section. What is the justification for the approach of the SDWA? Is this hybrid more or less stringent than what would result from a pure technology-based standard with the same definition of feasibility?

Under the hazardous air pollutant provision of the CAA, if one-in-a-million probability is considered the desirable goal, what is the justification for not weakening the technology-based standards if they would result in a lower probability of cancer?

Compare the CAA's approach to hazardous air pollutants to that of the SDWA. Under the former, a technology-based standard constitutes the first stage in the regulatory process; a health-based standard is the second step, which does not become effective until years later. In contrast, under the latter, the starting point is the health-based standard; at the second stage in the regulatory process, the enforceable, technology-based standard is promulgated. What factors might account for this different structure? For further discussion of risk management standards under the environmental statutes, see Harold P. Green, *The Role of Congress in Risk Management*, 16 ENVTL. L. REP. 10,220 (1986); *see also* Alon Rosenthal et al., *supra*.

What might explain the multiplicity of risk management frameworks under the federal environmental laws? Would some standardization be desirable?

21. The Precautionary Principle. Lave does not mention risk management predicated on the "precautionary principle," but this principle is one of the core environmental principles recognized by the European Community Treaty. *See* Treaty Establishing the European Community art. 174, Nov. 10, 1997, 1997 O.J. (C340) 3. This principle has been accepted as a risk management strategy to deal with cases "where there are reasonable grounds for concern that potential hazards may affect the environment or human, animal or plant health, and when at the same time the available data preclude a detailed risk evaluation." *Communication from the Commission on the Precautionary Principle*, at 8 COM (2000) 1 final (Feb. 2, 2000). In those circumstances, the precautionary principle "allows the competent public authority to take, on a provisional basis, preventive protective measures on what is as yet an incomplete scientific basis, pending the availability of additional scientific evidence." *Pfizer Animal Health SA v. Council of European Union*, Case t–13/99, 2002 E.C.R. II–03305, ¶ 387. What level of risk should be required to justify the enactment of regulation? Should every potential hazard be addressed? Consider the application of the precautionary principle to the use of nuclear energy. Nuclear power plants raise health and safety issues as well as the possibility that they could cause catastrophic harms. At the same time, the replacement of these plants with coal-fired power plants would create other risks such as air pollution and global warming. Which option should be chosen? Based on this and other examples, Cass R. Sunstein argues:

> Taken in this strong form, the precautionary principle should be rejected, not because it leads in bad directions, but because it leads in no direction at all. The principle is literally paralyzing— forbidding inaction, stringent regulation, and everything in between. The reason is that in the relevant cases, every step, including inaction, creates a risk to health, the environment, or both.

Cass R. Sunstein, *Beyond the Precautionary Principle*, 151 U. PA. L. REV. 1003, 1003 (2003). Do you find this opinion compelling? For an economic perspective on how to implement a precautionary principle for risk management, see Scott Farrow, *Using Risk Assessment, Benefit-Cost Analysis, and Real Options to Implement a Precautionary Principle*, 24 RISK ANALYSIS 727 (2004).

B. BALANCING ENVIRONMENTAL BENEFITS AND OTHER SOCIAL GOALS

i. AGENCY COST-BENEFIT ANALYSIS

Although an agency is required to conduct analyses of the costs and benefits of significant regulatory actions pursuant to Executive Order 12,866, it can rely on that cost-benefit analysis to justify its action only if allowed to do so by the statutory provision it is implementing. Sometimes statutes require cost-benefit analysis for implementing certain provisions. For example, under the Safe Drinking Water Act, EPA must calculate the "incremental costs and benefits associated with each alternative maximum contaminant level considered" and consider these costs and benefits when establishing a maximum contaminant level. 42 U.S.C. § 300g–1(b)(3)(C)(i). In other instances, a statute may prohibit an agency's reliance on cost-benefit analysis. For example, as discussed in Chapter V, the Supreme Court has held that the costs of pollution reduction cannot be taken into account in setting the NAAQS under the Clean Air Act. 42 U.S.C. § 7409(b). Many statutes, however, neither require nor prohibit cost-benefit analysis. In such instances, agency decisionmaking is often informed by the cost-benefit analysis conducted to comply with executive order requirements.

Cost-benefit analysis plays an important role in environmental decisionmaking, even though environmental regulations often affect "nonmarket" goods that may be difficult to quantify or monetize. Typical benefits of environmental regulation can be categorized as benefits to human life and health on the one hand and benefits to the environment on the other. The latter, in turn, are generally subdivided into three categories: use values, option values, and existence values. Use values arise with respect to environmental resources, such as pristine lakes that one values because one plans to actually use them. Option values arise with respect to resources that one does not currently use but that one may want to use in the future. Existence values, sometimes called non-use values, arise with respect to resources that one does not currently use or expect to use in the future but the existence of which nonetheless gives rise to utility. For example, one can derive utility from knowing that a wilderness area that one never plans to visit will remain pristine.

During the last few decades, economists have developed different techniques for valuing environmental benefits. Some of these techniques rely on "revealed preferences" to estimate society's willingness to pay for certain benefits. For example, EPA has adopted a "value of a statistical life" (VSL) measure to place a monetary value on mortality risk reduction that is largely based on revealed preferences. Generally speaking, the economic benefits associated with the reduction of mortality risks make up the largest component of all regulatory benefits. The VSL is calculated using information about workers' risk-wage tradeoffs in the labor market. A similar type of revealed preference methodology has been used to value local environmental amenities by analyzing how property values change as the environmental attributes of otherwise comparable properties change. Another type of revealed preference methodology is the travel-cost method, which can generate use values for environmental resources such as parks. The method estimates the value of such a site by analyzing the costs in terms of time and out-of-pocket expenses that individuals are willing to incur in order to visit the site.

Where revealed preference studies cannot be carried out, stated preference studies, such as contingent valuation methodologies, are used to obtain individuals' willingness to pay or accept specific changes in environmental quality by soliciting answers to hypothetical scenarios. In stated preference studies, individual valuations are determined by means of surveys, and the resulting figures are multiplied by the number of affected individuals. Stated preference approaches can be applied to value a wide range of environmental attributes, including use, option, and existence values.

Increasingly, an important benefit of many environmental regulations is the benefit of reducing greenhouse gas emissions that contribute to climate change. The "social cost of carbon" (SCC), for example, is the estimate of the damages of one ton of carbon dioxide emitted into the atmosphere. This estimate is based on complex integrated assessment models that link greenhouse gas emissions, temperature changes, and monetary damages. The SCC and related estimates play an important role in cost-benefit analyses as more agencies consider the ways in which their actions affect climate change.

Despite its prominence in agency decisionmaking, the use of cost-benefit analysis remains controversial, with economic and legal scholars raising conceptual and empirical objections. In this excerpt, W. Kip Viscusi describes his early experiences with agency cost-benefit analysis, focusing on the calculation and use of VSL estimates in the analysis.

W. Kip Viscusi, Pricing Lives: Guideposts for a Safer Society

1–2, 4–15 (2018).[*]

The Challenge of Valuing Morality Risks

"We can't do that. That's immoral." This was the reaction I got in 1980 when I suggested to a prominent Occupational Safety and Health Administration (QSHA) official that the agency monetize the reduced risks of death from job safety regulations using labor market estimates of workers' valuation of fatality risks. The values I advocated were based on the extra amounts workers are paid for each expected workplace death. Early studies often referred to these figures as the value of life, but the terminology used to describe this approach has evolved to be the

---

"value of a statistical life," which is both more accurate and somewhat less inflammatory.

The idea of monetizing the benefit of reduced worker fatality risks was not controversial. OSHA and other agencies had routinely attached dollar values to the expected lives that would be saved by regulations. In doing so, they followed the general approach patterned after that used by the courts in wrongful death cases, in which they equated the benefit of reduced risks of death to the value of lost earnings and medical expenses. This formulation enabled agencies to generate a mortality risk reduction benefit number and to be able to point to the use of a similar approach by the courts, thus providing some evidence of its reasonableness. However, there is a fundamental disconnect between these values and the core principle underlying benefit assessment, which is that benefit values for government policies should reflect society's willingness to pay for the benefit. An instructive way to ascertain these values is to examine the revealed preferences based on risk-taking behavior. The estimates of the value of a statistical life make such a connection by using the value that the workers themselves place on risks of death. . . .

The Triumph of the Value of a Statistical Life Approach: The Hazard Communication Policy Debate

. . . The most expensive major new initiative proposed in the early years of President Reagan's first term was the OSHA hazard communication regulation, which OSHA proposed in 1982. If this regulation was enacted, for the first time there would be regulatory requirements that firms label dangerous chemicals used in the workplace. Since these chemicals are often considerably more potent than household chemicals, the absence of any such labeling regulation more than a decade after OSHA's establishment was surprising. After having read these proposed chemical labels, workers would be aware of their chemical risk exposures and be able to take appropriate precautions, possibly including the decision to quit and seek safer employment. In addition, the regulation would require that firms maintain material safety data sheets so that if workers were exposed to a dangerous chemical, the medical personnel would be aware of the consequences of the exposure and know how to treat the worker.

OSHA's regulatory impact analysis for the hazard communication standards tallied the prospective costs and expected improvements in worker health and attached a dollar benefit to these health effects. The dominant benefit component for this regulation, as it is for most other health, safety, and environmental regulations, was the value of the mortality risk reduction. However, instead of using the value of a statistical life to monetize these effects, at that time OSHA and other agencies used the value of medical costs and lost earnings, or what they termed the "cost of death." After completing the analysis based on the costs of the deaths prevented by the regulation, OSHA submitted the proposed regulation to the OMB regulatory oversight group for the approval that was required before the regulation could be issued. Although OSHA's evaluation concluded that the regulation was desirable on balance, its economic assessment was flawed in several respects. Based on the critique of the regulatory impact analysis by the OMB economists, if OSHA had done a proper analysis, the result would have been that costs exceeded the benefits so that the regulation failed a benefit-cost test. As a result, OMB rejected OSHA's regulatory proposal.

OSHA nevertheless wished to pursue the possibility of issuing the regulation. The procedure that the Reagan administration had established for agency appeals was that in the event of a dispute, the regulatory agency could appeal the decision to then Vice President George H. W. Bush. The vice president characterized the disagreement as a technical economics dispute and suggested that an outside expert assess the merits of the competing arguments. I was asked to resolve the dispute after being approved by the Secretary of Labor and OMB. By that time, I had left the government and was then at Duke University, where my research continued to focus on risk regulation issues. The OMB regulatory oversight staff, most of whom were my former colleagues at the Council on Wage and Price Stability, raised a host of criticisms of OSHA's benefit estimates. All of these critiques were well founded. The result of adopting the OMB corrections to the analysis was that the calculated costs of the regulation exceeded the estimated benefits in terms of improved worker safety. In my assessment of the competing agency arguments, I accepted all of OMB's critiques as being sound.

Where my approach differed from that taken by both OSHA and OMB was with respect to how the expected lives saved would be valued. Both OSHA and OMB valued the lives saved based on what OSHA termed the "cost of death," or the present value of the medical costs and lost earnings that would be saved by preventing workers from being killed by chemical exposures. Under this approach, lives would have a value of several hundred thousand dollars, which was not a trivial amount, but was an arbitrary accounting measure that bore little relationship to how workers themselves valued risks of death. The approach I suggested utilized my labor market estimates of how much compensation workers required to face small risks of death. My estimate of the value of a statistical life at that time was $3 million per expected fatality prevented, or about $7.4 million adjusted for inflation. More recent estimates of the value of a statistical life generally place its value at between $9 million and $11 million. Using this estimate in the regulatory benefits analysis instead of the cost-of-death approach boosted benefits by an order of magnitude. Following a similar approach, I also attached values to the prevention of nonfatal worker injuries, but the driving force in the benefit assessment was the value of the fatalities prevented by the proposed regulation. The result of abandoning the cost-of-death approach was that benefits now exceeded the costs so that the hazard communication regulation would now pass OMB's economic test.

President Reagan approved the regulation almost immediately after my report in support of the regulation reached the White House.

The Genesis of Estimates of the Value of a Statistical Life

Where did this $3 million figure come from? The average annual worker fatality risk at that time was 1/10,000, which is more than double the current level of dangerousness. In return for bearing this risk, workers received an annual wage premium of $300, where this amount was estimated statistically controlling for other aspects of the job and worker characteristics. The result is that for a group of 10,000 workers, on average one of them would be killed on the job in the coming year. The amount of compensation that this group of 10,000 workers would receive for the one expected death is 10,000 × $300, or $3 million. Thus, the value of a statistical life is simply the total amount of compensation required per expected workplace death. The value of a statistical life reflects the values that the workers themselves believe that bearing these risks is worth rather than an accounting measure or an arbitrary number assigned by a government analyst.

But why should any finite value be applied to the expected lives saved? One could treat each expected life saved as having an infinite value. In that case, it would be desirable to expend the entire federal budget on safety measures that would eliminate a small chance of even one expected death. Given the multiple risks that we face and the limits on our financial resources, this uncompromising approach is infeasible. Consider data for 2014, the most recent year for which comprehensive accident data are available. There were 126,053 accidental deaths in the United States in 2014. If the entire gross domestic product of $17.4 trillion in 2014 were allocated to preventing accidents, it would only be possible to spend an average of $128 million per death to prevent these accidents, leaving nothing left to prevent illnesses or to provide for daily living expenses.

To motivate the reasonableness of using workers' wage-risk trade-offs as the guide, it is useful to ask people to conceptualize scenarios in which the reader makes similar decisions that do not reflect an unbounded commitment to safety, whether it involves living in a riskier but less expensive neighborhood or driving a car that doesn't have all possible safety enhancements. Most transportation choices and dietary decisions entail at least some risk. We do not plan our lives to minimize all possible risks. Through daily risk-taking decisions, people reveal that they place a finite value on reduced risks to their life. People's unwillingness to display an unbounded commitment to safety is consistent with a myriad of other risk-taking decisions that we make. The labor market estimates undertake a similar comparison in which the tradeoff is based on the extra wages that workers are paid for the additional risks posed by their jobs. . . .

Why Monetizing the Effects Matters

The monetization of the reduced mortality risks through application of the value of a statistical life is instrumental in the assessment of the benefits by the government, as it enables these effects to be put in the same terms as other economic impacts. The benefit-cost analysis procedure that lies at the heart of regulatory analyses involves a comparison of the benefits and the costs and a judgment that the benefits exceed the costs. To make such a comparison, at some point all effects must be put in comparable units, at least implicitly. Cost figures are dollar amounts that appear to be real economic consequences. Indeed, the regulatory oversight efforts in the Ford and Carter administrations were motivated primarily by a concern with the economic burdens arising from the inflationary effects of regulatory costs, not a concern with benefits or benefit-cost balance. Monetization of risk reduction benefits puts these effects on the same footing as the cost numbers, making clear that they are just as real economic effects as are regulatory costs. . . .

Failing to monetize the effects also limits the ability of benefit-cost analysis to provide a comprehensive index of the policy's attractiveness. By converting benefits into monetary terms, it is possible to compare the benefits and costs to assess the net attractiveness of the policy. Ultimately, any policy decision will implicitly make such a comparison even if the benefits are not monetized, so the failure to monetize risks disguises the hard choices being made but does not avoid the task of setting an implicit value on expected lives saved. Approval of a policy that costs $100 million and expects to save fifty lives implies that the government values lives at least at $2 million. Similarly, failure to move forward with a policy that costs $100 million but expects to save only ten lives indicates that the government values expected lives saved at less than $10 million. In instances in which there are multiple attributes that are not monetized, such as lives, cancer cases, and disabling injuries, it becomes more difficult to impute the specific implicit value of a statistical life that is incorporated in the policy decision. But whether the valuation is undertaken implicitly or explicitly, there is still some valuation judgment being made. . . .

Risk Awareness and Beliefs

The application of the VSL estimates appears to offer enormous potential dividends in a variety of contents, but is there any reason to believe the numbers are credible? Do workers even understand the risks posed by their jobs? This is an important question, since the VSL estimates are based on economic frameworks that assume that workers are aware of the risks they face. An assumption of fully informed workers seems unreasonable for hazardous exposures that cannot be readily monitored and that lead to illnesses not captured in accident statistics. However, the VSL estimates are based on acute fatality risks generally caused by accidents rather than deferred risks associated with occupational illnesses. Basing the VSL approach on a framework that presupposes awareness of the risk is reasonable for the types of hazards captured in labor market studies, which are the more visible risks, such as motor vehicle hazards and risks of fires and falls, rather than less apparent risks, such as the cancer risks of asbestos.

The evidence that workers' risk beliefs are plausible is quite strong. While the economic theory does not require that every worker can identify the job risks with pinpoint accuracy, workers' subjective risk perceptions do follow the expected patterns. Workers are more likely to believe their jobs expose them to dangerous or unhealthy conditions if they work in industries with higher reported accident rates. Whereas only 24 percent of workers in low-risk industries view their jobs as dangerous, all workers in the highest-risk industries believe that their jobs are dangerous. The most prominent hazards cited by workers are inherently dangerous materials, inherently hazardous equipment, inherently hazardous procedures, dangerous exposure to dust, and transportation hazards. A particularly striking result is that for my survey of hundreds of chemical workers . . . , workers' perceptions of the accident rate in their jobs were equal to the objective measure of the average injury risk in the chemical industry.

The sources of information about risks are quite diverse. Many hazards, such as the dangers of high-rise construction work, are readily apparent. Moreover, over two-fifths of all workplace fatalities are related to motor vehicles, which post quite familiar risks. Workers also learn through their on-the-job experiences. Workers who have experienced an on-the-job injury on their current job are more likely to regard their jobs as being dangerous, as 71 percent of those who have experienced such an injury view their jobs as dangerous. These patterns of risk beliefs are consistent with the notion that people learn about risks in a sensible way. If the wages paid for these perceived risks are inadequate, they may quit. My estimates have found that one-third of all manufacturing quit rates are attributable to this learning response to job risks. Moreover, after quitting these jobs, workers switch to positions for which they receive appropriate risk compensation in line with the VSL estimates.

How do estimates of the wage premiums workers receive for subjectively assessed risks compare with the economists' estimates derived using objective risk measures in the statistical analysis of compensation for risk? There are in fact strong parallels in terms of the wage-premium effects implied by objective measures of the risk and subjective worker assessments. The wage-premium estimates for risk that I obtained using fatality risk measures conditional on workers perceiving that their jobs exposed them to dangerous or unhealthy conditions were the same as the values obtained with empirical estimates based on objective industry risk measures. Also, if workers are completely ignorant of the hazards, there will be no market mechanism that generates wage premiums for risks, so the existence of observed wage differentials provides additional evidence of some underlying risk awareness. Situations in which there are gaps in the provision of such risk compensation, such as for immigrant workers in dangerous jobs, serve as a red flag that there is something amiss and more vigilant government regulation might be beneficial. . . .

NOTES AND QUESTIONS

1. **Cost-Benefit Analysis in Environmental Regulation.** Cost-benefit analysis as generally practiced by federal agencies involves explicitly listing, quantifying, and, when possible, monetizing the expected benefits and costs of various regulatory alternatives. The estimated costs are largely regulatory compliance costs, which approximate the social or opportunity costs of regulation. Social benefits, meanwhile, may include health improvements from cleaner air or water. To value these benefits, economists estimate society's willingness to pay (WTP) to reduce these risks. In some cases, benefits may be difficult or controversial to quantify or monetize. Is this a reason to avoid quantifying benefits or using cost-benefit analysis altogether in environmental decisionmaking? How would Viscusi defend the use of cost-benefit analysis in environmental decisionmaking? *See also* Richard L. Revesz, *Quantifying Regulatory Benefits*, 102 CAL. L. REV. 1423 (2014).

2. **The Influence of Cost-Benefit Analysis.** Viscusi describes a situation in which correctly "pricing" lives led to the adoption of more stringent regulation. Another example is the Reagan administration's imposition of a stricter standard for phasing out lead in gasoline than initially thought warranted, based on the results of a cost-benefit analysis. *See* Statement of Christopher DeMuth, *in* AMERICAN ECONOMIC POLICY IN THE 1980S, at 508 (Martin Feldstein ed., 1994) ("A very fine piece of analysis persuaded everyone that the health harms of leaded gasoline were far greater than we had thought, and we ended up adopting a much tighter program than the one we had inherited."). In particular, the final cost-benefit analysis estimated the total benefits of reducing blood-lead levels in children to be about $500 million in 1988, which was much higher than in initial estimates that left categories of these benefits "nonmonetized." *See* Albert L. Nichols, *Lead in Gasoline*, in ECONOMIC ANALYSIS AT EPA: ASSESSING REGULATORY IMPACT 49, 56, 74 (Richard D. Morgenstern ed., 1997) (describing the evolution of the analysis). Combined with benefits of reduced conventional pollutant emissions, decreased maintenance costs, increased fuel economy, and reduced blood-pressure health effects, the estimated benefits far exceeded the estimated costs. *See id.* at 74.

More recent studies suggest that the benefits of phasing out lead in gasoline were even higher than initially estimated. *See, e.g.*, Joel Schwartz, *Societal Benefits of Reducing Lead Exposure*, 66 ENVTL. RESEARCH 105 (1994) (estimating net benefits of $17.2 billion per year for each 1 microgram reduction in average blood lead concentrations); Debra J. Brody et al., *Blood Lead Levels in the US Population*, 272 JAMA 277 (1994) (estimating a 10 microgram decline in average blood-lead levels in children due in large part to the lead phasedown). What does this suggest about the accuracy of the EPA's estimates? Does this provide evidence for or against the use of cost-benefit analysis?

3.   An Attack on Cost-Benefit Analysis. Steven Kelman questions the frequent use of cost-benefit analysis in environmental, safety, and health regulation. Steven Kelman, *Cost-Benefit Analysis: An Ethical Critique*, REGULATION, Jan–Feb 1981, at 33. First, he argues that the methods used by economists to perform these valuations are invariably subject to criticism on technical grounds. Second, he challenges the valuation of benefits by ascertaining an individual's WTP for an environmental amenity, a measure which he argues is likely to understate the true value of the resource. In support of this position, he relies upon studies which suggest that one's WTP for a resource is inevitably lower than one's willingness to accept (WTA) compensation to give up a resource already in one's possession. Third, Kelman argues that it is inappropriate to use WTP values in making public policy, because there exists a difference between the attitudes that people express in public and in private. Fourth, he argues that the mere act of pricing certain non-market commodities reduces their value.

Assess the strength of Kelman's critique of cost-benefit analysis. How would Viscusi respond? Which view do you find more persuasive? What decisional framework do you think Kelman favors? Other critiques of cost-benefit analysis from different perspectives include Duncan Kennedy, *Cost-Benefit Analysis of Entitlement Problems: A Critique*, 33 STAN. L. REV. 387 (1981); Richard B. Stewart, *Regulation in a Liberal State: The Role of Non-Commodity Values*, 92 YALE L.J. 1537 (1983).

One of Kelman's primary objections is directed toward the monetization of environmental benefits. Should he then favor the risk-benefit (risk-cost) approach? Under this approach, how could he decide whether a particular expenditure is worthwhile if it saves a certain number of lives?

4.   The Value of a Statistical Life. Should a regulatory system attempt to value human life? If not, on what basis should it decide to regulate an environmental risk?

Even if human life is not explicitly valued in the regulatory process, one can determine what value was "imputed" to life (at least in cases in which there are no additional benefits to the environment) by dividing the cost of the regulation by the number of lives that it expects to save. Studies show that there is a wide disparity across regulatory programs, ranging from $10,000 to over $100 million. *See* STEPHEN BREYER, BREAKING THE VICIOUS CIRCLE: TOWARD EFFECTIVE RISK REGULATION 92 (1993). In light of these results, is it appropriate to insist on more stringent regulation for programs in which the imputed valuation is low, and less stringent regulation for programs in which it is high? Is such an inquiry a disguised form of cost-benefit analysis? Is consistency desirable? In this connection, consider the factors, discussed in the previous section, that affect risk perceptions. *See* Lewis A. Kornhauser, *The Value of Life*, 38 CLEV. ST. L. REV. 209 (1990).

5.   Willingness to Pay as a Value of Human Life. Consider the WTP approach to calculating VSL. How does one determine that two jobs are identical in all respects except for the fatality risk level? How does one determine the additional fatality risk of one of the jobs? Is it likely to be an expert or a lay assessment? How many people are induced to take risky jobs as a result of wage premiums? Are there problems with extrapolating to the population as a whole? Why is this issue significant? As discussed in the previous section, studies show that individuals undervalue voluntary risks relative to involuntary risks. How does this phenomenon affect the valuations? Consider the following criticism advanced by Kelman—that individuals who take risky jobs are likely to have unusually low valuations of risk, because of either unusually weak aversions to risk or unusually strong constraints on their choices. For more discussion of the WTP procedure, see W. Kip Viscusi, *The Value of Risks to Life and Health*, 31 J. ECON. LITERATURE 1912 (1993); Richard Zeckhauser, *Procedures for Valuing Lives*, 23 PUB. POL'Y 419 (1975).

6. Environmental Risks v. Fatality Risks. Are risks in the environmental context different? Unlike the acute fatality risks that underlie estimates of wage premiums, most environmental regulations do not protect against fatality risks but rather against cancers that might arise later and eventually result in death. Should cancer risks be evaluated differently? Do you think individuals would pay more or less to avoid cancer risks?

7. Social Cost of Carbon. Another important benefit of many environmental regulations is the benefit of reducing greenhouse gas emissions. In 2010, the Obama administration convened an Interagency Working Group (IWG) to determine the SCC, which is the estimate of the damages of one ton of carbon dioxide. *See* IWG, SOCIAL COST OF CARBON FOR REGULATORY IMPACT ANALYSIS UNDER EXECUTIVE ORDER 12,866 (2010). In 2016 the IWG released the most recent estimate of the SCC, finding that each ton of carbon dioxide causes at least $51 in quantifiable damages to the economy, with this number rising over time. *See* IWG, TECHNICAL UPDATE OF THE SOCIAL COST OF CARBON at 4 (2016). Related estimates quantify damages from other greenhouse gases; for example, the "social cost of methane" (SCM) estimates damages of $1470 per ton of methane emitted. IWG, ADDENDUM: APPLICATION OF THE METHODOLOGY TO ESTIMATE THE SOCIAL COST OF METHANE AND THE SOCIAL COST OF NITROUS OXIDE at 7 (2016). During the Obama administration, the IWG's estimates of the SCC and the SCM have been used across agencies in cost-benefit analyses for regulations that reduce greenhouse gas emissions.

The Trump administration has disbanded the IWG, *see* Exec. Order. No. 13,783, 82 Fed. Reg. 16,093 (2017), and agencies have since produced much lower "interim" estimates of the SCC and the SCM, *see* EPA, REGULATORY IMPACT ANALYSIS FOR THE REVIEW OF THE CLEAN POWER PLAN: PROPOSAL at 44 (2017) (estimating SCC at as low as $1 per ton); BUREAU OF LAND MGMT., REGULATORY IMPACT ANALYSIS FOR THE PROPOSED RULE TO SUSPEND OR DELAY CERTAIN REQUIREMENTS OF THE 2016 WASTE PREVENTION RULE at 26 (2017) (estimating the SCM at as low as $58 per ton). These estimates attempt to value only the U.S. effects of climate change and apply a much higher discount rate to climate damages spanning several generations. Are a new administration's changes to the SCC a legitimate exercise in democratic accountability or a problematic intrusion of politics into a technical process?

8.   Global v. Domestic Social Cost of Carbon. One of the most controversial normative questions surrounding the use of SCC and SCM estimates in agency cost-benefit analysis is whether the estimates should reflect global or domestic-only damages from climate change. On one hand, statutes and regulations are typically concerned with effects within the United States. On the other hand, climate change presents a significant challenge to the United States as well as other nations. It is a challenge that the United States will not be able to solve on its own, and each country benefits from reductions in other countries. Should the United States use an estimate that reflects global or domestic-only damages? If the United States shifts from global to domestic estimates of damages, how might other countries respond? *See* Matthew J. Kotchen, *Which Social Cost of Carbon? A Theoretical Perspective*, 5 J. ASS'N ENVTL. & RESOURCE ECONOMISTS 673 (2018). In addition, experts agree that existing economic models, which already suffer from considerable uncertainty given the complexity of linked climate-economy-society systems, cannot accurately calculate a domestic-only estimate that still takes into account the spillover effects of foreign climate damages into the United States. Does this change your answer? For more discussion of this issue, see Peter Howard & Jason Schwartz, *Think Global: International Reciprocity as Justification for a Global Social Cost of Carbon*, 42 COL. J. ENVTL. L. 203 (2017); Ted Gayer & W. Kip Viscusi, *Determining the Proper Scope of Climate Change Policy Benefits in U.S. Regulatory Analyses: Domestic versus Global Approaches*, 10 REV. ENVTL. ECON. & POL'Y 1 (2016); Arden Rowell, *Foreign Impacts and Climate Change*, 39 HARV. ENVTL. L. REV. 371 (2015); Jody Freeman & Andrew Guzman, *Climate Change and U.S. Interests*, 109 COLUM. L. REV. 1531 (2009).

9.   Existence Values. While the concept of existence values is now well established in the economic literature, consider the following attack:

> Perhaps the greatest conceptual problem with existence value is deciding which goods and service . . . of the world have an existence value. For example, why not expand the concept to continued . . . existence of the great American farmer. . . .

> The family farm is also just the tip of the iceberg for an expanded list of possible existence values. Other candidates include . . . coal mining jobs in West Virginia, automobile manufacturing jobs in Detroit, or jobs anywhere. Because of existence values, trade barriers may start to look more efficient as they generate large economic values by preserving the existence of readily identifiable American jobs. But then, of course, there is also an existence value to reducing poverty in Third World nations that may offset the existence value gains closer to home.

Donald H. Rosenthal & Robert H. Nelson, *Why Existence Value Should <u>Not</u> Be Used in Cost-Benefit Analysis*, 11 J. POL'Y ANALYSIS & MGM'T 116, 118 (1992).

How would you respond? *See* Raymond J. Kopp, *Why Existence Value <u>Should</u> Be Used in Cost-Benefit Analysis*, 11 J. POL'Y ANALYSIS & MGM'T 123

(1992). If people value jobs or the reduction of poverty, why should these factors not enter a cost-benefit analysis?

The procedure generally employed for valuing existence values, the contingent valuation methodology, is highly controversial. What are possible concerns? The issues are summarized in Paul R. Portney, *The Contingent Valuation Debate: Why Economists Should Care*, 8 J. ECON. PERSP. 3 (1994). *See also* RICHARD L. REVESZ & MICHAEL A. LIVERMORE, RETAKING RATIONALITY 125–26 (2008).

10. Scope of Cost-Benefit Analysis. When an agency seeks to regulate a specific substance, should it consider only the direct costs and direct benefits of regulating that substance? Imagine that regulating the substance would result in indirect costs, such as increased use of an even more hazardous substance. Should an agency consider these potential costs in its cost-benefit analysis? Alternatively, imagine that regulating the substance would produce indirect benefits, such as reductions in other hazardous substances. Should an agency consider these potential benefits, sometimes referred to as "co-benefits," in its cost-benefit analysis? How would including these indirect effects change the recommended level of regulatory stringency? Is there a reason to consider one and not the other?

Including indirect effects ensures that regulators base their risk management decisions on an accurate picture of the actual effects of regulatory action. Agency guidelines have instructed regulators to assess indirect effects. *See* OMB, CIRCULAR A-4 at 26 (2003); EPA, GUIDELINES FOR PREPARING ECONOMIC ANALYSIS at 11–2 (2010). And when agencies have relied on cost-benefit analysis, courts have reviewed whether agencies considered indirect costs. *See, e.g., Michigan v. EPA*, 135 S. Ct. 2699, 2707 (2015) (explaining that the advantages and disadvantages of regulation included not just direct compliance costs, but indirect "harms that regulation might do to human health or the environment"); *Corrosion Proof Fittings v. EPA*, 947 F.2d 1201, 1225 (5th Cir. 1991) (holding that EPA must consider the indirect safety effects of substitute options for car brakes when banning asbestos-based brakes under the Toxic Substances Control Act). It is difficult to argue that agencies should treat indirect benefits differently than indirect costs. *See* REVESZ & LIVERMORE, *supra*, at 55–66. This is especially true when a statute, while silent on the specific scope of the cost-benefit analysis, provides an agency with authority to regulate in the public welfare. *See U.S. Sugar Corp. v. EPA*, 830 F.3d 579, 625–26 (D.C. Cir. 2016) (explaining that the statutory "text does not foreclose the Agency from considering co-benefits and doing so is consistent with the [statute's] purpose"). Is it more efficient to regulate pollutants jointly or separately? Does it matter if the co-benefits of regulating a substance are much higher than the direct benefits? What if indirect costs are much higher than direct costs?

ii.   JUDICIAL REVIEW OF AGENCY COST-BENEFIT ANALYSIS

When litigants challenge the reasonableness of an agency's decisionmaking, and the agency relied on some type of cost-benefit analysis, the court may review the cost-benefit analysis and assess its reasonableness. In the absence of specific statutory guidance, a reviewing court will scrutinize the cost-benefit analysis using the "arbitrary or capricious" standard of review prescribed by the Administrative Procedure Act (APA). In *Motor Vehicle Manufacturers Ass'n of the United States, Inc. v. State Farm Mutual Automobile Insurance Co*, 463 U.S. 29 (1983), the Supreme Court stated that

> an agency rule would be arbitrary and capricious if the agency has relied on factors which Congress has not intended it to consider, entirely failed to consider an important aspect of the problem, offered an explanation for its decision that runs counter to the evidence before the agency, or is so implausible that it could not be ascribed to a difference in view or the product of agency expertise.

Id. at 43. Typical challenges to a cost-benefit analysis include whether the agency sufficiently considered all reasonable, or statutorily mandated, factors; whether the underlying assumptions or methodology in the analysis were reasonable, including the agency's choice of model for a particular phenomenon or choice of discount rate when evaluating future effects; and whether the agency provided sufficient explanation of the analysis's scope or methodology to provide for adequate opportunity for notice and comment and substantive judicial review. The cases that follow highlight the practical challenges of conducting cost-benefit analysis and raise questions about the effectiveness and desirability of judicial review.

Environmental Defense Fund, Inc. v. Environmental Protection Agency

548 F.2d 998 (D.C. Cir. 1976), *cert. denied*, 431 U.S. 925 (1977).

■ Before LEVENTHAL, ROBINSON, and WILKEY, CIRCUIT JUDGES.

■ LEVENTHAL, CIRCUIT JUDGE:

This case involves the pesticides heptachlor and chlordane. Consolidated petitions seek review of an order of the Environmental Protection Agency (EPA) suspending the registration of those pesticides under the [Federal Insecticide, Fungicide, and Rodenticide Act (FIFRA)] for certain uses. The Administrator of EPA issued an order on December 24, 1975. The order prohibited further production of these pesticides for the suspended uses, but permitted the pesticides' continued production and sale for limited minor uses. Even as to the suspended uses, the Order tempered its impact in certain respects: It delayed until August 1, 1976, the effective date of the prohibition of production for use on corn pests; and it permitted the continued sale and use of existing stocks of registered products formulated prior to July 29, 1975.

One petition to review was filed by Earl L. Butz, Secretary of Agriculture of the United States (U.S.D.A.). Secretary Butz and intervenor Velsicol Chemical Corporation, the sole manufacturer of heptachlor and chlordane, urge that the EPA order as to chlordane be set aside on both substantive and procedural grounds. They contend that substantial evidence does not support the Administrator's conclusion that continued use of chlordane poses an "imminent hazard" to human health, and that the Administrator made critical errors in assessing the burden of proof and in weighing the benefits against the risks of continued use of chlordane.

The other petition, filed by Environmental Defense Fund, urges that the Order did not go far enough to protect against the hazards of heptachlor and chlordane use. EDF sought an injunction against the provisions permitting continued production and use of the pesticides on corn pests until August 1, 1976. EDF also challenges the Administrator's decision to allow continued use of the stocks of the two pesticides existing as of July 29, 1975, contending that EPA should have provided for retrieval and controlled disposal of such stocks. EDF also contends that the Administrator erred in failing to suspend certain "minor uses" of chlordane and heptachlor.

I.   Statutory Framework and Standard of Review

. . . The Administrator is authorized to suspend the registration of a pesticide where he determines that an "imminent hazard" is posed by continued use during the time required for cancellation. Section 6(c) of FIFRA, 7 U.S.C. § 136d(c)(1). An "imminent hazard" exists where continued use during the time required for the cancellation proceeding would be likely to result in "unreasonable adverse effects on the environment." Section 2(l) of FIFRA, 7 U.S.C. § 136(l). The term "unreasonable adverse effects on the environment" is, in turn, defined as "any unreasonable risk to man or the environment, taking into account the economic, social, and environmental costs and benefits of the use of any pesticide." Section 2(bb) of FIFRA, 7 U.S.C.§ 136(bb). . . .

II.   Substantial Evidence Support for the
Administrator's Decision

To evaluate whether use of a pesticide poses an "unreasonable risk to man or the environment," the Administrator engages in a cost-benefit analysis that takes "into account the economic, social, and environmental costs and benefits of the use of any pesticide." 7 U.S.C. § 136(bb). We have previously recognized that in the "preliminary assessment of probabilities" involved in a suspension proceeding, "it is not necessary to have evidence on . . . a specific use or area in order to be able to conclude on the basis of substantial evidence that the use of [a pesticide] in general is hazardous." EDF v. EPA, 489 F.2d at 1254, quoted in EDF v. EPA [Shell Chemical Co.], 510 F.2d at 1301. "Reliance on general data, consideration of laboratory experiments on animals, etc." has been held a sufficient basis for an order cancelling or suspending the registration of a pesticide. Id. Once risk is shown, the responsibility to demonstrate that the benefits outweigh the risks is upon the proponents of continued registration. Conversely, the statute places a "heavy burden" of explanation on an Administrator who decides to permit the continued use of a chemical known to produce cancer in experimental animals. Applying these principles to the evidence adduced in this case, we conclude that the Administrator's decision to suspend most uses of heptachlor and chlordane and not to suspend others is supported by substantial evidence and is a rational exercise of his authority under FIFRA. . . .

[Velsicol and USDA argued that the laboratory tests on mice and rats do not "conclusively" demonstrate that chlordane is carcinogenic to those animals; that mice are too prone to tumors to be used in carcinogenicity testing in any case; and that human exposure to chlordane is insufficient to create a cancer risk. After evaluating the data presented, the Court affirmed the Administrator's conclusions, stating "[w]e have previously held that it is not necessary to have evidence on a specific use to be able to conclude that the use of a pesticide in general is hazardous. Once the initial showing of hazard is made for one mode of exposure in a suspension proceeding, and the pesticide is shown to be present in human tissues, the burden shifts to the registrant to rebut the inference that other modes of exposure may also pose a carcinogenic hazard for humans. Velsicol has totally failed to meet that burden here."]
. . .

B.   Benefits

Velsicol and USDA challenge the Administrator's finding that the benefits derived from the suspended uses of chlordane do not outweigh the harms done. EDF urges that the Administrator's decision to continue some uses was not justified by evidence that the risk of harm was outweighed by benefits from the continued uses.

1.   Use on Corn

Heptachlor and chlordane were used on an estimated 3.5% of the total corn acreage in the United States in 1975, largely in an effort to control black cutworm. Cutworms sporadically infest 2 to 8% of total U.S. corn farms, and occur most often in lowland, river bottom areas. Chlordane and heptachlor are used as preplant treatments to insure against possible infestations. The Administrator found, with record support, that no macroeconomic impact will occur as a result of suspending those pesticides. He also found that crop surveillance or "scouting" for infestations during the early weeks of plant growth, together with application of post-emergence baits or sprays where necessary, provide an effective alternative to the more indiscriminate prophylactic use of chlordane and heptachlor. Velsicol urges that this approach is not as effective as the persistent protection provided by chlordane. Especially in the absence of proof of a serious threat to the nation's corn, there is no requirement that a pesticide can be suspended only if alternatives to its use are absolutely equivalent in effectiveness. The Administrator reasonably took into account that a transition period

would be necessary to implement post-emergent techniques of control
and concluded that the challenged pesticides could continue in use for
corn protection until August 1, 1976. This evaluation of alternatives and
the time required to implement them is supported by substantial
evidence, and we find no basis to disturb the Administrator's balancing
of costs and benefits.

2. Miscellaneous Agricultural Uses

The Administrator suspended a number of agricultural uses where
the record was insufficient to support any finding that benefits outweigh
costs of continued use of heptachlor or chlordane on these crops. Possibly
the lack of benefits evidence reflected readily available alternatives,
possibly a relative lack of interest in lesser-volume uses. In any event,
the registrant's failure to carry its burden of adducing sufficient evidence
on benefits in effect leaves the Administrator nothing to weigh in his cost-
benefit analysis except the evidence that the use of the challenged
pesticides in general is hazardous. That evidence of general hazard is
sufficient to support a suspension of uses.

3. Non-Agricultural Uses Suspended by the Administrator

Chlordane is a common household, lawn, garden, and ornamental
turf insecticide, with over 7.5 million pounds (36% of total use) so
employed in 1974. The ALJ and Administrator found on the basis of
substantial evidence that the "efficaciousness of the substitutes for
control of household and lawn insects is not really at issue" and that
when lack of evidence of substantial benefits from continued use is
weighed against the special hazards of exposure presented by the
possibilities of inhalation, dermal absorption, and the increased dangers
associated with improper handling, suspension of those uses was
justified. Similarly, on the basis of evidence in the record, the
Administrator could reasonably find that the residual capacity of
chlordane was not necessary to control either structural pests or ticks
and chiggers, given the existence of effective alternatives to each of those
uses.

4. The Administrator's Refusal to Suspend Certain Uses

EDF challenges the Administrator's refusal to suspend use of
chlordane or heptachlor on strawberries, for seed treatment, pineapples,
the white fringed beetle, Florida citrus, white grubs in Michigan, narcissi
bulbs, harvester ants, imported fire ant, Japanese beetle quarantine, and
black vine weevil quarantine in Michigan. Following the
recommendations of the ALJ, the Administrator found that for each use
the benefits outweighed the risks for the limited time under
consideration, effective alternatives were generally not available, and
that the exposure risk arising from the use was minimal. EDF counters
that the total exposure resulting from these "minor" uses is in fact
significant, and that the Administrator continued these uses whenever a
"colorable" case of benefits had been made out.

Once the Administrator has found that a risk inheres in the use of a pesticide, he has an obligation to explain how the benefits of continued use outweigh that risk. We are satisfied that he has met that obligation here, and that substantial evidence supports his decision. We note, however, that we come to this conclusion in the context of a suspension proceeding where perforce the Administrator is engaged in making a "preliminary assessment" of the evidence; a more careful exploration of economic impact and available alternatives would be required to support continued registration in a cancellation proceeding.

C.   Continued Sale and Use of Existing Stocks of Chlordane and Heptachlor for Suspended Uses

Although we have no doubt that the Administrator has the power under FIFRA to exempt from a suspension order the use of existing stocks (in this case stocks existing as of July 29, 1975), the Administrator acted arbitrarily when he failed to even inquire into the amount of stocks left, and the problem of returning and disposing of them. *Some* evidence must be adduced before an exemption decision is made, and it is the responsibility of the registrant to provide it. It may be that the lapse of time has lessened the current significance of this issue but we are in no position to do other than remand for further consideration.

We affirm the Agency's suspension order of December 24, 1975, as clarified by the order of January 19, 1976, except for the exemption of the sale and use of existing stocks. The record is remanded for further consideration of that issue.

NOTES AND QUESTIONS

1.   "Imminent Hazard" and "Unreasonable Adverse Effects" Under FIFRA. How does FIFRA define an "imminent hazard"? How does FIFRA define "unreasonable adverse effects on the environment"? On what basis did EPA engage in cost-benefit analysis to determine whether heptachlor and chlordane gave rise to "unreasonable adverse effects on the environment"?

2.   Adequacy of EPA's Cost-Benefit Analysis. What was the subject of controversy in this case? On what basis did Velsicol and USDA challenge EPA's finding that the benefits derived from the suspended uses of chlordane did not outweigh the resulting harms? On what basis did EDF argue that EPA's decisions to allow the continuation of other uses were not justified?

Compare, for example, EPA's findings on corn crops with those on strawberry crops. On what basis did EPA find that the costs of using the pesticides on corn crops outweighed its benefits? Why did EPA reach the opposite conclusion with respect to strawberries? Why, in both cases, did the court uphold the Agency's findings? In either case, did the Agency quantify the costs and benefits of the proposed regulation? If not, on what basis was a comparison made? Was this of concern to the court?

3.   Impact of Executive Order 12,291. Recall that this decision predated the promulgation of Executive Order 12,291 by President Reagan in 1981. Would this Order, and the subsequent Order promulgated by President

Clinton, have had an impact on the manner in which the Agency conducted its various cost-benefit analyses in this case?

Corrosion Proof Fittings v. Environmental Protection Agency

947 F.2d 1201 (5th Cir. 1991).

■ Before BROWN, SMITH, and WIENER, CIRCUIT JUDGES.

■ SMITH, CIRCUIT JUDGE:

The Environmental Protection Agency (EPA) issued a final rule under section 6 of the Toxic Substances Control Act (TSCA) to prohibit the future manufacture, importation, processing, and distribution of asbestos in almost all products. . . .

Asbestos is a naturally occurring fibrous material that resists fire and most solvents. Its major uses include heat-resistant insulators, cements, building materials, fireproof gloves and clothing, and motor vehicle brake linings. Asbestos is a toxic material, and occupational exposure to asbestos dust can result in mesothelioma, asbestosis, and lung cancer. . . .

An EPA-appointed panel reviewed over one hundred studies of asbestos and conducted several public meetings. Based upon its studies and the public comments, the EPA concluded that asbestos is a potential carcinogen at all levels of exposure, regardless of the type of asbestos or the size of the fiber. The EPA concluded in 1986 that exposure to asbestos "poses an unreasonable risk to human health" and thus proposed at least four regulatory options for prohibiting or restricting the use of asbestos, including a mixed ban and phase-out of asbestos over ten years; a two-stage ban of asbestos, depending upon product usage; a three-stage ban on all asbestos products leading to a total ban in ten years; and labeling of all products containing asbestos. *Id.* at 29,460–61.

Over the next two years, the EPA updated its data, received further comments, and allowed cross-examination on the updated documents. In 1989, the EPA issued a final rule prohibiting the manufacture, importation, processing, and distribution in commerce of most asbestos-containing products. Finding that asbestos constituted an unreasonable risk to health and the environment, the EPA promulgated a staged ban of most commercial uses of asbestos. The EPA estimates that this rule will save either 202 or 148 lives, depending upon whether the benefits are discounted, at a cost of approximately $450–800 million, depending upon the price of substitutes. *Id.* at 29,468. . . .

. . . TSCA provides that a reviewing court "shall hold unlawful and set aside" a final rule promulgated under § 6(a) "if the court finds that the rule is not supported by substantial evidence in the rulemaking record . . . taken as a whole." 15 U.S.C. § 2618(c)(1)(B)(i).

. . . An agency may exercise its judgment without strictly relying upon quantifiable risks, costs, and benefits, but it must "cogently explain why it has exercised its discretion in a given manner" and "must offer a 'rational connection between the facts found and the choice made.'" *Id.* (quoting Motor Vehicle Mfrs. Ass'n v. State Farm Mut. Auto. Ins., 463 U.S. 29 (1983)). . . .

TSCA provides, in pertinent part, as follows:

(a) Scope of regulation.—If the Administrator finds that there is a *reasonable basis* to conclude that the manufacture, processing, distribution in commerce, use, or disposal of a chemical substance or mixture, or that any combination of such activities, presents or will present an *unreasonable risk of injury* to health or the environment, the Administrator shall by rule apply one or more of the following requirements to such substance or mixture to the extent necessary to *protect adequately* against such risk using the *least burdensome* requirements.

Id. (emphasis added). As the highlighted language shows, Congress did not enact TSCA as a zero-risk statute. The EPA, rather, was required to consider both alternatives to a ban and the costs of any proposed actions and to "carry out this chapter in a reasonable and prudent manner [after considering] the environmental, economic, and social impact of any action." 15 U.S.C. § 2601(c).

We conclude that the EPA has presented insufficient evidence to justify its asbestos ban. We base this conclusion upon two grounds: the failure of the EPA to consider all necessary evidence and its failure to give adequate weight to statutory language requiring it to promulgate the least burdensome, reasonable regulation required to protect the environment adequately. Because the EPA failed to address these concerns, and because the EPA is required to articulate a "reasoned basis" for its rules, we are compelled to return the regulation to the agency for reconsideration.

1. Least Burdensome and Reasonable.

TSCA requires that the EPA use the least burdensome regulation to achieve its goal of minimum reasonable risk. This statutory requirement can create problems in evaluating just what is a "reasonable risk." Congress's rejection of a no-risk policy, however, also means that in certain cases, the least burdensome yet still adequate solution may entail somewhat more risk than would other, known regulations that are far more burdensome on the industry and the economy. The very language of TSCA requires that the EPA, once it has determined what an acceptable level of non-zero risk is, choose the least burdensome method of reaching that level.

In this case, the EPA banned, for all practical purposes, all present and future uses of asbestos—a position the petitioners characterize as the "death penalty alternative," as this is the *most* burdensome of all possible alternatives listed as open to the EPA under TSCA. TSCA not only provides the EPA with a list of alternative actions, but also provides those alternatives in order of how burdensome they are. The regulations thus provide for EPA regulation ranging from labeling the least toxic chemicals to limiting the total amount of chemicals an industry may use. Total bans head the list as the most burdensome regulatory option.

By choosing the harshest remedy given to it under TSCA, the EPA assigned to itself the toughest burden in satisfying TSCA's requirement that its alternative be the least burdensome of all those offered to it. Since, both by definition and by the terms of TSCA, the complete ban of manufacturing is the most burdensome alternative—for even stringent regulation at least allows a manufacturer the chance to invest and meet the new, higher standard—the EPA's regulation cannot stand if there is any other regulation that would achieve an acceptable level of risk as mandated by TSCA. . . .

The EPA considered, and rejected, such options as labeling asbestos products, thereby warning users and workers involved in the manufacture of asbestos-containing products of the chemical's dangers, and stricter workplace rules. . . .

The EPA presented two comparisons in the record: a world with no further regulation under TSCA, and a world in which no manufacture of asbestos takes place. The EPA rejected calculating how many lives a less burdensome regulation would save, and at what cost. Furthermore the EPA, when calculating the benefits of its ban, explicitly refused to compare it to an improved workplace in which currently available control technology is utilized. *See* 54 Fed. Reg. at 29,474. This decision artificially inflated the purported benefits of the rule by using a baseline comparison substantially lower than what currently available technology could yield. . . .

This comparison of two static worlds is insufficient to satisfy the dictates of TSCA. While the EPA may have shown that a world with a complete ban of asbestos might be preferable to one in which there is only the current amount of regulation, the EPA has failed to show that there is not some intermediate state of regulation that would be superior to both the currently-regulated and the completely-banned world. Without showing that asbestos regulation would be ineffective, the EPA cannot discharge its TSCA burden of showing that its regulation is the least burdensome available to it.

Upon an initial showing of product danger, the proper course for the EPA to follow is to consider each regulatory option, beginning with the least burdensome, and the costs and benefits of regulation under each option. The EPA cannot simply skip several rungs, as it did in this case, for in doing so, it may skip a less-burdensome alternative mandated by TSCA. Here, although the EPA mentions the problems posed by intermediate levels of regulation, it takes no steps to calculate the costs and benefits of these intermediate levels. *See* 54 Fed. Reg. at 29,462, 29,474. Without doing this it is impossible, both for the EPA and for this court on review, to know that none of these alternatives was less burdensome than the ban in fact chosen by the agency. . . .

2.   The EPA's Calculations.

Furthermore, we are concerned about some of the methodology employed by the EPA in making various of the calculations that it did perform. In order to aid the EPA's reconsideration of this and other cases, we present our concerns here. . . .

Although various commentators dispute whether it ever is appropriate to discount benefits when they are measured in human lives, we note that it would skew the results to discount only costs without according similar treatment to the benefits side of the equation. Adopting the position of the commentators who advocate not discounting benefits would force the EPA similarly not to calculate costs in present discounted real terms, making comparisons difficult. Furthermore, in evaluating situations in which different options incur costs at varying time intervals, the EPA would not be able to take into account that soon-to-be-incurred costs are more harmful than postponable costs. Because the EPA must discount costs to perform its evaluations properly, the EPA also should discount benefits to preserve an apples-to-apples comparison, even if this entails discounting benefits of a non-monetary nature. *See What Price Posterity?*, The Economist, March 23, 1991, at 73 (explaining use of discount rates for non-monetary goods).

When the EPA does discount costs or benefits, however, it cannot choose an unreasonable time upon which to base its discount calculation. Instead of using the time of injury as the appropriate time from which to discount, as one might expect, the EPA instead used the time of exposure.

The difficulties inherent in the EPA's approach can be illustrated by an example. Suppose two workers will be exposed to asbestos in 1995, with worker X subjected to a tiny amount of asbestos that will have no adverse health effects, and worker Y exposed to massive amounts of asbestos that quickly will lead to an asbestos-related disease. Under the EPA's approach, which takes into account only the time of exposure rather than the time at which any injury manifests itself, both examples would be treated the same. The EPA's approach implicitly assumes that the day on which the risk of injury occurs is the same day the injury actually occurs. Such an approach might be proper when the exposure and injury are one and the same, such as when a person is exposed to an immediately fatal poison, but is inappropriate for discounting toxins in which exposure often is followed by a substantial lag time before manifestation of injuries.

Of more concern to us is the failure of the EPA to compute the costs and benefits of its proposed rule past the year 2000, and its double-counting of the costs of asbestos use. In performing its calculus, the EPA only included the number of lives saved over the next thirteen years, and counted any additional lives saved as simply "unquantified benefits." 54 Fed. Reg. at 29,486. The EPA and intervenors now seek to use these unquantified lives saved to justify calculations as to which the benefits seem far outweighed by the astronomical costs. For example, the EPA plans to save about three lives with its ban of asbestos pipe, at a cost of $128–227 million (*i.e.*, approximately $43–76 million per life saved). Although the EPA admits that the price tag is high, it claims that the lives saved past the year 2000 justify the price. *See generally id.* at 29,473 (explaining use of unquantified benefits).

Such calculations not only lessen the value of the EPA's cost analysis, but also make any meaningful judicial review impossible. While TSCA contemplates a useful place for unquantified benefits beyond the EPA's calculation, unquantified benefits never were intended as a trump card allowing the EPA to justify any cost calculus, no matter how high. . . .

Unquantified benefits can, at times, permissibly tip the balance in close cases. They cannot, however, be used to effect a wholesale shift on the balance beam. Such a use makes a mockery of the requirements of TSCA that the EPA weigh the costs of its actions before it chooses the least burdensome alternative.

We do not today determine what an appropriate period for the EPA's calculations would be, as this is a matter better left for agency discretion. *See Motor Vehicle Mfrs. Ass'n*, 463 U.S. at 53. We do note, however, that the choice of a thirteen-year period is so short as to make the unquantified period so unreasonably large that any EPA reliance upon it must be displaced. . . .

3.   Reasonable Basis.

In addition to showing that its regulation is the least burdensome one necessary to protect the environment adequately, the EPA also must show that it has a reasonable basis for the regulation. 15 U.S.C. § 2605(a). . . .

Most problematical to us is the EPA's ban of products for which no substitutes presently are available. In these cases, the EPA bears a tough burden indeed to show that under TSCA a ban is the least burdensome alternative, as TSCA explicitly instructs the EPA to consider "the benefits of such substance or mixture for various uses and the availability of substitutes for such uses." *Id.* § 2605(c)(1)(C). These words are particularly appropriate where the EPA actually has decided to ban a product, rather than simply restrict its use, for it is in these cases that the lack of an adequate substitute is most troubling under TSCA.

As the EPA itself states, "[w]hen no information is available for a product indicating that cost-effective substitutes exist, the estimated cost of a product ban is very high." 54 Fed. Reg. at 29,468. Because of this, the EPA did not ban certain uses of asbestos, such as its use in rocket engines and battery separators. The EPA, however, in several other instances, ignores its own arguments and attempts to justify its ban by stating that the ban itself will cause the development of low-cost, adequate substitute products.

As a general matter, we agree with the EPA that a product ban can lead to great innovation, and it is true that an agency under TSCA, as under other regulatory statutes, "is empowered to issue safety standards which require improvements in existing technology or which require the development of new technology." Chrysler Corp. v. Department of Transp., 472 F.2d 659, 673 (6th Cir. 1972). As even the EPA acknowledges, however, when no adequate substitutes currently exist, the EPA cannot fail to consider this lack when formulating its own guidelines. Under TSCA, therefore, the EPA must present a stronger case to justify the ban, as opposed to regulation, of products with no substitutes. . . .

We also are concerned with the EPA's evaluation of substitutes even in those instances in which the record shows that they are available. The EPA explicitly rejects considering the harm that may flow from the increased use of products designed to substitute for asbestos, even where the probable substitutes themselves are known carcinogens. *Id.* at 29,481–83. The EPA justifies this by stating that it has "more concern about the continued use and exposure to asbestos than it has for the future replacement of asbestos in the products subject to this rule with other fibrous substitutes." *Id.* at 29,481. The agency thus concludes that any "[r]egulatory decisions about asbestos which poses well-recognized, serious risks should not be delayed until the risk of all replacement materials are fully quantified." *Id.* at 29,483.

This presents two problems. First, TSCA instructs the EPA to consider the relative merits of its ban, as compared to the economic effects of its actions. The EPA cannot make this calculation if it fails to consider the effects that alternate substitutes will pose after a ban.

Second, the EPA cannot say with any assurance that its regulation will increase workplace safety when it refuses to evaluate the harm that will result from the increased use of substitute products. While the EPA may be correct in its conclusion that the alternate materials pose less risk than asbestos, we cannot say with any more assurance than that flowing from an educated guess that this conclusion is true.

Considering that many of the substitutes that the EPA itself concedes will be used in the place of asbestos have known carcinogenic effects, the EPA not only cannot assure this court that it has taken the least burdensome alternative, but cannot even prove that its regulations will increase workplace safety. Eager to douse the dangers of asbestos, the agency inadvertently actually may increase the risk of injury Americans face. The EPA's explicit failure to consider the toxicity of likely substitutes thus deprives its order of a reasonable basis. *Cf.* American Petroleum Inst. v. OSHA, 581 F.2d 493, 504 (5th Cir. 1978) (An agency is required to "regulate on the basis of knowledge rather than the unknown.").

Our opinion should not be construed to state that the EPA has an affirmative duty to seek out and test every workplace substitute for any product it seeks to regulate. TSCA does not place such a burden upon the agency. We do not think it unreasonable, however, once interested parties introduce credible studies and evidence showing the toxicity of workplace substitutes, or the decreased effectiveness of safety alternatives such as non-asbestos brakes, that the EPA then consider whether its regulations are even increasing workplace safety, and whether the increased risk occasioned by dangerous substitutes makes the proposed regulation no longer reasonable. In the words of the EPA's own release that initiated the asbestos rulemaking, we direct that the agency consider the adverse health effects of asbestos substitute "for comparison with the known hazards of asbestos," so that it can conduct, as it promised in 1979, a "balanced consideration of the environmental, economic, and social impact of any action taken by the agency." 44 Fed. Reg. at 60,065 (1979).

In short, a death is a death, whether occasioned by asbestos or by a toxic substitute product, and the EPA's decision not to evaluate the toxicity of known carcinogenic substitutes is not a reasonable action under TSCA. Once an interested party brings forth credible evidence suggesting the toxicity of the probable or only alternatives to a substance, the EPA must consider the comparative toxic costs of each. Its failure to do so in this case thus deprived its regulation of a reasonable basis, at least in regard to those products as to which petitioners introduced credible evidence of the dangers of the likely substitutes.

4. Unreasonable Risk of Injury.

The final requirement the EPA must satisfy before engaging in any TSCA rulemaking is that it only take steps designed to prevent "unreasonable" risks. In evaluating what is "unreasonable," the EPA is required to consider the costs of any proposed actions and to "carry out this chapter in a reasonable and prudent manner [after considering] the environmental, economic, and social impact of any action." 15 U.S.C. § 2601(c).

As the District of Columbia Circuit stated when evaluating similar language governing the Federal Hazardous Substances Act, "[t]he requirement that the risk be 'unreasonable' necessarily involves a balancing test like that familiar in tort law: The regulation may issue if the severity of the injury that may result from the product, factored by the likelihood of the injury, offsets the harm the regulation itself imposes upon manufacturers and consumers." Forester v. CPSC, 559 F.2d 774, 789 (D.C. Cir. 1977). We have quoted this language approvingly when evaluating other statutes using similar language. *See, e.g., Aqua Slide,* 569 F.2d at 839.

That the EPA must balance the costs of its regulations against their benefits further is reinforced by the requirement that it seek the least burdensome regulation. While Congress did not dictate that the EPA engage in an exhaustive, full-scale cost-benefit analysis, it did require the EPA to consider both sides of the regulatory equation, and it rejected the notion that the EPA should pursue the reduction of workplace risk at any cost. *See American Textile Mfrs. Inst.*, 452 U.S. at 510 n. 30 ("unreasonable risk" statutes require "a generalized balancing of costs and benefits" (citing *Aqua Slide*, 569 F.2d at 839)). Thus, "Congress also plainly intended the EPA to consider the economic impact of *any* actions taken by it under . . . TSCA." *Chemical Mfrs. Ass'n*, 899 F.2d at 348.

Even taking all of the EPA's figures as true, and evaluating them in the light most favorable to the agency's decision (non-discounted benefits, discounted costs, analogous exposure estimates included), the agency's analysis results in figures as high as $74 million per life saved. For example, the EPA states that its ban of asbestos pipe will save three lives over the next thirteen years, at a cost of $128–227 million ($43–76 million per life saved), depending upon the price of substitutes; that its ban of asbestos shingles will cost $23–34 million to save 0.32 statistical lives ($72–106 million per life saved); that its ban of asbestos coatings will cost $46–181 million to save 3.33 lives ($14–54 million per life saved); and that its ban of asbestos paper products will save 0.60 lives at a cost of $4–5 million ($7–8 million per life saved). *See* 54 Fed. Reg. at 29,484–85. . . .

While we do not sit as a regulatory agency that must make the difficult decision as to what an appropriate expenditure is to prevent someone from incurring the risk of an asbestos-related death, we do note that the EPA, in its zeal to ban any and all asbestos products, basically ignored the cost side of the TSCA equation. The EPA would have this court believe that Congress, when it enacted its requirement that the EPA consider the economic impacts of its regulations, thought that spending $200–300 million to save approximately seven lives (approximately $30–40 million per life) over thirteen years is reasonable.

As we stated in the OSHA context, until an agency "can provide substantial evidence that the benefits to be achieved by [a regulation] bear a reasonable relationship to the costs imposed by the reduction, it cannot show that the standard is reasonably necessary to provide safe or healthful workplaces." *American Petroleum Inst.*, 581 F.2d at 504. Although the OSHA statute differs in major respects from TSCA, the statute does require substantial evidence to support the EPA's contentions that its regulations both have a reasonable basis and are the least burdensome means to a reasonably safe workplace.

The EPA's willingness to argue that spending $23.7 million to save less than one-third of a life reveals that its economic review of its regulations, as required by TSCA, was meaningless. As the petitioners' brief and our review of EPA caselaw reveals, such high costs are rarely, if ever, used to support a safety regulation. If we were to allow such cavalier treatment of the EPA's duty to consider the economic effects of its decisions, we would have to excise entire sections and phrases from the language of TSCA. Because we are judges, not surgeons, we decline to do so. . . .

NOTES AND QUESTIONS

1.   **Applicable Risk Management Framework Under the TSCA.** At what level does TSCA require that EPA regulate asbestos? How did EPA justify its regulation? More specifically, what comparison did EPA make in deciding that a total ban on asbestos complied with the requirements of the TSCA? On what basis did the court find this comparison to be insufficient?

The court interpreted TSCA as requiring that EPA use the least burdensome regulation to achieve its goal of minimum reasonable risk. Is this requirement explicit in the statute? How else could EPA's duties under the TSCA be framed? What is the applicable standard of review in this case? In light of this standard, could it be argued that the court overreached in this case?

2.   **Unquantified Benefits.** The court identified a number of deficiencies in EPA's cost-benefit analysis, one of which was EPA's treatment of unquantified benefits. What category of benefits did EPA determine to be unquantifiable? On what basis did EPA make this determination? What role did EPA propose that unquantified benefits play in its cost-benefit analysis? How does the court describe the role of unquantified benefits in this case? Are there occasions when unquantified benefits may make the difference between two regulatory decisions? Is it desirable to push an agency to quantify all benefits of a proposed regulatory response? *See* Richard L. Revesz, *Quantifying Regulatory Benefits*, 102 CAL. L. REV. 1423 (2014).

3.   **Discounting Benefits to Present Value.** The court also criticized EPA's failure to discount benefits to present value. What feature of the human health effects of asbestos led the court to require the discounting of the benefits of the proposed regulation to present value? Is it appropriate to apply to human lives discounting techniques normally used for financial flows? What difficulties could you anticipate?

Interestingly, the appropriateness of discounting the value of human lives first received sustained attention in the regulatory proceeding that led to EPA's adoption of the ban on asbestos. The following account describes an attempt by OMB to discount to present value the cost of each cancer case avoided as a consequence of the adoption of a total ban, and the subsequent reaction within and outside of the agency:

> . . . In a March 1985 letter to A. James Barnes, EPA's acting Deputy Administrator, OMB raised questions about whether the benefits of the rule exceeded its costs. In performing a cost-benefit analysis, OMB used a value per cancer case avoided of $1 million and discounted this amount at a rate of 4% for the length of the latency period.

In October 1985, a subcommittee of the U.S. House of Representatives chastised OMB for its insistence on discounting the value of human lives. It noted that discounting at OMB's 10% discount rate [OMB's preferred discount rate] over a forty year latency period would reduce the $1 million value per life saved to just over $22,000. Thus, on cost-benefit terms, one could not justify a current expenditure of over $22,000 to save a life forty years in the future. Even at a 4% discount rate, the $1 million value of life would be reduced to about $208,000.

The subcommittee referred to the testimony of Don Clay, Director of EPA's Office of Toxic Substances, that EPA "never ha[d] used discounting over the latency period of a chronic hazard," and that, by reducing the value of benefits to such an extent, OMB's approach would prevent EPA from regulating any carcinogen with a long latency period. The subcommittee further reported that Clay "personally opposed the discounting of lives in the asbestos case on ethical grounds." It concluded that OMB's position with respect to the discounting of the value of life was "simply an outrage" and urged EPA to "reject the use of discounting over the latency period of diseases caused by chronic hazards."

Richard L. Revesz, *Environmental Regulation, Cost-Benefit Analysis, and the Discounting of Human Lives*, 99 COLUM. L. REV. 941, 950–51 (1999).

In determining whether it is appropriate to discount the value of human life to present value in performing cost-benefit analysis, consider whether a distinction should be drawn between environmental problems which result in harms with a latency period and those which result in harms that affect future generations. On what basis could it be argued that discounting is appropriate in the former scenario but not the latter? *See id.* at 999. *See also*, RICHARD L. REVESZ & MICHAEL A. LIVERMORE, RETAKING RATIONALITY 107–119 (2008).

4.   Ethical Considerations.

Consider an exceedingly simple economy with 100 units of resources. Two individuals, with identical utility functions, live in this economy: one from year 1 to year 50 and the other from year 51 to year 100. There is no possibility for productive activity; thus, the individuals will be able to derive utility only from the existing 100 units of resources.

In the absence of discounting for time preference, each individual would be allocated 50 units of resources. In the face of a positive rate of time preference, however, even a relatively modest one, the first individual would get the bulk of the resources.

Revesz, *supra*, at 998. Is it ethically appropriate that the first individual be privileged in this manner, merely because she lived fifty years earlier than the second individual? What possible justifications exist for discounting for time preference at a positive rate? Do you find these justifications compelling? *See id.* at 999.

5.   Marginal Consequences. EPA was also criticized for considering only the total consequences of its proposed ban—that is, the total benefits and total costs of its preferred policy response—in conducting its cost-benefit analysis. In circumstances where there are various policy responses open to the Agency, does this approach ensure the maximization of social welfare? Take, for example, a world in which there exist only three possible policy responses: no regulation, a partial ban (which would impose total costs of $400 million and result in total benefits of $500 million), and a total ban (which would impose costs of $800 million and result in benefits of $850 million). Which response would maximize social welfare? Which would EPA have adopted under its approach in *Corrosion Proof Fittings*?

6.   Countervailing Risks. Finally, the court criticized EPA for its failure to consider the countervailing risks posed by the ban. What countervailing risks may arise in these circumstances? Consider, for instance, the application of asbestos as a fire-retardant. What factors influence the magnitude of these countervailing risks? According to the court, how should these risks be taken into account in the cost-benefit analysis?

7.   Valuing Human Lives. The court faulted the agency for not weighing the costs of the regulation against its purported benefits—noting that the regulation would cost "$200–300 million to save approximately seven lives (approximately $30–40 million per life) over thirteen years." Does the court say what does constitute an appropriate value of life in these circumstances? On what basis then did the court find that this value was unreasonable? Why was the court unwilling to defer to the agency's actions in this instance?

8.   The Aftermath of *Corrosion Proof Fittings*. One effect of *Corrosion Proof Fittings* was that it significantly raised the bar for cost-benefit under the TSCA. EPA never revisited the analysis underlying its effort to ban asbestos. In fact, EPA altogether stopped using the law to restrict chemicals. In response to EPA's inaction, Congress in 2016 passed the Frank R. Lautenberg Chemical Safety for the 21st Century Act, amending several key provisions of the TSCA. In particular, the Lautenberg Act requires EPA to evaluate chemicals and address unreasonable risks, and it removes the requirement that EPA must choose the "least burdensome" way of addressing those risks. But the Act still requires EPA to conduct a cost-benefit analysis of any proposed restrictions and to use the results of that analysis to guide its decisionmaking. Do you think the court would have decided *Corrosion Proof Fittings* differently under the Lautenberg Act? What does this say about the desirability of judicial review of cost-benefit analysis?

9.   *Corrosion Proof Fittings* and *EDF v. EPA*. What may account for the differences between the approaches of the D.C. Circuit in *Environmental Defense Fund v. EPA* and the Fifth Circuit in *Corrosion Proof Fittings*, decided some 15 years apart? To what extent might they demonstrate the rise of cost-benefit analysis as the predominant risk management framework in environmental decisionmaking throughout this period? For more information about judicial review of cost-benefit analysis, see Caroline Cecot & W. Kip Viscusi, *Judicial Review of Agency Benefit-Cost Analysis*, 22 GEO. MASON L. REV. 575 (2015) (analyzing thirty-eight judicial decisions involving cost-benefit analysis).

3. DISTRIBUTION OF ENVIRONMENTAL RISKS

The preceding section described the rise of cost-benefit analysis as the prevailing risk management framework in contemporary environmental decisionmaking. Cost-benefit analysis is concerned with the aggregate net benefits of an environmental regulation. It is not concerned with the manner in which those benefits are distributed among the individuals affected by the regulation. A policy that maximizes net benefits across the whole population might nonetheless impose significant net costs on a subset of that population. The traditional economic perspective would not advocate modifying such a policy to reduce these inequities, preferring, instead, to deal with distributional questions through other policy instruments such as the tax system. For other perspectives, distributional issues are far more salient and would play an important role in the choice of the preferred policy.

The readings in this section address the central claims of the environmental justice movement—namely, that the poor and, primarily, persons of color are disproportionately affected by inadequate environmental quality. The focus is on the siting of locally undesirable land uses (LULUs), which has been one of the particular concerns of the environmental justice movement. The Section first examines various theoretical perspectives. Then it describes the legal theories that have been invoked in an attempt to address the disproportionate allocation of risks.

A. THEORIES OF ENVIRONMENTAL JUSTICE

The first article excerpted by Robert Bullard asserts that "racism plays a key factor in environmental planning and decision-making," and that, as a result, communities of color in urban locations "face some of the worst environmental devastation in the nation." He claims that the problem manifests itself in a variety of contexts, including the siting of waste disposal sites, the exposure of children in inner cities to high levels of lead, and the risks faced by workers in the oil, chemical, and nuclear industries. Bullard argues that the disparities in access to environmental quality cannot be explained solely by reference to income differences and that race plays an independent role.

In the 1980s, two influential studies by the U.S. General Accounting Office (now called the U.S. Government Accountability Office) (GAO) and the United Church of Christ's Committee for Racial Justice (CRJ) documented that hazardous waste facilities are disproportionately located in areas in which the surrounding communities have a high proportion of people of color and the poor. The next article, by Vicki Been, surveys those studies and questions whether the disparity is the product of disproportionate siting or of market dynamics. She notes that the GAO and CRJ studies both looked at the current demographic characteristics of the surrounding communities, rather than the characteristics at the time that the facilities were sited. It may be that the location of the LULU makes housing in the surrounding community less desirable and depresses housing markets. A disproportionate number of those who can afford to leave the neighborhood will then do so and will be replaced by individuals searching for relatively inexpensive housing or those with otherwise constrained housing options. Thus, it is possible that, even if there was no disparity in the racial and economic composition of the community at the time of the siting, market dynamics will subsequently make the community disproportionately composed of people of color and the poor.

An excerpt of another article by Vicki Been explores the meaning of fairness in connection with the siting of LULUs. She examines three different notions of fairness: fairness in the pattern of distribution, fairness as cost-internalization, and fairness as process. Fairness in the pattern of distribution could involve distributing the burdens of LULUs on a proportional basis over society as a whole by physically spreading the LULUs themselves among the different communities, by equalizing the probability that any community would be chosen as a location for the LULU, or by ensuring that any affected community is compensated. Alternatively, it could involve progressive siting, under which advantaged communities get more than their share of the burden. Fairness as cost-internalization requires that the generators of waste pay the full social cost that results from the disposal of this waste. Finally, fairness as process requires acceptable procedures for the distribution of burdens, but does not inquire about the substance of the allocations.

Robert Bullard, Anatomy of Environmental Racism and the Environmental Justice Movement

in CONFRONTING ENVIRONMENTAL RACISM, VOICES FROM THE GRASSROOTS 15
(Robert Bullard ed., 1993).*

Communities are not all created equal. In the United States, for example, some communities are routinely poisoned while the government looks the other way. Environmental regulations have not uniformly benefited all segments of society. People of color (African Americans, Latinos, Asians, Pacific Islanders, and Native Americans) are disproportionately harmed by industrial toxins on their jobs and in their neighborhoods. These groups must contend with dirty air and drinking water—the byproducts of municipal landfills, incinerators, polluting industries, and hazardous waste treatment, storage, and disposal facilities.

Why do some communities get "dumped on" while others escape? Why are environmental regulations vigorously enforced in some communities and not in others? Why are some workers protected from environmental threats to their health while others (such as migrant

---

* Reprinted with the permission of South End Press, copyright © 1993.

farmworkers) are still being poisoned? How can environmental justice be incorporated into the campaign for environmental protection? What institutional changes would enable the United States to become a just and sustainable society? What community organizing strategies are effective against environmental racism? . . .

Environmental Racism

Racism plays a key factor in environmental planning and decisionmaking. Indeed, environmental racism is reinforced by government, legal, economic, political, and military institutions. It is a fact of life in the United States that the mainstream environmental movement is only beginning to wake up to. Yet, without a doubt, racism influences the likelihood of exposure to environmental and health risks and the accessibility to health care. Racism provides whites of all class levels with an "edge" in gaining access to a healthy physical environment. This has been documented again and again.

Whether by conscious design or institutional neglect, communities of color in urban ghettos, in rural "poverty pockets," or on economically impoverished Native-American reservations face some of the worst environmental devastation in the nation. Clearly, racial discrimination was not legislated out of existence in the 1960s. While some significant progress was made during this decade, people of color continue to struggle for equal treatment in many areas, including environmental justice. Agencies at all levels of government, including the federal EPA, have done a poor job protecting people of color from the ravages of pollution and industrial encroachment. It has thus been an up-hill battle convincing white judges, juries, government officials, and policymakers that racism exists in environmental protection, enforcement, and policy formulation.

The most polluted urban communities are those with crumbling infrastructure, ongoing economic disinvestment, deteriorating housing, inadequate schools, chronic unemployment, a high poverty rate, and an overloaded health-care system. Riot-torn South Central Los Angeles typifies this urban neglect. It is not surprising that the "dirtiest" zip code in California belongs to the mostly African-American and Latino neighborhood in that part of the city. In the Los Angeles basin, over 71 percent of the African Americans and 50 percent of the Latinos live in areas with the most polluted air, while only 34 percent of the white population does. This pattern exists nationally as well. As researchers Wernette and Nieves note:

> In 1990, 437 of the 3,109 counties and independent cities failed to meet at least one of the EPA ambient air quality standards . . . 57 percent of whites, 65 percent of African Americans, and 80 percent of Hispanics live in 437 counties with substandard air quality. Out of the whole population, a total of 33 percent of whites, 50 percent of African Americans, and 60 percent of Hispanics live in the 136 counties in which two or more air

pollutants exceed standards. The percentage living in the 29 counties designated as nonattainment areas for three or more pollutants are 12 percent of whites, 20 percent of African Americans, and 31 percent of Hispanics.

[D.R. Wernette & L.A. Nieves, *Breaking Polluted Air*, EPA JOURNAL, March/ April 1992, at 16–17.]

Income alone does not account for these above-average percentages. Housing segregation and development patterns play a key role in determining where people live. Moreover, urban development and the "spatial configuration" of communities flow from the forces and relationships of industrial production which, in turn, are influenced and subsidized by government policy. There is widespread agreement that vestiges of race-based decisionmaking still influence housing, education, employment, and criminal justice. The same is true for municipal services such as garbage pickup and disposal, neighborhood sanitation, fire and police protection, and library services. Institutional racism influences decisions on local land use, enforcement of environmental regulations, industrial facility siting, management of economic vulnerability, and the paths of freeways and highways.

People skeptical of the assertion that poor people and people of color are targeted for waste-disposal sites should consider the report the Cerrell Associates provided the California Waste Management Board. In their 1984 report, *Political Difficulties Facing Waste-to-Energy Conversion Plant Siting*, they offered a detailed profile of those neighborhoods most likely to organize effective resistance against incinerators. The policy conclusion based on this analysis is clear. As the report states:

> All socioeconomic groupings tend to resent the nearby siting of major facilities, but middle and upper socioeconomic strata possess better resources to effectuate their opposition. Middle and higher socioeconomic strata neighborhoods should not fall within the one-mile and five-mile radius of the proposed site.

[Id. at 43.]

Where then will incinerators or other polluting facilities be sited? For Cerrell Associates, the answer is low-income, disempowered neighborhoods with a high concentration of nonvoters. The ideal site, according to their report, has nothing to do with environmental soundness but everything to do with lack of social power. Communities of color in California are far more likely to fit this profile than are their white counterparts.

Those still skeptical of the existence of environmental racism should also consider the fact that zoning boards and planning commissions are typically stacked with white developers. Generally, the decisions of these bodies reflect the special interests of the individuals who sit on these boards. People of color have been systematically excluded from these decisionmaking boards, commissions, and governmental agencies (or allowed only token representation). Grassroots leaders are now demanding a shared role in all the decisions that shape their communities. They are challenging the intended or unintended racist assumptions underlying environmental and industrial policies. . . .

Beyond the Race Versus Class Trap

Whether at home or abroad, the question of who pays and who *benefits* from current industrial and development policies is central to any analysis of environmental racism. In the United States, race interacts with class to create special environmental and health vulnerabilities. People of color, however, face elevated toxic exposure levels even when social class variables (income, education, and occupational status) are held constant. Race has been found to be an independent factor, not reducible to class, in predicting the distribution of (1) air pollution in our society; (2) contaminated fish consumption; (3) the location of municipal landfills and incinerators; (4) the location of abandoned toxic waste dumps; and (5) lead poisoning in children.

Lead poisoning is a classic case in which race, not just class, determines exposure. It affects between three and four million children in the United States—most of whom are African Americans and Latinos living in urban areas. Among children five years old and younger, the percentage of African Americans who have excessive levels of lead in their blood far exceeds the percentage of whites at all income levels.

The federal Agency for Toxic Substances and Disease Registry found that for families earning less than $6,000 annually an estimated 68 percent of African-American children had lead poisoning, compared with 36 percent for white children. For families with incomes exceeding $15,000, more than 38 percent of African-American children have been poisoned, compared with 12 percent of white children. African-American children are two to three times more likely than their white counterparts to suffer from lead poisoning independent of class factors.

One reason for this is that African Americans and whites do not have the same opportunities to "vote with their feet" by leaving unhealthy physical environments. The ability of an individual to escape a health-threatening environment is usually correlated with income. However, racial barriers make it even harder for millions of African Americans, Latinos, Asians, Pacific Islanders, and Native Americans to relocate. Housing discrimination, redlining, and other market forces make it difficult for millions of households to buy their way out of polluted environments. For example, an affluent African-American family (with an income of $50,000 or more) is as segregated as an African-American family with an annual income of $5,000. Thus, lead poisoning of African-American children is not just a "poverty thing."

White racism helped create our current separate and unequal communities. It defines the boundaries of the urban ghetto, *barrio*, and reservation, and influences the provision of environmental protection and other public services. Apartheid-type housing and development policies reduce neighborhood options, limit mobility, diminish job opportunities, and decrease environmental choices for millions of Americans. It is unlikely that this nation will ever achieve lasting solutions to its environmental problems unless it also addresses the system of racial injustice that helps sustain the existence of powerless communities forced to bear disproportionate environmental costs.

NOTES AND QUESTIONS

1. **Causes of Environmental Injustice.** Consider three different explanations for Bullard's claim that persons of color are disproportionately affected by inadequate environmental quality. First, it might be that before 1970, when environmental quality first began to be regulated in a comprehensive manner, the disparities were even greater than they are now and that the process of equalizing access to environmental quality is still ongoing. Second, it might be that environmental regulation has unintentionally exacerbated the disparities (a disparate impact claim). Third, it might be that environmental regulation has intentionally discriminated against poor and minority communities (an intentional discrimination claim). To which of these views does Bullard subscribe? Other representative works by environmental justice advocates include Luke W. Cole, *Empowerment as the Key to Environmental Protection: The Need for Environmental Poverty Law*, 19 ECOLOGY L.Q. 619 (1992); Paul Mohai & Bunyan Bryant, *Environmental Injustice: Weighing Race and Class as Factors in the Distribution of Environmental Hazards*, 63 U. COLO. L. REV. 921 (1992); KENNETH A. MANASTER, ENVIRONMENTAL PROTECTION AND JUSTICE (1995); THE LAW OF ENVIRONMENTAL JUSTICE: THEORIES AND PROCEDURES TO ADDRESS DISPROPORTIONATE RISKS (Michael Gerrard ed., 1999); and CLIFFORD RECHTSCHAFFEN & EILEEN GAUNA, ENVIRONMENTAL JUSTICE: LAW, POLICY & REGULATION (2002).

2. **Political v. Economic Disempowerment.** Is Bullard's claim that environmental injustice primarily reflects racial minorities' lack of political power or that it results from their lack of economic power? For discussion of the causes of environmental inequities, see Richard J. Lazarus, *Pursuing "Environmental Justice": The Distributional Effects of Environmental Protection*, 87 NW. U. L. REV. 787 (1993).

3. **Environmental Justice and Risk Assessment.** The environmental justice movement contends that risk assessments systematically understate the risks that affect people of color and the poor. It makes two different types of claims: (1) that these individuals are more likely to be exposed to risk, principally as a result of multiple exposures and synergistic effects; and (2) that they are more susceptible to risk, in part as a result of genetic differences and social inequalities. For discussion, see Brian D. Israel, *An Environmental Justice Critique of Risk Assessment*, 3 N.Y.U. ENVTL. L.J. 469 (1995). In particular, consider the claim that people of color and the poor are

more likely to be exposed to risk. In what ways, if any, should the risk assessment process be modified to address each of these concerns?

4.   Lay v. Expert Perceptions of Risk. Are racial and economic disparities in communities surrounding environmentally undesirable facilities problematic only if the risk resulting from the environmental exposure is serious? If so, what should be more relevant: the objective estimates of risk or the perceptions of risk on the part of the surrounding community?

5.   Environmental v. Non-Environmental LULUs. Does the siting of hazardous waste sites in poor or minority areas raise issues that are analytically different from the siting of highways or of homeless shelters? What are possible differences? Are these differences persuasive? Are the claims of the environmental justice movement simply a subset of claims about unfairness in the siting of any facility that a community might regard as undesirable, even if the effects of the facility are non-environmental?

6.   LULUs v. Disparate Allocation of Public Amenities. Does the disparate siting of undesirable uses (environmental or non-environmental) raise issues that are analytically different from the disparate allocation of public amenities, such as higher quality schools or parks?

7.   Cost and Siting Decisions. Is it appropriate for the price of land to be considered in decisions concerning the siting of LULUs? If so, is it inevitable that facilities will be disproportionately sited where land is cheapest? Are these areas likely to be disproportionately minority or poor?

8.   Income Disparity and Access to Housing. It is inevitable that income disparities will result in access to different qualities of housing. The following factors contribute to such disparities:

  (a) differences in the natural attractiveness of the location;

  (b) differences in publicly provided amenities;

  (c) differences in the allocation of non-environmentally undesirable uses; and

  (d) differences in the allocation of environmentally undesirable uses.

Which of these differences in housing quality ought to be permissible?

9.   Benefits and Environmental Justice. Some facilities may bring economic benefits in the form of jobs for the surrounding community. What is the argument for basing environmental justice claims solely on costs without considering possible benefits? To achieve environmental justice, should the siting of undesirable land uses take into account only the cost of the facility and not any of its benefits?

10. Compensation and Environmental Justice. Communities might also be compensated for accepting the siting of a LULU. Should they be prevented from striking a deal that they consider desirable? If so, why? Who should represent the interests of the affected community in the negotiations? By what means should one determine whether the community received fair compensation? *See* Vicki Been, *Compensated Siting Proposals: Is it Time to Pay Attention?*, 21 FORDHAM URB. L.J. 787 (1994).

11. Wages and Environmental Justice. Similarly, as was discussed previously in this chapter, workers generally get wage premiums for accepting more risky occupations. Does this form of compensation cure the environmental justice problem that would otherwise exist? Should environmental policy seek to reduce the disparities in exposure to risk even if the affected workers prefer the additional income? In a portion of his book that is not excerpted above, Bullard makes the following argument:

> Workers of color are especially vulnerable to job blackmail because of the greater threat of unemployment they face compared to whites and because of their concentration in low-paying, unskilled nonunionized occupations. . . . Fear of unemployment acts as a potent incentive for many African-American workers to accept and keep jobs they know are health threatening.

Robert D. Bullard, *Anatomy of Environmental Racism and the Environmental Justice Movement, in* CONFRONTING ENVIRONMENTAL RACISM, VOICES FROM THE GRASSROOTS 17, 23 (R. Bullard ed., 1993). How does this perspective affect the assessment of the adequacy of wage premiums or other forms of compensation? *See also* Joni Hersch & W. Kip Viscusi, *Immigrant Status and the Value of Statistical Life*, 45 J. HUM. RESOURCES 749 (2010).

12. Economic Perspective's Response to Disparities in Risk. The economic perspective should not be considered insensitive to the concerns of the environmental justice movement. But rather than allowing distributional consequences to inhibit the efficient allocation of resources, advocates of the economic perspective would argue that discrepancies in risk should be addressed by way of wealth redistribution in the form of a progressive taxation regime. To what extent do you consider this response adequate? Why might environmental justice advocates argue that progressive taxation regimes may in fact not adequately compensate those communities facing disparate environmental risk?

Consider the following critique of the ability of centralized redistributive mechanisms to adequately account for the distributional consequences of aggregate policy:

> For [a] centralized redistributive mechanism [based on a tax and transfer system] to work properly, there must be an understanding of the net distributive consequences of the regulatory system, that is, how the cumulative costs and benefits of regulations are borne by the American public and its many sub-populations. Absent information about how the large set of federal regulations affects the distribution of wealth in society, it is impossible for a central redistributional mechanism like the tax-and-transfer system to adequately achieve distributional goals. Simply attending to straightforward measures of inequality—such as income and wealth disparities—will fail to take into account the large number of ways the regulatory system can create inequalities in well-being

and quality of life enjoyed by different subpopulations within the United States. For example, measures of wealth and income don't capture important variables like life expectancy. Without specific information on how the regulatory state affects the distribution of wealth and welfare across the population, it is impossible for a redistributional program to make up for systematic regulatory bias, leading to serious questions about the fair distribution of social goods.

RICHARD L. REVESZ & MICHAEL A. LIVERMORE, RETAKING RATIONALITY 181 (2008). How difficult would it be for a government to obtain information pertaining to the "net distributive consequences of the regulatory system"?

Vicki Been, Locally Undesirable Land Uses in Minority Neighborhoods: Disproportionate Siting or Market Dynamics?
103 YALE L.J. 1383 (1994).[*]

The environmental justice movement contends that people of color and the poor are exposed to greater environmental risks than are whites and wealthier individuals. The movement charges that this disparity is due in part to racism and classism in the siting of environmental risks, the promulgation of environmental laws and regulations, the enforcement of environmental laws, and the attention given to the cleanup of polluted areas. To support the first charge—that the siting of waste dumps, polluting factories, and other locally undesirable land uses (LULUs) has been racist and classist—advocates for environmental justice have cited more than a dozen studies analyzing the relationship between neighborhoods' socioeconomic characteristics and the number of LULUs they host. The studies demonstrate that those neighborhoods in which LULUs are located have, on average, a higher percentage of racial minorities and are poorer than non-host communities.

That research does not, however, establish that the host communities were disproportionately minority or poor at the time the sites were selected. Most of the studies compare the *current* socioeconomic characteristics of communities that host various LULUs to those of communities that do not host such LULUs. This approach leaves open the possibility that the sites for LULUs were chosen fairly, but that subsequent events produced the current disproportion in the distribution of LULUs. In other words, the research fails to prove environmental justice advocates' claim that the disproportionate burden poor and minority communities now bear in hosting LULUs is the result of racism and classism in the *siting process* itself.

In addition, the research fails to explore an alternative or additional explanation for the proven correlation between the current demographics

---

[*]   Reprinted with the permission of The Yale Law Journal Company, Inc. and the Williams S. Hein Company Volume 103.

of communities and the likelihood that they host LULUs. Regardless of whether the LULUs originally were sited fairly, it could well be that neighborhoods surrounding LULUs became poorer and became home to a greater percentage of people of color over the years following the sitings. Such factors as poverty, housing discrimination, and the location of jobs, transportation, and other public services may have led the poor and racial minorities to "come to the nuisance"—to move to neighborhoods that host LULUs—because those neighborhoods offered the cheapest available housing. Despite the plausibility of that scenario, none of the existing research on environmental justice has examined how the siting of undesirable land uses has subsequently affected the socioeconomic characteristics of host communities. Because the research fails to prove that the siting process causes any of the disproportionate burden the poor and minorities now bear, and because the research has ignored the possibility that market dynamics may have played some role in the distribution of that burden, policymakers now have no way of knowing whether the siting process is "broke" and needs fixing. Nor can they know whether even an ideal siting system that ensured a perfectly fair initial distribution of LULUs would result in any long-term benefit to the poor or to people of color. . . .

Market Dynamics and the Distribution of LULUs

The residential housing market in the United States is extremely dynamic. Every year, approximately 17 percent to 20 percent of U.S. households move to a new home. Some of those people stay within the same neighborhood, but many move to different neighborhoods in the same city, or to different cities. Some people decide to move, at least in part, because they are dissatisfied with the quality of their current neighborhoods. Once a household decides to move, its choice of a new neighborhood usually depends somewhat on the cost of housing and the characteristics of the neighborhood. Those two factors are interrelated because the quality of the neighborhood affects the price of housing.

The siting of a LULU can influence the characteristics of the surrounding neighborhood in two ways. First, an undesirable land use may cause those who can afford to move to become dissatisfied and leave the neighborhood. Second, by making the neighborhood less desirable, the LULU may decrease the value of the neighborhood's property, making the housing more available to lower income households and less attractive to higher income households. The end result of both influences is likely to be that the neighborhood becomes poorer than it was before the siting of the LULU.

The neighborhood also is likely to become home to more people of color. Racial discrimination in the sale and rental of housing relegates people of color (especially African-Americans) to the least desirable neighborhoods, regardless of their income level. Moreover, once a neighborhood becomes a community of color, racial discrimination in the promulgation and enforcement of zoning and environmental protection laws, the provision of municipal services, and the lending practices of banks may cause neighborhood quality to decline further. That additional decline, in turn, will induce those who can leave the neighborhood—the least poor and those least subject to discrimination—to do so.

The dynamics of the housing market therefore are likely to cause the poor and people of color to move to or remain in the neighborhoods in which LULUs are located, regardless of the demographics of the communities when the LULUs were first sited. As long as the market allows the existing distribution of wealth to allocate goods and services, it would be surprising indeed if, over the long run, LULUs did not impose a disproportionate burden upon the poor. And as long as the market discriminates on the basis of race, it would be remarkable if LULUs did not eventually impose a disproportionate burden upon people of color.

By failing to address how LULUs have affected the demographics of their host communities, the current research has ignored the possibility that the correlation between the location of LULUs and the socioeconomic characteristics of neighborhoods may be a function of aspects of our free market system other than, or in addition to, the siting process. It is crucial to examine that possibility. Both the justice of the distribution of LULUs and the remedy for any injustice may differ if market dynamics play a significant role in the distribution.

If the siting process is primarily responsible for the correlation between the location of LULUs and the demographics of host neighborhoods, the process may be unjust under current constitutional doctrine, at least as to people of color. Siting processes that result in the selection of host neighborhoods that are disproportionately poor (but not disproportionately composed of people of color) would not be unconstitutional because the Supreme Court has been reluctant to recognize poverty as a suspect classification. A siting process motivated by racial prejudice, however, would be unconstitutional. A process that disproportionately affects people of color also would be unfair under some statutory schemes and some constitutional theories of discrimination.

On the other hand, if the disproportionate distribution of LULUs results from market forces which drive the poor, regardless of their race, to live in neighborhoods that offer cheaper housing because they host LULUs, then the fairness of the distribution becomes a question about the fairness of our market economy. Some might argue that the disproportionate burden is part and parcel of a free market economy that is, overall, fairer than alternative schemes, and that the costs of regulating the market to reduce the disproportionate burden outweigh the benefits of doing so. Others might argue that those moving to a host neighborhood are compensated through the market for the disproportionate burden they bear by lower housing costs, and therefore that the situation is just. Similarly, some might contend that while the poor suffer lower quality neighborhoods, they also suffer lower quality food, housing, and medical care, and that the systemic problem of poverty is better addressed through income redistribution programs than through changes in siting processes.

Even if decisionmakers were to agree that it is unfair to allow post-siting market dynamics to create disproportionate environmental risk for the poor or minorities, the remedy for that injustice would have to be much more fundamental than the remedy for unjust siting *decisions*. Indeed, if market forces are the primary cause of the correlation between the presence of LULUs and the current socioeconomic characteristics of a neighborhood, even a siting process radically revised to ensure that LULUs are distributed equally among all neighborhoods may have only a short-term effect. The areas surrounding LULUs distributed equitably will become less desirable neighborhoods, and thus may soon be left to people of color or the poor, recreating the pattern of inequitable siting. Accordingly, if a disproportionate burden results from or is exacerbated by market dynamics, an effective remedy might require such reforms as stricter enforcement of laws against housing discrimination, more serious efforts to achieve residential integration, changes in the processes of siting low and moderate income housing, changes in programs designed to aid the poor in securing decent housing, greater regulatory protection for those neighborhoods that are chosen to host LULUs, and changes in production and consumption processes to reduce the number of LULUs needed.

Information about the role market dynamics play in the distribution of LULUs would promote a better understanding of the nature of the problem of environmental injustice and help point the way to appropriate solutions for the problem. Nonetheless, market dynamics have been largely ignored by the current research on environmental justice.

The Evidence of Disproportionate Siting

Several recent studies have attempted to assess whether locally undesirable land uses are disproportionately located in neighborhoods that are populated by more people of color or are more poor than is normal. The most important of the studies was published in 1987 by the [CRJ]. The CRJ conducted a cross-sectional study of the racial and socioeconomic characteristics of residents of the zip code areas surrounding 415 commercial hazardous waste facilities and compared those characteristics to those of zip code areas which did not have such facilities. The study revealed a correlation between the number of commercial hazardous waste facilities in an area and the percentage of the "non white" population in the area. Areas that had one operating commercial hazardous waste facility, other than a landfill, had about twice as many people of color as a percentage of the population as those that had no such facility. Areas that had more than one operating facility, or had one of the five largest landfills, had more than three times the percentage of minority residents as areas that had no such facilities.

Several regional and local studies buttress the findings of the nationwide CRJ study. The most frequently cited of those studies, which is often credited for first giving the issue of environmental justice visibility, was conducted by the United States General Accounting Office (GAO). The GAO examined the racial and socioeconomic characteristics of the communities surrounding four hazardous waste landfills in the eight southeastern states that make up EPA's Region IV. The sites studied include some of the largest landfills in the United States.

The results of the study are summarized in Table A. In short, three of the four communities where such landfills were sited were majority African-American in 1980; African-Americans made up 52 percent, 66 percent, and 90 percent of the population in those three communities. In contrast, African-Americans made up between 22 percent and 30 percent of the host states' populations. The host communities were all disproportionately poor, with between 26 percent and 42 percent of the population living below the poverty level. In comparison, the host states' poverty rates ranged from 14 percent to 19 percent.

Table A   Summary of GAO's Findings

| Landfill | Population, % African-American | Mean Family Income | | Population Below Poverty Level, % |
		All Races	African-Americans	
Chemical Waste	90	$11,198	$10,752	42
SCA Services	38	16,371	6,781	31
Ind. Chem.	52	18,996	12,941	26
Warren Cty. PCB	66	10,367	9,285	32

Another frequently cited local study was conducted by sociologist Robert Bullard and formed important parts of his books, *Invisible Houston* and *Dumping in Dixie*. Professor Bullard found that although African-Americans made up only 28 percent of the Houston population in 1980, six of Houston's eight incinerators and mini-incinerators and fifteen of seventeen landfills were located in predominantly African-American neighborhoods. . . .

[N]one of the . . . studies addressed the question of which came first—the people of color and the poor, or the LULU. As noted by the CRJ, the studies "were not designed to show cause and effect," but only to explore the relationship between the current distribution of LULUs and host communities' demographics. The evidence of disproportionate siting is thus incomplete: it does not establish that *the siting* process had a disproportionate effect upon minorities or the poor. . . .

Did the Siting Disparities Revealed by the GAO and Professor Bullard Result from Siting Practices, Market Dynamics or Both?

To begin to fill the gaps in the literature, this Part expands the GAO and Bullard studies described above. First, it adds to those studies data regarding the socioeconomic characteristics of the host communities at the time the siting decisions were made. Second, it traces changes in the demographics of the host communities since the sitings. . . .

The extensions of the GAO and Bullard studies, . . . show the effect of using demographic data from the census closest to the actual siting or capacity change decision (rather than the latest census data). Tracing changes in the demographics from this baseline reveals a significant difference in the evidence the studies provide regarding the burden LULUs impose on minorities and the poor. These studies suggest that the siting process bears some responsibility for the disproportionate burden waste facilities now impose upon the poor and people of color. The extension of the GAO study suggests that market dynamics play no role in the distribution of the burden. The extension of the Bullard study, on the other hand, suggests that market dynamics do play a significant role in that distribution.

The different results obtained by the two extensions may be attributable to the generally slower rate of residential mobility in rural areas, such as those hosting the GAO sites, versus urban areas, such as those hosting the Houston sites. The difference also may be attributable to the size and nature of the facilities studied in the two extensions. The sites studied in the GAO report are quite large, and provide a substantial number of jobs to residents of the host counties. Persons moving to the area to take those jobs may have displaced the African-Americans who previously lived in the community. The sites at issue in Professor Bullard's study, on the other hand, were unlikely to have created many new jobs, and those jobs that were created would have been much less likely than the jobs at the GAO sites to induce people to move nearby in order to take them.

Conclusion

Significant evidence suggests that LULUs are disproportionately located in neighborhoods that are now home to more of the nation's people of color and poor than other neighborhoods. Efforts to address that disparity are hampered, however, by the lack of data about which came first—the people of color and poor or the LULU. If the neighborhoods were disproportionately populated by people of color or the poor at the time the siting decisions were made, a reasonable inference can be drawn that the siting process had a disproportionate effect upon the poor and people of color. In that case, changes in the siting process may be required.

On the other hand, if, after the LULU was built, the neighborhoods in which LULUs were sited became increasingly poor, or became home to an increasing percentage of people of color, the cure for the problem of disproportionate siting is likely to be much more complicated and difficult. The distribution of LULUs would then look more like a confluence of the forces of housing discrimination, poverty, and free market economics. Remedies would have to take those forces into account.

The preliminary evidence derived from this extension of two of the leading studies of environmental justice . . . shows that research examining the socioeconomic characteristics of host neighborhoods at the time they were selected, then tracing changes in those characteristics following the siting, would go a long way toward answering the question of which came first—the LULU or its minority or poor neighbors. Until that research is complete, proposed "solutions" to the problem of disproportionate siting run a substantial risk of missing the mark.

NOTES AND QUESTIONS

1. **Market Dynamics Hypothesis.** If the market dynamics hypothesis presented by Been were to explain an important part of the *current* disparities in the socioeconomic characteristics of host communities, what solutions are possible to reduce or eliminate these disparities? Would anything short of massive economic redistribution work?

2. **Market Dynamics Hypothesis and Disparate Impact.** Does the market dynamics hypothesis explain why communities surrounding hazardous waste sites are not only disproportionately poor but also, even after adjusting for income, disproportionately composed of people of color?

3. **Race and Income: CRJ Studies.** The first CRJ study found that race was more significant than income as a predictor of the location of hazardous waste sites. In 1994, the CRJ updated its study using the 1990 census data. The results of the 1994 study were consistent with the original study. It found that zip codes hosting one facility had more than twice the percentage of minorities as zip codes hosting no facilities. *See* BENJAMIN A. GOLDMAN ET AL., TOXIC WASTES AND RACE REVISITED: AN UPDATE OF THE 1987 REPORT ON THE RACIAL AND SOCIOECONOMIC CHARACTERISTICS OF COMMUNITIES WITH HAZARDOUS WASTE SITES 3 (1994). A 2007 update of the study reached similar conclusions. It found that the percentage of people of color was 1.9 times greater in neighborhoods hosting one facility than in neighborhoods hosting no facilities. *See* ROBERT D. BULLARD ET AL., TOXIC WASTES AND RACE AT TWENTY: 1987–2007, 52 (2007). What factors might explain this phenomenon? Consider the following explanations:

    (a)   differential political power;

    (b)   differential access to information;

(c)   differential mobility; and

(d)   discrimination in housing.

4.   Race and Income: SADRI Study. A study conducted by the Social and Demographic Research Institute (SADRI) at the University of Massachusetts-Amherst reached quite different conclusions. Examining the siting of the same facilities as CRJ, it found no significant difference in the percentage of African-Americans in census tracts with commercial hazardous waste facilities, as compared to tracts without such facilities. There was, however, a marginally significant difference between the percentage of Latinos in host and non-host tracts. *See* Douglas L. Anderton et al., *Environmental Equity: The Demographics of Dumping*, 31 DEMOGRAPHY 229 (1994). Whereas the 1994 CRJ study had used zip codes as its unit of analysis, the SADRI study used census tracts, reasoning that they are intended to have a relatively homogeneous population. The SADRI study found, however, that while the host census tracts and the immediately adjoining census tracts did not have important racial disparities, tracts further from the facility but within a two-and-a-half mile radius contained significantly higher percentages of people of color and the poor than the remainder of the metropolitan area. What are possible explanations for this pattern? For an overview of the evidence of disparate siting, see Vicki Been, *Environmental Justice and Equity Issues*, in PATRICK J. ROHAN, ZONING AND LAND USE CONTROLS, ch. 25D (1995). For analyses of how to define the affected neighborhood, see John J. Fahsbender, *An Analytical Approach to Defining the Affected Neighborhood in the Environmental Justice Context*, 5 N.Y.U. ENVTL. L.J. 120 (1996); Bradford C. Mank, *Proving an Environmental Justice Case: Determining an Appropriate Comparison Population*, 20 VA. ENVTL. L.J. 365 (2001).

5.   Compensation Under the Market Dynamics Hypothesis. How does the market dynamics hypothesis affect the evaluation of compensation schemes? Who should get the compensation:

(a)   current owners of housing?

(b)   current renters of housing?

(c)   future owners of housing?

(d)   future renters of housing?

(e)   community groups?

Vicki Been, What's Fairness Got to Do with It? Environmental Justice and the Siting of Locally Undesirable Land Uses

78 CORNELL L. REV. 1001 (1993).*

Fairness in the Pattern of Distribution

Fairness Requires Equal Division—A Per Capita or Proportional Distribution of the Burdens of LULUs

A broad conception of fairness in siting would require that a LULU's burdens be spread on a per capita or proportional basis over society as a whole. This fairness concept is implicit in the contention that LULUs are inequitably sited if the percentage of LULUs in minority neighborhoods is disproportionate to the percentage of minorities in the nation's population. It is also inherent in the calls by the environmental justice movement demanding that people of color receive an "equitable distribution of 'healthy' physical environments" and that no neighborhood bear more than its proportionate share of LULUs. . . .

Several means of distribution are plausible under the proportional distribution of burden theory. One scheme would impose a physical proportional distribution: LULUs themselves would be distributed equally among neighborhoods. This distribution could be either equal *ex post* or equal *ex ante*. In an *ex post* scheme, the facilities and the harms that they pose would be distributed proportionately among neighborhoods. For example, if New York City requires facilities for 10,000 homeless individuals and has 100 neighborhoods, all holding some land suitable for a facility, each neighborhood would receive one facility housing 100 individuals. In an *ex ante* scheme, each neighborhood has an equal chance of being selected for the site through a lottery process. For example, if New York City requires a sewage sludge treatment plant, each of the 100 neighborhoods would have a 1/100 chance of being selected for the site. The *ex ante* physical distribution scheme is particularly well suited to situations in which there are economies of scale in building and operating fewer but larger LULUs. Some types of hazardous waste, for example, are stored most efficiently in large, centralized facilities. To accommodate such efficiency considerations, most neighborhoods should be spared the burden of having the facility nearby. A lottery procedure can ensure that although most neighborhoods will not have to host the site, all have an equal chance of being selected as the host site. The lottery accordingly achieves equality of opportunity before the actual distribution.

Instead of either *ex ante* or *ex post* physical equality, a distribution might seek "compensated" equality. In this distribution scheme, all individuals or communities that gain a net benefit from a particular

---

LULU must compensate those who suffer a net loss. For example, if a sludge treatment plant imposed costs upon a neighborhood, each of the neighborhoods that benefitted from the plant, but did not suffer the detriment of close proximity, would have to pay a proportionate share of the costs. Compensated equality can operate either *ex ante* or *ex post*. In an *ex ante* scheme, the siting neighborhood would be compensated for the expected loss that the site might inflict, even though the loss might never occur. In an *ex post* scheme, the siting neighborhood would be compensated only as injuries occurred. Compensation could be in the form of cash, neighborhood amenities, insurance, or indemnification. Compensation also could include "risk substitution," involving commitments to reduce some other burden borne by the community, such as a landfill developer's promise to clean up existing waste dumps. The amount and nature of the compensation would be determined either by a government authority, such as an administrative agency, or by the affected neighborhood itself. . . .

Fairness Requires Progressive Siting

One could argue that a fair distribution of LULUs would require advantaged neighborhoods to bear more of the burden that LULUs impose than poor and minority neighborhoods. Such a distribution could involve either a physical siting scheme in which advantaged neighborhoods receive a disproportionately greater number of LULUs or a compensated siting scheme in which advantaged neighborhoods pay a greater share of the cost of LULUs. One rationale for such "progressive" siting would be compensatory justice: advantaged neighborhoods should bear more of the LULU burden in order to redress or remedy past discrimination against poor and minority neighborhoods.

Although the compensatory argument for progressive siting is backward-looking, at least four forward-looking justifications exist. First, progressive siting may be necessary to achieve equality of results, or equal impact of the burdens of LULUs. Because residents of poor and minority neighborhoods suffer from numerous disadvantages, such as poor health and barriers to mobility, a LULU in a disadvantaged neighborhood will have a greater impact than one in a more advantaged community. Thus, to achieve the same level of impact, advantaged communities must bear a greater share of the burden of LULUs. The environmental justice movement's focus on tailoring risk assessments and regulatory activities to account for the special health risks faced by low income or minority communities reflects this argument.

Second, if the marginal utility of environmental quality declines as neighborhoods receive more environmental amenities, LULUs would impose less disutility upon advantaged neighborhoods than upon poor and minority neighborhoods. Thus, progressive siting would induce equal sacrifice from all neighborhoods and impose the least damage to society as a whole. Third, progressive siting could maximize total utility if putting more LULUs in advantaged neighborhoods encouraged society to reduce the number of LULUs it requires.

Fourth, John Rawls' difference principle might justify progressive siting. Rawls' theory of justice does not directly apply to siting controversies because it addresses the design of fair institutional structures, not the fairness of individual distributional choices. Nevertheless, on a micro-level the difference principle requires the siting process to yield the greatest benefit, or the least burden, to the least advantaged. A progressive siting scheme is justified, in other words, if such siting would be more likely to improve the condition of the poorest members of society than one that either distributed the burden of LULUs equally or imposed the burden disproportionately upon the poor and minorities. . . .

Fairness Requires an Equal Initial Split and Competitive Bidding

A much different conception of fairness can be drawn from Ronald Dworkin's work on the meaning of equality. In exploring the ideal of equality of resources, Dworkin asks how resources should be distributed among shipwreck survivors washed up on a desert island. Dworkin's thought experiment is far removed from the problems of siting LULUs, but his analysis helps illuminate the notions of fairness inherent in several recent proposals that LULUs be "auctioned" among communities. Dworkin posits that equality of resources would result if each shipwreck survivor were assigned initially an equal share of clamshells that she could use to bid competitively for resources. He argues that a distribution is fair if no individual prefers the distribution that some other individual obtains. Competitive bidding among those with initially equal bidding currency will produce such a distribution.

Applied to the siting context, Dworkin's scheme requires that communities be given an equal number of bargaining chips with which to bid against LULUs. Society would decide which LULUs it would need for some period of time and put them on the auction block. Each community would then receive chips to buy its way out of particular LULUs essentially a currency of vetos.

For example, suppose there are five communities of equal population and land area and there are fifteen LULUs, ranging from a home for juvenile delinquents to a low-level radioactive waste dump. Each community would be allocated ten veto chips. The auctioneer would begin by announcing that a particular LULU would be randomly distributed among the communities, but the highest bidder could remove itself from the eligible pool. If community A bids two chips to avoid it, B bids three, and C bids four, C "wins" the veto, paying four of its chips to disqualify itself from the selection process. Communities A, B, D, and E are still eligible, unless one wants to bid again. Suppose that A and E each again bid two, and B bids three; B is then eliminated, and so on, until none of the eligible communities wishes to veto the LULU. It is then randomly distributed among them. The process repeats for the next LULU. Once a community spends its ten veto chips, it is eligible for all remaining LULUs. The auction ends once all LULUs have been distributed.

If communities change their minds about the LULUs they prefer, they may trade their LULUs with other willing communities. Suppose that through the auction community A receives a large oil refinery and a prison, while community B receives a low-level radioactive waste storage facility. If community B believes that its geographical characteristics and the qualifications of its work force would enable it to host the oil refinery and prison more efficiently than the radioactive waste facility, community B could seek to trade with community A.

Under this conception of fairness, an auction for LULUs involves an equitable distribution of veto power. Proposals to hold reverse auctions, in which the siting agency or developer offers to pay a specific sum of money to the first community that agrees to accept the LULU, then increases the amount until some community steps forward with an acceptable site, are not fair under this conception because they take advantage of any inequalities of wealth that existed prior to the auction. . . .

Fairness as Cost-Internalization

Many environmental justice advocates argue that fairness requires those who benefit from LULUs to bear the cost of the LULUs. Forcing the internalization of costs leads to greater fairness in two ways. First, it is fairer to hold individuals responsible for their actions than to let costs fall on innocent bystanders. Second, forcing the internalization of costs results in greater efficiency, and greater efficiency is likely to mean fewer LULUs. Purchasers of products that generate waste will reduce consumption once the prices of the products reflect the true cost of waste facilities. In turn, producers will develop more efficient means of production, given the cost of disposing the waste generated. The number of LULUs will thereby decrease to the socially optimal level—the level at which the marginal utility of the product necessitating the LULU equals its costs. . . .

The cost-internalization conception of fairness requires that those who consume a product or make an allocation decision bear the product's or decision's full costs. To attain that goal, the manufacturer whose product generates the need for a LULU could compensate the host neighborhood for the full damages that the LULU inflicts, and then pass that cost forward to the consumers of the product. However, those who advocate cost-internalization as a means of combatting disproportionate siting generally oppose compensatory schemes. Instead, they either support programs to physically distribute LULUs more evenly across all neighborhoods or favor blocking all LULUs to encourage pollution prevention that would make LULUs unnecessary.

A physical distribution scheme would be less effective than compensation, however, at forcing the full internalization of the product's costs. It would be nonsensical to distribute one LULU to each consumer; therefore, a physical distribution of sites would always allow most consumers to avoid the full costs of their consumption decisions. Additionally, a physical distribution scheme would usually be both overinclusive and underinclusive: some residents of the host neighborhood might never consume the product in question, yet bear its burdens, while heavy users of the product outside the host neighborhood would bear no burden at all. . . .

Fairness as Process

Rather than focusing on the distribution of burdens to determine whether the siting process is equitable, the fairness as process theory focuses on the procedures by which the burden is distributed. The most obvious theory of fairness as process would assert that a distribution is fair as long as it results from a process that was agreed upon in advance by all those potentially affected. Although there are examples of interstate siting compacts and regional intrastate siting agreements, in which all participants voluntarily agree to a particular siting process, most LULUs are sited in communities that had no opportunity to remove themselves from the selection process. Therefore, this Section focuses on theories of fairness as process that do not rest upon voluntary agreement for their legitimacy.

Fairness Requires a Lack of Intentional Discrimination

A siting decision motivated by hostility toward people of a particular race is unfair under almost any theory of justice, and would not be considered fair under the Constitution. Under the intentional discrimination theory, fairness requires that a decision to site a LULU be made without any intent to disadvantage people of color. . . .

Fairness Requires Treatment as Equals

Even if discrimination is unintentional or based upon characteristics that do not trigger strict scrutiny under the Equal Protection Clause, disproportionate siting arguably would be inappropriate if it stemmed from a siting process that failed to treat people with "equal concern and respect," instead valuing certain people less than others. Under this theory, if a siting process is more attentive to the interests of wealthier or white neighborhoods than to the interests of poor or minority neighborhoods, that process illegitimately treats the poor and people of color as unequal.

Thus, if two potential sites were otherwise identical but one was in a poor neighborhood and one was in a wealthier neighborhood, society could not take note of the costs that the siting would impose on the wealthy, ignore the costs it would impose on the poor, and consequently site the LULU in the poor neighborhood. Nor could the siting decision consider the impact that the LULU would have on the poor, but discount that impact on the ground that the value of being free from certain kinds of risks or harms is worth less to poor people. Instead, the siting decision would have to consider the interests of the poor just as fully and sympathetically as it considered the interests of the more wealthy. If the decision-maker then concluded that both neighborhoods faced equal risk or loss, the choice between the two neighborhoods would have to be made with the flip of a coin or some other lottery mechanism.

If the two potential sites were not identical, treatment as equals would require only that the harm that a site would cause to the poor be considered in exactly the same manner as the harm that a site would cause to the more affluent. Thus, if siting the LULU in the poor neighborhood would expose five neighbors to a particular risk while siting it in the wealthier area would expose twenty-five neighbors to risk, society would be justified under this theory in choosing the site in the poor neighborhood. . . .

NOTES AND QUESTIONS

1.   **Fairness and Economic Considerations.** Been writes that, under the fairness as equal division theory, "if New York City requires facilities for 10,000 homeless individuals and has 100 neighborhoods, all holding some land suitable for a facility, each neighborhood would receive one facility housing 100 individuals." Consider the relevance of the following:

   (a)   land in certain communities is a great deal cheaper than in others;

   (b)   certain communities offer better social services for the homeless;

   (c)   the optimal size of each facility is 200 individuals; and

   (d)   the facilities impose less disutility in some communities than in others.

More generally, to what extent should fairness notions trump economic considerations?

2.   **Fairness as Auctions.** How would one define what counts as a community for the purposes of an auction to allocate LULUs? How should a community's auction strategy be determined? Are the interests of all members of the community likely to be coextensive?

3.   **Fairness as Cost-Internalization.** The internalization of the costs associated with waste disposal is achieved if the disposal charge reflects the expected harm of the waste. Is cost-internalization fair even if the community surrounding the site is not compensated for this harm? In contrast, if the community is compensated for this harm, does it matter if the funds are being disbursed by the disposer of the wastes? Should cost-internalization be seen as an independent notion of fairness?

4.   **Fairness as the Minimization of Property Depreciation.** Evaluate the fairness of a process that allocates LULUs on the basis of where they will decrease property values the least and under which, on the basis of unimpeachable studies, the LULUs always get allocated to poor communities.

5.   Disparate Impacts in Enforcement. So far the focus of the discussion has been on the siting of LULUs as the subject of environmental justice concerns. However, the disparities that have given rise to the environmental justice movement manifest themselves in a number of different contexts. For example, in addition to the siting of LULUs, the environmental justice movement has focused a great deal of attention on the disparate enforcement of environmental statutes and regulations and on the disparate remediation of contaminated sites. *See* David J. Galalis, Note, *Environmental Justice and Title VI in the Wake of* Alexander v. Sandoval: *Disparate-Impact Regulations Still Valid Under* Chevron, 31 B.C. ENVTL. AFF. L. REV. 61, 63 (2004).

A study by the National Law Journal (NLJ) conducted in 1992 found significant disparities in the enforcement of environmental laws. For example, with respect to cleanups of hazardous waste sites under the Superfund statute, it found that sites in minority neighborhoods took longer to be listed on the National Priorities List (NPL), which would make them eligible for the expenditure of federal funds for remedial action, and that the cleanups of these sites were less extensive. *See* Marianne Lavelle & Marcia Coyle, *Unequal Protection: The Racial Divide in Environmental Law*, NAT'L L.J., Sept. 21, 1992, at S2. In contrast, researchers at the University of Maryland found no statistically significant racial disparities in the choice of cleanup levels. Unlike the NLJ study, the University of Maryland study controlled for other variables, such as whether the site is located in an urban or rural area, that might influence the choice of cleanup remedy. Skreekant Gupta et al., *Do Benefits and Costs Matter in Environmental Regulation? An Analysis of EPA Decisions Under Superfund*, *in* ANALYZING SUPERFUND: ECONOMICS, SCIENCE, AND LAW 83 (Richard L. Revesz & Richard B. Stewart, eds., 1995). What role should environmental justice concerns play in the setting of enforcement priorities?

6.   Distributional Consequences Under the CAA and the Clean Water Act. Other studies have examined the distributional consequences of environmental policies in different contexts. One such study was conducted by Henry Peskin in 1978, examining the distributional impact of the CAA of 1970. Henry M. Peskin, *Environmental Policy and the Distribution of Benefits and Costs*, *in* CURRENT ISSUES IN ENVIRONMENTAL POLICY 144 (Paul R. Portney ed., 1978). The study allocated the national benefits of the legislation to regions. Within a region, the study assumed that each individual received an equal share of the benefit. Costs were initially allocated to industries, governments, or households. It was assumed that industrial costs were borne by families in proportion to their consumption of the product (the production of which generated the pollution regulated by the CAA); that government costs were allocated on the basis of each family's relative tax burden; and that household costs, which are primarily the costs of pollution controls for automobiles, were allocated proportionately to the number of vehicles owned by each family. The Peskin study showed the costs of pollution control to be spread out relatively evenly throughout the country, and critically, the benefits of the Act to be concentrated in highly polluted areas. Aggregating benefits and costs, Peskin found that people of color were the only net gainers from the legislation, as a result of their lower average vehicle ownership, larger average family size, and disproportionate concentration in urban locations. With respect to income, he concluded that the net benefits of the CAA, which were negative for all groups, were neither progressively nor regressively distributed.

For a recent analysis in a similar vein (and with largely similar results), see Matthew E. Kahn, *The Beneficiaries of Clean Air Act Regulation*, REGULATION, Spring 2001, at 22. For a discussion of the distribution of costs in the context of federal water pollution control policies, see Leonard P. Gianessi & Henry M. Peskin, *The Distribution of the Costs of Federal Water Pollution Control Policy*, 56 LAND ECON. 85 (1978).

7. Retrospective v. Prospective Perspectives on Environmental Justice. The Peskin study showed that the greatest benefits of the CAA in its early years accrued to the dirtiest areas. It is likely, however, that despite the improvement, these areas continue to be dirtier than the norm. In evaluating the environmental laws from a justice perspective, should the focus be on the changes that have taken place since their adoption or on the inequities that remain?

8. Aggregation of Environmental Impacts. The Peskin study suggested that people of color are the greatest net beneficiaries of the CAA. They may, however, be disproportionately disadvantaged by other environmental programs. Is it appropriate to disaggregate the effects of the environmental laws and urge a massive restructuring of any program that has disproportionately negative effects on people of color or the poor? Why should the effects not be aggregated? Might it be appropriate to look even more broadly at the aggregate distributional consequences of all governmental programs, including taxes and transfer payments? For an argument that environmental impacts should be assessed in the aggregate, see Daveed Gartenstein-Ross, *An Analysis of the Rights-Based Justification for Federal Intervention in Environmental Regulation,* 14 DUKE ENVTL. L. & POL'Y F. 185 (2003).

9. Geographic Inequality. There is also geographic inequality in the distribution of environmental health impacts. Residential proximity to hazardous waste sites, industrial sites, and cropland treated with pesticides have all been associated with an increased risk of adverse health outcomes. Jean D. Brender et al., *Residential Proximity to Environmental Hazards and Health Outcomes*, 101 AM. J. PUB. HEALTH S37 (2011). The association between adverse health outcomes and geographic location has given rise to nicknames for areas perceived to have disproportionate environmental health impacts—Cancer Alley, in Louisiana, and Toxicana, in Texarkana, Texas. *See* Douglas A. McWilliams, *Environmental Justice and Industrial Redevelopment: Economics and Equality in Urban Revitalization*, 21 ECOLOGY L.Q. 705, 761 (1994). What are appropriate legal remedies to deal with geographic inequalities?

10. Disparate Impacts of Climate Change. A number of studies have shown that the detrimental effects of climate change are, and will continue to be, borne disproportionately by developing nations. *See, e.g.*, NICHOLAS STERN, THE ECONOMICS OF CLIMATE CHANGE (2006). For example, countries located in low-lying areas, as well as small-island states, will suffer disproportionately as a consequence of the projected rise in sea levels and the increased frequency and intensity of climate-related extreme weather events. More generally, the projected effects of climate change upon agricultural production will disproportionately affect developing nations, in which the agricultural sector comprises a relatively high component of Gross Domestic Product. Furthermore, the inability of developing nations to adapt to the impacts of climate change—as a consequence of a lack of economic resources, technology, information, skills, infrastructure, and functioning institutional regimes—exacerbates their vulnerability to the impacts of climate change.

The disparate impacts of climate change are not isolated to the divide between developing and developed nations; a divide can also be drawn between current and future generations. The impacts of climate change that have already been experienced are only a portion of the total impacts that are expected to occur in the future. Even in the absence of any further emissions, greenhouse gases presently in the atmosphere will significantly affect the future climate, resulting in an estimated rise in temperature of between 0.4–0.6 degrees Celsius by the year 2100. *See* Gerald A. Meehl et al., *How Much More Global Warming and Sea Level Rise?*, 307 SCIENCE 1769 (2005). Moreover, at projected levels of emissions, the impacts upon future generations are expected to be severe. For example, it is estimated that by 2080, an additional 29–50 million people will be affected each year by floods attributable to climate change. Heat waves are projected to increase in intensity and duration, causing thousands of heat-related deaths. By 2100, the number of people exposed to malaria in Africa will increase by 16–28 percent, and the number of people exposed to dengue fever will increase by between 20–30 percent. *See* Richard L. Revesz & Matthew R. Shahabian, *Climate Change and Future Generations*, 84 S. CAL. L. REV. 1097 (2011).

In recent years, as a consequence of the increased recognition of these disparities, a rich vein of academic literature has emerged championing the justice movement in the context of climate change. Representative works include EDWARD A. PAGE, CLIMATE CHANGE, JUSTICE AND FUTURE GENERATIONS (2006); and Neil Adger et al., *Towards Justice in Adaptation to Climate Change*, *in* FAIRNESS IN ADAPTATION TO CLIMATE CHANGE (2006). In what ways should the environmental justice movement in the international context be considered analytically different from the domestic environmental justice movement? How do each of the notions of fairness, discussed by Been above, apply in the international context? What should the international response to climate change learn from the domestic environmental justice movement?

B. LEGAL THEORIES FOR ADDRESSING DISPROPORTIONATE RISKS

The environmental justice movement has tried to establish environmental justice as an enforceable right in federal courts. As discussed below, early environmental justice litigation had focused on the

Equal Protection Clause of the U.S. Constitution, while more recent attempts have focused on Title VI to the Civil Rights Act of 1964.

While a series of recent decisions have led many commentators to suggest that private actions challenging agency actions in federal court are all but foreclosed, regulations promulgated by EPA pursuant to § 602 of the Civil Rights Act do nevertheless provide an avenue for administrative relief. In addition, Executive Order 12,898 issued by President Clinton on February 11, 1994 signaled a commitment to addressing environmental justice concerns. The Order remained in effect throughout the Bush and Obama administrations and remains in effect today.

i.   EQUAL PROTECTION CLAUSE

Even before the movement gained prominence in the academic literature, attempts to defeat perceived governmental discrimination on environmental justice grounds had been made for a number of years under the Fourteenth Amendment. A 1979 Texas civil rights case is recognized as the first instance of environmental justice litigation. In *Bean v. Southwestern Waste Management Corp.*, 482 F. Supp. 673 (S.D. Tex. 1979), plaintiffs claimed that the siting of a proposed waste containment facility by the City of Houston was unconstitutional because it discriminated against the mostly African-American residents of Northwood Manor. While the action was ultimately dismissed for failure to establish that the siting of the facility had been motivated by purposeful racial discrimination, the case is nevertheless widely attributed with providing the "inspiration for the legal piece to the environmental justice movement." Luke W. Cole, *Environmental Justice Litigation: Another Stone in David's Sling*, 21 FORDHAM URB. L.J. 523, 523 (1994).

In order to succeed under the Equal Protection Clause, which provides that "no state shall . . . deny to any person within its jurisdiction the equal protection of the laws," a claimant must establish both that persons similarly situated are treated differently and that defendants intended to discriminate. *Washington v. Davis*, 426 U.S. 229, 239 (1976). No environmental justice claim under the Fourteenth Amendment has ever prevailed. Invariably, just as in the *Bean* case, claims are defeated for failure to establish discriminatory intent. These difficulties are borne out in the following case.

East Bibb Twiggs Neighborhood Association v. Macon-Bibb County Planning & Zoning Commission

706 F. Supp. 880 (M.D. Ga. 1989).

■ OWENS, CHIEF JUDGE:

This case involves allegations that plaintiffs have been deprived of equal protection of the law by the Macon-Bibb County Planning & Zoning Commission (Commission). Specifically, plaintiffs allege that the Commission's decision to allow the creation of a private landfill in census tract No. 133.02 was motivated at least in part by considerations of race. Defendants vigorously contest that allegation. . . .

On or about May 14, 1986, defendants Mullis Tree Service, Inc. and Robert Mullis ("petitioners") applied to the Commission for a conditional use to operate a non-putrescible waste landfill at a site bounded at least in part by Davis and Donnan Davis Roads. The property in question is located in census tract No. 133.02, a tract containing five thousand five hundred twenty-seven (5,527) people, three thousand three hundred sixty-seven (3,367) of whom are black persons and two thousand one hundred forty-nine (2,149) of whom are white persons. The only other private landfill approved by the Commission is situated in the adjacent census tract No. 133.01, a tract having a population of one thousand three hundred sixty-nine (1,369) people, one thousand forty-five (1,045) of whom are white persons and three hundred twenty (320) of whom are black persons. . . .

"To prove a claim of discrimination in violation of the Equal Protection Clause a plaintiff must show not only that the state action complained of had a disproportionate or discriminatory impact but also that the defendant acted with the intent to discriminate." *United States v. Yonkers Board of Education,* 837 F.2d 1181, 1216 (2d Cir. 1987), *cert. denied,* 486 U.S. 1055 (1988); *see Washington v. Davis,* 426 U.S. 229 (1976); *E & T Realty v. Strickland,* 830 F.2d 1107 (11th Cir. 1987), *cert. denied,* 485 U.S. 961 (1988). A plaintiff need not establish that "the challenged action rested solely on racially discriminatory purposes. Rarely can it be said that a legislature or administrative body operating under a broad mandate made a decision motivated solely by a single concern, or even that a particular purpose was the 'dominant' or 'primary' one." *Village of Arlington Heights v. Metropolitan Housing Development Corp.,* 429 U.S. 252, 265 (1977). "Determining whether invidious discriminatory purpose was a motivating factor demands a sensitive inquiry into such circumstantial and direct evidence of intent as may be available." *Id.* at 266. Considerations include the following: (1) the impact of the official action—whether it bears more heavily on one race than upon another; (2) the historical background of the decision; (3) the specific sequence of events leading up to the challenged decision; (4) any departures, substantive or procedural, from the normal decision-making process; and (5) the legislative or administrative history of the challenged decision. *Id.* at 266–68.

Having considered all of the evidence in light of the above-identified factors, this court is convinced that the Commission's decision to approve the conditional use in question was not motivated by the intent to discriminate against black persons. Regarding the discriminatory impact of the Commission's decision, the court observes the obvious—a decision to approve a landfill in any particular census tract impacts more heavily upon that census tract than upon any other. Since census tract No. 133.02 contains a majority black population equaling roughly sixty percent (60%) of the total population, the decision to approve the landfill in census tract No. 133.02 of necessity impacts greater upon that majority population.

However, the court notes that the only other Commission approved landfill is located within census tract No. 133.01, a census tract containing a majority white population of roughly seventy-six percent (76%) of the total population. This decision by the Commission and the existence of the landfill in a predominantly white census tract tend to undermine the development of a "clean pattern, unexplainable on grounds other than race. . . ." *Village of Arlington Heights*, 429 U.S. at 266.

Plaintiffs hasten to point out that both census tracts, Nos. 133.01 and 133.02, are located within County Commission District No. 1, a district whose black residents compose roughly seventy percent (70%) of the total population. Based upon the above facts, the court finds that while the Commission's decision to approve the landfill for location in census tract No. 133.02 does of necessity impact to a somewhat larger degree upon the majority population therein, that decision fails to establish a clear pattern of racially motivated decisions.

Plaintiffs contend that the Commission's decision to locate the landfill in census tract No. 133.02 must be viewed against an historical background of locating undesirable land uses in black neighborhoods. First, the above discussion regarding the two Commission approved landfills rebuts any contention that such activities are always located in direct proximity to majority black areas. Further, the court notes that the Commission did not and indeed may not actively solicit this or any other landfill application. The Commission reacts to applications from private landowners for permission to use their property in a particular manner. The Commissioners observed during the course of these proceedings the necessity for a comprehensive scheme for the management of waste and for the location of landfills. In that such a scheme has yet to be introduced, the Commission is left to consider each request on its individual merits. In such a situation, this court finds it difficult to understand plaintiffs' contentions that this Commission's decision to approve a landowner's application for a private landfill is part of any pattern to place "undesirable uses" in black neighborhoods.

Second, a considerable portion of plaintiffs' evidence focused upon governmental decisions made by agencies other than the planning and zoning commission, evidence which sheds little if any light upon the alleged discriminatory intent of the Commission.

Finally, regarding the historical background of the Commission's decision, plaintiffs have submitted numerous exhibits consisting of newspaper articles reflecting various zoning decisions made by the Commission. The court has read each article, and it is unable to discern a series of official actions taken by the Commission for invidious purposes. *See Village of Arlington Heights*, 429 U.S. at 267. Of the more recent articles, the court notes that in many instances matters under consideration by the Commission attracted widespread attention and vocal opposition. The Commission oft times was responsive to the opposition and refused to permit the particular development under consideration, while on other occasions the Commission permitted the development to proceed in the face of opposition. Neither the articles nor the evidence presented during trial provides factual support for a determination of the underlying motivations, if any, of the Commission in making the decisions. In short, plaintiffs' evidence does not establish a background of discrimination in the Commission's decisions.

"The specific sequence of events leading up to the challenged decision also may shed some light on the decisionmaker's purpose." *Village of Arlington Heights*, 429 U.S. at 267. Plaintiff identifies as the key piece of evidence in this regard a statement contained in "Action Plan for Housing," a study of the status of housing in the Macon area conducted by the Macon-Bibb County Planning and Zoning Commission. The study states that "[r]acial and low income discrimination still exist in the community." The study was issued in March of 1974, and it constitutes a recognition *by* the Commission that racial discrimination still existed in the Macon community in 1974. That recognition in no way implies that racial discrimination affected the decision-making process of the Commission itself. Rather, the statement indicates the Commission's awareness that certain individuals and/or groups in society had yet to come to grips with the concept of equality before the law. The Commission's recognition of the situation does not constitute its adoption. Indeed, such recognition probably encourages that Commission to exercise vigilance in guarding against such unprincipled influence. The statements of the various Commissioners during their deliberations indicates a real concern about both the desires of the opposing citizens and the needs of the community in general.

In terms of other specific antecedent events, plaintiffs have not produced evidence of any such events nor has the court discerned any such events from its thorough review of the record. No sudden changes in the zoning classifications have been brought to the court's attention. Plaintiffs have not produced evidence showing a relaxation or other change in the standards applicable to the granting of a conditional use.

Thus, this court finds no specific antecedent events which support a determination that race was a motivating factor in the Commission's decision.

Plaintiffs contend that the Commission deviated from its "normal procedures" in several ways. First, plaintiffs point to the Commission's efforts to encourage input from the County and the City. These efforts do not constitute evidence that "improper purposes are playing a role" in the Commission's decision. The statements of the Commissioners make clear that such efforts had their genesis in the Commission's concerns about accountability to the public for certain controversial governmental decisions and about centralized planning for the area's present and future waste disposal problems.

Plaintiffs' contentions regarding other alleged procedural irregularities, including the requirement that the Commission make certain findings of fact and that a rehearing was improperly granted, are without merit. The court has examined the Comprehensive Land Development Resolution in light of the actions taken and has been unable to identify any procedural flaws.

The final factor identified in *Village of Arlington Heights* involves the legislative or administrative history, particularly the contemporary statements made by members of the Commission. Plaintiffs focus on the reasons offered by the Commission for the initial denial of petitioners' application, *i.e.*, that the landfill was adjacent to a residential area and that the approval of the landfill in that area would result in increased traffic and noise, and they insist that those reasons are still valid. Thus, plaintiffs reason, some invidious racial purpose must have motivated the Commission to reconsider its decision and to approve that use which was at first denied. This court, having read the comments of the individual commissioners, cannot agree with plaintiffs' arguments.

NOTES AND QUESTIONS

1. **Disparate Impact.** The *East Bibb Twiggs* court found that the siting of the landfill in question did result in disparate environmental impacts. How did the court articulate these disparities? Do you agree with the court's analysis that the siting of any landfill facility would necessarily result in disparate impacts to the local neighborhood?

2. **Discriminatory Intent.** On what basis did the court find the Commission's decision to approve the landfill in question not to be motivated by the intent to discriminate against persons of color? What evidence did the plaintiffs provide to the contrary?

3. *Arlington Heights* **Factors.** As the *East Bibb Twiggs* case demonstrates, it is particularly difficult for a plaintiff to satisfy the *Arlington Heights* discriminatory intent test in an environmental justice context. Consider each of the five factors in turn. What evidence would be necessary to satisfy the test? In light of your response, how likely is it that a plaintiff

will ever succeed in an environmental justice claim under the Fourteenth Amendment?

ii. TITLE VI OF THE CIVIL RIGHTS ACT

Section 601 of Title VI of the Civil Rights Act of 1964, which prohibits discrimination on the grounds of race, color, and national origin by "any program or activity receiving Federal financial assistance," offers an alternative avenue for legal challenge on environmental justice grounds. 42 U.S.C. § 2000d. The potential scope of Title VI is broad, given that virtually every state environmental agency receives some funding from EPA. Following the decision of the Supreme Court in *Guardians Association v. Civil Service Commission*, 463 U.S. 582 (1983), however, environmental justice actions under § 601 of the Civil Rights Act have been rendered largely impotent. Just as in the case of the Equal Protection Clause, the Supreme Court found that plaintiffs must establish proof of discriminatory intent on the part of government or industry in order to sustain a challenge under Title VI. For an account of the history of environmental justice actions brought under Title VI of the Civil Rights Act, see THE LAW OF ENVIRONMENTAL JUSTICE: THEORIES AND PROCEDURES TO ADDRESS DISPROPORTIONATE RISKS 23–68 (Michael Gerrard ed., 1999).

Section 602 of the Civil Rights Act requires that every federal agency promulgate regulations specifying how the agency will determine whether grant applications or recipients are engaging in racially discriminatory practices and providing a process for investigating and reviewing complaints of racial discrimination filed with the agency. 42 U.S.C. § 2000d–1. Pursuant to this authority, EPA promulgated "disparate-impact" regulations in 1973 prohibiting recipients of EPA funds from using "criteria or methods of administering its program or activity which have the effect of subjecting individuals to discrimination because of their race, color, national origin, or sex, or have the effect of defeating or substantially impairing accomplishment of the objectives of the program or activity with respect to individuals of a particular race, color, national origin, or sex." 40 C.F.R. § 7.35(b).

Initially, it had been thought that § 602 may give rise to a substantive cause of action pursuant to which environmental justice advocates could challenge the actions of federal agencies in the courts. This strategy was particularly attractive to environmental justice advocates, given that the "disparate-impact" regulations prohibited discrimination regardless of intent. Ultimately, however, this strategy was short lived. In 2001, the Supreme Court held that there was no implied private right of action to directly enforce an agency's "disparate-impact" regulations. *Alexander v. Sandoval*, 532 U.S. 275 (2001). Instead, it held that regulations of this type provide only an avenue of administrative complaint. *Id.* As a result, the majority of direct environmental justice claims are now pursued in administrative forums.

See Kyle W. La Londe, *Who Wants to Be an Environmental Justice Advocate?: Options for Bringing an Environmental Justice Complaint in the Wake of* Alexander v. Sandoval, 31 B.C. ENVTL. AFF. L. REV. 27 (2004).

Originally, the Office of Civil Rights (OCR) within the Office of the Administrator was responsible for administering EPA's "disparate-impact" regulations. After a reorganization in December 2016, these responsibilities are now handled by the External Civil Rights Compliance Office (ECRCO), located in the Office of General Counsel. The regulations contain a strict procedure for administrative complaints. First, a person alleging a violation of the regulations must file a complaint with ECRCO within 180 days of the alleged discriminatory event. 40 C.F.R. § 7.120(a). ECRCO is then required, within 20 days, to respond to the complaint by either accepting, rejecting or forwarding the complaint to the appropriate federal agency. *Id.* In the event that the complaint is accepted for investigation, all relevant parties are then notified and given an opportunity to respond to the complaint in writing. 40 C.F.R. § 7.120(d)(2)(i). Next, the regulations provide for ECRCO to attempt to broker informal settlement. *Id.* Provided that resolution is not achieved, ECRCO must then make a preliminary determination after conducting an internal investigation into the matter. 40 C.F.R. § 7.115(c)(1)(i). If ECRCO makes a preliminary finding of noncompliance, it must advise the contravening party of how voluntary compliance may be achieved and of its right to engage in compliance negotiation. *Id.* The regulations make provision for the contravening party to request a hearing before EPA's Administrative Law Judge (ALJ) to challenge ECRCO's preliminary finding. 40 C.F.R. § 7.130(b). In the event that the preliminary finding is upheld by the ALJ, ECRCO is then entitled to bring a proceeding to terminate the contravening party's EPA funding under 40 C.F.R. § 7.130(a)–(b). If a complaint is denied, the complainant may challenge this denial under the Administrative Procedure Act. 5 U.S.C. § 706.

On February 11, 1994, President Clinton issued Executive Order 12,898, dealing with environmental justice. Exec. Order No. 12,898, 59 Fed. Reg. 7629 (1994). In broad terms, the Executive Order and its accompanying memorandum (which remain in effect) direct agencies to specifically address their responsibilities under Title VI and to formulate an environmental justice strategy. More specifically, the Order provides:

> [E]ach agency shall develop an agency-wide environmental strategy . . . that identifies and addresses disproportionately high and adverse human health or environmental effects of its programs, policies, and activities on minority populations and low-income populations. The environmental justice strategy shall list programs, policies, planning and public participation processes, enforcement, and/or rulemaking related to human health or the environment that should be revised to, at a minimum: (1) promote enforcement of all health and environmental statutes in areas with minority populations and

> low-income populations; (2) ensure greater public participation;
> (3) improve research and data collection relating to the health
> of and environment of minority populations and low-income
> populations; and (4) identify differential patterns of
> consumption of natural resources among minority populations
> and low-income populations.

Id. The Order was understandably perceived by the environmental justice movement as a renewed commitment on the part of the administration to act on its responsibilities under Title VI— responsibilities that EPA had largely avoided prior to 1993 for fear of disrupting state and local recipient agencies from pursuing pollution reduction initiatives.

In the years following the issuance of the Executive Order, EPA had difficulty responding to the number of complaints that were filed pursuant to the "disparate-impact" regulations. By 1998, despite having spent more than $50 million on investigations, the agency had not resolved a single complaint. That year, EPA issued interim guidelines concerning the investigation of Title VI administrative complaints. EPA, INTERIM GUIDELINES FOR INVESTIGATING TITLE VI ADMINISTRATIVE COMPLAINTS CHALLENGING PERMITS (1998) (Interim Guidelines). EPA issued the Interim Guidelines at the same time as the Shintech controversy (discussed in Note 1 below)—which remains to this day the highest profile administrative challenge filed with OCR pursuant to the "disparate-impact" regulations. In 2000 EPA revised its Interim Guidelines in an attempt to provide greater certainty to recipients of federal funds of their obligations under Title VI. EPA, Draft Revised Guidance for Investigating Title VI Administrative Complaints Challenging Permits, 65 Fed. Reg. 39,650 (2000) (Revised Guidelines). Like the Interim Guidelines, the Revised Guidelines has been widely criticized and has yet to be formally adopted. *See, e.g.*, Eileen Gauna, *EPA at 30: Fairness in Environmental Protection*, 31 ENVTL. L. REP. 10528, 10540–41 (2001); Tseming Yang, *The Form and Substance of Environmental Justice: The Challenge of Title VI of the Civil Rights Act of 1964 for Environmental Regulation*, 29 B.C. ENVTL. AFF. L. REV. 143, 156 (2002). The issuance of the Revised Guidelines did not result in any improvement in the rate at which complaints are processed by EPA. As of August 2007, a total of 149 complaints had been lodged with EPA's OCR pursuant to Title VI, of which 70 percent were dismissed or referred to other agencies, 6 percent were resolved informally, and 24 percent were pending. ECRCO, which now handles these complaints, issued a Case Resolution Manual to provide procedural guidance to its case managers in order to ensure "prompt, effective, and efficient resolution of civil rights cases consistent with science and the civil rights laws." *See* EPA, CASE RESOLUTION MANUAL (2017). It remains to be seen whether these procedural changes will result in more efficient complaint processing.

Much to the exasperation of the environmental justice movement, prior to 2011, EPA did not find that a single recipient agency has acted in contravention of the "disparate-impact" regulations. For this reason, much contemporary environmental justice litigation attempts to defeat proposals on procedural grounds, rather than mounting a direct challenge against the disparate allocation of environmental risks.

NOTES AND QUESTIONS

1.   **Shintech.** In August 1996, Shintech, a Texas-based subsidiary of a Japanese chemical manufacturer, announced that it was considering construction of a $700 million polyvinyl chloride (PVC) plant on a sugar cane plantation along the Mississippi River in St. James Parish, Louisiana. St. James Parish is located in Louisiana's "Cancer Alley," the eighty-five-mile stretch along the Mississippi River from Baton Rouge to New Orleans. While the average American was exposed to around ten pounds of toxic releases per year (and the average resident within Louisiana 21 pounds), residents within St. James Parish were subjected to approximately 360 pounds of toxic air pollutants per year. The proposal was particularly controversial, given that the Shintech proposal would have emitted over 600,000 pounds of air pollutants annually (including 143,000 pounds of vinyl chloride) and 3.6 million gallons of wastewater.

In May 1997, the Tulane Law Clinic, on behalf of several citizens' groups, filed an administrative complaint under EPA's Title VI regulations, challenging the Louisiana Department of Environmental Quality's (LDEQ) approval of the Shintech Plant. The complaint made specific reference to the fact that 95 percent of the 300 people living within one mile of the proposed plant were black and that 49 percent of the households had incomes of less than $15,000. *See* THE LAW OF ENVIRONMENTAL JUSTICE: THEORIES AND PROCEDURES TO ADDRESS DISPROPORTIONATE RISKS 46 (Michael Gerrard ed. 1999). In response, Shintech argued that the St. James Parish site had been selected on the basis that it offered the best access to raw materials and infrastructure. EPA, for its part, treated the Shintech complaint as a test case, to determine the manner in which it would apply the "disparate-impact" regulations in light of Executive Order 12,898. *See* Angela M. Baggetta, *Environmental Justice: Black Caucus, EPA to Meet on Shintech; Dispute May Be Test Case on Title VI Suits*, DAILY ENV'T REP., Jul. 21, 1998, at A1.

As the following account demonstrates, the complaint quickly gave rise to a political controversy of national significance:

Environmental justice advocates strongly encouraged EPA to veto the proposed facility because of the cumulative burden of adding even one more plant to the already significant health risks in the area. Business interests and many Louisiana politicians, however, argued that rejection of the permit would cost jobs and make it much more difficult to build any industrial facilities in minority areas in the future.

Unfortunately, the disagreements between environmentalists and business interests over Shintech often became heated. The Tulane environmental law clinic donated thousands of hours to assist the Shintech complainants, but the clinic's involvement led Governor Foster to denounce the law students involved with the clinic as "outlaws". . . .

The minority community in St. James Parish and nationwide divided about whether the proposed facility's economic benefits outweighed the health risks. The Louisiana NAACP initially opposed the plant, but the St. James chapter supported its construction. The U.S. Chamber of Commerce and the Black Chamber of Commerce began working together for the first time to repeal the EPA's environmental justice program on the grounds that the agency's policies will prevent investment in minority communities. On the other hand, nearly all members of the Congressional Black Caucus, including Louisiana's only African American congressperson, William Jefferson, urged EPA to veto the Shintech permit.

Id. at 46–47. Against this political backdrop, in September 1997, EPA ordered the LDEQ to temporarily revoke the permits it had issued Shintech pursuant to the CAA on technical grounds. EPA deferred a decision on the environmental justice complaint, noting that these issues were the subject of ongoing investigations. However, before the OCR was able to reach a preliminary finding on this issue, Shintech finally bowed to the obstacles that impeded the development of the plant and moved their proposed site to Plaqueminne (an area with a significantly lower percentage of minority population).

The Shintech saga was hailed as a triumph for the environmental justice movement, despite the fact that EPA failed to reach a decision on the Title VI complaint. What lessons can environmental justice advocates take from the Shintech experience in mounting future challenges under the Title VI regulations?

In late 2015, news swept the nation that residents of Flint, Michigan, a majority-African American city, were exposed to severely elevated lead levels in their drinking water when the city changed water sources. How could advocates have challenged actions that contributed to the Flint crisis under the Title VI regulations? Chapter VI describes in more detail the events that led to the drinking water crisis in Flint.

2.   EPA's "Disparate-Impact" Regulations. What might explain the apparent hesitancy on the part of EPA to find that a recipient agency has acted in contravention of its Title VI regulations? Why may EPA be reluctant to revoke federal funding of state agencies?

3.   Inclusion of Community Groups. In April of 2011, in response to a complaint filed in 1999, EPA found that the California Department of Pesticide Regulation (CDPR) violated the disparate impact regulations by renewing the registration of the pesticide methyl bromide. The OCR concluded that the application of methyl bromide between 1995 and 2001 resulted in disparate impacts on Latino schoolchildren. While CDPR disputed this finding, CDPR entered into an agreement with EPA to resolve the complaint. This agreement requires CDPR and the California Air Resources Board to monitor certain locations through the end of 2013 and to perform public outreach to the Latino community in five counties with high methyl bromide use. The agreement notes that CDPR has independently implemented several new regulatory measures for methyl bromide since 2001. Is this an effective resolution of the complaint?

The complainants expressed dissatisfaction with the process by which EPA reached an agreement with CDPR. They particularly pointed to EPA's lack of consultation with the complainants in reaching an agreement. CTR. OF RACE, POVERTY & THE ENV'T, PRESS RELEASE: EPA FAILS TO ENFORCE CIVIL RIGHTS ACT (2011). EPA has given complainants an opportunity to submit recommendations in a subsequent Title VI settlement agreement. *See* Daria E. Neal, *Recent Developments in Federal Implementation of Executive Order 12,898 and Title VI of the Civil Rights Act*, 57 HOW. L.J 941, 956 (2014).

The Department of Justice has incorporated environmental justice considerations into some enforcement settlement agreements. In May 2012, citizen groups helped shape a settlement with BP Products North America Inc. regarding its Whiting, Indiana refinery. The agreement required BP to pay a civil penalty, spend $400 million on pollution controls, make fenceline monitoring data available to the public, and spend $9.5 million on projects to reduce carbon emissions. In 2011, the Missouri Coalition for the Environment was included in settlement negotiations with the St. Louis Metropolitan Sewer District. The resulting settlement will require the sewer district to invest in projects to alleviate sewer overflows in low-income areas and provide online updates to help low-income residents connect to the sewer. Jessica Coomes, *DOJ Says Government Has Incorporated Environmental Justice Into Settlements*, 43 ENV'T REP. 261 (2012).

Does giving complainants an opportunity to contribute to settlement negotiations provide an adequate process for resolution of complaints? What are potential pitfalls?

4. Combating Agency Delay. In addition to bringing suit against a denial of a complaint, a complainant may also sue EPA for failing to respond to a complaint within the deadlines provided by the regulations under 5 U.S.C. § 706(1). *Rosemere Neighborhood Ass'n v. EPA*, 581 F.3d 1169, 1172 (9th Cir. 2009). Discovery in *Rosemere* revealed that EPA did not respond to a single complaint within the deadlines in 2006 or 2007. *Id.* at 1175. The Ninth Circuit allowed the Rosemere Neighborhood Association to proceed with a suit for injunctive relief compelling EPA to respond to future complaints by the appropriate deadlines. *Id.* at 1172–76. Is this likely to be a widely useful remedy? The complaint in question in *Rosemere* was first filed in 2003, and the Association sued EPA for delay in 2005. This first lawsuit was dismissed as moot after EPA accepted the complaint. However, EPA continued to delay, and the Ninth Circuit ruling came from an appeal of a second lawsuit filed by the Association in 2007. *Id.* at 1171–72. Consider also that in 2012 EPA dismissed a Title VI complaint filed in 1994, following litigation by the complainants commenced in 2011. *See Padres Hacia Una Vida Mejor v. Jackson*, 922 F. Supp. 2d 1057, 1059 (E.D. Cal. 2013), *aff'd sub nom. Padres Hacia Una Vida Mejor v. McCarthy*, 614 F. App'x 895 (9th Cir. 2015).

5.   Administrative v. Judicial Enforcement. Consider the differences in bringing an action for administrative enforcement (under EPA's "disparate-impact" regulations) as opposed to an action for judicial enforcement (such as under the Equal Protection Clause or under § 601 of Title VI of the Civil Rights Act). What are the relative advantages of each avenue of enforcement? Which would prove less costly? Which would provide the greatest scope for public participation? What remedies are available under each avenue?

6.   Executive Order 12,898. What is the effect of Executive Order 12,898? In what ways does it affect the actions of federal agencies?

7.   Interagency   Working   Group   and   Memorandum   of Understanding. Executive Order 12,898 also established the Federal Interagency Working Group on Environmental Justice. In August 2011, ten executive departments and EPA signed a memorandum of understanding (MOU) committing each agency to create or update an Environmental Justice Strategy, to allow public comment on the Strategy, and to issue annual progress reports on the implementation of the Strategy. The MOU instructs agencies to focus on implementing the National Environmental Policy Act and Title VI of the Civil Rights Act of 1964, considering impacts from climate change and commercial transportation, and supporting infrastructure (such as highways and railroads). The MOU also established a Charter for the Interagency Working Group. The Charter provides for monthly meetings and a number of avenues for public participation and interagency cooperation.

8.   Plan EJ 2014. In 2011, EPA issued "Plan EJ 2014," a compilation of numerous strategies to better incorporate environmental justice into the decisionmaking of EPA and other agencies. The goals of the Plan are (1) to protect health in communities over-burdened by pollution, (2) to empower communities to take action to improve their health and environment, and (3) to establish partnerships with local, state, tribal, and federal organizations to achieve healthy and sustainable communities. The Plan contains five "cross-agency focus areas," four "tools development areas," and programs initiatives within EPA offices. The Plan calls upon the Agency to incorporate environmental justice in rulemakings, permitting, and compliance and enforcement decisions. In 2014, EPA issued a report describing its progress toward completing its commitments under Plan EJ 2014. EPA, PLAN EJ 2014 PROGRESS REPORT (2014). There is concern that EPA's environmental justice initiatives will be discontinued or deprioritized under the Trump administration. *See, e.g.*, Talia Buford, *Has the Moment for Environmental Justice Been Lost?*, PROREPUBLICA, July 24, 2017. What value do non-enforceable strategy documents have in this context? Will political actors be able to stop these agency initiatives? Or will they be perpetuated by other actors in the executive branch?

9.   Solid Waste and Environmental Justice. In January 2015, EPA finalized a rule altering the definition of solid waste under the Resource Recovery and Conservation Act for certain types of hazardous secondary materials. EPA, Definition of Solid Waste, 80 Fed. Reg. 1,694 (2015). To inform EPA's decisionmaking for this rulemaking, EPA conducted a new environmental justice analysis for solid waste. The analysis contained six steps:

1.   Hazard characterization;

2.   Identification of potentially affected communities;

3.   Demographics of potentially affected communities;

4.   Identify other factors that affect vulnerability in potentially affected communities;

5.   Assessment of disproportionate impact; and

6.   Identification of potential preventive and mitigation strategies.

EPA, Proposed Rule on Definition of Solid Waste, 76 Fed. Reg. 44,094, 44,103–04 (2011). Step 4 included two sub-steps: analyses of the ability to participate in the decisionmaking process and the potential for multiple and cumulative effects. *Id.* at 44,106–07. EPA explained that the result of an environmental justice analysis "can affect how EPA uses its policy discretion under applicable authorities to pursue specific regulatory options or provide opportunities to involve the public in the implementation of regulations." *Id.* at 44,103. Overall, EPA altered the definition of solid waste "to address the potential for adverse impacts to human health and the environment from discarded material, including disproportionate impacts to minority and low income communities." *Id.* at 44,107. Should the definition of solid waste depend on which communities are affected?

10.   State Environmental Justice Initiatives. A number of states have adopted programs designed to address environmental justice concerns. *See generally* Chuck D. Barlow, *State Environmental Justice Programs and Related Authorities, in* THE LAW OF ENVIRONMENTAL JUSTICE: THEORIES AND PROCEDURES TO ADDRESS DISPROPORTIONATE RISKS 140 (Michael Gerrard ed., 1999). Recognizing "the critical role that local land use procedures play in the distribution of undesirable land uses," state programs typically focus on planning and zoning processes, in addition to state environmental impact review and facility permitting procedures. ROBERT C. ELLICKSON & VICKI BEEN, LAND USE CONTROLS 759 (3d ed. 2005). For example, the Department of Environmental Conservation in the state of New York has adopted regulations that "increase opportunities for public participation in permitting processes, require scrutiny to identify permit applications that may affect low-income or minority communities, and enhance the opportunities for considering environmental justice concerns in the environmental impact review process." *Id.* How successful do you think such measures will be in addressing environmental justice concerns?

In 2012, California approved legislation that assigned 25 percent of proceeds collected from the state's greenhouse gas emissions cap-and-trade program to benefit disadvantaged communities that are disproportionately affected by climate change. The legislation followed litigation by environmental justice groups arguing that the cap-and-trade program would adversely affect communities living near large emission sources. Disadvantaged communities are identified on the basis of geographic, socioeconomic, public health, and environmental hazard criteria. *See* Vien Truong, *Addressing Poverty and Pollution: California's SB 535 Greenhouse Gas Reduction Fund*, 49 HARV. C.R.-C.L. L. REV. 493 (2014). Is this approach desirable?

CHAPTER III

REGULATORY TOOLS

1. INTRODUCTION

This chapter explores the choice among different tools for improving environmental quality. Since the 1970s, command-and-control regulation has been the tool most used by the federal environmental statutes. Under this technique, polluting sources must meet a regulatory standard, typically set for categories of similar sources (for example, cement plants), by reference to what can be achieved through the use of "best available technology" (BAT). Thus, for example, under the Clean Air Act (CAA), BAT standards are set for categories of new stationary sources of air pollutants. Under the Clean Water Act (CWA), similar standards apply to effluent discharges by both new and existing sources.

The article by Bruce Ackerman and Richard Stewart argues that the emphasis on command-and-control regulation is misplaced. The authors raise two principal objections. First, firms that meet the command-and-control standard have no incentives to reduce their pollution further. Second, command-and-control regulation is generally insensitive to differences in the costs of pollution abatement. Thus, the same standard might apply to a source that can reduce its emissions cheaply as to one that can do so only at great expense. The cost of meeting a given level of environmental quality would be lower if the former source were regulated more stringently than the latter. Ackerman and Stewart advocate the establishment of a marketable permit scheme, which is also referred to as a cap-and-trade system or an emissions or permit trading system. Under such a scheme, the regulator would determine only the aggregate amount of permissible pollution and, by reference to this amount, define the number of permits to be allocated. Individual sources would have to possess a permit for each unit of pollution that they emitted. Initially, the permits would be auctioned off by the regulator, and subsequently, they would be traded in a market. The authors show that such a scheme satisfies the cost-effectiveness criterion: it leads to the achievement of a given level of environmental quality at least cost. This property holds regardless of whether the level of environmental quality is chosen to maximize social welfare or, instead, by reference to some other criterion. In the latter scenario, the use of a marketable permit scheme is "second best" in that, even though it does not lead to the maximization of social welfare, it provides the cheapest method for achieving the desired level of environmental quality.

The excerpt from the book by William Baumol and Wallace Oates explains that effluent fees (taxes per unit of pollution, such as carbon taxes) can also lead to the achievement of environmental standards at least cost. The authors compare the properties of these two tools. For example, marketable permits reduce the uncertainty about whether a given level of environmental quality will be met: that level is determined by the number of permits, assuming effective enforcement. In contrast, the environmental quality that results from a system of effluent fees depends on the extent to which individual firms reduce their pollution as a result of the imposition of the fees. Over the last several years, the U.S. Congress has considered a wide variety of proposals to curb levels of greenhouse gas (GHG) emissions. The debate around these proposals puts the focus on the relative desirability of emissions trading schemes and emissions taxes. The chapter analyzes different legislative proposals to combat climate change and describes programs that have been implemented around the world and at the state level.

The excerpt from the book by Peter Bohm analyzes the use of deposit-refund systems, under which purchasers of certain types of products must pay a deposit, which is refunded to them when the product is properly disposed. These schemes are a combination of a tax at the time of purchase and a subsidy at the time of return. Bohm explains that in certain instances deposit-refund systems are the only tool likely to be effective. For example, he notes that it is difficult to detect the improper disposal of small items that damage the environment, such as cadmium batteries. Thus, a ban or tax on improper disposal are unlikely to be effective tools. In contrast, if the tax and subsidy are set at a sufficiently high level, users of such batteries will have an economic incentive to dispose of them properly.

The article by Steven Shavell compares regulation and liability as means of controlling environmental risk. Regulation operates prospectively (or *ex ante*): a polluter must meet a given standard or face fines and other penalties. In contrast, liability operates retrospectively (or *ex post*): the polluter can engage in the activity in whatever way it wants but may be liable for any resulting harm. Regulation controls the activity directly, at least as long as enforcement is sufficiently vigorous and the penalties for noncompliance are sufficiently high. In contrast, liability controls the activity indirectly: Because an actor's expected liability is a function of the risk of its activities, liability creates incentives for the reduction of risk. Shavell identifies four factors as relevant for the choice between regulation and liability. First, liability is preferable if private actors have better information than regulatory authorities about an activity's risk. Second, regulation is preferable if the actors causing risk might have insufficient assets to pay for the resulting harm. Third, regulation is preferable if there is a sufficient possibility that suits will not be brought in the event of damage from the risky activity. Fourth, the relative administrative costs of the two schemes are relevant to the choice between them.

Finally, the excerpt from the book by Wesley Magat and W. Kip Viscusi analyzes hazard-warning schemes. The authors describe instances in which the provision of information might be more effective than direct regulation. For example, certain health-and-safety risks are a function of the decisions of both the manufacturer of a product, who decides how much to spend in order to reduce risk; and of the product's consumer, who decides how to operate the product. Thus, safety is likely to be increased if the consumer understands how to operate the product properly. Advocates of informational approaches to regulation also note that individuals have different preferences for risk. For example, some workers might prefer to take a relatively riskier job if it pays a sufficiently high wage premium, whereas others might make the opposite decision. Similarly, some consumers might be willing to pay a premium for a safer product whereas others might not. With accurate information about risk, workers and consumers can make the decisions that are best in light of their preferences.

2. COMMAND-AND-CONTROL REGULATION AND MARKETABLE PERMIT SCHEMES

Bruce A. Ackerman & Richard B. Stewart, Reforming Environmental Law
37 STAN. L. REV. 1333 (1985).*

The Existing System

The existing system of pollution regulation . . . is primarily based on a Best Available Technology (BAT) strategy. If an industrial process or product generates some nontrivial risk, the responsible plant or industry must install whatever technology is available to reduce or eliminate this risk, so long as the costs of doing so will not cause a shutdown of the plant or industry. BAT requirements are largely determined through uniform federal regulations. Under the Clean Water Act's BAT strategy, the EPA adapts nationally uniform effluent limitations for some 500 different industries. A similar BAT strategy is deployed under the Clean Air Act for new industrial sources of air pollution, new automobiles, and industrial sources of toxic air pollutants. BAT strategies are also widely

---

used in many fields of environmental regulation other than air and water pollution. . . .

BAT was embraced by Congress and administrators in the early 1970s in order to impose immediate, readily enforceable federal controls on a relatively few widespread pollutants, while avoiding widespread industrial shutdowns. Subsequent experience and analysis has demonstrated:

1. Uniform BAT requirements waste many billions of dollars annually by ignoring variations among plants and industries in the cost of reducing pollution and by ignoring geographic variations in pollution effects. A more cost-effective strategy of risk reduction could free enormous resources for additional pollution reduction or other purposes.

2. BAT controls, and the litigation they provoke, impose disproportionate penalties on new products and processes. A BAT strategy typically imposes far more stringent controls on new sources because there is no risk of shutdown. Also, new plants and products must run the gauntlet of lengthy regulatory and legal proceedings to win approval; the resulting uncertainty and delay discourage new investment. By contrast, existing sources can use the delays and costs of the legal process to burden regulators and postpone or "water-down" compliance. BAT strategies also impose disproportionate burdens on more productive and profitable industries because these industries can "afford" more stringent controls. This "soak the rich" approach penalizes growth and international competitiveness.

3. BAT controls can ensure that established control technologies are installed. They do not, however, provide strong incentives for the development of new, environmentally superior strategies, and may actually discourage their development. Such innovations are essential for maintaining long-term economic growth without simultaneously increasing pollution and other forms of environmental degradation.

4. BAT involves the centralized determination of complex scientific, engineering, and economic issues regarding the feasibility of controls on hundreds of thousands of pollution sources. Such determinations impose massive information-gathering burdens on administrators, and provide a fertile ground for complex litigation in the form of massive adversary rulemaking proceedings and protracted judicial review. Given the high costs of regulatory compliance and the potential gains from litigation brought to defeat or delay regulatory requirements, it is often more cost-effective for industry to "invest" in such litigation rather than to comply.

5. A BAT strategy is inconsistent with intelligent priority setting. Simply regulating to the hilt whatever pollutants happen to get on

the regulatory agenda may preclude an agency from dealing adequately with more serious problems that come to scientific attention later. BAT also tends to reinforce regulatory inertia. Foreseeing that "all or nothing" regulation of a given substance under BAT will involve large administrative and compliance costs, and recognizing that resources are limited, agencies often seek to limit sharply the number of substances on the agenda for regulatory action.

This indictment is not idle speculation, but the product of years of patient study by lawyers, economists, and political scientists. There are, for example, no fewer than fifteen careful efforts to estimate the additional cost burden generated by a wide range of traditional legalistic BAT systems used to control a variety of air and water pollutants in different parts of the country. Of the twelve studies of different air pollutants—ranging from particulates to chlorofluorocarbons—seven indicated that traditional forms of regulation were more than 400 percent more expensive than the least-cost solution; four revealed that they were about 75 percent more expensive; one suggested a modest cost-overrun of 7 percent. Three studies of water pollution control in five different water sheds also indicate the serious inefficiency of traditional forms of command-and-control regulation. These careful studies of selected problems cannot be used to estimate precisely the total amount traditional forms of regulation are annually costing the American people. Nonetheless, very large magnitudes are at stake. Even if a reformed system could cut costs by "only" one-third, it could save more than $15 billion *a year* from the nation's annual expenditure of $50 billion on air and water pollution control alone. . . .

Implementation

A BAT system has an implicit environmental goal: achievement of the environmental quality level that would result if all sources installed BAT controls on their discharges. The usual means for implementing this goal are centralized, industry-uniform regulations that command specific amounts of cleanup from specific polluters. When a polluter receives an air or water permit under existing law, the piece of paper does not content itself, in the manner of Polonius, with the vague advice that he "use the best available technology." Instead, the permit tries to be as quantitatively precise as possible, telling each discharger how much of the regulated pollutants he may discharge.

. . . [O]ur reforms build upon, rather than abandon, this basic permit system. Indeed, we have only two, albeit far-reaching, objections to the existing permit mechanism. First, existing permits are free. This is bad because it gives the polluter no incentive to reduce his wastes below the permitted amount. Second, they are non-transferable. This is bad because polluter A is obliged to cut back his own wastes even if it is cheaper for him to pay his neighbor B to undertake the extra cleanup instead.

Our basic reform would respond to these deficiencies by allowing polluters to buy and sell each other's permits—thereby creating a powerful financial incentive for those who can clean up most cheaply to sell their permits to those whose treatment costs are highest. This reform will, at one stroke, cure many of the basic flaws of the existing command-and-control regulatory systems discussed earlier.

A system of tradeable rights will tend to bring about a least-cost allocation of control burdens, saving many billions of dollars annually. It will eliminate the disproportionate burdens that BAT imposes on new and more productive industries by treating all sources of the same pollutant on the same basis. It will provide positive economic rewards for polluters who develop environmentally superior products and processes. It will, as we show below, reduce the incentives for litigation, simplify the issues in controversy, and facilitate more intelligent setting of priorities.

Would allowing the sale of permits lead to a bureaucratic nightmare? Before proceeding to the new administrative burdens marketability will generate, it is wise to pause ... to consider marketability's great administrative advantages.

First, marketability would immediately eliminate most of the information-processing tasks that are presently overwhelming the federal and state bureaucracies. No longer would the EPA be required to conduct endless adversary proceedings to determine the best available control technologies in each major industry of the United States, and to defend its determinations before the courts; nor would federal and state officials be required to spend vast amounts of time and energy in adapting these changing national guidelines to the particular conditions of every important pollution source in the United States. Instead of giving the job of economic and technological assessment to bureaucrats, the marketable rights mechanism would put the information-processing burden precisely where it belongs: upon business managers and engineers who are in the best position to figure out how to cut back on their plants' pollution costs. If the managers operating plant A think they can clean up a pollutant more cheaply than those in charge of plant B, they should be expected to sell some of their pollution rights to B at a mutually advantageous price; cleanup will occur at the least cost without the need for constant bureaucratic decisions about the best available technology. . . .

Second, marketable permits would open up enormous financial resources for effective and informed regulation. While polluters would have the right to trade their permits among themselves during the n years they are valid, they would be obliged to buy new ones when their permits expired at an auction held by the EPA in each watershed and air quality control region. These auctions would raise substantial sums of money for the government on a continuing basis. While no study has yet attempted to make global estimates for the United States as a whole, existing work suggests that auction revenues could well *equal* the

amount polluters would spend in cost-minimizing control activities. Even
if revenues turned out to be a third of this amount, the government would
still be collecting more than $6 to 10 billion a year. Moreover, it seems
reasonable to suppose that Congress would allow the EPA (and
associated state agencies) to retain a substantial share of these revenues.
Since the current EPA operating budget is $1.3 billion, using even a
fraction of the auction fund to improve regulatory analyses, research, and
monitoring would allow a great leap forward in the sophistication of the
regulatory effort. . . . Given its revenue-raising potential, environmental
reform is hardly a politically unrealistic pipe dream. To the contrary, it
is only a matter of time before the enormous federal deficit forces
Congress and the President to consider the revenue-raising potential of
an auction scheme.

Third, the auction system would help correct one of the worst
weaknesses of the present system: the egregious failure of the EPA and
associated state agencies to enforce the laws on the books in a timely and
effective way. Part of the problem stems from the ability of existing
polluters to delay regulatory implementation by using legal proceedings
to challenge the economic and engineering bases of BAT regulations and
permit conditions. But agencies also invest so little in monitoring that
they must rely on polluters for the bulk of their data on discharges. Since
polluters are predictably reluctant to report their own violations, the
current system perpetuates a Panglossian view of regulatory reality. For
example, a [U.S. Government Accountability Office] investigation of 921
major air polluters officially considered to be in compliance revealed 200,
or 22 percent, to be violating their permits; in one region, the number not
complying was 52 percent. Even when illegal polluters are identified,
they are not effectively sanctioned: The EPA's Inspector General in 1984
found that it was a common practice for water pollution officials to
respond to violations by issuing administrative orders that effectively
legitimized excess discharges. Thus, while the system may, after
protracted litigation, eventually "work" to force the slow installation of
expensive control machinery, there is no reason to think this machinery
will run well when eventually installed. Although there are many
reasons for this appalling weakness in enforcement, one stands out above
all others: The present system does not put pressure on agency
policymakers to make the large investments in monitoring and personnel
that are required to make the tedious and unending work of credible
enforcement a bureaucratic reality.

The auction system would change existing compliance incentives
dramatically. It would reduce the opportunity and incentive of polluters
to use the legal system for delay and obstruction by finessing the complex
BAT issues, and it would limit dispute to the question of whether a
source's discharges exceeded its permits. It would also eliminate the
possibility of using the legal system to postpone implementation of
regulatory requirements by requiring the polluter that lost its legal

challenge to pay for the permits it would have been obliged to buy during the entire intervening period of noncompliance (plus interest).

The marketable permit system would also provide much stronger incentives for effective monitoring and enforcement. If polluters did not expect rigorous enforcement during the term of their permits, this fact would show up at the auction in dramatically lower bids: Why pay a lot for the right to pollute legally when one can pollute illegally without serious risk of detection? Under a marketable permit approach, this problem would be at the center of bureaucratic attention. For if, as we envisage, the size of the budget available to the EPA and state agencies would depend on total auction revenues, the bureaucracy's failure to invest adequately in enforcement would soon show up in a potentially dramatic drop in auction income available for the next budgetary period. This is not a prospect that top EPA administrators will take lightly. Monitoring and enforcement will become agency priorities of the first importance. Moreover, permit holders may themselves support strong enforcement in order to ensure that cheating by others does not depreciate the value of the permit holders' investments. . . .

The reformed system we have described involves the execution of four bureaucratic tasks. First, the agency must estimate how much pollution presently is permitted by law in each watershed and air quality region. Second, it must run a system of fair and efficient auctions in which polluters can regularly buy rights for limited terms. Third, it must run an efficient title registry in each region that will allow buyers and sellers to transfer rights in a legally effective way. Fourth, it must consistently penalize polluters who discharge more than their permitted amounts.

And that's that. So far as the fourth bureaucratic task is concerned, we have already given reasons to believe that the EPA would enforce the law far more effectively under the new regime than it does at present. So far as the first three management functions are concerned, we think that they are, in the aggregate, far *less* demanding than those they displace under the BAT system.

Taking the three functions in reverse order . . . a system of title registration is within the range of bureaucratic possibility. In contrast, the second task—running fair and efficient auctions—is a complicated affair, and it is easy to imagine such a system run incompetently or corruptly. Nonetheless, other agencies seem to have done similar jobs in satisfactory fashions: If the Department of Interior can auction off oil and gas leases competently, we see no reason the EPA could not do the same for pollution rights. Finally, there remains the task of estimating the total allowable wasteload permitted under existing law in each watershed and air control region. If the BAT system functioned properly, these numbers would be easy to obtain. EPA's regional administrators would simply have to add up the allowed amounts appearing in the permits that are in their filing cabinets. We have no illusions, however, about present realities: So much bureaucratic time and energy has been diverted into the counterproductive factfinding tasks generated by the BAT system, and so little attention has been paid to actual discharges, that even the data needed for these simple arithmetic operations may well be incomplete and inadequate. Nonetheless, total permitted emissions in a region can be approximated in order to get a system of permits and auctions started. Surely this start-up effort would be less complex than the unending inquiries into available technologies required by the existing system. . . .

Would a system of marketable rights preclude improvement of environmental quality? By no means. The initial stock of rights can be amortized on a fixed schedule in order to reach a targeted goal, or the government may decide not to reissue existing rights after they expire. Any such reductions will increase the price of rights by reducing supply. Prices will also automatically tend to rise over time as the economy grows and the demand for rights increases. Under a BAT approach, by contrast, regulators must consistently undertake new, difficult, and unpopular initiatives to impose ever more stringent BAT controls on existing sources in order to accommodate economic growth without increased pollution. The prospect of steady increases in the price of rights will be a powerful incentive—far more powerful than the patchwork efforts at "technology forcing" under the BAT system—for businesses to develop cleaner products and processes.

A more serious objection to our proposal is that it ignores the problem of defining the region within which trades are permitted. The short answer is that the EPA and the States have already divided the nation into several hundred air quality control regions; similarly, the states have delineated the watershed boundaries for pollution control and other water management purposes. Rather than starting from scratch, our proposal can proceed on the basis of these existing boundaries. Especially in the area of air pollution, however, we have no doubt that existing regional lines have been drawn in a way that is extremely insensitive to ecological realities. We strongly recommend, therefore, that a reformed statute provide a mechanism for the orderly reexamination of existing regional boundaries—although it may well be wiser to defer this question for five or ten years to allow the EPA to concentrate on the challenges involved in managing the transition to a marketable permit system. . . .

. . . [A] reformed implementation system would not easily solve all foreseeable regulatory problems. In particular, the market system we have described could allow the creation of relatively high concentrations of particular pollutants in small areas within the larger pollution control region. In tolerating "hot spots," of course, our reform proposal shares the defects of the existing BAT system, which also generates risk of "hot spots" by imposing the same controls on sources regardless of their location, the size of the human population affected by their discharges, and the nature and vulnerability of affected ecosystems. Nonetheless, the blindness of both systems to intraregional variation is a serious source of concern. The extensive literature on marketable permits . . . points to a variety of feasible means for dealing with the hot spot problem. We believe that a long-run strategy for institutional reform should strive to take advantage of these more sophisticated market solutions to the problem of intraregional variation. For the present, it will be enough to emphasize . . . that administrative feasibility is an important constraint on the degree of sophistication that we may reasonably expect.

The critical question here, however, is not whether our market reform fails to solve problems that the BAT system also fails to solve. It is whether the reformed implementation system will generate *new* problems that offset its great economic, environmental, and administrative advantages. . . . We can foresee situations in which existing polluters might try to manipulate the rights market to deter entry by new firms in a way that is inconsistent with the antitrust laws, by either monopolizing the pollution rights market itself, or using it to block entry by competitors. There is, however, a considerable literature in which problems like this are discussed, and we ourselves have worried about them.

NOTES AND QUESTIONS

1.   **Best Available Technology Standards.** BAT standards can take one of two forms. First, the regulator could require the use of the best available technology; such requirements are often referred to as equipment or design standards. Second, the regulator could require the attainment of standards set by reference to what the best available technology can accomplish, but allow each source to choose the actual technology that it intends to use in order to meet the standard; such standards are generally referred to as emission standards in the case of air and as effluent standards in the case of water. With few exceptions, the federal environmental laws follow the latter approach. The statutes sometimes specify explicitly (as is the case, for example, in § 111(h) of the CAA, 42 U.S.C. § 7411(h)) that the former approach can be followed only when it is infeasible to set a numerical limitation. Which type of BAT standard is preferable? In particular, consider two issues:

(a)   ease of enforcement; and

(b)   incentive effects.

2.   **BAT Standards: New and Existing Sources.** Are BAT standards for new sources open to the same criticisms as BAT standards for existing sources? What are the relevant differences? Is it likely to be cheaper to design plants to meet a given standard or to retrofit existing plants? What are possible explanations for the differences in compliance costs between new and existing sources? For a particular category of plants, for example, electric utilities, is there likely to be more variation in the costs of meeting a particular standard for new sources or existing sources?

3. BAT Standards: Technological Innovation. Ackerman and Stewart contend that BAT standards discourage technological innovation. Consider a contrary argument: nationally uniform BAT standards create a national market for new technology that is labeled "best" by the regulatory authority; in contrast, under a system of marketable permits, there is likely to be great variation across firms in the chosen levels of emissions, and, consequently, different firms are likely to favor different types of pollution control technology. Assess the strength of this argument. What steps could a regulatory authority take in order to maximize the incentives of BAT standards for technological innovation? From this perspective, are equipment or design standards more desirable than emission or effluent standards? For discussion of the effects of environmental regulation on technological innovation, see Nicholas A. Ashford et al., *Using Regulation to Change the Market for Innovation*, 9 HARV. ENVTL. L. REV. 419 (1985). For defenses of BAT, see Howard Latin, *Ideal Versus Real Regulatory Efficiency: Implementation of Uniform Standards and "Fine Tuning" Regulatory Reforms*, 37 STAN. L. REV. 1267 (1985); and Sidney A. Shapiro & Thomas O. McGarity, *Not So Paradoxical: The Rationale for Technology-Based Regulation*, 1991 DUKE L.J. 729.

4. BAT Standards and Marketable Permit Schemes. BAT standards are generally set as a function of a unit of output, for example, pounds of sulfur dioxide per million BTU of energy produced. In contrast, marketable permit schemes and effluent fees are directly linked to units of pollution. Under the former, a firm can emit one unit of pollution for each permit that it holds, whereas under the latter, the firm must pay a set tax or submit another permit for each unit of pollution. What are the implications of this difference between BAT standards on the one hand and marketable permit schemes and effluent fees on the other? *See* Gloria E. Helfand, *Standards Versus Standards: The Effects of Different Pollution Restrictions*, 81 AM. ECON. REV. 622 (1991).

5. Allocation of Permits. In the transition from command-and-control regulation to marketable permit schemes, should there be an initial auction of permits or should the permits be given for free to firms that previously had the right to pollute? The latter approach is generally followed in the acid rain provisions of the 1990 amendments to the CAA—the most extensive marketable permit scheme under the federal environmental statutes—which create a national market for the trading of permits to emit sulfur dioxide. *See* 42 U.S.C. § 7651. Which approach is more desirable? Consider the effects of transaction costs in trading, as well as equity issues between new and existing plants. Which allocation approach is likely to have more political support? This question is considered in more detail later in this chapter and in Chapter IV.

6. Hot Spots. How serious is the "hot spot" problem that might arise under marketable permit schemes? For what types of pollutants is this problem likely to be most serious? How does it depend on the size of the area in which trades are permitted? What competing factors affect the delimitation of this area? How are such hot spots avoided under command-and-control regulation? Might marketable permit schemes ameliorate hot spots? Under what conditions? As discussed in Chapter II, the environmental justice movement believes that environmentally undesirable effects disproportionately affect people of color and the poor. What are the environmental justice implications of hot spots? How do hot spots affect the claim that marketable permit schemes are a tool to meet a particular level of environmental quality at least cost? How should one trade better quality in some areas against worse quality at a hot spot? What if, as compared to a command-and-control regime, everyone benefited under a marketable permit scheme but some groups benefited more? *See* Meredith Fowlie et al., *What Do Emissions Markets Deliver and to Whom? Evidence from Southern California's NOx Trading Program*, 102 AM. ECON. REV. 965 (2012).

What particular problems would arise from the implementation of marketable permit schemes under the CAA, which has as its centerpiece the nationwide achievement of uniform ambient air quality standards (maximum permissible concentrations of pollutants)? The structure of the CAA is discussed in detail in Chapter V. Would you expect hot spots if a marketable permit scheme is layered on top of the existing structure of the CAA? What if there are holes in the CAA's application?

7. **Markets in Environmental Degradation.** Ackerman and Stewart propose a marketable permit scheme in units of emissions. How would the hot spot problem be avoided by markets in units of environmental degradation? What are the characteristics of such markets? Consider the following issues:

    (a)   the number of markets in which a single source would have to buy a permit;

    (b)   the problems of coordination raised by the need to purchase permits in several markets;

    (c)   scientific problems in translating units of emissions into units of environmental degradation; and

    (d)   the role of the regulator.

Are the latter problems any less serious in the case of a command-and-control approach to meeting the CAA's ambient standards?

The impact of emissions on environmental quality is often a product not only of the level of emissions but also, among other factors, of the geographic location, prevailing winds, stack height, and climatic conditions. How does this feature affect the relative desirability of permits in units of emissions versus permits in units of environmental degradation? For discussion of different types of marketable permit schemes, see David W. Montgomery, *Markets in Licenses and Efficient Pollution Control Programs*, 5 J. ECON. THEORY 395 (1972); and Thomas H. Tietenberg, *Transferable Discharge Permits and the Control of Stationary Source Air Pollution: A Survey and Synthesis,* 56 LAND ECON. 391 (1980).

8. **Effluent Fees.** The same issues are raised by effluent fees. Should such fees be geographically uniform or should they be differentiated to reflect that one unit of emissions can have different impacts on environmental degradation as a result of factors such as the geographic location, prevailing

winds, stack height, and climatic conditions? How difficult would it be to implement a system of differentiated effluent fees? For further discussion, see Susan Rose-Ackerman, *Effluent Charges: A Critique*, 6 CAN. J. ECON. 512 (1973); and Thomas H. Tietenberg, *Spatially Differentiated Air Pollutant Emission Charges: An Economic and Legal Analysis*, 54 LAND ECON. 265 (1978).

9. Constrained Trading. Scholars have offered several different design solutions to the problem of "hot spots" that might otherwise form under marketable permit schemes. The trick is to adequately control this potential problem without sacrificing too much in efficiency and introducing too much complexity. One innovative proposal is to require prospective buyers and sellers to receive approval from a specially designed website before they could consummate their trade. The website would use an atmospheric dispersion model to predict the impact of the emissions, as modified by the proposed trade, on ambient pollution levels. The website would reject any trade resulting in the violation of an applicable ambient standard. How would such a scheme compare to markets in units of degradation? For more detail on this proposal, see Jonathan R. Nash & Richard L. Revesz, *Markets and Geography: Designing Marketable Permit Schemes to Control Local and Regional Pollutants*, 28 ECOLOGY L.Q. 569 (2001).

10. Retiring Permits. In a marketable permit system, should environmental groups be able to purchase permits with the intention of retiring them from circulation, so as to reduce the aggregate amount of pollution? Such purchases are allowed under the acid rain provisions of the CAA, and the environmental law societies of several law schools have purchased permits at auctions. In light of such purchases, is it appropriate for the government to increase the number of permits in circulation? Do these answers depend on how the number of permits in circulation was initially determined? Consider two options:

    (a) determination by reference to the level that maximizes social welfare; and

    (b) determination through the political process, without a well-articulated rationale.

11. Hoarding Permits. In a marketable permit system, should brokers be permitted to buy permits as an investment and hold them out of circulation for a period of time? Should polluters be allowed to buy permits and hold them for possible future expansion of their operations? Should they be allowed to purchase permits with the objective of increasing the costs of their competitors? Does the legal system have adequate protections with respect to these matters?

12. Marketable Permit Schemes, Property Rights, and Regulatory Takings. How are permits like property rights? If, having established a marketable permit scheme, a regulatory authority decides to dismantle it and return to command-and-control regulation, do holders of permits have a Fifth Amendment takings claim? Does it matter whether the initial allocation was by auction? Does it matter whether the holder bought the permit or got it for free? Are the issues raised by the elimination of a marketable permit scheme conceptually different from those that arise if the regulator makes a BAT standard for existing sources substantially more stringent than the previously applicable standard, thereby making valueless a firm's investment in pollution control technology?

Consider the following statutory language, contained within the acid rain provisions of the CAA:

> An allowance allocated under this subchapter is a limited authorization to emit sulfur dioxide in accordance with the provisions of this subchapter. Such allowance does not constitute a property right. Nothing in this subchapter or in any other provision of law shall be construed to limit the authority of the United States to terminate or limit such authorization.

42 U.S.C. § 7651b(f). Why do you think the Act specifies this? Should this provision be dispositive with respect to a possible takings claim?

For the period starting in 2010, EPA changed the allowance trading ratio in the acid rain program to require more permits in order to emit one ton of sulfur dioxide. Why do you think EPA made this change? What effect do you think this change had on the trading market? *See* Terry L. Anderson & Gary D. Libecap, *Cap and Take*, THE DAILY CALLER, May 15, 2012.

13. Markets in Operation. Even before the passage of the 1990 amendments, which added the acid rain provisions, the CAA contained some marketable permit schemes. For example, a source wishing to locate in a nonattainment area (an area that did not meet the ambient standards) had to obtain offsets from existing sources in the area. Studies of the operation of these trading schemes show that they have been vastly underutilized. For discussion, see Robert W. Hahn & Gordon L. Hester, *Where Did All the Markets Go?: An Analysis of EPA's Emissions Trading Program*, 6 YALE J. ON REG. 109 (1989). Scholarship suggests that marketable permit schemes may have substantial transaction costs as a result, primarily, of the costs of search and information, bargaining and decision, and monitoring and enforcement. *See* Robert N. Stavins, *Transaction Costs and Tradeable Permits*, 29 J. ENVTL. ECON. & MGMT. 133 (1995). What steps can be taken to encourage trades? For prescriptions about how to make marketable permit schemes work, see Robert W. Hahn & Roger G. Noll, *Environmental Markets in the Year 2000*, 3 J. RISK & UNCERTAINTY 351 (1990).

14. Trading Through Bubbles. Under the CAA, EPA has also authorized intrafirm trades through the "bubble" program. *See* 40 C.F.R. § 51.18(j)(1). Under the program, a firm can place an imaginary bubble over its various emission points as long as they are contiguous. The firm can then increase its pollution at certain points, or add additional points, as long as it reduces its pollution elsewhere by an equivalent amount. Thus, for example, a utility can add another smokestack without having to meet the otherwise applicable BAT standards, if it sufficiently reduces (or closes down) another smokestack. *See generally* RICHARD A. LIROFF, REFORMING AIR POLLUTION REGULATION: THE TOIL AND TROUBLE OF EPA'S BUBBLE (1986). Is the bubble program desirable? As discussed in Chapter V, existing sources generally face far less stringent environmental standards than new sources. Under what conditions do bubbles therefore slow down environmental improvements? How do they affect the competitive position of new firms?

15. Markets and Morality. Marketable permit schemes are sometimes attacked as "licenses to pollute." BAT, however, gives away for free the permission to pollute. Are marketable permit schemes morally more suspect? If so, why? *See generally* STEVEN KELMAN, WHAT PRICE INCENTIVES?: ECONOMISTS AND THE ENVIRONMENT (1981).

16. Comparative Efficiencies. On what basis do proponents of market-based forms of regulation claim that market-based mechanisms are inevitably more efficient than traditional command-and-control regimes for environmental protection? In what circumstances will this not hold true? *See* Daniel H. Cole & Peter Z. Grossman, *When is Command-and-Control Efficient? Institutions, Technology, and the Comparative Efficiency of Alternative Regulatory Regimes for Environmental Protection*, 1999 WIS. L. REV. 887 (arguing that in certain circumstances, particularly prior to the development of continuous emissions monitoring technologies, the heightened monitoring costs associated with market-based mechanisms eclipse any efficiencies attributable to the adoption of such mechanisms).

17. Enforcement in Marketable Permit Schemes. Ackerman and Stewart argue that a marketable permit scheme would dramatically improve the enforcement incentives of environmental agencies. Does an auction actually bring this kind of incentive to individuals within an agency? Could we actually tell if regulated entities are cheating from auction prices that are too low? What if the expected price is $20 but the actual price is $10? What if the vast majority of permits are distributed for free? Existing marketable permit schemes have had very different enforcement records. Lesley McAllister has compared the enforcement experience in the Title IV Acid Rain Trading Program, a national program to control sulfur dioxide emissions, with RECLAIM, a program to reduce smog precursors in Southern California. Lesley K. McAllister, *Enforcing Cap-and-Trade: A Tale of Two Programs*, 2 SAN DIEGO J. CLIMATE & ENERGY L. 1 (2010). She argues that "Even though RECLAIM regulated far fewer emissions, far more enforcement actions were pursued and far more penalties were imposed on regulated entities. RECLAIM further suggests that, under some conditions, environmental agencies may find cap-and-trade programs more difficult and costly to enforce than traditional regulation." *Id.* at 27. Can a marketable permit scheme be designed so that enforcement costs are likely to be low? Or is this entirely dependent on the types of sources that are regulated by the program?

3. MARKETABLE PERMIT SCHEMES AND EFFLUENT FEES

A. MARKETS V. TAXES: RELATIVE MERITS

William J. Baumol & Wallace E. Oates, The Theory of Environmental Policy
178–81 (1988).[*]

Although both effluent fees and systems of marketable permits have the capacity to achieve a set of environmental standards at least cost, they are by no means equivalent policy instruments from the viewpoint of an environmental agency. We shall consider first the grounds on which the environmental authority might prefer such permits to fees and shall then turn to the case for fees.

The first, and a major, advantage of marketable permits over fees is that permits promise to reduce the uncertainty and adjustment costs involved in attaining legally required levels of environmental quality. The environmental authority cannot be completely sure of the response of polluters to a particular magnitude of an effluent charge; in particular, if the authority inadvertently sets the fee too low, environmental standards will not be met. . . . [T]he fee may have to be raised and then altered again to generate an iterative path converging toward the target level of emissions. This means costly adjustments and readjustments by polluters in their levels of waste discharges and the associated abatement technology. The need for repeated changes in the fee is also an unattractive prospect for administrators of the program. In contrast, under a permit scheme, the environmental agency directly sets the total quantity of emissions at the allowable standard; there is, in principle, no problem in achieving the target.

Second, and closely related to the issue just discussed, are the complications that result from economic growth and price inflation. Continuing inflation will erode the real value of a fee; similarly, expanding production of both old and new firms will increase the demand for waste emissions. Both of these will require the fee to be raised periodically if environmental standards are to be maintained. The burden of initiating such corrective action under a system of fees falls necessarily upon environmental officials; they are forced to choose between unpopular fee increases or nonattainment of standards. Under a system of permits, market forces automatically accommodate themselves to inflation and growth with no increase in pollution. The rise in demand for permits, real and nominal, simply translates itself directly into a higher price.

---

[*]   Reprinted with the permission of Cambridge University Press, copyright © 1988.

Third, the introduction of a system of effluent fees may involve enormous increases in costs to polluters *relative* to alternative regulatory policies. This point may seem somewhat paradoxical in light of the widespread recognition that systems of pricing incentives promise large savings in aggregate abatement costs. But the two are not inconsistent. Although a system of effluent charges will reduce total abatement costs, it will impose a new financial burden, the tax bill itself, on polluting firms. Although these taxes represent a transfer payment from the viewpoint of society, they are a cost of operation for the firm. Some recent evidence on this issue suggests that the figures can be rather staggering. One such study of the use of pricing incentives to restrict emissions of certain halocarbons into the atmosphere estimates that aggregate abatement costs under a realistic program of direct controls would total about $230 million; a system of fees or of marketable permits would reduce these costs to an estimated $110 million (a saving of roughly 50 percent). However, the cost of the fees or permits to polluters would total about $1,400 million so that, in spite of the substantial savings in abatement costs, a program of pricing incentives would, in this instance, increase the total cost to polluters by a factor of *six* relative to a program of direct controls! Some studies of other pollutants also suggest that fees can be a major source of new costs. It is true that a system of marketable permits *making use of an auction for the initial acquisition of these rights* is subject to the same problem, because sources face high prices for permits. However, there is an alternative that gets around the problem: A permit system can be initiated through a *free* initial distribution of the permits among current polluters. This version of the permit scheme effectively eliminates the added costs for existing firms without any necessarily adverse consequences for the efficiency properties of the program and with some obvious and major advantages for its political acceptability. It is interesting in this regard that existing systems of marketable permits in the United States embody a kind of "grandfathering" scheme involving an initial distribution of emission permits or "rights" among polluters based on historical levels of emissions.

Fourth, . . . there may be instances where geographical distinctions among polluters are important. In fact, for several important air and water pollutants, various studies indicate that it is imperative for the environmental authority to differentiate among polluters according to their location if environmental standards are to be realized in a cost-effective way. Sources at a highly polluted location within an air shed cannot be allowed to increase their emissions on a one-to-one basis in exchange for emissions reductions by other sources at a less-polluted point. As we have indicated, it can be administratively quite cumbersome to deal with the spatial problem under a system of effluent charges, for it will typically require the environmental agency to determine a separate effluent fee for each source, depending upon its location in the air shed or river basin (or alternatively, it will be necessary to introduce a system of zones with different charges). Such discrimination among sources in fee levels may either be explicitly illegal or politically infeasible. In contrast, a system of marketable permits can address these spatial dimensions of the pollution problem in a manner that is less objectionable.

Fifth, marketable permits may well be the more feasible approach on grounds of familiarity. The introduction of a system of effluent fees requires the adoption of a wholly new method of controlling pollution, new both to regulators and polluters. Such sharp departures from established practice are hard to sell; moreover, some real questions have been raised about the legality of charging for pollution. In contrast, permits already exist, and it may be a less-radical step to make these permits effectively marketable.

There is thus a strong case on administrative grounds for favoring marketable permits over effluent fees. But the case is far from ironclad. Where charges are feasible, they represent a most attractive source of revenues for the public sector. Most taxes in the economy have undesired side effects: they distort economic choices in various ways. Income taxes, for example, can induce individuals to choose untaxed leisure activities rather than work; excise taxes shift peoples' purchases away from the taxed goods; and so on. Such taxes generate an "excess burden" on the economy—a cost in addition to the reduced disposable income directly attributable to the revenues. Effluent fees, in contrast, have a beneficial side effect: They tend to correct distortions in the economy while at the same time generating public revenues. Such fees can be said to impose a "negative excess burden." Fees, then, to the extent they are feasible, are a very desirable source of public revenues in terms of economic efficiency. . . .

There is yet another argument favoring effluent fees—one that involves savings in certain transactions costs. A system of marketable emission permits requires an initial distribution of the permits. However, if this initial distribution is based on the grandfathering principle or some other mechanism that does not reflect the relative marginal abatement costs of the different sources, a series of transfers (purchases and sales) of permits will be required if the least-cost allocation is to be attained. The incentives for such transfers exist: Buyers who can reduce emissions only at a higher real cost will be willing to pay more than the reservation price of sellers. But there may well be significant search costs and elements of strategic behavior that impede the transfers of emissions entitlements that are necessary to achieve the least-cost outcome. In contrast, under a system of fees, no such transfers of permits are needed—each source simply responds directly to the incentive provided by the fee. It may thus prove easier in certain circumstances to attain the least-cost allocation of waste emissions under a set of fees than under a system of marketable permits.

NOTES AND QUESTIONS

1. **Regulating Effluent: BAT Standards.** An environmental regulator wants to obtain a total of six units of effluent reduction from two firms that manufacture the same product. Unregulated, these firms would each have effluents of five units. If the regulator imposed BAT standards, which are uniform across categories of similar polluters, it would require each firm to reduce its emissions by three units. Alternatively, it could set up a scheme of marketable permits or impose effluent fees. Each firm's total costs of effluent reduction are set forth in Table III.1:

Table III.1.

Units of Effluent Reduction	Cost of Effluent Reduction	
	Firm 1	Firm 2
0	0	0
1	1	2
2	3	6
3	6	12
4	10	20
5	15	30

What is the cost-minimizing allocation of the pollution control burden? How do the aggregate costs under the cost-minimizing allocation compare to the aggregate costs under BAT?

2. **Regulating Effluent: Marketable Permits.** Assume, again by reference to Table III.1, that there is a transition from BAT to a marketable permit system and that the initial permits are given out, for free, to those with rights to emit under BAT (which requires each firm to reduce by three units its unregulated emissions of five units). What trades will take place? At what prices will these trades take place?

3. **Regulating Effluent: Effluent Fees.** If effluent fees are imposed, consider the effect of a tax of $2.50 per unit of effluent. The first unit of emission reduction costs $1.00 to Firm 1; thus, Firm 1 will prefer to expend this money rather than pay the tax of $2.50. The second unit of emission reduction costs this firm $2.00, so it will choose to engage in this reduction as well. The third unit costs $3.00, so the firm will prefer to pay the tax. In summary, faced with a tax of $2.50, Firm 1 will reduce its emissions two units. Similar logic establishes that this tax leads Firm 2 to reduce its emissions by only one unit. Thus a tax of $2.50 per unit of effluent is too low to achieve the regulator's objective. What is the effect of a tax of $5.50? What tax should the regulator set to achieve an aggregate reduction of six units?

If the regulatory authority initially sets the wrong tax (so that either too much or too little pollution is produced), can it correct its mistakes? What are the costs of frequent modifications of the tax rates?

4. **Revenue Raising.** The excerpts by Ackerman & Stewart and Baumol & Oates reach different conclusions about the desirability of having the

regulatory authority raise substantial revenues through an initial auction. Which perspective do you find most convincing? These and other issues concerning the structuring of markets are discussed in THOMAS H. TIETENBERG, EMISSIONS TRADING: AN EXERCISE IN REFORMING POLLUTION POLICY (1985).

5.   Marketable Permit Schemes and Effluent Fees. How should one determine the relative desirability of marketable permit schemes and effluent fees? The former fix pollution control levels but leave cleanup costs uncertain. The latter fix the incremental (though not the total) cleanup costs but leave the quantity of pollution uncertain. Which is more desirable under the following circumstances:

(a)   a sharp increase in the damage of pollution as the level of pollution increases?

(b)   a sharp increase in the incremental cost of pollution abatement as the stringency of the controls increase?

For further discussion, see A. Michael Spence & Martin L. Weitzman, *Regulatory Strategies for Pollution Control, in* APPROACHES TO CONTROLLING AIR POLLUTION 199 (Ann F. Friedlaender ed., 1978); Martin L. Weitzman, *Prices vs. Quantities*, 41 REV. ECON. STUD. 477 (1974); and Gary W. Yohe, *Towards a General Comparison of Price Controls and Quantity Controls Under Uncertainty*, 45 REV. ECON. STUD. 229 (1978).

Does it matter whether the regulatory authority has accurate information about each firm's costs of pollution control? Which tool is preferable as a replacement for command-and-control regulation if the objective is to meet existing ambient standards? Which tool is preferable given the competition that firms face in global markets? In this connection, does it matter how the initial allocation is performed?

6.   Enforcement. Which of the following regulatory tools are more desirable from the perspective of ease of enforcement:

(a)   BAT standards?

(b)   marketable permits?

(c)   effluent fees?

What are the enforcement difficulties raised by each approach?

7.   Subsidies and Effluent Fees. Subsidies are an alternative to effluent fees. If there is no entry of new firms into the market, both approaches ought to have equal properties. Why? What incentives do subsidies create with respect to the entry of new firms into the market? Are such incentives desirable? This issue is discussed in depth in a portion of the Baumol and Oates book that is not excerpted. *See* BAUMOL & OATES, *supra*, at 212–13, 216–28.

8.   Nominal Fees, Inflation, and Politics. Once it is recognized that the real value of a fixed nominal fee will be eroded by inflation, is this any longer a serious obstacle? Legislators can schedule fees to increase over time to keep pace with inflation or any other measure they choose. If regulated entities understand that a marketable permit scheme is likely to result in automatic price increases over time, will such a scheme be less objectionable politically than a tax that increases over time?

B. MARKETS V. TAXES: DOMESTIC RESPONSE TO CLIMATE CHANGE

Between 2005 and 2010, the U.S. Congress considered a wide variety of bills to establish and implement a mandatory GHG reductions program. These proposed bills generally focused on flexible mechanisms, such as trading schemes and emissions taxes, which are widely acknowledged to minimize the costs of achieving a particular level of reduction. *See, e.g.*, Joseph E. Aldy & Robert N. Stavins, *Using the Market to Address Climate Change: Insights from Theory and Experience*, DAEDALUS, Spring 2012, at 45. However, this is where the agreement stopped. First, there is considerable disagreement about which of these two mechanisms should be preferred. Given the European Union's [EU's] decision in 2005 to create a cap-and-trade system as well as the successful implementation of other trading regimes in the United States, such as the Title IV Acid Rain Trading Program for sulfur dioxide under the Clean Air Act, the focus in Congress was on a cap-and-trade system. A significant group of economists, however, argued that a tax would be the superior policy. *See, e.g.*, N. Gregory Mankiw, *One Answer to Global Warming: A New Tax*, N.Y. TIMES, Sept. 16, 2007, at 6; Ian W. Parry, *Should We Abandon Cap and Trade in Favor of a CO_2 Tax?*, RESOURCES FOR THE FUTURE, Summer 2007, at 7. Second, within these two types of mechanisms, the proposals contained significant variation.

The federal climate change bill closest to becoming law in the United States was titled the American Clean Energy and Security Act. H.R. 2454, 111th Cong. (2009). The bill, also known as Waxman-Markey after two influential House Democrats, passed the House in June 2009 by a vote of 219 to 212. Eight Republicans voted for the bill and forty four Democrats voted against it. This bill was never directly considered by the Senate and various other proposals failed to gain traction in the Senate in 2010. The heart of Waxman-Markey was a cap-and-trade program covering most sectors of the economy: electric generation units, producers and importers of petroleum-based or coal-based liquid fuels, industrial sources, and natural gas distribution companies. The cap-and-trade program mandated reductions in GHGs, relative to 2005 emissions, of 20% by 2020 and 80% by 2050. While most sectors would be covered by the program starting in 2012, industrial sources would not be directly included until 2014 and natural gas distribution companies would not be covered until 2016. In the early years of the program, a significant portion of the permits would be allocated to electric utilities for the benefit of retail ratepayers. This allocation would be based in part on historical emissions data and in part on retail electricity deliveries. Special allocation provisions were also included for coal generators not owned by a public utility and for generators in long-term contracts.

Industrial sources in industries that are energy-intensive, GHG-intensive, or both would be eligible for "emission allowance rebates." The annual rebate for each source would be based on output for the two prior years by that source and the average greenhouse gas intensity for the industry. These rebates would be phased out gradually between 2025 and 2035. Permits were also designated for natural gas consumers, consumers of home heating oil, low-income consumers, petroleum refineries, investment in energy efficiency and renewable energy, worker adjustment assistance, adaptation to climate change, and deficit reduction. Over time, most free allocation would be phased out and permits would be auctioned. A significant amount of the auction revenue would be used for per capita income tax refunds. One feature of the auction was a reserve price which started at $10 in 2012 and would escalate at 5% plus the rate of inflation each year.

Several measures in the bill were designed to control prices or to provide alternative ways of acquiring permits. In addition to the normal auctions, the bill also authorized "strategic reserve auctions" four times per year. Permits would be specifically set aside for the strategic reserve and available at a relatively high minimum price. This minimum would start at $28 in 2012, increasing at 5% per year plus inflation in 2013 and 2014. In 2015 and thereafter, the minimum price would be set at 60% above the average price over the previous three years for permits allocated for that year. The bill provided authority to the Federal Energy Regulatory Commission (FERC) to regulate permit markets. It directed FERC to issue regulations prohibiting fraud, market manipulation, and excess speculation. The bill also directed FERC to issue regulations "to limit unreasonable fluctuation" in the price of permits. The bill would also allow regulated entities to comply by purchasing offsets, which represent reductions in emissions from non-regulated parts of the economy or international sources. Domestic offsets could be used to account for one ton of emissions but 1.25 tons of international offsets were required for each ton of emissions. The bill specified a limit of 2 billion tons worth of offsets per year. This amount was approximately 40% of the overall cap in the early years of the program and represented an increasing share over time. Banking, the use of permits saved in earlier years, and borrowing, the use of permits allocated for future years, were both allowed, albeit with several restrictions on borrowing.

In addition to the cap-and-trade program, Waxman-Markey contained numerous complementary policies. A combined energy efficiency and renewable energy standard for electric utilities required 20% of electricity sales be matched with generation of renewable energy or reductions in electricity consumption by 2020. The bill would have established programs promoting carbon capture and sequestration, electric vehicles and other clean vehicles, "smart" electric grids, and energy efficiency in buildings, lighting, and appliances.

The other prominently discussed regulatory tool, a carbon tax, would impose a fee on each ton of carbon dioxide that is contained in fossil fuels. Other GHG emissions, to the extent measurable, could also be taxed. The tax could be levied against fossil fuel producers and importers, raising their costs of production and forcing them to charge higher prices to electricity generators. These generators, in turn, would have to charge higher prices to utilities, which would have to charge higher rates to electricity consumers, who would decrease their electricity consumption in the face of these higher rates. The tax could be set at the level that reflects the cost to society of the higher global temperatures caused by each ton of CO_2 emitted into the atmosphere. The best estimate of this level, based on the most widely peer-reviewed models and best available data, was developed by the Interagency Working Group on the Social Cost of Greenhouse Gases (IWG). *See* Richard L. Revesz et al., *Best Cost Estimate of Greenhouse Gases*, 357 SCIENCE 655 (2017). The IWG's most recent central estimate, in 2017 dollars, was $50 in global damages per ton of CO_2, based on year 2020 emissions. *Id.* Even a modest tax of $10 per ton of CO_2 has been estimated to reduce annual CO_2 emissions by 5% and raise annual revenues of about $55 billion. Parry, *supra*. In addition, the political climate might have changed such that more attention is now paid to carbon taxes. *See* Trent Lott & John Breaux, *Here's How to Break the Impasse on Climate*, N.Y. TIMES, June 20, 2018.

There exist a number of precedents upon which a domestic carbon tax could be based. For example, Germany and the United Kingdom impose an electricity consumption tax assessed on a per kilowatt basis on electric utilities. Scandinavian nations have enforced a carbon tax system for more than a decade. *See* Inho Choi, *Global Climate Change and the Use of Economic Approaches: The Ideal Design Features of Domestic Greenhouse Gas Emissions Trading With an Analysis of the European Union's CO_2 Emissions Trading Directive and the Climate Stewardship Act*, 45 NAT. RESOURCES J. 865 (2005).

The following notes and questions consider the features of Waxman-Markey and other proposals in order to explore the different ways that marketable permit schemes and emissions taxes can be implemented in practice. The notes also discuss the regimes for GHGs that have been implemented in other countries and at the state and regional level within the United States.

NOTES AND QUESTIONS

1.   Point of Regulation: Producers/Importers v. Emitters. An important choice to be made in any GHG-reduction regime is what point in the supply chain should be directly regulated. For example, in the context of oil, regulation could be imposed on the companies that extract oil from the ground (or import it), on oil refineries, on retail sellers of oil, or on consumers who actually burn oil (or any combination of these four). The same level of GHG reduction can be achieved through regulation of any of these entities.

A permit regime that regulates "upstream" entities, like producers and importers, would limit the amount of oil that eventually makes it to oil consumers and is burned. Likewise, a tax on upstream entities would be passed on to downstream entities, eventually encouraging consumers to burn less oil because of higher prices. Conversely, a tax for oil products directly on consumers would impact upstream entities by reducing demand for the taxed products.

Many proposals considered by Congress differed in terms of whether they would regulate producers and importers of fossil fuels that contain CO_2 or emitters of CO_2. The type of coverage within the Waxman-Markey bill depended on the type of fuel and the sector. The bill would have directly covered liquid fuels at the level of producers and importers. Electricity sources and industrial sources would be directly regulated for emissions from coal and natural gas. Residential and commercial use of natural gas would be covered by requiring natural gas distribution companies to submit permits for sales to those customers. This combination of coverage would include the vast majority of fossil fuel emissions within the United States. Other congressional proposals would regulate all fuels at the level of producers and importers. Similarly, the main bills proposing carbon tax schemes would collect the tax at the producer and importer level for all fossil fuels.

Classical economic theory predicts that, in competitive markets, a tax on buyers of a particular good or service will have the same distributional consequences—what economists call the "tax incidence"—as a tax of equal size on sellers of that good or service. This prediction also holds in the context of permit trading schemes. *See* Michael Hanemann, *Cap-and-Trade: A Necessary or Sufficient Condition for Emissions Reduction?*, 26 OXFORD REV. ECON. POL'Y 225, 226 (2010). If this is true, does it matter whether a GHG reduction program regulates at the upstream or downstream level? Which is likely to cover a greater percentage of GHG emissions? Is there a risk of "too much" coverage? *See* Robert N. Stavins, *Addressing Climate Change with a Comprehensive U.S. Cap-and-Trade System*, 24 OXFORD REV. ECON. POL'Y 298, 304 (2008) (noting that a "small portion of fossil fuels . . . are not combusted" and also recommending that regulation at the upstream level exempt "fossil fuel exports so that they are not at a competitive disadvantage relative to supply from other countries that do not face any allowance requirements"). Other things being equal, if the purpose is to regulate further downstream, where more entities tend to be directly subject to regulation, is a tax preferable to a permit scheme? Would it be administratively feasible to impose a permit trading regime that applies directly to consumers? Is a permit trading regime more desirable when there are fewer entities that are directly subject to regulation? *See id.* On the other hand, might this situation present opportunities for firms with market power to hoard permits, thereby preventing new firms from entering the market? *See* Frank J. Convery & Luke Redmond, *Market and Price Developments in the European Union Emissions Trading Scheme*, 1 REV. ENVTL. ECON. & POL'Y 88, 101–02 (2007) (analyzing extent of market power in the European Union's Emissions Trading System market for permits). Is environmental law the best vehicle for addressing this potential problem, or are there other bodies of law well suited to the task?

2.   Free Permit Allocation and Economic Efficiency. In a Coasean world, would unconditional free permit allocation to existing sources distort economic incentives? In the real world? Are there certain types of actors that are more likely to act in a perfectly rational economic manner? Independent of the incentives of the recipient of free allocation, are there efficiency reasons to avoid free allocation? Is the generation of revenues through an auction desirable? *See* Stavins, *supra*, at 305–06. Would returning the proceeds of an auction to taxpayers slow down their behavioral adjustments as consumers? How different from the provision of free permits to private parties is the grandfathering of existing sources in command-and-control programs?

What is the impact of the phased auctioning approach contemplated by Waxman-Markey and other proposals? *See* Stavins, *supra*, at 307. Some proposals would leave the extent of free allocation to the discretion of the President. What level of free allocation is likely to result from this arrangement?

3.   Alternative Criteria for Free Permit Allocation. After deciding how many permits will be sold at auction and how many will be given away to existing firms, there is still the issue of how the free permits will be allocated among existing firms. Most proposals for allocation are based on measures of past performance (either before the beginning of the program or before the enactment of the program). Some proposals would base allocation of permits on the amount of energy generated annually or other measures of output for a given industry. Other proposals would base allocation on annual heat input. Still others would be based on GHG emissions. Which of these bases of allocation is more desirable? If the information used is purely historical, is this only a distributional question?

Alternatively, some allocation proposals are based on information generated after the start of program, often collectively referred to as "updating" approaches. These proposals act as a de facto subsidy for the criteria chosen (that is, updating allocations based on output would incentivize firms to increase their output to receive more free permits in the future). Any free allocation to sources that start operation after the enactment of a program must be of this type. Some approaches cut off the free allocation to facilities when they shut down. From a fairness perspective, this kind of approach may seem desirable because shut-down facilities no longer incur any costs for their emissions and no longer provide any societal benefit worthy of compensation (for example, employment). However, this approach may provide an inefficient subsidy for existing sources to continue operations. How would you manage this efficiency-fairness tradeoff? The Title IV Acid Rain Trading Program for sulfur dioxide granted free allocation to existing sources in perpetuity. *See* 42 U.S.C. § 7651B(a) ("[T]he removal of an existing affected unit or source from commercial operation . . . shall not terminate or otherwise affect the allocation of allowances . . . to which the unit is entitled."). Does this tradeoff make free permit allocation to industrial sources less appealing?

In some cases, incentivizing output through an allocation scheme may be desirable from an environmental perspective. Without such a subsidy, production from a trade-exposed industry within the United States may merely be transferred to a country without substantial GHG regulations. This phenomenon is known as "leakage." If the facilities in that country are less efficient than those within the United States, global greenhouse gas emissions could even increase on net as a result. Even if this is the case, would it make any sense to distinguish between existing and new sources within the United States?

4.   Permit Allocation and Distributional Equity. Many proposals distribute permits directly to the entities regulated by the program. But, in principle, the permits created for a marketable permit scheme can be given to anyone. Similarly, the proceeds of a permit auction can be distributed to anyone. Given that the imposition of a market-based regulatory program for GHGs will impose costs on virtually all actors in the economy, many different groups have plausible claims for compensation. One way to address distributional concerns is through a cap-and-dividend scheme. In July 2014 Representative Christopher Van Hollen introduced the Healthy Climate and Family Security Act, H.R. 2230, 113rd Cong. (2014), which establishes a cap-and-dividend scheme. Under the bill, carbon pollution permits are auctioned to the first sellers of oil, coal, and natural gas into the U.S. market. The full amount of revenue raised is then returned to individuals on a per capita basis as a "Healthy Climate Dividend." Households would pay more for energy, as the costs of the permits would be passed on to consumers, but would receive compensation through the dividend. Who are the net beneficiaries under this scheme? Who are the net losers?

One possible downside to this scheme is that the costs imposed won't be evenly distributed across the country. As Robert Nordhaus and Kyle Danish have observed:

> [a]ll other things being equal, a regulatory program that aims to reduce GHG emissions will tend to impose its largest costs on firms and households that produce fossil fuels or are heavily dependent on them. A GHG regulatory program also will tend to be relatively more costly for low-income individuals because they spend a greater proportion of their total income on energy.

Robert R. Nordhaus & Kyle W. Danish, *Assessing the Options for Designing a Mandatory U.S. Greenhouse Gas Reduction Program*, 32 B.C. ENVTL. AFF. L. REV. 97, 118 (2005). Partly because of this feature, Waxman-Markey contained a more complicated mechanism to protect consumers from increases in electricity prices. Half of the permits to retail electricity distributors would have been allocated on the basis of a measure of historical emissions. The other half of the permits would be distributed based on an updated measure of electricity sales. The bill required that the proceeds from the permits be used to benefit retail ratepayers. Economists often argue that the best use of permit revenue is reducing other distortionary taxes (such as income taxes or taxes on labor). Obviously, tax reductions (or prevention of tax increases) have distributional effects as well as efficiency ones. One carbon tax proposal provided for an expansion of the Earned Income Tax

Credit, a subsidy program for low-income households. Can there be a right answer to this question? Are certain forms of free permit distribution truly "wasteful spending"? How willing are you to make potentially inefficient side payments in exchange for a mandatory GHG policy?

5.   Windfall Profits. In 2005, the European Union launched its Emissions Trading System (EU ETS), the first international cap-and-trade system. *See* European Commission, Emissions Trading System, http://ec.europa.eu/ clima/policies/ets/index_en.htm (last visited June 14, 2018). One of the controversies from Phase I of the EU ETS was whether certain regulated parties, primarily electric generators, received "windfall profits" from the program because they were granted substantial amounts of free allocation and earned additional revenue from an increase in wholesale electricity prices. *See* A. DENNY ELLERMAN & PAUL L. JOSKOW, THE EUROPEAN UNION'S EMISSION TRADING SCHEME IN PERSPECTIVE 24–31 (2008). This combination of effects raised the possibility that these regulated entities had *higher* profits as a result of the enactment of the EU ETS. However, the effect on electricity prices depended on the state of electricity sector regulation in particular countries. Was this effect foreseeable? How difficult would it be to tailor free allocation amounts so that no regulated parties are ever better off as a result of a cap-and-trade program? Does it matter to you that some consumers might be better off under a cap-and-dividend scheme?

6.   Taxes and Distributional Equity. It is also possible to design carbon tax schemes to address distributional concerns. In February 2018, Senator Sheldon Whitehouse introduced the American Opportunity Carbon Fee Act, S. 2368, 115th Cong. (2018), which establishes a zero net revenue carbon tax scheme. Under the bill, major facilities would pay a fee, starting at $50 in 2019, per ton of carbon dioxide emitted. The full amount of revenue raised would then be returned to the American people through reductions to the corporate income tax rate, tax credits to workers, and additional benefits to retired and disabled Americans. Who are the net beneficiaries under this scheme? Who are the net losers?

Another carbon tax proposal considered by Congress had a provision allocating about 2.25% of annual revenues to assist displaced energy workers during the first ten years of the scheme. *See* Market Choice Act, H.R. 6463, 115th Cong. (2018). The bill would give the Secretary of Labor discretion to assist such workers through worker retraining, relocation expenses for those who move to find new employment, early retirement, health benefits, and other assistance. Should transition relief be provided to the industry or to its workers? Should transition relief be an important part of greenhouse gas taxing regimes? Is there a principled basis for distinguishing between taxes and cap-and-trade programs in this regard? Are there any features of free allocation that can't be mimicked through tax rebates or other measures?

7.   Offsets. Most of the cap-and-trade proposals considered by Congress provided for offsets, which would allow regulated entities that fund or implement projects that reduce CO_2 levels to use those reductions as an "offset" (thus eliminating the need for permits) against GHG emissions. Two of the carbon tax proposals would grant tax refunds to regulated entities that engage in certain activities that reduce carbon emissions, like sequestration.

These refunds are a form of offset because they offer regulated entities an alternative—sequestration—to paying the carbon tax for their CO_2 production or reducing their production.

Offsets are a form of marketable permits; if a regulated entity believes it can reduce GHG emissions more cheaply through, for example, carbon sequestration than by reducing its emissions, the availability of offsets encourages it to do so. If most proposals would implement a permit trading scheme, why do they also allow for offsets? How does this affect the overall permit market?

Offsets raise a number of important issues. Several of the cap-and-trade proposals allowed at least some offsets from foreign sources. What additional problems can you foresee in allowing international offsets? How easy are they likely to be to enforce? What information would be necessary to determine whether a particular offset is valid? Offsets are desirable only if they are additive—that is, if they achieve CO_2 reductions that would not otherwise be undertaken. What difficulties might this raise in the context of international offsets? Many of the proposals treated domestic offsets more favorably than international offsets. For example, Waxman-Markey would have required 1.25 international offsets for each ton of emissions from a regulated entity. Another bill would have placed no limits on domestic offsets but limited international offsets to 10% of the total economy-wide cap. Likewise, one of the tax proposals would have granted tax refunds to sources that implement domestic sequestration and HFC (an especially harmful type of GHG) destruction programs; the bill contained no analogous provisions for international programs.

Offsets are especially problematic in the context of uncertain technology. On the one hand, if new offset technologies like carbon capture and storage seem to offer opportunities to reduce CO_2 emissions cheaply, maximum efficiency will be achieved by allowing regulated entities to use these technologies to meet their GHG reduction obligations (as opposed to reducing output). On the other hand, many of these technologies have not been fully tested, giving rise to the possibility that these offsets will result in lower-than-anticipated GHG reductions. In the face of scientific uncertainty, how should a GHG reduction plan treat offsets? One proposal required that any sequestration used to offset CO_2 reduction obligations be re-verified every five years. Might a carbon tax be better suited to addressing these uncertainties than a cap-and-trade regime?

8.   Permit Tracking and Fraud. In early 2011, the EU ETS was struck by a series of frauds originating out of a "phishing" scam where owners of permits received emails asking them to re-register on a fake agency website. The information was then used to access these permits and sell them to third parties who likely did not know the dubious origins of their acquisitions. *See, e.g., Phishing Scam Cripples European Emissions Trading*, DER SPIEGEL, Feb. 3, 2010. Because each EU ETS permit is identified by a unique identification number, it is possible to determine who ended up with these stolen permits. Should they be returned to their original owners? Should the new owners be compensated if they are returned? Within the European Union, this question may be complicated by widely varying liability rules.

9. Emissions Certainty. In the event securing a particular GHG emissions target were a priority, which proposal should be favored? Does your answer depend on whether the cap-and-trade regime in question allows environmental groups to purchase permits and remove them from circulation? Under what circumstances is securing emissions certainty especially important? Are these circumstances present in the case of GHGs? *See* William A. Pizer, *Choosing Price or Quantity Controls for Greenhouse Gases, in* CLIMATE CHANGE ECONOMICS AND POLICY 99, 102–03 (Michael A. Toman ed., 2001).

10. Price Volatility. Emissions taxes define the "price" of emissions reduction. Permit markets, in contrast, define the "quantity" of emissions reduction. Changes in fuel prices and the demand for energy could result in fluctuating levels of demand for carbon permits. Because under a cap-and-trade regime the supply of permits is fixed by the government, fluctuations in demand translate into fluctuations in price. In other words, under a cap-and-trade system, the prices of permits can be volatile. What incentives would fluctuations in price create on the part of firms to undertake R & D efforts to develop cleaner technology in the future or CO_2-saving investments with high upfront capital costs? How could markets be framed to address problems in price fluctuations?

The first three years of the EU ETS saw significant price volatility. The market price for a permit ranged from virtually zero to more than € 30. ELLERMAN & JOSKOW, *supra*, at 12–16. Indeed, the market price for permits for Phase I fell from € 30 to € 15 in the course of a single week in 2006, before settling close to zero for most of 2007. *Id.*

The cap-and-trade schemes under congressional consideration proposed different means to combat price volatility. A number of these provisions were included in Waxman-Markey and discussed *supra*. However, there are a number of other methods for managing price volatility. One bill would have created a new federal entity, colloquially called the "Climate Fed" as an allusion to the U.S. Federal Reserve Board, with the power to relax restrictions on borrowing permits from future years or restrictions on the number of offsets that each source may use for compliance. Other bills have included a "safety valve" on the price of permits. This type of provision allows regulated entities to purchase additional permits from the government at a given price. This means that the market price of permits will never go above the safety valve price. Because these permits would be above and beyond the specified cap, safety valves result in a hybrid between a marketable permit scheme and a tax regime. How does this feature affect firms' incentive to find cleaner technologies? At what level should the safety valve be set? *See* Stavins, *supra*, at 305.

11. Emissions Certainty v. Price Volatility. In the context of addressing global climate change, do you consider it more important to achieve emissions certainty or price stability? What might influence your decision? In light of your answers to the previous questions, what is your preferred policy response?

12. Setting the Cap. One of the most significant problems with Phase I of the EU ETS was the lack of available data about each country's level of past emissions. *See* ELLERMAN & JOSKOW, *supra*, at 31–35. In conjunction with the modest ambitions for the schedule of reductions during Phase I, these data issues led to the combined cap for Phase I to be more generous than intended. *See id.* The collective discovery of this fact in 2006 led to major drops in the market price for Phase I permits. The price for these permits hovered close to zero for most of 2007. *Id.* at 13. However, this doesn't necessarily mean that Phase I resulted in no environmental benefits. Using a very simple method, Ellerman and Joskow observe that higher permit prices in 2005 and 2006 may have led to 50 to 100 million tons of GHG abatement in each year. *Id.* at 34. Furthermore, Phase I was explicitly designed as a trial period for the EU ETS and no banking of permits was allowed between Phase I and Phase II. This limited the environmental consequences of "over-allocation" in Phase I.

13. Setting the Tax. In 2015 alone, two carbon tax proposals considered by Congress varied in the size of the proposed tax (at least initially) from \$15 per metric ton of CO_2 to \$30 per metric ton of CO_2. *See* Carbon Tax Center, Bills, https://www.carbontax.org/bills/ (last visited June 15, 2018). For a carbon tax to be efficient, it should reflect the costs to society from the future global warming potential of CO_2. These costs encompass "damages to agriculture, protection of valuable coastal land against sea-level rises, health impacts from the spread of tropical disease, [and] the risk of extreme climate change scenarios." Parry, *supra*, at 7. Given that there remains "enormous uncertainty over future climate change scenarios," *id.*, how should the level of the carbon tax be set? Is the SCC, introduced in the previous chapter, relevant for setting the level of the tax? Is the disparity in carbon tax proposals merely a reflection of the uncertainty over future costs of current CO_2 emissions? Is it preferable to err by setting the initial tax too high or too low in the face of this uncertainty?

14. Scope of Coverage. The proposals considered by Congress varied significantly in terms of what industries would be covered. At the high end, the Waxman-Markey and other bills would have covered more than 80% of domestic GHG emissions. In contrast, other proposals would cover only the electricity sector, which comprises about one third of domestic GHG emissions. The main carbon tax proposals would apply to all fossil fuels, resulting in coverage of about 80% of domestic GHG emissions.

From an efficiency perspective, why might a regime that requires modest reductions from a broad range of industries be superior to a regime that requires more stringent reductions from a narrower range of industries? From a fairness perspective? From a public choice perspective?

15. Administrative Feasibility. Which of the proposed measures would likely be most easily administered? What administrative tasks are common to both regimes? What tasks are unique to each?

Given that the stabilization of GHG concentrations will ultimately require global efforts, which policy framework is most easily adapted to achieve coordination with other countries? How likely do you think it is that countries that employ cap-and-trade regimes without a price safety valve would be willing to link their regime to a U.S. cap-and-trade regime that does contain a safety valve? *See* Stavins, *supra*, at 11 (pointing out that despite the European Union's likely reluctance to link its Emissions Trading Scheme with a U.S. system containing a safety valve, significant cost savings are available from such linkage).

Several of the proposals before Congress contained measures to encourage commensurate reductions from other countries. Beginning in 2020, one bill would have required importers of carbon-intensive products to obtain permits for those imports if the country of origin lacks a comparable GHG-reductions policy. Another proposal contained a similar provision, where the permits for imports would come from a different pool than the permits for domestic allowances. Why do you think these proposals in Congress contain these provisions?

16. Cost Effectiveness from a Global Perspective. Even if other countries enact cap-and-trade regimes to achieve GHG reductions commensurate with proposed U.S. reductions, few of the cap-and-trade proposals before Congress contemplated permit trading across international borders. Why might this be? What effect do you think this might have on the cost effectiveness of achieving a given level of GHG reductions worldwide? Is this potential inefficiency likely to be small or large relative to the efficiency gains achieved by allowing permit trading among firms within each country? Waxman-Markey would have allowed the use of international permits, albeit with limitations at the discretion of the EPA administrator. How does a carbon tax avoid this problem?

17. Utility of Complementary Policies. In theory, the price signal from a cap-and-trade program can cost-effectively lead to significant decreases in emissions without complementary policies. The experience with SO_2 and the Acid Rain Trading Program can be viewed as evidence in favor of this theory. However, Michael Hanemann has argued that the experience with the Acid Rain Trading Program is due to fundamental characteristics of that issue and that these characteristics are not present with GHGs. *See* Hanemann, *supra*, at 243–48. Hanemann observes that previous reductions in emissions from cap-and-trade programs involved changes solely on the supply side, with polluters changing their production process or reformulating their product, without substantial price increases that significantly affected consumer behavior. *Id.* at 243–44. By contrast, Hanemann argues that any solution for climate change will necessarily involve changes in consumer behavior and that a price signal alone may not change consumer behavior optimally. In particular, Hanemann argues that the principal-agent problem for landlords and renters and even high implicit discount rates for homeowners constitute behavioral impediments to proper investment in efficient products. Similarly, many consumers have inadequate information about their options. *See id.* at 244–48. How does this insight affect the evaluation of the Waxman-Markey bill?

18. Domestic Political Currency. Politics, rather than economics, will dictate which of the competing models will be adopted in the event that the United States does introduce a mandatory emissions reduction program.

Why might a cap-and-trade bill be more politically palatable than a proposed carbon tax? Would your answer differ if the cap-and-trade bill did not initially compensate existing sources with free permits? What if the carbon tax proposals included a commitment to apply the revenues raised from the tax to directly offset income taxes or payroll taxes? *See, e.g.,* American Opportunity Carbon Fee Act of 2018, S. 2368, 115th Cong. (2018). Does political support for a cap-and-trade program depend on the perception that it is not a "tax"? When the Waxman-Markey bill was being considered in the House of Representatives, there was a concerted effort by opponents of the bill to re-brand "cap-and-trade" as "cap-and-tax." *See, e.g., The Cap and Tax Fiction,* WALL ST. J., June 26, 2009. Does political support for a carbon tax rely on a commitment to redistribute revenues back to the American people?

19. International Political Currency. A carbon tax may better suited than a cap-and-trade scheme to the international dimensions of the problem. *See* Mankiw, *supra.* Evaluate the following argument presented by N. Gregory Mankiw:

> [A]ny long term approach to global climate change will have to deal with the emerging economies of China and India. By some reports, China is now the world's leading emitter of carbon, in large part simply because it has so many people. . . . Agreement on a truly global cap-and-trade system, however, is hard to imagine. China is unlikely to be persuaded to accept fewer carbon allowances per person than the United States. Using a historical baseline to allocate allowances, as is often proposed, would reward the United States for having been a leading cause of the problem. . . .
>
> A global carbon tax would be easier to negotiate. All governments require revenue for public purposes. The world's nations could agree to use a carbon tax as one instrument to raise some of that revenue. No money needs to change hands across national borders. Each government could keep the revenue from its tax and use it to finance spending or whatever form of tax relief it considered best.

Id. How could a cap-and-trade regime be structured to solve this problem? Is Mankiw's argument for taxes persuasive? At what levels would the countries set their tax rates? What might they do with the revenues? How might such uses affect the effectiveness of the tax?

20. Subnational Permit Trading Schemes in the United States.

Regional Greenhouse Gas Initiative. Ten northeastern states joined together to form a joint cap-and-trade program for greenhouse gas emissions from the electric power sector. *See* Regional Greenhouse Gas Initiative, www.rggi.org (last visited June 15, 2018). The program, known as "RGGI," began in 2009 and entered its fourth control period on January 1, 2018. Average CO_2 emissions for RGGI's third control period were 75.5 million short tons, representing a more than 50% cut in RGGI power sector emissions since 2005. RGGI, PRESS RELEASE, RGGI STATES RELEASE THIRD CONTROL PERIOD COMPLIANCE REPORT (2018). While nearly all of the permits for the program are being auctioned, the prices during the first three years of the program were very low: initially just over $3 per ton but then falling below $2 per ton. Auction prices increased in 2013, and, with one exception, have been trading at $3 or more per ton since March 2014. RGGI, Auction Results: Allowance Prices and Volumes, https://www.rggi.org/Auctions/ Auction-Results/Prices-Volumes (last visited June 15, 2018). Despite low prices, the auctions have brought in more than $2.3 billion in revenue to the ten states from 2009 through December 2015. RGGI, THE INVESTMENT OF RGGI PROCEEDS IN 2015, at 14 (2017). Significant uses of this revenue include investments in energy efficiency, accelerating the deployment of renewable energy technology, and providing assistance to low-income ratepayers. *Id.* at 13.

In 2011 Governor Christie of New Jersey withdrew the state from RGGI and vetoed legislation in 2011 and 2012 that would have required the state to rejoin. Since the withdrawal, electricity prices in New Jersey have remained high because the state is part of a regional electricity market but it no longer receives any revenue from RGGI. It has also foregone an estimated $113.3 million in RGGI auction proceeds. *See id.* at 14; Coral Davenport, *With an Eye on 2016, Christie Resists Climate Change Plan*, N.Y. TIMES, Sept. 18, 2014; Elizabeth McGowan, *Analysts: New Jersey's Early RGGI Exit Cost the State Millions*, ENERGY NEWS NETWORK, Apr. 17, 2018. On January 29, 2018, Governor Phil Murphy signed an executive order setting into motion plans for New Jersey to rejoin RGGI. *See* PRESS RELEASE, GOVERNOR MURPHY SIGNS EXECUTIVE ORDER DIRECTING NEW JERSEY TO REENTER THE REGIONAL GREENHOUSE GAS INITIATIVE (2018). Virginia is also on track to becoming the first Southern state to join RGGI. *See* Robert Walton, *Virginia Advances Stricter Carbon Emissions Cap Rule*, UTILITY DIVE, Oct. 31, 2018.

California's AB 32/SB 32. In 2006 Governor Schwarzenegger of California signed into law the Global Warming Solutions Act, often known as "AB 32," an abbreviation of Assembly Bill 32. *See* California Air Resources Board, Assembly Bill 32: Global Warming Solutions Act, http://www.arb.ca. gov/cc/ab32/ab32.htm (last visited June 15, 2018). The most general requirement of AB 32 is that GHG emissions in California must be reduced to the same level as 1990 by 2020. CAL. HEALTH & SAFETY CODE § 38550. In 2016, with California on track to exceed AB 32's requirement, its legislature passed "SB 32," setting a new goal of reducing GHG emissions to 40% below 1990 levels by 2030. California Air Resources Board, AB 32 Scoping Plan, https://www.arb.ca.gov/cc/scopingplan/scopingplan.htm (last visited June 15, 2018). The California Air Resources Board (CARB), the agency responsible for determining how California will meet its targets, initially adopted a scoping plan for satisfying AB 32 in 2008, which was re-approved in 2011 and updated in 2014. *Id.* In 2017 CARB again updated the scoping plan to reflect SB 32's 2030 target. *Id.* While several complementary policies, including a renewable electricity standard and various requirements for mobile sources, have been adopted by CARB, the heart of CARB's strategy is a cap-and-trade program covering the vast majority of emissions in the state. *See* CAL. AIR RES. BD., CALIFORNIA'S 2017 CLIMATE CHANGE SCOPING PLAN (2017).

Some of the most sustained opposition to this strategy within California came from community groups associated with the cause of environmental justice. *See* Center on Race, Poverty, and the Environment, Cap and Trade in California, http://crpe-ej.org/resources/policy/cap-and-trade/ (last visited June 15, 2018); California Environmental Justice Alliance, New Report Highlights Equity Flaws in California's Cap-and-Trade Program, https://caleja.org/2016/09/new-report-highlights-equity-flaws-in-californias-cap-and-trade-program/ (last visited June 15, 2018). These groups argued that the cap-and-trade program allows major polluters to avoid reducing their GHG emissions in minority communities by buying permits. In this way, the polluters also avoid reducing emissions of local air pollutants, such as particulate matter, that are correlated with GHG emissions. In February 2017 the California Environmental Justice Advisory Committee, a body of environmental justice leaders created by AB 32 to advise CARB, recommended ending the cap-and-trade program. Notwithstanding this opposition, Governor Jerry Brown signed a law in July 2017 to extend the cap-and-trade program to 2030. While local reductions in toxic, smog, and particulate matter pollution may be justifiable goals, is it an appropriate strategy to leverage climate policy to achieve other environmental goals? Is this any different than how regulated entities argue for compensation in the form of free permits?

21. Permit Trading in Other Countries. As of 2017, 42 national and 25 subnational jurisdictions effectively price carbon through either an emissions trading scheme or a carbon tax. *See* WORLD BANK, STATE AND TRENDS OF CARBON PRICING 2017.

The EU ETS is the first international GHG permit trading system. Its third phase, from 2013 to 2020, initiated several major changes in the program. *See* EU Emissions Trading System (EU ETS), https://ec.europa.eu/clima/policies/ets_en (last visited June 26, 2018). Notably, the caps set by each country were replaced by a single cap for the entire program. And the share of permits being auctioned was increased to 40%. The major exception to this is the largely free allocation to industries that are both energy-intensive and trade-exposed, such as manufacturing and aviation. The program also started to cover additional sources of industrial process emissions, increasing coverage to about 45% of the total GHG emissions in the European Union. In 2017, the European Union and Switzerland signed an agreement to link their trading systems. *See* International Carbon Market, https://ec.europa.eu/clima/policies/ets/markets_en (last visited June 27, 2018). The European Union has also cooperated with efforts to establish emissions trading systems in China and South Korea. *Id.*

In 2013, China launched pilot carbon permit trading programs in seven provinces. *See* Huizhen Chen, *Inspection and Enforcement in Chinese Carbon Emissions Trading: Progress, Problems and Prospect* 44 ENVTL. L. REP. NEWS & ANALYSIS 10,596, 10,601 (2014). Each pilot was authorized by municipal or provincial administrative rules, without national coordination, resulting in variation in rules across pilot programs. *Id.* at 10,599. What might be the benefit to operating a variety of pilot schemes in different parts of the country? In December 2017, China announced that it was taking steps to establish a national carbon permit trading scheme. *See* People's Republic of China, National Development and Reform Commission, Circular on the Program for the Establishment of a National Carbon Emissions Trading Market (Power Generation Industry), https://chinaenergyportal.org/en/national-carbon-emissions-trading-market-establishment-program-power-generation-industry/ (last visited June 27, 2018). Once implemented, China's emissions trading system will be the largest emissions trading system in the world.

Would it be desirable to allow for interjurisdictional trades in permit trading schemes? What difficulties might linking emissions trading schemes across countries pose? Are there ways to safeguard against these difficulties? What is the promise of such linking?

22. Carbon Taxes in Other Countries. In 2008, British Columbia introduced a tax on carbon dioxide emissions from fossil fueled power plants. The tax applies only to the combustion of fossil fuels within the Province, excluding fuels that are exported or used outside of the jurisdiction, and is collected at the wholesale level by fuel distributors. The tax rate was initially set at $10 per ton of CO_2e emissions, with yearly increases until 2012. In April 2018 the tax rate was set at $35 per ton, with yearly increases of $5 per ton until the tax rate reaches $50 per ton in 2021. British Columbia's Carbon Tax, https://www2.gov.bc.ca/gov/content/environment/climate-change/planning-and-action/carbon-tax (last visited June 24, 2018). The tax is intended to be revenue neutral. All revenue raised is to be redistributed to individuals and businesses in the form of personal and corporate income tax cuts. Low-income households also receive tax credits. *See* David G. Duff, *Carbon Taxation in British Columbia*, 10 VT. J. ENVTL. LAW 87 (2008). Why do you think the tax was initially set at a low rate with scheduled yearly increases?

Other countries that have carbon taxes include France, Japan, and Sweden. *See* WORLD BANK, *supra*, at 1, 30. Prices per ton of carbon vary. For example, Japan has one of the lowest tax rates at $3 per ton of CO_2e emissions, while Sweden has one of the highest tax rates at $140 per ton of CO_2e emissions. *Id.* at 28. How do you explain this variation? Would linking the schemes of different countries be more difficult in the case of carbon taxes than in the case of permits?

23. Subnational Linkages. In 2012, Québec became the first Canadian province to adopt a cap-and-trade scheme for GHG emissions. In 2013, the California Air Resources Board and the Québec government entered into an agreement to integrate the respective cap-and-trade programs. The two programs became linked on January 1, 2014. The linked scheme has a central Compliance Instrument Tracking System Service, through which emission allowances either allocated by government or purchased at auction, as well as early reduction credits, may be traded. The allowances can be traded freely between Québec and California. Charles Kazaz & Anne-Catherine Boucher, *Québec's Cap-and-Trade System: Emitters Cautiously Testing the Waters*, ABA TRENDS, May/June 2014, at 2, 3, 5–6. Is the linking of subnational emission markets from different nation-states desirable? What special difficulties does linking such emission markets pose?

24. Repeal of Australia's Carbon Trading Scheme. In 2011, Australia enacted a significant measure to curb GHGs. For three years starting in 2012, the scheme set a price of 23 Australian dollars per ton of GHG emissions from the biggest sources and was then intended to transition to a cap-and-trade program with market pricing from July 2015. The measure used the revenue generated by the program primarily to decrease income taxes on people with moderate incomes. *See* Alison Rehn, *It's Official, Australia Has a Carbon Tax*, THE DAILY TELEGRAPH, Nov. 8, 2011. At the time of its introduction, the program was bitterly opposed by the Liberal Party. In 2014, following a change in government that brought this party to power, the program was repealed. The government proposed to instead achieve a 5% overall reduction in emissions by offering financial grants to companies and organizations that voluntarily reduce emissions. Lenore Taylor, *Australia Kills Off Carbon Tax,* THE GUARDIAN, Jul. 16, 2014. How does paying entities that reduce emissions differ from taxing entities that emit? Does this scheme adequately internalize the cost of pollution? The government's goal to reduce emissions by 5% has not been successful. In fact, official reports show emissions are rising. Michael Slezak, *Australia's Greenhouse Gas Emissions are Rising and Forecast to Miss 2030 Target*, THE GUARDIAN, Dec. 21, 2016.

25. Preferred Policy Response. What is your preferred policy response in the event that the United States does seek to implement a nationwide GHG reduction program?

4. DEPOSIT-REFUND SYSTEMS

Peter Bohm, Deposit-Refund Systems: Theory and Applications to Environmental, Conservation, and Consumer Policy
2–3, 5–8 (1981).*

A deposit-refund system is essentially a combination of a tax and a subsidy. To attain objectives in areas such as environmental, conservation, and consumer policy, a refund (subsidy) is offered to consumers or producers, or both, in order to stimulate activities that otherwise would not have been undertaken or to guide existing activities in time and space. For example, refund offers can be introduced to avoid having used objects such as beverage containers, discarded automobiles, and waste lubricating oil dumped in places where they would be harmful in one way or another. Or refund offers can be used as an instrument for reducing waste management costs to society and for recovering certain materials from waste when there are economies of scale in recovery operations or lags in adjustment of disposal behavior.

To avoid extensive distributional and budgetary effects and to create adequate incentives, the refund offer is coupled with a deposit (tax) that is introduced at an earlier point in the chain of transactions. Thus in a complete deposit-refund system the deposit is refunded if certain conditions are met by the decision maker. A complete deposit-refund system can now be seen to have a wider field of application than was suggested by the examples just given. The refunding of a deposit if a specific condition is met by the depositor provides an instrument for protecting certain rights that the government may wish to transfer to the buyers of a product. For example, deposits (or similar arrangements) made by producers could protect consumers from producers who fail to honor contracts or warranties because of bankruptcy. The system could also be used to correct for market failure in servicing consumer durables or in the provision of spare parts. It could be applied to help protect people from hazards that could arise from production sites left unattended after shutdown of production. In addition, deposit-refund systems could even be used to protect consumers of public services from unlimited delays or unfulfilled promises of service delivery. . . .

In some cases a deposit-refund system may be the only possible policy solution. For example, it is hardly likely that the authorities could catch a significant number of those people who throw away small hazardous products such as cadmium batteries and thus damage the environment. Therefore, neither a ban nor a tax on improper disposal could be expected to work in this case. In contrast, a deposit on the sale of such batteries and a refund for properly returned batteries could be designed to provide appropriate incentives to protect the environment.

To cite another example, assume that 90 percent of a returnable commodity or a kind of scrap is returned without the support of any government initiative. To introduce a subsidy to increase this figure to, say, 100 percent would rarely be worthwhile, given the "costs" of having to finance the subsidy of those 90 percent already being returned. Thus, to get the remaining 10 percent of the units returned, the actual cost would be the social costs of the total volume of subsidies. This cost may be too high for whatever increased returns are desired, and it has consequently been used as an argument against such subsidies.

A deposit-refund system could accomplish the same thing that a subsidy would, but at a much lower social cost. Those who already return their units will pay and receive the same amount (an appropriate rate of interest may be paid to the depositor, of course), and so no cost other than that of temporary forced saving in the amount of the deposit will hit them. The cost to the people who are not already returning their units will be the inconvenience of using this disposal alternative (in addition to the probably negligible cost of forced saving). But it will not cost the government anything more than the administrative effort. Thus, if administrative costs and inconvenience costs are small enough, it may pay to have recovery rates increased in this way.

In other cases a deposit-refund system may be the only realistic way to introduce economic incentives; hence it may be the only alternative to regulation. Assume, for example, that government would like to consider making those who burn oil and release sulfur dioxide into the atmosphere pay for their sulfur emissions. A charge on all actual emissions would presumably be ruled out because of prohibitive measurement costs. In contrast, an economic incentive system could be introduced consisting of a deposit on the sulfur content of the fuel and a refund on the sulfur recovered. For firms to qualify for refunds at rates far above the market price for sulfur, the authorities may in some cases need to check actual oil purchases and verify the existence of sulfur recovery devices. The control costs would still be small in comparison with the costs of administering a tax on sulfur emissions.

As was pointed out earlier, deposit-refund systems may provide the same economic incentives as taxes or subsidies and at the same time avoid some of the disadvantages of these alternatives. That deposit-refund systems have the same incentive effects is clear from the fact that the deposit becomes a fee if the decision maker's behavior does not qualify for a refund. In certain applications, such systems may provide stronger or more well-focused incentives or involve a smaller amount of policy costs (administrative, enforcement, and information costs) than alternative solutions. For example:

1. If a commodity on which a deposit has been paid is disposed of in a way that does not qualify for a refund, someone else may take care of it and get the refund; this would not happen with regulations or fees on an improper disposal.

2. In a deposit-refund system the owner of a commodity has an incentive to prove that the commodity has not been disposed of in an improper fashion; in alternative systems the owner may have an incentive to hide the fact that it has been disposed of in an improper fashion.

3. In some cases it is simpler and less expensive to administer deposit-refund systems in which one is paid for choosing a certain kind of activity or disposal than systems in which one has to pay for alternative kinds of activity or disposal.

4. It may be simpler in some cases to formulate the conditions under which there is a refund than to state the conditions under which it is forbidden to dispose of the commodity or under which there is a fee for doing so.

5. By paying a deposit or by being told about the refund prospect by the seller as a sales argument, the buyer or user is informed about the conditional refund and thus about (maximum) liability; making similar information available and effective is usually quite costly under alternative systems.

6. The collection costs in deposit-refund systems may in some cases be lower than the corresponding costs under a regulatory system or a system of charges that, to be effective, may require extensive checking operations, prosecution, and so on (see the cadmium battery example mentioned earlier).

Thus policy costs may be lower for deposit-refund systems than for alternative solutions. In addition, budgetary effects of deposit-refund systems may be more attractive to policy makers. Whereas subsidies and regulations with high policy costs create a need for additional government funds, and charges or other allocative taxes may be disliked by administrators when they give rise to an unstable volume of government revenue, deposit-refund systems tend to leave the budget intact to the extent that refunds (paid by the government) approach the volume of deposits (directly or indirectly paid to the government).

Because distributional considerations play a fundamental role in economic policy, such aspects of deposit-refund systems should be discussed in some detail at this point. Let us focus on a deposit-refund system designed to influence disposal behavior in order to reach a given policy goal. In the case in which refunds are set at a level such that a maximum return rate is achieved—say, all beverage containers are returned for a refund by the original buyers—there will be no effects on the net *money income* distribution. In the case in which less than a maximum return rate is achieved, the return rate may differ among income groups; for example, it may be higher for households with a low opportunity cost for time, that is, for low-income households. This means that the deposit-refund system would have a progressive distributional effect for deposits on commodities with unitary income elasticity. In contrast, a product charge or any other policy alternative of an excise tax type—say, in the amount of the expected average negative environmental effect—would be proportional to income under the same circumstances. It would, moreover, definitely raise commodity prices and so, for example, definitely hit households at or below the poverty line. And it would hit those who buy inexpensive versions of the affected commodity harder, relatively speaking, than those who buy luxury versions. Apart from the effects on different income groups, product charges would not differentiate between "bad" and "good" behavior, such as littering and nonlittering, and thus would not be as equitable as a refund would, in the normative sense implied here. Finally, the deposit informs the buyer about different disposal options and their costs at the time of purchase, in contrast to a tax on a nonreturn option or a subsidy on a return option, neither of which it is relevant to observe until the time of disposal. This increase of the information level in the economy could benefit, in particular, households that are uninformed because of poor education. . . .

NOTES AND QUESTIONS

1.   Determining Deposit Amounts. How should one set the deposit amounts in deposit-refund systems? What are the consequences of an amount that is too low? What are the consequences of an amount that is too high? Should the deposit and refund amounts always be identical?

2.   Incentives. Consider two different types of uses for deposit-refund systems:

 (a) to create incentives for the return of products that can be recycled; and

 (b) to create incentives for the disposal of waste that ought to be segregated from the remainder of the waste stream.

What factors are relevant to determining whether deposit-refund systems are attractive regulatory tools in each of these instances? What is the relevance of the costs of administering the system?

3.   Recyclable Amounts. With respect to the first category, how should one determine whether to use deposit-refund systems for newspapers, plastic bottles, and cans? Are the arguments for deposit-refund systems stronger for the second of the categories defined in the previous question? Is litter prevention important enough to be an independent justification? Why not just impose a tax on the products?

4.   Hazardous Materials. Consider the issues raised by the use of a deposit-refund system for hazardous substances. How could such a system deal with the following issues:

 (a) hazardous substances that are subsequently mixed with other hazardous substances, becoming either more or less hazardous?

 (b) hazardous substances that are subsequently mixed with nonhazardous substances?

 (c) hazardous substances purchased in other jurisdictions?

With respect to the disposal of hazardous substances, compare the relative desirability of deposit-refund systems and liability rules?

5.   States' Deposit-Refund Systems. In the United States, deposit-refund systems have been mainly used for the recovery of beverage containers for beer and soft drinks. According to EPA, ten states have container deposit systems, including California, Connecticut, Hawaii, Iowa, Maine, Massachusetts, Michigan, New York, Oregon and Vermont. EPA OFFICE OF SOLID WASTE, MUNICIPAL SOLID WASTE IN THE UNITED STATES: 2011 FACTS AND FIGURES (2011). Under these programs, when consumers purchase a beverage they pay a deposit ranging from 5 to 15 cents that is then refunded to them when they return the empty container. *See, e.g.*, CONN. GEN. STAT. §§ 22a–243 to –246; IOWA CODE § 455c.1–.17. California's program has an additional feature where beverage distributors also pay a per bottle fee. *See* CAL. PUB. RES. CODE § 14560; *see also* Richard L. Revesz, *Federalism and Environmental Regulation: A Public Choice Analysis*, 115 HARV. L. REV. 553, 613–14 (2001); Anthony R. DePaolo, *Plastics Recycling*

Legislation: Not Just the Same Old Garbage, 22 B.C. ENVTL. AFF. L. REV. 873, 880–81 (1995). Given the size of the deposit, how effective do you think these schemes would be? A 2001 report by EPA estimated return rates above 70% for most products in these states. EPA, THE UNITED STATES EXPERIENCE WITH ECONOMIC INCENTIVES FOR PROTECTING THE ENVIRONMENT 59 (2001). Michigan, with a bottle deposit of 10 cents, was estimated to have a return rate of 93%. However, this is likely an overestimate because of returns for products purchased outside of Michigan. The same EPA report stated that bottle return fraud costs Michigan over $16 million per year. *Id.* at 60. Through what mechanisms might containers be returned? Deposit-refund systems for beverage containers have been successfully used in the European Union, with return rates of or over 90% in Denmark, Netherlands, Norway, and Sweden. ORGANIZATION FOR ECONOMIC CO-OPERATION AND DEVELOPMENT, ECONOMIC INSTRUMENTS FOR POLLUTION CONTROL AND NATURAL RESOURCES MANAGEMENT IN OECD COUNTRIES: A SURVEY 39–41 (1999). However, the size of the deposit in these countries is much higher than in the United States reaching, depending on the container's size and value, 0.4€ in Denmark, 0.25€ in Netherlands, 0.32€ in Norway, and 0.22€ in Sweden. *See* CM CONSULTING, DEPOSIT SYSTEMS FOR ONE-WAY BEVERAGE CONTAINERS: GLOBAL OVERVIEW 1, 9, 23, 25, 27 (2017).

6. Bottle Refunds, Poverty, and Crime. It has been argued that an unintended consequence of the introduction of bottle refunds is a reduction in petty crime rates because people with extremely low incomes, including the homeless, "substitute time and effort away from illegal activity to legal and remunerative recycling activity." Bevin Ashenmiller, *Externalities from Recycling Laws: Evidence from Crime Rates*, 12 AM. L. & ECON. REV. 245, 245 (2010). The article uses the introduction of deposit-refund schemes at different times in different states to estimate that the introduction of the scheme lowers petty crime rates by 11% on average. *Id.* Is it a good idea to partly solve our litter problem by enlisting the homeless? Even if it reduces crime? Would there be extra benefits to hiring additional state or local employees to collect bottles?

7. States' Deposit-Refund Systems, Continued. In addition to beverage containers, states have implemented deposit-refund schemes with respect to lead-acid batteries, pesticide containers, and vehicle tires. *See* EPA, THE UNITED STATES EXPERIENCE WITH ECONOMIC INCENTIVES FOR PROTECTING THE ENVIRONMENT 64–66 (2001). For instance, consider Maine's regulation of lead-acid batteries:

> For the purposes of this section, "lead-acid battery" means a device designed and used to store electrical energy through chemical reactions involving lead and acid. . . .
>
> 2. Lead-acid battery retailers. A person selling or offering for retail sale lead-acid batteries shall:
>
> > A. Accept, at the point of transfer, used lead-acid batteries in reasonably clean and unbroken condition from customers in a quantity at least equal to the number of new batteries purchased;

B.   If a used lead-acid battery is not exchanged at the time of sale, collect a $10 deposit on the new battery.

(1)   The deposit shall be returned to the customer when the customer delivers a used lead-acid battery within 30 days of the date of sale.

ME. REV. STAT. ANN. tit. 38, § 1604. Do you think this scheme generates incentives for residents of other states to return batteries to Maine retailers in order to recover a deposit that they never paid? Does this system encourage theft of batteries? How can these negative effects be deterred?

8.   Deposit-Refund and Recycling Schemes for Household Batteries. Regular and rechargeable dry-cell (household) batteries can contain mercury, lead, cadmium, and lithium. If incinerated, those metals may be released into the air. If disposed of in landfill, the metals can leach into the soil and water. Despite the success of lead-acid battery deposit-refund schemes, no U.S. state has a similar scheme for household batteries. In 2006, a bill was introduced in California that would have required battery distributors to pay a deposit of 10 cents per battery, which would be used to make payments to battery collectors and recyclers, but the bill was never passed into law. *See* AB 2271, 2005–2006 Gen. Assemb. (Ca. 2006). Why are household batteries a good candidate for a deposit-refund scheme? Why have they not been the subject of a deposit-refund scheme?

The Resource Conservation and Recovery Act (RCRA) regulates hazardous waste, including reporting, handling, and transportation requirements. Because they can contain heavy metals, both regular and rechargeable dry-cell and sealed lead-acid batteries may be hazardous waste for the purposes of RCRA, which exempts only household and small business waste from RCRA regulations. What difficulties might the RCRA pose for battery recycling programs?

9.   Deposit-Refund Systems for Motor Vehicles. According to EPA, in the United States, each year over 10 million vehicles reach the end of their useful life. *See* EPA, Product Stewardship: Vehicles, https://archive.epa.gov/wastes/conserve/tools/stewardship/web/html/vehicles.html (last visited June 4, 2018). Could a deposit-refund system be used to ensure that these motor vehicles are appropriately disposed? What would be the main challenges of such a system? Several European countries have used deposit-refund systems to ensure an appropriate disposal of end-of-life vehicles. An example of such a system is provided by the 1975 Swedish Car Scrapping Law. In order to address the problem of end-of-life vehicles being abandoned in the countryside, the Swedish Government enacted the Car Scrapping Law, SFS 1975:343, and the Car Scrapping Ordinance, SFS 1975:348 (both currently repealed). *See* MALCOLM FERGUSSON, STUDY FOR THE EP COMMITTEE ON ENVIRONMENT PUBLIC HEALTH AND FOOD SAFETY: END OF LIFE VEHICLES (ELV) DIRECTIVE 49–51 (2007). According to these regulations, when a new or old car entered to the Swedish market, the producer or importer had to pay a "recycling fee" on behalf of the potential buyer. *See* Massimiliano Mazzanti & Roberto Zoboli, *Economic Instruments and Induced Innovation: The European Policies on End-of-Life Vehicles*, 58 ECOLOGICAL ECON. 318,

330 (2006). These fees were collected in a state fund and were then used to pay "scrapping premiums" to the final owner when the automobile was unregistered for scrapping. *Id.* Since there is usually a registration system for cars, wouldn't a command-and-control regulation be easier to implement? Why do you think Sweden chose a deposit-refund system instead? The system was abandoned in 2007 in order to fulfill the requirements established by European Union Directive 2000/53/EG on producers' responsibility. According to this directive, the producer should be responsible for the vehicle from the cradle to the grave, and therefore it was not suitable for the Swedish government to keep a deposit-refund system. Under the new system, Swedish car owners could leave their end-of-life vehicles at facilities spread geographically over Sweden and producers were responsible for their gathering, treatment, and disposal. Do you think this system could be successful in obtaining a high level of returned cars? Which of the two approaches is preferable?

10. Performance Bonds. Performance bonds are fees levied on companies that engage in activities that may harm the environment. The performance bond is refunded when a company fulfills certain specified obligations, such as land remediation or reforestation. They can therefore be viewed as a form of deposit-refund system. Performance bonds are commonly required for mining projects in the United States, Canada, and Australia. *See* ORGANIZATION FOR ECONOMIC CO-OPERATION AND DEVELOPMENT, ECONOMIC INSTRUMENTS FOR POLLUTION CONTROL AND NATURAL RESOURCES MANAGEMENT IN OECD COUNTRIES: A SURVEY 46 (1999). Concerned that the bonds being set aside were insufficient to meet the actual cost of rehabilitation, in 2012 the state of Western Australia moved from a performance bond system to imposing a levy that is contributed to a central rehabilitation fund. *See* Robyn Glindemann & Nicole Ortigosa, *A New Mine Rehabilitation Fund for Western Australia*, 28 AUST. ENV'T REV. 421 (2012).

Performance bonds have also been used in forestry projects in the Philippines. The Forest Guarantee Bond was a returnable bond designed to ensure that harvesters implemented actions that would improve the long-term sustainability of harvesting and that violations of forestry leases could be penalized. Introduced in 1991, the government suspended the program in 1995 when it became apparent that the scheme encouraged clear-cutting. EPA, International Experiences with Economic Incentives for Protecting the Environment 26 (2004). Harvesters simply forfeited the bond without implementing the required actions. Some scholars speculate that the bond payment might have been too low to ensure compliance. *See* Olli-Pekka Kuusela & Gregory S. Amacher, *A Review of Performance Bonding in Forest Policy Settings*, 2 CURRENT FORESTRY REP. 189 (2016). What do the experiences of Western Australia and the Philippines indicate about the applicability of deposit-refund-type schemes to industrial activities?

5. *EX ANTE* REGULATION AND *EX POST* LIABILITY

Steven Shavell, Liability for Harm
Versus Regulation of Safety
13 J. LEG. STUD. 357 (1984).*

Liability in tort and the regulation of safety represent two very different approaches for controlling activities that create risks of harm to others. Tort liability is private in nature and works not by social command but rather indirectly, through the deterrent effect of damage actions that may be brought once harm occurs. Standards, prohibitions, and other forms of safety regulation, in contrast, are public in character and modify behavior in an immediate way through requirements that are imposed before, or at least independently of, the actual occurrence of harm.

As a matter of simple description, it is apparent that liability and safety regulation are employed with an emphasis that varies considerably with the nature of the activity that is governed. Whether I run to catch a bus and thereby collide with another pedestrian will be influenced more by the possibility of my tort liability than by any prior regulation of my behavior (informal social sanctions and risk to self aside). Similarly, whether I cut down a tree that might fall on my neighbor's roof will be affected more by the prospect of a tort suit than by direct regulation. But other decisions—whether I drive my truck through a tunnel when it is loaded with explosives or mark the fire exits in my store, or whether an electric utility incorporates certain safety features in its nuclear power plant—are apt to be determined substantially, although not entirely, by safety regulation. There are also intermediate cases, of course; consider, for instance, the behavior of ordinary drivers on the road and the effects of tort sanctions and regulation of automobile use.

What has led society to adopt this varying pattern of liability and safety regulation? What is the socially desirable way to employ the two means of alleviating risks? These are the questions to be addressed here, and in answering them I use an instrumentalist, economic method of analysis, whereby the effects of liability rules and direct regulation are compared and then evaluated on a utilitarian basis, given the assumption that individual actors can normally be expected to act in their own interest. In making this evaluation, I have not counted compensation of injured parties as an independent factor on the grounds that first-party insurance (augmented if necessary by a public insurance program) can discharge the compensatory function no matter what the mix of liability and regulation. . . .

Theoretical Determinants of the Relative Desirability of Liability and Safety Regulation

To identify and assess the factors determining the social desirability of liability and regulation, it is necessary to set out a measure of social welfare; and here that measure is assumed to equal the benefits parties derive from engaging in their activities, less the sum of the costs of precautions, the harms done, and the administrative expenses associated with the means of social control. The formal problem is to employ the means of control to maximize the measure of welfare.

We can now examine four determinants that influence the solution to this problem. The first determinant is the possibility of a *difference in knowledge about risky activities* as between private parties and a regulatory authority. This difference could relate to the benefits of activities, the costs of reducing risks, or the probability or severity of the risks.

Where private parties have superior knowledge of these elements, it would be better for them to decide about the control of risks, indicating an advantage of liability rules, other things being equal. Consider, for instance, the situation where private parties possess perfect information about risky activities of which a regulator has poor knowledge. Then to vest in the regulator the power of control would create a great chance of error. If the regulator overestimates the potential for harm, its standard will be too stringent, and the same will be the case if it underestimates the value of the activity or the cost of reducing risk. If the regulator makes the reverse mistakes, moreover, it will announce standards that are lax.

Under liability, however, the outcome would likely be better. This is clear enough under a system of strict liability—whereby parties have to pay damages regardless of their negligence—for then they are motivated to balance the true costs of reducing risks against the expected savings in losses caused. Now assume that the form of liability is the negligence rule—according to which parties are held responsible for harm done only if their care falls short of a prescribed level of "due" care—and suppose further that once harm occurs, the courts could acquire enough information about the underlying event to formulate the appropriate level of due care. Then parties, anticipating this, would be led in principle to exercise due care. The situation is altered for the worse if the courts are unable to acquire sufficient information to determine the best level of due care; but the outcome would still be superior to that achievable under regulation if the information obtained ex post at trial would be better than that which a regulator could acquire and act upon ex ante.

These conclusions are reversed, of course, if the information possessed by a regulator is superior to private parties' and the courts'; converse reasoning then shows that the use of direct regulation would be more attractive than liability.

The question that remains, therefore, is when we can expect significant differences in information between private parties and regulators to exist. And the answer is that private parties should generally enjoy an inherent advantage in knowledge. They, after all, are the ones who are engaging in and deriving benefits from their activities; in consequence, they are in a naturally superior position to estimate these benefits and normally are in at least as good a position to estimate the nature of the risks created and the costs of their reduction. For a regulator to obtain comparable information would often require virtually continuous observation of parties' behavior, and thus would be a practical impossibility. Similarly, the courts—when called upon under a negligence system—should have an advantage, though a less decisive one, over a regulator. One would indeed expect courts to adjust the due care level to take into account the facts presented by litigating parties more easily than a regulator could individualize its prior standards or modify them to reflect changed conditions.

Yet this is not to say that private parties or the courts will necessarily possess information superior to that held by a regulatory authority. In certain contexts information about risk will not be an obvious by-product of engaging in risky activities but rather will require effort to develop or special expertise to evaluate. In these contexts a regulator might obtain information by committing social resources to the task, while private parties would have an insufficient incentive to do this for familiar reasons: A party who generates information will be unable to capture its full value if others can learn of the information without paying for it. For parties to undertake individually to acquire information might result in wasteful, duplicative expenditures, and a cooperative venture by parties might be stymied by the usual problems of inducing all to lend their support. Continuing, once a regulator obtains information, it may find the information difficult to communicate to private parties because of its technical nature or because the parties are hard to identify or are too numerous. Thus we can point to contexts where regulators might possess better information than private parties to whom it cannot easily be transmitted, even if the usual expectation would be for these parties to possess the superior information.

The second of the determinants of the relative desirability of liability and regulation is that *private parties might be incapable of paying for the full magnitude of harm done.* Where this is the case, liability would not furnish adequate incentives to control risk, because private parties would treat losses caused that exceed their assets as imposing liabilities only equal to their assets. But under regulation inability to pay for harm done would be irrelevant, assuming that parties would be made to take steps to reduce risk as a precondition for engaging in their activities.

In assessing the importance of this argument favoring regulation over liability, one factor that obviously needs to be taken into account is the size of parties' assets in relation to the probability distribution of the magnitude of harm; the greater the likelihood of harm much larger than assets, the greater the appeal of regulation.

Another factor of relevance concerns liability insurance. Here the first point to make is that a party's motive to purchase liability insurance against damage judgments exceeding his assets will be a diminished one, as the protection will in part be for losses that the party would not otherwise have to bear. A party with assets of $20,000 might not be eager to purchase coverage against a potential liability of $100,000, as four-fifths of the premium would be in payment for the $80,000 amount that he would not bear if he did not buy coverage. Hence, it might be rational for the party not to insure against the $100,000 risk. If this is the case, then the assertion that liability does not create an adequate motive to reduce risk is clearly unrebutted. . . .

Let us turn next to the third of the four general determinants, the chance that *parties would not face the threat of suit for harm done.* Like incapacity to pay for harm, such a possibility results in a dilution of the incentives to reduce risk created by liability, but it is of no import under regulation.

The weight to be attached to this factor depends in part upon the reasons why suit might not be brought. One reason that a defendant can escape tort liability is that the harms he generates are widely dispersed, making it unattractive for any victim individually to initiate legal action. This danger can be offset to a degree if victims are allowed to maintain class actions, whose application has problematic features, however. A second cause of failure to sue is the passage of a long period of time before harm manifests itself. This raises the possibility that by the time suit is contemplated, the evidence necessary for a successful action will be stale or the responsible parties out of business. A third reason for failure to sue is difficulty in attributing harm to the parties who are in fact responsible for producing it. This problem could arise from simple ignorance that a given harm or disease was caused by a human agency (as opposed to being "natural" in origin) or from inability to identify which one or several out of many parties was the cause of harm.

The problems here are aggravated when the potential liability rests on large firms, where complications analogous to those mentioned before exist. Namely, even if the harms can be attributed to an individual firm, the prospect of a successful suit may exert only slight influence on the behavior of corporate decisionmakers. With the passage of time, for example, there might be no clear way of determining which were the responsible employees, or those who were responsible may no longer be with the firm. The actual decisionmakers therefore may be beyond both the threat of suit and the prospect of sanctions internal to the firm.

The last of the determinants is the magnitude of the *administrative costs incurred by private parties and by the public* in using the tort system or direct regulation. Of course, the costs of the tort system must be broadly defined to include the time, effort, and legal expenses borne by private parties in the course of litigation or in coming to settlements, as well as the public expenses of conducting trials, employing judges, empaneling juries, and the like. Similarly, the administrative costs of regulation include the public expense of maintaining the regulatory establishment and the private costs of compliance.

With respect to these costs, there seems to be an underlying advantage in favor of liability, for most of its administrative costs are incurred only if harm occurs. As this will usually be infrequent, administrative costs will be low. Indeed, in the extreme case where the prospect of liability induces parties to take proper care and this happens to remove all possibility of harm, there would be no suits whatever and thus no administrative costs (other than certain fixed costs). Moreover, there are two reasons to believe that even when harm occurs administrative costs should not always be large. First, under a well-functioning negligence rule, defendants should in principle generally have been induced to take due care; injured parties should generally recognize this and thus should not bring suit. Second, suits should usually be capable of being settled cheaply by comparison to the cost of a trial. A final cost advantage of the liability system is that under it resources are naturally focused on controlling the behavior of the subgroup of parties most likely to cause harm; for because they are most likely to cause harm (and presumably most likely to be negligent), they are most likely to be sued.

Under regulation, unlike under liability, administrative costs are incurred whether or not harm occurs; even if the risk of a harm is eliminated by regulation, administrative costs will have been borne in the process. Also, in the absence of special knowledge about parties' categories of risk, there is no tendency for administrative costs to be focused on those most likely to cause harm, again because these costs are incurred before harm occurs. On the other hand, a savings in administrative costs can typically be achieved through the use of probabilistic means of enforcement. But there is a limit to these savings because there is some minimum frequency of verification necessary to insure adherence to regulatory requirements.

Joint Use of Liability and Regulation

Examination of the four determinants has thus shown that two generally favor liability—administrative costs and differential knowledge—and the other two favor regulation—incapacity to pay for harm done and escaping suit. This suggests not only that neither tort liability nor regulation could uniformly dominate the other as a solution to the problem of controlling risks, but also that they should not be viewed as mutually exclusive solutions to it. A complete solution to the problem of the control of risk evidently should involve the joint use of liability and regulation, with the balance between them reflecting the importance of the determinants.

If, then, some combination of liability and regulation is likely to be advantageous, two questions immediately arise: Should a party's adherence to regulation relieve him of liability in the event that harm comes to pass? On the other hand, should a party's failure to satisfy regulatory requirements result necessarily in his liability? Our theory suggests a negative answer to both questions.

As to the first, if compliance with regulation were to protect parties from liability, then none would do more than to meet the regulatory requirements. Yet since these requirements will be based on less than perfect knowledge of parties' situations, there will clearly be some parties who ought to do more than meet the requirements—because they present an above-average risk of doing harm, can take extra precautions more easily than most, or can take precautions not covered by regulation. As liability will induce many of these parties to take beneficial precautions beyond the required ones, its use as a supplement to regulation will be advantageous. At the same time, just because this is true, regulatory requirements need not be as rigorous as if regulation were the sole means of controlling risks.

A similar analysis is appropriate for the second question. If failure to satisfy regulatory requirements necessarily resulted in a finding of negligence, then some parties would be undesirably led to comply with them when they would not otherwise have done so. In particular, there will be some parties (a) who ought not to meet regulatory requirements because they face higher than usual costs of care or because they pose lower risks than normal and (b) who will not have been forced to satisfy regulatory requirements due to flaws in or probabilistic methods of enforcement. By allowing these parties to escape liability in view of their circumstances, the possibility that they would still be led to take the wasteful precautions can be avoided.

NOTES AND QUESTIONS

1. Regulation Under the CAA v. Liability Under Superfund. The CAA (discussed in Chapter V) imposes a regulatory approach to the control of air pollution, whereas the Superfund statute (discussed in Chapter VII) imposes liability for the release of hazardous substances into the environment, generally the soil, surface water, and groundwater. Can the choice of different policy tools in these contexts be explained by Shavell's four factors? For a general discussion of the relative merits of liability-based approaches and regulations in the context of controlling air pollution, see *Boomer v. Atlantic Cement Co.*, 26 N.Y.2d 219, 257 N.E.2d 870 (1970).

2. Maximizing Social Welfare. Under a negligence rule, a court must determine the appropriate standard of care. Shavell calls on courts to choose a standard that would maximize social welfare. Is a negligence rule likely to compare favorably to regulation? Is a negligence rule likely to compare favorably to strict liability?

3. Access to Information. Shavell states that in some cases private parties will not possess information superior to that held by regulatory authorities. In what instances is this likely to be the case?

4. Evading Liability. In connection with Shavell's third determinant, consider the following potential roadblocks to bringing suits for environmental harms:

(a) statutes of limitations;

(b) proof of causation; and

(c) free-rider problems among victims.

How can the legal system ameliorate these problems? For discussion of the shortcomings of the common law in the environmental area, see Peter Menell, *The Limitations of Legal Institutions for Addressing Environmental Risks*, J. ECON. PERSP., summer 1991, at 93.

5. Administrative Costs. Shavell notes that under a liability system administrative costs are incurred only in the face of harm. He adds: "As this will usually be infrequent, administrative costs will be low." To what extent is this likely to be true? Compare the administrative costs of negligence and strict liability rules. If few cases are, in fact, brought under negligence rules, how will the relevant actors know the standard of care? For further discussion of the choice between regulation and liability, see Michelle T. White & Donald Wittman, *A Comparison of Taxes, Regulation, and Liability Rules Under Imperfect Information*, 12 J. LEGAL STUD. 413 (1983); and Donald Wittman, *Prior Regulation Versus Post Liability: The Choice Between Input and Output Monitoring*, 6 J LEGAL STUD. 193 (1977).

6. Delayed Harm. Consider the relative desirability of regulatory schemes and liability rules from the perspective of a factory that is contemplating the purchase of new and expensive pollution control equipment to reduce the risk of a harm with a long latency period. Which rule is it likely to prefer? What factors are relevant to this choice?

7. Incentives Through Penalties. In discussing the joint use of liability and regulation, Shavell notes: "If failure to satisfy regulatory requirements necessarily resulted in a finding of negligence, then some parties would be undesirably led to comply with them when they would otherwise not have done so." What penalties should actors face when they fail to meet regulatory standards? Of course, if these penalties are sufficiently severe, the actors will have incentives to meet the regulatory standard regardless of whether the failure to meet this standard is conclusive evidence of negligence. The joint use of liability and regulation in connection with Superfund and the Resource Conservation and Recovery Act (RCRA) is considered in Chapter VII.

More generally, does the effect of regulatory standards on behavior depend exclusively on the penalty structure for noncompliance? Does a regulatory standard coupled with a particular penalty for noncompliance have the same effect as a tax of zero for risk below the standard and a tax equal to the penalty for risk above the standard? What view of regulatory standards is implicit in Shavell's discussion?

8.   Nuisance Law and Climate Change. In 2004, a group of States and environmental groups sued four private utilities and the Tennessee Valley Authority under federal common law of interstate nuisance for their contributions to climate change. *See Am. Elec. Power Co. v. Conn.*, 564 U.S. 410 (2011). The plaintiffs in this case asked for an injunctive remedy forcing emissions reductions from the defendants over the course of a decade. *Id.* at 2534. In 2011, the Supreme Court held that the federal theory of nuisance used by the plaintiffs had been displaced by the authority of EPA to regulate greenhouse gases under the Clean Air Act. *Id.* at 2535–40. Were the plaintiffs in this case asking for the judiciary to create their own regulatory solution for climate change? How do the factors described by Shavell differ between EPA and the judiciary? What if the plaintiffs were asking for money damages instead? What are the obstacles to the judiciary effectively creating a carbon tax through nuisance law?

9.   Liability and Analysis. Shavell argues that, under ideal conditions, tort liability will induce private parties to take the socially optimal level of risks. How do you think a jury would react to a defense based on an explicit analysis showing that the cost of precautions exceeded the cost of harm? *See, e.g.*, Andrew Pollack, *Paper Trail Haunts GM After It Loses Injury Suit: An Old Memo Hinted at the Price of Safety*, N.Y. TIMES, July 12, 1999. What incentives does this create for corporate risk analysis in the environmental context? Without some protection for companies that conduct risk analysis, can tort liability play a useful role in encouraging socially optimal corporate risk decisionmaking? *See* W. Kip Viscusi, *Pricing Lives for Corporate and Governmental Risk Decisions*, 6 J. BENEFIT-COST ANALYSIS 227 (2015).

6. INFORMATIONAL APPROACHES

Wesley A. Magat & W. Kip Viscusi, Informational Approaches to Regulation
4–5 (1992).[*]

Information as a Regulatory Tool

When government regulators are faced with a situation involving a risk, they have four policy options. The first is to do nothing, which is a desirable course of action in situations where the market functions effectively. The second option is to ban the product or activity generating the risk. The Food and Drug Administration, for example, screens new pharmaceutical products to ensure that drugs posing substantial risks are not marketed. Third, the government can undertake an action to directly alter the risk, as in the case of Occupational Safety and Health Administration regulations that control conditions of the workplace, or Environmental Protection Agency requirements on household pesticides that limit the potency of commercially marketed products.

A fourth option . . . is to adopt a hazard-warning program. From a political standpoint this policy option is often viewed as a compromise between taking no action at all and taking an extreme form of action such as a product ban. As an intermediate policy option it has political appeal that is somewhat independent of its merits.

There are . . . sound economic reasons why such an intermediate course might be preferred. Informational programs often are potentially more effective than taking no regulatory action. Such programs can potentially remedy the informational inadequacies in markets. A major source of market failure that is often cited in the case of health and safety regulations is that if consumers and workers are not fully informed of the risks they face, market compensation for risk will not produce efficient safety incentives, thus leading to a justification for a government intervention. If these informational problems can be solved directly through informational regulation, more stringent forms of regulation will not be required, so the market outcome will be efficient.

Informational regulation also may be a more effective means of promoting safety than direct technological controls. Most accident situations are the result of two sets of influences: (1) the technological characteristics of the accident context, such as whether a lawn mower has an engine cutoff device, and (2) the role of the potential accident victim. The manner of operation of the lawn mower and the choice of which family member is to operate the mower play a potentially important role. In most instances consumer precautions are required for the amount and nature in which a product is used, as well as for particular precautions and precautionary equipment that should be employed. Once the role of individual action in contributing to risks is recognized, the potential role for regulatory intervention through an informational approach is apparent. Altering behavior may be a more effective regulatory strategy than is the technological approach that dominated the first decade of social regulation in the 1970s.

Partly in recognition of this role of individual behavior and partly because of the increasing cost of technological controls to reduce risk, the emphasis of health, safety, and environmental regulations in the 1980s became increasingly shifted toward informational regulations. In addition there has been increasing pressure to engage individuals in decisions about the risks they face by right-to-know activists.

A further argument for informational remedies, rather than command-and-control regulation, applies to informational problems prevalent in both risk and non-risk-related decisions. Consumer and worker preferences differ, as do the stocks of existing goods that they own, implying that the optimal regulation should differ across them. A product "improvement," such as a lawnmower engine cutoff system which makes the product safer but more costly, is more likely to be desired by consumers who are wealthy, risk averse, and careless than those with limited incomes who are risk prone and carefully operate the product.

Similarly, a product requirement, such as the building code requiring adequate caulking around windows, is more likely to be desired by consumers who are wealthy and know little about new homes than those with less income who are well informed about building characteristics.

Although informational regulations have proliferated, they have not been without controversy. Informational regulations generally are not completely effective, and there are some circumstances in which they may not be effective at all. Not all people will read the information provided, and not all recipients of the information will act upon it. Perhaps the main difficulty is that informational regulations do not involve simple technological prescriptions to problems. There is an important human element involved in the processing of the information and in the decisions using the information, and one must take into account both this limitation and the decision-making orientation in which the information will be used. For informational regulations to be effective, they must provide new information that can potentially alter individual decisions. If the information cannot be processed reliably or is viewed as not contributing any new information or perspective on a decision, then the informational program will not be successful.

NOTES AND QUESTIONS

1. **Free-Market Environmentalism.** The free-market environmentalist movement contends that markets can take care of environmental problems without government regulation. First, it believes that cooperative organizations interested in environmental protection will be able to solve the free-rider problem, for example, by purchasing conservation easements. Second, it places faith in technological innovations that will make it easier in the future to privatize common resources. Third, it believes that common law courts can play an effective role in protecting private property. *See* TERRY L. ANDERSON & DONALD R. LEAL, FREE MARKET ENVIRONMENTALISM (1991). For criticism of this movement, see Peter S. Menell, *Institutional Fantasylands: From Scientific Management to Free Market Environmentalism*, 15 HARV. J.L. & PUB. POL'Y 489 (1992). What position are free-market environmentalists likely to have with respect to marketable permits and effluent fees? Why do they place trust in common law courts but distrust in the political branches of government?

2. **Hazard-Warning Systems.** For what kinds of risk is a hazard-warning system likely to be a desirable alternative to regulation? Consider the following possibilities:

    (a)   disperse air pollution;

    (b)   highly localized air pollution;

    (c)   indoor air quality at industrial plants;

    (d)   disposal of hazardous wastes;

    (e)   automobiles; and

    (f)   lawn mowers.

In these examples, to what extent are affected individuals able to benefit from the additional risks? To what extent do they impose risks on other individuals?

3.   Justifications for Hazard-Warning Systems. Magat and Viscusi give two distinct arguments for hazard-warning systems:

(a)   that some risks are, at least in part, a function of the victims' decisions; and

(b)   that different individuals have different preferences for risk, or more precisely, different trade-offs between the riskiness and compensation of an occupation or riskiness and price of a product.

Does the first argument call for informational approaches as an alternative to regulation or as an adjunct to regulation? With respect to the second approach, to what extent should well-informed individuals be permitted to accept high risks? In this context, reflect upon the environmental justice discussion in Chapter II.

4.   Lay v. Expert Perceptions of Risk. What are the implications for the desirability of informational approaches to regulation of the discrepancy between expert and lay perceptions of risk (discussed in Chapter II)?

5.   Political Appeal. Magat and Viscusi recognize that informational approaches to regulation hold a "political appeal that is somewhat independent of its merits." To what do they refer?

6.   Green Labeling. Green labeling plays an important role in advertising. Hazard-warning systems are designed to tell consumers about the risk of a product so that the consumer can make an informed decision about whether the positive attributes of the product outweigh its risk. In contrast, green labeling informs consumers about the positive effects on the environment of the *processes* by which the product is manufactured and disposed, so that the consumer can decide whether to value environmental benefits to society at large more than the product's added cost. Should the government promote green labeling? Should it police the accuracy of green labeling claims by private organizations? Is it likely that green labeling will be an effective tool of environmental policy? For discussion, see Jamie A. Grodsky, *Certified Green: The Law and Future of Environmental Labeling*, 10 YALE J. ON REG. 147 (1993); and Peter S. Menell, *Structuring a Market-Oriented Federal Eco-Information Policy*, 54 MD. L. REV. 1435 (1995).

7.   Welfare Effects. Does getting more information always improve welfare? Under what circumstances might getting more information actually reduce welfare? Consider, for example, detailed medical information on various health risks. Why might someone not welcome receiving such information? Federal law often requires or allows agencies to mandate information disclosure. How should agencies evaluate whether information disclosure will do more good than harm? For a discussion of some of the challenges involved in assessing the costs and benefits of informational approaches, see Cass R. Sunstein, *The Welfare Effects of Information*, J. RISK & UNCERTAINTY (forthcoming 2019).

8.   Informational Regulation Under NEPA. A different type of informational approach is embodied in the National Environmental Policy Act (NEPA), the first of the modern federal environmental statutes, which is analyzed in Chapter VIII. NEPA requires federal agencies to prepare an environmental impact statement (EIS) before engaging in environmentally destructive activity. The idea behind NEPA was that such information would lead government agencies to make better and more environmentally sensitive decisions. For discussion, see Michael Herz, *Parallel Universes: NEPA Lessons for the New Property*, 93 COLUM. L. REV. 1668 (1993); and Joseph Sax, *The (Unhappy) Truth About NEPA*, 26 OKLA. L. REV. 239 (1973). Do you believe that the preparation of EISs is likely to lead government agencies to make decisions that are environmentally more protective?

9.   Fuel Economy Labeling. In 2011, EPA revamped the fuel economy labels for new passenger vehicles. *See* EPA, Revisions and Additions to Motor Vehicle Fuel Economy Label, 76 Fed. Reg. 39,478 (2011). The new label contains an estimate of annual average fuel costs and an estimate of fuel savings over five years compared to a car with average fuel efficiency. The label also gives a "Fuel Economy & Greenhouse Gas Rating" and a "Smog Rating." Would you use this information when shopping for a car? How big a behavioral change does this information cause? If this is layered on top of federal fuel economy standards, does it make any difference at all? Or does it make compliance for automotive companies easier?

CHAPTER IV

POLITICAL CONTEXT FOR ENVIRONMENTAL REGULATION

1. Constitutional Limitations on Federal and State Powers.
   A. Limitations on Federal Power.
      i. Commerce Clause.
      ii. Tenth Amendment.
      iii. Eleventh Amendment.
   B. Limitations on State Power.
2. Allocating Regulatory Authority Between the Federal Government and the States.
3. Environmental Law and Public Choice.

1. CONSTITUTIONAL LIMITATIONS ON FEDERAL AND STATE POWERS

A. LIMITATIONS ON FEDERAL POWER

As a way to "ensure protection of our fundamental liberties," the Constitution created a federal government of limited and enumerated powers. *United States v. Lopez*, 514 U.S. 549, 552 (1995) (quoting *Gregory v. Ashcroft*, 501 U.S. 452, 458 (1991)). In the field of environmental law, three principal constitutional provisions limit Congress' authority to enact regulation: the Commerce Clause, the Tenth Amendment, and the Eleventh Amendment. During the last two decades, the Rehnquist Court's new federalism agenda has resulted in a contraction of the federal regulatory power, using these three constitutional provisions as its primary instruments. Robert L. Glicksman, *From Cooperative to Inoperative Federalism: The Perverse Mutation of Environmental Law and Policy*, 41 WAKE FOREST L. REV. 719, 755 (2006).

First, the Constitution grants to Congress the power "[t]o regulate Commerce with foreign Nations, and among the several States, and with the Indian Tribes." U.S. CONST. art. I, § 8. The Supreme Court has understood that this constitutional provision is "broad enough to permit congressional regulation of activities causing air or water pollution, or other environmental hazards that may have effects in more than one State." *Hodel v. Va. Surface Min. & Reclamation Ass'n, Inc.*, 452 U.S. 264, 282 (1981). However, the power granted to Congress under the Commerce Clause is subject to outer limits. *Lopez*, 514 U.S. at 556. Indeed, the Court has held that this power:

> must be considered in the light of our dual system of government
> and may not be extended so as to embrace effects upon

interstate commerce so indirect and remote that to embrace them, in view of our complex society, would effectually obliterate the distinction between what is national and what is local and create a completely centralized government.

NLRB v. Jones & Laughlin Steel Corp., 301 U.S. 1, 37 (1937).

Second, the Supreme Court has interpreted the Tenth Amendment—"[t]he powers not delegated to the United States by the Constitution, nor prohibited by it to the States, are reserved to the States respectively, or to the people"—as allowing Congress to use its power only to encourage states to regulate a particular field or a particular way, not to require them to do so. *See New York v. United States*, 505 U.S. 144, 161 (1992). Therefore, despite Congress' power to enact environmental regulations directly, the Court has understood that the Constitution does not grant to Congress the power to "commandee[r] the legislative processes of the States by directly compelling them to enact and enforce a federal regulatory program." *Hodel*, 452 U.S. at 288 (cited by *New York*, 505 U.S. at 162).

Finally, the states' immunity recognized by the Eleventh Amendment—"[t]he Judicial power of the United States shall not be construed to extend to any suit in law or equity, commenced or prosecuted against one of the United States by Citizens of another State, or by Citizens or Subjects of any Foreign State"—also presents a limit to Congress' power. Indeed, the Supreme Court has interpreted the text of this amendment as barring suits against the states by both its own citizens and citizens of another State. *See Edelman v. Jordan*, 415 U.S. 651, 662–63 (1974). The Court has also limited Congress' authority to abrogate this immunity; it can do so only by means of legislation enacted pursuant to § 5 of the Fourteenth Amendment. *See Seminole Tribe of Fla. v. Florida*, 517 U.S. 44, 65–66 (1996). Therefore, by protecting the states from unconsented suits in federal courts, the Eleventh Amendment limits Congress' power to allow private suits against the states.

i.   COMMERCE CLAUSE

National Association of Home Builders v. Babbitt

130 F.3d 1041 (D.C. Cir. 1997), *cert denied*, 524 U.S. 937 (1998).

■ Before WALD, SENTELLE and HENDERSON, CIRCUIT JUDGES.

■ WALD, CIRCUIT JUDGE:

This dispute arose when the Fish and Wildlife Service ("FWS") placed the . . . [Delhi Sands Flower-Loving Fly ("the Fly")], an insect that is native to the San Bernardino area of California, on the endangered species list. The listing of the Fly, the habitat of which is located entirely within . . . California, forced San Bernardino County to alter plans to construct a new hospital on a recently purchased site that the FWS had determined contained Fly habitat. . . . In November 1995, . . . the County notified the FWS that it planned to redesign a nearby intersection to improve emergency vehicle access to the hospital. The FWS informed the County that expansion of the intersection as planned would likely lead to a "taking" of the Fly in violation of ESA section 9(a). After brief unsuccessful negotiations between the County and FWS, the County filed suit. . . .

Appellants challenge the application of section 9(a)(1) of the [Endangered Species Act (ESA)], which makes it unlawful for any person to "take any [endangered or threatened] species within the United States or the territorial sea of the United States," 16 U.S.C. § 1538(a)(1), to the Delhi Sands Flower-Loving Fly. . . . Appellants argue that the federal government does not have the authority to regulate the use of non-federal lands in order to protect the Fly, which is found only within a single state. . . .

The district court held that the application of section 9(a)(1) of the ESA to the Fly is constitutional. . . . The court . . . concluded that the ESA provides for a regulatory scheme that is within the bounds of Congress' power under the Commerce Clause. . . . We affirm the district court's decision.

Appellants' Commerce Clause challenge to the application of section 9(a)(1) of the ESA to the Fly rests on the Supreme Court's decision in *United States v. Lopez*, 514 U.S. 549 (1995). In *Lopez*, the Court held that the Gun-Free School Zones Act of 1990, 18 U.S.C. § 922(q), which made possession of a gun within a school zone a federal offense, exceeded Congress' Commerce Clause authority. Drawing on its earlier Commerce Clause jurisprudence, . . . the *Lopez* Court explained that Congress could regulate three broad categories of activity: (1) "the use of the channels of interstate commerce," (2) "the instrumentalities of interstate commerce, or persons or things in interstate commerce, even though the threat may come only from intrastate activities," and (3) "those activities having a substantial relation to interstate commerce . . . i.e., those activities that substantially affect interstate commerce." *Lopez*, 514 U.S. at 558–59. . . .

It is clear that, in this instance, section 9(a)(1) of the ESA is not a regulation of the instrumentalities of interstate commerce or of persons or things in interstate commerce. As a result, only the first and the third categories of activity discussed in *Lopez* will be examined. In evaluating whether ESA section 9(a)(1) is a regulation of the use of the channels of interstate commerce or of activity that substantially affects interstate commerce, we may look not only to the effect of the extinction of the individual endangered species at issue in this case, but also to the aggregate effect of the extinction of all similarly situated endangered species. As the *Lopez* Court explained, " '*where a general regulatory statute bears a substantial relation to commerce*, the de minimis character of individual instances arising under the statute is of no consequence.' " *Lopez*, 514 U.S. at 558. If a statute regulates "a class of activities . . . within reach of the federal power," *Perez* [*v. United States*,

402 U.S. 146, 154 (1971)], the courts have "no power 'to excise, as trivial, individual instances' of the class," *id.* Because section 9(a)(1) of the ESA regulates a class of activities—takings of endangered species—that is within Congress' Commerce Clause power under both the first and third *Lopez* categories, application of section 9(a)(1) to the Fly is constitutional.

Application of section 9(a)(1) of the ESA to the Fly can be viewed as a proper exercise of Congress' Commerce Clause power over the first category of activity that the *Lopez* Court identified . . . for two reasons. First, the prohibition against takings of an endangered species is necessary to enable the government to control the transport of the endangered species in interstate commerce. Second, the prohibition on takings of endangered animals falls under Congress' authority " 'to keep the channels of interstate commerce free from immoral and injurious uses.' " *Id.* (quoting *Heart of Atlanta Motel, Inc. v. United States*, 379 U.S. 241, 256 (1964)).

The ESA's prohibition on takings of endangered species can be justified as a necessary aid to the prohibitions in the ESA on transporting and selling endangered species in interstate commerce. In this sense, the prohibition against takings of endangered species is analogous to the prohibition against transfer and possession of machine guns (including purely intrastate possession) of 18 U.S.C. § 922(*o*), which has been upheld by the Fifth, Sixth, Ninth, and Eleventh Circuits as a regulation of the channels of interstate commerce. In *United States v. Rambo,* 74 F.3d 948, 951 (9th Cir.), for instance, the Ninth Circuit upheld section 922(*o*) against a *Lopez*-inspired Commerce Clause challenge. The court held that the statute was a " 'regulation of the use of the channels of interstate commerce' " because "[b]y regulating the market in machineguns, including regulating intrastate machinegun possession, Congress has effectively regulated the interstate trafficking in machineguns." *Id.* at 952 (quoting *Lopez*, 514 U.S. at 559). Thus, section 922(*o*) is properly classified as a first category regulation because " 'federal regulation of intrastate incidents of transfer and possession is essential to effective control of the interstate incidents of such traffic.' " *Id.* . . . Similarly, the prohibition on "taking" endangered species is properly classified as a first category regulation because one of the most effective ways to prevent traffic in endangered species is to secure the habitat of the species from predatory invasion and destruction. . . .

The prohibition on takings of endangered animals also falls under Congress' authority to prevent the channels of interstate commerce from being used for immoral or injurious purposes. . . . In *Heart of Atlanta,* the Supreme Court upheld a prohibition on racial discrimination in places of public accommodation serving interstate travelers against a Commerce Clause challenge. . . . [T]he power of Congress over interstate commerce "also includes the power to regulate the local incidents thereof, including local activities in both the States of origin and destination, which might have a substantial and harmful effect upon that commerce." *Id.* This same principle was elaborated in the seminal case of *United States v. Darby,* 312 U.S. 100 (1941). . . . In *Darby,* the Court upheld federal wage and hour regulations against a Commerce Clause challenge, noting that such regulations were necessary to prevent states with higher regulatory standards from being disadvantaged vis-à-vis states with lower regulatory standards. In upholding the regulation, the Court explained that [ ]Congress . . . is free to exclude from commerce goods that will have injurious effects in the state in which they are produced or to which they are destined. *Id.* at 114. This is true even though the activity prohibited by the regulation at issue in *Darby* . . . might have had little or no direct effect outside the state in which the goods were produced.

This same reasoning that the Supreme Court applied in *Darby* and *Heart of Atlanta* is applicable to the case at hand. In those cases as well as here, Congress used its authority to rid the channels of interstate commerce of injurious uses to regulate the conditions under which goods are produced for interstate commerce. . . . [I]n this case, Congress used this authority to prevent the eradication of an endangered species by a hospital that is presumably being constructed using materials and people from outside the state and which will attract employees, patients, and students from both inside and outside the state. Thus, like regulations preventing racial discrimination or labor exploitation, regulations preventing the taking of endangered species prohibit interstate actors from using the channels of interstate commerce to "promot[e] or spread[ ] evil, whether of a physical, moral or economic nature." *North American Co. v. S.E.C.,* 327 U.S. 686, 705 (1946). . . .

The takings clause in the ESA can also be viewed as a regulation of the third category of activity that Congress may regulate under its commerce power. According to *Lopez,* the test . . . "requires an analysis of whether the regulated activity 'substantially affects' interstate commerce." 514 U.S. at 559. A class of activities can substantially affect interstate commerce regardless of whether the activity at issue . . . is commercial or noncommercial. As the *Lopez* Court . . . noted: "[E]ven if appellee's activity be local and though it may not be regarded as commerce, it may still, whatever its nature, be reached by Congress if it exerts a substantial economic effect on interstate commerce, and this irrespective of whether such effect is what might at some earlier time have been defined as 'direct' or 'indirect.' " *Lopez,* 514 U.S. at 556 (quoting *Wickard,* 317 U.S. at 125). . . .

In evaluating the effect of the regulated activity on interstate commerce, I begin . . . with the legislative history of the Act under challenge. . . .

The Committee Reports on the ESA reveal that one of the primary reasons that Congress sought to protect endangered species from "takings" was the importance of the continuing availability of a wide variety of species to interstate commerce. . . .

This legislative history distinguishes the ESA from the statute at issue in *Lopez*. . . . The *Lopez* Court found . . . that there were no "congressional findings [that] would enable [it] to evaluate the legislative judgment that the activity in question substantially affected interstate commerce." *Id.* at 563. In this case, in contrast, the committee reports on the ESA discuss the value of preserving genetic diversity and the potential for future commerce related to that diversity. . . .

These congressional findings, while highly informative, are of course not sufficient by themselves to make the statute constitutional. The courts . . . must determine that there was a rational basis for Congress' conclusion that a regulated activity substantially affects interstate commerce. . . . [S]*ee* . . . *Hodel v. Virginia Surface Mining & Reclamation Ass'n, Inc.*, 452 U.S. 264, 276 (1981) ("The task of a court that is asked to determine whether a particular exercise of congressional power is valid under the Commerce Clause is relatively narrow. The court must defer to a congressional finding that a regulated activity affects interstate commerce, if there is any rational basis for such a finding.") . . .

Congress could rationally conclude that the intrastate activity regulated by section 9 of the ESA substantially affects interstate commerce for two primary reasons. First, the provision prevents the destruction of biodiversity and thereby protects the current and future interstate commerce that relies upon it. Second, the provision controls adverse effects of interstate competition. . . .

. . . The elimination of all or even some of these endangered species would have a staggering effect on biodiversity—defined as the presence of a large number of species of animals and plants—in the United States and, thereby, on the current and future interstate commerce that relies on the availability of a diverse array of species. . . .

The taking of the Fly and other endangered animals can also be regulated by Congress as an activity that substantially affects interstate commerce because it is the product of destructive interstate competition. . . .

The case at hand bears a substantial similarity to the three cases in which the Supreme Court best articulated the principle that Congress may act to prevent interstate competition that has a destructive effect: *Hodel v. Virginia*, 452 U.S. 264, *Hodel v. Indiana*, 452 U.S. 314 (1981), and *United States v. Darby*, 312 U.S. 100 (1941). In *Hodel v. Virginia*, the Supreme Court considered a challenge to the constitutionality of the Surface Mining Control and Reclamation Act of 1977. The Surface Mining Act required mine operators to restore the land after mining to its prior condition . . . in order to "protect society and the environment from the adverse effects of surface coal mining operations." 452 U.S. at 268. . . . The Court held that the Act was a valid exercise of Congress' power under the Commerce Clause because "Congress rationally determined that regulation of surface coal mining is necessary to protect interstate commerce from adverse effects that may result from that activity." *Id.* at 281. . . .

The parallels between *Hodel v. Virginia* and the case at hand are obvious. The ESA and the Surface Mining Act both regulate activities . . . that are carried out entirely within a State and which are not themselves commercial in character. The activities, however, may be regulated because they have destructive effects, on environmental quality in one case and on the availability of a variety of species in the other, that are likely to affect more than one State. In each case, moreover, interstate competition provides incentives to states to adopt lower standards to gain an advantage vis-à-vis other states: In *Hodel v. Virginia,* 452 U.S. 264, the states were motivated to adopt lower environmental standards to improve the competitiveness of their coal production facilities, and in this case, the states are motivated to adopt lower standards of endangered species protection in order to attract development.

. . . [T]he Supreme Court's decision in *United States v. Darby* . . . upheld wage and hour regulations for employees engaged in the production of lumber for interstate commerce. . . . The Court . . . explained that "interstate commerce should not be made the instrument of competition in the distribution of goods produced under substandard labor conditions, which competition is injurious to the commerce and to the states from and to which the commerce flows." *Id.* at 115.

Like *Darby*, the case at hand involves a regulation of the conditions under which commercial activity takes place. . . . In both cases, Congress passed the statute in part to prevent states from gaining a competitive advantage by enacting lower regulatory standards than other states. . . . As the cases discussed above illustrate, the Court has long held that Congress has the power under the Commerce Clause to prevent destructive interstate commerce similar to that at issue in this case. I therefore find that Congress has the power to prevent interstate competition that will result in the destruction of endangered species just as it has the power to prevent interstate competition that will result in harm to the environment, *Hodel v. Virginia* . . . or the employment of people under substandard labor conditions, *Darby*.

We hold that the section 9(a)(1) of the Endangered Species Act is within Congress' Commerce Clause power and that the Fish and Wildlife Service's application of the provision to the Delhi Sands Flower-Loving Fly was therefore constitutional. . . .

NOTES AND QUESTIONS

1. **Channels of Interstate Commerce.** Why did Judge Wald find that § 9(a)(1) of the ESA, 16 U.S.C. § 1538(a)(1), is a proper regulation of the channels of interstate commerce? Is the regulation of machine guns distinguishable from the regulation of endangered species? Is it relevant that some endangered species don't have any commercial value? In her concurring opinion, Judge Henderson argued:

Judge Wald first asserts that section 9(a)(1) is a proper regulation of the "channels of commerce." In support she cites decisions upholding regulation of commercially marketable goods, such as machine guns and lumber, and public accommodations. In each case, the object of regulation was necessarily connected to movement of persons or things interstate and could therefore be characterized as regulation of the channels of commerce. Not so with an endangered species, as the facts here graphically demonstrate. The Delhi Sands Flower-Loving Flies . . . are . . . entirely *intra*state creatures. They do not move among states either on their own or through human agency. As a result, like the Gun-Free School Zones Act in *Lopez*, the statutory protection of the flies "is not a regulation of the use of the channels of interstate commerce." 514 U.S. at 559.

Judge Wald also justifies the protection of endangered species on the ground that the loss of biodiversity "substantially affects" interstate commerce because of the resulting loss of potential medical or economic benefit. . . . It may well be that no species endangered now or in the future will have any of the economic value proposed. Given that possibility, I do not see how we can say that the protection of an endangered species has any effect on interstate commerce (much less a substantial one) by virtue of an uncertain potential medical or economic value.

NAHB, 130 F.3d at 1057–58. Do you find this opinion compelling?

2.   Channels of Interstate Commerce, Continued. Why did Judge Wald find that § 9(a)(1) of the ESA also falls under Congress' authority to prevent the channels of interstate commerce from being used for immoral or injurious purposes? In his dissenting opinion, Judge Sentelle argued:

As Judge Wald notes, both *Darby* and *Heart of Atlanta* concerned congressional efforts to "rid the channels of interstate commerce of injurious uses." *Wald Op.* at 1048. But . . . preventing habitat destruction contributes nothing to the goal of eliminating the fly, or any other endangered species, from the channels of commerce. The fact that activities like the construction of a hospital might involve articles that have traveled across state lines cannot justify federal regulation of the incidental local effects of every local activity in which those articles are employed. Judge Wald seems to be trying to extend Congress' power over the channels of commerce to allow direct federal regulation of any local effects caused by any activity using those channels of commerce. She focuses not on the fly in the channels of commerce, but everything else moving in the channels of commerce that may affect the fly. But this improperly inverts the third prong of *Lopez* and extends it without limit. Under Judge Wald's theory, instead of being limited to activities that *substantially affect* commerce, Congress may also regulate anything that is *affected by* commerce.

NAHB, 130 F.3d at 1063. Assess the strength of the argument. Can *Darby* and *Heart of Atlanta* be distinguished from *NAHB*?

3.   "Substantial Effect" Test. In order to determine if an activity has a substantial relation to interstate commerce, the court should analyze "whether the regulated activity 'substantially affects' [it]." *NAHB*, 130 F.3d at 1049. Does the taking of endangered species "substantially affect" interstate commerce? In her concurring opinion, Justice Henderson argued:

> The interstate effect of a taking is particularly obvious here given the nature of the taking the County proposes. . . . Congress expressly found that "economic growth and development untempered by adequate concern and conservation" was the cause for "various species of fish, wildlife, and plants in the United States hav[ing] been rendered extinct." 16 U.S.C. § 1531(a)(1). It is plain, then, that at the time it passed ESA the Congress contemplated protecting endangered species through regulation of land and its development, which is precisely what the Department has attempted to do here. Such regulation, apart from the characteristics or range of the specific endangered species involved, has a plain and substantial effect on interstate commerce. In this case the regulation relates to both the proposed redesigned traffic intersection and the hospital it is intended to serve, each of which has an obvious connection with interstate commerce. *See Terry v. Reno*, 101 F.3d 1412, 1416–17 (D.C. Cir. 1996) (concluding abortion clinic activities substantially affect interstate commerce). . . . Insofar as application of section 9(a)(1) of ESA here acts to regulate commercial development of the land inhabited by the endangered species, "it may . . . be reached by Congress" because "it asserts a substantial economic effect on interstate commerce." *Wickard v. Filburn*, 317 U.S. 111, 125 (1942).

NAHB, 130 F.3d at 1059. How did Judge Wald's opinion differ on this point? What is the "regulated activity" in this case?

4.   "Substantial Effect" Test, Continued. In his dissenting opinion, Judge Sentelle argued:

> Because category (3) was the only category which even arguably could have permitted Congress to regulate the purely intrastate possession of firearms considered in *Lopez*, the Supreme Court afforded it a more thorough analysis than the other two categories and, in so doing, established three areas of inquiry necessitated by a claim of interstate commerce authority under the "substantial effects" category. Thus, in considering whether or not to uphold regulation under that rationale, we must examine whether:
>
> > — the regulation controls a commercial activity, or an activity necessary to the regulation of some commercial activity;
> >
> > — the statute includes a jurisdictional nexus requirement to ensure that each regulated instance of the activity affects interstate commerce; and

— the rationale offered to support the constitutionality of the statute (*i.e.*, statutory findings, legislative history, arguments of counsel, or a reviewing court's own attribution of purposes to the statute being challenged) has a logical stopping point so that the rationale is not so broad as to regulate on a similar basis all human endeavors, especially those traditionally regulated by the states.

None of the rationales offered by my colleagues pass this examination. . . .

NAHB, 130 F.3d at 1063–64. Which of the judges has the stronger argument? Does § 9(a)(1) of the ESA, 16 U.S.C. § 1538(a)(1), control a commercial activity? *See id.* at 1064 (arguing that "[n]either killing flies nor controlling weeds nor digging holes is either inherently or fundamentally commercial in any sense."). In *Lopez*, the Supreme Court noted the statute contained "no jurisdictional element which would ensure, through case-by-case inquiry, that the firearms possession in question affects interstate commerce." *Id.* at 1064 (citing *Lopez*, 514 U.S. at 561). Is the ESA distinguishable? Does the rationale offered by Judges Wald and Henderson have a logical stopping point? Before the Supreme Court decision in *Lopez*, the Commerce Clause had been applied to such a wide range of circumstances that Judge Kozinski "wonder[ed] why anyone would make the mistake of calling it the Commerce Clause instead of the 'Hey, you-can-do-whatever-you-feel-like Clause.' " Alex Kozinski, *Introduction to Volume Nineteen,* 19 HARV. J. L. PUB. POL. 1, 5 (1995) (cited by *NAHB*, 130 F.3d at 1061). Judge Sentelle argued: "If we uphold this statute under Judge Wald's ["biodiversity"] rationale, we have indeed not only ignored *Lopez* but made the Commerce Clause into what Judge Kozinski suggested: the 'Hey, you-can-do-whatever-you-feel-like Clause.' " *NAHB*, 130 F.3d at 1065. Do you find this opinion compelling?

5.　Race to the Bottom. Relying on *Hodel v. Virginia*, 452 U.S. 264 (1981) and *United States v. Darby*, 312 U.S. 100 (1941), Judge Wald argued "[t]he taking of the Fly and other endangered animals can . . . be regulated by Congress as an activity that substantially affects interstate commerce because it is the product of destructive interstate competition. . . ." *NAHB*, 130 F.3d at 1054. Is *NAHB* distinguishable from *Hodel v. Virginia* and *United States v. Darby*? On what grounds? Judge Sentelle considered these cases inapplicable:

Although she asserts "striking parallels" between those cases and the present one, I see no parallel at all. In each of those cases, Congress regulated arguably intrastate *commercial* activities, specifically mining and lumber production for interstate commerce. In each of those cases, the Supreme Court upheld the relevant statutes, noting that the regulated actors would either destroy other commercial activities or be able to unfairly compete with interstate competitors subject to higher regulatory standards protective of other elements of commerce. In the present case neither Congress nor the litigants, nor for that matter Judge Wald, has pointed to any commercial activity being regulated, any commercial competition being unfairly challenged, or any other sort of commerce being destroyed by the taking of the fly.

NAHB, 130 F.3d at 1066. Do you find this opinion compelling?

6. **Federal Regulation of Wetlands.** In *Solid Waste Agency of Northern Cook County v. U.S. Army Corps of Engineers*, 531 U.S. 159 (2001) (discussed in Chapter IX), a consortium of municipalities challenged the jurisdiction of the Army Corps of Engineers to regulate non-navigable, isolated, intrastate waters that provided habitats for migratory birds. Section 404(a) of the Clean Water Act (CWA), 33 U.S.C. § 1344(a), authorizes the Army Corps of Engineers to issue permits "for the discharge of dredge or fill material into the navigable waters at specified disposal sites." The Act defines "navigable waters" as "the waters of the United States, including the territorial seas," 33 U.S.C. § 1362(7), and the Corps had issued regulations defining the term "waters of the United States" to include intrastate waters which are or would be used as habitat by migratory birds. 51 Fed. Reg. 41,217. The Solid Waste Agency of Northern Cook County (SWANCC) argued that the Corps' rule had exceeded its statutory authority in interpreting the CWA to cover non-navigable, isolated, intrastate waters based upon the presence of migratory birds. *SWANCC*, 531 U.S. at 179. In the alternative, SWANCC argued that Congress lacked the power under the Commerce Clause to grant such jurisdiction. *Id.* The Court held that the "Migratory Bird Rule" was not supported by the CWA and therefore it did not address the constitutional question. *Id.* at 167. However, the Court referred to the Commerce Clause in dicta:

> [T]he grant of authority to Congress under the Commerce Clause, though broad, is not unlimited. *See* United States v. Morrison, 529 U.S. 598 (2000); *United States v. Lopez*, 514 U.S. 549 (1995). Respondents argue that the "Migratory Bird Rule" falls within Congress' power to regulate intrastate activities that "substantially affect" interstate commerce. They note that the protection of migratory birds is a "national interest of very nearly the first magnitude," *Missouri v. Holland*, 252 U.S. 416 (1920), and that, as the Court of Appeals found, millions of people spend over a billion dollars annually on recreational pursuits relating to migratory birds. These arguments raise significant constitutional questions. For example, we would have to evaluate the precise object or activity that, in the aggregate, substantially affects interstate commerce. This is not clear, for although the Corps has claimed jurisdiction over petitioner's land because it contains water areas used as habitat by migratory birds, respondents now, *post litem motam*, focus upon the fact that the regulated activity is petitioner's municipal landfill, which is "plainly of a commercial nature." Brief for Federal Respondents 43. But this is a far cry, indeed, from the "navigable waters" and "waters of the United States" to which the statute by its terms extends.

SWANCC, 531 U.S. at 173. Does the commercial activity need to be closely related to the object of the statutes in order to justify its regulation under the Commerce Clause? *See GDF Realty Invs., Ltd. v. Norton*, 326 F.3d 622,

633–35 (5th Cir. 2003), *cert. denied*, 545 U.S. 1114 (2005); *see also* Bradford C. Mank, *Can Congress Regulate Intrastate Endangered Species Under the Commerce Clause?*, 69 BROOK. L. REV. 923 (2004).

7.   **Post** *NAHB* **Cases.** In 2003, both the Fifth and the D.C. Circuits evaluated Congress' authority to regulate the taking of solely intrastate species. Even though both circuits upheld § 9 of the ESA, they did so under very different rationales. *See* Mank, *supra*, at 925. In *GDF Realty Investments v. Norton*, 326 F.3d 622 (5th Cir. 2003), the Fifth Circuit held that intrastate spiders and beetles have an impact on interstate commerce when their impact is aggregated with the impacts of all other protected species. *See id.* In so holding, the court rejected the government's argument that the appropriate focus of the test was the economic impact of the commercial development regulated under the statute. *Id.* In contrast, the government's position was adopted by the D.C. Circuit in *Rancho Viejo, LLC v. Norton*, 323 F.3d 1062 (D.C. Cir. 2003), *cert. denied*, 540 U.S. 1218 (2004), which held that the "regulated activity [was] Rancho Viejo's planned commercial development, not the arroyo toad that it threatens." *Id.* at 626. Which approach do you find more compelling? How does the choice between them affect the kind of projects that the ESA may regulate? *See Rancho Viejo*, 323 F.3d at 1080 (Ginsburg, J., concurring) ("The large-scale residential development that is the take in this case clearly does affect interstate commerce. . . . [H]owever, the lone hiker in the woods, or the homeowner who moves dirt in order to landscape his property, though he takes the toad, does not affect interstate commerce.")

8.   *Gonzales v. Raich.* In *Gonzales v. Raich*, 545 U.S. 1 (2005), users of marijuana for medical purposes pursuant to California law sought injunctive and declaratory relief prohibiting the enforcement of the federal Controlled Substances Act (CSA), 21 U.S.C. § 801 *et seq.*, to the extent it prevented them from possessing and manufacturing cannabis. *Id.* at 7. They argued that such provision, as applied to the intrastate manufacture and possession of marijuana for medical purposes, exceeds Congress' authority under the Commerce Clause. *Id.* at 15. The Court upheld the challenged provision:

> Our case law firmly establishes Congress' power to regulate purely local activities that are part of an economic "class of activities" that have a substantial effect on interstate commerce. *See, e.g., Perez*, 402 U.S. at 151; *Wickard v. Filburn*, 317 U.S. 111, 128–12 (1942). As we stated in *Wickard*, "even if appellee's activity be local and though it may not be regarded as commerce, it may still, whatever its nature, be reached by Congress if it exerts a substantial economic effect on interstate commerce." *Id.* at 125. We have never required Congress to legislate with scientific exactitude. When Congress decides that the " 'total incidence' " of a practice poses a threat to a national market, it may regulate the entire class. *See Perez*, 402 U.S. at 154–155 (quoting *Westfall v. United States*, 274 U.S. 256, 259 (1927) ("[W]hen it is necessary in order to prevent an evil to make the law embrace more than the precise thing to be prevented it may do so")). In this vein, we have reiterated that when " 'a general regulatory statute bears a substantial relation to

commerce, the de minimis character of individual instances arising under that statute is of no consequence.' " *E.g.*, *Lopez*, 514 U.S. at 558 (emphasis deleted) (quoting *Maryland v. Wirtz*, 392 U.S. 183, 196, n. 27 (1968)).

Id. at 17. Could the taking of endangered species be treated as a class? What kind of risks are posed by the use of marijuana for medical purposes? What is the effect on interstate commerce? Are endangered species without commercial value distinguishable? *See Alabama-Tombigbee Rivers Coal. v. Kempthorne*, 477 F.3d 1250, 1273 (11th Cir. 2007) ("If the process of listing endangered species is 'an essential part of a larger regulation of economic activity,' then whether that process 'ensnares some purely intrastate activity is of no moment.' "), *cert. denied*, 552 U.S. 1097 (2008).

9.   Federal Regulation of Drinking Water. The Safe Drinking Water Act (SDWA) directs EPA to promulgate standards limiting the amount of contaminants that could be allowed in drinking water from public water systems. 42 U.S.C. § 300g–1(b); *see Nebraska v. EPA*, 331 F.3d 995, 997 (D.C. Cir. 2003). Could Congress regulate the intrastate distribution and sale of drinking water? On what grounds? Would it be relevant that some water utilities sell drinking water across state lines? *See Nebraska*, 331 F.3d at 998 (holding that the SDWA does not exceed congressional authority under the Commerce Clause).

10.   Federal Regulation of Hazardous Waste Disposal. The purpose of the Comprehensive Environmental Response, Compensation and Liability Act (CERCLA) is "to provide for liability, compensation, cleanup, and emergency response for hazardous substances released into the environment and the cleanup of inactive hazardous waste disposal sites." Pub.L. No. 96–510, 94 Stat. 2767, 2767 (1980). Suppose a chemical manufacturer released hazardous waste into the environment contaminating only its own property. Could the manufacturer be required to pay for the cleanup of this entirely local contamination? Can Congress' regulation of purely intrastate, on-site disposal activities be justified under the Supreme Court's Commerce Clause Jurisprudence? On what grounds? *See United States v. Olin Corp.*, 107 F.3d 1506 (11th Cir. 1997) (holding that there was no commerce clause violation in application of CERCLA to a chemical manufacturer, even absent evidence that manufacturer's on-site disposal had caused off-site damage). Is *Gonzales v. Raich* applicable?

11.   Federal Regulation of Asbestos. Pursuant to §§ 112(b) and 112(h)(1) of the Clean Air Act (CAA), 42 U.S.C. § 7412(b), (h)(1), EPA has adopted a work practice standard for handling asbestos in building renovation sites. *See* 40 C.F.R. §§ 61.145, 61.150. Could the owner of a building be convicted of failure to comply with this standard, even though asbestos was never released from the building into the ambient ("interstate") air? *See United States v. Ho*, 311 F.3d 589, 601 (5th Cir. 2002) ("[W]e uphold, as a valid exercise of Congress' commerce power, the provisions of the CAA under which [the defendant] was convicted").

ii.   TENTH AMENDMENT

New York v. United States
505 U.S. 144 (1992).

■ JUSTICE O'CONNOR delivered the opinion of the Court:

. . . In these cases, we address the constitutionality of three provisions of the Low-Level Radioactive Waste Policy Amendments Act of 1985, Pub.L. 99–240, 99 Stat. 1842, 42 U.S.C. § 202 1b *et seq.* . . .

. . . The Act provides three types of incentives to encourage the States to comply with their statutory obligation to provide for the disposal of waste generated within their borders.

1.   *Monetary incentives.* One quarter of the surcharges collected by the sited States must be transferred to an escrow account held by the Secretary of Energy. § 2021e(d)(2)(A). The Secretary then makes payments from this account to each State that has complied with a series of deadlines. . . .

2.   *Access incentives.* The second type of incentive involves the denial of access to disposal sites. States that fail to meet the July 1986 deadline may be charged twice the ordinary surcharge for the remainder of 1986 and may be denied access to disposal facilities thereafter. § 2021e(e)(2)(A). . . .

3.   *The take title provision.* The third type of incentive is the most severe. The Act provides:

> "If a State (or, where applicable, a compact region) in which low-level radioactive waste is generated is unable to provide for the disposal of all such waste generated within such State or compact region by January 1, 1996, each State in which such waste is generated, upon the request of the generator or owner of the waste, shall take title to the waste, be obligated to take possession of the waste, and shall be liable for all damages directly or indirectly incurred by such generator or owner as a consequence of the failure of the State to take possession of the waste as soon after January 1, 1996, as the generator or owner notifies the State that the waste is available for shipment."

§ 2021e(d)(2)(C). These three incentives are the focus of petitioners' constitutional challenge. . . .

Petitioners—the State of New York and the two counties—filed this suit against the United States in 1990. They sought a declaratory judgment that the Act is inconsistent with the Tenth [Amendment] . . . to the Constitution. . . . The States of Washington, Nevada, and South Carolina intervened as defendants. The District Court dismissed the complaint. 757 F.Supp. 10 (N.D.N.Y. 1990). The Court of Appeals affirmed. 942 F.2d 114 (C.A.2 1991). . . .

Petitioners do not contend that Congress lacks the power to regulate the disposal of low level radioactive waste. Space in radioactive waste disposal sites is frequently sold by residents of one State to residents of another. Regulation of the resulting interstate market in waste disposal is therefore well within Congress' authority under the Commerce Clause. . . . Petitioners likewise do not dispute that under the Supremacy Clause Congress could, if it wished, pre-empt state radioactive waste regulation. Petitioners contend only that the Tenth Amendment limits the power of Congress to regulate in the way it has chosen. Rather than addressing the problem of waste disposal by directly regulating the generators and disposers of waste, petitioners argue, Congress has impermissibly directed the States to regulate in this field.

Most of our recent cases interpreting the Tenth Amendment have concerned the authority of Congress to subject state governments to generally applicable laws. The Court's jurisprudence in this area has traveled an unsteady path. *See Maryland v. Wirtz*, 392 U.S. 183 (1968) (state schools and hospitals are subject to Fair Labor Standards Act); *National League of Cities v. Usery*, 426 U.S. 833 (1976) (overruling *Wirtz*) (state employers are *not* subject to Fair Labor Standards Act); *Garcia v. San Antonio Metropolitan Transit Authority*, 469 U.S. 528 (1985) (overruling *National League of Cities*) (state employers are once again subject to Fair Labor Standards Act). . . . This litigation presents no occasion to apply or revisit the holdings of any of these cases, as this is not a case in which Congress has subjected a State to the same legislation applicable to private parties. Cf. *FERC v. Mississippi*, 456 U.S. 742, 758–759 (1982).

This litigation instead concerns the circumstances under which Congress may use the States as implements of regulation; that is, whether Congress may direct or otherwise motivate the States to regulate in a particular field or a particular way. Our cases have established a few principles that guide our resolution of the issue.

As an initial matter, Congress may not simply "commandee[r] the legislative processes of the States by directly compelling them to enact and enforce a federal regulatory program." *Hodel v. Virginia Surface Mining & Reclamation Assn., Inc.*, 452 U.S. 264, 288 (1981). . . .

. . . While Congress has substantial powers to govern the Nation directly, including in areas of intimate concern to the States, the Constitution has never been understood to confer upon Congress the ability to require the States to govern according to Congress' instructions. See *Coyle v. Smith*, 221 U.S. 559, 565 (1911). The Court has been explicit about this distinction. "Both the States and the United States existed before the Constitution. The people, through that instrument, established a more perfect union by substituting a national government, acting, with ample power, *directly upon the citizens*, instead of the Confederate government, which acted with powers, greatly restricted, only upon the States." *Lane County v. Oregon*, 7 Wall., at 76 (emphasis added). . . .

In providing for a stronger central government, therefore, the Framers explicitly chose a Constitution that confers upon Congress the power to regulate individuals, not States. As we have seen, the Court has consistently respected this choice. We have always understood that even where Congress has the authority under the Constitution to pass laws requiring or prohibiting certain acts, it lacks the power directly to compel the States to require or prohibit those acts. . . . The allocation of power contained in the Commerce Clause, for example, authorizes Congress to regulate interstate commerce directly; it does not authorize Congress to regulate state governments' regulation of interstate commerce.

This is not to say that Congress lacks the ability to encourage a State to regulate in a particular way, or that Congress may not hold out incentives to the States as a method of influencing a State's policy choices. Our cases have identified a variety of methods, short of outright coercion, by which Congress may urge a State to adopt a legislative program consistent with federal interests. Two of these methods are of particular relevance here.

First, under Congress' spending power, "Congress may attach conditions on the receipt of federal funds." *South Dakota v. Dole*, 483 U.S., at 206. Such conditions must (among other requirements) bear some relationship to the purpose of the federal spending, *id.*, at 207–208; otherwise, of course, the spending power could render academic the Constitution's other grants and limits of federal authority. Where the recipient of federal funds is a State, as is not unusual today, the conditions attached to the funds by Congress may influence a State's legislative choices. . . . *Dole* was one such case: The Court found no constitutional flaw in a federal statute directing the Secretary of Transportation to withhold federal highway funds from States failing to adopt Congress' choice of a minimum drinking age. . . .

Second, where Congress has the authority to regulate private activity under the Commerce Clause, we have recognized Congress' power to offer States the choice of regulating that activity according to federal standards or having state law pre-empted by federal regulation. *Hodel v. Virginia Surface Mining & Reclamation Assn., Inc.*, *supra*, 452 U.S., at 288, *see also FERC v. Mississippi*, *supra*, 456 U.S., at 764–765. This arrangement, which has been termed "a program of cooperative federalism," *Hodel*, *supra*, 452 U.S., at 289, is replicated in numerous federal statutory schemes. These include the Clean Water Act, 33 U.S.C. § 1251 *et seq.*, see *Arkansas v. Oklahoma*, 503 U.S. 91, 101 (1992) (Clean Water Act "anticipates a partnership between the States and the Federal Government, animated by a shared objective"); . . . [and] the Resource Conservation and Recovery Act of 1976, 42 U.S.C. § 6901 *et seq.*, see *Department of Energy v. Ohio*, 503 U.S. 607, 611–612 (1992). . . .

By either of these methods, as by any other permissible method of encouraging a State to conform to federal policy choices, the residents of the State retain the ultimate decision as to whether or not the State will comply. . . . Where Congress encourages state regulation rather than compelling it, state governments remain responsive to the local electorate's preferences; state officials remain accountable to the people.

By contrast, where the Federal Government compels States to regulate, the accountability of both state and federal officials is diminished. . . .

With these principles in mind, we turn to the three challenged provisions of the Low-Level Radioactive Waste Policy Amendments Act of 1985. . . .

The first set of incentives works in three steps. First, Congress has authorized States with disposal sites to impose a surcharge on radioactive waste received from other States. Second, the Secretary of Energy collects a portion of this surcharge and places the money in an escrow account. Third, States achieving a series of milestones receive portions of this fund.

The first of these steps is an unexceptionable exercise of Congress' power to authorize the States to burden interstate commerce. While the Commerce Clause has long been understood to limit the States' ability to discriminate against interstate commerce . . . , that limit may be lifted, as it has been here, by an expression of the "unambiguous intent" of Congress. *Wyoming, supra*, 502 U.S., at 458; *Prudential Ins. Co. v. Benjamin*, 328 U.S. 408, 427–431 (1946). Whether or not the States would be permitted to burden the interstate transport of low level radioactive waste in the absence of Congress' approval, the States can clearly do so *with* Congress' approval, which is what the Act gives them.

The second step, the Secretary's collection of a percentage of the surcharge, is no more than a federal tax on interstate commerce, which petitioners do not claim to be an invalid exercise of either Congress' commerce or taxing power. Cf. *United States v. Sanchez*, 340 U.S. 42, 44–45 (1950); *Steward Machine Co. v. Davis*, 301 U.S. 548, 581–583 (1937).

The third step is a conditional exercise of Congress' authority under the Spending Clause: Congress has placed conditions—the achievement of the milestones—on the receipt of federal funds. Petitioners do not contend that Congress has exceeded its authority in any of the four respects our cases have identified. See generally, *South Dakota v. Dole*, 483 U.S., at 207–208. . . .

Petitioners contend nevertheless that the *form* of these expenditures removes them from the scope of Congress' spending power. . . . Petitioners argue that because the money collected and redisbursed to the States is kept in an account separate from the general treasury, because the Secretary holds the funds only as a trustee, and because the States themselves are largely able to control whether they will pay into the escrow account or receive a share, the Act "in no manner calls for the spending of federal funds." Reply Brief for Petitioner State of New York 6.

The Constitution's grant to Congress of the authority to "pay the Debts and provide for the . . . general Welfare" has never, however, been thought to mandate a particular form of accounting. . . . The Spending Clause has never been construed to deprive Congress of the power to structure federal spending in this manner. . . .

The Act's first set of incentives, in which Congress has conditioned grants to the States upon the States' attainment of a series of milestones, is thus well within the authority of Congress under the Commerce and Spending Clauses. Because the first set of incentives is supported by affirmative constitutional grants of power to Congress, it is not inconsistent with the Tenth Amendment.

In the second set of incentives, Congress has authorized States and regional compacts with disposal sites gradually to increase the cost of access to the sites, and then to deny access altogether, to radioactive waste generated in States that do not meet federal deadlines. As a simple regulation, this provision would be within the power of Congress to authorize the States to discriminate against interstate commerce. See *Northeast Bancorp, Inc. v. Board of Governors, FRS*, 472 U.S. 159, 174–175 (1985). Where federal regulation of private activity is within the scope of the Commerce Clause, we have recognized the ability of Congress to offer States the choice of regulating that activity according to federal standards or having state law pre-empted by federal regulation. See *Hodel v. Virginia Surface Mining & Reclamation Assn., Inc.*, 452 U.S., at 288; *FERC v. Mississippi*, 456 U.S., at 764–765.

This is the choice presented to nonsited States by the Act's second set of incentives: States may either regulate the disposal of radioactive waste according to federal standards by attaining local or regional self-sufficiency, or their residents who produce radioactive waste will be subject to federal regulation authorizing sited States and regions to deny access to their disposal sites. The affected States are not compelled by Congress to regulate, because any burden caused by a State's refusal to regulate will fall on those who generate waste and find no outlet for its disposal, rather than on the State as a sovereign. A State whose citizens do not wish it to attain the Act's milestones may devote its attention and its resources to issues its citizens deem more worthy; the choice remains at all times with the residents of the State, not with Congress. . . .

The Act's second set of incentives thus represents a conditional exercise of Congress' commerce power, along the lines of those we have held to be within Congress' authority. As a result, the second set of incentives does not intrude on the sovereignty reserved to the States by the Tenth Amendment.

The take title provision is of a different character. This third so-called "incentive" offers States, as an alternative to regulating pursuant to Congress' direction, the option of taking title to and possession of the low level radioactive waste generated within their borders and becoming liable for all damages waste generators suffer as a result of the States' failure to do so promptly. In this provision, Congress has crossed the line distinguishing encouragement from coercion. . . .

The take title provision offers state governments a "choice" of either accepting ownership of waste or regulating according to the instructions of Congress. Respondents do not claim that the Constitution would authorize Congress to impose either option as a freestanding requirement. On one hand, the Constitution would not permit Congress simply to transfer radioactive waste from generators to state governments. Such a forced transfer, standing alone, would in principle be no different than a congressionally compelled subsidy from state governments to radioactive waste producers. The same is true of the provision requiring the States to become liable for the generators' damages. Standing alone, this provision would be indistinguishable from an Act of Congress directing the States to assume the liabilities of certain state residents. Either type of federal action would "commandeer" state governments into the service of federal regulatory purposes, and would for this reason be inconsistent with the Constitution's division of authority between federal and state governments. On the other hand, the second alternative held out to state governments—regulating pursuant to Congress' direction—would, standing alone, present a simple command to state governments to implement legislation enacted by Congress. As we have seen, the Constitution does not empower Congress to subject state governments to this type of instruction.

Because an instruction to state governments to take title to waste, standing alone, would be beyond the authority of Congress, and because a direct order to regulate, standing alone, would also be beyond the authority of Congress, it follows that Congress lacks the power to offer the States a choice between the two. Unlike the first two sets of incentives, the take title incentive does not represent the conditional exercise of any congressional power enumerated in the Constitution. In this provision, Congress has not held out the threat of exercising its spending power or its commerce power; it has instead held out the threat, should the States not regulate according to one federal instruction, of simply forcing the States to submit to another federal instruction. A choice between two unconstitutionally coercive regulatory techniques is no choice at all. Either way, "the Act commandeers the legislative processes of the States by directly compelling them to enact and enforce a federal regulatory program," *Hodel v. Virginia Surface Mining & Reclamation Assn., Inc., supra*, 452 U.S., at 288, an outcome that has never been understood to lie within the authority conferred upon Congress by the Constitution.

NOTES AND QUESTIONS

1.   **Incentives to Adopt Legislative Programs.** What methods may Congress use to encourage the states to adopt a legislative program? Why did the *New York* Court argue that these methods maintain state accountability? On what grounds did the Court uphold the first and second sets of incentives?

2.   **"Take Title Provision."** The Low-Level Radioactive Waste Policy Amendments Act of 1985, 42 U.S.C. § 2021b, was based largely on a proposal submitted by the National Governors' Association. *New York*, 505 U.S. at 151. Why did the Court find that the third set of incentives "crossed the line distinguishing encouragement from coercion"? *Id.* at 175. In his dissenting opinion, Justice White argued:

> Curiously absent from the Court's analysis is any effort to place the take title provision within the overall context of the legislation. . . . [T]he 1980 and 1985 statutes were enacted against a backdrop of national concern over the availability of additional low-level radioactive waste disposal facilities. Congress could have pre-empted the field by directly regulating the disposal of this waste pursuant to its powers under the Commerce and Spending Clauses, but instead it unanimously assented to the States' request for congressional ratification of agreements to which they had acceded. *See* 131 Cong. Rec. 35,252 (1985); *id.* at 38,425. As the floor statements of Members of Congress reveal, *see supra*, at 2437, the States wished to take the lead in achieving a solution to this problem and agreed among themselves to the various incentives and penalties implemented by Congress to ensure adherence to the various deadlines and goals. The chief executives of the States proposed this approach, and I am unmoved by the Court's vehemence in taking away Congress' authority to sanction a recalcitrant unsited State now that New York has reaped the benefits of the sited States' concessions.

Id. at 195–96 (White, J., dissenting). Could the "Take Title Provision" be considered coercive? Is the fact that the Act was proposed and formulated by the States relevant?

3.   *Garcia v. San Antonio Metropolitan Transit Authority.* In *Garcia*, 469 U.S. 528 (1985), the Court stated:

> [W]e are convinced that the fundamental limitation that the constitutional scheme imposes on the Commerce Clause to protect the "States as States" is one of process rather than one of result. Any substantive restraint on the exercise of Commerce Clause powers must find its justification in the procedural nature of this basic limitation, and it must be tailored to compensate for possible failings in the national political process rather than to dictate a "sacred province of state autonomy."

Id. at 554. How did the *New York* majority distinguish *Garcia*? Justice White disagreed with that distinction:

The Court's distinction between a federal statute's regulation of States and private parties for general purposes, as opposed to a regulation solely on the activities of States, is unsupported by our recent Tenth Amendment cases. In no case has the Court rested its holding on such a distinction. Moreover, the Court makes no effort to explain why this purported distinction should affect the analysis of Congress' power under general principles of federalism and the Tenth Amendment. . . . An incursion on state sovereignty hardly seems more constitutionally acceptable if the federal statute that "commands" specific action also applies to private parties. The alleged diminution in state authority over its own affairs is not any less because the federal mandate restricts the activities of private parties.

New York, 505 U.S. at 201–02. Do you find this opinion compelling? Could the majority achieve the same result by applying *Garcia*? *See* William A. Hazeltine, New York v. United States: *A New Restriction on Congressional Power Vis-a-Vis the States?*, 55 OHIO ST. L.J. 237, 251 (1994) (arguing that the "[l]ack of congressional accountability is, at least to an extent, a failure of the national political process").

4.   Interstate Compacts. The Low-Level Radioactive Waste Policy Act "authorizes States to 'enter into such [interstate] compacts as may be necessary to provide for the establishment and operation of regional disposal facilities for low-level radioactive waste.'" *New York*, 505 U.S. at 151–52 (quoting 42 U.S.C. § 2021d(a)(2)). Compacts are binding agreements between two or more states authorized by Congress according with the Compact Clause of the Constitution. U.S. CONST. art. I, § 10, cl. 3. How does the *New York* Court's holding affect these compacts among the states? In his dissenting opinion Justice Stevens argued:

Even if § 2021e(d)(2)(C) is "invalidated" insofar as it applies to the State of New York, it remains enforceable against the 44 States that have joined interstate compacts approved by Congress because the compacting States have, in their agreements, embraced that provision and given it independent effect. Congress' consent to the compacts was "granted subject to the provisions of the [Act] . . . and only for so long as the [entities] established in the compact comply with all the provisions of [the] Act." Appalachian States Low-Level Radioactive Waste Compact Consent Act, Pub.L. 100–319, 102 Stat. 471. Thus the compacts incorporated the provisions of the Act, including the take title provision. These compacts, the product of voluntary interstate cooperation, unquestionably survive the "invalidation" of § 2021e(d)(2)(C) as it applies to New York. Congress did not "direc[t]" the States to enter into these compacts and the decision of each compacting State to enter into a compact was not influenced by the existence of the take title provision: Whether a State went its own way or joined a compact, it was still subject to the take title provision.

New York, 505 U.S. at 213 n.3; *see also Petty v. Tennessee-Missouri Bridge Comm'n*, 359 U.S. 275, 281–82 (1959) (upholding provisions of an interstate compact).

5.   *Printz v. United States.* In *Printz*, 521 U.S. 898 (1997), the Court held that a federal statute requiring each state's chief law enforcement officer to conduct background checks on handgun purchasers imposed an unconstitutional obligation on state officers to execute federal law.

> We held in *New York* that Congress cannot compel the States to enact or enforce a federal regulatory program. Today we hold that Congress cannot circumvent that prohibition by conscripting the State's officers directly. The Federal Government may neither issue directives requiring the States to address particular problems, nor command the States' officers, or those of their political subdivisions, to administer or enforce a federal regulatory program. It matters not whether policymaking is involved, and no case-by-case weighing of the burdens or benefits is necessary; such commands are fundamentally incompatible with our constitutional system of dual sovereignty.

Id. at 935. Are there additional difficulties presented by applying the New York principle to executive officers?

Virginia v. Browner

80 F.3d 869 (4th Cir. 1996), *cert. denied*, 519 U.S. 1090 (1997).

■ Before MURNAGHAN and MICHAEL, CIRCUIT JUDGES, and JAMES H. MICHAEL, JR., SENIOR UNITED STATES DISTRICT JUDGE for the Western District of Virginia, sitting by designation.

■ MICHAEL, CIRCUIT JUDGE:

The Commonwealth of Virginia petitions for review of the Environmental Protection Agency's final action disapproving Virginia's proposed program for issuing air pollution permits. Specifically, Virginia challenges EPA's finding that Virginia has failed to comply with Title V of the 1990 Amendments to the Clean Air Act (sometimes "CAA" or the "Act"), CAA §§ 501–507, 42 U.S.C. §§ 7661–7661f, because Virginia's proposal lacks adequate provisions for judicial review of the Commonwealth's permitting decisions. Virginia also challenges the constitutionality of Title V and its sanctions provisions, CAA §§ 179(b) & 502(d), 42 U.S.C. §§ 7509(b) & 7661a(d). According to Virginia, these provisions improperly commandeer the legislative processes of the states, in violation of the Tenth Amendment and the Spending Clause, U.S. Const. art. I § 8, cl. 1. . . .

. . . Title V's key provision, CAA § 502, 42 U.S.C. § 7661a, prohibits major stationary sources of air pollution from operating either without a valid permit or in violation of the terms of a permit. . . . Title V of the Act contemplates that states will administer and enforce the permitting program. . . .

States are directed to submit for EPA approval their own programs for issuing permits. CAA § 502(d)(1), 42 U.S.C. § 7661(a)(d)(1). EPA may not approve a proposed permit program unless it meets certain minimum criteria set out in CAA § 502(b), 42 U.S.C. § 7661a(b). Among other things, states must . . . provide for review in state courts of permitting decisions (§ 502(b)(6)). [Virginia law grants standing to seek judicial review of permitting decisions to "[a]ny owner aggrieved by" such decisions. Va.Code § 10.1–1318(A). This provision satisfies CAA § 502(b)(6)'s requirement that the permit "applicant" be allowed to seek judicial review. But § 502(b)(6) also requires that states grant certain standing rights to members of the public, and Virginia's judicial review provision does not provide for such review.]

If a state fails to submit a permit program, or submits a permit program that EPA disapproves for failure to comply with CAA § 502(b), the state becomes subject to sanctions designed to encourage compliance. CAA § 502(d), 42 U.S.C. § 7661a(d).

One sanction deprives states of certain federal highway funds. CAA § 179(b)(1), 42 U.S.C. § 7509(b)(1). However, the state loses no funds that would be spent in regions that are in "attainment" within the meaning of the Act. CAA § 179(b)(1)(A), 42 U.S.C. § 7509(b)(1)(A). And, even within "nonattainment" areas, funds remain available for highway projects that "resolve a demonstrated safety problem and likely will result in a significant reduction in, or avoidance of, accidents." *Id*. Finally, federal funds may be spent on many other types of transportation projects within nonattainment areas. . . .

A second sanction increases the pollution offset requirements already imposed on private polluters within ozone nonattainment areas. . . .

A third sanction eliminates the state's ability to manage its own pollution control regime. If the state does not gain approval for its permit program, EPA develops and implements its own Title V permitting program within the noncomplying state. CAA § 502(d)(3), 42 U.S.C. § 7661a(d)(3). The state is not required to do anything to assist EPA in this effort; the federal government becomes wholly responsible. . . .

Having determined that EPA had a valid reason to disapprove Virginia's permit program, we now examine whether Title V and its sanctions provisions are constitutional. Virginia claims that Title V and its sanctions provisions are unconstitutional because they impinge upon a fundamental element of state sovereignty, the state's right to articulate its own rules of judicial standing. Even assuming *arguendo* the accuracy of Virginia's assertion that its standing rules are within the core of its sovereignty, we find no constitutional violation because federal law "may, indeed, be designed to induce state action in areas that otherwise would be beyond Congress' regulatory authority." *FERC v. Mississippi*, 456 U.S. 742, 766 (1982). . . .

. . . [W]e find that the CAA does not compel the states to modify their standing rules; it merely induces them to do so. The CAA is constitutional because although its sanctions provisions potentially burden the states, those sanctions amount to inducement rather than "outright coercion." *See New York*, 505 U.S. at 165–67. We examine each sanction separately to explain how we reach this conclusion. *See id.* at 169–71.

Two sources of Congressional power allow use of the highway sanction. Because the elimination of air pollution promotes the general welfare, Congress may tie the award of federal funds to the states' efforts to eliminate air pollution. "The Congress shall have Power to lay and collect Taxes, Duties, Imposts and Excises, to pay the Debts and provide for the common Defence and general Welfare of the United States." U.S. Const. art. I, § 8, cl. 1. Furthermore, the Commerce Clause, U.S. Const. art. I, § 8, cl. 3, gives Congress the power to regulate "activities causing air or water pollution, or other environmental hazards that may have effects in more than one State." *Hodel v. Virginia Surface Mining & Reclamation Ass'n*, 452 U.S. 264, 282 (1981).

Generally, Congress may use the power of the purse to encourage states to enact particular legislation. *New York*, 505 U.S. at 165–67. This power, however, is not limitless. Exercise of the power to the point of "outright coercion" violates the Constitution. *Id.* "[I]n some circumstances the financial inducement offered by Congress might be so coercive as to pass the point at which 'pressure turns into compulsion.' " *South Dakota v. Dole*, 483 U.S. 203, 211 (1987) (quoting *Steward Machine Co. v. Davis*, 301 U.S. 548, 590 (1937)). Also, it has been suggested that federal funds may be subject to conditions "only in ways reasonably related to the purpose for which the funds are expended." *South Dakota*, 483 U.S. at 213 (O'Connor, J., dissenting); see also *New York*, 505 U.S. at 171–73. No court, however, has ever struck down a federal statute on grounds that it exceeded the Spending Power. See *Nevada v. Skinner*, 884 F.2d 445, 448 (9th Cir.1989).

The highway sanction here does not rise to the level of "outright coercion." First, a state does not lose any highway funds that would be spent in areas of the state that are in attainment. CAA § 179(b)(1)(A), 42 U.S.C. § 7509(b)(1)(A). Second, even within nonattainment areas, federal highway funds may be spent on projects designed to promote safety or designed to reduce air pollution. CAA § 179(b)(1), 42 U.S.C. § 7509(b)(1). More severe funding restrictions than those at issue here have been upheld. . . .

Virginia concedes that it is allowed to spend federal money on safety projects, on projects that will reduce pollution, and on projects within areas that are in attainment. The Commonwealth contends, however, that because it is difficult to shift funds from one transportation project to another, these exemptions do not reduce the sanction's coercive effect. According to Virginia, it simply lacks the time to reallocate funds away from highway projects it has already planned for nonattainment areas.

To this argument we can only say that Title V was enacted in 1990, and the states have had more than five years either to comply or to prepare themselves for the consequences of noncompliance.

And contrary to what Virginia claims, the conditions on spending are reasonably related to the goal of reducing air pollution. The CAA as a whole is a comprehensive scheme to cope with the problem of air pollution from all sources. Congress may ensure that funds it allocates are not used to exacerbate the overall problem of air pollution. . . .

We hold that the highway sanction, CAA § 179(b)(1), is a valid exercise of the Spending Power. As a valid exercise of that power, it also comports with the requirements of the Tenth Amendment. *New York*, 505 U.S. at 173–75. . . .

The burden of the offset sanction falls on private parties. The more stringent offset requirements will likely make it more difficult for individual pollution sources (manufacturers, utilities, and the like) to upgrade or modify existing plants and equipment or to open new plants. Thus, although the sanction may burden some Virginia citizens, it does not burden Virginia as a *governmental* unit. For this reason, the sanction does not violate the principles of federalism embodied in the Tenth Amendment. *New York*, 505 U.S. at 174. . . . The offset sanction is constitutional.

The final sanction, federal permit program implementation, CAA § 502(d)(3), 42 U.S.C. § 7661a(d)(3), also is constitutional. The essence of a Tenth Amendment violation is that the state is commanded to regulate. Here, Virginia is not commanded to regulate; the Commonwealth may choose to do nothing and let the federal government promulgate and enforce its own permit program within Virginia. Because "the full regulatory burden will be borne by the Federal Government," the sanction is constitutional. *Hodel*, 452 U.S. at 288. . . .

Because Congress may choose to preempt state law completely, it may also take the less drastic step of allowing the states the ability to avoid preemption by adopting and implementing their own plans that sufficiently address congressional concerns. *Id*. at 290; *Mack*, 66 F.3d at 1029 ("The federal government may offer to preempt regulation in a given area and permit the states to avoid preemption if they regulate in a manner acceptable to Congress."). . . .

Finally, the CAA's sanctions provisions maintain unity between regulation and political accountability. If sanctions are imposed, it will be "the Federal Government that makes the decision in full view of the public, and it will be federal officials that suffer the consequences if the decision turns out to be detrimental or unpopular." *New York*, 505 U.S. at 168. The sanctions provisions are constitutional.

NOTES AND QUESTIONS

1. **Commandeering Legislative Processes.** Why did EPA disapprove Virginia's permit program? What were the consequences of such disapproval? Why did Virginia argue that these sanctions were unconstitutional? Can Congress induce state action in areas that are beyond its authority? Where is the line between incentives and coercion?

2. **Conditions on the Receipt of Federal Funds.** What conditions may Congress attach to the receipt of federal funds? According to the Supreme Court in *New York v. United States*, 505 U.S. 144, 167 (1992), Congress may attach conditions on the receipt of federal funds but such conditions must (among other requirements) "bear some relationship to the purpose of the federal spending." What does "some relationship" mean? Jonathan H. Adler contends:

> The connection between the CAA's purpose and transportation is . . . ambiguous, as states can lose their highway funding for failing to meet any of the CAA's myriad SIP requirements. Nothing in the CAA requires any connection to highways, mobile sources, or even the specific pollutants most associated with vehicular traffic. Failure to adopt a sufficiently rigorous stationary source permit scheme, sufficiently stringent emission regulations on dry cleaners, bakeries and other "area" sources, or even failure to provide adequate citizen suit access to state courts can provide the basis for rejecting an SIP and imposing sanctions.

Jonathan H. Adler, *Judicial Federalism and the Future of Federal Environmental Regulation*, 90 IOWA L. REV. 377, 449–50 (2005). Do you find this view compelling?

3. **State Permit Programs.** Why would Congress prefer to encourage states to enact their own programs instead of preempting state law completely? According to § 502(d)(3) of the CAA, 42 U.S.C. § 7661a(d)(3), if the state does not gain approval for its permit program, EPA must promulgate, administer, and enforce a program for that state. What kind of problems would EPA encounter in this endeavor?

4. **The Affordable Care Act, *NFIB v. Sebelius*, and Environmental Regulation.** The Affordable Care Act significantly expanded Medicaid, the public health insurance program that is state-administered but largely federally-funded. The Social Security Act contains a provision that allows the federal government to withhold Medicaid funds from states that fail to comply with any Medicaid requirement. In *National Federation of Independent Business v. Sebelius*, 567 U.S. 519 (2012), 26 states argued that requiring them to expand Medicaid, or risk losing federal funds that amounted to "over 20 percent of the average State's total budget," was unduly coercive. *Id.* at 581. According to the plurality opinion,

> We have upheld Congress's authority to condition the receipt of funds on the States' complying with restrictions on the use of those funds, because that is the means by which Congress ensures that the funds are spent according to its view of the "general Welfare." Conditions that do not here govern the use of the funds, however,

cannot be justified on that basis. When, for example, such conditions take the form of threats to terminate other significant independent grants, the conditions are properly viewed as a means of pressuring the States to accept policy changes.

Id. at 580. The plurality found that the expansion of Medicaid was so dramatic that it was a "shift in kind, not merely degree." *Id.* at 583. The threat of withdrawal of funding for Medicaid if a state refused to expand the program as required, therefore amounted to conditioning receipt of a grant upon conditions unrelated to the grant. That, combined with the entrenched nature of the existing Medicaid program and the value of the grants involved, rendered the scheme unduly coercive. *Id.* at 580.

How might the decision in *NFIB v. Sebelius* affect the federal government's ability to regulate environmental harm? Section 179 of the CAA requires that where states fail to adequately submit or implement a plan to regulate air pollution, the Department of Transport withhold funding for federal highway projects. On what basis might § 179 be in violation of the Spending Clause? How is it different to the Medicaid expansion considered in *NFIB v. Sebelius*? How might the decision in *NFIB v. Sebelius* alter the federal relationship in the environmental regulation context? *See* Erin Ryan, *The Spending Power and Environmental Law after Sebelius*, 85 U. COLO. L. REV. 1003 (2014).

iii. ELEVENTH AMENDMENT

Burnette v. Carothers

192 F.3d 52 (2d Cir. 1999), *cert. denied*, 531 U.S. 1052 (2000).

■ Before WINTER, CHIEF JUDGE, and NEWMAN and SOTOMAYOR, CIRCUIT JUDGES.

■ WINTER, CHIEF JUDGE:

This is an appeal from the dismissal of a citizen enforcement action brought pursuant to the citizen suit provisions of the Clean Water Act ("CWA"), 33 U.S.C. § 1365, the Resource Conservation and Recovery Act ("RCRA"), 42 U.S.C. § 6972, and the Comprehensive Environmental Response, Compensation and Liability Act ("CERCLA"), 42 U.S.C. § 9659. . . .

Appellants, Marie G. Burnette and Ralph G. Burnette, Jr. . . . are homeowners in the Rye Hill section of Somers, Connecticut. They filed this action against various state officers in their official capacities, claiming that hazardous substances had emanated, and continued to emanate, from the Connecticut Correctional Institute ("CCI"), a prison located north of Rye Hill and operated by the Connecticut Department of Corrections. Appellants alleged that these toxic substances had polluted and were continuing to pollute their on-site water wells. They sought injunctive and monetary relief. In addition, they sought reimbursement from defendants for response costs which were alleged to have been incurred as a result of "a release or threatened release of hazardous substances" from CCI. *See* 42 U.S.C. § 9607(a)(4)(B). The complaint also included claims under CERCLA for a declaratory judgment, future response costs, and contribution, pursuant to 42 U.S.C. § 9613(f)(1).

. . . The district court dismissed all claims, holding that the State and its agents were immune from suit under the Eleventh Amendment. In addition, the court granted appellees' motion for summary judgment, holding that appellants were not entitled to response costs from the State or to potential contribution costs because such recovery would violate the State's sovereign immunity. This appeal followed.

. . . The Eleventh Amendment provides that: "The Judicial power of the United States shall not be construed to extend to any suit in law or equity, commenced or prosecuted against one of the United States by Citizens of another State, or by Citizens or Subjects of any Foreign State." U.S. CONST. amend. XI. "While the Amendment by its terms does not bar suits against a State by its own citizens, [the Supreme] Court has consistently held that an unconsenting State is immune from suits brought in federal courts by her own citizens as well as by citizens of another State." *Edelman v. Jordan*, 415 U.S. 651, 662–63 (1974). State immunity extends to state agencies and to state officers who act on behalf of the state. *See Puerto Rico Aqueduct & Sewer Auth. v. Metcalf & Eddy, Inc.*, 506 U.S. 139, 142–47 (1993). Thus, when the state is the real party in interest, the Eleventh Amendment generally bars federal court jurisdiction over an action against a state official acting in his or her official capacity. *See Pennhurst State School & Hosp. v. Halderman*, 465 U.S. 89, 101–02 (1984).

In certain circumstances, however, Congress may abrogate the states' constitutionally secured immunity from suit in federal court. To do so, Congress must make " 'its intention unmistakably clear in the language of the statute.' " *Dellmuth v. Muth*, 491 U.S. 223, 228 (1989) (quoting *Atascadero State Hosp. v. Scanlon*, 473 U.S. 234, 242 (1985)). "A general authorization for suit in federal court is not the kind of unequivocal statutory language sufficient to abrogate the Eleventh Amendment. When Congress chooses to subject the States to federal jurisdiction, it must do so specifically." *Atascadero*, 473 U.S. at 246.

The CWA, RCRA, and CERCLA contain substantially identical provisions permitting citizens to sue as private attorneys general in circumstances where government authorities have, after notice, failed to take steps to remedy particular environmental harms. These provisions state that "any citizen may commence a civil action on his own behalf— (1) against any person (including (i) the United States, and (ii) any other governmental instrumentality or agency *to the extent permitted by the eleventh amendment to the Constitution*) who is alleged to be in violation of [the Act]." 33 U.S.C. § 1365(a)(1) (emphasis added); *see also* 42 U.S.C. § 6972; 42 U.S.C. § 9659. These provisions do not unequivocally express Congress's intent to abrogate sovereign immunity and subject states to suit. Far from evidencing a Congressional intent to do away with sovereign immunity, these provisions are expressly limited by the Eleventh Amendment. *See Natural Resources Defense Council v. California Dep't of Transp.*, 96 F.3d 420, 423 (9th Cir.1996) (district court properly dismissed all claims under CWA against state agency on Eleventh Amendment immunity ground). . . . The district court was, therefore, correct in holding that these citizen suit provisions do not abrogate Connecticut's sovereign immunity and that the state defendants are therefore entitled to immunity from suit in federal court.

Appellants assert, however, that even if a citizen suit would ordinarily be barred under the Eleventh Amendment, immunity does not apply here because the complaint is in the nature of a *qui tam* action and the United States is the real party in interest. We disagree. In *Connecticut Action Now, Inc. v. Roberts Plating Co.*, 457 F.2d 81 (2d Cir.1972), we held that "there is no common law right to maintain a *qui tam* action; authority must always be found in legislation. . . . [T]he terms and structure of the particular statute are decisive." *Id.* at 84. The statutes at issue do not grant citizens the right to sue on behalf of the United States nor do they establish a formula for recovering civil penalties. To the contrary, the citizen suit provisions authorize "any citizen [to] commence a civil action on his *own* behalf." 33 U.S.C. § 1365(a) (emphasis added); *see also* 42 U.S.C. § 6972; 42 U.S.C. § 9659. The United States is not, therefore, the real party in interest here.

Appellants suggest on appeal that some of their claims remain viable because they fit within the exception to Eleventh Amendment immunity established by *Ex parte Young*, 209 U.S. 123 (1908) (holding that suits against state officers, rather than against State itself, are permitted when seeking prospective relief). . . . However, appellants failed to raise this issue in the district court, even though they were then represented by counsel. Perceiving that no miscarriage of justice will result, we hold that their claim under *Ex parte Young* has been waived. *See Singleton v. Wulff*, 428 U.S. 106, 120–21 (1976). . . .

We turn therefore to their remaining claim for response costs under CERCLA Section 107(a), 42 U.S.C. § 9607(a). In *Seminole Tribe v. Florida*, 517 U.S. 44, 55 (1996), the Supreme Court held that Congress may abrogate the states' sovereign immunity if two conditions are met: (i) Congress "unequivocally expresse[d] its intent to abrogate the immunity" and (ii) Congress acted "pursuant to a valid exercise of power." (alteration in original) (internal quotation marks omitted). In the instant case, the first requirement has been satisfied. In *Pennsylvania v. Union Gas Co.*, the Supreme Court held that the provisions of CERCLA unmistakably express Congress's intent to divest the states of their Eleventh Amendment immunity. *See Union Gas*, 491 U.S. 1, 8 (1989), *overruled on other grounds by Seminole*, 517 U.S. 44. The sole remaining question is, therefore, whether Congress enacted CERCLA pursuant to a constitutional provision granting Congress the power to abrogate. We hold that it did not.

The Supreme Court in *Seminole* held that Congress could abrogate the states' Eleventh Amendment immunity only when acting under the power vested in it by Section 5 of the Fourteenth Amendment. *See* 517 U.S. at 59, 65–66. CERCLA, however, was enacted pursuant to the Commerce Clause, and any provision in it that makes a state liable to private parties is accordingly unenforceable. See *Seminole*, 517 U.S. at 62 (implicitly recognizing that CERCLA was enacted pursuant to Commerce Clause); *Union Gas*, 491 U.S. at 19–23 (CERCLA enacted pursuant to Commerce Clause). . . .

NOTES AND QUESTIONS

1. **State Violation of Federal Environmental Statutes.** Why did the appellants bring a citizen enforcement action against Connecticut's officials? What did they seek? On what grounds did the district court dismiss their claim? What did the appellants argue on appeal?

2. **State Immunity.** What is the extent of the immunity provided by the Eleventh Amendment? Could EPA bring a suit against the state? In *Alden v. Maine*, 527 U.S. 706 (1999), the Court explained:

> In ratifying the Constitution, the States consented to suits brought by other States or by the Federal Government. *Principality of Monaco* [*v. Mississippi, 292 U.S. 313,*] 328–329 [(1934)] (collecting cases). A suit which is commenced and prosecuted against a State in the name of the United States by those who are entrusted with the constitutional duty to "take Care that the Laws be faithfully executed," U.S. CONST. art. II, § 3, differs in kind from the suit of an individual: While the Constitution contemplates suits among the members of the federal system as an alternative to extralegal measures, the fear of private suits against nonconsenting States was the central reason given by the Founders who chose to preserve the States' sovereign immunity. Suits brought by the United States itself require the exercise of political responsibility for each suit prosecuted against a State, a control which is absent from a broad delegation to private persons to sue nonconsenting States.

Id. at 755–56. Does the states' immunity extend to formal adjudications before independent agencies? *See Fed. Maritime Comm'n v. S.C. State Ports Auth.*, 535 U.S. 743, 747 (2002) (holding that state sovereign immunity precludes the Federal Maritime Commission from adjudicating a private party's complaint against a state-run port). Does states' immunity under the Eleventh Amendment apply to municipalities and local governments? *See Alden*, 527 U.S. at 756 (holding that "[t]he immunity does not extend to suits prosecuted against a municipal corporation or other governmental entity which is not an arm of the State"). What is the impact of states' immunity on government accountability?

3. Suits Brought in State Courts and the Eleventh Amendment.
Can states be sued in state courts for violations of a federal law? In *Alden*,
petitioners sued the State of Maine in a state court, alleging a violation of
the Fair Labor Standard Act of 1938 (FLSA), 29 U.S.C. § 201 *et seq.* This act
authorizes private actions against States in their own courts without regard
to State consent. 29 U.S.C. §§ 216(b), 203(x). The Supreme Court held that
state sovereign immunity bars lawsuits against the states in their own
courts. *Alden*, 527 U.S. at 754. In so holding, the Court reasoned:

> [S]overeign immunity derives not from the Eleventh Amendment
> but from the structure of the original Constitution itself. . . . The
> Eleventh Amendment confirmed, rather than established,
> sovereign immunity as a constitutional principle; it follows that the
> scope of the States' immunity from suit is demarcated not by the
> text of the Amendment alone but by fundamental postulates
> implicit in the constitutional design. . . .
>
> While the constitutional principle of sovereign immunity does pose
> a bar to federal jurisdiction over suits against nonconsenting
> States, *see, e.g.*, *Principality of Monaco*, 292 U.S., at 322–323, this
> is not the only structural basis of sovereign immunity implicit in
> the constitutional design. Rather, "[t]here is also the postulate that
> States of the Union, still possessing attributes of sovereignty, shall
> be immune from suits, without their consent, save where there has
> been 'a surrender of this immunity in the plan of the convention.' "
> *Ibid.* (quoting The Federalist No. 81). . . .

Id. at 728–30. Consider this limit in conjunction with the other limits on
federal impositions on state government expounded in *New York*, *supra*, and
Printz, *supra*.

4. Abrogation of State Immunity. Can Congress abrogate the states'
sovereign immunity? If so, in what way? Why did the *Burnette* court find that
the citizen suit provisions did not abrogate Connecticut's sovereign
immunity? What did the appellants argue? Why did the court find an
unequivocal congressional intent to abrogate the immunity in CERCLA
§ 107(a), 42 U.S.C. § 9607(a)? What is the difference between the citizen suit
provisions and § 107(a)? Can states waive their immunity? Under what
circumstances? *See, e.g.*, *Lapides v. Bd. of Regents of the Univ. Sys. of Ga.*,
535 U.S. 613, 618–19 (2002) (holding that "[a] State waives [its] immunity
when it removes a case from state court to federal court"); *Gunter v. Atl.
Coast Line R. Co.*, 200 U.S. 273, 284 (1906) ("[W]here a State voluntarily
becomes a party to a cause and submits its rights for judicial determination,
it will be bound thereby and cannot escape the result of its own voluntary
act by invoking the prohibitions of the Eleventh Amendment."), *cited by
Lapides*, 535 U.S. at 619.

5. "A Valid Exercise of Power." According to the *Burnette* court,
"Congress may abrogate the states' sovereign immunity if two conditions are
met: (i) Congress 'unequivocally expresse[d] its intent to abrogate the
immunity' and (ii) Congress acted 'pursuant to a valid exercise of power.' "
Burnette, 192 F.3d at 58. What does "a valid exercise of power" mean? Is it

relevant whether the plaintiff seeks prospective injunctive relief rather than retroactive monetary relief? *See Seminole Tribe v. Florida*, 517 U.S. at 58 (finding that "the type of relief sought is irrelevant to whether Congress has power to abrogate States' immunity."). Under what constitutional provision may Congress abrogate states' immunity? In *Fitzpatrick v. Bitzer*, 427 U.S. 445 (1976), the Supreme Court held that "Congress may, in determining what is 'appropriate legislation' for the purpose of enforcing the provisions of the Fourteenth Amendment, provide for private suits against States or state officials which are constitutionally impermissible in other contexts." *Id.* at 456. However, during the last decade, the Supreme Court has narrowed the congressional authority under § 5 of the Fourteenth Amendment. *See* Jesse H. Choper & John C. Yoo, *Who's Afraid of the Eleventh Amendment? The Limited Impact of the Court's Sovereign Immunity Rulings*, 106 COLUM. L. REV. 213, 220 (2006). According to the Court, Congress cannot use this section as a subterfuge to work a "substantive change in the governing law." *Id.* (quoting *City of Boerne v. Flores*, 521 U.S. 507, 519 (1997)). To exercise its remedial power, Congress must show a history and pattern of constitutional violations, and the regulation must be congruent and proportional to the prevention and remedying of a constitutional wrong. *Id.* at 239–40.

6.   Suits Against State Officers: *Ex Parte Young*. In *Ex parte Young*, 209 U.S. 123 (1908), the Supreme Court recognized an exception to states' sovereign immunity. The Court held that "the Eleventh Amendment does not bar suits seeking prospective relief against state officials acting in violation of federal law because such action is not considered an action of the state." *Burnette*, 192 F.3d at 57 n.3 (citing *Ex parte Young*). Is it possible to request monetary relief against a state official? *See Alden, supra*, 527 U.S. at 757 ("Even a suit for money damages may be prosecuted against a state officer in his individual capacity for unconstitutional or wrongful conduct fairly attributable to the officer himself, so long as the relief is sought not from the state treasury but from the officer personally."); *see also Edelman v. Jordan*, 415 U.S. 651, 668 (1974) (holding that to order state officials to release benefits wrongfully withheld is in practical effect indistinguishable from an award of damages against the State since it will almost certainly be paid from state funds). For a discussion of suits against state officers, see John C. Jeffries, Jr., *In Praise of the Eleventh Amendment and Section 1983*, 84 VA. L. REV. 47 (1998); and Henry Paul Monaghan, *The Sovereign Immunity "Exception,"* 110 HARV. L. REV. 102 (1996).

7.   Eleventh Amendment and Citizen Suits. In *Burnette v. Carothers*, the appellants presented two claims: first, they sought injunctive and monetary relief under the citizen suit provisions of the CWA, RCRA, and CERCLA; and second, they also sought reimbursement for response costs that had been incurred as a result of a release of hazardous substances, and a declaratory judgment for future response costs and contribution under CERCLA. *See Burnette*, 192 F.3d at 55–56. Regarding their first claim, appellants argued that the action was not barred by the Eleventh Amendment, since the United States was the real party in interest:

When the US attorney commences a civil action, even against a State, he or she uses their own name, title and signature. . . . When fines are levied, the US attorney does not get the money, the United States Government, as the real party in interest, gets the money. No Eleventh Amendment bar is permitted because it is the United States not the person of the US attorney who is pursuing the civil action and seeking injunctive relief. Like the US attorney, Marie and Ralph Burnette are merely acting on behalf of United States and the manifest intent of the Congress to ensure the enforcement of the law as specifically provided by 42 USC § 6972. Neither a US attorney nor the Burnettes get any proceeds from any civil penalties—they all go to the Treasury of the United States. Had the Administrator of the EPA or a US attorney acted to enforce the law, there would have been no need or basis for the plaintiff-appellants to act to protect the interests of the United States.

Brief of Plaintiff-Appellants, 20–22, *Burnette v. Carothers*, 192 F.3d 52 (2d Cir. 1999) (No. 98–7835). On what grounds did the Second Circuit reject this argument?

8.   **Eleventh Amendment and Citizen Suits, Continued.** How does the Eleventh Amendment affect citizen suits? In evaluating the citizen suit provisions of environmental statutes, lower courts have found an implicit authorization to sue under *Ex parte Young*. In *NRDC v. California Department of Transportation*, 96 F.3d 420 (9th Cir. 1996), the Ninth Circuit explained:

When Congress enacted the Clean Water Act citizen suit provision, it specified that it was legislating to the extent permitted by the Eleventh Amendment. Congress intended to encourage and assist the public to participate in enforcing the standards promulgated to reduce water pollution. *See* 33 U.S.C. § 1251(e). To further that goal, Congress enacted the citizen suit provision so that "a citizen enforcement action might be brought against an individual or a government agency." S.Rep. No. 414, 92d Cong., 2d Sess. (1972). It would seem reasonable, then, that Congress implicitly intended to authorize citizens to bring *Ex parte Young* suits against state officials with the responsibility to comply with clean water standards and permits. Therefore, we find that the district court did not err when it refused to dismiss the plaintiffs' suit against [California Department of Transportation's Director].

NRDC, 96 F.3d at 424; *see also Strahan v. Coxe*, 127 F.3d 155 (1st Cir. 1997); *Cox v. City of Dallas*, 256 F.3d 281 (5th Cir. 2001); *Clean Air Council v. Mallory*, 226 F. Supp. 2d 705 (E.D. Pa. 2002). How does this holding affect the scope of the relief that plaintiff can seek under the citizen suit provision? What happens if the plaintiff is unable to identify a specific state official responsible for the violation of the act? *See Mich. Peat v. EPA*, 175 F.3d 422, 429 (6th Cir. 1999) (holding that Michigan Peat may not sue the Director of the Michigan Department of Environmental Quality under the doctrine of *Ex parte Young* since it failed to allege that the Director had individually taken actions that constituted continuing violations of federal law); *see also*

Sarah C. Rispin, *Cooperative Federalism and Constructive Waiver of State Sovereign Immunity*, 70 U. CHI. L. REV. 1639 (2003).

B. LIMITATIONS ON STATE POWER

The state power to enact environmental regulation is limited by two constitutional provisions: the Supremacy Clause and the Dormant Commerce Clause. *See* U.S. CONST. art. VI, cl. 2 ("This Constitution, and the Laws of the United States which shall be made in Pursuance thereof . . . shall be the supreme Law of the Land; and the Judges in every State shall be bound thereby, any Thing in the Constitution or Laws of any State to the Contrary notwithstanding."); U.S. CONST. art. I, § 8, cl. 3 (giving Congress the power "[t]o regulate Commerce with foreign Nations, and among the several States, and with the Indian Tribes"). According to the Supreme Court's jurisprudence, there are three ways in which federal law may preempt state law under the Supremacy Clause. *See Michigan Canners & Freezers Ass'n, Inc. v. Agricultural Mktg. & Bargaining Bd.*, 467 U.S. 461, 469 (1984).

First, a federal statute may explicitly establish the extent to which it intends to preempt state law. *Id.* Environmental statutes usually preempt less stringent state standards but allow states to enact more stringent ones. *See, e.g.*, 42 U.S.C. § 7416 (CAA); 33 U.S.C. § 1370 (CWA). For example, the Solid Waste Disposal Act establishes that

> no State or political subdivision may impose any requirements less stringent than those authorized under this subchapter respecting the same matter as governed by such regulations. . . . Nothing in this chapter shall be construed to prohibit any State or political subdivision thereof from imposing any requirements . . . which are more stringent than those imposed by such regulations.

42 U.S.C. § 6929. In other cases, however, the federal statutes preempt both more stringent and less stringent standards. *See, e.g.*, Toxic Substances Control Act, 15 U.S.C. § 2617; Federal Insecticide, Fungicide, and Rodenticide Act, 7 U.S.C. § 136v. For example, the CAA prohibits states from enacting any regulations with respect to emissions from new motor vehicles, as is discussed in detail in Chapter V. *See* 42 U.S.C. § 7543(a). Congress enacted this provision to preserve the economies of scale inherent in the uniform national production of automobiles. However, given California's pollution problems and regulatory regime in this field, Congress allowed this state to apply for a preemption waiver. *See* 42 U.S.C. § 7543(b)(1).

Second, "in the absence of express preemptive language, Congress may indicate an intent to occupy an entire field of regulation." *Mich. Canners & Freezers Ass'n*, 467 U.S. at 469. For instance, in *Jersey Central Power & Light Co. v. Township of Lacey*, 772 F.2d 1103 (3d Cir. 1985), an electric utility brought an action challenging the constitutionality of a township ordinance that regulates the importation of nuclear waste. The Third Circuit found that the township ordinance was preempted by the Atomic Energy Act of 1954 (AEA) and the Hazardous Materials Transportation Act:

> Inasmuch as Congress has specifically established this pervasive scheme of federal regulation . . . , and inasmuch as the legislative history of the AEA and the regulations implementing it establish beyond dispute that it is congressional intent that federal law should regulate the radiological safety aspects of the nuclear power industry . . . we find that the ordinances under review are unconstitutional.

Jersey Central Power & Light Co., 772 F.2d at 1112.

Finally, "if Congress has not displaced state regulation entirely, it may nonetheless preempt state law to the extent that the state law actually conflicts with federal law." *Mich. Canners & Freezers Ass'n*, 467 U.S. at 469. This may happen "where compliance with both federal and state regulations is a physical impossibility, or where the state law stands as an obstacle to the accomplishment and execution of the full purposes and objectives of Congress." *Ray v. Atl. Richfield Co.*, 435 U.S. 151, 158 (1978) (internal citations omitted). For instance, in *ENSCO, Inc. v. Dumas*, 807 F.2d 743 (8th Cir. 1986), a county enacted an ordinance prohibiting the storage, treatment or disposal of "acute hazardous waste" within its boundaries. *See id.* at 744. The court found that, even though the Resource Conservation and Recovery Act (RCRA) allows states and their political subdivisions to enact more stringent regulations, "state and local enactments are nullified to the extent they actually conflict with federal law." *Id.* at 745. According to the court, such a "conflict exists when the local enactment 'stands as an obstacle to the accomplishment and execution of the full purpose and objectives of Congress.'" *Id.* (quoting *Hillsborough County v. Automated Med. Labs.*, 471 U.S. 707 (1985)). The court reasoned:

> The conflict between Ordinance No. 171 and the purposes and objectives of the RCRA is clear. The RCRA emphasizes the need for safe disposal and treatment of hazardous waste and grants to the EPA the authority to develop and detail appropriate waste procedures and to outlaw less healthful practices. Ordinance No. 171, however, ignores that [EPA regulations governing incineration] do exist, and through its ban on storage, treatment, and disposal in essence mandates that these wastes in Union County will not be handled in the manner deemed safest by Congress and the EPA.

ENSCO, Inc., 807 F.2d at 745; *see also Geier v. Am. Honda Motor Co.*, 529 U.S. 861 (2000).

Even in the absence of federal regulation, state legislation may be unconstitutional under the Dormant Commerce Clause. Indeed, even though article I, § 8, cl. 3 of the Constitution provides only that "[t]he Congress shall have Power . . . to regulate Commerce . . . among the several states," the Supreme Court has interpreted this clause as an implicit restraint on the States authority to regulate interstate commerce. *Id.*; *see United Haulers Ass'n, Inc. v. Oneida-Herkimer Solid Waste Mgmt. Auth.*, 550 U.S. 330, 338–39 (2007). The Court explained:

> This principle that our economic unit is the Nation, which alone has the gamut of powers necessary to control of the economy, including the vital power of erecting customs barriers against foreign competition, has as its corollary that the states are not separable economic units. . . . [W]hat is ultimate is the principle that one state in its dealings with another may not place itself in a position of economic isolation.

C & A Carbone, Inc. v. Town of Clarkstown, N.Y., 511 U.S. 383, 401 (1994) (O'Connor, J., concurring) (quoting *H.P. Hood & Sons, Inc. v. Du Mond*, 336 U.S. 525, 537–38 (1949)).

The Dormant Commerce Clause "prohibits economic protectionism—that is, regulatory measures designed to benefit in-state economic interests by burdening out-of-state competitors." *Wyoming v. Oklahoma*, 502 U.S. 437, 454 (1992) (citations omitted). When a state statute or regulation clearly discriminates against interstate commerce, it will be struck down, unless the discrimination is demonstrably justified by a valid factor unrelated to economic protectionism. Indeed, when the state statute amounts to simple economic protectionism, a "virtually per se rule of invalidity" has applied. *Id.* Moreover, even when a state statute does not directly discriminate against out-of-state competitors, it may violate the Dormant Commerce Clause if it has indirect effects on interstate commerce and the burden on commerce exceeds the in-state benefits gained by the regulation. *See id.* at 455 n.12. The following case discusses whether a New Jersey Law banning the importation of waste is inconsistent with the Dormant Commerce Clause.

Philadelphia v. New Jersey
437 U.S. 617 (1978).

■ JUSTICE STEWART delivered the opinion of the Court:

A New Jersey law [ch. 363] prohibits the importation of most "solid or liquid waste which originated or was collected outside the territorial limits of the State. . . ." In this case we are required to decide whether this statutory prohibition violates the Commerce Clause of the United States Constitution. . . .

Immediately affected by these developments were the operators of private landfills in New Jersey, and several cities in other States that had agreements with these operators for waste disposal. They brought suit against New Jersey and its Department of Environmental Protection in state court, attacking the statute and regulations on a number of state and federal grounds. In an oral opinion granting the plaintiffs' motion for summary judgment, the trial court declared the law unconstitutional because it discriminated against interstate commerce. The New Jersey Supreme Court consolidated this case with another reaching the same conclusion, *Hackensack Meadowlands Development Comm'n v. Municipal Sanitary Landfill Auth.,* 127 N.J. Super. 160, and reversed, 68 N.J. 451. It found that ch. 363 advanced vital health and environmental objectives with no economic discrimination against, and with little burden upon, interstate commerce, and that the law was therefore permissible under the Commerce Clause of the Constitution. . . .

. . . The dispositive question . . . is whether the law is constitutionally permissible in light of the Commerce Clause of the Constitution.

Before it addressed the merits of the appellants' claim, the New Jersey Supreme Court questioned whether the interstate movement of those wastes banned by ch. 363 is "commerce" at all within the meaning of the Commerce Clause. . . .

The state court expressed the view that there may be two definitions of "commerce" for constitutional purposes. When relied on "to support some exertion of federal control or regulation," the Commerce Clause permits "a very sweeping concept" of commerce. 68 N.J., at 469, 348 A.2d, at 514. But when relied on "to strike down or restrict state legislation," that Clause and the term "commerce" have a "much more confined . . . reach." *Ibid.*

The state court reached this conclusion in an attempt to reconcile modern Commerce Clause concepts with several old cases of this Court holding that States can prohibit the importation of some objects because they "are not legitimate subjects of trade and commerce." *Bowman v. Chicago & Northwestern R. Co.,* 125 U.S. 465. These articles include items "which, on account of their existing condition, would bring in and spread disease, pestilence, and death, such as rags or other substances infected with the germs of yellow fever or the virus of small-pox, or cattle or meat or other provisions that are diseased or decayed, or otherwise, from their condition and quality, unfit for human use or consumption." *Ibid. See also Baldwin v. G. A. F. Seelig, Inc.,* 294 U.S. 511, 525 and cases cited therein. The state court found that ch. 363 . . . banned only "those wastes which can[not] be put to effective use," and therefore those wastes were not commerce at all, unless "the mere transportation and disposal of valueless waste between states constitutes interstate commerce within the meaning of the constitutional provision." 68 N.J., at 468.

We think the state court misread our cases, and thus erred in assuming that they require a two-tiered definition of commerce. In saying that innately harmful articles "are not legitimate subjects of trade and commerce," the *Bowman* Court was stating its conclusion, not the starting point of its reasoning. All objects of interstate trade merit Commerce Clause protection; none is excluded by definition at the outset.

In *Bowman* and similar cases, the Court held simply that because the articles' worth in interstate commerce was far outweighed by the dangers inhering in their very movement, States could prohibit their transportation across state lines. Hence, we reject the state court's suggestion that the banning of "valueless" out-of-state wastes by ch. 363 implicates no constitutional protection. Just as Congress has power to regulate the interstate movement of these wastes, States are not free from constitutional scrutiny when they restrict that movement. Cf. *Hughes v. Alexandria Scrap Corp.*, 426 U.S. 794, 802–814; *Meat Drivers v. United States*, 371 U.S. 94.

Although the Constitution gives Congress the power to regulate commerce among the States, many subjects of potential federal regulation under that power inevitably escape congressional attention "because of their local character and their number and diversity." *South Carolina State Highway Dept. v. Barnwell Bros., Inc.*, 303 U.S. 177. In the absence of federal legislation, these subjects are open to control by the States so long as they act within the restraints imposed by the Commerce Clause itself. See *Raymond Motor Transportation, Inc. v. Rice*, 434 U.S. 429, 440. The bounds of these restraints appear nowhere in the words of the Commerce Clause, but have emerged gradually in the decisions of this Court giving effect to its basic purpose . . . :

> "This principle that our economic unit is the Nation, which alone has the gamut of powers necessary to control of the economy, including the vital power of erecting customs barriers against foreign competition, has as its corollary that the states are not separable economic units. As the Court said in *Baldwin v. Seelig*, 294 U.S. 511, 527, 'what is ultimate is the principle that one state in its dealings with another may not place itself in a position of economic isolation.' "

[*H. P. Hood & Sons, Inc. v. Du Mond*, 336 U.S. 525, 537–38.] The opinions of the Court through the years have reflected an alertness to the evils of "economic isolation" and protectionism, while at the same time recognizing that incidental burdens on interstate commerce may be unavoidable when a State legislates to safeguard the health and safety of its people. Thus, where simple economic protectionism is effected by state legislation, a virtually *per se* rule of invalidity has been erected. . . . But where other legislative objectives are credibly advanced and there is no patent discrimination against interstate trade, the Court has adopted a much more flexible approach, the general contours of which were outlined in *Pike v. Bruce Church, Inc.*:

> "Where the statute regulates evenhandedly to effectuate a legitimate local public interest, and its effects on interstate commerce are only incidental, it will be upheld unless the burden imposed on such commerce is clearly excessive in relation to the putative local benefits. . . . If a legitimate local purpose is found, then the question becomes one of degree. And

the extent of the burden that will be tolerated will of course depend on the nature of the local interest involved, and on whether it could be promoted as well with a lesser impact on interstate activities."

397 U.S. 137. . . .

The crucial inquiry, therefore, must be directed to determining whether ch. 363 is basically a protectionist measure, or whether it can fairly be viewed as a law directed to legitimate local concerns, with effects upon interstate commerce that are only incidental.

. . . This dispute about ultimate legislative purpose need not be resolved, because its resolution would not be relevant to the constitutional issue to be decided in this case. Contrary to the evident assumption of the state court and the parties, the evil of protectionism can reside in legislative means as well as legislative ends. Thus, it does not matter whether the ultimate aim of ch. 363 is to reduce the waste disposal costs of New Jersey residents or to save remaining open lands from pollution, for we assume New Jersey has every right to protect its residents' pocketbooks as well as their environment. And it may be assumed as well that New Jersey may pursue those ends by slowing the flow of *all* waste into the State's remaining landfills, even though interstate commerce may incidentally be affected. But whatever New Jersey's ultimate purpose, it may not be accomplished by discriminating against articles of commerce coming from outside the State unless there is some reason, apart from their origin, to treat them differently. Both on its face and in its plain effect, ch. 363 violates this principle of nondiscrimination. . . .

. . . On its face, it imposes on out-of-state commercial interests the full burden of conserving the State's remaining landfill space. It is true that in our previous cases the scarce natural resource was itself the article of commerce, whereas here the scarce resource and the article of commerce are distinct. But that difference is without consequence. In both instances, the State has overtly moved to slow or freeze the flow of commerce for protectionist reasons. It does not matter that the State has shut the article of commerce inside the State in one case and outside the State in the other. What is crucial is the attempt by one State to isolate itself from a problem common to many by erecting a barrier against the movement of interstate trade.

The appellees argue that not all laws which facially discriminate against out-of-state commerce are forbidden protectionist regulations. In particular, they point to quarantine laws, which this Court has repeatedly upheld even though they appear to single out interstate commerce for special treatment. See *Baldwin v. G. A. F. Seelig, Inc.*, *supra*, 294 U.S. at 525; *Bowman v. Chicago & Northwestern R. Co.*, 125 U.S., at 489. In the appellees' view, ch. 363 is analogous to such health-protective measures, since it reduces the exposure of New Jersey residents to the allegedly harmful effects of landfill sites.

It is true that certain quarantine laws have not been considered forbidden protectionist measures, even though they were directed against out-of-state commerce. See *Asbell v. Kansas*, 209 U.S. 251; *Reid v. Colorado*, 187 U.S. 137; *Bowman v. Chicago & Northwestern R. Co.*, 125 U.S., at 489. But those quarantine laws banned the importation of articles such as diseased livestock that required destruction as soon as possible because their very movement risked contagion and other evils. Those laws thus did not discriminate against interstate commerce as such, but simply prevented traffic in noxious articles, whatever their origin.

The New Jersey statute is not such a quarantine law. There has been no claim here that the very movement of waste into or through New Jersey endangers health, or that waste must be disposed of as soon and as close to its point of generation as possible. The harms caused by waste are said to arise after its disposal in landfill sites, and at that point, as New Jersey concedes, there is no basis to distinguish out-of-state waste from domestic waste. If one is inherently harmful, so is the other. Yet New Jersey has banned the former while leaving its landfill sites open to the latter. The New Jersey law blocks the importation of waste in an obvious effort to saddle those outside the State with the entire burden of slowing the flow of refuse into New Jersey's remaining landfill sites. That legislative effort is clearly impermissible under the Commerce Clause of the Constitution. . . .

NOTES AND QUESTIONS

1. **Definition of Commerce.** Why did the New Jersey Supreme Court question whether the Commerce Clause was applicable to the interstate movement of waste? In *Bowman v. Chicago & Northwestern Ry. Co.*, 125 U.S. 465 (1888), the Supreme Court found that the states might prohibit the importation of objects that "are not legitimate subjects of trade and commerce." *Id.* at 489. This definition includes items that "would bring in and spread disease, pestilence, and death." *Id.* Why did the Court find this case inapplicable to *Philadelphia*?

2. **Discrimination Against Interstate Commerce.** The Supreme Court has adopted a two-tier approach to analyze state regulation under the "dormant" aspect of the Commerce Clause:

> To determine whether a law violates this so-called "dormant" aspect of the Commerce Clause, we first ask whether it discriminates on its face against interstate commerce. In this context, " 'discrimination' simply means differential treatment of in-state and out-of-state economic interests that benefits the former and burdens the latter." Discriminatory laws motivated by "simple economic protectionism" are subject to a "virtually per se rule of invalidity," which can only be overcome by a showing that the State has no other means to advance a legitimate local purpose.

United Haulers Ass'n Inc. v. Oneida-Herkimer Solid Waste Mgmt. Auth., 550 U.S. 330, 338–39 (2007) (internal citations omitted). Why did the *Philadelphia* Court find that ch. 363 discriminated against interstate commerce? In what way could New Jersey reduce waste disposal without discriminating against out-of-state commercial interests? Suppose a state regulation prohibits landfill operators from accepting solid waste that originates outside the county in which their facilities are located, unless authorized by the county. Would the regulation violate the Dormant Commerce Clause? *See Fort Gratiot Sanitary Landfill, Inc. v. Mich. Dep't of Natural Res.*, 504 U.S. 353, 361 (1992) ("[A] State (or one of its political subdivisions) may not avoid the strictures of the Commerce Clause by curtailing the movement of articles of commerce through subdivisions of the State, rather than through the State itself.").

3.   Quarantine Laws. In several cases, the Supreme Court has upheld state regulations prohibiting the importation of items that could endanger the state's population. *See Philadelphia*, 437 U.S. at 628 (citing *Asbell v. Kansas*, 209 U.S. 251 (1908); *Reid v. Colorado*, 187 U.S. 137 (1902); *Bowman v. Chicago & Nw. R. Co.*, 125 U.S. 465, 489 (1888)). How did the Court distinguish ch. 363 from the quarantine laws that were upheld in *Asbell v. Kansas*, *Reid v. Colorado*, and *Bowman v. Chicago & Northwestern R. Co.*? In his dissenting opinion, Justice Rehnquist argued:

> In my opinion, these cases are dispositive of the present one. Under them, New Jersey may require germ-infected rags or diseased meat to be disposed of as best as possible within the State, but at the same time prohibit the *importation* of such items for disposal at the facilities that are set up within New Jersey for disposal of such material generated *within* the State. The physical fact of life that New Jersey must somehow dispose of its own noxious items does not mean that it must serve as a depository for those of every other State. Similarly, New Jersey should be free under our past precedents to prohibit the importation of solid waste because of the health and safety problems that such waste poses to its citizens. The fact that New Jersey continues to, and indeed must continue to, dispose of its own solid waste does not mean that New Jersey may not prohibit the importation of even more solid waste into the State. I simply see no way to distinguish solid waste, on the record of this case, from germ-infected rags, diseased meat, and other noxious items.

Philadelphia, 437 U.S. at 632 (Rehnquist, J., dissenting). Do you find this opinion compelling?

4.   *Pike* Test. The Court has adopted a more flexible approach to deal with state legislation "directed to legitimate local concerns, with effects upon interstate commerce that are only incidental." *Philadelphia*, 437 U.S. at 624. These laws are upheld unless the burden imposed on commerce clearly outweighs their local benefits. *See Pike v. Bruce Church, Inc.*, 397 U.S. 137, 142 (1970). For instance, in *Minnesota v. Clover Leaf Creamery Co.*, 449 U.S. 456 (1981), milk sellers brought action challenging the constitutionality of a Minnesota statute banning retail sale of milk in plastic, non-returnable, nonrefillable containers. The Court found that the Minnesota statute did not discriminate against interstate commerce, since it applies equally to milk containers and sellers from inside and outside the state; and that the incidental burden it imposed on interstate commerce is not excessive in relation to its local benefits:

> The burden imposed on interstate commerce by the statute is relatively minor. Milk products may continue to move freely across the Minnesota border, and since most dairies package their products in more than one type of containers, the inconvenience of having to conform to different packaging requirements in Minnesota and the surrounding States should be slight. . . .

> Even granting that the out-of-state plastics industry is burdened relatively more heavily than the Minnesota pulpwood industry, we find that this burden is not "clearly excessive" in light of the substantial state interest in promoting conservation of energy and other natural resources and easing solid waste disposal problems. . . . We find these local benefits ample to support Minnesota's decision under the Commerce Clause. Moreover, we find that no approach with "a lesser impact on interstate activities," *Pike*, [397 U.S.] at 142 is available.

Minn. v. Clover Leaf Creamery Co., 449 U.S. at 471–72. When should the local benefits of a waste reduction or recycling law be deemed to outweigh the burdens it imposes on commerce? Should a state statute that prevents waste generators from using the state's landfills unless they generate waste in a region that has adopted an effective recycling program be upheld? *See Nat'l Solid Wastes Mgmt. Ass'n v. Meyer*, 63 F.3d 652 (7th Cir. 1995) (finding Wisconsin recycling statute unconstitutional). What about a state law prohibiting the shipping of industrial waste into the state unless the state of origin had enacted similar standards for waste disposal as the receiving state? *See Hardage v. Atkins*, 619 F.2d 871, 873 (10th Cir. 1980) (finding that "the substantially similar standards" requirement of the statute is a mandatory reciprocity provision that violates the Commerce Clause).

5. Post *Philadelphia v. New Jersey* Cases. After *Philadelphia*, the Court has analyzed two other types of state regulatory measures that intended to control the flow of interstate waste: discriminatory surcharges and flow control ordinances. Suppose that a state enacts legislation charging out-of-state waste with a disposal fee. Should this fee be treated differently than import bans? In *Chemical Waste Mgmt., Inc. v. Hunt*, 504 U.S. 334 (1992), the Supreme Court analyzed a state law imposing an additional disposal fee on hazardous waste generated outside the state. The Court stated:

> As found by the trial court, "[a]lthough the Legislature imposed an additional fee of $72.00 per ton on waste generated outside Alabama, there is absolutely no evidence before this Court that waste generated outside Alabama is more dangerous than waste generated in Alabama. The Court finds under the facts of this case that the only basis for the additional fee is the origin of the waste."

. . . In the face of such findings, invalidity under the Commerce Clause necessarily follows, for "whatever [Alabama's] ultimate purpose, it may not be accomplished by discriminating against articles of commerce coming from outside the State unless there is some reason, apart from their origin, to treat them differently." . . . The burden is on the State to show that "the discrimination is demonstrably justified by a valid factor unrelated to economic protectionism," and it has not carried this burden.

Chem. Waste Mgmt., Inc., 504 U.S. at 343–44 (citations omitted). Would the outcome be different if the fee was based on the costs that in-state waste paid through general taxation? Is the intent of the law relevant under the Court's Dormant Commerce Clause jurisprudence? *See Or. Waste Sys., Inc. v. Dep't of Envtl. Quality of Or.*, 511 U.S. 93, 104 (1994).

Flow control ordinances are regulations that require trash haulers to deliver solid waste to a particular waste processing facility. *See United Haulers Ass'n*, 550 U.S. at 334. In *C & A Carbone, Inc. v. Clarkstown*, 511 U.S. 383, 387 (1994), a flow control ordinance forced haulers to deliver all non-hazardous solid waste to a particular private facility upon payment of an above-market tipping fee. The Court found:

> [T]he flow control ordinance discriminates, for it allows only the favored operator to process waste that is within the limits of the town. The ordinance is no less discriminatory because in-state or in-town processors are also covered by the prohibition. . . .

> The essential vice in laws of this sort is that they bar the import of the processing service. Out-of-state [facilities] are deprived of access to local demand for their services. . . . The flow control ordinance . . . hoards solid waste, and the demand to get rid of it, for the benefit of the preferred processing facility.

Id. at 391. Would the outcome be different if the law had required haulers to bring waste to facilities owned and operated by a state-created public benefit corporation? *See United Haulers Ass'n*, 550 U.S. at 334 (holding that "[d]isposing of trash has been a traditional government activity for years, and laws that favor the government in such areas—but treat every private business, whether in-state or out-of-state, exactly the same—do not discriminate against interstate commerce for purposes of the Commerce Clause.").

6. Environmental Federalism and International Trade. Similar issues arise in the international trade regime operated by the World Trade Organization (WTO). Two differences between the domestic environmental regulatory context and the international trade context are salient:

- while the WTO serves as a central body, designed to supervise and liberalize world trade, its centralized decisionmaking powers are weak in comparison to the federal government in the U.S.; and

- while the Dormant Commerce Clause of the U.S. Constitution severely constrains states from imposing product limitations—which would preclude the importation of a particular product based on the environmental consequences of the product itself—and process standards—which would preclude the importation of a particular product based on the environmental consequences of the process that produced the product—the limitations imposed by the international trade regime are not of comparable stringency.

Under the WTO regime, should a country be permitted to prohibit importation of a product on the basis of the environmental consequences of that product? Should a country be permitted to prohibit the importation of a product based on the processes that generated that product, in circumstances where comparable products (generated by less environmentally harmful processes) are produced domestically? Should the distinction between products and processes matter? For examples of the WTO's resolution of trade disputes concerning process standards, see the "Shrimp-Turtle" case, Appellant Body Report, *United States—Import Prohibitions of Certain Shrimp and Shrimp Products,* WT/DS58/AB/R, (Oct. 12, 1998), and the "Tuna-Dolphin" case, Panel Report, *United States—Restrictions on Imports of Tuna,* WT/DS21/R (Sept. 3, 1991). For academic commentary concerning the intersection of environmental regulation and international trade, see Alan O. Sykes, *The Least Restrictive Means*, 70 U. CHI. L. REV. 403 (2003).

2. ALLOCATING REGULATORY AUTHORITY BETWEEN THE FEDERAL GOVERNMENT AND THE STATES

The allocation of responsibility over environmental regulation in the United States between the federal government and the states has been the subject of considerable academic debate over the past two decades. This section examines the three most prominent justifications that appear both in the academic literature and in the legislative history of the federal environmental statutes for vesting control over environmental regulation at the federal level. Other justifications, as well as arguments for decentralization, are explored in the notes.

The first article by Richard L. Revesz addresses the race-to-the-bottom justification for federal environmental regulation, which posits that, in an attempt to induce geographically mobile firms to locate within their jurisdictions, states will formulate suboptimally lax environmental standards. He shows that the race-to-the-bottom is a form of prisoner's dilemma (a concept that is introduced in the Notes and Questions to Chapter I), in which, as a result of their inability to coordinate their actions, two jurisdictions pick suboptimally lax environmental standards even though they would both be better off with more stringent standards.

Revesz then argues that the race-to-the-bottom justification encounters no support in the theoretical literature on interjurisdictional competition. In the absence of interstate externalities, a jurisdiction interested in maximizing the aggregate welfare of their citizens should properly trade-off the additional benefits, in terms of jobs and taxes, of attracting new industry against the resulting environmental harms suffered by its citizens. The article shows, moreover, that if a race-to-the-bottom exists, federal regulation will not solve the underlying problem: states will then set suboptimally lax standards in other regulatory areas, such as worker safety, and social welfare will similarly be impaired.

The second article by Richard L. Revesz addresses the interstate externality rationale for federal regulation. The problem of interstate externalities arises because a state that sends pollution to another state obtains the labor and fiscal benefits of the economic activity that generates the pollution but does not suffer the full costs of the activity. While he recognizes that the presence of interstate externalities provides a compelling argument for federal regulation under conditions in which Coasian bargaining is unlikely to occur, Revesz argues that the federal environmental statutes have been largely ineffective in constraining interstate externalities in a desirable manner. Indeed, he argues that some federal provisions may in fact exacerbate interstate externalities.

The third article by Richard L. Revesz addresses the public choice rationale for federal intervention, which maintains that federal regulation is necessary because public choice pathologies cause systematic underrepresentation of environmental interests at the state level. Revesz first challenges the theoretical argument that environmental groups are less disadvantaged at the federal level due to economies of scale in organization. He argues that the relevant analysis would instead look to the relative effectiveness of environmental and industry groups at the state and federal levels. An examination of conventional and more plausible public choice accounts of environmental regulation reveal little support for the proposition that public choice pathologies standing in the way of environmental regulation are likely to be systematically more serious at the state level than at the federal level.

Richard L. Revesz, Rehabilitating Interstate Competition: Rethinking the "Race-to-the-Bottom" Rationale for Federal Environmental Regulation
67 N.Y.U. L. REV. 1210 (1992).*

Perhaps the most widely accepted justification for environmental regulation at the federal level is that it prevents states from competing for industry by offering pollution control standards that are too lax. This competition is said to produce a "race to the bottom"—that is, a race from the desirable levels of environmental quality that states would pursue if they did not face competition for industry to the increasingly undesirable levels that they choose in the face of such competition. . . .

This Article challenges the accepted wisdom on the race to the bottom. It argues that, contrary to prevailing assumptions, competition among states for industry should not be expected to lead to a race that

---

*   Reprinted with the permission of the New York University Law Review.

decreases social welfare; indeed, as in other areas, such competition can be expected to produce an efficient allocation of industrial activity among the states. It shows, moreover, that federal regulation aimed at dealing with the asserted race-to-the-bottom, far from correcting evils of interstate competition, is likely to produce results that are undesirable.

This challenge to the validity of race to the bottom arguments should lead to serious questioning of the federal environmental statutes. While there are other rationales for regulation at the federal level, they rest upon different empirical foundations and justify different forms of federal intervention than does the race to the bottom rationale. Most importantly, the other prominent market-failure argument for federal environmental regulation is that, in the absence of such regulation, interstate externalities will lead states to underregulate because some of the benefits will accrue to other states. But interstate externalities explain only isolated parts of the federal environmental statutes, with a good portion of the remainder being justified on race to the bottom grounds. Alternatively, one might justify federal regulation on public-choice grounds by arguing that state political processes systematically undervalue the benefits of environmental protection or overvalue the corresponding costs, whereas at the federal level the calculus is more accurate. But this rationale rests upon an empirical claim about failures in the political process rather than failures in the market for industrial location. Thus, at the very least, a different predicate would have to be constructed to defend the federal statutes. . . .

The Race to the Bottom Over Environmental Regulation

Because commentators have not paid sufficient attention to the characteristics a race to the bottom over environmental regulation would have, I start by defining the elements of the race. . . .

First, consider an "island" jurisdiction—a single jurisdiction surrounded by ocean, which is unaffected by what occurs beyond its borders. This island jurisdiction has a number of firms engaged in industrial activity that produces air pollution. The citizens of the jurisdiction suffer adverse health effects as a result of the pollution.

In the absence of regulation, the firms will choose the level of pollution that maximizes their profits and, as is the case generally with externalities, will ignore the social costs produced by their activities—the costs borne by the citizens who must breathe air of poor quality. The firms will be able to produce their goods more cheaply and will pollute more than if they were forced to bear these social costs.

Traditional economic theory holds that the socially optimal level of pollution reduction is the level that maximizes the benefits that accrue from such reduction to the individuals who breathe the polluted air, minus the costs of pollution control. To achieve this optimal reduction, a regulator must force polluters to internalize the costs that they impose on breathers. For the purposes of this discussion, it does not matter whether the regulator achieves this goal through command-and-control regulation, Pigouvian taxes, marketable permit schemes, or other strategies. Finally, for comparative purposes, assume that in this island jurisdiction the level of pollution reduction chosen by the regulator does not affect entry into or exit from the market. Thus, the number of polluters in the jurisdiction will be independent of the actions of the regulator.

Second, consider instead a "competitive" jurisdiction. This jurisdiction is affected by the actions taken in other jurisdictions, and, in turn, its own actions have effects beyond its borders. I have in mind a state within a federal system.

In order to focus the discussion on the competition among states to attract industry, assume for now that there are no interjurisdictional pollution externalities. Assume further, for ease of exposition, that the total number of firms across jurisdictions remains fixed—that although firms can move from one jurisdiction to another, there is no entry into or exit from the national market. Within the national market then, other factors being equal, firms will try to reduce the costs of pollution control by moving to the jurisdiction that imposes the least stringent requirements. Industrial migration will occur whenever the reduction in the expected costs of complying with the environmental standards is lower than the transaction costs involved in moving.

As in the island situation, competitive jurisdictions will want to set a pollution reduction level that takes account of the benefits to its citizens of such reduction and of the costs to polluters in the jurisdiction of complying with this level. There will be, however, an additional factor to consider: the location of a firm can lead to the creation of jobs, and thus to increases in wages and taxes—important benefits for a state. As a result of this additional factor, competitive jurisdictions will consider the potential benefits, in terms of inflows of industrial activity, of setting standards that are less stringent than those of other jurisdictions, and, conversely, the potential costs, in terms of outflows of industrial activity, of setting more stringent standards.

With this background in mind, I present the structure of the race to the bottom argument. Remember, however, that I am not positing that a competitive jurisdiction will in fact engage in a race to the bottom. I am, instead, merely explaining the theoretical structure of race to the bottom claims.

The simplest example of the race to the bottom is one in which there are two identical jurisdictions. Assume that State 1 initially sets its level of pollution reduction at the level that would be optimal if it were an island. State 2 then considers whether setting its standard at the same level is as desirable as setting it at a less stringent level. Depending on the benefits of pollution reduction, costs on polluters, and benefits from the migration of industry, the less stringent standard may be preferable, and industrial migration from State 1 to State 2 will ensue.

To recover some of its loss of jobs and tax revenues, State 1 then considers relaxing its standard, and so on. This process of adjustment and readjustment continues until an equilibrium is reached, in which neither state has an incentive to change its standard further.

At the conclusion of this race, both states will end up with equally lax standards, and they will not experience any inflow or outflow of industry. Each of these competitive states will thus have the same level of industrial activity that it would have had as an island jurisdiction. Social welfare in these states, however, will be less than it would be in identical island jurisdictions, because, as a result of the race to the bottom, the states will have adopted suboptimally lax standards.

The race to the bottom is the result of non-cooperative action on the part of the states. If they could enter into an enforceable agreement to adopt the optimally stringent standard, they could maximize social welfare without the need for federal regulation.

An alternative to an agreement among the states is pressure by the states for federal regulation. Federal regulation is justified under the race to the bottom theory because it can eliminate the undesirable effects of the race. If the federal regulation sets the standard at the level that the states would find optimal if they were islands, the states will be precluded from competing for industry by offering less stringent standards. They will end up with optimal, rather than suboptimally lax, standards, and they will not suffer the resulting loss in social welfare. In short, both states will be better off as a result of the federal regulation. The problem can thus be described in principal-agent terms, in which the principals, the states, empower an agent, the federal government, to achieve their goal of obtaining protective environmental standards.

The race to the bottom is a form of the prisoner's dilemma. . . . First, each individual has a dominant strategy—a course of action that he follows regardless of what the other individual does. . . . Second, if each individual uses his dominant strategy, the final outcome is Pareto-inferior in that both would have been better off with another outcome. . . . Third, even if the individuals can communicate beforehand and agree to avoid the Pareto-inferior outcome, unless they can somehow enter into a binding agreement, they will ultimately defect and follow their dominant strategies.

To see the applicability of the prisoner's dilemma, consider a simple race to the bottom example in which each of two competitive jurisdictions has only two choices: it can either set the optimally stringent standard that it would choose if it were an island, or it can set a suboptimally lax standard. In the presence of a race to the bottom, if one jurisdiction sets the optimally stringent standard, the other will set the lax standard and will benefit from industrial migration; in contrast, if one jurisdiction sets a suboptimally lax standard, the other will do so as well to avoid the outflow of industry. Thus, where the jurisdictions must choose between only two environmental standards, the dominant strategy for each is to pick the suboptimally lax standard, even though they would both be better off picking the stringent standard. . . .

Finally, it is important to stress that the existence of interstate competition for industry is not sufficient, by itself, to produce a race to the bottom or, consequently, to justify federal regulation. Obviously, a race to the bottom requires not just the existence of a "race," but also that the race be "to the bottom." This latter element requires, first, that a competitive jurisdiction adopt a less stringent pollution control standard than an otherwise identical island jurisdiction would have adopted. Second, it requires that the less stringent standards that emerge from the competitive process be socially undesirable. . . .

The Uncertain Theoretical Foundation of Race to the Bottom Arguments

. . . Until now, the legal literature has done little more than assert in a conclusory fashion that interstate competition to attract industry will reduce a jurisdiction's social welfare. It has not shown why, when an island jurisdiction is placed in a competitive situation, it becomes a participant in a race to the bottom. This Part demonstrates that there is no support in the theoretical literature on interjurisdictional competition for the claim that, without federal intervention, there will be a race to the bottom over environmental standards.

An Initial Hurdle

Race to the bottom advocates must clear an initial hurdle: for the competition among states to attract industry to be a race-to-the-bottom, interstate competition must be socially undesirable. But interstate competition can be seen as competition among producers of a good—the right to locate within the jurisdiction. These producers compete to attract potential consumers of that good—firms interested in locating in the jurisdiction. Even though states might not have the legal authority to prevent firms from locating within their borders, such firms must comply with the fiscal and regulatory regime of the state; the resulting costs to the firms can be analogized to the sale price of a traditional good.

If one believes that competition among sellers of widgets is socially desirable, why is competition among sellers of location rights socially undesirable? If federal regulation mandating a supra-competitive price for widgets is socially undesirable, why is federal regulation mandating a supra-competitive price for location rights socially desirable? . . .

The Theoretical Literature

Rather than undertake the daunting task of describing the numerous economic models that shed some light on the race to the bottom question, I center my account of the development and current state of the literature on a discussion of three principal works. . . .

In his influential article published in 1956, Charles Tiebout argues that a decentralized governmental structure, with multiple jurisdictions competing for residents, produces a Pareto-optimal outcome.

Tiebout argues that individuals will sort themselves into the jurisdictions offering the mix of taxes and public services that they prefer and that these jurisdictions will be of the optimal size. He concludes that it is therefore preferable to provide public services at the local level, rather than at the federal level and, more pertinently, that interjurisdictional competition is desirable.

Two of Tiebout's assumptions are problematic for my purposes. His ... assumption that individuals do not consider the employment opportunities of their prospective communities and that no productive activities take place in those communities assumes away the issue that is central to the race to the bottom argument: the effects on the environment of efforts by jurisdictions to attract firms in order to provide jobs for their residents. Second, much of the legal literature has dismissed as unrealistic the assumption of perfect mobility by individuals. There may, indeed, be substantial transaction costs in exiting one jurisdiction and moving to another, particularly in a world in which individuals have jobs and do not live solely on dividend income.

In his article published in 1975, William Fischel extends the Tiebout analysis to deal with the problem of industrial location. In his model, firms are owned by outsiders to the jurisdiction, do not employ any of the jurisdiction's residents, and all of their production is for export from the jurisdiction. The environmental externalities produced by these firms are uniformly distributed over all the residents, and there are no interjurisdictional spillovers. . . .

Fischel contemplates that jurisdictions are able to exclude firms through zoning decisions. They will refuse to permit a firm to locate unless it makes a direct cash payment to the zoning board, to be divided equally among the residents. The minimum amount that a jurisdiction would demand for the deterioration of its environmental quality is equal to the environmental harm caused by the firm. Any amount over this minimum constitutes a "profit," which competition among jurisdictions will drive to zero. . . .

The Fischel model suggests that competition among jurisdictions leads to economically desirable results, rather than to a race to the bottom. Two of his assumptions, however, are troubling. First, under his model, firms do not hire residents of the jurisdiction in which they locate. Thus, like Tiebout, he assumes away one of the cornerstones of race to the bottom arguments: that jurisdictions will relax their environmental standards to suboptimal levels in order to provide jobs for their residents. Second, also like Tiebout, Fischel assumes that individuals are perfectly mobile.

These two shortcomings are addressed by Wallace Oates and Robert Schwab in an article published in 1988. In their model,

> jurisdictions compete for a mobile stock of capital by lowering taxes and relaxing environmental standards that would otherwise deflect capital elsewhere. In return for an increased capital stock, residents receive higher incomes in the form of higher wages. The community must, however, weigh the benefits of higher wages against the cost of foregone tax revenues and lower environmental quality.

Oates and Schwab envision jurisdictions that are large enough to allow individuals to live and work in the same jurisdiction. Moreover, they assume that there are no interjurisdictional externalities: pollution generated in one jurisdiction does not spill over into another.

Each jurisdiction produces the same single good, which is sold in a national market. The production of the good requires capital and labor and produces waste emissions. The instrument of environmental policy is command-and-control regulation: each jurisdiction sets the total amount of allowable emissions. In addition, each jurisdiction raises revenues by levying a tax on each unit of capital. Capital is perfectly mobile across jurisdictions and seeks to maximize its after-tax earnings.

Unlike capital, however, labor is perfectly immobile.[101] Each individual in the community, who is identical in both tastes and productive capacity, puts in a fixed period of work each week, and everyone is employed. Additional capital raises the productivity of workers and, therefore, their wages.

Oates and Schwab describe the role of an individual resident of a jurisdiction as follows:

> First, he is a consumer, seeking in the usual way to maximize utility over a bundle of goods and services that includes a local public good, environmental quality. And, second, he supplies labor for productive purposes in return for his income. From the latter perspective, residents have a clear incentive to encourage the entry of more capital as a means to increase their wages. But this jurisdiction must compete against other jurisdictions. To attract capital, the community must reduce taxes on capital (which lowers income and, therefore, indirectly lowers utility) and/or relax environmental standards (which lowers utility directly). These are the tradeoffs inherent in interjurisdictional competition.

---

[101] . . . In a companion, unpublished manuscript, Oates and Schwab argue that their conclusion that competition among states produces efficient outcomes holds even if individuals are mobile. . . . If individuals are mobile, they will sort out, as in the Tiebout model, by reference to their preferences for environmental protection. Individuals who are willing to trade off a great deal in wages for better environmental quality will move to jurisdictions that impose stringent controls on industry; individuals who attach less importance to environmental quality will go to dirtier areas. . . .

Each jurisdiction makes two policy decisions: it sets a tax rate on capital and an environmental standard. Oates and Schwab show that competitive jurisdictions will set a tax rate on capital of zero. For positive tax rates, the revenues are less than the loss in wages that results from the move of capital to other jurisdictions; subsidies would cost the jurisdiction more than the increase in wages that additional capital would generate.

In turn, competitive jurisdictions will set an environmental standard that is defined by equating the willingness to pay for an additional unit of environmental quality with the corresponding change in wages. Pollution beyond this level generates an increment to wage income that is less than the value of the damage to residents from the increased pollution; in contrast, less pollution creates a loss in wage income greater than the corresponding decrease in pollution damages.

Oates and Schwab show that these choices of tax rates and environmental standards are socially optimal. . . . With respect to the environmental standard, competitive jurisdictions equate the marginal private cost of improving environmental quality (measured in terms of forgone consumption) with the marginal private benefit. For tax rates of zero, the marginal private cost is, as noted above, the decrease in wage income produced by the marginal unit of environmental protection. This decrease is also the marginal social cost, since it represents society's forgone consumption. Oates and Schwab conclude that "competition among jurisdictions is thus conducive to efficient outcomes." Thus, there is no race to the bottom. . . .

In their model, Oates and Schwab assume that capital does not require the provision of public services, such as roads, and police and fire protection. If it does, the optimal tax rate on capital, rather than zero, is the rate that exactly covers the cost of these services. It follows from the preceding discussion that, for this rate of taxation, jurisdictions would set environmental standards at the optimal level. . . .

Lessons from the Theoretical Literature

The conclusions that emerge from this review of the theoretical literature point strongly against race to the bottom claims. Tiebout, Fischel, and Oates and Schwab all conclude, in situations progressively more analogous to the problem of this Article, that interstate competition is not inconsistent with the maximization of social welfare. There are no formal models supporting the proposition that competition among states creates a prisoner's dilemma in which states, contrary to their interests, compete for industry by offering progressively laxer standards. . . .

One should not overstate the nature of my claim against race to the bottom justifications for environmental regulation. The fact that there are no models consistent with race to the bottom claims does not rule out the possibility that further research will yield such models. Modeling, by necessity, involves making strong sets of assumptions. The Oates and

Schwab work, which has studied the problem in the most systematic way, is no exception. A theoretical literature evolves as assumptions are relaxed, often one at a time. It is certainly conceivable that the next generation of theoretical work will provide support for race to the bottom arguments. But the fact remains that race to the bottom arguments in the environmental area have been made for the last two decades with essentially no theoretical foundation.

The Implications of the Environmental Race to the Bottom

Having shown . . . that the race to the bottom hypothesis, though influential, lacks a sound theoretical basis, this Part shows that even if there *were* such a race in the environmental arena, federal regulation would not necessarily be an appropriate response. The analysis centers on two important consequences of race to the bottom arguments in favor of federal environmental regulation. First, if the premises underlying the race to the bottom hold, federal environmental regulation will have undesirable effects on other state regulatory or fiscal interests; the supposed benefits of federal environmental regulation should therefore be balanced against these undesirable effects. Second, logic compels the conclusion that arguments in favor of federal environmental regulation are a frontal challenge to federalism, because the problems that they seek to correct can be addressed only by exclusive federal regulatory and fiscal powers. Both these consequences, which have been unexplored in the literature, ought to cast even more doubt on the validity of race to the bottom arguments for federal environmental regulation.

Race to the bottom arguments appear to assume, at least implicitly, that jurisdictions compete over only one variable—in this case, environmental quality. So, jurisdictions that would choose to have stringent environmental quality standards in the absence of interstate competition adopt less stringent standards as a result of such competition, and, consequently, suffer a reduction in social welfare.

Consider, instead, the problem in a context in which states compete over two variables—for example, environmental protection and worker safety. Assume that, in the absence of federal regulation, State 1 chooses a low level of environmental protection and a high level of worker safety. State 2 does the opposite: it chooses a high level of environmental protection and a low level of worker safety protection. Both states are in a competitive equilibrium: industry is not migrating from one to the other.

Suppose that federal regulation then imposes on both states a high level of environmental protection. The federal scheme does not add to the costs imposed upon industry in State 2, but it does in State 1. Thus, the federal regulation will upset the competitive equilibrium, and unless State 1 responds, industry will migrate from State 1 to State 2. The logical response of State 1 is to adopt less stringent worker-safety standards. This response will mitigate the magnitude of the industrial migration that would otherwise occur.

Thus, federal environmental standards can have adverse effects on other state programs. Such secondary effects must be considered in evaluating the desirability of federal environmental regulation. Most importantly, the presence of such effects suggests that federal regulation will not be able to eliminate the negative effects of interstate competition. Recall that the central tenet of race to the bottom claims is that competition will lead to the reduction of social welfare; the assertion that states enact suboptimally lax environmental standards is simply a consequence of this more basic problem. In the face of federal environmental regulation, however, states will continue to compete for industry by adjusting the incentive structure of other state programs. Federal regulation thus will not solve the prisoner's dilemma. . . .

One might respond to these arguments by saying that worker safety should also be the subject of federal regulation. But states would then compete over minimum wage laws, fair labor standards, and so on. It is difficult to imagine a federal system in which all the regulatory requirements that impose costs on industry are mandated at the federal level.

Suppose, however, that this were the case. States impose burdens on industry not only through regulation but also through taxes, which fund a variety of state programs and functions. So, if all regulatory programs are federalized, states still will be able to compete through their fiscal powers. Consider, now, an example in which State 1 and State 2, as island states, would impose both stringent regulatory standards and high corporate taxes. When placed in a competitive situation, State 1 chooses stringent regulatory standards and low corporate taxes, whereas State 2 does the opposite. If the federal government then requires stringent regulatory standards, State 2 will respond by lowering its taxes, and by, say, decreasing the size of its income maintenance programs. This reduction is a direct by-product of the federal regulatory scheme.

Thus, even if all regulatory functions are federalized, federal regulation will continue to have an adverse effect on other issues of state concern—in this example, social welfare programs. Moreover, such a scheme will not eliminate the reduction in social welfare that results from competition among the states.

The next logical step, of course, is to suggest preemption of state taxes, because otherwise the supposedly evil effects of interstate competition will persist. The race to the bottom rationale for federal environmental regulation is, therefore, radically underinclusive. It seeks to solve a problem that can be addressed only by wholly eliminating state autonomy. The prisoner's dilemma will not be solved through federal environmental regulation alone, as the race to the bottom argument posits. States will simply respond by competing over another variable. Thus, the only logical answer is to eliminate the possibility of any competition altogether. In essence, then, the race to the bottom argument is an argument against federalism. . . .

Conclusion

This Article should not be read as a definitive refutation of race to the bottom arguments in the environmental area. It is intended, instead, to question the underpinnings of such arguments and to suggest that the forces of interstate competition, far from being conclusively undesirable, are at least presumptively beneficial. If this project proves successful, it will be followed, without a doubt, by studies attempting to define specific circumstances in which federal regulation could improve upon the results of interstate competition.

NOTES AND QUESTIONS

1. Challenging the Race-to-the-Bottom. Why do proponents of the race-to-the-bottom rationale for federal intervention argue that states are unable to adequately trade-off the competing objectives of securing industry and environmental quality? Why is this proposition inconsistent with the theoretical literature described by Revesz?

2. Federal Regulation as a Cure to the Race-to-the-Bottom. Revesz claims that even if there were a race-to-the-bottom, its undesirable effects would not be cured by federal regulation. Instead, federal environmental regulation would simply transfer the race to other regulatory areas, or to the fiscal arena, without any reason to expect social welfare gains. Are race-to-the-bottom advocates concerned only with environmental quality? If a race-to-the-bottom were to mandate federal intervention in environmental regulation, should it not equally mandate federal intervention in regulations concerning workers safety, or any other regulatory requirements that impose costs on industry?

Evaluate the following argument in response to Revesz's position:

Fundamentally, this line of analysis fails to recognize the technical complexity of environmental policymaking as well as the irreversible nature of some environmental harms. Thus, driving interstate competition out of the inherently obscure realm of environmental policy and into that of other governmental activities, where the costs and benefits of various policies are more easily compared, will be beneficial.

Daniel C. Esty, *Revitalizing Environmental Federalism*, 95 MICH. L. REV. 570, 638 n.255 (1996).

3. Uncertainty Giving Rise to Races-to-the-Bottom. Richard B. Stewart argues that there are ways in which a race-to-the-bottom might occur:

[One] . . . possibility is that [state] A is uncertain about the exact value that [state] B's political system places on environmental protection and how B's government will respond to A's choice of standard, and vice-versa. If each [state's] choice of standards depends on those chosen by other [states], if each is uncertain as to what choices others will make, and if each is unsure how others will

> respond to its choices, it is possible that each [state] might indeed adopt lower standards.

Richard B. Stewart, *Environmental Regulation and International Competitiveness*, 102 YALE L.J. 2039, 2059 (1993). Might this type of uncertainty also lead countries to adopt suboptimally stringent standards? If so, under what circumstances?

4.   Competition for Mobile Capital. An implication of the Oates and Schwab article, on which Revesz relies, is that if states set a positive tax rate on mobile capital (that exceeds the cost of providing public services), they will set suboptimally lax environmental standards, but if they give mobile capital a net subsidy, they will set suboptimally stringent environmental standards. Which outcome is more likely? The divisions in the economic literature on this question are reviewed in Peter Mieszkowski & George R. Zodrow, *Taxation and the Tiebout Model: The Differential Effects of Head Taxes, Taxes on Land Rents, and Property Taxes*, 27 J. ECON. LIT. 1098 (1989). For related discussion, see Susan Rose-Ackerman, *Environmental Policy and Federal Structure: A Comparison of the United States and Germany*, 47 VAND. L. REV. 1587 (1994).

5.   Strategic Behavior. Writing in response to Revesz's article, both Kirsten H. Engel and Daniel C. Esty raised the specter of game-theoretic behavior on the part of states in opposition to Revesz's call for competition among states for industry. *See* Kirsten H. Engel, *State Environmental Standard-Setting: Is There a "Race" and Is It "to the Bottom"?*, 48 HASTINGS L.J. 271 (1997); *see also* Esty, *supra*, at 630. By engaging in strategic behavior, both Engel and Esty suggest that competition among states for industry is undesirable because it would give rise to competition that is not welfare enhancing. Do you find this position persuasive? Would game-theoretic behavior on the part of states necessarily result in environmental underregulation? *See* Richard L. Revesz, *The Race to the Bottom and Federal Environmental Regulation: A Response to Critics*, 82 MINN. L. REV. 535, 547–49 (1997) [hereinafter Revesz, *Response*]. Could it lead to overregulation?

6.   Perfect and Imperfect Markets. It has been suggested that the presumption of perfect competition, upon which the Oates and Schwab model relies, is inapposite to the case of competition among states for mobile capital:

> Unlike firms in perfect competition, states in their regulatory mode are not pure price takers. They cannot ignore the fact that a slight reduction in environmental standards (the price of their location rights) might bring economic welfare gains in excess of any losses from the resulting environmental degradation. In contrast, perfectly competitive firms face no such incentive because they can sell any quantity that they choose at the market-clearing price.

Esty, *supra*, at 630–31; *see also* Engel, *supra*, at 271. What effect would imperfect market conditions have on the analysis of Revesz? For an argument that it could lead to either overregulation or underregulation, see Revesz, *Response*, *supra*, at 549–51.

7.   Existence Values. Joshua Sarnoff, arguing in favor of federal intervention, notes that that even in the absence of physical externalities, the level of environmental protection chosen by the citizens of a state is of interest to citizens of other states: "Tailoring requirements to local preferences will not necessarily increase social welfare, because such tailoring prevents citizens located outside a state from satisfying their preferences for in-state regulation." Joshua D. Sarnoff, *The Continuing Imperative (But Only from a National Perspective) for Federal Environmental Protection*, 7 DUKE ENVTL. L. & POL'Y F. 225, 232 (1997). Evaluate the merit of Sarnoff's concerns about the need to protect the existence values that citizens of one state attach to the level of environmental quality in other states. For what types resources are existence values likely to be high? Are existence values likely to be high for the health of people living in different states? For a skeptical reaction, see Revesz, *Response*, *supra*, at 561–63.

8.   Technological and Pecuniary Externalities. As a justification for federal intervention, Richard Stewart notes that "[a] state that encourages economic development at the expense of environmental quality may inflict economic loss (in the form of industrial migration or decreased economic growth) on other states that prefer a higher level of environmental quality." Richard B. Stewart, *Pyramids of Sacrifice? Problems of Federalism in Mandating State Implementation of National Environmental Policy*, 86 YALE L.J. 1196, 1215–16 (1977). A state that seeks to attract industry in this manner is essentially lowering the price for industrial location. Is its decision different from the decision of a manufacturer to lower the price of its product, where this price change has undesirable economic effects on a competitor?

Consider the following distinction between technological and pecuniary externalities:

> [N]ot all relationships that appear to involve externalities will produce resource misallocation. There is a category of pseudo-externalities, the *pecuniary externalities*, in which one individual's activity level affect the financial circumstances of another, but which need not produce a misallocation of resources in a world of pure competition. . . . Pecuniary externalities result from a change in the prices of some inputs or outputs in the economy. An increase in the number of shoes demanded raises the price of leather and hence affects the welfare of the purchasers of handbags. But unlike a true externality (. . . a *technological externality*), it does not generate a *shift* in the handbag production function.

WILLIAM J. BAUMOL & WALLACE E. OATES, THE THEORY OF ENVIRONMENTAL POLICY 29 (2d ed. 1988). Is the externality described by Stewart technological or pecuniary? Does it affect social welfare?

9.   Federal Regulation and Superfund. Consider the rationales for federal regulation in the following components of the Superfund statute (the statutory scheme is discussed in Chapter VII):

> (a)   the liability scheme, which, in the event of the release of hazardous substances from a site, imposes liability on

generators and transporters, as well as the site owner and certain former owners;

(b)   the cleanup standards, which specify the extent to which the contamination at hazardous waste sites must be remedied; and

(c)   the tax scheme, which raises revenues primarily from chemical and petroleum companies to finance cleanups at sites at which liable parties are either insolvent or cannot be found.

For which of these components are the claims for federal regulation most persuasive? Least persuasive?

10. Subsidiarity in the European Union. The European Union (then known as the European Economic Community) was established by the Treaty of Rome in 1957. This treaty did not contain any specific rules dealing with environmental protection. The Treaty of Rome was amended by the Single European Act in 1986 and by the Treaty on European Union (the Maastricht Treaty) in 1992. Now, Articles 100a and 130r through 130t explicitly deal with environmental protection.

The Maastricht Treaty also adopted a "subsidiarity" principle, which provides in Article 3b:

> In areas which do not fall within its exclusive competence, the Community shall take action, in accordance with the principle of subsidiarity, only if and in so far as the objectives of the proposed action cannot be sufficiently achieved by the Member States and can therefore, by reason of the scale or effects of the proposed action, be better achieved by the Community.

(A similar principle had applied exclusively to environmental regulation under the Single European Act.) What inquiry should be undertaken to determine whether a proposed directive is consistent with the subsidiarity principle? Does Article 3b constitutionalize the policy debate that is ongoing in the United States concerning which level of government should have responsibility for environmental regulation? Are there differences? *See* Richard L. Revesz, *Federalism and Environmental Regulation: Lessons for the European Union and the International Community*, 83 VA. L. REV. 1331, 1339–40 (1997).

For discussion of the application of the subsidiarity principle to environmental law, see L.V. Brinkhorst, *Subsidiarity and European Environmental Policy*, *in* PROCEEDINGS OF THE JACQUES DELORS COLLOQUIUM (1991); Wouter P. J. Wils, *Subsidiarity and EC Environmental Policy: Taking People's Concerns Seriously*, 6 J. ENVTL. L. 85 (1994). Wils argues that one basis for justifying regulation at the European Union level is the presence of "psychic spillovers." He states:

> Many people in Denmark or the Netherlands are affected by the hunting and trapping of birds in France, even if these birds are not migratory, and irrespective of any touristic interest. Similarly, a large number of EU citizens in various Member States are appalled by bullfighting in Spain and would derive satisfaction from a ban.

Id. at 89. Are Wils's "psychic spillovers" coextensive with existence values? How large must these spillovers be to justify communitywide regulation? How would an appropriate inquiry about the magnitude of these spillovers be made? Is subsidiarity likely to ever be a constraint under Wils's theory? If so, under what circumstances?

Richard L. Revesz, Federalism and Interstate Environmental Externalities

144 U. PA. L. REV. 2341 (1996).[*]

Introduction

. . . This Article . . . criticizes the various approaches that federal environmental laws have taken to address the problem of interstate externalities. [It] shows that the Clean Air Act—the statute designed to deal with the pollution that gives rise to the most serious problems of interstate externalities—has been unsuccessful at forcing the internalization of interstate externalities. Its core provisions cannot be justified by the need to control interstate externalities, and may have exacerbated the problem. Similarly, the relatively minor provisions directed at controlling interstate externalities have been wholly ineffective, largely as a result of the failure of the Environmental Protection Agency ("EPA") and the federal courts to define a coherent and logical body of law. In fact, despite congressional preoccupation with the problem and the existence of statutory provisions expressly designed to correct it, the downwind states have always been unsuccessful at constraining upwind pollution. A similar situation arises under the Clean Water Act. . . .

The central purpose of this Article, particularly in light of my prior work, is to refocus the attention of federal environmental regulation. Of the two most prominent reasons for vesting responsibility for environmental regulation at the federal level, the race-to-the-bottom rationale is analytically unsound, despite the fact that much of the legal regime is structured to redress this asserted evil. In contrast, the rationale for federal regulation premised on the problem of interstate externalities is analytically unimpeachable but has not been effectively redressed in the current pollution-control scheme. At a time when federal environmental regulation is under fierce political attack, it is critical to define clearly what tasks can best be accomplished at the federal level and to ensure that the resulting regulatory scheme in fact accomplishes those tasks. This Article shows why a great deal more attention needs to be paid to fashioning an effective federal response to the problem of interstate externalities. . . .

---

[*]   Reprinted with the permission of the University of Pennsylvania Law Review.

Impact of the [Clean Air Act] on Interstate Externalities

This section shows that the ambient and emissions standards [of the Clean Air Act], which form the core of the [Act], are an ineffective and poorly targeted means of dealing with the problem of interstate externalities. It also explains why these provisions may have exacerbated the interstate spillover problem. . . .

Ambient and Emissions Standards

The Clean Air Act's federal emissions standards for stationary sources—. . . as well as its federal emissions standards for automobiles—are not a good means by which to combat the problem of interstate externalities. These standards constrain the pollution from each source, but do not regulate the number of sources within any given state or the location of the sources.

Similarly, the various federal ambient air-quality standards of the Clean Air Act . . . also are not well-targeted means to address the problem of interstate externalities, because they are both overinclusive and underinclusive. From the perspective of constraining interstate externalities at a desirable level, ambient standards are overinclusive because they require a state to restrict pollution that has only in-state consequences. Concern about interstate externalities can be addressed by limiting the amount of pollution that is permitted to cross interstate borders. Such externalities can be controlled even if the upwind state chooses to have poor environmental quality within its borders.

Conversely, the federal ambient air-quality standards are underinclusive from the perspective of controlling interstate externalities because a state could meet the applicable ambient standards but nonetheless export a great deal of pollution to downwind states because the sources in the state have tall stacks and are located near the interstate border. In fact, a state might meet its ambient standards precisely because it exports a great deal of its pollution.

The federal ambient and emissions standards could perhaps be justified as a second-best means by which to reduce the problem of uncontrolled interstate externalities. One might believe that by reducing pollution across the board they reduce interstate externalities proportionately. So, for example, if they lead to the halving of the aggregate amount of pollution, one might think that they would also cut in half the pollution that crosses state lines.

Such a view, however, is incorrect as a matter of both theory and empirical observation. The amount of aggregate emissions is not the only variable that affects the level of interstate externalities; two other factors play important roles. The first is the height of the stack from which the pollution is emitted—the higher the stack, the lesser the impact close to the source and the greater the impact far from the source. Thus, absent a federal constraint, states have an incentive to encourage their sources to use tall stacks as a way to externalize both the health and environmental effects of the pollution, as well as the regulatory costs of complying with the federal ambient standards.

Second, the level of interstate externalities is affected by the location of the sources. In the eastern part of the United States, where the problem of interstate pollution is most serious, the prevailing winds blow from west to east. Thus, states have an incentive to induce their sources to locate close to their downwind borders, for example, through the use of tax incentives or subsidies, so that the bulk of the effects of the pollution is externalized.

The best evidence that states do indeed encourage sources to use tall stacks can be found in the provisions of the [State Implementation Plans (SIPs)] adopted by at least fifteen states in response to the enactment of the Clean Air Act in 1970. [SIPs are air pollution regulations and control strategies developed by the states to ensure that state air quality complies with the federal ambient standards]. These SIPs allowed sources to meet the [federal ambient standards] by using taller stacks rather than by reducing emissions. In those SIPs, the permissible level of emissions was an increasing function of the height of the stack. If the stack was sufficiently high, the effects would be felt only in the downwind states and would therefore have no impact on in-state ambient air-quality levels. Through these measures, the states created strong incentives for their firms to externalize the effects of their sources of pollution.

It is true that states had an incentive to externalize pollution even before the enactment of the Clean Air Act in 1970 because, by encouraging tall stacks, states could make other states bear the adverse health effects of pollution. The 1970 provisions, however, created an additional incentive. By encouraging the use of tall stacks, states could also externalize the regulatory impact of the standards, thereby availing themselves, for example, of the opportunity to attract additional sources without violating the [federal ambient standards].

Taller stacks entail higher costs of construction and, possibly, operation. It is therefore conceivable that a state that did not view the externalization of health effects as sufficient by itself to outweigh imposing such costs on in-state firms would reach a different conclusion when tall stacks lead to the externalization of both health and regulatory impacts. . . .

It is therefore not surprising that the use of tall stacks expanded considerably after 1970. For example, whereas in 1970 only two stacks in the United States were higher than 500 feet, by 1985 more than 180 stacks were higher than 500 feet and twenty-three were higher than 1000 feet.

In contrast to the experience with tall-stack provisions, my research has uncovered no direct evidence concerning whether states also provided incentives for sources to locate close to their downwind borders.

There is, however, literature suggesting that such incentives are present in the case of the siting of waste sites. It would not be implausible to believe that states acted in the same manner with respect to air pollution facilities.

In summary, the central components of the Clean Air Act are not an effective or well-targeted response to the problem of interstate externalities. As I argued elsewhere, vesting authority at the federal level to promulgate the ambient and emissions standards described above can best be explained by reference to the race-to-the-bottom justification—a justification that I have criticized—rather than to the interstate externality justification. . . .

Administrative and Judicial Interpretation of the Interstate Spillover Provisions

This section analyzes the substantive standards that the EPA and the courts have fashioned to guide proceedings under [the Clean Air Act's interstate spillover provisions, which prohibit interstate air pollution that "significantly contributes" to nonattainment of federal ambient standards.] . . .

To understand the administrative and judicial interpretations of the substantive standards, it is helpful to construct a taxonomy defined by reference to whether the downwind state would meet the federal ambient standards if it did not have to face pollution transported from the upwind state and whether the downwind state actually meets the federal ambient standards despite the upwind pollution. There are three relevant categories.

In the first category, the downwind state would meet the federal ambient standards without the upwind pollution, and meets these standards despite the upwind pollution. In the second category, the downwind state would not meet the federal ambient standards even if there were no upwind pollution and, of course, does not meet the standards with the upwind pollution. In the third category, the downwind state would meet the federal ambient standards in the absence of upwind pollution, but does not meet these standards with the upwind pollution; here, the upwind pollution is the but-for cause of the violation of the federal ambient standards. This taxonomy is summarized in Table I.

Table I: Taxonomy of Interstate Spillovers

	Violation Without Upwind Pollution	Violation with Upwind Pollution
Category I	No	No
Category II	Yes	Yes
Category III	No	Yes

As to each of these categories, two questions are relevant. First, should the federal government play a role in controlling the upwind pollution? Second, assuming that such a role is appropriate, how should the federal government determine the permissible amount of upwind pollution that can enter the downwind state? . . .

[T]hree principal rules emerge from the administrative and judicial interpretations of [the interstate spillover provisions]: upwind pollution is never constrained if the downwind state meets the federal ambient standards; upwind pollution that exacerbates a violation of the federal ambient standards in the downwind states is constrained only if the upwind sources "significantly contribute" to the violation; and upwind pollution that is the but-for cause of the violation of federal ambient standards in the downwind state is always constrained.

The combination of these rules leads to illogical and undesirable results. Consider first the Category I case of a downwind state that is not violating the [federal ambient standards]. The amount by which the downwind state's ambient air-quality levels are better than the federal ambient standards represents that state's margin for growth. If the downwind state is not able to attract new sources, because, for example, it is experiencing a temporary economic downturn, the rules allow an upwind state to consume the downwind state's margin for growth without constraint by adding additional sources. Indeed, the rules even allow an upwind state to consume the downwind state's margin for growth by amending its SIP to permit its existing sources to increase their emissions up to the point at which the federal ambient standards become constraining in the downwind state. Once the air-quality levels in the downwind state reach the level of the federal ambient standards (with the help of the upwind state), the downwind state will be unable to attract any sources without requiring emissions reductions from its existing sources. At the extreme, a downwind state with no existing industrial base would be precluded from ever acquiring one.

In contrast, if the downwind state consumes its margin for growth first, either by attracting new sources or by amending its SIP to allow existing sources to pollute more, any increase in the pollution that the upwind state sends downwind would be deemed a violation of [the spillover provisions]. An upwind state without an industrial base at the time that the downwind state reaches the federal ambient standards might be effectively precluded by this rule from attracting any polluting sources in the future if, as a result of the state's geography, any in-state emissions would be likely to migrate downwind.

Accordingly, the margin for growth in the downwind state would be allocated on a "first-come-first-served" basis. Such rules of capture are undesirable; they create incentives for both upwind and downwind states to use the downwind state's margin for growth at a faster rate than is economically desirable, and do not allocate this margin for growth to the state that values it most highly.

The discussion so far has focused on a downwind state that intends to use its margin for growth for economic expansion. Instead, states might set state ambient standards that are more stringent than the federal standards because they attach more value to environmental protection. The federal environmental laws emphasize . . . that federal standards are floors and not ceilings, and that states remain free to enact standards that are more stringent than the federal standards. Under the dominant race-to-the-bottom and interstate externality justifications for vesting responsibility for environmental regulation at the federal level, the evil to be remedied is underregulation on the part of the states, not overregulation. Under both of these rationales, states should be encouraged to regulate more stringently if their preferences for environmental protection are stronger than those reflected in the federal standards, or if their costs of pollution reduction are lower than average. . . . [M]ore stringent standards are undesirable only if they are an effort to externalize to other states the costs of pollution control.

Under the current administrative and judicial approach, however, more stringent state ambient standards can be used only to limit the emissions of in-state sources and cannot be invoked, under any circumstances, to constrain upwind emissions. Such a regime creates a disincentive for downwind states to have more stringent state ambient standards: downwind states bear all the costs of such standards (the costs of tougher emissions limitations for in-state sources), but the upwind states can appropriate the benefit by taking the additional opportunities created for the externalization of pollution.

The administrative and judicial approach to Category II situations, in which the upwind pollution aggravates a violation of the federal ambient standards, also is misguided. In Category II cases, the downwind state would be unable to constrain the upwind pollution unless the pollution was deemed a "significant contribution" to the violation. Under the nonattainment provisions of the Clean Air Act, however, the downwind state has an obligation to reduce its emissions until it meets the [federal ambient standards]. Thus, absent a "significant contribution" from upwind sources, the full burden of pollution reduction falls initially on the downwind sources, even if upwind reductions would be far less costly.

But once the downwind state made sufficient improvements so that it could meet the [federal ambient standards] were it not for the upwind pollution, the situation would change. The upwind pollution would then be the but-for cause of the violation of the [federal ambient standards] in the downwind state—a Category III problem. The upwind pollution would be enjoined as "prevent[ing] the attainment" of the [federal ambient standards], even if the costs to the upwind state of doing so were wholly disproportionate to the costs to the downwind state of somewhat more stringent pollution controls. As already indicated, in cases in which all emissions from the upwind state have at least some impact downwind, such a rule would prevent any polluting activity in the upwind state. The downwind state, by reducing its emissions to the point at which it could meet the [federal ambient standards] in the absence of the upwind pollution, but no further, could effectively destroy the upwind state's industrial base.

In summary, of the three rules articulated by the EPA and the courts to address the problem of interstate spillovers, two are overly lenient and one is too harsh. It is undesirable to have no constraints on upwind pollution absent a violation of the federal ambient standards. Further, at least in its application, the "significant contribution" rule has allowed excessive upwind pollution. In contrast, the rule banning any upwind pollution that is the but-for cause of a violation of the federal ambient standards is unduly stringent.

NOTES AND QUESTIONS

1. **Ambient and Emissions Standards and Interstate Externalities.** Why does Revesz suggest that compliance with the federal ambient standards does not necessarily reduce interstate externalities? On what basis does he suggest that compliance with emissions standards would prove equally ineffective? In what ways does he argue that the CAA regime actually exacerbates interstate spillovers?

2. **Rules to Enjoin Upwind Pollution.** Adopting the taxonomy of interstate spillovers described above, design a more desirable set of rules for determining when to enjoin upwind pollution. Consider specifically the following scenarios:

> Category I, in circumstances where the upwind pollution reduces the downwind state's margin for industrial growth;

> Category I, in circumstances where the upwind pollution causes the downwind state to violate a state ambient standard that is more stringent than the corresponding federal standard;

> Category II; and

> Category III.

In general, should the relative stringency of emissions regulations in the two states matter? In connection with the latter question, should it matter whether the downwind state has a substantial industrial base that will be affected by these standards, or whether, instead, the bulk of the burdens will be borne by the upwind state? *See generally* Revesz, *supra*, at 2374–94.

3. **Coasian Bargaining.** Why does the problem of interstate air pollution not lend itself to resolution by Coasian bargaining? What transaction costs would exist? How well defined are the relevant entitlements?

4. **Interstate Pollution and the Dormant Commerce Clause.** If a state could stop polluted air at its borders, as it can stop garbage, and if there were no federal regulation, the permissibility of restrictions on out-of-state air pollution would be governed by the Dormant Commerce Clause. Can the understanding of federalism implicit in the Dormant Commerce Clause

inform, as a matter of policy though not of constitutional law, the standards to be used under the interstate spillover provisions of the CAA? In connection with the Dormant Commerce Clause, the Supreme Court has repeatedly held that a state cannot ban the disposal of out-of-state garbage and that it cannot impose discriminatory conditions such as higher disposal fees on out-of-state garbage. (For a discussion of the Supreme Court's treatment of the Dormant Commerce Clause in this context, see Section 1.B. Limitations on State Power, *supra*.) How could this standard be translated to the air pollution context under the hypothetical scenario presented in this question?

5.   Promise of Marketable Permit Schemes. How might marketable permit schemes improve upon mechanisms such as the existing interstate spillover provisions of the CAA, which rely upon administrative and judicial determinations of the permissible amounts, in combating the problems of interstate externalities?

Contrast the effectiveness of markets in units of emissions and markets in units of environmental degradation. The former, such as the SO_2 trading scheme, allow market participants to trade credits that allow a certain amount of emissions. Sources of pollution must purchase credits equal to the amount of pollution that they emit. In contrast, the latter allow market participants to trade credits in units of environmental degradation in the downwind state. Under marketable permit schemes in units of environmental degradation, a source must purchase permits at each location at which its emission will have an impact on ambient air quality levels. For a discussion of the promise of markets in units of environmental degradation, see Revesz, *supra*, at 2410–14.

6.   Federal Regulation and the CAA. Consider the rationales for federal regulation in the following components of the CAA:

(a)   National Ambient Air Quality Standards (NAAQS), which impose minimum levels of ambient environmental quality nationwide;

(b)   prevention of significant deterioration (PSD), which imposes more stringent ambient standards in areas that have air quality that is better than that prescribed by the NAAQS;

(c)   new source performance standards (NSPS), which impose nationally uniform emission standards on certain categories of new sources, such as electric utilities;

(d)   emission standards for automobiles; and

(e)   acid rain provisions, which are designed to counteract the adverse effects from the long-distance transport of certain pollutants.

Which, if any, can be explained by the interstate externalities rationale for federal intervention?

Richard L. Revesz, Federalism and Environmental Regulation: A Public Choice Analysis

115 HARV. L. REV. 553 (2001).*

The dominant view in the legal academy on the allocation of responsibility for environmental regulation favors federal regulation on the ground that public choice pathologies cause environmental interests to be systematically underrepresented at the state level relative to business interests. In the past, other arguments for federal regulation also were prominent in the public policy debate: that states would "race to the bottom" by offering industrial sources excessively lax standards and that states would underregulate as a result of interstate externalities. In recent years, however, these arguments have somewhat receded from prominence. . . .

This Article refutes the orthodox view concerning the merits of centralized environmental regulation. It shows that the normative analysis underpinning this view is inadequate and presents extensive empirical evidence undercutting the orthodoxy's claims.

The analysis in this Article should interest the principal actors in the regulatory process. For example, to the extent that environmental groups come to understand that federal regulation is not a panacea, they will more effectively focus their energies at the state level. In addition, they will be able to mitigate two increasingly negative features of federal regulation: the threat of federal preemption of more stringent state standards and the unsympathetic reception that their arguments tend to get in the D.C. Circuit, which has primary responsibility for the review of federal environmental policy. . . .

Interest Groups and the Demand for Environmental Regulation

This Part deals with the argument that underregulation at the state level results from the discrepancies in resources and organizational structures between the environmental groups seeking more stringent regulation and the industry groups seeking less stringent regulation. The discussion is thus demand-based. It considers the pressures that groups interested in the stringency of environmental regulation place on the suppliers of such regulation: legislatures and administrative agencies. . . .

Assessing the Conventional Theory

Articulation of the Public Choice Claim.—The dominant claim among supporters of federal regulation on public choice grounds is that states adopt suboptimally lax environmental standards because industry groups that favor less stringent regulation are small and cohesive, whereas individuals who support more stringent regulation are a larger and more diffuse group. Underregulation thus follows from a central

---

tenet of public choice theory, generally traced to Mancur Olson's influential work.

Some commentators do not explain, however, why these public choice problems would be any less serious at the federal level. Others acknowledge that advocates of federal regulation on public choice grounds cannot simply say that state political processes undervalue the benefits of environmental regulation or overvalue the corresponding costs. Instead, for the outcome at the federal level to be more socially desirable, either there must be less underregulation at the federal level, or any overregulation that occurs at the federal level must lead to smaller social welfare losses than underregulation at the state level.

A number of commentators assert that there would be less underregulation at the federal level. Daniel Esty states that "[a]t the centralized level, environmental groups find it easier to reach critical mass and thereby to compete on more equal footing with industrial interests." He adds that "[t]he difficulty of mobilizing the public in many separate jurisdictions is well established." Along similar lines, Richard Stewart states:

> In order to have effective influence with respect to state and local decisions, environmental interests would be required to organize on a multiple basis, incurring overwhelming transaction costs. Given such barriers, environmental interests can exert far more leverage by organizing into one or a few units at the national level.

Stewart acknowledges that "[c]entralized decisionmaking may imply similar scale economies for industrial firms," although he says that "these are likely to be of lesser magnitude—particularly if such firms are already national in scope." He adds that "effective representation may be less a function of comparative resources than of attainment of a critical mass of skills, resources, and experience. . . . [A] national forum for decision may greatly lessen the barriers to environmental interests' achievement of organizational critical mass, sharply reducing the disparity in effective representation." . . .

Mancur Olson and the Logic of Collective Action.—There are several reasons to be skeptical about the soundness of these general claims. Indeed, the starting point for Mancur Olson's analysis—on which some advocates of the public choice justification for federal regulation rely without much evaluation—implies that acting at the federal level magnifies the free-rider problems that environmental groups face.

In fact, as an initial matter, Olson is skeptical of the feasibility of organizing any groups, regardless of size. He notes that "any group or organization, large or small, works for some collective benefit that by its very nature will benefit all of the members of the group in question." An individual understands, however, that if the other members pay for the collective benefit, this benefit will be provided regardless whether he pays for it as well. But if the other members do not pay, the benefit will not be provided regardless whether the individual pays for it. Under either scenario, then, the individual is better off not paying for the collective benefit. Thus, the logic of collective action establishes that a rational individual will not contribute to the formation of groups that provide collective benefits, at least not under a wide range of circumstances.

Olson underscores that this problem is common to both large and small groups:

> If this is a fundamental characteristic of all groups or organizations with an economic purpose, it would seem unlikely that large organizations would be much different from small ones, and unlikely that there is any more reason that a collective service would be provided for a small group than a large one.

Although these problems are common to both small and large groups, Olson is more hopeful that a small group can provide a collective benefit. In small groups, Olson observes, it is more likely that one member can gain sufficient utility to justify the cost of paying for the benefit by himself. Such an outcome is more likely when the potential members are unequally interested in the collective good.

Olson also explains why other members of a small group might contribute to the provision of collective goods. He observes that collective goods are likely to have high initial or fixed costs: "Sometimes a group must set up a formal organization before it can obtain a collective good, and the cost of establishing an organization entails that the first unit of a collective good obtained will be relatively expensive." If a member with a large stake in the outcome is willing to pay for the fixed costs (in addition to some variable costs), members with smaller stakes might decide, given their interest in the collective benefit, to contribute to the additional variable costs. . . .

Therefore, contrary to the assertions of those who espouse the public choice rationale in support of federal environmental regulation, the theory of collective action does not predict greater success for environmental groups at the federal level. Much the opposite: it suggests that, given the necessarily larger size of groups acting at the federal level, groups will in fact be less effective there than at the state level.

Moreover, the national aggregation of environmental interests results in the loss of homogeneity of interests, thereby further complicating organizational problems. For example, environmentalists in Massachusetts may care primarily about air quality, whereas environmentalists in Colorado may care more about limitations on logging on public lands. Other things being equal, state-based environmental groups seeking, respectively, better air quality in Massachusetts and more protection of public lands in Colorado are likely to be more effective than a national environmental group seeking both improvements at the federal level. . . .

Beyond Olson's Theory.—Although academics advocating federal regulation on public choice grounds rely heavily on Olson's theory, his work does not explain convincingly why large environmental groups exist at all. . . .

More recent works have focused on two . . . explanations for the existence of large groups. One explanation takes issue with Olson's conclusion that members of large groups have a smaller incentive to contribute to the provision of the collective good because they get a smaller share of the benefit. Olson's critics argue that this conclusion does not hold in the case of pure public goods—that is, goods that can be enjoyed by one member without reducing another member's enjoyment. The technical literature shows that for pure public goods the amount of the good supplied may increase as the number of members in the group rises. To achieve this result, however, there must be at least one member in the group willing to contribute to the collective good even if nobody else does. Because of that person's large stake in the outcome, it would not be in his interest to free-ride. . . .

A number of important environmental organizations, however, began with significant support from foundations. These foundations may therefore have played the role of the group member willing to contribute to the provision of the collective benefit regardless of the actions of individual members.

A second explanation for the existence of large groups focuses on the moral motivations of group members. Hardin maintains, for example, that "the bulk of the Sierra Club's political activity is supported by public-spirited donations that are not tied to reciprocal exclusive rewards to the donors," and that one cannot "sensibly construct rational arguments for individual contributions to Sierra Club political activities, at least not rational in the sense of narrowly self-interested."

These extensions of Olson's work may explain the existence of environmental groups. They do not, however, suggest (much less establish) a public choice explanation for why environmental groups would do better at the federal level. . . .

Effects of Centralization on the Relative Effectiveness of Industry and Environmental Groups.—Advocates of federal environmental regulation who advance the public choice rationale must deal not only with the question whether environmental groups would be effective at the state or federal level, but also, and more importantly, with the question of how the effectiveness of environmental groups in these two fora compares to the effectiveness of the regulated community in resisting their efforts. Public choice advocates largely ignore this question.

For many environmental problems, firms with nationwide operations comprise an important portion of the regulated community.

For such firms, participation in the policymaking process at the federal level does not give rise to any additional free-rider problems or to any reduction in the homogeneity of the relevant interests. Moreover, many industries are sufficiently concentrated that either one or a small number of firms is able to dominate a national trade association, thereby solving the free-rider problem that normally exists when trade associations represent the interests of member firms. As Olson himself notes, the national trade associations representing industrial interests are often dominated by a few large firms. . . .

Moreover, the decisionmaking authority in trade associations is not evenly distributed among its members. Typically, the extent to which a member controls an association's actions is linked to the member's contribution level. Olson reports a study showing that in almost half the trade associations, "nearly 50 per cent of the cost is borne by a handful of members.". . .

In contrast, environmental groups face additional collective action problems at the federal level. The relevant inquiry is whether these additional problems are outweighed by the benefits of unity and uniformity in the federal forum. Indeed, at the federal level the clash between interest groups takes place before a single legislature, before a single administrative agency, and, in part as a result of the exclusive venue of the D.C. Circuit over important environmental statutes, before a single court.

If one assumes that, beyond a certain threshold, additional resources do not increase a group's probability of success in the political process, and that, at the federal level, this threshold is sufficiently lower than the sum of the corresponding thresholds at the state levels, environmental groups may not be disadvantaged at the federal level even if they would be disadvantaged at the state level. In this case, the economies of scale of operating at the federal level would outweigh the increased collective action problems.

The assumptions behind such a model, however, are not particularly plausible. The threshold concept might hold for certain costs associated with effective participation in the regulatory process. For example, with respect to the regulation of a particular carcinogen, each group might need to hire a scientist to review the regulator's risk assessment. A certain minimum expenditure may secure the services of a competent scientist, and devoting additional resources to the problem may be of little, if any, use. Thus, for costs of this type, the marginal benefit of additional expenditures is zero, or close to zero, regardless of the expenditures of the group seeking the opposite policy outcome.

However, additional resources also make it possible for concentrated industry interests to participate in more proceedings than do dispersed consumer and environmental interests. A number of studies . . . all point in this direction. . . .

But even if the costs of effective participation in the regulatory process were consistent with the threshold model, the structure of other costs is likely to be quite different. For example, with respect to success in the legislative process, a standard public choice account is that the highest bidder prevails. Thus, the benefit a party receives from its expenditures is a function of the other party's expenditures. Unless the costs of this type are quite small, the economies of scale of operating at the federal level are unlikely to outweigh the additional collective action problems that exist in the larger forum.

Even under more sophisticated models of the political process, the quantity of resources expended in securing favorable legislation matters. For example, Arthur Denzau and Michael Munger developed a model in which the price at which legislators will supply a policy depends in part on the distaste of voters for that policy. Thus, the more distasteful the policy, the more resources legislators demand. But under this model, as under the simpler auction model, an interest group can increase its probability of success by expending additional resources. Thus, this account is inconsistent with the threshold model that underpins the public choice rationale for federal environmental regulation. . . .

NOTES AND QUESTIONS

1. **Relative Disadvantage.** What arguments exist for the proposition that environmental groups are relatively more disadvantaged than industrial groups at the state level than at the federal level? What arguments exist for the proposition that they are relatively more disadvantaged at the federal level? Which do you find more convincing?

2. **Large and Small Groups.** Why might the problems of collective action be more easily overcome by small groups than larger groups? Should this count in favor of, or against, federal intervention?

3. **Past State Action.** As evidence of public choice pathologies, advocates for federal intervention claim that states were inadequate environmental regulators before the era of extensive federal intervention that began in 1970. What else might explain the relative inaction on the part of states prior to 1970? For an argument that states did in fact take significant steps to combat those environmental problems that were reasonably well understood at the time, see Revesz, *supra*, at 578–83.

4. **Current State Action.** A substantial number of states have adopted innovative environmental policies extending beyond the requirements imposed by federal regulation, even when doing so has imposed non-trivial costs on in-state firms. Examples include California's automobile emissions standards (discussed in Chapter V); state superfund provisions (such as the New Jersey Spill Compensation and Control Act); and state environmental protection acts (such California's Environmental Quality Act, discussed in Chapter VIII). This pattern, however, is far from universal. What might explain why some states have taken environmentally protective measures while others have not? *See* Revesz, *supra*, at 630–41.

5.   Justifications for Federal Intervention: Economies of Scale. The preceding discussion has evaluated the three most common justifications for federal intervention: the race-to-the-bottom justification, the interstate externality justification, and the public choice justification. There exist, however, a number of other arguments which count in favor of federal environmental regulation.

First, advocates of federal regulation often maintain that centralization has strong economies of scale. They argue that efficiencies will result as a consequence of concentrating regulatory resources at the federal level, as states will not be required to perform duplicative tasks. With respect to which of the following regulatory activities, however, is the economies of scale argument most persuasive:

(a)   performing scientific studies of the adverse effects of pollution?

(b)   setting ambient standards?

(c)   setting emission standards?

(d)   enforcing emission standards?

6.   Justifications for Federal Intervention: Uniformity. For the most part, federal environmental standards are generally minimum standards. States remain free to impose more stringent standards if they wish. Some standards, such as automobile standards under the CAA (discussed in Chapter V), set both floors and ceilings: they pre-empt both more stringent and less stringent state standards. For what types of products is uniformity of this type desirable? Should a distinction be drawn between process standards, which govern the environmental consequences of the manner in which goods are produced rather than the consequences of the goods themselves, and product standards?

7.   Justifications for Federal Intervention: Protection of Minimum Levels of Public Health. Some proponents of federal intervention advance a rights-based justification:

> The rights-based justification holds that the federal government is obligated to control pollution levels because its citizens possess certain environmental rights. Commentators have advanced at least four distinct reasons for vesting environmental rights in U.S. citizens. The first reason is that individuals possess a right to bodily integrity that is violated by high levels of environmental pollution. The second reason is that all citizens possess the right to live in, and to enjoy, a clean environment. A third rationale is distributional in nature. Some commentators, pointing to studies that conclude that poor people and racial minorities are exposed to disproportionate levels of environmental risk, argue that the federal government should intervene to combat "environmental racism." A final argument underlying the rights-based justification focuses on the potentially catastrophic impacts of elevated pollution levels. Some authors argue that the great risks that environmental contamination poses to the planet and to future generations justifies federal intervention.

The rights-based justification's proponents utilize the justification in two ways. First, they use the justification as a reason to oppose devolution of responsibility for environmental protection to the states. Second, they proffer the justification as a reason for the federal government to implement additional regulations.

Daveed Gartenstein-Ross, *An Analysis of the Rights-Based Justification for Federal Intervention in Environmental Regulation*, 14 DUKE ENVTL. L. & POL'Y F. 185, 187 (2003).

Given that federal environmental regulation seeks to limit the risk of exposure to particular pollutants or from particular sources, rather than limiting aggregate levels of environmental risk, in what ways could the rights-based justification be considered both under- and over-inclusive? Furthermore, do you consider it incongruous that the federal government should have such a pre-eminent role in environmental regulation, when it does relatively little with respect to the provision of general health care? *See* Gartenstein-Ross, *supra*.

8.   **Justifications for Decentralization.** Consider now the following justifications for decentralization:

(a)   *Different Costs*—The cost of implementing uniform federal standards varies among states. Determinants may include, for example, a state's climate or geographical characteristics. A standard that is an efficient regulatory response to an environmental problem in one state may be grossly inefficient in another. Uniform federal standards do not distinguish between these conditions.

(b)   *Different Benefits*—Just as the cost of implementing a uniform federal standard may differ between states, so too may the benefits of that standard. For example, a regime that saves 1000 lives in State A may save only one life in State B. A uniform federal standard prevents State B from allocating its regulatory resources more effectively.

(c)   *Different Preferences*—In addition to the divergent costs and benefits of federal regulation, the citizens of different states may hold different preferences with respect to their preferred level of environmental quality. By imposing a federal standard, centralization removes a state's ability to determine its preferred level of environmental regulation.

(d)   *Different Geographical Characteristics*—The United States is a big country, encompassing a range of distinct geographical regions and climates. Different geographical conditions between states ensures that a single regulatory response to an environmental problem is unlikely to be optimal in each state.

Which of these reasons do you find most persuasive? Many of the above concerns could be ameliorated by non-uniform federal standards. What difficulties would administering a non-uniform regime entail? Should it nevertheless be preferred to independent state regimes?

9. Experimentation. One common justification for decentralization is that it promotes policy experimentation and learning, creating the opportunity for successful experiences to be adopted elsewhere. This justification for federalism is captured in the notion of the states as laboratories, introduced by Justice Brandeis in his famous dissent in *New State Ice Co. v. Liebmann*, 285 U.S. 262, 311 (1932) (Brandeis, J., dissenting). But are states actually well positioned to carry out useful experimentation? Some scholars have noted that states lack incentives to engage in policy innovation, preferring to free ride on the risks taken by others. *See* Susan Rose-Ackerman, *Risk Taking and Reelection: Does Federalism Promote Innovation?*, 9 J. LEGAL STUD. 593 (1980). In addition, because states choose their policies (rather than have them randomly assigned) assessing causal links between policies and outcomes can be difficult. Michael Abramowicz, et al., *Randomizing Law*, 159 U. PENN. L. REV. 929 (2011). Decentralization might even lead to the production of harmful information, such as how incumbent politicians can best entrench themselves or special interest groups can exploit public choice pathologies. Michael A. Livermore, *The Perils of Experimentation*, 126 YALE L.J. 636 (2017). Given these challenges, is experimentation a good justification for decentralizations? For an influential experimentalist endorsement of federalism, see Michael C. Dorf & Charles F. Sabel, *A Constitution of Democratic Experimentalism*, 98 COLUM. L. REV. 267 (1998).

10. Federal Policy Vacuum. One practical argument in favor of federalism is that states serve as a kind of backstop when partisan gridlock or other obstacles interfere with national-level policymaking. In the environmental area, climate change is the paradigmatic example: in the face of a decades-long standoff at the federal level over policies to control greenhouse gas emissions, states have taken a leading role through such policies as California's AB 32 and the Regional Greenhouse Gas Initiative (RGGI) undertaken by several Northeastern states. But, as noted by Ann Carlson, even in the case of a seeming policy vacuum, "the federal government's long history of environmental policymaking has shaped and enabled state responses to the regulation of carbon emissions." Ann E. Carlson, *Iterative Federalism and Climate Change*, 103 NW. U. L. REV. 1097 (2009).

11. Partisan Federalism. Jessica Bulman-Pozen has argued that party politics deeply affect how state leaders choose to use their powers under decentralized policy regimes, with state officials challenging decisions by federal officials of the other party, and states serving as "fora for national partisan fights." Jessica Bulman-Pozen, *Partisan Federalism*, 127 HARV. L. REV. 1077, 1079 (2014). With increased political polarization on environmental issues, might decentralization exacerbate partisan disagreement? Alternatively, could variation *within* political parties at the state level create opportunities for political experimentation that provides useful new perspectives on national issues?

12. Desirable Level of Federal Intervention. Having regard to the preceding arguments for and against centralization, what do you consider to be a desirable level of federal intervention?

3. ENVIRONMENTAL LAW AND PUBLIC CHOICE

So far, the book has generally taken a public interest view of environmental regulation. Under this view, governmental action is designed primarily to mitigate the social welfare losses that arise from the presence of externalities. In contrast, under a public choice view, environmental regulation is seen as the response to the pressure of powerful groups that seek to further their individual interests, generally at the expense of aggregate social welfare.

It is difficult to explain environmental regulation in public choice terms if such regulation is viewed simply as imposing costs in terms of pollution control requirements on industrial firms in order to provide benefits in the form of better health to the mass of citizens. Public choice theory would predict that the industrial firms would be able to organize more effectively than the mass of citizens: as a result of their smaller numbers and larger individual stakes in the legislative outcome, their free-rider problems would be less serious. Thus, they would be able to block the enactment of environmental legislation.

This account is limited for at least two reasons. First, it understates the ability of environmental organizations to advocate effectively for policies that generate broad public benefits. To be sure, such organizations face their own collective action challenges, and how they overcome them presents something of a puzzle for the standard public choice account. At the same time, the environmental movement has been criticized for being responsive to a small and unrepresentative subset of the U.S. public and for failing to attend to the costs of environmental protection.

Second, the simple public choice account of environmental policymaking ignores the fact that industrial firms might, in some circumstances, support environmental regulation. Often, environmental regulation protects firms from worse outcomes or imposes on them differential costs, creating some relative winners and some relative losers. Consistent with public choice theory, such regulation can be explained, at least in some instances, as the response to the pressures of the winners.

The readings in this section explore the political context of environmental policymaking. The article by Cary Coglianese examines how the contemporary environmental movement has changed since it became an important social force in the late 1960s. After the initial wave of successes, which resulted in landmark legislation such as the National Environmental Policy Act (NEPA) and CAA and the creation of the EPA, the incentives and tactics of the environmental movement shifted. With new laws that embodied their policy goals, many environmental groups devoted resources to developing the legal and technical expertise necessary to engage in the administrative and legal proceedings that implemented those landmark statutes to consolidate and protect the gains made in Congress. This change led to the institutionalization of the environmental movement inside the U.S. political order as an actor with an interest in protecting at least some features of the status quo.

The article by E. Donald Elliott, Bruce A. Ackerman, and John C. Millian seeks to explain the enactment of the federal Clean Air Act. Their argument proceeds in two steps. First, by the mid-1960s, state environmental regulation had begun to pose a serious threat to powerful groups, particularly the automobile and coal-mining industries. In response, these groups lobbied successfully for federal legislation as a means of either preempting state standards or diminishing the impetus for further state legislation. Second, in 1970, President Richard Nixon, who was preparing to seek reelection in 1972, and Senator Edmund Muskie, his likely opponent, competed to appear more pro-environmental than the other. The authors argue that, as a result of these two phenomena, stringent environmental legislation was adopted despite the weakness of environmental groups. Their account challenges two widely accepted tenets: (1) that federal regulation was a response to inaction on the part of the states, and (2) that industry opposed such regulation.

The excerpt from the book by Bruce A. Ackerman and William T. Hassler describes the forces that led to the 1977 amendments to § 111 of the CAA, which requires new sources to comply with NSPS set by reference to the emission reductions that can be achieved through the use of the best available technology (BAT). Under the regime established in 1970, coal-fired power plants could meet these standards in either of two ways: by burning untreated low-sulfur coal or by "scrubbing" high-sulfur coal. The result of these standards was to increase the relative market share of low-sulfur coal, which is primarily produced in the West, at the expense of Eastern high-sulfur coal. Ackerman and Hassler recount how the high-sulfur coal lobby fought to regain its lost market. Ultimately, aided by the intervention of some environmental groups, it prevailed in securing an amendment to § 111 requiring, in addition to an emission limitation, a percentage reduction over the emissions that would result from the burning of untreated coal. According to Ackerman and Hassler, this standard, though nominally more protective of the environment, in fact increased air pollution in parts of the country.

The excerpt from the article by Nathaniel O. Keohane, Richard L. Revesz, and Robert N. Stavins examines in more detail the circumstances in which firms, as opposed to environmentalists, labor or consumers, demand environmental regulation. The authors divide firm demand for environmental regulation into three categories: firm preferences for particular instruments given lower aggregate costs of compliance compared to the industry as a whole; the presence of rents and entry barriers; and differential costs of compliance across firms in a given industry. The authors then examine the circumstances in which industry will favor the implementation of different regulatory tools.

Cary Coglianese, Social Movements, Law, and Society: The Institutionalization of the Environmental Movement

150 U. PENN. L. REV. 85 (2001).*

The symbiotic nature of the relationships among social movements, law, and society is well illustrated by the history of the environmental movement. The environmental movement has contributed to dramatic changes in law and in public values in the United States, and, as a result, society has achieved notable improvements in some of its underlying environmental conditions. Yet the relationships among the environmental movement, law, and society have been decidedly interactive, not unidirectional, over the past three decades. The movement existed for much of the twentieth century as a small niche in American society, outside the mainstream of prevailing political discourse. Beginning around the early 1970s, however, the environmental movement began to transform both law and society. Congress created a large web of new federal environmental legislation along with new rights for citizens and environmental groups to file suits to enforce government regulation. Public opinion also shifted dramatically and the environment took a prominent, and seemingly permanent, place on the public agenda.

Following its transformational period in the early 1970s, the movement settled back into a pattern of more normal politics and law reform. Compared with the dramatic shift in the legal landscape that accompanied the transformational period, the movement has more recently sought discrete, even incremental change, with activists working as often to maintain past gains as to achieve new ones. Environmental organizations have grown in both size and number since the 1970s, and they now work within a society that generally accepts the values of environmentalism, and within a regulatory regime that entrenches those values in law. . . . Though the United States still confronts environmental challenges, the environmental movement has succeeded in achieving significant changes in law, social values, and certain environmental conditions.

Yet the very success of the environmental movement has also tended to constrain the movement in important ways. . . .

I. Environmentalism as a Social Movement

A. The Early Roots of the Environmental Movement

Environmentalism's roots in American political life extend at least as far back as the 1800s. In those early times, the movement manifested itself in two distinct, but sometimes related, strands. The first strand consisted of efforts principally by hunters, naturalists, and explorers to promote the conservation and preservation of the nation's forests and

---

*   Reprinted with the permission of Blackwell Publishing.

other natural resources. The second consisted of efforts by doctors, engineers, and urban reformers to develop sanitation systems, ensure clean water supplies, and improve the overall living conditions in America's growing cities.

The first manifestation of a concentrated environmental movement came in the late nineteenth and early twentieth centuries with efforts to improve the management of the nation's natural resources. Until this time, management of such resources was highly decentralized or, for some resources, entirely nonexistent. The rise of the Progressive era saw the expansion of the federal government into management of water, land, and wildlife. . . . Some of the earliest conservation groups came into existence during this period. John Muir founded the Sierra Club in 1892, and contemporaneous groups such as the Audubon Society, National Wildlife Federation, Ducks Unlimited, and the Izaak Walton League were organized by hunters and naturalists interested in the effective management of wildlife and forest resources. . . .

A second early strand of the environmental movement could be found in America's growing cities around the beginning of the twentieth century. The growth of American cities in the latter part of the nineteenth century brought with it greater concentrations of people, new challenges in managing waste, and large-scale industrial facilities generating increased amounts of air and water pollution. A sanitation movement emerged, prompting the development of municipal landfills and water and sewage treatment systems. By the early decades of the twentieth century, the movement for improved living conditions in the nation's cities began to fuse with the Progressive movement, which sought to clean up both city politics and the living and working conditions of urban residents. Civic reformers organized to promote the beautification of cities, establish parks, clean up streets, and reduce smog, soot, and other byproducts of industrialization. . . .

B. The Rise of Contemporary Environmentalism

In the 1960s, the American environmental movement reawakened. Controversies in the midcentury had erupted over public dams in the West and the dangers of nuclear conflict, but the movement's renaissance fully blossomed in the 1960s. In 1962, Rachel Carson published Silent Spring, dramatically warning of the long-term dangers of pesticide use. In succeeding years, Carson's book was joined by others that warned of environmental and social decay precipitated by unregulated industrial activity, including Stewart Udall's The Quiet Crisis, Ralph Nader's Unsafe at Any Speed, Paul Ehrlich's The Population Bomb, and Barry Commoner's Science and Survival.

These popular books of the time not only warned of dangers from industrial activities, but also provided the public with a new conceptual apparatus for understanding ecological relationships and for constructing a broad-scale political movement. Moreover, messages of ecological alarm and activism found a receptive audience during the sixties, when there was broader social unrest over civil rights and the Vietnam War. This sense of alarm was further fueled by several highly visible environmental disasters, including a major oil spill in Santa Barbara in 1969 and the infamous burning of the Cuyahoga River in Ohio.

The environmental movement that developed in the 1960s and early 1970s grew out of an extraordinary grassroots response to ecological disasters. Some of the tactics employed at the time fit into the anti-establishment mood of the period. Law reform tactics, similar in some respects to those used by the civil rights movement, figured prominently in the rise of the contemporary environmental movement. Some early reformers even held out hope of winning a transformational declaration of a constitutional right to a clean environment.

Although environmental law reformers never succeeded in securing constitutional protection for environmental quality, their early litigation efforts did result in landmark victories that opened up governmental decision-making processes that had been previously closed to the claims of environmentalists. . . .

The 1960s and 1970s not only saw the growth and resurgence of older environmental organizations, such as the Sierra Club, but also the creation of new environmental organizations, particularly those that specialized in litigation. A successful lawsuit against the spraying of pesticides on Long Island brought together a group of scientists and lawyers who created the Environmental Defense Fund (EDF) in 1967. Other new environmental groups included the Natural Resources Defense Council, the Friends of the Earth, the Sierra Club Legal Defense Fund, Environmental Action, and Greenpeace. Groups that had previously emphasized nature preservation, such as the Sierra Club, Wilderness Society, and the National Audubon Society, also worked together with the new environmental groups toward a common cause of environmental protection.

Unlike many of the conservation organizations founded at the turn of the twentieth century, environmental organizations of the 1960s and 1970s secured a broad base of public support. The number of organizations demanding social change for the environment grew from several hundred to over three thousand by the end of the 1970s. The number of citizens who joined environmental organizations also increased dramatically. The Sierra Club's membership grew nearly tenfold between 1952 and 1969. Membership in the twelve largest environmental organizations grew from about one hundred thousand in 1960 to more than one million by 1972. . . .

C.   Transformations in Law and Society

The resurgence of the environmental movement resulted in significant transformations in American society and law. Around the time of the 1970 Earth Day celebration, the environment secured a position at the top of the public's agenda. Over the course of two years—from 1968 to 1970—press coverage of the environment in the New York Times quadrupled, with that coverage remaining at the higher level for the next seven years. . . . Over the succeeding decades, a substantial majority of Americans remained sympathetic to the cause of environmentalism.

Dramatic changes also took place in American law. . . . Between 1970 and 1977, Congress adopted fourteen major environmental statutes, marking an enormous expansion of federal authority over the environment. In contrast, in the ensuing years, a period more than three times as long, Congress has only adopted four new, major environmental statutes. From the signing of NEPA in 1970 to the adoption of the Superfund law in 1980, the 1970s saw the enactment of what became, and still remains, virtually the entire environmental regulatory system in the United States. . . . These legal transformations have had a significant effect on environmental conditions and economic activity in the United States

II. The Institutionalization of Environmentalism

During the 1960s and early 1970s, the environmental movement not only helped to bring about a remarkable transformation in American law and public opinion, it also transformed itself from a movement serving a relatively small constituency into a major force in American society. By the middle of the 1970s, the movement had become a fully institutionalized presence in the political process. The movement did not continue the protest tactics exemplified by Earth Day but instead employed traditional insider political strategies. Litigation shifted away from the earlier attempts to transform governmental procedures and secure landmark victories, toward more routine, even defensive use of the courts. In the 1980s and 1990s, national environmental organizations succeeded in activating public opinion to resist counter-efforts aimed at undoing the legislative gains of the 1970s, but they have faced much greater difficulty in attempting to alter public opinion enough to move the environmentalist agenda forward. . . .

A. Bringing the Movement Inside

The creation of an extensive set of new environmental laws compelled the leaders of environmental organizations to strengthen their presence in Washington, D.C., to oversee the implementation of the new legislation. Perhaps the clearest indication of the ascendancy of environmentalism came in the mid- to late 1970s when a number of leaders from environmental organizations assumed positions in the Carter administration. President Carter appointed environmentalists to positions in the EPA, the Department of the Interior, and the Department of Justice. . . .

As environmental organizations broadened their connections within government, they deepened their reliance on the kinds of political and legal strategies employed by other established interest groups in Washington, D.C. Legislative and administrative lobbying, along with strategic use of the media and electoral efforts, became mainstays within the environmentalist toolkit. Grassroots mobilization, when employed, became integrated into the environmentalists' legislative agenda and was strategically targeted at specific members of Congress. . . .

Environmental organizations grew more professional, increasing both the size and the specialization of their staffs. In order to be effective participants in the realm of insider politics, environmental groups needed their own teams of scientists and economists, as well as lawyers. They also employed professional fundraisers, media consultants, and membership recruitment specialists. . . . The major environmental organizations, although fewer in number than corporations and trade associations, deployed resources and tactics on a par with business organizations. Environmentalism had grown to be one of the largest social movements in American history. Instead of existing as a minority voice in the political process, the environmental movement became a part of the American political and social fabric. Environmentalism had matured from a social movement to an extensive network of interest group organizations with a presence in Washington, D.C., like that of any other political lobby.

B. Reaction and Maintenance

In 1981, the Reagan administration took office with an agenda aimed at reducing the burdens of federal regulation. Several Reagan appointees, most notably James Watt as Secretary of the Interior and Anne Gorsuch Burford as EPA Administrator, stirred up much controversy among environmentalists and the public. . . .

In response to the Reagan administration's countermovement, the "Group of Ten" environmental groups joined together to coordinate a response. These major national organizations mobilized to oppose the actions of Secretary Watt and seek his removal from office, garnering over one million signatures on a petition urging Reagan to remove Watt from office. In 1983, after he made some further controversial remarks, Watt was forced by the White House to tender his resignation. Under a cloud of scandal at the EPA, Burford also resigned in 1983 and was replaced by the EPA's original administrator, William Ruckelshaus, who had an impeccable reputation for integrity. Numerous other senior officials at the EPA were also forced to leave as a result of the controversy.

In the subsequent years of the Reagan administration, Congress renewed every major environmental statute up for reauthorization, including the Resource Conservation and Recovery Act, Superfund, the Safe Drinking Water Act, and the Clean Water Act. The Superfund Amendments, for example, tightened clean-up requirements and led to a nationwide right-to-know program, which required industry to report publicly the use and release of toxic chemicals. The Asbestos Hazardous

Emergency Response Act of 1986 required every school to implement plans for asbestos inspection, management, and parent notification. The Clean Water Act of 1987 required states to adopt policies to address toxic water pollutants.

The environmentalists' successful response to the Reagan administration's countermovement campaign served to reveal the depth of public support for environmental values. Even in a period of otherwise popular support for President Reagan, the environmental movement not only managed to sustain itself and resist counter-efforts, but it actually thrived. The Reagan administration proved to be excellent for environmental organizations' membership recruitment. Between 1979 and 1983, the Sierra Club grew to 346,000 members, the Wilderness Society doubled its membership, and the Audubon Society added 200,000 members. By the end of the Reagan presidency, the environmental movement was probably stronger than ever. It had secured a national presence and had placed environmental issues within the American consciousness. In 1988, over ninety percent of Americans were comfortable calling themselves environmentalists. . . .

[P]ublic opinion polls in the early 1990s [however] appeared to indicate a weakening in public support for the environmental movement. Two years into the Clinton administration, Republicans captured both houses of Congress, running on a "Contract with America" that called for a reduction in federal regulation. After Congress proposed revisions in various environmental laws, environmentalists mobilized a strong public backlash. President Clinton . . . came to see the environment as a key issue on which to challenge the Republicans. Clinton adopted a hard-line position, twice allowing the government to shut down because he would not sign appropriations bills containing riders which environmentalists viewed as threatening public health.

Clinton's actions were widely favored by the public and the Republicans learned that they had miscalculated. In interpreting polling responses showing comparatively weak support for the environmental movement, Republican analysts fell into the trap of thinking these equated with opposition to environmental regulation. It became clear that even though the environment may not have been foremost in their minds during the early 1990s, Americans were still very much concerned about the environment. . . .

C. Divisions and Diffusion

Mainstream environmental organizations came together in the 1980s and again in the 1990s to resist countermovement efforts, but the environmental movement as a whole also experienced significant internal divisions during this same period. Indeed, as the movement has grown more institutionalized, divisions within it have become evident. Michael McCloskey, a former executive director and chairman of the Sierra Club, has observed that for most of the 1970s, "the environmental movement was remarkably free of stress over ideology. However, this changed . . . by the mid-1980s when a new radical wing emerged in the environmental movement." As they matured, the major movement organizations came to be perceived by some as insular, bureaucratized, and out of touch. Segments of the environmental community did not find their values well represented by the mainstream groups. . . .

In addition to divisions within the movement, the values of environmentalism began to diffuse throughout society and were captured by other kinds of political organizations, such as unions. Business even began to espouse green values. By the mid-1980s, the environmental movement confronted greater competition both from within its own ranks as well as from external groups. . . .

III. Steady-State Environmentalism?

. . . The history of environmentalism suggests that law reform by itself is not adequate to sustain a social movement's goals over the long term, especially in the face of resistance and counterattacks. Legal reform, if it is to have an enduring impact, needs to be accompanied by a genuine change in public values. Broad public support for the environment has helped to sustain the nation's basic institutional commitment to the environment as reflected in contemporary law. Public opinion, however, has not been so radically transformed as to propel the environmental agenda toward further social and legal transformation. Following the major transformations of the 1970s, environmentalism has settled into what appears to be a steady state that resists significant changes in the institutional status quo.

A. Latent Environmentalism

The environmental movement has been extraordinarily successful in transforming public opinion. . . . Yet even though large majorities of Americans support the values of environmentalism, and very few report being actively opposed to the movement, public support for the environment has not always been constant nor even necessarily deep. . . . While consistently strong, support for the environment expressed in public opinion polls has varied over time, with other issues frequently taking precedence.

More significantly, public support for environmentalism tends to be latent. In the absence of crises, environmentalism does not motivate the political behavior of any large segment of the public. . . . The latency of this support means, however, that public concern for the environment affects the political process mainly when the public is activated by an environmental crisis or when the public believes that existing institutions designed to protect the environment are under threat. Rather than propelling the movement forward, public opinion remains a potential resource for environmentalists and an obstacle for those who would seek to change existing environmental laws.

B. Change in Social Movements

All social movements face challenges in sustaining themselves and advancing their goals over time. Social movements often fail to capture much of the public's attention in the first place. But even among those that do capture the public's attention, the public cannot be mobilized for a long time around any particular social cause. Even the most successful social movements and their organizations tend to lose momentum over time. The very institutionalization of a successful social movement, such as environmentalism, can constrain the movement for several reasons.

First, once institutionalized, social movements need to maintain their gains and this tends to siphon off the time and resources of movement organizations and activists. It is time consuming to work within and maintain an existing institutional structure. The time spent on maintaining the status quo is time that cannot be spent on addressing new problems. Activists can come to emphasize the preservation and maintenance of past accomplishments, rather than the promotion of a still more progressive agenda. . . .

Second, successful social movements can be co-opted by their own success. Once institutions are created to address a social problem, it can become harder to mobilize the public. The existence of an extensive array of environmental laws and governmental institutions that deal with environmental issues makes less likely the kinds of environmental crises needed to activate public outrage. This is not to suggest that significant environmental concerns do not remain, but rather that many of the environmental problems that are most visible to the public—such as oil spills, bulging soot, or rivers caught on fire—have largely been addressed by existing laws and institutions. Even when a crisis does occur, the fact that government institutions exist to respond to it tends to reassure the public and allay its concerns. As a result, the very success of the environmental movement in creating laws and institutions tends to constrain its ability to generate public support for significant new laws.

Finally, social movements can confront countermovements that sometimes reverse their accomplishments. The environmental movement has hardly been immune to counter-efforts. . . . The environmental movement has experienced resistance from smaller but vocal "wise use" and "sagebrush rebellion" movements, principally in Western states, along with the resistance from the Reagan administration in the 1980s and Republican members of Congress in the 1990s. What has been remarkable is that the environmental movement, unlike other social movements, has not only prevailed in these times of counterattack, but has each time come back apparently strengthened by the encounter.

C. Sustaining Law Reform

Even in the face of adversity, division, and the normal process of decay, the environmental movement has maintained a profound presence in American public life. The movement has achieved its successes due to the broad transformation in both institutions and social values that it helped engender. The quasi-constitutional transformation of American law in the 1970s, along with the growth of national environmental organizations, has secured a place for environmental values in economic and governmental decision making, even during times when the environment has not been high on the public's agenda. . . .

But law is also not fully autonomous from society. As we have seen, the creation of the U.S. system of environmental law came about in the 1970s as a response to a major political mobilization and a burst of public concern. Just as environmental law came into existence due to politics, so too can it be changed due to politics. Since the creation of the broad sweep of environmental statutes in the 1970s, these laws have been applied in a politically charged environment. At key points during the past several decades, counter-efforts sought to mark a retreat from the environmentalists' agenda. In each major instance, the environmental movement was able to prevail because it could draw upon broad public support and successfully portray its opponents as threatening to undermine core environmental values. Had it not been for the public's deep, albeit latent, acceptance of environmentalism, the victories won by the law reformers of the 1970s could very well have been reversed or left to atrophy by the countermovements of the 1980s and 1990s.

Social movements need law reform to help achieve their goals of social change, but law reform itself needs a supportive social and political climate if it is to maintain its viability and effectiveness over time. The environmental movement has succeeded in providing this supportive climate. Just as the legal system helps sustain environmentalism during periods of public inattention, the system of environmental law is itself sustained by a broad social consensus in favor of environmental protection and by a latent environmentalism that stands ready to be activated by environmental groups.

Law reform is not simply a tool for changing society; rather, law reform is itself affected by society and its non-legal norms and values. To be successful, social movement reformers need not only seek changes in the law but changes in public values too. In the absence of direct changes to society's values, law reform efforts could prove at worst vacuous or at best vulnerable to counterattack or atrophy over time. The history of the U.S. environmental movement teaches that the leadership of governmental institutions can retreat from earlier commitments made to the values of a social movement. For a social movement to resist such a retreat, it is essential to draw upon a solid base of public support.

NOTES AND QUESTIONS

1. **Collective Action.** Robert Percival has noted the "puzzle over the sources of the tremendous growth in national environmental groups, particularly because it seems so inconsistent with the predictions of

[Mancur] Olson's theory [of collective action.]" Robert V. Percival, *Environmental Legislation and the Problem of Collective Action*, 9 DUKE ENVTL. L. & POL'Y FORUM 9, 13 (1998). Some of the solutions to the puzzle offered by scholars essentially reject a model of human behavior grounded in self-interest in favor of alternatives such as altruism, civic republicanism, or "postmaterial values." *See id.*; Russell J. Dalton, *The Greening of the Globe? Cross-national Levels of Environmental Group Membership*, 14 ENVTL. POLITICS 441 (2005). Within the rational utility maximizer paradigm, economist James Andreoni has argued that charitable giving can provide a "warm glow" benefit to donors, who enjoy psychological or social benefits from giving. James Andreoni, *Impure Altruism and Donations to Public Goods: A Theory of Warm-Glow Giving*, 100 ECON. J. 464 (1990). But a warm-glow theory must explain why some causes generate these effects and others do not. Richard Stewart has concluded that the strength of the environmental movement is "the result of historical, cultural, and political contingencies that have yet to be fully or satisfactorily explained." Richard B. Stewart, *Environmental Quality as a National Good in a Federal State*, 1997 U. CHI. LEGAL FORUM 199, 210 (1997). What accounts for the environmental movement's success at overcoming collective action challenges? During their early years in the 1960s and 1970s, many of the now-major environmental organizations received sustained funding from a small number of major donors, such as the Ford Foundation. *See* Kaen O'Connor & Lee Epstein, *Rebalancing the Scales of Justice: Assessment of Public Interest Law*, 7 HARV. J. L. & PUB. POL'Y 483, 488 (1984) (noting importance of Ford Foundation support for several leading groups); BURTON ALLEN WEISBROD, PUBLIC INTEREST LAW: AN ECONOMIC AND INSTITUTIONAL ANALYSIS (1978). Does this help explain how these groups could come into being, despite facing collective action challenges?

2. Diversity and Representation. Mainstream environmental organizations in the United States have faced criticism for a lack of diversity in their staff, management, and boards. Faith R. Rivers, *Bridging The Black-Green-White Divide: The Impact of Diversity in Environmental Nonprofit Organizations*, 33 WM. & MARY ENVTL. L. & POL'Y REV. 449 (2009); Luke W. Cole, *Empowerment as the Key to Environmental Protection: The Need for Environmental Poverty Law*, 19 ECOLOGY L. Q. 619 (1992). In 1990, these concerns led a group of environmental justice leaders to issue a letter to the "Group of Ten" organizations, stating that, "[a]lthough environmental organizations calling themselves the 'Group of Ten' often claim to represent our interests, in observing your activities it has become clear to us that your organizations play [a] . . . role in the disruption of our communities." *See* Rivers, *supra* (citing *The Letter that Shook a Movement*, SIERRA MAGAZINE, May/June 1993, at 54, *reprinted in* LOUIS S. WARREN, AMERICAN ENVIRONMENTAL HISTORY 322 (2003)). The letter also demanded that the groups "cease operation in communities of color" until major staff changes were made. *Id.* Issues of racism and exclusion have a long history within the environmental movement. *See* DORCETA E. TAYLOR, THE RISE OF THE AMERICAN CONSERVATION MOVEMENT: POWER, PRIVILEGE, AND ENVIRONMENTAL PROTECTION (2016). But, despite decades of criticism, recent research has found a "green ceiling" in mainstream environmental organizations that has limited the success of efforts to diversify the movement. DORCETA E. TAYLOR, THE STATE OF DIVERSITY IN ENVIRONMENTAL ORGANIZATIONS (July 2014). Why has the racial composition of traditional environmental groups remained largely consistent, despite growing diversity within the American population?

3. **Role of the Media.** Between 1968 and 1970, press coverage of the environment in the *New York Times* quadrupled. *See* W. Douglas Costain & James P. Lester, *The Evolution of Environmentalism, in* ENVIRONMENTAL POLITICS AND POLICY 15, 33 fig. 2.4 (1995). In April 1970, the first Earth Day was held with an estimated 20 million Americans taking part in Earth Day-associated activities across the country. *See* Joseph Lelyveld, *Millions Join In Earth Day Observances Across the Nation*, N.Y. TIMES, Apr. 23, 1970. Earth Day is often considered to mark the beginning of the modern environmental movement. *See* Jonathan Cannon & Jonathan Riehl, *Presidential Greenspeak: How Presidents Talk About the Environment and What It Means*, 23 STAN. ENVTL. L.J. 195, 201 (2004). Did increased media focus on the environment reflect popular concern, or did it play a role in popularizing environmentalism?

4. **Partisan Polarization.** The bipartisan support that environmental protection enjoyed during the hayday of the 1970s has faded considerably: there is a now a large and growing partisan divide over environmental policy. *See* Aaron M. McCright, Chenyang Xiao & Riley E. Dunlap, *Political Polarization on Support for Government Spending on Environmental Protection in the USA, 1974–2012*, 48 SOC. SCI. RESEARCH 251 (2014). Climate change is an issue that provokes particularly strong partisan divides, with Democrat and Republican affiliated voters holding strongly divergent views on the threat posed by greenhouse gas emissions. *See* Riley E. Dunlap et al., *The Political Divide on Climate Change: Partisan Polarization Widens in the U.S.*, 58 ENV'T: SCI. & POL'Y FOR SUSTAINABLE DEV. 4 (2016). Many reasons have been hypothesized for the growing polarization, ranging from the moral framing of environmental issues to the influence of regulated industry on conservative views. *Compare* Matthew Feinberg & Robb Willer, *The Moral Roots of Environmental Attitudes*, 24 PSYCH. SCI. 56 (2013) (testing relationship between moral framing of environmental issues and polarization), *with* Daniel A. Farber, *The Conservative as Environmentalist: From Goldwater and the Early Reagan to the 21st Century*, 59 ARIZ. L. REV. 1005 (2017) (examining the role of business interests and conservative think tanks in facilitating environmental polarization). Is there anything that the environmental movement could do to slow down or reverse this trend?

E. Donald Elliott, Bruce A. Ackerman & John C. Millian, Toward a Theory of Statutory Evolution: The Federalization of Environmental Law

1 J. L. ECON. & ORG. 313 (1985).*

Collective Action and Prisoners' Dilemma

The Problem of Collective Action

Modern theories of voluntary organization, derived from Mancur Olson, imply that national environmental groups will be difficult, if not impossible, to organize. Large numbers of citizens, each with only a small stake in clean air, will, if they are rational in the narrow economic sense, decline to invest their time or money in the cause of cleaning up the environment in the hope that they will be able to "free-ride" on the efforts of others. Since everyone will be inclined to "let George do it," it won't get done at all. The paradox, of course, is that everyone ends up worse off than they would have been if they had been able to organize their actions for their collective benefit.

It is a small step from Olson's theory of voluntary organizations to the political corollary that the interest of citizens in a clean environment will be systematically underrepresented in any lawmaking process in which interest group politics plays a significant role. Individual citizens who wish to breathe clean air are a classic example of a large, disorganized population seeking a collective good which will benefit each individual by only a small amount. The costs of environmental regulation, on the other hand, tend to fall heavily on a relatively small number of companies, which are already reasonably well-organized and thus presumably less subject to free-rider problems. According to most popular theories of political influence, well-organized industries would be systematically overrepresented and diffuse environmentalists systematically underrepresented in formulating policy. How, then, is one to explain the passage of strong environmental legislation in the late 1960s and early 1970s? . . .

Politicians' Dilemma

The answer, or at least a more complete answer, can be discovered by considering the problems of environmental organizing and passing environmental legislation as analogous to the game of Prisoners' Dilemma.

Prisoners' Dilemma gets its name from a story about two prisoners who are separately interrogated about a crime. The two were the only witnesses, so if they both refuse to testify, the worst that can happen to them is a one-year conviction for illegal possession of firearms. However, a clever prosecutor approaches each prisoner and offers him a proposition: "If you confess and testify against your partner, he'll get life

---

* Reprinted with the permission of Oxford University Press, with permission conveyed through Copyright Clearance Center, Inc.

but you'll go free; the only hitch is that if you both confess, you'll both get a sentence of six years for armed robbery. I should tell you that I'm offering the same deal to your partner."

Assuming that the game is played only a single time, and assuming further that the prisoners are rational and motivated only by self-interest, they will both confess—and get six years in jail, rather than keep quiet and get off with only a year. The paradox, of course, is that by pursuing their individual self-interest, the prisoners behave in a way that is contrary to their shared collective interest in shorter sentences. If they could only organize their actions for their common benefit, they would both be better off. . . .

This . . . perspective helps to explain the evolution of environmental law during the late 1960s and early 1970s. Not that the evolving institutional structure technically complied with all the conditions for the game of Prisoners' Dilemma—in contrast to the standard game, our story involves many relevant players, no single subset of which could have coordinated their strategies in a way that guaranteed them an optimal result. Nonetheless, like the prisoners, many of the key actors responded to institutional threats of terrible outcomes by rationally choosing strategies that were very far from first-best from their point of view. We shall, then, use the term *Politicians' Dilemma* to describe situations which are analogous to the game of Prisoners' Dilemma in that the structure of incentives facing the players creates a strong incentive for them to pursue a less than ideal outcome in order to avoid an even less desirable result. . . .

Politicians' Dilemma and Environmental Statutes

The first significant federal statutes regulating air pollution, the Motor Vehicle Pollution Control Act of 1965 and the Air Quality Act of 1967 were not passed because of the political power of environmentalists at the national level but because two well-organized industrial groups, the automobile industry and the soft coal industry, were threatened with a state of affairs even worse from their perspective than federal air pollution legislation—namely, inconsistent and progressively more stringent environmental laws at the state and local level. As a consequence of the structure of our federal lawmaking system, environmentalists were able to organize industry to do their bidding for them. Thus, the first federal legislation regulating air pollution was passed not because environmentalists solved their own organizational problems on the national level but because environmentalists exploited the organizational difficulties of their industrial adversaries at the state and local level.

The auto industry and the soft coal industry undoubtedly would have preferred no government regulation of air pollution rather than federal legislation. When faced with the threat of inconsistent and increasingly rigorous state laws, however, they resolved their Politicians' Dilemma by using their superior organizational capacities in Washington to preempt or control the environmentalists' legislative victories at the state level.

It does not matter to our argument whether environmentalists and industrialists were consciously pursuing the strategy we outline. Like the characters in the Prisoners' Dilemma, they may have been simply reacting rationally to the strategic implications of their situation. What we have found, in short, is empirical support for a paradox previously elaborated by theorists of federal systems.

We will analyze the dynamic by first showing why a federal system gives environmentalists important strategic advantages at the state level, then showing that the strategic situation at the national level was vastly preferable from the polluters' point of view, and finally showing how the strategic interests of polluters coincided with the pursuit of political self-interest by reelection-maximizers and presidential aspirants in the Congress. . . .

The Period of Political Cost-Externalization

The existence of states aids environmentalists in three ways. First, and most obvious, the existence of the states makes it possible for environmentalists to seek piecemeal solutions to their organizational difficulties. Not that the effort to transcend their free-ride problems will be easy—even in smaller states, thousands of people will have to be convinced to take seriously the signals activists are beaming in their direction, and states such as California and New York present the problem of organizing a population the size of Canada's. Nonetheless, even here, the demands on a variety of resources—from political savvy to hard cash do not compare with the challenges involved in achieving organizational credibility in a nation of a quarter of a billion. . . .

Second, federalism opens up the possibility of a distinctive credit-claiming strategy for aspiring politicians on the state level, which we call *cost-externalization*. Quite simply, dividing the nation into fifty geographic zones makes it almost inevitable that some pollution problems will be generated by out-of-staters. Since midwestern auto workers don't vote on whether California should ban the internal combustion engine to control smog and Appalachian coalminers don't vote on whether New York should ban coal to control sulfur oxides from power plant smoke stacks, these issues promise politicians on the state level the equivalent of a free lunch—"tough" legislation allows them to garner public credit for bringing a benefit to *their* constituents at somebody else's expense.

Finally, as scattered environmental victories begin to appear, this evidence of success will feed efforts in other states. Activists will be prompted to continue the fight, rather than seek out other issues; the media and the public will gradually begin to take greater notice and express increased interest. A bandwagon effect becomes possible: victories in one state may promote the marshalling of the resources necessary for victory in another. Indeed, legislation in one state can stimulate other states to adopt even more stringent laws. . . .

Preemptive Federalization

The Motor Vehicle Air Pollution Control Act of 1965. The first statute which gave the federal government regulatory power over air pollution was the Motor Vehicle Air Pollution Control Act of 1965. The roots of this federal legislation run deep into the California of the 1950s and 1960s. . . . Suffice it to say that through a combination of a cost-externalization strategy by California politicians, auto industry ineptitude, and local environmental organizing, state air pollution legislation had begun to pose a serious threat to the automobile industry by the middle 1960s. California had already adopted a regulatory program requiring the installation of emission controls on all new cars sold in the state, an auto emissions bill was pending in the Pennsylvania state legislature, and New York was considering an emission standards bill even more stringent than California's. . . .

Unlike most other industries, the automobile industry has strong reasons to prefer national legislation over state and local regulation of air pollution. Most manufacturing industries would rather have state and local governments set air pollution standards, because the political and economic costs of controlling their pollution are concentrated at the local level. It is a rare politician who is immune to the charge that a proposal will harm a local, job-creating industry. In addition, some manufacturing industries may be able to play one state off against another by threatening to move their factories out of states which set stringent air pollution standards (thereby creating a true Prisoners' Dilemma from the standpoint of the states).

The automobile industry is in a very different strategic position, however, because it is geographically concentrated and its product, not its factories, is the main source of its pollution. Local politicians can set strict antipollution standards for motor vehicles without fear of being accused of putting their constituents out of work. It is true that pollution controls tend to increase the price of new cars, but the connection between government action and particular price increases is only dimly perceived by voters. And unlike other industries, Detroit could not credibly threaten to stop selling cars in California or other states which established stringent pollution standards. Moreover, differing or inconsistent air pollution standards set at the state and local level were perceived as a serious threat to Detroit's assembly lines. Finally, the companies feared a kind of political domino effect, in which one state legislature after another would set more and more stringent emission standards without regard to the costs or technical difficulties involved.

Ideally the auto companies would have preferred to remain free of any substantial government regulation of pollution, but if they were going to be regulated, federal legislation was preferable to state legislation—particularly if federal standards were set based on technical presentations to an administrative agency rather than through symbolic appeals to cost-externalizing politicians.

During the early 1960s, the automobile industry successfully opposed federal emission standards for motor vehicles. In mid-1965, however, the industry abruptly reversed its position on the advice of Washington lawyer Lloyd Cutler: provided that the federal standards would be set by an administrative agency, and provided that they would preempt any state standards more stringent than California's, the industry would support federal legislation. As a result, Senator Muskie's pending bill to have the federal government set emission standards for motor vehicles was amended to provide that standards would be set by HEW,* rather than in the legislation itself, and legislative history was written to leave no doubt that more stringent state laws were preempted. . . .

The Air Quality Act of 1967. The Air Quality Act of 1967 was the first federal statute to give the federal government a significant role in regulating air pollution from stationary sources such as factories and powerplants. Under the 1967 act, the federal government was to promulgate criteria based on the latest scientific evidence concerning the adverse effects of air pollution. Each state was then to develop its own air pollution control plan based on the federal criteria. If any state failed to adopt a satisfactory plan, the federal government could promulgate one for it.

The story behind the Air Quality Act of 1967 is complicated, but here too the threat of state and local legislation provided the impetus for a crucial industry to acquiesce in federal legislation in the hope that it might dampen local legislative initiatives. Like the automobile industry, the high-sulfur, soft (bituminous) coal industry is geographically concentrated, and its product, not its factories, constitutes the primary source of its air pollution. Soft coal provided a logical target for local politicians anxious to place the blame for pollution on out-of-state sources.

During the mid-1960s, the soft coal industry faced increasingly strict air pollution regulations in the Northeast, which eventually threatened it with the loss of a major market. In 1965, Mayor John Lindsay of New York proposed—and despite strong opposition mounted by the coal industry, the city council eventually passed—a program to ban the use of coal as a heating fuel and to greatly restrict the sulfur content of coals used for other purposes. In 1966, New York, New Jersey, Pennsylvania, and Connecticut announced joint plans to combat air pollution. In March 1967, the threat of strict state legislation which would eliminate markets for high-sulfur coals in most major metropolitan areas increased when the federal HEW released an advisory criteria document reviewing the

---

* The Department of Health, Education, and Welfare, which had jurisdiction over environmental regulation before the establishment of the Environmental Protection Agency (EPA)—ED.

scientific literature on the health risks of sulfur dioxide, a pollutant which is formed when soft coal is burned.

Its unsuccessful campaign against pollution control legislation in New York City had taught the coal industry that it was virtually impotent in local political arenas. . . . Ideally, the soft coal industry, like the automobile industry, probably would have preferred that there be no government regulation of the pollution produced by its product. However, if there was going to be regulation, federal legislation offered distinct advantages to the coal industry over runaway state and local lawmaking. While the 1967 federal Air Quality Act did not forbid states from setting air pollution standards more stringent than those recommended by HEW, as a practical, political matter, the air quality criteria which HEW established based on the latest scientific evidence would tend to restrain state legislation. Advisory committees within the federal bureaucracy promised to be a far more hospitable forum for the coal industry than the politics of state and local legislatures. . . .

The Air Quality Act of 1967, like the Motor Vehicle Air Pollution Control Act of 1965, passed not because environmentalists were a well-organized pressure group at the federal level, but because their efforts, and the actions of local politicians, created a Politicians' Dilemma for a well-organized industry. Faced with the even less desirable alternative of a significant loss of markets through state and local legislation, the soft coal industry strongly supported passage of [the] bill.

Aspirational Lawmaking

A structurally similar process also accounts for some of the surprisingly stringent provisions of the Clean Air Amendments of 1970. In particular, the requirement that automobile manufacturers reduce their pollution by 90 percent within five years, and the stipulation that EPA ignore economic and technological feasibility, did not result from the success of environmentalists at organizing a strong lobbying presence of their own in Washington. Here too a Politicians' Dilemma was at work. The "prisoners" in this case were politicians, primarily Senator Edmund Muskie and President Richard Nixon. By strategically threatening these political entrepreneurs with the loss of political capital which they had previously worked to build, environmentalists were able to organize them to pass a statute more stringent than the politicians really wanted. In an ideal world both Nixon and Muskie probably would have preferred a compromise statute less likely to alienate either industry or environmentalists, but as in a Prisoners' Dilemma, they were confronted with a situation in which they both had to choose the least-worst situation politically.

The structural feature which creates the Politicians' Dilemma is the fragmentation of the lawmaking system between Congress and the Executive, between House and Senate, between legislative committee and legislative committee. This division of lawmaking authority creates a situation in which various politicians can credibly claim credit for any particular law. David Mayhew has argued persuasively that most members of Congress can be thought of as "reelection maximizers." For this breed of legislator, the costs of sponsoring broad legislation such as the Clean Air Act will generally outweigh the benefits. A smaller number of legislators, however, aspire to run for higher office. These aspirants may analyze the political costs and benefits involved in environmental lawmaking in terms that are very different from the simple reelection maximizer.

If he hopes one day to gain the presidency, the aspirant must, somehow or other, gain public recognition as a serious political leader throughout the United States. And to this end, it will not suffice to sprinkle the home district with dams, post offices, and similar goodies, or to help constituents with their Social Security checks, or to return to the district for weekend orgies of baby-kissing and speechifying. To make a national impact, the aspirant must project an image as a statesman seriously concerned with the good of all Americans. And from this perspective, it *may* make sense to invest heavily in environmental lawmaking. . . .

Throughout the 1960s, Senator Muskie carefully invested his time and legislative effort in the environment, long before the issue achieved great public attention. As the primary drafter of the federal air pollution statutes of 1965 and 1967, as well as several water pollution statutes, Muskie stood to gain from the rapid rise in importance which the voting public attached to environmental issues in the early 1970s. However, because of the separation of the lawmaking function into multiple bodies and the difficulty which the voting public has in monitoring all the lawmaking activities in Washington, Muskie was vulnerable to see "his" issue stolen by other politicians, particularly the one in the White House. In addition, because most voters do not bother to follow the details of what goes on in Washington that closely, Muskie was also vulnerable to charges from the embryonic environmental movement that he was really "Mr. Dirty," not "Mr. Clean."

The divisions of lawmaking authority, coupled with the difficulty of credibly communicating with the voters about the political significance of legislative activities, created a situation in which Nixon and Muskie were caught in a Politicians' Dilemma. The result was the passage of the Clean Air Act of 1970 in a form which was more stringent than either of them would have preferred.

The Clean Air Act of 1970. The Clean Air Amendments of 1970 is a complex statute. There is no denying that a number of strands came together to contribute to its passage. One factor was the realization that the Air Quality Act of 1967 had failed to achieve its goal of cleaning up the air. In addition, by 1970 there had been an enormous increase in popular concern about the environment, fueled in part by the attention which the issue was receiving in the press and on television. Finally, 1970 was different from 1967 in that a "loose coalition" of environmentalists was just beginning to organize on the national level, although environmentalists were still nowhere near a match for even a single auto company's lobbyists, either in terms of numbers or funding.

In this political environment, it would not have been surprising for Congress to pass additional air pollution legislation of an incremental sort perhaps an increase of funding here, or a realignment of federal and state authority there. In fact, on December 10, 1969, the leading proponent of federal air pollution legislation, Senator Muskie, introduced just such a bill, the Air Quality Improvement Act. . . .

One writer has used the term "policy escalation" to refer to the process by which Muskie's weak, original proposal was transformed into a more extreme final statute; another has called it "speculative augmentation." Whatever one calls it, what happened was essentially as follows: on February 10, 1970, two months after Muskie had introduced his Air Quality Improvement bill, President Nixon transmitted his own air pollution proposals to Congress. Nixon's proposals called for major structural changes in existing federal air pollution statutes, including national standards for extremely hazardous air pollutants and a requirement that states develop abatement plans to meet mandatory federal air quality standards within one year.

The next significant event occurred in May 1970, when a Ralph Nader task force published a report harshly criticizing Muskie as being soft on industry. The flavor of the report is summed up by a sentence displayed prominently on its dust jacket: "Sen. Muskie's sub-committee on pollution and the federal laws for which it was responsible have resulted in a 'business-as-usual' license to pollute for countless companies across the country." The Nader report went on to claim that Muskie should be "stripped of his title as 'Mr. Pollution Control'" and to demand that he resign his chairmanship of the air and water pollution subcommittee. Muskie was clearly stung by Nader's public criticism.

In August, Muskie's subcommittee reported out a revised air quality bill which essentially followed the outlines of Nixon's proposal but was tougher at every turn than what the president had proposed: where Nixon's proposal would have allowed states one year to develop their implementation plans, Muskie's bill allowed only nine months; where the administration proposed that the auto companies be given until 1980 to achieve a 90 percent reduction in emissions, Muskie's subcommittee cut the deadline to 1975; where Nixon proposed nationwide federal air quality standards, Muskie's subcommittee added the requirement for an additional "margin of safety" and the protection of especially sensitive groups; where Nixon had proposed that we do what "we can do within the limits of existing technology," Muskie deleted technological or economic feasibility as a constraint. . . .

Muskie wrote a "tough" pollution statute in 1970, one which ran a serious risk of alienating industry, only when he was threatened with an outcome which was even worse from his perspective—the loss of his reputation with the public as a crusader to clean up the environment; Nixon went along, reluctantly, because the adverse political consequences of vetoing the bill were perceived as greater than those of signing it. . . .

It is important to recognize that the surprisingly strong environmental legislation in 1970 did not result from superior organization by environmentalists. Indeed, it is possible to speculate that if environmentalists had been more tightly organized as a conventional pressure group in 1970, as they later became, the Clean Air Act amendments might have been less, rather than more, stringent. Had there been a well-organized environmental lobby in 1970, Muskie could have deflected Nader's charges by giving in to its demands. And it is quite likely that this lobby would have settled for far less than the Great Leap Forward achieved by the Clean Air Act. In 1970, however, no group yet existed with whom to bargain. In these circumstances, Muskie had no way of knowing how much would be enough. He did about all that he could have done to prove that he was more "pro-environmental" than Nixon: he proposed a bill which was essentially Nixon's, only more so on every point.

NOTES AND QUESTIONS

1. Politicians' Dilemma. Elliott, Ackerman, and Millian use the term "Politicians' Dilemma" to describe situations in which "the structure of incentives facing the players creates a strong incentive for them to pursue a less than ideal outcome in order to avoid an even less desirable result." Is the Politicians' Dilemma that Elliott and his colleagues ascribe to the automobile and soft-coal industries analogous to the prisoners' dilemma, which is explained in the notes and questions to Chapter I? Who are the actors in this game? What is the structure of their incentives? Is the Politicians' Dilemma that the authors ascribe to Nixon and Muskie analogous to the prisoners' dilemma? Is the Politicians' Dilemma label useful?

2. Federal and State Regulation. Is the preference of the automobile industry for federal regulation likely to be contingent on the federal standards being (1) less stringent than *all* state standards or (2) less stringent than at least some state standards? Why is the connection between more stringent standards and higher car prices "only dimly perceived by voters"? Under the 1990 amendments to the CAA, states can opt for either the federal standards or the more stringent California standards. *See* 42 U.S.C. § 7507. For some states, the impact on car prices of the California standards had an important effect on this choice. Had voters become more sophisticated by 1990?

3. Preemption. If the purpose of the Air Quality Act of 1967 was to prevent more stringent regulation at the state level, why did the statute not preempt more stringent state standards, as the Motor Vehicle Air Pollution Control Act of 1965 had done? Was there not a risk that the coal industry would get the worst possible outcome: regulation at the federal level coupled with more stringent regulation at the state level?

4. Cost-Externalization. Elliott, Ackerman, and Millian focus on the cost-externalization permitted by a federal system. They give the example of a ban by New York on the use of high-sulfur coal in power plants affecting coal miners in Appalachia. But there also is benefit-externalization: some of the benefits of lower power plant emissions will accrue to residents of other states. What accounts, then, for state regulation? Are Elliott and his co-authors likely to be advocates of "race-to-the-bottom" arguments for vesting responsibility for environmental regulation at the federal level? Are they likely to believe that federal regulation is desirable because environmental interests are systematically underrepresented at the state level?

5. Automobiles and Soft Coal. Were the plights of the automobile and soft-coal industries comparable? Do they both have the same interest in uniform regulation?

6. Politicians' Dilemma Revisited. Is the Politicians' Dilemma faced by Nixon and Muskie a distinctive feature of the American political system? Might similar competition for credit-claiming exist in parliamentary governments? Unlike the actors in the prisoners' dilemma, Nixon and Muskie were repeat players: the CAA was not the only piece on legislation about which they had a mutual interest. Game theory suggests that repeat players are more likely to be able to coordinate their actions. Why might such coordination not have been possible for Nixon and Muskie?

Bruce A. Ackerman & William T. Hassler, Clean Coal/Dirty Air

1–3, 13–19, 29–33, 35–37, 40, 48–54 (1981).[*]

Our study . . . focuses upon a crucial substantive policy issue: the future of the coal burning power plant. At present, these plants contribute 48 percent of all electric power produced in the United States. This share will grow over the next half century. With oil scarce, nuclear risky, solar embryonic, and hydro limited, the nation's rich and cheap coal reserves call for exploitation. At the same time, coal burning generates environmental burdens. Coal-fired power plants are major sources of several pollutants; they are currently the single most important source of sulfur oxides. As a result, the control of new coal burners has gradually emerged as one of the most pressing questions confronting the Environmental Protection Agency (EPA), leading it, in June 1979, to revise the "new source performance standards" (NSPS) it had previously imposed on sulfur emissions from new coal-burning power plants. . . . Our story begins with the way Congress set about to control the environment in 1970. . . .

---

[*]   Reprinted with the permission of Yale University Press, copyright © 1981.

From Statute to Policy

... Despite Congress's aggressive stand on NSPS, it remained for the EPA to translate the statute into practical policy. Its task was to establish a standard that, in the words of the statute, "reflects the degree of emission limitation achievable through the application of the best system of emission reduction which (taking into account the cost of achieving such reduction) the Administrator determines has been adequately demonstrated." As we shall show, however, setting such a standard would have been a tricky business at best—for in its desire to avoid the perils of expertise, Congress had adopted a simplistic formula that was exceedingly difficult to apply to the problem posed by coal burning. . . .

Technology in a Vacuum

By its very terms, two aspects of the statute invited, if they did not require, agency sophistication in setting a standard for new coal burners. First, there was the instruction that the administrator take cost "into account" in making his decision. . . . Second, a proposed system had to be "adequately demonstrated" before it became the basis for a clean-up requirement. . . .

To understand the bureaucracy's view of its own choices, we must consider the state of technology in the early 1970s. At that time, there existed two methods for reducing emissions from coal-fired plants: a relatively old-fashioned technique known as physical coal cleaning, or "coal washing," and an embryonic technology, flue gas desulfurization, commonly known as "scrubbing."

Physical cleaning removes sulfur from coal before the coal is burned. The simplest method involves equipment not much more advanced than a wire screen and garden hose: freshly mined coal is crushed, passed through a screen, and wetted, so that heavy sulfur-bearing fragments can settle out. These relatively simple processes can remove most of the sulfur-bearing particles, called pyrites, that are physically mixed with the coal as it comes from the mine. They cannot, however, remove sulfur that is chemically bonded to the coal. Nonetheless, the gains achieved by primitive washing techniques can be substantial, varying from 20 percent to 40 percent. Within these limits, physical coal cleaning is a cheap and reliable technology. Moreover, it was not obvious that potential gains from coal washing had been exhausted. By grinding coal into a fine slurry, it would be possible to wash more of the pyritic sulfur than could be reached by the primitive crush-and-hose methods practiced in the early 1970s.

Nonetheless, the EPA disregarded such humdrum possibilities and concerned itself exclusively with more symbolically satisfying technologies devices that, attached to a smokestack and paid for directly by the polluter, promised to cleanse the smoke produced by the boilers below. Among the technologies existing in 1971, the scrubber was the only one that performed this symbolic function. Its ability to perform as an actual control technology, though, was more problematic.

A scrubber does not rely on physical processes such as crushing and washing, but on the maintenance of a large-scale chemical reaction. It is a 70-foot test tube which on a typical day may consume 400 tons of limestone and thousands of gallons of water to remove over 200 tons of SO_2. As exhaust gases flow up a power plant smokestack, they are exposed to a lime or limestone solution that is sprayed in their path. Sulfur dioxide in the gas reacts with the spray and goes into solution, from which it is later removed, dewatered, and extruded in the form of sludge. Maintaining the proper conditions for this reaction requires continuous supervision. For example, the coal burned may contain elements such as chlorine that interrupt the desired reaction; or a variation in the amount of SO_2 in the flue gas may adversely affect the process. Even when the reaction is proceeding apace, the machines must operate in a very harsh environment. Unreacted SO_2 and water may combine to form sulfuric acid which corrodes the inside of the scrubber and smokestack. Reacted SO_2 may form compounds that travel beyond the scrubber and clog smokestacks, pipes, and pumps. While these problems were not difficult to solve under carefully controlled conditions, the early scrubbers were prone to frequent breakdown—operating less than half the time. When the administrator promulgated his new standard of performance in 1971, only three scrubbers were operating in the United States. The oldest, built in 1968, would be abandoned by the end of the year.

In short, the EPA squarely confronted the problem posed by any statute requiring that a system be "adequately demonstrated"—how to trade off certainty and economy against incentives for further technological development. Moreover, creative ways of mediating the tension were available; perhaps a standard based on improved washing should have been required in the intermediate term with reliance on scrubbers projected for a decade or more hence. Rather than give the statutory formula a creative interpretation, however, the language was used as an excuse for thought. The possibility of advanced coal washing was totally excluded and official documents narrowly focused their attention on the question of whether the scrubber was "available" in some engineering sense, divorced from other development opportunities. Such an approach justified the bureaucracy's spending its limited resources on engineering projections to determine if scrubbers could be made operational in the near future. On the basis of these projections, the administrator found that the scrubber's ability to eliminate about 70 percent of a coal burner's sulfur oxides had been "adequately demonstrated," and proceeded to the task of translating this engineering judgment into regulatory policy.

Squaring the Circle

At this point the agency was forced to confront the dilemmas imposed by its own impoverished reading of the statute. The embarrassing fact is that the agency's interpretation made it conceptually impossible to move from its engineering judgment about the scrubber's availability to a policy judgment defining the number of pounds of SO₂ a plant could emit for each MBTU of energy it produced. To see why, consider that a power plant's emissions are not exclusively determined by its treatment technology but are also a function of the amount of sulfur in the coal that the plant burns. The agency's engineering judgment about scrubbing could readily be translated into an emission limitation only if *all* of America's coal contained the same sulfur content. Only then could 70 percent be multiplied by a constant to yield a single nationwide limit on new plant discharges. But, alas, America's coal reserves range in sulfur content from 1 to more than 10 pounds. To make matters even more difficult for the administrator, these coals are distributed unevenly throughout the coal-producing regions. Roughly half of the nation's reserves lie west of the Mississippi in the Northern Great Plains and Mountain regions and consist largely of low-sulfur coal. Eastern reserves, primarily from the Midwest and the Appalachians, contain much larger proportions of higher sulfur coal. . . .

The agency's predicament was intensified by a final statutory artifact. Although the statute directed the administrator to look at the "best system" in defining applicable effluent standards, it did not authorize him to force polluters to install scrubbers if their power plants could meet the effluent limit in some other way. Thus, whatever ceiling the administrator might set, polluters might find it cheaper simply to burn low-sulfur coal than to install scrubbers. The threat of a massive shift away from high-sulfur coal would, in turn, generate powerful political pressures from eastern producers. The conceptual inadequacy of the engineering approach—its lack of explicit concern with the variability of polluting inputs—masked a potentially explosive political problem: how to parry the predictable counterattack by eastern coal?

Surely not by surrendering without a fight. After all, the whole point of environmental regulation is to force producers to bear the social costs of their enterprise. High-sulfur coal had previously gained an unfair competitive advantage over low-sulfur coal precisely because the extra harm it caused the environment had not been reflected in coal prices. A program of controlling sulfur oxides merely removed that advantage. . . .

Despite the conceptual impossibility and political unwisdom of moving immediately from its engineering judgment to regulatory standards, the agency tried to square the circle by treating the problem of coal variability as if it were a minor detail. The agency simply failed to recognize that its findings about scrubbing were compatible with an NSPS ceiling ranging all the way from 3 pounds per MBTU to 0.3 pounds per MBTU—depending on whether ten-pound eastern or one-pound western coal was being scrubbed at 70 percent efficiency. Apparently there was no effort, however rudimentary, to estimate the costs and benefits generated by a range of different possible emission ceilings. Instead the agency finessed its conceptual and political problems by announcing a number and making a few casual remarks in its support. The numerical ceiling was set at 1.2 pounds of SO_2 per MBTU; in support, the EPA merely stated that this ceiling would permit eastern power plants to comply by scrubbing 70 percent of the SO_2 out of the average eastern coal—which was said to contain roughly 4 pounds of SO_2 per MBTU ($[1.0-.70]$ x 4 pounds = 1.2 pounds). At the same time, the agency recognized that utilities might respond to this ceiling the natural way, by burning 1.2-pound coal. It failed, however, to estimate the impact such decisions would have on the eastern coal industry, let alone whether the benefits of the 1.2 standard outweighed its expected costs. Instead, it blandly proclaimed that burning low-sulfur coal would also satisfy the new standard. . . .

The House Proposals of 1976

. . . When amendments were initially proposed by the subcommittee, they contained . . . a barely perceptible alteration of Section 111.* The 1970 version of this section directed the agency to set performance standards that reflected "the degree of emission limitation achievable through the application of the best system of emission reduction. . . ." In contrast, the new House proposal required a standard which "reflects the degree of emission *reduction* achievable through the application of the best *technological* system of *continuous* emission reduction. . . ." (emphasis added).

The significance of this change was far from obvious, given a special definition of "technological system of continuous emission reduction" that also appeared in the House proposals. Rather than define the term to require an "add-on" pollution control technology, Section 111(a)(7) gave the term a technical meaning to include "a technological process for production or operation by any source which is inherently low-polluting or nonpolluting." The use of low-sulfur coal can reduce power plant emissions by 80–90 percent! If anything, this wording placed the use of low-sulfur coal on a more solid statutory footing. Turning to the House committee report, however, one enters a new world of meaning. It proclaims that scrubbing or some other add-on technology is required of all new coal burners. . . . This clear statement would bear fruit only if the EPA and the courts focused their attention upon the committee report, glancing at the statute itself only when the report's language was ambiguous. Unfortunately, however, this approach to statutory interpretation is hardly unprecedented. . . .

House staffers began to organize political support for the invisible amendment of Section 111.

---

* The NSPS section—ED.

Their search for politically potent allies for the "new" NSPS led in a surprising—but readily explicable—direction. Although universal scrubbing had only a problematic relation to clean air goals, there *was* an interest group that valued it for its own sake—the producers of high-sulfur coal in the eastern United States. For many years this group had fought and lost the good fight against "unnecessarily" stringent pollution standards. As far as they were concerned, the invisible amendment of Section 111 offered a new strategy that promised to further their basic interests more effectively. Once the eastern utilities were forced to install scrubbers, it would be possible for them to meet the 1.2 NSPS while continuing to use cheap high-sulfur coal. Only if utilities were allowed to substitute low-sulfur coal for scrubbers would a shift away from high-sulfur products be conceivable. Thus it made sense for the dirty coal producers to abandon their campaign to weaken pollution standards and take up the cudgels for the costliest possible clean air solution—universal scrubbing.

As a consequence, when House staffers made contact with eastern coal interests, they met with a sympathetic response. From the point of view of the United Mine Workers Union, the scrubbing issue was particularly straightforward. Because its membership is concentrated in the East, it had no difficulty coming out publicly for universal scrubbing. Politics were more complicated for the National Coal Association. Since western owners were naturally interested in maximizing sales of low-sulfur coal in the East, they would not take kindly to the national lobby endorsing a requirement that would freeze them out of a potentially rich market. Consequently, the National Coal Association refused to take a position on scrubbing, leaving it to eastern members to use their considerable political muscle in ways we shall describe.

The stage had been set for a bizarre coalition between clean air and dirty coal forces. . . . The consummation of this political marriage was evident as early as the 1976 House committee report, whose language was repeated in the House report the following year. Besides announcing that the "new" Section 111 had invisibly imposed a universal scrubbing requirement, the report justified the innovation by finding six flaws in the "old" NSPS:

1. The standards give a competitive advantage to those States with cheaper low-sulfur coal and create a disadvantage for Mid-western and Eastern states where predominantly higher sulfur coals are available.

2. These standards do not provide for maximum practicable emission reduction using locally available fuels, and therefore do not maximize potential for long-term growth.

3. These standards do not help to expand the energy resources (that is, higher sulfur coal) that could be burned in compliance with emission limits as intended.

4. These standards aggravate compliance problems for existing coal-burning stationary sources which cannot retrofit and which must compete with larger, new sources for low-sulfur coal.

5. These standards increase the risk of early plant shutdowns by existing plants (for the reasons stated above), with greater risk of unemployment.

6. These standards operate as a disincentive to the improvement of technology for new sources, since untreated fuels could be burned instead of using such new, more effective technology.

Although this pronunciamento was written by House staffers with strong environmentalist reputations, its authors might easily have come from a major coal company. While point 6 attempts an inadequate invocation of technology-forcing, the text employs the standard rhetoric of the eastern coal lobby—the need to eliminate unemployment by using "locally available fuels" and to defeat the energy crisis by burning high-sulfur coal. . . .

Political Convenience and Legal Ambiguity

While the House report established the foundation for a clean air-dirty coal alliance, it remained for the environmental lobby in Washington, D.C. to accept the political invitation. . . .

Instead of campaigning for a congressionally mandated reduction in the 1.2 standard, . . . public interest lawyers embraced the dirty coal rhetoric. For example, Joseph Brecher, on behalf of the Sierra Club, condemned the 1971 NSPS decision because "eastern high-sulfur coal, which is now available, is having a hard time getting a market because of the comparative cheapness of bringing in western low-sulfur coal." Richard Ayres, for the Natural Resources Defense Council, bemoaned the fact "that the Clean Air Act became a factor influencing the competition in the marketing for coal, encouraging practices such as shipping mountain state coal to Illinois and Louisiana, with attendant use of oil powering the diesel engines used to transport train after train of coal." These passages represent a remarkable rhetorical turn. Typically, environmentalists do not protest when a government initiative forces industry to discard "dirty" inputs and substitute "clean" ones. In so doing, government is simply eliminating market distortions and requiring the prices of high-polluting products to reflect their true social cost. Rather than condemn the advantage gained by clean coal as artificial, environmentalists characteristically applaud when the "true" costs of dirty coal have finally been revealed. No matter. With such rhetorical assistance, the peculiar coalition between the friends of clean air and dirty coal would be a powerful political force.

Yet rhetoric alone cannot overcome the fundamental conflicts concealed by a marriage of convenience. While both groups wanted scrubbers, they wanted them for different reasons. Environmentalists saw scrubbing as a technique for cutting new plant emissions below 1.2

pounds to even lower levels. For example, if a plant using one pound western coal were required to scrub at 90 percent efficiency, only 0.1 pound of SO_2 would be discharged. For eastern coal interests, however, scrubbing was desirable only as long as new plants could keep discharging at the old 1.2 level. If the administrator used scrubbing as a reason for lowering the emission standard dramatically below 1.2, high-sulfur coal producers would be frozen out of the new plant market once again. . . .

Low-Visibility Politics

. . . The invisible revision of Section 111 passed through the House untouched; its lack of salience was emphasized by the failure of the Senate committee to include a comparable revision in its legislative proposals. . . .

[T]he Senate bill . . . proposed *no* change in Section 111, and the Senate report contained nothing resembling the House committee's low-visibility pronunciamento on behalf of dirty coal. Moreover, the scrubbing lobby was content to evade explicit senatorial consideration . . . leaving it to the conference committee to reach a "compromise" in which the House's legislative history would once again expose the hidden meaning of Section 111.

Midnight Lawmaking

The Senate's approval of the Clean Air Act . . . was only a preliminary to the main event—where conferees from both the House and Senate committees would hammer out a final compromise after two years of disagreement.

. . . [T]he House achieved a formal victory. . . . Henceforth the statute would require the administrator to regulate power plants differently from other dischargers. Although the administrator is simply to tell everybody else to reach specified emission limits, an acceptable power plant standard also requires: "the achievement of a percentage reduction in the emissions from such category of sources from the emissions which would have resulted from the use of fuels which are not subject to treatment prior to combustion."

Given this provision, the administrator must not only require a power plant to discharge no more than X pounds of sulfur oxide per MBTU, but also to reduce the sulfur in the coal by Y percent. By setting the percentage reduction requirement at a level only scrubbers can achieve, 85 percent for example, the administrator could effectively force all coal burners to install scrubbers. But the statute falls far short of mandating such a high percentage. Indeed, it does not even require the administrator to establish the same percentage for all coal burners. Although each plant must be told "a percentage reduction" to achieve, another subsection, unchanged from 1970, expressly authorizes the administrator "to distinguish among classes, types, and sizes within categories of new sources for the purposes of establishing such [NSPS] standards." Hence, the administrator has the authority to tell users of low-sulfur coal to reduce their sulfur content by Y_1 percent and require high-sulfur burners to eliminate Y_2 percent. . . .

Indeed, when viewed within the framework of the section as a whole, the new provision does not even bar the administrator from establishing a reduction of zero percent for low-sulfur coal burners. . . .

Rather than try to bring the increasingly complex statutory language under control, the draftsmen turned to their first love: making legislative history. Once again, the House staff gained a victory within the conference report that it failed to achieve on the surface of the statute: "The Senate concurs in the House provision with minor amendments. The agreement . . . preclude[s] use of untreated low sulfur coal alone as a means of compliance." Yet midnight legislative history is a game any number can play. Aides for Senator Dominici were quick to add their own opinion in the next paragraph: "The conferees agreed that the Administrator may, in his discretion, set a range of pollutant reduction that reflects varying fuel characteristics." Given this threat, the House staffers counterattacked with another tack-on: "Any departure from the uniform national percentage reduction requirement, however, must be accompanied by a finding that such a departure does not undermine the basic purposes of the House provision and other provisions of the act, such as maximizing the use of locally available fuels." . . .

The incoherent quality of the legislative history was apparent to the amendment's supporters almost immediately. After spending all of August 3 compiling the conference report that had been completed at 2:20 that morning, the staffers thought it wise to spend the next day formulating a "Clarifying Statement" while both Houses were voting their approval of the statutory language. Among these clarifications is one that reflects the continuing effort to wrestle with the scrubbing confusion. This time it is said that

> while the conferees agree that the Administrator may set the percentage reduction requirement as a percentage range, the conferees expect the Administrator to be exceedingly cautious if he should elect to do so. Such range would be allowed only to reflect varying fuel characteristics and must be based on a carefully and completely documented finding . . . that [this] does not undermine the basic purpose[s] . . . of the House Report. . . .

In short, the draftsmen brewed a mix of statute and legislative history worthy of the occasion. Instead of integrating Section 111 into the basic structure of the act, their task was to avoid a potential conference impasse by writing a document whose legal meaning was hopelessly confused. The new Section 111 is easier to understand as an exercise in small group dynamics than as a serious effort to guide the bureaucratic management of a multibillion-dollar problem.

NOTES AND QUESTIONS

1.   Old-Plant Effect. By making new source standards more stringent, the 1979 regulations exacerbated the old-plant effect, that is, they created incentives for highly polluting existing plants to remain in business rather than be replaced by new, cleaner plants. Consider an example in which the annual operating costs of an existing plant, including pollution costs, is $100, and in which the plant emits 10 pounds of SO_2 per MBTU. The annual operating costs for a new plant with the same production capacity, including pollution control costs and capital costs, are $90 if it must meet a standard of 2 pounds per MBTU and $110 if it must meet a standard of 1 pound per MBTU. Thus, if the regulator chooses the less stringent new source standard, the old plant is replaced and the resulting emissions are 2 pounds per MBTU (as compared to the 10 pounds per MBTU emitted by the old plant). In contrast, if the regulator chooses the more stringent new source standard, the old plant continues in operation and the resulting emissions are 10 pounds per MBTU. Thus, the more stringent regulation leads to the worse environmental outcome. For further discussion of the old-plant effect, see Robert W. Crandall, *The Political Economy of Clean Air: Practical Constraints on White House Review, in* ENVIRONMENTAL POLICY UNDER REAGAN'S EXECUTIVE ORDER: THE ROLE OF BENEFIT-COST ANALYSIS 205, 212–14 (V. Kerry Smith ed., 1984). How should regulators attempt to avoid the old-plant effect? What information do they need? What is a desirable relationship between the standards imposed on new and existing plants, respectively?

2.   Low- and High-Sulfur Coal. Ackerman and Hassler's argument can be best understood by reference to a stylized example. Assume that all low-sulfur coal has 1.2 pounds of SO_2 per MBTU and is concentrated along the West Coast, and that all high-sulfur coal has 8 pounds of SO_2 and is concentrated along the East Coast. Consider the impact on the markets for low-sulfur and high-sulfur coal of the following policies: (1) the pre-1971 regime, under which power plant emissions are essentially unregulated; (2) the regime under the Clean Air Act Amendments of 1970, which led to the adoption of regulations in 1971 requiring new power plants to meet a standard of 1.2 pounds SO_2 per MBTU; (3) the regime under the administrator's proposed regulations published in 1978 pursuant to the Clean Air Act Amendments of 1977, which limited emissions to 1.2 pounds SO_2 per MBTU and required an 85 percent reduction from the emissions that would have resulted from the use of untreated fuel; (4) the regime under the administrator's final regulations, adopted in 1979, which imposed (a) a 1.2 pounds SO_2 per MBTU limitation and (b) a 70 percent reduction if the resulting emissions are no more than 0.6 pound SO_2 per MBTU, and a 90 percent reduction otherwise. Table IV.1 shows the effects of the various regulatory measures on coal markets. The various rectangles are proportional to the market shares of the two different types of coal.

Table IV.1.

Pre-1970 Regime

Low-sulfur coal 1.2 pounds per MBTU no scrubbing	High-sulfur coal 8 pounds per MBTU no scrubbing

1971 Regulations

Low-sulfur coal 1.2 pounds per MBTU no scrubbing	High-sulfur coal 1.2 pounds per MBTU 85 percent scrubbing

1978 Proposed Regulations

Low-sulfur coal 0.18 pounds per MBTU 85 percent scrubbing	High-sulfur coal 1.2 pounds per MBTU 85 percent scrubbing

1979 Final Regulations

Low-sulfur coal 0.36 pounds per MBTU 70 percent scrubbing	High-sulfur coal 0.8 pounds per MBTU 90 percent scrubbing

Before 1971, the relative markets for low-sulfur and high-sulfur coal were determined by the relative prices of the two types of coal and by transportation costs. On the line dividing the two regions, the total costs (purchase price plus transportation) of both types of coal are equal. To the west of this line, it is cheaper to use low-sulfur coal; conversely, to the east of this line it is cheaper to use high-sulfur coal. The 1971 regulations increase the cost of using high-sulfur coal by effectively requiring scrubbing for this coal to meet the 1.2 pounds per MBTU standard, but leave unchanged the cost of using low-sulfur coal. As a result, the line separating the two regions moves to the east, and high-sulfur coal producers lose part of their market.

In contrast, the 1978 proposed regulations increase the cost of using low-sulfur coal by effectively requiring scrubbing of such coal in order to meet the percentage reduction requirement, but leave unchanged the cost of using high-sulfur coal, which already had to be scrubbed as a result of the 1971 regulations. Thus, they expand the market for high-sulfur coal. In fact, assuming that the costs of scrubbing a given percentage of SO_2 are the same of low-sulfur and high-sulfur coal, the 1978 proposed regulations return the two markets to their pre-1971 division by imposing the same pollution control costs on both types of coal. (The final regulations, by imposing a differential scrubbing requirement, once again move the dividing line to the east, but not as far as the 1971 approach.) What regulatory scheme should the administrator have promulgated pursuant to the 1977 amendments? Was he constrained in his ability to adopt differential reduction requirements?

3. 1977 Amendments. The 1977 amendments had different environmental effects throughout the country. Table IV.2 summarizes, for the 1971 and 1979 regulations, respectively, the effects illustrated in Table IV.1.

Table IV.2.

Region	1971 Regulations	1979 Regulations
West	Low-sulfur, unscrubbed	Low-sulfur, scrubbed
Midwest	Low-sulfur, unscrubbed	High-sulfur, scrubbed
East	High-sulfur, scrubbed	High-sulfur, scrubbed

The 1977 amendments produced several potentially negative environmental effects. The old-plant effect is discussed above. In addition, scrubbers are likely to malfunction or not be used at full capacity; while scrubbed high-sulfur coal produces the same emissions as unscrubbed low-sulfur coal, if the scrubber malfunctions, the resulting emissions for high-sulfur coal will be 8 rather than 1.2 pounds per MBTU. Moreover, scrubbers produce sludge, creating a solid waste problem. The first two of these negative effects are felt not only in the Midwest, but also in the East. Indeed, as sulfur dioxide travels in the atmosphere, it gets transformed into sulfates, which in turn cause acid rain. Because prevailing winds blow from west to east, the adverse consequences of forced scrubbing in the Midwest exacerbated the acid rain problem in the East. *See* BRUCE A. ACKERMAN & WILLIAM T. HASSLER, CLEAN COAL/DIRTY AIR, 20, 67–68, 70–72 (1981).

What were the environmental effects in the West? Which environmental groups are more likely to have supported the amendments? Consider that sulfates impair visibility and that the reduced visibility in the Grand Canyon and other national parks in the West was an important environmental concern at the time of the passage of the 1977 amendments. Were there better ways to improve the air quality in the West? Was there a better national solution?

4. Legislative History. Ackerman and Hassler urge courts to give little weight to the legislative history of the NSPS. *Id.* at 108–09. They note:

> There can . . . be no doubt that the clean air-dirty coal coalition would have vastly preferred a single statutory phrase commanding full scrubbing to a ream of legislative history in praise of 'locally available coal.' The reason they settled for less is that they feared they would lose if they went for broke and forced a statutory showdown on NSPS.

Id. at 108.

The strategy of the lobbyists, however, must be analyzed against the prevailing techniques of statutory construction. It did not make sense to take the risks of placing the protection of high-sulfur coal in the statute (and perhaps fail in this attempt) because they were likely to achieve the same result through the use of legislative history. If the prevailing technique of statutory construction had ignored legislative histories, the high-sulfur lobby would have had nothing to lose by pushing for statutory language and might well have gotten it. The impact of rules of statutory construction cannot be evaluated statically. Rather, one must consider the problem dynamically: if the ground rules are different, the lobbying activities will probably be different as well. In light of this complication, are Ackerman and Hassler justified in urging courts to depart from the then-prevailing technique of statutory construction?

5.   NSPS Percentage Reduction Requirement. The NSPS percentage reduction requirement for power plants, which had been added in the 1977 amendments, was repealed in the 1990 amendments to the Clean Air Act. Can this repeal be explained in public choice terms?

6.   The Role of Self-Interest. B. Peter Pashigian has argued that political support for the application of more stringent air pollution controls in less industrialized parts of the country was driven, at least in part, by concern by more industrialized areas that uniform standards would lead to an exodus of industry seeking to avoid costly investments in pollution control technology. His analysis of votes on several Clean Air Act related amendments in the U.S. House of Representatives in 1976 and 1977 revealed that "House members from areas with relatively dirty air were staunch defenders of the relatively clean air in *other* parts of the country." B. Peter Pashigian, *Environmental Regulation: Whose Self-Interests Are Being Protect?* 23 ECON. INQUIRY 551, 562 (1985). Other than imposing costs on their competitors, are there reasons why the more heavily industrialized regions might favor more stringent controls in cleaner parts of the country? For another empirical study of congressional self-interest in voting on environmental legislation, see ROBERT W. CRANDALL, CONTROLLING INDUSTRIAL POLLUTION: THE ECONOMICS AND POLITICS OF CLEAN AIR (1983).

Nathaniel O. Keohane, Richard L. Revesz & Robert N. Stavins, The Choice of Regulatory Instruments in Environmental Policy

22 HARV. ENVTL. L. REV. 313 (1998).[*]

. . . Firms tend to demand the policy instruments promising the highest profits (or the lowest losses) from regulation. While all environmental regulation imposes costs of compliance on firms, not all instruments impose the same costs to achieve a given regulatory goal. Positive political economy explanations of firm demand for environmental regulation can be divided into three principal categories:

firm preferences for particular instruments given lower aggregate costs of compliance compared to the industry as a whole; the presence of rents and entry barriers; and differential costs of compliance across firms in a given industry.

Lower Aggregate Costs to an Industry as a Whole

All else being equal, firms will tend to prefer regulatory instruments with lower aggregate costs for the industry as a whole. As market-based approaches are likely more cost-effective than command-and-control instruments, the above would suggest that private industry as a whole would generally prefer market-based approaches. However, a crucial distinction exists between the aggregate cost for society and the aggregate cost for private industry. By definition, cost-effective instruments minimize costs to society; they may however vary in proportion of costs imposed on polluters. Accordingly, the use of market-based instruments does not guarantee that firms' compliance costs will be less than the compliance costs of command-and-control regulation.

It would then follow that firms would oppose regulatory instruments that shift a greater cost burden onto industry. For instance, the virtually unanimous opposition by private industry to pollution taxes results from the fact that, under such schemes, firms pay not only their private costs of compliance, but also the costs of tax payments to the government for any residual emissions. Similarly, under tradeable permit schemes, firms bear equivalent costs if the initial distribution of the permits is through an auction. In contrast, under a tradeable permit scheme with grandfathered permits, existing firms do not bear any cost for their residual emissions.

The above suggests that private industry as a whole would prefer grandfathered permits and standards to other instruments, since grandfathered permits are cost-effective *and* the burden placed on industry (at least on existing firms) is minimized. Emissions standards are usually worse for industry in terms of the total-cost criterion, but are likely to be preferred by firms to auctioned permits or taxes.

Generation of Rents and Erection of Entry Barriers

Certain types of regulations can actually augment firms' profits through the generation of rents and the erection of entry barriers. In general, firms earn rents if a regulatory instrument drives price above average cost. Assume the case of a command-and-control standard that sets an allowable level of aggregate pollution for each firm, where firms can meet the standard only by reducing output. Assume further that the industry is initially made up of many identical firms, each facing an identical demand, with classical average and marginal cost functions. In the absence of regulation, each firm would produce at the intersection of its marginal and average cost curves, making zero profits. The environmental standard reduces total production and therefore raises price along the aggregate demand curve. If the environmental restriction is not exceptionally severe, the new price will be above average cost for all firms. Firms, therefore, earn rent: the difference between the price they receive for their product and their cost of production. If entry is prohibited, existing firms will continue earning rents into the future; even if not, rents will last until enough new firms enter to reestablish competitive equilibrium at the new price. Hence, in the above model, firms may prefer standards to no regulation at all, and firms will prefer standards to taxes, since a tax charges for a resource that otherwise would be free.

Firms, however, are not limited to the single response of cutting output. They can also reduce emissions by adopting new technologies or by changing their input mix. In this more general and realistic scenario, depending on the stringency of the standards and other factors, command-and-control standards can still have the effect of providing rents to regulated firms. Here, too, under certain conditions, firms may prefer command-and-control standards to no regulation at all.

It is important to note that the enhanced industry profitability resulting from rents will be sustainable over the long term *only* in the presence of entry restrictions. Thus, firms regulated by a rent generating instrument, such as command-and-control standards, will benefit if that instrument is linked to a mechanism that imposes barriers to entry. In theory, such a mechanism might prohibit new entry outright; a more politically feasible approach would impose higher costs on new entrants.

The above body of theory explains why private firms (and their trade associations) may have a strong preference for command-and-control standards, which may create rents, and especially for considerably more stringent command-and-control standards for new pollution sources, which create barriers to entry. The indication that firms would support this form of regulation begins to explain the prevalence of such instruments in U.S. environmental law. Furthermore, the theory indicates that, under certain conditions, the regulated industry would be better off than without regulation.

Although the theoretical arguments are strong, there are no conclusive empirical validations of these demand-side propositions. Direct empirical tests of firm demand for regulatory instruments (such as analyses of resources devoted to lobbying for such instruments as a function of firms' stakes in an issue) are virtually nonexistent. Instead, most empirical work in this area simply seeks to measure the benefits an industry receives under regulation. Thus, the work examines not instrument demand itself, but rather the presumed product of such demand.

The above discussion also provides a positive political economy explanation for why market-based instruments have virtually always taken the form of grandfathered tradeable permits, or at least why private firms should be expected to have strong demands for this means of permit allocation. In tradeable permit schemes, grandfathering not only conveys scarcity rents to firms, since existing polluters are granted valuable economic resources for free, but also provides entry barriers, in that new entrants must purchase permits from existing holders.

The preceding discussion does not provide a compelling explanation for the prevalence of command-and-control standards over grandfathered tradeable permits. In principle, either instrument could provide sustainable rents to existing firms. The theory needs to be extended to explain this phenomenon.

Differential Costs Across Firms in an Industry

An alternate explanation for the landscape of environmental policy instruments arises from the existence of differential costs of environmental compliance across firms. Due to this heterogeneity, a firm may support policy instruments that impose costs on it, as long as those costs affect it less than the industry average, giving it a competitive advantage. For example, firms which could reduce lead content at relatively low costs (thanks to large refineries) tended to support the tradeable permit system by which the leaded content of gasoline was reduced in the 1980s, while firms with less efficient, smaller refineries were vehemently opposed. Other empirical work, however, has cast doubt on the proposition that firms advocate instruments based on inter-industry or intra-industry transfers.

Another form of cost differential arises as a result of barriers to entry. It is important to maintain the distinction between the entry of new firms and the expansion of existing firms. Entry barriers from environmental regulation generally apply to both situations. Within an industry, firms with no plans to expand would derive greater benefit from entry barriers, potentially discouraging further growth by their competitors.

Conversely, firms with ambitious expansion plans relative to their existing operations would benefit from weaker barriers. Such firms would also try to structure barriers in a manner giving them an advantage relative to newcomers. For example, the "bubble" program of the Clean Air Act creates barriers that are less onerous for existing firms because firms are allowed to engage in intra-firm emissions trading. Under this program, a firm can reduce the emissions of an existing source by an amount at least equal to the emissions of the new source, instead of having to take the more costly step of meeting the command-and-control standard otherwise applicable to new sources. The CAA's banking policies, which allow intra-firm trading across time periods, also make expansion by an incumbent easier than entry by a new firm.

The mechanism for allocating tradeable permits might also produce different winners and losers within an industry. Under a grandfathering scheme that allocates permits on the basis of emissions at the time of the scheme's establishment, firms investing in pollution abatement prior to regulation stand to lose relative to their more heavily polluting competitors. Although such investing and expanding firms might conceivably prefer the allocation of permits by means of an initial auction, smaller firms often prefer grandfathering out of concern that auctions will be dominated by larger players. . . .

NOTES AND QUESTIONS

1. **Aggregate Cost for Society and Aggregate Cost for Industry.** In the context of the first of the categories identified by Keohane, Revesz, and Stavins, what is the significance of the distinction between the aggregate cost for society and the aggregate cost for industry of the implementation of a particular regulatory tool? Does this distinction necessarily favor market-based mechanisms at the expense of command and control mechanisms?

2. **Generation of Rents.** In what circumstances will a firm earn rents following the implementation of a regulatory tool? In what circumstances may firms favor regulation to no regulation at all? To what extent may the second category of firms identified by Keohane, Revesz, and Stavins explain the prevalence of command-and-control standards in U.S. environmental law?

3. **Command-and-Control v. Marketable Permit Schemes.** With respect to the second category of firms, the authors note that: "The . . . discussion does not provide a compelling explanation for the prevalence of command-and-control standards over grandfathered tradeable permits. In principle, either instrument could provide sustainable rents to existing firms." *Id.* at 351. What theories may explain this phenomenon?

4. **Competitive Advantage.** Under what circumstances will a firm achieve a competitive advantage over other firms in an industry following the introduction of a regulatory standard? Under what circumstances will this advantage be most marked? What is the significance, in the context of the third category of firms, of the distinction drawn between the entry of new firms and the expansion of existing firms?

5. **Convincing Explanations.** Which of the readings in this chapter provides a better explanation for environmental regulation? What strengths and weaknesses does each have? How much of environmental regulation do the readings explain?

6. **Deviations from Economic Theory.** The article by Keohane, Revesz, and Stavins, from which the above excerpt is drawn, identifies three ways that environmental law departs from the prescriptions of economic theory. First, despite the well-known economic advantages of market-based instruments, command-and-control standards have been used much more frequently. Second, when command-and-control standards have been used, the required level of pollution abatement has generally been far more stringent for new sources than for existing sources. Third, in the relatively rare instances in which market-based instruments have been adopted, they have nearly always taken the form of tradeable permits rather than emission taxes; moreover, the initial distribution has been through grandfathering rather than through auctions. In what ways can these apparent paradoxes be attributed to public choice rationales?

CHAPTER V

CONTROL OF AIR POLLUTION

1.   CLEAN AIR ACT: INTRODUCTION

The first federal step into the field of air pollution regulation occurred in 1955, when Congress passed the Air Pollution Control Act, Pub. L. No. 84–159, 69 Stat. 322 (1955). The 1955 Act left responsibility for direct regulation of air pollution in the states' hands, but it empowered the Secretary of the Department of Health, Education, and Welfare (HEW) to propose and implement research programs to explore the effects of air pollution on human health and welfare. *See generally* Jeffrey Fromson, Comment, *A History of Federal Air Pollution Control*, 30 OHIO ST. L.J. 516, 519–20 (1969). The Motor Vehicle Act of 1960, Pub. L. No. 86–493, 74 Stat. 162 (1960), authorized further research into the effects and potential prevention of air pollution specifically caused by motor vehicles.

The next major step taken by the federal government was the Clean Air Act of 1963, Pub. L. No. 88–206, 77 Stat. 392 (1963). The 1963 Act continued to vest primary responsibility for abating air pollution with the states, but it also authorized the Secretary of HEW to collect scientific data on air pollution effects, to develop advisory air quality criteria, and to recommend that the Attorney General commence particular enforcement actions. However, the Secretary's recommendations under the Act were only advisory and could be issued only after the Secretary had held conferences with state and local authorities to discuss the threat. *See* Fromson, *supra*, at 526.

In 1965, Congress began to impose direct federal air pollution control regulation when it passed the Motor Vehicle Air Pollution Control Act, Pub. L. No. 89–272, 79 Stat. 992 (1965). The Act gave the Secretary of HEW the authority to establish uniform emissions standards for new vehicles on the basis of "technological feasibility and economic costs." 42 U.S.C. § 1857f–1(a) (1965).

However, the meager effectiveness of these early initiatives fueled a growing belief that primary reliance on state and local authorities to control air pollution was insufficient to achieve desired levels of air quality. A stronger federal role was thought to be needed. *See* Fromson, *supra*, at 529. As a result, Congress passed, and President Johnson signed, the Air Quality Act of 1967, Pub. L. No. 90–148, 81 Stat. 485 (1967), a statutory scheme whose structural features can be seen in the framework of the current Clean Air Act (CAA). The 1967 Act required HEW to divide the nation into "atmospheric regions" that were relatively homogenous in terms of weather patterns and geography. It also directed HEW to designate air quality regions, which could include multiple states or even parts of states. In what was then the most significant instance of direct federal regulation of air pollution, the Act required states to adopt ambient air quality standards in each air quality region for various pollutants based on HEW criteria documents. The Act empowered HEW to promulgate these standards in case a state failed to comply with this statutory directive. States also were required to adopt implementation plans sufficient to achieve the ambient standards. *See generally* Robert Martin & Lloyd Symington, *A Guide to the Air Quality Act of 1967*, 33 L. & CONTEMP. PROB. 239 (1968).

Despite the fact that the 1967 Act was by far the most significant federal effort to control air pollution, the Act was generally ineffective. *See* Martin & Symington, *supra*, at 250. The momentum was clearly towards a new regime with a stronger role for the federal government.

Adopted in its contemporary form in 1970, the CAA and its supporting regulations comprise one of the most intricate regulatory schemes in existence, comparable in complexity to the tax laws. Partly, this is due to the complexity of the problem of clean air itself. "Clean" from which pollutants? "Clean" to what level? "Clean" at what cost? "Clean" from what sources? "Clean" by whose standards? The statute has also been amended several times, generally adding layers of complexity each time. It is useful to start at the beginning with a high-level picture of the Act's scope and basic layout.

The National Ambient Air Quality Standards (NAAQS) are *ambient standards*; that is, they set a maximum concentration of pollutants that is acceptable for the air all around us. The NAAQS are nationally uniform and, by design, are set without reference to cost. There is a separate NAAQS set for each so-called "criteria pollutant." Certain criteria pollutants are specified by statute, and EPA may supplement that list.

Setting the NAAQS, however, is only the first step in the regulatory process. The ambient standard is typically translated into an individual *emissions standard*—that is, the level of pollution that a given polluter may emit, so that the ambient standards are met when all polluters are complying with their emissions standards. In the CAA, this is generally done through state implementation plans (SIPs). The states bear primary responsibility for determining how the NAAQS will be met, and retain great flexibility in the choice of the regulatory tools they may use to distribute the burden of clean air in their state—so long as their distribution of the pollution burden will achieve the federal air standard. SIPs must contain certain statutory features, including enforceable emissions limitations or other control measures, and a program to provide for enforcement. SIPs are particularly important because they are the primary means by which existing sources of air pollution are regulated. Generally, such sources are grandfathered into the system without federal emissions regulation, but states may elect to regulate those sources through their SIPs.

If a state fails to submit a SIP, however, or submits one that is defective, EPA must promulgate its own federal implementation plan (FIP) for the state. In the past, EPA has been very reluctant to issue such plans due to the difficulties that their enforcement would pose.

In addition to the state regulation of existing sources through SIPs, EPA sets federal emissions standards for new and modified stationary sources called the New Source Performance Standards (NSPS). The Administrator proposes a list of categories of stationary sources, distinguishing among classes, types, and sizes within categories; the Administrator periodically adds or subtracts items from this list as necessary. For each entry on the list, the Administrator sets a "standard of performance," defined by statute as the level of emissions reduction that can be achieved with the best available control technology, taking costs into account. All new or modified sources must then comply with the NSPS, but as noted above, old sources are "grandfathered" in, subject to no regulation beyond what the individual states may require of them in their SIPs. This scheme makes the definition of a "modified" source extremely important—a question that will be explored at length.

In 1977, amendments to the Act added some major new elements. The first was the Prevention of Significant Deterioration (PSD) program, requiring areas of the country with air better than the NAAQS to comply with special rules to avoid degrading air quality too much.

The PSD program itself has ambient and emissions components. The ambient standard for a PSD area is set by reference to a baseline, defined as the air quality that exists when the first major facility applies for a permit to begin operations in the area. The CAA then defines permissible "increments" setting out how much the air may be degraded past the baseline. Each state's SIP must contain provisions ensuring the state will comply with this ambient standard. At first glance, this regime appears somewhat odd: after all, the NAAQS are set (in theory, without reference to costs) at the level requisite to protect the public health allowing an adequate margin of safety, so why not let states degrade their air right up to the level permitted by the NAAQS? Explanations will be explored in the relevant section.

The PSD emissions standards are linked to a permitting process. All major emitting facilities must get a permit before construction or modification in a PSD area. The permit requires the facility to show it will not contribute to pollution in excess of the allowable increment, and also that the facility achieves emissions limitation equivalent to the best available control technology (BACT), taking costs into account. At first, this simply seems to reiterate the requirements of the NSPS, but the PSD permit program calculates BACT and relevant costs on a source-by-source basis, whereas the NSPS are set by reference to categories. The BACT standard cannot be less stringent than NSPS, but it can be more stringent.

The second major addition in 1977 was the nonattainment program. In 1970, Congress contemplated that all areas of the country would meet the NAAQS by 1975, but this did not occur. Whereas PSD addresses areas with air better than required by the NAAQS, nonattainment deals with areas in which the air quality remained worse than the NAAQS would allow. The goal is to steadily improve the air quality of a region without freezing all economic development. In nonattainment areas, states must demonstrate "reasonable further progress" (RFP) in their SIPs, with a goal of attaining the NAAQS by certain deadlines.

In addition, a permitting process exists for nonattainment areas, applying to all new or modified major stationary sources. Each permit must show that other reductions in emissions have been achieved that will more than "offset" those created by the new facility. Permit applicants must also show that their source complies with the lowest achievable emissions rate (LAER), the most stringent emissions limitation for the relevant category of source contained in any state implementation plan, unless those emissions limitations are not achievable. Finally, to get a permit, all of the facility owner's other stationary sources must be on schedule for compliance.

The CAA also contains interstate air pollution provisions. Rather than being at the centerpiece of a federal regulatory scheme (as the theoretical materials earlier in this book suggest would be wise), they are largely an afterthought added by the 1977 amendments. States are prohibited from contributing significantly to nonattainment in other regions, or interfering with maintenance of the relevant NAAQS/PSD requirements. If a state believes another state is in violation of this standard, it may petition the Administrator. Alternatively, the Administrator may make a determination that a SIP or a group of SIPs are deficient in this regard and issue a "SIP call," demanding the problem be rectified. States also retain the option to challenge another state's SIP at the time of its approval, on the ground that excessive pollution goes to other states.

These overlays can sometimes interact in subtle ways. For example, imagine a new source is to be constructed in a given area. What are the requirements for such a source? The answer will depend on whether it is a "major" emitting facility; whether the area is in attainment or not; what the applicable PSD requirements, if any, are; whether a NSPS has been set for the category of source; and so on. It is important to read the statutory language for each of these sections carefully as you study them and to refer to each section's definitions of terms as well as the general statutory definitions. Words in the CAA are often given definitions that are quite particular to the Act (consider the definition of "modification," for example).

The CAA also regulates mobile sources, principally automobiles. EPA sets "best available technology" standards for emissions. Other provisions of the statute preempt less stringent state standards but allow states to have standards that are more stringent than the federal standards. The mobile source provisions, in contrast, require uniformity, except that California can set more stringent standards if it applies for and receives a waiver from EPA. Other states can adopt those standards instead of the federal standards.

Hazardous air pollutants (HAPs)—pollutants known or suspected to cause cancer or other serious health effects—are subject to different regulatory treatment than "criteria pollutants," on which the prior discussion has focused. After twenty years of profound agency inaction, Congress, in the 1990 Clean Air Act amendments, required a technology-based approach to the regulation of HAPs, with a health-based standard as a backstop.

The CAA has been largely successful in reducing air pollution. From 1970 to 2012, aggregate national emissions of the six pollutants subject to NAAQS fell by 73 percent. EPA, OUR NATION'S AIR: AIR QUALITY IMPROVES AS AMERICA GROWS, STATUS AND TRENDS THROUGH 2018 (2018). Lead levels in the ambient air are 99 percent lower than they were in 1980. EPA, Air Quality—National Summary, https://www.epa.gov/air-trends/air-quality-national-summary (last visited Sept. 9, 2018). Air concentrations of sulfur dioxide, carbon monoxide, and nitrogen dioxide decreased by 90 percent, 84 percent, and 63 percent, respectively between 1980 and 2017. *Id.* Improvements in air quality have been achieved even in the most polluted parts of the country. Between 1980 and 1998, ambient sulfur dioxide levels fells by 8.9 percent per year in the Los Angeles basin, and ozone levels fell 12.3 percent per year. Matthew E. Kahn, *The Beneficiaries of Clean Air Act Regulation*, REGULATION, Spring 2001, at 34 (2001). The fine particles and ozone reduction programs are estimated to have prevented 160,000 premature deaths nationally by 2010, and are predicted to prevent 230,000 premature deaths by 2030. *Id.* Ultimately, EPA estimates that the economic benefits of the CAA exceed its costs by a factor of 30 to one. EPA, Second Prospective Study—1990 to 2020, https://www.epa.gov/clean-air-act-overview/benefits-and-costs-clean-air-act-1990-2020-second-prospective-study (last visited Mar. 9, 2019).

Today, one of the most significant issues regarding the CAA is its intersection with climate change. In the absence of national climate legislation, the CAA has emerged as the primary tool for addressing greenhouse gas (GHG) emissions at the federal level. The first major Supreme Court decision on the regulation of carbon dioxide under the CAA was *Massachusetts v. EPA*. Following this decision, EPA issued rules in partnership with the Department of Transportation regulating carbon dioxide under the CAA's mobile source provisions. EPA's application of GHG rules to stationary sources through the PSD program generated a number of legal challenges, leading to the Supreme Court's decision in *Utility Air Regulatory Group v. EPA*. During the Obama Administration, EPA undertook an ambitious effort to regulate the GHG emissions of both new and existing power plants under NSPS. The Trump Administration, however, has proposed weakening the standards for both vehicles and power plants.

2. NATIONAL AMBIENT AIR QUALITY STANDARDS

A. INTRODUCTION

The national ambient air quality standards (NAAQS) form the centerpiece of the CAA. They are nationally uniform ambient standards, limiting the amount of an air pollutant allowed in the air averaged over various intervals of time.* The first step toward setting the NAAQS is set forth in § 108, 42 U.S.C. § 7408, which directs the Administrator to publish a list of air pollutants which 1) in her judgment, cause or contribute to air pollution which may reasonably be anticipated to endanger public health or welfare; 2) are present in the air due to numerous or diverse mobile or stationary sources; and 3) for which air quality criteria had not been issued before enactment of the CAA of 1970, but for which the Administrator plans to issue criteria. 42 U.S.C. § 7408(a)(1). Once the Administrator includes an air pollutant on this list, she must issue air quality criteria for the pollutant within twelve months. 42 U.S.C. § 7408(a)(2). The air quality criteria are technical documents that identify the public health and welfare effects of the pollutant. *Id.*

Section 109, 42 U.S.C. § 7409, requires the Administrator to issue proposed primary and secondary NAAQS simultaneously with the issuance of air quality criteria. 42 U.S.C. § 7409(a)(2). Section 109 also requires the Administrator to propose NAAQS for pollutants for which air quality criteria had already been issued at the time of enactment in 1970. The primary NAAQS must be set at a level which, in the judgment

---

* An "air pollutant" is defined as "any air pollution agent or combination of such agents, including any physical, chemical, biological, radioactive (including source material, special nuclear material, and byproduct material) substance or matter which is emitted into or otherwise enters the ambient air. Such term includes any precursors to the formation of any air pollutant, to the extent the Administrator has identified such precursor or precursors for the particular purpose for which the term 'air pollutant' is used." 42 U.S.C. § 7602(g).

of the Administrator and based on the air quality criteria, is "requisite to protect the public health" and allows "an adequate margin of safety." 42 U.S.C. § 7409(b)(1). The secondary NAAQS must be set at a level which, in the judgment of the Administrator and based on the air quality criteria, "is requisite to protect the public welfare from any known or anticipated adverse effects associated with the presence of such air pollutant in the ambient air." 42 U.S.C. § 7409(b)(2). The term "welfare," used to set the secondary NAAQS, is described in the general definitional provision of the CAA:

> All language referring to effects on welfare includes, but is not limited to, effects on soils, water, crops, vegetation, manmade materials, animals, wildlife, weather, visibility, and climate, damage to and deterioration of property, and hazards to transportation, as well as effects on economic values and on personal comfort and well-being, whether caused by transformation, conversion, or combination with other air pollutants.

42 U.S.C. § 7602(h). Once the NAAQS have been established, the Administrator is required to review the air quality criteria at five-year intervals and to propose revisions according to the process established in § 108. 42 U.S.C. § 7409(d).

When the CAA was enacted in 1970, air quality criteria had already been promulgated for sulfur oxides, particulates, carbon monoxide, hydrocarbons and photochemical oxidants (now defined as ozone). *See* ENVTL. POL'Y DIV., LIBRARY OF CONG., A LEGISLATIVE HISTORY ON THE CLEAN AIR ACT AMENDMENTS OF 1970, at 454 (1974). The EPA added nitrogen oxides in 1971. *See id.* at 430, 432 (noting that "[w]ithin the 13-month deadline, the Congress expects criteria to be issued for nitrogen oxides. . . ."). Lead was added after a citizen suit in 1976. *NRDC v. Train*, 545 F.2d 320 (2d Cir. 1976). No additional pollutants have been added; however, several organizations recently petitioned EPA to set a NAAQS for carbon dioxide, as discussed further below.

EPA has revised the NAAQS for several of the pollutants. For example, in 2008 EPA issued a revised lead NAAQS that tightened the standard by an order of magnitude, from 1.5 µg/m³ to 0.15 µg/m³. *See* EPA, National Ambient Air Quality Standards for Lead, 73 Fed. Reg. 66,964 (2008). Not every review results in changes to the NAAQS. In 2016, EPA again reviewed the lead standards and decided to keep the 2008 NAAQS in place without revision. EPA, Review of the National Air Quality Standards for Lead, 81 Fed. Reg. 71,906 (2016). Table V.1 shows the current NAAQS.

Table V.1. National Ambient Air Quality Standards

Pollutant	Primary Standard	Averaging Times	Secondary Standards
Carbon Monoxide	9 ppm (10 mg/m^3)	8-hour	None
	35 ppm (40 mg/m^3)	1-hour	None
Lead	0.15 µg/m^3	Rolling 3-month Average	Same as Primary
Nitrogen Dioxide	0.053 ppm (100 Sg/m^3)	Annual	Same as Primary
	0.010 ppm	1-hour	None
Particulate Matter (PM$_{10}$ or 10 microns)	150µg/m^3	24-hour	Same as Primary
Particulate Matter (PM$_{2.5}$ or 2.5 microns)	12 µg/m^3	Annual (Arithmetic Mean)	15 µg/m^3
	35 µg/m^3	24-hour	Same as Primary
Ozone	0.070 ppm	8-hour	Same as Primary
Sulfur Oxides	0.075 ppm	1-hour	
		3-hour	0.5 ppm (1300 µg/m^3)

Section 108 states that the Administrator "shall" publish a list of air pollutants for which he plans to publish air quality criteria. In *NRDC v. Train*, 545 F.2d 320 (2d Cir. 1976), citizens sued to compel the Administrator to list lead as a criteria pollutant because he had made findings about the potential for lead to endanger the public health when promulgating a rule to require unleaded gasoline under § 211 of the CAA, 42 U.S.C. § 7511. The court held that the Administrator was required to list lead under § 108. It was within the Administrator's discretion to make a finding of adverse effect, but once he made that finding, he was compelled by § 108 to list lead as a criteria pollutant. *Id.* at 328.

However, when citizens attempted to compel the Administrator to revise the sulfur oxides NAAQS to address acid deposition, after EPA had issued a report that identified sulfur oxides as endangering the public welfare, the court distinguished *NRDC v. Train. See* Envtl. Def. Fund v.

Thomas, 870 F.2d 892 (2d Cir. 1989). The court held that although the report compelled the Administrator to take some action under § 108, he was not compelled to revise the sulfur oxides NAAQS. The court explained that the content of a revision was within the Administrator's discretion, unlike the ministerial duty to list a pollutant after finding it had adverse effects on public health. Thus, the Administrator retained discretion to decline to revise the standard. *Id.* at 899–901.

NOTES AND QUESTIONS

1. **Uniformity: Virtue or Vice?** Consider the following view:

> [U]niform national ambient air quality standards represent a fundamental error in our approach to air quality control. . . . To justify uniform standards as efficient in cost-minimization terms one would have to assume that the costs of a given level of pollution and a given level of control are the same across the nation. This assumption, however, is manifestly not valid.

James E. Krier, *The Irrational National Air Quality Standards: Macro- and Micro-Mistakes*, 22 UCLA L. REV. 323 (1974).

> Evaluate the strength of the following arguments for uniform NAAQS:
>
> 1. To prevent unequal conditions of competition among the states;
>
> 2. To ensure every individual in the country an equal level of air quality; and
>
> 3. To ensure every individual in the country a minimum level of air quality.

What other arguments are plausible? What are the strongest arguments for uniform NAAQS?

B. SETTING THE NAAQS STANDARD

The standard-setting process of §§ 108 and 109 involves significant scientific uncertainty, creating risk assessment and risk management challenges. The following excerpts explore two areas of dispute regarding the NAAQS standard-setting process: the level "necessary to protect the public health"; and whether the statute allows or requires the consideration of costs in setting the NAAQS.

Lead: Proposed National Ambient Air Quality Standard
42 Fed. Reg. 63,076 (1977).

Development of the National Ambient Air Quality Standard for lead requires certain judgments by EPA about the relationship between concentrations of lead in the air and possible adverse health effects experienced by the public. This relationship is greatly complicated by the fact that lead in the air is not the only source of lead exposure, that there is variability of response among individuals exposed to lead, and that there are numerous effects of lead on health, occurring at various levels of exposure which vary in public health significance.

In developing the standard, EPA has made judgments in five key areas.

1.   Determining the critically sensitive population.

2.   Determining the pivotal adverse health effect.

3.   Determining the mean population blood lead level which would be consistent with protection of the sensitive population.

4.   Determining the relationship between air lead exposure and resulting blood lead level.

5.   Determining the allowable blood lead increment from air.

Determining the Critically Sensitive Population

Certain subgroups within the general population differ in sensitivity to lead exposure. Protection of populations exhibiting the greatest sensitivity of response to lead is a major consideration in determining the level of the lead standard. From information presented in the Criteria Document, there are a number of populations for which lead exposure poses a greater risk: young children, pregnant women and the fetus; the occupationally exposed; and individuals suffering from dietary deficiencies or exhibiting the genetic inability to produce certain blood enzymes.

EPA believes that young children (ages 1–5 years) should be regarded as the foremost critically sensitive population for setting the lead standard. This is because hematologic and neurologic effects in children are shown to occur at lower thresholds than adults, and because children have a greater risk of exposure to non-food material containing lead, such as dust and soil, as the result of normal hand-to-mouth activity. . . .

Pregnant women and the fetus are at risk because of transplacental movement of lead to the fetus and the possibility of maternal complication at delivery. . . . However, available evidence does not indicate that pregnant women and the fetus would require a more stringent standard than young children.

Groups exposed to lead in the workplace also comprise a population at greater risk. Because members of such groups are generally healthy and do not have a greater physiological sensitivity to lead than young children, [exposed workers do not require a more stringent standard than young children].

Determining the Pivotal Adverse Health Effect

The toxic effects of lead resulting from high levels of exposure are well documented. Among the first effects noted historically were the severe and sometimes fatal consequences such as colic, palsy, and encephalopathy which followed acute occupational exposure in the mining and smelting industries. Exposure to high concentrations of lead in paints, inks, pesticides, and plumbing have similarly been implicated in cases of severe poisoning.

Recent widespread increase of lead in the environment as a result of human activities has stimulated research on the possible effects of the longer-term, low level exposure characteristic of the general population. Clinical and epidemiological studies have revealed that lead accumulates in the body throughout life, to a large extent immobilized in bone, but with a significant mobile fraction in the blood and soft tissues. Blood lead concentrations respond predictably to changes in the level of environmental exposure and, as a result, are generally accepted as good indicators of that exposure as well as of the internal dose of lead to which all body tissues are exposed. The threshold for a particular health effect is considered to be the blood lead level at which the effect is first detected. . . .

Erythrocyte Protoporphyrin Elevation

Above 15–20 µg Pb/dl, the Criteria Document notes a correlation between blood lead levels in children and the elevation of protoporphyrin in red blood cells. Unlike ALAD inhibition at 10µg Pb/dl, the accumulation of erythrocyte protoporphyrin (EP) indicates a functional impairment of the heme synthetic pathway. . . .

EPA is proposing that lead-induced elevation in children of EP should be accepted as the pivotal adverse effect of lead. Accordingly, the air lead standard should be designed to prevent the occurrence of EP elevation in children. EPA bases its determination that EP elevation due to lead should be regarded as an adverse health effect on the following points:

1. EP elevation indicates an abnormal impairment of various cell functions, which should not be allowed to persist as a chronic condition.

2. The impairment of cellular function indicated by EP elevation extends to all body cells, and may have particular implications for the functioning of neural and hepatic tissues.

3. The air lead standard is intended to establish a level of airborne lead which can be regarded as consistent with protecting the health over a lifetime of exposure. The pervasive biological involvement of lead in the body, and its demonstrated impairment of biological functions are a strong impetus to the Agency in adopting the lowest

threshold biological effect which can be considered adverse to health.

4. The Center for Disease Control has also used EP elevation as an indicator of undue lead exposure, although their guidelines published in 1975 are oriented to establishing an individual threshold for risk (30 μg Pb/dl) in populations of children exposed to high-dose lead sources such as lead-based paint rather than for establishing a safe mean population blood lead level with a margin of safety.

5. The Act intends that the air standard be precautionary. Taking the lowest adverse effect levels is compatible with the scientific uncertainty about the health consequences of prolonged low level lead exposure, and with the downward trend in levels of lead in the blood regarded as adverse to health by the public health community. . . .

Determining a Safe Blood Lead Level for Protection of the Sensitive Population

The third key area for judgment in the development of the proposed standard involves the determination of the mean population blood lead level for children at which EP elevation does not occur. EPA is proposing that this standard for lead be based on the judgment that the mean population blood lead for children not exceed 15 μg Pb/dl. . . . On the basis of present knowledge, EPA believes that a population mean of 15 μg Pb/dl can be regarded as an indicator of a safe level of total lead exposure for children. . . .

In selecting 15 μg Pb/dl mean population blood lead as a target, EPA wishes to stress that it is proposing a statistical measure of population exposure. EPA is not suggesting that individual blood lead levels in excess of 15 μg Pb/dl necessarily constitute a significant risk to health. . . . [A] population with a mean blood lead level of 15 μg Pb/dl will have individuals with higher and lower blood lead levels. There will also be a variation of EP levels for individuals with a given blood lead level. It is also true that the absence of statistical correlation of EP levels with blood lead levels below 15 μg Pb/dl does not necessarily mean that these lower blood lead levels are known to be without risk. However, the threshold of 15 μg Pb/dl does represent a point below which the sensitive population as a group has not been seen to show an elevation in EP due to lead and above which EP elevation has been demonstrated to rise with increasing implications for health. . . .

Using standard statistical techniques, it is possible to calculate the mean population blood lead level which would place a given percentage of the population below the level of an effects threshold. For example, a mean population blood lead level of 15 μg Pb/dl would place 99.5% of a population of children below the Center for Disease Control guidelines of 30 μg Pb/dl. . . .

Determining the Relationship Between Air Lead Exposure and Resulting Blood Lead Level

. . . The range of ratios for children's blood lead response to a one µg increase in air lead cited in the Criteria Document is from 1.2 to 2.3. The lower ratio comes from studies at Kellogg, Idaho, where dust levels of lead were separately correlated with blood lead. In view of the tendency of children to experience higher ratios due to greater intake and absorption of air lead, EPA has selected a ratio of 1:2 in calculating the impact of air lead levels on blood lead levels in children.

Determining the Allowable Blood Lead Increment from Air

The fifth area of judgments made by EPA in developing the proposed standard for lead is related to an aspect of lead which has not characterized any pollutant previously addressed by EPA under Section 109 of the Clean Air Act: That significant amounts of the pollutant result from sources that are not subject to control by implementing an air quality standard.

Some studies reported in the Criteria Document clearly show that levels of lead in the blood derive from non-air sources. For example, studies in areas with minimal air lead levels still show significant levels of lead in the blood. A study of children in Boston correlates blood lead levels with lead levels in water supplies.

Other studies demonstrate a strong relationship of blood lead level with air lead. Clinical studies on adult volunteers in chamber studies demonstrate changes of blood lead with changes of the concentration of lead in the air. Epidemiological studies show a general pattern of urban-rural difference where blood lead levels are higher in urban settings where air lead levels are also higher. Other epidemiological studies directly correlate air lead with blood lead. These include studies using personal dosimeters to accurately gauge lead exposure, and the extensive population studies conducted in the community around the smelter complex at Kellogg, Idaho.

Implications of Multiple Sources of Lead in Setting an Air Standard

The implications of multiple sources of environmental lead are difficult to reconcile with the concept of a National Ambient Air Quality Standard. If the air were the only source of lead, it would be a reasonably straightforward matter to identify a safe level and to require that, regardless of what prevailing levels of air lead are today, the safe level be achieved. However, since non-air sources contribute lead as well, the level of an ambient air quality standard which will protect public health is affected by the contribution of these non-air sources. If their contribution is far below the allowable level of blood lead, the air contribution can be permitted to be relatively high. However, if they alone contribute more than the allowable blood lead level, even a zero ambient air quality standard would not prevent EP elevation in children. . . .

Because of the factors just discussed, no National Ambient Air Quality Standard can be assured of being protective in all locations. Regardless of what the non-air contribution is assumed to be, the air standard will be overprotective in areas where lead from non-air sources is low and under protective in areas where it is high. EPA does not believe, however, that it is given the latitude to set area specific air quality standards under Section 109. EPA has, therefore, undertaken to make a single judgment as to what contribution to population blood levels derives from non-air sources. . . . The level for non-air contribution used in this proposal is EPA's best judgment as to the appropriate level based partly on what is known about non-air lead contribution from a limited number of studies and partly on what EPA believes is an appropriate goal for air pollution control, consistent with the Agency's responsibility to protect the public health. . . .

Basis for EPA's Estimate of Contribution to Blood Lead Levels from Non-Air Sources

The level of the standard is very strongly influenced by judgments made regarding the size of non-air contribution to total exposure. EPA has encountered difficulties in attempting to estimate exposure from various lead sources in order to determine the contribution of such sources to blood lead levels. . . .

From reviewing [various] areas of evidence, EPA concludes that:

1. In studies showing mean blood lead levels above 15 µg Pb/dl, it is probable that both air and non-air sources of lead contribute significantly to blood lead with the possibility that contributions from non-air sources exceed 15 µg Pb/dl.

2. Studies showing a sustained drop in air lead levels show a corresponding drop in blood lead levels, down to an apparent limit in the range of 10.2 to 14.4 µg Pb/dl. These studies show the rough range of the lowest blood lead levels that can be attributed to non-air sources.

3. Isotopic tracing studies show air contribution to blood lead to be 7–41 percent in one study and about 33 percent in another study.

In considering this evidence, EPA notes that if, from the isotopic studies, approximately two-thirds of blood lead is typically derived from non-air sources, a mean blood lead target of 15 µg Pb/dl would attribute 10 µg Pb/dl to non-air sources. On the other hand, the average blood lead level from studies EPA believes to represent the least amount of blood attributable to non-air sources is 12.7 µg/Pb. In the absence of more precise information, EPA is proposing that the lead standard be based on the assumption that in general, 12 µg Pb/dl of the blood lead level in children is derived from lead sources unaffected by the lead air quality standard. EPA is aware that actual population blood lead levels, either individually or as a population mean, may exceed this benchmark. However, if EPA were to use a larger estimate of non-air contribution to blood lead, the result would be an exceptionally stringent standard, which would not address the principal source of lead exposure. Conversely, EPA believes that it should not adopt an estimate of non-air contribution below the level shown in available studies to be the lowest mean blood lead level documented in the Criteria Document.

Because of the strong impact that adopting this goal for non-air sources has on the level of the standard, EPA welcomes information and judgments about the validity of the numerical value chosen for this factor, as well as views about alternative ways in which EPA could develop an air standard that takes into account other routes of exposure.

Calculation of the Air Standard

EPA has calculated the proposed standard based on the conclusions reached in the previous sections:

1. Sensitive population: children, ages 1–5.

2. Health basis (lowest detectable adverse effect): elevation of erythrocyte protoporphyrin (EP).

3. Effect threshold in sensitive population: 15 µg Pb/dl.

4. Assumed goal for contribution to blood lead from non-air sources: 12 µg Pb/dl.

5. Allowable contribution to blood lead from air sources: 15 µg Pb/dl–12 µg Pb/dl = 3 µg Pb/dl.

6. Air lead concentration consistent with blood lead contribution from air sources: 1.5 µg Pb/m3. . . .

Margin of Safety

EPA believes that the recommended standard incorporates a sufficient margin to protect the public health and welfare from the adverse effects of lead exposure deriving from lead in the air. Margin of safety considerations have entered into the development of the standard in several key areas:

1. The standard is based on protection of young children, a critically sensitive general subgroup within the population.

2. The standard is based on the lowest threshold for the first adverse effect occurring with increasing blood lead levels in children: elevation of protoporphyrin in red blood cells at a blood lead level of 15 µg Pb/dl.

3. In estimating the change in blood lead levels resulting from the change in air lead levels, EPA has selected a ratio at the protective end of the range provided in the Criteria Document. . . .

NOTES AND QUESTIONS

1. Lead Standard-Setting. What is the general approach for setting NAAQS? In setting the lead regulations, EPA was required to make the following determinations:

1. Find the most sensitive group (critical population). Might EPA have selected an even more sensitive group than young children? What about particular subgroups of young children, such as "young children with respiratory diseases"? Why would the EPA choose one subgroup as the "critically sensitive population" and not another?

2. Identify the lowest level health effect of pollutant (critical effects). Why isn't any lead in the blood an adverse health effect? What about the health effects at lower levels than the one EPA chose, such as ALAD inhibition?

3. Establish the safe lead level in blood. This step assumes there is such a level. What if scientific evidence established that the ideal level of lead in the blood is zero?

4. Establish how much of the lead in air comes from other sources (12 μg/dl). Are you convinced by EPA's reasoning for using 12 rather than a larger number?

5. Translate level of lead in air into level of lead in blood. How did EPA pick the relevant ratio?

6. Establish the margin of safety. EPA's argument is that each step already included a margin of safety. Are you convinced of this? Might there still be room for an additional margin at the end? How would you recommend deciding how much of a margin is too much?

2. The Stopping Point Problem. The lead regulation example illustrates some of the difficulties that arise under a no-risk approach. Environmental pollutants, particularly carcinogens, often lack ambient concentrations under which there is no risk of negative health consequences. Second, sensitivity and exposure to pollutants vary across a population such that there is no threshold below which no individual will experience a risk. Third, some pollutants cause observable biological responses, but it might not be clear whether those responses are negative. Fourth, in some instances, agencies choose stopping points within a scientifically uncertain range, without justifying their particular choice. Michael A. Livermore & Richard L. Revesz, *Rethinking Health-Based Environmental Standards*, 89 N.Y.U. L. REV. 1184, 1208 (2014), discussing EPA's choice of air to blood ratio when setting lead standards. Fifth, even where there is a LOEL, there may be no evidence as to whether there is a NOEL for a given pollutant. Sixth, even where pollutants have a biological threshold, background levels of the pollutant might exceed that threshold, such that any additional exposure results in negative health risks. Given these factors, how can EPA justify any NAAQS other than zero? How can EPA justify a NAAQS other than zero when it cannot take costs into account? What do you think is the result of requiring EPA to ignore costs when regulating pollutants with no known safe exposure level? *See* Livermore & Revesz, *supra.*

3.   NAAQS and Thresholds. When setting the lead standard in the 1970s, EPA used language, such as the "critical populations, critical effects" approach, that suggested the existence of a threshold below which there were no adverse health effects. That practice quickly changed:

> "[A]s scientific research accumulated showing adverse health effects at lower concentrations, the EPA quickly departed from this approach and the Agency has not treated criteria pollutants as threshold pollutants for several decades under administrations of both parties. First, the EPA has explicitly acknowledged in many NAAQS rulemakings that there is no evidence to support the view that specific criteria pollutants have a threshold. Further, the EPA has stopped using the "critical effects" language when setting NAAQS. Additionally, the EPA has calculated benefits for reducing criteria pollutants below NAAQS levels—a practice that is inconsistent with the notion of a threshold. The EPA's modern treatment of the NAAQS moved the Agency in line with current science on this question, which supports a non-threshold model."

Kimberly M. Castle & Richard L. Revesz, *Environmental Standards, Thresholds, and the Next Battleground of Environmental Regulations*, 103 MINN. L. REV. 1349, 1358 (2019) (citations omitted). How should the NAAQS be conceived in a world without thresholds?

4.   Listing Requirement. Section 108 states that the Administrator

"shall . . . publish . . . a list which includes each air pollutant

> (A)   emissions of which, in his judgment, cause or contribute to air pollution which may reasonably be anticipated to endanger public health or welfare;
>
> (B)   the presence of which in the ambient air results from numerous or diverse mobile or stationary sources; and
>
> (C)   for which air quality criteria had not been issued before December 31, 1970 but for which he plans to issue air quality criteria under this section."

Once EPA lists a pollutant, it must propose (and then promulgate) primary and secondary NAAQS. 42 U.S.C. § 7409(a)(2).

Though EPA had made a finding that lead endangered public health, when promulgating a rule to require unleaded gasoline under § 211 of the CAA, EPA declined to list lead as a criteria pollutant under § 108. In *NRDC v. Train*, 545 F.2d 320 (2d Cir. 1976), the Second Circuit held that it was within the Administrator's discretion to make a finding of adverse effect, but once he made that finding, he was compelled by § 108 to list lead as a criteria pollutant. There was no room for discretion in deciding whether to issue air quality criteria. *Id.* at 328. To interpret § 108(a) literally, and thus require that pollutants only be listed when EPA planned to issue air quality criteria, was contrary to the structure, legislative history and "judicial gloss" placed upon the CAA. *Id.* Why did EPA not want to list lead? Do you agree with the court's interpretation of § 108(a)?

5. *EDF v. Thomas,* **No Obligation to Revise NAAQS.** Following *NRDC v. Train,* citizens attempted to compel the Administrator to revise the sulfur oxides NAAQS to address acid deposition, after EPA had issued a report that identified sulfur oxides as endangering the public welfare, and the court distinguished *NRDC v. Train. See Envtl. Def. Fund v. Thomas,* 870 F.2d 892 (2d Cir. 1989). The court held that although the report compelled the Administrator to take some action under § 108, he was not compelled to revise the sulfur oxides NAAQS. The court explained that the content of a revision was within the Administrator's discretion, unlike the ministerial duty to list a pollutant after finding it had adverse effects on public health. Thus, the Administrator retained discretion to decline to revise the standard. *Id.* at 899–901. Does this distinction make sense?

6. Lead Standard-Setting: Round Two. In 2008, EPA issued a revised Lead NAAQS that increased the stringency of the primary standard by an order of magnitude, from 1.5 μg/m³ to 0.15 μg/m³. *See* EPA, National Ambient Air Quality Standards for Lead, 73 Fed. Reg. 66,964 (2008). In developing its new standard, EPA dealt differently with some of the steps addressed in its 1977 analysis:

1. Find the most sensitive group (critical population): EPA's rule discussed several particularly sensitive subgroups of children, including children with existing high blood levels from non-air lead exposure and children with particular nutritional and genetic characteristics. *Id.* at 66,976. EPA nonetheless concluded that "young children remain the sensitive population of primary focus in this review." *Id.* at 66,984. Why might EPA have chosen to focus on young children in general? Is this choice justifiable under § 109?

2. Identify the lowest level health effect of pollutant (critical effects): EPA's final rule did not explicitly identify a critical effect. However, its discussion focused on neurocognitive functions and, in particular, children's loss of IQ points. *Id.* Was EPA's choice to focus on IQ loss more or less protective versus identifying EP elevation as the critical effect? More or less justified?

3. Establish the safe lead level in blood: EPA's Staff Paper concluded that " 'there is now no recognized safe level of Pb in children's blood. . . .' " *Id.* How can EPA establish a "safe level of lead" if its own analysis acknowledges that there is no threshold?

4. Establish how much of the lead in air comes from other sources: EPA's Staff Paper determined that " 'the nonair contribution to blood Pb has declined, perhaps to a range of 1.0–1.4 μg/dl. . . .' " *Id.*

5. Translate level of lead in air into level of lead in blood: EPA's Staff Paper also found that " 'the air-to-blood ratio appears to

be higher at today's lower blood Pb levels than the estimates at the time the standard was set, with current estimates on the order of 1:3 to 1:5 and perhaps up to 1:10.'" *Id.*

6.   Establish the margin of safety: In discussing the decision of where to set the standard, EPA's rule stated that "[t]he NAAQS must be sufficient but not more stringent than necessary to achieve that result, and does not require a zero-risk standard. Considering the advice of [science advisors and public commenters], the Administrator proposed to conclude that an air-related population mean IQ loss within the range of 1 to 2 points could be significant from a public health perspective, and that a standard level should be selected to provide protection from air-related population mean IQ loss in excess of this range." *Id.* at 66,998. Would a standard set pursuant to this goal incorporate a "margin of safety"?

The EPA analysis concluded that "[u]sing the ratio of 1:7 identified [ ] as central within the reasonable range of air-to-blood ratios, the estimate of air-related blood Pb associated with a standard level of 0.15 μg/m³ would be approximately 1 μg/dl. Adding this to the mean total blood Pb level for the U.S. population would yield a mean total blood Pb estimate of 2.8 μg/dl." *Id.* at 67,002, n.81. Yet EPA had earlier found that "'studies appear to show adverse effects at population mean concurrent blood Pb levels as low as approximately 2 μg/dl.'" *Id.* at 66,984. Is the decision to apply a 0.15 μg/m³ standard consistent with the text of § 109?

Where did EPA's conclusions differ with its 1977 standard? Where did the agency's conclusions remain the same? Did EPA's changed conclusions justify the more stringent 0.15 μg/m³ standard? Did they justify an even lower standard? Did they adequately deal with any of the factors that lead to the stopping point problem?

7.   Averaging Periods. In the proposed rule, the averaging period for lead was 1 month; in the final rule, the averaging time was 3 months. What are the consequences of this change? What if the averaging time for a given pollutant were just one day? What if it were a year? Which is more restrictive to industry? Which is more protective of air quality?

This process is illustrative of notice-and-comment rulemaking, which is the predominant mechanism for setting environmental standards. EPA first proposes a rule, solicits comments, and then proposes a final rule in response to those comments. Both the proposed and final rules are published in the Federal Register.

Averaging periods can be set to address a pollutant's specific attributes and impacts. In its 2010 revision of the sulfur dioxide NAAQS, EPA chose to revoke the existing annual and 24-hour primary standards and replace them with a 1-hour standard after determining that short-term peaks in sulfur dioxide levels were particularly associated with respiratory symptoms. *See* EPA, Primary National Ambient Air Quality Standard for Sulfur Dioxide, 75 Fed. Reg. 35,520, 35,539 (2010).

Periods also can be set to take into account a pollutant's varied effects depending on the time of day and season of year. In 2007, EPA proposed to change the secondary NAAQS for ozone. EPA, National Ambient Air Quality Standards for Ozone, 72 Fed. Reg. 37,818, 37,899 (2007). One of the two replacement options proposed by EPA was a "cumulative, seasonal standard expressed as an index of the annual sum of weighted hourly concentrations, cumulated over 12 hours per day (8:00 a.m. to 8:00 p.m.) during the consecutive three month period within the [ozone] season. . . ." *Id.* By weighting concentrations at peak exposures, the standard would have better accounted for ozone impacts on plants, which are not only dependent on concentration. *See New Ambient Air Quality Standards for Ozone Proposed*, 17 AIR POLLUTION CONSULTANT 4.1 (2007). In 2015, EPA promulgated new standards for ozone. The revised standards lowered the allowed concentration of ozone in the air but retained traditional means of timing and averaging criteria to measure concentration. EPA, National Ambient Air Quality Standards for Ozone, 80 Fed. Reg. 65,292, 65,292 (2015).

Under significant pressure from the President, EPA eventually made the controversial decision to retain the secondary standard at the same level and in the same form as the primary standard. *See* Robert V. Percival, *Who's in Charge? Does the President Have Directive Authority over Agency Regulatory Decisions?*, 79 FORDHAM L. REV. 2487, 2520–21 (2011). Was this decision contrary to EPA's mandate to set the secondary standard at a level "requisite to protect the public welfare"? 42 U.S.C. § 7409(b)(2).

8.   The Role of the Clean Air Scientific Advisory Committee. Scientific risk assessment plays a significant role in informing EPA's choice in setting a NAAQS. In particular, EPA is required to form and consult with an "independent scientific review committee" under 42 U.S.C. § 7409(d)(2), now known as the Clean Air Scientific Advisory Committee (CASAC). One CASAC responsibility is to "recommend to the Administrator any new national ambient air quality standards and revisions of existing criteria and standards as may be appropriate. . . ." *Id.*

In its 2006 particulate matter NAAQS review, EPA decided to retain the annual standard for fine particulate matter at 15 µg/m^3. *See* EPA, National Ambient Air Quality Standards for Particulate Matter, 71 Fed. Reg. 61,144, 61,144 (2006). CASAC disagreed with EPA's decision, maintaining that scientific findings dictated that a standard of between 12 and 14 µg/m^3 was necessary to protect public health. *See Am. Farm Bureau Fed. v. EPA*, 559 F.3d 512, 518 (D.C. Cir. 2009). The D.C. Circuit subsequently rejected EPA's standard, stating that "[b]y statute the EPA must explain its rejection of the CASAC's recommendation" and finding that the agency failed to "adequately explain" why it did not select a standard within CASAC's suggested range of 12 to 14 µg/m^3. *Id.* at 527.

Examine the text of 42 U.S.C. § 7607(d)(3), which governs judicial review of EPA's treatment of CASAC recommendations. Does EPA have authority to issue a NAAQS standard that does not follow CASAC's recommendations? If so, what justifications might permit EPA to select a different standard? Should EPA have broader discretion in setting NAAQS?

9.   Risk Management. The risk management approach embodied in §§ 108 and 109 is a no-risk approach. Such an approach works only with threshold pollutants, because the no-risk approach assumes that there is some level of emissions below which no adverse effects will occur. Was the lead standard really a no-risk standard? If not, what was it? At the time the lead NAAQS were set, EPA believed that lead was a threshold pollutant. However, a majority of lead exposure came from sources other than air, making any additional contributions from air potentially harmful to public health. *See* Joseph M. Feller, *Non-Threshold Pollutants and Air Quality Standards*, 24 ENVTL. L. 821, 854 (1994) ("The non-air background dose can, in effect, turn a threshold pollutant into a non-threshold one.").

At several junctures, EPA made decisions that would lead to less than full protection for the most sensitive group. Why didn't EPA set a more stringent standard?

EPA was in a bind. First, three-fourths of lead exposure came from sources other than air (such as paint chips). EPA did not have statutory authority to regulate those sources. Second, the bulk of lead in air came from auto sources, which were already regulated. Only a very small percentage of the problem came from stationary sources regulated by NAAQS, as explained in the regulatory document excerpted above. What should EPA have done?

What if the pollutant were a non-threshold pollutant (as lead was later determined to be)? On what grounds could the Administrator justify setting the standard at a level other than zero? If Congress knew that most pollutants were non-threshold, why might it formulate the NAAQS this way?

10.   Lead Regulation After the NAAQS. The development of the catalytic converter was a turning point in the level of lead emissions in the air. Even before the NAAQS for lead were established, EPA had promulgated regulations requiring automobiles with catalytic converters to use unleaded gasoline. In 1995, EPA banned the use of leaded gasoline for highway vehicles. Thus, lead in the air from transportation sources has dramatically decreased. Between 1980 and 2017, average nationwide air concentrations of lead have decreased 99%, in large part due to EPA regulation of gasoline lead content. *See* EPA, National Trends in Lead Levels, https://www.epa.gov/air-trends/lead-trends (last visited Oct. 2, 2018).

The problem of lead poisoning has not gone away, however. Major remaining sources of lead emissions to the air include metals processing and aircraft operating on leaded aviation gasoline. *See* EPA, Basic Information About Lead Air Pollution, https://www.epa.gov/lead-air-pollution/basic-information-about-lead-air-pollution#how (last visited Sept. 9, 2018). Currently, 21 areas in 15 states are in nonattainment under the 2008 Lead NAAQS. EPA, Lead Designations—Final Nonattainment Designations Rounds 1 and 2, https://www.epa.gov/lead-designations/lead-designations-final-nonattainment-designations-rounds-1-and-2 (last visited Sept. 9, 2018).

Moreover, the lead NAAQS did not address other sources of lead exposure: lead in water and paint. Lead is present in water because older houses used high levels of lead in pipes. EPA regulates lead in drinking water under the Safe Drinking Water Act. *See* 42 U.S.C. 300f *et seq.* But perhaps the most intractable problem comes from children eating lead paint chips and being exposed to lead paint dust in older housing across the United States. In 1978, the Consumer Product Safety Commission banned the use of lead in paint marketed for residential use. In 1992, Congress amended the Toxic Substances Control Act (TSCA) to further reduce residential exposure to lead paint. Title X, "Residential Lead-Based Paint Hazard Reduction Act of 1992," Pub. L. No. 102–550; 106 Stat. 3672 (1992). The TSCA amendments impose substantive standards on federally owned or subsidized housing, but they do not directly regulate privately owned housing. Instead, the TSCA amendments require owners of private housing built before 1962 to disclose the presence (or potential presence) of lead paint on the premises to current occupants and potential purchasers. Some states have enacted additional legislation imposing substantive requirements on private owners of housing to address the problem of lead paint contamination. *See* Clifford L. Rechtschaffen, *The Lead Poisoning Challenge: An Approach for California and Other States*, 21 HARV. ENVTL. L. REV. 387 (1997) (describing federal regulation of lead paint, including disclosure requirements for housing built before 1978).

What is the best strategy to attack lead poisoning now? Has EPA done all it can? Does your answer to that question depend on what authority EPA has under other statutes besides the CAA?

11. Did Congress Duck on Lead? David Schoenbrod has argued that Congress' delegation of the lead issue to EPA "killed and maimed people on the scale of American casualties in the Vietnam War." *See* David Schoenbrod, *The EPA's Faustian Bargain*, REGULATION, Fall 2006, at 36, 39. He attributes this to political unwillingness to shoulder responsibility for a lead standard. *Id.* By delegating to the agency, with the attendant delay in regulation, rather than simply enacting a lead standard directly, there was a substantial delay in lead reductions: legal victories on lead did not translate into reductions for roughly five years. Had Congress regulated lead directly in 1970, six years worth of lead exposure could have been avoided. Should Congress have regulated lead directly? Should it have done the same for other pollutants? What would have been the advantages? The disadvantages?

C. COST CONSIDERATION AND THE NAAQS

Whitman v. American Trucking Associations
531 U.S. 457 (2001).

■ JUSTICE SCALIA delivered the opinion of the Court:

    . . . These cases arose when, on July 18, 1997, the Administrator revised the NAAQS for particulate matter and ozone. American Trucking Associations, Inc., . . . challenged the new standards in the Court of Appeals for the District of Columbia Circuit. . . .

Section 109(b)(1) instructs the EPA to set primary ambient air quality standards "the attainment and maintenance of which . . . are requisite to protect the public health" with "an adequate margin of safety." 42 U.S.C. § 7409(b)(1). Were it not for the hundreds of pages of briefing respondents have submitted on the issue, one would have thought it fairly clear that this text does not permit the EPA to consider costs in setting the standards. The language, as one scholar has noted, "is absolute." D. Currie, Air Pollution: Federal Law and Analysis 4–15 (1981). The EPA, "based on" the information about health effects contained in the technical "criteria" documents compiled under § 108(a)(2) is to identify the maximum airborne concentration of a pollutant that the public health can tolerate, decrease the concentration to provide an "adequate" margin of safety, and set the standard at that level. Nowhere are the costs of achieving such a standard made part of that initial calculation.

Against this most natural of readings, respondents make a lengthy, spirited, but ultimately unsuccessful attack. They begin with the object of § 109(b)(1)'s focus, the "public health." When the term first appeared in federal clean air legislation—in the Act of July 14, 1955 (1955 Act), which expressed "recognition of the dangers to the public health" from air pollution—its ordinary meaning was "[t]he health of the community." Webster's New International Dictionary 2005 (2d ed.1950). Respondents argue, however, that § 109(b)(1), as added by the Clean Air Amendments of 1970, meant to use the term's secondary meaning: "[t]he ways and means of conserving the health of the members of a community, as by preventive medicine, organized care of the sick, etc." [84 Stat. 1676]. Words that can have more than one meaning are given content, however, by their surroundings, and in the context of § 109(b)(1) this second definition makes no sense. Congress could not have meant to instruct the Administrator to set NAAQS at a level "requisite to protect" "the art and science dealing with the protection and improvement of community health." Webster's Third New International Dictionary 1836 (1981). We therefore revert to the primary definition of the term: the health of the public.

Even so, respondents argue, many more factors than air pollution affect public health. In particular, the economic cost of implementing a very stringent standard might produce health losses sufficient to offset the health gains achieved in cleaning the air—for example, by closing down whole industries and thereby impoverishing the workers and consumers dependent upon those industries. That is unquestionably true, and Congress was unquestionably aware of it. Thus, Congress had commissioned in the Air Quality Act of 1967 (1967 Act) "a detailed estimate of the cost of carrying out the provisions of this Act; a comprehensive study of the cost of program implementation by affected units of government; and a comprehensive study of the economic impact of air quality standards on the Nation's industries, communities, and other contributing sources of pollution." § 2, 81 Stat. 505. The 1970 Congress, armed with the results of this study, not only anticipated that compliance costs could injure the public health, but provided for that precise exigency. Section 110(f)(1) of the CAA permitted the Administrator to waive the compliance deadline for stationary sources if, *inter alia,* sufficient control measures were simply unavailable and "the continued operation of such sources is *essential . . . to the public health* or welfare." 84 Stat. 1683 (emphasis added). Other provisions explicitly permitted or required economic costs to be taken into account in implementing the air quality standards. Section 111(b)(1)(B), for example, commanded the Administrator to set "standards of performance" for certain new sources of emissions that as specified in § 111(a)(1) were to "reflec[t] the degree of emission limitation achievable through the application of the best system of emission reduction which (taking into account the cost of achieving such reduction) the Administrator determines has been adequately demonstrated." Section 202(a)(2) prescribed that emissions standards for automobiles could take effect only "after such period as the Administrator finds necessary to permit the development and application of the requisite technology, giving appropriate consideration to the cost of compliance within such period." 84 Stat. 1690. Subsequent amendments to the CAA have added many more provisions directing, in explicit language, that the Administrator consider costs in performing various duties. We have therefore refused to find implicit in ambiguous sections of the CAA an authorization to consider costs that has elsewhere, and so often, been expressly granted.

Accordingly, to prevail in their present challenge, respondents must show a textual commitment of authority to the EPA to consider costs in setting NAAQS under § 109(b)(1). And because § 109(b)(1) and the NAAQS for which it provides are the engine that drives nearly all of Title I of the CAA, that textual commitment must be a clear one. Congress, we have held, does not alter the fundamental details of a regulatory scheme in vague terms or ancillary provisions—it does not, one might say, hide elephants in mouseholes. Respondents' textual arguments ultimately founder upon this principle.

Their first claim is that § 109(b)(1)'s terms "adequate margin" and "requisite" leave room to pad health effects with cost concerns. . . . [W]e find it implausible that Congress would give to the EPA through these modest words the power to determine whether implementation costs should moderate national air quality standards.

The same defect inheres in respondents' next two arguments: that while the Administrator's judgment about what is requisite to protect the public health must be "based on [the] criteria" documents developed under § 108(a)(2), it need not be based *solely* on those criteria; and that those criteria themselves, while they must include "effects on public health or welfare which may be expected from the presence of such pollutant in the ambient air," are not necessarily *limited* to those effects. Even if we were to concede those premises, we still would not conclude that one of the unenumerated factors that the agency can consider in developing and applying the criteria is cost of implementation. That factor is *both* so indirectly related to public health *and* so full of potential for canceling the conclusions drawn from direct health effects that it would surely have been expressly mentioned in §§ 108 and 109 had Congress meant it to be considered. Yet while those provisions describe in detail how the health effects of pollutants in the ambient air are to be calculated and given effect, they say not a word about costs.

Respondents point, finally, to a number of provisions in the CAA that *do* require attainment cost data to be generated. Section 108(b)(1), for example, instructs the Administrator to "issue to the States," simultaneously with the criteria documents, "information on air pollution control techniques, which information shall include data relating to the cost of installation and operation." And § 109(d)(2)(C)(iv) requires the Clean Air Scientific Advisory Committee to "advise the Administrator of any adverse public health, welfare, social, economic, or energy effects which may result from various strategies for attainment and maintenance" of NAAQS. Respondents argue that these provisions make no sense unless costs are to be considered in setting the NAAQS. That is not so. These provisions enable the Administrator to assist the States in carrying out their statutory role as primary *implementers* of the NAAQS. It is to the States that the CAA assigns initial and primary responsibility for deciding what emissions reductions will be required from which sources. *See* 42 U.S.C. §§ 7407(a), 7410. It would be impossible to perform that task intelligently without considering which abatement technologies are most efficient, and most economically feasible—which is why we have said that "the most important forum for consideration of claims of economic and technological infeasibility is before the state agency formulating the implementation plan." *Union Elect. Co. v. EPA,* 427 U.S. 246, 266. Thus, federal clean air legislation has, from the very beginning, directed federal agencies to develop and transmit implementation data, including cost data, to the States. That Congress chose to carry forward this research program to assist States in choosing the means through which they would implement the standards is perfectly sensible, and has no bearing upon whether cost considerations are to be taken into account in formulating the standards. . . .

The text of § 109(b), interpreted in its statutory and historical context and with appreciation for its importance to the CAA as a whole, unambiguously bars cost considerations from the NAAQS-setting process, and thus ends the matter for us as well as the EPA.[4]

---

4   Respondents' speculation that the EPA is secretly considering the costs of attainment without telling anyone is irrelevant to our interpretive inquiry. If such an allegation could be

■ JUSTICE BREYER, concurring in part and concurring in the judgment:

I . . . agree with the Court's determination . . . that the Clean Air Act does not permit the Environmental Protection Agency to consider the economic costs of implementation when setting national ambient air quality standards under § 109(b)(1) of the Act. But I would not rest this conclusion solely upon § 109's language or upon a presumption, such as the Court's presumption that any authority the Act grants the EPA to consider costs must flow from a "textual commitment" that is "clear." *Ante,* at 900. In order better to achieve regulatory goals—for example, to allocate resources so that they save more lives or produce a cleaner environment—regulators must often take account of all of a proposed regulation's adverse effects, at least where those adverse effects clearly threaten serious and disproportionate public harm. Hence, I believe that, other things being equal, we should read silences or ambiguities in the language of regulatory statutes as permitting, not forbidding, this type of rational regulation.

In these cases, however, other things are not equal. Here, legislative history, along with the statute's structure, indicates that § 109's language reflects a congressional decision not to delegate to the agency the legal authority to consider economic costs of compliance. . . .

The Senate directly focused upon the technical feasibility and cost of implementing the Act's mandates. And it made clear that it intended the Administrator to develop air quality standards set independently of either. The Senate Report for the 1970 amendments explains:

> In the Committee discussions, considerable concern was expressed regarding the use of the concept of technical feasibility as the basis of ambient air standards. The Committee determined that 1) *the health of people is more important than the question of whether the early achievement of ambient air quality standards protective of health is technically feasible;* and, 2) the growth of pollution load in many areas, even with application of available technology, would still be deleterious to public health. . . .

> Therefore, the Committee determined that *existing sources of pollutants either should meet the standard of the law or be closed down.* . . .

S. Rep. No. 91–1196, pp. 2–3 (1970) (emphasis added). . . . Subsequent legislative history confirms that the technology-forcing goals of the 1970 amendments are still paramount in today's Act. . . .

To read this legislative history as meaning what it says does not impute to Congress an irrational intent. Technology-forcing hopes can prove realistic. Those persons, for example, who opposed the 1970 Act's insistence on a 90% reduction in auto emission pollutants, on the ground

---

proved, it would be grounds for vacating the NAAQS, because the Administrator had not followed the law. It would not, however, be grounds for this Court's changing the law.

of excessive cost, saw the development of catalytic converter technology that helped achieve substantial reductions without the economic catastrophe that some had feared.

At the same time, the statute's technology-forcing objective makes regulatory efforts to determine the costs of implementation both less important and more difficult. It means that the relevant economic costs are speculative, for they include the cost of unknown future technologies. It also means that efforts to take costs into account can breed time-consuming and potentially unresolvable arguments about the accuracy and significance of cost estimates. Congress could have thought such efforts not worth the delays and uncertainties that would accompany them. In any event, that is what the statute's history seems to say. And the matter is one for Congress to decide. . . .

Finally, contrary to the suggestion of the Court of Appeals and of some parties, this interpretation of § 109 does not require the EPA to eliminate every health risk, however slight, at any economic cost, however great, to the point of "hurtling" industry over "the brink of ruin," or even forcing "deindustrialization." *American Trucking Assns., Inc. v. EPA,* 175 F.3d 1027, 1037, 1038, n.4 (C.A.D.C.1999). The statute, by its express terms, does not compel the elimination of *all* risk; and it grants the Administrator sufficient flexibility to avoid setting ambient air quality standards ruinous to industry.

Section 109(b)(1) directs the Administrator to set standards that are "requisite to protect the public health" with "an adequate margin of safety." But these words do not describe a world that is free of all risk—an impossible and undesirable objective. Nor are the words "requisite" and "public health" to be understood independent of context. We consider football equipment "safe" even if its use entails a level of risk that would make drinking water "unsafe" for consumption. And what counts as "requisite" to protecting the public health will similarly vary with background circumstances, such as the public's ordinary tolerance of the particular health risk in the particular context at issue. The Administrator can consider such background circumstances when "decid[ing] what risks are acceptable in the world in which we live." *Natural Resources Defense Council, Inc. v. EPA,* 824 F.2d 1146, 1165 (C.A.D.C.1987).

The statute also permits the Administrator to take account of comparative health risks. That is to say, she may consider whether a proposed rule promotes safety overall. A rule likely to cause more harm to health than it prevents is not a rule that is "requisite to protect the public health." For example, as the Court of Appeals held and the parties do not contest, the Administrator has the authority to determine to what extent possible health risks stemming from reductions in tropospheric ozone (which, it is claimed, helps prevent cataracts and skin cancer) should be taken into account in setting the ambient air quality standard for ozone.

The statute ultimately specifies that the standard set must be "requisite to protect the public health" *"in the judgment of the Administrator,"* § 109(b)(1) (emphasis added), a phrase that grants the Administrator considerable discretionary standard-setting authority.

The statute's words, then, authorize the Administrator to consider the severity of a pollutant's potential adverse health effects, the number of those likely to be affected, the distribution of the adverse effects, and the uncertainties surrounding each estimate. They permit the Administrator to take account of comparative health consequences. They allow her to take account of context when determining the acceptability of small risks to health. And they give her considerable discretion when she does so.

This discretion would seem sufficient to avoid the extreme results that some of the industry parties fear. After all, the EPA, in setting standards that "protect the public health" with "an adequate margin of safety," retains discretionary authority to avoid regulating risks that it reasonably concludes are trivial in context. Nor need regulation lead to deindustrialization. Preindustrial society was not a very healthy society; hence a standard demanding the return of the Stone Age would not prove "requisite to protect the public health."

Although I rely more heavily than does the Court upon legislative history and alternative sources of statutory flexibility, I reach the same ultimate conclusion. Section 109 does not delegate to the EPA authority to base the national ambient air quality standards, in whole or in part, upon the economic costs of compliance.

NOTES AND QUESTIONS

1. **Setting the NAAQS.** Why is EPA forbidden from considering costs when formulating the NAAQS? What is the statutory support for the Court's position? Is it compelling? How could the Court have reached the opposite result?

2. **Cost Consideration: Inevitable?** Consider the following testimony of George Eads, then on the Council of Economic Advisors to the Carter Administration:

> When decisions having such enormous potential economic consequences for the country are being made, it is foolish to pretend that economic concerns will not enter into the decision-making process. Indeed, it is positively deceitful to require that the economic considerations which do influence the Administrator's decision be hidden from public view.

Clean Air Act Oversight: Hearings Before the Committee on Environment and Public Works, U.S. Senate, 97th Cong. 199 (1980). If Eads is correct, and EPA is secretly considering costs (contravening the requirements of the CAA), what—if anything—can or should be done in response?

Perhaps more importantly, if such a back-room cost-benefit analysis is occurring, what are the likely sources of information for EPA? Are environmental groups or industry groups better positioned to influence such a back-room process? Industry groups may have, for example, low-cost access to information about the effects of their industries. What advantages do environmental groups have in such a secretive process? Is the only solution to this problem increased disclosure and openness in whatever cost consideration process will inevitably occur?

3. **Cost Consideration: When?** Consider the following view:

> The costs of meeting primary air quality standards are best taken into account in determining what control programs should be implemented in specific areas of the country, not in establishing a national air quality standard to protect public health. Although the level of air pollution affecting public health generally does not vary in different locations, the costs of meeting any specific standard will vary substantially, depending upon the severity of existing pollution levels, from one area to another. Thus, if a national air quality standard were based in part on the costs of complying with it, the very high costs of meeting the standard in a few severely polluted areas would probably require that the standard be set at a less protective level than is achievable in a reasonable, economic fashion in most areas of the country. The most effective balance between the beneficial effects of good air quality on human health and the economic, social, energy, and other costs of meeting health-based standards will be achieved when conditions in particular areas can be considered in deciding when the standards should be met in the areas and what measures will be adopted to meet the standards.

NATIONAL COMMISSION ON AIR QUALITY, TO BREATHE CLEAN AIR 2.1–2 (1981).

Evaluate the argument. Does the CAA provide such flexibility? If not, should costs be taken into account in setting the NAAQS? Should the statute have provided for disuniform NAAQS? Are there other strategies that could address this concern?

4. **Cost Consideration for Lead.** Cost was not (explicitly) considered in the setting of the lead NAAQS. The lead industry challenged the standards on that ground in *Lead Industries Association v. EPA*, 647 F.2d 1130 (D.C. Cir. 1980). Writing for the court, J. Skelly Wright held that the argument that EPA's "adequate margin of safety" should have been a foothold for cost consideration was "totally without merit." Considering both the statute and its legislative history, the court concluded that "economic considerations play no part in the promulgation of ambient air quality standards under Section 109. Where Congress intended the Administrator to be concerned about economic and technological feasibility, it expressly so provided." This result is consistent with the "elephants in mouseholes" theory propounded by Justice Scalia in *American Trucking* (see note below). Were there reasons for

the much earlier *Lead Industries* opinion to come out the other way, even if one believes *American Trucking* was correct when it was decided?

5.   Nondelegation and the NAAQS. In a portion of the *American Trucking* opinion not excerpted above, the Supreme Court considered and rejected the D.C. Circuit's argument that, if the NAAQS was not read to include cost consideration, it would lack any intelligible principle to guide EPA's exercise of authority in setting the NAAQS and thus would effect an unconstitutional delegation of power by Congress. The Supreme Court ultimately found the scope of discretion of § 109(b)(1) "well within the outer limits of our nondelegation precedents." Do you agree? The Court defines "requisite to protect the public health" as "sufficient, but not more than necessary." How is EPA to decide what is "sufficient" or "necessary," if not by considering costs?

6.   Elephants in Mouseholes. In *American Trucking*, the majority held that the text of § 109 does not permit the consideration of costs, applying a presumption that Congress does not hide "elephants" like cost consideration in "mouseholes," or statutory silence and ambiguity. Justice Breyer, concurring in the judgment, argued that the Court should apply a presumption in favor of cost consideration in the absence of a clear statement by Congress. Justice Breyer found a clear statement against cost consideration in the structure and legislative history of the CAA; thus he concurred in the judgment. But for reasons of "rational" regulatory policy, he would read a statute to allow cost-benefit analysis when Congress has not spoken clearly on the subject. Which approach do you think is preferable?

Justice Breyer found the ban on cost-benefit analysis rational in the context of the CAA because the statute gave the Administrator discretion to consider risk tradeoffs in determining the level of pollution "requisite to protect the public health." Risk tradeoff analysis considers the regulation's secondary effects on ancillary risks as well as the primary effect on the targeted risk to determine whether the regulation is justified to protect the public health. Justice Breyer identified three types of risk tradeoffs that could be considered by the Administrator:

1.   Contextual risk tradeoffs, taking into account "the public's ordinary tolerance of a particular health risk." Justice Breyer uses the example of "safe" football equipment versus "safe" drinking water.

2.   Cost-induced health risk tradeoffs, or health risks resulting from the economic effects of regulation. Thus, the Administrator does not need to set a standard at a level that would cause deindustrialization, because "[p]reindustrial society was not a very healthy society."

3.   Comparative health risk tradeoffs, such as the effect of ground-level ozone regulation. Ground-level ozone causes respiratory illness, but it also blocks UV radiation from reaching the earth, which in turn prevents some skin cancers.

What if the level of pollution reduction required to meet the NAAQS would cause some areas of the country to return to preindustrial practices? *Cf.* EPA,

Approval and Promulgation of Implementation Plans; California—South Coast Air Basin; Ozone and Carbon Monoxide Plans, 53 Fed. Reg. 49,494, 49,496 (1988) (to meet the NAAQS within five years, the South Coast Air Basin "must include restrictions and prohibitions that effectively prevent from operating within the Basin, in the fifth year, almost all fossil-fuel powered vehicles; eliminate almost all aircraft and marine vessels from the basin; prohibit almost every industrial source from emitting any VOCs; dramatically reduce VOC emissions from commercial and residential solvents and fuel combustion; and substantially limit agricultural VOC emissions.").

Consider the following views:

Justice Breyer's concurrence marks the arrival of risk tradeoff analysis in general, and health-health tradeoff analysis in particular, in the Supreme Court. It can be expected to pave the way for future challenges based on risk tradeoffs. The opinion is also noteworthy for at least two other reasons. First, Justice Breyer drew attention to the manner in which risk tradeoff analysis, and in particular health-health tradeoff analysis, can serve as a proxy for cost-benefit analysis when it is prohibited by statute. Commentators have observed that risk tradeoff analysis emerged in part because of statutory limitations on the application of cost-benefit analysis. But because health-health analysis can, to some extent, serve as a functional substitute for cost-benefit analysis, one might argue that it should be prohibited whenever cost-benefit analysis is prohibited. Justice Breyer, while recognizing the utility of health-health tradeoffs functionally to accomplish what cost-benefit analysis would have done had its use been permitted, took the position that the methodologies are sufficiently different that the ban on one does not apply to the other. . . . To Justice Breyer, both a regulation that entails a significant direct risk tradeoff and one whose exorbitant cost brings about health risks appear to be instances of a "rule likely to cause more harm to health than it prevents" and so "not a rule that is 'requisite to protect the public health.'"

Samuel J. Rascoff & Richard L. Revesz, *The Biases of Risk Trade-off Analysis: Toward Parity in Environmental and Health-and-Safety Regulation*, 69 U. CHI. L. REV. 1763, 1789–90 (2002).

Plainly, Breyer considers it a mistake to ignore regulatory costs. In an off-the-bench discussion of American Trucking, he has explained that "Congress could not have intended" the "counterproductive results" that would flow from reading the Clean Air Act to forbid EPA ever to take cost into account and that, "probably because of my earlier work in the field of regulation, I thought it important to say so." In the opinion itself, he was at pains to demonstrate why Congress's inescapable decision to do so in section 109 was not, under all the circumstances, irrational. His argument is subtle. The statute was meant to force technological development; therefore, the costs of compliance should, if all goes according to plan, be a moving target, making their calculation "both less important and more difficult." Costs do come into play in many other settings under the Act, including in provisions for actually achieving the standards set under section 109, which reduces the impact of the cost-blind approach to setting them. Section 109 itself does not require elimination of all risks, regardless of their size or the costs of doing so; the "public health" will be protected if "unreasonable risks" are eliminated, leaving only "acceptable risks." And in determining whether a given standard will protect public health, the agency must take into account all of its health effects. Thus, Justice Breyer identifies a justification for ignoring compliance costs in setting a NAAQS and explains why the consequences of doing so are acceptable given the other ways in which costs are taken into account.

Michael Herz, *The Rehnquist Court and Administrative Law*, 99 NW. U. L. REV. 297, 343–44 (2004).

Which of these views do you find more compelling? Are you concerned about the possibility of the Supreme Court deciding what Congress intended by gauging the "counterproductivity" of the likely results? Are there alternatives to this stark choice that afford due deference to the legislative enactments of Congress while accounting for the modern realities of regulation? Does Justice Breyer's view represent, in your view, a compelling first move in that direction?

7. Congressional "Ratification" of EPA's Interpretation. In an amicus brief in *American Trucking*, Environmental Defense and the American Public Health Association argued that Congress had ratified the no-cost-consideration framework, through years of legislation against its backdrop without modification. EPA had consistently interpreted the CAA not to allow consideration of costs, and when Congress amended the Act in 1977 and 1990, it made no effort to change this interpretation.

How compelling is this argument? A version of it had already formed the basis for the Supreme Court's holding in *FDA v. Brown & Williamson Tobacco Corp.*, 529 U.S. 120 (2000). For the purposes of statutory interpretation, which intent matters: the intent of the enacting Congress? The Congress to most recently amend the bill? The present Congress? It is certainly true that, in the 30 years intervening between the original enactment of the Act and *American Trucking*, Congress had extensively debated cost consideration and yet left the statute unchanged. *See, e.g., Clean Air Oversight: Hearings Before the Senate Comm. on Environment and Public Works*, 97th Cong. 505 (1981) (proposal by the Business Roundtable that § 109(b) be amended to take costs into account).

8. Health-Wealth Tradeoffs and Cost-Benefit Analysis. Health-wealth tradeoffs are a form of risk tradeoff analysis that assess the impact of a health and safety regulation in light of its reduction of social wealth, and thus, in theory, its reduction of overall social health. *See* Rascoff & Revesz, *supra*, at 1778–80. Proponents of this form of risk tradeoff analysis assert that a regulation with a cost of more than $15 million per life will have counterproductive results—that is it will result in more statistical lives lost due to reduction of social wealth than statistical lives saved due to regulation. *See id.* (citing Randall Lutter et al., *The Cost-Per-Life-Saved Cutoff for Safety-Enhancing Regulations*, 37 ECON. INQ. 599, 605 (1999)). Such an analysis, as noted above, is basically a proxy for cost-benefit analysis, with a valuation of human life at $15 million instead of the approximately $6 million in 1999 dollars EPA uses in its formal cost-benefit analysis. *See* Rascoff & Revesz, *supra*, at 1790.

Advocates for health-wealth tradeoff analysis argue that if the government spends too much on environmental, health, and safety regulation, the public health will suffer. Revesz & Livermore question the analytical soundness of this argument:

> Proponents of health-wealth tradeoff analysis observe that there is a correlation between more wealth and more health. Wealthy people do in fact live longer. But then these proponents assume that correlation is causation, asserting that more wealth causes more health. Under this pseudo logic, they assert that because any regulation will impose costs on people, thereby decreasing their wealth, such regulations will also create the countervailing risk of diminishing people's health. In other words, health regulations should be abolished because they kill people.

> A statistics teacher would give that reasoning an F and move on. Unfortunately, that is impossible here, and the health-wealth argument has gained significant traction. It has been heard in the halls of the White House and in the chambers of the U.S. Supreme Court. If anything, its popularity continues to grow . . .

> The reason that both income and wealth seem to have a relationship with health is that education has a significant relationship to health—the more educated you are, the healthier you tend to be.

RICHARD L. REVESZ & MICHAEL A. LIVERMORE, RETAKING RATIONALITY 67, 73 (2008).

For further exploration of the impact of health-wealth tradeoff analysis on regulatory policy, see Cass R. Sunstein, *Health-Health Tradeoffs*, 63 U. CHI. L. REV. 1533 (1996); Ralph L. Keeney, *Mortality Risks Induced by Economic Expenditures*, 10 RISK ANAL. 147 (1990); AARON WILDAVSKY, SEARCHING FOR SAFETY (1988); Aaron Wildavsky, *Richer Is Safer*, 60 PUB. INT. 23 (1980).

9.   Inadequacy Paradox. The most recent rulemakings for each NAAQS pollutant, except carbon monoxide, have involved a regulatory impact analysis (RIA) that includes a cost-benefit analysis of the rulemaking. The RIA is prepared separately from the rulemaking, and is not considered in setting the NAAQS. For four of the five criteria pollutants for which RIAs were prepared, the standards set by EPA were *less* stringent than those that would have resulted from the application of cost-benefit analysis. For sulfur dioxide and nitrogen dioxide, a cost-benefit analysis that included ancillary benefits would have resulted in a more stringent standard than the NAAQS actually set. Why does this outcome occur? When setting NAAQS, EPA does not consider ancillary benefits of a standard, whereas the RIA is required to consider ancillary benefits. Does the inadequacy paradox justify abandoning EPA's health-based approach to setting NAAQS? Does *American Trucking v. EPA* foreclose consideration of costs in all circumstances? How could *American Trucking v. EPA* be read down to allow a cost-benefit analysis? Could cost-benefit analysis become a regulatory floor? Or health-based standards a regulatory trump? *See* Michael A. Livermore & Richard L. Revesz, *Rethinking Health-Based Environmental Standards*, 89 N.Y.U. L. REV. 1184 (2014). Similarly, in the case of the most recent NAAQS for ozone, the standard set by EPA was *less* stringent than the standard that would have resulted from the application of cost-benefit analysis. *See* Michael A. Livermore & Richard L. Revesz, *Rethinking Health-Based Environmental Standards and Cost-Benefit Analysis,* 46 ENVTL. L. REP. 10,674, 10,678–79 (2016).

10. Political Economy of Cost Consideration. The environmental movement widely regarded *American Trucking* as a success. Why might environmentalists prefer that costs not be taken into account when setting environmental policy? It is possible, of course, that a thorough cost-benefit analysis might reveal that pollution was being underregulated, and that cost consideration would result in more stringent regulation. What reasons exist to object to cost consideration, then?

Of course, it is possible that environmentalists believe their preferred policies are not socially optimal, and thus that a thorough cost-benefit analysis would result in less regulation than they prefer. On what basis would they want the standards to be set?

11. Amici in *American Trucking*. Filing briefs as amici curiae in support of petitioners were (among others) the American Lung Association, Environmental Defense, the State of New York, and the State of California. Filing briefs as amici curiae in support of respondents the American Trucking Association were (among others) the Manufacturers Alliance, American Crop Protection Association, Arthur Andersen LLP, KPMG LLP, the General Electric Company, and Senator Orrin Hatch. Why would Arthur Andersen, an accounting firm, support the respondents? Why would the State of New York (which, under the CAA, was free to set more stringent state regulations) care about the case?

12. Reconsideration and Cost Consideration. Similar to EPA's 2006 particulate matter standards, discussed *supra*, EPA's 2008 ozone NAAQS revision set a standard that was not within the range recommended by the Clean Air Scientific Advisory Committee. *See* EPA, National Ambient Air Quality Standards for Ozone 73 Fed. Reg. 16,436, 16,500 (2008). After *American Farm Bureau v. EPA* highlighted the legal vulnerability of NAAQS set contrary to CASAC recommendations, EPA decided to reconsider the ozone NAAQS to ensure that the standard "appropriately reflects the available science"; the agency subsequently issued an ozone NAAQS proposal in 2010. *See* EPA, National Ambient Air Quality Standards for Ozone, 75 Fed. Reg. 2938, 2943 (2010).

In 2011, President Obama requested that EPA's Administrator, Lisa Jackson, withdraw the draft ozone NAAQS, stating:

> ... I have continued to underscore the importance of reducing regulatory burdens and regulatory uncertainty, particularly as our economy continues to recover. With that in mind, and after careful consideration, I have requested that Administrator Jackson withdraw the draft Ozone National Ambient Air Quality Standards at this time.

The White House Office of the Press Secretary, Statement by the President on the Ozone National Ambient Air Quality Standards (Sept. 2, 2011).

Consider that EPA undertook the NAAQS reconsideration voluntarily, ahead of the revision schedule mandated under § 109(d). Should the decision of whether or not to postpone a NAAQS reconsideration be treated differently than the setting of a NAAQS standard? Does EPA have discretion to postpone consideration of a NAAQS revision because of economic considerations? Does it make any difference that EPA had already submitted finalized standards to the White House when President Obama announced their withdrawal? In 2015, EPA did eventually revise the ozone NAAQS to be more stringent. EPA, National Ambient Air Quality Standards for Ozone, 80 Fed. Reg. 65,292 (2015).

3. STATE IMPLEMENTATION PLANS

The CAA was designed as an experiment in "cooperative federalism": the federal government provided a goal for air quality and the state retained discretion to achieve that goal in a manner consistent with state and local priorities. When Congress enacted the CAA, it decided "that air pollution prevention . . . and air pollution control at its source is the primary responsibility of States and local governments . . . ." 42 U.S.C. § 7401(a)(3). Nevertheless, Congress also determined "that Federal financial assistance and leadership is essential for the development of cooperative Federal, State, regional, and local programs to prevent and control air pollution." 42 U.S.C. § 7401(a)(4). The NAAQS are the air quality goal provided by Congress and promulgated by the Administrator. 42 U.S.C. § 7409. In order to adequately protect the public health (as determined by the NAAQS), each state must submit a plan to the Administrator that provides for "implementation, maintenance, and enforcement" of the NAAQS in each air quality control region within the state. 42 U.S.C. § 7410(a)(1). The State Implementation Plan, or SIP, is the mechanism through which the state allocates pollution reduction burdens. Section 110 governs the development, adoption and revision of SIPs.

The SIP is a federally enforceable plan that describes the manner in which the state will ensure that the NAAQS are met within its borders. Section 110(a)(2) requires the state to adopt its SIP after notice and a public hearing. 42 U.S.C. § 7410(a)(2). The SIP must contain several elements:

- Enforceable emissions limits to meet the NAAQS and PSD or nonattainment requirements;

- Air quality monitoring and reporting systems;

- Enforcement mechanisms;

- Adequate provisions to prohibit interstate spillover;

- Assurances that the state has adequate funding and personnel to carry out the SIP;

- Requirements that sources monitor and report emissions to the State, as prescribed by the Administrator; and state capacity to correlate the source data to the emissions standards established by the SIP, NAAQS, and PSD or nonattainment provisions;

- Emergency powers to prevent emissions that cause "imminent harm or substantial endangerment";

- Mechanisms for revision of the SIP;

- Air quality modeling systems;

- Fee systems for air permits; and

- Consultation and participation by local political subdivisions affected by the plan.

42 U.S.C. § 7410(a)(2). Once the state submits the SIP to the Administrator, she must first determine whether the plan is complete. 42 U.S.C. § 7410(k)(1)(B). If the SIP is complete and meets all applicable CAA requirements, the Administrator must approve it as a whole. 42 U.S.C. § 7410(k)(3).

Occasional revisions are also submitted for EPA approval, as discussed further below. For these, the Administrator may disapprove a portion of a plan revision if it does not meet the requirements. If she disapproves a portion, the revision will not be treated as meeting the requirements until she approves the entire plan revision. *Id.* The Administrator may also grant conditional approval of a SIP if a state commits to adopt specific enforceable measures within one year of approval. 42 U.S.C. § 7410(k)(4). If the state fails to adopt the measures, the conditional approval becomes plan disapproval. *Id.*

The Administrator's duty to promulgate a Federal Implementation Plan (FIP) is triggered if the Administrator finds that a SIP is incomplete or that a state failed to make a required submission, or if she disapproves a SIP in whole or in part. 42 U.S.C. § 7410(c). The Administrator must promulgate a FIP within two years of disapproval, unless the state corrects the deficiency and the Administrator approves the SIP or SIP revision. *Id.* Some of the materials that follow consider whether FIPs are a useful way to ensure compliance with the NAAQS.

After a SIP is approved, if the Administrator subsequently finds that a SIP for any area is inadequate to attain or maintain the NAAQS, she does not have to wait for a state to decide to revise its SIP. She has authority to issue a SIP call, which notifies the state of the deficiency and requires the state to revise its SIP. 42 U.S.C. § 7410(k)(5). Once the Administrator issues a SIP call, the state must revise its SIP as necessary within eighteen months of the notice. *Id.*

The cases that follow explore the roles of the federal and state governments in SIP development, approval and enforcement.

A. STATE ROLE IN ESTABLISHING SIPs

Union Electric Co. v. Environmental Protection Agency
427 U.S. 246 (1976).

■ JUSTICE MARSHALL delivered the opinion of the Court:

. . . The heart of the [Clean Air Act] Amendments [of 1970] is the requirement that each State formulate, subject to EPA approval, an implementation plan designed to achieve national primary ambient air quality standards—those necessary to protect the public health—"as expeditiously as practicable but . . . in no case later than three years from the date of approval of such plan." § 110(a)(2)(A) of the Clean Air Act. . . . Each State is given wide discretion in formulating its plan, and the Act provides that the Administrator "shall approve" the proposed plan if it has been adopted after public notice and hearing and if it meets eight specified criteria. § 110(a)(2).

[EPA approved the State of Missouri's SIP. The SIP focused on reduction of SO_2 levels in the St. Louis Interstate Region. Emissions limitations were effective immediately, but under the terms of the SIP, the State could grant variances to particular sources that could not immediately comply. Union Electric did not challenge the SIP; instead it applied for, and received, one-year variances that could be extended upon reapplication. Two of Union Electric's variances had expired and it was applying for further extensions when EPA notified the company that its SO_2 levels violated the SIP. Union Electric then filed a petition for review of EPA's approval of the SIP in the Eighth Circuit, arguing that the Administrator did not properly consider the economic and technological feasibility of the pollution allocation under the SIP. The Eighth Circuit held that the Administrator could not consider feasibility when determining whether to approve a SIP, and thus the court was without jurisdiction to hear the case. The Supreme Court granted certiorari to resolve a split among the circuits regarding whether the Administrator could take into account economic and technological feasibility when deciding whether to approve a SIP.]

. . . [W]e agree [with the Administrator] that Congress intended claims of economic and technological infeasibility to be wholly foreign to the Administrator's consideration of a state implementation plan.

As we have previously recognized, the 1970 Amendments to the Clean Air Act were a drastic remedy to what was perceived as a serious and otherwise uncheckable problem of air pollution. The Amendments place the primary responsibility for formulating pollution control strategies on the States, but nonetheless subject the States to strict minimum compliance requirements. These requirements are of a "technology-forcing character," *Train v. NRDC, supra*, at 91 and are expressly designed to force regulated sources to develop pollution control devices that might at the time appear to be economically or technologically infeasible.

This approach is apparent on the face of § 110(a)(2). The provision sets out eight criteria that an implementation plan must satisfy, and provides that if these criteria are met and if the plan was adopted after reasonable notice and hearing, the Administrator "shall approve" the proposed state plan. The mandatory "shall" makes it quite clear that the Administrator is not to be concerned with factors other than those specified, *Train v. NRDC, supra*, at 71 n. 11, and none of the eight factors appears to permit consideration of technological or economic infeasibility.[5] Nonetheless, if a basis is to be found for allowing the Administrator to consider such claims, it must be among the eight criteria, and so it is here that the argument is focused.

It is suggested that consideration of claims of technological and economic infeasibility is required by the first criterion—that the primary air quality standards be met "as expeditiously as practicable but . . . in no case later than three years . . ." and that the secondary air quality standards be met within a "reasonable time." § 110(a)(2)(A). The argument is that what is "practicable" or "reasonable" cannot be determined without assessing whether what is proposed is possible. This argument does not survive analysis.

Section 110(a)(2)(A)'s three-year deadline for achieving primary air quality standards is central to the Amendments' regulatory scheme and, as both the language and the legislative history of the requirement make clear, it leaves no room for claims of technological or economic infeasibility. The 1970 congressional debate on the Amendments centered on whether technology forcing was necessary and desirable in framing and attaining air quality standards sufficient to protect the public health, standards later termed primary standards. The House version of the Amendments was quite moderate in approach, requiring only that health-related standards be met "within a reasonable time." H.R. 17255, 91st Cong., 2d Sess., § 108(c)(1)(C)(i) (1970). The Senate bill, on the other hand, flatly required that, possible or not, health-related standards be met "within three years." S. 4358, 91st Cong., 2d Sess., § 111(a)(2)(A) (1970). . . .

---

[5] Comparison of the eight criteria of § 110(a)(2) with other provisions of the Amendments bolsters this conclusion. Where Congress intended the Administrator to be concerned about economic and technological infeasibility, it expressly so provided . . .

This position reflected that of the Senate committee:

"In the Committee discussions, considerable concern was expressed regarding the use of the concept of technical feasibility as the basis of ambient air standards. The Committee determined that 1) the health of people is more important than the question of whether the early achievement of ambient air quality standards protective of health is technically feasible; and 2) the growth of pollution load in many areas, even with application of available technology, would still be deleterious to public health.

"Therefore, the Committee determined that existing sources of pollutants either should meet the standard of the law or be closed down. . . ."

S.Rep. No. 91–1196, pp. 2–3 (1970).

The Conference Committee and, ultimately, the entire Congress accepted the Senate's three-year mandate for the achievement of primary air quality standards, and the clear import of that decision is that the Administrator must approve a plan that provides for attainment of the primary standards in three years even if attainment does not appear feasible. In rejecting the House's version of reasonableness, however, the conferees strengthened the Senate version. The Conference Committee made clear that the States could not procrastinate until the deadline approached. Rather, the primary standards had to be met in less than three years if possible; they had to be met "as expeditiously as practicable." § 110(a)(2)(A). Whatever room there is for considering claims of infeasibility in the attainment of primary standards must lie in this phrase, which is, of course, relevant only in evaluating those implementation plans that attempt to achieve the primary standard in less than three years.

It is argued that when such a state plan calls for proceeding more rapidly than economics and the available technology appear to allow, the plan must be rejected as not "practicable." Whether this is a correct reading of § 110(a)(2)(A) depends on how that section's "as expeditiously as practicable" phrase is characterized. The Administrator's position is that § 110(a)(2)(A) sets only a minimum standard that the States may exceed in their discretion, so that he has no power to reject an infeasible state plan that surpasses the minimum federal requirements—a plan that reflects a state decision to engage in technology forcing on its own and to proceed more expeditiously than is practicable. On the other hand, petitioner and *amici* supporting its position argue that § 110(a)(2)(A) sets a mandatory standard that the States must meet precisely and conclude that the Administrator may reject a plan for being too strict as well as for being too lax. . . . The final Amendments also separated welfare-related standards from health-related standards, labeled them secondary air quality standards, and adopted the House's requirement that they be met within a "reasonable time." §§ 109(b), 110(a)(2)(A). Thus, technology forcing is not expressly required in achieving standards to protect the public welfare.

It does not necessarily follow, however, that the Administrator may consider claims of impossibility in assessing a state plan for achieving secondary standards. As with plans designed to achieve primary standards in less than three years, the scope of the Administrator's power to reject a plan depends on whether the State itself may decide to engage in technology forcing and adopt a plan more stringent than federal law demands.

Amici Appalachian Power Co. et al. argue that the Amendments do not give such broad power to the States. They claim that the States are precluded from submitting implementation plans more stringent than federal law demands by § 110(a)(2)'s second criterion—that the plan contain such control devices "as may be necessary" to achieve the primary and secondary air quality standards. § 110(a)(2)(B). The contention is that an overly restrictive plan is not "necessary" for attainment of the national standards and so must be rejected by the Administrator.

The principal support for this theory of *amici* lies in the fact that while the House and Senate versions of § 110(a)(2) both expressly provided that the States could submit for the Administrator's approval plans that were stricter than the national standards required, the section as enacted contains no such express language. *Amici* argue that the Conference Committee must have decided to require state implementation plans simply—and precisely—to meet the national standards. The argument of *amici* proves too much. A Conference Committee lacks power to make substantive changes on matters about which both Houses agree. . . . And while the final language of § 110(a)(2)(B) may be less explicit than the versions originally approved by the House and the Senate, the most natural reading of the "as may be necessary" phrase in context is simply that the Administrator must assure that the minimal, or "necessary," requirements are met, not that he detect and reject any state plan more demanding than federal law requires.

This reading is further supported by practical considerations. Section 116 provides that the States may adopt emission standards stricter than the national standards. *Amici* argue that such standards must be adopted and enforced independently of the EPA-approved state implementation plan. This construction of §§ 110 and 116, however, would not only require the Administrator to expend considerable time and energy determining whether a state plan was precisely tailored to meet the federal standards, but would simultaneously require States desiring stricter standards to enact and enforce two sets of emission standards, one federally approved plan and one stricter state plan. We find no basis in the Amendments for visiting such wasteful burdens upon the States and the Administrator, and so we reject the argument of *amici*.

We read the "as may be necessary" requirement of § 110(a)(2)(B) to demand only that the implementation plan submitted by the State meet the "minimum conditions" of the Amendments.[13] *Train v. NRDC*, 421 U.S., at 71 n. 11. Beyond that, if a State makes the legislative determination that it desires a particular air quality by a certain date and that it is willing to force technology to attain it—or lose a certain industry if attainment is not possible—such a determination is fully consistent with the structure and purpose of the Amendments, and § 110(a)(2)(B) provides no basis for the EPA Administrator to object to the determination on the ground of infeasibility.[14]

In sum, we have concluded that claims of economic or technological infeasibility may not be considered by the Administrator in evaluating a state requirement that primary ambient air quality standards be met in the mandatory three years. And, since we further conclude that the States may submit implementation plans more stringent than federal law requires and that the Administrator must approve such plans if they meet the minimum requirements of § 110(a)(2), it follows that the language of § 110(a)(2)(B) provides no basis for the Administrator ever to reject a state implementation plan on the ground that it is economically or technologically infeasible. Accordingly, a court of appeals reviewing an approved plan under § 307(b)(1) cannot set it aside on those grounds, no matter when they are raised. . . .

Perhaps the most important forum for consideration of claims of economic and technological infeasibility is before the state agency formulating the implementation plan. So long as the national standards are met, the State may select whatever mix of control devices it desires, and industries with particular economic or technological problems may seek special treatment in the plan itself. Moreover, if the industry is not exempted from, or accommodated by, the original plan, it may obtain a variance, as petitioner did in this case; and the variance, if granted after notice and a hearing, may be submitted to the EPA as a revision of the plan. § 110(a)(3)(A). Lastly, an industry denied an exemption from the implementation plan, or denied a subsequent variance, may be able to take its claims of economic or technological infeasibility to the state courts. *See, e.g.*, Mo.Rev.Stat. § 203.130 (1972).

---

[13] Economic and technological factors may be relevant in determining whether the minimum conditions are met. Thus, the Administrator may consider whether it is economically or technologically possible for the state plan to require more rapid progress than it does. If he determines that it is, he may reject the plan as not meeting the requirement that primary standards be achieved "as expeditiously as practicable" or as failing to provide for attaining secondary standards within "a reasonable time."

[14] In a literal sense, of course, no plan is infeasible since offending sources always have the option of shutting down if they cannot otherwise comply with the standard of the law. Thus, there is no need for the Administrator to reject an economically or technologically "infeasible" state plan on the ground that anticipated noncompliance will cause the State to fall short of the national standards. Sources objecting to such a state scheme must seek their relief from the State.

While the State has virtually absolute power in allocating emission limitations so long as the national standards are met, if the state plan cannot meet the national standards, the EPA is implicated in any postponement procedure. [The Court cites § 110(e) and 110(f), which authorize the Governor of a State to request postponement in certain circumstances.] . . .

Even if the State does not intervene on behalf of an emission source, technological and economic factors may be considered in at least one other circumstance. When a source is found to be in violation of the state implementation plan, the Administrator may, after a conference with the operator, issue a compliance order rather than seek civil or criminal enforcement. Such an order must specify a "reasonable" time for compliance with the relevant standard, taking into account the seriousness of the violation and "any good faith efforts to comply with applicable requirements." § 113(a)(4). Claims of technological or economic infeasibility, the Administrator agrees, are relevant to fashioning an appropriate compliance order under § 113(a)(4).

In short, the Amendments offer ample opportunity for consideration of claims of technological and economic infeasibility. Always, however, care is taken that consideration of such claims will not interfere substantially with the primary goal of prompt attainment of the national standards. Allowing such claims to be raised by appealing the Administrator's approval of an implementation plan, as petitioner suggests, would frustrate congressional intent. It would permit a proposed plan to be struck down as infeasible before it is given a chance to work, even though Congress clearly contemplated that some plans would be infeasible when proposed. And it would permit the Administrator or a federal court to reject a State's legislative choices in regulating air pollution, even though Congress plainly left with the States, so long as the national standards were met, the power to determine which sources would be burdened by regulation and to what extent. Technology forcing is a concept somewhat new to our national experience and it necessarily entails certain risks. But Congress considered those risks in passing the 1970 Amendments and decided that the dangers posed by uncontrolled air pollution made them worth taking. Petitioner's theory would render that considered legislative judgment a nullity, and that is a result we refuse to reach.

■ JUSTICE POWELL, with whom THE CHIEF JUSTICE joins, concurring:

I join the opinion of the Court because the statutory scheme and the legislative history, thoroughly described in the Court's opinion, demonstrate irrefutably that Congress did not intend to permit the Administrator of the Environmental Protection Agency to reject a proposed state implementation plan on the grounds of economic or technological infeasibility. Congress adopted this position despite its apparent awareness that in some cases existing sources that cannot meet the standard of the law must be closed down. . . .

Environmental concerns, long neglected, merit high priority, and Congress properly has made protection of the public health its paramount consideration. But the shutdown of an urban area's electrical service could have an even more serious impact on the health of the public than that created by a decline in ambient air quality. The result apparently required by this legislation in its present form could sacrifice the well-being of a large metropolitan area through the imposition of inflexible demands that may be technologically impossible to meet and indeed may no longer even be necessary to the attainment of the goal of clean air.

I believe that Congress, if fully aware of this Draconian possibility, would strike a different balance.

NOTES AND QUESTIONS

1.   **What Does "As May Be Necessary" Mean?** Section 110(a)(2) lays out what must be in a SIP. What does § 110(a)(2)(A) require? (Note that this section has been amended since 1976, though the essential structure remains the same.) What did industry, in *Union Electric*, argue "emission limitations . . . as may be necessary . . . to meet the applicable requirements of this Act" meant? If a state enacts more stringent emissions limitations than required to meet the NAAQS, can those fairly be characterized as "necessary to meet the applicable requirements"? How?

2.   **Retention of State Authority.** Section 116 provides that, except for auto emissions and certain other specified exceptions, "nothing in this Act shall preclude or deny the right of any State . . . to adopt or enforce (1) any standard or limitation respecting emissions of air pollutants or (2) any requirement respecting control or abatement of air pollution. . . ." Does this language compel the *Union Electric* majority's reading of § 110(a)(2)(A)? Is there a plausible reading of the statute that accommodates both § 116 and the industry's argument that § 110(a)(2)(A) creates a "ceiling" on restrictions that may be included in a valid SIP?

Is there a good policy reason to require states—which may adopt emissions regulations that are more stringent than the NAAQS under § 116—to keep their more stringent regulations out of their SIP? Or would it simply waste resources?

Should industry be allowed to challenge SIPs as "too restrictive" even if the state could concededly re-enact the exact same restrictions outside the context of a SIP? Why might industry value the ability to make such challenges?

3.   **Cooperative Federalism.** Why do we have federal NAAQS? The NAAQS are structured to prevent state under-regulation of air pollution. *Union Electric* is an attempt by industry to prevent what it perceived as state over-regulation of pollution.

One year before *Union Electric*, the Supreme Court considered whether the states retained control to determine their preferred modes of compliance with the NAAQS. In *Train v. NRDC*, 421 U.S. 60 (1975), the state of Georgia had included a variance procedure for in-state sources that could not come into compliance immediately. NRDC challenged the variance procedure because it believed it was inconsistent with another provision in § 110 that authorized the Governor of a state to apply for postponement of attainment. The Court held that "the Act gives the Agency no authority to question the wisdom of a State's choices of emission limitations if they are part of a plan which satisfies the standards of § 110(a)(2)." *Id.* at 79. Thus, as long as Georgia could demonstrate compliance with the NAAQS, it was free to allocate its pollution burden according to its own preferences. Why do the SIP provisions give such authority to the states? How does this flexibility benefit the states?

In *Union Electric*, Missouri's SIP had a similar variance provision. It appeared that the power plant failed to renew its variance and subsequently attempted to challenge the State's allocation of the pollution control burden in the SIP.

The power plant tried to limit the State's discretion in two ways. First, it argued that the Administrator was required to consider the economic and technological feasibility of the SIP before approving it. Second, amici argued that the Missouri SIP could not be designed to improve air quality above the NAAQS. How did the Court respond to each of these arguments?

Circuits had split on the issue of whether the Administrator was required to consider the economic and technological feasibility of a SIP before approving it. *See Union Elec. v. EPA*, 427 U.S. 246, 254 (1976). What language did the petitioners point to in § 110(a)(2) to support their argument? How does the language in § 110(a)(2) compare with the language and structure of § 109 addressed in *American Trucking*?

B. ROLE OF FEDERAL IMPLEMENTATION PLANS

Coalition for Clean Air v. Environmental Protection Agency

971 F.2d 219 (9th Cir. 1992), *cert. denied*, 507 U.S. 950 (1993).

■ Before GOODWIN, NORRIS, and NOONAN, JR., CIRCUIT JUDGES.

■ NORRIS, CIRCUIT JUDGE:

California's South Coast Air Basin has the dirtiest air in the United States. Twenty-two years have passed since Congress first enacted legislation requiring implementation plans to attain national air quality standards, and yet today the South Coast still lacks implementation plans for ozone and carbon monoxide. In 1989, EPA entered into a settlement agreement with appellants requiring it to perform its statutory duty and promulgate federal implementation plans for the South Coast on an expeditious schedule. EPA now argues that, when Congress passed the Clean Air Act Amendments of 1990, it relieved EPA of this obligation and returned the implementation plan process to square one. We disagree. . . .

[EPA disapproved several versions of a SIP for the South Coast Basin both before and after the 1977 Amendments. At one point before the 1977 Amendments, EPA proposed a series of FIPs that would require gas rationing and other extreme measures, but it subsequently withdrew the proposals, citing "the seriously disruptive social and economic consequences of such regulations." In 1984, EPA approved a revised carbon monoxide and ozone SIP for the South Coast Basin while deferring determination of whether the control measures would achieve attainment by the statutory deadline.]

In September 1984, a citizen timely petitioned this court for review of the EPA's 1984 decision. We held that "EPA exceeded its authority under the Clean Air Act by approving the control measures without determining whether those measures would demonstrate attainment by the December 31, 1987 statutory deadline." *Abramowitz*, 832 F.2d at 1072–73. We remanded "with the specific instruction that EPA disapprove the relevant portions of the SIP and face up to implementing the measures which are to be triggered by failure to meet attainment requirements." In compliance with our order, EPA disapproved the South Coast SIPs for ozone and CO on January 22, 1988, triggering once again EPA's statutory obligation to adopt FIPs for the South Coast Air Basin.

On February 22, 1988, appellants Coalition for Clean Air and the Sierra Club filed this citizens' suit to enforce EPA's obligation to promulgate ozone and CO FIPs for the South Coast. In March 1989, EPA entered into a settlement agreement with plaintiffs, which obligated it to prepare, propose, and promulgate final FIPs for the South Coast. Because of the 1989 San Francisco earthquake, the district court extended EPA's deadline for publishing the proposed FIPs from April 30 to July 31, 1990. EPA finally published the proposed FIPs on September 5, 1990, and agreed to finalize them by February 28, 1991.

In the meantime, EPA sought across-the-board relief from its statutory obligation to promulgate FIPs from Congress, which had begun to consider new amendments to the Clean Air Act. In September 1989, at EPA's urging, the Senate passed an amendment that would have left promulgation of FIPs to EPA's discretion. In May 1990, a House Committee deleted this language, which prompted a letter from EPA Administrator Reilly complaining that the House action would require promulgation of a FIP imposing "across-the-board, draconian measures devastating the country's largest industrial area," an obvious reference to the South Coast Air Basin. 136 Cong.Rec. H2771, H2887 (daily ed. May 23, 1990). However, Administrator Reilly's complaint went unheeded by Congress. The House language retaining EPA's mandatory obligation to promulgate a FIP whenever it disapproves a SIP was ultimately enacted by Congress and signed into law by President Bush on November 15, 1991 as part of the Clean Air Act Amendments of 1990.

On November 30, 1991, EPA filed a motion asking the district court to vacate the settlement agreement and dismiss the case on the basis of the 1990 Amendments. EPA argued that Congress could not have intended to continue EPA's obligation to promulgate FIPs for the South Coast under the settlement agreement because the 1990 Amendments contained new criteria and new timetables for attainment, which EPA claimed the states must address in the first instance. Under EPA's interpretation of the 1990 Amendments, its mandatory obligation to promulgate FIPs would be triggered only if California failed to submit adequate SIPs under the new deadlines. The earliest date FIPs would be required for the South Coast under this interpretation of the 1990 Amendments is April 15, 1998. The district court granted EPA's motion to vacate the settlement agreement and dismissed the case. This appeal followed. . . .

EPA's statutory obligation to promulgate FIPs is contained in § 110(c)(1) of the Clean Air Act, as amended in 1990:

> The Administrator shall promulgate a Federal implementation plan at any time within 2 years after the Administrator—
>
> (A) finds that a State has failed to make a required submission or finds that the plan or plan revision submitted by the State does not satisfy the minimum criteria established under section 7410(k) (1) (A) of this title, or
>
> (B) disapproves a State implementation plan submission in whole or in part, unless the State corrects the deficiency, and the Administrator approves the plan or plan revision, before the Administrator promulgates such Federal implementation plan.

CAA § 110(c)(1).

Appellants contend that under subsection (B), EPA is obligated to promulgate ozone and CO FIPs for South Coast based on its disapproval in January 1988 of California's proposed SIPs. EPA, on the other hand, contends that § 110(c)(1), as amended in 1990, was intended to operate prospectively only, so that EPA's obligation to promulgate a FIP for the South Coast will be triggered only if California fails to submit a SIP that meets the requirements of the Clean Air Act by the deadlines set forth in the 1990 Amendments.

We begin with the language of the provision: "The Administrator shall promulgate a Federal implementation plan at any time within 2 years after the Administrator . . . disapproves a State implementation plan submission in whole or in part." This language is not, by its terms, limited to EPA's disapproval of "newly submitted" SIPs or SIPs "submitted under the 1990 Amendments." Instead it refers to disapproval of state implementation plans generally, either in whole or in part. EPA must promulgate a FIP within two years of such disapproval, unless the state submits and EPA approves revisions to the SIP that correct the deficiency. Since EPA disapproved the South Coast

SIPs in January 1988, the statute on its face requires EPA to promulgate FIPs for the South Coast by January 1990.

We recognize that EPA's obligation under § 110(c)(1) is put in the future tense. However, the time referred to by the word "shall" is two years from any of the triggering events listed in the provision, not two years from enactment of the 1990 Amendments. Triggering event (A) actually includes two separate events: (1) EPA's finding that a state has failed to make a required submission, and (2) EPA's finding that a submission fails to meet the minimum criteria for completeness established under § 7410(k)(1)(A). Since § 7410(k)(1)(A) was added by the 1990 Amendments, it appears that the second of these findings could only occur after enactment of the 1990 Amendments. However, neither the first of these findings nor triggering event (B)—disapproval of "a State implementation plan submission in whole or in part"—contains any similar temporal limitation. Since these events could occur in the past or in the future, the use of the future tense "shall" to express EPA's obligation does not indicate Congress' intent that § 110(c)(1) operate prospectively only. In other words, if "disapproves" refers to past disapprovals as well as to future ones, "shall" is the appropriate word to describe obligations which may already have been triggered as well as those which may be triggered in the future.

In short, the plain language of § 110(c)(1)(B) supports appellants' contention that EPA is currently obligated to promulgate FIPs for the South Coast based on its January 1988 disapproval of California's proposed SIPs.

EPA also argues that requiring it to promulgate FIPs for the South Coast at this time would be inconsistent with the 1990 Amendments as a whole because those Amendments impose new deadlines and change certain requirements of the Clean Air Act. The district court found this argument persuasive. It reasoned that if the Act were interpreted to continue EPA's existing obligation to promulgate FIPs for the South Coast, "there would be the anomaly that the SIP prepared by the State under the former criteria and rejected is to be replaced by a FIP prepared under new criteria that the State has never had an opportunity to address." Of course, the proper contents of FIPs for the South Coast are not before us, and we need not decide whether EPA would be required to meet any additional requirements imposed by the 1990 Amendments in promulgating FIPs for the South Coast. The sole question on appeal is whether EPA's obligation to promulgate such FIPs survived the 1990 Amendments. We therefore consider the 1990 changes in the Act's deadlines and requirements for the limited purpose of deciding whether an "anomaly" would result from enforcing the plain language of § 110(c)(1)(B).

On closer inspection, we find that no such anomaly exists. EPA points to the fact that the 1990 Amendments extend the deadlines for attainment of ozone and CO standards for the South Coast until 2010 and 2000 respectively. Yet the FIP that EPA has proposed to adopt for the South Coast, ostensibly under the requirements of the old Clean Air Act, provided for attainment of these standards on precisely the same schedule. Thus, EPA cannot claim that continuing its obligation to promulgate a FIP for the South Coast will deny the region any extra time to which they would be entitled under the 1990 Amendments.

EPA also argues that the 1990 Amendments require new measures to control oxides of nitrogen (NOx) and volatile organic compounds (VOCs), which are precursors of ozone, which the state must address in the first instance. However, there is no reason the state may not propose these new measures as revisions to the FIP under the timetables provided in the 1990 Amendments just as the state would be required to do if a FIP had been in effect when those Amendments were adopted. *See* CAA § 1511a(e). Appellants have not argued that EPA's continuing obligation to promulgate FIPs relieves the state of any new obligations imposed by the 1990 Amendments.

Running throughout EPA's argument is the notion that federal involvement necessarily preempts state planning to control air pollution. However, this is a misconception. The Clean Air Act creates "a federal-state partnership for the control of air pollution," which continues after EPA's obligation to promulgate a FIP has been triggered. As we have just observed, the state may propose and EPA may approve revisions to a proposed SIP that meet the requirements of the Act at any time prior to the actual promulgation of a FIP. Even after a FIP is promulgated, the states remain responsible for submitting revisions to the FIP if EPA changes the air quality standards or if Congress changes the provisions of the Act. Thus, we fail to see how enforcing the plain terms of § 110(c)(1)(B) will create an unintended anomaly. . . .

EPA also argues that we should defer to its interpretation of the statute because it is the administering agency. Under *Chevron*, we are required first to exhaust the "traditional tools of statutory construction" to determine if Congress has spoken to the precise question at issue. "If the intent of Congress is clear, that is the end of the matter." In this case, the plain language of § 110(c)(1) expresses Congress' intent that EPA promulgate a FIP when it has previously disapproved a SIP.

However, even if we were to conclude that Congress had no intent on the question, it is doubtful that EPA's interpretation of § 110(c)(1) would be entitled to deference. Its current interpretation is in direct conflict with the interpretation that it expressed to Congress. This is not a case in which the agency's change of interpretation reflects accumulated experience or responds to changing circumstances. Nor has the agency justified this change with "reasoned analysis." This is simply a case in which the agency, having failed to get Congress to adopt its position, asks the court to do what Congress would not.

In sum, we hold that EPA is currently obligated to promulgate ozone and CO FIPs for the South Coast under the plain terms of § 110(c)(1)(B) based on its disapproval of California's proposed SIPs in January 1988. Accordingly, we reverse the decision of the district court. We remand with instructions that the district court reinstate the settlement agreement and establish an expeditious schedule for the promulgation of final FIPs for the South Coast. In establishing the schedule, the district court should bear in mind that promulgation of these FIPs has already been delayed far beyond the statutory deadline, that EPA has already published proposed FIPs for the South Coast, and that the deadline for promulgation of final FIPs was only three months away when EPA moved to vacate the settlement agreement.

NOTES AND QUESTIONS

1.   Mechanics of a Federal Implementation Plan. Where does the federal government get the authority to write a FIP? May it do so at any time? Is the exercise of this authority discretionary? The findings required to promulgate a FIP are made by the Administrator. What standards guide her discretion in making these findings?

How can a state, whose SIP has been disapproved by EPA, avoid having EPA promulgate a FIP? If the FIP is nonetheless issued, and the state doesn't like it, what can the state do?

2.   Congressional Intervention in the South Coast Air Basin. After *Coalition for Clean Air*, EPA promulgated a FIP for the South Coast Air Basin in accordance with the court's ruling. EPA, Approval and Promulgation of State and Federal Implementation Plans; California; Ozone, 59 Fed. Reg. 23,264 (1994). Shortly thereafter, Congress intervened, temporarily relieving EPA of its responsibility to promulgate a FIP for the South Coast Air Basin in an appropriations rider:

> The Congress finds that the 1990 amendments to the Clean Air Act (Public Law 101–549) superseded prior requirements of the Clean Air Act regarding the demonstration of attainment of national ambient air quality standards for the South Coast, Ventura, and Sacramento areas of California and thus eliminated the obligation of the Administrator of the Environmental Protection Agency to promulgate a Federal implementation plan under section 110(e) [sic] of the Clean Air Act for those areas. Upon the enactment of this Act, any Federal implementation plan that has been promulgated by the Administrator of the Environmental Protection Agency under the Clean Air Act for the South Coast, Ventura, or Sacramento areas of California pursuant to a court order or settlement shall be rescinded and shall have no further force and effect.

Defense Supplemental Appropriation, Pub. L. No. 104–6 (1995).

After the appropriations rider passed, EPA rescinded the FIP. EPA, Congressional Action Rescinding California Federal Implementation Plans, 60 Fed. Reg. 43,468 (1995). To avoid the imposition of the post-*Coalition for Clean Air* FIP on the South Coast, California had adopted a SIP and submitted it to EPA, before the appropriations rider took effect. EPA approved that SIP two years later. EPA, Approval and Promulgation of Implementation Plans; California—Ozone, 62 Fed. Reg. 1150 (1997). After EPA approved the SIP, the Southern California Air Quality Management District (SCAQMD) determined many of the measures to be "inappropriate" and submitted a SIP revision to EPA. EPA delayed action on the SIP revision. *Coal. for Clean Air v. S. Coast Air Quality Mgmt. Dist.*, 1999 WL 33842864.

In 1999, a federal district court proposed to impose an injunction on the SCAQMD for failure to implement the approved SIP. *Id.* at 6. The parties settled the dispute shortly thereafter, agreeing to several SCAQMD revisions to the SIP, expedited EPA review, and a timeline for implementation. *See* Settlement Agreement (Dec. 8, 1999), https://www.aqmd.gov/docs/default-source/clean-air-plans/air-quality-management-plans/1997-air-quality-management-plan/final-1999-amendment-to-the-1997-ozone-sip-settlement-agreement.pdf?sfvrsn=2. For further discussion of Congressional intervention and the role of the FIP in the South Coast Air Basin, see Alan C. Waltner, *Paradise Delayed—The Continuing Saga of the Los Angeles Basin Federal Clean Air Implementation Plan*, 14 UCLA J. ENVTL. L. & POL'Y 247 (1996).

As is evident from the case and from the subsequent events, EPA did not want to implement or enforce a FIP. Consider that promulgating a FIP creates new obligations for EPA to develop and enforce the regulation. Furthermore, states are typically resistant to FIPs; compare the federal oversight role in SIP approval with the direct federal regulation allowed under FIPs. Why else might EPA hesitate to exercise its authority under § 110(c)? Was EPA's reticence justified by the subsequent congressional action? What are the reasons Congress might have "bailed out" EPA in this fashion? Why might states sometimes prefer that local regulation occur under a FIP?

3.   Enforcing a FIP. In the 1970s, EPA promulgated FIPs for several major metropolitan areas that required states to pass laws or promulgate regulations to control pollution from mobile sources. *See, e.g.*, 38 Fed. Reg. 32,884 (1971) (Philadelphia); 38 Fed. Reg. 33,702 (1973) (Washington, D.C.); 38 Fed. Reg. 31,232, as corrected, 38 Fed. Reg. 34,124, 35,467 (1973); 39 Fed. Reg. 1025, 1848 (1974) (Los Angeles and other areas in California). The states objected strongly to what they saw as federal commandeering of state resources to enforce federal law, arguing that neither the CAA nor the Constitution authorized EPA to compel a state to enact legislation or to promulgate other regulatory measures pursuant to a FIP.

Three circuit courts agreed with the states, construing § 113 of the CAA, 42 U.S.C. § 7413, narrowly to avoid the Constitutional issues and holding that EPA was without authority to compel the state to enforce a FIP. *Brown v. EPA*, 521 F.2d 827 (9th Cir. 1975), *vacated and remanded, EPA v. Brown*, 431 U.S. 99 (1977); *Arizona v. EPA*, 521 F.2d 825 (9th Cir. 1975); *District of Columbia v. Train*, 521 F.2d 971 (D.C. Cir. 1975); *Maryland v. EPA*, 530 F.2d 215 (4th Cir. 1975).

After EPA's early conflicts with the states, it lost enthusiasm for promulgating FIPs. EPA spent most of the 1980s avoiding promulgation of a FIP for the South Coast Basin, as discussed *supra*.

At least one commentator argues that EPA should exercise more forcefully its authority to enforce a FIP directly against individual polluters in a state:

> It may be that the only credible way for EPA to send a message to recalcitrant states that the Federal Clean Air Act cannot be ignored is to take over the air quality planning process for a major metropolitan area. For example, EPA, not the state, could write the contracts with centralized I/M [inspection/maintenance] companies and send a strike force of federal officials to the area to exercise the federal government's authority to write field citations of up to $5000 to individual drivers who do not demonstrate proof of having successfully passed a biennial I/M test. The federal government will, of course, encounter resistance at the local level, as it did when it attempted to implement the federal civil rights laws in the 1960s. But most people will comply with the law, even at the cost of some personal inconvenience, if they are convinced that the law is being administered evenly in all states.
>
> An aggressive show of federal determination to implement the federal law in a major urban area will no doubt precipitate attempts to amend the Clean Air Act to take away the power to write FIPs or to remove the centralized I/M requirement for heavily polluted areas. A renewed national debate on the need for effective I/M programs or on the desirability of a strong federal implementation role is not, as some EPA officials apparently believe, something to be avoided at all costs.

Thomas O. McGarity, *Regulating Commuters to Clear the Air: Some Difficulties in Implementing a National Program at the Local Level*, 27 PAC. L.J. 1521, 1626–27 (1996).

The federal government has the power to enforce a FIP directly against polluters within a state as long as Congress can regulate consistent with the Commerce Clause. Do you agree that the federal government should enforce a FIP in this way?

4. Are SIPs Irrelevant? Arnold Reitze notes that the SIP has been successful at reducing air pollution: "Since 1970 the gross domestic product has increased by 164 percent and energy consumption is up forty-two percent, yet the aggregate emissions of the six criteria pollutants is down forty-eight percent." Arnold W. Reitze, Jr., *Air Quality Protection Using State Implementation Plans: Thirty-Seven Years of Increasing Complexity*, 15 VILL. ENVTL. L.J. 209, 365 (2004). Nevertheless, Reitze argues, SIPs are increasingly irrelevant because they are premised on the assumption that air pollution is largely a localized problem with little need for federal involvement. *Id.* Do you agree?

5. SIPs as Elements of Industrial Policy. Recall that the SIP is the mechanism by which states retain authority to allocate pollution control burdens to meet the NAAQS. Why might a state prefer to allocate these burdens? Might states sometimes prefer that the federal government make these difficult, and often unpopular, allocation decisions?

4. NEW SOURCE PERFORMANCE STANDARDS

In § 111, the CAA requires the Administrator to set uniform, technology-based emissions standards for new and modified air pollution sources. 42 U.S.C. § 7411. These are the federal New Source Performance Standards (NSPS), which apply nationwide. They are set by the EPA on a per-category basis for stationary sources. The Administrator has discretion to vary the standards within each category according to the class, type, and size of the source. 42 U.S.C. § 7411(b). In 2013, there were approximately 90 categories and subcategories of sources subject to the NSPS requirements. *See* 40 C.F.R. pt. 60; EPA, Demonstrating Compliance with New Source Performance Standards and State Implementation Plans, https://www.epa.gov/compliance/demonstrating-compliance-new-source-performance-standards-and-state-implementation-plans (last visited Sept. 9, 2018).

Although frequently referred to as a "best available technology" (BAT) or "best demonstrated technology" (BDT) standard, when setting the NSPS, the Administrator may not demand that a source use a particular technology. Rather, the Administrator sets a "standard of performance," defined as:

> a standard for emissions of air pollutants which reflects the degree of emission limitation achievable through the application of the best system of emission reduction which (taking into account the cost of achieving such reduction and any nonair quality health and environmental impact and energy requirements) the Administrator determines has been adequately demonstrated.

42 U.S.C. § 7411(a)(1). The NSPS, in other words, is a performance standard, not a design standard. *See* Chapter III, *supra*. Once the Administrator has set the NSPS for a category of sources, she is required to review and, if necessary, to revise the standard at least every eight years. 42 U.S.C. § 7411(b)(1)(B).

There are three criteria for the NSPS: (1) the technology chosen must be the "best system" of reduction (meaning that which provides the highest level of reduction); (2) costs must be "taken into account"; and (3) it must have been "adequately demonstrated." When the Administrator promulgates or revises an NSPS for a particular category of sources, there is always considerable controversy. Generally, the regulated industries will seize on the elements of cost and adequacy of demonstration, whereas environmentalists will focus on the "best system" of reduction. The following cases illustrate the typical dynamic.

Portland Cement Association v. Ruckelshaus

486 F.2d 375 (D.C. Cir. 1973), *cert. denied*, 417 U.S. 921 (1974).

■ Before FAHY, SENIOR CIRCUIT JUDGE, and LEVENTHAL and ROBB, CIRCUIT JUDGES.

■ LEVENTHAL, CIRCUIT JUDGE:

Portland Cement Association seeks review of the action of the Administrator of the Environmental Protection Agency (EPA) in promulgating stationary source standards for new or modified portland cement plants, pursuant to the provisions of Section 111 of the Clean Air Act. . . .

The "standards of performance" were adopted by a regulation, issued December 16, 1971, which requires, inter alia, that particulate matter emitted from portland cement plants shall not be:

(1) In excess of 0.30 lb. per ton of feed to the kiln (0.15 Kg. per metric ton), maximum 2-hour average. (2) Greater than 10% opacity, except that where the presence of uncombined water is the only reason for failure to meet the requirements for this subparagraph, such failure shall not be a violation of this section. . . .

The objecting companies contend that the Administrator has not complied with the mandate of § 111 of the Act, which requires him to "[take] into account the costs" of achieving the emission reductions he prescribes, a statutory provision that clearly refers to the possible economic impact of the promulgated standards. . . .

The Administrator found in the Background Document that, for a new wet-process plant with a capacity of 2.5 million barrels per year, the total investment for all installed air pollution control equipment will represent approximately 12 percent of the investment for the total facility. He also found that "[a]nnual operating costs for the control equipment will be approximately 7 percent of the total plant operating costs if a baghouse is used for the kiln, and 5 percent if an electrostatic precipitator is used."

Petitioners argue that this analysis is not enough—that the Administrator is required to prepare a quantified cost-benefit analysis, showing the benefit to ambient air conditions as measured against the cost of the pollution devices. However desirable in the abstract, such a requirement would conflict with the specific time constraints imposed on the administrator. The difficulty, if not impossibility, of quantifying the benefit to ambient air conditions, further militates against the imposition of such an imperative on the agency. Such studies should be considered by the Administrator, if adduced in comments, but we do not inject them as a necessary condition of action.

The EPA contention that economic costs to the industry have been taken into account, derives substantial support from a study prepared for

EPA. . . . It concluded that the additional costs of control equipment could be passed on without substantially affecting competition with construction substitutes such as steel, asphalt and aluminum, because "[d]emand for cement, derived for the most part from demand for public and private construction, is not highly elastic with regard to price and would not be very sensitive to small price changes." The study did note that individual mills may be closed in the years ahead, but observed that these plants were obsolete both from a cost and pollution point of view. . . .

Petitioners also challenge the cement standards as unfair in light of lower standards mandated for fossil-fuel-fired steam generating power plants and incinerators. . . .

The core of our response to petitioners is that the Administrator is not required to present affirmative justifications for different standards in different industries. Inter-industry comparisons of this kind are not generally required, or even productive; and they were not contemplated by Congress in this Act. The essential question is whether the mandated standards can be met by a particular industry for which they are set, and this can typically be decided on the basis of information concerning that industry alone. This is not to say that evidence collected about the functioning of emission devices in one industry may not have implications for another. Certainly such information may bear on technological capability. But there is no requirement of uniformity of specific standards for all industries. The Administrator applied the same general approach, of ascertaining for each industry what was feasible in that industry. It would be unmanageable if, in reviewing the cement standards, the court should have to consider whether or not there was a mistake in the incinerator standard, with all the differences in parties, practice, industry procedures, and record for decision. Of course, the standard for another industry can be attacked, as too generous, and hence arbitrary or unsupported on the record, by those concerned with excessive pollution by that industry. There is, therefore, an avenue of judicial review and correction if the agency does not proceed in good faith to implement its general approach. But this is different from the supposition that a claim to the same specific treatment can be advanced by one who is in neither the same nor a competitive industry.

There is, of course, a significant and proper scope for inter-industry comparison in the case of industries producing substitute or alternative products. This bears on the issue of "economic cost". But this comparison was utilized in arriving at the agency decision, and no contention is raised in this court that such competitive-industry impact was either ignored or assessed invalidly. . . .

[The court then addressed the petitioner's challenge concerning the achievability of the standard.] Section 111 of the Act requires "the degree of emission limitation achievable [which] . . . the Administrator determines has been adequately demonstrated." Petitioners contend that the promulgated standard for new stationary sources has not been "adequately demonstrated", raising issues as to the interpretation to be given to this requirement . . . and the scientific evidence upon which it was formulated. An examination of these questions requires a brief description of the process used to manufacture portland cement and the devices presently employed to control emissions.

In the manufacturing process for portland cement, the principal ingredients, limestone and clay, are combined, after having been reduced to a powdery fineness, to make a substance known as raw feed. The powdered limestone and clay are mixed by either the wet process or the dry process. In the wet process, water is added to the limestone and clay to make a slurry, which is then introduced into a kiln. In the dry process, the two substances are mixed mechanically and by use of air before the mix is introduced into a kiln. . . .

The two types of equipment principally used in removing particulate matter from the exhaust gas are electrostatic precipitators and glass fabric bags, impregnated with graphite, located in a "bag house." When the precipitator is used, dust particles are charged and pass through an electrical field of the opposite charge, thus causing the dust to be precipitated out of the exhaust gas and thereafter collected by the device. When glass fabric bags are used, the exhaust gas is cooled, sometimes by a water spray, so that the bags will operate without damage from excessive heat. The bag filters out the particulate dust, though sometimes the coolant combines with the dust to form a gummy substance as residue in the bags, which must be continuously cleaned out in order to avoid impairing the permeability of the bag. . . .

A troublesome aspect of this case is the identification of what, in fact, formed the basis for the standards promulgated by EPA—a question that must be probed prior to consideration of whether the basis or bases for the standards is reliable. Nominally, there would seem to be three major bases for the rule and its standards: (1) the tests run on the dry-process Dragon Cement Plant, (2) the tests run on the wet-process Oregon Cement Plant, and (3) literature sources. . . .

Two kilns were tested by the EPA contractor at the Dragon Cement Plant. A test of a dry-process kiln controlled with a baghouse is used for support of the standard since testing "showed particulate emissions of 0.20 pound per ton of feed, which is below the proposed standard." This particular plant was selected for testing on the basis that it was reportedly one of the 12 best controlled plants in the United States.

The first point raised by petitioner, and included in the comments by cement manufacturers presented to the agency on its proposed standard, was that a single test offered a weak basis for inferring that all new cement plants would be able to meet the proposed standards. As we stated in [an earlier case:] "It would . . . seem incumbent on the Administrator to estimate the possible degree of error [inherent] in his prediction." The significance of the lack of any indication of statistical reliability was underscored by T. E. Kreichelt, the author of [a] study relied upon by the Administrator, in a letter, by way of comment, on the proposed standard. He stated that "the emission limit was based on one (1) test, i. e. the fabric filter test. . . . I do not believe that the emission limits should be selected on only four tests, much less one test."

Mr. Kreichelt raised a second and related point addressed to the reliability of a prediction based on a successful dry-process plant, for a prediction that wet-process plants would be able to also meet the standard. He stated in this regard:

> Another outcome of basing emission limits on insufficient data is that the limit may represent only part of a given industrial classification. For example, is 0.30 lb/ton of feed attainable only for dry-process kilns? Or is it also attainable for wet-process kilns? Probably both, but there is not even one test to substantiate the limit for wet-process kilns. For each variation of each process of each source classification, the number of tests required should be sufficient (say, three tests within the limit) to result in statistically sound limits.

We are not here considering a regulation that was issued in the contemplation that all new cement plants will be dry-process, and controlled by baghouses on the theory that this is the "best system" of emission control. Possibly such an approach would be feasible, but in any event it would require underlying reasons, by EPA, to terminate the process which . . . had [been] identified as major now and in future projection. . . .

The Oregon plant was wet-process controlled by a baghouse. Three tests were made on the kiln operation. . . . [S]ampling was not conducted when "process operation was interrupted" and . . . sampling was only conducted during the periods of "normal operation". . . . The concern of the manufacturers is that "start-up" and "upset" conditions, due to plant or emission device malfunction, is an inescapable aspect of industrial life, and that allowance must be made for such factors in the standards that are promulgated. On August 18, 1972, some eight months after the issuance of the standards under review . . . the EPA proposed a new regulation to take "startup, shutdown and malfunction" problems into effect. The proposed regulation, which as yet has not been adopted, sets up a procedure by which emissions due to malfunction will not be the basis of an enforcement action. It requires reports from manufacturers in cases where emissions exceed standards, recording the "violation" and indicating what measures will be taken to correct or minimize the excess emission levels. . . .

If the EPA adopts, or intends to adopt, this proposed regulation, it may take the attendant flexibility into account, on remand, as pertinent to the manufacturers' objections, even though the new regulation has been proposed in a proceeding with a different docket number and caption. . . .

The principal source in the scientific literature used by EPA . . . is called into question by petitioner on the ground that the test methods used to compile the results of the study were at odds with those used by EPA in its own tests. . . .

In this connection, a comment on the proper use of scientific literature may be in order. If such literature is relied upon, the agency should indicate which particular findings of that literature are significant. A generalized reference, to a work as a whole, will avail the agency little if a problem arises on judicial review. On remand, any findings in the literature that are relied on by EPA should be specifically indicated. . . .[95]

We are quite aware that the standards promulgated and here under review are to be applied to *new* stationary sources. It would have been entirely appropriate if the Administrator had justified the standards, not on the basis of tests on existing sources or old test data in the literature, but on extrapolations from this data, on a reasoned basis responsive to comments, and on testimony from experts and vendors made part of the record. This course was not followed here. Instead, the Administrator in his statement of reasons relied on tests on existing plants and the literature. . . .

New York v. Reilly
969 F.2d 1147 (D.C. Cir. 1992).

■ Before SILBERMAN, HENDERSON, and RANDOLPH, CIRCUIT JUDGES.

■ HENDERSON, CIRCUIT JUDGE:

Petitioners State of New York and State of Florida (petitioners or petitioner States) challenge the decision of the Environmental Protection Agency (EPA or Agency) to forgo promulgation of two provisions of two proposed rules. The relevant provisions would have required incinerator operators to separate a percentage of certain types of waste from their waste streams before incineration and would have placed a ban on the incineration of lead-acid vehicle batteries. Because our review of the record demonstrates that EPA adequately supported its decision to drop the waste separation provision, we uphold this portion of the Agency's action.

Section 111 of the Clean Air Act (CAA or Act), authorizes EPA to regulate municipal incinerators (municipal waste combustors or MWCs) as sources of air pollution. . . . EPA has labeled its goal in setting a standard of performance as selection of the "best demonstrated technology" (BDT).

---

[95] There is evidence in the record furnished by vendors of emission control devices but not relied upon by the EPA to support its standard that, with proper allowance for malfunction problems, the standards can be met. . . . We note . . . that if vendor representations were to be a principal source of reliance by the agency, representations peculiarly subject to considerations of self-interest, more might be required than mere comments [to the proposed regulation].

EPA's BDT analysis of MWCs resulted in proposed rules which focused primarily on limiting emissions from incinerator smokestacks. [The rules] would have required operators of *new* sources of air pollution to achieve a twenty-five per cent reduction by weight of unprocessed waste by separating out some or all of the following recoverable/recyclable materials: paper and paperboard combined; ferrous materials; nonferrous metals; glass; plastics; household batteries; and yard waste.

On December 4, 1990, EPA submitted a package of final rules to the Office of Management and Budget (OMB) for review pursuant to Executive Order 12291. OMB did not approve the sections of the proposed rules covering materials separation and battery burning. EPA then appealed to the President's Council on Competitiveness (Council). In a "Fact Sheet," the Council rejected the proposed rules on materials separation as being inconsistent with "several of the Administration's regulatory principles," including their failure to "meet the benefit/cost requirements for regulatory policy laid out in Executive Order 12291." The Fact Sheet also noted the Council's opinion that the materials separation requirement did not constitute a "performance standard" and that it violated principles of federalism. EPA subsequently abandoned the materials separation and battery burning provisions when it promulgated its final rules. . . .

In determining the BDT for limiting harmful emissions, the EPA Administrator must "tak[e] into consideration the cost of achieving such emission reduction, and any nonair quality health and environmental impact and energy requirements." 42 U.S.C. § 7411(a)(1)(C). Because Congress did not assign the specific weight the Administrator should accord each of these factors, the Administrator is free to exercise his discretion in this area. We must therefore uphold EPA's decision to abandon the separation requirements if such action is supported on either air or nonair (including economic) grounds.

Under the CAA, promulgated rules must be accompanied by "an explanation of the reasons for any major changes in the promulgated rule from the proposed rule." 42 U.S.C. § 7607(d)(6)(A). The Act also requires the court to sustain the Administrator's actions unless they are "arbitrary, capricious, an abuse of discretion, or otherwise not in accordance with law . . ." 42 U.S.C. § 7607(d)(9)(A). We are particularly deferential when reviewing agency actions involving policy decisions based on uncertain technical information.

The petitioners attack the sufficiency of the evidence supporting EPA's conclusions regarding both air and nonair benefits. . . .

The petitioners next challenge whether EPA's conclusions regarding nonair benefits are adequately supported in the record. Both the proposed rules and the final rules note that requiring separation and recycling could lead to either a cost benefit or a cost detriment. While EPA *initially* forecast a likely benefit, in promulgating its final rules it determined that the record was too inconclusive to justify a materials separation rule. We must therefore determine whether EPA adequately supported its change in position. The preamble to the final rules recites that the Agency, based in part on its own analysis, agreed with those comments suggesting that the uncertainty over costs associated with separation and recycling might be even greater than EPA had originally believed. *See, e.g.*, Comments of The U.S. Conference of Mayors National Resource Recovery Association, JA 342 ("We estimate that, depending on the technology/program mix, total program costs are likely to range from $100 to more than $200 per ton of recycled product, including collecting, processing, and marketing the material"). We conclude that these comments, on which the Agency expressly relied to confirm its own views on cost uncertainty provide sufficient evidence to support its changed view.[7] . . .

Lastly, the petitioners claim that EPA acted improperly in relying on the opinion of the Council rather than exercising its own expertise. After reviewing the record, we conclude that EPA did exercise its expertise in this case. The procedural history of the rules at issue demonstrates that the Council's views were important in formulating EPA's final policy decision regarding materials separation. The fact that EPA reevaluated its conclusions in light of the Council's advice, however, does not mean that EPA failed to exercise its own expertise in promulgating the final rules.

In sum, EPA's change of position on the materials separation issue was not improper. We are extremely deferential to administrative agencies in cases involving technical rulemaking decisions, and EPA has supported its new view of the materials separation policy with adequate evidence. Because the CAA allows EPA to balance air and nonair benefits and costs, which it did, EPA's decision not to promulgate materials separation rules was neither arbitrary nor capricious.

NOTES AND QUESTIONS

1.   New Sources, Old Sources, and "Cooperative Federalism." Why might Congress choose to impose nationally uniform requirements on new sources, but allow states to allocate pollution among existing sources? What incentives does this create:

(a)   For state legislatures? By leaving the task of regulating the existing sources to the states, did Congress create a difficult

---

[7]   After issuing its proposed rules, EPA conducted two studies on the economic effect of materials separation. These studies produced varying estimates regarding the effect of separation on costs. EPA stated that it did not rely on these studies in promulgating its final rules because the studies were not available for public inspection during the comment period. But EPA specifically mentioned these studies in responding to comments on the materials separation issue. EPA also used the studies in its brief. As we noted, however, the final rules expressly rely on the comments and other analyses rather than the additional studies. EPA's references to the post-proposal studies, therefore, do not alter our conclusion that EPA's decision to omit the materials separation provision was supported by substantial evidence.

public choice problem, given the considerable local power of large plants?

(b)   For existing and new industry? Beyond the simple "industry pressures local legislature" dynamic, does the grandfathering of old sources create a more complex "existing industry v. new industry" dynamic? In whose interest is the mandatory regulation of yet-to-be-built competitor plants?

2.   Justifying the NSPS. What must the Administrator do to justify an NSPS? How extensively must existing sources be tested? At all? How much may "extrapolations from data" be relied upon? What is the mechanism by which the "cost consideration" mandated by statute is to be performed?

3.   Wet v. Dry and Adequate Demonstration. Could the best technology in *Portland Cement*, have been defined as dry kilns? Could wet and dry processes have been treated as separate classes? What would the consequences have been? Why did the court conclude there had not been an "adequate demonstration"? What else could the agency have done?

After *Portland Cement*, the D.C. Circuit returned to this question. The court stated that "the Agency [must] consider the representativeness for the industry as a whole of the tested plants on which it relies, *at least where its central argument is that the standard is achievable because it has been achieved* (at the tested plants)." *Nat'l Lime Ass'n v. EPA*, 627 F.2d 416, 432–33 (D.C. Cir. 1980) (emphasis added). It added:

> The showing we require does not mean that EPA must perform repeated tests on every plant operating within its regulatory jurisdiction. It does, however, mean that due consideration must be given to the possible impact on emissions of recognized variations in operations and some rationale offered for the achievability of the promulgated standard given the tests conducted and the relevant variables identified.

Id. at 434. In other words, if test data are used to show that a technology is adequately demonstrated, such data must be shown to be representative of the regulated industry.

In another case, however, the D.C. Circuit upheld EPA's authority to "extrapolate" from utility boiler data to determine an NSPS for coal-fired industrial boilers. *Lignite Energy Council v. EPA*, 198 F.3d 930, 934 (D.C. Cir. 1999) ("EPA may compensate for a shortage of data through the use of other qualitative methods, including the reasonable extrapolation of a technology's performance in other industries."). EPA may thus look to other industries when determining whether a particular technology is "adequately demonstrated"—but only if data are unavailable.

Do *National Lime* and *Lignite Energy*, read together, provide EPA an incentive to select a more stringent technology that has not been tested on industry, in order to avoid the burden of ensuring the "representativeness" of tested plants—in other words, to avoid decisions based on the most relevant possible test data? What is the likely impact of EPA's discretion in this area on cost considerations? On innovation? *See* Bruce A. Ackerman &

Richard B. Stewart, *Reforming Environmental Law*, 37 STAN. L. REV. 1333 (1985).

4.   Which Costs, Which Benefits, and Whose Analyses? Logically antecedent to any "cost consideration" is a series of decisions: What things must be counted as costs? Against which benefits (if any) must such things be weighed? By what mechanism must seemingly disparate things be compared?

One method of doing the latter is to monetize (by various methods, none of which are uncontroversial) all the costs and all the benefits and to compare the resultant figures. In *Portland Cement*, the industry appeared to want exactly this. The court, however, dismisses as an "impossibility" the notion of "quantifying the benefit to ambient air conditions." *Portland Cement*, 486 F.2d at 387. Is that really so? If the court is right, what else might the CAA's directive to take costs into account mean? If the court is wrong about the impossibility of the task, does that mean the industry is automatically right about its desirability?

After *Portland Cement* was decided, Congress amended § 111 in 1977 to broaden the range of factors the Administrator must "take into account" when setting the NSPS for a particular industry. The Administrator must consider the nonair quality health and environment impact and energy requirements, in addition to the costs of the emission reduction. Pub.L. 95–95, § 109(c)(1)(A), codified at 42 U.S.C. § 7411.

Judge Leventhal noted that interested parties could submit quantified estimates of costs and benefits in the comment period, but EPA would not be required to prepare such estimates. Industry has an incentive to quantify costs and to estimate those costs highly to deter regulation (within the bounds of credibility). The beneficiaries of the regulation are likely to be a diffuse group of citizens ("breathers"), who face a significant collective action problem. *See* Shi-Ling Hsu, *Fairness Versus Efficiency in Environmental Law*, 31 ECOLOGY L.Q. 303, 333 (2004) ("When arguing over what may be fairly required of regulated industries, information on marginal pollution abatement costs and the availability of substitutes is almost exclusively controlled by the regulated industries. Calls for more stringent regulation are thus invariably met with irrefutable assertions by regulated industries of infeasibility and unfairness."). Does this argument affect your thinking on whether EPA should prepare cost-benefit analyses itself rather than rely on those prepared by industry? If a public interest group wanted to prepare its own private study of regulation costs and submit it to EPA, how would it go about getting the information to prepare such analyses?

5.   Cost-Benefit Analysis v. Feasibility. There is considerable debate (and has been, since at least the 1970s) about whether feasibility or cost-benefit analysis is a more appropriate tool for determining whether a particular technology-based environmental regulation is advisable, particularly given the scientific uncertainties associated with health effects of air pollution and the difficulties of valuing human life. In *Portland Cement*, the court deferred to EPA's application of a feasibility principle. By 1992, when *New York v. Reilly* was decided, Executive Order 12,291 required

EPA to perform a "regulatory impact analysis" with increased emphasis on quantification of costs and benefits.

A feasibility standard requires the decisionmaker to analyze the cost of a regulation, but it does not require the benefits of the regulation to be quantified. The most optimistic conclusion of a feasibility study is nothing more than the finding that an industry subject to such a regulation would not go bankrupt. What are the benefits of phrasing the question in such terms? Might there be regulations that would not bankrupt any industries but that would still, on balance, do more harm than good? What reasons can you think of to adopt such regulations?

Might there be industries which, given the costs they impose on the public good, ought to be driven into bankruptcy? How might you go about answering these questions?

6.   Inter-Industry Cost Comparisons. Is EPA required to look at costs imposed on other types of sources in setting NSPS standards? Should it do so anyway?

Could a competitor challenge regulations for another industry as too lax, if they are damaging the competitor's industry? What if the agency had done inter-industry comparisons, and Portland Cement had challenged the way it used the information? How should the agency respond to comments that include inter-industry comparisons? If Industry A can abate more pollution per dollar than Industry B, how should EPA respond?

7.   Judicial Deference to EPA's Balancing of Factors Under § 111. In *New York v. Reilly*, the court deferred to the weight the Administrator assigned to the potential costs of the waste separation requirement. Section 307(d)(6)(A)(ii) requires a change between the proposed and final rule to be accompanied by "an explanation of the reasons for any major changes." Section 307, 42 U.S.C. § 7607(d)(6)(C), also forbids the Administrator from relying "(in part or whole) on any information or data which has not been placed in the docket as of the date of such promulgation." Which studies and reports did the court rely on to uphold the Administrator's decision in *New York v. Reilly*? What role did information that was not in the docket play in the court's decision?

8.   Political Oversight of EPA. In an interview in 1995, EPA Administrator William K. Reilly explained his decision to withdraw the waste separation requirements from the final rule at issue in *New York v. Reilly*:

> The [municipal solid waste] proposal was opposed by cities, and by Senate Democrats such as Senator Baucus. The cities resented what they saw as intrusion and overreaching by EPA. Baucus considered recycling inappropriate to pursue as a Clean Air Act matter. I thought you could make a reasonable argument for or against the proposal. The President was in favor of recycling; I espoused a national goal of 25 percent recycling of municipal waste; and the objective was achievable. But in deference to the critics, and frankly to give the Vice President a win on something, I

withdrew the proposal. So, that became a Competitiveness Council victory.

EPA, William K. Reilly: Oral History Interview (Sept. 1995). In other words, EPA had decided to issue a NSPS and was overruled by the Council on Competitiveness, a group "headed by Vice President Dan Quayle," who was "a self-proclaimed zealot when it [came] to deregulation, and the council was sharply critical of any regulation and deeply solicitous of business interests." RICHARD L. REVESZ & MICHAEL A. LIVERMORE, RETAKING RATIONALITY 30 (2008) (citations omitted).

Evaluate the overruling of EPA by the Council on Competitiveness. Whom does the CAA charge with implementing its mandates? To whom does the Constitution entrust the responsibility to "take Care that the Laws be faithfully executed"?

For a description of the role of the Council on Competitiveness in the municipal incinerator rulemaking at issue in *New York v. Reilly*, see Malcolm D. Woolf, *Clean Air or Hot Air? Lessons from the Quayle Competitiveness Council's Oversight of EPA*, 10 J.L. & POL. 97 (1993).

9. Federalism and the "Race-to-the-Bottom." At the time that *New York v. Reilly* was decided, New York and Florida had the greatest incinerator capacity in the country. Both states faced significant solid waste disposal capacity shortages, and both faced challenges from neighbors that threatened to block new landfills. *See* Arnold W. Reitze, Jr. & Andrew N. Davis, *Regulating Municipal Solid Waste Incinerators Under the Clean Air Act: History, Technology and Risks*, 21 B.C. ENVTL. AFF. L. REV. 1, 12 (1993) ("While the public demands state and local governments solve waste disposal problems, they simultaneously organize to block proposed solutions"). Why might two states in dire need of waste disposal capacity demand more stringent federal regulation of municipal waste incineration? Nothing prevented them from implementing more stringent regulations themselves. What might a uniform national solution have done, if anything, to resolve the crisis these states faced?

10. NSPS and Flexible Compliance. Section 111 regulations typically specify an emissions rate standard to which regulated entities must adhere. EPA could substantially decrease the cost of achieving the greenhouse gas emission reductions by instead allowing new or existing sources to comply by trading emission rate credits, or by establishing a cap-and-trade program.

EPA previously included a cap-and-trade program in its 2005 Clean Air Mercury Rule under both § 111(b) and (d). However, the D.C. Circuit subsequently vacated the rule on separate grounds, without addressing the legality of the cap-and-trade program. *See New Jersey v. EPA*, 517 F.3d 574, 584 (D.C. Cir. 2008). In its municipal waste combustors NSPS regulation, EPA permits states to establish programs allowing regulated entities to trade in emissions rate credits; however, a court has never ruled on the legality of this approach either. *See* 40 C.F.R. §§ 60.30b *et seq.* (subpt. CB).

Does EPA have authority to apply these flexible compliance mechanisms for new sources under § 111(b)? For existing sources under § 111(d)? Compare the text of § 111(b) and (d). Does the specific reference in

§ 111(d) to the SIP process contained in § 110 provide EPA with additional flexibility as compared to the text of § 111(b)?

5. PREVENTION OF SIGNIFICANT DETERIORATION

A. GENESIS

When Congress enacted the CAA in 1970, it did not include separate requirements for states that already had air quality better than required by the NAAQS. Recall that the Administrator is required to set the NAAQS at levels that protect the public health and welfare from the adverse effects of air pollution with an adequate margin of safety. *See* 42 U.S.C. § 7409. Prior to 1977, the SIP provision, 42 U.S.C. § 7410, explicitly required only that a SIP provide for attainment of the primary and secondary NAAQS. Pub. L. 91–604, 84 Stat. 1676, 1680 (1970). There is a certain logic to this approach: after all, if the NAAQS are supposed to be set without reference to costs and with an adequate margin of safety to protect human health, degradation up to the NAAQS ought not to be problematic. Of course, there was skepticism, then and now, that the NAAQS in fact provide such protection.

In 1972, the EPA Administrator stated before Congress that he believed he was without legal authority to require anything beyond compliance with the NAAQS. Thus, EPA's SIP regulations required only that the states adopt a plan to meet the NAAQS. States could, of course, choose to implement more stringent air pollution controls than the NAAQS under § 116.

Environmentalists were concerned that the costs of air pollution control, coupled with lax state standards, would encourage firms to locate in clean air areas and quickly degrade air quality to the NAAQS throughout the country. Invoking the broad purposes of the CAA, the Sierra Club brought suit to challenge the Administrator's interpretation of the CAA.

Sierra Club v. Ruckelshaus

344 F. Supp. 253 (D.D.C. 1972), *aff'd*, 4 E.R.C. 1815 (D.C. Cir.),
aff'd by an equally divided Court, 412 U.S. 541 (1973).

■ PRATT, DISTRICT JUDGE:

In Section 101(b) of the Clean Air Act, Congress states four basic purposes of the Act, the first of which is

> to protect and enhance the quality of the Nation's air resources so as to promote the public health and welfare and the productive capacity of its population.

42 U.S.C. § 1857(b)(1). On its face, this language would appear to declare Congress' intent to improve the quality of the nation's air and to prevent

deterioration of that air quality, no matter how presently pure that quality in some sections of the country happens to be. . . .

Turning now to the legislative history of the 1970 Act, we note at the outset that both Secretary Finch and Under Secretary Veneman of HEW testified before Congress that neither the 1967 Act nor the proposed Act would permit the quality of air to be degraded. Hearings on Air Pollution Before the Subcomm. on Air and Water Pollution of the Senate Public Works Comm., 91st Cong., 2d Sess., at 132–33, 143 (1970); Hearings on Air Pollution and Solid Waste. Recycling Before the Subcomm. on Public Health and Welfare of the House Interstate and Foreign Commerce Comm., 91st Cong., 2d Sess., at 280, 287 (1970).

More important, of course, is the language of the Senate Report accompanying the bill that became the Clean Air Act of 1970. The Senate Report, in pertinent part, states:

> In areas where current air pollution levels are already equal to or better than the air quality goals, the Secretary shall not approve any implementation plan which does not provide, to the maximum extent practicable, for the continued maintenance of such ambient air quality.

S. Rep. No. 1196, 91st Cong., 2d Sess., at 2 (1970). The House Report, although not as clear, does not appear to contradict the Senate Report. *See* H. Rep. No. 1146, 91st Cong., 2d Sess., at 1, 2 and 5 (1970), U.S. Code Cong. & Admin. News 1970, p. 5356. . . .

On the other hand, the present Administrator, in remarks made in January and February of 1972 before certain House and Senate Subcommittees, has taken the position that the 1970 Act allows degradation of clean air areas. Several Congressional leaders voiced their strong disagreement with the Administrator's interpretation. . . .

The Administrator's interpretation of the 1970 Act, as disclosed in his current regulations, appears to be self-contradictory. On the one hand, 40 C.F.R. § 50.2(c) (1970) provides:

> The promulgation of national primary and secondary air quality standards shall not be considered in any manner to allow significant deterioration of existing air quality in any portion of any State.

Yet, in 40 C.F.R. § 51.12(b), he states:

> In any region where measured or estimated ambient levels of a pollutant are below the levels specified by an applicable secondary standard, the State implementation plan shall set forth a control strategy which shall be adequate to prevent such ambient pollution levels from exceeding such secondary standard.

The former regulation appears to reflect a policy of nondegradation of clean air but the latter mirrors the Administrator's doubts as to his authority to impose such a policy upon the states in their implementation plans. In our view, these regulations are irreconcilable and they demonstrate the weakness of the Administrator's position in this case. . . .

Having considered the stated purpose of the Clean Air Act of 1970, the legislative history of the Act and its predecessor, and the past and present administrative interpretation of the Acts, it is our judgment that the Clean Air Act of 1970 is based in important part on a policy of nondegradation of existing clean air and that 40 C.F.R. § 51.12(b), in permitting the states to submit plans which allow pollution levels of clean air to rise to the secondary standard level of pollution, is contrary to the legislative policy of the Act and is, therefore, invalid. Accordingly, we hold that plaintiffs have made out a claim for relief.

NOTES AND QUESTIONS

1.   Statutory Structure. If Congress had intended to provide a PSD-type program in the 1970 Act, where might you expect to find the statutory segment? Does the court analyze this question? What do you make of the fact that Congress failed to include any reference to preventing deterioration of air quality in § 110?

2.   Senate Report. A nondegradation program in fact appeared in the Senate version of the bill, and was then deleted in the final version approved by the House and Senate. What implication would you draw from this deletion? In light of this background, evaluate the significance of the Senate Report cited by the court in *Sierra Club v. Ruckelshaus*.

3.   Congress' Failure to Speak. Consider the following excerpt from the Conference Report that accompanied the 1970 CAA amendments, reporting differences between the House and Senate bills:

> The Senate bill required that each state consider adoption of more stringent air quality standards than the national standards at its public hearing on the proposed implementation plan, unless a separate hearing was held for that purpose.

H.R. REP. NO. 91–1783 (1970) (Conf. Rep.). Does the failure of the 1970 Act to require states to consider more stringent air quality standards in their public hearings indicate anything about Congress' intent with regard to prevention of significant deterioration? How about the fact that Congress debated for five years before issuing a detailed set of PSD rules that reflected a compromise between Senate and House bills? *See* Matthew D. McCubbins et al., *Structure and Process, Politics and Policy; Administrative Arrangements and the Political Control of Agencies*, 75 VA. L. REV. 431, 451 (1989) (arguing that the *Ruckelshaus* decision was a judicial policy innovation "unanticipated by the policymaking branches"). *But see* Craig N. Oren, *Clearing the Air: The McCubbins-Weingast-Noll Hypothesis and the Clean Air Act*, 9 VA. ENVTL. L.J. 45, 51 (1989) (arguing that the legislative history shows that the question whether Congress intended to prevent significant deterioration was "a close one" and that McCubbins et al. misread the Congressional dynamics leading up to the 1977 amendments).

In the Supreme Court, the Justices initially voted 5–3 to reverse the district court in *Sierra Club v. Ruckelshaus* (Justice Powell did not participate). Justice Stewart's draft majority opinion rejected the district court's reading of the statute, observing that "Congress may have failed to impose the right requirements to accomplish its announced goal. But it is the duty of the courts to apply the law as it is written." Justice Marshall changed his vote on the day that Justice Douglas issued a draft dissent arguing that "[i]t is inconceivable to me that Congress in passing the Clean Air Act contemplated an administrative regime that would make possible the pollution of existing clean air basins." The Supreme Court thus affirmed the district court's decision by an equally divided court. *See* Robert V. Percival, *Environmental Law in the Supreme Court: Highlights from the Marshall Papers*, 23 ENVTL. L. REP. 10,606, 10,621 (1993).

Does something on the scale of the PSD program count as a statutory "elephant"? Is the "goals" section of a statute a "mousehole"? Considering the Supreme Court's strident textualism when it comes to some aspects of the CAA—in *American Trucking*, for example—would *Sierra Club v. Ruckleshaus* be decided the same way today? Considering the detailed provisions of the CAA, what do you make of the district court's exclusive reliance on the broad language of the preamble to reach its holding? What is the strongest argument against the Court's holding?

4.   Inconsistent Interpretations. Though the case was decided before *Chevron v. NRDC*, how would the Administrator's arguments have fared if *Chevron* were the governing legal standard? Do inconsistent interpretations make a difference?

5.   NAAQS, PSD, and Preferences. If the NAAQS are supposed to adequately protect health and welfare, what reasons might the federal government have for wanting to protect air quality from "significant deterioration" toward the NAAQS? Why might a state want the flexibility to degrade its air quality if it has air better than the NAAQS? What reasons would a state have for maintaining its good air quality in the absence of federal regulation? For a detailed analysis of these and other questions, see B. Peter Pashigian, *Environmental Regulation: Whose Self-Interests Are Being Protected?*, 23 ECON. INQUIRY 551 (1985).

6.   Who Decides? Had Congress not subsequently acted, the fate of the PSD program would have rested on a single district court opinion, given the summary affirmance by the D.C. Circuit and the Supreme Court's evenly divided affirmance. Is this merely an example of the courts prompting Congress to clarify unclear statutory language, or is it a more concerning reallocation of decisionmaking authority? How much degradation would the Court's opinion allow? Zero? Does the Court say?

7.   State Interests in a PSD Program. The vast majority of states that submitted amicus briefs did so in favor of a PSD program. Why might that be? What incentive would states have to support a program that constrained them?

B. PSD PERMITTING PROGRAM

Judge Pratt's interpretation of the CAA in *Sierra Club v. Ruckelshaus* required EPA, without a clear directive from Congress, to establish a program to prevent significant deterioration of air quality even in states that met the NAAQS. In response, EPA promulgated regulations, codified at 40 C.F.R. § 52.21 (1975). The regulations created three categories:

1. In Class I areas, any change in air quality is considered significant.

2. In Class II areas, "deterioration normally accompanying moderate well-controlled growth" is allowable.

3. In Class III, degradation up to the NAAQS is acceptable.

All areas were initially categorized as Class II areas. States were given authority to reclassify areas from Class II to Class I or III after a hearing and EPA approval based on the record of the hearing. 40 C.F.R. § 52.21(g) (1975). The regulations also added considerable burdens to the existing NSPS requirements for new sources. If a new source proposed to locate in a PSD area, it had to demonstrate compliance with a best available control technology (BACT) requirement, determined on a case-by-case basis. The source also had to perform a "source impact analysis" to demonstrate that it would not cause a violation of the "maximum allowable increase" in the area or of the NAAQS. 40 C.F.R. § 52.21 (1975).

In the 1977 Clean Air Act Amendments, Congress codified the prevention of significant deterioration (PSD) program. Clean Air Act Amendments of 1977, Pub. L. No. 95–95, §§ 160–178, 91 Stat. 685, 731–51 (1977). Despite significant differences between the House and Senate proposals and several rounds of compromise, the end result of Congress' intervention was a program very similar to EPA's 1975 regulations. *See* Matthew D. McCubbins et al., *Structure and Process, Politics and Policy; Administrative Arrangements and the Political Control of Agencies*, 75 VA. L. REV. 431, 463–66 (1989) (describing Congress' reaction to *Sierra Club v. Ruckelshaus* and offering an interpretation of the political process that led to statutory codification of the program). The resulting statute asserted that its goal, in part, was "to insure that economic growth will occur in a manner consistent with the preservation of existing clean air resources." 42 U.S.C. § 7470.

Under the PSD program, areas with air quality better than the NAAQS are designated "attainment areas." 42 U.S.C. § 7407(d). Section 165 requires "major emitting facilities" that want to locate within an attainment area to obtain a permit. The states, with EPA approval, administer the PSD permitting program. 42 U.S.C. §§ 7410(a)(2)(C), 7471. The permit application contains both an ambient and a technology-based component. In order to obtain a permit, the applicant must demonstrate: (1) that the emissions of the proposed construction or modification will not contribute to air pollution in excess of the applicable "increment" (see below) and the NAAQS; and (2) that the facility will comply with Best Available Control Technology (BACT). 42 U.S.C. § 7475(a)(3)–(4).

Not all new facilities that want to locate in an attainment area are subject to PSD requirements. The term "major emitting facility" is defined according to the source's "potential to emit" (PTE). 42 U.S.C. § 7479(1). For certain categories of sources, a PTE of more than 100 tons per year of an air pollutant triggers the PSD requirements. For all other sources, a PTE of 250 tons per year of an air pollutant triggers the PSD requirements. *Id.* The pollution thresholds are measured in terms of emissions of a single pollutant, rather than the aggregate of all regulated pollutants. 40 C.F.R. § 51.166(b)(1)(i).

To obtain a permit, major emitting facilities are required to install the best available control technology (BACT). Section 169 defines BACT as "an emission limitation based on the maximum degree of reduction of each pollutant . . . which the permitting authority, on a case-by-case basis, taking into account energy, environmental, and economic impacts and other costs, determines is achievable for such facility. . . ." BACT can be no less stringent than NSPS. Like NSPS, BACT is a performance standard and does not necessarily mandate the installation of a particular technology.

Unlike NSPS, which is set for classes and categories of sources, BACT is determined on a case-by-case basis. In some cases, BACT may be more stringent than the NSPS for a source that is subject to both requirements. EPA guidance provides the following instructions for determining BACT on a case-by-case basis:

> In brief, the top-down process provides that all available control technologies be ranked in descending order of control effectiveness. The PSD applicant first examines the most stringent—or "top"—alternative. That alternative is established as BACT unless the applicant demonstrates, and the permitting authority in its informed judgment agrees, that technical considerations, or energy, environmental, or economic impacts justify a conclusion that the most stringent technology is not "achievable" in that case. If the most stringent technology is eliminated in this fashion, then the next most stringent alternative is considered, and so on.

EPA, NEW SOURCE REVIEW WORKSHOP MANUAL B2 (1990).

This approach is known as "top-down BACT" because it requires the most stringent control to be ruled out by economic or environmental concerns before the agency considers the next-most-effective alternative.

NOTES AND QUESTIONS

1. **Threshold Requirements for PSD.** The PSD regime applies only to major sources. Why would Congress enact a scheme that regulates only

sources that emit a minimum level of pollutants? What incentives does this approach transmit? Are these incentives desirable?

2. Case-by-Case Assessment. Assessing what constitutes BACT on a case-by-case basis is far more resource-intensive than determining BACT for a given class of emission sources. What are the benefits of a case-by-case assessment process? Do these outweigh the burden of considering each facility individually?

3. Top-Down Analysis of BACT. The CAA does not require a top-down analysis of BACT. The top-down analysis process is a policy implemented by EPA. What are the benefits and downsides of a top down analysis? What other methods of assessing BACT might there be?

C. PSD AMBIENT STANDARD: BASELINE AND INCREMENT

i. BASELINE

The "baseline" for an area is set when the first new source proposes to locate in the attainment area after the PSD regulations are enacted. 42 U.S.C. § 7479(4). Under § 169(4), the baseline is defined as the amount of pollution in a region when the first major emitting facility proposes to locate there.

ii. INCREMENT

The applicable "increment" defines the amount of deterioration toward the NAAQS authorized for a particular attainment area. The "increment," on which so much of the PSD program turns, is calculated by reference to a baseline.

The statute initially divides attainment areas into either Class I or Class II areas. 42 U.S.C. § 7472. Class I areas are relatively pristine areas, including areas in national parks and wilderness areas. Class II areas include all areas within a state that are designated in attainment or unclassifiable and are not Class I areas. Class I areas are concentrated in the western states.

Section 163, 42 U.S.C. § 7473, specifies the allowable increments for particulate matter and sulfur dioxide in Class I, Class II and Class III areas. Suppose a major emitting facility (MEF) for particulate matter wants to locate in a Class II area. The source will have to demonstrate through air modeling that its emissions will not cause increases above the area's baseline particulate matter concentration in excess of: 1) an annual geometric mean of 19 micrograms per cubic meter; and 2) a twenty-four hour maximum of 37 micrograms per cubic meter. In addition, the source must demonstrate that its particulate matter emissions will not cause the area to violate the NAAQS for particulate matter. Recall that the NAAQS for particulate matter are set at a twenty-four hour maximum of 150 micrograms per cubic meter. The Class II increment represents 25 percent of the twenty-four hour maximum available under the particulate matter NAAQS.

iii. INCREMENTS FOR POLLUTANTS OTHER THAN PARTICULATE
MATTER AND SO_2

Section 166, 42 U.S.C. § 7476 directs EPA to promulgate regulations
to prevent significant deterioration for hydrocarbons, carbon monoxide,
ozone, and nitrogen oxides. EPA may choose to "provide specific
measures at least as effective as the increments . . . to fulfill [the] goals
and purposes" of the CAA and the PSD program, rather than setting
increments. 42 U.S.C. § 7476(d). Pursuant to this section, EPA has
chosen to promulgate an increment for nitrogen dioxide. 40 C.F.R.
§ 52.21. *See also* EPA, Prevention of Significant Deterioration for
Nitrogen Oxides, 70 Fed. Reg. 59,582 (2005) (retaining the existing
nitrogen oxide increment as part of a PSD strategy for nitrogen oxides).

There are no increments established for carbon monoxide or
hydrocarbons, probably because these pollutants are traditionally
associated with mobile sources addressed elsewhere in the CAA. In
addition, no increment has been set for ozone, which is controlled through
regulation of precursor pollutants (nitrogen oxides and volatile organic
compounds). Section 166 also authorizes EPA to exempt pollutants from
area designations and increments if the pollutants are at least as
adequately addressed elsewhere in a SIP. 42 U.S.C. § 7476(e).

In *Environmental Defense Fund v. EPA*, 898 F.2d 183 (D.C. Cir.
1990), EDF challenged the nitrogen dioxide (NO_2) increment
promulgated by EPA. EDF argued that the agency did not adequately
consider the goals of the PSD program and the CAA, as required by
§ 166(c), when it promulgated the increment. EPA used the percentages
employed by the existing particulate matter and sulfur dioxide
increments to set the NO_2 increment, arguing that because the NO_2
increment was "equally stringent" in numerical terms, it was "at least as
effective" under § 166(d) as the increments for particulate matter and
sulfur dioxide. *Envtl. Def. Fund*, 898 F.2d at 187–88. The court accepted
EPA's interpretation of § 166(d) as a "contingent safe harbor," but held
that EPA was required to assess whether a more stringent standard was
required under § 166(c), which "commands a broad weighing of factors"
consistent with §§ 101 and 160 of the Act. *Id.* at 189. Because EPA had
not performed a § 166(c) analysis, the court remanded the case to the
agency.

Initially, the court's holding in *Environmental Defense Fund* seemed
to indicate the possibility that more stringent increments could be
established for "Set II" pollutants like nitrogen dioxide. *See* Robert L.
Glicksman, *Pollution on the Federal Lands I: Air Pollution Law*, 12
UCLA J. ENVTL. L. & POL'Y 1 (1993) (arguing that *Environmental
Defense Fund* "may result in a tougher, more expansive PSD program in
the future"). Fourteen years later, under a court order to comply with the
court's instructions in *Environmental Defense Fund*, EPA promulgated a
rule that maintained the increment as it was originally proposed. EPA,
Prevention of Significant Deterioration of Nitrogen Oxides, 70 Fed. Reg.

59,582 (2005). The final rule makes clear that states are not required to use increments for NO_2, and that they may employ alternative means, such as a cap-and-trade system under the Clean Air Interstate Rule, to comply with the purpose and goals of the PSD program. EPA will approve a SIP that demonstrates compliance using alternative means. *Id.* at 59,585.

iv. REDESIGNATION

Section 164, 42 U.S.C. § 7474, authorizes states to redesignate Class II areas within their jurisdiction to either Class I areas (more protective of air quality) or Class III areas (less protective of air quality). National monuments, nature preserves, wildlife areas and the like may only be Class I or II. 42 U.S.C. § 7474(a)(1). In order to redesignate an area as a Class III area, a state must meet additional requirements, including approval by the Governor after consultation with the legislature and concurrence of a majority of the local governments of the area. 42 U.S.C. § 7474(a)(2).

The Administrator may disapprove a redesignation only if she finds that the procedures have not been followed or that the redesignation is inconsistent with the mandatory Class I designations of § 162 or the requirements of § 164(a). All redesignations must conform to certain procedures: an effects analysis, a public hearing, and notice to affected federal land managers. 42 U.S.C. § 7474(b).

Recall that the Class II designation for particulate matter authorizes an increment above the baseline of 25 percent of the NAAQS (twenty-four hour maximum). 42 U.S.C. § 7473. If the area were redesignated as a Class III area, the particulate matter increment above the baseline would be 50 percent of the NAAQS. To date, no state has redesignated an area as a Class III area. *See* Memorandum from Peter Tsirigotis, Dir. Office of Air Quality Planning and Standards to Regional Air Division Dirs. 16 n.43 (Apr. 27, 2018).

Although the requirements for redesignation from Class II to Class I are less onerous, only a handful of federal Indian tribes, and no states, have sought redesignation from Class II to Class I areas. Six tribes have been successful in gaining redesignation: the Flathead Indian Reservation (MT), Fort Peck Indian Reservation (MT), Northern Cheyenne Indian Reservation (MT), Spokane Indian Reservation (WA), the Yavapai-Apache Indian Reservation (AZ), and the Forest County Potawatomi Community (WI). *See* Arnold W. Reitze, Jr., *The Control of Air Pollution on Indian Reservations*, 46 ENVTL. L. 893, 914–16 (2017). Tribes have sometimes employed redesignation to constrain pollution sources outside their jurisdiction. *See* Jana B. Milford, *Tribal Authority Under the Clean Air Act: How is it Working?*, 44 NAT. RESOURCES J. 213, 231–33 (2004) (noting that these redesignations "can be a double-edged sword that can constrain tribal development efforts as well as off-reservation sources").

NOTES AND QUESTIONS

1. **Triggering the Baseline.** When is the baseline set? Do you see a problem with this approach? What if air is degraded by the successive location of many non-major emitting facilities? Is there a way around this problem? Could Congress simply have defined the "baseline" for any region as the amount of pollution at the time of the Act's passage? Why do you think it didn't?

2. **NSPS v. BACT.** If a new source proposes to locate in a PSD area, it has to demonstrate compliance with a best available control technology (BACT) requirement, determined on a case-by-case basis. Recall that the NSPS requirements are set by category, rather than using case-by-case evaluations. What difference does this make? Will there always be an NSPS for a given source? What about a BACT determination?

3. **Class III Redesignations and the Role of Increments.** What is the relationship between the NAAQS and the increments? Do the increments allow a little or a lot of pollution? As of 2018, no areas were designated as Class III. Memorandum from Peter Tsirigotis, Dir. Office of Air Quality Planning and Standards to Regional Air Division Dirs. 16 n.43 (Apr. 27, 2018). Why do you suppose no state has attempted to reclassify an attainment area to Class III?

Shortly after the statutory PSD program was implemented, the National Commission on Air Quality analyzed the program's effectiveness in reducing total atmospheric pollutant loading. The Commission found that the increment system generally did not affect the stringency of BACT determinations because Class II increments are relatively large and siting alternatives are usually available. The Council thus concluded that the increment system, outside of Class I areas, was an unnecessary element of the PSD program "if BACT determinations were made in a manner requiring the maximum degree of control considering cost and other factors." NATIONAL COMMISSION ON AIR QUALITY, TO BREATHE CLEAN AIR 3.5–4.7, 4.8 (1981). How would this analysis change over time?

Recall from the discussion of *Environmental Defense Fund* that establishing an increment for nitrogen dioxide took fourteen years of litigation, and that the increment is waivable if states use alternative means to achieve a similar pollution level. Air modeling to demonstrate compliance with an increment on a case-by-case basis is expensive and time-consuming. Should Congress abandon the increment system entirely? Would BACT alone be sufficient in Class II areas? What happens if too many sources try to locate in such areas, each using the best method of pollution abatement?

4. **Air Modeling v. Air Monitoring.** Because of its reliance on establishing baselines and evaluating the amount of pollution a source will contribute toward fulfilling the increment, the PSD program hinges on accurate determinations of current ambient air concentrations of pollutants. EPA, citing the limitations of air quality monitoring, has historically relied on air quality modeling to make these determinations. At least one commentator attributes the program's failure in part to this element of implementation:

Modeling has great value, but it is a mighty peculiar way to ascertain current ambient air quality. To consider just how peculiar, one need only ask how EPA's approach to PSD increment compliance would look if applied to the majestic ambient air standards—NAAQS—that lie at the heart of the CAA.

Imagine that SIP provisions establishing emissions limitations and transportation control plans all over the country are established— as they indeed are—on the basis of air quality modeling. The models tell EPA and the states that emissions limits and other SIP features must be designed in such and such a way to guarantee compliance with the NAAQS. This is a proper and wholly necessary use of models. Now, however, imagine that precisely the same models used to craft the SIP ingredients are run again and again to demonstrate that the ambient air in each of the nation's airsheds does, in fact, comply with all NAAQS. How do we know that? Because the models prove compliance!

John-Mark Stensvaag, *Preventing Significant Deterioration Under the Clean Air Act: Baselines, Increments, and Ceilings—Part II*, 36 ENVTL. L. REP. 10,017, 10,045 (2006). What solutions can you imagine for the problem he describes? Are there better alternatives?

5.   PSD and Public Health. Craig N. Oren suggests, that rather than concern with public health, the PSD program is rooted in the distinct value people attach to benefits they will have to pay to acquire versus benefits they already possess. Craig N. Oren, *Prevention of Significant Deterioration: Control-Compelling Versus Site-Shifting*, 74 IOWA L. REV. 1, 76 (1988). This is known as the "endowment effect": people value things they have more highly than things they do not have. The PSD program protects existing air quality, arguably (according to Oren) at a cost society would not bear to attain that air quality if we did not already have it.

The PSD program, he argues, may actually worsen public health impacts by encouraging additional development in densely populated areas with higher levels of pollution.

The increment system has considerable potential to misallocate public health and welfare protection beyond the standards. Hypothesize, for instance, an increment of twenty micrograms and area "Pure" with baseline of ten and area "Sullied" with baseline of fifty. The increment system treats the two areas equally, even though, with Pure's lower baseline concentration, less marginal damage can be expected to occur there from increasing air pollution concentrations. If Pure grows more quickly than Sullied and uses up its increment, the increment system allocates growth to Sullied even though Pure's air quality is better than Sullied. This result is difficult to justify as protecting health, since, after all, baseline and increment-consuming sources are indistinguishable in their effects. Moreover, it is likely that Pure, with the lower baseline, has fewer people than Sullied. Yet because the increment system disregards

the baseline concentration, it affords the greater overall protection
to Pure.

Oren, *supra*, at 33. Is this analysis compelling? Might there be value in
having areas of differing air quality to suit differing preferences, so long as
no area falls below some floor requisite to protect the public health—in other
words, the NAAQS? Are the PSD rules a sensible way to achieve that air
quality diversity, if you believe in such a goal?

D. STATE OVERSIGHT OF PSD PERMITTING

Alaska Department of Environmental Conservation v. Environmental Protection Agency

540 U.S. 461 (2004).

■ JUSTICE GINSBURG delivered the opinion of the Court:

[Cominco owned a zinc concentrate mine ("the Red Dog Mine") in
northwest Alaska, near two Native Alaskan villages; Cominco operated
five diesel electric generators and kept one on standby (MG–5) pursuant
to a PSD permit for nitrogen oxide (NO_X). In 1996, Cominco required
additional electric capacity. To meet its electricity needs, Cominco
proposed an additional generator (MG–17) and installation of low-NO_X
technology, which reduces NO_X by thirty percent, on all seven of its
generators. The Alaska Department of Environmental Conservation
(ADEC) accepted the company's proposed low-NO_X alternative, finding
that it "achieve[d] a similar maximum NO_X reduction as the most
stringent controls."

EPA wrote to ADEC on July 29, 1999, criticizing its failure to follow
top-down BACT procedures. After a failure on the part of ADEC to
respond meaningfully to these complaints, EPA issued multiple
enforcement orders, under § 113(a)(5) and § 167 of the Act, prohibiting
ADEC's issuance of the permit and Cominco's construction pursuant to
the permit. § 113(a)(5) authorizes EPA to issue an order prohibiting
construction or modification of a major source, issue an administrative
penalty or bring a civil action under § 113(b) whenever EPA finds that
the State is "not acting in compliance with any requirement or
prohibition of the chapter relating to the construction of new sources or
the modification of existing sources." CAA § 113(a)(5). Section 167
provides that "[t]he Administrator shall, and a State may" issue an order
or seek injunctive relief to prevent the construction of a major emitting
facility that does not conform to the PSD requirements or that is located
in an attainment area which does not have a SIP that conforms to the
PSD requirements.]

Centrally at issue in this case is the question whether EPA's
oversight role, described by Congress in CAA §§ 113(a)(5) and 167,
extends to ensuring that a state permitting authority's BACT
determination is reasonable in light of the statutory guides. Sections

113(a)(5) and 167 lodge in the Agency encompassing supervisory responsibility over the construction and modification of pollutant emitting facilities in areas covered by the PSD program. In notably capacious terms, Congress armed EPA with authority to issue orders stopping construction when "a State is not acting in compliance with any [CAA] requirement or prohibition . . . relating to the construction of new sources or the modification of existing sources," or when "construction or modification of a major emitting facility . . . does not conform to the requirements of [the PSD program]," § 7477.

. . . Noting that state permitting authorities' statutory discretion is constrained by CAA's strong, normative terms "maximum" and "achievable," EPA reads §§ 113(a)(5) and 167 to empower the federal Agency to check a state agency's unreasonably lax BACT designation. . . .

ADEC assails the Agency's construction of the Act on several grounds. Its arguments do not persuade us to reject as impermissible EPA's longstanding, consistently maintained interpretation.

ADEC argues that the statutory definition of BACT unambiguously assigns to "the permitting authority" alone determination of the control technology qualifying as "best available." Because the Act places responsibility for determining BACT with "the permitting authority," ADEC urges, CAA excludes federal Agency surveillance reaching the substance of the BACT decision. EPA's enforcement role, ADEC maintains, is restricted to the requirement "that the permit contain a BACT limitation."

Understandably, Congress entrusted state permitting authorities with initial responsibility to make BACT determinations "case-by-case." A state agency, no doubt, is best positioned to adjust for local differences in raw materials or plant configurations, differences that might make a technology "unavailable" in a particular area. But the fact that the relevant statutory guides—"maximum" pollution reduction, considerations of energy, environmental, and economic impacts—may not yield a "single, objectively 'correct' BACT determination," [Brief for Petitioner,] at 23, surely does not signify that there can be no *unreasonable* determinations. Nor does Congress' sensitivity to site-specific factors necessarily imply a design to preclude in this context meaningful EPA oversight under §§ 113(a)(5) and 167. EPA claims no prerogative to designate the correct BACT; the Agency asserts only the authority to guard against unreasonable designations. . . .

We emphasize, however, that EPA's rendition of the Act's less than crystalline text leaves the "permitting authority" considerable leeway. The Agency acknowledges "the need to accord appropriate deference" to States' BACT designations, and disclaims any intention to " 'second guess' state decisions." 63 Fed.Reg., at 13797. Only when a state agency's BACT determination is "not based on a reasoned analysis," may EPA step in to ensure that the statutory requirements are honored. EPA adhered to that limited role here, explaining why ADEC's BACT determination was "arbitrary" and contrary to ADEC's own findings. . . .

ADEC also points to 42 U.S.C. § 7475(a)(8), a provision of the Act expressly requiring, in a limited category of cases, EPA approval of a state permitting authority's BACT determination before a facility may be constructed. Had Congress intended EPA superintendence of BACT determinations, ADEC urges, Congress would have said so expressly by mandating Agency approval of all, not merely some, BACT determinations. ADEC's argument overlooks the obvious difference between a statutory *requirement, e.g.,* § 7475(a)(8), and a statutory *authorization.* Sections 113(a)(5) and 167 sensibly do not require EPA approval of all state BACT determinations, they simply authorize EPA to act in the unusual case in which a state permitting authority has determined BACT arbitrarily. EPA recognizes that its authorization to issue a stop order may be exercised only when a state permitting authority's decision is unreasonable; in contrast, a required approval may be withheld if EPA would come to a different determination on the merits. . . .

We turn finally, and more particularly, to the reasons why we conclude that EPA properly exercised its statutory authority in this case. . . .

[The Court recounts ADEC's top-down BACT determinations and its switch to support Cominco's Low-NOx proposal despite having found SCR economically and technically feasible.]

ADEC's basis for selecting Low NOx thus reduces to a readiness "[t]o support Cominco's Red Dog Mine Production Rate Increase Project, and its contributions to the region." This justification, however, hardly meets ADEC's own standard of a "source-specific . . . economic impac[t] which demonstrate[s] [SCR] to be inappropriate as BACT." In short, as the Ninth Circuit determined, EPA validly issued stop orders because ADEC's BACT designation simply did not qualify as reasonable in light of the statutory guides. . . .

We emphasize that today's disposition does not impede ADEC from revisiting the BACT determination in question. In letters and orders throughout the permitting process, EPA repeatedly commented that it was open to ADEC to prepare "an appropriate record" supporting its selection of Low NOx as BACT. . . . At oral argument, counsel for EPA reaffirmed that, "absolutely," ADEC could reconsider the matter and, on an "appropriate record," endeavor to support Low NOx as BACT. We see no reason not to take EPA at its word. . . .

■ JUSTICE KENNEDY, with whom THE CHIEF JUSTICE, JUSTICE SCALIA, and JUSTICE THOMAS join, dissenting:

The majority, in my respectful view, rests its holding on mistaken premises, for its reasoning conflicts with the express language of the Clean Air Act (CAA or Act), with sound rules of administrative law, and with principles that preserve the integrity of States in our federal system. The State of Alaska had in place procedures that were in full compliance with the governing statute and accompanying regulations promulgated by the Environmental Protection Agency (EPA). As I understand the opinion of the Court and the parties' submissions, there is no disagreement on this point. Alaska followed these procedures to determine the best available control technology (BACT). . . . The Court errs, in my judgment, by failing to hold that EPA, based on nothing more than its substantive disagreement with the State's discretionary judgment, exceeded its powers in setting aside Alaska's BACT determination. . . .

The majority holds that, under the CAA, state agencies are vested with "initial responsibility for identifying BACT in line with the Act's definition of that term" and that EPA has a "broad oversight role" to ensure that a State's BACT determination is "reasonably moored to the Act's provisions." The statute, however, contemplates no such arrangement. It directs the "permitting authority"—here, the Alaska Department of Environmental Conservation (ADEC)—to "determine" what constitutes BACT. To "determine" is not simply to make an initial recommendation that can later be overturned. It is "[t]o decide or settle . . . conclusively and authoritatively." American Heritage Dictionary 495 (4th ed. 2000).

The BACT definition presumes that the permitting authority will exercise discretion. It presumes, in addition, that the BACT decision will accord full consideration to the statutory factors and other relevant and necessary criteria. Contrary to the majority's holding, the statute does not direct the State to find as BACT the technology that results in the "maximum reduction of a pollutant achievable for [a] facility" in the abstract. . . .

To be sure, §§ 113(a)(5) and 167 authorize EPA to enforce requirements of the Act. These provisions, however, do not limit the States' latitude and responsibility to balance all the statutory factors in making their discretionary judgments. If a State has complied with the Act's requirements, §§ 113(a)(5) and 167 are not implicated and can supply no separate basis for EPA to exercise a supervisory role over a State's discretionary decision.

EPA insists it needs oversight authority to prevent a "race to the bottom," where jurisdictions compete with each other to lower environmental standards to attract new industries and keep existing businesses within their borders. Whatever the merits of these arguments as a general matter, EPA's distrust of state agencies is inconsistent with the Act's clear mandate that States bear the primary role in controlling pollution and, here, the exclusive role in making BACT determinations. In "cho[osing] not to dictate a Federal response to balancing sometimes conflicting goals" at the expense of "[m]aximum flexibility and State discretion," H.R. Rep. No. 95–294, p. 146 (1977) . . . Congress made the overriding judgment that States are more responsive to local conditions and can strike the right balance between preserving environmental quality and advancing competing objectives.

NOTES AND QUESTIONS

1. **Least-Cost Reductions.** In Alaska's view, its approach would have resulted in the same or lower emissions as top-down BACT. By allowing the firm to make the least-cost reductions to their output, the same emissions reductions would have been achieved but at lower cost to the firm. Why wasn't the case litigated that way? If it had been, how do you think it would have been decided? Why was EPA not sympathetic to this "least cost reduction" strategy?

2. **Cooperative Federalism in PSD Areas.** If states are empowered to allocate pollution control burdens in SIPs and to issue permits under the PSD program, why should EPA be able to intervene in individual BACT determinations? Are you convinced by the Court's oversight rationale? Does the Court give adequate consideration to Justice Kennedy's argument that BACT was intended to allow states discretion? Does the Court's "failure to provide a reasoned analysis" limitation sufficiently limit EPA's discretion to intervene in state BACT determinations?

3. **Who Decides?** When it was litigated, *ADEC v. EPA* was seen as a major federalism case. The case boils down to a question of who decides what counts as the BACT mandated by statute: Alaska argues that, as the permitting authority, it gets to decide; EPA argues that, as the agency charged with enforcing the statute, it gets to decide. What do you regard as EPA's strongest argument? What are the merits of § 113 versus § 167 as sources of the authority to determine BACT in this context?

4. **Regional Haze Program.** 42 U.S.C. § 7491 establishes a program to protect visibility in mandatory Class I federal areas. The goal of the program is "the prevention of any future, and the remedying of any existing, impairment of visibility in mandatory Class I Federal areas which impairment results from manmade air pollution." 42 U.S.C. § 7491(a)(1). The statute directs the Administrator to promulgate regulations to assure "reasonable progress" toward the national goal. 42 U.S.C. 7491(a)(3) requires the Administrator to conduct studies to identify sources and source regions of visibility impairment and to use these studies to carry out his duties.

42 U.S.C. § 7491(b) requires SIPs to contain provisions requiring certain major stationary sources to apply the best available retrofit technology (BART) to assure reasonable progress toward maintenance and remedying of visibility. In *American Corn Growers Ass'n v. EPA*, 291 F.3d 1, 8 (D.C. Cir. 2002), the D.C. Circuit held that that the statute required a source-by-source determination of contribution to visibility-impairing pollution.

In 2005, EPA issued a revised Haze Rule. EPA, Regional Haze Program, 70 Fed. Reg. 39,104 (2005). Under the Haze Rule, 26 categories of sources (including electric generating units, or EGUs) built between 1962 and 1977 that have the potential to emit more than 250 tons a year of visibility-impairing pollution are "BART-eligible" and may be required to install pollution controls. States are required to impose BART on EGUs with capacity of 750 megawatts or greater; EPA estimates that the controls will be cost-effective for EGUs with capacity greater than 200 megawatts. States may exclude existing sources they identify that will not reasonably contribute to haze in Class I areas.

In *Utility Air Regulatory Group v. EPA*, 471 F.3d 1333 (D.C. Cir. 2006) the court upheld the Haze Rule against challenges by industry groups (contending the Haze Rule included too many sources) and the National Parks Conservation Association (contending the rule allowed too many exemptions). The court also held that allowing states to participate in CAIR's cap-and-trade system as an alternative to BART was reasonable.

EPA has also issued a rule allowing states to satisfy BART requirements by applying a cap-and-trade program that meets or exceeds the visibility benefits resulting from BART. *See* EPA, Regional Haze Regulations; Revisions to Provisions Governing Alternative to Source-Specific Best Available Retrofit Technology (BART) Determinations, 71 Fed. Reg. 60,612 (2006).

Implementation of state haze plans has been slow. In 2008, the Environmental Defense Fund and the National Parks Conservation Association sued EPA to compel the agency to issue a formal finding that many states had failed to submit required haze plans. EPA subsequently issued a finding that 37 states had failed to submit plans to control regional haze. *See* EPA, Finding of Failure to Submit State Implementation Plans Required by the 1999 Regional Haze Rule, 74 Fed. Reg. 2392 (2009). In 2011, EPA agreed to a schedule for acting on state regional haze plans as part of a proposed consent decree. *See* Alan Kovski, *EPA Agrees to Schedule for Taking Action on State Plans to Control Regional Haze*, BNA DAILY ENV'T REP., Nov. 10, 2011.

But controversy continued. In December 2016, the Obama EPA issued a final rule that updated several aspects of the Regional Haze Rule, including requiring states to consider long-term effects earlier in the development of the SIPs. *See* EPA, Protection of Visibility: Amendments to Requirements for State Plans, 82 Fed. Reg. 3078, 3091 (2017). States, industry groups, and environmental groups subsequently petitioned for review of the rule. *See* Environmental Law at Harvard, Overview of the Regional Haze Program, https://eelp.law.harvard.edu/2018/04/regional-haze-rule/ (last visited Feb. 1, 2019). A case challenging the program was held in abeyance while the Trump EPA reconsidered the final rule. *See id.* In September 2018, the Trump EPA announced a Regional Haze Review Roadmap, a year-long initiative over which the EPA will release "implementation tools and guidance documents that will help focus states' efforts and reduce and streamline the time and resources needed to meet" the program's requirements. EPA, Press Release, EPA Announces Regional Haze Reform Roadmap to Continue Improving Visibility and Reduce Regulatory Burdens (Sept. 10, 2018), https://www.epa.gov/newsreleases/epa-announces-regional-haze-reform-roadmap-continue-improving-visibility-and-reduce.

Could the objective of addressing visibility be achieved through the PSD program, without a separate regional haze program? Or is the PSD program an overbroad and poorly targeted way to protect parks and other areas of environmental value? For a discussion of the PSD program's effects on parks, see Craig N. Oren, *The Protection of Parklands from Air Pollution: A Look at Current Policy*, 13 HARV. ENVTL. L. REV. 313 (1989).

6. NONATTAINMENT

When the CAA of 1970 was enacted, Congress intended all areas to meet at least the primary NAAQS within five years. This goal was not achieved. In 1977, Congress responded by amending the Act to include requirements for areas in "nonattainment." These provisions, often known as "Part D" (because they are codified in Title I, Part D of the CAA), are designed to improve air quality in nonattainment areas while allowing economic development to continue. Almost 50 years after the enactment of the 1970 Clean Air Act, a large majority of states still have at least one county designated nonattainment for at least one NAAQS pollutant. *See* EPA, Current Nonattainment Counties for All Criteria Pollutants, https://www3.epa.gov/airquality/greenbook/ancl.html (last visited Dec. 10, 2018).

Like the PSD program, Part D of the CAA contains both ambient standards for air quality as well as a permitting program. The following materials trace the history of attainment and nonattainment, and the Congressional response.

A. CLEAN AIR ACT OF 1970: A FIVE-YEAR PLAN

When Congress passed the CAA in 1970, it optimistically required that each state attain the primary NAAQS within three years of the date of the approval of a SIP. Pub. L. 91–604, 84 Stat. 1676, 1680 (1970). Although the Act may have been ambiguous with regard to prevention of significant deterioration, Congress clearly expected to ensure that each air quality control region within a state met the uniform NAAQS by 1975—even if it meant imposing burdensome land-use and transportation controls in an area. Pub. L. 91–604, 84 Stat. 1676, 1680 (1970) (SIPs must include emissions limitations that are "necessary to insure attainment and maintenance of such primary or secondary standard, including, but not limited to, land-use or transportation controls."). Indeed, the statute passed with little debate about the dramatic federalism implications of imposing land-use controls (including, perhaps, federally administered zoning regulations, or shutting down major emitting facilities altogether) on states with poor air quality regions. *See* John P. Dwyer, *The Practice of Federalism Under the Clean Air Act*, 54 MD. L. REV. 1183, 1199–1201 (1995).

However, states with intractable air quality problems soon became aware of the difficult choices facing them, and many of them refused to write SIPs that contained the necessary land use policies and transportation systems. EPA had to walk a tightrope between implementing Congress' intent and imposing politically and economically difficult restrictions on states with poor air quality. In recognition of its technical and political limitations, EPA chose the path of least resistance: delay. *See* 37 Fed. Reg. 10,842, 10,845 (1972) (granting extensions to many states whose SIPs failed to meet the NAAQS).

Initially, EPA attempted to "read the law in the light of the real world problems of implementing it. . . ." EPA, Approval and Promulgation of Implementation Plans, California, 53 Fed. Reg. 49,494, 49,496 (1988) (describing the history of enforcement of the SIP provision). But these efforts were in vain. In 1973, the D.C. Circuit held that Congress' intent to impose deadlines was clear, and that EPA had no authority to circumvent these mandatory deadlines. *NRDC v. EPA*, 475 F.2d 968 (D.C. Cir. 1973). Subsequently, the states were presented with two options: write infeasible SIPs that would attempt to meet the NAAQS by 1975, or let EPA author equally infeasible FIPs for them. Several states refused to write SIPs; EPA's efforts to impose land use and transportation controls in FIPs were challenged by the states and rejected by three circuit courts on statutory grounds. *Brown v. EPA*, 521 F.2d 827 (9th Cir. 1975); *Maryland v. EPA*, 530 F.2d 215 (4th Cir. 1975), *vacated*, 431 U.S. 99 (1977); *District of Columbia v. Train*, 521 F.2d 971 (D.C. Cir. 1975). *But see Pennsylvania v. EPA*, 500 F.2d 246, 256–63 (3d Cir. 1974) (holding that EPA could impose and enforce transportation controls in FIPs pursuant to both statutory and Commerce Clause power).

B. CLEAN AIR ACT AMENDMENTS OF 1977: PART D AND A FIVE- TO TEN-YEAR PLAN

When Congress amended the CAA in 1977, it removed the controversial requirement that states impose "necessary land use controls" and added a requirement that states unable to achieve the NAAQS immediately instead comply with the permit requirements in the newly-drafted Part D, "Plan Requirements for Nonattainment Areas." Pub. L. 95–95, 91 Stat. 685, 693 (1977). By enacting Part D, Congress acknowledged that many states had been unable to achieve the NAAQS by its original five-year deadline and granted extensions for attainment of all primary NAAQS until 1982. Congress also provided a possible extension to 1987 for ozone and carbon monoxide (pollutants primarily from mobile sources), although to take advantage of this deadline, states were required to comply with more stringent pollution controls. Clean Air Act Amendments of 1977, Pub. L. No. 95–95, 91 Stat. 685, 748 (1977).

In addition to extending the relevant statutory deadlines, Part D imposed construction and operating permit requirements on new and modified major stationary sources in nonattainment areas. *Id.* (codified at 42 U.S.C. § 7503). The structure of the nonattainment permit program was similar to the PSD program, but its goal was to improve, rather than to preserve, air quality in the relevant air quality control region. Specifically, in a nonattainment area, the permitting authority was required to find the following before issuing a permit to a new or modified major source of air pollution:

1. That the source would comply with the lowest achievable emissions rate (LAER);

2. That the total allowable emissions from sources in the region was sufficiently less than the total emissions allowed under the SIP prior to the application, so as to represent reasonable further progress (RFP) toward attainment of the NAAQS; and

3. That the owner of the source had demonstrated that all of the major stationary sources she owns were on a schedule for compliance with all applicable emissions limitations under the Act.

Id. at 748 (1977) (codified at 42 U.S.C. § 7503). The lowest achievable emissions rate (LAER) was defined in § 171. Unlike the best available control technology (BACT) determination in the PSD context, LAER is a category-wide determination that reflects "the most stringent emission limitation" contained in a SIP or achieved in practice, whichever is more stringent. Sources may demonstrate that an emission limitation contained in a SIP is not achievable, but in no case may a source emit a pollutant in excess of the amount allowed under the applicable NSPS. Pub. L. No. 95–95, 91 Stat. 685 (1977) (codified at 42 U.S.C. § 7501); 40 C.F.R. § 51.165(a)(xiii).

The 1977 Amendments defined "reasonable further progress" (RFP) as the "annual incremental reductions in emissions of the applicable air pollutant (including substantial reductions in the early years following approval or promulgation of plan provisions under this part and § 110(a)(2)(I) and regular reductions thereafter) which are sufficient in the judgment of the Administrator, to provide for attainment of the applicable national ambient air quality standard by the date required in § 172(a)." In the 1977 Amendments, Congress codified an interpretive regulation by EPA that established that a new source could demonstrate RFP by obtaining offsets, or decreases in emissions, from existing sources. *See* EPA, Emissions Offset Interpretative Ruling in December 1976, 41 Fed. Reg. 55,524 (1976). Congress authorized the Administrator to modify the regulation, but specified that "the baseline to be used for determination of appropriate emission offsets under such regulation shall be the applicable implementation plan of the State in effect at the time of application for a permit by a proposed major stationary source." Pub. L. 95–95, 91 Stat. 685, 748 (1977). EPA's offset policy was intended to strike a balance between economic and environmental protection interests by requiring sources proposing to locate in a nonattainment area to "offset" their emissions with emissions reductions from other sources. In this way, EPA intended to enable nonattainment areas to continue to develop economically while working toward attainment of the NAAQS. *See Chevron U.S.A. Inc. v. NRDC*, 467 U.S. 837, 847–48 (1984) (describing EPA's 1976 regulation).

C. CLEAN AIR ACT AMENDMENTS OF 1990: THREE- TO TWENTY-YEAR PLAN

Most nonattainment areas are major metropolitan areas, often the "economic engines" of the states in which they are located. Consider the map in Figure V.1, which shows (in black) counties that were in nonattainment for at least one criteria pollutant in July 2014.

Figure V.1: Areas in Nonattainment (as of Aug. 31, 2018).

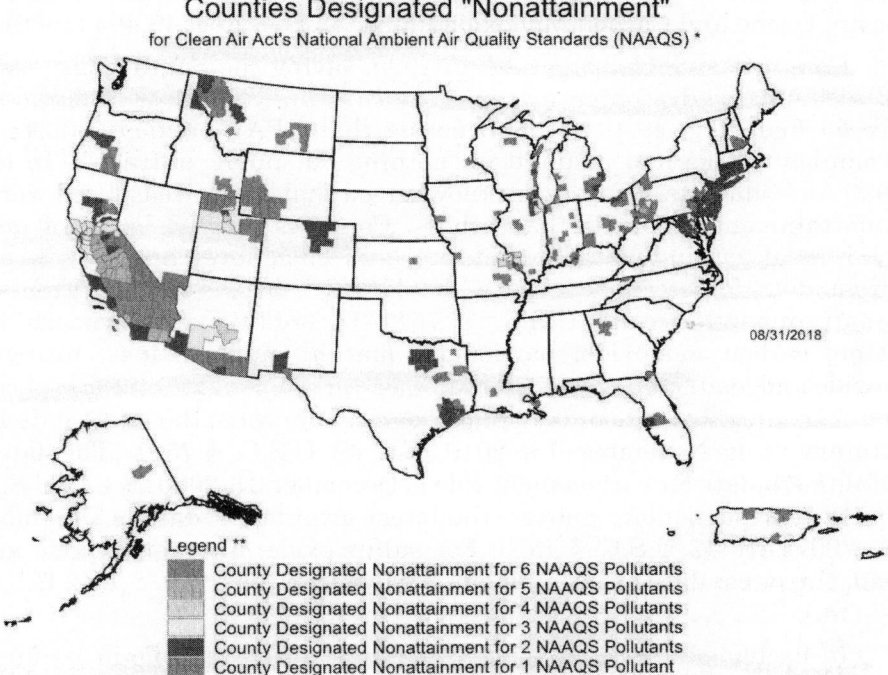

Guam - Piti and Tanguisson power stations are designated nonattainment for the SO2 (1971) NAAQS
Piti and Cabras power stations are designated nonattainment for the SO2 (2010) NAAQS

* The National Ambient Air Quality Standards (NAAQS) are health standards for Carbon Monoxide, Lead (1978 and 2008), Nitrogen Dioxide, 8-hour Ozone (2008), Particulate Matter (PM-10 and PM-2.5 (1997, 2006 and 2012), and Sulfur Dioxide.(1971 and 2010)

** Included in the counts are counties designated for NAAQS and revised NAAQS pollutants. Revoked 1-hour (1979) and 8-hour Ozone (1997) are excluded. Partial counties, those with part of the county designated nonattainment and part attainment, are shown as full counties on the map.

EPA, Counties Designated "Nonattainment", https://www3.epa.gov/airquality/ greenbook/map/mapnpoll.pdf (last visited Oct. 2, 2018).

The 1977 Amendments anticipated that all air quality control regions would attain the NAAQS by 1987. As the 1987 deadline approached, however, it became clear that some areas would not achieve attainment by the deadline. EPA hoped that Congress would provide relief from its enforcement duties, but also proposed a rule that would extend the deadlines for areas that did not meet the 1987 deadline. 52 Fed. Reg. 45,044 (1987). In *Abramowitz v. EPA*, 832 F.2d 1071 (9th Cir. 1987), the Ninth Circuit held that EPA could not approve a SIP for a nonattainment area that did not demonstrate compliance with the NAAQS for ozone and carbon monoxide by the 1987 deadline. Subsequently, EPA began the process of promulgating a FIP for the South Coast Air Quality Control Region, which includes the heavily polluted Los Angeles Basin, that predicted massive economic dislocation, including mass exodus of the population and the closing down of businesses due to lack of transportation options. EPA, Approval and Promulgation of Implementation Plans; California, South Coast Air Basin; Ozone and Carbon Monoxide Plans, 53 Fed. Reg. 49,494 (1988).

Congress amended the CAA in 1990, saving the South Coast—and EPA—from the draconian measures outlined in the 1988 FIP proposal. *See* 53 Fed. Reg. 49,494 (1988) (noting that EPA's previous efforts to promulgate FIPs had resulted in "nothing but public outrage"). In the 1990 Amendments, Congress acknowledged that some areas faced worse nonattainment problems than others. Congress created levels of non-attainment for individual pollutants, and each level had a different target date for compliance with the NAAQS, based on the extent of nonattainment. *See* 42 U.S.C. §§ 7511–14 (additional provisions for ozone, carbon monoxide, particulate matter, sulfur oxides, nitrogen dioxide and lead). The statutory deadlines vary depending on the severity of nonattainment and the type of pollutant. For ozone, the latest date for attainment is November 15, 2010. *See* 42 U.S.C. § 7511. The latest attainment date for carbon monoxide is December 31, 2000. *See* 42 U.S.C. § 7512. For particulate matter, the latest attainment date is December 31, 2001. *See* 42 U.S.C. § 7513. For sulfur oxide, nitrogen dioxide and lead, the latest date for attainment is November 16, 1995. *See* 42 U.S.C. § 7514.

In exchange for the extended deadlines, Congress again required additional measures to ensure that states were working toward attaining the NAAQS. States were required to demonstrate RFP in their SIPs, and the new source review trigger threshold was set lower than 100 tons per year in areas with more serious nonattainment problems. In addition, the offset ratio required to be demonstrated in the NSR permitting process increased with the severity of the nonattainment problem. *See* 42 U.S.C. §§ 7511–14.

The 1990 Amendments also revised the general nonattainment requirements in § 173. 42 U.S.C. § 7503. In addition to requiring RFP, LAER and compliance of the owner with all relevant emissions limits, a source had to demonstrate (1) that the Administrator had not found that the SIP was being inadequately implemented by the State; and (2) that an alternatives analysis demonstrated that the benefits of the proposed plant outweighed the costs.

The 1990 Amendments also added RACT, or Reasonably Available Control Technology; this measure is required, by § 172(c)(1), to be "adopted as expeditiously as possible" even on existing sources. This was the first federal regulation of existing sources in the CAA.

NOTES AND QUESTIONS

1.   Scope of Nonattainment Requirements. What types of facilities must apply for a permit? Must all new or modified stationary sources apply, or just some such sources? What is a "modified" source? What are the permitting requirements? How are they different from those in PSD areas?

2.   Major Emitting Facilities. What is the difference, if any, between a "major emitting facility" (the term used in the PSD program) and "major stationary source" (the term used in nonattainment)? The CAA's general definitions section, § 302, 42 U.S.C. § 7602, defines both terms. Are they defined differently for the purposes of PSD? For nonattainment? You should consult the definitions section of Part C (which is the PSD program) and Part D for the answers to these questions, as well as § 302, the general CAA definitional section.

As you will see, there is a difference in the definitions provided by the general definitional section and those provided by the PSD and nonattainment statutory sections. Which section controls?

3.   Types of Performance Standards. The nonattainment permits require the use of the "lowest achievable emissions rate," or LAER. How is LAER different from BACT, which is used in the PSD program? From the standard used in NSPS? From "reasonably available control technology"?

Is LAER more or less stringent than BACT? Under what conditions might top-down BACT be more stringent? Where does it seem more logical to have more stringent limitations on emissions: PSD areas (which have relatively unpolluted air), or nonattainment areas?

Why are there so many different verbal formulations of technology standards in the Act? There may be no clear answer to this question. Might the gradual evolution of the CAA, with repeated amendments in response to agency and court action, provide a part of the answer for this patchwork of technology standards?

4.   Offsets. What does it mean to offset emissions, as required by § 173(a)(1)? What strategies might a company use to achieve the required offsets if the company does not own other facilities? Which regulatory tool, among those discussed in Chapter II, do offsets resemble? How much progress is required to represent "reasonable further progress"?

5.   Ongoing Role of NSPS. What role does NSPS play anymore? Since any area must either be governed by PSD or nonattainment, each of which have independent permitting requirements, is it true to say that NSPS applies nowhere? How might NSPS be relevant even if it were never the governing standard?

Remember that NSPS standards set a floor for BACT and LAER determinations. Further, BACT and LAER apply only to "major emitting facilities" and "major stationary sources," respectively, while minor sources within an NSPS category would still be subject to NSPS. Minor sources outside of a listed NSPS category, however, would not be subject to any federal air quality regulation.

6.   Ongoing Role of the NAAQS, Continued. Consider the following proposition:

The country is divided into two categories of areas. Some are governed by PSD, and have air better than the NAAQS; they cannot degrade their air much. The others are governed by nonattainment, and have air worse than the NAAQS; they must steadily improve their air. Thus, the NAAQS are basically irrelevant; PSD and nonattainment do all the work.

Do you agree?

7.   NAAQS Revisions and Nonattainment Deadlines. The 1990 CAA Amendments created two types of nonattainment provisions: default provisions (in Subpart 1) and specific provisions for specific pollutants (in Subparts 2–5). Subpart 2, which addresses ozone nonattainment, is particularly comprehensive. The section spells out a wide variety of substantive requirements that EPA must implement and mandates specific nonattainment deadlines, the latest of which is November 15, 2010. 42 U.S.C. § 7511. In comparison, Subpart 1 includes only process requirements and its deadlines are set a specified number of years after a nonattainment determination is made. 42 U.S.C. § 7502(a)(2)(A).

As discussed above, many counties are still in nonattainment for ozone. How does this finding square with the unambiguous deadlines contained in Subpart 2?

In its 1997 ozone NAAQS revision, EPA announced its intention to phase out the existing 1-hour standard and stated that it would implement a new 8-hour standard under Subpart 1. EPA argued that the statute did not specify that Subpart 2 should apply to revised standards and that the ambiguity gave EPA discretion to apply Subpart 1. In a portion of the *American Trucking* opinion not excerpted above, the Supreme Court concluded that it was ambiguous under *Chevron* step one whether Subpart 2 was the exclusive remedy for revised standards but found under *Chevron* step two that EPA's decision to entirely abandon Subpart 2 was unreasonable. The Court remanded to EPA to craft a reasonable rule. 531 U.S. 457, 483–85 (2001).

In response, EPA issued a rule in 2004 that fully revoked the 1-hour NAAQS and established attainment dates and requirements for the 8-hour standard under Subpart 1. In *South Coast Air Quality Management District v. EPA*, the D.C. Circuit vacated the rule, concluding that § 172(e) (an anti-backsliding provision) required that areas that did not meet the original 1-hour standard must be regulated under Subpart 2, even if the 1-hour standard was revoked. 472 F.3d 882 (D.C. Cir. 2006).

Compare the statutory text of Subpart 1 to Subpart 2. Is it clear how Congress intended EPA to treat revised NAAQS? Did the courts in *American Trucking* and *South Coast* accurately interpret the congressional intent? Does EPA have flexibility to regulate revised NAAQS under Subpart 1? Should it?

8.   Nonattainment Fees. Under § 185 in Subpart 2, SIPs must include penalties for all major stationary sources in severe and extreme ozone nonattainment areas that fail to meet the statutory attainment deadlines contained in § 181. 42 U.S.C. § 7411d(a). Even after *South Coast* mandated that areas that did not meet the original 1-hour ozone NAAQS must be regulated under Subpart 2, EPA has continued to resist imposing the § 185 fee requirement.

EPA issued guidance in January 2010 that allowed states that would not meet attainment deadlines under the revoked 1-hour NAAQS to waive application of § 185 fees if the state established alternative attainment programs, arguing that it was within EPA's discretion to allow alternatives so long as they did not lead to backsliding under § 172(e). In *NRDC v. EPA*, the D.C. Circuit ruled against EPA on all points, concluding that Subpart 2 gave EPA no discretion to allow states to apply attainment alternatives in lieu of § 185 fees. 643 F.3d 311 (D.C. Cir. 2011). In a familiar refrain, the court stated that if EPA disagrees with the CAA, it should turn to Congress; in the meanwhile the agency must follow the statute.

In May 2012, EPA issued a rule that extended the deadline for compliance with the ozone NAAQS adopted in 2008. EPA, Implementation of the 2008 National Ambient Air Quality Standards for Ozone: Nonattainment Area Classifications Approach, Attainment Deadlines and Revocation of the 1997 Ozone Standards for Transportation Conformity Purposes, 77 Fed. Reg. 30,160 (2012). EPA justified the extension on the basis that it was absurd to require states to comply with the ozone NAAQS by the deadline set under the CAA, given that EPA had revised the ozone NAAQS in 2008 and the original dates for compliance have passed. The new deadline gives nonattainment areas the length of time granted by CAA § 181, but calculated from December 31, 2008. *Id.* at 30,165. Thus, the latest date for compliance for areas in extreme nonattainment is now December 31, 2032. *Id.*, 30,167. Was this a reasonable interpretation of § 181(a)?

In turn, in May 2018, EPA adopted a timeline for the ozone NAAQS adopted in 2015. Areas of extreme nonattainment have until May 2038 to come into compliance with these standards. EPA, Implementation of the 2015 National Ambient Air Quality Standards for Ozone: Nonattainment Area Classifications Approach, 83 Fed. Reg. 10,376, 10,380 (2018). This pattern shows that every time that EPA amends a standard, the compliance dates get extended. Is this approach desirable?

9.   Failure to Reach Attainment by Other Pollutant-Specific Deadlines. Currently, only the NAAQS for carbon monoxide and nitrogen dioxide have been achieved in all areas of the country. In 2010, EPA redesignated all nonattainment areas for the carbon monoxide NAAQS as maintenance areas. EPA, Green Book Carbon Monoxide Area Information, https://www.epa.gov/green-book/green-book-carbon-monoxide-1971-area-information (last visited Sept. 26, 2018). In 2012 EPA designated all areas of the country as being unclassifiable/in attainment with respect to the 2010 nitrogen dioxide NAAQS. EPA, Air Quality Designations for the 2010 Primary Nitrogen Dioxide (NO₂) National Ambient Air Quality Standards, 77 Fed. Reg. 9,532.

EPA issued nonattainment designations for the 2006 24-hour PM₂.₅ Standards in 2009. EPA completed designations for this standard in July 2018. *See* EPA, Additional Final Area Designations for the Annual Fine Particle Standard Established in 2012 for Areas in Florida.

As to sulfur dioxide, in 2013 EPA designated 29 areas as being in nonattainment for the 2010 sulfur dioxide NAAQS. The EPA has completed three rounds of designations under the 2010 sulfur dioxide NAAQS. In the second round, seven more nonattainment areas were designated. In the third round, published in January, 2018, the EPA designated six more nonattainment areas. *See* EPA, Air Quality Designations for the 2010 Sulfur Dioxide (SO₂) Primary National Ambient Air Quality Standard—Round 3, 83 Fed. Reg. 1098, 1099 (2018).

As to lead, in 2011 EPA published a rule designating 16 areas as being in nonattainment. The rule required that a state in which a nonattainment area is located revise its SIP by June 30, 2013, to provide for attainment of the lead NAAQS by December 31, 2016. EPA, Air Quality Designations for the 2008 Lead (Pb) National Ambient Air Quality Standards, 76 Fed. Reg. 72,097, 72,098 (2011). EPA has not revisited its lead designations since that deadline.

How can one justify EPA's actions concerning the nonattainment deadlines. What should it have done? Does the periodic revision of standards stand in the way of a serious focus on the nonattainment problem?

D. IMPLEMENTING NONATTAINMENT PROGRAMS

The cases that follow illustrate the interpretive and practical challenges in implementing the offset policy in nonattainment areas, as well as EPA's attempts to balance economic and environmental interests in interpreting the statute.

Citizens Against the Refinery's Effects, Inc. v. Environmental Protection Agency

643 F.2d 183 (4th Cir. 1981).

■ Before HALL, PHILLIPS, and SPROUSE, CIRCUIT JUDGES.

■ HALL, CIRCUIT JUDGE:

Citizens Against the Refinery's Effects (CARE) appeals from a final ruling by the Administrator of the Environmental Protection Agency (EPA) approving the Virginia State Implementation Plan (SIP) for reducing hydrocarbon pollutants. The plan requires the Virginia Highway Department to decrease usage of a certain type of asphalt, thereby reducing hydrocarbon pollution by more than enough to offset expected pollution from the Hampton Roads Energy Company's (HREC) proposed refinery. We affirm the action of the administrator in approving the state plan. . . .

. . . The offset program . . . permits the states to develop plans which allow construction of new pollution sources where accompanied by a corresponding reduction in an existing pollution source. In effect, a new emitting facility can be built if an existing pollution source decreases its emissions or ceases operations as long as a positive net air quality benefit occurs. . . .

The offset program has two other important requirements. First, a base time period must be determined in which to calculate how much reduction is needed in existing pollutants to offset the new source. This base period is defined as the first year of the SIP or, where the state has not yet developed a SIP, as the year in which a construction permit application is filed. Second, the offset program requires that the new source adopt the Lowest Achievable Emissions Rate (LAER) using the most modern technology available in the industry.

HREC proposes to build a petroleum refinery and offloading facility in Portsmouth, Virginia. Portsmouth has been unable to reduce air pollution enough to attain the national standard for one pollutant, photochemical oxidants, which is created when hydrocarbons are released into the atmosphere and react with other substances. Since a refinery is a major source of hydrocarbons, the Clean Air Act prevents construction of the HREC plant until the area attains the national standard.

In 1975, HREC applied to the Virginia State Air Pollution Control Board (VSAPCB) for a refinery construction permit. . . .

On November 28, 1977, the VSAPCB submitted a State Implementation Plan to EPA which included the HREC permit. The Virginia Board proposed to offset the new HREC hydrocarbon pollution by reducing the amount of cutback asphalt used for road paving operations in three highway districts by the Virginia Department of Highways. "Cutback" asphalt has a petroleum base which gives off great amounts of hydrocarbons. "Emulsified" asphalt uses a water base which evaporates, giving off no hydrocarbons. By switching from "cutback" to "emulsified" asphalt, the state can reduce hydrocarbon pollutants by the amount necessary to offset the pollutants from the proposed refinery. . . .

For several years, Virginia has pursued a policy of shifting from cutback asphalt to the less expensive emulsified asphalt in road-paving operations. The policy was initiated in an effort to save money, and was totally unrelated to a State Implementation Plan. Because of this policy, CARE argues that hydrocarbon emissions were decreasing independent of this SIP and therefore are not a proper offset against the refinery. They argue that there is not, in effect, an actual reduction in pollution.

The Virginia voluntary plan is not enforceable and therefore is not in compliance with the [requirement] which requires that the offset program be enforceable. The EPA, in approving the state plan, obtained a letter from the Deputy Attorney General of Virginia in which he stated that the requisites had been satisfied for establishing and enforcing the plan with the Department of Highways. Without such authority, no decrease in asphalt-produced pollution is guaranteed. In contrast to the voluntary plan, the offset plan guarantees a reduction in pollution resulting from roadpaving operations. . . .

NOTES AND QUESTIONS

1.   State Creativity in Implementing the Offset Requirements. Note that § 173(c)(2) prohibits states from using offsets that are already required by the CAA. Does § 173(c)(2) address the problem posed by the *CARE* case? Offsets create complicated markets because RFP has to be within the region with the nonattainment problem. Which are the set of potential offsetting sources? Why do you think the State of Virginia and HREC looked to the highway department for offsets?

2.   Incentives. The decision in *CARE* makes a state's pollution valuable: it can use reductions in it to accommodate industry that wants to locate in their state. What incentives does this give a state with regard to voluntary abatement measures? Is this likely to speed up attainment? Even if it is not, is this a justified concession to economic development?

Chevron U.S.A., Inc. v. Natural Resources Defense Council, Inc.

467 U.S. 837 (1984).

■ JUSTICE STEVENS delivered the opinion of the Court:

. . . The amended Clean Air Act required "nonattainment" States to establish a permit program regulating "new or modified major stationary sources" of air pollution. . . . The EPA regulation promulgated to implement this permit requirement allows a State to adopt a plantwide definition of the term "stationary source." Under this definition, an existing plant that contains several pollution-emitting devices may install or modify one piece of equipment without meeting the permit conditions if the alteration will not increase the total emissions from the plant. The question presented by these cases is whether EPA's decision to allow States to treat all of the pollution-emitting devices within the same industrial grouping as though they were encased within a single "bubble" is based on a reasonable construction of the statutory term "stationary source." . . .

The basic legal error of the Court of Appeals was to adopt a static judicial definition of the term "stationary source" when it had decided that Congress itself had not commanded that definition.

When a court reviews an agency's construction of the statute which it administers, it is confronted with two questions. First, always, is the question whether Congress has directly spoken to the precise question at issue. If the intent of Congress is clear, that is the end of the matter; for the court, as well as the agency, must give effect to the unambiguously expressed intent of Congress. If, however, the court determines Congress has not directly addressed the precise question at issue, the court does not simply impose its own construction on the statute, as would be necessary in the absence of an administrative interpretation. Rather, if the statute is silent or ambiguous with respect to the specific issue, the question for the court is whether the agency's answer is based on a permissible construction of the statute. . . .

The Clean Air Act Amendments of 1977 are a lengthy, detailed, technical, complex, and comprehensive response to a major social issue. A small portion of the statute [Part D] expressly deals with nonattainment areas. The focal point of this controversy is one phrase ["major stationary sources"] in that portion of the Amendments. . . .

The 1977 Amendments contain no specific reference to the "bubble concept." Nor do they contain a specific definition of the term "stationary source," though they did not disturb the definition of "stationary source" contained in § 111(a)(3), applicable by the terms of the Act to the NSPS program. Section 302(j), however, defines the term "major stationary source" as follows:

> (j)   Except as otherwise expressly provided, the terms "major stationary source" and "major emitting facility" mean any stationary facility or source of air pollutants which directly emits, or has the potential to emit, one hundred tons per year or more of any air pollutant (including any major emitting facility or source of fugitive emissions of any such pollutant, as determined by rule by the Administrator).

91 Stat. 770. . . .

In April, and again in September 1979, the EPA published additional comments in which it indicated that revised SIP's could adopt the plantwide definition of source in nonattainment areas in certain circumstances. . . .

In August 1980, however, . . . [t]he EPA took particular note of the two then-recent Court of Appeals decisions [*Alabama Power* and ASARCO], which had created the bright-line rule that the "bubble concept" should be employed in a program designed to maintain air quality but not in one designed to enhance air quality. Relying heavily on those cases, EPA adopted a dual definition of "source" for nonattainment areas that required a permit whenever a change in either the entire plant, or one of its components, would result in a significant increase in emissions even if the increase was completely offset by reductions elsewhere in the plant. . . .

In 1981 a new administration took office and initiated a "Government-wide reexamination of regulatory burdens and complexities." 46 Fed.Reg. 16281. In the context of that review, the EPA reevaluated the various arguments that had been advanced in connection with the proper definition of the term "source" and concluded that the term should be given the same definition in both nonattainment areas and PSD areas.

In explaining its conclusion, the EPA first noted that the definitional issue was not squarely addressed in either the statute or its legislative history and therefore that the issue involved an agency "judgment as how to best carry out the Act." *Ibid.* It then set forth several reasons for concluding that the plantwide definition was more appropriate. It pointed out that the dual definition "can act as a disincentive to new investment and modernization by discouraging modifications to existing facilities" and "can actually retard progress in air pollution control by discouraging replacement of older, dirtier processes or pieces of equipment with new, cleaner ones." *Ibid.* Moreover, the new definition "would simplify EPA's rules by using the same definition of 'source' for PSD, nonattainment new source review and the construction moratorium. This reduces confusion and inconsistency." *Ibid.* Finally, the agency explained that additional requirements that remained in place would accomplish the fundamental purposes of achieving attainment with NAAQS's as expeditiously as possible. . . .

The definition of the term "stationary source" in § 111(a)(3) refers to "any building, structure, facility, or installation" which emits air pollution. This definition is applicable only to the NSPS program by the express terms of the statute; the text of the statute does not make this definition applicable to the permit program. Petitioners therefore maintain that there is no statutory language even relevant to ascertaining the meaning of stationary source in the permit program aside from § 302(j), which defines the term "major stationary source." We disagree with petitioners on this point.

The definition in § 302(j) tells us what the word "major" means—a source must emit at least 100 tons of pollution to qualify—but it sheds virtually no light on the meaning of the term "stationary source." It does equate a source with a facility—a "major emitting facility" and a "major stationary source" are synonymous under § 302(j). The ordinary meaning of the term "facility" is some collection of integrated elements which has been designed and constructed to achieve some purpose. Moreover, it is certainly no affront to common English usage to take a reference to a major facility or a major source to connote an entire plant as opposed to its constituent parts. Basically, however, the language of § 302(j) simply does not compel any given interpretation of the term "source."

Respondents recognize that, and hence point to § 111(a)(3). Although the definition in that section is not literally applicable to the permit program, it sheds as much light on the meaning of the word "source" as anything in the statute. As respondents point out, use of the words "building, structure, facility, or installation," as the definition of source, could be read to impose the permit conditions on an individual building that is a part of a plant. A "word may have a character of its own not to be submerged by its association." *Russell Motor Co. v. United States*, 261 U.S. 514 (1923). On the other hand, the meaning of a word must be ascertained in the context of achieving particular objectives, and the words associated with it may indicate that the true meaning of the series is to convey a common idea. The language may reasonably be interpreted to impose the requirement on any discrete, but integrated, operation which pollutes. This gives meaning to all of the terms—a single building, not part of a larger operation, would be covered if it emits more than 100 tons of pollution, as would any facility, structure, or installation. Indeed, the language itself implies a "bubble concept" of sorts: each enumerated item would seem to be treated as if it were encased in a bubble. While respondents insist that each of these terms must be given a discrete meaning, they also argue that § 111(a)(3) defines "source" as that term is used in § 302(j). The latter section, however, equates a source with a facility, whereas the former defines "source" as a facility, among other items.

We are not persuaded that parsing of general terms in the text of the statute will reveal an actual intent of Congress. We know full well that this language is not dispositive; the terms are overlapping and the language is not precisely directed to the question of the applicability of a given term in the context of a larger operation. To the extent any congressional "intent" can be discerned from this language, it would appear that the listing of overlapping, illustrative terms was intended to enlarge, rather than to confine, the scope of the agency's power to regulate particular sources in order to effectuate the policies of the Act. . . .

Based on our examination of the legislative history, we agree with the Court of Appeals that it is unilluminating. The general remarks pointed to by respondents "were obviously not made with this narrow issue in mind and they cannot be said to demonstrate a Congressional desire. . . ." *Jewell Ridge Coal Corp. v. Mine Workers*, 325 U.S. 161, 168–169 (1945). We find that the legislative history as a whole is silent on the precise issue before us. It is, however, consistent with the view that the EPA should have broad discretion in implementing the policies of the 1977 Amendments.

More importantly, that history plainly identifies the policy concerns that motivated the enactment; the plantwide definition is fully consistent with one of those concerns—the allowance of reasonable economic growth—and, whether or not we believe it most effectively implements the other, we must recognize that the EPA has advanced a reasonable explanation for its conclusion that the regulations serve the environmental objectives as well.

Our review of the EPA's varying interpretations of the word "source"—both before and after the 1977 Amendments—convinces us that the agency primarily responsible for administering this important legislation has consistently interpreted it flexibly—not in a sterile textual vacuum, but in the context of implementing policy decisions in a technical and complex arena. The fact that the agency has from time to time changed its interpretation of the term "source" does not, as respondents argue, lead us to conclude that no deference should be accorded the agency's interpretation of the statute. An initial agency interpretation is not instantly carved in stone. On the contrary, the agency, to engage in informed rulemaking, must consider varying interpretations and the wisdom of its policy on a continuing basis. Moreover, the fact that the agency has adopted different definitions in different contexts adds force to the argument that the definition itself is flexible, particularly since Congress has never indicated any disapproval of a flexible reading of the statute. . . .

The arguments over policy that are advanced in the parties' briefs create the impression that respondents are now waging in a judicial forum a specific policy battle which they ultimately lost in the agency and in the 32 jurisdictions opting for the "bubble concept," but one which was never waged in the Congress. Such policy arguments are more properly addressed to legislators or administrators, not to judges.

In these cases, the Administrator's interpretation represents a reasonable accommodation of manifestly competing interests and is entitled to deference: the regulatory scheme is technical and complex, the agency considered the matter in a detailed and reasoned fashion, and the decision involves reconciling conflicting policies. Congress intended to accommodate both interests, but did not do so itself on the level of specificity presented by these cases. Perhaps that body consciously desired the Administrator to strike the balance at this level, thinking that those with great expertise and charged with responsibility for administering the provision would be in a better position to do so; perhaps it simply did not consider the question at this level; and perhaps Congress was unable to forge a coalition on either side of the question, and those on each side decided to take their chances with the scheme devised by the agency. For judicial purposes, it matters not which of these things occurred. . . .

We hold that the EPA's definition of the term "source" is a permissible construction of the statute which seeks to accommodate progress in reducing air pollution with economic growth. "The Regulations which the Administrator has adopted provide what the agency could allowably view as . . . [an] effective reconciliation of these twofold ends. . . ." *United States v. Shimer*, 367 U.S., at 383.

NOTES AND QUESTIONS

1. **Stakes of *Chevron*.** What was at stake, substantively, in *Chevron*? What is the difference between a "bubble" and an "offset"? Why is a bubble a more desirable deal for a source? How did EPA read the statute to enable "bubbling"?

A firm cannot "bubble" its emissions with another source across town, because the definition of "stationary source" in § 111 ("any building, structure, facility, or installation" that emits pollution) suggests contiguity. Existing firms benefit because of the contiguity requirement: They can often avoid new source requirements, while new sources of pollution do not have the "bubble" option. Thus, new sources of pollution that desire to locate in nonattainment areas will have to comply with the RFP requirement by obtaining offsets from existing sources. Offsets are not an alternative to regulation; rather, they are part of a system of broader regulation. The major differences between bubbles and offsets are outlined in Table V.2.

Table V.2. Bubbles v. Offsets

Bubble	Offset
Contiguous	Non-contiguous
Same owner	Different owners
Instead of the NSPS/BACT/LAER requirement	Additional requirement
No RFP	RFP

2. ***Chevron* Deference.** The *Chevron* case is famous for establishing the modern administrative law principle of judicial deference to an agency's interpretation of a statute it administers. The *Chevron* approach requires a two-step inquiry. First, the court asks whether Congress spoke directly and unambiguously to the issue in the statute itself. This step may include application of canons of statutory interpretation and investigation of legislative history, as illustrated by the *Chevron* case itself. If the court finds that Congress has not spoken directly to the issue in question, step two of the *Chevron* inquiry requires the court to defer to the agency's interpretation unless it finds that the agency's interpretation is an unreasonable construction of the statute.

Under this legal standard, was *Chevron* rightly decided? Which term or terms was EPA interpreting and the Court deferring to? Were the definitions clear enough to establish Congressional intent?

3. **Every Word Has Meaning?** The Carter Administration's interpretation of the CAA (modified by the Reagan Administration, and resulting in *Chevron*) gave two meanings to the term "source," depending on context. In the PSD context, it was defined plantwide, as a bubble; for nonattainment, however, it was not. The policy behind this was that, for nonattainment areas, the goal is not to maintain air quality, as it is in PSD areas; it is to steadily move toward the attainment of the NAAQS. This interpretation assigns two separate meanings to the same term, depending on the section of the statute being discussed. Is such an interpretation justifiable as a textual matter? *See Envtl. Def. v. Duke Energy Corp.*, 549 U.S. 561 (2007) (answering this question in the affirmative).

4.   Differing Interpretations. To what extent should the degree of deference be affected by the fact that the Reagan Administration departed from the Carter Administration's interpretation? To what extent does the answer depend on the rationales justifying deference?

Sierra Club v. Environmental Protection Agency
294 F.3d 155 (D.C. Cir. 2002).

■ Before GINSBURG, CHIEF JUDGE, and EDWARDS and SENTELLE, CIRCUIT JUDGES.

■ GINSBURG, CHIEF JUDGE:

The Sierra Club petitions for review of a decision by the Environmental Protection Agency approving revisions to the state implementation plans for ozone in the Washington, D.C. Metropolitan Area. The Club contends the EPA was without authority to approve revised SIPs that extend the Area's deadline for attainment. . . .

If an area "does not meet the NAAQS or it contributes to ambient air quality in a nearby area that does not meet the NAAQS," then the EPA designates the area as one of "nonattainment," and classifies the degree of nonattainment in the area as marginal, moderate, serious, severe, or extreme. This classification determines both the date by which the area must attain the NAAQS and the stringency of the measures that the area must implement in the meantime to reduce emissions of volatile organic compounds (VOCs) and oxides of nitrogen (NO_X), both of which are the precursors of ozone.

All states were required to revise their SIPs to bring any areas of "serious" nonattainment into attainment "as expeditiously as practicable but not later than" November 15, 1999. . . .

An area of serious nonattainment that failed to reach attainment by the deadline was to be reclassified by operation of law to "severe" nonattainment status. The deadline for attainment would then be extended until November 15, 2005, but the area would be required again to revise its SIP to implement still more rigorous programs for monitoring and reducing emissions.

The Washington, D.C. Metropolitan Area comprises the District of Columbia and several counties each in Maryland and Virginia. In 1991 the EPA declared the Washington Area to be in "serious" nonattainment of the NAAQS for ozone. In response, the District of Columbia

Department of Health, the Maryland Department of the Environment, and the Virginia Department of Environmental Quality (hereinafter referred to as "the States") submitted nonattainment SIPs for the Washington Area.

The three proposed SIPs did not provide for attainment by November 15, 1999. Instead, the States requested that the EPA extend the attainment deadline for the Washington Area until November 15, 2005 without reclassifying as "severe" the nonattainment status of the Area. The EPA previously had recognized that for certain "downwind areas, transport [of ozone] from upwind areas ha[d] interfered with their ability to demonstrate attainment" by the deadlines established in the Act. As a result, according to the EPA, many downwind areas "fac[ed] the prospect of being reclassified . . . to a higher nonattainment classification in spite of the fact that pollution that is beyond their control contributes to the levels of ozone they experience." With this in mind, the Agency granted the States' request for an extension, determining that the transport of ozone and its precursors into the Washington Area could delay the date by which the Area would reach attainment.

The States did not propose in their revised SIPs to adopt any [Reasonably Available Control Measures (RACM)], and the EPA concluded that none was warranted because "additional emission control measures would not advance the attainment date." [66 Fed. Reg.] at 608/1. Nor did the revised SIPs provide for annual rates of progress (ROP) in reducing emissions for the years after 1999; or for any contingency measures "to make up for any emission reduction shortfall, either in achievement of ROP milestones or for failure to attain" the NAAQS. The EPA determined that these omissions, too, were warranted. It deemed the ROP requirement "unreasonable" in light of the transport of ozone into the Washington Area, and it held that contingency measures are not mandatory elements of a SIP revision that establishes the attainment deadline and ROP for an area. Consequently, the Agency approved the revised SIPs. . . .

We agree with the Sierra Club that the plain terms of the Act preclude an extension of the sort the EPA granted here. Pursuant to § 181(a)(1), "each" area of "serious" nonattainment was required to meet the NAAQS by November 15, 1999. That deadline could be extended in certain limited circumstances or when an area was reclassified as one of "severe" nonattainment. In this case, the EPA neither determined that the Washington Area fit those limited circumstances nor acknowledged that the Area was reclassified as "severe."

The EPA characterizes the issue before the court as follows: "whether an attainment date extension is available without an accompanying reclassification to 'severe' nonattainment status where the Washington area's ability to attain has been demonstrably compromised by upwind emissions outside its control." Fair enough, but as the Sierra Club points out, the Act details the conditions in which the EPA may extend the attainment deadline, without reclassification, to account for upwind emissions that compromise an area's ability to come into attainment, and none of them is implicated here. For example, the Act exempts from the attainment deadlines any area that would be in attainment "but for emissions emanating from outside of the United States," 42 U.S.C. § 7509a(b); and "an[y] ozone nonattainment area that does not include, and is not adjacent to, any part of a Metropolitan Statistical Area," provided the "emissions within the area do not make a significant contribution to the ozone concentrations measured in the area or in other areas." We cannot but infer from the presence of these specific exemptions that the absence of any other exemption for the transport of ozone was deliberate, and that the Agency's attempt to grant such a dispensation is contrary to the intent of the Congress.

The EPA also contends the Approval "falls within this Court's parameters for when it will look beyond a 'literal' reading of a statute," but the Agency does not show that this is one of those "rare cases [in which] the literal application of a statute will produce a result demonstrably at odds with the intentions of its drafters." Because our "role is not to 'correct' the text so that it better serves the statute's purposes," we will not "ratify an interpretation that abrogates the enacted statutory text absent an extraordinarily convincing justification." Here the EPA asserts that "[a]s a matter of 'logic and statutory structure,' Congress 'almost surely' could not have meant to require" the Agency to treat the Washington Area as one of severe nonattainment merely because its "attainment has been temporarily stalled due to transported pollution." This assurance does nothing to persuade us that, although § 181(a)(1) as written sets a deadline without an exception for setbacks owing to ozone transport, "all the other evidence from the statute points the other way."

We reject also the EPA's argument that we must accept its interpretation of the Act in order to give effect to the "broader congressional intent not to punish downwind areas affected by ozone transport." The most reliable guide to congressional intent is the legislation the Congress enacted and, as we have seen, the Act itself reveals no intention to allow for an extension in circumstances like those affecting the Washington Area. Similarly, it is of no moment that the extension may be, as the Agency claims, "a reasonable accommodation of . . . the statutory attainment date and interstate transport provisions"; it is not the accommodation the Congress made. An agency may not disregard "the Congressional intent clearly expressed in the text simply by asserting that its preferred approach would be better policy." . . .

In sum, to permit an extension of the sort urged by the EPA would subvert the purposes of the Act. Therefore, we hold that the EPA was without authority in the Act or in our precedent to extend the attainment deadline for the Washington Area.

NOTES AND QUESTIONS

1. **Deadlines Are Deadlines.** The 1990 Amendments maintained both the uniform NAAQS and the deadline approach to the nonattainment problem, merely deferring confrontation of the difficult questions of interstate transport and unique geographical characteristics on pollution levels. In the same year that the D.C. Circuit decided that the D.C. area could not be granted an extension to attain the ozone NAAQS, the Seventh Circuit considered whether the St. Louis metropolitan area could be granted such an extension. In *Sierra Club v. EPA*, 311 F.3d 853 (7th Cir. 2002), the Seventh Circuit held that EPA had no authority to create an extension for St. Louis's "good behavior" and was required to redesignate the area as a serious ozone nonattainment area because St. Louis did not meet the required deadline. EPA had justified the extension on the fact that St. Louis was seriously affected by ozone transport and was expected to come into compliance once upwind pollution reductions occurred as a result of a federal air pollution program (the NOₓ SIP call, discussed in the Interstate Pollution subchapter, *infra*). *See* EPA, Extension of Attainment Dates for Downwind Transport Areas, 64 Fed. Reg. 14,441, 14,441–42 (1999). The court rejected this approach as an impermissible reading of the statute: "[W]e take issue with the EPA's most basic premise: that the CAA harbors within its structure a broad intent never to impose penalties on states burdened by transport." Is this the right approach to the interstate externality problem?

2. **Mission Accomplished: Reclassification.** In a follow-up case, the Seventh Circuit considered EPA's approval of St. Louis's application for reclassification to attainment for ozone. *Sierra Club v. EPA*, 375 F.3d 537 (7th Cir. 2004). Judge Easterbrook, writing for the court, upheld EPA's redesignation of the St. Louis metropolitan area as an ozone attainment area after approving the "applicable" implementation plan, § 107(d)(3)(E), which EPA interpreted to mean a plan including only the measures needed to achieve attainment, not the more onerous pre-attainment measures. Petitioners had argued that because St. Louis had been automatically "bumped up" to serious nonattainment for delay in meeting the NAAQS, it had to "use control measures appropriate to a serious nonattainment area as a condition of being designated as an attainment area." The court rejected this interpretation of the redesignation provision: "Under the Sierra Club's view, compliance does not have a payoff: the residents and businesses of St. Louis must take the same costly steps that would be required had the area been less successful." *Id.* at 541. Would incentives for compliance—a "payoff," as Judge Easterbrook put it—help solve the nonattainment problem?

3. **Deadlines Are Deadlines, Continued.** What happens when an area fails to attain the NAAQS for a specific pollutant by the required deadline, without having applied for an extension? After the San Joaquin Valley failed to attain the NAAQS for coarse particulate matter (PM–10) by the required deadline in 2001, EPA approved its new attainment plan revisions, which included a deadline extension to 2010. In *Association of Irritated Residents v. EPA*, 423 F.3d 989 (9th Cir. 2005), petitioners argued that EPA could only apply the more specific PM–10 "extension" provision, § 188(e), 42 U.S.C. § 7513(e), to extend the attainment deadline for a maximum of five years.

The court reasoned that the "overall statutory scheme" supported EPA's interpretation of the statute, because the longer deadline in § 179(d), 42 U.S.C. § 7509(d), unlike the PM–10-specific "extension" provision, was accompanied by a reduction quota and plan revision requirement, as punishment for missing the deadline without applying for an extension.

4.   Is Nonattainment So Bad? The nonattainment program provisions are premised on the idea that all states can and should attain the NAAQS. For an argument that forcing all areas to attain the NAAQS is economically inefficient, see Alan J. Krupnick & Paul R. Portney, *Controlling Urban Air Pollution: A Benefit-Cost Assessment*, 252 SCIENCE 522 (1991). The authors focus especially on the nonattainment problem in the South Coast Basin in California. For a critical review of the methodology of the epidemiological data underlying Krupnick and Portney's analysis, see Robert M. Friedman, *Air Pollution Benefit-Cost Assessment*, 253 SCIENCE 607 (1991). If attaining the NAAQS is not the proper goal, what should the goal be?

5.   Economic Incentive Plans. To promote attainment of the ozone and carbon monoxide NAAQS, §§ 182(g)(3) and 187(d)(3) encourage states to adopt economic incentive plans, or EIPs. Areas in "extreme" nonattainment of ozone and carbon monoxide standards are required to adopt EIPs. EPA has promulgated guidance for the EIPs, which can take the form of emissions trading programs, marketable permits, or fees. 40 C.F.R. §§ 51,492, 51,493 (2007). For a critical analysis of the South Coast Basin's implementation of EIPs, see Rachel Brasso Razon, *What is Good for the Market, Can Be Bad for Health: Emissions Trading Under SCAQMD's Rule 1610 and the Unjust Environmental Effects*, 29 GOLDEN GATE U. L. REV. 539 (1999).

7.   NEW SOURCE REVIEW

A.   OVERVIEW

Up to this point, you have seen how existing sources are regulated primarily through SIPs. You have also seen how the NSPS sets a uniform standard of performance for new sources, while both PSD and nonattainment have permitting requirements for new sources as well. Note, however, that the definition of a "new" source under NSPS, PSD, and nonattainment encompasses both "new" and "modified" sources.

The CAA's New Source Review (NSR) program is responsible for issuing permits for stationary source construction. The NSR program issues a permit for construction of a "new" facility only if it complies with applicable NSPS, PSD, and/or nonattainment regulations. *See* EPA, New Source Review (NSR) Permitting, https://www.epa.gov/nsr (last visited Sept. 26, 2018).

A key part of the NSR program is a determination whether the update of an existing facility qualifies as a "modification," prompting categorization as a "new" source. 42 U.S.C. § 7411(a)(4). Thus, New Source Review is a trigger for application of federal "new source" regulations to new sources and to "modified" existing sources that were previously regulated solely under SIPs.

The statutory definition of "modification" is given in § 111:

> The term "modification" means any physical change in, or change in the method of operation of, a stationary source which increases the amount of any air pollutant emitted by such source or which results in the emission of any air pollutant not previously emitted.

42 U.S.C. § 7411; *see also* 42 U.S.C. § 7501(4); 42 U.S.C. § 7479(2)(C). For a proposed facility update to qualify as a "modification," the statute thus requires both a physical change in a source and an increase in emissions of a pollutant. The materials that follow thus explore two basic questions: what counts as a "physical change," and what counts as an "increase in emissions."

At first glance, the statutory scheme seems fairly straightforward. But the questions of what constitutes a physical change and how to measure an increase in emissions have plagued EPA for the past twenty-five years. For a general overview of EPA's interpretation of "modification" and the resulting economic incentives, see RICHARD L. REVESZ & JACK LIENKE, STRUGGLING FOR AIR: POWER PLANTS AND THE "WAR ON COAL" 55–81 (2016); Richard L. Revesz & Allison L. Westfahl Kong, *Regulatory Change and Optimal Transition Relief*, 105 NW. U. L. REV. 1581 (2011); Jonathan Remy Nash & Richard L. Revesz, *Grandfathering & Environmental Regulation: The Law & Economics of New Source Review*, 101 NW. U. L. REV. 1677 (2007).

Early iterations of the regulatory definition of "modification" varied, even within the same rule. *See New York v. EPA*, 413 F.3d 3, 19–20 (D.C. Cir. 2005) (finding that NSPS regulations in force at time of 1977 CAA Amendments contained two definitions of modification). After the 1977 Amendments were enacted and legal challenges to EPA's initial attempt at a post-Amendments PSD rule were resolved in *Alabama Power Co. v. Costle*, 606 F.2d 1068 (D.C. Cir. 1979), EPA issued revised PSD and nonattainment rules in 1980 that contained new definitions of "modification." 45 Fed. Reg. 52,676 (1980) ("The 1980 rules"). The 1980 rules remained largely intact for over twenty years.

In the 1980 rules, EPA limited its regulatory authority to new construction and "major modifications." Major modifications were defined as the following:

> [A]ny physical change in or change in the method of operation of a major stationary source that would result in a significant net emissions increase of any pollutant subject to regulation under the Act.

40 C.F.R. § 52.24(f)(6)(i) (1980). The 1980 rules defined "physical change" in the negative, exempting (1) routine maintenance, repair and replacement; (2) use of alternative fuels in some situations; (3) increase

in the hours of operation or in the production rate; and (4) a change in ownership of the stationary source. 40 C.F.R. § 52.24(f)(6)(ii) (1980). Any other physical change qualified as a major modification, but only if it would also result in a significant net emissions increase of a pollutant.

As Nash and Revesz note:

These exceptions are inconsistent with the clear language of section 111, under which any increase in emissions, no matter how miniscule, triggers new source requirements. Nonetheless, the EPA viewed the routine maintenance exception as a "common-sense exclusion" from the statutory requirement; certainly the agency did not want to discourage basic maintenance.

Nash & Revesz, *supra* at 1685. As a result, what counted as "routine maintenance" became hotly contested. Because routine maintenance does not count as physical change for the purposes of the Act, it does not trigger NSR even if there is an increase in emissions, and the pollution source can avoid having to comply with the costly requirements of the NSPS or other standards.

The 1980 rules defined "net emissions increase" as "[a]ny increase in actual emissions from a particular physical change or change in the method of operation at a stationary source," taking into account any contemporaneous increases or decreases in emissions of the pollutant. Contemporaneous offsets were offsets that occurred within the five-year period before the physical change occurred. 40 C.F.R. § 52.24(f)(7) (1980). Finally, "significant" was defined in terms of a specific quantity of pollution, expressed in tons per year (tpy). Emissions increases that qualified as "significant" varied according to the pollutant.

Bolstered by early successes in enforcing NSR by applying its case-by-case "routine maintenance" determination (approved by the court in *WEPCO*, excerpted below), EPA collected data from several industries that indicated that many facilities were making major modifications to increase life expectancy without undergoing NSR. In the late 1990s, EPA began industry-wide enforcement of NSR for modifications to existing sources in the pulp and paper industry, the petroleum refining industry and electric utilities. *See* Christopher W. Armstrong, *EPA's New Source Review Enforcement Initiatives*, 14 NAT. RESOURCES & ENV'T 203 (2000).

These enforcement proceedings led to several large settlements that imposed penalties on sources and required them to install expensive pollution control equipment. In some cases, industry challenged EPA's interpretation of the CAA as a defense in the enforcement proceedings. *See, e.g.*, *United States v. Duke Energy Corp.*, 411 F.3d 539 (4th Cir. 2005) (holding that EPA's regulations defining "modification" differently in NSPS and NSR are not consistent with Congress' intent), *reversed sub nom.*, *Envtl. Def. v. Duke Energy Corp.*, 549 U.S. 561 (2007) (excerpted below).

Uncertainty surrounding implementation of the "modification" provisions, coupled with the rent-seeking of regulated industries as a result of disparate treatment of new and existing sources, led to a prolonged period of proposals for NSR reform. *See generally* Nash & Revesz, *supra*, at 1687–88 (describing EPA's efforts in the mid-1990s to rewrite NSR regulations through "NSR Simplification Workshops" and EPA's 2002 report to the President, which spurred a spate of new NSR rules). After 2002, EPA promulgated a series of NSR rules that radically altered its previous interpretation of "modification." These regulations, which are discussed below, have had a significant impact on the amount of pollution authorized under the NSR program.

B. "OLD PLANT" EFFECT

Commentators assert that Congress included modifications within the scope of NSR in order to expedite the installation of modern pollution controls on existing sources. *See, e.g.*, Deepa Varadarajan, Note, *Billboards and Big Utilities: Borrowing Land Use Concepts to Regulate "Nonconforming" Sources Under the Clean Air Act*, 112 YALE L.J. 2553, 2564 (2003) ("[L]egislators assumed that the natural turnover of power plants obviated the need for extensive old source regulation."); Shi-Ling Hsu, *Reducing Emissions from the Electricity Generation Industry: Can We Finally Do It?* 14 TUL. ENVTL. L.J. 427, 434 (2001) ("[P]olicy has been developed with the assumption that thirty-year-old plants would be soon phased out of production."). Courts have also adopted this rationale, citing legislative history that addressed the broad purposes of the CAA. *See, e.g.*, *Wis. Elec. Power Co. v. Reilly*, 893 F.2d 901, 919 (7th Cir. 1990) (noting that the purpose of the CAA was to "speed up, expand, and intensify the war against air pollution in the United States" (citing H.R. Rep. No. 1146, 91st Cong., 2nd Sess. 1, 1)).

Rather than fostering efficient modernization of pollution control, however, the grandfathering of existing sources in the CAA has provided an incentive to continue running existing facilities in order to avoid triggering the expensive and time-consuming requirements for new and modified facilities. Strict standards for new and modified plants, coupled with laxer standards for existing plants, may weight a source's cost-benefit calculus toward preserving an existing dirty plant longer than would otherwise be economically efficient. This "old plant effect" results from differential regulation of new and existing sources. For example, consider the case of *A*, the owner of a power-generating plant, who is contemplating upgrading or replacing the plant.

Situation 1: Absent Environmental Regulation

Annual Operating Cost of the Existing Facility (including annualized capital cost) = $100

Annual Operating Cost of a Comparable New Facility = $90 (including annualized capital cost)

Assuming that *A* acts economically, *A* will choose to construct a new facility.

Situation 2: With Environmental Regulation

Cost of Environmental Regulation for a New Facility = $20

Cost of Environmental Regulation for an Existing Facility = $0

Annual Operating Cost of the Existing Facility = $100

Annual Operating Cost of a New Facility = $110

A will now opt to retain her existing facility in operation.

Nash & Revesz, *supra*, at 1711.

Whether the "old plant" effect will in fact occur is an empirical question that is resolved by performing a cost comparison between the available options for a source. In some cases, when the cost of environmental regulation does not increase the annual operating cost of the new plant beyond that of the existing plant, the "old plant" effect will not occur.

But in other cases, such as in the example above, it will. The "old plant effect" means that clean air regulations may paradoxically make air quality problems worse by creating incentives to continue operating inefficient, out-of-date facilities. Furthermore, grandfathering can discourage existing plants from anticipating future changes in regulatory standards. Without regulation of existing sources, facilities that take early action to address emissions will not gain any competitive advantage over higher emitting facilities. *See* Revesz & Westfahl Kong, *supra*.

In the NSR context there is a third option: modification. Nash and Revesz explain the interaction of this third choice with the other two:

Say that the annual cost to A of a new plant is $90 (including annualized capital cost); of an existing plant subject to significant improvements is $95; and of an unmodified existing plant is $100. Further assume that environmental regulations will impose an additional $15 annual cost on a new [or modified] plant but no cost on an unmodified existing plant. In this case, A's ultimate decision as to how to proceed will depend upon whether the environmental regulations apply to a plant that has undergone significant improvements.

Nash & Revesz, *supra*, at 1713. For further discussion, see. REVESZ & LIENKE, *supra*, at 55–81.

In the case excerpted below, the Wisconsin Power Electric Company (WEPCO) challenged EPA's determination that WEPCO's proposed "life extension" project constituted a "major modification" for purposes of NSR. WEPCO argued that its project fell under the "routine maintenance" exclusion established by the 1980 NSR regulations.

Wisconsin Electric Power Co. v. Reilly

893 F.2d 901 (7th Cir. 1990) (as amended on denial of rehearing and
rehearing *en banc* Apr. 3, 1990).

■ Before CUDAHY and FLAUM, CIRCUIT JUDGES, and GRANT, SENIOR
DISTRICT JUDGE.

■ CUDAHY, CIRCUIT JUDGE:

... The EPA defines "modification" [for NSPS purposes] in substantially the same terms used by Congress. . . . To determine whether a physical change constitutes a modification for purposes of NSPS, the EPA must determine whether the change increases the facility's *hourly rate* of emission. For PSD purposes, current EPA regulations provide that an increase in the *total amount* of emissions activates the modification provisions of the regulations. 40 C.F.R. § 52.21(b)(3) (1988).

Even at first blush, the potential reach of these modification provisions is apparent: the most trivial activities—the replacement of leaky pipes, for example—may trigger the modification provisions if the change results in an increase in the emissions of a facility. As a result, the EPA promulgated specific exceptions to the modification provisions:

The following shall not, by themselves, be considered modifications under this part:

(1) Maintenance, repair, and replacement which the Administrator determines to be routine for a source category . . .

(2) An increase in production rate of an existing facility, if that increase can be accomplished without a capital expenditure on that facility.

(3) An increase in the hours of operation. . . .

40 C.F.R. § 60.14(e) (1988) (NSPS program). These regulations (and the statutes from which they derive) are the focal point of this case. . . .

WEPCO's Port Washington electric power plant is located on Lake Michigan north of Milwaukee, Wisconsin. The plant consists of five coal-fired steam generating units that were placed in operation between 1935 and 1950. . . .

[After performing a study and concluding that the plant needed extensive renovation], WEPCO submitted a proposed replacement program (which it termed a "life extension" project) to the Wisconsin Public Service Commission for its approval, as required by state law. WEPCO explained in its proposal that "[r]enovation is necessary to allow the Port Washington units to operate beyond their currently planned retirement dates of 1992 (units 1 and 2) and 1999 (units 3, 4 and 5) . . . [and that renovation would render the plant] capable of generating at its designed capability until year 2010. . . ." Cassidy Letter at 1–2. Among the renovations required were repair and replacement of the turbine-generators, boilers, mechanical and electrical auxiliaries and the common plant support facilities. . . .

. . . On September 9, 1988, EPA Acting Assistant Administrator Don R. Clay issued a memorandum in which he preliminarily concluded that the project would subject the plant to both NSPS and PSD requirements. . . . The Clay Memorandum pointed out that the project would constitute a "physical change" resulting in an increase of production and emissions, which would therefore subject the plant to the relevant strictures of the Clean Air Act. Further, the Clay Memorandum dismissed WEPCO's contention that the program was routine and was therefore exempt from the requirements of NSPS and PSD. . . .

. . . We must first consider whether WEPCO's Port Washington replacement program constitutes a modification under the terms of the controlling statute. Both parts of this definition—any physical change and an increase in emissions—must be satisfied before a replacement will be considered a "modification."

Certainly, under the plain terms of the Act, WEPCO's replacement program constitutes a "physical change." WEPCO proposes to replace rear steam drums on units 2, 3, 4 and 5. . . . In addition, WEPCO plans to replace another major component, the air heaters, in units 1–4. To implement this four-year program, WEPCO will need to make the replacements by taking the units successively out of service for nine-month periods. These steps clearly amount to a "physical change" in the Port Washington plant.

[WEPCO argued that "modification" means a "fundamental change," not including "like-kind replacement of the type it is proposing." The court rejected this argument, finding no support for it in either the statutory language nor in previous court determinations.]

Further, to adopt WEPCO's definition of "physical change" would open vistas of indefinite immunity from the provisions of NSPS and PSD. Were we to hold that the replacement of major generating station systems—including steam drums and air heaters—does not constitute a physical change (and is therefore not a modification), the application of NSPS and PSD to important facilities might be postponed into the indefinite future. There is no reason to believe that such a result was intended by Congress. The Clean Air Act Amendments were enacted to "speed up, expand, and intensify the war against air pollution in the United States with a view to assuring that the air we breathe throughout the Nation is wholesome once again." H.R. Rep. No. 91–1146, 91st Cong., 2d Sess. 1, 1. In particular, the permit program established by the 1977 Amendments to the Clean Air Act represented a balance between "the economic interests in permitting capital improvements to continue and the environmental interest in improving air quality." *Chevron*, 467 U.S. at 851. The House echoed this theme in its Committee report: "[The compliance program is designed, in part,] to allow reasonable economic growth to continue in an area while making reasonable further progress to assure attainment of the [pollution-control] standards by a fixed date. . . ." A too restrictive interpretation of "modification" might upset the economic-environmental balance in unintended ways.

. . . EPA regulations define "modification" as "any physical or operational change to an existing facility which results in an increase in the emission rate to the atmosphere of any pollutant to which a standard applies." However, the EPA has, in addition, used its regulations to exempt a number of activities from the broader definition. The exemption that may be relevant here is accomplished by the following language:

The following shall not, by themselves, be considered modifications under this part:

(1) Maintenance, repair, and replacement which the Administrator determines to be routine for a source category. . . .

40 C.F.R. § 60.14(e) (1998). WEPCO relies on this language to argue that, even if its repair and replacement program amounts to a physical change, it was specifically exempted by the regulations.

. . . In this connection, to determine whether proposed work at a facility is routine, "EPA makes a case-by-case determination by weighing the nature, extent, purpose, frequency, and cost of the work, as well as other relevant factors, to arrive at a common-sense finding." [citing the Clay Memorandum.] The EPA considered all these factors in determining that the Port Washington project was not routine; first, the EPA observed that the nature and extent of the project was substantial: WEPCO proposed to replace sixty-foot steam drums (in units 2, 3, 4 and 5) and air heaters (in units 1, 2, 3 and 4) during successive nine-month outages at each unit. Certainly, the magnitude of the project (as well as the down-time required to implement it) suggests that it is more than routine.

Further, the EPA points to WEPCO's admission in its application that "[work items] falling into the category of *repetitive maintenance that are normally performed* during scheduled equipment outages . . . *are not included in this application.*" Cassidy Letter at 1 (emphasis supplied). This admission suggests that WEPCO at first blush did not regard the repair and replacement project as ordinary or routine.

In addition, the EPA noted that far from being routine, the Port Washington project apparently was unprecedented. . . . We surmise, although the record is silent, that the "case of first impression" character of the project may reflect historical practice in the electric utility industry of replacing old plants (at the expiration of their useful lives) with new plants, employing improved technologies and achieving improved efficiencies. This was the typical practice, rather than the mere extension of life of existing plants through massive like-kind replacements. . . .

The purpose, frequency and cost of the work also support the EPA's decision here. . . . WEPCO reported that it had never previously replaced a steam drum or "header" of comparable size at any of its coal-fired electrical generating facilities. Further, the Port Washington renovation project will cost at least $70.5 million. These factors suggest that the project is not routine.

WEPCO urges that the EPA's conclusions are supported by neither the evidence nor the provisions of the Clean Air Act Amendments. WEPCO reasons that because *any* replacement project will presumably extend the life of a facility, the EPA's reliance on life extension as a factor in denying the "routine" nature of a project is overbroad. Although perhaps persuasive on its face, WEPCO's analysis is ultimately wide of the mark. While it is certainly true that the repair of deteriorated equipment will contribute to the useful life of any facility, it does not necessarily follow that the repairs in question would extend the *life expectancy* of the facility. The need for some repairs along the line is a given in determining in the first instance the life expectancy of a plant. WEPCO cannot seriously argue that its units' planned retirement dates of 1992 (units 1 and 2) and 1999 (units 3, 4 and 5) did not take into account at least minor equipment repairs and replacements. And WEPCO concedes that the Port Washington program will *extend* the life expectancy of the plant until 2010. The EPA concluded that the proposed project will increase the life expectancy of the Port Washington facility, and this conclusion was a factor in the finding that the work was not routine. These determinations were not arbitrary and capricious.

NOTES AND QUESTIONS

1. **Modifications in PSD and NSPS.** How are the definitions of "modification" different for the purposes of PSD and NSPS? For the current regulatory definitions of each, compare 40 C.F.R. § 52.21(b)(2)(i) and § 52.21(b)(21)(ii) (describing what constitutes a modification requiring a PSD permit) with 40 C.F.R. § 60.14(a) (defining modification for NSPS purposes). What differences result from measuring a modification by an increase in hourly emissions (NSPS) as compared to an increase in average annual emissions above the actual annual emissions for a prior two-year period (PSD)? Consider, for example, a modification that improves a plant's efficiency, allowing the plant to operate for longer hours and emit less of a pollutant per hour, but contributes through cumulative emissions to a higher annual level of pollution. For a more complete description of this scenario, and the effects of each regime on existing plants throughout the country, see Brian H. Potts, *The U.S. Supreme Court's New Dukedom: The Hour and Year, or a Proposal Quite Near*, 33 ECOLOGY L.Q. 517, 535–38 (2006).

2. **"Vistas of Indefinite Immunity."** Why is the *WEPCO* court reluctant to embrace industry's proposed definition of "modification"? What reasoning does it give? Is it convincing? Evaluate the court's prediction that a failure to apply regulations to all but the most "fundamental" modifications will allow those sources to escape regulation indefinitely. What incentives do regulations produce for those very same sources? What effect will failure to modify old sources have on air quality?

New York v. Environmental Protection Agency

413 F.3d 3 (D.C. Cir. 2005).

■ Before ROGERS and TATEL, CIRCUIT JUDGES, and WILLIAMS, SENIOR CIRCUIT JUDGE.

■ PER CURIAM:

. . . The Environmental Protection Agency ("EPA") has interpreted this rather terse definition [of "modification"] in numerous rules, including ones issued in 1980, 1992, and most recently in 2002. . . .

Industry, government, and environmental petitioners now challenge this 2002 rule, which departs sharply from prior rules in several significant respects . . .

[The court describes the 1970 CAA, 1977 Amendments, the 1980 NSR rule, and the 1992 NSR rule. The 1992 rule was issued in response to the court's ruling in *WEPCO*, and it applied an "actual-to-projected actual" emissions test to determine emissions increases for the utility industry. The 2002 rule extended this test to all sources.]

In 2002, EPA issued a new final rule to "reduce burden, maximize operating flexibility, improve environmental quality, provide additional certainty, and promote administrative efficiency." 67 Fed. Reg. at 80,189. This rule departed from the prior rules in several significant respects relevant to this litigation. . . . Under the 1980 rule, sources determined past actual emissions by averaging their annual emissions during the two years immediately prior to the change, though they could use either different, more representative periods or source-specific allowable emissions levels, if they could convince the permitting authorities. In contrast, under the 2002 rule, sources other than electric utilities determine past actual emissions by averaging annual emissions of *any* two consecutive years during the ten years prior to the change. . . .

Government and environmental petitioners raise two sets of challenges to the ten-year lookback period. First, they contend that the ten-year lookback period reflects an impermissible interpretation of the statutory term "increases" because it allows sources to increase their emissions beyond their most recent levels without triggering NSR. Second, they contend that EPA's selection of a ten-year lookback period is arbitrary and capricious because it contravenes the statutory purpose of protecting and enhancing air quality. For the following reasons, we conclude that petitioners' challenges to the ten-year lookback period fail to overcome the presumption of validity afforded to EPA regulations under the CAA. . . .

It is EPA's position that the ten-year lookback period is based on a permissible interpretation of the CAA because it "fulfills the statutory goal of balancing economic growth with the need to protect air quality." According to EPA, the ten-year lookback period promotes economic growth and administrative efficiency by affording sources the flexibility to respond rapidly to market changes, focusing limited regulatory resources on changes most likely to harm the environment, and eliminating conflicts over whether a proposed baseline period is "more representative of normal source operations." 67 Fed.Reg. at 80, 191–92. At the same time, EPA believes that the ten-year lookback period protects air quality by eliminating the regulatory disincentive to make physical or operational changes that improve efficiency and reduce emissions rates. *Id.* 80,192. We conclude that EPA supports these conclusions with "detailed and reasoned" analysis based on its experience and expertise. *Chevron*, 467 U.S. at 865.

In explaining the benefits of the ten-year lookback period, EPA appropriately refers to the problems experienced under the 1980 rule. EPA notes that under the 1980 rule, establishing a representative baseline period other than the two-year period immediately preceding the change was "complex and time-consuming" and often involved "disputed judgment calls." 61 Fed.Reg. at 38,258. EPA further notes that under the 1980 rule, sources experiencing periods of low production faced the unwelcome choice of either "surrendering capacity" by capping emissions at unrepresentative low levels or incurring the time and expense of securing NSR permits "for even small, non-excluded changes to a portion of the plant." *Id.* According to industry comments on the ten-year lookback period, this dilemma discourages sources from making economically efficient and environmentally beneficial changes during periods of low production. . . .

In response to these concerns, EPA commissioned a study of the business cycles of nine major emitting industries . . . The study examined industry output data from 1982 to 1994 and measured each industry's business cycle from peak to peak and from trough to trough. Peak-to-peak cycles ranged from three to six years, and trough-to-trough cycles ranged from three to eight years.

Government and environmental petitioners contend that the business cycle study does not support EPA's choice of a ten-year lookback period because none of the industries in the study had business cycles longer than eight years, and the study did not consider whether emissions vary with business cycles. However, petitioners ignore the study's conclusions that "business cycles differ markedly by industry" and that "a minimum of ten years of data is recommended to capture an entire industry cycle." [EASTERN RESEARCH GROUP INC., BUSINESS CYCLES IN MAJOR EMITTING SOURCE INDUSTRIES 16 (1997)]. Moreover, while the study did not track emissions, it did track output, which generally correlates with emissions. Hence, the business cycle study supports EPA's conclusion that a ten-year lookback period "is a fair and representative time frame for encompassing a source's normal business cycle." 67 Fed.Reg. at 80,200. . . .

EPA recognizes that "business cycles differ markedly by industry." 67 Fed.Reg. at 80,200. But in an effort to promote operational flexibility and administrative efficiency, EPA chose to apply a fixed ten-year lookback period to all sources in order to lend "clarity and certainty to the process" and to avoid the administrative burden of determining "representative" baselines on a case-by-case basis. 67 Fed.Reg. at 80,200. This policy choice, which reconciles conflicting interests in accuracy and efficiency, based on years of regulatory experience, is entitled to deference under *Chevron* Step 2, for petitioners fail to demonstrate that EPA's choice is impermissible under the CAA.

In enacting the NSR program, Congress did not specify how to calculate "increases" in emissions, leaving EPA to fill in that gap while balancing the economic and environmental goals of the statute. Based on its experience with the NSR program and its examination of the relevant data, EPA determined that a ten-year lookback period would alleviate the problems experienced under the 1980 rule and advance the economic and environmental goals of the CAA. Because we conclude that petitioners fail to demonstrate that EPA's policy determination is impermissible, we defer to EPA's statutory interpretation under *Chevron* Step 2, and we turn to petitioners' challenges to the environmental impact of the ten-year lookback period. . . .

Government petitioners maintain that the ten-year lookback period frustrates the purpose of the modification provision by allowing sources to restore their emissions capacities to historic levels without obtaining NSR permits. . . .

EPA acknowledges that fewer changes will trigger NSR under the 2002 rule than under the 1980 rule. However, based on its experience and its Environmental Impact Analysis, EPA "believe[s] that the environment will not be adversely affected" by the ten-year lookback period "and in some respects will benefit" from it, 67 Fed.Reg. at 80,192. As noted, it is EPA's position that the ten-year lookback period eliminates the regulatory disincentive for sources to implement changes that improve operating efficiency and reduce emissions rates. EPA further believes that the ten-year look-back period will not hinder states from achieving CAA air quality standards because NSR is not the primary mechanism for reducing emissions from existing sources. . . .

EPA concluded in its Environmental Impact Analysis that the "overall consequences" of the ten-year lookback period are "negligible" because it affects only "a very small number of facilities." Based on data from recent NSR permits, EPA's 1999 Trends Report, and the National Emissions Inventory, EPA estimated that 90% of the environmental benefits of the NSR program come from new sources, modifications at electric utilities, modifications at sources where emissions have been highest in recent years, and modifications at sources where emissions have been relatively stable—none of which are affected by the ten-year lookback period. EPA estimated that of the remaining 10% of sources where emissions have been lower in recent years, 70% are subject to legally enforceable emissions limitations that must be incorporated into their baselines and thus cannot claim higher baselines under the ten-year lookback period. . . .

To the extent that EPA's predictive judgment is supported by substantial evidence in the record, it is entitled to deference, as "the applicable standard of review allows the EPA considerable latitude to exercise its expertise through reasoned projections." *Natural Res. Def. Council, Inc. v. EPA*, 655 F.2d 318, 336 (D.C.Cir. 1981). EPA acknowledges that its Environmental Impact Analysis is based on incomplete data and thus cannot reasonably quantify the 2002 rule's impact on public health. . . .

For now, it suffices to conclude that EPA's predictive judgment is entitled to deference. Incomplete data does not necessarily render an agency decision arbitrary and capricious. . . .

■ WILLIAMS, SENIOR CIRCUIT JUDGE, concurring:

. . . [T]his case illustrates some of the painful consequences of reliance on command-and-control regulation in a world where emission control is typically far more expensive, per unit of pollution, when accomplished by retrofitting old plants than by including state-of-the-art control technology in new ones. In the interests of reasonable thrift, such regulation inevitably imposes more demanding standards on the new. But that provides an incentive for firms to string out the life of old plants. Indefinite plant life is impossible without modifications, however, so the statute conditions modifications on the firm's use of technological improvements. This in turn replicates the original dilemma: a broad concept of modification extends both the scope of the mandate for improved technology and the incentive to keep the old. By contrast, emissions charges or marketable pollution entitlements provide incentives for firms to use—*at any and every plant*—all pollution control methods that cost less per unit than the emissions charge or the market price of an entitlement, as the case may be.

NOTES AND QUESTIONS

1.   **Lookback Rule.** What is the logical limit of EPA's argument? Given the agency's position, wouldn't it be better to exempt all modifications? What is a defensible stopping point? How would a twenty-year lookback rule have fared?

2.   **"Routine Maintenance" Exception Clarified.** While EPA was still receiving comment on the 2002 "lookback" rule, it promulgated a rule that altered its application of the "routine maintenance" exclusion from NSR. EPA, Prevention of Significant Deterioration and Non-Attainment New Source Review, 68 Fed. Reg. 61,248, 61,250 (2003).

In its 2003 rulemaking, EPA sought to reduce the uncertainty created by the *WEPCO* case-by-case, four-factor approach to defining "routine maintenance." The 2003 rule established automatic exemptions for projects that met the following requirements:

> (1) [the project] involves replacement of any existing component(s) of a process unit with component(s) that are identical or that serve the same purpose as the replaced component(s); (2) the fixed capital cost of the replaced component, plus costs of any activities that are part of the replacement activity, does not exceed 20 percent of the current replacement value of the process unit; and (3) the replacement(s) does not alter the basic design parameters of the process unit or cause the process unit to exceed any emission limitation or operational limitation (that has the effect of constraining emissions) that applies to any component of the process unit and that is legally enforceable.

68 Fed. Reg. at 61,252 (the "twenty percent" rule). Whereas under the WEPCO four-factor test, EPA made *all* of its "routine maintenance" determinations on a case-by-case basis, the "twenty-percent" rule automatically exempts any projects that fall beneath the twenty percent threshold. The new rule was meant to supplement rather than to replace EPA's case-by-case approach to defining "routine maintenance," and projects that do not fall within the "twenty percent" rule will still be subject to *WEPCO's* multifactor test for determining whether the routine maintenance exclusion applies. What might be the benefits of such a rule? What might be the downsides? How should it deal with a succession of projects?

In response to outcry by states and environmental groups, the "twenty percent" rule was initially stayed by the D.C. Circuit. EPA subsequently decided to reconsider the rule, further delaying legal proceedings. Nearly one year later, EPA reissued the rule without change. 70 Fed. Reg. 33,838 (2005).

The petitioner states and environmental groups proceeded with their challenge. In March 2006, the D.C. Circuit vacated the "twenty percent rule," holding that it was inconsistent with the plain language of § 111(a)(4). *See New York v. EPA*, 443 F.3d 880 (D.C. Cir. 2006). Following Supreme Court precedent interpreting the word "any" and the specific regulatory history of the term "modification" in the CAA, the court refused to find ambiguity in the phrase "any physical change." *Id.* at 886. The court rejected EPA's argument that since Congress didn't list certain considerations as forbidden, EPA was free to consider them. *Id.* at 887 ("Only in a Humpty Dumpty world would Congress be required to use superfluous words while an agency could ignore an expansive word that Congress did use."). Would the "twenty percent" rule have made the "modification" inquiry more predictable? How could it have dealt with multiple projects?

3. **"Any" Physical Change?** Does the holding in *New York v. EPA* prove too much? If "any physical change" is not ambiguous, how can the "routine maintenance" exception be sustained in any form?

4. **A Mythological Analogy.** Consider the following questions in this ancient brainteaser, commonly known as the Ship of Theseus:

> Imagine a large wooden ship, in service for generations. As its planks decay, they are swapped out for new—but otherwise identical—timbers. Over time, every piece of the ship is replaced in this identical manner so that eventually not one of its original

planks remains. Is that the same ship? If not, when did it lose its
identity? When the first plank was replaced? The last? At some
point in between?

RICHARD L. REVESZ & JACK LIENKE, STRUGGLING FOR AIR: POWER PLANTS
AND THE "WAR ON COAL" 55 (2016).

5.   Additional Flaws of the "Twenty Percent" Rule. The D.C. Circuit
focused on statutory interpretation when invalidating the "twenty percent"
rule, but a review conducted by the Government Accountability Office (GAO),
focused on practical and informational flaws in the rule's structure. Among
other concerns, GAO cited informational problems resulting from emitters'
ability to select any 24-month period over the prior 10 years when
establishing an emissions baseline. According to GAO, "fewer facility
changes will require a federal permit and its related public participation
requirements." GAO, NEW SOURCE REVIEW REVISIONS COULD AFFECT
UTILITY ENFORCEMENT CASES AND PUBLIC ACCESS TO EMISSIONS DATA
(2003). Exacerbating the informational concern was a clause allowing
companies to determine whether there was a "reasonable possibility" that a
facility change would increase emissions enough to trigger new source
review. This policy essentially allowed emitters to police themselves and did
not require any sort of record keeping regarding how the "reasonable
possibility" determination was made. Since "reasonable possibility" was not
defined by the rule, companies would have been given substantial latitude
in determining whether they were subject to new source review.

    Why was GAO concerned with information about companies' emissions
and proposed changes being made publicly available? How could the public
have used this information to prevent potential harm? Is the public
awareness any more significant or effective than simply holding polluters to
new source review standards? In other words, are informational concerns as
important as making sure polluters are subject to the procedural
requirements of new source review?

6.   Transition Reliefs in NSR. The "grandfathering" of existing sources
is politically more palatable than subjecting them to the new standards,
particularly when these standards impose significant costs. Grandfathering
is a form of transition relief, a term that describes shielding existing sources
from a new legal regime. *See* Louis Kaplow, *An Economic Analysis of Legal
Transitions,* 99 HARV. L. REV. 509, 584–87 (1986). Transition relief is
generally undesirable because it discourages legal actors from anticipating
legal change and encourages rent-seeking behavior to preserve the relief
provided by the transition rule. *See* Jonathan Remy Nash & Richard L.
Revesz, *Grandfathering and Environmental Regulation: The Law and
Economics of New Source Review,* 102 NW. U.L. REV. 1677, 1724–32 (2007).
What are plausible arguments for some form of grandfathering? How broad
should it be?

7.   Sequential Optimization. Richard L. Revesz and Allison L. Westfahl
Kong criticize "the deep flaw" in the standard academic approach to setting
optimal regulatory standards. Richard L. Revesz & Allison L. Westfahl Kong,
Regulatory Change and Optimal Transition Relief, 105 NW. U. L. REV. 1581,

1582 (2011). Under this standard approach, the analysis "proceeds in two steps: (1) selecting the new standard solely by reference to new sources and (2) choosing the transition relief in light of that new source standard." *Id.* According to Revesz and Westfahl Kong, this approach "often yields a suboptimal result because there may be no new sources to meet the stringent standard, rendering the new standard entirely meaningless." *Id.* What is the solution?

8.   Modifications v. New Construction. Most commentators assume that the inclusion of modifications within the purview of NSR was an attempt to "bridge the gap" in the regulatory treatment of new and existing sources. Imposing NSR on "modifications" would result in the same level of pollution control on existing sources, eventually encouraging the construction of newer, cleaner plants—and eliminating the transition relief provided by the 1977 Amendments. As the *WEPCO* case demonstrates, however, firms found it in their economic interest to prolong the lives of existing plants rather than constructing new plants, often relying on the "routine maintenance" exclusion to justify avoidance of the strictures of NSR. In this regard, the uncertainty created by the case-by-case, four-factor test probably encouraged some sources to construct new plants when existing plants required extensive repairs.

In justifying the "twenty percent" rule, EPA argued that the *WEPCO* case-by-case approach was discouraging sources from making significant renovations—in other words, that it was exacerbating the "old plant effect." This argument assumed that the relevant choice was between not undertaking renovations and undertaking significant renovations. However, a third option exists: the construction of a new plant. *See* Nash & Revesz, *supra*, at 1707. On this view, the "twenty percent" rule exacerbates the distortion created by the "old plant effect" by artificially prolonging the lives of existing plants even longer than the original transition relief intended. *Id.* at 1709 n.188. Which scenario is more likely?

9.   Enforcement Discretion. After the "twenty percent" rule was invalidated by the D.C. Circuit, EPA announced it would nonetheless continue to use the rule in the case-by-case analysis of whether to bring enforcement actions, thus giving it de facto effect. *See Id.* at 1678–79. If EPA can simply decline to enforce NSR requirements part of the time, did the invalidation of the "twenty percent" rule in the D.C. Circuit achieve anything? What is the procedural difference between a regulation and an informal enforcement policy?

10.   New Defenses to NSR. Even after the implementation of more relaxed NSR regulations, EPA's remaining efforts to enforce NSR have faced strong headwinds.

In 1999, EPA commenced an enforcement initiative to find and sue sources that violate the new source review requirements. *United States v. EME Homer City Generation*, 727 F.3d 274, 281 (3d Cir. 2013). There have been some high-profile successes, such as a settlement with Tennessee Valley Authority in 2011 that required the Authority to retire 18 power plants and spend $3 billion to $5 billion on pollution controls. EPA,

Tennessee Valley Authority Clean Air Act Settlement, http://www2.epa. gov/enforcement/tennessee-valley-authority-clean-air-act-settlement (last visited Oct. 2, 2018). However, EPA has had less success before the courts. The Third, Seventh, Eighth and Tenth Circuits have all held that EPA cannot seek civil penalties against sources if it does not file suit within five years of the completion of the modification. *See United States v. EME Homer City Generation*, 727 F.3d 274 (3d Cir. 2013); *United States v. Midwest Generation*, 720 F.3d 644 (7th Cir. 2013); *Sierra Club v. Otter Tail Power Co.*, 615 F.3d 1008 (8th Cir. 2010); *National Parks & Conservation Ass'n v. Tennessee Valley Auth.*, 502 F.3d 1316 (11th Cir. 2007). Only the Sixth Circuit has held that an ongoing failure to comply with PSD requirements amounts to a series of discrete violations, and thus that EPA can seek civil penalties more than five years after the modification is completed. *See National Parks Conservation Association v. TVA*, 480 F.3d 410 (2007), but that decision rested on the specific language of the Tennessee SIP. *National Parks Conservation Association v. TVA*, 480 F.3d 410, 419 (2007).

Both the Third and Seventh Circuit cases involved claims concerning modifications made by former owners. The Third Circuit explained that "[w]hen more than five years have passed since the end of construction, and the facility has been taken over by new owners and operators, the Clean Air Act protects their reasonable investment expectations." *EME Homer City Generation*, 727 F.3d at 289. Should transfer of ownership make a difference to EPA's ability to seek financial penalties?

Courts have split on whether the failure to acquire a permit should be treated as a discrete violation or as a continuing violation. Which approach do you think is the right policy outcome? The right legal outcome? What is the best approach to successor liability for the failure to obtain a permit?

Though EPA loses the right to seek civil penalties if it does not commence an action within five years, the Third Circuit has held that EPA can still obtain an injunction requiring the source owner or operator to comply with PSD requirements. *See EME Homer City Generation*, 727 F.3d at 289. Is this remedy sufficient?

11. Pollution Control Projects. In *New York v. EPA*, environmental petitioners also challenged the 2002 rule's exemption of "environmentally beneficial" pollution control projects from NSR regulation. 413 F.3d at 40. Under the rule, a pollution control project that had the effect of decreasing a "primary" pollutant's emissions, while raising the emissions of a "collateral" pollutant, did not constitute a "change" triggering NSR if the project had a net "environmentally beneficial" effect. *Id.; see also* 67 Fed. Reg. 80,186, 80,232–33 (2002). The court found that because such projects literally constituted a "change," EPA was not authorized to exempt them from regulation. 413 F.3d at 40–42.

Environmental Defense v. Duke Energy Corp.

549 U.S. 561 (2007).

■ JUSTICE SOUTER delivered the opinion of the Court:

In the 1970s, Congress added two air pollution control schemes to the Clean Air Act: New Source Performance Standards (NSPS) and Prevention of Significant Deterioration (PSD), each of them covering modified, as well as new, stationary sources of air pollution. The NSPS provisions define the term "modification," 42 U.S.C. § 7411(a)(4), while the PSD provisions use that word "as defined in" NSPS, § 7479(2)(C). The Court of Appeals concluded that the statute requires the Environmental Protection Agency (EPA) to conform its PSD regulations on "modification" to their NSPS counterparts, and that EPA's 1980 PSD regulations can be given this conforming construction. We hold that the Court of Appeals's reading of the 1980 PSD regulations, intended to align them with NSPS, was inconsistent with their terms and effectively invalidated them; any such result must be shown to comport with the Act's restrictions on judicial review of EPA regulations for validity.

I

. . . The Court of Appeals held that Congress's provision defining a PSD modification by reference to an NSPS modification caught not only the statutory NSPS definition, but also whatever regulatory gloss EPA puts on that definition at any given time (for the purposes of the best technology requirement). When, therefore, EPA's PSD regulations specify the "change" that amounts to a "major modification" requiring a PSD permit, they must measure an increase in "the amount of any air pollutant emitted," 42 U.S.C. § 7411(a)(4), in terms of the hourly rate of discharge, just the way NSPS regulations do. Petitioners and the United States say, on the contrary, that when EPA addresses the object of the PSD scheme it is free to put a different regulatory interpretation on the common statutory core of "modification," by measuring increased emission not in terms of hourly rate but by the actual, annual discharge of a pollutant that will follow the modification, regardless of rate per hour. This disagreement is the nub of the case.

II

Respondent Duke Energy Corporation runs 30 coal-fired electric generating units at eight plants in North and South Carolina. *United States v. Duke Energy Corp.*, 411 F.3d 539, 544 (CA4 2005). The units were placed in service between 1940 and 1975, and each includes a boiler containing thousands of steel tubes arranged in sets. *Ibid.* Between 1988 and 2000, Duke replaced or redesigned 29 tube assemblies in order to extend the life of the units and allow them to run longer each day. *Ibid.* . . .

Duke moved for summary judgment, one of its positions being that none of the projects was a "major modification" requiring a PSD permit because none increased hourly rates of emissions. The District Court agreed with Duke's reading of the 1980 PSD regulations. . . .

The Court of Appeals for the Fourth Circuit affirmed, "albeit for somewhat different reasons." 411 F.3d, at 542. "The language and various interpretations of the PSD regulations . . . are largely irrelevant to the proper analysis of this case," reasoned the Court of Appeals, "because Congress' decision to create identical statutory definitions of the term 'modification' " in the NSPS and PSD provisions of the Clean Air Act "has affirmatively mandated that this term be interpreted identically" in the regulations promulgated under those provisions. *Id.*, at 547, n. 3, 550. The Court of Appeals relied principally on the authority of *Rowan Cos. v. United States*, 452 U.S. 247, 250 (1981), where we held against the Government's differing interpretations of the word "wages" in different tax provisions. 411 F.3d at 550. As the Court of Appeals saw it, Rowan establishes an "effectively irrebuttable" presumption that PSD regulations must contain the same conditions for a "modification" as the NSPS regulations, including an increase in the hourly rate of emissions. 411 F.3d at 550.

As the Court of Appeals said, Duke had not initially relied on *Rowan*, see 411 F.3d, at 547, n. 4, and when the Court *sua sponte* requested supplemental briefing on *Rowan*'s relevance, plaintiffs injected a new issue into the case. They argued that a claim that the 1980 PSD regulation exceeded statutory authority would be an attack on the validity of the regulation that could not be raised in an enforcement proceeding. Under § 307(b) of the Act, they said, judicial review for validity can be obtained only by a petition to the Court of Appeals for the District of Columbia Circuit, generally within 60 days of EPA's rulemaking.

The Court of Appeals rejected this argument. "Our choice of this interpretation of the PSD regulations . . . is not an invalidation of those regulations," it said, because "the PSD regulations can be interpreted" to require an increase in the hourly emissions rate as an element of a major "modification" triggering the permit requirement. 411 F.3d, at 549, n. 7. To show that the 1980 PSD regulations are open to this construction, the Court of Appeals cited the conclusions of the District Court and the Reich opinions.

We granted the petition for certiorari brought by intervenor-plaintiffs, 547 U.S. 1127 (2006), and now vacate.

III

The Court of Appeals understood that it was simply construing EPA's 1980 PSD regulations in a permissible way that left them in harmony with their NSPS counterpart and, hence, the Act's single definition of "modification." The plaintiffs say that the Court of Appeals was rewriting the PSD regulations in a way neither required by the Act nor consistent with their own text.

It is true that no precise line runs between a purposeful but permissible reading of the regulation adopted to bring it into harmony with the Court of Appeals's view of the statute, and a determination that the regulation as written is invalid. But the latter occurred here, for the Court of Appeals's efforts to trim the PSD regulations to match their different NSPS counterparts can only be seen as an implicit declaration that the PSD regulations were invalid as written.

A

In applying the 1980 PSD regulations to Duke's conduct, the Court of Appeals thought that, by defining the term "modification" identically in its NSPS and PSD provisions, the Act required EPA to conform its PSD interpretation of that definition to any such interpretation it reasonably adhered to under NSPS. But principles of statutory construction are not so rigid. Although we presume that the same term has the same meaning when it occurs here and there in a single statute, the Court of Appeals mischaracterized that presumption as "effectively irrebuttable." 411 F.3d, at 550. We also understand that "most words have different shades of meaning and consequently may be variously construed, not only when they occur in different statutes, but when used more than once in the same statute or even in the same section." *Atlantic Cleaners & Dyers, Inc. v. United States*, 286 U.S. 427, 433 (1932). Thus, the "natural presumption that identical words used in different parts of the same act are intended to have the same meaning . . . is not rigid and readily yields whenever there is such variation in the connection in which the words are used as reasonably to warrant the conclusion that they were employed in different parts of the act with different intent." *Ibid.* A given term in the same statute may take on distinct characters from association with distinct statutory objects calling for different implementation strategies.

The point is the same even when the terms share a common statutory definition, if it is general enough, as we recognized in *Robinson v. Shell Oil Co.*, 519 U.S. 337 (1997). There the question was whether the term "employees" in § 704(a) of Title VII of the Civil Rights Act of 1964 covered former employees. Title VII expressly defined the term "employee," 42 U.S.C. § 2000e(f), but the definition was "consistent with either current or past employment," 519 U.S., at 342, and we held that "each section" of Title VII "must be analyzed to determine whether the context gives the term a further meaning that would resolve the issue in dispute," *id.*, at 343–344. . . .

It is true that the Clean Air Act did not merely repeat the term "modification" or the same definition of that word in its NSPS and PSD sections; the PSD language referred back to the section defining "modification" for NSPS purposes. 42 U.S.C. § 7479(2)(C). But that did not matter in *Robinson*, and we do not see the distinction as making any difference here. Nothing in the text or the legislative history of the technical amendments that added the cross-reference to NSPS suggests that Congress had details of regulatory implementation in mind when it imposed PSD requirements on modified sources; the cross-reference alone is certainly no unambiguous congressional code for eliminating the customary agency discretion to resolve questions about a statutory definition by looking to the surroundings of the defined term, where it occurs. . . . Absent any iron rule to ignore the reasons for regulating PSD and NSPS "modifications" differently, EPA's construction need do no more than fall within the limits of what is reasonable, as set by the Act's common definition. . . .

■ JUSTICE THOMAS, concurring in part:

I join all but Part III-A of the Court's opinion. I write separately to note my disagreement with the dicta in that portion of the opinion, which states that the statutory cross-reference does not mandate a singular regulatory construction.

The Prevention of Significant Deterioration (PSD) statute explicitly links the definition of the term "modification" to that term's definition in the New Source Performance Standard (NSPS) statute:

> The term 'construction' when used in connection with any source or facility, includes the modification (as defined in section 7411(a) of this title) of any source or facility.

42 U.S.C. § 7479(2)(C). Section 7411(a) contains the NSPS definition of "modification," which the parties agree is the relevant statutory definition of the term for both PSD and NSPS. Because of the cross-reference, the definitions of "modification" in PSD and NSPS are one and the same. The term "modification" therefore has the same meaning despite contextual variations in the two admittedly different statutory schemes. Congress' explicit linkage of PSD's definition of "modification" to NSPS' prevents the Environmental Protection Agency (EPA) from adopting differing regulatory definitions of "modification" for PSD and NSPS. Cf. *IBP, Inc. v. Alvarez*, 546 U.S. 21, 34 (2005) (concluding that an "explicit reference" to a previous statutory definition prohibits interpreting the same word differently).

Section 7479(2)(C)'s cross-reference carries more meaning than the mere repetition of the same word in a different statutory context. When Congress repeats the same word in a different statutory context, it is possible that Congress might have intended the context to alter the meaning of the word. See *Atlantic Cleaners & Dyers, Inc. v. United States*, 286 U.S. 427, 433 (1932). No such possibility exists with § 7479(2)(C). By incorporating NSPS' definition of "modification," Congress demonstrated that it did not intend for PSD's definition of "modification" to hinge on contextual factors unique to the PSD statutory scheme. Thus, *United States v. Cleveland Indians Baseball Co.*, 532 U.S. 200 (2001), which analyzes the mere repetition of the same word in a different statutory context, carries little weight in this situation. . . .

Even if the cross-reference were merely the equivalent of repeating the words of the definition, we must still apply our usual presumption that the same words repeated in different parts of the same statute have the same meaning. See *Atlantic Cleaners, supra,* at 433; *ante,* at 9. That presumption has not been overcome here. While the broadly stated regulatory goals of PSD and NSPS differ, these contextual differences do not compel different definitions of "modification." That is, unlike in *Robinson*, reading the statutory definition in the separate contexts of PSD and NSPS does not require different interpretations of the term "modification." EPA demonstrated as much when it recently proposed regulations that would unify the regulatory definitions of "modification." *See* 70 Fed. Reg. 61,083, n. 3 (2005) (terming the proposal "an appropriate exercise of our discretion" and stating that the unified definition better serves PSD's goals).

The majority opinion does little to overcome the presumption that the same words, when repeated, carry the same meaning. Instead, it explains that this Court's cases do not compel identical language to be interpreted identically in all situations. Granting that point, the majority still has the burden of stating why our general presumption does not control the outcome here. It has not done so.

NOTES AND QUESTIONS

1. Same Word, Different Meanings? What is the Court's reason for stating that the same word, in the same place in the statute, can have different meanings in two regulatory contexts? Does this form part of the holding of the case?

What if EPA interpreted the word to mean the same thing in both contexts? Under the reasoning of *Chevron*, should that agency interpretation receive deference from the Court? Does such a result make sense when compared to the substantive (rather than standard of review) issues in *Chevron*? Can a court impose a different meaning on the same word in a statute even in the absence of an agency interpretation?

2. Judicial Review of a Petition for Review. Why is Justice Thomas' opinion—which disagrees with the majority and argues that the same word cannot have different meanings—a concurring, and not dissenting, opinion? Note that Justice Thomas agrees with Part II of the majority opinion, which rejects the Fourth Circuit's "implicit declaration that the PSD regulations were invalid as written."

Review the text of § 307(b), 42 U.S.C. § 9607(b), which delineates the procedures required to initiate a petition for review of an EPA regulation. Is it accurate to characterize the Fourth Circuit decision as invalidating EPA's PSD regulation? Did Duke Energy's challenge fail to fulfill any of the requirements for a petition for review under § 307(b)? Which requirements?

3. Effect of *Duke Energy*. The *Duke Energy* case had a large and immediate impact. American Electric Power, involved in a lawsuit that had been stayed pending the resolution of *Duke Energy*, subsequently settled its case, agreeing to spend $4.6 billion on emission reductions. *AEP Settles Lawsuit Alleging Violations*, ENV'T REP., Oct. 12, 2007, at 2165. Why might it have done so when *Duke Energy* was primarily a holding about jurisdiction?

8. INTERSTATE AIR POLLUTION

A. CONSTRAINING UPWIND POLLUTION

Air pollutants cross state borders. When a plant in one state creates pollution in another, the upwind state is externalizing harms: it emits pollution that causes adverse effects in downwind states. If transaction costs were zero, Coasian bargaining among states—limiting the level of interstate pollution to the amount each state was willing to pay to pollute or be paid to accept pollution—would solve interstate air pollution problems. However, transaction costs are sufficiently high to preclude such bargains. In addition, baseline entitlements are not well defined by statute; moreover, the beneficiaries of such bargains may change with the pollution problems. Compounding all of this are difficult questions of causation, as it is not trivial to determine which sources are having which effects on downwind states. *See* Richard L. Revesz, *Federalism and Interstate Environmental Externalities*, 144 U. PA. L. REV. 2341, 2375 n.123 (1996). In the absence of Coasian bargaining, interstate externalities are a compelling justification for federal regulation. Nonetheless, the original CAA was a poor tool to address such externalities. Ambient standards, such as the NAAQS, do not control interstate pollution effectively because the states are not forced to take into account pollution they cause in other states, so long as their local air quality meets the NAAQS. Emissions standards, such as NSPS, do not control the geographic placement of sources, the number of sources located in the state, or the size of each source. *See id.* at 2349–54.

State incentives to externalize the impacts of pollution were exacerbated by the 1970 CAA because states, by building tall stacks to disperse pollution, could externalize both the pollution impacts and the newly-created regulatory impacts, thus preserving flexibility to attract new sources without violating the NAAQS. *See id.* at 2352. Externalization allowed states to attract more industry without violating the NAAQS.

Subsequent amendments to the CAA attempted to address this problem. The 1977 amendments limited the use of "tall stacks" (which disperse pollution across state borders intentionally, to lower the amount of pollution in the state's borders). Section 123 constrained the amount of emissions credit a state can receive (that is, credit toward meeting emissions requirements) to the level consistent with a stack height built according to "good engineering practice." For a discussion of the additional incentives to build tall stacks created by the 1970 CAA, see *id.* at 2352–53 (noting that "whereas in 1970 only two stacks in the United

States were higher than 500 feet, by 1985 more than 180 stacks were higher than 500 feet and twenty-three were higher than 1000 feet."). Richard Revesz describes the perverse incentives created by the 1970 CAA with regard to interstate pollution: "The higher the stack, the less a source's emissions will affect ambient air-quality levels nearby, and the more they will affect ambient air-quality levels farther away." *Id.* at 2355.

Revesz argues that § 123 and the regulations that implement the "good engineering practice" standard are insufficient to deter a source from building a tall smoke stack when the pollution impacts are external to the state's decisionmaking process. This issue, however, became somewhat less salient after the acid rain provisions created a market in sulfur dioxide emissions. *See* Arnold W. Reitze, Jr., *State and Federal Command-and-Control Regulation of Emissions from Fossil-Fuel Electric Power Generating Plants*, 32 ENVTL. L. 369, 405–06 (2002).

The CAA amendments of 1977 added a substantive prohibition to § 110(a)(2), the statutory section setting out the requirements for a SIP, intended to address interstate air pollution. Subsection (D) requires a SIP to have provisions

> prohibiting . . . any source or other type of emissions activity within the State from emitting any air pollutant in amounts which will . . . contribute significantly to nonattainment in, or interfere with maintenance by, any other State with respect to any such national primary or secondary ambient air quality standard, or . . . interfere with measures [by] any other State under part C . . . to prevent significant deterioration of air quality. . . .

42 U.S.C. § 7410(a)(2)(D).

This single substantive standard is at the heart of the three methods in which interstate air pollution can be addressed under the CAA. A SIP may be challenged at the time of approval (of the original SIP or of a revision) for failing to meet this standard; states may file a petition under § 126, or the Administrator may make a SIP call for one or several states. Each of these methods are explained below.

i.   SIP CHALLENGE

If a state (or other person or entity) believes an upwind state's SIP is inadequate under § 110(a)(2)(D), it may challenge it, under amendments added in 1977. The utility of enforcing § 110(a)(2)(D) directly through the SIP approval process is limited by time constraints: The downwind state must sue within sixty days of approval of a SIP or SIP revision. 42 U.S.C. § 7607(b)(1).

Judicial interpretation further narrowed direct application of the provision. In *New York v. EPA*, 716 F.2d 440 (7th Cir. 1983), New York challenged EPA approval of an Illinois SIP revision that would increase the amount of sulfur dioxide emitted by a single source, Kincaid Power Station. New York argued that in reviewing Illinois's SIP revision for consistency with § 110(a)(2)(D), EPA was required to consider the effects of emissions from aggregate sources, not just the Kincaid Power Station; that EPA failed to consider sulfur dioxide contributions to total suspended particulates (TSP) concentrations; and that EPA did not adequately evaluate long-range interstate effects ascertainable by available air modeling systems. The court rejected all three of New York's arguments and upheld Illinois's SIP revision. The court held that agency review of SIP revisions should focus on emissions from the single pollution source proposed by the revision, not the emissions caused by aggregate sources.

New York v. EPA demonstrates the narrowness of the relief available directly under § 110(a)(2)(D). The court in *New York* observed that § 126 petitions provide "the proper forum in which to challenge revisions of emission levels from separate sources to determine if these aggregate emissions create an impermissible interstate impact." *Id.* at 445.

ii.   SECTION 126 PETITION

Section 126, added in 1977, authorizes a state to petition EPA for a finding that a major source or group of sources "emits or would emit any air pollutant in violation of the prohibition of § 110(a)(2)(D)(ii) of this title or this section." 42 U.S.C. § 7426(b). The text contains a scrivener's error; the prohibition actually referred to is § 110(a)(2)(D)(i). The notes following the *North Carolina v. EPA* case, *infra*, discuss this issue.

Within 60 days of receipt of a § 126 petition and after public hearing, the Administrator "shall make such a finding or deny the petition." If the Administrator finds a violation, he must set a schedule to bring the source into compliance "as expeditiously as practicable, but in no case later than three years after the date of such finding." 42 U.S.C. § 7426(c). Section 126 therefore provides for direct federal regulation of existing sources.

The provision also requires a state to provide written notice to nearby states when it proposes to build a new or modified source that is subject to the PSD requirements or might contribute significantly to nonattainment of the NAAQS in the downwind state. *See id.* States can petition EPA to make a finding under § 126 at any time. *See id.*

iii.   SIP CALL

Finally, under § 110(k)(5), added in 1990, the Administrator may issue a "SIP call" whenever he finds that the SIP for an area is substantially inadequate to maintain or attain the relevant NAAQS, "or to otherwise comply with any requirement of this chapter" of the CAA. When the Administrator issues a SIP call, the statute directs him to "require the State to revise the plan as necessary to correct such inadequacies." 42 U.S.C. § 7410(k)(5).

Air Pollution Control District of Jefferson County v. Environmental Protection Agency

739 F.2d 1071 (6th Cir. 1984).

■ Before ENGEL, MARTIN, and CONTIE, CIRCUIT JUDGES.

■ ENGEL, CIRCUIT JUDGE:

The Air Pollution Control District of Jefferson County, Kentucky, seeks review of an order of the Environmental Protection Agency ("EPA"). That order denied Jefferson County's petition for interstate pollution abatement, filed pursuant to section 126 of the Clean Air Act, CAA § 126(b). Jefferson County sought relief upon its claim that the Gallagher Power Station ("Gallagher") in southern Indiana emits air pollutants in violation of section 110 of the Act, CAA § 110(a)(2)(E)(i).* In that connection, Jefferson County sought a reduction of sulfur dioxide ("SO_2") emissions from the Gallagher generator. The County claimed that Gallagher's SO_2 emissions violated the provisions of the Clean Air Act which prohibit emissions in one state that prevent the attainment or maintenance of national ambient air quality standards ("NAAQSs") in another state. Jefferson County also maintained that Gallagher's emissions interfered with the margin for future industrial growth that the County had sought to create by placing strict controls on the emission of SO_2 by Kentucky sources.

The EPA denied Jefferson County's section 126 petition for interstate pollution abatement because it found that Gallagher did not "substantially contribute" to the violation of NAAQSs in Jefferson County. . . .

Jefferson County, Kentucky, and Floyd County, Indiana, share a common boundary on the Ohio River. The City of Louisville is located in the northwest portion of populous Jefferson County. In contrast, Floyd County is relatively undeveloped. However, since Jefferson County and Floyd County draw on the same air resources, they, along with Clark County, Indiana, were designated by the EPA as the Louisville Interstate Air Quality Control Region.

Because the structure of the Clean Air Act is state-oriented, each state is charged with implementing national clean air standards within its own political boundaries. Thus, although Floyd County and Jefferson County are in the same air quality control region, each county is subject to the implementation plan adopted by its respective state. Initially this was not a problem, since Indiana and Kentucky had adopted identical emission limitations for the pollutant at issue in this case, SO_2.

---

* At the time of the case, the provisions now contained in § 110(a)(2)(D) were in (a)(2)(E)— ED.

On May 14, 1973, EPA approved Indiana's SIP for Floyd County. This regulatory scheme set an emission limitation for the Gallagher Power Station of 1.2 pounds of SO_2 per million British Thermal Units ("lbs/MBTU") of heat input. Gallagher is situated less than a mile from the Indiana-Kentucky border and is the largest producer of SO_2 in Floyd County. In 1972, the EPA had approved Kentucky's SIP which set emission limitations of 1.2 lbs/MBTU of SO_2 for the major sources in Jefferson County: three power plants owned by Louisville Gas and Electric.

This uniformity of emission limitations in Floyd County and Jefferson County did not last long. In 1974, Indiana adopted new SO_2 regulations for Floyd County that completely exempted Gallagher from the 1.2 lbs/MBTU emission limitation, though the plant was required to keep on hand a two week supply of low-sulfur fuel should atmospheric conditions require lower SO_2 emissions. At first the EPA proposed to disapprove Indiana's regulation. However, when Indiana submitted technical data which showed that exempting Gallagher from limitations on the emission of SO_2 would not interfere with the attainment and maintenance of SO_2 standards in either Indiana or Kentucky, the EPA approved the regulation. In 1979, Indiana submitted a revision of the SO_2 portion of its SIP to the Agency. The new plan established an emission limitation for SO_2 of 6 lbs/MBTU heat input for most Indiana power plants, including Gallagher. This 6 lbs/MBTU limitation represents the amount of SO_2 currently emitted by the Gallagher plant without any controls; thus, the new "limitation" effectively maintains the status quo of uncontrolled SO_2 emission at Gallagher. On May 26, 1982, EPA proposed to approve the 6 lbs/MBTU limit with respect to the primary NAAQSs in Floyd County, but to disapprove it as to the secondary NAAQS.

Meanwhile, in Jefferson County the 1.2 lbs/MBTU emission limitation was generally enforced. In 1975 Louisville Gas and Electric negotiated consent orders whereby final compliance with the 1.2 lbs/MBTU limitation would be delayed until 1985. However, even with strict emission limitations, Jefferson County has yet to attain the NAAQSs for SO_2, and on February 23, 1978, Jefferson County was designated a Part D non-attainment area for both primary and secondary standards.

It can therefore be seen that a significant disparity exists between the permissible emission limits of power plants in Jefferson County, Kentucky, and the Gallagher plant in Floyd County, Indiana. Louisville Gas and Electric, the primary producer of SO_2 in Jefferson County, spent approximately $138 million installing scrubbers to remove SO_2 from its emissions, while across the river, Gallagher's SO_2 emissions were completely uncontrolled.

On May 14, 1979, the Air Pollution Control District of Jefferson County filed a petition for interstate pollution abatement under section

126 of the Clean Air Act, [CAA § 126]. The petition requested that EPA find (1) that SO_2 emissions from Gallagher are preventing attainment and maintenance of the NAAQSs for SO_2 in Jefferson County and (2) that once Jefferson County attains the NAAQSs for SO_2, Gallagher's emissions will interfere with Jefferson County's efforts to prevent significant deterioration of air quality under Part C of the Act. The petition sought tighter controls on Gallagher's SO_2 emissions. . . .

. . . EPA calculated that only about three percent of the SO_2 concentration at any location in Jefferson County where the NAAQSs are violated is attributable to Gallagher. However, an EPA modeling study also stated that:

> The highest second-highest predicted impact on a 24-hour average in Kentucky from Gallagher is 126 pg/m3 [micrograms per cubic meter], which is about 34.5% of the primary NAAQS. This is a substantial portion of the NAAQS and has the potential to limit the increment available to new sources in Louisville. The highest second-highest predicted 3-hour concentration in Kentucky resulting from the plant is 608 pg/m3. This represents 47% of the secondary NAAQS, and has a far more serious potential for limiting growth in Kentucky.

In fact, the EPA's study concluded that by 1985 Gallagher's emissions "will be the predominate [sic] influence upon air quality in Louisville, Kentucky."

Notwithstanding these determinations, the EPA, on February 16, 1982, finally denied Jefferson County's section 126 petition for interstate pollution abatement. The EPA concluded that "the Gallagher plant does not cause or substantially contribute to a violation of the SO_2 NAAQS." [47 Fed. Reg. 6624] at 6628.[11] . . .

Jefferson County asserts that Kentucky's SIP was designed to create a margin of clean air in Jefferson County by setting stringent emission standards that would leave the air cleaner than the NAAQSs require. Creation of this margin of clean air would allow further industrial growth in Jefferson County without the NAAQSs being violated. Since the operation of Gallagher without controls could in certain parts of Jefferson County contribute 47% of the secondary NAAQS for SO_2, the County contends that the margin for growth contemplated by the Kentucky SIP has been stolen by Gallagher to the economic disadvantage of Jefferson County. The County also seems to contend that once it attains the secondary NAAQS for SO_2, Gallagher's emissions will interfere with future measures to prevent significant deterioration of air quality in

---

[11] Although Gallagher contributes pollutants to Jefferson County, evidently its emissions impact most heavily on parts of the County that are not in violation of the NAAQS for SO_2. Consequently, the EPA concluded that Gallagher does not substantially contribute to a *violation* of the SO_2 NAAQS.

Jefferson County. Presently, no such measures are in place, since the County has not achieved the NAAQSs for SO_2.

The EPA's response to this "margin for growth" argument was seemingly inconsistent. Initially, in its notice of the proceedings on Jefferson County's section 126 petition, the EPA interpreted the interstate pollution abatement provisions as prohibiting interference with another state's margin for growth:

> The Agency considers that the degree of protection afforded by the interstate pollution provisions includes not only protection against NAAQS violations, but also protection against unreasonable interference with a maintenance program or margin for growth in the SIP. . . .

However, when the EPA rendered its final determination on Jefferson County's section 126 petition, the "margin for growth" argument was rejected. In referring to the problem of Gallagher consuming Jefferson County's future PSD increment, the EPA stated:

> *Comment.* One commentator objected to EPA's proposed finding that emissions from Gallagher do not interfere with PSD provisions and urged the Administrator to make a finding on the plant's potential impact on future PSD requirements in Jefferson County.

> *Response.* Jefferson County is a nonattainment area for SO_2, and the PSD regulations are not applicable. Consequently the Gallagher plant cannot interfere at this time with PSD requirements in Jefferson County. Section 126 only prohibits interference with PSD measures required by the Clean Air Act, and therefore EPA need not review possible future impacts on regulations not yet in place. Furthermore, Gallagher's emissions will not consume any future PSD increment since its emissions at the time the baseline date is set will be included in the baseline air quality in Jefferson County.

47 Fed. Reg. 6624, 6627 (Feb. 16, 1982).

The EPA contends that it is irrelevant to the petition brought by Jefferson County under section 126 whether Gallagher infringes on the margin for growth which the County asserts it needs for future industrial development. By utilizing section 126 to prevent upwind states from contributing SO_2 to air that is cleaner than the NAAQSs require, the County is in effect attempting to establish a local air quality standard that is more stringent than the national standard. The EPA argues that the literal language of sections 126(b) and 110(a)(2)(E), 42 U.S.C. §§ 7426(b), 7410(a)(2)(E), indicates that interstate pollution is prohibited only insofar as it prevents another state from attaining or maintaining "any such *national* primary or secondary ambient air quality standard." [CAA § 110(a)(2)(E)(i)] (emphasis added). Thus, in the EPA's view, the interstate pollution abatement provisions only protect against interference with national air quality standards, not with a margin for growth or any other "individually tailored" standard. . . .

Upon consideration of the statute and the relevant case law, we cannot say that the EPA's determination that the Act does not protect future margins for growth is unreasonable. Since Jefferson County has yet to achieve the NAAQSs for SO_2, any "interference" by Gallagher with the asserted margin for growth is necessarily conjectural. Also, the literal language of [CAA § 110(a)(2)(E)] supports the EPA's interpretation. . . . Thus, we decline to disturb the EPA's holding that the Clean Air Act does not require an upwind state to alter an otherwise valid SIP solely because a downwind state that has yet to comply with the NAAQSs has requested such an alteration to protect an asserted margin for growth. . . .

When it denied Jefferson County's petition, EPA interpreted the "prevent attainment or maintenance" language of section 7410 to mean that an interstate polluter, here Gallagher, must "cause or substantially contribute" to a violation of a NAAQS in another state before the pollution abatement provisions are triggered. 47 Fed. Reg. 6624, 6628 (Feb. 18, 1982). According to this interpretation, a section 126 petition may not be granted unless there is (a) a violation of the NAAQSs in one state and (b) pollution emissions in another state which substantially contribute to the violation. Jefferson County particularly objects to the use of the term "substantial contribution," describing it as "an unduly restrictive approach" which fails to consider the equitable elements of the Clean Air Act.

Essentially, Jefferson County's objection concerns the meaning of the word "prevent" in section 7410(a)(2)(E)(i). Since the Clean Air Act itself offers no guidance as to what levels of pollution "prevent attainment and maintenance" of the NAAQSs, this language is open to differing interpretations. The County disagrees with the EPA's conclusion that, since only about three percent of the pollutants in areas which violate the SO_2 NAAQSs in Kentucky are attributable to Gallagher, the plant does not "prevent attainment or maintenance" of the NAAQSs in Jefferson County. The County asserts that in effect the EPA has amended section 126 of the Act by adding a requirement that there be a showing that a polluting state "substantially contributes" to a violation of the NAAQSs in the downwind state before a section 126 petition can be granted. The County urges an approach whereby any contribution by a polluting state to a NAAQS violation in a receiving state would be forbidden under section 126: "If the sending state contributes 100% to a problem, then it will be required to contribute 100% of the solution. If the contribution is 1%, then the solution is 1% and any amounts in between." . . .

Upon examining the language of the Clean Air Act, we believe that the test probably intended by Congress is whether one state "significantly contributes" to NAAQS violations in another state. Although this test is not specifically incorporated into the statute, we do find reference to the phrase in section 126(a), [CAA § 126(a)], of the Act, which requires written notice to nearby states of interstate pollution. This new section of the Act provides that all nearby states are entitled to notice of any proposed new or modified source of pollution "which may significantly contribute to levels of air pollution in excess of the national ambient air quality standards in any air quality control region outside the state in which such source intends to locate (or makes such modifications)." *Id.* Since the purpose of written notice is to enable affected states to take action, it seems logical to infer that in enacting section 126, Congress intended to prohibit interstate pollution which does or will "significantly contribute to levels of air pollution in excess of the national air quality standards." We do not believe that Congress intended to prohibit even *de minimis* contributions by one state to NAAQS violations in another state because such a policy would in effect "hold one state hostage to another's failure to enact the pollution control strategies necessary to conform to the requirements of the Clean Air Act." *Connecticut v. EPA*, 696 F.2d 147, 164 (2d Cir.1982).

Having concluded that the proper test to be applied in evaluating the section 126 petition is whether Gallagher's emissions "significantly contribute" to NAAQS violations in Jefferson County, we must ascertain whether the EPA was correct in its determination that Gallagher's emissions are permissible. . . . For the purposes of this opinion, we decline to delve into the semantic distinctions between "substantial" and "significant" and choose to treat the terms as having the same meaning. We are convinced that the broad deference which we are statutorily required to accord to the findings of the Agency preclude our disturbing the EPA's determination, at least absent any other criteria established by the EPA, or found elsewhere in the Act, that would require a different result. Jefferson County points to the fact that, although Gallagher may contribute only three percent to actual NAAQS violations, Gallagher contributes a substantially greater percentage of the pollutants present in parts of the County where the NAAQSs are not violated. However, [CAA § 110(a)(2)(E)] appears to contemplate interstate pollution abatement actions only where interstate emissions prevent attainment of the NAAQSs, *i.e.*, only where the standards are violated. Thus, we believe that the EPA did not err in denying Jefferson County's section 126 petition.

NOTES AND QUESTIONS

1. Disparities in State Behavior. Jefferson County was in nonattainment. Louisville Gas & Electric had to install scrubbers (at a cost of $138 million) while its neighbor across the border, Gallagher, was polluting unrestrained. Should this disparity be relevant to the analysis?

2. PSD and Interstate Pollution. What would the result have been if Jefferson County had been designated a PSD area? What percent degradation would be "significant"?

3.   State Ambient Standards and Margins for Growth. What would have happened if Kentucky had enacted a more stringent ambient standard than the NAAQS? Could a downwind state make a more stringent state ambient standard to enjoin upwind pollution? Should it be able to do so? Should a state be able to "reserve" a margin for growth for its own sources?

4.   Nonattainment and Interstate Pollution. Why was the 3 percent contribution not deemed "significant"? What percentage would be considered significant? Why was the 47 percent contribution not relevant?

B.   A QUARTER CENTURY OF EFFORTS TO CONTROL REGIONAL POLLUTION

The Northeast region of the United States has some of the most severe ozone pollution in the country. Though ozone in the upper atmosphere provides protection from ultraviolet radiation, in the lower atmosphere and at ground level it has negative effects on plants and animals, and on human health. It is one of the pollutants that makes up smog. Ozone is not emitted directly into the atmosphere, but forms as a result of chemical reactions of ozone precursors, including NO_x and volatile organic compounds. Ozone is a regional pollutant, often affecting regions far from where ozone precursor pollutants were emitted. EPA observed that "the smog that causes health problems in New York City is the result, in part, of cars driven in Pennsylvania, Maryland and elsewhere in the northeast." EPA, Finding of Significant Contribution and Rulemaking for Certain States in the Ozone Transport Assessment Group Region for Purposes of Reducing Regional Transport of Ozone, 60 Fed. Reg. 4712, 4713 (1995). EPA estimated in 1998 that, along the Northeast corridor, cumulatively upwind states including adjacent states, contributed 83 percent of Washington, DC's nonattainment problem; 68 percent of Maryland's nonattainment problem; 65 percent of Pennsylvania's nonattainment problem; and 85 to 88 percent of each of New Jersey's, New York's, Connecticut's, and Massachusetts's nonattainment problems. EPA, Finding of Significant Contribution and Rulemaking for Certain States in the Ozone Transport Assessment Group Region for Purposes of Reducing Regional Transport of Ozone, 63 Fed. Reg. 57,356, 57,403–04 (1998). For the last quarter century, EPA has endeavored to bring this problem under control.

i.   LOW EMISSION VEHICLE PROGRAM FOR THE NORTHEAST OZONE TRANSPORT REGION

In 1990, Congress amended the CAA to address regional transport in the Northeastern states. *See* Pub. L. 101–549, 104 Stat. 2423 (1990). Section 184, established the Northeastern Ozone Transport Commission (NOTC) to coordinate reductions in air pollution in that region. NOTC recommended that the Northeastern states adopt California's motor vehicle emissions standards to address the ozone transport problem hazard. EPA subsequently issued a SIP call requiring all Northeastern states to adopt these standards. EPA, Final Rule on Ozone Transport Commission; Low Emission Vehicle Program for the Northeast Ozone Transport Region, 60 Fed. Reg. 4712, 4713 (1995). The Commonwealth of Virginia, a member of the NOTC that had voted against the NOTC's adoption of the California emissions standard, sued EPA, alleging that its SIP call violated both the CAA and the Constitution by directing the states to adopt a particular regulatory measure.

EPA argued that the 1990 amendments, which added § 110(k)(5), authorized it to issue SIP calls that proposed particular measures, because of the inclusion of the phrase "revise the plan as necessary." In *Virginia v. EPA*, 108 F.3d 1397, 1398 (D.C. Cir. 1997), the D.C. Circuit rejected EPA's interpretation of § 110(k)(5), and held that the CAA did not authorize EPA to condition SIP approval on the adoption of particular measures. *Id.* at 1410 ("We would have to see much clearer language to believe a statute allowed a federal agency to intrude so deeply into state political processes.").

ii.   NOx SIP CALL

In 1998, EPA issued a NOx SIP call affecting twenty-three Mid-Western and Eastern states that EPA identified as "significant" contributors to downwind nonattainment of NOx (an ozone precursor) emissions. EPA, Finding of Significant Contribution and Rulemaking for Certain States in the Ozone Transport Assessment Group Region for Purposes of Reducing Regional Transport of Ozone, 63 Fed. Reg. 57,359 (1998). EPA decided what pollution was "significant" in light of the magnitude, frequency and relative amount of pollution a state contributed to a downwind state's nonattainment; and the cost of reducing that pollution. As a result, the point at which emissions were "significant," whether measured in volume of NOx emitted or arriving in nonattainment areas, varied from state to state, depending on variations in control costs. Each state was then required to reduce its significant emissions by the amount achievable were the state to implement "highly cost effective controls" (*i.e.*, those reductions that could be achieved for less than $2000 per ton). Each state was given discretion in what mechanisms it used to actually achieve the required reductions, and was also given the option to enter a NOx budget trading program that allowed an emitter to purchase NOx "allowances" from sources that elected to over-control.

In *Michigan v. EPA*, 213 F.3d 663 (D.C. Cir. 2000), state, industry and labor petitioners argued that § 110(a)(2)(D) prohibited any consideration of costs or cost-effectiveness in determining which contributions are significant. The D.C. Circuit upheld the SIP call. The Court held that EPA could consider costs because "the term 'significant' does not in itself convey a thought that significance should be measured in only one dimension—here, in the petitioners' view, health alone." *Id.* at 677. It observed that there is "nothing in the text, structure or history of § 110(a)(2)(D) that bars EPA from considering cost in its application," and that "[w]ithout consideration of cost it is hard to see why *any* ozone-creating emissions should not be regarded as fatally 'significant' under § 110(a)(2)(D)(i)(I)." *Id.* at 678.

Judge Sentelle dissented, arguing that EPA had exceeded its statutory authority. He argued that § 110(a)(2)(D) empowered the EPA to base its actions on amounts of pollutants, to be measured in terms of significance of contribution to downwind nonattainment. "[N]o reasonable reading of the statutory provision in its entirety allows the term significantly to springboard costs of alleviation into EPA's statutorily-defined authority." *Id.* at 696.

Michigan v. EPA limited *Virginia v. EPA* to situations in which the states would be compelled to regulate in a particular way. The trading scheme was valid because the states had a "myriad of reasonably cost-effective options" available to them and were not required to participate in the NOx market to achieve their NOx emissions reductions. Nevertheless, all of the affected states ultimately chose to participate in the NOx market. *See* EPA, EVALUATING OZONE CONTROL PROGRAMS IN THE EASTERN UNITED STATES: FOCUS ON NOx BUDGET TRADING PROGRAM, 2004 (2004).

iii. CLEAN AIR INTERSTATE RULE

In 2005, EPA promulgated the Clean Air Interstate Rule (CAIR), to reduce or eliminate the impact of upwind sources on out-of-state downwind nonattainment of NAAQS for fine particulate matter ($PM_{2.5}$) and eight-hour ozone. Like the trading program considered in *Michigan v. EPA*, CAIR derived its statutory authority from § 110(a)(2)(D)(i)(I). The rule required 28 upwind states and the District of Columbia to revise their SIPs to include control measures to reduce emissions of SO_2 and NOx, which are precursors to $PM_{2.5}$ and ozone formation. CAIR provided that a state was subject to the rule if the state contributed 0.2 mg/m^3 or more of $PM_{2.5}$ to out-of-state downwind areas in nonattainment; or if it contributed more than 2 ppb or one percent of ozone concentration to a nonattainment area's ozone concentration level; and its contributions were significant in magnitude, frequency, or relative to the amount by which an area's ozone contribution was in nonattainment. If a state were deemed a "significant contributor," it would be required to reduce its emissions by the level of reduction that could be achieved by applying "highly cost-effective" emissions controls. *North Carolina v. EPA*, 531 F.3d 896, 904 (D.C. Cir. 2008). To implement CAIR's emission reductions, the rule also created an optional interstate trading program for each pollutant. All upwind sources were required to participate in the trading program unless they were located in a state that revised its SIP to achieve the emissions reductions required by CAIR. *See North Carolina v. EPA*, 531 F.3d 896 (D.C. Cir. 2008).

The D.C. Circuit, with Chief Judge Sentelle and Judges Rogers and Brown on the panel, struck down the rule for two reasons. First, it held that CAIR was invalid because the language of § 110(a)(2)(D)(i)(I) requires EPA to measure each upwind state's contribution to downwind nonattainment. In the absence of such information, EPA had no statutory authority for CAIR. Second, the Court held that § 110(a)(2)(D)(i)(I) required that any interstate pollution reduction program "must do more than achieve something measurable; it must actually require elimination of emissions from sources that contribute significantly and interfere with maintenance in downwind nonattainment areas." *Id.* at 908. The Court held that the cap-and-trade program set out in CAIR did not guarantee such a result. "Theoretically, sources in Alabama could purchase enough NO_x and SO_2 allowance to cover all their current emissions, resulting in no change in Alabama's contribution to Davidson County, North Carolina's nonattainment. CAIR only assures that the entire region's significant contribution will be eliminated." *Id.* at 907.

iv.   TRANSPORT RULE

In response to *North Carolina v. EPA*, EPA promulgated a new regulation to replace CAIR and address interstate pollution transport. *See* EPA, Federal Implementation Plans: Interstate Transport of Fine Particulate Matter and Ozone and Correction of SIP Approvals, 76 Fed. Reg. 48,208 (2011) (Transport Rule). Like CAIR, the Transport Rule (also referred to as the Cross-State Air Pollution Rule) is a SIP call for the Midwestern and Eastern United States, covering 27 states. Under the Transport Rule, a state is deemed to make a "significant contribution" to downwind pollution if it contributes at least one percent of emissions of a downwind state in nonattainment. The Transport Rule establishes state-specific emission budgets based on EPA's evaluation of each state's "significant contribution" to nonattainment of fine particulate matter ($PM_{2.5}$) and/or 8-hour ozone NAAQS in downwind states that could be eliminated at a cost of less than $500 per ton. *Id.* at 48,210. The rule allows for trading of emission allowances among covered states, but under the associated FIPs, trading is constrained by the requirement that each state limit its emissions to its individual budget. *See id.* at 48,212.

No state west of Texas is covered by the rule, while nearly all states east of Texas are. For a map of covered states, see EPA, Map of States Covered by CSAPR, https://www.epa.gov/airmarkets/map-states-covered-csapr (last visited Oct. 2, 2018).

Section 110(a)(2)(D)(i), also known as the Good Neighbor Provision, requires that states prohibit in-state sources "from emitting any air pollutant in amounts which will . . . contribute significantly" to downwind states' "nonattainment . . . , or interfere with maintenance," of any NAAQS, but leaves it to the states to determine how they comply with this requirement. EPA's Transport Rule requires that, to comply with the Good Neighbor Provision, states reduce particulate matter and 8-hour ozone from power plants to the levels set by the rule. At the same time that EPA promulgated the Transport Rule, it also issued a FIP for each state covered by the rule, on the grounds that none of those states had a SIP that complied with the Good Neighbor Provision. States were not given an opportunity to revise their SIPs to comply with the Transport Rule.

In *EME Homer City Generation v. EPA*, 696 F.3d 7 (D.C. Cir. 2012), the D.C. Circuit held that the Transport Rule, and the FIPs, were invalid because the states' emissions budgets were not calculated by reference to the "amounts" of emissions that "contribute significantly to nonattainment," but rather on region-wide modeling of the effect of the reduction that took into account the cost of reduction in various regions. The majority, comprising Judges Kavanaugh and Griffith, maintained that *Michigan v. EPA* allowed EPA to consider costs in order to "allow some upwind State to do *less* than their full fair share," but that it was impermissible to ask "one upwind State to eliminate *more* than its statutory fair share, [because] that State is necessarily being forced to clean up another upwind State's share of the mess in the downwind State." *Id.* at 27. Further, the Transport Rule impermissibly risked requiring a state to reduce its emissions by more than was required to achieve the NAAQS in the downwind states.

As to the FIPs, the D.C. Circuit held that under the Clean Air Act "the Federal Government establishes air quality standards, but States have primary responsibility for attaining those standards within their borders." *Id.* at 29. EPA's promulgation of a FIP at the same time that it issued the Transport Rule violated that statutory scheme. The structure and text of the CAA required that the EPA give the state an opportunity to comply with the Good Neighbor Provision (as quantified by the Transport Rule) before promulgating a FIP. Accordingly, the D.C. Circuit vacated the Transport Rule and the corresponding FIPs. Judge Rogers dissented, principally on the basis that for procedural reasons, the court did not have jurisdiction to hear the matter. The Supreme Court granted EPA's certiorari petition. *See EPA v. EME Homer City Generation*, 572 U.S. 489 (2014), *infra*.

NOTES AND QUESTIONS

1. *Michigan* **and** *North Carolina* **Compared.** What differences were there between the regulatory schemes in *Michigan* and *North Carolina*? How were costs taken into account in the NO$_X$ Rule? How were they taken into account under CAIR? If an upwind state's pollution reduction requirements are lessened by consideration of costs, how is the additional burden allocated? Is that a desirable outcome?

Judges Williams and Rogers formed the majority in *Michigan v. EPA*, with Judge Sentelle in dissent. *North Carolina v. EPA* was a unanimous decision of Chief Judge Sentelle and Judges Rogers and Brown. Recall the dissent of Judge Sentelle in *Michigan v. EPA*, discussed *supra*. To what extent is the decision in *North Carolina* foreshadowed by and consistent with his dissent in *Michigan v. EPA*? What difference do you think that the composition of the respective panels may have made to the outcome in each case? *See* Richard L. Revesz, *Environmental Regulation, Ideology, and the D.C. Circuit*, 83 VA. L. REV. 1717 (1997).

The *North Carolina* opinion states that in *Michigan v. EPA* the court "never passed on the lawfulness of the NOx SIP Call's trading program." *North Carolina v. EPA*, 531 F.3d at 908. In the *Michigan* opinion, the court mentions that "[o]f course we are able to assume the existence of EPA's allowance trading program only because no one has challenged its adoption." *Michigan v. EPA*, 213 F.3d at 676. Why might the petitioners in *Michigan* have declined to challenge the statutory authority for the NOx SIP Call trading program?

Under the court's reasoning in *North Carolina*, was the NOx SIP Call program at issue in *Michigan* lawful under § 110(k)? Can the state-specific budgets applied in the NOx SIP Call be distinguished from the regional approach taken by EPA in CAIR?

2.   Attitudes to Trading Schemes. In *North Carolina*, the court was concerned that "under CAIR, sources in Alabama, which contribute to nonattainment of $PM_{2.5}$ NAAQS in Davidson County, North Carolina, would not need to reduce their emissions at all. Theoretically, sources in Alabama could purchase enough NOx and SO_2 allowances to cover all their current emissions, resulting in no change in Alabama's contribution to Davidson County, North Carolina's nonattainment. CAIR only assures that the entire region's significant contribution will be eliminated." *North Carolina v. EPA*, 531 F.3d at 908. Is this an accurate characterization of the effect of an emissions trading scheme?

The D.C. Circuit compared CAIR to the emissions reduction scheme in *Michigan v. EPA*. It stated that in *Michigan*, the court "deferred to EPA's decision to apply uniform emissions controls to all upwind states despite different levels of contribution of NOx to nonattainment areas . . . because these effects flow ineluctably from the EPA's decision to draw the 'significant contribution' line on a basis of cost differentials." *Id.* at 908. Yet CAIR was invalid because EPA evaluated its emissions reductions at the regionwide level and "never measured the 'significant contribution' from sources within an individual state to downwind nonattainment areas. . . . Thus EPA's apportionment decisions have nothing to do with each state's 'significant contribution.' " *Id.* at 907. What is the difference between the calculation of state pollution budgets in *Michigan* and *North Carolina* that justifies the different outcomes? Or can the different outcomes only be explained on the basis that the *North Carolina* panel had an antipathy to an emissions trading scheme?

Neither the NOx Rule nor CAIR limited interstate trading of emissions allowances. The Transport Rule allows sources to trade allowances across state borders, so long as the trade does not cause a state to exceed its emissions budget. Why do you think that this limitation was introduced? Is such a constraint desirable? Is it necessary? How will it affect the market in emissions allowances?

3. ***North Carolina*** **and** ***American Trucking.*** Recall *American Trucking*, excerpted above in Section 2 of this chapter, which concluded that costs could not be considered in setting the NAAQS. *Michigan v. EPA* was decided the year before the *American Trucking* decision. In *American Trucking*, the Supreme Court, citing *Michigan*, held that "[n]one of the sections of the CAA in which the District of Columbia Circuit has found authority for the EPA to consider costs shares § 109(b)(1)'s prominence in the overall statutory scheme." *American Trucking*, 531 U.S. 457, 469 n.1. *North Carolina* was decided several years after *American Trucking*. The *North Carolina* opinion refers to *American Trucking* only once, concluding that "[a]ll the policy reasons in the world cannot justify reading a substantive provision out of a statute." *North Carolina*, 531 F.3d 896, 910 (D.C. Cir. 2008). What substantive provision did the D.C. Circuit think was being read out of the statute?

How might the *American Trucking* decision have influenced the *North Carolina* court? Compare the statutory text in § 109 that governs the setting of a NAAQS standard and was at issue in *American Trucking* with the text of § 110(a)(2)(D)(i)(I). Should it matter that § 109 sets a standard while § 110 prescribes part of the means to achieve the standard?

4.   Tenth Amendment. Consider the SIP call challenged in *Virginia*. Why did a SIP call, issued by a federal agency, requiring Midwestern and Northeastern states to adopt California's vehicle emissions standards, not violate the Tenth Amendment?

5.   Court's Remedy. In expectation of CAIR's application, downwind states had already incorporated the rule's pollution reductions into their air quality planning and many power companies had already made or planned pollution control investments to meet the rule's requirements. The court's decision in *North Carolina v. EPA* to vacate CAIR, setting aside its application and enforcement, threw these existing plans into disarray. *See* Del Quentin Wilber & Marc Kaufman, *Judges Toss EPA Rule To Reduce Smog, Soot; It Was Agency's Most Aggressive Air Measure*, WASH. POST, July 12, 2008, at A1.

In response, EPA filed a petition requesting that CAIR not be vacated during the remand. The court reversed its decision to vacate the rule, allowing EPA to apply the regulation until the agency promulgated a rule consistent with the court's opinion. *See North Carolina v. EPA*, 550 F.3d 1176 (D.C. Cir. 2008).

Given that the court initially found that the flaws in CAIR were not severable from the remaining portions of the rule, should the court have insisted on the rule's vacatur? Or was it appropriate to remand the rule to the agency, based on the disruption that would have resulted from vacatur? When is a remand without vacatur appropriate? For a discussion of when remand without vacatur is an appropriate remedy, see Kristina Daugirdas, Note, *Evaluating Remand Without Vacatur: A New Judicial Remedy for Defective Agency Rulemakings*, 80 N.Y.U. L. REV. 278 (2005). *See also* Admin.

Conf. of the U.S., *Remand Without Vacatur*, ADMIN. CONF. REC. 2013–16 (2013).

Environmental Protection Agency v. EME Homer City Generation

572 U.S. 489 (2014).

■ JUSTICE GINSBURG delivered the opinion of the Court:

These cases concern the efforts of Congress and the Environmental Protection Agency (EPA or Agency) to cope with a complex problem: air pollution emitted in one State, but causing harm in other States. Left unregulated, the emitting or upwind State reaps the benefits of the economic activity causing the pollution without bearing all the costs. See Revesz, Federalism and Interstate Environmental Externalities, 144 U. PA. L. REV. 2341, 2343 (1996). Conversely, downwind States to which the pollution travels are unable to achieve clean air because of the influx of out-of-state pollution they lack authority to control. To tackle the problem, Congress included a Good Neighbor Provision in the Clean Air Act (Act or CAA). That provision, in its current phrasing, instructs States to prohibit in-state sources "from emitting any air pollutant in amounts which will ... contribute significantly" to downwind States' "nonattainment ... , or interfere with maintenance," of any EPA-promulgated national air quality standard. 42 U.S.C. § 7410(a)(2)(D)(i).

Interpreting the Good Neighbor Provision, EPA adopted the Cross-State Air Pollution Rule (commonly and hereinafter called the Transport Rule). The rule calls for consideration of costs, among other factors, when determining the emission reductions an upwind State must make to improve air quality in polluted downwind areas. The Court of Appeals for the D.C. Circuit vacated the rule in its entirety. It held, 2 to 1, that the Good Neighbor Provision requires EPA to consider only each upwind State's physically proportionate responsibility for each downwind State's air quality problem. That reading is demanded, according to the D.C. Circuit, so that no State will be required to decrease its emissions by more than its ratable share of downwind-state pollution. . . .

The rule challenged here . . . is EPA's response to the D.C. Circuit's *North Carolina* decision. Finalized in August 2011, the Transport Rule curtails NO_X and SO_2 emissions of 27 upwind States to achieve downwind attainment of three different NAAQS: the two 1997 NAAQS previously addressed by CAIR, and the 2006 NAAQS for $PM_{2.5}$ levels measured on a daily basis.

Under the Transport Rule, EPA employed a "two-step approach" to determine when upwind States "contribute[d] significantly to nonattainment," *id.,* at 48254, and therefore in "amounts" that had to be eliminated. At step one, called the "screening" analysis, the Agency excluded as *de minimis* any upwind State that contributed less than one percent of the three NAAQS to any downwind State "receptor," a location at which EPA measures air quality. If all of an upwind State's contributions fell below the one-percent threshold, that State would be considered not to have "contribute[d] significantly" to the nonattainment of any downwind State. States in that category were screened out and exempted from regulation under the rule.

The remaining States were subjected to a second inquiry, which EPA called the "control" analysis. At this stage, the Agency sought to generate a cost-effective allocation of emission reductions among those upwind States "screened in" at step one.

The control analysis proceeded this way. EPA first calculated, for each upwind State, the quantity of emissions the State could eliminate at each of several cost thresholds. Cost for these purposes is measured as cost per ton of emissions prevented, for instance, by installing scrubbers on powerplant smokestacks. EPA estimated, for example, the amount each upwind State's NOx emissions would fall if all pollution sources within each State employed every control measure available at a cost of $500 per ton or less. The Agency then repeated that analysis at ascending cost thresholds. See *ibid* . . . "Moving beyond the $500 cost threshold," EPA concluded, "would result in only minimal additional . . . reductions [in emissions]."

Finally, EPA translated the cost thresholds it had selected into amounts of emissions upwind States would be required to eliminate.

Taken together, the screening and control inquiries defined EPA's understanding of which upwind emissions were within the Good Neighbor Provision's ambit. In short, under the Transport Rule, an upwind State "contribute[d] significantly" to downwind nonattainment to the extent its exported pollution both (1) produced one percent or more of a NAAQS in at least one downwind State (step one) and (2) could be eliminated cost-effectively, as determined by EPA (step two). Upwind States would be obliged to eliminate all and only emissions meeting both of these criteria.

For each State regulated by the Transport Rule, EPA contemporaneously promulgated a FIP allocating that State's emission budget among its in-state sources. For each of these States, EPA had determined that the State had failed to submit a SIP adequate for compliance with the Good Neighbor Provision. . . .

If EPA determines a SIP to be inadequate, the Agency's mandate to replace it with a FIP is no less absolute [than a State's obligation to adopt a SIP that satisfies the Good Neighbor Provision]:

"[EPA] shall promulgate a [FIP] at any time within 2 years after the [Agency]

"(A) finds that a State has failed to make a required submission or finds that the plan or plan revision submitted by the State does not satisfy the minimum [relevant] criteria . . . , or

"(B) disapproves a [SIP] in whole or in part,

"unless the State corrects the deficiency, and [EPA] approves the plan or plan revision, before the [Agency] promulgates such [FIP]." § 7410(c)(1).

In other words, once EPA has found a SIP inadequate, the Agency has a statutory duty to issue a FIP "at any time" within two years (unless the State first "corrects the deficiency," which no one contends occurred here). . . .

Nothing in the Act differentiates the Good Neighbor Provision from the several other matters a State must address in its SIP. Rather, the statute speaks without reservation: Once a NAAQS has been issued, a State "shall" propose a SIP within three years, § 7410(a)(1), and that SIP "shall" include, among other components, provisions adequate to satisfy the Good Neighbor Provision, § 7410(a)(2).

Nor does the Act condition the duty to promulgate a FIP on EPA's having first quantified an upwind State's good neighbor obligations . . . The Act empowers the Agency to promulgate a FIP "at any time" within the two-year limit. Carving out an exception to the Act's precise deadlines, as the D.C. Circuit did, "rewrites a decades-old statute whose plain text and structure establish a clear chronology of federal and State responsibilities." 696 F.3d, at 47 (Rogers, J., dissenting).

The practical difficulties cited by the Court of Appeals do not justify departure from the Act's plain text. See *Barnhart v. Sigmon Coal Co.*, 534 U.S. 438, 461–462 (2002) (We "must presume that a legislature says in a statute what it means and means in a statute what it says there."). When Congress elected to make EPA's input a prerequisite to state action under the Act, it did so expressly. States developing vehicle inspection and maintenance programs under the CAA, for example, must await EPA guidance before issuing SIPs. 42 U.S.C. § 7511a(c)(3)(B). A State's obligation to adopt a SIP, moreover, arises only after EPA has first set the NAAQS the State must meet. § 7410(a)(1). Had Congress intended similarly to defer States' discharge of their obligations under the Good Neighbor Provision, Congress, we take it, would have included a similar direction in that section. . . .

The statute requires States to eliminate those "amounts" of pollution that "contribute significantly to *nonattainment*" in downwind States. 42 U.S.C. § 7410(a)(2)(D)(i) (emphasis added). Thus, EPA's task is to reduce upwind pollution, but only in "amounts" that push a downwind State's pollution concentrations above the relevant NAAQS. As noted earlier, however, the nonattainment of downwind States results from the collective and interwoven contributions of multiple upwind States. The statute therefore calls upon the Agency to address a thorny causation problem: How should EPA allocate among multiple contributing upwind States responsibility for a downwind State's excess pollution?

A simplified example illustrates the puzzle EPA faced. Suppose the Agency sets a NAAQS, with respect to a particular pollutant, at 100 parts per billion (ppb), and that the level of the pollutant in the atmosphere of downwind State A is 130 ppb. Suppose further that EPA has determined that each of three upwind States—X, Y, and Z—contributes the equivalent of 30 ppb of the relevant pollutant to State A's airspace. The Good Neighbor Provision, as just observed, prohibits only upwind emissions that contribute significantly to downwind *nonattainment*. EPA's authority under the provision is therefore limited to eliminating a *total* of 30 ppb, *i.e.,* the overage caused by the collective contribution of States X, Y, and Z.

How is EPA to divide responsibility among the three States? Should the Agency allocate reductions proportionally (10 ppb each), on a per capita basis, on the basis of the cost of abatement, or by some other metric? The Good Neighbor Provision does not answer that question for EPA. Cf. *Chevron,* 467 U.S., at 860 ("[T]he language of [the CAA] simply does not compel any given interpretation of the term 'source.'"). . . .

[T]he Court of Appeals believed that the Act speaks clearly, requiring EPA to allocate responsibility for reducing emissions in "a manner proportional to" each State's "contributio[n]" to the problem. Nothing in the text of the Good Neighbor Provision propels EPA down this path. Understandably so, for as EPA notes, the D.C. Circuit's proportionality approach could scarcely be satisfied in practice. . . .

The dissent, for its part, strains to give meaning to the D.C. Circuit's proportionality constraint as applied to a world in which multiple upwind States contribute emissions to multiple downwind locations. . . . The dissent's formulation, however, does not account for the combined and cumulative effect of each upwind State's reductions on attainment in multiple downwind locations. See *ibid.* ("Under a proportional-reduction approach, State X would be required to eliminate emissions of that pollutant by whatever minimum amount reduces *both* State A's level by 0.2 unit and State B's by 0.7 unit." (emphasis added)). The result would be costly overregulation unnecessary to, indeed in conflict with, the Good Neighbor Provision's goal of attainment.

In the dissent's view, upwind States must eliminate emissions by "whatever minimum amount reduces" their share of the overage in each and every one of the downwind States to which they are linked. In practical terms, this means each upwind State will be required to reduce emissions by the amount necessary to eliminate that State's largest downwind contribution. The dissent's formulation, however, does not account for the combined and cumulative effect of each upwind State's reductions on attainment in multiple downwind locations: "Under a proportional-reduction approach, State X would be required to eliminate emissions of that pollutant by whatever minimum amount reduces *both* State A's level by 0.2 unit and State B's by 0.7 unit." (emphasis added).

The result would be costly overregulation unnecessary to, indeed in conflict with, the Good Neighbor Provision's goal of attainment. . . .

Persuaded that the Good Neighbor Provision does not dictate the particular allocation of emissions among contributing States advanced by the D.C. Circuit, we must next decide whether the allocation method chosen by EPA is a "permissible construction of the statute." *Chevron,* 467 U.S. 837, at 843. . . .

Using costs in the Transport Rule calculus, we agree with EPA, also makes good sense. Eliminating those amounts that can cost-effectively be reduced is an efficient and equitable solution to the allocation problem the Good Neighbor Provision requires the Agency to address. Efficient because EPA can achieve the levels of attainment, *i.e.,* of emission reductions, the proportional approach aims to achieve, but at a much lower overall cost. Equitable because, by imposing uniform cost thresholds on regulated States, EPA's rule subjects to stricter regulation those States that have done relatively less in the past to control their pollution. Upwind States that have not yet implemented pollution controls of the same stringency as their neighbors will be stopped from free riding on their neighbors' efforts to reduce pollution. They will have to bring down their emissions by installing devices of the kind in which neighboring States have already invested. . . .

Lacking a dispositive statutory instruction to guide it, EPA's decision, we conclude, is a "reasonable" way of filling the "gap left open by Congress." *Chevron,* 467 U.S., at 866. . . .

We agree with the Court of Appeals to this extent: EPA cannot require a State to reduce its output of pollution by more than is necessary to achieve attainment in every downwind State or at odds with the one-percent threshold the Agency has set. If EPA requires an upwind State to reduce emissions by more than the amount necessary to achieve attainment in *every* downwind State to which it is linked, the Agency will have overstepped its authority, under the Good Neighbor Provision, to eliminate those "amounts [that] contribute . . . to nonattainment." Nor can EPA demand reductions that would drive an upwind State's contribution to every downwind State to which it is linked below one percent of the relevant NAAQS. Doing so would be counter to step one of the Agency's interpretation of the Good Neighbor Provision. . . .

■ JUSTICE SCALIA, with whom JUSTICE THOMAS joins, dissenting:

I would affirm the judgment of the D.C. Circuit that EPA violated the law both in crafting the Transport Rule and in implementing it. . . .

As described in the Government's briefing:

"[T]he term 'significantly' . . . is ambiguous, and. . . EPA may permissibly determine the amount of a State's 'significant' contribution by reference to the amount of emissions reductions achievable through application of highly cost-effective controls."

. . .

But of course the statute does not focus on whether the upwind State has "achieved significantly"; it asks whether the State has "contributed significantly" to downwind pollution. The provision addresses the physical effects of physical causes, and it is only the magnitude of the relationship sufficient to trigger regulation that admits of some vagueness. Stated differently, the statute is ambiguous as to *how much* of a contribution to downwind pollution is "significant," but it is not at all ambiguous as to whether factors unrelated to the *amounts of pollutants* that make up a contribution affect the analysis. Just as "[i]t does not matter whether the word 'yellow' is ambiguous when the agency has interpreted it to mean 'purple,'" *United States v. Home Concrete & Supply, LLC,* 566 U.S. ___, ___, n. 1 (2012) (SCALIA, J., concurring in part and concurring in judgment), it does not matter whether the phrase "amounts which . . . contribute significantly [to downwind NAAQS nonattainment]" is ambiguous when EPA has interpreted it to mean "amounts which are inexpensive to eliminate."

It would be extraordinary for Congress, by use of the single word "significantly," to transmogrify a statute that assigns responsibility on the basis of amounts of pollutants emitted into a statute authorizing EPA to reduce interstate pollution in the manner that it believes most efficient. We have repeatedly said that Congress "does not alter the fundamental details of a regulatory scheme in vague terms or ancillary provisions—it does not, one might say, hide elephants in mouseholes." *Whitman v. American Trucking Assns., Inc.,* 531 U.S. 457, 468. . . .

The Good Neighbor Provision is one of the requirements with which SIPs must comply. § 7410(a)(2)(D)(i)(I). The statutory structure [of the *Clean Air Act*] . . . plainly demands that EPA afford States a meaningful opportunity to allocate reduction responsibilities among the sources within their borders. But the majority holds that EPA may in effect force the States to guess at what those responsibilities might be by requiring them to submit SIPs before learning what the Agency regards as a "significan[t]" contribution—with the consequence of losing their regulatory primacy if they guess wrong. . . .

The majority attempts to place the blame for hollowing out the core of the Clean Air Act on "the Act's plain text." The first textual element to which it refers is § 7410(c)'s requirement that after EPA has disapproved a SIP, it "shall promulgate a [FIP] at any time within 2 years." That is to say, the Agency has discretion whether to act at once or to defer action until some later point during the 2-year period. But it also has discretion to work within the prescribed timetable to respect the rightful role of States in the statutory scheme by delaying the issuance or enforcement of FIPs pending the resubmission and approval of SIPs—as EPA's conduct surrounding CAIR clearly demonstrates. And all of this assumes that the Agency insists on disapproving SIPs before promulgating the applicable good-neighbor standards—though in fact EPA has discretion to publicize those metrics before the window to submit SIPs closes in the first place.

NOTES AND QUESTIONS

1. **Significant Contribution and the Cost of Reduction.** How did the majority interpret the phrase "significant contribution"? How does the dissent respond? Which is more persuasive? Can the term "significant contribution" include a component related to the necessary effort? Is a contribution of $10,000 to a charity equally significant for Bill Gates as for a middle class person? Is this analogy relevant to the understanding of the case?

2. **Industry Petitioners' Argument.** In this matter, industry and labor petitioners argued that the EPA was not entitled to consider the cost of reduction when deciding what amounts to a "significant contribution." Counsel for industry petitioners argued that "there are always going to be legitimate policy arguments in favor of the least cost, most efficient solution to any problem. But we would also say that there are countervailing policy arguments at issue here." Transcript of Oral Argument at 58, *EPA v. EME Homer City*, 572 U.S. 489 (2013). Why do you think industry argued against a cost-minimization approach? In considering this question, consider that industry petitioners were principally power generators located in the Midwest.

3. **Proportionate Contribution to Nonattainment.** How was a "significant contribution" calculated under the Transport Rule, considered in *EPA v. EME Homer City*? How would the dissent have calculated a significant contribution? Recall *Jefferson County v. EPA, supra*. Can either the majority or dissenting position in *EPA v. EME Homer City* be reconciled with *Jefferson County v. EPA*? What role should proportionality play in determining whether an upwind state "contributes significantly" to nonattainment in a downwind state? To what extent is this issue one for EPA to figure out?

4. **Relevance of *American Trucking*.** In *American Trucking* the Court "refused to find implicit in ambiguous sections of the [CAA] an authorization to consider costs that has elsewhere, and so often, been expressly granted." *Whitman v. American Trucking*, 531 U.S. 457, 467 (2001). *American Trucking* considered § 109(b)(1) of the CAA, which instructs the EPA to set primary NAAQS which are "requisite to protect the public health" with "an adequate margin of safety." In his dissenting opinion in *EME Homer City*, Justice Scalia held that the Court's opinion "turns its back upon [*American Trucking*] and is incompatible with that opinion." The majority held that "[u]nlike the provision at issue in [*American Trucking*], which provides express criteria by which EPA is to set NAAQS, the Good Neighbor Provision . . . fails to provide *any* metric by which EPA can differentiate among the contributions of multiple upwind States." *EPA v. Homer City Generation,* 572 U.S. 489, 520 n.21 (2014). Why might it be justified to consider costs in determining the meaning of the phrase "contributes significantly," but not in determining what constitutes an "adequate margin of safety," or what is

"requisite to protect the public health"? Consider the language of each provision. Consider also the different purposes of the two provisions: one governs how the health-based NAAQS level is set, while the other governs an aspect of its implementation. How might the different roles of the two provisions justify distinct approaches to interpreting congressional silence?

5.   Over-Control of Interstate Pollution. Emissions from State A account for 5% of the concentration of an air pollutant in downwind State Y, which is in nonattainment. State A's emissions also contribute 1% to downwind State Z, which is also in nonattainment. If State A reduces its emissions by the amount required under the Transport Rule, State Z's pollution levels will incidentally be reduced below the maximum levels permitted by the NAAQS, at no expense to State Z. What might be the consequence of this result? Could a strictly proportional interpretation of the Good Neighbor Provision overcome this difficulty?

6.   Limits on Federal Control of Interstate Pollution. What limits did the Court place on the power of the EPA to require a state to reduce its pollution? Even within these limits, might there be incidental over-control of some areas in nonattainment?

7.   Allocation of the Cost of Pollution Reduction. If an upwind state can abate pollution more cheaply than a downwind state, which should bear the cost? Why? Are any fairness issues at stake?

8.   Timing of Promulgation of FIPs. Section 110(a)(2) of the CAA requires the EPA to issue a FIP "at any time" within two years of disapproving a SIP. Section 110(a)(a) requires states to submit SIPs "within 3 years" of each new or revised NAAQS "or such shorter period as [EPA] may prescribe." On what basis did the majority decide that a FIP may be promulgated simultaneously with the publication of an upwind state's Good Neighbor provisions? Does the structure of the CAA give any indication that the EPA must prescribe a certain minimum period?

Justice Scalia was concerned that the majority in *EME Homer City* paved the way for the EPA to prescribe a period that states submit SIPs "within a matter of days—or even hours—after a NAAQS" is published. Is such a scenario realistic? When, in his view, might the EPA promulgate a FIP?

9.   Scrivener's Error. Section 126 refers to § 110(a)(2)(D)(ii). In *Appalachian Power Company v. EPA*, 249 F.3d 1032 (D.C. Cir. 2001), the court determined this to be a scrivener's error, and that it should have referred to § 110(a)(2)(D)(i). If the amended § 126 were read literally, it would refer to the amended § 110(a)(2)(D)(ii), which requires the SIP to contain adequate provisions "insuring compliance with the applicable requirements of sections 7426 [§ 126] and 7415 [§ 115] of this title (relating to interstate and international pollution abatement)." Thus, § 126 would no longer authorize petitions for findings that sources in another state contribute significantly to the state's nonattainment problem, and the state would be without the remedy of direct federal regulation of the offending sources.

Acknowledging the high threshold to overcome the "seemingly clear" language of a statute, the court found that threshold met in the § 126 cross-reference; perhaps most critically, § 126 refers to the "prohibition" of § 110(a)(2)(D)(ii)—a section which does not actually contain a prohibition. The court upheld EPA's interpretation of the cross-reference as a scrivener's error and preserved the states' substantive right to compel direct federal regulation of polluting sources in other states.

The CAA is a complex statute, as you have come to appreciate, and even careful drafting may produce occasional errors such as the one highlighted in *Appalachian Power*. What method should the courts use when deciding questions like this one? How critical is a thorough understanding of the statute at a "high level" to deciding questions at a "low level" like "scrivener's errors"?

10. EPA's Use of § 126. In *Appalachian Power Company v. EPA*, 249 F.3d 1032 (D.C. Cir. 2001), the D.C. Circuit evaluated a challenge to EPA's grant of a § 126 petition.

Several downwind states had filed a § 126 petition with EPA at the same time that the agency was developing a SIP call to address the same pollution transport problems. In response to the § 126 petition, EPA made an "affirmative technical determination" that sources in upwind states were indeed contributing to nonattainment in downwind states. The agency nonetheless decided that it withhold a formal § 126 finding until the conclusion of the SIP call except, if any state's response to the SIP call was either unsatisfactory or untimely, the finding would be triggered automatically. A subsequent delay in processing the SIP call triggered the § 126 finding.

The court affirmed that § 126 provided for federal regulation of existing sources and operated independently of EPA's authority to issue a SIP call. The opinion rejected the petitioner's argument that the CAA was "animated by a commitment to 'cooperative federalism' " and thus direct federal regulation under § 126 should operate as a last resort where states could not or did not meet SIP requirements. *Appalachian Power*, 249 F.3d at 1047 ("EPA may not, as part of the 'section 110 process,' intervene in a state's choice of how to reach the NAAQS. We [do] not suggest that under § 110 states may develop their plans free of extrinsic legal constraints. . . . That § 126 imposes one such limitation—and it is surely not the only independent provision of federal law to do so—does not affect a state's discretion under § 110." (internal citations omitted)).

Appalachian Power affirms the role of § 126 petitions in constraining upwind pollution. In what ways is the power afforded to downwind states under § 126 still limited? Are the remedies available under § 126 and the SIP call equivalent?

C.   ACID DEPOSITION

It is a fair and reasonable demand on the part of a sovereign that the air over its territory should not be polluted on a great scale by sulphurous acid gas, that the forests on its mountains, be they better or worse, and whatever domestic destruction they have suffered, should not be further destroyed or threatened by the act of persons beyond its control. . . .

Georgia v. Tenn. Copper Co., 206 U.S. 230, 238 (1907) (opinion by Holmes, J.).

The United States depends heavily on coal-fired power generation for its electricity needs. One by-product of this dependence on coal is the emission of SO_2 and NO_X, criteria pollutants that cause acidification of soils and water, in addition to causing adverse health effects. *See* EPA, Acid Rain, http://www.epa.gov/acidrain/index.html (last visited Sept. 26, 2018). As Justice Holmes' words indicate, emissions of SO_2 and NO_X across state boundaries have long affected neighboring states.

The 1990 Amendments included a new program for the control of acid deposition. The acid deposition control provisions established a new market-based approach to pollution control, contained in Title IV of the CAA. The program set a permanent cap on the total amount of SO_2 that can be emitted nationwide from electric power plants. New and existing electric generating units (EGUs) are allocated a certain quantity of allowances based on historic fuel consumption and emission rates. Some allowances were made available as incentives for EGUs that demonstrated SO_2 emissions reductions prior to compliance obligations coming into force. About three per cent of all allowances available are auctioned on an annual basis. Allowances can also be bought, sold and traded between entities. An EGU must have allowances for each unit of emissions, but may not emit in excess of any other state or federal laws, even if it holds sufficient allowances to do so. The Program requires EGUs to account for each ton of emission, to ensure compliance. This requires continuous monitoring by EGUs, with the records audited by EPA. If an EGU's annual emissions exceed the number of allowances it holds, it must pay a penalty of $2,000 in 1990 dollars, adjusted each year for inflation. It must also offset the excess emissions by surrendering future year allowances. *See* HARV. ENVTL. ECON. PROGRAM, THE SO_2 ALLOWANCE TRADING SYSTEM AND THE CLEAN AIR ACT AMENDMENTS OF 1990 (2012).

The acid rain program distributed allowances in two phases. In the first phase, beginning in 1995, EPA distributed allowances to certain electric generating units (EGUs) at an emission rate of 2.5 pounds of SO_2/MMBtu (SO_2 per million Btu) of heat input, multiplied by the unit's baseline MMBtu. Phase I thus regulated the "big dirties." It did not put a total cap on emissions. In Phase II, beginning in 2000, allowances were distributed to a much broader range of EGUs and other emissions units, at an emission rate of 1.2 pounds of SO_2/MMBtu of heat input, multiplied by the unit's baseline. Phase II also instituted a total cap on SO_2/MMBtu emissions of 8.95 million pounds.

The market operated nationwide, so that emissions units in one state could trade allowances with emissions units in another state. The following cases illustrate the challenges faced by EPA and the states as they implemented the market-based approach to reducing interstate air pollution.

Alliance for Clean Coal v. Miller
44 F.3d 591 (7th Cir. 1995).

■ Before CUMMINGS, CUDAHY, and RIPPLE, CIRCUIT JUDGES.

■ CUMMINGS, CIRCUIT JUDGE:

Plaintiff Alliance for Clean Coal ("Alliance") is a Virginia trade association whose members include Colorado and Oregon coal companies and three railroads that transport coal. The defendants are the chairman and six commissioners of the Illinois Commerce Commission in charge of the administration and enforcement of the Illinois Public Utilities Act.

. . . Coal's sulfur content varies greatly depending on its geographical origin. Western coal, mined west of the Rocky Mountains, generally has the lowest sulfur content of any coal produced in the country. Coal mined in the "Illinois Basin," which includes most of Illinois and parts of Indiana and western Kentucky, is relatively high in sulfur. Burning coal emits sulfur dioxide in an amount proportional to the coal's sulfur content. In the 1970 Amendment to the Clean Air Act, Congress authorized the Environmental Protection Agency ("EPA") to set new standards to regulate various emissions, including sulfur dioxide. The EPA provided for two methods to control sulfur dioxide emissions: (1) the use of low sulfur coal; and (2) the use of pollution control devices ("scrubbers").

In 1977 Congress again amended the Clean Air Act, requiring new electric plants to build scrubbers. By requiring scrubbers regardless of the sulfur content of the coal burned, Congress essentially eliminated for new facilities the low-sulfur coal compliance option that had been available under the 1970 Amendment.

In 1990 Congress once again amended the Act, this time requiring a drastic two-stage reduction in industrial sulfur dioxide emissions in an attempt to combat acid rain. The 1990 Act implements a market-driven approach to emissions regulation, allowing for the free transfer of emission "allowances." The Act is aimed at reducing sulfur dioxide emissions in the most efficient manner and, like the 1970 Act, allows electric generating plants to meet the emission standards in the cheapest way possible. The principal methods of compliance now include installing new scrubbers, using low-sulfur coal, switching to another fuel source, or buying additional emission allowances.

The 1990 amendments meant the end of the salad days for high-sulfur coal-producing states such as Illinois. Low sulfur western coal once again offered a viable alternative to the continued burning of high-sulfur coal combined with the installation of expensive new scrubbers. Faced with potentially damaging competition for the local coal industry, in 1991 the Illinois General Assembly passed the Coal Act, an addition to the Utilities Act, concerning implementation and compliance with the 1990 Clean Air Act amendments. See 220 ILCS 5/8–402.1 Under the Coal Act, utilities must formulate Clean Air Act compliance plans which must be approved by the Illinois Commerce Commission. . . .

Alliance attacks the constitutionality of the Illinois Coal Act under the Commerce Clause of the Constitution. That clause provides that "the Congress shall have power . . . to regulate commerce . . . among the several states." Article I, Section 8, Clause 3. It has long been interpreted to have a "negative" aspect that denies the states the power to discriminate against or burden the interstate flow of articles of commerce. Two recent Supreme Court cases interpreting the negative Commerce Clause are controlling here. In *Oregon Waste Systems v. Department of Environmental Quality*, 511 U.S 93, the Court held that the negative Commerce Clause prohibited a state surcharge on the disposal of solid waste generated out of state. In *West Lynn Creamery, Inc. v. Healy*, 512 U.S 186, the Court struck down a Massachusetts milk-pricing order which employed a tax on all milk sold to fund a subsidy to in-state producers. Because the Illinois Coal Act, like the milk-pricing order in *West Lynn*, has the same effect as a "tariff or customs duty— neutralizing the advantage possessed by lower cost out of state producers," it too is repugnant to the Commerce Clause and the principle of a unitary national economy which that clause was intended to establish. *West Lynn*, 114 S.Ct. at 221.

The Illinois Coal Act is a none-too-subtle attempt to prevent Illinois electric utilities from switching to low-sulfur western coal as a Clean Air Act compliance option. Indeed, the statute itself states that the Illinois General Assembly determined that there was "the need to use coal mined in Illinois" and "the need to maintain and preserve as a valuable State resource the mining of coal in Illinois." 220 ILCS 5/8–402.1(a). The Act implements this protectionist policy in four ways. First, it tilts the overall playing field by requiring that commissioners take account of the effect on the local coal industry when considering compliance plans. Second, the Act requires that certain large generating units install scrubbers "to enable them to continue to burn Illinois coal." 220 ILCS 5/8–402.1(e). Third, the Act guarantees that the cost of these scrubbers can be included in the utility's rate base and passed through to consumers, even where the use of low-sulfur western coal would be a cheaper compliance option. Finally, the Act requires Commerce Commission approval before a utility can make a change in fuel that would result in a 10 percent or greater decrease in the utility's use of Illinois coal. In determining whether to grant approval, the Commerce Commission "shall consider the impact on employment related to the production of coal in Illinois." The intended effect of these provisions is to foreclose the use of low-sulfur western coal by Illinois utilities as a means of complying with the Clean Air Act. This of course amounts to discriminatory state action forbidden by the Commerce Clause.

Illinois seeks to save the Act by claiming that it merely "encourages" the local coal industry and does not in fact discriminate. This argument rings hollow. The Illinois Coal Act cannot continue to exist merely because it does not facially compel the use of Illinois coal or forbid the use of out-of-state coal. As recognized in *West Lynn Creamery*, even ingenious discrimination is forbidden by the Commerce Clause. 114 S.Ct. at 2215. By "encouraging" the use of Illinois coal, the Act discriminates against western coal by making it a less viable compliance option for Illinois generating plants. Moreover, the requirement that certain generators be equipped with scrubbers essentially mandates that these generators burn Illinois coal: that is the purpose of the scrubber requirement, and the Commerce Commission would likely not allow the pass-through of the then-unnecessary additional cost of low-sulfur western coal. Such a mandate runs directly afoul of *Wyoming v. Oklahoma*, 502 U.S. 437 (requirement that Oklahoma generating plants burn 10 percent Oklahoma coal held to violate the Commerce Clause). Similarly, the guaranteed pass-through of the scrubber cost to rate-payers is equivalent to the minimum price fixing for the benefit of local producers held unconstitutional in *Baldwin v. G.A.F. Seelig, Inc.*, 294 U.S. 511.

Illinois argues that it has merely "agreed to 'subsidize' the cost of generating electricity through the use of Illinois coal by requiring its own citizens to bear the cost of pollution control devices." First, the fact that Illinois rate-payers are footing the bill does not cure the discriminatory impact on western coal producers. As the Supreme Court noted in rejecting an identical argument in *West Lynn*, "[t]he cost of a tariff is also borne primarily by local consumers yet a tariff is the paradigmatic Commerce Clause violation." *West Lynn*, 114 S.Ct. at 2216–2217. Second, Illinois' characterization of the Act as an "agreement to subsidize" does not suffice to fit this case into the "market participant" exception to the negative Commerce Clause created in *Hughes v. Alexandria Scrap Corp.*, 426 U.S. 794. Illinois is not acting as a purchaser of either coal or electricity but as a regulator of utilities. The fact that its regulatory action "has the purpose and effect of subsidizing a particular industry . . . does not transform it into a form of state participation in the free market." *New Energy Co. of Indiana v. Limbach*, 486 U.S. 269, 277. . . .

Finally, defendants champion the Illinois Coal Act as a means of protecting Illinois and its citizens from economic harm that would result from a decline in the local coal industry. Such concerns do not justify discrimination against out-of-state producers. "Preservation of local industry by protecting it from the rigors of interstate competition is the hallmark of economic protection that the Commerce Clause prohibits." *West Lynn*, 114 S.Ct. 2217.

The purpose of the Illinois Coal Act was "to maintain and preserve . . . the mining of coal in Illinois" and to continue "to use Illinois coal as a fuel source." 220 ILCS 5/8–402.1(a). The Illinois Commerce Commission was required to take into account "the need to use coal mined in Illinois." *Id*. The obvious intent was to eliminate western coal use by Illinois generating plants, thus effectively discriminating against western coal. The Commerce Clause compels us to invalidate this statute, and consequently the compliance plans thereunder.

■ CUDAHY, CIRCUIT JUDGE, concurring:

Although the framework provided by the majority opinion is supportable, I believe that it is incomplete and, at the same time, may overstate the case. When all the conflicting considerations are weighed, there is some basis for concluding that Illinois has crossed the constitutional line, but its actions are probably only the first in a series of efforts to accommodate conflicting but important and legitimate public policies. . . .

The parties take issue starkly on the question whether a state may "encourage" local industry by indirect means. What is in part at issue is a form of state subsidy for the installation of "scrubbers"—a pollution abatement technology for dealing with the sulfur contained in coal. The Coal Act guarantees that the ratepayers will pay in their rates for the capital and operating costs of scrubbers, which the Act in effect mandates in certain cases. The ratepayers are substantially coterminous with the taxpayers and a mandate to place a charge on the ratepayers is in economic effect functionally equivalent to a subsidy financed from general revenues. . . .

The State's most effective argument is that we are dealing with a local (retail) ratemaking and electric operations problem over which the states have plenary authority. The basic principle under the Coal Act (as elsewhere) for the conduct of electric operations is to arrive at the "least cost" solution. The State argues, in accordance with unimpeachable economic theory, that "cost" means "social cost" and should include the cost of providing compensation for the sectors of society suffering injury from the lost Illinois coal business (such as the cost of unemployment compensation and loss of tax revenue). This is an "externality" not incorporated in ordinary commercial calculations but is a real cost to society nonetheless.

The answer to this argument seems to be that this is an externality that the states may not recognize since the Commerce Clause effectively precludes consideration of local economic damage as a legitimate reason to handicap interstate commerce. Another way of handling this problem would be to offset the externality of damage to the Illinois coal industry with the additional externality of the long-term *benefit* accruing to Illinois from the free trade bias of the Constitution. In any event, the external cost of damage to the Illinois coal industry is something that presumably may *not* be recognized in computation of "least cost" for present purposes. . . .

With respect to constitutional vulnerability it seems to me that the requirement that utilities get permission from the I.C.C. for any change that causes their use of Illinois coal to drop by ten percent or more is much more questionable than the rate base treatment of scrubbers or the injunction to consider the local coal industry as part of a determination of least cost. I am also inclined to consider this legislation as possibly vulnerable under the Supremacy Clause. In contrast to the 1978 law, when Congress ordered scrubbers for all new coal plants, in 1990 it presumably adopted a "market-driven" view. This approach is much in vogue currently, and it is at least plausible that Congress in 1990 would have accepted this characterization. Over the years, the scrubber problem has been hotly debated and in 1978 the Eastern coal interests and coal mine labor succeeded in securing a mandate for scrubbers. As indicated, in 1990 there seems to have been a disposition to leave the matter to the markets. It might be argued that Congress intended to "occupy the field" with a market-based approach, eschewing any mandatory measures. If this were the case, any "putting of thumbs on the scale" by the states might be preempted by the prescribed market-oriented methodology. The relevant Court cases, however, seem to make much easier the striking down of state legislation on Commerce Clause grounds, where relatively little burden on interstate commerce need be shown, than on grounds of preemption, where the requirements seem quite exacting.

These somewhat inconsistent considerations seem to create a conundrum in the case before us, whatever the standard for striking down state "encouragement" to local industry. In the end, I join, but with significant reservations, in the result reached by the majority opinion.

Clean Air Markets Group v. Pataki
338 F.3d 82 (2d Cir. 2003).

■ Before WINTER and CABRANES, CIRCUIT JUDGES, and AMON, DISTRICT JUDGE OF THE EASTERN DISTRICT OF NEW YORK.

■ CABRANES, CIRCUIT JUDGE:

. . . Title IV of the Clean Air Act Amendments of 1990 has the express purpose of "reducing the adverse effects of acid deposition through reductions in annual emissions of sulfur dioxide." [CAA § 1651(b)]. According to Title IV's statement of purpose, "it is the intent of [Title IV] to effectuate such reductions . . . through . . . an emission allocation and transfer system." In other words, the purpose of Title IV is to implement a "cap-and-trade" system in order to reduce sulfur dioxide ("SO_2") emission, which is a leading cause of "acid rain" and other forms of "acid deposition" that are harmful to the environment. Under the cap-and-trade system created by Title IV, electricity-generating utilities

("utilities") are each allocated a certain number of emission allowances per year, and each allowance authorizes the utility to emit one ton of SO_2. Every successive year, the total cap on allowable SO_2 emissions is reduced, and fewer allowances are allocated. Pursuant to the system created by Title IV, SO_2 allowances "may be transferred . . . [to] any other person who holds such allowances." [CAA § 1651b(b) (emphasis added).] By permitting the sale of unneeded allowances, the cap-and-trade system creates a financial incentive for utilities to reduce their SO_2 emissions.

Title IV's cap-and-trade system seeks to minimize acid deposition, the most common form of which is acid rain. Acid deposition has been a particular problem in the Adirondack region of New York State. The thin, calcium-poor soils and igneous rocks in this area make it highly susceptible to acidification. Acid deposition in this region has caused substantial harm to aquatic life and other natural resources.

Because SO_2 emissions can travel hundreds of miles in the wind, much of the acid deposition in the Adirondacks results not from SO_2 emissions in New York, but, rather, from SO_2 emissions in fourteen "upwind" states. These states include New Jersey, Pennsylvania, Maryland, Delaware, Virginia, North Carolina, Tennessee, West Virginia, Ohio, Michigan, Illinois, Kentucky, Indiana, and Wisconsin.

In 2000, the New York legislature sought to address this problem by passing the Air Pollution Mitigation Law, N.Y. Pub. Serv. L. § 66–k ("section 66–k"). Pursuant to this statute, the New York State Public Service Commission ("PSC") is required to assess "an air pollution mitigation offset" upon any New York utility whose SO_2 allowances are sold or traded to one of the fourteen upwind states. N.Y. Pub. Serv. L. § 66–k(2). The amount assessed is equal to the amount of money received by the New York utility in exchange for the allowances. Moreover, the assessment is made regardless of whether the allowances are sold directly to a utility in an upwind state or are subsequently transferred there. Accordingly, in order to avoid the assessment, New York utilities must attach a restrictive covenant to any allowances they sell that prohibits their subsequent transfer to any of the fourteen upwind states. . . .

On appeal, defendants first argue that the District Court erred in holding that section 66–k violates the Supremacy Clause of the Constitution. The Supreme Court has instructed that the Supremacy Clause "invalidates state laws that 'interfere with, or are contrary to,' federal law." *West Lynn*, 114 S.Ct. 2217. Federal law may supersede state laws under the Supremacy Clause in three ways. First, "Congress is empowered to pre-empt state law by so stating in express terms." *Id.* at 713. Second, preemption of all state law in a particular field "may be inferred where the scheme of federal regulation is sufficiently comprehensive to make reasonable the inference that Congress left no room for supplementary state regulation." *Id.* (internal quotation marks and citation omitted). Finally, "even where Congress has not completely displaced state regulation in a specific area, state law is nullified to the extent that it *actually conflicts* with federal law." *Id.* (emphasis added). Such a conflict necessarily arises where " 'compliance with both federal and state regulations is a physical impossibility.' " *Id.* Moreover, an actual conflict exists when a state law " 'stands as an obstacle to the accomplishment and execution of the full purposes and objectives of Congress,' " in enacting federal legislation. *Id.*

The District Court held that section 66–k is preempted by Title IV because section 66–k " 'stands as an obstacle to the accomplishment and execution of the full purposes and objectives of [Title IV].' " CAMG, 194 F.Supp.2d at 158. Defendants disagree, arguing that section 66–k supports the ultimate purpose of Title IV by helping to protect natural resources.

The Supreme Court has held, however, that "in determining whether [a state law] stands as an obstacle to the full implementation of [a federal statute], it is not enough to say that the ultimate goal of both federal and state law is [the same]." International Paper Co. v. Ouellette, 479 U.S. 481, 494 (1987). Even where federal and state statutes have a common goal, a state law will be preempted "if it interferes with the *methods* by which the federal statute was designed to reach this goal." *Id.* (emphasis added).

There can be no doubt that section 66–k interferes with the method selected by Congress for regulating SO_2 emissions. Title IV expressly states that "it is the intent of [Title IV] to effectuate [SO_2 emission] reductions . . . *through . . . an emission allocation and transfer system.*" [CAA § 1651(b) (emphasis added).] In creating this system, Congress sought to grant utilities "the opportunity to reallocate among themselves their total emissions reduction obligations *in the most efficient and cost-effective way possible.*" S. Rep. 101–228, at 303 (1989), reprinted in 1990 U.S.C.C.A.N. 3385, 3686 (emphasis added). In the words of the District of Columbia Circuit: "The basic idea of [Title IV's allowance trading system] is that if polluters for which cutbacks are relatively costly can buy pollution entitlements from ones for which cutbacks are relatively cheap, the nation can achieve a much greater overall cutback for a given expenditure of resources (or achieve a given cutback for a lower expenditure)." Texas Mun. Power Agency v. EPA, 89 F.3d 858, 861 (D.C. Cir. 1996) (emphasis added). In order to implement this scheme on a national scale, Title IV permits allowances to "be transferred . . . [to] *any other person* who holds such allowances." [CAA § 1651b(b) (emphasis added).]

The legislative history of Title IV provides further support for the fact that Congress intended the allowance transfer system to be nationwide. In implementing Title IV, the House of Representatives initially passed a bill that would have divided the nation into two geographic regions and would have required the transferring utility and the receiving utility to have been located in the same region. This geographic restriction also appeared in the bill passed by the Senate Committee on Environmental and Public Works. However, the bill passed by the Senate contained no geographic restrictions, instead providing for a national allowance trading system, S. Rep. 101–228, at 303 (1989), reprinted in 1990 U.S.C.C.A.N. 3385, 3686, and the bill that ultimately emerged from the House-Senate Conference, and that was signed by the President, also included no geographic restrictions on the allowance trading system. Instead, the enacted bill clearly states that allowances "may be transferred . . . [to] *any other person* who holds such allowances," [Pub. L. No. 101–549, 104 Stat. 2399, 2590–91 (emphasis added)], anywhere in the United States.

The regulations adopted by the Environmental Protection Agency ("EPA") in order to implement Title IV further support the conclusion that the nationwide allowance trading system is an essential element of Title IV. In particular, the EPA regulations expressly mandate that state programs for granting "acid rain permits" pursuant to Title V of the Clean Air Act Amendments "shall not restrict or interfere with allowance trading." 40 C.F.R. § 72.72(a). These regulations were adopted over the objection of New York State, which argued vigorously in favor of a scheme that permitted allowance trading to be geographically restricted. In rejecting New York's arguments, the EPA explained that "the national transfer of allowances was clearly contemplated by the drafters of the act." EPA, Acid Rain Program: General Provisions and Permits, Allowance System, Continuous Emissions Monitoring, Excess Emissions and Administrative Appeals, 58 Fed. Reg. 3590, 3614–15 (Jan. 11, 1993). Accordingly, the EPA structured the regulations implementing Title IV to "create . . . a national system of tradable pollution permits." Madison Gas & Elect. Co. v. EPA, 4 F.3d 529, 530 (7th Cir. 1993). Although section 66–k does not technically limit the authority of New York utilities to transfer their allowances, it clearly interferes with their ability to effectuate such transfers. First, by requiring utilities to forfeit one hundred percent of their proceeds from any allowance sale to a utility in an upwind state, section 66–k effectively bans such sales. Moreover, the only way for New York utilities to ensure that they will not be assessed pursuant to section 66–k is to attach to every allowance they sell a restrictive covenant that prohibits the subsequent transfer of the allowance to an upwind state. Because such a restrictive covenant indisputably decreases the value of the allowances, section 66–k clearly "restrict[s] or interfere[s] with allowance trading," 40 C.F.R. § 72.72(a).

In sum, section 66–k impermissibly "interferes with the *methods* by which [Title IV] was designed to reach [the] goal" of decreasing SO_2 emissions, and therefore it "stands as an obstacle" to the execution of Title IV's objectives. *International Paper*, 479 U.S. at 494 (emphasis added). . . .

In sum, section 66–k is preempted by Title IV of the Clean Air Act Amendments of 1990 because it impedes the execution of "the full purposes and objectives" of Title IV, *see Hillsborough County*, 471 U.S. at 713, and because it is not otherwise authorized by federal law. Accordingly, section 66–k violates the Supremacy Clause of the United States Constitution.

NOTES AND QUESTIONS

1.   **Allocation of Allowances Under the Acid Rain Provisions.** In an emissions trading scheme, should allowances be auctioned or distributed for free to emissions units? The acid rain program adopted the latter approach. *See* 42 U.S.C. §§ 7651c, 7651d. Although some commentators argued that an auction was the best way to allocate allowances, others report that the auction-only option was "not on the table in 1989 and 1990," perhaps because of lingering doubts about whether the market would work at all. *See* DENNY A. ELLERMAN ET AL., MARKETS FOR CLEAN AIR, 24–25 (2000). In what ways might an auction be preferable to free distribution? Who might prefer free distribution, and why? Was the acid rain program a grandfathering system, or a hybrid system? Why? Who were the losers in the acid rain program? Why?

Compare the allocation scheme created by the acid rain program with the allocation scheme proposed by the Regional Greenhouse Gas Initiative (RGGI). RGGI is a cap-and-trade marketable permit scheme designed to reduce carbon dioxide emissions in several northeastern states. *See* Regional Greenhouse Gas Initiative, Welcome, http://www.rggi.org (last visited Sept. 26, 2018). The 2005 Memorandum of Understanding (MOU) among the RGGI states proposed the following:

> Each signatory state may allocate allowances from its CO_2 emissions budget as determined appropriate by each Signatory State, provided:
>
> (1)   each Signatory State agrees that 25% of the allowances will be allocated for a consumer benefit or strategic energy purpose. Consumer benefit or strategic energy purposes include the use of allowances to promote energy efficiency, to directly mitigate electricity ratepayer impacts, to promote renewable or non-carbon-emitting energy technologies, to stimulate or reward investment in the development of innovative carbon emissions abatement technologies with significant carbon reduction potential, and/or to fund administration of this Program. . . .

Regional Greenhouse Gas Initiative, Memorandum of Understanding 6 (Dec. 20, 2005). This twenty-five percent allocation for consumer benefit will likely be achieved by auctioning allowances and using the revenue for one of the purposes listed in the MOU. Is this approach preferable to the one taken by the Acid Rain Program? Should governments be constrained in their use of revenue from an initial auction?

2.   **Allowance Prices.** Ellerman and Montero describe how "[w]hen acid rain legislation was being debated, sulfur dioxide emissions were expected to rise throughout the 1990s as a result of the increase in the demand for electricity and continuing reliance on coal-fired generation." Early estimates

of the trading price of allowances ranged from $250 to $400, but the first annual auction of sulfur dioxide allowances, in 1993, cleared at only $131. 26–27. Although coal-fired power generation increased throughout the early 1990s, by 1993 sulfur dioxide emissions were 7.3 percent below 1985 levels. A. Denny Ellerman & Juan-Pablo Montero, *The Declining Trend in Sulfur Dioxide Emissions: Implications for Allowance Prices*, 36 J. ENVTL. ECON. & MGMT. 26, 27–28 (1998). Why do you think this was? Ellerman and Montero argue that the principal reason for the reduction in emissions was that rail deregulation reduced rail freight prices, making it cheaper for low-sulfur coal to be transported from the west to power plants in the Midwest that had traditionally used high-sulfur coal. *Id.* at 28–29. Does that seem plausible?

3. **Impacts on Local Economies.** In *Alliance for Clean Coal v. Miller*, the Illinois legislature sought to reduce the economic impacts of the acid rain program on local high-sulfur coal producers and miners. What is the strongest argument for upholding its provisions? For a detailed discussion of local legislative responses to the acid rain program, see Russell Korobkin, *The Local Politics of Acid Rain: Public Versus Private Decisionmaking and the Dormant Commerce Clause in a New Era of Environmental Law*, 75 B.U. L. REV. 689, 696–701 (1995).

4. **Geography and Hot Spots.** In *Clean Air Markets*, New York attempted to provide additional protection for its forests and lakes by penalizing local utilities that sold Acid Rain Program allowances to upwind states. New York was concerned that the federal Acid Rain Program did not provide adequate environmental protection because it did not constrain the location of a trade. Thus, "big dirties" in the upwind states might purchase additional allowances rather than reducing emissions, resulting in higher levels of acid deposition in New York.

New York was particularly concerned because of its geography. New York borders the Atlantic Ocean, and is upwind of it; hence, local utilities that emit NO_x in New York mostly send that pollution out over the ocean where it does little harm. However, the same unit of pollution emitted upwind of New York may cause acid deposition in New York's forests and lakes. Thus, there is more social harm created when the same amount of pollution comes from Atlanta rather than Albany.

Given this, why would a national market be used for these pollutants? If a utility in Minnesota sells its emissions allowance to a firm in California, are the resulting emissions likely to ever cross the Rocky Mountains? If the social cost of a unit of pollution depends on the location of its source, why have a uniform national market?

The flexibility of emissions trading programs allows firms to make decisions about whether purchasing allowances or reducing emissions is the most economically efficient approach for them. However, a significant problem with this flexibility is the potential to create "hot spots," or areas where emissions are concentrated, thus disproportionately impacting the health and environment in the hot spot area.

Can you think of a solution to this problem? Is there a way to combine a market in pollutants with air modeling to ensure that no trade ever causes such a "hot spot?" Or is this the wrong paradigm altogether to think about solutions to the hot spot problem?

5.   Federal Limitations on State Regulation of Federal Markets. *Alliance for Clean Coal* and *Clean Air Markets Group* illustrate two legal doctrines that limit states' ability to regulate markets established under the CAA: the Dormant Commerce Clause and federal preemption, which are discussed in Chapter IV.

Recall that Congress has plenary authority to regulate interstate commerce under the Constitution. U.S. CONST. art. I, § 8, cl. 3. Dormant Commerce Clause jurisprudence establishes that this authority also contains a negative aspect, limiting states' ability to interfere with interstate commerce.

On which grounds did the court strike down the Illinois statute in *Alliance for Clean Coal*? How does the analysis of the concurrence differ from the majority? Compare these two approaches to that of the *Clean Air Markets Group* court.

6.   Title IV and Litigation. In many of the cases excerpted elsewhere in this casebook, parties challenged technology-based EPA regulations, arguing that the rule did not meet the relevant statutory standard. In contrast, EPA's application of the Title IV Acid Rain program was not the subject of significant litigation (though New York and Illinois' efforts to affect implementation of the program were subject to challenge, see *supra*).

Does the relative absence of litigation in implementation of Title IV constitute an additional benefit of market-based programs over technology-based standards? For a discussion of how technology-based standards lead to more litigation than emissions trading programs, see Bruce A. Ackerman & Richard B. Stewart, *Reforming Environmental Law: The Democratic Case for Market Incentives*, 13 COLUM. J. ENVTL. L. 171, 173–74 (1988).

Compare this outcome to the history of litigation under § 110(a)(2)(D), discussed *supra*, where the mandate for emissions trading is less explicit. What language in Title IV provides statutory authority for emissions trading? How does this language compare to the provision at issue in *North Carolina v. EPA*? How does the language compare to § 111(b) & (d), which provide authority for EPA's GHG NSPS?

7.   More Markets. The Acid Rain Program is widely considered a success in reducing overall SO_2 emissions, despite the hot spot problem identified above. Since Title IV was enacted, emissions trading approaches have been proposed or adopted by EPA to address interstate transport of NO_X (through the NO_X SIP Call and the Cross-State Air Pollution Rule), and proposed to address the problem of regional haze, caused by visibility-impairing pollutants, such as fine particulate matter ($PM_{2.5}$), and compounds which contribute to $PM_{2.5}$ formation, such as NO_X, SO_2, certain volatile organic compounds, and ammonia. A variety of market-based approaches were proposed in the United States to address climate change, including the American Clean Energy and Security Act, discussed in Chapter III, *supra*. In addition, market-based approaches have been adopted to address greenhouse gas emissions on both global and regional scales; for an illustrative example, see the EU Emissions Trading Scheme, discussed in Chapter III, *supra*, or the Kyoto Protocol. Conference of the Parties to the Framework Convention on Climate Change: Kyoto Protocol U.N. Doc. No. FCCC/CP/1997/L.7/Add.1 (Dec. 10, 1997).

9. MOBILE SOURCES

A. INTRODUCTION

i. IMPACT OF MOBILE SOURCES

Mobile sources of air pollution are vehicles and engines of all sizes, from ships and trains to hand-held lawn and garden equipment. EPA, Mobile Sources, https://www3.epa.gov/air/sat/mobile.html (last visited Oct. 2, 2018). Through engine combustion and fuel evaporation, mobile sources generate more than half of the air pollution in the United States, including approximately 80 percent of carbon monoxide emissions, 55 percent of NOx emissions, and 40 percent of fine particulate matter emissions. EPA, OUR NATION'S AIR: STATUS AND TRENDS THROUGH 2008, at 6 (2010). In addition, mobile source emissions of hazardous air pollutants (HAPs) are responsible for almost 50 percent of domestic cancer risk; in particular, mobile sources are a major source of benzene, the largest contributor to cancer risk of all chemicals quantitatively assessed by EPA. EPA, Control of Hazardous Air Pollutants from Mobile Sources, 72 Fed. Reg. 8428, 8434 (2007). Finally, mobile sources are a significant source of carbon dioxide emissions, accounting for 31 percent of carbon dioxide emissions in the United States—the largest percentage of any economic sector. EPA, INVENTORY OF GREENHOUSE GAS EMISSIONS AND SINKS: 1990–2009, at 2–9 (2011). Of that 31 percent, 65 percent is attributable to emissions from passenger cars and light-duty trucks. *Id.* at 2–22.

EPA estimates that automobiles emit 75 to 90 percent less pollution (per vehicle mile) today than they did in 1970, due to changes in technology partly spurred by Clean Air Act regulation. Nevertheless, air pollution from mobile sources continues to present one of the largest challenges to the achievement of air quality standards and other air pollution reduction objectives. More people are driving today than in 1970—and most are driving more vehicle miles. Technology-based standards, such as those imposed by Title II of the Clean Air Act (described below), do not cap the overall level of emissions. Thus, due largely to the nation's increased reliance on automobiles for transportation, air pollution from mobile sources continues to constitute more than half of the nation's air pollution problem, just as it did in 1970.

ii.   SETTING THE MOBILE SOURCE STANDARD

Title II of the Clean Air Act regulates emissions from mobile sources. The substantive standard for mobile source regulation is stated in CAA § 202:

> the Administrator is to promulgate standards which reflect the greatest degree of emission reduction achievable through the application of technology which the Administrator determines will be available for the model year to which such standards apply, giving appropriate consideration to cost, energy, and safety factors associated with the application of such technology.

42 U.S.C. § 7521.

The automobile industry claimed initially that the standards promulgated by the Administrator could not be met, and petitioned for a one-year waiver, which EPA denied. The first case below is the D.C. Circuit's treatment of this initial battle.

International Harvester Co. v. Ruckelshaus
478 F.2d 615 (D.C. Cir. 1973).

■ Before BAZELON, CHIEF JUDGE, and TAMM and LEVENTHAL, CIRCUIT JUDGES.

■ LEVENTHAL, CIRCUIT JUDGE:

These consolidated petitions of International Harvester and the three major auto companies, Ford, General Motors and Chrysler, seek review of a decision by the Administrator of the Environmental Protection Agency denying petitioners' applications, filed pursuant to Section 202 of the Clean Air Act, for one-year suspensions of the 1975 emission standards prescribed under the statute for light duty vehicles in the absence of suspension.

The tension of forces presented by the controversy over automobile emission standards may be focused by two central observations:

(1) The automobile is an essential pillar of the American economy. Some 28 per cent of the nonfarm workforce draws its livelihood from the automobile industry and its products.

(2) The automobile has had a devastating impact on the American environment. As of 1970, authoritative voices stated that "[a]utomotive pollution constitutes in excess of 60% of our national air pollution problem" and more than 80 per cent of the air pollutants in concentrated urban areas. . . .

On December 31, 1970, Congress grasped the nettle and amended the Clean Air Act to set a statutory standard for required reductions in levels of hydrocarbons (HC) and carbon monoxide (CO) which must be achieved for 1975 models of light duty vehicles. . . .

Congress was aware that these 1975 standards were "drastic medicine," designed to "force the state of the art." There was, naturally, concern whether the manufacturers would be able to achieve this goal. Therefore, Congress provided, in Senator Baker's phrase, a "realistic escape hatch": the manufacturers could petition the Administrator of the EPA for a one-year suspension of the 1975 requirements, and Congress took the precaution of directing the National Academy of Sciences to undertake an ongoing study of the feasibility of compliance with the emission standards. The "escape hatch" provision addressed itself to the possibility that the NAS study or other evidence might indicate that the standards would be unachievable despite all good faith efforts at compliance. This provision was limited to a one-year suspension, which would defer compliance with the 90% reduction requirement until 1976. Under section 202(b)(5)(D) of the Act, the Administrator is authorized to grant a one-year suspension

> only if he determines that (i) such suspension is essential to the public interest or the public health and welfare of the United States, (ii) all good faith efforts have been made to meet the standards established by this subsection, (iii) the applicant has established that effective control technology, processes, operating methods, or other alternatives are not available or have not been available for a sufficient period of time to achieve compliance prior to the effective date of such standards, and (iv) the study and investigation of the National Academy of Sciences conducted pursuant to subsection (c) of this section and other information available to him has not indicated that such technology, processes, or other alternatives are available to meet such standards. . . .

At the outset of his Decision, the Administrator determined that the most effective system so far developed was the noble metal oxidizing catalyst. Additionally, he stated that the "most effective systems typically include: improved carburetion; a fast-release choke; a device for promoting fuel vaporization during warm-up; more consistent and durable ignition systems; exhaust gas recirculation; and a system for injecting air into the engine exhaust manifold to cause further combustion of unburned gases and to create an oxidizing atmosphere for the catalyst." It was this system to which the data base was initially narrowed: only cars using this kind of system were to be considered in making the "available technology" determination.

The problem the Administrator faced in making a determination that technology was available, on the basis of these data, was that actual tests showed only one car with actual emissions which conformed to the standard prescribing a maximum of .41 grams, per mile, of HC and 3.4 grams per mile of CO. No car had actually been driven 50,000 miles, the statutory "useful life" of a vehicle and the time period for which conformity to the emission standards is required. In the view of the EPA

Administrator, however, the reasons for the high test readings were uncertain or ambivalent.

. . . With the data submitted and the above assumptions, the Administrator concluded that no showing had been made that requisite technology was not available. . . .

For purposes of judicial review, the initial EPA decision rests on the technology determination. . . . The Report made by the NAS, pursuant to its obligation under 202(b)(5)(D) of the Clean Air Act, had concluded: "The Committee finds that the technology necessary to meet the requirements of the Clean Air Act Amendments for 1975 model year light-duty motor vehicles is not available at this time."[33]

The Administrator apparently relied, however, on the NAS Report to bolster his conclusion that the applicants had not established that technology was unavailable. The same NAS Report had stated:

> . . . the status of development and rate of progress made it possible that the larger manufacturers will be able to produce vehicles that will qualify, provided that provisions are made for catalyst replacement and other maintenance, for averaging emissions of production vehicles, and for the general availability of fuel containing suitably low levels of catalyst poisons.

The Administrator pointed out that two of NAS's provisos—catalytic converter replacement and low lead levels—had been accounted for in his analysis of the auto company data, and provision therefor had been insured through regulation. As to the third, "averaging emissions of production vehicles," the Administrator offered two reasons for declining to make a judgment about this matter: (1) The significance of averaging related to possible assembly-line tests, as distinct from certification test procedure, and such tests had not yet been worked out. (2) If there were an appropriate assembly-line test it would be expected that each car's emissions could be in conformity, without a need for averaging, since the assembly line vehicles "equipped with fresh catalysts can be expected to have substantially lower emissions at zero miles than at 4000 miles." . . .

The Administrator did refer to the "severe driveability problems" underscored by the NAS Report, which in the judgment of NAS "could have significant safety implications," stating that he had not been presented with any evidence of "specific safety hazard" nor knew of any presented to the NAS. He did not address himself to the issue of performance problems falling short of specific safety hazards. . . .

Two principal considerations compete for our attention. On the one hand, if suspension is not granted, and the prediction of the EPA Administrator that effective technology will be available is proven incorrect, grave economic consequences could ensue. This is the problem

---

[33] Committee on Motor Vehicle Emissions, National Academy of Sciences, Semiannual Report to the Environmental Protection Agency, January 1, 1972 [hereinafter NAS Report] at 49.

Senator Griffin described as the "dangerous game of economic roulette." 116 Cong. Rec. 33,081 (1970). On the other hand, if suspension is granted, and it later be shown that the Administrator's prediction of feasibility was achievable in 1975 there may be irretrievable ecological costs. It is to this second possibility we first turn.

The most authoritative estimate in the record of the ecological costs of a one-year suspension is that of the NAS Report. Taking into account such "factors as the vehicle-age distribution among all automobiles, the decrease in vehicle miles driven per year, per car as vehicle age increases, the predicted nationwide growth in vehicle miles driven each year" and the effect of emission standards on exhaust control, NAS concluded that:

> . . . the effect on total emissions of a one-year suspension with no additional interim standards appears to be small. The effect is not more significant because the emission reduction now required of model year 1974 vehicles, as compared with uncontrolled vehicles (80 percent for HC and 69 percent for CO), is already so substantial.

. . . On balance the record indicates the environmental costs of a one-year suspension are likely to be relatively modest. This must be balanced against the potential economic costs—and ecological costs—if the Administrator's prediction on the availability of effective technology is incorrect.

. . . This case inevitably presents, to the court as to the Administrator, the need for a perspective on the suspension that is informed by an analysis which balances the costs of a "wrong decision" on feasibility against the gains of a correct one. These costs include the risks of grave maladjustments for the technological leader from the eleventh-hour grant of a suspension, and the impact on jobs and the economy from a decision which is only partially accurate, allowing companies to produce cars but at a significantly reduced level of output. Against this must be weighed the environmental savings from denial of suspension. The record indicates that these will be relatively modest. There is also the possibility that failure to grant a suspension may be counter-productive to the environment, if there is significant decline in performance characteristics. . . .

. . . The submission of the auto companies unquestionably showed that no car had actually been driven 50,000 miles and achieved conformity of emissions to the 1975 standards. The Administrator's position is that on the basis of the methodology outlined, he can predict that the auto companies can meet the standards, and that the ability to make a prediction saying the companies can comply means that the petitioners have failed to sustain their burden of proof that they cannot comply. . . .

The number of unexplained assumptions used by the Administrator, the variance in methodology from that of the Report of the National

Academy of Sciences, and the absence of an indication of the statistical reliability of the prediction, combine to generate grave doubts as to whether technology is available to meet the 1975 statutory standards. . . . We think the vehicle manufacturers established by a preponderance of the evidence, in the record before us, that technology was not available, within the meaning of the Act, when they adduced the tests on actual vehicles; that the Administrator's reliance on technological methodology to offset the actual tests raised serious doubts and failed to meet the burden of proof which in our view was properly assignable to him, in the light of accepted legal doctrine and the intent of Congress discerned, in part, by taking into account that the risk of an "erroneous" denial of suspension outweighed the risk of an "erroneous" grant of suspension. We do not use the burden of proof in the conventional sense of civil trials, but the Administrator must sustain the burden of adducing a reasoned presentation supporting the reliability of EPA's methodology.

. . . This statute was, indeed, deliberately designed as "shock treatment" to the industry. Our central difference with the Administrator, simply put, stems from our view concerning the Congressional intent underlying the one year suspension provision. That was a purposeful cushion—with the twin purpose of providing "escape hatch" relief for 1975, and thus establishing a context supportive of the rigor and firmness of the basic standards slated for no later than 1976. In our view the overall legislative firmness does not necessarily require a "hardnosed" approach to the application for suspension, as the Administrator apparently supposed, and may indeed be furthered by our more moderate view of the suspension issue, particularly in assigning to the Administrator the burden of producing a reasoned presentation of the reliability of his methodology. This is not a matter of clemency, but rather a benign approach that moderates the "shock treatment" so as to obviate excessive and unnecessary risk of harm.

[The Court remanded the decision, instructing the Administrator to reconsider the request for suspension, to reach relevant factors beyond technical feasibility, like "public interest," and to make a decision within 60 days.]

■ BAZELON, CHIEF JUDGE (concurring in result):

Socrates said that wisdom is the recognition of how much one does not know. I may be wise if that is wisdom, because I recognize that I do not know enough about dynamometer extrapolations, deterioration factor adjustments, and the like to decide whether or not the government's approach to these matters was statistically valid. Therein lies my disagreement with the majority.

The court's opinion today centers on a substantive evaluation of the Administrator's assumptions and methodology. I do not have the technical know-how to agree or disagree with that evaluation—at least on the basis of the present record. My grounds for remanding the case rest upon the Administrator's failure to employ a reasonable decision-making process for so critical and complex a matter. At this time I cannot say to what extent I could undertake an evaluation of the Administrator's findings if they were based on an adequate decisional process.

. . . I would have preferred to make the "public interest" factor . . . an independent ground for suspension. The court today deals with the public interest indirectly, through the device of burden of proof. I do not fully understand this approach, but I suspect it leads to essentially the same result I favor.

NOTES AND QUESTIONS

1.　**Perils of Technology-Forcing Legislation.** Early cases confronted the difficulty of imposing Title II's technology-forcing mandate on a powerful and powerfully reluctant automobile industry. To resolve the case, the court engaged in a balancing test and found that the risks of forcing the automobile industry to include a new technology that would potentially make cars less drivable outweighed the threat to the environment posed by a one-year waiver. In ruling for industry, the court effectively switched the statutorily-assigned burden of proof—from industry proving that achievement of the standard was not feasible to EPA proving that achievement was feasible. *See* Daniel A. Farber, *Statutory Interpretation and Legislative Supremacy*, 78 GEO. L.J. 281, 300 (1989). This early case illustrates the general tenor of regulation under Title II: increasingly stringent regulation of emissions and fuel content is met with feasibility-based challenges from the well-organized automobile industry.

In fact, industry has repeatedly met the deadlines imposed upon them even after predictions that they would be unable to do so. How solicitous should courts be to claims of industry infeasibility? Who is in the best position to analyze industry's readiness to meet standards? Where do the greatest incentives to distort that information lie?

B.　FEDERAL PREEMPTION OF STATE STANDARDS

An important feature of Title II is the broad power assumed by the federal government to regulate automobile emissions. Compare this approach with the regulation of stationary sources and the primary role states take using their SIPs.

Congress' overall approach is to require nationally uniform technology-based standards for vehicle emissions (§ 202) and fuel content (§ 211). These programs preempt state and local standards in both directions. That is, unlike the stationary source provisions considered so far, which establish a floor but allow state regulation more stringent than the floor, the mobile source provisions preempt state standards that are both more and less stringent than the federal requirements. *See* 42 U.S.C. § 7543(a).

An exception is made for California, which is authorized in § 209 to tailor its own mobile source emissions control program subject to a waiver by EPA. Section 209(b) requires the Administrator to waive preemption for any state "which has adopted standards (other than crankcase emission standards) for the control of emissions from new motor vehicle or new motor vehicle engines prior to March 30, 1966." 42 U.S.C. § 7543(b). California is the only state that had adopted such standards as of 1966. *See Motor & Equip. Mfr. Ass'n v. EPA*, 627 F.2d 1095, 1100 n.1 (D.C. Cir. 1979). Section 177 allows other states with nonattainment areas to adopt California's standards instead of the national standards.

The California exception has come to dominate the mobile sources debate. One reason is that California emissions standards are significantly more stringent than national standards. For example, in September 2004, the California Air Resources Board (CARB) adopted greenhouse gas emission standards for light-duty vehicles that would have resulted in a thirty percent reduction in greenhouse gas emissions from all light-duty vehicles by 2018. *See* CARB, Fact Sheet: Climate Change Emissions Control Regulations (Dec. 10, 2004), http://www.arb.ca.gov/cc/factsheets/cc_newfs.pdf. Sixteen states moved to adopt California's standards. *See* California Office of the Attorney General, *Brown Sues EPA for Illegally Blocking California's Plan to Curb Tailpipe Emissions*, Jan. 2, 2008. In May 2009, the Obama Administration announced that it had reached an agreement with automakers and states that would resolve pending litigation brought by automakers against the California standards; EPA and the Department of Transportation (DOT) would establish nationwide, coordinated greenhouse gas emission standards under § 202 and fuel efficiency standards under DOT statutory authority for model year 2012–2016 passenger vehicles. *See Report of the Climate Change and Emissions Committee*, 30 ENERGY L. J. 563, 573 (2009). See further discussion, *infra*, on regulation of carbon dioxide emissions from mobile sources.

To what extent can California standards established pursuant to a waiver under § 209 create pressure for stronger national standards? How does this dynamic compare to the "race-to-the-bottom" concerns discussed in Chapter IV, *supra*?

The cases below explore the scope of this preemption. The first case, *Motor & Equipment Manufacturers Association v. EPA*, establishes that the scope of EPA's waiver power for California under § 209(b) is coextensive with the preemption power under § 209(a). In other words, anything that is preempted by § 209(a) can be waived with respect to California under § 209(b), assuming the three statutory factors (arbitrary and capricious review of protectiveness, necessary and compelling need, and consistency with § 202(a) technological feasibility) are met.

Motor & Equipment Manufacturers Association v. Environmental Protection Agency

627 F.2d 1095 (D.C. Cir. 1979).

■ Before WRIGHT, CHIEF JUDGE, and MACKINNON and ROBB, CIRCUIT JUDGES.

■ MACKINNON, CIRCUIT JUDGE:

Section 209 of the Clean Air Act requires the Administrator of the Environmental Protection Agency (EPA) to waive federal preemption of motor vehicle emission control regulations for the State of California unless he makes certain findings that a waiver is inappropriate. In July 1978 the Administrator waived federal preemption for California regulations limiting the amount of maintenance that a manufacturer can require of motor vehicle purchasers in the written instructions which accompany new motor vehicles sold in that State.

. . . Section 202 of [the CAA] establishes nationwide motor vehicle emission standards applicable to certain model years for three major pollutants, carbon monoxide, hydrocarbons, and oxides of nitrogen. It also sets long-term goals for the control of emissions, and authorizes the EPA Administrator to prescribe standards consistent with those goals for model years not covered by the statute. These regulations can take effect at such time as the Administrator finds them to be technologically feasible, giving appropriate consideration to the costs of compliance.

Section 206 requires the Administrator to test or to have tested any new motor vehicle or new motor vehicle engine submitted by a manufacturer to determine whether the vehicle or engine conforms to the standards contained in section 202 and in the regulations promulgated under it. This "certification process" consists of various procedures which enable a manufacturer to demonstrate by use of a prototype that it has designed a class of motor vehicle which complies with the standards. One feature of this certification process is a durability test to determine the effects of deterioration on the functioning of the emission control system. The Administrator limits by regulation the amount of "scheduled maintenance" that can be performed on the prototype vehicle during this durability test. . . .

Section 207 imposes two types of warranty obligations on manufacturers which are directly related to the standards issued in section 202. First it requires manufacturers to warrant to purchasers that each new motor vehicle is designed, built, and equipped to conform to the section 202 standards, and further to warrant that each is free of defects in materials and workmanship which cause a motor vehicle to fail to conform to the standards for their useful life. This is the defect warranty. Second, it provides that the Administrator shall impose a "performance warranty" on manufacturers whereby manufacturers will bear the costs of remedying any nonconformity with section 202 emission standards on vehicles maintained in accordance with the written maintenance instructions required by the statute. The written maintenance instructions, which manufacturers must furnish with each new motor vehicle, must conform to regulations promulgated by the Administrator. If the purchaser fails to comply with the written instructions it relieves the manufacturer of his performance warranty obligations.

By virtue of the unique status it enjoys under section 209 of the Clean Air Act, California has an emissions control program that parallels the federal program in many respects. This litigation grew out of a decision made by the California Air Resources Board (CARB), which is California's version of the federal EPA in the area of emissions control regulations. In May 1977, the CARB adopted regulations limiting the amount of scheduled maintenance that can be performed on the prototype used in the durability testing during California's certification process. No party in this court challenges the application of these maintenance restrictions to the certification process. Rather the object of challenge is the CARB's simultaneous decision to limit the maintenance a manufacturer can require of purchasers in the written instructions manufacturers must furnish with each new motor vehicle. Under these "in-use maintenance regulations," a manufacturer cannot require a purchaser to perform maintenance beyond that which a manufacturer can perform during the certification process. The furnishing of written instructions which abide by the in-use maintenance regulations is a condition precedent to the initial retail sale of new motor vehicles in California. The regulations also define the manufacturers' warranty obligations. . . .

The first question for decision is whether section 209 empowers the Administrator to consider a waiver of federal preemption for California's in-use maintenance regulations. Petitioners argue that the in-use maintenance regulations are not aimed at emissions control performance of new motor vehicles but instead purport to regulate in-use performance and post-sale obligations of manufacturers. As such, they contend, the regulations intrude on the pervasive federal regulatory scheme embodied in section 207, and are not subject to waiver under subsection (b) of section 209. Petitioners acknowledge that absent some provision for waiver the regulations are preempted by subsection (a) of section 209. They thereby avoid any explicit suggestion that section 207 alone effects a preemption of the CARB's in-use maintenance regulations and exclusively rely on a theory that subsection (b)'s waiver power is circumscribed by section 207.

The Administrator rejected this claim on the ground that the only relevant preemption provision is the express terms of subsection (a) and that whatever is preempted therein is subject to waiver under subsection (b). We agree.

Nothing in section 209 supports petitioners' one-way approach to waiver of federal preemption for California. Subsection (b) provides that unless the Administrator makes certain findings he must "waive application of this *section*" to California. The underscored phrase has no conceivable meaning other than to refer to subsection (a). Subsection (a) forbids any state from "adopt[ing] or attempt[ing] to enforce" standards relating to emissions from new motor vehicles, and from imposing any requirements relating to same as a "condition precedent" to the initial retail sale of motor vehicles. California's in-use maintenance regulations are attempts to enforce California's emission standards, and compliance with the regulations is a condition precedent to the initial retail sale of motor vehicles in California. The in-use maintenance regulations are, therefore, preempted by subsection (a). Subsection (b) authorizes the Administrator to waive application of subsection (a) for California; it contains no suggestion that the scope of this authority is something other than that defined by subsection (a). Hence the Administrator is empowered to waive federal preemption for California's in-use maintenance regulations.

The plain meaning of the statute indicates that Congress intended to make the waiver power coextensive with the preemption provision. Petitioners' efforts to reduce the phrase "of this section" to a truism would, if successful, render the California waiver provision either meaningless or ineffectual.

First, if only the pervasiveness of section 207's regulation of in-use performance is sufficient to restrict the Administrator's waiver authority, there is no reason why on the same reasoning a comparable limitation could not be found in section 202's pervasive regulation of national motor vehicle emission standards or section 206's pervasive regulation of the federal certification process. Sections 202, 206 and 207 are all integral parts of a comprehensive federal program; all three are equally treated in section 209(a). Yet were the Administrator to regard sections 202 and 206 as petitioners urge him to regard section 207, he would be powerless to consider waiving federal preemption for California's emission standards and certification process. This lack of power would render the waiver provision—and indeed, the express preemption provision—mere surplusage. It is axiomatic that a statute must be construed to avoid that result so that no provision will be inoperative or superfluous.

Second, if instead petitioners divine the limit on the waiver authority from section 207's particular area of regulation—in-use performance—then their argument is that Congress did not intend California to have any interests in emissions control once new motor vehicles leave the assembly line. Certainly section 209 makes no distinction among different types of in-use performance regulation which operate as enforcement procedures and conditions precedent. Thus on petitioners' reading the statute permits California to establish emission standards and certification procedures, but forbids it from ensuring that the standards are effective once the motor vehicle leaves the showroom. Yet the only time that a new motor vehicle is capable of polluting the environment is when it is out on the road. The purpose of the Clean Air Act is to reach precisely that kind of pollution. Our duty is to "favor an interpretation which would render the statutory design effective in terms of the policies behind its enactment and to avoid an interpretation which would make such policies more difficult of fulfillment, particularly where, as here, that interpretation is consistent with the plain language of the statute." *National Petroleum Refiners Association v. FTC*, 157 U.S. App.D.C. 83, 100 (1973), *cert. denied*, 415 U.S. 951 (1974).

. . . Congress had an opportunity to restrict the waiver provision in making the 1977 amendments, and it instead elected to expand California's flexibility to adopt a complete program of motor vehicle emissions control. Under the 1977 amendments, California need only determine that its standards will be "in the aggregate, at least as protective of public health and welfare than applicable Federal standards," rather than the "more stringent" standard contained in the 1967 Act.

. . . Since the inception of the federal government's emissions control program it has drawn heavily on the California experience to fashion and to improve the national efforts at emissions control. The history of congressional consideration of the California waiver provision, from its original enactment up through 1977, indicates that Congress intended the State to continue and expand its pioneering efforts at adopting and enforcing motor vehicle emission standards different from and in large measure more advanced than the corresponding federal program; in short, to act as a kind of laboratory for innovation. Had Congress wanted to limit California's role to forbid its adoption of any program comparable to the federal scheme in section 207, it could have easily done so. It did not. For a court to do so despite the absence of such an indication would only frustrate the congressional intent.

. . . We accordingly hold that section 209(b) empowers the Administrator to consider a waiver request for in-use maintenance regulations. . . .

Engine Manufacturers Association v. South Coast Air Quality Management District

541 U.S. 246 (2004).

■ JUSTICE SCALIA delivered the opinion of the Court:

Respondent South Coast Air Quality Management District (District) is a political subdivision of California responsible for air pollution control in the Los Angeles metropolitan area and parts of surrounding counties that make up the South Coast Air Basin. It enacted six Fleet Rules that generally prohibit the purchase or lease by various public and private fleet operators of vehicles that do not comply with stringent emission requirements. The question in this case is whether these local Fleet Rules escape pre-emption under § 209(a) of the Clean Air Act (CAA) because they address the purchase of vehicles, rather than their manufacture or sale.

The District is responsible under state law for developing and implementing a "comprehensive basinwide air quality management plan" to reduce emission levels and thereby achieve and maintain "state and federal ambient air quality standards." Cal. Health & Safety Code Ann. § 40402(e) (West 1996). Between June and October 2000, the District adopted six Fleet Rules. The Rules govern operators of fleets of street sweepers, of passenger cars, light-duty trucks, and medium-duty vehicles, of public transit vehicles and urban buses, of solid waste collection vehicles, of airport passenger transportation vehicles, including shuttles and taxicabs picking up airline passengers, and of heavy-duty on-road vehicles. All six Rules apply to public operators; three apply to private operators as well.

The Fleet Rules contain detailed prescriptions regarding the types of vehicles that fleet operators must purchase or lease when adding or replacing fleet vehicles. Four of the Rules require the purchase or lease of "alternative-fuel vehicles," and the other two require the purchase or lease of either "alternative-fueled vehicles" or vehicles that meet certain emission specifications established by the California Air Resources Board (CARB).[3] . . .

In August 2000, petitioner Engine Manufacturers Association sued the District and its officials, also respondents, claiming that the Fleet Rules are pre-empted by § 209 of the CAA, which prohibits the adoption or attempted enforcement of any state or local "standard relating to the control of emissions from new motor vehicles or new motor vehicle engines." The District Court granted summary judgment to respondents, upholding the Rules in their entirety. It held that the Rules were not "standard[s]" under § 209(a) because they regulate only the purchase of vehicles that are otherwise certified for sale in California. . . . The Ninth Circuit affirmed on the reasoning of the District Court. We granted certiorari.

Section 209(a) of the CAA states:

No State or any political subdivision thereof shall adopt or attempt to enforce any standard relating to the control of emissions from new motor vehicles or new motor vehicle engines subject to this part. No State shall require certification,

---

[3] More specifically, Rules 1191(d), (e)(1), id., at 27–28, require that these vehicles comply with CARB's Low-Emission Vehicle (LEV), Ultra-Low-Emission Vehicle (ULEV), Super-Ultra-Low-Emission Vehicle (SULEV), or Zero-Emission Vehicle (ZEV) standards . . . The tiers are subject to varying emission limitations for carbon monoxide, formaldehyde, nonmethane organic gases, oxides of nitrogen, and particulate matter. No vehicle may be sold in California unless it meets the TLEV, LEV, ULEV, SULEV, or ZEV requirements. Additionally, manufacturers are obligated to meet overall "fleet average" emission requirements. The fleet average emission requirements decrease over time, requiring manufacturers to sell progressively cleaner mixes of vehicles. Manufacturers retain flexibility to decide how many vehicles in each emission tier to sell in order to meet the fleet average.

inspection, or any other approval relating to the control of emissions . . . as condition precedent to the initial retail sale, titling (if any), or registration of such motor vehicle, motor vehicle engine, or equipment.

The District Court's determination that this express pre-emption provision did not invalidate the Fleet Rules hinged on its interpretation of the word "standard" to include only regulations that compel manufacturers to meet specified emission limits. . . .

. . . Today, as in 1967 when § 209(a) became law, "standard" is defined as that which "is established by authority, custom, or general consent, as a model or example; criterion; test." Webster's Second New International Dictionary 2455 (1945). The criteria referred to in § 209(a) relate to the emission characteristics of a vehicle or engine. To meet them the vehicle or engine must not emit more than a certain amount of a given pollutant, must be equipped with a certain type of pollution-control device, or must have some other design feature related to the control of emissions. This interpretation is consistent with the use of "standard" throughout Title II of the CAA (which governs emissions from moving sources) to denote requirements such as numerical emission levels with which vehicles or engines must comply, e.g., 42 U.S.C. § 7521(a)(3)(B)(ii), or emission-control technology with which they must be equipped, e.g., § 7521(a)(6).

Respondents, like the courts below, engraft onto this meaning of "standard" a limiting component, defining it as only "[a] *production* mandat[e] that require[s] *manufacturers* to ensure that the vehicles they produce have particular emissions characteristics, whether individually or in the aggregate." Brief for Respondent South Coast Air Quality Management District 13 (emphasis added). This confuses standards with the means of enforcing standards. Manufacturers (or purchasers) can be made responsible for ensuring that vehicles *comply* with emission standards, but the standards themselves are separate from those enforcement techniques. While standards target vehicles or engines, standard-enforcement efforts that are proscribed by § 209 can be directed to manufacturers or purchasers.

The distinction between "standards," on the one hand, and methods of standard enforcement, on the other, is borne out in the provisions immediately following § 202. These separate provisions enforce the emission criteria—i.e., the § 202 standards. Section 203 prohibits manufacturers from selling any new motor vehicle that is not covered by a "certificate of conformity." Section 206 enables manufacturers to obtain such a certificate by demonstrating to the EPA that their vehicles or engines conform to the § 202 standards. Sections 204 and 205 subject manufacturers, dealers, and others who violate the CAA to fines imposed in civil or administrative enforcement actions. By defining "standard" as a "production mandate directed toward manufacturers," respondents lump together § 202 and these other distinct statutory provisions, acknowledging a standard to be such only when it is combined with a mandate that prevents manufacturers from selling noncomplying vehicles.

That a standard is a standard even when not enforced through manufacturer-directed regulation can be seen in Congress's use of the term in another portion of the CAA. As the District Court recognized, CAA § 246 (in conjunction with its accompanying provisions) requires state-adopted and federally approved "restrictions on the purchase of fleet vehicles *to meet clean-air standards.*" 158 F.Supp.2d, at 1118 (emphasis added). (Respondents do not defend the District's Fleet Rules as authorized by this provision; the Rules do not comply with all of the requirements that it contains.) Clearly, Congress contemplated the enforcement of emission standards through purchase requirements.

Respondents contend that their qualified meaning of "standard" is necessary to prevent § 209(a) from pre-empting "far too much" by "encompass[ing] a broad range of state-level clean-air initiatives" such as voluntary incentive programs. Brief for Respondent South Coast Air Quality Management District 29. But it is hard to see why limitation to mandates on manufacturers is necessary for this purpose; limitation to mandates on manufacturers and purchasers, or to mandates on *anyone*, would have the same salvific effect. We need not resolve application of § 209(a) to voluntary incentive programs in this case, since all the Fleet Rules are mandates.

In addition to having no basis in the text of the statute, treating sales restrictions and purchase restrictions differently for pre-emption purposes would make no sense. The manufacturer's right to sell federally approved vehicles is meaningless in the absence of a purchaser's right to buy them. It is true that the Fleet Rules at issue here cover only certain purchasers and certain federally certified vehicles, and thus do not eliminate all demand for covered vehicles. But if one State or political subdivision may enact such rules, then so may any other; and the end result would undo Congress's carefully calibrated regulatory scheme.

A command, accompanied by sanctions, that certain purchasers may buy only vehicles with particular emission characteristics is as much an "attempt to enforce" a "standard" as a command, accompanied by sanctions, that a certain percentage of a manufacturer's sales volume must consist of such vehicles. We decline to read into § 209(a) a purchase/sale distinction that is not to be found in the text of § 209(a) or the structure of the CAA.

. . . The language of § 209(a) is categorical. It is (as we have discussed) impossible to find in it an exception for standards imposed through purchase restrictions rather than directly upon manufacturers. . . .

. . . The dissent objects to our interpretive method, which neither invokes the "presumption against preemption" to determine the *scope* of pre-emption nor delves into legislative history. Application of those methods, on which not all Members of this Court agree, demonstrably makes no difference to resolution of the principal question, which the dissent (after applying them) answers the same as we. As for the additional question that the dissent reaches, we think the same is true: The textual obstacles to the strained interpretation that would validate the Rules by reason of the "commercial availability" provisos are insurmountable—principally, the categorical words of § 209(a). The dissent contends that giving these words their natural meaning of barring implementation of standards at the purchase and sale stage renders superfluous the second sentence of § 209(a), which provides: "No State shall require certification, inspection, or any other approval relating to the control of emissions from any new motor vehicle or new motor vehicle engine as condition precedent to the initial retail sale, titling (if any), or registration of such motor vehicle, motor vehicle engine, or equipment." We think it not superfluous, since it makes clear that the term "attempt to enforce" in the first sentence is not limited to the actual imposition of penalties for violation, but includes steps preliminary to that action.

. . . The courts below held all six of the Fleet Rules to be entirely outside the pre-emptive reach of § 209(a) based on reasoning that does not withstand scrutiny. In light of the principles articulated above, it appears likely that at least certain aspects of the Fleet Rules are pre-empted. For example, the District may have attempted to enforce CARB's ULEV, SULEV, and ZEV standards when it required 50% of new passenger-car and medium-duty-vehicle purchases by private airport-shuttle van operators to "meet ULEV, SULEV, or ZEV emission standards" after July 1, 2001, and 100% to meet those standards after July 1, 2002.

It does not necessarily follow, however, that the Fleet Rules are preempted *in toto*. We have not addressed a number of issues that may affect the ultimate disposition of petitioners' suit, including the scope of petitioners' challenge, whether some of the Fleet Rules (or some applications of them) can be characterized as internal state purchase decisions (and, if so, whether a different standard for pre-emption applies), and whether § 209(a) pre-empts the Fleet Rules even as applied beyond the purchase of new vehicles (*e.g.*, to lease arrangements or to the purchase of used vehicles). These questions were neither passed on below nor presented in the petition for certiorari. They are best addressed in the first instance by the lower courts in light of the principles articulated above.

■ JUSTICE SOUTER, dissenting:

The Court holds that preemption by the Clean Air Act prohibits one of the most polluted regions in the United States from requiring private fleet operators to buy clean engines that are readily available on the commercial market. I respectfully dissent and would hold that the South

Coast Air Quality Management District Fleet Rules are not preempted by the Act.

So far as it concerns this case, § 209(a) of the Act provides that "[n]o State or any political subdivision thereof shall adopt or attempt to enforce any standard relating to the control of emissions from new motor vehicles or new motor vehicle engines subject to [Title II of the Act]." The better reading of this provision rests on two interpretive principles the majority opinion does not address.

First, "[i]n all pre-emption cases, and particularly in those [where] Congress has legislated . . . in a field which the States have traditionally occupied, we start with the assumption that the historic police powers of the States were not to be superseded by the Federal Act unless that was the clear and manifest purpose of Congress." . . .

Second, legislative history should inform interpretive choice, and the legislative history of this preemption provision shows that Congress's purpose in passing it was to stop States from imposing regulatory requirements that directly limited what manufacturers could sell. . . .

NOTES AND QUESTIONS

1. Basics of Title II Regulation. What does § 202 require in the establishment of standards? How does § 207 set rules for compliance by vehicles in actual use? What does § 209 say about state standards that are less stringent than the standards promulgated pursuant to § 202? What about those that are more stringent?

2. Scope of § 209 Preemption. The two cases above establish the basic outlines of the scope of federal preemption power under § 209: § 209(a) preempts any pre-sale regulation of motor vehicles—even if a state is merely attempting to enforce a federal standard or enforcement mechanism through state regulation. *See, e.g., In re Detroit Diesel Corp. v. Attorney Gen. of N.Y.,* 709 N.Y.S.2d 1 (App. Div. 2000) ("In light of the CAA's broad preemption provision, States are barred from providing their own regulatory or judicial remedies for conduct prohibited or arguably prohibited by Federal law."); *see also Metropolitan Taxicab Bd. of Trade v. City of New York,* 615 F.3d 152 (2d Cir. 2010) (affirming the grant of a preliminary injunction against enforcement of New York City taxicab lease rates that would incentivize use of fuel-efficient vehicles because the rules were preempted by DOT statutory authority, but declining to reach the question of whether the rules were preempted by CAA § 209. New York unsuccessfully sought to argue that a scale of lease rates that were higher for hybrid vehicles was not a fuel efficiency standard, but a mechanism to internalize the cost of fuel for vehicle owners), *cert. denied,* 562 U.S. 1264 (2011).

EMA v. SCAQMD establishes the limits of what is preempted by § 209(a) by defining "standard" broadly to mean any criterion related to the emission characteristics of a vehicle or engine and holding that preemption of "attempts to enforce" such "standards" may be directed to either manufacturers or purchasers. *Cf. Sims v. State of Fla., Dept. of Highway*

Safety & Motor Vehicles, 862 F.2d 1449, 1455–58 (11th Cir. 1989) (holding that a Florida statute that was directed toward purchasers of vehicles was not preempted).

3.   **Voluntary Incentive Programs.** One question left open by the Court in *EMA v. SCAQMD* is whether voluntary incentive programs *(e.g.,* providing rebates or other incentives for purchasers of clean fuel vehicles) fall within the scope of § 209(a). Is it at least arguable that such programs do not "attempt to enforce" a "standard"? The Supreme Court has distinguished between voluntary *contractual* agreements and state-imposed regulations, holding that the former are not within the scope of an express preemption statute. *See, e.g., Am. Airlines v. Wolens*, 513 U.S. 219 (1995) ("We do not read the ADA's preemption clause, however, to shelter airlines from suits alleging no violation of state-imposed obligations, but seeking recovery solely for the airline's alleged breach of its own, self-imposed undertakings.").

What if "self-imposed undertakings" are contracts with the state that are the result of a state regulation providing incentives for production or purchase of low-emissions vehicles (LEVs)? *Cf. Ass'n of Int'l Auto. Mfrs. v. Mass. Dep't of Envtl. Prot.*, 208 F.3d 1 (1st Cir. 2000) (holding that memoranda of agreement between California and automobile manufacturers are not "standards" for purposes of § 209 and thus Massachusetts could not adopt them pursuant to § 177).

4.   **Supreme Court's Preemption Jurisprudence.** At least one commentator has noted the inconsistency of the Supreme Court's preemption jurisprudence with its generally pro-federalism agenda:

> So far as I am aware, no commentator has affirmatively linked the Supreme Court's preemption cases to its federalism agenda. The explanation resides partly in preemption doctrine's entrenched tenets. The doctrine has long expressed a pro-federalism presumption against inferring preemption, especially in areas of traditional state regulation. But part of the explanation, too, involves the unwillingness of the Rehnquist Court consistently to enforce a robust presumption against preemption. Over the decade since Clarence Thomas joined the Court and produced the current pro-federalism five-member majority, the Court has decided thirty-five preemption cases and found state statutes or causes of action to be preempted, either in whole or in part, in twenty-two. Indeed, during the Court's 1999 and 2000 Terms, the Court decided seven preemption cases and held that federal law preempted state law in all of them. . . .

> Whereas one might expect pro-federalism Justices to disfavor claims of federal preemption of state law, substantive conservatism may help to explain why the Court has so frequently upheld preemption claims in recent years. Because federal preemption eliminates state regulatory burdens, preemption rulings have a tendency—welcome to substantive conservatives—to minimize the regulatory requirements to which businesses are subject. As noted above, the Court held that state law was preempted in every one of

its seven preemption cases during the 1999 and 2000 Terms. Four of the Court's five most conservative, generally pro-federalism justices—Chief Justice Rehnquist and Justices O'Connor, Scalia, and Kennedy—found federal preemption in each instance, and Justice Thomas agreed in every case but one.

Richard H. Fallon, Jr., *The "Conservative" Paths of the Rehnquist Court's Federalism Decisions*, 69 U. CHI. L. REV. 429, 462–63, 471–72 (2002).

In *EMA v. SCAQMD*, eight of the justices agreed that the purchasing restrictions were preempted by § 209(a). Justice Scalia's analysis focused on the plain language of the statute and rejected application of the presumption against preemption advocated by the dissent. Was this the right approach? Is it consistent with the spirit of "cooperative federalism" that informs the CAA? Is there a clear textual answer to these questions? If not, how should they be answered? How do you think the Court is answering them? *See also* Lisa Heinzerling, *Climate, Preemption, and the Executive Branches*, 50 ARIZ. L. REV. 925, 927 (2008) (discussing executive and judicial branch treatment of preemption issues with respect to state greenhouse gas regulation).

5.   Standards in California. The CAA generally prohibits the states from adopting any vehicle emissions standards. 42 U.S.C. § 7543(a). However, § 209(b) provides that the Administrator may waive application of the prohibition to any state that adopted new motor vehicle emission standards prior to March 30, 1966, so long as the state determines that its standards will be "at least as protective of public health and welfare as applicable Federal standards." 42 U.S.C. § 7543(b). The Administrator may not grant a waiver if the state's determination is arbitrary and capricious, the state's standards are not necessary "to meet compelling and extraordinary circumstances," or the state's standards are inconsistent with certain CAA provisions relating to technical feasibility and lead time to be given to manufacturers. 42 U.S.C. § 7543(b)(c). California is the only state that adopted vehicle emissions standards prior to 1966, and thus is the only state that can seek a § 209(b) waiver. GAO, CLEAN AIR ACT; HISTORICAL INFORMATION ON EPA'S PROCESS FOR REVIEWING CALIFORNIA WAIVER REQUESTS (2009). California has requested, and been granted, more than 50 waivers. *Id.* Why does the Clean Air Act provide a mechanism for California to introduce more stringent vehicle standards? Is it appropriate that California remains the only state that can seek a waiver? Should the expression "extraordinary and compelling circumstances" be interpreted to mean the general circumstances that led to the inclusion in the CAA of a mechanism for California to seek a waiver, or should it be more narrowly interpreted as the direct circumstances that have driven California to seek each particular waiver?

In 2005, California sought a waiver from EPA that would allow California to regulate motor vehicle emissions of greenhouse gases. EPA delayed deciding California's waiver request pending the decision in *Massachusetts v. EPA*, 549 U.S. 497 (2007). In 2008, under the Bush administration, the Administrator formally refused California's waiver on the ground that California did not have any "compelling and extraordinary circumstances"—the first time that EPA had denied a formal waiver request outright. *Id* at 2. In January 2009, the Obama administration directed EPA to reconsider California's waiver request. *See* Memorandum from President Barack Obama to Administrator of the EPA, State of California Request for Waiver Under U.S.C. 7543(b), the Clean Air Act (2009). The waiver was granted in June 2009. *See* 74 Fed. Reg. 32,744 (2009).

On what basis might the Administrator have determined that California did not have any compelling and extraordinary circumstances that justified the waiver?

6.   Adoption of California Standards by Other States. Section 177 authorizes other states with nonattainment areas to adopt California's mobile source standards in lieu of the federal standards as long as two conditions are met: "(1) such standards are identical to the California standards for which a waiver has been granted for such model year, and (2) California and such State adopt such standards at least two years before commencement of such model year (as determined by regulations of the Administrator)." 42 U.S.C. § 7507. As of August 2018, 36 states, plus the District of Columbia, Puerto Rico, and Guam, have at least one county that is in nonattainment for at least one criteria pollutant. *See* EPA, Current Nonattainment Counties for All Criteria Pollutants, https://www3.epa.gov/airquality/greenbook/ancl.html (last visited Sept. 26, 2018).

The auto industry has successfully challenged states' adoption of California's standards on the grounds that the state's regulations are not "identical" to California's. For example, after obtaining a waiver from EPA, California adopted sales restrictions that required certain percentages of LEVs and zero emissions vehicles (ZEVs) to be sold within the state. Several states, including Massachusetts and New York, subsequently adopted these sales restrictions pursuant to § 177. Later, however, California abandoned the ZEV requirement and instead entered into memoranda of agreement (MOAs) with automakers to produce a certain number of ZEVs for the state. Industry then sued Massachusetts and New York, arguing that their standards were no longer "identical" to California's and thus were preempted by § 209(a). The First and Second Circuits agreed. *See Am. Auto. Mfr. Ass'n v. Cahill*, 152 F.3d 196, 200–01 (2d Cir. 1998) (holding that regardless of the MOAs, New York's standards were no longer "identical"); *Ass'n of Int'l Auto. Mfrs. v. Mass. Dep't of Envtl. Prot.*, 208 F.3d 1 (1st Cir. 2000) (holding that MOAs are not "standards" and thus Massachusetts could not adopt them pursuant to § 177).

Is this the right result? What if it could be shown that industry entered into the MOAs precisely in order to change its regulatory obligations in other states? Should this matter? What if industry refuses to even consider such MOAs with other states? In what position does this put California? What public policy goals, if any, are promoted by this approach?

In September of 2007, the district court of Vermont ruled in *Green Mt. Chrysler v. Crombie*, 508 F. Supp. 2d 295 (D. Vt. 2007) that Vermont's state regulation of greenhouse gas emissions was not preempted. The court relied on the fact that Vermont's regulations were identical to California's greenhouse gas standards. Does § 177 require states seeking to adopt

California standards to make any specific findings about the effects of emissions in their jurisdictions? Why don't other states have to make the findings that California must when it seeks a waiver?

7. California Standards Influence the Federal Program. Following California's adoption of emissions standards that are more stringent that the federal program requires, other states considered the choice between the Californian and the federal standards. In 1991, the states comprising the Ozone Transport Commission (the 12 northeastern states, the District of Columbia, Texas, Michigan, Illinois and Wisconsin) agreed that each would take steps to adopt California's standards. Only Massachusetts and New York actually went on to adopt the standards. In 1993, the OTC recommended to EPA that all states within the OTC be required to adopt California's vehicle emission standards beginning in model year 1999. In 1995, EPA approved the OTC's recommendation. At the same time it announced it would attempt to develop a voluntary national LEV program, even though the CAA precluded it from requiring vehicle manufacturers to meet more stringent standards before model year 2004. Though it was voluntary for vehicle manufacturers to enter the national program, once they did so, EPA could enforce the standard like any other binding standard. The California standards would be applied if the national LEV program failed. Even though the D.C. Circuit held that EPA lacked authority to require OTC states to adopt the California standards (*Virginia v. EPA*, 108 F.3d 1397, 1415, modified on other grounds, 116 F.3d 499, 501 (D.C. Cir. 1997)), EPA succeeded in developing a national LEV program that applied to northeastern states from model year 1999, and nationally from model year 2001. All automobile manufacturers in the country entered into the agreement, which provided for less stringent standards than California applies. *See* Richard L. Revesz, *Federalism and Environmental Regulation: A Public Choice Analysis* 115 HARV. L. REV 553, 588–90 (2001). As of 2018, 12 other states and the District of Columbia have adopted California's stricter emissions standards. *See* Timothy Gardner, *U.S. States Vow to Defend Auto Fuel Efficiency Standards*, REUTERS, Apr. 3, 2018. What role did the California standards play in the development of national standards? What is the possible effect of having two sets of vehicle emissions standards applicable in different states?

8. Market Participant Exception to Preemption. Recall that the Court left open the possibility that SCAQMD could adopt some of its fleet rules pursuant to the market participant exception to preemption. The market participant exception recognizes that states as market actors may make internal purchasing or other business decisions to further their competitiveness in the regulated field. *See Building & Constr. Trades Council v. Associated Builders & Contractors*, 507 U.S. 218, 227 (1993) ("When a State owns and manages property . . . it must interact with private participants in the marketplace. . . . [T]he State is not subject to pre-emption . . . because pre-emption doctrines apply only to state *regulation*."). To qualify for this exception, the government must be acting as a proprietor, rather than a regulator. The Ninth Circuit has applied the following test to make the proprietor-regulator determination:

To determine whether a government entity is acting in a proprietary or a regulatory capacity, we consider whether the challenged action essentially reflect[s] the entity's own interest in its efficient procurement of needed goods and services, as measured by comparison with the typical behavior of private parties in similar circumstances and whether the narrow scope of the challenged action defeat[s] an inference that its primary goal was to encourage a general policy rather than address a specific proprietary problem.

Olympic Pipe Line Co. v. City of Seattle, 437 F.3d 872, 881 (9th Cir. 2006) (quotation marks omitted).

On remand, the District Court upheld SCAQMD's regulations as applied to state and local fleets pursuant to the market participant exception to preemption; the Ninth Circuit affirmed this finding. *See Engine Mfrs. Ass'n v. S. Coast Air Quality Mgmt. Dist.*, 498 F.3d 1031, 1050 (9th Cir. 2007). The Ninth Circuit reasoned that the rules' express goal of increasing fuel efficiency was not "fatal," because the action in question qualified as market participation. *Id.* at 1046 ("That a state or local governmental entity may have policy goals that it seeks to further through its participation in the market does not preclude the doctrine's application, so long as the action in question is the state's own market participation."). Is this result a fair interpretation of the Supreme Court's opinion? Is it a fair interpretation of Congress' intent in enacting § 209?

SCAQMD also requested that CARB apply for a waiver of preemption from EPA. *See* SCAQMD, Fleet Rules, http://www.aqmd.gov/home/rules-compliance/rules/fleet-rules (last visited Oct. 2, 2018). Before CARB can apply for a waiver, it must adopt the SCAQMD's findings of compelling need and go through a state administrative process. *See* Letter from Barry R. Wallerstein, SCAQMD, to Catherine Witherspoon, CARB, Jan. 28, 2005. Why do you suppose SCAQMD did not go through CARB to request a waiver from EPA in the first instance?

10. HAZARDOUS AIR POLLUTANTS

A. GENERAL PROVISIONS

Hazardous air pollutants (HAPs) are air pollutants "known or suspected to cause cancer or other serious health effects, such as reproductive effects or birth defects, or adverse environmental effects." EPA, About Air Toxics, http://www.epa.gov/ttn/atw/allabout.html (last visited Sept. 26, 2018). Examples include asbestos, benzene, vinyl chloride, and mercury. Many HAPs are non-threshold pollutants, for which no "safe" level of human exposure exists. Sources of HAPs are pervasive in everyday life, ranging from coal-fired power plants and steel mills to dry cleaners and automobiles.

EPA regulates stationary HAP sources separately from criteria pollutants, pursuant to § 112. Before 1990, § 112 directed the

Administrator to identify HAPs and to set emissions standards "at the level which in his judgment provides an ample margin of safety to protect the public health from such hazardous air pollutant." 42 U.S.C. § 7412 (1982). Thus, the pre-1990 § 112 envisioned a two-step approach to regulation of HAPs:

> The approach chosen by Congress for control of hazardous air pollutants, while based on the same theory of environmental rights that characterizes the entire Act, differs somewhat from the approach chosen for other types of air pollutants. The cornerstone of the Clean Air Act Amendments of 1970 was the complex federal/state relationship established for control of the so-called "criteria" pollutants under sections 108 through 110. Section 112 is one of the major exceptions to this federalist approach to pollution control. The point of section 112 is to allow the EPA to bypass the unwieldy process of establishing ambient standards and reviewing state implementation plans. The toxic air pollutants to be regulated under section 112 were supposed to be more dangerous—that is, more severe in their health effects—than the criteria pollutants, thus justifying direct EPA control of emission sources. In light of the dangers involved, Congress created a simple two-step rulemaking process: A specific pollutant is first listed as hazardous, based on a consideration of relevant scientific data; then, uniform national emission standards are established for each source category.

John D. Graham, *The Failure of Agency-Forcing: The Regulation of Airborne Carcinogens Under Section 112 of the Clean Air Act*, 1985 DUKE L.J. 100, 107–08. Once the Administrator listed a pollutant as a HAP, he was required to propose emissions standards within 180 days and finalize the standards within another 180 days. 42 U.S.C. § 7412 (1982).

As the court observed in *Sierra Club v. EPA*, 353 F.3d 976, 979 (D.C. Cir. 2004) "[t]his approach proved to be disappointing." In fact, in the twenty years after the initial passage of the 1970 CAA, EPA listed and promulgated standards for only seven pollutants: asbestos, beryllium, mercury, vinyl chloride, benzene, inorganic arsenic, and radionuclides. *See NRDC v. Thomas*, 885 F.2d 1067, 1071 (2d Cir. 1989). Even these pollutants were regulated somewhat haphazardly. For example, the mercury standards exempted electric utilities despite the significant contribution of power plants to mercury pollution in the Great Lakes. *See* Arnold W. Reitze, Jr. & Randy Lowell, *Control of Hazardous Air Pollution*, 28 B.C. ENVTL. AFF. L. REV. 229, 238 (2001). For these reasons, regulation under the pre-1990 § 112 is often cited as the quintessential example of ineffective health-based standard-setting. *See, e.g.*, Graham, *supra*, at 148–50; Wendy E. Wagner, *The Science Charade in Toxic Risk Regulation*, 95 COLUM. L. REV. 1613, 1678–70 (1995).

While most commentators attribute the ultimate failure of pre-1990 § 112 to statutory design, the courts also played a role both in complicating an already difficult standard-setting process and facilitating agency foot-dragging. In *NRDC v. EPA*, the D.C. Circuit rejected EPA's attempt to establish standards explicitly based on technical and economic feasibility. 824 F.2d 1146, 1163 (D.C. Cir. 1987) (en banc). EPA considered itself faced with two choices for regulation of non-threshold pollutants: either set the emissions standard at zero-exposure and risk closure of entire industries, or take into account technical and economic feasibility and set the standard accordingly. In effect, the second approach replaced a health-based standard with a technology-based standard. *See id.* The petitioners argued that EPA could not consider non-statutorily identified factors at all and was required to consider only the public health; EPA argued that the broad language of § 112 gave the Administrator discretion to base his decision on feasibility considerations. The court agreed that EPA could consider feasibility, but restricted the feasibility analysis to determining the "ample margin of safety." Because the statute was primarily concerned with public health, the Administrator first had to make a health-based determination of the "safe" level of exposure. (The court noted, however, that "safe" does not mean risk-free.) Only then, when considering at what level to set the "ample margin of safety," could the Administrator consider technical and economic feasibility. *Id.* at 1164–65. The two-step analysis established by *NRDC v. EPA* thus blocked what was clearly an attempt by the Administrator to dodge the difficult value judgments involved in health-based standard setting by transforming § 112 into a technology-based standard. The result, however, was even greater reluctance on EPA's part to promulgate standards.

In *NRDC v. Thomas*, 885 F.2d 1067, 1068–69 (2d Cir. 1989), the Second Circuit upheld the trial court's dismissal of a case that sought to compel the Administrator to list eight pollutants for which he had issued notices that each pollutant was a probable or known carcinogen.* Petitioners argued that the Administrator had failed to perform a non-discretionary duty, reviewable in the district court pursuant to § 304, by not listing the pollutants after issuing the notice of his findings. The Second Circuit held that the notices were not the "functional equivalent" of a finding that the pollutants were HAPs:

> For the most part, the Notices indicate that more data is being compiled, or that the available testing methodology is limited. Moreover, these conclusions, as pointed out in the Notices, are based upon experiments on laboratory animals, or upon the epidemiological studies of workers exposed to unusually high levels of the Pollutants, leaving open to further investigation the overall effects of the Pollutants upon the general human population.

---

*   The eight pollutants were cadmium, hexavalent chromium, acrylonitrile, carbon tetrachloride, chloroform, ethylene oxide, 1,3–butadiene, and ethylene dichloride.

. . . We conclude that the Notices are not, as NRDC contends, the "functional equivalent" of determinations by the Administrator that the Pollutants are "hazardous air pollutants," a term whose statutory definition in section 112(b)(1)(A) expressly incorporates the *judgment* of the Administrator as to health effects. In rendering this judgment, the Administrator must have the flexibility to analyze a great deal of information in an area which " 'is on the frontiers of scientific knowledge.' "

Id. at 1074–75 (citations omitted). Thus, in *NRDC v. Thomas*, EPA was authorized to continue its pattern of delay based on scientific uncertainty.

Finally, after twenty years of profound agency inaction, Congress overhauled § 112 in the 1990 CAA amendments. Pub. L. No. 101–549, 104 Stat. 2531 (1990). The amended § 112 adopts a technology-based approach to regulation of HAPs, with a health-based standard as a backstop. Section 112(b) establishes an initial list of 189 pollutants that Congress identified and defined as HAPs. 42 U.S.C. § 7412(b).

Section 112(c) requires the Administrator to establish a list of "source categories" for HAPs, consistent to the extent practicable with the source categories established under the NSPS of § 111. 42 U.S.C. § 7412(c). For each source category, the Administrator must establish an emission standard according to the schedules set forth in § 112. The guidelines for establishing these emissions standards are set forth in § 112(d). For major sources (defined in § 112(a) as sources having the potential to emit (PTE) 10 tons per year (TPY) of any HAP or 25 TPY of any combination of HAPs), the Administrator is required to set the standard according to the maximum available control technology (MACT). 42 U.S.C. § 7412(d). The "MACT floor," or the minimum standard for major sources, is the "the average emission limitation achieved by the best performing 12 percent of the existing sources," or, for categories containing fewer than 30 sources, the emission limitation achieved by the best performing five sources. 42 U.S.C. § 7412(d)(3). Once EPA defines the floor of the proposed MACT standard, it next examines the possibility of enacting more stringent standards—known as "beyond-the-floor" standards. In determining whether "beyond-the-floor" standards are achievable, the Administrator must take into consideration "the cost . . . and any non-air quality health and environmental impacts and energy requirements." 42 U.S.C. § 7412(d)(2). For area sources (defined in § 112(a) as all sources that are not major), the Administrator may set the standard according to generally available control technology (GACT) in lieu of applying a MACT standard. 42 U.S.C. § 7412(d)(5).

The 1990 amendments preserved the health-based standard as a backstop in § 112(f), which requires the Administrator, in the absence of congressional action, to consider promulgation of a health-based standard to address residual risks eight years after the development of the initial standards under § 112(d). *See* 42 U.S.C. § 7412(f). This health-based standard "shall provide an ample margin of safety to protect public health . . . unless the Administrator determines that a more stringent standard is necessary to prevent, taking into consideration costs, energy, safety, and other relevant factors, an adverse environmental effect." *Id.*

Despite the introduction of technology-based regulation of HAPs in the 1990 amendments, EPA has continued to drag its feet. In August 2006, a federal district court ordered EPA to promulgate regulations for several area source categories according to a judicially-determined schedule. The court stated that EPA had been "grossly delinquent" in fulfilling its mandatory duties under § 112, and noted that "the history of regulation under Section[ ] 112(c) . . . shows that EPA has fulfilled its statutory duties only when forced by litigation to do so." *Sierra Club v. Johnson*, 444 F. Supp. 2d 46, 58 (D.D.C. 2006).

In 2011, over twenty years after the 1990 amendments, EPA finalized hazardous air pollution regulations for two categories of major sources, incinerators and industrial boilers. 76 Fed. Reg. 28,662 (2011). At the same time that it issued these rules, however, EPA stayed their effectiveness for an indefinite period pending reconsideration by the agency. *Id.* In 2012, EPA finalized regulations for hazardous air pollution from power plants. 77 Fed. Reg. 9304 (2012). The regulation of power plants is discussed further in Section 11.

The following cases explore the definitions of "major source" and "potential to emit" and the elements of a MACT determination under § 112.

National Mining Association v. Environmental Protection Agency
59 F.3d 1351 (D.C. Cir. 1995).

■ Before SILBERMAN, GINSBURG, and RANDOLPH, CIRCUIT JUDGES.

■ PER CURIAM:

. . . Under the Act, "major sources" of hazardous air pollutants are potentially subject to stricter regulatory control than are "area sources." For example, major sources must comply with technology-based emission standards requiring the maximum degree of reduction in emissions EPA deems achievable, often referred to as "maximum achievable control technology" or MACT standards. 42 U.S.C. § 7412(d)(1)–(2). In order to obtain an operating permit under title V of the Act, §§ 501–507, major sources must comply with extensive monitoring, reporting and record-keeping requirements. 42 U.S.C. §§ 7661–7661f. Further, § 112(g) generally conditions the modification, construction or reconstruction of a major source on the source's meeting MACT emission limitations. 42 U.S.C. § 7412(g).

... EPA proposed a rule codifying the "procedures and criteria needed to implement" emission standards for hazardous air pollutants. It promulgated a final rule, which is the subject of this dispute, adopting these general provisions on March 16, 1994. 59 Fed. Reg. 12,408 (1994).

Among other things, the general provisions rule implements § 112(a)(1)'s definition of "major source." The rule defines "major source" in terms nearly identical to those in § 112(a)(1) of the Clean Air Act:

> Major source means any stationary source or group of stationary sources located within a contiguous area and under common control that emits or has the potential to emit considering controls, in the aggregate, 10 tons per year or more of any hazardous air pollutant or 25 tons per year or more of any combination of hazardous air pollutants, unless the Administrator establishes a lesser quantity, or in the case of radionuclides, different criteria from those specified in this sentence.

59 Fed. Reg. at 12,433–34. A "stationary source" is "any building, structure, facility or installation which emits or may emit any air pollutant." *Id.* An "area source [is] any stationary source . . . that is not a major source." *Id.* . . .

In the preamble to the final rule, EPA made clear that in determining whether a source is major, emissions from all sources of hazardous air pollutants within a plant site must be aggregated, so long as the sources are geographically adjacent and under common control. As a result, if the total annual emissions of hazardous air pollutants from a plant site exceed the designated thresholds, each source emitting pollutants at the site must comply with the stricter MACT emission standards applicable to sources under § 112(d)(2), and with other requirements applicable to major sources.

Petitioners read § 112(a)(1) more restrictively. In their view, EPA's approach will impermissibly regulate "minor facilities" that happen to be located at an industrial site with annual emissions of hazardous air pollutants that, in the aggregate, exceed the major source thresholds. They contend that EPA may require aggregation of emissions from sources only if those sources fall within a single source category— General Electric's argument, or the same two-digit SIC Code—National Mining Association's contention. . . .

If § 112(a)(1) is viewed in isolation, EPA's reading of the provision is not simply consistent with the provision; it is nearly compelled by the statutory language. Section 112(a)(1) states that a "group of stationary sources" need meet only three conditions to be termed a "major source": (1) sources within the group must be "located within a contiguous area"; (2) they must be "under common control"; and (3) in the aggregate, they must emit or, considering controls, have the potential to emit 10 or more tons per year of a single hazardous air pollutant or 25 or more tons per year of any combination of hazardous air pollutants. Section 112(a)(1) says nothing about combining emissions only from sources within the same source categories or SIC Codes. In this respect, EPA's definition of "major source," set forth in the preamble to the final rule, is faithful to the language of § 112 (a) (1). . . .

In addition to alleging inconsistencies between EPA's definition of "major source" and § 112's other provisions, General Electric insists that EPA's implementation of § 112(a)(1) is at odds with other aspects of the Clean Air Act. It points to § 112(a)(3)'s provision that "stationary source" has the same meaning as it does in § 111 of the Act, 42 U.S.C. § 7411, which deals with performance standards applicable to new sources. In *Alabama Power Co. v. Costle*, General Electric notes, this court rejected EPA's definition of "stationary source" as used in § 111(a)(3) as a "combination" of "buildings, structures, facilities, or installations." To be sure, *Alabama Power* struck down EPA's defining "source" for purposes of its preventing significant deterioration in air quality program, as any "structure, building, facility equipment, installation or operation *(or combination thereof)*" 636 F.2d at 394, 395–96 (italics added). But that was because EPA had unlawfully expanded § 111(a)(3), which defines "stationary source" as "any building, structure, facility or installation which emits or may emit any air pollutant," without reference to combinations of these things. 636 F.2d at 396. That is not the case here. Section § 112(a)(1) expressly provides that a "major source" is "any stationary source *or group of stationary sources* 'with emissions exceeding certain limits.' [CAA § 1412(a)(1) (italics added).] Indeed, one could infer from § 112(a)(1) a congressional intent, in the context of hazardous air pollution regulation, to override *Alabama Power*. . . ."

. . . [I]n determining whether a source is to be categorized as a "major source" of emissions (or by default an "area" source), EPA was directed by Congress to calculate the amount of hazardous air pollutants a stationary source "emits or has the potential to emit *considering controls*." Clean Air Act § 112(a)(1) (emphasis added). In its final rule, EPA defined a source's "potential to emit" as its "maximum capacity . . . to emit a pollutant under its physical and operational design." 59 Fed. Reg. at 12,434. To comply with the statutory directive to "consider[ ] controls" while determining emissions capacities, the rule also provides:

> Any physical or operational limitation on the capacity of the stationary source to emit a pollutant, including air pollution control equipment and restrictions on hours of operation or on the type or amount or material combusted, stored, or processed, shall be treated as part of its design *if the limitation or the effect it would have on emissions is federally enforceable.*

Id. (emphasis added). Under the rule, a control is deemed to be "federally enforceable" if it is "enforceable by the Administrator and citizens under the Act or . . . under other statutes administered by the Administrator."

[The court describes a decade-long battle between the agency and industry over whether controls must be federally enforceable in order to reduce a source's PTE for purposes of major source determinations.]

. . . Congress thus acted in 1990 against a backdrop of over a decade of skirmishing between the agency and affected companies, during which the issue of whether and to what extent state and local controls were to be credited in calculating a source's "potential to emit" was very much in the forefront. In drafting § 112 Congress specifically directed EPA to consider controls in determining which producers should be classified as "major sources," but conspicuously did not limit controls to those that are federally enforceable.

. . . [I]t is certainly permissible for EPA to have refused to take into account ineffective controls (indeed, it is likely that a contrary interpretation would be impermissible). But is it also open to EPA under the statute to refuse to consider controls on grounds other than their lack of effectiveness? To qualify as "federally enforceable," (as best we can determine) controls are required, in addition to being effective as a practical matter, to have been approved by EPA and integrated into the state implementation plan, or SIP, drawn up by each state to enforce substantive restrictions under the Clean Air Act and submitted to the Administrator for approval under § 110. Once included within the SIP, a state control becomes enforceable not only by the state which is its primary regulating authority, but also by the Administrator under § 113 of Act, and, in certain settings, by private citizens, who can bring suit for noncompliance with federal pollution control programs under § 304.

. . . What EPA has not explained is how its refusal to consider limitations other than those that are "federally enforceable" serves the statute's directive to "consider[ ] controls" when it results in a refusal to credit controls imposed by a state or locality even if they are unquestionably effective. Under EPA's regime, even a state program of unassailable effectiveness would not qualify in computing a source's capacity to emit unless it had been submitted not only for EPA approval, but also for inclusion in the SIP. In doing so, EPA would sacrifice a statutory objective in pursuit of ends that, at least as presented in argument to us, have not been justified, either in terms of § 112 or other provisions of the Act. EPA has not explained why it is essential that a control be included within a SIP. It is not apparent why a state's or locality's controls, when demonstrably effective, should not be credited in determining whether a source subject to those controls should be classified as a major or area source.

. . . EPA's core justifications for its federal enforceability policy are the need to avoid the administrative burden that EPA would have to bear were it obligated to evaluate the effectiveness of state and local controls and the desirability of uniformity in environmental enforcement. These, of course, are not illegitimate agency objectives. Administrative problems, in particular, can under certain circumstances inform an agency's construction of imprecise statutory language. Here, however, EPA would have us accept a rather strained interpretation of the statute based on what appears to be only its unwillingness to evaluate any state or local controls that are not federalized. If there is a closer fit between the notion of "federal enforceability" and § 112's concern with crediting effective controls it is not evident on this record.

As for national uniformity, the government contends that "one of Congress' driving concerns in amending the hazardous air pollutants provision in the Act in 1990 was to remedy the haphazard state of air toxic regulations. . . . The states' approaches to regulation varied widely," creating " 'a patchwork of differing standards' " (citing H.R. REP. NO. 490(I), 101st Cong., 2d Sess. 232 (1990)). Just so; but the amendments do create a national substantive standard, namely categories of sources (major and area) and corresponding technological compliance measures. By no means does that suggest that Congress necessarily intended for state emissions controls to be disregarded in determining whether a source is classified as "major" or "area" under that national standard. Nor did Congress mandate that EPA assume the administration and enforcement of all governmental efforts at emissions limits. If such administration and enforcement is necessary to ensure that controls are effective in the context of the extant regulatory environment, EPA has certainly not made that case and has not indicated how that consideration supports its claim that its interpretation of the statute is reasonable.

In sum, EPA's definition of "major source" without respect to source categories or two-digit SIC codes is reasonable, as is its requirement that fugitive emissions be included in a source's aggregate emissions in determining whether the source is major . . . However, EPA has not explained why the criteria for federal approval and the consequences of that approval are related to ensuring the practical effectiveness of state controls such that the set of controls considered under § 112 should be limited in that fashion.

NOTES AND QUESTIONS

1.   **Sorting out Pollutants.** What is a "hazardous" air pollutant? What is a "criteria" pollutant? How do you tell one from another? Some pollutants are regulated as both criteria pollutants and HAPs. Lead, for example, is listed as a criteria pollutant, *see* EPA, Six Common Air Pollutants, https://www.epa.gov/criteria-air-pollutants (last visited Sept. 27, 2018), and lead compounds are listed as HAPs, *see* EPA, Original List of Hazardous Air Pollutants, http://www.epa.gov/ttn/atw/orig189.html (last visited Sept. 27, 2018). Why would this be the case?

Section 112(b)(1) of the CAA contains a list of substances that Congress determined to be HAPs. 42 U.S.C. 7412(b)(1). Section 112(b)(2) requires the Administrator to periodically review that list by adding pollutants which "may present, through inhalation or other routes of exposure, a threat of adverse human health effects. . . or adverse environmental effects." 42 U.S.C. § 4712(b)(2). Further, any person may petition the Administrator to modify the list of HAPs to add or remove a substance. The Administrator must add a substance if the petitioner shows, or the Administrator determines, that a substance is an air pollutant that "may reasonably be anticipated to cause adverse effects to human health or adverse environmental effects." 42 U.S.C. § 7412(b)(3)(A). The Administrator must delete a substance from the list if a petitioner shows, or the Administrator determines, that there is "adequate data on the health and environmental effects of the substance to determine that. . . the substance may not reasonably be anticipated to cause any adverse effects to the human health or adverse environmental effects." 42 U.S.C. § 7412(b)(3)(B). What is the difference between the standard of proof required to list a substance, and the standard required to delist a substance?

2. **Cost Considerations Revisited.** Compare the health-based statutory standards in §§ 109 and 112 (pre-1990 amendments) of the CAA:

> § 109(b)(1): National primary ambient air quality standards, prescribed, under subsection (a) shall be ambient air quality standards the attainment and maintenance of which in the judgment of the Administrator, based on such criteria and allowing an adequate margin of safety, are requisite to protect the public health. . . .

> § 112(b)(1)(B): The Administrator shall establish any such standard at the level which in his judgment provides an ample margin of safety to protect the public health from such air pollutant.

42 U.S.C. §§ 7409(b)(1), 7412(b)(1)(B).

Recall judicial interpretations of § 109 in *Lead Industries* and *American Trucking* that refused to allow cost considerations in setting the NAAQS. *NRDC v. EPA*, 824 F.2d 1146 (D.C. Cir. 1987) (en banc) (Bork, Circuit Judge), distinguished *Lead Industries* in the following way:

> In Lead Industries, we held that the Administrator is not required to consider cost and technology under the mandate in section 109 of the Clean Air Act to promulgate primary air quality standards which "allow[ ] an adequate margin of safety . . . to protect the public health." CAA § 1409(b)(1) (1982). The NRDC argues that the decision in Lead Industries, which involved the more permissive language "adequate," rather than "ample," "margin of safety," compels the conclusion that section 112 precludes consideration of economic and technological feasibility. We think not.

> The Lead Industries court did note that the statute on its face does not allow consideration of technological or economic feasibility, but the court based its decision that section 109 does not allow consideration of these factors in part on structural aspects of the ambient air pollution provisions that are not present here. First, besides "allowing an adequate margin of safety," ambient air standards set under section 109(b) must be based on "air quality

criteria," which section 108 defines as comprising several elements, all related to health. *See* CAA § 108(a)(2)(A), (B) & (C) (1982). The court reasoned that the exclusion of economic and technological feasibility considerations from air quality criteria also foreclosed reliance on such factors in setting the ambient air quality standards based on those criteria. The court also relied on the fact that state implementation plans, the means of enforcement of ambient air standards, could not take into account economic and technological feasibility if such consideration interfered with the timely attainment of ambient air standards, and that the Administrator could not consider such feasibility factors in deciding whether to approve the state plans. This provided further grounds for the court to believe that Congress simply did not intend the economics of pollution control to be considered in the scheme of ambient air regulations.

Id. at 1158–59. How persuasive is this distinction?

How would § 112 have fared under Justice Scalia's "no elephants in mouseholes" approach in *American Trucking*? Recall that Justice Scalia required that there be an explicit textual commitment to cost consideration, since "[w]e have . . . refused to find implicit in ambiguous sections of the CAA an authorization to consider costs that has elsewhere, and so often, been expressly granted." *Whitman v. Am. Trucking Ass'n*, 531 U.S. 457, 467 (2001).

How would § 112 fare under Justice Breyer's "statutory silence means cost consideration is acceptable" approach in *American Trucking*? *See id.* at 490–96 (Breyer, J., concurring in part, concurring in the judgment). Which approach would you have chosen in the context of § 112? Was the *NRDC v. EPA* court's compromise, which required the initial "safe level" determination to be made on the basis of health risk only, statutorily compelled? Did it show the appropriate level of deference to EPA under *Chevron*?

3. Definitions of "Major Source." In *National Mining*, industry was arguing for an "anti-bubble" major source determination under § 112, similar to the major source determination used for § 111. In other words, industry wanted the major source determination to apply to each unit within the plant, rather than to the total emissions of the plant as a whole. Presumably fewer individual units would meet the 10 TPY minimum if EPA did not aggregate emissions, and thus more sources would be categorized as "area sources," triggering a lower regulatory standard.

Recall that in *Chevron*, the Court upheld EPA's plantwide, or "bubble" definition of stationary source for purposes of determining whether new construction or modification triggered NSR in nonattainment areas. In that case, bubbling worked to industry's advantage, since it could avoid triggering NSR by reducing emissions in a more cost-effective manner within the plant. Should the differential effect on industry make a difference in the outcome of the cases?

4. "Federally Enforceable" in the Context of Cooperative Federalism. In *National Mining*, the D.C. Circuit rejected EPA's use of the "federally enforceable" limitation in PTE determinations for purposes of triggering regulation as a major source. The court subsequently struck down the federally enforceable limitations in PTE determinations in the PSD/nonattainment, NSR, and Title V operating permit contexts, basing its orders on the decision in *National Mining. See Chem. Mfrs. Assoc. v. EPA*, 70 F.3d 637 (D.C. Cir. 1995); *Clean Air Implementation Project v. EPA*, 1996 WL 393118 (D.C. Cir. 1996) (unpublished opinion).

Does the court strike the right balance in the context of the CAA's cooperative federalism principle? What are some of the practical problems EPA might face in including effective state and local controls in its PTE determinations? Is the court correct that failing to include effective state and local controls "would sacrifice a statutory objective"? What about the objective of ensuring pollution reduction? Compare the court's deference to state and local controls in this context with the grant of EPA review of BACT determinations in *Alaska Department of Environmental Conservation v. EPA, supra*, Section 5.D. Why is the court willing to defer to state and local standards but not state BACT determinations?

5. Implementation of 1990 Amendments. In 2006, a GAO report examined EPA's late and ineffective implementation of HAP program requirements set forth in the 1990 Amendments to the CAA. GAO cited a number of reasons for EPA's difficulty in regulating air toxics. A major stumbling block was the air toxics program's low priority compared to other CAA tasks—only around 18–19 percent of clean air funding went to the hazardous air pollutant program from 2000–2003, and that figure dropped to 15 percent in 2004 and 12 percent in 2005. GAO believed that programs dealing with NAAQS, climate change, and indoor air quality all received higher priority because they were viewed as obtaining more significant health benefits at lower costs. Why else might these other programs be receiving a higher proportion of funds than the HAP program? Why might the proportion of funds devoted to hazardous air pollutants be decreasing?

GAO also pointed out that EPA had done a poor job of updating its index of toxic chemicals; essentially the agency was only reacting to petitions rather than proactively assessing chemicals in the market. Given the limited funding allocated to the hazardous air pollutant program, is it troubling that EPA has shied away from acting in areas where it has limited information, or from taking assertive action to survey new chemicals on the market? Or is it better and more cost-effective to regulate in the areas with the most readily available information and allow private parties to bring to the agency's attention new chemicals that may need to be added to the index? *See* GAO, EPA SHOULD IMPROVE THE MANAGEMENT OF ITS AIR TOXICS PROGRAM (2006).

Sierra Club v. Environmental Protection Agency
353 F.3d 976 (D.C. Cir. 2004).

■ Before HENDERSON, TATEL, and ROBERTS, CIRCUIT JUDGES.

■ ROBERTS, CIRCUIT JUDGE:

Petitioner Sierra Club challenges the Environmental Protection Agency's promulgation, pursuant to Section 112 of the Clean Air Act, of regulations governing the emission of hazardous air pollutants from primary copper smelters.

. . . The issues in this case focus on the first phase of emission standards promulgation [MACT]. Within that phase, there are two steps. Step one requires EPA to establish what has come to be known as the MACT floor—the minimum level of reduction required by statute. For existing sources, EPA sets the MACT floor at "the average emission limitation achieved by the best performing 5 sources" in a category "with fewer than 30 sources." [CAA 112(d)(3)(B).] Once EPA has set the MACT floor, it may then impose stricter standards—so-called "beyond-the-floor" limits—if the Administrator determines them to be achievable after "taking into consideration the cost . . . and any non-air quality health and environmental impacts and energy requirements." *Id.* § [112(d)(2).] These "beyond-the-floor" limits in phase one under Section 112(d)(2) are distinct from the risk-based limits to be set eight years later under Section [112(f)(2)] during phase two.

[The court describes the copper smelting process, which involves melting refined copper sulfide ore and removing the "slag" that floats to the top of the molten ore, leaving pure copper behind.]

. . . Melting rocks and minerals at nearly 2,000 degrees Fahrenheit not surprisingly produces exhaust gas, which EPA refers to as "off-gases." The off-gases . . . contain metallic impurities—including lead and arsenic—that had been trapped in the ore but are released during smelting in the form of particulate matter (PM) in the off-gases. These metallic impurities released during the smelting process are the HAPs that are the focus of the subject rulemaking.

Copper smelters use several different methods of PM control to regulate process emissions. Exhaust streams from copper dryers are vented to either a baghouse or an electrostatic precipitator (ESP) to reduce PM emissions. . . . After surveying the technology used at the various locations, EPA determined that copper smelters used PM control devices to reduce HAP emissions. EPA accordingly set standards for HAP emissions in terms of PM, rather than setting individual limits for each HAP.

. . . Sierra Club alleges that EPA refused to consider "non-air quality health and environmental impacts," as required under Section 7412(d)(2). Sierra Club interprets this provision to require EPA to consider the "impacts of deposition, persistence, toxicity and bioaccumulation of metal HAP emissions on people, wildlife and the environment." Pet. Br. at 36. In other words, "non-air quality . . . impacts" are just like air quality impacts, except that the impact is not delivered directly through the air but instead, for example, by "deposition"—the eventual settling of HAPs on the ground. EPA takes a different view—that " 'non-air quality . . . impacts' refers to any health and environmental impacts . . . that may result directly or indirectly from measures that will achieve the emission reductions." Resp. Br. at 31. In other words, "nonair quality . . . impacts" are those that result from the required efforts to *control* the air quality impacts of the underlying manufacturing process.

Congress did not define "non-air quality . . . impacts," so we will defer to EPA's construction of the ambiguous statutory language, so long as it is reasonable. It is. The statute groups consideration of "non-air quality . . . impacts" with consideration of "the cost of achieving such emission reduction" and "energy requirements." [CAA § 112(d)(2).] This context strongly supports EPA's interpretation of "nonair quality . . . impacts" to mean the by-products of the control technology just as additional cost or energy needs are by-products of controlling air quality impacts.

Second, there is no apparent reason to suppose that Congress would have required immediate consideration of health and environmental impacts caused by, say, deposition of HAPs, while postponing consideration of the more direct health and environmental impacts caused by emission of HAPs into the air until the second stage of standard promulgation under the CAA. As discussed, the 1990 Amendments established a two-phase approach to promulgating emission standards. The first phase—at issue in this case—requires a technology-based approach. *See* [CAA § 1412(d).] The second phase occurs eight years later and involves a risk-based approach. *See id.* § 7412(f)(2)(A) ("Emissions standards promulgated under this subsection shall provide an ample margin of safety to protect public health. . . ."). That risk-based analysis requires EPA to consider, *inter alia*, public health and adverse environmental effects, *id.*—precisely what Sierra Club contends EPA must consider *now* with respect to non-air quality impacts. Sierra Club's interpretation would collapse the technology-based/risk-based distinction at the heart of the Act, undermining the central purpose of the 1990 Amendments—to facilitate the near-term implementation of emission standards through technology-based solutions. In doing so, that interpretation would reintroduce the very problem Congress sought to exorcize—that the pursuit of the perfect (risk-based standards) had defeated timely achievement of the good (technology-based standards). EPA's reading of the statute is reasonable.

NOTES AND QUESTIONS

1.   **Non-Air Quality Impacts.** What type of impacts did the Sierra Club assert should be considered "non-air quality impacts"? What was EPA's position? On what basis did the court find in favor of EPA? To what extent did deference to the agency's construction of the statute influence the holding of the court? Were EPA to have favored Sierra Club's interpretation of § 112(d), would it likely have survived challenge from industry?

2.   **MACT.** In setting the MACT standard, EPA must determine "the average emission limitation achieved by the best performing 12 percent of the existing sources," or, for categories containing fewer than 30 sources, the emission limitation achieved by the best performing five sources. 42 U.S.C. § 7412(d)(3). Having established the MACT floor, EPA must next consider whether more stringent standards are achievable, "taking into consideration the cost . . . and any non-air quality health and environmental impacts and energy requirements." 42 U.S.C. § 9612(d)(2). Like BACT and LAER, MACT is a technology-based standard. Why then would Congress only prescribe a two-step process in the case of determining the MACT standard?

3.   **Achievable v. Achieved.** In *Cement Kiln Recycling Coalition v. EPA*, 255 F.3d 855 (D.C. Cir. 2001), the court ruled that EPA air pollution standards for hazardous waste combustors did not reflect the "emissions achieved in practice by the best-performing sources," as the Act requires. EPA had set floors it considered "achievable" by all sources, rather than a standard reflecting what had actually been "achieved" by the best sources. EPA argued that it was required to do so by the language of § 112(d)(2), which directs EPA to require the "maximum emission reduction" that it determines achievable. Section 112(d)(3), however, directs that this shall not be deemed less stringent than what the best-performing sources "achieve."

In *Sierra Club v. EPA*, 479 F.3d 875 (D.C. Cir. 2007), the D.C. Circuit again vacated EPA MACT regulations. The court concluded that EPA had failed to heed the court's interpretation in *Cement Kiln Recycling*, pointing to the agency's "fundamental failure to set floors at the emission levels actually achieved by the best-performing sources." *Id.* at 881. The court rejected EPA's argument that it had "reasonably construe[d] the term best performing . . . to allow it to consider whether retrofitting kilns with a particular pollution control technology is technically feasible." *Id.* at 880 (quotation marks omitted).

Who was right? Section 112(d)(3)'s language is clear. However, what is the point of having § 112(d)(2) if it is rendered irrelevant by § 112(d)(3)? Is it in fact rendered irrelevant? Is there room for consideration of feasibility in § 112(d)?

4.   **Comparison of Technology-Based Standards in the CAA.** Table V.3 compares the language and structure of the four major technology-based standards in the CAA.

Table V.3. Comparison of Technology-Based Standards			
BAT **[§ 111(a)(1)]**	**MACT** **[§ 112(d)(2)]**	**BACT** **[§ 169(a)(3)]**	**LAER** **[§ 171(3)]**
• Best system of emission reduction. • Adequately demonstrated. • Cost, nonair quality health and environmental impact and energy requirements taken into account.	• Maximum degree of reduction emission achievable. • Includes a prohibition on such emissions, wherever achievable. • Cost, nonair quality health and environmental impact and energy requirements taken into account.	• Maximum degree of reduction of each pollutant. • Case-by-case basis achievability analysis. • Cost, nonair quality health and environmental impact and energy requirements taken into account.	The more stringent of the following: • Most stringent emission limitation which is contained in SIP of any State for such category of source (unless owner demonstrates not achievable). • Or most stringent emissions limitation which is achieved in practice by such class or category of source.

How are each of these technology standards different from one another? Are the differences in these technology-based standards compelled by policy objectives? The statutory structure? Relevant differences in pollutant characteristics?

Which standard seems the most stringent to you? Why? Recall the discussion of BACT in *Alaska Dept. of Environmental Conservation v. EPA*, 540 U.S. 461 (2004), and EPA's authority to override a state BACT determination. Compare the Court's review of the agency's override of the state's BACT determination with the *Cement Kiln* court's review of the EPA's MACT standard for hazardous waste combustors. Which standard gives the Administrator the most discretion?

5.　Start Up, Shut Down, and Malfunction. How should EPA enforce emission requirements during periods of start up, shut down, and malfunction (SSM), when facility emissions may rise? In a 1994 rule, EPA concluded that excess emissions during SSM periods were not violations of CAA emissions standards, so long as the regulated entity prepared and complied with an SSM plan that detailed operating procedures during SSMs, was publicly available, and was subject to approval by the EPA. *See* 59 Fed. Reg. 12,408 (1994). Over the course of rulemakings in 2002, 2003, and 2006,

EPA loosened its SSM policy for HAPs, finally concluding that a facility's legal requirement was solely to adhere to a general duty to minimize emissions during SSMs.

Under § 112, EPA must promulgate "emissions standards" that include MACT. The general definition section of the CAA defines an "emissions standard" as "a requirement . . . which limits the quantity, rate, or concentration of emissions of air pollutants on a continuous basis. . . ." 42 U.S.C. § 7602(k). In *Sierra Club v. EPA*, the D.C. Circuit vacated EPA's SSM policy, finding that "[b]ecause the general duty is the only standard that applies during SSM events—and accordingly no section 112 standard governs these events—the SSM exemption violates the [Clean Air Act] requirement that some section 112 standard apply continuously." 551 F.3d 1019, 1028 (D.C. Cir. 2008).

Should the MACT standard apply during start ups, shut downs, and malfunctions? Should a modified form of the standard apply? Does the statute provide any discretion for EPA to apply a modified form of the standard during SSMs?

6.   **Residual Risk Program.** Section 112(f)(1) required EPA to report to Congress within six years after passage of the 1990 amendments to describe its methodology for assessing risk, evaluate the health risks likely to remain after installation of MACT for each category of sources, and propose legislation to address such risks. EPA presented its report in 1999; however, the agency largely limited its discussion to describing its methodology for risk assessment. EPA argued that it could not evaluate risk at the level requested by Congress and noted that it would evaluate risk in each individual residual risk assessment as required by § 112(f)(2). The agency also asserted that it had sufficient regulatory authority to achieve the goals of § 112(f) and thus did not propose any legislative changes. *See* EPA, RESIDUAL RISK REPORT TO CONGRESS 21–23 (1999).

Section 112(f)(2) requires EPA to promulgate new health-based standards within eight years after the initial MACT standard is set for a category of sources "if promulgation of such standards is required in order to provide an ample margin of safety to protect public health." 42 U.S.C. § 7412. In *NRDC v. EPA*, NRDC challenged a residual risk rulemaking where EPA had determined, by rule, not to change its existing standard for facilities that use or produce synthetic organic chemicals. 529 F.3d 1077 (D.C. Cir. 2008). The D.C. Circuit held that EPA reasonably interpreted § 112(f)(2)(A) as only mandating an additional round of rulemaking and not requiring the agency to set a standard that achieves the statute's one-in-one-million lifetime excess cancer risk benchmark. *Id.* at 1086. Do you agree with the court's interpretation of § 112(f)(2)(A)?

7.   **Cumulative Risk and Environmental Justice.** Recall Chapter II's discussion of environmental justice and EPA's Plan EJ 2014. As part of Plan EJ 2014, EPA issued its INTERIM GUIDANCE ON CONSIDERING ENVIRONMENTAL JUSTICE DURING THE DEVELOPMENT OF AN ACTION (2010). The guidance highlighted the need to consider cumulative risks in rulemakings, finding that "[n]umerous empirical studies and anecdotal

accounts describe minority, low-income, and indigenous communities that are impacted by multiple environmental hazards." The Guidance concluded that "[a]nalyzing cumulative effects from multiple stressors allows a more realistic evaluation of a population's risk to pollutants." *Id.* at 8.

When setting a residual risk standard for one category of sources, should EPA consider the existing level of health risk generated by other § 112 categories when deciding what emissions limitation will provide an "ample margin of safety"? Does the agency have statutory authority to do so? Does the agency have authority to consider risks from other environmental hazards?

B. REGULATING POWER PLANTS

The 1990 Amendments to the CAA required EPA to take action with respect to the hazardous air pollutant emissions of power plants. First, the agency was tasked with performing a study of "the hazards to public health reasonably anticipated to occur" as a result of the emission of hazardous air pollutants from power plants and with reporting the results of this study to Congress within three years. 42 U.S.C § 7412(n)(1)(A). EPA was then required to regulate the plants if it found, after considering the results of its study, that such regulation was "appropriate and necessary." *Id.*

Despite the three-year statutory deadline, EPA failed to complete the required study. In 1995, following litigation by environmental groups, EPA entered into a settlement agreement to complete the study. It was finally published in 1998. *See New Jersey v. EPA*, 517 F.3d 574, 579 (D.C. Cir. 2008). The study concluded that while power plants emit a number of hazardous air pollutants, mercury was "of greatest concern" because it is "highly toxic, persistent, and bioaccumulates in food chains." *See* EPA, Regulatory Finding on the Emissions of Hazardous Air Pollutants From Electric Utility Steam Generating Units, 65 Fed. Reg. 79,825, 79,827 (2000).

Despite the results of EPA's 1998 study, it took a further two years for EPA to conclude that regulating plants' mercury emissions under § 112 was "appropriate and necessary" because the emissions "present[ed] significant hazards to public health and the environment." *Id.* at 79,826, 79,830. However, EPA's intent to regulate mercury emissions from EGUs under § 112 was short-lived. In March 2005, EPA announced that it was removing EGUs from the § 112(c)(1) list. 70 Fed. Reg. 15,994 (2005). Instead of regulating mercury pursuant to § 112, EPA finalized the Clean Air Mercury Rule (CAMR), which proposed to create a cap-and-trade program for mercury emissions under § 111. *See* EPA, Standards of Performance for New and Existing Electric Utility Steam Generating Units, 71 Fed. Reg. 33,388, 33,395 (2006). EPA estimated that when fully implemented, CAMR would result in mercury reductions of nearly seventy percent from EGUs. *See* EPA, Clean Air Mercury Rule:

Basic Information, https://archive.epa.gov/mercuryrule/web/html/basic.html (last visited Sept. 27, 2018).

EPA's Inspector General issued a report criticizing the agency's finding that the CAMR would not result in "hotspots" of mercury pollution in certain water bodies located near EGUs. EPA, OFFICE OF INSPECTOR GENERAL, REPORT NO. 2006–P–00025, MONITORING NEEDED TO ASSESS IMPACT OF EPA'S CLEAN AIR MERCURY RULE ON POTENTIAL HOTSPOTS (2006). In the final rule, EPA responded that it still believed that no hotspots would result but noted that the agency would monitor the situation. 71 Fed. Reg. at 33,393.

Fourteen states and several environmental groups filed suit to challenge CAMR. They maintained that EPA violated the plain text and structure of § 112 when it delisted EGUs without complying with the requirements of § 112(c)(9).

Section 112(c)(9) provides that:

> The Administrator may delete any source category from the [section 112(c)(1) list] . . . whenever the Administrator . . . [determines] that emissions from no source in the category or subcategory concerned . . . exceed a level which is adequate to protect public health with an ample margin of safety and no adverse environmental effect will result from emissions from any source.

42 U.S.C. § 7412(c)(9). EPA conceded that it had not complied with the express requirements of § 112(c)(9). Instead, the agency argued that its finding that it was no longer "necessary and appropriate" to regulate EGUs under § 112 meant that the agency was not required to make the § 112(c)(9) determination. "[I]f EPA makes a determination under section 112(n)(1)(A) that power plants should not be regulated at all under section 112 . . . [then] this determination *ipso facto* must result in removal of power plants from the section 112(c) list." Brief of Respondent at 26, *New Jersey v. EPA*, 517 F.3d 574 (D.C. Cir. 2008).

The D.C. Circuit dismissed this argument and upheld the petitioners' challenge to the 2006 rule delisting EGUs and finalizing CAMR. *New Jersey v. EPA*, 517 F.3d 574, 582 (2008). Because EPA could "point to no persuasive evidence suggesting that section 112(c)(9)'s plain text is ambiguous," *id.*, the court held that EPA was unable to avoid the literal application of § 112(c)(9) at *Chevron* step one.

Three years later, in 2011, the Obama administration proposed the Mercury and Air Toxics Standards (MATS), under § 112. MATS was finalized in February 2012. EPA, National Emission Standards for Hazardous Air Pollutants From Coal- and Oil-Fired Electric Utility Steam Generating Units, 77 Fed. Reg. 9304 (2012).

By March 2015, the rule was expected to cut mercury emissions from coal- and oil-fired power plants by 90 percent and to achieve significant reductions in emissions of other toxic pollutants like arsenic. *Id.* at 9306.

NOTES AND QUESTIONS

1. Regulation of Mercury Emissions Under § 111 of the CAA. Was EPA's attempt to regulate mercury emissions under § 111 appropriate? Does § 112 provide a better method? Why or why not?

2. Findings Required to Delist Power Plants. What differences are there between the findings required under § 112(n)(1)(A) and § 112(c)(9)? Why did EPA not simply make the § 112(c)(9) determination, having determined that it was no longer "necessary and appropriate" to regulate EGUs pursuant to § 112? Do you agree with the *New Jersey v. EPA* court that, despite § 112(n)(1)(A), the statutory language in § 112(c)(9) gives rise to no ambiguities?

Michigan v. Environmental Protection Agency
135 S. Ct. 2699 (2015).

■ JUSTICE SCALIA delivered the opinion of the Court:

The Clean Air Act directs the Environmental Protection Agency to regulate emissions of hazardous air pollutants from power plants if the Agency finds regulation "appropriate and necessary." We must decide whether it was reasonable for EPA to refuse to consider cost when making this finding.

I

The Clean Air Act establishes a series of regulatory programs to control air pollution from stationary sources (such as refineries and factories) and moving sources (such as cars and airplanes). 69 Stat. 322, as amended, 42 U. S. C. §§ 7401–7671q. One of these is the National Emissions Standards for Hazardous Air Pollutants Program—the hazardous-air-pollutants program, for short. Established in its current form by the Clean Air Act Amendments of 1990, 104 Stat. 2531, this program targets for regulation stationary-source emissions of more than 180 specified "hazardous air pollutants." § 7412(b). . . .

. . . Congress established a unique procedure to determine the applicability of the program to fossil-fuel-fired power plants. The Act refers to these plants as electric utility steam generating units, but we will simply call them power plants. Quite apart from the hazardous-air-pollutants program, the Clean Air Act Amendments of 1990 subjected power plants to various regulatory requirements. The parties agree that these requirements were expected to have the collateral effect of reducing power plants' emissions of hazardous air pollutants, although the extent of the reduction was unclear. Congress directed the Agency to "perform a study of the hazards to public health reasonably anticipated to occur as a result of emissions by [power plants] of [hazardous air pollutants] after imposition of the requirements of this chapter." § 7412(n)(1)(A). If the Agency "finds . . . regulation is appropriate and necessary after considering the results of the study," it "shall regulate [power plants] under [§ 7412]." Ibid. . . .

. . . EPA must first divide sources covered by the program into categories and sub-categories in accordance with statutory criteria. § 7412(c)(1). For each category or subcategory, the Agency must promulgate certain minimum emission regulations, known as floor standards. § 7412(d)(1), (3). The statute generally calibrates the floor standards to reflect the emissions limitations already achieved by the best-performing 12% of sources within the category or subcategory. § 7412(d)(3). In some circumstances, the Agency may also impose more stringent emission regulations, known as beyond-the-floor standards. The statute expressly requires the Agency to consider cost (alongside other specified factors) when imposing beyond-the-floor standards. § 7412(d)(2).

EPA completed the study required by § 7412(n)(1)(A) in 1998, 65 Fed. Reg. 79826 (2000), and concluded that regulation of coal-and-oil-fired power plants was "appropriate and necessary" in 2000, id., at 79830. In 2012, it reaffirmed the appropriate-and-necessary finding, divided power plants into subcategories, and promulgated floor standards. The Agency found regulation "appropriate" because (1) power plants' emissions of mercury and other hazardous air pollutants posed risks to human health and the environment and (2) controls were available to reduce these emissions. 77 Fed. Reg. 9363. It found regulation "necessary" because the imposition of the Act's other requirements did not eliminate these risks. Ibid. EPA concluded that "costs should not be considered" when deciding whether power plants should be regulated under § 7412. Id., at 9326.

In accordance with Executive Order, the Agency issued a "Regulatory Impact Analysis" alongside its regulation. This analysis estimated that the regulation would force power plants to bear costs of $9.6 billion per year. Id., at 9306. The Agency could not fully quantify the benefits of reducing power plants' emissions of hazardous air pollutants; to the extent it could, it estimated that these benefits were worth $4 to $6 million per year. Ibid. The costs to power plants were thus between 1,600 and 2,400 times as great as the quantifiable benefits from reduced emissions of hazardous air pollutants. The Agency continued that its regulations would have ancillary benefits—including cutting power plants' emissions of particulate matter and sulfur dioxide, substances that are not covered by the hazardous-air-pollutants program. Although the Agency's appropriate-and-necessary finding did not rest on these ancillary effects, id., at 9320, the regulatory impact analysis took them into account, increasing the Agency's estimate of the quantifiable benefits of its regulation to $37 to $90 billion per year, id., at 9306. EPA concedes that the regulatory impact analysis "played no role" in its appropriate-and-necessary finding. Brief for Federal Respondents 14.

Petitioners (who include 23 States) sought review of EPA's rule in the Court of Appeals for the D. C. Circuit. As relevant here, they challenged the Agency's refusal to consider cost when deciding whether to regulate power plants. The Court of Appeals upheld the Agency's decision not to consider cost, with Judge Kavanaugh concurring in part and dissenting in part. White Stallion Energy Center, LLC v. EPA, 748 F. 3d 1222 (2014) (per curiam). We granted certiorari. 574 U. S. (2014). . . .

EPA's decision to regulate power plants under § 7412 allowed the Agency to reduce power plants' emissions of hazardous air pollutants and thus to improve public health and the environment. But the decision also ultimately cost power plants, according to the Agency's own estimate, nearly $10 billion a year. EPA refused to consider whether the costs of its decision outweighed the benefits. The Agency gave cost no thought *at all*, because it considered cost irrelevant to its initial decision to regulate.

EPA's disregard of cost rested on its interpretation of § 7412(n)(1)(A), which, to repeat, directs the Agency to regulate power plants if it "finds such regulation is appropriate and necessary." The Agency accepts that it *could* have interpreted this provision to mean that cost is relevant to the decision to add power plants to the program. Tr. of Oral Arg. 44. But it chose to read the statute to mean that cost makes no difference to the initial decision to regulate. See 76 Fed. Reg. 24988 (2011) ("We further interpret the term 'appropriate' to not allow for the consideration of costs"); 77 Fed. Reg. 9327 ("Cost does not have to be read into the definition of 'appropriate' ").

We review this interpretation under the standard set out in Chevron U. S. A. Inc. v. Natural Resources Defense Council, Inc., 467 U. S. 837 (1984). Chevron directs courts to accept an agency's reasonable resolution of an ambiguity in a statute that the agency administers. Id., at 842–843. Even under this deferential standard, however, "agencies must operate within the bounds of reasonable interpretation." Utility Air Regulatory Group v. EPA, 573 U. S. , (2014) (slip op., at 16) (internal quotation marks omitted). EPA strayed far beyond those bounds when it read § 7412(n)(1) to mean that it could ignore cost when deciding whether to regulate power plants.

A

The Clean Air Act treats power plants differently from other sources for purposes of the hazardous-air-pollutants program. Elsewhere in § 7412, Congress established cabined criteria for EPA to apply when deciding whether to include sources in the program. It required the Agency to regulate sources whose emissions exceed specified numerical thresholds (major sources). It also required the Agency to regulate sources whose emissions fall short of these thresholds (area sources) if they "presen[t] a threat of adverse effects to human health or the environment . . . warranting regulation." § 7412(c)(3). In stark contrast, Congress instructed EPA to add power plants to the program if (but only

if) the Agency finds regulation "appropriate and necessary."
§ 7412(n)(1)(A). . . .

Read naturally in the present context, the phrase "appropriate and
necessary" requires at least some attention to cost. One would not say
that it is even rational, never mind "appropriate," to impose billions of
dollars in economic costs in return for a few dollars in health or
environmental benefits. In addition, "cost" includes more than the
expense of complying with regulations; any disadvantage could be
termed a cost. EPA's interpretation precludes the Agency from
considering any type of cost—including, for instance, harms that
regulation might do to human health or the environment. The
Government concedes that if the Agency were to find that emissions from
power plants do damage to human health, but that the technologies
needed to eliminate these emissions do even more damage to human
health, it would *still* deem regulation appropriate. No regulation is
"appropriate" if it does significantly more harm than good.

There are undoubtedly settings in which the phrase "appropriate
and necessary" does not encompass cost. But this is not one of them.
Section 7412(n)(1)(A) directs EPA to determine whether *regulation* is
appropriate and necessary." (Emphasis added.) Agencies have long
treated cost as a centrally relevant factor when deciding whether to
regulate. Consideration of cost reflects the understanding that
reasonable regulation ordinarily requires paying attention to the
advantages *and* the disadvantages of agency decisions. It also reflects the
reality that "too much wasteful expenditure devoted to one problem may
well mean considerably fewer resources available to deal effectively with
other (perhaps more serious) problems." Entergy Corp. v. Riverkeeper,
Inc., 556 U. S. 208, 233 (2009) (BREYER, J., concurring in part and
dissenting in part). Against the backdrop of this established
administrative practice, it is unreasonable to read an instruction to an
administrative agency to determine whether "regulation is appropriate
and necessary" as an invitation to ignore cost.

Statutory context reinforces the relevance of cost. The procedures
governing power plants that we consider today appear in § 7412(n)(1),
which bears the caption "Electric utility steam generating units." In
subparagraph (A), the part of the law that has occupied our attention so
far, Congress required EPA to study the hazards to public health posed
by power plants and to determine whether regulation is appropriate and
necessary. But in subparagraphs (B) and (C), Congress called for two
additional studies. One of them, a study into mercury emissions from
power plants and other sources, must consider "the health and
environmental effects of such emissions, technologies which are available
to control such emissions, *and the costs of such technologies."*
§ 7412(n)(1)(B) (emphasis added). This directive to EPA to study cost is
a further indication of the relevance of cost to the decision to regulate. . . .

B

EPA identifies a handful of reasons to interpret § 7412(n)(1)(A) to mean that cost is irrelevant to the initial decision to regulate. We find those reasons unpersuasive. EPA points out that other parts of the Clean Air Act expressly mention cost, while § 7412(n)(1)(A) does not. But this observation shows only that § 7412(n)(1)(A)'s broad reference to appropriateness encompasses *multiple* relevant factors (which include but are not limited to cost); other provisions' specific references to cost encompass just cost. It is unreasonable to infer that, by expressly making cost relevant to other decisions, the Act implicitly makes cost irrelevant to the appropriateness of regulating power plants. (By way of analogy, the Fourth Amendment's Reasonableness Clause requires searches to be "[r]easonable," while its Warrant Clause requires warrants to be supported by "probable cause." Nobody would argue that, by expressly making level of suspicion relevant to the validity of a warrant, the Fourth Amendment implicitly makes level of suspicion categorically *irrelevant* to the reasonableness of a search. To the contrary, all would agree that the expansive word "reasonable" encompasses degree of suspicion alongside other relevant circumstances.) Other parts of the Clean Air Act also expressly mention environmental effects, while § 7412(n)(1)(A) does not. Yet that did not stop EPA from deeming environmental effects relevant to the appropriateness of regulating power plants.

Along similar lines, EPA seeks support in this Court's decision in Whitman v. American Trucking Assns., Inc., 531 U. S. 457 (2001). There, the Court addressed a provision of the Clean Air Act requiring EPA to set ambient air quality standards at levels "requisite to protect the public health" with an "adequate margin of safety." 42 U. S. C. § 7409(b). Read naturally, that discrete criterion does not encompass cost; it encompasses health and safety. The Court refused to read that provision as carrying with it an implicit authorization to consider cost, in part because authority to consider cost had "elsewhere, and so often, been expressly granted." 531 U. S., at 467. American Trucking thus establishes the modest principle that where the Clean Air Act expressly directs EPA to regulate on the basis of a factor that on its face does not include cost, the Act normally should not be read as implicitly allowing the Agency to consider cost anyway. That principle has no application here. "Appropriate and necessary" is a far more comprehensive criterion than "requisite to protect the public health"; read fairly and in context, as we have explained, the term plainly subsumes consideration of cost.

Turning to the mechanics of the hazardous-air-pollutants program, EPA argues that it need not consider cost when first deciding *whether* to regulate power plants because it can consider cost later when deciding *how much* to regulate them. The question before us, however, is the meaning of the "appropriate and necessary" standard that governs the initial decision to regulate. And as we have discussed, context establishes that this expansive standard encompasses cost. Cost may become relevant again at a later stage of the regulatory process, but that possibility does not establish its irrelevance at *this* stage. In addition, once the Agency decides to regulate power plants, it must promulgate certain minimum or floor standards no matter the cost (here, nearly $10 billion a year); the Agency may consider cost only when imposing regulations *beyond* these minimum standards. By EPA's logic, someone could decide whether it is "appropriate" to buy a Ferrari without thinking about cost, because he plans to think about cost later when deciding whether to upgrade the sound system.

EPA argues that the Clean Air Act makes cost irrelevant to the initial decision to regulate sources other than power plants. The Agency claims that it is reasonable to interpret § 7412(n)(1)(A) in a way that "harmonizes" the program's treatment of power plants with its treatment of other sources. This line of reasoning overlooks the whole point of having a separate provision about power plants: treating power plants *differently* from other stationary sources. Congress crafted narrow standards for EPA to apply when deciding whether to regulate other sources; in general, these standards concern the volume of pollution emitted by the source, § 7412(c)(1), and the threat posed by the source "to human health or the environment," § 7412(c)(3). But Congress wrote the provision before us more expansively, directing the Agency to regulate power plants if "appropriate and necessary." "That congressional election settles this case. [The Agency's] preference for symmetry cannot trump an asymmetrical statute." CSX Transp., Inc. v. Alabama Dept. of Revenue, 562 U. S. 277, 296 (2011).

EPA persists that Congress treated power plants differently from other sources because of uncertainty about whether regulation of power plants would still be needed after the application of the rest of the Act's requirements. That is undoubtedly *one* of the reasons Congress treated power plants differently; hence § 7412(n)(1)(A)'s requirement to study hazards posed by power plants' emissions "after imposition of the requirements of [the rest of the Act]." But if uncertainty about the need for regulation were the *only* reason to treat power plants differently, Congress would have required the Agency to decide only whether regulation remains "necessary," not whether regulation is "appropriate *and* necessary." In any event, EPA stated when it adopted the rule that "Congress did not limit [the] appropriate and necessary inquiry to [the study mentioned in § 7412(n)(1)(A)]." 77 Fed. Reg. 9325. The Agency instead decided that the appropriate-and- necessary finding should be understood in light of all three studies required by § 7412(n)(1), and as we have discussed, one of those three studies reflects concern about cost.

C

The dissent does not embrace EPA's far-reaching claim that Congress made costs altogether irrelevant to the decision to regulate power plants. Instead, it maintains that EPA need not "explicitly analyze costs" before deeming regulation appropriate, because other features of the regulatory program will on their own ensure the cost-effectiveness of regulation. Post, at 2 (opinion of KAGAN, J.). This line of reasoning contradicts the foundational principle of administrative law that a court may uphold agency action only on the grounds that the agency invoked when it took the action. SEC v. Chenery Corp., 318 U. S. 80, 87 (1943). When it deemed regulation of power plants appropriate, EPA said that cost was *irrelevant* to that determination—not that cost-benefit analysis would be deferred until later. Much *less* did it say (what the dissent now concludes) that the consideration of cost at subsequent stages will ensure that the costs are not disproportionate to the benefits. What it said is that cost is irrelevant to the decision to regulate.

That is enough to decide these cases. But for what it is worth, the dissent vastly overstates the influence of cost at later stages of the regulatory process. For example, the dissent claims that the floor standards—which the Act calibrates to reflect emissions limitations already achieved by the best-performing sources in the industry—reflect cost considerations, because the best-performing power plants "must have considered costs in arriving at their emissions outputs." Post, at 10. EPA did not rely on this argument, and it is not obvious that it is correct. Because power plants are regulated under other federal and state laws, the best-performing power plants' emissions limitations might reflect cost-blind regulation rather than cost-conscious decisions. Similarly, the dissent suggests that EPA may consider cost when dividing sources into categories and subcategories. Post, at 11–12. Yet according to EPA, "it is *not* appropriate to premise subcategorization on costs." 77 Fed. Reg. 9395 (emphasis added). That statement presumably explains the dissent's carefully worded observation that EPA considered "technological, geographic, and other factors" when drawing categories, post, at 13, n.4, which factors were in turn "related to costs" in some way, post, at 11. Attenuated connections such as these hardly support the assertion that EPA's regulatory process featured "exhaustive consideration of costs," post, at 2.

All in all, the dissent has at most shown that some elements of the regulatory scheme mitigate cost in limited ways; it has not shown that these elements ensure cost-effectiveness. If (to take a hypothetical example) regulating power plants would yield $5 million in benefits, the prospect of mitigating cost from $11 billion to $10 billion at later stages of the program would not by itself make regulation appropriate. In all events, we need not pursue these points, because EPA did not say that the parts of the regulatory program mentioned by the dissent prevent the imposition of costs far in excess of benefits. "[EPA's] action must be measured by what [it] did, not by what it might have done." Chenery, supra, at 93–94.

D

Our reasoning so far establishes that it was unreasonable for EPA to read § 7412(n)(1)(A) to mean that cost is irrelevant to the initial decision to regulate power plants. The Agency must consider cost—including, most importantly, cost of compliance—before deciding whether regulation is appropriate and necessary. We need not and do not hold that the law unambiguously required the Agency, when making this preliminary estimate, to conduct a formal cost-benefit analysis in which each advantage and disadvantage is assigned a monetary value. It will be up to the Agency to decide (as always, within the limits of reasonable interpretation) how to account for cost.

Some of the respondents supporting EPA ask us to uphold EPA's action because the accompanying regulatory impact analysis shows that, once the rule's ancillary benefits are considered, benefits plainly outweigh costs. The dissent similarly relies on these ancillary benefits when insisting that "the outcome here [was] a rule whose benefits exceed its costs." Post, at 16. As we have just explained, however, we may uphold agency action only upon the grounds on which the agency acted. Even if the Agency *could* have considered ancillary benefits when deciding whether regulation is appropriate and necessary—a point we need not address—it plainly did not do so here. In the Agency's own words, the administrative record "utterly refutes [the] assertion that [ancillary benefits] form the basis for the appropriate and necessary finding." 77 Fed. Reg. 9323. The Government concedes, moreover, that "EPA did not rely on the [regulatory impact analysis] when deciding to regulate power plants," and that "[e]ven if EPA had considered costs, it would not necessarily have adopted . . . the approach set forth in [that analysis]." Brief for Federal Respondents 53–54.

■ JUSTICE KAGAN, with whom JUSTICE GINSBURG, JUSTICE BREYER, and JUSTICE SOTOMAYOR join, dissenting:

The Environmental Protection Agency placed emissions limits on coal and oil power plants following a lengthy regulatory process during which the Agency carefully considered costs. At the outset, EPA determined that regulating plants' emissions of hazardous air pollutants is "appropriate and necessary" given the harm they cause, and explained that it would take costs into account in developing suitable emissions standards. Next, EPA divided power plants into groups based on technological and other characteristics bearing significantly on their cost structures. It required plants in each group to match the emissions levels already achieved by the best-performing members of the same group—benchmarks necessarily reflecting those plants' own cost analyses. EPA then adopted a host of measures designed to make compliance with its proposed emissions limits less costly for plants that needed to catch up with their cleaner peers. And with only one narrow exception, EPA decided not to impose any more stringent standards (beyond what some plants had already achieved on their own) because it found that doing so would not be cost-effective. After all that, EPA conducted a formal cost-benefit study which found that the quantifiable benefits of its regulation would exceed the costs up to nine times over—by as much as $80 billion each year. Those benefits include as many as 11,000 fewer premature deaths annually, along with a far greater number of avoided illnesses.

Despite that exhaustive consideration of costs, the Court strikes down EPA's rule on the ground that the Agency "unreasonably . . . deemed cost irrelevant." Ante, at 15. On the majority's theory, the rule is invalid because EPA did not explicitly analyze costs at the very first stage of the regulatory process, when making its "appropriate and necessary" finding. And that is so even though EPA later took costs into account again and again and . . . so on. The majority thinks entirely immaterial, and so entirely ignores, all the subsequent times and ways EPA considered costs in deciding what any regulation would look like.

That is a peculiarly blinkered way for a court to assess the lawfulness of an agency's rulemaking. I agree with the majority—let there be no doubt about this—that EPA's power plant regulation would be unreasonable if "[t]he Agency gave cost no thought *at all*." Ante, at 5 (emphasis in original). But that is just not what happened here. Over more than a decade, EPA took costs into account at multiple stages and through multiple means as it set emissions limits for power plants. And when making its initial "appropriate and necessary" finding, EPA knew it would do exactly that—knew it would thoroughly consider the cost-effectiveness of emissions standards later on. That context matters. The Agency acted well within its authority in declining to consider costs at the opening bell of the regulatory process given that it would do so in every round thereafter—and given that the emissions limits finally issued would depend crucially on those accountings. Indeed, EPA could not have measured costs at the process's initial stage with any accuracy. And the regulatory path EPA chose parallels the one it has trod in setting emissions limits, at Congress's explicit direction, for every other source of hazardous air pollutants over two decades. The majority's decision that EPA cannot take the same approach here—its micromanagement of EPA's rulemaking, based on little more than the word "appropriate"— runs counter to Congress's allocation of authority between the Agency and the courts. Because EPA reasonably found that it was "appropriate" to decline to analyze costs at a single stage of a regulatory proceeding otherwise imbued with cost concerns, I respectfully dissent. . . .

II A

In the years after its "appropriate and necessary" finding, EPA made good on its promise to account for costs "[a]s a part of developing a regulation." 65 Fed. Reg. 79830; see supra, at 7. For more than a decade, as EPA deliberated on and then set emissions limits, costs came into the calculus at nearly every turn. Reflecting that consideration, EPA's final rule noted that steps taken during the regulatory process had focused on "flexib[ility] and cost-effective[ness]" and had succeeded in making "the rule less costly and compliance more readily manageable." 77 Fed. Reg. 9306, 9376. And the regulation concluded that "the benefits of th[e] rule" to public health and the environment "far outweigh the costs." Id., at 9306.

Consistent with the statutory framework, EPA initially calculated floor standards: emissions levels of the best-performing 12% of power plants in a given category or subcategory. The majority misperceives this part of the rulemaking process. It insists that EPA "must promulgate certain . . . floor standards no matter the cost." Ante, at 11. But that ignores two crucial features of the top-12% limits: first, the way in which any such standard intrinsically accounts for costs, and second, the way in which the Agency's categorization decisions yield different standards for plants with different cost structures.

The initial point is a fact of life in a market economy: Costs necessarily play a role in any standard that uses power plants' existing emissions levels as a benchmark. After all, the best-performing 12% of power plants must have considered costs in arriving at their emissions outputs; that is how profit-seeking enterprises make decisions. And in doing so, they must have selected achievable levels; else, they would have gone out of business. (The same would be true even if other regulations influenced some of those choices, as the majority casually speculates. See ante, at 13.) Indeed, this automatic accounting for costs is why Congress adopted a market-leader-based standard. As the Senate Report accompanying the 1990 amendments explained: "Cost considerations are reflected in the selection of emissions limitations which have been achieved in practice (rather than those which are merely theoretical) by sources of a similar type or character." S. Rep. No. 101–228, pp. 168–169 (1989). Of course, such a standard remains technology-forcing: It requires laggards in the industry to catch up with frontrunners, sometimes at significant expense. But the benchmark is, by definition, one that some power plants have achieved economically. And when EPA made its "appropriate and necessary" finding, it knew that fact—knew that the consequence of doing so was to generate floor standards with cost considerations baked right in.

Still more, EPA recognized that in making categorization decisions, it could take account of multiple factors related to costs of compliance—and so avoid impracticable regulatory burdens. Suppose, to use a simple example, that curbing emissions is more technologically difficult—and therefore more costly—for plants burning coal than for plants burning oil. EPA can then place those two types of plants in different categories, so that coal plants need only match other coal plants rather than having to incur the added costs of meeting the top oil plants' levels. Now multiply and complexify that example many times over. As the Agency noted when making its "appropriate and necessary" finding, EPA "build[s] flexibility" into the regulatory regime by "bas[ing] subcategorization on . . . the size of a facility; the type of fuel used at the facility; and the plant type," and also "may consider other relevant factors such as geographic conditions." 65 Fed. Reg. 79830; see S. Rep. No. 101–228, at 166 (listing similar factors and noting that "[t]he proper definition of categories . . . will assure maximum protection of public health and the environment while minimizing costs imposed on the regulated community"). Using that classification tool, EPA can ensure that plants have to attain only the emissions levels previously achieved by peers facing comparable cost constraints, so as to further protect plants from unrealistic floor standards.

And that is exactly what EPA did over the course of its rulemaking process, insisting on apples-to-apples comparisons that bring floor standards within reach of diverse kinds of power plants. Even in making its "appropriate and necessary" finding, the Agency announced it would divide plants into the two categories mentioned above: "coal-fired" and "oil-fired." 65 Fed. Reg. 79830. Then, as the rulemaking progressed, EPA went further. [The dissent goes on to describe the subcategories EPA established to spare power plants from having to retrofit or redesign their facilities, as well as EPA's decision that regulating natural gas plants was not appropriate or necessary because regulation would have negligible impacts on pollution.] . . .

With all that cost-consideration under its belt, EPA next assessed whether to set beyond-the-floor standards, and here too, as it knew it would, the Agency took costs into account. For the vast majority of coal and oil plants, EPA decided that beyond-the-floor standards would not be "reasonable after considering costs." Id., at 9331. The Agency set such a standard for only a single kind of plant, and only after determining that the technology needed to meet the more lenient limit would also achieve the more stringent one. See id., at 9393; 76 Fed. Reg. 25046–25047. Otherwise, EPA determined, the market-leader-based standards were enough.

Finally, as required by Executive Order and as anticipated at the time of the "appropriate and necessary" finding, EPA conducted a formal cost-benefit analysis of its new emissions standards and incorporated those findings into its proposed and final rules. See id., at 25072–25078; 77 Fed. Reg. 9305–9306, 9424–9432. That analysis estimated that the regulation's yearly costs would come in at under $10 billion, while its annual measurable benefits would total many times more—between $37 and $90 billion. See id., at 9305–9306; ante, at 4. On the costs side, EPA acknowledged that plants' compliance with the rule would likely cause electricity prices to rise by about 3%, but projected that those prices would remain lower than they had been as recently as 2010. See 77 Fed. Reg. 9413–9414. EPA also thought the rule's impact on jobs would be about a wash, with jobs lost at some high-emitting plants but gained both at cleaner plants and in the pollution control industry. See ibid. On the benefits side, EPA noted that it could not quantify many of the health gains that would result from reduced mercury exposure. See id., at 9306. But even putting those aside, the rule's annual benefits would include between 4,200 and 11,000 fewer premature deaths from respiratory and cardiovascular causes, 3,100 fewer emergency room visits for asthmatic children, 4,700 fewer non-fatal heart attacks, and 540,000 fewer days of lost work. See id., at 9429.

Those concrete findings matter to these cases—which, after all, turn on whether EPA reasonably took costs into account in regulating plants' emissions of hazardous air pollutants. The majority insists that it may ignore EPA's cost-benefit analysis because "EPA did not rely on" it when issuing the initial "appropriate and necessary" finding. Ante, at 15 (quoting Solicitor General); see also SEC v. Chenery Corp., 318 U. S. 80, 87, 93–94 (1943). At one level, that description is true—indeed, a simple function of chronology: The kick-off finding preceded the cost-benefit analysis by years and so could not have taken its conclusions into account. But more fundamentally, the majority's account is off, because EPA knew when it made that finding that it would consider costs at every subsequent stage, culminating in a formal cost-benefit study. And EPA knew that, absent unusual circumstances, the rule would need to pass that cost-benefit review in order to issue. See Exec. Order No. 12866, 58 Fed. Reg. 51736 ("Each agency shall . . . adopt a regulation only upon a reasoned determination that the benefits of the intended regulation justify its costs"). The reasonableness of the Agency's decision to consider only the harms of emissions at the threshold stage must be evaluated in that broader context. . . .

Still more, EPA could not have accurately assessed costs at the time of its "appropriate and necessary" finding. See 8 Mercury Study, at 6–2 (noting the "many uncertainties" in any early-stage analysis of pollution control costs). Under the statutory scheme, that finding comes before— years before—the Agency designs emissions standards. And until EPA knows what standards it will establish, it cannot know what costs they will impose. Nor can those standards even be reasonably guesstimated at such an early stage. Consider what it takes to set floor standards alone. First, EPA must divide power plants into categories and subcategories; as explained earlier, those classification decisions significantly affect what floors are established. See supra, at 4, and n. 1, 11–12. And then, EPA must figure out the average emissions level already achieved by the top 12% in each class so as to set the new standards. None of that can realistically be accomplished in advance of the Agency's regulatory process: Indeed, those steps are the very stuff of the rulemaking. Similarly, until EPA knows what "compliance options" it will develop, it cannot know how they will mitigate the costs plants must incur to meet the floor standards. See supra, at 13–14. And again, deciding on those options takes substantial time. So there is good reason for different considerations to go into the threshold finding than into the final rule. Simply put, calculating costs before starting to write a regulation would put the cart before the horse. . . .

NOTES AND QUESTIONS

1. Special Treatment for Power Plants Under the CAA. Power plants are given unusual treatment under the CAA. The EPA cannot list power plants under section 112(c) as the agency would any other source of hazardous air pollutants; the statute requires the agency to first determine that regulating power plants is "appropriate and necessary." 42 U.S.C. § 7412(n)(1). Why would Congress give power plants this special treatment? One possibility is that in 1990, when Congress added the carveout for power plants, legislators might have thought the new federal acid rain program would address power plant pollution. If power plants installed scrubbers to comply with acid rain requirements, they might also significantly reduce other forms of air pollution, making further regulation unnecessary. Why else might power plants have received special treatment?

2. Understanding the EPA's Approach to Decisionmaking. EPA argued that although cost could affect how the agency decided to regulate power plants, cost considerations could not influence whether the decision to regulate was "appropriate." Does this reasoning make sense?

Perhaps the EPA's approach can be understood by reference to an analogy. If your friend down the street gets sick, it might be "appropriate" to send a get well card. Sending get well cards to sick friends is generally considered an appropriate thing to do. But what if a different friend living overseas gets sick? You might choose not to send a card because of the cost of shipping. This does not necessarily mean it is inappropriate to send a card. Rather, even though sending a card would be an appropriate thing to do, given other considerations, like cost, you decide sending the card doesn't make sense. Does this example shed doubt on the idea that "appropriate" must always implicate all relevant factors of a decision? How well does the analogy hold up in the context of the CAA, given that EPA is required to set regulatory floors for sources of hazardous air pollutants?

3. "Appropriate" and Kavanaugh's Influence. Part of the oral arguments for *Michigan v. EPA* dwelt on whether "appropriate" as used in § 7412(n)(1) has a distinct meaning from "necessary," or whether the two terms combine to communicate a single, unified legal standard, as is the case with "arbitrary and capricious." *See* Transcript of Oral Argument at 9–12, *Michigan v. EPA*, 135 S. Ct. 2699 (2015) (No. 14-46). The majority opinion determined "appropriate" requires the consideration of cost. *See* 135 S. Ct. at 2702. This reasoning comes from a lower court dissent by Judge Kavanaugh for the D.C. Circuit. In a portion not excerpted above, Justice Scalia quoted Judge Kavanaugh, describing "appropriate" as "the classic broad and all-encompassing term that naturally and traditionally includes consideration of all the relevant factors." *Id.* (quoting *White Stallion v. EPA*, 748 F. 3d, at 1266) (opinion of Kavanaugh, J., dissenting). Citing the "centrality of cost consideration to proper regulatory decisionmaking," as well as its "common sense" relevance to the appropriateness of regulation, Judge Kavanaugh argued EPA had acted unreasonably in deciding to regulate power plants without first considering cost. 748 F. 3d at 1261.

In 2018, Justice Kavanaugh was confirmed to the U.S. Supreme Court. Does his dissent in *White Stallion* suggest agencies need to focus not only on *whether* to consider cost in a decisionmaking process, but also on *when* to consider cost? What would be a narrow interpretation of his concerns in *White Stallion*? How might his dissent be construed broadly?

4.   Hypotheticals in a One-off Rule. Even though the total benefits of EPA's rule significantly outweighed its costs, Justice Scalia repeatedly cited hypotheticals where failure to consider cost in threshold regulatory decisions could lead to pernicious results. For example, he said: "If (to take a hypothetical example) regulating power plants would yield $5 million in benefits, the prospect of mitigating cost from $11 billion to $10 billion at later stages of the program would not by itself make regulation appropriate." 135 S. Ct. at 2711. But at the time of the Justice's writing, these hypotheticals were unlikely to come to fruition. Section 7412(n)(1) and its "appropriate and necessary" language only apply to power plants. After deciding to regulate power plants, EPA would not need to return to § 7412(n)(1) to regulate other sources. Because EPA would not need to rely on this provision again after deciding to regulate power plants, scenarios like the hypothetical above would not arise. If none of Justice Scalia's hypothetical concerns arose in EPA's promulgation of this specific rule, and if this was the only time the agency would make such a decision under this statutory provision, are the hypotheticals relevant?

5.   Timing of Cost Consideration: How Early Is Too Early? The dissent points out that EPA could not have effectively considered cost in its threshold decision even if the agency wanted to do so. The reason is that subsequent decisions after the threshold determination, like establishing regulatory subcategories of power plants, have a significant effect on the ultimate costs of a rule. One way the agency could try to evaluate cost early in the decisionmaking process would be to have specific regulatory regimes in mind and try to estimate associated costs as part of its threshold decision to regulate. This would require the agency to frontload a lot of its work in the decisionmaking process. What would be the benefits and drawbacks of such an approach?

6.   Fully Accounting for Benefits. The dissent emphasizes that EPA's cost-benefit analysis shows the agency's regulation of power plants is extremely cost-justified, with annual costs under $10 billion and quantifiable annual benefits ranging from $37–$90 billion. The majority, however, emphasizes that direct benefits from regulating hazardous air pollutants amount to only $4–$6 million per year. The estimate of direct benefits was lower than the rule's overall benefits for a couple of reasons. First, the agency was unable to quantify all of the direct health benefits of regulating hazardous air pollutants. EPA described these benefits qualitatively, but did not include them in its monetary estimate of benefits. *See* EPA, National Emissions Standards for Hazardous Air Pollutants from Coal- and Oil-Fired Electric Utility Steam Generating Units, 77 Fed. Reg. 9304, 9306 (2012). Second, the bulk of the rule's anticipated benefits came from reducing pollutants other than those covered by § 7412. *See id.* at 9305. These benefits are termed "ancillary benefits" or "co-benefits" because they are benefits outside the specific purpose of the authorizing statutory provision.

The majority did not reach the issue of whether co-benefits could be considered in determining whether rules were cost-justified. What are the pros and cons of considering co-benefits? Does the size of direct benefits relative to co-benefits matter? What if a rule has zero direct benefits, but huge co-benefits?

7.   Subsequent History of the Case. After the Supreme Court's decision, the D.C. Circuit remanded the case without vacatur. *See* Jonathan H. Adler, Opinion, *EPA Mercury Rule to Remain in Place While Agency Considers* Costs, WASH. POST, Dec. 15, 2015. The Obama Administration's EPA subsequently made the threshold finding that regulating power plants was appropriate, taking cost into account. *See* Coral Davenport, *E.P.A. to Reconsider Obama-Era Curbs on Mercury Emissions by Power Plants*, N.Y. TIMES, Aug. 29, 2018. Industry challenged the finding, and after President Trump's election, EPA successfully asked the D.C. Circuit to place the case in abeyance so the agency could reconsider its finding. *See* Sonal Patel, *D.C. Circuit Halts Clean Power Plan, Mercury Rule Litigation*, POWER, Apr. 28, 2017. In February 2019, EPA proposed to withdraw the "appropriate and necessary" finding but to keep the rule's standards in place. *See* EPA, National Emissions Standards for Hazardous Air Pollutants: Coal- and Oil-Fired Electric Utility Steam Generating Units, 84 Fed. Reg. 2670 (2019). Why would EPA make this decision? Consider the fact that by now, most regulated power plants have already bought the equipment necessary to comply with the Obama-era regulation. *See* Davenport, *supra*. These firms might not be able to recover costs from consumers if the requirements no longer apply to the whole industry. What if a non-compliant firm challenges EPA's approach and claims that the standards are illegal without an appropriate and necessary finding? Does the agency's approach seem legally vulnerable?

11. GREENHOUSE GAS EMISSIONS

A. REGULATION OF CARBON DIOXIDE EMISSIONS FROM MOBILE SOURCES

Since the enactment of the original CAA, climate change has grown enormously in political prominence, and the scientific consensus on the adverse consequences of climate change is much greater than it was 40 years ago. The first major case to consider the applicability of the CAA to carbon dioxide emissions was a Title II case.

Massachusetts v. Environmental Protection Agency
549 U.S. 497 (2007).

■ JUSTICE STEVENS delivered the opinion of the Court:

A well-documented rise in global temperatures has coincided with a significant increase in the concentration of carbon dioxide in the atmosphere. Respected scientists believe the two trends are related. For when carbon dioxide is released into the atmosphere, it acts like the ceiling of a greenhouse, trapping solar energy and retarding the escape of reflected heat. It is therefore a species—the most important species—of a "greenhouse gas."

Calling global warming "the most pressing environmental challenge of our time," a group of States, local governments, and private organizations alleged in a petition for certiorari that the Environmental Protection Agency (EPA) has abdicated its responsibility under the Clean Air Act to regulate the emissions of four greenhouse gases, including carbon dioxide. Specifically, petitioners asked us to answer two questions concerning the meaning of § 202(a)(1) of the Act: whether EPA has the statutory authority to regulate greenhouse gas emissions from new motor vehicles; and if so, whether its stated reasons for refusing to do so are consistent with the statute. . . .

I

Section 202(a)(1) of the Clean Air Act . . . provides:

"The [EPA] Administrator shall by regulation prescribe (and from time to time revise) in accordance with the provisions of this section, standards applicable to the emission of any air pollutant from any class or classes of new motor vehicles or new motor vehicle engines, which in his judgment cause, or contribute to, air pollution which may reasonably be anticipated to endanger public health or welfare. . . ."

The Act defines "air pollutant" to include "any air pollution agent or combination of such agents, including any physical, chemical, biological, radioactive . . . substance or matter which is emitted into or otherwise enters the ambient air." [§ 302(g).] "Welfare" is also defined broadly: among other things, it includes "effects on . . . weather . . . and climate." [§ 302(h).]

When Congress enacted these provisions, the study of climate change was in its infancy. In 1959, shortly after the U.S. Weather Bureau began monitoring atmospheric carbon dioxide levels, an observatory in Mauna Loa, Hawaii, recorded a mean level of 316 parts per million. This was well above the highest carbon dioxide concentration—no more than 300 parts per million—revealed in the 420,000-year-old ice-core record. By the time Congress drafted § 202(a)(1) in 1970, carbon dioxide levels had reached 325 parts per million. . . .

... In 1990, the Intergovernmental Panel on Climate Change (IPCC), a multinational scientific body organized under the auspices of the United Nations, published its first comprehensive report on the topic. Drawing on expert opinions from across the globe, the IPCC concluded that "emissions resulting from human activities are substantially increasing the atmospheric concentrations of ... greenhouse gases [which] will enhance the greenhouse effect, resulting on average in an additional warming of the Earth's surface." ...

II

On October 20, 1999, a group of 19 private organizations filed a rulemaking petition asking EPA to regulate "greenhouse gas emissions from new motor vehicles under § 202 of the Clean Air Act." App. S. ...

Fifteen months after the petition's submission, EPA requested public comment on "all the issues raised in [the] petition," adding a "particular" request for comments on "any scientific, technical, legal, economic or other aspect of these issues that may be relevant to EPA's consideration of this petition." 66 Fed. Reg. 7486, 7487 (2001). EPA received more than 50,000 comments over the next five months. See 68 Fed. Reg. 52,924 (2003). ...

On September 8, 2003, EPA entered an order denying the rulemaking petition. 68 Fed. Reg. 52,922. The agency gave two reasons for its decision: (1) that contrary to the opinions of its former general counsels, the Clean Air Act does not authorize EPA to issue mandatory regulations to address global climate change, see *id.*, at 52,925–52,929; and (2) that even if the agency had the authority to set greenhouse gas emission standards, it would be unwise to do so at this time, *id.*, at 52,929–52,931.

In concluding that it lacked statutory authority over greenhouse gases, EPA observed that Congress "was well aware of the global climate change issue when it last comprehensively amended the [Clean Air Act] in 1990," yet it declined to adopt a proposed amendment establishing binding emissions limitations. *Id.* Congress instead chose to authorize further investigation into climate change. ... EPA further reasoned that Congress' "specially tailored solutions to global atmospheric issues," 68 Fed. Reg. 52,926—in particular, its 1990 enactment of a comprehensive scheme to regulate pollutants that depleted the ozone layer—counseled against reading the general authorization of § 202(a)(1) to confer regulatory authority over greenhouse gases. ...

... In essence, EPA concluded that climate change was so important that unless Congress spoke with exacting specificity, it could not have meant the agency to address it.

Having reached that conclusion, EPA believed it followed that greenhouse gases cannot be "air pollutants" within the meaning of the Act. ...

Even assuming that it had authority over greenhouse gases, EPA explained in detail why it would refuse to exercise that authority. The agency began by recognizing that the concentration of greenhouse gases has dramatically increased as a result of human activities, and acknowledged the attendant increase in global surface air temperatures. EPA nevertheless gave controlling importance to the NRC Report's statement that a causal link between the two " 'cannot be unequivocally established.' " Given that residual uncertainty, EPA concluded that regulating greenhouse gas emissions would be unwise. 68 Fed. Reg. 52,930. . . .

III

Petitioners, now joined by intervenor States and local governments, sought review of EPA's order in the United States Court of Appeals for the District of Columbia Circuit. Although each of the three judges on the panel wrote a separate opinion, two judges agreed "that the EPA Administrator properly exercised his discretion under § 202(a)(1) in denying the petition for rule making." 415 F.3d 50, 58 (2005). The court therefore denied the petition for review. . . .

V

The scope of our review of the merits of the statutory issues is narrow. As we have repeated time and again, an agency has broad discretion to choose how best to marshal its limited resources and personnel to carry out its delegated responsibilities. That discretion is at its height when the agency decides not to bring an enforcement action. . . . Some debate remains, however, as to the rigor with which we review an agency's denial of a petition for rulemaking. . . .

. . . In contrast to nonenforcement decisions, agency refusals to initiate rulemaking "are less frequent, more apt to involve legal as opposed to factual analysis, and subject to special formalities, including a public explanation." [American Horse Protection Ass'n, Inc. v. Lyng, 812 F.2d 1, 4 (D.C.Cir. 1987)] They moreover arise out of denials of petitions for rulemaking which (at least in the circumstances here) the affected party had an undoubted procedural right to file in the first instance. Refusals to promulgate rules are thus susceptible to judicial review, though such review is "extremely limited" and "highly deferential." National Customs Brokers & Forwarders Ass'n v. United States, 883 F.2d 93, 96 (CADC 1989).

EPA concluded in its denial of the petition for rulemaking that it lacked authority under [CAA § 202(a)(1)] to regulate new vehicle emissions because carbon dioxide is not an "air pollutant" as that term is defined in [§ 302.] In the alternative, it concluded that even if it possessed authority, it would decline to do so because regulation would conflict with other administration priorities. As discussed earlier, the Clean Air Act expressly permits review of such an action. § 7607(b)(1). We therefore "may reverse any such action found to be . . . arbitrary, capricious, an

abuse of discretion, or otherwise not in accordance with law."
§ 7607(d)(9).

VI

On the merits, the first question is whether § 202(a)(1) of the Clean
Air Act authorizes EPA to regulate greenhouse gas emissions from new
motor vehicles in the event that it forms a "judgment" that such
emissions contribute to climate change. We have little trouble concluding
that it does. In relevant part, § 202(a)(1) provides that EPA "shall by
regulation prescribe . . . standards applicable to the emission of any air
pollutant from any class or classes of new motor vehicles or new motor
vehicle engines, which in [the Administrator's] judgment cause, or
contribute to, air pollution which may reasonably be anticipated to
endanger public health or welfare." Because EPA believes that Congress
did not intend it to regulate substances that contribute to climate change,
the agency maintains that carbon dioxide is not an "air pollutant" within
the meaning of the provision.

The statutory text forecloses EPA's reading. The Clean Air Act's
sweeping definition of "air pollutant" includes "*any* air pollution agent or
combination of such agents, including *any* physical, chemical . . .
substance or matter which is emitted into or otherwise enters the
ambient air. . . ." [§ 302(g)] (emphasis added). On its face, the definition
embraces all airborne compounds of whatever stripe, and underscores
that intent through the repeated use of the word "any." Carbon dioxide,
methane, nitrous oxide, and hydrofluorocarbons are without a doubt
"physical [and] chemical . . . substance[s] which [are] emitted into . . . the
ambient air." The statute is unambiguous.

Rather than relying on statutory text, EPA invokes postenactment
congressional actions and deliberations it views as tantamount to a
congressional command to refrain from regulating greenhouse gas
emissions. Even if such postenactment legislative history could shed light
on the meaning of an otherwise-unambiguous statute, EPA never
identifies any action remotely suggesting that Congress meant to curtail
its power to treat greenhouse gases as air pollutants. That subsequent
Congresses have eschewed enacting binding emissions limitations to
combat global warming tells us nothing about what Congress meant
when it amended § 202(a)(1) in 1970 and 1977. And unlike EPA, we have
no difficulty reconciling Congress' various efforts to promote interagency
collaboration and research to better understand climate change with the
agency's pre-existing mandate to regulate "any air pollutant" that may
endanger the public welfare. Collaboration and research do not conflict
with any thoughtful regulatory effort; they complement it. . . .

EPA finally argues that it cannot regulate carbon dioxide emissions
from motor vehicles because doing so would require it to tighten mileage
standards, a job (according to EPA) that Congress has assigned to DOT.
See 68 Fed. Reg. 52,929. But that DOT sets mileage standards in no way
licenses EPA to shirk its environmental responsibilities. EPA has been

charged with protecting the public's "health" and "welfare," 42 U.S.C. § 7521(a)(1), a statutory obligation wholly independent of DOT's mandate to promote energy efficiency. See Energy Policy and Conservation Act, § 2(5), 89 Stat. 874, 42 U.S.C. § 6201(5). The two obligations may overlap, but there is no reason to think the two agencies cannot both administer their obligations and yet avoid inconsistency.

While the Congresses that drafted § 202(a)(1) might not have appreciated the possibility that burning fossil fuels could lead to global warming, they did understand that without regulatory flexibility, changing circumstances and scientific developments would soon render the Clean Air Act obsolete. The broad language of § 202(a)(1) reflects an intentional effort to confer the flexibility necessary to forestall such obsolescence. Because greenhouse gases fit well within the Clean Air Act's capacious definition of "air pollutant," we hold that EPA has the statutory authority to regulate the emission of such gases from new motor vehicles.

VII

The alternative basis for EPA's decision—that even if it does have statutory authority to regulate greenhouse gases, it would be unwise to do so at this time—rests on reasoning divorced from the statutory text. While the statute does condition the exercise of EPA's authority on its formation of a "judgment," 42 U.S.C. § 7521(a)(1), that judgment must relate to whether an air pollutant "cause[s], or contribute[s] to, air pollution which may reasonably be anticipated to endanger public health or welfare," *ibid.* Put another way, the use of the word "judgment" is not a roving license to ignore the statutory text. It is but a direction to exercise discretion within defined statutory limits.

If EPA makes a finding of endangerment, the Clean Air Act requires the agency to regulate emissions of the deleterious pollutant from new motor vehicles. *Ibid.* (stating that "[EPA] shall by regulation prescribe . . . standards applicable to the emission of any air pollutant from any class of new motor vehicles"). EPA no doubt has significant latitude as to the manner, timing, content, and coordination of its regulations with those of other agencies. But once EPA has responded to a petition for rulemaking, its reasons for action or inaction must conform to the authorizing statute. Under the clear terms of the Clean Air Act, EPA can avoid taking further action only if it determines that greenhouse gases do not contribute to climate change or if it provides some reasonable explanation as to why it cannot or will not exercise its discretion to determine whether they do. To the extent that this constrains agency discretion to pursue other priorities of the Administrator or the President, this is the congressional design.

EPA has refused to comply with this clear statutory command. Instead, it has offered a laundry list of reasons not to regulate. For example, EPA said that a number of voluntary executive branch programs already provide an effective response to the threat of global warming, 68 Fed. Reg. 52,932, that regulating greenhouse gases might impair the President's ability to negotiate with "key developing nations" to reduce emissions, *id.*, at 52,931, and that curtailing motor-vehicle emissions would reflect "an inefficient, piecemeal approach to address the climate change issue," *ibid.*

Although we have neither the expertise nor the authority to evaluate these policy judgments, it is evident they have nothing to do with whether greenhouse gas emissions contribute to climate change. Still less do they amount to a reasoned justification for declining to form a scientific judgment. . . .

Nor can EPA avoid its statutory obligation by noting the uncertainty surrounding various features of climate change and concluding that it would therefore be better not to regulate at this time. If the scientific uncertainty is so profound that it precludes EPA from making a reasoned judgment as to whether greenhouse gases contribute to global warming, EPA must say so. That EPA would prefer not to regulate greenhouse gases because of some residual uncertainty—which, contrary to Justice SCALIA's apparent belief, is in fact all that it said, see 68 Fed. Reg. 52,929 ("We do not believe . . . that it would be either effective or appropriate for EPA *to establish [greenhouse gas] standards for motor vehicles* at this time" (emphasis added))—is irrelevant. The statutory question is whether sufficient information exists to make an endangerment finding.

In short, EPA has offered no reasoned explanation for its refusal to decide whether greenhouse gases cause or contribute to climate change. Its action was therefore "arbitrary, capricious, . . . or otherwise not in accordance with law." We need not and do not reach the question whether on remand EPA must make an endangerment finding, or whether policy concerns can inform EPA's actions in the event that it makes such a finding. Cf. *Chevron U.S.A. Inc. v. NRDC*, 467 U.S. 837, 843–844 (1984). We hold only that EPA must ground its reasons for action or inaction in the statute. . . .

■ JUSTICE SCALIA, with whom THE CHIEF JUSTICE, JUSTICE THOMAS, and JUSTICE ALITO join, dissenting:

I

The provision of law at the heart of this case is § 202(a)(1) of the Clean Air Act (CAA), which provides that the Administrator of the Environmental Protection Agency (EPA) "shall by regulation prescribe . . . standards applicable to the emission of any air pollutant from any class or classes of new motor vehicles or new motor vehicle engines, which *in his judgment* cause, or contribute to, air pollution which may reasonably be anticipated to endanger public health or welfare." As the Court recognizes, the statute "condition[s] the exercise of EPA's authority on its formation of a 'judgment.'" *Ante*, at 30. There is no dispute that the Administrator has made no such judgment in this case. See *ante*, at

32 ("We need not and do not reach the question whether on remand EPA must make an endangerment finding"); 68 Fed. 52929 (2003) ("[N]o Administrator has made a finding under any of the CAA's regulatory provisions that CO_2 meets the applicable statutory criteria for regulation").

The question thus arises: Does anything *require* the Administrator to make a "judgment" whenever a petition for rulemaking is filed? Without citation of the statute or any other authority, the Court says yes. Why is that so? When Congress wishes to make private action force an agency's hand, it knows how to do so. See, *e.g.*, *Brock v. Pierce County*, 476 U.S. 253 (1986) (discussing the Comprehensive Employment and Training Act (CETA), 92 Stat. 1926, 29 U.S.C. § 816(b) (1976 ed., Supp. V), which "provide[d] that the Secretary of Labor 'shall' issue a final determination as to the misuse of CETA funds by a grant recipient within 120 days after receiving a complaint alleging such misuse"). Where does the CAA say that the EPA Administrator is required to come to a decision on this question whenever a rulemaking petition is filed? The Court points to no such provision because none exists.

Instead, the Court invents a multiple-choice question that the EPA Administrator must answer when a petition for rulemaking is filed. The Administrator must exercise his judgment in one of three ways: (a) by concluding that the pollutant *does* cause, or contribute to, air pollution that endangers public welfare (in which case EPA is required to regulate); (b) by concluding that the pollutant *does not* cause, or contribute to, air pollution that endangers public welfare (in which case EPA is *not* required to regulate); or (c) by "provid[ing] some reasonable explanation as to why it cannot or will not exercise its discretion to determine whether" greenhouse gases endanger public welfare (in which case EPA is *not* required to regulate).

I am willing to assume, for the sake of argument, that the Administrator's discretion in this regard is not entirely unbounded—that if he has no reasonable basis for deferring judgment he must grasp the nettle at once. The Court, however, with no basis in text or precedent, rejects all of EPA's stated "policy judgments" as not "amount[ing] to a reasoned justification," *ante*, at 31, effectively narrowing the universe of potential reasonable bases to a single one: Judgment can be delayed *only* if the Administrator concludes that "the scientific uncertainty is [too] profound." *Ibid.* The Administrator is precluded from concluding *for other reasons* "that it would . . . be better not to regulate at this time." *Ibid.* Such other reasons—perfectly valid reasons—were set forth in the agency's statement. . . .

The Court dismisses this analysis as "rest[ing] on reasoning divorced from the statutory text." *Ante* at 30. "While the statute does condition the exercise of EPA's authority on its formation of a 'judgment,' . . . that judgment must relate to whether an air pollutant 'cause[s], or contribute[s] to, air pollution which may reasonably be anticipated to endanger public health or welfare.' " *Ibid*. True but irrelevant. When the Administrator *makes* a judgment whether to regulate greenhouse gases, that judgment must relate to whether they are air pollutants that "cause, or contribute to, air pollution which may reasonably be anticipated to endanger public health or welfare." But the statute says *nothing at all* about the reasons for which the Administrator may *defer* making a judgment—the permissible reasons for deciding not to grapple with the issue at the present time. Thus, the various "policy" rationales that the Court criticizes are not "divorced from the statutory text," *ante*, at 30, except in the sense that the statutory text is silent, as texts are often silent about permissible reasons for the exercise of agency discretion. The reasons the EPA gave are surely considerations executive agencies *regularly* take into account (and *ought* to take into account) when deciding whether to consider entering a new field: the impact such entry would have on other Executive Branch programs and on foreign policy. There is no basis in law for the Court's imposed limitation.

EPA's interpretation of the discretion conferred by the statutory reference to "its judgment" is not only reasonable, it is the most natural reading of the text. The Court nowhere explains why this interpretation is incorrect, let alone why it is not entitled to deference under *Chevron*. . . . I would uphold the decision to deny the rulemaking petition on that ground alone.

Even on the Court's own terms, however, the same conclusion follows. As mentioned above, the Court gives EPA the option of determining that the science is too uncertain to allow it to form a "judgment" as to whether greenhouse gases endanger public welfare. Attached to this option (on what basis is unclear) is an essay requirement: "If," the Court says, "the scientific uncertainty is so profound that it precludes EPA from making a reasoned judgment as to whether greenhouse gases contribute to global warming, EPA must say so." *Ante*, at 31. But EPA has said precisely that—and at great length, based on information contained in a 2001 report by the National Research Council (NRC) entitled Climate Change Science: An Analysis of Some Key Questions:

[Justice Scalia quotes at length from EPA's discussion of the NRC report, including the observation that "there is considerable uncertainty in current understanding of how the climate system varies naturally and reacts to emissions of [GHGs] and aerosols."]

I simply cannot conceive of what else the Court would like EPA to say.

II

Even before reaching its discussion of the word "judgment," the Court makes another significant error when it concludes that "§ 202(a)(1) of the Clean Air Act *authorizes* EPA to regulate greenhouse gas emissions from new motor vehicles in the event that it forms a 'judgment' that such emissions contribute to climate change." *Ante*, at 25 (emphasis added). For such authorization, the Court relies on what it calls "the Clean Air Act's capacious definition of 'air pollutant.'" *Ante*, at 30.

"Air pollutant" is defined by the Act as "any air pollution agent or combination of such agents, including any physical, chemical, . . . substance or matter which is emitted into or otherwise enters the ambient air." [§ 302(g).] The Court is correct that "[c]arbon dioxide, methane, nitrous oxide, and hydrofluorocarbons," fit within the second half of that definition: They are "physical, chemical, . . . substance[s] or matter which [are] emitted into or otherwise ente[r] the ambient air." But the Court mistakenly believes this to be the end of the analysis. In order to be an "air pollutant" under the Act's definition, the "substance or matter [being] emitted into . . . the ambient air" must also meet the *first* half of the definition—namely, it must be an "air pollution agent or combination of such agents." The Court simply pretends this half of the definition does not exist.

The Court's analysis faithfully follows the argument advanced by petitioners, which focuses on the word "including" in the statutory definition of "air pollutant." As that argument goes, anything that *follows* the word "including" must necessarily be a subset of whatever *precedes* it. Thus, if greenhouse gases qualify under the phrase following the word "including," they must qualify under the phrase preceding it. Since greenhouse gases come within the capacious phrase "any physical, chemical, . . . substance or matter which is emitted into or otherwise enters the ambient air," they must also be "air pollution agent[s] or combination[s] of such agents," and therefore meet the definition of "air pollutant[s.]"

That is certainly one possible interpretation of the statutory definition. The word "including" can indeed indicate that what follows will be an "illustrative" sampling of the general category that precedes the word. *Federal Land Bank of St. Paul v. Bismarck Lumber Co.*, 314 U.S. 95, 100 (1941). Often, however, the examples standing alone are broader than the general category, and must be viewed as limited in light of that category. The Government provides a helpful (and unanswered) example: "The phrase 'any American automobile, including any truck or minivan,' would not naturally be construed to encompass a foreign-manufactured [truck or] minivan." The general principle enunciated—that the speaker is talking about *American* automobiles—carries forward to the illustrative examples (trucks and minivans), and limits them accordingly, even though in isolation they are broader. Congress often uses the word "including" in this manner. In 28 U.S.C. § 1782(a), for example, it refers to "a proceeding in a foreign or international tribunal, including criminal investigations conducted before formal accusation." Certainly this provision would not encompass criminal investigations underway in a *domestic* tribunal. See also, *e.g.*, 2 U.S.C. § 54(a) ("The Clerk of the House of Representatives shall, at the request of a Member of the House of Representatives, furnish to the Member, for official use only, one set of a privately published annotated version of the United States Code, including supplements and pocket parts"); 22 U.S.C. § 2304(b)(1) ("the relevant findings of appropriate international organizations, including nongovernmental organizations").

In short, the word "including" does not require the Court's (or the petitioners') result. It is perfectly reasonable to view the definition of "air pollutant" in its entirety: An air pollutant *can* be "any physical, chemical, . . . substance or matter which is emitted into or otherwise enters the ambient air," but only if it retains the general characteristic of being an "air pollution agent or combination of such agents." This is precisely the conclusion EPA reached: "[A] substance does not meet the CAA definition of 'air pollutant' simply because it is a 'physical, chemical, . . . substance or matter which is emitted into or otherwise enters the ambient air.' It must also be an 'air pollution agent.'" . . . Once again, in the face of textual ambiguity, the Court's application of *Chevron* deference to EPA's interpretation of the word "including" is nowhere to be found. . . .

Using (as we ought to) EPA's interpretation of the definition of "air pollutant," we must next determine whether greenhouse gases are "agent[s]" of "air pollution." If so, the statute would authorize regulation; if not, EPA would lack authority.

Unlike "air pollutants," the term "air pollution" is not itself defined by the CAA; thus, once again we must accept EPA's interpretation of that ambiguous term, provided its interpretation is a "permissible construction of the statute." *Chevron*, 467 U.S., at 843. In this case, the petition for rulemaking asked EPA for "regulation of [greenhouse gas] emissions from motor vehicles to reduce the risk of global climate change." 68 Fed. Reg. 52925. Thus, in deciding whether it had authority to regulate, EPA had to determine whether the concentration of greenhouse gases assertedly responsible for "global climate change" qualifies as "air pollution." EPA began with the commonsense observation that the "[p]roblems associated with atmospheric concentrations of CO_2," *Id.* at 52927, bear little resemblance to what would naturally be termed "air pollution":

> EPA's prior use of the CAA's general regulatory provisions provides an important context. Since the inception of the Act, EPA has used these provisions to address air pollution problems that occur primarily at ground level or near the surface of the earth. For example, national ambient air quality standards (NAAQS) established under CAA section 109 address concentrations of substances in the ambient air and the related public health and welfare problems. This has meant setting NAAQS for concentrations of ozone, carbon monoxide, particulate matter and other substances in the air near the surface of the earth, not higher in the atmosphere. . . . CO_2, by

contrast, is fairly consistent in concentration throughout the world's atmosphere up to approximately the lower stratosphere.

Id. at 52926–52927. In other words, regulating the buildup of CO_2 and other greenhouse gases in the upper reaches of the atmosphere, which is alleged to be causing global climate change, is not akin to regulating the concentration of some substance that is *polluting* the *air*.

We need look no further than the dictionary for confirmation that this interpretation of "air pollution" is eminently reasonable. The definition of "pollute," of course, is "[t]o make or render impure or unclean." Webster's New International Dictionary 1910 (2d Ed. 1949). And the first three definitions of "air" are as follows: (1) "[t]he invisible, odorless, and tasteless mixture of gases which surrounds the earth"; (2) "[t]he body of the earth's atmosphere; esp., the part of it near the earth, as distinguished from the upper rarefied part"; (3) "[a] portion of air or of the air considered with respect to physical characteristics or as affecting the senses." EPA's conception of "air pollution"—focusing on impurities in the "ambient air" "at ground level or near the surface of the earth"—is perfectly consistent with the natural meaning of that term.

In the end, EPA concluded that since "CAA authorization to regulate is generally based on a finding that an air pollutant causes or contributes to air pollution," 68 Fed. Reg. 52928, the concentrations of CO_2 and other greenhouse gases allegedly affecting the global climate are beyond the scope of CAA's authorization to regulate. "[T]he term 'air pollution' as used in the regulatory provisions cannot be interpreted to encompass global climate change." *Ibid.* Once again, the Court utterly fails to explain why this interpretation is incorrect, let alone so unreasonable as to be unworthy of *Chevron* deference.

The Court's alarm over global warming may or may not be justified, but it ought not distort the outcome of this litigation. This is a straightforward administrative-law case, in which Congress has passed a malleable statute giving broad discretion, not to us but to an executive agency. No matter how important the underlying policy issues at stake, this Court has no business substituting its own desired outcome for the reasoned judgment of the responsible agency.

NOTES AND QUESTIONS

1. **Defining Pollutants and Pollution.** How does the majority go about defining a "pollutant"? How does the dissent respond? Which is more persuasive? The dissent insists it would "def[y] common sense" to define pollutants as the majority does. Does the majority's interpretation of "pollution" really mean, as the dissent charges, that everything from "Frisbees to flatulence" counts as "pollution"? If a sudden onslaught of, say, methane emissions from cows was threatening the public health, is there a statutory reason EPA shouldn't have to do anything about it in response to a petition? Or is this characterizing the dissent's argument unfairly?

How do the majoring and dissent define "air pollution agent?" Which interpretation is more compelling?

Once a pollutant is defined, what further steps are required of the Administrator before regulations are issued for mobile sources? Which of those steps are discretionary and which are essentially required? In making judgments, what factors may the Administrator consider, and what factors may she not consider? Does *Massachusetts v. EPA* make it harder for EPA to "do nothing"? Is that wise?

2. Responses to Petitions. Justice Scalia's dissent argues that EPA is not required to make a judgment about the harmfulness of a given substance any time it is faced with a petition for rulemaking about that substance. Does the majority effectively respond to this argument? What are the risks of requiring EPA to analyze the risks of compounds in the ambient air any time a petition asking them to do so is filed? What are the risks of allowing inaction? Under Justice Scalia's understanding of the statute, must EPA ever make such judgments in response to petitions?

Does the majority, as charged by the dissent, put EPA in a "multiple choice" conundrum where it must either judge the pollutant harmful, harmless, or explain some reason for not making a judgment? Is this the essence of the disagreement between the two opinions?

3. Greenhouse Gases and Fuel Efficiency. In addition to EPA's authority to regulate vehicle emissions under § 202, the Department of Transportation (DOT) has authority under the Energy Policy and Conservation Act (EPCA) to regulate vehicle fuel efficiency. Justice Stevens noted in *Massachusetts v. EPA* that "[t]he two obligations may overlap, but there is no reason to think the two agencies cannot both administer their obligations and yet avoid inconsistency." 549 U.S. at 532. In what ways can vehicle GHG emissions be reduced that do not involve fuel efficiency? Should the degree of overlap be a factor in deciding whether EPA has authority to act?

After EPA issued its endangerment finding, EPA and DOT issued coordinated greenhouse gas and fuel efficiency standards for model year 2012–2016 light-duty vehicles. EPA, Light-Duty Vehicle Greenhouse Gas Emission Standards and Corporate Average Fuel Economy Standards, 75 Fed. Reg. 25,324 (2010). More recently, EPA and DOT have established standards for future model years and for heavy-duty vehicles that will achieve additional, substantial GHG reductions. *See* The White House, *White House Announces First Ever Oil Savings Standards for Heavy Duty Trucks, Buses,* Aug. 9, 2011.

How can fuel efficiency standards be used to address climate change within the framework of the CAA? Is EPA or DOT better positioned to take the lead, or is a coordinated approach best? *See* Jody Freeman & Adrian Vermeule, *Massachusetts v. EPA: From Politics to Expertise,* 2007 SUP. CT. REV. 51 (2007). How do these subsequent events affect your evaluation of the arguments EPA made in *Massachusetts v. EPA*? How do these subsequent events affect your evaluation of the arguments EPA made in *Massachusetts v. EPA*?

4.   Regulation of Fuel. Section 211 authorizes the Administrator to require registration of fuels or fuel additives and to control or prohibit the manufacture or sale of any fuel or fuel additive "if in the judgment of the Administrator any emission product of such fuel or fuel additive causes, or contributes, to air pollution which may reasonably be anticipated to endanger the public health or welfare." *See* 42 U.S.C. § 7545(a)–(c). Section 211(k) establishes a reformulated gasoline (RFG) program for certain nonattainment areas, particularly those in nonattainment for ozone. *See* 42 U.S.C. § 7545(k). The Administrator was required to publish RFG requirements within one year after passage of the 1990 CAA Amendments, requiring "the greatest reduction in emissions of ozone forming volatile organic compounds (during the high ozone season) and emissions of toxic air pollutants (during the entire year) achievable through the reformulation of conventional gasoline, taking into consideration the cost of achieving such emission reductions, any nonair-quality and other air-quality related health and environmental impacts and energy requirements." 42 U.S.C. § 7545(k).

At first, gasoline manufacturers met the RFG requirements using an oxygenate additive called methyl tertiary-butyl ether (MTBE). The addition of MTBE to gasoline in nonattainment areas resulted in significant improvements in air quality. However, cities in these areas began noticing the foul-smelling MTBE in local water supplies—the result of leaking underground storage tanks (regulated by the Comprehensive Environmental Response, Compensation, and Liability Act). MTBE is a suspected human carcinogen. Several cities have sued the gasoline manufacturers and obtained large settlements for groundwater contamination. In 1999, California became the first state to ban MTBE as a gasoline additive. For an account of EPA's role in authorizing the use of MTBE, as well as the challenges of regulating a multi-media pollutant, see Thomas O. McGarity, *MTBE: A Precautionary Tale*, 28 HARV. ENVTL. L. REV. 281 (2004).

Ethanol, which also serves as an oxygenate additive, has emerged as the dominant replacement for MTBE. *See* James A. Duffield et al., *Ethanol Policy: Past, Present, and Future*, 53 S.D. L. REV. 425, 436 (2008). Should EPA's fuel regulation be coordinated with national gasoline supply policy?

5.   Climate Change and California. The issue of EPA's authority to regulate carbon dioxide under the CAA has implications for California's regulation of GHG emissions from motor vehicles. For example, if carbon dioxide is not a "pollutant," California may face preemption from regulating CO_2 emissions under the Energy Policy and Conservation Act, which preempts states from issuing regulations that "relate to fuel economy standards." 49 U.S.C. § 32919(a). If carbon dioxide is a pollutant, California may only regulate CO_2 emissions in the event that EPA grants it a waiver under § 209. For discussion of these and other questions raised by issues in the *Massachusetts v. EPA* case, see Ann E. Carlson, *Federalism, Preemption, and Greenhouse Gas Emissions,* 37 U.C. DAVIS L. REV. 281 (2003); Rachel L. Chanin, Note, *California's Authority to Regulate Mobile Source Greenhouse Gas Emissions*, 58 N.Y.U. ANN. SURV. AM. L. 699 (2003). *See also Central Valley Chrysler-Jeep, Inc. v. Goldstene*, 529 F. Supp. 2d 1151 (E.D. Cal. 2007) (holding that EPCA did not preempt California from regulating greenhouse gas emissions under a CAA § 209 waiver).

Now that EPA does regulate carbon dioxide, consider whether California can regulate it more stringently. Can California argue that state-specific regulation is justified because California faces "compelling and extraordinary" conditions from a global problem such as climate change? California, with its long coastline, might plausibly have an interest in rising sea levels greater than, say, Missouri. Is that relevant? *See* Jonathan Martel, *Climate Change Law and Litigation in the Aftermath of* Massachusetts v. EPA, ENV'T REP., Nov. 9, 2007, at 2424.

In 2004, when the California Air Resources Board (CARB) issued its GHG emissions standards for automobiles, it applied to EPA for a waiver to put those emissions standards into effect. In December 2007, EPA denied the waiver, claiming that the 2007 Energy Security and Independence Act constituted a comprehensive federal solution. In January 2008, California filed suit against EPA's denial of the waiver and asked EPA for a more detailed explanation of its denial of the waiver. EPA denied the request for further explanation, claiming executive privilege.

Recall that § 209(b) of the CAA directs the Administrator to grant California's waiver request if it is at least as protective of public health as the federal standard, unless one of three conditions applies. The Administrator is to deny the waiver if he finds that:

A.   California's request is arbitrary and capricious;

B.   California does not need the proposed standards to meet compelling and extraordinary conditions; or

C.   California's standards and accompanying enforcement procedures are not consistent with § 202(a).

42 U.S.C. § 7543(a). Bearing these standards in mind, how should California's challenge to EPA's waiver denial have been resolved?

Before litigation over the waiver denial was resolved, EPA withdrew its denial and granted California's waiver request. EPA, California State Motor Vehicle Pollution Control Standards, 74 Fed. Reg. 32,744 (2009). EPA concluded that opponents of the waiver had not met their burden in demonstrating that California's coastline vulnerabilities, among others, did not create "compelling and extraordinary conditions," and that in the alternative, EPA "interpreted the 'compelling and extraordinary conditions' criterion to not properly include a consideration of whether the impacts from climate change are compelling and extraordinary in California." *Id*. at 32,746. Does this interpretation accord with congressional intent to grant broad discretion to California, or does it render the "compelling and extraordinary conditions" requirement hollow?

6.   Withdrawal of a Waiver. When President Obama took office, he announced not only an auto industry bailout, but also new national standards on greenhouse gas emissions from cars. Robinson Meyer, *The Coming Clean Air War Between Trump and California*, ATLANTIC, Mar. 6, 2017. EPA also granted California's waiver under CAA § 209(b). *Id*. The

Trump Administration changed course in August 2018. EPA proposed to weaken federal greenhouse gas emission standards and revoke California's waiver to maintain its own greenhouse gas and zero emission vehicle standards. EPA & NHTSA, The Safer Affordable Fuel-Efficient Vehicles Rule for Model Years 2021–2026 Passenger Cars and Light Trucks, 83 Fed. Reg. 42,986, 42,999 (2018).

EPA has never revoked a waiver before. DENISE A. GRAB ET AL., INST. POL'Y INTEGRITY, NO TURNING BACK i (2018). The text of § 209 is silent as to whether the agency has authority to revoke a waiver once granted. In contrast, other sections of the CAA, like Title V, lay out when and how EPA can revoke authority delegated to states. 42 U.S.C. § 7661a(i)(1),(4). Even if revoking a § 209 waiver is permitted under certain circumstances, revocation might be impermissible in this case. When EPA granted California's waiver to regulate greenhouse gases in 2009, it suggested that it might be able to withdraw the waiver later, but only if "[f]ederal greenhouse gas standards are promulgated in the future," and such standards render California's regulations comparatively less protective. EPA, Notice of Decision Granting a Waiver of Clean Air Act Preemption for California's 2009 and Subsequent Model Year Greenhouse Gas Emission Standards for New Motor Vehicles, 74 Fed. Reg. 32,744, 32,752 (2009). EPA does not now claim that California's standards are insufficiently protective relative to federal standards, but instead argues that revocation is justified because 1) the National Highway Traffic Safety Administration has proposed to find that California's standards are preempted under the Energy Policy and Conservation Act, 2) California no longer needs its greenhouse gas standards to meet compelling and extraordinary circumstances, and 3) California's standards are technically infeasible. 83 Fed. Reg. at 43,240. According to GRAB ET AL., *supra*, at 16–20, as to the first claim, "another agency's finding as to the preemptive effect of an entirely separate statute would not be permissible grounds for revocation" and the factual contentions for the other two claims are "flatly unreasonable."

If § 209 is silent as to revocation power, courts might rely on non-textual considerations to interpret the provision. When analyzing another CAA provision silent on revoking waivers, § 211(f), the D.C. Circuit found no authority to revoke, citing among its considerations the "legitimate expectations" of regulated parties that waivers were non-revocable. *Am. Methyl Corp. v. EPA*, 749 F.2d 826, 839–40 (D.C. Cir. 1984). If EPA can revoke § 209 waivers, how might that affect states and industries that rely on them? Would revoking the waiver be worse for California than denying the waiver at the outset? Relatedly, courts sometimes consider federalism in reaching decisions. The Supreme Court has long recognized the "historic primacy of state regulation of matters of health and safety." *Medtronic, Inc. v. Lohr*, 518 U.S. 470, 485 (1996). How would the ability to revoke § 209 waivers affect the balance of power between states and the national government?

American Electrical Power Co. v. Connecticut

564 U.S. 410 (2011).

■ JUSTICE GINSBURG delivered the opinion of the Court:

We address in this opinion the question whether the plaintiffs (several States, the city of New York, and three private land trusts) can maintain federal common law public nuisance claims against carbon-dioxide emitters (four private power companies and the federal Tennessee Valley Authority). . . . The Clean Air Act and the Environmental Protection Agency action the Act authorizes, we hold, displace the claims the plaintiffs seek to pursue. . . .

In July 2004, two groups of plaintiffs filed separate complaints in the Southern District of New York against the same five major electric power companies. The first group of plaintiffs included eight States and New York City, the second joined three nonprofit land trusts; both groups are respondents here. The defendants, now petitioners, are four private companies and the Tennessee Valley Authority, a federally owned corporation that operates fossil-fuel fired power plants in several States. According to the complaints, the defendants "are the five largest emitters of carbon dioxide in the United States." Their collective annual emissions of 650 million tons constitute 25 percent of emissions from the domestic electric power sector, 10 percent of emissions from all domestic human activities, *ibid.,* and 2.5 percent of all anthropogenic emissions worldwide. . . . All plaintiffs sought injunctive relief requiring each defendant "to cap its carbon dioxide emissions and then reduce them by a specified percentage each year for at least a decade." . . .

We need not address the parties' dispute [as to whether private citizens or political subdivisions of a State may invoke the federal common law of nuisance to abate out-of-state pollution]. For it is an academic question whether, in the absence of the Clean Air Act and the EPA actions the Act authorizes, the plaintiffs could state a federal common law claim for curtailment of greenhouse gas emissions because of their contribution to global warming. Any such claim would be displaced by the federal legislation authorizing EPA to regulate carbon-dioxide emissions.

"[W]hen Congress addresses a question previously governed by a decision rested on federal common law," the Court has explained, "the need for such an unusual exercise of law-making by federal courts disappears." *Milwaukee II,* 451 U.S. 304, 314 (1981) (holding that amendments to the Clean Water Act displaced the nuisance claim recognized in *Milwaukee I*). Legislative displacement of federal common law does not require the "same sort of evidence of a clear and manifest [congressional] purpose" demanded for preemption of state law. *Id.,* at 317. " '[D]ue regard for the presuppositions of our embracing federal system . . . as a promoter of democracy,' " *id.,* at 316, does not enter the calculus, for it is primarily the office of Congress, not the federal courts, to prescribe national policy in areas of special federal interest. *TVA v. Hill,* 437 U.S. 153, 194 (1978). The test for whether congressional legislation excludes the declaration of federal common law is simply whether the statute "speak[s] directly to [the] question" at issue. *Mobil Oil Corp. v. Higginbotham,* 436 U.S. 618, 625 (1978); see *Milwaukee II,* 451 U.S. 304, 315 (1981); *County of Oneida v. Oneida Indian Nation of N. Y.,* 470 U.S. 226, 236–237 (1985).

We hold that the Clean Air Act and the EPA actions it authorizes displace any federal common law right to seek abatement of carbon-dioxide emissions from fossil-fuel fired power plants. *Massachusetts* made plain that emissions of carbon dioxide qualify as air pollution subject to regulation under the Act. 549 U.S., at 528–529. And we think it equally plain that the Act "speaks directly" to emissions of carbon dioxide from the defendants' plants.

Section 111 of the Act directs the EPA Administrator to list "categories of stationary sources" that "in [her] judgment . . . caus[e], or contribut[e] significantly to, air pollution which may reasonably be anticipated to endanger public health or welfare." § 7411(b)(1)(A). Once EPA lists a category, the agency must establish standards of performance for emission of pollutants from new or modified sources within that category. § 7411(b)(1)(B); see also § 7411(a)(2). And, most relevant here, § 7411(d) then requires regulation of existing sources within the same category. For existing sources, EPA issues emissions guidelines, see 40 C.F.R. § 60.22, .23 (2009); in compliance with those guidelines and subject to federal oversight, the States then issue performance standards for stationary sources within their jurisdiction, § 7411(d)(1).

The Act provides multiple avenues for enforcement. See *County of Oneida,* 470 U.S., at 237–239 (reach of remedial provisions is important to determination whether statute displaces federal common law). EPA may delegate implementation and enforcement authority to the States, § 7411(c)(1), (d)(1), but the agency retains the power to inspect and monitor regulated sources, to impose administrative penalties for noncompliance, and to commence civil actions against polluters in federal court. §§ 7411(c)(2), (d)(2), 7413, 7414. In specified circumstances, the Act imposes criminal penalties on any person who knowingly violates emissions standards issued under § 7411. See § 7413(c). And the Act provides for private enforcement. If States (or EPA) fail to enforce emissions limits against regulated sources, the Act permits "any person" to bring a civil enforcement action in federal court. § 7604(a).

If EPA does not *set* emissions limits for a particular pollutant or source of pollution, States and private parties may petition for a rulemaking on the matter, and EPA's response will be reviewable in federal court. See § 7607(b)(1); *Massachusetts,* 549 U.S. 497, 516–517, 529. . . . We see no room for a parallel track.

The plaintiffs argue, as the Second Circuit held, that federal common law is not displaced until EPA actually exercises its regulatory authority, *i.e.*, until it sets standards governing emissions from the defendants' plants. We disagree.

The sewage discharges at issue in *Milwaukee II* . . . were subject to effluent limits set by EPA; under the displacing statute, "[e]very point source discharge" of water pollution was "prohibited unless covered by a permit." 451 U.S., at 318–320 (emphasis deleted). As *Milwaukee II* made clear, however, the relevant question for purposes of displacement is "whether the field has been occupied, not whether it has been occupied in a particular manner." *Id.*, at 324. Of necessity, Congress selects different regulatory regimes to address different problems. Congress could hardly preemptively prohibit every discharge of carbon dioxide unless covered by a permit. After all, we each emit carbon dioxide merely by breathing.

The Clean Air Act is no less an exercise of the legislature's "considered judgment" concerning the regulation of air pollution because it permits emissions *until* EPA acts. See *Middlesex County Sewerage Authority v. National Sea Clammers Assn.*, 453 U.S. 1, 22, n.32 (1981) (finding displacement although Congress "allowed some continued dumping of sludge" prior to a certain date). The critical point is that Congress delegated to EPA the decision whether and how to regulate carbon-dioxide emissions from power plants; the delegation is what displaces federal common law. Indeed, were EPA to decline to regulate carbon-dioxide emissions altogether at the conclusion of its ongoing § 7411 rulemaking, the federal courts would have no warrant to employ the federal common law of nuisance to upset the agency's expert determination.

EPA's judgment, we hasten to add, would not escape judicial review. Federal courts, we earlier observed, . . . can review agency action (or a final rule declining to take action) to ensure compliance with the statute Congress enacted. As we have noted, . . . the Clean Air Act directs EPA to establish emissions standards for categories of stationary sources that, "in [the Administrator's] judgment," "caus[e], or contribut[e] significantly to, air pollution which may reasonably be anticipated to endanger public health or welfare." § 7411(b)(1)(A). "[T]he use of the word 'judgment,'" we explained in *Massachusetts*, "is not a roving license to ignore the statutory text." 549 U.S., at 533. "It is but a direction to exercise discretion within defined statutory limits." *Ibid.* EPA may not decline to regulate carbon-dioxide emissions from power plants if refusal to act would be "arbitrary, capricious, an abuse of discretion, or otherwise not in accordance with law." § 7607(d)(9)(A). If the plaintiffs in this case are dissatisfied with the outcome of EPA's forthcoming rulemaking, their recourse under federal law is to seek Court of Appeals review, and, ultimately, to petition for certiorari in this Court.

Indeed, this prescribed order of decisionmaking—the first decider under the Act is the expert administrative agency, the second, federal judges—is yet another reason to resist setting emissions standards by judicial decree under federal tort law. The appropriate amount of regulation in any particular greenhouse gas-producing sector cannot be prescribed in a vacuum: as with other questions of national or international policy, informed assessment of competing interests is required. Along with the environmental benefit potentially achievable, our Nation's energy needs and the possibility of economic disruption must weigh in the balance.

The Clean Air Act entrusts such complex balancing to EPA in the first instance, in combination with state regulators. Each "standard of performance" EPA sets must "tak[e] into account the cost of achieving [emissions] reduction and any nonair quality health and environmental impact and energy requirements." § 7411(a)(1), (b)(1)(B), (d)(1); see also 40 C.F.R. § 60.24(f) (EPA may permit state plans to deviate from generally applicable emissions standards upon demonstration that costs are "[u]n-reasonable"). EPA may "distinguish among classes, types, and sizes" of stationary sources in apportioning responsibility for emissions reductions. § 7411(b)(2), (d); see also 40 C.F.R. § 60.22(b)(5). And the agency may waive compliance with emission limits to permit a facility to test drive an "innovative technological system" that has "not [yet] been adequately demonstrated." § 7411(j)(1)(A). The Act envisions extensive cooperation between federal and state authorities, see § 7401(a), (b), generally permitting each State to take the first cut at determining how best to achieve EPA emissions standards within its domain, see § 7411(c)(1), (d)(1)–(2).

It is altogether fitting that Congress designated an expert agency, here, EPA, as best suited to serve as primary regulator of greenhouse gas emissions. The expert agency is surely better equipped to do the job than individual district judges issuing ad hoc, case-by-case injunctions. Federal judges lack the scientific, economic, and technological resources an agency can utilize in coping with issues of this order. See generally *Chevron U.S.A. Inc. v. Natural Resources Defense Council, Inc.*, 467 U.S. 837, 865–866 (1984). Judges may not commission scientific studies or convene groups of experts for advice, or issue rules under notice-and-comment procedures inviting input by any interested person, or seek the counsel of regulators in the States where the defendants are located. Rather, judges are confined by a record comprising the evidence the parties present. Moreover, federal district judges, sitting as sole adjudicators, lack authority to render precedential decisions binding other judges, even members of the same court. . . .

■ JUSTICE SOTOMAYOR took no part in the consideration or decision of this case.

■ JUSTICE ALITO, with whom JUSTICE THOMAS joins, concurring in part and concurring in the judgment:

I concur in the judgment, and I agree with the Court's displacement analysis on the assumption (which I make for the sake of argument because no party contends otherwise) that the interpretation of the Clean

Air Act, 42 U.S.C. § 7401 *et seq.*, adopted by the majority in *Massachusetts v. EPA*, 549 U.S. 497, is correct.

NOTES AND QUESTIONS

1. GHGs, the CAA and the Common Law. What difficulties does a tort action based on emission by GHGs pose? Are there other air pollutants that might be better suited to a tort action? Recall that in *Massachusetts* EPA's position was that it had no authority to regulate GHGs under the CAA, because climate change was so important that it could not regulate unless "Congress spoke with exacting specificity." Does the CAA adequately deal with the harm that the plaintiffs sought to redress?

2. Comprehensive Structure of the CAA. Which provisions did the Court focus on when deciding that the CAA and EPA action that the CAA authorizes displace any federal common law right to seek abatement of carbon dioxide emissions from power plants? Why did the Court think that these provisions displaced the plaintiffs' common law rights?

3. Federal Common Law v. State Common Law. Why was this case brought under the federal common law rather than state common law? Are the state common law rules of nuisance preempted? In *Bell v. Cheswick Generating Station*, 734 F.3d 188 (3d Cir. 2013), petitioners argued that though *American Electric Power Co. v. Connecticut*, 564 U.S. 410 (2011) held that the CAA preempted federal common law nuisance claims, it left open the question of whether state common law claims are available. The Third Circuit agreed, holding that the CAA does not preempt nuisance, negligence or trespass claims made under state law. The Supreme Court denied certiorari. *Genon Power Midwest, L.P. v. Bell*, 572 U.S. 1149 (2014).

B. GREENHOUSE GAS REGULATION AFTER *MASSACHUSETTS V. EPA*

i. ENDANGERMENT FINDING

Recall that the Supreme Court in *Massachusetts v. EPA* did not compel EPA to regulate greenhouse gases (GHGs). The Court held only that GHGs are an "air pollutant" for the purpose of § 202 of the CAA and that EPA did not have a discretion to decline to make, or delay making, a judgment as to whether GHGs endanger public health or welfare. Accordingly, following *Massachusetts v. EPA*, President Bush issued an Executive Order stating that it was "the policy of the United States . . . to protect the environment with respect to greenhouse gas emissions" from mobile sources "in a manner consistent with sound science, analysis of benefits and costs, public safety, and economic growth." Cooperation Among Agencies in Protecting the Environment With Respect to Greenhouse Gas Emissions From Motor Vehicles, Nonroad Vehicles, and Nonroad Engines, 72 Fed. Reg. 27,717 (2007). EPA commenced consideration of whether GHGs required regulation.

In December 2007 EPA prepared a document concluding that GHGs are pollutants that must be controlled. The report was e-mailed to the Office of Management and Budget. Unnamed sources alleged that minutes after the e-mail was sent, White House officials contacted EPA and asked that the e-mail be recalled. An unnamed official reported that when EPA refused to do so, the White House refused to open the e-mail containing the finding. On July 30, 2008, EPA issued an Advanced Notice of Proposed Rulemaking that solicited further input but declined to make a judgment as to whether greenhouse gases endanger human health and welfare. *See* Nina A. Mendelson, *Disclosing "Political" Oversight of Agency Decision Making*, 108 MICH. L. REV. 1127, 1153 (2010). At the end of the Bush administration, EPA had not made an endangerment finding.

EPA finally issued an endangerment finding for GHGs on December 15, 2009, under the Obama administration. EPA, Endangerment and Cause or Contribute Findings for Greenhouse Gases Under Section 202(a) of the Clean Air Act, 74 Fed. Reg. 66,496 (2009). The Administrator found that "six greenhouse gases taken in combination endanger both the public health and the public welfare of current and future generations." The Administrator also found that, for the purpose of § 202(a), GHGs from new motor vehicles contributed to the GHG pollution that endangered public health and welfare.

ii.   TAILPIPE RULE

Section 202(a) requires that EPA establish motor-vehicle emission standards for "any air pollutant . . . which may reasonably be anticipated to endanger public health or welfare." After EPA issued its endangerment finding, EPA and DOT issued coordinated greenhouse gas and fuel efficiency standards for model year 2012–2016 light-duty vehicles. The standards set an emissions limit of 250 grams per mile of carbon dioxide equivalent emissions by 2016, which equated to a fuel efficiency standard of 35.5 miles per gallon if the emissions limit were met through fuel efficiency measures alone. EPA, Light-Duty Vehicle Greenhouse Gas Emission Standards and Corporate Average Fuel Economy Standards, 75 Fed. Reg. 25,324 (2010) (the Tailpipe Rule). In 2014, EPA and DOT established standards for future model years and for heavy-duty vehicles that require fuel consumption reductions of between 10 and 20 percent, depending upon vehicle class. *See* EPA, Greenhouse Gas Emissions Standards and Fuel Efficiency Standards for Medium- and Heavy-Duty Engines and Vehicles, 76 Fed. Reg. 57,106 (2011); Dan Utech, *Kicking Vehicle Efficiency into High Gear,* THE WHITE HOUSE BLOG (Feb. 18, 2014), http://www.whitehouse.gov/blog/2014/02/18/kicking-vehicle-efficiency-high-gear.

More recently, the Trump EPA has proposed a rule to roll back the Obama-era emissions standards for 2021–2026, asserting that new information has shown the Obama-era standards are in fact infeasible. *See* EPA & NHTSA, The Safer Affordable Fuel-Efficient (SAFE) Vehicles

Rule for Model Years 2021–2026 Passenger Cars and Light Trucks, 83 Fed. Reg. 42,986, 42,990–91 (2018). When the White House announced plans to revise the rule, automakers publicly criticized the decision. *See* Robinson Meyer, *How the Carmakers Trumped Themselves*, ATLANTIC, June 20, 2018. Why would automakers object to the EPA's proposed rollback?

iii. TAILORING RULE AND TIMING RULE

The decision in *Massachusetts*, and the subsequent endangerment finding, "spurred a cascading series of greenhouse gas-related rules and regulations." *Coalition for Responsible Regulation v. EPA*, 684 F.3d 102, 114 (D.C. Cir. 2012). Under PSD, new or modified major sources "in any area to which this part applies" must apply BACT for "each pollutant subject to regulation" under the CAA. 42 U.S.C. § 7475(a)(4). In EPA's view, the expression "each air pollutant" meant any air pollutant that is regulated under the CAA, not only those pollutants for which there are NAAQS. *See* EPA, Prevention of Significant Deterioration and Title V Greenhouse Gas Tailoring Rule ("Tailoring Rule"), 75 Fed. Reg. 31,514, 31,553–54 (2010).

What qualifies as "in any area to which this part applies" for the purposes of PSD? According to EPA:

> At the time that Congress enacted the PSD provisions in 1977, every area of the nation was designated attainment or unclassifiable for at least one air pollutant, and that has remained the case to the present time. Accordingly, at all times, PSD has applied in every area of the country. The PSD requirements clearly cover all air pollutants emitted by the source, and provide a process for reviewing those emissions and determining BACT for them under CAA section 165(a)(4). It is true that at the time Congress adopted the PSD provisions, it was primarily concerned about the NAAQS pollutants . . . . But its overall purpose was broad enough to cover additional pollutants; the process it enacted for establishing BACT was broad enough to encompass additional pollutants; and the applicability provisions it established were phrased broadly enough to encompass additional pollutants, *see* section 169(1). As a result, we believe that the PSD applicability provisions, which, again, refer to, as we have interpreted them, "any air pollutant [subject to regulation under the CAA]," should be seen as "capacious" and therefore encompass GHG sources, in much the same manner as the U.S. Supreme Court viewed the definition of "air pollutant" to be "capacious" and therefore encompass GHGs. Massachusetts v. EPA, 549 U.S. 497, 533 (2007).

75 Fed. Reg. 31,514, 31,561 (2010). Reread the text of §§ 165 and 169. Do you agree with EPA's interpretation? How else might you interpret these provisions?

What qualifies as a "subject to regulation" for the purposes of PSD? EPA answered this question in a rulemaking that defined a pollutant as "subject to regulation" when a regulatory requirement to control emissions of that pollutant "takes effect," rather than when some other form of regulation, such as reporting requirements, goes into effect. *See* EPA, Reconsideration of Interpretation of Regulations That Determine Pollutants Covered by Clean Air Act Permitting Programs, 75 Fed. Reg. 17,004, 17,004, 17,010 (2010) ("Timing Rule").

These decisions meant that regulation of GHGs under PSD was triggered on January 2, 2011, when EPA's GHG emissions standards for light-duty vehicles took effect (the vehicle standards are discussed in Section 9 of this chapter, which reviews regulation of mobile sources under the CAA). As of January 2, 2011, all new or modified major sources were required to apply BACT controls for GHG emissions.

According to § 169(1), a "major emitting facility" subject to PSD regulations includes any stationary source that has the potential to emit 250 tons per year of any air pollutant and, for certain enumerated categories, any stationary source that has the potential to emit 100 tons per year of any air pollutant. Few sources emit this quantity of conventional pollutants, like carbon monoxide or lead: EPA's permitting program for NSPS, PSD and nonattainment regulations covers fewer than 15,000 sources. In contrast, EPA estimated that over six million sources, many of them residential, met the emission threshold of 100 tons per year for GHGs. *See* EPA, Prevention of Significant Deterioration and Title V Greenhouse Gas Tailoring Rule, 75 Fed. Reg. 31,514, 31,523 (2010). The average cost of complying with the permitting regime was estimated to be $23,175, and permitting authorities would be required to hire an additional 230,000 full-time employees to manage the influx of applications. *Id* at 31,562. The annual administrative cost of the program would expand from $62 million to approximately $21 billion. *Id*.

EPA considered that three doctrines justified its modifying the application of the PSD to GHGs. First, it considered that the "absurd result" of a literal application of the law authorized it to apply the statutory requirements differently. Second, the "administrative necessity" doctrine authorized EPA to apply statutory requirements in a way that avoids impossible burdens. Third, the "one-step-at-a-time" doctrine authorized EPA to implement statutory requirements in stages. *Id* at 31,541. Accordingly, it tailored the scope of PSD regulation. In the agency's "Tailoring Rule," EPA established phased-in emissions thresholds for GHGs. *Id.* at 31,516 (2010). Under the Tailoring Rule, for six months after January 2, 2011, only new and modified sources already required to control emissions of other air pollutants were required to control GHG emissions. After that period, only new stationary sources with GHG emissions exceeding 100,000 tons per year and modified existing sources with GHG emissions above 75,000 tons per year were required to control emissions. EPA committed to considering permanently excluding some sources from the program and/or lowering the thresholds below 100,000 tons per year, but only after the agency studied and evaluated the first two phases of the program. *Id.* at 31,596. The Tailoring Rule was intended to "reliev[e the] overwhelming permitting burdens that would, in the absence of this rule, fall on permitting authorities and sources." *Id.* at 31,516 (2010).

iv. LEGAL CHALLENGES TO EPA'S RULES

A number of states and industry groups petitioned for review of the endangerment finding, the Tailpipe Rule, the Timing Rule and the Tailoring Rule. In *Coalition for Responsible Regulation v. EPA*, 684 F.3d 102 (D.C. Cir. 2012), the D.C. Circuit, with Chief Judge Sentelle and Judges Rogers and Tatel on the panel, upheld the validity of the endangerment finding and the Tailpipe Rule, and dismissed the challenges to the Timing and Tailoring Rules.

Petitioners argued that EPA erred in restricting the endangerment finding to a science-based judgment devoid of policy considerations. They asserted that EPA should have considered the consequences of making the endangerment finding. That is, EPA should have conducted a cost-benefit analysis for the regulation of GHGs that would flow from the finding, should have considered the effectiveness of the regulations that would be triggered by the endangerment finding, and should have considered the potential for societal adaptation to climate change. The court rejected the petitioners' argument, holding that the plain language of § 202(a)(1) "does not leave room for EPA to consider as part of the endangerment inquiry the stationary-source regulation triggered by an endangerment finding, even if the degree of regulation triggered might at a later stage be characterized as 'absurd.'" *Id.* at 119. The plain language of the statute required that EPA decide only whether GHGs "may reasonably be anticipated to endanger public health or welfare," and whether motor-vehicle emissions "cause or contribute to" that endangerment.

As to the Tailpipe Rule, petitioners argued that had EPA considered the cost to industry and government that would flow from the PSD program and Title V permitting requirements, required to be imposed as a consequence of the Tailpipe Rule, EPA would have been forced to exclude carbon dioxide from the scope of the emission standards. The D.C. Circuit held that the mandatory language of § 202(a)(1), and the decision in *Massachusetts v. EPA*, prohibited EPA from declining to make, or deferring, regulation of GHG emissions from vehicles, once it made the endangerment finding. *Id.* at 134.

Petitioners also argued that the Timing and Tailoring Rules should be vacated. The D.C. Circuit found that the petitioners failed to make "any real arguments" against the Timing Rule, but argued that nothing in the CAA permitted EPA to depart from the clear, numerical permitting thresholds. *Id.* at 144. The court dismissed the challenge to these rules on the basis that Petitioners had not suffered an injury that would give them standing to challenge the rules. As the D.C. Circuit observed, the Timing and Tailoring Rules actually mitigated any purported injury caused by the introduction of the GHG permitting regime. *Id.* at 146.

NOTES AND QUESTIONS

1. EPA's Endangerment Finding. If EPA had simply published a notice in the *Federal Register* concluding that greenhouse gases do not endanger public health and welfare, how could that decision be challenged?

How is "welfare" defined for these purposes?

2. Endangerment Finding and Policy Considerations. Recall *American Trucking* and *Massachusetts v. EPA.* How does the Court's interpretation of § 202(a)(1) fit with those decisions? The D.C. Circuit reaches its decision without reference to *American Trucking*, relying only on *Massachusetts v. EPA* to justify its position. Do you think that *Massachusetts v. EPA* alone is authority for the court's decision?

3. Supreme Court Challenge. Following the decision in *Coalition for Responsible Regulation*, nine petitions for writs of certiorari were filed in the Supreme Court. The Supreme Court denied the petitions that sought to overturn the endangerment finding or that challenged EPA's failure to reconsider the finding, and one that challenged the legal sufficiency of the Tailpipe Rule. The Supreme Court did grant certiorari to the petitioners challenging EPA's regulation of stationary sources under the PSD program. Those petitions presented several questions for review concerning the rulemaking, but the Supreme Court limited the question to whether the regulation of GHGs from motor vehicles triggered permitting requirements for stationary sources. Why did the Court grant certiorari only on that issue?

Utility Air Regulatory Group v. Environmental Protection Agency

573 U.S. 302 (2014).

■ JUSTICE SCALIA announced the judgment of the Court and delivered the opinion of the Court with respect to Parts I and II:

Acting pursuant to the Clean Air Act, the Environmental Protection Agency recently set standards for emissions of "greenhouse gases" (substances it believes contribute to "global climate change") from new motor vehicles. We must decide whether it was permissible for EPA to determine that its motor-vehicle greenhouse-gas regulations automatically triggered permitting requirements under the Act for stationary sources that emit greenhouse gases.

I. Background

. . . Title I charges EPA with formulating national ambient air quality standards (NAAQS) for air pollutants. §§ 7408–7409. To date, EPA has issued NAAQS for six pollutants: sulfur dioxide, particulate matter, nitrogen dioxide, carbon monoxide, ozone, and lead. Clean Air Act Handbook 125 (J. Domike & A. Zacaroli eds., 3d ed. 2011); see generally 40 C.F.R. pt. 50 (2013). States have primary responsibility for implementing the NAAQS by developing "State implementation plans." 42 U.S.C. § 7410. A State must designate every area within its borders as "attainment," "nonattainment," or "unclassifiable" with respect to each NAAQS, § 7407(d), and the State's implementation plan must include permitting programs for stationary sources that vary according to the classification of the area where the source is or is proposed to be located. § 7410(a)(2)(C), (I).

Stationary sources in areas designated attainment or unclassifiable are subject to the Act's provisions relating to "Prevention of Significant Deterioration" (PSD). §§ 7470–7492. EPA interprets the PSD provisions to apply to sources located in areas that are designated attainment or unclassifiable for *any* NAAQS pollutant, regardless of whether the source emits that specific pollutant. Since the inception of the PSD program, every area of the country has been designated attainment or unclassifiable for at least one NAAQS pollutant; thus, on EPA's view, all stationary sources are potentially subject to PSD review.

It is unlawful to construct or modify a "major emitting facility" in "any area to which [the PSD program] applies" without first obtaining a permit. §§ 7475(a)(1), 7479(2)(C). To qualify for a permit, the facility must not cause or contribute to the violation of any applicable air-quality standard, § 7475(a)(3), and it must comply with emissions limitations that reflect the "best available control technology" (or BACT) for "each pollutant subject to regulation under" the Act. § 7475(a)(4). The Act defines a "major emitting facility" as any stationary source with the potential to emit 250 tons per year of "any air pollutant" (or 100 tons per year for certain types of sources). § 7479(1). It defines "modification" as a physical or operational change that causes the facility to emit more of "any air pollutant." § 7411(a)(4).

II. Analysis

This litigation presents two distinct challenges to EPA's stance on greenhouse-gas permitting for stationary sources. First, we must decide whether EPA permissibly determined that a source may be subject to the PSD and Title V permitting requirements on the sole basis of the source's potential to emit greenhouse gases. Second, we must decide whether EPA permissibly determined that a source already subject to the PSD program because of its emission of conventional pollutants (an "anyway" source) may be required to limit its greenhouse-gas emissions by employing the "best available control technology" for greenhouse gases. The Solicitor General joins issue on both points but evidently regards the second as more important; he informs us that "anyway" sources account for roughly 83% of American stationary-source greenhouse-gas emissions, compared to just 3% for the additional, non-"anyway" sources EPA sought to regulate at Steps 2 and 3 of the Tailoring Rule. . . .

A. The PSD and Title V Triggers

We first decide whether EPA permissibly interpreted the statute to provide that a source may be required to obtain a PSD or Title V permit on the sole basis of its potential greenhouse-gas emissions.

The Act-wide definition says that an air pollutant is "any air pollution agent or combination of such agents, including any physical, chemical, biological, [or] radioactive . . . substance or matter which is emitted into or otherwise enters the ambient air." § 7602(g). In *Massachusetts,* the Court held that the Act-wide definition includes greenhouse gases because it is all-encompassing; it "embraces all airborne compounds of whatever stripe." 549 U.S., at 529. But where the term "air pollutant" appears in the Act's operative provisions, EPA has routinely given it a narrower, context-appropriate meaning.

That is certainly true of the provisions that require PSD and Title V permitting for major emitters of "any air pollutant." Since 1978, EPA's regulations have interpreted "air pollutant" in the PSD permitting trigger as limited to *regulated* air pollutants. And since 1993 EPA has informally taken the same position with regard to the Title V permitting trigger, a position the Agency ultimately incorporated into some of the regulations at issue here. Those interpretations were appropriate: It is plain as day that the Act does not envision an elaborate, burdensome permitting process for major emitters of steam, oxygen, or other harmless airborne substances. It takes some cheek for EPA to insist that it cannot possibly give "air pollutant" a reasonable, context-appropriate meaning in the PSD and Title V contexts when it has been doing precisely that for decades.

Nor are those the only places in the Act where EPA has inferred from statutory context that a generic reference to air pollutants does not encompass every substance falling within the Act-wide definition. Other examples abound:

- The Act authorizes EPA to enforce new source performance standards (NSPS) against a pre-existing source if, after promulgation of the standards, the source undergoes a physical or operational change that increases its emission of "any air pollutant." § 7411(a)(2), (4), (b)(1)(B). EPA interprets that provision as limited to air pollutants *for which EPA has promulgated new source performance standards.*

- The Act requires a permit for the construction or operation in a nonattainment area of a source with the potential to emit 100 tons per year of "any air pollutant." §§ 7502(c)(5),

7602(j). EPA interprets that provision as limited to pollutants *for which the area is designated nonattainment.*

- The Act directs EPA to require "enhanced monitoring and submission of compliance certifications" for any source with the potential to emit 100 tons per year of "any air pollutant." §§ 7414(a)(3), 7602(j). EPA interprets that provision as limited to *regulated* pollutants.

- The Act requires certain sources of air pollutants that interfere with visibility to undergo retrofitting if they have the potential to emit 250 tons per year of "any pollutant." § 7491(b)(2)(A), (g)(7). EPA interprets that provision as limited to *visibility-impairing* air pollutants.

Although these limitations are nowhere to be found in the Act-wide definition, in each instance EPA has concluded—as it has in the PSD and Title V context—that the statute is not using "air pollutant" in *Massachusetts'* broad sense to mean any airborne substance whatsoever.

Massachusetts did not invalidate all these longstanding constructions. That case did not hold that EPA must always regulate greenhouse gases as an "air pollutant" everywhere that term appears in the statute, but only that EPA must "ground its reasons for action *or inaction* in the statute," 549 U.S., at 535, (emphasis added), rather than on "reasoning divorced from the statutory text," *id.,* at 532. EPA's inaction with regard to Title II was not sufficiently grounded in the statute, the Court said, in part because nothing in the Act suggested that regulating greenhouse gases under that Title would conflict with the statutory design. Title II would not compel EPA to regulate in any way that would be "extreme," "counterintuitive," or contrary to " 'common sense.' " *Id.,* at 531. At most, it would require EPA to take the modest step of adding greenhouse-gas standards to the roster of new-motor-vehicle emission regulations. *Ibid.*

Massachusetts does not strip EPA of authority to exclude greenhouse gases from the class of regulable air pollutants under other parts of the Act where their inclusion would be inconsistent with the statutory scheme. . . . As certain *amici* felicitously put it, while *Massachusetts* "rejected EPA's categorical contention that greenhouse gases *could not* be 'air pollutants' for any purposes of the Act," it did not "embrace EPA's current, equally categorical position that greenhouse gases *must* be air pollutants for all purposes" regardless of the statutory context.

To be sure, Congress's profligate use of "air pollutant" where what is meant is obviously narrower than the Act-wide definition is not conducive to clarity. One ordinarily assumes " 'that identical words used in different parts of the same act are intended to have the same meaning.' " *Environmental Defense v. Duke Energy Corp.*, 549 U.S. 561, 574 (2007). In this respect (as in countless others), the Act is far from a *chef d'oeuvre* of legislative draftsmanship. But we, and EPA, must do our best, bearing in mind the "fundamental canon of statutory construction that the words of a statute must be read in their context and with a view to their place in the overall statutory scheme." *FDA v. Brown & Williamson Tobacco Corp.*, 529 U.S. 120, 133 (2000). As we reiterated the same day we decided *Massachusetts*, the presumption of consistent usage "readily yields" to context, and a statutory term—even one defined in the statute—"may take on distinct characters from association with distinct statutory objects calling for different implementation strategies." *Duke Energy, supra*, at 574.

We need not, and do not, pass on the validity of all the limiting constructions EPA has given the term "air pollutant" throughout the Act. We merely observe that taken together, they belie EPA's rigid insistence that when interpreting the PSD and Title V permitting requirements it is bound by the Act-wide definition's inclusion of greenhouse gases, no matter how incompatible that inclusion is with those programs' regulatory structure.

In sum, there is no insuperable textual barrier to EPA's interpreting "any air pollutant" in the permitting triggers of PSD and Title V to encompass only pollutants emitted in quantities that enable them to be sensibly regulated at the statutory thresholds, and to exclude those atypical pollutants that, like greenhouse gases, are emitted in such vast quantities that their inclusion would radically transform those programs and render them unworkable as written.

Having determined that EPA was mistaken in thinking the Act *compelled* a greenhouse-gas-inclusive interpretation of the PSD and Title V triggers, we next consider the Agency's alternative position that its interpretation was justified as an exercise of its "discretion" to adopt "a reasonable construction of the statute." Tailoring Rule 31517. We conclude that EPA's interpretation is not permissible. . . .

Like EPA, we think it beyond reasonable debate that requiring permits for sources based solely on their emission of greenhouse gases at the 100- and 250-tons-per-year levels set forth in the statute would be "incompatible" with "the substance of Congress' regulatory scheme." *Brown & Williamson*, 529 U.S., at 156. A brief review of the relevant statutory provisions leaves no doubt that the PSD program and Title V are designed to apply to, and cannot rationally be extended beyond, a relative handful of large sources capable of shouldering heavy substantive and procedural burdens. . . .

The fact that EPA's greenhouse-gas-inclusive interpretation of the PSD and Title V triggers would place plainly excessive demands on limited governmental resources is alone a good reason for rejecting it; but that is not the only reason. EPA's interpretation is also unreasonable because it would bring about an enormous and transformative expansion in EPA's regulatory authority without clear congressional authorization. When an agency claims to discover in a long-extant statute an unheralded power to regulate "a significant portion of the American economy," *Brown & Williamson,* 529 U.S., at 159, we typically greet its announcement with a measure of skepticism. We expect Congress to speak clearly if it wishes to assign to an agency decisions of vast "economic and political significance." *Id.,* at 160; see also *MCI Telecommunications Corp. v. American Telephone & Telegraph Co.,* 512 U.S. 218, 231 (1994); *Industrial Union Dept., AFL-CIO v. American Petroleum Institute,* 448 U.S. 607, 645–646 (1980) (plurality opinion). The power to require permits for the construction and modification of tens of thousands, and the operation of millions, of small sources nationwide falls comfortably within the class of authorizations that we have been reluctant to read into ambiguous statutory text. Moreover, in EPA's assertion of that authority, we confront a singular situation: an agency laying claim to extravagant statutory power over the national economy while at the same time strenuously asserting that the authority claimed would render the statute "unrecognizable to the Congress that designed" it. Since, as we hold above, the statute does not compel EPA's interpretation, it would be patently unreasonable—not to say outrageous—for EPA to insist on seizing expansive power that it admits the statute is not designed to grant.

EPA thought that despite the foregoing problems, it could make its interpretation reasonable by adjusting the levels at which a source's greenhouse-gas emissions would oblige it to undergo PSD and Title V permitting. Although the Act, in no uncertain terms, requires permits for sources with the potential to emit more than 100 or 250 tons per year of a relevant pollutant, EPA in its Tailoring Rule wrote a new threshold of *100,000* tons per year for greenhouse gases. Since the Court of Appeals thought the statute unambiguously made greenhouse gases capable of triggering PSD and Title V, it held that petitioners lacked Article III standing to challenge the Tailoring Rule because that rule did not injure petitioners but merely relaxed the pre-existing statutory requirements. Because we, however, hold that EPA's greenhouse-gas-inclusive interpretation of the triggers was *not* compelled, and because EPA has essentially admitted that its interpretation would be unreasonable without "tailoring," we consider the validity of the Tailoring Rule.

We conclude that EPA's rewriting of the statutory thresholds was impermissible and therefore could not validate the Agency's interpretation of the triggering provisions. An agency has no power to "tailor" legislation to bureaucratic policy goals by rewriting unambiguous statutory terms. Agencies exercise discretion only in the interstices created by statutory silence or ambiguity; they must always " 'give effect to the unambiguously expressed intent of Congress.' " *National Assn. of Home Builders v. Defenders of Wildlife,* 551 U.S. 644, 665 (2007). It is hard to imagine a statutory term less ambiguous than the precise numerical thresholds at which the Act requires PSD and Title V permitting. When EPA replaced those numbers with others of its own choosing, it went well beyond the "bounds of its statutory authority." *Arlington,* 569 U.S., at ___, (emphasis deleted).

The Solicitor General does not, and cannot, defend the Tailoring Rule as an exercise of EPA's enforcement discretion. The Tailoring Rule is not just an announcement of EPA's refusal to enforce the statutory permitting requirements; it purports to *alter* those requirements and to establish with the force of law that otherwise-prohibited conduct will not violate the Act. This alteration of the statutory requirements was crucial to EPA's "tailoring" efforts. Without it, small entities with the potential to emit greenhouse gases in amounts exceeding the statutory thresholds would have remained subject to citizen suits—authorized by the Act—to enjoin their construction, modification, or operation and to impose civil penalties of up to $37,500 per day of violation. §§ 7413(b), 7604(a), (f)(4); 40 C.F.R. § 19.4. . . .

Because the Tailoring Rule cannot save EPA's interpretation of the triggers, that interpretation was impermissible under *Chevron.*

B.   BACT for "Anyway" Sources

For the reasons we have given, EPA overstepped its statutory authority when it decided that a source could become subject to PSD or Title V permitting by reason of its greenhouse-gas emissions. But what about "anyway" sources, those that would need permits based on their emissions of more conventional pollutants (such as particulate matter)? We now consider whether EPA reasonably interpreted the Act to require those sources to comply with "best available control technology" emission standards for greenhouse gases. . . .

2

. . . The text of the BACT provision is far less open-ended than the text of the PSD and Title V permitting triggers. It states that BACT is required "for each pollutant subject to regulation under this chapter" (*i.e.,* the entire Act), § 7475(a)(4), a phrase that—as the D.C. Circuit wrote 35 years ago—"would not seem readily susceptible [of] misinterpretation." *Alabama Power Co. v. Costle,* 636 F.2d 323, 404 (1979). Whereas the dubious breadth of "any air pollutant" in the permitting triggers suggests a role for agency judgment in identifying the subset of pollutants covered by the particular regulatory program at issue, the more specific phrasing of the BACT provision suggests that the necessary judgment has already been made by Congress. The wider statutory context likewise does not suggest that the BACT provision can bear a narrowing construction: There is no indication that the Act elsewhere uses, or that EPA has interpreted, "each pollutant subject to regulation under this chapter" to mean anything other than what it says.

Even if the text were not clear, applying BACT to greenhouse gases is not so disastrously unworkable, and need not result in such a dramatic expansion of agency authority, as to convince us that EPA's interpretation is unreasonable. We are not talking about extending EPA jurisdiction over millions of previously unregulated entities, but about moderately increasing the demands EPA (or a state permitting authority) can make of entities already subject to its regulation. And it is not yet clear that EPA's demands will be of a significantly different character from those traditionally associated with PSD review. In short, the record before us does not establish that the BACT provision as written is incapable of being sensibly applied to greenhouse gases. . . .

However, EPA may require an "anyway" source to comply with greenhouse-gas BACT only if the source emits more than a *de minimis* amount of greenhouse gases. As noted above, the Tailoring Rule applies BACT only if a source emits greenhouse gases in excess of 75,000 tons per year CO_2e, but the Rule makes clear that EPA did not arrive at that number by identifying the *de minimis* level. EPA may establish an appropriate *de minimis* threshold below which BACT is not required for a source's greenhouse-gas emissions. We do not hold that 75,000 tons per year CO2e necessarily exceeds a true *de minimis* level, only that EPA must justify its selection on proper grounds.

■ JUSTICE BREYER, with whom JUSTICE GINSBURG, JUSTICE SOTOMAYOR, and JUSTICE KAGAN join, concurring in part and dissenting in part:

. . . These cases take as a given our decision in *Massachusetts* that the Act's *general definition* of "air pollutant" includes greenhouse gases. One of the questions posed by these cases is whether those gases fall within the scope of the phrase "any air pollutant" as that phrase is used in the more specific provisions of the Act here at issue. The Court's answer is "no." I disagree. . . .

The Tailoring Rule solves the practical problems that would have been caused by the 250 tpy threshold. But what are we to do about the statute's language? The statute specifies a definite number—250, not 100,000—and it says that facilities that are covered by that number must meet the program's requirements. The statute says nothing about agency discretion to change that number. What is to be done? How, given the statute's language, can the EPA exempt from regulation sources that emit more than 250 but less than 100,000 tpy of greenhouse gases (and that also do not emit other regulated pollutants at threshold levels)?

The Court answers by (1) pointing out that regulation at the 250 tpy threshold would produce absurd results, (2) refusing to read the statute as compelling such results, and (3) consequently interpreting the phrase "any air pollutant" as containing an implicit exception for greenhouse gases. (Emphasis added.) Put differently, the Court reads the statute as defining "major emitting facility" to mean "stationary sources that have the potential to emit two hundred fifty tons per year or more of any air pollutant *except for those air pollutants, such as carbon dioxide, with respect to which regulation at that threshold would be impractical or absurd or would sweep in smaller sources that Congress did not mean to cover*." See *ante,* at 2442 ("[T]here is no insuperable textual barrier to EPA's interpreting 'any air pollutant' in the permitting triggers of PSD and Title V to encompass only pollutants emitted in quantities that enable them to be sensibly regulated at the statutory thresholds, and to exclude those atypical pollutants that, like greenhouse gases, are emitted in such vast quantities that their inclusion would radically transform those programs and render them unworkable as written"). . . .

I do not agree with the Court that the only way to avoid an absurd or otherwise impermissible result in these cases is to create an atextual greenhouse gas exception to the phrase "any air pollutant." After all, the word "any" makes an earlier appearance in the definitional provision, which defines "major emitting facility" to mean "*any* . . . source with the potential to emit two hundred and fifty tons per year or more of any air pollutant." § 7479(1) (emphasis added). As a linguistic matter, one can just as easily read an implicit exception for small-scale greenhouse gas emissions into the phrase "any source" as into the phrase "any air pollutant." And given the purposes of the PSD program and the Act as a whole, as well as the specific roles of the different parts of the statutory definition, finding flexibility in "any source" is far more sensible than the Court's route of finding it in "any air pollutant."

The implicit exception I propose reads almost word for word the same as the Court's, except that the location of the exception has shifted. To repeat, the Court reads the definition of "major emitting facility" as if it referred to "any source with the potential to emit two hundred fifty tons per year or more of any air pollutant *except for those air pollutants, such as carbon dioxide, with respect to which regulation at that threshold would be impractical or absurd or would sweep in smaller sources that Congress did not mean to cover.*" I would simply move the implicit exception, which I've italicized, so that it applies to "source" rather than "air pollutant": "any *source* with the potential to emit two hundred fifty tons per year or more of any air pollutant *except for those sources, such as those emitting unmanageably small amounts of greenhouse gases, with respect to which regulation at that threshold would be impractical or absurd or would sweep in smaller sources that Congress did not mean to cover.*"

From a legal, administrative, and functional perspective—that is, from a perspective that assumes that Congress was not merely trying to arrange words on paper but was seeking to achieve a real-world *purpose*—my way of reading the statute is the more sensible one. For one thing, my reading is consistent with the specific purpose underlying the 250 tpy threshold specified by the statute. The purpose of that number was not to prevent the regulation of dangerous air pollutants that cannot be sensibly regulated at that particular threshold, though that is the effect that the Court's reading gives the threshold. Rather, the purpose was to limit the PSD program's obligations to larger sources while exempting the many small sources whose emissions are low enough that imposing burdensome regulatory requirements on them would be senseless. . . .

An implicit source-related exception would serve this statutory purpose while going no further. The implicit exception that the Court reads into the phrase "any air pollutant," by contrast, goes well beyond the limited congressional objective. Nothing in the statutory text, the legislative history, or common sense suggests that Congress, when it imposed the 250 tpy threshold, was trying to undermine its own deliberate decision to use the broad language "any air pollutant" by removing some substances (rather than some facilities) from the PSD program's coverage. . . .

The Court's decision to read greenhouse gases out of the PSD program drains the Act of its flexibility and chips away at our decision in *Massachusetts*. What sense does it make to read the Act as generally granting the EPA the authority to regulate greenhouse gas emissions and then to read it as denying that power with respect to the programs for large stationary sources at issue here? It is anomalous to read the Act to require the EPA to regulate air pollutants that pose previously unforeseen threats to human health and welfare where "250 tons per year" is a sensible regulatory line but not where, by chemical or regulatory happenstance, a higher line must be drawn. And it is anomalous to read an unwritten exception into the more important phrase of the statutory definition ("any air pollutant") when a similar unwritten exception to less important language (the particular number used by the statute) will do just as well. The implicit exception preferred by the Court produces all of these anomalies, while the source-related exception I propose creates none of them. . . .

I agree with the Court's holding that stationary sources that are subject to the PSD program because they emit other (non-greenhouse-gas) pollutants in quantities above the statutory threshold—those facilities that the Court refers to as "anyway" sources—must meet the "best available control technology" requirement of § 7475(a)(4) with respect to greenhouse gas emissions. I therefore join Part II-B-2 of the Court's opinion. But as for the Court's holding that the EPA cannot interpret the language at issue here to cover facilities that emit more than 100,000 tpy of greenhouse gases by virtue of those emissions, I respectfully dissent.

■ JUSTICE ALITO, with whom JUSTICE THOMAS joins, concurring in part and dissenting in part:

In *Massachusetts v. EPA,* 549 U.S. 497 (2007), this Court considered whether greenhouse gases fall within the Clean Air Act's general definition of an air "pollutant." *Id.,* at 528–529. . . . I believed *Massachusetts v. EPA* was wrongly decided at the time, and these cases further expose the flaws with that decision.

As the present cases now show, trying to fit greenhouse gases into "key provisions" of the Clean Air Act involves more than a "little trouble." . . . I agree with the Court that the EPA is neither required nor permitted to take this extraordinary step, and I therefore join Parts I and II-A of the Court's Opinion. . . . I do not agree, however, with the Court's conclusion that what it terms "anyway sources," *i.e.*, sources that are subject to PSD and Title V permitting as the result of the emission of conventional pollutants, must install "best available control technology" (BACT) for greenhouse gases. As is the case with the PSD and Title V thresholds, trying to fit greenhouse gases into the BACT analysis badly distorts the scheme that Congress adopted. . . .

With respect to the text, it is curious that the Court, having departed from a literal interpretation of the term "pollutant" in Part II-A, turns on its heels and adopts a literal interpretation in Part II-B. The coverage thresholds at issue in Part II-A apply to any "pollutant." The Act's general definition of this term is broad, and in *Massachusetts v. EPA*, *supra*, the Court held that this definition covers greenhouse gases. The Court does not disturb that holding, but it nevertheless concludes that, as used in the provision triggering PSD coverage, the term "pollutant" actually means "pollutant, other than a greenhouse gas."

In Part II-B, the relevant statutory provision says that BACT must be installed for any "pollutant subject to regulation under [the Act]." § 7475(a)(4). If the term "pollutant" means "pollutant, other than a greenhouse gas," as the Court effectively concludes in Part II-A, the term "pollutant subject to regulation under [the Act]" in § 7475(a)(4) should mean "pollutant, other than a greenhouse gas, subject to regulation under [the Act], and that is subject to regulation under [the Act]." The Court's literalism is selective, and it results in a strange and disjointed regulatory scheme.

Under the Court's interpretation, a source can emit an unlimited quantity of greenhouse gases without triggering the need for a PSD permit. Why might Congress have wanted to allow this? The most likely explanation is that the PSD permitting process is simply not suited for use in regulating this particular pollutant. And if that is so, it makes little sense to require the installation of BACT for greenhouse gases in those instances in which a source happens to be required to obtain a permit due to the emission of a qualifying quantity of some other pollutant that is regulated under the Act.

The Court's second reason for holding that BACT applies to "anyway" sources is its belief that this can be done without disastrous consequences. Only time will tell whether this hope is well founded, but it seems clear that BACT analysis is fundamentally incompatible with the regulation of greenhouse-gas emissions for at least two important reasons.

First, BACT looks to the effects of covered pollutants in the area in which a source is located. The PSD program is implemented through "emission limitations and such other measures" as are "necessary . . . to prevent significant deterioration of air quality *in each region.*" § 7471 (emphasis added). The Clean Air Act provides that BACT must be identified "on a case-by-case basis," § 7479(3), and this necessarily means that local conditions must be taken into account. For this reason, the Act instructs the EPA to issue regulations requiring an analysis of "the ambient air quality . . . *at the site of the proposed major emitting facility and in the area potentially affected* by the emissions from such facility for each pollutant regulated under [the Act]." § 7475(e)(3)(B) (emphasis added). The Act also requires a public hearing on "the air quality *at the proposed site and in areas which may be affected* by emissions from such facility for each pollutant subject to regulation under [the Act] which will be emitted from such facility." §§ 7475(a)(2), (e)(1) (emphasis added). Accordingly, if BACT is required for greenhouse gases, the Act demands that the impact of these gases in the area surrounding a site must be monitored, explored at a public hearing, and considered as part of the permitting process. The effects of greenhouse gases, however, are global, not local. As a result, the EPA has declared that PSD permit applicants and permitting officials may disregard these provisions of the Act.

Second, as part of the case-by-case analysis required by BACT, a permitting authority must balance the environmental benefit expected to result from the installation of an available control measure against adverse consequences that may result, including any negative impact on the environment, energy conservation, and the economy. And the EPA itself has admitted that this cannot be done on a case-by-case basis with respect to greenhouse gases.

The Clean Air Act makes it clear that BACT must be determined on a "case-by-case basis, taking into account energy, environmental, and economic impacts and other costs." § 7479(3). To implement this directive, the EPA adopted a five-step framework for making a BACT determination. Under the fourth step of this analysis, potentially applicable and feasible control technologies that are candidates for selection as BACT for a particular source are eliminated from consideration based on their "collateral impacts," such as any adverse environmental effects or adverse effects on energy consumption or the economy.

More recently, the EPA provided guidance to permitting authorities regarding the treatment of greenhouse-gas emissions under this framework, and the EPA's guidance demonstrates the insuperable problem that results when an attempt is made to apply this framework to greenhouse gas emissions. . . . Suppose, for example, that a permitting authority must decide whether to mandate a change that both decreases a source's emission of greenhouse gases and increases its emission of a conventional pollutant that has a negative effect on public health. How should a permitting authority decide whether to require this change? Here is the EPA's advice:

> "[W]hen considering the trade-offs between the environmental impacts of a particular level of GHG [greenhouse gas] reduction and a collateral increase in another regulated NSR pollutant, rather than attempting to determine or characterize specific

environmental impacts from GHGs emitted at particular locations, EPA recommends that permitting authorities focus on the amount of GHG emission reductions that may be gained or lost by employing a particular control strategy and how that compares to the environmental or other impacts resulting from the collateral emissions increase of other regulated NSR pollutants."

As best I can make out, what this means is that permitting authorities should not even try to assess the net impact on public health. Instead of comparing the positive and negative public health effects of a particular option, permitting authorities are instructed to compare the adverse public health effects of increasing the emissions of the conventional pollutants with the amount of the reduction of the source's emissions of greenhouse gases. But without knowing the positive effects of the latter, this is a meaningless comparison.

The EPA tries to ameliorate this problem by noting that permitting authorities are entitled to "a great deal of discretion," Guidance 41, but without a comprehensible standard, what this will mean is arbitrary and inconsistent decisionmaking. . . . [I] respectfully dissent from Part II-B-2 of the opinion of the Court.

NOTES AND QUESTIONS

1.   **Supreme Court Split.** Which Justices joined which propositions? The excerpt above excludes the following portion of Justice Scalia's opinion: Part I, which provides the statutory and regulatory background, and a concluding paragraph following Part II. Why did Justice Scalia deliver the opinion of the Court only with respect to Parts I and II?

2.   **Statutory Interpretation.** On what basis do Justices Scalia's and Alito's opinions, respectively, find that "any air pollutant" could not include GHGs? Why did they not defer to EPA's discretion? What was Justice Breyer's response? Is Justice Breyer's limiting construction more consistent with the statute than Justice Scalia's? Consider Justice Scalia's examples of other CAA provisions that EPA has interpreted as having a narrower scope than a literal reading would suggest. Do these examples support his opinion's approach?

3.   *Massachusetts v. EPA.* How do Justices Scalia and Alito distinguish it? Does either opinion cast doubt on its validity? Recall that the CAA requires that the Administrator set automobile emissions standards for "any air pollutant . . . which in [the EPA Administrator's] judgment cause, or contribute to, air pollution which may reasonably be anticipated to endanger public health or welfare." Section 221(a)(1) is silent as to consideration of costs when deciding whether an air pollutant is one for which standards must be set. However, in determining the standards, the Administrator must consider the cost of compliance. *See* 42 U.S.C. § 7521(a). Justice Alito expresses concern about how to estimate the benefits of GHG reductions. Is

this problem limited to the determination of BACT under the PSD program? How could such tradeoffs be evaluated?

4. **Writ of Certiorari.** Recall that the Supreme Court granted certiorari to address only the question of whether the regulation of GHGs from motor vehicles triggered permitting requirements for stationary sources. Why did the Court address a broader set of issues in its opinion, given the limited nature of the grant of certiorari?

5. **Defending the Tailoring Rule.** EPA defended the Tailoring Rule on three grounds. Which of those grounds is most compelling? Which theory gives most support for Justice Scalia's position? For Justice Breyer's? Would EPA have been better off with a single theory?

6. **Justice Scalia's Interpretation.** Which statutory provisions does Justice Scalia identify as the trigger for the requirement to obtain a PSD permit? Which provisions is he interpreting when considering when BACT is required? Which provisions do Justices Breyer and Alito interpret in the portions of their opinions in which they do not join Justice Scalia?

7. **Enforcement Discretion.** To what extent is the Tailoring Rule different from a decision not to bring enforcement actions in certain cases? Does Justice Scalia raise a compelling point on this score?

8. **EPA's Interpretation of "Air Pollutant."** Recall that in *Massachusetts v. EPA*, the Supreme Court rejected a narrow interpretation of "air pollutant," finding that the definition was "capacious." Is EPA's interpretation of the phrase "any air pollutant" consistent with that decision? Section 202(a) regulates "any air pollutant . . . which cause[s] or contribute[s] to air pollution which may reasonably be anticipated to endanger public health or welfare." On what basis might the expression "any air pollutant" as used in reference to the PSD program and Title V permit schemes be distinguished from the phrase "air pollutant" in § 202 of the CAA? How did EPA define the terms? How did the Supreme Court?

9. **Justice Alito's Consideration of Tradeoffs.** Justice Alito describes how the CAA requires that the permitting authority balance the environmental benefit of installing a control measure against adverse consequences that may result from the installation. What adverse consequences does Justice Alito identify? What problem does he identify in the context of permitting GHGs? How does EPA normally deal with such tradeoffs?

10. **Consequences of *UARG* for Other Pollutants.** GHGs were not the only non-NAAQS pollutant regulated under the PSD program. Fluorides; sulfuric acid mist; hydrogen sulfide; total reduced sulfur; reduced sulfur compounds; municipal waste combustor organics, metals and acid gases; municipal waste landfill emissions; and ozone-depleting chemicals were also regulated. 40 C.F.R. §§ 51.166(b)(23)(i), 52.21(b)(5). What will be the consequence to regulation of these pollutants following *UARG*? How will the case affect the possible regulation of other non-NAAQS pollutants in the future? In this respect, what consequences would follow from Justice Alito's approach? In particular, how would Justice Alito treat ozone-depleting chemicals, which are global pollutants?

11. Interaction of PSD and NSPS. Recall § 111, which requires that the Administrator promulgate New Source Performance Standards for categories of stationary sources which "in his judgment [cause], or [contribute] significantly to, air pollution which may reasonably be anticipated to endanger public health or welfare." Given that EPA's endangerment finding for GHGs in motor vehicles was upheld, must the Administrator publish New Source Performance Standards for sources that emit GHGs? How is the Administrator to decide what level of emissions are required before a source is subject to the New Source Performance Standards? Prior to the decision in *UARG*, EPA had released guidance on applying GHG BACT requirements to refineries, cement plants, paper and pulp plants, landfills, nitric acid plants, iron and steel plants and other industrial emitters. *See* EPA, Clean Air Act Permitting for Greenhouse Gases, https://www.epa.gov/nsr/clean-air-act-permitting-greenhouse-gases (last visited Sept. 27, 2018).

EPA has issued guidance for permitting agencies charged with regulating GHG emissions under PSD that delineates how an agency should carry out a BACT analysis for GHGs. *See* EPA, PSD AND TITLE V PERMITTING GUIDANCE FOR GHGS (2011). In its discussion of potential BACT technologies, the guidance focuses primarily on methods to increase the energy efficiency of the facility in question and also discusses "add on" technologies to reduce GHG emissions, like carbon capture and storage.

What role do the PSD permitting provisions and BACT play given the NSPS provision? Is the duplication desirable? If so, what principal purpose does it serve?

12. Relative Stringency of BACT and NSPS. Does the relative stringency of the two standards differ? Does the order in which they are set matter? Does it make sense, in the case of GHGs, for BACT to focus on energy efficiency?

13. Construction, Modification and Regulatory Flexibility. In response to a comment on the 1989 rule on New Source Review, EPA explained that the PSD program serves a special role, in that it addresses risks posed by air pollutants with "an inherent speed and flexibility in its ability to protect public health and welfare" that other CAA "programs lack." EPA, Requirements for Implementation Plans; Air Quality New Source Review, 54 Fed. Reg. 27,286, 27,297 (1989). How does the decision in *UARG* affect EPA's ability to respond to dangers to public health and welfare? How important is the ability to respond with "speed and flexibility"?

Consider the CAA as a carefully structured scheme under which existing sources are relieved from the expense of retrofitting pollution controls, but are required to come into compliance as they undertake "any physical change" that "increases the amount of any air pollutant emitted." § 111(a)(4). How does the decision in *UARG* affect that scheme?

14. NAAQS for GHGs? In 2009, two organizations petitioned EPA to set a NAAQS for carbon dioxide. *See* Center for Biological Diversity and 350.org, *Petition to Establish National Pollution Limits for Greenhouse Gases Pursuant to the Clean Air Act* (Dec. 2, 2009). Recall that under § 108, the

Administrator shall publish a list of each air pollutant, emissions of which "cause or contribute to air pollution which may reasonably be anticipated to endanger public health or welfare." How does the language in § 108 differ from that in § 202? Once an endangerment finding has been made with respect to an air pollutant for the purpose of § 202, must the Administrator include that air pollutant on the § 108 list? Must the Administrator then go on to issue NAAQS for that air pollutant under § 109?

How would EPA set appropriate NAAQS for GHGs? How could a state write an appropriate SIP? What regulatory mechanisms are likely to be contained in these SIPs? Why? If it became necessary, how should EPA implement a nonattainment program for carbon dioxide? If states fail to include required SIP components, would the federal government be any better suited to address NAAQS attainment through FIPs? Does the criteria pollutant model make sense for carbon dioxide?

15. Sections 115, 615 and International Air Pollution. Section 115 provides that where, upon receiving reports, surveys or studies from an "international agency," the Administrator has reason to believe that air pollutants endanger public health or welfare in a foreign country, the Administrator shall notify the Governor of the State in which the emissions originate. CAA § 115(a). The notice to the Governor is deemed a SIP call requiring a plan revision "with respect to so much of the applicable implementation plan as is inadequate to prevent or eliminate the endangerment." CAA § 115(b). Any affected foreign country is to be invited to appear at any public hearing associated with any revision. CAA § 115(b).

EPA's endangerment finding relied in part on the reports of the Intergovernmental Panel on Climate Change. EPA reasoned that it did not need to independently review the Panel's reports because EPA took "an active part in [their] review, writing and approval," and that the Panel's assessments "have been reviewed and formally accepted by, commissioned by, or in some cases authorized by, U.S. government agencies and individual government scientists." EPA, Endangerment and Cause or Contribute Findings for Greenhouse Gases Under Section 202(a) of the Clean Air Act, 74 Fed. Reg. 66,496, 66,511 (2009). Are these reports from an "international agency"? Two cases—both dealing with acid rain pollution drifting into Canada from Midwestern states—have considered § 115. *See Thomas v. New York*, 802 F.2d 1443 (D.C. Cir. 1986); *Her Majesty the Queen v. EPA*, 912 F.2d 1525 (D.C. Cir. 1990). In those cases, the D.C. Circuit found that the International Joint Commission was a "duly constituted international agency," focusing on the fact that the Commission was established by treaty. Does EPA's endangerment finding mean that EPA must conclude, or even has already concluded, that GHGs endanger public health or welfare in foreign countries?

Section 115 requires reciprocity before any obligation to regulate arises. It applies only to a foreign country "which the Administrator determines has given the United States essentially the same rights with respect to the prevention or control of air pollution . . . as is given that country by this section." CAA § 115(c). How similar must the reciprocal rights be? What kind of regulatory scheme must be in place?

16. Stratospheric Ozone. Title VI of the CAA deals with Stratospheric Ozone Protection. Section 615 of the CAA provides that if, in the Administrator's judgment, any substance, practice, process or activity "may reasonably be anticipated to affect the stratosphere, especially ozone in the stratosphere, and such effect may reasonably be anticipated to endanger public health or welfare," the Administrator shall "promptly" promulgate regulations respecting the control of such substance, process or activity. Stratospheric ozone may be affected by increases in concentration of GHGs. U.N. ENVIRONMENT PROGRAMME, ENVIRONMENTAL EFFECTS OF OZONE DEPLETION AND ITS INTERACTIONS WITH CLIMATE CHANGE: 2010 ASSESSMENT 1 (2010). Nitrous oxides and methane can enhance the destruction of ozone in the upper stratosphere. *Id.* at 43. *See also* U.N. ENVIRONMENT PROGRAMME, QUESTIONS AND ANSWERS ABOUT THE ENVIRONMENTAL EFFECTS OF THE OZONE LAWYER DEPLETION AND CLIMATE CHANGE 2010 UPDATE 17 (2010). Is EPA obliged to regulate GHGs under § 615? How might this interfere with, or complement, regulatory efforts under other CAA provisions?

v.   REGULATING POWER PLANTS

In October 2015, EPA published, pursuant to § 111(b), carbon dioxide pollution standards for new coal- and gas-fired power plants. EPA, Standards of Performance for Greenhouse Gas Emissions From New Stationary Sources: Electric Utility Generating Units, 80 Fed. Reg. 64,510 (2015). The standards for coal-fired plants are based on partial implementation of carbon capture and storage as the "best system of emission reduction . . . adequately demonstrated" to limit pollution. CAA § 111(b). The standards for gas-fired plants are based on natural gas combined cycle technology. Under the standards, new coal-fired units need to meet a limit of 1400 pounds of CO_2 per megawatt-hour. Large natural gas-fired turbines will need to meet a limit of 1000 pounds of CO_2 per megawatt-hour. *Id.* at 64,512–13. In December 2018, EPA proposed weakening the standard for new coal-fired power plants, determining that the "best system of emission reduction" is not carbon capture and storage. EPA, Review of Standards of Performance for Greenhouse Gas Emissions from New, Modified, and Reconstructed Stationary Sources: Electric Utility Generating Units, 83 Fed. Reg. 65,424 (2018).

Also in October 2015, EPA promulgated the "Clean Power Plan" (CPP)—a set of "emission guidelines" for *existing* power plants fueled by coal or gas—under § 111(d) of the Clean Air Act. EPA, Carbon Pollution Emissions Guidelines for Existing Stationary Sources: Electric Utility Generating Units, 80 Fed. Reg. 64,662 (2015). Twenty-six states immediately challenged the CPP, and in February 2016, the U.S. Supreme Court stayed the rule's effectiveness for the duration of the litigation. Brook J. Detterman et al., *Will EPA 'ACE' Its Attempt to Replace the Clean Power Plan? A Deeper Dive into EPA's Proposed Affordable Clean Energy Rule*, NAT'L L. REV., Nov. 3, 2018. In September 2016, the D.C. Circuit heard the case en banc. Jonathan H. Adler,

Opinion, *The En Banc D.C. Circuit Meets the Clean Power Plan*, WASH. POST, Sept. 28, 2016. The case was still pending when President Trump took office, and under the new administration, EPA moved to have the case placed in abeyance while the agency reconsidered the CPP. Detterman et al., *supra*. The D.C. Circuit granted the motion. *Id.* After first proposing a clean repeal of the rule, EPA eventually proposed replacing it with the "Affordable Clean Energy Rule" (ACE). EPA, Emissions Guidelines for Greenhouse Gas Emissions from Existing Electric Utility Generating Units, 83 Fed. Reg. 44,746 (2018).

The CPP and ACE are different in several significant ways. Under the CPP, the "best system of emission reduction" (BSER) for existing power plants was defined as a combination of three "building blocks": (1) improving the heat rate at coal-fired steam plants; (2) substituting generation from lower-emitting existing natural gas combined cycle plants for generation from higher-emitting steam plants, which are primarily coal-fired; and (3) substituting generation from new zero-emitting renewable generating capacity for generation from both coal- and gas-fired plants. 80 Fed. Reg. at 64,667. Thus, the CPP called not only for increasing efficiency at coal-powered plants, but also for shifting production to natural gas plants and renewable energy sources. These steps were consistent with those the industry generally took independently when complying with other emissions regulations. *Id.* at 64,709. In contrast, in the more recent ACE proposal, EPA takes a different approach. The agency argues that BSER only permits measures that can be applied to or at a given source, not those that the source's owner or operator can implement at another location. 83 Fed. Reg. at 44,752. Accordingly, EPA limits its BSER to the CPP's first step: heat rate improvements. *Id.*

The ACE rule would also loosen regulations governing state implementation of § 111(d) emission guidelines. For example, the CPP, like all prior § 111(d) rules, set numerical emissions targets for each state to meet through SIP-like implementation plans, but the ACE rule does not provide any guidance on the *amount* of emission reduction that states are expected to achieve. *Id.* at 44,753. Instead, ACE provides more general guidance on strategies for improving heat rates, and leaves it to each state to decide when, whether, and how to apply each of those techniques to the state's existing plants. *Id.* at 44,750.

EPA also proposes changing New Source Review (NSR) in its ACE rule. Currently New Source Review is triggered when a source undertakes a physical or operational change that increases its annual emissions above a given threshold in PSD and nonattainment circumstances. *Id.* at 44,774. But EPA claims in the ACE rule that some projects undertaken to improve power plants' heat rates could lead to an annual increase in emissions, thereby triggering NSR and its attendant costs. *Id.* at 44,775. According to EPA, these costs might discourage power plants from pursuing heat rate improvements in the first place.

Therefore, EPA proposes adding an hourly emissions rate test in addition to its annual test. *Id.* at 44,780–81. Sources whose hourly rate does not increase would be excused from NSR, even if their annual emissions rate increases significantly. *Id.* In proposing this change, EPA discusses the incremental costs to power plants of NSR compliance, but does not focus on the incremental health and environmental benefits that would accompany such compliance. Institute for Policy Integrity, Comments on Emissions Guidelines for Greenhouse Gas Emissions from Existing Electric Utility Generating Units 19–20 (2018).

EPA's own analysis shows that by 2030, the ACE rule could lead to as many as 1,400 deaths that would not occur if the CPP were kept in place. Lisa Friedman, *Cost of New EPA Coal Rules: Up to 1,400 More Deaths a Year*, N.Y. TIMES, Aug. 21, 2018. The agency further finds that these forgone benefits would outweigh any compliance cost savings by up to tens of billions of dollars annually. Richard L. Revesz, *Trump's EPA Chooses Coal Over the American People*, THE HILL, Sept. 13, 2018. Why might EPA propose such a rule?

NOTES AND QUESTIONS

1. **"Beyond the Fenceline" Requirements and BSER.** EPA claims that it must replace the CPP because the CPP's BSER assumes that power plants can reduce emissions not only by improving efficiency on site, but also by shifting production to other forms of energy off site. According to EPA, setting the stringency of emission guidelines based on offsite changes exceeds the agency's statutory authority to select the best system of emissions reduction. ACE, 83 Fed. Reg. at 44,752. According to EPA's new proposed interpretation, BSER may only legally include changes that "can be applied to or at the source." EPA, Repeal of Carbon Pollution Guidelines for Existing Stationary Sources: Electric Utility Generating Units, 82 Fed. Reg. 48,035, 48,039 (2017) (CPP Repeal). To support this contention, EPA claims that it has traditionally based BSERs on techniques that reduce pollution rates, not the overall amount of a type of production. ACE, 83 Fed. Reg. at 44,752. Notably, EPA considers requiring coal plants to "co-fire" natural gas on site but declines to include this technique in the BSER because it might be infeasible or costly for some sources. *Id.* at 44,762.

EPA also argues its new BSER interpretation is supported by the language of the CAA. For example, the agency notes that § 111(d) requires that standards be established *"for* any existing source," not for other sources or entities. CPP Repeal, 82 Fed. Reg. at 48,039. The text of § 111(a) and § 111(d), however, does not explicitly limit BSER to changes on site. Moreover, the legislative history suggests lawmakers drafting and amending § 111 took a broad view of possible definitions of BSER and acknowledged that the best system of emissions reduction was "not necessarily technological," but might involve other kinds of changes. *See id.* at 64,765 (quoting H.R. Rep. No. 95–294 (1977)); Clean Air Act Amendments of 1990, Pub. L. 101–549, § 403, 104 Stat. 2399, 2631 (Nov. 15, 1990).

Finally, there is precedent for considering generation shifting when setting pollution limits for regulated entities. The Clean Air Mercury Rule, promulgated under § 111(d), set emissions limits that took a cap-and-trade program into account, anticipating industry's shifting production across parties through trade. EPA, Standards of Performance for New and Existing Stationary Sources: Electric Utility Steam Generating Units, 70 Fed. Reg. 28,606, 28,617 (2015). EPA also considered trade when setting state emissions caps for the Transport Rule promulgated under the Good Neighbor Provision, § 110(a)(2)(d). EPA, Federal Implementation Plans: Interstate Transport of Fine Particulate Matter and Ozone and Correction of SIP Approvals, 76 Fed. Reg. 48,208, 48,261 (2011). Section 111(d) expressly directs EPA to follow "a procedure similar to that provided by" § 110, and the latter expressly allows marketable permits. CAA § 110 and § 111; Richard L. Revesz et al., *Familiar Territory: A Survey of Legal Precedents for the Clean Power Plan*, 46 ENVTL. L. REP. 10,190, 10,192 (2016).

As discussed above, the building block model EPA chose in the CPP aligned with the approach industry followed of its own accord when responding to other regulations, a seeming confirmation of the approach's feasibility. CPP, 80 Fed. Reg. at 64,709. Does industry use of these practices strengthen the case for CPP's BSER definition?

2.   Trading Schemes and Existing Power Plants. The Obama EPA's standards for new and modified power plants did not refer to trading schemes as part of the "best system of emission reduction" for those sources. Why might EPA have suggested trading schemes as a mechanism for emissions reductions only for existing power plants? In the proposed ACE rule, EPA has solicited comments on whether states should be allowed to permit power plants to comply with heat rate-based emission standards through the trading of emissions credits. CPP Repeal, 83 Fed. Reg. at 44,767. How might this be in tension with the agency's objection to the CPP's approach to BSER?

3.   Carbon Sequestration and the Energy Policy Act of 2005. Section 111 authorizes EPA to set emissions standards that require the use of certain technologies only if those technologies have been "adequately demonstrated." The proposed NSPS for new coal-fired power plants is based on the emissions reductions that can be achieved with carbon capture and sequestration technology. In its 2012 proposal for NSPS for power plants, EPA referenced three carbon sequestration projects in the United States to prove that carbon sequestration is "adequately demonstrated." On November 15, 2013, four members of the House Committee on Energy and Commerce sent a letter to the EPA Administrator asking her to withdraw the proposed standards for new plants on the grounds that they go beyond the scope of EPA's legal authority. The members argued that EPA relied on legally impermissible evidence. They cited § 402 of the Energy Policy Act of 2005, which provides that "[n]o technology, or level of emission reduction, solely by reason of the use of the technology, or the achievement of the emission reduction, by 1 or more facilities receiving assistance under this Act, shall be considered to be . . . adequately demonstrated for purposes of [§ 111 of the CAA]." Each of the carbon sequestration projects EPA relied upon received subsidies pursuant to the Energy Policy Act. Letter from Rep. Fred Upton, Chair, H. Comm. on Energy & Commerce, et al., to Gina McCarthy, Admin., EPA (Nov. 15, 2013), citing 42 U.S.C. § 15962. EPA re-proposed the rule in 2014, stating that it considered the emissions reductions achievable with no carbon capture, partial carbon capture, and full carbon capture. It referred to several U.S. power plants and a global database of power plants using carbon capture and sequestration technology before concluding that "[p]artial [carbon capture] . . . has been implemented successfully in a number of facilities over many years." EPA, Standards of Performance for Greenhouse Gas Emissions From New Stationary Sources: Electric Utility Generating Units, 79 Fed. Reg. 1430, 1435–36 (2014). At what point is a technology "adequately demonstrated"?

A challenge to the standards for new power plants is currently pending in the D.C. Circuit. If the new-source standards were to be struck down, what implication would that have for the validity of the CPP or its replacement? What role do the standards for modified power plants play in this analysis?

Under the Trump Administration, EPA has also begun reconsidering the rules for new sources. EPA, Review of the Standards of Performance for Greenhouse Gas Emissions from New, Modified, and Reconstructed Stationary Sources: Electric Generating Units, 82 Fed. Reg. 16,330 (2017).

4. Existing Sources, §§ 111 and 112, and Drafting Controversy. Section 111 is typically employed to establish a federal standard for pollution from new or modified sources. However, § 111(d)(1) addresses existing sources, but only with respect to pollutants for which NAAQS have not been set and which are not regulated as "hazardous air pollutants" under § 112. Under this provision, EPA is required to promulgate guidelines establishing "a procedure similar to that provided by section 110 under which each State shall submit to the Administrator a plan" that establishes performance standards for emissions of any pollutant from any existing source that would be subject to a § 111(b) standard were it a new source. Thus, the regulation of categories of pollution sources under § 111(d)(1) and § 111(b) maintains the division of federal-state responsibilities that occurs for criteria pollutants listed under § 108. In either case, the federal government establishes national standards for new sources under § 111(b) while states are responsible for regulation of existing sources, either through a SIP under § 110 or under § 111(d)(1) guidelines.

As part of the 1990 amendments to the CAA, the House of Representatives passed a version of Section 111(d)(1)(A) that prohibited the Administrator from setting "standards of performance for any existing source for any air pollutant . . . emitted from a source category which is regulated under section [112]." The version of the amending bill passed by the Senate did not include this language, instead prohibiting regulation under § 111(d)(1)(A) for any *pollutant* regulated by § 112. The Conference Committee, which would ordinarily reconcile the discrepancies between the bills passed by the House and the Senate, failed to reconcile this discrepancy. Thus the Statutes at Large contain both amending provisions. The House version of § 111(d)(1)(A) was the one published in the U.S. Code.

In 2012, EPA regulated mercury emissions from power plants pursuant to § 112. EPA, National Emission Standards for Hazardous Air Pollutants From Coal- and Oil-Fired Electric Utility Steam Generating Units and Standards of Performance for Fossil-Fuel-Fired Electric Utility, Industrial-Commercial-Institutional, and Small Industrial-Commercial-Institutional Steam Generating Units, 77 Fed. Reg. 9304 (2012). In their D.C. Circuit challenge to the CPP, certain states argued that EPA cannot regulate GHG emissions from power plants because they are a source category regulated under § 112. Brief of the States of West Virginia, et al. as Amici Curiae in Support of the Petitioner, In Re: Murray Energy Corporation, No. 14–1112 (D.C. Cir. June 25, 2014). EPA argued that the Statutes at Large control where there is an inconsistency with the Code, and that it has authority to reasonably interpret the CAA in the face of the inconsistent language in the Statutes at Large. EPA, Legal Memorandum for Proposed Carbon Pollution Emission Guidelines for Existing Electric Utility Generating Units (2014). Accordingly, EPA has interpreted § 111(d)(1)(A) as consistent with the Senate bill, and it therefore maintains it has the power to promulgate the standards. Is this position justified?

Consider that in EPA's view "it would be difficult to identify any pollutant that is not emitted from at least one source category that is regulated under 112." If § 111(d)(1)(A) is read literally, what role is there for § 111 as a source of standards for sources other than power plants? What role does *American Electric Power* play in this inquiry? Even under the Trump administration, EPA's proposed ACE rule implicitly assumes the agency has authority to regulate existing power plants under § 111(d). Although the proposed regulations are less stringent, they nonetheless apply to existing power plants, despite the fact that such plants are already subject to limits on their mercury emissions under § 112.

12. REVIEW PROBLEMS

1.   First Cement. First Cement Co. has a Portland Cement plant (Plant 1), originally built in 1950, which emits a total of 150 tons per year of pollutants. Its emissions of particulates are 0.28 kilograms per metric ton of feed (dry basis). The plant is contemplating a replacement of its outdated equipment with state of the art technology. One wall of the building in which the machinery is located would have to be torn down to permit the removal of the old machinery and introduction of the new machinery. The wall would then be rebuilt.

With the new technology in place, First Cement's emissions (including emissions of criteria pollutants) per metric ton of feed will be halved. At the same time, however, the plant's hourly production capacity will be 80 percent higher. In addition, shutdowns caused by malfunctioning of the machinery will be far less frequent. The new technology will also make it possible for First Cement to extend the length of its daily shift.

First Cement is located in Lincoln County, which has been classified pursuant to § 107(d)(1)(A)(ii) of the CAA. It has never been reclassified.

The baseline concentration in Lincoln County was set in the mid-1980s; since then, the concentration of particulates in the county has increased as follows, in micrograms per cubic meter:

(a)   Annual geometric mean: 19.

(b)   Twenty-four hour maximum: 37.

First Cement also has a plant at the other end of the County (Plant 2). For a number of years, this plant has been out of compliance with the provisions of the SIP, and First Cement is planning to close it.

Discuss all non-trivial CAA issues raised by the possible replacement of First Cement's equipment in Plant 1. Would your analysis be different if Lincoln County had been classified under § 107(d)(1)(A)(i) of the CAA? To what extent can Plant 2's closure ease the regulatory requirements on Plant 1?

2.   Best Electric. Best Electric, an electric utility, is looking to expand its operations by building a new coal fired generating unit at Brown Corners, a three-acre site that it owns in Columbia County. The new unit would emit 180 tons per year of pollutants, including 90 tons of sulfur dioxide and 80 tons of particulates. The proposed unit, Unit X, would have a stack height of 500 feet.

The site already contains an older generating unit, Unit A, which emits 170 tons of sulfur dioxide and 200 tons of particulates, through a stack that is 800 feet tall. In addition, Best Electric also operates Unit B, which is identical to Unit A, but is located twenty miles downwind of Unit A and about 2 miles upwind of the state border. For both Units A and B, Best Electric would be able to cut in half the emissions of sulfur dioxide and particulates, if necessary.

Columbia County has been classified under § 107(d)(1)(A)(i) for sulfur dioxide, and under § 107(d)(1)(A)(ii) for particulates. The proposed unit would be the first new source to locate in the county in more than 35 years.

Discuss the Clean Air Act issues.

3.   NAAQS for Carbon Dioxide. Several organizations have filed actions seeking to compel EPA to promulgate NAAQS for carbon dioxide-the most prevalent of the greenhouse gases responsible for the problem of climate change.

(a)   What should the outcome be?

(b)   Assume that the organizations prevail. What difficulties will EPA have in setting NAAQS for carbon dioxide? How should it resolve these difficulties?

(c)   How should the states set the SIPs for carbon dioxide? What difficulties would they face? What regulatory mechanisms are likely to be contained in these SIPs? Why?

(d) How should EPA implement the nonattainment and PSD programs for carbon dioxide?

(e) How does the listing of carbon dioxide affect the definition of "major" sources for the purposes of the PSD and nonattainment programs?

Assume, for the purposes of your answer, that the organizations have standing to bring their suits.

CHAPTER VI

CONTROL OF WATER POLLUTION

1. INTRODUCTION

Federal regulation of water pollution did not begin on a clean slate with the passage of the Clean Water Act (CWA) in 1972. A quarter century earlier, increased levels of water pollution resulting from intensive industrial production during World War II, combined with a diversion of resources from wastewater treatment to the war effort, prompted Congress to pass the Water Pollution Control Act of 1948, Pub. L. No. 80–845, 62 Stat. 1155 (1948). *See generally* William L. Andreen, *The Evolution of Water Pollution Control in the United States—State, Local, and Federal Efforts, 1789–1972: Part II*, 22 STAN. ENVTL. L.J. 215, 235–37 (2003). Like early federal efforts in the field of air pollution control, the 1948 Act left primary responsibility for water pollution regulation with the states. The role of the federal government under the Act was limited to the provision of technical advice and funding to state regulatory efforts and very weak enforcement authority over the most egregious instances of interstate pollution, subject to the veto of the states involved. *Id.* at 237. The Act was amended in 1956 to increase federal funding of state programs and to remove the provision allowing states to veto federal enforcement actions. *See* Water Pollution Control Act Amendments of 1956, Pub. L. No. 84–660, 70 Stat. 498 (1956); *see also* Andreen, *supra*, at 240–41. Congress amended the Act again in 1961 to extend federal enforcement authority to some instances of intrastate water pollution, but this authority was subject to state veto. *See* Federal Water Pollution Control Act Amendments of 1961, Pub. L. No. 87–88, 75 Stat. 204 (1961); *see also* Andreen, *supra*, at 242–43.

Four years later, Congress passed the Water Quality Act of 1965, Pub. L. No. 89–234, 79 Stat. 903 (1965). *See* Andreen, *supra*, at 248. The 1965 Act required states to adopt water quality standards and implementation plans sufficient to meet those standards. Pub. L. No. 89–234, § 5(a). The federal government was given the authority to disapprove standards that did not adequately protect interstate waters. *Id.* Federal enforcement authority remained weak under the 1965 Act, with federal enforcement proceedings allowed only after the Attorney General had provided the polluter 180 days notice of noncompliance. *Id.* One year later, Congress supplemented this regime with additional funding in the Clean Water Restoration Act of 1966, Pub. L. No. 89–753, 80 Stat. 1246 (1966). *See also* Andreen, *supra*, at 252.

Four years later, in response to several highly publicized oil spills, Congress passed the Water Quality Improvement Act (WQIA) of 1970, Pub. L. No. 91–224, 84 Stat. 91 (1970), which prohibited oil discharges into the navigable waters of the United States and made violators of this prohibition strictly liable for cleanup costs incurred by the federal government. The WQIA also regulated the discharges of parties that applied for federal permits or licenses. *See* Andreen, *supra*, at 257.

Despite the increasing federal regulatory role for water pollution control in each successive statute, the statutes' failure to include significant provisions for aggressive federal enforcement rendered their success limited. As in the context of air pollution control, the solution was seen to be a much more substantial role for the federal government. *See id.*; *see also* N. William Hines, *Nor Any Drop to Drink: Public Regulation of Water Quality Part III: The Federal Effort*, 52 IOWA L. REV. 799 (1967).

In 1972, Congress enacted the Federal Water Pollution Control Act Amendments, better known as the Clean Water Act (CWA), "to restore and maintain the chemical, physical, and biological integrity of the Nation's waters." 33 U.S.C. § 1251(a). In order to achieve its goal of eliminating all discharges of pollutants into the navigable waters of the United States, *see* 33 U.S.C. § 1251(a)(1), the CWA establishes a permitting system, known as the National Permit Discharge Elimination System (NPDES). *See* 33 U.S.C. § 1342. Section 301(a) of the CWA prohibits the discharge of all pollutants from point sources of pollution, except in compliance with a permit issued under the NPDES. 33 U.S.C. § 1311(a). NPDES permits contain both federal effluent limitations, which are technology-based standards—the principal means by which water pollution is controlled under the CWA—as well as limitations necessary to achieve state water quality standards.

The CWA adopts a similar approach to the Clean Air Act (CAA) for new sources, requiring all new point sources of water pollution to meet strict federally set standards of performance. These standards are to reflect "the greatest degree of effluent reduction . . . achievable through application of the best available demonstrated control technology." 33 U.S.C. § 1316(a)(1). However, rather than "grandfathering" existing sources like the CAA, the CWA adopted a phased approach to the setting of federal standards for existing sources, such that EPA was directed to set increasingly stringent effluent limitations for point sources over time. The first round of standards, to be met by 1977, required the use of the "best practicable control technology currently available" (BPT). 33 U.S.C. § 1311(b)(1)(A). The second round, to be met by 1983 (a deadline that was subsequently extended to 1987), required existing point sources of pollution to adopt the "best available technology economically achievable for such category or class" (BAT). 33 U.S.C. § 1311(b)(2)(A). The CWA contains guidance for how EPA must go about setting the new source, BPT, and BAT standards. 33 U.S.C. § 1314.

In addition to the focus on effluent limitations for point sources, the CWA envisions controls on nonpoint sources of water pollution. A typical example of a point source is a pipe dumping pollutants from a factory into a stream. In contrast, a nonpoint source will typically involve pollution attributable to a diffuse area, such as contaminated runoff from agricultural land or leakage from mining operations. The regulation of nonpoint sources presents different challenges to those posed by point sources, calling for a different statutory response. Instead of specifying targets and timetables for effluent limitations, the CWA approach to controlling non-point sources includes the development of areawide waste treatment plans (that address the municipal and industrial waste treatment needs of a region, 33 U.S.C. § 1288) and state management programs (that mandate the implementation of best management practices for different forms of nonpoint sources, 33 U.S.C. § 1329(b)). More recently, the use of marketable permit schemes, known as water quality trading schemes, has grown in prominence. Proponents of market-based approaches argue that water quality trading schemes are superior to traditional command-and-control regulations, on the grounds that they can achieve pollution reduction at lower cost. The implementation of successful trading schemes presents challenges, however, including defining what will be traded and how each unit will be measured.

Despite these initiatives, the regulation of nonpoint sources has proven problematic, given the inherent difficulties in detection and enforcement. As a result, following the sequential implementation of the BPT and BAT effluent standards on existing point sources, pollution from nonpoint sources has grown in proportion to the total level of watercourse pollution nationwide. If further gains are to be achieved in water quality in the coming decade, they will have to come from the enhanced regulation of nonpoint sources.

In addition to the imposition of effluent limitations on point sources and the various controls on nonpoint sources, the CWA also provides an alternative means for controlling water pollution. The EPA can require polluters (by way of conditions on NPDES permits) to meet more stringent limitations necessary to attain state water quality standards. 33 U.S.C. § 1311(b)(1)(C). Water quality standards are comprised of two parts: the designated uses of the navigable water body and the water quality criteria necessary to support those uses. *See* 33 U.S.C. § 1313(c)(2)(A). As an interim goal in achieving the objectives of the Act, § 101(a)(2) targeted, by July 1, 1983, the achievement of national water quality at a level "which provides for the protection and propagation of fish, shellfish, and wildlife and . . . for recreation in and on the water." 33 U.S.C. § 1251(a)(2). States were allowed to designate lesser uses, however, in circumstances where this level was demonstrated to be unattainable. Despite the stated objectives of the Act, many of these lesser designations have persisted to this day. Once a use is designated for a particular body of water, states must determine the water quality criteria necessary to support the designated use. This might involve numerical criteria (such as the allowable concentration of individual pollutants) or less precise narrative criteria. In a process highly analogous to the setting of SIPs under the CAA, where technology-based effluent limitations or other pollution control mechanisms are insufficient to implement the water quality standards, states are required to develop Total Maximum Daily Load (TMDL) limits in order to allocate the additional pollution reduction burdens among the various sources. 33 U.S.C. § 1313(d)(1)(C).

Of the fifty states that comprise the United States, only Alaska and Hawaii do not share ground or surface water resources with another state. The extent of common water resources gives rise to the potential for significant conflict, as effluent discharges from sources within an upstream state may affect the water quality of downstream states. Just as in the CAA, the CWA provides a means for controlling interstate water pollution, although the attention is not as great as might be expected from a federal statute. With EPA support, a downstream state may be able to enforce its water quality standards against upstream sources of pollution, in circumstances where upstream pollution results in a detectable or measurable impact upon the violation of downstream water quality standards.

Throughout this chapter, many comparisons will be drawn between the regimes established under the CAA and the CWA. The two regimes address similar environmental problems in quite different ways. For example, under the CAA, the federal government sets ambient standards and emissions standards for new sources, whereas the states set emissions standards for existing sources. In contrast, under the CWA, the federal government sets effluent limitations for both new and existing sources (the CWA equivalent of emissions standards) whereas water quality standards (the CWA equivalent of ambient standards) are set by the states. In reading this chapter, note the many differences between the two regimes, and consider what characteristics of air and water pollution, if any, may justify these differences.

2. EFFLUENT LIMITATIONS

E.I. du Pont de Nemours & Co. v. Train
430 U.S. 112 (1977).

■ JUSTICE STEVENS delivered the opinion of the Court:

. . . These cases present . . . important questions of statutory construction concerning the Federal Water Pollution Control Act: whether EPA has the authority under § 301 of the Act to issue industrywide regulations limiting discharges by existing plants; . . . and whether the new-source standards issued under § 306 must allow variances for individual plants. . . .

The statute, enacted on October 18, 1972, authorized a series of steps to be taken to achieve the goal of eliminating all discharges of pollutants into the Nation's waters by 1985, § 101(a)(1).

The first steps required by the Act are described in § 304, which directs the Administrator to develop and publish various kinds of technical data to provide guidance in carrying out responsibilities imposed by other sections of the Act. Thus, within 60 days, 120 days, and 180 days after the date of enactment, the Administrator was to promulgate a series of guidelines to assist the States in developing and carrying out permit programs pursuant to § 402. §§ 304(h), (f), (g). Within 270 days, he was to develop the information to be used in formulating standards for new plants pursuant to § 306. § 304(c). And within one year he was to publish regulations providing guidance for effluent limitations on existing point sources. Section § 304(b) goes into great detail concerning the contents of these regulations. They must identify the degree of effluent reduction attainable through use of the best practicable or best available technology for a class of plants. The guidelines must also specify factors to be taken into account in determining the control measures applicable to point sources within these classes. A list of factors to be considered then follows. The Administrator was also directed to develop and publish, within one year, elaborate criteria for water quality accurately reflecting the most current scientific knowledge, and also technical information on factors necessary to restore and maintain water quality. § 304(a). The title of § 304 describes it as the "information and guidelines" portion of the statute.

Section 301 is captioned "effluent limitations." Section 301(a) makes the discharge of any pollutant unlawful unless the discharge is in compliance with certain enumerated sections of the Act. The enumerated sections which are relevant to this case are § 301 itself, § 306, and § 402. . . .

Section 402 authorizes the Administrator to issue permits for individual point sources, and also authorizes him to review and approve the plan of any State desiring to administer its own permit program. These permits serve "to transform generally applicable effluent limitations . . . into the obligations (including a timetable for compliance) of the individual discharger(s). . . ." *EPA v. California ex rel. State Water Resources Control Board*, 426 U.S. 200, 205. Petitioner chemical companies' position in this litigation is that § 402 provides the only statutory authority for the issuance of enforceable limitations on the discharge of pollutants by existing plants. It is noteworthy, however, that although this section authorizes the imposition of limitations in individual permits, the section itself does not mandate either the Administrator or the States to use permits as the method of prescribing effluent limitations.

Section 306 directs the Administrator to publish within 90 days a list of categories of sources discharging pollutants and, within one year thereafter, to publish regulations establishing national standards of performance for new sources within each category. Section 306 contains no provision for exceptions from the standards for individual plants; on the contrary, subsection (e) expressly makes it unlawful to operate a new source in violation of the applicable standard of performance after its effective date. The statute provides that the new-source standards shall reflect the greatest degree of effluent reduction achievable through application of the best available demonstrated control technology.

Section 301(b) defines the effluent limitations that shall be achieved by existing point sources in two stages. By July 1, 1977, the effluent limitations shall require the application of the best *practicable* control technology currently available; by July 1, 1983, the limitations shall require application of the best *available* technology economically achievable. The statute expressly provides that the limitations which are to become effective in 1983 are applicable to "categories and classes of point sources"; this phrase is omitted from the description of the 1977 limitations. While § 301 states that these limitations "shall be achieved," it fails to state who will establish the limitations.

Section 301(c) authorizes the Administrator to grant variances from the 1983 limitations. Section 301(e) states that effluent limitations established pursuant to § 301 shall be applied to all point sources.

To summarize, § 301(b) requires the achievement of effluent limitations requiring use of the "best practicable" or "best available" technology. It refers to § 304 for a definition of these terms. Section 304 requires the publication of "regulations, providing guidelines for effluent limitations." Finally, permits issued under § 402 must require compliance with § 301 effluent limitations. Nowhere are we told who sets the § 301 effluent limitations, or precisely how they relate to § 304 guidelines and § 402 permits.

The various deadlines imposed on the Administrator were too ambitious for him to meet. For that reason, the procedure which he followed in adopting the regulations applicable to the inorganic chemical industry and to other classes of point sources is somewhat different from that apparently contemplated by the statute. Specifically, as will appear, he did not adopt guidelines pursuant to § 304 before defining the effluent limitations for existing sources described in § 301(b) or the national standards for new sources described in § 306. . . .

EPA began by engaging a private contractor to prepare a Development Document. This document provided a detailed technical study of pollution control in the industry. The study first divided the industry into categories. For each category, present levels of pollution were measured and plants with exemplary pollution control were investigated. Based on this information, other technical data, and economic studies, a determination was made of the degree of pollution control which could be achieved by the various levels of technology mandated by the statute. The study was made available to the public and circulated to interested persons. It formed the basis of "effluent limitation guideline" regulations issued by EPA after receiving public comment on proposed regulations. These regulations divide the industry into 22 subcategories. Within each subcategory, precise numerical limits are set for various pollutants. The regulations for each subcategory contain a variance clause, applicable only to the 1977 limitations.[10]. . .

The broad outlines of the parties' respective theories may be stated briefly. EPA contends that § 301(b) authorizes it to issue regulations establishing effluent limitations for classes of plants. The permits granted under § 402, in EPA's view, simply incorporate these across-the-board limitations, except for the limited variances allowed by the regulations themselves and by § 301(c). The § 304(b) guidelines, according to EPA, were intended to guide it in later establishing § 301 effluent-limitation regulations. Because the process proved more time consuming than Congress assumed when it established this two-stage process, EPA condensed the two stages into a single regulation. In contrast, petitioners contend that § 301 is not an independent source of authority for setting effluent limitations by regulation. Instead, § 301 is seen as merely a description of the effluent limitations which are set for each plant on an individual basis during the permit-issuance process.

---

[10] These limitations may be made "either more or less stringent" to the extent that "factors relating to the equipment or facilities involved, the process applied, or other such factors related to such discharger are fundamentally different from the factors considered" in establishing the limitations. . . .

Under the industry view, the § 304 guidelines serve the function of guiding the permit issuer in setting the effluent limitations.

The jurisdictional issue is subsidiary to the critical question whether EPA has the power to issue effluent limitations by regulation. Section 509(b)(1) provides that "[r]eview of the Administrator's action . . . (E) in approving or promulgating any effluent limitation . . . under § 301" may be had in the courts of appeals. On the other hand, the Act does not provide for judicial review of § 304 guidelines. If EPA is correct that its regulations are "effluent limitation(s) under § 301," the regulations are directly reviewable in the Court of Appeals. If industry is correct that the regulations can only be considered § 304 guidelines, suit to review the regulations could probably be brought only in the District Court, if anywhere. Thus, the issue of jurisdiction to review the regulations is intertwined with the issue of EPA's power to issue the regulations.

We think § 301 itself is the key to the problem. The statutory language concerning the 1983 limitation, in particular, leaves no doubt that these limitations are to be set by regulation. Subsection (b)(2)(A) of § 301 states that by 1983 "effluent limitations *for categories and classes* of point sources" are to be achieved which will require "application of the best available technology economically achievable *for such category or class*." (Emphasis added.) These effluent limitations are to require elimination of all discharges if "such elimination is technologically and economically achievable for a *category or class* of point sources." (Emphasis added.) This is "language difficult to reconcile with the view that individual effluent limitations are to be set when each permit is issued." *American Meat Institute v. EPA*, 526 F.2d 442, 450 (C.A.7 1975). The statute thus focuses expressly on the characteristics of the "category or class" rather than the characteristics of individual point sources. Normally, such classwide determinations would be made by regulation, not in the course of issuing a permit to one member of the class.

Thus, we find that § 301 unambiguously provides for the use of regulations to establish the 1983 effluent limitations. Different language is used in § 301 with respect to the 1977 limitations. Here, the statute speaks of "effluent limitations for point sources," rather than "effluent limitations for categories and classes of point sources." Nothing elsewhere in the Act, however, suggests any radical difference in the mechanism used to impose limitations for the 1977 and 1983 deadlines. For instance, there is no indication in either § 301 or § 304 that the § 304 guidelines play a different role in setting 1977 limitations. Moreover, it would be highly anomalous if the 1983 regulations and the new-source standards were directly reviewable in the Court of Appeals, while the 1977 regulations based on the same administrative record were reviewable only in the District Court. The magnitude and highly technical character of the administrative record involved with these regulations makes it almost inconceivable that Congress would have required duplicate review in the first instance by different courts. We conclude that the statute authorizes the 1977 limitations as well as the 1983 limitations to be set by regulation, so long as some allowance is made for variations in individual plants, as EPA has done by including a variance clause in its 1977 limitations.

The question of the form of § 301 limitations is tied to the question whether the Act requires the Administrator or the permit issuer to establish the limitations. Section 301 does not itself answer this question, for it speaks only in the passive voice of the achievement and establishment of the limitations. But other parts of the statute leave little doubt on this score. Section 304(b) states that "(f)or the purpose of adopting or revising effluent limitations . . . the Administrator shall" issue guideline regulations; while the judicial-review section, § 509(b)(1), speaks of "the Administrator's action . . . in approving or promulgating any effluent limitation or other limitation under § 301. . . ." *See, infra,* at 979. And § 101(d) requires us to resolve any ambiguity on this score in favor of the Administrator. It provides that "(e)xcept as otherwise *expressly* provided in this Act, the Administrator of the Environmental Protection Agency . . . shall administer this Act." (emphasis added) In sum, the language of the statute supports the view that § 301 limitations are to be adopted by the Administrator, that they are to be based primarily on classes and categories, and that they are to take the form of regulations. . . .

What, then, is the function of the § 304(b) guidelines? As we noted earlier, § 304(b) requires EPA to identify the amount of effluent reduction attainable through use of the best practicable or available technology and to "specify factors to be taken into account" in determining the pollution control methods "to be applicable to point sources . . . within such categories or classes." These guidelines are to be issued "(f)or the purpose of adopting or revising effluent limitations under this Act." As we read it, § 304 requires that the guidelines survey the practicable or available pollution-control technology for an industry and assess its effectiveness. The guidelines are then to describe the methodology EPA intends to use in the § 301 regulations to determine the effluent limitations for particular plants. If the technical complexity of the task had not prevented EPA from issuing the guidelines within the statutory deadline, they could have provided valuable guidance to permit issuers, industry, and the public, prior to the issuance of the § 301 regulations. . . .

. . . The petitioners' view of the Act would place an impossible burden on EPA. It would require EPA to give individual consideration to the circumstances of each of the more than 42,000 dischargers who have applied for permits, and to issue or approve all these permits well in advance of the 1977 deadline in order to give industry time to install the necessary pollution-control equipment. We do not believe that Congress would have failed so conspicuously to provide EPA with the authority needed to achieve the statutory goals. . . .

The remaining issue in this case concerns new plants. Under § 306, EPA is to promulgate "regulations establishing Federal standards of performance for new sources. . . ." § 306(b)(1)(B). A "standard of performance" is a "standard for the control of the discharge of pollutants which reflects the greatest degree of effluent reduction which the Administrator determines to be achievable through application of the best available demonstrated control technology, . . . including, where practicable, a standard permitting no discharge of pollutants." § 306(a)(1). In setting the standard, "(t)he Administrator may distinguish among classes, types, and sizes within categories of new sources . . . and shall consider the type of process employed (including whether batch or continuous)." § 306(b)(2). As the House Report states, the standard must reflect the best technology for "that category of sources, and for class, types, and sizes within categories." H.R. Rep.No. 92–911, p. 111 (1972).

The Court of Appeals held:

"Neither the Act nor the regulations contain any variance provision for new sources. The rule of presumptive applicability applies to new sources as well as existing sources. On remand EPA should come forward with some limited escape mechanism for new sources." *Du Pont II*, 541 F.2d, at 1028.

The court's rationale was that "(p)rovisions for variances, modifications, and exceptions are appropriate to the regulatory process." *Ibid.*

The question, however, is not what a court thinks is generally appropriate to the regulatory process; it is what Congress intended for *these* regulations. . . . In striking contrast to § 301(c), there is no statutory provision for variances, and a variance provision would be inappropriate in a standard that was intended to insure national uniformity and "maximum feasible control of new sources." S.Rep. No. 92–414, p. 58 (1971).

NOTES AND QUESTIONS

1.   **The *Du Pont* Formulation.** What view did EPA have of §§ 301, 304, and 402? What view did the petitioners have? Do you agree with the *Du Pont* Court's resolution of this dispute? What role did deference to EPA's interpretation of the CWA play in the Court's decision?

2.   **Alternative Construction.** One can imagine, given the ambiguity on the face of the statute, that the *Du Pont* Court could have framed key provisions of the CWA differently? How would this have looked? What would be the consequences of a regime framed on these terms?

3.   **Role of EPA.** Does it make sense for Congress to have created the requirement that EPA both create guidelines and set effluent standards? Could § 301 be interpreted to impose regulatory responsibilities upon states? Given that this matter is integral to the implementation of the Act, why would Congress simply not specify who was to set the standards?

4.   Effluent Limitations Under the CWA. As discussed by the *Du Pont* Court, the CWA makes provision for three primary technology based effluent limitations applicable to point sources: the BPT standard, § 301(b)(1); the BAT standard, § 301(b)(2); and the new source standard, § 306(b)(1)(B).

In each case, are the standards to be set by the federal government or by the states? Which of the standards are to set for categories of point sources as opposed to individual point sources? To what extent do the express provisions of the CWA resolve these issues? To what extent do you rely on the formulation of the CWA presented by the *Du Pont* Court?

Consider next the applicability of variance provisions to each of the standards. What purpose are these provisions designed to serve? To which standards do the statutory variance provisions of §§ 301(c) and 301(g) apply? To what standard, and in what circumstances, did the variance provision contained within EPA's regulations apply? Following *Du Pont*, is it possible to obtain a variance from the requirements of the new source standards?

5.   Categories of Sources: BPT and BAT. Are effluent standards set for individual sources likely to be more or less stringent than effluent standards set for categories of sources? In light of the timeline for implementation of the BPT and BAT standards under the CWA, on what basis could it be argued that it is appropriate for BPT standards be set for individual sources, while BAT standards be set for categories of sources? On what basis did the *Du Pont* Court reject this argument?

6.   Case-by-Case Evaluation of Sources. In certain instances, it might not be technically feasible to set standards by reference to categories of sources. In these situations, the CWA allows EPA to regulate sources on a case-by-case basis. For example, the Second Circuit upheld an EPA regulation, promulgated pursuant to § 306 of the CWA, that allowed effluent limitations to be set for water cooling structures in smaller facilities on a case-by-case basis. *See Riverkeeper, Inc. v. EPA*, 358 F.3d 174, 203 (2d Cir. 2004). When is such an approach reasonable?

7.   Other Types of Effluent Limitations: Best Management Practices. The typical effluent limitation is a numerical limit on the quantity of a pollutant that can be discharged from a point source. Because this type of limitation is not compatible with all sources of pollution, regulators must occasionally take a different approach to deal with important sources of pollution. One of these approaches is to specify the best management practices (BMPs) that will minimize the amount of the pollutant being discharged into the environment. BMPs fit within the CWA definition of "effluent limitation," as "any restriction" on discharges of pollutants from point sources, "including schedules of compliance." 33 U.S.C. § 1362(11). This approach has been upheld repeatedly by the courts. *See Citizens Coal Council v. EPA*, 447 F.3d 879, 895–96 (6th Cir. 2006) (involving regulation of coal mining point sources). For what types of point sources would BMPs constitute a more appropriate form of effluent limitation than numerical limitations?

8.   Other Types of Effluent Limitations: Best Conventional Technology. Section 304(a)(4) of the Act requires that the Administrator publish information identifying conventional pollutants, "including but not limited to, pollutants classified as biological oxygen demanding, suspended solids, fecal coliform and pH." In turn, § 301(b)(2)(E) requires, with respect to these pollutants, that point sources comply with "effluent limitations for categories and classes of point sources . . . [which] require application of the best conventional pollutant control technology" (BCT) as determined by the Administrator. 33 U.S.C. § 1311(b)(2)(E). In what ways is the BCT standard likely to differ from the BPT and BAT standards? For a discussion of BCT, see *American Paper Inst. v. EPA*, 660 F.2d 954 (1981).

9.   **Technology Forcing.** The legislative history of the CWA emphasizes the technology forcing characteristics of the regime. Should the CWA's technology forcing character count in favor of or against federal regulation?

A. BPT STANDARDS

As discussed by the *Du Pont* Court, as a first step in addressing water pollution, Congress mandated that EPA issue standards reflecting the best practicable control technology currently available. This standard had to be met by existing point sources no later than July 1, 1977. 33 U.S.C. § 1311(b)(1)(A). BPT standards were to be set not for individual sources applying for a discharge permit, but rather for a category or class of point sources. *See U.S. Steel Corp. v. Train*, 556 F.2d 822 (7th Cir. 1977). The following case deals with the manner in which EPA considered costs in the setting of BPT standards.

Weyerhaeuser Co. v. Costle
590 F.2d 1011 (D.C. Cir. 1978).

■ Before MCGOWAN and TAMM, CIRCUIT JUDGES, and RICHEY, DISTRICT JUDGE.

■ MCGOWAN, CIRCUIT JUDGE:

Under the aegis of the Federal Water Pollution Control Act Amendments of 1972 (the Act), the Environmental Protection Agency has embarked upon a step-by-step process of issuing effluent limitations for each industry that discharges pollutants into the waters of the United States. By these consolidated petitions, members of one such industry, American pulp and paper makers, challenge the validity of EPA regulations limiting the 1977–83 effluent discharges of many pulp, paper, and paperboard mills. We are satisfied that EPA properly construed and rationally exercised the authority delegated to it by Congress and that, with one exception, it did so according to the appropriate procedures. Accordingly, we uphold the resulting effluent limitations in all but one instance. . . .

Petitioners . . . challenge EPA's manner of assessing two factors that all parties agree must be considered: cost and non-water quality environmental impacts. They contend that the Agency should have more carefully balanced costs versus the effluent reduction benefits of the regulations, and that it should have also balanced those benefits against the non-water quality environmental impacts to arrive at a "net" environmental benefit conclusion. Petitioners base their arguments on certain comments made by the Conferees for the Act, and on the fact that the Act lists non-water quality environmental impacts as a factor the Agency must "take into account."

In order to discuss petitioners' challenges, we must first identify the relevant statutory standard. Section 304(b)(1)(B) of the Act, identifies the factors bearing on BPCTCA ["best practicable control technology currently available"] in two groups. First, the factors shall "include consideration of the total cost of application of technology in relation to the effluent reduction benefits to be achieved from such application," and second, they "shall also take into account the age of equipment and facilities involved, the process employed, the engineering aspects of the application of various types of control techniques, process changes, non-water quality environmental impact (including energy requirements), and such other factors as the Administrator deems appropriate."

The first group consists of two factors that EPA must compare: total cost versus effluent reduction benefits. We shall call these the "comparison factors." The other group is a list of many factors that EPA must "take into account:" age, process, engineering aspects, process changes, environmental impacts (including energy), and any others EPA deems appropriate. We shall call these the "consideration factors." Notably, section 304(b)(2)(B) of the Act, which delineates the factors relevant to setting 1983 BATEA ["best available technology economically achievable"] limitations, tracks the 1977 BPCTCA provision before us except in one regard: in the 1983 section, *all* factors, including costs and benefits, are consideration factors, and no factors are separated out for comparison.

Based on our examination of the statutory language and the legislative history, we conclude that Congress mandated a particular structure and weight for the 1977 comparison factors, that is to say, a "limited" balancing test. In contrast, Congress did not mandate any particular structure or weight for the many consideration factors. Rather, it left EPA with discretion to decide how to account for the consideration factors, and how much weight to give each factor. In response to these divergent congressional approaches, we conclude that, on the one hand, we should examine EPA's treatment of cost and benefit under the 1977 standard to assure that the Agency complied with Congress' "limited" balancing directive. On the other hand, our scrutiny of the Agency's treatment of the several consideration factors seeks to assure that the Agency informed itself as to their magnitude, and reached its own express and considered conclusion about their bearing. More particularly, we do not believe that EPA is required to use any specific structure such as a balancing test in assessing the consideration factors, nor do we believe that EPA is required to give each consideration factor any specific weight.

Our conclusions are based initially on the section's wording and apparent logic. By singling out two factors (the comparison factors) for separate treatment, and by requiring that they be considered "in relation to" each other, Congress elevated them to a level of greater attention and rigor. Moreover, the comparison factors are a closed set of two, making it possible to have a definite structure and weight in considering them and preventing extraneous factors from intruding on the balance.

By contrast, the statute directs the Agency only to "take into account" the consideration factors, without prescribing any structure for EPA's deliberations. As to this latter group of factors, the section cannot logically be interpreted to impose on EPA a specific structure of consideration or set of weights because it gave EPA authority to "upset" any such structure by exercising its discretion to add new factors to the mix. Instead, the listing of factors seems aimed at noting all of the matters that Congress considered worthy of study before making limitation decisions, without preventing EPA from identifying other factors that it considers worthy of study. So long as EPA pays some attention to the congressionally specified factors, the section on its face lets EPA relate the various factors as it deems necessary. . . .

Consequently, we must review the comparison factors to determine if EPA weighed them through the "limited" balancing test as intended by Congress. On the other hand, we may review the consideration factors only to determine if EPA was fully aware of them and reached its own express conclusions about them. Since the two types of factors are separate, we divide our discussion accordingly.

Petitioners do not challenge the cost-benefit analysis for the whole industry. They do, however, challenge the analysis for the sulfite sector, contending that EPA used an "overall" instead of an "incremental" method of balancing, and that its figures on the cost of BPCTCA for the dissolving sulfite subcategory were underestimates. We uphold EPA's determination against both contentions.

EPA's approach was similar to the one we upheld in *American Paper Inst.* [*v. Train*, 543 F.2d 328, 338–39 (D.C. Cir. 1976)]. The Agency assessed the costs of internal and external effluent treatment measures, not only for the industry, but also for each subcategory. This included a separate cost assessment for the sulfite subcategories. An economic analysis was prepared to determine the impact of the costs on the industry. It found that the industry as a whole would readily absorb the cost of compliance with the 1977 standards, estimated at $1.6 billion. Out of 270 mills employing 120,000 people, eight mills would likely be closed and 1800 people laid off. The Agency noted that the impact on the three heavily polluting sulfite subcategories would be the greatest. Of less than 30 sulfite mills, three would probably close, resulting in 550 people being laid off.

Against these costs, EPA balanced the main effluent reduction benefit: overall 5,000 fewer tons per day of BOD [biochemical oxygen demand] discharged into the nation's waters. EPA refined this balance by calculating the cost per pound of BOD removed for each subcategory. Although sulfite mills must make large investments in waste treatment facilities, the cost-benefit balance is favorable for the limitations on these mills, because of the large volume of waste they produce and thus the greater treatment efficiency.

Petitioners' first contention is that EPA not only should have calculated the overall cost-benefit balance, but also should have made an "incremental" calculation of that balance. More precisely, they contend that EPA must undertake to measure the costs and benefits of each additional increment of waste treatment control, from bare minimum up to complete pollution removal. In support of this contention, they point to Senator Muskie's description of cost-benefit balancing, which suggests a focus on the "additional degree" or "marginal" amount of effluent reduction. Petitioners concede that we accepted EPA's calculation of the overall cost-benefit balance, without any further marginal or incremental analysis, in *American Paper Inst.*, 543 F.2d at 338. Nonetheless, they suggest that the present case can be distinguished, because in these proceedings, unlike in *American Paper Inst.*, industry representatives submitted an incremental breakdown of costs and benefits to the Agency.

The failure of *American Paper Inst.* to require EPA to perform its own incremental analysis is justified for a number of reasons beyond some oversight on the part of paper industry petitioners in that case. While EPA has no discretion to avoid cost-benefit balancing for its 1977 standards, it does have some discretion to decide how it will perform the cost-benefit balancing task. "[E]ven with th[e] 1977 standard, the cost of compliance was not a factor to be given primary importance," *American Iron & Steel Inst.* [*v. EPA* 526 F.2d 1027, 1051 (3d Cir. 1976)], and, as such, cost need not be balanced against benefits with pinpoint precision. A requirement that EPA perform the elaborate task of calculating incremental balances would bog the Agency down in burdensome proceedings on a relatively subsidiary task. Hence, the Agency need not on its own undertake more than a net cost-benefit balancing to fulfill its obligation under section 304.

However, when an incremental analysis has been performed by industry and submitted to EPA, it is worthy of scrutiny by the Agency, for it may "avoid the risk of hidden imbalances between cost and benefit." *Id.* at 1076 n. 19. (Adams, J. concurring). If such a "hidden imbalance" were revealed here, and if the Agency had ignored it, we might remand for further consideration. But in this case the incremental analysis proffered by industry showed that the last and most expensive increment of BOD treated in sulfite mills cost less than $.15 per pound of BOD removed, which is below the average cost of treatment in most of the industry's subcategories. We would be reluctant to find that EPA had ignored a "hidden imbalance" when the most unfavorable incremental cost-benefit balance that is challenged falls well within the range of averages for the industry as a whole.

Petitioners' next contention is that EPA underestimated the cost of BPCTCA for the dissolving sulfite subcategory, by misfiguring the cost of SSL [spent sulphate liquor] recovery. We have examined petitioners' contention, *bearing in mind* that we do not review EPA's cost figuring *de novo*, but accord EPA discretion to arrive at a cost figure within a broad zone of reasonable estimate. Petitioners' complaint revolves around the Agency's refusal to include the capital cost of installing SSL recovery in some of its cost calculations. As EPA notes, five out of six dissolving sulfite mills have already installed SSL recovery. Where, as here, most of a cost element has been incurred already, or will be incurred for a purpose other than meeting federal effluent limitations, EPA may exclude that element from the cost of BPCTCA. Accordingly, we uphold EPA's estimate of the cost of BPCTCA.

"[N]on-water quality environmental impact[s] (including energy requirements)" are among the "consideration factors" listed in § 304, and are the sole factors of that kind on which petitioners premise a challenge to the limitations. We have already seen that the Act does not specify a particular structure for EPA's treatment of the consideration factors but instead leaves the Agency with discretion in deciding how they will be "taken into account." In exercising that discretion, it is clear that EPA devoted considerable attention to assessing environmental impact and adequately set forth its conclusions with respect thereto. Most crucially, in view of the Act's emphasis in listing "energy requirements" as part of environmental impacts, EPA developed estimates of the new energy demands for the industry as a whole—about 2.4% of the industry's total energy use—and for each industry subcategory. For the sulfite subcategories, with their higher waste loads requiring greater waste treatment, the figure was an 18% increase in energy demand. EPA also developed estimates of the sludge disposal problem, which is the reverse side of effluent reduction benefit, because the waste that is removed from effluent must be disposed of as sludge. We are consequently convinced that EPA took adequately into account the environmental impacts of its regulations.

Petitioners assert, however, that we must impose on EPA a further and special requirement to engage in environmental balancing. They cite allegedly dramatic examples of negative environmental impacts from the air pollution and sludge disposal incident to waste treatment, and contend that EPA failed to give these enough "weight" in the balance. As we have discussed, we believe Congress entrusted the manner of deliberation about all of the "consideration factors" to EPA's discretion, and we are prepared to uphold EPA on that basis alone. Nonetheless, the special policies in the Act with respect to environmental protection warrant some additional comments.

NOTES AND QUESTIONS

1. **Consideration of Cost.** BPT standards must be set with "consideration of the total cost of application of technology in relation to the effluent reduction benefits." 33 U.S.C. § 1314(b)(1)(B). In contrast, in setting BAT standards, "the cost of achieving such effluent reduction" is merely specified as one of the "factors relating to the assessment of best available technology." 33 U.S.C. § 1314(b)(2)(B). What is the significance of this distinction? Why might Congress have placed such an emphasis on cost?

2. **Cost-Benefit Analysis and BPT.** Consider the ways in which the truncated cost-benefit analysis required by the *Weyerhaeuser* court differs from a comprehensive cost-benefit analysis? How does the *Weyerhaeuser* court justify these differences? Contrast the court's decision in *Weyerhaeuser* with the decision of the *Corrosion Proof Fittings* court (discussed in Chapter II). Why did the courts require that the Agency perform an incremental cost-benefit analysis in the context of one statutory scheme but not another?

3. **A Case for More Comprehensive Cost-Benefit Analysis.** It is likely that the cost of performing an incremental cost-benefit analysis would not significantly exceed the cost of conducting the truncated cost-benefit analysis prescribed by the *Weyerhaeuser* court. As a result, could the EPA regulations have been challenged on the basis that they were irrational, contrary to § 706(2)(A) of the Administrative Procedure Act? Similarly, could it be argued that EPA had acted irrationally in not taking the industry incremental cost-benefit analysis into account? Were this case to be argued today, what would be the effect of Executive Order 12,866 "Regulatory Planning and Review"? Exec. Order No. 12,866, 58 Fed. Reg. 51,735 (1993) (discussed in Chapter II).

B. BAT STANDARDS

EPA was required to issue standards reflecting the best available technology economically achievable. Existing point sources were required to comply with these standards within 6 years of the date when the BPT standards had to be met. This deadline was subsequently extended by 4 years to 1987. *See* 33 U.S.C. § 1311(b)(2)(A). BAT standards are set for categories or classes of point sources. *Id*. As the following case demonstrates, unlike challenges to BPT standards (which typically involved an overt challenge to the Administrator's consideration of cost), challenges to BAT standards typically turn on the Administrator's determination of what constitutes "available technology" for the purposes of § 301(b)(2).

Kennecott v. EPA

780 F.2d 445 (4th Cir. 1985), *cert. denied*, 479 U.S. 814 (1986).

■ Before PHILLIPS, MURNAGHAN, and WILKINSON, CIRCUIT JUDGES.

■ WILKINSON, CIRCUIT JUDGE:

Petitioners challenge the effluent limitations set by the Environmental Protection Agency for the non-ferrous metals manufacturing industry. . . . We have reviewed with care petitioners' challenges to these regulations. We conclude, however, that EPA has properly discharged the task it is required by Congress to perform.

The instant action reflects the tensions recurrent in every case of environmental regulation. The . . . petitioners here produce substantial amounts of the country's primary copper, lead, and zinc. . . . The [petitioners] contend that the effluent limitations adopted by EPA in the name of the Act are unachievable and will impose widespread costs upon the industries themselves and upon those who depend for their economic livelihood upon non-ferrous metals use.

EPA in turn states that petitioners discharge massive amounts of pollutants, over 3 million pounds annually, including "some of the most toxic metals found in industrial waste streams . . . lead, cadmium, arsenic, antimony, and zinc." It contends these pollutants create "a variety of serious adverse health and environmental effects, including cancer, brain damage, and kidney failure." The effluent limits are, in EPA's view, based upon achievable technologies and must be met promptly to fulfill the basic purposes of the Clean Water Act. . . .

For the purposes of this case, the non-ferrous metals industry was generally subject to BAT requirements. Defining Best Available Technology requires substantial technical expertise in evaluating both the efficiency of advanced technologies and the adaptability of those technologies to the production processes of the companies in this case. Our review of the EPA rulemaking is appropriately cautious. As this court has previously noted, "The scope of our review is further colored by the policy of the Clean Water Act and the sophisticated data evaluations mandated by that lengthy and complicated statute. . . . Further, technological and scientific issues, such as those presented in this case, are by their very nature difficult to resolve by traditional principles of judicial decisionmaking." . . .

To achieve a reasoned result in a dispute over technologies, EPA is bound to consider industry data, but it is not bound to accept it. Any other resolution would undermine the integrity of agency decision-making. For obvious reasons, this court should be loathe to compel an agency to accept data submitted by a regulated industry. That does not imply we are blind to the capacities of agencies to enthrone their own agendas and dismiss contending views. In considering petitioners' challenges to the non-ferrous metals rulemaking, we ask whether EPA's technical judgments find support in the record and whether they reflect the rule of reason, not the imposition of fiat. . . .

EPA did not approach casually the task of non-ferrous metals rulemaking. In 1977, the agency began gathering data for the proposed rules which it published on February 17, 1983. Data was obtained from plant visits, plant samplings, studies of scientific journals, and consultations with industry. Three hundred and nineteen firms, operating 416 facilities, received questionnaires from EPA asking for information on flow rates, production rates, wastewater treatment, and costs. Each plant visited by EPA also received an opportunity to comment on the trip report prepared by the agency. Various of the petitioners met with EPA both before and after publication of the proposed rules.

The resulting record ran 24,000 pages. EPA solicited public comment on all aspects of the regulations, highlighting points on which the agency wanted additional information. The initial comment period lasted eleven weeks. EPA reopened the comment period twice and accepted late-filed comments from one of the petitioners.

The agency considered the comments and contacted each petitioner with follow-up inquiries. The comments led EPA to re-examine its selections of model technologies and data bases. EPA likewise considered additional data on the treatment of lead and ammonia, as well as continuing to request and evaluate data from plants that had not previously submitted data. The long process of gathering data and the ongoing dialogue with the industry culminated in the final rule promulgated March 8, 1984.

We do not imply, in detailing this lengthy consideration, that a matter of the magnitude and complexity of non-ferrous metals rulemaking deserved anything less. We note only that an appellate court cannot be oblivious to the expenditure of effort that preceded its consideration and that, if the process has been a fair one, a time does come when rulemaking may cease and compliance must commence.

. . . Kennecott objects to the non-ferrous metals rulemaking, arguing [amongst other things] that the agency's data base was flawed [and] that petitioners were not given the opportunity to comment on part of the model technology, sulfide precipitation. . . . After carefully considering petitioners' numerous and specific objections, we have concluded that EPA acted within the bounds of its discretion when it set effluent limits for the primary metals industry.

When it set effluent limits for the primary metals industry, EPA used as its model technology a waste treatment process called lime, settle and filtration (L, S & F). Briefly, this treatment technique works in the following way: adding lime to wastewater increases the pH; it makes the wastewater more alkaline. At different pHs, different metals precipitate, that is, emerge from solution and become suspended as solids in the wastewater. Eventually, most solids settle at the bottom of the tank. The precipitate can then be disposed of separately from the wastewater. The wastewater is often subsequently filtered through coal or sand in order to remove additional suspended solids.

A number of industries use lime and settle. Beginning in the late 1970s, EPA collected data from six such industries (aluminum forming, battery manufacturing, secondary lead, coil coating, copper forming, and porcelain enameling). After deleting unreliable data, EPA compiled the Combined Metals Data Base (CMDB). The agency then used the CMDB to calculate achievable effluent limitations for several related industries, including the primary base metals industry.

Kennecott objects to EPA's use of the CMDB. It argues that the CMDB data was limited, that the wastewaters of CMDB plants differed significantly from those of the primary metals plants, and that EPA should not have rejected data submitted by the primary metals industry.

Kennecott's basic objection is that EPA used data from the waste treatment systems of other industries (the CMDB) rather than using data submitted by the primary metals industry. Specifically, Kennecott makes the following argument: EPA's data base was limited, containing only 300 raw and treated data points from nineteen plants. EPA did not obtain samples from any given plants over a long term; therefore, the data cannot accurately reflect long-term performance. Kennecott contends that longterm data is necessary because fluctuations in pollutant concentrations occur even in properly operated treatment facilities due to "seasonal changes in temperature and precipitation, production surges or slow downs" and other variables. Because EPA did not collect enough samples, over a long enough period of time, Kennecott contends that the data does not accurately reflect achievable concentrations. Therefore, Kennecott says, petitioners will not be able to meet the effluent limitations.

In response, EPA notes that courts customarily defer to an agency's choice of data, and that in any case, EPA could use the CMDB to predict long-term performance accurately. On the first point, the agency is indisputably correct. This court has consistently given EPA a reasonable leeway in its selection of data and statistical methods. "[W]e note that an agency's data selection and choice of statistical methods are entitled to great deference . . . and its conclusions with respect to data and analysis need only fall within a 'zone of reasonableness'." *Reynolds Metals* [*v. U.S.E.P.A.*, 760 F.2d 549, 559 (4th Cir. 1985)] (citations omitted). The question is thus whether EPA acted reasonably in basing effluent limitations for the primary base metals industry on the CMDB.

EPA contends that it does not necessarily need long-term data to predict long-term performance. It notes that the data base at issue here has been used in regulations in a number of other metals industries. By using well-established statistical methods, EPA could factor in the variability one would expect in an optimally operating plant. It is true that prediction of long-term performance would not account for fluctuations resulting from operational failures. However, the agency argues that plants with operating problems do not represent the Act's goal of Best Available Technology. *FMC Corp. v. Train*, 539 F.2d [973, 986 (4th Cir. 1976)]. ("The purpose of these variability factors is to account for the routine fluctuations that occur in plant operation, not to allow for poor performances.") Moreover, the agency contends that the addition of second-step sulfide precipitation to the model technology further reduces the variability of lime and settle treatment. *See* subsection IIB, *infra*. Courts have traditionally respected the agency's selection of a data base in the face of challenges that the data failed to account for variable pollution loads, *Ass'n of Pac. Fisheries v. EPA*, 615 F.2d 794, 812–13 (9th Cir.1980); *American Petroleum Inst. v. EPA*, 540 F.2d 1023, 1035–36 (10th Cir.1976). The number of data points here is not insignificant, and there must exist some reasonable termination point in the process of data collection.

Kennecott responds that even if EPA collected a sufficient number of data points, the CMDB remains flawed. It argues that the CMDB wastewater is so different from the wastewater in the primary metals industries that EPA cannot use the CMDB to set effluent limits that would apply to Kennecott. Without quantifying its claim, Kennecott says that the base metals industry has "huge amounts of wastewater," "tremendously high concentrations of metals," and a "very large variety of different metals" in the wastewater. EPA's similarly unquantified response is that the wastewaters in the CMDB industries and those of the primary base metals industry are indeed comparable. The agency agrees that the differences in concentration of metals may be statistically significant. However, there is evidence to show that the treatability of wastewater depends on the solubility of the pollutants, not on their concentrations. A difference in concentration of influents would thus not affect the concentration of effluents. *See* Proposed Rules, 48 Fed.Reg. 7050 (Feb. 17, 1983). This judgment constitutes a reasonable basis for EPA's belief that the wastewaters are comparable. We cannot say that EPA has acted arbitrarily or capriciously in using the CMDB to set effluent limitations for the primary metals industries. . . .

EPA had originally proposed lime, settle and filtration as the BAT for treating wastewater in the primary base metals industry. Commenters objected that they would not be able to meet the proposed effluent limitations. In the Final Rules, EPA responded that any plant unable to meet the effluent limitations by using the model lime, settle and filtration technology could add an additional step: sulfide precipitation. . . .

Sulfide precipitation works on the same principle as lime and settle. When sulfide is added to wastewater, certain pollutants precipitate out and become suspended as solids in the wastewater. The wastewater is held in tanks until most of the precipitated metals have settled to the bottom. Filtration will remove additional suspended solids. When sulfide precipitation precedes L, S & F, it is called "sulfide pretreatment." When sulfide precipitation follows L, S & F, it is called "sulfide polishing." . . .

There remains the question of whether EPA acted arbitrarily in selecting sulfide precipitation as part of the Best Available Technology. Kennecott argues that sulfide precipitation will not reduce effluent concentrations to the required levels. Specifically, Kennecott charges that data from the model plants which currently use sulfide precipitation (Ashio, Japan; Boliden, Sweden; AMAX Ft. Madison) cannot be used to predict achievable concentrations at Kennecott's plants, because conditions at the two groups of plants are so different. Kennecott notes that the plant in Ashio, Japan, for example, uses sulfide precipitation to produce arsenic trioxide as an end-product, rather than to treat wastewater. EPA replies that the ultimate disposition of the solid precipitate is irrelevant, as long as the concentration levels of pollutants in the wastewater are acceptable.

The model technology may exist at a plant not within the primary base metals industry. Congress contemplated that EPA might use technology from other industries to establish the Best Available Technology. *Reynolds Metals*, 760 F.2d at 562. Progress would be slowed if EPA were invariably limited to treatment schemes already in force at the plants which are the subject of the rulemaking. Congress envisioned the scanning of broader horizons and asked EPA to survey related industries and current research to find technologies which might be used to decrease the discharge of pollutants. Leg.Hist. at 170.

To determine that technology from one industry can be applied to another, the agency must:

(1) show that the transfer technology is available outside the industry;

(2) determine that the technology is transferable to the industry;

(3) make a reasonable prediction that the technology if used in the industry will be capable of removing the increment required by the effluent standards.

Tanners' Council of America, Inc. v. Train, 540 F.2d 1188, 1192 (4th Cir.1976) (using the standard set out by the Eighth Circuit in *CPC Int'l Inc. v. Train,* 515 F.2d 1032, 1048 (8th Cir.1975)).

EPA has demonstrated that sulfide precipitation—a process it terms "familiar" and "well established"—is available outside the primary base metals industry and that the technology is transferable to that industry. The agency notes that "the low solubility of metal sulfides" has made sulfide precipitation a more effective treatment than the conventional lime and settle process. We do not think it disqualifying that the Ashio plant, for example, uses sulfide precipitation to produce an end-product rather than to clean its wastewater, so long as the process adequately reduces pollutant concentrations in wastewater. Again, granting the agency a proper measure of deference in technical judgments, it was not arbitrary for EPA to decide that sulfide precipitation would remove pollutants to the degree required by the effluent limitations.

Kennecott discusses two other differences between the sulfide precipitation process at the model plants and the process at the primary base metals plants. Kennecott points out that the Ashio plant treats wastewater in batches, while the primary base metals plants treat wastewater continuously. EPA answers that the choice of the batch or continuous processes affects only cost, not effectiveness, and that study demonstrates the installation and operation of sulfide precipitation is economically achievable.

Kennecott also notes that all three model plants use sulfide pretreatment, rather than sulfide polishing. Again, EPA believes that the difference is irrelevant; whether sulfide precipitation is the step before or after L,S & F will not affect the achievability of the desired effluent limitations. The critical matter, in the agency's judgment, is the application of the proper amount of precipitant and the maintenance of proper levels of pH, factors entirely independent of the timing of wastewater treatment.

We hold that EPA had a reasonable basis for deciding that the sulfide precipitation technology is transferable. We are unable to conclude the agency acted arbitrarily or capriciously in selecting sulfide precipitation as part of the Best Available Technology for the primary base metals industry. . . .

NOTES AND QUESTIONS

1. **EPA's Non-Ferrous Metals Standard.** On what basis did industry challenge EPA's adoption of L, S & F as the model waste treatment technology in the setting of the non-ferrous metals standard? Was this the same basis that industry challenged the sulfide precipitation component of the standard? How did EPA respond to each challenge? On what basis did the court find in favor of EPA in each instance?

2. **Determination of Available Technology.** In light of the decision of the *Kennecott* court, consider what is required for EPA to make a determination of BAT for a particular category of point sources. Must the technology be demonstrated widely at a number of facilities within the category? Can demonstration at a single facility be sufficient to establish BAT? Must the facility be operating in the normal course of business? Would demonstration at a test facility be sufficient?

Consistent with the *Kennecott* decision, courts have upheld EPA regulations setting standards based on studies of data at a single facility. *See Ass'n of Pac. Fisheries v. EPA*, 615 F.2d 794, 816–17 (9th Cir. 1980) (upholding BAT regulation of effluent at fish canning and processing plants based on statistics from a single plant). Additionally, EPA could even assess technology that had not been applied in practice, so long as it was reasonable to believe the technology would be available by the 1983 deadline. *See Tanners' Council of Am. v. Train*, 540 F.2d 1188 (4th Cir. 1976).

3.   Applicable Technology Between Industries. The *Kennecott* court, following *Tanners' Council of America,* 540 F.2d at 1192, cites three conditions that must be satisfied in order for technology in one industry to be deemed applicable in another:

(i)   that the transfer technology is available outside the industry;

(ii)   that the technology is transferable to the industry; and

(iii)   that (based on a reasonable prediction) the technology is capable of removing the increment required by the effluent standards.

Do you think that these conditions would prove difficult to establish in the majority of circumstances?

4.   Cost and BAT. While cost is to be considered by EPA in setting BAT, it is afforded significantly less weight than in determining BPT. *See Rybachek v. EPA*, 904 F.2d 1276 (9th Cir. 1990). EPA need not conduct a cost-benefit analysis in setting the standard—it need simply take cost into account. *See Am. Meat Inst. v. EPA*, 526 F.2d 442 (7th Cir. 1975). In what ways is this approach consistent with the structure of the CWA?

5.   Industry Data. The *Kennecott* court held that

[t]o achieve a reasoned result in a dispute over technologies, EPA is bound to consider industry data, but it is not bound to accept it. Any other resolution would undermine the integrity of agency decision-making. For obvious reasons, this court should be loathe to compel an agency to accept data submitted by a regulated industry.

Compare this approach with the approach of the *Weyerhauser* court.

C.   NEW SOURCE STANDARDS

While BPT and BAT were implemented as a phased approach for dealing with existing sources, all new point sources were required to meet the new source performance standards from the moment they began operation. The CWA defines the new source standard to be "a standard for the control of the discharge of pollutants which reflects the greatest degree of effluent reduction which the Administrator determines to be achievable through application of the best available demonstrated control technology." 33 U.S.C. § 1316(a)(1). These standards are to be set for categories of sources. *See* 33 U.S.C. § 1316(b). As the following case demonstrates, challenges to new source standards by industry typically mimic the character of challenges to BAT standards by existing sources.

CPC International, Inc. v. Train

540 F.2d 1329 (8th Cir. 1976), *cert. denied*, 430 U.S. 966 (1977).

■ Before MATTHES, SENIOR CIRCUIT JUDGE, and HEANEY and WEBSTER, CIRCUIT JUDGES.

■ HEANEY, CIRCUIT JUDGE:

The petitioners, representatives of the corn wet milling industry, seek direct review of regulations promulgated by the Environmental Protection Agency setting forth standards of effluent discharges for new plants in this industry under § 306 of the Federal Water Pollution Control Act Amendments of 1972. 33 U.S.C. § 1316. . . .

The EPA has proposed that a new plant in the corn wet milling industry shall achieve an average of daily values for thirty consecutive days that shall not exceed an effluent level of 20 pounds of BOD_5 and 10 pounds of TSS per MSBu.* This standard is to be reached through the use of a complete activated sludge system to reduce the wasteload to 50 pounds each of BOD_5 and TSS per MSBu, the 1977 guidelines, and a subsequent reduction of 30 pounds of BOD_5 and 40 pounds of TSS per MSBu through the addition of a deep bed filtration system. The EPA asserts that the experience of the Clinton corn plant treatment facility, which includes the use of deep bed filtration, supports the new source standards. [Clinton corn was a large corn wet milling plant at which a new waste treatment facility had been constructed. It utilized much of EPA's proposed technology, including deep bed filtration. The Clinton treatment facility began operations on January 1, 1974, and data for the period from November, 1974, to September, 1975, was utilized by EPA in setting the proposed standards.] It contends that deep bed filtration is a demonstrated technology in the treatment of wastewater in municipal and industrial plants and its use has resulted in effluent discharges containing essentially no suspended solids. It finally asserts that deep bed filtration technology can be transferred to the corn wet milling industry with approximately the same successful rate of BOD_5 and TSS effluent level reduction. The petitioners deny these assertions.

A. BOD_5

We consider initially whether the conclusion of the EPA that the 20-pound BOD_5 standard can be met, is arbitrary and capricious. . . .

In preparation of the standards, the EPA synthesized a model corn wet milling plant and corresponding treatment facility from data received from the corn wet milling industry and from other industries

---

*   Corn wet milling is the process of chemically or biochemically separating corn into chemical components using water, grinding, and centrifugation. BOD_5 is a pollutant measurement of five-day biochemical oxygen demand. It reflects the oxygen-consuming capability of organic matter which will be fulfilled as the matter in the wastewater decomposes. It is a common measurement employed in the field of water quality. TSS is the pollutant measurement of the total amount of suspended solids, inorganic and organic, in the wastewater. One MSBu is equal to one thousand standard bushels of corn processed—a common measure of corn weighing approximately 26 kilograms.—ED.

that encounter similar wastewater. The model contained most of the best technology and procedures presently used or practiced in the industry. It is from this model and its estimated ability to reduce the projected wasteloads that the EPA set the proposed new plant standards.

The petitioners challenge two of the projections made by the EPA in synthesizing its model plant. First, they assert that the EPA erred in not considering the additional wastewater flows of between 90 and 250 pounds of BOD_5 per MSBu that result from the use of wet water scrubbers. Second, they assert that the EPA erred in failing to accurately account for the higher concentrations of BOD_5 that result from the production of modified starches. These errors, they assert, render the effluent-level reductions inaccurate.

The petitioners do not dispute that the alleged additional wastewater flows could not be effectively treated by the proposed technology. They argue only that the capacity of the model treatment plant may be insufficient to handle the volumes or concentrations of this additional wastewater.

Our review of the record discloses that the petitioners' conclusion on the increased wastewater generated by the wet water scrubbers is based upon preliminary and conflicting data. The most persuasive of these inconclusive estimates is that an additional flow of 90 pounds of BOD_5 per MSBu may be created. . . . [T]he Clinton treatment facility has consistently achieved a 98% BOD_5 reduction over an eleven-month period during which the influent has varied considerably in terms of concentration and amount. If this additional 90 pounds were treated at the Clinton facility, the seven months BOD_5 effluent averages of 4.5 of the EPA and 7.5 of the petitioners would be increased to 6.3 and 9.3, respectively. Both of these figures remain well below the EPA proposed standard of 20 pounds of BOD_5 per MSBu.

The record also discloses that the EPA did take into consideration the increased wasteloads generated by the production of modified starches. The EPA compiled data of actual performance results from newer existing mills that produce both conventional corn syrups and modified starches and also the projections for new plants, submitted by the industry, in order to determine the wastewater flow and influent levels for the model plant. Moreover, it is undisputed that the Clinton plant produces a variety of end products including modified starches. Both the Clinton wastewater load and influent levels of BOD_5 approximate the projections set out for the EPA's model plant.

Furthermore, the data relied upon by the petitioners to show increased wasteloads because of modified starch production must be contrasted with other data showing no appreciable influent increase. As stated by a representative of CPC in a report to the EPA, there were a number of occasions when the production of modified starches increased the wasteload substantially and:

about an equal number of times when there did not seem to be any effect. No explanation has been found for this problem.

Letter from R. L. Hap of CPC International to Dr. H. E. Schwartz, Jr., June 25, 1975.

Based on the model plant data, we cannot say that the EPA ignored the effects of additional waste produced by the production of modified starches nor did it act in an arbitrary or capricious manner in calculating the effect of this waste in preparing its model plant. . . .

B. TSS

We turn to a consideration of whether the conclusion of the EPA that the 10-pound TSS standard can be met is arbitrary and capricious. . . .

Recognizing the lack of support for its proposed TSS standards from results within the corn wet milling industry, the EPA points to the use of deep bed filtration in other industries. It argues that these results support the proposed TSS standards for the corn wet milling industry. In our judgment, the results from other industries indicate that deep bed filtration will remove suspended solids but not with the efficiency or the consistency necessary to satisfy the proposed TSS standard for this industry.

The studies relating to municipal treatment plants indicate that deep bed filtration will remove an average of 70% of the suspended solids in the wastewater. However, the record also establishes that the removal rates range from a low of 20% to a high of 95% with no indication of consistency. Moreover, the level of suspended solid influent in most municipal treatment plants is considerably less than that found in the corn wet milling industry.

The record indicates that the strength or concentration of the influent wastewater substantially affects the success of deep bed filtration. If the wastewater has been effectively pretreated in a biological treatment system, deep bed filtration will remove a substantial percentage of the remaining suspended solids. However, one cannot say that a properly functioning system will reduce the TSS level below that of the BOD_5 level. In the winery industry, for example, treatment of heavily concentrated wastewaters similar to those found in the corn wet milling industry produce TSS levels that exceed the BOD_5 level by as much as 48 mg/1. Moreover, the deep bed filtration system there appears to remove less than 40% of the suspended solids.

Data from the brewery and edible oil industries is largely unusable because it is set forth in milligrams per liter and because it is not clear whether deep bed filtration is used or not in these industries. This data gives some support to the finding that corn wet milling plants can meet the 1977 existing plant guidelines but little or no support that 1983 or new source standards can be met. Again, TSS levels are often higher than BOD_5 levels.

The data from Morton Frozen Foods indicates only that TSS levels are often higher than BOD_5 levels and that there are wide variations in TSS levels between the minimum and maximum days. . . .

The decision of the EPA that new corn wet milling plants can meet a TSS standard of 10 pounds per MSBu is an arbitrary and capricious one. . . .

[The Court next considered the role of cost-benefit analysis in setting the new source standard.] The new source standards are to attain the "greatest degree of effluent reduction" achievable through the use of the "best available demonstrated control technology." Section 306(a)(1), 33 U.S.C. § 1316(a)(1). This standard exceeds the effluent level reduction of that required in the 1977 existing plant guidelines for the corn wet milling industry while the proposed 1983 existing plant guidelines are the same as the new source standards. The legislative history indicates that Congress felt that new plants could realize effluent level reductions at a lower cost than existing sources because of the lower cost of constructing a new plant in comparison to retrofitting an existing facility and because technical alternatives may be made available for new plants which would not be suited for existing plants.

There is no language in § 306 requiring a cost-benefit analysis. Rather, the EPA is required only to take costs under "consideration." We conclude, therefore, that a cost-benefit analysis is not required in determining the reasonableness of the cost of achieving the new source standards. What is required for new source standards is a thorough study of initial and annual costs and an affirmative conclusion that these costs can be reasonably borne by the industry.

NOTES AND QUESTIONS

1. **New Source Standards for the Corn Wet Milling Industry.** On what basis did industry challenge the new source standard for BOD_5? On what basis did it challenge the standard for TSS? Why was the court willing to uphold the BOD_5 component but strike down the TSS component?

2. **Setting the New Source Standard.** New source performance standards must be based on technology demonstrated to be presently available, although it need not be in wide use. Consistent with the holding of the *CPC International* court, a standard can be justified by reference to the performance of a single plant or of pilot plants. *See Am. Iron & Steel Inst. v. EPA*, 526 F.2d 1027 (3d Cir. 1975).

A standard may also be set by reference to the use of the applicable technology in other industries. Compare the approach of the *CPC International* court (with respect to the applicability of the use of deep bed filtration in other industries) with the approach of the *Kennecott* court (with respect to the applicability of the use of sulfide precipitation in other industries). Are these approaches consistent?

3. Consideration of Cost. How does the consideration of the cost of compliance under the new source standards differ from that under the BPT and BAT standards? How may these differences best be explained?

4. New Sources Under the CWA and the CAA. Under the CAA, new source review extends to modifications to existing sources. Are comparable provisions contained within the CWA? If not, why might Congress not have been as concerned with this loophole in the context of the CWA?

5. Effluent Limitations Under the CWA v. Emissions Limitations Under the CAA. Compare how BPT, BAT, and new source standards are set under the CWA with how BACT, LAER, and NSPS standards are set under the CAA. How are the approaches different? What may account for the differences?

3. COOLING TOWERS

Entergy Corp. v. Riverkeeper, Inc.
556 U.S. 208 (2009).

■ JUSTICE SCALIA delivered the opinion of the Court:

These cases concern a set of regulations adopted by the Environmental Protection Agency (EPA or agency) under § 316(b) of the Clean Water Act, 33 U.S.C. § 1326(b). 69 Fed. Reg. 41576 (2004). Respondents—environmental groups and various States—challenged those regulations, and the Second Circuit set them aside. *Riverkeeper, Inc. v. EPA*, 475 F.3d 83, 99–100 (2007). The issue for our decision is whether, as the Second Circuit held, the EPA is not permitted to use cost-benefit analysis in determining the content of regulations promulgated under § 1326(b).

I

Petitioners operate—or represent those who operate—large powerplants. . . . To cool their facilities, petitioners employ "cooling water intake structures" that extract water from nearby water sources. These structures pose various threats to the environment, chief among them the squashing against intake screens (elegantly called "impingement") or suction into the cooling system ("entrainment") of aquatic organisms that live in the affected water sources. Accordingly, the facilities are subject to regulation under the Clean Water Act, 33 U.S.C. § 1251 *et seq.*, which mandates: "Any standard established pursuant to section 1311 of this title or section 1316 of this title and applicable to a point source shall require that the location, design, construction, and capacity of cooling water intake structures reflect the best technology available for minimizing adverse environmental impact." § 1326(b).

Sections 1311 and 1316, in turn, employ a variety of "best technology" standards to regulate the discharge of effluents into the Nation's waters.

The § 1326(b) regulations at issue here were promulgated by the EPA after nearly three decades in which the determination of the "best technology available for minimizing [cooling water intake structures'] adverse environmental impact" was made by permit-issuing authorities on a case-by-case basis, without benefit of a governing regulation. . . .

In 1995, the EPA entered into a consent decree which, as subsequently amended, set a multiphase timetable for the EPA to promulgate regulations under § 1326(b). In the first phase the EPA adopted regulations governing certain new, large cooling water intake structures. . . . These regulations were upheld in large part by the Second Circuit in *Riverkeeper, Inc. v. EPA*, 358 F.3d 174 (2004).

The EPA then adopted the so-called "Phase II" rules at issue here. They apply to existing facilities that are point sources, whose primary activity is the generation and transmission (or sale for transmission) of electricity, and whose water-intake flow is more than 50 million gallons of water per day, at least 25 percent of which is used for cooling purposes. Over 500 facilities, accounting for approximately 53 percent of the Nation's electric-power generating capacity, fall within Phase II's ambit. Those facilities remove on average more than 214 billion gallons of water per day, causing impingement and entrainment of over 3.4 billion aquatic organisms per year.

To address those environmental impacts, the EPA set "national performance standards," requiring Phase II facilities (with some exceptions) to reduce "impingement mortality for all life stages of fish and shellfish by 80 to 95 percent from the calculation baseline"; a subset of facilities must also reduce entrainment of such aquatic organisms by "60 to 90 percent from the calculation baseline." Those targets are based on the environmental improvements achievable through deployment of a mix of remedial technology, which the EPA determined were "commercially available and economically practicable."

In its Phase II rules, however, the EPA expressly declined to mandate adoption of closed-cycle cooling systems or equivalent reductions in impingement and entrainment, as it had done for new facilities subject to the Phase I rules. It refused to take that step in part because of the "generally high costs" of converting existing facilities to closed-cycle operation, and because "other technologies approach the performance of this option." Thus, while closed-cycle cooling systems could reduce impingement and entrainment mortality by up to 98 percent, . . . the cost of rendering all Phase II facilities closed-cycle-compliant would be approximately $3.5 billion per year, nine times the estimated cost of compliance with the Phase II performance standards. . . .

The regulations permit the issuance of site-specific variances from the national performance standards if a facility can demonstrate either that the costs of compliance are "significantly greater than" the costs considered by the agency in setting the standards, or that the costs of compliance "would be significantly greater than the benefits of complying with the applicable performance standards." Where a variance is warranted, the permit-issuing authority must impose remedial measures that yield results "as close as practicable to the applicable performance standards."

Respondents challenged the EPA's Phase II regulations, and the Second Circuit granted their petition for review and remanded the regulations to the EPA. The Second Circuit identified two ways in which the EPA could permissibly consider costs under 33 U.S.C. § 1326(b): (1) in determining whether the costs of remediation "can be 'reasonably borne' by the industry," and (2) in determining which remedial technologies are the most cost-effective, that is, the technologies that reach a specified level of benefit at the lowest cost. It concluded, however, that cost-benefit analysis, which "compares the costs and benefits of various ends, and chooses the end with the best net benefits," is impermissible under § 1326(b).

The Court of Appeals held the site-specific cost-benefit variance provision to be unlawful. Finding it unclear whether the EPA had relied on cost-benefit analysis in setting the national performance standards, or had only used cost-effectiveness analysis, it remanded to the agency for clarification of that point. (The remand was also based on other grounds which are not at issue here.) The EPA suspended operation of the Phase II rules pending further rulemaking. We then granted certiorari limited to the following question: "Whether [§ 1326(b)] . . . authorizes the [EPA] to compare costs with benefits in determining 'the best technology available for minimizing adverse environmental impact' at cooling water intake structures."

II

In setting the Phase II national performance standards and providing for site-specific cost-benefit variances, the EPA relied on its view that § 1326(b)'s "best technology available" standard permits consideration of the technology's costs, and of the relationship between those costs and the environmental benefits produced. That view governs if it is a reasonable interpretation of the statute—not necessarily the only possible interpretation, nor even the interpretation deemed *most* reasonable by the courts. *Chevron U.S.A. Inc. v. Natural Resources Defense Council, Inc.*, 467 U.S. 837, 843–844 (1984).

As we have described, § 1326(b) instructs the EPA to set standards for cooling water intake structures that reflect "the best technology available for minimizing adverse environmental impact." The Second Circuit took that language to mean the technology that achieves the greatest reduction in adverse environmental impacts at a cost that can reasonably be borne by the industry. That is certainly a plausible interpretation of the statute. The "best" technology—that which is "most advantageous," Webster's New International Dictionary 258 (2d ed. 1953)—may well be the one that produces the most of some good, here a reduction in adverse environmental impact. But "best technology" may also describe the technology that *most efficiently* produces some good. In common parlance one could certainly use the phrase "best technology" to refer to that which produces a good at the lowest per-unit cost, even if it produces a lesser quantity of that good than other available technologies.

Respondents contend that this latter reading is precluded by the statute's use of the phrase "for minimizing adverse environmental impact." Minimizing, they argue, means reducing to the smallest amount possible, and the "best technology available for minimizing adverse environmental impacts," must be the economically feasible technology that achieves the greatest possible reduction in environmental harm. But "minimize" is a term that admits of degree and is not necessarily used to refer exclusively to the "greatest possible reduction." For example, elsewhere in the Clean Water Act, Congress declared that the procedures implementing the Act "shall encourage the drastic minimization of paperwork and interagency decision procedures." 33 U.S.C. § 1251(f). If respondents' definition of the term "minimize" is correct, the statute's use of the modifier "drastic" is superfluous.

Other provisions in the Clean Water Act also suggest the agency's interpretation. When Congress wished to mandate the greatest feasible reduction in water pollution, it did so in plain language: The provision governing the discharge of toxic pollutants into the Nation's waters requires the EPA to set "effluent limitations [which] shall require the *elimination* of discharges of all pollutants if the Administrator finds . . . that such elimination is technologically and economically achievable," § 1311(b)(2)(A) (emphasis added). Section 1326(b)'s use of the less ambitious goal of "minimizing adverse environmental impact" suggests, we think, that the agency retains some discretion to determine the extent of reduction that is warranted under the circumstances. That determination could plausibly involve a consideration of the benefits derived from reductions and the costs of achieving them. It seems to us, therefore, that the phrase "best technology available," even with the added specification "for minimizing adverse environmental impact," does not unambiguously preclude cost-benefit analysis.

Respondents' alternative (and, alas, also more complex) argument rests upon the structure of the Clean Water Act. . . .

[Justice Scalia next examined the varying pollution control technologies mandated by other provisions of the CWA for various categories of point sources: the "best practicable control technology currently available" (BPT) standard from § 1311(b)(1)(A); the "best available technology economically achievable" (BATEA) standard contained in § 1311(b)(2)(A); the "best conventional-pollutant control technology" (BCT) standard from § 1311(b)(2)(E); and the "best available demonstrated control technology" (BADT) standard from § 1316(a)(1).]

The Second Circuit, in rejecting the EPA's use of cost-benefit analysis, relied in part on the propositions that (1) cost-benefit analysis is precluded under the BATEA and BADT tests; and (2) that, insofar as the permissibility of cost-benefit analysis is concerned, the BTA test (the one at issue here) is to be treated the same as those two. It is not obvious to us that the first of these propositions is correct, but we need not pursue that point, since we assuredly do not agree with the second. It is certainly reasonable for the agency to conclude that the BTA test need not be interpreted to permit only what those other two tests permit. Its text is not identical to theirs. It has the relatively modest goal of "minimizing adverse environmental impact" as compared with the BATEA's goal of "eliminating the discharge of all pollutants." And it is unencumbered by specified statutory factors of the sort provided for those other two tests, which omission can reasonably be interpreted to suggest that the EPA is accorded greater discretion in determining its precise content.

Respondents and the dissent argue that the mere fact that § 1326(b) does not expressly authorize cost-benefit analysis for the BTA test, though it does so for two of the other tests, displays an intent to forbid its use. This surely proves too much. For while it is true that two of the other tests authorize cost-benefit analysis, it is also true that *all four* of the other tests expressly authorize *some* consideration of costs. Thus, if respondents' and the dissent's conclusion regarding the import of § 1326(b)'s silence is correct, it is *a fortiori* true that the BTA test permits *no consideration of cost whatsoever*, not even the "cost-effectiveness" and "feasibility" analysis that the Second Circuit approved, that the dissent would approve, and that respondents acknowledge. The inference that respondents and the dissent would draw from the silence is, in any event, implausible, as § 1326(b) is silent not only with respect to cost-benefit analysis but with respect to all potentially relevant factors. If silence here implies prohibition, then the EPA could not consider *any* factors in implementing § 1326(b)—an obvious logical impossibility. It is eminently reasonable to conclude that § 1326(b)'s silence is meant to convey nothing more than a refusal to tie the agency's hands as to whether cost-benefit analysis should be used, and if so to what degree.

Contrary to the dissent's suggestion, our decision[ ] in *Whitman v. American Trucking Assns., Inc.*, 531 U.S. 457 (2001) . . . do[es] not undermine this conclusion. In *American Trucking*, we held that the text of § 109 of the Clean Air Act, "interpreted in its statutory and historical context . . . unambiguously bars cost considerations" in setting air quality standards under that provision. The relevant "statutory context" included other provisions in the Clean Air Act that expressly authorized consideration of costs, whereas § 109 did not. *American Trucking* thus stands for the rather unremarkable proposition that sometimes statutory silence, when viewed in context, is best interpreted as limiting agency discretion. For the reasons discussed earlier, § 1326(b)'s silence cannot bear that interpretation. . . .

While not conclusive, it surely tends to show that the EPA's current practice is a reasonable and hence legitimate exercise of its discretion to weigh benefits against costs that the agency has been proceeding in essentially this fashion for over 30 years. . . .

Indeed, in its review of the EPA's Phase I regulations, the Second Circuit seemed to recognize that § 1326(b) permits some form of cost-benefit analysis. In considering a challenge to the EPA's rejection of dry cooling systems as the "best technology available" for Phase I facilities the Second Circuit noted that "while it certainly sounds substantial that dry cooling is 95 percent more effective than closed-cycle cooling, it is undeniably relevant that that difference represents a relatively small improvement over closed-cycle cooling at a very significant cost." . . .

In the last analysis, even respondents ultimately recognize that some form of cost-benefit analysis is permissible. They acknowledge that the statute's language is "plainly not so constricted as to require EPA to require industry petitioners to spend billions to save one more fish or plankton." This concedes the principle—the permissibility of at least some cost-benefit analysis—and we see no statutory basis for limiting its use to situations where the benefits are *de minimis* rather than significantly disproportionate.

* * *

We conclude that the EPA permissibly relied on cost-benefit analysis in setting the national performance standards and in providing for cost-benefit variances from those standards as part of the Phase II regulations. . . . The judgment of the Court of Appeals is reversed, and the cases are remanded for further proceedings consistent with this opinion.

■ JUSTICE BREYER, concurring in part and dissenting in part:

[After examining statements made by the Act's principal sponsor, Senator Edmund Muskie, Justice Breyer agreed with the majority in part, finding that the EPA is permitted to take costs and benefits into account under § 1326(b). He dissented, however, regarding the issue of variances. Justice Breyer would have struck down the EPA's rule that allows variances from national standards to be issued "if a facility demonstrates that its costs would be 'significantly greater than the benefits of complying.'" According to Justice Breyer, "[t]he words 'significantly greater' differ from the words the EPA has traditionally used to describe its standard, namely, 'wholly disproportionate.' Perhaps the EPA does not mean to make much of that difference. But if it means the new words to set forth a new and different test, the EPA must adequately explain why it has changed its standard."]

■ JUSTICE STEVENS, with whom JUSTICE SOUTER and JUSTICE GINSBURG join, dissenting:

. . . Like the Court of Appeals, I am convinced that the EPA has misinterpreted the plain text of § 316(b). Unless costs are so high that the best technology is not "available," Congress has decided that they are outweighed by the benefits of minimizing adverse environmental impact. Section 316(b) neither expressly nor implicitly authorizes the EPA to use cost-benefit analysis when setting regulatory standards; fairly read, it prohibits such use.

I

As typically performed by the EPA, cost-benefit analysis requires the Agency to first monetize the costs and benefits of a regulation, balance the results, and then choose the regulation with the greatest net benefits. The process is particularly controversial in the environmental context in which a regulation's financial costs are often more obvious and easier to quantify than its environmental benefits. And cost-benefit analysis often, if not always, yields a result that does not maximize environmental protection. . . .

Because benefits can be more accurately monetized in some industries than in others, Congress typically decides whether it is appropriate for an agency to use cost-benefit analysis in crafting regulations. Indeed, this Court has recognized that "[w]hen Congress has intended that an agency engage in cost-benefit analysis, it has clearly indicated such intent on the face of the statute." *American Textile Mfrs. Institute, Inc. v. Donovan*, 452 U.S. 490, 510 (1981). Accordingly, we should not treat a provision's silence as an implicit source of cost-benefit authority, particularly when such authority is elsewhere expressly granted and it has the potential to fundamentally alter an agency's approach to regulation. Congress, we have noted, "does not alter the fundamental details of a regulatory scheme in vague terms or ancillary provisions—it does not, one might say, hide elephants in mouseholes." *Whitman v. American Trucking Assns., Inc.*, 531 U.S. 457, 467–468 (2001).

When interpreting statutory silence in the past, we have sought guidance from a statute's other provisions. Evidence that Congress confronted an issue in some parts of a statute, while leaving it unaddressed in others, can demonstrate that Congress meant its silence to be decisive. We concluded as much in *American Trucking*. . . .

American Trucking's approach should have guided the Court's reading of § 316(b). Nowhere in the text of § 316(b) does Congress explicitly authorize the use of cost-benefit analysis as it does elsewhere in the CWA. And the use of cost-benefit analysis, like the consideration of implementation costs in *American Trucking*, "pad[s]" § 316(b)'s environmental mandate with tangential economic efficiency concerns. *Id.*, at 468. Yet the majority fails to follow *American Trucking* despite that case's obvious relevance to our inquiry.

II

In 1972, Congress amended the CWA to strike a careful balance between the country's energy demands and its desire to protect the environment. . . . Although Congress realized that technology standards would necessarily put some firms out of business, see *EPA v. National Crushed Stone Assn.*, 449 U.S. 64, 79 (1980), the statute's steady march was toward stricter rules and potentially higher costs.

Section § 316(b) was an integral part of the statutory scheme. The provision instructs that "[a]ny standard established pursuant to section 1311 of this title or section 1316 of this title and applicable to a point source shall require that the location, design, construction, and capacity of cooling water intake structures reflect the *best technology available for minimizing adverse environmental impact*." 33 U.S.C. § 1326(b) (2006 ed.) (emphasis added). The "best technology available," or "BTA," standard delivers a clear command: To minimize the adverse environmental impact of water intake structures, the EPA must require industry to adopt the best technology available.

Based largely on the observation that § 316(b)'s text offers little guidance and therefore delegates some amount of gap-filling authority to the EPA, the Court concludes that the Agency has discretion to rely on cost-benefit analysis The Court assumes that, by not specifying how the EPA is to determine BTA, Congress intended to give considerable discretion to the EPA to decide how to proceed. Silence, in the majority's view, represents ambiguity and an invitation for the Agency to decide for itself which factors should govern its regulatory approach.

The appropriate analysis requires full consideration of the CWA's structure and legislative history to determine whether Congress contemplated cost-benefit analysis and, if so, under what circumstances it directed the EPA to utilize it. This approach reveals that Congress granted the EPA authority to use cost-benefit analysis in some contexts but not others, and that Congress intend to control, not delegate, when cost-benefit analysis should be used. See *Chevron U.S.A. Inc. v. Natural Resources Defense Council, Inc.*, 467 U.S. 837, 842–843 (1984).

Powerful evidence of Congress' decision not to authorize cost-benefit analysis in the BTA standard lies in the series of standards adopted to regulate the outflow, or effluent, from industrial powerplants. Passed at the same time as the BTA standard at issue here, the effluent limitation standards imposed increasingly strict technology requirements on industry. In each effluent limitation provision, Congress distinguished its willingness to allow the EPA to consider costs from its willingness to allow the Agency to conduct a cost-benefit analysis. And to the extent Congress permitted cost-benefit analysis, its use was intended to be temporary and exceptional.

The first tier of technology standards applied to existing plants—facilities for which retrofitting would be particularly costly. Congress required these plants to adopt "effluent limitations . . . which shall require the application of the best practicable control technology currently available." 33 U.S.C. § 1311(b)(1)(A). . . . Congress gave BPT two unique features: First, it would be temporary, remaining in effect only until July 1, 1983. Second, it specified that the EPA was to conduct a cost-benefit analysis in setting BPT requirements by considering "the total cost of application of technology in relation to the effluent reduction benefits to be achieved from such application." § 1314(b)(1)(B). Permitting cost-benefit analysis in BPT gave the EPA the ability to cushion the new technology requirement. For a limited time, a technology with costs that exceeded its benefits would not be considered "best."

The second tier of technology standards required existing powerplants to adopt the "best available technology economically achievable" to advance "the national goal of eliminating the discharge of all pollutants." § 1311(b)(2)(A). In setting this "best available technology," or "BAT," standard, Congress gave the EPA a notably different command for deciding what technology would qualify as "best": The EPA was to consider, among other factors, "the cost of achieving such effluent reduction," but Congress did not grant it authority to balance costs with the benefits of stricter regulation. § 1314(b)(2)(B). Indeed, in *Crushed Stone* this Court explained that the difference between BPT and BAT was the existence of cost-benefit authority in the first and the absence of that authority in the second.

The BAT standard's legislative history strongly supports the view that Congress purposefully withheld cost-benefit authority for this tier of regulation. . . .

The third and strictest regulatory tier was reserved for new point sources—facilities that could incorporate technology improvements into their initial design. These new facilities were required to adopt "the best available demonstrated control technology," or "BADT," which Congress described as "a standard . . . which reflect[s] the greatest degree of effluent reduction." § 1316(a)(1). In administering BADT, Congress directed the EPA to consider "the cost of achieving such effluent reduction." § 1316(b)(1)(B). But because BADT was meant to be the most stringent standard of all, Congress made no mention of cost-benefit analysis. Again, the silence was intentional. The House's version of BADT originally contained an exemption for point sources for which "the economic, social, and environmental costs bear no reasonable relationship to the economic, social, and environmental benefit to be obtained." That this exemption did not appear in the final legislation demonstrates that Congress considered, and rejected, reliance on cost-benefit analysis for BADT.

It is in this light that the BTA standard regulating water intake structures must be viewed. The use of cost-benefit analysis was a critical component of the CWA's structure and a key concern in the legislative process. We should therefore conclude that Congress intended to forbid cost-benefit analysis in one provision of the Act in which it was silent on the matter when it expressly authorized its use in another. See, *e.g.*, *Allison Engine Co. v. United States ex rel. Sanders*, 553 U.S. 662 (2008); *Russello v. United States*, 464 U.S. 16, 23 (1983). This is particularly true given Congress' decision that cost-benefit analysis would play a temporary and exceptional role in the CWA to help existing plants transition to the Act's ambitious environmental standards. Allowing cost-benefit analysis in the BTA standard, a permanent mandate applicable to all powerplants, serves no such purpose and instead fundamentally weakens the provision's mandate.

Accordingly, I would hold that the EPA is without authority to perform cost-benefit analysis in setting BTA standards. To the extent the EPA relied on cost-benefit analysis in establishing its BTA regulations, that action was contrary to law, for Congress directly foreclosed such reliance in the statute itself. *Chevron*, 467 U.S., at 843. Because we granted certiorari to decide only whether the EPA has authority to conduct cost-benefit analysis, there is no need to define the universe of considerations upon which the EPA can properly rely in administering the BTA standard. I would leave it to the Agency to decide how to proceed in the first instance.

NOTES AND QUESTIONS

1. ***Entergy* and *American Trucking*.** Is Justice Scalia's effort to distinguish the Court's decision in *American Trucking* from the virtually identical question presented in *Entergy* convincing? Are the differences between the CAA and the CWA in terms of their "statutory and historical context" significant enough to warrant the opposite answer to this question, as Justice Scalia believes? After *Entergy* (but keeping in mind *American Trucking*, which was not overruled), how should the EPA (or any other agency charged with implementing an environmental statute) determine whether statutory silence allows it to perform a cost-benefit analysis or not?

2. ***Entergy* and *Chevron*.** Does Justice Stevens disagree with the *Entergy* court regarding how to conduct a *Chevron* analysis of the agency interpretation or does he agree with the method of analysis under *Chevron* but come to a different conclusion in applying the test? In a footnote to the dissenting opinion not reproduced above, Justice Stevens admonishes the majority for "announc[ing] at the outset that the EPA's reading of the BTA standard 'governs if it is a reasonable interpretation of the statute.' " Justice Stevens calls this "puzzling in light of the commonly understood practice that, as a first step, we ask 'whether Congress has directly spoken to the precise question at issue.' " (quoting *Chevron*, 467 U.S., at 842). Justice Scalia replies, also in a footnote omitted above, that "surely if Congress has directly spoken to an issue then any agency interpretation contradicting what Congress has said would be unreasonable." Which interpretation of *Chevron* is more persuasive? How important is this difference to the ultimate decision to either uphold or strike down the agency's interpretation?

3. **Statutory Analysis.** The *Entergy* majority primarily utilizes textual and intertextual arguments to conclude that the EPA is free to use cost-benefit analysis under § 1326(b). The dissent, on the other hand, relies on the structure of the CWA to support their opposing conclusion. Which argument is more persuasive? Is the majority or the dissent more convincing

in addressing the arguments against their preferred interpretation of the statute?

4. Costs and Benefits. In 2014, EPA promulgated a final rule establishing national standards for cooling water intake structures (CWIS). (The rule was upheld in *Cooling Water Intake Structure Coal. v. United States EPA*, 905 F.3d 49 (2d Cir. 2018).) EPA estimated that societal costs of the 2014 CWIS regulation would be approximately $297 million annually. *See* 79 Fed. Reg. 48,300, 48,303–04 (2014). For its economic analysis of the rule, EPA conducted a stated preference survey to estimate nonuse benefits. EPA designed the stated preference survey as a choice experiment, which estimated individuals' values for certain policy outcomes, and sent surveys to thousands of people across the country. The estimated household willingness to pay for the final rule ranged from $0.69 to $27.57, depending on region, with an estimated annual social benefit of $1.1 billion. However, EPA decided not to include these results in its final economic analysis, leaving nonuse benefits largely unquantified. *See* EPA, EPA-821-R-14-005, BENEFITS ANALYSIS FOR THE FINAL SECTION 316(B) EXISTING FACILITIES RULE (2014). Would it have been better for the agency to include the results from a stated preference survey in its economic analysis?

4. VARIANCES

By authorizing EPA to create effluent limitations for categories of new and existing point sources, the CWA takes a different approach to the CAA, where certain standards (such as BACT under PSD and LAER under nonattainment) are set on a case-by-case basis. The CWA deals with the inevitable variation among individual sources by allowing the granting of variances when circumstances justify an exemption from an otherwise applicable effluent limitation. The three main types of variances are § 301(c) variances (allowing modifications of BAT standards on the basis of economic capability), § 301(g) variances (allowing modification to BAT standards on water quality grounds), and fundamentally different factor (FDF) variances (allowing modifications to individual point sources that demonstrate characteristics that are fundamentally different from those which define the category in which the source is placed). These variances, however, are granted only to existing sources: Recall that the *Du Pont* Court held that § 306 precludes new sources from obtaining variances.

The cases that follow address different elements of the variance provisions of the CWA. First, in *EPA v. National Crushed Stone Association*, 449 U.S. 64 (1980), the Supreme Court considered the applicability of the § 301(c) variance to the 1977 BPT standard. Second, in *Chemical Manufacturers Association v. NRDC*, 470 U.S. 116 (1985), the Supreme Court considered the application of the FDF variance.

Environmental Protection Agency v. National Crushed Stone Association

449 U.S. 64 (1980).

■ JUSTICE WHITE delivered the opinion of the Court:

. . . [T]he Environmental Protection Agency (EPA) . . . promulgated pollution discharge limitations for [existing sources in] the coal mining industry and [in] that portion of the mineral mining and processing industry comprising the crushed-stone, construction-sand, and gravel categories. Although the Act does not expressly authorize or require variances from the 1977 limitation, each set of regulations contained a variance provision. . . .

To obtain a variance from the 1977 [BPT] uniform discharge limitations a discharger must demonstrate that the "factors relating to the equipment or facilities involved, the process applied, or other such factors relating to such discharger are fundamentally different from the factors considered in the establishment of the guidelines." Although a greater than normal cost of implementation will be considered in acting on a request for a variance, economic ability to meet the costs will not be considered. A variance, therefore, will not be granted on the basis of the applicant's economic inability to meet the costs of implementing the uniform standard. . . .

Section 301(c) of the Act explicitly provides for modifying the 1987 (BAT) effluent limitations with respect to individual point sources. A variance under § 301(c) may be obtained upon a showing "that such modified requirements (1) will represent the maximum use of technology within the economic capability of the owner or operator; and (2) will result in reasonable further progress toward the elimination of the discharge of pollutants." Thus, the economic ability of the individual operator to meet the costs of effluent reductions may in some circumstances justify granting a variance from the 1987 limitations.

No such explicit variance provision exists with respect to BPT standards, but in *E. I. du Pont de Nemours & Co. v. Train*, 430 U.S. 112 (1977), we indicated that a variance provision was a necessary aspect of BPT limitations applicable by regulations to classes and categories of point sources. The issue in this case is whether the BPT variance provision must allow consideration of the economic capability of an individual discharger to afford the costs of the BPT limitation. . . .

. . . Section 301(c) is limited on its face to modifications of the 1987 BAT limitations. It says nothing about relief from the 1977 BPT requirements. Nor does the language of the Act support the position that although § 301(c) is not itself applicable to BPT standards, it requires that the affordability of the prescribed 1977 technology be considered in BPT variance decisions. This would be a logical reading of the statute only if the factors listed in § 301(c) bore a substantial relationship to the considerations underlying the 1977 limitations as they do to those controlling the 1987 regulations. This is not the case.

The two factors listed in § 301(c)—"maximum use of technology within the economic capability of the owner or operator" and "reasonable further progress toward the elimination of the discharge of pollutants"— parallel the general definition of BAT standards as limitations that "require application of the best available technology economically achievable for such category or class, which will result in reasonable further progress toward . . . eliminating the discharge of all pollutants. . . ." § 301(b)(2). A § 301(c) variance, thus, creates for a particular point source a BAT standard that represents for it the same sort of economic and technological commitment as the general BAT standard creates for the class. As with the general BAT standard, the variance assumes that the 1977 BPT standard has been met by the point source and that the modification represents a commitment of the maximum resources economically possible to the ultimate goal of eliminating all polluting discharges. No one who can afford the best available technology can secure a variance.

There is no similar connection between § 301(c) and the considerations underlying the establishment of the 1977 BPT limitations. First, § 301(c)'s requirement of "reasonable further progress" must have reference to some prior standard. BPT serves as the prior standard with respect to BAT. There is, however, no comparable, prior standard with respect to BPT limitations. Second, BPT limitations do not require an industrial category to commit the maximum economic resources possible to pollution control, even if affordable. Those point sources already using a satisfactory pollution control technology need take no additional steps at all. The § 301(c) variance factor, the "maximum use of technology within the economic capability of the owner or operator," would therefore be inapposite in the BPT context. It would not have the same effect there that it has with respect to BAT's, *i.e.*, it would not apply the general requirements to an individual point source.

More importantly, to allow a variance based on the maximum technology affordable by the point source, even if that technology fails to meet BPT effluent limitations, would undercut the purpose and function of BPT limitations. Rather than the 1987 requirement of the best measures economically and technologically feasible, the statutory provisions for 1977 contemplate regulations prohibiting discharges from any point source in excess of the effluent produced by the best practicable technology currently available in the industry. The Administrator was referred to the industry and to existing practices to determine BPT. He was to categorize point sources, examine control practices in exemplary plants in each category, and, after weighing benefits and costs and considering other factors specified by § 304, determine and define the best practicable technology at a level that would effect the obvious statutory goal for 1977 of substantially reducing the total pollution produced by each category of the industry. Necessarily, if pollution is to be diminished, limitations based on BPT must forbid the level of effluent produced by the most pollution-prone segment of the industry, that segment not measuring up to "the average of the best existing performance." So understood, the statute contemplated regulations that would require a substantial number of point sources with the poorest performances either to conform to BPT standards or to cease production. To allow a variance based on economic capability and not to require adherence to the prescribed minimum technology would permit the employment of the very practices that the Administrator had rejected in establishing the best practicable technology currently in use in the industry. . . .

Nor did Congress restrict the reach of § 301(c) without understanding the economic hardships that uniform standards would impose. Prior to passage of the Act, Congress had before it a report jointly prepared by EPA, the Commerce Department, and the Council on Environmental Quality on the impact of the pollution control measures on industry. That report estimated that there would be 200 to 300 plant closings caused by the first set of pollution limitations. Comments in the Senate debate were explicit: "There is no doubt that we will suffer some disruptions in our economy because of our efforts; many marginal plants may be forced to close." Leg. Hist. 1282 (Sen. Bentsen). The House managers explained the Conference position as follows:

> If the owner or operator of a given point source determines that he would rather go out of business than meet the 1977 requirements, the managers clearly expect that any discharge issued in the interim would reflect the fact that all discharges not in compliance with such 'best practicable technology currently available' would cease by June 30, 1977. . . .

Id., at 231. In rejecting EPA's interpretation of the BPT variance provision, the Court of Appeals relied on a mistaken conception of the relation between BPT and BAT standards. The court erroneously believed that since BAT limitations are to be more stringent than BPT limitations, the variance provision for the latter must be at least as flexible as that for the former with respect to affordability. The variances permitted by § 301(c) from the 1987 limitations, however, can reasonably be understood to represent a cost in decreased effluent reductions that can only be afforded once the minimal standard expressed in the BPT limitation has been reached.

NOTES AND QUESTIONS

1. **Section 301(c) Variances from BPT and BAT.** The *National Crushed Stone* Court's decision contemplates the granting of statutory variances from the more stringent BAT standards in the case of economic hardship, but not from the less stringent BPT standards. Why? What role

does the *National Crushed Stone* Court envisage the BPT standard playing under the CWA?

2.   Variances. Does it make sense to have different variance requirements for BPT, BAT, and new source limitations? Do these variances somewhat lessen the seemingly harsh approach taken by Congress toward existing sources under the CWA? Could it be argued that the CWA effectively replicates the grandfathering provisions for existing sources under the CAA?

3.   Application of BPT to Existing Sources. Should an existing source be eligible for a variance on the ground that it cannot afford to meet the BPT standard? The *Du Pont* Court read in the requirement of variances based on FDFs as a necessary component of a regulatory system that created effluent limitations for categories of sources. The variance provisions of § 301(c) and (g), however, clearly contemplate that some existing sources must shut down if they cannot comply with BPT. Why should BPT standards be treated differently than BAT standards?

4.   Cost and FDF Variances. Why did the appellee in *National Crushed Stone* pursue a variance under § 301(c) of the CWA rather than an FDF variance? Why should the fact that the appellee faces bankruptcy as a consequence of implementing the regulatory standard not be sufficient to support an FDF variance? What showing would the appellee have to make in order to obtain an FDF variance?

Chemical Manufacturers Association v. Natural Resources Defense Council, Inc.

470 U.S. 116 (1985).

■ JUSTICE WHITE delivered the opinion of the Court:

As part of a consolidated lawsuit, respondent Natural Resources Defense Council (NRDC) [seeks] a declaration that § 301(*l*) of the Clean Water Act, 33 U.S.C. § 1311(*l*), prohibit[s] EPA from issuing "fundamentally different factor" (FDF) variances for pollutants listed as toxic under the Act.

[Section 301(*l*), which was introduced as part of the 1977 amendments to the CWA, was said to "reflect[ ] Congress' increased concern with the dangers of toxic pollutants." *Id.* at 122. As at the time of the *Chemical Manufacturers* case, § 301(*l*) provided that "[t]he Administrator may not modify any requirement of this section as it applies to any specific pollutant which is on the toxic pollutant list under § 307(a)(1) of this Act." 91 Stat. 1590. (For reasons described in the notes and questions that follow, § 301(*l*) was subsequently amended to reflect the introduction of § 301(n)). While EPA recognized that § 301(*l*) precluded the application of the § 301(c) and 301(g) variance provisions, it nevertheless continued its practice of granting FDF variances with respect to effluent limitations applicable to toxic pollutants. NRDC claimed that the § 301(*l*) preclusion on modifications extended to FDF variances.]

. . . [The] view of the agency charged with administering the statute is entitled to considerable deference; and to sustain it, we need not find that it is the only permissible construction that EPA might have adopted but only that EPA's understanding of this very "complex statute" is a sufficiently rational one to preclude a court from substituting its judgment for that of EPA. Of course, if Congress has clearly expressed an intent contrary to that of the Agency, our duty is to enforce the will of Congress.

NRDC insists that the language of § 301(*l*) is itself enough to require affirmance of the Court of Appeals, since on its face it forbids any modifications of the effluent limitations that EPA must promulgate for toxic pollutants. If the word "modify" in § 301(*l*) is read in its broadest sense, that is, to encompass any change or alteration in the standards, NRDC is correct. But it makes little sense to construe the section to forbid EPA to amend its own standards, even to correct an error or to impose stricter requirements. Furthermore, reading § 301(*l*) in this manner would forbid what § 307(b)(2) expressly directs: EPA is there required to "revise" its pretreatment standards "from time to time, as control technology, processes, operating methods, or other alternatives change." As NRDC does and must concede, § 301(*l*) cannot be read to forbid every change in the toxic waste standards. The word "modify" thus has no plain meaning as used in § 301(*l*), and is the proper subject of construction by EPA and the courts. NRDC would construe it to forbid the kind of alteration involved in a FDF variance, while the Agency would confine the section to prohibiting the partial modifications that § 301(c) would otherwise permit. Since EPA asserts that the FDF variance is more like a revision permitted by § 307 than it is like a § 301(c) or (g) modification, and since, as will become evident, we think there is a reasonable basis for such a position, we conclude that the statutory language does not foreclose the Agency's view of the statute. . . .

Neither are we convinced that FDF variances threaten to frustrate the goals and operation of the statutory scheme set up by Congress. The nature of FDF variances has been spelled out both by this Court and by the Agency itself. The regulation explains that its purpose is to remedy categories which were not accurately drawn because information was either not available to or not considered by the Administrator in setting the original categories and limitations. An FDF variance does not excuse compliance with a correct requirement, but instead represents an acknowledgment that not all relevant factors were taken sufficiently into account in framing that requirement originally, and that those relevant factors, properly considered, would have justified—indeed, required—the creation of a subcategory for the discharger in question. As we have recognized, the FDF variance is a laudable corrective mechanism, "an acknowledgement that the uniform . . . limitation was set without reference to the full range of current practices, to which the Administrator was to refer." *EPA v. National Crushed Stone Ass'n*, 449

U.S. 64, 77–78 (1980). It is, essentially, not an exception to the standard-setting process, but rather a more fine-tuned application of it.

We are not persuaded by NRDC's argument that granting FDF variances is inconsistent with the goal of uniform effluent limitations under the Act. Congress did intend uniformity among sources in the same category, demanding that "similar point sources with similar characteristics . . . meet similar effluent limitations," S.Rep. No. 92–1236, p. 126 (1972). EPA, however, was admonished to take into account the diversity within each industry by establishing appropriate subcategories. Leg.Hist. 455.

NRDC concedes that EPA could promulgate rules under § 307 of the Act creating a subcategory for each source which is fundamentally different from the rest of the class under the factors the EPA must consider in drawing categories. The same result is produced by the issuance of a FDF variance for the same failure properly to subdivide a broad category. Since the dispute is therefore reduced to an argument over the means used by EPA to define subcategories of indirect dischargers in order to achieve the goals of the Act, these are particularly persuasive cases for deference to the Agency's interpretation. Cf. *Vermont Yankee Nuclear Power Corp. v. NRDC*, 435 U.S. 519, 543 (1978). . . .

NRDC argues, echoing the concern of the Court of Appeals below, that allowing FDF variances will render meaningless the § 301(*l*) prohibition against modifications on the basis of economic and water-quality factors. That argument ignores the clear difference between the purpose of FDF waivers and that of §§ 301(c) and (g) modifications, a difference we explained in *National Crushed Stone*. A discharger that satisfies the requirements of § 301(c) qualifies for a variance "simply because [it] could not afford a compliance cost that is not fundamentally different from those the Administrator has already considered" in creating a category and setting an effluent limitation. 449 U.S., at 78. A § 301(c) modification forces "a displacement of calculations already performed, not because those calculations were incomplete or had unexpected effects, but only because the costs happened to fall on one particular operator, rather than on another who might be economically better off." *Ibid.* FDF variances are specifically unavailable for the grounds that would justify the statutory modifications. 40 CFR §§ 403.13(e)(3) and (4) (1984). Both a source's inability to pay the foreseen costs, grounds for a § 301(c) modification, and the lack of a significant impact on water quality, grounds for a § 301(g) modification, are irrelevant under FDF variance procedures. *Ibid.*; see also *Crown Simpson Pulp Co. v. Castle*, 642 F.2d 323 (CA9), *cert. denied*, 454 U.S. 1053 (1981). . . .

Viewed in its entirety, neither the language nor the legislative history of the Act demonstrates a clear congressional intent to forbid EPA's sensible variance mechanism for tailoring the categories it promulgates. In the absence of a congressional directive to the contrary, we accept EPA's conclusion that § 301(*l*) does not prohibit FDF variances. That interpretation gives the term "modify" a consistent meaning in §§ 301(c), (g), and (*l*), and draws support from the legislative evolution of § 301(*l*) and from congressional silence on whether it intended to forbid FDF variances altogether and thus to obviate our decision in *du Pont*. . . .

■ JUSTICE MARSHALL, with whom JUSTICE BLACKMUN and JUSTICE STEVENS join, and with whom JUSTICE O'CONNOR joins as to Parts I, II, and III, dissenting:

. . . The Court today defers to EPA's interpretation of the Clean Water Act even though that interpretation is inconsistent with the clear intent of Congress, as evidenced by the statutory language, history, structure, and purpose. I had not read our cases to permit judicial deference to an agency's construction of a statute when that construction is inconsistent with the clear intent of Congress. . . .

III

. . . EPA argues that FDF variances do not excuse compliance with the correct standards, but instead provide a means for setting more appropriate standards. It is clear that, pursuant to § 307(b)(2), EPA can "revise" the pretreatment standards, as long as it does so "following the procedure established . . . for the promulgation of such standards." The statute contemplates that the standards will be set and revised through notice-and-comment rulemaking and will be applicable to categories of sources. See §§ 307(b)(2), (3); see also Brief for EPA 9. EPA argues that such a "revision," which is clearly not proscribed by § 301(*l*), would be substantively indistinguishable from an FDF variance. Thus, according to the Agency, NRDC's concern stems not from the result achieved when an FDF variance is granted, but rather from the procedure employed in reaching that result. EPA relies on *Vermont Yankee Nuclear Power Corp. v. NRDC*, 435 U.S. 519 (1978), for the proposition that an agency is free to choose between two procedures for reaching the same substantive ends. See Brief for EPA 11, 36.

To support its argument, EPA points out that the factors that may justify an FDF variance are the same factors that may be taken into account in setting and revising the national pretreatment standards. Compare § 304(b)(2) (statutory standard) with 40 CFR § 403.13(d) (1984) (FDF variance provision). EPA also points out that, in considering whether an FDF variance will be granted, it cannot take into account factors that could not have justified a change in the national standards. See Brief for EPA 31; 40 CFR § 403.13(e) (1984). EPA acknowledges that the statute requires that the national pretreatment standards be established—and therefore revised—for "categories" of dischargers, see § 307(b)(3) (pretreatment standards); Brief for EPA 11; see also § 307(a)(2) (toxic standards), and not on a case-by-case basis. It argues, however, that nothing in the Clean Water Act precludes EPA from defining a subcategory that has only one discharger. See Brief for EPA 31.

The logic of EPA's position is superficially powerful. If EPA can, through rulemaking, define a subcategory that includes only one discharger, why should it not be able to do so through a variance procedure? In fact, if rulemaking and the variance procedure were alternative means to the same end, I might have no quarrel with EPA's position, which the Court has accepted. *Ante*, at 1111–1112. Indeed, "[a]bsent constitutional constraints or extremely compelling circumstances the administrative agencies should be free to fashion their own rules of procedure and to pursue methods of inquiry capable of permitting them to discharge their multitudinous duties." *Vermont Yankee, supra*, at 543 (citations omitted); see also *SEC v. Chenery Corp.*, 332 U.S. 194 (1947).

However, the Agency's position does not withstand more than superficial analysis. An examination of the legislative history of the 1972 amendments to the Clean Water Act—the relevance of which both the Court and EPA ignore—reveals that Congress attached great *substantive* significance to the method used for establishing pollution control requirements. . . .

The FDF variance procedure leads to substantive results that are different in two fundamental ways from those attained through the rule-making for categories of dischargers contemplated in § 307(b). First, it is less protective of the environment. If, for example, a discharger shows that its production processes—and, as a result, its costs of compliance—are significantly different from those taken into account in setting the categorical standards, that discharger would be eligible for an FDF variance, and EPA could set a new requirement based on the applicant's peculiar situation. See 40 CFR § 403.13(d)(5), (6) (1984); Tr. of Oral Arg. 14. It may turn out, however, that there are many other dischargers in the same situation, and that all of these dischargers use production processes that make pollution control possible at a much lower cost. If EPA took into account the production processes of these more efficient dischargers—as it presumably would have to do if it proceeded through rulemaking on a categorical scale—it would set a requirement far more stringent than that adopted as part of the FDF variance mechanism.

In the aggregate, if EPA defines a new pretreatment subcategory through rulemaking, the BAT-level pollution control requirement of each discharger would be determined by reference to the capability of the "best performer." In contrast, if EPA provides individual variances to each plant in this group, only one discharger would have a requirement based on the capability of the best performer—the best performer itself. The others would necessarily be subject to less stringent standards.

The second important difference is that FDF variances do not spur technological innovation to the same extent as § 307(b) revisions. In the preceding example, the discharger with environmentally unsound production processes would probably be compelled to purchase new technology if it were subjected to a pollution control requirement set by reference to the characteristics of the "best" discharger. Under the less stringent requirement adopted through the FDF variance procedure, it might not need to do so. The additional demand for new technology that results from the § 307(b) procedures creates incentives for technological innovation. In the long run, such innovation would lead to even better technology and to the possibility of further tightening of the pollution control requirements, as such technology became cheaper. In fact, Congress envisioned that this iterative procedure would ultimately lead to an elimination of harmful discharges. See 118 Cong.Rec. 33696 (1972), 1972 Leg.Hist. 170 (Sen. Muskie).

It is true, of course, that even the statutory revision procedure might identify a subcategory with only one discharger. That procedure, however, will have established that this discharger is indeed uniquely situated. In contrast, an FDF variance sets an individual requirement even where there may be similarly situated dischargers.

In summary, whatever else FDF variances might do, they do not further the same congressional goals as the notice-and-comment rulemaking required for § 307(b) revisions. *Vermont Yankee* is simply inapposite; Congress intended, for substantive reasons, that the pretreatment standards be set and revised through rulemaking for categories of dischargers. The Court's conclusion to the contrary stems exclusively from its failure to consider why Congress chose to require categorical standards. . . .

NOTES AND QUESTIONS

1. **Meaning of Modification.** At the heart of the *Chemical Manufacturers* case is the interpretation of the word "modify" as it appears in the § 301(*l*) prohibition. More particularly, the majority and dissenting opinions differ on the question of whether an FDF variance constitutes a "modification" of a standard.

In distinguishing between the opinions of the majority and the dissent, consider whether § 301(*l*) could have been interpreted in such broad terms as to prohibit any modifications to categorical standards? Why did both the majority and dissent find that this was not the intention of Congress?

Given the consensus between the majority and the dissent that the term modify should not be attributed its broadest meaning, on what point did they disagree? How did the majority characterize FDF variances? In what ways did this differ from the characterization of the dissent?

2. **Notice-and-Comment Rulemaking for Subcategories.** The *Chemical Manufacturers* Court agreed with EPA that FDF variances are subcategories and not modifications to existing standards. In the opinion of the dissent, however, what important differences exist between the creation of subcategories and the granting of FDF variances?

Consider whether the grant of an FDF variance is equivalent to the creation of a category of one point source. In granting an FDF variance, for example, need EPA consider the characteristics of similarly situated firms? Need EPA consider these other firms in establishing a category under § 307(b)(2)? What is the consequence of this distinction in the opinion of the dissent? What procedural differences exist between the two processes?

3. **Technology Forcing.** The dissent notes that "[b]y requiring that the standards be set by reference to either the 'average of the best' or very 'best' technology, the Act seeks to foster technological innovation." 470 U.S. at 155–56. To what extent does the majority opinion erode the technology forcing nature of the regime?

4. **Role of *Chevron* Analysis.** The *Chemical Manufacturers* case was decided one year after *Chevron*. It is clear that deference to EPA's interpretation of the CWA played a large part in the decision of the majority. What role did *Chevron* play in the dissent? Consider the following passage from Justice Marshall's dissent:

> The determination that Congress clearly intended that § 301(*l*) do more than just ban modifications otherwise permitted by §§ 301(c) and (g) compels the conclusion that EPA's construction to the contrary cannot stand. As this Court has repeatedly stated:
>
>> The interpretation put on the statute by the agency charged with administering it is entitled to deference, but the courts are the final authorities on issues of statutory construction. They must reject administrative constructions of the statute, whether reached by adjudication or by rulemaking, that are inconsistent with the statutory mandate or that frustrate the policy that Congress sought to implement. *FEC v. Democratic Senatorial Campaign Committee*, 454 U.S. 27, 31–32 (1981) (citations omitted).

Id. at 151. Does the disagreement between the majority and dissent center on a reading of *Chevron*? If not, how can the different applications of the *Chevron* doctrine be reconciled?

5. **Small Exception, Big Consequences.** In a further section of the dissent not reproduced above, Justice Marshall commented that "[e]xceptions . . . are not without costs. For example, they are inappropriate where small errors could lead to irreversible or catastrophic results. In such cases, individual equity should give way to comprehensive rationality." *Id.* at 159–60. In what circumstances could a small error with respect to toxic pollutants lead to irreversible or catastrophic results? Does this count in favor of the majority's limited definition of "modification" or the dissent's broader definition? In what other statutory regimes has Congress disallowed exceptions, even in the absence of an explicit statutory ban, on the grounds that it has attached great importance on the attainment and maintenance of certain environmental goals?

6. **Hardship Exceptions and Fairness Exceptions.** A footnote to the opinion of Justice Marshall notes that:

[c]ommentators have identified two categories of exceptions that are relevant in these cases: hardship exceptions and fairness exceptions. See, e.g., [Alfred] Aman, Administrative Equity: An Analysis of Exceptions to Administrative Rules, 1982 DUKE L.J. 277, 293–294; [Martin] Shapiro, Administrative Discretion: The Next Stage, 92 YALE L.J. 1487, 1504 (1983); [Peter] Schuck, When the Exception Becomes the Rule: Regulatory Equity and the Formulation of Energy Policy Through an Exceptions Process, 1984 DUKE L.J. 163, 283–289.

Id. at 163, n.21. How would you characterize the FDF variance under this dichotomy? Does this differ from your characterization of the § 301(c) and (g) variances? Is this distinction of any consequence?

7.   Adjustments or Exceptions. EPA points out that the factors for determining an FDF variance are the same as the factors used in setting and revising the national pretreatment standards. Compare the FDF variance factors in 40 C.F.R. § 403.13(c)–(e) with the statutory factors in § 304(b)(2) of the CWA. How similar are they? In what ways do they differ? Is their similarity convincing evidence that FDF variances are more akin to an adjustment of the national standard rather than an exception to that standard? How important is it to the Court's ruling that the regulation also prohibits the consideration of certain factors for FDF variance determinations? *See* 40 C.F.R. § 403.13(e) (listing four prohibited factors).

8.   Congressional Response: § 301(n). In the aftermath of the decision in the *Chemical Manufacturers* case, Congress enacted § 301(n), which limits the circumstances in which FDF variances can be granted. 33 U.S.C. § 1311(n). A source may seek an FDF variance based only on information that was submitted to EPA during the rulemaking establishing the relevant effluent limitation, unless such information was not reasonably available at the time of the rulemaking. *See* 33 U.S.C. § 1311(n)(1)(B). Significantly, § 301(n) provides that cost is not a factor that can be taken into account in granting an FDF variance. What are the consequences of this provision?

Section § 301(*l*) was also amended following the introduction of 301(n). It now provides that: *"[o]ther than as provided in subsection (n) of this section*, the Administrator may not modify any requirement of this section as it applies to any specific pollutant which is on the toxic pollutant list under § 1317(a)(1) of this Act." 33 U.S.C. § 1311(*l*) (emphasis added).

5.   CONTROL OF NONPOINT SOURCES

The regulatory regime for controlling point sources has proven highly successful, resulting in a significant improvement in the quality of national watercourses. The same cannot be said, however, for the regulation of nonpoint sources. EPA estimates that nonpoint source pollution is the "nation's largest source of water quality problems." EPA, EPA-841-F-96-0041, NONPOINT SOURCE POLLUTION: THE NATION'S LARGEST WATER QUALITY PROBLEM (1996). It is the "main reason that approximately forty percent of [the nation's] surveyed rivers, lakes, and estuaries are not clean enough to meet basic uses such as fishing or swimming." *Id.* The most recent National Water Quality Report to Congress submitted by the EPA in 2017 found significant impairment of a large portion of our nation's waters. EPA, NATIONAL WATER QUALITY INVENTORY: REPORT TO CONGRESS (2017). Of the bodies of water assessed by the study, 55 percent of rivers and streams, 70 percent of lakes, and 78 percent of bays and estuaries were found to be impaired. However, 69 percent of streams and rivers, 55 percent of lakes, and 61 percent of bays and estuaries have not been assessed. *Id.* For all of these different types of bodies of water, nonpoint source pollution was determined to be a leading cause of impairment. *Id.* It is clear that in the event that further reduction in the pollution of national watercourses is to be achieved, the regulation of nonpoint sources must be improved.

The distinction between point and nonpoint sources is central to federal water quality regulation. It can be traced to § 301(a) of the CWA, which proclaims the discharge of any pollution (defined to include only "point source" pollution) to be unlawful unless it takes place pursuant to a permit. In turn, the CWA defines "point source" to mean "any discernible, confined and discrete conveyance, including but not limited to any pipe, ditch, channel, tunnel, conduit, well, discrete fissure, container, rolling stock, concentrated animal feeding operation, or vessel or other floating craft, from which pollutants are or may be discharged." 33 U.S.C. § 1362(14). In contrast, the term "nonpoint source" is not defined in the Act, but has been interpreted to encompass all sources of pollution that are not point sources. Typical examples of point sources include a pipe dumping pollutants from a factory into a stream, or discharges from wastewater treatment plants. Nonpoint source pollution typically consists of runoff from a diffuse area that cannot be traced to any discrete, individual source. Categories of nonpoint sources recognized by EPA include agriculture, forestry, acid mine drainage, roads/highways/bridges, and marinas/boating. *See* EPA, Sources of Nonpoint Source Pollution, https://www.epa.gov/nps/sources-nonpoint-source-pollution (last visited Feb. 14, 2019).

It is not always easy to determine whether a particular source of pollution should be characterized as a point source or a nonpoint source. One problem is that pollution may change in character over time. For example, contaminated runoff that originates as a nonpoint source may later be channeled, thereby adopting many of the characteristics of a point source. As a consequence, there exists considerable overlap and ambiguity between programs designed to control point and nonpoint source pollution. In addition, while many sources of pollution fit easily within the framework of a "discernible, confined, and discrete conveyance," 33 U.S.C. § 1362(14), others do not. For example, concentrated animal feeding operations (CAFOs) are expressly defined as point sources pursuant to § 502(14), but seem to be more in keeping with agricultural practices, which are specifically excluded from the § 502(14) "point source" definition.

The regulation of nonpoint sources presents different challenges from those posed by point sources. Most notably, difficulties in identifying the origin of nonpoint source pollution, coupled with problems associated with measurement and enforcement, have significantly hampered attempts to curtail nonpoint source pollution. Whereas the CWA provides for enforceable effluent limitations for point sources, it addresses pollution from nonpoint sources in different ways. Rather than imposing controls upon outputs, measures designed to curtail nonpoint source pollution typically focus upon the regulation of inputs. A prominent example is the creation of state management programs. *See* 33 U.S.C. § 1329(b)(2)(B). More recently, there have been attempts to address nonpoint source pollution through the creation of marketable permit schemes known as water quality trading schemes.

NOTES AND QUESTIONS

1. **Difficulties in Classification.** The case of *Concerned Area Residents for the Env't v. Southview Farm*, 34 F.3d 114 (2d Cir. 1994), demonstrates the complexities in identifying whether pollution is attributable to point or nonpoint sources. In that case, the court distinguished between pollution generated by the use of vehicles to spread manure on a field, and the contaminated runoff from that field. While the runoff was classified as nonpoint source pollution, because the manure was never "collected" by human activity, the court held that the vehicles used to spread the manure on the fields did constitute point sources. *Id.* at 118.

Sierra Club v. Abston Construction Co., 620 F.2d 41 (5th Cir. 1980), further illustrates these complexities. In that case, the Fifth Circuit was called upon to determine whether a point source existed in the absence of any "direct action" on the part of the defendant, which operated a strip coal mine adjacent to the Black Warrior River, in Tuscaloosa County, Alabama. *Id.* at 45. The question before the court was whether overflow from the mine's sediment basin, following heavy rainfall events, as well as the erosion of piles of discarded materials, constituted point sources for the purpose of § 502(14). A witness for the mine operator testified that in some areas, drainage basins were constructed along a naturally occurring drainage course and that, following a precipitation event, "water and small amounts of sediment would drain through the sediment basin outflow." *Id.* at 43. Finding that each source constituted a point source, the court stated that

> [n]othing in the [CWA] relieves miners from liability simply because the operators did not actually construct those conveyances, so long as they are reasonably likely to be the means by which pollutants are ultimately deposited into a navigable body of water. Conveyances of pollution formed either as a result of natural erosion or by material means, and which constitute a component of a mine drainage system, may fit the statutory definition and thereby subject the operators to liability under the Act.

Id. In reaching this conclusion, however, the court did note that "[s]imple erosion over the material surface, resulting in the discharge of water and other materials into navigable waters, does not constitute a point source discharge." *Id.* at 44–45.

The following are examples of cases in which courts have classified sources of pollution as "point sources" under the CWA: *Nw. Envtl. Def. Ctr. v. Brown*, 640 F.3d 1063 (9th Cir. 2011) (stormwater runoff from logging roads and adjacent ditches, channels, and culverts); *Parker v. Scrap Metal Processors, Inc.*, 386 F.3d 993 (11th Cir. 2004) (piles of debris); *Carr v. Alta Verde Indus., Inc.*, 931 F.2d 1055 (5th Cir. 1991) (cattle feedlot); *Nat'l Wildlife Fed'n v. Gorsuch*, 693 F.2d 156 (D.C. Cir. 1982) (pipes or spillways connecting a reservoir through dam to a downstream river); *Sierra Club v. Abston Const. Co.*, 620 F.2d 41 (5th Cir. 1980) (mining spoil piles); *N.C. Shellfish Growers Ass'n v. Holly Ridge Assocs.*, 278 F. Supp. 2d 654 (E.D.N.C. 2003) (ditches dug by landowner collecting and channeling storm water runoff); *PIRG v. Atl. Salmon of Me.*, 215 F. Supp. 2d 239 (D. Me. 2002) (salmon farm's offshore net pens).

Conversely, the following are examples of nonpoint source pollution, explicitly recognized by the CWA: agricultural and silvicultural activities, including runoff from fields and crop and forest lands, § 304(f)(A); mining activities, including runoff and siltation from new, currently operating, and abandoned surface and underground mines, § 304(f)(B); all construction activity, including runoff from the facilities resulting from such construction, § 304(f)(C); the disposal of pollutants in wells or in subsurface excavations, § 304(f)(D); salt water intrusion resulting from reductions of fresh water flow from any cause, including extraction of ground water, irrigation, obstruction, and diversion, § 304(f)(E); and changes in the movement, flow, or circulation of dams, levees, channels, causeways, or flow diversion facilities, § 304(f)(F).

2. Direct v. Indirect Discharge of Pollutants. In order for a facility to qualify as a point source of pollution, must it discharge pollutants directly into navigable waters? Several cases have held that this is not required. For example, a plant that sent its wastewater to a publicly-owned treatment works (POTW) for treatment before it was discharged into a river, nevertheless qualified as a point source and was required to comply with CWA requirements. *RSR Corp. v. Browner*, 924 F. Supp. 504 (S.D.N.Y. 1996).

3. Groundwater Discharges. Two federal circuit courts have held that pollutants discharged by a point source were subject to the point source provisions of the CWA, where the discharges were to groundwater and the pollutants traveled through the groundwater to a navigable water. In *Upstate Forever v. Kinder Morgan Energy Partners, L.P.*, 887 F.3d 637 (4th Cir. 2018), the Fourth Circuit held that an energy company, whose underground pipeline burst, spilling oil, had violated the point source discharge provisions of the CWA. Oil from the pipeline traveled through groundwater and seeped into a nearby surface waters. In *Hawai'i Wildlife Fund v. County of Maui*, 881 F.3d 754 (9th Cir. 2018), the Ninth Circuit held that discharges from an underground injection well required a NPDES permit when the pollutants from those discharges traveled through groundwater and were released to the Pacific Ocean. *But see Kentucky Waterways Alliance v. Kentucky Utilities Co.*, 905 F.3d 925, 933 (6th Cir. 2018) (disagreeing with *Upstate Forever* and *Hawai'i Wildlife Fund*, and holding that there was no violation of the CWA when coal ash from settling ponds was transported to a navigable surface water via groundwater). At the time of publication, the Supreme Court had granted certiorari in *Hawai'i Wildlife Fund*, to consider whether the CWA requires a permit when pollutants are discharged from a point source but are convenyed to navigable waters by a nonpoint source. *Cty. of Maui v. Hawaii Wildlife Fund*, No. 18-260, 2019 WL 659786, at *1 (U.S. Feb. 19, 2019).

4.   The Stream Protection Rule. The Surface Mining Control and Reclamation Act (SMCRA) was passed in 1977 to provide for comprehensive regulation of coal mining operations. P.L. 95–87 (Aug. 3, 1977); 30 U.S.C. § 1201, *et seq.* The Act set out minimum performance standards for environmental protection and public health and safety at coal mining and reclamation sites and created the Office of Surface Mining Reclamation and Enforcement (OSM), which was empowered to promulgate regulations implementing and enforcing the Act. *See* 30 U.S.C. §§ 1211, 1251. Stream protection was specifically identified as a fundamental purpose of the Act. 30 U.S.C. § 1201(c).

In 2016, OSM finalized a rule to update stream protection requirements, and generally update the regulations under SMCRA. The 2016 rule would have replaced a 1983 rule, which was the last rule left in place after a long series of litigation over proposed updates. *See* 80 Fed. Reg. 44,435, 44,447–51 (2015). The final rule altered permitting requirements, established data collection protocols, and updated restoration standards and fish and wildlife protections. In addition, the rule prohibited mining through intermittent or perennial streams unless the permit applicant demonstrated that the stream could be restored to its approximate pre-mining condition, and required that the permittee establish a 100-foot-wide riparian corridor on each side of every stream following the completion of mining activities. *See* Stream Protection Rule, 81 Fed. Reg. 93,065, 93,068–69 (2016).

The final Stream Protection Rule faced stiff opposition by regulated industry. The House and Senate, using the Congressional Review Act (CRA), 5 U.S.C. §§ 801–08, passed a joint resolution repealing the final rule, which was signed by the President on February 23, 2017. The CRA allows Congress to use an expedited process to repeal agency rules before they go into effect and prevents the agency from promulgating a substantially similar rule unless there has been a change in federal law. *See* Paul J. Larkin, Jr., *Reawakening the Congressional Review Act*, 41 HARV. J.L. & PUB. POL'Y 187 (2018). This was only the second time in history that the CRA had been used to repeal a rule. Since the 2016 Stream Protection Rule was repealed, the regulations revert to the 1983 rule. *See* Stephen Lee, *Trump Repeals Stream Protection Rule*, BNA ENV'T REP., Feb. 24, 2017.

5.   The Water Transfer Rule and the Unitary Water Theory. Should all the navigable waters of the United States be considered a single, unitary body of water, such that the "discharge of a pollutant" is considered to refer only to the initial introduction of the pollutant into a body of water and not to the subsequent transfer of the now polluted water into another body of water? This question has sparked considerable debate. Prior to 2008 this narrow conception of "discharge of a pollutant" was advanced by the EPA in several memorandums and guidelines. However, when these informal policies were challenged, courts did not grant them *Chevron* deference and they were consistently struck down as contrary to the goals of the CWA. *See Catskill Mountains Chapter of Trout Unlimited, Inc. v. City of New York (Catskills II)*, 451 F.3d 77, 81–82 (2d Cir. 2006); *Catskill Mountains Chapter of Trout Unlimited, Inc. v. City of New York (Catskills I)*, 273 F.3d 481, 492 (2d Cir. 2001).

In 2008 the EPA issued a final rule, again interpreting "discharge of a pollutant" in conformity with the unitary water theory, exempting "discharges from water transfer" from NPDES permitting requirements. 40 C.F.R. § 122.3(i). The rule was upheld by the Eleventh Circuit in *Friends of the Everglades v. South Florida Water Management District*, 570 F.3d 1210 (11th Cir. 2009), *cert. denied*, 562 U.S. 1082 (2010). The court applied *Chevron* deference and stated that while it "might agree with the Friends of the Everglades that the unitary waters theory does not comport with the broad, general goals of the [CWA] . . . there are other provisions of the [CWA] that [also] do not comport with its broad purpose of restoring and maintaining the chemical, physical and biological integrity of the Nation's waters." *Id.* at 1226. *See also Catskill Mountains Chapter of Trout Unlimited, Inc. v. EPA (Catskills III)*, 846 F.3d 492 (2d Cir. 2017) (upholding rule), *cert. denied*, 138 S. Ct. 1164–65 (2018).

The rule has far reaching effects, especially in western states, but also throughout the country. Thousands of water transfers, through tunnels, channels, or other means, are routinely conducted by federal, state, and local agencies for such purposes as providing public water supply, irrigation, power generation, flood control, and environmental restoration. If the unitary water theory is discarded and "discharge of a pollutant" is defined broadly to include all of these transfers the relevant authorities will need to obtain many thousands of additional NPDES permits. What should the rule regarding water transfers be?

A. MANAGEMENT PROGRAMS

The earliest approach to addressing pollution from nonpoint sources, contained in § 208, requires the identification of areas with substantial water quality control problems and the creation of "Areawide Waste Treatment" plans. *See* 33 U.S.C. § 1288. These plans, adopted by the states, must contain a comprehensive program for the treatment of wastewater and for controlling water pollution from all point and nonpoint sources. *Id.* Each plan must identify treatment works necessary to meet the anticipated municipal and industrial waste treatment needs of the area over a twenty-year period. *Id.*

The CWA was later amended to include another section dealing with nonpoint sources of pollution. Section 319 lays out the requirements for state management programs, which must be approved by EPA, like SIPs under the CAA. *See* 33 U.S.C. § 1329(b)(1). One of the major features of state management programs is the requirement for the development of "best management practices" (BMPs) designed to reduce the amount of pollution from the various nonpoint sources. 33 U.S.C. § 1329(b)(2)(B). Typically, BMPs are applied to agricultural lands or other sources of pollution for which measuring the effluent is impractical. In this context, these plans might involve regulating the application of pesticides or fertilizer to ensure that farmers are not using excessive quantities, or they may require certain land use controls that will lessen the amount of pollutants that escape, particularly in times of heavy rain. As an incentive for states to adopt management programs, EPA provides funding of up to 60 percent to those programs that demonstrate the attainment of annual milestones. EPA, NATIONAL NONPOINT SOURCE PROGRAM (2016).

These programs have failed to significantly curb the level of nonpoint source pollution as a consequence of the inherent difficulties in measuring nonpoint source pollution and in ensuring compliance with the various regimes.

NOTES AND QUESTIONS

1.   **Enforcement of State Management Programs.** Consider what additional challenges the enforcement of standards for nonpoint sources pose beyond the enforcement of standards for point sources. What difficulties can you anticipate in identifying noncompliance with a state management program? Using the example of contaminated agricultural runoff attributable to the use of a particular pesticide, consider how variables such as wind, rain, and different farming practices may complicate detection? Why are these variables not as significant in the detection of noncompliance with point source standards? What other variables may complicate the detection of nonpoint source pollution?

2.   **Measurement of Inputs.** Rather than focusing on the measurement of outputs, could noncompliance with nonpoint source standards be addressed by focusing upon inputs? Using the example of contaminated agricultural runoff attributable to pesticides, how could an enforcement regime be constructed on these terms? Might such a scheme be preferable?

3.   **Failure of State Management Programs.** If the regulation of inputs, as opposed to outputs, could solve some of the problems associated with detecting noncompliance, what might explain the relative lack of success of state management programs in curbing the level of nonpoint source pollution? What disincentives may states face in enforcing the terms of state management programs?

4.   **EPA Approval of State Management Programs.** State management programs are required under 33 U.S.C. § 1329(a)(1) to identify navigable waters within the state that "without additional action to control nonpoint sources of pollution, cannot reasonably be expected to attain or maintain applicable water quality standards;" to "identify those categories and subcategories of nonpoint sources" that contribute to nonattainment; to "describe[ ] the process . . . for identifying best management practices and measures which will be undertaken to reduce pollutant loadings resulting from each category, subcategory, or particular nonpoint source;" and to

"identif[y] and describ[e] State and local programs for controlling pollution added from nonpoint sources to . . . navigable waters." *Id.* § 1329(a)(1)(A)–(D).

Further statutorily required components of state management programs include "identification of the best management practices and measures" to be undertaken; "identification of programs . . . to achieve implementation of the best management practices;" "a schedule containing annual milestones . . . [that] shall provide for utilization of the best management practices at the earliest practicable date;" and identification of "[s]ources of Federal and other assistance and funding." *Id.* § 1329(b)(2)(A)–(F).

The EPA expanded upon these statutory requirements in a guidance document that enumerates the "key elements" that "characterize an effective and dynamic State nonpoint source program." EPA, NONPOINT SOURCE PROGRAM AND GRANTS GUIDELINES FOR STATES AND TERRITORIES, at app. A (2013). The "key elements" include: (1) developing "explicit short- and long-term goals, objectives and strategies to protect surface and groundwater;" (2) strengthening "working partnerships" with "appropriate State, interstate, Tribal, regional and local entities . . . , private sector groups, citizens groups, and Federal agencies;" (3) balancing statewide nonpoint source programs with "on-the-ground management of individual watersheds;" (4) preventing threats to water quality from developing in the first place; (5) conducting regular, detailed assessments to determine impaired and at risk bodies of water; (6) including "flexible, targeted, and iterative approaches to achieve and maintain beneficial uses of water as expeditiously as practicable" including "[a] mix of water quality-based and/or technology-based programs" and "[a] mix of regulatory, non-regulatory, financial and technical assistance;" (7) identifying federal lands and activities that are "not managed consistently" with the state plan and seeking EPA assistance to resolve these issues; (8) managing and implementing state programs "efficiently and effectively, including necessary financial management;" (9) reviewing and revising the management program at least every five years using "environmental and functional measures of success." *Id.*

Do these "key elements," in conjunction with the statutory requirements, provide sufficient guidance to states in the process of designing and implementing state management programs to address nonpoint source pollution? What other requirements or considerations might make state management programs more effective? Rather than serving as guidance to states, should these "key elements" be made mandatory for EPA approval of state plans under 33 U.S.C. § 1329? How else might state management programs be made more effective in addressing nonpoint source pollution?

5. **State Management Programs and SIPs.** In many respects, state management programs are the equivalent of SIPs under the CAA. Section 110 of the CAA directs each state to prepare a plan for the "implementation, maintenance, and enforcement" of the NAAQS set by EPA. 42 U.S.C. § 7410(a)(1). EPA has power to either approve or disapprove the SIPs formulated by the states. 42 U.S.C. § 7410. If approved, both the state and

EPA are entitled to enforce the provisions of the SIP. In what further ways are SIPs and state management programs similar? In what ways do they differ?

B. WATER QUALITY TRADING SCHEMES

Marketable permit schemes, in the form of water quality trading schemes, constitute an alternative approach to the control of nonpoint source pollution. Given the disparity between the stringency of the controls applicable to point sources and nonpoint sources of pollution, market-based solutions hold obvious appeal. While the CWA does not specifically prescribe the adoption of market-based mechanisms in the furtherance of its objectives, EPA actively encourages states to adopt water quality trading schemes to achieve water quality improvements at reduced cost. EPA, WATER QUALITY TRADING POLICY 2 (2003).

A marketable permit scheme could take one of two forms. First, in keeping with the highly successful SO_2 trading program under the CAA, a cap-and-trade system could be created. Under a cap-and-trade regime, permits totaling allowable discharges, as determined by EPA, would be distributed among existing polluters, either by way of auction, lottery, or by grandfathering existing sources. Assuming perfect market conditions, trading among sources would lead to the most efficient allocation of permits. Second, a credit trading program could be established, under which market participants generate credits by polluting at levels below a predetermined legal limit. Credits generated in this manner, usually expressed in pounds of pollutant per day, month or year, could then be traded among market participants. Of the two options, the majority of water quality trading markets established to date have adopted the credit trading model. *See* Lynda Hall, *Water Quality Trading: Where Do We Go from Here?*, 20 NAT. RESOURCES & ENV'T. 38, 38 (2005).

Facilitating trades between nonpoint sources and point sources gives rise to a significant challenge in the design of water quality trading schemes. An integrated approach has the potential for great efficiency. Because nonpoint sources are presently regulated less stringently than point sources, they face a lower marginal cost in reducing a given level of effluent. This disparity gives rise to the potential for trade between point and nonpoint sources—point sources will seek to ease their regulatory burden by purchasing credits generated by nonpoint sources. *See* EPA, WATER QUALITY TRADING ASSESSMENT HANDBOOK: CAN WATER QUALITY TRADING ADVANCE YOUR WATERSHED GOALS? (2004). EPA has estimated that annual savings could amount to as much as $900 million. *See* EPA, WATER QUALITY TRADING POLICY (2003). This assessment appears conservative, in light of the findings of a finance panel examining the potential for trade in the Chesapeake Bay region, that "[water quality trading programs] . . . could save an estimated $1 billion in wastewater treatment costs" in that region alone. CHESAPEAKE BAY BLUE RIBBON FINANCE PANEL, SAVING A NATIONAL TREASURE: FINANCING THE

CLEANUP OF THE CHESAPEAKE BAY 30 (2004). The now familiar problems of measurement and detection of nonpoint source pollution constitute significant hurdles in establishing a functional market encompassing both point and nonpoint sources.

In order for a market to operate effectively, a common unit of currency must be established—trades must not involve the exchange of apples for oranges. Nonpoint source pollution takes a number of different forms, including nutrients, phosphates, and other chemical compounds. As a general rule, EPA favors markets trading in only one type of pollutant. *See* EPA, Water Quality Trading Policy, 68 Fed. Reg. 1608 (2003). As an alternative, marketable permits could conceivably be designed so that polluters could transact in units of environmental degradation, so that the relative harms of various types of pollutants could be measured in one common metric. (Markets trading in units of environmental degradation are discussed in Chapter III). Reducing upstream nutrient levels to offset a downstream biochemical oxygen demand or to improve a depressed in-stream dissolved oxygen level are examples of cross-pollutant trading. *See id.* Such schemes require the calculation of defined translation ratios, based upon the relative impact of each pollutant on the environment. Because these calculations pose higher level[s] of risk, EPA demands that they "receive a higher level of scrutiny" and be evaluated on a case-by-case basis. *See id.*

Participation in a water quality trading scheme does not take the place of any of the other requirements of the Act. For example, "sources and activities that are required to obtain a [NPDES permit] must do so to participate in a trade or trading program." *Id.* Permits may make provision for trading either by way of general condition (authorizing trading and describing appropriate conditions and restrictions) or by specifying variable permit limits that may be adjusted up or down based on the quantity of credits generated or used. *See id.*

The adoption of water quality trading schemes has increased markedly in recent years. According to the EPA, as of 2017, 21 states have regulations or policies in place to facilitate water quality trading. EPA, Water Quality Trading, https://www.epa.gov/npdes/water-quality-trading (last visited Aug. 22, 2018). Credits for temperature, nutrients, sediment and BOD are being traded. *Id.* In 2014, according to a GAO report, there were 19 trading programs across 11 states. GAO, WATER POLLUTION, SOME STATES HAVE TRADING PROGRAMS TO HELP ADDRESS NUTRIENT POLLUTION, BUT USE HAS BEEN LIMITED 37 (Oct. 2017).

EPA has attempted to facilitate this expansion by issuing the Water Quality Trading Policy in 2003 and Water Quality Trading Assessment Handbook in 2004. Recognizing that "progress made towards restoring and maintaining the chemical, physical, and biological integrity of the nation's waters under the 1972 [CWA] and its [NPDES] permits has been incomplete," EPA "specifically endorses the use of 'water quality trading' for certain pollutants where it can help achieve [CWA] goals." *See* EPA,

WATER QUALITY TRADING ASSESSMENT HANDBOOK, *supra*; *see also* EPA, WATER QUALITY TRADING TOOLKIT FOR PERMIT WRITERS (updated June, 2009). In addition, a number of states (including Colorado, Idaho, Maryland, Michigan, Oregon, Pennsylvania, Virginia, West Virginia, and Wisconsin) have adopted trading policy frameworks, to guide the development of marketable permit schemes within multiple watersheds. Policies differ among states with respect to the types of pollution covered and the nature of the trading regime adopted. While most of the early initiatives have involved point-to-point trading, more recent schemes have increasingly incorporated point-to-nonpoint trading. Most of these trades occurred within a single facility, but one of the goals (and challenges) of the program is to extend more of the point-to-nonpoint trades to the watershed scale. *See* Environmental Trading Network, State Programs, http://www.envtn.org/water-quality-trading/state-programs (last visited Aug. 27, 2018).

There has not been a comprehensive study of potential water quality trading cost savings since the 2003 EPA Policy was released. However, a 2008 EPA study estimated that the Long Island Sound Nitrogen Credit Trading program resulted in a capital cost savings of $200 million, while nutrient credit trading in the Great Miami River Basin would save $385 million. EPA, WATER QUALITY TRADING EVALUATION, FINAL REPORT 3–14 (2008); *see also* EPA and USDA Pledge Actions to Support America's Growing Water Quality Trading Markets, EPA Blog (Aug. 1, 2016), https://blog.epa.gov/blog/2016/08/epa-and-usda-pledge-actions-to-support-americas-growing-water-quality-trading-markets/.

NOTES AND QUESTIONS

1.   **Cap-and-Trade v. Credit Trading.** As discussed above, markets can either be framed around a cap-and-trade model or a credit trading model. Under what conditions would each of the systems produce the same outcomes? How likely are these conditions? Which alternative should be preferred? *See* Donald Dewees, *Emissions Trading: ERCs or Allowances?*, 77 LAND ECON. 513, 513–26 (2001).

2.   **Efficiency Gains.** Why are there considerable efficiency gains associated with point-to-nonpoint trading? What are the risks in establishing a market on these terms? In what way could measurement problems result in leakage from the market? Could point-to-nonpoint trades imperil the advances previously secured through the implementation of the CWA effluent limitations?

3.   **Unit of Trade.** Why does EPA favor markets trading in single pollutants? What are the drawbacks in creating markets on these terms? Should potential efficiency gains be sacrificed in the face of the uncertainty inherent in calculating translation ratios among different pollutants?

4.   **Peculiarities of Water Quality Trading Schemes.** What challenges do water quality trading schemes pose that other forms of marketable permit schemes (such as the SO_2 trading scheme discussed in Chapter V) do not?

What is the consequence of many pollutants being threshold pollutants? How would this feature influence the structure of the scheme, including the unit of trade? What should determine the scope of the market? Are water quality trading schemes likely to give rise to hot spots? What are their likely implications for environmental justice?

5.   Markets to Address Urban Nonpoint Source Pollution. After pollution from agricultural activities, contaminated runoff from urban land uses constitutes one of the leading sources of nonpoint source pollution. *See* EPA, NATIONAL WATER QUALITY INVENTORY REPORT: REPORT TO CONGRESS 10, 17, 18 (2002). Would it be possible to create a water quality trading scheme to address contaminated urban runoff? What form would this scheme take? How would it differ from marketable permit schemes designed for areas in which the principal form of nonpoint source pollution is attributable to agricultural activities?

6.   Strange Bedfellows. Consider the incentives that point sources, such as individual industrial polluters, have to participate in water quality trading schemes. How do these incentives differ from those attributable to nonpoint sources, such as farmers, municipalities, and small businesses? What are the likely costs and benefits faced by point and nonpoint sources upon entering a marketable permit scheme? Consider also the incentives for non-market participants, such as environmental advocacy groups and litigation attorneys, to support the creation of water quality trading schemes. Are these incentives likely to result in "strange bedfellows"? For a discussion of these issues, see Darin Lowder, *Strange Watershed Bedfellows? Will the EPA Water Quality Trading Policy Encourage Unlikely Clean Water Alliances?*, 13 GEO. MASON L. REV. 411 (2005).

6. WATER QUALITY STANDARDS

While national standards for air quality are the cornerstone of the CAA, effluent limitations for point sources are the cornerstone of the CWA. As indicated in section 1, prior to the passage of the CWA in 1972, however, water quality standards, similar in operation to the NAAQS, constituted the principal regulatory response to national watercourse pollution (pursuant to the Water Quality Act of 1965, Pub.L. No. 89–234, 79 Stat. 903). The regime, under which water quality standards were set by individual states and enforced by the federal government, ultimately proved ineffective as water quality continued to decline throughout the late 1960s. Rather than jettison the regime entirely, the authors of the CWA retained water quality standards as a safety net to the NPDES permit system, to be pursued as a secondary priority in the event that effluent limitations failed to achieve the objectives of the Act. For a discussion of the circumstances leading to the retention of water quality standards within the CWA, see OLIVER HOUCK, THE CLEAN WATER ACT TMDL PROGRAM: LAW, POLICY, AND IMPLEMENTATION 24 (1999). In recent years, the prominence of water quality standards has risen. They have become the principal means of obtaining further improvements in the quality of national watercourses, following the successful implementation of the BPT and BAT effluent standards. Throughout the mid-to-latter parts of the 1980s, a spate of citizen suits under the CWA aimed at forcing states and EPA to adopt water quality standards, served to reinvigorate the scheme, which had lain largely dormant up until that time. *See id.*

Water quality standards are composed of two principal components: the designated uses of the water body and the water quality criteria necessary to support those uses. 33 U.S.C. § 1313(c)(2)(A). The goals of the CWA indicate that, "wherever attainable, . . . water quality [should] provide[ ] for the protection and propagation of fish, shellfish, and wildlife and provide[ ] for recreation in and on the water" (the so called "fishable/swimmable" standard). 33 U.S.C. § 1251(a)(2). Section 303, however, contemplates that uses other than fishable/swimmable may be designated—including agricultural and industrial uses. 33 U.S.C. § 1313(c)(2)(A). Additionally, states are required to adopt an antidegradation policy to protect existing uses and high quality waters. 33 U.S.C. § 1313(d)(4)(B). For a description of the statutory requirements for water quality standards, see *NRDC v. EPA*, 16 F.3d 1395, 1399–1400 (4th Cir. 1993).

The major statutory provision specifying the role of water quality standards is § 303. 33 U.S.C. § 1313. Section 303(a)(3)(A) requires states to adopt water quality standards for all waters within their jurisdiction and to submit them to EPA for approval. 33 U.S.C. § 1313(a)(3)(A). EPA has the authority to reject those standards if they are inconsistent with the applicable requirements of the Act. 33 U.S.C. § 1313(a)(3)(C). If a state fails to submit its own standards to EPA for approval, EPA may then issue water quality standards for that state. 33 U.S.C. § 1313(b)(1)(A). Thus, while EPA and the states both play a role, the primary responsibility falls on the states to set the water quality standards. Section 302 of the CWA requires the establishment of effluent limitations sufficient to meet state water quality standards in circumstances where the technology-based BAT limitations are unable to achieve these standards. *See* 33 U.S.C. § 1312(a).

EPA has promulgated detailed regulations to guide the process of setting water quality standards and to clarify the roles of the state and federal governments. 40 C.F.R. § 131.1–.22 (WQS Regulations). The WQS Regulations, discussed in the sections that follow, were first adopted in 1975 and most recently updated in 2015. *See* EPA, WATER QUALITY STANDARDS REGULATORY REVISIONS FINAL RULE FACT SHEET (2015).

A. DESIGNATED USES, WATER QUALITY CRITERIA, AND ANTIDEGRADATION

i.   DESIGNATED USES

In designating a use for a particular body of water, a state must first determine what use is attainable for that body of water. The WQS Regulations provide that "[t]he classification of the waters of the State must take into consideration the use and value of water for public water supplies, protection and propagation of fish, shellfish and wildlife, recreation in and on the water, agricultural, industrial, and other purposes including navigation." 40 C.F.R. § 131.10(a). As a minimum, a use is deemed attainable if it can be achieved by the imposition of the CWA's technology-based effluent limitations for point sources or cost-effective and reasonable BMPs for nonpoint source control. 40 C.F.R. § 131.10(d). Further, in designating uses for a water body, a state must take into consideration the water quality standards of downstream waters and ensure that "its water quality standards provide for the attainment and maintenance of the water quality standards of downstream waters." 40 C.F.R. § 131.10(b).

In order to designate a use lower than fishable/swimmable, a state must demonstrate that:

(1) Naturally occurring pollutant concentrations prevent the attainment of the use; or

(2) Natural, ephemeral, intermittent or low flow conditions or water levels prevent the attainment of the use, unless these conditions may be compensated for by the discharge of sufficient volume of effluent discharges without violating State water conservation requirements to enable uses to be met; or

(3) Human caused conditions or sources of pollution prevent the attainment of the use and cannot be remedied or would cause more environmental damage to correct than to leave in place; or

(4) Dams, diversions or other types of hydrologic modifications preclude the attainment of the use, and it is not feasible to restore the water body to its original condition or to operate such modification in a way that would result in the attainment of the use; or

(5) Physical conditions related to the natural features of the water body, such as the lack of a proper substrate, cover, flow, depth, pools, riffles, and the like, unrelated to water quality, preclude attainment of aquatic life protection uses; or

    (6)   Controls more stringent than those required by sections 301(b) and 306 of the Act would result in substantial and widespread economic and social impact.

40 C.F.R. § 131.10(g). In evaluating these factors, a state must undertake a use attainability analysis (UAA)—"a structured scientific assessment of the factors affecting the attainment of the use which may include physical, chemical, biological, and economic factors as described in § 131.10(g)." 40 C.F.R. § 131.10(j). Conversely, a UAA is not required in circumstances where a state seeks to designate a body of water as being fishable/swimmable, consistent with § 102(a) of the CWA. 40 C.F.R. § 131.10(k).

The WQS Regulations prohibit certain uses, regardless of the outcome of UAA. For instance, states may not designate a body of water for use in waste disposal. 40 C.F.R. § 131.10(a). More importantly, as a result of the antidegradation requirement, a state may not designate a use for a body of water below its existing use. 40 C.F.R. § 131.10(i). An existing use is one that is "actually attained in [a] water body . . . whether or not [it is] included in the water quality standards." 40 C.F.R. § 131.3(e). A state may, however, adopt seasonal uses as an alternative to periodically reclassifying a water body. 40 C.F.R. § 131. 10(f).

The following case examines the extent to which the CWA gives rise to a "rebuttable presumption" in favor of the designation of fishable/swimmable uses.

Idaho Mining Association, Inc. v. Browner

90 F. Supp. 2d 1078 (D. Idaho. 2000).

■ WILLIAMS, CHIEF MAGISTRATE JUDGE:

[In this case, EPA had promulgated revised water quality standards for three bodies of water in Idaho, following the state's failure to promulgate standards which complied with the WQS Regulations. An association of mining interests challenged the new water quality standards and EPA's use of a rebuttable presumption in favor of fishable/swimmable uses.]

. . . The CWA does not impose upon states the obligation to designate any particular use(s) for water bodies. At a minimum, however, states must revise their water quality standards to reflect existing uses, i.e. those uses which are actually being attained. 40 C.F.R. § 131.10(i); 40 C.F.R. § 131.10(e). Furthermore, fishable/swimmable uses are favored. Section 101(a)(2), 33 U.S.C. § 1251(a)(2). Thus, where a state fails to designate a water body for fishable/swimmable uses, the state must conduct a [UAA] in accordance with the provisions of the CWA. 40 C.F.R. § 131.10(j)(1). Conversely, a UAA is not required whenever fishable/swimmable uses are designated. 40 C.F.R. § 131.10(k). . . .

The regulatory provisions upon which the EPA relies are codified at 40 C.F.R. §§ 131.10(j) and (k). Specifically, § 131.10(j) provides that a state must conduct a use attainability analysis anytime the state fails to designate a water body for fishable/swimmable uses. Section 131.10(k), on the other hand, provides that a state is not required to conduct a use attainability analysis whenever the state designates fishable/swimmable uses. According to the EPA, the net effect of these two provisions is to require that water quality standards provide for fishable/swimmable uses unless those uses have been shown by a use attainability analysis to be unattainable. . . .

Despite the foregoing, Plaintiff contends that the EPA's "presumptive use" interpretation is contrary to its own regulations. In particular, Plaintiff points to 40 C.F.R. § 131.10(d), a water quality standards regulation which it contends explicitly establishes a presumption regarding use attainability. That regulation states:

> At a minimum, uses are deemed attainable if they can be achieved by the imposition of effluent limits required under §§ 301(b) and 306 of the Act and cost effective and reasonable best management practices for nonpoint source control.

Id. Plaintiff argues that this regulation explicitly creates a presumption that uses are not attainable unless they can be achieved by the imposition of technology-based point source controls and best management practices for nonpoint source controls. Thus, under Plaintiff's interpretation, the EPA would have been required to find that the imposition of point source and nonpoint source pollution controls on the affected waters would result in the attainment of fishable/swimmable uses before it actually established fishable/swimmable use designations for those waters. . . . Unfortunately, Plaintiff's argument not only misconstrues the applicability of 40 C.F.R. § 131.10(d), but it also completely ignores other pertinent water quality standards regulations.

Although not entirely clear on its face, § 131.10(d) is not a generally applicable provision defining the requirements of attainability. Rather, it is a provision which applies in the context of a UAA to prohibit states from downgrading existing designated uses when those uses can be attained by imposing pollution controls in the form of effluent limits for point sources and cost-effective and reasonable best management practices for nonpoint sources. *See* 47 Fed.Reg. 49234, 49236 (Oct. 29, 1982). Thus, while § 131.10(d) establishes the parameters by which states are allowed to make unattainability determinations, it does not impose upon states the obligation to conduct a UAA every time the state establishes a new beneficial use designation. On the contrary, 40 C.F.R. § 131.10(k) expressly provides that a state is not required to conduct a UAA so long as the state adopts water quality standards that protect fishable/swimmable uses in and on the water. This is a point even Plaintiff concedes.

While Plaintiff expressly acknowledges that subsection (k) of 40 C.F.R. § 131.10 authorizes states to establish fishable/swimmable use designations without performing a UAA, it nevertheless argues that the EPA does not have that same authority. However, as both Defendants and the Intervenors point out, this argument carries little force. Because Idaho failed to correct the deficiencies in its 1994 water quality standards, the EPA was under a mandatory duty pursuant to § 303(c) of the CWA to promptly adopt replacement standards for those standards which it had disapproved. Section 303(c)(4)(A); 33 U.S.C. § 1313(c)(4)(A); 40 C.F.R. § 131.22(a). *See also, Arkansas v. Oklahoma*, 503 U.S. 91, 101 (1992); *Idaho Conservation League, Inc. v. Russell*, 946 F.2d 717, 720 (9th Cir.1991); *ICL v. Browner*, 968 F. Supp. 546, 549 (W.D. Wash. 1997). In doing so, the EPA was "subject to the same policies, procedures, analyses, and public participation requirements established for States in [the WQS Regulations]." 40 C.F.R. § 131.22(c). Thus, despite Plaintiff's assertions to the contrary, § 131.10(k) authorized the EPA to establish aquatic life uses for the affected waters without performing a UAA. . . .

Based upon the foregoing, the Court concludes that the EPA permissibly relied upon a rebuttable presumption of fishable/swimmable use attainability in promulgating the challenged rule. The use of the rebuttable presumption in favor of fishable/swimmable uses was not a new and unauthorized interpretation of the CWA but was instead a reasonable interpretation of the EPA's existing regulations at 40 C.F.R. § 131.10(j) and (k). Furthermore, although the CWA does not require fishable/swimmable use designations for all waters of the United States, the EPA clearly acted within the bounds of its statutory authority in creating the presumption to further the mandatory goals and purposes of the Act. Thus, the Court finds that the actions of the EPA in relying on the rebuttable presumption in this case were neither arbitrary and capricious nor an abuse of discretion.

NOTES AND QUESTIONS

1.   **EPA Determination of Uses.** EPA may promulgate water quality standards only in limited circumstances. It may act only when: (1) it determines that a state's proposed new or revised standard does not comply with the CWA requirements and the state refuses to accept EPA-proposed revisions to the standard (as in *Idaho Mining*); or (2) a state does not act to promulgate or update a standard but, in EPA's view, a new or revised standard is necessary to meet CWA muster. 33 U.S.C. § 1313(c)(3)–(4).

In a part of the *Idaho Mining* opinion not excerpted above, the court discusses EPA's response after it denied Idaho water quality standards for those waters where the state did not designate fishable/swimmable uses. *Id.* at 1084. EPA gave Idaho the option of either conducting acceptable UAAs showing why fishable/swimmable waters could not be attained or of adopting designated uses that provide for fishable/swimmable waters. *Id.* When the state failed to comply with either of those options, EPA designated fishable/swimmable uses. What might explain Idaho's reticence to act in these circumstances?

2.   Stratification of Uses. The traditional categorizations of designated uses, which revolve around the CWA's fishable/swimmable goals, may be too vague. The National Academy of Sciences recommends that the states develop more specific categorizations of designated uses: "[I]n order for designated uses to reflect the range of scientific information and social desires for water quality, there must be substantial stratification and refinement of designated uses." NATIONAL ACADEMY OF SCIENCES, ASSESSING THE TMDL APPROACH TO WATER QUALITY MANAGEMENT 22 (2001). How could the WQS Regulations deal with this matter?

3.   State Adoption of Lower Use. In the above case, if Idaho had sought to designate a less protective use, such as an agricultural or industrial use, it would have needed to conduct a UAA showing that one of the § 131.10(g) factors prevented attainment of fishable/swimmable waters. Consider the six factors contained within § 131.10(g). How difficult would each be to establish? What types of evidence may be relevant to each factor?

4.   Widespread Economic and Social Interest. Section 131.10(g)(6) of the WQS Regulations provides that a state may remove a designated use that is not an existing use if the state can demonstrate that attaining the designated use is not feasible because "[c]ontrols more stringent than those required by sections 301(b) and 306 of the Act would result in substantial and widespread economic and social impact." How difficult would it be for states to meet this standard? How should "widespread economic and social impact" be measured?

The EPA INTERIM ECONOMIC GUIDANCE FOR WATER QUALITY STANDARDS WORKBOOK (1995) (Workbook), attempts to provide guidance on these questions. In order to establish "substantial and widespread economic and social impact," the Workbook requires that an analysis demonstrate:

- that the polluting entity, whether privately or publicly owned, would face substantial financial impacts due to the costs of the necessary pollution controls, and

- that the affected community will bear significant adverse impacts if the entity is required to meet existing or proposed water quality standards.

Id. at 1–2. To determine whether an impact would be substantial, the Workbook distinguishes between public and private dischargers of pollution:

If the entity is publicly-owned (e.g., a municipal sewage treatment plant), the households in the community will bear the cost either through an increase in user fees, an increase in taxes or a combination of both. The burden to households resulting from total annual pollution control costs must be estimated. In addition, the financial impact analysis must consider the community's ability to obtain financing and the general economic health of the community.

> If the entity is privately-owned (e.g., a manufacturing facility), the analysis should consider factors such as the entity's ability to secure financing and the degree to which it will be able to pass the cost of pollution control on to its customers in the form of higher prices. The financial impact analysis of private-sector entities employs a variety of financial ratios and tests. Some of these ratios and tests include benchmark values to help in the analysis.

Id. at 1–5. The Workbook also provides that reference should also be had to "changes in factors such as median household income, unemployment, and overall net debt as a percent of full market value of taxable property." *Id.* at 1–6.

To determine whether an impact is widespread, it is first necessary to define the geographic area which is affected by the designation. The Workbook notes that the affected area may be a "town, city, region, county or some combination of these geographical units." *Id.* at 1–6.

Does this standard amount to a cost-benefit test? Could a state choose not to remove a designated use in circumstances where the costs to the community exceeded the benefits to the water quality?

5. Inappropriate Use Designations. For many states, faced with the requirement that they specify designated uses in order to receive federal CWA grant funding, the initial process of designating uses in the 1970s was made without adequate data. *See* GAO, WATER QUALITY: IMPROVED EPA GUIDANCE AND SUPPORT CAN HELP STATES DEVELOP STANDARDS THAT BETTER TARGET CLEANUP EFFORTS 26 (2003). For example, Utah admits to having set designated uses for its water bodies in a period of four or five days using best professional judgment rather than data collection and analysis. *Id.* at 26–27. Inappropriate designations persist. In 2003, nearly all U.S. states reported that the designated uses for one or more of their water bodies were either under- or over-inclusive—designated use changes were needed for 1–20 percent of water bodies in 28 states, 21–50 percent of water bodies in 11 states, and for more than 50 percent of water bodies in 5 states. *Id.* Are there plausible solutions to this problem?

6. Race-to-the-Bottom. Why was Congress, in drafting the CWA, not as concerned about a race-to-the-bottom as it was when drafting the CAA? As we have seen in previous sections, the CWA requires all point sources, both existing and new, to meet federal minimum effluent limitations. Why might this feature of the CWA regime largely allay concerns over a potential race-to-the-bottom?

ii. WATER QUALITY CRITERIA

Once states have designated uses for their waters, they must establish the water quality criteria necessary to achieve and maintain those uses. 33 U.S.C. § 1313(c)(2)(A); 40 C.F.R. § 131.11(a). Criteria are defined as "elements of State water quality standards, expressed as constituent concentrations, levels, or narrative statements, representing a quality of water that supports a particular use." 40 C.F.R. § 131.3(b). These criteria may be either numeric, based on EPA guidance issued under § 304(a) of the CWA (or other scientifically defensible methods), or narrative (where it is not possible to specify numeric criteria). 40 C.F.R. § 131.11(b).

Shortly after the passage of the CWA, EPA issued a guidance document, which became known as the "Red Book." *See* EPA, QUALITY CRITERIA FOR WATER (1976). EPA initially established a policy of requiring that states justify their standards whenever they proposed criteria less stringent than those contained in the Red Book.

EPA's current version of water quality criteria guidance is known as the "Gold Book." *See* EPA, QUALITY CRITERIA FOR WATER 1986 (1986). EPA has now abandoned the approach of requiring that state standards follow federal guidance. Instead, EPA looks to whether the state criteria have sound scientific support. *See* 40 C.F.R. § 131.11. Although some environmental groups have sought to compel EPA to conduct more thorough and searching reviews of the criteria component of state water quality standards, EPA has taken a limited approach to its review and approval process. EPA approves those state water quality standards it determines to be scientifically defensible and protective of designated uses. Thus, EPA often does not insist that states set criteria that meet the federal guidance. Courts have deferred to EPA's interpretation of its duty under the CWA. *See, e.g., NRDC v. EPA*, 16 F.3d 1395 (4th Cir. 1993).

NOTES AND QUESTIONS

1.   Numeric and Narrative Criteria. As discussed above, the WQS Regulations allow for either numerical or narrative criteria. The latter are used when the setting of numerical criteria is impractical. A particular body of water may have multiple criteria for different pollutants or for different designated uses; the aggregate criteria must be sufficient to meet the most sensitive use. *See* 40 C.F.R. § 131.11.

Some polluters have challenged narrative criteria as being so vague that they result in a deprivation of due process under the Constitution. For example, the City of Albuquerque challenged the narrative criteria issued by a Native American tribe on this basis. *See City of Albuquerque v. Browner*, 97 F.3d 415, 429 (10th Cir. 1996). The court ultimately upheld criteria prohibiting "objectionable . . . floating materials" or "[materials] impart[ing] unpalatable flavor to fish," on the grounds that administrative procedures were in place through which the City would have notice of the specific enforceable standards that it was required to meet. Environmental groups have also challenged narrative criteria as being inadequate to protect water bodies. *See Florida Wildlife Federation v. Jackson*, 853 F. Supp. 2d 1138, 1157 (N.D. Fla. 2012).

2.   Putting Narrative Criteria into Practice. Because of the ambiguity inherent in narrative criteria, EPA promulgated regulations requiring that permits use one of three mechanisms for translating narrative criteria into numerical effluent limitations for point sources: (1) a calculated numeric water quality criterion derived from such tools as a proposed state numeric criterion or an "explicit state policy or regulation interpreting its narrative water quality criterion"; (2) an EPA approved numeric water quality criterion, to be applied only on a "case-by-case basis" and "supplemented where necessary by other relevant information"; and/or (3) assuming that certain conditions were met, limitations on the discharge of an "indicator parameter," *i.e.*, a different pollutant found in the point source's effluent. 40 C.F.R. § 122.44(d)(1)(vi). These rules were challenged on the grounds that they infringed on the state role in setting water quality standards, but were upheld as a reasonable and practical approach to converting the narrative criteria into specific effluent limitations. *See Am. Paper Inst. v. EPA*, 996 F.2d 346 (D.C. Cir. 1993).

3.   How Far May States Go to Force Technology? Need states have any regard of the limitations of existing technology in setting water quality standards? This question was addressed by the Seventh Circuit in *U.S. Steel Corp. v. Train*, 556 F.2d 822 (7th Cir. 1977). In that case, the owner of a steel works argued that the water quality standards on which certain limitations were based were invalid on the grounds that they were "impossible to achieve with present technology." *Id.* at 838. In rejecting this argument, the court stated:

> It is clear from §§ 301 and 510 of the Act, and the legislative history, that the states are free to force technology. Although the Indiana Board considered technology in setting some of [the] limitations, it was not required to do so. Only the federal effluent limitations must be technology-based, and they represent the minimum level of pollution reduction required by the Act. If the states wish to achieve better water quality, they may, even at the cost of economic and social dislocations caused by plant closings.

Id. at 838. Compare the holding of the Seventh Circuit in *U.S. Steel*, with the holding of the Supreme Court in *Union Electric Co. v. EPA*, 427 U.S. 246 (1976) (concerning the stringency of emissions standards set by states pursuant to SIPs under the CAA).

iii.   ANTIDEGRADATION

The EPA regulations require that states "develop and adopt a statewide antidegradation policy." 40 C.F.R. § 131.12(a). At a minimum, the antidegradation policy and implementation methods must be consistent with the following:

(1)   Existing instream water uses and the level of water quality necessary to protect the existing uses shall be maintained and protected.

(2)   Where the quality of the waters exceed levels necessary to support propagation of fish, shellfish, and wildlife and recreation in and on the water, that quality shall be maintained and protected unless the State finds, after full satisfaction of the intergovernmental coordination and

public participation provisions of the State's continuing planning process, that allowing lower water quality is necessary to accommodate important economic or social development in the area in which the waters are located. In allowing such degradation or lower water quality, the State shall assure water quality adequate to protect existing uses fully. Further, the State shall assure that there shall be achieved the highest statutory and regulatory requirements for all new and existing point sources and all cost-effective and reasonable best management practices for nonpoint source control.

(3) Where high quality waters constitute an outstanding National resource, such as waters of National and State parks and wildlife refuges and waters of exceptional recreational or ecological significance, that water quality shall be maintained and protected. . . .

Id. These three provisions establish what are commonly referred to as the three "tiers" of antidegradation protection. *See Am. Wildlands v. Browner*, 260 F.3d 1192, 1194 (10th Cir. 2001). Tier 1 applies to all waters, and requires that existing water uses be protected. 40 C.F.R. § 131.12(a)(1). Tier 2 applies to high quality waters, defined as waters "[w]here the quality of the waters exceed levels necessary to support propagation of fish, shellfish, and wildlife and recreation in and on the water." 40 C.F.R. § 131.12(a)(2). In Tier 2 waters, water quality (as opposed to uses) "shall be maintained and protected" unless the State finds, after a process of public participation, "that allowing lower water quality is necessary to accommodate important economic or social development in the area in which the waters are located." *Id.* § 131.12(a)(2)(ii). Tier 3 applies to high quality waters that "constitute an outstanding National resource, such as waters of National and State parks and wildlife refuges and waters of exceptional recreational or ecological significance." 40 C.F.R. § 131.12(a)(3). In Tier 3 waters, "water quality shall be maintained and protected," with no exception for economic or social necessity. *Id.*

The following case involves a series of challenges to the antidegradation policy of West Virginia, which had been approved by EPA.

Ohio Valley Environmental Coalition v. Horinko

279 F. Supp. 2d 732 (S.D.W.Va. 2003).

■ GOODWIN, DISTRICT JUDGE:

This case involves a challenge to the [EPA's] decision, pursuant to its authority under § 303(c) of the Clean Water Act, 33 U.S.C. § 1313(c), to approve the State of West Virginia's antidegradation implementation procedures, a set of procedures designed to prevent the degradation of the State waters. For the reasons that follow, the court concludes that the EPA acted arbitrarily and capriciously in approving West Virginia's antidegradation procedures. . . .

[The Ohio Valley Environmental Coalition mounted various challenges to EPA approval of the antidegradation policy. The remainder of the excerpt, however, focuses only on two specific complaints: the classification of certain segments of the Kanawha and Monongahela rivers as Tier 1 (as opposed to Tier 2) waterways; and the consistency of a proposed water quality trading scheme with the CWA and the EPA regulations.]

Classification of segments of the Kanawha and Monongahela Rivers as Tier 1 waterways

Section 60–5–4.3 of West Virginia's antidegradation implementation procedures provides that:

> In determining whether a water segment is afforded only Tier 1 protection, the agency will focus on whether the water segment is meeting or failing to meet minimum uses, except that, notwithstanding any other provision of this rule, the main stems of the Monongahela River, and the Kanawha River from milepoint 72 to the confluence with the Ohio River shall be afforded Tier 1 protection only.

The plaintiffs argue that there is insufficient evidence in the administrative record to permit the EPA to conclude that these segments of the Monongahela and Kanawha Rivers are not entitled to Tier 2 protection. In fact, the plaintiffs state that the only evidence in the record regarding the water quality levels in these river segments indicates that they should be categorized as Tier 2 waterways. The plaintiffs point to a letter by Jeffrey Towner of the United State Fish and Wildlife Service (USFWS) written to the EPA in response to the EPA's request for comments on West Virginia's proposed antidegradation implementation procedures. In this letter, the USFWS objects to the classification of these river segments as Tier 1 waters, stating that "water quality parameters in these waters exceed levels necessary to support minimum use and [the waters] are therefore Tier 2 waters." AR 633.

In response, the EPA argues that "EPA's antidegradation regulation gives states the discretion regarding how to identify 'high quality waters' that are afforded Tier 2 protection." EPA Op. Br. at 48. Specifically, the EPA argues that states may choose to use either a "pollutant-by-pollutant" approach or a "water body-by-water body" approach to classifying water segments. The court agrees with the EPA that its regulations give states some discretion in how they identify waters as Tier 2 waters. The EPA discusses its approach to Tier 2 waters in its advanced notice of proposed rulemaking (ANPRM) for 40 C.F.R. Part 131. *See* Water Quality Standards Regulation, 63 Fed.Reg. 63,742 (proposed July 7, 1998) (to be codified at 40 C.F.R. pt. 131); AR 514–79.

In the ANPRM, the EPA states that § 131.12(a)(2), the regulation establishing the Tier 2 designation, "does not include specific guidelines for identifying high quality waters." 63 Fed.Reg. 63,742, 36,782; AR 555. The EPA notes that various EPA guidance documents "make a variety of suggestions concerning approaches to defining tier 2 waters," and that "States and Tribes have developed various ways to identify tier 2 waters." *Id.* In particular, the EPA states that the various approaches to classifying waters "fall into two basic categories: (1) pollutant-by-pollutant approaches; and (2) water body-by-water body approaches." *Id.*

Under the pollutant-by-pollutant approach, the State makes a classification for each pollutant in a given water body. The water body is classified as Tier 2 for those pollutants for which "water quality is better than applicable criteria. . . ." *Id.* The same water body therefore could be classified as Tier 2 for certain pollutants and Tier 1 for other pollutants: "available assimilative capacity for any given pollutant is always subject to tier 2 protection, regardless of whether the criteria for other pollutants are satisfied." *Id.* Under the water body-by-water body approach, States "weigh a variety of factors to judge a water body segment's overall quality." *Id.* Tier 2 classification is based on the overall quality of the water body segment, not on individual pollutants. *Id.* The EPA stated that "[t]here are advantages and disadvantages to each approach," and that "either, when properly implemented, is acceptable." *Id.* The pollutant-by-pollutant approach may be "easier to implement because the need for an overall assessment considering various factors is avoided" and "may result in more waters receiving some degree of tier 2 protection" because the overall quality need not be high. *Id.* On the other hand, the water body-by-water body approach "allows for a weighted assessment of chemical, physical, biological, and other information (e.g., unique ecological or scenic attributes)," and thus "may be better suited to EPA's stated vision for the water quality standards program: refined designated uses with tailored criteria, complete information on uses and use attainability, and clear national norms." 63 Fed.Reg. 63,742, 36,783; AR 556. A danger in the water body-by-water body approach is that a State might not "develop inclusive qualification criteria" but might define overall water quality so as to include only a "narrow universe of waters," excluding "many deserving high quality waters." *Id.*

While the plaintiffs do not concede that the water body-by-water body approach is an acceptable manner of classifying waters, they spend the bulk of their energies arguing that even assuming this approach is permissible in general, West Virginia's designation of the main segments of the Kanawha and Monongahela Rivers in this case is unsupported by evidence. . . .

The court is satisfied that the water body-by-water body approach permits a State to make an overall classification of a particular water body without needing to make a classification for each individual pollutant, and that this approach has the benefit of allowing a State to focus its resources on overall high quality waters. The question remains, however, whether the segments of the Kanawha and Monongahela Rivers at issue here are, overall, the sort of "high quality" water bodies deserving of Tier 2 protection. To answer this question, one must know something about the quality of water in those rivers.

. . . EPA points to only *one* piece of evidence that pertains directly to the water quality in the Kanawha and Monongahela Rivers. That evidence is the fact that both river segments are on a list of impaired waters prepared by the [West Virginia Department of Environmental Protection (WVDEP)] for submission to the EPA under § 303(d) of the Clean Water Act. Section 303(d) requires States to submit to the EPA a list of waters that fail to meet water quality standards for at least one pollutant parameter. *See* 33 U.S.C. § 1313(d). . . .

The EPA has not even attempted to explain why the Kanawha and Monongahela's appearance on the § 303(d) list means that those rivers are not, overall, high quality waters. The EPA itself warned of the risk under the water body-by-water body approach of failing to develop adequate "inclusive qualification criteria" for identifying Tier 2 waters, 63 Fed.Reg. 63,742, 36,783; AR 556, but that is precisely what seems to have occurred here. Apart from the § 303(d) listing, neither the EPA nor the WVDEP has identified *any* qualification criteria—such as chemical, physical, biological, ecological, scenic, or other attributes—against which these river segments (and others) can be judged and classified as Tier 1 or Tier 2. In short, there may be legitimate reasons why these two river segments are classified as Tier 1 bodies, but the EPA has not offered any such reasons or identified *anything* in the record (or, in the case of the § 303(d) list, outside of the record) that would support this classification. . . .

In light of the total absence of *any* evidence about the quality of water in these river segments apart from their listing on the § 303(d) list, the court concludes that the EPA's approval of section 4.3's classification of these segments of the Kanawha and Monongahela Rivers as Tier 1 waters was arbitrary and capricious. . . .

Trading provisions

The plaintiffs' final challenge to the EPA's approval of West Virginia's antidegradation implementation procedures concerns certain water quality trading provisions. The trading provisions state that a proposed new or expanded discharge will be allowed, without triggering antidegradation review, "where the applicant agrees to implement or finance upstream controls of point or nonpoint sources sufficient to offset the water quality effects of the proposed activity from the same parameters and insure an improvement in water quality as a result of the trade. . . . A trade may be made between more than one stream segment where removing a discharge in one stream segment directly results in improved water quality in another stream segment." Section

5.6.f. These trading provisions are present in the regulations governing all . . . Tiers of protection. . . .

The plaintiffs raise several objections to these trading provisions. First, the plaintiffs argue that the trading provisions permit a new or expanded source to discharge into a water segment that does not meet water quality standards. This violates EPA regulations regarding NPDES permits, the plaintiffs argue, which prohibit further discharges into non-compliant water quality segments unless certain strict controls are in place. *See* 40 C.F.R. §§ 122.4(i), 122.44(d). In response, the EPA agrees with the plaintiffs' statement regarding its NPDES regulations, but disagrees that the antidegradation trading provisions authorize West Virginia to permit discharges that would otherwise violate NPDES standards. The court agrees that the antidegradation trading provisions merely permit a new or expanded discharge to satisfy *antidegradation* requirements in certain circumstances; those provisions do not purport to exempt (and do not exempt) those discharges from limits imposed by other regulations, such as NPDES permit regulations.

Second, the plaintiffs argue that the trading provisions are illegal because they permit an applicant to offset new or expanded point source discharge with a reduction in nonpoint source discharge. Because West Virginia has neither developed nor implemented a system for quantifying nonpoint source pollution, the plaintiffs argue, it cannot permit an applicant to trade some unquantified reduction in nonpoint source pollution for a quantified increase in point source pollution. To put it another way, the plaintiffs argue that it will be impossible for West Virginia to ensure that a reduction in nonpoint source pollution truly offsets an increase in point source pollution, because West Virginia has no method of quantifying nonpoint source pollution. In response, the EPA argues that this objection is premature, as it pertains to the implementation of the trading provisions rather than the provisions themselves. The EPA notes that its approval of this program "does not mean that West Virginia will attempt to use these provisions without first developing a quantification method to ensure that trades with nonpoint sources meet the conditions specified in the trading provisions. . . . EPA understands that West Virginia is developing that method now and EPA expects that West Virginia will not use these trading provisions until that method has been developed." EPA Op. Br. at 46 n. 50.

The court agrees with the EPA that the plaintiffs' objection in this regard pertains to the implementation of these provisions, not to the validity of the provisions themselves. The trading provisions require, among other things, that the reduced upstream pollution be "sufficient to offset the water quality effects of the proposed activity," that "where uncertainty exists regarding the effluent trade, an adequate margin of safety will be required," and that "the trades must be enforceable." Section 5.6.f. If West Virginia were to permit trading between point sources and nonpoint sources without any means of quantifying the reduction in nonpoint source pollution, it would clearly be violating these parts of its own regulation. Thus, the EPA is entirely reasonable in interpreting West Virginia's trading provisions as requiring that nonpoint source pollution reduction be quantifiable before any trading with nonpoint sources will be permitted. This objection is therefore without merit.

Finally, the plaintiffs argue that the trading provisions for Tiers 2, 2.5 and 3 are inconsistent with EPA regulations because they permit trading between two different stream segments without requiring an improvement in the same stream segment where the new or expanded discharge occurs. That is, the plaintiffs argue that under the trading provisions, an individual would be permitted to lower the water quality in one stream segment without antidegradation review so long as that individual improves another, different stream segment. The EPA agrees with the plaintiffs that its regulations do not permit the degradation of one stream segment without antidegradation review simply because another, different stream segment is improved. The EPA states that trading without antidegradation review is only permissible when the stream segment where the new or expanded discharge occurs experiences a net improvement in water quality. The EPA argues, however, that the West Virginia trading provisions are consistent with this approach.

The trading provisions state that trading is permissible when "upstream controls of point or nonpoint sources [are] sufficient to offset the water quality effects of the proposed activity from the same parameters and insure an improvement in water quality as a result of the trade." Section 5.6.f. In addition, the provision states that "[a] trade may be made between more than one stream segment where removing a discharge in one stream segment directly results in improved water quality in another stream segment." Section 5.6.f. The court concludes that these statements, taken together, are ambiguous as to whether the improvement must occur in the same stream segment where the discharge takes place, or whether an improvement in one stream segment may be traded for a decrease in quality in another stream segment. The EPA's conclusion that the trading provisions mean the former is a reasonable interpretation of those provisions, and thus the court will defer to that interpretation. The part of section 5.6.f that refers to improvement in quality in "another stream segment" seems to suggest that one segment may be degraded if *another* segment is improved. This statement must be read in light of the first part of section 5.6.f, however, which provides that the reduction must be "sufficient to *offset* the water quality effects of the proposed activity," and that the trade must "insure an *improvement* in water quality." These provisions can reasonably be read to mean that the trade must result in an improvement in water quality in the water segment where the new or expanded discharge is located. Because this interpretation of the trading provisions is reasonable, the EPA's approval of these provisions was not arbitrary or capricious.

NOTES AND QUESTIONS

1. Tier 1 v. Tier 2 Classifications. What is the consequence of classifying a certain body of water as Tier 1 as opposed to Tier 2? What are the differences between the "pollutant-by-pollutant" approach to classification and the "water body-by-water body" approach? On what basis did the Ohio Valley Environmental Coalition object to the classification of the Kanawha and Monongahela rivers? On what basis did the court sustain this challenge? What was the applicable standard of review? What evidence would EPA have had to produce in order for the court to have upheld the classifications?

2. Water Quality Trading Schemes and Antidegradation. On what grounds did the Ohio Valley Environmental Coalition object to the use of a water quality trading scheme in the context of the West Virginia Antidegredation Policy? To what extent are the plaintiffs' challenges applicable to all water quality trading schemes (as opposed to those which operate in the context of an antidegradation policy)? On what basis did the *Horinko* court reject each of the challenges?

In what ways does the trading scheme described in *Horinko* mirror the offset provisions of the nonattainment regime under the CAA? In what ways does it differ from that regime?

3. Role of the Federal Government in Setting Antidegradation Policies. The WQS Regulations prescribe that it is the responsibility of the states to develop antidegradation policies. Compare this with the role played by the states in setting PSD standards under the CAA. What features of the respective regimes may account for this disparity? What are the substantive differences between the regimes?

B. TOTAL MAXIMUM DAILY LOADS (TMDLs)

Section 303(d) of the Act establishes the TMDL process, to provide for more stringent water quality-based controls in circumstances where technology-based controls are inadequate to achieve state water quality standards. 33 U.S.C. § 1313(d). As a first step in setting TMDLs, the CWA requires that states list bodies of water that have failed to attain applicable water quality standards. 33 U.S.C. § 1313(d)(1)(A). This list must establish a priority ranking for such waters, taking into account the severity of the pollution and the uses to be made of such waters. *Id.* States must then set TMDLs for each pollutant—defining the maximum amount of a pollutant that can be discharged into the water segment without violating the water quality standard. 33 U.S.C. § 1313(d)(1)(C). In a process highly analogous to SIPs under the CAA, states must next allocate the TMDLs among dischargers. Allocations may either take the form of waste load allocations (WLAs—applicable to point sources of pollution) or load allocations (LAs—applicable to nonpoint sources).

WLAs, which are incorporated into NPDES permits, are the maximum load of pollutants that each discharger of waste is allowed to release into a particular waterway. LAs, which are typically given effect as components of state management programs, are the portion of a receiving water loading capacity that is attributable to existing or future nonpoint sources of pollution. In addition, a margin of safety is added to account for any uncertainty concerning the relationship between effluent limitations and water quality. Models accounting for conditions within a watershed (such as water flow, ambient water quality, point and nonpoint source pollution and land use) are used to determine the allocation of TMDLs among dischargers. In 2001, a report prepared by the National Research Council (NRC) developed eight criteria for model selection. *See* NATIONAL RESEARCH COUNCIL, ASSESSING THE TMDL APPROACH TO WATER QUALITY MANAGEMENT, REPORT TO THE COMMITTEE TO ASSESS THE SCIENTIFIC BASIS OF THE TOTAL MAXIMUM DAILY LOAD APPROACH TO WATER POLLUTION REDUCTION (2001). To date EPA has not promulgated any formal regulations concerning the adoption of these criteria.

Mirroring their inaction in setting water quality standards under § 303(a), states were also recalcitrant in setting TMDLs under § 303(d). A series of federal court cases in the late 1980s and early 1990s, which in the words of one commentator "[caught] EPA and the states by surprise," forced a rapid reversal of this position. OLIVER A. HOUCK, THE CLEAN WATER ACT TMDL PROGRAM: LAW, POLICY, AND IMPLEMENTATION 5 (2d ed. 2002). The consequences of this litigation, designed to force states to act on their statutory responsibilities under § 303(d), have been described in the following terms:

> [The litigation, progressing state by state, compelled] listings of impaired waters and schedules for first-ever TMDLs. The listings were daunting. Idaho rose from 16 impaired waters to 962. The schedules were tight, as early as five years. EPA scrambled forward with § 303(d) guidance and memoranda as fast as they could be proposed and convened a Federal Advisory Committee Act panel of state agencies, industry dischargers, and environmentalists to seek a consensus on goals, mechanisms, and timetables for the program. Consensus would not be easy. Nonpoint sources, largely responsible for the pollution at issue and largely immune to date from the requirements of the CWA, were openly hostile to abatement requirements. Municipal and industrial sources were no happier with the prospect of being tagged with nonpoint sources' share. Environmentalists, meanwhile, were spurring the action forward. A few states accepted the challenge. Others bunkered down and looked to Congress for relief. As the heat turned up on the TMDL program it was easy to forget that the reason the CWA retained such an approach, and directed its use for the

upgrade of polluted waters, is that both the states and pollution dischargers insisted on it. In a very real sense, this is the ghost they wanted.

Id. The following case addresses a challenge by agricultural groups to EPA's TMDL for nutrients and sediment in the Chesapeake Bay. The case analyzes whether EPA's approach to setting a TMDL was permissible under the statutory language of the CWA.

American Farm Bureau Federation v. Environmental Protection Agency

792 F.3d 281 (3d. Cir. 2015), *cert. denied*, 136 S. Ct. 1246 (2016).

■ Before AMBRO, SCIRICA, and ROTH, CIRCUIT JUDGES.

■ AMBRO, CIRCUIT JUDGE:

The Environmental Protection Agency ("EPA") published in 2010 the "total maximum daily load" ("TMDL") of nitrogen, phosphorous, and sediment that can be released into the Chesapeake Bay (the "Bay") to comply with the Clean Water Act, 33 U.S.C. § 1251 et seq. The TMDL is a comprehensive framework for pollution reduction designed to "restore and maintain the chemical, physical, and biological integrity" of the Bay, 33 U.S.C. § 1251, the subject of much ecological concern over several decades.

Trade associations with members who will be affected by the TMDL's implementation. . . sued. They allege that all aspects of the TMDL that go beyond an allowable sum of pollutants (i.e., the most nitrogen, phosphorous, and sediment the Bay can safely absorb per day) exceeded the scope of the EPA's authority to regulate, largely because the agency may intrude on states' traditional role in regulating land use.

Background

The EPA and seven states—Virginia, West Virginia, Maryland, Delaware, Pennsylvania, New York, and the District of Columbia, which is a "state" for Clean Water Act purposes, 33 U.S.C. § 1362(3)—have engaged in a decades-long process to develop a plan to improve the quality of the water in the Chesapeake Bay, the largest estuary in North America. The Bay's watershed area of 64,000 square miles contains tens of thousands of lakes, rivers, streams and creeks. The Bay itself has a surface area of 4,500 square miles, and it has 11,684 miles of shoreline, longer than the coastline from San Diego, California to Seattle, Washington. . . .

In 1972, [Congress] passed major revisions to federal water pollution legislation known as the Clean Water Act. Under that law, the EPA and the states participate in a "cooperative federalism" framework working together to clean the Nation's waters.

We deal primarily with one provision of this complex statute, which calls for the establishment of a "total maximum daily load" of pollution for certain waters. 33 U.S.C. § 1313(d)(1)(C). The parties dispute what those words mean. They are not defined in the Act, but the EPA has interpreted them to require publication of a comprehensive framework for pollution reduction in a given body of water. When we discuss this comprehensive document, we refer to it by the acronym "TMDL"; by contrast, when we analyze the statutory text, we refer to the words "total maximum daily load."

The Act provides that states set a total maximum daily load, and the EPA approves or disapproves it. If the EPA disapproves, it must create the TMDL itself. In this case, the Chesapeake Bay watershed jurisdictions agreed that they would not submit TMDLs, and the EPA would do so in the first instance.

To understand the parties' arguments, we consider the statutory context in which the words "total maximum daily load" arise. The Clean Water Act does not simply direct the publication of the TMDL; it is one step in a process with several layers, each placing primary responsibility for pollution controls in state hands with "backstop authority" vested in the EPA. TMDLs happen after a state enacts pursuant to its law (but required by the Clean Water Act) "water quality standards." The state designates a use for each relevant water (e.g., recreation or fishing) and sets a target water quality based on that use. *Id.* § (c)(1) & (2). The EPA must approve or disapprove the water quality standards. If the latter, it must promulgate its own water quality standard for the state. 33 U.S.C. § 1313(a)(3)(A)–(C) & (b).

Once water quality standards are in effect, the EPA and the states share responsibility for making sure that pollutants discharged into waters do not violate those standards. . . . The Clean Water Act gives the EPA primary responsibility for regulating point sources by establishing "effluent limitations," 33 U.SC. § 1311(b)(1)(A), which are pollution caps that by statutory definition apply only to point sources. *Id.* § 1362(11). States in turn regulate nonpoint sources. There is significant input and oversight from the EPA, but it does not regulate nonpoint sources directly. *Id.* § 1329(b) & (e).

Section 1313 anticipates that effluent limitations on point sources will be the front line of the defense against water pollution. But, acknowledging that effluent limitations may not be enough, § 1313(d) requires the states to submit to the EPA a list of all bodies of water (or, by regulation, any segment of a body of water) for which effluent limitations and technology-based point source controls are insufficient to meet the applicable water quality standard. These areas are known as "water quality limited segment[s]," 40 C.F.R. § 131.3(h), and the list on which they appear often goes by the "Section 303(d) list" after the part of the uncodified Clean Water Act to which 33 U.S.C. § 1313(d) corresponds.

Together with the Section 303(d) list, states must submit "total maximum daily loads" for those pollutants that cannot be brought to an acceptable level by point source controls. 33 U.S.C. § 1313(d)(1)(A) & (C). After a state submits its Section 303(d) list and TMDL, the EPA must approve or disapprove them; if it disapproves, it must create its own list and TMDL. 33 U.S.C. § 1313(d)(2).

To recap: states set water quality standards for the waters within their borders, and they must submit to the EPA a list of those waters for which point-source pollution limitations alone are not enough to make the water meet the applicable quality standard; for all the waters on that list, a state must submit a TMDL. If the EPA disapproves a state submission, it takes responsibility for the unmet requirement(s). As noted, for the Chesapeake Bay the relevant states and the EPA agreed that the EPA would draft the TMDL in the first instance.

This case primarily concerns the meaning of "total maximum daily load," words that occur in the part of the Clean Water Act that requires states (or, in this case, the EPA) to:

> establish . . . the total maximum daily load[ ] for those pollutants which the Administrator identifies under section 1314(a)(2) of this title as suitable for such calculation. Such load shall be established at a level necessary to implement the applicable water quality standards with seasonal variations and a margin of safety which takes into account any lack of knowledge concerning the relationship between effluent limitations and water quality. 33 U.S.C. § 1313(d)(1)(C).

The Act directed states to include "total maximum daily load[s]" in their required "continuing planning process[es]" no later than February 15, 1973. 33 U.S.C. § 1313(e)(2).

Definition and Development of TMDLs, 1972–2000

This deadline, it turns out, was overly optimistic, as both states and the EPA have been slow in establishing TMDLs. . . . [The court goes on to review the history of litigation over failure to issue TMDLs.] The lawsuits of the 1990s were followed by the actual drafting of thousands of TMDLs, which the EPA has described as "the technical backbone" of its approach to cleaning the Nation's waters. EPA Office of Water, Total Maximum Daily Load (TMDL) Program Draft TMDL Program Implementation Strategy § 1.2 (1996). TMDLs are now thorough "informational tools that allow the states to proceed from the identification of waters requiring additional planning to the required plans." *Pronsolino v. Nastri*, 291 F.3d 1123, 1129 (9th Cir.2002). TMDLs are not self-executing, but they serve as the cornerstones for pollution-reduction plans that do create enforceable rights and obligations.[4]

---

[4] The parties debate what precisely TMDLs are. Our understanding of them as informational tools is supported by every case and piece of scholarship to consider them as well as the language of the Chesapeake Bay TMDL itself. *See City of Arcadia v. EPA*, 411 F.3d 1103,

The Chesapeake Bay TMDL, 2000–2010

Development of the Chesapeake Bay TMDL began in earnest with the Chesapeake 2000 Agreement, whereby the EPA and political backers from the Bay states made commitments geared to reducing pollution in the Bay. This Agreement eventually gave way to states' submission to the EPA of "Phase I Watershed Improvement Plans," which were drafts proposing target pollutant limitations and how the states would achieve them. The EPA developed the Chesapeake Bay TMDL in reliance on these plans and did so only after approving the pollutant limitations and concluding that each state had given "reasonable assurance" of actually meeting the targets in its Watershed Improvement Plan. . . . [EPA] determined that the final draft Phase I Watershed Improvement Plans provided reasonable assurance in all respects save two sources of pollution (Pennsylvania urban stormwater and West Virginia agriculture), and it imposed a "backstop adjustment," meaning that it will require greater reductions from point sources in Pennsylvania and West Virginia if those states cannot meet their projected load allocations. . . .

After making these adjustments to the states' Watershed Improvement Plans, the EPA incorporated them into the final Chesapeake Bay TMDL. It is detailed, as it includes point- and nonpoint-source limitations on nitrogen, phosphorous, and sediment for 92 segments of the Bay identified as overpolluted and further allocates those limits to specific point sources and to nonpoint source sectors. The TMDL sets target dates, anticipating that 60% of its proposed actions will be complete by 2017, with all pollution control measures in place by 2025. The next step, yet to happen, is for the states to develop their Phase II Watershed Improvement Plans to implement the TMDL.

On December 29, 2010, the EPA promulgated the TMDL through the notice-and-comment rulemaking process of the Administrative Procedure Act ("APA"). See 5 U.S.C. § 553. Over 45 days, the EPA held 18 public meetings (at which 2,500 members of the public attended), and

---

1105 (9th Cir. 2005); Sierra Club v. Meiburg, 296 F.3d 1021, 1025 (11th Cir. 2002) ("Each TMDL serves as the goal for the level of that pollutant in the waterbody to which that TMDL applies."); Bravos v. Green, 306 F. Supp. 2d 48, 56 (D.D.C. 2004) ("EPA's approval of a State's TMDL does not translate into approval of the State's implementation plan."); City of Arcadia v. EPA, 265 F. Supp. 2d 1142, 1144 (N.D. Cal. 2003) ("TMDLs established under Section 303(d)(1) of the CWA function primarily as planning devices and are not self-executing."); Idaho Sportsmen's Coal. v. Browner, 951 F. Supp. 962, 966 (W.D. Wash. 1996) ("TMDL development in itself does not reduce pollution. It is only a step toward bringing [water quality limited segments] into compliance with water quality standards; TMDLs inform the design and implementation of pollution control measures."); Corey Longhurst, *Where Is the Point? Water Quality Trading's Inability to Deal with Nonpoint Source Agricultural Pollution*, 17 DRAKE J. AGRIC. L. 175, 187 (2012); Jan G. Laitos & Heidi Ruckriegle, *The Clean Water Act and the Challenge of Agricultural Pollution*, 37 VT. L. REV. 1033, 1054–57 (2013) (criticizing courts for the limited legal effect they have given to TMDLs); J.A. 1113 ("The cornerstone of the accountability framework is the jurisdictions' development of [Watershed Improvement Plans], which serve as roadmaps for how and when a jurisdiction plans to meet its pollutant allocations under the TMDL.").

it received more than 14,000 comments. It took these comments and meetings into account when publishing the final TMDL.

Procedural Background, 2011–Present

As discussed above, TMDLs have long been the subject of litigation. Environmental groups continue to press the EPA to promulgate more stringent TMDLs. Not to be left on the sidelines, commercial concerns took to the courts to air their grievances with the EPA—this time not for acting too slowly, but for acting at all. Our case is of this most recent variety.

In January 2011, Farm Bureau sued the EPA under the APA and the citizen-suit provision of the Clean Water Act. It asserted that the EPA exceeded its statutory authority by including deadlines and allocations in the TMDL and by requiring "reasonable assurance" from the states in drafting that document. The District Court granted summary judgment in favor of the EPA, and this appeal followed. . . .

Merits

Farm Bureau interprets the words "total maximum daily load" in the Clean Water Act as unambiguous: a TMDL can consist only of a number representing the amount of a pollutant that can be discharged into a particular segment of water and nothing more. Thus it argues that the EPA overstepped its statutory authority in drafting the Chesapeake Bay TMDL when the agency (1) included in the TMDL allocations of permissible levels of nitrogen, phosphorous, and sediment among different kinds of sources of these pollutants, (2) promulgated target dates for reducing discharges to the level the TMDL envisions, and (3) obtained assurance from the seven affected states that they would fulfill the TMDL's objectives. In Farm Bureau's view, even if allocations, target dates, and reasonable assurance are useful in calculating the number that is the TMDL, the final document may not specify a distribution of pollutants from point and nonpoint sources or deadlines for meeting the target reductions in pollutant discharge, nor may the EPA in drafting the document obtain any assurance from states that they will meet the targets.

The parties agree that this case is governed by *Chevron v. NRDC*, 467 U.S. 837 (1984). . . .

Farm Bureau concludes that the statute unambiguously forecloses the EPA's interpretation and hence the agency is not entitled to deference. Several considerations persuade us otherwise. . . .

Statutory Text

Farm Bureau's strongest argument is that Congress specifically authorized the EPA to publish "*total* maximum daily *load* [s] . . . at a *level* necessary to implement the applicable water quality standards. . . ." 33 U.S.C. § 1313(d)(1)(C) (emphases added). Under Farm Bureau's reading, a "total load" is just a number, like the "total" at the bottom of a restaurant receipt. This ordinary understanding of the word "total" is supported, the argument continues, because the load is to be established at a "level," which can be high or low (so long as it is necessary to implement the water quality standards); in any event it should not be expressed as a comprehensive framework, and in no event can a TMDL include allocations among point and nonpoint sources, deadlines, and the reasonable assurance requirement.

This argument has some intuitive appeal, but other readings are possible. Our most significant textual concern is that Farm Bureau's analysis makes the word "total" redundant. "Maximum daily load[s]. . . . established at a level necessary to implement the applicable water standard" would mean the same thing that Farm Bureau argues "total maximum daily load" means: a number set at a level needed to alleviate water pollution. Applying the canon against surplusage, a plausible understanding of "total" is that it means the sum of the constituent parts of the load. The load is still set at the level necessary to fight pollutants, but it is expressed in terms of a total of the different relevant allocations. . . .

Additionally, although Congress explicitly required the EPA to establish "total maximum daily loads," it nowhere prescribed how the EPA is to do so. The agency has chosen to lay out in detail (1) how and why it arrived at the number it chose; (2) how it thinks it and affected jurisdictions will be able to achieve that number; (3) why that number is "necessary to implement the applicable water quality standard[ ]," *id.* § 1313(d)(1)(C); (4) when it expects the TMDL to achieve the applicable water quality standard; and (5) what it will do if the water quality standard is not met. As the EPA has chosen to use notice-and-comment rulemaking to promulgate TMDLs, the APA likely requires the EPA to provide sufficient information in connection with the TMDL for the public adequately to comment on the agency's judgment and to make suggestions where appropriate. . . .

The EPA's approach also fits the statute's requirement that the load be established in light of "seasonal variations and a margin of safety which takes into account any lack of knowledge concerning the relationship between effluent limitations and water quality." 33 U.S.C. § 1313(d)(1)(C). Under Farm Bureau's approach, these factors that affect the EPA's calculation would need to remain absent from the TMDL. It would be strange to require the EPA to take into account these specific considerations but at the same time command the agency to excise them from its final product. . . .

Farm Bureau's textual argument . . . fails to persuade us that Congress excluded everything other than the sum of pollutants from a TMDL. . . .

Statutory Structure and Purpose

Turning from the text of the provision, we consider the structure and purpose of the Clean Water Act. Broadly speaking, it "anticipates a partnership between the States and the Federal Government, animated by a shared objective: 'to restore and maintain the chemical, physical, and biological integrity of the Nation's waters.' 33 U.S.C. § 1251(a)." *Arkansas v. Oklahoma*, 503 U.S. 91 (1992). This goal informs our understanding that "total maximum daily load" is broad enough to include allocations, target dates, and reasonable assurance.

1. Allocations Between Point and Nonpoint Sources

As noted, the Act assigns the primary responsibility for regulating point sources to the EPA and nonpoint sources to the states. The EPA sets limits on pollution that may come from point sources via a permitting process (which can be delegated to the states) known as the National Pollutant Discharge Elimination System. 33 U.S.C. § 1342. Nonetheless, in drafting a TMDL the Clean Water Act unambiguously requires the author (here, the EPA) to take into account nonpoint sources (though whether those sources must be expressed is not obvious). This conclusion follows when we consider the steps that precede and culminate in a TMDL.

1. Each state must designate a use for each body of water within its borders and set a target water quality based on that use. 33 U.S.C. § 1313(c)(1) & (2). The state must then enact "water quality standards" pursuant to state law. *Id.* § 1313(a) & (b).

2. In order to meet water quality standards, the EPA (or the states to which the EPA has delegated this responsibility) sets "effluent limitations," which are pollution limits on point sources. *Id.* §§ 1311(b)(1)(A) & 1362(11).

3. States must submit to the EPA a list of the waters within their boundaries for which effluent limitations (a.k.a. point-source pollution limits) are, by themselves, inadequate to attain the applicable water quality standard—i.e., those waters for which both point source and nonpoint source limitations will be necessary. *Id.* § 1313(d).

4. It is only for these waters, for which point source effluent limitations alone are insufficient, that a state must establish a TMDL.

5. TMDLs set the maximum amount of pollution a water body can absorb before violating applicable water quality standards. In the statutory context noted above, it is impossible to meet those standards by point-source reductions alone. Therefore, the Clean Water Act requires the drafter of a TMDL to consider nonpoint-source pollution.

"As should be apparent, TMDLs are central to the Clean Water Act's water-quality scheme because . . . they tie together point-source and nonpoint-source pollution issues in a manner that addresses the whole health of the water." *Meiburg*, 296 F.3d at 1025. As far as allocations are concerned, the EPA's construction of the TMDL requirement comports well with the Clean Water Act's structure and purpose. Specifically allocating the pollution load between point sources (primarily the EPA's responsibility) and nonpoint sources (the states' dominion) is a commonsense first step to achieve the target water quality.

Because TMDLs only relate to bodies of water for which point source limitations are insufficient, they must take into account pollution from both point and nonpoint sources. We believe the congressional silence on how to promulgate a TMDL and the congressional command that a TMDL be established only for waters that cannot be cleaned by point-source limitations alone (necessarily implying that, whatever form the TMDL takes, it must incorporate nonpoint source limitations) combine to authorize the EPA to express load and waste load allocations. To be sure, the statute does not command the EPA's final regulation to allocate explicitly parts of a load among different kinds of sources, but we agree with the EPA that it may do so.

2.   "Deadlines" or "Target Dates"

Similarly, it is common sense that a timeline complements the Clean Water Act's requirement that all impaired waters achieve applicable water quality standards. The amount of acceptable pollution in a body of water is necessarily tied to the date at which the EPA and the states believe the water should meet its quality standard; if the target date is 100 years from now, more pollution per day will be allowable than if the target date is five years from now. Additionally, any meaningful pollution-reduction plan needs to take into account the dynamic nature of watersheds, particularly the fact that they change over time. As promulgating an accurate TMDL—that is, one that states a pollutant load "necessary to implement the applicable water quality standards," 33 U.S.C. § 1313(d)(1)(C)—requires consideration of a timeline and of changes over time, it is more consistent with the purpose of the Clean Water Act to express the deadline that the EPA relied on in calculating the TMDL than to make states and the public guess what it is.

3.   Reasonable Assurance

Farm Bureau's argument that the Act forbids the EPA from seeking reasonable assurance from the states that their Watershed Improvement Plans will meet their stated goals is also inconsistent with the purpose and structure of the Clean Water Act. The TMDL must be set "at a level necessary to implement the applicable water quality standards." 33 U.S.C. § 1313(d)(1)(C). The EPA chose to set the TMDL with substantial input from the states but, in order to comply with the Clean Water Act and the APA, the EPA would not blindly accept states' submissions. Instead it decided to satisfy itself that the states' proposals would actually "implement the applicable water quality standards." Id. This requirement made sure that the EPA could exercise "reasoned judgment" in evaluating the states' proposed standards and was thus consistent with the Clean Water Act. *Ctr. for Biological Diversity v. EPA*, 749 F.3d 1079, 1087 (D.C. Cir. 2014).

4. Summary of Structure and Purpose

The point of the TMDL is to take into consideration nonpoint-source pollution; no meaningful decision about limiting pollution can be made without specifying a time frame within which pollution is to be eliminated; and the Clean Water Act envisions assurance of effective pollution controls. Preventing the EPA from expressing allocations and timelines and from obtaining reasonable assurance from affected states appears to frustrate those goals, and thus the phrase "total maximum daily load" has enough play in the joints to allow the EPA to consider and express these factors in its final action. . . .

Conclusion

Water pollution in the Chesapeake Bay is a complex problem currently affecting at least 17,000,000 people (with more to come). Any solution to it will result in winners and losers. To judge from the arguments and the amici briefs filed in this case, the winners are environmental groups, the states that border the Bay, tourists, fishermen, municipal waste water treatment works, and urban centers. The losers are rural counties with farming operations, nonpoint source polluters, the agricultural industry, and those states that would prefer a lighter touch from the EPA. Congress made a judgment in the Clean Water Act that the states and the EPA could, working together, best allocate the benefits and burdens of lowering pollution. The Chesapeake Bay TMDL will require sacrifice by many, but that is a consequence of the tremendous effort it will take to restore health to the Bay—to make it once again a part of our "land of living," Robert Frost, *The Gift Outright* line 10—a goal our elected representatives have repeatedly endorsed. Farm Bureau's arguments to the contrary are unpersuasive, and thus we affirm the careful and thorough opinion of the District Court.

NOTES AND QUESTIONS

1.   The Chesapeake Bay. The Chesapeake Bay watershed covers 64,000 square miles across six states and the District of Columbia. The watershed provides significant ecological, economic, recreational, historic, and cultural value to the region, which has been estimated to exceed $1 trillion. *See American Farm Bureau Federation ("AFBF") v. U.S. E.P.A.*, 984 F. Supp. 2d 289, 299 (M.D. Pa. 2013). Unfortunately, the water quality of the Bay has been seriously degraded by excess nutrient and sediment pollution, which causes hypoxic conditions in the Bay. *Id.* at 300 n.5.

The Bay TMDL was not the first step in attempts to clean up the Bay. In the early 1970's Congress sponsored a five-year study to analyze the Bay's loss of aquatic life. In 1983, the governors of Maryland, Pennsylvania, and Virginia, as well as the Mayor of D.C., the chairman of the Chesapeake Bay Commission, and the EPA Administrator signed the first Chesapeake Bay Agreement. This agreement was the first multi-state coordinated effort to clean up the Bay. The agreement has been renewed multiple times, most recently in 2014. In 2000 the "headwater states," Delaware, New York, and West Virginia, joined the agreement. Each agreement added to the efforts to restore the Bay. *See id.* Congress, enacted section 177 of the CWA in 1987, specifically recognizing the unique value of the Bay, and directing EPA to "coordinate state and federal efforts to improve Bay water quality." *See* 33 U.S.C. § 1267. In 2009, President Obama issued an Executive Order recognizing the importance of the Chesapeake Bay and creating a Federal Leadership Committee charged with overseeing restoration efforts of the Bay. Exec. Order No. 13,508, 74 Fed. Reg. 23,099 (2009).

Like the Bay, the Chesapeake Bay TMDL is unique in many ways. It is the largest TMDL ever developed by EPA. Unlike most TMDLs, which are developed by a particular state, or EPA after disproving the State's TMDL, the Bay states agreed that EPA would develop the Bay TMDL with input from the states. *See AFBF*, 984 F. Supp. 2d at 302–03. The Bay TMDL is actually a combination of 92 smaller TMDLs for individual watershed segments. EPA, CHESAPEAKE BAY TMDL, EXECUTIVE SUMMARY ES-3 (2010). Finally, the Bay TMDL requires the Bay States to develop and submit updated Watershed Implementation Plans, which are road maps for the States' individual pollution reductions. *Id.* at ES-8. For a more in-depth discussion of the creation of the Chesapeake Bay TMDL, and a discussion challenging some of the court's assumptions in *AFBF*, *see* Jamison E. Colburn, *Coercing Collaboration: The Chesapeake Bay Experience*, 40 WM. & MARY ENVTL. L. & POL'Y REV. 677 (2016).

2.   EPA Duty to Promulgate TMDLs. The citizen suit provisions of many environmental statutes, including the CWA, enable private citizens to compel the EPA Administrator to take action on non-discretionary or mandatory duties. *See* 33 U.S.C. § 1365(a)(2). Section 303(d) of the CWA requires states to submit lists of waters with insufficient controls to meet the water quality standards and develop TMDLs for the waters on the list. EPA is then required to either approve or disapprove the lists and TMDLs within 30 days of submission. 33 U.S.C. § 1313(d)(2). If EPA disapproves the submission, it must create its own list of waters and TMDLs necessary to meet the water quality standards. *Id.* Citizen suits seeking to compel EPA action on TMDLs thus focus on whether § 303(d) creates a non-discretionary duty on the part of EPA to act in the face of limited or insufficient state action.

3.   Constructive Submission. The *AFBF* court noted that during the TMDL litigation of the 1990's, courts held that "a state's failure to submit a TMDL should be deemed a 'constructive submission' that no TMDL is needed, triggering the EPA's duty to accept that conclusion or promulgate its own TMDL." 792 F.3d at 290. In *San Francisco BayKeeper v. Whitman*, 297 F.3d 877 (9th Cir. 2002), BayKeeper argued that California's failure to submit a TMDL for approval between 1980 and 1994 should be a "constructive submission" that no TMDL was needed, triggering EPA's non-discretionary duty to create TMDLs for California waters. *Id.* at 881. The court found that California had submitted eighteen TMDLs and had established a schedule for completing the remaining TMDLs, which prevented application of the constructive submission doctrine. *Id.* at 883. Based on the *BayKeeper* reading, how hard would it be for states to take steps to defeat the constructive submission doctrine?

4.   EPA Authority to Create TMDLs. The court in *AFBF* said that "courts have recognized the EPA's authority to fill the Clean Water Act's considerable gaps on how to promulgate a 'total maximum daily load.' " 792 F.3d at 296. The court was analyzing the agency's interpretation of the CWA under *Chevron.* Courts often rely on the CWA's broad purpose to determine if an agency's construction is permissible. *See Nat. Res. Def. Council, Inc. v. Muszynski,* 268 F.3d 91, 98 (2d Cir. 2001) ("[Plaintiff's] overly narrow reading of the statute loses sight of the overall structure and purpose of the CWA.") For example, *Pronsolino v. Nastri,* 291 F.3d 1123, 1139 (9th Cir. 2002), held that EPA had the authority to set a TMDL for waterbodies polluted only by nonpoint sources, finding that:

> Nothing in the statutory structure—or purpose—suggests that Congress meant to distinguish, as to § 303(d)(1) lists and TMDLs, between waters with one insignificant point source and substantial nonpoint source pollution and waters with only nonpoint source pollution. Such a distinction would, for no apparent reason, require the states or the EPA to monitor waters to determine whether a point source had been added or removed, and to adjust the § 303(d)(1) list and establish TMDLs accordingly. There is no statutory basis for concluding that Congress intended such an irrational regime.

5.   Federal Power to Enforce TMDLs. In another portion of its opinion, the court in *Pronsolino,* described TMDLs as "primarily informational tools" and as such "implementation and monitoring are state responsibilities." *Id.* at 1129, 1140 (internal quotes omitted). The court went on to say that "[s]tates must implement TMDLs only to the extent that they seek to avoid losing federal grant money; there is no pertinent statutory provision otherwise requiring implementation of § 303 plans or providing for their enforcement." *Id.* at 40. Following the *Pronsolino* decision, at least one commentator referred to section 303 as "toothless" because states still had discretion to implement and enforce the pollution reduction goals outlined in the TMDL. Jocelyn B. Garovoy, *"A Breathtaking Assertion of Power"? Not Quite.*, 30 ECOLOGY L.Q. 543, 555 (2003).

Yet, in *AFBF,* the EPA had set target dates and reasonable assurance provisions, in the TMDL, to ensure that the state watershed implementation plans met the pollution reduction goals. 792 F.3d at 300–01. The court interpreted these provisions as being within the permissible scope of defining the TMDL. *Id.* The agency also described other steps it would take to meet pollution load reductions if the states failed to achieve those reductions through their own implementation plans. These steps include expanding coverage of NPDES permits, increasing oversight of state-issued NPDES permits, prohibiting new or expanded pollution discharges, revising water quality standards, among others. See EPA, CHESAPEAKE BAY TMDL, EXECUTIVE SUMMARY ES-13 (2010).

Is section 303 really as "toothless" as Jocelyn Garovoy suggested, or did the court in *AFBF* allow the agency to give the section some bite? Arguably, in crafting the TMDL enforcement mechanism, EPA was relying on existing statutory authority under the point source and water quality standards provisions of the CWA. *See* 33 U.S.C. §§ 1313(b), 1342. Does EPA's use of its various authorities to encourage the states to meet the pollution reduction targets outlined in the Bay TMDL make it more than an informational document?

6.   Federalism Concerns. The plaintiffs in both *AFBF* and *Pronsolino* raised federalism concerns about the agency's TMDLs. The *Pronsolino* court did not believe the TMDL upset the cooperative federalism balance of the CWA because California had ultimate authority for implementing the TMDL. *See* 291 F.3d at 1140. The court in *AFBF* viewed the TMDL as not threatening the federalism balance, because it was clearly "within the agency's jurisdiction" to establish the TMDL. 792 F.3d at 302. Given the TMDL enforcement mechanisms found in *AFBF*, do these responses to the federalism objections hold water?

7.   TMDLs and Climate Change. Climate change adversely affects water quality in a number of ways, increasing the likelihood that water bodies will be listed as impaired under § 303(d). For example, incorporating climate change into models used for setting water quality standards and TMDLs will anticipate greater ocean acidification—a drop in pH caused primarily by water absorbing carbon dioxide. *See* Memorandum from Denise Keehner, Dir. Office of Wetlands, Oceans and Watersheds, EPA, Integrated Reporting and Listing Decisions Related to Ocean Acidification (Nov. 15, 2010) (encouraging states to list waters that fail to meet pH standards due to, *inter alia*, climate change). For reasons independent of climate change, other types of pollution, such as nutrient enrichment (largely from nonpoint sources), can also lead to decreases in marine pH. *Id.* at 9. When setting TMDLs, unless such standards can reflect carbon emissions, the burden may fall on producers of other types of pollution. In this way, TMDLs may become a means of promoting ecological restoration in response to climate change rather than a means of internalizing the costs of degradation to those polluters directly contributing to acidification by emitting greenhouse gases. Is this result inevitable under the CWA? Is it undesirable?

8.   Funding Gap. The National Academy of Public Administration estimates state CWA funding needs at between $1.5 billion and $1.7 billion annually. *See* NATIONAL ACADEMY OF PUBLIC ADMINISTRATION, UNDERSTANDING WHAT STATES NEED TO PROTECT WATER QUALITY (2002). At the time, states spent between $722 million to $805 million per year on water quality programs—less than half of the requisite amount. *Id.* Budget woes have become so serious that states such as Missouri, Kansas, and Iowa had considered giving up primacy over their NPDES programs. Clifford Rechtschaffen, *Enforcing the Clean Water Act in the Twenty-First Century*, 55 ALA. L. REV. 775, 789 (2004). Additionally, EPA has been petitioned by citizens and environmental groups to withdraw NPDES program authorizations for the states of Alabama, Florida, Indiana, Kansas, Louisiana, Michigan, Nevada, Tennessee, and Virginia because of inadequate state level program management. EPA, Letter of Ronald Kreizenbeck, Acting Regional Administrator to Hon. Frank Murkowski, Governor of Alaska (Aug. 1, 2006).

According to a GAO report, states have not allocated adequate funding to fully implement 86 percent of long-established TMDLs addressing nonpoint source pollution. GAO, CHANGES NEEDED IF KEY EPA PROGRAM IS TO HELP FULFILL THE NATION'S WATER QUALITY GOALS 60 (Dec. 2013). Further, EPA has estimated that at current funding levels and restoration rates it would take longer than 1,000 years to restore all waterbodies that are now impaired by nonpoint source pollution. *Id.* at 2.

9. Land Use Change. Farm Bureau had argued that the Chesapeake Bay TMDL impermissibly intruded on the states' authority to regulate land use. EPA estimated that 44 percent of the nutrient loads and 65 percent of the sediment loads delivered to the Bay came from nonpoint source agricultural lands. *See* EPA, CHESAPEAKE BAY TMDL, SOURCES OF NITROGEN, PHOSPHORUS, AND SEDIMENT TO THE CHESAPEAKE BAY 4–28 (2010). So, at least in theory, agriculture would have to take steps to significantly reduce its contribution of nutrients and sediment to the Bay. EPA had indicated that financial incentives, voluntary programs, and state-specific regulatory programs would have to be used to achieve nonpoint source pollution reduction. EPA, CHESAPEAKE BAY TMDL, EXECUTIVE SUMMARY ES-8 (2010). The court dismissed Farm Bureau's arguments because it thought the states would make the ultimate decision about how to regulate nonpoint source discharges. Even though the state is implementing regulations to meet the TMDL pollution reduction requirements, is there an argument that the TMDL itself is requiring the land-use change?

10. TMDL Models and Agency Discretion. Calculating pollution loads to a watershed in order to set the TMDL can be an extremely complex undertaking. EPA has developed a series of models to assist with this process. *See* EPA, COMPENDIUM OF TOOLS FOR WATERSHED ASSESSMENT AND TMDL DEVELOPMENT (1997). The Chesapeake Bay TMDL relies on a complex model to determine pollution loading from each source category and geographic region and allocate reduction targets. *See* Chesapeake Bay Program, Modeling, https://www.chesapeakebay.net/what/programs/ modeling (last visited Feb. 15, 2019). In the district court, Farm Bureau alleged that EPA had improperly withheld documentation about the models and had relied on flawed data inputs in crafting the Bay TMDL. *AFBF*, 984 F. Supp. 2d at 334–44. The court ultimately rejected these claims after finding that the Agency had provided a rational basis for its choice of models and data. *Id.*

Similarly, in *Natural Resource Defense Council, Inc. v. Muszynski*, 268 F.3d 91 (2d Cir. 2001), NRDC had challenged EPA's approval of New York's TMDLs for phosphorus in New York City's reservoirs. The CWA requires that the TMDL be established "at a level necessary to implement the applicable water quality standards with . . . a margin of safety which takes into account any lack of knowledge concerning the relationship between effluent limitations and water quality." *Id.* at 97. New York, partially relying on a model of phosphorus loading to the reservoirs had set a ten percent margin of safety (MOS). NRDC argued that the MOS failed to meet "the clearly delineated Congressional specifications" because there were not adequate findings in the record that the MOS used would address "any lack of knowledge concerning the relationship between effluent limitations and water quality" *Id.* at 102. In upholding EPA's approval the court stated:

> NRDC takes issue with the adoption of a ten percent margin of safety, arguing that no scientific or mathematical basis prescribed this percentage as opposed to any other. As EPA explained, because "there is no 'standard' or guideline for choosing a specific margin of safety, best professional judgment and the available information are used in setting [it]." While the MOS may thus be set with an uncomfortable degree of discretion, requiring that EPA show a rigorous scientific methodology dictates one course of action as opposed to another and would effectively prevent the agency from acting in situations where action is required in the face of a clear public health or environmental danger but the magnitude of that danger cannot be effectively quantified. "[A]s long as Congress delegates power to an agency to regulate on the borders of the unknown, courts cannot interfere with reasonable interpretations of equivocal evidence." *Public Citizen Health Research Group v. Tyson*, 796 F.2d 1479, 1505 (D.C. Cir. 1986). Were it clear, for instance, that a widely used and reliable scientific methodology was applicable to determining a margin of safety and that EPA had turned a blind eye to recommendations based on such a methodology, NRDC's challenge would have more force. But simply to reject EPA's efforts to implement the CWA because it must respond to real water quality problems without the guidance of a rigorously precise methodology would essentially nullify the exercise of agency discretion in the form of 'best professional judgment.' *Id.* at 102–03.

11. Scope of Agency Discretion. The *Muszynski* court commented that "as long as Congress delegates power to an agency to regulate on the borders of the unknown, courts cannot interfere with reasonable interpretations of equivocal evidence." *Id.* at 101. In this case, however, the court upheld EPA's actions, even though neither EPA nor New York provided a scientific or mathematical justification for the margin. On what basis, then, did the court choose to uphold EPA's decision?

12. "Daily" Limits. Courts may read "total maximum daily load" as an ambiguous term and give deference to EPA's interpretation. But, as the *AFBF* court noted:

> The only time a court has considered an aspect of the phrase "total maximum daily load" unambiguous was in response to a challenge to the EPA's practice of promulgating total maximum seasonal or annual loads. The D.C. Circuit held that the word "daily" was unambiguous, though it did not consider the above phrase

unambiguous in all respects. *Friends of Earth, Inc. v. EPA*, 446 F.3d 140, 144 (D.C. Cir. 2006). The Second Circuit disagrees with the D.C. Circuit on this point, *Muszynski*, 268 F.3d at 98–99, and even after *Friends of Earth* the District of D.C. has allowed the EPA to issue total maximum annual or seasonal loads in addition to daily loads because, although the statute is explicit about the requirement for a daily load, it is silent on whether another timeframe may be used when that would be more appropriate for the particular pollutant at issue. *Anacostia Riverkeeper, Inc. v. Jackson,* 798 F. Supp. 2d 210, 245 (D.D.C. 2011).

792 F.3d at 296.

In *Friends of the Earth v. EPA*, 446 F.3d 140 (2006), *cert. denied*, 549 U.S. 1175 (2007), the D.C. Circuit rejected EPA's argument that the CWA left room for setting seasonal or annual loads for pollutants that are poorly suited to daily load recognition. In that case, EPA had approved one TMDL limiting the *annual* discharge of oxygen-depleting pollutants into the Anacostia River (which was one of the 10 most polluted rivers in the country), and another limiting the *seasonal* discharge of pollutants contributing to turbidity. In the wake of the *Friends of the Earth* decision, EPA issued a memorandum clarifying the formation of TMDL "daily" loads. *See* EPA, *Memo Clarifying EPA Position on the Use of Daily Time Increment When Establishing Total Maximum Daily Loads for Pollutants*, BNA ENV'T REP., Nov. 2006. The memorandum, which applies nationwide, proposed three bases upon which TMDLs can be expressed:

- If consistent with the applicable water quality standard and technically suitable for the pollutant and water body type in question, a TMDL and associated load allocations and wasteload allocations may be expressed as both minimum and, maximum daily loads, or as average daily loads. For example, a TMDL for the pollutant parameter pH may include both minimum and maximum values consistent with how the applicable WQS for the parameter pH is expressed (commonly as a range.)

- If technically appropriate and consistent with the applicable water quality standard, it may also be appropriate for the TMDL and associated load allocations and wasteload allocations to be expressed in terms of differing maximum daily values depending on the season of the year, stream flow (e.g., wet v. dry weather conditions) or other factors. In situations where pollutant loads, water body flows, or other environmental factors are highly dynamic, it may be appropriate for TMDLs and associated allocations to be expressed as functions of controlling factors such as water body flow. For example, a load-duration curve approach to expressing a TMDL and associated allocations might be appropriate, provided it clearly identifies the allowable daily pollutant load for any given day as a function of the flow occurring that day. Using the load-duration curve approach also has the advantage of addressing seasonal variations as required by the statute and the regulations.

- For TMDLs that are expressed as a concentration of a pollutant, a possible approach would be to use a table and/or graph to express the TMDL as daily loads for a range of possible daily stream flows. The in-stream water quality criterion multiplied by daily stream flow and the appropriate conversion factor would translate the applicable criterion into a daily target (TMDL).

Id. at 2465. Is the *Friends of the Earth* court likely to find this construction acceptable? Does it adequately serve EPA's interests?

Subsequent to the issue of the EPA memorandum, the D.C. Water & Sewer Authority filed a petition with the Supreme Court, seeking review of the ruling of the D.C. Circuit in *Freinds of the Earth*. In its petition, the D.C. Utility claimed that the D.C. Circuit's literal interpretation should not be upheld, on the basis that it was overly rigid. In response, EPA argued that the case did not warrant Supreme Court review, on the grounds that the EPA memorandum would ensure an adequate degree of flexibility to state permitting agencies and to clean water permit holders in applying daily limits for TMDLs. The Supreme Court ultimately sided with EPA and denied the petition for review. In an attempt to quell industry fears, EPA has declared that it expects that daily limits for TMDLs will result in less stringent controls than annual or seasonal limits, given that they "would account for all of the conditions that a river could potentially experience in a given day." *See* Armena H. Saiyid, *EPA Official Says Daily TMDL Limit Unlikely to Exceed Annual Seasonal Limit*, BNA ENV'T REP., May 5, 2006.

13. Nutrient Pollution. The CWA has been highly successful at addressing many forms of pollution. But one major category of pollutants it has not been able to address are nutrients. Nitrogen and phosphorus are both foundational nutrients for producing food and supporting healthy ecosystems. However, when too much nitrogen or phosphorus get into aquatic ecosystems they can cause excess algal growth which can lead to hypoxic zones. Nitrogen in the form of nitrate is also a pollutant of concern in drinking water. The Chesapeake Bay TMDL was designed to reduce nutrient pollution in the Bay. EPA has described nutrient pollution as "one of the greatest challenges to our Nation's water quality." Memorandum from Joel Beauvais, Deputy Assistant Administrator, EPA, Renewed Call to Action to Reduce Nutrient Pollution and Support for Incremental Actions to Protect Water Quality and Public Health (Sept. 22, 2016).

The Gulf Hypoxia Task Force is a collaborative effort of federal and state agencies to address nutrient pollution that causes hypoxia in the Gulf of Mexico each summer. MISSISSIPPI RIVER/GULF OF MEXICO WATERSHED NUTRIENT TASK FORCE, 2017 REPORT TO CONGRESS (Aug. 2017). In addition to TMDLs the states within the task force have established strategies to reduce nutrient pollution from both point and nonpoint sources. *Id.* at 38. These strategies are developed cooperatively with the federal agencies and implement similar programs and regulations as would be used to meet the pollution goals of a TMDL. *Id.*; *see also* ASSOC. OF CLEAN WATER ADMINISTRATORS, NUTRIENT REDUCTION PROGRESS TRACKER (March 2018).

7. INTERSTATE WATER POLLUTION

Other than Alaska and Hawaii, every U.S. state shares ground or surface water with another state. The following case examines the recourse available to downstream states in which water quality has been compromised by pollution originating from upstream states.

Arkansas v. Oklahoma
503 U.S. 91 (1992).

■ JUSTICE STEVENS delivered the opinion for a unanimous Court:

. . . In 1985, the city of Fayetteville, Arkansas, applied to the EPA, seeking a permit for the city's new sewage treatment plant under the National Pollution Discharge Elimination System (NPDES). After the appropriate procedures, the EPA, pursuant to § 402(a)(1) of the Act, 33 U.S.C. § 1342(a)(1), issued a permit authorizing the plant to discharge up to half of its effluent (to a limit of 6.1 million gallons per day) into an unnamed stream in northwestern Arkansas. That flow passes through a series of three creeks for about 17 miles, and then enters the Illinois River at a point 22 miles upstream from the Arkansas-Oklahoma border.

The permit imposed specific limitations on the quantity, content, and character of the discharge and also included a number of special conditions, including a provision that if a study then underway indicated that more stringent limitations were necessary to ensure compliance with Oklahoma's water quality standards, the permit would be modified to incorporate those limits.

Respondents challenged this permit before the EPA, alleging, *inter alia*, that the discharge violated the Oklahoma water quality standards. Those standards provide that "no degradation [of water quality] shall be allowed" in the upper Illinois River, including the portion of the river immediately downstream from the state line.

Following a hearing, the Administrative Law Judge (ALJ) concluded that the Oklahoma standards would not be implicated unless the contested discharge had "something more than a mere *de minimis* impact" on the State's waters. He found that the discharge would not have an "undue impact" on Oklahoma's waters and, accordingly, affirmed the issuance of the permit.

On a petition for review, the EPA's Chief Judicial Officer first ruled that § 301(b)(1)(C) of the Clean Water Act "requires an NPDES permit to impose any effluent limitations necessary to comply with applicable state water quality standards." He then held that the Act and EPA regulations offered greater protection for the downstream State than the ALJ's "undue impact" standard suggested. He explained the proper standard as follows:

> [A] mere theoretical impairment of Oklahoma's water quality standards—*i.e.,* an infinitesimal impairment predicted through modeling but not expected to be actually detectable or measurable—should not by itself block the issuance of the permit. In this case, the permit should be upheld if the record shows by a preponderance of the evidence that the authorized discharges would not cause an actual *detectable* violation of Oklahoma's water quality standards. (emphasis in original).

On remand, the ALJ made detailed findings of fact and concluded that the city had satisfied the standard set forth by the Chief Judicial Officer. Specifically, the ALJ found that there would be no detectable violation of any of the components of Oklahoma's water quality standards. The Chief Judicial Officer sustained the issuance of the permit.

Both the petitioners (collectively Arkansas) and the respondents in this litigation sought judicial review. Arkansas argued that the Clean Water Act did not require an Arkansas point source to comply with Oklahoma's water quality standards. Oklahoma challenged the EPA's determination that the Fayetteville discharge would not produce a detectable violation of the Oklahoma standards.

The Court of Appeals did not accept either of these arguments. The court agreed with the EPA that the statute required compliance with Oklahoma's water quality standards, and did not disagree with the Agency's determination that the discharges from the Fayetteville plant would not produce a detectable violation of those standards. Nevertheless, relying on a theory that neither party had advanced, the Court of Appeals reversed the Agency's issuance of the Fayetteville permit. The court first ruled that the statute requires that "where a proposed source would discharge effluents that would contribute to conditions currently constituting a violation of applicable water quality standards, such [a] proposed source may not be permitted." Then the court found that the Illinois River in Oklahoma was "already degraded," that the Fayetteville effluent would reach the Illinois River in Oklahoma, and that that effluent could "be expected to contribute to the ongoing deterioration of the scenic [Illinois R]iver" in Oklahoma even though it would not detectably affect the river's water quality. . . .

The parties have argued three analytically distinct questions concerning the interpretation of the Clean Water Act. First, does the Act require the EPA, in crafting and issuing a permit to a point source in one State, to apply the water quality standards of downstream States? Second, even if the Act does not *require* as much, does the Agency have the statutory authority to mandate such compliance? Third, does the Act provide, as the Court of Appeals held, that once a body of water fails to meet water quality standards no discharge that yields effluent that reach the degraded waters will be permitted?

In these cases, it is neither necessary nor prudent for us to resolve the first of these questions. In issuing the Fayetteville permit, the EPA assumed it was obligated by both the Act and its own regulations to ensure that the Fayetteville discharge would not violate Oklahoma standards. As we discuss below, this assumption was permissible and reasonable and therefore there is no need for us to address whether the Act requires as much. Moreover, much of the analysis and argument in the briefs of the parties relies on statutory provisions that govern not only federal permits issued pursuant to §§ 401(a) and 402(a), but also state permits issued under § 402(b). It seems unwise to evaluate those arguments in a case such as these, which only involve a federal permit.

Our decision not to determine at this time the scope of the Agency's statutory *obligations* does not affect our resolution of the second question, which concerns the Agency's statutory *authority*. Even if the Clean Water Act itself does not require the Fayetteville discharge to comply with Oklahoma's water quality standards, the statute clearly does not limit the EPA's authority to mandate such compliance.

Since 1973, EPA regulations have provided that an NPDES permit shall not be issued "[w]hen the imposition of conditions cannot ensure compliance with the applicable water quality requirements of all affected States." 40 CFR § 122.4(d) (1991). Those regulations—relied upon by the EPA in the issuance of the Fayetteville permit—constitute a reasonable exercise of the Agency's statutory authority.

Congress has vested in the Administrator broad discretion to establish conditions for NPDES permits. Section 402(a)(2) provides that for EPA-issued permits "[t]he Administrator shall prescribe conditions . . . to assure compliance with the requirements of [§ 402(a)(1)] and *such other requirements as he deems appropriate.*" 33 U.S.C. § 1342(a)(2). (emphasis added). Similarly, Congress preserved for the Administrator broad authority to oversee state permit programs:

> No permit shall issue . . . if the Administrator . . . objects in writing to the issuance of such permit as being outside the guidelines and requirements of this chapter.

33 U.S.C. § 1342(d)(2). The regulations relied on by the EPA were a perfectly reasonable exercise of the Agency's statutory discretion. The application of state water quality standards in the interstate context is wholly consistent with the Act's broad purpose "to restore and maintain the chemical, physical, and biological integrity of the Nation's waters." 33 U.S.C. § 1251(a). Moreover, as noted above, § 301(b)(1)(C) expressly identifies the achievement of state water quality standards as one of the Act's central objectives. The Agency's regulations conditioning NPDES permits are a well-tailored means of achieving this goal.

Notwithstanding this apparent reasonableness, Arkansas argues that our description in *Ouellette* of the role of affected States in the permit process and our characterization of the affected States' position as "subordinate," see 479 U.S., at 490–491, indicates that the EPA's application of the Oklahoma standards was error. We disagree. Our statement in *Ouellette* concerned only an affected State's input into the permit process; that input is clearly limited by the plain language of § 402(b). Limits on an affected State's direct participation in permitting decisions, however, do not in any way constrain the *EPA's* authority to require a point source to comply with downstream water quality standards.

Arkansas also argues that regulations requiring compliance with downstream standards are at odds with the legislative history of the Act and with the statutory scheme established by the Act. Although we agree with Arkansas that the Act's legislative history indicates that Congress intended to grant the Administrator discretion in his oversight of the issuance of NPDES permits, we find nothing in that history to indicate that Congress intended to preclude the EPA from establishing a general requirement that such permits be conditioned to ensure compliance with downstream water quality standards.

Similarly, we agree with Arkansas that in the Clean Water Act Congress struck a careful balance among competing policies and interests, but do not find the EPA regulations concerning the application of downstream water quality standards at all incompatible with that balance. Congress, in crafting the Act, protected certain sovereign interests of the States; for example, § 510 allows States to adopt more demanding pollution-control standards than those established under the Act. Arkansas emphasizes that § 510 preserves such state authority only as it is applied to the waters of the regulating State. Even assuming Arkansas' construction of § 510 is correct, that section only concerns *state* authority and does not constrain the *EPA's* authority to promulgate reasonable regulations requiring point sources in one State to comply with water quality standards in downstream States.

For these reasons, we find the EPA's requirement that the Fayetteville discharge comply with Oklahoma's water quality standards to be a reasonable exercise of the Agency's substantial statutory discretion.

The Court of Appeals construed the Clean Water Act to prohibit any discharge of effluent that would reach waters already in violation of existing water quality standards. We find nothing in the Act to support this reading.

The interpretation of the statute adopted by the court had not been advanced by any party during the Agency or court proceedings. Moreover, the Court of Appeals candidly acknowledged that its theory "has apparently never before been addressed by a federal court." 908 F.2d, at 620, n. 39. The only statutory provision the court cited to support its legal analysis was § 402(h), which merely authorizes the EPA (or a state permit program) to prohibit a publicly owned treatment plant that is violating a condition of its NPDES permit from accepting any additional pollutants for treatment until the ongoing violation has been corrected.

Although the Act contains several provisions directing compliance with state water quality standards, the parties have pointed to nothing that mandates a complete ban on discharges into a waterway that is in violation of those standards. The statute does, however, contain provisions designed to remedy existing water quality violations and to allocate the burden of reducing undesirable discharges between existing sources and new sources. Thus, rather than establishing the categorical ban announced by the Court of Appeals—which might frustrate the construction of new plants that would improve existing conditions—the Clean Water Act vests in the EPA and the States broad authority to develop long-range, area-wide programs to alleviate and eliminate existing pollution.

To the extent that the Court of Appeals relied on its interpretation of the Act to reverse the EPA's permitting decision, that reliance was misplaced.

The Court of Appeals also concluded that the EPA's issuance of the Fayetteville permit was arbitrary and capricious because the Agency misinterpreted Oklahoma's water quality standards. The primary difference between the court's and the Agency's interpretation of the standards derives from the court's construction of the Act. Contrary to the EPA's interpretation of the Oklahoma standards, the Court of Appeals read those standards as containing the same categorical ban on new discharges that the court had found in the Clean Water Act itself. Although we do not believe the text of the Oklahoma standards supports the court's reading (indeed, we note that Oklahoma itself had not advanced that interpretation in its briefs in the Court of Appeals), we reject it for a more fundamental reason—namely, that the Court of Appeals exceeded the legitimate scope of judicial review of an agency adjudication. To emphasize the importance of this point, we shall first briefly assess the soundness of the EPA's interpretation and application of the Oklahoma standards and then comment more specifically on the Court of Appeals' approach.

As discussed above, an EPA regulation requires an NPDES permit to comply "with the applicable water quality requirements of all affected States." 40 CFR § 122.4(d) (1991). This regulation effectively incorporates into federal law those state-law standards the Agency reasonably determines to be "applicable." In such a situation, then, state water quality standards—promulgated by the States with substantial guidance from the EPA and approved by the Agency—are part of the federal law of water pollution control.

Two features of the body of law governing water pollution support this conclusion. First, as discussed more thoroughly above, we have long recognized that interstate water pollution is controlled by *federal* law. Recognizing that the system of federally approved state standards as applied in the interstate context constitutes federal law is wholly consistent with this principle. Second, treating state standards in interstate controversies as federal law accords with the Act's purpose of authorizing the EPA to create and manage a uniform system of interstate water pollution regulation.

Because we recognize that, at least insofar as they affect the issuance of a permit in another State, the Oklahoma standards have a federal character, the EPA's reasonable, consistently held interpretation of those standards is entitled to substantial deference. In these cases, the Chief Judicial Officer ruled that the Oklahoma standards—which require that there be "no degradation" of the upper Illinois River—would only be violated if the discharge effected an "actually detectable or measurable" change in water quality.

This interpretation of the Oklahoma standards is certainly reasonable and consistent with the purposes and principles of the Clean Water Act. As the Chief Judicial Officer noted, "unless there is some method for measuring compliance, there is no way to ensure compliance." Moreover, this interpretation of the Oklahoma standards makes eminent sense in the interstate context: If every discharge that had some theoretical impact on a downstream State were interpreted as "degrading" the downstream waters, downstream States might wield an effective veto over upstream discharges.

The EPA's application of those standards in these cases was also sound. On remand, the ALJ scrutinized the record and made explicit factual findings regarding four primary measures of water quality under the Oklahoma standards: eutrophication, esthetics, dissolved oxygen, and metals. In each case, the ALJ found that the Fayetteville discharge would not lead to a detectable change in water quality. He therefore concluded that the Fayetteville discharge would not violate the Oklahoma water quality standards. Because we agree with the Agency's Chief Judicial Officer that these findings are supported by substantial evidence, we conclude that the Court of Appeals should have affirmed both the EPA's construction of the regulations and the issuance of the Fayetteville permit. . . .

As we have often recognized, an agency ruling is "arbitrary and capricious if the agency has . . . entirely failed to consider an important aspect of the problem." *Motor Vehicle Mfrs. Assn. of United States, Inc. v. State Farm Mut. Automobile Ins. Co.*, 463 U.S. 29, 43 (1983). However, in these cases, the degraded status of the river is only an "important aspect" because of the Court of Appeals' novel and erroneous interpretation of the controlling law. Under the EPA's interpretation of that law, what matters is not the river's current status, but rather whether the proposed discharge will have a "detectable effect" on that status. If the Court of Appeals had been properly respectful of the

Agency's permissible reading of the Act and the Oklahoma standards, the court would not have adjudged the Agency's decision arbitrary and capricious for this reason.

In sum, the Court of Appeals made a policy choice that it was not authorized to make. Arguably, as that court suggested, it might be wise to prohibit any discharge into the Illinois River, even if that discharge would have no adverse impact on water quality. But it was surely not arbitrary for the EPA to conclude—given the benefits to the river from the increased flow of relatively clean water and the benefits achieved in Arkansas by allowing the new plant to operate as designed—that allowing the discharge would be even wiser. It is not our role, or that of the Court of Appeals, to decide which policy choice is the better one, for it is clear that Congress has entrusted such decisions to the Environmental Protection Agency.

NOTES AND QUESTIONS

1.   What Is Detectable? The *Arkansas* Court expresses concern that if any theoretical impact were interpreted as "degrading" downstream waters, then downstream states would effectively have a veto on upstream discharges. Instead, the Court authorized EPA's approach that only "actually detectable or measurable" impacts could violate downstream water quality standards. What are the practical difficulties that might be involved in connecting some detectable downstream impact to a particular upstream discharge? Does this requirement essentially provide a loophole enabling upstream states to prevent downstream states from attaining their water quality standards?

If you were designing a system to determine under what circumstances an impact is excessive, what might you do? Would you require that a source significantly contribute to the violation of a water quality standard? Alternatively, would you adopt a "but-for" test? EPA's Water Quality Guidance for the Great Lakes System (Guidance) addresses these issues. *See* EPA, Final Water Quality Guidance for the Great Lakes System to Prohibit Mixing Zones for Bioaccumulative Chemicals of Concern, 65 Fed. Reg. 67,638 (2000). Procedure 5.F of the Guidance provides that where pollution levels in fish tissue samples exceed water quality criteria, then "each facility that discharges detectable levels of such pollutant to that water has the reasonable potential to cause or contribute to" the violation of the water quality standard. *Id.* at 67,642. EPA's approach has been upheld, over industry opposition, on the grounds that discharge of the pollutant in this situation has a "reasonable potential" to cause exceedance of the water quality standard. *See Am. Iron & Steel Inst. v. EPA*, 115 F.3d 979, 1000 (D.C. Cir. 1997).

2.   Mandatory v. Discretionary Duties. The *Arkansas* Court expressly declined to decide whether EPA must ensure that any permits issued do not violate the water quality standards of another state. The Court was able to avoid this decision because EPA had assumed it was obliged to ensure that the permit did not violate the downstream state water quality standards.

What would happen if EPA issued a permit where it was shown that the discharges would have a significant detectable impact on the downstream state? What would happen if the permit had instead been issued by the upstream state?

3.   Other Examples of Interstate Litigation. The conflicts between Arkansas and Oklahoma did not end with the resolution of this case by the Supreme Court. In 2006, another dispute arose between the states, this time over pollution from chicken farms in Arkansas. Of particular concern were high levels of phosphorus from fertilizer (chicken waste) applied to farms near the river, which led to the emergence of high levels of algae. The algae kills fish, clouds the water, and sometimes emits a foul odor, which officials in Oklahoma assert damages the region's tourist industry.

Another conflict between states involved discharge of briny water from strip mining into a river near the border. EPA approved Virginia's plan to allow this discharge, and in 2006 the Kentucky Attorney General was considering suing Virginia. *See* Juliet Eilperin, *Pollution in the Water, Lawsuits in the Air*, WASH. POST, Aug. 28, 2006, at A3.

4.   Common Law Nuisance. In *City of Milwaukee v. Illinois*, 451 U.S. 304, 317 (1981), the Supreme Court held that the CWA preempted the federal common law of nuisance. In *International Paper Co. v. Ouellette*, 479 U.S. 481, 494 (1987), the Court held that the CWA preempted state nuisance actions brought under the common law of the affected state. Under *Ouellette*, actions can be maintained only under the common law of the source state. *See id.* at 493–99. What incentive would this rule create on the part of states to externalize interstate water pollution?

5.   CWA v. CAA: "Actual Detection and Measurement" v. "Significant Contribution." Compare the control of interstate water pollution under the CWA with the control of interstate air pollution under the CAA. How does the "actually detectable or measurable" impact test developed by the *Arkansas* Court compare with the "significant contribution" test developed by the *Air Pollution Control District of Jefferson County* court? Which is more stringent? Could an upwind state's contribution to the violation of a downwind state's NAAQS be "actually detectable or measurable," but not "significant"? Conversely, could an upstream state's contribution to the violation of a downstream state's water quality standards be "significant," but not "actually detectable or measurable"? Which measure should be preferred?

6.   CWA v. CAA: Stringent State Standards. Under the CAA, states are entitled to set ambient standards at levels more stringent than the NAAQS. *Union Elec. v. EPA*, 427 U.S. 246 (1976). They are not, however, entitled to enjoin upwind states that contribute to a violation of those standards. Under the CWA, states are similarly able to set water quality standards at levels that are more stringent than the federal standards. Are downstream states able to enjoin upstream states that violate such heightened standards? Which regime is preferable?

7.   CWA in Practice. It is not entirely clear how much of an impact a more stringent downstream water quality standard has on upstream polluters in neighboring states. While the *Arkansas* Court declined to determine whether EPA had a mandatory duty to apply downstream water quality standards to upstream polluters, the Court accepted as reasonable EPA regulations requiring as much. In practice, however, downstream water quality standards may not have a significant impact on interstate pollution. Consider this view:

> The EPA has rarely taken formal action on interstate water pollution pursuant to the CWA. This is likely because the Environmental Protection Agency, like other federal agencies, is reluctant to take on heated interstate controversies. This suggests that relying on the federal government, and specifically on federal agencies, to resolve contentious interstate environmental impact disputes may not be the most politically realistic solution, regardless of statutory authority.

Noah D. Hall, *Political Externalities, Federalism, and a Proposal for Interstate Environmental Impact Assessment Policy*, 32 HARV. ENVTL. L. REV. 49, 75 (2008). What else might explain EPA's hesitance to take formal action? Are there other ways in which the CWA requirements might limit interstate water pollution?

In *City of Albuquerque v. Browner*, 97 F.3d 415 (10th Cir. 1996), the court upheld EPA's approval of a downstream water quality standard for a Native American tribe—considered a "state" under these circumstances— against a challenge by upstream polluters. EPA mediated a negotiation between the tribe and the upstream state to establish permits that would respect the tribe's designation of a "ceremonial use" for the water body, which had resulted in something akin to a fishable/swimmable standard. EPA did not have to resort to its formal authority to deny permits issued by the upstream state. Is the mere threat of formal action by EPA sufficient for a workable interstate regime? How might the interstate provisions better account for the political costs in denying upstream permits?

8. DRINKING WATER

Every day, millions of people receive drinking water from their local water systems. There are over 170,000 public drinking water systems in the United States. EPA, UNDERSTANDING THE SAFE DRINKING WATER ACT (2009). Some of these systems are privately owned; others are owned and operated by public agencies. Though the quality of American drinking water is generally quite high, that quality cannot be taken for granted, as there are a number of threats to the quality of drinking water: Animal waste, human waste, pesticides, and chemicals can all threaten public health by contaminating the local water supply.

The Safe Drinking Water Act (SDWA), 42 U.S.C. § 300f *et seq.*, was originally enacted by Congress in 1974, and has been subsequently amended in 1986 and 1996. The SDWA requires EPA to work cooperatively with states to ensure the quality of local drinking water. The SDWA does not regulate bottled water, which is regulated by the

Food and Drug Administration under the Federal Food, Drug, and Cosmetic Act, 21 U.S.C. § 301 *et seq.*

Regulation under the SDWA begins with the identification of contaminants for listing. Under the SDWA, a "contaminant" is "any physical, chemical, biological, or radiological substance or matter in water." 42 U.S.C. § 300f(6). Contaminants are regulated if the Administrator determines that the contaminant "may have an adverse effect on the health of persons," "is known to occur . . . in public water systems with a frequency and at levels of public health concern," and that regulation of such contaminant "presents a meaningful opportunity for health risk reduction." 42 U.S.C. § 300g–1(b)(1)(A).

For each contaminant, EPA must set a "maximum contaminant level goal" (MCLG). The MCLG is to be set at "the level at which no known or anticipated adverse effects on the health of persons occur and which allows an adequate margin of safety." 42 U.S.C. § 300g–1(b)(4)(A). EPA then sets primary drinking water regulations. These regulations must specify a "maximum contaminant level" (MCL) if it is "economically and technologically feasible to ascertain the level of such contaminant in water." 42 U.S.C. § 300f(1)(C)(i). For those contaminants for which it is not feasible to ascertain the level, the regulations must specify treatment techniques. The MCL is to be set "as close to the maximum contaminant level goal as is feasible," 42 U.S.C. § 300g–1(b)(4)(B), and is "the maximum permissible level of a contaminant in water which is delivered to any user of a public water system," 42 U.S.C. § 300f(3).

In the 1996 amendments to the SDWA, Congress incorporated provisions requiring the use of cost-benefit analysis. Prior to 1996, when setting the MCL, the Administrator was required to set it at "as close to the [MCLG] as is feasible." 42 U.S.C. § 300g–1(b)(4) (amended 1996). The amendments required the Administrator to determine whether "the benefits of the maximum contaminant level justify, or do not justify, the costs." Pub. L. No. 104–182, § 104(a), 110 Stat. 1613, 1623 (1996) (codified at 42 U.S.C. § 300g–1(b)(4)(C) (2000)). If the benefits do not outweigh the costs, the Administrator may set a less stringent standard. For further discussion of the 1996 amendments, see Richard Revesz, *Federalism and Environmental Regulation: A Public Choice Analysis*, 115 HARV. L. REV. 553, 631–32 (2001).

NOTES AND QUESTIONS

1.   **Regulating Drinking Water at the Source.** About 130 million people in the United States rely on groundwater for their drinking water and groundwater accounts for 98 percent of self-supplied domestic water (*i.e.* private wells). NANCY L. BARBER ET AL., UNITED STATES GEOLOGICAL SURVEY, CIRCULAR 1405, ESTIMATED USE OF WATER IN THE UNITED STATES IN 2010 (2014). In its most recent report on groundwater quality the United States Geological Survey found samples taken from 22 percent of the wells sampled contained at least one contaminant above the drinking water MCL.

Most of these contaminants were from geological sources (*e.g.*, arsenic, manganese, or uranium). Nitrate was the only contaminant from manmade sources that exceeded the MCL in more than one percent of sampled wells. However, human caused contaminants (*e.g.*, dissolved solids, chloride, or nitrate) increased in two-thirds of the wells sampled between the early 1990s and 2010. Additionally, pesticides and other manmade chemicals are now observed more frequently in shallow groundwater beneath agricultural and urban land. These chemicals may migrate to the deeper aquifers where most drinking water is drawn from. Deep aquifer contamination can take decades to address. LESLIE A. DESIMONE ET AL., UNITED STATES GEOLOGICAL SURVEY, CIRCULAR 1360, WATER QUALITY IN PRINCIPAL AQUIFERS OF THE UNITED STATE, 1991–2010 (2014).

There is no comprehensive federal law protecting the United States' groundwater resources. In the most recent attempt to clarify federal jurisdiction over "waters of the United States" under the CWA, the EPA and Army Corps expressly excluded groundwater from CWA jurisdiction. Clean Water Rule: Definition of "Waters of the United States," 80 Fed. Reg. 37,054, 37,125 (2015). As discussed above, some courts have held that the CWA regulates point source pollutant discharges to groundwater, when those discharges contaminate jurisdictional surface waters. However, most regulation of groundwater quality is left to the states. *See* Michael C. Blumm & Steven M. Thiel, *(Ground)waters of the United States: Unlawfully Excluding Tributary Groundwater from Clean Water Act Jurisdiction*, 46 ENVTL. L. 333, 340–42 (2016).

The SDWA, Resource Conservation and Recovery Act (RCRA), and Comprehensive Environmental Response, Compensation, and Liability Act (CERCLA) all include some provisions aimed at preventing groundwater contamination, but none of them provide comprehensive protection. The SDWA requires that operators of underground injection wells obtain permits and do not inject any effluent which would endanger a public drinking water supply. *See* 42 U.S.C. § 300h; 40 C.F.R. Parts 144–48. The SDWA also authorizes the EPA Administrator to provide grants to states for state groundwater protection efforts. 42 U.S.C. § 300h–8. The RCRA requires that underground storage tanks at facilities handling hazardous wastes are constructed and maintained to national standards to prevent leakage. *See* 80 Fed. Reg. 41,566, 41,568 (2015). Leaking underground storage tanks are a significant source of groundwater contamination. *Id.* The RCRA also requires operators of facilities handling hazardous wastes to clean up spills and the entire facility upon closure to prevent contamination of soil and groundwater. *See* 42 U.S.C. § 6907(a)(2); 40 C.F.R. Parts 264–65. The CERCLA does not prevent new sources of groundwater contamination but does help clean up existing contaminated sites, which would otherwise serve as a source of groundwater contamination. *See* 42 U.S.C. § 9604(a)(1).

2. Underground Injection and Hydraulic Fracturing. As noted above, the SDWA requires EPA to regulate underground injection of effluent that may endanger public water systems. In 2005 Congress passed an amendment to the SDWA exempting "the underground injection of fluids or propping agents (other than diesel fuels) pursuant to hydraulic fracturing operations related to oil, gas, or geothermal production activities." *See* 42 U.S.C. § 300h(d)(1)(B)(ii); David B. Spence, *Federalism, Regulatory Lags, and the Political Economy of Energy Production*, 161 U. PA. L. REV. 431, 449–50 (2013). This exemption prevents EPA from regulating the injection of non-diesel containing fluids used in hydraulic fracturing for natural gas and oil production. The EPA also exempted oil and gas drilling muds and oil production brines from regulation under RCRA in 1988. *See* Spence, *supra*, at 452 n.107. The EPA does have authority to regulate the underground injection of diesel containing hydraulic fracturing fluids under the SDWA. *See* EPA, OFFICE OF WATER, 816-R-14-001, PERMITTING GUIDANCE FOR OIL AND GAS HYDRAULIC FRACTURING ACTIVITIES USING DIESEL FUELS: UNDERGROUND INJECTION CONTROL PROGRAM GUIDANCE #84 (Feb., 2014).

3.   MTBE Groundwater Contamination. Methyl Tertiary-butyl Ether (MTBE) is a fuel additive that was used to increase the oxygen level of gasoline to improve vehicle performance and reduce emissions of air pollutants. Fuel companies began adding MTBE to gasoline in the late 1970s to replace tetra-ethyl lead. MTBE use increased significantly in the late 1980s as fuel manufacturers used it to reduce carbon monoxide emissions in NAAQS non-attainment areas. Finally, fuel manufacturers relied on MTBE to comply with the Clean Air Act Amendments of 1990, which required producers to add oxygenates to gasoline to reduce ozone emissions in large metropolitan areas. *See* Thomas O. McGarity, *MTBE: A Precautionary Tale*, 28 HARV. ENVTL. L REV. 281, 284–85 (2004).

MTBE is very water soluble and does not easily degrade in the environment. It also has a foul turpentine-like taste and odor that is detectable by humans at levels of one to two parts per billion (ppb) and is also considered a possible carcinogen by EPA. Many underground storage tank systems at retail gas stations were corroded and leaked gasoline. While the gasoline largely stayed in the soil near the tank, the MTBE, due to its solubility, rapidly moved through the soil into the groundwater. This led to contamination of many drinking water systems in areas where reformulated gasoline was used. *See In re Methyl Tertiary Butyl Ether (MTBE) Products Liability Litigation*, 725 F.3d 65 (2d Cir. 2013).

The MTBE contamination sparked hundreds of lawsuits. *Id.* at 78; McGarity, *supra*, at 282. A few lawsuits were based on federal law claims under RCRA or TSCA, however most of the lawsuits relied on state law claims, specifically state common law tort, nuisance, and trespass claims. *See In re Methyl Tertiary Butyl Ether (MTBE) Products Liability Litigation*, 725 F.3d at 79. In response to MTBE contamination, and public concern about leaking underground storage tanks, Congress amended RCRA to require EPA to regulate underground storage tank systems in 1988. McGarity, *supra*, at 302–04. Congress eventually ended the gasoline reformulation requirements in 2005, and many states banned MTBE in gasoline. *Id.* at 289; *In re Methyl Tertiary Butyl Ether (MTBE) Products Liability Litigation*, 725 F.3d at 78.

International Fabricare Institute v. Environmental Protection Agency

972 F.2d 384 (D.C. Cir. 1992).

▪ Before BUCKLEY, SENTELLE, and RANDOLPH, CIRCUIT JUDGES.

▪ PER CURIAM:

In these consolidated cases, petitioners challenge regulations promulgated by the Environmental Protection Agency pursuant to the Safe Drinking Water Act. The regulations establish permissible concentration levels for contaminants occurring in drinking water. Petitioners claim that the EPA committed both substantive and procedural errors in formulating the regulations. . . .

Petitioners raise a general challenge to the EPA policy rejecting the existence of safe threshold levels for carcinogens in the absence of contrary evidence. Petitioners then present procedural and substantive challenges to the permissible concentration levels established for two contaminants—dibromochloropropane and ethylene dibromide. Petitioners also allege procedural defects in the regulations pertaining to perchloroethylene. . . .

The EPA promulgated the disputed regulations to implement the Safe Drinking Water Act, 42 U.S.C. §§ 300f–300j–25 (1988), which requires the Agency to establish national drinking water standards and to issue regulations to prevent the harmful contamination of public water systems. The regulations are to identify contaminants occurring in drinking water that may have an adverse effect on health, and to regulate them to the extent cost and technology permit. The regulations are to establish a "maximum contaminant level goal" ("MCLG") for each identified contaminant. *Id.* § 300g–1(a)(3). An MCLG is a non-enforceable goal that is to be set "at the level at which no known or anticipated adverse effects on the health of persons occur and which allows an adequate margin of safety." *Id.* § 300g–1(b)(4). The regulations for most contaminants also specify an enforceable "maximum contaminant level" ("MCL") that sets the maximum permissible level of the contaminant in water delivered to any user of a public water system. *See id.* § 300f(3). MCLs must be set "as close to the [MCLG] as is feasible." *Id.* § 300g–1(b)(4). "Feasible" means using "the best technology, treatment techniques and other means . . . available (taking cost into consideration)." *Id.* § 300g–1(b)(5).

On November 13, 1985, the EPA published a notice of proposed rulemaking for the regulation of specific water contaminants. *See National Primary Drinking Water Regulations; Synthetic Organic Chemicals, Inorganic Chemicals and Microorganisms*, 50 Fed. Reg. 46,936 (1985) ("1985 Proposed Rule"). The EPA resubmitted the rulemaking on May 22, 1989, to reflect revisions to the Act made by Congress in amendments enacted in 1986. *See National Primary and Secondary Drinking Water Regulations*, 54 Fed. Reg. 22,062, 22,068

(1989) ("Proposed Rule"). This revised proposal contained MCLGs and MCLs for thirty-eight organic and inorganic chemicals. *Id.* at 22,064. The Proposed Rule also responded to the comments the EPA had received on the 1985 proposal. . . .

On March 28, 1991, several petitioners filed challenges to the final regulations. The petitions involve four contaminants. Petitioners Dow Chemical Company, Shell Oil Company, and Occidental Chemical Corporation seek review of the MCLs and MCLGs for 1,2 dibromo–3–chloropropane ("DBCP"). Dow also challenges the regulation with respect to ethylene dibromide ("EDB"). International Fabricare Institute ("IFI") and intervenor Halogenated Solvents Industry Alliance ("HSIA") ask us to set aside the regulations concerning tetrachloroethylene, also known as perchloroethylene ("perc"). Finally, National Electrical Manufacturers Association ("NEMA") and Chemical Manufacturers Association ("CMA") seek review of the rule relating to polychlorinated biphenyls ("PCBs"). . . .

As part of its methodology for establishing MCLGs, the EPA has developed a classification scheme that sorts contaminants into "Groups" (A to E) and "Categories" (I to III). See Final Rule, 56 Fed. Reg. at 3,532. Group A contaminants are considered to be known human carcinogens based on sufficient human epidemiologic evidence. *Id.* Group B1 substances are considered probable human carcinogens based on limited human epidemiological evidence. *Id.* Group B2 chemicals are classified as probable human carcinogens "based on a combination of sufficient evidence in animals and inadequate data in humans." *Id.* Group C contaminants are defined as "[p]ossible human [c]arcinogens based on limited evidence of carcinogenicity in animals [and] the absence of human data." *Id.* Group D is reserved for substances that the EPA finds to be unclassifiable due to lack of data or inadequate evidence of carcinogenicity. *Id.* Finally, Group E chemicals are those for which the EPA finds no evidence of carcinogenicity based on adequate animal tests or animal and human epidemiological studies. *Id.*

In most cases, the EPA places Group A, B1, and B2 contaminants into Category I, Group C into Category II, and Groups D and E into Category III. *Id.* The EPA sets MCLGs for Category I chemicals at zero because it assumes, "in the absence of other data, that there is no known threshold" at which these known or probable carcinogens can be safely tolerated. *Id.* at 3,533. In contrast, Category II and III substances are set at levels "likely to be without an appreciable risk of deleterious health effects during a lifetime." . . .

The Act requires the EPA to set "[e]ach maximum contaminant level goal . . . at the level at which no known or anticipated adverse effects on the health of persons occur and which allows an adequate margin of safety." 42 U.S.C. § 300g–1(b)(4). Consistent with its past practice, see, e.g., NRDC v. EPA, 824 F.2d 1211, 1214–16 (D.C. Cir. 1987); 50 Fed. Reg. 46,895 (1985), the EPA here set a goal of zero for each chemical it considered a known or probable human carcinogen (Category I contaminants).

The EPA previously adopted the zero goal approach in another rulemaking under this statute. *See National Primary Drinking Water Regulations; Volatile Synthetic Organic Chemicals*, 50 Fed. Reg. 46,880 (1985). It did so in part based on its reading of the legislative history of the Act, *see id.* at 46,884 col. 2 (quoting H.R. Rep. No. 1185, 93d Cong., 2d Sess. 20 (1974)), and in part based on a conclusion that, since current science could not ascertain exactly how a carcinogen caused cancer, "it was conservatively believed" that exposure to any dose could have adverse health effects. *Id.* On petition for review, this court determined that, in adopting its zero goal approach, the "EPA made an expert judgment" based on a "reasoned determination." *NRDC v. EPA*, 824 F.2d at 1215. We upheld that judgment. *Id.*

Perhaps in light of the foregoing, petitioners today argue neither that the EPA's use of a zero goal approach is precluded by Congress's clear intent as expressed in the Act, nor that it is *per se* an impermissible exercise of the agency's discretion under the Act. Rather, they assert that new scientific evidence exists that might make the EPA's approach untenable, and the agency arbitrarily and capriciously failed to consider and address that evidence.

The evidence consisted primarily of a three-page letter to the editor, written by Drs. Bruce N. Ames and Lois Swirsky Gold of the University of California at Berkeley, published in *Science* magazine. Ames & Gold, Pesticides, Risk, and Applesauce, 244 *Science* 755 (May 19, 1989). The only other evidence submitted was the declaration of Dr. Gori. Comment to the EPA, Declaration of Dr. Gio Batta Gori (Aug. 17, 1989), *reprinted in* J.A. at 320–36. Both admitted that the causes of human cancer were still unknown. 244 *Science* at 757; Gori Decl. at 4, *reprinted in* J.A. at 323. The Ames letter advanced the argument that "low doses of carcinogens appear to be . . . less hazardous than is generally thought," 244 *Science* at 757; Gori pointed out the difficulties inherent in drawing conclusions about humans from studies done on animals. Gori Decl. at 6–10, *reprinted in* J.A. at 325–29.

Neither document, however, reflected the results of any new empirical studies or laboratory experiments. Neither offered a new statistical analysis of existing data. Both simply pointed out certain shortcomings in the methods and data generally relied on by the scientific establishment. (Ames's letter was substantially similar to his 1985 submission to the California Legislature regarding a bill then under consideration. Letter from Dr. Bruce N. Ames to Hon. Art Torres (Nov. 11, 1985), *reprinted in* J.A. at 352–54.) The "new scientific evidence" petitioners point to, *see* Brief for Petitioners at 31, boils down to the opinions of a few scientists who, however qualified, are in their own words at odds with what is "generally thought" about the subject. 244 *Science* at 757; *cf.* Gori Decl. at 9, *reprinted in* J.A. at 328.

In the context of the EPA's treatment of carcinogens generally, and its rulemakings under this statute in particular, we find the Agency's response to the comments adequate. After noting that it had heard before most of what was now being said, Final Rule, 56 Fed. Reg. at 3,533, the EPA stated that it was sticking with its zero goal policy "when current scientific data do not show a safe threshold." *Id.* at 3,535. Necessarily implicit in that statement, we think, is an Agency conclusion that the Gori declaration and the Ames letter did not require a contrary result. The EPA stated that it would continue to consider "whether it is possible to define levels that have little or no meaning in terms of cancer risk," and that if such levels were found it would reconsider its zero goal approach. *Id.* While in some circumstances an agency must undertake a more detailed re justification of its prior position, *see, e.g., Bechtel v. FCC*, 957 F.2d 873 (D.C. Cir. 1992) when the agency's decision is as recent (and as recently upheld) as this one, that duty cannot be triggered by the submission of comments consisting of little more than assertions that in the opinions of the commenters the agency got it wrong. Given that neither submission here presented any "data," Final Rule, 56 Fed. Reg. at 3,535, we cannot fault the EPA for not paying more attention to them. . . .

In ruling on these petitions, our responsibility is limited to determining whether the EPA's interpretations of the Safe Drinking Water Act are permissible, and whether in applying the Act, the Agency has abided by the requirements of the Administrative Procedure Act. As we are not scientists and must defer to the Agency's judgments on matters within its technical competence, our task is to assure that they be reasoned, not that they be right. Because we find that the EPA's interpretations of the Act are permissible, that it has complied with the procedures mandated by the APA, and that its conclusions have been neither arbitrary nor capricious, we deny the petitions for review.

NOTES AND QUESTIONS

1.   **Deciding What to Regulate.** The SDWA features a listing mechanism and some discretion by the Administrator in regulating pollutants in drinking water. *See* 42 U.S.C. § 300g–1(b)(1)(B)(i). What differences does the contaminant listing process have to the criteria pollutant listing process in the CAA? With other statutes you have encountered thus far? Study the text of the statute: If an interested party wanted to compel regulation of a given pollutant in court, would that be possible? See *id.* If an interested party wanted to challenge the regulation of a pollutant as improper (not the particular regulations, but the decision to regulate), would that be possible? *See id.*

The 1996 amendments reduced the frequency with which the Administrator must publish regulations of listed contaminants from no fewer than twenty-five every three years to no fewer than five every five years. *See* 42 U.S.C. § 300g–1(b)(1)(B)(ii). The SDWA requires EPA, "[i]n selecting unregulated contaminants for consideration under subparagraph

(B), [to] select contaminants that present the greatest public health concern."
42 U.S.C. § 300g–1(b)(1)(C). Since the 1996 amendments, EPA has decided
to not regulate 20 listed contaminants; most of the existing drinking water
regulations were promulgated under the framework of the 1986
amendments. In early 2011, EPA reversed its 2008 preliminary decision to
not regulate perchlorate, marking the first time that a contaminant was
recommended for regulation since the 1996 amendments. For an analysis of
EPA regulations under the SDWA since the 1996 amendments, see GAO,
SAFE DRINKING WATER ACT: EPA SHOULD IMPROVE IMPLEMENTATION OF
REQUIREMENTS ON WHETHER TO REGULATE ADDITIONAL CONTAMINANTS
(2011). The GAO report found that

> EPA has not developed policies or guidance providing its
> interpretation of, or guiding personnel in how to implement, the
> broad statutory criteria for selecting contaminants and making
> regulatory determinations on them. Moreover, the credibility of
> some of EPA's regulatory determinations is reduced because of a
> lack of transparency, clarity, and consistency in the regulatory
> determination notices and primary support documents.

Id. at 17. What might explain EPA's recent decisions to not regulate listed
contaminants?

2.   Improving the Public Health. EPA must conclude, to regulate a
pollutant under the SDWA, that regulating such pollutant presents
"meaningful opportunity for health risk reduction." 42 U.S.C. § 300g–
1(b)(1)(A)(iii). Is this simply duplicative of the requirement that
contaminants have an adverse effect on the health of persons, or does it add
some independent meaning? What is 'meaningful' in this context—a net
beneficial outcome under a cost-benefit standard? Something less stringent?

3.   No Threshold Contaminants. In *International Fabricare*, EPA had
decided on a policy of setting the MCLG for most carcinogens at zero. Why?
This policy was initially upheld in *NRDC v. EPA*, 824 F.2d 1211 (D.C. Cir.
1987). In that case, some petitioners argued that EPA was required to make
a threshold finding of significant risk (under the *Benzene* decision) before it
could regulate a contaminant at a given level. The court rejected this
argument as inconsistent with the text of the statute, directing the
Administrator to establish a recommended level for a contaminant which
"may have any adverse effect" on human health. Is this rejection correct?
Recall that the *Benzene* decision was based on the statutory text of OSHA.

How does the "no threshold" approach EPA takes in SDWA regulation
different from its approach in the CAA/CWA? It may help to consider how
MCLGs are different from (and similar to) the NAAQS. Under the SDWA, at
what point must EPA abandon its "no threshold" policy? For an example of
where the SDWA was held to limit EPA's discretion in this regard, see
Chlorine Chemistry Council v. EPA, 206 F.3d 1286 (D.C. Cir. 2000). In that
case, EPA's use of a default assumption of linearity and zero MCLG for
chloroform was held to violate the SDWA.

City of Waukesha v. Environmental Protection Agency

320 F.3d 228 (D.C. Cir. 2003).

■ Before HENDERSON, ROGERS, and GARLAND, CIRCUIT JUDGES.

■ PER CURIAM:

The petitioners—the City of Waukesha and its water utility customer Bruce Zivney, trade associations Nuclear Energy Institute ("NEI") and National Mining Association ("NMA"), and advocacy group Radiation, Science & Health ("RSH")—seek review of regulations promulgated by the Environmental Protection Agency ("EPA") pursuant to the Safe Drinking Water Act of 1970 ("SDWA" or "Act"), 42 U.S.C. § 300f *et seq.* The challenged regulations establish standards governing radionuclide levels in public water systems. Specifically, they set the maximum contaminant level goal ("MCLG") and the maximum contaminant level ("MCL") for radium-226 and radium-228, naturally occurring uranium, and various beta/photon emitters. . . .

In 1976 EPA promulgated interim regulations that established MCLGs and MCLs for radionuclides, which are materials that emit radiation as they decay from one elemental form to another. The regulations established an MCL of 5 picocuries/Liter (pCi/L) for the isotopes radium-226 and radium-228; a combined MCL of 4 millirems (mrem) 2 for all beta/photon emitters; and no MCL for naturally-occurring uranium. *See* National Interim Primary Drinking Water Regulations, 41 Fed. Reg. 28,402, 28,404 (July 9, 1976).

In 1991 EPA proposed new MCLs for the radionuclides: 20 pCi/L for radium-226 and-228; 4 mrem effective dose equivalent ("ede") for the beta/photon emitters; and 20 micrograms per liter (mpg/L) or 30 pCi/L for naturally occurring uranium. *See* National Primary Drinking Water Regulations; Radionuclides, Notice of Proposed Rulemaking, 56 Fed. Reg. 33,050, 33,051 (July 18, 1991).

In 1996 the Congress amended the SDWA to, *inter alia,* add an "anti-backsliding" provision requiring that any water regulation revision "maintain, or provide for greater, protection of the health of persons," 42 U.S.C. § 300g–1(b)(9), and to require the agency to consider the relative costs and benefits in setting each MCL, *id.* § 300g–1(b)(3)(C), (4)(C). . . .

In December 2000 EPA issued the final radionuclides rule, National Primary Drinking Water Regulations; Radionuclides, 65 Fed. Reg. 76,708 (Dec. 7, 2000) (Final Rule). As it had proposed, EPA retained the 1976 standards for radium-226 and-228 and for beta/photon emitters and instituted the separate radium isotope monitoring requirement. 65 Fed. Reg. at 76,710–11. For uranium, however, the final rule set the MCL at 30 mpg/L. 65 Fed. Reg. at 76,710. Petitioners filed timely petitions for review of the final rule. . . .

By contrast to the 2000 radium and beta/photon regulations, the uranium MCL issued in that year represented a "new" standard, as there was no pre-existing MCL for uranium. *See* 65 Fed. Reg. at 76,708. Section 1412(b)(3)(C)(i) therefore required EPA to prepare and publish a cost-benefit analysis, and it did so. Petitioners contend that EPA's analysis failed to satisfy the requirements of that section and the APA.

Petitioners' first argument is that EPA failed to comply with § (b)(3)(C)(i) because it did not analyze the costs and benefits associated with compliance with the uranium MCL in contexts other than the SDWA. In particular, petitioners assert that EPA failed to evaluate the costs and benefits arising from compliance with the MCLs at hazardous waste sites governed by CERCLA. EPA counters that the SDWA does not require it to analyze such costs.

EPA again has the better of the argument. Section (b)(3)(C)(i)(III) requires EPA to analyze:

> Quantifiable and nonquantifiable costs for which there is a factual basis in the rulemaking record to conclude that such costs are likely to occur *solely as a result of compliance with the maximum contaminant level*, including monitoring, treatment, and other costs and *excluding costs resulting from compliance with other proposed or promulgated regulations*.

42 U.S.C. § 300g–1(b)(3)(C)(i)(III) (emphasis added). EPA reasonably reads the italicized words, particularly the phrase "excluding costs resulting from compliance with other . . . regulations," as excluding costs associated with compliance with regulatory regimes other than the SDWA itself. As EPA argues, the purpose of the MCLs is to protect the public, as much as feasible, from the adverse health effects of drinking contaminated water. *See id.* § 300g–1(b)(4)(A), (B). That purpose would be undermined if the cost-benefit balance were skewed by consideration of the additional costs imposed by other uses of the MCLs, unrelated to protecting consumers of drinking water.

Petitioners attack EPA's view on a number of grounds. First, they note that the cited exclusion refers only to costs resulting from compliance with other "regulations." CERCLA, they correctly point out, is not a regulation but a statute—one that specifically instructs that the clean-up of hazardous waste sites must satisfy contamination standards promulgated under the SDWA. *See* 42 U.S.C. § 9621(d)(2)(A). But EPA, equally correctly, points out that like most statutes, CERCLA's mandate is implemented by regulations, which, among other things, set forth the circumstances under which MCLGs and MCLs of the SDWA are to be used as clean-up standards, as well as the circumstances under which compliance with them can be waived. *See* 40 C.F.R. § 300.430(e), (f); *see generally* 40 C.F.R. pt. 300. Moreover, as EPA further notes, CERCLA itself imposes no requirement that EPA consider the costs and benefits of compliance with MCLs as an element of clean-up standards, and certainly no requirement that the agency do so as part of its obligations under a separate statute like the SDWA.

Second, petitioners contend that the legislative history of the SDWA indicates that the exclusion of consideration of the costs of compliance with other regulations applies only to those regulations that are themselves the product of cost-benefit analysis. This argument relies on a single sentence from a Senate report: "The Administrator is not to consider the benefits (or costs) that are attributable to compliance with other proposed or promulgated regulations, if those benefits and costs are considered in a determination as to whether benefits justify costs under those regulations." S. Rep. No. 104–169, at 29–30. But as EPA notes, while this passage mandates that the agency may not consider benefits and costs under such circumstances, it does not state that the agency *must* do so under all other circumstances. Since the statute itself contains no such qualification on its exclusion of the consideration of the costs and benefits of other regulations, that is hardly an unreasonable view for the agency to take.

Third, petitioners assert that even if the SDWA does exclude consideration of the costs associated with the application of MCLs in other contexts, the Act does not also exclude consideration of the benefits of applying MCLs under other regulatory regimes. In support, petitioners point to the benefits provision of § 1412(b)(3)(C)(i)(I), which, unlike the costs provision of § (b)(3)(C)(i)(III), contains no exclusion relating to compliance with other regulations. Without qualification, the benefits provision requires an analysis of "quantifiable and nonquantifiable health risk reduction benefits . . . likely to occur as the result of treatment to comply with each level." 42 U.S.C. § 300g–1(b)(3)(C)(i)(I). But while it is true that § (b)(3)(C)(i)(I) contains no exclusion, in context it is also clear that the section's use of the phrase "the result of treatment" refers to *drinking water* treatment, and not to treatment of contaminants for other purposes. *See id.* § 300g–1(b)(3)(C)(ii); *id.* § 300g–4(e)(3). Moreover, we do not understand what petitioners hope to gain by requiring EPA to add further to the benefits (but not to the costs) of MCLs in conducting its cost-benefit analysis; such a calculus would only increase the justification for the MCLs actually promulgated by EPA, as compared to the higher levels favored by petitioners.

Finally, petitioners contend that EPA has itself "acknowledged the necessity of evaluating benefits and costs of MCLs at CERCLA sites." Petitioners' Br. at 26. It is true that EPA's preliminary cost-benefit analysis stated that "the impact of the regulations on other programs, such as the use of MCLs in site clean-up decisions," was a "factor[ ] . . . of interest to decision-makers and will be taken into account in the final selection of the regulatory options to be implemented." PHRRCA, at 6–8. But regarding something as a factor "of interest" is not the same as regarding it as a statutory obligation, and nothing else in the agency's statements suggests that EPA has regarded the consideration of CERCLA costs and benefits as mandatory.

American Water Works Association v. Environmental Protection Agency

40 F.3d 1266 (D.C. Cir. 1994).

■ Before GINSBURG and RANDOLPH, CIRCUIT JUDGES, and SHADUR, SENIOR DISTRICT JUDGE.

■ GINSBURG, CIRCUIT JUDGE:

The American Water Works Association [(AWWA)] and the Natural Resources Defense Council [(NRDC)] separately petition for review of the Environmental Protection Agency's final rule under the Safe Drinking Water Act promulgating a national primary drinking water regulation for lead. The NRDC challenges the EPA's decisions establishing a treatment technique instead of a maximum contaminant level (MCL) for lead . . . .

I. Background

The Safe Drinking Water Act requires the EPA to promulgate drinking water regulations designed to prevent contamination of public water systems. 42 U.S.C. § 300g–1(b). A national primary drinking water regulation (NPDWR) is one that specifies for a contaminant with an adverse effect upon human health either an MCL or a treatment technique, and establishes the procedures and criteria necessary to ensure a supply of drinking water that complies with that MCL or treatment technique. 42 U.S.C. § 300f(1). An NPDWR is an enforceable standard applicable to all public water systems nationwide. In most of the NPDWRs promulgated to date the EPA has set an MCL for the particular contaminant being regulated. The EPA has the authority, however, to specify a treatment technique in lieu of an MCL if the Administrator finds that it is not "economically or technologically feasible" to determine the level of the particular contaminant in a public water system. 42 U.S.C. § 300f(1)(C)(ii).

It is particularly difficult to determine the level of lead in a public water system. Less than one percent of all public water systems draw source water containing any lead. *Notice of Proposed Rulemaking: Drinking Water Regulations; Maximum Contaminant Level Goals and National Primary Drinking Water Regulations for Lead and Copper*, 53 Fed.Reg. 31,516, 31,526–27 (1988). Instead, most lead enters a public water system through corrosion of service lines and plumbing materials containing lead, such as brass faucets and lead solder connecting copper pipes, that are privately owned and thus beyond the EPA's regulatory reach under the Act. System-wide measurement is made still more difficult because the degree to which plumbing materials leach lead varies greatly with such factors as the age of the material, the temperature of the water, the presence of other chemicals in the water, and the length of time the water is in contact with the leaded material. *Final Rule: Maximum Contaminant Level Goals and National Primary Drinking Water Regulations for Lead and Copper*, 56 Fed.Reg. 26,460, 26,463–66, 26,473–76 (1991). Indeed, lead levels in samples drawn consecutively from a single source can vary significantly. *Id.* at 26,473–76. Measurement difficulties aside, treatment is made problematic because chemicals added to the drinking water supply in order to reduce the corrosion of pipes can increase the levels of other contaminants subject to MCLs. *Id.* at 26,486–87.

Recognizing the peculiar difficulty of establishing an MCL for lead in public water systems, the EPA proposed regulations that distinguish between control of lead in source water and control of lead due to corrosion. First, the EPA proposed an MCL for lead in source water, to be measured at the point where the water enters the distribution system. Second, the EPA proposed to require a treatment technique—an "optimal corrosion control treatment" supplemented with a program of public education—to be tailored specifically by each public water system in such a way as to minimize lead contamination in drinking water without increasing the level of any other contaminant to the point where it violates the NPDWR for that substance. 53 Fed.Reg. at 31,537–38.

In the final rule the EPA abandoned [this] two-part monitoring and treatment proposal in favor of a rule under which all large water systems must institute corrosion control treatment, while smaller systems must do so only if representative sampling indicates that lead in the water exceeds a designated "action level." 56 Fed.Reg. at 26,550 (to be codified at 40 C.F.R. § 141.81(d) & (e)). The EPA required larger systems to come into compliance sooner than smaller systems because they are generally more sophisticated technically and have a greater impact upon the purity of drinking water; also the states, which are responsible for implementing the regulation, would benefit from experience gained with larger systems before reviewing treatment plans for smaller systems.

Unlike the proposed rule, the final rule requires each public water system to replace each year at least 7% of the lead service lines it controls that when tested exceed a designated action level. 40 C.F.R. § 141.84(b) & (d). A public water system is said to "control" a service line if it has

> authority to set standards for construction, repair, or maintenance of the line, authority to replace, repair, or maintain the service line, or ownership of the service line.

40 C.F.R. § 141.84(e). The rule establishes a presumption that the public water system controls every service line up to the wall of the building it serves; the system can rebut the presumption only by demonstrating that its control is limited by state statute, local ordinance, public service contract, or other legal authority. 40 C.F.R. § 141.84(e). A public water system that controls only part of a service line must replace the portion under its control and must offer to replace the remaining

portion, although not necessarily at the system's expense. 40 C.F.R. § 141.84(d).

II. Analysis

... The NRDC [ ] contends that, because it is economically and technologically feasible to ascertain the level of lead in water, the Safe Drinking Water Act requires that the EPA set an MCL for lead. See 42 U.S.C. § 300f(1)(C); 42 U.S.C. § 300g–1(b)(7). Further, because the tap is the delivery point to the user of a public water system, the NRDC concludes that the MCL must be set at the tap.

At bottom the NRDC and the EPA disagree over the meaning of the word "feasible" as it applies to ascertaining the level of lead in drinking water. The NRDC argues that the Congress clearly expressed its intent that "feasible" be understood to mean "physically capable of being done at reasonable cost". . . . For its part, the EPA does not dispute that it is "feasible" to monitor lead under the definition advanced by the NRDC; instead the agency interprets "feasible" to mean "capable of being accomplished in a manner consistent with the Act." The agency argues that if public water systems were required to comply with an MCL for lead, they would have to undertake aggressive corrosion control techniques that might reduce the amount of lead leached from customers' plumbing but would also increase the levels of other contaminants. The EPA argues that because the Congress apparently did not anticipate a situation in which monitoring for one contaminant, although possible, is not conducive to overall water quality, it impliedly delegated to the agency the discretion to specify a treatment technique instead of an MCL.

We agree with the EPA that the meaning of "feasible" is not as plain as the NRDC suggests. . . .

The Congress clearly contemplated that an MCL would be a standard by which both the quality of the drinking water and the public water system's efforts to reduce the contaminant could be measured. See 42 U.S.C. § 300g–1(b)(5). Because lead generally enters drinking water from corrosion in pipes owned by customers of the water system, an MCL for lead would be neither; ascertaining the level of lead in water at the meter (i.e. where it enters the customer's premises) would measure the public water system's success in controlling the contaminant but not the quality of the public's drinking water (because lead may still leach into the water from the customer's plumbing), while ascertaining the level of lead in water at the tap would accurately reflect water quality but effectively hold the public water system responsible for lead leached from plumbing owned by its customers.

We must defer to the EPA's interpretation of "feasible" if it is reasonable, *Chevron v. NRDC*, 467 U.S. 837, 842–43 (1984), and we think that it is. A single national standard (i.e., an MCL) for lead is not suitable for every public water system because the condition of plumbing materials, which are the major source of lead in drinking water, varies across systems and the systems generally do not have control over the sources of lead in their water. In this circumstance the EPA suggests that requiring public water systems to design and implement custom corrosion control plans for lead will result in optimal treatment of drinking water overall, i.e. treatment that deals adequately with lead without causing public water systems to violate drinking water regulations for other contaminants. 56 Fed. Reg. 26,487.

Viewing the Act as a whole, we cannot say that the statute demonstrates a clear congressional intent to require that the EPA set an MCL for a contaminant merely because it can be measured at a reasonable cost. In light of the purpose of the Act to promote safe drinking water generally, we conclude that the EPA's interpretation of the term "feasible" so as to require a treatment technique instead of an MCL for lead is reasonable. . . .

For the foregoing reasons, we deny the petition of the NRDC insofar as it challenges [ ] the EPA's decision to require a treatment technique in lieu of an MCL for lead.

NOTES AND QUESTIONS

1.   **Feasibility.** The plaintiffs in both *City of Waukesha* and *American Water Works Association* challenged the Agency's interpretation of "feasible" in setting, or declining to set, an MCL. How did the Agency's interpretation differ between the two cases? What should "feasibility" mean in the context of the SDWA? How does the MCLG/MCL scheme compare to BAT standards under the CWA?

2.   **MCL v. Treatment Technique Regulations.** Lead and copper are two of only nine contaminants for which the EPA has required a treatment technique instead of an MCL. *See* 40 C.F.R. §§ 141.70, 141.111, 141.710–14. The SDWA allows EPA to establish a treatment technique where the Administrator determines that it is not economically or technologically feasible to ascertain the level of a contaminant in the water system. 42 U.S.C. § 300g–1(b)(7)(A). In addition to the treatment technique for lead, EPA also established an action level for lead at 0.015 mg/L (15 ppb) in no more than 10 percent of the samples. *See* Maximum Contaminant Level Goals and National Primary Drinking Water Regulations for Lead and Copper, 56 Fed. Reg. 26,460, 26,478–79 (1991). The action level for lead was set at what the agency believed was the most health protective level, which corrosion control technology could achieve. *Id.* at 26490. Unlike an MCL, which cannot be exceeded without violating the NPDWR, an action level is a screening tool to determine if additional treatment technique controls are needed.

The SDWA allows EPA to set a less stringent MCL when the Administrator determines that the costs of complying with the more stringent MCL would outweigh the benefits. In that case the agency must set the MCL at a level "that maximizes health risk reduction benefits at a cost that is justified by the benefits." 42 U.S.C. § 300g–1(b)(6)(A). However, following a deadly outbreak of Cryptosporidium in Milwaukee, Wisconsin, Congress amended the SDWA to prohibit EPA from using cost-benefit analysis in setting an MCL for Cryptosporidium. 42 U.S.C. § 300g–1(b)(6)(C). The amendment was silent as to treatment techniques, however, the court in *City of Portland v. EPA,* extended Congress' reasoning to prohibit cost-benefit analysis in setting a less strict treatment technique for Cryptosporidium. 507 F.3d. 706, 710–11 (D.C. Cir. 2007). Why would Congress want to allow cost-benefit analysis for other contaminants, but not for Cryptosporidium?

3.   Lead and Copper Rule (LCR). As discussed in *American Water Works Association*, the primary source for lead in drinking water is corrosion of lead pipes and plumbing fixtures, which are used to deliver water to the tap. Congress did not ban lead service lines (LSL), which are the pipes that carry the water from the water main to the home, until 1986. It is estimated that between 6.5 to 10 million homes are still served by lead service lines across the country. EPA promulgated the original LCR in 1991. The rule applies to 68,000 public water systems nationwide. Exceedances of the 15ppb action level by large water systems have been reduced by 90 percent since the LCR was implemented. *See* EPA, OFFICE OF WATER, LEAD AND COPPER RULE REVISIONS WHITE PAPER (Oct. 2016).

Since the LCR's original promulgation, EPA made minor changes to the Rule in 2000 and 2007, while recognizing that significant strengthening of the LCR was needed. The drinking water crisis in Flint, Michigan (discussed below) drew national focus to the need to update the LCR. The LCR is one of the most complicated SDWA regulations for drinking water systems due to complex sampling and treatment technique requirements. Unlike other rules, which require sampling at the point of distribution (*e.g.*, where the water leaves the treatment facility), the LCR requires sampling at the consumer's faucet. The LCR also requires corrosion control techniques, which if not implemented correctly may increase other contaminants in the water system.

In 2016, EPA, relying on recommendations from the National Drinking Water Advisory Council, issued a white paper outlining changes to strengthen the LCR. Some of the changes involve consumer focused improvements, such as establishing a more robust public education requirement for consumers receiving water from LSLs and establishing household action levels which would trigger reporting to consumers. Some of the changes are technology focused, such as improving corrosion control treatment, and tailoring water quality parameters by the treatment system. The white paper also proposes improving monitoring requirements and requiring proactive LSL replacement. *Id.*

4.   Lead Service Line Replacement. Today, many public water systems do not know exactly how many LSLs are in their distribution systems. David Cornwell et al., *National Survey of Lead Service Line Occurrence*, 108:4 J. AMER. WATER WORKS ASSOC. 182 (April, 2016). Under the current regulations, water treatment systems are only required to replace LSLs after an exceedance of the action level. EPA, OFFICE OF WATER, LEAD AND COPPER RULE REVISIONS WHITE PAPER 8 (Oct. 2016). The estimated cost of replacing a single LSL ranges from $2,500 to $8,000. With an estimated 6.5 to 10 million LSLs nationwide the potential cost of replacement could range from $16 to $80 billion. *Id.*

An additional challenge to replacing LSLs is that the public water systems may own the line only up to the private homeowner's property boundary. An issue, which was excluded from *American Water Works Association* excerpt above, was the definition of "control." In the final rule EPA had established a rebuttable presumption that the public water system owned the LSL up to the wall of the building. The AWWA challenged that definition, and EPA has since revised the regulations to include only the portion of the LSL that the public water service actually owns, typically up to the property line. The EPA's Science Advisory Board found that partial replacement of LSLs was not shown to reliably reduce drinking water lead levels in the short term (up to months) and may actually elevate short term lead levels. *Id.* For a LSL replacement to be effective the entire LSL needs to be replaced, and lead bearing plumbing fixtures in the home may also need to be replaced.

The costs of replacing LSLs may also fall disproportionately on low-income communities, raising social justice concerns. For example, Detroit, where 40 percent of the population is below the poverty line, has an estimated 100,000 LSLs. *Id.* The goal of the SDWA is to ensure safe drinking water across the nation, in the context of lead the most effective way to achieve that outcome would be to replace the LSLs and lead bearing plumbing fixtures. However, the cost of LSL replacement is prohibitively high, especially for low income communities. How should EPA and state agencies implementing the SDWA balance the costs and benefits of replacing LSLs? Ultimately, rate payers often bear the cost of increased regulatory requirements. They also gain the benefits of cleaner water. Should a community's willingness to pay be used to determine which lead reduction efforts the Agency should require?

9. THE FLINT CRISIS

In late 2015, a crisis that had been brewing in Flint, Michigan, for over a year burst onto the national stage. Due to a change in source water and failures at multiple levels of government, Flint residents were exposed to severely elevated lead levels in their drinking water. The Flint crisis demonstrates the challenges of cooperative federalism and implementing a complex regulatory regime like the LCR.

Flint, Michigan, is a majority-African American city, with a population of slightly less than 100,000, in southeastern Michigan. Over 40 percent of the population of Flint lives below the federal poverty line. Flint was placed in state receivership in 2011 and an emergency manager was assigned to run the city. See *Concerned Pastors for Soc. Action v. Khouri*, 217 F. Supp. 3d 960, 968 (E.D. Mich. 2016).

Prior to 2014, Flint had purchased its water from the City of Detroit. Detroit treated its water with orthophosphate to control corrosion and prevent leaching of lead from the lead water pipes carrying the water. Flint had planned to switch its water supply from Detroit to the Karegondi Water Authority (KWA), which would have resulted in significant cost savings. Flint had notified Detroit that it planned to terminate its contract for water in April, 2014; however, the pipeline for the KWA was not complete when the contract ended. Instead of renegotiating the contract with Detroit, the emergency manager and city officials decided to begin using water from the Flint River to supply the city's drinking water needs. Flint processed the Flint River water through its water treatment facility, which it had maintained in case of an emergency. However, the city failed to add corrosion control treatment, as required by the LCR, to the water. This was because the Michigan Department of Environmental Quality (DEQ) had incorrectly determined that corrosion control not needed until two six-month monitoring periods had passed. FLINT WATER ADVISORY TASK FORCE, FINAL REPORT 15–16 (March, 2016).

Soon after the city began treating its own water, residents began complaining of its odor, taste, and appearance. Numerous operational challenges and water quality problems resulted in violations of the SDWA regulations related to E. Coli contamination and disinfection by-products. *Id.* In February 2015, a city test returned high lead levels in at least one resident's home. The resident contacted EPA with concerns. EPA reached out to MDEQ after the initial contact, but it was not until April that the MDEQ confirmed with EPA that the City had never implemented corrosion control technology to prevent lead leaching. Despite internal EPA concerns, MDEQ officials maintained that the water was safe. By September, Virginia Tech scientists had tested water from hundreds of homes and found elevated lead levels. The same month a study found that the number of children with elevated lead levels in their blood had increased since the change in source water. *Id.* at 18, 21.

In September, the city issued a lead advisory, but maintained that it was in full compliance with the SDWA. In early October, Michigan Governor Rick Snyder released an action plan and said that the city and State would provide free filters and water testing to residents. Shortly after, the city switched back to the Detroit water supply. In December the mayor declared a state of emergency, followed in January by a declaration of a state of emergency by the Governor and President Obama. *Id.*

Michigan DEQ officials initially cited confusion about the federal SDWA regulations when the water supply was switched. However, subsequent investigation by an independent task force found that, in addition to failures at all levels of government, MDEQ officials had misrepresented the LCR, misapplied its requirements, and waited months before accepting assistance from EPA. The task force also found that EPA was hesitant and slow to insist on LCR compliance. *Id.* at 6, 8–9. Eventually nine city and state officials would have criminal charges brought against them for misconduct, neglect of duty, and conspiracy. The crisis also spawned numerous lawsuits against the city and state. *See* Merrit Kennedy, *Lead-Laced Water In Flint: A Step-By-Step Look At The Makings Of A Crisis*, NAT'L PUB. RADIO (April 20, 2016).

NOTES AND QUESTIONS

1. **Remedies for Flint Residents.** One of the lawsuits that was brought following the Flint crisis was *Concerned Pastors for Soc. Action v. Khouri*, 217 F. Supp. 3d 960 (E.D. Mich. 2016). The plaintiffs in *Concerned Pastors* brought citizen suit claims against the City and the State for violations of the LCR and SDWA. The plaintiffs requested a preliminary injunction requiring the city to deliver bottled water door-to-door, ensure filters were properly installed, and provide additional public education on the unsafe nature of the City's water. The district court granted the preliminary injunction and ordered the city to deliver bottled water to the almost 100,000 Flint residents, unless officials had confirmed that a residence had a properly installed water filter. The estimated cost of the water delivery program was $9.4 million per month, which was $6 million more than was already being spent on bottled water.

The Sixth Circuit upheld the preliminary injunction over a dissent by Judge Sutton. *Concerned Pastors for Social Action v. Khouri*, 844 F.3d 546 (6th Cir. 2016). In his dissent, Judge Sutton questioned whether bottled water delivery was the most effective way to address the problem. Instead, Judge Sutton suggested the district court should have ordered the city to ensure filters were installed correctly, and that no violations of the SDWA were occurring, leaving bottled water delivery as a backstop. Due to the resource intensive requirements of bottled water delivery, Judge Sutton argued it would be better to use the City's limited resources by addressing the underlying problem. 844 F.3d at 550–551 (J. Sutton, dissenting).

2. **Water Quality Monitoring.** One of the violations noted in *Concerned Pastors* was a failure by the city to comply with the LCR monitoring requirements. Most SDWA regulations require sampling where water enters the distribution system. *See* 40 C.F.R. § 141.23. The LCR requires monitoring from faucets in residences. Prior to the change in source water, Flint had been sampling from designated residences as prescribed by the LCR. After the change in source water, the city reached out to the general public to request sampling sites instead of using the historical sampling sites. By the end of 2015 the City had only collected 39 of the required 100 samples. *Concerned Pastors*, 217 F. Supp. 3d at 967.

3. **Costs Comparison of SDWA Regulations.** One of the biggest challenges facing an updated LCR is the cost of replacing LSLs. As discussed above, LSL replacement is estimated to cost between $16 and $80 billion nationally. This is both a very high cost, and a broad range. How might the EPA estimate how much a new rule is going to cost?

The SDWA Amendments of 1996 require the EPA to perform a Health Risk Reduction and Cost Analysis (HRRCA) for each regulation the Agency promulgates under the Act. The HRRCA is effectively a cost-benefit analysis.

On the cost side, the agency considers the number of drinking water systems impacted by the rule, the cost of treatment technology, the operation and maintenance cost of that technology, and costs to states to implement the rule, among many other factors. On the benefit side, the agency considers both tangible and intangible benefits. Tangible benefits include reduced disease occurrence and healthcare costs. The intangible benefits, may actually have a very real value but may be more difficult to calculate than tangible benefits. These include avoided material damage to water systems, enhanced aesthetic qualities, and avoided cost of averting behavior. The SDWA doesn't require benefits to outweigh costs, only that the regulatory requirement (MCL or treatment technology) be "feasible" considering the benefits and costs. See EPA, ECONOMIC ANALYSIS AND STATUTORY REQUIREMENTS (Feb. 22, 2017).

The Surface Water Treatment Rule (SWTR), 54 Fed. Reg. 27,486 (1989), was one of the first major rules promulgated under the SDWA, it required water systems to control infectious diseases in their water. At the time, EPA estimated that the national capital costs of implementing the SWTR would be $6.31 billion and the national annualized costs would be $1.03 billion per year.[1] Capital costs represent the costs of physical system upgrades and technology installation. Annualized costs include the costs of operation and maintenance of the upgraded system, monitoring costs, and the costs of financing capital improvements. All annualized costs are based on a 20-year effective-life of the capital upgrades.

Two more major rules promulgated under the SDWA had very different capital costs, but similar annualized costs. The original LCR, 56 Fed. Reg. 26,460 (1991), was estimated to have national capital costs of $9.32 billion and national annualized costs of $1.18 billion. The Stage 1 Disinfection By-Products Rule (DBPR), 63 Fed. Reg. 69,389 (1998), was estimated to have national capital costs of $3.51 billion and national annualized costs of $1.06 billion. Why would the annualized costs for these rules be similar when the capital costs are so different?

Another way the EPA represents costs is by estimating how much the rule will increase the cost of treating 1,000 gallons of water. For instance, in the SWTR the Agency estimated that the cost of treating 1,000 gallons of water would increase between $0.98 and $4.21 depending on system size. In the Radionuclide Rule, which was challenged in *City of Waukesha*, the agency estimated that costs to treat 1,000 gallons of water would increase by $0.25 to $0.41 for large systems. Under the rule, some small systems would face costs of up to $4.41 per 1,000 gallons. The estimated annualized costs for the Radionuclides Rule was only $119 million. Why would some systems have similar per 1,000 gallon treatment costs under the Radionuclide Rule as under the SWTR, even though annualized costs under the SWTR were far higher?

---

[1]   All values in this section have been converted to 2018 dollars. The U.S. Department of Labor, Bureau of Labor Statistics, Inflation Calculator, available at https://www.bls.gov/data/inflation_calculator.htm, was used to calculate all current dollar values for SDWA regulations. The date of rule promulgation was used as the base year, unless the rule specified otherwise. January, 2018 was used for the current value.

Small systems treat significantly less water and have fewer customers than large systems. Large systems have a large customer base to spread the costs of upgrades and treatment measures across, while customers of small systems will bear a higher marginal cost for SDWA regulations. To account for this discrepancy, another way the agency calculates costs is per-household. For the DBPR it was estimated that 95 percent of households would incur less than $1.50 per month in additional costs due to the rule, 4 percent would incur between $1.50 and $15 per month cost increase, and one percent would experience cost increases of between $15 and $50 per month. The final one percent still represents 1 million households according to agency estimates. The agency estimated that the per household costs for large systems under the Radionuclide Rule would range from $20 to $33 per month, while small systems would experience per household costs of between $29 and $368 per month. The Radionuclide Rule had estimated annualized costs of $119 million, which are low compared to the $1.06 billion in annualized costs of the DBPR. How can per household costs in the Radionuclide rule be larger, especially in large systems than the DBPR. At least part of the answer is that the Radionuclide Rule only applied to community water systems that serve smaller populations (<10,000 people), while the DBPR covers water systems that serve over one million customers.

On the benefits side, the agency, in the SWTR estimated that 90 percent of water system customers would receive positive benefits from the rule, while the costs would outweigh the benefits for 10 percent of customers. The Agency however declined to put an exact dollar figure on the benefits of the rule because the risk of contracting a waterborne illness from drinking water was speculative. In the LCR the Agency estimated that the benefit-cost ratio would be at least 2:1, but again declined to put an exact figure on the benefits due to intangible benefits of reducing corrosion to water systems and reducing lead exposure. In the Radionuclide rule, the Agency only quantified benefits for monitoring radium-228, which it estimated at $1.7 million, and acknowledged that costs would outweigh quantified benefits. The Agency declined to quantify benefits of the MCL because they were difficult to monetize, since the number of kidney toxicity cases avoided could not be estimated with current risk models.

4.   Using the SDWA for Watershed Protection. The New York City Watershed is the largest unfiltered water supply in the United States, encompassing 2,000 square miles. It provides 1.2 billion gallons of water to nine million people in New York City and surrounding counties every day. *See* New York State, Department of Lands Conservation, New York City Water Supply, https://www.dec.ny.gov/lands/25599.html (last visited Mar. 19, 2018).

Prompted by development in the watershed and degrading water quality, the EPA in 1989, under authority of the SDWA, ordered the City to either protect the watershed or build a filtration plant. It was estimated that the filtration plant would cost approximately $8 billion to build, with operation costs of $1 million per day. The high cost of, and desire to avoid, filtration prompted the City and State to engage in a multi-year negotiation with watershed communities and stakeholders to protect the New York City

Watershed. In 1997, New York City signed a landmark agreement with the State, EPA, local municipalities, and stakeholders to protect the watershed. The New York City Watershed Agreement committed the City to invest about $1.5 billion over ten years to restore and protect the watershed and fund improvement projects for watershed residents. Michael C. Finnegan, *New York City's Watershed Agreement: A Lesson in Sharing Responsibility*, 14 PACE ENVTL. L. REV. 577 (1997).

An important component of the agreement was a land acquisition and protection program. As of December 2017, the City had obtained easements on, or directly purchased, 140,000 acres of land in the watershed. This land is permanently protected from development and managed to protect water quality. Other watershed protection measures included upgrades to waste water treatment plants, septic tanks, and stormwater controls in the watershed and stream management aimed at reducing erosion and riparian degradation. The agreement also created task forces to identify and implement agricultural and forestry best management practices aimed at protecting water quality. *See* NEW YORK STATE DEPARTMENT OF HEALTH, NEW YORK CITY FILTRATION AVOIDANCE DETERMINATION (December, 2017).

The agreement is one of the largest programs implementing payments by beneficiaries of watershed services to providers of those services. All of the land acquisitions conducted by the City have been at fair market value, and the City continues paying property tax on those properties, supporting watershed communities. The City, through fees on water users, also pays for implementation of many of the watershed protection measures described above. The watershed protection measures implemented by the agreement benefit water users, upstream communities, and more broadly improve environmental quality throughout the watershed.

The CWA is typically thought of as protecting the environment, while the SDWA is thought of as protecting end-of-tap water quality. However, in this example the SDWA played a significant role in protecting a large watershed. A filtration plant likely would have achieved the same end-of-tap outcomes as the watershed agreement, but it would have cost significantly more and would not have generated the same environmental benefits. The watershed agreement creates a program, by which New Yorkers pay for upstream ecosystem services that benefit their water quality. *See* Thomas C. Brown et al., *Defining, Valuing, and Providing Ecosystem Goods and Services*, 47 NAT. RESOURCES J. 329, 342 (2007).

CHAPTER VII

CONTROL OF HAZARDOUS SUBSTANCES

1. INTRODUCTION: *EX ANTE* REGULATION V. *EX POST* LIABILITY

This chapter examines the two statutes that deal primarily with the regulation of hazardous wastes and substances in the United States—the Resource Conservation and Recovery Act (RCRA), 42 U.S.C. 6901 *et seq.*, and the Comprehensive Environmental Response, Compensation, and Liability Act (CERCLA or Superfund), 42 U.S.C. § 9601 *et seq.* RCRA establishes an *ex ante* regulatory regime, under which generators and transporters of hazardous waste, along with facilities that treat, store or dispose of hazardous waste, are required to comply with "cradle to grave" standards designed to prevent damages to human health and the environment. In contrast, CERCLA establishes an *ex post* liability regime, designed to impose liability upon parties responsible for the contamination of land by hazardous substances. Whereas RCRA is a forward-looking statute, directed towards addressing present hazardous waste activities, CERCLA is a backward-looking statute, directed toward the remediation of past activities.

As an introduction to both regimes, the excerpt from the essay by Richard L. Revesz and Lewis A. Kornhauser discusses the incentives transmitted by *ex ante* and *ex post* instruments in the context of hazardous waste regulation. The Supreme Court's opinion in *Meghrig v. KFC Western, Inc.*, 516 U.S. 479 (1996), which follows, discusses in broad terms the roles played by each regime.

Lewis A. Kornhauser & Richard L. Revesz, Regulation of Hazardous Wastes

in 3 THE NEW PALGRAVE DICTIONARY OF ECONOMICS AND THE LAW, 238–39
(Peter Newman ed., 1998).[*]

. . . [C]onsider the incentives that a liability regime can transmit to generators of hazardous wastes and owners of hazardous waste sites. First, a generator must determine the volume of hazardous wastes that it will produce. Because the wastes are a by-product of profitable economic activity, this decision is affected by the costs of different production processes as well as the expected liability associated with the wastes. So, for example, a generator must trade off the costs of more expensive production processes that would yield a smaller amount of wastes per unit of useful output against the higher costs, including the expected liability, of disposing a larger amount of wastes.

Second, a generator must determine whether to recycle, to treat (i.e., render non-hazardous), or to dispose of the wastes. Each of these processes has certain immediate costs and gives rise to different levels of expected liability.

---

[*]   Internal citations have been omitted. Reprinted with the permission of Macmillan Reference Limited, copyright © 1998, all rights reserved.

Third, a generator must choose a level of care for the handling of the wastes in the pre-disposal phase. More care raises the cost of disposal but decreases the generator's expected liability.

Fourth, for wastes that it chooses to dispose, a generator must choose a disposal site. Similarly, the owner of the disposal site must determine what types of wastes it will accept. Different sites might charge different fees, present different risks that at some point hazardous wastes will be released into the environment, and give rise to different cleanup costs in the event of a release.

Fifth, the owner of the site must determine the level of effort that it will expend to prevent the contamination of the environment. Similarly, a generator must decide the effort that it will expend in monitoring the disposal site to detect releases of the wastes into the environment. Such monitoring is desirable because cleanup costs can rise rapidly if the problem is left unattended.

Sixth, a liability regime can provide incentives for a generator or site owner to expend efforts to ensure that the cleanup is performed in a cost-effective manner. The savings can be substantial. There are estimates indicating that cleanup costs are about 20% lower when actions are undertaken by [private parties] rather than by the government.

A prospective liability regime—a regime that applies to conduct occurring after the adoption of the liability provisions—can create appropriate incentives with respect to all six decisions. In contrast, while a retroactive regime, applying to conduct occurring prior to the passage of the statute, typically cannot transmit incentives with respect to the first four steps, which will be complete, it can transmit incentives for the monitoring of sites and for cost-effective cleanups. (Retroactive liability, however, can create disincentives for the purchase and remediation of contaminated property.)

The problem with liability regimes, however, is that they work well only as long as the parties have sufficient solvency, at the time that they make the various decisions, and have no plans to shed their solvency thereafter. Also, liability regimes can be less desirable than alternative schemes for transmitting incentives if their transaction costs are too high.

Now, consider the effects of an *ex ante* regulatory system. In theory, a system of *ex ante* regulation could be designed to provide the correct incentives with respect to all six decisions. For example, it could prescribe the maximum permissible amount of hazardous waste per unit, say, of output; the types and proportions of wastes that should be recycled or reused; and the site to which the wastes should be sent. It could also, in principle, include monitoring requirements, as well as requirements that generators perform any necessary cleanup.

In practice, it would be exceedingly hard to structure an *ex ante* regulatory system that would transmit proper incentives with respect to each of these decisions. For example, setting the permissible amount of hazardous waste per unit of output would require a staggering amount of information. . . .

A hybrid scheme of *ex ante* regulation and *ex post* liability is likely to be more desirable than either pure system. *Ex post* liability can transmit incentives with respect to a broader set of decisions, but is hampered by the problem of potential insolvency. *Ex ante* regulation, as a practical matter, can only influence a subset of relevant decisions, and, when it takes the form of command-and-control regulation, is likely to be economically inefficient, but it is not disabled by the lack of solvency. The hybrid regime in the United States is therefore at least potentially attractive. The broad *ex post* liability provisions of the Superfund statute are coupled with *ex ante* licensing requirements imposed by RCRA. RCRA also aids the functioning of the Superfund system through elaborate record-keeping requirements, which should make it easier to trace responsible parties in the future, and through financial responsibility requirements. . . .

NOTES AND QUESTIONS

1. **Incentives Generated by *Ex Post* Instruments.** *Ex post* liability instruments do not prescribe particular conduct. Instead, they transmit incentives through the deterrent effect of damages actions that may be brought if harm occurs. *See* Steven Shavell, *Liability for Harm Versus Regulation of Safety*, 13 J. LEG. STUD. 357, 357 (1984) (excerpted in Chapter III). Under what circumstances will the threat of damage actions carry no deterrent effect?

2. **Information Generated by *Ex Ante* Instruments.** Kornhauser and Revesz note that, in theory, an *ex ante* regulatory regime could transmit the same incentives with respect to each of the six decisions facing generators and owners of hazardous wastes as an *ex post* regulatory regime. In practice, however, Kornhauser and Revesz argue that the information necessary to achieve this parity would be too difficult to obtain. For each of the six decisions, what information would be required to operate an efficient *ex ante* regime? How difficult would this information be to obtain?

3. **Transaction Costs.** Kornhauser and Revesz note that "liability regimes can be less desirable than alternative schemes for transmitting incentives if their transaction costs are too high." In the context of the management of hazardous waste, what are the likely transaction costs associated with *ex post* instruments? How high are these costs likely to be?

4. **Knowledge.** As discussed in Chapter III, one determinant in the relative appeal of *ex post* and *ex ante* regulatory instruments is the relative knowledge about risky activities held by private parties and by the regulatory authority. *See* Shavell, *supra*, at 360. In the context of the management of hazardous materials, should this factor count against or in favor of *ex post* instruments?

5. Administrative Costs. What administrative costs would an *ex post* regime impose on private parties and on the public? How do these differ from the costs imposed under an *ex ante* regime? *See* Shavell, *supra*, at 368. In the context of the management of hazardous materials, which regime should be preferred with respect to this factor?

6. Hybrid System. Evaluate the basis upon which Kornhauser and Revesz claim that "[a] hybrid scheme of *ex ante* regulation and *ex post* liability is likely to be more desirable than either pure system." What factors would be relevant to the design of an optimal hybrid system?

Consider, for example, the two questions concerning hybrid regimes raised by Professor Shavell in Chapter III: "Should a party's adherence to regulation relieve him of liability in the event that harm comes to pass? On the other hand, should a party's failure to satisfy regulatory requirements result necessarily in his liability?" 13 J. LEG. STUD. at 365. How would you answer each question in the context of the management of hazardous materials?

Meghrig v. KFC Western, Inc.

516 U.S. 479 (1996).

■ JUSTICE O'CONNOR delivered the opinion of the Court:

. . . Respondent KFC Western, Inc. (KFC), owns and operates a "Kentucky Fried Chicken" restaurant on a parcel of property in Los Angeles. In 1988, KFC discovered during the course of a construction project that the property was contaminated with petroleum. The County of Los Angeles Department of Health Services ordered KFC to attend to the problem, and KFC spent $211,000 removing and disposing of the oil-tainted soil.

Three years later, KFC brought this suit under the citizen suit provision of RCRA, 42 U.S.C. § 6972(a),* seeking to recover these cleanup costs from petitioners Alan and Margaret Meghrig.

KFC claimed that the contaminated soil was . . . covered by RCRA, . . . and that the Meghrigs were responsible for "equitable restitution" of KFC's cleanup costs under § 6972(a) because, as prior owners of the

---

* Section 6972(a) provides, in relevant part:

"Except as provided in subsection (b) or (c) of this section, any person may commence a civil action on his own behalf—

(1)(B) against any person, including . . . any past or present generator, past or present transporter, or past or present owner or operator of a treatment, storage, or disposal facility, who has contributed or who is contributing to the past or present handling, storage, treatment, transportation, or disposal of any solid or hazardous waste which may present an imminent and substantial endangerment to health or the environment. . . .

The district court shall have jurisdiction . . . to restrain any person who has contributed or who is contributing to the past or present handling, storage, treatment, transportation, or disposal of any solid or hazardous waste referred to in paragraph (1)(B), to order such person to take such other action as may be necessary, or both. . . ."

property, they had contributed to the waste's "past or present handling, storage, treatment, transportation, or disposal." See App. 12–19.

RCRA is a comprehensive environmental statute that governs the treatment, storage, and disposal of solid and hazardous waste. Unlike the Comprehensive Environmental Response, Compensation, and Liability Act of 1980 (CERCLA), RCRA is not principally designed to effectuate the cleanup of toxic waste sites or to compensate those who have attended to the remediation of environmental hazards. RCRA's primary purpose, rather, is to reduce the generation of hazardous waste and to ensure the proper treatment, storage, and disposal of that waste which is nonetheless generated, "so as to minimize the present and future threat to human health and the environment." 42 U.S.C. § 6902(b).

Chief responsibility for the implementation and enforcement of RCRA rests with the Administrator of the Environmental Protection Agency (EPA), see §§ 6928, 6973, but like other environmental laws, RCRA contains a citizen suit provision, § 6972, which permits private citizens to enforce its provisions in some circumstances.

Two requirements of § 6972(a) defeat KFC's suit against the Meghrigs. The first concerns the necessary timing of a citizen suit brought under § 6972(a)(1)(B): That section permits a private party to bring suit against certain responsible persons, including former owners, "who ha[ve] contributed or who [are] contributing to the past or present handling, storage, treatment, transportation, or disposal of any solid or hazardous waste which *may present* an *imminent* and substantial endangerment to health or the environment." (Emphasis added.) The second defines the remedies a district court can award in a suit brought under § 6972(a)(1)(B): Section 6972(a) authorizes district courts "*to restrain* any person who has contributed or who is contributing to the past or present handling, storage, treatment, transportation, or disposal of any solid or hazardous waste . . . , *to order such person to take such other action as may be necessary*, or both." (Emphasis added.)

It is apparent from the two remedies described in § 6972(a) that RCRA's citizen suit provision is not directed at providing compensation for past cleanup efforts. Under a plain reading of this remedial scheme, a private citizen suing under § 6972(a)(1)(B) could seek a mandatory injunction, *i.e.*, one that orders a responsible party to "take action" by attending to the cleanup and proper disposal of toxic waste, or a prohibitory injunction, *i.e.*, one that "restrains" a responsible party from further violating RCRA. Neither remedy . . . contemplates the award of past cleanup costs, whether these are denominated "damages" or "equitable restitution." In this regard, a comparison between the relief available under RCRA's citizen suit provision and that which Congress has provided in the analogous, but not parallel, provisions of CERCLA is telling. CERCLA was passed several years after RCRA went into effect, and it is designed to address many of the same toxic waste problems that inspired the passage of RCRA. Compare 42 U.S.C. § 6903(5) (RCRA definition of "hazardous waste") and § 6903(27) (RCRA definition of "solid waste") with § 9601(14) (CERCLA provision incorporating certain "hazardous substance[s]," but specifically excluding petroleum). CERCLA differs markedly from RCRA, however, in the remedies it provides. CERCLA's citizen suit provision mimics § 6972(a) in providing district courts with the authority "to order such action as may be necessary to correct the violation" of any CERCLA standard or regulation. 42 U.S.C. § 9659(c). But CERCLA expressly permits the Government to recover "all costs of removal or remedial action," § 9607(a)(4)(A), and it expressly permits the recovery of any "necessary costs of response, incurred by any . . . person consistent with the national contingency plan," § 9607(a)(4)(B). CERCLA also provides that "[a]ny person may seek contribution from any other person who is liable or potentially liable" for these response costs. See § 9613(f)(1). Congress thus demonstrated in CERCLA that it knew how to provide for the recovery of cleanup costs, and that the language used to define the remedies under RCRA does not provide that remedy. . . .

. . . [W]e agree with the Meghrigs that a private party cannot recover the cost of a *past* cleanup effort under RCRA. . . . Section 6972(a) does not contemplate the award of past cleanup costs, and § 6972(a)(1)(B) permits a private party to bring suit only upon an allegation that the contaminated site presently poses an "imminent and substantial endangerment to health or the environment," and not upon an allegation that it posed such an endangerment at some time in the past.

NOTES AND QUESTIONS

1. RCRA and CERCLA. How did the *Meghrig* Court describe the roles played by RCRA and CERCLA in the management of hazardous substances in the U.S.? In what way is this characterization consistent with the characterization of RCRA as an *ex ante* regime and CERCLA as an *ex post* regime?

2. Recovery of Costs. Why did the *Meghrig* Court find that the cleanup costs could not be recovered under RCRA? What would need to have been the case for the recovery action to fall within the ambit of RCRA?

3. Citizen Suit Provisions. The *Meghrig* Court was persuaded, in part, by a comparison between the relief available under the citizen suit provisions of RCRA and CERCLA. What did this comparison reveal? Why was it significant?

4. Imminent and Substantial Endangerment. As the *Meghrig* court noted, RCRA's citizen suit provision allows private parties to bring suit only if a contaminated site presently poses an "imminent and substantial endangerment to health or the environment." 42 U.S.C. § 6972(a)(1)(B). What point in time should courts look to when deciding if the "imminence" requirement is met? Should it be when the endangerment arose, the time of trial, or the time of filing? *See Am. Int'l Specialty Lines Ins. Co. v. 7-Eleven, Inc.*, 2010 WL 184444 (N.D. Tex. 2010) (holding that courts should examine the nature of the threat at the time of filing). Courts have interpreted "substantial" leniently, such that it is satisfied by reasonable medical or scientific concern. *Me. People's Alliance v. Mallinckrodt*, 471 F.3d 277 (1st Cir. 2006), *cert. denied*, 552 U.S. 816 (2007).

5.   Citizen Suits and Enforcement Actions. RCRA citizen suits and government enforcement suits often overlap. When does agency action preempt a citizen suit? *See Mallinckrodt*, 471 F.3d at 292–93 (describing the four ways the EPA can preempt a citizen suit); 42 U.S.C. § 6972(b)(2)(B). If an enforcement action is filed subsequent to a citizen suit, should the citizen be able to intervene? Why is this significant? *United States v. Doe Run Res. Corp.*, 2011 WL 1771007 (E.D. Mo. 2011). For a further discussion of these issues, see Chapter X.

2.   *EX ANTE* APPROACH: RESOURCE CONSERVATION RECOVERY ACT

A.   HISTORY AND OVERVIEW

RCRA was enacted in 1976, several years after the passage of the Clean Air Act (CAA) and the Clean Water Act (CWA). The House Report accompanying the Act noted that air and water pollutants were strictly regulated, but that the same pollutants could be disposed of on land in an environmentally unsound manner—which in turn could lead to increased air and water pollution. *See* H.R. REP. NO. 94–1491(I), at 4 (1976). Regulating the disposal of solid wastes on land, in addition to air and water pollution, would allow "the environmental laws to function in a coordinated and effective way," and would "eliminate [ ] the last remaining loophole in environmental law." *Id.* RCRA was amended in the Solid Waste Disposal Act Amendments of 1980, Pub. L. No. 96–482, and again in the Hazardous and Solid Waste Amendments of 1984, Pub. L. No. 98–616.

RCRA applies only to "solid wastes," as defined in § 1004(27). 42 U.S.C. § 6903(27). This definition is broad, however, encompassing any "garbage, refuse, sludge from a waste treatment plant, water supply treatment plant, or air pollution control facility and other discarded material, including solid, liquid, semisolid, or contained gaseous material resulting from industrial, commercial, mining, and agricultural operations." *Id.* RCRA contains two broad regulatory schemes administered by EPA: one for hazardous wastes, covered by Subtitle C, *see* 42 U.S.C. §§ 6921–6939e, and one for nonhazardous wastes, covered by Subtitle D, *see* 42 U.S.C. §§ 6941–6949a. The more burdensome requirements of Subtitle C apply only to "hazardous waste," defined in § 1004(5) to mean any solid waste, which because of its quality, concentration, or physical, chemical, or infectious characteristics, may: "(A) cause, or significantly contribute to an increase in mortality or an increase in serious irreversible, or incapacitating reversible, illness; or (B) pose a substantial present or potential hazard to human health or the environment when improperly treated, stored, transported, or disposed." 42 U.S.C. § 6903(5).

The centerpiece of the Subtitle C regime is the manifest system, which tracks hazardous wastes from "cradle to grave." Pursuant to this regime, each generator of hazardous waste must prepare a Uniform Hazardous Waste Manifest whenever it transports or offers for transport any hazardous waste for off-site treatment, storage, recycling, or disposal. 40 C.F.R. § 262.20. The manifest contains information and instructions on the characteristics of the waste being transported and is required to accompany the waste from its first transfer until its final disposal. *See* EPA, Hazardous Waste Manifest System, http://www.epa. gov/hwgenerators/hazardous-waste-manifest-system (last visited Oct. 24, 2018). Each party is required to maintain a copy of the manifest, establishing a paper trail. 40 C.F.R. § 262.20. Once the waste reaches its final destination, a copy of the manifest is returned to the generator to confirm that the waste has arrived. *Id.* In June 2018, EPA began transitioning to an electronic-based reporting system by launching the e-Manifest system, an electronic alternative to paper-based tracking. *See* EPA, Learn About the Hazardous Waste Electronic Management System (e-Manifest), http://www.epa.gov/e-manifest/learn-about-hazardous-waste-electronic-manifest-system-e-manifest (last visited Oct. 24, 2018).

Under the relevant provisions of Subtitle C, EPA has promulgated standards governing hazardous waste generators and transporters, *see* 42 U.S.C. §§ 6922–6923, and owners and operators of hazardous waste treatment, storage, and disposal facilities (TSD Facilities), *see* 42 U.S.C. § 6924.

A generator is any person, or site, whose processes and actions create hazardous waste. 40 C.F.R. § 260.10. Pursuant to § 3002, EPA has enacted regulations establishing handling, record-keeping, storage, and monitoring requirements for generators. *See* 42 U.S.C. § 6922; 40 C.F.R. pt. 262. Before treating, storing, disposing, transporting, or offering hazardous waste for transportation, the generator must obtain an EPA identification number from the Administrator. 40 C.F.R. § 262.18(a). If she decides to transport the hazardous waste for offsite treatment, storage, or disposal, a generator must comply with the packaging, labeling, and marking requirements established by the Department of Transportation. *See* 40 C.F.R. §§ 262.31–.33; 49 C.F.R. pts. 172–73, 178–79. Besides these requirements, a generator must prepare a manifest in which she identifies the type and quantity of the hazardous waste being shipped, designates the facilities that are permitted to handle the waste, and certifies that she has complied with the waste minimization practices, among other requirements established by EPA or state regulations. *See* 40 C.F.R. § 263.20–.22, .25. Generators must maintain a copy of the manifest signed by the transporter until the TSD facility returns the last copy, which in turn must be kept for three years. *See* 40 C.F.R. § 262.40(a). If a generator does not receive a copy of the manifest within a certain period of time from the shipment day, she must contact the transporter and/or TSD facility to determine the status of the waste and must notify EPA. 40 C.F.R. § 262.42.

EPA has also established stringent regulations regarding the accumulation of waste, waste storage, personnel training, and emergency procedures to deal with spills and other emergencies. *See* 40 C.F.R. § 262.16–.17. According to these regulations, generators can only accumulate waste for 90 or 180 days without a permit, depending on the size of the generator. *Id.* If they exceed this time limit, they are deemed to be storage facilities and must obtain a permit and comply with all the applicable requirements. 40 C.F.R. § 262.10. Waste should be accumulated in containers, tanks, or drip pads that meet the storage and labeling requirements established by EPA regulations. 40 C.F.R. § 262.16–.17. Moreover, facility personnel must successfully complete a training program that meets the requirements established under 40 C.F.R. § 264.16.

Hazardous waste transporters are individuals or entities that move hazardous waste from one site to another by highway, rail, water, or air, including the transportation of hazardous waste from a generator's site to a TSD facility or to a recycling plant. 40 C.F.R. § 260.10. Pursuant to 40 C.F.R. § 263.11, transporters of hazardous waste are required to obtain an EPA identification number before starting their operations. They can accept hazardous waste only if it is accompanied by the manifest; when the shipment is delivered, they must retain one copy for themselves and give the remaining copies to the designated facility. *See* 40 C.F.R. § 263.20. They are obligated to deliver the shipment to one of the facilities designated in the manifest, and if for some reason, other than rejection, the hazardous waste cannot be delivered to any of those facilities, a transporter must contact the generator for further instructions. *See* 40 C.F.R. § 263.21. Transporters can store hazardous waste shipments in containers that meet the requirements of 40 C.F.R. § 262.30 at a transfer facility for up to 10 days. 40 C.F.R. § 263.12. But if they exceed that period, they will be obligated to comply with the TSD facility regulations. *Id.* Besides complying with EPA regulations, transporters must fulfill the requirements established by the Department of Transportation hazardous material standards. *See* 49 C.F.R. pt. 171.

If a discharge of hazardous waste occurs during transportation, the transporter must take appropriate immediate action to protect human health and the environment, including proper notification to the local authorities. 40 C.F.R. § 263.30. Besides these immediate actions, transporters must clean up the hazardous waste discharge or take the actions required or approved at the federal or state level so that the discharge no longer presents a hazard to human health or the environment. 40 C.F.R. § 263.31.

TSD facilities are subject to much more stringent regulation than either generators or transporters. The term "treatment" is defined broadly to include any method, technique, or process designed to neutralize the waste, to recover energy or material resources from it, or to render it non-hazardous, less hazardous, safer, amenable for recovery or storage, or reduced in volume. *See* 40 C.F.R. § 260.10. "Storage" is further defined as the holding of hazardous waste for a temporary period, at the end of which it will be treated, disposed, or stored elsewhere. *Id.* Finally, "disposal" comprises virtually any act as a result of which hazardous waste gets into the air, water, or land. *Id.*

Owners or operators are required to obtain a permit to operate a TSD facility. *See* 40 C.F.R. § 270.10. The permitting process has two parts. Part A contains basic information about the facility, owner or operator, hazardous waste handled, and treatment processes. 40 C.F.R. § 270.13. Part B requires more detailed information on how the facility will meet substantive and technical federal standards promulgated under 40 C.F.R. pt. 264. *See* 40 C.F.R. § 270.14–.28.

An owner or operator of a TSD facility must meet the general standards established under 40 C.F.R. Part 264, by obtaining an EPA identification number and by fulfilling the information, training, security, and inspection requirements. Besides that, the regulation establishes specific requirements relating to the location and construction of the TSD facility and the management of waste. *See* 40 C.F.R. § 264.13, .17–.19. In order to minimize the possibility of fire, explosion, or any other situation that may result in the unplanned release of hazardous waste, Subpart C of 40 C.F.R. Part 264 provides the standards for "preparedness and prevention." *See* 40 C.F.R. § 264.30–.37. These regulations establish extremely detailed requirements regarding the construction and operation of the TSD facilities. *Id.* Besides these requirements, and in order to address the possibility of an accident occuring, TSD owners or operators are required to develop a contingency plan and emergency procedures to deal with accidents. *See* 40 C.F.R. § 264.51. When hazardous waste is recovered through the implementation of these procedures, the TSD owner or operator becomes a generator of such a waste, and, therefore, is subjected to the applicable regulations. *See* 40 C.F.R. § 264.56(g). In order to ensure that the TSD owner or operator will be able to afford compensation for the damages that the release of hazardous waste may cause, 40 C.F.R. § 264.147(a) requires the owner or operator to obtain and maintain liability coverage for sudden accidental occurrences in the amount of at least $1 million per occurrence with an annual aggregate of at least $2 million, exclusive of legal defense costs.

Requirements for closure and post-closure care are established under 40 C.F.R. § 264.111–.116 and 264.117–.120. The main purpose of these requirements is to ensure that the facility will not pose a threat to human health or the environment, and to prevent the development of new Superfund sites. As part of the requirements for obtaining permit approval, owners or operators of TSD facilities must present a closure plan. *See* 40 C.F.R. § 270.14(b)(13). Once the closure process has been completed, a certification of closure must be submitted and signed by a professional engineer and by the facility operator. *See* 40 C.F.R. § 264.115. If the owner and operator completely remove all waste that was treated, stored, or disposed in the facility (Clean Closure), she is exempt from complying with the post-closure regulations. *See* EPA, RCRA ORIENTATION MANUAL 74–76 (2014). In order to establish a Clean Closure, the owner or operator must show that the levels of hazardous contaminants at the facility do not exceed EPA-recommended exposure levels. *Id.* When a Clean Closure is not feasible, post-closure care should be provided in order to avoid future releases: for 30 years after the receipt of the closure certification, monitoring and maintenance activities must be undertaken according to the provisions of the post-closure plan submitted with the permit application. *See* 40 C.F.R. § 264.117–.118.

RCRA Subtitle D delegates primary authority for regulating the disposal of nonhazardous solid wastes to the states, with EPA acting in a supervisory role. 42 U.S.C. § 6941. Subtitle D requires states to adopt minimum standards for the disposal of nonhazardous solid wastes, contains a list of factors that states must consider in developing their solid waste disposal standards, and requires that states prohibit open waste dumps. 42 U.S.C. § 6943. The state standards adopted pursuant to Subtitle D must be approved by EPA. 42 U.S.C. § 6947. The stringency of the obligations contained in the Subtitle C hazardous waste regime far exceed those contained in Subtitle D. For this reason, RCRA creates considerable incentives for generators and transporters of waste, as well as TSD facilities, to structure their operations so as not to fall within the ambit of Subtitle C.

B. DEFINING WASTE

In order for a substance to be covered by Subtitle C of RCRA, it must be both a solid waste, for the purpose of § 1004(27), as well as a hazardous waste, for the purpose of § 1004(5). This section examines the difficulties inherent in characterizing substances pursuant to these definitions.

i. SOLID WASTE

Both the Subtitle C and Subtitle D regimes operate only with respect to solid waste. Despite its nominal limitation to solid substances, the § 1004(27) solid waste definition applies to wastes that demonstrate a wide variety of physical properties—including solids, liquids, and contained gases. *See* 42 U.S.C. § 6903(27). Of greater controversy, in determining the scope of the Act, is in what circumstances a particular substance generated in the course of an industrial process may be considered a waste product for the purposes of § 1004(27).

American Petroleum Institute v. Environmental Protection Agency

216 F.3d 50 (D.C. Cir. 2000).

■ Before WILLIAMS, SENTELLE, and ROGERS, CIRCUIT JUDGES.

■ PER CURIAM:

. . . RCRA is a comprehensive environmental statute granting EPA authority to regulate solid and hazardous wastes. "Solid wastes" are governed by Subtitle D of RCRA, and are generally subject to less stringent management standards than "hazardous wastes" which are regulated under Subtitle C. For purposes of RCRA, Congress defined solid waste as follows:

> The term "solid waste" means any garbage, refuse, sludge from a waste treatment plant, water supply treatment plant, or air pollution control facility and other discarded material, including solid, liquid, semisolid, or contained gaseous material resulting from industrial, commercial, mining, and agricultural operations, and from community activities. . . .

42 U.S.C. § 6903(27).

In pursuit of its congressionally conferred duty and authority to regulate solid waste under RCRA, the EPA has adopted regulations defining solid waste for purposes of its hazardous waste regulations: "A solid waste is any discarded material," 40 C.F.R. § 261.2(a)(1) (1999), subject to a number of exclusions enumerated in § 261.4(a) and case-by-case variances under §§ 260.30 and 260.31. The term "discarded material" for purposes of the regulation means any material which is abandoned, recycled, or considered inherently wastelike. 40 C.F.R. § 261.2(a)(2).

In 1994 and 1998 rulemakings in pursuit of its RCRA obligations, the EPA examined the production processes of the petroleum refining industry. As pertinent to the issue before us, EPA considered whether to exclude from the definition of solid waste two secondary materials: oil-bearing wastewaters generated by the petroleum refining industry and recovered oil produced by the petrochemical manufacturing industry. EPA determined that oil-bearing wastewaters are solid waste for purposes of RCRA regulation. . . . Industry petitioners challenge [this] conclusion[ ].

In petroleum refining, impurities are removed and usable hydrocarbon fractions are isolated from crude oil feedstock. Large quantities of water are used, and the resulting wastewaters contain a small percentage of residual oil. These "oilbearing wastewaters" are destined for ultimate discharge, but only after a three-step treatment process is first applied. The first phase of treatment, known as "primary treatment," removes certain materials including the oil. This phase has at least two beneficial consequences: (1) it meets a Clean Water Act requirement that refineries remove oil from their wastewater, and (2) it allows refineries to recover a not insignificant quantity of oil (which industry claims can range up to 1,000 barrels a day at certain refineries) which is cycled back into the refinery production process.

Industry petitioners and EPA disagree over when these wastewaters become discarded for purposes of the solid waste definition. While no one disputes that discard has certainly occurred by the time the wastewaters move into the later phases of treatment, the question is whether discard happens before primary treatment, allowing regulation of wastewater as solid waste at that point, or not until primary treatment is complete and oil has been recovered for further processing.

EPA's initial proposal excluded oil-bearing wastewaters. However, it changed its mind in 1994 and concluded that even before the oil is recovered in primary treatment, "the wastewaters are discarded materials and hence solid wastes subject to regulation under RCRA." 59 Fed.Reg. 38,540/1. EPA stated: "Primary wastewater treatment operations exist to treat plant wastewaters." *Id.* at 38,539/3. It noted that the percentage of oil in the wastewater is very small and "not significant in the context of a refinery's overall production activities," and that the Clean Water Act mandates such treatment. For these stated reasons, EPA concluded that "[c]learly, wastewater treatment is the main purpose of the systems in question, and any oil recovery is of secondary import." *Id.* at 38,539/3. . . .

Industry petitioners . . . contend that . . . oil-bearing wastewaters cannot be regulated because they are . . . unquestionably in-process materials not yet discarded. Alternately, even if the status of oil-bearing wastewaters is not so plain, petitioners assert that EPA's conclusion is arbitrary and capricious because it is not based on reasoned decisionmaking. *See, e.g., Motor Vehicle Mfrs. Ass'n of United States, Inc. v. State Farm Mut. Auto. Ins. Co.,* 463 U.S. 29, 43 (1983) (agency must "articulate a satisfactory explanation for its action including a rational connection between the facts found and the choice made") (internal quotation marks omitted). Petitioners emphasize that primary treatment yields valuable oil that is reinserted into the refining processes in a continuous operation. They also claim that oil recovery operations began long before Clean Water Act regulations required it. In sum, they contend that oil recovery in primary treatment is a part of in-process oil production.

At bottom, the parties disagree over the proper characterization of primary treatment. Is it simply a step in the act of discarding? Or is it the last step in a production process before discard? Our prior cases have not had to draw a line for deciding when discard has occurred. . . .

It may be permissible for EPA to determine that the predominant purpose of primary treatment is discard. Legal abandonment of property is premised on determining the intent to abandon, which requires an inquiry into facts and circumstances. Where an industrial by-product may be characterized as discarded or "in process" material, EPA's choice of characterization is entitled to deference. However, the record must reflect that EPA engaged in reasoned decisionmaking to decide which characterization is appropriate. The record in this case is deficient in that regard. EPA has noted two purposes of primary treatment and concludes, "[c]learly, wastewater treatment is the main purpose." 1994 Rule, 59 Fed.Reg. 38,539/3. As English teachers have long taught, a conclusion is not "clear" or "obvious" merely because one says so.

EPA points out that primary treatment only recovers a small amount of oil relative to the entire output of a typical refining facility. However, the oil is still valuable and usable, so that reason alone cannot show discard. The rock of a diamond mine may only contain a tiny portion of precious carbon, but that is enough to keep miners busy. According to claims by the refining industry, the net amount of oil recovered may reach 1,000 barrels a day for certain refineries. It is plausible to claim, as industry petitioners do, that refiners engage in primary treatment first and foremost to recover this usable resource. At the very least, EPA cannot merely rely on the small relative amount of oil recovered from primary treatment without further explanation.

EPA also notes that the Clean Water Act requires primary treatment before discharge. If refiners got nothing from primary treatment, this might be a compelling rationale because it would be hard to explain why, other than to discard, refiners would engage in a costly treatment activity with no economic benefits. However, petitioners claim they would engage in primary treatment regardless of the treatment standards in order to recover the desired oil. EPA does not explain why this possibly valid motivation is not compelling. EPA makes no attempt to balance the costs and benefits of primary treatment, or otherwise to explain why the Clean Water Act requirements are the real motivation behind primary treatment. Indeed, without further explanation, it is not inherently certain why a substance is definitively "discarded" if its possessor is continuing to process it, even though the possessor's decision to continue processing may have been influenced, or even predominantly motivated, by some external factor. Otherwise put, it is not so obvious as EPA would have us hold that if the industry petitioners conceded that their overriding motivation in further processing the wastewaters was compliance with Clean Water Act regulations that they would then conclusively be discarding the material in question even while further processing it. If the non-Clean Water Act benefits of the initial treatment are enough to justify firms' incurring the costs (petitioners point to material in the record that may support such a proposition), the EPA would have to reconcile that fact with any conclusion that the Clean Water Act purpose was primary.

In short, EPA has not set forth why it has concluded that the compliance motivation predominates over the reclamation motivation. Perhaps equally importantly it has not explained why that conclusion, even if validly reached, compels the further conclusion that the wastewater has been discarded. Therefore, because the agency has failed to provide a rational explanation for its decision, we hold the decision to be arbitrary and capricious. *See State Farm*, 463 U.S. at 46–57. We therefore vacate the portion of EPA's decision declining to exclude oil-bearing wastewaters from the statutory definition of solid waste, and remand for further proceedings. We do not suggest any particular result on remand, only a reasoned one demonstrating when discard occurs if EPA wishes to assert jurisdiction.

NOTES AND QUESTIONS

1.   **Primary Treatment.** What is at issue in this case? Is it the industry petitioners' position that oil-bearing waste-waters should never be considered solid waste for the purposes of the Act? What, in the eyes of the industry petitioners, is significant about the process of primary treatment, such that the wastewater should not be considered solid waste during this phase of treatment?

2.   **Primary Purpose.** In finding for the industry petitioners, did the *American Petroleum Institute* court hold that the main purpose of the primary treatment of oil-bearing waste-waters is oil extraction? Why then did the court side with the industry petitioners? What did EPA need to show in order to establish that the primary purpose of this process was the discarding of the wastewaters? Why would such a finding be dispositive in light of the definition of solid waste?

3.   **Discarding and Recycling.** As we have seen, pursuant to the § 1004(27) definition, whether a substance can be considered a "solid waste" for the purposes of the Act often turns on whether it can be considered "discarded material." Is it desirable to treat recyclable material as "discarded material" for the purposes of the Act?

If material can be reused or recycled, why would it ever make sense to regulate it as a waste? Wouldn't exempting reused and recycled materials encourage recycling and reduce land disposal of wastes? On the other hand, if reused or recycled materials are not regulated as wastes, then could the mismanagement of recyclable materials during the recycling process lead to unchecked environmental damage? What difficulties can you anticipate EPA would face in distinguishing between waste and recyclable material?

4.   **What Constitutes Recycling?** For the purposes of RCRA, on what basis should the distinction between recycling and disposal be made? Consider the following three scenarios in which hazardous substances are produced during an industrial process—first, where those substances are immediately used as inputs in the ongoing production process; second, where those substances are first stored on site for a period of 30 days, until such time as an adequate amount is produced and then fed back into the production process; and third, where those substances are stored indefinitely on site, to be harnessed in the future in the event that production processes evolve. Characterization of the first and third scenarios, as recycling and disposal, respectively, appears easy. How would you characterize the second

scenario? Would your answer change if the substances were stored for 60, 90, or 180 days? What if material was used for a secondary purpose off-site? At what point does the material become "spent" and thus discarded? EPA defines spent material as material that can no longer serve "the purpose for which it was produced without processing." Yet if the material is re-used for a secondary purpose, which purpose governs? *See Howmet Corp. v. EPA*, 614 F.3d 544 (D.C. Cir. 2010) (upholding EPA's interpretation, which focused on the material's initial use to determine its purpose and, thus, whether it was spent).

5.   **Recycling: Case Law.** Just as in the *American Petroleum Institute* case, there often exists controversy concerning to what extent the § 1004(27) definition covers recyclable material. Consider the following questions that have arisen in different courts.

Should the line between discarded wastes that are regulated, and recycled substances that are not, turn on whether the generator reuses the materials itself in an on-site, continuous process? *Am. Mining Congress v. EPA*, 824 F.2d 1177 (D.C. Cir. 1987) (holding that EPA was not entitled to regulate in-process secondary materials). *Cf. Oklahoma v. Tyson Foods, Inc.*, 2010 WL 653032 (N.D. Okla. 2010) (noting that *Am. Mining Congress* did not mean that poultry litter destined for agriculture fertilizer was necessarily discarded if used in a process by another industry). What if the materials are sent by a generator to a recycling facility? Does it make any sense to regulate waste that is recycled by a third party, but not waste that is recycled by the generator? *See Am. Petroleum Inst. v. EPA*, 906 F.2d 729 (D.C. Cir. 1990) (holding that slag removed from ovens and recycled by a third party must be regulated, but slag left in ovens and burned off later in the production process was not).

Should the timeframe within which the materials will be reused or recycled make a difference? Should generators be able to escape regulation under RCRA entirely by storing waste on-site indefinitely and claiming that at some point in the future the materials will be reused or recycled? Should materials that are stored only for a few days before they are reused be regulated as solid waste? How quickly must materials be reused in order to escape regulation as wastes? *See Ass'n of Battery Recyclers, Inc. v. EPA*, 208 F.3d 1047 (D.C. Cir. 2000).

6.   **Recycling: Regulations.** EPA has promulgated regulations in an attempt to clarify the application of the solid waste definition to recyclable materials. *See* 40 C.F.R. pt. 261. These regulations, in effect, separate recyclable hazardous secondary materials into 2 categories—those which can be reused directly as effective substitutes for commercial products or directly in industrial processes, 40 C.F.R. § 261.2, and those which must be significantly processed before they can be reused in a manner similar to products in commerce, 40 C.F.R. § 261.1. It is only the latter category of materials that EPA considers to be sufficiently "waste-like," and subject to the RCRA regime. *Id.* More specifically, recycling practices that are considered to produce solid waste for the purposes of the act include the recycling of "inherently waste-like" materials (as defined by the regulations), 40 C.F.R. § 261.2(d), recycling of materials that are "[u]sed in a manner

constituting disposal," or "[u]sed to produce products that are applied to or placed on the land," 40 C.F.R. § 261.2(c)(1), and the "[b]urning for energy recovery" or those that are "used to produce a fuel or are otherwise contained in fuels," 40 C.F.R. § 261.2(c)(2).

In an attempt to encourage further recycling on the part of industry, EPA has begun to issue rules that exclude certain recycled materials from the definition of solid waste under RCRA. A 2002 rule, for example, exempted some secondary materials used to make fertilizer from the definition of solid waste, though the exempted materials are still subject to some handling, storage, and reporting conditions. *See* 67 Fed. Reg. 48,393; *Safe Food & Fertilizer v. EPA*, 350 F.3d 1263 (D.C. Cir. 2003) (upholding EPA's fertilizer exclusion).

7. Recycling: Regulations, Continued. In 2008, EPA issued a final rule with a new definition of solid waste that excluded two categories of hazardous secondary material from regulatory control. Hazardous secondary materials are defined as those that would be a hazardous waste subject to regulation if discarded. 40 C.F.R. § 260.10. The first exclusion is for hazardous secondary materials generated and reclaimed by the generator itself; the second, known as the transfer-based exclusion, excludes materials transferred to a third party for reclamation. *See* 40 C.F.R. § 261.4(23), (24). What reasons are there for excluding these two categories of materials? Is this good policy?

In order to operate under either exclusion, generators and third party reclamation facilities have to meet several conditions. First, materials must be "legitimately recycled" or serve a useful contribution to a recycling process or to a product. 40 C.F.R. §§ 261.4(23), (24), 260.43. Second, materials cannot be speculatively accumulated. 40 C.F.R. § 261.4(23), (24). What is the purpose of these two conditions? Third, materials must be "contained," meaning: (1) the unit must be in good condition with no leaks or other continuing or intermittent releases; (2) the unit is properly labeled or has a system to immediately identify the hazardous secondary materials in it; and (3) the unit does not hold incompatible materials and addresses any potential risks of fire or explosion. 40 C.F.R. § 260.10. If a hazardous secondary material is in a unit with leaks or other releases, the material is considered discarded and solid waste. 40 C.F.R. § 261.4(24)(v)(a). Finally, under the transfer-based exclusion, the generator is required to make "reasonable efforts" to ensure materials would be safely and legitimately recycled by third parties. 40 C.F.R. § 261.4(24)(B). What problems do you see with the incentives created by these exclusions? These exclusions are self-implementing, so generators and reclamation facilities simply notify the relevant regulatory authority before operating under the exclusion and then use the exclusion. Why would EPA make the exclusions self-implementing? Is this problematic? What benefits are there to this approach?

8. Recycling: A New Approach. In *Rethinking Recycling*, 38 ENVTL. L. 1053 (2008), Jeffrey M. Gaba suggests a new approach for dealing with recycling under RCRA. Gaba argues that the current RCRA regulatory scheme for recycling lacks a consistent rationale for classifying "solid wastes," is poorly drafted and confusing, and unnecessarily includes materials involved in legitimate recycling. In order to provide a more coherent regulatory scheme that properly balances the objectives of RCRA, Gaba suggests that EPA should assert broad authority under the statutory definition of solid waste to include all materials no longer part of a continuous industrial process. This would allow EPA to employ reporting and liability provisions to regulate recycled materials under RCRA, without regulating them as hazardous wastes under Subtitle C. Second, Gaba suggests that EPA should develop a narrow regulatory definition of solid waste under Subtitle C that includes materials recycled through land application or burning of wastes, and "sham" recycling. Gaba suggests this combination will allow EPA to enforce and regulate recycling based on possible risks and benefits, rather than whether the material is discarded. Do you agree with Gaba's approach?

ii.   HAZARDOUS WASTE

In order to be subject to the requirements of Subtitle C, a substance must also be considered a hazardous waste. RCRA does not include a list of hazardous wastes or a specific method for determining whether a waste is hazardous. Instead, the statute defines "hazardous waste" generally as a solid waste, or combination of solid wastes, which because of its quantity, concentration, or physical, chemical, or infectious characteristics may:

(A)   cause, or significantly contribute to an increase in mortality or an increase in serious irreversible, or incapacitating reversible, illness; or

(B)   pose a substantial present or potential hazard to human health or the environment when improperly treated, stored, transported, or disposed of, or otherwise managed.

42 U.S.C. § 6903(5). Having set out this general definition, Congress delegated to EPA the duty to "promulgate regulations identifying the characteristics of hazardous waste, and listing particular hazardous wastes . . . which shall be subject to the provisions of [Subtitle C]." 42 U.S.C. § 6921(b)(1). Thus, Congress directed EPA to identify hazardous wastes in one of two ways. First a waste may be hazardous if it possesses certain characteristics—toxicity, ignitability, corrosivity, and reactivity, as defined by EPA regulations. *See* 40 C.F.R. §§ 261.21, 261.22, 261.23, and 261.24. The first case excerpted below, *United States v. Elias*, 269 F.3d 1003 (9th Cir. 2001), concerns a challenge to a determination by EPA that a particular substance is hazardous because it exhibits reactive characteristics. Second, a waste may be hazardous if EPA individually lists the waste as hazardous, as a result of a determination that the waste invariably presents a substantial threat of mortality, serious illness, or other significant hazard to human health or the environment. The second excerpt below revisits *American Petroleum Institute v. EPA*, *supra*. It concerns a separate challenge brought by the petitioners to a decision of EPA to list a particular substance as hazardous pursuant to § 1004(5)(B).

The characterization of mixed waste streams—substances containing both hazardous and non-hazardous materials—under the RCRA hazardous waste definition raises a number of additional complications. The third case, *American Chemistry Council v. EPA*, 337 F.3d 1060 (D.C. Cir. 2003), addresses EPA's "mixed waste" rule, which treats as hazardous any substance that is either mixed with or derived from a listed hazardous waste.

United States v. Elias

269 F.3d 1003 (9th Cir. 2001), *cert. denied*, 537 U.S. 812 (2002).

■ Before WALLACE, HALL, and T.G. NELSON, CIRCUIT JUDGES.

■ T.G. NELSON, CIRCUIT JUDGE:

After a three-and-a-half-week trial, a jury convicted Allen Elias of four [RCRA] offenses, the most serious of which was disposing of hazardous waste without a permit, knowing that his actions placed others in imminent danger of death or serious bodily injury in violation of 42 U.S.C. § 6928(e). Elias appeals [on the ground that the substance disposed of should not be considered a hazardous waste for the purposes of RCRA]. . . .

Allen Elias owned Evergreen Resources, a fertilizer company located near Soda Springs, Idaho. In August 1996, Elias decided to transfer sulfuric acid from two railroad cars into a stationary 25,000-gallon tank that he had transported to Evergreen from his previous business, AEI.

At AEI, Elias had used the thirty-six-foot-long, eleven-foot-high tank as a storage tank for byproducts of a cyanide leaching process he had patented. Elias realized that his process resulted in the transfer of cyanide-laced solids into the tank. He admitted, moreover, that there were one to two tons of cyanide-laced sludge left in the tank when he shipped it to Evergreen in the early 1990s. This sludge did not preclude Elias from using the tank for some purposes. In 1996, however, Elias decided that the sludge, which was hardened and more than a foot deep, had to be cleaned out of the tank before he could store the sulfuric acid in it.

On August 26, 1996, Elias ordered four of his employees, Bryan Smith, Gene Thornock, Darrin Weaver, and Scott Dominguez, to enter the tank and wash the sludge out a valve opening in the end. Despite Smith's repeated requests, Elias failed to provide any safety equipment for this task. Consequently, Dominguez and Weaver entered the tank wearing only their regular work clothes. After about fifteen minutes, they realized that the sludge could not be washed out the small hole in the end of the tank, and they exited. Both complained of sore throats and nasal passages.

The next morning, on August 27, 1996, Elias met with his employees, who told him of the difficulties of the day before and the health effects they suffered. Smith again insisted on the necessary safety equipment. Elias said he would get it, but told his employees to proceed anyway and that he expected the tank to be cleaned out that morning. Although he instructed his employees to "do it by the book," Elias provided none of the safety equipment or training needed for them to do so.

After cutting a bigger hole in the end of the tank, Dominguez and Weaver again entered the tank with no safety equipment. About 45 minutes later, after they had emptied about one-third of the sludge through the hole onto the ground, Weaver shouted that Dominguez had collapsed. Thornock and Smith unsuccessfully tried to get Dominguez out of the tank, which had only a 22-inch manhole at the top. When firefighters got to Dominguez, he was in severe respiratory distress and in danger of dying.

After extricating Dominguez, the fire chief asked Elias whether cyanide could be in the tank. Elias insisted that he had no knowledge of anything in the tank other than water and sludge, which the fire chief understood to mean mud.

After Dominguez was rushed to the hospital in Soda Springs, the treating physician there concluded that the most likely cause of his condition was cyanide poisoning. He called Elias and asked him whether there was a possibility that there was cyanide in the tank, to which Elias again replied no. The doctor nonetheless asked the LifeFlight helicopter from Pocatello to bring a cyanide antidote kit to Soda Springs. After the doctor administered it, Dominguez responded positively. Blood drawn while Dominguez was in the Soda Springs hospital revealed extremely toxic levels of cyanide in his body. . . .

To obtain convictions [against Elias under RCRA], the Government had to prove that Elias transported or disposed of "hazardous waste." [*See* 42 U.S.C. § 6928(d), (e).] The governing regulations provide that "hazardous waste" includes wastes that exhibit the characteristic of reactivity and that "[a] solid waste exhibits the characteristic of reactivity if a representative sample of [it] . . . is a cyanide or sulfide bearing waste which, when exposed to pH conditions between 2 and 12.5, can generate toxic gases, vapors or fumes in a quantity sufficient to present a danger to human health or the environment." A "representative sample" is "a sample of a universe or whole (e.g., waste pile, lagoon, ground water) which can be expected to exhibit the average properties of the universe or whole." [40 C.F.R. §§ 261.3(a)(2), 261.20–.24.]

Elias argues that there was insufficient evidence for the jury to convict him of disposing of "hazardous waste" because the Government presented no evidence that the samples it took from a three-foot radius inside the tank and from outside the tank exhibited the average properties of the entire tank. This analysis misses the mark for two reasons. First, it assumes that to prove Elias guilty of disposing of hazardous waste, the Government had to prove that the entire tank was hazardous. That is incorrect. As the EPA's Environmental Appeals Board explained in *In re Electric Service Co.*,

> proof of the disposal violations does not hinge on accurately describing the condition or quality of some larger body. Instead, it hinges on proof of an uncontrolled discharge. . . . Under such circumstances, the sample itself is the uncontrolled discharge, the improper disposal, or, so to speak, the corpus delicti. Therefore, the violations may be established by simply proving two things: (1) that the samples themselves contain [reactive cyanide]; and (2) that the [reactive cyanide] w[as] not disposed of properly, a conclusion which may be inferred from where the [samples] were found.

[1 E.A.D. 947 (Env. App. Bd. 1985), *available at* 1985 WL 57155.]

In this case, EPA investigators took at least one sample from sludge located outside the tank. By definition, therefore, this sludge sample had been disposed of.[38] It was reactive and tested positive for cyanide. No further evidence is necessary. Thus, whether this hazardous sludge sample bears the same characteristics of the tank waste Dominguez had not yet gotten to before he collapsed is legally beside the point.

On a more basic level, we think Elias's hypertechnical interpretation contravenes common sense. As the Government's witness, Dr. Lowery, explained, if the Government or a waste generator is trying to prove the negative, i.e., that cyanide is not present, relying on just one or two samples would be dangerous. Rather, the generator would need to do the more extensive sampling contemplated by the regulations to guard against obtaining a false negative from potentially striated waste. By contrast, if the Government is trying to prove a positive, i.e., that there is cyanide within, "it's not necessary to go to every inch of the tank to see if there's more cyanide there."

This explanation, which the EPA has advanced elsewhere, makes perfect sense. If a sample from one part of the tank contains wastes reactive enough to cause brain damage to someone, there can be no conceivable purpose in sending other people into the tank to excerpt more samples. Indeed, under these circumstances, retrieving additional samples would actually disserve RCRA's objectives. . . .

NOTES AND QUESTIONS

1.   **Reactivity.** EPA regulations provide that "[a] solid waste exhibits the characteristic of reactivity if a representative sample of [it] . . . is a cyanide or sulfide bearing waste which, when exposed to pH conditions between 2 and 12.5, can generate toxic gases, vapors or fumes in a quantity sufficient

---

[38] *See* 40 C.F.R. § 260.10 ("Disposal means the discharge, deposit, injection, dumping, spilling, leaking, or placing of any solid waste or hazardous waste into or on any land . . . so that such solid waste or hazardous waste or any constituent thereof may enter the environment. . . .").

to present a danger to human health or the environment." 40 C.F.R. § 261.23. In turn, a "representative sample" is "a sample of a universe or whole . . . which can be expected to exhibit the average properties of the universe or whole." 40 C.F.R. § 260.10. What samples did EPA take? On what basis did the *Elias* court consider this to constitute a "representative sample"? Do you agree with the court's reasoning?

2.   Representation. According to the *Elias* court: ". . . EPA investigators took at least one sample from sludge located outside the tank. By definition, therefore, this sludge sample had been disposed of. It was reactive and tested positive for cyanide. No further evidence is necessary." 269 F.3d at 1013–14. Why did the *Elias* court not deem it necessary to determine whether the sludge sample taken by EPA was representative of the discarded material?

3.   Common Sense. On what basis does the *Elias* court claim its decision to be consistent with common sense? Can you envisage a situation in which the court's common sense approach could result in an unsatisfactory outcome?

4.   Federalism and RCRA. Under RCRA, a state may enact its own hazardous waste program and impose "more stringent" requirements than the federal program. 42 U.S.C. §§ 6926(b), 6929; 40 C.F.R. § 271.1(i). The federal government can enforce an authorized state RCRA program, unless it has a greater scope of coverage than the federal program. 40 C.F.R. § 271.1(i)(2). The line between "greater scope of coverage" and "more stringent" has been the subject of substantial debate. In *United States v. Southern Union Co.*, 630 F.3d 17, 28–30 (1st Cir. 2010), *rev'd and remanded on other grounds*, 567 U.S. 343 (2012), the court held that Rhode Island's decision not to recognize a federal exemption for small generators was "more stringent" as opposed to a "greater scope of coverage." The court observed that small generators were required to meet several conditions to qualify for the federal exemption. Since small generators started out as regulated entities under the federal scheme, Rhode Island's program did not have a broader scope, because it also regulated the small generators, but it was "more stringent."

American Petroleum Institute v. Environmental Protection Agency

216 F.3d 50 (D.C. Cir. 2000).

■ Before WILLIAMS, SENTELLE, and ROGERS, CIRCUIT JUDGES.

■ PER CURIAM:

[In addition to the petitioners' challenge of EPA's classification of oil-bearing wastewaters as solid waste (discussed in Section 2.B.i above), petitioners challenged EPA's listing of certain refinery residuals as hazardous wastes. EPA had listed these materials pursuant to § 1004(5)(B) after concluding that the refinery residuals constituted a substantial present hazard to human health.]

. . . Industry petitioners allege that the listed refinery residuals do not pose a *"substantial* present or potential hazard to human health or the environment," RCRA § 1004(5)(B), 42 U.S.C. § 6903(5)(B); 40 C.F.R. § 261.11(a)(3) (emphasis added), and thus were improperly listed as "hazardous waste." Their argument is based on EPA's explicit recognition that for some of the wastestreams at issue "population risk" is "near zero." Notice of Proposed Rulemaking: Hazardous Waste Management System, 60 Fed.Reg. 57,747, 57,789/2 (1995). Our disposition of this claim turns on the relationship between "individual risk," which EPA regarded as substantial, and "population risk," which for some wastestreams it acknowledged as negligible. Until a letter filed after oral argument, petitioners did *not* attack the EPA's characterization of the individual risks, and thus we have no occasion to consider whether the agency lawfully characterized such risks as substantial.

Before considering this claim, we pause for a brief explication of these concepts. "Population risk" is, as its name suggests, the risk of the population at large, generally calculated as an "upper bound" estimate of risk for the population overall. It is commonly measured in terms of health effects cases over a given time period (e.g., cancer deaths caused per year). Draft Report: Assessments of Risks From the Management of Petroleum Refining Wastes: Background Document 2–25 (October 1995) ("Draft Report"). "Individual risk" is calculated variously as a "bounding estimate," a "central tendency estimate," or a "high-end estimate," for a member of a particular segment of the population. *Id.* at 2–33. (For high-end estimates, the agency set the two most sensitive parameters at the high end (90th percentile point on the distribution), and set the others at their central tendency. Final Rule, 63 Fed.Reg. at 42,117/2, 42,120 (Table IV-2) (1998).) Unlike population risk, individual risk is commonly measured in terms of *lifetime* risk. As the term population risk seems to imply, it is an aggregate, calculated either by "summing the estimated individual risk over all of the individuals in the population," Draft Report at 2–34, or by estimating methods aimed at the same goal, *id.* EPA counsel confirmed at oral argument that population risk aggregates individual risk.

Suppose, for example, that a particular waste poses an individual 1-in-100,000 lifetime risk of death from cancer to 100 people. The estimated annual population risk is 1 in 100,000 divided by 70, since the "individual" risk estimate assumes a 70-year lifespan, and multiplied by 100, to reflect the 100 persons exposed; thus the estimated additional annual cancer incidence for this population is $100 \times 1/7,000,000 = 1.4 \times 10^{-5}$ (or, 1.4 cases every 100,000 years). Of course any other cancer cases estimated to result from exposure to the waste across the overall population would be added in to produce the complete population risk estimate.

According to established EPA practice, wastestreams with "high-end individual cancer-risk level[s]" of 1 in 100,000 lifetimes or higher "generally are considered initial candidates" for listing, and those that pose a risk of at least 1 in 10,000 lifetimes are "presumptively assumed" to merit listing. Notice of Proposed Rulemaking: Hazardous Waste Management System, 59 Fed.Reg. 66,072, 66,077 (1994). EPA found that the risks posed by the refinery residuals generally met at least the candidate level for listing. *See* Final Rule, 63 Fed.Reg. at 42,150–55. But in the case of one subcategory of clarified slurry oil ("CSO") sediment, namely landfilled sediments, EPA appears to acknowledge that high-end individual risk was actually as low as 4×10^{-6}, i.e., 4 cancer deaths in one million lifetimes of exposure, *id.* at 42,152/2 (expressed as "4E–6"), and "that the incremental [population] risk in terms of cancer cases avoided would be near zero." Notice of Proposed Rulemaking: Hazardous Waste Management System, 60 Fed.Reg. 57,747, 57,789 (1995). Petitioners argue that EPA's failure to consider the "near zero" population risk, which by their calculations based on EPA's figures ranged from 0.3 cancer cases in 10,000 years to 0.7 cases in 1 million years, API's Initial Br. at 34, rendered its listing unlawful. 5 U.S.C. § 706(2)(A).

Were population risk a factor that EPA had to weigh with and against individual risk to determine whether a particular hazard was "substantial," the Agency would have to provide a reason for ignoring it in this instance. *Dithiocarbamate Task Force v. EPA*, 98 F.3d 1394, 1398–99 (D.C.Cir.1996). But neither the statute nor the regulation identifies population risk per se as one of the mandatory factors that the Agency must consider. *See* 42 U.S.C. § 6921(a); 40 C.F.R. § 261.11(a)(3). Under EPA's regulations, the Administrator must "consider[ ]" "[t]he nature and severity of the human health and environmental damage that has occurred" from mismanagement of the waste, 40 C.F.R. § 261.11(a)(3)(ix); but this does not necessarily imply that substantial individual risk alone, without high population risk, cannot be enough to constitute a "substantial . . . hazard."

Much of what EPA has written could be taken as requiring substantial population risk. Thus, here it observed, "Population risk is only one of many factors to be considered," Final Rule, 63 Fed.Reg. at 42,138/3, arguably suggesting that it always "consider[s]" it, so that zero or near-zero population risk would exonerate, or tend to exonerate, a wastestream. In context, however, we believe we may discern the Agency's path to its conclusion that individual risk alone may be enough to justify a hazardous waste listing, regardless of population risk. *Motor Vehicle Mfrs. Ass'n of the United States, Inc. v. State Farm Mut. Auto. Ins. Co.*, 463 U.S. 29, 43 (1983). EPA states, for instance, that it "does not believe that it is appropriate to allow contamination from waste management units to cause substantial risk *to nearby residents* simply because there are few wells in the immediate area" and that its "decision to list these wastes is based primarily on the concern over risks to those individuals who are significantly exposed, even if there are relatively few of them." Final Rule, 63 Fed.Reg. at 42,138/3 (emphasis added). These justifications are consistent with its 1995 Guidance for Risk Characterization, which states that when small populations are exposed (and thus population risk is low), "individual risk estimates will usually be a more meaningful parameter for decision-makers." *Id.* Moreover, EPA cited instances (primarily in the Superfund context) in which, consistent with this reasoning, it "rejected using population risk as the point of departure" and took action because of the high individual risk even though population risk was low. *Id.* at 42,139/1. We thus read EPA as saying—in consonance with both the governing statute and regulation—that it will regulate a waste that poses a substantial risk to highly exposed individuals, even if that risk poses a relatively small risk to the population at large. . . .

NOTES AND QUESTIONS

1.   Population Risk and Individual Risk. What is the difference between population risk and individual risk? How are they related? Which is a better indicator of whether a chemical poses a substantial hazard to human health for the purposes of § 1004(5)? In what circumstances should one be favored as a measure of substantial hazard over the other?

2.   Substantial Hazard. Why, in the above case, did the court uphold EPA's listing of clarified slurry oil as a hazardous waste despite the fact that the population risk was negligible? Do you think it is appropriate to impose arduous industry-wide standards upon substances that pose no threat to the population at large? Does the court's holding stand for the proposition that substantial hazard should be found in any circumstance where population risk is negligible, provided that individual risk is high?

3.   Beyond Listing. Like most major environmental statutes (including the CAA and the CWA), RCRA's basic approach to regulation is to list a number of pollutants and regulate them comprehensively. Chemicals that are regulated in one medium might not be regulated in another—for example, a chemical that is considered hazardous when disposed in land might not be regulated at all when emitted into the ambient air—and non-listed pollutants are not regulated at all. In some cases, such discrepancies are explicable because of the pollutants' differing effects; in other cases the choice to regulate one medium but not another, or one pollutant but not another, seems arbitrary. Would environmental regulation be improved by a more comprehensive approach to regulating pollutants across mediums? How would you structure a more integrated approach? *See* John C. Dernbach, *The Unfocused Regulation of Toxic and Hazardous Pollutants*, 21 HARV. ENVTL. L. REV. 1 (1997).

4.   Climate Change and RCRA. In order to facilitate development and utilization of geological sequestration, EPA promulgated a rule that conditionally excludes hazardous carbon dioxide streams produced for sequestration from the definition of hazardous waste and, therefore, RCRA regulation. *See* EPA, Hazardous Waste Management System: Identification and Listing of Hazardous Waste: Carbon Dioxide Streams in Geologic

Sequestration Activities, 76 Fed. Reg. 48,073 (2011). In support of the rule, EPA argued that this exclusion will not present a substantial risk to human health or the environment, because the construction, operation, and monitoring of wells and transportation pipelines are already regulated under the Safe Drinking Water Act and Department of Transportation regulations regarding transport of hazardous materials respectively. Generators and operator/owners of the wells are required to annually certify that the carbon dioxide stream meets all the conditions under the exclusion and keep the certification on site. However, there is no tracking mechanism for transportation of the streams. Do you think this is a good policy? Will it create the incentives EPA hopes for?

American Chemistry Council v. Environmental Protection Agency
337 F.3d 1060 (D.C. Cir. 2003).

■ Before GINSBURG, CHIEF JUDGE, and SENTELLE and RANDOLPH, CIRCUIT JUDGES.

■ GINSBURG, CHIEF JUDGE:

The American Chemistry Council (ACC) petitions for review of a rule promulgated by the Environmental Protection Agency pursuant to the Resource Conservation and Recovery Act of 1976, 42 U.S.C. §§ 6901–6992(k), treating as a "hazardous waste" any substance that is either mixed with or derived from a listed hazardous waste. The effect is to render such mixtures and derivatives subject to the stringent standards for the management of hazardous waste. We reject the ACC's argument that the EPA lacked authority for the rule under the RCRA and hence we deny the petition for review. . . .

Both characteristic hazardous wastes and listed hazardous wastes are subject to regulation under Subtitle C of the RCRA, which applies stringent management standards to the generation, transportation, treatment, storage, and disposal of hazardous waste. *See* 42 U.S.C. §§ 6921–6925. Under the "delisting process" provided in the Act, a listed hazardous waste will be deemed non-hazardous at a particular facility if a petitioner demonstrates that the waste no longer meets any of the criteria for which it was listed, and that it is not hazardous because of any other factor reasonably identified by the EPA. 42 U.S.C. § 6921(f), 40 C.F.R. § 260.22.

In the proceeding here under review, the EPA modified the regulatory definition of "hazardous waste" to include, subject to certain exceptions, "a mixture of solid waste and one or more hazardous wastes," 40 C.F.R. § 261.3(a)(2)(iv), and "any solid waste generated from the treatment, storage, or disposal of a hazardous waste, including any sludge, spill residue, ash emission control dust, or leachate." 40 C.F.R. § 261.3(c)(2)(i). The EPA's new definition went into effect on an interim basis in 1992. 57 Fed.Reg. 7628 (Mar. 3). In 1999 the EPA proposed in substance to make permanent the 1992 rule, with some minor alterations not relevant to this case. 64 Fed.Reg. 63,382 (Nov. 19). The EPA issued the Final Rule so doing on May 16, 2001. 66 Fed.Reg. 27,266.

We review the Agency's interpretation of a statute it is charged with administering under the two-step analysis of *Chevron U.S.A., Inc. v. Natural Resources Defense Council, Inc.*, 467 U.S. 837 (1984). First we must determine "whether Congress has directly spoken to the precise question at issue," *id.* at 842—here, whether, as the ACC argues, the statutory definition of "hazardous waste" excludes substances mixed with or derived from such waste. If the Congress has so spoken, then "the court, as well as the agency, must give effect to the unambiguously expressed intent of Congress." *Id.* at 842–43. If, however, "the statute is silent or ambiguous with respect to the specific issue," then we must go on to determine "whether the agency's answer is based on a permissible construction of the statute." *Id.* at 843.

A.   *Chevron* step one

The ACC argues first that the EPA's interpretation is inconsistent with the statutory definition of hazardous waste, 42 U.S.C. § 6903(5), because the rule brings within that definition substances that do not exhibit a harmful "characteristic." The ACC points to the "EPA['s] acknowledge[ment] that not all mixtures and derivatives pose hazards to human health and the environment." Final Rule, 66 Fed.Reg. at 27,276. According to the ACC, the Congress could not possibly have meant to include in the definition of hazardous waste solid wastes that do not pose a threat to human health or the environment. *See Natural Resources Defense Council, Inc. v. United States EPA*, 907 F.2d 1146, 1159 (D.C.Cir.1990) ("A hazardous waste . . . is such only if various factors, including the *concentration* of hazardous constituents, actually make it hazardous to human health or the environment") (internal citation omitted).

In our view, however, the Congress did not speak directly, let alone clearly, to this issue. As the EPA points out, the definition of "hazardous waste" in the statute has a broad sweep. *See Environmental Defense Fund*, 210 F.3d at 397. It includes not only those solid wastes that do pose hazards to human health or the environment, but also those that "may" do so. In addition, the definition includes those wastes in which the "potential hazard" becomes an actual hazard only if the waste is "improperly treated, stored, transported, or disposed of, or otherwise managed." 42 U.S.C. § 6903(5)(B). This provision does not make mixtures and derivatives clearly hazardous wastes or clearly non-hazardous wastes. The element of judgment imported into the definition of hazardous waste by the use of "may" and the inclusion of waste that may be hazardous only if mismanaged necessarily makes the statute ambiguous on this score.

The ACC argues nonetheless that the Final Rule simply cannot be squared with the Act because it allows the EPA to classify a substance as hazardous without "taking into account toxicity, persistence, and degradability in nature, potential for accumulation in tissue, and other related factors," as required by § 6921(a). Amicus American Petroleum Institute adds that the legislative history of § 6921 indicates the EPA must follow a two-step process in order to regulate a solid waste as hazardous: it must first determine the characteristics of a hazardous waste and then show that a particular solid waste has at least one such characteristic. *See* H.R.Rep. No. 1491, 94th Cong., 2d Sess. 25, *reprinted in* 1976 U.S.C.C.A.N. 6238, 6263 ("Only after the criteria for determining what is hazardous has [sic] been developed can the Administrator determine which specific wastes are hazardous").

According to the EPA, however, when it lists a waste as hazardous it could, in principle, automatically list its mixtures and derivatives as well. That is, the mixture rule and the derived-from rule are consistent with § 6921 because mixtures and derivatives are "a second generation of the listed hazardous wastes from which they originate, [and] it is reasonable to presume, until demonstrated otherwise, that these wastes are also hazardous."

We think the EPA's response is sufficient, at the least, to demonstrate that the statute does not directly answer the issue before us. For the reason just quoted, § 6921 cannot be understood to preclude the EPA from regulating mixtures and derivatives until such time as they may be shown to be non-hazardous. Some—perhaps most— mixtures and derivatives maintain the characteristics of their parent hazardous waste. *See* Final Rule, 66 Fed.Reg. at 27,274–75 (citing Mark Eads, Office of Solid Waste, EPA, *Analysis of RCRA "Mixtures and Derived-From" Hazardous Waste Constituent Data*, which analyzed the EPA's National Hazardous Waste Constituent Survey Database); *Chemical Waste Management, Inc. v. EPA*, 869 F.2d 1526, 1539 (D.C.Cir.1989) ("a hazardous waste does not lose its hazardous character simply because it changes form or is combined with other substances"). Any mixture or derivative that does not remain hazardous may be exonerated either by an explicit exclusion in the initial listing or through the delisting process of § 6921(f).

In sum, neither the definition of "hazardous waste" nor § 6921 answers the question whether that definition or any other provision of the RCRA authorizes the EPA to regulate a mixture or derivative that may be, but has not yet been shown to be, a hazardous waste. We must go on to determine, therefore, whether the EPA's interpretation of 42 U.S.C. § 6903(5) is reasonable.

B.   *Chevron* step two

The EPA persuasively argues that it reasonably interpreted the term "hazardous waste" presumptively to include mixtures and derivatives: "[The Final Rule] assure[s] that hazardous mixtures and derivatives do not imprudently escape Subtitle C requirements." We agree. The Final Rule fulfills the purpose for which the Congress passed the RCRA, namely to subject hazardous waste to "cradle-to-grave" regulation in order to protect public health and the environment. *United Technologies*, 821 F.2d at 716. To that end, too, the Congress "requir[ed] that hazardous waste be properly managed in the first instance thereby reducing the need for corrective action at a future date." 42 U.S.C. § 6902(a)(5). We also agree that, because many mixtures of and derivatives from hazardous wastes are themselves hazardous, it is reasonable for the EPA to assume that all such mixtures and derivatives are hazardous until shown otherwise. For that reason we have already endorsed a similar action by the EPA with respect to hazardous wastes that mix with soil and groundwater. *See Chemical Waste Management*, 869 F.2d at 1540. Placing the burden upon the regulated entity to show the lack of a hazardous characteristic in a mixture or derivative it manages avoids placing upon the EPA what the agency persuasively describes as "the nearly impossible affirmative burden of anticipating and analyzing, in a listing decision, the hazardousness or non-hazardousness [of] every conceivable mixture or derivative that a generator might create." In addition, the dozen or more exceptions already contained in the rule—such as those for used oil, 40 C.F.R. § 261.3(a)(2)(v), certain laboratory wastewaters, *id.* § 261.3(a)(2)(iv)(E), and certain carbamate [an organic compound found in pesticides] wastewaters, *id.* § 261.3(a)(2)(iv)(F)–(G)—prevent it from casting too wide a net over nonhazardous mixtures and derivatives.

The ACC objects that the delisting mechanism does not provide any realistic relief to the potential over-inclusiveness of the rule because it is "slow, onerous, ineffective, and at times controversial." OFFICE OF SOLID WASTE AND EMERGENCY RESPONSE, ENVIRONMENTAL PROTECTION AGENCY, THE NATION'S HAZARDOUS WASTE MANAGEMENT PROGRAM AT A CROSSROADS: THE RCRA IMPLEMENTATION STUDY 39 (1990). The cumbersome nature of the delisting process, however, says nothing about the reasonableness of the EPA's interpretation of the statute. And in any event, even if the delisting process were impossibly cumbersome, a party could still head off the initial listing of the mixture or derivative by proposing that the initial listing of a particular waste as hazardous include the qualification that certain specified mixtures and derivatives are not included in the listing.

The ACC claims the EPA has available to it other "lawful and adequate alternatives to the mixture rule and the derived-from rule," such as adopting broader listings or modifying the current prohibition on dilution of hazardous waste. *See* 40 C.F.R. § 268.3. We disagree because the EPA has shown not only that the Final Rule prevents hazardous mixtures and derivatives from evading proper treatment under the RCRA but also that the alternatives proposed by the ACC would not be as effective. For example, using broader listings would place upon the EPA the very administrative burden we deemed above to be impractical; the Agency would have to identify not only the hazardous waste but also to determine whether all second-generation wastes are hazardous. The anti-dilution rule makes unlawful the expedient of simply diluting hazardous waste in order to lower the concentration of hazardous constituents and thereby circumvent regulation under the RCRA. The ACC does not explain how modifying the anti-dilution rule would make it an effective substitute for the Final Rule.

Finally, the ACC argues that the Final Rule imposes a significant cost upon industry without any showing of a concomitant public benefit. The ACC, however, does not identify any provision of the RCRA requiring the benefits of a regulation to equal or exceed its costs. And the EPA has submitted evidence that some mixtures and derivatives display the hazardous characteristics of their parent waste, *see* Final Rule, 66 Fed.Reg. at 22,274–75, which suggests the rule will provide at least some added protection of the environment and public health.

We think the Congress wanted the EPA, in deciding which substances to regulate as "hazardous" under the RCRA, to err on the side of caution, *see* 42 U.S.C. § 6901(b)(6); the Final Rule is a reasonable exercise of such caution. Therefore, we cannot say the rule is an unreasonable interpretation of the agency's statutory mandate comprehensively to regulate hazardous waste.

NOTES AND QUESTIONS

1.   Mixtures and Derivatives. EPA expressly acknowledged that not all mixtures and derivatives pose hazards to human health and the environment. Some mixtures may, for example, contain only minimal volumes of hazardous substances in comparison with nonhazardous substances. Some may simply not demonstrate the characteristics of a hazardous waste. How then can the EPA mixtures and derivatives rule be reconciled with the stated purpose of Subtitle C? On what basis did the *American Chemistry Council* court find against the petitioners on *Chevron* step one?

2.   Administrative Burden. What is the motivation for EPA's mixtures and derivatives rule? What would be the consequences of presumptively not including mixtures and derivatives in the definition of hazardous waste? What burdens would it place on EPA? How important were these considerations to the *American Chemistry Council* court?

3.   Exemptions. As noted by the *American Chemistry Council* court, EPA's mixtures and derivatives rule provides specific exemptions for certain types of mixed waste—most notably those for used oil, 40 C.F.R. § 261.3(a)(2)(v), certain laboratory wastewaters, *id.* § 261.3(a)(2)(iv)(E), and certain carbamate wastewaters, 40 C.F.R. § 261.3(a)(2)(iv)(F)–(G). Would the court have upheld EPA's rule without these exemptions?

3. *EX POST* APPROACH: COMPREHENSIVE ENVIRONMENTAL RESPONSE, COMPENSATION, AND LIABILITY ACT

A. INTRODUCTION

i. OVERVIEW

The materials in this section examine CERCLA, popularly known as Superfund, which imposes liability for environmental problems associated with the disposal of hazardous substances. Superfund is among the most controversial of the federal environmental statutes and has led to frequent and often lengthy litigation. One set of complaints centers around the breadth of its liability scheme: strict liability, joint and several liability, weak causation requirements, and limited defenses. Superfund is also criticized for the high cost of cleanups, which average about $30 million for sites on the National Priorities List (NPL)—the list of the most hazardous sites. The following article provides an overview of the structure of the statute.

Richard L. Revesz & Richard B. Stewart, The Superfund Debate
in ANALYZING SUPERFUND: ECONOMICS, SCIENCE, AND LAW 3, 3–4, 6–13
(Richard L. Revesz & Richard B. Stewart eds., 1995).[*]

During the last decade, the Superfund approach to environmental liability and remediation has become highly controversial. The costs of remedying the environmental problems caused by hazardous substances are great, although Superfund is far from the most costly U.S. environmental program. Its annual costs are in the range of $3 to $5 billion—a fraction of the costs of the federal air or water pollution regulation programs.

Much of the controversy generated by Superfund stems from its far-reaching statutory system of liabilities, which goes far beyond that of the common law. . . .

The broad net of Superfund liability includes current and past owners and operators of waste sites and waste generators and transporters. Defendants at Superfund sites include not only large industrial firms, but also a broad array of other entities—municipalities, local dry cleaners, hospitals, and a myriad of small businesses. As a result of this expansive liability regime, Superfund also has had significant effects on the real estate, banking, and insurance industries, as well as on the legal profession.

---

[*] Reprinted with the permission of Resources for the Future, copyright © 1995, with permission conveyed through Copyright Clearance Center, Inc.

Defendants have criticized the cleanup levels demanded by the U.S. Environmental Protection Agency (EPA) as excessively stringent and costly. Superfund is also widely regarded as a wasteful and inefficient program, plagued by high transaction costs, serious administrative deficiencies, and long delays in cleaning up sites. . . .

The Liability and Taxing Regimes

Under Superfund, the cleanup of hazardous waste sites is funded by two separate sources: a liability regime and a taxing regime.

The Liability Regime

Superfund contains an extensive and far-reaching liability scheme. Liability is triggered when the government or a private party incurs response costs in dealing with a release or threatened release of hazardous substances into the groundwater, surface water, soil, or air. In the event of such a release, the following categories of parties, often referred to as *potentially responsible parties* (PRPs), are liable: the current owner or operator of the site at which the release occurs; prior owners and operators during whose period of ownership there was disposal of hazardous substances at the site; generators of the hazardous substances; and transporters of the hazardous substances who had responsibility for selecting the site. Liability is also imposed on an owner of the site who, though not otherwise liable, obtains knowledge of the release or threatened release and subsequently transfers the property without disclosing such knowledge.

The liability standard under the statute is strict liability, rather than negligence. Thus, a PRP cannot avoid liability by showing that it met the regulatory or common law standards of care applicable at the time that it engaged in the activity, or even that it was also complying with hazardous waste regulatory standards currently in force.

Liability under Superfund is both retroactive and prospective. In addition to imposing liability for cleanup costs attributable to generation, transportation, treatment, storage, or disposal of hazardous substances undertaken before the passage of the statute, it also attaches cleanup costs for wastes disposed after the passage of the statute.

The defenses to liability are extremely limited. A PRP can escape liability only if it can show that the release or threatened release was caused solely by an act of God, an act of war, an act or omission of a third party, or a combination of these causes. Not surprisingly, only the third-party defense has been of practical significance, and the Superfund statute imposes significant limitations on it. Although this defense is the source of considerable litigation, very few PRPs have successfully established it.

A PRP seeking to defend on this ground must show that the third party was the sole cause of the harm, and that the third party was not the PRP's employee or agent. Moreover, these acts or omissions cannot occur in connection with a direct or indirect contractual relationship between the third party and the PRP asserting the defense. Thus, for example, a generator cannot raise the defense if the need for a cleanup arose as a result of the actions of either its transporter or the operator of the site where the wastes were eventually deposited. The party raising the defense must also show that it exercised due care with respect to the hazardous substances and that it took precautions against foreseeable acts or omissions of the third party.

Moreover, the courts have held that PRPs are jointly-and-severally liable if the harm at the site is indivisible—that is, if the wastes are sufficiently commingled that it is not possible to determine which wastes were responsible for the release. PRPs have the burden of showing that the waste and corresponding cleanup costs for which they are responsible are divisible from those attributable to other parties.

Joint-and-several liability is coupled with a *right of contribution*, so that if one PRP had to pay the full cleanup costs at a site, it could require other PRPs to pay their equitable shares of the liability. The right of contribution, however, is unavailing if other PRPs are insolvent or cannot be located. Accordingly, the solvent PRPs, as a group, must absorb the "orphan" shares of insolvent or absent PRPs. The existence of joint-and-several liability is especially significant in the Superfund context. Because significant periods of time—often several decades—can elapse between the disposal of hazardous substances and the cleanup, it is particularly likely that some PRPs will not be found or will be insolvent once they are found.

The Superfund statute also has causation requirements that are highly attenuated. Thus, a PRP can be liable even if it cannot be shown that its hazardous substances were the ones implicated in the release or threatened release that gave rise to cleanup costs. Liability can be imposed upon a PRP if its hazardous substances at some point were present at a site at which there was later a release or threatened release of the same or even another hazardous substance.

In addition to its cleanup provisions, CERCLA authorizes federal, state, and Indian tribe authorities who manage or control natural resources to sue for damages to such resources resulting from the release of a hazardous substance. The categories of persons liable are the same, and the principles of liability are generally the same, as in the cleanup program. Thus, for example, contamination at a site might lead to the impairment or destruction of wetlands. Following a cleanup that removes the hazardous substances from the site, the PRPs could remain liable for *natural resource damages* (NRD) in connection with any residual damage to the wetlands.

The Taxing Regime

The Superfund taxing provisions are an adjunct to the liability scheme. Currently, three separate taxes are levied on chemicals, petroleum products, and general corporate profits to finance the

Hazardous Substances Superfund (the trust fund), which gives the statute its popular name. This fund is used for two primary purposes: to pay for cleanups at sites at which all the PRPs are either insolvent or unknown, and to advance money for EPA cleanups at other sites pending EPA's recovery of cleanup costs from the PRPs. Thus, the fund is a revolving as well as residual form of financing, which covers cleanup costs that cannot be recovered through the liability scheme. At the time of the passage of CERCLA in 1980, Congress authorized a $1.6 billion fund, with the money to be raised over five years. The 1986 SARA amendments provided for an additional $8.5 billion, also to be raised over five years. When Congress reauthorized the statute in 1990, it provided for a funding level of $5.1 billion between October 1, 1991, and September 30, 1994. The total costs of cleaning up sites potentially subject to Superfund have been estimated at $100 billion or more.

Impact of the Liability Regime

The Superfund liability scheme has transformed vast sectors of the U.S. economy and has had effects far beyond the PRPs at Superfund sites. Our discussion in this regard focuses on the real estate, banking, and insurance industries, as well as on municipalities and the legal profession, where the impact of Superfund has been particularly significant.

The Real Estate Industry

Purchasers of real estate face the threat that they will buy contaminated land and that, at some point in the future, they will face liability as the current owners of the land. CERCLA recognizes an "innocent landowner" defense to owner liability. In order to assert this defense, an owner must establish that at the time it acquired the facility it did not know and had no reason to know about the hazardous substances responsible for the release or threatened release. Having "no reason to know" is further defined as undertaking "all appropriate inquiry . . . consistent with good commercial or customary practice." In order for purchasers to take advantage of this defense and avoid potentially far-reaching liabilities, it is now customary in the context of transfers of commercial real estate for purchasers to undertake environmental assessments, which, depending on the circumstances, can include extensive testing of soil and groundwater.

The Banking Industry

With respect to the banking industry, the statute, somewhat confusingly, exempts from liability "a person, who, without participating in the management of a [site], holds indicia of ownership primarily to protect his security interest." Two categories of cases involving mortgage lenders are relevant. First, if the borrower defaults and the lender forecloses, taking title to the property, logic would suggest that because the lender then acquires full indicia of ownership it can no longer qualify for the exemption and would face liability as a current owner. Second, preforeclosure liability arises when the bank becomes sufficiently involved in the activities of the debtor—for example, by monitoring the debtor's operations—that it is deemed to participate in the debtor's management. Unfortunately, the courts have been quite divided about what constitutes too much involvement, and a regulation by EPA attempting to clarify the issue was recently struck down in the courts as beyond EPA's authority.

As a result, banks routinely perform, or require the performance of, environmental assessments before they approve mortgages for commercial real estate. Moreover, critics of Superfund claim that the potential liability of banks, and, perhaps more importantly, the considerable uncertainty surrounding the scope of such liability, has undesirably increased the cost and reduced the availability of credit, especially for small businesses.

The Insurance Industry

The insurance industry also has been centrally affected by the Superfund statute. Between 1973 and 1986 the standard *comprehensive general liability* (CGL) policy held by individuals and corporations included a pollution exclusion clause which provided that insurance would not cover bodily injury or property damage arising out of pollution except if the release was "sudden and accidental." In large part as a result of Superfund, insurers amended this clause in 1986, explicitly excluding any pollution-related liability. The impact of Superfund on the insurance industry is manifested in two distinct ways.

First, firms interested in protecting against liability for pollution must now purchase specialized insurance, which, to the extent it is available at all, carries high premiums, high deductibles, high coinsurance rates, and low caps. Moreover, the availability of such insurance is quite limited. Thus, many firms have had little option but to self-insure, sometimes risking bankruptcy in the event of an environmental accident.

Second, Superfund has raised an enormous amount of contentious litigation concerning the liability of insurers under policies written before the 1986 change in the pollution exclusion clause. PRPs in Superfund actions routinely seek indemnification from their CGL insurers. The interpretation of insurance contracts is a matter of state law, and the state supreme courts that have addressed the issue have split almost evenly on whether the release or threatened release of hazardous substances at Superfund sites is "sudden and accidental" and meets the other terms of policy coverage. The litigation on this matter between insureds and insurers has consumed exceedingly high transaction costs and has led to proposals for the establishment of a fund (to supplement the existing trust fund), financed by assessments on insurance companies, to pay for a portion of Superfund cleanup costs in place of case-by-case litigation between insureds and insurers.

Municipalities

Municipalities also have been caught in the Superfund web. Typically, municipal solid waste contains a small percentage of hazardous substances. Some municipalities disposed of this waste at sites also used by industrial generators. If liability is apportioned proportionally to the aggregate amount of waste contributed by each PRP, on the premise that cleanup costs are roughly proportional to the volume of waste to be cleaned up, the municipalities will generally bear a high percentage of the costs. If, instead, the relevant criterion is the amount of hazardous substances in the waste contributed by each PRP, the bulk of the burden will be placed on the industrial generators. Judicial decisions adopting the former approach have threatened to imperil the financial stability of small towns.

The Legal Profession

The legal profession has also been powerfully affected by the Superfund liability scheme. In the 1970s, the bulk of environmental law practice consisted in large part of challenging EPA and state command-and-control regulations and the implementation of those regulations. Typical lawsuits pitted industrial firms or environmental groups on one side against the federal government on the other. The specialized environmental bar was disproportionately located in Washington, D.C. Largely as a result of Superfund, environmental disputes now routinely involve controversies among industrial and commercial firms that are PRPs at the same site, and between such firms and insurers and banks. The federal government is sometimes both the enforcer of the law and a polluter responsible for cleanup costs at a site. As a result of the broad scope of Superfund liability, environmental law has become a standard component of legal practice nationwide.

The Cleanup Process

[The process of cleaning up hazardous waste sites is governed by the National Contingency Plan (NCP). 40 C.F.R. § 300. The NCP provides guidelines and procedures for responses to releases and threatened releases of hazardous substances, pollutants, or contaminants.] The process [established under the NCP] . . . is cumbersome and slow, and consists of several stages. First, EPA must become aware of a site's existence. Generally, a site is brought to the agency's attention by a state or municipality, or by citizen complaints; there is no federal discovery program. EPA then places the site in the CERCLA Information system (CERCLIS)—the inventory of locations that potentially require cleanup. [In 2014, the CERCLIS database was replaced by the Superfund Enterprise Management System (SEMS), which contains 12,890 active sites as of October 2018. *See* EPA, Superfund Data and Reports, https://www.epa.gov/superfund/superfund-data-and-reports (last visited Nov. 23, 2018).]

Second, EPA conducts a Preliminary Assessment (PA) to ascertain the risks posed by the site. If warranted, a Site Inspection (SI) then follows. At each of these stages, many sites are classified as sufficiently harmless to warrant no further attention.

Third, EPA ranks sites under the Hazard Ranking System (HRS). [The HRS is a composite score that measures the risk of the site by reference to four possible routes of human exposure: groundwater, surface water, soil exposure, and air.]

Fourth, sites that receive a score above a given cut-off are placed on the National Priorities List (NPL); currently there are over 1,200 sites on the NPL. Only sites listed on the NPL are eligible for the expenditure of money by EPA for long-term remedial action from the trust fund. This limitation, however, does not apply to EPA removal actions (quicker and less extensive measures often undertaken in the face of emergencies).

For sites on the NPL, the fifth stage of the process involves the preparation of a Remedial Investigation/Feasibility Study (RI/FS). This stage consists of a more detailed examination of the site and a preliminary study of possible remedies.

Sixth, EPA issues a Record of Decision (ROD). This document contains an analysis of alternative remedies, with their expected costs, and selects the remedy that will be implemented at the site.

Seventh, comes the Remedial Design/Remedial Action (RD/RA). The former is a more detailed design of the remediation technique chosen in the ROD; the latter is the actual cleanup of the site.

The process, however, does not always occur in this linear fashion. Cleanup activities at a site are often divided into separate parcels known as operable units; one unit, for example, might involve soil removal and another, groundwater treatment. The different operable units may progress at different rates: one might be at the RD/RA stage whereas the other might be at the RI/FS stage.

A RAND study completed in 1989 . . . showed that, for a site that ultimately gets listed on the NPL, it takes on average forty-three months between the time EPA becomes aware of a site's existence and its listing. Twenty months then elapse until the beginning of the RI/FS, thirty-eight additional months until the issuance of the ROD; the RD/RA takes an additional forty-three months. Thus, on average, the time elapsed between listing on CERCLIS and the completion of the RD/RA is twelve years; eight-and-a-half years elapse between the listing on the NPL and the completion of the RD/RA.

Typically, EPA or a state in which a site is located is responsible for the stages leading to listing on the NPL. Of the later stages, the RI/FS and the RD/RA can be conducted by EPA or the state, or by a group of PRPs. In contrast, the issuance of the ROD is the sole responsibility of EPA.

In the early years of the Superfund program, EPA followed a "fund lead" strategy for cleanup. It hired contractors to carry out cleanup activities, paid them out of the fund, and then sought reimbursement from PRPs. The limited size of the fund and the delays and difficulties in obtaining reimbursement led EPA to make increasing use of an "enforcement lead" approach. Under this approach, EPA uses its CERCLA authority to issue an administrative order to PRPs or seek a court order requiring the PRPs to undertake the cleanup. Currently, PRPs are undertaking the bulk of RI/FSs and RD/RAs, typically as a result of settlements with EPA. Evidence suggests that the cost of a given cleanup is about 20 percent lower when it is undertaken by the PRPs rather than by EPA, presumably because private PRPs have stronger incentives to minimize costs and can supervise contractors more effectively.

The Determination of Cleanup Standards

The most important decision at any NPL site is the determination of the extent of the cleanup and the choice of cleanup technology. If the site's soil is contaminated, should the site simply be capped to reduce the probability of releases into the groundwater, or should the soil be removed and incinerated off-site? The first option will typically be a great deal cheaper, but might pose some long-term risks. Similarly, in the face of groundwater contamination, is it sufficient to prevent migration of the contaminated groundwater through containment measures and secure an alternative source of drinking water (or do nothing at all if the contaminated groundwater is not used for drinking), or instead should one undertake a "pump and treat" program? The latter course of action will be far more expensive, and there is substantial question about its long-term effectiveness. Unfortunately, the statute says little that is helpful in answering these questions, and a wide range of remedies has been used in actual cleanups at NPL sites.

CERCLA contains two sets of provisions dealing with cleanup standards. First, it directs EPA to select remedies protective of "human health and the environment." In making this determination, EPA is to consider a wide range of factors. For example, remedial actions must be "cost effective," but must also "to the maximum extent practicable" utilize "permanent solutions" and technologies that will result "in a permanent and significant decrease" in the volume, toxicity, and mobility of contaminants. These provisions leave EPA with considerable discretion. EPA has tended to emphasize more permanent and costly remedies, such as treating contaminated groundwater rather than simply taking steps to prevent its migration.

Second, CERCLA requires that sites be cleaned in accordance with any "legally applicable" or "relevant and appropriate" standards (ARARs or applicable or relevant and appropriate requirements), where such standards exist. Any standard promulgated under a federal environmental law is "legally applicable" and therefore automatically an

ARAR; more stringent state standards are ARARs, if certain procedural conditions are met. The statute, however, does not define when standards are "relevant and appropriate," and therefore also ARARs.

The ARAR prescription is particularly problematic in the case of groundwater contamination. The Safe Drinking Water Act (SDWA) defines permissible levels of various pollutants in publicly supplied drinking water. If groundwater at a Superfund site is contaminated by such a pollutant, the SDWA standard probably will not be deemed "legally applicable" if this groundwater is not used as the source of publicly supplied drinking water, or if it is treated before its distribution to households. The standard might, however, be deemed "relevant and appropriate" and therefore qualify as an ARAR. The Superfund statute provides that where SDWA standards are "relevant and appropriate," the cleanups must at least achieve the Maximum Contaminant Level Goals (MCLGs) under the SDWA. (The SDWA provides that MCLGs "be set at the level at which no known or anticipated adverse effects on the health of persons occur and which allows an adequate margin of safety." MCLGs are aspirational goals; the enforceable standards or Maximum Containment Levels (MCLs) must be set to MCLGs "as is feasible.") In the case of known or probable carcinogens, MCLGs require a zero concentration of pollution—probably an unattainable objective in groundwater remediation.

The requirement that Superfund cleanups satisfy ARARs, however, is subject to significant exceptions. In the case of groundwater remediation, ARARs need not be used in a variety of circumstances, including "the remedial action includes enforceable measures that will preclude human exposure to the contaminated groundwater." More generally, for any remediation financed solely by the trust fund, exceptions from ARARs are appropriate on the basis of a balance between "the need for protection of public health and welfare and the environment at the facility," and the availability of amounts from the trust fund to respond to other sites. Moreover, ARARs generally do not exist for soil remediation, which is a major element in many cleanups.

NOTES AND QUESTIONS

1. **Who Should Pay?** CERCLA creates broad liability for PRPs to finance the cleanup of hazardous sites. PRPs may be held liable for the cost of cleanup even if they did not cause the harm at the site, and they may also be held liable for the entire cost of cleanup even if they caused only a small portion of the harm. (These issues are discussed in greater detail in the section on Joint and Several Liability, *infra*.) Many PRPs have attacked CERCLA as unfair for these reasons.

Who should pay for the cleanup of hazardous sites? Would it be fairer to hold PRPs liable only for the harm that they caused? In most CERCLA cases, it would be nearly impossible to prove causation. Should this difficulty of proof change whether causation is a requirement for liability? If PRPs were held liable only for the harm that they caused, how should the remainder of the cleanup costs be funded? Through a tax on all polluters, so that the costs of cleanup are spread more widely? Through general appropriations, so that the costs of cleanup are spread among all taxpayers? What incentives would these various options create for PRPs to take care in their handling of hazardous substances?

2.   **An Alternative Regime.** Evaluate the following argument advanced in favor of replacing CERCLA's entire liability system with a system of taxation:

> . . . [T]he process of encouraging or forcing responsible parties, either initially or subsequently, to finance the cleanup of hazardous waste sites tends to significantly impede overall progress towards CERCLA's primary goal of eliminating the immediate and long-term threats to human health and the environment posed by the nation's worst hazardous waste sites. The substantial transaction costs which arise from the government's efforts to have responsible parties bear site cleanup costs in effect impose enormous but unseen opportunity costs on society by shifting resources which might have been used to finance cleanup efforts to the process of imposing legal and financial responsibility for cleanup costs on responsible parties.

> These transaction costs, consisting primarily of fees paid to lawyers and to scientific consultants, are a natural consequence of the choice made and the method selected by Congress to shift the primary financial burden of cleaning up the worst hazardous waste sites from the public treasury to private parties who had a hand in the creation of the problem. . . . One estimate indicates that these costs could exceed $8 billion.

> What is forgone when transaction costs are paid is the opportunity for society to use those resources to actually achieve environmental results. . . . These transaction costs have their origins in Congress' choice to finance CERCLA response actions, when possible, through a liability system. The alternative is fairly obvious: funding should be derived exclusively through a system of taxation, especially when one considers the inequitable results created as a consequence of EPA's enforcement. . . .

John J. Lyons, *Deep Pockets and CERCLA: Should Superfund Liability Be Abolished?*, 6 STAN. ENVTL. L.J. 271, 271–73 (1987). Lyons' principal objection to the present liability regime appears to be the resultant transaction costs. What transaction costs would attach to Lyons' preferred plan? How would they likely compare to the transaction costs under the existing regime?

3.   **Superfund Tax.** Much of the rest of this chapter focuses on the CERCLA liability regime, under which PRPs may be held liable for the costs of cleaning up a contaminated site. As discussed in the above overview, CERCLA also provides for a fund, known as the Superfund, that is used to finance cleanups at sites where there are no known or solvent parties to hold

liable and to advance the costs for cleanup pending recovery from liable parties. From its inception until 1995, the Superfund was financed in large part by taxes on chemical feedstock and crude oil, and a corporate environmental tax. In 1995, however, the taxes expired and Congress has not yet reauthorized them. Since the expiration of these taxes, the funding available for government cleanup actions has decreased significantly. *See* Letter from United States General Accounting Office to James M. Jeffords, United States Senator (May 14, 2004).

In 2010, legislation was introduced in the House and Senate to reinstate the Superfund taxes, *see* H.R. 564, H.R. 832, S. 3164, and S. 3125, 111th Cong., and EPA indicated its support of such legislation, *see* Press Release, Environmental Protection Agency, EPA Supports Superfund "Polluter Pays" Provision (June 21, 2010). The bills would have reinstated the corporate environmental tax as well as the taxes on crude oil and certain chemical products. The taxes would be set at the level they were at upon expiration in 1995, but with a 50 percent increase for the next five years. The funding from the 50 percent increase would go directly to a new a special account within the general Superfund, the Megasites and High Risk Sites Cleanup Account, and would be earmarked for the cleanup of sites that are expected to cost more than $50 million or that pose high health risks. EPA has the resources to initiate cleanup actions only for a very small number of Superfund sites and must choose which sites deserve cleanup. Generally, sites that are very large or that pose serious health risks are the only sites that stand a significant chance of being the target of a government cleanup. If megasites and high risk sites are the sites that EPA is already more likely to clean up, then why create a new, separate account for these sites?

4.   Status of Superfund in 1999: The 20 Year Reports. The Government Accountability Office (then called the General Accounting Office) released a number of studies in 1999, as part of an assessment of CERCLA's progress during its first 20 years. GAO found that, after 20 years, 595 of the 1,231 NPL sites had been cleaned up or had comprehensive remedies in place. An additional 424 sites had at least one remedy selected, underway, or completed. According to the report, EPA expected the pace of cleanups to increase as sites began to move to later stages in the cleanup process, and managers asserted that 87 percent of remedies would be constructed or implemented by 2010. GAO, HALF THE SITES HAVE ALL CLEANUP REMEDIES IN PLACE OR COMPLETED (1999). Why would EPA assume that the number of sites on the NPL would decrease over time?

GAO also noted that some of the most significant problems in early implementation of CERCLA were: difficulty controlling costs, failure to recover cleanup funds from PRPs, and selection of sites for cleanup without assurance that they presented the greatest threats. GAO attributed some of these problems to the fact that EPA managers had little experience devising cost estimates and, as a result, struggled to control contractor overheads. GAO, PROGRESS, PROBLEMS, AND FUTURE OUTLOOK (1999).

5.   Status of Superfund in 2003: Financial Constraints. GAO again reviewed the overall health of the Superfund program in 2003. At that point, it noted that the Superfund trust fund had been dwindling since 1999, while additional sites continued to be added to the NPL. Specifically, the trust fund received over $2 billion in 1995—when the Superfund tax was still in effect—but only $370 million in 2002, yet overall expenditures had remained steady over that period. In order to continue operating, Superfund projects increasingly relied on general appropriations. Prior to the expiration of the Superfund tax, tax revenues were the primary source of income for the trust fund, but, once the tax expired, the main source of income became cost recoveries from PRPs.

Overall, the number of sites on the NPL stayed fairly steady, but GAO noted that many of them had progressed to later stages of cleanup. This coincided with an emerging EPA practice of taking the lead in earlier stages of the process and having PRPs play a more prominent role later in cleanups. In fact, between 2000 and 2003, PRPs funded around 70 percent of remedial actions.

State cleanup programs, on the other hand, did not provide much of a supplement to EPA's actions. Because state programs generally had small fund balances (usually under $25 million in 2003, and decreasing), state programs could play only a role in cleaning up sites if there was a cooperative, solvent PRP with whom to work. GAO noted that, since states took on most of the projects with identifiable, cooperative, and solvent PRPs, 42 of the 54 sites proposed to the NPL in 2001 and 2002 did not have a viable or cooperative PRP or were simply too expensive or complicated for a state to handle. GAO, CURRENT STATUS AND FUTURE FISCAL CHALLENGES (2003). What strategies might EPA have to implement if its trust fund is dwindling, but the sites being added to the NPL are primarily those with no solvent PRP identified? Are there any steps EPA could take to ensure that it would have adequate funding to continue meeting its cleanup responsibilities? Would re-implementing the Superfund tax be the best way to provide funding to cleanup programs?

ii. CERCLA'S LIABILITY SCHEME

CERCLA was enacted by Congress on December 11, 1980, in the final months of the Carter Administration. Pub. L. No. 96–510, 94 Stat. 2767 (1980). The statute was significantly amended in 1986, in the Superfund Amendments and Reauthorization Act (SARA), Pub. L. No. 99–499, 100 Stat. 1613 (1986). While there have been a number of amendments, its core liability provisions have not changed significantly since 1986.

At the time of its original passage, CERCLA garnered strong bipartisan support, in large part due to public outrage at the Love Canal disaster. In the 1940s and 1950s, a chemical company dumped countless drums of hazardous waste in an abandoned canal (the "Love Canal") in upstate New York. The chemical company then filled over the canal and sold it to the city for an elementary school and playground, and a number of homes were built in the immediate vicinity. Several decades later, a New York State Health Department investigation revealed that toxic chemicals had percolated into the basements of many of these homes, and the area's residents were experiencing health problems including "birth defects, miscarriages, epilepsy, liver abnormalities, sores, rectal bleeding, [and] headaches—not to mention undiscovered but possible latent illnesses." S. REP. NO. 96–848, at 9 (1980). The entire area was subsequently evacuated. At the time CERCLA was passed, it was estimated that it would cost at least $125 million to clean up the site.

The Love Canal disaster brought into stark relief the problem of irresponsible disposal of hazardous waste and the inadequacy of existing laws to address the problem. While a "patchwork of other existing Federal statutes . . . ostensibly deal with hazardous substance problems," existing statutes and common law left many gaps that made imposing liability on the owners or disposers of hazardous substances uncertain and complex. S. REP. NO. 96–848, *supra*, at 11. CERCLA was designed to close these gaps, ensuring that persons involved in handling hazardous waste could be held liable, and to create incentives for private parties to dispose of hazardous waste as safely as possible.

Shore Realty is one of the earliest cases interpreting CERCLA. Its approach is typical of the courts' interpretations of CERCLA's liability scheme. Later sections of this chapter deal with specific aspects of CERCLA's liability scheme in greater detail.

New York v. Shore Realty Corp.
759 F.2d 1032 (2d Cir. 1985).

■ Before FEINBERG, CHIEF JUDGE, and OAKES and NEWMAN, CIRCUIT JUDGES.

■ OAKES, CIRCUIT JUDGE:

. . . On February 29, 1984, the State of New York brought suit against Shore Realty Corp. ("Shore") and Donald LeoGrande, its officer and stockholder, to clean up a hazardous waste disposal site at One Shore Road, Glenwood Landing, New York, which Shore had acquired for land development purposes. At the time of the acquisition, LeoGrande knew that hazardous waste was stored on the site and that cleanup would be expensive, though neither Shore nor LeoGrande had participated in the generation or transportation of the nearly 700,000 gallons of hazardous waste now on the premises. . . .

[LeoGrande planned to use the Shore site for a condominium development, and was aware that the previous tenants used the site for hazardous waste disposal. Prior to finalizing the purchase, Shore retained an environmental consultant, whose study of the site found that it was in extremely poor condition and "concluded that if the current tenants 'close up the operation and leave the material at the site,' the [new] owners would be left with a 'potential time bomb.'" Shore nonetheless proceeded to acquire the property. Soon after, state officials inspected the site and ordered Shore to begin cleanup under the State's supervision. The State then brought suit to recover costs.]

We hold that the district court properly awarded the State response costs under section 9607(a)(4)(A). The State's costs in assessing the conditions of the site and supervising the removal of the drums of hazardous waste squarely fall within CERCLA's definition of response costs, even though the State is not undertaking to do the removal. *See id.* §§ 9601(23), (24), (25). . . .

CERCLA holds liable four classes of persons:

(1) the owner and operator of a vessel (otherwise subject to the jurisdiction of the United States) or a facility,

(2) any person who at the time of disposal of any hazardous substance owned or operated any facility at which such hazardous substances were disposed of,

(3) any person who by contract, agreement, or otherwise arranged for disposal or treatment, or arranged with a transporter for transport for disposal or treatment, of hazardous substances owned or possessed by such person, by any other party or entity, at any facility owned or operated by another party or entity and containing such hazardous substances, and

(4) any person who accepts or accepted any hazardous substances for transport to disposal or treatment facilities or sites selected by such person.

42 U.S.C. § 9607(a). As noted above, section 9607 makes these persons liable, if "there is a release, or a threatened release which causes the incurrence of response costs, of a hazardous substance" from the facility,[16] for, among other things, "all costs of removal or remedial action incurred by the United States Government or a State not inconsistent with the national contingency plan."

Shore argues that it is not covered by section 9607(a)(1) because it neither owned the site at the time of disposal nor caused the presence or the release of the hazardous waste at the facility. While section 9607(a)(1) appears to cover Shore, Shore attempts to infuse ambiguity into the statutory scheme, claiming that section 9607(a)(1) could not have been intended to include all owners, because the word "owned" in section 9607(a)(2) would be unnecessary since an owner "at the time of disposal" would necessarily be included in section 9607(a)(1). Shore claims that Congress intended that the scope of section 9607(a)(1) be no greater than that of section 9607(a)(2) and that both should be limited by the "at the time of disposal" language. By extension, Shore argues that both

---

[16] The phrase "from which there is a release, or a threatened release which causes the incurrence of response costs, of a hazardous substance" is incorporated in and seems to flow as if it were a part only of subparagraph (4), but it is quite apparent that it also modifies subparagraphs (1)–(3) inclusive. . . .

provisions should be interpreted as requiring a showing of causation. We agree with the State, however, that section 9607(a)(1) unequivocally imposes strict liability on the current owner of a facility from which there is a release or threat of release, without regard to causation.

Shore's claims of ambiguity are illusory; section 9607(a)'s structure is clear. Congress intended to cover different classes of persons differently. Section 9607(a)(1) applies to all current owners and operators, while section 9607(a)(2) primarily covers prior owners and operators. Moreover, section 9607(a)(2)'s scope is more limited than that of section 9607(a)(1). Prior owners and operators are liable only if they owned or operated the facility "at the time of disposal of any hazardous substance"; this limitation does not apply to current owners, like Shore. . . .

Shore's causation argument is also at odds with the structure of the statute. Interpreting section 9607(a)(1) as including a causation requirement makes superfluous the affirmative defenses provided in section 9607(b), each of which carves out from liability an exception based on causation. Without a clear congressional command otherwise, we will not construe a statute in any way that makes some of its provisions surplusage. . . .

Furthermore, as the State points out, accepting Shore's arguments would open a huge loophole in CERCLA's coverage. It is quite clear that if the current owner of a site could avoid liability merely by having purchased the site after chemical dumping had ceased, waste sites certainly would be sold, following the cessation of dumping, to new owners who could avoid the liability otherwise required by CERCLA. Congress had well in mind that persons who dump or store hazardous waste sometimes cannot be located or may be deceased or judgment-proof. *See, e.g.*, Senate Report, *supra*, at 16. We will not interpret section 9607(a) in any way that apparently frustrates the statute's goals, in the absence of a specific congressional intention otherwise.

NOTES AND QUESTIONS

1. **Current and Prior Owners.** The *Shore Realty* court found that "Congress intended to cover different classes of persons differently. . . . Prior owners and operators are liable only if they owned or operated the facility 'at the time of disposal of any hazardous substance'; this limitation does not apply to current owners, like Shore." 759 F.2d at 1044. What reasons are there to treat current and prior owners differently in this regard? What incentives does this create for owners who discover contamination on their property that predates their ownership?

2. **Retroactivity.** One of the main issues in early CERCLA litigation was whether CERCLA applied retroactively. In *United States v. Monsanto Co.*, 858 F.2d 160 (4th Cir. 1988), *cert. denied*, 490 U.S. 1106 (1989), defendant generators (held liable under the "arranged for" prong of § 107(a)) argued that they were not liable under CERCLA because all of the hazardous waste

at the site at issue had been placed there before CERCLA was enacted. The Fourth Circuit held that CERCLA did apply retroactively, finding that Congress intended to create liability for pre-enactment disposal of hazardous waste, and that its retroactive application did not violate the due process clause of the U.S. Constitution. *Id.* at 173–74.

In *United States v. Northeastern Pharmaceutical & Chemical Co., Inc.*, 810 F.2d 726 (8th Cir. 1986), *cert. denied*, 484 U.S. 848 (1987), the Eighth Circuit addressed the retroactive application of CERCLA to both pre-enactment disposal and pre-enactment response costs. Like the Fourth Circuit, the Eighth Circuit held that Congress did intend for CERCLA to create liability for pre-enactment disposal of hazardous waste, and that such retroactive application was constitutional. *Id.* at 732–34. On the issue of costs incurred prior to CERCLA's enactment, the court held that CERCLA did apply retroactively to response costs incurred by the United States or a state, *see* 42 U.S.C. § 9607(a)(4)(A), and to response costs incurred by private parties, *see* 42 U.S.C. § 9607(a)(4)(B), but held that CERCA did *not* apply retroactively to natural resource damages, *see* 42 U.S.C. § 9607(a)(4)(C), that occurred wholly before CERCLA's enactment. *Id.* at 734–37; *see also Ohio ex rel. Brown v. Georgeoff*, 562 F. Supp. 1300 (N.D. Ohio 1983). What could justify this distinction?

Applying CERCLA liability to pre-enactment disposal and response costs furthers the Congressional objective of holding the handlers of hazardous waste liable for harm caused by the waste. Does CERCLA's retroactive application also create desirable incentives, even though it cannot alter the manner in which the waste was disposed? For a discussion of this and other implications of CERCLA's retrospective application, see Jennifer R. Yelin, *Retroactivity Revisited: A Critical Appraisal of CERCLA's Retroactive Liability Scheme in Light of* Landgraf v. USI Film Products *and* Eastern Enterprises v. Apfel, 8 N.Y.U. ENVTL. L.J. 94 (1999).

3. Strict Liability. The standard of liability under CERCLA is somewhat elusively defined in § 101(32) as "the standard of liability . . . under [§ 311 of the CWA]." 42 U.S.C. § 9601(32). While § 311 of the CWA does not expressly specify a strict liability standard, it has repeatedly been interpreted in this fashion by the courts. *See, e.g., Steuart Transp. Co. v. Allied Towing Corp.*, 596 F.2d 609, 613 (4th Cir. 1979). If Congress "intended that responsible parties be held strictly liable," as the *Shore* court contends, *see* 759 F.2d at 1041, why does CERCLA's standard of liability reference the standard of liability under the CWA, rather than explicitly stating a precise standard? *Cf. United States v. Chem-Dyne Corp.*, 572 F. Supp. 802, 805 (S.D. Ohio 1983) (finding that CERCLA imposes a "strict liability standard" through analyzing its legislative history).

4. Defining Releases and Threatened Releases. As the *Shore* court discusses, CERCLA makes four categories of listed parties liable if there has been a release or threatened release of a hazardous substance that causes response costs to be incurred. "Release" is broadly defined to include any "spilling, leaking, pumping, pouring, emitting, emptying, discharging, injecting, escaping, leaching, dumping, or disposing into the environment. . . ." 42 U.S.C. § 9601(22); *see also Saline River Props., LLC v.*

Johnson Controls, Inc., 823 F. Supp. 2d 670 (E.D. Mich. 2011) (finding a potential release when a development company broke a concrete slab, allowing rainwater to mix with contaminated materials which migrated into additional areas). *But see infra* Section 3.C.iii (discussing passive migration). "Environment" is also defined broadly, and includes any "ambient air within the United States." 42 U.S.C. § 9601(8). Should releases into the air of a building or a structure that does not reach the outside air constitute a release "into the environment"? *See Reading Co. v. City of Philadelphia*, 823 F. Supp. 1218, 1238 (E.D. Pa. 1993) (holding that such releases are not releases "into the environment," so no liability attaches); *Cyker v. Four Seasons Hotels Ltd.*, 1991 WL 1401 (D. Mass. 1991) (holding that releases into an indoor swimming pool could not be considered releases "into the environment").

"Release" is defined in § 101(22), but "threatened" is not. *See* 42 U.S.C. § 9601. What actions should constitute a threatened release? If there is always some risk that hazardous substances will leak or corrode their containers, is any disposal necessarily a threatened release? What if the only corrosion is one or two leaks the size of a pinhole, and there is conclusive evidence that any emissions through such a pinhole leak would evaporate too quickly to pose any threat? *See O'Neil v. Picillo*, 682 F. Supp. 706, 724 (D.R.I. 1988) (holding that pinhole leak is threatened release), *aff'd*, 883 F.2d 176 (1st Cir. 1989), *cert. denied*, 493 U.S. 1071 (1990). Should the presence of hazardous substances that do not pose any immediate danger combined with abandonment of a site constitute a threatened release? *See United States v. Northernaire Plating Co.*, 670 F. Supp. 742, 747 (W.D. Mich. 1987) (holding such a situation is a threatened release), *aff'd sub nom. United States v. R.W. Meyer, Inc.*, 889 F.2d 1497 (6th Cir. 1989), *cert. denied*, 494 U.S. 1057 (1990). Should the fact that a storage tank contains hazardous materials and is at least 20 years old constitute a threatened release, if there is no indication other than the tank's age that it might leak? *See Nurad, Inc. v. William E. Hooper & Sons Co.*, 966 F.2d 837 (4th Cir. 1992) (holding such a situation to be a threatened release), *cert. denied*, 506 U.S. 940 (1992).

5. Removal Actions, Remedial Actions, and Natural Resource Damages. CERCLA liability is triggered only if a release or threatened release causes someone to incur response costs. *See* 42 U.S.C. § 9607(a)(4). "Response" is defined in § 101(25), 42 U.S.C. § 9601(25), and includes both removal actions, defined in § 101(23), 42 U.S.C. § 9601(23), and remedial actions, defined in § 101(24), 42 U.S.C. § 9601(24). Removal actions are generally short-term and constitute an immediate response to a developing problem, such as removing leaking barrels from a site. Remedial actions are generally long-term actions meant to deal with the environmental consequences of contamination, such as removing and incinerating contaminated soil, or groundwater remediation. (Removal and remedial actions are discussed in greater detail in the section on Cleanup, *infra*.)

The incurrence of response costs is what triggers liability. Once liability is triggered, however, PRPs may be held liable for an even broader range of costs. *See* 42 U.S.C. § 9607(a)(4)(A). First, PRPs may be liable for all removal or remedial costs incurred by a government, 42 U.S.C. § 9607(a)(4)(A), or a private party, 42 U.S.C. § 9607(a)(4)(B). CERCLA allows federal or state governments to recover costs for actions "not inconsistent with" the NCP, 42 U.S.C. § 9607(a)(4)(A), while private parties may recover costs for actions "consistent with" the NCP, 42 U.S.C. § 9607(a)(4)(B). What might explain this distinction? *See United States v. Ne. Pharm. & Chem. Co.*, 810 F.2d 726, 747–48 (8th Cir. 1986), *cert. denied*, 484 U.S. 848 (1987); *United States v. Ward*, 618 F. Supp. 884, 899 (E.D.N.C. 1985).

In addition, PRPs may be liable for "damages for injury to, destruction of, or loss of natural resources." 42 U.S.C. § 9607(a)(4)(C) (discussed in the section on Natural Resource Damages, *infra*). "Natural resources" is defined in § 101(16), and includes only natural resources owned or controlled by the federal government, a state government, or an Indian tribe. 42 U.S.C. § 9601(16). How are natural resource damages different from long-term remediation actions? Why are PRPs only liable for natural resource damages on publicly controlled land?

6. Cleanup by Private Parties. As mentioned in the previous note, CERCLA allows the government to recover costs of cleanup, and also allows private parties that independently clean up hazardous waste sites to recover costs. 42 U.S.C. § 9607(a)(4)(A)–(B). Why might it be desirable to encourage private parties to undertake their own cleanup efforts? Why might it be undesirable? What incentives and disincentives are there for a private party to independently initiate cleanup of a site? These questions are explored further in the section on Joint and Several Liability, *infra*.

7. Compensation for Injured Parties. As discussed above, CERCLA creates liability for a wide range of costs; nowhere, however, does it contain any provision for compensation for individuals who experience adverse health effects from a hazardous waste spill. What other avenues are there for individuals to recover for these types of adverse health effects? Will these other avenues be limited by some of the same difficulties (*e.g.*, difficulty in proving causation) that limited the avenues to recover cleanup costs prior to CERCLA's passage? The Senate Report accompanying CERCLA, S. REP. NO. 96–848 (1980), states that one of the goals in passing a comprehensive environmental response act would be to provide "prompt and adequate compensation for injured parties." Why might Congress ultimately have chosen not to create liability for individual harms in CERCLA?

8. Statutes of Limitation, Statutes of Repose and Preemption. Statutes of limitation and statutes of repose both limit the duration of a person's liability for a tort. A statute of limitation creates a time limit for suing in a civil case (usually measured from the time that a cause of action accrues). A statute of repose provides that a party has no right to bring a civil action after a certain period of time has passed, and is measured from the date of the last culpable act or omission of the defendant. 42 U.S.C. § 9658(a)(1) provides that:

> [i]n the case of any action brought under State law for personal injury, or property damages, which are caused or contributed to by exposure to any hazardous substance, or pollutant or contaminant, released into the environment from a facility, if the applicable limitations period for such action (as specified in the State statute

of limitations or under common law) provides a commencement date which is earlier than the federally required commencement date, such period shall commence at the federally required commencement date. . .

The "federally required commencement date" is "the date the plaintiff knew (or reasonably should have known) that the personal injury or property damage . . . were caused or contributed to by the hazardous substance or pollutant or contaminant concerned." 42 U.S.C. § 9658(b)(4)(A). In *CTS Corp. v. Waldburger*, 573 U.S. 1 (2014), the plaintiffs sued 24 years after purchasing land with contaminated well water from CTS Corp. They discovered that the water was contaminated, and allegedly contaminated by petitioners, only two years before filing suit. *Id.* at 6. North Carolina law contains a statute of repose that prevents subjecting a defendant to a tort suit brought more than 10 years after the last culpable act of the defendant. N.C. GEN. STAT. ANN. § 1–52(16). The Court held that § 9658 only preempts state statutes of limitation, not statutes of repose. It distinguished statutes of limitation, which "require plaintiffs to pursue 'diligent prosecution of known claims,'" with statutes of repose, which "effect a legislative judgment that a defendant should 'be free from liability after the legislatively determined period of time.'" *CTS Corp.*, 573 U.S. at 9. The Court found that at the time of the SARA amendments, Congress was aware of the difference between statutes of limitation and statutes of repose, and would have expressly referred to the latter if it had intended statutes of repose to be preempted. *Id.* at 15.

How does this case fit with the purpose of CERCLA as described by the Senate Report discussed in the previous note? Justice Ginsburg, joined by Justice Breyer, in dissent, stated that "[i]nstead of encouraging prompt identification and remediation of toxic contamination before it can kill, the Court's decision gives contaminators an incentive to conceal the hazards they have created until the repose period has run its full course." *Id.* at 23–24. Do you agree?

9.   Causation. In a typical action under tort, a plaintiff must first prove that the defendant's conduct caused the harm suffered. Under CERCLA, however, § 107 does not require that a plaintiff prove causation. As will be discussed in greater detail below, § 107(a) imposes joint liability without a plaintiff demonstrating that a particular PRP's release of hazardous substances caused the incurrence of response costs. PRPs may defend against liability only if they can establish, by a preponderance of the evidence, that the release or threatened release and resulting damages were caused solely by: (1) an act of God; (2) an act of war; or (3) an act or omission of a third party. 42 U.S.C. § 9607(b). What are the consequences of CERCLA's causation requirements? What might justify CERCLA's divergence from the common law traditions of tort? For a discussion of CERCLA's causation requirements, see Lisa C. Goodheart & Karen A. McGuire, *Environmental Law: CERCLA Causation and Apportionment*, 85 MASS. L. REV. 39 (2000).

10.   "Act of God." As noted above, PRPs may defend against liability if they can establish that the release or threatened release and resulting damages were caused solely by an "Act of God." 42 U.S.C. § 9607(b)(1). "Act of God" is defined in § 101(1) as an unforeseeable grave natural disaster of an "exceptional, inevitable, and irresistible character, the effects of which could not have been prevented or avoided by the exercise of due care or foresight," and the defense is available only if the act of God is the sole cause of the release or threatened release. 42 U.S.C. §§ 9601(1), 9607(b)(1).

How often will it be the case that natural disasters are completely unforeseeable, and that no steps could have been taken that would have avoided or mitigated the harm? Should unusually heavy rainfall count as an act of God? If drainage channels that would be unnecessary for normal levels of rainfall could have prevented or mitigated the release, does failing to install the drains make the defense unavailable because of a lack of due care or foresight? *See United States v. Stringfellow*, 661 F. Supp. 1053 (C.D. Cal. 1987) (holding Act of God defense unavailable in such circumstances). What if the heavy rainfall is associated with a hurricane? Should it matter if the hurricane hits an inland area far out of the normal path of hurricanes? *See United States v. Alcan Aluminum Corp.*, 892 F. Supp. 648, 658 (M.D. Pa. 1995) (holding act of God defense unavailable), *aff'd*, 96 F.3d 1434 (3d Cir. 1996), *cert. denied*, 521 U.S. 1103 (1997). Should releases or threatened releases of hazardous substances caused by Hurricane Katrina, the storm that devastated New Orleans in 2005, fall under the Act of God defense? Should it matter that weather experts could track the storm and project its point of impact and magnitude several days in advance? *See* Casey P. Kaplan, Note, *The Act of God Defense: Why Hurricane Katrina and Noah's Flood Don't Qualify*, 26 REV. LITIG. 155 (2007); Joel Eagle, *Divine Intervention: Re-examining the "Act of God" Defense in a Post-Katrina World*, 82 CHI.-KENT L. REV. 459 (2007).

11. "Act of War." In addition to the "Act of God" defense, PRPs can avoid liability if they establish that the release or threatened release was caused solely by an "Act of War." 42 U.S.C. § 9607(b)(2). "Act of War" is not defined in CERCLA. *See id.* § 9601. Should the Act of War defense extend to private actions that are authorized or compelled by the federal government during a time of war for the production of necessary war supplies? Should it matter whether the government actions are taken under the authority of the War Powers Clause? In *United States v. Shell Oil Co.*, 294 F.3d 1045, 1061–62 (9th Cir. 2002), *cert. denied*, 537 U.S. 1147 (2003), the Ninth Circuit held that Shell could not rely on the act of war clause to shield it from liability for dumping acid waste from its aviation fuel refineries during World War II. Although the federal government regulated petroleum activity during the war, the defense was held not to be so broad as to shield any governmental act taken by authority of the War Powers Clause of the Constitution.

What about release of hazardous waste as a result of terrorist attacks? In *In re September 11 Litigation*, 751 F.3d 86 (2d Cir.), *cert. denied*, 135 S. Ct. 742 (2014), the Second Circuit held that, although the September 11 attacks on the World Trade Center were not carried out by a state or government, they nonetheless amounted to an act of war, and the owners of the World Trade Center and the airlines involved were therefore not liable for pollution caused by the release of dust from the buildings. *Id.* at 92.

Observing that CERCLA is intended to be broadly interpreted to accomplish its remedial goals, the Second Circuit held that the September 11 attacks "wrested from the defendants all control over the planes and the buildings . . . and located sole responsibility for the event and the environmental consequences on fanatics whose acts the defendants were not bound by CERCLA to anticipate or prevent." *Id.* at 91.

12. Acts or Omissions of Third Parties. Of the three defenses, the third party defense in § 107(b)(3), 42 U.S.C. § 9607(b)(3), has been the subject of the most litigation, and is discussed in greater detail in the section on Land Transactions, *infra*. To establish the third party defense, a PRP must prove that the release or threatened release was caused solely by a third party; that the third party was not an employee, agent, or in a contractual relationship with the PRP; that the PRP exercised due care with regard to the hazardous substance; and that the PRP took precautions against foreseeable acts by the third party.

What does it mean for actions to occur in connection with a contractual relationship? Consider a scenario in which a generator of hazardous waste enters into a contractual relationship with a transporter, to dispose of hazardous waste at a particular waste disposal facility. If the transporter instead chooses to dump the waste by the side of a road, having accepted payment from the generator, can the generator prevail in the third party defense?

Consider now whether the defense covers a landowner who suddenly discovers that someone has placed hazardous substances on her property? What precautions should landowners reasonably be expected to take against the unauthorized dumping of hazardous substances on their land?

What justifies PRPs not being able to invoke the defense in circumstances where the release or threatened release was caused by an individual or firm in a contractual relationship with the PRP?

B. PRPs

The central component of Superfund is a set of provisions imposing liability on a large number of potentially responsible parties at each site, under expansive liability rules with weak causation requirements and limited defenses. Section 107(a) contains CERCLA's basic liability provision: it establishes both which parties may be held liable and the costs for which they may be responsible. 42 U.S.C. § 9607(a).

As discussed above, § 107(a) holds liable four classes of persons: current owners and operators, in § 107(a)(1); owners and operators at the time of disposal, in § 107(a)(2); any person who arranges for the disposal of hazardous waste, in § 107(a)(3); and transporters that transport hazardous wastes to sites they select, in § 107(a)(4). Each of these categories of PRPs is discussed below. Issues surrounding the costs for which PRPs may be held liable are discussed further in the section on Cleanup, *infra*.

i. OWNER AND OPERATOR LIABILITY

As the *Shore Realty* court explained, *supra*, § 107(a)(1) creates liability for all current owners of contaminated property, while § 107(a)(2) creates liability for past owners who owned the site "at the time of disposal of any hazardous substance." (See the section on Land Transactions, *infra*, for a discussion of the meaning of "disposal" in § 107(a)(2).) Both of these sections also impose liability on "operators." The following Supreme Court case discusses the scope of operator liability.

United States v. Bestfoods

524 U.S. 51 (1998).

■ JUSTICE SOUTER delivered the opinion for a unanimous Court:

The United States brought this action for the costs of cleaning up industrial waste generated by a chemical plant. The issue before us, under the Comprehensive Environmental Response, Compensation, and Liability Act of 1980 (CERCLA), 94 Stat. 2767, as amended, 42 U.S.C. § 9601 *et seq.*, is whether a parent corporation that actively participated in, and exercised control over, the operations of a subsidiary may, without more, be held liable as an operator of a polluting facility owned or operated by the subsidiary. We answer no, unless the corporate veil may be pierced. But a corporate parent that actively participated in, and exercised control over, the operations of the facility itself may be held directly liable in its own right as an operator of the facility.

In 1980, CERCLA was enacted in response to the serious environmental and health risks posed by industrial pollution. "As its name implies, CERCLA is a comprehensive statute that grants the President broad power to command government agencies and private parties to clean up hazardous waste sites." *Key Tronic Corp. v. United States*, 511 U.S. 809, 814 (1994). If it satisfies certain statutory conditions, the United States may, for instance, use the "Hazardous Substance Superfund" to finance cleanup efforts, see 42 U.S.C. §§ 9601(11), 9604; 26 U.S.C. § 9507, which it may then replenish by suits brought under § 107 of the Act against, among others, "any person who at the time of disposal of any hazardous substance owned or operated any facility." 42 U.S.C. § 9607(a)(2). So, those actually "responsible for any damage, environmental harm, or injury from chemical poisons [may be tagged with] the cost of their actions," S.Rep. No. 96–848, pp. 6119, 13, U.S.Code Cong. & Admin.News 1980, p. 6119 (1980). The term "person" is defined in CERCLA to include corporations and other business organizations, see 42 U.S.C. § 9601(21), and the term "facility" enjoys a broad and detailed definition as well, see § 9601(9). The phrase "owner or operator" is defined only by tautology, however, as "any person owning or operating" a facility, § 9601(20)(A)(ii), and it is this bit of circularity that prompts our review.

In 1957, Ott Chemical Co. (Ott I) began manufacturing chemicals at a plant near Muskegon, Michigan, and its intentional and unintentional dumping of hazardous substances significantly polluted the soil and ground water at the site. In 1965, respondent CPC International Inc. incorporated a wholly owned subsidiary to buy Ott I's assets in exchange for CPC stock. The new company, also dubbed Ott Chemical Co. (Ott II), continued chemical manufacturing at the site, and continued to pollute its surroundings. CPC kept the managers of Ott I, including its founder, president, and principal shareholder, Arnold Ott, on board as officers of Ott II. Arnold Ott and several other Ott II officers and directors were also given positions at CPC, and they performed duties for both corporations. . . .

By 1981, the federal Environmental Protection Agency had undertaken to see the site cleaned up, and its long-term remedial plan called for expenditures well into the tens of millions of dollars. To recover some of that money, the United States filed this action under § 107 in 1989, naming [defendant CPC as a responsible party. The only issue at trial and on appeal was] whether CPC, as the parent corporation[ ] of Ott II, had "owned or operated" the facility within the meaning of § 107(a)(2).

The District Court said that operator liability may attach to a parent corporation both directly, when the parent itself operates the facility, and indirectly, when the corporate veil can be pierced under state law. . . . Applying that test to the facts of this case, the District Court held [CPC] liable under § 107(a)(2) as [an] operator. . . .

After a divided panel of the Court of Appeals for the Sixth Circuit reversed in part, that court granted rehearing en banc and vacated the panel decision. This time, 7 judges to 6, the court again reversed the District Court in part. The majority remarked on the possibility that a parent company might be held directly liable as an operator of a facility owned by its subsidiary: "At least conceivably, a parent might independently operate the facility in the stead of its subsidiary; or, as a sort of joint venturer, actually operate the facility alongside its subsidiary." . . . Applying Michigan veil-piercing law, the Court of Appeals decided that [CPC was not] liable for controlling the actions of its subsidiaries, since the parent and subsidiary corporations maintained separate personalities and [CPC] did not utilize the subsidiary corporate form to perpetrate fraud or subvert justice.

We granted certiorari to resolve a conflict among the Circuits over the extent to which parent corporations may be held liable under CERCLA for operating facilities ostensibly under the control of their subsidiaries. We now vacate and remand. . . .

If the Act rested liability entirely on ownership of a polluting facility, this opinion might end here; but CERCLA liability may turn on operation as well as ownership, and nothing in the statute's terms bars a parent corporation from direct liability for its own actions in operating a facility owned by its subsidiary. . . .

This much is easy to say: the difficulty comes in defining actions sufficient to constitute direct parental "operation." Here of course we may again rue the uselessness of CERCLA's definition of a facility's "operator" as "any person . . . operating" the facility, 42 U.S.C. § 9601(20)(A)(ii), which leaves us to do the best we can to give the term its "ordinary or natural meaning." Bailey v. United States, 516 U.S. 137, 145 (1995). . . . [I]n the organizational sense more obviously intended by CERCLA, the word ordinarily means "[t]o conduct the affairs of; manage: *operate a business.*" American Heritage Dictionary, *supra,* at 1268; see also Webster's New International Dictionary, *supra,* at 1707 ("to manage"). So, under CERCLA, an operator is simply someone who directs the workings of, manages, or conducts the affairs of a facility. To sharpen the definition for purposes of CERCLA's concern with environmental contamination, an operator must manage, direct, or conduct operations specifically related to pollution, that is, operations having to do with the leakage or disposal of hazardous waste, or decisions about compliance with environmental regulations.

With this understanding, we are satisfied that the Court of Appeals correctly rejected the District Court's analysis of direct liability. But we also think that the appeals court erred in limiting direct liability under the statute to a parent's sole or joint venture operation, so as to eliminate any possible finding that CPC is liable as an operator on the facts of this case.

By emphasizing that "CPC is directly liable under § 107(a)(2) as an operator because CPC actively participated in and exerted significant control over Ott II's business and decision-making," 777 F. Supp. at 574, the District Court applied the "actual control" test of whether the parent "actually operated the business of its subsidiary," *id.,* at 573.

The well-taken objection to the actual control test, however, is its fusion of direct and indirect liability; the test is administered by asking a question about the relationship between the two corporations (an issue going to indirect liability) instead of a question about the parent's interaction with the subsidiary's facility (the source of any direct liability). If, however, direct liability for the parent's operation of the facility is to be kept distinct from derivative liability for the subsidiary's own operation, the focus of the enquiry must necessarily be different under the two tests. "The question is not whether the parent operates the subsidiary, but rather whether it operates the facility, and that operation is evidenced by participation in the activities of the facility, not the subsidiary. Control of the subsidiary, if extensive enough, gives rise to indirect liability under piercing doctrine, not direct liability under the statutory language." [Oswald, Bifurcation of the Owner and Operator Analysis under CERCLA, 72 Wash. U.L.Q. 223, 269 (1994).] The District Court was therefore mistaken to rest its analysis on CPC's relationship with Ott II, premising liability on little more than "CPC's 100-percent ownership of Ott II" and "CPC's active participation in, and at times majority control over, Ott II's board of directors." 777 F. Supp., at 575. The analysis should instead have rested on the relationship between CPC and the Muskegon facility itself. . . .

We accordingly agree with the Court of Appeals that a participation-and-control test looking to the parent's supervision over the subsidiary, especially one that assumes that dual officers always act on behalf of the parent, cannot be used to identify operation of a facility resulting in direct parental liability. Nonetheless, a return to the ordinary meaning of the word "operate" in the organizational sense will indicate why we think that the Sixth Circuit stopped short when it confined its examples of direct parental operation to exclusive or joint ventures, and declined to find at least the possibility of direct operation by CPC in this case.

In our enquiry into the meaning Congress presumably had in mind when it used the verb "to operate," we recognized that the statute obviously meant something more than mere mechanical activation of pumps and valves, and must be read to contemplate "operation" as including the exercise of direction over the facility's activities. The Court of Appeals recognized this by indicating that a parent can be held directly liable when the parent operates the facility in the stead of its subsidiary or alongside the subsidiary in some sort of a joint venture. We anticipated a further possibility above, however, when we observed that a dual officer or director might depart so far from the norms of parental influence exercised through dual officeholding as to serve the parent, even when ostensibly acting on behalf of the subsidiary in operating the facility. Yet another possibility, suggested by the facts of this case, is that an agent of the parent with no hat to wear but the parent's hat might manage or direct activities at the facility.

Identifying such an occurrence calls for line-drawing yet again, since the acts of direct operation that give rise to parental liability must necessarily be distinguished from the interference that stems from the normal relationship between parent and subsidiary. Again norms of corporate behavior (undisturbed by any CERCLA provision) are crucial reference points. Just as we may look to such norms in identifying the limits of the presumption that a dual officeholder acts in his ostensible capacity, so here we may refer to them in distinguishing a parental officer's oversight of a subsidiary from such an officer's control over the operation of the subsidiary's facility. "[A]ctivities that involve the facility but which are consistent with the parent's investor status, such as monitoring of the subsidiary's performance, supervision of the subsidiary's finance and capital budget decisions, and articulation of general policies and procedures, should not give rise to direct liability." Oswald 282. The critical question is whether, in degree and detail, actions directed to the facility by an agent of the parent alone are eccentric under accepted norms of parental oversight of a subsidiary's facility.

There is, in fact, some evidence that CPC engaged in just this type and degree of activity at the Muskegon plant. The District Court's opinion speaks of an agent of CPC alone who played a conspicuous part in dealing with the toxic risks emanating from the operation of the plant. G.R.D. Williams worked only for CPC; he was not an employee, officer, or director of Ott II, and thus, his actions were of necessity taken only on behalf of CPC. The District Court found that "CPC became directly involved in environmental and regulatory matters through the work of . . . Williams, CPC's governmental and environmental affairs director. Williams . . . became heavily involved in environmental issues at Ott II." 777 F. Supp., at 561. He "actively participated in and exerted control over a variety of Ott II environmental matters," and he "issued directives regarding Ott II's responses to regulatory inquiries," *id.*, at 575.

We think that these findings are enough to raise an issue of CPC's operation of the facility through Williams's actions, though we would draw no ultimate conclusion from these findings at this point. [Because Williams' role was not fully established by the trial court, the case is remanded], on the theory of direct operation set out here, for reevaluation of Williams's role, and of the role of any other CPC agent who might be said to have had a part in operating the Muskegon facility. . . .

NOTES AND QUESTIONS

1. Actual Control v. Participation-and-Control. Distinguish between the actual control test, favored by the District Court, and the participation-and-control test, favored by the Court of Appeals. Which did the Supreme Court favor in determining operator liability? Why?

2. Scope of Operator Liability. How involved should a parent company have to be in the activities of its subsidiary to trigger operator liability? *Bestfoods* held that activities that are "consistent with the parent's investor status" such as performance monitoring or financial supervision will not trigger operator liability. What activities would be "consistent with the parent's investor status" once the parent learns of activities by the subsidiary that could lead to CERCLA liability? If too much involvement by the parent could lead to operator liability, does this create incentives for parent corporations to avoid stepping in to prevent subsidiaries from behaving irresponsibly? Could more hazardous waste releases be prevented if parent corporations were able to exert more control over subsidiaries without incurring liability? If parent corporations could get extensively involved in preventing subsidiaries from incurring CERCLA liability without themselves incurring operator liability, what incentives would this create for corporations to create subsidiaries whose only "assets" relate to those activities that might lead to CERCLA liability?

Perhaps with these policy considerations in mind, the Second Circuit relied on *Bestfoods* in affirming a district court decision that a parent company did not manage, direct, or operate plants that produced wastes at various sites. The court wrote:

> Plaintiffs have marshaled an impressive volume of contemporaneous corporate records—including board and committee meeting minutes, correspondence, and internal reports—illustrating the extent of UGI's involvement in the business of its Connecticut subsidiaries. As the district court reasonably found, this evidence shows that UGI "was a vigilant parent that conducted detailed—yet not eccentric—oversight of the operations of its subsidiaries in Connecticut"; "provided assistance to CL & P from time to time when CL & P requested it"; and "carefully oversaw the operations of CL & P, consistent with UGI's status as a corporate parent." [Yankee Gas Servs. Co. v. UGI Utils., Inc., 616 F. Supp. 2d 228, 233 (D. Conn. 2009).] Such assistance did not, as a matter of law, equate to managing, directing, or operating the facilities in the stead of CL & P or in some sort of joint venture with it.

Yankee Gas Servs. Co. v. UGI Utils. Inc., 428 F. App'x 18, 21 (2d Cir. 2011).

3.   Piercing the Corporate Veil. Under state common law, a parent corporation may be liable for the acts of its subsidiary where it exerts over the subsidiary "[c]ontrol, not mere majority or complete stock control, but complete domination, not only of finances, but of policy and business practice in respect to the transaction attacked so that the corporate entity as to this transaction had at the time no separate mind, will or existence of its own." *Lowendahl v. Baltimore & O. R. Co.*, 287 N.Y.S. 62, 76 (App. Div. 1936), *aff'd*, 272 N.Y. 360, 6 N.E.2d 56 (1936). In an omitted portion of the opinion, the *Bestfoods* Court held that nothing in CERCLA purports to change state corporate law, and so parent corporations could only incur *owner* liability for the acts of their subsidiaries when the corporate veil is pierced. Under *Bestfoods*, does operator liability reach a significantly larger group of parent corporations than those that already could be held liable under the common law of veil piercing? Should it?

4.   State or Federal Common Law? *Bestfoods* holds that parent corporations may be held liable as owners only if the corporate veil is pierced. The Court noted, but did not resolve, the "significant disagreement among courts and commentators over whether, in enforcing CERCLA's indirect liability, courts should borrow state law, or instead apply a federal common law of veil piercing." *Bestfoods*, 524 U.S. at 64 n.9. Should state law apply, since corporate law is traditionally an area of state law? Or is there a sufficiently strong interest in uniformity that federal law should apply? *Compare United States v. Davis*, 261 F.3d 1, 54 (1st Cir. 2001) (applying state common law), *with United States v. Gen. Battery Corp.*, 423 F.3d 294, 303–04 (3d Cir. 2005) (applying federal common law), *cert. denied*, 549 U.S. 941 (2006).

5.   Successor Liability. If one corporation purchases the assets of another corporation, should the successor corporation inherit the first corporation's CERCLA liability? Under the common law of corporate successor liability, generally the successor corporation does not inherit the liability of the first corporation unless one of four exceptions applies: "(1) the successor expressly or impliedly agrees to assume the liabilities; (2) a *de facto* merger or consolidation occurs; (3) the successor is a mere continuation of the predecessor; or (4) the transfer to the successor corporation is a fraudulent attempt to escape liability." *K.C. 1986 Ltd. P'ship v. Reade Mfg.*, 472 F.3d 1009, 1021 (8th Cir. 2007). What incentives would be created if corporate successors were held liable in a broader set of circumstances? Would beneficial corporate restructuring be prevented? Would corporations have stronger incentives not to incur CERCLA liability that might later limit their ability to sell assets?

Several circuits have expanded the "mere continuation" common law exception and will find successor liability under the "substantial continuity" test, which imposes liability on a successor corporation in a broader set of circumstances; these circuits have considered a long list of factors such as retention of the same employees and continuity of business assets to determine whether sufficient continuity exists to hold the successor liable. *See United States v. Carolina Transformer Co.*, 978 F.2d 832 (4th Cir. 1992); *United States v. Mexico Feed & Seed Co.*, 980 F.2d 478 (8th Cir. 1992). Other circuits have rejected the "substantial continuity" test, finding corporate successors liable only if they fall under the standard four common law exceptions. *See, e.g., Gen. Battery Corp.*, 423 F.3d 294; *Davis*, 261 F.3d 1.

Does the Supreme Court's statement in *Bestfoods* that nothing in CERCLA purports to rewrite the settled rules of state corporate law call into question the "substantial continuity" test for successor liability—a test that extends state common law and that has been created by the federal courts? *Bestfoods*, 524 U.S. at 63–64; *see also Reade Mfg.*, 472 F.3d at 1022. For a detailed discussion of the substantial continuity test and corporate successor liability under CERCLA, see Kenneth K. Kilbert, *Successor Liability Under CERCLA: Wither Substantial Continuity?*, 14 PENN. ST. ENVTL. L. REV. 1 (2005).

6. When Owner and Operator Status Is Determined. The definition of "owner and operator" in CERCLA does not indicate from when ownership of a vessel or facility that causes contamination is to be measured. In *California Dep't of Toxic Substances Control v. Hearthside Residential Corp.*, 613 F.3d 910 (9th Cir. 2010), Hearthside purchased land that it knew was contaminated with polychlorinated biphenyls (PCBs). The Department alleged that PCB contamination on an adjacent site resulted from PCBs leaking from Hearthside's site. Hearthside disagreed that it bore any responsibility for the adjacent site. It remediated the land that it purchased, and sold it. Subsequently, the Department filed suit against Hearthside for costs incurred in remediating the adjacent site, on the basis that Hearthside was the current owner at the time of the cleanup. The Ninth Circuit rejected Hearthside's argument that ownership should be measured from the date that suit was filed. It found that the expression "owner and operator" means the owner of the vessel or facility at the time that cleanup costs are incurred (and the cause of action under CERCLA accrues). *Id.* at 916. The court considered that interpreting § 107(a)(1) as limited to the current owner at the time the suit was filed would give owners an incentive to delay the cleanup process, and therefore the filing of a recovery action, until the owner had sold the property. *Id.* at 915. It was also contrary to CERCLA's purpose of encouraging early settlement. *Id.* at 916.

7.   Owner *and* Operator. Section 107(a)(1) holds liable "the owner *and* operator" of a facility, whereas § 107(a)(2) holds liable "any person who . . . owned *or* operated" a facility. 42 U.S.C. § 9607(a)(1), (2) (emphasis added). Should this mean that, to be held liable under § 107(a)(1), an entity need both be the owner and the operator? If this were the case, how would the *Bestfoods* case have been decided? Although the "owner and operator" language of § 107(a)(1) is in the conjunctive, courts have consistently construed this language in the disjunctive. *See United States v. Md. Bank & Trust Co.*, 632 F. Supp. 573, 577–78 (D. Md. 1986); *United States v. Fleet Factors Corp.*, 901 F.2d 1550, 1554 n.3 (11th Cir. 1990); *Artesian Water Co. v. Gov't of New Castle Cty.*, 659 F. Supp. 1269, 1280–81 (D. Del. 1987), *aff'd*, 851 F.2d 643 (3d Cir. 1988).

8.   Liability of Lenders. As originally enacted, § 101(20)(A) of CERCLA exempts from owner and operator liability "a person, who, without participating in the management of a vessel or facility, holds indicia of ownership primarily to protect his security interest in the vessel or facility." 42 U.S.C. § 9601(20)(A). Under this exception, financial institutions that lend to owners and operators of hazardous waste sites are not liable for cleanup costs unless they "participate in the management" of the site. Determining what actions a lender may take prior to foreclosure before liability attaches, and determining whether the act of foreclosure in and of itself allows liability to attach, has given rise to some confusion.

Prior to 1996, courts generally held that a lender that took full title of a property through foreclosure did not fall within the exception to liability. *See United States v. Md. Bank & Trust Co.*, 632 F. Supp. 573, 580 (D. Md. 1986) (holding lender liable as owner after it had foreclosed and taken full title to property). *But see United States v. McLamb*, 5 F.3d 69 (4th Cir. 1993) (lender was not liable as owner even after foreclosure because lender only acquired title to protect security interest).

There was a great deal of uncertainty over when a lender was liable *before* foreclosure by virtue of "participating in the management" of the facility, a term then undefined in CERCLA. *Compare United States v. Fleet Factors Corp.*, 901 F.2d 1550, 1557–58 (11th Cir. 1990) (holding that "a secured creditor will be liable if its involvement with the management of the facility is sufficiently broad to support the inference that it could affect hazardous waste disposal decisions if it so chose" and that actual management of the facility was not necessary for creditor liability), *cert. denied*, 498 U.S. 1046 (1991), *with In re Bergsoe Metal Corp.*, 910 F.2d 668, 672 (9th Cir. 1990) ("[T]here must be *some* actual management of the facility before a secured creditor will [be liable under CERCLA]."). In 1992, EPA promulgated a rule defining what constituted participation in management; however, the D.C. Circuit held that EPA did not have the authority to issue rules interpreting the scope of lender liability. *Kelley ex rel. Michigan v. EPA*, 25 F.3d 1088 (D.C. Cir.), *cert. denied*, 513 U.S. 1110 (1995).

In 1996, Congress responded by amending CERCLA in the Asset Conservation, Lender Liability, and Deposit Insurance Protection Act of 1996. Pub. L. No. 104–208, §§ 2501–2505 (1996). The 1996 amendment addresses what liability attaches after foreclosure and clarifies what activities constitute "participating in management" prior to foreclosure. "Participating in management" does *not* include having the capability to influence, or the unexercised right to control, the facility. 42 U.S.C. § 9601(20)(G)(i). More specifically, activities that do *not* constitute participating in management include: "monitoring or undertaking 1 or more inspections of the vessel or facility"; "including in the terms of an extension of credit . . . a covenant, warranty, or other term or condition that relates to environmental compliance"; "requiring a response action or other lawful means of addressing the release or threatened release of a hazardous substance in connection with the vessel or facility prior to, during, or on the expiration of the term of the extension of credit"; "providing financial or other advice or counseling in an effort to mitigate, prevent, or cure default or diminution in the value of the vessel or facility"; and "conducting a response action under § 9607(d) of this title or under the direction of an on-scene coordinator appointed under the National Contingency Plan." 42 U.S.C. § 9601(20)(G)(iv). How do these provisions modify the prior case law interpreting participation in management? What would classify as "participating in management" for the purposes of § 101(20)(G)(i)?

The 1996 amendments also provide guidance on when a lender may foreclose without incurring owner liability: A lender is not liable after foreclosure if it did not participate in management prior to foreclosure, and if the lender seeks to sell the facility "at the earliest practicable, commercially reasonable time, on commercially reasonable terms, taking into account market conditions and legal and regulatory requirements." 42 U.S.C. § 9601(20)(F)(ii). How soon is it practicable to expect a lender to be able to sell a contaminated Superfund site for which the new owner will be liable? If the lender continues to seek to sell the site indefinitely, but no buyer materializes, is this sufficient to avoid liability under the amendments? What actions must a lender take to be deemed to have attempted to sell a facility? Is mere advertising sufficient? If no other solvent PRPs can be located and the site is eventually cleaned up using funds from the Superfund, is it fair that the lender will then reap a windfall from the increase in the value of the property resulting from the cleanup? What reasons are there for Congress to have provided such a broad exemption from liability for lenders?

Overall, the 1996 amendments limit liability for lenders to a fairly narrow set of circumstances. Why not exempt lenders entirely? Would it have been more appropriate for Congress to expand lender liability? As repeat market players, lending institutions may have substantial experience assessing environmental contamination and risk. What rules surrounding lender liability give lenders the best incentives to lend only to parties who will handle hazardous waste responsibly? What rules take the best advantage of lenders' potentially greater experience in assessing and managing environmental problems? *See generally* Roslyn Tom, Note, *Interpreting the Meaning of Lender Management Under Section 101(20)(A)* of *CERCLA*, 98 YALE L.J. 925 (1989) (discussing incentives for lenders before passage of 1996 amendments).

ii. ARRANGER LIABILITY

Section 107(a)(3) holds liable parties who "arrange for disposal" of hazardous wastes; it is through this provision that generators of hazardous waste are held liable. 42 U.S.C. § 9607(a)(3). "Arrange for" is not defined in CERCLA. In the absence of a Supreme Court decision on the matter, different circuits took different positions on what actions constitute arranging for disposal within the meaning of the statute. Some circuits required a showing that the PRP intended to dispose of hazardous substances to trigger arranger liability, while others did not. Circuits also split over whether a PRP must own the hazardous substance or whether control over the hazardous substance is sufficient to establish liability.

Amcast Indus. Corp. v. Detrex Corp., 2 F.3d 746 (7th Cir. 1993) (Posner, J.), *cert. denied*, 510 U.S. 1044 (1994), found intent to dispose of a waste to be a necessary element of arranger liability. In *Amcast*, a chemical manufacturer itself both delivered and hired a transport service to deliver its product to a regular customer, a copper manufacturer. The evidence indicated that both the transport service and the chemical manufacturer's own drivers spilled chemicals while unloading them into the copper manufacturer's storage tanks. The issue on appeal was whether the chemical manufacturer could be found to have arranged for the disposal of hazardous substances by hiring the transport service to deliver the chemical product to the copper manufacturer.

The Seventh Circuit held that the chemical manufacturer could not be found liable, stating:

> [t]he words ["arranged for"] imply intentional action. The only thing that [the chemical manufacturer] arranged for Transport Services to do was to deliver TCE to [the copper manufacturer's] storage tanks. It did not arrange for spilling the stuff on the ground. . . . [W]hen the shipper is not trying to arrange for the disposal of hazardous wastes, but is arranging for the delivery of a useful product, he is not a responsible person within the meaning of the statute and if a mishap occurs en route his liability is governed by other legal doctrines.

Id. at 751. The Seventh Circuit concluded that the chemical manufacturer was responsible for the spillage from its own trucks but not the spillage from the trucks of the transporter. *Id.*

The Eleventh Circuit, in *South Florida Water Management District v. Montalvo*, 84 F.3d 402 (11th Cir. 1996), found both intent to dispose of a waste and ownership of the waste to be relevant but not necessary to arranger liability. The court adopted a case-by-case approach, finding that factors such as intent, ownership, and knowledge were all useful but not dispositive in determining whether a party had "arranged for" the disposal of hazardous substances. *Id.* at 406–07.

In the first case excerpted below, the Eighth Circuit does not require a finding that a PRP intended to dispose of a waste to find that they "arranged for" its disposal. This approach has become known as "broad" arranger liability. The second case, *Burlington Northern & Santa Fe Railway Co. v. United States*, is the Supreme Court's only decision on arranger liability.

United States v. Aceto Agricultural Chemicals Corp.

872 F.2d 1373 (8th Cir. 1989).

■ Before HEANEY and BEAM, CIRCUIT JUDGES, and LARSON, SENIOR DISTRICT JUDGE.

■ LARSON, SENIOR DISTRICT JUDGE:

[Eight pesticide manufacturers, including Aceto Agricultural Chemicals Corporation, hired a formulator, Aidex Corporation, to convert their technical grade pesticides into commercial grade pesticides. The complaint alleged that the manufacturers owned the hazardous material at all points in the formulation process and that the manufacturers knew that generation of hazardous materials was an inherent part of the process. EPA commenced cleanup at the Aidex facility and sought recovery of its response costs from the manufacturers. The Eighth Circuit took up the question of whether the complaint alleged sufficient facts that six of the eight manufacturers could be held liable as arrangers of the waste that contaminated Aidex's property.]

. . . At issue in this appeal is whether the defendants "arranged for" the disposal of hazardous substances under the Act, and thus fall within the class of responsible persons described in § 9607(a)(3). In finding plaintiffs' allegations sufficient to hold defendants liable as responsible persons, the district court relied on the principle that CERCLA should be broadly interpreted and took guidance from common law rules regarding vicarious liability.

The six CERCLA defendants challenge the district court's decision on appeal, arguing . . . that Aidex, not they, "owned the hazardous waste and made the crucial decision how it would be disposed of or treated, and by whom." *United States v. A & F Materials Co.*, 582 F. Supp. at 842, 845 (S.D. Ill. 1984). They argue Aidex was hired "to formulate, not to dispose," and that imposition of liability under CERCLA on these facts would lead to "limitless" liability. Finally, defendants assert the plain meaning of the statute requires an intent to dispose of some waste, or, at the very least, the authority to control the disposal process, and that neither are alleged by plaintiffs here.

The plaintiffs counter that defendants' ownership of the technical grade pesticide, the work in process, and the commercial grade product establishes the requisite authority to control Aidex's operations. Plaintiffs argue that because the generation of pesticide-containing wastes is *inherent* in the pesticide formulation process, Aidex could not formulate defendants' pesticides without wasting and disposing of some portion of them. Thus, plaintiffs argue, defendants could not have hired Aidex to formulate their pesticides without also "arranging for" the disposal of the waste.

We begin our analysis with the language of the CERCLA statute. Section 9607(a)(3) provides in relevant part:

> Notwithstanding any other provision or rule of law, and subject only to the defenses set forth in subsection (b) of this section—
>
> (3)   any person who by contract, agreement, or otherwise arranged for disposal or treatment, or arranged with a transporter for transport for disposal or treatment, of hazardous substances owned or possessed by such person, by any other party or entity, at any facility or incineration vessel owned or operated by another party or entity and containing such hazardous substances . . .
>
> . . . from which there is a release, or a threatened release which causes the incurrence of response costs, of a hazardous substance, shall be liable for—
>
> (A)   all costs of removal or remedial action incurred by the United States Government or a State . . . not inconsistent with the national contingency plan.

42 U.S.C. § 9607(a).

Citing dictionary definitions of the word "arrange," defendants argue they can be liable under section 9607(a)(3) only if they intended to dispose of a waste. Defendants argue further the complaint alleges only an intent to arrange for formulation of a valuable product, and no intent to arrange for the disposal of a waste can be inferred from these allegations. We reject defendants' narrow reading of both the complaint and the statute.

Congress used broad language in providing for liability for persons who "by contract, agreement, *or otherwise arranged for*" the disposal of hazardous substances. *See A & F Materials*, 582 F. Supp. at 845. While the legislative history of CERCLA sheds little light on the intended meaning of this phrase, courts have concluded that a liberal judicial interpretation is consistent with CERCLA's "overwhelmingly remedial" statutory scheme. *NEPACCO*, 810 F.2d at 733.

We thus interpret the phrase "otherwise arranged for" in view of the two essential purposes of CERCLA:

> First, Congress intended that the federal government be immediately given the tools necessary for a prompt and effective

response to the problems of national magnitude resulting from
hazardous waste disposal. Second, Congress intended that those
responsible for problems caused by the disposal of chemical
poisons bear the costs and responsibility for remedying the
harmful conditions they created.

Dedham Water Co., 805 F.2d at 1081 (citing *United States v. Reilly Tar
& Chemical Corp.*, 546 F. Supp. 1100, 1112 (D. Minn. 1982)).

The second goal—that those responsible should pay for clean up—
would be thwarted by acceptance of defendants' argument that the
allegations in plaintiffs' complaint do not sufficiently allege they
"arranged for" disposal of their hazardous substances. While defendants
characterize their relationship with Aidex as pertaining solely to
formulation of a useful product, courts have not hesitated to look beyond
defendants' characterizations to determine whether a transaction in fact
involves an arrangement for the disposal of a hazardous substance. In
Conservation Chemical, for example, the court found defendants' sale of
lime slurry and fly ash byproducts to neutralize and treat other
hazardous substances at a hazardous waste site could constitute
"arranging for disposal" of the lime slurry and fly ash. 619 F.Supp. at
237–41. Denying defendants' motions for summary judgment, the court
reasoned that defendants contracted with the owner of the site "for
deposit or placement" of their hazardous substances on the site, and thus
could be found liable under the statute. *Id.*, at 241.

Other courts have imposed CERCLA liability where defendants
sought to characterize their arrangement with another party who
disposed of their hazardous substances as a "sale" rather than a
"disposal." *See New York v. General Electric Co.*, 592 F. Supp. 291, 297
(N.D.N.Y.1984). . . .

Courts have, however, refused to impose liability where a "useful"
substance is sold to another party, who then incorporates it into a
product, which is later disposed of. *E.g.*, *Florida Power & Light Co. v.
Allis Chalmers Corp.*, 27 Env't Rep.Cas. (BNA) 1558 (S.D. Fla. 1988). *See
also Edward Hines Lumber Co. v. Vulcan Materials Co.*, 685 F. Supp.
651, 654–57 (N.D. Ill.), *aff'd on other grounds*, 861 F.2d 155 (7th Cir.
1988). Defendants attempt to analogize the present case to those cited
above, but the analogy fails. Not only is there no transfer of ownership of
the hazardous substances in this case (defendants retain ownership
throughout), but the activity undertaken by Aidex is significantly
different from the activity undertaken by, for example, Florida Power &
Light. Aidex is performing a process on products owned by defendants for
defendants' benefit and at their direction; waste is generated and
disposed of contemporaneously with the process. Florida Power & Light,
on the other hand, purchased electrical transformers containing mineral
oil with PCBs from defendant Allis Chalmers, used the transformers for
approximately 40 years, and then made the decision to dispose of them

at the site in question. Allis Chalmers was thus far more removed from the disposal than the defendants are in this case.

Defendants nonetheless contend they should escape liability because they had no authority to control Aidex's operations, and our *NEPACCO* decision states "[i]t is the authority to control the handling and disposal of hazardous substances that is critical under the statutory scheme." *NEPACCO*, 810 F.2d at 743. In *NEPACCO,* we were confronted with the argument that only individuals who *owned* or *possessed* hazardous substances could be liable under CERCLA. We rejected that notion and imposed liability, in addition, on those who had the authority to control the disposal, even without ownership or possession. *Id.* at 743–44. Defendants in this case, of course, actually owned the hazardous substances, as well as the work in process. *NEPACCO* does not mandate dismissal of plaintiffs' complaint under these circumstances. . . .

For all of the reasons discussed above, accepting plaintiffs' allegations in this case as true and giving them the benefit of all reasonable inferences therefrom, we agree with the district court that the complaint states a claim upon which relief can be granted under CERCLA. Any other decision, under the circumstances of this case, would allow defendants to simply "close their eyes" to the method of disposal of their hazardous substances, a result contrary to the policies underlying CERCLA. *See Ward*, 618 F. Supp. at 895. Accordingly, we affirm the court's judgment denying defendants' motion to dismiss for failure to state a claim upon which relief can be granted.

Burlington Northern & Santa Fe Railroad Co. v. United States

556 U.S. 599 (2009).

■ JUSTICE STEVENS delivered the opinion of the court:

. . . In 1960, Brown & Bryant, Inc. (B & B), began operating an agricultural chemical distribution business, purchasing pesticides and other chemical products from suppliers such as Shell Oil Company (Shell). Using its own equipment, B & B applied its products to customers' farms. B & B opened its business on a 3.8 acre parcel of former farmland in Arvin, California, and in 1975, expanded operations onto an adjacent .9 acre parcel of land. . . . Both parcels of the Arvin facility were graded toward a sump and drainage pond located on the southeast corner of the primary parcel. See Appendix, *infra*. Neither the sump nor the drainage pond was lined until 1979, allowing waste water and chemical runoff from the facility to seep into the ground water below.

During its years of operation, B & B stored and distributed various hazardous chemicals on its property. Among these were the herbicide dinoseb, sold by Dow Chemicals, and the pesticides D-D and Nemagon, both sold by Shell. Dinoseb was stored in 55-gallon drums and 5-gallon containers on a concrete slab outside B & B's warehouse. Nemagon was stored in 30-gallon drums and 5-gallon containers inside the warehouse. Originally, B & B purchased D-D in 55-gallon drums; beginning in the mid-1960s, however, Shell began requiring its distributors to maintain bulk storage facilities for D-D. From that time onward, B & B purchased D-D in bulk.[1]

When B & B purchased D-D, Shell would arrange for delivery by common carrier, f.o.b. destination.[2] When the product arrived, it was transferred from tanker trucks to a bulk storage tank located on B & B's primary parcel. From there, the chemical was transferred to bobtail trucks, nurse tanks, and pull rigs. During each of these transfers leaks and spills could—and often did—occur. Although the common carrier and B & B used buckets to catch spills from hoses and gaskets connecting the tanker trucks to its bulk storage tank, the buckets sometimes overflowed or were knocked over, causing D-D to spill onto the ground during the transfer process.

Aware that spills of D-D were commonplace among its distributors, in the late 1970's Shell took several steps to encourage the safe handling of its products. Shell provided distributors with detailed safety manuals and instituted a voluntary discount program for distributors that made improvements in their bulk handling and safety facilities. Later, Shell revised its program to require distributors to obtain an inspection by a qualified engineer and provide self-certification of compliance with applicable laws and regulations. B & B's Arvin facility was inspected twice, and in 1981, B & B certified to Shell that it had made a number of recommended improvements to its facilities.

Despite these improvements, B & B remained a " '[s]loppy' [o]perator." App. to Pet. for Cert. in No. 07–1601, p. 130a. Over the course of B & B's 28 years of operation, delivery spills, equipment failures, and the rinsing of tanks and trucks allowed Nemagon, D-D, and dinoseb to seep into the soil and upper levels of ground water of the Arvin facility. In 1983, the California Department of Toxic Substances Control (DTSC) began investigating B & B's violation of hazardous waste laws, and the United States Environmental Protection Agency (EPA) soon followed suit, discovering significant contamination of soil and ground water. Of particular concern was a plume of contaminated ground water located under the facility that threatened to leach into an adjacent supply of potential drinking water. . . .

[After an EPA-ordered cleanup, the owners of the property] brought suit against B & B in the United States District Court for the Eastern

---

[1] Because D-D is corrosive, bulk storage of the chemical led to numerous tank failures and spills as the chemical rusted tanks and eroded valves.

[2] F.o.b. destination means "the seller must at his own expense and risk transport the goods to [the destination] and there tender delivery of them. . . ." U.C.C. § 2–319(1)(b) (2001). The District Court found that B & B assumed "stewardship" over the D-D as soon as the common carrier entered the Arvin facility. App. to Pet. for Cert. in No. 07–1601, p. 124a.

District of California. In 1996, that lawsuit was consolidated with two recovery actions brought by DTSC and EPA against Shell. . . .

The District Court conducted a 6-week bench trial in 1999 and . . . held that . . . Shell [was a] potentially responsible part[y (PRP)] under CERCLA . . . because it had "arranged for" the disposal of hazardous substances through its sale and delivery of D-D, see § 9607(a)(3).

. . . The Governments appealed the District Court's apportionment, and Shell cross-appealed the court's finding of liability. The Court of Appeals acknowledged that Shell did not qualify as a "traditional" arranger under § 9607(a)(3), insofar as it had not contracted with B & B to directly dispose of a hazardous waste product. 520 F.3d 918, 948 (C.A.9 2008). Nevertheless, the court stated that Shell could still be held liable under a " 'broader' category of arranger liability" if the "disposal of hazardous wastes [wa]s a foreseeable byproduct of, but not the purpose of, the transaction giving rise to" arranger liability. *Ibid.* Relying on CERCLA's definition of "disposal," which covers acts such as "leaking" and "spilling," 42 U.S.C. § 6903(3), the Ninth Circuit concluded that an entity could arrange for "disposal" "even if it did not intend to dispose" of a hazardous substance. 520 F.3d, at 949.

Applying that theory of arranger liability to the District Court's findings of fact, the Ninth Circuit held that Shell arranged for the disposal of a hazardous substance through its sale and delivery of D-D:

> "Shell arranged for delivery of the substances to the site by its subcontractors; was aware of, and to some degree dictated, the transfer arrangements; knew that some leakage was likely in the transfer process; and provided advice and supervision concerning safe transfer and storage. Disposal of a hazardous substance was thus a necessary part of the sale and delivery process." *Id.,* at 950.

Under such circumstances, the court concluded, arranger liability was not precluded by the fact that the purpose of Shell's action had been to transport a useful and previously unused product to B & B for sale.

. . . We granted certiorari to determine whether Shell was properly held liable as an entity that had "arranged for disposal" of hazardous substances within the meaning of § 9607(a)(3). . . .

To determine whether Shell may be held liable as an arranger, we begin with the language of the statute. As relevant here, § 9607(a)(3) applies to an entity that "arrange[s] for disposal . . . of hazardous substances." It is plain from the language of the statute that CERCLA liability would attach under § 9607(a)(3) if an entity were to enter into a transaction for the sole purpose of discarding a used and no longer useful hazardous substance. It is similarly clear that an entity could not be held liable as an arranger merely for selling a new and useful product if the purchaser of that product later, and unbeknownst to the seller, disposed of the product in a way that led to contamination. See *Freeman v. Glaxo*

Wellcome, Inc., 189 F.3d 160, 164 (C.A.2 1999); *Florida Power & Light Co. v. Allis Chalmers Corp.*, 893 F.2d 1313, 1318 (C.A.11 1990). Less clear is the liability attaching to the many permutations of "arrangements" that fall between these two extremes—cases in which the seller has some knowledge of the buyers' planned disposal or whose motives for the "sale" of a hazardous substance are less than clear. In such cases, courts have concluded that the determination whether an entity is an arranger requires a fact-intensive inquiry that looks beyond the parties' characterization of the transaction as a "disposal" or a "sale" and seeks to discern whether the arrangement was one Congress intended to fall within the scope of CERCLA's strict-liability provisions. See *Freeman*, 189 F.3d, at 164; *Pneumo Abex Corp. v. High Point, Thomasville & Denton R. Co.*, 142 F.3d 769, 775 (C.A.4 1998) (" '[T]here is no bright line between a sale and a disposal under CERCLA. A party's responsibility . . . must by necessity turn on a fact-specific inquiry into the nature of the transaction' " (quoting *United States v. Petersen Sand & Gravel*, 806 F.Supp. 1346, 1354 (N.D.Ill.1992))); *Florida Power & Light Co.*, 893 F.2d, at 1318.

Although we agree that the question whether § 9607(a)(3) liability attaches is fact intensive and case specific, such liability may not extend beyond the limits of the statute itself. Because CERCLA does not specifically define what it means to "arrang[e] for" disposal of a hazardous substance, . . . we give the phrase its ordinary meaning. In common parlance, the word "arrange" implies action directed to a specific purpose. See Merriam-Webster's Collegiate Dictionary 64 (10th ed.1993) (defining "arrange" as "to make preparations for: plan[;] . . . to bring about an agreement or understanding concerning"); see also *Amcast Indus. Corp.*, 2 F.3d, at 751 (words " 'arranged for' . . . imply intentional action"). Consequently, under the plain language of the statute, an entity may qualify as an arranger under § 9607(a)(3) when it takes intentional steps to dispose of a hazardous substance. See *Cello-Foil Prods., Inc.*, 100 F.3d, at 1231 ("[I]t would be error for us not to recognize the indispensable role that state of mind must play in determining whether a party has 'otherwise arranged for disposal . . . of hazardous substances' ").

The Governments do not deny that the statute requires an entity to "arrang[e] for" disposal; however, they interpret that phrase by reference to the statutory term "disposal," which the Act broadly defines as "the discharge, deposit, injection, dumping, spilling, leaking, or placing of any solid waste or hazardous waste into or on any land or water." 42 U.S.C. § 6903(3); see also § 9601(29) (adopting the definition of "disposal" contained in the Solid Waste Disposal Act).[7] The Governments assert that by including unintentional acts such as "spilling" and "leaking" in

---

[7] "Hazardous waste" is defined as "a solid waste, or combination of solid wastes, which . . . may . . . pose a substantial present or potential hazard to human health or the environment when improperly treated, stored, transported, or disposed of, or otherwise managed." § 6903(5)(B); § 9601(29).

the definition of disposal, Congress intended to impose liability on entities not only when they directly dispose of waste products but also when they engage in legitimate sales of hazardous substances . . . knowing that some disposal may occur as a collateral consequence of the sale itself. Applying that reading of the statute, the Governments contend that Shell arranged for the disposal of D-D within the meaning of § 9607(a)(3) by shipping D-D to B & B under conditions it knew would result in the spilling of a portion of the hazardous substance by the purchaser or common carrier. See Brief for United States 24 ("Although the delivery of a useful product was the ultimate purpose of the arrangement, Shell's continued participation in the delivery, with knowledge that spills and leaks would result, was sufficient to establish Shell's intent to dispose of hazardous substances"). Because these spills resulted in wasted D-D, a result Shell anticipated, the Governments insist that Shell was properly found to have arranged for the disposal of D-D.

While it is true that in some instances an entity's knowledge that its product will be leaked, spilled, dumped, or otherwise discarded may provide evidence of the entity's intent to dispose of its hazardous wastes, knowledge alone is insufficient to prove that an entity "planned for" the disposal, particularly when the disposal occurs as a peripheral result of the legitimate sale of an unused, useful product. In order to qualify as an arranger, Shell must have entered into the sale of D-D with the intention that at least a portion of the product be disposed of during the transfer process by one or more of the methods described in § 6903(3). Here, the facts found by the District Court do not support such a conclusion.

Although the evidence adduced at trial showed that Shell was aware that minor, accidental spills occurred during the transfer of D-D from the common carrier to B & B's bulk storage tanks after the product had arrived at the Arvin facility and had come under B & B's stewardship, the evidence does not support an inference that Shell intended such spills to occur. To the contrary, the evidence revealed that Shell took numerous steps to encourage its distributors to reduce the likelihood of such spills, providing them with detailed safety manuals, requiring them to maintain adequate storage facilities, and providing discounts for those that took safety precautions. Although Shell's efforts were less than wholly successful, given these facts, Shell's mere knowledge that spills and leaks continued to occur is insufficient grounds for concluding that Shell "arranged for" the disposal of D-D within the meaning of § 9607(a)(3). Accordingly, we conclude that Shell was not liable as an arranger for the contamination that occurred at B & B's Arvin facility. . . .

NOTES AND QUESTIONS

1.   **Intent to Dispose.** If intent to dispose of a hazardous substance is an element of arranger liability, as the Supreme Court held, will only

straightforward transactions in which a producer pays a third party to dispose of its hazardous substances trigger CERCLA arranger liability? Courts have treated knowledge as a threshold requirement for a finding of intent. *See Bonnieview Homeowners Ass'n v. Woodmont Builders, L.L.C.*, 655 F. Supp. 2d 473, 493 (D.N.J. 2009) (finding no evidence that the defendant took intentional steps when the defendant did not know topsoil it spread over a property was contaminated with pesticides). The Supreme Court said in *Burlington Northern* that knowledge can provide evidence of a company's intent to dispose of waste, but knowledge alone is not enough to trigger liability.

What other types of evidence should courts look to in inferring intent from knowledge? One district court held that a dry cleaner manufacturer whose operating instructions directed users to discharge hazardous substances into the environment was not an arranger. While the manufacturer knew that its manual directed that wastewater flow into an open drain, the court found that "plaintiffs' points of intentional PCE disposal are negated by the absence of . . . allegations that [the manufacturer] installed the Multimatic machine, connected it to floor drains, directed waste disposal from the Multimatic machine, or inspected the Multimatic machine and its waste disposal." *Hinds Invs., L.P. v. Team Enters.*, 2010 WL 922416, at *6 (E.D. Cal. 2010), *aff'd sub nom. Hinds Invs., L.P v. Anglioli*, 445 F. App'x 917 (9th Cir. 2011). If a court is required to find that a defendant took intentional steps, which of the circuit tests discussed above are still good law after *Burlington Northern*? *Amcast*? *Montalvo*? *Aceto*?

2.   Ginsburg's Dissent. Justice Ginsburg was the only justice who did not join the majority decision. In a sharply written dissent, Ginsburg warned against undermining CERCLA's purpose:

> Given the control rein held by Shell over the mode of delivery and transfer, 520 F.3d, at 950–951, the lower courts held and I agree, Shell was properly ranked an arranger. Relieving Shell of any obligation to pay for the cleanup undertaken by the United States and California is hardly commanded by CERCLA's text, and is surely at odds with CERCLA's objective—to place the cost of remediation on persons whose activities contributed to the contamination rather than on the taxpaying public.

556 U.S. at 622. In *Aceto*, the Eighth Circuit made a similar argument, finding arranger liability because "[a]ny other decision . . . would allow defendants to simply 'close their eyes' to the method of disposal of their hazardous substances, a result contrary to the policies underlying CERCLA." 872 F.2d at 1382. Is the inquiry into intent to dispose inconsistent with CERCLA's imposition of strict liability? Does it allow generators to manipulate their disposal practices to escape liability by outsourcing the stages of their production process that produce the most hazardous waste?

Moving forward, what incentives does a company like Shell have to attempt to minimize releases? *See, e.g., Hinds Invs.*, 2010 WL 922416 (finding no arranger liability for a dry cleaner manufacturer whose instruction manual advised purchasers to flush PCE-contaminated water down an open drain). On the other hand, if intent to dispose is not an element of arranger liability, is the sale of any commercial product containing hazardous material (such as batteries) enough to expose the seller to CERCLA liability, since the commercial product will eventually be disposed of by the purchaser? What if a producer sells a product that has a long useful life, but contains hazardous substances that will eventually be disposed of once the product finally reaches the end of its usefulness—should this count as an arrangement to dispose of hazardous substances? *See, e.g., 3550 Stevens Creek Assocs. v. Barclays Bank of Cal.*, 915 F.2d 1355 (9th Cir. 1990), *cert. denied*, 500 U.S. 917 (1991); *Fla. Power & Light Co. v. Allis Chalmers Corp.*, 893 F.2d 1313 (11th Cir. 1990).

3. **Ownership and Control.** Prior to the Supreme Court's decision in *Burlington Northern*, the circuits split on whether ownership of or authority to control the hazardous substances was necessary in order to establish arranger liability. The Eighth Circuit held that ownership or possession of the hazardous substances was not necessary to establish arranger liability; arranger liability could also attach to those with authority to control the disposal of hazardous substances. *See United States v. Ne. Pharm. & Chem. Co.*, 810 F.2d 726 (8th Cir. 1986), *cert. denied*, 484 U.S. 848 (1987). If ownership is not necessary and control is sufficient to establish arranger liability, then is it necessary for the arranger actually to have controlled the process by which hazardous substances were produced, or is the authority to control the process enough, regardless of whether that authority was exercised? *See United States v. Shell Oil Co.*, 294 F.3d 1045 (9th Cir. 2002), *cert. denied*, 537 U.S. 1147 (2003).

In contrast, the Third Circuit held that both either ownership or possession of the hazardous substance *and* either control or knowledge is necessary to establish arranger liability:

> Ownership or possession of the hazardous substance must be demonstrated, but this factor alone will not suffice to establish liability. A plaintiff must also demonstrate either control over the process that results in a release of hazardous waste *or* knowledge that such a release will occur during the process.

Morton Int'l v. A.E. Staley Mfg. Co., 343 F.3d 669, 677 (3d Cir. 2003). Should arranger liability attach only if the generator owned the product at the time that hazardous substances were produced as a byproduct? The *Aceto* court found that Aceto had retained ownership of the product while it was processed by Aidex; under the Third Circuit's rule, could Aceto have avoided liability by selling the product to Aidex and then repurchasing it after it had been processed?

While *Burlington Northern* did not directly address the issue, some courts have held that ownership and/or control is a threshold inquiry that must be satisfied before applying the Supreme Court's intent analysis. *See Voggenthaler v. Md. Square, LLC*, 2011 WL 693267, at *8 (D. Nev. 2011) ("Because Hoyt is not subject to liability in the absence of allegations of its ownership, possession or control of hazardous substances at disposal or otherwise, the CERCLA claims must be dismissed for failure to state a claim."). *But see Wells Fargo Bank v. Renz*, 2011 WL 97649, at *6 (N.D. Cal. 2011) (holding that "questions of ownership, possession, and control are relevant where a claim of liability is based on a 'broad' arranger theory, i.e., where it is not found that the accused party had direct involvement in arrangements for the disposal of waste").

If ownership is required for arranger liability, then can brokers who arrange for the disposal of hazardous substances ever be held liable? If an independent broker is hired by a generator to select the disposal site and set up contracts with the site and with transporters, and the broker makes a profit off of this service, should the broker escape liability because he never owned or possessed the hazardous substances? *See Am. Cyanamid Co. v. Capuano*, 381 F.3d 6, 24–25 (1st Cir. 2004); *Gould, Inc. v. A & M Battery & Tire Serv.*, 954 F. Supp. 1020 (M.D. Pa. 1997).

4.   Municipal Liability. Consider different ways in which Superfund might treat municipalities that disposed of their wastes at sites also used by industrial generators:

(a)   exempt from liability;

(b)   subject to liability, with damages apportioned proportionally to the total amount of waste dumped; or

(c)   subject to liability, with damages apportioned proportionally to the amount of hazardous waste dumped.

Which rule is most desirable from a fairness perspective? Which is more desirable from an efficiency perspective? Consider separately the questions of prospective and retroactive liability.

5.   Hazardous Car Batteries. Consider the implications of arranger liability under CERCLA in the context of the disposal of hazardous car batteries.

First, consider a scenario in which you send your used car to a junkyard. Over time, the dealership accumulates a number of cars, culminating in the discharge of hazardous battery acid on the site. In this case, the owner of the site is clearly a PRP, by virtue of her status as a § 107(a)(1) owner. Should you be considered an arranger for the purposes of § 107(a)(3)? What factors are relevant to this determination?

Second, consider a scenario in which the junkyard operator removes the battery from the car upon taking possession of your vehicle and sends it to a facility specifically designed to accept used car batteries. Would the junkyard operator be considered an arranger for the purposes of § 107(a)(3) in the event that a discharge occurred at the second facility? Would your answer depend on whether the facility harnessed the secondary materials in the battery for productive purposes? Would it matter if the price of disposal was negative (that is, the junkyard owner was paid for the used battery) or positive (the junkyard owner paid for disposal of the battery)? Would you, as the owner of the car, be considered an arranger for the purposes of § 107(a)(3) in these circumstances?

Third, consider whether the manufacturer of the car that you ultimately dispose of should be considered an arranger for the purposes of § 107(a)(3). What arguments exist in favor of this designation? Why might this outcome be desirable from a policy perspective? In practice, the car manufacturer would likely have purchased the battery from another manufacturer, which in turn would have purchased the hazardous chemicals from another. If you were willing to consider the car manufacturer an arranger for the purposes of § 107(a)(3), should these secondary participants be treated similarly?

If you were designing a system from scratch, where would you draw the line in determining arranger liability? What incentives are created by different levels of coverage?

iii. TRANSPORTER LIABILITY

Finally, § 107(a)(4) holds liable any person who "accepts . . . any hazardous substances for transport" and transports these substances to sites "selected by such person." 42 U.S.C. § 9607(a)(4). As courts have interpreted this limitation, "a transporter selects the disposal facility when it actively and substantially participates in the decision-making process which ultimately identifies a facility for disposal." *Tippins Inc. v. USX Corp.*, 37 F.3d 87, 90 (3d Cir. 1994). Therefore, a transporter need not have independently made the ultimate decision to select a particular site to be liable, but a transporter cannot be held liable without having had a significant voice in the site-selection process.

NOTES AND QUESTIONS

1. Limited Liability of Transporters. Generators of hazardous substances may be subject to arranger liability regardless of whether they select the site at which the waste is disposed. What reasons are there to limit transporter liability to those transporters that have some voice in selecting the waste disposal site?

2. What Counts as a "Site"? Transporters are liable if they transport hazardous substances to a site that they have helped select. If contaminated soil from one part of a site is excavated and spread over another part of the same site, does this count as transportation to a site? Or is the on-site dispersal of hazardous substances beyond the reach of transporter liability? *See Kaiser Aluminum & Chem. Corp. v. Catellus Dev. Corp.*, 976 F.2d 1338, 1343 (9th Cir. 1992). What if wastes leak out of a truck on the side of a highway?

3. Accepting Hazardous Substances for Transport. Section 107(a)(4) holds liable persons who "accept" hazardous substances for transport. If a generator transports hazardous substances that it has produced, has it "accepted" hazardous substances from itself? Does it make more sense to read transporter liability as attaching only to third party transporters? *See Pakootas v. Teck Cominco Metals, Ltd.*, 452 F.3d 1066, 1081 (9th Cir. 2006) (suggesting generator that transports its own waste could be liable as a transporter), *cert. denied*, 552 U.S. 1095 (2008).

Section 107(a)(3), the arranger liability provision, also seems to contemplate a third-party relationship by creating liability for "any person who . . . arranged for disposal or treatment, of hazardous substances owned or possessed by such person, by any other party or entity." Does this language imply that generators that arrange for their own transportation and disposal of hazardous substances, without "any other party or entity," can escape liability as arrangers? *See Am. Cyanamid Co. v. Capuano*, 381 F.3d 6, 24 (1st Cir. 2004) ("The clause 'by any other party or entity' clarifies that, for arranger liability to attach, the disposal or treatment must be performed by another party or entity. . . ."). What other portion of the arranger liability provision could the clause "by any other party or entity" modify? *See id.* (citing *United States v. Mottolo*, 629 F. Supp. 56, 60 (D.N.H. 1984)).

If generators are not liable as transporters because they cannot "accept" hazardous substances from themselves, are not liable as arrangers because they perform the disposal of the hazardous substances without "any other party or entity," and are not liable as owners because they dispose of the hazardous substances on another's property, then generators could escape liability entirely by not outsourcing the transportation or disposal of the hazardous substances that they produce. Does it make sense to read the arranger and transporter liability provisions to allow generators who transport and dispose of their own hazardous substances to escape liability under both provisions? *See Pakootas*, 452 F.3d at 1081–82 (finding that to so hold would run counter to congressional intent).

4.   Failure to Collect Cleanup Funds from PRPs. EPA faces a number of challenges in holding PRPs responsible for the costs of cleaning up hazardous sites. One serious challenge, addressed in a 2005 GAO report, is the risk that PRPs will go bankrupt or transfer assets to avoid liability. GAO, EPA SHOULD DO MORE TO ENSURE THAT LIABLE PARTIES MEET THEIR CLEANUP OBLIGATIONS (2005). Technically, EPA can make claims to recover cleanup costs in bankruptcy proceedings, but those claims are generally accorded low priority and, accordingly, are unlikely to garner significant payouts. *Id.* at 4, 27. GAO criticized EPA for frequently being unaware when its debtors went bankrupt and, therefore, missing out on a chance to make a claim in the bankruptcy proceeding. *Id.* at 29. GAO cited EPA's poor system for monitoring bankruptcies (which relies almost entirely on staff knowledge of which companies filing for bankruptcy are indebted to EPA), the inherent difficulty in monitoring bankruptcies of small businesses not reported in the press, and the challenge of stating a claim in a bankruptcy proceeding when EPA does not have a precise estimate of cleanup costs at a given site, as factors preventing EPA from recovering all of the funds to which it is entitled. *Id.* at 26, 29–30.

To counteract the characteristics of bankruptcy proceedings and corporate structuring that can make it difficult for EPA to find a solvent PRP, GAO recommended that EPA implement an underutilized requirement of CERCLA. Specifically, § 108(b) instructs EPA to require businesses handling hazardous substances to maintain financial assurances adequate to demonstrate their ability to pay for a cleanup in the event of a spill. *Id.* at

33. Even in the limited instances where EPA had requested assurances at the time of the report, GAO found that EPA generally accepts the assurance of the company's choice without considering the risk involved and the company's history of payment and default. *Id.* at 41. Furthermore, GAO found that only 30 percent of assurances existing at the time of the study were in compliance. *Id.* at 50. Thus, not only did GAO recommend that EPA fully implement the assurance program and use it more frequently, it also recommended that EPA do a more thorough job monitoring assurances to make sure they are in compliance. *Id.* at 50–51.

In addition to assurances, GAO recommended that EPA use tax offsets as a means to recover cleanup funds from insolvent parties. *Id.* at 54. By identifying money owed to an insolvent PRP by the government, and claiming it instead, EPA could efficiently recover at least some of the funds it spent during cleanup. *Id.* at 54–55. GAO also recommended more frequent use of liens on company property as an alternative method of compensation. *Id.* at 56–58.

During the economic crisis beginning in 2008, EPA made a concerted effort to pursue debtors in bankruptcy. Some of the largest bankruptcies of the past few years, including the Lyondell Chemical Company bankruptcy, the General Motors bankruptcy, the Chemturna bankruptcy, and the Chrysler bankruptcy, involved settlements of environmental claims under CERCLA worth hundreds of millions of dollars. *See* Civil Cases and Settlements, EPA, Office of Enf't & Compliance Assurance, http://cfpub.epa. gov/compliance/cases/index.cfm (last visited Oct. 24, 2018). In the case of the General Motors bankruptcy, for example, the S.D.N.Y. bankruptcy court confirmed a plan that created a $641 million environmental trust for continuing remediation of the remaining GM properties. *See* Second Amended Joint Chapter 11 Plan, at 11, *confirmed by In re Motors Liquidation Co.*, No. 09–50026 (REG) (Bankr. S.D.N.Y. Mar. 29, 2011).

Is the assurance system advocated by GAO more effective than taxing businesses that handle hazardous chemicals and using the tax revenues to provide adequate funding for potential cleanups? What different incentives would companies have under each system?

C. LAND TRANSACTIONS

i.   INNOCENT LANDOWNER DEFENSE

As discussed above, § 107(b)(3) provides PRPs with a defense to liability, for acts or omissions of third parties, other than those made in connection with a contractual relationship. Before the SARA Amendments in 1986, some courts read this third-party defense to be unavailable to current owners of property that had become contaminated solely as a consequence of the acts or omissions of previous owners. This was because, as a purchaser of the property, current owners were taken to have a "contractual relationship" with all predecessors in title by virtue of the deed through which the property was sold. *See M & M Realty Co. v. Eberton Terminal Corp.*, 977 F. Supp. 683, 686 (M.D. Pa. 1997)

(§ 107(b)(3) defense was unavailable to current owners before SARA amendments). Other courts had allowed current owners to assert the defense. *See United States v. Mirabile*, 1985 WL 97, at *16–17 (E.D. Pa. 1985) (§ 107(b)(3) defense is available to current owners who purchased the site from PRP).

As part of the 1986 SARA amendments, Congress added § 101(35) to CERCLA, which is referred to as the "innocent landowner defense." (Calling it a defense is generally a misnomer, since § 101(35) does not create a new defense to liability; instead, it defines the term "contractual liability" as used in the preexisting § 107(b)(3) defense.) Section 101(35) first provides that the term "contractual relationship . . . includes, but is not limited to, land contracts." 42 U.S.C. § 9601(35). It then provides an exception in circumstances where the owner acquired the property after the disposal of the hazardous substances, and where, at the time of acquisition, "the [owner] did not know and had no reason to know that any hazardous substance . . . was disposed of on, in, or at the facility." *Id.* For the purposes of the Act, an owner has no reason to know of the presence of hazardous substances if "on or before the date on which [she] acquired the facility, [she] carried out all appropriate inquiries." 42 U.S.C. § 9601(35)(B)(i)(I). Section 101(35) also exempts governments that acquire contaminated land through escheat and individuals who acquire contaminated property by inheritance or bequest from liability. 42 U.S.C. § 9601(35)(A)(ii)–(iii). If the requirements of § 101(35) are satisfied, the land contract is deemed non-contractual for the purposes of § 107(b)(3), but the owner must still establish all other elements of the § 107(b)(3) defense.

The level of inquiry that should satisfy the "all appropriate inquiry" requirement was an important question left open in the SARA Amendments. Generally the appropriate level of inquiry varied based on the norms at the time of purchase and the level of sophistication of the purchaser. For example, commercial purchasers would be held to a higher standard than individual homeowners. The following case addresses the question of how much (or little) inquiry satisfies the "all appropriate inquiry" requirement. (Subsequently, Congress amended the statute to add more guidance. *See infra*.)

United States v. Pacific Hide & Fur Depot, Inc.

716 F. Supp. 1341 (D. Idaho 1989).

■ CALLISTER, DISTRICT JUDGE:

In this action, the United States of America (Government) has sued . . . to recoup costs incurred in cleaning up a recycling yard contaminated with polychlorinated biphenyls (PCBs). . . . The individual defendants have filed a motion for partial summary judgment seeking to dismiss . . . part of the claim under the Comprehensive Environmental Response, Compensation and Liability Act of 1980 (CERCLA), 42 U.S.C. § 9601 *et seq.* The individual defendants characterize themselves as "innocent landowners" entitled to protection from CERCLA's provisions exposing them to liability for the cleanup cost. The Government has filed a cross-motion asserting that the innocent landowner defense is not available to these defendants. . . .

Defendant McCarty's, Inc., was formed in 1949 by Samuel McCarty for the purpose of operating a metal recycling scrapyard on a seventeen-acre parcel of property in Pocatello. In 1949, the only two shareholders of McCarty's, Inc., were Samuel and his wife. When Samuel passed away in 1966, a portion of the stock was devised to his children, S.R. McCarty, William McCarty, Richard McCarty, and Pat Eddy. In 1970, when Samuel McCarty's wife died, the remaining shares were distributed to S.R. McCarty, William McCarty and Richard McCarty. In 1975, McCarty's, Inc., redeemed Pat Eddy's shares leaving only three shareholders: S.R. McCarty, William McCarty and Richard McCarty.

Between 1970 and 1973, about 600 capacitors containing PCBs were disposed of in the recycling yard, specifically in an area known as the "gravel pit." During this time, the scrapyard was operated primarily by William and S.R. McCarty. The third shareholder, Richard, worked briefly in 1971 as an employee of McCarty's Inc., sorting copper. But after this, Richard was—to risk understatement—otherwise involved, as his affidavit establishes:

> Shortly after 1971 I went to school in New Jersey and as a conscientious objector worked in a nursing home. Then, I went to Panama and studied archeology, returning again to New Jersey and attending Temple University in Philadelphia until 1976. Then I went to the University of Nevada at Las Vegas.
>
> During the summer of 1976 I did work at the McCarty's site constructing a log cabin. I worked on the site for one and one-half months during the summer and had nothing to do with the salvage business at all.
>
> From May through October 1979, I worked with the United States Forest Service as the forest archeologist for the Humboldt Forest in Nevada. . . .

This arrangement whereby S.R. McCarty and William McCarty operated the scrapyard in Richard's absence, continued until 1979 when a deal was struck with Pacific Hide & Fur, Inc., to sell a portion of the scrapyard property. . . . Richard was then elected as a director of McCarty's, Inc., to facilitate the sale to Pacific Hide & Fur Depot, Inc.:

> The chairman [William McCarty] advised that inasmuch as a substantial portion of McCarty's, Inc., was to be sold that Richard L. McCarty should be elected as a director of said company to serve with the existing directors of said company being William H. McCarty, Samuel R. McCarty and Ralph H. Jones, Jr. . . . and after discussion thereof, it was unanimously

resolved to increase the board of directors of said company from
three directors to four directors and Richard L. McCarty was
unanimously elected as a director to serve with the existing
board.

Richard's own affidavit then goes on to detail his duties after being
elected director:

> Even after being elected a director and officer of the corporation,
> I was not involved in the management or operations of the
> corporate affairs. At that time, McCarty's, Inc., had ceased doing
> business, selling most of its assets to Pacific Hide & Fur Depot,
> Inc., except for some of the site property.

> When the corporation redeemed the shareholders' stock in
> September 1982 by quitclaiming some of the site property to the
> shareholders, I received an interest in the site real property
> equal to my percentage of stock ownership. Both prior to
> receiving an interest in the real property and, thereafter, I did
> not know and had no reason to know that electrical
> transformers or capacitors had been brought onto the site, and
> I did not know and had no reason to know that such equipment
> contained PCBs which have been alleged to be a toxic or
> hazardous substance. At all times I believed that McCarty's,
> Inc., was solely involved in the salvage of scrap metal and
> animal hides.

> I have no knowledge of the actual operations of McCarty's, Inc.,
> scrap metal business and at no time did I go to the piece of
> property where the dumping of the PCBs is alleged to have
> occurred.

In the 1979 sale transaction, Pacific Hide & Fur Depot, Inc.,
purchased the main office buildings and the rights to salvage any ferrous
metals located in the gravel pit for four years. McCarty's, Inc., retained
ownership of the gravel pit.

In March 1981, S.R. McCarty died. His stock in McCarty's, Inc., his
separate property, was devised to his wife, Dayna McCarty. . . .

In April 1982, William McCarty made a gift of one share of
McCarty's, Inc., stock to each of his three children, Terry, Sherry, and
Michael McCarty. During this time, McCarty's, Inc., was winding up its
affairs. It had forfeited its charter in November of 1981, and in
September 1982 it transferred its assets—including ownership of the
gravel pit—to existing shareholders in return for redemption of their
shares. . . . In December 1982, William McCarty transferred all of his
interest in the property to Terry, Sherry and Michael McCarty by
warranty deed. . . .

In March 1983, about six months after the stock transfer took place,
federal agents discovered the capacitors in the gravel pit and found that
"many of the PCB capacitors have been or were leaking PCB-laden liquid

into the porous soil of the gravel pit." The EPA began clean-up efforts and removed 590 capacitors, twenty drums of waste, and "substantial amounts of PCB-contaminated soil" from the gravel pit. . . . The Government filed this suit seeking to recoup those costs and enjoin the defendants from any further PCB disposal. . . .

. . . The defendants Richard McCarty, Dayna McCarty, Terry, Sherry and Michael McCarty are all current owners. There has been no argument that the site is not a "facility" and that a release of a "hazardous substance" has not occurred. The Government has therefore made out a *prima facie* case of liability under 42 U.S.C. § 9607(a)(1) against Richard and Dayna McCarty, and Terry, Sherry and Michael McCarty. The individual defendants argue, however, that the "innocent landowner" defense protects them from liability as current owners of the facility. . . .

Turning first to Terry, Sherry and Michael McCarty, it is clear that the PCB release was caused "solely by an act or omission of a third party," and not by these three defendants. The Court also finds that these defendants had no reason to suspect that PCBs were on the property. As established by the affidavits of these three defendants discussed earlier, the defendants had no knowledge of any PCB release on the property until the EPA moved onto the site. When the defendants were teenagers, they did some sporadic labor at the site, but did almost nothing beyond working in a retail outlet and participating in construction of a log cabin in 1976. Their involvement came not as a result of any commercial transaction, but rather because their father gave them a gift of one share of McCarty's, Inc., stock. At the time of this gift, the three defendants were in their early-20s and had no connection with the operation of the site. While it is true that the shares of stock were redeemed by the three defendants for a percentage ownership in the property, that transaction does not change the nature of their innocent involvement. The redemption was precipitated by the corporation as part of its dissolution. Terry, Sherry and Michael McCarty were simply along for the ride because of a gift made earlier by their father.

The legislative history behind the SARA amendments shows that commercial transactions are to be treated differently than private transactions and inheritances. In fact, that legislative history establishes a three-tier system: Commercial transactions are held to the strictest standard; private transactions are given a little more leniency; and inheritances and bequests are treated the most leniently of these three situations. The present case is actually more like an inheritance than a private transaction. Certainly these three defendants did not obtain their interest in an arms-length private sales transaction—they obtained their initial interest by familial gift and their ultimate interest by a corporate event beyond their control. All of this occurred when they were barely out of their teenage years. This is precisely the situation designed to be covered by the innocent landowner defense.

It is also important under 42 U.S.C. § 9601(35)(B) to examine the "obviousness or the presence or likely presence of contamination of the property." . . . While there is evidence in the present case that some of the defendants had holes eaten in their clothes by battery acid, this case was brought over PCBs, not battery acid, and there is no evidence that the PCBs were obvious.

Title 42 U.S.C. § 9601(35)(B) also directs this Court to examine whether the defendants had any "specialized knowledge or experience." As previously discussed, the three McCarty children had no specialized knowledge or experience concerning PCBs or any hazardous wastes.

The Government argues, however, that "no inquiry" can never constitute "all appropriate inquiry" under 42 U.S.C. § 9601(35)(A). The Government argues that Congress intended everyone, under any conceivable circumstance, to make some inquiry about the existence of hazardous wastes when obtaining an interest in real property. . . . It would have been easy to draft into the statute the very requirements sought by the Government: Congress could have simply said that some inquiry must be made in every case. But Congress did not do so. Instead, Congress used terms like "appropriate" and "reasonable" in describing the necessary inquiry. The choice of such terms indicates to this Court that Congress was not laying down the bright line rule asserted by the Government. Rather, Congress recognized that each case would be different and must be analyzed on its facts. Under the facts of the present case, the conduct of defendants Terry, Sherry and Michael McCarty was reasonable under all the circumstances. The Court therefore finds that these three defendants cannot be liable under 42 U.S.C. § 9607(a)(1), the "current owner or operator" prong of the Government's complaint.

The Court turns next to defendant Dayna McCarty and finds her level of involvement similar to that of the three McCarty children. Dayna McCarty initially received her shares through an inheritance from her late husband. Her affidavit . . . shows that she had no knowledge of PCBs on the property until the EPA clean-up efforts. While she did become a secretary of the corporation, this occurred at a time when the corporation had basically ceased doing business and was in the process of dissolution. She was never involved in the operation of the site and had no knowledge about the presence of capacitors. She had no specialized knowledge or experience that would put her on notice. Under these circumstances, the Court finds that Dayna McCarty has proven the elements of the "innocent landowner" defense by a preponderance of the evidence and shall not be liable under 42 U.S.C. § 9607(a)(1), the "current owner or operator" prong of the Government's complaint.

The Court turns next to defendant Richard McCarty. His affidavit, quoted earlier, shows that he had no hand in the operation of the site. Although he had an ownership interest in the site for a longer period than Dayna or the McCarty children, he was absent most of that time either at school, working in a nursing home, or working for the Forest Service.

He had no knowledge of PCBs or capacitors on the site. While he was made a director and officer of McCarty's, Inc., in 1979, his elevation to these offices was done solely to facilitate the Pacific Hide deal. For all these reasons, the Court finds that Richard McCarty has proven the elements of the "innocent landowner" defense by a preponderance of the evidence and thus is not liable under 42 U.S.C. § 9607(a)(1), the "current owner or operator" prong of the Government's complaint.

NOTES AND QUESTIONS

1.   **No Inquiry.** When, as in the *Pacific Hide* case, does no inquiry constitute "all appropriate inquiry" for the purposes of § 101(35)? How convincing do you find the *Pacific Hide* court's assessment of Richard McCarty's duties as director of Pacific Hide? This case was decided in 1989. Do you think that the court would reach the same conclusion today?

2.   **Land Contracts.** What burdens does a current owner of land have in establishing the innocent landowner defense? Does a contract for the sale of land give rise to contractual relations for the purposes of § 101(35)? Is the document itself relevant? What then determines the existence of a contractual relationship?

3.   **Innocent Landowner Liability and Incentives.** Is it desirable for Superfund to impose liability on individuals who unknowingly purchase contaminated real estate? Consider the following issues:

   (a)   incentives for detection of the environmental problem;

   (b)   likelihood that detection will lead to a cleanup;

   (c)   potential for unjust enrichment; and

   (d)   avoidance of loopholes that would frustrate the statutory scheme.

For a discussion of the relationship between causation and responsibility under Superfund, see John Copeland Nagle, *CERCLA, Causation and Responsibility*, 78 MINN. L. REV. 1493 (1994).

4.   **Inquiries Once Some Contamination Is Found.** If an initial investigation reveals either some level of contamination or reason to believe that the property might be contaminated, what further inquiries are required? In *AMCAL Multi-Housing, Inc. v. Pac. Clay Prods.*, 457 F. Supp. 2d 1016 (C.D. Cal. 2006), AMCAL purchased property that it knew had been used as a clay product and ceramic manufacturing facility in the past. AMCAL hired an environmental consultant to conduct a site assessment, which revealed some contamination on the property. AMCAL went ahead with the purchase, but once it began to develop the property, it became clear that the contamination was far more extensive than had been revealed by the site assessment. The court explained:

   [T]he allegations in its complaint clearly show that [AMCAL] should have known about the contamination at the site—the environmental consultant hired by them "disclosed the presence of," among other things, "lead and other heavy metals in areas throughout the site"—thereby precluding application of the innocent landowner defense. At oral argument counsel for the AMCAL entities explained that the lead mentioned only concerned that found in superficial level of the soil, but that the lead contamination cleanup costs comprising the "vast majority" of those sought to be recovered in the present action were those associated with the lead putty found buried under brick tunnels placed underground at the site by Pacific Clay which, their environmental consultants will testify, was "virtually impossible to discover . . . by conventional means of investigating properties." Counsel explained that the brick tunnels in question were "constructed long before [the city] started requiring as-built drawings of things, so there were no documents on file" evincing the existence of these tunnels. The fact that the tunnels were made out of brick also made it unreasonable to uncover the lead putty's existence as any effort in excavating those portions of the site where the tunnels laid buried would cause drill-bit refusal when a drill struck the tunnel leaving the impression that the drill had struck bedrock. As explained by counsel: "We swiss-cheesed the site.[ ] However, we suffered what we call drill-bit refusal in a number of places that we were attempting to excavate the site, which simply means that as we sent our drill down to take borings, the drill bit would not go any further. That happens fairly often, and it typically happens when you run into bedrock . . . ; and so the environmental consultants in this instance concluded 'we're getting drill refusal; it looks like we're hitting bedrock; we're not going to be able to take soil samples out of bedrock; we've investigated this soil as fully as we can investigate it.'"

Id. at 1028–29. Should AMCAL be liable for all of the costs at the site, or only those that they knew about when they purchased the property? Was it reasonable for AMCAL to assume that the contamination in the superficial levels of the soil was the only contamination at the site? If further testing was not possible because the drill bit would not go through the brick, what further measures would it be reasonable to expect AMCAL to take? In general, how much testing should be required?

5.   All Appropriate Inquiry. In 2002, Congress amended § 101(35) to define more precisely what constitutes "all appropriate inquiry." Pub. L. No. 107–118 (2002). The amendment requires EPA to issue regulations defining "all appropriate inquiry," and, in the interim, provides that the "all appropriate inquiry" requirement is satisfied if the purchaser complies with certain standards set by the American Society for Testing and Materials. *See* 42 U.S.C. § 9601(35)(B). In 2005, EPA published its final rule defining "all appropriate inquiry." 40 C.F.R. § 312. The rule defines the level of due diligence required to satisfy the "reason to know" requirement under § 101(35)(B) that can lead to the establishment of the § 107(b)(3) third-party defense; it also applies to the *bona fide* prospective purchaser defense (discussed *infra* in the Brownfields section), *see* 42 U.S.C. §§ 9607(r),

9601(40); and the contiguous property owner defense, *see* 42 U.S.C. § 9607(q).

Under the EPA rule, many of the tasks required as part of "all appropriate inquiries" must be undertaken by an "environmental professional." 40 C.F.R. § 312.10(b). The environmental professional and/or purchaser are required to investigate the current and past property uses and occupancies; current and past uses of hazardous substances; waste management and disposal activities; and properties adjoining or located nearby the subject property, among other issues. In investigating these matters, the professional and/or purchaser are expected to gather information that is publicly available and reasonably obtainable; to review and evaluate the reliability of the information gathered; and to identify any data gaps and the significance of these data gaps. *See* 40 C.F.R. § 312.20(e)–(f). Environmental professionals are required to conduct interviews of past and present owners, operators, and occupants to the extent necessary to "achieve[ ] the objectives and performance factors" of the inquiry. *Id.* § 312.23(a). How is the interview scope different for parties interested in brownfield redevelopment as opposed to the innocent landowners defense? *See id.* § 312.23(b). What happens if the prior owners have abandoned the property? § 312.23(d). How might an environmental professional's particular level of knowledge and/or area of expertise influence the scope of the interview? *See, e.g.*, Michelle Weiler, *The Environmental Protection Agency's New Standard for CERCLA All Appropriate Inquiry: More Time and Money for Compliance, But Well Worth the Cost to Avoid CERCLA Liability*, 14 U. BALT. J. ENVTL. L. 159, 174–75, 184 (2007) (discussing impact of EPA's new rule on the interview scope).

The EPA rule is certainly far more specific than the entirely open-ended inquiry into the reasonableness of the inquiries (or lack thereof) undertaken by the *Pacific Hide* court. Are there ways in which the level of inquiry under the EPA rule is still ambiguous? For example, how difficult does it have to be to obtain information before it is no longer reasonably obtainable? How significant must a data gap be to warrant a recommendation of further inquiry to fill the gap? How much money must be spent in the investigation? In how many different parts of a property must soil samples be taken?

6.   Purchasing Property. Consider the implications of the requirement to undertake appropriate inquiries in the following scenario. You are interested in purchasing a parcel of land for residential purposes. While you are aware that the previous owner had used the land for residential purposes, you also believe that at an earlier time the land had been zoned for industrial use. What is the minimum that you have to do to satisfy the "all appropriate inquiries" standard? If, in the course of your investigations, you discover that the land had previously been used for industrial purposes, what further inquiries (if any) would you need to undertake? Would your answers to these questions differ if, instead of you, the potential purchaser was a property developer?

What would be the consequences, if having taken "all appropriate inquiries" in the purchase of your property, you subsequently discover, while constructing your residence, that your land is contaminated? Would you still be able to rely on the innocent landowner defense? What actions would you need to take to ensure that this is the case?

7. Retroactivity. CERCLA liability is retroactive: PRPs are liable for activities that pre-date CERCLA's enactment. *See, e.g., United States v. Monsanto Co.*, 858 F.2d 160, 173–75 (4th Cir. 1988), *cert. denied*, 490 U.S. 1106 (1989). However, courts have held that the new standards for "all appropriate inquiries" contained in the 2002 amendments to CERCLA do not apply retroactively. *See, e.g., R.E. Goodson Constr. Co. v. Int'l Paper Co.*, 2006 WL 1677136, at *5 (D.S.C. 2006); *1325 "G" Street Assocs., LP v. Rockwood Pigments NA*, 2004 WL 2191709, at *10 (D. Md. 2004); *United States v. Domenic Lombardi Realty, Inc.*, 290 F. Supp. 2d 198, 210 (D.R.I. 2003). Why would Congress choose not to make the new "all appropriate inquiry" standards retroactive? What effect would retroactivity have on the availability of the defense if the new standards do constitute a significant change from previous due diligence practices?

8. Due Care. Even if a landowner establishes that it is not in a "contractual relationship" because it falls within one of the exceptions in § 101(35)(A), all that it has established is that the § 107(b)(3) defense is not *unavailable* because of the presence of a contractual relationship. To actually escape liability, the landowner still must establish a number of other elements, including that the release was caused *solely* by the third party, and that the landowner took due care with respect to the hazardous substances concerned, and took precautions against the foreseeable acts or omissions of third parties.

What steps should landowners be required to take to satisfy the requirement of due care? Publicly owned treatment works (POTWs)—*i.e.*, city sewers—have often argued that they should not be held liable for hazardous substances that leak from sewer pipes when the hazardous substances have been poured into the sewer system by third parties. What precautions should POTWs have to take against the possibility that third parties will pour hazardous substances into the sewer system? Does failing to ensure that there are no leaks in the sewage pipes constitute a lack of due care? *Compare Westfarm Assocs. v. Wash. Suburban Sanitary Comm'n*, 66 F.3d 669, 682–83 (4th Cir. 1995) (holding that municipal operator of a sewer system could not establish due care and reasonable precautions because the municipal operator knew of the discharge of hazardous substances into the sewer and knew that cracks were present in the sewer), *cert. denied*, 517 U.S. 1103 (1996), *with Lincoln Props., Ltd. v. Higgins*, 823 F. Supp. 1528, 1539–44 (E.D. Cal. 1992) (holding that a municipal operator of a sewer system that leaked hazardous waste had established third party defense because "no evidence [existed] that the County could or should have foreseen the releases."). *See also* Robert M. Frye, Note, *Municipal Sewer Authority Liability Under CERCLA: Should Taxpayers Be Liable for Superfund Cleanup Costs?*, 14 STAN. ENVTL. L.J. 61 (1995) (criticizing the *Westfarm* decision and arguing that municipalities should not bear CERCLA liability for operating sewer systems because some leakage from sewers is unavoidable and the party dumping chemicals into the sewer, not the operator of the sewer, is the responsible party).

9. Foreseeable Precautions. Consider now what should constitute "precautions against the foreseeable acts or omissions of third parties" for the purposes of the § 107(b)(3) defense. In the case of *United States v. Monsanto*, 858 F.2d 160 (1988), the Fourth Circuit noted that the foreseeable precautions requirement precluded "willful or negligent blindness" on the part of PRPs. *Id.* at 169. In that case, land owned by Monsanto had been contaminated, following the discharge of hazardous substances by a chemical manufacturing company leasing the land. The court dismissed Monsanto's argument that it was eligible to escape liability under the § 107(b)(3) third party defense because, although they were aware that the tenant was a chemical manufacturing company, it was completely ignorant of all waste disposal activities at the facility. What constitutes "willful or negligent blindness"? What foreseeable precautions should Monsanto have taken in this instance?

10. "Sole" Cause. The § 107(b)(3) defense is available only if the release or threatened release was caused solely by a third-party. Does this mean that a PRP can establish the defense only if it can prove that it was not a but-for cause of the release? Or is it sufficient to prove that they were not a proximate cause? Will owners of a facility ever be able to prove that they were not the but-for cause of a release, since but for the existence of the facility that they own, the release would not have occurred? Courts and commentators have taken different positions on whether but-for or proximate cause should be required to establish the § 107(b)(3) defense. *Compare Lincoln Props., Ltd. v. Higgins*, 823 F. Supp. 1528, 1540–42 (E.D. Cal. 1992) ("If the defendant's release was not foreseeable, and if its conduct—including acts as well as omissions—was 'so indirect and insubstantial' in the chain of events leading to the release, then the defendant's conduct was not the proximate cause of the release and the third-party defense may be available."), *and Advanced Tech. Corp. v. Eliskim, Inc.*, 96 F. Supp. 2d 715, 718 (N.D. Ohio 2000) (following *Lincoln Properties*); *United States v. Meyer*, 120 F. Supp. 2d 635, 640 (W.D. Mich. 1999) (same); *United States v. Iron Mountain Mines, Inc.*, 987 F. Supp. 1263, 1274 (E.D. Cal. 1997) (same), *with United States v. Poly-Carb, Inc.*, 951 F. Supp. 1518, 1530–31 (D. Nev. 1996) ("We adopt the customary legal principle: 'but for' causation. In other words, if the spill would not have happened but for Defendant's sale of caustic to Poly-Carb, then an intervening third-party act will not exonerate Defendant."). *See also* James R. MacAyeal, *The Comprehensive Environmental Response, Compensation, and Liability Act: The Correct Paradigm of Strict Liability and the Problem of Individual Causation*, 18 UCLA J. ENVTL. L. & POL'Y 217, 316 (2001) (arguing that incorporating proximate causation into the third-party defense is "blatantly inconsistent with CERCLA's strict liability structure").

11. Government Entities. A land contract is not a contract for the purposes of the § 107(b)(3) defense if the defendant is a "government entity which acquired the facility by escheat, or through any other involuntary transfer or acquisition, or through the exercise of eminent domain authority by purchase or condemnation." 42 U.S.C. § 9601(35)(A)(ii). Unlike escheat or other involuntary transfers, in which governments may be forced to acquire contaminated property, governments may choose whether to acquire property by eminent domain. Why should the innocent landowner defense be available for property that a government entity voluntarily acquires through eminent domain? *See* Hope Whitney, *Cities and Super-fund: Encouraging Brownfield Redevelopment*, 30 ECOLOGY L.Q. 59 (2003). Why not exempt property acquired by government entities regardless of how it is acquired?

Acquiring properties "through the exercise of eminent domain authority by purchase or condemnation" does not give rise to a "contractual relationship" under § 107(b)(3). What does it mean to acquire a facility "through" the exercise of eminent domain authority by purchase or condemnation? Does a government entity actually have to exercise their power of eminent domain, or is a sale that was induced by the threat of eminent domain sufficient? If the state's eminent domain laws require government entities to attempt to negotiate the purchase of property as a prerequisite to the exercise of eminent domain, does it make sense to exclude such purchases from the exemption for property acquired by eminent domain? *Compare City of Toledo v. Beazer Materials & Servs., Inc.*, 923 F. Supp. 1013, 1020–21 (N.D. Ohio 1996) (finding that a sale pursuant to negotiations required as a prerequisite to the exercise of eminent domain does not fall within § 101(35)(A)(ii)), *and City of Wichita v. Aero Holdings, Inc.*, 177 F. Supp. 2d 1153, 1168 n.15 (D. Kan. 2000) (same), *with Emeryville v. Elementis Pigments*, 2001 WL 964230, at *8 (N.D. Cal. 2001) (formal exercise of eminent domain not required under § 101(35)(A)(ii)). Does requiring an actual exercise of eminent domain lead to needless eminent domain litigation costs? *See* Whitney, *supra*, at 91–93. Since it is virtually always possible for government entities to acquire property by eminent domain, *see Kelo v. City of New London*, 545 U.S. 469 (2005), if the threat of eminent domain satisfies the requirements of § 101(35)(A)(ii), does this effectively exempt all property purchased by government entities so long as the government mentions that it *could* condemn the property before purchasing it?

12. State and Local Government. In addition to the specific provisions of the "innocent landowner" defense, state and local governments are exempt from the definition of "owner or operator" in circumstances where they "acquired ownership or control through seizure or otherwise in connection with law enforcement activity, or through bankruptcy, tax delinquency, abandonment, or other circumstances in which the government acquires title by virtue of its function as sovereign." 42 U.S.C. § 9601(20)(D). This exemption does not preclude state and local government liability in circumstances where they had previously caused or contributed to the release or threatened release of hazardous substances. *Id.*

13. Disclosure and Cleanup as a Condition of Transfer. Under § 101(35)(C), any defendant who "obtained actual knowledge of the release or threatened release . . . when the defendant owned the real property and then subsequently transferred ownership of the property . . . without disclosing such knowledge" is liable under § 107(a), and the § 107(b)(3) defense is not available. 42 U.S.C. § 9601(35)(C). What must defendants disclose before transferring property under CERCLA if they want to maintain the possibility of asserting the § 107(b)(3) defense? If not all disposal of hazardous substances constitutes a "release or threatened release," then may landowners transfer property on which hazardous wastes have been stored without disclosing the presence of the wastes to the purchaser, so long as no release of hazardous substances seems imminent? Is it a good idea to allow the transfer of property containing hazardous substances without disclosure to the new owner? If the new owner does not know of hazardous substances that are stored on her property, does this make it more likely that she may inadvertently cause a release? What other obligations discussed in this section might lead the new owner to discover that hazardous substances are stored on her property?

14. State Laws on Disclosure and Cleanup. Some state laws go much further than CERCLA in requiring disclosure and even cleanup as a condition of transfer. Many state laws require full disclosure of any known hazardous substances as a condition of transfer, though the disclosure obligations sometimes differ for commercial and residential property. A much smaller number of states require actual cleanup as a condition of transfer. New Jersey's Environmental Cleanup Responsibility Act (ECRA) (later replaced with the Industrial Site Recovery Act (ISRA)), originally passed in 1983, requires both disclosure and cleanup as a condition of transfer; Connecticut and Hawaii later passed statutes that also require some level of cleanup as a condition of transfer. *See generally* JOHN PENDERGRASS, ENVIRONMENTAL LAW INSTITUTE, AN ANALYSIS OF STATE SUPERFUND PROGRAMS: A 50 STATE STUDY, 2001 UPDATE (2002).

New Jersey's ISRA is the strictest of the state statutes, requiring both disclosure and cleanup as a condition of transfer:

> ISRA is triggered by "transfer[al] [of] ownership or operations" at an "industrial establishment." The seller must notify the New Jersey Department of Environmental Protection (NJDEP) of the transaction "within five days after the execution of an agreement to transfer ownership or operations." Before the transaction can proceed, the seller must obtain the NJDEP's approval of either a "negative declaration" that the land is not contaminated, or in the case of contaminated land, a "remedial action workplan" describing a proposed cleanup. In the latter situation, the seller is obligated to remedy the contamination in a manner that meets the "health risk or environmental standards" set by the NJDEP. The seller must also establish a "remediation funding source," such as a trust fund, insurance policy, line of credit, or self-guarantee, to pay for the cleanup.

Richard L. Revesz, *Federalism and Environmental Regulation: A Public Choice Analysis*, 115 HARV. L. REV. 553, 605–06 (2001). Is requiring cleanup as a condition of transfer desirable? New Jersey courts have held that some corporate mergers trigger ISRA, necessitating NJDEP approval before a merger can proceed if either party to the merger owns an industrial facility in New Jersey. *See id.* at 606–07. Should corporate mergers be contingent on cleanup of contaminated sites?

ii.   Past and Future Owners

Section 101(35) establishes when a land contract is a "contractual relationship" for the purposes of § 107(b)(3). If, under § 101(35), a given land contract is not a "contractual relationship," then a purchaser may attempt to establish the other elements of the affirmative defense to escape liability, as the defendants in *Pacific Hide*, *supra*, were able to do. Section 107(b)(3), however, precludes the availability of the third-party defense based on the existence of a contractual relationship only if the act or omission of a third-party occurred "in connection with" that contractual relationship—leaving open the possibility that even if a land contract is a contractual relationship under § 101(35), a defendant could still establish the § 107(b)(3) defense by proving that a third-party's act or omission did not occur "in connection with" the contract.

Westwood Pharmaceuticals, Inc. v. National Fuel Gas Distribution Corp.

964 F.2d 85 (2d Cir. 1992).

■ Before FEINBERG, TIMBERS, and MINER, CIRCUIT JUDGES.

■ TIMBERS, CIRCUIT JUDGE:

. . . On October 14, 1988, Westwood commenced this action against National Fuel seeking to recover costs incurred in investigating and remedying chemical contamination at certain premises in Buffalo it had purchased from National Fuel's predecessor in interest, Iroquois Gas Corporation (Iroquois). . . .

The site which is the subject matter of this action was purchased in 1925 by Iroquois. Iroquois conducted gas manufacturing and storage operations on the land through 1951. For several years thereafter it continued to use the site for gas compression and storage. During these operations Iroquois placed or used various underground pipes and structures at the site. In 1968, Iroquois demolished certain structures on the northeast portion of the site, but left other structures on the site standing.

Iroquois sold the site to Westwood in 1972 for $60,100. Westwood demolished the remaining structures on the site and constructed a warehouse on the southern portion of the site. During these construction activities and associated soil testing, Westwood discovered various subsurface contaminants. In the instant action Westwood seeks to recover the response costs—the costs of cleaning up the contaminants—for which it claims National Fuel is liable. . . .

The district court held that National Fuel had raised a triable issue of fact by contending that, under the "third-party defense" of CERCLA § 107(b)(3), it was not liable on Westwood's CERCLA claims. . . .

National Fuel did not dispute the fact that its 1972 sales contract with Westwood was a "contractual relationship", since CERCLA

§ 101(35)(A) provides that "[t]he term 'contractual relationship', for the purpose of § 9607(b)(3) of this title includes, but is not limited to, land contracts, deeds or other instruments transferring title or possession. . . ." National Fuel asserted, however, that Westwood's construction activities were not undertaken by Westwood "in connection with" the contractual relationship between National Fuel and Westwood. Furthermore, National Fuel asserted that, if in fact it placed hazardous substances at the site, it exercised due care with respect to such substances and took precautions against the foreseeable acts or omissions of third persons. Specifically, National Fuel asserted that any such substances that were not eventually removed from the premises for off-site use or disposal were left inside secure subsurface receptacles. Moreover, National Fuel asserted that the structural integrity of these subsurface receptacles left at the site would not have been breached and therefore hazardous substances would not have escaped but for the unforeseeable construction activities of Westwood.

The district court held that the phrase "in connection with" in § 107(b)(3) requires that there be some relationship between the disposal/releasing activity and the contract with the defendant for the defendant to be barred from raising the third-party defense of § 107(b)(3). . . .

Other cases considering this or similar questions also have indicated that something more than a mere contractual relationship is required. In *United States v. Hooker Chemicals & Plastics Corp.*, 680 F. Supp. 546 (W.D.N.Y.1988), the court held that defendants' contractual relationship with the present landowner—defendants had deeded the land to the City—precluded defendant from raising the third-party defense of § 107(b)(3) since "[defendant] was able to control the acts of these subsequent purchasers because of the nature of its relationship with these defendants in this case." *Id.* at 558. In *Shapiro v. Alexanderson*, 743 F. Supp. 268 (S.D.N.Y.1990), the court held that the contractual relationship clause of § 107(b)(3) does not embrace "all acts by a third party with any contractual relationship with a defendant. Such a construction would render the language 'in connection with' mere surplusage." *Id.* at 271. "The act or omission must occur in a context so that there is a connection between the acts and the contractual relationship." *Id.* In *Shapiro*, the court described the "classic scenario" in which a landowner would be precluded from asserting a § 107(b)(3) defense: when the third party is operating a landfill pursuant to a contract with the owner. *Id.*

We agree with the district court that a landowner is precluded from raising the third-party defense only if the contract between the landowner and the third party somehow is connected with the handling of hazardous substances. The result would be the same if the contract allows the landowner to exert some control over the third party's actions so that the landowner fairly can be held liable for the release or threatened release of hazardous substances caused solely by the actions of the third party. The mere existence of a contractual relationship between the owner of land on which hazardous substances are or have been disposed and a third party whose act or omission was the *sole* cause of the release or threatened release of such hazardous substances into the environment does not foreclose the owner of the land from escaping liability, provided that the owner satisfies the additional requirements of § 107(b)(3)(a) and (b).

NOTES AND QUESTIONS

1. Land Contracts and Sellers. In circumstances such as *Westwood*, where a seller is asserting the third-party defense, when should a land contract be taken to give rise to a contractual relationship for the purposes of § 101(35)? Is there any evidence that Congress contemplated a seller of land advancing the third-party defense when it drafted § 101(35)? Consider specifically § 101(35)(A)(i), which specifies that a contract of land may give rise to a contractual relationship if, *inter alia*, "at the time the defendant *acquired* the facility. . . ." 42 U.S.C. § 9601(35)(A)(i) (emphasis added).

2. Act or Omission. *Westwood* excused a seller of land from liability for the actions of the purchaser. What, in this case, was the "act or omission by a third party" upon which the seller relies in establishing its defense under § 107(b)(3)?

3. "In Connection with." On what basis did the *Westwood* court find the act or omission of the third-party not to have occurred in connection with the contractual relationship?

Subsequent Second Circuit cases have extended *Westwood*'s reading of the "in connection with" requirement to excuse purchasers as well. In *New York v. Lashins Arcade Co.*, 91 F.3d 353 (2d Cir. 1996), the court noted that "[i]n *Westwood*, the seller of the contaminated site sought exoneration from the buyer's conduct, whereas in this case the buyer seeks exoneration from the seller's activities, but this is surely an immaterial distinction in terms of the *Westwood* rationale." *Id.* at 360. The court then proceeded to consider the requirement under § 107(b)(3) that the defendant have taken adequate precautions against foreseeable acts or omissions of third parties, and found that "[g]iven that the last release in the instant case happened more than fifteen years before Lashins' purchase of the Arcade, there was obviously nothing Lashins could have done to prevent actions leading to a release." *Id.*; *see also Major v. Astrazeneca, Inc.*, 2006 WL 2640622, at *26 (N.D.N.Y. 2006) (finding that "the Second Circuit has interpreted 'in connection with' . . . to prevent a party from being liable for response costs merely because it purchased property from a potentially responsible party" and that the purchaser could not have taken precautions against foreseeable acts or omissions because the contamination occurred before she purchased the property).

Is the *Lashins* court right that the distinction between purchasers and sellers is "immaterial"? If *purchasers* of contaminated land are allowed to escape liability on the grounds that the contract for the sale of land was not related to the past disposal of hazardous substances on the property, how often will current owners of contaminated property be held liable? Does this give rise to a massive loophole? If this loophole were to stand, what incentives would it create on the part of prospective purchasers to undertake all appropriate inquiries? If you disagree with the *Lashins* court must you necessarily disagree with the *Westwood* court?

4.　Closing the Loophole. How do the arguments that a release or threatened release did not occur "in connection with" a land contract differ if asserted by a prior owner, as opposed to a current owner? If events occurring before the sale of the property are capitalized into its price, is it ever fair for a current owner to argue that these events did not occur in connection with the land contract? Similarly, if the hazardous substances were released prior to the sale, could it be argued that the relevant act or omission occurred "in connection with" the sales contract because the purchaser necessarily purchased the land and everything contained therein? In what ways do these arguments distinguish between past and present owners for the purposes of the § 107(b)(3) defense?

At least one other circuit court has interpreted § 107(b)(3) in the same way as the court in *Lashins. See United States v. Cordova Chem. Co. of Mich.*, 113 F.3d 572, 583 (6th Cir. 1997) (en banc), *rev'd in part and remanded on other grounds*, 524 U.S. 51 (1998). In contrast, the Ninth Circuit held that the "in connection with" language is intended only to address situations where the prior owner's acts or omissions were "unrelated to its status as a landowner" and provided an example:

> Imagine, for instance, that an owner, *A*, sold uncontaminated land to *B* and that, years after the sale, a truck owned by *A* happened to overturn near the land, causing contamination with hazardous pollutants. If *B* were to be sued under CERCLA, it could assert a third-party defense notwithstanding its contractual relationship with *A*, because the truck's turning over was in no way related to *A*'s status as the owner of the land—it occurred long after *A* had parted with its interest in the land, and it did not occur while *A* was using the land in its capacity as an owner.

Cal. Dep't of Toxic Substances Control v. Westside Delivery, LLC, 888 F.3d 1085, 1101 (9th Cir. 2018). Courts in other circuits have similarly limited the application of the third party defense by a subsequent purchaser of contaminated land, finding that the prior contamination of the land occurred in connection with a contractual relationship between the purchaser and its predecessors in title. *See, e.g., United States v. Domenic Lombardi Realty, Inc.*, 204 F. Supp. 2d 318, 331–32 (D.R.I. 2002) (finding that to follow *Westwood* "would render the explicit language of the statutory definition inoperative."); *M & M Realty Co. v. Eberton Terminal Corp.*, 977 F. Supp. 683, 686–87 (M.D. Pa. 1997). For a criticism of the *Lashins* and *Cordova* line of cases, see Craig N. Johnston, *Current Landowner Liability Under CERCLA: Restoring the Need for Due Diligence*, 9 FORDHAM ENVTL. L.J. 401 (1998).

5.   Incentives for Sellers. If activity by future owners was always found to be "in connection with" the contract for the sale of the property, this would create a strong incentive for sellers to ensure that future owners used the land responsibly. Would this be desirable? Are sellers the persons in the best position to monitor buyers' future use of land?

6.   Indemnification Agreements. The *Lashins* decision highlights why sellers may seek legal indemnification from purchasers. Section 107(e)(1), however, provides that "[n]o indemnification . . . shall be effective to transfer from [one PRP] . . . to any other person the liability imposed under [§ 107(a)]." 42 U.S.C. § 9607(e)(1). This provision prevents sellers from evading liability as PRPs. It does not, however, prevent sellers from pursuing an action against the purchaser under the indemnification agreement. Why might such an agreement nonetheless not be particularly valuable?

7.   Actual Knowledge. Section 101(35)(C) provides that a defendant who "obtained actual knowledge of the release or threatened release of a hazardous substance at such facility when the defendant owned the real property and then subsequently transferred ownership of the property to another person without disclosing such knowledge" is liable as a PRP and may not assert the § 107(b)(3) defense. 42 U.S.C. § 9601(35)(C). Section 101(35)(D) provides that a defendant who "caused or contributed to the release or threatened release of a hazardous substance" may not assert the § 107(b)(3) defense. 42 U.S.C. § 9601(35)(D).

The seller, found not to be liable in *Westwood*, admitted to disposing hazardous waste at the site in question for many years. Should the disposal of hazardous waste constitute actual knowledge of a threatened release, since there is always a possibility that the waste might leak or be released in the future? Should it constitute causing or contributing to a threatened release? The following section addresses a similar question.

iii.   PASSIVE MIGRATION AND LEAKING

CERCLA holds liable owners and operators "at the time of disposal," § 107(a)(2), which has been interpreted to create liability for past owners, *see Shore Realty, supra*. If a past owner can prove that it was not an owner "at the time of disposal," however, it is not liable under § 107(a)(2). "Disposal" is defined to include "the discharge, deposit, injection, dumping, spilling, leaking, or placing of any solid waste or hazardous waste into or on any land or water." 42 U.S.C. § 9601(29). The following case deals with the meaning of "disposal" and the liability of past owners.

United States v. CDMG Realty Co.
96 F.3d 706 (3d Cir. 1996).

■ Before BECKER, MCKEE, and MCKAY, CIRCUIT JUDGES.

■ BECKER, CIRCUIT JUDGE:

. . . The property at issue in this case, a ten-acre parcel of land in Morris County, New Jersey, was once part of the Sharkey's Farm Landfill

(Sharkey's Landfill). Sharkey's Landfill operated as a municipal landfill from 1945 until 1972 [during which time it received and disposed of hazardous chemical waste and municipal solid waste from multiple sources].

In December 1981, Dowel purchased the property. The land was vacant at the time of purchase, and it remained vacant during Dowel's ownership. Neither Dowel nor any other person deposited waste at the site during Dowel's term of ownership. Dowel's only activity on the land was a soil investigation, conducted in September 1981 (three months prior to finalizing its purchase) to determine the land's ability to support construction. The soil investigation, which was performed by Thor Engineering, involved nine drill borings, each twelve to eighteen feet into the ground. Thor's logs show that its equipment bored through various waste materials and groundwater and that several of the boreholes "caved" during the testing. . . .

In 1987, Dowel sold the property to [HMAT Associates, Inc (HMAT), a plaintiff]. In the contract of sale, Dowel fully disclosed that the property was part of the Sharkey Landfill, that the landfill was under investigation by state and federal environmental authorities, and that the property was part of a possible Superfund site.

In October 1989, EPA and [New Jersey Department of Environmental Protection and Energy (NJDEPE)] commenced actions against parties potentially liable for the costs of cleaning up the Sharkey Landfill and seeking a declaration of future liability. HMAT, as the current owner of the property, was named as a defendant under CERCLA § 107(a)(1), 42 U.S.C. § 9607(a)(1). Dowel was not sued. However, HMAT filed a third-party suit against Dowel, seeking contribution from Dowel as a former owner of the property "at the time of disposal" pursuant to CERCLA §§ 107(a)(2) and 113(f). . . .

Dowel moved for summary judgment, arguing that under CERCLA, prior owners are only liable if they actively engage in waste disposal during their ownership of the property. HMAT also moved for summary judgment. HMAT challenged Dowel's reading of CERCLA, contending that prior owners are liable if they fail to stop the migration of contaminants on their property. . . .

The definition of disposal begins with "the discharge, deposit, injection, dumping, spilling, leaking, or placing of any solid waste or hazardous waste into or on any land or water." 42 U.S.C. § 6903(3). Courts holding that passive migration can constitute disposal have focused on the words "leaking" and "spilling," terms that generally do not denote active conduct. *See CPC International, Inc. v. Aerojet-General Corp.,* 759 F. Supp. 1269, 1278 (W.D.Mich.1991); *United States v. Price,* 523 F. Supp. 1055, 1071 (D.N.J.1981), *aff'd,* 688 F.2d 204 (3d Cir.1982).

We think there is a strong argument, however, that in the context of this definition, "leaking" and "spilling" should be read to require affirmative human action. Both "leaking" and "spilling" also have meanings that require some active human conduct. "Leak" can be defined as "to permit to enter or escape through a leak." *Webster's Third New International Dictionary, Unabridged* 1285 (Philip Babcock Gove & the Mirriam-Webster Editorial Staff eds., 1986) [hereinafter *Webster's*]. Similarly, "spill" can mean "to cause or allow to pour, splash, or fall out." *Id.* at 2195. Meaning derives from context, hence the constructional canon *noscitur a sociis*, which states that one may infer meaning by examining the surrounding words. The words surrounding "leaking" and "spilling"—"discharge," "deposit," "injection," "dumping," and "placing"— all envision a human actor. In the context of these other words, then, Congress may have intended active meanings of "leaking" and "spilling." *See Ecodyne Corp. v. Shah*, 718 F. Supp. 1454, 1457 (N.D. Cal. 1989). . . .

It is especially unjustified to stretch the meanings of "leaking" and "spilling" to encompass the passive migration that generally occurs in landfills in view of the fact that another word used in CERCLA, "release," shows that Congress knew precisely how to refer to this spreading of waste. A prior owner who owned a waste site at the time of "disposal" is only liable in the event of a "release" or "threatened release." 42 U.S.C. § 9607. CERCLA defines release in relevant part as follows:

> The term "release" means any spilling, leaking, pumping, pouring, emitting, emptying, discharging, injecting, escaping, leaching, dumping, or disposing into the environment (including the abandonment or discarding of barrels, containers, and other closed receptacles containing any hazardous substance or pollutant or contaminant). . . .

Id. § 9601(22). The definition of "release" is thus broader than that of "disposal": "release" encompasses "disposing" and some elements of the "disposal" definition and also includes some additional terms. . . .

Our conclusion that the meaning of the words in the "disposal" definition cannot cover the passive migration alleged in this case is buttressed by the language of CERCLA's liability provision. If the spreading of contaminants is constant, as HMAT would have us assume, characterizing liable parties as "any person who at the time of disposal . . . owned or operated any facility," 42 U.S.C. § 9607(a)(2), would be a rather complicated way of making liable all people who owned or operated a facility after the introduction of waste into the facility.

Our conclusion that the language of CERCLA's definition of "disposal" does not include the passive migration alleged here is also supported by a significant aspect of CERCLA's liability scheme, the innocent owner defense. Since the 1986 Superfund Amendments and Reauthorization Act (SARA), Pub.L. No. 99–499, 100 Stat. 1613 (1986) (codified at 42 U.S.C. §§ 9601–9675), CERCLA has exempted certain "innocent owners" from liability.

CERCLA provides a defense to liability if the defendant can prove that the release or threatened release was caused solely by an act or omission of a third party. 42 U.S.C. § 9607(b)(3). The defense is generally not available if the third party causing the release is in the chain of title with the defendant. *See id.* § 9601(35)(A). However, the defense is available in such circumstances if the person claiming the defense is an "innocent owner." To establish the innocent owner defense, the defendant must show that "the real property on which the facility is located was acquired by the defendant after the disposal or placement of the hazardous substance on, in, or at the facility" and that "[a]t the time the defendant acquired the facility the defendant did not know and had no reason to know that any hazardous substance which is the subject of the release or threatened release was disposed of on, in, or at the facility."
. . .

The innocent owner defense's apparent limitation to current owners also supports the conclusion that "disposal" does not encompass the passive spreading alleged here. The provision establishing the innocent owner defense states: "Nothing in this paragraph or in section 9607(b)(3) of this title[, which provides the causation defenses including the third party defense,] shall diminish the liability of any previous owner or operator who would be otherwise liable under this chapter." 42 U.S.C. § 9601(35)(C). This language certainly suggests that the innocent owner defense is unavailable to prior owners or operators.[8]

While the question whether the innocent owner defense is available only to present owners is not before us—and we do not decide the issue—we note that such a limitation makes sense only if passive spreading of waste in a landfill is not included in disposal. If passive migration is excluded from "disposal," past owners will generally only be liable as owners "at the time of disposal" when they have committed or allowed affirmative acts of disposal on their property. They would thus have little need for the innocent owner defense, which requires, inter alia, that a defendant did not "cause[ ] or contribute [ ] to the release or threatened release," 42 U.S.C. § 9601(35)(D); "exercised due care with respect to the hazardous substance concerned," *id.* § 9607(b)(3)(a); and "took precautions against foreseeable acts or omissions of any such third party [causing the release] and the consequences that could foreseeably result from such acts or omissions," *id.* § 9607(b)(3)(b). On the other hand, if prior owners were liable because waste spread during their tenure and the innocent owner defense is available only to current owners, prior owners would be in a significantly worse position than current owners: they would be liable for passive migration of waste even if they had no reason to know of the waste's presence. We do not believe that this was Congress's intent.

---

[8]   Despite this plain language, the Second Circuit has suggested that the innocent owner defense is available to prior owners. *See Westwood Pharmaceuticals, Inc. v. National Fuel Gas Distrib. Corp.*, 964 F.2d 85, 91 (2d Cir.1992). We need not decide that issue in this case.

. . . [O]ur holding will not undermine the goal of facilitating the cleanup of potentially dangerous hazardous waste sites. Even if owners of previously contaminated land can evade liability by transferring the land, ample incentives remain to promote cleanup. *See United States v. Petersen Sand and Gravel, Inc.,* 806 F. Supp. 1346, 1353 (N.D.Ill.1992); Bronston, *supra* at 637–40. Present owners and operators remain strictly liable for the costs of cleanup, 42 U.S.C. § 9607(a)(1), as do some prior owners, *id.* § 9607(a)(2), people who arranged for disposal, *id.* § 9607(a)(3), and transporters of hazardous substances, *id.* § 9607(a)(4). Moreover, a number of provisions ensure that contamination will be discovered and the fact of contamination disclosed if the land is transferred. CERCLA imposes criminal liability (including prison sentences) for failure to report a "release" of hazardous substances above a certain threshold. *See id.* § 9603. As mentioned, if an owner transfers land that it knows to be contaminated without disclosing the contamination, it remains liable even after the transfer. *Id.* § 9601(35)(C). In addition, the innocent owner defense encourages potential buyers to investigate the possibility of contamination before a purchase. *See id.* § 9601(35)(B) (in order to claim the innocent owner defense, a defendant must have undertaken all appropriate inquiry).

[The court concluded that, for the above reasons, passive migration does not constitute disposal under CERCLA.]

NOTES AND QUESTIONS

1.   Cleanup Incentives. The *CDMG Realty* court believed that its holding that passive migration does not constitute leaking "[would] not undermine the goal of facilitating the cleanup of potentially dangerous hazardous waste sites." 96 F.3d at 718. In *Nurad, Inc. v. William E. Hooper & Sons Co.*, 966 F.2d 837 (4th Cir.), *cert. denied*, 506 U.S. 940 (1992), the Fourth Circuit reached the opposite conclusion, finding that the passive migration of hazardous waste was encompassed within the meaning of "leaking." The Fourth Circuit found that adopting the contrary view would mean that

> an owner could avoid liability simply by standing idle while an environmental hazard festers on his property, . . . so long as he transfers the property before any response costs are incurred. . . .
> A CERCLA regime which rewards indifference to environmental hazards and discourages voluntary efforts at waste cleanup cannot be what Congress had in mind.

Id. at 845–46. Which position is more compelling?

2.   Soil Investigation as Disposal. In an omitted portion of *CDMG Realty Co.*, the court addressed the argument that the defendant's drill borings, which were part of the environmental testing at the site, exacerbated contamination by "mixing, shifting, and spreading waste materials," and that this drill boring should constitute disposal under CERCLA. While normally dispersal (such as shifting and spreading) does constitute disposal, the court held that a non-negligent soil investigation does not constitute disposal. What are the court's likely motivations in drawing this distinction?

3. Previous Owners and Operators. In dicta, the *CDMG Realty* court suggested that the "innocent landowner" defense may not be available to previous owners and operators of contaminated property because § 101(35)(C) contains a savings clause that states that "[n]othing in this paragraph or in § [107(b)(3)] shall diminish the liability of any previous owner or operator of such facility who otherwise would be liable under this chapter." 96 F.3d at 717. Does this language preclude a seller of contaminated property from asserting the § 107(b)(3) defense? Do you agree with the *CDMG Realty* court's suggestion that this language seems inconsistent with the Second Circuit's holding in *Westwood*?

4. Structural Arguments and Differing Definitions. The *CDMG Realty* court supports its interpretation of "disposal" by making a structural argument: If disposal included passive migration, then the innocent landowner defense would, as a practical matter, be unavailable in virtually every case because it is only available to defendants that purchased property "after the disposal" of the hazardous substances on the property. 42 U.S.C. § 9601(35)(A). This structural argument makes sense only if "disposal" has the same meaning in § 107(a)(2) as it does in § 101(35)(A).

In *Environmental Defense v. Duke Energy Corp.*, 549 U.S. 561 (2007), the Supreme Court held that EPA was not required to interpret the term "modification" consistently in its regulations governing the Prevention of Significant Deterioration (PSD) program under the CAA and its regulations governing the New Source Performance Standards (NSPS) under the CAA. Does this call into question the *CDMG Realty* court's implicit assumption that "disposal" must have the same meaning in both scenarios? What differences are there between the two uses of "disposal" in CERCLA and the two uses of "modification" in the CAA that could lead to the conclusion that "disposal" must have the same meaning, whereas "modification" might not?

iv. BROWNFIELDS

The liability that CERCLA imposes on current owners of contaminated land creates a strong disincentive to acquire any parcel of land that might be contaminated. If a site appears to be polluted, prospective purchasers might be unwilling to spend the money to conduct environmental testing to determine whether the site actually contains hazardous waste that could subject them to CERCLA liability. Even if environmental testing reveals that a site is not contaminated or is only minimally contaminated, the risk that further pollutants will be discovered later, subjecting the purchaser to liability for the full cost of cleanup, may be enough to deter prospective purchasers from acquiring polluted or potentially polluted sites. These unwanted sites are known as brownfields, defined as "real property, the expansion, redevelopment, or reuse of which may be complicated by the presence or potential presence of a hazardous substance, pollutant, or contaminant." 42 U.S.C. § 9601(39)(A).

Brownfields are problematic for a number of reasons. The level of contamination at brownfields varies significantly, and the more heavily contaminated brownfield sites may pose serious health risks to nearby residents. But even sites that do not pose significant health risks from contamination can harm surrounding communities. Left vacant and untended, brownfields may become hotbeds for crime. Brownfields are also often located in otherwise desirable urban commercial areas; not putting these sites to productive use forgoes an opportunity for economic growth. Rather than redeveloping unused urban brownfields, developers might instead seek out new "greenfield" sites further out in the suburbs, contributing to urban sprawl and leading to environmental problems including increased air pollution and reduction of habitat for local species. *See* S. REP. NO. 107–2 (2001).

Often the level of contamination in brownfields is not significant enough to warrant attention from EPA, but prospective owners may nevertheless be wary of acquiring brownfield property even if the value of the property exceeds the cost of the cleanup. Current owners of brownfields may prefer to fence off the site and leave it unused rather than take any action that could lead to a CERCLA suit. Recognizing these problems, EPA attempted to encourage the redevelopment of brownfields through "comfort letters" and "prospective purchaser agreements." *See* 54 Fed. Reg. 34,235 (1989) (authorizing use of prospective purchaser agreements in limited circumstances); 60 Fed. Reg. 34,792 (1995) (expanding use of prospective purchaser agreements and comfort letters). Comfort letters are assurances from EPA to current owners that EPA does not intend to pursue further CERCLA actions at a given site. Prospective purchaser agreements provide similar assurances, usually contingent on some level of cleanup by the purchaser. However, EPA is not bound by comfort letters, so if future administrators adopted different policies, owners could still be held liable for cleanup costs. Moreover, these letters did not preclude actions by other parties, such as states or other PRPs. Prospective purchaser agreements, negotiated on a case-by-case basis, proved to be time-consuming and cumbersome, and so were not well suited to incentivize redevelopment at any significant portion of the estimated 450,000 brown-fields nationwide. *See* S. REP. NO. 107–2 (2001).

In 2002, Congress amended CERCLA in the Small Business Relief and Brownfield Revitalization Act, Pub. L. No. 107–118, which created the *bona fide* prospective purchaser exemption from liability. The *bona fide* prospective purchaser provision entirely exempts owners or operators from liability under § 107(a) if they meet certain requirements. *See* 42 U.S.C. §§ 9601(40), 9607(r)(1). Unlike the "innocent landowner" defense, *see* 42 U.S.C. §§ 9601(35), 9607(b)(3), a *bona fide* prospective purchaser may qualify for the exemption even if it has actual knowledge of contamination at the site before acquiring it.

An owner or operator must meet a number of requirements to qualify as a *bona fide* prospective purchaser. *See* 42 U.S.C. § 9601(40). All disposal of hazardous substances must have occurred before the person acquired the facility, 42 U.S.C. § 9601(40)(B)(i), and the person must have made "all appropriate inquiries into the previous ownership and uses of the facility," 42 U.S.C. § 9601(40)(B)(ii). The person must take affirmative steps to stop any continuing harm and limit future harm, 42 U.S.C. § 9601(40)(B)(iv), and must cooperate and assist in response actions or natural resource restorations, 42 U.S.C. §§ 9601(40)(B)(v), 9607(r)(1). The person must also provide certain notices and information on request, 42 U.S.C. § 9601(40)(B)(iii) & (vii), and must be in compliance with applicable land use restrictions, § 9601(40)(B)(vi). Finally, the owner must not be affiliated with any person who is potentially liable for response costs at the facility through any familial or contractual relationship. 42 U.S.C. § 9601(40)(B)(viii). The *bona fide* prospective purchaser has the burden of proving all of these elements by a preponderance of the evidence. 42 U.S.C. § 9601(40)(A). Land need not meet CERCLA's definition of a brownfield in § 101(39) for the *bona fide* prospective purchaser exception to be available; the brownfields definition instead is used to determine the availability of federal grant money for site assessments and limited cleanup efforts.

The *bona fide* prospective purchaser provision prevents brownfield owners from reaping windfalls if their land is cleaned up using federal funds. Under § 107(r)(2) and (3), if the United States incurs response costs at a facility, and if the response action increases the fair market value of the facility, then the United States shall have a lien on the facility for the unrecovered response costs. However, the lien may only be in the amount of the increase in the fair market value that is attributable to the response action. 42 U.S.C. § 9607(r)(4)(A).

Even before the passage of the federal Small Business Relief and Brownfield Revitalization Act, many states and cities had begun to address the problems of brownfields. By the end of 2000, 45 states had programs in place to clean up and redevelop brownfields, and the number of sites addressed had been increasing in recent years in many states. Some states require cleanup to the same standards for their brownfields programs as for state-led or enforcement sites (though the level of cleanup required under state Superfund laws can differ from the level required under CERCLA), while others allow lower levels of cleanup based on the future uses of the site.

Many states provide liability relief or protection as part of their brownfields programs, and many also provided financial incentives such as grants, loans, and tax incentives. *See* ENVIRONMENTAL LAW INSTITUTE, AN ANALYSIS OF STATE SUPERFUND PROGRAMS: 50-STATE STUDY, 2001 UPDATE 41–44 & tbls. IV-17, IV-18 (2002); ICF Consulting, Inc., Assessment of State Initiatives to Promote Redevelopment of Brownfields (1999) (prepared for the U.S. Department of Housing and

Urban Development); *see also* Jessica Higgins, Note, *Evaluating the Chicago Brownfields Initiative: The Effects of City-Initiated Brownfield Redevelopment on Surrounding Communities*, 3 NW. J. L. & SOC. POL'Y 240 (2008) (discussing the city of Chicago's brownfields program); Joel B. Eisen, *Brownfields at 20: A Critical Reevaluation*, 34 FORDHAM URB. L.J. 721 (2007) (describing and evaluating New Jersey's brownfields program); Emily A. Green, *The Rustbelt and the Revitalization of Detroit: A Commentary and Criticism of Michigan Brownfield Legislation*, 5 J.L. SOC. 571 (2004) (discussing state brownfield programs in Michigan, Pennsylvania, Ohio, Indiana, and New York). EPA has entered into agreements with various states in which it promises not to pursue cleanup actions against properties cleaned under voluntary programs; however, like comfort letters, these agreements are nonbinding. *See, e.g.*, Superfund Memorandum of Agreement Between the Wyoming Department of Environmental Quality and the U.S. Environmental Protection Agency, Region VIII (Jan. 28, 2002); Superfund Memorandum of Agreement Between the Kansas Department of Health and Environment and the U.S. Environmental Protection Agency, Region VII (Mar. 2, 2001); Superfund Memorandum of Agreement Between the Illinois Environmental Protection Agency and the U.S. Environmental Protection Agency, Region V (Apr. 6, 1995).

NOTES AND QUESTIONS

1. Innocent Landowners and *Bona Fide* Prospective Purchasers. There are many similarities, as well as several critical differences, between the "innocent landowner defense" and the *bona fide* prospective purchaser exemption from liability. Both require that the disposal of hazardous substances have taken place before the owner acquired the property. 42 U.S.C. §§ 9601(35)(A), 9601(40)(B)(i). Both require that the owner exercise care with regard to the hazardous substances and take affirmative steps to stop any continuing release and prevent future releases. 42 U.S.C. §§ 9601(35)(B)(i)(II), 9601(40)(B)(iv), 9607(b)(3)(a). Both require that the owner not have a contractual relationship with the person who caused the release (excluding the deed through which the property is conveyed, if other conditions are satisfied). 42 U.S.C. §§ 9601(40)(B)(viii), 9607(b)(3). Both require that the owner provide access and assistance to persons authorized to conduct response actions. 42 U.S.C. §§ 9601(35)(A), 9601(40)(B)(v). And, both require that the owner make "all appropriate inquiries" into the previous uses of the property. 42 U.S.C. §§ 9601(35)(B), 9601(40)(B)(ii). The EPA rule defining "all appropriate inquiry" applies to both the innocent landowner defense and the *bona fide* prospective purchaser defense, so the level of inquiry required is the same under both. 40 C.F.R. § 312.1.

The critical difference between the two defenses is that, under the innocent landowner defense, the owner must not know or have reason to know of the hazardous substances, § 101(35)(A)(i), while a *bona fide* prospective purchaser may have knowledge of the hazardous substances. *Bona fide* prospective purchasers also must meet certain notice, information, and land use compliance requirements that are not applicable under § 101(35). *See* 42 U.S.C. § 9601(40)(B)(iii), (vi), (vii).

What are the consequences of asserting the *bona fide* prospective purchaser exemption as opposed to the "innocent landowner" defense? Where do the burdens of proof lie in each case?

2.   Appropriate Sites. For what type of sites will the Brownfields Act incentivize redevelopment and use? What will determine whether a *bona fide* purchaser is willing to acquire contaminated land?

3.   Disposal Prior to Acquisition. In order to establish the *bona fide* purchaser exemption, § 101(40)(B)(i) provides that "[a]ll disposal of hazardous substances at the facility [must have] occurred before the person acquired the facility." 42 U.S.C. § 9601(40)(B)(i). What does "disposal" mean for the purpose of § 101(40)(B)(i)? Could the leaking of hazardous waste already on the site constitute disposal? Contrast the holding of the *CDMG Realty* court with the holding of the *Nurad* court, discussed above. How does the Brownfields Act, enacted after these cases were decided, strengthen the statutory interpretation favored by the *CDMG Realty* court?

4.   Federal Funding for State Brownfield Cleanups. In addition to creating the *bona fide* purchaser exemption, the 2002 Brownfields Act also authorized small federal grants to state and local governments for brownfield redevelopment. *See* 42 U.S.C. § 9628. These small grants are meant to provide the funding to initiate redevelopment:

> Many . . . brownfield sites may be ripe for redevelopment, and merely lack a site assessment that confirms that a site is not contaminated. Often, funding is unavailable to conduct these site assessments or site characterizations. If the site assessment does confirm contamination at a brownfield site, private funding is often unavailable, but a small amount of Federal seed money can leverage other moneys that can be used for remediation.

S. REP. NO. 107–2, at 5. Why are only state and local governments, as opposed to potential developers, allowed to apply for federal grants for site assessments? Wouldn't allowing developers to pick which sites to assess make it even more likely that a site assessment finding little or no contamination would lead to redevelopment?

The federal government does, however, provide a number of other programs and tax incentives to developers for brownfields redevelopment. EPA, BROWNFIELDS FEDERAL PROGRAMS GUIDE (2017).

5.   City, State, and Federal Roles in Brownfield Redevelopment. CERCLA was designed to address the problem of highly contaminated sites—such as the site at Love Canal that prompted the statute's passage—and much of CERCLA's structure is geared towards addressing a relatively small number of major NPL sites. In 2004, for example, EPA reported that it had listed 11 new Superfund sites on the NPL and had proposed another 26 for listing, and that over 52 percent of the Superfund obligations for long-term, ongoing cleanup work were committed to just 9 sites. *See* EPA, FISCAL YEAR 2004 SUPERFUND ANNUAL REPORT (2005). In total, less than 1500 sites have been listed on the NPL; in contrast, there are estimated to be more than

450,000 brownfield sites nationwide. *See* S. REP. NO. 107–2, *supra*, at 2–3. Is CERCLA an effective tool for addressing the problem of brownfields, or is its usefulness limited to major sites such as the Love Canal? Will the *bona fide* prospective purchaser exemption and funding for local site assessments be enough to prompt the cleanup of the nearly half-million brownfields nationwide? Are they at least sufficient to remove the disincentive of potential CERCLA liability? Or will the exception be expansive enough to eviscerate the CERCLA liability scheme?

Is the problem of brownfields one best addressed at the federal, state, or local level? *See* Richard L. Revesz, *Federalism and Environmental Regulation: A Public Choice Analysis*, 115 HARV. L. REV. 553, 598–603 (2001) (noting that states have taken the lead in brownfield cleanup, while federal government has played only a limited role); *see also* Matthew D. Fortney, *Devolving Control Over Mildly Contaminated Property: The Local Cleanup Program*, 100 NW. U. L. REV. 1863 (2006) (arguing for local control); Hope Whitney, *Cities and Superfund: Encouraging Brownfield Redevelopment*, 30 ECOLOGY L.Q. 59 (2003) ("[C]ities—not private parties, not states, and not the federal government—are in the best position to clean up contaminated properties within their borders."); D. Evan Van Hook, *Area-Wide Brownfields Planning, Remediation and Development*, 11 FORDHAM ENVTL. L.J. 743 (2000) (arguing for regional model); Joel B. Eisen, *Brownfield Policies for Sustainable Cities*, 9 DUKE ENVTL. L. & POL'Y F. 187 (1999) (arguing for strong federal oversight of state brownfield redevelopment programs); William W. Buzbee, *Brownfields, Environmental Federalism, and Institutional Determinism*, 21 WM. & MARY ENVTL. L. & POL'Y REV. 1 (1997) (discussing dynamic role of federal and state governments in brownfield redevelopment).

6. How Clean Is Clean? Under the Brownfields Act, the funding available for site assessments includes a requirement that an ensuing cleanup comply with the National Contingency Plan "only to the extent that the requirement is relevant and appropriate to the program . . . as determined by the Administrator," 42 U.S.C. § 9604(k)(10)(A), and a requirement that the resulting cleanup comply with all applicable federal and state laws and be protective of human health and the environment, 42 U.S.C. § 9604(k)(10)(B). Because the Brownfields Act is relatively recent, there is little consensus over the level of cleanup that EPA and courts will require under this provision. *See* Richard G. Opper, *The Brownfield Manifesto*, 37 URB. LAW. 163 (2005) (discussing uncertainty over cleanup standards and other requirements under Brownfields Act). State brownfield programs differ in the level of cleanup they require. Some require cleanup to a level as stringent as for enforcement actions under the state Superfund laws, while others allow for reduced levels of cleanup based on the future uses of the property.

Does requiring a less stringent level of cleanup for some brownfield sites make sense? What if the health risks posed by a less stringent level of cleanup are small? Should potential developers be required to clean up brownfield sites to meet all ARARs? If not, what other standard should be deemed to be "protective of human health and the environment"? Is the full

NCP process of studying and planning a cleanup appropriate for every abandoned former gas station? How does the uncertainty over the level of cleanup that will be required under the federal Brownfields Act affect incentives to acquire and redevelop brownfields?

7.   Brownfields, Cleanup Standards, and Environmental Justice. In many cities, the residential areas near brownfields are comprised mainly of lower-income and/or minority residents. Where this is the case, does requiring a less stringent level of cleanup raise environmental justice concerns? How should brownfield redevelopment policies take into consideration the fact that many lower-income and/or minority communities are exposed to disproportionately high cumulative levels of environmental risk? If brownfields are usually located in lower-income and/or minority neighborhoods, do programs requiring a less stringent level of cleanup for brownfields condemn these residents to an unjust level of exposure to environmental hazards? If more stringent levels of cleanup are required and, as a result, a smaller number of sites are actually cleaned up, is the exposure from the neglected sites worse for these neighborhoods than a cleanup that actually takes place, but to a lower level? How should the environmental risks posed by a lower level of cleanup be balanced against the prospect of increased jobs that a redevelopment might be able to offer?

The questions of whether brownfield redevelopment benefits or harms nearby low-income and minority communities and how to balance brownfield redevelopment with a fair distribution of environmental risk have been the subject of significant controversy. *See, e.g.,* Catherine A. O'Neill, *Risk Avoidance, Cultural Discrimination, and Environmental Justice for Indigenous Peoples*, 30 ECOLOGY L.Q. 1 (2003) (exploring environmental justice implications of risk avoidance, as opposed to risk reduction, in indigenous communities); Bradford C. Mank, *Reforming State Brownfield Programs to Comply with Title VI*, 24 HARV. ENVTL. L. REV. 115 (2000) (discussing environmental justice concerns with brownfield redevelopment and analyzing whether brownfield redevelopment programs violate Title VI); Lincoln L. Davies, Note, *Working Toward a Common Goal? Three Case Studies of Brownfields Redevelopment in Environmental Justice Communities*, 18 STAN. ENVTL. L.J. 285, 291–92 (1999) (arguing for increased community participation in brownfields redevelopment); Paul Skanton Kibel, *The Urban Nexus: Open Space, Brownfields, and Justice*, 25 B.C. ENVTL. AFF. L. REV. 589 (1998); Tara Burns Koch, Comment, *Betting on Brownfields—Does Florida's Brownfields Redevelopment Act Transform Liability Into Opportunity?*, 28 STETSON L. REV. 171 (1998) (arguing that brownfields redevelopment improves both public health and economic conditions of surrounding neighborhoods); Kirsten H. Engel, *Brownfield Incentives and Environmental Justice: Second-Class Cleanups or Market-Based Equity?*, 13 J. NAT. RESOURCES & ENVTL. L. 317 (1997–1998) (comparing market-based and rights-based approaches to brownfield cleanup); Georgette C. Poindexter, *Separate and Unequal: A Comment on the Urban Development Aspect of Brownfields Programs*, 24 FORDHAM URB. L.J. 1 (1996) (arguing that "the potential inconsistency in environmental standards created by Brownfields Programs will result in long-term environmental apartheid").

8. Brownfields, Greenfields, and the Costs of Suburban Sprawl. One of the reasons that encouraging brownfield redevelopment can be difficult is that developers often have the option of developing "green-fields," or undeveloped sites that have no history of contamination, often located far from the city center. Developers may prefer this option in order to avoid environmental liability, but greenfield development can pose a number of environmental problems.

> Development at the suburban fringe—on 'greenfields'—consumes agricultural land, destroys natural habitat, and uses a disproportionate share of municipal resources. Building industrial and commercial facilities on greenfields requires that roads, sewers, schools, and residences be developed anew, which will require the formation of new units of government formed to levy the taxes to pay for them. Commuters driving to homes in the suburbs consume more gasoline than urban residents and cause congestion, which in turn leads to the combustion of more fossil fuels and poor air quality.
>
> In contrast, brownfield sites already have much of the development infrastructure in place, potentially saving fiscal and environmental resources, although such savings have not been quantified. Endangered species are normally located on greenfields, not brownfields. Brownfield redevelopment can potentially slow new greenfield development, protecting open space and the species that depend upon it.

Hope Whitney, *Cities and Superfund: Encouraging Brownfield Redevelopment*, 30 Ecology L.Q. 59, 66–67 (2003).

In addition to encouraging the redevelopment of brownfields, should governments take steps to discourage the development of greenfields? What would these steps look like? Are prohibitions on greenfield development desirable? Should greenfield developers be forced to bear more of the costs of greenfield development? For a comparison of brownfield programs and restrictions on greenfield development in the United States and Europe, see Andrew O. Guglielmi, Comment, *Recreating the Western City in a Post-Industrialized World: European Brownfield Policy and an American Comparison*, 53 Buff. L. Rev. 1273 (2005).

9. Retroactivity. Unlike CERCLA's liability provisions generally, which apply to actions that took place before CERCLA's enactment, the Brownfields Act explicitly provides that the *bona fide* purchaser exemption is available only to owners who purchased land after the amendment was enacted. 42 U.S.C. § 9601(40); *see also City of Wichita v. Trustees of the APCO Oil Corp. Liquidating Trust*, 306 F. Supp. 2d 1040, 1051–52 (D. Kan. 2003). Why might Congress have chosen to limit the *bona fide* purchaser exemption to purchases that occurred after the amendment?

10. Affiliation. Under § 101(40)(B)(viii), a party seeking protection as a *bona fide* purchaser cannot be "affiliated with" a potential PRP. CERCLA includes exemptions for affiliations created by "the instruments by which title to the facility is conveyed or financed . . . or by a contract for a sale of goods or services." 42 U.S.C. § 9601(40)(B)(viii)(I)(bb). Despite the exemption, the affiliation language is broad and could encompass many familial and corporate relationships. In September 2011, EPA used its enforcement discretion to create additional exceptions, including relationships at other properties, relationships that developed post-acquisition, relationships created during the transfer of the title, and relationships established between a tenant and owner during a lease when the tenant then seeks to purchase the property. Memorandum, EPA, Enforcement Discretion Guidance Regarding the Affiliation Language of CERCLA's Bona Fide Prospective Purchaser and Contiguous Property Owner Liability Protections (Sept. 21, 2011).

11. Appropriate Level of Incentives? The Brownfields Act creates strong incentives for the redevelopment of brownfield sites. Do you think the regime strikes an appropriate balance between the cleanup of contaminated sites and the prevention of the problems associated with brownfields? How much incentive would you provide for redevelopment?

D. JOINT AND SEVERAL LIABILITY

i.   STANDARD OF LIABILITY

CERCLA does not explicitly impose joint and several liability on PRPs. Courts, however, have routinely held PRPs jointly and severally liable. They have relied both on common law principles and on strong indications that Congress intended for joint and several liability to apply in at least some circumstances. *See* S. REP. 96–848 (1980).

The legislative history of CERCLA reveals that Congress contemplated that liability under CERCLA would be joint and several. Rather than impose joint and several liability in all cases by setting a statutory standard of liability, however, Congress chose to leave the standard of liability to the courts, with the understanding that common law principles would dictate the imposition of joint and several liability in most cases. *See United States v. Chem-Dyne Corp., infra.*

More recent amendments to CERCLA confirm this conclusion. The right to contribution contained in § 113, which was passed as part of the SARA Amendments in 1986, clearly demonstrates that Congress intended for PRPs to be held jointly and severally liable in at least some circumstances—a right to contribution is only necessary if PRPs may be held liable for *more* than their individual share of response costs.

The consequences of joint and several liability are significant. Under joint and several liability, any single PRP may be held liable for all of the costs of cleanup at a contaminated site, regardless of how many other PRPs may have contributed to the contamination. A PRP that has been held liable for more than its fair share of the costs, however, may bring an action against other PRPs to force them to contribute to the costs of the cleanup. 42 U.S.C. § 9613(f)(1). The determination of whether PRPs are jointly and severally liable is an inquiry into causation—if the court cannot determine which PRPs caused which portion of the contamination, then all PRPs should be held jointly and severally liable. *See, e.g., Chem-Dyne, infra.* In contrast, the determination of what amount each liable PRP should contribute to the total cost of cleanup is an equitable inquiry. *See United States v. Township of Brighton*, 153 F.3d 307, 319 (6th Cir. 1998). These two inquiries—liability and contribution—are conceptually distinct, *see United States v. Hercules, Inc.*, 247 F.3d 706, 717–18 (8th Cir.), *cert. denied*, 534 U.S. 1065 (2001), but they are easy to confuse. The distinction between these issues is addressed in the sections that follow.

Chem-Dyne, infra, was the first major opinion on the standard of liability under CERCLA, has been cited in many subsequent cases, and is still considered the seminal opinion on apportionment. *See Burlington Northern*, 556 U.S. at 613. When Congress enacted the SARA Amendments to CERCLA in 1986, *see* Pub. L. No. 99–499, 100 Stat. 1613, *Chem-Dyne* was cited approvingly in the legislative history. *See In re Bell Petroleum Servs., Inc.*, 3 F.3d 889, 897 (5th Cir. 1993).

United States v. Chem-Dyne Corp.

572 F. Supp. 802 (S.D. Ohio 1983).

■ CARL B. RUBIN, CHIEF JUDGE:

This matter is before the Court on the Motion of the defendants for Partial Summary Judgment under the Comprehensive Environmental Response, Compensation and Liability Act, 42 U.S.C. § 9607 ("CERCLA"). Plaintiff United States has sued 24 defendants, who allegedly generated or transported the hazardous substances located at the Chem-Dyne treatment facility, for reimbursement of the superfund money expended to institute remedial action at the site. In order to expedite discovery and trial preparation, the defendants have moved for an early determination that they are not jointly and severally liable for the clean-up costs at Chem-Dyne.

The defendants have moved for a determination of the scope of liability under CERCLA, 42 U.S.C. § 9607 which is a matter of first impression to this Court. At present, there is no case authority specifically addressing this point. . . .

The liability section lists the classes of persons potentially liable under the Act for the costs incurred by government removal or remedial action. In contrast to plaintiff's assertion that joint and several liability is clear from the express statutory language, the Court finds the language ambiguous with regard to the scope of liability. Consequently, in an attempt to discern the Congressional intent, the Court will review and weigh the legislative history of the Act. . . .

As background, two different superfund bills proceeded simultaneously through the House and Senate. On November 24, 1980, the Senate made its final amendment to its bill, thereby eliminating the term strict, joint and several liability from its provisions. Subsequently, on December 3, 1980, the House struck the language in its bill and substituted the language of the Senate bill, which was later enacted. . . .

Senator Stafford, sponsor of the bill, succinctly noted that there was an [elimination] of the term joint and several liability. . . . Senator Randolph, sponsor, explained the significance of the[ ] modification[ ]:

> [W]e have deleted any reference to joint and several liability, relying on common law principles to determine when parties should be severally liable. . . . The changes were made in recognition of the difficulty in prescribing in statutory terms liability standards which will be applicable in individual cases. The changes do not reflect a rejection of the standards in the earlier bill.

[126 Cong.Rec. S14969 (Nov. 24, 1980).]

. . . A reading of the entire legislative history in context reveals that the scope of liability and term joint and several liability were deleted to avoid a mandatory legislative standard applicable in all situations which might produce inequitable results in some cases. 126 Cong.Rec. at S14964, S15004, H11787, H11799. The deletion was not intended as a rejection of joint and several liability. Rather, the term was omitted in order to have the scope of liability determined under common law principles, where a court performing a case by case evaluation of the complex factual scenarios associated with multiple-generator waste sites will assess the propriety of applying joint and several liability on an individual basis.

The question of whether the defendants are jointly or severally liable for the clean-up costs turns on a fairly complex factual determination. Read in the light most favorable to the plaintiff, the following facts illustrate the nature of the problem. The Chem-Dyne facility contains a variety of hazardous waste from 289 generators or transporters, consisting of about 608,000 pounds of material. Some of the wastes have commingled but the identities of the sources of these wastes remain unascertained. The fact of the mixing of the wastes raises an issue as to the divisibility of the harm. Further, a dispute exists over which of the wastes have contaminated the ground water, the degree of their migration and concomitant health hazard. Finally, the volume of waste of a particular generator is not an accurate predictor of the risk associated with the waste because the toxicity or migratory potential of a particular hazardous substance generally varies independently with the volume of the waste.

This case, as do most pollution cases, turns on the issue of whether the harm caused at Chem-Dyne is "divisible" or "indivisible." If the harm is divisible and if there is a reasonable basis for apportionment of damages, each defendant is liable only for the portion of harm he himself caused. Restatement (Second) of Torts, §§ 443A, 881. In this situation, the burden of proof as to apportionment is upon each defendant. *Id.* at § 433B. On the other hand, if the defendants caused an indivisible harm, each is subject to liability for the entire harm. *Id.* at § 875. The defendants have not carried their burden of demonstrating the divisibility of the harm and the degrees to which each defendant is responsible. . . .

NOTES AND QUESTIONS

1. **Effects of Insolvency.** Under joint and several liability, each PRP is potentially liable for the entire harm caused. This means that if some of the PRPs cannot be located or are insolvent, then the PRPs that are found liable will have to pay for their share of the cleanup costs. If it becomes more likely that some PRPs will not be found or will become insolvent as time elapses between the contamination of a site and its eventual cleanup, what incentives does joint and several liability create for PRPs to initiate cleanup actions? How does the likelihood that the government or another PRP will eventually initiate a cleanup action and sue for cost recovery or contribution affect these incentives? If all potential PRPs can be found and are solvent, does it make any difference whether liability is joint and several or not? Which alternative will be less expensive and time consuming for the government?

2. **Relationships Among PRPs.** Because liability under CERCLA is strict and generally joint and several, generators of hazardous substances will often be held liable for the costs of cleanup at sites where the contamination was caused by the irresponsible behavior of the present or past owners of the site, transporters, or other PRPs who also disposed of hazardous substances at the same site. PRPs, however, may defend against liability if they can prove that a third party was the *sole* cause of the release, *see* § 107(b)(3), but this defense is unavailable for parties that are in a contractual relationship with this third party and where the act or omission of the third party occurs in connection with that contractual relationship. If generators of hazardous substances know that the actions of the transporters, owners of disposal sites, and other generators that contribute to disposal sites that they use may subject them to extensive liability, what incentives does this create for generators?

3. **Distinct and Divisible.** The *Chem-Dyne Corp.* court refers to the Restatement (Second) of Torts in determining the circumstances in which joint and several liability applies under CERCLA. Under the Restatement (Second) of Torts, there are two grounds on which PRPs can avoid joint and several liability: Courts should apportion the harm where either "(a) there are distinct harms, or (b) there is a reasonable basis for determining the contribution of each cause to a single harm." RESTATEMENT (SECOND) OF TORTS § 433A (1965). What is the difference between distinct harms and divisible harms?

4.   **Distinct Harms.** Most CERCLA cases, including *Bell Petroleum* and *Burlington Northern*, discussed below, focus on the divisibility of harm. Under what set of facts, however, might PRPs have a colorable argument that they have caused separate, distinct harms? What if there are two non-contiguous geographical areas of soil contamination, or separate subterranean plumes of groundwater that were contaminated? *See Akzo Coatings, Inc. v. Aigner Corp.*, 881 F. Supp. 1202, 1210 (N.D. Ind. 1994), *clarified on reconsid.*, 909 F. Supp. 1154 (N.D. Ind. 1995); *United States v. Broderick Inv. Co.*, 862 F. Supp. 272, 277 (D. Colo. 1994). If a site has been divided into multiple geographic units for the purposes of cleanup and remediation, should the contamination in each individual unit constitute a separate, distinct harm? *See United States v. Vertac Chem. Corp.*, 364 F. Supp. 2d 941 (E.D. Ark. 2005), *aff'd*, 453 F.3d 1031 (8th Cir. 2006), *cert. denied*, 550 U.S. 903 (2007).

ii.   DIVISIBILITY

Under CERCLA, joint and several liability applies only in those circumstances where the harm from contamination cannot be apportioned between the various PRPs. As noted above, the Restatement (Second) of Torts provides that "[d]amages for harm are to be apportioned among two or more causes where (a) there are distinct harms, or (b) there is a reasonable basis for determining the contribution of each cause to a single harm." RESTATEMENT (SECOND) OF TORTS § 433A (1965). The comments to this section note that harms that are not distinct, but "are still capable of division upon a reasonable and rational basis" should be apportioned. *Id.* PRPs frequently argue that the harm in their case is divisible and so should be apportioned, because such a finding allows PRPs to avoid bearing any portion of the costs of the harm caused by other PRPs that are insolvent or cannot be located. Until recently, most courts have held that proving divisibility under CERCLA is a "very difficult proposition," *United States v. Hercules, Inc.*, 247 F.3d 706, 717 (8th Cir.), *cert. denied*, 534 U.S. 1065 (2001), although the Supreme Court's decision in *Burlington Northern* suggests that this may no longer be the case.

PRPs have frequently argued that liability should be divisible on the basis of the volume of hazardous waste that each PRP contributed to a site; however, courts have typically refused to apportion liability volumetrically. *See United States v. Monsanto Co.*, 858 F.2d 160, 172–73 (4th Cir. 1988), *cert. denied*, 490 U.S. 1106 (1989); *Pakootas v. Teck Cominco Metals, Ltd.*, 905 F.3d 565, 594–96 (9th Cir. 2018). In *Monsanto*, the generator defendants argued that because each generator sent a potentially identifiable volume of waste to the disposal site at issue, liability should have been apportioned according to the volume of waste contributed by each generator as compared to the total volume of waste disposed at the site. The court rejected this argument.

Most courts have agreed with the *Monsanto* court that the volume of hazardous substances contributed by different PRPs should not be sufficient to find a harm divisible, because the volume of hazardous substances contributed by each PRP does not necessarily correspond to the contamination caused by each. Under certain circumstances, however, courts have been willing to apportion liability based on the relative volume of hazardous substances contributed by multiple defendants. The first two cases excerpted below, *United States v. Monsanto* and *In re Bell Petroleum Services, Inc.*, address volumetric divisibility. The third case, *Burlington Northern & Santa Fe Railway Co. v. United States*, deals with a different set of arguments for divisibility.

United States v. Monsanto Co.

858 F.2d 160 (4th Cir. 1988), *cert. denied*, 490 U.S. 1106 (1989).

■ Before WIDENER, SPROUSE, and ERVIN, CIRCUIT JUDGES.

■ SPROUSE, CIRCUIT JUDGE:

Oscar Seidenberg and Harvey Hutchinson (the site-owners) and Allied Corporation, Monsanto Company, and EM Industries, Inc. (the generator defendants), appeal from the district court's entry of summary judgment holding them liable to the United States and the State of South Carolina (the governments) under § 107(a) of the Comprehensive Environmental Response, Compensation, and Liability Act of 1980 (CERCLA). 42 U.S.C.A. § 9607(a) (West Supp. 1987). The court determined that the defendants were liable jointly and severally for $1,813,624 in response costs accrued from the partial removal of hazardous waste from a disposal facility located near Columbia, South Carolina. . . .

The appellants . . . challenge the district court's imposition of joint and several liability for the governments' response costs.[22] The court concluded that joint and several liability was appropriate because the environmental harm at Bluff Road was "indivisible" and the appellants had "failed to meet their burden of proving otherwise." *SCRDI*, 653 F. Supp. at 994. We agree with its conclusion.

While CERCLA does not mandate the imposition of joint and several liability, it permits it in cases of indivisible harm. *See Shore Realty*, 759 F.2d at 1042 n. 13; *United States v. Chem-Dyne*, 572 F. Supp. 802, 810–11 (S.D.Ohio 1983). In each case, the court must consider traditional and evolving principles of federal common law,[23] which Congress has left to the courts to supply interstitially.

---

[22] The site-owners limit their joint and several liability argument to the contention that it is inequitable under the circumstances of this case, *i.e.*, their limited degree of participation in waste disposal activities at Bluff Road. As we have stated, however, such equitable factors are relevant in subsequent actions for contribution. They are not pertinent to the question of joint and several liability, which focuses principally on the divisibility among responsible parties of the harm to the environment.

[23] As many courts have noted, a proposed requirement that joint and several liability be imposed in all CERCLA cases was deleted from the final version of the bill. *See, e.g., Chem-Dyne*, 572 F. Supp. at 806. "The deletion," however, "was not intended as a rejection of joint and

Under common law rules, when two or more persons act independently to cause a single harm for which there is a reasonable basis of apportionment according to the contribution of each, each is held liable only for the portion of harm that he causes. *Edmonds v. Compagnie Generale Transatlantique,* 443 U.S. 256, 260 n.8 (1979). When such persons cause a single and indivisible harm, however, they are held liable jointly and severally for the entire harm. *Id.* (citing Restatement (Second) of Torts § 433A (1965)). We think these principles, as reflected in the Restatement (Second) of Torts, represent the correct and uniform federal rules applicable to CERCLA cases.

Section 433A of the Restatement provides:

(1) Damages for harm are to be apportioned among two or more causes where

(a) there are distinct harms, or

(b) there is a reasonable basis for determining the contribution of each cause to a single harm.

(2) Damages for any other harm cannot be apportioned among two or more causes.

Restatement (Second) of Torts § 433A (1965).

Placing their argument into the Restatement framework, the generator defendants concede that the environmental damage at Bluff Road constituted a "single harm," but contend that there was a reasonable basis for apportioning the harm. They observe that each of the off-site generators with whom SCRDI contracted sent a potentially identifiable volume of waste to the Bluff Road site, and they maintain that liability should have been apportioned according to the volume they deposited as compared to the total volume disposed of there by all parties. In light of the conditions at Bluff Road, we cannot accept this method as a basis for apportionment.

The generator defendants bore the burden of establishing a reasonable basis for apportioning liability among responsible parties. *Chem-Dyne,* 572 F. Supp. at 810; Restatement (Second) of Torts § 433B (1965).[24] To meet this burden, the generator defendants had to establish that the environmental harm at Bluff Road was divisible among responsible parties. They presented no evidence, however, showing a

---

several liability," but rather "to have the scope of liability determined under common law principles." *Id.* at 808. We adopt the *Chem-Dyne* court's thorough discussion of CERCLA's legislative history with respect to joint and several liability. We note that the approach taken in *Chem-Dyne* was subsequently confirmed as correct by Congress in its consideration of SARA's contribution provisions. *See* H.R.Rep. No. 253(I), 99th Cong.2d Sess., 79–80 (1985), *reprinted in* 1986 U.S.Code Cong. & Admin. News at 2835, 2861–62.

[24] Section 433(B)(2) of the Restatement provides:

Where the tortious conduct of two or more actors has combined to bring about harm to the plaintiff, and one or more of the actors seeks to limit his liability on the ground that the harm is capable of apportionment among them, the burden of proof as to the apportionment is upon each such actor.

Restatement (Second) of Torts § 433(B)(2) (1965).

relationship between waste volume, the release of hazardous substances, and the harm at the site.[25] Further, in light of the commingling of hazardous substances, the district court could not have reasonably apportioned liability without some evidence disclosing the individual and interactive qualities of the substances deposited there. Common sense counsels that a million gallons of certain substances could be mixed together without significant consequences, whereas a few pints of others improperly mixed could result in disastrous consequences.[26] Under other circumstances proportionate volumes of hazardous substances may well be probative of contributory harm.[27] In this case, however, volume could not establish the effective contribution of each waste generator to the harm at the Bluff Road site.

Although we find no error in the trial court's imposition of joint and several liability, we share the appellants' concern that they not be ultimately responsible for reimbursing more than their just portion of the governments' response costs. In its refusal to apportion liability, the district court likewise recognized the validity of their demand that they not be required to shoulder a disproportionate amount of the costs. It ruled, however, that making the governments whole for response costs was the primary consideration and that cost allocation was a matter "more appropriately considered in an action for contribution between responsible parties after plaintiff has been made whole." *SCRDI*, 653 F. Supp. at 995 & n.8. Had we sat in place of the district court, we would have ruled as it did on the apportionment issue, but may well have retained the action to dispose of the contribution questions. *See* 42 U.S.C.A. § 9613(f) (West Supp. 1987). That procedural course, however, was committed to the trial court's discretion and we find no abuse of it. As we have stated, the defendants still have the right to sue responsible parties for contribution, and in that action they may assert both legal and equitable theories of cost allocation.

---

[25] At minimum, such evidence was crucial to demonstrate that a volumetric apportionment scheme was reasonable. The governments presented considerable evidence identifying numerous hazardous substances found at Bluff Road. An EPA investigator reported, for example, that in the first cleanup phase RAD Services encountered substances "in every hazard class, including explosives such as crystallized dynamite and nitroglycerine. Numerous examples were found of oxidizers, flammable and nonflammable liquids, poisons, corrosives, containerized gases, and even a small amount of radioactive material." Under these circumstances, volumetric apportionment based on the overall quantity of waste, as opposed to the quantity and quality of hazardous substances contained in the waste would have made little sense.

[26] We agree with the district court that evidence disclosing the relative toxicity, migratory potential, and synergistic capacity of the hazardous substances at the site would be relevant to establishing divisibility of harm.

[27] Volumetric contributions provide a reasonable basis for apportioning liability only if it can be reasonably assumed, or it has been demonstrated, that independent factors had no substantial effect on the harm to the environment. *Cf.* Restatement (Second) of Torts § 433A comment d, illustrations 4, 5 (1965).

In re Bell Petroleum Services, Inc.

3 F.3d 889 (5th Cir. 1993).

■ Before JOLLY and DUHÉ, CIRCUIT JUDGES, and PARKER, DISTRICT JUDGE.

■ JOLLY, CIRCUIT JUDGE:

The Environmental Protection Agency (EPA) seeks to recover its response costs under the Comprehensive Environmental Response, Compensation and Liability Act (CERCLA) because of a discharge of chromium waste that contaminated a local water supply. Sequa Corporation appeals from the imposition of joint and several liability. . . . We REVERSE the portion of the judgment imposing joint and several liability, and REMAND for further proceedings. . . .

In the district court, the EPA contended that there was no reasonable basis for apportionment, because the harm to the Trinity Aquifer was a single harm, and that a single harm is the equivalent of an indivisible harm, thus mandating the imposition of joint and several liability. Apparently now recognizing the lack of support for that position, the EPA on appeal acknowledges that apportionment is available, at least theoretically, when there is a reasonable basis for determining the contribution of each cause to a single harm. It asserts, however, that Sequa failed to meet its burden of proof on that issue. Sequa responds that the district court was misled by the EPA's incorrect view of the law, and erroneously required it to prove a *certain*—as opposed to *reasonable*—basis for apportionment.

Essentially, the question whether there is a reasonable basis for apportionment depends on whether there is sufficient evidence from which the court can determine the amount of harm caused by each defendant. If the expert testimony and other evidence establishes a factual basis for making a reasonable estimate that will fairly apportion liability, joint and several liability should not be imposed in the absence of exceptional circumstances. The fact that apportionment may be difficult, because each defendant's exact contribution to the harm cannot be proved to an absolute certainty, or the fact that it will require weighing the evidence and making credibility determinations, are inadequate grounds upon which to impose joint and several liability. . . .

As is evident from our previous discussion of the jurisprudence, most CERCLA cost-recovery actions involve numerous, commingled hazardous substances with synergistic effects and unknown toxicity. In contrast, this case involves only one hazardous substance—chromium— and no synergistic effects. The chromium entered the groundwater as the result of similar operations by three parties who operated at mutually exclusive times. Here, it is reasonable to assume that the respective harm done by each of the defendants is proportionate to the volume of chromium-contaminated water each discharged into the environment.

Even though it is not possible to determine with absolute certainty the exact amount of chromium each defendant introduced into the groundwater, there is sufficient evidence from which a reasonable and rational approximation of each defendant's individual contribution to the contamination can be made. The evidence demonstrates that Leigh owned the real property at the site from 1967 through 1981, and conducted chrome-plating activities there in 1971 and 1972. In 1972, Bell purchased the assets of the shop and leased the property from Leigh. It continued to conduct similar, but more extensive, chrome-plating activities there until mid-1976. In August 1976, Sequa purchased the assets from Bell, leased the property from Leigh, and conducted similar chrome-plating activities at the site until late 1977. In response to the EPA's motion for summary judgment, Sequa introduced evidence regarding chrome flake purchases during each operator's tenure. It also introduced evidence with respect to the value of the chrome-plating done by each, as well as summaries of sales. Given the number of years that had passed since the activities were conducted, the records of these activities were not complete. However, there was testimony from various witnesses regarding the rinsing and wastewater disposal practices of each defendant, and the amount of chrome-plating activity conducted by each.

During the Phase III hearing, Sequa introduced expert testimony regarding a volumetric approach to apportionment. The first expert, Henderson, calculated the total amount of chromium that had been introduced into the environment by Leigh, Bell, and Sequa, collectively and individually. The second expert, Mooney, calculated the amount of chromium that would have been introduced into the environment by each operator on the basis of electrical usage records.

In addition to rejecting apportionment because of competing theories, the district court also rejected volume as a basis for apportionment, because there was no method of dividing the liability among the defendants which would rise to any level of fairness above mere speculation. It stated that each of the proposed apportionment methods involved significant assumption factors, because records had been lost, and because the theories differed significantly.

The existence of competing theories of apportionment is an insufficient reason to reject all of those theories. It is true, as the district court noted, that the records of chrome-plating activity were incomplete. However, under the facts and circumstances of this case, and in the light of the other evidence that is available, that factor may be taken into account in apportioning Sequa's share of the liability. Finally, the fact that Sequa's experts relied on certain assumptions in forming their opinions is not fatal to Sequa's ability to prove that there is a reasonable basis for apportionment. Expert opinions frequently include assumptions. If those assumptions are well-founded and reasonable, and not inconsistent with the facts as established by other competent evidence, they may be sufficiently reliable to support a conclusion that a reasonable basis for apportionment exists.

In sum, we conclude that the district court erred in imposing joint and several liability, because Sequa met its burden of proving that there is a reasonable basis for apportioning liability among the defendants on a volumetric basis. We therefore remand the case to the district court for apportionment.

■ PARKER, DISTRICT JUDGE, concurring in part and dissenting in part:

I cannot agree with the majority's holding on the joint and several liability/quantitative apportionment issue in this case. I do agree that the determination of whether the type [of] harm involved in this case is *capable* of quantitative apportionment is a question of law. And the majority is correct that the single chromium harm suffered by the Trinity Aquifer is the sort theoretically *capable* of apportionment. However, while Sequa met its *legal* burden of establishing that the type [of] harm involved is capable of apportionment, it failed to meet its factual burden relative to apportionment. If proof exists by which the fact-finder could determine, on a reasonable basis, the extent of environmental injury attributable to a party, then certainly that party is entitled to escape the heavy hand of joint and several liability and to have its liability restricted to its actual, quantitative contribution to the single harm. The majority correctly places the burden of proof on the party seeking such a finding, to produce credible evidence to meet its burden. But the majority confuses the distinction between the *legal* burden [of proving] that the single harm at issue caused is of a type capable of apportionment, and the *factual* burden of proving the amount of harm attributable to a particular party. *See* majority opinion at 903. ("Our review of the record convinces us that Sequa met its burden of proving that, as a matter of law, there is a reasonable basis for apportionment." This case is closely analogous to the *Restatement's* illustrations in which apportionment of liability is appropriate.).

The gist of the majority opinion is this legal fallacy: because the evidence is clear that Sequa did not cause 100% of the harm to the aquifer, Sequa *must* be entitled to a finding by the district court apportioning the amount of harm attributable to it under the *Restatement (Second) of Torts,* § 433. We are not to approach our analytical task from that end. The majority's "rule of thumb" miscasts the role of the district court and eviscerates the very concept of joint and several liability.

Burlington Northern & Santa Fe Railway Co. v. United States

556 U.S. 599 (2009).

■ JUSTICE STEVENS delivered the opinion of the Court:

[See the excerpt of the case in Section 3.B.ii for more of the facts of *Burlington Northern*. Burlington Northern and Santa Fe Railway Company and Union Pacific Railroad Company owned the land on which the contamination occurred, and EPA brought suit against them to recover cleanup costs. The district court determined that the Railroads had been responsible for 9% of the costs; the Ninth Circuit found that there were insufficient facts to determine apportionment and held the Railroads joint and severally liable for full costs.]

. . . We must, however, determine whether the Railroads were properly held jointly and severally liable for the full cost of the Governments' response efforts.

The seminal opinion on the subject of apportionment in CERCLA actions was written in 1983 by Chief Judge Carl Rubin of the United States District Court for the Southern District of Ohio. *United States v. Chem-Dyne Corp.*, 572 F.Supp. 802. After reviewing CERCLA's history, Chief Judge Rubin concluded that although the Act imposed a "strict liability standard," *id.*, at 805, it did not mandate "joint and several" liability in every case. See *id.*, at 807. Rather, Congress intended the scope of liability to "be determined from traditional and evolving principles of common law[.]" *Id.*, at 808. The *Chem-Dyne* approach has been fully embraced by the Courts of Appeals. . . .

Following *Chem-Dyne*, the courts of appeals have acknowledged that "[t]he universal starting point for divisibility of harm analyses in CERCLA cases" is § 433A of the Restatement (Second) of Torts. *United States v. Hercules, Inc.*, 247 F.3d 706, 717 (C.A.8 2001); *Chem-Nuclear Systems, Inc. v. Bush*, 292 F.3d 254, 259 (C.A.D.C.2002); *United States v. R.W. Meyer, Inc.*, 889 F.2d 1497, 1507 (C.A.6 1989). Under the Restatement, . . . apportionment is proper when "there is a reasonable basis for determining the contribution of each cause to a single harm." Restatement (Second) of Torts § 433A(1)(b), p. 434 (1963–1964).

Not all harms are capable of apportionment, however, and CERCLA defendants seeking to avoid joint and several liability bear the burden of proving that a reasonable basis for apportionment exists. See *Chem-Dyne Corp.*, 572 F.Supp., at 810 (citing Restatement (Second) of Torts § 433B (1976)) (placing burden of proof on party seeking apportionment). When two or more causes produce a single, indivisible harm, "courts have refused to make an arbitrary apportionment for its own sake, and each of the causes is charged with responsibility for the entire harm." Restatement (Second) of Torts § 433A, Comment i, p. 440 (1963–1964).

Neither the parties nor the lower courts dispute the principles that govern apportionment in CERCLA cases, and both the District Court and Court of Appeals agreed that the harm created by the contamination of the Arvin site, although singular, was theoretically capable of apportionment. The question then is whether the record provided a reasonable basis for the District Court's conclusion that the Railroads were liable for only 9% of the harm caused by contamination at the Arvin facility.

The District Court criticized the Railroads for taking a " 'scorched earth,' all-or-nothing approach to liability," failing to acknowledge any responsibility for the release of hazardous substances that occurred on their parcel throughout the 13-year period of B & B's lease. According to the District Court, the Railroads' position on liability, combined with the Governments' refusal to acknowledge the potential divisibility of the harm, complicated the apportioning of liability. . . . Yet despite the parties' failure to assist the court in linking the evidence supporting apportionment to the proper allocation of liability, the District Court ultimately concluded that this was "a classic 'divisible in terms of degree' case, both as to the time period in which defendants' conduct occurred, and ownership existed, and as to the estimated maximum contribution of each party's activities that released hazardous substances that caused Site contamination." *Id.*, at 239a. Consequently, the District Court apportioned liability, assigning the Railroads 9% of the total remediation costs.

The District Court calculated the Railroads' liability based on three figures. First, the court noted that the Railroad parcel constituted only 19% of the surface area of the Arvin site. Second, the court observed that the Railroads had leased their parcel to B & B for 13 years, which was only 45% of the time B & B operated the Arvin facility. Finally, the court found that the volume of hazardous-substance-releasing activities on the B & B property was at least 10 times greater than the releases that occurred on the Railroad parcel, and it concluded that only spills of two chemicals, Nemagon and dinoseb (not D-D), substantially contributed to the contamination that had originated on the Railroad parcel and that those two chemicals had contributed to two-thirds of the overall site contamination requiring remediation. The court then multiplied .19 by .45 by .66 (two-thirds) and rounded up to determine that the Railroads were responsible for approximately 6% of the remediation costs. "Allowing for calculation errors up to 50%," the court concluded that the Railroads could be held responsible for 9% of the total CERCLA response cost for the Arvin site. *Id.*, at 252a.

The Court of Appeals criticized the evidence on which the District Court's conclusions rested, finding a lack of sufficient data to establish the precise proportion of contamination that occurred on the relative portions of the Arvin facility and the rate of contamination in the years prior to B & B's addition of the Railroad parcel. The court noted that neither the duration of the lease nor the size of the leased area alone was a reliable measure of the harm caused by activities on the property owned by the Railroads, and—as the court's upward adjustment confirmed—the court had relied on estimates rather than specific and detailed records as a basis for its conclusions.

Despite these criticisms, we conclude that the facts contained in the record reasonably supported the apportionment of liability. The District Court's detailed findings make it abundantly clear that the primary pollution at the Arvin facility was contained in an unlined sump and an unlined pond in the southeastern portion of the facility most distant from the Railroads' parcel and that the spills of hazardous chemicals that occurred on the Railroad parcel contributed to no more than 10% of the total site contamination, see *id.*, at 247a–248a, some of which did not require remediation. With those background facts in mind, we are persuaded that it was reasonable for the court to use the size of the leased parcel and the duration of the lease as the starting point for its analysis. Although the Court of Appeals faulted the District Court for relying on the "simplest of considerations: percentages of land area, time of ownership, and types of hazardous products," 520 F.3d, at 943, these were the same factors the court had earlier acknowledged were relevant to the apportionment analysis. See *id.*, at 936, n. 18 ("We of course agree with our sister circuits that, if adequate information is available, divisibility may be established by 'volumetric, chronological, or other types of evidence,' including appropriate geographic considerations" (citations omitted)).

The Court of Appeals also criticized the District Court's assumption that spills of Nemagon and dinoseb were responsible for only two-thirds of the chemical spills requiring remediation, observing that each PRP's share of the total harm was not necessarily equal to the quantity of pollutants that were deposited on its portion of the total facility. Although the evidence adduced by the parties did not allow the court to calculate precisely the amount of hazardous chemicals contributed by the Railroad parcel to the total site contamination or the exact percentage of harm caused by each chemical, the evidence did show that fewer spills occurred on the Railroad parcel and that of those spills that occurred, not all were carried across the Railroad parcel to the B & B sump and pond from which most of the contamination originated. The fact that no D-D spills on the Railroad parcel required remediation lends strength to the District Court's conclusion that the Railroad parcel contributed only Nemagon and dinoseb in quantities requiring remediation.

The District Court's conclusion that those two chemicals accounted for only two-thirds of the contamination requiring remediation finds less support in the record; however, any miscalculation on that point is harmless in light of the District Court's ultimate allocation of liability, which included a 50% margin of error equal to the 3% reduction in liability the District Court provided based on its assessment of the effect of the Nemagon and dinoseb spills. Had the District Court limited its apportionment calculations to the amount of time the Railroad parcel was in use and the percentage of the facility located on that parcel, it would have assigned the Railroads 9% of the response cost. By including a two-thirds reduction in liability for the Nemagon and dinoseb with a 50% "margin of error," the District Court reached the same result. Because the District Court's ultimate allocation of liability is supported by the evidence and comports with the apportionment principles outlined above, we reverse the Court of Appeals' conclusion that the Railroads are subject to joint and several liability for all response costs arising out of the contamination of the Arvin facility.

NOTES AND QUESTIONS

1.   **Illustrations of Divisibility.** As an illustration of the concept of divisibility, determine the liability of A, B, and where appropriate, C, in each of the following examples contained in the Restatement (Second) of Torts:

> Five dogs owned by A and B enter C's farm and kill ten of C's sheep. There is evidence that three of the dogs are owned by A and two by B, and that all of the dogs are of the same general size and ferocity. . . .

> Through the negligence of A, B, and C, water escapes from irrigation ditches on their land, and floods a part of D's farm. There is evidence that 50 per cent of the water came from A's ditch, 30 per cent from B's and 20 per cent from C's. . . .

> Oil is negligently discharged from two factories, owned by A and B, onto the surface of a stream. As a result C, a lower riparian owner, is deprived of the use of the water for his own industrial purposes. There is evidence that 70 per cent of the oil has come from A's factory, and 30 per cent from B's. . . .

RESTATEMENT (SECOND) OF TORTS § 433A cmt. d, illus. 3–5 (1965).

2.   **Illustrations of Divisibility: Superfund Context.** Consider now the following illustrations of divisibility in the Superfund context:

> Multiple generators send different kinds of hazardous substances to a facility. Over time, these substances are released, merge, and result in the contamination of the site.

> Multiple generators send the same kind of hazardous substances to a facility. Over time, these substances are released, leading to the contamination of the site.

When should joint and several liability be deemed to apply? What other factors might inform your answer?

3.   **Relevant Factors: Superfund Context.** Consider the following factors relevant in determining divisibility in the Superfund context:

> • Whether each PRP contributes the same or different hazardous substances;

- Whether the volumetric contributions by the PRPs are known or unknown;

- Whether the harm function of the hazardous substance is linear (*i.e.* damages are directly proportional to the amount of the hazardous substance) or nonlinear (*i.e.* convex or concave harm functions).

Different combinations of these factors give rise to eight different scenarios. In which of these eight scenarios should joint and several liability attach? What is the combination of factors that lends itself most to divisibility? What is the combination of factors that lends itself least to divisibility?

4.   Case Law. Where possible, in each of *United States v. Monsanto Co.*, *In re Bell Petroleum Services, Inc.*, and *Burlington Northern & Santa Fe Railway v. United States*, identify which of the characteristics outlined above are evident. What was the outcome of each case?

5.   Evidentiary Burden. The dissenting judge in *Bell Petroleum* found that the PRPs had met their legal burden of proving that, in theory, theirs was a case where apportionment would be possible. Judge Berzon disagreed, however, because the PRPs had not met their factual burden of proving the amount of harm attributable to each PRP. Different circuits have taken different positions on how precisely a PRP must prove the relative amounts of harm attributable to different PRPs. Some circuits, for example, have held that a defendant cannot simply rely on a chain of inferences. *See Chem-Nuclear Sys., Inc. v. Bush*, 292 F.3d 254, 260 (D.C. Cir. 2002). *Bell Petroleum*, in contrast, did allow apportionment based on some estimations. Was this decision correct?

In *Burlington Northern*, the Ninth Circuit found that, "although most of the numbers the district court used were sufficiently exact, they bore insufficient logical connection to the pertinent question: What part of the contaminants found on the Arvin parcel were attributable to the presence of toxic substances or to activities on the Railroad parcel?" 479 F.3d 1113, 1136 (9th Cir. 2007). The Supreme Court reversed, holding that the district court's assumptions were both reasonable and reasonably supported by evidence in the record. To what extent does *Burlington Northern* relax the evidentiary burden of PRPs? *Compare Appleton Papers Inc. v. George A. Whiting Paper Co.*, 2009 WL 3931036, at *1 (E.D. Wis. 2009) ("*Burlington Northern* is indeed a watershed apportionment case—it significantly eases the burden on defendants who seek to avoid joint and several liability. . . ."), *with 3000 E. Imperial, LLC v. Robertshaw Controls Co.*, 2010 WL 5464296, at *10 (C.D. Cal. 2010) ("*Burlington* did not relieve Defendant from supporting its divisibility arguments with evidence that these figures bear a relationship to amount of harm that it caused . . . although it did not seem to require the exact fit which some previous cases had held was necessary.").

6.   Apportionment Post-*Burlington Northern*. A number of academics predicted that, as a result of *Burlington Northern*, "joint and several liability in CERCLA actions will become the exception and not the rule." Aaron Gershonowitz, *The End of Joint and Several Liability in Superfund Litigation: From Chem-Dyne to Burlington Northern*, 50 DUQ. L. Rev. 83, 83–

85 (2012), quoted in Derek Wetmore, *Joint and Several Liability After Burlington Northern: Alive and Well*, 32 VA. ENVTL. L.J. 27, 39 (2014). *See also id.* at 39 n.82. Yet in the four years following the decision in *Burlington Northern*, of the more than 20 lower court cases that refer to *Burlington Northern* in the context of CERCLA apportionment, only two apportion liability. *Id.* at 40–41. Why have so few cases apportioned liability?

7. *United States v. Alcan Aluminum Corp.* In *United States v. Alcan Aluminum Corp.*, 990 F.2d 711 (2d Cir. 1993), the court held that Alcan could escape liability entirely because its pollutants had contributed no more than the pre-existing background level of hazardous substances. The United States had argued that CERCLA does not require that a PRP contribute some threshold level of hazardous substances, and so Alcan should not be able to escape liability. The court rejected this argument:

> In [remanding the case for further consideration] we candidly admit that causation is being brought back into the case—through the backdoor, after being denied entry at the front door—at the apportionment stage. We hasten to add nonetheless that causation—with the burden on defendant—is reintroduced only to permit a defendant to escape payment where its pollutants did not contribute more than background contamination and also cannot concentrate. To state this standard in other words, we adopt a special exception to the usual absence of a causation requirement, but the exception is applicable only to claims, like Alcan's, where background levels are not exceeded.

Id. at 722. Some circuits have adopted the *Alcan* exception to liability for PRPs that contributed no more than the background level of pollutants, *see Acushnet Co. v. Mohasco Corp.*, 191 F.3d 69, 77 (1st Cir. 1999), while other circuits have rejected similar causation-based liability defenses beyond those explicitly created in the statute, holding that such considerations are only relevant in a claim for contribution under § 113, *see W. Props. Serv. Corp. v. Shell Oil Co.*, 358 F.3d 678, 692 (9th Cir. 2004). CERCLA contains no requirement that PRPs contribute a certain threshold level of pollutants to be held liable. Should courts carve out an exception for PRPs such as Alcan? *Compare* Lynda J. Oswald, *New Directions in Joint and Several Liability Under CERCLA?*, 28 U.C. DAVIS L. REV. 299 (1995) (praising *Alcan* and arguing for a more moderate approach to joint and several liability under CERCLA), *with* James R. MacAyeal, *The Comprehensive Environmental Response, Compensation, and Liability Act: The Correct Paradigm of Strict Liability and the Problem of Individual Causation*, 18 UCLA J. ENVTL. L. & POL'Y 217 (2000–2001) (criticizing *Alcan* and arguing that courts should only relieve PRPs from liability if they fall within the terms of the third-party defense).

iii. CONTRIBUTION

The above cases address when a PRP may avoid joint and several liability by proving that the harm caused is divisible. If the harm is not divisible, all PRPs are jointly and severally liable, and so each is

potentially liable for the entire amount of damages—often a very large
amount, and one that may be disproportionate to an individual
defendant's role in causing the harm. Contribution actions, however,
provide avenues through which damages may be equitably shared among
multiple jointly and severally liable defendants. Contribution "is a
standard legal term that refers to a claim by and between jointly and
severally liable parties for an appropriate division of the payment one of
them has been compelled to make." *New Castle Cty. v. Halliburton NUS
Corp.*, 111 F.3d 1116, 1121 (3d Cir. 1997) (internal quotations omitted).

When Congress enacted CERCLA in 1980, the statute did not
contain an explicit right to contribution. As case law under CERCLA
developed, some courts interpreted the language of § 107 to find an
implied cause of action for contribution allowing PRPs that had paid
more than their fair share of the cleanup costs to recover from other
PRPs. *See, e.g.*, *Pinole Point Props. v. Bethlehem Steel Corp.*, 596 F. Supp.
283, 290–91 (N.D. Cal. 1984) (holding that current landowner, who was
a PRP for purposes of § 107, nevertheless had standing to bring action
under § 107 to recover cleanup costs from other PRPs); *see also Wehner
v. Syntex Agribusiness, Inc.*, 616 F. Supp. 27, 31 (E.D. Mo. 1985) (finding
an implied right of contribution under federal common law when one PRP
sues another under § 107); *Colorado v. ASARCO, Inc.*, 608 F. Supp. 1484
(D. Colo. 1985) (same). Meanwhile, the Supreme Court struck down an
implied right of contribution in several unrelated statutory contexts.
Texas Indus. v. Radcliff Materials, Inc., 451 U.S. 630, 639–40 (1981)
(finding no federal common law right to contribution under the Sherman
Act antitrust laws); *Nw. Airlines v. Transport Workers Union of Am.*, 451
U.S. 77, 91–95 (1981) (finding no implied right to contribution under the
Equal Pay Act or Title VII of the Civil Rights Act). Because the right to
contribution under CERCLA relied solely on interpretations finding an
implied cause of action, a PRP's ability to recover some portion of their
costs from other PRPs seemed to rest on uncertain grounds.

As part of the 1986 SARA Amendments, Congress explicitly created
a right to contribution for PRPs by adding § 113(f) to CERCLA. Pub. L.
No. 99–499, § 113(b), 100 Stat. 1613, 1647–48 (1986). Section 113
authorized "[a]ny person . . . who is liable or potentially liable" under
§ 107 to seek contribution "during or following any civil action under
§ 9606 [§ 106] of this title or under § 9607(a) [§ 107(a)] of this title." 42
U.S.C. § 9613(f)(1). Section 113 authorized the court to use equitable
factors to allocate response costs among PRPs. *Id.*

Under § 113, courts have broad discretion to allocate costs among
PRPs in a contribution action. The case below addresses the equitable
distribution of costs among PRPs.

United States v. Consolidation Coal Co.

345 F.3d 409 (6th Cir. 2003).

■ Before DAUGHTREY and GILMAN, CIRCUIT JUDGES, and CALDWELL, DISTRICT JUDGE.

■ DAUGHTREY, CIRCUIT JUDGE:

Third-party defendant Neville Chemical Company appeals a district court decision holding it liable for a portion of the past and future costs of cleanup at the Buckeye Reclamation Landfill in Belmont County, Ohio. The landfill has been on the National Priorities List as a Superfund site since 1983. Third-party plaintiffs Consolidation Coal Company (referred to throughout the record as Consol) and Triangle Wire & Cable, Inc., brought an action under § 113 of the Comprehensive Environmental Response, Compensation, and Liability Act of 1980, as amended by the Superfund Amendments and Reauthorization Act of 1986 (CERCLA), 42 U.S.C. §§ 9601 *et seq.,* seeking a declaration of liability and equitable allocation of response costs to Neville Chemical. Although the chemical company stipulated that it had deposited 472,000 gallons of wastewater sludge from its Pennsylvania treatment plant in the landfill between December 1978 and February 1979, Neville Chemical claims that the district court was unreasonable in imposing any of the cleanup costs on it because the wastewater caused no harm. The district court found Neville Chemical liable under CERCLA and determined its equitable share of past and future response costs for cleanup of the landfill to be 6%. *See United States v. Consolidation Coal Co.,* 184 F. Supp.2d 723, 752 (S.D. Ohio 2002).

The district court . . . recognized the broad discretion it had in making CERCLA contribution allocations using "such equitable factors as the court determines are appropriate." 42 U.S.C. § 9613(f)(1). It discussed commonly used equitable factors, including the six so-called "Gore factors" considered by Congress in enacting the law and the four "critical factors" identified by Judge Torre in *United States v. Davis,* 31 F. Supp.2d 45, 63 (D.R.I. 1998), *aff'd,* 261 F.3d 1 (1st Cir. 2001). Neither of these lists is intended to be exhaustive or exclusive, and "in any given case, a court may consider several factors, a few factors, or only one determining factor . . . depending on the totality of the circumstances presented to the court." *See Environmental Trans. Sys., Inc. v. ENSCO, Inc.,* 969 F.2d 503, 509 (7th Cir.1992).

Although both Consol and Neville Chemical argued that the district court had to determine only Neville Chemical's equitable share, and not the share of any other PRP, the district court rejected that argument, reasoning that a fair and equitable allocation could only be achieved by comparing Neville's role as a PRP to other PRPs. The district court then divided the PRPs into four categories: generators and transporters of industrial waste; owners and operators of the landfill; Consol as the generator of the gob; and generators and transporters of the municipal solid waste. In allocating response costs, the district court focused primarily on the second "critical factor" from *Davis*, the PRP's varying levels of culpability, and two of the "Gore factors," the amount of waste and cooperation with the government, after carefully explaining why other factors were not helpful in deciding this particular case.

The court determined the equitable allocation across the four groups in the following way. First, the court assigned the industrial generators and transporters, including Neville Chemical, an equitable share of 60% of past and future costs, finding they were the most culpable. Their culpability arose from the fact that they knew or should have known, of the hazardous substances present in their waste, yet they disposed of their waste without seeking the permission required by the Belmont County Board of Commissioners. Second, the court assigned the owners and operators of the landfill a 25% equitable share of the response costs based on their lesser culpability, but also on their irresponsibility in not doing more to prevent the disposal of industrial wastes. Third, the court assigned Consol as generator of the "gob" a 10% equitable share, finding that Consol had knowledge that it contained hazardous substances, but recognizing at the same time that the material was deposited at the site between 1934 and 1952, at a time when there was nothing to prohibit such disposal. Finally, the court assigned the generators and transporters of municipal solid waste a 5% equitable share, because the group had little or no knowledge that the waste contained hazardous substances and because they were required to dispose of the waste at the landfill by rule of the Belmont County Board of Commissioners.

Within the 60% equitable share assigned to the industrial generators and transporters, the court used percentage weight of the waste as a fair and equitable way of determining individual shares. The parties stipulated that Neville Chemical was responsible for 4.78% of the industrial waste by percentage weight. The court rounded Neville's 4.78% share up to 5% based on the fact that Neville did not seek prior written approval of the Belmont County Board of Commissioners, as the county regulations required it to do. Triangle Wire is the only industrial generator which did seek prior approval, and the court found that this fact made that company marginally less culpable than its percentage weight would reflect. By rounding up Neville Chemical's individual share and decreasing Triangle Wire's share, the district court adjusted for Neville Chemical's violation of applicable local regulation and Triangle Wire's compliance. Thus, at this point in the court's analysis, Neville Chemical had an individual share of 5% of 60%, or 3%, of the past and future response costs.

The court considered one additional equitable factor in its analysis: cooperation with the government. The court concluded that Neville Chemical did not cooperate with the [Ohio Environmental Protection Agency (OEPA)] or the [EPA] and that it did not participate in any efforts of the other PRPs to work with the government to investigate the site, design a remedy, abide by the remedy. In sum, the district court found that "Neville did not meaningfully cooperate in any phase of the CERCLA process in this case, although it was given ample opportunity to do so." Because of this "persistent, pervasive, and unjustified" lack of cooperation when Neville Chemical knew or should have known that its sludge had been deposited at the site, the court doubled the company's share of response costs from 3% to 6%. The court also noted that because the cooperating PRPs had negotiated a remedy that was half the cost of the originally approved remedy, doubling Neville Chemical's individual share would avoid the possibility of a windfall to that company, based on the successful efforts of the cooperating PRPs to find a less costly solution.

Neville Chemical argues on appeal that the district court abused its discretion in this allocation of chemical costs, given the opinion of Neville Chemical's expert that the company's waste caused no harm. However, the district court found the opinion of the expert unreliable because it was not based on conditions similar to those that existed in the waste pit.

Neville Chemical also argues that the district court abused its direction in allocating 60% of the response costs to the industrial generators and 5% of that share to Neville Chemical. Finally, the company argues that the district court abused its discretion in doubling Neville Chemical's share from 3% to 6%. However, all these arguments boil down to a disagreement with the particular equitable factors the district court chose to use and how the court applied them. After an independent review, we conclude that nothing in Neville's arguments leads us to a "definite and firm conviction that the trial court committed a clear error of judgment." *Kalamazoo River Study Group v. Rockwell Int'l Corp.*, 274 F.3d at 1047.

NOTES AND QUESTIONS

1.   **Equitable Factors.** Section 113(f)(1) provides that, "[i]n resolving contribution claims, the court may allocate response costs among liable parties using such equitable factors as the court determines are appropriate." 42 U.S.C. § 9613(f)(1). What equitable factors did the *Consolidation Coal* court apply? What other factors may be relevant? Do you agree with the court's balancing of these factors?

2.   **"Gore" Factors.** Under § 113, courts have broad discretion to determine what equitable factors to consider in allocating cleanup costs between PRPs. Many courts consider some or all of the six "Gore factors," which are "(1) the ability of the parties to demonstrate that their contribution to the site can be distinguished; (2) the amount of hazardous waste involved; (3) the degree of toxicity of the hazardous waste involved; (4) the degree of involvement by the parties in the generation, transportation, treatment, storage or disposal of the hazardous waste; (5) the degree of care exercised by the parties with respect to the hazardous waste concerned, taking into account the characteristic of such waste; and (6) the degree of cooperation by

the parties with federal, state or local officials to prevent any harm to the public health or the environment." *See, e.g., Seneca Meadows, Inc. v. ECI Liquidating, Inc.*, 427 F. Supp. 2d 279, 292 (W.D.N.Y. 2006). The Gore factors, named for then-Congressman Al Gore, were part of a proposed amendment to CERCLA that would have made the Gore factors the basis for allocating liability. *Id.* at 292 n.10. Given that these factors were considered, but ultimately removed as a part of the proposed amendment, is it appropriate that courts make reference to them?

Other factors courts have considered include "the financial resources of the liable parties; the extent of the benefit that the parties received from the hazardous waste disposal practices; the extent of the parties' knowledge and awareness of the environmental contamination of the site; the efforts made, if any, to prevent environmental harm; and the efforts made to settle the case." *Id.* at 292. Finally, some courts distill these many factors into four "critical factors": (1) the extent to which cleanup costs are attributable to wastes for which a party is responsible; (2) the party's level of culpability; (3) the degree to which the party benefited from disposal of the waste; and (4) the party's ability to pay its share of the cost. *See United States v. Davis*, 31 F. Supp. 2d 45, 63 (D.R.I. 1998), *aff'd*, 261 F.3d 1 (2001).

Which of these factors should courts weigh most heavily in determining each PRP's equitable share of response costs? The *Consolidation Coal* court relied only on some of these factors, and doubled one PRP's equitable share because it had not cooperated with the government's cleanup efforts. Would it be preferable for courts to take a more uniform approach to equitable allocation, so that PRPs could anticipate what actions might lessen their required contribution? For example, if all courts doubled a PRP's contribution for failure to cooperate with a government cleanup effort, would this ensure cooperation from more PRPs? Or would a standardized approach prevent courts from taking into account the facts and circumstances of each individual case?

3.   Divisibility and Contribution. Courts routinely hold PRPs jointly and severally liable after determining that the harm caused is indivisible, and then proceed to allocate responsibility for cleanup costs in contribution actions. Does it make sense to say that a harm is indivisible and therefore not capable of apportionment for the purposes of determining whether joint and several liability attaches, but nonetheless is capable of apportionment in a contribution action?

4.   Role of Equitable Factors. Most courts have held that equitable factors have no role in determining whether joint and several liability attaches. The only place that equitable factors are considered are in actions for contribution. *See, e.g., United States v. Hercules, Inc.*, 247 F.3d 706, 717–18 (8th Cir.), *cert. denied*, 534 U.S. 1065 (2001); *United States v. Burlington Northern & Santa Fe Ry. Co.*, 502 F.3d 781, 799–800 (9th Cir. 2007) ("Assuring fairness among PRPs is the proper subject of the contribution stage, not of apportionment at the liability stage. . . . Any court-created structure that would allow PRPs to whittle their share to little or nothing and leave the taxpayers holding the bag may seem more equitable to some PRPs but would violate the basic structure of the CERCLA statutory scheme."). However, a few courts have incorporated the Gore factors into the divisibility inquiry, including *Bell Petroleum*, where the court considered volume, which is one of the Gore factors, at the liability stage. *See United States v. A & F Materials Co.*, 578 F. Supp. 1249, 1256–57 (S.D. Ill. 1984); *Allied Corp. v. Acme Solvents Reclaiming, Inc.*, 691 F. Supp. 1100, 1116–17 (N.D. Ill. 1988). If equitable factors are considered at the divisibility stage, how does this affect whether PRPs or taxpayers will wind up paying for the contamination caused by PRPs that are insolvent or cannot be located?

5.   Allocations of Zero. There are a number of cases in which courts have allocated no response costs at all to a party that is liable as a PRP. *See, e.g.*, *PMC, Inc. v. Sherwin-Williams Co.*, 151 F.3d 610, 616 (7th Cir. 1998) (allocating no costs to one PRP even though that PRP was responsible for some dumping at the site), *cert. denied*, 525 U.S. 1104 (1999); *Envtl. Transp. Sys., Inc. v. ENSCO, Inc.*, 969 F.2d 503 (7th Cir. 1992) (allocating all of the response costs to one PRP because that PRP was the sole cause of the release). In what ways is this different to finding that the harm is divisible at the liability stage?

6.   Recovery of Costs Incurred in Cleanup by a Private Non-PRP. *NCR Corp. v. George A. Whiting Paper Co.*, 768 F.3d 682 (7th Cir. 2014), dealt in part with a situation where a corporation that was not a PRP contributed to cleanup costs. Appvion was identified by EPA as a PRP with respect to certain pollution in the Fox River, Wisconsin. Pursuant to an administrative order, it contributed towards the cost of cleanup. However, Appvion was later found by the district court not be a PRP. The issue was how Appvion was to recover the amount it had paid from other PRPs. The court held that a § 113(f) action was not available, as a right of contribution only exists between joint tortfeasors, and Appvion was not liable as a tortfeasor. *Id.* at 690–91. Ordinarily, a party that has resolved its liability to the United States or a state in an administrative or judicial settlement cannot proceed under § 107(a). *See Bernstein v. Bankert*, 733 F.3d 190, 201–02 (7th Cir. 2012), *cert. denied*, 571 U.S. 1175 (2014). Nonetheless, the court found that Appvion could sue under § 107(a), on the basis that Appvion was not legally obligated to contribute towards the cleanup. Its contribution was therefore best characterized, in retrospect, as "wholly voluntary." *NCR Corp.* at 694. Does § 107(a) allow such a result?

iv.   SETTLEMENT

Superfund has been criticized for generating protracted, inefficient multiple-party litigation, which often gives rise to costs far in excess of the costs of remediation. *See* Marc L. Frohman, *Rethinking the Partial Settlement Credit Rule in Private Party CERCLA Actions: An Argument in Support of the Pro Tanto Credit Rule*, 66 U. COLO. L. REV. 711, 712 (1995). Rather than participate in complex litigation of this nature, there exist significant incentives on the part of individual PRPs and plaintiffs to reach settlement. In the context of multiple-party actions, however, when a plaintiff enters into settlement with fewer than all defendants, a question arises concerning how the liability of the remaining defendants will be reduced.

There exist two methods by which residual liability may be reduced. Under the *pro tanto* approach, residual liability is reduced by the amount of the settlement—meaning that if the plaintiff settles with some defendants for less than their share, the other PRPs are responsible for all remaining costs should the plaintiff succeed in the litigation against them. Under the *proportionate share* approach, residual liability is reduced by the share of the total fault attributed to the settling defendants—meaning that the plaintiff must bear the cost of any reduced settlements. *See Akzo Nobel Coatings, Inc. v. Aigner Corp.*, 197 F.3d 302, 306–08 (7th Cir. 1999) (discussing *pro tanto* and proportionate share rules); *see also* Lewis A. Kornhauser & Richard L. Revesz, *Sharing Damages Among Multiple Tortfeasors*, 98 YALE L.J. 831, 842–43 (1989). In the words of one commentator, the application of these methods "directly influences the likelihood that settlement will occur, the equitable effect of the partial settlement on the settlor, the plaintiff, and the non-settlors, and judicial economy." Frohman, *supra*, at 714.

Section 113(f)(2) governs settlements between PRPs and the government. It prescribes the *pro tanto* approach, providing that ". . . [partial settlement] does not discharge any of the other [PRPs] unless its terms so provide, but it reduces the potential liability of the others by the amount of the settlement." 42 U.S.C. § 9613(f)(2). Settlements between PRPs in private cost recovery actions (discussed in Section 3.E below) and in private contribution actions, however, are not governed by § 113(f)(2). In these contexts, courts have, for the most part, rejected the *pro tanto* approach and adopted instead the proportionate share approach. *See, e.g., Edward Hines Lumber Co. v. Vulcan Materials Co.*, 685 F. Supp. 651 (N.D. Ill. 1988), *aff'd*, 861 F.2d 155 (7th Cir. 1988); *Lyncott Corp. v. Chem. Waste Mgmt.*, 690 F. Supp. 1409 (E.D. Pa. 1988); *United States v. W. Processing Co.*, 756 F. Supp. 1424 (W.D. Wash. 1990). The following case, *Atlantic Richfield Co. v. American Airlines, Inc.*, 836 F. Supp. 763 (N.D. Okla. 1993), is one of the few examples in which courts have adopted the *pro tanto* approach in this context.

Atlantic Richfield Co. v. American Airlines, Inc.

836 F. Supp. 763 (N.D. Okla. 1993).

■ BRETT, DISTRICT JUDGE:

[In 1988, the plaintiff entered into a consent decree with EPA under which it agreed to perform site cleanup and reimburse EPA for its oversight costs. The plaintiff, in turn, filed response cost and contribution claims against approximately 400 PRPs. The majority of these were settled on the basis of volume contribution. Five years after the consent agreement was entered into, a U.S. Magistrate Judge considered and granted the plaintiff's motion to adopt the *pro tanto* credit rule with respect to the residual liability. Fairness hearings were conducted with respect to each of the settlement agreements and no evidence of collusion or unfair settlement was detected. According to the magistrate, because the plaintiff had agreed, pursuant to its consent order, to perform a cleanup that was "in the first instance the burden of the United States, equity dictates that it should be afforded the same consideration" of settlement under the *pro tanto* rule. The defendants appealed to the district court.]

. . . The issue before the Court is the proper credit rule to apply to any future recovery against non-settling defendants. A number of courts have discussed the application of the *pro tanto* and proportionate credit rules as they apply to cases brought pursuant to the Comprehensive Environmental, Response, Compensation, and Liability Act ("CERCLA"). *See* Magistrate's Report and Recommendation of March 3, 1993, pp. 6–7. The *pro tanto* approach is contained in the Uniform Contribution Among Tortfeasors Act (UCATA), which provides contribution protection to all settling parties and reduces the amount of the non-settling parties' liability by the dollar amount of the settlements. This approach requires the Court to conduct a "fairness hearing" prior to approving a partial settlement.

The proportionate approach is used in the Uniform Comparative Fault Act (UCFA) to handle partial settlements. This approach results in the reduction of the plaintiff's claim by the percentage of the settling defendant's causal fault, which must be determined at trial, where total damages and the percentage of the settling defendants' proportionate fault are found.

The Magistrate's Report and Recommendation includes a thorough explanation of the development of the case law and discusses the practical and policy considerations relevant to this issue. The Magistrate concluded that the application of the proportionate or *pro tanto* approach is a matter left to the Court's discretion and should be determined on a case by case basis in an effort to both reach an equitable result and further the goals of CERCLA. . . .

Prior to 1986, CERCLA did not include a provision dealing with settlements or the proper apportionment methodology to be used when plaintiffs entered into partial settlements. *United States v. Conservation Chemical Co.*, 628 F. Supp. 391 (W.D.Mo.1985). Congress subsequently provided some guidance on the issue in the Superfund Amendments and Reauthorization Act of 1986 ("SARA"), Pub.L. 99–499, § 113(f), which provides in pertinent part:

> . . . A person who has resolved its liability to the United States or a State in an administrative or judicially approved settlement shall not be liable for claims for contribution regarding matters addressed in the settlement. Such settlement does not discharge any of the other potentially liable persons unless its terms so provide, but it reduces the potential liability of the others by the amount of the settlement.

This amendment clearly adopted the contribution bar and *pro tanto* credit rule for administrative or judicially approved settlements involving the United States or a State. However, it did not explicitly provide which credit rule should be applied to settlements when the cost recovery action is brought by a private party, rather than the United States or a State.

Several courts have continued to follow the analysis and reasoning of *Conservation Chemical* and have applied the proportionate credit rule to settlements involving private parties, despite Congress' express adoption of the *pro tanto* rule for partial settlements with the government. *E.g. Edward Hines Lumber Co. v. Vulcan Materials Co.*, 685 F. Supp. 651 (D.C.Ill.1988), *aff'd*, 861 F.2d 155 (7th Cir.1988); *Lyncott Corp. v. Chemical Waste Management*, 690 F. Supp. 1409 (E.D.Pa.1988); and *United States v. Western Processing Co., Inc.*, 756 F. Supp. 1424 (W.D.Wash.1990). These courts concluded that Congress only intended for the *pro tanto* rule to be applied in actions brought by the Government and that policy and practical considerations still favored the application of the proportionate rule in actions brought by private parties.

Other courts have viewed the passage of SARA as an indication that Congress has rejected the UCFA approach and the proportionate credit rule. *Allied Corp. v. Frola*, 730 F. Supp. 626 (D.N.J.1990); *United States v. Cannons Engr. Corp.*, 720 F. Supp. 1027 (D.C.Mass.1989), *aff'd*, 899 F.2d 79 (1st Cir.1990); and *United States v. Rohm & Haas Co.*, 721 F. Supp. 666 (D.N.J.1989). Neither the Tenth Circuit Court of Appeals nor this Court has yet addressed the issue of the proper credit rule to be applied in CERCLA cases brought by private parties.

Although the majority of Courts that have been faced with this issue have applied the proportionate rule, this Court concludes that it has the discretion to apply the credit rule which under the facts of the instant case will best achieve the overriding objectives of CERCLA. Upon consideration of all the facts and circumstances of this particular case, the Court concludes the *pro tanto* rule is superior to the proportionate rule in this instance. . . .

Adoption of the proportionate rule in this case would substantially complicate Plaintiff's trial task and expose Plaintiff to the risk of a less than full recovery. On the other hand, adoption of the *pro tanto* approach in this case will assure Plaintiff of a full recovery and apparently will not leave the non-settling defendants with an inequitable share of the costs. The Court does not share Defendants concern that application of the *pro tanto* rule will result in the non-settling defendants being assessed an inequitable portion of the response costs.

Furthermore, the prospect of conducting "fairness hearings" does not dissuade this Court from applying the *pro tanto* credit rule in this case. The Court has conducted an evidentiary hearing on the fairness of the [previous settlement] and has concluded that the settlement was in good faith and is fair to the non-settling defendants. The Court has also previously found that the settlements were entered into in good faith and with certain minor exceptions, the parties have stipulated the . . . settlements were fair. Although "fairness hearings" do take the Court's time, they also simplify trial.

In summary, the Court concludes the selection of the proper credit rule is a matter that has been left to the Court's discretion, to be evaluated on a case-by-case basis. In this particular instance, the Court concludes application of the *pro tanto* rule will best achieve the objectives of CERCLA by encouraging settlement, simplifying trial and equitably distributing cost.

NOTES AND QUESTIONS

1.   ***Pro Tanto* Rule and Incentives to Settle.** According to the *Atlantic Richfield (ARCO)* court, one of the potential benefits of the *pro tanto* rule is that it would provide better incentives for settlement. Why would this be the case? Under what circumstances, however, may the *pro tanto* approach give rise to incentives on the part of defendants to hold out from settlement? Would these same incentives be created under the proportionate share approach?

2.   ***Pro Tanto* and Equity.** The *pro tanto* rule is often criticized on the basis that it undermines equitable apportionment, because the dollar-for-dollar credit results in a distribution of losses among defendants that is not based upon comparative fault. Why was this not a concern to the *ARCO* court? On what evidentiary finding of the magistrate did the district court rely? Why do proponents of the proportionate share approach claim it to be superior to the *pro tanto* approach on grounds of equity?

3.   ***Pro Tanto* and Collusion.** In what way may the *pro tanto* approach encourage collusion between the plaintiff and the settlor? Was this considered by the *ARCO* court? In what way was the *ARCO* court satisfied that there was no collusion in that instance? Do the evidentiary inquiries necessary to dispel collusion outweigh the efficiency gains attributed to the *pro tanto* approach by the *ARCO* court? Is there scope for the proportionate share approach to be manipulated by collusion?

4.   ***Pro Tanto* and Proportionate Share.** The *ARCO* court did not declare the *pro tanto* approach to be superior to the proportionate share approach in all circumstances. Instead, it called for an evaluation of the appropriate response on a case-by-case basis. What factors would be relevant to this determination? In what circumstances should courts apply the *pro tanto* approach? When should courts apply the proportionate share approach?

5.   **Joint Tortfeasors and Joint and Several Liability.** In *United States v. Atlantic Research Corp.*, the Supreme Court recognized that there may be "overlap" cases, where a forced remediator has a cause of action under both § 107(a)'s cost recovery provision and § 113(f)'s right of contribution. 551 U.S. 128, 139 n.6 (2007). The Court stated: "We do not decide whether these compelled costs of response are recoverable under

§ 113(f), § 107(a), or both." *Id.* The Court also declined to decide, in footnote 7, whether § 107(a) provides for joint and several liability although it assumed that it does. *Id.* at 140 n.7. The *Atlantic Research* Court thus left open the possibility that a § 113(f) contribution counterclaim by a joint tortfeasor could wipe-out joint and several liability under § 107(a); or conversely, that joint and several liability could preclude a contribution counterclaim allowing the § 107(a) plaintiff full recovery of response costs.

Post-*Atlantic Research*, two district courts have adopted a middle-of-the-road approach. Both held that private parties liable under CERCLA, for whom a § 113(f) contribution claim was an option, could pursue § 107(a) claims imposing joint and severable liability on other liable parties. *Raytheon Aircraft Co. v. United States*, 532 F. Supp. 2d 1306 (D. Kan. 2007); *In re Dana Corp.*, 379 B.R. 449 (S.D.N.Y. 2007). Both courts found that § 113(f) counterclaims by § 107(a) defendants would not defeat joint and several liability, but that contribution counterclaims could be used to equitably address concerns regarding the § 107(a) plaintiff's own liability. *Raytheon Aircraft*, 532 F. Supp. 2d at 1310–11; *In re Dana Corp.*, 379 B.R. at 460.

6. Contribution Protection for Settling Parties. Section 113(f)(2) provides that parties who settle with the government "shall not be liable for claims for contribution regarding matters addressed in the settlement." 42 U.S.C. § 9613(f)(2). The Supreme Court's decision in *Atlantic Research* opened the door for § 107 actions against settling parties, which the government argued would reduce incentives for parties to settle. Notably, § 107's imposition of joint and several liability exposes settling parties to liability for potentially significant "orphan shares" of cleanup costs assumed by other PRPs or third parties. This issue highlights the tensions between Congress' intent to encourage rapid cleanups through the promise of § 107 cost recovery and its intent under SARA to protect settling parties from open-ended liability.

If significant orphan shares exist, are settlement incentives retained for PRPs when a non-PRP makes a § 107(a) cost recovery claim against parties that have settled their liability with the government? How does a § 113(f) contribution counterclaim against other PRPs that have been found joint and severally liable affect the issue of orphan share liability for settling parties?

7. Settlement Incentives. Joint and several liability creates different incentives for plaintiffs and defendants to settle before trial under different circumstances, depending on whether the probability that the plaintiff will prevail against one defendant is independent from, or correlated to, the probability that the plaintiff will prevail against the other defendant. To illustrate the incentives created by these two different scenarios, assume a hypothetical with one plaintiff, P; two fully solvent, non-collusive defendants, A and B; total cleanup costs of $100; joint and several liability; and litigation costs of zero.

First assume that there is no correlation in the probabilities that P will prevail against A and B—that is, whether or not P wins against A does not affect the likelihood that P will win against B. Assume that there is a 50%

likelihood that P will prevail against each defendant. If P litigates against both A and B, there are four possible outcomes: P wins against both; P loses against both; P wins against A but loses against B; or P wins against B but loses against A. If P wins against one or more defendant—as is the case in three of the four possible outcomes—then P will recover the full $100, because with joint and several liability each defendant is potentially liable for the full cost of cleanup. So, because each of the four possible outcomes is equally likely, A has a 75 percent chance of recovering $100. Its expected recovery is therefore $75.

If P's expected recovery is $75, then P would be willing to settle with both A and B for $37.50 each, assuming P is risk neutral. However, if P first settles only with A for $37.50, then the most that B could be held liable for at trial under the *pro tanto* settlement rule is $62.50. Because there is still a 50 percent likelihood that P will prevail against B, this means that P's expected recovery at trial, and B's expected loss, is now only $31.25. So if P offers B the same settlement that P offered A—$37.50—B will reject it. Moreover, P's total recovery has now been reduced by settling with one defendant: P will now get the $37.50 from the settlement with A, and an expected recovery of $31.25 from going to trial with B. So, where P's expected recovery before settling was $75, P's expected recovery after settling with one defendant is reduced to $68.75. If P realizes that settling with A will have the effect of reducing P's total recovery, then P will not make a settlement offer to A in the first place. Accordingly, under joint and several liability, where both defendants are solvent and there is no correlation in the probabilities that P will prevail against each defendant, there are disincentives to settle and cases will go to trial if transaction costs are sufficiently low.

Now assume that the probabilities that P will prevail against each defendant are perfectly correlated—that is, if P wins against one defendant P will always also win against the other, and if P loses against one P will always also lose against the other. Again assume that there is a 50% likelihood that P will prevail against each defendant. If P litigates against A and B, there are now only two possible outcomes: either P wins against both A and B, or loses against both. If P wins against both defendants, P will recover the full $100, and if P loses against both, P will recover nothing. Because each outcome is equally likely, under this scenario P's expected recovery is only $50.

If P's expected recovery is $50, then P would be willing to settle with both A and B for $25 each (again assuming that P is risk neutral). If P settles with A first for $25, then the most that B could be held liable for at trial is $75. Because there is still a 50% likelihood that P will prevail against B, this means that P's expected recovery at trial, and B's expected loss, has now increased to $37.50. So, if P offers B a settlement of $37.50, B will accept it. P's total recovery has now increased to $62.50 ($25 from the settlement with A plus $37.50 from the settlement with B), and if P realizes that settling will increase P's expected recovery, then P will make settlement offers to both A and B. Accordingly, under joint and several liability, where both defendants are solvent and there is perfect correlation in the probabilities that P will prevail against each defendant, there are incentives to settle.

Which of these scenarios seems more likely: that the probabilities of P's success against two defendants will be correlated, or that they will not? How would these outcomes change if one or more of the defendants was not fully solvent? How would they change if litigation costs were taken into account? Or if the defendants' shares of the total liability are very dissimilar? *See* Lewis A. Kornhauser & Richard L. Revesz, *Multidefendant Settlements: The Impact of Joint and Several Liability*, 23 J. LEGAL STUD. 41 (1994); Lewis A. Kornhauser & Richard L. Revesz, *Multidefendant Settlements Under Joint and Several Liability: The Problem of Insolvency*, 23 J. LEGAL STUD. 517 (1994). How would the incentives look under the proportionate share rule?

8. *De Minimis* **Settlement Provisions.** Courts have found ways to limit the CERCLA liability of parties that have contributed only minimally to the contamination at a hazardous waste site—for example, through finding that the harm is divisible with respect to a given party's contribution, as in *Alcan*, *supra*, or by limiting or eliminating a party's share of the costs in a contribution action. However, resolving these issues through litigation may be time-consuming and involve very large litigation costs; these costs can be particularly crippling to small businesses that contributed only nominally to an environmental harm and do not have the resources for extensive litigation. Recognizing this problem, Congress in 1986 added a *de minimis* settlement provision to CERCLA. Pub. L. No. 99–499, § 113(b), 100 Stat. 1613, 1648 (codified at 42 U.S.C. § 122(g) (1986)). Under the *de minimis* settlement provision, the government is encouraged to reach a settlement with PRPs if either of two sets of conditions are met: First, both the amount and the toxic or hazardous effects of the substances contributed by the PRP are minimal; or second, the PRP is a landowner that did not conduct or permit the disposal of hazardous substances on their property and did not contribute to the release or threatened release. 42 U.S.C. § 9622(g).

EPA was initially slow to pursue *de minimis* settlements under § 122(g), *see* Lewis A. Kornhauser & Richard L. Revesz, *De Minimis Settlements Under Superfund: An Empirical Study*, in ANALYZING SUPERFUND: ECONOMICS, SCIENCE, AND LAW 187 (Richard L. Revesz & Richard B. Stewart eds., 1995), but has since begun using the *de minimis* settlement provisions more frequently. In addition to the *de minimis* settlement provisions, in 2002 Congress added a "*de micromis*" settlement provision to CERCLA as part of the Small Business Liability Relief and Brownfields Revitalization Act, Pub. L. No. 107–118, § 102, 115 Stat. 2356, 2356–57 (2002). The *de micromis* settlement provisions entirely exempt from liability generators or transporters who contribute less than a certain minimum amount of waste to a given facility. 42 U.S.C. § 9607(o).

Because Congress has explicitly created avenues to resolve the liability of PRPs that are less culpable, should courts relieve less culpable PRPs from liability on different grounds, as the *Alcan* court did? Or should the avenues provided by Congress be the sole means for less culpable PRPs to resolve their liability? Remember that even if a PRP is found to be liable, in a contribution action a court may find that their equitable share of the costs is small or even nothing. *See, e.g., Seneca Meadows, Inc. v. ECI Liquidating, Inc.*, 427 F. Supp. 2d 279, 292 (W.D.N.Y. 2006).

9.   *Pioneer Metals*: The Effect of Settlement on Contribution Actions. Once a PRP defendant enters into a settlement with the United States or a state, it is no longer liable to other PRPs in an action for contribution. 42 U.S.C. § 9613(f)(2). This protection from liability applies only to costs that are the subject of the settlement; a PRP may still be pursued in a contribution action for other categories of costs arising from the same facility or incident. *See Am. Cyanamid Co. v. Capuano*, 381 F.3d 6, 18 (1st Cir. 2004) (PRP was immune from contribution actions for past response costs that were the subject of a settlement, but could still be held liable in contribution actions for future response costs at the same site). While settling parties are immune from further contribution actions, a settling party may itself pursue other non-settling parties for contribution, provided their claims do not interfere with cost-recovery actions by the United States or a state. 42 U.S.C. § 9613(f)(3). Sections 113(f)(3) and 113(f)(1), which authorizes contribution actions "during or following" a civil action, provide two distinct avenues for contribution; therefore, a PRP that does not meet the civil action requirement of § 113(f)(1) may still potentially seek contribution under § 113(f)(3). *See Pioneer Metals, Inc. v. Univar USA, Inc.*, 168 Fed. Appx. 335 (11th Cir. 2006). Why should a party that has entered into a settlement with the government for a specific amount be allowed to pursue other PRPs for a portion of their settlement costs?

10.   Court Scrutiny of Proposed Settlements. In 2010, Arizona entered into early settlement agreements with 18 of 22 PRPs with respect to a hazardous waste site in Tucson, Arizona. Consistent with § 113(f)(2), the agreements also released the settling parties from any obligation to pay a contribution to non-settling parties in the future. Arizona's motion to enter consent decrees explained that the total cost of remediation was estimated to be $75 million, and the liability of the settling parties was estimated to be 0.01 to 0.2 percent of the total costs. In approving the consent decrees, the district court did not discuss the parties' individual or aggregate settlement amounts, deferring to the state's judgment that "the public interest is best served through the entry of th[e] agreement[s]." *Arizona v. City of Tuscon*, 761 F.3d 1005, 1009 (9th Cir. 2014), *cert. denied*, 136 S. Ct. 30 (2015). The approval of the consent decrees was overturned on appeal.

The Ninth Circuit held that in approving a CERCLA consent decree, a court has an "obligation to independently scrutinize the terms of [the agreement]." *Id.* at 1012. To do so, the court must "gauge the adequacy of settlement amounts to be paid by settling [parties by comparing] the proportion of total projected costs to be paid by the settlors with the proportion of liability attributable to them, and then . . . factor into the equation any reasonable discount for litigation risks, time savings, and the like." *Id.* It noted that greater deference might be shown to federal agencies than to state entities. *Id.* at 1014. How might the obligation on a court to scrutinize a consent decree affect the settlement negotiations?

In dissent, Judge Callahan stated that the majority's decision will "significantly restrict state agencies' ability to enter into early CERCLA consent decrees to the detriment of the environment, the statutory framework envisioned by Congress, and PRPs seeking to resolve their liability early in the process." *Id.* at 1027. Are these concerns well-founded? Are there countervailing concerns?

11. Estimating Cleanup Costs. In 2001, GAO reviewed EPA procedures for estimating cleanup costs at Superfund sites. Generally, when settling with a PRP, EPA and the PRP must agree on the cost of a cleanup before they can reach a settlement regarding which party will be responsible for each portion of the cost. GAO criticized EPA for essentially accepting contractors' estimates of how much the work would cost. GAO argued that EPA could get a better price from contractors if EPA managers calculated their own cost estimates and used those figures in negotiations with contractors. GAO also pointed out that it would be advisable for EPA to collect and store data on the prices awarded for contracts to see where its money was being spent, and so that future project managers would have an idea of how much certain projects should cost. GAO, EPA'S COST-ESTIMATING INITIATIVES SHOW PROMISE AND SHOULD BE MONITORED (2001).

12. Designing Joint and Several Liability Regimes. This part has described the application of joint and several liability under CERCLA. The CERCLA regime could, however, have been designed differently. The following passage identifies seven choices in designing a legal regime, each of which can affect the economic analysis of the consequences of joint and several liability:

> First, a right of contribution permits a defendant that has paid a disproportionately large share of the plaintiff's damages as a result of the application of joint and several liability to obtain compensation from a defendant that has paid a disproportionately small share of these damages. Absent a right of contribution, such reallocation is not possible. Second, contribution shares are usually determined either *pro rata* (equal division among the defendants) or by reference to comparative fault.
>
> Third, the question of an appropriate set-off rule arises when the plaintiff settles with one defendant and litigates against the other. Under the *pro tanto* set-off rule, the plaintiff's claim against the non-settling defendant is reduced by the amount of the settlement. In contrast, under the apportioned share set-off rule (sometimes referred to as a proportional set-off rule), the plaintiff's claim against the non-settling defendant is reduced by the share of the liability attributable to the settling defendant.
>
> Fourth, under the *pro tanto* set-off rule, when one defendant settles and the other litigates and ultimately loses, the question arises whether the settling defendant is protected from contribution actions. Fifth, the legal regime must also specify whether settling defendants are entitled to bring contribution actions against defendants who settled for less than their share of the liability.
>
> Sixth, under the *pro tanto* set-off, if the plaintiff enters into an inadequately low settlement with one defendant, the other

defendant is responsible for the shortfall if it litigates and loses. To protect the interests of non-settling defendants, courts sometimes require "good faith" hearings on the adequacy of settlements.

Seventh, if the plaintiff joins all the joint tortfeasors in a single suit, its claims against all of them will be adjudicated in the same proceeding. If the plaintiff chooses not to join all the tortfeasors as defendants, the question arises whether a named defendant can join another tortfeasor as a third-party defendant. Otherwise, the named defendant would have to file a separate action for contribution after the adjudication of its liability to the plaintiff.

Lewis A. Kornhauser & Richard L. Revesz, *Joint and Several Liability, in* 2 THE NEW PALGRAVE DICTIONARY OF ECONOMICS AND THE LAW 371 (Peter Newman ed., 1998). Consider each of the seven choices in turn. What choices have been made in the context of CERCLA? Specify in each case whether your answer has been informed by CERCLA, by case law concerning CERCLA, or by a different body of law altogether. Do you think that the choices made in the context of CERCLA give rise to optimal economic incentives? What choices provide better deterrent effects? What choices create better incentives for proper and efficient cleanups?

13. Joint and Several Liability and Fairness. Should a system of joint and several liability be considered superior to a system of non-joint liability on grounds of fairness?

Lewis A. Kornhauser and Richard L. Revesz identify four principal issues relevant to this question. The first three arise in circumstances in which the defendants are fully solvent:

    (i)   the size of the plaintiff's expected recovery when she litigates against the defendants;

    (ii)   the division of the plaintiff's recovery among litigating defendants; and

    (iii) the effects of settlements.

The fourth issue arises in circumstances in which the defendants have limited solvency:

    (iv) the division of the burden of insolvency between the plaintiff and the solvent defendant.

See Lewis A. Kornhauser & Richard L. Revesz, *Joint Tortfeasors, in* ENCYCLOPEDIA OF LAW AND ECONOMICS 637 (Boudewijn Bouckaert & Gerrit D. Geest eds., 2000). As noted by Kornhauser and Revesz: "[a] question relevant to all four issues is whether one should assess fairness *ex ante* (in terms of the parties' expected payments) or *ex post* (in terms of the actual payments in particular cases)." *Id.* at 637.

With respect to the first issue, it is clear that unless the plaintiff's probabilities of success against the defendants are perfectly correlated, joint and several liability leads to a higher expected recovery than non-joint liability. As a consequence, this will result in a transfer of resources from the defendants to the plaintiff. When will this transfer be fair? Contrast the circumstance in which the defendants are liable and the plaintiff has difficulty proving liability, against the circumstance in which there exists true uncertainty about whether the defendants are liable.

With respect to the second issue, Kornhauser and Revesz conclude that "joint and several liability performs badly." *Id.* at 638. Why would this be the case?

With respect to the third issue, consider the implications of the *pro tanto* set-off rule. Which party will bear a disproportionate burden of the liability? Which party benefits from the application of the rule? How does this differ from a non-joint liability regime? Which regime produces fairer outcomes? *See id.* at 639–40.

With respect to the fourth issue, contrast the circumstance in which the plaintiff's probabilities of success against each defendant are perfectly correlated, against the circumstance in which the plaintiff's probabilities of success against each defendant are not correlated. In each case, which party will bear the shortfall of the insolvent defendant? What are the fairness implications in terms of allocating liability among defendants? What are the fairness implications in terms of allocating liability between the plaintiff on the one hand and the defendants on the other? How does this compare with non-joint liability? *See id.* at 640–41.

E. PRIVATE COST RECOVERY ACTIONS

This section addresses those circumstances in which a PRP voluntarily undertakes the cleanup of a Superfund site and subsequently seeks to recover a portion of those costs from other PRPs. As discussed above, following the enactment of SARA, courts read CERCLA as providing two distinct remedies: a cost recovery remedy under § 107 and a contribution remedy under § 113. *See, e.g., United Techs. Corp. v. Browning-Ferris Indus.*, 33 F.3d 96, 98–100 (1st Cir. 1994) ("CERCLA and SARA together create two different kinds of legal actions by which parties can recoup some or all of the costs associated with cleanups."), *cert. denied*, 513 U.S. 1183 (1995). There are several critical differences between liability under §§ 107 and 113—most importantly, a cost recovery action under § 107 imposes joint and several liability on the defendants, unless the defendant can demonstrate that the causes of the harm are divisible. An action for contribution under § 113, on the other hand, invokes the court's equitable powers to determine the appropriate allocation of liability and cannot impose joint and several liability. *Elementis Chromium L.P. v. Coastal States Petroleum Co.*, 450 F.3d 607, 612 (5th Cir. 2006).

With both of these remedies available, courts were confronted with questions of which remedy was available when, and to which parties. A party that was not a PRP was clearly entitled to recover costs under § 107. Courts were concerned, however, that allowing a PRP to proceed under the § 107 cost recovery provision would enable that PRP to become immune from joint and several liability while imposing it upon other PRPs. Proceeding under § 107 would also enable a PRP to evade the shorter three-year statute of limitations that governed actions for contribution under § 113(g). *See, e.g., New Castle Cty. v. Halliburton NUS Corp.*, 111 F.3d 1116, 1123 (3d Cir. 1997); *Pinal Creek Grp. v. Newmont Mining Corp.*, 118 F.3d 1298, 1304 (9th Cir. 1997), *cert. denied*, 524 U.S. 937 (1998).

Following SARA, many circuits held that PRPs could not bring an action against other PRPs for cost recovery under § 107. *See, e.g., Bedford Affiliates v. Sills*, 156 F.3d 416, 423–24 (2d Cir. 1998); *Centerior Serv. Co. v. Acme Scrap Iron & Metal Corp.*, 153 F.3d 344, 349–56 (6th Cir. 1998); *Pneumo Abex Corp. v. High Point, Thomasville & Denton R.R.*, 142 F.3d 769, 776 (4th Cir.), *cert. denied*, 525 U.S. 963 (1998); *Pinal Creek Grp.*, 118 F.3d at 1301–06; *New Castle Cty.*, 111 F.3d at 1120–24; *Redwing Carriers, Inc. v. Saraland Apartments*, 94 F.3d 1489, 1496 & n.7 (11th Cir. 1996); *United States v. Colorado & E. R.R.*, 50 F.3d 1530, 1534–36 (10th Cir. 1995); *United Techs. Corp.*, 33 F.3d at 98–103. While these courts found that PRPs could not bring cost recovery actions under § 107, there was some confusion over whether a PRP that did not satisfy the civil action requirement of § 113—that the action be brought in or during a civil action under § 107(a)—could nevertheless demand contribution from other PRPs under § 107. *See United Techs. Corp.*, 33 F.3d at 99 n.8 (acknowledging that "[i]t is possible that, although falling outside the statutory parameters established for an express cause of action for contribution [under § 113(f)] . . . a PRP who spontaneously initiates a cleanup without governmental prodding might be able to pursue an implied right of action for contribution under [§ 107]").

In 2004, the Supreme Court held that PRPs that did not satisfy the civil action requirement of § 113(f) could not bring a contribution action under that provision. *Cooper Indus. v. Aviall Servs.*, 543 U.S. 157 (2004). The Court was silent, however, concerning whether § 107 was available, and if so, whether the available action under § 107 was a cost recovery action or an implied right to contribution.

Following *Aviall*, courts took three different positions on how cost-sharing actions should be structured in the context of a voluntary cleanup by a PRP. First, some courts found that § 107 did not authorize any type of cost recovery by PRPs, and that § 113 was the sole avenue through which PRPs may recover costs from other PRPs. This meant that a PRP that voluntarily cleaned up a contaminated site had no way of recovering any portion of the costs of the cleanup. This was the position taken by the district court that originally decided the *Aviall* case, following the remand by the Supreme Court. *Aviall Servs. v. Cooper Indus.*, 2006 WL 2263305 (N.D. Tex. 2006), *vacated*, 2007 WL 5704042 (N.D. Tex. 2007). The Third Circuit also adopted this position. *See E.I. DuPont v. United States*, 460 F.3d 515 (3d Cir. 2006), *vacated*, 551 U.S. 1129 (2007).

Second, some courts held that PRPs could not pursue cost recovery actions under § 107, but they could pursue contribution actions through an implied right to contribution under § 107. In this case, PRPs that voluntarily clean up may always recover costs, but may not impose joint and several liability on other PRPs. *See Pinal Creek Grp.*, 118 F.3d 1298; *W. Props. Serv. Corp. v. Shell Oil Co.*, 358 F.3d 678 (9th Cir. 2004); *Ferguson v. Arcata Redwood Co.*, 2005 WL 1869445 (N.D. Cal.) (citing *Pinal Creek Grp.* for the proposition that the Ninth Circuit "recognized a PRP's right to bring a contribution claim under § 107").

Third, some courts held that a PRP may bring a cost recovery action under § 107. The PRPs that are the subject of that action could then bring a counterclaim for contribution under § 113, since the original suit under § 107 will satisfy the "civil action" requirement of § 113. While allowing PRPs to pursue cost recovery actions under § 107 might enable them to impose joint and several liability on other PRPs without being subject to joint and several liability themselves, if the sued PRPs bring a counterclaim for contribution under § 113, the court can employ equitable factors to distribute costs between all parties, avoiding this problematic result. *See Consol. Edison Co. of N.Y. v. UGI Utils., Inc.*, 423 F.3d 90, 100 n.9, 102 (2d Cir. 2005), *cert. denied*, 551 U.S. 1130 (2007); *Schaefer v. Town of Victor*, 457 F.3d 188 (2d Cir. 2006); *see also* Richard O. Faulk & Cynthia J. Bishop, *There and Back Again: The Progression and Regression of Contribution Actions Under CERCLA*, 18 TUL. ENVTL. L.J. 323, 336 (arguing that the "proper solution may be to revert to the pre-SARA interpretation of § 107 and allow a PRP to file a cost recovery action," triggering the threshold civil action requirement for the defendant PRPs, which can then file a counterclaim for contribution under § 113).

In the following case, the Supreme Court addressed the question that it had left open in *Aviall*: whether PRPs that do not meet the requirements of § 113 may bring a cost recovery action under § 107.

United States v. Atlantic Research Corp.
551 U.S. 128 (2007).

■ JUSTICE THOMAS delivered the opinion for a unanimous Court:

Two provisions of the Comprehensive Environmental Response, Compensation, and Liability Act of 1980 (CERCLA)—§§ 107(a) and 113(f)—allow private parties to recover expenses associated with cleaning up contaminated sites. 42 U.S.C. §§ 9607(a), 9613(f). In this case, we must decide a question left open in *Cooper Industries, Inc. v. Aviall Services, Inc.*, 543 U.S. 157, 161 (2004): whether § 107(a) provides so-called potentially responsible parties (PRPs), 42 U.S.C. §§ 9607(a)(1)–(4), with a cause of action to recover costs from other PRPs. We hold that it does.

The parties' dispute centers on what "other person[s]" may sue under § 107(a)(4)(B). The Government argues that "any other person" refers to any person not identified as a PRP in §§ 107(a)(1)–(4). In other words, subparagraph (B) permits suit only by non-PRPs and thus bars Atlantic Research's claim. Atlantic Research counters that subparagraph (B) takes its cue from subparagraph (A), not the earlier paragraph (1)–(4). In accord with the Court of Appeals, Atlantic Research believes that subparagraph (B) provides a cause of action to anyone except the United States, a State, or an Indian tribe—the persons listed in subparagraph (A). We agree with Atlantic Research.

Statutes must "be read as a whole." *King v. St. Vincent's Hospital*, 502 U.S. 215, 221 (1991). Applying that maxim, the language of subparagraph (B) can be understood only with reference to subparagraph (A). The provisions are adjacent and have remarkably similar structures. Each concerns certain costs that have been incurred by certain entities and that bear a specified relationship to the national contingency plan. Bolstering the structural link, the text also denotes a relationship between the two provisions. By using the phrase "other necessary costs," subparagraph (B) refers to and differentiates the relevant costs from those listed in subparagraph (A).

In light of the relationship between the subparagraphs, it is natural to read the phrase "any other person" by referring to the immediately preceding subparagraph (A), which permits suit only by the United States, a State, or an Indian tribe. The phrase "any other person" therefore means any person other than those three. See 42 U.S.C. § 9601(21) (defining "person" to include the United States and the various States). Consequently, the plain language of subparagraph (B) authorizes cost-recovery actions by any private party, including PRPs. *See Keytronic*, 511 U.S., at 818.

Section 113(f) explicitly grants PRPs a right to contribution. Contribution is defined as the "tortfeasor's right to collect from others responsible for the same tort after the tortfeasor has paid more than his or her proportionate share, the shares being determined as a percentage of fault." Black's Law Dictionary 353 (8th ed.1999). Nothing in § 113(f) suggests that Congress used the term "contribution" in anything other than this traditional sense. The statute authorizes a PRP to seek contribution "during or following" a suit under § 106 or § 107(a). 42 U.S.C. § 9613(f)(1). Thus, § 113(f)(1) permits suit before or after the establishment of common liability. In either case, a PRP's right to contribution under § 113(f)(1) is contingent upon an inequitable distribution of common liability among liable parties.

By contrast, § 107(a) permits recovery of cleanup costs but does not create a right to contribution. A private party may recover under § 107(a) without any establishment of liability to a third party. Moreover, § 107(a) permits a PRP to recover only the costs it has "incurred" in cleaning up a site. 42 U.S.C. § 9607(a)(4)(B). When a party pays to satisfy a settlement agreement or a court judgment, it does not incur its own costs of response. Rather, it reimburses other parties for costs that those parties incurred.

Accordingly, the remedies available in §§ 107(a) and 113(f) complement each other by providing causes of action "to persons in different procedural circumstances." *Consolidated Edison*, 423 F.3d at 99. Section 113(f)(1) authorizes a contribution action to PRPs with common liability stemming from an action instituted under § 106 or § 107(a). And § 107(a) permits cost recovery (as distinct from contribution) by a private party that has itself incurred cleanup costs. Hence, a PRP that pays money to satisfy a settlement agreement or a court judgment may pursue § 113(f) contribution. But by reimbursing response costs paid by other parties, the PRP has not incurred its own costs of response and therefore cannot recover under § 107(a). As a result, though eligible to seek contribution under § 113(f)(1), the PRP cannot simultaneously seek to recover the same expenses under § 107(a). Thus, at least in the case of reimbursement, the PRP cannot choose the 6-year statute of limitations for cost-recovery actions over the shorter limitations period for § 113(f) contribution claims.

For similar reasons, a PRP could not avoid § 113(f)'s equitable distribution of reimbursement costs among PRPs by instead choosing to impose joint and several liability on another PRP in an action under § 107(a).[7] The choice of remedies simply does not exist. In any event, a defendant PRP in such a § 107(a) suit could blunt any inequitable distribution of costs by filing a § 113(f) counterclaim. 459 F.3d at 835. Resolution of a § 113(f) counter-claim would necessitate the equitable apportionment of costs among the liable parties, including the PRP that filed the § 107(a) action. 42 U.S.C. § 9613(f)(a) ("In resolving contribution claims, the court may allocate response costs among liable parties using such equitable factors as the court determines are appropriate").

Because the plain terms of § 107(a)(4)(B) allow a PRP to recover costs from other PRPs, the statute provides Atlantic Research with a cause of action. We therefore affirm the judgment of the Court of Appeals.

NOTES AND QUESTIONS

1. Voluntary Cleanup. In what circumstances would it be in a PRP's interest to voluntarily cleanup a contaminated site? What incentives do each of the three positions outlined above create on the part of PRPs contemplating voluntary cleanup? The Eighth Circuit held that a party that incurs costs pursuant to an administrative order or judicially approved consent decree does not undertake voluntary cleanup under § 107 and thus can only recover under § 113. *Morrison Enters., LLC v. Dravo Corp.*, 638 F.3d 594 (8th Cir.), *cert. denied*, 565 U.S. 879 (2011).

2. Cost Recovery and Contribution. The differences between cost recovery and contribution actions were discussed above. What is the significance of these differences in the context of private parties undertaking voluntary cleanup?

---

[7]   We assume without deciding that § 107(a) provides for joint and several liability.

3. PRPs and Cost Recovery. On what basis did the *Atlantic Research* Court determine that CERCLA allows PRPs to bring cost recovery actions under § 107(a) following voluntary cleanup? Do you agree with the reasoning of the Court?

4. Voluntariness as an Equitable Factor. The effect of allowing cross-claims under § 113(f) is to transform the original cost recovery action into "one for contribution, subject to equitable factors. . . ." *See* Richard O. Faulk & Cynthia J. Bishop, *There and Back Again: The Progression and Regression of Contribution Actions Under CERCLA*, 18 TUL. ENVTL. L.J. 323, 337 (2005). In apportioning liability according to these equitable factors, should courts take into account the fact that the cleanup was undertaken voluntarily? In other words, should the PRP that voluntarily incurred costs be rewarded in the apportionment process? *See id.* Would this create desirable incentives?

F. CLEANUP

In addition to its liability provisions, CERCLA provides guidance on both the process of cleaning up hazardous waste sites and the degree of cleanup required. The process of cleaning up a Superfund site is lengthy, and the environmental standards that the cleanup must meet are high. As you read the materials in this section, consider whether Superfund strikes the right balance between environmental protection and costs.

i. CLEANUP PROCESS

The process of cleaning up hazardous waste sites is governed by the National Contingency Plan (NCP). 40 C.F.R. § 300. The NCP provides the guidelines and procedures for responses to releases and threatened releases of hazardous substances, pollutants, or contaminants. As part of the NCP, CERCLA also requires the establishment of a National Priorities List (NPL) of the hazardous waste sites throughout the country presenting the greatest risk to health, welfare, or the environment. 42 U.S.C. § 9605(a)(8). CERCLA directs EPA to revise the NCP regularly. 42 U.S.C. § 9605(a); *see also* Exec. Order No. 12,580, 52 Fed. Reg. 2923 (1987) (delegating President's authority under CERCLA to EPA, including responsibility for NCP). Under CERCLA, the costs of cleaning up a hazardous waste site are divided into two categories: removal costs, defined at § 101(23), and remedial costs, defined at § 101(24). 42 U.S.C. § 9601(23), (24). Removal actions are short-term cleanup actions that alleviate immediate risks to the public health and environment, § 101(23), while remedial actions are long-term cleanup actions designed to permanently clean up a site to the maximum extent possible, § 101(24). EPA may spend Superfund money on removal actions at any site that poses an imminent risk, but may spend on remedial actions only for sites that have been placed on the NPL. 42 U.S.C. § 9604.

The process of placing sites on the NPL and subsequently initiating remedial actions is lengthy and involves many steps. It is described in the excerpt by Richard L. Revesz and Richard B. Stewart at the beginning of this chapter. In brief, the process begins when EPA is notified, generally by a private party or state agency, of a potential Superfund site. EPA then enters the site into the Superfund Enterprise Management System (SEMS), which, in 2014, replaced EPA's previous inventory of hazardous sites, the Comprehensive Environmental Response, Compensation, and Liability Information System (CERCLIS). As of October 2018, there were 12,890 active sites listed on SEMS. *See* EPA, Superfund Data and Reports, https://www.epa.gov/superfund/ superfund-data-and-reports (last visited Nov. 23, 2018).

EPA then assesses the site to determine whether the contamination is serious enough to warrant placing the site on the NPL. This process involves the following steps (described in Revesz & Stewart, *supra*):

- the Preliminary Assessment and Site Inspection (PA/SI): an initial, limited investigation designed to distinguish between sites that pose little or no threat to human health and the environment and sites that may pose a threat and require further investigation; and

- the calculation of a score pursuant to the Hazard Ranking System (HRS)—a score based on information gained during the PA/SI, representing the risk the site poses, and determining whether the site is eligible to be entered in the NPL, and its ranking within the NPL, *see* 40 C.F.R. § 300.425(c).

In the event that the site is not assigned to the NPL, it is "archived" for the purposes of SEMS. The archive designation means that, to the best of EPA's knowledge, assessment at a site has been completed and that EPA has determined no further steps will be taken to list this site on the NPL. This decision does not necessarily mean that there is no hazard associated with a given site; only that, based upon available information, the location is not judged to be a potential NPL site. As of October 2018, there were 40,081 archived sites on SEMS. *See* EPA, Superfund Data and Reports, https://www.epa.gov/superfund/superfund-data-and-reports (last visited Nov. 23, 2018).

In the event that the site is assigned to the NPL, a further series of procedures are conducted:

- the Remedial Investigation and Feasibility Study (RI/FS): designed to inform the nature of appropriate cleanup processes;

- the Record of Decision (ROD): a public document that explains which cleanup processes will be used to remediate the site; and

- the Remedial Design (RD): a plan that details the technical specifications for cleanup remedies.

Having completed these steps, the cleanup process—or Remedial Action (RA)—is then undertaken. Under § 106, EPA has the power to issue orders, called unilateral administrative orders (UAOs), instructing PRPs to clean up hazardous waste; it can also order treble damages for companies that fail to comply with the UAO. *See Gen. Elec. Co. v. Jackson*, 610 F.3d 110 (D.C. Cir. 2010) (holding that UAO process does not violate Due Process), *cert. denied*, 563 U.S. 1032 (2011).

Of the 12,890 sites listed on SEMS as of October 2018, 1,338 are contained on the NPL. *See* EPA, Superfund Data and Reports, https://www.epa.gov/superfund/superfund-data-and-reports (last visited Nov. 23, 2018); EPA, NPL Site Totals by Status and Milestone, http://www.epa.gov/superfund/npl-site-totals-status-and-milestone (last visited Oct. 24, 2018). A 1994 study by the Congressional Budget Office estimated that the national average for the time it takes from when a site is first listed on the NPL until the major stages of cleanup are completed is twelve years. *See* CBO, ANALYZING THE DURATION OF CLEANUP AT SITES ON SUPERFUND'S NATIONAL PRIORITIES LIST 2 (1994). Empirical evidence suggests that the average costs of a Superfund cleanup run between 20 and 30 million dollars. *See* JAMES LIS & MELINDA WARREN, REFORMING SUPERFUND 10 (1994). In the 1994 fiscal year alone, it is estimated that compliance with CERCLA (including remediation costs, but not including corporate legal costs) led to an estimated $28 billion of expenditures. *See* RICHARD J. MAHONEY, SUPERFUND: THIS TIME LET'S GET IT RIGHT 1 (1995). Since the inception of the NPL, a total of 412 sites have been removed from the list. EPA, NPL Site Totals by Status and Milestone, http://www.epa.gov/superfund/npl-site-totals-status-and-milestone (last visited Oct. 24, 2018).

NOTES AND QUESTIONS

1.   **Twelve Years to Clean up?** As discussed above, there are many steps involved in an EPA cleanup of a NPL site. While short-term removal actions are available to address the environmental problems posing the most immediate and serious risks, at least some of the environmental risks addressed by long-term remediation actions may become worse (and more costly to cleanup) in the time between the release of hazardous substances and the time that cleanup actually begins at the site. For example, if hazardous substances eventually seep down into the groundwater, remediation can become much more costly and difficult.

The 1994 Congressional Budget Office report on the duration of Superfund cleanups analyzed data obtained from interviewing Regional Project Managers about the speed of their cleanup projects and their perceived reasons for why they proceeded slowly or quickly. *See* CBO, ANALYZING THE DURATION OF CLEANUP AT SITES ON SUPERFUND'S NATIONAL PRIORITIES LIST (1994). The major reasons given for slow cleanups fell into two categories. First, there were problems intrinsic to the contaminated site, namely size and amount of contamination. *Id.* at 2. Second, there were legal and enforcement problems, such as negotiations with PRPs, and shifts in cleanup management between EPA and the PRPs. *Id.* These problems were heavily correlated with sites that had a large number of PRPs, high expected costs to PRPs, and certain land uses like chemical manufacturing and mixed-waste landfills. *Id.* at 3. While the most common answer for why a cleanup went more quickly than average was the size and simplicity of the contamination, many project managers also cited the use of CERCLA settlement tools and unusually good compliance by PRPs as important factors. *Id.* at 13.

Does the cleanup process strike a good balance between, on the one hand, thoroughly assessing the environmental risks and possible cleanup alternatives at a site before beginning the invariably expensive process of remediation, and, on the other hand, addressing environmental problems before they become even more serious? Do the problems that cause cleanup delays point to any measures that might speed up the process?

2. Costs of Superfund Cleanups. In 1994, the Congressional Budget Office also published a report on cleanup costs. Its estimates varied, but it predicted a baseline of additional Superfund costs of $74 billion, with a top estimate going up to $120 billion, dependent largely on how many sites will ultimately be listed on the NPL. The report also predicted that Superfund cleanups could continue through 2070. CBO, THE TOTAL COSTS OF CLEANING UP NONFEDERAL SUPERFUND SITES 13 (1994).

Though it announced very high predictions for future costs, the CBO report was actually more moderate than at least one other major cost prediction, largely because it assumed that individual site cleanups would decrease in average cost over time. *Id.* at 36. This assumption is based on the argument that larger and more highly polluted sites will be the first to come to the EPA's attention, will be the most pressing in need for action, and will be the most expensive to clean up on average. Therefore, as time goes along, CBO assumed that cleanups will be "scraping the bottom of the barrel" in cost and seriousness. *Id.* at 20. Nevertheless, CBO concluded, in all but its least expensive scenario, that the current EPA approach to Superfund would not have sufficient funding to maintain the pace of cleanup. *Id.* at 39.

Note that this report was before the expiration of the Superfund taxes. With the pace of cleanup now determined primarily by the cooperation and contribution of PRPs, is there reason to be more or less optimistic about future cleanups? Should Congress be willing to accept a slower pace of cleanup if it means that only the PRPs, instead of corporate and chemical taxpayers, are footing the bill?

3. Criticisms of EPA Policy. The 1994 CBO reports criticized the EPA's approach to enforcing CERCLA for not providing enough solid data to make predictions about the number of remaining cleanup sites, future costs, or cleanup durations. EPA had not conducted any kind of comprehensive site-discovery effort, instead relying on a policy of passive discovery, in which outside parties bring contaminated sites to the attention of the EPA. CBO, THE TOTAL COSTS OF CLEANING UP NONFEDERAL SUPERFUND SITES 37 (1994). As a result, CBO's estimates for the total number of sites to be placed on the

NPL ranged from 2300 to 7800, leaving a great deal of uncertainty in how to build future policy. *Id.* at 13.

In practice, the EPA also divides most cleanup sites into two or more "operable units." These units generally correspond to different areas or different media, like soil and groundwater, which need cleaning. CBO complains that data on the progress of sites is clouded by the fact that one site may be the subject of multiple cleanup actions. This confusion is compounded by the fact that the EPA only provided management reports at the individual project level. The CBO believes that, to build sound policy, the EPA needs to provide and track data both on individual projects and entire sites. CBO, ANALYZING THE DURATION OF CLEANUP AT SITES ON SUPERFUND'S NATIONAL PRIORITIES LIST 4 (1994).

EPA's usual response to such criticisms is that, because its policy of passive discovery was already bringing in a workload that they could not keep up with, there was no reason to expend more resources on data such as site discovery. CBO, THE TOTAL COSTS OF CLEANING UP NONFEDERAL SUPERFUND SITES 37 (1994). Is this a sufficient rationale? What important policy decisions do you think could, or should, change if the information about future costs and time commitment were better known?

4.   Coeur D'Alene River Basin Study. The National Research Council conducted an independent, in-depth assessment of EPA's scientific and technical practices in Superfund cleanups by examining the cleanup process of a major Superfund site in northern Idaho, the Coeur D'Alene River Basin. *See* NATIONAL RESEARCH COUNCIL, SUPERFUND AND MINING MEGASITES: LESSONS FROM THE COEUR D'ALENE RIVER BASIN (2005). One of the areas the report addresses is remedy selection. The NCP requires that any remedial action selected must meet the threshold criteria of protecting public health and the environment and satisfying ARARs. In its conclusions, the report questions whether the NCP's threshold criteria should be applicable in all cases: In the case of the Coeur D'Alene River basin, the EPA modeling studies predict that it will take several hundred years to meet these requirements, regardless of how much remediation is performed. *Id.* at 418. Is it reasonable to prepare a several hundred year long remediation plan before beginning the cleanup of a major site like the Coeur D'Alene? Should the requirement that the remediation satisfy all ARARs apply to the Coeur D'Alene?

5.   PRP Led Cleanups. The length and cost involved in the cleanup of sites listed on the NPL highlight the benefits of PRP led cleanups. These benefits have been described in the following terms:

> . . . [P]rivate cleanup is preferred because it too helps conserve the Superfund's relatively scarce resources. Private cleanup requires less total cost per site and is thus more efficient than an EPA cleanup. First, a private cleanup reduces the administrative costs inherent to any large scale governmental action. Second, even if strict monitoring by the EPA is required or otherwise desirable to avoid unnecessary delays or inadequate cleanup, the private cleanup would be less expensive. Third, as the plaintiff must bear

the initial out-of-pocket expenses of cleanup, there is a significant incentive to conduct cost-effective response actions, a factor not present in governmental responses as the EPA has no duty to engage in cost effective response, or even to mitigate its costs. Fourth, the expertise of private parties may allow private cleanups to be conducted more cost-effectively than government cleanups.

Additionally, because private parties are significantly less constrained by bureaucratic, administrative, and statutory limits on response authority than the EPA, private parties can begin cleanup much sooner than the government. By expediting cleanup, private cleanup decreases the amount of time that the environment is exposed to the hazardous waste, which reduces not only the cost of cleanup, but also the potential for environmental and human injury resulting from prolonged exposure to toxins. Eliminating the potential for injury is precisely the reason Congress enacted CERCLA in the first place.

Joseph A. Fischer, Comment, *All CERCLA Plaintiffs Are Not Created Equal: Private Parties, Settlements, and the UCATA*, 30 HOUS. L. REV. 1979, 1991–92 (1994). What incentives does the present regime provide to PRPs to undertake cleanups? How else could private parties be encouraged to initiate cleanups? What problems might arise in PRPs leading the cleanup process?

6.   Significance of Listing on the NPL. As noted above, the legal significance of listing a site on the NPL is to authorize the government to undertake remedial cleanup actions. The NCP expressly provides that "[o]nly those releases included on the NPL shall be considered eligible for Fund-finance remedial actions," 40 C.F.R. § 300.425(b), though listing a site on the NPL does not mean that remedial action will be taken, only that it may be taken. In the event that a site is not listed on the NPL, the government can spend Superfund money solely on removal actions. In addition to the legal significance, what is the practical and political significance of listing a site on the NPL? *See* Fischer, *supra*, at 1991.

7.   Management of Places Not on the National Priority List. In 2013, GAO reviewed the status of sites not on the NPL. As of December 2012, of 3,402 sites EPA had identified as potentially eligible, it had deferred 1,984 sites to cleanup approaches outside the Superfund program. The cleanup of 1,766 of those sites was deferred to states and other entities as "Other Cleanup Activity" (OCA). EPA managed 67 sites under the "Superfund Alternative" (SA) approach (where a PRP conducts the cleanup), and at least 38 sites were managed under other, undefined, non-NPL approaches. GAO, EPA SHOULD TAKE STEPS TO IMPROVE ITS MANAGEMENT OF ALTERNATIVES TO PLACING SITES ON THE NATIONAL PRIORITIES LIST 1 (2012). While EPA has issued guidelines for managing NPL and SA sites, it does not currently provide program guidance for OCAs. GAO recommended that EPA clearly define each type of OCA deferral and the documentation that should be obtained to support a decision to defer. *Id.* GAO also found, when comparing NPL and SA sites, mixed results in the average time to complete negotiations with PRPs and conduct specific cleanup activities. Although SA sites tended to be in earlier phases of the cleanup process, GAO attributed this to the fact that the SA approach began more recently that the NPL approach. *Id.* Is it preferable that site cleanups proceed without program guidance and a documented process, or that cleanups not commence until such guidance is developed? What are the benefits of allowing a PRP to conduct the cleanup? What are the risks? How can those risks be managed?

8. **Availability and Timing of Citizen Suits.** CERCLA contains a broad citizen suit provision, *see* 42 U.S.C. § 9659, that was modified by the 1986 SARA Amendments, *see* 42 U.S.C. § 9613(h). Under § 113(h)(4), citizens may bring suit to challenge the adequacy of a removal or remedial action, but only once the removal or remedial action is complete. 42 U.S.C. § 9613(h)(4). Does it make sense to limit review of removal and remedial actions until the action is complete? Would allowing judicial review of ongoing remedial actions delay cleanup, increasing exposure to hazardous substances? What if a misguided remedial action threatens to irremediably harm public health and the environment? *Compare Frey v. EPA*, 403 F.3d 828 (7th Cir. 2005) (holding that judicial review of remedial action was not barred under § 113(h), even though EPA insisted that some remedial measures were still ongoing), *with Hanford Downwinders Coal., Inc. v. Dowdle*, 71 F.3d 1469, 1484 (9th Cir. 1995) (holding that § 113(h) may permanently foreclose judicial review, regardless of irreparable harm to important interests). *See also* Megan A. Jennings, Frey v. Environmental Protection Agency: *A Small Step Toward Preventing Irreparable Harm in CERCLA Actions*, 33 ECOLOGY L.Q. 675 (2006).

9. **Institutional Controls.** Occasionally sites cannot be completely cleaned up, so EPA must implement post-cleanup controls to prevent the sites from posing a danger to the population and the environment. The use of such institutional controls has increased over time (from 10 percent of sites cleaned up between 1991 and 1993 to 53 percent of sites cleaned up between 2001 and 2003). GAO, IMPROVED EFFECTIVENESS OF CONTROLS AT SITES COULD BETTER PROTECT THE PUBLIC (2005). In its review of EPA's use of institutional controls, GAO identified four different types of controls. *Id.* at 8–9. Government controls use regulatory authority to impose restrictions, and EPA generally has to rely on state or local governments to establish such controls. *Id.* at 8. Proprietary controls are legal instruments placed in the chain of title of the site, such as easements and covenants. *Id.* Enforcement and permit tools with institutional control components can be issued or negotiated to compel site owners to limit the site to certain activities. *Id.* Informational devices are designed to warn the public about the risks inherent in using the property in question. *Id.* at 9. Which of these controls seems most effective? What problems might EPA face in using the different methods of institutional controls?

GAO noted that covenants and consent decrees were used most frequently by EPA, but criticized EPA for not adequately monitoring the institutional controls it put in place. *Id.* at 5, 16. Specifically, it found that some controls that had been previously agreed to were never implemented. *Id.* at 5. GAO also reported that reviewing institutional controls every five years, as required by CERCLA, is not sufficient to ensure that institutional controls are being implemented adequately so that the public is protected from the residual risks at the sites in question. *Id.* at 6. Overall, GAO recommended that EPA take more time to consider the controls' objectives and consider different types of controls before selecting any particular one. GAO also advocated consideration of the timing and duration of the controls' implementation, and who would be responsible for monitoring and enforcing the controls. *Id.*

Why have institutional controls been used more frequently in recent years than the early years of Superfund cleanups? Why might EPA have used covenants and consent decrees more frequently than the other institutional controls categorized by GAO?

ii. CLEANUP STANDARDS

As originally enacted, CERCLA provided little guidance on the degree of cleanup required. In the 1986 SARA amendments, however, Congress added § 121, which sets out general standards for Superfund cleanups. *See* Casey Scott Padgett, *Selecting Remedies at Superfund Sites: How Should "Clean" Be Determined?*, 18 VT. L. REV. 361 (1994) (discussing cleanup standards under the original Superfund statute and SARA amendments). Under § 121, remedial actions must be protective of the human health and environment, cost effective (taking into consideration both short- and long-term costs), and permanent to the maximum extent practicable. 42 U.S.C. § 9621(a)–(b). Remedial actions must also clean up a site to the level required by any legally applicable or relevant and appropriate standard or requirement under federal or state law; these standards are collectively referred to as "ARARs." 42 U.S.C. § 9621(d).

After Congress passed § 121, EPA revised the NCP to incorporate and expand upon the new cleanup standards. These provisions of the NCP were challenged by a number of states in the following case.

Ohio v. Environmental Protection Agency
997 F.2d 1520 (D.C. Cir. 1993).

■ Before MIKVA, CHIEF JUDGE, and EDWARDS and RANDOLPH, CIRCUIT JUDGES.

■ PER CURIAM:

These consolidated petitions present a multifarious challenge to Environmental Protection Agency ("EPA") regulations promulgated under the Comprehensive Environmental Response, Compensation, and Liability Act of 1980 ("CERCLA"), 42 U.S.C. §§ 9601–9675, as amended by the Superfund Amendments and Reauthorization Act of 1986 ("SARA"), Pub.L. No. 99–499, 100 Stat. 1613. The regulations under review are portions of the National Oil and Hazardous Substances Pollution Contingency Plan, 40 C.F.R. Part 300, commonly known as the "NCP."

Before Congress created the Environmental Protection Agency ("EPA" or "the Agency"), and long before Congress enacted the Comprehensive Environmental Response, Compensation, and Liability Act of 1980 ("CERCLA"), 42 U.S.C. §§ 9601–9675, there was a National Contingency Plan ("NCP"). . . .

Of particular importance to this case is the prominent role of the NCP under CERCLA. Section 104(a)(1) of CERCLA authorizes the President "to act, consistent with the national contingency plan, to remove or arrange for the removal of, and provide for remedial action relating to such hazardous substance, pollutant, or contaminant at any time . . . , or take any other response measure consistent with the national contingency plan which the President deems necessary to protect the public health or welfare or the environment." 42 U.S.C. § 9604(a)(1). The NCP thus "provide[s] the organizational structure and procedures" for responding to hazardous waste threats. 40 C.F.R. § 300.1. It is the means by which EPA implements CERCLA.

When Congress enacted CERCLA in 1980, it directed the President to revise and republish the NCP in light of the new law. 42 U.S.C. § 9605(a). Pursuant to section 115 of CERCLA, the President assigned EPA the responsibility of amending the NCP. *See* 42 U.S.C. § 9615; Exec. Order No. 12,316, 46 Fed.Reg. 42,237 (1981); Exec. Order No. 12,580, 52 Fed.Reg. 2923 (1987). In 1982, EPA issued a new version of the NCP. 47 Fed.Reg. 31,180 (1982). EPA revised the NCP again in 1985. 50 Fed.Reg. 47,912 (1985). When Congress passed the Superfund Amendments and Reauthorization Act of 1986 ("SARA"), Pub.L. No. 99–499, 100 Stat. 1613, which significantly revised the statute, Congress directed the President to revise the NCP again to reflect the changes in CERCLA. 42 U.S.C. § 9605(b). EPA issued these revisions to the NCP in 1990. 55 Fed.Reg. 8666 (1990).

Petitioners, whom we shall call "the States," include both states and private parties contending that EPA's changes to the NCP in 1985 and 1990 are inconsistent with the requirements of CERCLA. . . .

The States first challenge several elements of the NCP definition of legally "applicable" or "relevant and appropriate" environmental standards, known as "ARARs." CERCLA does not define ARARs, but the statute does require that remedial actions at Superfund sites result in a level of cleanup or standard of control that at least meets the legally applicable or otherwise relevant and appropriate federal (or stricter state) requirements. 42 U.S.C. § 9621(d)(2)(A). The NCP defines "applicable requirements" as follows:

> *Applicable requirements* means those cleanup standards, standards of control, and other substantive requirements, criteria, or limitations promulgated under federal environmental or state environmental or facility siting laws that specifically address a hazardous substance, pollutant, contaminant, remedial action, location, or other circumstance

found at a CERCLA site. Only those state standards that are identified by a state in a timely manner and that are more stringent than federal requirements may be applicable.

40 C.F.R. § 300.5. "Relevant and appropriate requirements" are those substantive requirements that, while not "applicable," nonetheless "address problems or situations sufficiently similar to those encountered at the CERCLA site that their use is well suited to the particular site." *Id.* . . .

Does the NCP improperly fail to apply zero-level Maximum Contaminant Level Goals ("MCLGs") as ARARs?

The States challenge EPA's decision that Maximum Contaminant Level Goals ("MCLGs") established under the Safe Drinking Water Act ("SDWA"), 42 U.S.C. §§ 300f to 300j–26, do not have to be attained for contaminants whose MCLG has been set at a level of zero. 40 C.F.R. § 300.430(e)(2)(i)(C). The States contend that EPA lacks authority to depart from a statutory requirement to achieve MCLGs, and in the alternative, that even if EPA possesses this authority, it has failed to provide a reasoned basis for its departure.

The SDWA is specifically referenced in section 121(d)(2)(A) of CERCLA as one of the federal laws containing ARARs for Superfund cleanups. 42 U.S.C. § 9621(d)(2)(A). The SDWA identifies two standards for exposure to contaminants. The first, Maximum Contaminant Level Goals ("MCLGs"), are generally unenforceable goals that reflect the level for a given contaminant at which "no known or anticipated adverse effects on the health of persons occur and which allows an adequate margin of safety." 42 U.S.C. § 300g–1(b)(4). Many MCLGs for carcinogens are set at zero. 55 Fed.Reg. 8750 (1990). The second type of standards, Maximum Contaminant Levels ("MCLs")—the actual maximum permissible concentration levels under the SDWA—must be set as close as "feasible" to their corresponding MCLGs, taking into account available technology and cost. 42 U.S.C. § 300g–1(b)(4)–(5).

While MCLGs are unenforceable under the SDWA, section 121 of CERCLA converts them into enforceable goals, providing:

> Such remedial action shall require a level or standard of control which at least attains Maximum Contaminant Level Goals established under the Safe Drinking Water Act . . . where such goals or criteria are relevant and appropriate under the circumstances of the release or threatened release.

42 U.S.C. § 9621(d)(2)(A). Consistent with this requirement, the NCP generally requires the attainment of MCLGs. 40 C.F.R. § 300.430(e)(2)(i)(B). When the MCLG for a contaminant has been set at a level of zero, however, the NCP requires only that the MCL be attained. In essence, EPA has made a categorical determination that MCLGs set

at a level of zero are never "relevant and appropriate under the circumstances" of a release.

This determination was based on EPA's conclusion "that it is impossible to detect whether 'true' zero has actually been attained." 55 Fed.Reg. 8752 (1990). During rulemaking to promulgate MCLGs under the SDWA, EPA "emphasized that . . . zero is not a measurable level in scientific terms." 50 Fed.Reg. 46,884, 46,896 (1985). "Due to limitations in analytical techniques, it will always be impossible to say with certainty that the substance is not present. In theory, RMCLs [Recommended Maximum Contaminant Levels] at zero will always be unachievable (or at least not demonstrable)." 49 Fed.Reg. 24,330, 24,347 (1984).

The States contend that EPA's decision concerning zero-level MCLGs is inconsistent with CERCLA's mandate that all remedial actions attain MCLGs. This argument ignores the full language of the section, which imposes the requirement "where such goals . . . are relevant and appropriate under the circumstances of the release or threatened release." 42 U.S.C. § 9621(d)(2)(A). This language leaves EPA with discretion to determine when MCLGs are relevant and appropriate. The States contend, though, that such discretion cannot be exercised in a categorical manner, but instead must be based on a case-specific determination at individual sites. Hence, there is no reason for EPA to make an individualized determination of what they have concluded can never be relevant and appropriate.

The States also contend that even if EPA has discretion to conclude that zero-level MCLGs are never relevant and appropriate, it has not justified the decision to do so in this case. But EPA articulated a number of justifications, *see* 55 Fed.Reg. 8750–52 (1990), and we find its reliance on the fact that true zero levels can never be detected to provide adequate support for the Agency's decision. As we understand EPA's scientific analysis, one can never prove a true zero level. If the measuring device indicates zero, this shows only that the device is not sufficiently sensitive to detect the presence of any contaminants. It does not show the total absence of the contaminants. In other words, if one asserts that zero contaminants are present, this can be *falsified* by showing the presence of some detectable level, but it can never be shown to be *true*. EPA chose to set MCLGs for carcinogens at zero under the SDWA because they "are goals which may or may not be practically achievable and the practicality of these goals should be factored into the MCLs," not the MCLGs. 50 Fed.Reg. 46,896 (1985). In contrast, EPA concluded that "ARARs must be measurable and attainable since their purpose is to set a standard that an actual remedy will attain." 55 Fed.Reg. 8752 (1990).

The States do not contest EPA's scientific conclusion that zero-level MCLGs are not achievable. Instead, they argue that EPA could select a method of measurement approximating zero by setting "a goal of achieving the analytical detection limits for specific carcinogens." Final Amended Joint Brief of Petitioning States at 68. That EPA could do this, however, does not mean it is required to do so. Section 121 requires the selection of MCLs where MCLGs are unattainable. That is what the NCP does. That conclusion is reasonable given EPA's discretion to determine when ARARs are relevant and appropriate.

The next set of challenges by the States addresses a variety of issues concerning remedy selection: the role of cost-benefit analysis in remedy selection; the requirement that selected remedies are permanent to the maximum extent practicable; [and] the use of a cancer risk range in remedy selection. . . .

Does the NCP establish an improper cost-benefit analysis in the remedy selection process?

Section 121 of CERCLA, added by SARA, requires the selection of remedial actions "at a minimum which assures protection of human health and the environment." 42 U.S.C. § 9621(d)(1). Although a different provision of section 121 requires the selection of remedial actions that are also cost-effective, 42 U.S.C. § 9621(b)(1), the States interpret section 121(d)(1) to prohibit EPA from considering the cost of a remedial action when it determines the level of protectiveness to be achieved by that remedial action. EPA is in full agreement with the States' interpretation of § 121(d)(1). *See* 55 Fed.Reg. 8726 (1990). The States contend, however, that two provisions in the NCP implicitly authorize the use of cost-benefit analysis, thereby permitting cost to be considered in determining the level of protectiveness to be achieved by a remedial action. In making this argument, the States distort the language of the NCP, which is carefully structured so "that protection of human health and the environment will not be compromised by other selection factors, such as cost." *Id*.

The States first point to a provision in the NCP authorizing EPA to balance nine different criteria, including both protection of human health and cost, in selecting a remedy. 40 C.F.R. § 300.430(f)(1)(i)(A). But while the NCP identifies nine criteria to be used in selecting a remedy, all of the criteria are not given equal weight. Instead, they are divided into three classifications: threshold criteria, primary balancing criteria, and modifying criteria. Under this structure, "[o]verall protection of human health and the environment and compliance with ARARs (unless a specific ARAR is waived) are threshold requirements that each alternative must meet in order to be eligible for selection." 40 C.F.R. § 300.430(f)(1)(i)(A). EPA explained in the preamble to the NCP that remedial alternatives "must be demonstrated to be protective . . . in order to be eligible for consideration in the balancing process by which the remedy is selected." 55 Fed.Reg. 8726 (1990). The identification of threshold criteria therefore undermines the States' claim that by listing nine criteria, the NCP permits the level of protectiveness to be affected by cost.

The States also point us to the NCP's definition of "cost-effectiveness," which states that "[a] remedy shall be cost-effective if its costs are proportional to its overall effectiveness." 40 C.F.R.

§ 300.430(f)(1)(ii)(D). The States contend that this language actually authorizes the use of cost benefit analysis. In making this argument, though, the States ignore the first sentence of the same section of the NCP that they are challenging. It states: "Each remedial action shall be cost-effective, provided that it first satisfies the threshold criteria set forth in § 300.430(f)(1)(ii)(A) and (B)." *Id.; see also* 55 Fed.Reg. 8727 (1990). Thus, consistent with the creation of threshold criteria, the NCP explicitly prohibits consideration of costs in the manner complained of by the States.

Does the NCP improperly fail to require the selection of permanent remedies to the maximum extent practicable?

The States next argue that the NCP is inconsistent with section 121(b)(1)'s requirement that the President select remedial actions "that utilize[ ] permanent solutions . . . to the maximum extent practicable." 42 U.S.C. § 9621(b)(1). The NCP classifies permanence as one of the five primary balancing criteria, along with reduction of toxicity, mobility, or volume; short-term effectiveness; implementability; and cost. 40 C.F.R. § 300.430(f)(1)(i)(B). The States reason that because the selection of permanent remedies "is one of the overarching statutory principles of remedy selection under CERCLA," Final Amended Joint Brief of Petitioning States at 27, the other balancing criteria, particularly cost, should play no role in EPA's determination whether a permanent remedy is to be selected. In essence, the States would like permanence to be treated as an additional threshold criterion that must be evaluated independently of cost.

The flaw in the States' argument is in the premise that permanence is an overarching statutory principle. This premise is not supported by the statutory language. 42 U.S.C. § 9621(b)(1), which the States rely upon, requires the President to "select a remedial action that is protective of human health and the environment, that is cost effective, and that utilizes permanent solutions and alternative treatment technologies or resource recovery technologies to the maximum extent practicable." 42 U.S.C. § 9621(b)(1). The statutory language places as much emphasis on the selection of cost-effective remedies as it does on the selection of permanent remedies. Although the NCP elevates protection of human health and the environment to a threshold criterion, a different provision in section 121 provides the basis for that treatment. 42 U.S.C. § 9621(d)(1); *see supra* p. 1531. But there is nothing in section 121 to suggest that selecting permanent remedies is more important than selecting cost-effective remedies. . . .

Does the NCP cancer risk range improperly fail to protect human health and the environment without regard to cost?

The States next challenge EPA's use of a cancer risk range between 10^{-6} and 10^{-4} in the NCP, arguing that an exposure level greater than

10^{-6} is never appropriate. A 10^{-4} risk subjects the surrounding population to an increased lifetime cancer risk of 1 in 10,000. A 10^{-6} risk subjects the surrounding population to an increased lifetime cancer risk of 1 in 1,000,000. When EPA develops objectives for a remedial action at a site, it selects a remediation goal that "establish[es] acceptable exposure levels that are protective of human health." 40 C.F.R. § 300.430(e)(2)(i). EPA attempts to use health-based ARARs to set the goal, but if ARARs are nonexistent or unsuitable for use, EPA establishes the goal based on criteria in the NCP. 55 Fed.Reg. 8712 (1990). "For known or suspected carcinogens, acceptable exposure levels are generally concentration levels that represent an excess upper bound lifetime cancer risk to an individual of between 10^{-6} and 10^{-4}...." 40 C.F.R. § 300.430(e)(2)(i)(A)(2). The NCP expresses a preference for remedial actions that achieve a level of 10^{-6}; however, the ultimate decision depends on a balancing of nine criteria, including cost. *Id.*; 55 Fed.Reg. 8718 (1990).

The States contend that by permitting cost to play a role in determining the level of exposure, the cancer risk range fails to meet the requirement in § 9621 that remedial actions be "protective of human health." 42 U.S.C. § 9621(b)(1); *see also* 42 U.S.C. § 9621(d)(1). The States' argument necessarily depends, though, on the notion that an exposure level greater than 10^{-6} is not protective of human health. CERCLA requires the selection of remedial actions "that are protective of human health," not as protective as conceivably possible. A "risk range of 10^{-4} to 10^{-6} represents EPA's opinion on what are generally acceptable levels." 55 Fed.Reg. 8716 (1990). Although cost cannot be used to justify the selection of a remedy that is not protective of human health and the environment, it can be considered in selecting from options that are adequately protective.

The States also argue that the actual risk range selected is not adequately protective. EPA concluded, though, that all levels of exposure within the risk range are protective of human health. *Id.* EPA has used 10^{-4} as an upper bound for establishing risk levels in the past, *see* 53 Fed.Reg. 51,394, 51,426 (1988), and "[m]any ARARs, which Congress specifically intended be used as cleanup standards at Superfund sites, are set at risk levels less stringent than 10^{-6}," 55 Fed.Reg. 8717 (1990). The States offer no evidence challenging EPA's position that 10^{-4} represents a safe level of exposure, and in any event, we give EPA's findings on this point significant deference. *See* New York v. EPA, 852 F.2d 574, 580 (D.C. Cir.1988), *cert. denied*, 489 U.S. 1065 (1989).

NOTES AND QUESTIONS

1. Applicable Requirements and Relevant and Appropriate Requirements. What is the difference between "applicable" requirements and "relevant and appropriate" requirements? When would a standard not be applicable, but be relevant and appropriate?

2.   MCLGs. What is the difference between MCLGs and MCLs under the SDWA? How are MCLGs and MCLs determined? Given this distinction, why would § 121(d)(2)(A) of CERCLA make reference to MCLGs as opposed to MCLs? In doing so, does CERCLA elevate the attainment of MCLGs at Superfund sites above the aspirations of the SDWA? In other words, given that most entirely unpolluted waters do not achieve MCLGs, does requiring cleanup to a level more stringent than even that of drinking water make sense?

3.   MCLGs as ARARs. In what limited circumstances would MCLGs be considered applicable requirements? On what basis did the *Ohio v. EPA* court find that EPA has discretion to determine in what circumstances MCLGs are relevant and appropriate requirements? Is this reconcilable with the express terms of § 121(d)(2)(A)? What justification did EPA provide for its determination in this case?

4.   Absolute Zero. In *Ohio v. EPA*, EPA argued that MCLGs established under the SDWA were never relevant or appropriate (and so were not ARARs) when the MCLG was set at zero, because it is scientifically impossible to detect whether "true zero" has been attained. Is this argument persuasive? If this is the only reason to reject zero-level MCLGs, why not accept the states' argument that concentrations for these MCLGs could be found to be at zero when they can no longer be detected by a specified measuring instrument? In what circumstances would the lowest detectable level of pollution be a more stringent standard than MCLs?

5.   Consideration of Costs. What do you consider to be EPA's true motivations in determining that zero-level MCLGs can never constitute ARARs? Was EPA entitled to consider costs in making this determination?

6.   Appropriate Standard? Given the previous discussion concerning brownfields, on what basis may one argue that § 121(d)(2)(A) prescribes a level of cleanup that is overly stringent?

7.   Threshold Criteria, Primary Balancing Criteria, and Modifying Criteria. Another controversy in the *Ohio v. EPA* case concerns whether EPA adopts an improper cost-benefit analysis in the remedy selection process. In resolving this controversy, the *Ohio v. EPA* court introduces the concepts of threshold criteria, primary balancing criteria, and modifying criteria. What are the differences between these three categories? How does the court divide the various requirements of 42 U.S.C. § 9621(d) among these categories? What role do these categories play in the court's determination?

8.   Protective of Human Health and the Environment. According to the *Ohio v. EPA* court, the first threshold in determining the level of cleanup is the level necessary to protect the human health and environment. 42 U.S.C. § 9621(d)(1). Does this call for a no risk framework? If not, what is the appropriate risk management framework (as discussed in Chapter II)?

9.   Cost Effectiveness and Cost-Benefit Analysis. Section 121(a) requires that the level of cleanup be cost-effective. On what basis did the States contend that this provision, coupled with the NCP's definition of cost-effectiveness, authorized the use of cost-benefit analysis? Why was this argument rejected by the court?

10. Cost and Permanence. The *Ohio v. EPA* court found that "there is nothing in § 121 to suggest that selecting permanent remedies is more important than selecting cost-effective remedies." The court based this conclusion on its reading of § 121(b)(1), which requires the President to "select a remedial action that is ... cost effective, and that utilizes permanent solutions and alternative treatment technologies or resource recovery technologies to the maximum extent practicable." 997 F.2d at 1532. Does the court suggest that Congress intended costs to play a more prominent role than permanence?

11. Permissible Risk Range. In *Ohio v. EPA*, the States argued that an exposure level greater than 10^{-6} is never protective of human health and the environment. What evidence did the States provide in support of this proposition? What evidence could the States have provided?

The *Ohio v. EPA* court was satisfied that EPA's preferred range of 10^{-6} to 10^{-4} did constitute a permissible range. How did EPA pick this range? Why are ARARs relevant to the determination of what constitutes the threshold level necessary to protect human health and the environment? Under the court's reasoning, could EPA have selected another range?

12. Selecting a Point Within the Range. How is EPA to select a point within the permissible risk range? Do the nine selection criteria identified by the court enable EPA to conduct some form of limited cost-benefit analysis in making this determination?

iii. ARARs

A state environmental requirement or standard is an ARAR if it is (1) properly promulgated, (2) more stringent than federal standards, (3) legally applicable or relevant and appropriate, and (4) timely identified. *See* 42 U.S.C. § 9621(d). The following case discusses each of these requirements.

United States v. Akzo Coatings of America, Inc.
949 F.2d 1409 (6th Cir. 1991).

■ Before JONES, CIRCUIT JUDGE, ENGEL, and WELLFORD, SENIOR CIRCUIT JUDGES.

■ ENGEL, SENIOR CIRCUIT JUDGE:

This is an appeal by the State of Michigan from the entry of a consent decree between the United States Environmental Protection Agency ("EPA") and twelve defendants pursuant to the Comprehensive Environmental Response, Compensation, and Liability Act of 1980 ("CERCLA"), as amended by the Superfund Amendments and Reauthorization Act of 1986 ("SARA"), 42 U.S.C. § 9601 *et seq.* The consent decree would require the defendants, or potentially responsible parties ("PRPs"), to engage in remedial work to clean up a hazardous waste site in Rose Township, Oakland County, Michigan ("Rose Site"). The proposed remedial plan at the Rose Site calls for the excavation and incineration of surface soils contaminated with polychlorinated biphenyls ("PCBs"), lead, arsenic and other toxic materials and the flushing of the subsurface soils contaminated with a variety of volatile and semi-volatile organic compounds.

The state challenges the legality of the remedial action, and seeks to prevent entry of the consent decree. . . .

The State of Michigan and amici curiae contend that the proposed remedy is not in accordance with the law because it does not meet the state's ARARs. Under CERCLA, the remedial action selected must comply with identified state ARARs that are more stringent than applicable federal standards unless the ARARs are waived. The relevant provision provides in part:

> With respect to any hazardous substance, pollutant or contaminant that will remain onsite, if (i) any standard, requirement, criteria, or limitation under any Federal environmental law, . . . or (ii) any promulgated standard, requirement, criteria, or limitation under a State environmental . . . law that is more stringent than any Federal standard, . . . is legally applicable to the hazardous substance or pollutant or contaminant concerned or is relevant and appropriate under the circumstances, . . . the remedial action selected . . . shall require, at the completion of the remedial action, a level or standard of control for such hazardous substance or pollutant or contaminant which at least attains such legally applicable or relevant and appropriate standard, requirement, criteria, or limitation.

42 U.S.C. § 9621(d)(2)(A). Before deciding whether the decree must comply with such laws, we need to determine whether there are any state ARARs applicable to the Rose Site.

The district court found that the Michigan Water Resources Commission Act ("WRCA"), and its corresponding agency rules, Mich. Admin. Code R. 323.2201 (1980), *et seq.*, ("Part 22 Rules") satisfy each of the criteria for ARARs to which a proposed remedy must comply under § 9621(d). Section 6(a) of the WRCA provides, in part:

> It shall be unlawful for any persons directly or indirectly to discharge into the waters of the state any substance *which is or may become injurious* to the public health, safety, or welfare; or which is or may become injurious to domestic, commercial, industrial, agricultural, recreational or other uses which are being or may be made of such waters. . . .

M.C.L.A. § 323.6(a) (emphasis added). The corresponding agency rules, the Part 22 Rules, provide for the nondegradation of groundwater in usable aquifers. Mich.Admin.Code R. 323.2205 (1980). Defendants challenge the district court's conclusion that said Michigan law and rules, collectively referred to as Michigan's anti-degradation law, qualify as a state ARAR.

Under 42 U.S.C. § 9621(d), *supra*, a state environmental requirement or standard constitutes a state ARAR to which the remedy must comply if it is (1) properly promulgated, (2) more stringent than federal standards, (3) legally applicable or relevant and appropriate, and (4) timely identified.

1.   Whether Michigan's Anti-degradation Law is Properly Promulgated

To be considered an ARAR, the anti-degradation law must be "promulgated." 42 U.S.C. § 9621(d)(2)(A)(ii). According to EPA, "promulgated" as used in § 9621 refers to "laws imposed by state legislative bodies and regulations developed by state agencies that are of general applicability and are legally enforceable." EPA, *Superfund Program; Interim Guidance on Compliance with Applicable or Relevant and Appropriate Requirements; Notice of Guidance,* 52 Fed.Reg. 32495, 32498 (Aug. 27, 1987) [hereinafter *Interim Guidance*]. *See also* Preamble, *National Oil and Hazardous Substances Pollution Contingency Plan,* 55 Fed.Reg. 8666, 8841 (Mar. 8, 1990) (codified at 40 C.F.R. § 300.400(g)(4)) [hereinafter *NCP, Final Rule*]. EPA evidently desired to differentiate "advisories, guidance, or other non-binding policies, as well as standards that are not of general application," *Interim Guidance,* 52 Fed.Reg. at 32498, from laws or rules promulgated by state legislatures or agencies that are imposed on all citizens of a particular state, which is the case with Michigan's anti-degradation law since it was enacted by the Michigan legislature, and the accompanying administrative rules were properly developed by the Michigan Water Resources Commission. *Akzo Coatings,* 719 F. Supp. at 583.

While defendants concede that Michigan's anti-degradation law has general applicability, they contend that it was not properly promulgated because its vagueness and lack of a quantifiable standard render it legally unenforceable. . . . [The Court rejected the argument that the anti-degradation law was unconstitutionally vague.]

Defendants emphasize that EPA, in its proposed rules, requires "general state goals" to be implemented by means of "specific requirements," which Michigan's current implementing regulations fail to do, as they only prohibit "degradations" of the "local background groundwater quality." However, as evidenced by its proposed rules *as a whole*, EPA is not limiting the validity of general state goals solely to those which are implemented via specific numerical standards promulgated in corresponding agency rules. Rather, the type of standard provided is one of several factors courts should consider in deciding whether a state goal is an ARAR. EPA's proposed rules state:

General State goals that are contained in a promulgated statute and implemented via specific requirements found in the statute *or* in other promulgated regulations are potential ARARs. For example, a State antidegradation statute which prohibits degradation of surface waters below specific levels of quality *or* in ways that *preclude certain uses of that water* would be a potential ARAR. *Where such promulgated goals are general in scope,* e.g., a general prohibition against discharges to surface waters of "toxic materials in toxic amounts," *compliance must be interpreted within the context of implementing regulations, the specific circumstances of the site, and the remedial alternatives being considered.*

EPA, *National Oil and Hazardous Substances Pollution Contingency Plan; Proposed Rule*, 53 Fed.Reg. 51394, 51,438 (Dec. 21, 1988) [hereinafter *Proposed Rule*] (emphasis added). EPA's final revisions are even clearer: "Even if a state has not promulgated implementing regulations, a general goal can be an ARAR if it meets the eligibility criteria for state ARARs. However, EPA would have considerable latitude in determining how to comply with the goal in the absence of implementing regulations." *NCP, Final Rule*, 55 Fed.Reg. at 8746. Hence, EPA's own publications recognize that general requirements containing no specific numerical standards, or any implementing regulations at all for that matter, can be enforceable ARARs.[33]

Other Michigan cases demonstrate that Michigan's anti-degradation law is legally enforceable. . . . In sum, the WRCA and the Part 22 Rules are legally enforceable, and thus "promulgated" within the meaning of 42 U.S.C. § 9621(d)(2)(A)(ii).

2. Whether Michigan's Anti-degradation Law is More Stringent than Federal Standards

Section 9621(d)(2)(A)(ii) also requires that for state standards to apply to a remedial action plan, they must be "more stringent than any Federal standard, requirement, criteria or limitation. . . ." The district court summarily concluded that

> [a]lthough it is difficult to compare a federal statute containing specific requirements with a state agency rule that contains a broad prohibition, this Court finds that the broad prohibition is more stringent than the federal statute setting minimal standards. Accordingly, Michigan's anti-degradation law also complies with this aspect of 42 U.S.C. § 9621(d).

---

[33] Defendants also contend that the vagueness and unenforceability of Michigan's anti-degradation law is evident in the inconsistency of its application. . . . [W]hile under CERCLA an ARAR's inconsistent application allows EPA to "waive" compliance with that ARAR, *see* section 9621(d)(4), it is not determinative of whether the state requirement is in fact an ARAR. Therefore, the fact that courts have required, according to defendants, differing levels of cleanup under the WRCA does not affect the determination of whether such a law is a state ARAR if that law is otherwise enforceable. Indeed, as local background groundwater quality naturally varies from acquifer [sic] to acquifer [sic], some variation in cleanup requirements is to be expected.

Akzo Coatings, 719 F. Supp. at 584. The district court, however, is not left without authority for its conclusion. In its proposed revision of the NCP, EPA stated: "Where no Federal ARAR exists for a chemical, location, or action, but a State ARAR does exist, or where a state ARAR is broader in scope than the Federal ARAR, the State ARAR is considered more stringent." *Proposed Rule*, 53 Fed.Reg. at 51435. Senator Mitchell, one of the principal authors of § 9621, similarly explained during the debate on SARA that a "more stringent" state requirement within the meaning of section 9621(d)(2)(A) "includes *any* State requirement where there is no comparable Federal requirement." 132 Cong.Rec. S14,915 (Oct. 3, 1986) (emphasis added).

We find that no comparable federal statute or rule identified by the parties broadly regulates direct or indirect discharges of any injurious or potentially injurious substance into groundwater resources as does section 6(a) of the WRCA. The WRCA is not directly comparable to the federal Safe Drinking Water Act ("SDWA"), 42 U.S.C. § 300g–1(a)(2) because it is broader in coverage and, depending on the site, as or more demanding in terms of cleanup requirements than the SDWA. We believe, therefore, that the WRCA is more stringent than the SDWA. . . .

3. Whether Michigan's Anti-degradation Law is Legally Applicable to the Rose Site or Relevant and Appropriate to the Remedial Action Selected

The third requirement under section 9621(d) is that the potential ARARs be "legally applicable to the hazardous substance or pollutant or contaminant concerned or [ ] relevant and appropriate under the circumstances of the release or remedial action selected. . . ."[38] To determine whether this requirement is satisfied, we must re-examine the scope of Michigan's anti-degradation law. Section 6(a) of the WRCA prohibits persons from discharging, "directly or indirectly," certain substances into the groundwaters. The Part 22 Rules define "discharges" to be "the addition of materials to ground waters from any facility or operation which acts as a discreet or diffuse source. . . ." Mich.Admin.Code R. 323.2202(j).

The record in this case clearly establishes an ongoing, indirect discharge of injurious substances from the soil into the groundwater at the Site caused by the natural infiltration of water through contaminated soils, which in turn results in the leaching of contaminants. The RI/FS (Exh. 3.1a, at 20), the 1987 ROD (Exh. 3.1c, at 11), the 1987 Responsiveness Summary (Exh. 3.1c, at 17–18), and the amended ROD (Exh. 3.22a, at 3) all reflect that soils contaminated with toxic chemicals

---

[38] "Applicable requirements" are those standards promulgated under federal or state law that specifically address a hazardous substance, pollutant, contaminant, remedial action, or other circumstance at a CERCLA site. In contrast, "relevant and appropriate requirements" are those standards which, while not applicable to a CERCLA remedial action, are promulgated under federal or state law and address problems or situations sufficiently similar to those encountered at a site that their use is well situated to that site. 300 C.F.R. § 300.6; *Interim Guidance*, 52 Fed.Reg. at 32497; *NCP Final Rule*, 55 Fed.Reg. at 8742.

on site will, unless remediated, act as a "continual source of groundwater degradation." Exh. 3.22a, ROD Amendment, at 3. The record also establishes that the nature and distribution of these contaminants is such that they are or may become "injurious to the public health, safety or welfare . . . or [to] uses which are being made or may be made of such waters. . . ." M.C.L.A. § 323.6(a). *Cf. United States Aviex Co. v. Travelers Ins. Co.*, 125 Mich.App. 579, 336 N.W.2d 838 (1983) (court held that property owner was subject to liability to the state under WRCA for discharge of pollutants into groundwater under his property as a result of contaminated water used to extinguish a fire at a chemical plant above ground).

We thus agree with the district court that "because soil flushing diffusely discharges toxicants from the soil into the ground water, the anti-degradation rules are legally applicable to the clean up of the Rose Township site" and to soil flushing in particular. *Akzo Coatings*, 719 F. Supp. at 584 (citing to Mich.Admin.Code R. 323.2202(j)). *See also* Exh. 3.18, Explanation of Significant Differences, at 2 (The effect of soil flushing "would be to 'mimic' the natural precipitation infiltration process which is currently leaching chemicals into the groundwater."). For reasons previously stated, we do not accept the argument that Michigan's anti-degradation law is inapplicable to soil flushing because it is "prospective" and thus only covers further degradation of groundwaters. Michigan's anti-degradation law provides for the protection from degradation of "background," not "existing," groundwater and thus requires, assuming it is an ARAR, that the PRPs restore the groundwater at the site to the local background groundwater quality, whatever that may be. *Cf. Thomas Solvent Co.*, 146 Mich. App. at 64, 380 N.W.2d 53 (The court explained that the "status quo" to be protected by the injunction under the WRCA was "an unpolluted environment . . . [and] the maintenance of uncontaminated groundwater and soil."). . . .

Even if Michigan's anti-degradation law were not applicable to this site, its consideration would certainly be "relevant and appropriate." Among possible factors to be considered, the environmental media ("groundwater"), the type of substance ("injurious") and the objective of the potential ARAR ("protecting aquifers from actual or potential degradation)," are all "relevant" in this case because they pertain to the conditions of the Rose Site. Moreover, considering the aforementioned factors, the use of Michigan's anti-degradation law is well-suited to the site at issue and therefore "appropriate" in this case. *See Proposed Rule*, 53 Fed.Reg. at 51436; 40 C.F.R. § 300.400(g)(2) (1990).

Accordingly, we conclude that Michigan's anti-degradation law is properly promulgated, more stringent than the federal standard, legally applicable or relevant and appropriate, as well as timely identified (the latter factor not having been argued on appeal), and therefore constitutes an ARAR within the meaning of 42 U.S.C. § 9621(d)(2).

NOTES AND QUESTIONS

1. Michigan's Anti-Degradation Law. On what basis did the *Akzo* court determine the Michigan anti-degradation law to be an ARAR? What were the relevant federal anti-degradation standards? In circumstances where there are no federal standards, will state standards always be ARARs? What factors are relevant to this determination?

2. Cleanup Standard. Having determined that Michigan's anti-degradation law did constitute an ARAR, what cleanup standard applies? In the event that the anti-degradation law was not considered an ARAR, at what level would cleanup standards be set? What is the significance of determining the anti-degradation law to be an ARAR?

3. Waiving ARARs. EPA has the option of waiving compliance with an ARAR under certain circumstances, including when the response action that would attain the ARAR would result in greater risk to human health and the environment than a response action that would not attain the ARAR; when compliance with the ARAR is technically impracticable from an engineering perspective; or when a state has not consistently applied its own standard or requirement. 42 U.S.C. § 9621(d)(4). Are there other circumstances in which EPA should have the option of waiving compliance with an ARAR?

4. Preemption of State Law. Should state environmental laws that are not found to be ARARs be preempted by CERCLA? *Compare United States v. Colorado*, 990 F.2d 1565 (10th Cir. 1993) (CERCLA does not preempt state laws dealing with the handling of hazardous waste), *cert. denied*, 510 U.S. 1092 (1994), *with R.I. Res. Recovery Corp. v. R.I. Dep't of Envtl. Mgmt.*, 2006 WL 2128904 (D.R.I. 2006) (state environmental laws not incorporated as ARARs may not be enforced against a PRP as to the Superfund site). The NCP standards governing cleanups under CERCLA are already fairly detailed and complex. Would allowing non-ARAR state laws to apply to Superfund cleanups in addition to the NCP requirements unnecessarily complicate the cleanup process? Would finding state laws to be preempted create inconsistent environmental regulation within the state, and unnecessarily deprive states of authority to regulate in one of their traditional areas of sovereignty?

iv. ENVIRONMENTAL RISKS AND CLEANUP COSTS

The costs of a full CERCLA cleanup are often extremely high. The following study examines the risks that a CERCLA cleanup reduces, and questions whether the mitigation of all of these risks is always worth the cost.

James T. Hamilton & W. Kip Viscusi, The Magnitude and Policy Implications of Health Risks from Hazardous Waste Sites

in ANALYZING SUPERFUND: ECONOMICS, SCIENCE, AND LAW 55, 55–83
(Richard L. Revesz & Richard B. Stewart eds., 1995).[*]

Identifying the Risks: An Overview of Our Analysis

. . . Our analysis represents the first systematic effort to document the character of the risks addressed by Superfund. Which population groups are most affected? How do these risks arise? What is the magnitude of the risks that are present? Are the risks in fact trivial, or are there serious threats to public health?

Most important from a policy standpoint, should we expand the range of policy options being considered? For instance, should we continue to favor the more "permanent" options of hazard treatment and removal over on-site containment and land-use restrictions? Although our analysis does not assess all attributes of hazardous waste policies, it does highlight a key dimension—the pathway by which the risks arise. Limited policy options, such as capping and fencing a site or restricting land use, can eliminate some mechanisms by which risks arise. Our analysis documents the nature of these risk pathways and provides startling evidence on the way in which these risks arise.

The character of the risks is in many respects quite surprising. Whereas risks to current residents have played a pivotal role in generating political support for the Superfund program, *the overwhelming preponderance of the risks is to future populations* for land uses that represent departures from current behavior. In our database of seventy-eight sites, there are thirty-five sites where future residential pathway risks occur despite the absence of any current residential risks exceeding the 10^{-6} cutoff level used in this analysis. The detailed analysis of the character of the risks, which leads to a wide variety of similar insights, is particularly instructive in highlighting how different policy mechanisms can influence the pathways responsible for generating the risk.

The Scope of Our Analysis

To address these issues, we analyze the human health risk assessments conducted at seventy-eight Superfund sites that had Records of Decision (RODs) signed in 1991 or 1992. We focus on the distribution of these risks across different categories of analysis in risk assessments. These categories of analysis include:

- time frame of exposure (current use or potential future uses)

- location of exposure (on-site or off-site)

- population type (residential, worker, recreational, trespasser)

- exposure medium (such as soil or groundwater)

- exposure route (such as ingestion, dermal contact, inhalation) . . .

Risk Assessments at Superfund Sites

Risk Assessment Pathways

Part of the decisions involved in conducting the baseline risk assessments lies in determining what pathways to evaluate to derive quantitative estimates of cancer and noncancer risks. Our database defines the pathways in risk assessments by a number of different category variables: time scenario of exposure, exposed population, age group, location of population, location of medium, exposure medium, and exposure route.

The *time scenario* variable refers generally to whether land use envisioned in the risk assessment corresponds to the current use or is related to a projected use in the future. Current land use is determined by the risk assessor according to site inspection data, zoning information, census data, and aerial photographs. Our designation of a pathway as a current or future scenario is determined by whether the risk assessment defined the pathway as current or future. Note that not all current risks are risk pathways that actually represent a risk today. Some assessments are based on current potential scenarios where the land use in an area does not change but other things may change, such as the size of a groundwater contamination plume so that wells not currently contaminated are assumed to become contaminated. These "current potential" risks are defined as current risks in our analysis if the risk assessors described them as such risks.

Future risks are generally those associated with changes in land use or activities. The guidance provided by the RAGS [Risk Assessment Guidance for Superfund] encourages risk assessors to consider a scenario where land that is currently not residential is brought into residential use in the future. The guidance document states:

> Because residential land use is most often associated with the greatest exposures, it is generally the most conservative choice to make when deciding what type of alternative land use may occur in the future. Assume future residential land use if it seems possible based on the evaluation of the available information.

Thus, future residential risks may be estimated at sites that are currently undeveloped or industrial and that have a low probability of future residential use. In our database of seventy-eight sites, there are thirty-five where future residential pathway risks occur despite the absence of any current residential risks exceeding the 10^{-6} cutoff level used in this analysis.

Exposed populations for which pathways are estimated include residents; workers; recreational users, such as swimmers or hunters; and trespassers. Though risk assessments are often conducted with very specific age group designations for the particular pathway described, we have (for this analysis) generally collapsed the different age groupings into adult (ages eighteen and higher) and child (ages less than eighteen).

The risk assessment category for the *location of population* generally refers to where the particular population is exposed to the contaminant (for residents, location of population refers to where they live).

Location of medium refers to whether the contaminant for which the pathway is estimated is on-site or off-site.

Exposure medium describes in what medium the individual is exposed to the contaminant (such as air, groundwater, soil, or biota, that is, plants or animals containing chemicals that are later consumed by humans).

Exposure route details how a person comes into contact with the chemical. For example, soil contaminants may enter the body through ingestion or through dermal contact or through inhalation.

Categories of Cancer and Noncancer Pathways

In our analysis, we break down the description of cancer and noncancer pathways by risk assessment categories. Determining the relative magnitudes of current versus future risks is important in distinguishing how estimates of human health risks at Superfund sites are affected by assumptions about future land use. Designating whether risks involve residents, workers, recreational users, or trespassers is a necessary step in analyzing the efficacy of different policy options for reducing human health risks. Similarly, analyzing whether the populations exposed are on-site or off-site and whether the contaminants are on-site or off-site is a necessary part of evaluating the impact of remedies at Superfund sites.

We also analyze the contribution of specific chemicals to the risks posed. Since uncertainty may exist over the toxicity of particular chemicals, consideration of the relative frequency of these chemicals at sites and their estimated contribution to pathway risks may help determine where additional resources could be devoted to defining the risks of these chemicals or developing remedies to deal with particular types of contaminants. . . .

Risk Pathway Mechanisms

An examination of the distribution of pathways is instructive to get a sense of the frequency with which alternative risk exposure mechanisms are operative. However, one should be cautious in proceeding from a pathway count to making inferences about the total level of the risk associated with a particular grouping of pathways. The risk associated with a set of pathways is governed not only by the number of such pathways but also by the magnitude of the risk associated with them. Pathways for which there is a high probability of an adverse outcome consequently pose greater risk than those with a lower probability. . . .

Distribution of Pathways by Risk Assessment Categories

Table 1 provides a comprehensive overview of the distribution of the risk pathways by various categories of analysis. The columns of statistics in the table provide the pertinent breakdowns within the risk assessment categories for all 1,430 pathways, for the 1,015 cancer pathways, and for the 415 noncancer pathways in the sample.

The first distinction in the table, which is perhaps the most salient result of the study, pertains to the breakdown between risks arising from current uses of the land and risks arising from future uses. This distinction pertains not to the time period of the risk but rather to the nature of the context in which the risks will arise. For example, future risks to current residents are generally captured under the "current" timeframe designation, but new uses, such as the decision to build a residential area on land that is now a Superfund site, would be a "future" risk. The striking result of Table 1 is that the great majority of the risk pathways pertain to such future risk exposures as opposed to risks associated with current uses. Overall, 70 percent of the cancer pathways, 79 percent of the noncancer pathways, and 72 percent of the total pathways pertain to future as opposed to current uses.

Of the exposed population types, the most important in terms of the risk pathways is that of residential populations. Approximately three-fourths of all pathways pertain to residential populations, with the next most important group being workers, for whom only 17 percent of the pathways are pertinent. Recreational users, such as those who fish in streams on Superfund sites, account for a very small fraction of all the risk pathways.

In terms of the age distribution of those affected by the risk pathways, most of the risk pathways (over 60 percent) are to adult populations, and just over one-third of the risk pathways pertain to children (that is, those under eighteen years of age). The main difference between these figures and the overall age distribution of the U.S. population is that whereas 37 percent of the risks are to the child age population, this group comprises only 26 percent of the U.S. population overall. Thus, the pathways affecting children occur almost 1.5 times as often as the representation of children in the population.

Table 1. Distribution of Pathways by Risk Assessment Categories (%)

Risk Assessment Category	Total Pathways ($N = 1,430$)	Cancer Pathways ($N = 1,015$)	Noncancer Pathways ($N = 415$)
Scenario			
Current	27.8	30.5	21.0
Future	72.2	69.5	79.0
Exposed population type			
Residential	73.2	71.2	78.1
Worker	17.4	17.8	16.4
Recreational	3.6	3.8	3.1
Trespasser	5.8	7.2	2.4
Age group			
Adult	62.7	65.3	56.4
Child	37.3	34.7	43.6
Location of population			
On-site	69.2	70.2	66.7
Off-site	23.2	23.3	22.9
Not indicated	7.6	6.5	10.4
Location of Medium			
On-site	79.6	80.3	77.8
Off-site	13.7	14.3	12.3
Not indicated	6.7	5.4	9.9
Exposure Medium			
Air (from soil)	9.0	9.0	8.9
Air (from water)	9.0	10.4	5.3
Soil	33.6	38.2	22.2
Groundwater	37.2	30.8	52.8
Surface water	1.0	1.1	0.7
Sediment	5.2	5.7	3.9
Biota	3.6	2.9	5.3
Structures	0.1	0.2	—
Sludge	0.8	0.9	0.5
Combination	0.3	0.4	—
Leachate	0.1	0.2	—
Mothers' milk	0.3	0.2	0.5
Exposure Route			
Ingestion	58.4	53.7	69.9
Dermal contact	22.6	25.7	14.9
Inhalation (vapor phase chemicals)	13.0	14.6	9.4
Inhalation (dust)	5.7	5.8	5.3
Dermal contact and inhalation	0.3	0.2	0.5

The location where the risks arise is also of substantial interest, particularly as it relates to the potential efficacy of policy options that limit future uses of land at or near Superfund sites. Both the location of the populations and the location of the medium (that is, the location of the medium from which the risks arise) are heavily concentrated toward on-site risks. Of the total pathways, 69 percent pertain to risks to on-site populations; 80 percent of the media associated with the pathways pertain to on-site media. The particular media that appear to be most prominent are soil and groundwater, as each of these accounts for over one-third of all pathways. The other relatively important exposure media are air (from soil), air (from water), and sediment, each of which accounts for 5 percent to 10 percent of all pathways. If the two air pathway mechanisms are aggregated, they account for almost one-fifth of all pathways.

The final component of Table 1 lists the exposure route by which the risk arises. The dominant exposure route is that of ingestion, such as drinking contaminated groundwater or ingesting dirt, where this category gives rise to 58 percent of all pathways. Dermal contact accounts for 23 percent of all of the different exposure routes, and inhalation of vapor phase chemicals and dust are next in importance.

For the exposure routes as well as for most of the other components of the table, the distribution of pathways is fairly similar for both cancer pathways and noncancer pathways. The major distinctions are that the noncancer pathways play a more prominent role in the future risk scenarios, are more likely to affect residential populations, are less likely to affect adults, are more likely to involve groundwater exposure rather than soil, and are more likely to arise from ingestion rather than dermal contact.

Distribution of Pathways by Scenario and Exposed Population

Table 2 analyzes the distribution of the exposed population and the location of the exposed population for each of the two land use scenarios. Overall, the great majority of the pathways are accounted for by residents based on future risk scenarios, which account for 59 percent of the pathways. In contrast, current risks to current residents, as well as future populations in current residential areas, account for only 14 percent of the risk. The next most prevalent category, that of workers, also has a greater number of pathways for future scenarios as opposed to current time frames, but the difference is not as stark as in the case of the residential risks.

Table 2. Distribution of Pathways

Distribution by Exposed Population Type

Scenario	Residential	Worker	Recreational	Trespasser
Current	13.85	6.43	1.96	5.52
Future	59.37	10.91	1.68	0.28

Distribution by Population Location

Scenario	On-site	Off-site	Not Indicated
Current	15.38	10.91	1.47
Future	53.78	12.31	6.15

Note: All figures are a percentage of total pathways, where
$N = 1,430$

There is also a substantial difference in the character of the risks with respect to their population location and the time frame for the analysis. On-site risks under current scenarios account for 15 percent of the pathways, which is only somewhat greater than the current off-site risks of 11 percent. For the future based scenarios, however, on-site risks escalate to account for 54 percent of the pathways, which is more than four times as great as the 12 percent of the pathways due to future off-site risks. Overall, 90 percent of current pathways are on-site residential pathways, 59 percent of future pathways are on-site residential, and future on-site residential pathways account for 43 percent of all pathways in the sample. *The dominant exposure to risks consequently arises from the expected future residential exposures on Superfund sites.*

In the case of residents, the chief risks arise from ingestion of either groundwater or soil. Resident ingestion of groundwater accounts for a quarter of all total pathways. Although Superfund anecdotes frequently highlight the importance of children who eat dirt, it is noteworthy that ingestion of soil plays a much greater proportional role in the risk pathways for workers than it does for residents. Dermal contact with soil and ingestion of groundwater also account for a substantial share of the risks to workers and a significant share of all total pathways.

The risk pathways for recreational users and trespassers account for a very small percentage of all pathways in the sample, but the distribution within these groups is nevertheless of interest. The primary risk to recreational users is that from dermal contact with soil, with ingestion of soil and inhalation of the vapor phase chemicals from soil being next in importance. For trespassers, the major risks are from ingestion of soil and ingestion of sediment, which together account for almost half of all the risks to trespassers. . . .

Risk Levels Associated with Pathways

Risk-Weighted Shares of Cancer Pathway Risks

Analysis of the frequency of risk pathways gives a sense of how often the pathways are pertinent; consideration of the risk levels associated with the pathways indicates the magnitudes of the risk per pathway. However, the overall level of the risk that will be generated at a Superfund site will reflect the combined influence of the frequency with which particular types of risk pathways occur as well as the levels of the risk associated with different types of pathways. . . .

To convey information concerning both the frequency and magnitude of pathway cancer risks, Table 6 provides statistics on the risk-weighted shares of the different cancer risk pathways. Rather than simply determining the fraction of the pathways represented by particular types of exposures, such as risk to future generations, each of these pathways is weighted by the total magnitude of the risk estimated for that pathway and the risk-weighted pathways are then summed for the entire sample. The statistics in Table 6 provide information on the percentage of the total risk-weighted pathways accounted for by each pathway type.

The principal purpose of combining the influence of the frequency of pathway occurrence with the magnitude of the risk is to generate a hybrid of the two influences discussed above. For example, in the case of future risk scenarios, we found that future risk pathways were not only more prevalent than pathways based on current risk scenarios, but that these pathways posed a greater risk level per pathway as well. The compounding of these influences is borne out in the statistics in Table 6, as 91 percent of all total cancer pathway risks are attributable to future risk scenarios. This emphasis on future risks is much greater than the unweighted share of future pathways, which we found in Table 1 to be only 72 percent.

Table 6. Risk-Weighted Shares of Cancer Pathway Risks (%)

Risk Assessment Category	Total Cancer Pathway Risk	Future Cancer Pathway Risk	Current Cancer Pathway Risk
Scenario			
Current	8.8	——	100.0
Future	91.2	100.0	——
Age group			
Adult	74.9	74.5	78.5
Child	25.1	25.5	21.5
Exposed population type			
Residential	87.3	89.4	65.6
Worker	11.0	9.4	27.7
Recreational	1.4	1.2	3.6
Trespasser	0.2	0.0	3.1
Location of population			
On-site	77.5	81.0	40.9
Off-site	19.9	17.4	45.4
Not indicated	2.7	1.6	13.7
Exposure Medium			
Air (from soil)	4.5	4.2	7.3
Air (from water)	2.1	2.0	3.1
Soil	32.9	34.2	19.4
Groundwater	47.7	49.1	32.8
Surface water	0.0	0.0	0.0
Sediment	0.5	0.5	1.0
Biota	10.0	7.5	36.5
Structures	0.0	0.0	0.0
Sludge	0.3	0.3	0.0
Combination	0.0	0.0	0.0
Leachate	0.0	0.0	0.0
Mothers' milk	1.8	2.0	0.0
Exposure Route			
Ingestion	65.4	64.6	74.1
Dermal exposure	28.0	29.2	15.6
Inhalation (vapor phase chemicals)	6.2	5.9	9.4
Inhalation (dust)	0.3	0.3	0.9
Ingestion and dermal	——	——	——
Inhalation and dermal	0.0	——	——

The other statistics in the table are presented for total cancer pathway risks, future cancer pathway risks, and current cancer pathway risks. In terms of the distribution of risks, by far the largest risk share is for adults for current pathways and for future pathways.

A very strong contrast arises with respect to risks to the various exposed populations. Residential populations account for 66 percent of the current cancer pathway risks, and this figure escalates to 89 percent for future risk pathways. Similarly, exposures to workers account for 28 percent of current cancer pathway risks, and this figure drops to only 9 percent for future risk pathways.

The location of the populations affected by these risks also changes dramatically depending on the time frame for the risk scenario. The percentage role of on-site population risks rises from 41 percent to 81 percent when one moves to the future risk scenarios, and the role of offsite drops from 45 percent to 17 percent. The implications of the exposed population and location of population results is that future risk scenarios put a much greater weight on risks posed to on-site residential areas. Of the exposure media listed in Table 6 the most noteworthy pattern is that groundwater risks account for almost half of the future cancer risk pathways, as contrasted with about one-third of these pathways for current cancer risk assessments. . . .

Conclusion

Most of the political pressures that generated the impetus for the Superfund program arose because of the concern of existing populations for the risks that they believe these sites currently pose. Consideration of the risk assessments for Superfund sites indicates, however, that it is not the existing risks that are most salient. Rather, the dominant risks arise from future risk scenarios that generally involve alternative uses of the land. Indeed, these future risks account for 90 percent of all the risk-weighted pathways for the Superfund sites in our sample. Chief among these future risks is that of future residents living on-site. The underlying assumption driving the EPA risk analyses is that there will be new residential areas on existing future Superfund sites where there are currently no such residential areas.

Analysis of the structure of risks is of fundamental importance with respect to the choice of different possible modes of government intervention. If some mechanism were available that could eliminate these future risks, such as the use of various use restrictions and containment options, then the great preponderance of the risks analyzed in human health assessments at Superfund sites would be eliminated. Indeed, examination of the risk pathways suggested that many of the risks likely to remain with such containment and land-use restriction options, such as that to trespassers, are very low even without adopting policies, such as fencing, to reduce these risks. . . .

NOTES AND QUESTIONS

1. **Burden of Risks.** According to Hamilton and Viscusi, which group of people suffer the greatest risk from Superfund sites? What proportion of the risk does this group face?

2.　Selection of Remedies. How should the Hamilton and Viscusi study influence the selection of Superfund remedies? Is it likely that deed restrictions will be respected in the future? What is the likely impact of containment and fencing (rather than a permanent cleanup) on land use development around the site? Would the racial and demographic characteristics of the surrounding communities affect your views on this matter? How would you view the choice between extensive cleanup that would make the site suitable for future residential use and less extensive cleanup that would permit only industrial use? Does your answer depend on how the surrounding land is currently used?

States have begun to adopt legislation such as the Uniform Environmental Covenants Act to make it easier to enforce land use restrictions on contaminated property. This legislation is intended to spur redevelopment at sites where full remediation is impossible or economically infeasible. *See* Linda Roeder, *States Adopting Model Law to Help Enforce Land-Use Restrictions at Contaminated Sites*, 38 BNA ENV'T REP., Oct. 12, 2007, at 2207. Will covenants effectively ensure that the contaminated land will never be put to a use in which the contamination might lead to serious health risks? Will covenants provide enough of a guarantee against future inappropriate uses that developers will be willing to acquire contaminated land? Can complementary zoning restrictions adequately safeguard future interests?

Currently, private parties undertaking a cleanup and seeking to recover costs must determine a site's baseline risk by assessing "current and potential threats to human health and the environment." 40 C.F.R. § 300.430(d)(4). How might a baseline risk assessment and the subsequent establishment of acceptable exposure levels influence the development of remedial options for a site?

3.　Risk Avoidance and Risk Reduction. There are two main methods of limiting the health risks posed by environmental contamination. One, risk reduction, is comprised of cleanups that reduce the levels of contamination. The other, risk avoidance, is comprised of strategies that rely on changes in behavior to avoid environmental risk, such as restricting contaminated areas to future industrial uses or fencing-off a contaminated area and posting signs warning residents of the environmental risk. Risk avoidance may often be far less expensive than risk reduction—cleaning up a site to comply with all ARARs can cost millions of dollars, whereas putting up a fence or restricting the use of a site is relatively inexpensive. Is it a better use of limited resources to lower the level of cleanup at some sites and restrict them to industrial uses in the future, or to fence off certain areas and post signs warning residents of the contamination? Do we want to live in communities where we have to avoid nearby contaminated areas to avoid exposing ourselves to environmental risks? What about possible ecological harm stemming from a reduced level of cleanup? As discussed above, is there any way to guarantee that contaminated sites will not be put to residential use at some point in the future? For a criticism of over-reliance on risk avoidance, see Catherine A. O'Neill, *No Mud Pies: Risk Avoidance as Risk Reduction*, 31 VT. L. REV. 273 (2007).

4.   Brownfields. How are the brownfields provisions of CERCLA, discussed above, consistent with the findings of Hamilton and Viscusi?

5.   Effect of Population Size. Hamilton and Viscusi did not consider the size of the populations affected at a Superfund site or the costs of achieving risk reductions. Another empirical study found that EPA did not tolerate higher risks to surrounding populations at sites with higher cleanup costs. Shreekant Gupta, George Van Houtven & Maureen L. Cropper, *Do Benefits and Costs Matter in Environmental Regulation?: An Analysis of EPA Decisions Under Superfund, in* ANALYZING SUPERFUND: ECONOMICS, SCIENCE, AND LAW 83 (Richard L. Revesz & Richard B. Stewart eds., 1995). This study also found, somewhat paradoxically, that higher risks are selected in urban areas, which are more densely populated, than in rural areas. The authors speculate that EPA may be reluctant to excavate soils in urban areas and that sites in urban areas might be intended for industrial use, for which extensive cleanups might be less necessary. Finally the study also found that the racial and economic composition of the surrounding population is not a factor in the choice of target risk.

Should factors such as the size of the affected population or the magnitude of cleanup costs be considered in deciding how much to spend on cleanups? Are the arguments raised by this question comparable to those relevant to the assessment of the desirability of uniform ambient standards under the CAA? Consider the more localized nature of the effects of hazardous waste contamination.

6.   Cleanup Standards and Community Choice. Should communities surrounding a Superfund site be able to agree to less extensive cleanups than would otherwise be required in return for the financing of other projects that reduce health risks? For example, consider two possible uses for $30 million in an isolated community:

(a)   a $30 million cleanup, which would reduce to one in a million the probability that a resident would contract cancer from exposure to the site; and

(b)   a cleanup costing $5 million, which would reduce this probability to one in a hundred thousand, coupled with $25 million for a clinic.

If it is undisputed that the latter option produces a larger improvement in the health of the community, should EPA be able to defer to the community's preference for the latter option? For further discussion, see John D. Graham & March Sadowitz, *Superfund Reform: Reducing Risks Through Community Choice*, ISSUES IN SCI. & TECH., Summer 1994, at 35. Should EPA be able to choose the latter option if the community desires the former? How should the analysis be affected if, instead of using the $25 million for a clinic, the community wishes to use the money for a school or to reduce taxes? These issues are discussed at length in Chapter II.

7.   Groundwater Remediation. The most expensive part of cleanups is generally groundwater remediation. Should such remediation be undertaken if the surrounding communities do not currently use the water for drinking and if there exist abundant alternative supplies to meet future demand? Is it desirable to undertake such cleanups if they can be justified only by reference to existence values? Is it likely that such valuations would be high in the case of groundwater? In what way does the outcome of the *Ohio v. EPA* case influence your answers?

v. COMPLIANCE WITH THE NCP

Under CERCLA, PRPs may be held liable for response costs incurred by the federal government or a state that are "not inconsistent with" the NCP, 42 U.S.C. § 9607(a)(4)(A), and response costs incurred by private parties that are "consistent with" the NCP, 42 U.S.C. § 9607(a)(4)(B). In a § 113 contribution action, PRPs may recover costs from other PRPs who are liable under the terms of § 107(a). 42 U.S.C. § 9613(f)(1). As a result, both cost recovery and contribution actions are available only for cleanup actions that comply with the NCP.

Costs incurred by EPA need only be "not inconsistent with" the NCP to be recoverable. 42 U.S.C. § 9607(a)(4)(A). CERCLA instructs the courts to review EPA's choice of response actions deferentially: Section 113 provides that a reviewing court "shall uphold the President's decision in selecting the response action unless the objecting party can demonstrate, on the administrative record, that the decision was arbitrary and capricious or otherwise not in accordance with law." 42 U.S.C. § 9613(j)(2); *see also City of Bangor v. Citizens Commc'ns Co.*, 532 F.3d 70, 91 (1st Cir. 2008) ("Actions undertaken by the federal or a state government are presumed not to be inconsistent with the NCP. . . ."); *United States v. Hardage*, 982 F.2d 1436, 1442 (10th Cir. 1992) (burden is on objecting party to demonstrate inconsistency with NCP and standard of review is arbitrary and capricious), *cert. denied*, 510 U.S. 913 (1993). Under this deferential standard of review, EPA's choice of response action is almost always sufficient to support a § 107(a)(4)(A) cost recovery action.

Costs incurred by private parties must be "consistent with" the NCP to support a cost recovery action, 42 U.S.C. § 9607(a)(4)(B), and the burden is on the party seeking such recovery to prove that its actions were consistent with the NCP. The following case deals with the requirements the NCP imposes on private cleanup actions.

Raytheon Constructors, Inc. v. ASARCO, Inc.

2000 WL 1635482 (D. Colo. 2000), *rev'd on other grounds*, 368 F.3d 1214 (10th Cir. 2003).

■ NOTTINGHAM, DISTRICT JUDGE:

"No good deed goes unpunished." This declaratory judgment action is before the court for findings of fact and conclusions of law on the issue of the amount of damages for which Plaintiff Raytheon Constructors, Inc. ("Raytheon") is liable to Defendant ASARCO Incorporated ("ASARCO") under the Comprehensive Environmental Response, Compensation, and

Liability Act, 42 U.S.C.A. §§ 9601–9675 (West 1995 & Supp.1999) [hereinafter "CERCLA"]. . . .

. . . In the first phase of this litigation, I held that Raytheon, as the corporate successor in interest to Stearns-Roger Manufacturing Company ("Stearns-Roger"), is liable to ASARCO for forty percent of the cleanup costs at the Rawley Mine and Rawley Mill (collectively "the Rawley Site") on three grounds: (1) as an "operator" under CERCLA, 42 U.S.C.A. § 9607(a)(2); (2) as an "arranger" under CERCLA, 42 U.S.C.A. § 9607(a)(3); and/or (3) as a joint tortfeasor under the Colorado Uniform Contribution Among Tortfeasors Act, Colo.Rev.Stat. § 13–50.5–101 to 106 (West 1999) [hereinafter "UCATA"]. (Liability Order.) In this phase of the litigation, Raytheon seeks to avoid paying any of the forty percent of the cleanup costs for which I held it was liable in the first phase of these proceedings. . . .

The primary remaining dispute in the present protracted litigation is whether ASARCO's response costs were incurred in compliance with the NCP. The NCP is a series of regulations which provide a roadmap for performing a "CERCLA quality cleanup." *County Line Inv. Co. v. Tinney,* 933 F.2d 1508, 1514 (10th Cir. 1991) (citation omitted). The NCP "sets performance standards, identifies methods for investigating the environmental impact of a release or threatened release, and establishes criteria for determining the appropriate extent of response activities." *OHM Remediation Servs.,* 116 F.3d at 1579; 40 C.F.R. § 300 (1998). Where the party seeking recovery or contribution for response costs is the United States, a State, or an Indian tribe, there is a presumption that the costs were incurred in a fashion consistent with the NCP. *United States v. Hardage,* 982 F.2d 1436, 1442 (10th Cir. 1992). In contrast, any "other party" seeking costs from a PRP bears the burden of proving that its actions were consistent with the NCP. *Id.; accord Washington State Dep't of Transp. v. Washington Natural Gas Co., Pacificorp,* 59 F.3d 793, 799 (9th Cir. 1995). Thus, ASARCO bears the burden of proving the consistency of its response actions with the NCP before it may obtain contribution from Raytheon. *See Public Serv. Co. of Colo.,* 175 F.3d at 1181 n. 5 ("Consistency with the NCP is not only an essential element of proof under § 9607[a] but also becomes the lynchpin for § 9613[f] contribution."); *County Line Inv. Co.,* 933 F.2d at 1516 (holding that "absent a showing that [a party's] response costs were incurred consistent with the NCP, no right to contribution for these costs exists under CERCLA"); *see also Bancamerica Comm. Corp. v. Mosher Steel of Kan., Inc.,* 100 F.3d 792, 796 (10th Cir. 1996) ("In order for [the PRP who financed the cleanup] to obtain contribution from [another PRP], [its] response actions must have been 'consistent with the [NCP].' ") (quoting 42 U.S.C.A. § 9607[a][4][B]) (footnote omitted). The NCP regulations currently in force provide that "[a] private party response action will be considered 'consistent with the NCP' if the action, when evaluated as a whole, is in *substantial compliance* with the applicable requirements in paragraphs (5) and (6) of this section and results in a CERCLA-quality clean-up. . . ." 40 C.F.R. § 300.700(c)(3)(1). Section 300.700(c)(3)(1) defines "consistent with the NCP" to require substantial compliance when the response is evaluated as a whole. "Immaterial or insubstantial deviations" from the provisions of 40 C.F.R. part 300 "will not be considered not consistent with the NCP." 40 C.F.R. § 300.700(c)(4). Thus, it is through the lens of substantial compliance with the NCP that ASARCO's actions must be viewed. . . .

The NCP regarding private remedial actions has four primary requirements, each of which is detailed through extensive regulation: (1) identification of applicable or relevant and appropriate requirements ("ARARs"), as mandated by 40 C.F.R. § 300.400(g); (2) remedial site evaluation, which may consist of two steps, including a remedial preliminary assessment ("PA") and a remedial site inspection ("SI"), as required by 40 C.F.R. § 300.420; (3) remedial investigation/feasibility study and selection of remedy, as required by 40 C.F.R. § 300.430; and (4) remedial design ("RD")/remedial action ("RA"), operation, and maintenance of selected remedy, as required by 40 C.F.R. § 300.435. In addition, the statute provides a whole separate section of regulations under the "public comment" aegis. *See* 40 C.F.R. § 300.700(c)(6) (outlining a panoply of public comment requirements for each stage of the remedial process, according to 40 C.F.R. §§ 300.415, 300.430, and 300.435). Finally, as noted above, for a private party to obtain contribution for a response action, it must also demonstrate that the action resulted in a "CERCLA-quality cleanup." Several of the "CERCLA-quality" standards are similar to those already mandated by the NCP provisions, although they speak more to the end-product than the process used to arrive there. In its preamble to the 1990 revisions to the NCP, the EPA culled the revised CERCLA statute to define a "CERCLA-quality cleanup" by private actors. To reach such a standard, the remedial action must:

(1) be "protective of human health and the environment," utilize "permanent solutions and alternative treatment technologies or resource recovery technologies to the maximum extent practicable," and be "cost-effective"[;]

(2) attain applicable and relevant and appropriate requirements (ARARs) [; and]

(3) provide for meaningful public participation.

40 C.F.R. § 300.430(f)(1)(ii)(A), (D), and (E); *see also County Line Inv. Co.,* 933 F.2d at 1514 (citing same).

Raytheon contends that ASARCO should not be able to recover the majority of its costs because (1) ASARCO failed to conduct an RI/FS; and (2) ASARCO failed to provide a meaningful opportunity for public participation. (Raytheon's Trial Br. At 16–18.) ASARCO acknowledges that it produced no actual RI/FS study document, but contends that the

Initial Work Plan and other associated documents are the functional equivalent of an RI/FS and thus substantially comply with the RI/FS requirement. (Def. ASARCO's Trial Br. at 24–25.) The regulations state that the purpose of the remedial investigation is "to collect data necessary to adequately characterize the site for the purpose of developing and evaluating effective remedial alternatives." 40 C.F.R. § 300.430(d)(1).

As noted above, the NCP for remedial actions provide for remedial site evaluation, remedial investigation, and analysis of remedial alternatives. See 40 C.F.R. § 300.700(c)(5)(vii)–(viii). Substantial compliance with the detailed provisions of § 300.430 is required in order to satisfy the requirement. Section 300.700(c)(5)(viii) directs private parties to compile an RI/FS in accordance with § 300.430 before conducting a cleanup. The RI/FS process requires the private party to "conduct field investigations, including treatability studies, and conduct a baseline risk assessment" in order to provide information for the analysis of the initial threat of the contamination to health, welfare, and the environment and to support the development, evaluation, and selection of the appropriate response actions. *Id.* § 300.430(d)(1). The investigation must also take into account numerous factors ranging from the physical characteristics of the site and of the waste to the potential exposure pathway through environmental media in deciding the type of remedial action to be taken. *Id.* § 300.430(d)(2)(i)–(vii).

Next, the alternatives generated must undergo a feasibility evaluation. *Id.* § 300.430(e). The feasibility study is intended to ensure that "appropriate remedial alternatives are developed and evaluated such that relevant information concerning the remedial action options can be presented to a decision-maker and an appropriate remedy selected." *Id.* § 300.430(e)(1). Alternatives that protect human health and the environment are then developed. *Id.* § 300.430(e)(2). In developing and screening the alternatives, the NCP mandates that the lead agency or private party: (1) establish remedial action objectives which specify contaminants and media of concern, potential exposure pathways, and remediation goals; (2) identify and evaluate potentially suitable technologies; and (3) assemble the suitable technologies into alternative remedial actions. *Id.* § 300.430(e)(i)–(iii). The remedial alternatives are then screened against three criteria: effectiveness, implementability, and cost. *Id.* § 300.430(e)(7)(i)–(iii).[3]

---

[3] The effectiveness criterion focuses on "the degree to which an alternative reduces toxicity, mobility, or volume through treatment, minimizes residual risks and affords long-term protection, complies with ARARs, minimizes short-term impacts, and how quickly it achieves protection." 40 C.F.R. § 300.430(e)(7)(i). The implementability criterion considers "the technical feasibility and availability of the technologies each alternative would employ and the administrative feasibility of implementing the alternative." *Id.* § 300.430(e)(7)(ii). The cost criterion considers construction costs as well as any long-term costs to operate and maintain the alternatives considered. *Id.* § 300.430(e)(7)(iii).

At the next stage, the NCP mandates a further "detailed analysis of alternatives" on a limited number of alternatives "that represent viable approaches to remedial action." 40 C.F.R. § 300.430(e)(9)(i)–(ii). The analysis must consider the following factors (in order of importance): (1) overall protection of human health and the environment; (2) compliance with ARARS; (3) long-term effectiveness and permanence; (4) reduction of toxicity, mobility or volume through treatment; (5) short-term effectiveness; (6) implementability; (7) cost; (8) state acceptance; and (9) community acceptance. 40 C.F.R. § 300.430(e)(9)(iii). After completing the detailed analysis of the various alternatives, the process proceeds to a selection of remedies phase. A preferred alternative response is identified and public comment is solicited and reviewed. *Id.* § 300.430(f)(1). A proposed plan is then presented to the public. *Id.* § 300.430(f)(2). The proposed plan provides a brief summary description of the various alternatives evaluated during the screening process, identifies and provides a discussion of the rationale supporting the preferred alternative, and summarizes any formal comments received from government agencies. *Id.* § 300.430(f)(2)(i)–(iv). After publication and a comment period on the proposed plan, a final remedy is selected. *Id.* § 300.430(f)(3)–(4). The decision is then documented in accordance with the provisions of § 300.430(f)(5).

ASARCO contends that the Initial Work Plan and subsequent documents are functionally equivalent to an RI/FS. (ASARCO's Trial. Br. at 24–25.) The Initial Work Plan collects the results of a year's worth of surface-water sampling which McCulley, Frick & Gilman conducted and also contains a review of past studies conducted in the Bonanza Mining District. (Def. ASARCO's Exs., Ex. I–2 [Initial Work Plan at 2–3 to 2–6].) The Initial Work Plan also includes a site characterization of the Rawley Site based upon historical studies performed on the Bonanza Mining District, and the Rawley Site in particular, including, *inter alia*, EPA's 1984 Preliminary Assessment, the 1991 Target Assessment, the SSI, and McCulley, Frick & Gilman's own surface-water sampling and analysis program. (*Id.*, Ex. I–2 [Initial Work Plan at 4–1 to 4–28].) Based upon this site characterization, the Initial Work Plan screened a variety of alternatives for the Rawley Site cleanup. (*Id.*, Ex. I–2 [Initial Work Plan at 5–1 to 5–22].) The primary criteria against which remedial alternatives were screened were: (1) overall protection of human health and the environment; (2) long-term effectiveness and permanence; (3) reduction of toxicity, mobility, and volume of hazardous substances; (4) short-term effectiveness; (5) implementability; and (6) cost. (*Id.*, Ex. I–2 [Initial Work Plan at 5–3].) The Initial Work Plan then discussed various potential alternative responses to the Rawley 12 Adit acid mine drainage discharge and tailings deposits. (*Id.*, Ex. I–2 [Initial Work Plan at 5–15 to 5–22].)

Raytheon contends that ASARCO's analysis does not substantially comply with the NCP requirements for an RI/FS. I agree. The feasibility study alternatives which are generated during the remedial investigation "must be evaluated against three criteria—effectiveness, implementability, and cost—each of which is then described at length." *Public Serv. Co.*, 22 F. Supp. 2d at 1194; 40 C.F.R. § 300.430(e)(7). The Initial Work Plan does not evaluate the alternative remedies "at length" based upon these criteria. For example, the Initial Work Plan contains only general statements about costs and no detailed cost comparison. Instead, there are only two short paragraphs comparing the costs of in very general terms—*i.e.*, that the costs were high or low. (Def. ASARCO's Exs., Ex. I–2 [Initial Work Plan at 5–21].) In addition, the Initial Work Plan devotes just over one page of double-spaced text to the comparison and selection of alternatives, which is hardly the type of detailed evaluation which the NCP contemplates. (*Id.*, Ex. I–2 [Initial Work Plan at 5–21 to 5–22].) It also appears that ASARCO failed to screen the alternatives which it considered against ARARs, as ARARs were not identified until after the Initial Work Plan had been created. Finally, after the alternative screening process, the Initial Work Plan did not evaluate the alternatives and select a remedy based upon the nine evaluative criteria set forth in § 40 C.F.R. § 300.430(e)(9)(iii). To the contrary, the Initial Work Plan contained a short discussion touching in quite general terms upon six of the mandated nine criteria. While this analysis suggests *some* compliance, I do not find it suggestive of *substantial* compliance with the NCP.

As I noted in *Public Service Company*, CERCLA is underlaid with "competing policies which complicate application of the NCP standards." *Public Serv. Co. of Colo.*, 22 F. Supp. 2d at 1190. Congress intended CERCLA cost recovery actions—both full recovery and contribution—to encourage private parties to "undertake hazardous waste cleanups with greater speed and at lower cost" than a government-run cleanup, particularly in light of the reality that "there are simply more private parties than there are government officials." *Channel Master*, 748 F. Supp. at 394 (quoting [Jeffrey M.] Gaba, *Recovering Hazardous Waste Cleanup Costs: The Private Cause of Action Under CERCLA*, 13 Ecology L.Q. 181, 231 [1986]). Certainly, this implies a need for flexibility in allowing private parties to initiate and conduct their own cleanups. Indeed, the NCP's preamble cautions that "an omission based on lack of experience with the Superfund program should not be grounds for defeating an otherwise valid cost recovery action, assuming the omission does not affect the quality of the cleanup." National Oil and Hazardous Substances Pollution Contingency Plan, 55 Fed.Reg. at 8793. Nonetheless, the complex and detailed regulatory scheme reveals that the purpose of requiring private parties to comply with NCP guidance "is to give some consistency and cohesiveness to response planning and actions," given the risks involved for the environment and the surrounding communities. *Channel Master*, 748 F. Supp. at 394 (quoting H.R.Rep. No. 96–1016, Pt. I at 30 [1980] *reprinted in* 1980 U.S.C.C.A.N. at 6133).

Courts have deemed noncompliance with NCP requirements important enough to deny relief to individual parties seeking response costs, even where several parties may have been liable for causing the environmental damage. *See, e.g., County Line Inv. Co.*, 933 F.2d at 1517; *VME Am. Inc.*, 946 F. Supp. at 692 (denying party relief under CERCLA for failure to substantially comply with the NCP); *Yellow Freight Sys., Inc. v. ACF Indus., Inc.*, 909 F. Supp. 1290 (E.D.Mo.1995) (same); *Channel Master*, 748 F. Supp. at 393 (same). I am quite cognizant that, by holding that certain of ASARCO's actions were inconsistent with the NCP, I am reaching a result that holds ASARCO, which has unquestionably acted in a considerably more responsible fashion than Raytheon, liable for more than its fair share of the costs of cleaning up its own mess and that of Raytheon at the Rawley Site. I am also convinced that Raytheon would be petulant and complaining no matter how ASARCO had gone about cleaning up the Rawley Site. Unfortunately, Raytheon's complaints about ASARCO's conduct at the Rawley site are meritorious. As unpalatable as allowing Raytheon to dodge full responsibility is, to hold otherwise would do a measure of violence to the careful outline of the NCP. The incentive which CERCLA gives to private parties to conduct cleanups "is not . . . without its costs. Unchaining private forces to begin digging up and moving hazardous wastes does, of course, raise concerns of § [9607](a)(4)(B). . . . The NCP rel[ies] almost exclusively on private judgments about complex and ambiguous environmental standards." *Channel Master Satellite Sys.*, 748 F. Supp. at 394 (quoting Gaba, *supra*, at 231–32). In this case, ASARCO is subject to the higher, remedial cleanup standard because it had the opportunity to plan for more contingencies and to engage the affected community. "[S]ince [ASARCO] seeks recovery under the CERCLA statute, [ASARCO] is required to comply with the specific requirements of that statutory claim, as set forth in the regulations and caselaw." *Id.* ASARCO fell short of this gauge and it therefore may not obtain full contribution from Raytheon. . . .

NOTES AND QUESTIONS

1. **"No Good Deed Goes Unpunished."** The *ASARCO* court begins its opinion by apologizing for the unfairness of allowing Raytheon to avoid contribution. In omitted portions of the opinion, the court describes in detail the long-term cleanup effort that ASARCO conducted. Some of the technical studies relied on in ASARCO's Initial Work Plan (which ASARCO claimed was the functional equivalent of a RI/FS) were conducted by EPA and the U.S. Forest Service; throughout the cleanup, ASARCO communicated and collaborated with various federal and state officials and kept them appraised of the cleanup choices made at the site; and at no point did any state or federal official request that ASARCO prepare a more comprehensive RI/FS. ASARCO also informed surrounding residents of the cleanup and took precautions that the cleanup process would not endanger them. Raytheon refused to participate in any of the cleanup activities over the course of the

many years that ASARCO conducted the site cleanup. Should ASARCO's cleanup have been found to be in "substantial compliance" with the NCP in order to allow it to collect contribution from Raytheon? Would so holding allow other private parties in future private cleanup actions to intentionally cut corners to minimize their own costs, potentially increasing environmental contamination and health risks at the site?

2. Competing Objectives. The *ASARCO* decision attempts to balance two competing policy objectives. On the one hand, the court is conscious of not creating incentives for private parties to cut corners in the performance of cleanup actions. On the other hand, the court understands that in finding against ASARCO, it will create disincentives for private parties to undertake cleanup actions in the first place. Which objective do you consider to be most important in the context of the Superfund regime as a whole? Do you think the decision of the *ASARCO* court adequately balances these competing objectives?

3. Working with Environmental Agencies. As discussed above, courts presume that actions undertaken by federal or state governments are consistent with the NCP. *E.g.*, *City of Bangor v. Citizens Commc'ns Co.*, 532 F.3d 70, 91 (1st Cir. 2008). What about actions taken by private parties that are monitored and approved by federal or state environmental agencies? A few circuits have held that work carried out under the aegis of a federal or state environmental agency is entitled to the same deference as work undertaken by federal and state governments directly. *See Niagara Mohawk Power Corp. v. Chevron USA Inc.*, 596 F.3d 112, 137 (2d Cir. 2010); *NutraSweet Co. v. X-L Eng'g Co.*, 227 F.3d 776, 791 (7th Cir. 2000). One district court held that a company's failure to comply fully with a remedial action plan does not mandate dismissal of its cost recovery claim when the county health department took part in the cleanup and it acted under a consent order with the state environmental agency. *Rococo Assocs., Inc. v. Award Packaging Corp.*, 803 F. Supp. 2d 184 (E.D.N.Y. 2011).

4. Remedial and Removal Actions. In another omitted portion of the opinion, the *ASARCO* court examined each phase of ASARCO's cleanup efforts and classified each as either removal or remedial actions. In deciding whether each phase of the cleanup should be considered a removal or remedial action, the court considered several factors:

> (a) the nature of the action taken; (b) the imminence of the release or threatened release; (c) whether a federal or state agency has found the existence of a threat to public health and safety or to the environment; (d) whether an agency has recommended a course of action to eliminate the threat [;] and (e) the cost, complexity[,] and duration of the activity.

ASARCO, 2000 WL 1635482, at *15 (citing *Hatco Corp. v. W.R. Grace & Co.*, 849 F. Supp. 931 (D.N.J. 1994)). The NCP's requirements for removal actions are much less detailed than for remedial actions. For example, remedial actions must be cost-effective, can only be conducted after a site assessment, and must allow opportunity for public comment on alternative remedial actions; none of these requirements apply to removal actions. *See* 40 C.F.R.

§§ 300.435, 300.415. The *ASARCO* court found that ASARCO had complied with the NCP's requirements, and so could recover costs, for those portions of the cleanup that the court determined constituted removal actions, rather than remedial actions. *ASARCO*, 2000 WL 1635482, at *24.

When EPA conducts a cleanup and then seeks to recover costs, it also must demonstrate that its actions were not inconsistent with the NCP as a prerequisite to recovering costs. 42 U.S.C. § 9607(a)(4)(A). As discussed above, courts review EPA's choice of remedial actions deferentially. However, should courts also defer to EPA's characterization of cleanup actions as removal or remedial, given the significant difference in the NCP requirements for the two types of actions? *See United States v. W.R. Grace & Co.*, 429 F.3d 1224 (9th Cir. 2005) (deferring to EPA's interpretation), *cert. denied*, 549 U.S. 951 (2006); *see also* Amy L. Ohnemus, Note, *The Strong Arm of CERCLA: EPA Allowed Free Reign to Recoup Cleanup Costs*, 14 Mo. ENVTL. L. & POL'Y REV. 239 (2006).

5.   **Opportunity for Public Comment.** The NCP provides that "[p]rivate parties undertaking response actions should provide an opportunity for public comment concerning the selection of the response action." 40 C.F.R. § 300.700(c)(6). The preamble to the NCP emphasizes the importance of this requirement: "The public—both PRPs and concerned citizens—have a strong interest in participating in cleanup decisions that may affect them, and their involvement helps to ensure that these cleanups—which are performed without governmental supervision—are carried out in an environmentally sound manner." National Oil and Hazardous Substances Pollution Contingency Plan, 55 Fed. Reg. 8666, 8795 (1990). As discussed in *ASARCO*, *supra*, private parties whose actions are not "consistent with" the NCP are unable to recover costs from other PRPs in a contribution action. Should failure to provide an opportunity for public comment preclude a PRP from bringing a contribution action, under the "substantial compliance" standard promulgated by EPA? Some courts have held that it does bar a contribution action. *See, e.g., Cty. Line Inv. Co. v. Tinney*, 933 F.2d 1508 (10th Cir. 1991). The Second Circuit, however, has held that "[w]here a state agency responsible for overseeing remediation of hazardous wastes gives comprehensive input, and the private parties involved act pursuant to those instructions, the state participation may fulfill the public participation requirement." *Bedford Affiliates v. Sills*, 156 F.3d 416, 428 (2d Cir. 1998). The Eighth Circuit has held that the participation of a state agency could, under some circumstances, fill the public participation requirement, but not if the cost and quality of the remedy are disputed. *See Union Pac. R.R. v. Reilly Indus., Inc.*, 215 F.3d 830 (8th Cir. 2000).

6.   **Selecting a Cleanup Remedy.** The NCP requires that private parties undertaking a cleanup conduct a rigorous remedial investigation and feasibility study. *See* 40 C.F.R. § 300.430(d), (e). How might the baseline risk assessment conducted as part of the remedial investigation affect the selection of a remedy? What specific criteria are considered in the development and screening of other remedial alternatives? *See id.* § 300.430(e)(7). Why is a "no-action" alternative required?

Alternatives must be thoroughly discussed before a remedy is selected. *Id.* § 300.430(e)(9). *See also Carson Harbor Vill., Ltd. v. County of Los Angeles*, 433 F.3d 1260, 1268–69 (9th Cir. 2006) (holding feasibility study fully analyzing only one remedial alternative did not substantially comply with NCP). How does the process balance or weight the effectiveness of a particular remedy against community acceptance of a different remedy? Can a remedy ever be selected that does not meet an ARAR? How and when is the cost of a remedy taken into account?

7. Consistency and Flexibility. One court has described the evaluation of compliance with the NCP (for the purposes of determining whether to allow cost recovery and contribution) as beset by competing policies:

> CERCLA cost recovery actions . . . were designed to encourage private parties to undertake hazardous waste cleanups with greater speed and at lower cost than a government-run cleanup. . . . This would imply a need for flexibility in allowing private parties to initiate their own cleanups. . . . At the same time, the complex and detailed regulations reveal that the purpose of the mandatory NCP component is to give some consistency and cohesiveness to response planning and actions, given the risks involved for the environment and the surrounding communities.

Pub. Serv. Co. of Colo. v. Gates Rubber Co., 22 F. Supp. 2d 1180, 1190 (D. Colo. 1997) (internal citations omitted), *aff'd*, 175 F.3d 1177 (10th Cir. 1999). Does the case law discussed above strike the right balance between these two competing considerations?

G. NATURAL RESOURCE DAMAGES

In addition to the provisions designed to ensure the cleanup of contaminated sites across the United States, CERCLA imposes liability for damages to natural resources resulting from the release of hazardous substances. 42 U.S.C. § 9607(a)(4)(C). While these provisions are less salient, liability for damages to natural resources may often far exceed liability for cleanup costs, amounting in some cases to tens of millions of dollars. The provisions are designed to ensure that natural resources are restored to their original condition following the contamination of a site—an objective that is not necessarily accomplished through a site's decontamination. For example, in the event that hazardous substances are released into a forest, remediation works may adequately safeguard against ongoing dangers to public health, but may not adequately rectify the damage sustained by the trees and other natural resources which inhabit the forest.

Section 107(a)(4)(C) provides that, in addition to liability for remediation costs, PRPs will be liable for "damages for injury to, destruction of, or loss of natural resources, including the reasonable costs of assessing such injury, destruction, or loss" which result as a consequence of the release of a hazardous substance from a facility. 42 U.S.C. § 9607(a)(4)(C). The term "natural resources" is defined broadly under CERCLA to include "land, fish, wildlife, biota, air, water, ground water, drinking water supplies, and other such resources belonging to, managed by, held in trust by, appertaining to, or otherwise controlled by the United States[,] . . . any State or local government, any foreign government, [or] any Indian tribe. . . ." 42 U.S.C. § 9601(16). Even though CERCLA does not create a private right of recovery for damages suffered by natural resources, the scope of § 107(a)(4)(C) liability nevertheless extends beyond those natural resources owned by the Government on public lands. By defining natural resources as those "belonging to, managed by, held in trust by, appertaining to, or otherwise controlled by the United States . . . ," Congress clearly intended to extend liability to other types of government interests in privately owned property. *Id.* The precise scope of government interests covered by the § 101(16) "natural resources" definition is discussed in *Ohio v. U.S. Dep't of the Interior*, 880 F.2d 432 (D.C. Cir. 1989), excerpted below.

Just as in the case of liability for cleanup costs, § 107(a)(4)(C) provides for strict liability, and courts have routinely held PRPs jointly and severally liable for damages to natural resources. Similarly, the § 107(b) defenses of (1) an act of God, (2) an act of war, or (3) a third party act or omission, are open to PRPs facing liability for natural resource damages. 42 U.S.C. § 9607(b).

Pursuant to § 107(f)(2)(a), the President is required to designate federal officials to act as public trustees for those natural resources under federal control. 42 U.S.C. § 9607(f)(2)(A). The President designated the Secretaries of the Department of the Interior (DOI) and the Department of Commerce (DOC) to act in this capacity. In addition to those trustees designated by the states to oversee the natural resources under state control, DOI and DOC are charged with holding § 101(16) natural resources in trust for the public and future generations, and for pursuing claims under § 107(a)(4)(C) on the public's behalf. Section 107(f)(1) provides that any sum recovered by a trustee for natural resource damages must be used to restore, replace, rehabilitate, or acquire equivalent natural resources. 42 U.S.C. § 9607(f)(1).

Section 301(c) of CERCLA required the passage of regulations for the assessment of natural resource damages, specifying a standard procedure for simplified assessments, as well as alternative protocols for assessments in individual cases. 42 U.S.C. § 9651(c)(1)–(2). The regulations are required to identify the best available procedures for determining damages to natural resources, including replacement value, use value, and the ability of the ecosystem or resource to recover. *Id.* Although a trustee is not strictly required to adhere to the regulations, § 107(f)(2)(C), an assessment conducted in accordance with the regulations has a rebuttable presumption of validity in any administrative or judicial proceeding. *See* 42 U.S.C. § 9607(f)(2)(C). The responsibility for this rulemaking was delegated to DOI by the President in Executive Order 12,580. 52 Fed. Reg. 2923 (1987).

DOI's regulations, first promulgated in 1986, draw a distinction between coastal and marine environments (Type A) and all other environments (Type B). With respect to Type A environments, the regulations prescribe the use of a computer model to assess damages that result from chemical or oil discharges. With respect to Type B environments, the regulations require that an individual approach be adopted and tailored to each case. In broad terms, however, both the Type A and Type B regulations call for the following four stages in each Natural Resource Damage Assessment (NRDA):

- Pre-assessment Screen: Trustees must first conduct an initial screen to determine whether an injury has occurred and whether a pathway of exposure exists;

- Assessment Plan: Trustees must next confirm the exposure of § 101(16) natural resources and develop an Assessment Plan to identify how the potential damages will be evaluated. The nature and content of the Assessment Plan will vary depending on whether the resource is Type A or B;

- Assessment Implementation: Trustees must next gather the data necessary to quantify the injuries to the natural resources and to determine damages. This process consists of three steps: (1) injury determination; (2) quantification; and (3) damage determination;

- Post-Assessment: Finally, trustees must prepare a Report of Assessment detailing the results of the Assessment Implementation phase. The report must contain a reasonable number of restoration alternatives, including natural attenuation. A preferred alternative is then selected, based on several factors, including technical feasibility, relationship of costs to benefits, and consistency with response actions.

43 C.F.R. § 11. Section 107(f)(1) authorizes trustees to pursue claims to recover damages identified in a NRDA. 42 U.S.C. § 9607(f)(1).

The following case describes challenges to DOI's Type B regulations promulgated in 1986.

Ohio v. Department of the Interior
880 F.2d 432 (D.C. Cir. 1989).

■ Before Wald, Chief Judge, and Robinson and Mikva, Circuit Judges.

■ Mikva, Circuit Judge:

Petitioners are 10 states, three environmental organizations ("State and Environmental Petitioners"), a chemical industry trade association, a manufacturing company and a utility company ("Industry Petitioners"), who seek review of regulations promulgated by the Department of the Interior ("DOI" or "Interior") pursuant to § 301(c)(1)–(3) of the Comprehensive Environmental Response, Compensation and Liability Act of 1980 ("CERCLA" or the "Act"), as amended, 42 U.S.C. § 9651(c). The regulations govern the recovery of money damages from persons responsible for spills and leaks of oil and hazardous substances, to compensate for injuries such releases inflict on natural resources. Damages may be recovered by state and in some cases the federal governments, as trustees for those natural resources.

Petitioners challenge many aspects of those regulations. State and Environmental Petitioners raise ten issues, all of which essentially focus on the regulations' alleged undervaluation of the damages recoverable from parties responsible for hazardous materials spills that despoil natural resources. Industry Petitioners attack the regulations from a different vantage point, claiming they will permit or encourage overstated damages. In addition, three public interest organizations ("Environmental Intervenors") defend the regulations from the attacks of Industry Petitioners, and a collection of corporations and industry groups ("Industry Intervenors") defend the regulations from the attacks of State and Environmental Petitioners. . . .

The "Lesser-Of" Rule

The most significant issue in this case concerns the validity of the regulation providing that damages for despoilment of natural resources shall be "the *Lesser-of*: restoration or replacement costs; or diminution of use values." 43 C.F.R. § 11.35(b)(2) (1987) (emphasis added).

State and Environmental Petitioners challenge Interior's "Lesser-of" rule, insisting that CERCLA requires damages to be at least sufficient to pay the cost in every case of restoring, replacing or acquiring the equivalent of the damaged resource (hereinafter referred to shorthandedly as "restoration"). Because in some—probably a majority of—cases lost-use-value will be lower than the cost of restoration, Interior's rule will result in damages award[s] too small to pay for the costs or restoration. Petitioners point to a section of CERCLA providing that recovered damages must be spent only on restoration as evidence that Congress intended restoration cost-based damages to be the norm. As further proof of such a norm, the same section goes on to state that the measure of damages "shall not be limited by" the sums which can be used for restoration. Petitioners maintain that the "shall not be limited by" language clearly establishes restoration costs as a "floor" measure of damages. Petitioners also rely on the legislative history of CERCLA and of SARA, claiming that it reinforces the sense of the text and documents Congress' primary emphasis on restoration of natural resources. In particular, they point to a House report on SARA, insisting that it, together with the other statutory indicators, proves conclusively that Congress intended restoration costs to be a minimum measure of damages in natural resource cases.

Interior defends its rule by arguing that CERCLA does not prescribe any floor for damages but instead leaves to Interior the decision of what the measure of damages will be. DOI acknowledges that all recovered damages must be spent on restoration but argues that the amount recovered from the responsible parties need not be sufficient to complete the job. DOI suggests two alternative meanings of the "shall not be limited by" phrase that do not construe it as a damages floor. Finally, DOI argues that the legislative history, like the statutory text, is ambiguous and that Interior's rule for measuring damages is a reasonable one.

Although our resolution of the dispute submerges us in the minutiae of CERCLA text and legislative materials, we initially stress the enormous practical significance of the "Lesser-of" rule. A hypothetical example will illustrate the point: imagine a hazardous substance spill that kills a rookery of fur seals and destroys a habitat for seabirds at a sealife reserve. The lost use value of the seals and seabird habitat would be measured by the market value of the fur seals' pelts (which would be approximately $15 each) plus the selling price per acre of land comparable in value to that on which the spoiled bird habitat was located. Even if, as likely, that use value turns out to be far less than the cost of restoring the rookery and seabird habitat, it would nonetheless be the only measure of damages eligible for the presumption of recoverability under the Interior rule.

After examining the language and purpose of CERCLA, as well as its legislative history, we conclude that Interior's "Lesser-of" rule is directly contrary to the expressed intent of Congress. . . .

Our reading of the complex of relevant provisions concerning damages under CERCLA convinces us that Congress established a distinct preference for restoration cost as the measure of recovery in natural resource damage cases. This is not to say that DOI may not establish some class of cases where other considerations—*i.e.*, infeasibility of restoration or grossly disproportionate cost to use value— warrant a different standard. We hold the "Lesser-of" rule based on comparing costs alone, however, to be an invalid determinant of whether or not to deviate from Congress' preference

The Public Ownership Rule

The second issue raised by State and Environmental Petitioners is whether the regulations invalidly limit the availability of natural resource damages to cases where the resources harmed (such as land, water, air, fish and wildlife) are owned by federal, state, local or foreign governments, rather than by private parties. The critical language in the DOI regulations mirrors the language of the statute, but State and Environmental Petitioners complain that DOI's comments accompanying the publication of the regulations articulate an understanding of the regulation that is inconsistent with the statute. The issue is further complicated by the statements of DOI counsel at oral argument, which put yet another interpretive gloss on the regulation. . . .

The critical language is contained in CERCLA's definition of the term "natural resources." The statute provides that responsible parties shall be liable for "damages for injury to, destruction of, or loss of natural resources." § 107(a)(C), 42 U.S.C. § 9607(a)(C). In the "definitions" sections, the statute provides that "natural resources" are resources "belonging to, managed by, held in trust by, appertaining to, or otherwise controlled by the United States[,] . . . any State or local government, any foreign government, any Indian tribe, or, if such resources are subject to a trust restriction on alienation, any member of an Indian tribe." § 101(16), 42 U.S.C. § 9601(16). The difficult questions, obviously, center around the series of phrases: "belonging to, managed by, held in trust by, appertaining to, or otherwise controlled by" a state or federal or foreign government.

Initially we deal with one argument presented by State and Environmental Petitioners that is without merit. They point to a section of CERCLA providing that liability for harm to natural resources "shall be to the United States Government and to any State *for natural resources within the State* or belong[ing] to, managed by, controlled by, or appertaining to such State" and to Indian tribes and their members in some circumstances. 42 U.S.C. § 9607(f)(1) (emphasis added). State and Environmental Petitioners argue on the basis of this section that CERCLA covers injuries to any land, water, air, fish and wildlife that exist "within [a] State"—a reading which, if true, would establish natural resource damage liability for harm to all private as well as public property. This interpretation, however, rips the "within the State" phrase out of its statutory context. "[N]atural resources within the State" incorporates § 101(16)'s definition of "natural resources" as resources "belonging to, managed by, held in trust by, appertaining to, or otherwise controlled by" the state. Thus it is this series of phrases, and not the "within the State" language, that controls the issue.[43] . . .

It should be noted, however, that while the statute excludes purely private resources, it clearly does not limit the definition of "natural resources" to resources *owned* by a government. If that were the meaning of § 101(16), then all the phrases other than "belonging to" would be surplusage. If the words "managed by, held in trust by, appertaining to, or otherwise controlled by" mean anything at all, they must refer to

---

[43] . . . For reasons set out below, we do not believe Congress held such a view. Rather, the expression "within the State" permits a state to recover damages not only for resources owned by, managed by, appertaining to or otherwise controlled by the state government, but also for resources owned by, managed by, appertaining to or otherwise controlled by a local government or a foreign government—if those resources exist "within the State." This makes sense because the definition of "natural resources" in § 101(16) includes resources appertaining to local and foreign governments, while the liability provision of § 107(f)(1) does not empower those governments to bring actions for damages.

certain types of governmental (federal, state or local) interests in privately-owned property.

The legislative history of CERCLA further illustrates that damage to private property—absent any government involvement, management or control—is not covered by the natural resource damage provisions of the statute. Early drafts of CERCLA would have covered private property. *See* H.R. 7020, 96th Cong., 2d Sess. § 5 (1980), *reprinted in* 2 *Legislative History, supra* note 19, at 40 (damages to include "all damages for personal injury, injury to real or personal property, and economic loss, resulting from such release or threatened release"); H.R. 85, 96th Cong., 1st Sess. § 103(a)(2), *reprinted in* 2 *Legislative History* at 487 (damages to include "injury to, or destruction of, real or personal property"); S. 1480, 96th Cong., 1st Sess. § 4(a)(2)(A), *reprinted in* 1 *Legislative History* at 169 (damages to include "any injury to, destruction of, or loss of any real or personal property"). Each of these proposed provisions was rejected and the statute's "natural resources" formulation was adopted instead. Congress quite deliberately excluded purely private property from the ambit of the natural resource damage provisions. . . .

The Hierarchy of Assessment Methods

The regulations establish a rigid hierarchy of permissible methods for determining "use values," limiting recovery to the price commanded by the resource on the open market, unless the trustee finds that "the market for the resource is not reasonably competitive." 43 C.F.R. § 11.83(c)(1). If the trustee makes such a finding, it may "appraise" the market value in accordance with the relevant sections of the "Uniform Appraisal Standards for Federal Land Acquisition," *see* 43 C.F.R. § 11.83(c)(2). Only when neither the market value nor the appraisal method is "appropriate" can other methods of determining use value be employed, *see* 43 C.F.R. § 11.83(d).

Environmental petitioners maintain that Interior's emphasis on market value is an unreasonable interpretation of the statute, under the so-called "second prong" of *Chevron U.S.A., Inc. v. Natural Resources Defense Council, Inc.*, 467 U.S. 837, 845 (1984), and we agree. While it is not irrational to look to market price as one factor in determining the use value of a resource, it is unreasonable to view market price as the *exclusive* factor, or even the predominant one. From the bald eagle to the blue whale and snail darter, natural resources have values that are not fully captured by the market system. *See Commonwealth of Puerto Rico v. SS Zoe Colocotroni*, 628 F.2d 652, 673–74 (1st Cir.1980), *cert. denied*, 450 U.S. 912 (1981). DOI's own CERCLA 301 Project Team recognized that "most government resources, particularly resources for which natural resource damages would be sought[,] may often have no market." DOI has failed to explain its departure from this view. Indeed, many of the materials in the record on which DOI relied in developing its rules regarding contingent valuation expressed the same idea; it is the incompleteness of market processes that gives rise to the need for contingent valuation techniques. Courts have long stressed that market prices are not to be used as surrogates for value "when the market value has been too difficult to find, or when its application would result in manifest injustice to owner or public," *United States v. Commodities Trading Corp.*, 339 U.S. 121, 123 (1950); see also *United States v. Cors*, 337 U.S. 325, 332 (1949) (warning against making "a fetish" of market value, "since that may not be the best measure of value in some cases"). As we have previously noted in the context of the "Lesser-of" rule, *see supra* note 40, market prices are not acceptable as primary measures of the use values of natural resources. *See generally* Anderson, *Natural Resource Damages, Superfund, and the Courts*, 16 Envtl.Aff. 405, 442–46 (1989). We find that DOI erred by establishing "a strong presumption in favor of market price and appraisal methodologies." 51 Fed. Reg. 27,720 (1986). . . .

Contingent Valuation

When a natural resource is injured by a discharge of oil or release of a hazardous substance, an authorized official assesses the damages resulting. DOI has prescribed methodologies for estimating in any such instance the amount of money to be sought as recompense. Either DOI's restoration methodology or one of its use methodologies must be employed in calculations of damages. The issue we now address concerns one of the latter.

DOI's natural resource damage assessment regulations define "use value" as

> the value to the public of recreational or other public uses of the resource, as measured by changes in consumer surplus, any fees or other payments collectable by the government or Indian tribe for a private party's use of the natural resource, and any economic rent accruing to a private party because the government or Indian tribe does not charge a fee or price for the use of the resource.

[43 C.F.R. § 11.83(b)(1).] The regulations provide several approaches to use valuation. When the injured resource is traded in a market, the lost use value is the diminution in market price. When that is not precisely the case, but similar resources are traded in a market, an appraisal technique may be utilized to determine damages. When, however, neither of these two situations obtains, non-marketed resource methodologies are available. One of these is "contingent valuation" (CV), the subject of controversy here.

The CV process "includes all techniques that set up hypothetical markets to elicit an individual's economic valuation of a natural resource." CV involves a series of interviews with individuals for the purpose of ascertaining the values they respectively attach to particular changes in particular resources. Among the several formats available to an interviewer in developing the hypothetical scenario embodied in a CV survey are direct questioning, by which the interviewer learns how much the interviewee is willing to pay for the resource; bidding formats, for example, the interviewee is asked whether he or she would pay a given amount for a resource and, depending upon the response, the bid is set higher or lower until a final price is derived; and a "take or leave it" format, in which the interviewee decides whether or not he or she is willing to pay a designated amount of money for the resource. CV methodology thus enables ascertainment of individually-expressed values for different levels of quality of resources, and dollar values of individuals' changes in well-being. The regulations also sanction resort to CV methodology in determining "option" and "existence" values. . . .

The primary argument of Industry Petitioners is that the possibility of bias is inherent in CV methodology, and disqualifies it as a "best available procedure." In evaluating the utility of CV methodology in assessing damages for impairment of natural resources, DOI surveyed a number of studies which analyzed the methodology, addressed the shortcomings of various questionnaires, and recommended steps needed to fashion reliable CV assessments. For example, an early study by the Water Resources Council advised that questions in CV surveys be "carefully designed and pretested," a warning DOI was quick to heed.

Industry Petitioners urge, however, that even assuming that questions are artfully drafted and carefully circumscribed, there is such a high degree of variation in size of the groups surveyed, and such a concomitant fluctuation in aggregations of damages, that CV methodology cannot be considered a "best available procedure." We think this attack on CV methodology is insufficient in a facial challenge to invalidate CV as an available assessment technique. The extent of damage to natural resources from releases of oil and hazardous substances varies greatly, and though the impact may be widespread and severe, it is in the mission of CERCLA to assess the public loss. Certainly nothing in CV methodology itself shapes the injury inflicted by an environmental disaster, or influences identification of the population affected thereby. The argument of Industry Petitioners strikes at CERCLA, not CV's implementation, and can appropriately be considered only by Congress.

Similarly, we find wanting Industry Petitioners' protest that CV does not rise to the status of a "best available procedure" because willingness-to-pay—a factor prominent in CV methodology—can lead to overestimates by survey respondents. The premise of this argument is that respondents do not actually pay money, and likely will overstate their willingness-to-pay. One study relied upon by Industry Petitioners hypothesizes that respondents may "respond in ways that are more indicative of what they would like to see done than how they would behave in an actual market," and also observes that the converse is possible. The simple and obvious safeguard against overstatement, however, is more sophisticated questioning. Even as matters now stand, the risk of overestimation has not been shown to produce such egregious results as to justify judicial overruling of DOI's careful estimate of the caliber and worth of CV methodology.

Industry Petitioners[] also challenge the use of CV *after* an oil leak or a hazardous waste release has occurred. They fear that application of CV methodology in those circumstances is fraught with a significant bias leading to overvaluation of the damaged resources. As a practical matter, it would be prohibitively expensive, if not physically impossible, to solicit individual valuations of each and every natural resource, or even a sizeable number thereof, in order to avoid any upward bias in the event that the resource is later damaged. Moreover, in light of CERCLA's preference for restoration, it would be a terrible waste of time and energy to conduct broad-scale valuation interviewing beforehand. While, depending on whether interviewing occurs before or after damage, the results may differ somewhat, that alone does not reduce CV methodology to something less than a "best available procedure." We have no cause to overturn DOI's considered judgment that CV methodology, when properly applied, can be structured so as to eliminate undue upward biases.

We sustain DOI in its conclusion that CV methodology is a "best available procedure." As such, its conclusion in the Natural Resource Damage Assessment regulations was entirely proper. . . .

Conclusion

DOI's Type B Natural Resource Damage Assessment Regulations are upheld on review as to the following issues: . . . the adoption of contingent valuation methodology (Part XIII). We grant the petition for review with respect to the "Lesser-of" rule (Part III) and the hierarchy of assessment methods (Part VI). We also remand the public ownership rule (Part IV) for DOI's reasoned consideration and explanation. We instruct DOI to proceed as expeditiously as possible in issuing new regulations in conformance with this opinion.

NOTES AND QUESTIONS

1. **"Lesser-of" Rule.** On what basis did the court hold the "lesser-of" rule to be invalid? Does the court's ruling stand for the proposition that trustees may recover the costs to restore injured resources to their baseline, regardless of the extent to which this amount may exceed the value of the resource?

2. **Resource Valuation.** The "lesser-of" rule pitted restoration and replacement costs against diminutions in use value. How were use values to be measured under the proposed rule? Recall the discussion in Chapter II concerning use values (the value of using a resource now), option values (the value of being able to use a resource in the future), and existence values (the value in the resource's existence, independent of use). Is the prescribed valuation methodology likely to adequately account for a resource's true value? Does it adequately take into account a resource's option or existence

values? What other valuation methods might better take into account a resource's true value? What is the court's determination in this respect?

3. Restoration Costs. The *Ohio v. DOI* court concluded that "[o]ur reading of the complex of relevant provisions concerning damages under CERCLA convinces us that Congress established a distinct preference for restoration cost as the measure of recovery in natural resource damage cases." *Id.* at 459. Central to this "complex" of provisions is § 107(f)(1), which provides that any sum recovered by a trustee must be "retained . . . without further appropriation, for use only to restore, replace, or acquire the equivalent of such natural resources." 42 U.S.C. § 9607(f)(1). Does this provision necessarily suggest that restoration cost-based damages should be the norm?

In order to determine the amount of restoration costs, it is first necessary to determine the resource's baseline condition—that is, the condition that would have existed but for the release of the hazardous substance. In determining a natural resource's baseline, trustees are required to take into account factors that may have adversely affected the resource's condition, but that are wholly unrelated to the release of the hazardous substance. What difficulties might trustees face in determining a resource's baseline?

4. Private Actions for Damages to Natural Resources. "Natural resources" are defined in § 101(16) as those resources "belonging to, managed by, held in trust by, appertaining to, or otherwise controlled by the United States[,] . . . any State or local government, any foreign government, any Indian tribe, or, if such resources are subject to a trust restriction on alienation, any member of an Indian tribe." 42 U.S.C. § 9601(16). Given that § 107(f)(1) provides that liability for natural resource damages "shall be to the United States Government and to any State for natural resources within the State," 42 U.S.C. § 9607(f)(1), why does the *Ohio v. DOI* court hold that natural resource damages (NRD) liability does not apply to private lands?

Following *Ohio v. DOI*, how else could citizens recover damages for injury suffered to privately owned natural resources? Consider the numerous causes of action open to private citizens under state law for pollution damage sustained by their resources, including actions under state negligence, strict liability, or other statutory theories. Compare the legal regimes applicable to actions under the common law and under § 107(a)(4)(C). Which is more burdensome upon the plaintiff?

5. Defining "Injury" to Natural Resources. The DOI regulations define "injury" to a natural resource as a "measurable adverse change" brought on by a release or discharge of oil or a hazardous substance. 43 C.F.R. § 11.14(v). Does that mean that any change, even a *de minimis* one, would trigger a natural resource damage award? Note also that exceedance of a regulatory standard under, for example, the CWA may constitute an injury. *See id.* § 11.62. What if the contaminant level in a body of water exceeded regulatory standards prior to the release? *See, e.g.,* § 11.62(b)(1)(i)–(iii). If information is lacking about the baseline condition of a resource, might it be difficult to show that an injury has occurred?

6.   Contingent Valuation. Under both the Type A and Type B Regulations, there exist a number of valuation methodologies available to trustees to determine "compensable values" for interim lost public uses. These include market methodologies (such as market price and/or appraisal) and non-market methodologies (such as factor income, travel cost, hedonic pricing, contingent valuation, or unit values). 43 C.F.R. § 11.83. What happens if a portion of the injury to the natural resource, but not all, can be calculated using market-based methodologies? *See id.* § 11.83(c)(2). When is an estimate of option and existence values, as opposed to use values, authorized? *See id.* § 11.83(c)(1)(iii), (c)(2)(vii)(B). What restrictions exist on other valuation methodologies not explicitly listed in the regulation? *See id.* § 11.83(c)(3).

The *Ohio v. DOI* court considered, at length, the validity of the contingent valuation methodology. How persuasive are industries' concerns that the application of the contingent valuation methodology "is fraught with a significant bias leading to overvaluation of the damaged resources"? What problems arise in using contingent valuation methods to value damages in natural resource damages cases? *See* Dale B. Thompson, *Valuing the Environment: Courts' Struggles with Natural Resource Damages*, 32 ENVTL. L. 57, 58–61 (2002).

7.   Natural Resource Liability. In addition to the defenses in § 107(b) of the Act, CERCLA provides two additional defenses to natural resource liability in circumstances where the damages were authorized by permit. First, § 107(f)(1) provides that a PRP is not liable for natural resource damages in circumstances where it can demonstrate that the damages complained of "were specifically identified as an irreversible and irretrievable commitment of natural resources in an environmental impact statement," and that the commitment was also authorized by the permit or license issued. 42 U.S.C. § 9607(f)(1). Second, § 107(j) provides that "recovery by any person . . . for response costs or damages resulting from a federally permitted release shall be pursuant to existing law in lieu of [§ 107]." 42 U.S.C. § 9607(j). A federally permitted release is defined in § 101(10) to include discharges in compliance with permits issued under each of the CAA, CWA, RCRA, and under other federal statutes such as the Atomic Energy Act, Marine Protection, Research and Sanctuaries Act, and the SDWA. 42 U.S.C. § 9601(10).

8.   Retroactivity. Unlike the cleanup cost provisions, the natural resource damage provisions of § 107 do not apply retroactively. Section 107(f)(1) specifically provides that "[t]here shall be no recovery under the authority of [§ 107(a)(4)(C)] where such damages and the release of a hazardous substance from which such damages resulted have occurred wholly before December 11, 1980." 42 U.S.C. § 9607(f)(1). What is the justification for drawing a distinction between the retroactive application of the cleanup cost and natural resource damage provisions of § 107?

9.   Time Limitations. Section 113(g)(1) of the Act provides that actions for natural resource damages must be commenced no later than three years after "(A) [t]he date of the discovery of the loss and its connection with the release in question" or "(B) the date on which [the Type A and B regulations were promulgated by DOI]." 42 U.S.C. § 9613(g). Furthermore, with respect to any facility listed on the NPL, § 113(g) provides that "an action for [natural resource] damages . . . must be commenced within 3 years after the completion of the remedial action (excluding operation and maintenance activities)" in lieu of the timeframes listed above. *Id.* Actions for remedial actions associated with the cleanup of a contaminated site, however, may be commenced within six years of the initiation of the action. *Id.* Why would Congress have made this distinction?

10. Dollar Limitations. Section 107(c) provides that liability under § 107(a)(4)(C) shall not exceed $50,000,000. 42 U.S.C. § 9607(c). Critical to the operation of this provision is determining what constitutes a single "release" for the purposes of § 107(c). In *California v. Montrose Chem. Corp.*, 104 F.3d 1507 (9th Cir. 1997), the Ninth Circuit found that a series of releases occurring over a short time period could be considered as one release for the purpose of § 107(c). What other factors may be relevant to this determination?

11. Double Recovery. Because liability for natural resource damages is independent of liability for cleanup costs, there is scope for overlap between the two regimes—that is, where cleanup costs partly or wholly address damages for natural resources. For this reason, the delegated authority of trustees is limited to the recovery of *costs beyond cleanup* to restore or replace natural resources to the conditions that would have existed but for the release of a hazardous material. 42 U.S.C. § 9607(f)(1); 40 C.F.R. § 300.615(c)(3). How easy is it likely to be to distinguish between the costs necessary for cleanup and the costs necessary to remediate damages to natural resources?

Furthermore, CERCLA precludes trustees from recovering the same damages twice, meaning that if a trustee has received damages for a particular natural resource loss or injury caused by a release or discharge, that trustee cannot sue in the same or in a different court for additional damages for the same loss or injury. *See* 42 U.S.C. § 9607(f)(1).

In other circumstances, there may be multiple trustees for the same resource, because of a coexisting or contiguous natural resource or concurrent jurisdictions. In these circumstances, 40 C.F.R. § 300.615(a) requires that the trustees coordinate and cooperate in carrying out their shared responsibilities.

12. Section 111(b). In addition to § 107(a)(4)(C), § 111(b) separately permits trustees to bring claims against the Superfund for injury to or destruction of natural resources, including costs for damage assessment. 42 U.S.C. § 9611(b). Section 111(c) further specifies that the Superfund may be used for "(1) [t]he costs of assessing . . . natural resource [injuries]", and "(2) the costs of Federal or State . . . efforts in the restoration, rehabilitation, or replacement or acquiring the equivalent of any [injured] natural resources." 42 U.S.C. § 9611(c). Section 111(e)(2) limits Superfund reimbursement of natural resource claims to fifteen percent of the fund. 42 U.S.C. § 9611(e)(2). What is the purpose of § 111(b)? How does it compliment the § 107(a)(4)(C) regime?

13. Beyond Tort. Consider the following critique of the NRD regime offered by Professor Richard Stewart:

> The NRD regime represents an extension of traditional tort liability to public natural resources and is based upon a simple and appealing logic. Private owners obtain compensation and redress for injury to their property. Property damage liability also serves important deterrent functions. The public commons deserves at least as much protection as does private property.
>
> The effort to protect the commons through statutory extension of tort liability has, however, created a number of novel, difficult, and unresolved legal issues, including the standards for determining injury and causation and the measure of damages, the availability of jury trial, and the principles governing court review of trustee damage assessments. Resolving issues of injury, causation, and damages also involves extraordinarily difficult and contentious factual issues at the frontiers of science. The validity and reliability of contingent valuation methodology in assessing nonuse values is sharply disputed. These difficulties are merely symptomatic of a more fundamental problem, stemming from the hybrid character of the NRD scheme and the flaws inherent in the attempt to adapt private tort liability to public natural resource injury.
>
> The NRD statutory programs represent a novel hybrid, composed of elements of tort, trust, and administrative law. In imposing tort liability for public natural resource injury, Congress went far beyond the common law by adopting rules of near-absolute strict, retroactive, joint-and-several liability against a wide range of parties. Another significant departure from the common law is the rejection of market measures of damages; instead, damage claims have been based on restoration costs, lost use values, and nonuse values as measured by contingent value methodology. . . .
>
> In large part because of its novel hybrid character and the effort to adapt private tort liability to public natural resources, the current NRD system involves large transaction costs, ubiquitous factual and legal uncertainty, bureaucratic waste, and the persistent threat of arbitrary and grossly inflated liabilities. These difficulties cannot be solved without fundamental rethinking and restructuring of the current system. Natural resources should be protected by means other than the private tort model. These means include criminal sanctions and civil penalties, trust funds generated by imposing taxes or fees on risk-creating activities or scheduled liability assessments following the model of workers' compensation.

Richard B. Stewart, *Liability for Natural Resource Injury: Beyond Tort, in* ANALYZING SUPERFUND—ECONOMICS, SCIENCE AND LAW 219, 220–22 (Richard L. Revesz & Richard B. Stewart eds., 1995).

Consider the validity of Professor Stewart's claim that private tort liability is an inappropriate model to apply in the context of public natural resources. Could either of the two dominant rationales that support the model—namely corrective justice and welfare maximization—apply in the present context? As alternatives to the present regime, Stewart proposes (i) an NRD system of scheduled damages; (ii) a restoration trust fund for a scheduled NRD system, and (iii) an enhancement of civil penalties. How would such a system operate? *See id.* at 241–44. Would it be more desirable than the current regime?

H. REVIEW PROBLEMS

1. **Toxic Farms.** A cleanup is underway at a hazardous waste site in upstate New York known as Toxic Farms. Consider the possible liability of the following parties under CERCLA:

    (a) ABC Chemical Co. sold hazardous substances to an industrial solvents distributor, Solvents, Inc.

    (b) Solvents, Inc. sold its products to a variety of firms around the country. It contracted with Fast Trucks to dispose of the hazardous residue at a licensed site, Safe Disposal.

    (c) Fast Trucks instead took the residue to Toxic Farms.

    (d) The contract between Solvents, Inc. and Fast Trucks specified that Fast Trucks would indemnify Solvents, Inc. for any Superfund liability that might be imposed against Solvents, Inc.

    (e) After receiving these wastes, the owner of Toxic Farms stopped paying property taxes. As a result of this tax delinquency, title to the site passed to the State of New York, which held the property for a year. The State of New York never undertook an inspection of the property. It was aware, however, that hazardous substances had been received at the site. At the time of the sale, it made no disclosures concerning the condition of the property.

    (f) After holding the property for a year, the State of New York sold it to American Realty, an industrial developer. American Realty began a cleanup at the property and brought actions under §§ 107 and 113 of CERCLA against ABC Chemical Co., Solvents, Inc., Fast Trucks, Toxic Farms, and the State of New York.

    (g) Fast Trucks offered a settlement under § 113(f)(2) for $50,000, its total solvency, which American Realty accepted.

    (h) A year after the commencement of American Realty's actions, EPA listed the site on the National Priorities list and sued American Realty for the recovery of the costs associated with the site investigation and for a declaratory judgment establishing American Realty's liability for the cost of the cleanup.

2.   Chessell and Saulino. Chessell sold a parcel of agricultural land to Saulino. The sale contract provided that Chessell would indemnify Saulino for any liability that Saulino might suffer as a result of the condition of the land at the time of the sale. Chessell did not inform Saulino of the presence of any hazardous substances on the land. Saulino undertook a title search and a visual inspection at the time of the purchase.

Years later, as a result of an economic downturn, Saulino decided to build condominiums at the site. During the course of excavation work, one of Saulino's employees noticed a greenish liquid bubbling in the soil. Saulino called an environmental consultant who removed some soil and did not find any further contamination in the surrounding area.

Saulino then brought in heavy construction equipment and began to build the foundations of the condominiums. Saulino's equipment pierced several barrels that bore the clear legend "Chessell." Tests revealed that the liquid in the barrels had strong carcinogenic properties.

EPA brought an action under CERCLA against Chessell and Saulino to recover the cleanup costs. How should the case be decided?

Assume now that it is litigated before the enactment of § 101(40). The cleanup costs are $10 million. Chessell is in a precarious financial condition, and EPA settles with Chessell for $1 million. What is the effect of the settlement? Would the analysis be different if the action to recover cleanup costs had been brought by Saulino instead of EPA?

3.   Toxicacre. Until 1950, the site now known as Toxicacre was a farm in upstate New York. The site was then acquired by the ABC Chemical Company (ABC), which used the property to bury, in metal drums, various hazardous wastes produced by its industrial processes.

In 1960, the Sunny Homes Realty Company (Sunny Homes) acquired the property. At the time, Sunny Homes checked the chain of title and conducted a visual survey of the property, but did not learn about the presence of the buried drums. The purchase of the property was financed through a mortgage extended by the First National Bank (First National). Shortly after the purchase, Sunny Homes began excavating the property in order to build a residential subdivision.

On August 1965, during the excavation, Jim Green (Green), a worker on the construction crew, inadvertently punctured a drum. He had to be rushed to the hospital with severe burns on his face.

That same month, Sunny Homes began experiencing severe financial difficulties as a result of the downturn in the real estate market. First National took steps to help Sunny Homes avoid bankruptcy. In particular, it extended the period for repayment of the mortgage, required that every expenditure of over $1000 be approved by a First

National officer, and made available to Sunny Homes a consultant on the construction of low-cost housing.

In January 1966, the Sunny Homes president, John Smith (Smith) ordered that the area excavated by Green be filled. Work on the development then resumed, but on another part of the property. Without any further incident, the construction of the first house was completed in 1970. In January 1971, Sunny Homes defaulted on its mortgage payments, and the bank foreclosed on the property.

Within a few months, the bank advertised the property for sale and on January 1972, transferred it to another developer, Vacation Homes, Inc. (Vacation Homes). Internal bank records indicate that at the time of the sale, bank officers knew that the property had previously been used to store hazardous waste drums. This fact was not disclosed to Vacation Homes, which did not learn about any contamination at the time of the purchase (or at any time during its period of ownership) despite a title search and visual inspection.

Vacation Homes took no steps to develop the property. In January 1975, it transferred half of Toxicacre to Robert James (James), who intended to build a vacation home. James did not take any steps at the time of the purchase to determine whether hazardous substances were present on the property. James continues to own the property, but has not built the home and remained unaware of the contamination until the site was listed on the NPL.

In 1976, the City of Jefferson (City) took control of the other half of Toxicacre as a result of the tax delinquency of Vacation Homes. The City then used part of the property to dispose of old car batteries, which were sent to the site by Jefferson Cars, Inc. (Jefferson Cars). The batteries had originally been manufactured by the Best Battery Corporation (Best Battery). The City did not take any precautions in connection with the disposal.

The City became aware of the presence of hazardous substances on its portion of Toxicacre in January 1978, when torrential rainfalls—in fact, the greatest precipitation in the century—led to a large increase in the concentration of several hazardous pollutants on a pond in the property, causing the death of large numbers of fish and the destruction of vegetation. Chemical tests of the pond did not reveal the presence of any hazardous substances normally found in car batteries. At that time, the City closed the battery facility. The City, which was prevented from raising any additional tax revenues as a result of a state ban on tax increases, could not afford to devote any further resources to the problem. In 1981, shortly after the passage of Superfund, the City informed EPA of the contamination.

EPA did nothing until the mid-1980s. Subsequently, EPA began the process for placing the site on the NPL. EPA is now seeking the recovery of response costs to finance the excavation of the property and the transportation of any contaminated soil for incineration off-site. The possibility of groundwater remediation is also contemplated, though the extent, if any, of this problem is not yet known.

Discuss the CERCLA theories under which each of the parties might be held liable. What defenses to liability is each party likely to raise? Assess the strength of each defense.

4.   Alco, RSR, Quemetco, Davis, Pasminco, and PKM. The State of New York has brought a cost recovery action under CERCLA, seeking cleanup costs arising from the release of hazardous substances at a former lead processing facility operated by Defendant Alco Pacific, Inc. (Alco). The State asserts that Defendants RSR Corporation (RSR), Quemetco, Inc. (Quemetco), Davis Wire Corporation (Davis), Pasminco, Inc. (Pasminco), and P. Kay Metal Supply, Inc. (PKM) sold lead content materials to Alco and thus are subject to liability for contamination of the site under CERCLA.

Alco operated a lead processing facility on the site from approximately 1950 to 1990. During that period Alco refined and reclaimed lead from raw materials acquired from thousands of sources. These materials included lead ingots, automobile batteries, scrap metal, wheel weights, dross, and slag. The latter two materials are particularly important in the context of the instant appeal. "Dross" is the material that rises to the surface of melted metal that is not perfectly pure. Dross typically is skimmed off the molten metal and stored for later use or disposal. Depending on the care taken in skimming, the dross thus removed may contain a significant percentage of the metal itself. "Slag" also results from the separation of impurities from metal during the smelting and refining process. Alco purchased high lead content dross and slag that were by-products of other lead processors' operations. Material was deemed to have high lead content if it contained approximately thirty percent recoverable lead. The price Alco paid for the dross, slag, and other raw materials it purchased was based upon an analysis of the lead content of the material and the published market price of lead at the time of the transaction, as measured by the commodities price index quoted in daily newspapers.

After processing the materials supplied by Defendants and others, Alco sold the resulting refined and reclaimed lead in various forms. For example, Alco cast lead sailboat keels and produced sheet metal and lead anodes. Alco also sold lead in the form of ingots or babbitts. Alco disposed of the waste material resulting from its operations—low lead content slag—at a facility authorized to accept hazardous wastes. Alco did not dispose of dross generated during its operations, but rather used the dross again in its smelting process.

Defendants RSR and Quemetco

RSR is the parent corporation of Quemetco. RSR did not sell or transfer any materials to Alco, but it allegedly arranged for the sale of materials to Alco on behalf of Quemetco. Quemetco is a lead smelter that reclaims lead from scrap and lead-acid automobile batteries. Though Quemetco sold several different types of lead content materials to Alco, the parties have focused on sales of lead content slag.

Quemetco generates three types of slag: "first run slag" or "reverb slag," which is produced during the initial processing of scrap through a reverberatory furnace; "second run slag" or "rerun slag," which has been processed a second time; and "inert slag" or "waste slag," which has been processed at least twice and is ready for disposal. On October 25, 1988, Quemetco sold to Alco 47,920 pounds of "rerun antimonial lead slag." On October 31, 1988, Quemetco sold to Alco 49,580 pounds of "rerun antimonial lead slag." Alco paid seven cents per pound on both transactions, resulting in total payments of $3,354.40 on the first purchase and $3,470.60 on the second purchase.

Defendant Davis

Davis operated a wire manufacturing company that used molten lead to treat wire. A by-product of this process was lead content dross that was composed of lead and coke. Between 1978 and 1988, Davis periodically sold lead content dross to Alco at varying prices, depending on the amount of lead contained in the particular shipment. Alco paid Davis at least $110,000 for lead content dross during this period.

Defendant Pasminco

Pasminco operated a zinc smelting facility. Between 1978 and 1983, Pasminco periodically sold lead content dross and other materials to Alco.

Defendant PKM

PKM operates a solder manufacturing facility, reclaiming tin and lead in a manner similar to that used by Alco. PKM reclaims tin, lead and other metals and converts them into solder that it sells to others. PKM sold various materials to Alco, including lead dross, solder dross and antimonial lead dies. The parties have focused on the dross transactions. Between 1982 and 1989, PKM periodically sold lead and solder dross to Alco at varying prices. PKM characterizes these transactions as part of a "conversion" agreement whereby Alco processed the dross to strip it of impurities and then returned the extracted refined metal to PKM. PKM paid a fee for this conversion process.

Contamination of the Site

During Alco's operations, molten lead, slag and other materials, including dust and residue from the materials, occasionally spilled or otherwise were deposited onto the ground at the site. Additionally, solidified lead and slag were stored on the ground at least temporarily. The State determined that surface dust, soils, and slag piles at the site were contaminated with lead. It incurred significant cleanup costs at the site.

Assess the possible CERCLA liability of each of the defendants.

5.   Joint and Several Liability. EPA is considering the promulgation of regulations clarifying the applicability of joint and several liability under CERCLA. What should these regulations be? For each regulatory provision, present commentary on its rationale as well as a relevant example. Focus only on the case of generators. Be as specific as possible.

How would these regulations differ from the current case law? How are the courts likely to deal with a challenge to these regulations?

CHAPTER VIII

DISCLOSURE OF ENVIRONMENTAL RISKS

1. INTRODUCTION

A. OVERVIEW

Each of the federal environmental regimes discussed in Chapters V, VI, and VII have incorporated a different mix of regulatory tools in an attempt to achieve their stated objectives. These include traditional command-and-control regulations (such as the technology-based standards under the CAA and CWA), market-based initiatives (such as the SO_2 market under CAIR and the various water quality trading schemes under the CWA), and liability rules (such as the liability provisions of CERCLA). This chapter will primarily discuss the National Environmental Policy Act (NEPA) that adopts a different regulatory approach. Rather than compelling a substantive outcome, NEPA creates procedures and standards for the production, collection, and dissemination of environmental information.

Regulations of this type are broadly known as informational regulations and are typically designed to influence either consumer choices or government decisionmaking. Students of torts or products liability law will be familiar with the first type of informational regulation: manufacturers' safety notices, nutrition facts labels, and the Food and Drug Administration's cigarette warnings are designed to provide consumers with the tools they need to make informed decisions about the products that they purchase and how they will use them. The benefits and limits of consumer based regulations of this type were discussed in the article by Wesley A. Magat and W. Kip Viscusi in Chapter III. NEPA, the focus of this chapter, constitutes an example of the second type of informational regulation. It seeks to influence government decisionmaking by requiring the assessment and disclosure of the potential environmental impacts of proposed federal actions.

Two other prominent federal statutes, the Toxic Substances Control Act (TSCA) of 1976 and the Emergency Planning and Community Right-to-Know Act (EPCRA) of 1986, are designed to provide information on environmental and public health risks to governmental actors and the public. TSCA provides EPA with the authority, upon making certain determinations, to collect information about the hazards posed by chemical substances and to take action to control unreasonable risks by either preventing dangerous chemicals from making their way into use or placing restrictions on those already in commerce. 15 U.S.C. §§ 2601–2629. TSCA generally places the burden of obtaining data on existing chemicals on EPA, rather than on the companies that produce the chemicals. *Id.* §§ 2603–2610. As a result, EPA does not routinely assess the risks of the roughly 80,000 industrial chemicals in use. Moreover, TSCA does not require chemical companies to test the approximately 700 new chemicals introduced into commerce annually for their toxicity, and companies generally do not voluntarily perform such testing. *See* GAO, OPTIONS FOR ENHANCING THE EFFECTIVENESS OF THE TOXIC SUBSTANCES CONTROL ACT (Feb. 26, 2009). In 2016, Congress passed the Frank R. Lautenberg Chemical Safety for the 21st Century Act, amending several key provisions of the TSCA. The amendments require EPA to evaluate existing chemicals and address unreasonable risks, and it removes the requirement that EPA must choose the "least burdensome" way of addressing those risks. The Act still requires EPA to conduct a cost-benefit analysis of any proposed restrictions and to use the results of that analysis to guide its decisionmaking. *See* 15 U.S.C. § 2605(c)(2)(A)(iv).

In passing EPCRA in 1986, Congress required facilities to disclose information on hazardous substances to their communities. EPCRA is organized around four focal areas: emergency planning, 42 U.S.C. §§ 301–303; reporting of hazardous chemical inventories, §§ 311–312; notification of chemical accidents and releases, § 304; and reporting of toxic chemical releases, § 313. *See* 42 U.S.C. §§ 11001–11004, 11021–11023. One of EPCRA's best known and most important feature is the Toxics Release Inventory (TRI). 42 U.S.C. § 11023. The TRI requires facilities of a certain size and minimum emissions level to report, on a yearly basis, all releases of listed toxic pollutants to EPA. 42 U.S.C. § 11023(b), (f). Releases must be made available to the public through an internet database. 42 U.S.C. § 11023(g), (j). Facilities are required to provide their location and contact information, the maximum amount of the chemical onsite every year, and the amount and type of release. In addition to industry disclosures, chemicals have been added by citizen petition and by legislative action. Currently, more than 600 chemicals are covered by the TRI.

Informational regulation is by no means a recent development in the regulatory environment. NEPA, passed in 1969, is the oldest and (in many respects) most ambitious environmental statute. While NEPA, TSCA, and EPCRA remain the most prominent examples of informational regulatory regimes in the environmental context, the application of informational regulations is not limited to these regimes. Many of the major command-and-control regimes contain informational components—section 402(j) of the CWA, for example, requires that pollution discharge permits, as well as the information submitted in support of those permits, be made available to the public. 33 U.S.C. § 1342(j).

States have also taken steps to address the disclosure of risks related to hazardous chemicals. California's Proposition 65 is one of the most well known examples. In a 1986 general election, Californian voters overwhelmingly approved a proposition creating a broad warning requirement in situations involving the exposure of California residents to carcinogens and reproductive toxins. *See* CAL. HEALTH & SAFETY CODE § 25249.5 *et seq.* Proposition 65, titled "Safe Drinking Water and Toxic Enforcement Act," provides that "[n]o person in the course of doing business shall knowingly and intentionally expose any individual to a chemical known to the state to cause cancer or reproductive toxicity without first giving clear and reasonable warning to such individual. . . ." *Id.* § 25249.6. Like EPCRA, Proposition 65 establishes a list of hazardous chemicals. *Id.* § 25249.8. However, Proposition 65 applies to a much broader list of chemicals than EPCRA and is not limited to industrial facilities; the Proposition 65 list includes about 900 chemicals, about 300 of which have been granted a "safe harbor" level of exposure by the state regulatory agency, below which there is no requirement to provide a warning. *See* California Office of Environmental Health Hazard Assessment, The Proposition 65 List, https://oehha.ca.gov/proposition-65/proposition-65-list (last visited Nov. 19, 2018).

This chapter will discuss the various rationales for informational regulation before examining NEPA in detail.

B. RATIONALES FOR INFORMATIONAL REGULATION

Proponents of informational approaches to regulation argue that they enhance market efficiency, create incentives for self-policing, improve the effectiveness of command-and-control regulation, and promote democratic values by making information available to the public.

As has been noted in the context of corporate financial governance, "you manage what you measure." Louis Lowenstein, *Financial Transparency and Corporate Governance: You Manage What You Measure*, 96 COLUM. L. REV. 1335, 1342–43 (1996). Informational approaches require regulated actors to collect and disclose data that they may never have systematically examined—or even produced—in the past. Managers cannot correct a problem of which they are unaware. It is impossible to manage an agency, corporation, or project for better environmental performance without a clear understanding of baseline conditions and performance metrics. *See* Bradley C. Karkkainen, *Information as Environmental Regulation: TRI and Performance Benchmarking, Precursor to a New Paradigm*, 89 GEO. L.J. 257, 296–303 (2001).

Once regulated parties are aware of their level of performance and know that information about their performance has been made public, they have strong incentives to self-police, even if the governing statute creates no substantive requirements. *See id.* Managers are aware that poor environmental performance may provoke public calls for coercive regulation or erode congressional support for a federal program. *See* David W. Case, *Corporate Environmental Reporting as Informational Regulation: A Law and Economics Perspective*, 76 U. COLO. L. REV. 379, 421–22 (2005). Investors and insurers may perceive that companies with poor environmental performance present greater risks due to the possibility of future litigation or regulation. *Id.* at 407–11 (describing SEC regulation of the disclosure of environmental liabilities); *see, e.g.*, Christina Ross et al., *Limiting Liability in the Greenhouse: Insurance Risk Management Strategies in the Context of Global Climate Change*, 43 STAN. J. INT'L L. 251, 305–10 (2007). Furthermore, the disclosure of negative environmental information may damage a corporation's brand image, particularly for corporations that perceive and market themselves as progressive or environmentally friendly. Finally, consumers may react to the disclosure of negative information by changing their purchasing habits. *See* Cass R. Sunstein, *Informational Regulation and Informational Standing:* Akins *and Beyond*, 147 U. PA. L. REV. 613, 624–26 (1999). Therefore, even in the absence of substantive law requirements, the regulated entity will strive to improve environmental performance.

Informational regulation benefits democratic values by lowering informational barriers to citizen participation in government decisionmaking. Individuals and many nonprofit groups are at a considerable disadvantage in collecting information about corporate or agency actions, which may be proprietary, expensive, unwieldy, or simply difficult to acquire. Informational regulations, by making data available to citizens, enable them to fulfill their roles as monitors of government activity. *Id.*; *see also* ROBERT G. DREHER, NEPA UNDER SIEGE: THE POLITICAL ASSAULT ON THE NATIONAL ENVIRONMENTAL POLICY ACT 2–4, 6 (2005).

Finally, informational approaches may improve the effectiveness of other types of regulation and policymaking. Informational gaps hinder efforts to set optimal pollution limits and to design appropriate control measures. Lack of information also makes it difficult for agencies to monitor the effectiveness of regulation, impedes enforcement, and renders the design of effective control programs for certain types of pollutants (such as non-point source water pollution) incredibly difficult.

Daniel C. Esty, *Environmental Protection in the Information Age*, 79 N.Y.U. L. REV. 115, 167 (2004).

Professor Esty argues that the technological development of the Information Age will have a dramatic impact on environmental regulation. Existing regulatory regimes are shaped by persistent information gaps. However, technological innovation has increased our ability to pinpoint sources of pollutants, enabling us to create more tightly focused environmental laws. Furthermore, high-speed global communications networks enable information to be shared quickly and efficiently among large numbers of people, "undermin[ing] the governmental monopoly over decision-making." *Id.* EPCRA is one of the first statutes to make use of new information technologies, requiring EPA to make information gathered under the Toxic Release Inventory program available to the public on the internet.

Furthermore, newer technology like geospatial analysis, data visualization, and computer-based modeling can help government and private actors identify optimal locations for siting new development or setting boundaries for protected lands, among other uses. *See generally* Dave Owen, *Mapping, Modeling, and the Fragmentation of Environmental Law*, 2013 UTAH L. REV. 219 (2013). These technologies are transforming how researchers conceptualize environmental systems and how policymakers analyze potential environmental, social, and economic outcomes. *Id.* at 219, 221.

However, information is not an unabashed good. Information can be costly, inefficient, or difficult to obtain. Its availability, accuracy, cost, and timeliness are constraints on the capacity of regulators to use information to cure real-world problems. *See* Bradley C. Karkkainen, *Information As Environmental Regulation: Tri and Performance Benchmarking, Precursor to A New Paradigm?*, 89 GEO. L.J. 257, 270 (2001). Striking the appropriate balance of information provided to the public is also difficult. Provide too little context, and people will be unable to use information effectively; provide too much information, and people may become overwhelmed and not pay attention to the warnings they receive. Even when the correct informational balance is struck, those receiving the information may lack the educational, cultural, or linguistic background necessary to make use of these informational resources. This is particularly true in the case of warnings that convey complex, highly technical information. *See* Alexander Volokh, *The Pitfalls of the Environmental Right-to-Know*, 2 UTAH L. REV. 805, 814–24 (2002). Furthermore, as was discussed in Chapter II, individuals experience great difficulty in determining how best to weigh the risks of low-probability events and may often treat such events as much more dangerous than they actually are. Finally, in some cases, despite taking advantage of the economies of scale inherent in centralized data collection and dissemination, the costs of informational regulation may outweigh the benefits in terms of lives saved or exposures avoided. *See*

Cass R. Sunstein, *supra*, at 626–27 (describing costs of the Occupational Safety and Health Agency's hazard communication policy).

2.   THE NATIONAL ENVIRONMENTAL POLICY ACT

A.   INTRODUCTION

NEPA became law on New Year's Day, 1970, and was the first major environmental statute of the modern era. Its purpose is

> [t]o declare a national policy which will encourage productive and enjoyable harmony between man and his environment; to promote efforts which will prevent or eliminate damage to the environment and biosphere and stimulate the health and welfare of man; to enrich the understanding of the ecological systems and natural resources important to the Nation; and to establish a Council on Environmental Quality.

42 U.S.C. § 4321. Notwithstanding the breadth of the Act's objectives, NEPA has been interpreted as introducing only procedural requirements upon federal agencies. *See, e.g., Strycker's Bay Neighborhood Council, Inc. v. Karlen*, 444 U.S. 223 (1980). Most significantly, NEPA requires the preparation of environmental impact statements (EIS) for major federal actions that have a significant environmental impact on the human environment. 42 U.S.C. § 4332(2)(C). In addition, it requires that agencies consider "alternatives" to proposed actions, even with respect to those actions that do not require the preparation of an EIS. 42 U.S.C. § 4332(2)(E). Despite not containing any substantive components, the impact of NEPA upon federal decisionmaking has been immense. Each year, federal agencies prepare more than 50,000 assessments pursuant to the Act, ranging in cost from $250,000 to $2,000,000 for an EIS, to $5,000 to $200,000 for an EA. *See* THE NEPA TASK FORCE, REPORT TO THE COUNCIL ON ENVIRONMENTAL QUALITY: MODERNIZING NEPA IMPLEMENTATION 65–66 (2003). The Act has created impetus for change in the composition of federal agencies—in order to comply with NEPA's procedural requirements, agencies have been forced to incorporate younger, more liberal employees to provide environmental expertise. *See* WENDY NELSON ESPELAND, THE STRUGGLE FOR WATER: POLITICS, RATIONALITY, AND IDENTITY IN THE AMERICAN SOUTHWEST 146 (1998). The Act promotes political feedback and public participation, ensuring that environmental issues are brought to an agency's attention prior to the commencement of an action.

Section 101 of the Act contains the Congressional Declaration of National Environmental Policy. Recognizing "the profound impact of man's activity on the interrelations of all components of the natural environment," § 101(a) provides that

> it is the continuing policy of the Federal Government, in cooperation with State and local governments, and other

concerned public and private organizations, to use all practicable means and measures, including financial and technical assistance, in a manner calculated to foster and promote the general welfare, to create and maintain conditions under which man and nature can exist in productive harmony, and fulfill the social, economic, and other requirements of present and future generations of Americans.

42 U.S.C. § 4331(a). In order to achieve this policy, § 101(b) requires that the federal government coordinate its actions so as to:

1. fulfill the responsibilities of each generation as trustee of the environment for succeeding generations;

2. assure for all Americans safe, healthful, productive, and esthetically and culturally pleasing surroundings;

3. attain the widest range of beneficial uses of the environment without degradation, risk to health or safety, or other undesirable and unintended consequences;

4. preserve important historic, cultural, and natural aspects of our national heritage, and maintain, wherever possible, an environment which supports diversity, and variety of individual choice;

5. achieve a balance between population and resource use which will permit high standards of living and a wide sharing of life's amenities; and

6. enhance the quality of renewable resources and approach the maximum attainable recycling of depletable resources.

42 U.S.C. § 4331(b). Section 102 constitutes the main operative provision of the Act. It requires that federal agencies prepare a detailed statement with respect to all "proposals for legislation and other major Federal actions significantly affecting the quality of the human environment." 42 U.S.C. § 4332(2)(C). Each statement must contain an evaluation of:

(i)   the environmental impact of the proposed action,

(ii)   any adverse environmental effects which cannot be avoided should the proposal be implemented,

(iii) alternatives to the proposed action,

(iv)   the relationship between local short-term uses of man's environment and the maintenance and enhancement of long-term productivity, and

(v)   any irreversible and irretrievable commitments of resources which would be involved in the proposed action should it be implemented.

Id. Responsibility for the preparation of an EIS falls upon the federal agency undertaking the federal action. An EIS must be prepared with respect to all federal actions (including all state and private actions that demonstrate a "federal nexus" by virtue of federal funding or involvement) and proposals for legislation that significantly affect the quality of the human environment. *Id.* NEPA's impact statement procedure has been held to apply where a federal agency approves a lease of land to private parties, grants licenses and permits to private parties, or approves and funds state highway projects. In this way, NEPA can be seen to act "as an environmental full disclosure law, providing information which Congress thought the public should have concerning the particular environmental costs involved in a project." *Silva v. Lynn*, 482 F.2d 1282, 1284 (1st Cir. 1973). As noted above, an EIS must describe the environmental impact of the proposed action, adverse environmental harms resulting from its implementation, and alternatives to the proposal. The discussion of environmental impacts should address both beneficial and detrimental, as well as direct and indirect, impacts. 40 C.F.R. § 1508.8. The alternatives described in the EIS must incorporate a "no-action alternative," under which the proposed action does not take place. *See* 40 C.F.R. § 1502.14(d).

Section 202 of the Act establishes the Council on Environmental Quality (CEQ), within the Executive Office of the President. 42 U.S.C. § 4342. The CEQ is responsible for promulgating regulations interpreting NEPA, *see* Exec. Order No. 11,991, 42 Fed. Reg. 26,967 (1977), as well as preparing an annual environmental report to the President "on the state and condition of the environment," 42 U.S.C. § 4344. The CEQ has created a multi-step process for determining the circumstances in which an EIS is required. First, an agency must determine whether the proposal normally requires an EIS. 40 C.F.R. § 1501.4(a)(1). If it does, the agency must prepare an EIS unless it can demonstrate that there exists no potential for significant impact. Conversely, if the agency determines that the proposal does not normally require an EIS, the project is deemed to fall within a categorical exclusion, thereby not requiring the preparation of an EIS (unless there exists substantial evidence to suggest that there is potential for significant impact). 40 C.F.R. § 1501.4(a)(2). If the proposal does not fall neatly within either category, the agency is required to conduct an environmental assessment (EA)—a truncated EIS designed to provide sufficient evidence and analysis for determining whether the preparation of an EIS is warranted. 40 C.F.R. §§ 1501.4(a)–(c), 1508.9. An EA must include an assessment of the environmental impacts of the proposed action, as well as a description of its appropriate alternatives and their environmental impacts. 40 C.F.R. § 1508.9. These include direct, indirect, and cumulative effects. *See Ctr. for Envtl. Law & Policy v. U.S. Bureau of Reclamation*, 655 F.3d 1000, 1006 (9th Cir. 2011). After the EA is completed, an agency must either issue a finding of no significant impact (FONSI) or a notice of intent to conduct an EIS (NOI). 40 C.F.R. § 1501.4(c)–(e). Agencies may also apply a categorical exclusion (CE) to certain activities, which exempts them from many NEPA requirements, including preparation of an EA or EIS. 40 C.F.R. § 1508.4.

The vast majority of agency actions subject to NEPA review do not involve preparation of an EIS. The Government Accountability Office estimated that about 94 percent of all NEPA decisions fall under categorical exclusions; about 5 percent are EAs; and less than 1 percent are reviewed under EISs. GAO, NATIONAL ENVIRONMENTAL POLICY ACT: LITTLE INFORMATION EXISTS ON NEPA ANALYSES 8–9 (April 2014).

In the event that an EIS is deemed necessary, the responsible agency must first publish the NOI in the Federal Register, thereby signaling the initiation of the process. A draft EIS is then prepared, providing a detailed description of the proposal, its purpose and need, the reasonable alternatives, the affected environment, and the anticipated beneficial and adverse environmental effects of each alternative. Following a formal comment period, a final EIS is prepared and issued. The final EIS addresses the comments on the draft EIS and identifies, based on analysis and comments, the agency's preferred alternative. Finally, a Record of Decision is issued, identifying the selected alternative and presenting the basis for the decision.

Despite NEPA's broad aspirational provisions and specific procedural requirements, it fails to provide citizens a private right of action that would allow them to challenge agency noncompliance and to enforce NEPA provisions. Thus, litigants can gain judicial review of an agency's action only under the terms of the Administrative Procedure Act (APA).

* * *

NEPA introduced new requirements on the way federal agencies addressed the environment in their decisionmaking. Immediately following its implementation, however, the scope of those obligations was uncertain—different federal agencies sought to give effect to the Act in different ways. The following case was the first major decision interpreting the scope of NEPA's provisions.

Calvert Cliffs' Coordinating Committee, Inc. v. United States Atomic Energy Commission

449 F.2d 1109 (D.C. Cir. 1971).

■ Before WRIGHT, TAMM, and ROBINSON, CIRCUIT JUDGES.

■ WRIGHT, CIRCUIT JUDGE:

[In response to the passage of NEPA, the Atomic Energy Commission [AEC] promulgated rules regarding the consideration of non-radiological matter in the issuance of construction permits or operating licenses for nuclear power facilities. In broad terms, the rules required that each applicant for a construction permit submit an "environmental report" to the AEC, which was to form the basis of the AEC's own "detailed statement" concerning the environmental costs, benefits, and alternatives of the proposal. While the detailed statement was to be submitted to the hearing board charged with evaluating the permit application, the rules provided that it was only to be considered by the board in the event that it was specifically raised by a party to the proceeding. If a party did not raise any environmental issue in the course of the hearing, the environmental report and detailed statement would accompany the application through the review process but not be taken into evidence. The plaintiffs argued that these procedures, while technically consistent with the procedural requirements of NEPA, fell short of the Congressional mandate.]

These cases are only the beginning of what promises to become a flood of new litigation—litigation seeking judicial assistance in protecting our natural environment. Several recently enacted statutes attest to the commitment of the Government to control, at long last, the destructive engine of material "progress." But it remains to be seen whether the promise of this legislation will become a reality. Therein lies the judicial role. In these cases, we must for the first time interpret the broadest and perhaps most important of the recent statutes: the National Environmental Policy Act of 1969 (NEPA). We must assess claims that one of the agencies charged with its administration has failed to live up to the congressional mandate. Our duty, in short, is to see that important legislative purposes, heralded in the halls of Congress, are not lost or misdirected in the vast hallways of the federal bureaucracy.

NEPA, like so much other reform legislation of the last 40 years, is cast in terms of a general mandate and broad delegation of authority to new and old administrative agencies. It takes the major step of requiring all federal agencies to consider values of environmental preservation in their spheres of activity, and it prescribes certain procedural measures to ensure that those values are in fact fully respected. Petitioners argue that rules recently adopted by the Atomic Energy Commission to govern consideration of environmental matters fail to satisfy the rigor demanded by NEPA. The Commission, on the other hand, contends that the vagueness of the NEPA mandate and delegation leaves much room for discretion and that the rules challenged by petitioners fall well within the broad scope of the Act. We find the policies embodied in NEPA to be a good deal clearer and more demanding than does the Commission. We conclude that the Commission's procedural rules do not comply with the congressional policy. Hence we remand these cases for further rule making.

We begin our analysis with an examination of NEPA's structure and approach and of the Atomic Energy Commission rules which are said to conflict with the requirements of the Act. The relevant portion of NEPA is Title I, consisting of five sections. Section 101 sets forth the Act's basic substantive policy: that the federal government "use all practicable means and measures" to protect environmental values. Congress did not establish environmental protection as an exclusive goal; rather, it desired a reordering of priorities, so that environmental costs and benefits will assume their proper place along with other considerations. In Section 101(b), imposing an explicit duty on federal officials, the Act provides that "it is the continuing responsibility of the Federal Government to use all practicable means, consistent with other essential considerations of national policy," to avoid environmental degradation, preserve "historic, cultural, and natural" resources, and promote "the widest range of beneficial uses of the environment without . . . undesirable and unintended consequences."

Thus the general substantive policy of the Act is a flexible one. It leaves room for a responsible exercise of discretion and may not require particular substantive results in particular problematic instances. However, the Act also contains very important "procedural" provisions— provisions which are designed to see that all federal agencies do in fact exercise the substantive discretion given them. These provisions are not highly flexible. Indeed, they establish a strict standard of compliance.

NEPA, first of all, makes environmental protection a part of the mandate of every federal agency and department. The Atomic Energy Commission, for example, had continually asserted, prior to NEPA, that it had no statutory authority to concern itself with the adverse environmental effects of its actions. Now, however, its hands are no longer tied. It is not only permitted, but compelled, to take environmental values into account. Perhaps the greatest importance of NEPA is to require the Atomic Energy Commission and other agencies to consider environmental issues just as they consider other matters within their mandates. This compulsion is most plainly stated in Section 102. There, "Congress authorizes and directs that, to the fullest extent possible: (1) the policies, regulations, and public laws of the United States shall be interpreted and administered in accordance with the policies set forth in this Act. . . ." Congress also "authorizes and directs" that "(2) all agencies of the Federal Government shall" follow certain rigorous procedures in considering environmental values. Senator Jackson, NEPA's principal sponsor, stated that "[n]o agency will [now] be able to maintain that it has no mandate or no requirement to consider the environmental consequences of its actions." He characterized the requirements of Section 102 as "action-forcing" and stated that "[o]therwise, these lofty declarations [in § 101] are nothing more than that."

. . . Section 102(2)(C) requires that responsible officials of all agencies prepare a "detailed statement" covering the impact of particular actions on the environment, the environmental costs which might be avoided, and alternative measures which might alter the cost-benefit equation. The apparent purpose of the "detailed statement" is to aid in the agencies' own decision making process and to advise other interested agencies and the public of the environmental consequences of planned federal action. Beyond the "detailed statement," Section 102(2)(D) requires all agencies specifically to "study, develop, and describe appropriate alternatives to recommended courses of action in any proposal which involves unresolved conflicts concerning alternative uses of available resources." This requirement, like the "detailed statement" requirement, seeks to ensure that each agency decision maker has before him and takes into proper account all possible approaches to a particular project (including total abandonment of the project) which would alter the environmental impact and the cost-benefit balance. Only in that fashion is it likely that the most intelligent, optimally beneficial decision will ultimately be made. Moreover, by compelling a formal "detailed statement" and a description of alternatives, NEPA provides evidence that the mandated decision making process has in fact taken place and, most importantly, allows those removed from the initial process to evaluate and balance the factors on their own.

Of course, all of these Section 102 duties are qualified by the phrase "to the fullest extent possible." We must stress as forcefully as possible that this language does not provide an escape hatch for footdragging agencies; it does not make NEPA's procedural requirements somehow "discretionary." Congress did not intend the Act to be such a paper tiger. Indeed, the requirement of environmental consideration "to the fullest extent possible" sets a high standard for the agencies, a standard which must be rigorously enforced by the reviewing courts. . . .

. . . [T]he Section 102 duties are not inherently flexible. They must be complied with to the fullest extent, unless there is a clear conflict of *statutory* authority. Considerations of administrative difficulty, delay or economic cost will not suffice to strip the section of its fundamental importance. . . .

We conclude, then, that Section 102 of NEPA mandates a particular sort of careful and informed decisionmaking process and creates judicially enforceable duties. The reviewing courts probably cannot reverse a substantive decision on its merits, under Section 101, unless it be shown that the actual balance of costs and benefits that was struck was arbitrary or clearly gave insufficient weight to environmental values. But if the decision was reached procedurally without individualized consideration and balancing of environmental factors—conducted fully and in good faith—it is the responsibility of the courts to reverse. As one District Court has said of Section 102 requirements: "It is hard to imagine a clearer or stronger mandate to the Courts." Texas Committee on Natural Resources v. United States, W.D.Tex., 1 Envir. Rpts.—Cass. 1303, 1304 (1970).

In the cases before us now, we do not have to review a particular decision by the Atomic Energy Commission granting a construction permit or an operating license. Rather, we must review the Commission's recently promulgated rules which govern consideration of environmental values in all such individual decisions. The rules were devised strictly in order to comply with the NEPA procedural requirements—but petitioners argue that they fall far short of the congressional mandate. . . .

The procedure for environmental study and consideration set up by the [AEC rules] is as follows: Each applicant for an initial construction permit must submit to the Commission his own "environmental report," presenting his assessment of the environmental impact of the planned facility and possible alternatives which would alter the impact. When construction is completed and the applicant applies for a license to operate the new facility, he must again submit an "environmental report" noting any factors which have changed since the original report. At each stage, the Commission's regulatory staff must take the applicant's report and prepare its own "detailed statement" of environmental costs, benefits and alternatives. The statement will then be circulated to other interested and responsible agencies and made available to the public. After comments are received from those sources, the staff must prepare a final "detailed statement" and make a final recommendation on the application for a construction permit or operating license.

Up to this point in the [AEC] rules petitioners have raised no challenge. However, they do attack . . . other, specific parts of the rules which, they say, violate the requirements of Section 102 of NEPA. Each of these parts in some way limits full consideration and individualized balancing of environmental values in the Commission's decision making process. (1) Although environmental factors must be considered by the agency's regulatory staff under the rules, such factors need not be considered by the hearing board conducting an independent review of staff recommendations, unless affirmatively raised by outside parties or staff members. (2) Another part of the procedural rules prohibits any such party from raising nonradiological environmental issues at any hearing if the notice for that hearing appeared in the Federal Register before March 4, 1971. . . .

NEPA makes only one specific reference to consideration of environmental values in agency review processes. Section 102(2)(C) provides that copies of the staff's "detailed statement" and comments thereon "shall accompany the proposal through the existing agency review processes." The Atomic Energy Commission's rules may seem in technical compliance with the letter of that provision. . . . The question here is whether the Commission is correct in thinking that its NEPA responsibilities may "be carried out in toto outside the hearing process"— whether it is enough that environmental data and evaluations merely "accompany" an application through the review process, but receive no consideration whatever from the hearing board.

We believe that the Commission's crabbed interpretation of NEPA makes a mockery of the Act. What possible purpose could there be in the Section 102(2)(C) requirement (that the "detailed statement" accompany proposals through agency review processes) if "accompany" means no more than physical proximity—mandating no more than the physical act of passing certain folders and papers, unopened, to reviewing officials along with other folders and papers? What possible purpose could there be in requiring the "detailed statement" to be before hearing boards, if the boards are free to ignore entirely the contents of the statement? NEPA was meant to do more than regulate the flow of papers in the federal bureaucracy. The word "accompany" in Section 102(2)(C) must not be read so narrowly as to make the Act ludicrous. It must, rather, be read to indicate a congressional intent that environmental factors, as compiled in the "detailed statement," be *considered* through agency review processes.

Beyond Section 102(2)(C), NEPA requires that agencies consider the environmental impact of their actions "to the fullest extent possible." The Act is addressed to agencies as a whole, not only to their professional staffs. Compliance to the "*fullest*" possible extent would seem to demand that environmental issues be considered at every important stage in the decision making process concerning a particular action—at every stage where an overall balancing of environmental and nonenvironmental factors is appropriate and where alterations might be made in the proposed action to minimize environmental costs. . . .

The rationale of the Commission's limitation of environmental issues to hearings in which parties affirmatively raise those issues may have been one of economy. It may have been supposed that, whenever there are serious environmental costs overlooked or uncorrected by the staff, some party will intervene to bring those costs to the hearing board's attention. Of course, independent review of the "detailed statement" and independent balancing of factors in an uncontested hearing will take some time. If it is done properly, it will take a significant amount of time. But all of the NEPA procedures take time. Such administrative costs are not enough to undercut the Act's requirement that environmental protection be considered "to the fullest extent possible." . . . [The] responsibility [of the agency] is not simply to sit back, like an umpire, and resolve adversary contentions at the hearing stage. Rather, it must itself take the initiative of considering environmental values at every distinctive and comprehensive stage of the process beyond the staff's evaluation and recommendation. . . .

The sweep of NEPA is extraordinarily broad, compelling consideration of any and all types of environmental impact of federal action. . . . We believe the Commission's rule is in fundamental conflict with the basic purpose of the Act. NEPA mandates a case-by-case balancing judgment on the part of federal agencies. In each individual case, the particular economic and technical benefits of planned action must be assessed and then weighed against the environmental costs; alternatives must be considered which would affect the balance of values. The magnitude of possible benefits and possible costs may lie anywhere on a broad spectrum. Much will depend on the particular magnitudes involved in particular cases. In some cases, the benefits will be great enough to justify a certain quantum of environmental costs; in other cases, they will not be so great and the proposed action may have to be abandoned or significantly altered so as to bring the benefits and costs into a proper balance. The point of the individualized balancing analysis is to ensure that, with possible alterations, the optimally beneficial action is finally taken.

Certification by another agency that its own environmental standards are satisfied involves an entirely different kind of judgment. Such agencies, without overall responsibility for the particular federal action in question, attend only to one aspect of the problem: the magnitude of certain environmental costs. They simply determine whether those costs exceed an allowable amount. Their certification does not mean that they found no environmental damage whatever. In fact, there may be significant environmental damage (*e.g.*, water pollution), but not quite enough to violate applicable (*e.g.*, water quality) standards. Certifying agencies do not attempt to weigh that damage against the opposing benefits. Thus the balancing analysis remains to be done. It may be that the environmental costs, though passing prescribed standards, are nonetheless great enough to outweigh the particular economic and technical benefits involved in the planned action. The only agency in a position to make such a judgment is the agency with overall responsibility for the proposed federal action—the agency to which NEPA is specifically directed. . . .

The Commission appears to recognize the severe limitation which its rules impose on environmental protection. Yet it argues that full NEPA consideration of alternatives and independent action would cause too much delay at the preoperating license stage. It justifies its rules as the most that is "practicable, in the light of environmental needs and 'other essential considerations of national policy'." . . .

. . . NEPA requires that an agency must—to the *fullest* extent possible under its other statutory obligations—consider alternatives to its actions which would reduce environmental damage. That principle establishes that consideration of environmental matters must be more than a *pro forma* ritual. Clearly, it is pointless to "consider" environmental costs without also seriously considering action to avoid them. Such a full exercise of substantive discretion is required at every important, appropriate and nonduplicative stage of an agency's proceedings. . . .

NOTES AND QUESTIONS

1. **Major Federal Action.** Section 102(2)(C) requires that an agency prepare an EIS in circumstances where it undertakes a "major federal action[ ] significantly affecting the quality of the human environment." 42 U.S.C. § 4332(2)(C). In *Calvert Cliffs*, did the AEC suggest that the granting of an operating permit or construction license to a nuclear power facility did not constitute a major federal action? What then was the nature of the dispute?

2.   Accompanying the Proposal. Section 102(2)(C) requires that copies of an EIS "accompany the proposal through the existing agency review processes." 42 U.S.C. § 4332(2)(C). On what basis did the AEC contend that the regulations in question complied with the requirements of § 102(2)(C)? Was it the AEC's position that the EIS would simply accompany the proposal throughout the licensing process and never be considered? In many respects, the AEC's regulations mirrored the responsibilities of an appellate court—which does not face an independent obligation to scrutinize matters beyond those grounds of complaint raised by an appellant. Why then did the *Calvert Cliffs* court find that the regulations "made a mockery of the Act"? What statutory support exists for the *Calvert Cliffs* court's finding that NEPA requires an agency to consider the environmental impacts of a proposed action, regardless of whether those issues are raised by a third party?

3.   To the "Fullest Extent Possible." Federal agencies are required to comply with the requirements of § 102(2)(C) "to the fullest extent possible." 42 U.S.C. § 4332. How does the *Calvert Cliffs* court interpret this legislative provision? Why was the court concerned that this provision could render the Act a "paper tiger"? To what extent are agencies entitled to rely on considerations of administrative difficulty, delay, or economic cost, in choosing not to prepare an EIS?

4.   Substantive Force? The *Calvert Cliffs* court expressly recognized that NEPA requires that federal agencies "consider values of environmental preservation." It found "the policies embodied in NEPA to be a good deal . . . more demanding than . . . the Commission," 449 F.2d at 1111, and that a reviewing court could reverse a decision of an agency where it had "clearly [given] insufficient weight to environmental values." *Id.* To what extent was the *Calvert Cliffs* court willing to recognize a substantive component in NEPA?

5.   Fox Guarding the Henhouse. Does it make sense that federal agencies responsible for the action in question also be responsible for evaluating its environmental impacts? Some commentators, such as Wendy B. Davis, suggest that this should not be the case:

> Federal agencies, which lack environmental expertise, and whose mission is not environmental protection, should not have the power to determine whether their proposed projects will harm the environment. Agencies with environmental expertise, such as the Environmental Protection Agency (EPA), should be involved in the environmental assessment process. Foreseeable adverse environmental impact should result in a judicial finding that any proposed action pursuant to an [EIS] is arbitrary and capricious. . . .
>
> Pursuant to NEPA, . . . even if [a] federal agency has no environmental expertise, the agency will have authority to decide (a) whether the project will result in a major federal action with a significant environmental impact so that an EIS is required, (b) what other federal agencies, if any, may cooperate and assist in the preparation of the EIS, and (c) whether to continue with the project

notwithstanding the disapproval of environmental expert or the predicted adverse environmental impact.

Wendy B. Davis, *The Fox Is Guarding the Henhouse: Enhancing the Role of the EPA in FONSI Determinations Pursuant to NEPA*, 39 AKRON L. REV. 35, 35–36 (2006).

How convincing do you find Davis' argument? For what reasons would it make sense for the federal agencies responsible for the action to be responsible for evaluating its environmental impacts? Given that there are in excess of 100,000 categorical exclusions, 6,000 EAs, and 400 EISs prepared each year (including draft, supplemental, and final documents in each category), how plausible is it to suggest that EPA should be "involved in the assessment process"? *See* GAO, NATIONAL ENVIRONMENTAL POLICY ACT: LITTLE INFORMATION EXISTS ON NEPA ANALYSES 9 (April 2014).

B. PROCEDURE V. SUBSTANCE

Throughout the 1970s, federal courts interpreted the provisions of NEPA expansively. Decisions such as *Calvert Cliffs* suggested that NEPA contained a substantive component, pursuant to which agency decisionmaking could be struck down on the basis that it did not accord sufficient weight to environmental concerns. In the early 1980s, however, it became evident that the Supreme Court preferred a more restrictive interpretation of the Act. In the following cases, the Supreme Court rejects the notion that NEPA contains a substantive component, finding instead that its provisions simply prescribe a particular process to be adopted by agencies in the course of decisionmaking. In contrast, however, as the notes and questions that follow these cases discuss, many of the environmental policy statutes adopted by the states (mirroring the federal NEPA) do create substantive obligations on the part of state agencies to consider the environmental impacts of a proposed action.

Strycker's Bay Neighborhood Council, Inc. v. Karlen

444 U.S. 223 (1980).

■ PER CURIAM:

[Plaintiffs challenged the U.S. Department of Housing and Urban Development's (HUD) approval of a low-income housing project on the Upper West Side of Manhattan (at what is referred to in the case as "Site 30"). The Court of Appeals found that although an EIS was not required, HUD had violated NEPA because it had not considered appropriate alternatives. The Court of Appeals remanded the case to HUD to come up with a list of alternatives.]

On remand, HUD prepared a lengthy report entitled Special Environmental Clearance (1977). After marshaling the data, the report asserted that, "while the choice of Site 30 for development as a 100 percent low-income project has raised valid questions about the potential social environmental impacts involved, the problems associated with the impact on social fabric and community structures are not considered so serious as to require that this component be rated as unacceptable." The last portion of the report incorporated a study wherein the [New York City Planning] Commission evaluated nine alternative locations for the project and found none of them acceptable. While HUD's report conceded that this study may not have considered all possible alternatives, it credited the Commission's conclusion that any relocation of the units would entail an unacceptable delay of two years or more. According to HUD, "[m]easured against the environmental costs associated with the minimum two-year delay, the benefits seem insufficient to justify a mandated substitution of sites." *Id.*, at 54.

After soliciting the parties' comments on HUD's report, the District Court again entered judgment in favor of petitioners. See *Trinity Episcopal School Corp. v. Harris*, 445 F.Supp. 204 (1978). The court was "impressed with [HUD's analysis] as being thorough and exhaustive," *id.*, at 209–210, and found that "HUD's consideration of the alternatives was neither arbitrary nor capricious"; on the contrary, "[i]t was done in good faith and in full accordance with the law." *Id.*, at 220.

On appeal, the Second Circuit vacated and remanded again. *Karlen v. Harris*, 590 F.2d 39 (1978). The appellate court focused upon that part of HUD's report where the agency considered and rejected alternative sites, and in particular upon HUD's reliance on the delay such a relocation would entail. The Court of Appeals purported to recognize that its role in reviewing HUD's decision was defined by the Administrative Procedure Act (APA), 5 U.S.C. § 706(2)(A), which provides that agency actions should be set aside if found to be "arbitrary, capricious, an abuse of discretion, or otherwise not in accordance with law. . . ." Additionally, however, the Court of Appeals looked to "[t]he provisions of NEPA" for "the substantive standards necessary to review the merits of agency decisions. . . ." 590 F.2d, at 43. The Court of Appeals conceded that HUD had "given 'consideration' to alternatives" to redesignating the site. *Id.*, at 44. Nevertheless, the court believed that " 'consideration' is not an end in itself." *Ibid.* Concentrating on HUD's finding that development of an alternative location would entail an unacceptable delay, the appellate court held that such delay could not be "an overriding factor" in HUD's decision to proceed with the development. *Ibid.* According to the court, when HUD considers such projects, "environmental factors, such as crowding low-income housing into a concentrated area, should be given determinative weight." *Ibid.* The Court of Appeals therefore remanded the case to the District Court, instructing HUD to attack the shortage of low-income housing in a manner that would avoid the "concentration" of such housing on Site 30. *Id.*, at 45.

In *Vermont Yankee Nuclear Power Corp. v. NRDC*, 435 U.S. 519, 558 (1978), we stated that NEPA, while establishing "significant substantive goals for the Nation," imposes upon agencies duties that are "essentially procedural." As we stressed in that case, NEPA was designed "to insure a fully informed and well-considered decision," but not necessarily "a decision the judges of the Court of Appeals or of this Court would have reached had they been members of the decisionmaking unit of the agency." *Ibid. Vermont Yankee* cuts sharply against the Court of Appeals' conclusion that an agency, in selecting a course of action, must elevate environmental concerns over other appropriate considerations. On the contrary, once an agency has made a decision subject to NEPA's procedural requirements, the only role for a court is to insure that the agency has considered the environmental consequences; it cannot "interject itself within the area of discretion of the executive as to the choice of the action to be taken." *Kleppe v. Sierra Club*, 427 U.S. 390, 410, n. 21 (1976). See also *FPC v. Transcontinental Gas Pipe Line Corp.*, 423 U.S. 326 (1976).

In the present litigation there is no doubt that HUD considered the environmental consequences of its decision to redesignate the proposed site for low-income housing. NEPA requires no more. The petitions for certiorari are granted, and the judgment of the Court of Appeals is therefore *reversed*.

■ JUSTICE MARSHALL, dissenting:

The issue raised by these cases is far more difficult than the *per curiam* opinion suggests. . . .

The issue before the Court of Appeals . . . was whether HUD was free under NEPA to reject an alternative acknowledged to be environmentally preferable solely on the ground that any change in sites would cause delay. This was hardly a "peripheral issue" in the case. Whether NEPA, which sets forth "significant substantive goals," *Vermont Yankee Nuclear Power Corp. v. NRDC, supra*, at 558, permits a projected two-year time difference to be controlling over environmental superiority is by no means clear. Resolution of the issue, however, is certainly within the normal scope of review of agency action to determine if it is arbitrary, capricious, or an abuse of discretion. The question whether HUD can make delay the paramount concern over environmental superiority is essentially a restatement of the question whether HUD in considering the environmental consequences of its proposed action gave those consequences a "hard look," which is exactly the proper question for the reviewing court to ask. *Kleppe v. Sierra Club, supra*, at 410, n. 21.

The issue of whether the Secretary's decision was arbitrary or capricious is sufficiently difficult and important to merit plenary consideration in this Court. Further, I do not subscribe to the Court's apparent suggestion that *Vermont Yankee* limits the reviewing court to the essentially mindless task of determining whether an agency "considered" environmental factors even if that agency may have effectively decided to ignore those factors in reaching its conclusion. Indeed, I cannot believe that the Court would adhere to that position in a different factual setting. Our cases establish that the arbitrary-or-capricious standard prescribes a "searching and careful" judicial inquiry designed to ensure that the agency has not exercised its discretion in an unreasonable manner. *Citizens to Preserve Overton Park, Inc. v. Volpe*, 401 U.S. 402, 416 (1971). Believing that today's summary reversal represents a departure from that principle, I respectfully dissent.

Robertson v. Methow Valley Citizens Council
490 U.S. 332 (1989).

■ JUSTICE STEVENS delivered the opinion for a unanimous Court:

[Petitioners challenged the validity of an EIS prepared by the Forest Service in connection with its decision to issue to Methow Recreation, Inc. (MRI), a special use permit to develop and operate a proposed ski resort on federally owned land (known as Sandy Butte) adjacent to a National Forest. The EIS prepared by the Forest Service identified that the proposed action would result in adverse effects on air quality and on local mule deer herds, primarily as a consequence of off-site development. It outlined certain steps that might be taken to mitigate adverse effects, but indicated that these proposed steps were merely conceptual and "[would] be made more specific as part of the design and implementation stages of the planning process." Among other things, the petitioners claimed that NEPA gave rise to substantive requirements on the part of the Forest Service to formulate and adopt a specific and detailed mitigation plan with respect to the proposed action.]

. . . The statutory requirement that a federal agency contemplating a major action prepare [ ] an environmental impact statement serves NEPA's "action-forcing" purpose in two important respects. See *Baltimore Gas & Electric Co. v. Natural Resources Defense Council, Inc.*, 462 U.S. 87, 97 (1983); *Weinberger v. Catholic Action of Hawaii/Peace Education Project*, 454 U.S. 139, 143 (1981). It ensures that the agency, in reaching its decision, will have available, and will carefully consider, detailed information concerning significant environmental impacts; it also guarantees that the relevant information will be made available to the larger audience that may also play a role in both the decisionmaking process and the implementation of that decision.

Simply by focusing the agency's attention on the environmental consequences of a proposed project, NEPA ensures that important effects will not be overlooked or underestimated only to be discovered after resources have been committed or the die otherwise cast. See *ibid.*; *Kleppe, supra*, 427 U.S., at 409. Moreover, the strong precatory language of § 101 of the Act and the requirement that agencies prepare detailed impact statements inevitably bring pressure to bear on agencies "to respond to the needs of environmental quality." 115 Cong.Rec. 40425 (1969) (remarks of Sen. Muskie).

Publication of an EIS, both in draft and final form, also serves a larger informational role. It gives the public the assurance that the agency "has indeed considered environmental concerns in its decisionmaking process," *Baltimore Gas & Electric Co.*, *supra*, 462 U.S., at 97, and, perhaps more significantly, provides a springboard for public comment, see L. Caldwell, Science and the National Environmental Policy Act 72 (1982). Thus, in this case the final draft of the [Forest Service EIS] reflects not only the work of the Forest Service itself, but also the critical views of the Washington State Department of Game, the Methow Valley Citizens Council, and Friends of the Earth, as well as many others, to whom copies of the draft Study were circulated. See Early Winters Study, Appendix D. Moreover, with respect to a development such as Sandy Butte, where the adverse effects on air quality and the mule deer herd are primarily attributable to predicted off-site development that will be subject to regulation by other governmental bodies, the EIS serves the function of offering those bodies adequate notice of the expected consequences and the opportunity to plan and implement corrective measures in a timely manner.

The sweeping policy goals announced in § 101 of NEPA are thus realized through a set of "action-forcing" procedures that require that agencies take a " 'hard look' at environmental consequences," *Kleppe*, 427 U.S., at 410, n. 21, (citation omitted), and that provide for broad dissemination of relevant environmental information. Although these procedures are almost certain to affect the agency's substantive decision, it is now well settled that NEPA itself does not mandate particular results, but simply prescribes the necessary process. See *Strycker's Bay Neighborhood Council, Inc. v. Karlen*, 444 U.S. 223, 227–228 (1980) (*per curiam*); *Vermont Yankee Nuclear Power Corp. v. Natural Resources Defense Council, Inc.*, 435 U.S. 519, 558 (1978). If the adverse environmental effects of the proposed action are adequately identified and evaluated, the agency is not constrained by NEPA from deciding that other values outweigh the environmental costs. See *ibid.*; *Strycker's Bay Neighborhood Council, Inc.*, *supra*, 444 U.S., at 227–228; *Kleppe*, *supra*, 427 U.S., at 410, n. 21. In this case, for example, it would not have violated NEPA if the Forest Service, after complying with the Act's procedural prerequisites, had decided that the benefits to be derived from downhill skiing at Sandy Butte justified the issuance of a special use permit, notwithstanding the loss of 15 percent, 50 percent, or even 100 percent of the mule deer herd. Other statutes may impose substantive environmental obligations on federal agencies, but NEPA merely prohibits uninformed—rather than unwise—agency action.

To be sure, one important ingredient of an EIS is the discussion of steps that can be taken to mitigate adverse environmental consequences. The requirement that an EIS contain a detailed discussion of possible mitigation measures flows both from the language of the Act and, more expressly, from CEQ's implementing regulations. Implicit in NEPA's demand that an agency prepare a detailed statement on "any adverse environmental effects which cannot be avoided should the proposal be implemented," 42 U.S.C. § 4332(C)(ii), is an understanding that the EIS will discuss the extent to which adverse effects can be avoided. See D. Mandelker, NEPA Law and Litigation § 10:38 (1984). More generally, omission of a reasonably complete discussion of possible mitigation measures would undermine the "action-forcing" function of NEPA. Without such a discussion, neither the agency nor other interested groups and individuals can properly evaluate the severity of the adverse effects. An adverse effect that can be fully remedied by, for example, an inconsequential public expenditure is certainly not as serious as a similar effect that can only be modestly ameliorated through the commitment of vast public and private resources. Recognizing the importance of such a discussion in guaranteeing that the agency has taken a "hard look" at the environmental consequences of proposed federal action, CEQ regulations require that the agency discuss possible mitigation measures in defining the scope of the EIS, 40 CFR § 1508.25(b) (1987), in discussing alternatives to the proposed action, § 1502.14(f), and consequences of that action, § 1502.16(h), and in explaining its ultimate decision, § 1505.2(c).

There is a fundamental distinction, however, between a requirement that mitigation be discussed in sufficient detail to ensure that environmental consequences have been fairly evaluated, on the one hand, and a substantive requirement that a complete mitigation plan be actually formulated and adopted, on the other. In this case, the off-site effects on air quality and on the mule deer herd cannot be mitigated unless nonfederal government agencies take appropriate action. Since it is those state and local governmental bodies that have jurisdiction over the area in which the adverse effects need be addressed and since they have the authority to mitigate them, it would be incongruous to conclude that the Forest Service has no power to act until the local agencies have reached a final conclusion on what mitigating measures they consider necessary. Even more significantly, it would be inconsistent with NEPA's reliance on procedural mechanisms—as opposed to substantive, result-based standards—to demand the presence of a fully developed plan that will mitigate environmental harm before an agency can act. Cf. *Baltimore Gas & Electric Co.*, 462 U.S., at 100, 103 ("NEPA does not require agencies to adopt any particular internal decisionmaking structure").

We thus conclude that the Court of Appeals erred, first, in assuming that "NEPA requires that 'action be taken to mitigate the adverse effects of major federal actions,'" 833 F.2d, at 819 (quoting *Stop H-3 Assn. v. Brinegar*, 389 F.Supp., at 1111), and, second, in finding that this substantive requirement entails the further duty to include in every EIS "a detailed explanation of specific measures which *will* be employed to mitigate the adverse impacts of a proposed action," 833 F.2d, at 819 (emphasis supplied).

NOTES AND QUESTIONS

1.   Environmental Impacts. What was at stake in the *Strycker's Bay* and *Methow Valley* cases? What types of environmental impacts were identified in the EISs prepared by the respective agencies? Why did each agency nevertheless decide to proceed with the projects in question, notwithstanding the contents of the EISs?

2.   Procedure v. Substance. Central to the *Strycker's Bay* and *Methow Valley* cases is the question of what happens when an EIS reveals that a proposed agency action will result in adverse environmental consequences.

      What were the findings of the *Strycker's Bay* and *Methow Valley* Courts in this respect? Where did the respective courts derive support for their conclusion that NEPA contains no substantive component? Upon what statutory provisions did the respective courts rely in concluding that NEPA does not require a balancing of environmental harms and economic benefits?

3.   *Vermont Yankee*. Both the *Strycker's Bay* and *Methow Valley* Courts rely, in part, upon the decision of the Supreme Court in *Vermont Yankee Nuclear Power Corp. v. NRDC*, 435 U.S. 519 (1978), in support of their finding that NEPA does not contain substantive requirements. *Vermont Yankee* (discussed in Section E below) related primarily to the adequacy of an Agency's alternatives analysis under § 102(2)(C)(iii) rather than the substantive nature of the Act. In concluding that "NEPA does set forth significant substantive goals for the Nation, but its mandate to the agencies is essentially procedural," the *Vermont Yankee* Court did not undertake a detailed statutory analysis, referring only to § 102 and an earlier decision of *Aberdeen & Rockfish R. Co. v. SCRAP*, 422 U.S. 289 (1975) (which in turn did not contain a detailed statutory analysis). 435 U.S. at 558. Are you satisfied then with the level of analysis undertaken by the *Strycker's Bay* and *Methow Valley* Courts?

4.   A Different Regime. Could NEPA have been interpreted differently— so as to contain a substantive component? Consider specifically § 101(b) of the Act. Could this provision, when read in conjunction with § 102(2)(C), be interpreted so as to require that an agency undertake a balancing of costs and benefits?

5.   Justice Marshall's Dissent. Per curiam decisions of the Supreme Court, such as *Strycker's Bay*, are generally handed down only in unanimous cases. They are generally, as in the case of *Strycker's Bay*, cases in which there was no oral argument before the Court. For this reason, the dissenting opinion of Justice Marshall in *Strycker's Bay* is peculiar. What is the nature of Justice Marshall's dissent? Does it disagree with the per curiam decision's interpretation of NEPA, or does it deal with the separate questions of the application of "arbitrary and capricious" review under the APA?

6.   NEPA and the APA. Following *Strycker's Bay* and *Methow Valley*, are there any circumstances in which a plaintiff can challenge the manner in which an agency weighs a particular substantive factor in circumstances where the relevant agency has complied with the procedural requirements of NEPA? For example, could a petitioner challenge a proposed agency action under the APA, on the basis that an EIS has revealed that the environmental harm of the action would significantly outweigh the benefits of the proposed action? How else could a challenge be mounted against the proposed action in these circumstances?

One commentator argues that formally including environmental factors in decisionmaking documents without paying them any real heed may violate the "arbitrary and capricious" standard under the APA. Jason J. Czarnezki, *Revisiting the Tense Relationship Between the U.S. Supreme Court, Administrative Procedure, and the National Environmental Policy Act*, 25 STAN. ENVTL. L.J. 3 (2006). Would it be "arbitrary and capricious" to give no weight to environmental factors in light of NEPA's requirement that agencies use "all practicable means" to protect the environment? Or because the agency action reduces social welfare? Czarnezki proposes that agency decisions should be overturned as "arbitrary and capricious" in circumstances where an agency ignores scientific data, makes irretrievable commitments, or exhibits tunnel vision. *Id.* at 20–21. How likely is it that claims of this type will succeed?

7.   Does NEPA Matter? If the requirements of NEPA are purely procedural, is NEPA merely an empty vessel? Evaluate and assess the significance of the following three arguments as to why this may not be the case.

First, NEPA provides a procedural framework that encourages political feedback and public participation. NEPA ensures that environmental issues are brought into the agency process before the project begins. But it is not just the agency that becomes informed through the EIS. The public also gains access to large amounts of information regarding agency projects. These procedural protections can also influence the substance of agency decisions. *See* Michael Herz, *Parallel Universes: NEPA Lessons for the New Property*, 93 COLUM. L. REV. 1668, 1690–92 (1993).

Second, the advent of NEPA caused a change in the composition of federal agencies. In order to comply with NEPA, agencies were forced to hire younger, more environmentally-conscious employees who could provide environmental expertise. *See* WENDY NELSON ESPELAND, THE STRUGGLE FOR WATER: POLITICS, RATIONALITY, AND IDENTITY IN THE AMERICAN SOUTHWEST 146 (1998). Changing agency culture from the inside out may have proven to be one of the more influential legacies of NEPA.

Third, the high cost of complying with the NEPA process has had a significant impact on agency behavior. The preparation of an EIS can cost as much as $2,000,000 and take as long as 6 years. *See* THE NEPA TASK FORCE, REPORT TO THE COUNCIL ON ENVIRONMENTAL QUALITY: MODERNIZING NEPA IMPLEMENTATION 66 (2003). This creates incentives on the part of agencies to reach creative solutions. The fear of delay, which necessarily accompanies challenges under NEPA, creates incentives for compromises to be struck between agencies proposing major federal actions and others who are concerned with the way in which those actions will affect the environment. The large costs associated with the preparation of an EIS has also given rise to the profession of environmental consulting. Using consultants to prepare an EIS is permitted as long as there is sufficient agency control over the work product. *See NRDC v. Callaway*, 524 F.2d 79 (2d Cir. 1975). The large costs of an EIS may also incentivize agencies to mitigate the environmental impacts of their actions from the outset. *See* Bradley C. Karkkainen, *Breaking the Logjam: Environmental Reform for the New Congress and Administration*, 17 N.Y.U. ENVTL. L.J. 75, 86 (2008).

Which of NEPA's impacts described above do you consider most significant? What other impacts do you think NEPA may have had?

8.   EPA and the ESA. Contrast the aspirational goals of NEPA with the substantive provisions of the Endangered Species Act (ESA) of 1973, 87 Stat. 892 (discussed in Chapter IX). Strikingly, the ESA requires that every federal agency "insure that any action authorized, funded, or carried out by such agency . . . is not likely to jeopardize the continued existence of any endangered species or threatened species." 16 U.S.C. § 1536(a)(2). Why do you think that the Supreme Court was so hesitant to interpret NEPA as containing any substantive component, when Congress had specifically provided for comparable requirements in other legislation?

9.   Substantive Standards Under State NEPAs. At least fifteen states and the District of Columbia have adopted environmental policy acts modeled on NEPA, an additional ten have statutes of limited applicability and six have administratively promulgated NEPA-like programs. State NEPAs typically apply to state actions but not to private actions. While the scope and operation of each state equivalent differ, all adopt the basic imprint of the federal scheme.

In stark contrast to NEPA after *Strycker's Bay*, some state NEPAs create substantive obligations on the part of state agencies to consider the environmental impacts of a proposed action. The extent to which states have chosen to implement more stringent environmental controls in the context of NEPA requirements is discussed in Richard L. Revesz, *Federalism and Environmental Regulation: A Public Choice Analysis*, 115 HARV. L. REV. 553 (2001).

For example, the New York Supreme Court has described the substantive component of the New York State Environmental Quality Review Act (SEQRA) in the following terms:

> Substantively, SEQRA and applicable regulations list general categories of information that must be analyzed in an EIS: an EIS must set forth a description of the proposed action, including its environmental impact and any unavoidable adverse environmental effects (ECL 8–0109[2][a]–[c]; 6 NYCRR 617.14[f][1]–[4]); alternatives to the proposed action (ECL 8–0109[2][d]), including a "no-action alternative" (6 NYCRR 617.14[f][5]); and mitigation measures proposed to minimize the environmental impact (ECL 8–0109[2][f]; 6 NYCRR 617.14[f][7]). In addition, SEQRA requires agencies to "act and choose alternatives which, consistent with social, economic and other essential considerations, to the maximum extent practicable, minimize or avoid adverse environmental effects" (ECL 8–0109[1]). An agency may not approve an action unless it makes "an explicit finding that the

requirements of [SEQRA] have been met and that consistent with social, economic and other essential considerations, to the maximum extent practicable, adverse environmental effects revealed in the environmental impact statement process will be minimized or avoided" (ECL 8–0109[8]; see, 6 NYCRR 617.9[c][2][i]), and that, "consistent with social, economic and other essential considerations, to the maximum extent practicable, adverse environmental effects revealed in the environmental impact statement process will be minimized or avoided by incorporating as conditions to the decision those mitigative measures which were identified as practicable" (6 NYCRR 617.9[c][2][ii]).

Jackson v. N.Y. State Urban Dev. Corp., 67 N.Y.2d 400, 416, 494 N.E.2d 429 (1986). How does SEQRA's substantive mandate, concerning in particular the obligation to consider and impose practicable mitigation measures "to the maximum extent possible . . . consistent with social, economic and other essential considerations," compare with the "hard look" requirement discussed by the *Methow Valley* Court? To what extent do you think the New York SEQRA imposes more meaningful burdens on state agencies?

It has been suggested that "[w]hen, as is often the case, an involved agency strongly favors the project, [SEQRA] often fails to achieve its purpose of ensuring that agencies regulate . . . activities so that due consideration is given to preventing environmental damage." John W. Caffry, *The Substantive Reach of SEQRA: Aesthetics, Findings, and Non-Enforcement of SEQRA's Substantive Mandate*, 65 ALB. L. REV. 393, 410 (2002) (internal quotations omitted). Why might this be the case, despite the explicit provisions of SEQRA?

10. California's Approach. The California Environmental Quality Act (CEQA) also contains substantive requirements. It requires state and local agencies to prepare an EIS for "any project they propose to carry out or approve which may have a significant effect on the environment." CAL. PUB. RES. CODE § 21100. It is designed to act principally as an "informational document" that state agencies must consider before approving or disproving the project. CAL. PUB. RES. CODE § 21061. CEQA is more demanding than NEPA, in that it requires consideration of "growth-inducing" effects and energy conservation mitigation measures. CAL. PUB. RES. CODE § 21100. Furthermore, state agencies, as a condition for project approval under CEQA, must substantively adopt mitigation to remove significant environmental impacts: "The Legislature finds and declares that it is the policy of the state that public agencies should not approve projects as proposed if there are feasible alternatives or feasible mitigation measures available which would substantially lessen the significant environmental effects of such projects. . . ." CAL. PUB. RES. CODE § 21002. An agency may, however, approve or carry out a project if "economic, legal, social, technological, or other considerations" make mitigation measures or project alternatives "infeasible" so the mitigation requirement has little substantive effect. CAL. PUB. RES. CODE § 21081.

How do the substantive requirements under CEQA differ from those under SEQRA? Which are likely to be more stringent?

11. Social Environment. In *Strycker's Bay*, HUD weighed concerns about the impact of a low-income housing project on the social fabric and community structures on the Upper West Side of Manhattan. Can the impact on a community from a proposal be considered to pertain to the "environment" for the purposes of NEPA? If so, how broad is the term "human environment"?

The CEQ regulations provide only limited guidance on what may be considered part of the "human environment." Specifically, § 1508.14 provides that the human environment

> shall be interpreted comprehensively to include the natural and physical environment and the relationship of people with that environment. . . . This means that economic or social effects are not intended by themselves to require preparation of an environmental impact statement. When an environmental impact statement is prepared and economic or social and natural or physical environmental effects are interrelated, then the environmental impact statement will discuss all of these effects on the human environment.

40 C.F.R. § 1508.14.

The preamble to the 1978 CEQ Regulations provides further guidance on what should be considered part of the "human environment":

> In its proposed form § 1508.14 stated that the term "human environment" shall be interpreted comprehensively to include the natural and physical environment and the interaction of people with that environment. A few commentators expressed concern that this definition could be interpreted as being limited to the natural and physical aspects of the environment. This is not the Council's intention. . . .

> The only line we draw is one drawn by the cases. Section 1508.14 stated that economic or social effects are not intended by themselves to require preparation of an environmental impact statement. A few commentators sought further explanation of this provision. This provision reflects the Council's determination, which accords with the case law, that NEPA was not intended to require an environmental impact statement where the closing of a military base, for example, only affects such things as the composition of the population or the level of personal income in a region.

43 Fed. Reg. 55,988 (1978). In *Metropolitan Energy Co. v. People Against Nuclear Energy*, 460 U.S. 766 (1983), the Supreme Court considered whether the Nuclear Regulatory Commission (NRC) was required under NEPA to prepare an EIS for a proposal to reopen a nuclear power reactor at Three Mile Island, following the serious malfunction that occurred at a different part of the facility in March 28, 1979. The petitioners claimed that the proposal triggered the § 102(2)(C) EIS requirement, given that "restarting

[the facility] would cause both severe psychological health damage to persons living in the vicinity, and serious damage to the stability, cohesiveness, and well-being of the neighboring communities." *Id.* at 769.

Justice Rehnquist couched the issue before the Court in the following terms:

> Our understanding of the congressional concerns that led to the enactment of NEPA suggests that the terms "environmental effect" and "environmental impact" in § 102 be read to include a requirement of a reasonably close causal relationship between a change in the physical environment and the effect at issue. This requirement is like the familiar doctrine of proximate cause from tort law. See generally W. Prosser, Law of Torts ch. 7 (4th ed. 1971).

Id. at 774. In finding against the petitioners, the Court concluded that

> [i]f contentions of psychological health damage caused by risk were cognizable under NEPA, agencies would, at the very least, be obliged to expend considerable resources developing psychiatric expertise that is not otherwise relevant to their congressionally assigned functions. The available resources may be spread so thin that agencies are unable adequately to pursue protection of the physical environment and natural resources. As we said in another context in *United States v. Dow,* 357 U.S. 17, 25 (1958), [w]e cannot attribute to Congress the intention to . . . open the door to such obvious incongruities and undesirable possibilities.

Id. at 776 (internal quotations omitted).

C. TIMING AND SCOPE UNDER NEPA

Under NEPA, an EIS must be completed at the time that a federal agency makes a recommendation or report on a proposal for major federal action. *See* 42 U.S.C. § 4332(2)(C). Despite this seemingly precise statutory rule, it can sometimes be difficult for agencies to determine the appropriate timing for the preparation of an EIS. Determining the scope of an EIS is equally difficult, particularly in circumstances where a federal program operates at both a national and local level, as in *Kleppe v. Sierra Club,* 427 U.S. 390 (1976) (the first of the cases excerpted below). Further complications arise, as in *Thomas v. Peterson,* 753 F.2d 754 (9th Cir. 1985) (the second of the cases excerpted below), when a proposed action has a number of component parts.

Kleppe v. Sierra Club
427 U.S. 390 (1976).

■ JUSTICE POWELL delivered the opinion of the Court:

[At issue was the development of coal reserves on federal land in a region encompassing parts of Wyoming, Montana, North Dakota, and South Dakota (the Northern Great Plains Region). The Department of the Interior (DOI) had conducted three studies in the region, including one study that was devoted entirely to the environment (it did not, however, constitute an EIS). The DOI did prepare an EIS for the national coal program (entitled the "Coal Programmatic EIS"), however, as well as specific EISs for each of the local actions within the region (including the issuing of a lease and right-of-way permit and the approval of a mining plan). Plaintiffs claimed that development of the coal reserves could not continue without the preparation of an EIS at the regional level. The Court of Appeals agreed, holding that a four-factor balancing test should govern when a programmatic test must be commenced and remanding to the DOI.]

     . . . The major issue remains the one with which the suit began: whether NEPA requires petitioners to prepare an environmental impact statement on the entire Northern Great Plains region. Petitioners, arguing the negative, rely squarely upon the facts of the case and the language of § 102(2)(C) of NEPA. We find their reliance well placed.

     . . . § 102(2)(C) requires an impact statement "in every recommendation or report on proposals for legislation and other major Federal actions significantly affecting the quality of the human environment." Since no one has suggested that petitioners have proposed legislation on respondents' region, the controlling phrase in this section of the Act, for this case, is "major Federal actions." Respondents can prevail only if there has been a report or recommendation on a proposal for major federal action with respect to the Northern Great Plains region. . . . [T]here has been none; instead, all proposals are for actions of either local or national scope.

     . . . [T]here is no evidence in the record of an action or a proposal for an action of regional scope. The District Court, in fact, expressly found that there was no existing or proposed plan or program on the part of the Federal Government for the regional development of the area described in respondents' complaint. It found also that the three studies initiated by the Department in areas either included within or inclusive of respondents' region . . . were not parts of any plan or program to develop or encourage development of the Northern Great Plains. That court found no evidence that the individual coal development projects undertaken or proposed by private industry and public utilities in that part of the country are integrated into a plan or otherwise interrelated. . . .

Quite apart from the fact that the statutory language requires an impact statement only in the event of a proposed action, respondents' desire for a regional environmental impact statement cannot be met for practical reasons. In the absence of a proposal for a regional plan of development, there is nothing that could be the subject of the analysis envisioned by the statute for an impact statement. Section 102(2)(C) requires that an impact statement contain, in essence, a detailed statement of the expected adverse environmental consequences of an action, the resource commitments involved in it, and the alternatives to it. Absent an overall plan for regional development, it is impossible to predict the level of coal-related activity that will occur in the region identified by respondents, and thus impossible to analyze the environmental consequences and the resource commitments involved in, and the alternatives to, such activity. A regional plan would define fairly precisely the scope and limits of the proposed development of the region. Where no such plan exists, any attempt to produce an impact statement would be little more than a study . . . containing estimates of potential development and attendant environmental consequences. There would be no factual predicate for the production of an environmental impact statement of the type envisioned by NEPA.

The Court of Appeals . . . accepted all of the District Court's findings of fact, but concluded nevertheless that the petitioners "contemplated" a regional plan or program. . . .

. . . Even had the record justified a finding that a regional program was contemplated by the petitioners, the legal conclusion drawn by the Court of Appeals cannot be squared with the Act. The court recognized that the mere "contemplation" of certain action is not sufficient to require an impact statement. But it believed the statute nevertheless empowers a court to require the preparation of an impact statement to begin at some point prior to the formal recommendation or report on a proposal. . . .

The Court's reasoning and action find no support in the language or legislative history of NEPA. The statute clearly states when an impact statement is required. . . . Under the first sentence of § 102(2)(C) the moment at which an agency must have a final statement ready "is the time at which it makes a recommendation or report on a proposal for federal action." *Aberdeen & Rockfish R.C. v. SCRAP*, 422 U.S. 289, 320 (1975) (SCRAP II) (emphasis in original). The procedural duty imposed upon agencies by this section is quite precise, and the role of the courts in enforcing that duty is similarly precise. A court has no authority to depart from the statutory language and . . . determine a point during the germination process of a potential proposal at which an impact statement *should be prepared*. Such an assertion of judicial authority would leave the agencies uncertain as to their procedural duties under NEPA, would invite judicial involvement in the day-to-day decisionmaking process of the agencies, and would invite litigation. . . .

. . . Respondents insist that, even without a comprehensive federal plan for the development of the Northern Great Plains, a "regional" impact statement nevertheless is required on all coal-related projects in the region because they are intimately related.

. . . [Section] 102(2)(C) may require a comprehensive impact statement in certain situations where several proposed actions are pending at the same time . . . when several proposals for coal-related actions that will have cumulative or synergistic environmental impact upon a region are pending concurrently before an agency, their environmental consequences must be considered together. Only through comprehensive consideration of pending proposals can the agency evaluate different courses of action.

Agreement to this extent with respondents' premise, however, does not require acceptance of their conclusion that all proposed coal-related actions in the Northern Great Plains region are so "related" as to require their analysis in a single comprehensive impact statement. . . .

. . . Cumulative environmental impacts are, indeed, what require a comprehensive impact statement. But determination of the extent and effect of these factors, and particularly identification of the geographic area within which they may occur, is a task assigned to the special competency of the appropriate agencies. Petitioners dispute respondents' contentions that the interrelationship of environmental impacts is regionwide and, as respondents' own submissions indicate, petitioners appear to have determined that the appropriate scope of comprehensive statements should be based on basins, drainage areas, and other factors.

We cannot say that petitioners' choices are arbitrary. . . .

In sum, respondents' contention as to the relationships between all proposed coal-related projects in the Northern Great Plains region does not require that petitioners prepare one comprehensive impact statement covering all before proceeding to approve specific pending applications. As we already have determined that there exists no proposal for regionwide action that could require a regional impact statement, the judgment of the Court of Appeals must be reversed, and the judgment of the District Court reinstated and affirmed. . . .

NOTES AND QUESTIONS

1.   **Timing.** In *Kleppe v. Sierra Club*, there were three different times when DOI might have prepared the EIS. It could have been prepared for the national program of coal development, the regional program under the umbrella of the national program, or the individual decisions on coal exploitation. What was DOI's position concerning when the EIS should be prepared? Why did the Sierra Club want a regional EIS prepared when an EIS had been prepared at the national level and would be prepared for each individual project? What arguments exist for and against preparing an EIS for a regional plan? What position did the Court adopt?

Following *Kleppe*, are agencies more or less likely to conduct a regional EIS in a similar situation? Was it clear that DOI was actually going to prepare an individual EIS for each subsequent coal exploitation? Could DOI argue that an EIS is not required for individual leases?

2.   **Taking NEPA Seriously at the Beginning of the Process.** Why is it important for the procedural requirements of NEPA to operate at the beginning of the planning process? In what way may an agency's cost-benefit calculus be affected by the timing of an EIS? How does the decision in *Strycker's Bay* (discussed in the Section B) serve to emphasize this point?

Consider *Monsanto Co. v. Geertson Seed Farms*, 561 U.S. 139 (2010), which concerned the deregulation of a genetically-modified crop, Roundup Ready Alfalfa. The district court had granted an injunction to stop deregulation until the agency completed an EIS. *Id.* at 2746. The Supreme Court reversed, holding that while a full deregulation may indeed require an EIS, the agency could proceed with a partial deregulation based on an EA and FONSI even as the EIS for the full deregulation went forward. *Id.* at 2750. In dissent, Justice Stevens argued that "partial deregulation would undermine the agency's eventual decision" and make a mockery of the EIS process, "converting it from analysis to rationalization." *Id.* at 2768–69 (Stevens, J., dissenting). Who has the better argument? If a partial action proceeds, is it likely to change the agency's analysis of the full action? Does this create a loophole in NEPA or simply give agencies some flexibility in fulfilling their statutory responsibilities?

3.   **Finality of Decision.** In *Kleppe*, the Court held that an EIS is not required until the agency has made a formal and final proposal. Similarly, in *Public Citizen, Inc. v. NRC*, 940 F.2d 679 (D.C. Cir. 1991), the D.C. Circuit held that an EIS was not required for the issuance of a policy statement, preliminary to a formal rulemaking. *See also Envtl. Def. Fund, Inc. v. Alexander*, 501 F. Supp. 742 (N.D. Miss. 1980) (holding that the U.S. Army Corps of Engineers was not required to prepare an EIS with respect to a feasibility study it conducted in order to evaluate the need for a proposed action). Is it always going to be easy to identify when an agency has made a final decision with respect to a particular action?

For a critique of agency attempts to defer NEPA responsibilities until later in the planning process, see Oliver A. Houck, *How'd We Get Divorced?: The Curious Case of NEPA and Planning*, 39 ENVTL. L. REP. NEWS & ANALYSIS 10645 (2009).

4.   **Personal Investment.** A major federal project requires significant commitments of time and effort from many individuals within an agency before it is completed, and often before it begins. The proposed Orme Dam, a hydroelectric project in the Southwest, required decades of planning from staff at the Bureau of Reclamation before it was ultimately scrapped. The longest-serving staff had invested more than half of their careers in the Dam effort; not surprisingly, they were its most forceful advocates throughout the NEPA process. *See* WENDY NELSON ESPELAND, THE STRUGGLE FOR WATER: POLITICS, RATIONALITY, AND IDENTITY IN THE AMERICAN SOUTHWEST 16 (1998). While NEPA demands a detached analysis, human psychology and investment in a project inevitably come into play. How does this factor affect the timing of an EIS? Given that an EIS itself can take several years, do you see a conflict?

5.   **Programmatic EISs and Tiering.** Programmatic EISs, such as the Coal Programmatic EIS considered in *Kleppe*, are prepared for broad federal actions. Site-specific EISs, such as the EISs prepared with respect to each local action in *Kleppe*, are intended to supplement the programmatic EIS. The preparation of multiple EISs in this fashion is known as "tiering." While NEPA doesn't refer either to programmatic EISs or to tiering, the CEQ regulations provide that "[a]gencies shall reduce excessive paperwork by . . .

[u]sing program, policy, or plan environmental impact statements and tiering from statements of broad scope to those of narrower scope, to eliminate repetitive discussions of the same issues." 40 C.F.R. § 1500.4. Furthermore, § 1502.20 provides:

> Agencies are encouraged to tier their environmental impact statements to eliminate repetitive discussions of the same issues and to focus on the actual issues ripe for decision at each level of environmental review (§ 1508.28). Whenever a broad environmental impact statement has been prepared (such as a program or policy statement) and a subsequent statement or environmental assessment is then prepared on an action included within the entire program or policy (such as a site specific action) the subsequent statement or environmental assessment need only summarize the issues discussed in the broader statement and incorporate discussions from the broader statement by reference and shall concentrate on the issues specific to the subsequent action. The subsequent document shall state where the earlier document is available. Tiering may also be appropriate for different stages of actions.

40 C.F.R. § 1502.20. What are the potential pitfalls of tiering?

Thomas v. Peterson
753 F.2d 754 (9th Cir. 1985).

■ Before WRIGHT, SNEED, and ALARCON, CIRCUIT JUDGES.

■ SNEED, CIRCUIT JUDGE:

[Conservation groups sought to enjoin construction of a road that would allow access to timber in a formerly undeveloped National Forest area. Plaintiffs alleged violations of NEPA and other environmental laws. The Forest Service prepared an EA for the road but did not prepare an EIS after making a FONSI. Following the FONSI for the road, the Forest Service issued EAs and FONSIs for two timber sales located in the area that the road was servicing.]

. . . The central question that plaintiffs' NEPA claim presents is whether the road and the timber sales are sufficiently related so as to require combined treatment in a single EIS that covers the cumulative effects of the road and the sales. If so, the Forest Service has proceeded improperly. An EIS must be prepared and considered by the Forest Service before the road can be approved. If not, the Forest Service may go ahead with the road, and later consider the environmental impacts of the timber sales.

Section 102(2)(C) of NEPA requires an EIS for "major Federal actions significantly affecting the quality of the human environment." 42 U.S.C. § 4332(2)(C) (1982). While it is true that administrative agencies must be given considerable discretion in defining the scope of environmental impact statements, *see Kleppe v. Sierra Club*, 427 U.S.

390, 412–415 (1976), there are situations in which an agency is required to consider several related actions in a single EIS, *see id.* at 409–410. Not to require this would permit dividing a project into multiple "actions," each of which individually has an insignificant environmental impact, but which collectively have a substantial impact. *See Alpine Lakes Protection Society v. Schlapfer*, 518 F.2d 1089, 1090 (9th Cir.1975).

Since the Supreme Court decided the *Kleppe* case, the Council on Environmental Quality (CEQ) has issued regulations that define the circumstances under which multiple related actions must be covered by a single EIS. The regulations are made binding on federal administrative agencies by Executive Order. *See* Exec. Order No. 11,991, 42 Fed. Reg. 42 FR 26,967 (1977); *Andrus v. Sierra Club*, 442 U.S. 347, 357–58 (1979). The CEQ regulations and this court's precedents both require the Forest Service to prepare an EIS analyzing the combined environmental impacts of the road and the timber sales.

The CEQ regulations require "connected actions" to be considered together in a single EIS. *See* 40 C.F.R. § 1508.25(a)(1) (1984). "Connected actions" are defined, in a somewhat redundant fashion, as actions that

> "(i) Automatically trigger other actions which may require environmental impact statements.
>
> (ii) Cannot or will not proceed unless other actions are taken previously or simultaneously.
>
> (iii) Are interdependent parts of a larger action and depend on the larger action for their justification."

Id.

The construction of the road and the sale of the timber in the Jersey Jack area meet the second and third, as well as perhaps the first, of these criteria. It is clear that the timber sales cannot proceed without the road, and the road would not be built but for the contemplated timber sales. This much is revealed by the Forest Service's characterization of the road as a "logging road," and by the first page of the environmental assessment for the road, which states that "[t]he need for a transportation route in the assessment area is to access the timber lands to be developed over the next twenty years." Moreover, the environmental assessment for the road rejected a "no action" alternative because that alternative would not provide the needed timber access. The Forest Service's cost-benefit analysis of the road considered the timber to be the benefit of the road, and while the Service has stated that the road will yield other benefits, it does not claim that such other benefits would justify the road in the absence of the timber sales. Finally, the close interdependence of the road and the timber sales is indicated by an August 1981 letter in the record from the Regional Forester to the Forest Supervisor. It states, "We understand that sales in the immediate future will be dependent on the early completion of portions of the Jersey Jack Road. It would be advisable to divide the road into segments and establish separate completion dates for those portions to be used for those sales." E.R. 111.

We conclude, therefore, that the road construction and the contemplated timber sales are inextricably intertwined, and that they are "connected actions" within the meaning of the CEQ regulations.

The CEQ regulations also require that "cumulative actions" be considered together in a single EIS. 40 C.F.R. § 1508.25(a)(2). "Cumulative actions" are defined as actions "which when viewed with other proposed actions have cumulatively significant impacts." *Id.* The record in this case contains considerable evidence to suggest that the road and the timber sales will have cumulatively significant impacts. The U.S. Fish & Wildlife Service, the Environmental Protection Agency, and the Idaho Department of Fish & Game have asserted that the road and the timber sales will have significant cumulative effects that should be considered in an EIS. The primary cumulative effects, according to these agencies, are the deposit of sediments in the Salmon River to the detriment of that river's population of salmon and steelhead trout and the destruction of critical habitat for the endangered Rocky Mountain Gray Wolf. These agencies have criticized the Forest Service for not producing an EIS that considers the cumulative impacts of the Jersey Jack road and the timber sales. For example, the Fish & Wildlife Service has written, "Separate documentation of related and cumulative potential impacts may be leading to aquatic habitat degradation unaccounted for in individual EA's (i.e., undocumented cumulative effects). . . . Lack of an overall effort to document cumulative impacts could be having present and future detrimental effects on wolf recovery potential." [E.R.] at 3. These comments are sufficient to raise "substantial questions" as to whether the road and the timber sales will have significant cumulative environmental effects. Therefore, on this basis also, the Forest Service is required to prepare an EIS analyzing such effects. *See Foundation for North American Wild Sheep v. United States Dept. of Agriculture*, 681 F.2d 1172, 1178 (9th Cir.1982). . . .

The Forest Service argues that the cumulative environmental effects of the road and the timber sales will be adequately analyzed and considered in the EA's and/or EIS's that it will prepare on the individual timber sales. The EA or EIS on each action, it contends, will document the cumulative impacts of that action and all previous actions.

We believe that consideration of cumulative impacts after the road has already been approved is insufficient to fulfill the mandate of NEPA. A central purpose of an EIS is to force the consideration of environmental impacts in the decisionmaking process. That purpose requires that the NEPA process be integrated with agency planning "at the earliest possible time," 40 C.F.R. § 1501.2, and the purpose cannot be fully served if consideration of the cumulative effects of successive, interdependent steps is delayed until the first step has already been taken.

The location, the timing, or other aspects of the timber sales, or even the decision whether to sell any timber at all affects the location, routing, construction techniques, and other aspects of the road, or even the need for its construction. But the consideration of cumulative impacts will serve little purpose if the road has already been built. Building the road swings the balance decidedly in favor of timber sales even if such sales would have been disfavored had road and sales been considered together before the road was built. Only by selling timber can the bulk of the expense of building the road be recovered. Not to sell timber after building the road constitutes the "irrational" result that Trout Unlimited's standard is intended to avoid. Therefore, the cumulative environmental impacts of the road and the timber sales must be assessed before the road is approved.

The Forest Service argues that the sales are too uncertain and too far in the future for their impacts to be analyzed along with that of the road. This comes close to saying that building the road now is itself irrational. We decline to accept that conclusion. Rather, we believe that if the sales are sufficiently certain to justify construction of the road, then they are sufficiently certain for their environmental impacts to be analyzed along with those of the road. *Cf. City of Davis v. Coleman*, 521 F.2d 661, 667–76 (9th Cir.1975) (EIS for a road must analyze the impacts of industrial development that the road is designed to accommodate). Where agency actions are sufficiently related so as to be "connected" within the meaning of the CEQ regulations, the agency may not escape compliance with the regulations by proceeding with one action while characterizing the others as remote or speculative.

NOTES AND QUESTIONS

1.   Loophole of Connected Actions. The *Thomas v. Peterson* court identified a potential loophole in the operation of NEPA, under which an applicant may "[divide] a project into multiple 'actions,' each of which individually has an insignificant environmental impact, but which collectively have a substantial impact." 753 F.2d at 758. For example, in that case, assuming that neither the road nor the timber sales would result in a significant impact on the human environment, the agency would be able to avoid preparation of an EIS by treating each action separately.

The CEQ regulations attempt to address this loophole. First, they require that "connected actions" be considered together in a single EIS. Connected actions are defined as actions that: "(i) [a]utomatically trigger other actions which may require environmental impact statements; (ii) [c]annot or will not proceed unless other actions are taken previously or simultaneously; (iii) [a]re interdependent parts of a larger action and depend on the larger action for their justification." 40 C.F.R. § 1508.25(a)(1).

Are the road and timber sales in *Thomas v. Peterson* connected actions under the CEQ regulations? How would the CEQ regulations (which were promulgated in 1984) have applied to the regional program contemplated in the *Kleppe* case (heard in 1976)?

2. Connected v. Cumulative Actions. Are the two timber sales in *Thomas v. Peterson* cumulative actions? What is the difference between connected and cumulative actions? In what circumstances would projects be considered "cumulative" but not "connected" for the purposes of the CEQ regulations?

For another example of connected actions requiring a single EIS, see *Blue Ocean Preservation Society v. Watkins*, 754 F. Supp. 1450 (D. Haw. 1991) (holding that even if the four phases of a geothermal energy project in Hawaii were considered separate actions triggering separate NEPA obligations, the four phases were sufficiently connected to require that they all be evaluated in a single EIS).

3. Which Cumulative Impacts Count? The CEQ regulations define "cumulative impact" as:

> the impact on the environment which results from the incremental impact of the action when added to other past, present, and reasonably foreseeable future actions regardless of what agency (Federal or non-Federal) or person undertakes such other actions. Cumulative impacts can result from individually minor but collectively significant actions taking place over a period of time.

40 C.F.R. § 1508.7. Agencies must consider "ecological . . . , aesthetic, historic, cultural, economic, social, or health [effects]." 40 C.F.R. § 1508.8. At what point are cumulative impacts no longer "reasonably foreseeable"? For those impacts that are foreseeable, how much consideration must they be given? For examples of courts grappling with these and other related questions, see *Wyoming v. USDA*, 661 F.3d 1209, 1250–53 (10th Cir. 2011); and *Klamath-Siskiyou Wildlands Ctr. v. BLM*, 387 F.3d 989 (9th Cir. 2004). In *Wyoming*, the agency had anticipated the cumulative impact of other related rules but had declined to address the magnitude or degree of these impacts since those rules would be implemented in response to specific development proposals in the future. The court held that "because the agency could not reasonably predict what specific actions and decisions would be taken under the other three rulemakings in the future . . . , the precise cumulative impacts flowing from these other coordinated rulemakings were only speculative in nature; that is, they were not 'reasonably foreseeable' at that time." *Id.* at 1253. In *Klamath*, the EAs for two timber sales proposed by the agency did not satisfy NEPA because insufficient attention was paid to cumulative impact. The court held that the BLM did not sufficiently identify or discuss the incremental impact of each successive timber sale or how those individual sales might have combined or synergistically interacted with each other to affect the environment. Are these cases consistent? How might they be distinguished?

D. DETERMINING SIGNIFICANCE UNDER NEPA

An EIS need only be prepared for major federal actions and proposals for legislation that significantly affect the human environment.

42 U.S.C. § 4332(2)(C). In light of the high cost and lengthy delays involved in preparing an EIS, a great deal rests on determinations of significance under § 102(2)(C).

Section 1508.27 of the CEQ regulations provides that "[s]ignificantly, as used in NEPA, requires consideration of both context and intensity." 40 C.F.R. § 1508.27. With respect to context, the regulations provide that "the significance of an action must be analyzed . . . [with respect to] society as a whole (human, national), the affected region, the affected interests, and the locality." 40 C.F.R. § 1058.27(a). Significance, it is noted, varies with the setting of the proposed action. *See id.* With respect to intensity, the regulations require consideration of (among other things) the impact of the proposal upon public health or safety, the unique characteristics of the geographic area affected by the proposal, the controversy associated with the proposal, and the degree to which the possible effects on the human environment are uncertain. 40 C.F.R. § 1508.27(b).

As the introduction to this section explained, agencies must prepare an EA with respect to those actions that they cannot establish have no potential to significantly impact the environment. 40 C.F.R. § 1501.4(b). Having conducted an EA, an agency must then make a determination on a projects potential significance—either resulting in the issuance of a FONSI, or in the preparation of an EIS. The first case excerpted below, *Hanly v. Kleindienst*, 471 F.2d 823 (2d Cir. 1972), *cert. denied*, 412 U.S. 908 (1973), focuses on the relationship between an EA and an EIS. 40 C.F.R. § 1501.4(c), (e). The second case, *Anderson v. Evans*, 371 F.3d 475 (9th Cir. 2004), examines the concepts of context and intensity as they appear in § 1508.27 of the CEQ regulations. The third case, *Center for Biological Diversity v. NHTSA*, 538 F.3d 1172 (9th Cir. 2008), deals with the determination of significance in the context of climate change. The fourth case, *National Audubon Society v. Hoffman*, 132 F.3d 7 (2d Cir. 1997), examines to what extent federal agencies can take mitigating factors into account in reaching determinations of significance under § 102(2)(C).

Hanly v. Kleindienst
471 F.2d 823 (2d Cir. 1972), *cert. denied*, 412 U.S. 908 (1973).

■ Before FRIENDLY, CHIEF JUDGE, and MANSFIELD and TIMBERS, CIRCUIT JUDGES.

■ MANSFIELD, CIRCUIT JUDGE:

[The General Services Administration (GSA) concluded that an EIS was not needed for the construction of a jail and office building as an annex to the federal courthouse in Manhattan. In *Hanly v. Mitchell*, 460 F.2d 640 (2d Cir. 1972) (*Hanly I*) the Second Circuit held that the GSA must more fully explore the effects on the "human environment" of the jail before concluding that an EIS was not required. The GSA responded with a twenty five page "Assessment of the Environmental Impact" and decided, again, that an EIS was not required. Local community members again filed suit and the district court denied an injunction. The community members appealed.]

Upon attempting, according to the ["arbitrary and capricious"] standard, to interpret the amorphous term "significantly," as it is used in § 102(2)(C), we are faced with the fact that almost every major federal action, no matter how limited in scope, has *some* adverse effect on the human environment. It is equally clear that an action which is environmentally important to one neighbor may be of no consequence to another. Congress could have decided that every major federal action must therefore be the subject of a detailed impact statement prepared according to the procedure prescribed by § 102(2)(C). By adding the word "significantly," however, it demonstrated that before the agency in charge triggered that procedure, it should conclude that a greater environmental impact would result than from "any major federal action." Yet the limits of the key term have not been adequately defined by Congress or by guidelines issued by the CEQ and other responsible federal agencies vested with broad discretionary powers under NEPA. Congress apparently was willing to depend principally upon the agency's good faith determination as to what conduct would be sufficiently serious from an ecological stand-point to require use of the full-scale procedure.

Guidelines issued by the CEQ, which are echoed in rules for implementation published by the Public Buildings Service, the branch of GSA concerned with the construction of the [Metropolitan Convention Center (MCC)], suggest that a formal impact statement should be prepared with respect to "proposed actions, the environmental impact of which is likely to be highly controversial." See Council on Environmental Quality, Statements on Proposed Federal Actions Affecting the Environment, Guidelines § 5(b), 36 Fed.Reg. 7724 (April 23, 1971). However, the term "controversial" apparently refers to cases where a substantial dispute exists as to the size, nature or effect of the major federal action rather than to the existence of opposition to a use, the effect of which is relatively undisputed. This Court in *Hanly I*, for instance, did not require a formal impact statement with respect to the office building portion of the Annex despite the existence of neighborhood opposition to it. The suggestion that "controversial" must be equated with neighborhood opposition has also been rejected by others.[9A]

In the absence of any Congressional or administrative interpretation of the term, we are persuaded that in deciding whether a major federal action will "significantly" affect the quality of the human environment

---

[9A] To require an impact statement whenever a threshold determination dispensing with one is likely to face a court challenge, as the dissent suggests, would surrender the determination to opponents of a major federal action, no matter how insignificant its environmental effect when viewed objectively. Experience in local zoning disputes demonstrates that it is the rare case where some neighbors do not oppose a project, no matter how beneficial, and that their opposition is usually accompanied by threats of litigation.

the agency in charge, although vested with broad discretion, should normally be required to review the proposed action in the light of at least two relevant factors: (1) the extent to which the action will cause adverse environmental effects in excess of those created by existing uses in the area affected by it, and (2) the absolute quantitative adverse environmental effects of the action itself, including the cumulative harm that results from its contribution to existing adverse conditions or uses in the affected area. Where conduct conforms to existing uses, its adverse consequences will usually be less significant than when it represents a radical change. Absent some showing that an entire neighborhood is in the process of redevelopment, its existing environment, though frequently below an ideal standard, represents a norm that cannot be ignored. . . .

Although the existing environment of the area which is the site of a major federal action constitutes one criterion to be considered, it must be recognized that even a slight increase in adverse conditions that form an existing environmental milieu may sometimes threaten harm that is significant. One more factory polluting air and water in an area zoned for industrial use may represent the straw that breaks the back of the environmental camel. Hence the absolute, as well as comparative, effects of a major federal action must be considered.

Chief Judge Friendly's thoughtful dissent, while conceding that we (and governmental agencies) face a difficult problem in determining the meaning of the vague and amorphous term "significantly" as used in § 102(2)(C), offers no solution other than to suggest that an impact statement should be required whenever a major federal action might be "arguably" or "potentially" significant and that such an interpretation would insure the preparation of impact statements except in cases of "true" insignificance. In our view this suggestion merely substitutes one form of semantical vagueness for another. By failure to use more precise standards it would leave the agency, which admittedly must make the determination, in the very quandary faced in this case and only serve to prolong and proliferate uncertainty as to when a threshold determination should be accepted. The problem is not resolved by use of terms [such as] "*obviously* insignificant," "minor," "*arguably* significant," a "*fairly arguable*" adverse impact, or the like, or by reference to "grey" areas or characterization of our opinion as "raising the floor" to permit agencies to escape an impact statement.

. . . Rather than encourage agencies to dispense with impact statements, we believe that application of the foregoing objective standards, coupled with compliance with minimum procedural requirements (specified below), which are designed to assure consideration of relevant facts, will lead agencies in doubtful cases (so-called "grey" areas) to obtain impact statements rather than to risk the delay and expense of protracted litigation. . . .

. . . Now that the GSA has made and submitted its redetermination in the form of a 25-page "Assessment," our task is to determine (1) whether it satisfies the foregoing tests as to environmental significance, and (2) whether GSA, in making its assessment and determination, has observed "procedure required by law" as that term is used in § 10 of the APA, 5 U.S.C. § 706(2)(D).

The Assessment closely parallels in form a detailed impact statement. . . .

Appellants contend that the Assessment is merely a "rewrite" of GSA's earlier February 23, 1971 "Environmental Statement" found inadequate in *Hanly I*, and that GSA has failed to take into consideration certain adverse facts. A comparison of the 25-page detailed Assessment with the earlier statement reveals that the former is far more than a "rewrite" and that it furnishes detailed findings with respect to most of the relevant factors unmentioned in the earlier statement. On its face the Assessment indicates that GSA has redetermined the environmental impact of the MCC with care and thoroughness. In the absence of contrary factual proof, we would have no hesitancy in upholding it. . . .

. . . We do not share the Government's view that the procedural mandates of § 102(A), (B), and (D), 42 U.S.C. § 4332(2)(A), (B) and (D), apply only to actions found by the agency itself to have a significant environmental effect. While these sections are somewhat opaque, they are not expressly limited to "major Federal actions significantly affecting the quality of the human environment." Indeed if they were so limited § 102(D), which requires the agency to develop appropriate alternatives to the recommended course of action, would be duplicative since § 102(C), which does apply to actions "significantly affecting" the environment, specifies that the detailed impact statement must deal with "alternatives to the proposed action." 42 U.S.C. § 4332(2)(C)(iii). . . . [W]e find that § 102 (2)(D) was complied with insofar as the GSA specifically considered the alternatives to continuing operation at the present facility at West Street and evaluated the selected site as compared with other specified possibilities. Although the assessment of the alternative sites was not as intensive as we might hope, its failure to analyze them in further detail does not warrant reversal.

A more serious question is raised by the GSA's failure to comply with § 102(2)(B), which requires the agency to "identify and develop methods and procedures . . . which will insure that presently unquantified environmental amenities and values may be given appropriate consideration in decision-making along with economic and technical considerations." 42 U.S.C. § 4332 (2)(B). Since an agency, in making a threshold determination as to the "significance" of an action, is called upon to review in a general fashion the same factors that would be studied in depth for preparation of a detailed environmental impact statement, § 102(2)(B) requires that some rudimentary procedures be designed to assure a fair and informed preliminary decision. Otherwise the agency, lacking essential information, might frustrate the purpose of NEPA by a threshold determination that an impact statement is unnecessary. Furthermore, an adequate record serves to preclude later changes in use without consideration of their environmental significance as required by NEPA.

Where a proposed major federal action may affect the sensibilities of a neighborhood, the prudent course would be for the agency in charge, before making a threshold decision, to give notice to the community of the contemplated action and to accept all pertinent information proffered by concerned citizens with respect to it. Furthermore, in line with the procedure usually followed in zoning disputes, particularly where emotions are likely to be aroused by fears, or rumors of misinformation, a public hearing serves the dual purpose of enabling the agency to obtain all relevant data and to satisfy the community that its views are being considered. However, neither NEPA nor any other federal statute mandates the specific type of procedure to be followed by federal agencies. . . .

Notwithstanding the absence of statutory or administrative provisions on the subject, this Court has already held in *Hanly I* at 647 that federal agencies must "affirmatively develop a reviewable environmental record . . . even for purposes of a threshold section 102 (2)(C) determination." We now go further and hold that before a preliminary or threshold determination of significance is made the responsible agency must give notice to the public of the proposed major federal action and an opportunity to submit relevant facts which might bear upon the agency's threshold decision. We do not suggest that a full-fledged formal hearing must be provided before each such determination is made, although it should be apparent that in many cases such a hearing would be advisable for reasons already indicated. The necessity for a hearing will depend greatly upon the circumstances surrounding the particular proposed action and upon the likelihood that a hearing will be more effective than other methods in developing relevant information and an understanding of the proposed action. The precise procedural steps to be adopted are better left to the agency, which should be in a better position than the court to determine whether solution of the problems faced with respect to a specific major federal action can better be achieved through a hearing or by informal acceptance of relevant data. . . .

[Case remanded for GSA to make specific findings in regards to the jail including a potential increase in crime and to accept additional evidence offered by the appellants and concerned citizens. After completing these tasks, GSA was to decide again whether an EIS was necessary.]

■ FRIENDLY, CHIEF JUDGE, dissenting:

The learned opinion of my brother Mansfield gives these plaintiffs . . . both too little and too much. It gives too little because it raises the floor of what constitutes "major Federal actions significantly affecting the quality of the human environment," 42 U.S.C. § 4332 (2)(C), higher than I believe Congress intended. It gives too much because it requires that before making a threshold determination that no impact statement is demanded, the agency must go through procedures which I think are needed only when an impact statement must be made. The upshot is that a threshold determination that a proposal does not constitute major Federal action significantly affecting the quality of the human environment becomes a kind of mini-impact statement. The preparation of such a statement under the conditions laid down by the majority is unduly burdensome when the action is truly minor or insignificant. On the other hand, there is a danger that if the threshold determination is this elaborate, it may come to replace the impact statement in the grey area between actions which, though "major" in a monetary sense, are obviously insignificant (such as the construction of the proposed office building) and actions that are obviously significant (such as the construction of an atomic power plant). We would better serve the purposes of Congress by keeping the threshold low enough to insure that impact statements are prepared for actions in this grey area and thus to permit the determination that no statement is required to be made quite informally in cases of true insignificance. . . .

It is not readily conceivable that Congress meant to allow agencies to avoid [the EIS] requirement by reading "significant" to mean only "important," "momentous," or the like. One of the purposes of the impact statement is to insure that the relevant environmental data are before the agency and considered by it prior to the decision to commit Federal resources to the project; the statute must not be construed so as to allow the agency to make its decision in a doubtful case without the relevant data or a detailed study of it. This is particularly clear because of the absence from the statute of any procedural requirement upon an agency in making the threshold determination that an impact statement is not demanded, although the majority has managed to contrive one. What Congress was trying to say was "You don't need to make an impact statement, with the consequent expense and delay, when there is no sensible reason for making one." I thus agree with Judge J. Skelly Wright's view that "a statement is required whenever the action *arguably* will have an adverse environmental impact," Students Challenging Regulatory Agency Procedures (S.C.R.A.P.) v. United States, 346 F.Supp. 189, 201 (D.D.C.1972) (three-judge court) (emphasis in original), prob. juris. noted, 409 U.S. 1073, with the qualification, doubtless intended, that the matter must be *fairly* arguable. . . .

[The CEQ Guidelines] provide that "if there is *potential* that the environment may be significantly affected, the statement is to be prepared." Guidelines § 5(b), 36 Fed. Reg. 7,724 (1971) (emphasis added). And they state further, in a remark highly relevant to this case:

> Proposed actions, the environmental impact of which is likely to
> be highly controversial, should be covered in all cases.

Id. This Guideline has been expressly adopted by the GSA in its own regulations. With respect, I see no basis for reading this as limited to cases where there is a dispute over what the environmental effects actually will be. Rather, I would think it clear that this includes action which the agency should know is likely to arouse intense opposition, even if the actual environmental impact is readily apparent. Apart from the former being the natural meaning of the words, the CEQ may well have had in mind that when action having some environmental impact "is likely to be highly controversial," an agency assessment that the action does not constitute major Federal action significantly affecting the environment is almost certain to evoke challenge in the courts. The CEQ could well have believed that rather than to incur the delay incident to such a suit, and the further delay if a court sustains the challenge—both vividly illustrated in this case where nearly two years have elapsed since the initial assessment that an impact statement was not required and a further remand is being directed—the agency would do better to prepare an impact statement in the first instance. In addition to possibly providing new information making reconsideration or modification of the project appropriate, such a policy has the added benefits of allowing opponents to blow off steam and giving them the sense that their objections have been considered—an important purpose of NEPA, as it is of the British statutory inquiry.

. . . The energies my brothers would require GSA to devote to still a third assessment designed to show that an impact statement is not needed would better be devoted to making one.

I would reverse and direct the issuance of an injunction until a reasonable period after the making of an impact statement.

NOTES AND QUESTIONS

1. **EAs and EISs.** An EIS must be prepared for actions that significantly affect the human environment. 42 U.S.C. § 4332(2)(c). As the majority notes, "almost every major federal action, no matter how limited in scope, has some adverse effect on the human environment." 471 F.2d at 830. How does the majority propose that an agency make an initial determination of significance? How does Chief Judge Friendly propose that this determination be made?

2. **Over- and Under-Inclusiveness.** What is Chief Judge Friendly most concerned about in his dissent? In what ways does the EA favored by the *Hanly* majority differ from an EIS? On what basis did Chief Judge Friendly describe the process favored by the majority as being at once both over- and under-inclusive? Do you agree with Chief Judge Friendly that the purposes of the Act would be better served by setting a low threshold in determining whether a proposal constitutes a significant action?

3. Agency Incentives. What incentives does the regime favored by the *Hanly* majority create for federal agencies contemplating major actions? Are these incentives desirable? Are they likely to lead to an enhanced consideration of environmental issues in cases of significance?

4. Time and Money. The preparation of an EIS is both time-consuming and costly. The 2003 CEQ NEPA Task Force Report reported that EISs typically range from between 200 and 2000 pages in length, take between one and six years to prepare, and cost between $250,000 and $2,000,000. *See* THE NEPA TASK FORCE, REPORT TO THE COUNCIL ON ENVIRONMENTAL QUALITY: MODERNIZING NEPA IMPLEMENTATION 66 (2003) (Task Force Report). The Task Force Report also reported that those EAs designed to meet the minimum requirements of the CEQ regulations (small EAs) usually range in length from 10 to 30 pages, take between two weeks and two months to prepare, and cost between $5,000 and $25,000. *Id.* at 65. Large EAs, associated with more controversial or high profile projects, range from between 50 and 200 pages, require between nine and eighteen months to prepare, and cost between $50,000 and $200,000. *See id.*

What incentives do you think these discrepancies in price create for federal agencies?

5. Lengthy EAs. Should the preparation of a large and detailed EA by a federal agency with respect to a proposed action suggest that an EIS would be the more appropriate assessment method? In *Heartwood, Inc. v. U.S. Forest Service*, 380 F.3d 428 (8th Cir. 2004), plaintiffs challenged a decision by the Forest Service to issue a FONSI with respect to a large logging project in the Mark Twain National Forest in Missouri. The EA prepared by the Forest Service was detailed and lengthy and included scoping and other public involvement activities. It thoroughly considered a number of potential impacts including impacts on endangered and threatened species, biological diversity, and recreation, as well as the future health of the forests in the project area. The plaintiffs argued that the length and detail of the EA itself suggested that an EIS should have been prepared. In response, the court held that the agency was not required to prepare an EIS simply because it chose to issue a detailed EA that included EIS-like information about its decision process: "[a] rule requiring an EIS whenever an EA is longer than [a certain length] would encourage agencies to prepare bare-bones EAs. . . . What ultimately determines whether an EIS rather than an EA is required is the scope of the project itself, not the length of the agency's report." 380 F.3d at 434.

Anderson v. Evans
371 F.3d 475 (9th Cir. 2004).

■ Before HILL, GOULD and BERZON, CIRCUIT JUDGES.

■ BERZON, CIRCUIT JUDGE:

[A traditional Northwest Indian whale hunting tribe (the Makah Tribe), which had given up hunting in the 1920s, sought permission from the U.S. Government to re-commence the hunting of grey whales for cultural reasons. The Tribe proposed a limited annual harvest (of 5 whales per year), to be conducted in the Strait of Juan de Fuca off the coast of Washington. While there was some disagreement about the precise composition of the whale population, it was generally agreed that there existed a fairly small number of whales that spent some or all of the summer in the general area of the planned Tribe hunt, and that some of these whales returned to the area for more than one summer, albeit not necessarily in successive years. The U.S. Government prepared an EA for the proposal and concluded that it would not give rise to a significant impact on the overall Californian gray whale population or on the environment. Permission was subsequently granted to the Tribe to undertake a limited annual harvest. The plaintiffs, citizens and animal conservation groups, challenged (among other things) the government's failure to prepare an EIS, on the grounds that it had failed to adequately assess the significance of the proposal on the local population of gray whales.]

. . . Under the CEQ regulations, we must consider whether the effects of the Tribe's whaling on the human environment are "likely to be highly controversial," 40 C.F.R. § 1508.27(b)(4), and also whether the "possible effects . . . are highly uncertain or involve unique or unknown risks." 40 C.F.R. § 1508.27(b)(5). A proposal is highly controversial when there is "a substantial dispute [about] the size, nature, or effect of the major Federal action rather than the existence of opposition to a use." *Blue Mountains*, 161 F.3d at 1212 (quoting *Greenpeace Action v. Franklin*, 14 F.3d 1324, 1335 (9th Cir. 1993)). Put another way, a proposal can be considered controversial if "substantial questions are raised as to whether a project . . . may cause significant degradation of some human environmental factor." *Nat'l Parks*, 241 F.3d at 736 (quoting *Northwest Envtl. Def. Ctr. v. Bonneville Power Admin.*, 117 F.3d 1520, 1539 (9th Cir. 1997) (Reinhardt, J., concurring in part and dissenting in part)).

There is no disagreement in this case concerning the EA's conclusion that the impact of the Makah Tribe's hunt on the overall California gray whale population will not be significant. What is in hot dispute is the possible impact on the whale population in the local area where the Tribe wants to hunt. In our view, the answer to this question—of greatly increased importance [given that the proposed management plan expressly contemplates the] hunting of local nonmigrating animals—is sufficiently uncertain and controversial to require the full EIS protocol.

Our reasoning in this regard is as follows: The government agrees that a relatively small group of whales comes into the area of the Tribe's hunt each summer, and that about sixty percent of them are returning whales (although, again, not necessarily whales returning annually). Even if the eastern Pacific gray whales overall or the smaller PCFA group of whales are not significantly impacted by the Makah Tribe's whaling, the summer whale population in the *local* Washington area may be significantly affected. [The Pacific Coast Feeding Aggregation of whales (PCFA) is a subgroup of whales that the Government believed did not migrate all the way north for the summer but ranged over a long stretch of the Pacific Coast from California to Southern Alaska.] Such local effects are a basis for a finding that there will be a significant impact from the Tribe's hunts. *See* 40 C.F.R. § 1508.27(a). Thus, if there are substantial questions about the impact on the number of whales who frequent the Strait of Juan de Fuca and the northern Washington Coast, an EIS must be prepared.

The crucial question, therefore, is whether the hunting, striking, and taking of whales from this smaller group could significantly affect the environment in the local area. The answer to this question is, we are convinced, both uncertain and controversial within the meaning of NEPA. No one, including the government's retained scientists, has a firm idea what will happen to the local whale population if the Tribe is allowed to hunt and kill whales pursuant to the approved quota and Makah Management Plan. There is at least a substantial question whether killing five whales from this group either annually or every two years, which the quota would allow, could have a significant impact on the environment.

The government estimates that a conservative allowable take from a group of 222 to 269 whales is 2.5 whales per year, while a less conservative approach would allow killing up to six whales per year from the PCFA. Final EA at 57. Thus, with a smaller group, it would appear that a take of less than 2.5 whales per year could exceed the allowable Potential Biological Removal level or "PBR" established under the MMPA's [Marine Mammal Protection Act's] standards.

Some of the scientists relied upon by the government worry that takes from the local resident whale population may deplete the number of local whales in the area off the coast of Washington State and in and around the Strait of Juan de Fuca. . . .

The government tries in two ways to minimize the importance of the possible local impact. First, the government maintains that the PCFA—or summer resident whale group, if one exists—is not genetically distinct from the other California gray whales. For purposes of applying the CEQ regulations, this consideration is irrelevant. If California gray whales disappear from the area of the Strait of Juan de Fuca . . . that would be a significant environmental impact even if the PCFA whales populating the rest of the Pacific Coast in the summer are genetically identical to the local whales, and even if the PCFA whales are genetically identical to the migrating whales.

Second, the government implies that any whales taken from the local resident group will be replaced in the local area by other whales from the PCFA, so the number of whales locally will not decline. The EA describes the PCFA as composed of whales that move from one feeding area to another rather than staying in one locale for all the summer months.

That some of the whales who return, whether annually or intermittently, to the area of the proposed hunt also visit other areas of the coast cannot, however, eliminate concern about the local impact. The fact remains that a majority of the fairly small number of whales identified in the Makah Tribe's hunting area have been there in previous years, wherever else they have also journeyed. Whether there will be fewer or no whales in the pertinent local area if the hunt is permitted depends not on whether the whales who frequent that area also travel elsewhere, but upon the opposite inquiry: whether whales who heretofore have *not* visited the area will do so, thereby replenishing the summer whale population in the area, if some of the returning whales are killed.

It is on this latter question that the scientific uncertainty is at its apogee. Almost all of the scientific experts relied upon in the EA state that the effect of taking whales who demonstrate some site fidelity within the Tribe's hunting area is uncertain. Quan, for example, suggests that much depends on how whales are recruited to the area, an open question requiring further study. *See* Quan, *supra*, at 11–13. If the local whales are recruited randomly, removing four whales annually from the Tribe's hunt area should not have any long-term impact. If the whales are recruited familially, however, "the annual removal of four gray whales could directly [affect the number of whales] observed and utilizing the area." Quan, *supra*, at 13.

Similarly, Darling states that "the recruitment mechanism that influences or maintains the resident group of gray whales found in Washington is not known. As a result, it is difficult to predict at this time how the harvesting of resident whales could affect the resident population." Darling Decl. ¶ 10. *See also* Calambokidis et al., *Range and Movements*, *supra*, at 4 ("It is unclear how loyal these [seasonal resident] animals are to the feeding grounds, how they adopt this alternate feeding strategy, and their range of movements."); *Review of Studies*, at 20 ("Relatively little is known about how individuals choose feeding grounds throughout their lives. . . . It is plausible that females may learn their migration route and preferred feeding areas from their mothers. . . . A summer hunt that is localized and very coastal has the potential to adversely affect such localized feeding groups and could lead to distributional changes and local extirpation.").

The EA's *only* substantive attempt to address the impact of the Tribe's whaling on the number of whales in the area of the . . . Strait of Juan de Fuca is as follows: "With the extreme movements of whales in the [PCFA] both within and between seasons . . . a limit of five strikes over two years should also alleviate any potential local depletion issues." Final EA at 58. The EA's conclusion simply does not follow from its premise: That PCFA whales do not spend all summer or every summer in the area of the Tribe's hunt does not eliminate the possibility that the killing of returning whales present in any given year may lead to a depletion of whales in the local area. Obviously, with the demise of some returning whales, fewer whales with the habit of returning to that area in the summer will survive. As the underlying studies establish, the local impact of the Tribe's whaling therefore turns on whether different PCFA whales will fill in for the killed, struck, or frightened whales no longer in the area. This critical question is never analyzed, numerically or otherwise, in the EA.

In short, the record establishes that there are "substantial questions" as to the significance of the effect on the *local* area. Despite the commendable care with which the EA addresses other questions, the EA simply does not adequately address the highly uncertain impact of the Tribe's whaling on the *local* whale population and the local ecosystem. This major analytical lapse is, we conclude, a sufficient basis for holding that the agencies' finding of no significant impact cannot survive the level of scrutiny applicable in this case. And because the EA simply does not adequately address the local impact of the Tribe's hunt, an EIS is required. See *Blue Mountains*, 161 F.3d at 1213 (ordering the Forest Service to prepare an EIS where the EA's treatment of one important environmental factor was "cursory and inconsistent"); *Nat'l Parks*, 241 F.3d at 735–36 (requiring preparation of an EIS when the EA admitted that it was not known how serious the dangers of the proposed action were and the EA failed adequately to address opposing expert studies). . . .

In sum, given the substantial uncertainty and controversy over the local impact of the Makah Tribe's whaling . . . , an EIS should have been prepared. Of course scientific inquiry rarely yields certainty. But here the agencies' inquiry itself was deficient. Thus, an EIS is required.

There is no doubt that the government put much effort into preparing the lengthy environmental assessment now before us. While a notable attribute of the creatures we discuss in this opinion, girth is not a measure of the analytical soundness of an environmental assessment. No matter how thorough, an EA can never substitute for preparation of an EIS, if the proposed action could significantly affect the environment. *See Sierra Club v. Marsh*, 769 F.2d 868, 874–76 (1st Cir.1985).

We stress in this regard that an EIS serves different purposes from an EA. An EA simply assesses whether there will be a significant impact on the environment. An EIS weighs any significant negative impacts of the proposed action against the positive objectives of the project. Preparation of an EIS thus ensures that decision-makers know that there is a risk of significant environmental impact and take that impact into consideration. As such, an EIS is more likely to attract the time and attention of both policymakers and the public.

In addition, there is generally a longer time period for the public to comment on an EIS as opposed to an EA, and public hearings are often held. *See id.* at 875–76. Furthermore, preparation of an EIS could allow additional study of a key scientific issue, the local recruitment scheme of the whales in the Makah Tribe's hunting area. See, e.g., Review of

Studies at 21 ("A better understanding of site fidelity and potential stock structure will be gained through continuation and expansion of photographic identification and satellite tagging research on the feeding grounds. . . .").

Because the agencies have not complied with NEPA, we set aside the FONSI, suspend implementation of the Agreement with the Makah Tribe, and vacate the approved whaling quota for the Tribe. . . .

NOTES AND QUESTIONS

1.   **Significance.** Was it the plaintiffs' position that the tribe's proposed hunt would result in a significant impact upon the local whale population? Was this the holding of the *Anderson* court? On what basis did the *Anderson* court determine that the proposal should be considered significant for the purposes of § 102(2)(C)?

2.   **Controversy in *Anderson*.** Under the CEQ regulations, in determining whether a proposal is significant for the purposes of § 102(2)(C), an agency must consider whether it is "likely to be highly controversial." 40 C.F.R. § 1508.27(b)(4). The *Anderson* court's determination that the proposal was highly controversial was a key factor in its decision. What was the nature of the controversy in this case? Was it scientific controversy? Was it deemed controversial as a consequence of the widespread public outcry concerning the resumption of whaling?

3.   **Controversy Generally.** For the purposes of 40 C.F.R. § 1508.27(b)(4), what should count as a "highly controversial" proposal? Should the simple fact that there is opposition to a proposal warrant a determination of controversy? Should the amount of opposition to a proposal be relevant? Wouldn't determining the existence of controversy merely by reference to the amount of opposition "be the environmental counterpart to the 'heckler's veto' of the First Amendment law"? *River Rd. Alliance, Inc. v. U.S. Army Corps of Eng'rs*, 764 F.2d 445, 451 (7th Cir. 1985), *cert. denied*, 475 U.S. 1055 (1986). If the amount of opposition is relevant, how is an agency to draw the line between uncontroversial and controversial proposals? *See Nat'l Parks & Conservation Ass'n v. Babbitt*, 241 F.3d 722, 736–37 (9th Cir. 2001), *cert. denied*, 534 U.S. 1104 (2002). What factors may be relevant to this determination? How may concepts of public choice theory, discussed in Chapter IV, play out in this context?

4.   **Uncertainty in *Anderson*.** The CEQ regulations also provide that a proposed action should be considered significant in circumstances where its "possible effects . . . are highly uncertain or involve unique or unknown risks." 40 C.F.R. § 1508.27(b)(5). To what extent did considerations of uncertainty influence the holding of the *Anderson* court? Were the issues in dispute uncertain because of a lack of scientific consensus or because the U.S. Government had simply failed to adequately evaluate the impacts of the proposal on the relevant subpopulation of whales? If it were merely the latter of these two scenarios, why was the U.S. Government not required to undertake a supplemental EA, as opposed to a full scale EIS?

Center for Biological Diversity v. National Highway Traffic Safety Administration

538 F.3d 1172 (9th Cir. 2008).

■ Before B. FLETCHER, SILER, JR., and HAWKINS, CIRCUIT JUDGES.

■ BETTY B. FLETCHER, CIRCUIT JUDGE:

[The National Highway Traffic Safety Administration (NHTSA) issued a final rule to update corporate average fuel economy (CAFE) standards for cars and light trucks, as required by the Energy Policy and Conservation Act (EPCA). NHTSA had also raised light truck fuel economy standards in an earlier rule. The agency conducted an EA for the new rule, which included the cumulative impacts of the previous rule, and nevertheless issued a FONSI. Eleven states, District of Columbia, city and public interest organizations petitioned for review of the rule, seeking more stringent standards. The court found the cumulative impacts analysis in the EA to be inadequate under NEPA, however, since the rules would still allow net GHG emissions from cars and light trucks to increase: the projected increase in total cars and light trucks on the road, and their respective emissions, would exceed the emission reductions from the new rules. The agency had therefore failed to assess whether the impact of that net emissions increase was significant, among other errors. The court began its analysis with the EPCA requirements before moving on to NEPA and the question of significance.]

. . . With respect to non-passenger automobiles (i.e., light trucks), the [EPCA] fuel economy standard "shall be the maximum feasible average fuel economy level that the Secretary decides the manufacturers can achieve in that model year." 49 U.S.C. § 32902(a). "Maximum feasible" is not defined in the EPCA. . . .

Even if NHTSA may use a cost-benefit analysis to determine the "maximum feasible" fuel economy standard, it cannot put a thumb on the scale by undervaluing the benefits and overvaluing the costs of more stringent standards. NHTSA fails to include in its analysis the benefit of carbon emissions reduction in either quantitative or qualitative form. It did, however, include an analysis of the employment and sales impacts of more stringent standards on manufacturers. *See* 71 Fed. Reg. at 17,590–91. . . .

Under [its] methodology, the values that NHTSA assigns to benefits are critical. Yet, NHTSA assigned no value to the most significant benefit of more stringent CAFE standards: reduction in carbon emissions. . . .

. . . While the record shows that there is a range of values, the value of carbon emissions reduction is certainly not zero. [Noting that NHTSA had monetized other "uncertain" benefits in setting the new fuel economy standard under the EPCA, the court concluded that the failure to monetize the net benefit of reducing carbon emissions was arbitrary and capricious.]

. . . Petitioners argue that the evidence raises a substantial question as to whether the Final Rule *may have* a significant impact on the environment and that NHTSA failed to provide a convincing statement of reasons for why a small decrease (rather than a larger decrease) in the growth of CO_2 emissions would not have a significant impact on the environment. Petitioners note that NHTSA has never evaluated the impacts of carbon emissions from light trucks or other vehicles, much less the effect of any reduction or increase in those emissions on climate change. Petitioners presented evidence that continued increase in greenhouse gas emissions may change the climate in a sudden and non-linear way. Without some analysis, it would be "impossible for NHTSA to know . . . whether a change in GHG emissions of 0.2% or 1% or 5% or 10% . . . will be a significant step toward averting the 'tipping point' " and irreversible adverse climate change. States' Gray Br. at 6. . . .

Petitioners have raised a "substantial question" as to whether the CAFE standards for light trucks . . . "may cause significant degradation of some human environmental factor," *Idaho Sporting Cong.*, 137 F.3d at 1149, particularly in light of the compelling scientific evidence concerning "positive feedback mechanisms" in the atmosphere. Among the evidence Petitioners presented to the agency was the following:

— The [Intergovernmental Panel on Climate Change (IPCC)] Third Assessment Report, which discusses the history of anthropogenic interference with the climate system, the projected increase in climate variability and extreme weather events, and the projected effects on various ecological systems. *See* IPCC Third Assessment Report at 2–33. The IPCC found:

Changes in climate could increase the risk of abrupt and non-linear changes in many ecosystems, which would affect their function, biodiversity, and productivity. The greater the magnitude and rate of the change, the greater the risk of adverse impacts. For example:

Changes in disturbance regimes and shifts in the location of suitable climatically defined habitats may lead to abrupt breakdown of terrestrial and marine ecosystems with significant changes in composition and function and increased risk of extinctions.

Sustained increases in water temperatures of as little as 1°C, alone or in combination with any of several stresses . . . can lead to corals ejecting their algae (coral bleaching) and the eventual death of some corals. . . . Inertia is a widespread inherent characteristic of the interacting climate, ecological, and socioeconomic systems. Thus *some impacts of anthropogenic climate change may be slow to become apparent, and some*

> *could be irreversible if climate change is not limited in both rate and magnitude before associated thresholds, whose positions may be poorly known, are crossed.*

IPCC Third Assessment Report at 16 (emphasis added); *see also id.* at 15 (Table SPM-2 shows "[e]xamples of climate variability and extreme climate events and examples of their impacts.").

— The IPCC Working Group I Technical Summary provided: "The possibility for rapid and irreversible changes in the climate system exists, but there is a large degree of uncertainty about the mechanisms involved and hence also about the likelihood or time-scales of such transitions. The climate system involves many processes and feedbacks that interact in complex non-linear ways. *This interaction can give rise to thresholds in the climate system that can be crossed if the system is perturbed sufficiently.*" Technical Summary of IPCC Working Group I Report at 53 (emphasis added); *see also id.* at 46–53 (discussion of positive feedback mechanism).

— "The American [Meteorological] Society, the American Geophysical Union, and the American Association for Advancement of Science, among many, many other scientific organizations have all concluded that the evidence of human induced warming is compelling. . . . In an April 2004 article, leading NASA and Department of Energy scientists stated that emissions of carbon dioxide and other heat-trapping gases have warmed the oceans and led to an energy imbalance that is causing and will continue to cause, significant warming, increasing the urgency of reducing CO_2 emissions." States' Cmt. at 9 (citing essay that reviewed 928 peer-reviewed scientific papers).

— The Climate Change Futures Report published by the Center for Health and the Global Environment at Harvard Medical School, which analyzed in detail climate change scenarios that "will affect the health of humans as well as the ecosystems and species on which we depend." Climate Change Futures Report at 5; *see generally id.* at 32–90 (case studies involving infectious and respiratory diseases, extreme weather events, and natural and managed systems).

Finally, Petitioners have satisfied several of the "intensity" factors listed in 40 C.F.R. § 1508.27(b) for determining "significant effect." For example, the Final Rule clearly may have an "individually insignificant but cumulatively significant" impact with respect to global warming. Evidence that Petitioners submitted in the record also shows that global warming will have an effect on public health and safety. Climate Change

Futures Report at 6–90. Petitioners do not claim (nor do they have to show) that NHTSA's Final Rule would be the *sole* cause of global warming, and that is NHTSA's only response on this point.

Petitioners have also satisfied the "controversy" factor. *See* 40 C.F.R. § 1508.27(b)(4); *see Blue Mountains Biodiversity Project*, 161 F.3d at 1212 (" 'controversial' is 'a substantial dispute [about] the size, nature, or effect of the major Federal action rather than the existence of opposition to a use.' " (alteration in original)). NHTSA received over 45,000 individual submissions on its proposal. *See* 71 Fed. Reg. at 17,577; *see also Nat'l Parks & Conservation Ass'n*, 241 F.3d at 736 (four-hundred and fifty comments, 85% of which opposed the agency's preferred alternative was "more than sufficient to meet the 'outpouring of public protest' discussed in [prior case law]. More important, to the extent the comments urged that the EA's analysis was incomplete, . . . they cast substantial doubt on the adequacy of the Parks Service's methodology and data."). . . .

Nowhere does the EA provide a "statement of reasons" for a finding of no significant impact, much less a "convincing statement of reasons." For example, the EA discusses the amount of CO_2 emissions expected from the Rule, but does not discuss the potential impact of such emissions on climate change. In the "Affected Environment" section of the EA, NHTSA states that "[i]ncreasing concentrations of greenhouse gases are likely to accelerate the rate of climate change." . . .

NHTSA's EA "shunted aside [significant questions] with merely conclusory statements," failed to "directly address[ ]" "substantial questions," and most importantly, "provide[d] no foundation" for the important inference NHTSA draws between a decrease in the rate of carbon emissions growth and its finding of no significant impact. *Found. for N. Am. Wild Sheep*, 681 F.2d at 1179. NHTSA makes "vague and conclusory statements" unaccompanied by "supporting data," and the EA "do[es] not constitute a 'hard look' at the environmental consequences of the action as required by NEPA." *Great Basin Mine Watch v. Hankins*, 456 F.3d 955, 973 (9th Cir. 2006). Thus, the FONSI is arbitrary and capricious. *See Klamath-Siskiyou Wildlands Center*, 387 F.3d at 994 ("[T]he problem with the entire table is that it does not provide any objective quantification of the impacts. Instead, the reader is informed only that a particular environmental factor will be 'unchanged,' 'improved,' or 'degraded' and whether that change will be 'minor' or 'major.' The reader is not told what data the conclusion was based on, or why objective data cannot be provided."). . . .

In light of the emergent consensus on global warming, Chief Judge Wald's reasoning in her dissent in *City of Los Angeles* is not only prescient but persuasive:

> While NHTSA did the calculations necessary to determine how much extra carbon dioxide would be emitted, it failed completely to discuss in any detail the global warming phenomenon itself, or to explain the benchmark for its determination of

insignificance in relation to that environmental danger. Had the emissions been slightly over one percent, would that have been significant? Without some articulated criteria for significance in terms of contribution to global warming that is grounded in the record and available scientific evidence, NHTSA's bald conclusion that the mere magnitude of the percentage increase is enough to alleviate its burden of conducting a more thorough investigation cannot carry the day.

912 F.2d at 500.

Petitioners have raised a substantial question of whether the Final Rule may significantly affect the environment. NHTSA acknowledges that carbon emissions contribute to global warming, and it does not dispute the scientific evidence that Petitioners presented concerning the significant effect of incremental increases in greenhouses gases. Instead of providing the required "convincing statement of reasons," *Blue Mountains Biodiversity Project*, 161 F.3d at 1211, NHTSA simply asserts that the insignificance of the effects is "self-evident[.]"

Finally, we must decide the appropriate remedy given NHTSA's inadequate EA. . . .

Whether to require an EIS now is a very close question. Petitioners' evidence demonstrates, overwhelmingly, the environmental significance of CO_2 emissions and the effect of those emissions on global warming. How NHTSA can, on remand, prepare an EA that takes proper account of this evidence and still conclude that the 2006 Final Rule has no significant environmental impact is questionable. *See* 40 C.F.R. § 1508.13 (FONSI is a document "presenting the reasons why an action . . . *will not* have a significant effect on the human environment and for which an [EIS] therefore will not be prepared" (emphasis added)). We nonetheless give the benefit of the doubt to NHTSA and decline to order the immediate preparation of an EIS for two reasons. . . .

[The court found that (1) the agency should have the opportunity to rebut Petitioners' evidence that the impacts of the rule change would be environmentally significant and (2) since a recently enacted federal law required a further increase in fuel economy standards, and NHTSA had already begun an EIS for that rulemaking, that process would further inform the agency as to whether it required an EIS in this case.]

NOTES AND QUESTIONS

1.   **Monetizing Costs and Benefits.** The court found that NHTSA could use a cost-benefit analysis to determine the "maximum feasible" fuel economy standard, but that its failure to monetize the benefits of reducing CO_2 emissions was arbitrary and capricious. Why? If the agency had used a different approach to risk management, would the omission of CO_2 reduction benefits be allowable? Note that this part of the opinion reviewed compliance

with the EPCA requirements. Could the court have found the failure to monetize these "uncertain" benefits to be a NEPA violation?

2.   Monetization Using the Social Cost of Carbon. In response to *CBD v. NHTSA*, the federal government convened an interagency working group to develop a metric to monetize the cost of CO_2 emissions, based on the best available peer-reviewed science and economic models. Following the development of the Interagency Working Group's "social cost of carbon" (SCC) (discussed in Chapter II), several federal courts have held that agencies violate NEPA when they fail to monetize greenhouse gas emissions in NEPA reviews where they monetized at least some economic benefits of the proposed federal action.

In *High County Conservation Advocates v. U.S. Forest Service*, a U.S. district court considered a NEPA challenge to a BLM-issued Final EIS approving a coal lease modification. 52 F. Supp. 3d 1174, 1184, 1189 (D. Colo. 2014). The court noted that "[b]eyond quantifying the amount of emissions relative to state and national emissions and giving general discussion to the impacts of global climate change, [the FEIS] did not discuss the impacts caused by [greenhouse gas emissions]." *Id.* at 1190. However, the FEIS did include a dollar value quantification of the economic benefits of the proposed lease modification. *Id.* at 1188, 1191. The court concluded that, "[e]ven though NEPA does not require a cost-benefit analysis, it was nonetheless arbitrary and capricious to quantify the *benefits* of the lease modifications and then explain that a similar analysis of the *costs* was impossible when such an analysis was in fact possible and was included in an earlier draft EIS." *Id.* at 1191 (emphasis in original). Do you agree with the court's reasoning? Do you think the result would have been the same if the agency had not included monetized climate costs in its earlier draft EIS?

In *Montana Environmental Information Center v. U.S. Office of Surface Mining,* 274 F. Supp. 3d 1074 (D. Mont. 2017), the Office of Surface Mining argued that its Mining Plan EA adequately considered the impact of greenhouse gas emissions by quantifying the emissions that would be released if the mine expansion were approved and comparing that amount to the emissions of the entire United States. The EA adopted a socioeconomic analysis that concluded that the mine "generates a monthly payroll in Montana of over $400,000, adding much needed revenue and employment to the local economy," and that "the proposed project could contribute $23,816,000 million [sic] annually in tax revenues to the states." *Id.* at 1096. The court held that it was arbitrary and capricious for the Mining Plan EA to adopt a quantitative analysis of the benefits of the proposed action without considering the quantifiable costs, including the social cost of greenhouse gases. *Id.* at 1098.

How might agencies change their future NEPA analyses in light of these cases?

3.   NEPA Regulations on Cost-Benefit Analysis. NEPA's implementing regulations describe some conditions in which cost-benefit analysis may be incorporated into NEPA analysis:

If a cost-benefit analysis relevant to the choice among environmentally different alternatives is being considered for the proposed action, it shall be incorporated by reference or appended to the statement as an aid in evaluating the environmental consequences. . . . For purposes of complying with the Act, the weighing of the merits and drawbacks of the various alternatives need not be displayed in a monetary cost-benefit analysis and should not be when there are important qualitative considerations. In any event, an environmental impact statement should at least indicate those considerations, including factors not related to environmental quality, which are likely to be relevant and important to a decision.

40 C.F.R. § 1502.23. Is this regulation consistent with the decisions in *CBD v. NHTSA, High County Conservation Advocates*, and *Montana Environmental Information Center*?

4.   Uncertainty and the Climate "Tipping Point." What facts does the court in *CBD v. NHTSA* rely on to find uncertainty? How is the uncertainty here different from the uncertainty in *Anderson*? Recall that in *Anderson* the court seemed concerned with the apparent lack of scientific consensus on the local impacts of whale hunting. In *CBD v. NHTSA*, the scientific community appears unified on many of the risks of climate change, yet uncertainty remains. 538 F.3d at 1221–22. Given the positive feedback loops and the possibility of crossing a "threshold" that leads to irreversible climate change impacts, *id.* at 1221, is it possible to account for this uncertainty? Did NHTSA need to eliminate the uncertainty or simply deal with it more concretely in order to satisfy NEPA? If the level of the tipping point were known with substantial certainty, would the court's decision have come out differently?

5.   Cumulative Climate Effects. In order to reach the question of significance under NEPA, the court in *CBD v. NHTSA* first found a deficiency in the agency's analysis of cumulative impacts of two recent fuel economy rules. While the rules would decrease individual vehicles' emissions, the projected rise in the total number of vehicles on the road meant that total GHG emissions would still increase under the rules. Thus, the percentage reduction on a vehicle-by-vehicle basis was an important component of the analysis, but it alone did not sufficiently describe "the *actual* environmental effects" from the emissions. *Id.* (quoting *Klamath-Siskiyou Wildlands Ctr. v. BLM*, 387 F.3d 989, 995 (9th Cir. 2004)). Furthermore, NHTSA had to look beyond the cumulative impact of its own two rulemaking actions:

The fact that "climate change is largely a global phenomenon that includes actions that are outside of [the agency's] control . . . does not release the agency from the duty of assessing the effects of *its* actions on global warming within the context of other actions that also affect global warming." The cumulative impacts regulation specifically provides that the agency must assess the "impact of the action when added to other past, present, and reasonably foreseeable future actions regardless of what agency *(Federal or non-Federal) or person undertakes such other actions."*

Id. at 1217 (citing 40 C.F.R. § 1508.7) (emphasis in original). How wide is the scope of activities that an agency must analyze in its cumulative impacts analysis? The answer could turn on what actions are "reasonably foreseeable" or on the range of individuals whose actions must be taken into account. From an atmospheric perspective, all global greenhouse gas emissions are cumulative and contribute equally to climate change, but this literal approach may be unworkable. Two commentators argue that a cumulative impacts analysis on climate change under NEPA is "not realistically possible." Kevin Haroff & Katherine Moore, *Global Climate Change and the National Environmental Policy Act*, 42 U.S.F.L. REV. 155, 174–77 (2007).

Generally speaking, do you think that federal agencies are competent to assess global climate change impacts, particularly when they must account for other reasonably foreseeable future actions? (If not, what makes climate change different than any other environmental risk that must be assessed under NEPA?)

6.   CEQ Guidance and 25,000 Metric Ton Threshold. CEQ issued draft guidance in February 2010 to advise agencies on how to assess the significance of climate change effects and GHG emissions in their NEPA analyses. *See* Nancy H. Sutley, Chair, CEQ, Memorandum for Heads of Federal Departments and Agencies on Draft NEPA Guidance on Consideration of the Effects Climate Change and Greenhouse Gas Emissions (Feb. 18, 2010). CEQ guidance is not binding on agencies, unlike CEQ's NEPA regulations, which are legally binding. The guidance suggested a minimum annual level of GHG emissions—25,000 metric tons of CO_2-equivalent emissions per year—that should serve as a useful proxy for significance. *Id.* at 3. Do you think this a useful threshold for significance?

CEQ issued revised draft guidance in 2014. *See* Revised Draft Guidance for Federal Departments and Agencies on Consideration of Greenhouse Gas Emissions and the Effects of Climate Change in NEPA Reviews, 79 Fed. Reg. 77,802 (2014). The 2014 draft guidance maintained the 25,000 metric tons of CO_2-equivalent annual emissions as a reference point, under which a quantitative analysis of GHG emissions would not be warranted. But CEQ emphasized that the reference point was not intended to be equivalent to a determination of significance, stating that the ultimate determination of significance requires consideration of context and intensity, as set forth in CEQ's NEPA regulations. *Id.* at 77,827–28. Which guidance do you find more useful? In the 2014 draft guidance, CEQ also indicated that, where an agency determines that a cost-benefit analysis is appropriate, it should use the federal social cost of carbon to monetize GHG emissions. *See id.* at 77,827.

7.   Final CEQ Guidance on Climate Change Impacts. In August 2016, CEQ released final guidance for federal agencies on how to consider climate change impacts in NEPA analysis. 81 Fed. Reg. 51,866 (2016). The final guidance removed the 25,000 metric tons of CO_2-equivalent annual emissions reference point. It recommended that agencies "quantify a proposed agency action's projected direct and indirect GHG emissions, taking into account available data and GHG quantification tools that are suitable for the proposed agency action." *Id.* at 51,866. The final guidance noted that NEPA does not require cost-benefit analysis, but when "an agency determines that a monetized assessment of the impacts of greenhouse gas emissions or a monetary cost-benefit analysis is appropriate," that such analysis may be "an aid in evaluating the environmental consequences." Christina Goldfuss, CEQ, Memorandum for Heads of Federal Departments and Agencies: Final Guidance for Federal Departments and Agencies on Consideration of Greenhouse Gas Emissions and the Effects of Climate Change in National Environmental Policy Act Reviews 33 (Aug. 1, 2016). The final guidance also noted that the Interagency Working Group's SCC "provides a harmonized, interagency metric that can give decision makers and the public useful information for their NEPA review." *Id.* Why might CEQ have eliminated any reference to the 25,000 metric ton threshold? What are the benefits of agencies using the Interagency Working Group's SCC? Is it important that all agencies use the same metric to monetize emissions?

8.   Rescission of CEQ's Climate Guidance. In March 2017, President Trump issued an executive order directing CEQ to rescind its final guidance on climate change and NEPA reviews. Exec. Order No. 13,783, 82 Fed. Reg. 16,093 (2017). CEQ subsequently withdrew the guidance. CEQ, Withdrawal of Final Guidance for Federal Departments and Agencies on Consideration of Greenhouse Gas Emissions and the Effects of Climate Change in National Environmental Policy Act Reviews, 82 Fed. Reg. 16,576 (2017).

What effect, if any, do you think the withdrawal of CEQ's guidance will have on agencies' NEPA reviews? Could rescinding the guidance create more legal risk for agencies?

9.   Codifying Climate Change Guidance? In 2014, CEQ denied a petition to amend its NEPA regulations to address the impacts of climate change directly. CEQ advised petitioners that in its view the regulations "already encompass consideration of climate effects and it is not the best use of CEQ's resources at this time. . . ." Letter from Michael J. Boots, Acting Chair of CEQ, to Joseph Mendelson, III., Int'l Center for Tech. Assessment (2014). Would such an amendment make a difference? Without the CEQ's guidance on greenhouse gas emissions, which was withdrawn by the Trump administration, is it true that the regulations already encompass consideration of climate effects?

10. The Courts Weigh in: Combustion Emissions Are Indirect Effects. Notwithstanding the withdrawal of CEQ's climate change guidance, a growing number of federal courts have held that combustion emissions are an indirect effect of an agency's decision to extract fossil fuel resources that must be analyzed in NEPA analysis. *See San Juan Citizens All. v. United States Bureau of Land Mgmt.*, 326 F. Supp. 3d 1227, 1241–45 (D.N.M. 2018); *W. Org. of Res. Councils v. U.S. Bureau of Land Mgmt.*, No. CV 16-21 GF-BMM, 2018 WL 1475470, *13 (D. Mont. March 26, 2018) ("In light of the degree of foreseeability and specificity of information available to the agency while completing the EIS, NEPA requires BLM to consider in the EIS the environmental consequences of the downstream combustion of the coal, oil and gas resources potentially open to development under these RMPs"); *Sierra Club v. Fed. Energy Regulatory Comm'n*, 867 F.3d 1357, 1374 (D.C. Cir. 2017) (stating that greenhouse gas emissions from the combustion of gas "are an indirect effect of authorizing this [pipeline] project, which [the agency] could reasonably foresee" and "conclud[ing] that the EIS for the . . . Pipelines Project should have either given a quantitative estimate of the downstream greenhouse emissions that will result from burning the natural gas that the pipelines will transport or explained more specifically why it could not have done so"); *Montana Envtl. Info. Ctr. v. U.S. Office of Surface Mining*, 274 F. Supp. 3d 1074 (D. Mont. 2017) (stating that indirect effects from coal trains include "the effects of the estimated 23.16 million metric tons of greenhouse gas emissions the Mining Plan EA concluded would result from combustion of the coal that would be extracted from the Mine"); *Diné Citizens Against Ruining Our Env't v. U.S. Office of Surface Mine Reclamation & Enforcement*, 82 F. Supp. 3d 1201, 1213 (D. Colo. 2015) ("find[ing] that the coal combustion-related impacts of [the mine's] proposed expansion are an 'indirect effect' requiring NEPA analysis"), *vacated as moot by* 643 Fed. Appx. 799 (10th Cir. 2016); *WildEarth Guardians v. United States Office of Surface Mining, Reclamation & Enforcement*, 104 F. Supp. 3d 1208, 1229–30 (D. Colo. 2015) (rejecting the argument that "coal combustion is not an actual [indirect] 'effect' of the mining plan within the meaning of NEPA because a mining plan does not cause coal combustion").

Do these decisions render the CEQ climate change guidance unnecessary? If CEQ were to issue new guidance that contradicts the holdings in these cases—stating that analysis of downstream combustion emissions is not necessary pursuant to NEPA—what should agencies do?

11. What Difference? Would you expect NHTSA to change its fuel economy rule if the revised EA or EIS reveals that the emissions increase is significant? Recall that NEPA merely forces "a recognition, not a reduction" in climate impacts. Haroff & Moore, *supra*, at 169.

Indeed, a recent study shows that agencies increasingly acknowledge the climate impacts of an action, but those impacts appear to carry little or no weight in the final agency decision. Amy Stein, *Climate Change Under NEPA: Avoiding Cursory Consideration of Greenhouse Gases*, 81 U. COLO. L. REV. 473 (2010). In one telling example from Stein's study, the Bureau of Land Management (BLM) had proposed a large power plant complex. In its EIS, the agency discussed global climate change, noted that burning fossil fuels causes GHG emissions, and estimated that the proposed plant would produce over seven million tons of CO_2 emissions per year. This suggests serious consideration of climate impacts, but

> the BLM failed to require or even consider mitigation of any of the seven million annual metric tons of carbon dioxide emissions in the EIS. The agency went through the motions of considering climate change, but the outcome failed to reflect NEPA's purposes. As a result, the United States is left with more paperwork and more GHG emissions.

Id. at 476–77. The other EISs in this small sample varied in their attention to climate impacts, but with little change in the outcomes.

> Of the thirty-five BLM EISs issued during [2007–2008] that evaluate coal, oil, gas, or mining activities, thirteen fail to contain any mention of climate change or GHGs. Seven EISs contain nothing more than stock language about climate change or a cursory mention that GHG emissions are negligible. Fifteen EISs quantify GHG emissions, but only three of these discuss GHG mitigation. This assessment suggests an outcome NEPA cannot possibly have intended: sporadic and superficial climate change analysis.

Id. at 477. Stein argues that a clear and consistent threshold for significance of climate impacts will force agencies into more meaningful consideration of alternatives or mitigation. *Id.* at 478.

12. Worst Case Scenarios. In *Anderson* and *CBD v. NHTSA*, the courts dealt with uncertainty in both local and global impacts and in areas of both scientific dispute and scientific consensus. But agencies must also make decisions in the face of a different type of uncertainty: the probability of a given impact. In particular, an action may carry the risk of a highly unlikely, worst case scenario. Should an agency be required to assess its effects? What if the probability of that worst case scenario was one in a million? One in a billion?

Consideration of worst case scenarios was originally required but later revoked by CEQ regulations. *See Robertson v. Methow Valley Citizens Council*, 490 U.S. 332, 359 (1989) (holding that NEPA "does not require a 'worst case analysis' "). The current regulations require NEPA analysis only if the risk is reasonably foreseeable, is "supported by credible scientific evidence and is not based on pure conjecture, and is within the rule of reason." 40 C.F.R. § 1502.22. How should this apply in situations like the Deepwater Horizon oil spill disaster in the Gulf of Mexico, a nuclear meltdown like the Fukushima Daiichi reactor in Japan, or terrorism?

In 2006, the Ninth Circuit ruled that the Nuclear Regulatory Commission (NRC) violated NEPA by failing to account for terrorist sabotage in conducting an EA of a proposed new storage facility at a nuclear plant in California. *See San Luis Obispo Mothers for Peace v. NRC*, 449 F.3d 1016 (9th Cir. 2006), *cert. denied*, 549 U.S. 1166 (2007). The Ninth Circuit said terror risks should be assessed even if they cannot be quantified. On the whole, however, courts have read the CEQ regulations to require relatively little analysis of low-probability, high-risk effects in an EIS, according to one critic. *See* Daniel A. Farber, *Confronting Uncertainty under NEPA*, ISSUES IN LEGAL SCHOLARSHIP, Vol. 8, Issue 3, at 21–27 (2009) (adding that the few recent decisions to reject an EIS for failing to properly deal with uncertainty did little to change the final agency decision on the projects at issue); *see also* Oliver Houck, *Worst Case and the Deepwater Horizon Blowout: There Ought to Be a Law*, 40 ENVTL. L. REP. 11033, 11039 (2010) (arguing for restoration of the worst-case scenario requirement and elimination of the "reasonably foreseeable" limitation on required analyses of catastrophic effects under NEPA).

Agencies may also apply a categorical exclusion (CE) to certain activities, which allows a reprieve from NEPA requirements. 40 C.F.R. § 1508.4. The Deepwater Horizon oil well was one such activity, and assuredly a worst-case scenario, which has led to calls for reforming and limiting the use of CEs. *See* CENTER FOR OCEAN SOLUTIONS, THE NATIONAL ENVIRONMENTAL POLICY ACT (NEPA) AND A REVIEW OF MMS NEPA DOCUMENTS 15–16 (Oct. 19, 2010). CEs are discussed further in Section G.

National Audubon Society v. Hoffman
132 F.3d 7 (2d Cir. 1997).

■ Before WINTER, CHIEF JUDGE, and CARDAMONE and CABRANES, CIRCUIT JUDGES.

■ CARDAMONE, CIRCUIT JUDGE:

[The Forest Service issued an EA concerning a logging project in part of Vermont's Green Mountain National Forest. The logging project was part of a larger National Forest Plan. One month later, the agency made a FONSI. The logging project consisted of a timber management program, the improvement of two existing roads, and improving conditions for all terrain vehicles. The Forest Service proposed a number of ways to mitigate the project's potential negative affect on black bears, into whose habitat the proposed project encroached. In June of 1994, plaintiffs (a coalition of environmental groups) filed suit against the Forest Service alleging a violation of NEPA for failing to take into account the negative effect the project would have on black bears (in a state-designated critical bear habitat) and migratory bird populations. The district court granted summary judgment for the plaintiffs, finding that the Forest Service violated NEPA by not preparing a site-specific EIS. The Forest Service appealed].

. . . The question before us [is] . . . whether the Forest Service's decision to implement this proposed action has met the procedural requirements of the National Environmental Policy Act (NEPA). . . .

Congress has charged the United States Forest Service with the responsibility of managing our national forests. The Forest Service's decisionmaking process is governed by NEPA, which requires certain procedures to ensure that the agency fully considers the environmental consequences of its decisions prior to their implementation. The federal judiciary's responsibility to review an agency's decisions generally does not extend to finding facts and drawing conclusions that would infringe on the authority Congress delegated to the agency to make independent decisions in its area of expertise. Instead, for a court in an environmental case, the expression "Let's look at the record" means that judicial attention is focused on the agency's compliance with NEPA's procedure-forcing steps in an effort to ensure that environmental concerns are fully considered. Such consideration, it is hoped, will prevent needless damage to our natural resources and promote "enjoyable harmony" between humans and their environment. . . .

When the determination that a significant impact will or will not result from the proposed action is a close call, an EIS should be prepared. . . . It is only when the proposed action "*will not* have a significant effect on the human environment," 40 C.F.R. § 1508.13 (emphasis added), that an EIS is not required. . . .

A forest plan for an entire national forest unit is implemented through a series of individual site-specific projects. These projects are proposed and assessed to determine whether they are consistent with the forest plan. At this stage, the agency also conducts the NEPA analysis described above to evaluate the environmental impact of the *specific* project. . . .

The Forest Service followed this two-part NEPA/National Forest Act scheme in the case at hand. The EA expressly states that it is part of the "second, and final, level of decisionmaking . . . [which] involves site-specific analysis to meet the requirements of the National Environmental Policy Act and specific on-site resource needs." The Forest Service, however, does not urge that its programmatic EIS was sufficient to obviate the need for any additional environmental analysis under NEPA. In fact, it has not even submitted the programmatic EIS as part of the appellate record. The question before us therefore is whether the Forest Service violated the action-forcing process mandated by NEPA when it determined that [this] project will not "significantly" affect the quality of the human environment in that area.

. . . [I]n reviewing an administrative decision not to issue an EIS, a federal court must undertake a two-step analysis. First, we must consider whether the agency took a "hard look" at the possible effects of the proposed action. *See Village of Grand View v. Skinner*, 947 F.2d 651, 657 (2d Cir. 1991). Second, if the agency has taken a "hard look," we must ask whether the agency's decision was arbitrary or capricious. *See Grand View*, 947 F.2d at 657. . . .

The district court determined that the Forest Service's finding of no significant environmental impact violated NEPA for two reasons: (1) the agency's EA failed to take a "hard look" at all the relevant effects of the proposed action, and (2) had the Forest Service taken a hard look, it necessarily would have decided that the project could result in a significant impact, thereby requiring completion of a site-specific EIS. 917 F. Supp. at 288–89. We turn to an analysis of these rulings. . . .

In support of his finding that the agency failed to take a hard look, the trial judge focused primarily on the Forest Service's failure to quantify the amount of unauthorized traffic that will occur as a result of the lengthening and improvement of [one of the roads]. In the EA, the Forest Service conceded that the unauthorized use by [All Terrain

Vehicles (ATVs)] is a problem, that the amount of such use is unknown, and that it would likely increase with the improvements to [the road] and its extension. Moreover, one of its experts notes that "[i]f increased permanent public access during the spring, summer, and fall results from this action then I would concur that there would be a strong potential for the creation of an adverse impact to black bears." The Forest Service's proposed mitigation measure to counter the impact of the unauthorized traffic calls for the "obliterat[ion]" of a section of [the road] at a point near its current end, thereby hopefully causing unauthorized users to believe that the road stops there. But a question remains: whether it is sufficient for the agency to propose mitigation measures—the efficacy of which are seriously disputed—to support its finding of no significant impact.

When the adequacy of proposed mitigation measures is supported by substantial evidence, the agency may use those measures as a mechanism to reduce environmental impacts below the level of significance that would require an EIS. . . .

We emphasize the requirement that mitigation measures be supported by substantial evidence in order to avoid creating a temptation for federal agencies to rely on mitigation proposals as a way to avoid preparation of an EIS. That is to say, agencies should define "significance" broadly and not rely on proposed mitigation measures as an excuse to avoid preparing an EIS. *Abenaki*, 805 F. Supp. at 244. In this case, we have no assurance of [the proposed mitigation measure's] efficacy. The Forest Service conducted no study of its likely effects, proposed no monitoring to determine how effective the proposed mitigation would be, and did not consider alternatives in the event [the proposed mitigation measure] fails. Although the Forest Service affidavits considered by the district court suggest that additional measures may be used to control illegal ATV use, there is no indication that the agency reviewed these measures at the time of its decision, or that it afforded the public an opportunity to comment on them. Absent substantial evidence to support the efficacy of [the proposed mitigation measure], we, like the district court, are left with the firm conviction that the Forest Service could not have adequately considered the significance of its proposed action's impact on the environment. Because this factor alone convinces us that the Forest Service failed to take a hard look, we need not address the district court's remaining objections to the agency's environmental assessment.

The mode of analysis employed in this case is intended to allow an agency to omit the preparation of an EIS when it determines that a mitigation measure will sufficiently limit the negative environmental impact of a proposed project. In the instant case, for example, had [the proposed mitigation measure] included a program to monitor and ensure its effectiveness, there would then have been substantial evidence to support it. We hope our holding that the Forest Service's attempt to moderate one of the anticipated impacts of its proposed logging project was not supported by substantial evidence will ensure that such agencies in NEPA cases propose mitigation measures supported by studies and/or procedures to monitor their effectiveness.

In sum, we agree that the Forest Service violated NEPA by failing to adequately consider all relevant environmental factors prior to making its finding of no significant impact.

In addition to concluding that the agency failed to consider all relevant factors, the district court found that the agency's finding of no significant impact was arbitrary. It ruled that had the Forest Service taken a hard look "at the context and intensity of its proposal," it necessarily would have decided to prepare an EIS.

As discussed earlier, when it is a close call whether there will be a significant environmental impact from a proposed action, an EIS should be prepared. This view is reinforced by the CEQ Guideline's direction to agencies to consider "[t]he degree to which the effects on the quality of the human environment are likely to be highly controversial" when determining significance. 40 C.F.R. § 1508.27(b)(4). Moreover, we think NEPA's policy goals require agencies to err in favor of preparation of an EIS when the proposed action is likely to have a significant environmental impact. Consequently, we agree with the district court that a party challenging the agency's decision not to prepare an EIS must show only that there is a substantial possibility that the action may have a significant impact on the environment, not that it clearly will have such an impact. See *Foundation for N. Am. Wild Sheep*, 681 F.2d at 1177–78. The Forest Service's determination that preparation of an EIS was not necessary, based on the record before it, was therefore arbitrary and capricious.

Our agreement with the legal standard employed by the district court does not necessitate agreement with its application. The relevant question is whether the proposed action may have a significant impact on the environment. The district court undertook to answer the question, despite an incomplete record, holding that the impact of the proposed action was potentially significant. The question is substantive, and consequently not one within the purview of the district court. Rather, it is one the Forest Service must decide.

The Forest Service's failure to weigh the factors related to its project's environmental impact is a flaw that precludes a definitive determination as to whether the project may have a significant impact. What impact the Forest Service's proposed action will have on the birds, the bears, and the existence value of [the affected area] is not clear because the scope of current and future ATV use is unknown. We also take notice of possible gaps in the administrative record with respect to [the road's] future use and maintenance, as highlighted by the district court. The district court overstepped the narrow confines of judicial review of an agency's decision when it jumped to the conclusion that the impact of the project would be "arguably significant" and, on that basis, ordered the agency to prepare an EIS.

Because the question of whether the project may have significant adverse impacts is one that the Forest Service must decide, the appropriate remedy is to remand the case to the agency to correct the deficiencies in the record and in its analysis. The Forest Service should reconsider the issues which we have held were inadequately addressed in its initial environmental assessment, and it should also address additional possible shortcomings raised by the district court which we have elected not to explore here. After doing so, it should reconsider its finding of no significant impact in light of its additional investigation and the applicable legal standard.

Plaintiffs declare that a remand to the agency may result in nothing more than a new rationalization for the same result, rather than a "hard look" at the potential effects of the proposed action. *See* Louis L. Jaffe, *Judicial Control of Administrative Action* 589 (1965); *see also Louisiana v. Lee,* 758 F.2d 1081, 1085 (5th Cir.1985) (EA revised in response to challenge of agency's finding of no significant impact is *post-hoc* rationalization that should be reviewed critically). Nonetheless, NEPA is a procedural statute and an agency's substantive decisions are intended to be largely insulated from judicial review. Our task is to ensure NEPA compliance with the environmental policies and the law without infringing upon the agency's decisions in areas where it has expertise.

Consequently, a remand for reconsideration of the EA carefully balances the need for judicial review of the procedures followed with the need to recognize the agency's independent decisionmaking power regarding the substantive issues before it. Moreover, a remand in this case may improve the agency's decisionmaking processes and encourage NEPA compliance in the long run by inducing the agency to make a better initial investigation with respect to the impact of a proposed action. *See* Jaffe, *supra,* at 589. . . .

Accordingly, for the reasons stated, we affirm the judgment insofar as it found the Forest Service's environmental assessment inadequate under NEPA. The judgment is reversed to the extent that the district court made a finding of potentially significant impact and ordered the Forest Service to prepare a site-specific environmental impact statement, and the case is remanded to the district court with instructions that it order the Forest Service to address the issues discussed and reassess the environmental significance of the Project in light of these issues. . . .

NOTES AND QUESTIONS

1.   **Mitigation.** On what basis did the Forest Service determine that the project would not "significantly" affect the quality of the human environment in the area? What was the Forest Service's proposed mitigation measure in response to the prospect of unauthorized traffic? How effective do you think this measure would be?

2. Substantial Evidence. Against what practice on the part of federal agencies was the *National Audubon Society* court trying to safeguard, by requiring that proposed mitigation measures be supported by sufficient evidence? On what basis did the *National Audubon Society* court find that the Forest Service had failed to provide sufficient evidence? For an example of an agency's proposed mitigation measures being found to be based on sufficient evidence, see *Roanoke River Basin Ass'n v. Hudson*, 940 F.2d 58, 62 (4th Cir. 1991) ("[i]f a mitigation condition eliminates all significant environmental effects, no EIS is required." (citing *C.A.R.E. Now, Inc. v. FAA*, 844 F.2d 1569, 1573 (11th Cir. 1988))), *cert. denied*, 502 U.S. 1092 (1992).

3. Litigation Strategy. On what alternative basis could the plaintiffs in *National Audubon Society* have litigated this case? Based on the findings of the court, what would the likely outcome have been?

4. Consequences. Does anything actually turn on the finding of the court in this case? Is the Forest Service simply required to conduct a large— instead of truncated—assessment of environmental impacts? What are the procedural consequences of having to prepare an EIS rather than an EA? What are the consequences in terms of public participation?

The court sought to keep mitigation measures from becoming a way for agencies to avoid an EIS. 132 F.3d at 17. Indeed, according to one commentator, the prohibitive cost of producing an EIS has had precisely that "backhanded" effect. Bradley C. Karkkainen, *Breaking the Logjam: Environmental Reform for the New Congress and Administration*, 17 N.Y.U. ENVTL. L.J. 75, 86 (2008) (describing the incentive for agencies to avoid the need to produce a costly EIS by adding mitigation measures to a project). Karkkainen notes that this "circuitous and unexpected" route to greater mitigation actually leads to environmental benefits, *id.*, but consider whether those benefits outweigh the procedural benefits of the more robust NEPA analysis in an EIS.

5. Accountability. What if the mitigation fails, either immediately or over time? The *National Audubon Society* court suggested that to assure the efficacy of a mitigation measure, the agency should study it, propose a monitoring plan, and consider alternatives if it fails. CEQ recently issued a Guidance that pushes agencies to go further by making a binding commitment to proposed mitigation measures, including full funding, monitoring systems, and public participation, even for a FONSI. CEQ, Final Guidance for Federal Departments and Agencies on the Appropriate Use of Mitigation and Monitoring and Clarifying the Appropriate Use of Mitigated Findings of No Significant Impact, 76 Fed. Reg. 3,843, 3,852 (2011).

6. Significant Positive Environmental Impacts. Should an agency be compelled to prepare an EIS with respect to projects that will result in a significant positive environmental impact? In *Friends of Fiery Gizzard v. Farmers Home Administration*, 61 F.3d 501 (6th Cir. 1995), the court reviewed a decision of the Farmers Home Administration (FHA) not to prepare an EIS with respect to a water treatment project. After completing an EA with respect to the proposed action, the FHA concluded that "[t]he project will have a positive impact on the living environment of the residents of the area because they would be provided with a dependable, sanitary water supply." Plaintiffs sued, claiming that the existence of "significant" beneficial impacts required the preparation of an EIS. Affirming the lower court decision, the *Friends of Fiery Gizzard* court held that if an agency reasonably concludes on the basis of an environmental assessment that the project will have no significant adverse environmental consequences, an EIS is not required. The court based its conclusion on its reading of NEPA and the CEQ regulations: "It was in keeping with this philosophy that the environmental assessment process was devised to screen projects where the preparation of an expensive and time-consuming environmental impact statement would serve no useful purpose." 61 F.3d at 505. Is this decision consistent with the express provisions of the Act?

E. ADEQUACY UNDER NEPA

Section 102(2) of the Act contains the procedural requirements designed to compel federal agencies contemplating major federal actions or proposals for legislation to consider NEPA's substantive policies and goals as enunciated in § 101. The effectiveness of the Act, therefore, turns on compliance with these procedural duties "to the fullest extent possible." *Sierra Club v. Froehlke*, 534 F.2d 1289, 1299 (8th Cir. 1976). Disputes often arise concerning whether an agency has adequately performed its duties pursuant to § 102 of the Act. In resolving disputes of this type, courts typically consider whether the agency in question has "reached its decision after a full, good faith consideration and balancing of environmental factors." *Envtl. Def. Fund, Inc. v. U.S. Army Corps of Eng'rs*, 470 F.2d 289, 300 (8th Cir. 1972), *cert. denied*, 412 U.S. 931 (1973).

The decisions that follow canvas a range of different challenges to the adequacy of EISs prepared pursuant to NEPA. The first, *Vermont Yankee Nuclear Power Corp. v. NRDC*, 435 U.S. 519 (1978), centers on the adequacy of the alternatives considered by an agency. The second, *State of Alaska v. Andrus*, 580 F.2d 465 (D.C. Cir. 1978), addresses the adequacy of the information relied upon by an agency in the preparation of an EIS. The third, *Sierra Club v. U.S. Army Corps of Engineers*, 701 F.2d 1011 (2d Cir. 1983), explores an agency's obligations in circumstances where new information arises during the preparation of an EIS. The fourth, *Marsh v. Oregon Natural Resources Council*, 490 U.S. 360 (1989), examines circumstances in which new information arises after an EIS was completed. In each case, consider the balance struck by the court in reconciling the competing objectives of ensuring that an agency is not permitted to avoid its obligations under the Act on the one hand, and ensuring that the Act does not impose an impossible standard on the other.

Vermont Yankee Nuclear Power Corp. v. Natural Resources Defense Council, Inc.

435 U.S. 519 (1978).

■ JUSTICE REHNQUIST delivered the opinion of the Court:

[The AEC granted a permit to the Vermont Yankee Nuclear Power Corp. to operate a nuclear power plant. After the permit had been granted, the CEQ promulgated regulations requiring, for the first time, that energy conservation should be considered as an alternative during the NEPA process. One of the intervenors (Saginaw) moved to reopen the permit proceedings to consider energy conservation. The AEC, in considering Saginaw's proposal, first ruled that it was required to consider only those energy conservation alternatives that satisfied the following 3 threshold tests: that the measures were reasonably available, that they would curtail demand for electricity to a level at which the proposed facility would not be needed, and that they satisfied a reasonable degree of proof. It then determined, after a thorough examination of the record, that Saginaw's proposal did not meet these threshold tests. The Court of Appeals for the District of Columbia, held that the "rejection of energy conservation on the basis of the 'threshold test' was capricious and arbitrary," and remanded the decision of the AEC to grant a license to the petitioner.]

. . . The Court of Appeals ruled that the Commission's "threshold test" for the presentation of energy conservation contentions was inconsistent with NEPA's basic mandate to the Commission. 547 F.2d, at 627. The Commission, the court reasoned, is something more than an umpire who sits back and resolves adversary contentions at the hearing stage. 547 F.2d, at 627. And when an intervenor's comments "bring 'sufficient attention to the issue to stimulate the Commission's consideration of it,'" the Commission must "undertake its own preliminary investigation of the proffered alternative sufficient to reach a rational judgment whether it is worthy of detailed consideration in the EIS. Moreover, the Commission must explain the basis for each conclusion that further consideration of a suggested alternative is unwarranted." 547 F.2d, at 628, quoting from *Indiana & Michigan Electric Co. v. FPC*, 502 F.2d 336, 339 (1974), *cert. denied*, 420 U.S. 946 (1975).

While the court's rationale is not entirely unappealing as an abstract proposition, as applied to this case we think it basically misconceives not only the scope of the agency's statutory responsibility, but also the nature of the administrative process, the thrust of the agency's decision, and the type of issues the intervenors were trying to raise. . . .

NEPA, of course, has altered slightly the statutory balance, requiring "a detailed statement by the responsible official on . . . alternatives to the proposed action." 42 U.S.C. § 4332(C). But, as should be obvious even upon a moment's reflection, the term "alternatives" is not self-defining. To make an impact statement something more than an exercise in frivolous boilerplate the concept of alternatives must be bounded by some notion of feasibility. As the Court of Appeals for the District of Columbia Circuit has itself recognized:

> There is reason for concluding that NEPA was not meant to require detailed discussion of the environmental effects of "alternatives" put forward in comments when these effects cannot be readily ascertained and the alternatives are deemed only remote and speculative possibilities, in view of basic changes required in statutes and policies of other agencies—making them available, if at all, only after protracted debate and litigation not meaningfully compatible with the time-frame of the needs to which the underlying proposal is addressed.

Natural Resources Defense Council v. Morton, 458 F.2d 827, 837–838 (1972). Common sense also teaches us that the "detailed statement of alternatives" cannot be found wanting simply because the agency failed to include every alternative device and thought conceivable by the mind of man. Time and resources are simply too limited to hold that an impact statement fails because the agency failed to ferret out every possible alternative, regardless of how uncommon or unknown that alternative may have been at the time the project was approved.

With these principles in mind we now turn to the notion of "energy conservation," an alternative the omission of which was thought by the Court of Appeals to have been "forcefully pointed out by Saginaw in its comments on the draft EIS." 547 F.2d, at 625. Again, as the Commission pointed out, "the phrase 'energy conservation' has a deceptively simple ring in this context. Taken literally, the phrase suggests a virtually limitless range of possible actions and developments that might, in one way or another, ultimately reduce projected demands for electricity from a particular proposed plant." Moreover, as a practical matter, it is hard to dispute the observation that it is largely the events of recent years that have emphasized not only the need but also a large variety of alternatives for energy conservation. Prior to the drastic oil shortages incurred by the United States in 1973, there was little serious thought in most Government circles of energy conservation alternatives. Indeed, the Council on Environmental Quality did not promulgate regulations which even remotely suggested the need to consider energy conservation in impact statements until August 1, 1973. See 40 CFR § 1500.8(a)(4) (1977); 38 Fed.Reg. 20554 (1973). And even then the guidelines were not made applicable to draft and final statements filed with the Council before January 28, 1974. *Id.*, at 20557, 21265. The Federal Power Commission likewise did not require consideration of energy conservation in applications to build hydroelectric facilities until June 19, 1973. 18 CFR pt. 2, App. A., § 8.2 (1977); 38 Fed.Reg. 15946, 15949 (1973). And these regulations were not made retroactive either. *Id.* at 15946. All this occurred over a year and a half after the draft environmental statement for [the relevant facility] had been prepared, and over a year after the final environmental statement had been prepared and the hearings completed.

We think these facts amply demonstrate that the concept of "alternatives" is an evolving one, requiring the agency to explore more or fewer alternatives as they become better known and understood. This was well understood by the Commission, which, unlike the Court of Appeals, recognized that the Licensing Board's decision had to be judged by the information then available to it. And judged in that light we have little doubt the Board's actions were well within the proper bounds of its statutory authority. Not only did the record before the agency give every indication that the project was actually needed, but also there was nothing before the Board to indicate to the contrary.

We also think the court's criticism of the Commission's "threshold test" displays a lack of understanding of the historical setting within which the agency action took place and of the nature of the test itself. In the first place, while it is true that NEPA places upon an agency the obligation to consider every significant aspect of the environmental impact of a proposed action, it is still incumbent upon intervenors who wish to participate to structure their participation so that it is meaningful, so that it alerts the agency to the intervenors' position and contentions. This is especially true when the intervenors are requesting the agency to embark upon an exploration of unchartered territory, as was the question of energy conservation in the late 1960s and early 1970s. . . . Indeed, administrative proceedings should not be a game or a forum to engage in unjustified obstructionism by making cryptic and obscure reference to matters that "ought to be" considered and then, after failing to do more to bring the matter to the agency's attention, seeking to have that agency determination vacated on the ground that the agency failed to consider matters "forcefully presented." In fact, here the agency continually invited further clarification of Saginaw's contentions. Even without such clarification it indicated a willingness to receive evidence on the matters. But not only did Saginaw decline to further focus its contentions, it virtually declined to participate, indicating that it had "no conventional findings of fact to set forth" and that it had not "chosen to search the record and respond to this proceeding by submitting citations of matter which we believe were proved or disproved."

. . . The proposed plant underwent an incredibly extensive review. The reports filed and reviewed literally fill books. The proceedings took years, and the actual hearings themselves over two weeks. To then nullify that effort seven years later because one report refers to other problems, which problems admittedly have been discussed at length in other reports available to the public, borders on the Kafkaesque. . . . NEPA does set forth significant substantive goals for the Nation, but its mandate to the agencies is essentially procedural. See 42 U.S.C. § 4332. It is to insure a fully informed and well-considered decision, not necessarily a decision the judges of the Court of Appeals or of this Court would have reached had they been members of the decisionmaking unit of the agency. Administrative decisions should be set aside in this context, as in every other, only for substantial procedural or substantive reasons as mandated by statute, not simply because the court is unhappy with the result reached. And a single alleged oversight on a peripheral issue, urged by parties who never fully cooperated or indeed raised the issue below, must not be made the basis for overturning a decision properly made after an otherwise exhaustive proceeding.

NOTES AND QUESTIONS

1.   **Alternatives Analysis.** The requirement that agencies consider the alternatives to a proposed action in an EIS is contained in § 102(2)(C)(iii) of the Act. How is an agency to draw the line in determining what alternatives to consider under § 102(2)(C)(iii)? Section 1502.14 of the CEQ regulations requires that agencies must consider all "reasonable alternatives." 40 C.F.R. § 1502.14. How is an agency to determine whether an alternative is reasonable until such time as it has examined the alternative?

   Agencies must also consider alternatives under § 102(2)(E) of the Act, which extends the requirement to EAs. How do the two alternative-review provisions differ? Do you think that alternatives review in an EA should be more extensive than in an EIS, or less? EAs have grown increasingly detailed over time: recall that in *CBD v. NHTSA* the court rejected the alternatives assessment in an EA. Courts have typically treated the requirements under § 102(2)(C)(iii) and (E) as identical, however, despite the variations in their text. *See* Jeremy Suttenberg et al., *Unresolved Conflicts: How Revisiting NEPA Section 102(2)(E) Could Increase Efficiency, Simplify Government, and Save Taxpayers Money*, 18 N.Y.U. ENVTL. L.J. 156 (2010) (arguing that NEPA should require EISs to review a broader range of alternatives than in an EA, but with less depth).

2.   **Energy Conservation Alternative.** On what basis did the Court find that the AEC was not required to consider energy conservation alternatives? Does the court's holding stand for the proposition that the AEC is not required to consider any alternatives beyond its jurisdiction? Would the outcome of the case have differed had Saginaw expressly brought the issue of energy conservation to the AEC's attention prior to the completion of the EIS?

3.   **Evolving Alternatives.** What did Justice Rehnquist mean when he described the concept of alternatives as evolving? How did this play into the holding of the Court? Would you expect the outcome of this case to have differed if the EIS had been prepared after 1973? What if the case were to be re-litigated with respect to an EIS prepared in 2012?

4.   **No Action Alternative.** Section 1502.14(d) of the CEQ regulations requires that an agency consider the "no action" option as one of the alternatives. Under what circumstances should an agency be required to consider alternatives beyond the no action alternative? *See Citizens Against Burlington, Inc. v. Busey*, 938 F.2d 190 (D.C. Cir. 1991) (EIS conducted by

the Federal Aviation Administration acceptable even though it considered only two options: adding a cargo hub at the Toledo Airport or not undertaking the project at all), *cert. denied*, 502 U.S. 994 (1991).

5.   The "No Action" Alternative and Fossil Fuel Leasing. In a 2010 EIS for four large coal leases in the Powder River Basin, BLM reasoned that if it were to select the "no action" alternative (not leasing the coal), other coal mines in the country would increase production to entirely replace all 2 billion tons of coal anticipated from the leases. BLM, FINAL ENVIRONMENTAL IMPACT STATEMENT FOR THE WRIGHT AREA COAL LEASE APPLICATIONS, VOL. 1, at 4–141 (2010). As a result, it predicted that the amount of coal burned in the United States—and the resulting carbon dioxide and methane emissions—would be identical whether or not the leases were approved. *Id.*

In September 2017, the U.S. Court of Appeals for the 10th Circuit found BLM's "perfect substitution" assumption to be arbitrary and capricious, as it lacked support in the record and was contrary to basic economic principles of supply and demand, as well as the empirical state of knowledge concerning the U.S. coal market. *WildEarth Guardians v. U.S. Bureau of Land Mgmt.*, 870 F.3d 1222 (10th Cir. 2017). The leases at issue would have produced up to 230 million tons of coal per year—more than 20 percent of the total U.S. coal used for electricity in 2010. Plaintiffs argued that removing over 20 percent of total U.S. production would be a non-marginal change that would affect coal prices, demand, and greenhouse gas emissions. The Court agreed, holding that it was an "abuse of discretion to rely on an economic assumption [perfect substitution of coal], which contradicted basic economic principles, as the basis for distinguishing between the no action alternative and the preferred alternative." *WildEarth Guardians*, 870 F.3d at 1237–38. Do you agree with the 10th Circuit? What are the implications of this opinion?

Other federal agencies, including the Surface Transportation Board and the State Department, have more fully analyzed the effects of their energy management decisions in NEPA reviews, and have had those decisions upheld by federal courts. *See Mayo Found. v. Surface Transp. Bd.*, 472 F.3d 545, 555 (8th Cir. 2006); *Sierra Club v. Clinton*, 746 F. Supp. 2d 1025, 1046 (D. Minn. 2010).

Alaska v. Andrus

580 F.2d 465 (D.C. Cir. 1978).

■ Before BAZELON, CHIEF JUDGE, and LEVENTHAL and WILKEY, CIRCUIT JUDGES.

■ BAZELON, CHIEF JUDGE:

. . . On January 23, 1974, former President Nixon announced that as part of "Project Independence" he was directing the Secretary of the Interior "to increase the acreage leased on the Outer Continental Shelf [OCS] to 10 million acres beginning in 1975, more than tripling what had originally been planned." The President ordered the Secretary, in carrying out this directive, "to ensure that . . . environmental safeguards are observed." In addition, the President pointed out that there would be "no decision on leasing on the Outer Continental Shelf in the Atlantic and in the Gulf of Alaska until the Council on Environmental Quality (CEQ) completes its current environmental study of those areas."

The CEQ study to which the President referred was released on April 18, 1974. That study concluded that the environmental risks associated with OCS development varied from region to region but that of the regions studied, development in the Eastern Gulf of Alaska would post the *highest* level of environmental risks. Indeed, CEQ concluded that the "conditions in the Gulf of Alaska are more severe than the (oil and gas) industry has yet experienced anywhere in the world."

On October 18, DOI published a draft programmatic EIS analyzing the President's proposed acceleration of OCS leasing to 10 million acres per year. . . . [The programmatic EIS was submitted to EPA for review pursuant to § 309 of the CAA. Section 309 requires that the Administrator of EPA "review and comment in writing on the environmental impact" of those federal actions that relate to "duties and responsibilities granted pursuant to the CAA." If the Administrator should determine that a proposed action is environmentally "unsatisfactory," § 309(b) requires him to publish his determination and refer the matter to CEQ.] The statement, in EPA's view, had failed to address "key policy options and managerial issues pertaining to an accelerated OCS oil and gas leasing program." EPA was especially critical of the proposed inclusion of Alaskan OCS areas in the leasing schedule:

> The CEQ Task Force on the OCS, in which DOI participated, states that the petroleum industry would encounter a higher environmental risk in the development of the Gulf of Alaska than in any other area. DOI has not been able to demonstrate that the benefit in oil development outweighs the environmental cost. *In fact, DOI's own data . . . show conclusively that because of material constraints, there is no relative advantage to leasing Alaskan OCS areas at this time despite the magnitude of Alaska's reserves. EPA's position is therefore that leasing in Alaskan waters should not be considered at this time and that substantial technical and biological research is required.* Although we expect that as a result of that research, exploration and subsequent production will be feasible at some point in the future, EPA believes that the point cannot be predicted at this time. *In our opinion, it is therefore neither necessary nor prudent for Alaskan OCS areas to be placed on the leasing schedule at this time.* We think that the future decision should be based on (1) baseline and biological effects research, most of which has not been funded or planned at this time, (2) coastal zone planning, and (3) assessment of operating experience with advanced technologies which can be tested in other OCS areas. . . .

[DOI subsequently prepared a project specific EIS with respect to the proposal to lease parts of the Alaskan OCS. The project specific EIS was again submitted to EPA for review pursuant to § 309 of the CAA.]

On December 18, [1975,] the Administrator (having reviewed the project specific EIS) informed the Secretary that EPA had concluded that . . . the sale should be delayed in order to allow, inter alia, the completion of [further] environmental studies. Accordingly, under the terms of § 309(b), the Administrator referred the question of [the Alaskan OCS lease] to CEQ.

Following this § 309 referral, the [CEQ] . . . engaged in an "intensive review of the objections raised by Administrator Train. . . ." Based on this review, CEQ informed the Secretary that it agreed with EPA that "it would be most desirable, from an environmental point of view, to delay the sale. . . ."

On [February 17, 1976], the Secretary informed CEQ of his decision to proceed with the sale [of 1.1 million acres of Alaskan OCS] as scheduled. In response to the suggestions that the sale be delayed, the Secretary indicated that, in his "considered judgment,"

> delays of . . . (several years) in the lease sale would not gain us enough to be worth the cost in postponement of development of the resources. I am convinced that we already know what the major hazards are in oil and gas development of the Gulf of Alaska; further studies will refine that knowledge, but they are unlikely to change it fundamentally. . . .

. . . Appellants [argue] that the information available to the Secretary in April, 1976, was insufficient, as a matter of law, to permit a decision to proceed with the sale at that time. . . . [More particularly] [t]hey argue that even though the EIS may have been based on the best information available as of the date of its preparation, under NEPA the "best available information" may not be good enough. They contend that NEPA imposes on agencies affirmative information-gathering obligations; and until those obligations have been satisfactorily carried out—until, that is, sufficient data has been amassed "to provide a factual basis for responsible impact prediction or mitigation," Appt.'s Br. at 31— NEPA imposes an absolute bar to proceeding with a given project. *Id.* at 31–2.

Appellants conceded, of course, that these information-gathering obligations, like an agency's other NEPA obligations, are necessarily bounded by a "rule of reason;" but they contend that Interior's action here was clearly "unreasonable." They agree that agencies need not "wait forever to fathom the unfathomable, or arrive at definitive answers on questions far beyond the existing state of scientific or technological ability." Appt. Br. at 35. Where, however, the data deficiencies are substantial, and where the present level of scientific ability is adequate to cure those deficiencies within a reasonable period of time, appellants contend that those deficiencies *must* be rectified before the project may be allowed to proceed. Thus, in the present case, appellants argue that the Secretary really had no discretion to reject the suggestions of CEQ and others that the sale be delayed in order to allow further progress in the ongoing environmental research program. The data to be obtained from that additional research were, in appellants' view, an essential prerequisite to the Secretary's lease-sale decision.

As a preliminary matter, we note that NEPA does, unquestionably, impose on agencies an affirmative obligation to seek out information concerning the environmental consequences of proposed federal actions. Indeed, this is one of NEPA's most important functions. As this court has held, "the basic thrust of an agency's responsibilities under NEPA is to predict the environmental effects of proposed action before the action is taken and those effects fully known." *Scientists' Institute for Public Information, Inc. v. AEC (SIPI)*, 481 F.2d 1079, 1092 (1973). And prediction—or, at least, *informed* prediction—is only possible after an agency has conducted a thorough inquiry into all aspects of the contemplated project and the area to be affected.

Predictions, however, by their very nature, can never be perfect; and the information available to an agency could always be augmented. The question in each case is, "How much information is enough?" And that is not a question to which NEPA provides a clear, firm answer. Certainly, NEPA cannot be

> read as a requirement that *complete* information concerning the environmental impact of a project must be obtained before action may be taken. If we were to impose a requirement that an impact statement can never be prepared until *all* relevant environmental effects were known, it is doubtful that any project could ever be initiated.

[*Jicarilla Apache Tribe of Indians v. Morton*, 471 F.2d 1275, 1280 (9th Cir. 1973).]

Some element of "speculation" is "implicit in NEPA." And just as agencies may not be allowed "to shirk their responsibilities under NEPA by labeling any and all discussion of future environmental effects as 'crystal ball inquiry,'" so also agencies may not be precluded from proceeding with particular projects merely because the environmental effects of that project remain to some extent speculative. NEPA simply does not specify the quantum of information that must be in the hands of a decisionmaker before that decisionmaker may decide to proceed with a given project. Rather,

> NEPA was intended to ensure that decisions about federal actions would be made only after responsible decisionmakers had fully adverted to the environmental consequences of the actions, and had decided that the public benefits flowing from the actions outweighed their environmental costs.

[*Jones v. District of Columbia Redevelopment Land Agency*, 499 F.2d 502, 512 (1974).]

One of the costs that must be weighed by decisionmakers is the cost of uncertainty—*i.e.*, the costs of proceeding without more and better information. Where that cost *has* been considered, and where the responsible decisionmaker has decided that it is outweighed by the benefits of proceeding with the project without further delay, the courts may not substitute their judgment for that of the decisionmaker and insist that the project be delayed while more information is sought. *Kleppe v. Sierra Club*, 427 U.S. 390, 410 n. 21 (1976).

We thus hold that the Secretary was not required, as a matter of law, to await the results of the ongoing studies before deciding to proceed with the lease sale. Even though the "alternative of delay" was vigorously advocated by CEQ, EPA, and others, it is the Secretary of the Interior who has been charged by Congress with the responsibility for deciding whether, and when, to lease portions of the OCS; in making those decisions, the Secretary *did* have the discretion to reject the advice that had been offered to him. . . .

NOTES AND QUESTIONS

1. Affirmative Obligations. The *Andrus* court recognized that NEPA, "unquestionably, impose[s] on agencies an affirmative obligation to seek out information concerning the environmental consequences of proposed federal actions." 580 F.2d at 473. Why then did the court find that DOI need not conduct the further research deemed necessary by both EPA and CEQ?

2. How Much Information Is Enough? In determining how much information is adequate to inform an EIS, the *Andrus* court identified two competing policy concerns: that to permit agencies to proceed without adequate information would be to allow them to "shirk their responsibilities under NEPA," whereas to require agencies to obtain all relevant environmental information before proceeding with a project would be to significantly curtail their ability to perform their statutory duties. *Id.* Do you think the *Andrus* court's decision strikes an appropriate balance between these competing concerns?

3. Cost of Uncertainty. The *Andrus* court recognizes that "one of the costs that must be weighed by decisionmakers is the cost of uncertainty." 580 F.2d at 473. How might decisionmakers go about weighing this cost? In the *Andrus* decision, do you think DOI made an adequate attempt to weigh the cost of uncertainty? Should its evaluation have been afforded the degree of deference ultimately granted by the court, in light of the strenuous objections of both EPA and CEQ? For one approach to weighing uncertainty, see the discussion of option value and *Center for Sustainable Economy v. Jewell*, 779 F.3d 588 (D.C. Cir. 2015) in Chapter IX.

4. *Jicarilla Apache Tribe of Indians v. Morton.* In *Jicarilla Apache Tribe of Indians v. Morton*, 471 F.2d 1275 (9th Cir. 1973), the Ninth Circuit considered the adequacy of information relied upon by an agency in support of an EIS. In that case, appellants challenged a decision by DOI in connection with the construction of electric-generating facilities in the southwestern United States on the basis that the Secretary of the Interior had failed to consider adequate information in the preparation of the supporting EIS—namely, the views of the public concerning elements of the proposal. In reaching a conclusion similar to the *Andrus* court, the *Jicarilla* court held:

> . . . Neither § 102(2)(B) nor (C) can be read as a requirement that complete information concerning the environmental impact of a project must be obtained before action may be taken. If we were to impose a requirement that an impact statement can never be prepared until all relevant environmental effects were known, it is doubtful that any project could ever be initiated. While appellants here have limited their argument to one specific piece of information, that does not solve the larger problem. At any point in time, there are likely to be any number of studies underway concerning a host of environmental or other societal problems. What appellants seek is for this Court to substitute its judgment for that of the Secretary, who is charged by NEPA with preparing a thorough statement of the environmental consequences of a proposed project, as to what particular information will be required to complete that statement. We decline to assume that role.

Id. at 1280–81. In light of the *Andrus* and *Jicarilla Apache Tribe* decisions, when would a court invalidate an agency's EIS on the basis of inadequate information?

5. NEPA and Hurricane Katrina. It has been suggested that the requirement that an EIS contain adequate information may have played a part in the Hurricane Katrina disaster. Indeed, some argue that the levee system would have protected New Orleans if a NEPA lawsuit had not been brought in the 1970s. In 1976, an environmental organization and a group of fishermen sued the Army Corps of Engineers for allegedly preparing an inadequate EIS for part of a levee project in New Orleans. In 1977, a federal district court found the EIS inadequate in part due to the fact that the EIS was based on obsolete studies and that the biological analysis in the EIS relied on a single conversation between a member of the agency and a marine biologist. The court issued an injunction preventing further work on the levees until an adequate EIS was prepared. After the injunction, the Corps eventually decided to implement a different levee plan. *See* Douglas A. Kysar & Thomas O. McGarity, *Did NEPA Drown New Orleans? The Levees, the Blame Game, and the Hazards of Hindsight*, 56 DUKE L.J. 179 (2006). Kysar and McGarity convincingly argue that the original plan prevented by the NEPA litigation would not have prevented the catastrophe in New Orleans.

Sierra Club v. United States Army Corps of Engineers

701 F.2d 1011 (2d Cir. 1983).

■ Before OAKES, MESKILL, and KEARSE, CIRCUIT JUDGES.

■ KEARSE, CIRCUIT JUDGE:

[Plaintiffs challenged plans to construct a New York City highway known as "Westway," which was intended to replace the southernmost portion of the Westside Highway. Plaintiffs argued that the United States Army Corps of Engineers (Corps) violated NEPA, the CWA, and the Rivers and Harbors Act, by making inadequate investigations and disclosures regarding the impact of the related Westway landfill project on fisheries in the Hudson River. These complaints were premised upon information indicating the presence of a juvenile striped bass population in the Hudson River, which came to light during the preparation of the relevant EIS. The Corps, anxious to proceed with the development, did not prepare a supplemental EIS, despite the fact that EPA, Fisheries Service, and Wildlife Service (with whom the Corps was required to consult pursuant to provisions of the CWA) all raised concerns regarding the adequacy of the EIS in terms of its impact upon fisheries. In particular, information came to light suggesting that the proposed development would result in the loss of habitat for the local striped bass population. The District Court enjoined the project pending preparation of a supplemental EIS. The Corps appealed.]

. . . As the Supreme Court has stated repeatedly, although NEPA established " 'significant substantive goals for the Nation,' " the balancing of the substantive environmental issues is consigned to the judgment of the executive agencies involved, and the judicially reviewable duties that are imposed on the agencies are " 'essentially procedural.' " *Strycker's Bay Neighborhood Council, Inc. v. Karlen*, 444 U.S. 223, 227 (1980) (quoting *Vermont Yankee Nuclear Power Corp. v. Natural Resources Defense Council, Inc.*, 435 U.S. 519, 558 (1978) (*Vermont Yankee*)). "The only role for a court is to insure that the agency has taken a 'hard look' at environmental consequences; it cannot 'interject itself within the area of discretion of the executive as to the choice of the action to be taken.' " *Kleppe v. Sierra Club*, 427 U.S. 390, 410 n. 21 (1976) (quoting *Natural Resources Defense Council, Inc. v. Morton*, 458 F.2d 827, 838 (D.C.Cir.1972)). . . .

Given the role of the EIS and the narrow scope of permissible judicial review, the court may not rule an EIS inadequate if the agency has made an adequate compilation of relevant information, has analyzed it reasonably, has not ignored pertinent data, and has made disclosures to the public. . . .

In the present case the district court's rulings on the merits of plaintiffs' NEPA claims were consonant with the proper scope of its review and the proper view of the obligations imposed on [the Federal

Highway Administration (FHWA)] and the Corps. With respect to the fisheries issues, the court found, *inter alia*, that the [Final Environmental Impact Statement (FEIS)] contained false statements depicting the interpier region as "biologically impoverished" and as a "biological wasteland," when in fact the interpier area in winter harbored a concentration of juvenile striped bass. The court found that the FEIS statements regarding aquatic impact had not been compiled in "objective good faith." Notwithstanding [the New York State Department of Transport's (NYSDOT's)] contention that "the FEIS set forth the relevant facts that were known about the interpier area and the surrounding Hudson estuary at the time it was prepared . . . ," the court's findings to the contrary are amply supported by the record.

For example, after the [Draft Environmental Impact Statement (DEIS)] was issued, the Project received critical comments regarding fisheries impact from Fisheries Service, Wildlife Service, and EPA to the effect that the fish life had been underestimated and that the information provided was inadequate. Although the FEIS purported to respond to these comments, no new studies were performed, no additional information was collected, no further inquiry was made; and the FEIS essentially reiterated or adopted the statements in the DEIS. Employees of the Project and FHWA testified that they knew before getting any data from the Lawler study that the Project's 1973 sampling had been faulty in both timing and technique and that these flaws were the reason the earlier study had revealed virtually no fish in the interpier area. Yet the Water Report, prepared in the wake of comments to the DEIS and appended to the FEIS, simply relied on the 1973 data. [The project's Executive Director, Lowell K.] Bridwell, who was responsible for the preparation of the FEIS's fisheries discussion[,] testified that he was aware that the Water Report had not attempted to make any thorough or investigative inquiry into the existence of fish in the interpier area. He stated that the Water Report had attempted to verify only the existing literature on fish life in that area. It is not clear that even this academic study was performed: the Water Report neither identified any existing literature on the subject nor stated that there was no such literature; Bridwell himself was unaware of whether any literature existed. The evidence at trial suggested that there was no literature upon which the Report could have based its conclusion that the interpier area was biologically impoverished. . . .

In short, we concur in the district court's view that the FEIS did not reasonably adequately compile relevant information with respect to fisheries impact. The evidence as to the cavalier manner in which the Project had reached its conclusion that the interpier area was a biological wasteland, and as to FHWA's failure to make an independent evaluation or to react in any way to sister agencies' pointed comments that the draft EIS did not provide adequate information for a reasoned assessment of impact on fisheries, easily supports the district court's findings (1) that the FEIS's fisheries conclusions lacked a "substantial basis in fact," and (2) that a decisionmaker relying on the January 1977 EIS could not have fully considered and balanced the environmental factors. In the circumstances, we agree that FHWA's issuance of the FEIS, and the Corps's reliance on the FEIS, violated NEPA. . . .

. . . [T]he record revealed that the authors of the FEIS had not made an adequate compilation of fisheries data, had not compiled information in objective good faith, had paid no heed to the experts' warnings that they lacked needed information, and hence had reached the erroneous conclusion that the interpier area was a biological wasteland. This baseless and erroneous factual conclusion then became a false premise in the decision-makers' evaluations of the overall environmental impact of Westway and their balancing of the expected benefits of the proposed action against the risks of harm to the environment. Thus, the January 1977 EIS provided no valid "outward sign that environmental values and consequences [had] been considered" with respect to fisheries issues, *Andrus v. Sierra Club, supra*, 442 U.S. at 350, and hence furnished no assurance that the Westway approvals had been given on a reasoned basis.

Enforcement of NEPA requires that the responsible agencies be compelled to prepare a new EIS on those issues, based on adequately compiled information, analyzed in a reasonable fashion. Only if such a document is forthcoming can the public be appropriately informed and have any confidence that the decisionmakers have in fact considered the relevant factors and not merely swept difficult problems under the rug. Accordingly, we uphold the district court's requirement that before Westway landfill may proceed, FHWA or the Corps must prepare a new EIS on fisheries issues. . . .

Our ruling on this point is not, however, an expansive one. We do not intend to suggest that inaccuracies in an EIS will always, or even usually, warrant a court's ordering the preparation of a supplemental EIS. Had the January 1977 EIS contained a reasoned analysis of fisheries data reasonably adequately compiled, and merely drawn an erroneous factual conclusion, we would not believe it proper to order FHWA or the Corps to prepare a [Supplementary Environmental Impact Statement (SEIS)]. *See Hanly v. Kleindienst*, 471 F.2d 823 (2d Cir.1972), *cert. denied*, 412 U.S. 908 (1973). Or had reasonable investigative efforts resulted in less accurate data than later became available, the determination as to whether the later data warranted preparation of a SEIS, *see* 33 C.F.R. § 230.11(b) (1981); *see also* 33 C.F.R. § 209.410(g)(1) (1977); would be a matter committed to the discretion of the responsible agencies, not to the judgment of the court.

Nor do we express any view as to whether the decisionmakers' overall evaluation of the benefits and detriments of Westway was "wrong." We hold simply that a decision made in reliance on false information, developed without an effort in objective good faith to obtain accurate information, cannot be accepted as a "reasoned" decision.

NOTES AND QUESTIONS

1. **Supplemental EIS.** Why didn't the Corps simply prepare a supplemental EIS upon the information concerning the local striped bass population coming to light? The Corps does not possess expertise in evaluating the likely impact of a proposed action on fish populations. Why then, contrary to the express advice of EPA and the Fisheries Service (which do possess such expertise), would it have sought to commence the project without conducting further studies? Had the Corps prepared a supplemental EIS, and determined that the benefits of the proposal nevertheless outweighed the costs to the environment, would the plaintiffs have been successful in challenging the proposed action?

2. **New Information.** Does the holding in the *Westway* case stand for the proposition that an agency must go back and prepare a new study each time that it receives new information during the course of preparing an EIS? Under what circumstances does the Second Circuit find this necessary? What would be the consequences of requiring that a supplemental EIS be prepared each time that new information came to light?

3. **Demise of Westway.** Following *Sierra Club v. U.S. Army Corps of Engineers*, 701 F.2d 1011 (2d Cir. 1983), the Corps took steps to prepare a supplementary EIS (SEIS). Despite the Corps' District Engineer's recommendation that a nineteen-month, two-winter study be undertaken into fisheries impacts, the draft SEIS completed by the Corps was informed only by a four-month impact study. Notwithstanding the curtailed assessment, the draft SEIS found that the Westway project could have significant adverse impacts upon the striped bass fishery. More specifically, it concluded that "[i]t would . . . be imprudent to consider any such habitat loss as projected by the Westway landfill to be either minimal, insignificant, or sustainable at current population levels. Some measurable long-term reduction in the overall stock along with a reduced recovery rate would be a reasonable expectation." *Sierra Club v. U.S. Army Corps of Eng'rs*, 614 F. Supp. 1475, 1493 (S.D.N.Y. 1985). In stark contrast to this conclusion, however, the final SEIS issued by the Corps concluded that Westway would not have any significant adverse impacts upon the striped bass fishery, and the relevant permits were again issued.

NRDC again mounted a challenge in the federal courts, which culminated in the Second Circuit finding that the action of Corps in issuing the SEIS was "arbitrary and capricious" and that the accompanying permit grants were therefore unlawful. *See id.* The court's decision centered on the failure on the part of the Corps to account for the discrepancies between the draft SEIS and the final SEIS with respect to the impact of the proposal upon the striped bass fishery.

At the same time, the Westway project began to lose federal support:

New Jersey representatives, concerned that a Westway project might lead to denial of their own waterfront projects, persuaded colleagues to vote to cut off federal Westway landfill funds. Without such landfill funds, the Westway project, with its transportation, landfill, park and redevelopment components, would have had to be completely rethought and scaled back. Westway opponents also succeeded in defeating any change to an impending legislative deadline for a trade-in of interstate highway dollars. New York City now stood at risk of losing Westway and the alternative of federally funded, improved mass transit. Confronted with this difficult choice between long odds on a reversal of Judge Griesa's order and losing all federal dollars, Mayor Koch and Governor Cuomo surrendered, accepting the trade-in dollars.

A scaled down project called Hudson River Park, combined with a more rudimentary highway resurfacing, is now underway in the area. This Park, too, has engendered citizen opposition and regulatory skirmishing, but no court litigation has been filed attacking it for failure to prepare any EIS. Its prospects hinge largely on finding government and private funding to build paths, refurbish piers, and build a smaller scale river-edge park.

William W. Buzbee, *The Regulatory Fragmentation Continuum, Westway and the Challenges of Regional Growth*, 21 J.L. & POL. 323, 339–40 (2005).

As the preceding account demonstrates, the delay caused by litigation under NEPA ultimately killed the Westway project. In many instances, NEPA is harnessed strategically by opponents to a proposal as a technique to force delay. How could such strategic behavior be curtailed?

Marsh v. Oregon Natural Resources Council
490 U.S. 360 (1989).

■ JUSTICE STEVENS delivered the opinion for a unanimous Court:

[The Corps released an EIS in 1971 and a supplemental EIS in 1980 for a dam project on the Rogue River Basin in southwest Oregon. After construction on the dam began, the Corps rejected undertaking a further supplemental EIS, despite new information becoming available (in the form of a memorandum prepared by biologists from the Oregon Department of Fish and Wildlife (ODFW)) suggesting that the Corps may have underestimated the environmental impact of the dam upon downstream fisheries and turbidity. Instead, the Corps prepared a Supplemental Information Report (SIR) with respect to the memorandum, concluding that ". . . this information . . . does not require additional NEPA documentation." The district court upheld this claim but the Court of Appeals reversed, concluding that the new information was significant and that the Corps failed to evaluate it with significant care.]

. . . The subject of postdecision supplemental environmental impact statements is not expressly addressed in NEPA. Preparation of such statements, however, is at times necessary to satisfy the Act's "action-forcing" purpose. NEPA does not work by mandating that agencies achieve particular substantive environmental results. Rather, NEPA promotes its sweeping commitment to "prevent or eliminate damage to the environment and biosphere" by focusing Government and public attention on the environmental effects of proposed agency action. 42 U.S.C. § 4321. By so focusing agency attention, NEPA ensures that the agency will not act on incomplete information, only to regret its decision after it is too late to correct. Similarly, the broad dissemination of information mandated by NEPA permits the public and other government agencies to react to the effects of a proposed action at a meaningful time. It would be incongruous with this approach to environmental protection, and with the Act's manifest concern with preventing uninformed action, for the blinders to adverse environmental effects, once unequivocally removed, to be restored prior to the completion of agency action simply because the relevant proposal has received initial approval. As we explained in *TVA v. Hill*, 437 U.S. 153, 188, n. 34 (1978), although "it would make sense to hold NEPA inapplicable at some point in the life of a project, because the agency would no longer have a meaningful opportunity to *weigh* the benefits of the project versus the detrimental effects on the environment," up to that point, "NEPA cases have generally required agencies to file environmental impact statements when the remaining governmental action would be environmentally 'significant.'"

. . . [A]n agency need not supplement an EIS every time new information comes to light after the EIS is finalized. To require otherwise would render agency decisionmaking intractable, always awaiting updated information only to find the new information outdated by the time a decision is made. On the other hand, and as [the Corps] concedes, NEPA does require that agencies take a "hard look" at the environmental effects of their planned action, even after a proposal has received initial approval. Application of the "rule of reason" thus turns on the value of the new information to the still pending decisionmaking process. In this respect the decision whether to prepare a supplemental EIS is similar to the decision whether to prepare an EIS in the first instance: If there remains "major Federal actio[n]" to occur, and if the new information is sufficient to show that the remaining action will "affec[t] the quality of the human environment" in a significant manner or to a significant extent not already considered, a supplemental EIS must be prepared. Cf. 42 U.S.C. § 4332(2)(C).

The parties disagree, however, on the standard that should be applied by a court that is asked to review the agency's decision. [The government] argue[s] that the reviewing court need only decide whether the agency decision was "arbitrary and capricious," whereas respondents argue that the reviewing court must make its own determination of reasonableness to ascertain whether the agency action complied with the law. . . .

. . . Because analysis of the relevant documents "requires a high level of technical expertise," we must defer to "the informed discretion of the responsible federal agencies." *Kleppe v. Sierra Club*, 427 U.S. 390, 412 (1976). Under these circumstances, we cannot accept respondents' supposition that review is of a legal question and that the Corps' decision "deserves no deference." Accordingly, as long as the Corps' decision not to supplement the FEIS[ ] was not "arbitrary or capricious," it should not be set aside.

. . . When specialists express conflicting views, an agency must have discretion to rely on the reasonable opinions of its own qualified experts even if, as an original matter, a court might find contrary views more persuasive. On the other hand, in the context of reviewing a decision not to supplement an EIS, courts should not automatically defer to the agency's express reliance on an interest in finality without carefully reviewing the record and satisfying themselves that the agency has made a reasoned decision based on its evaluation of the significance—or lack of significance—of the new information. A contrary approach would not simply render judicial review generally meaningless, but would be contrary to the demand that courts ensure that agency decisions are founded on a reasoned evaluation "of the relevant factors."

. . . [R]egardless of its eventual assessment of the significance of this information, the Corps had a duty to take a hard look at the proffered evidence. However, having done so and having determined based on careful scientific analysis that the new information was of exaggerated importance, the Corps acted within the dictates of NEPA in concluding that supplementation was unnecessary. Even if another decisionmaker might have reached a contrary result, it was surely not "a clear error of judgment" for the Corps to have found that the new and accurate information contained in the documents was not significant and that the significant information was not new and accurate. As the SIR demonstrates, the Corps conducted a reasoned evaluation of the relevant information and reached a decision that, although perhaps disputable, was not "arbitrary or capricious." . . .

NOTES AND QUESTIONS

1.   **New Information and Supplemental EISs.** Given the fact that the ODFW memorandum was available prior to the completion of the project, why didn't the *Marsh* Court hold that the new information required the preparation of a supplemental EIS? How is an agency to determine the significance of new information without conducting a supplemental EIS? Under what circumstances would the preparation of a supplemental EIS have been required? Would the *Marsh* Court's decision have differed if it had considered the ODFW memorandum to be more compelling?

2.   **New Information: Before and After the Commencement of Federal Actions.** Compare the decision of the *Marsh* Court (in which new information arose after the Corps had commenced the federal action in

question) with the decision of the *Westway* court (in which new information arose prior to the commencement of the federal action). Are there substantive differences in the approaches of the courts in determining an agency's obligation to consider new information arising before and after the commencement of a federal action? Is the only difference between the cases the "significance" of the new information?

3.   **Role of the Courts.** The *Marsh* Court deferred to the Corps in part because of the high level of technical expertise of its members. 490 U.S. at 377 (finding that where "analysis of the relevant documents requires a high level of technical expertise," the Court should defer to the discretion of the agency (internal quotations omitted)). Is it likely that the Corps would possess the expertise necessary to adequately evaluate the memorandum prepared by the biologists at the ODFW? Is it appropriate then that the Court adopt such a deferential approach?

4.   **Requirement That Agencies "Take a Hard Look."** The *Marsh* Court recognized that NEPA requires "that agencies take a 'hard look' at the environmental effects of their planned action, even after a proposal has received initial approval." 490 U.S. at 368. What does this mean?

In *Marble Mountain Audubon Society v. Rice*, 914 F.2d 179 (9th Cir. 1990), the Ninth Circuit held that a final EIS prepared by the Forest Service, calling for the salvage and harvest of timber in an area ravaged by a forest fire, was inadequate on the basis that it did not take a "hard look" at the impact of selected alternatives on a biological corridor connecting two wilderness areas. Specifically, the court found that the Forest Service's conclusion that the preservation of the biological corridor in question would be sufficient was "without any apparent study or supporting documentation" in the EIS. *Id.* at 182.

Similarly, in *Center for Biological Diversity v. U.S. Forest Service*, 349 F.3d 1157, 1165 (9th Cir. 2003), the Ninth Circuit held that the Forest Service had failed to take a "hard look" at pertinent scientific studies (concerning the Northern Goshawk) in reaching its position with respect to a Forest Land and Management Plan for the Southwest Region of the United States. More specifically, "[b]ecause the commenters' evidence and opinions directly challenge the scientific basis upon which the Final EIS rests and which is central to it, we hold that Appellees were required to disclose and respond to such viewpoints in the final impact statement itself." *Id.* at 1167; *see also Pit River Tribe v. U.S. Forest Serv.*, 469 F.3d 768 (9th Cir. 2006) (Bureau of Land Management and U.S. Forest Service were found to have violated NEPA by failing to take a "hard look" at the environmental consequences of extending leases to a power company in California); *Barnes v. U.S. Dep't of Transp.*, 655 F.3d 1124, 1138 (9th Cir. 2011) (holding that the agencies failed to take the required "hard look" at the indirect effects of a proposed airport expansion).

5.   **Rule of Reason.** The *Marsh* Court makes specific reference to the "rule of reason." 490 U.S. at 363. What role is the rule playing in this case? Is the rule of reason consistent with the provisions of the statute? Is the *Marsh*

Court's application of this principle consistent with the approach of the other decisions in this section?

F. PROPOSALS FOR LEGISLATION AND EIS

Preparation of an EIS is required not only when an agency conducts a major federal action, but when an agency makes a "proposal[ ] for legislation . . . significantly affecting the quality of the human environment." 42 U.S.C. § 4332(2)(C). The CEQ regulations define what counts as a "proposal" for the purposes of § 102(2)(C). First, they define legislation to mean "a bill or legislative proposal to Congress developed by or with the significant cooperation and support of a Federal Agency." 40 C.F.R. § 1508.17. Second, they direct that significant cooperation should be determined by reference to "whether the proposal is in fact predominantly that of the agency rather than another source. Drafting does not by itself constitute significant cooperation." *Id.* As discussed in the notes and questions below, because congressional lawmaking does not always follow a well defined path, it is not always clear in what circumstances a proposal for legislation is "predominantly that of an Agency."

The preparation of EISs in connection with proposals for legislation are rare. One example in the early 1990s involved the North American Free Trade Agreement (NAFTA). In 1992, the United States, Mexico, and Canada reached an agreement to provide a free trade zone in North America through NAFTA. The Office of the United States Trade Representative (OTR) drafted the legislation without preparing an EIS. Public Citizen first sued the OTR to compel the preparation of an EIS in 1991 while NAFTA was still being negotiated. Given that NEPA does not create a private right of action, Public Citizen filed suit under the APA—a necessary precondition of which being that the agency action in question must constitute a "final agency action." 5 U.S.C. § 704. At the time of the first challenge by Public Citizen, the D.C. Circuit ruled that there was no final action upon which to base jurisdiction under the APA because NAFTA was still being negotiated. *Public Citizen v. Office of the U.S. Trade Representative*, 970 F.2d 916 (D.C. Cir. 1992), *cert. denied*, 510 U.S. 1041 (1994). Public Citizen again sued OTR after the President signed and released a final draft of NAFTA. The case again turned on whether this constituted a "final agency action" for the purposes of the APA.

Public Citizen v. United States
Trade Representative

5 F.3d 549 (D.C. Cir. 1993), *cert. denied*, 510 U.S. 1041 (1994).

■ Before MIKVA, CHIEF JUDGE, and WALD and RANDOLPH, CIRCUIT JUDGES.

■ MIKVA, CHIEF JUDGE:

Appellees Public Citizen, Friends of the Earth, Inc., and the Sierra Club (collectively "Public Citizen") sued the Office of the United States Trade Representative, claiming that an environmental impact statement was required for [NAFTA]. The district court granted Public Citizen's motion for summary judgment and ordered that an impact statement be prepared "forthwith." In its appeal of that ruling, the government contends that the Trade Representative's preparation of NAFTA without an impact statement is not "final agency action" under the Administrative Procedure Act (APA) and therefore is not reviewable by this court. Because we conclude that NAFTA is not "final agency action" under the APA, we reverse the decision of the district court and express no view on the government's other contentions.

In 1990, the United States, Mexico, and Canada initiated negotiations on [NAFTA]. NAFTA creates a "free trade zone" encompassing the three countries by eliminating or reducing tariffs and "non-tariff" barriers to trade on thousands of items of commerce. After two years of negotiations, the leaders of the three countries signed the agreement on December 17, 1992. NAFTA has not yet been transmitted to Congress. If approved by Congress, NAFTA is scheduled to take effect on January 1, 1994.

Negotiations on behalf of the United States were conducted primarily by [OTR]. OTR, located "within the Executive Office of the President," 19 U.S.C. § 2171(a) ("Trade Act of 1974" or "Trade Acts"), is the United States' chief negotiator for trade matters. OTR "report[s] directly to the President and the Congress, and [is] responsible to the President and the Congress for the administration of trade agreements . . ." *Id.* § (c)(1)(B).

Under the Trade Acts and congressional rules, NAFTA is entitled to "fast-track" enactment procedures which provide that Congress must vote on the agreement, without amendment, within ninety legislative days after transmittal by the President. The current version of NAFTA, once submitted, will therefore be identical to the version on which Congress will vote. President Clinton has indicated, however, that he will not submit NAFTA to Congress until negotiations have been completed on several side agreements regarding, among other things, compliance with environmental laws. . . .

The National Environmental Policy Act ("NEPA") requires federal agencies to include an EIS "in every recommendation or report on proposals for legislation and other major Federal actions significantly affecting the quality of the human environment. . . ." 42 U.S.C. § 4332(2)(C). In drafting NEPA, however, Congress did not create a private right of action. Accordingly, Public Citizen must rest its claim for judicial review on the Administrative Procedure Act. Section 702 of the APA confers an action for injunctive relief on persons "adversely affected or aggrieved by agency action within the meaning of a relevant statute." 5 U.S.C. § 702; *see Public Citizen I*, 970 F.2d at 918. Section 704, however, allows review only of "*final* agency action." 5 U.S.C. § 704 (emphasis added); *see Lujan v. National Wildlife Fed'n*, 497 U.S. 871, 882 (1990). The central question in this appeal then is whether Public Citizen has identified some agency action that is final upon which to base APA review.

[The Court then examines the Supreme Court decision of *Franklin v. Massachusetts*, 505 U.S. 788 (1992). In that case, the Supreme Court held that it could not review the method used by the Secretary of Commerce to calculate the 1990 census under the APA, on the basis that the final action under the reapportionment statute (being the transmittal of the apportionment to Congress) was that of the President, and the President is not an agency.]

. . . Even though the OTR has completed negotiations on NAFTA, the agreement will have no effect on Public Citizen's members unless and until the President submits it to Congress. Like the reapportionment statute in *Franklin*, the Trade Acts involve the President at the final stage of the process by providing for him to submit to Congress the final legal text of the agreement, a draft of the implementing legislation, and supporting information. 19 U.S.C. § 2903(a)(1)(B). The President is not obligated to submit any agreement to Congress, and until he does there is no final action. If and when the agreement is submitted to Congress, it will be the result of action by the President, action clearly not reviewable under the APA.

The district court attempts to distinguish *Franklin* by noting that unlike the census report (which the President was authorized to amend before submitting to Congress), NAFTA is no longer a "moving target" because the "final product . . . will not be changed before submission to Congress." 822 F. Supp. at 26. The district court goes on to say that NAFTA "shall" be submitted to Congress. *Id.* This distinction is unpersuasive. NAFTA is just as much a "moving target" as the census report in *Franklin* because in both cases the President has statutory discretion to exercise supervisory power over the agency's action. It is completely within the President's discretion, for example, to renegotiate portions of NAFTA before submitting it to Congress or to refuse to submit the agreement at all. In fact, President Clinton has conditioned the submission of NAFTA on the successful negotiation of side agreements on the environment, labor, and import surges. The President's position that the version of NAFTA negotiated by the OTR is the one that he "will" submit to Congress is irrelevant under *Franklin*. . . .

. . . Public Citizen argues that applying *Franklin* in this case would effectively nullify NEPA's EIS requirement because often "some other step must be taken before" otherwise final agency actions will result in environmental harm. Public Citizen Br. at 43. In support of this position, it catalogs a number of cases in which courts have reviewed NEPA challenges to agency actions that require the involvement of some other governmental or private entity before becoming final. Public Citizen Br. at 40–44. Although we acknowledge the stringency of *Franklin*'s "direct effect" requirement, we disagree that it represents the death knell of the legislative EIS. *Franklin* is limited to those cases in which the President has final constitutional or statutory responsibility for the final step necessary for the agency action directly to affect the parties. Moreover, *Franklin* notes explicitly the importance of the President's role in the "integrity of the process" at issue. *Franklin*, 505 U.S. at 800. Congress involved the President and the Secretary of Commerce in the reapportionment process to avoid stalemates resulting from congressional battles over the method for calculating reapportionment. *Id.* at 791–92. Similarly, the requirement that the President, and not OTR, initiate trade negotiations and submit trade agreements and their implementing legislation to Congress indicates that Congress deemed the President's involvement essential to the integrity of international trade negotiations. When the President's role is not essential to the integrity of the process, however, APA review of otherwise final agency actions may well be available. . . .

In sum, under the reasoning and language of *Franklin v. Massachusetts,* the "final agency action" challenged in this case is the submission of NAFTA to Congress by the President. Because the Trade Acts vest in the President the discretion to renegotiate NAFTA before submitting it to Congress or to refuse to submit it at all, his action, and not that of the OTR, will directly affect Public Citizen's members. The President's actions are not "agency action" and thus cannot be reviewed under the APA. The district court's grant of summary judgment in favor of Public Citizen is, therefore, Reversed.

■ RANDOLPH, CIRCUIT JUDGE, concurring:

I agree with my colleagues that the injunction against the United States Trade Representative must be set aside. . . .

. . . But I get a bit concerned when the opinion announces that it is too early to toll the bell for judicial review in a "legislative EIS" case and then starts trying to limit *Franklin* (maj. op. at 552–53). The idea behind this is that proposing legislation to Congress can constitute "final . . . action," and that when an "agency" rather than the President does the proposing, § 704 of the APA will be satisfied (maj. op. at 552–53). I am not so sure. *Franklin* held not only that the President is outside the APA's definition of "agency," but also that "action" cannot be considered "final" under the APA unless it "will directly affect the parties." 505 U.S. at 796–97. When the alleged "action" consists of a *proposal* for legislation, how can this condition for judicial review be satisfied? In *Franklin*, the President's submission to Congress directly affected the parties because, under the "automatic reapportionment statute," congressional action was not required. 505 U.S. at 792. In general, however, it is difficult to see how the act of proposing legislation could generate direct effects on parties, or anyone else for that matter. The head of an independent agency, a member of the President's Cabinet, or the President himself may send a letter to the Speaker of the House and the President of the Senate transmitting a draft of proposed legislation. Such "executive communications" are commonplace. *See* HOW OUR LAWS ARE MADE, H.R.DOC. NO. 139, 101st Cong., 2d Sess. 4 (1989). Yet only a Member of Congress may introduce a bill embodying the proposal, and even then no one will be affected, directly or otherwise, unless and until Congress passes the bill and the President signs it into law. If one takes *Franklin* at its word, a legislative proposal's lack of any direct effects would seem to mean that there can be no final action sufficient to permit judicial review under the APA. Of course, there is a big difference between saying that APA review is unavailable and saying that officials do not have to comply with NEPA when they suggest legislation. If Congress believed an agency had not lived up to its obligation to prepare an impact statement, it could always refuse to consider the agency's proposal. Or, if Congress wanted to evaluate environmental impacts before putting the measure to a vote, congressional committees could hold hearings on the subject. This is how a large proportion of legislative proposals already must be treated. NEPA's impact statement requirement applies only to federal agencies. Members of Congress, who alone introduce bills and offer amendments, are not covered. Neither are private individuals, corporations, labor unions, citizen groups or other organizations, all of which frequently avail themselves of their First Amendment right to petition the government.

I am therefore not prepared to say whether in NEPA cases, the act of proposing legislation constitutes final action under § 704 of the APA, as *Franklin* has interpreted that provision. This is a troublesome question, bound to arise in future cases, and we should not stake out a position on it here. The nub of the problem is that judicial review under the APA demands "final agency action" whereas the duty to prepare an impact statement arises earlier. The main objective of an impact statement is to ensure that the decisionmaker considers environmental effects prior to taking action. This is why in *Kleppe v. Sierra Club*, 427 U.S. 390, 406 n.15 (1976), the Court—without mentioning § 704 of the APA—identified the "time at which a court enters the process" to be "when the report or recommendation on the proposal is made, and someone protests either the absence or the adequacy of the final impact statement." *Franklin*'s direct-effects-on-the-parties test, as applied to NEPA suits, may have to be reconciled with the portion of *Kleppe v.*

Sierra Club just quoted. But there is no need to make the attempt in this case. It is enough to hold that regardless of whether the President's submission of NAFTA to Congress would be final action, there is no "final" action that can be attributed to an "agency."

NOTES AND QUESTIONS

1. **NAFTA.** What was the sequence of events that led to the passage of NAFTA? Who first drafted the proposal for NAFTA? What happened next? Who ultimately submitted NAFTA to Congress? Is this a typical sequence of events in giving effect to international agreements? What was the significance of this sequence in the decisions of Chief Judge Mikva and Judge Randolph?

2. **Final Agency Action.** To determine whether an agency action is final, for the purpose of the APA, "[t]he core question is whether the agency has completed its decisionmaking process, *and* whether the result of that process is one that will directly affect the parties." *Franklin v. Massachusetts*, 505 U.S. 788, 797 (1992) (emphasis added).

On what basis did Chief Judge Mikva hold that OTR's preparation of NAFTA did not constitute a final agency action for the purposes of the APA? Would Chief Judge Mikva regard the President's action in sending NAFTA to Congress as a final agency action? Why was the President not required to prepare an EIS for that action?

3. **"Death Knell of the Legislative EIS"?** In what way did Chief Judge Mikva find the OTR's actions with respect to NAFTA to differ from other proposals for legislation? On what basis did Chief Judge Mikva claim that the *Public Citizen* case should not be taken to "represent the death knell of the legislative EIS"? Do you agree?

4. **"Direct Effect."** Contrast the opinion of Chief Judge Mikva with the concurring opinion of Judge Randolph. On what basis does Judge Randolph take issue with Chief Judge Mikva's handling of the *Franklin* decision? In what circumstances, if any, would Judge Randolph recognize a direct effect following a proposal for legislation by an agency? What then are the consequences of Judge Randolph's opinion on parties seeking review of an agency's treatment of legislative proposals under NEPA?

Consider a proposal sent by EPA to Congress to amend key provisions of the CAA. Could this proposal, according to the opinion of Judge Randolph, ever constitute a final agency action for the purposes of the APA? Could it ever be taken to directly affect the parties? If not, why? What position would Chief Judge Mikva adopt? With whom do you agree?

5. **Non-Reviewable Obligations.** How convincing do you find Judge Randolph's conclusion that there exists a "big difference between saying that APA review is unavailable and saying that officials do not have to comply with NEPA when they suggest legislation"? *Public Citizen*, 5 F.3d at 554 (Randolph, J., concurring). If judicial review were not available, are there any other ways that an agency could be compelled to comply with the terms of NEPA? Are there other examples of non-reviewable agency obligations?

6.   Executive Order 13,141. On November 16, 1999, President Clinton issued an executive order that provides for environmental review of trade agreements. Exec. Order No. 13,141, 64 Fed. Reg. 63,169 (1999). The Executive Order requires that the OTR conduct environmental reviews (comparable in scope and character to an EIS under NEPA) for all comprehensive multilateral trade rounds, bilateral or plurilateral free trade agreements, and major new trade liberalization agreements in natural resource sectors. The Executive Order does not, however, give rise to a private right of action pursuable in the courts. What is the significance of the Executive Order? Does it add anything beyond the express terms of NEPA?

G.   LIMITS ON NEPA

At first glance, NEPA's procedural mandate appears broad—applying, "to the fullest extent possible," to all "proposals for legislation and major federal actions" that significantly affect the human environment. 42 U.S.C. § 4332(2)(C). Early judicial pronouncements, such as *Calvert Cliffs' Coordinating Committee, Inc. v. U.S. Atomic Energy Commission*, 449 F.2d 1109 (D.C. Cir. 1971) (discussed in Section A), sought to give effect to the Act's provisions, by holding that this language requires absolute compliance with NEPA unless there exists "clear conflict" of statutory authority. *Id.* at 1115. In more recent times, however, a combination of judicial decisions, congressional intervention and regulations promulgated by the CEQ have cumulatively served to curtail NEPA's reach.

The first of the cases excerpted below, *Department of Transportation v. Public Citizen*, 541 U.S. 752 (2004), falls within the first of these categories of limitations. It concerns an agency's obligation to prepare an EIS with respect to nondiscretionary duties. The second case, *Merrell v. Thomas*, 807 F.2d 776 (9th Cir. 1986), *cert. denied*, 484 U.S. 848 (1987), examines the second category—and more particularly, the circumstances in which Congress can be taken to have passed legislation in direct conflict with NEPA. The notes and questions that follow the cases examine the third category—the manner in which the CEQ regulations limit the operation of the Act.

Department of Transportation v. Public Citizen
541 U.S. 752 (2004).

■ JUSTICE THOMAS delivered the opinion for a unanimous Court:

[Respondents challenged the failure on the part of the Federal Motor Carrier Safety Administration (FMCSA) to prepare an EIS with respect to the passage of regulations allowing Mexican trucks to operate in the United States. The passage of the regulations followed a decision by the President to lift a moratorium on Mexican trucks operating within the United States, on the basis that it contravened NAFTA. FMCSA prepared an EA on the regulations but did not consider the environmental effects of additional Mexican trade volume with Mexico because it concluded that any such increase would result from the President's lifting of the moratorium, not from the adoption of the regulations.]

. . . [R]espondents have only one complaint with respect to the EA: It did not take into account the environmental effects of increased cross-border operations of Mexican motor carriers. Respondents' argument that FMCSA was required to consider these effects is simple. Under § 350, FMCSA is barred from expending any funds to process or review any applications by Mexican motor carriers until FMCSA implemented a variety of specific application and safety-monitoring requirements for Mexican carriers. This expenditure bar makes it impossible for any Mexican motor carrier to receive authorization to operate within the United States until FMCSA issued the regulations challenged here. The promulgation of the regulations, the argument goes, would "caus[e]" the entry of Mexican trucks (and hence also cause any emissions such trucks would produce), and the entry of the trucks is "reasonably foreseeable." 40 CFR § 1508.8 (2003). Thus, the argument concludes, under the relevant CEQ regulations, FMCSA must take these emissions into account in its EA when evaluating whether to produce an EIS.

Respondents' argument, however, overlooks a critical feature of this case: FMCSA has no ability to countermand the President's lifting of the moratorium or otherwise categorically to exclude Mexican motor carriers from operating within the United States. To be sure, § 350 did restrict the ability of FMCSA to authorize cross-border operations of Mexican motor carriers, but Congress did not otherwise modify FMCSA's statutory mandates. In particular, FMCSA remains subject to the mandate of 49 U.S.C. § 13902(a)(1), that FMCSA "*shall* register a person to provide transportation . . . as a motor carrier if [it] finds that the person is willing and able to comply with" the safety and financial responsibility requirements established by DOT. (Emphasis added.) Under FMCSA's entirely reasonable reading of this provision, it must certify *any* motor carrier that can show that it is willing and able to comply with the various substantive requirements for safety and financial responsibility contained in DOT regulations; only the moratorium prevented it from doing so for Mexican motor carriers before 2001. App. 51–55. Thus, upon the lifting of the moratorium, if FMCSA refused to authorize a Mexican motor carrier for cross-border services, where the Mexican motor carrier was willing and able to comply with the various substantive safety and financial responsibilities rules, it would violate § 13902(a)(1).

If it were truly impossible for FMCSA to comply with both § 350 and § 13902(a)(1), then we would be presented with an irreconcilable conflict of laws. As the later enacted provision, § 350 would quite possibly win out. See *Posadas v. National City Bank*, 296 U.S. 497, 503 (1936). But FMCSA can easily satisfy both mandates: It can issue the application and safety inspection rules required by § 350, and start processing applications by Mexican motor carriers and authorize those that satisfy § 13902(a)(1)'s conditions. Without a conflict, then, FMCSA must comply with all of its statutory mandates.

Respondents must rest, then, on a particularly unyielding variation of "but for" causation, where an agency's action is considered a cause of an environmental effect even when the agency has no authority to prevent the effect. However, a "but for" causal relationship is insufficient to make an agency responsible for a particular effect under NEPA and the relevant regulations. As this Court held in *Metropolitan Edison Co. v. People Against Nuclear Energy*, 460 U.S. 766, 774 (1983), NEPA requires "a reasonably close causal relationship" between the environmental effect and the alleged cause. The Court analogized this requirement to the "familiar doctrine of proximate cause from tort law." *Ibid.* In particular, "courts must look to the underlying policies or legislative intent in order to draw a manageable line between those causal changes that may make an actor responsible for an effect and those that do not." *Id.*, at 774, n. 7. See also W. Keeton, D. Dobbs, R. Keeton & D. Owen, Prosser and Keeton on Law of Torts 264, 274–275 (5th ed.1984) (proximate cause analysis turns on policy considerations and considerations of the "legal responsibility" of actors).

Also, inherent in NEPA and its implementing regulations is a " 'rule of reason,' " which ensures that agencies determine whether and to what extent to prepare an EIS based on the usefulness of any new potential information to the decisionmaking process. See *Marsh*, 490 U.S., at 373–374. Where the preparation of an EIS would serve "no purpose" in light of NEPA's regulatory scheme as a whole, no rule of reason worthy of that title would require an agency to prepare an EIS. See *Aberdeen & Rockfish R. Co. v. Students Challenging Regulatory Agency Procedures (SCRAP)*, 422 U.S. 289, 325 (1975); see also 40 CFR §§ 1500.1(b)–(c) (2003).

In these circumstances, the underlying policies behind NEPA and Congress' intent, as informed by the "rule of reason," make clear that the causal connection between FMCSA's issuance of the proposed regulations and the entry of the Mexican trucks is insufficient to make FMCSA responsible under NEPA to consider the environmental effects of the entry. The NEPA EIS requirement serves two purposes. First, "[i]t ensures that the agency, in reaching its decision, will have available, and will carefully consider, detailed information concerning significant environmental impacts." *Robertson*, 490 U.S., at 349. Second, it "guarantees that the relevant information will be made available to the larger audience that may also play a role in both the decisionmaking process and the implementation of that decision." *Ibid.* Requiring FMCSA to consider the environmental effects of the entry of Mexican trucks would fulfill neither of these statutory purposes. Since FMCSA has no ability categorically to prevent the cross-border operations of Mexican motor carriers, the environmental impact of the cross-border operations would have no effect on FMCSA's decisionmaking—FMCSA simply lacks the power to act on whatever information might be contained in the EIS.

Similarly, the informational purpose is not served. The "informational role" of an EIS is to "giv[e] the public the assurance that the agency 'has indeed considered environmental concerns in its decisionmaking process,' *Baltimore Gas & Electric Co. [v. Natural Resources Defense Council, Inc.*, 462 U.S. 87, 97 (1983)], and, perhaps more significantly, provid[e] a springboard for public comment" in the agency decisionmaking process itself, *ibid.* The purpose here is to ensure that the "larger audience," *ibid.*, can provide input as necessary to the agency making the relevant decisions. See 40 CFR § 1500.1(c) (2003) ("NEPA's purpose is not to generate paperwork—even excellent paperwork—but to foster excellent action. The NEPA process is intended to help public officials make decisions that are based on understanding of environmental consequences, and take actions that protect, restore, and enhance the environment"); § 1502.1 ("The primary purpose of an environmental impact statement is to serve as an action-forcing device to insure that the policies and goals defined in the Act are infused into the ongoing programs and actions of the Federal Government"). But here, the "larger audience" can have no impact on FMCSA's decisionmaking, since, as just noted, FMCSA simply could not act on whatever input this "larger audience" could provide.

It would not, therefore, satisfy NEPA's "rule of reason" to require an agency to prepare a full EIS due to the environmental impact of an action it could not refuse to perform. Put another way, the legally relevant cause of the entry of the Mexican trucks is *not* FMCSA's action, but instead the actions of the President in lifting the moratorium and those of Congress in granting the President this authority while simultaneously limiting FMCSA's discretion.

NOTES AND QUESTIONS

1. **Major Federal Action.** Was it the *Department of Transportation* Court's position that the FMCSA's act of passing the regulations in question did not constitute a major federal action? Did the *Department of Transportation* Court find that the action would not result in a significant impact upon the human environment? Why then, in light of the express provisions of § 102(2)(C), did the Court find that the FMCSA was not required to consider the increased cross-border operations of the Mexican motor carriers?

2. **Nondiscretionary Duties.** Why should the actions of the President have any bearing on the FMSCA's duties under NEPA? On what statutory provisions did the Supreme Court rely in finding that an agency's nondiscretionary duties are not subject to the Act? How could the opposite conclusion be supported?

3. Ramifications. How wide is the loophole created by the *Department of Transportation* Court? Can Congress simply evade review under NEPA by delegating decisions to the President instead of to a federal agency? What happens in those circumstances when an agency simply implements decisions of the President?

4. Rule of Reason. Consistent with the holding of the *Marsh* Court (discussed in Section E), the *Department of Transportation* Court claims that "inherent in NEPA . . . is a 'rule of reason,' which ensures that agencies determine whether and to what extent to prepare an EIS based on the usefulness of any new potential information to the decisionmaking process." 541 U.S. at 767. Does the court justify this contention with reference to the statute? What role does the "rule of reason" play in the Court's decision?

5. Federal Energy Regulatory Commission and "Nondiscretionary Duties." In three cases applying the rule from *Department of Transportation*, the D.C. Circuit found that the Federal Energy Regulatory Commission (FERC), in licensing physical upgrades for a liquefied natural gas (LNG) terminal, was acting pursuant to narrow, delegated authority from the Department of Energy and had no legal authority to consider the environmental effects of LNG exports. According to the Court, because FERC had no authority to deny an upgrade license based on the climate effects of LNG exports, it had no NEPA obligation to evaluate the climate change effects of exporting natural gas. *Sierra Club v. FERC*, 827 F.3d 36 (D.C. Cir. 2016); *Sierra Club v. FERC*, 827 F.3d 59 (D.C. Cir. 2016); *EarthReports, Inc. v. FERC*, 828 F.3d 949 (D.C. Cir. 2016).

By contrast, the D.C. Circuit held in *Sierra Club v. FERC*, 867 F.3d 1357, 1372 (D.C. Cir. 2017) ("Sabal Trail")—decided after the three cases described above—that because FERC does have legal authority to consider climate change effects in its Natural Gas Act pipeline certificate determinations, FERC *must* properly analyze those effects pursuant to NEPA. The D.C. Circuit held that because "FERC could deny a pipeline certificate on the ground that the pipeline would be too harmful to the environment, the agency is a 'legally relevant cause' of the direct and indirect environmental effects of pipelines it approves." *Sabal Trail*, 867 F.3d at 1373. Are you persuaded by the Court's distinction between the agency action in *Sabal Trail* and the agency action in the line of cases following the rule from *Department of Transportation*?

Merrell v. Thomas

807 F.2d 776 (9th Cir. 1986), *cert. denied*, 484 U.S. 848 (1987).

■ Before SNEED, KENNEDY, and KOZINSKI, CIRCUIT JUDGES.

■ SNEED, CIRCUIT JUDGE:

This appeal raises a single legal issue: whether the Environmental Protection Agency (EPA) must comply with the National Environmental Policy Act of 1969 (NEPA), 42 U.S.C. §§ 4321–4370a, when it registers pesticides under the Federal Insecticide, Fungicide, and Rodenticide Act (FIFRA), 7 U.S.C. §§ 136–136y. The district court, 608 F.Supp. 644, ruled that it need not. After examining FIFRA's registration procedure, its registration standard, and the applicable review procedures, we conclude that Congress did not intend that EPA should comply with NEPA. Therefore, we affirm.

Appellant Paul E. Merrell, plaintiff below, sued to enjoin EPA from continuing to register seven herbicides which his local road department sprayed along the road leading to his wife's farm. Merrell charged that the registrations were invalid because EPA and its predecessor agency had not made public the information on which they were based. Merrell alleged that EPA thereby violated NEPA and its implementing regulations, 40 C.F.R. §§ 1500.1–1508.28, particularly insofar as EPA failed either to prepare a site-specific environmental impact statement (EIS) for each right-of-way use registration, or to explain why no EIS was necessary under 42 U.S.C. § 4332(2)(C). Complaint for Injunctive Relief, Excerpt of Record (E.R.) at 1–10. . . .

Since 1947, pesticides that move in interstate commerce have had to be registered with the Federal Government. FIFRA, Pub. L. No. 80–104, § 4(a), 61 Stat. 163, 167 (1947). To register a pesticide, an applicant had to submit its name, its label, the claims made for it and, "if requested," a description of tests made and their results. *Id.* Under the original act, an applicant who failed to meet even these minimal standards could nevertheless obtain a "protest registration" for his product. *Id.* § 4(c), 61 Stat. at 168. In 1964, Congress eliminated the protest registration. A disappointed applicant could instead request a referral to an advisory committee or a public hearing. Act of May 12, 1964, Pub. L. No. 88–305, § 3, 78 Stat. 190, 190–91. Otherwise, there was no opportunity for public participation.

In 1970, when FIFRA's pesticide registration procedure was as described above, Congress passed NEPA, Pub. L. No. 91–190, 83 Stat. 852 (1970). . . . The question before us is, did Congress intend to superimpose NEPA's procedures on top of the FIFRA registration procedure?

After 1970, EPA did not change its FIFRA regulations to require preparation of EIS's. In 1972, Congress comprehensively amended FIFRA, in part in response to "increasing public concern over the uses and application of pesticides [reflecting] expanded interest in environmental protection by many citizens." H.R. Rep. No. 511, 92d Cong., 1st Sess. 4 (1971). Yet Congress gave no indication that it thought NEPA would apply. Instead, Congress created a registration procedure within FIFRA to ensure consideration of environmental impact—a procedure that apparently made NEPA superfluous. Congress also created limited opportunities for public notice and public participation in FIFRA's registration procedure. But the 1972 amendments did not make FIFRA a carbon copy of NEPA. It reflected a compromise between environmentalists, farmers, and manufacturers. *Id.* at 5. The differences between FIFRA's registration procedure and NEPA's requirements indicate that Congress did not intend that NEPA apply.

First, if an application for a pesticide registration involved a new active ingredient or a changed use pattern, the 1972 amendments required the Administrator to place a notice in the Federal Register before he made his decision. Federal Environmental Pesticide Control Act of 1972, Pub. L. No. 92–516, § 2, 86 Stat. 973, 980 (amending FIFRA section 3(c)(4)). This is the only provision for public notice prior to a decision to register a pesticide. It obviously falls short of an EIS requirement, both because the Administrator will not have to publish the notice with respect to many applications, and because the notice does not contain the information contained in an EIS.

Second, the 1972 amendments required the Administrator to act "as expeditiously as possible" on an application, *id.*, 86 Stat. at 980 (amending FIFRA section 3(c)(3)), and Congress expected him to reach a decision within three months of receiving an application, H.R. Rep. No. 511, 92d Cong., 1st Sess. 20 (1971). Such a time frame is incompatible with the lengthy research and hearings that are ordinarily part of preparing an EIS. *Compare Flint Ridge Dev. Co. v. Scenic Rivers Ass'n*, 426 U.S. 776, 788–91 & 789 n.10 (1976) (statutory requirement that filing take effect in thirty days means that NEPA cannot apply) with *Jones v. Gordon*, 792 F.2d 821, 826–27 (9th Cir.1986) (agency regulation requiring publication of notice "as soon as practicable" after application is deemed sufficient does not prevent NEPA from applying).

Third, the 1972 amendments provided that the Administrator would make available to the public the information on which he based a decision to register a pesticide within thirty days of that decision. Federal Environmental Pesticide Control Act of 1972, § 2, 86 Stat. at 980 (amending FIFRA section 3(c)(2)). But the Administrator would not release information if it was test data for which a subsequent user would have to compensate an applicant, or if it contained trade secrets. *Id.*, 86 Stat. at 979–80, 989 (amending FIFRA sections 3(c)(1)(D), 3(c)(2), 10(b)). NEPA does not contain equivalent restrictions.

Thus, when Congress revised FIFRA in 1972, it designed a registration procedure with public notice and public participation provisions that differ materially from those that NEPA would require.

When Congress amended FIFRA in 1975, 1978, and 1984, EPA had interpreted FIFRA so as not to require compliance with NEPA. And "when Congress revisits a statute giving rise to a longstanding administrative interpretation without pertinent change, the 'congressional failure to revise or repeal the agency's interpretation is persuasive evidence that the interpretation is the one intended by Congress.'" *Commodity Futures Trading Comm'n v. Schor*, 478 U.S. 833 (1986) (quoting *NLRB v. Bell Aerospace Co.*, 416 U.S. 267, 274–75 (1974) (footnotes omitted)). . . .

NOTES AND QUESTIONS

1.   Legislative Compromise. The *Merrell* court held that the 1972 amendments to FIFRA reflected a compromise between "environmentalists, farmers, and manufacturers," and that to apply the provisions of NEPA would be to upset that compromise. 807 F.2d at 778. Why, given that NEPA was in effect prior to 1972, should NEPA not be taken to constitute a part of that compromise?

2.   Express Repudiation. The *Merrell* court presents three reasons why the 1972 amendments to FIFRA should preclude NEPA's application. None of these reasons explain why Congress would not simply preclude NEPA's operation by way of an express provision in FIFRA, if this were its intention. What would be the likely response of the *Merrell* court in this respect?

3.   "To the Fullest Extent Possible." Recall that federal agencies are required to comply with the requirements of § 102(2)(C) "to the fullest extent possible." 42 U.S.C. § 4332. Do you think that the *Merrell* court paid adequate regard to this provision?

4.   Recent Legislation Limiting NEPA. In addition to implied limitations, Congress has on a number of occasions expressly limited NEPA review through legislation. EPA, for instance, has been exempted from complying with NEPA with respect to its duties under the CAA, 15 U.S.C. § 793(c)(1), and many of its duties under the CWA, 33 U.S.C. § 1371(c)(1). In recent years, Congress has taken a number of additional steps to limit NEPA's application. NEPA doesn't apply to regional transportation plans developed with federal assistance under The Transportation Equity Act for the 21st Century (2005). The Healthy Forests Restoration Act of 2003 expedites environmental reviews under NEPA for authorized hazardous fuel reduction projects in national forests such as thinning, the establishment of strategic fuel breaks, and prescribed fires. This legislation limits both alternatives and judicial review. The Safe, Accountable, Flexible, Efficient Transportation Act (2005) included a 150-day statute of limitations for judicial review that runs after the publication of a Federal Register notice announcing that a permit, license or approval is final. 23 U.S.C. § 139(*l*). It has been suggested that specific legislative exemptions threaten to make NEPA obsolete, given the apparent willingness on the part of Congress to limit its operation by way of express legislative pronouncement. *See* Aaron Ehrlich, *In Hidden Places: Congressional Legislation that Limits the Scope of the National Environmental Policy Act*, 13 HASTINGS W.-NW. J. ENVTL. L. & POL'Y 285, 302 (2007).

5.   Express Limitation by Way of Appropriations Riders. Express exemptions to the operation of NEPA are also often contained in riders to congressional appropriations. Appropriations legislation is necessary to fund many of the federal programs that are subject to NEPA. It can be contrasted, in broad terms, with authorization legislation (which creates federal programs). For the simple reason that federal programs cannot operate without funding

> appropriations legislation presents a lawmaking opportunity to legislators who are . . . willing to hold . . . legislation hostage in a

game of legislative "chicken" with their colleagues. Because everyone knows that Congress must pass [appropriations] legislation, it is tempting to try to attach incidental provisions that otherwise might lack the political momentum (or even majority support) necessary for passage.

Richard J. Lazarus, *Congressional Descent: The Demise of Deliberative Democracy in Environmental Law*, 94 GEO. L.J. 619, 635 (2006). These incidental provisions, known as appropriations riders, often preclude the operation of NEPA and other environmental statutes to particular federal projects or programs. In the 1998, 1999, and 2000 fiscal years, for example, Congress considered 197, and enacted at least 143, appropriations riders limiting the operation of environmental statutes. *Id.* at 643. While the promulgation of procedural rules by both the House and the Senate has somewhat curbed the application of appropriations riders in this fashion, their use remains a considerable constraint on the operation of NEPA.

What are the procedural and substantive differences in precluding the operation of NEPA by way of an appropriations rider as opposed to an express statutory pronouncement in authorization legislation? Evaluate the following critique of the use of appropriations riders in environmental lawmaking:

Simply stated, the legislative process surrounding appropriations legislation does not provide for the kind of meaningful public debate and deliberation that proved so important in the fashioning of the comprehensive environmental protection laws of the 1970s and 1980s. Indeed, the very reason appropriations legislation has risen in significance is its ability to feed off the perverse political incentives created when Congress is otherwise incapable of passing needed laws through the normal authorization committee lawmaking processes. The upshot has been the kind of ad hoc, incoherent lawmaking resulting from closed-door appropriations deal-making that is of questionable efficacy for any area of law, but especially for environmental law because of its widespread distributional consequences. Congress has displayed no ability to engage in the deliberate policymaking essential to thoughtful resolution of the difficult economic, social, and moral issues raised by environmental lawmaking.

Id. at 632–33.

6. Implied Limitation by Way of Appropriations Riders. An interesting question arises as to what extent ongoing congressional appropriations, such as those necessary to finance large infrastructure projects constructed over many years, can be taken to constitute an implicit exemption to the application of NEPA. The Supreme Court, in the case of *TVA v. Hill*, 437 U.S. 153 (1978) (discussed at length in Chapter IX), considered this issue as it applied to the application of the Endangered Species Act. In finding that continued appropriations did not constitute an implicit exemption, the Supreme Court held "[w]hen voting on appropriations measures, legislators are entitled to operate under the assumption that the funds will be devoted to purposes which are lawful and not for any purpose forbidden. Without such an assurance, every appropriations measure would be pregnant with prospects of altering substantive legislation." *Id.* at 190. This reasoning has repeatedly been adopted by lower federal courts in the context of ongoing congressional appropriations and NEPA. *See, e.g., Envtl. Def. Fund, Inc. v. Froehlke*, 473 F.2d 346 (8th Cir. 1972). For a detailed discussion of the impact of ongoing congressional appropriations on NEPA's action forcing mandate, see DANIEL R. MANDELKER, NEPA LAW AND LITIGATION § 5:7 (2011).

7. Proposals for NEPA Reform. For decades, policymakers and stakeholders have issued calls for NEPA reform. Suggestions have included, among others: capping the time allowed for an agency to complete EISs and EAs; capping page counts for EISs and EAs; streamlining NEPA requirements for certain categories of "environmentally beneficial" projects; revising CEQ's NEPA regulations to contain more specific criteria differentiating EISs from EAs; eliminating the requirement to comply with NEPA if a project passes muster under a state statute functionally equivalent to NEPA; and placing limits on who can bring NEPA litigation, and under what circumstances. Congress has not adopted any of these proposals, to-date. What reforms to NEPA, or its regulations, do you think may be warranted? Which potential reforms may have the greatest chance of success?

8. Categorical Exclusions. The application of NEPA is also limited by way of categorical exclusions under the CEQ regulations. The CEQ regulations define categorical exclusions (CEs) as "categor[ies] of actions which do not individually or cumulatively have a significant effect on the human environment and which have been found to have no such effect in procedures adopted by a federal agency in implementation of these regulations." 40 C.F.R. § 1508.4. An agency is not required to prepare an EIS or an EA for a proposed action falling within a CE unless there exists information suggesting that the proposed action will have a significant effect on the human environment.

The CEQ issued a guidance document on the application of CEs under NEPA, which explains that "[t]he purpose of a [CE] is to eliminate the need for unnecessary paperwork and effort under NEPA for categories of actions that normally do not warrant preparation of an environmental impact statement (EIS) or environmental assessment (EA)." CEQ, The National Environmental Protection Act—Guidance on Categorical Exclusions, 71 Fed. Reg. 54,816 (2006). More recently, in a draft guidance, CEQ noted an "expansion of the number and range of activities categorically excluded combined with the extensive use of [CEs]," and warned that "an inappropriate reliance on [CEs] may thwart the purposes of NEPA." Memorandum from Nancy Sutley on Establishing and Applying Categorical Exclusions Under the National Environmental Policy Act 2 (Feb. 18, 2010). Indeed, CEs have become "the most frequently employed method of complying with NEPA." *Id.* CEQ's final guidance on CEs provides "methods for substantiating categorical exclusions, clarifies the process for establishing categorical exclusions, [and] outlines how agencies should engage the public when establishing and using categorical exclusions." 75 Fed. Reg. 75,628 (2010). One of the most significant CEs is for oil and gas exploration and development on the Outer Continental Shelf, which notoriously allowed the Deepwater Horizon oil well to be exempt from NEPA review. *See* Notice of Intent to Conduct a Review of Categorical Exclusions for Outer Continental Shelf Decisions, 75 Fed. Reg. 62,418 (2010). While the federal agency overseeing offshore drilling announced plans to review and likely revise its CEs, it never completed this review. *See id.*; Bureau of Ocean Energy Management, Categorical Exclusion Reviews, https://www.boem.gov/Categorical-Exclusion-Reviews/ (last visited Feb. 10, 2019). The Forest Service has also used CEs extensively, although a CE that it adopted for proposals to change land management plans was struck down as inappropriate for the scope and magnitude of nationwide forest planning decisions. *See Citizens for Better Forestry v. USDA*, 481 F. Supp. 2d 1059, 1087 (N.D. Cal. 2007).

Recalling that the *Hanly* court recognized that "almost every major federal action, no matter how limited in scope, has some adverse effect on the human environment," 471 F.2d at 830, what difficulties can you anticipate in defining a CE under § 1508.4? Given their wide use, does it seem likely that agencies are adopting varied definitions?

9.   Reasoned Decision. An agency must be capable of demonstrating that it made a "reasoned decision" with respect to the creation of a CE. *See Marsh v. Or. Natural Res. Council*, 490 U.S. 360, 378 (1989). What does this require of an agency? *See, e.g., Sierra Club v. Bosworth*, 510 F.3d 1016 (9th Cir. 2007) (Forest Service failed to demonstrate a "reasoned decision" in creating CE for forest burns up to 4,500 acres given that it conducted "data call" after it had decided to establish exclusion).

After the oil well blowout that caused the Deepwater Horizon disaster in the Gulf of Mexico, the Oil Spill Commission report noted that the risk of a blowout was never analyzed by the federal agency (formerly the Minerals Management Service (MMS)) that approved the drilling. It had exempted the well's exploration plan (EP) and application for a permit to drill (APD) from NEPA analysis based on CEs. *See* Nat'l Comm'n on the BP Deepwater Horizon Oil Spill & Offshore Drilling, *The National Environmental Policy Act and Outer Continental Shelf Oil and Gas Activities* 29–30 (Staff Working Paper No. 12, 2011), *available at* http://permanent.access.gpo.gov/gpo8613/The%20National%20Environmental%20Policy%20Act%20and%20Outer%20Continental%20Shelf%20Oil%20and%20Gas%20Activities.pdf. The report states:

> The notion that the largest oil spill in American history resulted from a blowout on a well that had been defined by the agency as exempt from NEPA because it is an action "which do[es] not have a significant effect on the human environment" indicates that the application of the CEQ definition was off-kilter and the exceptions were not sufficiently examined.... The exceptions to the application of a CE include actions which "[h]ave highly uncertain and potentially significant environmental effects or involve unique or unknown environmental risks." The May 2000 Gulf of Mexico

Deepwater Operations and Activities EA expressly discussed the potential for a deepwater spill and the length of time needed to control one (60–120 days); it concluded that "further investigation is needed" to evaluation the consequences of a deepwater blowout. Given the actual events after the blowout took place, it is clear that such investigation was never completed. How a deepwater EP escaped NEPA review under the exception to CEs is difficult to understand.

Id. at 31 (internal citations omitted). Note that CEQ regulations no longer require an analysis of worst-case scenarios (discussed briefly in Section D). Does the agency's use of CEs seem to fit with the language of § 1508.4 or the *Marsh* court's notion of a "reasoned decision"?

10. Emergency Exemptions. In addition to categorical exclusions under § 1508.14, the CEQ regulations also allow the circumvention of NEPA's procedural mandate in cases of emergency:

Where emergency circumstances make it necessary to take an action with significant environmental impact without observing the provisions of [the CEQ] regulations, the Federal agency taking the action should consult with the Council about alternative arrangements. Agencies and the Council will limit such arrangements to actions necessary to control the immediate impacts of the emergency. Other actions remain subject to NEPA review.

40 C.F.R. § 1506.11. The CEQ regulations are silent on what should constitute an emergency for the purposes of the § 1506.11 exemption. It has been suggested that this represents a danger to the EIS process:

NEPA commands federal agencies to prepare an EIS, and does not provide any exception for emergencies. Section 1506.11, a purely regulatory provision, thus modifies the statute. Today, once an "emergency" exists, the clear command of NEPA becomes blurred, and then a federal agency may cut short the EIS process or take a major action before completing the EIS process. Such an interpretation represents a novel precedent that blunts the EIS procedure required by NEPA and could severely harm consideration of environmental factors in agency decision making.

Robert Orsi, *Emergency Exceptions From NEPA: Who Should Decide?*, 14 B.C. ENVTL. AFF. L. REV. 481, 484 (1987). Do you consider this criticism to be well founded?

11. National Security. When the Nuclear Regulatory Commission (NRC) approved an interim spent fuel storage installation at the Diablo Canyon nuclear power plant in California, it refused to disclose the information it relied upon in making a FONSI. *See San Luis Obispo Mothers for Peace v. NRC*, 635 F.3d 1109, 1116 (9th Cir. 2011). The NRC argued that the security risks in releasing the documents outweighed the benefits of disclosure under NEPA. *Id.* at 1114. NEPA's public disclosure requirements are coextensive with the Freedom of Information Act (FOIA). *Id.* at 1115. The Ninth Circuit agreed with the NRC, finding that "NEPA does not require the Commission to disclose sensitive information in a closed hearing." *Id*. at 1117. Given that the disclosure requirements are governed by FOIA, does this create a loophole in NEPA disclosure for agencies that can claim national security concerns?

Recall that in an earlier case with the same two parties, the Ninth Circuit held that NEPA may require agencies to consider terrorism risks, even if they need not analyze every worst-case scenario. *See San Luis Obispo Mothers For Peace v. NRC*, 449 F.3d 1016 (9th Cir. 2006), *cert. denied*, 549 U.S. 1166 (2007) (discussed briefly in Section D). Do these two decisions conflict?

CHAPTER IX

MANAGEMENT OF NATURAL RESOURCES

1. PROTECTION OF ENDANGERED SPECIES

A. INTRODUCTION

i. OVERVIEW

The Endangered Species Act (ESA) was enacted in 1973 in response to Congress' increased recognition of the importance of biological diversity and the inadequacy of existing protections. While earlier federal legislation provided some protection to endangered species, by the time the ESA was passed it was clear that existing legislation was not sufficient to protect species from extinction: the rate of extinction had increased to the point that, on average, one species disappeared each year. *See* S. REP. NO. 93–307, at 2990 (1973).

The two main ways that the ESA protects endangered species are through its prohibition on federal actions that jeopardize endangered or threatened species, § 7(a)(2), and its prohibition on private takings of endangered species, § 9(a)(1)(B), discussed in later sections of this chapter. 16 U.S.C. §§ 1536(a)(2), 1538(a)(1)(B).

The operative provisions of the ESA are triggered when the Secretaries of Interior or Commerce list a species as endangered or threatened under § 4(a). 16 U.S.C. § 1533(a). The Secretary may list species on her own initiative or interested persons may petition the Secretary to list a species; the Secretary must take action on such petitions within twelve months. 16 U.S.C. § 1533(b)(3). The Secretary is also required to designate a "critical habitat," 16 U.S.C. § 1532(5), for endangered and threatened species when the species is first listed, 16 U.S.C. § 1533(a)(3). A species is "endangered" if it is "in danger of extinction throughout all or a significant portion of its range," 16 U.S.C. § 1532(6), and is "threatened" if it is likely to become endangered in the "foreseeable future," 16 U.S.C. § 1532(20). The determination that a species is endangered or threatened is made "solely on the basis of the best scientific and commercial data available," without consideration of the cost of protecting the species. 16 U.S.C. § 1533(b)(1)(A). "Critical habitat" is defined as the "specific areas within the geographical area occupied by [a] species . . . on which are found . . . physical or biological features (I) essential to the conservation of the species and (II) which may require special management considerations. . . ." 16 U.S.C. § 1532(5)(A)(i). The designation of critical habitat may take "economic impact" and "any other relevant impact" into consideration. 16 U.S.C. § 1533(b)(2).

The ESA contains provisions for both civil penalties, 16 U.S.C. § 1540(a), and criminal penalties, 16 U.S.C. § 1540(b). Section 11(g) authorizes citizen suits against individuals in violation of the Act, 16 U.S.C. § 1540(g)(1)(A), and against the Secretary for failure to perform any nondiscretionary duty under the Act, 16 U.S.C. § 1540(g)(1)(C).

The ESA grants authority to both the Secretary of Commerce, for marine species, and the Secretary of Interior, for all other species. 16 U.S.C. § 1532(15). The Secretary of Interior has delegated the administration of the ESA to the Fish and Wildlife Service (FWS), and the Secretary of Commerce has similarly delegated authority to the National Marine Fisheries Service (NMFS), a division of the National Oceanographic and Atmospheric Administration (NOAA) (also known as NOAA Fisheries). Thus, the FWS and the NMFS are the federal agencies with the most responsibility for enforcing the ESA, though the law also calls upon all federal agencies to support that effort. Current information about the ESA, lists of endangered and protected species, and information on the ESA's provisions are available at the FWS's web site at http://www.fws.gov/endangered (last visited Nov. 26, 2018).

NOTES AND QUESTIONS

1. Human-Centered or Nature-Centered? The Congressional declaration of purpose in the ESA states that species are "of esthetic, ecological, educational, historical, recreational, and scientific value to the Nation and its people." 16 U.S.C. § 1531(a)(3). The value of species is also briefly addressed in the Senate Report accompanying the ESA:

> Consideration of this need to protect endangered species goes beyond the aesthetic. In hearings before the Subcommittee on the Environment it was shown that many of these animals perform vital biological services to maintain a "balance of nature" within their environments. Also revealed was the need for biological diversity for scientific purposes.

S. REP. NO. 93–307, at 2990 (1973). Do these reasons support a human-centered or nature-centered approach to the need to protect species? What benefit do humans derive from protecting species under the ESA? Should we protect only those species that are useful to us, such as those that are of high scientific value? Does the fact that the ESA does not make this distinction—protecting all species found to be endangered, regardless of their "value"—evidence either a human-centered or nature-centered approach? If the ESA were truly to adopt a nature-centered perspective, does it make sense to protect species rather than each individual member of the species? Is there a nature-centered justification for an act entitled the *Endangered* Species Act?

2. All or Nothing. The protections of the ESA apply only to species that are listed as "endangered" or "threatened." Unlisted species receive no protection under the ESA. Would it make more sense to provide some protection to all species, with increasing protection for species that are more threatened or endangered? What problems would such an approach pose? Are there other ways that we could, or should, protect species that are not listed under the ESA?

3. Species v. Ecosystem Protection. The first purpose described in the ESA is to "provide a means whereby the ecosystems upon which endangered species and threatened species depend may be conserved. . . ." 16 U.S.C. § 1531(b). Does the ESA accomplish this? Is ecosystem protection feasible? Is it preferable to protecting individual species? How could Congress have achieved this goal more effectively? If this was Congress' primary concern, how can the current structure of the ESA best be explained?

4. Objectivity in Listing Decisions. Recall that the decision to list a species as endangered or threatened must be made "solely on the basis of the best scientific and commercial data available. . . ." 16 U.S.C. § 1533(b)(1)(A). The word "solely" implies that listing decisions are to be made without reference to policy concerns. Is this a realistic expectation? In what ways might listing decisions necessarily involve policy judgments? For further discussion, see Holly Doremus, *Listing Decisions Under the Endangered Species Act: Why Better Science Isn't Always Better Policy*, 75 WASH. U. L.Q. 1029, 1035 (1997) (arguing that "the ESA's current requirement that listing decisions rest solely on science . . . has forced the listing agencies into a 'science charade,' in which they must pretend to make non-scientific decisions entirely on the basis of science").

There are two major concerns with couching non-scientific judgments in seemingly objective language. When policy considerations are unacknowledged, there are costs to democratic accountability and scientific progress—improperly making politics appear scientific. *See* Holly Doremus, *Science Plays Defense: Natural Resource Management in the Bush Administration*, 32 ECOLOGY L.Q. 249, 297–304 (2005). Relatedly, by creating the expectation that listing decisions are to be strictly objective, the ESA may invite scientists to become policy advocates themselves—shaping the scientific process by means of politics. *See* Rob R. Ramey II, *On the Origin of Specious Species*, *in* INSTITUTIONS AND INCENTIVES IN REGULATORY SCIENCE 77 (Jason Scott Johnston ed., 2012). How might the ESA be amended to create a more desirable balance between science and policy?

B. FEDERAL ACTIONS

i. LISTING AND DISTINCT POPULATION SEGMENTS

The ESA contains two procedures for the consideration of whether a species should be listed. First, the FWS or the NMFS can initiate the process itself based on information collected by agency scientists. 16 U.S.C. § 1533(a). Alternately, any interested person may petition the appropriate agency to list a species. *Id.* § 1533(b)(3).

The ESA directs the Secretary of the Interior to apply five factors in determining whether a "species" is endangered or threatened: (i) "the present or threatened destruction, modification, or curtailment of [the species'] habitat or range"; (ii) "overutilization [of the species] for commercial, recreational, scientific, or educational purposes"; (iii) "disease or predation"; (iv) "the inadequacy of existing regulatory mechanisms"; or (v) "other natural or manmade factors affecting [the species'] continued existence." 16 U.S.C. § 1533(a)(1). In making that determination, the Secretary must rely on "the best scientific and commercial data available." *Id.* § 1533(b)(1)(A).

As of October 2018, a total of 2,344 species are listed under the ESA, including plants and animals. There are 1,868 endangered species and 476 threatened species. 1,661 of those endangered and threatened species live in the United States; the rest live in foreign countries. (For current totals, see the FWS website at https://ecos.fws.gov/ecp0/reports/box-score-report.

The ESA defines "species" to include subspecies and distinct population segments. 16 U.S.C. § 1532(16). Neither "subspecies" nor "distinct population segment" are defined by the Act. The following case discusses the definition of distinct population segments (DPS) adopted by the FWS in policy guidance and the circumstances under which a DPS is entitled to protection under the Act.

National Association of Home Builders v. Norton
340 F.3d 835 (9th Cir. 2003).

■ Before NOONAN, TASHIMA, and WARDLAW, CIRCUIT JUDGES.

■ TASHIMA, CIRCUIT JUDGE:

. . . The cactus ferruginous pygmy-owl (*Glaucidium brasilianum cactorum*) is a small bird, about 6.75 inches in length, that can be reddish-brown or gray. It is one of four subspecies of the ferruginous pygmy-owl. The range of the cactus ferruginous pygmy-owl ("pygmy-owl") extends "from lowland central Arizona south through western Mexico, to the States of Colima and Michoacan, and from southern Texas south through the Mexican States of Tamaulipas and Nuevo Leon." The pygmy-owls in Arizona represent the northernmost edge of the subspecies' range. . . .

On May 26, 1992, conservation organizations petitioned the FWS to list the pygmy-owls in the United States and Mexico as an endangered species and to designate a critical habitat for them. Following a status review, the FWS proposed listing the pygmy-owl as endangered with critical habitat in Arizona and threatened in Texas. After a notice and comment period, the FWS issued a final rule listing the Arizona pygmy-owls as endangered (but not listing the Texas pygmy-owls as threatened). . . .

In the Listing Rule, the FWS designated the Arizona pygmy-owls as a DPS. The ESA permits the FWS to designate a population of a species as a DPS and to list it as an endangered species. *See* 16 U.S.C. §§ 1532(16), 1533(a)(1). To designate a DPS under the *DPS Policy,* the FWS must find that a population is discrete "in relation to the remainder of the species to which it belongs" and significant "to the species to which it belongs." 61 Fed. Reg. at 4725. In making this designation in the Listing Rule, the FWS first found that the pygmy-owl populations in the east (southeast Texas south through northeastern Mexico) and west (central Arizona south through northwestern Mexico) are (1) discrete "based on geographic isolation, distribution and status of habitat, and potential morphological and genetic distinctness," and (2) significant because the loss of either population would create a significant gap in the range of the subspecies. 62 Fed. Reg. at 10,731.

Next, the FWS further subdivided the western pygmy-owl DPS into an Arizona population and a northwestern Mexico population. According to the Listing Rule, the Arizona pygmy-owls are discrete from the northwestern Mexico pygmy-owls because they are "delimited by international boundaries" and "the status of the species in Arizona is different from that in Sonora [Mexico], with records currently indicating a higher number of individuals in Sonora." *Id.* at 10,737. The FWS also found that the discrete population of Arizona pygmy-owls is significant to its taxon because [s]hould the loss of either the Arizona or Texas populations occur, the remaining population would not fill the resulting gap as the remaining population would not be genetically or morphologically identical, and would require different habitat parameters. The loss of either population also would decrease the genetic variability of the taxon and would result in a significant gap in the range. 62 Fed. Reg. 10,730, 10,737.

Home Builders sued to vacate the Listing Rule and the designation of critical habitat. The district court granted summary judgment to the FWS. The district court held that the "FWS' decision to divide the 'western population,' at the international border between Arizona and Mexico in order to protect the population segment facing extinction within the United States" was permissible and consistent with ESA policy. . . .

On appeal, Home Builders argue that the FWS violated the *DPS Policy* by designating the Arizona pygmy-owls as a DPS. . . .

Preliminarily, it is helpful to note what is not at issue in this case. First, Home Builders do not challenge the *DPS Policy* itself; they agree that the policy is valid and entitled to *Chevron* deference. The challenge here is only to the FWS' application of the *DPS Policy*. Second, Home Builders do not challenge the FWS' determination that, once severed from the rest of the western pygmy-owl population, the Arizona pygmy-owls could be considered endangered. Home Builders only challenge their designation as a DPS. Third, Home Builders do not contest the designation of the eastern and western pygmy-owls as DPSs, only the subdivision of the western pygmy-owls into the Arizona DPS and the northwestern Mexico population.[7] Thus, the question we must decide is whether the FWS violated its *DPS Policy* by finding that the Arizona pygmy-owls are a discrete and significant population.

The FWS Acted Arbitrarily and Capriciously in Designating the Arizona Pygmy Owls as a DPS

The ESA definition of species "includes any subspecies of fish or wildlife or plants, and any *distinct population segment* of any species of vertebrate fish or wildlife which interbreeds when mature." 16 U.S.C. § 1532(16) (emphasis added). Thus, under the ESA, the FWS can designate a particular population of a species as a DPS and then consider

---

[7] Home Builders also do not challenge the well-established propositions that (1) international borders can divide protected and unprotected populations; and (2) the United States can protect endangered populations within its borders even if other populations of the same species are more abundant in other countries. In fact, the *DPS Policy* incorporates those propositions.

that DPS as a species for listing purposes. 16 U.S.C. §§ 1532(16), 1533(a)(1).

The ability to designate and list DPSs allows the FWS to provide different levels of protection to different populations of the same species. The FWS does not have to list an entire species as endangered when only one of its populations faces extinction.

Since the ESA does not define the term "distinct population segment," the FWS and the National Marine Fisheries Service jointly promulgated the *DPS Policy* to ensure consistency in their respective DPS designations. Under the *DPS Policy*, a DPS must be discrete "in relation to the remainder of the species to which it belongs" and significant "to the species to which it belongs." *DPS Policy*, 61 Fed. Reg. 4722, 4725. A DPS must be both discrete and significant, because "[t]he interests of conserving genetic diversity would not be well served by efforts directed at either well-defined but insignificant units or entities believed to be significant but around which boundaries cannot be recognized." *Id.* at 4724.

A. *The FWS Did Not Arbitrarily and Capriciously Find That the Arizona Pygmy-Owl Population is Discrete*

The purpose of the discreteness standard is to ensure that a DPS is "adequately defined and described," allowing for the effective administration of the ESA. *Id.* This standard distinguishes a population from other members of its species, but does not require "absolute separation." A population is discrete if (1) "[i]t is markedly separated from other populations of the same taxon as a consequence of physical, physiological, ecological, or behavioral factors"; or (2) "[i]t is delimited by international governmental boundaries within which differences in control of exploitation, management of habitat, conservation status, or regulatory mechanisms exist that are significant in light of section 4(a)(1)(D) of the Act." *Id.* at 4725. Although the use of international borders "may introduce an artificial and non-biological element" into the discreteness standard, "it appears to be reasonable for national legislation . . . to recognize units delimited by international boundaries when these coincide with differences in the management, status, or exploitation of a species." *Id.* at 4723.

In the Listing Rule, the FWS found that the Arizona pygmy-owls are discrete from the northwestern Mexico pygmy-owls because the international border divides the two populations and significant differences in conservation status exist between those populations. *See* 62 Fed. Reg. at 10,737 ("[T]he Service believes the status of the species in Arizona is different from that in Sonora, [Mexico,] with records currently indicating a higher number of individuals in Sonora. . . ."). Home Builders contend that the FWS failed to demonstrate any differences in the conservation status of pygmy-owls in Arizona and northwestern Mexico. The issue here, therefore, is whether the FWS acted arbitrarily in determining that significant differences in conservation status exist across the international boundary.

The *DPS Policy* does not define the term "conservation status." The FWS argues that the term "conservation status" means "the number of individuals left in the population." As a consequence, "differences in conservation status" mean "differences in the number of owls" on either side of the border. . . .

Comparing the "conservation status" of pygmy-owls across the border, the FWS found that pygmy-owls were abundant in parts of northwestern Mexico but were rare and declining in Arizona. [The Court upheld this finding as not arbitrary and capricious.] . . .

B.   *The FWS Has Not Demonstrated a Rational Basis in the Listing Rule For its Finding That the Arizona Pygmy Owl Population is Significant to its Taxon*

If a population is discrete, the FWS then considers the "biological and ecological significance" of the population to the taxon to which it belongs. The purpose of the significance element is "to carry out the expressed congressional intent that this authority [to list DPSs] be exercised sparingly as well as to concentrate conservation efforts undertaken under the Act on avoiding important losses of genetic diversity." 61 Fed. Reg. at 4724, 4725; *See also* S. Rep. No. 96–151, at 7 ("[T]he committee is aware of the great potential for abuse of this authority [to list DPSs] and expects the FWS to use the ability to list populations sparingly and only when the biological evidence indicates that such action is warranted."). The FWS determines the significance of a discrete population by considering the following non-exclusive factors:

1. Persistence of the discrete population segment in an ecological setting unusual or unique for the taxon,

2. Evidence that loss of the discrete population segment would result in a significant gap in the range of a taxon,

3. Evidence that the discrete population segment represents the only surviving natural occurrence of a taxon that may be more abundant elsewhere as an introduced population outside its historic range, or

4. Evidence that the discrete population segment differs markedly from other populations of the species in its genetic characteristics.

61 Fed. Reg. at 4725. In the Listing Rule, the FWS found that the discrete population of Arizona pygmy-owls is significant because

> [s]hould the loss of either the Arizona or Texas populations occur, the remaining population would not fill the resulting gap as the remaining population would not be genetically or morphologically identical, and would require different habitat parameters. The loss of either population also would decrease

the genetic variability of the taxon and would result in a significant gap in the range.

62 Fed. Reg. at 10,737. The FWS argues that it found the Arizona pygmy-owl population to be significant to its taxon in the Listing Rule based on the second and fourth significance factors.

1. The Second Significance Factor

In the Listing Rule, the FWS concluded that the loss of the Arizona pygmy-owls "would result in a significant gap in the range" of their taxon. 62 Fed.Reg. at 10,737. The question, then, is whether the FWS arbitrarily determined that the loss of the discrete Arizona pygmy-owl population would cause a gap in the range of its taxon and that such a gap would be significant. *See DPS Policy,* 61 Fed.Reg. at 4725.

a. Whether the Loss of the Arizona Pygmy Owl Population Would Cause a Gap in the Range of the Taxon

The FWS noted in the Listing Rule that the Arizona pygmy-owls "represent the northernmost portion of the pygmy-owl's range." 62 Fed. Reg. at 10,734. The parties disagree over whether the loss of a peripheral population (*i.e.,* a population at the edge of a species' range) could create a gap in the range of a taxon. The parties analogize to "a gap in a fence" to support their respective definitions of a gap in the range of a taxon. Home Builders argue that "a 'gap,' by definition, occurs in the middle of the fence, not at its end," so that only the loss of a population that severs a taxon into isolated parts would create a gap. The FWS argues that "the gap in a fence is just as great if it occurs at the end as in the middle," so that the loss of a peripheral population would create a gap in a taxon's range.

The *DPS Policy* does not define what constitutes a "gap" for the purposes of the second significance factor. *See* 61 Fed.Reg. at 4725. The ordinary dictionary definition of "gap" is "a hole or opening, as in a wall or fence, made by breaking or parting," which does not by itself resolve the ambiguity of this issue. *Webster's New World Dictionary of American English* at 555 (3d ed.1994). Since the definition of gap is ambiguous, the FWS is entitled to deference in interpreting its own regulations, unless that interpretation is plainly erroneous. *Stinson,* 508 U.S. at 45. The FWS has previously found a "gap in the middle of the fence." *See* 63 Fed.Reg. at 13,136 ("The loss of Peninsular bighorn sheep in the United States would isolate bighorn sheep populations in Mexico . . . from all other bighorn sheep. . . ."). In other listing rules, however, the FWS has interpreted the term "gap" to include the loss of peripheral populations. . . .

We defer to the FWS' interpretation of a "gap at the end of the fence" because it is not plainly erroneous. Even the loss of a peripheral population, however small, would create an empty geographic space in the range of the taxon. Regardless of the size of such a gap, a gap would exist. To satisfy the second significance factor, however, the gap must be significant, to which question we now turn.

b. Whether the Gap Would be Significant

Since the loss of the Arizona pygmy-owls would create a gap in the range of the taxon, we now consider whether that gap is significant. The *DPS Policy* intended the term "significant" to have its "commonly understood" meaning, which is "important." 61 Fed.Reg. at 4723; *Webster's New World Dictionary* at 1248. The plain language of the second significance factor does not limit how a gap could be important, *see DPS Policy,* 61 Fed.Reg. at 4725, and, as discussed *infra,* the FWS has given different reasons for the importance of gaps in various listing rules. . . .

The FWS argues that it found the gap to be significant in the Listing Rule because the loss of the Arizona pygmy-owls would (1) decrease the genetic variability of the taxon; (2) reduce the current range of the taxon; (3) reduce the historic range of the taxon; and (4) extirpate the western pygmy-owls from the United States. We therefore must examine whether the FWS had a rational basis in its Listing Rule to base a significance finding on any of these grounds or whether the FWS' arguments here are only *post hoc* rationalizations.

(1) Decrease the Genetic Variability of the Taxon

. . . We cannot defer to the FWS' argument on appeal that the Arizona pygmy-owls are genetically distinct from and important to the central population of northwestern Mexico pygmy-owls because the FWS did not make such a finding in the Listing Rule. Since the Listing Rule does not contain evidence of genetic variability between the Arizona and northwestern Mexico pygmy-owls, the argument that the loss of the Arizona population is significant because it would "decrease the genetic variability of the taxon," 62 Fed. Reg. at 10,737, appears to be a *post hoc* rationalization. While the FWS can draw conclusions based on less than conclusive scientific evidence, *Southwest Ctr. for Biological Diversity v. Babbitt,* 215 F.3d 58, 60 (D.C.Cir. 2000), it cannot base its conclusions on no evidence. *See Bennett v. Spear*, 520 U.S. 154, 176 (1997) ("The obvious purpose of the requirement that each agency 'use the best scientific and commercial evidence available' is to ensure that the ESA not be implemented haphazardly, on the basis of speculation or surmise.").

(2) Reduce the Current Range of the Taxon

The FWS argues that the gap would be significant because the loss of the Arizona pygmy-owls would reduce the current range of its taxon. In other listing rules, the FWS has found two ways in which the loss of a discrete population could reduce the current range of its taxon.

First, the loss of a discrete population could reduce the geographic size of the taxon's range. . . . These listing rules suggest that finding a gap significant based on the curtailment of a taxon's current range requires the loss of a geographic area that amounts to a substantial reduction of a taxon's range. *See* 62 Fed. Reg. at 59,609; 66 Fed. Reg. at 38,622. The FWS found in the Listing Rule, however, that the Arizona pygmy-owls represented only "a small percentage" of the total range of the western pygmy-owls. 62 Fed. Reg. at 10,737. It did not find that the loss of this "small percentage" of the western pygmy-owls' current range would substantially curtail that range.

Second, the loss of a discrete population that is numerous and constitutes a large percentage of the total number of taxon members could be considered a significant curtailment of a taxon's current range. *See Proposed Endangered Status for a Distinct Population Segment of Smalltooth Sawfish in the United States*, 66 Fed. Reg. 19,414, 19,416 (proposed Apr. 16, 2001) (finding that a gap caused by the loss of the smalltooth sawfish population in the United States would be significant because that population was very large and other populations of smalltooth sawfish in the world were small and declining). Here, the FWS found that the Arizona pygmy-owls number between 20 and 40 individuals. *See Home Builders,* 2001 WL 1876349, at *4. The FWS did not find, however, that the loss of these 20 to 40 individuals would significantly curtail the western pygmy-owls' current range, which consists mostly of the more-numerous northwestern Mexico pygmy-owl population. *See* Listing Rule, 62 Fed. Reg. at 10,741.

(3)　Reduce the Historic Range of the Taxon

The FWS argues that the gap would be significant because the loss of the Arizona pygmy-owls would reduce the historical range of its taxon. Other listing rules have found a gap to be significant on these grounds. . . .

The issue here is whether the FWS provided a rational basis in the Listing Rule for its conclusion that the loss of the Arizona pygmy-owl population would significantly reduce the historical range of its taxon. . . .

While the Arizona range might possibly be significant to its taxon's historic range despite its existence as a stable population at the periphery of that range, the FWS did not articulate a reasoned basis in the Listing Rule as to why that is so. We cannot supply a reasoned basis here "to make up for deficiencies in the agency's decision," nor can we defer to the FWS when its path of reasoning is not clear. *See Dioxin/ Organochlorine Ctr.*, 57 F.3d at 1525.

(4)　Extirpation of the Western Pygmy Owl
from the United States

Finally, the FWS argues that the gap would be significant because it would deprive the United States of its portion of the western pygmy-owl's range. Similarly, Intervenors-Appellees argue that the Arizona pygmy-owl's range is significant because of its location in the United States, where it and the owl can receive ESA protection.

This argument misconstrues the second significance factor. In designating a DPS under the *DPS Policy*, the FWS must find that a discrete population is significant to its taxon as a whole, not to the United States. *See* 61 Fed. Reg. at 4725. Extirpation of the western pygmy-owl from the United States is certainly significant to the United States, but that does not mean that the loss of the Arizona pygmy-owl population is significant to its taxon. The gap caused by the loss of the pygmy-owl's Arizona range cannot be significant to the range of the taxon as a whole simply because that range is in the United States. There must also be some significance to the entire taxon. . . .

In sum, we conclude that the FWS did not articulate a reasoned basis in the Listing Rule for finding that the gap created by the loss of the discrete Arizona pygmy-owl population would be significant to the taxon as a whole.

2. The Fourth Significance Factor

A discrete population can be significant to its taxon based on evidence that it "differs markedly from other populations of the species in its genetic characteristics." 61 Fed. Reg. at 4725. The FWS argues that since the eastern and western pygmy-owls had potentially different genetic characteristics, the loss of the Arizona pygmy-owls would extirpate the genetic distinctness of the western pygmy-owls from the United States. As argued by the FWS, such a loss would contravene the ESA's policy of conserving genetic resources.

In the Listing Rule, the FWS divided the Arizona pygmy-owls and the northwestern Mexico pygmy-owls into separate populations. Therefore, under the plain language of the fourth significance factor, the FWS needed to show that the Arizona pygmy-owls differed markedly in their genetic characteristics from the northwestern Mexico pygmy-owls. Yet neither the Listing Rule nor the record presented any evidence of marked genetic differences between the pygmy-owls in Arizona and northwestern Mexico. The FWS attempts to argue around this lack of evidence by citing to the finding that the western and eastern pygmy-owls had potential genetic differences and then arguing that the conservation policy incorporated in the significance element mandated the protection of the western pygmy-owls within the United States. We reject this argument because (1) the FWS only found potential, rather than marked, genetic differences between the eastern and western pygmy-owls, and (2) the FWS must find that a discrete population is significant to its taxon, not to the United States.

The FWS found in the Listing Rule that "[t]he potential for genetic distinctness" exists between the western and eastern pygmy-owls. 62 Fed. Reg. at 10,731. The Listing Rule highlighted two facts to support this determination. First, non-migratory pygmy-owls are "separated by the basin-and-range mountains and intervening Chihuahuan Desert basins of southeastern Arizona, southern New Mexico, and western Texas" in the United States and "by the highlands of the Sierra Madre

Oriental and Occidental, and the Mexican Plateau" in Mexico. *Id.* This separation suggests infrequent genetic mixing between the two pygmy-owl populations. *Id.* Second, the Listing Rule found that "considerable variation in plumage between regional populations has been noted, including specific distinctions between Arizona and Texas pygmy-owls." *Id.* The literature cited by the Listing Rule does contain evidence of "specific distinctions" in plumage between Arizona and Texas pygmy-owls. Based in part on this "potential morphological and genetic distinctness," the FWS divided the pygmy-owls into eastern and western pygmy-owl populations. *Id.*

We conclude that this analysis fails to meet the requirement of the fourth significance factor. Under the *DPS Policy*, "markedly" is given its common meaning, which in this context is "appreciably." 61 Fed. Reg. at 4723; *Webster's New World Dictionary* at 828 (defining "marked"). Here, after examining all the evidence described above, the FWS only found that potential (*i.e.*, possible) genetic differences exist between the western and eastern pygmy-owl populations. The fourth significance factor, however, requires not only actual genetic differences, but that those actual genetic differences be appreciable. In this case, the FWS was not even sure if the genetic differences between the eastern and western pygmy-owl populations were actual, let alone appreciable. Moreover, the only genetic study conducted on the pygmy-owls found "very little genetic difference" between the Texas and northeastern Mexico pygmy-owls. *See id.* This study did not evaluate genetic differences between western and eastern pygmy-owls, and the finding of "low levels of genetic variation" among eastern pygmy-owls certainly does nothing to show that genetic differences between the western and eastern pygmy-owls are more than just a possibility. . . .

The FWS also contends that the policy behind the significance element of the *DPS Policy* mandates the conservation of the genetic diversity of the United States population of the western pygmy-owls. The FWS argues that:

> [w]ithout the Arizona population, the United States would have lost one of its two pygmy-owl populations, and the chance it had to conserve the western population. Conservation of the western range would then be entirely in the hands of Mexico, because the U.S. has no ability to protect the species outside its borders.

[Appellee's Brief at 28.] Under the *DPS Policy*, a discrete population segment must be significant "to the taxon to which it belongs." 61 Fed. Reg. at 4725. The FWS' argument, however, emphasizes the significance of the Arizona pygmy-owls to the United States, not to its taxon. . . .

The FWS promulgated the *DPS Policy* consistently to designate DPSs "in light of Congressional guidance . . . that the authority to list DPS's [sic] be used '. . . sparingly' while encouraging the conservation of genetic diversity." *Id.* Having chosen to promulgate the *DPS Policy*, the FWS must follow that policy. *Steenholdt v. FAA*, 314 F.3d 633, 639 (D.C.

Cir. 2003) (noting that federal agencies must follow their own rules). As such, to meet this fourth significance factor, the FWS must find significance to the taxon as a whole, not just to the United States. It did not do so in this case.

We conclude, therefore, that the FWS did not articulate a rational basis in the Listing Rule for its finding that the discrete Arizona pygmy-owl population is significant to its taxon as a whole under . . . [the] fourth significance factor. . . .

NOTES AND QUESTIONS

1. **Discreteness and International Boundaries.** The DPS policy promulgated jointly by FWS and NMFS requires a finding that a DPS be both discrete and significant to its taxon before it may be listed under the ESA. 61 Fed. Reg. at 4725. International boundaries may only be considered in the discreteness prong of the DPS inquiry. A population may be considered discrete if "[i]t is delimited by international governmental boundaries within which differences in control of exploitation, management of habitat, conservation status, or regulatory mechanisms exist. . . ." *Id.* The *Norton* court upheld the FWS finding that the Arizona pygmy-owl population was discrete, deferring to the FWS interpretation of "conservation status" as meaning simply "the number of individuals left in the population." 340 F.3d at 843. Because there were different numbers of individuals in the Mexico and Arizona populations of pygmy owls, with the Mexican population being more abundant, the Arizona population was discrete. Is this a desirable interpretation of the term "conservation status"? If all that is required for a United States population to be discrete is that it exist in different numbers than a foreign population, is this a meaningful requirement? Does the ESA contemplate listing a species anytime it is threatened or endangered within the U.S., even if it is abundant in other parts of the world? Should there be a requirement that the foreign population of a species be less numerous than the United States population before it can be listed under the ESA? Should the foreign population have to be threatened or endangered before the U.S. population can be listed? What if there is actually a single, contiguous population, such that individuals regularly cross the border separating the two countries? Would it be more coherent to look at the conservation efforts each country makes to protect the species, either alone, or in conjunction with, the species abundance in each country? Can the ESA be understood as a United States species self-sufficiency statute, expressing the desire that the United States retain a viable population of a species regardless of its abundance in the rest of the world?

2. **Significance to Its Taxon and International Populations.** In a footnote, the *Norton* court stated that it is well-established that "the United States can protect endangered populations within its borders even if other populations of the same species are more abundant in other countries." 340 F.3d at 841 n.7. Under the DPS Policy issued by FWS, however, a distinct population segment may be protected only if it is significant to its taxon. Citing this language, the *Norton* court rejected the argument that the

Arizona pygmy-owl should be protected because it constituted the only population of western pygmy-owls in the United States. The court instead reasoned that a finding of significance required "significance to the taxon as a whole, not just to the United States." *Id.* at 852. Is the court's holding on this issue consistent with its earlier statement in footnote seven? How often is it likely to be the case that a DPS is "significant to the taxon as a whole, not just to the United States" if "other populations of the species are . . . abundant in other countries"? Conversely, if the foreign population is threatened or endangered, is the United States population automatically "significant to its taxon" by default?

In *Northwest Ecosystem Alliance v. U.S. Fish and Wildlife Service*, 475 F.3d 1136 (9th Cir. 2007), the court upheld the DPS policy when conservation groups argued that the "significant to the taxon" requirement violated the ESA. The Ninth Circuit first found the term "distinct population segment" to be ambiguous. The issue then became what level of deference the DPS policy was due. FWS had considered adopting the DPS policy as a legislative rule but in the end issued only a policy statement. Nevertheless, the court granted the DPS policy Chevron deference, highlighting the fact that it had been issued after a notice-and-comment procedure, even though it escaped many of the other rigors of the rulemaking process. Is the requirement that a DPS be "significant to its taxon" consistent with the purposes of the ESA— to protect species because they are "of esthetic, ecological, educational, historical, recreational, and scientific value to the Nation and its people"? 16 U.S.C. § 1531(a)(3). What practical effect is this decision likely to have on agency rulemaking in the future?

3. DPS Policy and the Best Available Science Mandate. The DPS policy justifies the consideration of international boundaries in listing decisions with the rationale that "it appears to be reasonable for national legislation, which has its principal effects on a national scale, to recognize units delimited by international boundaries when these coincide with differences in the management, status, or exploitation of a species." 61 Fed. Reg. at 4723. The ESA, however, requires that listing decisions be based "solely on the basis of the best scientific and commercial data available." 16 U.S.C. § 1533(b)(1)(A). Is the use of international political boundaries under the DPS policy consistent with the strictly scientific mandate of the ESA? Can the two be reconciled?

Compounding this issue is the fact that "distinct population segment" is a statutory term that is not defined in the ESA. Is it even possible to rely "solely" on the best scientific evidence available in defining a DPS when scientists do not utilize the term? Furthermore, scientists often disagree on whether different populations of an organism represent different species, and even on how to define what a species is. *E.g.*, R. L. Mayden, *A Hierarchy of Species Concepts: The Denouement in the Saga of the Species Problem*, *in* SPECIES: THE UNITS OF BIODIVERSITY 381 (Michael F. Claridge et al. eds., 1997) (noting over twenty concepts of species in modern scientific literature). Was the inclusion of DPSs in the ESA a tacit acknowledgement by Congress that reliance on science alone is insufficient to protect domestic plant and animal populations? Was it a recognition of the uncertainty inherent in science? Could it be interpreted as an attempt to circumvent the best available science standard?

4.   Significant Gap Under the Second Significance Factor. The FWS argued that the Arizona DPS was significant, *inter alia*, because the loss of the Arizona DPS would result in a significant gap in the range of the taxon. On what basis did FWS argue that the loss of the Arizona population segment would constitute a gap in the range of the taxon? Why did Home Builders argue that the loss of the Arizona population could not constitute a "gap"? Which argument do you find most convincing?

On what grounds did the FWS argue that the gap in the taxon should be considered significant? Why did the *Norton* court dismiss each of these arguments?

5.   Genetic Variation Under the Fourth Significance Factor. Pursuant to the fourth significance factor, a DPS is considered significant if there exists evidence "that the [DPS] differs markedly from other populations of the species in its genetic characteristics." 61 Fed. Reg. at 4725. In *Norton*, FWS found that there was the *potential* for genetic distinctness between western and eastern pygmy owls, but the agency had not shown that this genetic distinctness actually existed. The only existing study on genetic variation in pygmy owls looked at genetic variation among eastern pygmy owls, but did not address the differences between eastern and western owls. The court found the FWS's finding of potential for genetic distinctness to be inadequate, and found that FWS would have to prove actual genetic distinctness for that to be the basis for protecting the DPS. Should FWS be required to undertake its own extensive genetic study before a DPS can be protected? If the results of such a study are inconclusive or contain some level of uncertainty, should FWS be allowed to protect the DPS?

6.   DPS and Delisting. The ESA authorizes FWS to list, delist and reclassify "species," a category that includes DPSs. In *Humane Soc'y of the United States v. Jewell*, 76 F. Supp. 3d 69, 76 (D.D.C. 2014), the court held that an agency may not designate a DPS for the purpose of immediately *delisting* that DPS from the ESA. The court explained that "whether a group of organisms is a 'species' within the meaning of 16 U.S.C. § 1532(16), a definition that includes DPSs, is of no legal consequence under the ESA until a determination is made that the group is an endangered or threatened species." *Id.* at 111. The court concluded that "the creation or initial designation of a DPS operates as a one-way ratchet to provide ESA protections to the covered vertebrates. Only after a DPS has been created to afford protection to the covered vertebrates may the DPS be revised and the covered vertebrates down-listed." *Id.* at 112.

The D.C. Circuit disagreed with the lower court. The Court explained:

> . . . the statutory text leaves room for the Service, at the initial stage, to list most of a species as threatened, while dividing out a distinct population segment for listing as endangered based on its unique circumstances and conditions. That same language would also permit the Service at the outset to list a segment as threatened even if the remainder of the taxon is endangered. *See* 16 U.S.C.

§ 1532(16) (defining "species" in non-exhaustive terms). . . .
Because the statutory text and purposes can be read to permit such
a divided listing on the front end of the listing process, the Service
likewise can reasonably read the statute to permit similar
determinations at the revision stage. The statutory text does not
have to be treated like a one-way street leading only to uplisting.

Humane Soc'y of United States v. Zinke, 865 F.3d 585, 597–98 (D.C. Cir.
2017). The Court held that FWS permissibly concluded that the ESA allows
the assignment of a different conservation status to a DPS if the statutory
criteria for uplisting, downlisting, or delisting are met. *Id.* at 600. Do you
agree with the D.C. Circuit's conclusion? Does it further the ESA's objectives
to allow the use of DPSs in delisting?

The D.C. Circuit ultimately rejected the FWS's delisting of the Western
Great Lakes segment of the gray wolf population, holding that the agency's
analysis of the DPS' status wrongly omitted all consideration of the species'
lost historical range, and was arbitrary and capricious. *Id.* at 605.

7.   Perverse Incentives for Private Landowners? There is evidence
that some landowners facing potential land use restrictions from the ESA
may have reduced incentives to maintain or improve habitat, and in fact,
may destroy it in order to preempt regulation. Landowner incentives
generated by the ESA, as well as informational asymmetries between
landowners and the government, have been examined in the theoretical and
empirical literature. *See* Robert Innes, et al., *Takings, Compensation and
Endangered Species Protection on Private Lands*, 12 J. ECON. PERSPECTIVES,
No. 3, 35–52 (1998); Stephen Polasky & Holly Doremus, *When the Truth
Hurts: Endangered Species Policy on Private Land with Imperfect
Information*, 35 J. ENVT'L. ECON. & MGMT. 22–47 (1998); Robert Innes, *The
Economics of Takings and Compensation When Land and Its Public Use
Value Are in Private Hands*, 76 LAND ECON., No. 2, 195–212 (2000). One case
study that provides empirical evidence of such behavior involves the Arizona
pygmy owl at issue in *Norton*.

As recounted in *Norton*, the FWS listed the Arizona pygmy owl as a DPS
under the ESA in 1997. The FWS proposed critical habitat for the DPS
covering 1.2 million acres in 1998, and finalized it in 1999. An empirical
study used the time gap between the announcement and designation of
critical habitat to examine changes in the timing of development permit
applications inside and outside of proposed critical habitat areas. The study
found that parcels within critical habitat were developed approximately one
year earlier and sold for roughly 22 percent less than noncritical habitat
parcels, supporting the hypothesis of preemptive behavior by private
landowners. John A. List et al., *Is the Endangered Species Act Endangering
Species?* 22, 25 (Nat'l Bureau of Econ. Research, Working Paper No. 1277,
2007).

The authors noted that leading up to the designation of critical habitat,
public hearings and public attention to the possibility of critical habitat
designation can drive private landowners to take more aggressive
development activities than they would otherwise. What can be done, if

anything, to limit the perverse incentive to accelerate development in order to preempt critical habitat designation?

As a result of the decision in *Norton*, the FWS withdrew the designation of the Arizona DPS of the pygmy owl from the federal list of endangered and threatened wildlife and removed designated critical habitat for the DPS.

ii. "NOT LIKELY TO JEOPARDIZE"

The ESA imposes requirements on both federal and private actions, but the requirements for federal actions are significantly more stringent than the requirements for private actions. Section 7 of the ESA requires each federal agency to insure that any agency action is "not likely to jeopardize" the continued existence of any endangered or threatened species or result in the destruction or adverse modification of their critical habitat. The case below discusses the application of this requirement to the building of a major federal dam that was well underway before the passage of the ESA.

Tennessee Valley Authority v. Hill
437 U.S. 153 (1978).

■ CHIEF JUSTICE BURGER delivered the opinion of the Court:

The questions presented in this case are (a) whether the Endangered Species Act of 1973 requires a court to enjoin the operation of a virtually completed federal dam—which had been authorized prior to 1973—when, pursuant to authority vested in him by Congress, the Secretary of the Interior has determined that operation of the dam would eradicate an endangered species; and (b) whether continued congressional appropriations for the dam after 1973 constituted an implied repeal of the Endangered Species Act, at least as to the particular dam.

The Little Tennessee River originates in the mountains of northern Georgia and flows through the national forest lands of North Carolina into Tennessee, where it converges with the Big Tennessee River near Knoxville. The lower 33 miles of the Little Tennessee takes the river's clear, free-flowing waters through an area of great natural beauty. Among other environmental amenities, this stretch of river is said to contain abundant trout. Considerable historical importance attaches to the areas immediately adjacent to this portion of the Little Tennessee's banks. To the south of the river's edge lies Fort Loudon, established in 1756 as England's southwestern outpost in the French and Indian War. Nearby are also the ancient sites of several native American villages, the archeological stores of which are to a large extent unexplored. These include the Cherokee towns of Echota and Tennase, the former being the sacred capital of the Cherokee Nation as early as the 16th century and the latter providing the linguistic basis from which the State of Tennessee derives its name.

In this area of the Little Tennessee River the Tennessee Valley Authority, a wholly owned public corporation of the United States, began constructing the Tellico Dam and Reservoir Project in 1967, shortly after Congress appropriated initial funds for its development. Tellico is a multi-purpose regional development project designed principally to stimulate shoreline development, generate sufficient electric current to heat 20,000 homes, and provide flatwater recreation and flood control, as well as improve economic conditions in "an area characterized by underutilization of human resources and outmigration of young people." Hearings on Public Works for Power and Energy Research Appropriation Bill, 1977, before a Subcommittee of the House Committee on Appropriations, 94th Cong., 2d Sess., pt. 5, p. 261 (1976). Of particular relevance to this case is one aspect of the project, a dam which TVA determined to place on the Little Tennessee, a short distance from where the river's waters meet with the Big Tennessee. When fully operational, the dam would impound water covering some 16,500 acres—much of which represents valuable and productive farmland—thereby converting the river's shallow, fast-flowing waters into a deep reservoir over 30 miles in length.

The Tellico Dam has never opened, however, despite the fact that construction has been virtually completed and the dam is essentially ready for operation. Although Congress has appropriated monies for Tellico every year since 1967, progress was delayed, and ultimately stopped, by a tangle of lawsuits and administrative proceedings. [The project was initially delayed by a lawsuit challenging the adequacy of the project's environmental impact statement under NEPA.]

A few months prior to the District Court's decision dissolving the NEPA injunction, a discovery was made in the waters of the Little Tennessee which would profoundly affect the Tellico Project. Exploring the area around Coytee Springs, which is about seven miles from the mouth of the river, a University of Tennessee ichthyologist, Dr. David A. Etnier, found a previously unknown species of perch, the snail darter, or *Percina (Imostoma) tanasi*. This three-inch, tannish-colored fish, whose numbers are estimated to be in the range of 10,000 to 15,000, would soon engage the attention of environmentalists, the TVA, the Department of the Interior, the Congress of the United States, and ultimately the federal courts, as a new and additional basis to halt construction of the dam.

Until recently the finding of a new species of animal life would hardly generate a cause célèbre. This is particularly so in the case of darters, of which there are approximately 130 known species, 8 to 10 of these having been identified only in the last five years.[7] The moving force

---

[7]   In Tennessee alone there are 85 to 90 species of darters, of which upward to 45 live in the Tennessee River system. New species of darters are being constantly discovered and classified—at the rate of about one per year. This is a difficult task for even trained ichthyologists since species of darters are often hard to differentiate from one another.

behind the snail darter's sudden fame came some four months after its discovery, when the Congress passed the Endangered Species Act of 1973 (Act), 16 U.S.C. § 1531 *et seq.* This legislation, among other things, authorizes the Secretary of the Interior to declare species of animal life "endangered" and to identify the "critical habitat" of these creatures. When a species or its habitat is so listed, the following portion of the Act—relevant here—becomes effective:

> The Secretary [of the Interior] shall review other programs administered by him and utilize such programs in furtherance of the purposes of this chapter. All other Federal departments and agencies shall, in consultation with and with the assistance of the Secretary, utilize their authorities in furtherance of the purposes of this chapter by carrying out programs for the conservation of endangered species and threatened species listed pursuant to section 1533 of this title and *by taking such action necessary to insure that actions authorized, funded, or carried out by them do not jeopardize the continued existence of such endangered species and threatened species or result in the destruction or modification of habitat of such species* which is determined by the Secretary, after consultation as appropriate with the affected States, to be critical.

16 U.S.C. § 1536 (emphasis added). In January 1975, the respondents in this case [a regional association of biological scientists, a Tennessee conservation group, and individuals who were citizens or users of the Little Tennessee Valley] and others petitioned the Secretary of the Interior to list the snail darter as an endangered species. After receiving comments form [sic] various interested parties, including TVA and the State of Tennessee, the Secretary formally listed the snail darter as an endangered species on October 8, 1975. In so acting, it was noted that "the snail darter is a living entity which is genetically distinct and reproductively isolated from other fishes." 40 Fed. Reg. 47,505. More important for the purposes of this case, the Secretary determined that the snail darter apparently lives only in that portion of the Little Tennessee River which would be completely inundated by the reservoir created as a consequence of the Tellico Dam's completion. *Id.* at 47,506. The Secretary went on to explain the significance of the dam to the habitat of the snail darter:

> [T]he snail darter occurs only in the swifter portions of shoals over clean gravel substrate in cool, low-turbidity water. Food of the snail darter is almost exclusively snails which require a clean gravel substrate for their survival. *The proposed impoundment of water behind the proposed Tellico Dam would result in total destruction of the snail darter's habitat.*

Ibid. (emphasis added). Subsequent to this determination, the Secretary declared the area of the Little Tennessee which would be affected by the Tellico Dam to be the "critical habitat" of the snail darter. Using these determinations as a predicate, and notwithstanding the near completion of the dam, the Secretary declared that pursuant to § 7 of the Act, "all Federal agencies must take such action as is necessary to insure that actions authorized, funded, or carried out by them do not result in the destruction or modification of this critical habitat area." 41 Fed. Reg. 13,928 (1976). This notice, of course, was pointedly directed at TVA and clearly aimed at halting completion or operation of the dam. . . .

In February 1976, pursuant to § 11(g) of the Endangered Species Act, 16 U.S.C. § 1540(g), respondents filed the case now under review, seeking to enjoin completion of the dam and impoundment of the reservoir on the ground that those actions would violate the Act by directly causing the extinction of the species *Percina (Imostoma) tanasi*. . . .

We begin with the premise that operation of the Tellico Dam will either eradicate the known population of snail darters or destroy their critical habitat. Petitioner does not now seriously dispute this fact. In any event, under § 4(a)(1) of the Act, 16 U.S.C. § 1533(a)(1), the Secretary of the Interior is vested with exclusive authority to determine whether a species such as the snail darter is "endangered" or "threatened" and to ascertain the factors which have led to such a precarious existence. By § 4(d) Congress has authorized—indeed commanded—the Secretary to "issue such regulations as he deems necessary and advisable to provide for the conservation of such species." 16 U.S.C. § 1533(d). As we have seen, the Secretary promulgated regulations which declared the snail darter an endangered species whose critical habitat would be destroyed by creation of the Tellico Dam. . . .

Starting from the above premise, two questions are presented: (a) Would TVA be in violation of the Act if it completed and operated the Tellico Dam as planned? (b) If TVA's actions would offend the Act, is an injunction the appropriate remedy for the violation? For the reasons stated hereinafter, we hold that both questions must be answered in the affirmative.

It may seem curious to some that the survival of a relatively small number of three-inch fish among all the countless millions of species extant would require the permanent halting of a virtually completed dam for which Congress has expended more than $100 million. The paradox is not minimized by the fact that Congress continued to appropriate large sums of public money for the project, even after congressional Appropriations Committees were apprised of its apparent impact upon the survival of the snail darter. We conclude, however, that the explicit provisions of the Endangered Species Act require precisely that result.

One would be hard pressed to find a statutory provision whose terms were any plainer than those in § 7 of the Endangered Species Act. Its very words affirmatively command all federal agencies "to *insure* that actions *authorized, funded,* or *carried out* by them do not *jeopardize* the continued existence" of an endangered species or "*result* in the destruction or modification of habitat of such species. . . ." 16 U.S.C. § 1536 (emphasis added). This language admits of no exception. Nonetheless, petitioner urges, as do the dissenters, that the Act cannot reasonably be interpreted as applying to a federal project which was well under way when Congress passed the Endangered Species Act of 1973. To sustain that position, however, we would be forced to ignore the ordinary meaning of plain language. It has not been shown, for example, how TVA can close the gates of the Tellico Dam without "carrying out" an action that has been "authorized" and "funded" by a federal agency. Nor can we understand how such action will *insure* that the snail darter's habitat is not disrupted.[18] Accepting the Secretary's determinations, as we must, it is clear that TVA's proposed operation of the dam will have precisely the opposite effect, namely the *eradication* of an endangered species.

Concededly, this view of the Act will produce results requiring the sacrifice of the anticipated benefits of the project and of many millions of dollars in public funds. But examination of the language, history, and structure of the legislation under review here indicates beyond doubt that Congress intended endangered species to be afforded the highest of priorities. . . .

. . . The plain intent of Congress in enacting this statute was to halt and reverse the trend toward species extinction, whatever the cost. This is reflected not only in the stated policies of the Act, but in literally every section of the statute. . . .

One might . . . [say] that in this case the burden on the public through the loss of millions of unrecoverable dollars would greatly outweigh the loss of the snail darter. But neither the Endangered Species Act nor Art. III of the Constitution provides federal courts with authority to make such fine utilitarian calculations. On the contrary, the plain language of the Act, buttressed by its legislative history, shows clearly that Congress viewed the value of endangered species as "incalculable." Quite obviously, it would be difficult for a court to balance the loss of a sum certain—even $100 million—against a congressionally declared "incalculable" value, even assuming we had the power to engage in such a weighing process, which we emphatically do not.

In passing the Endangered Species Act of 1973, Congress was also aware of certain instances in which exceptions to the statute's broad sweep would be necessary. Thus, § 10, 16 U.S.C. § 1539, creates a number

---

[18] In dissent, Mr. Justice POWELL argues that the meaning of "actions" in § 7 is "far from 'plain,' " and that "it seems evident that the 'actions' referred to are not all actions that an agency can ever take, but rather actions that the agency is *deciding whether* to authorize, to fund, or to carry out." 437 U.S. at 205 (Powell, J., dissenting). . . . [T]he dissent's reading of § 7 is flawed on several counts. First, under its view, the words "or carry out" in § 7 would be superfluous since all prospective actions of an agency remain to be "authorized" or "funded." Second, the dissent's position logically means that an agency would be obligated to comply with § 7 only when a project is in the planning stage. But if Congress had meant to so limit the Act, it surely would have used words to that effect, as it did in the National Environmental Policy Act, 42 U.S.C. §§ 4332(2)(A), (C).

of limited "hardship exemptions," none of which would even remotely apply to the Tellico Project. In fact, there are no exemptions in the Endangered Species Act for federal agencies, meaning that under the maxim *expressio unius est exclusio alterius*, we must presume that these were the only "hardship cases" Congress intended to exempt.

Notwithstanding Congress' expression of intent in 1973, we are urged to find that the continuing appropriations for Tellico Dam constitute an implied repeal of the 1973 Act, at least insofar as it applies to the Tellico Project. In support of this view, TVA points to the statements found in various House and Senate Appropriations Committees' Reports . . . [that] generally reflected the attitude of the *Committees* either that the Act did not apply to Tellico or that the dam should be completed regardless of the provisions of the Act. Since we are unwilling to assume that these latter Committee statements constituted advice to ignore the provisions of a duly enacted law, we assume that these Committees believed that the Act simply was not applicable in this situation. But even under this interpretation of the Committees' actions, we are unable to conclude that the Act has been in any respect amended or repealed.

There is nothing in the appropriations measures, as passed, which states that the Tellico Project was to be completed irrespective of the requirements of the Endangered Species Act. These appropriations, in fact, represented relatively minor components of the lump-sum amounts for the *entire* TVA budget.[35] To find a repeal of the Endangered Species Act under these circumstances would surely do violence to the " 'cardinal rule . . . that repeals by implication are not favored.' " *Morton v. Mancari*, 417 U.S. 535, 549 (1974) (quoting *Posadas v. National City Bank*, 296 U.S. 497, 503 (1936)). In *Posadas* this Court held, in no uncertain terms, that "the intention of the legislature to repeal must be clear and manifest." *Ibid*. In practical terms, this "cardinal rule" means that "[i]n the absence of some affirmative showing of an intention to repeal, the only permissible justification for a repeal by implication is when the earlier and later statutes are irreconcilable." *Mancari*, 417 U.S. at 550.

The doctrine disfavoring repeals by implication "applies with full vigor when . . . the subsequent legislation is an appropriations measure." *Committee for Nuclear Responsibility v. Seaborg*, 463 F.2d 783, 785 (D.C. Cir. 1971) (emphasis added); *Environmental Defense Fund v. Froehlke*, 473 F.2d 346, 355 (8th Cir. 1972). This is perhaps an understatement since it would be more accurate to say that the policy applies with even *greater* force when the claimed repeal rests solely on an Appropriations Act. We recognize that both substantive enactments and appropriations measures are "Acts of Congress," but the latter have the limited and

---

[35] The Appropriations Acts did not themselves identify the projects for which the sums had been appropriated; identification of these projects requires reference to the legislative history. Thus, unless a Member scrutinized in detail the Committee proceedings concerning the appropriations, he would have no knowledge of the possible conflict between the continued funding and the Endangered Species Act.

specific purpose of providing funds for authorized programs. When voting on appropriations measures, legislators are entitled to operate under the assumption that the funds will be devoted to purposes which are lawful and not for any purpose forbidden. Without such an assurance, every appropriations measure would be pregnant with prospects of altering substantive legislation, repealing by implication any prior statute which might prohibit the expenditure. Not only would this lead to the absurd result of requiring Members to review exhaustively the background of every authorization before voting on an appropriation, but it would flout the very rules the Congress carefully adopted to avoid this need. House Rule XXI(2), for instance, specifically provides:

> No appropriation shall be reported in any general appropriation bill, or be in order as an amendment thereto, for any expenditure not previously authorized by law, unless in continuation of appropriations for such public works as are already in progress. *Nor shall any provision in any such bill or amendment thereto changing existing law be in order.*

(Emphasis added). See also Standing Rules of the Senate, Rule 16.4. Thus, to sustain petitioner's position, we would be obliged to assume that Congress meant to repeal *pro tanto* § 7 of the Act by means of a procedure expressly prohibited under the rules of Congress.

Perhaps mindful of the fact that it is "swimming upstream" against a strong current of well-established precedent, TVA argues for an exception to the rule against implied repealers in a circumstance where, as here, Appropriations Committees have expressly stated their "understanding" that the earlier legislation would not prohibit the proposed expenditure. We cannot accept such a proposition. Expressions of committees dealing with requests for appropriations cannot be equated with statutes enacted by Congress, particularly not in the circumstances presented by this case. First, the Appropriations Committees had no jurisdiction over the subject of endangered species, much less did they conduct the type of extensive hearings which preceded passage of the earlier Endangered Species Acts, especially the 1973 Act. We venture to suggest that the House Committee on Merchant Marine and Fisheries and the Senate Committee on Commerce would be somewhat surprised to learn that their careful work on the substantive legislation had been undone by the simple-and brief-insertion of some inconsistent language in Appropriations Committees' Reports.

Second, there is no indication that Congress as a whole was aware of TVA's position, although the Appropriations Committees apparently agreed with petitioner's views. Only recently in *SEC v. Sloan,* 436 U.S. 103 (1978), we declined to presume general congressional acquiescence in a 34-year-old practice of the Securities and Exchange Commission, despite the fact that the Senate Committee *having jurisdiction over the Commission's activities* had long expressed approval of the practice. Mr. Justice REHNQUIST, speaking for the Court, observed that we should be "extremely hesitant to presume general congressional awareness of the Commission's construction based only upon a few isolated statements in the thousands of pages of legislative documents." *Id.*, at 121. *A fortiori,* we should not assume that petitioner's views—and the Appropriations Committees' acceptance of them—were any better known, especially when the TVA is not the agency with primary responsibility for administering the Endangered Species Act.

Quite apart from the foregoing factors, we would still be unable to find that in this case "the earlier and later statutes are irreconcilable," *Mancari*, 417 U.S. at 551; here it is entirely possible "to regard each as effective." *Id.* at 550. The starting point in this analysis must be the legislative proceedings leading to the 1977 appropriations since the earlier funding of the dam occurred prior to the listing of the snail darter as an endangered species. In all successive years, TVA confidently reported to the Appropriations Committees that efforts to transplant the snail darter appeared to be successful; this surely gave those Committees some basis for the impression that there was no direct conflict between the Tellico Project and the Endangered Species Act. Indeed, the special appropriation for 1978 of $2 million for transplantation of endangered species supports the view that the Committees saw such relocation as the means whereby collision between Tellico and the Endangered Species Act could be avoided. . . . [T]he Committees understandably advised TVA to cooperate with the Department of the Interior "to relocate the endangered species to another suitable habitat so as to permit the project to proceed as rapidly as possible." H.R. Rep. No. 95–379, p. 11 (1977). It is true that the Committees repeated their earlier expressed "view" that the Act did not prevent completion of the Tellico Project. Considering these statements in context, however, it is evident that they " 'represent only the personal views of these legislators,' " and "however explicit, [they] cannot serve to change the legislative intent of Congress expressed before the Act's passage." *Regional Rail Reorganization Act Cases*, 419 U.S. 102, 132 (1974).

Having determined that there is an irreconcilable conflict between operation of the Tellico Dam and the explicit provisions of § 7 of the Endangered Species Act, we must now consider what remedy, if any, is appropriate. . . .

Here we are urged to view the Endangered Species Act "reasonably," and hence shape a remedy "that accords with some modicum of common sense and the public weal." 437 U.S. at 196 (Powell, J., dissenting). But is that our function? We have no expert knowledge on the subject of endangered species, much less do we have a mandate from the people to strike a balance of equities on the side of the Tellico Dam. Congress has spoken in the plainest of words, making it abundantly clear that the balance has been struck in favor of affording endangered species the highest of priorities, thereby adopting a policy which it described as "institutionalized caution." . . .

We agree with the Court of Appeals that in our constitutional system the commitment to the separation of powers is too fundamental for us to pre-empt congressional action by judicially decreeing what accords with "common sense and the public weal." Our Constitution vests such responsibilities in the political branches.

NOTES AND QUESTIONS

1. **Agency "Action."** The ESA applies to "any *action* authorized, funded, or carried out by [any federal] agency." 16 U.S.C. § 1536(a)(2) (emphasis added). In dissent, Justice Powell (joined by Justice Blackmun) argued that the completion of the Tellico dam should not constitute an "action" within the meaning of the statute:

> In terms of planning and executing various activities, it seems evident that the "actions" referred to are not all actions that an agency can ever take, but rather actions that the agency is *deciding whether* to authorize, to fund, or to carry out. In short, these words reasonably may be read as applying only to *prospective actions, i.e.,* actions with respect to which the agency has reasonable decisionmaking alternatives still available, actions *not yet* carried out. At the time respondents brought this lawsuit, the Tellico Project was 80% complete at a cost of more than $78 million. . . . Thus, under a prospective reading of § 7, the action already had been "carried out" in terms of any remaining reasonable decisionmaking power.

437 U.S. at 205 (Powell, J., dissenting). The majority argued that such a reading of "action" would make "the words 'or carry out' in § 7 . . . superfluous" since any prospective federal action would need to be authorized and funded. *Id.* at 173 n.18. Which argument do you find more persuasive? What should the term "action" encompass? If the dam had been entirely completed, does commencing its operation constitute an action? Does continuing its operation constitute an action?

2. **Effect of Continuing Congressional Appropriations.** Should the statements by the congressional appropriations committees that the ESA does not apply to the Tellico project carry any weight? The Court stated that "[e]xpressions of committees dealing with requests for appropriations cannot be equated with statutes enacted by Congress." 437 U.S. at 191. Do you agree in this case? What about the fact that the continued appropriation of funds for Tellico was approved by the full Congress? Why are repeals by implication even more suspect when they are the product of appropriations?

3. **Conflicting Statutes and Discretionary Actions.** In *National Association of Homebuilders v. Defenders of Wildlife*, 551 U.S. 644 (2007), the Supreme Court was charged with reconciling two seemingly conflicting statutory provisions, § 7(a)(2) of the ESA and § 402(b) of the CWA. Under the CWA, EPA initially administers each State's water pollution discharge permitting program, but § 402(b) of the CWA states that EPA "shall approve" the transfer of this permitting authority to a State if nine specified criteria are satisfied. *See* 33 U.S.C. § 1342(b). Arizona had applied to EPA and was

granted authority to issue water pollution discharge permits. 551 U.S. at 653–55. Defenders of Wildlife (DOW) challenged EPA's decision to transfer this permitting authority to Arizona as arbitrary and capricious. *Id.* at 655. The Ninth Circuit agreed with DOW, finding that § 7(a)(2) of the ESA imposed an affirmative duty on EPA to insure that its transfer decision would not jeopardize any listed species, regardless of the fact that Arizona had met the nine criteria specified in § 402(b) of the CWA and the "shall approve" language therein. *Id.* at 655–57. The Supreme Court, in a 5–4 decision, disagreed, holding that EPA's transfer decision under § 402(b) of the CWA was not subject to § 7(a)(2) of the ESA because it was not a discretionary agency action.

Justice Alito, writing for the majority, found the text of the two statutory provisions to be in conflict. Concerning § 402(b) of the CWA, he wrote that "[b]y its terms, the statutory language is mandatory and the list exclusive; if the nine specified criteria are satisfied, EPA does not have the discretion to deny a transfer application." 551 U.S. at 660–62. Requiring EPA to heed § 7(a)(2) of the ESA and insure that its transfer decision would not jeopardize any listed species would "effectively repeal § 402(b)'s statutory mandate by engrafting a tenth criterion onto the CWA. . . . § 402(b) does not just set forth *minimum* requirements for the transfer of permitting authority; it affirmatively mandates that the transfer 'shall' be approved if the specified criteria are met." *Id.* at 662–64. The majority invoked the canon of statutory interpretation disfavoring implied repeals in support of it position that it was improper to read the ESA as having altered § 402(b) of the CWA, expressing a concern that "[r]eading [§ 7(a)(2)] broadly would thus partially override every federal statute mandating agency action by subjecting such action to the further condition that it pose no jeopardy to endangered species." *Id.* at 664. The majority found a means to "harmonize[ ] the statutes" by way of a joint FWS/NMFS regulation, 50 C.F.R. § 402.03, which states that, "Section 7 [of the ESA] and the requirements of this Part apply to all actions in which there is *discretionary* Federal involvement or control." *Id.* at 664–65 (quoting 50 C.F.R. § 402.03) (emphasis added). Applying *Chevron*, the majority deferred to the regulation as a reasonable interpretation of § 7(a)(2) of the ESA. *Id.* at 644–68. Since the decision to transfer water pollution permitting authority to Arizona was a non-discretionary act that EPA was required to undertake under § 402(b) of the CWA once the nine specified criteria were met, § 7(a)(2) of the ESA was not applicable. *Id.* at 673.

The majority in *Defenders of Wildlife* determined that the ESA was not meant to implicitly repeal or amend other statutes. Do you agree? Do you share the majority's concern that a broad reading of § 7(a)(2) would "partially override every federal statute mandating agency action?" *Id.* at 664. Is the decision in *Defenders of Wildlife* consistent with the purpose of the ESA? Is it consistent with the strong language in *TVA v. Hill* that § 7(a)(2) of the ESA "admits of no exception," 437 U.S. at 173, and "reveals a conscious decision by Congress to give endangered species priority over the 'primary missions' of federal agencies"? *Id.* at 185. Is the joint FWS/NMFS regulation, 50 C.F.R. § 402.03, stating that § 7 of the ESA applies only to discretionary agency action consistent with the text of § 7(a)(2)? Is the regulation consistent with the Supreme Court's earlier interpretation of § 7 in *TVA v. Hill*? Is the regulation due deference by the Court? Is EPA's decision to transfer water pollution permitting authority to a state really non-discretionary? Doesn't EPA have to use some discretion in determining if the State has met the nine criteria specified in § 402(b) of the CWA, or is this not the type of discretion that would make EPA's transfer decision a discretionary agency action subject to the commands of § 7(a)(2) of the ESA? Was the agency action in *TVA v. Hill* discretionary? Do the continued Congressional appropriations directing that money be utilized to build the Tellico dam matter? If *TVA v. Hill* were to come before the Supreme Court that decided *Defenders of Wildlife*, do you think they would find § 7(a)(2) of the ESA applicable to the Tellico project?

In a portion of his dissenting opinion, Justice Stevens attempts to give the CWA and the ESA "full effect without privileging one statute over the other." 551 U.S. at 684 (Stevens, J., dissenting). Do you think that this is possible? Can the two statutes truly be reconciled? Can you think of any ways this might be accomplished? Justice Stevens notes that even after EPA transfers permitting authority to a State, it still retains the authority to oversee the State's permitting program. *Id.* at 688–89. Because a State must enter into a Memorandum of Agreement (MOA) laying out the parameters of EPA's oversight duties, Justice Stevens suggests that EPA

> [use] the MOA process to structure its later oversight in a way that will allow it to protect endangered species in accordance with § 7(a)(2) of the ESA. EPA might negotiate a provision in the MOA that would require a State to abide by the ESA requirements when issuing pollution permits. . . . Or the MOA might be drafted in a way that would allow the agency to object to state permits that would jeopardize any and all endangered species.

Id. at 689–90. Does Justice Stevens' proposal accomplish his task of giving full effect to both the CWA and the ESA? Does it add a tenth criterion to § 402(b) of the CWA?

4.   State Actions. Because the ESA applies to actions "authorized" or "funded" by federal agencies, 16 U.S.C. § 1536(a)(2), actions undertaken by private parties that require federal permits or that are partially supported by federal funding are covered by the "no jeopardy" requirement. Under a number of major environmental statutes, a federal agency may delegate some portion of the statute's administration to individual states—for example, under § 402(b) of the CWA, EPA delegates the authority to issue permits for the discharge of pollutants to a state if the state meets certain criteria. Should states' authorization of actions (such as the granting of a discharge permit) pursuant to a federal statute trigger the requirements of the ESA? *See* John W. Steiger, *The Consultation Provision of Section 7(a)(2) of the Endangered Species Act and Its Application to Delegable Federal Programs*, 21 ECOLOGY L.Q. 243 (1994).

iii. "GOD SQUAD" EXEMPTION PROCESS

Following the Court's opinion in *TVA v. Hill*, Congress amended the ESA to provide a process for granting exemptions from its requirements for federal agency actions. The amendment created the Endangered Species Committee, 16 U.S.C. § 1536(e), and authorized the Committee to exempt certain agency actions from the "no jeopardy" requirement, 16 U.S.C. § 1536(h). The Committee, popularly known as the "God Squad" because of its authority to determine whether a species survives, is comprised of the Secretary of Agriculture, the Secretary of the Army, the Chairperson of the Council of Economic Advisors, the Administrator of the Environmental Protection Agency, the Secretary of the Interior, the Administrator of the National Oceanic and Atmospheric Administration, and one member from each affected state to be appointed by the President. 16 U.S.C. § 1536(e)(3). A supermajority of five of the seven members must vote in favor of an exemption for one to be authorized. 16 U.S.C. § 1536(h)(1).

A federal agency, the Governor of the state in which the proposed agency action will occur, or a permit or license applicant are the only parties authorized to apply for an exemption from the Committee, 16 U.S.C. § 1536(g)(1), and the application must pass a series of threshold requirements before it reaches the Committee. *See* 16 U.S.C. § 1536(g)(3). The Committee may grant an exemption only if it finds that:

(i) [T]here are no reasonable and prudent alternatives to the agency action;

(ii) the benefits of such action clearly outweigh the benefits of alternative courses of action consistent with conserving the species or its critical habitat, and such action is in the public interest;

(iii) the action is of regional or national significance; and

(iv) neither the Federal agency concerned nor the exemption applicant made any irreversible or irretrievable commitment of resources prohibited by subsection (d) of this section. . . .

16 U.S.C. § 1536(h)(1)(A). The Committee must also formulate "such reasonable mitigation and enhancement measures . . . as are necessary and appropriate to minimize the adverse effects of the agency action upon the [species]." 16 U.S.C. § 1536(h)(1)(B). A Committee decision may be appealed in the United States Court of Appeals for the circuit where the proposed action will be carried out. 16 U.S.C. § 1536(n).

Congress directed the Endangered Species Committee to convene and rule on exemption applications for Tellico dam and another project, Grayrocks dam. 16 U.S.C. § 1539(i)(1) (Supp. III 1979). The Committee promptly denied the exemption for the Tellico project in a unanimous vote. As Charles Schultze, Chairman of the Council of Economic

Advisors, remarked: "[t]he interesting phenomenon is that here is a project that is 95 percent complete, and if one takes just the cost of finishing it against the total benefits and does it properly, it doesn't pay, which says something about the original design!" WILLIAM BRUCE WHEELER & MICHAEL J. MCDONALD, TVA AND THE TELLICO DAM 1936–1979: A BUREAUCRATIC CRISIS IN POST-INDUSTRIAL AMERICA 211 (1986). Secretary of the Interior Cecil Andrus, serving as Chairman of the Committee, added, "[f]rankly, I hate to see the snail darter get the credit for stopping a project that was ill-conceived and uneconomical in the first place." *Id.* Congress responded by directing in an appropriations rider that the ESA would not apply to the Tellico dam project. Energy and Water Appropriations Act for Fiscal Year 1980, Pub. L. No. 96–69, 93 Stat. 437. Shortly thereafter, snail darter populations were discovered in nearby rivers and creeks, and in 1984 the snail darter was reclassified from an endangered to a threatened species. 49 Fed. Reg. 27,510 (1984).

The Committee unanimously granted the exemption for Grayrocks dam on the Laramie River in Wyoming, which was designed to provide power to portions of eight states. Jared des Rosiers, Note, *The Exemption Process Under the Endangered Species Act: How the "God Squad" Works and Why*, 66 NOTRE DAME L. REV. 825, 846 n.144 (1991) (quoting Note, *Environmental Law—The Endangered Species Act Amendments of 1978: Congress Responds to* Tennessee Valley Authority v. Hill, 25 WAYNE L. REV. 1327, 1339 n.74 (1979)). The FWS found that the project would adversely modify the seasonal habitat utilized by endangered whooping cranes on their migration route over more than 300 miles downstream of the dam on the Platte River by reducing annual stream flow. *Id.* The Committee required mitigation measures, including the establishment of an irrevocable trust fund used to maintain whooping crane critical habitat, and controlling water releases from the dam as part of its exemption decision. *Id.* at 846–47 (citing ENDANGERED SPECIES COMMITTEE DECISION ON GRAYROCKS DAM AND RESERVOIR APPLICATION FOR EXEMPTION (Feb. 7, 1979)).

The only other final decision rendered by the Committee is outlined in the following case, in which several environmental groups successfully challenged the Committee's 5–2 vote to exempt timber sales in Oregon from the requirements of the ESA. In three other instances, the process was initiated but cancelled before a decision was reached. CONG. RES. SERV., ENDANGERED SPECIES ACT (ESA): THE EXEMPTION PROCESS (Jan. 27, 2017).

Portland Audubon Society v. Endangered Species Committee

984 F.2d 1534 (9th Cir. 1993).

■ Before GOODWIN, D.W. NELSON, and REINHARDT, CIRCUIT JUDGES.

■ REINHARDT, CIRCUIT JUDGE:

We consider here a motion filed in a most important and controversial case. The motion itself raises a significant issue of first impression. In the underlying proceeding, petitioners Portland Audubon Society *et al.* (collectively "the environmental groups") challenge the decision of the statutorily-created Endangered Species Committee ("the Committee"), known popularly as "The God Squad," to grant an exemption from the requirements of the Endangered Species Act [as it applies to the protection of the Northern Spotted Owl, an endangered species under the Act] to the Bureau of Land Management for thirteen timber sales in western Oregon. The environmental groups complain of numerous procedural and substantive flaws in the Committee's decision. . . .

The Endangered Species Act requires that "[e]ach Federal agency shall . . . insure that any action authorized, funded or carried out by such agency . . . is not likely to jeopardize the continued existence of any endangered species . . . or result in the destruction or adverse modification of [critical] habitat of such species." 16 U.S.C. § 1536(a)(2) (1988). However, if the Secretary of the Interior (Secretary) finds that a proposed agency action would violate § 1536(a)(2), an agency may apply to the Committee for an exemption from the Endangered Species Act. §§ 1536(a)(2), (g)(1)–(2). The Committee was created by the Endangered Species Act for the sole purpose of making final decisions on applications for exemptions from the Act, § 1536(e), and it is composed of high level officials. Because it is the ultimate arbiter of the fate of an endangered species, the Committee is known as "The God Squad."

The Secretary must initially consider any exemption application, publish a notice and summary of the application in the Federal Register, and determine whether certain threshold requirements have been met. 16 U.S.C. §§ 1536(g)(1)–(3). If so, the Secretary shall, in consultation with the other members of the Committee, hold a hearing on the application (which is conducted by an ALJ), and prepare a written report to the Committee. § 1536(g)(4); 50 C.F.R. § 452.05(a)(2) (Oct. 1, 1991). Within thirty days of receiving the Secretary's report, the Committee shall make a final determination whether or not to grant the exemption from the Endangered Species Act based on the report, the record of the Secretary's hearing, and any additional hearings or written submissions for which the Committee itself may call. § 1536(h)(1)(A); 50 C.F.R. § 453.04. An exemption requires the approval of five of the seven members of the Committee. § 1536(h)(1).

On May 15, 1992, the Committee approved an exemption for the Bureau of Land Management for thirteen of forty-four timber sales. It was only the second exemption ever granted by the Committee. The environmental groups filed a timely petition for review in this court on June 10, 1992. . . .

Both in their petition and in this motion the environmental groups contend that improper ex parte contacts between the White House and members of the Committee tainted the decision-making process. They base their charges on two press reports, one by Associated Press (AP) and one by Reuters, and on the facts stated in the declaration of Victor Sher, lead counsel for the environmental groups. Published on May 6, 1992, the AP and Reuters accounts reported that, according to two anonymous administration sources, at least three Committee members had been "summoned" to the White House and pressured to vote for the exemption. In his declaration filed August 25, 1992, Sher stated that his conversations with "several sources within the Administration," who asked for anonymity, revealed that the media reports were accurate, and further that the pressure exerted by the White House may have changed the vote of at least one Committee member. Sher declared that his sources indicated that, in addition to in-person meetings, at least one Committee member had "substantial on-going contacts with White House staff concerning the substance of his decision on the application for exemption by telephone and facsimile, as well as through staff intermediaries." He also declared that he had learned from his sources that White House staff members had made substantial comments and recommendations on draft versions of the "Endangered Species Committee Amendment," a part of the Committee's final decision. For the purposes of the present motion, the Committee neither admits nor denies that these communications occurred. . . .

The environmental groups contend that the Endangered Species Act incorporates by reference the ex parte communications ban of the APA and forbids ex parte contacts with members of the Committee regarding an exemption application. The ex parte prohibition is set forth at 5 U.S.C. § 557(d)(1). Section 557(d)(1) is a broad provision that prohibits any ex parte communications relevant to the merits of an agency proceeding between "any member of the body comprising the agency" or any agency employee who "is or may reasonably be expected to be involved in the decisional process" and any "interested person outside the agency." 5 U.S.C. §§ 557(d)(1)(A)–(B); *see North Carolina, Envtl. Policy Inst. v. Environmental Protection Agency*, 881 F.2d 1250, 1257–58 (4th Cir. 1989) (interpreting § 557(d)(1) broadly "to include anyone who was involved in the decisional process but is no longer an agency employee or has recused himself or herself from further involvement"). The purpose of the ex parte communications prohibition is to ensure that " 'agency decisions required to be made on a public record are not influenced by private, off-the-record communications from those personally interested in the outcome.' " *Raz*

Inland Navigation Co. v. Interstate Commerce Comm'n, 625 F.2d 258, 260 (9th Cir. 1980) (quoting legislative history). . . .

[T]he ex parte communications prohibition applies whenever the three requirements set forth in APA § 554(a) are satisfied: The administrative proceeding must be 1) an adjudication; 2) determined on the record; and 3) after the opportunity for an agency hearing. The question is, therefore, are those three conditions met here? We find our answer primarily in the language of § 1536(h)(1)(A) of the Endangered Species Act.

We conclude that the first requirement of APA § 554(a) is satisfied. Certain administrative decisions closely resemble judicial determinations and, in the interests of fairness, require similar procedural protections. *Marathon Oil Co. v. EPA,* 564 F.2d 1253, 1261 (1977). Where an agency's task is "to adjudicate disputed facts in particular cases," an administrative determination is quasi-judicial. *See id.* at 1262 (internal quotations omitted). By contrast, rulemaking concerns policy judgments to be applied generally in cases that may arise in the future; it is *sometimes* guided by more informal procedures. *See id.* Under the Endangered Species Act the Committee decides whether to grant or deny specific requests for exemptions based upon specific factual showings. Thus, the Committee's determinations are quasi-judicial. Accordingly, they constitute "adjudications" within the meaning of § 554(a).

The legislative history of the Endangered Species Act confirms our conclusion in this respect. The Senate committee report accompanying the 1982 amendments to the Endangered Species Act stated that "the Endangered Species Committee is designed to function as an *administrative court of last resort.*" S. Rep. No. 418, 97th Congress, 2d Sess. 17 (1982) (emphasis added). The Report states that the Committee's decision will be based, in part, upon a "formal adjudicatory hearing." *Id.* at 18. The Report also makes clear that the Committee's duty is to be the ultimate arbiter of conflicts that the parties involved have been unable to resolve. *Id.* at 16–17.

The language of the Endangered Species Act explicitly meets the second requirement of § 554(a). Section 1536(h)(1)(A) of the Act mandates that the Committee make its final determination of an exemption application "on the record." . . .

It is equally clear that the third requirement of APA § 554(a) is satisfied here. Section 1536(h)(1)(A) of the Endangered Species Act also requires that the Committee's final decision be "*based on* the report of the Secretary, *the hearing* held under (g)(4) of this section [(the Secretary's hearing)] and on such other testimony or evidence as it may receive." 16 U.S.C. § 1536(h)(1)(A) (emphasis added). Wherever the outer bounds of the "after opportunity for an agency hearing" requirement may lie, we hold that where, as here, a statute provides that an adjudication be determined at least in part *based on* an agency hearing, that requirement is fulfilled.

Because Committee decisions are adjudicatory in nature, are required to be on the record, and are made after an opportunity for an agency hearing, we conclude that the APA's ex parte communication prohibition is applicable. . . .

NOTES AND QUESTIONS

1. Valuing Species. The Endangered Species Committee may only approve an exemption if the benefits of the project clearly outweigh the benefits of alternative projects that do not jeopardize the species. 16 U.S.C. § 1536(h)(1)(A)(ii). How should the Committee go about making this determination? If the Committee is required to value the species, how should the Committee determine its value? What factors should be relevant? Is it necessary to place a monetary value on the existence of the species at issue in order to determine whether the benefits of the project clearly outweigh the benefits of preserving the species?

In practice, FWS attempted to value the Northern Spotted Owl using contingent valuation surveys, though the surveys did not ask directly about preserving the owl, but rather about old-growth forests, the owl's habitat. DOI, REPORT OF THE SECRETARY OF THE INTERIOR TO THE ENDANGERED SPECIES COMMITTEE 2–29, 30 (1992). FWS sent surveys to 1,000 households to evaluate their willingness to pay higher taxes and higher prices for timber products in exchange for preserving old-growth forests. *Id.* The surveys were designed to monetize the existence value that people placed on the old-growth forest ecosystem, the option value people placed on the possibility of future recreational use of the ecosystem, and the option value people placed on the possibility of future timber harvesting after collecting additional scientific and economic data. *Id.* FWS created a 95 percent confidence interval for the mean amount that each household was willing to pay to preserve old-growth forests, and chose the lower limit of this confidence interval as its estimate. *Id.* at 2–30. This value was then reduced by 19 percent, based on the assumption that the 19 percent of households that did not respond to the survey placed no value on the preservation of old-growth forests. *Id.* In the end, FWS calculated that each of the 96 million households in the United States was willing to pay at least $47.93 to preserve old-growth forests. *Id.* It was noted that estimates of non-market benefits are difficult to monetize and that the survey asked about preserving old-growth forests in general, not the specific tracts of forest at issue in the Committee's decision. *Id.* at 2–31. Perhaps because of these problems, the Committee appeared not to place any emphasis on the estimated value that each American household was willing to pay to preserve old-growth forests, instead basing its decision primarily on the more-easily quantified economic benefits associated with the timber harvests versus the economic benefits of the various alternatives. *See* Endangered Species Committee Decision on the Application for Exemption by the Bureau of Land Management to Conduct 44 Timber Sales in Western Oregon, 57 Fed. Reg. 23,405, 23,407 (1992). When the benefits of preserving the owl and its habitat were taken into account, it was on a qualitative, rather than quantitative basis. *See id.* Do you think that willingness-to-pay surveys of this type are reliable? What difficulties might be associated with the use of these surveys? Why might FWS have chosen the lower end of the mean 95 percent confidence interval as the basis for its estimate? Do you agree with this decision? Is the assumption that all households that did not answer the survey place no value on the preservation of old-growth forests valid? Are there other possible explanations for why a household would not answer the survey? Was the Committee justified in ignoring the FWS's monetary estimate from the willingness-to-pay surveys in making its final decision? Why might the Committee have done this?

2.   Presidential Powers. The *Portland Audubon* court's finding that the Endangered Species Committee's decision was quasi-judicial, and thus an adjudication, led it to the conclusion that the APA was applicable to the Committee's proceedings. 984 F.2d at 1540–41. Do you agree with the court's finding that that the Committee's decision was an adjudication? In what other way could it have been characterized?

After determining that the APA applied to the Endangered Species Committee, in a later portion of the opinion omitted above, the court found that the APA's ban on *ex parte* contacts—off-the-record contacts between administrative agencies and parties to agency proceedings—applies to the President and White House staff. The APA prohibits any interested person from outside the agency from making an *ex parte* contact relevant to the proceeding to an agency employee involved in the decisionmaking process. 5 U.S.C. § 557(d)(1)(A). This rule applies both in formal rulemakings and in adjudications, though not expressly in informal rulemaking. (A decision of the D.C. Circuit, *Home Box Office, Inc. v. FCC*, 567 F.2d 9 (D.C. Cir. 1977), has recognized a narrow application of the prohibition against *ex parte* contacts in informal rulemaking). The court first found that the President was an "interested person" under the APA. 984 F.2d at 1543–45. The court also determined that the President was "outside the agency," despite the fact six of the seven Committee members are Executive Branch officials who serve solely at the President's pleasure. *Id.* at 1545–46. Lastly, the court held that subjecting presidential communications to the APA's ban on *ex parte* contacts would not violate the separation of powers doctrine. *Id.* at 1546–48. Do you agree with these determinations?

The government argued that subjecting the President and White House staff to the APA's ban on *ex parte* communications "would represent Congressional interference with the President's constitutional duty to provide . . . supervision and guidance to inferior officials." *Id.* at 1546. The court rejected this argument out of hand, stating, "carried to its logical conclusion the government's position would effectively destroy the integrity of all federal agency adjudications." *Id.* Do you agree with this concern? Why shouldn't the President be able to communicate with members of his cabinet who serve at his pleasure? Isn't the government correct that applying the APA's ban on *ex parte* contacts to the President will interfere with the performance of his presidential duties? Is the President barred from meeting with the members of the Committee about unrelated matters when they are deciding whether to grant an exemption? If he is allowed to meet with them, how is it possible to ensure that the Committee's proceedings are not discussed? Could the President dismiss all of the Committee members and appoint people more inclined to support his position to their posts?

3.   Composition of the God Squad. In looking at the composition of the God Squad, which members seem likely to place a high value on the existence of endangered or threatened species? Which seem likely to place a high value on major federal projects that jeopardize a species? How often would you anticipate that the Committee would grant exemptions?

iv. CRITICAL HABITAT

Critical habitat is defined as the "specific areas within the geographical area occupied by the species . . . on which are found . . . physical or biological features (I) essential to the conservation of the species and (II) which may require special management considerations." 16 U.S.C. § 1532(5)(A)(i). Areas outside the geographical area occupied by the species may be listed as critical habitat "upon a determination by the Secretary that such areas are essential for the conservation of the species." 16 U.S.C. § 1532(5)(A)(ii). Conservation is defined as "the use of all methods and procedures which are necessary to bring any endangered species or threatened species to the point at which the measures provided pursuant to this chapter are no longer necessary." 16 U.S.C. § 1532(3). Unless the Secretary determines otherwise, critical habitat "shall not include the entire geographical area which can be occupied by the . . . species." 16 U.S.C. § 1532(5)(C).

FWS and NMFS have promulgated joint regulations specifying that the Secretary shall:

> Identify physical and biological features essential to the conservation of the species at an appropriate level of specificity using the best available scientific data. This analysis will vary between species and may include consideration of the appropriate quality, quantity, and spatial and temporal arrangements of such features in the context of the life history, status, and conservation needs of the species.

50 C.F.R. § 424.12(b)(1)(ii).

Critical habitat is to be designated concurrent to a species being listed as threatened or endangered, 16 U.S.C. § 1533(a)(3), and is to be determined "on the basis of the best scientific data available and after taking into consideration the economic impact, the impact on national security, and any other relevant impact, of specifying any particular area as critical habitat." 16 U.S.C. § 1533(b)(2). Once critical habitat has been designated, federal agencies must ensure that their actions are "not likely to . . . result in the destruction or adverse modification of" critical habitat. 16 U.S.C. § 1536(a)(2).

The following cases discuss the critical habitat designation process, particularly the consideration that must be given to the economic impact of designating a critical habitat.

New Mexico Cattle Growers Association v. United States Fish and Wildlife Service

248 F.3d 1277 (10th Cir. 2001).

■ Before TACHA, CHIEF JUDGE, KELLY, CIRCUIT JUDGE, and LUNGSTRUM, DISTRICT JUDGE FOR THE DISTRICT OF KANSAS.

■ TACHA, CHIEF JUDGE:

. . . The Southwestern Willow Flycatcher (flycatcher), *empidonax traillii extimus,* is one of four sub-species of the willow flycatcher, a small bird that nests in riparian areas along river beds. On July 23, 1993, the FWS published its "Proposed Rule to List the Southwestern Willow Flycatcher as Endangered With Critical Habitat," 58 Fed. Reg. 39,495. On February 27, 1995, the FWS issued its "Final Rule Determining Endangered Status for the Southwestern Willow Flycatcher." 60 Fed. Reg. 10,694. The Final Rule listed the flycatcher as endangered, but deferred the critical habitat designation (CHD) in order to gather more information. However, the FWS did not, on its own initiative, move forward with the CHD for the flycatcher.

On March 20, 1997, the U.S. District Court for the District of Arizona, in the case of *Southwest Ctr. for Biological Diversity v. Babbitt,* Civ. No. 96–1874–PHX–RGS (D. Ariz. March 20, 1997), ordered the FWS to complete the CHD for the flycatcher within 120 days. Pursuant to the court order, the FWS issued its CHD for the flycatcher on July 22, 1997. At that time, the known population of the flycatcher was between 300 and 500 nesting pairs spread across seven states and parts of Mexico. The CHD designated eighteen critical habitat units, including four in New Mexico, totaling 599 miles of stream and river beds.

The Endangered Species Act (ESA), which controls CHDs, requires the FWS to perform an economic analysis of the effects of the CHD before making a final designation. 16 U.S.C. § 1533(b)(2). In order to determine what the "economic impact" of a CHD will be, the FWS has adopted an incremental baseline approach (the baseline approach). The baseline approach utilized by the FWS is premised on the idea that the listing of the species (which will occur prior to or simultaneously with the CHD) will have economic impacts that are not to be considered. The primary statutory rationale for this position comes from 16 U.S.C. § 1533(b)(1)(A), which states that listing determinations be made "solely on the basis of the best scientific and commercial data available." Thus, the baseline approach moves any economic impact that can be attributed to listing below the baseline and, when making the CHD, takes into account only those economic impacts rising above the baseline. Using the baseline approach, the FWS determined that the flycatcher CHD resulted in no economic impact, stating that "[c]ritical habitat designation will . . . result in no additional protection for the flycatcher nor have any additional economic effects beyond those that may have been caused by listing and by other statutes." Division of Economics, U.S. Fish and Wildlife Service, *Economic Analysis of Critical Habitat Designation for the Southwestern Flycatcher,* S3 (1997). . . .

[The appellants argue] that the FWS's adoption of the baseline approach to measuring the economic impact of the flycatcher CHD is an erroneous construction and, thus, a violation of the ESA. . . .

Normally, when the agency decision at issue involves interpretations of federal statutes, we owe deference to that decision as set forth in *Chevron U.S.A., Inc. v. Natural Resources Def. Council, Inc.,* 467 U.S. 837, 842–43 (1984). Indeed, the district court in this case, applying *Chevron* deference to the FWS's use of the baseline approach, did not find it to be a violation of the ESA. The appellants, however, argue that *Chevron* deference is not applicable in this case. We agree.

The FWS concedes, in fact, that *Chevron* deference is not due the FWS's use of the baseline approach in making CHDs. Because the statutory interpretation resulting in the baseline approach has never undergone the formal rulemaking process, it remains an informal interpretation not entitled to deference. *Hunnicutt v. Hawk,* 229 F.3d 997, 1000 (10th Cir. 2000) ("Where the agency's interpretation of the statute is made informally, however, such as by a 'program statement,' the interpretation is not entitled to . . . deference." (quoting *Fristoe v. Thompson,* 144 F.3d 627, 631 (10th Cir. 1998))). Instead, we simply ask if the agency's interpretation is "well reasoned" and has the "power to persuade." *Fristoe,* 144 F.3d at 631 (quoting *S. Ute Indian Tribe v. Amoco Prod. Co.,* 119 F.3d 816, 834 (10th Cir. 1997), *overruled on other grounds by Amoco Prod. Co. v. S. Ute Indian Tribe,* 526 U.S. 865 (1999)). . . .

In addition to the protections afforded listed species by the ESA, the Act requires the agency to designate "critical habitat" for all listed species, to the extent determinable. 16 U.S.C. § 1533(a)(3). Critical habitat is defined as:

> (i) the specific areas within the geographic area occupied by the species, at the time it is listed . . . on which are found those physical or biological features (I) essential to the conservation of the species and (II) which may require special management considerations or protection; and (ii) specific areas outside the geographic area occupied by the species at the time it is listed . . . upon a determination by the Secretary that such areas are essential for the conservation of the species.

16 U.S.C. § 1532(5)(A). Thus, the CHD may include specific areas found both inside of and outside of the geographic area occupied by the species.

The CHD is required to be based on "the best scientific data available" considering "the economic impact, and any other relevant impact, of specifying any particular area as critical habitat." 16 U.S.C. § 1533(b)(2). The agency "may exclude" a particular area from the CHD if the agency determines that "the benefits of such exclusion outweigh the benefits of specifying such area as part of the critical habitat, unless . . . the failure to designate such area . . . will result in the extinction of the species concerned." *Id.* Once critical habitat is designated, federal agencies must consult with the FWS to "insure that any action authorized, funded, or carried out by such agency . . . is not likely to . . . result in the destruction or adverse modification of [designated critical] habitat." 16 U.S.C. § 1536(a)(2). Thus, agency action that is prohibited is both (1) action that is likely to jeopardize the existence of a listed species and (2) action that is likely to result in the adverse modification of any area within a CHD.

The crux of the statutory dispute is in determining the meaning of "economic impact" in 16 U.S.C. § 1533(b)(2). The baseline approach adopted by the FWS utilizes a "but for" method for determining what economic impacts flow from the CHD. Thus, unless an economic impact would not result but for the CHD, that impact is attributable to a different cause (typically listing) and is not an "economic impact . . . of specifying any particular area as critical habitat." Conversely, the approach advocated by the appellants would take into account all of the economic impact of the CHD, regardless of whether those impacts are caused co-extensively by any other agency action (such as listing) and even if those impacts would remain in the absence of the CHD. The issue presented is a question of first impression in this circuit and, to our knowledge, has not been decided by any of our sister circuits.

The root of the problem lies in the FWS's long held policy position that CHDs are unhelpful, duplicative, and unnecessary. Between April 1996 and July 1999, more than 250 species had been listed pursuant to the ESA, yet CHDs had been made for only two. S. Rep. No. 106–126, at 2 (1999). Further, while we have held that making a CHD is mandatory once a species is listed, *Forest Guardians v. Babbitt*, 174 F.3d 1178, 1186 (10th Cir. 1999), the FWS has typically put off doing so until forced to do so by court order. S. Rep. No. 106–126, at 2 (1999).

In turn, the policy position of the FWS finds its root in the regulations promulgated by the FWS in 1986 defining the meaning of both the "jeopardy standard" (applied in the context of listing) and the "adverse modification standard" (applied in the context of designated critical habitat). Action violating the jeopardy standard is action reasonably expected "to reduce appreciably the likelihood of both the survival and recovery of a listed species." 50 C.F.R. § 402.02. Action violating the adverse modification standard is action "that appreciably diminishes the value of critical habitat for both the survival and recovery of a listed species." *Id.* Thus, the standards are defined as virtually identical, or, if not identical, one (adverse modification) is subsumed by the other (jeopardy). *See Am. Rivers v. Nat'l Marine Fisheries Serv.*, 1999

U.S. App. LEXIS 3860 *5 (9th Cir. Jan. 11, 1999) (agreeing with the agency that " 'jeopardy' and 'critical habitat' . . . are 'closely related,' and [thus] the jeopardy discussion properly 'encompasses' the critical habitat analysis"). While these regulatory definitions are not before us today, they have been the cause of much confusion in that they inform the FWS's interpretation of the ESA's economic impact language.[2]

Consistent with its long standing position, the FWS argues in the instant case that the impacts of the flycatcher listing and the flycatcher CHD are co-extensive. The FWS stated in its economic analysis that, because all actions "that result in adverse modification of critical habitat will also result in a jeopardy decision, designation of critical habitat for the flycatcher is not expected to result in any incremental restrictions on agency activities." Division of Economics, U.S. Fish and Wildlife Service, *Economic Analysis of Critical Habitat Designation for the Southwestern Flycatcher*, S3 (1997). The CHD itself states that "[c]ommon to both [the jeopardy standard and the adverse modification standard] is an appreciable detrimental effect on both survival and recovery of a listed species," and thus "actions satisfying the standard for adverse modification are nearly always found to also jeopardize the species concerned, and the existence of a critical habitat designation does not materially affect the outcome of consultation." 60 Fed. Reg. 39,131 (July 22, 1997). Moreover, the FWS continues to assert that agency action that is "likely to adversely modify critical habitat but not to jeopardize the species for which it is designated are extremely rare historically, and none have been issued in recent years." Appellee's Brief at 31.

However, as we have previously said, the fact that the FWS says that no real impact flows from the CHD does not make it so. *Catron County Bd. of Comm'rs v. United States Fish & Wildlife Serv.*, 75 F.3d 1429, 1436 (10th Cir. 1996) ("[W]e disagree with the [Ninth Circuit] that no actual impact flows from the critical habitat designation. Merely because the Secretary says it does not make it so. The record in this case suggests that the impact will be immediate and the consequences could be disastrous."). Because *Catron County* dealt with whether an environmental impact statement had to be prepared pursuant to NEPA when the FWS made a CHD, the court was dealing specifically with the environmental impacts of the CHD rather than its economic impacts. However, our holding in that case casts doubt on the FWS's position in this case.

In fact, the district court in this case, by granting the appellants standing to challenge the CHD, implicitly acknowledged that they have been impacted by the flycatcher CHD. *N.M. Cattle Growers Ass'n v. United States Fish & Wildlife Serv.*, 81 F.Supp.2d 1141, 1153 (D.N.M.

---

[2]   Though these regulatory definitions are not before us today, federal courts have begun to recognize that the results they produce are inconsistent with the intent and language of the ESA. *See, e.g., Sierra Club v. U.S. Fish and Wildlife Service*, 245 F.3d 434 (5th Cir. 2001) (holding that the adverse modification standard of 50 C.F.R. 402.02 is inconsistent with the ESA).

1999) (holding that the appellants had alleged an injury in fact flowing from the flycatcher CHD). If none of the impacts of the CHD are actually attributable to the CHD, the district court's standing decision is rendered incoherent. If the injury alleged is attributable wholly to listing, then the appellants suffer no injury from the CHD, and cannot establish standing to challenge it. The district court's standing determination further points to the inconsistency between the policy position of the FWS and the language of the ESA itself. But the question of whether the impacts of listing and a CHD are co-extensive is not the precise question before us. Rather, the question is whether the FWS must analyze all of the economic impacts of critical habitat designation (regardless of whether the impacts are coextensive with other causes), or only those impacts that are a "but for" result of the CHD.

It is true that the ESA clearly bars economic considerations from having a seat at the table when the listing determination is being made. "The addition of the word 'solely' is intended to remove from the process of the listing or delisting of species any factor not related to the biological status of the species. . . . [E]conomic considerations have no relevance to determinations regarding the status of species." H.R. Rep. No. 97–567, pt. 1, at 29 (1982), *reprinted in* 1982 U.S.C.C.A.N. 2807. However, Congress clearly intended that economic factors were to be considered in connection with the CHD. 16 U.S.C. § 1533(b)(2).

The statutory language is plain in requiring some kind of consideration of economic impact in the CHD phase. Although 50 C.F.R. 402.02 is not at issue here, the regulation's definition of the jeopardy standard as fully encompassing the adverse modification standard renders any purported economic analysis done utilizing the baseline approach virtually meaningless. We are compelled by the canons of statutory interpretation to give some effect to the congressional directive that economic impacts be considered at the time of critical habitat designation. *Bridger Coal Co./Pac. Minerals, Inc. v. Dir., Office of Workers' Compensation Programs,* 927 F.2d 1150, 1153 (10th Cir. 1991) ("We will not construe a statute in a way that renders words or phrases meaningless, redundant, or superfluous."). Because economic analysis done using the FWS's baseline model is rendered essentially without meaning by 50 C.F.R. § 402.02, we conclude Congress intended that the FWS conduct a full analysis of all of the economic impacts of a critical habitat designation, regardless of whether those impacts are attributable co-extensively to other causes. Thus, we hold the baseline approach to economic analysis is not in accord with the language or intent of the ESA.

The FWS contends that should they be forced to abandon the baseline approach and consider all of the economic impact of a CHD, even if that impact is attributable co-extensively to another cause, they will be injecting economic analysis improperly into the listing process. The only two federal courts to consider this question come to essentially the same conclusion. *N.M. Cattle Growers Ass'n,* 81 F.Supp.2d at 1158; *Trinity*

County Concerned Citizens v. Babbitt, 1993 WL 650393 *4 (D.D.C. Sept. 20, 1993) (holding that absent the baseline approach, "the Secretary would be required to include . . . certain costs that might have already been incurred as a result of the listing of the species, for example, through the ESA's jeopardy and take provisions," even though "the Secretary is expressly forbidden from considering such economic costs in making the decision to list species"). We cannot agree.

Requiring that the FWS comply with the intent of the legislative body by considering economic impacts at a point subsequent to listing does not inject economic considerations into the listing process, but rather, situates those considerations in precisely the spot intended by Congress. Moreover, should this ruling result in certain areas being excluded from future CHDs, it will not undermine congressional intent that economic factors be excluded from the listing decision. The listing of the species will remain in effect and the significant protections afforded a species by listing will not be undermined. Indeed, if the FWS's position that the protections afforded by a CHD are subsumed by the protections of listing is accepted, this ruling will result in no decreased protection for endangered species or their habitat.

As set forth above, the baseline approach to economic analysis pursuant the 16 U.S.C. § 1533(b)(2) is expressly rejected. The flycatcher CHD is thus set aside and the FWS is instructed to issue a new flycatcher CHD in compliance with this opinion as required by the ESA.

Arizona Cattle Growers' Association v. Salazar
606 F.3d 1160 (9th Cir. 2010), *cert. denied*, 562 U.S. 1216 (2011).

■ Before FLETCHER, CANBY, and GRABER, CIRCUIT JUDGES.

■ FLETCHER, CIRCUIT JUDGE:

In 1993 the Mexican Spotted Owl was listed as a threatened species under the Endangered Species Act ("ESA"). The listing decision prompted a series of lawsuits alternately seeking to compel the [United States Fish and Wildlife Service's ("FWS")] to designate critical habitat for the owl and, following the FWS's designation of habitat, attacking that designation. . . .

[Arizona Cattle Growers' Association ("Arizona Cattle")] challenges the FWS's determination of the economic impacts of the designation, arguing primarily that the FWS applied an impermissible "baseline" approach that did not account for economic impacts of the critical habitat designation that are also attributable to the listing decision. The district court rejected Arizona Cattle's arguments and granted the Appellees' cross-motions for summary judgment. . . .

The decision to list a species as endangered or threatened is made without reference to the economic effects of that decision. *See N.M. Cattle Growers Ass'n v. U.S. Fish & Wildlife Serv.*, 248 F.3d 1277, 1282 (10th

Cir. 2001). Listing alone results in certain protections for the species, including a requirement that federal agencies "insure that any action authorized, funded, or carried out by such agency . . . is not likely to jeopardize the continued existence of any endangered species or threatened species." 16 U.S.C. § 1536(a)(2); *see also, e.g., id.* § 1538. These protections may impose economic burdens.

In contrast to the listing decision, under the ESA the agency may designate critical habitat only after considering the economic impact of the designation on any particular area. *Id.* § 1533(b)(2). The agency has discretion to exclude any area from the designation if the agency determines "that the benefits of such exclusion outweigh the benefits of specifying such area as part of the critical habitat," unless exclusion would result in extinction of the species. *Id.* This can be a delicate balancing act. After critical habitat is designated, the ESA requires that federal agencies "insure that any action authorized, funded, or carried out by such agency . . . is not likely to . . . result in the destruction or adverse modification" of critical habitat. *Id.* § 1536(a)(2).

The crux of the parties' dispute over the FWS's economic analysis is whether the FWS was required to attribute to the critical habitat designation economic burdens that would exist even in the absence of that designation. The parties agree that the FWS applied the "baseline" approach to the economic analysis. Under this approach, any economic impacts of protecting the owl that will occur regardless of the critical habitat designation—in particular, the burdens imposed by listing the owl—are treated as part of the regulatory "baseline" and are not factored into the economic analysis of the effects of the critical habitat designation.[12] Arizona Cattle, relying on the Tenth Circuit's decision in *New Mexico Cattle Growers Association*, argues that this was error and that the FWS was required to apply a "co-extensive" approach to the economic analysis. Under the co-extensive approach, the agency must ignore the protection of a species that results from the listing decision in considering whether to designate an area as critical habitat. Any economic burden that designating an area would cause must be counted in the economic analysis, even if the same burden is already imposed by listing the species and, therefore, would exist even if the area were not designated.

In *New Mexico Cattle Growers Association* the Tenth Circuit held that the baseline approach was impermissible under the ESA. *See* 248 F.3d at 1285. It did so, however, relying on an FWS regulation that defined "destruction or adverse modification" as effectively identical to the standard for determining whether an agency action places a species

---

[12] For example, suppose that the decision to list the owl as endangered resulted in a ban on logging in a particular area, and that designating that area as critical habitat would independently result in the same ban. Because the listing decision would result in the logging ban even if the agency did not designate critical habitat in that area, the baseline approach would not treat the ban as a burden that was imposed by the critical habitat designation.

in "jeopardy." *See id.* at 1283–85.[13] The Tenth Circuit held that this regulation rendered an economic analysis relying on the baseline approach "virtually meaningless" because it allowed the agency, in all cases, to find no economic impact to the critical habitat designation. *See id.* Our court and others have since found the agency's definition of "adverse modification" too narrow. *See Gifford Pinchot Task Force v. U.S. Fish & Wildlife Serv.*, 378 F.3d 1059, 1070 (9th Cir. 2004). We therefore reject the Tenth Circuit's approach in *New Mexico Cattle Growers Association* as relying on a faulty premise and hold that the FWS may employ the baseline approach in analyzing the critical habitat designation.

The baseline approach is, if anything, more logical than the co-extensive approach. The very notion of conducting a cost/benefit analysis is undercut by incorporating in that analysis costs that will exist regardless of the decision made.[14] Moreover, the practical relevance of the economic analysis under the ESA is to determine the benefits of excluding or including an area in the critical habitat designation: if there is no net benefit (such as a reduction in economic impacts) to excluding the area, the agency must designate it. *See* 16 U.S.C. § 1533(b)(2). The baseline approach, in contrast to the co-extensive approach, reflects this purpose.

Congress has directed the FWS to list species, and thus impose a regulatory burden, without consideration of the costs of doing so. *See* 16 U.S.C. § 1533(a); *N.M. Cattle Growers*, 248 F.3d at 1282. It would be strange to conclude that Congress intended the FWS to consider costs at the critical habitat phase that the agency was barred from considering at the listing phase where, as a result, the analysis would bear little relationship to reality.[15] It would also be strange to conclude that Congress intended to use the critical habitat designation to require the agency to consider the previously irrelevant costs of listing the species, particularly given that the decision to exclude an area from critical habitat for economic reasons is discretionary. *See* 16 U.S.C. § 1533(b)(2); *Bennett v. Spear*, 520 U.S. 154, 172 (1997). The simpler explanation is that the economic analysis of the critical habitat designation is exactly what it sounds like and is not intended to incorporate the burdens imposed by listing the species.

---

[13] The Tenth Circuit declined to address whether the FWS's definition of "adverse modification" was invalid. *See N.M. Cattle Growers*, 248 F.3d at 1283–85.

[14] We note further the confusion engendered by the co-extensive approach on the "benefit" side of the equation. If the FWS must consider "burdens" imposed by the critical habitat designation as if there were no protections imposed by the listing decision, must it also assume that in the absence of the critical habitat designation the species is entirely unprotected in considering the "benefits" of designating a particular area? The co-extensive approach runs the risk of becoming a purely academic exercise.

[15] Although the Tenth Circuit is likely correct that inclusion of the costs of listing in the critical habitat analysis does not affect the FWS's *listing* process, *see N.M. Cattle Growers*, 248 F.3d at 1285, it has clear potential to distort the critical habitat analysis.

Arizona Cattle argues that if the FWS designated critical habitat at the same time as it listed the species, *see* 16 U.S.C. § 1533(a)(3), there would be no baseline to which to compare the critical habitat designation. Even if the FWS lists the species concurrently with designating critical habitat, however, listing the species is a necessary antecedent to designating habitat. We see little inconsistency with the FWS's considering the burdens imposed by the critical habitat designation while taking into account those necessarily imposed by the listing decision even in these circumstances.

Finally, Arizona Cattle argues that the baseline approach allows the FWS to treat the economic analysis as a mere procedural formality. We reject the argument that, as a matter of course, the FWS will neglect its duty to perform a thorough economic analysis. To hold otherwise would amount to a presumption that the FWS will act in an arbitrary and capricious fashion, a presumption that is inconsistent with the deference the court affords agencies. *See, e.g., Smith v. U.S. Forest Serv.*, 33 F.3d 1072, 1077 n. 2 (9th Cir. 1994). Furthermore, contrary to Arizona Cattle's contention that the impact of designating critical habitat cannot be negligible, the costs of a critical habitat designation could, in fact, be subsumed by the burdens imposed by listing the species—any burden that is entirely "co-extensive" with the listing decision will reflect exactly such a case.

We hold that the FWS permissibly applied the baseline approach in conducting the economic analysis of the effects of the designation. . . .

NOTES AND QUESTIONS

1. Economic Impact of Critical Habitat Designation. The *New Mexico Cattle Growers* court struck down the baseline economic model, finding that it caused FWS to undervalue the full economic impact of a critical habitat designation, thereby violating § 4(b)(2), which requires that the economic impact of designating critical habitat be considered. *Arizona Cattle Growers' Association* rejected this reasoning and approved the use of the baseline approach, finding that it could not have been Congress' intent for "the FWS to consider costs at the critical habitat phase that the agency was barred from considering at the listing phase." 606 F.3d 1160, 1173. With which court's analysis do you agree? How did the court in *Arizona Cattle Growers' Association* distinguish its analysis from the earlier analysis in *New Mexico Cattle Growers*?

2. "Destruction or Adverse Modification." The ESA defines critical habitat as "the specific areas . . . essential to the *conservation* of the species. . . ." 16 U.S.C. § 1532(5)(A)(i) (emphasis added). Conservation means "the use of all methods and procedures which are necessary to bring any endangered species or threatened species to the point at which the measures provided pursuant to this chapter are no longer necessary." 16 U.S.C. § 1532(3). Thus, the ESA defines critical habitat with reference to the recovery of a species, not just its continued survival. The ESA also requires that federal agencies ensure their actions do not "result in the destruction or adverse modification of critical habitat." 16 U.S.C. § 1536(a)(2). This standard is not defined in the ESA, but the FWS had at one time defined "destruction or adverse modification" as a "direct or indirect alteration that appreciably diminishes the value of critical habitat for *both* the survival and recovery of a listed species." 50 C.F.R. § 402.02 (emphasis added).

The validity of the regulations was not before the court in *New Mexico Cattle Growers*. Nonetheless, in a footnote, the court noted that other courts had found the FWS regulations defining "destruction or adverse modification" to be inconsistent with the ESA. 248 F.3d at 1283 n.2. In *Sierra Club*, the Fifth Circuit determined that the "destruction or adverse modification" standard "sets the bar too high" because it requires consultation only when a federal agency action affects *both* the recovery and survival of a listed species, whereas, "the ESA requires consultation where an action affects recovery alone; it is not necessary for an action to affect the survival of a species." 245 F.3d at 441–42. The Ninth Circuit agreed, stating that "[t]he agency's controlling regulation on critical habitat thus offends the ESA because the ESA was enacted not merely to forestall the extinction of species (*i.e.*, promote a species survival), but to allow a species to recover to the point where it may be delisted." *Gifford Pinchot Task Force v. FWS*, 378 F.3d 1059, 1070 (9th Cir. 2004).

Following *Gifford Pinchot*, the FWS abandoned its regulatory definition when analyzing whether an action is likely to destroy or adversely modify critical habitat. In 2016, the FWS, as part of an interagency process with NMFS and NOAA, finalized a rule that amended the definition of "destruction or adverse modification" to mean:

> a direct or indirect alteration that appreciably diminishes the value of critical habitat for the conservation of a listed species. Such alterations may include, but are not limited to, those that alter the physical or biological features essential to the conservation of a species or that preclude or significantly delay development of such features.

Interagency Cooperation—Endangered Species Act of 1973, as Amended; Definition of Destruction or Adverse Modification of Critical Habitat, 81 Fed. Reg. 7214, 7216 (2016). Does the new definition adequately address the concerns of the *Gifford Pinchot* court?

3.   Unoccupied Critical Habitat and Economic Considerations. In *Weyerhaeuser Co. v. U.S. Fish and Wildlife Service*, 139 S. Ct. 361 (2018), landowners claimed that the Fish & Wildlife Service exceeded its statutory authority and acted arbitrarily and capriciously in designating an area of privately-owned land in Louisiana as a critical habitat for the endangered dusky gopher frog. The area had not been occupied by the frog in decades but contained historic breeding grounds and ephemeral ponds that the Service found were "essential" to the conservation of the species. *Id.* at 366. Petitioners contended that the area could not be critical habitat for the dusky gopher frog because the frog could not survive there without replacing the closed-canopy timber plantation encircling the ponds with an open-canopy longleaf pine forest. *Id.* at 367. Petitioners also argued that it was arbitrary and capricious for the Service to designate the area as critical habitat in light of the potential economic harms, estimated at up to $33.9 million over 20 years in loss of development value. *Id.*

The Fifth Circuit upheld the designation and rejected the imposition of any "habitability requirement" for critical habitat, as the ESA explicitly discusses occupied and unoccupied lands in the context of critical habitat designation. *Markle Interest, LLC v. United States Fish and Wildlife Service,* 827 F.3d 452, 466–68 (5th Cir. 2016). The court held that the land satisfied the statutory definition of unoccupied critical habitat, which requires only that the FWS deem the it "essential for the conservation [of] the species." *Id.* The Fifth Circuit also held that once the agency fulfills its statutory obligation to consider economic impacts, as required by 16 U.S.C. § 1533(b)(2), its decision not to exclude an area as critical habitat is discretionary and unreviewable by courts. *Id.* at 474–75.

The U.S. Supreme Court granted certiorari to answer two questions: (1) "whether 'critical habitat' under the ESA must also be 'habitat'," and (2) whether an agency decision not to exclude an area from critical habitat is subject to judicial review. *Weyerhaeuser,* 139 S. Ct. at 368. The Court issued a narrow opinion, authored by Chief Justice Roberts for a unanimous Court (without Justice Kavanaugh's participation), vacating and remanding the Fifth Circuit's judgment. The Court found that Section 4(a)(3)(A)(i) of the ESA, which the lower courts did not analyze, states that when the Secretary lists a species as endangered he must also "designate *any habitat* of such species which is then considered to be critical habitat." 16 U.S.C. § 1533(a)(3)(A)(i) (emphasis added). The Court held that only the "habitat" of the endangered species is eligible for designation as critical habitat, notwithstanding the statutory definition of critical habitat as encompassing unoccupied habitat "essential for the conservation [of] the species." *Id.* at 368. The Service argued that "habitat" can include areas like the land in question, which would require some modification in order to support a sustainable population of a species. Weyerhaeuser argued that habitat cannot include areas where a species could not currently survive. The Service also disputed the premise that the administrative record shows that the frog could not survive in the land unit. The Supreme Court remanded the issue to the Fifth Circuit, which did not interpret the term "habitat" in § 1533(a)(3)(A)(i), and did not assess the Service's administrative findings regarding the land in question. *Id.* at 368–69.

The Court also held that the Secretary's decision not to exclude an area from critical habitat under § 1533(b)(2) is subject to judicial review. The Court held that the statute is not "drawn so that a court would have no meaningful standard against which to judge the [Secretary's] exercise of [his] discretion." *Weyerhaeuser,* 139 S. Ct. at 372 (internal citations omitted). The Court held that the Fifth Circuit should consider in the first instance whether the Service's assessment of the costs and benefits of designation and resulting decision not to exclude the land unit was arbitrary, capricious, or an abuse of discretion. *Id.* at 369–72.

Habitat loss and degradation are the leading causes of species endangerment in North America. Given this, how should "habitat" be defined in order to best effectuate the purpose of the ESA? In your view, can the land area in question be "habitat" for the dusky gopher frog?

4.   What Does "Recovery" Mean? Species may be delisted when they are recovered. The agency has defined "recovery" as an "improvement in the status of listed species to the point at which listing is no longer appropriate under the criteria set out in section 4(a)(1) of the Act." 50 C.F.R. § 402.02. A species that is delisted must be monitored for at least five years to ensure that the recovery has indeed taken place. 16 U.S.C. § 1533(g)(1).

Additionally, agencies are directed to develop recovery plans for the conservation and survival of listed species. 16 U.S.C. § 1533(f). These plans shall include criteria to assess when and how recovery goals are to be met. *Id.* The plans may help an agency both to establish critical habitat and to assess when adverse modification is likely to occur. *See, e.g.*, NMFS, INTERIM ENDANGERED AND THREATENED SPECIES RECOVERY PLANNING GUIDANCE VERSION 1.3 (June 2010). In what ways might recovery be measured? Is it enough to say that a species is recovered when it no longer meets the listing criteria? For further discussion, see Dale D. Goble, *The Endangered Species Act: What We Talk About When We Talk About Recovery*, 49 NAT. RESOURCES J. 1 (2009) (describing "recovery" as having both biological components, such as numerical criteria, and legal components, such as reasonable assurances and risk-management mechanisms).

5.   "A Hard Case Making Bad Law." In *Cape Hatteras Access Preservation Alliance v. Department of the Interior*, 344 F. Supp. 2d 108 (D.D.C. 2004), the court examined both the baseline model and the regulatory definition of "destruction or adverse modification." It found the decision in *New Mexico Cattle Growers* to be "ill advised" and classified it as "an instance of a hard case making bad law." *Id.* at 129–30. The *Cape Hatteras* court concluded that "while the Tenth Circuit's rejection of the baseline approach is unfounded, the Fifth and Ninth Circuit's rejection of the regulation" defining "destruction or adverse modification" is "well reasoned." *Id.* at 130. If the Tenth Circuit had the regulation defining "adverse modification" before it or if *New Mexico Cattle Growers* had post-dated the *Gifford Pinchot-Cape Hatteras* line of cases, would the court still have found the baseline economic model to be inconsistent with the ESA?

6.   "Destruction or Adverse Modification" v. "Not Likely to Jeopardize." The *New Mexico Cattle Growers* court points out that FWS had a "long held policy position that CHDs are unhelpful, duplicative, and unnecessary." 248 F.3d at 1283. FWS supported this policy position by stating that "species protection benefits from a critical habitat designation largely duplicate those already in place as a result of the species being listed." FWS, CRITICAL HABITAT—QUESTIONS AND ANSWERS 1 (2003). Section 7(a)(2) of the ESA imposes two distinct duties on federal agencies: to ensure that their actions are "not likely to jeopardize the continued existence" of a listed species, and to ensure that they do not cause the "destruction or adverse modification" of the species' critical habitat. 16 U.S.C. § 1536(a)(2). Critics pointed out that FWS was able to maintain its policy only because its regulations improperly defined the "destruction or adverse modification" of critical habitat by reference to the survival of a species. *See, e.g.,* Michael Senatore et al., *Critical Habitat at the Crossroads: Responding to the G.W. Bush Administration's Attacks on Critical Habitat Designation Under the ESA*, 33 GOLDEN GATE U. L. REV. 447, 467 (2003); Amanda R. Garcia, Student Article, *The Sage Grouse Debate: Cost-Benefit Analysis and the Discourse of the Endangered Species Act*, 14 N.Y.U. ENVTL. L.J. 572, 600–01 (2006). "Critical habitat" is defined in the ESA as the habitat necessary for the "conservation" of the species. 16 U.S.C. § 1532(5)(A). The FWS's mandate under § 7(a)(2) with respect to critical habitat, then, extends beyond survival and is geared toward recovery.

Does the 2016 FWS definition of "destruction or adverse modification of critical habitat" extend beyond survival to encompass species recovery? What would be the consequence of FWS revising its definition of "destruction or adverse modification" to encompass a recovery standard even more explicitly?

7.   Towards Quantification and Cost-Benefit Analysis. Amy Sinden performed an in-depth examination of FWS's response to the *New Mexico Cattle Growers* decision, particularly concerning the economic analysis FWS has adopted. Amy Sinden, *The Economics of Endangered Species: Why Less Is More in the Economic Analysis of Critical Habitat Designations*, 28 HARV. ENVTL. L. REV. 129 (2004). She notes that since the *New Mexico Cattle Growers* decision, FWS analyses of the economic impacts of critical habitat designation have increasingly quantified costs and benefits, attempting to express them in monetary terms, in an approach more resembling a formal cost-benefit analysis than was practiced previously. *Id.* at 174–75. She points out that the costs of critical habitat designation have been monetized in all recent FWS reports, requiring FWS

> to make innumerable guesses and simplifying assumptions about, *inter alia*, the nature and extent of future development in the area, the extent to which future development projects are likely to have a federal nexus and therefore trigger Section 7 consultations, the procedural and substantive costs likely to be imposed by such consultations, and whether those costs would have been imposed anyway as a result of the listing or can be attributed solely to the critical habitat designation.

Id. at 175–76. "Thus, even accepting FWS's overall framework of analysis, there is substantial room for disagreement on any given case. . . . [A] comprehensive analysis of costs should also take into account the indirect economic impacts on, for example, labor markets, property values, and municipal tax revenues." *Id.* at 179–80. FWS has also begun a move towards monetizing the benefits of critical habitat designation, but so far has been more reluctant to do so than in the case of monetizing costs. *Id.* at 180–81. FWS takes care to note that quantifying benefits is particularly difficult and that it "believes that the benefits of critical habitat designation are best expressed in biological terms that can be weighed against the expected cost impacts of the rulemaking." *Id.* at 181 (quoting FWS, DRAFT ECONOMIC ANALYSIS OF CRITICAL HABITAT DESIGNATION FOR THE GULF STURGEON 1, 65

(2002)). This position was repeated in 2006. *See* INDUSTRIAL ECONOMICS, INC., FINAL REPORT: ECONOMIC ANALYSIS OF CRITICAL HABITAT DESIGNATION FOR THE CHOCTAWHATCHEE, PERDIDO KEY, AND ST. ANDREW BEACH MICE, prepared for Division of Economics, U.S. Fish and Wildlife Service (Sept. 8, 2006). Nevertheless, Sinden notes an increased reliance on willingness-to-pay surveys to measure the potential benefits of critical habitat designation, and concludes that this "at least suggests, and indeed seems to endorse, a methodology that could be used to monetize the benefits of critical habitat." *Id.* at 181. In 2007, for instance, FWS used willingness-to-pay surveys as one component of critical habitat analysis. *See* U.S. Fish and Wildlife Service, Endangered and Threatened Wildlife and Plants; Designation of Critical Habitat for Five Endangered and Two Threatened Mussels in Four Northeast Gulf of Mexico Drainages; Final Rule, 72 Fed. Reg. 64,285, 64,295 (2007).

Sinden is critical of this move towards monetization and formal cost-benefit analyses in the context of the ESA and preserving endangered species. Do you agree? Can the FWS sufficiently consider the economic impacts of a critical habitat designation without quantifying the impacts into dollar values? Without performing a full cost-benefit analysis? What are the possible alternatives? Is it possible to sufficiently value the benefit of preserving an endangered species in economic terms? Does the ESA contemplate doing this? Would doing so be inconsistent with the structure and purpose of the ESA?

8. Delays in Designating Critical Habitat. Prior to abandoning its policy position that CHDs are duplicative, FWS touted the importance of active conservation measures, stating:

> The ESA can compel agencies and landowners or managers not to harm listed species or not to adversely impact their designated critical habitat. It cannot compel them to take the positive steps needed to recover most species. Those must be done voluntarily. Inasmuch as most listed species are found in whole or part on State and private lands, and we have found both to be generally strongly opposed to having their property designated as critical habitat, "critical habitat" has become a significant obstacle to obtaining landowner cooperation in species conservation. As such, it is an obstacle to recovery for many species. This is a classic example of good intentions failing the test of reality.

FWS, CRITICAL HABITAT—QUESTIONS AND ANSWERS, *supra*, at 1. Is this reasoning persuasive? Do you agree that people taking voluntary, positive steps to recover species would be dissuaded if their property came to be designated as critical habitat? If only federal agencies are bound by the requirement not to destroy or adversely modify critical habitat, why would people care if their property was designated critical habitat in the first place?

FWS explains why the designation of critical habitat remains a low priority, stating, "[d]esignating critical habitat for species already on the endangered species list provides little conservation benefit to species." FWS, CRITICAL HABITAT—QUESTIONS AND ANSWERS, *supra*, at 1. Does the FWS position on critical habitat justify ignoring the statutory commands of the ESA that the Secretary "shall . . . designate . . . critical habitat"? If the ESA commands FWS to designate critical habitat regardless, why does FWS make its distaste for critical habitat known publicly?

9.   How Other Agencies View Critical Habitat. Compare the FWS view expressed above in Note 8—that critical habitat designation generally provides little conservation benefit to the species—to that evinced by another federal agency, the Federal Energy Regulatory Commission (FERC), which oversees interstate oil and natural gas pipeline approvals. In reviewing a recent EA for compliance with NEPA requirements, FERC pointed to the lack of critical habitat within the project area as supporting a finding of no significance under NEPA, and ultimately, to approval of the new pipeline. *See* FERC, Order Denying Rehearing and Dismissing Clarification, Docket No. CP15-77-001, 163 FERC ¶ 61,190 at *6 (June 12, 2018). Does this change your view of the importance of critical habitat designation?

10.   "To the Maximum Extent Prudent and Determinable." The ESA contains the caveat that critical habitat be designated "to the maximum extent prudent and determinable." 16 U.S.C. § 1533(a)(3). Joint FWS and NMFS regulations define when a critical habitat designation is not prudent or not determinable:

> (1)   A designation of critical habitat is not prudent when any of the following situations exist:
>
> > (i)   The species is threatened by taking or other human activity, and identification of critical habitat can be expected to increase the degree of such threat to the species; or
> >
> > (ii)   Such designation of critical habitat would not be beneficial to the species. In determining whether a designation would not be beneficial, the factors the Services may consider include but are not limited to: Whether the present or threatened destruction, modification, or curtailment of a species' habitat or range is not a threat to the species, or whether any areas meet the definition of "critical habitat."
>
> (2)   Critical habitat is not determinable when one or both of the following situations exist:
>
> > (i)   Data sufficient to perform required analyses are lacking; or
> >
> > (ii)   The biological needs of the species are not sufficiently well known to identify any area that meets the definition of "critical habitat."

50 C.F.R. § 424.12(a). Currently, critical habitat is designated for less than half of all listed species. *See* FWS, Critical Habitat, Frequently Asked Questions, https://www.fws.gov/endangered/what-we-do/critical-habitats-faq.html (last visited Feb. 19, 2019). FWS routinely justifies its decision not to designate critical habitat on the grounds that doing so would not be

prudent, or that critical habitat is not determinable. Courts have become increasingly skeptical of these justifications, particularly in light of FWS's general disdain for critical habitat. *See, e.g., NRDC v. DOI*, 113 F.3d 1121 (9th Cir. 1997) (finding FWS decision that it was "not prudent" to designate critical habitat for the California gnatcatcher to be arbitrary and capricious because FWS failed to consider the possible benefits of critical habitat designation to the species when it concluded that such designation would lead to increased takings); *Conservation Council for Haw. v. Babbitt*, 2 F. Supp. 2d 1280 (D. Haw. 1998) (rejecting FWS's determination that designating critical habitat for rare Hawaiian plants would not be prudent because it would lead to increased takings since FWS failed to provide any evidence of prior takings); *N. Spotted Owl v. Lujan*, 758 F. Supp. 621 (W.D. Wash. 1991) (holding that FWS determination that critical habitat was not determinable was arbitrary and capricious because FWS failed to explain the basis for its decision).

FWS has also attempted to justify its failure to designate critical habitat on the grounds that it lacked the necessary funding to do so. This issue became particularly contentious in the mid-1990s when Congress cut funding to the FWS and prohibited the expenditure of funds on listing decisions and critical habitat designations. Despite the actions of Congress, in *Forest Guardians v. Babbitt*, 174 F.3d 1178, 1187 (10th Cir. 1999), the court held that a lack of funding could not overcome FWS's mandatory, non-discretionary duty to designate critical habitat under the ESA.

Could the actions of Congress in the mid-1990s be seen as a temporary *de facto* repeal of the critical habitat sections of the ESA? Should courts be more receptive to agency budgetary restraints? If the agency decides that it is more cost effective to spend limited money on active conservation measures or listing species than it is on designating critical habitat, should a court defer to this decision? Isn't the agency in the best position to make this decision? Does the ESA mandate that critical habitat designations be placed above all other FWS responsibilities? *See generally* Thomas F. Darin, Comment, *Designating Critical Habitat Under the Endangered Species Act: Habitat Protection Versus Agency Discretion*, 24 HARV. ENVTL. L. REV. 209 (2000) (discussing FWS justifications for failing to designate critical habitat and the courts' response).

v. THE CONSULTATION PROCESS

The ESA requires an elaborate consultation process between the agency contemplating a project and the agency that administers the ESA (NMFS for marine species and FWS for all other species) to determine whether a project is "likely to jeopardize the continued existence" of a listed species or "result in the destruction or adverse modification" of critical habitat. 16 U.S.C. § 1536(a)(4). The next case discusses this consultation process.

Thomas v. Peterson

753 F.2d 754 (9th Cir. 1985).

■ Before WRIGHT, SNEED, and ALARCON, CIRCUIT JUDGES.

■ SNEED, CIRCUIT JUDGE:

. . . Plaintiffs—landowners, ranchers, outfitters, miners, hunters, fishermen, recreational users, and conservation and recreation organizations—challenge actions of the United States Forest Service in planning and approving a timber road in the Jersey Jack area of the Nezperce National Forest in Idaho. . . . The area lies in a "recovery corridor" identified by the U.S. Fish & Wildlife Service for the Rocky Mountain Gray Wolf, an endangered species. . . .

In November, 1980, the Forest Service solicited public comments and held a public hearing on a proposed gravel road that would provide access to timber to be sold. The Forest Service prepared an environmental assessment (EA), *see* 40 C.F.R. § 1508.9 (1984), to determine whether an EIS would be required for the road. . . . The decision notice stated that "no known threatened or endangered plant or animal species have been found" within the area, but the EA contained no discussion of endangered species.

. . . [Plaintiffs allege that the road] is likely to affect the Rocky Mountain Gray Wolf, an endangered species, and the Forest Service has failed to follow procedures mandated by the Endangered Species Act, 16 U.S.C. §§ 1531–1543.

After briefing and oral argument, the district court granted summary judgment for the Forest Service on all claims. *Thomas v. Peterson* (D. Idaho 1984) (hereinafter cited as Memorandum Decision). . . . [The district court] found that, although the Forest Service had not complied with the procedural requirements of the Endangered Species Act, it had "undertaken sufficient study and action to further the purposes" of the Act, *id.* at 1149, E.R. 103, and the court therefore declined to enjoin construction of the road. . . .

The plaintiffs' . . . claim concerns the Forest Service's alleged failure to comply with the Endangered Species Act (ESA) in considering the effects of the road and timber sales on the endangered Rocky Mountain Gray Wolf.

The ESA contains both substantive and procedural provisions. Substantively, the Act prohibits the taking or importation of endangered species, *see* 16 U.S.C. § 1538, and requires federal agencies to ensure that their actions are not "likely to jeopardize the continued existence of any endangered species or threatened species or result in the destruction or adverse modification" of critical habitat of such species. *See* 16 U.S.C. § 1536(a)(2).

The Act prescribes a three-step process to ensure compliance with its substantive provisions by federal agencies. Each of the first two steps serves a screening function to determine if the successive steps are required. The steps are:

(1) An agency proposing to take an action must inquire of the Fish & Wildlife Service (F & WS) whether any threatened or endangered species "may be present" in the area of the proposed action. *See* 16 U.S.C. § 1536(c)(1).

(2) If the answer is affirmative, the agency must prepare a "biological assessment" to determine whether such species "is likely to be affected" by the action. *Id.* The biological assessment may be part of an environmental impact statement or environmental assessment. *Id.*

(3) If the assessment determines that a threatened or endangered species "is likely to be affected," the agency must formally consult with the F & WS. 16 U.S.C. § 1536(a)(2). The formal consultation results in a "biological opinion" issued by the F & WS. *See* 16 U.S.C. § 1536(b). If the biological opinion concludes that the proposed action would jeopardize the species or destroy or adversely modify critical habitat, *see* 16 U.S.C. § 1536(a)(2), then the action may not go forward unless the F & WS can suggest an alternative that avoids such jeopardization, destruction, or adverse modification. 16 U.S.C. § 1536(b)(3)(A). If the opinion concludes that the action will not violate the Act, the F & WS may still require measures to minimize its impact. 16 U.S.C. § 1536(b)(4)(ii)–(iii).

Plaintiffs first allege that, with respect to the Jersey Jack road, the Forest Service did not undertake step (1), a formal request to the F & WS. The district court found that to be the case, but concluded that the procedural violation was insignificant because the Forest Service was already aware that wolves may be present in the area. The court therefore refused to enjoin the construction of the road. . . .

Once an agency is aware that an endangered species may be present in the area of its proposed action, the ESA requires it to prepare a biological assessment to determine whether the proposed action "is likely to affect" the species and therefore requires formal consultation with the F & WS. *See supra.* The Forest Service did not prepare such an assessment prior to its decision to build the Jersey Jack road. Without a biological assessment, it cannot be determined whether the proposed project will result in a violation of the ESA's substantive provisions. A failure to prepare a biological assessment for a project in an area in which it has been determined that an endangered species may be present cannot be considered a *de minimis* violation of the ESA.

The district court found that the Forest Service had "undertaken sufficient study and action to further the purposes of the ESA," Memorandum Decision at 1149, E.R. 103. Its finding was based on affidavits submitted by the Forest Service for the litigation. *See* Memorandum Decision at 1148, E.R. 99. These do not constitute a substitute for the preparation of the biological assessment required by the ESA.

Given a substantial procedural violation of the ESA in connection with a federal project, the remedy must be an injunction of the project pending compliance with the ESA. The procedural requirements of the ESA are analogous to those of NEPA: under NEPA, agencies are required to evaluate the environmental impact of federal projects "significantly affecting the quality of the human environment," 42 U.S.C. § 4332(2)(C); under the ESA, agencies are required to assess the effect on endangered species of projects in areas where such species may be present. 16 U.S.C. § 1536(c). A failure to prepare a biological assessment is comparable to a failure to prepare an environmental impact statement.

Our cases repeatedly have held that, absent "unusual circumstances," an injunction is the appropriate remedy for a violation of NEPA's procedural requirements. *See Save Our Ecosystems v. Clark,* 747 F.2d 1240, 1250 (9th Cir. 1984); *Alpine Lakes Protection Society v. Schlapfer,* 518 F.2d 1089 (9th Cir. 1975); *Lathan v. Volpe,* 455 F.2d 1111, 1116–17 (9th Cir. 1971). Irreparable damage is presumed to flow from a failure properly to evaluate the environmental impact of a major federal action. *Save Our Ecosystems,* 747 F.2d at 1250; *Friends of the Earth, Inc. v. Coleman,* 518 F.2d 323, 330 (9th Cir. 1975). We see no reason that the same principle should not apply to procedural violations of the ESA.

The Forest Service argues that the procedural requirements of the ESA should be enforced less stringently than those of NEPA because, unlike NEPA, the ESA also contains substantive provisions. We acknowledge that the ESA's substantive provisions distinguish it from NEPA, but the distinction acts the other way. If anything, the strict substantive provisions of the ESA justify *more* stringent enforcement of its procedural requirements, because the procedural requirements are designed to ensure compliance with the substantive provisions. The ESA's procedural requirements call for a systematic determination of the effects of a federal project on endangered species. If a project is allowed to proceed without substantial compliance with those procedural requirements, there can be no assurance that a violation of the ESA's substantive provisions will not result. The latter, of course, is impermissible. *See TVA v. Hill,* 437 U.S. 153 (1978). . . .

The Forest Service would require the district court, absent proof by the plaintiffs to the contrary, to make a finding that the Jersey Jack road is not likely to effect [sic] the Rocky Mountain Gray Wolf, and that therefore any failure to comply with ESA procedures is harmless. This is not a finding appropriate to the district court at the present time. Congress has assigned to the agencies and to the Fish & Wildlife Service the responsibility for evaluation of the impact of agency actions on endangered species, and has prescribed procedures for such evaluation.

Only by following the procedures can proper evaluations be made. It is not the responsibility of the plaintiffs to prove, nor the function of the courts to judge, the effect of a proposed action on an endangered species when proper procedures have not been followed. *Cf. City of Davis v. Coleman*, 521 F.2d 661, 671 (9th Cir. 1975) (under NEPA, agency, not plaintiff, is responsible for investigating the environmental effects of a proposed action).

We therefore hold that the district court erred in declining to enjoin construction of the Jersey Jack road pending compliance with the ESA. . . .

NOTES AND QUESTIONS

1.   ESA's Procedural Mandate. On what basis was it suggested that the Forest Service had failed to comply with the procedural requirements of the ESA? Given that the Forest Service had conducted an EA that concluded that there were no known threatened or endangered plant and animal species within the area, would it not have been a waste of time to make inquiries of the FWS? Is this relevant? Did the court find that the actions of the Forest Service would necessarily breach the substantive provisions of the ESA? Following *Thomas v. Peterson*, are there any circumstances in which a court would uphold the actions of an agency that failed to comply with the procedural requirements of the Act, provided that it met the Act's substantive mandate? For example, what would have happened if the Forest Service had prepared a biological assessment (without having first made initial inquiries of FWS) that suggested that an endangered species was likely to be affected by the proposed action. If FWS had then prepared a biological opinion permitting the proposed action, could the action nevertheless be enjoined for the Forest Service's failure to comply with the first step of the ESA process?

2.   Agency Expertise: NEPA and ESA. Under the ESA, FWS is responsible for the ultimate assessment of the impact of the federal action on the species (in the form of a Biological Assessment). Conversely, under NEPA, the agency that proposes the project at issue (the project agency) is responsible for the final impact assessment (in the form of an EIS). Which model is preferable? Is it desirable that an agency with relevant environmental expertise (such as FWS) issue the final opinion on a project's impact, despite not possessing the most information about the project? Alternatively, is it desirable that an agency that wants to undertake a specific project, but which has little or no environmental expertise, assess the project's impact? What might explain the different approaches in the respective regimes?

Is the consultation process contemplated by the ESA a preferable compromise between the two extremes set out above? Is it an efficient procedure? What are its benefits? What are its drawbacks?

3.   Substantive and Procedural Requirements. Unlike NEPA, the ESA contains both a substantive and procedural component. Substantively, the Act prohibits any federal action that is likely to jeopardize endangered or threatened species. 16 U.S.C. § 1536(a)(2). Procedurally, the Act requires federal agencies to consult with FWS. 16 U.S.C. §§ 1536(a)(2), 1536(b)(3)(A), 1536(c). These requirements are distinct, but an agency's compliance with the procedural requirements will almost always satisfy its substantive obligations as well, so long as the agency then acts in compliance with the FWS biological opinion:

> [W]hile consultation with the FWS may have satisfied the [agency's] procedural obligations under the ESA, the [agency] may not rely solely on a FWS biological opinion to establish conclusively its compliance with its substantive obligations under § 7(a)(2). A federal agency cannot abrogate its responsibility to ensure that its actions will not jeopardize a listed species; its decision to rely on a FWS biological opinion must not have been arbitrary or capricious. Nonetheless, even when the FWS's opinion is based on "admittedly weak" information, another agency's reliance on that opinion will satisfy its obligations under the Act if a challenging party can point to no "new" information—*i.e.*, information the Service did not take into account—which challenges the opinion's conclusions.

> [Plaintiff] argues at length that the FWS's biological opinions which contain the "no jeopardy" findings are based on faulty analyses. . . . [Plaintiff's] argument misses the mark, however, because the FWS is not a party to this action. The FWS's actions, or lack thereof, in preparing its opinions are relevant on appeal only to the extent that they demonstrate whether the [agency's] reliance on the reports is "arbitrary and capricious."

Pyramid Lake Paiute Tribe v. U.S. Navy, 898 F.2d 1410, 1415 (9th Cir. 1990) (citations omitted). Why would Congress have included a substantive component in ESA, when it had chosen not to in designing NEPA? What differences in the regimes may explain this discrepancy?

4.   Injunctive Relief for ESA Violations. In *Thomas v. Peterson*, the Ninth Circuit held that the Forest Service violated the procedural requirements of the ESA, and issued an injunction preventing construction of the road pending compliance with the ESA. 753 F.2d 754, 764 (9th Cir. 1985). In issuing this remedy, the Ninth Circuit recognized an exception to the traditional test for injunctive relief when addressing procedural violations under the ESA. A plaintiff seeking permanent injunctive relief must traditionally satisfy a four-factor test by showing that: (1) it has suffered an irreparable injury; (2) remedies available at law, such as monetary damages, are inadequate to compensate for that injury; (3) considering the balance of hardships between the plaintiff and defendant, a remedy in equity is warranted; and (4) the public interest would not be disserved by a permanent injunction. *eBay Inc. v. MercExchange, L.L.C.,* 547 U.S. 388, 391 (2006).

But in *Thomas*, the Court analogized to the NEPA context, where it had held that because "[i]rreparable damage is presumed to flow from a failure properly to evaluate" environmental impacts of an agency action, an injunction is typically the appropriate remedy. *Thomas*, 753 F.2d at 764. The

Court held that "[w]e see no reason that the same principle should not apply to procedural violations of the ESA." *Id.* The *Thomas* Court's presumption of irreparable harm supporting injunctive relief in ESA consultation cases remained the law in the Ninth Circuit until 2015, when it was overruled in *Cottonwood Environmental Law Center v. U.S. Forest Service*, 789 F.3d 1075 (9th Cir. 2015).

In *Cottonwood*, the Court explained that two recent Supreme Court cases addressing injunctive relief in the context of NEPA called its prior presumption into question. In one of those cases, the Supreme Court explained that there is nothing in NEPA that allows courts considering injunctive relief to put their "thumb on the scales" in favor of plaintiffs. *Monsanto Co. v. Geertson Seed Farms*, 561 U.S. 139, 157 (2010); *see also Winter v. Natural Resources Defense Council*, 555 U.S. 7, 22 (2008) (rejecting the Ninth Circuit test for preliminary injunctive relief in NEPA cases as "too lenient."). The Ninth Circuit ultimately held that the ESA, like NEPA, does not allow courts to put their "thumb on the scales" in evaluating whether plaintiffs have suffered an irreparable injury. *Cottonwood*, 789 F.3d at 1090. Do you find the *Cottonwood* or *Thomas* courts' approach to injunctive relief in ESA cases preferable?

5.   Consultation in Competition with Recovery. According to the GAO, between 2001 and 2003, FWS and NMFS had to conduct over 1,500 consultations. Of the consultations requested in that period, 40 percent could not be finished on time and some were over a year late. GAO found that many agencies feel pressured to consult with EPA out of fear of litigation, whether or not they believe the consultation is actually appropriate. GAO, MORE FEDERAL MANAGEMENT ATTENTION IS NEEDED TO IMPROVE THE CONSULTATION PROCESS (2004).

Another GAO study focused on the allocation of the Services' time and money. Looking specifically at 2001, GAO found that 42 percent of the Services' time was spent on consultations, 28 percent on recovery, 13 percent on candidate conservation, 10 percent on listing, and 6 percent on landowner incentive programs. Of the time spent on recovery, 34 percent of that consisted of developing plans, 62 percent involved implementation of the plans (most frequently by contracting out the recovery work), and 4 percent of the time was devoted to delisting activities. Funding allocations showed slightly different priorities. Recovery spending was around $60 million, consultation spending was $43 million, candidate conservation received $7 million, listing received $6 million, and landowner incentive programs received $5 million. GAO, INFORMATION ON HOW FUNDS ARE ALLOCATED AND WHAT ACTIVITIES ARE EMPHASIZED (2002).

How could so much more money be spent on recovery than consultation even though consultation represents a significantly higher portion of the Services' workload? Since consultations are initiated largely by other federal agencies, they essentially control the direction of the largest portion of the Services' endangered species workload. Is it advisable to allow other agencies set the Services' priorities? What alternatives could be implemented that might strike a different balance between allowing the Services to use their expertise to implement their own priorities while still ensuring that activities engaged in by other federal agencies will not threaten protected species?

vi.   The Obligation to Conserve

In addition to its prohibition on federal actions that jeopardize endangered or threatened species, 16 U.S.C. § 1536(a)(2), the ESA also states that all federal agencies "shall . . . carry[ ] out programs for the conservation of endangered species and threatened species." 16 U.S.C. § 1536(a)(1). The term "conserve" is defined as "the use of all methods and procedures which are necessary to bring any endangered species or threatened species to the point at which the measures provided pursuant to this chapter are no longer necessary." 16 U.S.C. § 1532(3). The following case examines what affirmative actions these provisions require agencies to undertake.

Pyramid Lake Paiute Tribe of Indians v. United States Department of Navy

898 F.2d 1410 (9th Cir. 1990).

■ Before TANG, CANBY, and O'SCANNLAIN, CIRCUIT JUDGES.

■ O'SCANNLAIN, CIRCUIT JUDGE:

We must determine whether certain practices of the Department of the Navy in leasing acreage and contiguous water rights to local farmers in Nevada violate federal law. The Pyramid Lake Paiute Tribe of Indians alleges that these practices seriously threaten the continued viability of an endangered species of fish, the cui-ui, in violation of the Endangered Species Act. . . .

The Department of the Navy (the "Navy") owns and operates Fallon Naval Air Station ("Fallon") in Nevada. . . .

The Navy conducts extensive flight training throughout most of the year at Fallon. . . . Fallon faces certain unique dangers . . . because of the desert conditions. For example, the Navy must contend with poor visibility caused by dust storms, damage to aircraft engines from foreign objects, and an increased risk of fire.

To diminish the risk of these dangers occurring, the Navy has surrounded the runways with "buffer zones" containing irrigated vegetation. These zones work to minimize the dangerous conditions and therefore lessen the risk of injury or death to Navy pilots. . . .

The diversion of water used to irrigate the land involved in the outlease program . . . occurs as follows:

> [The Project] diverts water from the Truckee River into the Truckee Canal at Derby Dam. The diverted water flows through the Truckee Canal into Lahontan Reservoir, where it is merged with water from the Carson River. Of course, any water that is

diverted into Lahontan Reservoir does not enter Pyramid Lake. . . .

Pyramid Lake is located on the Pyramid Lake Indian Reservation, which is inhabited by the [Tribe]. Drainage from the Truckee River into Lahontan Reservoir has significantly reduced the size of Pyramid Lake.

Truckee-Carson Irrigation Dist. v. Department of Interior, 742 F.2d 527, 529 (9th Cir. 1984), *cert. denied*, 472 U.S. 1007 (1985).

Before the upstream diversions for the Project as well as for other irrigation and municipal and industrial uses began, the Truckee River maintained the lake's level and provided river spawning flows for the cui-ui, a species of fish which has as its exclusive habitat Pyramid Lake. The Secretary of the Interior (the "Secretary") has categorized the cui-ui (pronounced "kwee-wee") as an endangered species under the Endangered Species Act (the "Act" or "ESA"). 32 Fed. Reg. 4001 (1967). The parties do not dispute this categorization; indeed, they stipulate that "inadequate flows" of the Truckee River into Pyramid Lake have led to a "precarious condition" for the cui-ui. . . .

The [Endangered Species] Act . . . provides, in § 7(a)(1), that federal agencies outside the Interior Department shall execute their programs in a manner consistent with the conservation of endangered and threatened species. ESA § 7(a)(1), 16 U.S.C. § 1536(a)(1). In full, § 7(a)(1) provides:

> The Secretary shall review other programs administered by him and utilize such programs in furtherance of the purposes of this chapter. *All other federal agencies* shall, in consultation with and with the assistance of the Secretary, utilize their authorities in furtherance of the purposes of [the Act] by carrying out programs for the conservation of endangered species and threatened species listed pursuant to § 1553 of this title.

16 U.S.C. § 1536(a)(1) (emphasis added). Similar mandates are laid down in other sections of the Act. *See Carson-Truckee Water Conservancy Dist. v. Clark*, 741 F.2d 257, 261–62 & n. 3 (9th Cir. 1984), *cert. denied,* 470 U.S. 1083 (hereinafter "*Carson-Truckee WCD*"); ESA §§ 2(b), (c) & 3(3), 16 U.S.C. §§ 1531(b), (c) & 1532(3).[14] The key term in these sections, "conservation," means "to use and the use of all methods and procedures which are necessary to bring any endangered species or threatened species to the point at which the measures provided pursuant to [the Act]

---

[14] Section 2(b) states that the purposes of the Act are: "to provide a means whereby the ecosystems upon which endangered species and threatened species depend may be *conserved*, [and] to provide a program for the *conservation* of such endangered species and threatened species. . . ." 16 U.S.C. § 1531(b) (emphasis added).

Section 2(c) of the Act provides in pertinent part that: "all Federal departments and agencies shall seek to *conserve* endangered species and threatened species and shall utilize their authorities in furtherance of the purposes of [the Act]." 16 U.S.C. § 1531(c) (emphasis added).

are no longer necessary." ESA § 3(3), 16 U.S.C. § 1532(3). This court has recognized that agencies have affirmative obligations to conserve under § 7(a)(1), but has not had occasion to consider the scope of those obligations. *Carson-Truckee WCD,* 741 F.2d at 262 n. 5.

The Tribe asserts that if an alternative to the challenged action would be equally as effective at serving the government's interest, and at the same time would enhance conservation to an equal or greater degree than does the challenged action, then the agency must adopt the alternative. The Tribe suggests in essence that § 7(a)(1) requires an agency to adopt the "least burdensome alternative," to borrow a phrase from constitutional law. The Tribe notes that it proposed an alternative to the current outlease program that would both require the use of less Project water and further the Navy's interest in pilot safety to the same degree. The Navy's refusal to adopt the proposal, the Tribe argues, violates the Navy's affirmative obligation to conserve under § 7(a)(1). The Navy responds that while § 7(a)(1) requires agencies to develop programs that will operate to conserve listed species, the agencies need do so only in a manner consistent with the accomplishment of the agencies' primary goals. . . .

. . . [T]he Navy's "primary mission" construction is not viable because it understates the Navy's duty to conserve. The Navy concedes that § 7(a)(1) contains a congressional directive that agencies must act affirmatively in the interest of listed species, but qualifies the declaration by stating that the section was not "intended to frustrate the agencies' accomplishment of their primary missions." Appellee's Brief at 20. The Court in *TVA* rejected such a proposition as being inconsistent with congressional intent. *TVA v. Hill,* 437 U.S. 153, 181–83 (1978) (noting that Congress "carefully omitted" from the final version of the Act all proposed language which tempered federal agencies' duty to conserve (*e.g.,* language which extended the duty only "*insofar as is practicable and consistent with the[ir] primary purposes*")).

On the other hand, the Tribe's interpretation overstates the Navy's duty, for it would work to divest an agency of virtually all discretion in deciding how to fulfill its duty to conserve. We have recognized that the Secretary is to be afforded some discretion in ascertaining how best to fulfill the mandate to conserve under § 7(a)(1). *See Carson-Truckee WCD,* 741 F.2d at 262. That some discretion should be allowed is also evident from the regulations promulgated under the Act. For example, a non-Interior agency is given discretion to decide whether to implement conservation recommendations put forth by the FWS. 50 C.F.R. § 402.14(j) (1988). The interpretation of a statute by the agency charged with its administration is entitled to deference. *Chevron U.S.A., Inc.,* 467 U.S. 837, 844 (1984). . . .

Even were we to adopt the stringent standard of duty the Tribe would impose, we would be hard-pressed to rule that the Navy has violated § 7(a)(1) given the district court's findings of fact. Our reasoning hinges primarily on the court's finding that the Tribe's proposals would be of "insignificant effect upon the availability of water in the lower Truckee River for the preservation of the cui-ui." . . .

[I]n light of our earlier discussion of the Navy's duty under § 7(a)(1), [we do not] agree that any slight conservation effect, however insignificant, requires the Navy to accept the Tribe's proposal. . . .

We hold that the district court's finding relating to the insignificant impact of the conservation measures the Tribe has proposed is not clearly erroneous. We therefore affirm the court's holding that the Navy has not violated § 7(a)(1).

NOTES AND QUESTIONS

1.   **Conservation.** Conservation is defined in § 3(3) of the Act as

> the use of all methods and procedures which are necessary to bring any endangered species or threatened species to the point at which the measures provided pursuant to this chapter are no longer necessary. Such methods and procedures include, but are not limited to, all activities associated with scientific resources management such as research, census, law enforcement, habitat acquisition and maintenance, propagation, live trapping, and transplantation. . . .

16 U.S.C. § 1532(3). Which of these methods or procedures appears to have been implicated in the *Pyramid Lake Piute Tribe* decision? How did the *Pyramid Lake* court define the Navy's obligations under § 7(a)(1)? On what basis did the *Pyramid Lake* court determine the Navy's actions to be in compliance with § 7(a)(1)?

2.   **Scope of § 7(a)(1).** Imagine a slightly different scenario to the one which gave rise to the *Pyramid Lakes* controversy, in which the Navy's proposed action would have appreciably affected the ability of the cui-ui to reproduce (though not to such an extent as to constitute jeopardy under § 7(a)(2)) thereby impeding its ability to overcome its threatened status. Under this scenario, would the holding of the *Pyramid Lake* court have differed? What should the Navy's obligations under § 7(a)(1) be in these circumstances?

There is very little case law on this question. Courts seem to agree that § 7(a)(1) "imposes only a general requirement [to conserve and that] the specifics of any given conservation plan are subject to the discretionary authority of each federal agency." *Fla. Key Deer v. Paulison*, 522 F.3d 1133, 1146 (11th Cir. 2008) (citing *Pyramid Lake*, 898 F.2d 1410, 1418 (9th Cir. 1990); *Defenders of Wildlife v. Babbitt*, 130 F. Supp. 2d 121, 135 (D.D.C. 2001); *Northwest Envtl. Advocates v. EPA*, 268 F. Supp. 2d 1255, 1273 (D. Or. 2003)). This discretion, however, is not limitless, and total inaction on the part of the agency or conservation actions so insignificant as to qualify as inaction are not allowed. *See Fla. Key Deer*, 522 F.3d at 1146–48 (holding that a program intended to incentivize the creation of conservation plans but that in fact did not result in any such plans amounted to inaction). At a minimum, then, agencies "must in fact carry out a program to conserve, and not an 'insignificant' measure that does not, or is not reasonably likely to, conserve endangered or threatened species." *Id.*

Bearing in mind the literal interpretation of § 7(a)(2) favored by the *TVA v. Hill* Court, how expansively could § 7(a)(1) be interpreted? How expansively should it be interpreted? For example, should an agency proposing an action with no impact on an endangered species be forced to improve conditions for an endangered species? Should an agency that has not proposed any action at all be forced to do so? Should the cost of undertaking a conservation measure be a factor in assessing the application of § 7(a)(1)? If so, why? Do you favor the least burdensome alternative standard advanced by the Tribe in *Pyramid Lake*? Would this be a meaningful standard in applying § 7(a)(1)?

3. Relationship Between §§ 7(a)(1) and 7(a)(2). Consider the relationship between §§ 7(a)(1) and 7(a)(2). Section 7(a)(2) prohibits actions that are likely to jeopardize the continued existence of any endangered or threatened species or result in the destruction or adverse modification of critical habitat. 16 U.S.C. § 1536(a)(2). Section 7(a)(1) requires that federal agencies utilize their authorities in furtherance of the Act's conservation objectives. 16 U.S.C. § 1536(a)(1). Should the scope of § 7(a)(1) be read in light of the relatively limited scope of § 7(a)(2)? Should an agency's obligations to conserve threatened and endangered species exceed its obligations not to jeopardize their continued existence?

4. Responsibilities of FWS and Other Federal Agencies. Sections 7(a)(1) and 2(c)(1) both impose obligations to conserve on all federal agencies. 16 U.S.C. §§ 1536(a)(1), 1531(c)(1). Section 2(c)(1) does so directly: It applies to "all Federal departments and agencies," including FWS. 16 U.S.C. § 1531(c)(1). Section 7(a)(1) distinguishes between the Secretary and "all other federal agencies," but imposes similar requirements on both. 16 U.S.C. § 1536(a)(1). Should the FWS, an agency with environmental expertise and charged with the administration of the ESA, and all other federal agencies have identical obligations to take affirmative steps to conserve endangered species, or should FWS have a greater obligation to initiate affirmative conservation efforts? *See Pyramid Lake*, 898 F.2d at 1417 n.15.

In *Defenders of Wildlife v. U.S. Fish and Wildlife Service*, the district court held that while the United States Forest Service (USFS) "has [a] responsibility, equal to that of the [FWS], to use its authorities in furtherance of the conservation of the Mexican gray wolf," it was not required to develop or implement its own conservation program for the Mexican gray wolf when a program developed by the FWS already existed. 797 F. Supp. 2d 949, 957 (2011). The court goes on to find that the rubberstamping of an FWS conservation program is not permitted and that USFS is "independently responsible for the sufficiency of the [FWS] programs it adopts as its own. . . . [I]f [FWS's] recommendations [are] arbitrary and capricious then reliance on them by the action agency is likewise arbitrary and capricious." *Id.* at 959 (internal quotations omitted). Under this reasoning, FWS does not have the sole or final say in the development or implementation of a conservation program. Given the agency's expertise, is this reasonable?

5.   Consultation. Section 7(a)(1) directs other federal agencies to consult with FWS in carrying out programs for the conservation of endangered species; does it follow from this consultation requirement that an agency must follow FWS's conservation recommendations, or is the agency free to pursue alternative conservation measures? What if the agency's chosen conservation measures are less stringent than those recommended by FWS?

C. PRIVATE ACTIONS

i.   PRIVATE TAKINGS

Section 9(a)(1)(B) provides that it is unlawful for any person to "take" any endangered species listed under the Act. 16 U.S.C. § 1538(a)(1)(B). Regulations issued by the FWS have extended the operation of this provision to threatened species. *See* 50 C.F.R. § 17.31(a). In 2018, FWS proposed to revise its regulations extending most of the prohibitions for activities involving endangered species to threatened species. The proposed regulations would require the Service, pursuant to section 4(d) of the Endangered Species Act, to determine what, if any, protective regulations are appropriate for species that the Service in the future determines to be threatened. Endangered and Threatened Wildlife and Plants; Revision of the Regulations for Prohibitions to Threatened Wildlife and Plants, 83 Fed. Reg. 35,174 (2018). If this rule is finalized, species listed or reclassified as a threatened species after the rule's effective date would have protective regulations only if the Service promulgates a species-specific rule. *Id.* at 35,175.

"Take" is defined in § 3(19), and includes a list of actions such as "harass," "harm," "shoot," and "capture." 16 U.S.C. § 1532(19). The § 9 prohibition on takings is more lenient than the no jeopardy requirement of § 7 in several ways. First, private parties may apply for permits for actions that would otherwise violate § 9 under § 10(a), which allows exceptions to the taking prohibition in a significantly broader range of circumstances than the § 7(h) "God Squad" exemption process. 16 U.S.C. § 1539(a). Second, § 7 applies to actions that might possibly harm endangered species, whereas § 9 is only triggered if a taking actually occurs. Third, § 7 contains an affirmative obligation to conserve endangered species, whereas § 9 imposes no comparable obligation. Thus, the ESA imposes significantly less stringent requirements on private actors than on government actors.

Based on the statute's definition of "take," it is clear that shooting an endangered species, for example, is unlawful under § 9(a)(1)(B). The meaning of "harm," however, is less clear. If a developer builds a series of new houses on previously undeveloped land and these structures change or destroy part of the natural habitat of an endangered species, does this constitute "harm" within the meaning of the Act? Does it matter if certain identifiable animals have been harmed, or is harm to a habitat that could support an endangered species that is known to be in the area sufficient? FWS developed a regulation defining "harm" relatively broadly, to include adverse habitat modification that actually kills or injures endangered species. This regulation was challenged in the following case.

Babbitt v. Sweet Home Chapter of Communities for a Great Oregon

515 U.S. 687 (1995).

■ JUSTICE STEVENS delivered the opinion of the Court:

The Endangered Species Act of 1973 (ESA or Act), 87 Stat. 884, 16 U.S.C. § 1531 (1988 ed. and Supp. V), contains a variety of protections designed to save from extinction species that the Secretary of the Interior designates as endangered or threatened. Section 9 of the Act makes it unlawful for any person to "take" any endangered or threatened species. The Secretary has promulgated a regulation that defines the statute's prohibition on takings to include "significant habitat modification or degradation where it actually kills or injures wildlife." This case presents the question whether the Secretary exceeded his authority under the Act by promulgating that regulation.

Section 9(a)(1) of the Act provides the following protection for endangered species:

Except as provided in sections 1535(g)(2) and 1539 of this title, with respect to any endangered species of fish or wildlife listed pursuant to section 1533 of this title it is unlawful for any person subject to the jurisdiction of the United States to—

(B) take any such species within the United States or the territorial sea of the United States.

16 U.S.C. § 1538(a)(1). Section 3(19) of the Act defines the statutory term "take":

The term "take" means to harass, harm, pursue, hunt, shoot, wound, kill, trap, capture, or collect, or to attempt to engage in any such conduct.

16 U.S.C. § 1532(19). The Act does not further define the terms it uses to define "take." The Interior Department regulations that implement the statute, however, define the statutory term "harm":

Harm in the definition of 'take' in the Act means an act which actually kills or injures wildlife. Such act may include significant habitat modification or degradation where it actually kills or injures wildlife by significantly impairing essential behavioral patterns, including breeding, feeding, or sheltering.

50 CFR § 17.3 (1994). This regulation has been in place since 1975.

A limitation on the § 9 "take" prohibition appears in § 10(a)(1)(B) of the Act, which Congress added by amendment in 1982. That section authorizes the Secretary to grant a permit for any taking otherwise prohibited by § 9(a)(1)(B) "if such taking is incidental to, and not the purpose of, the carrying out of an otherwise lawful activity." 16 U.S.C. § 1539(a)(1)(B). . . .

Respondents in this action are small landowners, logging companies, and families dependent on the forest products industries in the Pacific Northwest and in the Southeast, and organizations that represent their interests. They . . . challenge the statutory validity of the Secretary's regulation defining "harm," particularly the inclusion of habitat modification and degradation in the definition. Respondents challenged the regulation on its face. . . .

Because this case was decided on motions for summary judgment . . . we must assume, *arguendo,* that [Respondents'] activities will have the effect, even though unintended, of detrimentally changing the natural habitat of both listed species and that, as a consequence, members of those species will be killed or injured. Under respondents' view of the law, the Secretary's only means of forestalling that grave result—even when the actor knows it is certain to occur—is to use his § 5 authority to purchase the lands on which the survival of the species depends. The Secretary, on the other hand, submits that the § 9 prohibition on takings, which Congress defined to include "harm," places on respondents a duty to avoid harm that habitat alteration will cause the birds unless respondents first obtain a permit pursuant to § 10.

The text of the Act provides three reasons for concluding that the Secretary's interpretation is reasonable. First, an ordinary understanding of the word "harm" supports it. The dictionary definition of the verb form of "harm" is "to cause hurt or damage to: injure." WEBSTER'S THIRD NEW INTERNATIONAL DICTIONARY 1034 (1966). In the context of the ESA, that definition naturally encompasses habitat modification that results in actual injury or death to members of an endangered or threatened species.

Respondents argue that the Secretary should have limited the purview of "harm" to direct applications of force against protected species, but the dictionary definition does not include the word "directly" or suggest in any way that only direct or willful action that leads to injury constitutes "harm."[10] Moreover, unless the statutory term "harm"

---

[10] Respondents and the dissent emphasize what they portray as the "established meaning" of "take" in the sense of a "wildlife take," a meaning respondents argue extends only to "the effort to exercise dominion over some creature, and the concrete effect of [*sic*] that creature." Brief for Respondents 19; see 515 U.S. at 717–18 (Scalia, J., dissenting). This limitation ill serves the statutory text, which forbids not taking "some creature" but "tak[ing] any [endangered] *species*"—a formidable task for even the most rapacious feudal lord. More importantly, Congress explicitly defined the operative term "take" in the ESA, no matter how much the dissent wishes otherwise, *see id.* at 716–724, thereby obviating the need for us to probe its meaning as we must probe the meaning of the undefined subsidiary term "harm." Finally, Congress' definition of "take" includes several words—most obviously "harass," "pursue," and "wound," in addition to "harm" itself—that fit respondents' and the dissent's definition of "take" no better than does "significant habitat modification or degradation."

encompasses indirect as well as direct injuries, the word has no meaning that does not duplicate the meaning of other words that § 3 uses to define "take." A reluctance to treat statutory terms as surplusage supports the reasonableness of the Secretary's interpretation. See, *e.g.*, *Mackey v. Lanier Collection Agency & Service, Inc.*, 486 U.S. 825, 837, and n. 11 (1988).[11]

Second, the broad purpose of the ESA supports the Secretary's decision to extend protection against activities that cause the precise harms Congress enacted the statute to avoid. . . . Congress' intent to provide comprehensive protection for endangered and threatened species supports the permissibility of the Secretary's "harm" regulation. . . .

Third, the fact that Congress in 1982 authorized the Secretary to issue permits for takings that § 9(a)(1)(B) would otherwise prohibit, "if such taking is incidental to, and not the purpose of, the carrying out of an otherwise lawful activity," 16 U.S.C. § 1539(a)(1)(B), strongly suggests that Congress understood § 9(a)(1)(B) to prohibit indirect as well as deliberate takings. *Cf. NLRB v. Bell Aerospace Co.*, 416 U.S. 267, 274–275 (1974). The permit process requires the applicant to prepare a "conservation plan" that specifies how he intends to "minimize and mitigate" the "impact" of his activity on endangered and threatened species, 16 U.S.C. § 1539(a)(2)(A), making clear that Congress had in mind foreseeable rather than merely accidental effects on listed species. No one could seriously request an "incidental" take permit to avert § 9 liability for direct, deliberate action against a member of an endangered or threatened species, but respondents would read "harm" so narrowly that the permit procedure would have little more than that absurd purpose. "When Congress acts to amend a statute, we presume it intends its amendment to have real and substantial effect." *Stone v. INS*, 514 U.S. 386, 397 (1995). Congress' addition of the § 10 permit provision supports the Secretary's conclusion that activities not intended to harm an endangered species, such as habitat modification, may constitute unlawful takings under the ESA unless the Secretary permits them. . . .

We need not decide whether the statutory definition of "take" compels the Secretary's interpretation of "harm," because our conclusions that Congress did not unambiguously manifest its intent to adopt respondents' view and that the Secretary's interpretation is reasonable suffice to decide this case. See generally *Chevron U.S.A., Inc. v. Natural Resources Defense Council, Inc.*, 467 U.S. 837 (1984). The latitude the ESA gives the Secretary in enforcing the statute, together with the degree of regulatory expertise necessary to its enforcement, establishes that we owe some degree of deference to the Secretary's reasonable

---

[11] In contrast, if the statutory term "harm" encompasses such indirect means of killing and injuring wildlife as habitat modification, the other terms listed in § 3—"harass," "pursue," "hunt," "shoot," "wound," "kill," "trap," "capture," and "collect"—generally retain independent meanings. Most of those terms refer to deliberate actions more frequently than does "harm," and they therefore do not duplicate the sense of indirect causation that "harm" adds to the statute.

interpretation. See Breyer, Judicial Review of Questions of Law and Policy, 38 ADMIN. L. REV. 363, 373 (1986). . . .

■ JUSTICE O'CONNOR, concurring:

My agreement with the Court is founded on two understandings. First, the challenged regulation is limited to significant habitat modification that causes actual, as opposed to hypothetical or speculative, death or injury to identifiable protected animals. Second, even setting aside difficult questions of scienter, the regulation's application is limited by ordinary principles of proximate causation, which introduce notions of foreseeability. . . . Because there is no need to strike a regulation on a facial challenge out of concern that it is susceptible of erroneous application, however, and because there are many habitat-related circumstances in which the regulation might validly apply, I join the opinion of the Court. . . .

. . . The regulation has clear application, for example, to significant habitat modification that kills or physically injures animals which, because they are in a vulnerable breeding state, do not or cannot flee or defend themselves, or to environmental pollutants that cause an animal to suffer physical complications during gestation. Breeding, feeding, and sheltering are what animals do. If significant habitat modification, by interfering with these essential behaviors, actually kills or injures an animal protected by the Act, it causes "harm" within the meaning of the regulation. . . .

By the dissent's reckoning, the regulation at issue here, in conjunction with 16 U.S.C. § 1540(a)(1), imposes liability for any habitat-modifying conduct that ultimately results in the death of a protected animal, "regardless of whether that result is intended or even foreseeable, and no matter how long the chain of causality between modification and injury." Even if § 1540(a)(1) does create a strict liability regime (a question we need not decide at this juncture), I see no indication that Congress, in enacting that section, intended to dispense with ordinary principles of proximate causation. Strict liability means liability without regard to fault; it does not normally mean liability for every consequence, however remote, of one's conduct. See generally W. KEETON, D. DOBBS, R. KEETON & D. OWEN, PROSSER AND KEETON ON LAW OF TORTS 559–560 (5th ed. 1984) (describing "practical necessity for the restriction of liability within some reasonable bounds" in the strict liability context). I would not lightly assume that Congress, in enacting a strict liability statute that is silent on the causation question, has dispensed with this well-entrenched principle. In the absence of congressional abrogation of traditional principles of causation, then, private parties should be held liable under § 1540(a)(1) only if their habitat-modifying actions proximately cause death or injury to protected animals. The regulation, of course, does not contradict the presumption or notion that ordinary principles of causation apply here. Indeed, by use of the word "actually," the regulation clearly rejects speculative or conjectural effects, and thus itself *invokes* principles of proximate causation.

Proximate causation is not a concept susceptible of precise definition. See KEETON, supra, at 280–281. It is easy enough, of course, to identify the extremes. The farmer whose fertilizer is lifted by a tornado from tilled fields and deposited miles away in a wildlife refuge cannot, by any stretch of the term, be considered the proximate cause of death or injury to protected species occasioned thereby. At the same time, the landowner who drains a pond on his property, killing endangered fish in the process, would likely satisfy any formulation of the principle. We have recently said that proximate causation "normally eliminates the bizarre," *Jerome B. Grubart, Inc. v. Great Lakes Dredge & Dock Co.*, 513 U.S. 527, 536 (1995), and have noted its "functionally equivalent" alternative characterizations in terms of foreseeability, see *Milwaukee & St. Paul Ry. Co. v. Kellogg*, 94 U.S. 469, 475 (1877) ("natural and probable consequence"), and duty, see *Palsgraf v. Long Island R.R. Co.*, 162 N.E. 99 (NY 1928). Proximate causation depends to a great extent on considerations of the fairness of imposing liability for remote consequences. The task of determining whether proximate causation exists in the limitless fact patterns sure to arise is best left to lower courts. But I note, at the least, that proximate cause principles inject a foreseeability element into the statute, and hence, the regulation, that would appear to alleviate some of the problems noted by the dissent. See, *e.g.*, *post*, at 2423 (describing "a farmer who tills his field and causes erosion that makes silt run into a nearby river which depletes oxygen and thereby [injures] protected fish").

In my view, then, the "harm" regulation applies where significant habitat modification, by impairing essential behaviors, proximately (foreseeably) causes actual death or injury to identifiable animals that are protected under the Endangered Species Act. . . .

■ JUSTICE SCALIA, with whom THE CHIEF JUSTICE and JUSTICE THOMAS join, dissenting:

I think it unmistakably clear that the legislation at issue here (1) forbade the hunting and killing of endangered animals, and (2) provided federal lands and federal funds *for the acquisition of private lands*, to preserve the habitat of endangered animals. The Court's holding that the hunting and killing prohibition incidentally preserves habitat on private lands imposes unfairness to the point of financial ruin—not just upon the rich, but upon the simplest farmer who finds his land conscripted to national zoological use. I respectfully dissent. . . .

. . . If "take" were not elsewhere defined in the Act, none could dispute what it means, for the term is as old as the law itself. To "take," when applied to wild animals, means to reduce those animals, by killing or capturing, to human control. See, *e.g.,* 11 OXFORD ENGLISH DICTIONARY (1933) ("Take . . . To catch, capture (a wild beast, bird, fish, etc.)"); WEBSTER'S NEW INTERNATIONAL DICTIONARY OF THE ENGLISH

LANGUAGE (2d ed. 1949) (take defined as "to catch or capture by trapping, snaring, etc., or as prey"); *Geer v. Connecticut*, 161 U.S. 519, 523 (1896) (" '[A]ll the animals which can be taken upon the earth, in the sea, or in the air, that is to say, wild animals, belong to those who take them' ") (quoting the Digest of Justinian); 2 W. BLACKSTONE, COMMENTARIES 411 (1766) ("Every man . . . has an equal right of pursuing and taking to his own use all such creatures as are *ferae naturae*"). This is just the sense in which "take" is used elsewhere in federal legislation and treaty. See, *e.g.*, Migratory Bird Treaty Act, 16 U.S.C. § 703 (1988 ed., Supp. V) (no person may "pursue, hunt, take, capture, kill, [or] attempt to take, capture, or kill" any migratory bird); Agreement on the Conservation of Polar Bears, Nov. 15, 1973, Art. I, 27 U.S.T. 3918, 3921, T.I.A.S. No. 8409 (defining "taking" as "hunting, killing and capturing"). And that meaning fits neatly with the rest of § 1538(a)(1), which makes it unlawful not only to take protected species, but also to import or export them, § 1538(a)(1)(A); to possess, sell, deliver, carry, transport, or ship any taken species, § 1538(a)(1)(D); and to transport, sell, or offer to sell them in interstate or foreign commerce, §§ 1538(a)(1)(E), (F). The taking prohibition, in other words, is only part of the regulatory plan of § 1538(a)(1), which covers all the stages of the process by which protected wildlife is reduced to man's dominion and made the object of profit. It is obvious that "take" in this sense—a term of art deeply embedded in the statutory and common law concerning wildlife—describes a class of acts (not omissions) done directly and intentionally (not indirectly and by accident) to particular animals (not populations of animals).

The Act's definition of "take" does expand the word slightly (and not unusually), so as to make clear that it includes not just a completed taking, but the process of taking, and all of the acts that are customarily identified with or accompany that process ("to harass, harm, pursue, hunt, shoot, wound, kill, trap, capture, or collect"); and so as to include attempts. § 1532(19). The tempting fallacy—which the Court commits with abandon, see *ante,* at 2413, n. 10—is to assume that *once defined,* "take" loses any significance, and it is only the definition that matters. The Court treats the statute as though Congress had directly enacted the § 1532(19) definition as a self-executing prohibition, and had not enacted § 1538(a)(1)(B) at all. But § 1538(a)(1)(B) *is* there, and if the terms contained in the definitional section are susceptible of two readings, one of which comports with the standard meaning of "take" as used in application to wildlife, and one of which does not, an agency regulation that adopts the latter reading is necessarily unreasonable, for it reads the defined term "take"—the only operative term—out of the statute altogether.

That is what has occurred here. The verb "harm" has a *range* of meaning: "to cause injury" at its broadest, "to do hurt or damage" in a narrower and more direct sense. See, *e.g.,* 1 N. WEBSTER, AN AMERICAN DICTIONARY OF THE ENGLISH LANGUAGE (1828) ("Harm, *v.t.* To hurt; to injure; to damage; *to impair soundness of body, either animal* or vegetable") (emphasis added); AMERICAN COLLEGE DICTIONARY 551 (1970) ("harm . . . *n.* injury; damage; hurt: *to do him bodily harm*"). In fact the more directed sense of "harm" is a somewhat more common and preferred usage; "*harm* has in it a little of the idea of specially focused hurt or injury, as if a personal injury has been anticipated and intended." J. OPDYCKE, MARK MY WORDS: A GUIDE TO MODERN USAGE AND EXPRESSION 330 (1949). See also AMERICAN HERITAGE DICTIONARY 662 (1985) ("*Injure* has the widest range. . . . *Harm* and *hurt* refer principally to what causes physical or mental distress to living things"). To define "harm" as an act or omission that, however remotely, "actually kills or injures" a population of wildlife through habitat modification is to choose a meaning that makes nonsense of the word that "harm" defines— requiring us to accept that a farmer who tills his field and causes erosion that makes silt run into a nearby river which depletes oxygen and thereby "impairs [the] breeding" of protected fish has "taken" or "attempted to take" the fish. It should take the strongest evidence to make us believe that Congress has defined a term in a manner repugnant to its ordinary and traditional sense.

Here the evidence shows the opposite. "Harm" is merely one of 10 prohibitory words in § 1532(19), and the other 9 fit the ordinary meaning of "take" perfectly. To "harass, pursue, hunt, shoot, wound, kill, trap, capture, or collect" are all affirmative acts (the provision itself describes them as "conduct," see § 1532(19)) which are directed immediately and intentionally against a particular animal—not acts or omissions that indirectly and accidentally cause injury to a population of animals. The Court points out that several of the words ("harass," "pursue," "wound," and "kill") "refer to actions or effects that do not require direct *applications of force.*" *Ante,* at 2414 (emphasis added). That is true enough, but force is not the point. Even "taking" activities in the narrowest sense, activities traditionally engaged in by hunters and trappers, do not all consist of direct applications of force; pursuit and harassment are part of the business of "taking" the prey even before it has been touched. What the nine other words in § 1532(19) have in common—and share with the narrower meaning of "harm" described above, but not with the Secretary's ruthless dilation of the word—is the sense of affirmative conduct intentionally directed against a particular animal or animals. . . .

. . . I would call it *noscitur a sociis.* . . . The fact that "several items in a list share an attribute counsels in favor of interpreting the other items as possessing that attribute as well," *Beecham v. United States,* 511 U.S. 368, 371 (1994). The Court contends that the canon cannot be applied to deprive a word of all its "independent meaning," *ante,* at 2415. That proposition is questionable to begin with, especially as applied to long lawyers' listings such as this. If it were true, we ought to give the word "trap" in the definition its rare meaning of "to clothe" (whence "trappings")—since otherwise it adds nothing to the word "capture." See *Moskal v. United States,* 498 U.S. 103, 120 (1990) (SCALIA, J., dissenting). In any event, the Court's contention that "harm" in the narrow sense adds nothing to the other words underestimates the ingenuity of our own species in a way that Congress did not. To feed an animal poison, to spray it with mace, to chop down the very tree in which it is nesting, or even to destroy its entire habitat in order to take it (as by draining a pond to get at a turtle), might neither wound nor kill, but would directly and intentionally harm. . . .

So far I have discussed only the immediate statutory text bearing on the regulation. But the definition of "take" in § 1532(19) applies "[f]or the purposes of this chapter," that is, it governs the meaning of the word *as used everywhere in the Act.* Thus, the Secretary's interpretation of "harm" is wrong if it does not fit with the use of "take" throughout the Act. And it does not. In § 1540(e)(4)(B), for example, Congress provided for the forfeiture of "[a]ll guns, traps, nets, and other equipment . . . used to aid the taking, possessing, selling, [etc.]" of protected animals. This listing plainly relates to "taking" in the ordinary sense. If environmental modification were part (and necessarily a major part) of taking, as the Secretary maintains, one would have expected the list to include "plows, bulldozers, and backhoes." As another example, § 1539(e)(1) exempts "the taking of any endangered species" by Alaskan Indians and Eskimos "if such taking is primarily for subsistence purposes"; and provides that "[n]on-edible byproducts of species taken pursuant to this section may be sold . . . when made into authentic native articles of handicrafts and clothing." Surely these provisions apply to taking only in the ordinary sense, and are meaningless as applied to species injured by environmental modification. The Act is full of like examples. See, *e.g.,* § 1538(a)(1)(D) (prohibiting possession, sale, and transport of "species taken in violation" of the Act). "[I]f the Act is to be interpreted as a symmetrical and coherent regulatory scheme, one in which the operative words have a consistent meaning throughout," *Gustafson v. Alloyd Co.,* 513 U.S. 561, 569 (1995), the regulation must fall. . . .

. . . [T]he Court seeks support from a provision that was added to the Act in 1982, the year after the Secretary promulgated the current regulation. The provision states:

> [T]he Secretary may permit, under such terms and conditions as he shall prescribe . . . any taking otherwise prohibited by section 1538(a)(1)(B) . . . if such taking is incidental to, and not the purpose of, the carrying out of an otherwise lawful activity.

16 U.S.C. § 1539(a)(1)(B). This provision does not, of course, implicate our doctrine that reenactment of a statutory provision ratifies an extant judicial or administrative interpretation, for neither the taking prohibition in § 1538(a)(1)(B) nor the definition in § 1532(19) was reenacted. See *Central Bank of Denver, N.A. v. First Interstate Bank of Denver, N.A.,* 511 U.S. 164, 185 (1994). The Court claims, however, that

the provision "strongly suggests that Congress understood [§ 1538(a)(1)(B)] to prohibit indirect as well as deliberate takings." 515 U.S. at 700 (majority opinion). That would be a valid inference if habitat modification were the only substantial "otherwise lawful activity" that might incidentally and nonpurposefully cause a prohibited "taking." Of course it is not. This provision applies to the many otherwise lawful takings that incidentally take a protected species—as when fishing for unprotected salmon also takes an endangered species of salmon, see *Pacific Northwest Generating Cooperative v. Brown*, 38 F.3d 1058, 1067 (9th Cir. 1994). Congress has referred to such "incidental takings" in other statutes as well—for example, a statute referring to "the incidental taking of . . . sea turtles in the course of . . . harvesting [shrimp]" and to the "rate of incidental taking of sea turtles by United States vessels in the course of such harvesting," 103 Stat. 1038, § 609(b)(2), note following 16 U.S.C. § 1537 (1988 ed., Supp. V); and a statute referring to "the incidental taking of marine mammals in the course of commercial fishing operations," 108 Stat. 546, § 118(a). The Court shows that it misunderstands the question when it says that "[n]o one could seriously request an 'incidental' take permit to avert . . . liability for direct, deliberate action *against a member of an endangered or threatened species*." 515 U.S. at 700–01 (majority opinion) (emphasis added). That is not an *incidental* take at all.[4]

This is enough to show, in my view, that the 1982 permit provision does not support the regulation. I must acknowledge that the Senate Committee Report on this provision, and the House Conference Committee Report, clearly contemplate that it will enable the Secretary to permit environmental modification. *See* S. Rep. No. 97–418, p. 10 (1982); H.R. Conf. Rep. No. 97–835, pp. 30–32 (1982). But the *text* of the amendment cannot possibly bear that asserted meaning, when placed within the context of an Act that must be interpreted (as we have seen) not to prohibit private environmental modification. The neutral language of the amendment cannot possibly alter that interpretation, nor can its legislative history be summoned forth to contradict, rather than clarify, what is in its totality an unambiguous statutory text. See *Chicago v. Environmental Defense Fund*, 511 U.S. 328 (1994). There is little fear, of course, that giving no effect to the relevant portions of the Committee Reports will frustrate the real-life expectations of a majority of the Members of Congress. If they read and relied on such tedious detail on such an obscure point (it was not, after all, presented as a revision of the statute's prohibitory scope, but as a discretionary-waiver provision) the Republic would be in grave peril. . . .

---

[4] The statutory requirement of a "conservation plan" is as consistent with this construction as with the Court's. *See* 515 U.S. at 700–01, and n. 14 (majority opinion). The commercial fisherman who is in danger of incidentally sweeping up protected fish in his nets can quite reasonably be required to "minimize and mitigate" the "impact" of his activity. 16 U.S.C. § 1539(a)(2)(A).

NOTES AND QUESTIONS

1.   Competing Constructions of Harm. The dispute between the majority and the dissent in *Sweet Home* turns on the definition of harm. The majority, in upholding the definition of the Interior Department ("Interior"), favors a broad definition of "harm," including indirect harms through habitat modification. The dissent interprets the term narrowly, with reference to the remainder of the terms listed in § 3(19), to include only direct harms.

In distinguishing between the competing definitions of harm advanced by the majority and dissent, consider the following four scenarios involving an endangered species of bird. First, the shooting of a bird in a tree. Second, the logging of a tree directly resulting in the death of a bird. Third, the logging of a tree containing a nest, resulting in an impact upon the longevity of a bird and its ability to reproduce, but not resulting in its direct or immediate death. Finally, the logging of a tree containing a nest with eggs.

With respect to the second scenario, would the intentions of the logger have any bearing on Justice Scalia's classification? Is it analogous to the scenario described by Justice Scalia concerning the incidental taking of endangered salmon? With respect to the third and fourth scenarios, would the majority be willing to find indirect harm? The Interior regulations define harm to include significant habitat modification only in circumstances in which it "actually kills or injures wildlife." 50 C.F.R. § 17.3. In the third scenario, has the bird actually suffered injury? In the fourth scenario, has any bird suffered injury? For a discussion of the shortcomings of the textual approaches used by both the majority and the dissent, see Richard A. Epstein, Babbitt v. Sweet Home Chapters of Oregon*: The Law and Economics of Habitat Preservation*, 5 SUP. CT. ECON. REV. 1, 10–16 (1997). Epstein argues that the narrow focus of the majority and dissent on the definition of harm caused both sides to create artificial and unsatisfactory interpretations of the takings prohibition. For instance, the majority ignored interpretations of harm that allow for an independent meaning of the word without extending the prohibition to habitat modification, such as with poisoning. *Id.* at 10–11. On the other side, Epstein argues that the dissent unnecessarily restricted its definition of harm only to acts done directly and intentionally, ignoring the strict liability aspect of the statute. *Id.* at 15.

2.   Canons of Construction. Both the majority and the dissent employ canons of statutory construction in support of their respective interpretations of the word "harm." The majority argues that harm should be interpreted so as not to be redundant in the context of the other words that constitute a "taking" for the purposes of § 3(19) of the Act (harass, pursue, hunt, shoot, wound, kill, trap, capture, or collect). For this reason, the majority suggests that the term should necessarily encompass indirect harms. The dissent argues that harm should be interpreted in light of the words that surround it in § 3(19). Since the surrounding words all constitute types of direct harms, the term harm should be interpreted in its direct sense as well.

How should courts go about reconciling competing canons of statutory construction? In the present case, which construction do you find most convincing? Do you agree with the majority that the term "harm" would become redundant were it given only the narrow meaning advocated by the dissent? Do you agree with the dissent that Congress intended the Secretary be able to stop the detrimental consequences of habitat modification only by exercising her authority under § 5 of the ESA—by purchasing the lands on which the survival of the species depends?

3.   ***Chevron* and Canons of Construction.** The *Sweet Home* case concerns an agency's interpretation of its own statutory mandate. What role did *Chevron* deference play in the opinion of the majority? What might explain it not being given greater emphasis in the majority's decision? As discussed in the preceding note, in finding against the Agency's interpretation, Justice Scalia relied upon an established canon of statutory construction. In what circumstances should canons of statutory construction outweigh *Chevron* deference? Are the two reconcilable in the context of Justice Scalia's dissent? *See generally* Denise DeFranco, *Chevron and Canons of Statutory Construction*, 58 GEO. WASH. L. REV. 829 (1990); David A. Schlesinger, *Chevron Unlatined: The Inapplicability of the Canon Noscitur A Sociis Under Prong One of the Chevron Framework*, 5 N.Y.U. ENVTL. L.J. 638 (1996).

4.   **Statutory Solution.** Bearing in mind that the term "harm" appears in the middle of a long list of terms defining "take," what small modifications could be made to § 3(19) to remove any ambiguity in favor of the majority's interpretation? What small modifications could be made in favor of the dissent's interpretation?

5.   **Palila Decisions.** The palila, an endangered finch endemic to Hawaii, had been the subject of an earlier series of lawsuits implicating the definition of "harm." At issue in the second round of Palila cases was whether the presence of mouflon sheep in the habitat occupied by the palila constituted a "taking" of the palila. *Palila v. Haw. Dep't of Land & Natural Res.*, 649 F. Supp. 1070 (D. Haw. 1986), *aff'd*, 852 F.2d 1106 (9th Cir. 1988). The sheep, which had been introduced by the State as quarry for recreational hunters, ate mamane tree seedlings, which the palila utilized for feeding, sheltering, and breeding when the trees were full-grown. Thus, the plaintiffs claimed that the actions of the mouflon sheep impaired the essential behavioral patterns of the palila, thus harming them and constituting a taking. The district court stated:

> A finding of "harm" does not require death to individual members of the species; nor does it require a finding that habitat degradation is presently driving the species toward extinction. Habitat destruction that prevents the recovery of the species by affecting essential behavioral patterns causes actual injury to the species and effects a taking under section 9 of the Act.

649 F. Supp. at 1075. The Ninth Circuit affirmed the district court's conclusion that the continued presence of the mouflon sheep constituted a "taking" of the palila, but noted that:

> Under this resolution of the appeal, we do not reach the issue of whether harm includes habitat degradation that merely retards

recovery. The district court's (and the Secretary's) interpretation of harm as including habitat destruction that could result in extinction, and findings to that effect are enough to sustain an order for the removal of the mouflon sheep.

852 F.2d at 1110. The Ninth Circuit bolstered its Palila decisions one year prior to the decision in *Sweet Home*, in a case where it did not find a "taking," but reiterated that the definition of harm could be met upon a showing of a "*significant impairment* of the species' breeding or feeding habits and [proof] that the habitat degradation prevents, or possibly retards, recovery of the species." *Nat'l Wildlife Fed'n v. Burlington N. R.R.*, 23 F.3d 1508, 1513 (9th Cir. 1994) (emphasis added).

In a portion omitted from the excerpt above, Justice O'Connor expressly questioned the Palila cases. 515 U.S. at 708–14. The grounds on which she joined the majority opinion were "actual, as opposed to hypothetical or speculative, death or injury to identifiable protected animals" [emphasis added] and the "ordinary principles of proximate causation" that limit the regulation's application. *Id.* at 708–09. Consequently, Justice O'Connor disagreed with the *Palila* decision because "[d]estruction of the seedlings did not proximately cause actual death or injury to identifiable birds; it merely prevented the regeneration of forest land not currently sustaining actual birds." *Id.* at 714.

Which interpretation of the definition of harm do you agree with: the one described in the Palila decisions, or the one espoused by Justice O'Connor? Which is more faithful to the actual text of the regulatory definition of harm? Which is more consistent with the overall purposes of the ESA? Under Justice O'Connor's view, if all of the mature mamane trees died, and then the sheep ate all of the seedlings, would this qualify as "harm"? Would it matter if the sheep ate all of the seedlings and then all of the mature trees died? In response to arguments stemming from Justice O'Connor's position in *Sweet Home*, the Ninth Circuit stated that "five Justices affirmed *Palila* in all respects." *Seattle Audubon Soc'y v. Moseley*, 80 F.3d 1401, 1405 (9th Cir. 1996).

6.   Impaired Breeding, Feeding, and Sheltering: Cases Since *Sweet Home*. In *Sweet Home*, Justice Scalia and Justice O'Connor disagreed on the issue of whether a habitat modification that significantly impaired the breeding of endangered species constituted harm to an actual animal. In an omitted portion of the dissenting opinion, Justice Scalia argued that impaired breeding does not actually harm an identifiable animal but rather harms only the general population, and since harms to the general population are not contemplated by the Act, the regulation defining harm to include impaired breeding was not permissible. 515 U.S. at 715–17, 734 & n.5 (Scalia, J., dissenting). In her concurrence, Justice O'Connor argued that impaired breeding does injure individual animals in addition to the general population. *Id.* at 709–10 (O'Connor, J., concurring). Specifically, she stated that "to make it impossible for an animal to reproduce is to impair its most essential physical functions and to render that animal, and its genetic material, biologically obsolete. This, in my view, is actual injury." *Id.* at 710. The majority opinion did not directly address this issue and lower courts have taken differing positions on whether a showing of impairment of breeding, feeding, or sheltering constitutes an actionable harm.

The Ninth Circuit has found that a habitat modification that impairs the breeding of a species does constitute a harm. *Marbled Murrelet v. Babbitt*, 83 F.3d 1060, 1067 (9th Cir. 1996) ("[U]nder Sweet Home, a habitat modification which significantly impairs the breeding and sheltering of a protected species amounts to 'harm' under the ESA."), *cert. denied*, 519 U.S. 1108 (1997). A district court in the Virgin Islands, on the other hand, refused to find that a habitat modification that impaired the feeding and sheltering patterns of endangered sea turtles and tree boa constrictors constituted harm. The court determined that there was significant modification of habitat for both species, and that these modifications had impaired the species' feeding and sheltering patterns. *Hawksbill Sea Turtle v. FEMA*, 11 F. Supp. 2d 529, 553–54 (D.V.I. 1998). However, the court focused on the fact that "[p]laintiffs have provided no direct evidence that Tree Boas have died or been injured as a result of changes in their feeding and sheltering patterns. Furthermore, they provide no evidence of any general decline in the population of the Tree Boa." *Id.* at 554. Although the plaintiffs produced two dead tree boas, the court found that they had "provide[d] insufficient evidence to establish a causal relationship between the habitat modification caused by the Project and the actual harm to these two Tree Boas." *Id.* Similarly, with respect to the sea turtles, the court held that the "[p]laintiffs have failed to provide evidence of one dead or injured Sea Turtle." *Id.*

Do habitat modifications that impair breeding, feeding, and sheltering patterns of endangered species necessarily harm at least some members of these species? Should plaintiffs under the ESA be able to show harm to a species by showing impairment to essential behavioral patterns, on the theory that these invariably harm identifiable animals? Or must plaintiffs actually produce dead or injured animals to show harm? How easy will it be for plaintiffs to identify the specific animals that are harmed when a species' essential behavioral patterns are impaired? For plaintiffs to prove that the harm was due to the habitat modification?

7. **"Actually Kills or Injures."** In a case decided less than one month before *Sweet Home* was argued in the Supreme Court, the Ninth Circuit decided a case that turned on the meaning of the word "actually" in the definition of harm. *Forest Conservation Council v. Rosboro Lumber Co.*, 50 F.3d 781 (9th Cir. 1995). The plaintiffs sought an injunction to prevent logging in an area that was home to the northern spotted owl, which had been listed as a threatened species. *Id.* at 782. The defendants in *Rosboro* argued that an injunction could not issue because the term "actually kills or injures wildlife" in the definition of "harm" required a past or presently occurring injury for the plaintiffs claim to be cognizable—since they had not yet begun logging, any injury was prospective. The Ninth Circuit ruled that "use of the term 'actually' was not intended to foreclose claims of an imminent threat of injury," but rather "to preclude claims that only involve habitat modification without any attendant requirement of death or injury to protected wildlife." *Id.* at 784. The court concluded that "a showing of an

imminent threat of injury to wildlife suffices" for the issuance of an injunction. *Id.*

In omitted portions of the *Sweet Home* majority opinion, Justice Stevens wrote that "every term in the regulation's definition of 'harm' is subservient to the phrase 'an act which actually kills or injures wildlife.' " 515 U.S. at 700 (majority opinion). He also stated that "the Government cannot enforce the § 9 prohibition until an animal has actually been killed or injured." *Id.* at 703.

Seizing on this language, the appellant in *Marbled Murrelet v. Babbitt*, 83 F.3d 1060 (9th Cir. 1996), argued that the decision in Sweet Home effectively overruled *Rosboro*, renewing the argument that an injunction could not issue until an animal had actually been injured. 83 F.3d at 1063–64. The Ninth Circuit responded:

> The facts of *Sweet Home* did not require the Court to address the question whether a showing of a threat of future harm is sufficient for an injunction. The case involved a facial challenge to the Secretary's definition of "harm." To the extent the *Sweet Home* opinion may be read to say past injury is required before an injunction may issue, such a statement is dictum.
>
> Furthermore, the remainder of the *Sweet Home* opinion indicates that the Court did not intend to alter case law which held that an injunction may issue upon a showing of a threat of imminent harm. The Court explicitly found the Secretary's interpretation of the law reasonable. . . .
>
> We conclude that the Supreme Court's decision in *Sweet Home* does not overrule *Rosboro*. A reasonably certain threat of imminent harm to a protected species is sufficient for issuance of an injunction under section 9 of the ESA.

Id. at 1065–66 (citations omitted). Based on the definition of the word "harm," should a party be granted relief when an animal has not yet been injured? Does the nature of injunctive relief compel the result in *Rosboro*? Do you agree with the reasoning in *Marbled Murrelet* that *Sweet Home* did not overrule *Rosboro*? What other meaning could be given to the quotes taken from the majority opinion in *Sweet Home*?

8. Captive Animals and the ESA. In 2015, NOAA Fisheries found that killer whales held in captivity, such as those in zoos and aquariums, are not precluded from being listed as threatened or endangered species under the ESA. *See* NOAA Fisheries, Listing Endangered or Threatened Species: Amendment to the Endangered Species Act Listing of the Southern Resident Killer Whale, 80 Fed. Reg. 7380 (2015). Accordingly, NOAA Fisheries removed the previously-existing exclusion for captive killer whales from the regulatory language describing the Southern Resident killer whale DPS.

NOAA had previously identified captive members as part of an ESA-listed unit during some listing actions in the past, such as for endangered smalltooth sawfish, Atlantic sturgeon, and five species of foreign sturgeon. But the agency has no policy requiring it to do so as a general matter. Do you think captive animals should be treated the as wild for purposes of the ESA?

Following the regulatory change for captive killer whales in 2015, animal rights organizations, led by People for the Ethical Treatment of Animals (PETA), filed a lawsuit against the Miami Seaquarium, alleging that the marine park was harming and/or harassing Lolita, a captive killer whale held in captivity at the facility, in violation of the ESA. *See People for Ethical Treatment of Animals, Inc. v. Miami Seaquarium*, 879 F.3d 1142 (11th Cir. 2018). Plaintiffs sought a declaration that conditions of confinement of the killer whale amounted to a take, in violation of ESA section 9(a)(1)(B), and sought an injunction requiring the park to forfeit possession of the killer whale and to transfer it to a sea pen. Based on the Court's opinion in *Sweet Home* and your reading of ESA section 9(a)(1)(B), how would you expect the court to rule in *Miami Seaquarium*?

The Eleventh Circuit concluded that "harm" and "harass" should be read as referring to conduct that poses a threat of serious harm. *Id.* at 1150. PETA claimed that the whale was unable to engage in normal swimming and diving behaviors in her small tank, suffered psychological injury attributable to the absence of a socially compatible companion, developed an eye condition caused by over exposure to ultraviolet radiation from the sun, and suffered general unhealthiness illustrated by a mild kidney impairment and past treatment for respiratory infections. The court found that none of these conditions posed a "threat of serious harm" to the animal, who had lived in captivity for longer than a killer whale's normal lifespan of 50 years. Do you agree with the court's interpretation of "harm" and "harass"? Do you think the result would have been different if Lolita had died 10 or 20 years earlier than the average killer whale? Lolita is the last known survivor of a group of more than 50 killer whales captured 47 years ago off Puget Sound along the coast of Washington.

9. Acquisition of Land Under § 5. In omitted portions of the *Sweet Home* opinion, the majority and the dissent addressed the argument that § 9 should not be extended to prohibit private habitat modification because the ESA also includes § 5, which authorizes the Secretary to acquire land for the preservation of endangered species. Respondents argued that § 5 is the only avenue created by the statute for habitat conservation, and that if the Secretary could instead impose the obligation to conserve habitat on private parties under § 9, there would be no need for the government to acquire land for habitat conservation. The majority opinion argues that there are a number of ways in which the Secretary's § 5 land acquisition authority is still important even if § 9 prohibits habitat modification—for example, "the § 5 procedure allows for protection of habitat before the seller's activity has harmed any endangered animal, whereas the Government cannot enforce the § 9 prohibition until an animal has actually been killed or injured." 515 U.S. at 702–03. What effect do you think the § 5 land acquisition provision should have on the meaning of "harm" under § 9?

10. Takings by Federal Agencies. The § 9(a)(1)(B) prohibition precludes any "person" from "taking" an endangered species. 16 U.S.C. 1538(a)(1)(B). "Person" is defined broadly in § 3(13) to mean an "individual, corporation, partnership, trust, association, or any other private entity; or any officer, employee, agent, department, or instrumentality of the Federal

Government. . . ." 16 U.S.C. § 1532(13). Consider the circumstance in which a federal agency has received permission from the God Squad to undertake an action that jeopardizes a threatened or endangered species. What if, in undertaking that action, an employee of the Federal Government "takes" a threatened or endangered species in contravention of § 9(a)(1)(B). Should the government action (sanctioned by the God Squad) nevertheless be precluded by the operation of § 9? Section 7(*o*)(1) attempts to close this loophole. It provides:

> any action for which an exemption is granted [by the God Squad] . . . shall not be considered to be a taking of any endangered species or threatened species with respect to any activity which is necessary to carry out such action. . . .

16 U.S.C. § 1536(*o*)(1).

11. Endangered Plants. The ESA applies to endangered plants as well as endangered animals; however, the level of protection provided for plants is lower than that provided for animals. The ESA generally requires the federal government to protect endangered plants, but leaves the choice of whether to protect endangered plants on private property largely to the states. Section 7 applies equally to plants and animals, so federal agencies may not take actions that jeopardize endangered plants. Section 9(a)(2) lists the protection afforded endangered plant species on private lands; unlike § 9(a)(1), § 9(a)(2) does *not* prohibit the taking of endangered plants by private parties on their own property. Section 9 does provide some protection to endangered plants: § 9(a)(2)(B) makes it unlawful to remove or maliciously damage endangered plants on federal lands, and § 9(a)(2)(A), (C), and (D) prohibit commerce in endangered plants.

Section 9(a)(2)(B) also makes it illegal to remove or damage endangered plants on any land in knowing violation of any state law. There is significant variation among state laws in the protection afforded endangered plant species—some do not protect endangered plants at all, while others forbid private landowners from killing or adversely modifying the habitat of any endangered plant. *See* Jeffrey J. Rachlinski, *Protecting Endangered Species Without Regulating Private Landowners: The Case of Endangered Plants*, 8 CORNELL J.L. & PUB. POL'Y 1 (1998).

12. Section 9 and Threatened Species. The ESA allows FWS to promulgate rules that "provide for the conservation" of threatened species. 16 U.S.C. § 1533(d). In order to conserve threatened species, regulations promulgated by FWS under Section 9 extend the prohibition on taking any endangered wildlife in the United States to threatened wildlife as well. 50 C.F.R. § 17.31(a); *see, e.g.*, *Animal Welfare Inst. v. Martin*, 588 F. Supp. 2d 70, 98 (D. Me. 2008) (holding that under § 9, taking a Canada lynx, a threatened species, was prohibited). As described earlier in this section, in 2018, the FWS proposed to revise its regulation that extends most of the prohibitions for activities involving endangered species to threatened species. 83 Fed. Reg. 35,174, 35,175 (2018). In addition, expressly excluded from extending to threatened species is § 17.21(c)(5), which enables a qualified employee or agent of a State Conservation Agency . . . when acting in the course of his official duties [to] take those endangered species . . . provided that such taking is not reasonably anticipated to result in the death or permanent disabling of the specimen; the removal of the specimen from the State where the taking occurred; the introduction of the specimen so taken, or of any progeny derived from such a specimen, into an area beyond the historical range of the species; or the holding of the specimen in captivity for a period of more than 45 consecutive days.

50 C.F.R. §§ 17.31(a), 17.21(c)(5). Instead, § 17.31(b) simply provides that such employee or agent "may, when acting in the course of his official duties, take those threatened species of wildlife which are covered by an approved cooperative agreement to carry out conservation programs." 50 C.F.R. § 17.31(b).

13. Section 9 and CITES. The United States is a signatory to the Convention on International Trade in Endangered Species of Wild Fauna and Flora (CITES). Convention on International Trade in Endangered Species of Wild Fauna and Flora, Mar. 3, 1973, 27 U.S.T. 1087. CITES regulates the international trade in species presently or potentially "threatened with extinction which are or may be affected by trade." *Id.* art. II. Trade is defined broadly to include "export, re-export, import and introduction from the sea." *Id.* art. I(c). Trade in endangered species may be undertaken only in accordance with permits issued under CITES. *See id.* arts. III–V. Permits will be granted only in a limited set of circumstances, including circumstances in which "a Scientific Authority of the State of export has advised that such export will not be detrimental to the survival of that species." *Id.*

CITES has given rise to substantive requirements in the ESA. Specifically, § 9(c) renders it unlawful to "engage in any trade in any specimens," or "possess any specimens traded," contrary to the provisions of CITES. 16 U.S.C. § 1538(c). Section 9(a)(1) makes it unlawful to "import any [endangered or threatened] species . . . the United States" or "take any such species within the United States or the territorial sea of the United States." 16 U.S.C. § 1538(a)(1)(A)–(B).

ii.   INCIDENTAL TAKE PERMITS AND HABITAT CONSERVATION PLANS

The § 9 prohibition on private takings of endangered species is not absolute: § 10 provides a process for granting exemptions from the prohibition. Section 10(a) authorizes the Secretary to issue permits for any otherwise proscribed taking if such taking is "incidental to . . . the carrying out of an otherwise lawful activity." 16 U.S.C. § 1539(a)(1)(B). Exemptions may also be granted for scientific purposes. 16 U.S.C. § 1539(a)(1)(A). The incidental take provision was added to the ESA in 1982 to ease the hardship that a strict no takings requirement might impose on private landowners seeking to develop their property. Endangered Species Act Amendments of 1982, Pub. L. No. 97–304, 96 Stat. 1411 (1982). A condition of the issuance of an incidental take permit is that the permit applicant must submit a conservation plan that will "minimize and mitigate" the impact of the taking that will be authorized by the permit. 16 U.S.C. § 1539(a)(2)(A)(ii).

The incidental take provision essentially allows a private party wishing to engage in actions that would result in an impermissible taking to be granted permission for the taking so long as it undertakes some other action that will benefit the species. The ESA does not define what actions may be taken pursuant to a habitat conservation plan to "minimize and mitigate" the impact of a taking, but the most typical conservation plans involve a commitment by a developer to acquire and conserve some amount of land that provides a suitable habitat for the species at issue in return for a permit to develop land that currently constitutes part of the species' habitat.

National Wildlife Federation v. Norton

2005 WL 2175874 (E.D. Cal. 2005).

■ LEVI, DISTRICT JUDGE:

Plaintiffs National Wildlife Federation, Friends of the Swainson's Hawk, Planning and Conservation League, and Sierra Club allege that the Secretary of the Interior violated the Endangered Species Act by approving the Natomas Basin Habitat Conservation Plan and issuing incidental take permits to the City of Sacramento and Sutter County. . . .

This is the second time that the court has been asked to review a habitat conservation plan for the Basin. *See Nat'l Wildlife Fed'n v. Babbitt*, 128 F.Supp.2d 1274 (E.D. Cal. 2000) (*Natomas I*). In *Natomas I*, the court held that the habitat conservation plan was inadequate. For the reasons that follow, the court now finds that the revised plan satisfies the requirements of the Endangered Species Act (ESA).

The Natomas Basin is a low-lying region of approximately 53,000 acres in Sacramento and Sutter Counties. (Administrative Record (AR) 59.) The Basin is home to the Giant Garter Snake (GGS) and the Swainson's Hawk, the two species of greatest concern in this litigation. . . .

The ESA conditions the Secretary's issuance of an incidental take permit (ITP) upon her approval of a habitat conservation plan (HCP). The ITP allows activity, here development, that could injure or harm—"take" in the language of the statute—an endangered or threatened species. Without an ITP, developers would be subject to serious penalties, including criminal prosecution, for any injury to an endangered or threatened species. 16 U.S.C. §§ 1538, 1540. The history of the development of the Natomas Basin HCP is outlined in *Natomas I* and need not be repeated here in detail. *See Nat'l Wildlife Fed'n v. Babbitt*, 128 F.Supp.2d at 1277–78. In brief, the first HCP for the Basin was a regional conservation plan designed to cover development in the entire

Basin. *Id.* at 1279. . . . The HCP was designed to permit development of 17,500 acres of Basin land over the 50-year life of the ITPs, with mitigation lands acquired at a .5-to-1 ratio as land was developed. *Id.* at 1280. The acquisitions were to be funded with mitigation fees paid by developers in the relevant jurisdictions. *Id.* . . .

The Secretary's issuance of an ITP to the City was challenged by various organizations, among whom were the plaintiffs in the present action. On August 15, 2000, the court found that several of the Secretary's findings were unreasonable and violated the ESA, thereby setting aside the Secretary's issuance of the ITP. *Id.* at 1292–1300. . . .

After the 1997 ITP was set aside, the City revised the HCP to address the flaws identified by the court. Currently before the court is a revised HCP, covering development only by the City and Sutter. This second Natomas Basin HCP (NBHCP) was approved by the Secretary in April 2003. . . .

The purpose of the NBHCP is to "promote biological conservation in conjunction with economic and urban development within the permit area." (AR 19.) . . . The NBHCP covers 22 species, with particular attention to the GGS and the Swainson's Hawk, since they are prominent in the Basin, listed as threatened under state or federal law, and occupy habitat that will also benefit other covered species. (*Id.* at 64.) . . .

Like the 1997 HCP, the primary mitigation measure relied on in the NBHCP is acquisition and enhancement of reserve properties at a .5-to-1 ratio for all of the lost habitat, to be funded by developer fees. (*Id.* at 36, 169–98.) . . .

The NBHCP also imposes monitoring and review obligations designed to ensure that the plan will achieve the desired conservation objectives and goals. . . .

The purpose of the ESA is to "conserve ecosystems upon which endangered and threatened species depend" and "to provide a program for the conservation of such endangered species." 16 U.S.C. § 1531(b). As a means of achieving this goal, Section 9 of the ESA prohibits private individuals from "taking" endangered or threatened species. 16 U.S.C. § 1538(a)(1)(B). The ESA defines "take" to include "harm" to animals. 16 U.S.C. § 1532(19). The Service has defined "harm," within the meaning of "take," to include "significant habitat modification or degradation where it actually kills or injures wildlife," a definition that has been upheld by the Supreme Court. 50 C.F.R. § 17.3 (2004); *Babbitt v. Sweet Home Chapter for Cmtys. for a Great Or.,* 515 U.S. 687, 696 (1995).

The broad scope of Section 9 is limited by several exceptions, found in Section 10. Specifically, Section 10 authorizes the Secretary to issue a permit, an ITP, for any taking that is incidental to the carrying out of an otherwise lawful activity. 16 U.S.C. § 1539(a)(1)(B). To receive an ITP, the permit applicant must submit an HCP that specifies: (i) the impact which will likely result from such taking; (ii) what steps the applicant will take to minimize and mitigate such impacts, and the funding that will be available to implement such steps; (iii) what alternative actions to such taking that the applicant considered and the reasons why such alternatives were not selected; and (iv) such other measures that the Secretary may require as necessary or appropriate for the purposes of the plan. 16 U.S.C. § 1539(a)(2)(A); 50 C.F.R. § 17.22 (2004). The Secretary must issue an ITP upon finding that: (i) the taking will be incidental; (ii) the applicant will, to the maximum extent practicable, minimize and mitigate the impacts of the taking; (iii) the applicant has ensured adequate funding for the HCP; (iv) the taking will not appreciably reduce the likelihood of the survival and recovery of the species in the wild; and (v) any additional measures required by the Secretary will be undertaken. 16 U.S.C. § 1539(a)(2)(B).

Section 7 of the ESA applies to federal actions, and requires federal agencies, through consultation with the Service, "to insure that any action authorized, funded, or carried out" by the agency is "not likely to jeopardize the continued existence of any endangered species or threatened species." 16 U.S.C. § 1536(a)(2). Issuance of an ITP is an agency action that requires the Service to engage in internal consultation and prepare a [Biological Opinion (BiOp)] evaluating whether issuance of the ITP will result in jeopardy to any endangered or threatened species. 16 U.S.C. § 1536(b). An action will result in "jeopardy" if it will "reduce appreciably the likelihood of both the survival and recovery of a listed species in the wild. . . ." 50 C.F.R. § 402.02 (2004). The required jeopardy analysis under Section 7(a)(2) is identical in almost all respects to the inquiry under Section 10(a)(2)(B)(iv). *Natomas I*, 128 F.Supp.2d at 1286. In considering whether the action will jeopardize a species, the Service must evaluate the effects of the action and any cumulative effects on the listed species. 50 C.F.R. § 402.14(g) (2004). . . .

Prior to issuing an ITP, the Secretary must determine that the permit applicant will, to the maximum extent practicable, minimize and mitigate the impacts of the taking. 16 U.S.C. § 1539(a)(2)(B)(ii). There are two components to this finding: (1) the adequacy of the mitigation program in proportion to the level of injury—take—that will result; and (2) whether the mitigation is the maximum that can be practically implemented by the applicant. *Metro Air Park*, 306 F.Supp.2d at 927–28. These two factors are evaluated on a sliding scale, such that a stronger showing on one factor may compensate for a weaker showing on the other. *Id.* For instance, where the habitat lost is of minimal or no value to the covered species and the mitigation plan more than compensates for the level of injury, the applicant need not do more, even if it would be financially feasible. *Id.* at 928. Here, plaintiffs assert that the Service's findings on both aspects are arbitrary and capricious.

Plaintiffs argue that the Service erred in finding that the .5-to-1 mitigation ratio sufficiently compensates for the injury that will occur to the GGS and the Swainson's Hawk as a result of the development authorized by the ITPs. (Pls.' Mot. at 35.)

As a result of the development authorized by the ITPs, 8,512 acres of GGS snake habitat will be destroyed. (AR 1021.) The Service determined that, if unmitigated, this would result in considerable harm to the GGS. (*Id.* at 1190.) However, this habitat will be replaced by 2,187 acres of restored marshlands and 4,375 acres of rice habitat, resulting in an effective mitigation ratio, for the GGS, of approximately .75-to-1. (*Id.* at 1191.)

The Service offers several reasons why the reserve lands adequately compensate for the loss of some habitat. Unlike existing habitat, reserve habitat: (1) will be protected in perpetuity; (2) will be actively managed for the snake; (3) will not be subject to the continual disturbance caused by farming or canal maintenance; (4) will be available year round; (5) will not be unavailable to the snake because of canal maintenance activities; and (6) will be relatively free of human intrusion. (*Id.* 1026, 1191.) The restored marsh is considered particularly valuable replacement habitat, as it is the preferred habitat for the GGS. (*Id.* at 1191.) The Service also emphasizes the provisions of the NBHCP that preserve connectivity and minimize disturbances during construction activity. (*Id.* at 1190–92.) The Service concludes that the combination of on-site minimization measures and the new high-quality wetland habitat will effectively mitigate for the harm to the GGS of the development permitted by the ITP and the NBHCP. (*Id.* at 1192.) The Service's analysis considers the relevant issues and is a reasoned explanation as to why the mitigation measures are proportionate to the possible injury or take.

Two types of Swainson's Hawk habitat will be affected by the development authorized by the ITPs: nesting habitat and foraging habitat. (*Id.* at 1188–89.) Approximately 80% of the nesting habitat in the Basin, most of it in the Swainson's Hawk Zone, will remain after the authorized development. (*Id.* at 1032.) Although four nest trees will be removed as a result of the authorized development, the City has committed to planting 60 replacement nesting trees. (*Id.* at 1033.) The Service determined that this was adequate to mitigate for the removal of nest trees and the small loss of nesting habitat, particularly given that most of the nesting trees in the area of authorized development are not active. (*Id.* at 1034.) Plaintiffs do not point to any evidence in the record to contradict this conclusion, or any evidence that the Service should have considered, but did not. The Service evaluated the available scientific information and reached a reasonable conclusion that the effects to nesting habitat would be fully mitigated.

The impact to Swainson's Hawk foraging habitat is quantitatively more significant. Approximately 40% of the Basin's potential foraging habitat, some 9,188 acres, will be lost as a result of the authorized development. (*Id.* at 1034.) The NBHCP provides for acquisition of 2,187.5 acres of high-quality upland foraging habitat. (*Id.* at 731.)

Approximately 1,000 acres of additional foraging habitat will be available through the fallowed rice lands and upland components of the managed marsh. (*Id.* at 732.) However, even with the reserve lands, there will be a net loss of approximately 6,000 acres of potential foraging habitat.

Nonetheless, the Service concludes, for reasons discussed at length in the BiOp, the Findings and Recommendations, and an Addendum to the EIR/EIS, that the loss of this habitat would result in a low level of harm to the hawk if mitigated as required by the NBHCP. (*Id.* at 1034–39, 1189–90, 726–47.) The Service concludes that despite the quantitative losses in habitat, the replacement habitat will likely be qualitatively equivalent. (*Id.*) The technical memorandum identifies at least three reasons why the Swainson's Hawk will not be negatively affected by the loss of habitat. First, the 2,187.5 acres of replacement habitat will all be of high quality, managed specifically for the hawk. (*Id.* at 731.) Even under the worst-case implementation scenario, where more than half of the reserve lands would consist of current high-value habitat, rather than newly created high-value habitat, the NBHCP will result in an increase of 353 acres of high-value habitat. (*Id.* at 742.)

Second, under the NBHCP, the temporal availability of foraging opportunities would be maintained or improved. (*Id.*) Under current conditions, much of potential foraging habitat is available in September, when row crops such as corn are harvested, and in June. (*Id.* at 737.) By contrast, relatively little foraging habitat is available during the other months the Swainson's Hawk is in the Basin—April, May, July, and August. (*Id.*) Under the most likely implementation scenarios for the NBHCP, foraging opportunities would be increased during the months of April, May, and June, with the anticipated effect of increasing nesting density and reproductive success. (*Id.* at 740–41, 744.)

Third, the acquired reserves will likely be in closer proximity to nesting trees. (*Id.* at 745.) A primary acquisition criteria for upland reserves is proximity to known or potential nesting trees. (*Id.* at 156.) Proximity of foraging habitat to nesting trees has been linked to reproductive success for the Swainson's Hawk. (*Id.* at 738.) For all of these reasons, the Service concludes that any harm to the Swainson's Hawk as a result of lost foraging lands will be effectively mitigated by the reserve lands. The Service considered the relevant scientific evidence in the record and articulated reasons for its ultimate conclusion that the mitigation was sufficient. . . .

Based on the evidence in the record, the Secretary's determination that the mitigation was proportionate to the expected take of the GGS and Swainson's Hawk is not arbitrary or capricious. . . .

NOTES AND QUESTIONS

1. **ITP Issuance Standards.** FWS can issue an ITP only if "the taking will not appreciably reduce the likelihood of the species' survival and

recovery in the wild." 16 U.S.C. § 1539(a)(2)(B). FWS notes that the statutory language "does not explicitly require an HCP to recover listed species, or contribute to their recovery objectives outlined in a recovery plan," reflecting "the fact that HCPs were designed by Congress to authorize incidental take, not to be mandatory recovery tools." FWS & NMFS, ENDANGERED SPECIES HABITAT CONSERVATION PLANNING HANDBOOK 3–20 (1996) (HCP Handbook). Why does the ESA have ITP/HCP provisions? Are they consistent with the overall purposes of the statute? What is the best explanation that can be given for why a statute designed to protect endangered species allows "takings" of those species by private individuals? Do you agree with FWS's interpretation of the statute that HCPs do not have to lead to the recovery of a listed species? Should HCPs be required to provide a net benefit to the listed species?

2.   Measuring Harm and Conservation. Proponents of habitat conservation plans have argued that they allow for a more efficient allocation of resources because they provide flexibility to developers while maintaining the desired level of protection for endangered species. Critics have argued that the mitigating measures taken pursuant to habitat conservation plans are frequently inadequate to offset the harm caused by the taking. What metric should be used to determine whether critics are correct that mitigation measures are inadequate or whether proponents are correct that they maintain equivalent measures of protection? If habitat conservation protects some number of acres of land and the taking harms some number of animals, how should the two be compared? What factors did the *National Wildlife Federation* court rely on in determining that the conservation plan adequately mitigated the harm to the species?

3.   Incidental Take Statements for Plants? In *Center for Biological Diversity v. Bureau of Land Management*, the Ninth Circuit held that the Bureau of Land Management did not violate the ESA when its analysis of plans to expand access for off-road vehicles in the Imperial Sand Dunes Special Recreation Area in California did not include a Biological Opinion with an "Incidental Take Statement" for the threatened Pierson's milkvetch plant. 833 F.3d 1136 (9th Cir. 2016). The Court held that the "incidental take" requirements under sections 7 and 9 of the ESA do not apply to listed plant species; rather, the incidental take provisions apply only to listed fish and wildlife species. The Court explained:

> Section 9(a)(2) contains separate protections for plants, but does not use the term "take." *See* 16 U.S.C. § 1538(a)(2). Section 9 thus demonstrates that when Congress uses the word "take," it means to describe an adverse action against animals, not plants. And, as the district court noted, unlike the section 9(a)(1) protections for "fish or wildlife," the section 9(a)(2) prohibitions relating to plants require "deliberate or malicious conduct." Incidental takings, by definition, are not deliberate. Given that one cannot be held liable for the taking of a plant, it is difficult to conceive how an incidental take "safe harbor" would be necessary for plants.

833 F.3d at 1143. Why do you think the ESA distinguishes between endangered plants and endangered fish and wildlife species?

4. Minimization and Mitigation to the Maximum Extent Practicable. As discussed in *National Wildlife Federation*, prior to issuing an ITP, the Secretary must determine that the permit applicant will, to the maximum extent practicable, minimize and mitigate the impacts of the taking. 16 U.S.C. § 1539(a)(2)(B)(ii). FWS and NMFS produced the HCP Handbook, clarifying that in determining whether an applicant has minimized and mitigated the impacts of the taking to the maximum extent practicable, they will consider two factors: (1) the adequacy of the minimization and mitigation program, and (2) whether it is the maximum extent that can be practically implemented by the applicant. HCP Handbook, *supra*, at 7–2. The HCP Handbook explains that "where the adequacy of mitigation is a close call, the record must contain some basis to conclude that the proposed program is the maximum that can be reasonably required by that applicant." *Id.* at 7–3. The HCP Handbook has been updated several times since it was issued in 1996; most recently in 2016. The 2016 edition contains information on the "burden of proving maximum extent practicable," stating that if the proposed minimization and mitigation will leave impacts that are not fully offset, the applicant must provide "a clear justification to the Services documenting the reasons no more mitigation is practicable." FWS & NMFS, ENDANGERED SPECIES HABITAT CONSERVATION PLANNING HANDBOOK 9–34 (2016). The handbook states that such justification could be financial hardship from additional mitigation, or that there are "insufficient implementation options." *Id.* at 9–35. Does this mean that wealthier applicants will have to spend more money on mitigation and minimization? What would the practical effects of a requirement like this be? Does this standard require that an applicant spend money on minimization and mitigation up until the point that project would no longer be economically feasible? Why should the fact that a program is the maximum extent of minimization and mitigation that can reasonably be required of an applicant make up for any shortcomings in the adequacy of the program? Is this approach consistent with the rest of the ESA?

5. "No Surprises" Policy. FWS has adopted a "No Surprises" policy concerning HCPs and their associated ITPs. Habitat Conservation Plan Assurances ("No Surprises") Rule, 63 Fed. Reg. 8859 (1998). The "No Surprises" rule provides private parties with assurances that as long as they are properly implementing a valid HCP, if unforeseen circumstances arise, FWS will not require "commitment[s] of additional land, water or financial compensation or additional restrictions on the use of the land, water . . . or other natural resources" without the permittee's consent. *Id.* at 8868. If an unforeseen circumstance does arise, "the primary obligation for implementing additional conservation measures would be the responsibility of the Federal government, other government agencies, or other non-Federal landowners who have not yet developed an HCP." *Id.* at 8867. FWS can, however, revoke an ITP if the taking will "appreciably reduce the likelihood of the survival and recovery of the species in the wild," though FWS makes clear that this is an "unexpected and unlikely situation" that serves as "a last resort." Endangered Species Act Incidental Take Permit Revocation Regulations, 69 Fed. Reg. 71,723, 71,724 (2004). Why does FWS provide "No

Surprises" assurances to private parties? How do "No Surprises" assurances enhance HCPs?

6. Issuance of ITPs and Section 7. As noted by the court in *National Wildlife Federation*, the issuance of an ITP (and the approval of the HCP) implicates the limitations on federal action in § 7, namely the "no jeopardy" clause and the requirement to issue a BiOp. While the ESA, then, seems to provide a check on the cumulative impact that ITPs might have on a species, the effectiveness of the "no jeopardy" clause hinges on the quality and comprehensiveness of the science relied on by the agency. *See Nw. Envtl. Def. Ctr. v. NMFS, 647 F. Supp. 2d 1221 (D. Or. 2009)* (upholding issuance of ITP against challenge based on adequacy of § 7 findings). As ITPs are issued with a greater frequency, cover a greater area, and last for a greater length of time (100 years is not uncommon), any potential shortcomings in ITPs become more problematic. Each ITP carries with it a significant risk of error in its estimates, and this margin of error is further exacerbated by the "No Surprises" policy and longer period for which the ITP is issued. *See* Patrick Duggan, *Incidental Extinction: How the Endangered Species Act's Incidental Take Permits Fail to Account for Population Loss*, 41 ENVTL. L. REP. NEWS & ANALYSIS 10628 (2011).

7. Alternative Approaches. Jonathan Nash has labeled the ESA "a clumsy command-and-control approach" to species and habitat preservation. Jonathan Remy Nash, *Trading Species: A New Direction for Habitat Trading Programs*, 32 COLUM. J. ENVTL. L. 1, 2 (2007). He urges a shift towards a marketable permit scheme, where permits to develop land could be traded amongst end-users, and where "[t]he initial allocation of development permits would be loaded onto a computer website, along with all data necessary for a computer model to predict how development of various plots would affect the population of various species." *Id.* at 38. Would such a scheme for habitat be similar to a marketable permit scheme for air pollution? How would it be different? Would the value of different plots of land and their constituent habitat have to be converted to a single metric? How could this be done? What could the metric be? What variables would need to be considered in the valuation of a particular piece of land? Would such a system create incentives for the restoration of degraded habitat and the creation of new habitat? Could it? Should it?

D. ENDANGERED SPECIES AND CLIMATE CHANGE

Each of the core provisions of the ESA discussed so far—the listing provisions (including critical habitat designation and recovery plans), interagency consultation and the jeopardy prohibition, the take prohibition, and incidental take permits—are implicated when the conservation of species is threatened by pollution. Global pollutants, and the effects of climate change in particular, present especially difficult problems for agencies attempting to conserve species. When reading the following cases and memorandum, pay particular attention to how climate change is implicated in each.

Natural Resources Defense Council v. Kempthorne

506 F. Supp. 2d 322 (E.D. Cal. 2007).

■ WANGER, DISTRICT JUDGE:

This case concerns the effect on a threatened species of fish, the Delta smelt (*Hypomesus transpacificus*), of the coordinated operation of the federally-managed Central Valley Project ("CVP") and the State of California's State Water Project ("SWP"), among the world's largest water diversion projects. Both projects divert large volumes of water from the California Bay (Sacramento-San Joaquin) Delta ("Delta") and use the Delta to store water.

For over thirty years, the projects have been operated pursuant to a series of cooperation agreements. In addition, the projects are subject to ever-evolving statutory, regulatory, contractual, and judicially-imposed requirements. The Long-Term Central Valley Project and State Water Project Operations Criteria and Plan ("2004 OCAP" or "OCAP") surveys how the projects are currently managed in light of these evolving circumstances. At issue in this case is a 2005 biological opinion ("BiOp"), issued by the United States Fish and Wildlife Service ("FWS" or "Service") pursuant to the Endangered Species Act ("ESA"), which concludes that current project operations described in the OCAP and certain planned future actions will not jeopardize the continued existence of the Delta smelt or adversely modify its critical habitat. . . .

[Plaintiffs move for summary judgment, asking the court to invalidate the BiOp as arbitrary and capricious, on the ground that] the BiOp did not utilize the Best Available Science by . . . failing to consider the possible effects that climate change might have on the smelt's habitat. . . .

The § 7 formal consultation process is designed to "insure" that any agency action "is not likely to jeopardize the continued existence of any endangered species or threatened species or result in the destruction or adverse modification of habitat of such species which is determined . . . to be critical. . . ." 16 U.S.C. § 1536(a)(2). "In fulfilling the requirements of this paragraph each agency shall use the best scientific and commercial data available." *Id.*

An agency has wide discretion to determine what is "the best scientific and commercial data available." *San Luis v. Badgley*, 136 F.Supp.2d 1136, 1151 (E.D. Cal. 2000). Yet, an agency must make its decision about jeopardy based on the best science available at the time of the decision, and may not defer that jeopardy analysis by promising future studies to assess whether jeopardy is occurring. While uncertainty is not necessarily fatal to an agency decision, an agency may not entirely fail to develop appropriate projections where data "was available but [was] simply not analyzed[.]" *Greenpeace v. NMFS*, 80 F.Supp.2d 1137, 1149–50 (W.D. Wash. 2000) (where agency totally failed to develop any projections regarding population viability, it could not use as an excuse the fact that relevant data had not been analyzed). Here, [FWS] maintains the necessary data cannot be obtained. . . .

Plaintiffs . . . argue that the BiOp ignored data about Global Climate Change that will adversely affect the Delta smelt and its habitat. This is potentially significant because the BiOp's conclusions are based in part on the assumption that the hydrology of the water bodies affected by the OCAP will follow historical patterns for the next 20 years.

In a July 28, 2004 comment letter, Plaintiff NRDC directed FWS's attention to several studies on the potential effects of climate change on water supply reliability, urging that the issue be considered in the BiOp. The comment letter stated:

> The best scientific data available today establishes that global climate change is occurring and will affect western hydrology. At least half a dozen models predict warming in the western United States of several degrees Celsius over the next 100 years. Such sophisticated regional climate models must be considered as part of the FWS' consideration of the best available scientific data.

> Unfortunately, the Biological Assessment provided by the Bureau to FWS entirely ignores global climate change and existing climate change models. Instead, the BA projects future project impacts in explicit reliance on seventy-two years of historical records. In effect, the Biological Assessment assumes that neither climate nor hydrology will change. This assumption is not supportable.

> In California, a significant percentage of annual precipitation falls as snow in the high Sierra Nevada mountains. Snowpack acts as a form of water storage by melting to release water later in the spring and early summer months. The effects of global climate change are expected to have a profound effect on this dynamic. *Among other things, more precipitation will occur as rain rather than snow, less water will be released slowly from snowpack "storage" during spring and summer months, and flooding is expected to increase. These developments will make it more difficult to fill the large reservoirs in most years, reducing reservoir yields and will magnify the effect of CVP operations on downstream fishes.* These developments will also dramatically increase the cost of surface storage relative to other water supply options, such as conservation.

> While the precise magnitude of these changes remains uncertain, judgments about the likely range of impacts can and have been made. *See e.g.*, U.S. Global Climate Action Report— 2002; Third National Communication of the United States Under the United Nations Framework Convention on Climate Change at 82, 101 (2002). The Service can and must evaluate

how that range of likely impacts would affect CVP operations and impacts, including the Bureau's ability to provide water to contractors while complying with environmental standards. We therefore request that the Service review and consider the work cited above, as well as the background and Dettinger presentation at a recent climate change conference held in Sacramento, June 9–11, 2004 and climate change reports.

(emphasis added).

[Following the climate change conference held in June, 2004, Michael Dettinger gave a second presentation at a joint meeting of federal and state regulators and] concluded that "warming is already underway . . ."; that this would result in earlier flows, more floods, and drier summers; and that "California water supplies/ecosystems are likely to experience [ ] changes earliest and most intensely." Following Dettinger's presentation, members of CALFED noted "the need to reevaluate water storage policies and ERP [Ecosystem Recovery Program] recovery strategies, all of which would be affected by projected climate changes." The record reflects that extreme water temperatures can have dramatic impacts upon smelt abundance.

In addition to the specific studies and data cited by NRDC, FWS scientists recognized the issue of climate change warranted further consideration. At a June 2003 symposium entitled "Framing the issues for Environmental and Ecological Effects of Proposed Changes in Water Operations: Science Symposium on the State of Knowledge," a number of questions regarding climate change were raised, including: "How does the proposed operations plan account for the potential effects of climate change (e.g., El Nino or La Nina, long term changes in precipitation and runoff patters, or increases in water temperature)?"

Plaintiffs argue that, despite this evidence that climate change could seriously impact the smelt by changing Delta hydrology and temperature, the BiOp "did not so much as mention the probable effects of climate change on the delta smelt, its habitat, or the magnitude of impacts that could be expected from the 2004 OCAP operations, much less analyze those effects." Defendants and Defendant-Intervenors respond by arguing . . . that the evidence before FWS at the time the BiOp was issued was inconclusive about the impacts of climate change. . . . ; and (2) that, far from ignoring climate change, the issue is built into the BiOp's analysis through the use of [water salinity] as a proxy for the location and distribution of Delta smelt.

Federal Defendants and the State Water Contractors characterize Mr. Dettinger's presentation, as reflecting "a great deal of uncertainty that climate change will impact future precipitation." . . . Dettinger acknowledges that, although current climate models "yield consistent warming scenarios for California," there is no similar consensus regarding the impact of warming on future precipitation. Federal Defendants suggest that FWS "responsibly refused to engage in sheer guesswork, and properly declined to speculate as to how global warming might affect delta smelt." But, the NRDC letter cited a number of studies in addition to Mr. Dettinger's presentations, all of which predict that anticipated climate change will adversely impact future water availability in the Western United States.

At the very least, these studies suggest that climate change will be an "important aspect of the problem" meriting analysis in the BiOp. However, . . . the climate change issue was not meaningfully discussed in the biological opinion, making it impossible to determine whether the information was rationally discounted because of its inconclusive nature, or arbitrarily ignored. . . .

The State Water Contractors argue that the approaches taken in the [adaptive management plan] are "more than adequate to deal with the projected impacts of climate change—assuming they occur." For example, Plaintiffs' suggestion that climate change will produce earlier flows, more floods, and drier summers is addressed by the [plan's water salinity] trigger. Flow level changes will be reflected in the position of [specific salt concentrations]. If climate change alters water temperatures, [the plan] also includes a temperature trigger, that monitors the temperature range within which successful Delta smelt spawning occurs.

The [plan] offers no assurance that any mitigating fish protection actions will be implemented if the [salinity] criteria is triggered. That [salinity] indirectly monitors climate change does not assuage Plaintiffs' concerns that the BiOp has not adequately analyzed the potential impact of climate change on the smelt.

The BiOp does not gauge the potential effect of various climate change scenarios on Delta hydrology. Assuming, *arguendo*, a lawful adaptive management approach, there is no discussion when and how climate change impacts will be addressed, whether existing take limits will remain, and the probable impacts on CVP-SWP operations.

FWS acted arbitrarily and capriciously by failing to address the issue of climate change in the BiOp. This absence of *any* discussion in the BiOp of how to deal with any climate change is a failure to analyze a potentially "important aspect of the problem."

Plaintiffs' motion for summary adjudication is GRANTED as to this claim.

Alaska Oil & Gas Ass'n v. Pritzker

840 F.3d 671 (9th Cir. 2016).

■ Before FISHER, PAEZ and HURWITZ, CIRCUIT JUDGES.

■ PAEZ, CIRCUIT JUDGE:

The National Marine Fisheries Service ("NMFS") used climate projections to determine that the loss of sea ice over shallow waters in the Arctic would leave the Pacific bearded seal subspecies (*Erignathus barbatus nauticus*) endangered by the year 2095. This case turns on one issue: When NMFS determines that a species that is not presently endangered will lose its habitat due to climate change by the end of the century, may NMFS list that species as threatened under the Endangered Species Act? The district court answered in the negative, ruling that NMFS's listing decision was arbitrary and capricious. We hold that on the basis of the administrative record, NMFS's listing decision is reasonable. Accordingly, we reverse the district court's grant of summary judgment in favor of Plaintiffs. . . .

After a lengthy administrative process that included two rounds of peer review, several rounds of public notice and comment, and public hearings, NMFS concluded that the Okhotsk and Beringia distinct population segments ("DPS") of the Pacific bearded seal subspecies (*Erignathus barbatus nauticus*) were "likely to become . . . endangered species within the foreseeable future throughout . . . a significant portion of [their] range." 16 U.S.C. § 1532(20); Listing Rule, 77 Fed. Reg. at 76,740.

Plaintiffs Alaska Oil and Gas Association ("AOGA"), the State of Alaska, and North Slope Borough (collectively, "Plaintiffs") filed separate lawsuits challenging the listing decision under the ESA's citizen suit provision, 16 U.S.C. § 1540(g), and the Administrative Procedure Act ("APA"), 5 U.S.C. § 706. Plaintiffs alleged, *inter alia*, that the listing decision was not based on the "best scientific and commercial data available" in violation of 16 U.S.C. § 1533(b)(1)(A); the population of bearded seals was plentiful; a lack of reliable population data made it impossible to determine an extinction threshold; NMFS's use of predictive climate projections beyond 2050 were speculative; NMFS had unreasonably "changed tack" from its previous Arctic sea-ice listing decisions; and NMFS had failed to demonstrate a causal connection between the loss of sea ice and the impact of that loss to the Okhotsk and Beringia DPS's viability. . . .

In October 2009, NMFS established a Biological Review Team of eight marine mammal biologists, a fishery biologist, a marine chemist, and a climate scientist to review the status of the "best scientific and commercial data available" regarding bearded seals. Listing Rule, 77 Fed. Reg. at 76,740. NMFS solicited four scientists to conduct independent peer reviews of the Review Team's report. *Id.* at 76,740 & 76,750. Based on the Review Team's assessment and the peer reviewers' comments, NMFS published a proposed rule listing the Beringia and Okhotsk bearded seal DPSs as threatened under the ESA. . . .

Using observational and predictive data from the Intergovernmental Panel on Climate Change's ("IPCC") Fourth Assessment Report, NMFS used six climate models to determine when the Beringia DPS's sea ice habitat would degrade to such an extent that it would render the Beringia DPS endangered, and it made available for public review its methodology and data. Proposed Rule, 75 Fed. Reg. at 77,497. All independent peer reviewers agreed that the Beringia DPS's continued viability depended on the availability of sea ice in the Bering and Barents Seas during crucial life stages. . . .

Having concluded that the availability of sea ice in shallow water was crucial to the Beringia DPS's viability, NMFS evaluated several climate models to determine the magnitude and timing of climate change's impact on the availability of sea ice in areas inhabited by the Beringia DPS. *Id.* at 76,744. Those projections indicated that by 2095, sea ice in several regions where the Beringia DPS whelps will have disappeared entirely during the mating, nursing, and birthing season (April through June). *Id.* . . .

The Endangered Species Act seeks to recover endangered and threatened species and to "reverse the trend towards species extinction, whatever the cost." *Jewell*, 815 F.3d at 550–51 (quoting *Tenn. Valley Auth. v. Hill*, 437 U.S. 153, 184, 98 S.Ct. 2279, 57 L.Ed.2d 117 (1978)); 16 U.S.C. § 1531(b). To achieve that purpose, the ESA requires the Secretary of Commerce, or her designee, to identify and list endangered or threatened species. *See* 16 U.S.C. § 1533(a)(1) & (2); *see also Nw. Ecosys. All.*, 475 F.3d at 1137. When determining whether to list a species, the reviewing agency must make its decision "solely on the basis of the best scientific and commercial data available." 16 U.S.C. § 1533(b)(1)(A). . . .

Plaintiffs contend that NMFS used climate models that cannot reliably predict the degree of global warming beyond 2050 or the effect of that warming on a subregion, such as the Arctic. Although Plaintiffs frame their arguments as challenging long-term climate projections, they seek to undermine NMFS's use of climate change projections as the basis for ESA listings. Plaintiffs' contention is unavailing; in *Alaska Oil and Gas Association v. Jewell*, we adopted the D.C. Circuit's holding that the IPCC climate models constituted the "best available science" and reasonably supported the determination that a species reliant on sea ice likely would become endangered in the foreseeable future. 815 F.3d at 558–59; *In re Polar Bear Litig.*, 709 F.3d at 4–6, 9–11.

We have stressed that we "must defer to the agency's interpretation of complex scientific data" so long as the agency provides a reasonable explanation for adopting its approach and discloses the limitations of that approach. *Nw. Ecosys. All.*, 475 F.3d at 1150; *see also San Luis & Delta-Mendota Water Auth. v. Jewell*, 747 F.3d 581, 602 (9th Cir. 2014) ("The determination of what constitutes the *best* scientific data available belongs to the agency's special expertise. . . . [and w]hen examining this kind of scientific determination . . . a reviewing court must generally be at its most deferential." (internal quotation marks omitted)). NMFS provided ample evidence of significant sea ice loss from 2007 to 2050, a period in which specific data supports the IPCC climate projections. Proposed Rule, 75 Fed. Reg. at 77,503–05. Those projections indicate that during months in which bearded seals used that ice for "critical life events" such as mating, birthing, and nursing, most Beringia DPS habitats will have lost most, if not all, of their sea ice. *Id.* at 77,504. By September 2010, observational data confirmed that the amount of summer sea ice in the areas populated by the Beringia DPS was 40% below the long-term average. *Id.* at 77,503. NMFS has provided a reasonable explanation, based on the best available scientific and commercial data, for relying on those projections in its listing decision.

NMFS's projections for the second-half of the century are also reasonable, scientifically sound, and supported by evidence. There is no debate that temperatures will continue to increase over the remainder of the century and that the effects will be particularly acute in the Arctic. The current scientific consensus is that Arctic sea ice will continue to recede through 2100, and NMFS considered the best available research to reach that conclusion. . . . A second peer reviewer opined that it was "more likely than not that the *uncertainty* attaching to 80-year predictions of how changing climate will affect bearded seals and their habitat has been, is being, and will be greatly underestimated." Excerpts of R. at 118, ECF No. 10. All parties agree that there will be sea ice melt; the only uncertainty is the magnitude of warming, the speed with which warming will take place, and the severity of its effect.

The fact that climate projections for 2050 through 2100 may be volatile does not deprive those projections of value in the rulemaking process. The ESA does not require NMFS to make listing decisions only if underlying research is ironclad and absolute. *See San Luis & Delta-Mendota Water Auth.*, 747 F.3d at 602 ("[W]here the information is not readily available, we cannot insist on perfection: [T]he best scientific . . . data *available*, does not mean the best scientific data *possible*." (internal quotation marks omitted) (emphasis added)). The ESA directs NMFS to make its determinations "solely on the basis of the best scientific and commercial data available . . . after conducting a review of the status of the species." 16 U.S.C. § 1533(b)(1)(A). After conducting that assessment, if NMFS finds it likely that a species will "become an endangered species within the foreseeable future throughout all or a significant portion of its range," it must list that species as threatened. 16 U.S.C. §§ 1532(20), 1533(b)(1)(B)(ii). NMFS provided a reasonable and scientifically supported methodology for addressing volatility in its long-term climate projections, and it represented fairly the shortcomings of those projections—that is all the ESA requires. *See Jewell*, 815 F.3d at 558 ("To the extent that Plaintiffs demand greater scientific specificity than available data could provide, [they] echo the district court's error in demanding too high a standard of scientific proof.").

The majority of independent peer reviewers agreed that NMFS's long-term climate projections were based on the "best scientific and commercial data available," that there was scientific consensus regarding the "direction and effect" of climate change, that there would be significant sea ice loss in the Beringia DPS's habitat, and that such a significant loss of habitat would almost certainly have a negative effect on the bearded seal's survival. Moreover, under NMFS's 2007 to 2050 climate projections, even if global warming plateaued in the second-half of the century, devastating sea ice losses would still result during months that are currently critical to the bearded seal's propagation. Proposed Rule, 75 Fed. Reg. at 77,501–06.

Further, climate studies released and noticed for public comment after the publication of the Proposed Listing Rule indicated that the Arctic was warming at a much faster rate than anticipated by the IPCC mid-century projections. . . .

The ESA does not require NMFS to base its decision on ironclad evidence when it determines that a species is likely to become endangered in the foreseeable future; it simply requires the agency to consider the best and most reliable scientific and commercial data and to identify the limits of that data when making a listing determination. In light of the data available to it during the rulemaking process, NMFS reasonably concluded that there would be continued sea ice loss over shallow waters, resulting in habitat loss that would almost certainly threaten the Beringia DPS's survival. NMFS has provided a rational and reasonable basis for evaluating the bearded seal's viability over 50 and 100 years, and it has candidly disclosed the limitations of the available data and its analysis. The ESA does not require more, and NMFS did not act arbitrarily or capriciously in concluding that the effects of global climate change on sea ice would endanger the Beringia DPS in the foreseeable future. . . .

Next, Plaintiffs contend that NMFS failed to provide an evidence-based explanation for the relationship between habitat loss and the bearded seal's survival. They argue that NMFS has not provided sufficient evidence to demonstrate a nexus between the loss of sea ice and the bearded seal's risk of future extinction. They note that at the time NMFS issued its final listing rule, the bearded seal had not suffered population losses, and they argue NMFS should have adopted a "wait and see" approach before determining whether to list the bearded seal.

Similarly, the district court took issue with NMFS's disclosure that it could only provide a range for the Beringia DPS baseline population, which would make it difficult to measure the relationship between population declines and loss of access to sea ice. *Pritzker*, 2014 WL 3726121, at *15. The district court concluded that NMFS was unable to provide a predicted "population reduction," "extinction threshold," or "probability of reaching that threshold," and that without that information, there was no reasonable basis for listing the Beringia DPS as threatened. *Id.* & n.69. The district court expressed doubt that NMFS was able to conduct a reasonable risk assessment supported by evidence when the agency could not provide population information on the current state of the species. *Id.*

The district court's effort to impose requirements for which data is unavailable or does not exist is at odds with the ESA. NMFS demonstrated that, based on the best data available at the time of listing, a decrease in sea ice availability would likely have a significant adverse effect on the bearded seal population. In rejecting the Beringia DPS final listing rule, the district court imposed ad hoc requirements that exceed the ESA's provisions. The district court's request for unobtainable, highly specified data would require NMFS to wait until it had quantitative data reflecting a species' decline, its population tipping point, and the exact year in which that tipping point would occur before it could adopt conservation policies to prevent that species' decline. . . .

The judgment of the district court is REVERSED.

Guidance on the Applicability of the Endangered Species Act's Consultation Requirements to Proposed Actions Involving the Emission of Greenhouse Gases

Memorandum from David Longly Bernhardt, Solicitor, Department of the Interior, to Dirk Kempthorne, Secretary of the Interior, October 3, 2008.

On May 14, 2008, the U.S. Geological Survey (USGS) . . . [announced] the following conclusion:

> It is currently beyond the scope of existing science to identify a specific source of CO_2 emissions and designate it as the cause of specific climate impacts at an exact location.

In response, the [FWS] issued guidance laying out an analytical framework within which the Service would be able to assist Federal action agencies (including the Service itself when intra-Service consultation is appropriate) in achieving procedural and substantive compliance with the Act. In that memorandum, the FWS Director stated:

> GHG that are projected to be emitted from a facility would not, in and of themselves, trigger section 7 consultation for a particular action unless it is established that the emissions from the proposed action cause an indirect effect to listed species or critical habitat. To constitute an indirect effect, the impact to the species must be later in time, must be caused by the proposed action, and must be reasonably certain to occur.

Based on the above statement by USGS, I concur with the guidance provided by the FWS and conclude, for the reasons explained below, that where the effects at issue result from climate change potentially induced by GHGs, a proposed action that will involve the emission of GHG cannot pass the "may affect" test, and is not subject to consultation under the ESA and its implementing regulations.

I.   The "May Affect" Test

. . . [N]ot all proposed actions of Federal agencies are subject to the consultation requirement. The section 7 regulations state that consultation is required only when a Federal agency determines that its proposed action "may affect listed species or critical habitat." 50 C.F.R. § 402.1 4(a).

The regulations do not establish any criteria for determining when the "may affect" test is satisfied. The Final ESA Section 7 Handbook describes "may affect" as:

"The appropriate conclusion when a proposed action may pose any effects on listed species or designated critical habitat."

Based in part on this guidance, it is generally understood that a proposed action passes the "may affect" test when an agency determines there is some likelihood the proposed action will have an effect on listed species or designated critical habitat. Effects of a proposed action on listed species or critical habitat that are "beneficial, discountable or insignificant," are still considered to be effects of the action.

In determining whether a proposed action "may affect" a listed species, or, conversely, whether there will be "no effect," a Federal agency must go through a multi-step process. . . . [I]t must determine, in at least a preliminary way, what the effects of those activities are likely to be on the environment[, and it] must determine whether those effects will "pose any effects" on a listed species or critical habitat—i.e., whether there are listed species or critical habitat within the reach of those effects. . . .

II.   The "May Affect" Test and GHG Emissions

As the primary administrator of the Clean Air Act, the Environmental Protection Agency (EPA) has developed considerable expertise in current global climate change research and has substantial expertise in using the available models to analyze the fate of GHG emissions. Before applying the legal framework discussed above to a proposed action that will involve the emission of GHGs, we note as background the following statement that was recently made by the EPA:

To date, research on how emissions of CO_2 and other GHGs influence global climate change and associated effects has focused on the overall impact of emissions from aggregate regional or global sources. This is primarily because GHG emissions from single sources are small relative to aggregate emissions, and GHGs, once emitted from a given source, become well mixed in the global atmosphere and have a long atmospheric lifetime. The climate change research community has not yet developed tools specifically intended for evaluating or quantifying end-point impacts attributable to the emissions of GHGs from a single source, and we are not aware of any scientific literature to draw from regarding the climate effects of individual, facility-level GHG emissions.

A. Direct effects

For climate change to be considered a "direct effect" of a proposed action involving the emission of GHGs, it would have to be an immediate effect that will result from that emission. [A]t the "may affect" stage, the direct effects of the proposed action are considered and define the action area along with the indirect effects. While the emission of GHGs from a single source may ultimately constitute an extremely small constituent of the aggregate global concentration of GHGs, such an emission by itself does not have a direct or immediate climate change effect. That being the case, it is proper to conclude, for purposes of the "may affect" test, that there will be no "direct effect" in the form of climate change from such emissions.

B. Indirect effects

For climate change to be considered an "indirect effect" on a member of a listed species or its habitat from a proposed action, the observed effect would have to be "caused by" the proposed action, occur later in time than the "direct effects" of the proposed action, and be "reasonably certain to occur." 50 C.F.R. § 402.02. When these three tests are met, an agency considers the indirect effects of the proposed action and uses those effects, along with the direct effects, to define the action area. As with "direct effects," however, "indirect effects" are considered in determining if an agency action "may affect a listed species or critical habitat" while "cumulative effects," that are not a part of the agency action are evaluated in the subsequent formal consultation, once the "may effect" determination has been made. . . . [T]he "cumulative effects" are effects from independent actions that are "reasonably certain to occur" within the action area defined by the direct and indirect effects. 50 C.F.R. § 402.14(c) and (g)(4).

The statement from the Director of the USGS quoted at the outset of this memorandum indicates that the requisite causal connections cannot be made between the emissions of GHGs from a proposed agency action and specific localized climate change as it impacts listed species or critical habitat. Given the nature of the complex and independent processes active in the atmosphere and the ocean acting on GHGs, the causal link simply cannot currently be made between emissions from a proposed action and specific effects on a listed species or its critical habitat. Specifically, science cannot say that a tiny incremental global temperature rise that might be produced by an action under consideration would manifest itself in the location of a listed species or its habitat. Similarly, any observed climate change effect on a member of a particular listed species or its critical habitat cannot be attributed to the emissions from any particular source. Rather it would be the consequence of the collective greenhouse gas accumulation from natural sources and the world-wide anthropogenically produced GHG emissions since at least the beginning of the industrial revolution.

Moreover, even if a theoretical link between emissions and effects is hypothesized, a question arises as to the magnitude of the effect that might occur from that emission at the location of the listed species. The EPA has recently modeled global climate change impacts from a model source emitting 20% more GHGs than a 1500 MW coal-fired steam electric generating plant. It estimated a hypothetical maximum mean global temperature value increase resulting from such a project. The results ranged from 0.00022 and 0.00035 degrees Celsius occurring approximately 50 years after the facility begins operation. These values provide a way of understanding the scale of the issues involved. Not only are these modeled changes extremely small, the downsizing of these results to interpolate local applications would be a novel and untested application of the model, with even greater uncertainly [sic] in the predicted outcomes. The EPA concluded that even assuming such an increase in temperature could be downscaled to a particular location, it "would be too small to physically measure or detect."

III. Conclusion

Based on the USGS statement, and its continued scientific validity, we conclude that where the effect at issue is climate change in the form of increased temperatures, a proposed action that will involve the emission of GHG cannot pass the "may affect" test and is not subject to consultation under the ESA and its implementing regulations.

NOTES AND QUESTIONS

1. **The Polar Bear Listing and Agency Actions.** In 2008, responding to a 2005 petition by the Center for Biological Diversity, the NMFS listed the polar bear as a "threatened" species. The listing was challenged both as not going far enough—polar bears should be considered endangered—and as going too far—polar bears are not threatened. Both the district court and D.C. Circuit rejected the challenges, deferring to the agency and upholding the regulation as reasoned and based on the best available science. *See In re Polar Bear Endangered Species Act Listing & Section 4(d) Rule Litig.*, MDL No. 1993, 709 F.3d 1, 8–9 (D.C. Cir. 2013); *In re Polar Bear Endangered Species Act Listing & § 4(d) Rule Litig.*, 794 F. Supp. 2d 65 (D.D.C. 2011). The D.C. Circuit explained:

> The Listing Rule is the product of FWS's careful and comprehensive study and analysis. Its scientific conclusions are amply supported by data and well within the mainstream on climate science and polar bear biology. . . . [S]everal of Appellants' challenges rely on portions of the record taken out of context and blatantly ignore FWS's published explanations. Others, as the District Court correctly explained, "amount to nothing more than competing views about policy and science," on which we defer to the agency.

In re Polar Bear, 709 F.3d at 8. The Court upheld the listing of the polar bear as a threatened species under the ESA due to the projected loss of its sea ice habitat due to climate change.

Within a year of any such listing, the ESA requires federal officials to designate habitat critical to the conservation of the species. The government did so in this instance. The energy industry, concerned that the habitat designation would compromise their Arctic oil and gas exploration efforts, sued to challenge the habitat designation as excessive in scope. In *Alaska Oil and Gas Assn. v. Jewell*, however, the Ninth Circuit upheld the government's polar bear habitat designation as neither arbitrary, capricious, nor in contravention of applicable ESA provisions. 815 F.3d 544 (9th Cir. 2016).

2.   Polar Bear Listing: Choice of Threatened v. Endangered. The choice of threatened, rather than endangered, is important because it gave the NMFS more discretion in designing regulation; in particular, the § 9 take provisions do not automatically apply. Section 9, by its terms, extends only to endangered species, and in 2018, the FWS proposed to revise its regulation that had extended most of the prohibitions for activities involving endangered species to threatened species. 83 Fed. Reg. 35,174, 35,175 (2018). Given that the polar bear listing was in response to concern about loss of habitat due to climate change, the listing triggered two critical questions. First, would actions that caused or authorized emissions of greenhouse gases be "likely to jeopardize" under § 7? The "Guidance on the Applicability of the Endangered Species Act's Consultation Requirements to Proposed Actions Involving the Emission of Greenhouse Gases" [hereinafter Solicitor's letter], along with a series of other guidance documents and, eventually, regulations, answered this question definitively in the negative. *See* Interagency Cooperation Under the Endangered Species Act, 73 Fed. Reg. 76,272 (2008) (establishing that greenhouse gas emissions would neither require formal consultation nor lead to jeopardy findings). In 2009, the Obama administration rescinded these regulations and requested public comment on whether changes needed to be made to the now-reinstated pre-2008 rules. Interagency Cooperation Under the Endangered Species Act, 74 Fed. Reg. 20,421 (2009). The Obama administration did not embark upon a new rulemaking and instead continued the informal policy announced in the Solicitor's letter, explaining that "[i]t is currently not possible to directly link the emission of greenhouse gases from a specific power plant, etc. to effects on specific bears or bear populations. This direct 'connect the dots' standard is required under the Act and court rulings. Therefore, the [FWS]'s policy guidance to its field staff is not to require such consultations." *See* FWS, POLAR BEAR 4(D) RULE—Q'S AND A'S (Oct. 22, 2009).

Second, would "takes" resulting from greenhouse gas emissions be prohibited under § 9? The Bush administration issued a regulation finding that GHG-emitting activities occurring outside the polar bear's range would not be "takes." Endangered and Threatened Wildlife and Plants; Special Rule for the Polar Bear, 73 Fed. Reg. 76,249, 76,269 (2008). When the Obama administration opted to preserve this rule, Secretary of the Interior Ken Salazar noted that "the Endangered Species Act is not the proper mechanism for controlling our nation's carbon emissions." New Release, Department of the Interior, Salazar Retains Conservation Rule for Polar Bears Underlines Need for Comprehensive Energy and Climate Change Legislation (May 8, 2000). The rule was challenged on both ESA and NEPA grounds. *See In re*

Polar Bear Endangered Species Act Listing & § 4(d) Rule Litig., 818 F. Supp. 2d 214 (D.D.C. 2011). On the NEPA challenge, the rule was vacated (reinstating the interim rule) because the Administration failed to conduct an environmental assessment. On the ESA challenge, plaintiffs argued the rule violated the ESA because, in failing to address global greenhouse gas emissions, the rule does not provide for the conservation of the polar bear. The court held, under a deferential standard of review, that the FWS "reasonably concluded that [the listing rule] provides for the conservation of the polar bear even if it does not reverse the trend of Arctic sea ice loss." *Id.* at 219. The court stayed clear of commenting on whether the ESA is an effective or prudent tool for managing climate change, noting only that the plaintiffs failed to show that the "complementary management regime encompassing the MMPA, CITES, and the ESA" developed by the FWS was arbitrary and capricious. *Id.* at 233.

3.   Trump Administration Seeks to Narrow "Foreseeable Future." In 2018, FWS proposed to add a new regulatory framework for determining whether a species is likely to become an endangered species within the foreseeable future. The agency proposed to add a new paragraph to its regulations explaining that:

> The term foreseeable future extends *only so far into the future as the Services can reasonably determine that the conditions potentially posing a danger of extinction in the foreseeable future are probable.* The Services will describe the foreseeable future on a case-by-case basis, using the best available data and taking into account considerations such as the species' life-history characteristics, threat-projection timeframes, and environmental variability. The Services need not identify the "foreseeable future" in terms of a specific period of time, but may instead explain the extent to which they can reasonably determine that both the future threats and the species' responses to those threats are probable.

Endangered and Threatened Wildlife and Plants; Revision of the Regulations for Listing Species and Designating Critical Habitat, 83 Fed. Reg. 35,193, 35,195 (2018) (emphasis added). In describing its proposal, FWS states, "[t]he Services will avoid speculating as to what is hypothetically possible." *Id.* at 35,196.

Do you think this proposed rule, if issued, will limit the ability of agencies to use climate modelling to assess threatened and endangered status? Would the agency's analysis at issue in *Alaska Oil and Gas v. Pritzger* pass muster according to this framework? Recall that in *Pritzger*, the court noted that, "[t]he ESA does not require NMFS to base its decision on ironclad evidence when it determines that a species is likely to become endangered in the foreseeable future." *Alaska Oil & Gas*, 840 F.3d at 681. Is the proposed regulation at odds with the *Pritzger* court's holding? With the purpose of the ESA?

4.   Mitigation: GHG Regulation? Is the Interior Department's guidance document, excerpted above, consistent with the court's holding in *NRDC v. Kempthorne*? The consultation in *Kempthorne* dealt with water diversion, not with greenhouse gas emissions. The court's primary concern was with the FWS's failure to consider how climate change would impact the project rather than with any failure to consider how the project would cause climate change. This is an essential distinction. Could climate change causes, that is, GHG emissions, be regulated through enforcement of §§ 7 and 9? Would such regulation be statutorily permissible? Would it be desirable? Consider the following analysis:

> [T]he problem with fitting climate change into the consultation framework is that it exhibits more certainty at macro levels than at micro levels. Consider for example, the proposed coal-fired power plant in Florida and its effects on the pika [a rabbit-like, high-altitude mammal] in the Sierra Nevada Mountains. It would seem quite a stretch to conclude that the power plant emissions will jeopardize the pika. Yet, at a macro level the analysis is rather straightforward: the power plant emits greenhouse gases (a direct effect of the action), greenhouse gases are reasonably certain to warm the troposphere (an indirect effect of the action), a warming troposphere is reasonably expected to adversely alter ecological conditions for the pika, and it is reasonably expected that such ecological changes will bring an end to the pika. At a micro level, however, it becomes difficult to link the *individual* plant's emissions as the jeopardizing agent for the pika, given that *all* greenhouse gas emissions worldwide are subject to the same macro analysis. Other than quantity of emissions, the FWS would have no reasoned basis for distinguishing between the power plant in Florida, a farm in Kansas, or an elementary school in Oregon.

J.B. Ruhl, *Climate Change and the Endangered Species Act: Building Bridges to the No-Analog Future*, 88 B.U. L. REV. 1, 46–47 (2008). Does Ruhl's analysis cut for or against regulation? Why? What causation standard should the agencies and courts apply? Would a court find "harm" under the *Sweet Home* standard? Is *Massachusetts v. EPA* relevant here?

For the argument that regulation would not be statutorily permissible, see Steven P. Quarles & Thomas R. Lundquist, *The Endangered Species Act and Greenhouse Emissions—Species, Projects, and Statute at Risk,* SR021 ALI-ABA 169, 191–95 (2009). For the argument the ESA allows for such regulation, see Anna T. Moritz et al., *Biodiversity Baking and Boiling: Endangered Species Act turning Down the Heat*, 44 TULSA L. REV. 205 (2008); and Ari N. Sommer, Note, *Taking the Pit Bull Off the Leash: Siccing the Endangered Species Act on Climate Change*, 36 B.C. ENVTL. AFF. L. REV. 273 (2009) (exploring the possibility of a citizen suit to force greenhouse gas regulation).

5. Adaptation: A Statute on the Verge of Extinction? Scientists predict that climate change may wipe out as many as thirty percent of the world's species. INTERGOVERNMENTAL PANEL ON CLIMATE CHANGE, FOURTH ASSESSMENT REPORT: CLIMATE CHANGE 2007, WORKING GROUP II REPORT: IMPACTS, ADAPTATION AND VULNERABILITY. Given the scope of this loss and the unlikelihood that the ESA can play a role in slowing climate change, what is the Act's relevance?

One commentator has suggested that, accepting the Act has little to no role to play in preventing climate change causes, administrators must turn their focus to how to save species from climate change effects. *See* J.B. Ruhl, *Keeping the Endangered Species Act Relevant*, 19 DUKE ENVTL L. & POL'Y F. 275 (2009). The FWS and the NMFS are not free to do nothing; they must continue to respond to petitions to list species and, in doing so, must apply the best available science. According to *NRDC v. Klempthorne* and *Alaska Oil & Gas v. Pritzger*, this includes consideration of climate change. Indeed, in addition to polar bears and Pacific bearded seals, the agencies have also listed several species of coral that are threatened by rising ocean temperatures. Endangered and Threatened Wildlife and Plants: Final Listing Determinations on Proposal To List 66 Reef-Building Coral Species and To Reclassify Elkhorn and Staghorn Corals, 79 Fed. Reg. 53,851 (2014) (listing 20 reef coral species as threatened due to ocean warming). But how will these listings provide protection? One possibility is that in designating critical habitat, the agencies could plan for shifts in species' ranges that will result from changing temperature patterns. In essence, the agencies could protect future habitat, as they did with respect to critical polar bear habitat, the agency action upheld in *Alaska Oil & Gas Ass'n v. Jewell. See* 815 F.3d at 555; *see also* Ruhl, *Climate Change and the Endangered Species Act, supra*, at 36. Making such determinations, or compelling agencies to do so, however, can be difficult. *See, e.g., Alliance for Wild Rockies v. Lyder*, 728 F. Supp. 2d 1126, 1140–43 (D. Mont. 2010) ("[T]he science does not provide the specificity needed to identify the location of lynx habitat in the future, the Service did not act arbitrarily or unreasonably in not designating unoccupied lynx habitat to account for climate change."); *Weyerhaeuser Co. v. U.S. Fish and Wildlife Service*, 139 S. Ct. 361 (2018) (remanding case to the Court of Appeals to decide in the first instance whether an area of land not presently occupied by a species can be deemed critical habitat for that endangered species).

Another related possibility is the use of assisted migration programs. Under § 10(j), the FWS can transport and release members of a threatened or endangered species to an area outside its current range if the agency "determines that such release will further the conservation of such species." Ruhl, *Climate Change and the Endangered Species Act, supra*, at 36.

6.   People v. Endangered Species. Like endangered species, people will also need to adapt to climate change. What happens when our needs for adaptation conflict with the needs of endangered species? For example, climate change is likely to increase incidence of drought. Current ESA provisions allow state and federal agencies to restrict water rights in order to protect listed species. *See United States v. Glenn-Colusa Irr. Dist.*, 788 F. Supp. 1126 (E.D. Cal. 1992) (discussing 16 U.S.C. § 1531(c)(2)); Linda R. Larson & Jessica K. Ferrell, *Precautionary Resources Management and Climate Change*, 24 NAT. RESOURCES & ENVT. 51 (2009). How far should this go? What happens if this policy begins to threaten food supplies? For an example of conflicting priorities concerning water management and endangered species, see Reed D. Benson, *New Adventures of the Old Bureau:*

Modern-Day   Reclamation   Statutes   and   Congress's   Unfinished Environmental Business, 48 HARV. J. ON LEGIS. 137, 179–80 (2011).

7.   Return to the Question: Human-Centered or Nature-Centered? Does the potential scale of climate changed-related extinction change the nature of this debate? Do people have a moral obligation toward species that are threatened by climate change? What, aside from ecosystem functioning, is lost when a species goes extinct? When many species go extinct at once? For further discussion, see Clare Palmer, *Harm to Species? Species, Ethics, and Climate Change: The Case of the Polar Bear*, 23 NOTRE DAME J.L. ETHICS & PUB. POL'Y 587 (2009).

8.   Differences in Degree or in Kind. Are GHGs merely a subset of emissions in general? If agencies are capable of applying the ESA in other pollution contexts, such as with habitat destruction due to nitrogen deposition, are the issues discussed in this section due only to limitations in science? For a discussion of how to understand where GHGs fit within a broader pollution category, see Zdravka Tzankova et al., *Can the ESA Address the Threats of Atmospheric Nitrogen Deposition? Insights from the Case of the Bay Checkerspot Butterfly*, 35 HARV. ENVTL. L. REV. 433, 456 (2011).

9.   Existing Statutory Options: A Comparison. How does the ESA fare as a tool to mitigate and adapt to climate change? Relative to the CAA? Relative to the CWA? If Congress continues to stall on climate change legislation, should Interior pursue the more dramatic policy options discussed above? Should its decision depend on whether the EPA regulates greenhouse gases under the CAA?

2.   PROTECTION OF WETLANDS UNDER THE CWA

Wetlands are transition zones, forming a link between land and water. They are defined by EPA as "areas that are inundated or saturated by surface or groundwater at a frequency and duration sufficient to support . . . a prevalence of vegetation typically adapted for life in saturated soil conditions." 40 C.F.R. § 122.2. Within this broad definition, wetlands vary dramatically with respect to soil composition, landscape, climate, and vegetation—ranging from the salt water lagoons and tundra of Alaska in the north to the freshwater marshes of the Everglades of Florida in the south. They are rich in ecological value, providing wildlife habitat for a wide range of terrestrial and semi-aquatic animals and numerous plant species, as well as nesting habitat for many migratory bird species. In addition, they serve to remove pollutants from surface runoff and small streams by retaining sediment and toxic pollutants, as well as to slow and retain surface water, providing storage and shoreline stabilization.

While the ecological values of wetlands are now well understood, more than half of the wetlands within the United States have been destroyed in the course of the past century—drained and converted to farmland, filled for housing developments and industrial facilities, or used to dispose of household and industrial waste. *See* T.E. DAHL, WETLANDS LOSSES IN THE UNITED STATES 1780'S TO 1980'S, U.S. DEPARTMENT OF THE INTERIOR, FISH AND WILDLIFE SERVICE (1990). Section 404 of the CWA, 33 U.S.C. § 1344, is an attempt to regulate the destruction of wetlands. In broad terms, § 404 establishes a permit program, jointly administered by the U.S. Army Corps of Engineers (the Corps) and EPA, designed to regulate the discharge of dredged or fill material into the navigable waters of the United States.

A. SCOPE OF THE CWA WETLANDS REGIME

The § 404 permit program operates in a similar fashion to the National Permit Discharge Elimination System (NPDES) permit program (discussed in Chapter VI), insofar as it authorizes the discharge of certain materials into the waters of the United States that would otherwise be subject to the § 301(a) prohibition against the "discharge of any pollutant by any person." 33 U.S.C. § 1311(a). In order to fall within the ambit of the § 404 permit program, a person must seek to discharge "dredged or fill materials" into the "navigable waters." 33 U.S.C. § 1344(a). Dredged material is defined by EPA and the Corps as "material that is excavated or dredged from the waters of the United States," 33 C.F.R. § 323.2(c), whereas fill material is defined as "material used for the primary purpose of replacing an aquatic area with dry land or of changing the bottom elevation of a water body." 33 C.F.R. § 323.2(e)(1). The term "navigable waters" is defined in § 502(7) of the CWA as "the waters of the United States, including the territorial sea." 33 U.S.C. § 1362(7). Given that approximately 98 percent of the nation's water bodies are not waters that would traditionally be considered navigable, the meaning attributed the phrase "waters of the United States" has a significant impact upon the jurisdictional limits of § 404. In particular, the extent to which many wetlands may be considered "waters of the United States" for the purpose of § 502(7) is the subject of considerable controversy.

In *United States v. Riverside Bayview Homes, Inc.*, 474 U.S. 121 (1985), the Supreme Court held that the Corps did possess § 404(a) jurisdiction over wetlands that abutted a navigable waterway. In so doing, the Court noted that the term "navigable" is of "limited import" in the context of § 502(7) and that Congress evidenced its intent to "regulate at least some waters that would not be deemed 'navigable' under the classical understanding of that term." *Id.* at 133. The Court's holding was based in large part on Congress' unequivocal acquiescence to, and approval of, the Corps' regulations interpreting the CWA to cover wetlands adjacent to navigable waters. *See id.* at 135–39. The *Riverside Bayview Homes* Court found that Congress' concern for the protection of water quality and aquatic ecosystems indicated its intent to regulate wetlands "inseparably bound up with the waters of the United States." *Id.* at 134.

In the later decision of *Solid Waste Agency of Northern Cook County v. U.S. Army Corps of Engineers*, 531 U.S. 159 (2001) (*SWANCC*), the Supreme Court considered the authority of the Corps to regulate discharges of fill material into wetlands not adjacent to bodies of open water. At issue in this case was the Corps' jurisdiction over intrastate waters used as habitat by birds protected by migratory bird treaties. More particularly, the petitioner (a consortium of 23 suburban Chicago cities and villages that sought to establish a nonhazardous waste site) asserted that the Corps did not possess § 404 jurisdiction over an abandoned sand and gravel pit mine, in which excavation trenches had developed into permanent and seasonal ponds of varying sizes and depths. Initially, the Corps ruled that it did not possess § 404 jurisdiction on the basis that the mine site was wholly isolated from any open waterway. It subsequently reversed this determination, however, upon being advised by the Illinois Natural Preserves Commission that over 121 species of migratory birds had been observed on the site. In reaching this conclusion, the Corps conceded that the waters could not be considered navigable waters, but determined that they nevertheless constituted "waters of the United States" for the purposes of § 502(7) of the CWA. The *SWANCC* Court ruled against the Corps on the following grounds:

> We . . . decline [the Corps'] invitation to take what they see as the next ineluctable step after Riverside Bayview Homes: holding that isolated ponds, some only seasonal, wholly located within two Illinois counties, fall under § 404(a)'s definition of "navigable waters" because they serve as habitat for migratory birds. As counsel for respondents conceded at oral argument, such a ruling would assume that "the use of the word navigable in the statute . . . does not have any independent significance." Tr. of Oral Arg. 28. We cannot agree that Congress' separate definitional use of the phrase "waters of the United States" constitutes a basis for reading the term "navigable waters" out of the statute. We said in Riverside Bayview Homes that the word "navigable" in the statute was of "limited import" 474 U.S., at 133, and went on to hold that § 404(a) extended to nonnavigable wetlands adjacent to open waters. But it is one thing to give a word limited effect and quite another to give it no effect whatever. The term "navigable" has at least the import of showing us what Congress had in mind as its authority for enacting the CWA: its traditional jurisdiction over waters that were or had been navigable in fact or which could reasonably be so made. *See, e.g., United States v. Appalachian Elec. Power Co.*, 311 U.S. 377, 407–408 (1940).

Id. at 171–72. Recently, the § 404 jurisdiction of the Corps was again called into question. In the following case, the Supreme Court examines whether wetlands not "inseparably bound up with waters of the United

States" could nevertheless be considered "navigable waters" for the purposes of § 404(a).

Rapanos v. United States
547 U.S. 715 (2006).

■ JUSTICE SCALIA announced the judgment of the Court, and delivered an opinion, in which THE CHIEF JUSTICE, JUSTICE THOMAS, and JUSTICE ALITO joined:

In April 1989, petitioner John A. Rapanos backfilled wetlands on a parcel of land in Michigan that he owned and sought to develop. This parcel included 54 acres of land with sometimes-saturated soil conditions. The nearest body of navigable water was 11 to 20 miles away. 339 F.3d 447, 449 (C.A.6 2003) (*Rapanos I*). Regulators had informed Mr. Rapanos that his saturated fields were "waters of the United States," 33 U.S.C. § 1362(7), that could not be filled without a permit. Twelve years of criminal and civil litigation ensued.

The burden of federal regulation on those who would deposit fill material in locations denominated "waters of the United States" is not trivial. In deciding whether to grant or deny a permit, the U.S. Army Corps of Engineers (Corps) exercises the discretion of an enlightened despot, relying on such factors as "economics," "aesthetics," "recreation," and "in general, the needs and welfare of the people," 33 CFR § 320.4(a) (2004). The average applicant for an individual permit spends 788 days and $271,596 in completing the process, and the average applicant for a nationwide permit spends 313 days and $28,915—not counting costs of mitigation or design changes. Sunding & Zilberman, The Economics of Environmental Regulation by Licensing: An Assessment of Recent Changes to the Wetland Permitting Process, 42 Natural Resources J. 59, 74–76 (2002). "[O]ver $1.7 billion is spent each year by the private and public sectors obtaining wetlands permits." *Id.*, at 81. These costs cannot be avoided, because the Clean Water Act "impose[s] criminal liability," as well as steep civil fines, "on a broad range of ordinary industrial and commercial activities." *Hanousek v. United States*, 528 U.S. 1102, 1103 (2000) (THOMAS, J., dissenting from denial of certiorari). In this litigation, for example, for backfilling his own wet fields, Mr. Rapanos faced 63 months in prison and hundreds of thousands of dollars in criminal and civil fines. See *United States v. Rapanos*, 235 F.3d 256, 260 (C.A.6 2000).

The enforcement proceedings against Mr. Rapanos are a small part of the immense expansion of federal regulation of land use that has occurred under the Clean Water Act—without any change in the governing statute—during the past five Presidential administrations. In the last three decades, the Corps and the Environmental Protection Agency (EPA) have interpreted their jurisdiction over "the waters of the United States" to cover 270-to-300 million acres of swampy lands in the

United States—including half of Alaska and an area the size of California in the lower 48 States. And that was just the beginning. The Corps has also asserted jurisdiction over virtually any parcel of land containing a channel or conduit—whether manmade or natural, broad or narrow, permanent or ephemeral—through which rainwater or drainage may occasionally or intermittently flow. On this view, the federally regulated "waters of the United States" include storm drains, roadside ditches, ripples of sand in the desert that may contain water once a year, and lands that are covered by floodwaters once every 100 years. Because they include the land containing storm sewers and desert washes, the statutory "waters of the United States" engulf entire cities and immense arid wastelands. In fact, the entire land area of the United States lies in some drainage basin, and an endless network of visible channels furrows the entire surface, containing water ephemerally wherever the rain falls. Any plot of land containing such a channel may potentially be regulated as a "water of the United States." . . .

Following our decision in SWANCC, the Corps did not significantly revise its theory of federal jurisdiction under § 1344(a). The Corps provided notice of a proposed rulemaking in light of SWANCC, 68 Fed.Reg.1991 (2003), but ultimately did not amend its published regulations. Because SWANCC did not directly address tributaries, the Corps notified its field staff that they "should continue to assert jurisdiction over traditional navigable waters . . . and, generally speaking, their tributary systems (and adjacent wetlands)." 68 Fed.Reg.1998. In addition, because SWANCC did not overrule *Riverside Bayview*, the Corps continues to assert jurisdiction over waters " 'neighboring' " traditional navigable waters and their tributaries. 68 Fed.Reg.1997 (quoting 33 CFR § 328.3(c) (2003)). . . .

In addition to "tributaries," the Corps and the lower courts have also continued to define "adjacent" wetlands broadly after SWANCC. For example, some of the Corps' district offices have concluded that wetlands are "adjacent" to covered waters if they are hydrologically connected "through directional sheet flow during storm events," GAO Report 18, or if they lie within the "100-year floodplain" of a body of water—that is, they are connected to the navigable water by flooding, on average, once every 100 years, *Id.*, at 17, and n. 16. Others have concluded that presence within 200 feet of a tributary automatically renders a wetland "adjacent" and jurisdictional. *Id.*, at 19. And the Corps has successfully defended such theories of "adjacency" in the courts, even after SWANCC's excision of "isolated" waters and wetlands from the Act's coverage. . . .

In [this case], we consider whether . . . Michigan wetlands, which lie near ditches or man-made drains that eventually empty into traditional navigable waters, constitute "waters of the United States" within the meaning of the Act. Petitioners in No. 04–1034, the Rapanos and their affiliated businesses, deposited fill material without a permit into wetlands on three sites near Midland, Michigan: the "Salzburg site," the "Hines Road site," and the "Pine River site." The wetlands at the Salzburg site are connected to a man-made drain, which drains into Hoppler Creek, which flows into the Kawkawlin River, which empties into Saginaw Bay and Lake Huron. See Brief for United States in No. 04–1034, p. 11; 339 F.3d, at 449. The wetlands at the Hines Road site are connected to something called the "Rose Drain," which has a surface connection to the Tittabawassee River. App. to Pet. for Cert. in No. 04–1034, pp. A23, B20. And the wetlands at the Pine River site have a surface connection to the Pine River, which flows into Lake Huron. *Id.*, at A23–A24, B26. It is not clear whether the connections between these wetlands and the nearby drains and ditches are continuous or intermittent, or whether the nearby drains and ditches contain continuous or merely occasional flows of water.

The United States brought civil enforcement proceedings against the Rapanos petitioners. The District Court found that the three described wetlands were "within federal jurisdiction" because they were "adjacent to other waters of the United States," and held petitioners liable for violations of the CWA at those sites. *Id.*, at B32–B35. On appeal, the United States Court of Appeals for the Sixth Circuit affirmed, holding that there was federal jurisdiction over the wetlands at all three sites because "there were hydrological connections between all three sites and corresponding adjacent tributaries of navigable waters." 376 F.3d, at 643. . . .

The . . . petitioners contend that the terms "navigable waters" and "waters of the United States" in the Act must be limited to the traditional definition of *The Daniel Ball*, which required that the "waters" be navigable in fact, or susceptible of being rendered so. See 10 Wall., at 563. But this definition cannot be applied wholesale to the CWA. The Act uses the phrase "navigable waters" as a *defined* term, and the definition is simply "the waters of the United States." 33 U.S.C. § 1362(7). Moreover, the Act provides, in certain circumstances, for the substitution of state for federal jurisdiction over "navigable waters . . . *other than* those waters which are presently used, or are susceptible to use in their natural condition or by reasonable improvement as a means to transport interstate or foreign commerce . . . including wetlands adjacent thereto." § 1344(g)(1) (emphasis added). This provision shows that the Act's term "navigable waters" includes something more than traditional navigable waters. We have twice stated that the meaning of "navigable waters" in the Act is broader than the traditional understanding of that term, *SWANCC*, 531 U.S., at 167; *Riverside Bayview*, 474 U.S., at 133. We have also emphasized, however, that the qualifier "navigable" is not devoid of significance, *SWANCC*, *supra*, at 172.

We need not decide the precise extent to which the qualifiers "navigable" and "of the United States" restrict the coverage of the Act. Whatever the scope of these qualifiers, the CWA authorizes federal jurisdiction only over "waters." 33 U.S.C. § 1362(7). The only natural definition of the term "waters," our prior and subsequent judicial constructions of it, clear evidence from other provisions of the statute, and this Court's canons of construction all confirm that "the waters of the United States" in § 1362(7) cannot bear the expansive meaning that the Corps would give it.

The Corps' expansive approach might be arguable if the CWA defined "navigable waters" as "water of the United States." But "the waters of the United States" is something else. The use of the definite article (the) and the plural number (waters) show plainly that § 1362(7) does not refer to water in general. In this form, "the waters" refers more narrowly to water "[a]s found in streams and bodies forming geographical features such as oceans, rivers, [and] lakes," or "the flowing or moving masses, as of waves or floods, making up such streams or bodies." Webster's New International Dictionary 2882 (2d ed.1954) (hereinafter Webster's Second). On this definition, "the waters of the United States" include only relatively permanent, standing or flowing bodies of water. The definition refers to water as found in "streams," "oceans," "rivers," "lakes," and "bodies" of water "forming geographical features." *Ibid.* All of these terms connote continuously present, fixed bodies of water, as opposed to ordinarily dry channels through which water occasionally or intermittently flows. Even the least substantial of the definition's terms, namely "streams," connotes a continuous flow of water in a permanent channel—especially when used in company with other terms such as "rivers," "lakes," and "oceans." None of these terms encompasses transitory puddles or ephemeral flows of water. . . .

The restriction of "the waters of the United States" to exclude channels containing merely intermittent or ephemeral flow also accords with the commonsense understanding of the term. In applying the definition to "ephemeral streams," "wet meadows," storm sewers and culverts, "directional sheet flow during storm events," drain tiles, man-made drainage ditches, and dry arroyos in the middle of the desert, the Corps has stretched the term "waters of the United States" beyond parody. The plain language of the statute simply does not authorize this "Land Is Waters" approach to federal jurisdiction.

In addition, the Act's use of the traditional phrase "navigable waters" (the defined term) further confirms that it confers jurisdiction only over relatively *permanent* bodies of water. The Act adopted that traditional term from its predecessor statutes. See *SWANCC*, 531 U.S., at 180 (STEVENS, J., dissenting). . . .

Our subsequent interpretation of the phrase "the waters of the United States" in the CWA likewise confirms this limitation of its scope. In *Riverside Bayview*, we stated that the phrase in the Act referred primarily to "rivers, streams, and other *hydrographic features more conventionally identifiable as 'waters' "* than the wetlands adjacent to such features. 474 U.S., at 131 (emphasis added). We thus echoed the dictionary definition of "waters" as referring to "streams and bodies *forming geographical features* such as oceans, rivers, [and] lakes." Webster's Second 2882 (emphasis added). Though we upheld in that case the inclusion of wetlands abutting such a "hydrographic featur[e]"—principally due to the difficulty of drawing any clear boundary between the two, see 474 U.S., at 132, Part IV, infra—nowhere did we suggest that "the waters of the United States" should be expanded to include, in their own right, entities other than "hydrographic features more conventionally identifiable as 'waters.'" Likewise, in both *Riverside Bayview* and *SWANCC*, we repeatedly described the "navigable waters" covered by the Act as "open water" and "open waters." *See Riverside Bayview*, *supra*, at 132, and n. 8, 134; *SWANCC*, *supra*, at 167, 172. Under no rational interpretation are typically dry channels described as "*open waters.*"

Most significant of all, the CWA itself categorizes the channels and conduits that typically carry intermittent flows of water separately from "navigable waters," by including them in the definition of "'point source.'" The Act defines "'point source'" as "any discernible, confined and discrete conveyance, including but not limited to any pipe, ditch, channel, tunnel, conduit, well, discrete fissure, container, rolling stock, concentrated animal feeding operation, or vessel or other floating craft, from which pollutants are or may be discharged." 33 U.S.C. § 1362(14). It also defines "'discharge of a pollutant'" as "any addition of any pollutant *to* navigable waters *from* any point source." § 1362(12)(A) (emphases added). The definitions thus conceive of "point sources" and "navigable waters" as separate and distinct categories. The definition of "discharge" would make little sense if the two categories were significantly overlapping. The separate classification of "ditch[es], channel[s], and conduit[s]"—which are terms ordinarily used to describe the watercourses through which *intermittent* waters typically flow—shows that these are, by and large, *not* "waters of the United States." . . .

In sum, on its only plausible interpretation, the phrase "the waters of the United States" includes only those relatively permanent, standing or continuously flowing bodies of water "forming geographic features" that are described in ordinary parlance as "streams[,] . . . oceans, rivers, [and] lakes." See Webster's Second 2882. The phrase does not include channels through which water flows intermittently or ephemerally, or channels that periodically provide drainage for rainfall. The Corps' expansive interpretation of the "the waters of the United States" is thus not "based on a permissible construction of the statute." *Chevron U.S.A. Inc. v. Natural Resources Defense Council, Inc.*, 467 U.S. 837, 843 (1984). . . .

When we characterized the holding of *Riverside Bayview* in *SWANCC*, we referred to the close connection between waters and the wetlands that they gradually blend into: "It was the *significant* nexus between the wetlands and 'navigable waters' that informed our reading of the CWA in *Riverside Bayview Homes*." 531 U.S., at 167. In particular, *SWANCC* rejected the notion that the ecological considerations upon which the Corps relied in *Riverside Bayview*—and upon which the dissent repeatedly relies today . . .—provided an *independent* basis for including entities like "wetlands" (or "ephemeral streams") within the phrase "the waters of the United States." *SWANCC* found such ecological considerations irrelevant to the question whether physically isolated waters come within the Corps' jurisdiction. It thus confirmed that *Riverside Bayview* rested upon the inherent ambiguity in defining where water ends and abutting (adjacent) wetlands begin, permitting the Corps' reliance on ecological considerations *only to resolve that ambiguity* in favor of treating all abutting wetlands as waters. Isolated ponds were not "waters of the United States" in their own right, see 531 U.S., at 167, 171, and presented no boundary-drawing problem that would have justified the invocation of ecological factors to treat them as such.

Therefore, *only* those wetlands with a continuous surface connection to bodies that are "waters of the United States" in their own right, so that there is no clear demarcation between "waters" and wetlands, are "adjacent to" such waters and covered by the Act. Wetlands with only an intermittent, physically remote hydrologic connection to "waters of the United States" do not implicate the boundary-drawing problem of *Riverside Bayview*, and thus lack the necessary connection to covered waters that we described as a "significant nexus" in *SWANCC*. 531 U.S., at 167. Thus, establishing that wetlands such as those at the Rapanos . . . site [is] covered by the Act requires two findings: First, that the adjacent channel contains a "wate[r] of the United States," (*i.e.*, a relatively permanent body of water connected to traditional interstate navigable waters); and second, that the wetland has a continuous surface connection with that water, making it difficult to determine where the "water" ends and the "wetland" begins. . . .

Because the Sixth Circuit applied the wrong standard to determine if these wetlands are covered "waters of the United States," and because of the paucity of the record in both of these cases, the lower courts should determine, in the first instance, whether the ditches or drains near each wetland are "waters" in the ordinary sense of containing a relatively permanent flow; and (if they are) whether the wetlands in question are "adjacent" to these "waters" in the sense of possessing a continuous surface connection that creates the boundary-drawing problem we addressed in *Riverside Bayview*. . . .

■ JUSTICE STEVENS, with whom JUSTICE SOUTER, JUSTICE GINSBURG, and JUSTICE BREYER join, dissenting:

. . . The narrow question presented . . . is whether wetlands adjacent to tributaries of traditionally navigable waters are "waters of the United States" subject to the jurisdiction of the Army Corps; . . . . The broader question is whether regulations that have protected the quality of our waters for decades, that were implicitly approved by Congress, and that have been repeatedly enforced in case after case, must now be revised in light of the creative criticisms voiced by the plurality and Justice KENNEDY today. Rejecting more than 30 years of practice by the Army Corps, the plurality disregards the nature of the congressional delegation to the agency and the technical and complex character of the issues at stake. Justice KENNEDY similarly fails to defer sufficiently to the Corps, though his approach is far more faithful to our precedents and to principles of statutory interpretation than is the plurality's.

In my view, the proper analysis is straightforward. The Army Corps has determined that wetlands adjacent to tributaries of traditionally navigable waters preserve the quality of our Nation's waters by, among other things, providing habitat for aquatic animals, keeping excessive sediment and toxic pollutants out of adjacent waters, and reducing downstream flooding by absorbing water at times of high flow. The Corps' resulting decision to treat these wetlands as encompassed within the term "waters of the United States" is a quintessential example of the Executive's reasonable interpretation of a statutory provision. See *Chevron U.S.A. Inc. v. Natural Resources Defense Council, Inc.*, 467 U.S. 837, 842–845 (1984).

Our unanimous decision in *United States v. Riverside Bayview Homes, Inc.*, 474 U.S. 121 (1985), was faithful to our duty to respect the work product of the Legislative and Executive Branches of our Government. Today's judicial amendment of the Clean Water Act is not. . . .

Even setting aside the plurality's dramatic departure from our reasoning and holding in *Riverside Bayview*, its creative opinion is utterly unpersuasive. The plurality imposes two novel conditions on the exercise of the Corps' jurisdiction that can only muddy the jurisdictional waters. As Justice KENNEDY observes, "these limitations . . . are without support in the language and purposes of the Act or in our cases interpreting it." *Ante*, at 2242 (opinion concurring in judgment). The impropriety of crafting these new conditions is highlighted by the fact that *no* party or *amicus* has suggested either of them.

First, ignoring the importance of preserving jurisdiction over water beds that are periodically dry, the plurality imposes a requirement that only tributaries with the "relatively permanent" presence of water fall within the Corps' jurisdiction. *Ante*, at 2221. Under the plurality's view, then, the Corps can regulate polluters who dump dredge into a stream that flows year round but may not be able to regulate polluters who dump into a neighboring stream that flows for only 290 days of the year—even if the dredge in this second stream would have the same effect on downstream waters as the dredge in the year-round one. *Ante*, at 2221, n. 5. . . .

Most importantly, the plurality disregards the fundamental significance of the Clean Water Act. As then-Justice Rehnquist explained when writing for the Court in 1981, the Act was "not merely another law" but rather was "viewed by Congress as a 'total restructuring' and 'complete rewriting' of the existing water pollution legislation." *Milwaukee v. Illinois*, 451 U.S. 304, 317. "Congress' intent in enacting the [Act] was clearly to establish an all-encompassing program of water pollution regulation," and "the most casual perusal of the legislative history demonstrates that . . . views on the comprehensive nature of the legislation were practically universal." *Id.*, at 318, and n. 12; see also 531 U.S., at 177–181 (STEVENS, J., dissenting). The Corps has concluded that it must regulate pollutants at the time they enter ditches or streams with ordinary high-water marks—whether perennial, intermittent, or ephemeral—in order to properly control water pollution. 65 Fed.Reg. 12823 (2000). Because there is ambiguity in the phrase "waters of the United States" and because interpreting it broadly to cover such ditches and streams advances the purpose of the Act, the Corps' approach should command our deference. Intermittent streams can carry pollutants just as perennial streams can, and their regulation may prove as important for flood control purposes. The inclusion of all identifiable tributaries that ultimately drain into large bodies of water within the mantle of federal protection is surely wise.

The plurality's second statutory invention is as arbitrary as its first. Trivializing the significance of changing conditions in wetlands environments, the plurality imposes a separate requirement that "the wetland has a continuous surface connection" with its abutting waterway such that it is "difficult to determine where the 'water' ends and the 'wetland' begins." *Ante*, at 2227. An "intermittent, physically remote hydrologic connection" between the wetland and other waters is not enough. *Ibid.* Under this view, wetlands that border traditionally navigable waters or their tributaries and perform the essential function of soaking up overflow waters during hurricane season—thus reducing flooding downstream—can be filled in by developers with impunity, as long as the wetlands lack a surface connection with the adjacent waterway the rest of the year. . . .

The plurality . . . define[s] " 'adjacent to' " as meaning "with a continuous surface connection to" other water. *Ante*, at 2225–2227. It is unclear how the plurality reached this conclusion, though it plainly neglected to consult a dictionary. Even its preferred Webster's Second defines the term as "[l]ying near, close, or contiguous; neighboring; bordering on" and acknowledges that "[o]bjects are ADJACENT when they lie close to each other, but *not necessarily in actual contact*." Webster's Second 32 (emphasis added); see also Webster's Third 26. In any event, the proper question is not how the plurality would define "adjacent," but whether the Corps' definition is reasonable.

The Corps defines "adjacent" as "bordering, contiguous, or neighboring," and specifies that "[w]etlands separated from other waters of the United States by man-made dikes or barriers, natural river berms, beach dunes and the like are 'adjacent wetlands.' " 33 CFR § 328.3(c)

(2005). This definition is plainly reasonable, both on its face and in terms of the purposes of the Act. While wetlands that are physically separated from other waters may perform less valuable functions, this is a matter for the Corps to evaluate in its permitting decisions. . . .

As I explained in *SWANCC*, Congress passed the Clean Water Act in response to wide-spread recognition—based on events like the 1969 burning of the Cuyahoga River in Cleveland—that our waters had become appallingly polluted. 531 U.S., at 174–175 (dissenting opinion). The Act has largely succeeded in restoring the quality of our Nation's waters. Where the Cuyahoga River was once coated with industrial waste, "[t]oday, that location is lined with restaurants and pleasure boat slips." EPA, A BENEFITS ASSESSMENT OF THE WATER POLLUTION CONTROL PROGRAMS SINCE 1972, p. 1–2 (Jan. 2000), *available at* http://water.epa.gov/lawsregs/lawsguidance/cwa/316b/upload/2000_04_17_economics_assessment.pdf. By curtailing the Corps' jurisdiction of more than 30 years, the plurality needlessly jeopardizes the quality of our waters. In doing so, the plurality disregards the deference it owes the Executive, the congressional acquiescence in the Executive's position that we recognized in *Riverside Bayview*, and its own obligation to interpret laws rather than to make them. . . .

NOTES AND QUESTIONS

1. **Where Water Ends and Land Begins.** What are the difficulties in determining where water ends and land begins? How do the plurality and dissenting opinions differ in drawing this distinction? How do they differ in their interpretation of both the *Riverside Bayview* and *SWANCC* decisions? Which position do you find most convincing, having regard to the statutory language and previous decisions of the Court?

2. **Navigable Waters.** Neither the plurality nor the dissent limit the term "navigable waters" solely by reference to navigability in fact. Under the plurality's interpretation, what role does the phrase "the waters of the United States" play in giving meaning to this term? What distinction does the plurality draw between "the waters of the United States" and the "water of the United States"? Do you find this distinction meaningful? For a detailed examination of the statutory construction favored by the plurality and the dissent, see Courtney Covington, Rapanos v. United States: *Evaluating the Efficacy of Textualism in Interpreting Environmental Laws*, 34 ECOLOGY L.Q. 801 (2007).

3. **Relative Permanence.** The plurality found that only those bodies of water that are relatively permanent fall under the scope of the § 404 permit program. What does this mean? Should a body of water that is full 11 months of the year be considered "relatively permanent"? What about 6 months of the year? How is the Corps to make determinations in this respect? What factors would be relevant? What view does the dissenting opinion take with respect to relative permanence? Which view do you think best gives effect to the intent of Congress?

4.   Continuous Surface Connection. On what basis does the plurality limit the scope of the § 404 regime to those wetlands that demonstrate a "continuous surface connection" with abutting waterways? 547 U.S. at 717. Why does the dissent claim that this requirement "trivializ[es] the significance of changing conditions in wetlands environments"? 547 U.S. at 804. Do you agree? What does it mean to have a continuous surface connection with an abutting waterway? In the view of the plurality, would a wetland that was connected to a waterway only in occurrences of extreme flood be subject to the § 402 regime? Would the dissent classify such wetlands differently?

5.   Kennedy's Middle Ground. Justice Kennedy, in a concurring opinion not excerpted above, found in favor of the petitioners, albeit on very different grounds to the plurality:

> Consistent with *SWANCC* and *Riverside Bayview* and with the need to give the term "navigable" some meaning, the Corps' jurisdiction over wetlands depends upon the existence of a significant nexus between the wetlands in question and navigable waters in the traditional sense. The required nexus must be assessed in terms of the statute's goals and purposes. Congress enacted the law to "restore and maintain the chemical, physical, and biological integrity of the Nation's waters," 33 U.S.C. § 1251(a), and it pursued that objective by restricting dumping and filling in "navigable waters," §§ 1311(a), 1362(12). With respect to wetlands, the rationale for Clean Water Act regulation is, as the Corps has recognized, that wetlands can perform critical functions related to the integrity of other waters—functions such as pollutant trapping, flood control, and runoff storage. 33 CFR § 320.4(b)(2). Accordingly, wetlands possess the requisite nexus, and thus come within the statutory phrase "navigable waters," if the wetlands, either alone or in combination with similarly situated lands in the region, significantly affect the chemical, physical, and biological integrity of other covered waters more readily understood as "navigable." When, in contrast, wetlands' effects on water quality are speculative or insubstantial, they fall outside the zone fairly encompassed by the statutory term "navigable waters."

> Although the dissent acknowledges that wetlands' ecological functions vis-á-vis other covered waters are the basis for the Corps' regulation of them, *post,* at 2256–2257, it concludes that the ambiguity in the phrase "navigable waters" allows the Corps to construe the statute as reaching all "non-isolated wetlands," just as it construed the Act to reach the wetlands adjacent to navigable-in-fact waters in *Riverside Bayview,* see *post,* at 2257. This, though, seems incorrect. The Corps' theory of jurisdiction in these consolidated cases—adjacency to tributaries, however remote and insubstantial—raises concerns that go beyond the holding of *Riverside Bayview;* and so the Corps' assertion of jurisdiction cannot rest on that case. . . .

In both the consolidated cases before the Court the record contains evidence suggesting the possible existence of a significant nexus according to the principles outlined above. Thus the end result in these cases and many others to be considered by the Corps may be the same as that suggested by the dissent, namely, that the Corps' assertion of jurisdiction is valid. Given, however, that neither the agency nor the reviewing courts properly considered the issue, a remand is appropriate, in my view, for application of the controlling legal standard.

547 U.S. at 779–82. How does Justice Kennedy's "significant nexus" requirement relate to the holdings of the plurality and the dissent? What factors would be relevant in determining the existence of a "significant nexus"? Is Justice Kennedy's position attractive?

6. Roberts' Lament. Chief Justice Roberts, in a concurring opinion not excerpted above, lamented "how readily the situation could have been avoided." 547 U.S. at 758. He suggests that had the Corps passed new regulations following *SWANCC*, clarifying the scope of § 404, there would be less scope for judicial intervention. Why would this be the case?

It is clear that Chief Justice Roberts is dissatisfied with the split 4–1–4 outcome of the case. He noted that, "[l]ower courts and regulated entities will now have to feel their way on a case-by-case basis." *Id.*

7. Agency Response: "Waters of the United States" Rule. In 2015, EPA and the Corps jointly promulgated a final rule defining the "waters of the United States" that are protected under the Clean Water Act. Clean Water Rule: Definition of "Waters of the United States," 80 Fed. Reg. 37,053, 37,054 (2015). The agencies' final rule was significantly informed by Justice Kennedy's concurrence in *Rapanos*, which outlined a "significant nexus" standard; recall, "a water or wetland must possess a 'significant nexus' to waters that are or were navigable in fact or that could reasonably be made so." *Id.* at 37,056 (citing *Rapanos v. United States*, 547 U.S. 715, 759 (2006)). In effect, the agencies affirmed that, in order to properly protect the navigable waters, interstate waters, and territorial seas that are traditionally covered by the CWA, one must also protect waters that have a "significant nexus" with these waters. *Id.* at 37,057. According to the agencies, identifying the "significant nexus" for given bodies of water involved not only peer-reviewed science, but practical experience with CWA implementation, policy judgement, and legal interpretation. *Id.*

As defined in the 2015 rule, U.S. waters are split into three groups: (i) waters that are always jurisdictional; (ii) waters that are excluded from coverage; and (iii) waters that are subject to a case-by-case analysis. 80 Fed. Reg. at 37,057. Traditional navigable waters, interstate waters (including interstate wetlands), territorial seas, and impoundments of jurisdictional waters are jurisdictional waters, as they were under the old regulatory scheme. *Id.* at 37,058, 37,104; EPA, Clean Water Rule Factsheet, https://19 january2017snapshot.epa.gov/sites/production/files/2015-05/documents/fact _sheet_summary_final_1.pdf (last visited Feb. 19, 2019). In addition, tributaries and "adjacent" waters, as defined in the 2015 final rule, are jurisdictional in all cases because they meet the significant nexus standard. 80 Fed. Reg. at 37,058. The rule also designates several classes of waters that will qualify as CWA covered waters only after a case-by-case significant nexus analysis; these include specific categories, such as "waters within the 100-year floodplain of a traditional navigable water, interstate water, or the territorial seas." *Id.* at 37,058–59. Lastly, certain waters are excluded from the definition of "waters of the United States," including waste treatment systems, converted cropland, and certain ditches with ephemeral or intermittent flow. *Id.* at 37,105. Under this framework, is the plurality test irrelevant?

The 2015 rule defined "significant nexus" to mean a water, including wetlands, that either alone or in combination with other similarly situated waters in the region, significantly affects the chemical, physical, or biological integrity of a primary water. 80 Fed. Reg. at 37,106. Is this definition consistent with Justice Kennedy's concurrence in *Rapanos*?

In support of its position that all tributaries have a significant nexus to traditional navigable waters, interstate waters, or territorial sea, EPA and the Corps relied on the Connectivity Report, a report issued by EPA in 2015 that summarizes the agency's scientific findings on the connections between upland streams, wetlands and water bodies, and traditional navigable waters. EPA, CONNECTIVITY OF STREAMS AND WETLANDS TO DOWNSTREAM WATERS: A REVIEW AND SYNTHESIS OF THE SCIENTIFIC EVIDENCE (Jan. 2015). Critics of the proposed rule complained that it would "place virtually every river, creek, stream, along with vast amounts of neighboring lands, under . . . CWA jurisdiction." Letter from Attorneys General of West Virginia and others, to Gina McCarthy, Administrator of EPA (Oct. 8, 2014). Do you agree with this assertion, or does the significant nexus test impose discernable limits on CWA jurisdiction?

8. Legal Challenges and 2018 "Waters of the United States" Proposed Rule. The final "Waters of the United States" rule was met with objection from a number of groups. Twenty-seven states challenged the rule almost immediately; in October 2015, the Sixth Circuit, hearing a consolidated case from eighteen of the challenging states, ordered a nationwide stay of the rule, pending judicial action on a jurisdictional dispute. *In re EPA*, 803 F.3d 804 (6th Cir. 2015). The Supreme Court later found that the Sixth Circuit did not have jurisdiction over the case, leading to vacatur of the nationwide stay. *Nat'l Ass'n of Mfrs. v. Dep't of Defense*, 138 S. Ct. 617 (2018). Litigation challenging the rule proceeds in multiple district courts across the country. Due to stays issued in some of these courts, as of December 2018, 22 states are subject to the 2015 Clean Water Rule, while the remaining 28 are operating under the previous regulatory definition from 1988. David LaRoss, *CWA Rollback Adopts Narrower New Jurisdiction Test than Current Rules*, INSIDEEPA.COM, Dec. 11, 2018.

In July 2018, EPA and the Corps issued a proposed rule to repeal the Waters of the United States rule, asserting that "the 2015 Rule is not compelled and raises significant legal questions." 83 Fed. Reg. 32,228 (2018). In February 2019, the agencies proposed a new rule to replace the 2015 rule. The proposed rule would create a narrower jurisdictional test than the existing "significant nexus" standard, by limiting CWA jurisdiction over tributaries and wetlands to features that contribute flow to navigable waterways in "a typical year." The proposal is intended to establish "categorical bright lines that provide clarity and predictability" by defining "waters of the United States" to include the following: "traditional navigable waters, including the territorial seas; tributaries of such waters; certain ditches; certain lakes and ponds; impoundments of otherwise jurisdictional waters; and wetlands adjacent to other jurisdictional waters." Proposed Rule: Revised Definition of "Waters of the United States," 81 Fed. Reg. 4,154, 4,170 (2019). The agencies propose to eliminate the case-by-case application of Justice Kennedy's significant nexus test. *Id.*

The proposed rule would impose new requirements for several of these categories; for example, tributaries, lakes, and ponds must contribute perennial or intermittent flow to a traditional navigable water or territorial sea "in a typical year" in order to be jurisdictional; ephemeral features (defined as "surface water flowing or pooling only in direct response to precipitation") would not qualify under the proposal. *Id.* at 72, 105, 188. The proposed rule also details what are not "waters of the United States," such as features that only contain water during or in response to rainfall (*e.g.*, ephemeral features); groundwater; many ditches, including most roadside or farm ditches; prior converted cropland; stormwater control features; and waste treatment systems. *Id.* at 133.

How are tributaries treated differently in the 2019 proposed rule as compared to the 2015 rule? Is the proposed rule consistent with the plurality opinion in *Rapanos*? Is it consistent with the purpose of the CWA?

9.   Legislative Amendment of § 404. In *Sackett v. EPA*, 566 U.S. 120 (2012), Justice Alito stated:

> Real relief requires Congress to do what it should have done in the first place: provide a reasonably clear rule regarding the reach of the Clean Water Act. When Congress passed the Clean Water Act in 1972, it provided that the Act covers "the waters of the United States." But Congress did not define what it meant by "the waters of the United States"; the phrase was not a term of art with a known meaning; and the words themselves are hopelessly indeterminate. Unsurprisingly, the EPA and the Army Corps of Engineers interpreted the phrase as an essentially limitless grant of authority. We rejected that boundless view, but the precise reach of the Act remains unclear. For 40 years, Congress has done nothing to resolve this critical ambiguity, and the EPA has not seen fit to promulgate a rule providing a clear and sufficiently limited definition of the phrase. Instead, the agency has relied on informal guidance. But far from providing clarity and predictability, the agency's [2011] guidance advises property owners that many jurisdictional determinations concerning wetlands can only be made on a case-by-case basis by EPA field staff. Allowing aggrieved property owners to [seek judicial review of orders declaring certain waters to be "waters of the United States"] is better than nothing,

but only clarification of the reach of the Clean Water Act can rectify the underlying problem.

At 133. Could Congress resolve the lack of certainty as to what constitutes "waters of the United States"?

10. Implications Beyond § 404. Recall that the term navigable waters is equally determinative in defining EPA's jurisdiction under the § 402 NPDES permit program. Pursuant to § 301(a), permits under that program are required only in circumstances where there has been a "discharge of a pollutant." The term "discharge of a pollutant," in turn, is defined in § 502(12) to mean "any addition of any pollutant to *navigable waters* from any point source. . . ." 33 U.S.C. § 1362(12) (emphasis added). By adopting a limited interpretation of the term "navigable waters" for the purposes of § 404, could it be that the *Rapanos* Court has inadvertently curtailed the operation of the § 402 program? Justice Scalia, in a section of the plurality's opinion not excerpted above, suggests that this will not be the case:

> . . . there is no reason to suppose that our construction today significantly affects the enforcement of § 1342, inasmuch as lower courts applying § 1342 have not characterized intermittent channels as "waters of the United States." The Act does not forbid the "addition of any pollutant *directly* to navigable waters from any point source," but rather the "addition of any pollutant *to* navigable waters." § 1362(12)(A) (emphasis added); § 1311(a). Thus, from the time of the CWA's enactment, lower courts have held that the discharge into intermittent channels of any pollutant *that naturally washes downstream* likely violates § 1311(a), even if the pollutants discharged from a point source do not emit "directly into" covered waters, but pass "through conveyances" in between. . . .

> In contrast to the pollutants normally covered by the permitting requirement of § 1342(a), "dredged or fill material," which is typically deposited for the sole purpose of staying put, does not normally wash downstream, and thus does not normally constitute an "addition . . . to navigable waters" when deposited in upstream isolated wetlands. §§ 1344(a), 1362(12). The Act recognizes this distinction by providing a separate permitting program for such discharges in § 1344(a). It does not appear, therefore, that the interpretation we adopt today significantly reduces the scope of § 1342 of the Act.

547 U.S. at 743. How convincing do you find Justice Scalia's suggestion that the *Rapanos* decision would not have a significant impact on the NPDES program? Might it have some effect?

Consider the following retort contained in the dissent (not excerpted above):

> . . . EPA's authority over pollutants (other than dredged and fill materials) stems from the identical statutory language that gives rise to the Corps' § 404 jurisdiction. The plurality claims that there is a practical difference, asserting that dredged and fill material "does not normally wash downstream." Ante, at 2228. While more

of this material will probably stay put than is true of soluble pollutants, the very existence of words like "alluvium" and "silt" in our language, see Webster's Third 59, 2119, suggests that at least some fill makes its way downstream. *See also, e.g., United States v. Deaton*, 332 F.3d 698, 707 (C.A.4 2003) ("Any pollutant or fill material that degrades water quality in a tributary has the potential to move downstream and degrade the quality of the navigable waters themselves"). Moreover, such fill can harm the biological integrity of downstream waters even if it largely stays put upstream. The Act's purpose of protecting fish, see 33 U.S.C. § 1251(a)(2); *S.D. Warren Co.*, 547 U.S. at 374–76, could be seriously impaired by sediment in upstream waters where fish spawn, since excessive sediment can "smother bottom-dwelling invertebrates and impair fish spawning," OTA 48.

Id. at 806–07.

In *Upstate Forever v. Kinder Morgan Energy Partners*, the Fourth Circuit considered whether the Clean Water Act requires a discharge directly from a point source into navigable waters in order for the discharge to constitute a violation of the CWA. 887 F.3d 637 (4th Cir. 2018). The Court answered in the negative, holding that the Act does *not* require a discharge directly from a point source into navigable waters in order for the discharge to constitute a violation. The Court further held that a plaintiff must allege a direct hydrological connection between ground water and navigable waters in order to state a claim under the Clean Water Act for a discharge of a pollutant that passes through ground water; it found that plaintiffs had done so in the case before it. *Id.* at 649–50.

11. Triggering § 404: Discharge of Dredged and Fill Material. In addition to controversy surrounding the scope of the Corps § 404(a) jurisdiction, there often arise disputes concerning whether a particular action triggers § 404 and, more particularly, whether an action constitutes the "discharge" of "dredged or fill" materials for the purposes of § 404. In *Save Our Community v. EPA,* 971 F.2d 1155 (5th Cir. 1992), for instance, the Fifth Circuit found that the drainage of a wetland did not require a § 404 permit, because it did not involve the "discharge" of any material into the wetland. For the most part, however, the term "discharge" has been interpreted broadly by the Corps and by the Courts. In *Avoyelles Sportsmen's League v. Marsh*, 715 F.2d 897 (5th Cir. 1983), for instance, the Fifth Circuit held that land-clearing activities that resulted in the substantial redeposit of wetland material constituted a "discharge" of dredged material. Similarly, in *United States v. Deaton*, 209 F.3d 331 (4th Cir. 2000), the Fourth Circuit held that the process of sidecasting fill material into wetlands, in the course of excavation, constituted a "discharge" for the purpose of § 404.

12. Statutory Exemptions. The scope of the § 404 permit program is also limited by § 404(f) of the CWA, which exempts releases of dredged or fill material:

(A) from normal farming, silviculture, and ranching activities such as plowing, seeding, cultivating, minor drainage, harvesting for the production of food, fiber, and forest products, or upland soil and water conservation practices;

(B) for the purpose of maintenance, including emergency reconstruction of recently damaged parts, of currently serviceable structures such as dikes, dams, levees, groins, riprap, breakwaters, causeways, and bridge abutments or approaches, and transportation structures;

(C) for the purpose of construction or maintenance of farm or stock ponds or irrigation ditches, or the maintenance of drainage ditches;

(D) for the purpose of construction of temporary sedimentation basins on a construction site which does not include placement of fill material into the navigable waters;

(E) for the purpose of construction or maintenance of farm roads or forest roads, or temporary roads for moving mining equipment, where such roads are constructed and maintained, in accordance with best management practices, to assure that flow and circulation patterns and chemical and biological characteristics of the navigable waters are not impaired, that the reach of the navigable waters is not reduced, and that any adverse effect on the aquatic environment will be otherwise minimized; . . .

33 U.S.C. § 1344(f)(1). The scope of the § 404(f)(1)(A) "normal farming" exemption was considered by the Ninth Circuit in *Borden Ranch Partnership v. U.S. Army Corps of Engineers*, 261 F.3d 810 (9th Cir. 2001). In that case, a property developer sought to establish a vineyard on agricultural land (containing a wetland) previously used for the purposes of rangeland and cattle grazing. This required a procedure known as "deep ripping," in which four- to seven-foot long metal prongs were dragged through the soil behind a tractor, disgorging soil that was then dragged behind the ripper. The developer failed to obtain a § 404 permit authorizing these works. He argued, however, that his actions fell within the § 404(f)(1)(A) "normal farming" exemption. In dismissing this argument, that court held that:

Converting ranch land to orchards and vineyards is clearly bringing the land "into a use to which it was not previously subject," and there is a clear basis in this record to conclude that the destruction of the soil layer at issue here constitutes an impairment of the flow of nearby navigable waters.

Although the Corps cannot regulate a farmer who desires "merely to change from one wetland crop to another," activities that require "substantial hydrological alterations" require a permit. *United States v. Akers*, 785 F.2d 814, 820 (9th Cir. 1986). As we have explained, "the intent of Congress in enacting the Act was to prevent conversion of wetlands to dry lands," and we have classified "as non-exempt those activities which change a wetland's hydrological regime." *Akers*, 785 F.2d at 822. In this case, [the developer's] activities were not intended simply to substitute one wetland crop for another; rather they radically altered the hydrological regime of the protected wetlands. Accordingly, it was entirely proper for the Corps and EPA to exercise jurisdiction over [the developer's] activities.

Id. at 815–16.

B. OPERATION OF THE CWA WETLANDS REGIME

EPA has promulgated guidelines under § 404(b)(1) of the CWA that the Corps must follow in administering the § 404(a) permit program. These guidelines provide that a permit may not be issued with respect to a proposed discharge: (a) "if there is a practicable alternative to the proposed discharge which would have less adverse impact on the aquatic ecosystem, so long as the alternative does not have other significant adverse environmental consequences"; (b) if it "[c]auses or contributes. . .to violations of any applicable State water quality standard"; (c) if it would "cause or contribute to significant degradation of the waters of the United States"; or (d) "unless appropriate and practicable steps have been taken which will minimize potential adverse impacts of the discharge on the aquatic ecosystem." 40 C.F.R. § 230.10(a)–(d).

In addition to these four criteria, the guidelines retain in the Corps the discretion to deny any permit application that it deems to be "contrary to the public interest." 33 C.F.R. § 320.4(a). In determining what constitutes the public interest in any given case, the guidelines "require[ ] a careful weighing of all those factors which become relevant in each particular case," which may entail consideration of issues as diverse as

> conservation, economics, aesthetics, general environmental concerns, wetlands, historic properties, fish and wildlife values, flood hazards, floodplain values, land use, navigation, shore erosion and accretion, recreation, water supply and conservation, water quality, energy needs, safety, food and fiber production, mineral needs, considerations of property ownership and, in general, the needs and welfare of the people.

Id.

The following cases examine those elements of the § 404 permitting process that are most frequently the subject of challenge. The first, *Hoosier Environmental Council, Inc. v. U.S. Army Corps of Engineers*, 105 F. Supp. 2d 953 (S.D. Ind. 2000), concerns a challenge to the Corps' balancing of the § 320.4(a) factors. The second, *Greater Yellowstone Coalition v. Flowers*, 359 F.3d 1257 (10th Cir. 2004), concerns a challenge to the adequacy of the Corps alternatives analysis pursuant to § 230.10(a).

Hoosier Environmental Council, Inc. v. United States Army Corps of Engineers

105 F. Supp. 2d 953 (S.D. Ind. 2000).

■ McKINNEY, DISTRICT JUDGE:

[On 10 February, 1998, the Corps issued a permit to RDI/Caesars Riverboat Casino, L.L.C. (Caesars), pursuant to § 404 of the CWA. The permit authorized the placement of fill material in the Ohio River (in Harrison County, Indiana) so as to facilitate the development of a permanent mooring facility required to service a riverboat casino. Opponents of the casino challenged the proposal on a number of grounds, including a challenge to the adequacy of the Corps public interest review pursuant to 33 C.F.R. § 320.4(a).] . . .

When any environmental impacts of a project such as the riverboat casino have been identified, the [Corps is] obligated to also conduct a public interest review before issuing a permit. 33 C.F.R. § 320.4(a); *Van Abbema,* 807 F.2d at 638. The process of collecting comments from the public and from other agencies and experts, holding public hearings, conducting interagency meetings, and reviewing all of the relevant materials forms the basis for the [Corps'] public interest review of a proposed action. Specifically, the regulations provide that:

> All factors *which may be relevant to the proposal* must be considered including the cumulative effects thereof: among those are conservation, economics, aesthetics, general environmental concerns, wetlands, historic properties, fish and wildlife values, flood hazards, floodplain values, land use, navigation, shore erosion and accretion, recreation, water supply and conservation, water quality, energy needs, safety, food and fiber production, mineral needs, considerations of property ownership and, in general, the needs and welfare of the people.

33 C.F.R. § 320.4(a)(1) (emphasis added). This review calls for a balancing of negative and positive impacts of the proposed project in light of the public interest. The agency is in the best position to determine which impacts are relevant to performing the balance, *Kleppe,* 427 U.S. at 414, but the court is expected to review the agency's determination for an abuse of discretion. *Marita,* 46 F.3d at 619 (citing *Citizens to Preserve Overton Park, Inc. v. Volpe,* 401 U.S. 402, 416 (1971)).

Even though a court is required to conduct a searching and thorough review of the agency's exercise of discretion, it is not allowed to substitute its own judgment for that of the agency. *Marita,* 46 F.3d at 619. Instead, the court is charged with assessing whether the agency "relied on factors which Congress has not intended it to consider, entirely failed to consider an important aspect of the problem, [or] offered an explanation for its decision that runs counter to the evidence before the agency, or is so implausible that it could not be ascribed to a difference in view or the product of agency expertise." *Id.* (citing *Motor Veh. Mfrs. Assoc. v. State Farm Mut. Auto. Ins. Co.,* 463 U.S. 29, 43 (1983)). Given that the Court's review here occurs in the context of a challenge to agency action under the APA, the plaintiffs, Hoosier, POW and PORE, bear the burden of proving that the agency made any of these mistakes in conducting its review of the permit application. *Id.*; *see also Holmes v. Department of Veterans Aff.,* 58 F.3d 628, 632 (Fed.Cir.1995); *Sierra Club v. United States Army Corps of Eng.,* 935 F.Supp. 1556, 1565 (S.D.Ala.1996) (a logical corollary of the APA's deferential standard of review and the "presumption of regularity" that attaches to agency decisions is that a party challenging agency action must bear the burden of establishing the agency acted in an arbitrary or capricious manner).

The [Corps] must balance the impacts in light of the twenty enumerated factors in the regulations listed above. The specific weight to be given any one factor depends on its "importance and relevance to the particular proposal," as determined by the District Engineer. *Id.* In determining the relative weight to be assigned the factors, the District Engineer is to give "full consideration and appropriate weight" to "all comments, including those of federal, state, and local agencies, and other experts on matters within their expertise." 33 C.F.R. § 320.4(a)(3). The balancing of all these factors enables the [Corps] to decide whether to issue a permit, and what conditions should be attached to it. 33 C.F.R. § 320.4(a). . . .

. . . The plaintiffs argue that the public interest review failed to consider the socio-economic costs of gambling. Those costs, they assert, include the impacts of compulsive gambling, alcohol consumption, crime, and other social issues related to gambling. Noting that the District Engineer specifically declined to discuss the relative desirability of gambling, the plaintiffs argue that he ignored the projects' social impacts.

The Court cannot agree. The relative value of legalized gambling to the citizens of Indiana has been decided by the General Assembly, and the citizens of Harrison County, who voted in favor of a riverboat gambling casino in their county. As the [Corps] has noted, the primary responsibility for deciding land use issues lies with the state and local governments, unless there are significant issues of overriding national concern. No such issues were identified for the District Engineer or this Court. On the contrary, the materials designated by the plaintiffs as proof of the socioeconomic cost of gambling serve instead to demonstrate a lack of consensus among experts as to the relative effect of gambling on society and the economy. It is not the task of the [Corps], however, to resolve disagreements among experts. *Marsh,* 490 U.S. at 378. Rather, the [Corps] must be informed about the disputes and give whatever weight to this factor that he deems warranted. *Id.* The Court's job is to determine if the District Engineer's decision about this factor is arbitrary or capricious, not whether it is wrong. *Id.* It is not the job of the Court to second-guess the District Engineer's decisions. *Simmons,* 120 F.3d at

669; *Van Abbema*, 807 F.2d at 636. Moreover, the mere existence of a dispute or controversy about a factor does not mean that the [Corps] reached a decision that is arbitrary or capricious. None of the materials cited by the plaintiff suffice to render the [Corps'] reliance on the expertise and decisions of the Indiana General Assembly, the [Indiana Gaming Commission (IGC)] and the citizens of Harrison County arbitrary and capricious with respect to gambling. . . .

[T]he plaintiffs [also] assert that the [Corps] failed to undertake any meaningful consideration of the economic impacts of the proposal, relying instead on the fact that a business is presumed to have determined that a proposed project would be economically viable. *See* 33 C.F.R. § 320.4(q). Claiming that the riverboat will have a dramatic and unprecedented economic impact on Southeast Indiana, the plaintiffs accuse the [Corps] of failing to balance that impact with the others. Primarily, they point to a finding in which the District Engineer included "economics" in a list of factors he considered and found that the proposed project would not significantly impact. *See* Findings at 59. When considered in the context of the entire section, however, the reference to economics appears to imply that he found no significant adverse impacts to economics. This reading is consistent with the District Engineer's specific finding elsewhere that "economic benefits would accrue from" the Caesars' project in Harrison County. No amount of emphasis on the positioning of economics in that listing would convince this Court that the [Corps] failed to consider, much less balance, the economic impacts of the project.

As the [Corps] has noted, the record contains sufficient evidence, which the District Engineer is presumed to have considered, showing economic benefits from the proposed project. *See Motor Veh. Mfrs. Assoc.,* 463 U.S. at 44, 103 (noting presumption of regularity afforded agency that is fulfilling its statutory mandate); *Akiak Native Comm.,* 213 F.3d 1140 (same). The Center for Urban Policy at Indiana University documented the fiscal benefits expected to flow to the county if the Caesars project were constructed. AR Vol. VIII, Tab 65, Sec. IV, p. 44. This study was performed for the IGC prior to its issuance of a Certificate of Suitability to Caesars. In addition, Harrison County commissioned a task force to study, among other things, the potential economic benefits of riverboat gambling to the county. AR Vol. VIII, Tab 65, Att. "Harrison County Riverboat Casino Task Force Report." It documented the contributions such a casino would be expected to make to the county and its citizens. *Id.* at 7 (Economic Impact). Finally, the IGC selected the Caesars' project from among four competing riverboat gaming proposals for Harrison County to be awarded a Certificate of Suitability. Such a certificate communicates a finding that the Caesars project is expected to offer the most economic development in its home dock area and best serve the interests of the citizens of Indiana.

The process used by the IGC for selecting an applicant to be awarded a Certificate is intended to achieve this result. Specifically, the IGC is required to perform a "background investigation, including economic development analysis of the applicant. . . ." Ind. Admin. Code, tit. 68, r. 2–1–5(a)(2) (2000). After the background check, the IGC must conduct a public hearing, at which the IGC and members of the public may "question the applicant on any aspect of its application and presentation." *Id.* 2–1–5(b). During the course of its presentation, the applicant "must present evidence that it meets or possesses" certain designated standards, qualifications or criteria. *Id.* 2–1–5(c). Those include the qualifications set forth in the Indiana gaming law, possession of a "high level of skill, experience, or knowledge necessary to conduct a riverboat gambling operation," and proof of the "positive economic impact that the applicant's plan will have on the entire state of Indiana." *Id.* The first step an applicant usually takes after obtaining a Certificate of Suitability is to apply for a permit to develop its riverboat operation from the [Corps]. *Id.* 2–1–5(e). That is precisely what Caesars did. Given the obvious goals of the process for determining a Certificate of Suitability, the [Corps] cannot be said to have acted arbitrarily or to have abused its discretion by considering this Certificate when determining the economic impact of the proposed project.

. . . The plaintiffs have not succeeded in proving to the Court that the [Corps'] decision to issue a permit to Caesars was uninformed, despite their extensive efforts to show that it was unwise.

NOTES AND QUESTIONS

1.   **Public Interest Review.** Section 320.4(a) of the guidelines specifies no less than 20 factors to be considered by the Corps, as appropriate, in conducting assessments of public interest. How does the *Hoosier* court propose that the Corps go about weighing these various factors? How do the guidelines propose the Corps should determine "the relative weight to be assigned the factors"? Does the standard amount to a cost-benefit analysis? Could the Corps grant a permit in circumstances when the costs of the proposal outweighed the benefits?

2.   **Socio-Economic Considerations.** On what basis did the plaintiffs challenge the Corps's consideration of the socio-economic costs of gambling? What specific socio-economic costs did the plaintiffs claim the Corps had failed to take into account? Why did the Corps find that the permit would not be contrary to the public interest? On what basis did the *Hoosier* court uphold this determination?

3.   **Economic Considerations.** On what basis did the plaintiffs claim the Corps had failed to undertake any meaningful consideration of the economic impacts of the proposal? Upon what evidence did the Corps rely in making its determination with respect to economic impact? To what extent did the Corps conduct any independent analysis into the sufficiency of this data? Do you consider this to be adequate?

4.   **Scope of § 320.4(a) Review.** In the context of their determination under § 320.4(a), why was the Corps required to consider the economic and

socio-economic costs of the Riverboat Casino at all, when the permission granted under § 404 of the CWA related only to the construction of the permanent mooring facility?

Greater Yellowstone Coalition v. Flowers

359 F.3d 1257 (10th Cir. 2004).

■ Before EBEL, ANDERSON, and MURPHY, CIRCUIT JUDGES.

■ ANDERSON, CIRCUIT JUDGE:

In this case we consider . . . challenges to a CWA § 404 "dredge and fill" permit, issued by the [Corps] to Canyon Club, Inc. (Canyon Club), a development company. The permit authorizes Canyon Club to proceed with constructing an upscale housing development and championship golf course on ranch land previously owned by Mr. L. Richard Edgcomb, Canyon Club's president and primary shareholder. The land lies along the Snake River in Teton County, Wyoming, in the vicinity of highly productive bald eagle nesting territory.

Two environmental groups, the Greater Yellowstone Coalition and the Jackson Hole Conservation Alliance (collectively referred to as the appellants), brought this suit against Corps officials (collectively referred to as the federal appellees) and Canyon Club, challenging the Corps' issuance of the permit as a final agency action and seeking a preliminary injunction on construction activities. . . .

In this appeal, the appellants ask us to set aside the permit because, they argue [among other things that] the Corps' consideration of alternatives to Canyon Club's proposal did not meet the requirements of . . . the CWA. . . .

The 359-acre Canyon Club development property lies seventeen miles south of Jackson, Wyoming, in the Snake River Canyon, across the river from U.S. Highway 26/89. The property is part of a "1,222-acre conglomerate of private land" that includes a 544-acre segment of the River Bend Ranch on the Canyon Club property's north side, the 195-acre Snake River Canyon Ranch to the north of that, and a 125-acre segment of the River Bend Ranch to the south, on the other side of a strip of National Forest land. Appellants' App. Vol. 3 at 419. Together, these properties "represent the largest private land-development opportunity in the upper portion of the Snake River Canyon." *Id.*

While upstream levees have negatively impacted the Snake River's riparian habitat closer to Jackson, the area surrounding the Canyon Club property "currently supports an intact and healthy riparian ecosystem" that includes important wintering, foraging, and nesting habitat for bald eagles. *Id.* Vol. 1 at 35. Three bald eagle nesting territories lie on or in the immediate vicinity of the Canyon Club property. Two of these—the Dog Creek and the Cabin Creek territories—have been highly productive, together yielding at least fifty-six fledglings since the bald eagle's 1978 listing as "endangered" under the Endangered Species Act (ESA), 16 U.S.C. §§ 1531–44. The pair occupying the third territory—Martin Creek—have produced fledglings only once since constructing their nest in 1995. The area's habitat also supports moose, elk, mule deer, black bears, mountain lions, trumpeter swans, and Snake River cutthroat trout, among other species. . . .

In the course of its decisionmaking process, the Corps asked Canyon Club to submit three documents—a biological assessment (BA), an environmental assessment (EA), and a § 404(b)(1) analysis. All three documents were prepared by Pioneer Environmental Services, Inc., an environmental consulting firm.

[The BA concluded that the project "may affect, and is likely to adversely affect bald eagles." As a consequence, the Corps sought the advice of the FWS pursuant to § 7 of the ESA. FWS issued a biological opinion (BiOp) which concluded that the proposed development "[was] not likely to jeopardize the continued existence of the bald eagle" as a species, even if up to three breeding pairs were lost. Attached to the BiOp was FWS's incidental take statement, indicating that FWS "anticipate[d] the loss of 3 bald eagle nesting territories . . . as a result of the proposed action." The incidental take statement allowed the Corps to issue a § 404 permit authorizing the project without violating the ESA, provided that the Corps ensured Canyon Club's compliance with a number of terms and conditions. These included the requirements that construction activities be completed within two years, that construction be regulated so that no activity would take place within 400 meters of a nest containing eagle chicks less than three weeks old, and that the effects of the project on the eagle nests be closely monitored by qualified biologists, both during construction and for five years after its completion.]

. . . [O]n June 14, 2002, the Corps issued its decision granting the § 404 permit. The decision document was also designated as constituting the Corps' environmental assessment, statement of findings, public interest review, and NEPA compliance determination, and incorporated the Pioneer § 404(b)(1) analysis, EA, and BA, attaching these as appendices.

The decision document stated its agreement with the Pioneer § 404(b)(1) analysis' conclusion that the proposed action "is the least damaging practicable on-site alternative." Appellants' App. Vol. 2 at 224. The Pioneer § 404(b)(1) analysis had noted that its determination of what was "practicable" took into account limitations imposed by golf course design requirements, Teton County [Land Development Regulations (LDRs)], and the project's stated purpose, which included the preservation of River Bend Ranch. It then described five alternatives, including a no-action alternative, a nine-hole golf course, [a proposal covering 286-acres (originally submitted to the Corps)], [a modified 286 acre proposal], and the current 359-acre proposal. The analysis concluded that the no-action alternative would have a greater environmental impact than the proposed action because it would likely lead to the sale of the entire River Bend Ranch to Canyon Club and the construction of a 250-house residential development on the property. The analysis determined that the nine-hole golf course alternative was impracticable because the resulting reduced value of the associated residences and the lower demand for such a golf course would not cover golf course operation expenses or provide the required financial support to River Bend Ranch. The 286-acre alternatives were also deemed impracticable because they did not comply with Teton County LDRs. The analysis concluded that the proposed action "is the least damaging practicable alternative that satisfies the project purpose." *Id.* at 322.

The Corps had also conducted an independent analysis of whether other real estate sites in Teton County were practicable alternative sites for the project. The Corps found only two properties on the market that could support such a project and determined that locating the project at these locations would have a similar impact on wetlands while entailing a much higher cost than the proposed action. The Corps concluded that the proposed action "is the least environmentally damaging practicable alternative available." *Id.* at 225. . . .

. . . In granting the § 404 permit, the Corps established certain mandatory conditions and, in particular, noted that the permit authorization was conditional upon Canyon Club's compliance with the terms and conditions imposed by FWS's incidental take statement. . . .

We review the Corps' compliance with . . . the CWA pursuant to the Administrative Procedure Act, 5 U.S.C. §§ 701–06, which "empowers a reviewing court to hold unlawful and set aside [final] agency action, findings, and conclusions found to be arbitrary, capricious, an abuse of discretion, or otherwise not in accordance with law." *Utahns for Better Transp. v. U.S. Dep't of Transp.*, 305 F.3d 1152, 1164 (10th Cir.2002), *modified on reh'g*, 319 F.3d 1207 (10th Cir.2003). In considering whether to overturn the Corps' decision to issue the § 404 permit, we apply the same deferential standard to the administrative record as did the district court; the Corps' determinations "may be set aside only for substantial procedural or substantive reasons." *Id.* . . .

CWA § 404, 33 U.S.C. § 1344, prohibits dredging or filling waters of the United States, including wetlands, without a permit from the Corps authorizing the dredge or fill activity. 33 U.S.C. § 1344(a), (d). The Corps may not issue a § 404(b)(1) permit "if there is a practicable alternative to the proposed discharge which would have less adverse impact on the aquatic ecosystem," unless the alternative has "other significant adverse environmental consequences." 40 C.F.R. § 230.10(a). A "practicable" alternative is one that is "available and capable of being done after taking into consideration cost, existing technology, and logistics in light of overall project purposes." *Id.* § 230.10(a)(2).

The Corps' burden in finding the least damaging practicable alternative under the CWA guidelines is heaviest for non-water dependent projects planned for a "special aquatic site," such as a wetlands area. *See Holy Cross Wilderness Fund v. Madigan*, 960 F.2d 1515, 1524 (10th Cir. 1992). There, the presumption is that there are "practicable alternatives that do not involve special aquatic sites" and that these alternatives do "have less adverse impact on the aquatic ecosystem." 40 C.F.R. § 230.10(a)(3). These presumptions hold unless "clearly demonstrated otherwise." *Id.* We have thus held that in such a case, the Corps may not issue a § 404 permit unless the applicant, "with independent verification by the [Corps], . . . provide[s] detailed, clear and convincing information *proving*" that an alternative with less adverse impact is "impracticable." *Utahns for Better Transp.*, 305 F.3d at 1186–87 (requiring denial of a permit "where insufficient information is provided to determine compliance"); *see also Greater Yellowstone I*, 321 F.3d at 1262 n. 12 ("[U]nder the CWA, it is not sufficient for the Corps to consider a range of alternatives to the proposed project: the Corps must rebut the presumption that there are practicable alternatives with less adverse environmental impact.").

Citing *Utahns for Better Transportation*, the appellants argue that the Corps violated 40 C.F.R. § 230.10 by "fail[ing] to require 'detailed, clear and convincing information' proving that there was no practicable alternative to the Canyon Club developer's proposal" and "ignor[ing] obvious alternatives with fewer adverse impacts on the 'aquatic ecosystem.' " Appellants' Br. at 27. Specifically, the appellants contend that the Corps failed to consider whether the Canyon Club property could be expanded so that certain features of the golf course and housing development could be relocated to the north, on what until now has remained part of the River Bend Ranch, "so as to avoid dredging and filling jurisdictional wetlands, constructing weirs in the Snake River, and related impacts to bald eagles." *Id.* at 28. The appellants also suggest the Corps should have considered whether wetland and bald eagle impacts could have been reduced by decreasing the number of home sites in the planned housing development.

The appellees respond that the Corps need not have considered these alternatives because, first, they do not serve the project's purpose of preserving the River Bend Ranch as an operating ranch, and second, the Corps' analysis reflects an adequate level of effort and documentation in light of the proposal's expected impact. We uphold the Corps' § 404(b)(1) alternatives analysis on the latter basis.

We first recognize that the Corps, in determining whether to issue a § 404 permit, " 'has a duty to take into account the objectives of the applicant's project,' " *Sylvester v. U.S. Army Corps of Eng'rs*, 882 F.2d 407, 409 (9th Cir. 1989) (quoting *La. Wildlife Fed'n, Inc. v. York*, 761 F.2d 1044, 1048 (5th Cir. 1985) (per curiam)), as long as this objective is " 'legitimate,' " *id.* (quoting *Friends of the Earth v. Hintz*, 800 F.2d 822, 833 (9th Cir. 1986)). *See Nat'l Wildlife Fed'n v. Whistler*, 27 F.3d 1341, 1346 (8th Cir. 1994) (noting the Corps should not permit developers to "artificially constrain the Corps' alternatives analysis by defining the projects' purpose in an overly narrow manner"). However, the burden of proving that a given alternative does not meet the applicant's objective remains on the applicant when 40 C.F.R. § 230.10(a)(3) applies, and the applicant's assessment must be critically evaluated by the Corps. . . .

Here, it is true that one of Canyon Club's stated purposes in developing the golf course and housing complex was to "[s]upplement ranching operations on the adjacent River Bend Ranch with income from the Canyon Club in order to continue the working ranch operations." Appellants' App. Vol. 2 at 220. The Pioneer § 404(b)(1) analysis, adopted by the Corps, proceeded to explain that:

> [t]he total amount of acreage available for development by the Canyon Club Development is limited by ownership and availability. Any additional commitment of land to the development would have to be made available by the River Bend Ranch. Any action that reduces the size of the River Bend Ranch to the status of a non-viable ranch operation would trigger the full allowable build-out of all remaining undeveloped property for both the River Bend Ranch and the Canyon Club properties. . . . Therefore, one of the factors for meeting the purpose and need of the project was to optimize the amount of land required for the project without compromising the viability of the remaining undeveloped property as a working ranch.

Id. at 317–18.

This statement implies that there is a limit to the amount of Ranch property that could be used for the Canyon Club development without compromising the Ranch's viability. Yet, none of the alternatives that were considered led Canyon Club or the Corps to examine whether any commitment of Ranch property beyond the 359 acres would exceed this limit, nor does the administrative record contain any evidentiary support for such a conclusion.

Nevertheless, under the circumstances of this case, we do not hold that the Corps' failure to require Canyon Club to prove the impracticability of committing more Ranch property to the development renders its decision arbitrary and capricious. The CWA guidelines instruct the Corps to "recognize the different levels of effort that should be associated with varying degrees of impact and require or prepare commensurate documentation. The level of documentation should reflect the significance and complexity of the discharge activity." 40 C.F.R. § 230.6(b). They further state that "[a]lthough all requirements in § 230.10 must be met, the compliance evaluation procedures will vary to reflect the seriousness of the potential for adverse impacts on the aquatic ecosystems posed by specific dredged or fill material discharge activities." *Id.* § 230.10.

Here, the Corps' level of effort and documentation was in accord with this standard. As required by the CWA guidelines, the Pioneer § 404(b)(1) analysis includes detailed factual determinations on "the nature and degree of effect that the proposed discharge will have . . . on the structure and function of the aquatic ecosystem and organisms," in particular on the "physical, chemical, and biological components of the aquatic environment." 40 C.F.R. § 230.11(e). Overall, while 1.45 acres of wetlands would be eliminated through fill for construction of golf features and home sites, the function and vegetation diversity of remaining jurisdictional wetlands, comprising 32.65 acres, would improve due to the removal of cattle grazing. Additional wetlands would be added as part of the project's mitigation efforts; a Snake River tributary, Martin Creek, would be restored, providing new trout spawning habitat; and the bendway weirs, if installed, were predicted to increase riffle and pool complexes on the Snake River, considered a beneficial effect.

The Corps also concluded that "all of the alternatives [considered] would have similar effects on . . . bald eagles" and that these impacts were not "unacceptable." Appellants' App. Vol. 2 at 227. This conclusion was partly based on the Corps' assessment that the possibility of an "incidental take" of bald eagles was "greatly reduced" by the terms and conditions imposed by FWS on the Canyon Club development. *Id.* As described above, these restrictions would prohibit construction within 400 meters of a nest containing eagle chicks for the first three weeks after hatching and would otherwise require construction work near the Snake River during nesting season to take place only between 9 am and 6 pm in order to reduce impacts on eagle foraging activities. Any bendway weir construction would have to take place outside the nesting season.

Apart from these restrictions, which the Corps legitimately took into account, we understand the Corps' conclusion to reflect its recognition that the primary cause of the predicted adverse impact on eagles— increased human activity resulting from development on the property— was in a large sense unavoidable. The record indicates that the bald eagles and their progeny cannot be fully protected simply by moving all dredge and fill activities more than 400 meters away from all nests. FWS' BiOp states that while the area within 400 meters of an occupied eagle nest is the "most sensitive to human disturbance," the recommended buffer around nests is one mile. Appellants' App. Vol. 4 at 837. The BiOp indicates that all three nesting territories could be negatively impacted by the proposed action, due to "increased recreational activity, increased overall human intrusion, and changes in habitat quality," even though no golf course features or housing lots were planned within 400 meters of the active Cabin Creek nest, and only a portion of one hole would lie within 400 meters of the Dog Creek nest. *Id.* at 847.

The Pioneer § 404(b)(1) analysis similarly states that "[d]evelopment of the Canyon Club property would facilitate activities that could have indirect effects on nesting bald eagles due to disturbance from construction, operation, use of the Canyon Club golf course, and housing development and occupation." *Id.* Vol. 2 at 333. These effects would occur under "any of the action alternatives" and would not be "the direct result of filling within wetlands." *Id.*

Even the "no-action" alternative was predicted to have similar, if not worse, impacts, in light of Canyon Club's clear assertion throughout the permit application process that were the Corps to deny it a § 404 permit, the River Bend Ranch would likely be dismantled, and its remaining property, along with the Canyon Club property, would likely be converted into a residential development containing up to 250 houses. Although these houses would not be constructed on top of wetlands or (under the terms of Teton County LDRs) within 400 meters of bald eagle nests, the human intrusion would at least equal that expected from the Canyon Club 359-acre proposal. Moreover, the 332 acres of conservation easements that are associated with the 359-acre proposal and are intended primarily "to provide secure habitat for bald eagles," *id.* Vol. 4 at 834, would not be established, and other mitigation measures, such as the use restrictions drafted for the Canyon Club Declaration, might also be abandoned.

Thus, even assuming that the appellants' suggested alternatives may incrementally reduce impacts to bald eagles by removing specific features from the 400-meter radius around their nests, the record suggests that these measures would not be significant relative to the impact on eagles of the development as a whole. We therefore hold that the Corps' level of effort and documentation in its CWA alternatives analysis and its conclusion that the 359-acre proposal was the least damaging practicable alternative were not arbitrary or capricious. . . .

NOTES AND QUESTIONS

1.   Practicable Alternative. Pursuant to § 230.10 of the regulations, a practicable alternative is one that is "available and capable of being done after taking into consideration cost, existing technology, and logistics in light of overall project purposes." 40 C.F.R. § 230.10(a)(2). Consider each of the no-action alternative, the nine-hole alternative, the original 286-acre alternative, and the modified 286-acre alternative in turn. On what basis was each dismissed by the Corps? In light of § 230.10, do you think that it would have been possible for the Corps to have reached the opposite conclusion with respect to the practicability of any of these alternatives? Based on the demonstrated approach of the *Greater Yellowstone* court, would the court likely have upheld a decision on these terms?

2.   Rebuttable Presumption. As the *Greater Yellowstone* court notes, "under the CWA, it is not sufficient for the Corps to consider a range of alternatives to the proposed project: the Corps must rebut the presumption that there are practicable alternatives with less adverse environmental impact." 359 F.3d at 1269. How does this compare with the requirement that agencies consider alternatives in performing their assessments under NEPA and the ESA? Would you agree with the conclusion of the *Greater Yellowstone* court that the Corps had done enough to satisfy this burden?

3.   Level of Analysis. How is the Corps to determine at what level of documentation and effort to conduct alternatives analysis under the CWA? If the level is to be defined with reference to the purpose of the project, how can the Corps prevent developers "artificially constrain[ing] the Corps's alternatives analysis by defining the projects' purpose in an overly narrow manner"? 359 F.3d at 1270. In the *Greater Yellowstone* case, how could the purpose of the proposed project be described differently, so that a more detailed alternatives analysis would have been warranted?

4.   Timing of the Alternatives Analysis. Study the language of § 230.10(a)(2) excerpted in Note 1 above. When conducting the alternatives analysis, at what point in time should the availability of practicable alternatives be determined? What are the implications or incentives created by positioning the analysis at different points in time? *See Bersani v. EPA*, 850 F.2d 36 (2d Cir. 1988) (upholding EPA's examination of available alternatives at the time the applicant entered the market for a site instead of at the time it applied for a permit), *cert. denied*, 489 U.S. 1089 (1989).

3.   MANAGEMENT OF NATURAL RESOURCES ON PUBLIC LAND

A.   INTRODUCTION

The first two sections of this chapter have addressed specific regimes designed to safeguard particular natural resources—namely; endangered species and wetlands. The remainder of this chapter is devoted to examining the manner in which each of the main federal land management agencies—the Forest Service, the Bureau of Land Management ("BLM"), the Bureau of Ocean Energy Management ("BOEM") the National Park Service ("NPS"), and the Fish and Wildlife Service ("FWS")—manage natural resources located on public lands. This section provides an overview of several federal land management regimes: national forests, rangelands, onshore and offshore mineral leasing, national parks, national monuments, wilderness, and national wildlife refuges. There is no single federal land policy guiding the management of natural resources on public lands. Several federal land units, such as national forests and BLM lands eligible for mineral leasing, are managed pursuant to a "multiple use" mandate, dictating that these public lands be managed to accommodate a variety of prescribed public uses. Others, such as national parks and national wildlife refuges, can be considered subject to a "dominant use" philosophy, dictating that certain uses be prioritized over other allowable uses. Still others are subject to a single prescribed use, such as wilderness conservation. The different federal land management agencies are also subject to unique federal statutes. However, they share the perpetual challenge of seeking to balance allowable uses, including intense human uses, against resource conservation and environmental protection.

The Forest Service, housed within the U.S. Department of Agriculture, is responsible for managing over 193 million acres of federally owned forests and grasslands, contained within 154 national forests (188 million acres) and 20 national grasslands (4 million acres). *See* Forest Service, National and Regional Areas Summary, Table 1 (2018), https://www.fs.fed.us/land/staff/lar/LAR2018/LARTable01.pdf (last visited Sept. 30, 2018). While these lands are concentrated predominantly in the West, the Forest Service manages more federal land in other parts of the country than all other federal agencies combined (a total of 12 million acres in the East and 13 million acres in the South). *Id.* Pursuant to the Multiple-Use-Sustained-Yield Act, 16 U.S.C. §§ 528–531, the Forest Service is required to manage the resources under its control for "outdoor recreation, range, timber, watershed, and wildlife and fish purposes," in a manner that best meets the needs of the American people. 16 U.S.C. § 528. The Agency's organic statute, the National Forest Management Act of 1976, 16 U.S.C. § 1600 *et seq.*, along with the Renewable Resources Planning Act of 1974, 16 U.S.C. §§ 1601–1610, establish a long-term planning process for the management of the Natural Forest System.

Within the Department of Interior, BLM, formed in 1946 following the consolidation of the General Land Office and the U.S. Grazing Service, operates pursuant to several statutes, including its organic act, the Federal Land Policy Management Act ("FLPMA"). 43 U.S.C. § 1761 *et seq.* BLM is responsible for managing over 245 million onshore surface acres (all of which are located in the West, other than 89 million acres located in Alaska) and 700 million acres of subsurface mineral estate—totaling more than 40 percent of all land managed by the federal government. *See* BLM, About the BLM, https://www.blm.gov/about/data (last visited Feb. 15, 2019). Like the Forest Service, BLM is subject to a multiple use and sustained yield mandate. BLM is responsible for the management of approximately 160 million acres of rangelands under federal control, which are primarily used for livestock grazing. BLM, Livestock Grazing on Public Lands, https://www.blm.gov/programs/natural-resources/rangelands-and-grazing/livestock-grazing (last visited Feb. 15, 2019). The Forest Service administers an additional 96 million acres of rangelands on Forest Service lands. *See* Forest Service, Rangeland Management, https://www.fs.fed.us/rangeland-management/aboutus/index.shtml (last visited Feb. 15, 2019).

BLM also manages onshore mineral resources, including the leasing of public lands to private developers for coal, oil, and natural gas extraction, subject to the requirements of FLPMA, the Mineral Leasing Act of 1920, and additional federal laws and regulations. While not covered in depth in this book, BLM is also responsible for hard rock mining, as well as managing renewable resources, including geothermal energy, solar, and wind resources on public lands.

A different bureau within Interior, BOEM, oversees more than 1.7 billion acres offshore in the waters of the U.S. Outer Continental Shelf. BOEM manages offshore lands pursuant to the requirements of the Outer Continental Shelf Lands Act ("OCSLA"), 43 U.S.C. § 1331 *et seq.*, which sets forth procedural and substantive requirements for offshore oil and natural gas leasing.

After addressing national forests, rangelands, and onshore and offshore mineral leasing, this section will next describe four categories of protected lands: national parks, national monuments, wilderness, and national wildlife refuges.

NPS, created in 1916, is the bureau of Interior responsible for the management of the 417 units that comprise the National Park System, including national parks, national monuments and historic sites, and national recreation areas. NPS, National Park System, https://www.nps.gov/aboutus/national-park-system.htm (last visited Sept. 14, 2018). Unlike the Forest Service and BLM, NPS does not operate pursuant to a multiple-use sustainable yield mandate. Instead, it is responsible for managing the 84 million acre National Park System so as to "to conserve the scenery, natural and historic objects, and wild life in the System units and to provide for the enjoyment of the scenery, natural and historic objects, and wild life in such manner and by such means as will leave them unimpaired for the enjoyment of future generations." 54 U.S.C.A. § 100101(a) (formerly cited as 16 U.S.C. § 1). The inherent tension between these competing objectives is explored in the subsection below on national parks.

NPS also manages the vast majority of the national monuments on public lands. National monuments are areas of federal land set aside by the President, under authority of the Antiquities Act of 1906, to protect prominent or important features of the national landscape. *See* 54 U.S.C. § 320301 (formerly cited as 16 U.S.C. § 431). Sixteen Presidents have declared 157 national monuments totaling more than 800 million acres. *See* CAROL HARDY VINCENT & LAURA A. HANSON, CONG. RESEARCH SERV., EXECUTIVE ORDER FOR REVIEW OF NATIONAL MONUMENTS: BACKGROUND AND DATA 1 (2017).

The Wilderness Act of 1964 established the National Wilderness Preservation System, composed of federally owned areas designated by Congress as "wilderness areas," and directed that these areas "be administered for the use and enjoyment of the American people in such manner as will leave them unimpaired for future use and enjoyment as wilderness." 16 U.S.C. § 1131(a). Wilderness areas are managed by four federal agencies: the Forest Service, BLM, NPS, and FWS.

Finally, the FWS, in addition to administering the ESA and some wilderness lands, is the bureau of Interior charged with managing the

National Wildlife Refuge System ("NWRS")—a network of over 494 wildlife refuges dedicated primarily to the conservation of animals and plants. While NWRS refuges are contained in 50 states, the vast majority of the land under FWS control is located in Alaska. FWS, NATIONAL WILDLIFE REFUGE SYSTEM, 2017 ANNUAL LANDS REPORT (2017). The Agency's organic statute (the National Wildlife Refuge System Improvement Act, 16 U.S.C. §§ 668dd–668ee), provides that conservation goals dominate the Service's management mandate. The FWS is entitled, however, to issue a permit allowing any use within a refuge area, provided that the proposed use is compatible with the major purposes for which the refuge was established.

In reading the sections below, consider how the different agencies go about striking a balance between the competing demands upon the natural resources under their control. Consider the agencies' distinct planning regimes, and whether the agencies are equally well suited to addressing modern challenges such as climate change. Further, consider whether the agencies and other relevant actors—including Congress, the President, relevant industries, and the general public—have appropriate incentives and opportunities to help achieve an optimal allocation of the nation's natural resources.

NOTES AND QUESTIONS

1. Why the Need for Public Lands? The federal government presently owns approximately 28 percent of all land within the United States *See* GEORGE C. COGGINS ET AL., FEDERAL PUBLIC LAND AND RESOURCES LAW 8 (5th ed. 2002). This, however, has not always been the case. The guiding principles of federal land management in the United States have changed significantly over the nation's history and have been described as encompassing four eras: acquisition, disposition, retention, and management. *Id.* With the exception of the original thirteen colonies, Texas, and Hawaii, the federal government at one point owned nearly all land within the present borders of the United States *Id.* at 7. Throughout the 19th and 20th centuries, in an attempt to encourage the expansion and settlement of the nation, the majority of this land was privatized or given to states for education, transport, and other purposes. *Id.* at 34. This practice continued largely unabated until the turn of the 20th century, when a shift in public consciousness, following the revelation that the process of public land disposition was "often tainted by maladministration and chicanery," prompted the government to begin withdrawing specific tracts of public land for specified national purposes. *Id.* Growing public concern about fraud and the waste of natural resources in the early 20th century led to "an accelerated trend toward national retention of ownership." *Id.* By 1934, the federal government had largely ceased the disposition of public lands, and its land holding has remained relatively constant ever since. *Id.*

Part of the federal government's motivation in ceasing the disposition of public lands was a desire to safeguard the nation's natural resources. Is public ownership necessary, however, to secure this objective? Could the same objective be secured under a system of private ownership? If so, what role would the federal government play? How would claims among the competing uses of national resources be resolved? What would be the advantages of privatization? *See generally* RICHARD L. STROUP & JOHN A. BADEN, NATURAL RESOURCES: BUREAUCRATIC MYTHS AND ENVIRONMENTAL MANAGEMENT (1983). What would be the disadvantages? *See generally* Amy Sinden, *The Tragedy of the Commons and the Myth of a Private Property Solution*, 78 U. COLO. L. REV. 533 (2007).

If you were to design a system from scratch, what types of natural resources would you place under private control (subject to federal regulation) and what types of resources would you place under public control? Do you think the present balance between public and private resource allocation is optimal? Would you favor more or less privatization?

2. Efficiency. Consider the following argument in favor of the privatization of the natural resources under the Forest Service's control:

> When well-trained economists look at the [Forest Service] planning process, they see many problems in the way values are assigned, in the way criteria are set, and in the lack of distinction between the two. These problems can be easily explained. They are caused by the lack of good data inherent in a failure to price outputs as well as inputs, in a failure to recognize the opportunity cost of capital, and to the pressures that must come to bear when decision makers are held accountable only through the political system. The wonder is that the national forests have been managed as well as they have.

> Privatizing the national forests should end many of the obstacles to good management. Not only would decision makers be given larger amounts of validated and continuously updated information, but political obstacles to efficient management would largely disappear. Perhaps just as important, environmentalists, timber producers, miners, recreationists, and others who make demands on the Forest Service would quickly move away from their carping and faultfinding toward positive and constructive accommodation.

STROUP & BADEN, *supra*, at 118. Do you find this argument persuasive? Stroup and Baden attribute the failings of the Forest Service, in part, to its inability to gather accurate information on the price of inputs and outputs. Why would this be the case? Why would private actors be in a better position to gather more accurate information? What do you think Stroup and Baden mean when they claim that part of the failure of the Forest Service is attributable to the "pressures that must come to bear when decision makers are held accountable only through the political system"? *Id.* How would these differ from those pressures that would come to bear upon decisionmakers under a market system?

3. Ecosystem Services. Ecosystem services and ecosystem services markets involve assigning or recognizing value in what is typically thought of as free byproducts flowing from the natural environment. These byproducts encompass a broad range of environmental benefits, including clean drinking water, waste decomposition, carbon storage, and many

others. *See* The Millennium Ecosystem Assessment, https://www.
millenniumassessment.org/en/index.html (last visited Feb. 19, 2019).
Sometimes ecosystem services directly benefit discrete parties. For instance,
it may be more cost effective to pay upstream landowners to reduce erosion
than to dredge sediment downstream. In other situations, however,
government action may be needed to create a market for ecosystem services
or to protect the services themselves, such as with biodiversity. *See, e.g.*,
James Salzman, *Creating Markets for Ecosystem Services: Notes from the
Field*, 80 N.Y.U. L. REV. 870, 883 (2005). What are the implications of
ecosystem services for the debate over privatization? In the federal statutes
discussed in this casebook, can you think of areas where ecosystem services
or markets in them may be helpful?

4.   **Equal Access.** A retort to the call for privatization is that the nation's
natural resources should be made available for the benefit of all Americans.
How might advocates of privatization respond to this criticism? How may the
application of revenues derived as a consequence of privatization address
such concerns? Are concerns over access necessarily solved under a system
of public land ownership? Are they necessarily warranted under a system of
private land ownership?

5.   **Public Choice.** Why might decisions with respect to the management
of natural resources be particularly susceptible to manipulation by special
interests? Consider, for example, the nation's timber, grazing, and mineral
resources. What types of actors have special interests in these resources? Are
they likely to be well organized? For what types of natural resources will the
existence of special interests be less marked? How should this influence an
approach to the management of these resources?

6.   **Management of Natural Resources on Private Land.** When should
the federal government step in to regulate use of resources on private land?
What types of regulatory mechanisms would be appropriate in this context?
Consider the Farm and Ranchlands Protection Program, which is a
voluntary and incentive-based federal program designed to prevent
conversion of farm and ranchlands to other more intensive uses. Could or
should the federal government use more direct regulatory mechanisms such
as zoning to shape these types of private land use decisions? For an argument
for comprehensive land use planning, see Jess M. Krannich, *A Modern
Disaster: Agricultural Land, Urban Growth, and the Need for a Federally
Organized Comprehensive Land Use Planning Model*, 16 CORNELL J. L. &
PUB. POL'Y 57 (2006).

B. NATIONAL FORESTS

In 1630, at the beginning of the European settlement of the North
American continent in what is now the United States, forests covered
about 46 percent of the total land area. By 1907, as a result of logging
and agricultural clearing, the area of forest land had declined to about 34
percent. U.S. DEPT. OF AGRIC., U.S. FOREST FACT AND HISTORICAL
TRENDS (2001). In 1997, 302 million hectares—or 33 percent of the total
land area of the United States—was forest land. *Id.* However, not all of

the presently remaining forest land is original or "virgin" forest; much of it has been transformed through grazing, cutting, burning, and other modifications.

As early as 1830, federally-owned forest was frequently subject to unauthorized logging, prompting Congress to pass laws against the practice. In 1891, Congress passed an amendment to the General Revision Act that authorized the President to "from time to time, set apart and reserve, in any State or Territory... any part of the public lands wholly or in part covered with timber or undergrowth, whether of commercial value or not, as public reservations." 26 Stat. 1095, 1103 (1891).

The Organic Act of 1897 established general guidelines for the administration of forests on federal lands, and served as the primary authority for federal regulation of forests until it was supplemented by the Multiple Use-Sustained Yield Act in 1960. *See* Act of June 4, 1897, c. 2, § 1, 30 Stat. 35 (codified as amended at 16 U.S.C. §§ 473–551; 16 U.S.C. § 528, *et seq.*). In 1905, Congress formally transferred the forest reserves from the Department of the Interior to the Department of Agriculture and created the U.S. Forest Service. GEORGE C. COGGINS ET AL., FEDERAL PUBLIC LAND AND RESOURCES LAW 684 (6th ed. 2007). The Department of Agriculture began prohibiting the grazing of cattle, sheep and livestock on forest reserves as one of its first administrative policies. The ability of the Secretary of Agriculture to pass such laws—including the right to impose grazing permits and fees for the use of public land—was challenged in two separate cases. In *Light v. United States*, the Supreme Court affirmed the authority of the United States to enjoin a defendant from pasturing his cattle on public land without authorization, noting that the "United States can prohibit absolutely or fix the terms on which its property may be used." 220 U.S. 523, 536 (1911). In *United States v. Grimaud*, the Supreme Court held that Congress acted within its constitutional power in delegating to the Secretary of Agriculture the power to make rules for the lawful use of forest reservations. 220 U.S. 506, 517 (1911).

For the first several decades of the Forest Service's existence, congressional directives were generally interpreted as allowing the agency to harvest timber within national forests where, when, and how it saw fit. COGGINS ET AL., FEDERAL PUBLIC LAND, at 684. Under one of the agency's first leaders, Gifford Pinchot—who popularized the concept of utilitarian conservation—the Forest Service was organized into a group of professionally trained forest managers who exercised decentralized authority over the national forests. Pinchot viewed sustainable timber production as the dominant use of forests. In his seminal 1905 letter on management of national forest reserves, he explained:

> In the administration of the forest reserves ... all land is to be
> devoted to its most productive use for the permanent good of the

whole people, and not for the temporary benefit of individuals or companies. All the resources of the reserves are for use . . . under such restrictions only as will insure the permanence of the resources. . . . [W]here conflicting interests must be reconciled the question will always be decided from the standpoint of the greatest good of the greatest number in the long run. . . . [T]he administration of each reserve is left very largely in the hands of local officers, under the eye of thoroughly trained and competent inspectors.

Letter from Secretary James Wilson, Dept. of Agriculture, to Foresters, U.S. Forest Service (Feb. 1, 1905) (Pinchot wrote the letter and then brought it to James Wilson, Secretary of Agriculture, to sign). Pinchot's utilitarian philosophy matured into the Forest Service's multiple use, sustained yield concepts, which have been carried over to other public resource policy regimes, such as BLM's management of energy resources. *See* George Cameron Coggins, *The Developing Law of Land Use Planning on the Federal Lands*, 61 U. COLO. L. REV. 307, 308 (1990).

The National Forest System's Organic Act of 1897 was updated by the Multiple Use-Sustained Yield Act of 1960, and later, the National Forest Management Act ("NFMA") of 1976. These laws were proposed and passed, in part, to reflect changing societal attitudes about national forest management.

Today, pursuant to the NFMA, national forests are subject to relatively elaborate unit-level planning requirements. National forests are unique among other federal lands in that they have clear statutory requirements for system-wide planning. The greater attention paid to long-term planning for national forests, relative to other types of land, makes some practical sense. As one legal commentator observed:

> Forest management is a paradigm case of the need to consider long-term consequences in near-term decisionmaking. Trees take decades to reach commercial logging size. Groves take centuries to mature into old growth. Soils need millennia to develop. Fish and wildlife species, plants, and ecological communities evolve over millions of years. The short time horizons utilized day-to-day by many people and most business models are ill-suited to dealing with these processes. Take the short view and in short order you may wind up with no forest at all.

Nathaniel S.W. Lawrence, *A Forest of Objections: The Effort to Drop NEPA Review for National Forest Management Act Plans*, 39 ENVTL. L. REP. NEWS & ANALYSIS 10,651 (2009).

NFMA mandates adoption, and regular revision at no more than 15-year intervals, of comprehensive, unified management plans, for each unit of the National Forest System. 16 U.S.C. § 1604(f). The Act prescribes minimum procedural standards for planning, including three months of public review for proposed plans and preparation by an interdisciplinary team. *Id.* § 1604(d), (f)(3). It further requires that plans determine management systems and harvesting levels in light of the statutory multiple uses of national forests. *Id.* § 1604(e)(2), (f)(2).

NFMA also sets forth requirements for the contents of the Forest Service's planning regulations. The Act directs that the regulations assure that "plans are prepared in accordance with the National Environmental Policy Act." *Id.* § 1604(g)(1). The regulations are also required to "provide for the diversity of plant and animal communities," ensure against irreversible soil and slope damage, protect water bodies, limit clearcutting to carefully specified uses, and mandate monitoring, among other requirements. *See id.* § 1604(g). NFMA also directs that: "Resource plans and permits, contracts, and other instruments for the use and occupancy of National Forest System lands shall be consistent with the land management plans." *Id.* § 1604(i).

Under the NFMA, the Forest Service has adopted and revised forest-wide management plans more than 150 times. Lawrence, *A Forest of Objections*, 39 ENVTL. L. REP. at 10,652. Virtually all of these planning exercises have followed detailed regulations adopted in 1982, though the Forest Service has four times since then attempted comprehensive revisions, most recently in 2012, with minor revisions in 2016. *See* Forest Service, National Forest System Land Management Planning: Final Rule, 81 Fed. Reg. 90,723 (2016); Forest Service, National Forest System Land Management Planning: Final Rule, 77 Fed. Reg. 21,161 (2012). The planning rules contain procedural and substantive standards extending beyond those directly specified in the statute itself. Among the best known of these provisions is the requirement that plans provide for biological diversity by including "plan components, including standards or guidelines, to maintain or restore the diversity of ecosystems and habitat types throughout the plan area." 36 C.F.R. § 219.9. In doing so, the plan must include components to maintain or restore: "(i) Key characteristics associated with terrestrial and aquatic ecosystem types; (ii) Rare aquatic and terrestrial plant and animal communities; and (iii) The diversity of native tree species similar to that existing in the plan area." *Id.* And, in order to comply with NEPA, these plans must be accompanied by EISs.

In addition to the NFMA, the Forest and Rangeland Renewable Resources Planning Act of 1974 (commonly known as the Resources Planning Act) requires the Forest Service to prepare system-wide, five-year program documents, based on assessments of the system. 16 U.S.C. § 1602. Some of the required elements of the program include "evaluat[ing] objectives for the major Forest Service programs in order that multiple-use and sustained-yield relationships among and within the renewable resources can be determined," and issuing recommendations that "recognize the fundamental need to protect and, where appropriate, improve the quality of soil, water, and air resources. . ." *Id.* However, these documents are often very general.

Today, the Forest Service manages and develops land management plans for 154 national forests, 20 grasslands, and 1 prairie that comprise the 193-million-acre National Forest System. Forest Service, National Forest System Land Management Planning: Final Rule, 81 Fed. Reg. 90,723, 90,723 (2016). While annual timber harvests on national forests increased through the mid-20th century, spurred by the demands of World War II and the postwar construction boom, the annual timber harvest has declined markedly since the early 1990s. COGGINS ET AL., FEDERAL PUBLIC LAND AND RESOURCES LAW, *supra*, at 684. The decline is the result of several factors, including: (a) Endangered Species Act protections; (b) adoption and maturation of the planning process required by the NFMA; (c) growing public opposition to the practice of clearcutting; (d) a sharp decrease in building new roads within national forests; and (e) increasing timber production in private timber farms in the southeast, which shifted the core of the industry away from public lands in the west. *Id.*

The case below concerns management plans for two national forests, and specifically, the Forest Service's "diversity mandate."

<h1 style="text-align:center">Sierra Club v. Marita</h1>
46 F.3d 606 (7th Cir. 1995).

■ Before CUMMINGS, FLAUM, and RIPPLE, CIRCUIT JUDGES.

■ FLAUM, CIRCUIT JUDGE:

Plaintiffs Sierra Club, Wisconsin Forest Conservation Task Force, and Wisconsin Audubon Council, Inc. (collectively, Sierra Club) brought suit against defendant United States Forest Service (Service) seeking to enjoin timber harvesting, road construction or reconstruction, and the creation of wildlife openings at two national forests in northern Wisconsin. The Sierra Club claimed that the Service violated a number of environmental statutes and regulations in developing forest management plans for the two national forests by failing to consider properly certain ecological principles of biological diversity. The district court determined that the plaintiffs' claims were justiciable but then granted the Service summary judgment on the merits of those claims. We affirm.

The National Forest Management Act (NFMA) requires the Secretary of Agriculture, who is responsible for the Forest Service, to develop "land and resource management plans" to guide the maintenance and use of resources within national forests. 16 U.S.C. §§ 1601–1604. In developing these plans the Secretary must determine the environmental impact these plans will have and discuss alternative plans, pursuant to the National Environmental Policy Act (NEPA), 42 U.S.C. § 4321 *et seq.*

The Secretary must also consider the "multiple use and sustained yield of the several products and services obtained" from the forests, pursuant to the Multiple-Use Sustained Yield Act (MUSYA), 16 U.S.C. §§ 528–531. . . .

The present case concerns management plans developed for two forests: Nicolet National Forest (Nicolet) and Chequamegon (She-WA-me-gon) National Forest (Chequamegon). Nicolet spreads over 973,000 acres, of which 655,000 acres are National Forest Land, in northeastern Wisconsin, while Chequamegon encompasses 845,000 publicly-owned acres in northwestern and north-central Wisconsin. Collectively, the Nicolet and the Chequamegon contain hundreds of lakes and streams, thousands of miles of roads and trails, and serve a wide variety of uses, including hiking, skiing, snowmobiling, logging, fishing, hunting, sightseeing, and scientific research. The forests are important for both the tourism and the forest product industries in northern Wisconsin. . . .

The Sierra Club claims that the Service violated the NFMA . . . by using scientifically unsupported techniques to address diversity concerns in its management plans and by arbitrarily disregarding certain principles of conservation biology in developing those plans. . . . According to the Sierra Club, the Service, rather than address the important ecological issues the plaintiffs raised, stuck its head in the sand. The result, the Sierra Club argues, was a plan with "predictions about diversity directly at odds with the prevailing scientific literature." Several statutes and regulations mandate consideration of diversity in preparing forest management plans. Section 6(g) of the NFMA, the primary statute at issue, directs the Secretary of Agriculture in preparing a forest management plan to, among other things,

> provide for diversity of plant and animal communities based on the suitability and capability of the specific land area in order to meet overall multiple-use objectives, and within the multiple-use objectives of a land management plan adopted pursuant to this section, provide, where appropriate, to the degree practicable, for steps to be taken to preserve the diversity of tree species similar to that existing in the region controlled by the plan[.]

16 U.S.C. § 1604(g)(3)(B).

A number of regulations guide the application of this statute. The most general one stipulates that:

> Forest planning shall provide for diversity of plant and animal communities and tree species consistent with the overall multiple-use objectives of the planning area. Such diversity shall be considered throughout the planning process. Inventories shall include quantitative data making possible the evaluation of diversity in terms of its prior and present condition. For each planning alternative, the interdisciplinary

team shall consider how diversity will be affected by various mixes of resource outputs and uses, including proposed management practices.

36 C.F.R. § 219.26. . . .

. . . Diversity is defined for the purposes of these regulations as "[t]he distribution and abundance of different plant and animal communities and species within the area covered by a land and resource management plan." 36 C.F.R. § 219.3. . . .

The NFMA diversity statute does not provide much guidance as to its execution; "it is difficult to discern any concrete legal standards on the face of the provision." Wilkinson and Anderson, *supra* at 296. However, "when the section is read in light of the historical context and overall purposes of the NFMA, as well as the legislative history of the section, it is evident that section 6(g)(3)(B) requires Forest Service planners to treat the wildlife resource as a controlling, co-equal factor in forest management and, in particular, as a substantive limitation on timber production." *Id.* . . .

The Service addressed diversity concerns in the Nicolet and Chequamegon in largely similar ways, both of which are extensively detailed in the district court opinions issued below. *See Nicolet*, 843 F.Supp. at 1533–40; *Chequamegon*, 845 F.Supp. at 1322–28. The Service defined diversity as "[t]he distribution and abundance of different plant and animal communities and species within the area covered by the Land and Resource Management Plan." The Service assumed that "an increase in the diversity of habitats increases the potential livelihood of diverse kinds of organisms."

The Service focused its attention first on vegetative diversity. Diversity of vegetation was measured within tree stands as well as throughout the forest, noting that such diversity is "desirable for diverse wildlife habitat, visual variety, and as an aid to protecting the area from wildfire, insects, and disease." The Service assessed vegetative diversity based on vegetative types, age class structure of timber types, within-stand diversity of tree species, and the spacial distribution pattern of all these elements across the particular forest. The Service also factored in other considerations, including the desirability of "large areas of low human disturbance" and amount of "old-growth" forest, into its evaluations. Using these guidelines, the Service gathered and analyzed data on the current and historical composition of the forests to project an optimal vegetative diversity.

The Service assessed animal diversity primarily on the basis of vegetative diversity. Pursuant to the regulations, the Service identified all rare and uncommon vertebrate wildlife species as well as those species identified with a particular habitat and subject to significant change through planning alternatives. The Service grouped these species with a particular habitat type, identifying 14 categories in the Nicolet and 25 (reduced to 10 similar types) in the Chequamegon. For each of these habitat types, the Service selected [Management Indicator Species (MIS)] (33 in the Nicolet and 18 in the Chequamegon) to determine the impact of management practices on these species in particular and, by proxy, on other species in general. For each MIS, the Service calculated the minimum viable population necessary in order to ensure the continued reproductive vitality of the species. Factors involved in this calculation included a determination of population size, the spatial distribution across the forest needed to ensure fitness and resilience, and the kinds, amounts and pattern of habitats needed to support the population.

Taking its diversity analysis into consideration, along with its numerous other mandates, the Service developed a number of plan alternatives for each of the forests (eight in the Nicolet and nine in the Chequamegon). Each alternative emphasized a different aspect of forest management, including cost efficiency, wildlife habitat, recreation, and hunting, although all were considered to be "environmentally, technically, and legally feasible." In the Nicolet, the Service selected the alternative emphasizing resource outputs associated with large diameter hardwood and softwood vegetation; in the Chequamegon an alternative emphasizing recreational opportunities, quality saw-timber, and aspen management was chosen.

The Sierra Club argues that the diversity statute and regulations . . . required the Service to consider and apply certain principles of conservation biology in developing the forest plan. These principles, the Sierra Club asserts, dictate that diversity is not comprehensible solely through analysis of the numbers of plants and animals and the variety of species in a given area. Rather, diversity also requires an understanding of the relationships between differing landscape patterns and among various habitats. That understanding, the Sierra Club says, has led to the prediction that the size of a habitat—the "patch size"—tends to affect directly the survival of the habitat and the diversity of plant and animal species within that habitat.

A basic generalization of conservation biology is that smaller patches of habitat will not support life as well as one larger patch of that habitat, even if the total area of the smaller patches equals the total area of the large patch. This generalization derives from a number of observations and predictions. First, whereas a large-scale disturbance will wipe out many populations in a smaller patch, those in a larger patch have a better chance of survival. Second, smaller patches are subject to destruction through "edge effects." Edge effects occur when one habitat's environment suffers because it is surrounded by different type of habitat. Given basic geometry, among other factors, the smaller the patch size of the surrounded habitat, the greater the chance that a surrounding habitat will invade and devastate the surrounded habitat. Third, the more isolated similar habitats are from one another, the less chance organisms can migrate from one habitat to another in the event of a local disturbance. Consequently, fewer organisms will survive such a disturbance and diversity will decline. This third factor is known as the theory of "island biogeography." Thus, the mere fact that a given area contains diverse habitats does not ensure diversity at all; a "fragmented forest" is a recipe for ecological trouble. On the basis of these submissions, the Sierra Club desires us to rule that

> [t]o perform a legally adequate hard look at the environmental consequences of landscape manipulation across the hundreds of thousands of hectares of a National Forest, a federal agency must apply in some reasonable fashion the ecological principles identified by well accepted conservation biology. Species-by-species techniques are simply no longer enough. Ecology must be applied in the analysis, and it will be used as a criterion for the substantive results.

Nicolet Appellant's Br. at 7; Chequamegon Appellant's Br. at 7; *see generally* Nicolet Appellant's App. 273–336; Chequamegon Appellant's App. 223–280 (describing principles of conservation biology).

As a way of putting conservation biology into practice, the Sierra Club suggested that large blocks of land (at least 30,000 to 50,000 acres per block), so-called "Diversity Maintenance Areas" (DMAs), be set aside in each of the forests. The Sierra Club proposed and mapped three DMAs for the Nicolet and two for the Chequamegon. In these areas, which would have included about 25% of each forest, habitats were to be undisturbed by new roads, timber sales, or wildlife openings. Neither forest plan, however, ultimately contained a DMA; the Chequamegon Forest Supervisor initially did include two DMAs, but the Regional Forester removed them from the final Chequamegon plan.

The Sierra Club contends that the Service ignored its submissions. . . .

The Service replies that it correctly considered the implications of conservation biology for both the Nicolet and Chequamegon and appropriately declined to apply the science. The Service asserts that it duly noted the "concern [of the Sierra Club and others] that fragmentation of the . . . forest canopy through timber harvesting and road building is detrimental to certain plant and animal species." The Service decided that the theory had "not been applied to forest management in the Lake States" and that the subject was worthy of further study. However, the Service found in both cases that while the theories of conservation biology in general and of island biogeography in particular were "of interest, . . . there is not sufficient justification at this time to make research of the theory a Forest Service priority." Given its otherwise extensive analysis of diversity, as well as the deference owed its interpretation of applicable statutory and regulatory requirements, the Service contends that it clearly met all the "diversity" obligations imposed on it.

The case now turns to whether the Service was required to apply conservation biology in its analysis and whether the Service otherwise complied with its statutory mandates and regulatory prescriptions regarding diversity in national forests. We hold that the Service met all legal requirements in addressing the concerns the Sierra Club raises. . . .

The Sierra Club's arguments regarding the inadequacy of the Service's plans . . . can be distilled into five basic allegations, each of which we address in turn. First, the Sierra Club asserts that the law "treats ecosystems and ecological relationships as a separately cognizable issue from the species by species concepts driving game and timber issues." The Sierra Club relies on the NFMA's diversity language to argue that the NFMA treats diversity in two distinct respects: diversity of plant and animal communities and diversity of tree species. See 16 U.S.C. § 1604(g)(3)(B). . . . The Sierra Club concludes from these statutes and regulations that the Service was obligated to apply an ecological approach to forest management and failed to do so. In the Sierra Club's view, MISs and population viability analyses present only half the picture, a picture that the addition of conservation biology would make complete.

The Sierra Club errs in these assertions because it sees requirements in the NFMA . . . that simply do not exist. The drafters of the NFMA diversity regulations themselves recognized that diversity was a complex term and declined to adopt any particular means or methodology of providing for diversity. Report of the Committee of Scientists to the Secretary of Agriculture Regarding Regulations Proposed by the United States Forest Service to Implement Section 6 of the National Forest Management Act of 1976, 44 Fed.Reg. 26,599, 26,609 (1979). We agree with the district court that "[i]n view of the committee's decision not to prescribe a particular methodology and its failure to mention the principles that plaintiffs claim were by then well established, the court cannot fairly read those principles into the NFMA. . . ." *Nicolet*, 843 F.Supp. at 1542; *Chequamegon*, 845 F.Supp. at 1330. Thus, conservation biology is not a necessary element of diversity analysis insofar as the regulations do not dictate that the service analyze diversity in any specific way. . . .

In a second and related argument, the Sierra Club submits that the substantive law of diversity necessitated the set-aside of large, unfragmented habitats to protect at least some old-growth forest communities. The Sierra Club points out that 36 C.F.R. § 219.27(g) requires that "where appropriate and to the extent practicable" the Service "shall preserve and enhance the diversity of plant and animal communities . . . so that it is at least as great as that which would be expected in a natural forest. . . ." Furthermore, "[r]eductions in diversity of plant and animal communities and tree species from that which would be expected in a natural forest or from that similar to the existing diversity in the planning area[ ] may be prescribed only where needed to meet overall multiple-use objectives." *Id.* Diversity, the Sierra Club asserts, requires the Service to maintain a range of different, ecologically viable communities. Because it is simply not possible to ensure the survival of any old-growth forest communities without these large, undisturbed patches of land, the Service has therefore reduced diversity. The Service was thus bound to protect and enhance the natural forest or explain why other forest uses prevented the Service from doing so. The Sierra Club believes the Service did neither.

The Sierra Club asserts that the diversity regulations require a certain procedure and that because the substantive result of the Service's choices will produce, in the Sierra Club's view, results adverse to "natural forest" diversity, the Service has violated its mandate. However, as the Service points out, the regulations do not actually require the promotion of "natural forest" diversity but rather the promotion of diversity at least as great as that found in a natural forest. The Service maintains that it did provide for such diversity in the ways discussed above. Additionally, the Service did consider the maintenance of some old-growth forest, even though the Sierra Club disputes that the Service's efforts will have any positive effects. And to the extent the Service's final choice did not promote "natural diversity" above all else, the Service acted well within its regulatory discretion. *See Sierra Club v. Espy*, 38 F.3d 792, 800 (5th Cir.1994) (That [NFMA diversity] protection means something less than the preservation of the status quo but something more than eradication of species suggests that this is just the type of policy-oriented decision Congress wisely left to the discretion of the experts-here, the Forest Service.) . . .

Fourth, the Sierra Club contends that the rejection of its "high quality" science argument on the basis of "uncertainty" in the application of conservation biology was unscrupulous. The Sierra Club asserts that conservation biology represented well-accepted and well-respected science even at the time the Service developed its management plans in the mid-1980s and that this evidence was before the Service when it drafted the forest plans. Thus, if the Service's only argument against applying the "high quality" science of conservation biology was its uncertainty, the Service has utterly failed to respond to the challenge of conservation biology.

A brief look at available evidence suggests that the district court's understanding of uncertainty was correct and the Service's explanation principled. The Service, in looking at island biogeography, noted that it had been developed as a result of research on actual islands or in the predominantly old-growth forests of the Pacific Northwest and therefore did not necessarily lend itself to application in the forests of Wisconsin. Literature submitted by the Sierra Club to the Service was not unequivocal in stipulating how to apply conservation biology principles in the Nicolet and Chequamegon. Likewise, a Sierra Club group member suggested during meetings regarding the Chequamegon that "the Forest

Service should be a leader and incorporate this concept into the Plan. He indicated that it would set a precedent for other Forests and Regions." Pl. Brief App. I at 95. The Chequamegon Forest Supervisor also originally decided to include the DMAs in his forest plan not because science so compelled but as a way to research an as yet untested theory. Even recent literature has recognized that "new legislation may be necessary" in order to force the Service to adopt conservation biology. Robert B. Keiter, *Conservation Biology and the Law: Assessing the Challenges Ahead*, 69 Chi.Kent L.Rev. 911, 916 (1994). Perhaps the Service "ha[s] the ability to reinterpret [its] own governing mandates to give species protection priority over visitor services and other concerns," *id.* at 921, but that is not and was not required.

The amici scientific societies suggest that the district court misunderstood the nature of scientific uncertainty. Their argument on this point boils down to the assertion that all scientific propositions are inherently unverifiable and at most falsifiable. *See Daubert*, 509 U.S. at 590 (1993) ("[I]t would be unreasonable to conclude that the subject of scientific testimony must be 'known' to a certainty; arguable there are no certainties in science."); Richard A. Posner, THE PROBLEMS OF JURISPRUDENCE 367 (Harvard 1990) ("[B]ecause of the possibility of ever really 'confirming' a scientific hypothesis it might be best to view all scientific knowledge as conjectural"). Hence, amici argue, allowing the Service to ignore the theories of conservation biology because they are "uncertain" would, on the same logic, allow the Service to ignore the theory of gravity.

Amici, like the Sierra Club, misapprehend the "uncertainty" of which the Service and the district court spoke. We agree that an agency decision to avoid a science should not escape review merely because a theory is not certain. But, however valid a general theory may be, it does not translate into a management tool unless one can apply it to a concrete situation. The Service acknowledged the developments in conservation biology but did not think that they had been shown definitively applicable to forests like the Nicolet or the Chequamegon. Thus, circumstances did not warrant setting aside a large portion of these forests to study island biogeography and related theories at the expense of other forest-plan objectives. Given that uncertainty, we appropriately defer to the agency's method of measuring and maintaining diversity. *See Baltimore Gas & Elec. Co. v. Natural Resources Defense Council, Inc.*, 462 U.S. 87, 103 (1983). . . .

The creation of a forest plan requires the Forest Service to make tradeoffs among competing interests. *See Sierra Club v. Espy*, 38 F.3d at 802. The NFMA's diversity provisions do substantively limit the Forest Service's ability to sacrifice diversity in those trades, and NEPA does require that decisions regarding diversity comply with certain procedural requirements. However, the Service neither ignored nor abused those limits in the present case. Thus, while the Sierra Club did have standing to challenge the choices made by the Service, the Service made those choices within the boundaries of the applicable statutes and regulations.

NOTES AND QUESTIONS

1.   **NFMA's Diversity Mandate.** Section 1604(g)(3)(B) of the NFMA requires that Land Management Plans:

> . . . provide for diversity of plant and animal communities based on the suitability and capability of the specific land area in order to meet overall multiple-use objectives, and within the multiple-use objective of a land management plan adopted pursuant to this section, provide, where appropriate, to the degree practicable, for steps to be taken to preserve the diversity of tree species similar to that existing in the region controlled by the plan. . . .

16 U.S.C. § 1604(g)(3)(B). What type of legal hook does this provision give petitioners, such as the Sierra Club, in seeking to force the Forest Service to adopt certain practices? In what way did the Forest Service incorporate diversity considerations into its regional management plans? On what basis did the Sierra Club argue that this provision required the Forest Service to adopt conservation biology in the preparation of regional management plans?

2.   **Conservation Biology.** Did the Forest Service reject the science of conservation biology? In preparing plans that provided for the fragmentation of forest resources, is the Forest Service effectively precluding its application in the future? The court expressly noted that the theories of island biogeography had been developed from studies conducted in the Pacific Northwest. Would the court's decision have differed if the plans in question had been prepared with respect to national forests within those regions?

In the event that the Forest Service had adopted conservation biology in formulating the regional management plans, would logging interests likely have succeeded in challenging its application?

The agency made several attempts to promulgate a new planning rule, before issuing one in 2012. In a proposed rule in 2011, the agency incorporated the language of conservation biology, acknowledging that since the promulgation of the 1982 rule,

> much has changed in our understanding of how to create and implement effective land management plans. The body of science that informs land management planning in areas such as conservation biology and ecology has advanced considerably since 1982, as has our understanding of the values and benefits of NFS lands, and the challenges and stressors that may impact resources on the unit (including climate change).

National Forest System Land Management Planning; Proposed Rule, 72 Fed. Reg. 22,717 (2011). Do you find the agency's assertion that the adoption of conservation biology reflects a change in its understanding of the science satisfactory? Are other factors, such as shifting policy preferences, effectively hidden from view in these disputes over science?

In the final amended planning rule, adopted in 2012 and further amended in 2016, the terminology used by the agency is principally in terms of "connectivity" and "ecosystems." For instance, the revised diversity regulation requires that, "the plan must include plan components, including standards or guidelines, to maintain or restore the ecological integrity of terrestrial and aquatic ecosystems and watersheds in the plan area, including plan components to maintain or restore their structure, function, composition, and connectivity." 36 C.F.R. § 219.9. Further, the regulation states that, "[t]he plan must include plan components, including standards or guidelines, to maintain or restore the diversity of ecosystems and habitat types throughout the plan area." *Id.* The term "ecosystems" is defined as a "spatially explicit, relatively homogeneous unit of the Earth that includes all interacting organisms and elements of the abiotic environment within its boundaries." 36 C.F.R. § 219.19.

3.   Denying Gravity. Amici in *Marita* argue that the logic adopted by the Forest Service in denying the application of conservation biology would also allow the Service to ignore the theory of gravity. 46 F.3d at 622. Do you agree with the amici's position?

On what basis did the court draw a distinction between scientific uncertainty, on the one hand, and the uncertainty of applying scientific principles in a particular context, on the other? Do you find this distinction convincing? Evaluate the following criticism of the court's ruling in this regard:

> The Seventh Circuit's distinction between scientific uncertainty and uncertainty of application is meaningless and allows the Forest Service to do exactly what the amici foretold: to insulate itself from scientific advances in the name of uncertainty. Scientific propositions are always uncertain because the nature of science is to pose a hypothesis and then to attempt to disprove that hypothesis through experimentation and study. If the hypothesis is not disproved, it is accepted to the extent that it has been tested. Put another way, "all scientific knowledge [is] conjectural" because not every possible permutation can be explored. In essence, the Seventh Circuit's distinction is really nothing more than a recognition that the theory of island biogeography has not been tested in every possible location. One wonders how far the Forest Service could take that logic. Could it reject a scientific theory tested and verified in an adjacent forest but not yet tested in the forest for which it is making plans? Presumably the agency would need to support the decision with some rationale, but given that "[e]cosystems are not only more complex than we think, but more complex than we can think," and that judicial deference is highest in areas of technical expertise, it is not hard to imagine that the Forest Service will almost always be able to articulate some rationale for its decision. The upshot of Sierra Club v. Marita may be that the Forest Service has expanded its already broad discretion to the point that it can pick and choose among scientific

theories to find the rationale that best supports its particular land-management goals.

Greg D. Corbin, *The United States Forest Service's Response to Biodiversity Science*, 29 ENVTL. L. 377, 406–07 (1999).

4. Trade-offs Under the National Forest Management Act. The *Marita* court expressly recognizes that "[t]he creation of a forest plan requires the Forest Service to make trade-offs among competing interests." 46 F.3d at 624. These interests may include recreational interests (such as hiking, skiing, snowmobiling, hunting, or fishing), commercial interests (such as logging), scientific interests, or environmental interests (such as biological diversity). How does the *Marita* court envisage the Forest Service should go about reconciling these competing interests? Does the Sierra Club suggest that the Forest Service's diversity mandate should take precedence? Is there support for this proposition in the NFMA?

5. Roadless Rule Saga. During the final days of the Clinton administration, the Forest Service announced a rule prohibiting most road construction within roadless areas of national forests. The State of Wyoming challenged the rule as an implied designation of wilderness in violation of Section 2(a) of the Wilderness Act. A federal district court agreed because "[t]o allow the Secretary of Agriculture and the Forest Service to establish their own system of de facto administrative wilderness through administrative rulemaking negates the system of wilderness designation established by Congress." *Wyoming v. U.S. Dep't of Agric.*, 277 F. Supp. 2d 1197, 1236 (D. Wyo. 2003) ("*Wyoming I*"). The dispute became moot when the Forest Service substituted a different rule the day after oral argument on the appeal in the Tenth Circuit. *See Wyoming v. U.S. Dep't of Agric.*, 414 F.3d 1207 (10th Cir. 2005). However, the Bush administration's replacement rule was successfully challenged under NEPA and the Administrative Procedure Act, leading to reinstatement of the 2001 roadless rule. *See California ex rel. Lockyer v. U.S. Dep't of Agric.*, 459 F. Supp. 2d 874, 879 (N.D. Cal. 2006). As a result, the State of Wyoming renewed its NEPA and Wilderness Act challenges to the 2001 rule.

In *Wyoming v. USDA* ("*Wyoming II*"), the same district judge again concluded that the 2001 Roadless Rule violated the Wilderness Act, as well as NEPA. 570 F. Supp. 2d 1309, 1318 (D. Wyo. 2008). A unanimous panel of the Tenth Circuit reversed the district court, concluding that the 2001 Roadless Rule complied with NEPA and did not violate the Wilderness Act. *Wyoming v. U.S. Dep't of Agric.*, 661 F.3d 1209, 1272 (10th Cir. 2011). The court observed that the 2001 rule allowed some motorized uses and development, compared with far more restrictive Wilderness Act provisions, stating, "wilderness areas governed by the Wilderness Act and [roadless areas] governed by the Roadless Rule are not only distinct, but that the Wilderness Act is more restrictive and prohibitive than the Roadless Rule." *Id.* at 1233; *see also* Michael C. Blumm & Andrew B. Erickson, *Federal Wild Lands Policy in the Twenty-First Century: What A Long, Strange Trip It's Been*, 25 COLO. NAT. RES., ENERGY & ENVTL L. REV. 1, 28 (2014).

Do you agree with the Tenth Circuit? Should an agency such as the Forest Service or BLM, each subject to a "multiple use" mandate, be able to designate large areas of roadless public lands where timber production and mining are prohibited, without explicit statutory authority to do so? At present, about 58 million acres of roadless lands in national forests qualify as wilderness, but Congress has not passed legislation designating most of these areas as wilderness. Blumm & Erickson, *Federal Wild Lands Policy, supra*, at 5.

C. RANGELANDS

In the nineteenth and early twentieth centuries, federal rangelands were essentially unregulated; settlers freely grazed livestock on public lands and paid no fees to the federal government for the use of rangeland. But by the early twentieth century, the federal rangelands were suffering from overuse, causing ecological degradation and exacerbating tensions among ranchers competing for remaining rangelands.

Congress responded by passing the Taylor Grazing Act of 1934, which established a federal grazing program, to be managed by the Secretary of the Interior. The Act directs the Secretary to "promote the highest use of the public lands" and authorizes the Secretary to create grazing districts from any part of the unreserved federal public domain which are not in national forests, national parks, or national monuments, and which in his opinion "are chiefly valuable for grazing and raising forage crops." 43 U.S.C. § 315. It further directs that the Secretary:

> shall make such rules and regulations and establish such service, enter into such cooperative agreements, and do any and all things necessary to accomplish the purposes of this subchapter and to insure the objects of such grazing districts, namely, to regulate their occupancy and use, to preserve the land and its resources from destruction or unnecessary injury, [and] to provide for the orderly use, improvement, and development of the range. . . .

43 U.S.C. § 315a.

The Taylor Act authorized the Secretary of the Interior to issue grazing permits and to charge annual fees, with permit preference given to "those within or near a district who are landowners engaged in the livestock business, bona fide occupants or settlers, or owners of water or water rights, as may be necessary to permit the proper use of lands, water or water rights owned, occupied, or leased by them. . ." 43 U.S.C. § 315b.

Today, fees are charged for grazing on approximately 160 million acres of BLM land and 81 million acres of Forest Service land under a fee formula established in the Public Rangelands Improvement Act of 1978 and continued administratively. *See* 43 U.S.C. §§ 1901, 1905; Carol Hardy Vincent, *Grazing Fees: Overview and Issues*, Congressional Research Service 1 (June 19, 2012).

Charging fees for grazing private livestock on federal lands is a contentious practice. In general, livestock producers who use federal lands want to keep fees low, while conservation groups and others believe fees should be increased. The formula for determining grazing fees uses a base value adjusted annually by the lease rates for grazing on private lands, beef cattle prices, and the cost of livestock production. *Id.* at 3. The fee does not factor in any environmental or social externalities associated with grazing on public lands. The federal grazing program is expensive for agencies to administer and often costs far more in administrative expenses than it generates in revenue. *Id.* at 2. The collected fees are divided among the Treasury, states, and federal agencies. Grazing fee reform was attempted but never adopted in the 1990s, due to political headwinds. As you read the case below, consider the amount of discretion federal agencies have to set federal grazing policy.

Public Lands Council v. Babbitt
529 U.S. 728 (2000).

■ JUSTICE BREYER delivered the opinion of the Court:

This case requires us to interpret several provisions of the 1934 Taylor Grazing Act, 48 Stat. 1269, 43 U.S.C. § 315 *et seq.* The petitioners claim that each of three grazing regulations, 43 C.F.R. §§ 4100.0–5, 4110.1(a), and 4120.3–2 (1998), exceeds the authority that this statute grants the Secretary of the Interior. We disagree and hold that the three regulations do not violate the Act. . . .

By the 1930's, opposition to federal regulation of the federal range had significantly diminished. Population growth, forage competition, and inadequate range control all began to have consequences both serious and apparent. With a horrifying drought came 'dawns without day' as dust storms swept the range. The devastating storms of the Dust Bowl were in the words of one Senator "the most tragic, the most impressive lobbyist, that ha[s] ever come to this Capitol." Congress acted; and on June 28, 1934, President Franklin Roosevelt signed the Taylor Grazing Act into law. . . .

The Taylor Act seeks to "promote the highest use of the public lands." 43 U.S.C. § 315. Its specific goals are to "stop injury" to the lands from "overgrazing and soil deterioration," to "provide for their use, improvement and development," and "to stabilize the livestock industry dependent on the public range." 48 Stat. 1269. The Act grants the Secretary of the Interior authority to divide the public range-lands into grazing districts, to specify the amount of grazing permitted in each district, to issue leases or permits "to graze livestock," and to charge "reasonable fees" for use of the land. 43 U.S.C. §§ 315, 315a, 315b. It specifies that preference in respect to grazing permits "shall be given . . . to those within or near" a grazing district "who are landowners engaged in the livestock business, bona fide occupants or settlers, or owners of water or water rights." § 315b. And, as particularly relevant here, it adds:

> So far as consistent with the purposes and provisions of this subchapter, grazing privileges recognized and acknowledged shall be adequately safeguarded, but the creation of a grazing district or the issuance of a permit . . . shall not create any right, title, interest, or estate in or to the lands.

Ibid. . . .

This case arises out of a 1995 set of Interior Department amendments to the federal grazing regulations. 60 Fed.Reg. 9894 (1995) (Final Rule). The amendments represent a stated effort to "accelerate restoration" of the rangeland, make the rangeland management program "more compatible with ecosystem management," "streamline certain administrative functions," and "obtain for the public fair and reasonable compensation for the grazing of livestock on public lands." 58 Fed.Reg. 43208 (1993) (Proposed Rule). The amendments in final form emphasize individual "stewardship" of the public land by increasing the accountability of grazing permit holders; broaden membership on the district advisory boards; change certain title rules; and change administrative rules and practice of the Bureau of Land Management to bring them into closer conformity with related Forest Service management practices. See 60 Fed.Reg. 9900–9906 (1995). . . .

The ranchers attack the new "grazing preference" regulations first and foremost. Their attack relies upon the provision in the Taylor Act stating that "grazing privileges recognized and acknowledged shall be adequately safeguarded. . . ." 43 U.S.C. § 315b. Before 1995 the regulations defined the term "grazing preference" in terms of the *AUM-denominated amount* of grazing privileges that a permit granted. [An AUM is an "Animal Unit Month"—the right to obtain the forage needed to sustain one cow (or five sheep) for one month.] The regulations then defined "grazing preference" as

> the total number of animal unit months of livestock grazing on public lands apportioned and attached to base property owned or controlled by a permittee or lessee.

43 CFR § 4100.0–5 (1994). The 1995 regulations changed this definition, however, so that it now no longer refers to grazing privileges "apportioned," nor does it speak in terms of AUMs. The new definition defines "grazing preference" as

> a superior or priority position against others for the purpose of receiving a grazing permit or lease. This priority is attached to base property owned or controlled by the permittee or lessee.

43 CFR § 4100.0–5 (1995). [The term "base property" refers to private land (or water rights) sufficient to partially support herds.] The new definition "omits reference to a specified quantity of forage." 60 Fed.Reg. 9921 (1995). It refers only to a priority, not to a specific number of AUMs

attached to a base property. But at the same time the new regulations add a new term, "permitted use," which the Secretary defines as

> the forage allocated by, or under the guidance of, an applicable land use plan for livestock grazing in an allotment under a permit or lease and is expressed in AUMs.

43 CFR § 4100.0–5 (1995). This new "permitted use," like the old "grazing preference," is defined in terms of allocated rights, and it refers to AUMs. But this new term as defined refers, not to a rancher's forage priority, but to forage "allocated by, or under the guidance of *an applicable land use plan*." *Ibid.* (emphasis added). And therein lies the ranchers' concern.

The ranchers refer us to the administrative history of Taylor Act regulations. . . . In the ranchers' view, history has created expectations in respect to the security of "grazing privileges"; they have relied upon those expectations; and the statute requires the Secretary to "safeguar[d]" that reliance. Supported by various farm credit associations, they argue that defining their privileges in relation to land use plans will undermine that security. They say that the content of land use plans is difficult to predict and easily changed. Fearing that the resulting uncertainty will discourage lenders from taking mortgages on ranches as security for their loans, they conclude that the new regulations threaten the stability, and possibly the economic viability, of their ranches, and thus fail to "safeguard" the "grazing privileges" that Department regulations previously "recognized and acknowledged." Brief for Petitioners 22–23.

We are not persuaded by the ranchers' argument for three basic reasons. First, the statute qualifies the duty to "safeguard" by referring directly to the Act's various goals and the Secretary's efforts to implement them. The full subsection says:

> *So far as consistent with the purposes and provisions of this subchapter,* grazing privileges recognized and acknowledged shall be adequately safeguarded, *but* the creation of a grazing district or the issuance of a permit pursuant to the provisions of this subchapter shall *not* create any right, title, interest or estate in or to the lands.

43 U.S.C. § 315b (emphasis added). The words "so far as consistent with the purposes . . . of this subchapter" and the warning that "issuance of a permit" creates no "right, title, interest or estate" make clear that the ranchers' interest in permit stability cannot be absolute; and that the Secretary is free reasonably to determine just how, and the extent to which, "grazing privileges" shall be safeguarded, in light of the Act's basic purposes. Of course, those purposes include "stabiliz[ing] the livestock industry," but they also include "stop[ping] injury to the public grazing lands by preventing overgrazing and soil deterioration," and "provid[ing] for th[e] orderly use, improvement, and development" of the public range. 48 Stat. 1269; see *supra,* at 1819.

Moreover, Congress itself has directed development of land use plans, and their use in the allocation process, in order to preserve, improve, and develop the public rangelands. See 43 U.S.C. §§ 1701(a)(2), 1712. That being so, it is difficult to see how a definitional change that simply refers to the use of such plans could violate the Taylor Act by itself, without more. Given the broad discretionary powers that the Taylor Act grants the Secretary, we must read that Act as here granting the Secretary at least ordinary administrative leeway to assess "safeguard[ing]" in terms of the Act's other purposes and provisions. Cf. §§ 315, 315a (authorizing Secretary to establish grazing districts "*in his discretion*" (emphasis added), and to "make provision for protection, administration, regulation, and improvement of such grazing districts.")

Second, the pre-1995 AUM system that the ranchers seek to "safeguard" did not offer them anything like absolute security—not even in respect to the proportionate shares of grazing land privileges that the "active/suspended" system suggested. As discussed above, the Secretary has long had the power to reduce an individual permit's AUMs or cancel the permit if the permit holder did not use the grazing privileges, did not use the base property, or violated the Range Code. See *supra*, at 1820 (collecting CFR citations 1938–1998). And the Secretary has always had the statutory authority under the Taylor Act and later FLPMA to reclassify and withdraw rangeland from grazing use, see 43 U.S.C. § 315f (authorizing Secretary, "in his discretion, to examine and classify any lands . . . which are more valuable or suitable for the production of agricultural crops . . . or any other use than [grazing]); §§ 1712, 1752(c) (authorizing renewal of permits "so long as the lands . . . remain available for domestic livestock grazing *in accordance with land use plans*" (emphasis added)). The Secretary has consistently reserved the authority to cancel or modify grazing permits accordingly. See supra, at 1820–1821 (collecting CFR citations). Given these well-established pre-1995 Secretarial powers to cancel, modify, or decline to renew individual permits, *including the power to do so pursuant to the adoption of a land use plan*, the ranchers' diminishment-of-security point is at best a matter of degree.

Third, the new definitional regulations by themselves do not automatically bring about a self-executing change that would significantly diminish the security of granted grazing privileges. The Department has said that the new definitions do "not cancel preference," and that any change is "merely a clarification of terminology." 60 Fed.Reg. 9922 (1995). It now assures us through the Solicitor General that the definitional changes "preserve all elements of preference" and "merely clarify the regulations within the statutory framework." See Brief in Opposition 13, 14.

The Secretary did consider making a more sweeping change by eliminating the concept of "suspended use"; a change that might have more reasonably prompted the ranchers' concerns. But after receiving comments, he changed his mind. See 59 Fed.Reg. 14323 (1994). The Department has instead said that "suspended" AUMs will

> continue to be recognized and have a priority for additional grazing use within the allotment. Suspended use provides an important accounting of past grazing use for the ranching community and is an insignificant administrative workload to the agency. Bureau of Land Management, Rangeland Reform '94: Final Environmental Impact Statement 144 (1994).

Of course, the new definitions seem to tie grazing privileges to land use plans more explicitly than did the old. But, as we have pointed out, the Secretary has since 1976 had the authority to use land use plans to determine the amount of permissible grazing, 43 U.S.C. § 1712. The Secretary also points out that since development of land use plans began nearly 20 years ago, "all BLM lands in the lower 48 States are covered by land use plans," and "all grazing permits in those States have now been issued or renewed in accordance with such plans, or must now conform to them." Brief for Respondents 26. Yet the ranchers have not provided us with a single example in which interaction of plan and permit has jeopardized or might yet jeopardize permit security. An *amicus* brief filed by a group of Farm Credit Institutions says that the definitional change will "threate[n]" their "lending policies." Brief for Farm Credit Institutions as *Amicus Curiae* 3. But they do not explain *why* that is so, nor do they state that the new definitions will, in fact, lead them to stop lending to ranchers.

We recognize that a particular land use plan could change pre-existing grazing allocation in a particular district. And that change might arguably lead to a denial of grazing privileges that the pre-1995 regulations would have provided. But the affected permit holder remains free to challenge such an individual effect on grazing privileges, and the courts remain free to determine its lawfulness in context. We here consider only whether the changes in the definitions by themselves violate the Taylor Act's requirement that recognized grazing privileges be "adequately safeguarded." Given the leeway that the statute confers upon the Secretary, the less-than-absolute pre-1995 security that permit holders enjoyed, and the relatively small differences that the new definitions create, we conclude that the new definitions do not violate that law. . . .

■ JUSTICE O'CONNOR, with whom JUSTICE THOMAS joins, concurring:

I join the Court's opinion. I write separately to make the following observations concerning the Court's decision.

. . . [T]he Court holds that the Secretary did not exceed his authority under the Taylor Grazing Act by promulgating the new "grazing preference" and "permitted use" rules. I agree with that holding but would place special emphasis on the Court's third reason for rejecting petitioners' facial challenge to the regulations. Petitioners have not shown how the new regulations themselves—rather than specific actions the Secretary might take pursuant to those regulations—violate the Taylor Grazing Act's requirement that "grazing privileges recognized and acknowledged . . . be adequately safeguarded." 43 U.S.C. § 315b. It is of particular importance, as the Court notes, *ante*, at 1824, that the Secretary has assured us that the new regulations do not in actual practice "alter the active use/suspended use formula in grazing permits" and that " 'present suspended use would continue to be recognized and have a priority for additional grazing use within the allotment.' " Brief for Respondents 22 (quoting Bureau of Land Management, Rangeland Reform '94: Final Environmental Impact Statement 144 (1994)). For these reasons, petitioners' facial challenge to the regulations must fail. Should a permit holder find, however, that the Secretary's specific application of the new regulations deviates from the above assurances and in the process deprives the permit holder of grazing privileges to such an extent that the Secretary's conduct can be termed a failure to adequately safeguard such privileges, the permit holder may bring an as-applied challenge to the Secretary's action at that time. The Court's holding today in no way forecloses such a challenge. See *ante*, at 1825 ("[T]he affected permit holder remains free to challenge such an individual [denial of] grazing privileges, and the courts remain free to determine its lawfulness in context"). . . .

NOTES AND QUESTIONS

1.   Taylor Grazing Act. As Justice Breyer noted, the purposes of the Taylor Grazing Act range from "stop[ping] injury" to the lands "from overgrazing and soil deterioration," to "provid[ing] for their use, improvement and development," and to "stabiliz[ing] the livestock industry dependent on the public range." 529 U.S. at 733. Does the ruling of the *Public Lands Council* Court suggest that these goals are not of equal importance? How should the BLM go about weighing these (sometimes) competing interests?

2.   What Is at Stake? What type of interest did a permit issued under the Taylor Grazing Act bestow upon a rancher? How did the regulations at issue in the *Public Lands Council* decision alter those interests? Were the ranchers arguing that the BLM did not have authority to reduce their grazing rights in order to protect the rangeland? If not, what was the substance of the ranchers' claim? What was motivating the ranchers in this case?

3.   Ranchers' Revenge. Despite being unsuccessful before the *Public Lands Council* Court, it was not long before the ranchers succeeded in having the 1995 BLM regulations replaced. In July 2006, the BLM promulgated new grazing regulations which, for the most part, reinstated the pre-1995 status quo. *See* 43 C.F.R. § 4100 (2006). The new regulations redefined grazing "preference" with reference to quantity of grazing; allowed ranchers to obtain water rights in their own names; required that the BLM monitor existing practices before it; ordered improved grazing practices to protect rangeland health; and reduced the opportunity for the public to have input in agency grazing decisions at various points in the process. Why do you suppose the policy was changed?

In 2010, the Ninth Circuit held that the BLM violated provisions of NEPA and the ESA when promulgating the new regulations. *W. Watersheds Project v. Kraayenbrink*, 632 F.3d 472 (9th Cir. 2011). As a result, the regulations were enjoined and the pre-2006 rules reinstated.

4.   Grazing Fees. The introduction of "grazing preference" regulations, which were the subject of the *Public Lands Council* case, was only one part of a major overhaul of the grazing system undertaken during the early 1990s. Led by Bruce Babbitt, Secretary of the Interior throughout the Clinton Administration, Interior made the reform of public lands ranching a key initiative. A major focus of this initiative was an attempt to alter the grazing fee structure. Unlike the grazing preference proposal, however, the fee structure proposal was ultimately abandoned by Interior in the face of intense political resistance.

The problems with grazing fee have been described in the following terms:

> The present grazing fee makes very little sense economically. First, as the United States General Accounting Office (GAO) has concluded, the grazing fee "significantly understates the market value of grazing on federal lands," which is inconsistent with the predominant policy objectives of the grazing administration statutes, as discussed above, as well as sound fiscal policy. Second, the revenue created by the grazing fee is substantially less than the administration, management, and improvement costs of the grazing program paid by the federal government. In 1999, grazing fee receipts totaled $14,022,995, while the costs of the grazing program were estimated at $200,000,000. Third, administering the grazing program costs the federal government more than the "ranchers who use the federal lands make in profits." Indeed, "[a]s long as administrative costs are so high, it would pay to abolish the existing grazing regime and buy out all grazing rights." Notably, receipts generated by various other activities on BLM lands well exceed the revenues from grazing fees: in fiscal year 1999, sales of land generated $21,956,883; mining claim fees produced $25,318,963; and even helium revenues amounted to $16,100,000. A further area of criticism is the existence of other subsidies inherent in the grazing program, such as insecticide application and predator "control," which the BLM provides at no additional cost to public lands ranchers. Finally, because no property right is conferred by the permit or lease, ranchers are not required to pay any property taxes for their allotment, which represents a sizable advantage over owner-utilized pasture.

Michelle M. Campana, *Public Lands Grazing Fee Reform: Welfare Cowboys and Rolex Ranchers Wrangling with the New West*, 10 N.Y.U. ENVTL. L.J. 403, 433–34 (2002). In the face of these criticisms, Babbitt's proposed reform was relatively simple—an increase in the grazing fee (of $1.86 per AUM) to reflect market prices (of $4.28 per AUM). *See* Scott Nicoll, *The Death of Rangeland Reform*, 21 J. ENVTL. L. & LITIG. 47, 65 (2006). While the proposal was generally well received, it was strongly opposed by westerners in the Senate and by ranching interests. *See* Campana, *supra*, at 442. Indeed, as noted by Campana,

> [t]he Senate went so far as to pass a bill that would have limited DOI appropriations if the agency proceeded with the rulemaking as it then appeared. . . . Although the DOI appropriations bill was eventually passed without any limitations, this episode, in conjunction with the western opposition, essentially rendered the reform proposal a failure.

Id.

The disparity between grazing revenue and administrative costs persists today. In 2009, BLM estimated appropriations for grazing management at $49.3 million, while grazing receipts were only $11.9 million. The Forest Service had estimated appropriations for grazing management at $72.1 million, while receipts were approximately $5.2 million. Vincent, *Grazing Fees, supra,* at 2. The grazing fee has ranged from $1.35 to $2.31 per year since 1981; in 2018, the fee was $1.41 per AUM. *Id.* at 3; BLM, Instruction Memorandum: 2018 Grazing Fee, Surcharge Rates, and Penalty for Unauthorized Grazing Use Rates (Feb. 26, 2018). Moreover, environmentalists note that low grazing fees fail to account for many externalities including degraded soil quality, water use, greenhouse gas emissions, and negative effects on wildlife habitat.

What can explain the artificially low grazing fee presently implemented by the BLM and the Forest Service? What are its consequences? What incentives does the present fee structure create on the part of ranchers? How would these incentives differ in the face of an appropriately structured fee? To what extent can the failed reform of the grazing fee be explained by public choice theory? Do public choice pathologies also explain the "rancher's revenge" described in the preceding note?

For a discussion of Babbitt's attempts to reform federal management of the national rangelands, and other natural resources under Interior's control, *see* John D. Leshy, *The Babbitt Legacy at the Department of the Interior: A Preliminary View*, 31 ENVTL. L. 199 (2001).

5.   Tragedy of the Commons. In many respects, the circumstances that led to the passage of the Taylor Grazing Act mirror the classic illustration of Hardin's "tragedy of the commons" (discussed in Chapter I). Recall that Hardin, in response to the "tragedy," suggested a number of different treatments of the commons:

> We might sell them off as private property. We might keep them as public property, but allocate the right to enter them. The allocation might be on the basis of wealth, by the use of an auction system. It might be on the basis of merit, as defined by some agreed-upon standards. It might be by lottery. Or it might be on a first-come first-served basis, administered to long queues. These, I think, are

all the reasonable possibilities. They are all objectionable. But we must choose, or acquiesce in the destruction of the commons. . . .

Garnett Hardin, *The Tragedy of the Commons*, 162 SCIENCE 1243, 1245 (1968). How would you characterize the approach adopted in the Taylor Grazing Act under these alternatives? In what ways could this approach be considered "objectionable"? In what other ways could the Act have been structured?

6.   Alternative Approaches. As the Hardin excerpt suggests, there exist a number of different approaches to dealing with the tragedy of the commons. One proposal contemplates the introduction of conservation permits (CPs). *See* David G. Alderson, *Buyouts and Conservation Permits: A Market Approach to Address the Federal Public Land Grazing Problem*, 12 N.Y.U. ENVTL. L.J. 903 (2005). A conservation permit has been described in the following terms:

> A [CP] confers the right to conduct ecologically valuable activities on a defined piece of federal land. Just as grazing permits entitle ranchers to graze livestock on specific sections of federal land, CPs [would] authorize their owners to perform conservation-oriented activities on the land.

Id. at 930. The CP system would operate as a form of buyout procedure. A citizen or environmental organization would first identify a controversial or environmentally valuable piece of land, on which grazing is undertaken. The group would then approach the holder of the grazing permit and negotiate a price for the permit. Having taken control of the permit, the citizen or environmental organization could then exchange that permit for a CP. *See id.* What are the advantages of proposed market based mechanisms such as the CP system? What are the disadvantages? What incentives would it create on the part of relevant actors, such as ranchers, preservationists and other users of the rangelands? *See id.* Would the system create perverse incentives on the part of existing permit holders? How do these incentives compare with those that would be created by the privatization of the land?

7.   FLPMA and Grazing. As noted in *Public Lands Council*, FLPMA was passed in 1976, and is BLM's "organic act," directing it manage public lands according to the principles of "multiple use" and "sustained yield." 43 U.S.C. §§ 1701, 1702(c). In addition to setting forth broadly applicable standards for public lands and requiring land use planning, FLPMA addresses grazing specifically. These provisions supplement BLM's authority under the Taylor Act, as well as the Public Rangelands Improvement Act of 1978, 43 U.S.C. §§ 1901, *et seq.*

FLPMA provides that livestock grazing permits and leases:

> [S]hall be for a term of ten years subject to such terms and conditions the Secretary concerned deems appropriate and consistent with the governing law, including, but not limited to, the authority of the Secretary concerned to cancel, suspend, or modify a grazing permit or lease, in whole or in part, pursuant to the terms and conditions thereof, or to cancel or suspend a grazing permit or

lease for any violation of a grazing regulation or of any term or condition of such grazing permit or lease.

43 U.S.C. § 1752(a). The Secretary can issue permits for *less* than ten years where the land is pending disposal, the land will be devoted to another public purpose sooner than ten years, or if a shorter term is "in the best interest of sound land management." *Id.* § 1752(b). Holders of expiring permits or leases have first priority in renewing said permits or leases, provided that the Secretary agrees to renew, and subject to all conditions of the permit or lease. *Id.* § 1752(c).

How does FLPMA change BLM's role in administering leasing? Given that BLM is subject to the Taylor Act, FLPMA, and the Public Rangelands Improvement Act (not detailed here, but mandating that BLM inventory and monitor range conditions, and seek to "improve range conditions"), do you see any potential conflicts in the statutory directives contained in each statute?

8.   Unauthorized Grazing. Another challenge for federal agencies managing extensive, and often remote, land holdings is the unauthorized use of public lands. In 2016, the U.S. Government Accountability Office found that the frequency and extent of unauthorized grazing on BLM and Forest Service lands was "largely unknown because according to agency officials, the agencies prefer to handle most incidents informally (e.g., with a telephone call) and do not record them." GAO, UNAUTHORIZED GRAZING: ACTIONS NEEDED TO IMPROVE TRACKING AND DETERRENCE EFFORTS (July 2016).

On what other types of public land might you expected unauthorized use to be a problem? What can federal agencies do to deter and combat this? With respect to unauthorized grazing, GAO offered several recommendations, including recording all incidents, amending regulations to reflect practices for resolving such incidents, and strengthening enforcement of unauthorized grazing. *Id.* at 31–32.

9.   States and Sagebrush Rebellions. "Sagebrush Rebels" is a general term coined for those who want the federal government to give more control of federally-owned western lands to state and local authorities. One legal commentator characterized the Sagebrush Rebellion as stemming from backlash in western states to the passage of FLPMA in 1976, which ended the largescale disposal of unappropriated federal lands to the states and placed restrictions on mining, ranching, and other commercial interests. John Leshy, *Unraveling the Sagebrush Rebellion: Law, Politics and Federal Lands*, 14 U.C. DAVIS L. REV. 317, 341, 343 (1980). Ronald Reagan declared himself a sagebrush rebel in an August 1980 campaign speech in Salt Lake City. James Coates, *'Sagebrush Rebellion' On Hold, Group Lights Other Legal Fires*, CHICAGO TRIBUNE, Mar. 16, 1986.

The sentiment has endured well into the 21st century with pressure from politicians and organized interest groups with respect to livestock grazing, mineral extraction, and other economic development of federal lands in the West. In 2014, cattle rancher Cliven Bundy, contravening court orders, refused to pay $1.2 million in grazing fees for using federal land in southeastern Nevada to graze his cattle for 20 years. BLM moved to confiscate some of his cattle, and an armed standoff ensued. Brian Feldman, *Armed Standoff Over Cattle Grazing Comes to an End*, THE ATLANTIC, Apr. 14, 2014.

Why do you think the Sagebrush Rebellion has endured, in some form, for decades? Is there any merit to the argument that bureaucrats in Washington, D.C. should not dictate how western lands are used? What are the pros and cons of the current system? BLM provides states with 50 percent of all revenue from federal mineral extraction on public lands within their borders. *See* 30 U.S.C. § 191(a). Further, BLM and the Forest Service allocate grazing revenue to the states: 12.5% to 50% for BLM lands and 25% for Forest Service lands. 43 U.S.C. § 315(i); 16 U.S.C. § 500. For both agencies, the money allocated to states is to be used to benefit the counties from which the fees were generated. Does the existence of these longstanding revenue share provisions change your view on the fairness of federal control of public lands within states?

10. Climate Change and Grazing. What effect does the scientific consensus around human-caused climate change have on federal management of the rangelands? Grazing livestock on public lands contributes to climate change in the form of methane, a potent greenhouse gas released through the digestive process of ruminant animals. U.S. EPA, *Sources of Greenhouse Gas Emissions: Agriculture Sector Emissions*, https://www.epa.gov/ghgemissions/sources-greenhouse-gas-emissions (last visited Dec. 1, 2018) ("Livestock, especially ruminants such as cattle, produce methane as part of their normal digestive processes. This process is called enteric fermentation, and it represents almost one third of the emissions from the Agriculture economic sector."). In addition, the BLM and Forest Service make land use decisions concerning grazing on more than 200 million acres of public lands, which also affect greenhouse gas emissions. How might BLM adjust its grazing policies to account for climate change effects?

Hillary Hoffman notes that federal agencies can use adaptive management techniques to better manage grazing in an era of climate change:

> . . . agencies like the BLM and Forest Service know that temperatures will warm by several degrees in the southwestern states, which will impact forage and water availability in somewhat predicable ways (less forage and less surface water). Thus, when revising land or resource management plans under FLPMA, the agencies could use that outcome to lower the Animal Unit Month ("AUM") levels on all allotments in the southwestern states, to a degree that might maintain adequate forage. Then, the agencies can develop plans to monitor forage availability in light of temperatures and water supply to determine if the across-the-board decision to lower AUMs was effective, conduct the monitoring, and make any necessary adjustments in AUMs based on the results.

Hillary M. Hoffmann, *Climate Change and the Decline of the Federal Range: Is Adaptive Management the Solution?*, 15 VT. J. ENVTL. L. 36, 288 (2014). What other policies should federal agencies consider?

D. MINERAL LEASING

The U.S. Department of the Interior ("Interior") oversees more than 260 million surface acres and 700 million subsurface acres of mineral resources onshore, and more than 1.7 billion acres offshore. GAO, NO. GAO-14-50, OIL AND GAS RESOURCES: ACTIONS NEEDED FOR INTERIOR TO BETTER ENSURE A FAIR RETURN 2 (2013). Interior's Bureau of Land Management ("BLM") manages onshore mineral resources including coal, oil, and natural gas. Offshore in the waters of the U.S. Outer Continental Shelf, Interior's Bureau of Ocean Energy Management ("BOEM") manages oil and gas leasing. This section addresses onshore and offshore mineral leasing in turn, focusing on the statutory duties of each agency that center on balancing resource development and environmental protection.

i. ONSHORE MINERAL LEASING

The vast majority of public lands that BLM manages are located in 12 western states. These diverse lands include arctic, desert, range, and timber lands, valued for a wide spectrum of uses including mineral and renewable energy production, as well as scenic, wildlife, wilderness, historic, and recreational values.

At the turn of the 20th century, the growing economic importance of coal led many to question the federal government's lax oversight over coal-rich lands, which had enabled fraudulent private acquisition and unregulated development. In 1906, President Theodore Roosevelt authorized the reservation of 66 million acres of coal-rich lands to the federal government, so that the U.S. Geological Survey could determine the best use for the lands. Sylvia L. Harrison, *Disposition of the Mineral Estate on United States Public Lands: A Historical Perspective*, 10 PUB. LAND L. REV. 131, 148 (1989). Roosevelt's successors followed suit by reserving federal lands containing oil and gas minerals, as well as phosphate, nitrate, potash, and asphaltic minerals. In 1920, Congress passed the Mineral Leasing Act ("MLA"), allowing individuals and companies to prospect for and develop minerals on federal public lands, while the federal government retained title to the land. *See* 30 U.S.C. §§ 181 et seq.

In the MLA, Congress outlined the federal authority to lease lands for mineral development and manage exploration and production, and established a system to collect royalties and rents from private developers. BLM was created in 1946, when Interior merged two older agencies: the General Land Office, created in 1800 to sell public lands and encourage settlement; and the Grazing Service, created in 1934 to manage grazing on public lands. Michael C. Blumm & Andrew B.

Erickson, *Federal Wild Lands Policy in the Twenty-First Century: What
A Long, Strange Trip It's Been*, 25 COLO. NAT. RES., ENERGY & ENVTL L.
REV. 1, 32 (2014). BLM continued issuing mineral leases on public lands.
For several decades, BLM lacked a legal mandate and was viewed as an
agency with the "nebulous and unenviable task" of overseeing the
"leftover" public lands—lands that were never privatized through
homesteading or any of the other land disposal policies and yet were not
"adopted" by the more structured federal land management agencies,
such as the Forest Service, National Park Service, or Fish and Wildlife
Service. Sarah Krakoff, *Settling the Wilderness*, 75 U. COLO. L. REV.
1159, 1163 (2004).

In 1976, Congress passed FLPMA, which provided BLM with an
organic act to guide its land management priorities and practices. 43
U.S.C. §§ 1701–1787. FLPMA provides that federal lands are to be used
only for the advancement of the national interest. 43 U.S.C. § 1701(a)(1).
The Act declares that:

> [P]ublic lands be managed in a manner that will protect the
> quality of scientific, scenic, historical, ecological, environmental,
> air and atmospheric, water resource, and archeological values;
> that, where appropriate, will preserve and protect certain public
> lands in their natural condition; that will provide food and
> habitat for fish and wildlife and domestic animals; and that will
> provide for outdoor recreation and human occupancy and use.

Id. § 1701(a)(8). The Act sets forth BLM's dual mandate of development
and preservation. BLM must both protect the environment and manage
federal lands in such a way as to "recognize[] the Nation's need for
domestic sources of minerals, food, timber, and fiber from the public
lands." *Id.* § 1701(a)(12).

FLPMA requires agencies to develop land use plans, and to manage
public lands in accordance with the "principles of multiple use and
sustained yield." 43 U.S.C. § 1712(a)–(c)(1). The Act defines "multiple
use" as:

> [T]he management of the public lands and their various
> resource values so that they are utilized in the combination that
> will best meet the present and future needs of the American
> people; . . . the use of some land for less than all of the resources;
> a combination of balanced and diverse resource uses that takes
> into account the long-term needs of future generations for
> renewable and nonrenewable resources, including, but not
> limited to, recreation, range, timber, minerals, watershed,
> wildlife and fish, and natural scenic, scientific and historical
> values.

43 U.S.C. § 1702(c). "Multiple use" also refers to the "harmonious and
coordinated management of the various resources without permanent
impairment of the productivity of the land and the quality of the

environment with consideration being given to the relative values of the resources and not necessarily to the combination of uses that will give the greatest economic return or the greatest unit output." *Id.*

FLPMA defines "sustained yield" as: "the achievement and maintenance in perpetuity of a high-level annual or regular periodic output of the various renewable resources of the public lands consistent with multiple use." *Id.* § 1702(h). The Act also tasks Interior with "tak[ing] any action necessary to prevent unnecessary or undue degradation of the lands." *Id.* § 1732(b).

Section 202 of FLPMA authorized BLM to identify areas of critical environmental concern ("ACEC") through its planning process. ACECs are defined as areas "within the public lands where special management attention is required" to protect "important historic, cultural or scenic areas, fish and wildlife resources, or other natural systems or processes, or to protect life and safety from natural hazards. . . ." 43 U.S.C. § 1702(a).

Pursuant to FLPMA and the MLA, all federal oil, natural gas, and coal leases must provide the American people with "fair market value" for the "use of the public lands and their resources." 43 U.S.C. § 1701(a)(9); 30 U.S.C. § 201(a)(1). BLM receives revenue from coal, oil, and natural gas leasing in three ways: (1) a bonus bid that is paid at the time BLM issues a lease; (2) rental fees paid until production begins; and (3) production royalties. Royalty rates are set by statute and regulation at not less than 12.5 percent for surface coal mines, oil, and natural gas, and 8 percent for underground coal mines.

BLM undertakes a three-step process to lease federal coal, oil and natural gas resources. First, in the planning phase, BLM identifies geographic areas that are suitable for leasing by preparing a Resource Management Plan ("RMP"). Next, BLM identifies specific parcels within the RMP to make available to producers through competitive lease sales, and reviews the environmental impact of the proposed leases. If BLM finds the leases will not significantly impact the environment, it proceeds with the sales. Finally, in the permitting stage, developers apply for a permit to drill or mine from the agency. *See Ctr. for Biological Diversity v. Bureau of Land Mgmt.*, 937 F. Supp. 2d 1140, 1146 (N.D. Cal. 2013). Leases are subject to the terms and conditions of the standard lease form and any additional stipulations or lease notices identified in the relevant RMP or in site-specific environmental analysis.

Other Interior bureaus, in particular the Office of Natural Resources Revenue ("ONRR"), also have responsibilities in administering mineral development. ONRR collects, disburses, and verifies revenues from leases, including bonus bids, royalties, and rental payments, and distributes those funds evenly between the Federal Treasury and the states where the mineral resources are located. 30 U.S.C. § 191(a)–(b). One exception is Alaska, which is entitled to 90 percent of federal royalties for oil, gas, and coal production in the state. 30 U.S.C. § 191(a).

For coal mining, Interior's Office of Surface Mining Reclamation and Enforcement ("OSMRE") carries out the requirements of the Surface Mining Control and Reclamation Act ("SMCRA") in cooperation with states and tribes. OSMRE's primary objectives are to ensure that coal mines are operated in a manner that protects citizens and the environment during mining, ensure that the land is restored to beneficial use following mining, and to mitigate the effects of past mining by pursuing reclamation of abandoned coal mines. *See* 30 U.S.C. §§ 1201; 1211; 1231–1279.

Some of BLM's fiscal terms—including royalty rates for onshore oil and gas production—have not changed since 1920. The U.S. Government Accountability Office has repeatedly called for Interior to reform its fiscal system, which may be depriving tax payers of hundreds of millions of dollars each year from domestic energy production. *See* GAO, NO. GAO-14-50, OIL AND GAS RESOURCES: ACTIONS NEEDED FOR INTERIOR TO BETTER ENSURE A FAIR RETURN (2013). Further, some legal commentators observe that because Interior excludes many environmental and social considerations when setting lease terms, federal leases are undervalued from a social welfare-maximizing perspective. *See* Jayni Foley Hein, *Federal Lands and Fossil Fuel: Maximizing Social Welfare in Federal Energy Leasing*, 42 HARV. ENVTL. L. REV. 1, 12 (2018).

Today, coal produced on federal lands accounts for about 40 percent of total U.S. coal production; crude oil and natural gas produced from federal lands account for about 25 percent of U.S. production. OFFICE OF POLICY ANALYSIS, U.S. DEP'T OF THE INTERIOR, U.S. DEPARTMENT OF THE INTERIOR ECONOMIC REPORT FY 2015 1 (2016). Federal oil and gas production has been decreasing as a share of total U.S. production, as new technology like fracking has greatly increased production in shale basins under state and private ownership. Coal mining on federal lands, by contrast, has grown as a proportion of the domestic total as demand for low-sulfur coal produced predominantly in federal basins increased over the past decade, in response to air quality regulations. *See* CONG. RESEARCH SERV., R42432, U.S. CRUDE OIL AND NATURAL GAS PRODUCTION IN FEDERAL AND NON-FEDERAL AREAS (2014); U.S. ENERGY INFO. ADMIN., SALES OF FOSSIL FUELS PRODUCED FROM FEDERAL AND INDIAN LANDS, FY 2003 THROUGH FY 2014 (2015). Federal coal produced from the Powder River Basin in Montana and Wyoming accounts for over 85 percent of that federal coal production, and federal coal was used to generate about 14 percent of the Nation's electricity in 2015. SECRETARY OF THE INTERIOR, SECRETARIAL ORDER NO. 3338 (Jan. 16, 2015).

The case below addresses a challenge under the statutory requirement to obtain "fair market value" for coal leases. The next passage is an excerpt from Secretarial Order 3338, issued by former Interior Secretary Sally Jewell in 2016, which outlined priorities for reevaluating the federal coal program through a programmatic environmental review. The Secretarial Order was rescinded in 2017, at the beginning of the Trump administration, but remains illustrative of modern critiques of the federal mineral leasing system and recent efforts at reform.

Nat'l Wildlife Fed'n v. Burford

871 F.2d 849 (9th Cir. 1989).

■ Before HUG, NORRIS and THOMPSON, CIRCUIT JUDGES.

■ HUG, CIRCUIT JUDGE:

The National Wildlife Federation ("NWF"), Montana Wildlife Federation, Northern Plains Resource Council, and the Powder River Basin Resource Council appeal the district court's entry of summary judgment on count 1 of their amended complaint. Count 1 alleged that the Secretary of the Interior violated 30 U.S.C. § 201(a)(1) (1982) by accepting coal lease bids that fell below fair market value ("FMV"). The district court properly held that NWF had standing to bring its suit and properly concluded that the Secretary had acted within the law in selling the leases. We affirm the summary judgment.

In 1982, NWF initiated this action challenging the Department of Interior's ("DOI") sale of coal leases in the Powder River Basin area of Montana and Wyoming. The sale involved approximately 1.6 billion tons of coal distributed over 23,000 acres of public land. NWF alleged a variety of federal statutory violations surrounding the sale and sued under the Administrative Procedure Act ("APA"), 5 U.S.C. §§ 551–706 (1982).

. . . 30 U.S.C. § 201(a)(1) (1982) provides that no bid on land offered for leasing "shall be accepted which is less than the fair market value, *as determined by the Secretary,* of the coal subject to the lease" (emphasis added). The Secretary "shall award leases . . . by competitive bidding." *Id.* Defined in 43 C.F.R. § 3400.0–5(n) (1981), fair market value is "that amount in cash, or on terms reasonably equivalent to cash, for which in all probability the coal deposit would be sold or leased by a knowledgeable owner willing but not obligated to sell or lease to a knowledgeable purchaser who desires but is not obligated to buy or lease."

In light of the language contained in section 201(a)(1) and the interpretative regulation, NWF's task is to show that DOI did not receive FMV for its leases in the Powder River Basin area. Since agency action is presumed to be justified, *Wilderness Public Rights,* 608 F.2d at 1254, and the Secretary need present only a reasonable explanation for his actions, NWF's burden of proof is considerable.

The district court, after a careful review of the administrative record, concluded that the Secretary acted reasonably, although possibly not supremely wisely, in accepting the Powder River lease bids. He found specifically that the shift to an entry level bid ("ELB") system which

allowed lower initial bids than the prior minimum acceptable bid
("MAB") system, was satisfactorily explained in the record by
information attesting to declining coal prices; that FMV refers to receipt
of a fair return, and not to the procedures used (citing California v. Watt,
712 F.2d 584, 606 (D.C. Cir. 1983)); that nine of the eleven tracts up for
lease received high bids that met or exceeded the pre-sale estimates of
FMV; and that the process used to calculate the pre-sale FMV figures,
which involved approximately 4,000 hours of work, was not unsound.

NWF raises two major attacks on the district court's finding of
reasonableness. First, it contends that the shift to the ELB system was
irrational and insufficiently explained in the record. The ELB procedure
guaranteed, according to NWF, the receipt of less than FMV. Second,
NWF argues that the MABs used in the sales were skewed by the DOI's
reliance on a prior coal lease sale not comparable to the Powder River
Basin sale. Use of these MABs as benchmarks of FMV, consequently, was
improper.

The claim based on deficiencies in the ELB system is unpersuasive.
First, the ELB system is not in itself arbitrary or capricious. The basis
for the bidding procedure, as NWF repeatedly points out, is the
presumption of competitive bidding. As section 201(a)(1) makes clear,
leases shall be sold by the Secretary "by competitive bidding." The
Secretary contends the ELB system stimulates competitive bidding. The
Secretary can hardly be faulted for using a sales system whose purpose
is to implement the statute's mandate. Second, the shift from the MAB
to ELB procedure did not constitute an abrupt or unexplained departure
from settled policy. As the administrative record shows, DOI had begun
to consider use of the ELB system in coal lease sales in 1981. The decision
to implement this system in the Powder River lease sale occurred as a
result of studies suggesting a decline in the western coal market. The use
of the ELB to stimulate competitive bidding at the time of a softening
market cannot be said to be arbitrary and capricious. Finally, despite
whatever flaws may have existed in the ELB system, actual high bids on
nine out of the eleven available tracts met or exceeded the pre-sale
estimate of FMV. It is the result of the bidding procedure that is
important: whether the high bid represented fair market value.

NWF's second contention is that the MABs used in the pre-sale
estimates were defective, and did not represent fair market value. NWF
claims that in calculating pre-sale FMV, DOI used data from one prior
sale, the "AB" sale, that was not comparable while ignoring data from a
comparable sale, the "CD" sale. Choice of comparable sales figures and
the calculation of MABs is a technical issue subject to analysis by trained
specialists. The reviewing court's task is not to resolve disagreements
between differing technical perspectives. Instead, its duty "is the limited
one of ascertaining that the choices made by the [Secretary] were
reasonable and supported by the record. . . . That the evidence in the
record may support other conclusions, even those that are inconsistent

with the [Secretary's], does not prevent us from concluding that his decisions were rational and supported by the record." *Lead Indus. Ass'n, Inc. v. EPA*, 647 F.2d 1130, 1160 (D.C. Cir.), *cert. denied*, 449 U.S. 1042 (1980). The administrative record suggests that the Economic Evaluation Committee's appraisal of the AB sales led to the conclusion that the AB figures best suited the type of leases available in the Powder River Basin. DOI had a reasonable basis for its Powder River MABs and for its conclusion that the lease price for the tracts which equaled or exceeded the pre-sale MABs represented fair market value.

Finally, NWF contends that a variety of procedural irregularities corrupted the bid process. NWF states that pre-bid pricing leaks to industry representatives, the Secretary's quick announcement that the sale was successful, and other events of a similar nature irretrievably corrupted the sale. Although these irregularities may have occurred, NWF has not met its burden of showing that the leases did not sell for a fair return as a result of these problems. Given that the pre-sale FMV figures were reasonable and that nine out of the ten leases went to bidders who met or exceeded those figures, NWF's procedural argument is unpersuasive.

NWF has not demonstrated that DOI received less than FMV for its Powder River leases and that the Secretary's decision to accept the leases was arbitrary or capricious. The district court's summary judgment ruling, consequently, is AFFIRMED.

Secretary of the Interior, Secretarial Order No. 3338 (Jan. 16, 2015)

Subject: Discretionary Programmatic Environmental Impact Statement to Modernize the Federal Coal Program

Sec. 1 Purpose. The Department of the Interior (Department) is entrusted with overseeing Federal land and resources for the benefit of current and future generations. This responsibility includes advancing the safe and responsible development of our energy resources, while also promoting the conservation of our Federal lands and the protection of their scientific, historic, and environmental values for generations to come. The production of federally managed coal presently accounts for approximately 41 percent of the coal produced in the Nation. However, the existing regulatory and programmatic scheme for leasing that coal has been in place, with only relatively minor adjustments, since 1979. It was established at a time when market conditions, environmental concerns, and energy infrastructure were considerably different from today. To help determine whether and how the current system for developing Federal coal should be modernized, this Secretarial Order directs the Bureau of Land Management (BLM) to prepare a discretionary Programmatic Environmental Impact Statement (PEIS) that analyzes potential leasing and management reforms to the current

Federal coal program. The PEIS will provide a vehicle for the Department to undertake a comprehensive review of the program and consider whether and how the program may be improved and modernized to foster the orderly development of BLM administered coal on Federal lands in a manner that gives proper consideration to the impact of that development on important stewardship values, while also ensuring a fair return to the American public. . . .

Of [the public] concerns [raised through listening sessions and written comments], three aspects of the current coal program received the most attention. First, numerous stakeholders are concerned that American taxpayers are not receiving a fair return on public coal resources. Second, many stakeholders are concerned that the Federal coal program conflicts with the Administration's climate policy and our national climate goals, making it more difficult for us to achieve those goals. Third, there are numerous and varying concerns about the structure of the Federal coal program in light of current market conditions, including how implementation of the Federal leasing program affects current and future coal markets, coal-dependent communities and companies, and the reclamation of mined lands. . . .

i. Concerns about Fair Return. In 2013, both GAO and OIG [Office of Inspector General] issued reports expressing concerns about the Federal coal program, particularly with respect to the leasing process and fair market value. . . .

These concerns arise, at least in part, because there is currently very little competition for Federal coal leases. About 90 percent of lease sales receive bids from only one bidder, typically the operator of a mine adjacent to the new lease, given the investment required to open a new mine. While the BLM conducts a peer-reviewed analysis to determine the "fair market value" of the coal and will not sell a lease unless the bid meets or exceeds that value, commenters have questioned whether an accurate fair market value can be identified in the absence of a truly competitive marketplace.

Commenters also raised concerns about the royalty rates set in Federal leases, which are set by regulation at a fixed 8 percent for underground mines and not less than 12.5 percent for surface mines. Many stakeholders believe that these rates do not adequately compensate the public for the removal of the coal and the externalities associated with its use. Still others have suggested that the impact of Federal coal sales, which currently represent approximately 41 percent of total domestic production, artificially lowers market prices, further reducing the amount of royalties received.

Stakeholders also criticize the Federal coal program for obtaining even lower returns through certain types of leasing actions, such as lease modifications, and through royalty rate reductions, which may result in royalty rates as low as 2 percent. In addition, stakeholders have noted that the $100 acre minimum bid requirement, which is rarely applicable due to fair market value requirements, but occasionally relevant, is outdated.

ii. Concerns about Climate Change. The second broad category of concerns about the Federal coal program relates to its impacts on climate change. The United States has pledged to the United Nations Framework Convention on Climate Change (UNFCCC) to reduce its greenhouse gas (GHG) emissions by 26–28 percent below 2005 levels by 2025. The Obama Administration has made, and is continuing to make, unprecedented efforts to reduce GHG emissions in line with this target through numerous measures. Numerous scientific studies indicate that reducing GHG emissions from coal use worldwide is critical to addressing climate change.

At the same time, as noted above, the Federal coal program is a significant component of overall United States' coal production. Federal coal represents approximately 41 percent of the coal produced in the United States, and when combusted, it contributes roughly 10 percent of the total U.S. GHG emissions.

Many stakeholders highlighted the tension between producing very large quantities of Federal coal while pursuing policies to reduce U.S. GHG emissions substantially, including from coal combustion. Critics also noted that the current leasing system does not provide a way to systematically consider the climate impacts and costs to taxpayers of Federal coal development. . . .

Sec. 4 Discretionary Programmatic Environmental Impact Statement. Given the broad range of issues raised over the course of the past year (and beyond) and the lack of any recent analysis of the Federal coal program as a whole, a more comprehensive, programmatic review is in order, building on the BLM's public listening sessions. Accordingly, to meaningfully address the breadth and complexity of the issues raised by commenters regarding the Federal coal program, I hereby direct the BLM to conduct a broad, programmatic review of the Federal coal program it administers through the preparation of a PEIS under NEPA.

The Department is authorized to undertake this effort in its stewardship role as a proprietor and sovereign regulator which is charged by Congress with managing and overseeing mineral development on the public lands, not only for the purpose of ensuring safe and responsible development of mineral resources, but also to ensure conservation of the public lands, the protection of their scientific, historic, and environmental values, and compliance with applicable environmental laws. Additionally, the Department has the statutory duty to ensure a fair return to the taxpayer and broad discretionary authority to decide where, when, and under what terms and conditions, mineral development should occur, including with regard to the issuance of Federal coal leases. . . .

While the precise issues to be assessed in the PEIS will be determined through the public scoping process, the PEIS should at a minimum address the following topics:

a. How, When and Where to Lease. The regional leasing program authorized in the 1979 regulations has not worked as envisioned and, instead, BLM has conducted leasing only in response to industry applications. Given concerns about the lack of competition in the lease-by-application system, as well as consideration of environmental goals, the PEIS should examine whether the current regulatory framework should be changed to provide a better mechanism or mechanisms to decide which coal resources should be made available and how the leasing process should work.

As part of this evaluation, the PEIS should explicitly examine the issue of when to lease. Some leasing programs for other Federal resources operate with an established schedule for leasing or consideration of leasing (e.g., BLM holds onshore oil and gas lease sales on a quarterly basis if parcels are available; offshore oil and gas leasing occurs using a schedule established in a five-year plan). The PEIS should examine whether scheduled sales should be used for Federal coal.

The PEIS should also examine where to lease. In other contexts, the Department has identified areas to promote certain kinds of resource development. For example, the BLM's Solar PEIS (Western Solar Plan) amended land use plans across six southwestern states and established preferred locations for solar development. The PEIS should examine whether a similar approach would be useful for coal to minimize potential user conflicts and streamline leasing decisions.

b. Fair Return. The PEIS should address whether the bonus bids, rents, and royalties received under the Federal coal program are successfully securing a fair return to the American public for Federal coal, and, if not, what adjustments could be made to provide such compensation. As part of this analysis, the PEIS should examine whether the decision to lease large amounts of relatively low cost coal artificially drives down pricing in the U.S. market and, if so, how the taxpayer may best be compensated for the reduced royalties due to artificially low prices. The PEIS should also examine whether the BLM estimates of fair market value for purposes of establishing minimum bids successfully substitute for competition in the bidding process, and if not, how to better estimate fair market value.

c. Climate Impacts. With respect to the climate impacts of the Federal coal program, the PEIS should examine how best to assess the climate impacts of continued Federal coal production and combustion and how to address those impacts in the management of the program to meet both the Nation's energy needs and its climate goals, as well as how best to protect the public lands from climate change impacts.

d. Socio-Economic Considerations. Beyond the issue of fair market value, the PEIS should assess whether the current Federal coal leasing program adequately accounts for externalities related to Federal coal production, including environmental and social impacts. It should more broadly examine how the administration, availability, and pricing of Federal coal affect regional and national economies (including job impacts), and energy markets in general, including the pricing and viability of other coal resources (both domestic and foreign) and other energy sources. The impact of possible program alternatives on the projected fuel mix and cost of electricity in the United States should also be examined.

e. Exports. The PEIS should address whether leasing decisions should consider whether the coal to be produced from a given tract would be for domestic use or export. In consultation with other applicable executive branch offices, the PEIS should examine how to estimate export potential, particularly given potential differences between the estimates of industry and independent economic experts about the prospects for exports in a given circumstance.

f. Energy Needs. Finally, the PEIS should examine the degree to which Federal coal supports, or should support, fulfilling the energy needs of the United States. The evaluation should include an assessment of how the administration, availability, and pricing of Federal coal impacts electricity generation in the United States, particularly in light of other regulatory influences, and what other sources of energy supply (including efficiency) are projected to be available. . . .

NOTES AND QUESTIONS

1. Uncompetitive Leasing. The Mineral Leasing Act of 1920 and Federal Coal Leasing Amendments Act of 1976 require that federal oil, gas, and coal leases be offered by competitive bidding. 30 U.S.C. § 226(b)(1)(A); 30 U.S.C. § 201(a)(1). In 2013, GAO found that approximately 90 percent of all federal coal lease sales since 1990 attracted only one bidder. GAO, OIL AND GAS RESOURCES: ACTIONS NEEDED FOR INTERIOR TO BETTER ENSURE A FAIR RETURN (2013). This is likely the result of a structural issue: coal companies frequently nominate tracts for lease adjacent to their existing coal mines and operations. While this may be efficient from a private company perspective, it all but ensures that there will be minimal competition for new coal leases from different companies, for whom the cost to mine the lease would be much greater.

Low competition is not unique to federal coal; about 40 percent of oil and gas leases in effect as of 2015 were issued noncompetitively, for the minimum bid price of $2 per acre. BLM, Advance Notice of Proposed Rulemaking: Oil and Gas Leasing; Royalty on Production, Rental Payments, Minimum Acceptable Bids, Bonding Requirements, and Civil Penalty Assessments, 80 Fed. Reg. 22,148 (2015). Further, all onshore coal, oil, and gas leasing is done by application, which allows private companies to design lease boundaries.

BLM, Coal Operations (2016), https://www.blm.gov/programs/energy-and-minerals/coal/lease-by-application-process (last visited Mar. 20, 2019). What are some potential reforms that BLM could consider to increase competition when leasing?

2.   Prevention of Waste. In 2016, BLM finalized a "Waste Prevention Rule," designed to limit methane emissions from oil and gas production on public lands. *See* Waste Prevention, Production Subject to Royalties, and Resource Conservation, 81 Fed. Reg. 83,008, 83,020 (2016). The Trump administration rescinded the rule and issued an alternative, less stringent rule. BLM now argues that the 2016 rule "was based on the premise that essentially any losses of gas at the production site could be regulated as 'waste,' without regard to the economics of conserving that lost gas." Final Rule: Waste Prevention, Production Subject to Royalties, and Resource Conservation; Rescission or Revision of Certain Requirements, 83 Fed. Reg. 49,184, 49,186 (2018). BLM's 2018 rule added an economic limitation: waste does not occur "where the cost of conserving the oil or gas exceeds the monetary value of that oil or gas." *Id.* at 49,197. The Waste Prevention Rule and the Trump administration's replacement rule have spurred multiple legal challenges. Should BLM consider the loss of *any* methane—the primary component of natural gas and also a potent greenhouse gas pollutant—to be "waste" pursuant to the MLA, or must it limit "waste" to that which the operator can economically capture and market as natural gas?

The 2016 Waste Prevention Rule was found to deliver net social benefits; the Obama Administration included both the value of captured marketable natural gas as well as prevented methane releases (calculated using the Social Cost of Methane) on the benefits side of the ledger in its cost-benefit analysis. *Id.* at 49,187.

3.   Fair Market Value and Climate Change Costs. Interior, under the Obama administration, followed the directive in Secretarial Order 3338, excerpted above, and released a coal PEIS scoping report in January 2017, days before the change in Presidential administrations. INTERIOR, FEDERAL COAL PROGRAM PROGRAMMATIC EIS SCOPING REPORT (Jan. 2017). The report articulated potential alternatives to the current system of coal leasing designed to improve receipt of "fair market value" and address climate change effects.

What changes to Interior's fiscal terms do you think might be warranted in order to ensure receipt of fair market value? How can Interior better account for climate change impacts in its coal, oil, and gas programs? Can the two goals of fair market value and addressing climate change impacts be addressed jointly? One legal scholar has argued that Interior should seek to maximize social welfare in federal energy leasing by adjusting royalty rates upwards to account for climate change costs. Jayni Foley Hein, *Federal Lands and Fossil Fuel: Maximizing Social Welfare in Federal Energy Leasing*, 42 HARV. ENVTL. L. REV. 1, 12 (2018).

4.   "Energy Dominance" and Coal Reform. In early 2017, the Trump administration rescinded Secretarial Order 3338 and lifted the corresponding moratorium on new coal leasing that the Obama administration enacted while the coal PEIS was in progress. Exec. Order No. 13783, 82 Fed. Reg. 16,093 (2017). The same year, Interior also repealed Interior's Coal Valuation Rule, which was designed to close a loophole in coal valuation that had afforded industry a windfall by allowing them to report coal sales to affiliates, rather than true "arm's length" sales for royalty valuation purposes. These changes, in addition to others, were made as part of the Trump administration's "energy dominance" strategy. Is such an "energy dominance" strategy compatible with Interior's "multiple use" and "sustained yield" mandates? Is it compatible with other MLA and FLPMA requirements?

5.   Areas of Critical Environmental Concern. FLPMA directs the Secretary of Interior to "prepare and maintain on a continuing basis an inventory of all public lands and their resource and other values (including, but not limited to outdoor recreation and scenic values), *giving priority to areas of critical environmental concern.*" 43 U.S.C. § 1711 (emphasis added). It further instructs the Secretary to "give priority to the designation and protection of areas of critical environmental concern" in developing and revising land use plans. 43 U.S.C. § 1712(c)(3). The ACEC provisions not only afford BLM the opportunity to implement conservation measures, but they direct that the agency do so in its planning for and administration of these areas. Karin P. Sheldon & Pamela Baldwin, *Areas of Critical Environmental Concern: FLPMA's Unfulfilled Conservation Mandate*, 28 COLO. NAT. RES., ENERGY & ENVTL L. REV. 1, 9 (2017). However, one set of legal scholars has termed the ACEC provision BLM's "unfulfilled conservation mandate," as BLM does not inventory or collect data on areas with possible ACEC resources and values, has no detailed implementing regulations regarding how to meet this mandate, and fails to give priority to ACECs in most land use plans. *Id.* at 33–40. As a result, there is considerable inconsistency in how BLM field offices treat ACECs in their RMPs. *Id.* at 50. If BLM were to amend its regulations to provide more detail on carrying out its ACEC mandate, what should those regulations contain? Consider when and where in the planning process ACECs should be identified and addressed, how they could be managed, and the activities (or uses) that should be allowed within them.

6.   Renewable Energy on BLM Lands. While this section focuses on mineral resources, in recent years, wind and solar energy have joined the list of energy sources derived from BLM lands. Several factors have contributed to the rise of wind and solar energy, including state renewable portfolio standards, federal tax credits, a decrease in the cost of renewable energy technology, and improvements in federal siting and permitting. For instance, in 2012, BLM and the Department of Energy released a Solar Programmatic Environmental Impact Statement, a roadmap for large-scale solar energy development on lands managed by BLM in Arizona, California, Colorado, Nevada, New Mexico, and Utah. The Solar PEIS identified 17 solar energy zones, which are priority development areas for utility-scale solar energy facilities. *See* BLM & DEPT. OF ENERGY, FINAL PROGRAMMATIC ENVIRONMENTAL IMPACT STATEMENT FOR SOLAR ENERGY DEVELOPMENT IN SIX SOUTHWESTERN STATES, Volume 1 (July 2012).

How does development of wind and solar resources fit within BLM's statutory mandates? Could BLM announce a policy that gives priority to development of these resources over fossil fuels on all public lands, and if so, what statutory or regulatory support could it cite for such a policy? Would such a policy be susceptible to legal challenges?

ii.   OFFSHORE MINERAL LEASING

The Outer Continental Shelf ("OCS") of the United States is a vast underwater expanse nearly equal in size to the Australian continent. Beginning a few miles from the U.S. coast, the OCS extends roughly 200 miles into the ocean to the seaward limit of the U.S. Exclusive Economic Zone ("EEZ") of the United States. *See* 43 U.S.C. §§ 1331(a), 1301(a). The federal government manages the submerged lands, subsoil, and seabed of the OCS between the seaward extent of the states' jurisdiction (three to nine miles, depending on the state) and the seaward extent of federal jurisdiction. *Id.*

The Outer Continental Shelf contains abundant oil, natural gas, and other mineral resources. Federal offshore oil reserves represent about 11% of all oil reserves in the United States. MARC HUMPHRIES, CONG. RESEARCH SERV., U.S. CRUDE OIL AND NATURAL GAS PRODUCTION IN FEDERAL AND NONFEDERAL AREAS 2 (2016). Developing and managing these fossil fuel reserves was a primary motivation behind the passage of OCLSA in 1953. *See* Pub. L. No. 83–212, 67 Stat. 462 (1953), codified as amended at 43 U.S.C. § 1331 *et seq.*

OCSLA empowered Interior to grant leases, but it did not establish statutory guidelines to govern the Secretary's decisions. *California v. Watt ("Watt I")*, 668 F.2d 1290, 1295 (D.C. Cir. 1981). In 1978, Congress amended OCSLA in response to growing awareness of the need for environmental protection of offshore resources, as well as a desire to produce more domestic energy sources. The 1978 Amendments reflect both of these goals, promoting "expedited exploration and development of the Outer Continental Shelf in order to achieve national economic and energy policy goals, assure national security, reduce dependence on foreign sources, and maintain a favorable balance of payments in world trade," while also ensuring "protection of the human, marine, and coastal environments." Pub. L. No. 95–372, 92 Stat. 629 (1978), codified at 43 U.S.C. § 1802.

OCSLA establishes both a procedural framework and a set of substantive requirements that govern where, when, and how Interior may open up areas of the OCS for resource development. *See* 43 U.S.C. §§ 1334, 1337; *Ctr. for Biological Diversity v. U.S. Dep't of Interior*, 563 F.3d 466, 472 (D.C. Cir. 2009). Procedurally, Interior must undertake a four-stage process before allowing offshore leasing and development, with each stage more specific than the last. In the first stage—the most general—Interior prepares and approves a five-year program of proposed lease sales across the whole OCS. *See* 43 U.S.C. § 1344. It does not need to include proposed lease sales in every OCS region. In the second stage, Interior issues leases—granted to the highest responsible qualified bidder or bidders by competitive bidding—in accordance with the approved program. *Id.* § 1337(a). Leases begin with a fixed term of 5 to 10 years, but can continue as long as drilling continues to take place. Once production begins, lessees pay royalties to the federal government (a portion of which are shared with coastal states closest to production); royalties are currently set at 18.75% for deepwater drilling and 12.5% for shallow water drilling. In the third stage, Interior reviews lessees' exploration plans. *Id.* § 1340. In the fourth stage, Interior and affected state and local governments review lessees' development plans. *Id.* § 1351.

As is apparent from the foregoing summary, the procedures embodied in the 1978 amendments are pyramidic in structure, proceeding from broad-based planning to an increasingly narrower focus as actual development grows more imminent. *Watt I*, 668 F.2d at 1297. OCSLA Section 18 establishes a process by which the Secretary of Interior weighs energy potential and other benefits against environmental and other risks in determining how, when and where oil and gas should be made available from the various Outer Continental Shelf areas to meet national energy needs. *Id.* It requires the Secretary to prepare, maintain and periodically revise a leasing program consisting of a schedule of proposed lease sales, indicating, "as precisely as possible, the size, timing and location of leasing activity which he determines will best meet national energy needs for the five-year period following its approval or reapproval." 43 U.S.C. § 1344(a).

The Secretary must prepare and maintain the program consistent with four basic principles, laid out in Section 18(a):

(1) Management of the outer Continental Shelf shall be conducted in a manner which considers economic, social, and environmental values of the renewable and nonrenewable resources contained in the outer Continental Shelf, and the potential impact of oil and gas exploration on other resource values of the outer Continental Shelf and the marine, coastal, and human environments.

(2) Timing and location of exploration, development, and production of oil and gas among the oil- and gas-bearing physiographic regions of the outer Continental Shelf shall be based on a consideration of—

(A) existing information concerning the geographical, geological, and ecological characteristics of such regions;

(B) an equitable sharing of developmental benefits and environmental risks among the various regions;

(C) the location of such regions with respect to, and the relative needs of, regional and national energy markets;

(D) the location of such regions with respect to other uses of the sea and seabed, including fisheries, navigation, existing or proposed sealanes, potential sites of deepwater ports, and other anticipated uses of the resources and space of the outer Continental Shelf;

(E) the interest of potential oil and gas producers in the development of oil and gas resources as indicated by exploration or nomination;

(F) laws, goals, and policies of affected States which have been specifically identified by the Governors of such States as relevant matters for the Secretary's consideration;

(G) the relative environmental sensitivity and marine productivity of different areas of the outer Continental Shelf; and

(H) relevant environmental and predictive information for different areas of the outer Continental Shelf.

(3) The Secretary shall select the timing and location of leasing, to the maximum extent practicable, so as to obtain a proper balance between the potential for environmental damage, the potential for the discovery of oil and gas, and the potential for adverse impact on the coastal zone.

(4) Leasing activities shall be conducted to assure receipt of fair market value for the lands leased and the rights conveyed by the Federal Government.

43 U.S.C. § 1344(a).

Interior is directed to consider economic, social, and environmental values of OCS resources at every phase in its four-step process. In reviewing a lessee's exploration plans at the third stage, for example, Interior must ensure that, among other things, such plans "will not be unduly harmful to aquatic life in the area, result in pollution, create hazardous or unsafe conditions, unreasonably interfere with other uses of the area, or disturb any site, structure, or object of historical or archeological significance." *Id.* § 1340(g)(3). In analyzing a lessee's development plans at the fourth stage, Interior must ensure, among other things, that such development will not "probably cause serious harm or damage . . . to the marine, coastal or human environments." *Id.* § 1351(h)(1)(D)(i).

Drilling on the OCS can have potentially devastating effects on the environment, including on the sea floor, water, and coastal areas. One of the greatest risks of offshore oil and gas development is the risk of an oil spill, with its attendant effects on wildlife, fishing stocks, water quality, and coastal economies. More common effects include discharge of oil, wastewater, and debris; air pollution, including greenhouse gas emissions; infrastructure impacts such as pipeline trenching on the seafloor; and increased vessel traffic to and from production and exploration sites—all of which can negatively affect aquatic wildlife and ecosystems. Jayni Foley Hein, *Monumental Decisions: One-Way Levers Towards Preservation in the Antiquities Act and Outer Continental Shelf Lands Act*, 48 ENVTL. L. 125, 133–34 (2018). Concerns about the OCS's ecological vulnerability and potential harm to coastal tourism led to moratoriums on OCS drilling in the Atlantic, the Pacific, parts of the Gulf of Mexico, and parts of Alaska for more than a quarter of a century, from 1982 until the moratoriums were partially lifted in 2009. *Ctr. for Sustainable Econ. v. Jewell,* 779 F.3d 588, 592 (D.C. Cir. 2015). In 2010, the BP Deepwater Horizon disaster renewed debate about the safety of offshore drilling. BP was drilling in mile-deep water 52 miles from shore when a subsea well ruptured and caused an oil spill spreading over thousands of square miles, damaging local economies, sensitive coastlines, and valuable wildlife throughout the region. *Id.* (citing DEP'T OF INTERIOR, INCREASED SAFETY MEASURES FOR ENERGY DEVELOPMENT ON THE OUTER CONTINENTAL SHELF 1 (2010)).

In addition to OCSLA, offshore drilling and other development on the OCS, such as offshore wind, is also subject to the requirements of additional environmental laws including NEPA, the Coastal Zone Management Act (requiring state review of federal actions that affect the land and water use of the coastal zone), the Clean Water Act (through the issuance of National Pollutant Discharge and Elimination System permits, regulating the discharge of toxic and nontoxic pollutants into surface waters), the Clean Air Act, the Marine Mammals Protection Act (providing for the protection and conservation of all marine mammals and their habitats), and the Endangered Species Act.

The case below concerns a challenge to Interior's 2012–1017 offshore leasing program. Petitioners alleged violations of OCSLA and NEPA; the excerpt below focuses on one of their OCSLA claims.

Center for Sustainable Economy v. Jewell
779 F.3d 588 (D.C. Cir. 2015).

■ Before GARLAND, PILLARD, and SENTELLE, CIRCUIT JUDGES.

■ PILLARD, CIRCUIT JUDGE:

. . . . The Outer Continental Shelf Lands Act (OCSLA) created a framework to facilitate the orderly and environmentally responsible exploration and extraction of oil and gas deposits on the OCS. It charges the Secretary of the Interior with preparing a program every five years containing a schedule of proposed leases for OCS resource exploration and development. In light of the potential benefits and costs of OCS development, the Secretary's program must balance competing economic, social, and environmental values in determining when and where to make leases available. Those obligations are set forth in Section 18 of OCSLA, 43 U.S.C. § 1344.

The Center for Sustainable Economy (CSE) . . . challenges the Department of the Interior's latest leasing program on the ground that the 2012–2017 leasing schedule fails to comply with the provisions of Section 18(a), which governs how Interior is to balance competing economic, social, and environmental values, *id.* § 1344(a)(1), (3), quantify and assess environmental and ecological impact, *id.* § 1344(a)(2)(A), (H), and ensure an equitable distribution of benefits and costs between OCS regions and stakeholders, *id.* § 1344(a)(2)(B)–(G). CSE argues that Interior's economic analysis violates OCSLA's express terms by failing properly to consider environmental and market effects that the agency is required to address at the planning stage, and arbitrarily and irrationally fails to quantify many of the Program's costs and benefits. . . .

A program is required to "indicat[e], as precisely as possible, the size, timing, and location of leasing activity . . . for the five-year period following its approval," *id.* § 1344(a), and is to be prepared in a manner consistent with four principles set out in numbered paragraphs in Section 18(a). Briefly stated, those four principles are that Interior must: (1) account for all relevant "economic, social, and environmental values," *id.* § 1344(a)(1); (2) use "existing" and "predictive" information to account for the interests of all relevant regions and stakeholders, *id.* § 1344(a)(2); (3) strike a "proper balance" between resource potential and environmental impact, *id.* § 1344(a)(3), and (4) assure that the Federal Government receives "fair market value for the lands leased and the rights conveyed," *id.* § 1344(a)(4).

This first stage, involving approval of a leasing program, carries enormous "practical and legal significance." *Watt I,* 668 F.2d at 1299. The key national decisions as to the size, timing, and location of OCS leasing—as well as the basic economic analyses and justifications for such decisions—are made at this first stage. *See* 43 U.S.C. § 1344(d)(3). The Program also creates important reliance interests. . . .

At issue here is the 2012–2017 Program, the eighth five-year program Interior has prepared pursuant to the 1978 Amendment. That Program includes 15 potential lease sales in six OCS planning areas: the Western and Central Gulf of Mexico, the portion of the Eastern Gulf of Mexico not currently under congressional moratorium, and the Chukchi Sea, Beaufort Sea, and Cook Inlet planning areas off the coast of Alaska. Twelve of the sales are planned for the Gulf of Mexico, and one sale each is planned for the three Alaskan areas. . . .

Our analysis of the most recent Program is informed and guided by our four prior decisions regarding earlier leasing-program challenges. *See CBD,* 563 F.3d 466 (challenging the 2007–2012 Program); *Natural Res. Def. Council, Inc. v. Hodel ("Hodel"),* 865 F.2d 288 (D.C.Cir.1988) (challenging the 1987–1992 Program); *California v. Watt ("Watt II"),* 712 F.2d 584 (D.C.Cir.1983) (challenging the 1982–1987 Program); *Watt I,* 668 F.2d 1290 (challenging the 1980–1985 Program). . . .

CSE raises six distinct challenges to Interior's adoption of the 2012–2017 Program. All six are grounded in the same basic claims: that Interior either violated the dictates of Section 18(a) of OCSLA, or failed rationally to strike an appropriate balance between environmental costs and national energy needs as required under the Administrative Procedure Act, or both. Two of those challenges are forfeited because they were not properly raised before the agency; the other four fail on their merits. . . .

CSE argues that Section 18 of OCSLA required Interior explicitly to quantify the "informational value," also known as the "option value," of delaying OCS leasing. Section 18 requires Interior to schedule the leasing of OCS mineral resources at the time that best meets national energy needs. *See* 43 U.S.C. § 1344(a). Interior could authorize new leasing this year, next year, or in fifty years. Every day that Interior waits has a cost insofar as valuable fuel that could be used today instead lies dormant. *See Watt I*, 668 F.2d at 1320. But waiting also has benefits, including what is referred to as informational value. More is learned with the passage of time: Technology improves. Drilling becomes cheaper, safer, and less environmentally damaging. Better tanker technology renders oil tanker spills less likely and less damaging. The true costs of tapping OCS energy resources are better understood as more becomes known about the damaging effects of fossil fuel pollutants. Development of energy efficiencies and renewable energy sources reduces the need to rely on fossil fuels. As safer techniques and more effective technologies continue to be developed, the costs associated with drilling decline. There is therefore a tangible present economic benefit to delaying the decision to drill for fossil fuels to preserve the opportunity to see what new technologies develop and what new information comes to light. Economists have crafted techniques for quantifying, in at least some situations, such informational value or option value of delaying decisions.

CSE builds its informational-value claim out of two principles articulated in Section 18 and our prior opinions. First, Section 18 requires Interior to evaluate the advantages and disadvantages of delaying and forgoing leasing in determining when leases should issue. *See* 43 U.S.C. § 1344(a)(3), (a)(2)(H). Second, Interior must quantify costs when possible, especially where those costs are "not inherently insusceptible of quantitative analysis." *Watt I*, 668 F.2d at 1319. CSE contends that, because the informational value of delay is a relevant cost and it is susceptible of quantification, Interior acted irrationally in failing to quantify it.

We are not persuaded that the informational value of delay is yet so readily quantifiable that Interior acted unreasonably in choosing not to quantify it in this planning cycle. Rather than assign a specific dollar value in the 2012–2017 Program to delaying leasing on the OCS, Interior qualitatively considered the informational value of delay. In its evaluation of alternatives in the Programmatic EIS, for example, Interior considered whether to "[d]elay sales until further evaluation of oil spill response, drilling safety reform, and baseline environmental conditions [were] collected and analyzed," "[d]efer deepwater leasing in the [Gulf of Mexico] planning areas," and "[d]evelop alternative/renewable energy sources as a complete or partial substitute for oil and gas leasing on the OCS." The Proposed Final Program also described the process Interior is developing to "continue to use incoming scientific information and stakeholder feedback to proactively determine, in advance of any potential sale, which specific areas offer the greatest resource potential while minimizing potential conflicts with environmental and subsistence considerations." In part on the basis of its qualitative assessment of the informational value of delay, Interior chose to postpone leasing in the Chukchi and Beaufort Sea program areas until late in the Program to allow gathering of additional information.

CSE does not dispute that Interior qualitatively considered the informational value of delay; it argues that Interior's failure to assess the informational value of delay quantitatively was irrational. We are persuaded, however, that the methodology for valuing the informational advantages of delaying offshore oil development is not sufficiently well established to render irrational Interior's decision not to use it in the 2012–2017 Program. Our decisions afford greater leeway to Interior to evaluate qualitatively costs that are difficult to quantify. *See, e.g., Watt I*, 668 F.2d at 1317–18. "Where existing methodology or research in a new area of regulation is deficient, the agency necessarily enjoys broad discretion to attempt to formulate a solution to the best of its ability on the basis of available information." *Watt II*, 712 F.2d at 600 (quoting *Watt I*, 668 F.2d at 1301 n. 18). To that end, in making timing decisions, Interior is generally "free to choose any methodology so long as it is not irrational." *CBD*, 563 F.3d at 488 (internal quotation marks omitted).

CSE neither identifies in the record, nor itself puts forward, a methodology for pricing the informational value of delay in the context of offshore oil and gas leasing that is sufficiently established to render arbitrary or irrational Interior's decision to opt instead for a qualitative analysis. When reviewing the rationality of Interior's methodological selections, we have looked to, among other factors, whether the methodology has been "performed extensively in the past." *Watt II*, 712 F.2d at 600. CSE acknowledges that there is no established practice of quantifying informational values stemming from environmental impacts in the petroleum industry, and that Interior has never before sought to undertake such an analysis.

The difficulties in undertaking such a quantitative analysis are great. Pricing the value of delay would require Interior to make complex estimates of the pace and nature of likely future trends in the development of various technological and scientific fields affecting drilling, transportation, oceanography, and alternative energy. Interior would also be required to attempt to quantify the value of future, as-yet-unknown benefits and harms of OCS development, and the probability of countervailing developments that could enhance those benefits or mitigate those harms. Many difficult choices would need to be made and justified, and a "substantial amount of data" would need to be gathered. Michael A. Livermore, *Patience Is an Economic Virtue: Real Options, Natural Resources, and Offshore Oil*, 84 U. COLO. L. REV. 581, 639 (2013). Even if Interior had an adequate methodology in hand, it might rationally have viewed such an unprecedented analysis as unduly time-consuming and error-prone. As we have explained in prior opinions, "the final decision as to how much analysis is necessary in view of the available data must be the agency's, subject to judicial review only for obviously incorrect results or methodology." *Watt II*, 712 F.2d at 600 (quoting *Watt I*, 668 F.2d at 1317 n. 224); *see also Hodel*, 865 F.2d at 309. So, too, here. Interior acted reasonably in employing qualitative, rather than quantitative, measures of the informational value of delay.

Our holding is a narrow one. In preparing a five-year program, the agency is not permitted to substitute qualitative assessments for well-established quantitative methods whenever it deems such substitutions convenient. *See Hodel*, 865 F.2d at 308–09. But Interior permissibly concluded that Section 18 does not require it to employ methods of cost-benefit analysis at the "frontiers of scientific knowledge." *See Watt II*, 712 F.2d at 600 (quoting *Watt I*, 668 F.2d at 1301). Had the path been well worn, it might have been irrational for Interior not to follow it. Under the circumstances it faced, Interior might permissibly have blazed a new trail. It was not, however, required to do so. We therefore reject CSE's argument that Interior acted irrationally in failing to quantify the informational value of delay. We are satisfied that Interior's qualitative analysis of the benefits of delaying leasing was adequate, and that methods for quantifying the time value of delaying leasing on the OCS are not yet so well established that Interior was required to use them in developing the 2012–2017 Leasing Program. . . .

For the foregoing reasons, we deny the petition for review.

NOTES AND QUESTIONS

1. **Waiting to Drill.** The option to wait is valuable in situations where future costs and benefits of a project are uncertain, decisions are irreversible, and delaying will generate additional information. Michael A. Livermore, *Patience Is an Economic Virtue: Real Options, Natural Resources, and Offshore Oil*, 84 U. COLO. L. REV. 581, 589 (2013). The value associated with waiting to act in such contexts is called the "real option value." *Id.* Private oil and gas companies routinely account for option value, as they purchase leases that have a 5–10-year initial term, and time their production to be optimal from a private-welfare perspective, taking market prices and technology costs into account, for example. But as Michael Livermore explains, the federal government fails to account for environmental, social, and economic option value both when scheduling offshore lease sales and

setting minimum bids. Failure to account for this option value "leads to over-early exploitation of these resources, reduces economic returns for the American public, and exposes agency decisions to litigation risk." *Id.* at 588. Livermore argues that in the offshore oil context, Interior can incorporate option value at two stages of its decisionmaking process. First, when evaluating the costs and benefits of opening lands for leasing. And second, during the bid adequacy process, where the government can set a higher minimum bid price, "reflecting the option value of the land, both to ensure that the private benefits of extraction exceed the public benefits of delay, and to secure adequate compensation for the American public for the right that is being transferred." *Id.*

What are some of the relevant environmental and social uncertainties that have option value in the offshore drilling context? Based on your reading of OCSLA, is Interior required to account for these uncertainties when managing offshore leasing? What was the Court's holding with respect to option value in *CSE v. Jewell*?

2. **Option Value Beyond *CSE v. Jewell*.** While the Court denied petitioner's request for review in *CSE v. Jewell*, the litigation and related advocacy prompted a change in federal offshore leasing policy. In the government's subsequent offshore leasing plan for 2017–2022, it added a 12-page section on environmental, social, and economic uncertainty, including a robust qualitative discussion of option value and its relevance to offshore leasing decisions and bid prices. *See* BOEM, 2017–2022 OUTER CONTINENTAL SHELF OIL AND GAS LEASING DRAFT PROPOSED PROGRAM 8-3–8-16 (Jan. 2015).

If applied to the government's future leasing decisions, what would you expect the effect of accounting for option value to be? Do you think option value is equally applicable to onshore leasing? Is option value greater in certain types of locations?

3. **Previous Legal Challenges.** *CSE v. Jewell* was not the first challenge to a five-year OCS leasing program. In *Watt I*, cited in *CSE v. Jewell*, petitioners brought a successful challenge under OCSLA Section 18. *California v. Watt ("Watt I")*, 668 F.2d 1290 (D.C. Cir. 1981). The D.C. Circuit held that "Congress intended the Secretary to consider all factors listed in section 18(a)(2) in developing the leasing program, and did not envision the deferral thereof until some later date," and "the Secretary must base the leasing program upon the result of his consideration of these factors." *Id.* at 1305. Further, the court held that Secretary Watt failed to give proper consideration to the mandate of section 18(a)(2)(B) that environmental risks be "equitabl(y) shar(ed)" among the various OCS regions. *Id.* at 1307–08. Finally, the court held that the Secretary failed to comply with Section 18(a)(2)(G), requiring him to consider the relative environmental sensitivity and marine productivity of OCS regions. The court noted that "[l]ack of information, lack of time, and methodological imperfections all may make the consideration highly speculative, as will the difficulties inherent in comparing . . . [but] [a]ll that is required is that the Secretary make a good faith determination . . . based upon the best 'existing information' available to him." *Id.* at 1313. The court noted the presence of relevant data and

information in the record that could have assisted Interior in calculating the relative environmental sensitivities of the regions to oil spills and other effects. *Id.* at 1312.

In a 2009 decision, the D.C. Circuit ruled in favor of petitioners on one of its claims against Interior's 2007–2012 leasing program, on the ground that the program's environmental sensitivity rankings were irrational. *Ctr. for Biological Diversity v. U.S. Dep't of Interior*, 563 F.3d 466, 472, 488–89 (D.C. Cir. 2009) ("*CBD*"). The court found that the leasing program violated OCSLA Section 18(a)(2)(G) because it incorrectly assessed the environmental sensitivity of each OCS planning area. *See id.*; 43 U.S.C. § 1344(a)(2)(G). The court first reiterated that the Secretary was " free to choose any methodology so long as it is not irrational," citing *Watt I*, 668 F.2d at 1320, and that the Secretary's decision would not be irrational so long as it is "based on a consideration of the relevant factors." *Id.* at 488 (citing *Watt I*, 668 F.2d at 1317) (internal citations omitted). But, the court held that the Secretary's interpretation of Section 18(a)(2)(G) was irrational because it was not based on a consideration of the relevant factors set forth in the statute, which states that an agency must assess the environmental sensitivity of "different areas *of the outer Continental Shelf*" in order to make its determination of when and where to explore and develop additional areas for oil. *See* 43 U.S.C. § 1344(a)(2)(G) (emphasis added). Instead, Interior had used one NOAA study that assessed the effects of oil spills on *shorelines* only—but not on the OCS areas themselves, which are "distant" from the shoreline. *See CBD*, 563 F.3d at 488.

Watt I, CBD, and *CSE v. Jewell* each discuss lack of information and imperfect methodologies. Is *CSE v. Jewell* consistent with *Watt I* and *CBD*? Based on these decisions, to what extent must a methodology be developed in order for a court to hold that an agency must use it? Does the answer depend upon the specific analysis called for in the statute? If petitioners in *CSE v. Jewell* had commented on the draft offshore leasing plan by quantifying the environmental, social, and economic option value of delaying lease sales in each OCS region, do you think the court would have reached the same result? Would Interior have had discretion to reject petitioners' proposed quantitative methodology?

4.   **OCSLA and Climate Change.** In *CBD v. Interior*, petitioners also brought two climate change-related OCSLA claims. They argued that the Secretary violated sections 18(a)(1) and (a)(3) of OCSLA by failing to account for the environmental costs resulting from consumption of the fossil fuels extracted from the OCS. They also contended that Interior violated section 18(a)(2) by failing to adequately consider the present and future effect of climate change caused by consumption of these fossil fuels on OCS areas, as section 18(a)(2)(H) requires. The D.C. Circuit rejected both claims. It held that "OCSLA does not require Interior to consider the global environmental impact of oil and gas consumption before approving a Leasing Program." *CBD*, 563 F.3d at 484. Furthermore, it held that "OCSLA does not require Interior to consider the further derivative environmental impact that oil and gas consumption has on OCS areas." *Id.*

Do you agree with the court's holding in *CBD* with respect to the effect of fossil fuel consumption associated with the proposed oil and gas leases? Review the OCSLA Section 18 requirements. Are there any other possible avenues for bringing climate change-related OCSLA challenges to a leasing program? Are climate change effects better dealt with in environmental impact statements, prepared pursuant to NEPA, that accompany five-year offshore leasing plans?

5.   Offshore Leasing Withdrawals. Driven by environmental concerns, both Congress and the President, at various times, have declared moratoria on offshore leasing and development in areas of the OCS, or withdrawn areas from leasing eligibility. OCSLA Section 12(a) is titled "Reservation of lands and rights" and states, in full: "The President of the United States may, from time to time, withdraw from disposition any of the unleased lands of the outer Continental Shelf." 43 U.S.C. § 1341(a). Section 12(a) has been used by six presidents spanning sixty-seven years, including to withdraw as much as several hundred million acres at a time from offshore leasing eligibility. *See* Jayni Foley Hein, *Monumental Decisions: One-Way Levers Towards Preservation in the Antiquities Act and Outer Continental Shelf Lands Act*, 48 ENVTL. L. 125, 132 (2018). Section 12(a) withdrawals can be time-limited, or, as President Obama used the provision on several occasions, "for a time period without specific expiration." *Id.* (citing Memorandum on Withdrawal of Certain Portions of the United States Arctic Outer Continental Shelf from Mineral Leasing, 2016 Daily Comp. Pres. Doc. 1 (Dec. 20, 2016)). On April 28, 2017, President Trump issued an executive order rescinding President Obama's offshore leasing withdrawals made pursuant to OCSLA section 12(a). Exec. Order No. 13,795, 82 Fed. Reg. 20,815, 20,816 (2017). Environmental groups sued, alleging that OCSLA provides presidents with the power to protect OCS lands, but not to overturn those protections. *See* Complaint for Declaratory & Injunctive Relief at 2, *League of Conservation Voters v. Trump*, No. 3:17-cv-00101-SLG (D. Alaska filed May 3, 2017). Until President Trump, no president had ever rescinded a Section 12(a) withdrawal made for "a time period without specific expiration," and the issue is a matter of first impression for the federal court hearing the case. Based on the text of Section 12(a) and your understanding of OCSLA, how do you think a court should rule on this question?

For the view of that such withdrawals cannot be rescinded by a subsequent president (but could be reversed by Congress, pursuant to legislation), *see* Hein, *Monumental Decisions*, 48 ENVTL L. at 132–48; Kevin O. Leske, *"Un-Shelfing" Lands Under the Outer Continental Shelf Lands Act (OCSLA): Can a Prior Executive Withdrawal Under Section 12(a) Be Trumped by a Subsequent President?*, 26 N.Y.U. ENVTL. L.J. 1 (2017).

6.   Revised Five-Year Plans. It is fairly common for new presidential administrations to revise and issue new offshore leasing plans upon the change in political leadership. In January 2018, Interior released a new draft program for offshore drilling, to replace the program prepared during the Obama Administration. *See* BOEM, 2019–2024 NATIONAL OUTER CONTINENTAL SHELF OIL AND GAS LEASING DRAFT PROPOSED PROGRAM (Jan. 2018). The Trump Administration's draft program proposed to make over

90% of federal offshore lands available for future exploration and development (including areas withdrawn by President Obama pursuant to his Section 12(a) authority), and to hold the largest number of lease sales in U.S. history. The previous program offered roughly 6% of available offshore acreage for lease. Lisa Friedman, *Trump Moves to Open Nearly All Offshore Waters to Drilling*, N.Y. TIMES (Jan. 4, 2018). Governors and members of Congress from several coastal states, on both sides of the aisle, voiced opposition to the proposal, as coastal states dependent on tourism and fishing face serious risks from offshore oil spills. The plan will likely be revised as it moves towards a proposed program, and then a final program.

If you were the governor of South Carolina, how would you comment on a proposed plan that would include a first-of-its-kind lease sale in the Atlantic OCS region, 20 miles from the South Carolina coast? What constituents would you consult, what concerns would you weigh, and how would you try to persuade BOEM, which ultimately decides whether to hold the lease sale?

7. Changes in the Wake of Deepwater Horizon. Following the *Deepwater Horizon* disaster, Interior disbanded the Mineral Management Service ("MMS"), which had previously overseen all aspects of offshore leasing and OCS management, and replaced it with three independent successor agencies: BOEM, the Bureau of Safety and Environmental Enforcement ("BSEE"), and the Office of Natural Resources Revenue ("ONRR"). This change was intended to improve Interior's performance with respect to ensuring: (1) balanced and responsible development of energy resources on the OCS; (2) safe and environmentally responsible exploration and production and enforcement of applicable regulations; and (3) fair return to the taxpayer from offshore royalty and revenue collection and disbursement activities.

Some legal scholars have called for further reforms, for instance, recommending that BOEM issue new regulations that contain more detail on how the agency should carry-out its OCSLA requirements. *See* Andrew Hartsig et al., *Next Steps to Reform the Regulations Governing Offshore Oil and Gas Planning and Leasing*, 33 ALASKA L. REV. 1, 10 (2016). They note that unlike other federal agencies, BOEM does not have its own guidance or regulations defining the way in which it fulfills its NEPA obligations. *Id.* at 10. This lack of specific guidance has contributed to calls from the National Commission on the BP Deepwater Horizon Disaster, CEQ, and others for reforms to how Interior addresses its NEPA obligations with regard to OCS activities. Effective regulations would clarify the way in which BOEM complies with NEPA requirements at each stage of the OCSLA process. *Id.*

What other issues could more specific implementing regulations cover? Would such regulations be preferable to the agency relying on court decisions to interpret or clarify its statutory mandates under OCSLA?

E. PROTECTED LANDS

i.   NATIONAL PARKS

The national park system began with the establishment of Yellowstone National Park in 1872. *See* 16 U.S.C. § 21. In 1916, Congress passed the National Park Service Organic Act of 1916 (the "Organic Act"). 54 U.S.C.A. § 100101, *et seq.* (formerly cited as 16 U.S.C. § 1). The Organic Act created the National Park Service ("NPS"), a new bureau within the Department of the Interior, for the purpose of:

> promot[ing] and regulat[ing] the use of the National Park System by means and measures that conform to the fundamental purpose of the System units, which purpose is to conserve the scenery, natural and historic objects, and wild life in the System units and to provide for the enjoyment of the scenery, natural and historic objects, and wild life in such manner and by such means as will leave them unimpaired for the enjoyment of future generations.

54 U.S.C.A. § 100101. The Act not only created NPS, but provided authority to organize disparate park units into a more unified National Park System.

Today, NPS manages 418 individual units covering more than 84 million acres in all 50 states, the District of Columbia, and U.S. territories. NPS, National Park System, https://www.nps.gov/aboutus/national-park-system.htm (last visited Dec. 13, 2018). Additions to the National Park System are generally made through acts of Congress, and new national parks can be created only through such legislation. Further, many national parks have specific establishment statutes that apply only to them; such specific statutory guidance generally controls over the more general terms of the Organic Act when the two differ. *See, e.g.,* 16 U.S.C.A. § 396b (establishment of Haleakalā National Park); Robert L. Fischman, *The Problem of Statutory Detail in National Park Establishment Legislation and Its Relationship to Pollution Control Law*, 74 DENV. U. L. REV. 779, 780 (1997) (describing the "general trend in environmental law for Congress, through greater statutory detail, to assume an ever larger role in specifying how agencies should implement delegated programs," including national parks).

For decades, NPS has grappled with its dual mission of preservation and public enjoyment, a delicate balance that is reflected in the cases discussed below. As the number of annual national park visitors has grown, this challenge has become increasingly salient. Joseph Sax aptly observed, "most conflict over national park policy does not really turn on whether we ought to have nature reserves (for that is widely agreed), but on the uses that people will make of those places—which is neither a subject of general agreement nor capable of resolution by reference to ecological principles." JOSEPH L. SAX, MOUNTAINS WITHOUT HANDRAILS: REFLECTIONS ON THE NATIONAL PARKS 103 (1980).

How should NPS carry-out its dual mission? Are there any principles it should employ as it attempts to strike a balance between conservation and enjoyment? Consider these questions as you read the case below, concerning the Park Service's management of a road reconstruction project in Yosemite National Park.

Sierra Club v. Babbitt
69 F. Supp. 2d 1202 (E.D. Cal. 1999).

■ ISHII, DISTRICT JUDGE:

[On January 2, 1997, a winter storm caused Yosemite National Park to suffer damage, including Highway 140 from Yosemite National Park's western border to the Pohono Bridge (El Portal Road). Plaintiffs sought to enjoin the National Park Service (NPS) from taking any steps towards reconstructing the El Portal Road (Project) until the NPS had undertaken "all necessary consideration of all significant environmental effects in compliance with [among other pieces of legislation] the National Park Organic Act."] . . .

The National Park Service Organic Act (the Organic Act) of 1916 establishes the National Park Service to "promote and regulate the use of the Federal areas known as national parks, monuments and reservations hereinafter specified, . . . to conserve the scenery and the natural and historic objects and the wild life therein and to provide for the enjoyment of the same in such manner and by such means as will leave them unimpaired for the enjoyment of future generations." 16 U.S.C. § 1. Plaintiffs allege Defendants have violated the Organic Act because "construction involved in expanding the El Portal Road is permanently altering the Merced River Canyon, within the boundaries of Yosemite National Park, inconsistent with the mandates and limitations imposed on the National Park Service by the Organic Act, 16 U.S.C. § 1 *et seq.* and by the regulations and policies promulgated thereunder." Plaintiffs' Memorandum at 44.

The Organic Act commits the NPS to the protection and furtherance of two fundamentally competing values; the preservation of natural and cultural resources and the facilitation of public use and enjoyment. These competing values of conservation and public use have been actively in conflict since before the establishment of the NPS. The Organic Act did not resolve the conflict in favor of one side or the other. *See* Nathan L. Scheg, *Preservationists vs. Recreationists in Our National Parks*, HASTINGS W.-N.W. J. ENVTL. L. & POL'Y 47 (1998). Rather, the Organic Act acknowledges the conflict and, saying nothing about how to achieve resolution, grants deference to NPS in balancing the competing and conflicting values.

Plaintiffs cite 16 U.S.C. § 20 which states "development shall be limited to those that are necessary and appropriate for public use and enjoyment of the National Park area in which they are located and that are consistent to the highest practical degree with the preservation and conservation of the areas." Defendants correctly point out that the language cited in Section 20 comes from Subchapter IV which is titled "Concessions for Accommodations, Facilities, and Services in Areas Administered by National Park Service" and is part of the National Park System Concessions Policy Act, not the National Parks Organic Act. The purpose of the Concessions Act is to assure that concessionaire development "be limited to those that are necessary and appropriate for public use and enjoyment of the national park area in which they are located. . . ." 16 U.S.C. § 20. Thus, the Concessions Act language Plaintiffs cite is directed primarily at regulating the development of in-park amenities, accommodations and services provided by concessionaires rather than at park infrastructure elements such as roads and drainage. Since the repair of a road does not represent the types of activities of concessionaires contemplated by Section 20, reliance on this section is misplaced in seeking injunctive relief for the activities involved in the Project.

The Organic Act is set forth in Section 1, Section 1 notes 2–4, and Sections 22, and 43 of Subchapter I of Title 16 of the United States Code. Taken together, the provisions of the Organic Act establish the National Park Service and provide that the national parks be administered so as to "*conserve* the scenery and the natural and historic objects and the wild life therein *and* to *provide for the enjoyment* of the same in such a manner and by such means as will leave them unimpaired to the enjoyment of future generations." 16 U.S.C. § 1 (emphasis added). Section I recognizes, both implicitly and explicitly the tension between conservation and providing for public enjoyment. Courts have consistently recognized the discretion that the Organic Act accords NPS. *See Bicycle Trails Council of Marin v. Babbitt*, 82 F.3d 1445, 1454 (9th Cir. 1996) (noting several courts have accorded NPS authority to determine what uses of park resources are proper and which avenues best achieve the Organic Act's mandates.). The Organic Act itself does not mandate that the balance in any particular decision reflect one value over the other. For that reason, the Organic Act does not serve as basis for a cause of action when the issue is confined to the Agency's exercise of discretion in attempting to balance valid, competing values. The Organic Act would serve as a basis for a cause of action were the NPS to allow use of a national park in a way that was not in the interests of either conservation or public enjoyment or in a way that was clearly against the interests of future generations. The current action does not fall in either category. The current action concerns how best to preserve access to the park while at the same time preserving the values for which the Yosemite Valley and the Merced River corridor were declared a national park. How NPS does that is within its discretion and the Organic Act offers no basis for the court to conclude that Defendants have violated the Act on the basis of NPS's exercise of discretion to decide that El Portal Road should be repaired in a certain manner. . . .

NOTES AND QUESTIONS

1. **The Organic Act.** Recall the Organic Act's text directing the Park Service to "to conserve the scenery, natural and historic objects, and wild life in the System units and to provide for the enjoyment of the scenery, natural and historic objects, and wild life in such manner and by such means as will leave them unimpaired for the enjoyment of future generations." 54 U.S.C.A. § 100101.

Is there a contradictory mandate embedded within this directive in the Organic Act? Does the Act provide any guidance in addressing the road repair at issue in *Sierra Club v. Babbitt*?

2. **Mountains Without Handrails.** Joseph Sax titled his book on national parks "Mountains Without Handrails." Today, the park system contains plenty of mountains without handrails, and an ample number with. The establishment and maintenance of national parks require NPS to constantly assess what level of human influence to allow within parks, monuments, and other protected areas within the park system. Consider the following examples.

At the turn of the 20th century, Frederick Law Olmsted (Sr.), while manager of the Mariposa Estate and a frequent visitor to the Yosemite Valley, advocated for the construction in Yosemite Valley of arched bridges in the manner of Central Park in order to "humanize" the landscape. *See* Robin Winks, *The National Park Service Act of 1916: "A Contradictory Mandate"?*, 74 DENV. U. L. REV. 575, 612 (1997). No such arched bridges were constructed. However, today, Yosemite's iconic granite monolith Half Dome is lined with a narrow stretch of cables (similar to handrails) for visitor safety. In addition, permits to hike to the top of Half Dome are required seven days per week, "in order to protect wilderness character, reduce crowding, protect natural and cultural resources, and improve safety." National Park Service, Half Dome Permits for Day Hikers, https://www.nps.gov/yose/plan yourvisit/hdpermits.htm (last visited Dec. 3, 2018). A maximum of 300 hikers are allowed each day on the Half Dome Trail beyond the base of the subdome; permits are $20 and distributed by a phone and internet lottery system. *Id.* Are the cables appropriate? Are the permits an appropriate measure to reduce crowding while allowing for public enjoyment?

3. **Concessions Act.** In 1965, Congress passed the Concessions Act, noted in *Sierra Club v. Babbit*. The Act, as amended, provides that:

> It is the policy of Congress that the development of public accommodations, facilities, and services in System units shall be limited to accommodations, facilities, and services that—(1) are necessary and appropriate for public use and enjoyment of the System unit in which they are located; and (2) are consistent to the highest practicable degree with the preservation and conservation of the resources and values of the System unit.

54 U.S.C. § 101912.

Today, several hotels exist within national parks, including Yosemite and Yellowstone. The Yellowstone Park Hotel, opened in 1891, is situated on the shore of Yellowstone Lake in the Yellowstone Valley. Today, it contains typical modern amenities such as wireless internet, a business center, restaurant, and room service. Are such hotels compatible with the Organic Act's charge to "conserve[e] the scenery" of parks? Are they compatible with the statement of policy in the Concessions Act?

NPS has issued regulations, codified in title 36 of the Code of Federal Regulations, addressing some of the most common subjects potentially affecting parks, such as boating, fishing, vehicles, and concessions. It has also issued management policies, which are not legally enforceable, but which are designed to improve the internal management of the National Park Service. *See* NATIONAL PARK SERVICE, MANAGEMENT POLICIES 2006: THE GUIDE TO MANAGING THE NATIONAL PARK SYSTEM (Aug. 31, 2006).

4.   **Limits on Agency Action.** In *Sierra Club v. Babbitt*, the court expressly recognizes that "the Organic Act itself does not mandate that the balance [between conservation and recreation values] in any particular decision reflect one value over the other." It goes on to observe that the courts have consistently recognized the discretion that the Organic Act accords NPS in reconciling competing objectives. Are the actions of the Park Service then, in managing the natural resources contained within the National Park System, wholly insulated from challenge? How else might the Organic Act be interpreted? Compare the emphasis used by the court when reading the Organic Act in *Sierra Club v. Babbitt* with the following interpretation:

> [W]hile it is true that "enjoyment" is also a fundamental purpose of the parks, enjoyment is qualified in the Organic Act in a way that conservation is not. The Organic Act charges NPS with the duty to "provide for the enjoyment" of the parks' resources and values in "such manner and by such means as will leave them unimpaired for the enjoyment of future generations." This is not blanket permission to have fun in the parks in any way the NPS sees fit. . . . [T]he "enjoyment" referenced in the Organic Act is not enjoyment for its own sake, or even enjoyment of the parks generally, but rather the enjoyment of "the scenery and natural and historic objects and the wild life" in the parks in a manner that will allow future generations to enjoy them as well. Accordingly, while NPS has the discretion to balance the sometimes conflicting policies of resource conservation and visitor enjoyment in determining what activities should be permitted or prohibited, that discretion is bounded by the terms of the Organic Act itself. NPS cannot circumvent this limitation through conclusory declarations that certain adverse impacts are acceptable, without explaining why those impacts are necessary and appropriate to fulfill the purposes of the park.

Greater Yellowstone Coal. v. Kempthorne, 577 F. Supp. 2d 183, 192–93 (D.D.C. 2008) (internal citations omitted). Which approach is more persuasive?

5.   Cause of Action Under the Organic Act. Under what circumstances does the court recognize that the Organic Act could serve as a basis for a cause of action? What circumstances might there be under a different reading of the Act?

6.   National Parks and Climate Change. The effects of climate change are already being felt in national parks. In a 2012 memorandum entitled, "Applying National Park Service Management Policies in the Context of Climate Change," former NPS director Jonathan Jarvis stated, "[w]idespread, cascading effects from climate change challenge park managers in ways unimaginable even a few decades ago." Memorandum from Jonathan Jarvis, NPS Director, to All NPS Employees (Mar. 6, 2012). The memorandum addressed emergent questions regarding the influence of climate change on the guiding principles of park natural resource management, including the NPS directive to maintain "natural" conditions and processes within parks:

> *Management Policies 2006* defines "natural condition" as "the condition of resources that would occur *in the absence of human dominance* over the landscape" (Ch. 4 Introduction, italics added). Considering that current science tells us that climate change is linked in large measure to human activity, and that the rate of climate change will continue to accelerate, achieving natural conditions is a challenging directive. Although "natural conditions" may be both increasingly difficult to characterize and ineffective as a guide for desired future conditions, traditional practices targeted to maintain "natural conditions" in parks—such as removing invasive species and other stressors; maintaining natural processes and disturbance regimes; restoring naturally functioning ecosystems; supporting biodiversity and landscape connectivity; and continuing other actions that build and support system resilience—remain as viable management strategies that are also consistent with our need to adapt to climate change.

Id. at 2. The NPS Climate Change Action Plan, released in 2012, lists high-priority actions for NPS to undertake in the near-term in order to address climate change in national parks. Eight "emphasis areas for action" are described in the plan in broad contours, as follows: (1) enhance workforce climate literacy; (2) engage youth and their families; (3) develop effective planning frameworks and guidance; (4) provide climate change science to parks; (5) implement the *Green Parks Plan;* (6) foster robust partnerships; (7) apply appropriate adaptation tools and options; and (8) strengthen communication. NPS, NATIONAL PARK SERVICE CLIMATE CHANGE ACTION PLAN 2012–2014 (2012).

Can you think of other potential "emphasis areas for action"? How can NPS best apply its statutory mandates in order to address climate change within the park system?

ii.   NATIONAL MONUMENTS

The Antiquities Act has served as another important avenue for protecting lands in the United States. Enacted in 1906, the Antiquities Act authorizes the President:

> in the President's discretion, [to] declare by public proclamation historic landmarks, historic and prehistoric structures, and other objects of historic or scientific interest that are situated on land owned or controlled by the Federal Government to be national monuments. . . . The President may reserve parcels of land as a part of the national monuments. The limits of the parcels shall be confined to the smallest area compatible with the proper care and management of the objects to be protected.

54 U.S.C. § 320301.

Proposed initially to address the loss of archaeological artifacts in the West, the Antiquities Act has played a central role in several Presidents' conservation efforts. *See* Sandra Zellmer, *A Preservation Paradox: Political Prestidigitation and an Enduring Resource of Wildness*, 34 ENVTL. L. 1015 (2004); Mark Squillace, *The Monumental Legacy of the Antiquities Act of 1906*, 37 GA. L. REV. 473 (2003). Sixteen Presidents, from both political parties, have declared 157 national monuments totaling more than 800 million acres, protecting everything from natural wonders such as the Grand Canyon and Natural Bridges, to diverse cultural and historical sites such as Chimney Rock, Birmingham Civil Rights, and Stonewall (the first national monument focused on LGBT history). *See* CAROL HARDY VINCENT & LAURA A. HANSON, CONG. RESEARCH SERV., EXECUTIVE ORDER FOR REVIEW OF NATIONAL MONUMENTS: BACKGROUND AND DATA 1 (2017).

Despite the Act's direction that the preserved public lands "be confined to the smallest area compatible with the proper care and management of the objects to be protected," Presidents have designated large land masses as national monuments since the Act's inception. President Theodore Roosevelt created 17 monuments, including the 808,120-acre Grand Canyon National Monument. While Presidents Theodore Roosevelt and Bill Clinton were known for their prodigious use of Antiquities Act authority, President Barack Obama surpassed them both by protecting more than 550 million acres of federal lands and waters pursuant to Antiquities Act authority. Congress has also established national monuments through legislation, independent of the Antiquities Act's delegation of authority to the President. Congress has also converted some national monuments to national parks, through legislation. *See, e.g.,* Gates of the Arctic National Park, Pub. L. 96–487, Title VII, § 701(2), Dec. 2, 1980, 94 Stat. 2417.

When Presidents designate national monuments, they typically proclaim the existence of the monument and establish restrictions on activities within the monument area. Many national monument designations prohibit new coal mining, hard rock mining, and oil and natural gas production, as well as other activities like commercial fishing and use of off-road vehicles. *See, e.g.*, Proclamation No. 9558, 82 Fed. Reg. 1139, 1143 (2017) (prohibiting mining and mineral leasing in Bears Ears National Monument); Proclamation No. 9478, 81 Fed. Reg. 60,227, 60,231 (2016) (prohibiting commercial fishing, drilling, and mining in the Papahānaumokuākea Marine National Monument); Proclamation No. 7397, 66 Fed. Reg. 7,354, 7,356 (2001) (prohibiting mining, mineral leasing, and off-road vehicles in Sonoran Desert National Monument, while allowing some grazing to continue if BLM determines that grazing is compatible with the "paramount purpose" of protecting the monument).

Monument designations have often been controversial. Designating large swaths of public land as off-limits to extractive and other commercial interests has the potential to spark strong local and state opposition. Moreover, the President can make such decisions alone, without any requirement to consult with Congress, states, or local interest groups. Presidents thus receive credit for new monument designations, as well as potentially potent ire. The case below considers one contentious monument designation, made by President Clinton shortly before the conclusion of his final term.

Utah Assoc. of Counties v. Bush

316 F. Supp. 2d 1172 (D. Utah 2004), *appeal dismissed*,
455 F.3d 1094 (10th Cir. 2006).

■ BENSON, DISTRICT JUDGE:

On September 18, 1996, President William Jefferson Clinton, invoking his authority under the Antiquities Act, designated 1.7 million acres of federal land in southeastern Utah as the Grand Staircase-Escalante National Monument. On June 23, 1997, the Utah Association of Counties, (UAC) filed this lawsuit challenging the President's actions. . . .

The Antiquities Act of 1906, 16 U.S.C. § 431, gives the President authority to create national monuments. Since its enactment, presidents have used the Antiquities Act more than 100 times to withdraw lands from the public domain as national monuments. President Clinton's use of the Antiquities Act to create the Grand Staircase Monument in 1996 was the first use of the Antiquities Act in more than two decades. The Antiquities Act authorizes the President, "in his discretion," to establish as national monuments "objects of historic or scientific interest that are situated upon the lands owned or controlled by the government of the United States." *Id.* The Act requires the president to reserve land confined to the "smallest area compatible with the proper care and management of the objects to be protected." *Id.* For purposes of this litigation, it is helpful to look to the creation of the Act and how it has been used and interpreted since its creation in 1906.

The original purpose of the proposed Act was to protect objects of antiquity. The substance of the Act, developed over a period of more than six years, was created in response to the demands of archaeological organizations. Although the scope of the archaeological organizations' proposals was limited to preservation of antiquities on federal lands, the United States Department of the Interior proposed adding the protection of scenic and scientific resources to the Act. . . .

Edgar Lee Hewitt, a prominent archaeologist, drafted the bill that was finally enacted in 1906. Government officials persuaded Hewitt to broaden the scope of his draft by including the phrase "other objects of historic or scientific interest." This phrase essentially allowed the Department of the Interior's proposal, which Congress had previously rejected, to be included in the final bill. In addition, while earlier proposals had limited the reservations to 320 or at the most 640 acres, Hewitt's draft allowed the limit to be set according to "the smallest area compatible with the proper care and management of the objects to be protected." Despite the presence of this broader language, there is some support for the proposition that Congress intended to limit the creation of national monuments to small land areas surrounding specific objects. Illustrative of this intent is House Report No. 2224, which states "[t]here are scattered throughout the southwest quite a large number of very interesting ruins . . . [t]he bill proposes to create small reservations reserving only so much land as may be absolutely necessary for the preservation of these interesting relics." H.R. Rep. No. 2224, 59th Congress, 1st sess. at 1 (1906).

Despite what may have been the intent of some members of Congress, use of the Antiquities Act has clearly expanded beyond the protection of antiquities and "small reservations" of "interesting ruins." Nothing in the language of the Act specifically authorizes the creation of national monuments for scenic purposes or for general conservation purposes. Nonetheless, several presidents have used the Act to withdraw large land areas for scenic and general conservation purposes. President Theodore Roosevelt was the first president to withdraw land under the Act, establishing a precedent other presidents later followed to create large scenic monuments. Within two years of enactment of the Act, President Roosevelt made eighteen withdrawals of land. . . .

Coincidentally, during the 1930s, the Franklin D. Roosevelt administration considered the creation of a monument in virtually the same area as the Grand Staircase Monument. President Roosevelt received a recommendation to withdraw 4.4. million acres of Utah's red rock country, creating Escalante National Monument. The Roosevelt administration ultimately rejected the idea, in large part because of local opposition. . . .

Most of the presidential withdrawals have been uncontroversial. However, there have been several legal challenges to presidential monument designations under the Antiquities Act. Every challenge to date has been unsuccessful. *See Cameron v. United States*, 252 U.S. 450 (1920) (the President's designation of the Grand Canyon as a national monument was a valid use of his authority under the Antiquities Act); *Wyoming v. Franke*, 58 F.Supp. 890 (D. Wyo. 1945) (the proclamation creating the Jackson Hole National Monument complied with the standards set forth in the Antiquities Act); *Cappaert v. United States*, 426 U.S. 128 (1976) (presidential proclamation withdrawing the Devil's Hole tract of land and accompanying water from the public domain and combining it with the Death Valley National Monument, explicitly reserved water rights to the federal Government and constituted a valid exercise of presidential authority under the Antiquities Act); *Anaconda Copper Co. v. Andrus*, No. A79–101 (D. Alaska, 1980); *Alaska v. Carter*, 462 F. Supp. 1155 (D. Alaska 1978) (president not subject to requirements of National Environmental Policy Act when proclaiming national monuments under the Antiquities Act). . . .

Plaintiffs assert, and the record appears to support, that another driving force behind Secretary Babbitt's, the DOI's, and eventually the President's efforts to create the Grand Staircase Monument was to prevent the proposed Andalex Smoky Hollow coal mining operation in Kane County, Utah from coming to fruition. Besides supporting Congressman Hinchey's proposed wilderness designation, which would encompass the property proposed for the Smoky Hollow Mine, Secretary Babbitt and the DOI also attacked the validity of the federal Smoky Hollow coal leases by attempting to cancel the suspension in the interest of conservation granted to the holders of the coal leases several years earlier by the Utah BLM State Director. . . .

From the exhibits submitted by plaintiffs, the majority of which were secured by congressional subpoena, it appears that in early 1996, efforts involving various officials within the executive branch of government began discussing the possibility of creating a national monument in Utah by way of a presidential proclamation. Internal memoranda indicate that as early as March 1996, the DOI requested that CEQ or White House officials send a letter to Secretary Babbitt under the President's signature requesting an investigation and recommendations for a Utah national monument. Plaintiffs assert that the reasoning behind the request was to enable defendants to avoid having to comply with NEPA and FLPMA, because the President is not a federal agency and not subject to either NEPA or FLPMA. . . .

From March 1996 to September 18, 1996, DOI officials worked closely with CEQ Director Kathleen McGinty and others to identify the lands to include in the proclamation and the actions needed to ensure that the proclamation would survive judicial scrutiny. In August 1996, the DOI conducted a database and bibliography search to prepare a record to support the proclamation. Some of the reasons for creating Grand Staircase Monument focused on the proposed Smoky Hollow coal mine and contentions that the mine would irreversibly damage the environment and Utah's public lands. . . .

Following this history, the Proclamation itself took place on September 18, 1996, when President Clinton stood at the south rim of the Grand Canyon in Arizona and announced the establishment of the 1.7 million acre Utah monument. There was virtually no advance consultation with Utah's federal or state officials, which may explain the decision to make the announcement in Arizona. The monument created a good deal of controversy, heightened even more because the presidential election was less than 8 weeks away. In making the announcement, President Clinton emphasized his "concern[ ] about a large coal mine proposed for the area" and his belief that "we shouldn't have mines that threaten our national treasures." Remarks Announcing the Establishment of the Grand Staircase-Escalate National Monument, 32 Weekly Comp. Pres. Doc. 1785 (Sept. 23, 1996). . . .

The record is undisputed that the President of the United States used his authority under the Antiquities Act to designate the Grand Staircase Monument. The record is also undisputed that in doing so the President complied with the Antiquities Act's two requirements, 1) designating, in his discretion, objects of scientific or historic value, and 2) setting aside, in his discretion, the smallest area necessary to protect the objects. With little additional discussion, these facts compel a finding in favor of the President's actions in creating the monument. That is essentially the end of the legal analysis. Clearly established Supreme Court precedent instructs that the Court's judicial review in these circumstances is at best limited to ascertaining that the President in fact invoked his powers under the Antiquities Act. Beyond such a facial review the Court is not permitted to go. . . . When the President is given such a broad grant of discretion as in the Antiquities Act, the courts have no authority to determine whether the President abused his discretion. . . . To do so would impermissibly replace the President's discretion with that of the judiciary. . . .

"It is evident from the language of the Proclamation that the President exercised the discretion lawfully delegated to him by Congress under the Antiquities Act, and that finding demarcates the outer limit of judicial review. Whether the President's designation best fulfilled the general congressional intention embodied in the Antiquities Act is not a matter for judicial inquiry. This Court declines plaintiffs' invitation to substitute its judgment for that of the President, particularly in an arena in which the congressional intent most clearly manifest is an intention to delegate decision-making to the sound discretion of the President." (At 1186).

While there has been some debate among the United States Supreme Court justices as to whether judicial review of executive actions by the President are subject to judicial review at all, recent judgments have indicated the Court's willingness to engage in a narrowly circumscribed form of judicial review. This willingness does not, however, allow judicial review of sufficient scope to assist plaintiffs' cause; long-standing United States Supreme Court precedent has clearly foreclosed the broad review for which plaintiffs contend: "Whenever a statute gives a discretionary power to any person, to be exercised by him upon his own opinion of certain facts, it is a sound rule of construction, that the statute constitutes him the sole and exclusive judge of the existence of those facts." For the judiciary to probe the reasoning which underlies this Proclamation would amount to a clear invasion of the legislative and executive domains. *United States v. George S. Bush & Co.*, 310 U.S. 371 (1940) (quoting *Martin v. Mott*, 25 U.S. 19 (1827). A grant of discretion to the President to make particular judgments forecloses judicial review of the substance of those judgments altogether. . . .

Although judicial review is not available to assess a particular exercise of presidential discretion, a Court may ensure that a president was in fact exercising the authority conferred by the act at issue. Thus, although this Court is without jurisdiction to second-guess the reasons underlying the President's designation of a particular monument, the Court may still inquire into whether the President, when designating this Monument, acted pursuant to the Antiquities Act.

The Antiquities Act offers two principles to guide the President in making a designation under the Act:

> The President of the United States is authorized, in his discretion, to declare by public proclamation . . . objects of historic or scientific interest . . . to be national monuments, and may reserve as a part thereof parcels of land, the limits of which in all cases shall be confined to the smallest area compatible with the proper care and management of the objects to be protected.

16 U.S.C. § 431. The Proclamation of which plaintiffs complain speaks in detail of the Monument's natural and archeological resources and indicates that the designated area is the smallest consistent with the protection of those resources. The language of the Proclamation clearly indicates that the President considered the principles that Congress required him to consider: he used his discretion in designating objects of scientific or historic value, and used his discretion in setting aside the smallest area necessary to protect those objects.

It is evident from the language of the Proclamation that the President exercised the discretion lawfully delegated to him by Congress under the Antiquities Act, and that finding demarcates the outer limit of judicial review. Whether the President's designation best fulfilled the general congressional intention embodied in the Antiquities Act is not a matter for judicial inquiry. This Court declines plaintiffs' invitation to substitute its judgment for that of the President, particularly in an arena in which the congressional intent most clearly manifest is an intention to delegate decision-making to the sound discretion of the President. . . .

NOTES AND QUESTIONS

1.   **The Role of Congress.** Grand Staircase-Escalante was not the first, nor the last, controversial national monument created by a President. In 1943, President Franklin D. Roosevelt designated the Jackson Hole National Monument, against the State of Wyoming's and many members of Congress' wishes. In *Wyoming v. Franke*, the court upheld the monument designation, stating:

> If there be evidence in the case of a substantial character upon which the President may have acted in declaring that there were objects of historic or scientific interest included within the area, it is sufficient upon which he may have based a discretion. For example, if a monument were to be created on a bare stretch of sage-brush prairie in regard to which there was no substantial evidence that it contained objects of historic or scientific interest, the action in attempting to establish it by proclamation as a monument, would undoubtedly be arbitrary and capricious and clearly outside the scope and purpose of the Monument Act. . . .

> [I]f the Congress presumes to delegate its inherent authority to Executive Departments which exercise acquisitive proclivities not actually intended, the burden is on the Congress to pass such remedial legislation as may obviate any injustice brought about as the power and control over and disposition of government lands inherently rests in its Legislative branch. What has been said with reference to the objects of historic and scientific interest applies equally to the discretion of the Executive in defining the area compatible with the proper care and management of the objects to be protected.

58 F. Supp. 890, 895–96 (D. Wyo. 1945). What does the court view as the role of Congress with respect to national monuments? What recourse does Congress have if it is unhappy with a Presidential monument proclamation?

2.   **"Objects of Historic or Scientific Interest."** What types of objects qualify for national monument designation? A unique geologic formation? Historic trails spanning several miles? An extensive underwater reef home to hundreds of endemic species? Past presidential monument proclamations identified each of these components and more, and explained their significance. Are there any meaningful limits on what can be protected as a national monument? Are all public lands of some scientific or historic interest?

What does the court in *Wyoming v. Franke*, in Note 1 above, say about possible limits on monument designation? How much deference should a court give to the executive to decide the boundaries of the "smallest area compatible with the proper care and management of the objects to be protected"? *See* 54 U.S.C. § 320301(b).

3.   **State and Local Consultation.** The Antiquities Act is silent with respect to any required or recommended consultation with states or local interests before creating a new national monument. Thinking back to the history of the Antiquities Act, why might this be the case? Given the scale of many monument designations, do you view this as a sound policy choice, or if even the chance, would you amend the Antiquities Act to discuss consultation in some form? Does it matter to your views on consultation that Presidential monument proclamations are not subject to NEPA, because the President is not an agency, as noted by the court in *Utah Association of Counties*?

4.   **Monuments at Sea.** Does the Antiquities Act give the President authority to designate national monuments offshore? Several Presidents have designated such monuments, including George W. Bush's creation of the Northwest Hawaiian Islands Marine National Monument in 2006 (renamed as Papahānaumokuākea in 2007). President Obama later expanded the size of Papahānaumokuākea by nearly four times, issuing a new proclamation with respect to the additions. The expanded monument became the world's largest marine protected area. *See* NOAA, Papahānaumokuākea Expands, Now Largest Conservation Area on Earth, (Aug. 2016), https://sanctuaries.noaa.gov/news/aug16/president-announced-expansion-of-papahanaumokuakea-marine-national-monument.html (last visited Feb. 19, 2019). Commercial fishing and other resource extraction activities are prohibited within the monument. *Id.*

President Obama also proclaimed the Northeast Canyons and Seamounts Marine National Monument, in the Atlantic Ocean 150 miles southeast of Cape Cod, Massachusetts. The monument protects a cluster of four extinct undersea volcanoes (known as seamounts) and three undersea canyons, each one deeper than the Grand Canyon. Motivated by the area's "unique ecological resources that have long been the subject of scientific interest," including a diverse range of endemic and migratory sea life, the President sought to protect the area for future use and study. Proclamation No. 9496, 3 C.F.R. § 262 (2016). As with Papahānaumokuākea, commercial fishing and resource extraction are prohibited within the monument. *Id.*

Plaintiffs from the commercial fishing industry sued, challenging the designation of the Northeast Canyons and Seamounts monument. They alleged that the President had no power to designate the monument for three reasons: first, because the submerged lands of the Canyons and Seamounts are not "lands" under the Antiquities Act; second, because the federal government does not "control" the lands on which the Canyons and Seamounts lie; and third, because the amount of land reserved as part of the monument is not the smallest compatible with its management. *See Massachusetts Lobstermen's Ass'n v. Ross,* 349 F. Supp. 3d 48, 51 (D.D.C. 2018).

The federal district court rejected each of these challenges. It held that the Antiquities Act does reach submerged lands and the water associated with them, an interpretation supported by legal precedent, executive practice, and ordinary meaning. *Id.* at 56. For instance, in *Alaska v. United States*, the Supreme Court concluded that the federal government had title to the submerged lands in Glacier Bay National Monument off the coast of Alaska. 545 U.S. 75, 101–03 (2005). Second, the court held that the United States sufficiently controls the Exclusive Economic Zone ("EEZ")—where the Northeast Canyons and Seamounts National Marine Monument is located—to empower the President under the Antiquities Act. *Id.* at 63–64. And third, it held that to obtain judicial review of claims about a monument's size, "plaintiffs must offer specific, nonconclusory factual allegations establishing a problem with its boundaries," which it failed to do. *Id.* at 67.

Which of plaintiffs' claims do you find most compelling? If you were representing the federal government defending the President's monument designation, what arguments would you make to support the claim that the United States exercises sufficient control over the EEZ to empower an offshore monument designation? And could you draw on any language in OCSLA (addressed in the preceding section on offshore mineral leasing) to support the government's position with respect to the EEZ in this case?

5. Power to Diminish Monuments? On April 26, 2017, President Trump signed an executive order directing the Secretary of the Interior, Ryan Zinke, to review national monuments designated by previous presidents under the Antiquities Act, to assess whether to rescind or reduce the boundaries of some of these national monuments. In December 2017, President Trump issued two proclamations, downsizing Bears Ears National Monument by 85 percent and Grand Staircase-Escalante National Monument by nearly 50 percent. Native American tribes and conservation groups sued, challenging these actions under the Antiquities Act, the U.S. Constitution, and the Administrative Procedure Act. As of October 2018, the litigation is ongoing.

Does the President have authority to undo or downsize a national monument designation made by a preceding President? While past presidents have altered monuments before, including shrinking monument boundaries a handful of times, none of those changes were ever challenged in court. Is such power delegated by Congress to the executive branch in the text of the Antiquities Act? Can such a power be implied?

Several legal scholars have analyzed this question, with the majority finding no presidential power to undo or significantly diminish an existing monument; such power is reserved to Congress, alone. *See* Jayni Foley Hein, *Monumental Decisions: One-Way Levers Towards Preservation in the Antiquities Act and Outer Continental Shelf Lands Act*, 48 ENVTL L. 125, 128–131 (2018); Mark Squillace et al., *Presidents Lack the Authority to Abolish or Diminish National Monuments*, 103 VA. L. REV. ONLINE 55, 70–71 (2017); ALEXANDRA M. WYATT, CONG. RESEARCH SERV., R44687, ANTIQUITIES ACT: SCOPE OF AUTHORITY FOR MODIFICATION OF NATIONAL MONUMENTS 4 (2016). For the competing view that Presidents can modify and even rescind existing monuments, *see* JOHN YOO & TODD GAZIANO, AM. ENTER. INST., PRESIDENTIAL AUTHORITY TO REVOKE OR REDUCE NATIONAL MONUMENT DESIGNATIONS (2017).

iii. WILDERNESS

Congress enacted the Wilderness Act in 1964, after nearly a decade of debate. Many western officials and economic interests opposed wilderness legislation when it was first introduced during the 1950's, fearing that development restrictions in lands designated as wilderness would deprive local interests of the ability to provide for their economic well-being. John Copeland Nagle, *Wilderness Exceptions*, 44 ENVTL. L. 373, 379 (2014). Congress responded, in part, by providing that "no Federal lands shall be designated as 'wilderness areas' except as provided for in this chapter or by a subsequent Act." 16 U.S.C. § 1131(a). This placed the creation of new wilderness areas firmly within Congressional control, and helped to assuage the concerns of lawmakers desiring to recapture more authority over public lands from the executive branch. Indeed, in the decades before passage of the Act, the Forest Service had designated several areas of national forest as wilderness on its own accord. *See* ROSS W. GORTE, CONG. RESEARCH SERV., WILDERNESS: OVERVIEW AND STATISTICS 1 (2010).

The creation of new wilderness areas is thus dependent upon congressional legislation. The Wilderness Act itself designated nine million acres of Forest Service land as wilderness. "Wilderness" is defined in the Act as:

> . . .an area where the earth and its community of life are untrammeled by man, where man himself is a visitor who does not remain. An area of wilderness is further defined to mean in this Act an area of undeveloped Federal land retaining its primeval character and influence, without permanent improvements or human habitation, which is protected and managed so as to preserve its natural conditions and which (1) generally appears to have been affected primarily by the forces of nature, with the imprint of man's work substantially unnoticeable; (2) has outstanding opportunities for solitude or a primitive and unconfined type of recreation; (3) has at least five thousand acres of land or is of sufficient size as to make practicable its preservation and use in an unimpaired condition; and (4) may also contain ecological, geological, or other features of scientific, educational, scenic, or historical value.

16 U.S.C. § 1131(c). The Act established a National Wilderness Preservation System, composed of federally owned areas designated by Congress as wilderness areas, and directed that these areas "shall be administered for the use and enjoyment of the American people in such manner as will leave them unimpaired for future use and enjoyment as wilderness, and so as to provide for the protection of these areas, the preservation of their wilderness character, and for the gathering and dissemination of information regarding their use and enjoyment as wilderness." *Id.* § 1131(a). The Act also prohibits certain activities within designated wilderness, including "commercial enterprise, permanent or

temporary roads, mechanical transports, and structures or installations," with exceptions for necessary area administration and emergencies *Id.* § 1133(b). The Act's restrictions can also be waived for "the control of fire, insects and diseases." *Id.* § 1133(d).

Wilderness designations have resulted in protection of over 109 million acres of public land. Congress designated additional wilderness areas in the eastern United States through the Eastern Wilderness Act of 1975; in the west through the California Desert Protection Act of 1994; and in several states in 2009. *See, e.g.,* 16 U.S.C. §§ 410aaa–410aaa–83; Omnibus Public Land Management Act of 2009, Pub. L. No. 111–11, 123 Stat. 991, §§ 1001–1983 (2009). However, other wilderness proposals await congressional approval, and many observers object to the slow pace of wilderness designations. *See, e.g.,* Sandra Zellmer, *A Preservation Paradox: Political Prestidigitation and an Enduring Resource of Wildness,* 34 ENVTL. L. 1015, 1017–18 (2004) (asserting that "the cumbersome and compromise-ridden legislative process has not fulfilled the Wilderness Act's goal of 'securing an enduring resource of wilderness' ").

Wilderness areas are managed by four federal agencies: the Forest Service, BLM, NPS, and FWS. The case that follows addresses BLM's management of wilderness areas, including its statutory duties under both FLPMA and the Wilderness Act.

Norton v. Southern Utah Wilderness Alliance

542 U.S. 55 (2004).

■ JUSTICE SCALIA delivered the opinion of the Court.

In this case, we must decide whether the authority of a federal court under the Administrative Procedure Act (APA) to "compel agency action unlawfully withheld or unreasonably delayed," 5 U.S.C. § 706(1), extends to the review of the United States Bureau of Land Management's stewardship of public lands under certain statutory provisions and its own planning documents.

Almost half the State of Utah, about 23 million acres, is federal land administered by the Bureau of Land Management (BLM), an agency within the Department of Interior. For nearly 30 years, BLM's management of public lands has been governed by the Federal Land Policy and Management Act of 1976 (FLPMA), 90 Stat. 2744, 43 U.S.C. § 1701 et seq., which "established a policy in favor of retaining public lands for multiple use management." *Lujan v. Nat'l Wildlife Fed'n,* 497 U.S. 871, 877 (1990). . . . FLPMA establishes a dual regime of inventory and planning. Sections 1711 and 1712, respectively, provide for a comprehensive, ongoing inventory of federal lands, and for a land use planning process that "project[s]" "present and future use," § 1701(a)(2), given the lands' inventoried characteristics.

Of course, not all uses are compatible. Congress made the judgment that some lands should be set aside as wilderness at the expense of commercial and recreational uses. A pre-FLPMA enactment, the Wilderness Act of 1964, 78 Stat. 890, provides that designated wilderness areas, subject to certain exceptions, "shall [have] no commercial enterprise and no permanent road," no motorized vehicles, and no manmade structures. 16 U.S.C. § 1133(c). The designation of a wilderness area can be made only by Act of Congress, *see* 43 U.S.C. § 1782(b).

Pursuant to § 1782, the Secretary of the Interior has identified so-called "wilderness study areas" (WSAs), roadless lands of 5,000 acres or more that possess "wilderness characteristics," as determined in the Secretary's land inventory. § 1782(a); *see* 16 U.S.C. § 1131(c). As the name suggests, WSAs (as well as certain wild lands identified prior to the passage of FLPMA) have been subjected to further examination and public comment in order to evaluate their suitability for designation as wilderness. In 1991, out of 3.3 million acres in Utah that had been identified for study, 2 million were recommended as suitable for wilderness designation. 1 U.S. Dept. of Interior, BLM, Utah Statewide Wilderness Study Report 3 (Oct. 1991). This recommendation was forwarded to Congress, which has not yet acted upon it. Until Congress acts one way or the other, FLPMA provides that "the Secretary shall continue to manage such lands . . . in a manner so as not to impair the suitability of such areas for preservation as wilderness." 43 U.S.C. § 1782(c). This nonimpairment mandate applies to all WSAs identified under § 1782, including lands considered unsuitable by the Secretary.

Aside from identification of WSAs, the main tool that BLM employs to balance wilderness protection against other uses is a land use plan— what BLM regulations call a "resource management plan." 43 C.F.R. § 1601.0–5(k) (2003). Land use plans, adopted after notice and comment, are "designed to guide and control future management actions," § 1601.0–2. *See* 43 U.S.C. § 1712; 43 C.F.R. § 1610.2 (2003). Generally, a land use plan describes, for a particular area, allowable uses, goals for future condition of the land, and specific next steps. § 1601.0–5(k). Under FLPMA, "[t]he Secretary shall manage the public lands under principles of multiple use and sustained yield, in accordance with the land use plans . . . when they are available." 43 U.S.C. § 1732(a).

Protection of wilderness has come into increasing conflict with another element of multiple use, recreational use of so-called off-road vehicles (ORVs), which include vehicles primarily designed for off-road use, such as lightweight, four-wheel "all-terrain vehicles," and vehicles capable of such use, such as sport utility vehicles. *See* 43 C.F.R. § 8340.0–5(a) (2003). According to the United States Forest Service's most recent estimates, some 42 million Americans participate in off-road travel each year, more than double the number two decades ago. United States sales of all-terrain vehicles alone have roughly doubled in the past five years, reaching almost 900,000 in 2003. The use of ORVs on federal land has negative environmental consequences, including soil disruption and compaction, harassment of animals, and annoyance of wilderness lovers. Thus, BLM faces a classic land use dilemma of sharply inconsistent uses, in a context of scarce resources and congressional silence with respect to wilderness designation.

In 1999, respondents Southern Utah Wilderness Alliance and other organizations (collectively SUWA) filed this action in the United States District Court for Utah against petitioners BLM, its Director, and the Secretary. In its second amended complaint, SUWA sought declaratory and injunctive relief for BLM's failure to act to protect public lands in Utah from damage caused by ORV use. SUWA made three claims that are relevant here: (1) that BLM had violated its nonimpairment obligation under § 1782(a) by allowing degradation in certain WSAs; (2) that BLM had failed to implement provisions in its land use plans relating to ORV use; (3) that BLM had failed to take a "hard look" at whether, pursuant to the National Environmental Policy Act of 1969 (NEPA), 42 U.S.C. § 4321 *et seq.*, it should undertake supplemental environmental analyses for areas in which ORV use had increased. SUWA contended that it could sue to remedy these three failures to act pursuant to the APA's provision of a cause of action to "compel agency action unlawfully withheld or unreasonably delayed." 5 U.S.C. § 706(1). The District Court [dismissed SUWA's three claims, but a divided panel of the Tenth Circuit reversed].

All three claims at issue here involve assertions that BLM failed to take action with respect to ORV use that it was required to take. Failures to act are sometimes remediable under the APA, but not always. . . . [A] claim under § 706(1) can proceed only where a plaintiff asserts that an agency failed to take a *discrete* agency action that it is *required to take.* . . .

With these principles in mind, we turn to SUWA's first claim, that by permitting ORV use in certain WSAs, BLM violated its mandate to "continue to manage [WSAs] . . . in a manner so as not to impair the suitability of such areas for preservation as wilderness," 43 U.S.C. § 1782(c). SUWA relies not only upon § 1782(c) but also upon a provision of BLM's Interim Management Policy for Lands Under Wilderness Review, which interprets the nonimpairment mandate to require BLM to manage WSAs so as to prevent them from being "degraded so far, compared with the area's values for other purposes, as to significantly constrain the Congress's prerogative to either designate [it] as wilderness or release it for other uses."

Section 1782(c) is mandatory as to the object to be achieved, but it leaves BLM a great deal of discretion in deciding how to achieve it. It assuredly does not mandate, with the clarity necessary to support judicial action under § 706(1), the total exclusion of ORV use.

SUWA argues that § 1782 *does* contain a categorical imperative, namely the command to comply with the nonimpairment mandate. It contends that a federal court could simply enter a general order compelling compliance with that mandate, without suggesting any particular manner of compliance. It relies upon the language from the Attorney General's Manual quoted earlier, that a court can "take action upon a matter, without directing how [the agency] shall act," and upon language in a case cited by the Manual noting that "mandamus will lie . . . even though the act required involves the exercise of judgment and discretion." *Safeway Stores v. Brown*, 138 F.2d 278, 280 (Emerg. Ct. App. 1943). The action referred to in these excerpts, however, is discrete agency action, as we have discussed above. General deficiencies in compliance, unlike the failure to issue a ruling that was discussed in *Safeway Stores*, lack the specificity requisite for agency action.

The principal purpose of the APA limitations we have discussed— and of the traditional limitations upon mandamus from which they were derived—is to protect agencies from undue judicial interference with their lawful discretion, and to avoid judicial entanglement in abstract policy disagreements which courts lack both expertise and information to resolve. If courts were empowered to enter general orders compelling compliance with broad statutory mandates, they would necessarily be empowered, as well, to determine whether compliance was achieved— which would mean that it would ultimately become the task of the supervising court, rather than the agency, to work out compliance with the broad statutory mandate, injecting the judge into day-to-day agency management. To take just a few examples from federal resources management, a plaintiff might allege that the Secretary had failed to "manage wild free-roaming horses and burros in a manner that is designed to achieve and maintain a thriving natural ecological balance," or to "manage the [New Orleans Jazz National] [H]istorical [P]ark in such a manner as will preserve and perpetuate knowledge and understanding of the history of jazz," or to "manage the [Steens Mountain] Cooperative Management and Protection Area for the benefit of present and future generations." 16 U.S.C. §§ 1333(a), 410bbb–2(a)(1), 460nnn–12(b). The prospect of pervasive oversight by federal courts over the manner and pace of agency compliance with such congressional directives is not contemplated by the APA.

SUWA's second claim is that BLM failed to comply with certain provisions in its land use plans, thus contravening the requirement that "[t]he Secretary shall manage the public lands . . . in accordance with the land use plans . . . when they are available." 43 U.S.C. § 1732(a); *see also* 43 C.F.R. § 1610.5–3(a) (2003) ("All future resource management authorizations and actions . . . and subsequent more detailed or specific planning, shall conform to the approved plan"). . . .

SUWA does not contest BLM's assertion in the court below that informal monitoring has taken place for some years, but it demands continuing implementation of a monitoring *program*. By this it apparently means to insist upon adherence to the plan's general discussion of "Use Supervision and Monitoring" in designated areas, which (in addition to calling for the use supervision files that have already been created) provides that "[r]esource damage will be documented and recommendations made for corrective action," "[m]onitoring in open areas will focus on determining damage which may necessitate a change in designation," and "emphasis on use supervision will be placed on [limited and closed areas]." *Id.*, at 149. . . .

The statutory directive that BLM manage "in accordance with" land use plans, and the regulatory requirement that authorizations and actions "conform to" those plans, prevent BLM from taking actions inconsistent with the provisions of a land use plan. Unless and until the plan is amended, such actions can be set aside as contrary to law pursuant to 5 U.S.C. § 706(2). The claim presently under discussion, however, would have us go further, and conclude that a statement in a plan that BLM "will" take this, that, or the other action, is a binding commitment that can be compelled under § 706(1). In our view it is not— at least absent clear indication of binding commitment in the terms of the plan.

FLPMA describes land use plans as tools by which "present and future use is *projected*." 43 U.S.C. § 1701(a)(2) (emphasis added). The implementing regulations make clear that land use plans are a preliminary step in the overall process of managing public lands— "designed to guide and control future management actions and the development of subsequent, more detailed and limited scope plans for resources and uses." 43 C.F.R. § 1601.0–2 (2003). The statute and regulations confirm that a land use plan is not ordinarily the medium for affirmative decisions that implement the agency's "project[ions]." Title 43 U.S.C. § 1712(e) provides that "[t]he Secretary may issue management decisions to implement land use plans"—the decisions, that is, are distinct from the plan itself. Picking up the same theme, the regulation defining a land use plan declares that a plan "is not a final implementation decision on actions which require further specific plans, process steps, or decisions under specific provisions of law and regulations." 43 C.F.R. § 1601.0–5(k) (2003). The BLM's Land Use Planning Handbook specifies that land use plans are normally not used to make site-specific implementation decisions.

Plans also receive a different agency review process from implementation decisions. Appeal to the Department's Board of Land Appeals is available for "a specific action being proposed to implement some portion of a resource management plan or amendment." 43 C.F.R. § 1610.5–3(b). However, the Board, which reviews "decisions rendered by Departmental officials relating to . . . [t]he use and disposition of public lands and their resources," § 4.1(b)(3)(i), does not review the approval of a plan, since it regards a plan as a policy determination, not an implementation decision. . . .

Quite unlike a specific statutory command requiring an agency to promulgate regulations by a certain date, a land use plan is generally a statement of priorities; it guides and constrains actions, but does not (at least in the usual case) prescribe them. It would be unreasonable to think that either Congress or the agency intended otherwise, since land use plans nationwide would commit the agency to actions far in the future, for which funds have not yet been appropriated. Some plans make explicit that implementation of their programmatic content is subject to budgetary constraints. While the Henry Mountains plan does not contain such a specification, we think it must reasonably be implied. A statement by BLM about what it plans to do, at some point, provided it has the funds and there are not more pressing priorities, cannot be plucked out of context and made a basis for suit under § 706(1).

Of course, an action called for in a plan may be compelled when the plan merely reiterates duties the agency is already obligated to perform, or perhaps when language in the plan itself creates a commitment binding on the agency. But allowing general enforcement of plan terms would lead to pervasive interference with BLM's own ordering of priorities. For example, a judicial decree compelling immediate preparation of all of the detailed plans called for in the San Rafael plan would divert BLM's energies from other projects throughout the country that are in fact more pressing. And while such a decree might please the environmental plaintiffs in the present case, it would ultimately operate to the detriment of sound environmental management. Its predictable consequence would be much vaguer plans from BLM in the future—making coordination with other agencies more difficult, and depriving the public of important information concerning the agency's long-range intentions.

We therefore hold that the Henry Mountains plan's statements to the effect that BLM will conduct "use supervision and monitoring" in designated areas—like other "will do" projections of agency action set forth in land use plans—are not a legally binding commitment enforceable under § 706(1). That being so, we find it unnecessary to consider whether the action envisioned by the statements is sufficiently discrete to be amenable to compulsion under the APA. . . .

NOTES AND QUESTIONS

1. **John Muir on Wilderness.** John Muir, writing in 1901, described the value of wilderness and other protected lands in characteristic lofty prose:

> The tendency nowadays to wander in wildernesses is delightful to see. Thousands of tired, nerve-shaken, over-civilized people are beginning to find out that going to the mountains is going home; that wildness is a necessity; and that mountain parks and reservations are useful not only as fountains of timber and

irrigating rivers, but as fountains of life. Awakening from the stupefying effects of the vice of over-industry and the deadly apathy of luxury, they are trying as best they can to mix and enrich their own little ongoings with those of Nature, and to get rid of rust and disease. Briskly venturing and roaming, some are washing off sins and cobweb cares of the devil's spinning in all-day storms on mountains; sauntering in rosiny pinewoods or in gentian meadows, brushing through chaparral, bending down and parting sweet, flowery sprays; tracing rivers to their sources, getting in touch with the nerves of Mother Earth; jumping from rock to rock, feeling the life of them, learning the songs of them, panting in whole-souled exercise, and rejoicing in deep, long-drawn breaths of pure wildness. This is fine and natural and full of promise. So also is the growing interest in the care and preservation of forests and wild places in general, and in the half wild parks and gardens of towns. . . .

Under the control of the vast mysterious forces of the interior of the earth all the continents and islands are slowly rising or sinking. . . . Man, too, is making many far-reaching changes. This most influential half animal, half angel is rapidly multiplying and spreading, covering the seas and lakes with ships, the land with huts, hotels, cathedrals, and clustered city shops and homes, so that soon, it would seem, we may have to go farther than Nansen to find a good sound solitude. None of Nature's landscapes are ugly so long as they are wild; and much, we can say comfortingly, must always be in great part wild, particularly the sea and the sky, the floods of light from the stars, and the warm, unspoilable heart of the earth, infinitely beautiful, though only dimly visible to the eye of imagination. The geysers, too, spouting from the hot underworld; the steady, long-lasting glaciers on the mountains, obedient only to the sun; Yosemite domes and the tremendous grandeur of rocky cañons[sic] and mountains in general,—these must always be wild, for man can change them and mar them hardly more than can the butterflies that hover above them. But the continent's outer beauty is fast passing away, especially the plant part of it, the most destructible and most universally charming of all. . . .

JOHN MUIR, OUR NATIONAL PARKS, Chapter 1 (1901). What benefits does Muir ascribe to wilderness? Do you find his description of wilderness, and the benefits it confers, equally valid today as it was in 1901? Muir helped inspire President Theodore Roosevelt's innovative conservation programs, including establishing the first national monuments by proclamation, and Yosemite National Park by congressional action. The Sierra Club, The John Muir Exhibit: Who Was John Muir?, https://vault.sierraclub.org/john_muir_exhibit/about/default.aspx (last visited Dec. 8, 2018).

2.   Definition of Wilderness. Reread the definition of wilderness in the Wilderness Act. Does the definition, alone, foreclose all mining, timber harvesting, grazing, or mechanical transport? Would an area of public forest that was logged 60 years ago, but has grown back and is largely indistinguishable from virgin forest (to a non-expert's eye) qualify as wilderness? What about an area of wild forest bordering an urban area, where some of the lights of the city are within view from certain areas of the forest? Consider the use of the word "untrammeled" in the definition—and look the word up in a dictionary if you an uncertain of its meaning. Why might the Act's drafters have selected this word as opposed to "undisturbed" or "pristine" in the first sentence of the definition?

3.   Agency Discretion and "Wilderness Study Areas." If the land in question in *Norton v. SUWA* had been designated as wilderness, could BLM allow ORV use? Could it allow mountain biking or boating? What is the policy rationale for treating "wilderness study areas" differently from designated wilderness? Do you find this persuasive, or would you offer a different management approach for wilderness study areas?

4.   Causes of Action. According to the unanimous court's decision, when, if ever, could SUWA sue to challenge BLM's policies with respect to ORVs in wilderness study areas? Under what circumstances could SUWA sue to enforce compliance with an existing land use plan?

5.   The Wilderness Act and Agency Discretion. The Wilderness Act is much more restrictive than the broad multiple-use standards that apply to BLM and Forest Service lands. And the Park Service has significant discretion under its Organic Act. *See, e.g., Sierra Club v. Babbitt*, 69 F. Supp. 2d 1202, 1247 (E.D. Cal. 1999) (rejecting Organic Act challenge to Park Service road reconstruction project); *Int'l Snowmobile Mfrs. Ass'n. v. Norton*, 340 F. Supp. 2d 1249, 1266 (D. Wyo. 2004) (rejecting claim that restrictions on snowmobiles in Yellowstone National Park violated the Organic Act).

Further, courts have been willing to enforce the Wilderness Act's restrictions against federal land management agencies. Elisabeth Long & Eric Biber, *The Wilderness Act and Climate Change Adaptation*, 44 ENVTL. L. 623, 631 (2014) (noting that "courts have prevented agencies from conducting timber projects, fish hatchery projects, motorized transport of tourists, and maintenance of dams in wilderness areas."). For example, in *Wilderness Society v. U.S. Fish & Wildlife Service*, the Ninth Circuit held that a salmon enhancement project using a commercial fish hatchery within a wilderness area violated the Wilderness Act's prohibition of commercial enterprise in wilderness. 353 F.3d 1051, 1066–67 (9th Cir. 2003), *amended in part*, *Wilderness Soc'y v. U.S. Fish & Wildlife Serv.*, 360 F.3d 1374 (9th Cir. 2004). In *Wilderness Watch v. Mainella*, the Eleventh Circuit held that the Wilderness Act prohibits "the Park Service from offering motorized transportation to park visitors through the wilderness area." 375 F.3d 1085, 1094 (11th Cir. 2004).

Who should decide what activities are allowed in wilderness: federal agencies or federal courts? Are these decisions consistent with principles of deference normally accorded to agencies? Does the Wilderness Act alter the level of deference agencies should receive?

6.   Wilderness and Climate Change. Due to global climate change, humans have a pervasive influence on the planet, including in wilderness areas. In the era of climate change, is any part of nature truly "untrammeled" or "primeval" in character? Should climate change affect how agencies manage wilderness areas?

Eric Biber and Elisabeth Long point out the dichotomy between the Wilderness Act, which "establish[es] that passive, recreational use was to be one of the dominant uses of federal public lands," and the potential need to *actively* manage these lands in order to respond and adapt to climate change, because "hands-off management is no longer a guarantee that natural processes will dominate in wilderness areas." Elisabeth Long & Eric Biber, *The Wilderness Act and Climate Change Adaptation*, 44 ENVTL. L. 623, 626 (2014). For instance, there have been several proposals to aggressively use timber harvests to respond to climate change-induced pine beetle infestations. *Id.* Long and Biber argue that the Act's procedural and substantive hurdles to active management for climate change adaptation in wilderness areas "are an important check against this impulse to 'do something.' They encourage more thoughtful, reflective responses that reduce the risk of agency action that produces ineffectual or counterproductive active management steps, and also reduce negative impacts on other wilderness values." *Id.* at 690.

Compare this view to that of another set of scholars, David Cole and Laurie Young, who write, "Because of those pervasive human impacts on all wilderness areas—particularly climate change—active human intervention in wilderness areas will be necessary to retain desired natural features, protect biodiversity, and maintain functioning ecosystems." David N. Cole & Laurie Yung, *Park and Wilderness Stewardship: The Dilemma of Management Intervention, in* BEYOND NATURALNESS: RETHINKING PARK AND WILDERNESS STEWARDSHIP IN AN ERA OF RAPID CHANGE 1 (David N. Cole & Laurie Yung eds., 2010). Which view do you agree with more? What kind of active management might be compatible with managing wilderness pursuant to the Wilderness Act's directives?

iv. NATIONAL WILDLIFE REFUGES

The National Wildlife Refuge System includes over 550 refuges and 150 million acres of protected land. The Department of the Interior, acting through the U.S. Fish and Wildlife Service ("FWS"), manages these lands pursuant to the National Wildlife Refuge Administration Act, as amended by the National Wildlife Refuge System Improvement Act ("Improvement Act"). *See* 16 U.S.C. §§ 668dd–668ee.

The FWS traces its lineage back to two predecessor bureaus—the Bureau of Fisheries and the Bureau of Biological Survey, within the Departments of Commerce and Agriculture, respectively. Systematic protection of federal wildlife habitat began in earnest during Theodore Roosevelt's Presidency. An ornithologist, hunter, and conservationist, by the end of his Presidency in 1909, Roosevelt had created 55 bird and game reservations, which became the foundation of the National Wildlife Refuge System. FWS, *Service Organization and History*, Part 29: History (Aug. 2009), https://www.fws.gov/policy/029fw1.pdf (last visited Dec. 12, 2018).

Over the next two decades the refuge system continued to expand, adding new refuges for migratory waterfowl and other wildlife. The Migratory Bird Conservation Act of 1929 authorized the ongoing purchase of land to serve as waterfowl refuges. *See* 16 U.S.C. §§ 715–715r; Robert L. Fischman, *The National Wildlife Refuge System and the Hallmarks of Modern Organic Legislation,* 29 ECOLOGY L.Q. 457, 473 (2002). Responding to declining waterfowl populations due to overhunting, agricultural land use, and drought, in 1934, Congress passed the Migratory Bird Hunting and Conservation Stamp Act (popularly known as the Duck Stamp Act). The Act required each waterfowl hunter to possess a valid federal hunting stamp; the Act provided substantial funding for the purchase and protection of wetlands across the country. Fischman, *supra,* at 474; 16 U.S.C. §§ 718a–718k. Along with the Land and Water Conservation Fund Act of 1964, which collects revenue from federal offshore oil and gas leases, the Duck Stamp Act's funding mechanism remains the major source of revenue for purchasing expansions to the National Wildlife Refuge System. GEORGE C. COGGINS ET AL., FEDERAL PUBLIC LAND AND RESOURCES LAW 846–47 (6th ed. 2007).

In 1940, Interior merged the Bureau of Fisheries and Bureau of Biological Survey to create the Fish and Wildlife Service. Fischman, *supra,* at 475–76 (citing Reorganization Plan No. 3, 54 Stat. 1232 (1940)). The 1962 Refuge Recreation Act allowed increased recreational uses on refuges as long as they did not interfere with the refuge's primary mission. 16 U.S.C. § 460k. The National Wildlife Refuge System Administration Act of 1966 systematized the diverse units of wildlife protection (*e.g.,* game ranges, waterfowl protection areas, wildlife ranges) under the refuge system and allowed for multiple uses on refuges as long as they were compatible with the establishing legislation. Pub. L. No. 89–669, § 1(a), 80 Stat. 926 (1966) (codified as amended at 16 U.S.C. § 668dd(d)(1)(a)). In 1966, the Endangered Species Preservation Act directed the FWS to begin creating a list of endangered species and to acquire refuges for these species. Pub. L. No. 89–669, §§ 1–3, 80 Stat. 926 (repealed 1973). Congress took a more comprehensive approach in 1973 by passing the Endangered Species Act ("ESA"), detailed in Section 1 of this chapter, *infra.*

The National Wildlife Refuge System existed for 94 years without an "organic act" or comprehensive legislation outlining how it should be managed and used. In managing wildlife refuges, the FWS has more varied responsibilities and confronts more resource conflicts than the NPS does with respect to national parks, because all uses are potentially permissible on wildlife refuges. *See* George Cameron Coggins, *The Developing Law of Land Use Planning on the Federal Lands,* 61 U. COLO. L. REV. 307, 313 (1990). The agency's lack of a consistent planning structure also meant that FWS decisions were often made on an ad hoc basis. *Id.* at 314.

Passed in 1997, the Improvement Act established a unifying mission for the refuge system, a new process for determining compatibility of uses on refuges, and a requirement that each refuge be managed under a Comprehensive Conservation Plan, developed through an open public process. The Act defined the refuge system's mission as "the conservation, management, and where appropriate, restoration of the fish, wildlife and plant resources and their habitats within the United States for the benefit of present and future generations of Americans." 16 U.S.C. § 668dd(a)(2). The Act requires that each refuge be managed to fulfill the refuge system mission as well as the specific purpose(s) for which the particular refuge was established. *Id.* § 668dd(a)(3)(A). The Act also declares that "compatible wildlife-dependent recreational uses are the priority general public uses of the System and shall receive priority consideration in refuge planning and management." *Id.* § 668dd(a)(3)(B). Six uses—hunting, fishing, wildlife observation and photography, and environmental education and interpretation—receive enhanced consideration in planning and management over all other general public uses of the Refuge System. *See* Executive Order No. 12996, Management and General Public Use of the National Wildlife Refuge System, 61 Fed. Reg. 13,647, 13,647 (1996).

The following case is illustrative of the type of judgment calls that the FWS regularly makes with respect to wildlife refuge management.

McGrail & Rowley, Inc. v. Babbitt

986 F. Supp. 1386 (S.D. Fla. 1997), *aff'd*, 226 F.3d 646 (11th Cir. 2000).

■ ROETTGER, DISTRICT JUDGE:

This action was brought by McGrail and Rowley, Inc. (MRI), a corporation in the business of operating catamarans out of Key West, Florida, . . . against the Secretary of the United States Department of the Interior and several other officials of the United States Fish and Wildlife Service (FWS). MRI brought this action to challenge the Fish and Wildlife Service's denial of MRI's application for a special use permit to transport passengers to Boca Grande Key, an island within the Key West National Wildlife Refuge. (KWNWR). . . .

The KWNWR was established in 1908 by President Theodore Roosevelt's Executive Order 923 to provide "a preserve and breeding ground for native birds." The administration of the Refuge is governed by the Refuge Administration Act of 1966, (Refuge Act), 16 U.S.C. § 668dd *et seq.*, and administered by the Secretary of the Interior through the Fish and Wildlife Service. Federally owned islands within the Refuge were designated as part of the National Wilderness Preservation System (NWPS) pursuant to the Wildlife Act of 1964. Pub. Law 88–577. Congress intended the NWPS to be "administered for the use and enjoyment of the American people in such manner as will leave them unimpaired for future use and enjoyment as wilderness. . . ." 16 U.S.C. § 1131(a).

"Wilderness" is defined to be "an area where the earth and its community of life are untrammeled by man, where man himself is a visitor who does not remain." 16 U.S.C. § 1131(c).

Boca Grande Key is a small island located within the Key West NWR. The island features a narrow beach on the west and southwest sides. The only part of the beach providing access at any tide is a 700-foot section on the northeast side. The island provides a habitat for a variety of wildlife, including federally-listed threatened and endangered species: piping plover, peregrine falcon, and bald eagle. Green, loggerhead and hawksbill turtles, which are all endangered or threatened, nest or have nested on the beach and dune areas of Boca Grande. State-listed endangered sea lavender grows adjacent to the beach on the southwest side.

In 1992 the FWS and the State of Florida, Department of Natural Resources adopted a Management Plan entitled, "Management Agreement for Submerged Lands Within Boundaries of the Key West and Great Heron National Wildlife Refuges." The purpose of the Plan was to identify the resource problems in protecting certain islands and their associated wildlife.

The Plan cited damage to the wilderness values in certain areas of the Refuge and adopted certain actions to curtail the damage, including a recognition that greater enforcement of existing regulations was necessary, and that law enforcement efforts should be bolstered. With respect to commercial use of refuge islands, the Plan provided as follows: "The regulations governing commercial use of refuge islands will be followed. Commercial use of refuge islands requires a permit. Permit requests will be evaluated on a case-by-case basis for compatibility with the purposes for which the refuges were established."

It is official FWS policy to permit private parties to visit Boca Grande Key; only a portion of the 700 foot beach is restricted to visitors. Boca Grande Key is identified in the Management Plan as having a "chronic history of public use problems (large scale littering, vegetation clearing, and cooking fires) and . . . crowds in excess of 40 persons." Said crowding was feared to cause a "greater chance of degradation of natural resources and noncompliance with established regulations." . . .

For more than a year prior to the commencement of this action, MRI had been taking passengers to the public beach on Boca Grande Key in a Sebago catamaran. MRI had not been issued a permit for this activity. The Refuge Manager for the Key West NWR, defendant Jon Andrew, met with the president of MRI, Paul McGrail, in January, 1994, regarding commercial use of the refuge islands. After the meeting, Andrew sent McGrail a letter dated March 4, 1994, describing the permitting process and a document entitled "Information and Guidelines for Permit Applicants."

On June 23, 1994, MRI submitted its permit application, entitled "Proposal for Limited Commercial Access of Boca Grande in the Key West National Wildlife Refuge." The application sought a permit to bring tours of "less [sic] than 50" people to Boca Grande Key four days a week, for about an hour. The 65-foot catamaran would be anchored in the deep water channel on the northwest end. Passengers would wade ashore, advised to stay below the high tide mark. Some would travel by kayak around the north side of the island. Other passengers would be provided kites, paddleballs and frisbees for play in the water.

In a letter dated August 3, 1994, from Refuge Manager Jon Andrew, the FWS denied MRI's permit application, finding, *inter alia*, that the proposed activities were "incompatible with the purposes of the refuge." Andrew requested that MRI cease its commercial activities at Boca Grande Key, and notified MRI of its right to an appeal. Andrew telephoned Paul McGrail on August 10 to discuss the permit denial and appeal process. MRI continued to bring passengers to Boca Grande after the permit denial.

On October 13, 1994, MRI submitted its appeal. The Assistant Regional Director for Refuges and Wildlife, defendant Geoffrey Haskett, wrote MRI's then-counsel a letter dated November 9, 1994, acknowledging receipt of MRI's appeal and informing counsel that "an appeal is meaningless" as long as MRI continued to use the refuge for commercial purposes without a permit. The FWS did not process MRI's appeal.

Plaintiff filed this action on March 10, 1995, asking the court to order defendants to provide MRI an appeal pursuant to the applicable regulations (Count I), and seeking a declaratory judgment regarding a variety of issues surrounding the permitting process and the authority of the FWS to regulate the commercial use of Boca Grande Key (Count II).

Plaintiffs filed an emergency motion seeking a temporary restraining order (TRO), and the court held a brief hearing. The parties agreed to the entry of two TROs. The March 21, 1995, TROs prohibited the government from seizing any of plaintiffs' vessels or arresting the vessels' captains for activity related to transporting passengers to and from public beaches at Boca Grande and Woman Key, and prohibited plaintiffs from violating any federal law applicable to the Key West National Wildlife Refuge.

After the entry of the dual TROs, the FWS sent a letter to MRI indicating that in light of the court's order forbidding MRI from violating federal laws on the refuge, the service would process MRI's appeal. MRI was invited to contact Haskett to arrange an oral presentation and to submit written material in support of its appeal, but it failed to do so. Without further participation from MRI, the FWS Regional Director upheld the Refuge Manager's denial of a permit by letter dated May 22, 1995. This constituted the final decision of the agency pursuant to 50 C.F.R. § 25.45(d). . . .

A review of the administrative record reveals that the agency's decision to deny MRI's permit application was made after considering the relevant factors, and that it did not make a clear error in judgment. Section 668dd(d)(1)(A) of the Refuge Act requires the agency to determine whether a permit is compatible with the major purposes for which the area is established. Neither the Refuge Act nor FWS regulations define "compatible," but the refuge manual contains the Service's interpretation. The manual states: "A use may be determined to be compatible if it will not materially interfere with or detract from the purpose(s) for which the refuge was established." The document entitled "Information and Guidelines for Permit Applicants" sent by refuge manager Jon Andrew to MRI president Paul McGrail states that applications are "strictly reviewed for the impacts of the activity on wildlife and their habitat."

The agency actor relied on various laws, regulations and internal guidelines in determining compatibility, including President Theodore Roosevelt's 1908 Executive Order establishing the refuge. The Order set aside the islands "as a preserve and breeding ground for native birds." The Wilderness Act, as discussed previously, requires agencies to "manage designated [w]ilderness so as to insure that wilderness character is preserved and protected."

The refuge manager also relied on Wildlife Biologist Tom Wilmers' assessment of MRI's proposal. Wilmers' memorandum, dated July 7, 1994, conveyed his "very serious concerns" about MRI's operations in this "very sensitive . . . area." Wilmers addressed the potential damage to Boca Grande Key, which he describes as "one of the premier islands for wildlife in the entire lower Florida Keys." Of particular concern to the biologist were preservation of nesting areas for green turtles (all nests had been found in dunes located very near the area to be used by MRI's customers), damage to the shoreline from excessive public use (nearly 10,000 passengers annually), and the regular use of kites, paddleballs and frisbees, which he suggested is incompatible with the wilderness character of the island.

Wilmers is a dedicated biologist whose testimony about Boca Grande Key—clearly "the apple of his eye" among the islands in the Refuge—was at times a bit emotional. He gives lip service to the Agency position that the public is welcome to come by private boat to the Refuge islands, but the court feels he does not believe it. He clearly dislikes the visitors who picnic, wade in the water by the beach, and especially the kayakers.

In his August 3, 1994, letter to Paul McGrail officially denying the permit application, refuge manager Andrew makes explicit his reasoning. Andrew found, *inter alia*, that MRI's proposed activities would adversely affect wilderness values and were incompatible with refuge purposes. He also states that refuge resources were inadequate to administer and manage the proposed use, and that he was "reluctant to issue several permits until a reliable evaluation of costs can be made."

Further, "[t]he small size of the beach and the concentration of current public use activities" caused the refuge manager concern about conflicts among groups using the island. Finally, the refuge manager points out that MRI engaged in its commercial activities without a permit despite actual notice from the agency that a permit was required. The agency perceived this as a demonstration of "bad faith" on the part of MRI, and "raise[d] questions about [MRI's] future performance under a special use permit."

Plaintiff argues that FWS's decision to permit another commercial use of Woman Key, a nearby refuge island, that of Adventure Catamaran Tours, Inc. (Stars & Stripes), while denying MRI's application is evidence that the agency's decision was arbitrary and capricious. A review of the administrative record establishes that the decisions were rationally based. The refuge manager specifically found that the Stars & Stripes tour was, unlike that of MRI, "passive and education oriented." Further, Stars & Stripes passengers had not been observed entering closed areas, as had MRI's passengers. The record supports the agency's decision based on relevant factors, and therefore this court may not set it aside as arbitrary and capricious, although the court is dubious about FWS's appraisal of Stars & Stripes and this court might well have come to different conclusions, if writing on a clean slate. . . .

NOTES AND QUESTIONS

1.   Refuges and National Parks. Compare the mandate of the Park Service under the National Park Organic Act and the FWS under the Refuge Act. How do they differ?

2.   Compatibility. The Plan prepared by the FWS with respect to the Key West National Wildlife Refuge provides that "[p]ermit requests will be evaluated on a case-by-case basis for compatibility with the purposes for which the refuges were established." For what purpose was the Key West National Wildlife Refuge created? In light of the particular afflictions attributable to the Boca Grande Key, under what circumstances could commercial uses be considered "compatible" with this objective?

3.   Restated Compatibility Test. In 1997, after the relevant permit application had been lodged in the *McGrail & Rowley* case, Congress enacted the National Wildlife Refuge System Improvement Act ("Improvement Act"). 16 U.S.C. §§ 668dd–668ee. Under the Improvement Act, the compatibility test was restated in the following terms: " 'compatible use' means a wildlife-dependent recreational use or any other use of a refuge that, in the sound professional judgment of the Director, will not materially interfere with or detract from the fulfillment of the mission of the System or the purposes of the refuge." 16 U.S.C. § 668ee(1). In turn, "sound professional judgment" is defined to mean "a finding, determination, or decision that is consistent with principles of sound fish and wildlife management and administration, available science and resources, and adherence to the requirements of the this Act and other applicable laws." 16 U.S.C. § 668ee(3). Do you think the *McGrail & Rowley* court would have reached similar conclusions concerning compatibility under the restated standard? How much discretion does this standard afford the FWS in making determinations of compatibility?

4.   Arbitrary and Capricious Review. On what basis did the plaintiff claim that the FWS had acted arbitrarily and capriciously with respect to the processing of the permit application? Why, despite being "troubled" by the Agency's actions, did the court dismiss this claim?

On what basis did the plaintiff claim that the FWS had acted arbitrarily and capriciously with respect to its permitting of other commercial operations within the Key West National Wildlife Refuge? Given that the court noted that it was "dubious about FWS's appraisal of Stars & Stripes" and that it "might well have come to different conclusions" with respect to that proposal "if writing on a clean slate," why did it nonetheless dismiss the plaintiff's claim?

What would the plaintiff have to have shown in order to succeed in its challenge under the APA?

5.   Refuge Management Plans. The National Elk Refuge is part of the National Wildlife Refuge System. Located just north of Jackson, Wyoming, and adjacent to Grand Teton National Park, the Refuge was established in 1912 as a "winter game (elk) reserve." Act of Aug. 10, 1912, Pub.L. No. 62–261, 37 Stat. 293 (codified as amended at 16 U.S.C. § 673). As required by the Improvement Act, the FWS and NPS devised a plan to manage the elk and bison populations in the National Elk Refuge and Grand Teton National Park. *See* BISON AND ELK MANAGEMENT PLAN: NATIONAL ELK REFUGE AND GRAND TETON NATIONAL PARK 129–34 (Apr. 2007). Part of this plan includes ending the longstanding agency practice of feeding these animals during the winter—a practice known as "supplemental feeding," which can contribute to disease outbreaks by bringing together large numbers of elk for feeding. In *Defenders of Wildlife v. Salazar*, plaintiffs challenged the plan because it failed to include a deadline for ending the practice. 651 F.3d 112 (D.C. Cir. 2011).

Defenders of Wildlife preferred an alternative to the agencies' chosen plan that would have committed the Secretary to end supplemental feeding within five years. Plaintiffs argued that the plan's failure to commit to a deadline for ending supplemental feeding was arbitrary and capricious given the Secretary's duty under the Improvement Act to "provide for the conservation of . . . wildlife" and "ensure that the biological integrity, diversity, and environmental health of the [wildlife refuge system] are maintained." *Defs. of Wildlife*, 651 F.3d at 115 (citing 16 U.S.C. § 668dd(a)(4)(A)(B)).

The Court, while acknowledging that the Refuge "can hardly provide such a sanctuary if, every winter, elk and bison are drawn by the siren song of human-provided food to what becomes, through the act of gathering, a miasmic zone of life-threatening diseases," sided with the federal government. *Id.* at 116. The Court explained:

> There is no doubt that unmitigated continuation of supplemental feeding would undermine the conservation purpose of the National Wildlife Refuge System. But we cannot conclude that the agencies

acted unlawfully by adopting a plan that contained no deadline for ending the practice, and that is the only issue before us. The record amply demonstrates that the agencies collected the relevant data, identified the dangers posed by supplemental feeding, and adopted a plan to mitigate those dangers. That they also determined that the many objectives of the Act, including conservation, could best be met without implementation of a fixed deadline for stopping supplemental feeding was not arbitrary or capricious.

Id. at 117. Does this decision give the FWS and NPS *carte blanche* to continue supplemental feeding indefinitely? Why might the agencies have wanted to avoid committing to a five-year deadline for ending supplemental feeding?

6. Alaskan Wildlife Refuges. President Theodore Roosevelt first set aside refuge lands in southwestern Alaska in 1909. In 1980, President Jimmy Carter signed the Alaska National Interest Lands Conservation Act ("ANILCA") into law. 16 U.S.C. § 3101, *et seq.* ANILCA added nine new wildlife refuges, expanded seven refuges, and added 53.7 million acres to the refuge system, nearly tripling the acreage of refuge lands. FWS, *Service Organization and History*, Part 29. The expanded refuges included the nation's largest refuge, the 19.6 million acre Arctic National Wildlife Refuge (ANWR) in northeastern Alaska. ANICLA provided four purposes that guide management of the Refuge: to conserve animals and plants in their natural diversity, ensure a place for hunting and gathering activities, protect water quality and quantity, and fulfill international wildlife treaty obligations. Today, the eleven largest national wildlife refuges are all in the state of Alaska. FWS, NATIONAL WILDLIFE REFUGE SYSTEM, 2017 ANNUAL LANDS REPORT (2017).

In late 2017, Congress voted to lift a ban that had been in place since 1980 on oil and gas drilling in ANWR. The ban was removed as part of the Republican tax-reform package: a rider was inserted into the Tax Act of 2017 directing BLM to hold two lease sales, of not fewer than 400,000 acres each, within the Coastal Plain of ANWR within 10 years. Tax Cuts and Jobs Act of 2017, Pub. L. No. 115–97, 131 Stat. 2054 (2017).

Legal scholars have argued that the appropriations process is not a proper vehicle for substantive policymaking. For example, Neal Devins has argued that the "use of the appropriations process to accomplish substantive objectives that have not been considered previously or that contravene established statutory objectives may prevent the appropriate authorizing committee from applying its expertise. Exacerbating this problem, appropriations are often acted on quickly, providing little opportunity for thoughtful deliberation of the issues raised by such measures." Neal E. Devins, *Regulation of Government Agencies Through Limitation Riders*, 1987 DUKE L. J. 456, 458. Do you agree? Is an appropriations rider a suitable mechanism by which to open ANWR to drilling?

The Coastal Plain of ANWR, where drilling would occur, contains nesting habitat for about 200 species of migratory birds and critical denning habitat for threatened polar bears, in addition to other wildlife and habitat.

The 2017 Tax Act did not exempt BLM from existing laws, such as NEPA and the ESA. In 2018, BLM initiated a NEPA scoping process for implementation of a possible oil and gas leasing program within ANWR. BLM, COASTAL PLAIN OIL AND GAS LEASING PROGRAM EIS (Apr. 20, 2018). As it undertakes its NEPA analysis, what alternatives should BLM consider? Consider BLM's available discretion with respect to lease sale size, location, timing, and stipulations. What provisions of the ESA are applicable to BLM's potential actions?

CHAPTER X

ENFORCEMENT OF ENVIRONMENTAL STANDARDS

1. Mechanisms of Enforcement.
    A. Civil Penalties.
    B. Voluntary Audits.
    C. Overfiling.
    D. Environmental Crimes.
    E. Citizen Suits.
    F. Settlements.
2. Access to the Courts.
    A. Standing.
    B. Ripeness and Exclusive Pre-Enforcement Review.

1. MECHANISMS OF ENFORCEMENT

Enforcement of the environmental statutes is critical to their effectiveness. John C. Cruden and Bruce S. Gelber argue that, from a quantitative perspective, the structure of environmental enforcement could be described as a pyramid of actions. *See* John C. Cruden & Bruce S. Gelber, *Federal Civil Environmental Enforcement—Processes, Actors, and Trends*, SM072 A.L.I.-A.B.A. 695 (2007). The base of the pyramid is formed by state, tribal, local prosecutors and attorneys general, state agencies, and citizen groups that engage in a variety of enforcement actions including compliance orders, permit revocations, and civil and criminal proceedings before administrative tribunals and state or federal courts. *See id.* at 697–98. It has been estimated that state actors bring nearly 70 percent of all enforcement actions and conduct the great majority of environmental inspections. Mark Seidenfeld & Janna Satz Nugent, *"The Friendship of the People": Citizen Participation in Environmental Enforcement*, 73 GEO. WASH. L. REV. 269, 272 (2005).

The next level is comprised of the federal agencies, among which EPA exercises the primary enforcement responsibility for most of the federal environmental statutes, including the Clean Air Act (CAA), the Clean Water Act (CWA), the Resource Conservation and Recovery Act (RCRA), and the Comprehensive Environmental Response, Compensation and Liability Act (CERCLA), among others. *See* Cruden & Gelber, *supra*, at 698.

Once EPA detects a violation of an environmental statute it either notifies the state of the detected violation or takes over the enforcement action. *See, e.g.*, 42 U.S.C. § 7413(a) (CAA), 33 U.S.C. § 1319(a) (CWA). *See* Seidenfeld & Nugent, *supra*, at 272. However, if after 30 days of such notification the state has not commenced an appropriate enforcement action, EPA can do so. Under certain circumstances, EPA may prosecute an alleged violator even though the state has already initiated its own enforcement action. *See* William Daniel Benton, *Application of Res Judicata and Collateral Estoppel to EPA Overfiling*, 16 B.C. ENVTL. AFF. L. REV. 199, 203–04 (1988). This practice is known as overfiling and will be discussed in Section 1.C, *infra*.

In bringing enforcement actions, EPA may choose between administrative, civil, or criminal enforcement mechanisms based on the severity of the violation and the particular circumstances. *See* Seidenfeld & Nugent, *supra*, at 272–73; *see, e.g.*, 33 U.S.C. § 1319(a)(3) (CWA). Administrative enforcement tools include compliance orders and civil penalties. *See* Seidenfeld & Nugent, *supra*, at 274. In the first case, a compliance order is served on the violator specifying the nature of the violation and a time for compliance. *See id.*; *see, e.g.*, 33 U.S.C. § 1319(a)(3)–(5) (CWA). A copy of such an order must be sent immediately by the Administrator to the state in which the violation occurs and other affected states. 33 U.S.C. § 1319(a)(4) (CWA). However, if the circumstances require more than a compliance order, the Administrator may assess an administrative penalty. *See* Seidenfeld & Nugent, *supra*, at 275; *see, e.g.*, 33 U.S.C. § 1319(g) (CWA).

The proceedings for assessing these penalties may vary depending on the kind of violation and the amount of the penalty. For example, the CWA establishes different procedures for Class I penalties and Class II penalties. *See* 33 U.S.C. § 1319(g)(2). Class I penalties are those that do not exceed an amount set at $25,000 in 1972. *See* 33 U.S.C. § 1319(g)(2)(A). This amount is periodically adjusted for inflation, as discussed in Section 1.A, *infra*. To impose Class I penalties, the Administrator must notify the alleged violator, who must have the opportunity to request a hearing on the proposed order. *See id.* Class II penalties are those that do not exceed $125,000, adjusted for inflation. *See* 33 U.S.C. § 1319(g)(2)(B). To impose Class II penalties, EPA must provide notice and a formal hearing as established in the Administrative Procedure Act (APA). *See* 33 U.S.C. § 1319(g)(2)(B); *see also* Seidenfeld & Nugent, *supra*, at 275. The violator may seek judicial review of the penalty assessment. *See* 33 U.S.C. § 1319(g)(8). However, the court may set aside or remand such orders only if there is not substantial evidence in the record to support the finding of a violation, or if EPA's assessment of the penalty constitutes an abuse of discretion. *See id.*

Instead of pursuing an administrative remedy, EPA may decide to sue the alleged violator in federal court in order to obtain a permanent or temporary injunction, to assess and recover a civil penalty larger than the one available in administrative proceedings, or to obtain a reimbursement of the government expenses in responding to a polluting event. *See, e.g.*, 33 U.S.C. § 1319(b) (CWA); 42 U.S.C. § 7413(b) (CAA). *See* Seidenfeld & Nugent, *supra*, at 276; *see also* Cruden & Gelber, *supra*, at 707. "The threat of a civil suit provides EPA with added leverage as district courts have authority to grant relief beyond that which is available in administrative enforcement, including issuing a temporary or permanent injunction, . . . and collecting fees owed to the United States." Seidenfeld & Nugent, *supra*, at 276; *see, e.g.*, 33 U.S.C. § 1319(b) (CWA) ("[S]uch court shall have jurisdiction to restrain such violations and to require compliance"); 42 U.S.C. § 7413(b) (CAA) (The district court "shall have jurisdiction to restrain such violation, to require compliance, to assess such civil penalty, to collect any fees owed . . . and any noncompliance assessment and nonpayment penalty owed . . . and to award any other appropriate relief.").

At the top of the pyramid are federal criminal actions, which are authorized by most environmental statutes as a way to address the most significant violations of their provisions. *See* Cruden & Gelber, *supra*, at 699 (citing 42 U.S.C. § 7413(c) (CAA); 33 U.S.C. § 1319(c) (CWA); 42 U.S.C. § 9603 (CERCLA)). "Because of the severity of the punishment, criminal prosecutions of environmental violations usually focus on conduct that presents an endangerment, demonstrates a disregard for human safety or environmental integrity, or reflects a pattern of dishonest or false conduct." *Id*. As a result, criminal prosecutions are relatively infrequent. *See id*.

A. CIVIL PENALTIES

Civil penalties can be assessed by either using administrative enforcement mechanisms or bringing a civil suit in federal court. The CAA and CWA specify a *maximum* penalty of $25,000 per day of violation, periodically adjusted for inflation, as discussed *infra*. *See* 42 U.S.C. § 7413(b) (CAA); 33 U.S.C. § 1319(d) (CWA). Under this formula, the statutory maximum penalty can become extremely large because many violations last for years. Thus, the EPA and courts have significant discretion as to the actual penalty amount imposed. When determining the appropriate penalty, the CAA requires the court to consider "the size of the business, the economic impact of the penalty on the business, the violator's full compliance history and good faith efforts to comply, the duration of the violation . . . [,] the economic benefit of noncompliance, and the seriousness of the violation." 42 U.S.C. § 7413(e)(1). The CWA has similar statutory factors that must be considered when determining a civil penalty. *See* 33 U.S.C. § 1319(d). The following case demonstrates the method one court used to come up with what it thought of as an appropriate penalty under the CWA.

Sierra Club v. Cedar Point Oil Co.

73 F.3d 546 (5th Cir. 1996), *cert. denied*, 519 U.S. 811 (1996).

■ Before GARZA, KING, and HIGGINBOTHAM, CIRCUIT JUDGES.

■ KING, CIRCUIT JUDGE:

. . . The CWA directs district courts to assess civil penalties for violations of the CWA. 33 U.S.C. § 1319(d). Specifically, the statute states that violators "shall be subject to a civil penalty not to exceed $25,000 per day for each violation." *Id*. Aside from this maximum amount, the statute guides the court's discretion in setting the penalty as follows:

> In determining the amount of a civil penalty the court shall consider the seriousness of the violation or violations, the economic benefit (if any) resulting from the violation, any history of such violations, any good-faith efforts to comply with the applicable requirements, the economic impact of the penalty on the violator, and such other matters as justice may require.

Id. The Eleventh Circuit has taken these statutory directives and developed a procedural framework for calculating penalties under the CWA. *Tyson Foods*, 897 F.2d at 1142. First, the court is to calculate the maximum penalty that could be assessed against the violator. *Id*. Using that maximum as a starting point, the court should then determine if the penalty should be reduced from the maximum by reference to the statutory factors. *Id*.

The district court followed the *Tyson Foods* framework in this case. The parties had stipulated that there were 797 days of unpermitted discharge of produced water prior to trial. The judgment was entered twelve days later, during which time the discharge presumably continued. Accordingly, the court multiplied the statutory figure of $25,000 per day by 809 days of unpermitted discharge to arrive at [a] maximum penalty of $20,225,000.

The district court then made findings of fact with respect to the statutory factors. First, the court found that the violation was moderately serious because of the effect of the discharge on benthic organisms and the lack of monitoring and reporting with respect to the discharge. Second, the court found that the economic benefit to Cedar Point from the violation was $186,070, which the court determined was the amount that Cedar Point saved by not disposing of its produced water in a reinjection well. Third, the court found that Cedar Point had been violating the CWA since it began operating state well 1876. Fourth, the court found that Cedar Point had not demonstrated good faith in attempting to comply with the CWA. In this regard, the court noted that, although Cedar Point had attempted to obtain a NPDES permit for its discharge, it had not explored other ways to comply with the CWA. Finally, the court reviewed Cedar Point's financial position and expected future profits from the Cedar Point field and determined that Cedar

Point could at least afford a penalty equal to the economic benefit attained from the violation.

In weighing these facts and calculating the penalty, the district court held that the maximum penalty of $20,225,000 was inappropriate. The court determined, however, that the penalty should at a minimum recapture the savings realized by Cedar Point because of the violation. Although the court's findings with respect to the other statutory factors were also not favorable to Cedar Point, the court apparently chose not to accord these factors any weight because it did not increase the penalty beyond what it found to be the economic benefit to Cedar Point. Accordingly, the court assessed a penalty of $186,070. . . .

. . . [W]e do not think that the district court abused its discretion in assessing a penalty in an amount that reflected only the economic benefit to Cedar Point. The Supreme Court has described the process of weighing the statutory factors in calculating civil penalties under the CWA as "highly discretionary" with the trial court. *Tull v. United States*, 481 U.S. 412, 427 (1987). It is clear from the district court's Memorandum Opinion that it considered all of the statutory factors before settling on an amount based only on economic benefit. Considering that the court could have imposed a penalty as high as $20,225,000, this appears to be a fair and just result. As such, we perceive no abuse of discretion. Therefore, we affirm the district court's assessment of a penalty in the amount of $186,070 for Cedar Point's violation of the CWA.

NOTES AND QUESTIONS

1. **Calculation of Civil Penalties.** How should an agency or court determine the amount of a civil penalty? What was the amount of the civil penalty determined by the district court? Did the factual findings support such a determination? What does the term "consider" mean in the context of § 1319(d)? Could the district court have said: "We considered all the relevant factors and decided that the proper penalty is zero"? Could the district court have established a civil penalty equal to the statutory maximum? Is such wide discretion desirable? If Congress wanted to improve this provision, what wording should it use? The court of appeals found that the district court decision not to give weight to any factor aside from the economic benefit to the violator was not an abuse of discretion. How can that conclusion be justified?

Over the past several decades agencies have used the value of a statistical life (VSL) to monetize the benefits of lifesaving regulations and help determine their stringency. Despite its widespread use in regulatory decisionmaking, agencies do not use the VSL in setting penalty levels for violations that lead to death. W. Kip Viscusi, *How Regulatory Agencies Undervalue Life*, REGULATORY REVIEW (Sept. 11, 2018). To provide an example, after releasing chemicals into the Kanawha River in West Virginia killing one person, DuPont was forced to pay $1.3 million, whereas the VSL is currently $10 million. *Id.* Similarly, BP Oil Refinery was required to pay only $21 million for an explosion killing 15 and injuring 170. Viscusi argues that "penalties for fatalities should create efficient incentives for deterrence to ensure that regulated entities assume the costs required to provide efficient levels of health and safety." *Id.* Do you agree with his argument?

2.   Deterrence and Economic Benefit. Suppose that you use the subway without paying the fare: What should be the amount of the fine? Should it be equal to the amount of the fare? What is the deterrent effect of a penalty that recovers only the economic benefit gained from violating an environmental law? How high should the penalty be in order to create deterrence? Do attorneys' fees, time spent on litigation, and negative public exposure provide an additional disincentive to violations?

According to the Fifth Circuit's analysis, as long as the district court "considers" the requisite statutory factors, it is free to choose "not to accord these factors any weight," given that the process of weighing the statutory factors in calculating civil penalties is "highly discretionary." Other courts have found differently. *See United States v. Gulf Park Water Co.*, 14 F. Supp. 2d 854, 862 (S.D. Miss. 1998) ("In order for the penalty to serve the purpose of deterrence, it should exceed the economic benefit enjoyed by the defendants."); *Student PIRG of N.J. v. Monsanto Co.*, 1988 WL 156691 (D.N.J. 1988) (holding that some additional penalty over and beyond the economic benefit should be imposed to discourage other and future violations); *see also United States v. Mun. Auth. of Union Twp.*, 929 F. Supp. 800, 806–09 (M.D. Pa. 1996) (assessing a total penalty of $4,031,000 for a violation which incurred economic benefits of $2,015,000, the court noted that without imposing a penalty exceeding economic benefit, "those regulated by the Clean Water Act would understand that they have nothing to lose by violating it."). What would an appropriate penalty have been in *Cedar Point Oil*? Instead of looking at the economic benefit of non-compliance in determining the penalty, would it have been better to look at the cost imposed on others due to the violation? Should an additional amount for deterrence be added?

3.   Civil Penalties and Taxes. To what extent should the polluter treat civil penalties like effluent taxes? Under an effluent tax regime, a polluter seeks to minimize the sum of the taxes and the costs of environmental controls: it will reduce its pollution until the cost of an additional unit of reduction is equal to the tax. Are civil penalties analogous? Or is there a moral reason for complying with standards and therefore not being subject to penalties even when it is economically advantageous to pay such penalties? What might account for the difference between taxes and civil penalties?

4.   EPA Penalty Calculation Methodology. EPA has, since 1984, provided general guidance for how penalties should be calculated for the purpose of administrative penalty assessments and civil judicial settlement negotiations. *See* EPA, POLICY ON CIVIL PENALTIES, GENERAL ENFORCEMENT POLICY #GM–21 (1984); *see also* EPA, A FRAMEWORK FOR STATUTE-SPECIFIC APPROACHES TO PENALTY ASSESSMENTS, GENERAL ENFORCEMENT POLICY #GM–22 (1984). This general policy lays out the three goals of penalty assessment, each informing the ultimate calculation. "The first goal of penalty assessment is to deter people from violating the law." EPA, POLICY

ON CIVIL PENALTIES, *supra*, at 3. This goal is effectuated through a minimum penalty of the economic benefit of the violation, plus a gravity factor to provide additional deterrence. *Id.* This gravity factor can be adjusted to account for needed additional general deterrence, such as a regulatory program with a history of noncompliance. This amount is called the "preliminary deterrence amount." The second goal of penalty assessment is "the fair and equitable treatment of the regulated community," defined as consistent yet flexible penalties. *Id.* at 4. This is effectuated by adjusting penalties up or down based on "[the] degree of willfulness and/or negligence, [a] history of noncompliance, [the] ability to pay, [the] degree of cooperation . . . [,] and other unique factors." *Id.* at 5. When combined with the preliminary deterrence amount, this figure is the "initial penalty target figure" and should be the administrative penalty amount or the first offer in civil judicial settlement negotiations. The third goal of penalty assessment is "the swift resolution of environmental programs." *Id.* Based on this goal, penalty figures can take into account remedial action taken and delaying tactics which prolong environmental degradation. *Id.* at 6.

5.   EPA Penalty Calculation Methodology, CWA. The above guidance documents do not create any specific penalty policies. Instead, they are used by EPA as guidance in the design of useable policies for each environmental law. The specific policy for the Clean Water Act calculates the penalty as:

> Penalty = Economic Benefit + Gravity + / − Gravity Adjustment Factors − Litigation Considerations − Ability to Pay − Supplemental Environmental Projects

EPA, INTERIM CWA SETTLEMENT PENALTY POLICY 4 (1995). The calculation of economic benefit is intended to put violators "in the same financial position as they would have been if they complied on time." *Id.* The gravity component is intended to meet the requirements of deterrence and fundamental fairness that the violator be worse off than if she had complied on time. *Id.* at 6. The penalty may also be adjusted upwards for bad faith or delay in remedying a violation, or downwards for quick settlement. *Id.* at 12–13. Litigation considerations are intended to reflect the risk of achieving lesser penalties at trial, perhaps due to mitigating factors, although general weaknesses in a case are not a sufficient justification for reducing the penalty calculation. *Id.* at 13–14. Absent certain aggravating factors, EPA will not seek to jeopardize a violator's financial viability by imposing penalties that the violator is clearly unable to pay and still continue operations and achieve compliance. *Id.* at 21. Supplemental Environmental Projects are discussed in greater detail in Section 1.F, *infra*. Does this specific methodology match the general 1984 policy? Does it sufficiently account for the probability that an enforcement action would not be brought?

6.   Top-Down or Bottom-up Penalty Calculation? In *United States v. Municipal Authority of Union Township*, 150 F.3d 259 (3d Cir. 1998), in the context of determining a CWA civil penalty, the Third Circuit observed that "[s]ome courts have employed a 'top down' approach in which the maximum possible penalty is first established, then reduced following an examination of the six 'mitigating' factors. . . . Other courts have used a 'bottom up' approach whereby the economic benefit a violator gained by noncompliance is established and adjusted upward or downward using the remaining five factors in § 1319(d). . . . Because the statute does not prescribe either method, it appears that a court is free to use its discretion in choosing the appropriate method." *Id.* at 265 (citations omitted). Which approach is preferable? Which approach does the EPA Penalty Calculation Methodology for the CWA take?

7.   Penalty Calculation: Comparing the CWA and CAA. In 2009, EPA implemented a similar methodology for calculating penalties for administrative settlement agreements under Title II of the Clean Air Act:

> Penalty = Preliminary Deterrence Amount (Adjusted Economic Benefit + Adjusted Gravity) + / − Flexibility/Consistency Adjustment (Willfulness/Negligence, Cooperation, History of Noncompliance Factors) − Ability to Pay − Litigation Risk

EPA, CLEAN AIR ACT MOBILE SOURCE CIVIL PENALTY POLICY—VEHICLE AND ENGINE CERTIFICATION REQUIREMENTS (2009). However, whereas this methodology is used for administrative and civil settlements under the Clean Water Act, it is explicitly used only for administrative settlements for Clean Air Act violations. *Id.* at 3. "It is EPA's policy, in judicial actions, to assert a claim for up to the maximum penalty allowable under the Act." *Id.* Is your assessment of the methodology for calculating penalties affected by whether it applies to administrative versus civil actions?

8.   Civil Monetary Penalty Inflation Adjustment Rule. In order to preserve the deterrent effect of monetary penalties in environmental law, the Debt Collection Improvement Act of 1996 increased the statutory limits to account for inflation. Pub. L. No. 104–134, tit. III, § 31001, 110 Stat. 1321–58 (1996). EPA promulgated a final rule on setting the new limits for Clean Water Act penalties: $27,500 for violations between January 31, 1997, and March 15, 2004; $32,000 for violations between March 15, 2004, and January 12, 2009; $37,500 for violations after January 12, 2009; and $37,500 for violations after December 6, 2013. *See* EPA, Civil Monetary Penalty Inflation Adjustment Rule, 78 Fed. Reg. 66,643, 66,647 (2013). EPA retained the same penalty in the 2013 revision, because the low cost-of-living adjustment between 2008 and 2013 meant that when mandatory rounding rules were applied, the adjusted amount was insufficient to warrant an increase. Memorandum from Cynthia Giles, Assistant Administrator, EPA, Amendments to EPA's Civil Penalty Policies to Account for Inflation (Dec. 6, 2013). In 2015, Congress passed the Bipartisan Budget Act, which requires "each federal agency to publish annual adjustments to all civil penalties under the laws implemented by the agency" by January 15 of each year, beginning in 2017. *See* EPA, Civil Monetary Penalty Inflation Adjustment Rule, 83 Fed. Reg. 1190, 1191 (2018). In accordance with the Act, EPA published rules on January 12, 2017 and January 10, 2018, respectively, increasing penalties based on inflation. *Id.*; *see also* Memorandum from Susan Parker Bodine, Assistant Administrator, EPA, Amendments to the EPA's Civil Penalty Policies to Account for Inflation (effective January 15, 2018) and Transmittal of the 2018 Civil Monetary Penalty Inflation Adjustment Rule (Jan. 11, 2018).

9.   EPA Enforcement Involving Federal Agencies. Under the "unitary executive" theory, the President, as head of the Executive Branch, is seen as ultimately accountable for all actions of the Executive Branch. This theory implies that as a result of the Case or Controversy Clause of Article III of the Constitution, executive agencies cannot sue each other because they are in effect the same party. *See* Nelson D. Cary, *A Primer on Federal Facility Compliance with Environmental Laws: Where Do We Go from Here*, 50 WASH. & LEE L. REV. 801, 828–32 (1993). The Executive Branch's adherence to the "unitary executive" principle complicates the enforcement of CERCLA by EPA against federal agencies considered potentially responsible parties (PRPs) at Superfund sites. *See* William C. Tucker, *The Manacled Octopus: The Unitary Executive and EPA Enforcement Involving Federal Agencies,* 16 VILL. ENVTL. L.J. 149 (2005). The Executive Branch has consistently taken the position that EPA cannot independently enforce CERCLA in the federal courts against federal agency PRPs without violating the Constitution. *Id*. at 149–50. Yet even with that policy in place, due to the nature of CERCLA enforcement actions, EPA frequently finds itself a plaintiff in enforcement actions involving federal agency PRPs. *See id.* When this happens, the Department of Justice often represents both EPA and the federal PRPs in the same CERCLA litigation and acts as a sort of arbitrator. *See id.*

When the DOJ represents both EPA and the defendant federal PRP, it must choose between the interests of one client party and the opposing interests of the other client party in order to present a unified government position. *See* Tucker, *supra*, at 158. In addition to forcing the government to choose one policy concern over another, the unitary executive principle in practice leads federal PRPs to receive more favorable settlement agreement terms than private PRPs. *Id*. at 156. This in turn can undermine settlement negotiations with private PRPs. *Id*. at 157.

Can two federal agencies be seen as distinct parties regardless of the fact that the President is ultimately responsible for both? The Supreme Court has consistently held that one must look beyond the names of the parties in determining whether a case presents an Article III case or controversy, susceptible to judicial resolution. *See United States v. Nixon*, 418 U.S. 683, 693–94 (1974) ("The mere assertion of a claim of an 'intrabranch dispute,' without more, has never operated to defeat federal jurisdiction; justiciability does not depend on such a surface inquiry."); *United States v. Interstate Commerce Comm'n*, 337 U.S. 426, 430 (1949) ("[C]ourts must look behind names that symbolize the parties to determine whether a justiciable case or controversy is presented."); *see also TVA v. United States*, 13 Cl. Ct. 692, 697 (1987) (concluding that dispute between two executive agencies was justiciable); *Dean v. Herrington*, 668 F. Supp. 646, 651 (E.D. Tenn. 1987) (finding suit between two executive agencies justiciable).

The courts do not usually have a problem finding intergovernmental suits justiciable, but because the DOJ controls most agency litigation, it is able to keep potential inter-agency suits from ever reaching the courts. *See* Michael Herz, *United States v. United States: When Can the Federal Government Sue Itself?*, 32 WM. & MARY L. REV. 893, 896–97 (1991). Would an inter-agency adjudication without the conflict of interest inherent in having the DOJ represent adversarial parties be the preferred method of dispute resolution? *See* Neal Devins & Michael Herz, *The Uneasy Case for Department of Justice Control of Federal Litigation*, 5 U. PA. J. CONST. L. 558 (2003) (arguing that in petitions for judicial review of regulations, litigation authority should be transferred from the DOJ to agency lawyers.)

If inter-agency disputes are justiciable under the Constitution, then adherence to the unitary executive principle would be a matter of policy, one that traditionally is said "to strengthen the executive by preserving its policy-making prerogative." Tucker, *supra*, at 151. Instead of accepting this justification, Tucker presents another perspective:

> Such a rationale, while persuasive in the context of policy development, is less persuasive when applied to enforcement of environmental laws by one agency against another. It is often assumed that a "unitary" executive, hierarchical and centralized, is strongest. However, in the enforcement context, this Article proposed a paradigm of the modern executive as a complex organism whose various departments and agencies function as multiple appendages: an octopus, if you will. The strength of such an executive depends not upon rigid central control, but upon the untrammeled, vigorous and independent operation of its agency "arms." In the CERCLA enforcement context, restricting the free use of enforcement discretion (as well as defense capability) of executive agencies by exercising centralized control of the type usually associated with policy development, in effect, manacles the octopus, rendering the executive weaker and less effective.

Id. (footnotes omitted). Is this account of the Executive Branch more attractive? For further discussion of the unitary executive principle in general, see Michael Herz, *supra*, 893 (taking the position that when one part of the government enforces a statutory scheme and another part is either regulated by or is a beneficiary of such scheme, the two are sufficiently opposed to support judicial resolution, notwithstanding the framers' adoption of a unitary executive); Cass R. Sunstein, *The Myth of the Unitary Executive*, 7 ADMIN. L.J. AM. U. 299 (1993) (arguing that the framers never intended the President to necessarily have hierarchical control of the administration); Morton Rosenberg, *Congress's Prerogative over Agencies and Agency Decisionmakers: The Rise and Demise of the Reagan Administration's Theory of the Unitary Executive*, 57 GEO. WASH. L. REV. 627, 634 (1989) (arguing that the theory of the unitary executive is a "myth concocted by the Reagan administration to provide a semblance of legal respectability for an aggressive administrative strategy designed to accomplish what its failed legislative agenda could not").

B. VOLUNTARY AUDITS

Environmental audits are "internal programs and measures a firm employs to ensure that its activities conform to environmental regulations." Jay P. Kesan, *Encouraging Firms to Police Themselves:*

Strategic Prescriptions to Promote Corporate Self-Auditing, 2000 U. ILL. L. REV. 155, 156. These procedures have a number of advantages. They allow the firm to collect information about its performance and operations and may help it to identify unknown environmental and health risks earlier, to detect noncompliance, and to facilitate remedial actions. *See* Miri Berlin, *Environmental Auditing: Entering the Eco-Information Highway*, 6 N.Y.U. ENVTL. L.J. 618, 620–21 (1998); *see also* Kesan, *supra*, at 156. At the same time, governmental agencies have a strong interest in promoting self-compliance and auditing practices within the firms, given their limited resources for enforcement and monitoring.

In addition to these incentives to self-audit, firms also face a number of disincentives. Companies may fear that the audits will uncover a violation that will result in civil or criminal sanctions, or that those results could be used against them in enforcement procedures or citizen suits. *See* Berlin, *supra*, at 622. There have been different approaches to address these concerns including immunity, evidentiary privileges, and enforcement leniency. *See id.* As of 2018, 28 states have enacted privilege and/or immunity laws that specifically provide varying degrees of protection for environmental compliance audit results and/or immunities from civil and criminal action. EPA, State Audit Privilege and Immunity Laws & Self-Disclosure Laws and Policies, https://www.epa.gov/ compliance/state-audit-privilege-and-immunity-laws-self-disclosure-laws-and-policies (last visited Feb. 1, 2019). State privilege laws usually provide a qualified privilege for environmental audit reports and related documents. *See* David Sorenson, *The U.S. Environmental Protection Agency's Recent Environmental Auditing Policy and Potential Conflict with State-Created Environmental Audit Privilege Laws*, 9 TUL. ENVTL. L.J. 483, 493 (1996) (citing ARK. CODE ANN. §§ 8–1–301, 8–1–302; COLO. REV. STAT. § 13–25–126.5; 1995 Kan. Sess. Laws 204; KY. REV. STAT. ANN. § 224.01–040; MISS. CODE ANN. § 49–2–71; OR. REV. STAT. § 468.963; UTAH CODE ANN. §§ 19–7–103, 19–7–107; VA. CODE ANN. § 10.1–1198). The applicability of this privilege can be challenged, and state law usually provides for an *in camera* review process in those cases. *See* Sorenson, *supra*, at 494. Generally, the courts have decided, in accordance with the applicable statutory provisions, that documents are not privileged if the regulated entity has not taken appropriate steps to address the lack of compliance. *See id.* This approach aims to avoid the use of the audit privilege to hide inappropriate or non-existent corrective measures. *See id.*

In addition to a qualified privilege, some state laws provide immunity from civil and criminal prosecution if the company discloses its violations. *See id.* at 497 (citing 1995 Idaho Sess. Laws 359 (sunset 12/97); 1995 Kan. Sess. Laws 204; 1995 Minn. Sess. Laws 168; VA. CODE ANN. § 10.1–1198; WYO. STAT. §§ 35–11–1105, 35–11–1106). For example, Wyoming's statute provides that "[i]f an owner or operator of a facility . . . voluntarily reports to the department a violation . . . the department shall not seek civil penalties or injunctive relief for the violation reported." WYO. STAT. § 35–11–1106. However, immunity is not provided if "the facility is under investigation for any violation of this act at the time the violation is reported," if "[t]he violation is the result of gross negligence or recklessness," or if waiving the penalty would result in violation of a state or federal program. *Id.*

EPA first developed and issued a policy regarding environmental auditing in 1986 (1986 Policy). *See* EPA Auditing Policy Statement, 51 Fed. Reg. 25,004 (1986). According to this policy, EPA would not "routinely request environmental audit reports." *See id.* at 25,007. The 1986 Policy, however, did not specify when an audit would be requested nor did it promise a reduction in inspections or enforcement when an audit was forthcoming. *See* Berlin, *supra*, at 622–23. In 1994, partially in response to the new state legislation providing for environmental audit privileges and penalty immunity, EPA amended its policy, expressing its strong opposition to "self-evaluative" privileges:

> Four States (Colorado, Indiana, Kentucky, and Oregon) have recently enacted legislation which, with some variations, creates a "self-evaluative" privilege for audit reports. EPA has consistently opposed this approach, principally because of the risk of weakening State enforcement programs, the imposition of unnecessary transaction costs and delays in enforcement actions, and the potential increase in the number of situations requiring the expenditure of scarce Agency resources, including the "overfiling" of State enforcement actions.

59 Fed. Reg. 38,455, 38,459 (1994). Moreover, in 1995, EPA announced an interim audit policy. *See* 60 Fed. Reg. 16,877 (1995). This policy indicated that "[the agency] will scrutinize enforcement more closely in states with audit privilege and/or penalty immunity laws." *See id.* at 16,878. EPA can also refuse to approve delegation of enforcement authority over federal environmental programs to states with immunity and privilege laws that are too expansive. *See* Memorandum from Steven A. Herman, Assistant Administrator, Office of Enforcement and Compliance Assurance, EPA, Statement of Principles: Effect of State Audit Immunity/Privilege Laws on Enforcement Authority for Federal Programs (2003).

The following excerpt from EPA's 2000 Policy describes the agency's current approach to auditing.

The EPA Audit Policy

65 Fed. Reg. 19,618 (2000).

I.   Explanation of Policy

. . .

B.   *Background and History*

The Audit Policy provides incentives for regulated entities to detect, promptly disclose, and expeditiously correct violations of Federal environmental requirements. The Policy contains nine conditions, and entities that meet all of them are eligible for 100% mitigation of any gravity-based penalties that otherwise could be assessed. ("Gravity-based" refers to that portion of the penalty over and above the portion that represents the entity's economic gain from noncompliance, known as the "economic benefit.") Regulated entities that do not meet the first condition—systematic discovery of violations—but meet the other eight conditions are eligible for 75% mitigation of any gravity-based civil penalties. On the criminal side, EPA will generally elect not to recommend criminal prosecution by DOJ or any other prosecuting authority for a disclosing entity that meets at least conditions two through nine—regardless of whether it meets the systematic discovery requirement—as long as its self-policing, discovery and disclosure were conducted in good faith and the entity adopts a systematic approach to preventing recurrence of the violation.

The Policy includes important safeguards to deter violations and protect public health and the environment. For example, the Policy requires entities to act to prevent recurrence of violations and to remedy any environmental harm that may have occurred. Repeat violations, those that result in actual harm to the environment, and those that may present an imminent and substantial endangerment are not eligible for relief under this Policy. Companies will not be allowed to gain an economic advantage over their competitors by delaying their investment in compliance. And entities remain criminally liable for violations that result from conscious disregard of or willful blindness to their obligations under the law, and individuals remain liable for their criminal misconduct. . . .

C.   *Purpose*

The revised Policy . . . is designed to encourage greater compliance with Federal laws and regulations that protect human health and the environment. It promotes a higher standard of self-policing by waiving gravity-based penalties for violations that are promptly disclosed and corrected, and which were discovered systematically—that is, through voluntary audits or compliance management systems. To provide an incentive for entities to disclose and correct violations regardless of how they were detected, the Policy reduces gravity-based penalties by 75% for violations that are voluntarily discovered and promptly disclosed and corrected, even if not discovered systematically.

EPA's enforcement program provides a strong incentive for compliance by imposing stiff sanctions for noncompliance. Enforcement has contributed to the dramatic expansion of environmental auditing as measured in numerous recent surveys. For example, in a 1995 survey by Price Waterhouse LLP, more than 90% of corporate respondents who conduct audits identified one of the reasons for doing so as the desire to find and correct violations before government inspectors discover them.

At the same time, because government resources are limited, universal compliance cannot be achieved without active efforts by the regulated community to police themselves. More than half of the respondents to the same 1995 Price Waterhouse survey said that they would expand environmental auditing in exchange for reduced penalties for violations discovered and corrected. While many companies already audit or have compliance management programs in place, EPA believes that the incentives offered in this Policy will improve the frequency and quality of these self-policing efforts. . . .

F.   *Opposition to Audit Privilege and Immunity*

The Agency believes that the Audit Policy provides effective incentives for self-policing without impairing law enforcement, putting the environment at risk or hiding environmental compliance information from the public. Although EPA encourages environmental auditing, it must do so without compromising the integrity and enforceability of environmental laws. It is important to distinguish between EPA's Audit Policy and the audit privilege and immunity laws that exist in some States. The Agency remains firmly opposed to statutory and regulatory audit privileges and immunity. Privilege laws shield evidence of wrongdoing and prevent States from investigating even the most serious environmental violations. Immunity laws prevent States from obtaining penalties that are appropriate to the seriousness of the violation, as they are required to do under Federal law. Audit privilege and immunity laws are unnecessary, undermine law enforcement, impair protection of human health and the environment, and interfere with the public's right to know of potential and existing environmental hazards. . . .

II. Statement of Policy—Incentives for Self-Policing: Discovery, Disclosure, Correction and Prevention of Violations

C.   *Incentives for Self-Policing*

1.   No Gravity-Based Penalties

If a regulated entity establishes that it satisfies all of the conditions of Section D of this Policy, EPA will not seek gravity-based penalties for violations of Federal environmental requirements discovered and disclosed by the entity.

2. Reduction of Gravity-Based Penalties by 75%

If a regulated entity establishes that it satisfies all of the conditions of Section D of this Policy except for D(1)—systematic discovery—EPA will reduce by 75% gravity-based penalties for violations of Federal environmental requirements discovered and disclosed by the entity.

3. No Recommendation for Criminal Prosecution

(a) If a regulated entity establishes that it satisfies at least conditions D(2) through D(9) of this Policy, EPA will not recommend to the U.S. Department of Justice or other prosecuting authority that criminal charges be brought against the disclosing entity, as long as EPA determines that the violation is not part of a pattern or practice that demonstrates or involves:

(i) A prevalent management philosophy or practice that conceals or condones environmental violations; or

(ii) High-level corporate officials' or managers' conscious involvement in, or willful blindness to, violations of Federal environmental law;

(b) Whether or not EPA recommends the regulated entity for criminal prosecution under this section, the Agency may recommend for prosecution the criminal acts of individual managers or employees under existing policies guiding the exercise of enforcement discretion.

4. No Routine Request for Environmental Audit Reports

EPA will neither request nor use an environmental audit report to initiate a civil or criminal investigation of an entity. For example, EPA will not request an environmental audit report in routine inspections. If the Agency has independent reason to believe that a violation has occurred, however, EPA may seek any information relevant to identifying violations or determining liability or extent of harm.

D. *Conditions*

1. Systematic Discovery

The violation was discovered through:

(a) An environmental audit; or

(b) A compliance management system reflecting the regulated entity's due diligence in preventing, detecting, and correcting violations. The regulated entity must provide accurate and complete documentation to the Agency as to how its compliance management system meets the criteria for due diligence outlined in Section B and how the regulated entity discovered the violation through its compliance management system. EPA may require the regulated entity to make publicly available a description of its compliance management system.

2.   Voluntary Discovery

The violation was discovered voluntarily and not through a legally mandated monitoring or sampling requirement prescribed by statute, regulation, permit, judicial or administrative order, or consent agreement. For example, the Policy does not apply to:

(a)   Emissions violations detected through a continuous emissions monitor (or alternative monitor established in a permit) where any such monitoring is required;

(b)   Violations of National Pollutant Discharge Elimination System (NPDES) discharge limits detected through required sampling or monitoring; or

(c)   Violations discovered through a compliance audit required to be performed by the terms of a consent order or settlement agreement, unless the audit is a component of agreement terms to implement a comprehensive environmental management system.

3.   Prompt Disclosure

The regulated entity fully discloses the specific violation in writing to EPA within 21 days (or within such shorter time as may be required by law) after the entity discovered that the violation has, or may have, occurred. The time at which the entity discovers that a violation has, or may have, occurred begins when any officer, director, employee or agent of the facility has an objectively reasonable basis for believing that a violation has, or may have, occurred.

4.   Discovery and Disclosure Independent of Government or Third-Party Plaintiff

(a)   The regulated entity discovers and discloses the potential violation to EPA prior to:

(i)   The commencement of a Federal, State or local agency inspection or investigation, or the issuance by such agency of an information request to the regulated entity (where EPA determines that the facility did not know that it was under civil investigation, and EPA determines that the entity is otherwise acting in good faith, the Agency may exercise its discretion to reduce or waive civil penalties in accordance with this Policy);

(ii)   Notice of a citizen suit;

(iii)   The filing of a complaint by a third party;

(iv)   The reporting of the violation to EPA (or other government agency) by a "whistleblower" employee, rather than by one authorized to speak on behalf of the regulated entity; or

(v)   imminent discovery of the violation by a regulatory agency.

(b)   For entities that own or operate multiple facilities, the fact that one facility is already the subject of an investigation, inspection, information request or third-party complaint does not preclude the

Agency from exercising its discretion to make the Audit Policy available for violations self-discovered at other facilities owned or operated by the same regulated entity.

5.   Correction and Remediation

The regulated entity corrects the violation within 60 calendar days from the date of discovery, certifies in writing that the violation has been corrected, and takes appropriate measures as determined by EPA to remedy any environmental or human harm due to the violation. EPA retains the authority to order an entity to correct a violation within a specific time period shorter than 60 days whenever correction in such shorter period of time is feasible and necessary to protect public health and the environment adequately. If more than 60 days will be needed to correct the violation, the regulated entity must so notify EPA in writing before the 60-day period has passed. Where appropriate, to satisfy conditions D(5) and D(6), EPA may require a regulated entity to enter into a publicly available written agreement, administrative consent order or judicial consent decree as a condition of obtaining relief under the Audit Policy, particularly where compliance or remedial measures are complex or a lengthy schedule for attaining and maintaining compliance or remediating harm is required.

6.   Prevent Recurrence

The regulated entity agrees in writing to take steps to prevent a recurrence of the violation. Such steps may include improvements to its environmental auditing or compliance management system.

7.   No Repeat Violations

The specific violation (or a closely related violation) has not occurred previously within the past three years at the same facility, and has not occurred within the past five years as part of a pattern at multiple facilities owned or operated by the same entity. For the purposes of this section, a violation is:

(a)   Any violation of Federal, State or local environmental law identified in a judicial or administrative order, consent agreement or order, complaint, or notice of violation, conviction or plea agreement; or

(b)   Any act or omission for which the regulated entity has previously received penalty mitigation from EPA or a State or local agency.

8.   Other Violations Excluded

The violation is not one which (a) resulted in serious actual harm, or may have presented an imminent and substantial endangerment, to human health or the environment, or (b) violates the specific terms of any judicial or administrative order, or consent agreement.

9. Cooperation

The regulated entity cooperates as requested by EPA and provides such information as is necessary and requested by EPA to determine applicability of this Policy.

E. Economic Benefit

EPA retains its full discretion to recover any economic benefit gained as a result of noncompliance to preserve a "level playing field" in which violators do not gain a competitive advantage over regulated entities that do comply. EPA may forgive the entire penalty for violations that meet conditions D(1) through D(9) and, in the Agency's opinion, do not merit any penalty due to the insignificant amount of any economic benefit.

F. Effect on State Law, Regulation or Policy

EPA will work closely with States to encourage their adoption and implementation of policies that reflect the incentives and conditions outlined in this Policy. EPA remains firmly opposed to statutory environmental audit privileges that shield evidence of environmental violations and undermine the public's right to know, as well as to blanket immunities, particularly immunities for violations that reflect criminal conduct, present serious threats or actual harm to health and the environment, allow noncomplying companies to gain an economic advantage over their competitors, or reflect a repeated failure to comply with Federal law. EPA will work with States to address any provisions of State audit privilege or immunity laws that are inconsistent with this Policy and that may prevent a timely and appropriate response to significant environmental violations. The Agency reserves its right to take necessary actions to protect public health or the environment by enforcing against any violations of Federal law.

G. Applicability

(1) This Policy applies to settlement of claims for civil penalties for any violations under all of the Federal environmental statutes that EPA administers, and supersedes any inconsistent provisions in media-specific penalty or enforcement policies and EPA's 1995 Policy on "Incentives for Self-Policing: Discovery, Disclosure, Correction and Prevention of Violations." . . .

(3) This Policy sets forth factors for consideration that will guide the Agency in the exercise of its enforcement discretion. It states the Agency's views as to the proper allocation of its enforcement resources. The Policy is not final agency action and is intended as guidance. This Policy is not intended, nor can it be relied upon, to create any rights enforceable by any party in litigation with the United States. As with the 1995 Audit Policy, EPA may decide to follow guidance provided in this document or to act at variance with it based on its analysis of the specific facts presented. . . .

NOTES AND QUESTIONS

1. Goals of Self-Auditing. Self-auditing can be considered to have two conceptually related, but distinct, goals: first, it can decrease the amount the government has to spend on enforcement by shifting some of that burden to the firms themselves; second, it can reduce the overall level of violations by making compliance auditing a visible deterrent for anyone considering a violation.

Under a traditional strict vicarious liability system, there might not be sufficient incentives for voluntary auditing. The incentives for collecting information, detecting and remedying noncompliance, deterring employee violations, and promoting a positive public reputation might not be sufficient to dominate the disincentives in the form of a greater probability of civil or criminal penalties, the cost of auditing, and the possible loss of trade secrets when firms turn over their private information. *See, e.g.*, Daniel C. Esty, *Environmental Protection in the Information Age*, 79 N.Y.U. L. REV. 115, 202 (2004). Jodi Short and Michael Toffel confirm this in their 2008 article finding that facilities disclose only after regulators spend a significant amount of resources on investigation and prosecution, potentially mitigating the *ex ante* resource savings for such regulators. *See* Jodi L. Short & Michael W. Toffel, *Coerced Confessions: Self-policing in the Shadow of the Regulator*, 24 J.L. & ECON. 45 (2008).

Jennifer Arlen and Reinier Kraakman note another significant problem for firms considering a self-audit regime under traditional strict liability: the "credibility problem." This problem arises because employees might not believe their employers' threats of self-auditing. Employers might want to benefit from the deterrence and reputational effects of having an auditing policy, but then save money by not following through with an effective audit protocol. Understanding this incentive, employees might continue to violate the regulatory requirements. *See* Jennifer Arlen & Reinier Kraakman, *Controlling Corporate Misconduct: An Analysis of Corporate Liability Regimes*, 72 N.Y.U. L. REV. 687, 712–17 (1997).

A strict liability scheme potentially also suffers from the problem of detection avoidance. Robert Innes argues that increasing government enforcement or penalties for violations could have the perverse effect of giving firms incentives to spend resources on not getting caught, rather than on compliance or auditing. *See* Robert Innes, *Violator Avoidance Activities and Self-Reporting in Optimal Law Enforcement*, 17 J.L. ECON. & ORG. 239 (2001).

As a result, to be effective, self-reporting is likely to need some kind of encouragement. The government can eliminate the credibility problem at the employee level by giving teeth to companies' threats to audit and eliminate the detection avoidance problem by making it less costly to audit than to attempt to escape penalties altogether. There are three primary ways in which governments attempt to encourage greater auditing: evidentiary privilege, which prevents audit documents from being used against the firm; immunity, which shields firms completely from liability for violations discovered through auditing; and mitigation, which, like EPA policy, decreases penalties for firms that engage in auditing. In thinking about the strengths and weaknesses of each type of policy, consider how they each affect both the efficiency of enforcement and the deterrence of violations.

2.   **Incentives for Self-Policing.** What are the incentives for engaging in voluntary audits under EPA's policy? Which factors need a regulated entity satisfy to be eligible for a reduction in civil penalties? What does "systematic discovery" mean? Could a firm satisfy the first requirement by accidentally finding a violation? How often does the company need to do it? What would happen if you violated any of the other factors? Why does the policy distinguish between the "systematic discovery" requirement and the other eight factors?

3.   **Effects of Self Audits.** The biggest problem in using mitigation of penalties to encourage self-policing is that it requires careful calculation. Unlike privileges and immunities, which are essentially all-or-nothing, mitigation can encourage reporting only when the resulting reduction in penalties creates a benefit that is greater than the cost of auditing. *See* Jennifer Arlen, *The Potentially Perverse Effects of Corporate Criminal Liability*, 23 J. LEGAL STUD. 833, 863 (1994).

Robert Innes would counsel caution with respect to attempts to increase reporting at all costs. The optimal level of penalty that will deter future violations while still encouraging reporting depends both on the harm caused by the violation and the likelihood of being caught. Therefore, because not all firms have the same chance of being caught for the same violation, it is impossible to set penalties, or penalty reductions, that either deter all violations equally or equally convince all firms to report. Innes still counsels for severely reduced penalties, however, because the decrease in deterrence is likely to be small compared to the great benefit in enforcement efficiency of more companies self-reporting. *See* Robert Innes, *Self-Reporting in Optimal Law Enforcement When Violators Have Heterogeneous Probabilities of Apprehension*, 29 J. LEG. STUD. 287 (2000).

Are the reduced penalties offered by EPA enough of an incentive to report violations? Do the regulators gain enough in the form of increased compliance to justify forfeiting some enforcement powers to the regulated entities? Given the reality that not every firm will be driven to report at the same level, how far should EPA go in rewarding self-reporting?

4.   **Criticisms of EPA Audit Policy.** The most common criticism of EPA Audit Policy is that it does not go far enough to convince firms that they will benefit from auditing. Despite the penalty reductions, firms would still have to bear penalties equal to the economic benefit they derived from the violation and could be liable to injured plaintiffs. Even though the overall liability for firms conducting audits is decreased significantly, critics argue that the remaining penalties and risks may be substantial enough to cause firms to prefer taking the chances of getting caught. *See* Alexander Pfaff & Chris Sanchirico, *Big Field, Small Potatoes: An Empirical Assessment of EPA's Self-Audit Policy,* 23 J. POL'Y ANALYSIS & MGMT. 415, 416–17 (2004).

From a perspective of administrative ease, reducing penalties further would certainly result in more firms auditing and thus less effort required for the government in enforcement. Might there be a danger, however, that if penalties are lowered further, there will be a loss of deterrence and the number of violations will increase? *See* Jennifer Arlen & Reinier Kraakman, *When Companies Come Clean: Mitigation is Better Than Environmental Audit Privileges*, BUSINESS LAW TODAY, Jan.–Feb. 2000, at 9. How should EPA strike the right balance?

Are there additional problems with the Audit Policy aside from effectiveness concerns? *See* Sarah L. Stafford, *Outsourcing Enforcement: Principles to Guide Self-Policing Regimes*, 32 CARDOZO L. REV. 2293, 2309–13 (2011) (discussing concerns such as accountability, inherently governmental functions, reduced governmental capacity, and corruption).

Alexander Pfaff and Chris Sanchirico argue that the EPA policy of only rewarding audits that end in the prompt correction of any violations limits the actual occurrence of self-reporting because it prevents firms from being able to choose the most efficient expenditures after they discover a violation. Sometimes, they argue, even after conducting an audit, it makes sense for a firm not to attempt to meet EPA's strict remediation requirements. Instead, the authors suggest that an audit policy should reduce penalties based on a firm's investigative effort, creating some penalty reductions even when there is no remediation. Firms would then have an incentive to turn over their audit reports to the government even when they do not immediately take the prescribed remedial action. Alexander S.P. Pfaff & Chris W. Sanchirico, *Environmental Self-Auditing: Setting the Proper Incentives for Discovery and Correction of Environmental Harm*, 16 J.L. ECON. & ORG. 189 (2000). Is this test workable? Is the loss of the full remediation requirement too much to trade for more information? Why might EPA want to require full remediation?

5.   **Analysis and Effects of the Audit Policy.** Pfaff and Sanchirico also present data showing that, despite EPA's claims that the Audit Policy has been a great success, most of the self-reporting it has prompted has been about very minor compliance violations that can easily be fixed. Pfaff & Sanchirico, *Big Field, Small Potatoes*, *supra*. On the other hand, self-reporting of actual emissions violations has been rare, despite the fact that they are perhaps the most commonly discovered violations through government investigation. *Id.* at 417. In this light, the claims of the Audit Policy's success may be severely misleading.

Because EPA policy reduces gravity-based damages, firms conducting an audit may have a disproportionate incentive to report those violations for which gravity-based damages are the biggest parts of the total penalty, while refusing to report their discoveries of major violations that would subject them to significant non-gravity damages. *See id.* at 426. This incentive could explain why there are so many reports of minor violations, such as reporting and recording unrelated to an emissions violation. *See id.* at 417. Sarah Stafford presents another explanation for this phenomenon: One purpose of the Audit Policy is to encourage firms to discover violations so that the enforcement system can serve as a disincentive to future violation. By encouraging self-policing among those who might otherwise be unaware of their violations, more firms face the incentives of the enforcement system.

These otherwise unaware violators, however, are the firms one might most expect to have minor violations such as reporting errors. *Outsourcing Enforcement, supra* at 2306. In either case, is this necessarily a serious problem, or might it be a natural result of increasing overall reporting? If there is a problem here, how could the Audit Policy be altered to encourage reporting of more serious violations?

Looking both at participants and non-participants in EPA's self-policing program, Michael W. Toffel and Jodi L. Short recently conducted a study of facilities' compliance behavior and regulators' inspection behavior in the context of enforcing the CAA. *See* Michael W. Toffel & Jodi L. Short, *Coming Clean and Cleaning Up: Does Voluntary Self-Reporting Indicate Effective Self-Policing?*, 54 J.L. & ECON. 609 (2011). They found that with respect to the CAA, self-policing is associated both with improved compliance and reduced scrutiny over firms that self police. *See id.* at 638–39. However, the same is not necessarily true with respect to RCRA. Sarah Stafford has found that the Audit Policy had no measurable impact on the compliance of hazardous waste regulations. Sarah Stafford, *Does Self-Policing Help the Environment? EPA's Audit Policy and Hazardous Waste Compliance*, 6 VT. J. ENVTL. L. 14 (2005). She has, however, confirmed Toffel and Short's findings that the Audit Policy leads to reduced inspection in future years: finding a four-fifths decrease for firms that disclosed hazardous waste violations. Sarah L. Stafford, *Should You Turn Yourself In? The Consequences of Environmental Self-Policing*, 26 J. POL'Y ANALYSIS & MGMT. 305 (2007).

6. EPA Audit Policy as Applied to New Owners. In 2008 EPA promulgated the Interim Approach to Applying the Audit Policy to New Owners, a policy that provides additional incentives for environmental reporting and remediation to new owners of facilities that have been in environmental noncompliance prior to the ownership change. EPA, Interim Approach to Applying the Audit Policy to New Owners, 73 Fed. Reg. 44,991 (2008). The Interim Approach expands the incentives for voluntary self-disclosure and modifies five of the nine conditions required to take advantage of the Audit Policy. The Interim Policy defines a "new owner" as one who certifies:

(a) Prior to the transaction, the new owner was not responsible for environmental compliance at the facility which is the subject of the disclosure, did not cause the violations being disclosed and could not have prevented their occurrence;

(b) The violation which is the subject of the disclosure originated with the prior owner; and

(c) Prior to the transaction, neither the buyer nor the seller had the largest ownership share of the other entity, and they did not have a common corporate parent.

Id. at 44,995. How is this definition different from the analogous definition of *bona fide* prospective purchaser under CERCLA? What are the potential impacts of having both policies in place?

New owners who, within nine months of the transaction closing, (a) disclose violations to the EPA or enter into an audit agreement and (b) meet the modified Audit Policy conditions (see below), receive additional penalty mitigation, including (1) no penalties assessed for violations prior to the ownership change, (2) economic benefit penalties only assessed from the date of ownership change, and (3) no penalty due to the economic benefit of delayed capital expenditure or unfair competitive advantage assessed if violations are corrected within 60 days of discovery. *Id.* at 44,998.

The Interim New Owner Policy also modifies five of the nine Audit Policy conditions for new owners:

- Condition 1—Systematic Discovery: New owners need only conduct pre-closing due diligence on the property, rather than periodic discovery, to qualify.

- Condition 2—Voluntary Discovery: Legally mandated disclosure will not disqualify a new owner who disclose prior to the first instance of such legally mandated disclosure.

- Condition 3—Prompt Disclosure: The disclosure period is extended to 45 days after closing, from 21 days after discovery.

- Condition 8—Excluded Violations: Violations that, before the transfer of ownership, resulted in serious actual harm or substantial endangerment, which would not otherwise be eligible for mitigation under the Audit Policy, are eligible for new owners, as long as they did not result in a fatality, community evacuation, or other catastrophic event.

- Condition 9—Cooperation: New owners must cooperate with EPA in determining if these modified Audit Policy conditions have been met.

Id. at 44,999–45,004. While the Interim Approach attempts to increase the reporting of serious violations by allowing new purchasers to start with a "clean slate," the policy does not completely close off risks to new owners who report violations. EPA refused to provide any penalty mitigation to sellers who knew of violations prior to sale, even if those sellers have indemnification agreements with the new owner. These provisions will potentially serve as a continued disincentive for new owners to report violations. *See* Patrick J. Paul, *Incentives for New Owners under EPA's Audit Policy*, 23 NAT. RESOURCES & ENV'T 65, 66–67 (2009).

7. Example of a State Audit Privilege and Immunity Law. Colorado has one of the broader environmental audit privilege and immunity laws. The immunity section provides that voluntary disclosures of violations of State environmental laws and regulations will not result in the assessment of monetary penalties if all of the following conditions are met: the disclosure must be made promptly after knowledge of the noncompliance; the disclosure must arise out of a self-initiated assessment, audit, or review, not otherwise expressly required by law; the requester pursues compliance with due diligence and corrects the noncompliance within two years; and the requester fully cooperates with the Colorado Department of Public Health and Environment (CDPHE). *See* COLO. REV. STAT. §§ 25–1–114.5, 25–1–114.6;

Colorado Department of Public Health and Environment, Environmental Self Audit Reporting, https://www.colorado.gov/pacific/cdphe/environmental-self-audit-reporting (last visited Aug. 28, 2018). In determining whether penalty immunity is appropriate in a given situation, the CDPHE has the discretion to consider whether the activities disclosed may create imminent and substantial endangerment of public health and the environment and whether the activities disclosed conferred an unfair or excessive economic benefit on the disclosing entity. *Id.*

The Colorado law also creates an evidentiary privilege for information developed through voluntary self-evaluation. The privilege does not apply to information required to be developed, maintained, or reported by any applicable law, regulation, permit, or order; information obtained by a regulatory agency; information developed or obtained from an independent source; documents existing prior to or prepared subsequent to the voluntary self-evaluations; documents developed or maintained in the regular course of business; and information disclosed in association with a request for penalty immunity, which constitutes waiver of the privilege for that information. *Id.*; COLO. REV. STAT. § 13–25–126.5.

The privilege does not exist when a court or administrative law judge determines that the identified violations have not been addressed and a return to compliance has not been achieved, or there to be a clear, present, and impending off-site danger to human health and the environment. *Id.* Further, if an investigation was imminent or underway or a court or administrative judge determines that there are compelling reasons to divulge the privileged information, then once again the privilege will not be deemed to exist. *Id.* Finally, the Colorado privilege and immunity law does not affect public access to any information currently available under the Colorado Open Records Act. *Id.* Are these exceptions desirable?

What is the difference between privilege and immunity? What happens with systematic violators? Could the agency base an enforcement action on its own inspection? What could the polluter argue?

8. Privilege, Immunity, and Incentives. As indicated in the excerpt above, EPA objects to privilege and immunity laws because they are "unnecessary, undermine law enforcement, impair protection of human health and the environment, and interfere with the public's right to know of potential and existing environmental hazards." EPA Audit Policy, *supra.* While this argument is mostly that privileges deprive the government of the information it requires for efficient enforcement, there are also other reasons to believe that privilege and immunity laws do not effectively deter violations.

Arlen and Kraakman articulate several problems with audit privilege schemes in the environmental context. First, they argue that privileges take away the information that EPA needs to pursue action against individual managers and employees guilty of violations. Audit privileges will also not achieve optimal reduction in violations because they make audits too valuable in relation to other enforcement expenditures; as a result, firms will not spend sufficient money on prevention and other policing mechanisms.

Additionally, even if a privilege system were to work extremely well and encourage auditing and reporting, fewer sanctions would be levied against firms; in turn, each of these sanctions would need to be much more severe, leading to a greater risk of insolvency that would in turn reduce the incentives for compliance with the regulatory standards. *See* Jennifer Arlen & Reinier Kraakman, *Controlling Corporate Misconduct: An Analysis of Corporate Liability Regimes*, 72 N.Y.U. L. REV. 687, 742–44 (1997). A 2008 study finds some support for these concerns, showing that state legislation providing for complete immunity results in reduced rates of Clean Air Act inspections but an increase in toxic emissions. *See* Santiago Guerrero & Robert Innes, *Statutory Rewards to Environmental Self-Auditing: Do They Reduce Pollution and Save Regulatory Costs? Evidence from a Cross-State Panel* (2008) (unpublished manuscript), http://ageconsearch.umn.edu/bitstream/6204/2/467771.pdf.

What do states see as the benefit of privilege and immunity laws? What is the proper balance between privilege, immunities, and penalties? Is privilege protection necessary to provide incentives for corporate self-evaluation and remediation? Jay P. Kesan argues:

> [A]lthough the self-evaluative privilege removes the disincentives, it does not create any positive incentives for companies to police themselves. . . . [A] multipronged approach, which permits regulator access to audit materials, provides mitigated penalties for self-policing firms, and limits third-party use of audit materials, is the most effective legal regime to encourage firms to police themselves. Such regime minimizes the fear of self-incrimination but maintains the positive incentives to self-police that regulatory access provides.

Jay P. Kesan, *Encouraging Firms to Police Themselves: Strategic Prescriptions to Promote Corporate Self-Auditing*, 2000 U. ILL. L. REV. 155, 155. Do you find his view compelling? Might there still be a place for some kind of limited privilege or immunity in light of the alleged failures of EPA Audit Policy to convince firms that they will not be worse off by auditing?

9. State Audit Immunity, Privilege Laws and Delegated Enforcement Authority. When a state has expansive audit immunity and privilege laws, EPA can refuse to approve the delegation of enforcement authority over federal environmental programs. With regard to audit immunity laws, in order for EPA to consider a state to have adequate enforcement authority, the state must at a minimum have the ability to:

1. Obtain immediate and complete injunctive relief;

2. Recover civil penalties for: (i) significant economic benefit; (ii) repeat violations and violations of judicial or administrative orders; (iii) serious harm; (iv) activities that may present imminent and substantial endangerment;

3. Obtain criminal fines/sanctions for willful and knowing violations of federal law and for violations that result from gross negligence under the Clean Water Act.

Memorandum from Steven A. Herman, Assistant Administrator, Office of Enforcement and Compliance Assurance, EPA, Statement of Principles: Effect of State Audit Immunity/Privilege Laws on Enforcement Authority for Federal Programs (May 21, 2003). Are these conditions desirable?

In determining whether to authorize or approve a program in a state with an audit privilege law, EPA expects the state to:

1. retain information-gathering authority it is required to have under the specific requirements of regulations governing authorized or delegated programs;

2. avoid making the privilege applicable to criminal investigations, grand jury proceedings, and prosecutions, or exempted evidence of criminal conduct from the scope of privilege;

3. preserve the right of the public to obtain information about noncompliance, report violations, and bring enforcement actions for violations of federal environmental law.

Id. Does this policy strike the right balance?

10. Voluntary Environmental Programs. EPA's self-auditing policy is not the only voluntary environmental program available to firms today. Richard D. Morgenstern and William A. Pizer separate voluntary programs into three distinct types:

Unilateral agreements by industrial firms. Business-led corporate programs fall under this heading, as do commitments or reduction targets chosen by firms or industry associations. Examples of such agreements in the United States include the Chemical Manufacturers Association's "Responsible Care" program for reducing chemical hazards, and McDonald's replacement of its Styrofoam "clamshell" containers with paper packaging. . . .

Public voluntary programs. Participating firms agree to protocols that have been developed by environmental agencies or other public bodies. Although the public agencies may promote the programs to industry, they do not generally negotiate over the specific terms. Eligibility criteria, rewards, obligations, and other elements are established by the public agencies. . . .

Negotiated agreements. Consisting of a target and timetable for attaining the agreed-upon environmental objectives, these are created out of a negotiation between government authorities and a firm or industry group over specific terms. In some cases, participating firms also receive relief from an otherwise burdensome tax, making the voluntary notion of the program somewhat hazy. . . .

Richard D. Morgenstern & William A. Pizer, *Introduction: The Challenge of Evaluating Voluntary Programs*, *in* REALITY CHECK: THE NATURE AND PERFORMANCE OF ENVIRONMENTAL PROGRAMS IN THE UNITED STATES, EUROPE, AND JAPAN 1, 4–5 (Richard D. Morgenstern & William A. Pizer eds. 2007). Morgenstern and Pizer discuss the growth of these programs:

> The explosive growth in voluntary environmental programs since the early 1990s in the United States, Europe, and Japan reflects, in part, changing societal attitudes on the environment and a growing optimism about the possibility of enhanced cooperation between government and business. It also reflects the widespread frustration with the long and expensive battles often associated with new environmental regulations. In most cases, voluntary programs are being used to control pollutants that have not yet been regulated and for which legislative authority may be difficult to obtain. Unlike market-based approaches to environmental management, where the conceptual roots are largely academic, voluntary programs have emerged as a pragmatic response to the needs for more flexible ways to protect the environment.

Id. at 1. Are these programs desirable?

11. Voluntary Programs: EPA's Performance Track. The most prominent national voluntary environmental program in the United States has been the EPA's National Environmental Performance Track ("Performance Track"). Based on a 1999 EPA report, "Aiming for Excellence," Performance Track was created in 2000 to recognize and encourage firms to go beyond the current environmental regulatory requirements. Scott Hassell et al., RAND Corp., An Assessment of the U.S. Environmental Protection Agency's National Environmental Track Program 14 (2010). Participating firms had to meet stringent admissions criteria to be accepted into the program, including:

(1) implementing an environmental management system (EMS);

(2) setting three-year "stretch goals," developed in coordination with EPA, which went beyond legal requirements;

(3) demonstrating a sustained record of compliance with environmental laws; and,

(4) publicly reporting performance and engaging in community outreach.

Id. at 14–18. Members, in one of two tracks, agreed to make various levels of environmental improvement beyond legally required compliance, and in exchange received a number of benefits including:

- regulatory benefits (reduced frequency of compliance investigations, reduced frequency of reporting, expedited permit review),

- information sharing benefits (best practice information from other members through national and regional conferences, meetings, and seminars), and

- recognition (use of Performance Track Logo, listed on EPA website, included in public service and promotional materials).

Id. at 19. By 2009, Performance Track had 547 members and claimed "reductions in water use by 2.87 billion gallons, greenhouse gas emission reductions of 366,948 metric tons of carbon dioxide equivalent, and conservation of 24,864 acres of habitat." EPA, Performance Track Final

PROGRESS REPORT (May 2009). Following a significant decrease in Performance Track's budget in the Omnibus Appropriations Act of 2009, *id.* at 3, and an exposé claiming that the program gave members benefits without verifying actual improvements, John Sullivan & John Shiffman, *Green Club an EPA Charade: The EPA Touts the Perk-filled Program but has Recruited Some Firms with Dismal Environmental Records*, PHILADELPHIA INQUIRER, Dec. 9, 2008, at A1, EPA Administrator Lisa Jackson suspended the program to "pause and reflect on . . . achievements and opportunities." *See* Memorandum from Lisa Jackson, Administrator, EPA, Next Steps for Environmental Performance Track Program and the Future of Environmental Leadership Programs (2009). The program was formally cancelled in May 2009. EPA, Notice to Terminate the National Environmental Performance Track Program, 74 Fed. Reg. 22,741 (2009). For a comprehensive evaluation of Performance Track, see HASSELL ET AL., *supra.*

How is the Performance Track program similar and/or different from the Audit Policy? What is the impact of having both policies? Is one preferable to the other?

While Performance Track was terminated, states continue to implement and expand similar two-tier voluntary Environmental Programs. *See, e.g.,* Wis. Dep't Of Natural Res., Overview of the Green Tier Program, http://dnr.wi.gov/topic/GreenTier/Overview.html (last visited May 25, 2018). Are the concerns that caused Performance Track to be terminated (lack of verified environmental improvement, excessive regulatory reductions) also applicable to these state level programs?

C. OVERFILING

Federal environmental law statutes usually require EPA to promulgate federal regulations that provide national substantive minimum requirements. The statutes also empower EPA to delegate to the states the day-to-day implementation and enforcement of the requirements, including the issuance of permits and the prosecution and settlement of violations. *See* Markus G. Puder & John A. Veil, *Overfiling in the Cooperative Federalism Balance: A Search Forever Incomplete and Incompletable*, 29 COLUM. J. ENVTL. L. 119, 121 (2004); *see, e.g.,* 42 U.S.C. §§ 7410, 7413 (CAA); 33 U.S.C. §§ 1319, 1342 (CWA); 42 U.S.C. § 6926(b) (RCRA). Even when a state program approved by EPA is in place, the Agency retains the power to enforce its provisions. For example, under § 309(a) of the CWA, EPA may enforce a permit issued by a state directly; or, if after 30 days of EPA's notification, the state does not commence an "appropriate enforcement action." *See* William Daniel Benton, *Application of Res Judicata and Collateral Estoppel to EPA Overfiling*, 16 B.C. ENVTL. AFF. L. REV. 199, 209 (1988).

Overfiling occurs when "EPA exercises its authority to prosecute an alleged violator in an approved state that has already initiated its own enforcement action for the same requirement against the same defendant." Benton, *supra*, at 203–04. "The EPA policy is that overfiling is appropriate 'when the state fails to take timely and appropriate action' or when the 'state's action is clearly inadequate.' " *Id.* at 204. The following case addresses the question of whether this practice is allowed under RCRA.

Harmon Industries, Inc. v. Browner
191 F.3d 894 (8th Cir. 1999).

■ Before BEAM and HANSEN, CIRCUIT JUDGES, and MOODY, DISTRICT JUDGE.

■ HANSEN, CIRCUIT JUDGE:

Harmon Industries operates a plant in Grain Valley, Missouri, which it utilizes to assemble circuit boards for railroad control and safety equipment. In November 1987, Harmon's personnel manager discovered that maintenance workers at Harmon routinely discarded volatile solvent residue behind Harmon's Grain Valley plant. This practice apparently began in 1973 and continued until November 1987. Harmon's management was unaware of its employees' practices until the personnel manager filed his report in November 1987. Following the report, Harmon ceased its disposal activities and voluntarily contacted the Missouri Department of Natural Resources (MDNR). The MDNR investigated and concluded that Harmon's past disposal practices did not pose a threat to either human health or the environment. The MDNR and Harmon created a plan whereby Harmon would clean up the disposal area. Harmon implemented the clean up plan. While Harmon was cooperating with the MDNR, the EPA initiated an administrative enforcement action against Harmon in which the federal agency sought $2,343,706 in penalties. Meanwhile, Harmon and the MDNR continued to establish a voluntary compliance plan. In harmonizing the details of the plan, Harmon asked the MDNR not to impose civil penalties. Harmon based its request in part on the fact that it voluntarily self-reported the environmental violations and cooperated fully with the MDNR.

On March 5, 1993, while the EPA's administrative enforcement action was pending, a Missouri state court judge approved a consent decree entered into by the MDNR and Harmon. In the decree, MDNR acknowledged full accord and satisfaction and released Harmon from any claim for monetary penalties. MDNR based its decision to release Harmon on the fact that the company promptly self-reported its violation and cooperated in all aspects of the investigation. After the filing of the consent decree, Harmon litigated the EPA claim before an administrative law judge (ALJ). The ALJ found that a civil penalty against Harmon was appropriate in this case. The ALJ rejected the EPA's request for a penalty in excess of $2 million but the ALJ did impose a civil fine of $586,716 against Harmon. A three-person Environmental Appeals Board panel affirmed the ALJ's monetary penalty. Harmon filed a complaint challenging the EPA's decision in federal district court on June 6, 1997.

In its August 25, 1998, summary judgment order, the district court found that the EPA's decision to impose civil penalties violated the Resource Conservation and Recovery Act and contravened principles of res judicata. The EPA appeals to this court. . . .

The Resource Conservation and Recovery Act (RCRA) permits states to apply to the EPA for authorization to administer and enforce a hazardous waste program. *See* 42 U.S.C. § 6926(b). If authorization is granted, the state's program then operates "in lieu of" the federal government's hazardous waste program. *Id.* The EPA authorization also allows states to issue and enforce permits for the treatment, storage, and disposal of hazardous wastes. *Id.* "Any action taken by a State under a hazardous waste program authorized under [the RCRA] [has] the same force and effect as action taken by the [EPA] under this subchapter." 42 U.S.C. § 6926(d). Once authorization is granted by the EPA, it cannot be rescinded unless the EPA finds that (1) the state program is not equivalent to the federal program, (2) the state program is not consistent with federal or state programs in other states, or (3) the state program is failing to provide adequate enforcement of compliance in accordance with the requirements of federal law. *See* 42 U.S.C. § 6926(b). Before withdrawing a state's authorization to administer a hazardous waste program, the EPA must hold a public hearing and allow the state a reasonable period of time to correct the perceived deficiency. *See* 42 U.S.C. § 6926(e).

Missouri, like many other states, is authorized to administer and enforce a hazardous waste program pursuant to the RCRA. Despite having authorized a state to act, the EPA frequently files its own enforcement actions against suspected environmental violators even after the commencement of a state-initiated enforcement action. *See* Bryan S. Miller, *Harmonizing RCRA's Enforcement Provisions: RCRA Overfiling in Light of Harmon Industries v. Browner,* 5 ENVTL. L. 585 (1999). The EPA's process of duplicating enforcement actions is known as overfiling. *See id.* The permissibility of overfiling apparently is a question of first impression in the federal circuit courts. After examining this apparent issue of first impression, the district court concluded that the plain language of section 6926(b) dictates that the state program operate "in lieu" of the federal program and with the "same force and effect" as EPA action. Accordingly, the district court found that, in this case, the RCRA precludes the EPA from assessing its own penalty against Harmon.

The EPA contends that the district court's interpretation runs contrary to the plain language of the RCRA. Specifically, the EPA cites section 6928 of the RCRA, which states that:

(1)   Except as provided in paragraph (2), whenever on the basis of any information the [EPA] determines that any person has violated or is in violation of any requirement of this subchapter, the [EPA] may issue an order assessing a civil

penalty for any past or current violation, requiring compliance immediately or within a specified time period, or both, or the [EPA] may commence a civil action in the United States district court in the district in which the violation occurred for appropriate relief, including a temporary or permanent injunction.

(2) In the case of a violation of any requirement of [the RCRA] where such violation occurs in a State which is authorized to carry out a hazardous waste program under section 6926 of this title, the [EPA] shall give notice to the State in which such violation has occurred prior to issuing an order or commencing a civil action under this section.

42 U.S.C. § 6928(a)(1) and (2).

The EPA argues that the plain language of section 6928 allows the federal agency to initiate an enforcement action against an environmental violator even in states that have received authorization pursuant to the RCRA. The EPA contends that Harmon and the district court misinterpreted the phrases "in lieu of" and "same force and effect" as contained in the RCRA. According to the EPA, the phrase "in lieu of" refers to which regulations are to be enforced in an authorized state rather than who is responsible for enforcing the regulations. The EPA argues that the phrase "same force and effect" refers only to the effect of state issued permits. The EPA contends that the RCRA, taken as a whole, authorizes either the state or the EPA to enforce the state's regulations, which are in compliance with the regulations of the EPA. The only requirement, according to the EPA, is that the EPA notify the state in writing if it intends to initiate an enforcement action against an alleged violator.

Both parties argue that the plain language of the RCRA supports their interpretation of the statute. We also are ever mindful of the long-established plain language rule of statutory interpretation, *see Walker v. Dilworth*, 2 U.S. (2 Dall.) 257, 259 (1796), as we inquire into the scope of the EPA's enforcement powers under the RCRA. Such an inquiry requires examining the text of the statute as a whole by considering its context, "object, and policy." *Pelofsky v. Wallace*, 102 F.3d 350, 353 (8th Cir. 1996).

An examination of the statute as a whole supports the district court's interpretation. The RCRA specifically allows states that have received authorization from the federal government to administer and enforce a program that operates "in lieu of" the EPA's regulatory program. While the EPA is correct that the "in lieu of" language refers to the program itself, the administration and enforcement of the program are inexorably intertwined.

The RCRA gives authority to the states to create and implement their own hazardous waste program. The plain "in lieu of" language contained in the RCRA reveals a congressional intent for an authorized state program to supplant the federal hazardous waste program in all respects including enforcement. Congressional intent is evinced within the authorization language of section 6926(b) of the RCRA. Specifically, the statute permits the EPA to repeal a state's authorization if the state's program "does not provide adequate enforcement of compliance with the requirements of" the RCRA. *Id.* This language indicates that Congress intended to grant states the primary role of enforcing their own hazardous waste program. Such an indication is not undermined, as the EPA suggests, by the language of section 6928. Again, section 6928(a)(1) allows the EPA to initiate enforcement actions against suspected environmental violators, except as provided in section 6928(a)(2). Section 6928(a)(2) permits the EPA to enforce the hazardous waste laws contained in the RCRA if the agency gives written notice to the state. Section 6928(a)(1) and (2), however, must be interpreted within the context of the entire Act. Harmonizing the section 6928(a)(1) and (2) language that allows the EPA to bring an enforcement action in certain circumstances with section 6926(b)'s provision that the EPA has the right to withdraw state authorization if the state's enforcement is inadequate manifests a congressional intent to give the EPA a secondary enforcement right in those cases where a state has been authorized to act that is triggered only after state authorization is rescinded or if the state fails to initiate an enforcement action. Rather than serving as an affirmative grant of federal enforcement power as the EPA suggests, we conclude that the notice requirement of section 6928(a)(2) reinforces the primacy of a state's enforcement rights under RCRA. Taken in the context of the statute as a whole, the notice requirement operates as a means to allow a state the first chance opportunity to initiate the statutorily-permitted enforcement action. If the state fails to initiate any action, then the EPA may institute its own action. Thus, the notice requirement is an indicator of the fact that Congress intended to give states that are authorized to act, the lead role in enforcement under RCRA.

The "same force and effect" language of section 6926(d) provides additional support for the primacy of states' enforcement rights under the RCRA when the EPA has authorized a state to act in lieu of it. The EPA argues that the "same force and effect" language is limited to state permits because the words appear under a heading that reads: "Effect of State Permit." The EPA contends that the "same force and effect" language indicates only that state-issued permits will have the same force and effect as permits issued by the federal government. The EPA claims that the district court was incorrect when it applied the "same force and effect" language to encompass the statute's enforcement mechanism. We disagree.

Regardless of the title or heading, the plain language of section 6926(d) states that "[a]ny action taken by a State under a hazardous waste program authorized under this section shall have the same force and effect as action taken by the [EPA] under this subchapter." In this context, the meaning of the text is plain and obvious. "Any action" under this provision broadly applies to any action authorized by the subchapter, and this language is not limited to the issuance of permits. The state authorization provision substitutes state action (not excluding enforcement action) for federal action. It would be incongruous to conclude that the RCRA authorizes states to implement and administer a hazardous waste program "in lieu of" the federal program where only the issuance of permits is accorded the same force and effect as an action taken by the federal government. Contrary to the EPA's assertions, the statute specifically provides that a "[s]tate is authorized to carry out [its hazardous waste program] in lieu of the Federal program . . . and to issue and enforce permits." 42 U.S.C. § 6926(b). Issuance and enforcement are two of the functions authorized as part of the state's hazardous waste enforcement program under the RCRA. Nothing in the statute suggests that the "same force and effect" language is limited to the issuance of permits but not their enforcement. We believe that if Congress had intended such a peculiar result, it would have stated its preference in a clear and unambiguous manner. Absent such an unambiguous directive, we will apply a common sense meaning to the text of the statute and interpret its provisions in a manner logically consistent with the Act as whole. . . .

Even assuming some ambiguity exists in the statutory language, the primacy of the states' enforcement rights, once the EPA has authorized a state to act, is illustrated further through the RCRA's legislative history. The United States House of Representatives stated after its hearings that, through the RCRA, it intended to vest primary enforcement authority in the states. *See* H.R. Rep. 1491, 94th Cong., 2nd Sess. 24, *reprinted in* 1976 U.S.C.C.A.N. 6262 ("It is the Committee's intention that the States are to have primary enforcement authority and if at any time a State wishes to take over the hazardous waste program it is permitted to do so, provided that the State laws meet the Federal minimum requirements for both administering and enforcing the law"). The House Report states that although the "legislation permits the states to take the lead in the enforcement of the hazardous wastes [sic] laws [,] . . . the Administrator [of the EPA] is not prohibited from acting in those cases where the state fails to act, or from withdrawing approval of the state hazardous waste plan and implementing the federal hazardous waste program pursuant to . . . this act." 1976 U.S.C.C.A.N. 6269. The House Report also states that the EPA, "after giving the appropriate notice to a state that is authorized to implement the state hazardous waste program, that violations of this Act are occurring and the state [is] failing to take action against such violations, is authorized to take appropriate action against those persons in such state not in compliance with the hazardous waste title." *Id.* at 6270. The House Report thus supports our interpretation of the statute—that the federal government's right to pursue an enforcement action under the RCRA attaches only when a state's authorization is revoked or when a state fails to initiate any enforcement action. . . .

. . . Without question, the EPA can initiate an enforcement action if it deems the state's enforcement action inadequate. Before initiating such an action, however, the EPA must allow the state an opportunity to correct its deficiency and the EPA must withdraw its authorization. Consistent with the text of the statute and its legislative history, the EPA also may initiate an enforcement action after providing written notice to the state when the authorized state fails to initiate any enforcement action. The EPA may not, however, simply fill the perceived gaps it sees in a state's enforcement action by initiating a second enforcement action without allowing the state an opportunity to correct the deficiency and then withdrawing the state's authorization.

A contrary interpretation would result in two separate enforcement actions. Such an interpretation, as explained above, would derogate the RCRA's plain language and legislative history. Companies that reach an agreement through negotiations with a state authorized by the EPA to act in its place may find the agreement undermined by a later separate enforcement action by the EPA. While, generally speaking, two separate sovereigns can institute two separate enforcement actions, those actions can cause vastly different and potentially contradictory results. Such a potential schism runs afoul of the principles of comity and federalism so clearly embedded in the text and history of the RCRA. When enacting the RCRA, Congress intended to delegate the primary enforcement of EPA-approved hazardous waste programs to the states. *See* 1976 U.S.C.C.A.N. 6262, 6270. In fact, as we have noted above, the states' enforcement action has the "same force and effect as an action taken by" the EPA. *See* 42 U.S.C. § 6926(d). In EPA authorized states, the EPA's action is an alternative method of enforcement that is permitted to operate only when certain conditions are satisfied. *See* 42 U.S.C. § 6926(b) and (e); 42 U.S.C. § 6928(b). The EPA's interpretation simply is not consistent with the plain language of the statute, its legislative history, or its declared purpose. Hence, it is also an unreasonable interpretation to which we accord no deference. Therefore, we find that the EPA's practice of overfiling, in those states where it has authorized the state to act, oversteps the federal agency's authority under the RCRA.

NOTES AND QUESTIONS

1.   **Statutory Interpretation and *Chevron* Deference.** How did the district court interpret § 3006 of RCRA? What did EPA argue? Why did the court of appeals find that the "statute as a whole supports the district court's interpretation"? 191 F.3d at 899. How did the court interpret § 3008(a)(2)? According to *Chevron*, when interpreting a statute, "if the intent of Congress is clear, that is the end of the matter; for the court, as well as the agency, must give effect to the unambiguously expressed intent of Congress."

Chevron U.S.A., Inc. v. Nat. Res. Def. Council, Inc., 467 U.S. 837, 842–43 (1984). Was the *Harmon* court correct in finding the statute's language unambiguous? 191 F.3d at 901. Once EPA grants a state authorization to administer and enforce a hazardous waste program, the state's program then operates "in lieu of" the federal government's program. 42 U.S.C. § 6926(b) (RCRA). Does that language clearly foreclose the possibility for duplicate enforcement actions? Congress explicitly prohibits citizens from duplicating a federal or state RCRA action in § 6972(b)(1), whereas § 6928 conditions EPA enforcement on providing notice to an authorized state. Is the lack of an express prohibition evidence of congressional intent to allow duplicate suits? Are both arguments plausible, leading to the conclusion that the statute is ambiguous and that deference should be given to the interpretation of the administrative agency?

While the Eighth Circuit held that overfiling was not allowed under RCRA, there is a split among the circuits on this issue, and several subsequent decisions in other circuits have rejected the *Harmon* court's reasoning or distinguished the facts. The Tenth Circuit in *United States v. Power Engineering Co.*, 303 F.3d 1232 (10th Cir. 2002), *cert. denied*, 538 U.S. 1012 (2003), held that EPA's construction of RCRA, purporting to authorize the filing of EPA actions for financial assurances from alleged polluters, notwithstanding the existence of independent state enforcement actions, was based on a reasonable interpretation of the statute, and thus was entitled to deference by the court. *Power Eng'g Co.*, 303 F.3d at 1237–38. While the *Harmon* court had found that the plain language of the statute allowed overfiling only if EPA withdrew authorization from the state or if the state failed to initiate an enforcement action, the *Power Engineering* court disagreed. *See id.* The Tenth Circuit found the language of the statute to be ambiguous and therefore EPA's interpretation was entitled to deference under *Chevron*. *See id.* For a discussion of several other federal court cases on the issue, see Joel A. Mintz, *Enforcement "Overfiling" in the Federal Courts: Some Thoughts on the Post-*Harmon *Cases*, 21 VA. ENVTL. L.J. 425, 433–47 (2003).

2.   **Collateral Estoppel and Res Judicata.** In *Harmon*, "[a]s an alternative basis to support its grant of summary judgment, the district court concluded that principles of res judicata also bar the EPA's enforcement action by reason of the Missouri state court consent decree." 191 F.3d at 902. William Benton analyzes the application of the doctrines of collateral estoppel and res judicata to EPA overfiling:

> Historically, defendants facing multiple prosecutions arising from a single transaction may find some relief in the common law doctrines of res judicata and collateral estoppel when subsequent suits are brought by the same plaintiff or a different party in privity with that plaintiff. It has been suggested that these doctrines apply with equal force and effect in the field of environmental law without any particular refinement or distinction. Even a critic of the application of collateral estoppel to concurrent enforcement situations concedes that preclusion and related stay and abstention

doctrines ought to be used by a court in its discretion to avoid jurisdictional strife.

Application of either res judicata or collateral estoppel in a situation where the state and federal governments have concurrent enforcement authority generally depends upon a finding that governments were in privity with one another. Otherwise, the violator of an environmental law is generally in the same position as any other person in a federal system. He would be subject to concurrent regulation by both federal and state authorities, like a bank robber whose single act can lead to simultaneous prosecutions in both jurisdictions.

William Daniel Benton, *Application of Res Judicata and Collateral Estoppel to EPA Overfiling*, 16 B.C. ENVTL. AFF. L. REV. 199, 200–01 (1988) (footnotes omitted). According to the Ninth Circuit in *ITT Rayonier*, "[t]he doctrine of privity extends the conclusive effect of a judgment to nonparties who are in privity with parties to an earlier action. . . . [T]he Supreme Court characterized the relationship as one of 'substantial identity' between parties." *United States v. ITT Rayonier, Inc.*, 627 F.2d 996, 1003 (9th Cir. 1980). In *Harmon*, could EPA be considered privy to the prior state court action? Do the provisions of RCRA support that interpretation? *See* 191 F.3d at 903 ("The plain language of the RCRA permits the State of Missouri to act in lieu of the EPA. When such a situation occurs, Missouri's action has the same force and effect as an action initiated by the EPA. . . . [P]rivity under Missouri law is satisfied when the two parties represent the same legal right."). *But see Power Eng'g Co.*, 303 F.3d at 1240–41 ("Unlike the Eighth Circuit in Harmon, we have found that states act in lieu of the EPA only with respect to administration of the program and issuance of permits. The EPA's connection to the state's litigation is therefore more limited than in Harmon."). Could a state be considered to be in privity with a prior EPA court action? *See State Water Control Bd. v. Smithfield Foods, Inc.*, 542 S.E.2d 766, 770 (Va. 2001) (holding that the state agency was in privity with EPA and, therefore, precluded from pursuing its own claim for NPDES permit violations because "the Board and the EPA determined that their interests . . . would be protected by the permits issued by the Board pursuant to this joint program. Thus, the Board and the EPA share an identity of interest in the permit . . . such that the Board's legal right was represented by the EPA in the federal action when the EPA sought to enforce the provisions of the permit.").

3.   Policy Questions. From a policy perspective, should overfiling be allowed? Is it a solution to a possible race-to-the-bottom among the states? If overfiling is not allowed, then EPA's options in cases where a state has not taken an appropriate response to a particular environmental violation would be severely constrained. Under RCRA, EPA has the ability to revoke the state's authorization, but that would mean that EPA is then wholly responsible for both administration and enforcement of the hazardous waste program in that state, which might be difficult given EPA's limited resources. EPA would obviously much rather let the state do the bulk of the administration and enforcement and only intercede in particular instances.

Does that limited interference undermine the state's authority? Is it desirable? Would disallowing EPA actions undermine the ability of the agency to implement important national enforcement priorities? Is the threat of an additional federal enforcement action an important bargaining chip in the hands of the state enforcement officer? Additionally, could relying entirely on the state to implement and enforce the environmental laws lead to a race-to-the-bottom, where facilities flock to the state that is granted authority to implement and enforce the environmental laws, but is less than vigilant in the manner they go about it?

4.   Overfiling in CAA Enforcement Actions. The court in *Harmon* paid particular attention to the "in lieu of" language in RCRA. The CAA does not have this same language and many courts have upheld EPA's enforcement of SIP violations even when state enforcement proceedings were also pending or had occurred. *See, e.g., United States v. LTV Steel Co.*, 118 F. Supp. 2d 827 (N.D. Ohio 2000); *United States v. Murphy Oil USA, Inc.*, 143 F. Supp. 2d 1054 (W.D. Wis. 2001). Moreover, the CAA contains language that seems to contemplate overfiling. The Act states that "in determining the amount of any penalty to be assessed under this section . . . the court [ ] shall take into consideration . . . payment by the violator of penalties previously assessed for the same violation." *See* 42 U.S.C. § 7413(e).

However, where a state has issued a permit to a facility, EPA may not bring an enforcement action where the owner has met the terms of the permit, even if EPA argues that the permit was improperly granted. *See United States v. Solar Turbines, Inc.*, 732 F. Supp. 535 (M.D. Pa. 1989). This "permit shield," however, may not apply if the state permit was granted due to the owner's failure to disclose material facts. *See United States v. East Ky. Power Coop., Inc.*, 498 F. Supp. 2d 1010 (E.D. Ky. 2007) (holding that EPA could challenge a state granted Title V permit when the plant operator failed to disclose major modifications to its plant that might reasonably subject it to PSD requirements).

5.   Overfiling in CWA Enforcement Actions. Courts have allowed for overfiling under the CWA. Like the CAA, the CWA does not include the "in lieu of" or "same force and effect" language of RCRA. Instead, courts have found that the language of § 402(i) authorizes EPA to retain enforcement power even in states that have a delegated NPDES program. *See* 33 U.S.C. § 1342(i). The CWA states that "Federal enforcement [is] not limited. Nothing in this section shall be construed to limit the authority of the Administrator to take action pursuant to section 1319 of this title [the enforcement section]." *Id.; see, e.g., S. Ohio Coal Co. v. Office of Surface Min., Reclamation & Enforcement, Dept. of Interior*, 20 F.3d 1418, 1428 (6th Cir. 1994) ("[The]EPA retains independent enforcement authority in primacy states, 33 U.S.C. § 1342(i). . . ."), *cert. denied*, 513 U.S. 927 (1994); *United States v. City of Rock Island*, 182 F. Supp. 2d 690, 694 (C.D. Ill. 2001) ("*Harmon* relies heavily upon language in RCRA which does not appear in the Clean Water Act. The Clean Water Act has no 'in lieu of' or 'same force and effect' language."); *United States v. City of Youngstown*, 109 F. Supp. 2d 739, 741 (N.D. Ohio 2000) ("The language of CWA, on the other hand, compels the opposite conclusion.").

The enforcement section of the CWA, however, contains a limit on the civil penalty actions that can be brought by EPA. Section 309(g)(6)(A) reads:

Action taken by the Administrator or the Secretary, as the case may be, under this subsection shall not affect or limit the Administrator's or Secretary's authority to enforce any provision of this chapter; except that any violation—

(i)   with respect to which the Administrator or the Secretary has commenced and is diligently prosecuting an action under this subsection,

(ii)   with respect to which a State has commenced and is diligently prosecuting an action under a State law comparable to this subsection, or

(iii) for which the Administrator, the Secretary, or the State has issued a final order not subject to further judicial review and the violator has paid a penalty assessed under this subsection, or such comparable State law, as the case may be,

shall not be subject of a civil penalty action under subsection (d) of this section or section 1321(b) of this title or section 1365 of this title.

33 U.S.C. § 1319(g)(6)(A). Notwithstanding the apparent prohibition on overfiling when an action has been "commenced and is [being] diligently prosecut[ed]," there do not seem to be any cases which have disallowed overfiling on these (or any other) grounds. *See United States v. Smithfield Foods, Inc.*, 191 F.3d 516 (4th Cir. 1999) (finding that the state's enforcement scheme was not sufficiently comparable to the federal scheme to preclude EPA from bringing the federal action), *cert. denied*, 531 U.S. 813 (2000).

D. ENVIRONMENTAL CRIMES

Most environmental statutes criminalize the knowing violation of their provisions. *See, e.g.*, 16 U.S.C. § 1540(b)(1) (ESA); 33 U.S.C. § 1319(c)(2) (CWA); 42 U.S.C. § 6928(d) (RCRA); 42 U.S.C. § 7413(c)(1) (CAA); 42 U.S.C. § 9603(b) (CERCLA). Yet, even in these cases, a criminal prosecution need not necessarily be initiated. Instead, DOJ and EPA could decide to bring a civil or administrative action.

In deciding whether to bring a criminal prosecution for a violation of a federal environmental statute, DOJ considers several factors. Besides the specific criminal act, the DOJ may consider: (1) voluntary disclosure; (2) the degree and timeliness of cooperation; (3) preventative measures and compliance programs; (4) pervasive non-compliance; (5) disciplinary systems to punish employees who violate compliance policies; and (6) subsequent compliance efforts. DOJ, FACTORS IN DECISIONS ON CRIMINAL PROSECUTIONS FOR ENVIRONMENTAL VIOLATIONS IN THE CONTEXT OF SIGNIFICANT VOLUNTARY COMPLIANCE OR DISCLOSURE EFFORTS BY THE VIOLATOR (1991).

Historically, EPA's prevailing view has long been that criminal prosecutions for environmental violations should be brought only in the most egregious cases. Over the last few decades, however, EPA's criminal program has gained a position of greater prominence within the agency. The George W. Bush administration increased its focus on environmental criminal enforcement, while other environmental enforcement efforts were deemphasized. *See* David M. Uhlmann, *Strange Bedfellows*, 25 ENVTL. F. 3, May–June 2008, at 40–43. The Obama administration continued this growth, increasing the number of new criminal investigators to 200. *See* Steven P. Solow & Anne M Carpenter, *The State of Environmental Crime Enforcement: A Survey of Developments in 2010*, BNA ENV'T REP., Mar. 18, 2011.

Whereas in the past it was unlikely that a large civil case would be referred for a criminal investigation unless a civil investigation revealed unusually troubling details, while President Obama was in office, many large civil cases received at least an initial review for possible criminal investigation. *See* Steven P. Solow, *The State of Environmental Crime Enforcement: A Survey of Developments in 2006*, BNA ENV'T REP., Mar. 2, 2007. The Obama EPA prioritized criminal enforcement for high impact, complex cases that seriously threatened human health and the environment. *See* EPA, FISCAL YEAR 2015 EPA ENFORCEMENT AND COMPLIANCE ANNUAL REPORT.

The Trump administration, however, appears to have reversed course. During fiscal year 2017, EPA opened fewer criminal cases and charged fewer defendants than it had in any year during the prior decade. *See* EPA, ENFORCEMENT ANNUAL RESULTS ANALYSIS AND TRENDS FOR FISCAL YEAR 2017. The total amount of criminal fines collected was higher than in previous years, though this is mostly due to criminal actions against BP, Duke Energy, and Volkswagen, which had been brought under prior administrations. *See id.* Furthermore, early estimates of fiscal year 2018 indicate that the Trump EPA is on track to prosecute the fewest environmental crimes in one year in at least two decades. Laura Peterson, *Enforcement of Environmental Laws Drops Under Trump Administration*, POGO.ORG, Feb. 20, 2018.

The following case details the type of scenario in which EPA may decide to bring a criminal enforcement action and a court's corresponding analysis.

United States v. Hansen

262 F.3d 1217 (11th Cir. 2001), *cert. denied*, 535 U.S. 1111 (2002).

■ Before BIRCH and DUBINA, CIRCUIT JUDGES, and HANCOCK, DISTRICT JUDGE.

■ PER CURIAM:

[This case involved workplace exposure to hazardous substances including mercury occurring at a LCP Chemicals-Georgia (LCP) plant. Hansen was the President and CEO of the company operating the plant for much of the relevant time period, and he also served as the plant manager for two months. Randall, Hansen's son, became an Executive Vice President of the company and then took over as CEO. Taylor served as plant manager for several months. After discussing the background facts and the procedural posture, the court turned to a discussion of the knowledge requirements in environmental crimes.]

Δ's arguments

... Hansen, Randall, and Taylor argue that the evidence was insufficient to convict them for knowing endangerment. They acknowledge that the government may have shown that they "could have been aware" of the inherent dangers of working in a chlor-alkali plant, but argue that it failed to show that they knew and had an actual belief that the conduct which allegedly violated the environmental laws was substantially certain to cause death or serious bodily injury to others. Specifically, they maintain that, while the evidence showed that the employees were exposed to mercury, the evidence did not show that they were endangered due to any RCRA violation. They contend that the evidence of the employees' exposure to caustic was not sufficient to support the conviction for knowing endangerment. They claim that the government did not show that they had actual knowledge that their conduct in causing the RCRA violation was at that time substantially certain to place the employees in imminent danger of death or serious bodily injury. They also posit that there was no evidence that they were participants in any alleged conspiracy.

S.o.R.

For a conviction of knowing endangerment under the RCRA, the government must prove that the defendants knowingly caused the illegal treatment, storage, or disposal of hazardous wastes while knowing that such conduct placed others in imminent danger of death or serious injury. 42 U.S.C. § 6928(e). A defendant acts "knowingly" "if he is aware or believes that his conduct is substantially certain to cause danger of death or serious bodily injury." *Id.* at 6928(f)(1)(C). The defendant must have possessed "actual awareness or actual belief." *Id.* at 6928(f)(2)(A). Circumstantial evidence, "including evidence that the defendant took affirmative steps to shield himself from relevant information," may be used to prove the defendant's awareness or belief. *Id.* The knowing endangerment statute was drafted to "assure to the extent possible that persons are not prosecuted or convicted unjustly for making difficult business judgments where such judgments are made without the necessary scienter" "however dire may be the danger in fact created." The penalties imposed by the knowing endangerment section were "designed for the occasional case where the defendant's knowing conduct shows that his respect for human life is utterly lacking and it is merely fortuitous that his conduct may not have caused a disaster." We have held that "[t]he government need only prove that a defendant had knowledge of the general hazardous character of the chemical" and knew "that the chemicals have the potential to be harmful to others or to the environment." *United States v. Goldsmith*, 978 F.2d 643, 645–646 (11th Cir.1992). "[W]hile knowledge of prior illegal activity is not conclusive as to whether a defendant possessed the requisite knowledge of later illegal activity, it most certainly provides circumstantial evidence of the defendant's later knowledge from which the jury may draw the necessary inference." *Self*, 2 F.3d at 1088.

The statute defines "serious bodily injury" as "(A) bodily injury which involves a substantial risk of death; (B) unconsciousness; (C) extreme physical pain; (D) protracted and obvious disfigurement; or (E) protracted loss or impairment of the function of a bodily member, organ, or mental faculty." 42 U.S.C. § 6928(f)(6). A condition which may cause one of the statutorily defined conditions is sufficient to show "serious bodily injury." *See United States v. Protex Industries, Inc.*, 874 F.2d 740, 743 (10th Cir.1989).

The Evidence of Endangerment

Former . . . employees testified that they suffered serious skin and respiratory conditions from the wastewater on the cellroom floors. A November 1992 memorandum from Taylor to Randall showed Taylor's concern for needed repairs "to avert severe safety and environmental problems." The urinalysis testing on employees showed "an increase" in the number with mercury levels which exceeded the 150 action level from 1986 to 1993. Taylor admitted that most of the employees in the cellroom were removed to other plant locations "before any medical condition occurred" but said that he did not see any "reason to draw any correlation between" the rise in the number of employees exposed to excess mercury and the dumping of hazardous wastes and mercury.

Expert testimony and reports linked exposure to mercury and caustic to a variety of serious health problems. The National Institute for Occupational Safety and Health (NIOSH) report on sodium hydroxide caustic indicated that local contact with caustic could result in "extensive damage to tissues, with resultant blindness, cutaneous burns, and perforations of the alimentary tract," with potential for development of "squamous cell carcinomas." The NIOSH report on inorganic mercury warned of the effects of mercury and mercury vapors to the central nervous system. Dr. Teitelbaum testified that exposure to caustic could cause burns ranging from first-to third-degree and could be lethal, and that exposure to mercury could cause mild tremors, personality changes, some detectable neurological abnormalities, changes in kidney function to severe kidney damage with potential death, and immune system problems. Dr. Teitelbaum opined that the employees were "in danger of death or serious bodily injury." The evidence was sufficient for the jury to find that the defendants placed others in danger of death or serious bodily injury.

The Evidence of *Mens Rea*

The evidence showed that Hansen, Randall, and Taylor knew that the conditions of the plant were dangerous and that the conditions posed a serious danger to the employees. LCP former employee Wilbur Duane Outhwaite testified that he voiced his opposition to the use of the Bunker "C" storage with Hansen, and that Hansen responded that it was "his decision to make, and he decided to use them." LCP acting plant manager Hugh Croom discussed his concerns regarding the dangerous conditions in the cellroom and the danger to the employees with Randall. Croom and LCP former employee Outhwaite testified that Randall received daily reports from the plant managers concerning plant operations and "safety problems." Randall was aware of the water on the cellroom floor and "wouldn't say that [he] wasn't unaware of the hazard," but thought that the walkway was "an acceptable resolution" to "eliminating the hazard to the employees while we worked to dry the cellroom floor." He conceded that he was aware that the company was cited for willful violation of OSHA safety regulations as a result of water on cellroom floors. Jesse Jones, a former LCP employee and a union representative, met with Randall to discuss the employees' safety issues, and Randall promised the needed repairs. He said that he discussed the safety concerns, specifically "the water condition, the deterioration of the plant with the pipes, the leaks, and the safety equipment[ ]" with Hansen and Taylor. Between 3 August 1993, and 4 February 1994, Randall was sent 22 reports listing 110 different violations of the NPDES standards. As LCP's environmental manager, Brent Hanson regularly advised Randall of the plant's environmental problems "[w]henever he was interested in things" and by monthly reports.

As early as 1988, NIOSH informed Taylor that the plant employees had "extremely high" levels of mercury in their bodies which created "an unacceptably high potential for health effects," and that the mercury-contaminated wastes should be kept in vapor-proof containers. Despite this, the employees' exposure to high levels of mercury continued. In 1992, Taylor addressed his concerns about "severe safety" problems in a memorandum to Randall. Taylor was aware that, during the spring of 1993, 23 cellroom employees were removed from their duty in the cellrooms due to their high levels of mercury and that the mercury level in the workplace increased. Taylor was aware of and concerned by the mercury-contaminated waste which was stored in drums in the cellrooms' basement and which was emitting elevated levels of mercury fumes. He admitted that the mercury-contaminated mud on the cellroom floors posed a health risk and needed to be monitored. He testified that, on occasion, he would get into the water wearing protective equipment to make repairs and improvements to the pumps, and admitted that, if the wastewater got onto bare skin and was caustic, "you would start to feel a little burning or a little heat sensation" but that it could be neutralized by washing with the safety solution. He said that such burns were "not unusual" in a caustic soda manufacturing plant through employee carelessness and equipment failures.

Consent to the Risks

The RCRA knowing endangerment provision can be affirmatively defended if "the conduct charged was consented to by the person endangered and that the danger and conduct charged were reasonably foreseeable hazards of—(A) an occupation, a business, or a profession." 42 U.S.C. § 6928(f)(3). The evidence showed that the plant's environmental violations seriously endangered the employees and were not typical to chloralkali plants. Hugh Croom, the plant manager for the LCP chlor-alkali plant in North Carolina, testified that the dangerous conditions in the Brunswick plant were not present in the North Carolina plant because the North Carolina plant had adequate waste treatment equipment and facility maintenance. He said that he discussed his concerns regarding the environmental issues, the wastewater treatment system issues, and the dangers to the employees with Randall and with Taylor. LCP environmental manager Brent Hanson noted that, although covering mercury with water to limit mercury vapors was an accepted practice within the chlor-alkali industry, it was usually practiced "in a little more confined manner" than the condition of the cellrooms, it was not an industry practice to allow such quantities of mercury to accumulate on the cellroom floors, and he knew of no other chlor-alkali plants that permitted such a condition to exist. Dr. Teitelbaum testified that, although he did not think that "you can get a zero risk" in a chlor-alkali plant, he thought "you can make chlor-alkali plants safe so that workers under everyday conditions are extremely unlikely to be hurt." The employees also did not freely consent to conditions at the plant.

They complained to management, including Hansen, Randall, and Taylor, about the dangerous working conditions, and refused to work in the cellrooms. Union representative and former plant employee Jesse Jones testified that LCP suspended nine employees who refused to "go underneath the cellroom to repair the pump" because of the wastewater on the cellroom floor. Jones said that he discussed his concerns about the working conditions with Hansen, Randall, and Taylor. Former employee Larry Barwick said that he complained "to whoever would listen," including the LCP management, about the fumes and visible mercury in the cell buildings. He refused to go into the cellrooms, and was once sent home for the day based on his refusal. The evidence, therefore, was sufficient to show that the defendants knew that the plant's violations of the CWA and RCRA violations were inevitable, that the plant was incapable of complying with environmental standards, and that the employees were endangered while working within this environment without consenting to the risk. . . .

Knowledge of the Substantive Offenses

Randall argues that the district court erred in denying his motion for acquittal because the government failed to show that he had the requisite "knowledge" of the CWA and RCRA violations on the specific dates when they occurred. He contends that his knowledge after the violations had occurred was not sufficient. The statutes for the violations under which Randall was indicted contain explicit knowledge requirements. For a conviction under [the CWA], the defendant must be shown to have "knowingly" violated various sections of the CWA or permit conditions or limitations. For a conviction under [RCRA], the defendant must be shown to have "knowingly" treated, stored, or disposed of an identified hazardous waste without a permit. We have held that the knowledge element is satisfied where a defendant, who may not have "directly" caused a hazardous waste violation but had "approved of previous dumpings as a way to meet storage squeezes," "effectively ordered" a subsequent violation when he instructed a subordinate to "handle" hazardous waste. *United States v. Greer*, 850 F.2d 1447, 1451–52 (11th Cir.1988).

Here, although Randall did not directly cause the violations, he knew that the plant was violating its permit on an almost daily basis, accumulating wastes that it could not treat, and was frequently releasing the wastes from the cellrooms as needed to keep the plant operational. He received 22 written reports between 3 August 1993 and 4 February 1994 advising him of a total of 110 different violations of the NPDES permit. He received frequent and sometimes daily oral and written reports from the various plant managers of the plant's operations and safety concerns. He knew that the plant was incapable of complying with the environmental standards and knew that the violations were inevitable. We conclude that the evidence that Randall permitted the plant employees to process the hazardous wastes as they had in the past despite his knowledge that the procedures were in violation of environmental regulations was sufficient to show that Randall acted "knowingly." . . .

NOTES AND QUESTIONS

1. **Civil v. Criminal Prosecutions.** Whereas most civil actions are premised on strict liability, environmental crimes have a *scienter* requirement. What is the nature of this requirement? What must a defendant have knowledge of? Does she need to know that she was in violation of a permit or other environmental regulation? Is knowledge of the predicate facts sufficient? What if the defendant intentionally kept herself from knowing what was going on even though she should have known? What amount of knowledge is sufficient for a criminal prosecution of a specific violation? Does the defendant need to know that she placed an individual, or

the environment, in danger? In *Hansen*, the court held that "[w]hile knowledge of prior illegal activity is not conclusive as to whether a defendant possessed the requisite knowledge of later illegal activity, it most certainly provides circumstantial evidence of the defendant's later knowledge from which the jury may draw the necessary inference." 262 F.3d at 1243. Is this approach desirable or will it lead to too many criminal prosecutions?

EPA says that criminal enforcement actions will be used in situations where violations are knowingly and willfully committed. *But see United States v. Ortiz*, 427 F.3d 1278, 1279 (10th Cir. 2005) ("[T]he plain language of the Clean Water Act criminalizes any act of ordinary negligence that leads to the discharge of a pollutant into the navigable waters of the United States."). What principle should justify a criminal prosecution being brought instead of a civil enforcement action?

2.   EPA Policy on Investigating Environmental Crimes. While the Justice Department may exercise prosecutorial discretion with respect to environmental crimes, EPA also plays a role in focusing enforcement resources through the use of "investigative discretion." Memorandum from Earl E. Devaney, Director, Office of Criminal Enforcement, EPA, The Exercise of Investigative Discretion, at 3 (Jan. 12, 1994). EPA has identified several factors to guide the use of this discretion under its policy of selecting "high impact" cases that provide the greatest potential to protect human health and the environment. Specifically, EPA focuses on significant environmental harms and culpable conduct. Evidence of a significant environmental harm can be shown both by the presence of an illegal discharge or emission that has an identifiable and significant harmful impact on human health or the environment, and by the threat of such harm. *Id.* at 4. Failure to report an incident makes investigation more likely, and criminal enforcement will also be used when there is a "trend or common attitude" within the regulated community in order to deter the community as a whole from committing a violation. *Id.*

The EPA guidance also identifies several factors that indicate culpable conduct. These include history of repeated violations, deliberate misconduct, concealment or falsification of records, tampering with monitoring or control equipment, and operating without a license. *Id.* at 5. Are criminal prosecutions appropriate in these cases?

In 2010, EPA formally implemented a targeting methodology to prioritize its cases, with a focus on health and environmental impacts, release characteristics (such as continuing violations), and subject characteristics (such as repeat violators). *See* EPA, COMPLIANCE AND ENFORCEMENT ANNUAL RESULTS 2011 FISCAL YEAR, STRATEGIC PROGRAM MANAGEMENT: CRIMINAL ENFORCEMENT CASE SELECTION METHODOLOGY. The Agency's goal was to reduce the number of prosecutions but increase the impact of those prosecutions. To date, this approach seems successful: from 2011 to 2015, the number of investigations opened decreased while the sentence increased. EPA, FISCAL YEAR 2015 EPA ENFORCEMENT AND COMPLIANCE ANNUAL RESULTS. What is the right tradeoff between the number of cases brought and the severity of the cases? Is your answer different for criminal versus civil cases?

3.   Public Reporting of Environmental Crimes. EPA has continued to increase its effort to enhance public reporting of environmental violations. EPA maintains a tip reporting webpage (www.epa.gov/tips). According to EPA, in 2006 more than 4,000 reports flowed in, 500 of which were related to possible criminal violations. *See* Steven P. Solow, *The State of Environmental Crime Enforcement: Survey of Developments in 2006,* BNA ENV'T REP., Mar. 2, 2007, at 2. In December 2008, EPA also launched a Fugitive Website (http://www2.epa.gov/enforcement/epa-fugitives) in order to enable the public to report information on the whereabouts of defendants charged with environmental crimes. Are these tools likely to be effective?

4.   Measuring Enforcement Success. Joel A. Mintz identifies three metrics by which the success of EPA's enforcement activities can be measured. The first are outcome measures, such as the number of pounds of pollutants that will no longer be discharged, or the amount of money that would have been spent on health care by persons exposed to the illegal pollutants. The second are output measures, or the activity levels of enforcement personnel, such as the number of enforcement proceedings, years of incarceration, and amounts of penalties paid. The third are organizational measures, such as the extent to which EPA is sufficiently well-staffed, experienced, and able to handle its workload. Joel A. Mintz, *Measuring Environmental Enforcement Success: The Elusive Search for Objectivity,* 44 ENVTL. L. REP. NEWS & ANALYSIS 10751 (2014). Which of these metrics is most appropriate for measuring EPA's success?

5.   Intersection of Environmental and Criminal Law. Environmental crimes inhabit an unusual position in our legal system. Indeed, there is some debate over whether they are part of environmental law or criminal law. *See* Michael Herz, *Structures of Environmental Criminal Enforcement,* 7 FORDHAM ENVTL. L.J. 679 (1996) (noting that while most other bodies of law have integrated environmental law, criminal law has not). Historically, environmental crimes have been treated as another tool for environmental enforcement with added deterrent effect. *Id.* at 680. Herz argues that the failure to see criminal enforcement as essentially different from other enforcement tools leads to inappropriate prosecutions. *Id.* Why would that be so? Is it because the goal of deterrence drives criminal enforcement in the environmental context? Is it appropriate to punish a few as a way to keep the community in compliance? Is that how criminal law normally works?

Although public support for prosecuting environmental crimes is quite high, the regulated community expresses deep concerns about the prosecution of environmental crimes. Is the concern justified? Richard Lazarus has argued that the overwhelming complexity of environmental law makes it difficult to fairly integrate with criminal law. *See* Richard J. Lazarus, *Meeting the Demand of Integration in the Evolution of Environmental Law: Reforming Environmental Criminal Law,* 83 GEO. L.J. 2407, 2445–85 (1995). Some commentators see this concern as overstated. *See, e.g.,* David M. Uhlmann, *Environmental Crime Comes of Age: The Evolution of Criminal Enforcement in the Environmental Regulatory Scheme,* 2009 UTAH L. REV. 1223, 1233 (arguing that prosecutorial discretion should limit the pursuit of cases where compliance with the law was uncertain and that sufficient safeguards exist to ensure the proper use of such discretion); Kathleen F. Brickey, *Environmental Crime at the Crossroads: The Intersection of Environmental and Criminal Law Theory*, 71 TUL. L. REV. 487 (1996) (arguing that because environmental law critics approach environmental crime primarily as an abstraction, their concerns about the fairness of environmental criminal enforcement are greatly exaggerated).

6.   Moral Culpability and Environmental Crimes. Much of the concern over the appropriate use of environmental criminal enforcement revolves around the question of when a defendant is morally culpable for causing damage to the environment. Richard Lazarus has framed the issue in the following terms:

> Defining the outer reach of criminal sanctions for violations of regulatory laws, like environmental protection laws, necessarily raises a tension between these two aims of criminal law functions: deterring regulatory violations and expressing moral culpability. . . . For just as criminal sanctions can be justified by norms of moral culpability, so too may the imposition of criminal sanctions in the absence of such culpability itself run afoul of those very same norms of morality. There are limits beyond which something cannot be deemed immoral because it is criminal. And, when it fails to recognize those limits, the criminal law itself risks moral condemnation.

Richard J. Lazarus, *Mens Rea in Environmental Criminal Law: Reading Supreme Court Tea Leaves*, 7 FORDHAM ENVTL. L.J. 861, 867–68 (1996). Might the public's perceptions of the morality of environmental violations have become sufficiently ingrained as to justify the expansion of criminal environmental law? *See* Uhlmann, *supra*, at 1231. Should we trust EPA's criminal investigators and DOJ's prosecutors to be able to tell the difference between a negligent violation that requires only a civil enforcement action, and one that deserves a criminal prosecution? Might the decision be arbitrary? *See id.* at 1242–52.

7.   Corporations and Criminal Sanctions. Section 309(c)(2) of the CWA establishes that "[a]ny person who knowingly violates . . . shall be punished by a fine of not less than $5000 nor more than $50,000 per day of violation, or by imprisonment for not more than 3 years, or both." Who should be considered a person for the purpose of this provision? Does the definition of "person" include corporations? *See United States v. Chemetco, Inc.*, 274 F.3d 1154 (7th Cir. 2001) (affirming district court sentence that convicted a corporation for discharging pollutants without a permit, in violation of CWA, and sentenced it to a fine of $3,327,500). What is the impact of corporate criminal liability?

8.   Over-Criminalization and the Erosion of the *Mens Rea* Requirement? Should the *mens rea* of an employee be imputed to officers in a company's management in a type of modified respondent superior doctrine? Should corporate officers be held criminally liable in the absence of any actual knowledge of criminal violations? For a discussion of these questions, see Ruth Ann Weidel et al., *The Erosion of Mens Rea in Environmental Criminal Prosecutions*, 21 SETON HALL L. REV. 1100 (1991) (discussing the many different ways in which the traditional criminal law definitions of *mens rea* have been significantly eroded in environmental enforcement). *See also* David C. Fortney, Note, *Thinking Outside the "Black Box": Tailored Enforcement in Environmental Criminal Law*, 81 TEX. L. REV. 1609, 1623–28 (2003) (exploring the debate over criminal enforcement of environmental laws, arguing that the current regime is fatally flawed).

Do the benefits of criminal prosecutions outweigh the social cost to the business community? *See* John C. Coffee, Jr., *Does "Unlawful" Mean "Criminal"?: Reflections on the Disappearing Tort/Crime Distinction in American Law*, 71 B.U. L. REV. 193, 219–20 (1991) (contending that harsh environmental sanctions entangle a large proportion of the American workforce with criminal law and create undesirable levels of anxiety); *see also* Stuart P. Green, *Why It's a Crime to Tear the Tag Off a Mattress: Overcriminalization and the Moral Content of Regulatory Offenses*, 46 EMORY L.J. 1533, 1535 (1997) (positing that the over-criminalization of regulatory crimes undermines the efficacy of punishment, wastes enforcement resources, and invites selective prosecution).

What are the practical implications of the broad criminal net created by the environmental statutes? To what extent is the critique of environmental criminal regimes motivated by the substantive content of the broad and ambitious statutes they are designed to enforce rather than by the criminal regimes themselves? For a discussion of these questions and the role that prosecutorial discretion plays, see David A. Barker, Note, *Environmental Crimes, Prosecutorial Discretion, and the Civil/Criminal Line*, 88 VA. L. REV. 1387 (2002) (arguing that the wide discretion afforded to prosecutors is not evidence that environmental crimes do not fit within the criminal law scheme, but instead is typical of both state and federal criminal law).

9.   Criminal Law and Deepwater Horizon. The most significant oil spill in U.S. history occurred when 200 million gallons of oil flowed into the Gulf of Mexico before the blown well caused by the explosion of the Deepwater Horizon oil rig could be capped. DOJ brought several criminal charges against BP, including one count of violating the Migratory Bird Treaty Act, "11 counts of felony manslaughter for the death of crew members on the Deepwater Horizon rig[,] . . . one count of felony obstruction of Congress[,] and one count of violating the Clean Water Act." BP pleaded guilty and settled for four billion dollars "in criminal fines and penalties—the largest criminal resolution in United States history." U.S. Fish and Wildlife Service Office of Law Enforcement, Deepwater Horizon Criminal Task Force, https://www.fws.gov/le/pdf/press-release-fws-role-in-deepwater-horizon-criminal-investigation.pdf. (last visited June 6, 2018). Although DOJ did not allege intentional wrongdoing, the court found that the discharge of oil constituted gross negligence and willful misconduct, elevating the penalty under the Clean Water Act. *See In re Oil Spill by Oil Rig Deepwater Horizon in Gulf of Mexico,* 21 F. Supp. 3d 657, 737 (E.D. La. 2014). Combined with the civil penalties, the BP oil spill resulted in a $20.8 billion settlement, which was the largest environmental settlement in U.S. history. *See* NOAA, Deepwater

Horizon Oil Spill Settlement: Where the Money Went, http://www.noaa.gov/
explainers/deepwater-horizon-oil-spill-settlements-where-money-went (last
visited June 17, 2018).

10. Attorney-Client Privilege. For the past few years, there has been a
debate between federal prosecutors and the regulated community and its
outside counsel concerning the attorney-client privilege. The debate largely
came out of the U.S. Sentencing Commission's 2004 position regarding
waiver of the attorney-client privilege and work-product protections. The
Commission had stated that waiver of privilege by the subject of a
government investigation could be an appropriate factor in determining
whether a company "cooperated" with the government investigation and
thus receive more lenient treatment under the Sentencing Guidelines. Such
a waiver could also potentially affect the DOJ's decision to bring criminal
charges against a corporation. *See* Steven P. Solow, *The State of
Environmental Crime Enforcement: An Annual Survey*, BNA ENV'T REP.,
Mar. 3, 2006, at 1. In addressing this issue, Steven P. Solow raises a number
of important concerns, including:

> The degree to which the regulated community relies upon the
> attorney-client privilege and the work-product doctrine to enhance
> their ability to conduct corporate self-investigations and maintain
> effective compliance programs, and the degree to which those
> investigations and programs would be hampered if
> communications with counsel were known to be subject to review
> by the government.

> Whether or to what degree invasion of the privilege will interfere
> with the routine use of lawyers to provide legal advice regarding a
> company's day-to-day business activities, legal advice that can be
> crucial in ensuring that a company's activities conform with the
> requirements of the law.

Id. at 3. Is it appropriate for federal prosecutors to be allowed to seek
privileged or work-product materials in the course of criminal prosecutions?
The regulated community describes these requests as routine, while the
federal investigators contend that such requests are rare. Does it matter how
frequent or infrequent such requests are? Isn't any request coercive? Would
allowing prosecutors to make such requests encourage the regulated entities
to not keep written accounts of their compliance programs?

On April 5, 2006, the U.S. Sentencing Commission voted to remove
language from the sentencing guidelines that identified waiver of the
attorney-client privilege as a part of "meaningful cooperation" with a
government investigation or prosecution. *See* Steven P. Solow, *The State of
Environmental Crime Enforcement: Survey of Developments in 2006*, BNA
ENV'T REP., Mar. 2, 2007, at 1, 3. In response the Justice Department issued
new guidelines requiring federal prosecutors to establish a legitimate need
for privileged information and to seek approval from senior officials in the
department before requesting a waiver of attorney-client privilege and work
product protection in criminal investigations. *Id.* How difficult will it be for
a prosecutor to show a legitimate need for privileged information?

11. Civil and Criminal Actions. Under most environmental statutes, civil, administrative, and criminal penalties can be imposed for the same violation of a statutory provision. *See, e.g.,* 42 U.S.C. § 7413(a)–(d) (CAA). In which cases should a civil action be preferred to a criminal one? "Parallel proceedings" means "overlapping criminal and civil or administrative enforcement activities with respect to the same or related parties and that deal with the same or a related course of conduct." DOJ, DIRECTIVE NO. 2008–02, PARALLEL PROCEEDINGS POLICY (2008). Under what circumstances would parallel enforcement proceedings be desirable? EPA identifies two main scenarios where parallel proceedings are appropriate: (1) commonly, where criminal remedies also require a civil, administrative, or cleanup order to fully protect the environment, and (2) rarely, where conduct is sufficiently egregious to warrant both criminal and civil penalties. Memorandum from Granta Y. Nakayama, Assistant Administrator, EPA, Parallel Proceedings Policy, at 2 (Sept. 24, 2007). EPA and DOJ guidance outlines a specific set of procedures that must be followed when engaging in a parallel proceeding. *See id.* at 6–9; *see also* DOJ, DIRECTIVE NO. 2008–02, *supra,* at 4–8. What kind of difficulties do parallel enforcement procedures present? *See id.*

E. CITIZEN SUITS

To supplement the federal and state enforcement efforts, many environmental statutes authorize citizen suits. *See, e.g.,* 16 U.S.C. § 1540(g) (ESA); 33 U.S.C. § 1365 (CWA); 42 U.S.C. § 6972 (RCRA); 42 U.S.C. § 7604 (CAA); 42 U.S.C. § 9659 (CERCLA). These provisions usually allow citizens to seek injunctions and penalties payable to the U.S. Treasury against alleged violators of the environmental statutes and to file suit against a federal agency for failing to perform a non-discretionary duty. *See, e.g.,* 33 U.S.C. § 1365(a) (CWA); 42 U.S.C. § 6972(a) (RCRA); 42 U.S.C. § 7604(a) (CAA). Challenge to other agency actions that do not involve a non-discretionary duty cannot be brought under these provisions. Instead, they must be brought under the judicial review provision of the applicable statute. Not all environmental acts, however, contains citizen suit provisions. An important exception is NEPA. *See* 42 U.S.C. §§ 4321–4370(f).

As a prerequisite to starting a citizen suit, the plaintiff must give notice of the alleged violation to the Administrator, to the state in which the alleged violation occurs, and to any alleged violator. 33 U.S.C. § 1365(b)(1)(A) (CWA); 42 U.S.C. § 6972(b)(1)(A) (RCRA); 42 U.S.C. § 7604(b)(1)(A) (CAA); 42 U.S.C. § 9659(d)(1) (CERCLA). In cases where the action is directed against a federal agency for failing to perform a non-discretionary duty, the plaintiff must give notice of such action to the Administrator. 33 U.S.C. § 1365(b)(2) (CWA); 42 U.S.C. § 6972(c) (RCRA); 42 U.S.C. § 7604(b)(2) (CAA). The plaintiff will be able to commence a citizen suit only after a certain period of time of filing such notice or notices, although some exceptions may apply. 33 U.S.C. § 1365(b)(1)–(2) (CWA) (60-days notice); 42 U.S.C. § 6972(b)(1)(A)

(RCRA) (60-days notice), (b)(2)(A) (90-days notice), (c) (60-days notice); 42 U.S.C. § 7604(b) (CAA) (60-days notice); 42 U.S.C. § 9659(e) (CERCLA) (60-days notice). Citizen suits may not be commenced if the Administrator or the state has already commenced and is diligently prosecuting a civil or criminal action in a federal or state court to require compliance with the standard, limitation, or order. 33 U.S.C. § 1365(b)(1)(B) (CWA); 42 U.S.C. § 6972(b)(1)(B) (RCRA); 42 U.S.C. § 7604(b)(1)(B) (CAA); 42 U.S.C. § 9659(d)(2) (CERCLA).

To encourage these suits, Congress has authorized the courts to award the cost of litigation, including reasonable attorney and expert witness fees, "whenever the court determines such award is appropriate." 33 U.S.C. § 1365(d) (CWA); 42 U.S.C. § 6972(e) (RCRA); 42 U.S.C. § 7604(d) (CAA); 42 U.S.C. § 9659(f) (CERCLA). Nevertheless, cost and resource considerations highly influence the number of citizen suits that are brought, resulting in many fewer citizen suits than state and federal enforcement actions. *See* Barton H. Thompson, Jr., *The Continuing Innovation of Citizen Enforcement*, 2000 U. ILL. L. REV. 185, 204. It is not surprising that the majority of citizen-initiated litigation has been brought under the CWA under which dischargers must file periodic discharge reports that plaintiffs can then use as the basis for their claims, lowering costs. *See id.*

The next case discusses whether citizen suits can be brought for past violations. The standing of the plaintiff to bring a citizen suit may also be an issue, as explored in Section 2.A, *infra*.

Gwaltney of Smithfield, Ltd. v. Chesapeake Bay Foundation, Inc.

484 U.S. 49 (1987).

■ JUSTICE MARSHALL delivered the opinion of the Court:

In this case, we must decide whether § 505(a) of the Clean Water Act . . . confers federal jurisdiction over citizen suits for wholly past violations. . . .

I

The holder of a federal NPDES [National Pollutant Discharge Elimination System] permit is subject to enforcement action by the Administrator for failure to comply with the conditions of the permit. The Administrator's enforcement arsenal includes administrative, civil, and criminal sanctions. The holder of a state NPDES permit is subject to both federal and state enforcement action for failure to comply. In the absence of federal or state enforcement, private citizens may commence civil actions against any person "alleged to be in violation of" the conditions of either a federal or state NPDES permit. If the citizen prevails in such an action, the court may order injunctive relief and/or impose civil penalties payable to the United States Treasury.

The Commonwealth of Virginia established a federally approved state NPDES program administered by the Virginia State Water Control Board (Board). In 1974, the Board issued a NPDES permit to ITT-Gwaltney authorizing the discharge of seven pollutants from the company's meatpacking plant on the Pagan River in Smithfield, Virginia. The permit, which was reissued in 1979 and modified in 1980, established effluent limitations, monitoring requirements, and other conditions of discharge. In 1981, petitioner Gwaltney of Smithfield acquired the assets of ITT-Gwaltney and assumed obligations under the permit.

Between 1981 and 1984, petitioner repeatedly violated the conditions of the permit by exceeding effluent limitations on five of the seven pollutants covered. These violations are chronicled in the Discharge Monitoring Reports that the permit required petitioner to maintain. The most substantial of the violations concerned the pollutants fecal coliform, chlorine, and total Kjeldahl nitrogen (TKN). Between October 27, 1981, and August 30, 1984, petitioner violated its TKN limitation 87 times, its chlorine limitation 34 times, and its fecal coliform limitation 31 times. Petitioner installed new equipment to improve its chlorination system in March 1982, and its last reported chlorine violation occurred in October 1982. The new chlorination system also helped to control the discharge of fecal coliform, and the last recorded fecal coliform violation occurred in February 1984. Petitioner installed an upgraded wastewater treatment system in October 1983, and its last reported TKN violation occurred on May 15, 1984.

Respondents Chesapeake Bay Foundation and Natural Resources Defense Council, two nonprofit corporations dedicated to the protection of natural resources, sent notice in February 1984 to Gwaltney, the Administrator of EPA, and the Virginia State Water Control Board, indicating respondents' intention to commence a citizen suit under the Act based on petitioner's violations of its permit conditions. Respondents proceeded to file this suit in June 1984, alleging that petitioner "has violated ... [and] will continue to violate its NPDES permit." Respondents requested that the District Court provide declaratory and injunctive relief, impose civil penalties, and award attorney's fees and costs. The District Court granted partial summary judgment for respondents in August 1984, declaring Gwaltney "to have violated and to be in violation" of the Act. The District Court then held a trial to determine the appropriate remedy.

Before the District Court reached a decision, Gwaltney moved in May 1985 for dismissal of the action for want of subject-matter jurisdiction under the Act. Gwaltney argued that the language of § 505(a), which permits private citizens to bring suit against any person "alleged to be in violation" of the Act, requires that a defendant be violating the Act at the time of suit. Gwaltney urged the District Court to adopt the analysis of the Fifth Circuit in *Hamker v. Diamond*

Shamrock Chemical Co., 756 F.2d 392 (1985), which held that "a complaint brought under [§ 505] must allege a violation occurring at the time the complaint is filed." *Id.*, at 395. Gwaltney contended that because its last recorded violation occurred several weeks before respondents filed their complaint, the District Court lacked subject-matter jurisdiction over respondents' action.

The District Court rejected Gwaltney's argument, concluding that § 505 authorizes citizens to bring enforcement actions on the basis of wholly past violations. . . .

The Court of Appeals affirmed, expressly rejecting the Fifth Circuit's approach in *Hamker* and holding that § 505 "can be read to comprehend unlawful conduct that occurred only prior to the filing of a lawsuit as well as unlawful conduct that continues into the present." 791 F.2d 304, 309 (CA4 1986). The Court of Appeals concluded that its reading of § 505 was consistent with the Act's structure, legislative history, and purpose. Although it observed that "[a] very sound argument can be made that [respondents'] allegations of continuing violations were made in good faith," the Court of Appeals declined to rule on the District Court's alternative holding, finding it unnecessary to the disposition of the case. *Id.*, at 308, n. 9. . . .

II

Respondents urge that the choice of the phrase "to be in violation," rather than phrasing more clearly directed to the past, is a "careless accident," the result of a "debatable lapse of syntactical precision." See, *e.g.*, Clean Air Act, 42 U.S.C. § 7604; Resource Conservation and Recovery Act of 1976, 42 U.S.C. § 6972. But the prospective orientation of that phrase could not have escaped Congress' attention. Congress used identical language in the citizen suit provisions of several other environmental statutes that authorize only prospective relief. Moreover, Congress has demonstrated in yet other statutory provisions that it knows how to avoid this prospective implication by using language that explicitly targets wholly past violations. . . .

Our reading of the "to be in violation" language of § 505(a) is bolstered by the language and structure of the rest of the citizen suit provisions in § 505 of the Act. These provisions together make plain that the interest of the citizen-plaintiff is primarily forward-looking.

One of the most striking indicia of the prospective orientation of the citizen suit is the pervasive use of the present tense throughout § 505. A citizen suit may be brought only for violation of a permit limitation "which is in effect" under the Act. 33 U.S.C. § 1365(f). Citizen-plaintiffs must give notice to the alleged violator, the Administrator of EPA, and the State in which the alleged violation "occurs." § 1365(b)(1)(A). A Governor of a State may sue as a citizen when the Administrator fails to enforce an effluent limitation "the violation of which is occurring in another State and is causing an adverse effect on the public health or welfare in his State." § 1365(h). The most telling use of the present tense is in the definition of "citizen" as "a person . . . having an interest which is or may be adversely affected" by the defendant's violations of the Act. § 1365(g). This definition makes plain what the undeviating use of the present tense strongly suggests: the harm sought to be addressed by the citizen suit lies in the present or the future, not in the past.

Any other conclusion would render incomprehensible § 505's notice provision, which requires citizens to give 60 days' notice of their intent to sue to the alleged violator as well as to the Administrator and the State. § 1365(b)(1)(A). If the Administrator or the State commences enforcement action within that 60-day period, the citizen suit is barred, presumably because governmental action has rendered it unnecessary. § 1365(b)(1)(B). It follows logically that the purpose of notice to the alleged violator is to give it an opportunity to bring itself into complete compliance with the Act and thus likewise render unnecessary a citizen suit. If we assume, as respondents urge, that citizen suits may target wholly past violations, the requirement of notice to the alleged violator becomes gratuitous. Indeed, respondents, in propounding their interpretation of the Act, can think of no reason for Congress to require such notice other than that "it seemed right" to inform an alleged violator that it was about to be sued.

Adopting respondents' interpretation of § 505's jurisdictional grant would create a second and even more disturbing anomaly. The bar on citizen suits when governmental enforcement action is under way suggests that the citizen suit is meant to supplement rather than to supplant governmental action. The legislative history of the Act reinforces this view of the role of the citizen suit. The Senate Report noted that "[t]he Committee intends the great volume of enforcement actions [to] be brought by the State," and that citizen suits are proper only "if the Federal, State, and local agencies fail to exercise their enforcement responsibility." Permitting citizen suits for wholly past violations of the Act could undermine the supplementary role envisioned for the citizen suit. This danger is best illustrated by an example. Suppose that the Administrator identified a violator of the Act and issued a compliance order under § 309(a). Suppose further that the Administrator agreed not to assess or otherwise seek civil penalties on the condition that the violator take some extreme corrective action, such as to install particularly effective but expensive machinery, that it otherwise would not be obliged to take. If citizens could file suit, months or years later, in order to seek the civil penalties that the Administrator chose to forgo, then the Administrator's discretion to enforce the Act in the public interest would be curtailed considerably. The same might be said of the discretion of state enforcement authorities. Respondents' interpretation of the scope of the citizen suit would change the nature of the citizen's role from interstitial to potentially intrusive. We cannot agree that Congress intended such a result. . . .

III

Our conclusion that § 505 does not permit citizen suits for wholly past violations does not necessarily dispose of this lawsuit, as both lower courts recognized. The District Court found persuasive the fact that "[respondents'] allegation in the complaint, that Gwaltney was continuing to violate its NPDES permit when plaintiffs filed suit[,] appears to have been made fully in good faith." 611 F. Supp. at 1549, n. 8. On this basis, the District Court explicitly held, albeit in a footnote, that "even if Gwaltney were correct that a district court has no jurisdiction over citizen suits based entirely on unlawful conduct that occurred entirely in the past, the Court would still have jurisdiction here." *Ibid.* The Court of Appeals acknowledged, also in a footnote, that "[a] very sound argument can be made that [respondents'] allegations of continuing violations were made in good faith," 791 F.2d, at 308, n. 9, but expressly declined to rule on this alternative holding. Because we agree that § 505 confers jurisdiction over citizen suits when the citizen-plaintiffs make a good-faith allegation of continuous or intermittent violation, we remand the case to the Court of Appeals for further consideration.

Petitioner argues that citizen-plaintiffs must prove their allegations of ongoing noncompliance before jurisdiction attaches under § 505. We cannot agree. The statute does not require that a defendant "be in violation" of the Act at the commencement of suit; rather, the statute requires that a defendant be *alleged* to be in violation." Petitioner's construction of the Act reads the word "alleged" out of § 505. As petitioner itself is quick to note in other contexts, there is no reason to believe that Congress' drafting of § 505 was sloppy or haphazard. We agree with the Solicitor General that "Congress's use of the phrase 'alleged to be in violation' reflects a conscious sensitivity to the practical difficulties of detecting and proving chronic episodic violations of environmental standards." Our acknowledgment that Congress intended a good-faith allegation to suffice for jurisdictional purposes, however, does not give litigants license to flood the courts with suits premised on baseless allegations. Rule 11 of the Federal Rules of Civil Procedure, which requires pleadings to be based on a good-faith belief, formed after reasonable inquiry, that they are "well grounded in fact," adequately protects defendants from frivolous allegations. . . .

Petitioner also worries that our construction of § 505 would permit citizen-plaintiffs, if their allegations of ongoing noncompliance become false at some later point in the litigation because the defendant begins to comply with the Act, to continue nonetheless to press their suit to conclusion. According to petitioner, such a result would contravene both the prospective purpose of the citizen suit provisions and the "case or controversy" requirement of Article III. Longstanding principles of mootness, however, prevent the maintenance of suit when "there is no reasonable expectation that the wrong will be repeated." *United States v.*

W.T. Grant Co., 345 U.S. 629, 633 (1953). In seeking to have a case dismissed as moot, however, the defendant's burden "is a heavy one." 345 U.S., at 633. The defendant must demonstrate that it is *"absolutely clear that the allegedly wrongful behavior could not reasonably be expected to recur." United States v. Phosphate Export Assn., Inc.*, 393 U.S. 199, 203 (1968). Mootness doctrine thus protects defendants from the maintenance of suit under the Clean Water Act based solely on violations wholly unconnected to any present or future wrongdoing, while it also protects plaintiffs from defendants who seek to evade sanction by predictable "protestations of repentance and reform." United States v. Oregon State Medical Society, 343 U.S. 326, 333 (1952).

Because the court below erroneously concluded that respondents could maintain an action based on wholly past violations of the Act, it declined to decide whether respondents' complaint contained a good-faith allegation of ongoing violation by petitioner. We therefore remand the case for consideration of this question.

■ JUSTICE SCALIA, with whom JUSTICE STEVENS and JUSTICE O'CONNOR join, concurring in part and concurring in the judgment:

I join Parts I and II of the Court's opinion. I cannot join Part III because I believe it misreads the statute to create a peculiar new form of subject-matter jurisdiction.

The Court concludes that subject-matter jurisdiction exists under § 505 if there is a good-faith allegation that the defendant is "in violation." Thereafter, according to the Court's interpretation, the plaintiff can never be called on to prove that jurisdictional allegation. This creates a regime that is not only extraordinary, but to my knowledge unique. I can think of no other context in which, in order to carry a lawsuit to judgment, allegations are necessary but proof of those allegations (if they are contested) is not. The Court thinks it necessary to find that Congress produced this jurisprudential anomaly because any other conclusion, in its view, would read the word "alleged" out of § 505. It seems to me that, quite to the contrary, it is the Court's interpretation that ignores the words of the statute.

Section 505(a) states that "any citizen may *commence* a civil action on his own behalf . . . against any person . . . who is alleged to be in violation . . ." (emphasis added). There is of course nothing unusual in the proposition that only an allegation is required to *commence* a lawsuit. Proof is never required, and could not practicably be required, at that stage. From this clear and unexceptionable language of the statute, one of two further inferences can be made: (1) The inference the Court chooses, that the requirement for commencing a suit is the same as the requirement for maintaining it, or (2) the inference that, in order to maintain a suit the allegations that are required to commence it must, if contested, be proved. It seems to me that to favor the first inference over the second is to prefer the eccentric to the routine. It is well ingrained in the law that subject-matter jurisdiction can be called into question *either* by challenging the sufficiency of the allegation or by challenging the accuracy of the jurisdictional facts alleged. *See, e.g., Land v. Dollar*, 330 U.S. 731, 735, n. 4 (1947). Had Congress intended us to eliminate the second form of challenge, and to create an extraordinary regime in which the jurisdictional fact consists of a good-faith belief, it seems to me it would have delivered those instructions in more clear fashion than merely specifying how a lawsuit can be commenced.

In my view, therefore, the issue to be resolved by the Court of Appeals on remand of this suit is not whether the allegation of a continuing violation on the day suit was brought was made in good faith after reasonable inquiry, but whether petitioner was in fact "in violation" on the date suit was brought. The phrase in § 505(a), "to be in violation," unlike the phrase "to be violating" or "to have committed a violation," suggests a state rather than an act—the opposite of a state of compliance. A good or lucky day is not a state of compliance. Nor is the dubious state in which a past effluent problem is not recurring at the moment but the cause of that problem has not been completely and clearly eradicated. When a company has violated an effluent standard or limitation, it remains, for purposes of § 505(a), "in violation" of that standard or limitation so long as it has not put in place remedial measures that clearly eliminate the cause of the violation. It does not suffice to defeat subject-matter jurisdiction that the success of the attempted remedies becomes clear months or even weeks after the suit is filed. Subject-matter jurisdiction "depends on the state of things at the time of the action brought"; if it existed when the suit was brought, "subsequent events" cannot "ous[t]" the court of jurisdiction. *Mullan v. Torrance*, 9 Wheat 537, 539 (1824). It is this requirement of clarity of cure for a past violation, contained in the phrase "to be in violation," rather than a novel theory of subject-matter jurisdiction by good-faith allegation, that meets the Court's concern for "the practical difficulties of detecting and proving chronic episodic violations."

Thus, I think the question on remand should be whether petitioner had taken remedial steps that had clearly achieved the effect of curing all past violations by the time suit was brought. I cannot claim that the Court's standard and mine would differ greatly in their practical application. They would, for example, almost certainly produce identical results in this lawsuit. This practical insignificance, however, makes all the more puzzling the Court's willingness to impute to Congress creation of an unprecedented scheme where that which must be alleged need not be proved.

NOTES AND QUESTIONS

1. **Allegations and Proof.** Why did Justice Scalia write separately in *Gwaltney*? What is the difference between his approach and Justice Marshall's? What proof would Justice Scalia require? What proof would Justice Marshall require? Could a plaintiff prevail under Justice Marshall's

approach but not under Justice Scalia's approach? Could the opposite happen? Under what circumstances?

2. **Establishing an Ongoing Violation Following *Gwaltney*.** In the aftermath of *Gwaltney*, courts have attempted to more clearly define the requirements for an ongoing violation. Citizen plaintiffs can establish an ongoing violation sufficient to confer jurisdiction in a variety of ways. *See, e.g., Friends of Sakonnet v. Dutra*, 738 F. Supp. 623 (D.R.I. 1990) (continued discharge sufficient even for previous owners); *PIRG of N.J., Inc. v. N.J. Expressway Auth.*, 822 F. Supp. 174 (D.N.J. 1992) (good faith allegations of continuing discharges sufficient); *Informed Citizens United, Inc. v. USX Corp.*, 36 F. Supp. 2d 375 (S.D. Tex. 1999) (illegally dumped fill material constitutes ongoing violation until removed). At the same time, many courts have denied theories for establishing ongoing violations on other grounds. *See, e.g., Conn. Coastal Fishermen's Ass'n v. Remington Arms Co.*, 989 F.2d 1305 (2d Cir. 1993) (decomposition of lead shot and clay targets not an ongoing violation); *Allen Cty. Citizens for the Env't, Inc. v. BP Oil Co.*, 762 F. Supp. 733 (N.D. Ohio 1991) (single, isolated exceedance insufficient as matter of law to be continuing violation), *aff'd*, 966 F.2d 1451 (6th Cir. 1992). Compliance after a suit is filed but before judgment is entered is sufficient to moot a suit for injunctive relief, but civil penalties could still be imposed for any violations ongoing at the time the complaint was filed or subsequent violations. *See Atl. States Legal Found., Inc. v. Pan Am. Tanning Corp.*, 993 F.2d 1017 (2d Cir. 1993). Similarly, a government enforcement action may moot a citizen's claim for injunctive relief but not a claim for civil penalties based on ongoing violations. *See Comfort Lake Ass'n, Inc. v. Dresel Contracting, Inc.*, 138 F.3d 351, 356 (8th Cir. 1998). For a more complete discussion of these cases, see Deborah F. Buckman, Annotation, *Requirement that There Be Continuing Violation to Maintain Citizen Suit Under Federal Environmental Protection Statutes—Post-Gwaltney Cases*, 158 A.L.R. FED. 519 (1999).

3. **Past Violations: CAA Amendments of 1990.** Following the *Gwaltney* decision, Congress amended the CAA in 1990 to explicitly allow citizen suits based solely on prior violations. Under the current version of the CAA citizen suit provision, a citizen suit may be brought "against any person . . . who is alleged to have violated (if there is evidence that the alleged violation has been repeated) or to be in violation of (A) an emission standard or limitation under this chapter or (B) an order issued by the Administrator or a State with respect to such a standard or limitation." 42 U.S.C. § 7604(a)(1). Is it difficult to prove an ongoing violation? If a citizen suit cannot be brought for a wholly past violation, does that undermine the punitive goals of environmental laws? Note that the federal or state government has always been able to bring suit for a past violation under the CAA and the CWA. What added benefit does the citizen suit provision bring?

4. **Citizen Suits Under RCRA.** RCRA contains two citizen suit provisions. The first, called the "citizen enforcement action," *Marrero Hernandez v. Esso Standard Oil Co.*, 597 F. Supp. 2d 272, 279 (D.P.R. 2009), has the same "to be in violation" language as the CWA. 42 U.S.C. § 6972(a)(1)(A). Courts, therefore, have interpreted that section to require

that plaintiffs establish that the defendant is currently in violation of a "permit, standard, regulation, condition, requirement, prohibition, or order" for jurisdiction to be found. *See ABB Indus. Sys., Inc. v. Prime Tech., Inc.*, 120 F.3d 351 (2d Cir. 1997); *see also Conn. Coastal Fishermen's Ass'n*, 989 F.2d 1305 (dismissing claim under § 6972(a)(1)(A) because the "claim alleges a 'wholly past' RCRA violation"). The citizen enforcement action provision also presents a question as to who can be considered a defendant. There is currently a split between district courts regarding whether suits can be brought against former owners for a continuing violation. *Compare Bd. of County Comm'rs v. Brown Group Retail, Inc.*, 598 F. Supp. 2d 1185, 1201 (D. Colo. 2009) (holding former owners cannot "be in violation," and therefore cannot be subject to a citizen suit), *with Scarlett & Assocs., Inc. v. Briarcliff Ctr. Partners, LLC*, 2009 WL 3151089, at *12 (N.D. Ga. 2009) (holding that violations which continue after sale can subject former owners to citizen suits). For a discussion of this conflict and its basis in the majority's reasoning in *Gwaltney*, see Michael F. Hearn, Note, *One Person's Waste is Another Person's Liability: Closing the Liability Loophole in RCRA's Citizen Enforcement Action*, 42 McGeorge L. Rev. 467 (2010–2011).

The second citizen suit provision of RCRA authorizes citizen suits to be brought against any violator "who has contributed or who is contributing to the past or present handling, storage, treatment, transportation, or disposal of any solid or hazardous waste which may present an imminent and substantial endangerment to health or the environment." 42 U.S.C. § 6972(a)(1)(B). This provision, added to RCRA by the Hazardous and Solid Waste Amendments of 1984, Pub. L. No. 98–616, 98 Stat. 3221, is modeled on a similar provision giving EPA authority to bring suit when disposal presents an "imminent and substantial endangerment to public health or the environment." 42 U.S.C. § 6973(a). Courts have found that the language of this section ("may . . . endanger") requires only "a reasonable prospect of future harm . . . to engage the gears of RCRA." *Me. People's Alliance v. Mallinckrodt, Inc.*, 471 F.3d 277, 296 (1st Cir. 2006).

5.   Citizen Suits Under EPCRA. The language used in the citizen suit provision of EPCRA is not the same as that used in the CWA and RCRA. It lacks the "pervasive use of the present tense throughout" found to be significant in *Gwaltney*. 484 U.S. at 59. The venue provision even refers to violations that have allegedly "occurred." 42 U.S.C. § 11046(b)(1). This language has been interpreted by a number of lower courts to mean that the provision should be interpreted to allow suits for past violations despite *Gwaltney*. *See Atl. States Legal Found., Inc. v. Whiting Roll-Up Door Mfg. Corp.*, 772 F. Supp. 745 (W.D.N.Y. 1991) (holding that EPCRA citizen suit provision does provide jurisdiction for wholly past violations); *Del. Valley Toxics Coal. v. Kurz-Hastings, Inc.*, 813 F. Supp. 1132 (E.D. Pa. 1993) (same). What explains the inconsistency in Congress providing for citizen suits for past violations under some statutes but not under others? Is the lack of consistency likely to be an oversight or is it intentional?

6.   Citizen Suits and Preclusion. The Court in *Gwaltney* argued that "[p]ermitting citizen suits for wholly past violations of the [Clean Water] Act could undermine the supplementary role envisioned for the citizen suit."

Gwaltney, 484 U.S. at 60. The Court argued that if a citizen could bring suit for civil penalties months or years after EPA or the state, in an action for the same violation, intentionally chose to forgo seeking civil penalties on the condition that the entity in violation take some extreme corrective action that would not otherwise be required, then that would severely limit EPA and state enforcement agencies discretion to choose alternative enforcement solutions. *See id.* Why does the Court think that a citizen suit would be barred had EPA or the state enforcement agency previously imposed civil penalties, but not if they chose a different type of settlement? Is it because with that sort of settlement, the bar to commencement of citizen suits when "the Administrator or State has commenced and is diligently prosecuting a civil action in a court" will not be met?

Most of the citizen suit provisions in environmental statutes are based on the CAA. These provisions include a bar to citizen suits where "the Administrator or a State has commenced and is diligently prosecuting a civil action in a court of the United States or a State to require compliance." 42 U.S.C. § 7604(b)(1)(B). There is some variation among the statutes, however, as described by Jeffrey Miller:

> There are ... four variations among the bar elements of the preclusion device in the citizen suit provisions. First, the citizen suit provisions of statutes not envisioning a state implementation role do not bar citizen suits because of a state action. Second, several of the citizen suit provisions bar citizen suits when EPA has commenced and is diligently prosecuting a criminal action. Third, some citizen suit provisions bar citizen suits if EPA has commenced assessing an administrative penalty or has commenced and is diligently prosecuting the assessment of an administrative penalty. Finally, RCRA bars some citizen suits if EPA or states have commenced one of a variety of judicial or administrative remedial actions under either RCRA or CERCLA.

Jeffrey G. Miller, *Theme and Variations in Statutory Preclusions Against Successive Environmental Enforcement Actions by EPA and Citizens: Part I: Statutory Bars in Citizen Suit Provisions*, 28 HARV. ENVTL. L. REV. 401, 419 (2004) (footnotes omitted). Miller further suggests that the diligent prosecution requirement actually raises five distinct questions:

> (1) What government entities may act to bar a citizen suit? (2) What government actions may bar a citizen suit? (3) When must the government commence an action to bar a citizen suit? (4) How diligently must the government prosecute an action to bar a citizen suit? (5) What citizen suits may a government action bar?

Id. at 427. While only a civil action will preclude a citizen suit under the CAA, RCRA gives preclusive effect to a range of federal and state actions. *Id.* at 435. Determining whether federal or state authorities are diligently prosecuting an action is largely a factual determination, and "[t]he real question . . . is whether the government is moving steadily, with reasonable speed, energy, effectiveness and professionalism to secure compliance, a question that courts are in a uniquely experienced position to determine." *Id.*

at 464–65 (footnotes omitted); *see also Me. People's Alliance v. Mallinckrodt*, 471 F.3d 277 (1st Cir. 2006) (describing the four ways the EPA can preempt a RCRA citizen suit), *cert. denied*, 552 U.S. 816 (2007). If an enforcement action is filed subsequent to a citizen suit, should the citizen be able to intervene? Why is this significant? *See United States v. Doe Run Res. Corp.*, 2011 WL 1771007 (E.D. Mo. 2011) (holding that allowing citizen to intervene in enforcement action would give citizens "multiple days in court on the same issue"). Might there be strategic reasons to intervene rather than try to maintain a separate suit? *See* Steven C. Anderson, Note, *Stop Swinging for the Fences: An Argument for Citizen Intervention in CWA Enforcement Actions*, 29 J. LAND RESOURCES & ENVTL. L. 377 (2009). For a discussion of how the "diligent prosecution" standard limits citizen suits, see Will Reisinger et al., *Environmental Enforcement and the Limits of Cooperative Federalism: Will Courts Allow Citizen Suits to Pick up the Slack*, 20 DUKE ENVTL. L. & POL'Y F. 1, 51–56 (2010).

Under CERCLA, an analogous provision bars citizen suits until after remedial action has been completed. 42 U.S.C. § 9613(h). While the language of this section merely bars "challenges" to removal and remediation orders, courts have found that citizen suits seeking civil penalties count as a "challenge." *See, e.g.*, *Pakootas v. Teck Cominco Metals, Ltd.*, 646 F.3d 1214, 1223 (9th Cir. 2011). What happens when such actions span decades? One court has found that decades of testing, with no remedial action plan, is not sufficient to bar a citizen suit for CERCLA violations. *Frey v. EPA*, 403 F.3d 828 (7th Cir. 2005) ("EPA cannot preclude review by simply pointing to ongoing testing and investigation, with no clear end in sight."). Other courts, however, have refused to follow the Seventh Circuit's approach. *See Cannon v. Gates*, 538 F.3d 1328 (10th Cir. 2008), cert. denied, 556 U.S. 1151 (2009). What complications might arise under *Gwaltney* if citizen suits are barred both during remediation, under § 113(h), and after violations have occurred? For a discussion of these issues, see Theresa Sauer, Note, *DANGER! Bombs May Be Present. See also* Cannon v. Gates*: A Jammed* Cannon *Preempts Citizen Suit Indefinitely*, 86 DENV. U. L. REV. 1215 (2008–2009).

What happens when a citizen believes that the civil penalty or other remedial aspect of the administrative or judicial decree or settlement, resulting from a prior enforcement action, is unacceptably low? Where the statute allows citizen suits to be brought for wholly past violations, does the common law doctrine of claim preclusion keep citizens from suing under these circumstances? *See Atl. States Legal Found., Inc. v. Eastman Kodak Co.*, 933 F.2d 124, 127 (2d Cir. 1991) ("A citizen suing pursuant to Section 505 of the Act . . . may not revisit the terms of a settlement reached by competent state authorities without regard to the probability of a continuation of the violations alleged in its complaint."); *see also Comfort Lake Ass'n, Inc. v. Dresel Contracting, Inc.*, 138 F.3d 351, 357 (8th Cir. 1998) ("[A]n administrative enforcement agreement between EPA or [the state agency] and the polluter will preclude a pending citizen suit claim for civil penalties if the agreement is the result of a diligently prosecuted enforcement process, however informal."). What if a citizen brings a suit that results in a settlement that is unacceptable to the government? *See* 42 U.S.C.

§ 7604(c)(2) (CAA); *see also, Sierra Club, Inc. v. Elec. Controls Design, Inc.*, 909 F.2d 1350, 1356 n.8 (9th Cir. 1990) ("The legislative history [of § 505(c)(3) of the CWA] indicates only that Congress rejected a clause specifically disclaiming that the United States could be bound by judgments in cases to which it is not a party because the proposed clause restated current law and was unnecessary. . . . Accordingly, the United States would not be bound by the proposed consent judgment in this action and could bring its own enforcement action at any time."). For a discussion of these and other issues see William V. Luneburg, *Claim Preclusion as it Affects Non-Parties to Clean Air Act Enforcement Actions: The Ghosts of* Gwaltney, 10 WIDENER L. REV. 113 (2003). *See also* Justin Vickers, *Res Judicata Claim Preclusion of Properly Filed Citizen Suits*, 104 NW. U. L. REV. 1623 (2010).

7.   Citizen Suits for Non-Discretionary Agency Action. In addition to citizen suits for damages or injunctive relief, as described *supra*, many citizen suit provisions in environmental statutes allow for suits against the Administrator for a failure to perform non-discretionary duties. *See, e.g.*, 42 U.S.C. § 1365(a)(2) (CWA); 42 U.S.C. § 6972(a)(2) (RCRA); 42 U.S.C. § 7604(a)(2) (CAA), 42 U.S.C. § 9659(a)(2) (CERCLA). What counts as a non-discretionary duty? While there is no clear rule, the failure to bring a particular enforcement action is almost certainly not a non-discretionary duty. *See, e.g., Sierra Club v. Whitman*, 268 F.3d 898 (9th Cir. 2001) ("[T]he Clean Water Act leaves it to the discretion of the EPA Administrator whether to find violations and to take enforcement action, and that these discretionary decisions are not subject to judicial review."). The D.C. Circuit has refused to decide whether a date-specific deadline is necessary to create a non-discretionary duty, or whether agency regulations can create non-discretionary duties for the purpose of citizen suits. *See Sierra Club v. EPA*, 475 F. Supp. 2d 29, 33 (D.D.C. 2007); *Nat'l Wildlife Fed'n v. Browner*, 127 F.3d 1126, 1128 (D.C. Cir. 1997). For a discussion of the impact and potential advantages and disadvantages of these "agency-forcing" citizen suits, see Robert L. Glicksman, *The Value of Agency-Forcing Citizen Suits to Enforce Nondiscretionary Duties*, 10 WIDENER L. REV. 353 (2004). Note that these provisions are different than the more general judicial review provisions of environmental statutes, which are subject to pre-enforcement review, discussed Section 2.B, *infra*.

8.   Citizen Suits and Sovereign Immunity. In addition to acting as enforcers of environmental laws, federal and state actors that contribute to pollution could be potential defendants in citizen suit enforcement actions. The doctrine of sovereign immunity, embodied in the Eleventh Amendment to the U.S. Constitution, however, places limits on when citizens can sue federal and state governments. When Congress has unequivocally waived its immunity, suits may proceed against the federal government. *See United States v. Mitchell*, 445 U.S. 535 (1980). The Supreme Court has found that the citizen suit provisions of environmental laws have been sufficiently unequivocal to waive sovereign immunity against the federal government. *See U.S. Dept. of Energy v. Ohio*, 503 U.S. 607, 613–14 (1992) (holding that, for the CWA and RCRA, the "explicit authorizations for suits against the United States will likewise be effective, since those sections concededly authorize coercive sanctions against the National Government"). However, courts have been more likely to grant sovereign immunity to individual states sued under the citizen suit provisions of the environmental laws. *See* Reisinger et al., *supra*, at 42–51 (analyzing a 4th Circuit decision, *Bragg v. West Virginia Coal Ass'n*, 248 F.3d 275, 298 (4th Cir. 2001), limiting Clean Water Act citizen suits against states); Hope Babcock, *The Effect of the United States Supreme Court's Eleventh Amendment Jurisprudence on Clean Water Act Citizen Suits: Muddied Waters*, 83 ORE. L. REV. 47 (2004) (arguing that the 11th Amendment continues to bar citizen suits against state governments).

9. Remedies in Citizen Suits. As in the case of enforcement actions brought by the federal or state governments, the remedies available for successful citizen suit enforcement actions are generally penalties or injunctive relief. *See, e.g.*, 33 U.S.C. 1365 (CWA) ("The district courts shall have jurisdiction . . . to enforce such an effluent standard or limitation, or such an order, or to order the Administrator to perform such act or duty, as the case may be, and to apply any appropriate civil penalties. . . ."). The Seventh Circuit has affirmed that courts have discretion to grant either or both remedies in citizen suit cases. *See Sierra Club v. Franklin County Power of Ill.*, 546 F.3d 918, 935 (7th Cir. 2008) (interpreting CAA remedy language, which is identical to the corresponding CWA language), *cert. denied*, 557 U.S. 936 (2009). However, like federal and state enforcement actions, any penalties collected through citizen suits go to the U.S. Treasury and not to the citizen that brought suit. *See Friends of the Earth v. Laidlaw Envtl. Servs.*, 528 U.S. 167, 201 (2000) ("[T]he remedy is a statutorily specified 'penalty' for past violations, payable entirely to the United States Treasury."). How might this requirement change incentives for diligent enforcement?

Unlike other environmental laws, RCRA does not provide for a general damages remedy. *Meghrig v. KFC Western, Inc.*, 516 U.S. 479 (1996). Some courts, however, have found a way around this limit, holding that citizen enforcers can, through injunction, recover cleanup costs for the remediation of immediate and substantial endangerment following a RCRA violation. *See, e.g.*, *Gilroy Canning Co. v. Cal. Canners & Growers*, 15 F. Supp. 2d 943 (N.D. Cal. 1998). Other courts, however, have rejected such reasoning. *See Avondale Fed. Savings Bank v. Amoco Oil Co.*, 997 F. Supp. 1073, 1076 (N.D. Ill. 1998), *aff'd*, 170 F.3d 692 (7th Cir. 1999).

10. Citizen Suits and Attorneys' Fees. If environmental organizations are not entitled to monetary awards, even if successful, why might they bring citizen suits anyhow? In addition to a public-interest motivation, publicity benefits, and the potential for injunctive relief to mitigate harm to members (which may not alone be sufficient to sustain these non-profits during expensive multi-year litigation), environmental organizations are generally eligible to collect attorneys' fees. *See, e.g.*, 42 U.S.C. § 1365(d) (CWA); 42 U.S.C. § 7604(d) (CAA); 42 U.S.C. § 9659(f) (CERCLA). In fact, the threshold for an award of attorneys' fees in environmental litigation is relatively low. Unlike in civil rights statutes, a party need not prevail to collect attorneys' fees. Interpreting the language of the Clean Air Act allowing for fees "whenever the court determines such award is appropriate," the Supreme Court has held that unsuccessful plaintiffs may not be awarded fees but partially successful plaintiffs may. *Ruckelshaus v. Sierra Club*, 463 U.S. 680 (1983). Should unsuccessful parties be allowed to collect attorneys' fees? Partially successful parties? Would a requirement of success discourage socially beneficial suits? Or does the lack of a requirement encourage frivolous litigation? For a discussion of how this interpretation has affected citizen suit enforcement, see Reisinger et al., *supra*, at 29–34. For a discussion of the circuit split in interpreting similar language in the Clean Water Act, see Joshua E. Hollander, *Fee-Shifting Provisions in Environmental Statutes: What They Are, How They Are Interpreted, and Why They Matter*, 23 GEO. J. LEGAL ETHICS 633 (2010).

Are there additional concerns with allowing citizen suit plaintiffs to collect fees? The Ninth Circuit has refused to award attorneys' fees to plaintiffs who have a financial interest in citizen suit litigation. *See Western States Petroleum Ass'n v. EPA*, 87 F.3d 280 (9th Cir. 1996) (arguing that Congress did not intend the award of attorneys' fees to benefit economically advantaged parties who would have litigated anyway). The Tenth Circuit disagreed in *Pound v. Airosol Co.*, 498 F.3d 1089 (10th Cir. 2007). In that case a producer of insecticide sued a competitor for failing to meet CAA standards relating to ozone-depleting products. The court held that such suits, regardless of intent, are in the public interest of enforcing the nation's environmental laws and therefore should not be barred. Should the motive of a citizen suit matter in the award of fees? For a discussion of these issues, see Michel Lee, *Attorneys' Fees in Environmental Citizen Suits and the Economically Benefited Plaintiff: When are Attorneys' Fees and Costs Appropriate*, 26 PACE ENVTL. L. REV. 495 (2009). *See also* Caroline C. Owings, Pound v. Airosol Co.: *Are Attorney Fees Appropriate When a Claimant Brings Suit for Personal Economic Reasons Rather Than to Promote the Goals of the Clean Air Act*, 31 AM. J. TRIAL ADVOC. 441 (2007–2008); Mark Tannahill, Note, *Fee-Shifting Provisions and the Clean Air Act: Should Financially-Motivated Plaintiffs be Barred from Recovering Fees*, 49 SANTA CLARA L. REV. 863 (2009).

11. Citizen Suits and Politics. Beyond the award of attorneys' fees, environmental groups could be motivated to bring citizen suits in order to force agencies shirking their responsibilities to act. Even before taking office, President Trump's administration has promised to roll back environmental regulations. King and Spalding, Client Alert: Environmental Citizen Suits— A Growing Trend Under the Trump Administration (Nov. 16, 2017). Given this campaign promise, environmental groups have received record amounts of new donations, which has resulted in increased resources to bring citizen suits. James Smith, *Private Environmental Litigation: Will We See A Trump/Pruitt Effect?*, 17 AM. BAR. ASS'N SECTION ENV'T, ENERGY, & RESOURCES 14, 15 (2018). These new resources have already brought about more—and more creative—citizen suits under CWA, CAA, and RCRA. *Id.*; *see, e.g., Ohio Valley Envtl. Coal. v. Fola Coal Co.*, 845 F.3d 133 (4th Cir. 2017) (suing under CWA citizen suit provision to enforce company's water quality permit); *Sierra Club v. Chesapeake Operating, LLC*, 248 F. Supp. 3d

1194 (W.D. Okla. 2017) (suing under RCRA citizen suit provision, arguing that earthquakes caused by fracking create "imminent and substantial endangerment"); *see generally* Sara Mogharabi et al., *Environmental Citizen Suits in the Trump Era*, 32 NAT. RESOURCES & ENV'T 3 (2017). What are the limitations to relying on citizen suits to enforce environmental regulations?

F. SETTLEMENTS

The standard remedy for a violation of the environmental statutes is monetary penalties paid to the U.S. Treasury. Plaintiffs in citizen suits tend to dislike this remedy because it does not address the local harm caused by the offense. They generally prefer that the violator fund local projects that benefit the environment. Thus, the parties to the litigation often reach settlement agreements prior to the issuance of a final judgment. These agreements do not always include a civil penalty paid to the Treasury. The following case addresses this practice.

Sierra Club, Inc. v. Electronic Controls Design, Inc.
909 F.2d 1350 (9th Cir. 1990).

■ Before GOODWIN, CHIEF JUDGE, and FERGUSON and FERNANDEZ, CIRCUIT JUDGES.

■ GOODWIN, CHIEF JUDGE:

Sierra Club, Inc. appeals the refusal to enter a proposed consent judgment in its citizens' suit against Electronic Controls Design (ECD) for alleged violations of the Federal Water Pollution Control Act ("Clean Water Act" or "the Act"), 33 U.S.C. § 1365 (1988). We reverse.

On February 23, 1987, the Sierra Club filed a citizens' suit against ECD under section 505 of the Clean Water Act, 33 U.S.C. § 1365. The complaint alleged that ECD violated section 301(a) of the Act, 33 U.S.C. § 1311(a), by discharging pollutants from its printed circuit board manufacturing plant into the Molalla River via Milk Creek, in violation of the terms of ECD's National Pollutant Discharge Elimination System (NPDES) permit.

On September 30, 1988, the parties filed a Stipulation for Entry of Consent Judgment. In the proposed judgment, ECD agreed to: (1) comply with the terms of its NPDES permit and to terminate all discharges if it violates its permit after June 1, 1989; (2) pay $45,000 to various identified private environmental organizations for their efforts to maintain and protect water quality in Oregon; (3) pay additional sums to these organizations if ECD violates its permit between September 1, 1988, and June 1, 1989; and (4) pay $5000 to the Sierra Club for attorney and expert witness fees. In the consent judgment ECD did not admit any violation, and none was established.

The United States filed an objection to the proposed consent judgment, arguing that the proposed judgment was illegal because it contained no requirement that ECD make payments to the U.S. treasury. The Clean Water Act authorizes the imposition of civil penalties only if paid to the U.S. Treasury. The district court concluded that the payments to be made under the proposed consent judgment were civil penalties within the meaning of the Act and therefore refused to enter the order.

Recognizing "that Congress encourages settlements that put money directly to use in protecting the environment", the court also reasoned that a settlement could dictate that money be "channeled towards environmental projects, but perhaps not through private entities [such as those in this proposed consent judgment]." Accordingly, the court indicated that it would approve a consent judgment designating the Oregon Water Quality Program as the "civil penalty recipient." . . .

We agree with the district court that if the payments required under the proposed consent decree are civil penalties within the meaning of the Clean Water Act, they may be paid only to the U.S. treasury. We disagree, however, that the payments are civil penalties. No violation of the Act was found or determined by the proposed settlement judgment. When a defendant agrees before trial to make payments to environmental organizations without admitting liability, the agreement is simply part of an out-of-court settlement which the parties are free to make. . . .

While it is clear that a court cannot order a defendant in a citizens' suit to make payments to an organization other than the U.S. treasury, this prohibition does not extend to a settlement agreement whereby the defendant does not admit liability and the court is not ordering non-consensual monetary relief. "[C]onsent decrees bear some of the earmarks of judgments entered after litigation. At the same time, because their terms are arrived at through mutual agreement of the parties, consent decrees also closely resemble contracts." *Local No. 93, International Ass'n of Firefighters, AFL-CIO v. City of Cleveland*, 478 U.S. 501, 519 (1986).

Because of the unique aspects of settlements, a district court should enter a proposed consent judgment if the court decides that it is fair, reasonable and equitable and does not violate the law or public policy. *See Citizens for a Better Environment v. Gorsuch*, 718 F.2d 1117, 1125–26 (D.C.Cir. 1983), *cert. denied*, 467 U.S. 1219 (1984); *cf. Davis v. City and County of San Francisco*, 890 F.2d 1438, 1444–45 (9th Cir. 1989) (district court reviews proposed consent decree in a class action suit brought under Fed. R. Civ. P. 23(c) to determine whether the settlement is "fundamentally fair, adequate and reasonable").

In *Local No. 93*, the Supreme Court upheld a district court's order entering a consent decree that went beyond the type of relief provided by the civil rights statute under which the suit had been brought. 478 U.S. 501. The Court stated that "a federal court is not necessarily barred from entering a consent decree merely because the decree provides broader relief than the court could have awarded after a trial." 478 U.S. at 525.

As long as the consent decree comes " 'within the general scope of the case made by the pleadings,' " furthers "the objectives upon which the law is based," and does not "violate[ ] the statute upon which the complaint was based," the parties' agreement may be entered by the court. *Id.* at 525–26 (quoting *Pacific R. Co. v. Ketchum*, 101 U.S. 289, 297, 25 L. Ed. 932 (1880) (citations omitted)).

The consent decree agreed to by the Sierra Club and ECD comes within the scope of the pleadings, furthers the broad objectives upon which the complaint was based and does not violate the Clean Water Act. The Sierra Club's complaint was based upon the allegation that ECD was not in compliance with the Clean Water Act and was polluting the Oregon waters. The district court found that compelling ECD to comply with the terms of its permit or cease all discharges is "in the public interest." *Sierra Club*, 703 F. Supp. at 878. It also acknowledged that the environmental organizations that will receive funds under the proposed consent judgment "will apply the money in ways that will help further the goals of the Act." *Id.* Moreover, as the court noted, "Congress 'encourages' settlements of this type 'which preserve the punitive nature of enforcement actions while putting the funds collected to use on behalf of environmental protection.' " *Id.* at 877.

The Clean Water Act also does not render the proposed consent judgment unlawful. The provisions of the Act provide no limitation on the type of payments to which parties to citizens' suits can agree in a settlement. There is no indication that where a defendant agrees to a settlement it must also agree to pay penalties to the treasury. Likewise, the Act's legislative history reveals no Congressional intent that private parties be precluded from entering into settlements which do not require the defendant to tender civil penalties to the United States.

In 1987, Congress amended the Act to give the government more power to oversee and monitor the entry of consent judgments in citizens' suits. *See* 33 U.S.C. § 1365(c)(3). The new provision prohibits a court from entering proposed consent judgments in citizens' suit where the United States is not a party until forty-five days after the Attorney General and the Administrator of the EPA receive copies of the proposed consent. Congress did not take this opportunity to comment on the type of relief permitted in citizens' suit settlements and did not indicate that the settlements must include payment of civil penalties to the U.S. treasury. *See* 33 U.S.C. § 1365(c)(3).

We therefore find that the proposed consent decree furthers the purpose of the statute upon which the complaint was based and does not violate its terms or policy. The payments to the environmental organizations are not in recognition of liability under the Clean Water Act and are not civil penalties. No liability was ever judicially established. The district court abused its discretion in failing to enter the proposed consent judgment. *See Citizens for a Better Environment*, 718 F.2d at 1125–26 (district court should enter proposed consent decree if it is fair, reasonable and equitable and does not violate the law or public policy). Upon remand, the district court should enter the consent decree proposed by the Sierra Club and ECD and award costs and attorney fees pursuant to the decree.

NOTES AND QUESTIONS

1. **Settlement of Citizen Suits.** The settlement of citizen suits raises a number of important issues. When citizen suit provisions were first proposed, most of the opposition to them relied on a concern that they would lead to harassing or frivolous lawsuits, which the defendants would be forced to pay to settle rather than defend through costly litigation. In the end, the supporters of citizen suits were able to convince enough detractors that this situation would not occur.

Because the penalties imposed pursuant to a citizen suit are paid directly to the U.S. Treasury, citizen groups often might prefer settlement if they can reach favorable terms. Once penalties are paid into the Treasury, Congress has control over how that money will be spent. Citizen groups retain much more control over the terms of their settlements, so they can direct that funds be spent directly on remedying the environmental harm or on other environmentally beneficial activities. In whose interest might it be not to settle?

Is there potential for collusion between the parties? Could a citizen plaintiff settle for a smaller private benefit as opposed to a larger settlement that would benefit the environment more? Recall that citizens are entitled to claim attorneys' fees when they bring a successful (and sometimes even a partially successful) citizen suit. *See* Section 1.E, *supra*. Similarly, citizens can also often obtain attorneys' fees in their settlements. Should there be a concern that attorneys will encourage premature settlement in order to secure fees?

When citizen suits are initiated under most environmental statutes, the plaintiff is required to send the DOJ copies of their complaint when it is filed in federal court. The citizen suit provisions of the CAA and the CWA provide that consent judgments cannot be entered by the court until 45 days after a copy of the proposed consent judgment has been received by the Attorney General and the Administrator. *See* 42 U.S.C. § 7604(c)(3) (CAA); 33 U.S.C. § 1365(c)(3) (CWA). As a result, the government can intervene as a matter of right. Do these provisions solve the problem?

2. **Supplemental Environmental Projects.** Supplemental Environmental Projects (SEPs) are widely seen as a better outcome in many instances both for the environment and for the defendant. Because most penalties are paid directly to the U.S. Treasury, there is no direct benefit to the environment. While court-imposed stiff penalties may enhance deterrence, which may benefit the environment prospectively, such penalties would not address the harm that has already been done. Defendants may prefer to implement a SEP because it avoids costly litigation and also makes for improved public relations, particularly when the SEP provides a benefit to the local community.

EPA encourages the use of SEPs but has set out a number of constraints on what may be considered a SEP. For example, all of the projects must be environmentally beneficial, which means that they "must improve, protect, or reduce risk to public health or environment." EPA, SUPPLEMENTAL ENVIRONMENTAL PROJECTS POLICY 2015 UPDATE (2015). In determining whether a project has an environmental benefit, EPA identifies seven categories of projects qualifying as SEPs: public health, pollution prevention, pollution reduction, environmental restoration and protection, assessments and audits, environmental compliance promotion, and emergency planning and preparedness. *Id.* Additionally, EPA requires that projects have an adequate nexus to the violation, and may not be activities that the violator is otherwise legally required to perform by law. *Id.* EPA also identifies projects that are not allowable as SEPs, such as general public education and environmental awareness, studies that do not require the violator to further address the issues identified in the study, and donations or contributions. *Id.*

The nexus requirement is a very important component of any SEP. A project must meet one of the following criteria to be approved as a SEP:

> The project must be designed to reduce the likelihood of similar violations recurring in the future; or

> The project must reduce the adverse environmental or public health impact of the violation; or

> The project must reduce the overall risk to public health or the environment caused by the violation.

Memorandum from Walker B. Smith, Director, Office of Enforcement and Compliance Assurance, EPA, Importance of the Nexus Requirement in the Supplemental Environmental Projects Policy (2002). These limits have had a significant impact on the use of SEPs. According to a study by Kenneth Kristl, only 12 percent of 1992–2006 settlements that involve penalties used SEPs, a proportion that has decreased since the mid-1990s. *See* Kenneth T. Kristl, *Making a Good Idea Even Better: Rethinking the Limits on Supplemental Environmental Projects*, 31 VT. L. REV. 217, 244 (2007). Kristl argues that the nexus requirement has been one of the causes of the diminishing use of SEPs and argues for their abolition. *Id; see also* Benne C. Hutson & Amanda K. Short, *The Nexus Requirement for Supplemental Environmental Projects—The Emperor's New Clothes of Environmental Enforcement,* 3 CHARLOTTE L. REV. 67 (2011) (explaining the difficulties of the nexus requirement as it relates to TSCA violations). Do you agree? Are there any benefits to this requirement?

According to a 2005 study of the SEPs and practices of the fifty states, thirty states have instituted formal, published SEP policies in the form of legislation, executive agency regulation, or guidelines. Steven Bonorris et al., *Environmental Enforcement in the Fifty States: The Promise and Pitfalls of Supplemental Environmental Projects*, 11 HASTINGS W.-NW. J. ENVTL. L. & POL'Y 185, 188 (2005). Additionally, only two states have rejected the use of SEPs in settlements as a matter of policy or law. *Id.* In 1997, when the prior survey of state SEP practices was conducted, there were only nineteen states with formal policies or practices. *Id.* What does this trend show? Does it simply imply that the states are bowing to the inevitability of SEPs due to EPA's adoption of them as a favored settlement provision? Or is it evidence that the states agree that SEPs can benefit all parties, including the affected communities, industry, and regulators?

3. Tax Treatment of Settlements. Under the Internal Revenue Code, deductions to a business' taxable income can be made for "the ordinary and necessary expenses" incurred during the taxable year. 26 U.S.C. § 162(a). Section 162(f) provides, however, that "no deduction shall be allowed under subsection (a) for any fine or similar penalty paid to a government for the violation of any law." 26 U.S.C. § 162(f). Does this prohibition apply to settlements paid to a party other than the government? *See* John C. Smith, *Should Environmental Monetary Sanctions Be Tax Deductible?*, 26 B.C. ENVTL. AFF. L. REV. 435, 451 (1999); *see also Bailey v. Comm'r of Internal Revenue*, 756 F.2d 44, 46 (6th Cir. 1985) (finding that "the fact that the . . . district court, . . . permitted [the tax payer] to apply the . . . civil penalty toward the settlement of his potential liabilities in the multidistrict class action does not change the status of the payment as a civil penalty"); Rev. Rul. 74–148, 1974–1 C.B. 138 (concluding that a court-directed payment to a charitable organization instead of a government was a nondeductible fine under § 162(f)) (cited by Smith, *supra*, at 452). Additionally, the Treasury Regulations specifically include as a "fine or similar penalty," any amount "paid in settlement of the taxpayer's actual or potential liability for a fine or penalty." *See* Treas. Reg. § 1.162–21(b)(1)(iii). After reviewing the statute and the Internal Revenue Service's regulations, John C. Smith put forth the following summary:

> From the tax perspective, which environmental monetary sanctions are deductible is straight-forward, at least in theory. Criminal fines clearly are not deductible. On the other hand, compensatory payments clearly are deductible. If the statute giving rise to the claim has multiple purposes, the court must determine which purpose will govern. If a monetary sanction is comprised of two or more components, the tax treatment of each component of the monetary sanction must be determined separately. Generally, civil penalties imposed for purposes of enforcing the law and as punishment for the violation thereof are nondeductible payments under section 162(f), while civil penalties imposed to encourage prompt compliance with a requirement of the law, or as a remedial measure to compensate another party for expenses incurred as a result of the violation, fall outside the scope of the deduction prohibition in section 162(f).

Smith, *supra*, at 468 (footnotes omitted). From a policy perspective should a tax deduction be allowed for money spent on establishing SEPs? Wouldn't that be consistent with the purposes of the environmental statutes since it would allow for larger settlement agreements to remediate the harm and provide relief to the victims, while not changing the underlying economic burden on the violator? *See id.* at 437 (arguing "that it is better for the environment to allow a tax deductible $1,000,000 monetary sanction paid to establish a beneficial environmental project (*e.g.* a [SEP]) to remediate the harm caused by the violation, than it is to pay $650,000 into the U.S. Treasury.").

4. Settling Citizen Suits Against EPA. During the Trump administration, former EPA Administrator Scott Pruitt issued a directive ending "sue-and-settle" agreements. EPA, NEWS RELEASE, ADMINISTRATOR PRUITT ISSUES DIRECTIVE TO END EPA "SUE & SETTLE" (2017). Prior to this directive, EPA frequently entered into settlements in citizen suits when EPA had missed setting statutory deadlines. *See* Pat Gallagher, *Scott Pruitt and the Myth of "Sue and Settle,"* SIERRA, Oct. 18, 2017. How could this policy be advantageous to the agency?

2. ACCESS TO THE COURTS

A. STANDING

The law of standing establishes whether a litigant is entitled to have the court decide a particular case or controversy. *See Warth v. Seldin*, 422 U.S. 490, 498 (1975). Standing requirements are based on the concern about the proper role of the courts in a democratic society. They involve both constitutional limitations on federal-court jurisdiction and prudential limitations on its exercise. *See id.*

"In its constitutional dimension, standing imports justiciability: whether the plaintiff has made out a 'case or controversy' between himself and the defendant within the meaning of Art. III. This is the threshold question in every federal case, determining the power of the court to entertain the suit." *Id.* The Supreme Court has established that the "irreducible constitutional minimum of standing contains three elements": injury in fact, causal connection, and redressability. *Lujan v. Defenders of Wildlife*, 504 U.S. 555, 560 (1992). First, the plaintiff must allege and prove that she has suffered a harm that is concrete, particularized, and "actual or imminent, not 'conjectural' or 'hypothetical.'" *Id.* Second, the injury has to be "fairly . . . trace[able] to the challenged action of the defendant, and not . . . th[e] result [of] the independent action of some third party not before the court." *Simon v. E. Ky. Welfare Rights Org.*, 426 U.S. 26, 41–42 (1976). Third, the injury must likely be redressed by a court's favorable decision. *Id.,* at 38, 43.

Beyond the constitutional limitations, standing is limited by a set of principles that had traditionally been treated as prudential. *See Valley Forge Christian Coll. v. Americans United for Separation of Church & State*, 454 U.S. 464, 474 (1982). First, "the plaintiff generally must assert his own legal rights and interests, and cannot rest his claim to relief on the legal rights or interests of third parties." *Id.* (quoting *Warth*, 422 U.S. at 499). Second, "the Court has refrained from adjudicating 'abstract questions of wide public significance' which amount to 'generalized grievances,' pervasively shared and most appropriately addressed in the representative branches." *Id.* (quoting *Warth*, 422 U.S. at 499–500). "Finally, the Court has required that the plaintiff's complaint fall within 'the zone of interests to be protected or regulated by the statute or constitutional guarantee in question.' " *Id.* at 475 (quoting *Ass'n of Data Processing Serv. Orgs. v. Camp*, 397 U.S. 150, 153 (1970)). These principles are also founded in concerns about the proper role of the courts in a democratic society, "but unlike their constitutional counterparts, they can be modified or abrogated by Congress." *Bennett v. Spear*, 520 U.S. 154, 162 (1997) (citing *Warth*, 422 U.S. at 501).

In *Lexmark, Int'l, Inc. v. Static Control Components*, 572 U.S. 118, 127 (2014), the Supreme Court clarified the status of the "zone of interests" requirement: "Although we admittedly have placed that test under the 'prudential' rubric in the past, it does not belong there. . . . Whether a plaintiff comes within the 'zone of interests' is an issue that requires us to determine, using traditional tools of statutory interpretation, whether a legislatively conferred cause of action encompasses a particular plaintiff's claim." (citations omitted).

Several environmental acts contain citizen suit provisions, which typically state that "any person" can bring an action. *See, e.g.*, 33 U.S.C. § 1365 (1994) (CWA); 42 U.S.C. § 7604 (CAA); 42 U.S.C. § 11046(a)(1) (EPCRA); 42 U.S.C. § 6972 (RCRA); 42 U.S.C. § 300j–8 (SDWA); 16 U.S.C. § 1540(g) (ESA). These provisions have been held to abrogate or modify prudential standing principles. *See Bennett v. Spear*, 520 U.S. at 164 ("ESA's citizen-suit provision . . . negates the zone-of-interests test"); *Covington v. Jefferson County*, 358 F.3d 626, 638 n.13 (9th Cir. 2004) ("There is no prudential standing issue here because Congress has authorized citizen suit provisions for the violations of RCRA and CAA that the Covingtons alleged."); *Am. Soc'y for Prevention of Cruelty to Animals v. Ringling Bros. & Barnum & Bailey Circus*, 317 F.3d 334, 336 (D.C. Cir. 2003) ("The citizen-suit provision in the Endangered Species Act, by specifying that 'any person' may be a plaintiff, eliminates any prudential standing requirement.").

In his last decade on the Court, Justice Scalia attempted to convert the doctrine of "generalized grievance" from a prudential principle into a constitutional requirement grounded principally in Articles II and III. *See Lujan v. Defenders of Wildlife*, 504 U.S. 555, 573–78 (1992); *Friends of the Earth v. Laidlaw Envtl. Servs.*, 528 U.S. 167, 203 (2000) (Scalia, J., dissenting); *Hein v. Freedom From Religion Foundation, Inc.*, 551 U.S. 587, 619–20 (2007) (Scalia, J., concurring); *see also* Mark Gabel, *Generalized Grievances and Judicial Discretion*, 58 HASTINGS L.J. 1331 (2007). Under this approach, such congressional intent to allow citizens to sue without proving a concrete distinctive harm constitutes an affront to the President's constitutional duty to "take care that the Laws be faithfully executed." Article II § 3; *see Defenders of Wildlife*, 504 U.S. at 573–78. The following cases focus on the injury in fact and redressability requirements, as well as the treatment of "generalized grievances."

Lujan v. National Wildlife Federation

497 U.S. 871 (1990).

■ JUSTICE SCALIA delivered the opinion of the Court:

In this case we must decide whether respondent, the National Wildlife Federation (hereinafter respondent), is a proper party to challenge actions of the Federal Government relating to certain public lands.

Respondent filed this action in 1985 in the United States District Court for the District of Columbia against petitioners the United States Department of the Interior, the Secretary of the Interior, and the Director of the Bureau of Land Management (BLM), an agency within the Department. In its amended complaint, respondent alleged that petitioners had violated the Federal Land Policy and Management Act of 1976 (FLPMA), 43 U.S.C. § 1701 *et seq.* (1982 ed.), the National Environmental Policy Act of 1969 (NEPA) 42 U.S.C. § 4321 *et seq.*, and § 10(e) of the Administrative Procedure Act (APA), 5 U.S.C. § 706, in the course of administering what the complaint called the "land withdrawal review program" of the BLM. . . .

In 1976, Congress passed the FLPMA, which repealed many of the miscellaneous laws governing disposal of public land, 43 U.S.C. § 1701 *et seq.* (1982 ed.), and established a policy in favor of retaining public lands for multiple use management. It directed the Secretary to "prepare and maintain on a continuing basis an inventory of all public lands and their resource and other values," § 1711(a), required land use planning for public lands, and established criteria to be used for that purpose, § 1712. It provided that existing classifications of public lands were subject to review in the land use planning process, and that the Secretary could "modify or terminate any such classification consistent with such land use plans." § 1712(d). It also authorized the Secretary to "make, modify, extend or revoke" withdrawals. § 1714(a).* Finally it directed the Secretary, within 15 years, to review withdrawals in existence in 1976 in 11 Western States, § 1714(*l*)(1), and to "determine whether, and for how long, the continuation of the existing withdrawal of the lands would be, in his judgment, consistent with the statutory objectives of the programs for which the lands were dedicated and of the other relevant programs," § 1714(*l*)(2). The activities undertaken by the BLM to comply with these various provisions constitute what respondent's amended complaint styles the BLM's "land withdrawal review program," which is the subject of the current litigation. . . .

---

*   "The term 'withdrawal' means with-holding an area of Federal land from settlement, sale, location, or entry, under some or all of the general land laws, for the purpose of limiting activities under those laws in order to maintain other public values in the area or reserving the area for a particular public purpose or program; or transferring jurisdiction over an area of Federal land, other than 'property' governed by the Federal Property and Administrative Services Act, as amended from one department, bureau or agency to another department, bureau or agency." 43 U.S.C. § 1702(j).—ED.

In its complaint, respondent averred generally that the reclassification of some withdrawn lands and the return of others to the public domain would open the lands up to mining activities, thereby destroying their natural beauty. Respondent alleged that petitioners, in the course of administering the Nation's public lands, had violated the FLPMA by failing to "develop, maintain, and, when appropriate, revise land use plans which provide by tracts or areas for the use of the public lands," 43 U.S.C. § 1712(a) (1982 ed.); failing to submit recommendations as to withdrawals in the 11 Western States to the President, § 1714(*l*); failing to consider multiple uses for the disputed lands, § 1732(a), focusing inordinately on such uses as mineral exploitation and development; and failing to provide public notice of decisions, §§ 1701(a)(5), 1712(c)(9), 1712(f), and 1739(e). Respondent also claimed that petitioners had violated NEPA, which requires federal agencies to "include in every recommendation or report on . . . major Federal actions significantly affecting the quality of the human environment, a detailed statement by the responsible official on . . . the environmental impact of the proposed action." 42 U.S.C. § 4332(2)(C) (1982 ed.). Finally, respondent alleged that all of the above actions were "arbitrary, capricious, an abuse of discretion, or otherwise not in accordance with law," and should therefore be set aside pursuant to § 10(e) of the APA, 5 U.S.C. § 706. . . .

[T]he [district] court denied petitioners' motion under Rule 12(b) of the Federal Rules of Civil Procedure to dismiss the complaint for failure to demonstrate standing to challenge petitioners' actions under the APA, 5 U.S.C. § 702. App. to Pet. for Cert. 183a. The Court of Appeals affirmed both orders. *National Wildlife Federation v. Burford*, 835 F.2d 305 (1987). As to the motion to dismiss, the Court of Appeals found sufficient to survive the motion the general allegation in the amended complaint that respondent's members used environmental resources that would be damaged by petitioners' actions. *See id.*, at 312. It held that this allegation, fairly read along with the balance of the complaint, both identified particular land-status actions that respondent sought to challenge—since at least some of the actions complained of were listed in the complaint's appendix of Federal Register references—and asserted harm to respondent's members attributable to those particular actions. *Id.*, at 313. To support the latter point, the Court of Appeals pointed to the affidavits of two of respondent's members, Peggy Kay Peterson and Richard Erman, which claimed use of land "in the vicinity" of the land covered by two of the listed actions. Thus, the Court of Appeals concluded, there was "concrete indication that [respondent's] members use specific lands covered by the agency's Program and will be adversely affected by the agency's actions," and the complaint was "sufficiently specific for purposes of a motion to dismiss." *Ibid.* On petitions for rehearing, the Court of Appeals stood by its denial of the motion to dismiss and directed the parties and the District Court "to proceed with this litigation with dispatch." *National Wildlife Federation v. Burford*, 844 F.2d 889, 890 (1988).

Back before the District Court, petitioners again claimed, this time by means of a motion for summary judgment under Rule 56 of the Federal Rules of Civil Procedure . . . , that respondent had no standing to seek judicial review of petitioners' actions under the APA. After argument on this motion, and in purported response to the court's postargument request for additional briefing, respondent submitted four additional member affidavits pertaining to the issue of standing. The District Court rejected them as untimely, vacated the injunction and granted the Rule 56 motion to dismiss. . . . It found the Peterson and Erman affidavits insufficient to withstand the Rule 56 motion, even as to judicial review of the particular classification decisions to which they pertained. And even if they had been adequate for that limited purpose, the court said, they could not support respondent's attempted APA challenge to "each of the 1250 or so individual classification terminations and withdrawal revocations" effected under the land withdrawal review program. *National Wildlife Federation v. Burford*, 699 F.Supp. 327, 332 (DC 1988).

This time the Court of Appeals reversed. *National Wildlife Federation v. Burford*, 878 F.2d 422 (1989). It both found the Peterson and Erman affidavits sufficient in themselves and held that it was an abuse of discretion not to consider the four additional affidavits as well. The Court of Appeals also concluded that standing to challenge individual classification and withdrawal decisions conferred standing to challenge all such decisions under the land withdrawal review program. We granted certiorari. 493 U.S. 1042 (1990).

We first address respondent's claim that the Peterson and Erman affidavits alone suffice to establish respondent's right to judicial review of petitioners' actions. . . . [R]espondent claims a right to judicial review under § 10(a) of the APA, which provides:

"A person suffering legal wrong because of agency action, or adversely affected or aggrieved by agency action within the meaning of a relevant statute, is entitled to judicial review thereof." 5 U.S.C. § 702.

This provision contains two separate requirements. First, the person claiming a right to sue must identify some "agency action" that affects him in the specified fashion; it is judicial review "thereof" to which he is entitled. . . .

Second, the party seeking review under § 702 must show that he has "suffer[ed] legal wrong" because of the challenged agency action, or is "adversely affected or aggrieved" by that action "within the meaning of a relevant statute." Respondent does not assert that it has suffered "legal wrong," so we need only discuss the meaning of "adversely affected or aggrieved . . . *within the meaning of a relevant statute.*" . . . [W]e have said that to be "adversely affected or aggrieved . . . within the meaning" of a statute, the plaintiff must establish that the injury he complains of (*his* aggrievement, or the adverse effect *upon him*) falls within the "zone of interests" sought to be protected by the statutory provision whose violation forms the legal basis for his complaint. *See Clarke v. Securities Industry Assn.*, 479 U.S. 388, 396–397 (1987). . . .

We turn, then, to whether the specific facts alleged in the two affidavits considered by the District Court raised a genuine issue of fact as to whether an "agency action" taken by petitioners caused respondent to be "adversely affected or aggrieved . . . within the meaning of a relevant statute." . . .

The Peterson affidavit averred:

"My recreational use and aesthetic enjoyment of federal lands, particularly those in the vicinity of South Pass-Green Mountain, Wyoming have been and continue to be adversely affected in fact by the unlawful actions of the Bureau and the Department. In particular, the South Pass-Green Mountain area of Wyoming has been opened to the staking of mining claims and oil and gas leasing, an action which threatens the aesthetic beauty and wildlife habitat potential of these lands." App. to Pet. for Cert. 191a.

Erman's affidavit was substantially the same as Peterson's, with respect to all except the area involved; he claimed use of land "in the vicinity of Grand Canyon National Park, the Arizona Strip (Kanab Plateau), and the Kaibab National Forest." *Id.,* at 187a.

The District Court found the Peterson affidavit inadequate for the following reasons:

". . . This decision [W–6228] opened up to mining approximately 4500 acres within a two million acre area, the balance of which, with the exception of 2000 acres, has always been open to mineral leasing and mining. . . . There is no showing that Peterson's recreational use and enjoyment extends to the particular 4500 acres covered by the decision to terminate classification to the remainder of the two million acres affected by the termination. All she claims is that she uses lands 'in the vicinity.' The affidavit on its face contains only a bare allegation of injury, and fails to show specific facts supporting the affiant's allegation." 699 F. Supp., at 331 (emphasis in original).

The District Court found the Erman affidavit "similarly flawed."

"The magnitude of Erman's claimed injury stretches the imagination. . . . [T]he Arizona Strip consists of all lands in Arizona north and west of the Colorado River on approximately 5.5 million acres, an area one-eighth the size of the State of Arizona. Furthermore, virtually the entire Strip is and for many years has been open to uranium and other metalliferous mining. The revocation of withdrawal [in Public Land Order 6156] concerned only non-metalliferous mining in the western one-third of the Arizona Strip, an area possessing no potential for non-metalliferous mining." *Id.,* at 332.

The Court of Appeals disagreed with the District Court's assessment as to the Peterson affidavit (and thus found it unnecessary to consider the Erman affidavit) for the following reason:

> "If Peterson was not referring to lands in this 4500-acre affected area, her allegation of impairment to her use and enjoyment would be meaningless, or perjurious. . . . [T]he trial court overlooks the fact that unless Peterson's language is read to refer to the lands affected by the Program, the affidavit is, at best, a meaningless document.

> "At a minimum, Peterson's affidavit is ambiguous regarding whether the adversely affected lands are the ones she uses. When presented with ambiguity on a motion for summary judgment, a District Court must resolve any factual issues of controversy in favor of the nonmoving party. . . ." 878 F.2d, at 431.

That is not the law. In ruling upon a Rule 56 motion, "a District Court must resolve any factual issues of controversy in favor of the non-moving party" only in the sense that, where the facts specifically averred by that party contradict facts specifically averred by the movant, the motion must be denied. That is a world apart from "assuming" that general averments embrace the "specific facts" needed to sustain the complaint. As set forth above, Rule 56(e) provides that judgment "shall be entered" against the nonmoving party unless affidavits or other evidence "set forth specific facts showing that there is a genuine issue for trial." . . .

At the margins there is some room for debate as to how "specific" must be the "specific facts" that Rule 56(e) requires in a particular case. But where the fact in question is the one put in issue by the § 702 challenge here—whether one of respondent's members has been, or is threatened to be, "adversely affected or aggrieved" by Government action—Rule 56(e) is assuredly not satisfied by averments which state only that one of respondent's members uses unspecified portions of an immense tract of territory, on some portions of which mining activity has occurred or probably will occur by virtue of the governmental action. It will not do to "presume" the missing facts because without them the affidavits would not establish the injury that they generally allege. . . .

■ JUSTICE BLACKMUN, with whom JUSTICE BRENNAN, JUSTICE MARSHALL, and JUSTICE STEVENS join, dissenting:

In my view, the affidavits of Peggy Kay Peterson and Richard Loren Erman, in conjunction with other record evidence before the District Court on the motions for summary judgment, were sufficient to establish the standing of the National Wildlife Federation (Federation or NWF) to bring this suit. I also conclude that the District Court abused its discretion by refusing to consider supplemental affidavits filed after the hearing on the parties' cross-motions for summary judgment. I therefore would affirm the judgment of the Court of Appeals.

The Federation's asserted injury in this case rested upon its claim that the Government actions challenged here would lead to increased mining on public lands; that the mining would result in damage to the environment; and that the recreational opportunities of NWF's members would consequently be diminished. Abundant record evidence supported the Federation's assertion that on lands newly opened for mining, mining in fact would occur. Similarly, the record furnishes ample support for NWF's contention that mining activities can be expected to cause severe environmental damage to the affected lands. The District Court held, however, that the Federation had not adequately identified particular members who were harmed by the consequences of the Government's actions. . . . The majority, like the District Court, holds that the averments of Peterson and Erman were insufficiently specific to withstand a motion for summary judgment. Although these affidavits were not models of precision, I believe that they were adequate at least to create a genuine issue of fact as to the organization's injury. . . .

The requirement that evidence be submitted is satisfied here: The Federation has offered the sworn statements of two of its members. There remains the question whether the allegations in these affidavits were sufficiently precise to satisfy the requirements of Rule 56(e). The line of demarcation between "specific" and "conclusory" allegations is hardly a bright one. But, to my mind, the allegations contained in the Peterson and Erman affidavits, in the context of the record as a whole, were adequate to defeat a motion for summary judgment. These affidavits, as the majority acknowledges, were at least sufficiently precise to enable Bureau of Land Management (BLM) officials to identify the particular termination orders to which the affiants referred. See *ante*, at 3187. And the affiants averred that their "recreational use and aesthetic enjoyment of federal lands . . . have been and continue to be adversely affected in fact by the unlawful actions of the Bureau and the Department." App. to Pet. for Cert. 188a (Erman affidavit), 191a (Peterson affidavit). The question, it should be emphasized, is not whether the NWF has *proved* that it has standing to bring this action, but simply whether the materials before the District Court established "that there is a genuine issue for trial," see Rule 56(e), concerning the Federation's standing. In light of the principle that "[o]n summary judgment the inferences to be drawn from the underlying facts contained in [evidentiary] materials must be viewed in the light most favorable to the party opposing the motion," *United States v. Diebold, Inc.*, 369 U.S. 654, 655 (1962), I believe that the evidence before the District Court raised a genuine factual issue as to NWF's standing to sue.

No contrary conclusion is compelled by the fact that Peterson alleged that she uses federal lands "in the vicinity of South Pass-Green Mountain, Wyoming," App. to Pet. for Cert. 191a, rather than averring that she uses the precise tract that was recently opened to mining. The agency itself has repeatedly referred to the "South Pass-Green Mountain area" in describing the region newly opened to mining. Peterson's assertion that her use and enjoyment of federal lands *have been* adversely affected by the agency's decision to permit more extensive mining is, as the Court of Appeals stated, *National Wildlife Federation v. Burford*, 878 F.2d 422, 431 (1989), "meaningless, or perjurious" if the lands she uses do not include those harmed by mining undertaken pursuant to termination order W–6228. To read particular assertions within the affidavit in light of the document as a whole is, as the majority might put it, "a world apart" from "presuming" facts that are neither stated nor implied simply because without them the plaintiff would lack standing. The Peterson and Erman affidavits doubtless could have been more artfully drafted, but they definitely were sufficient to withstand the federal parties' summary judgment motion.

Lujan v. Defenders of Wildlife
504 U.S. 555 (1992).

■ JUSTICE SCALIA delivered the opinion of the Court with respect to Parts I, II, III-A, and IV, and an opinion with respect to Part III-B, in which THE CHIEF JUSTICE, JUSTICE WHITE, and JUSTICE THOMAS join:

This case involves a challenge to a rule promulgated by the Secretary of the Interior interpreting § 7 of the Endangered Species Act of 1973 (ESA), 87 Stat. 884, 892, as amended, 16 U.S.C. § 1536, in such fashion as to render it applicable only to actions within the United States or on the high seas. The . . . issue . . . is whether respondents here [(organizations dedicated to wildlife conservation and other environmental causes)] have standing to seek judicial review of the rule.

I

. . . The ESA instructs the Secretary of the Interior to promulgate by regulation a list of those species which are either endangered or threatened under enumerated criteria, and to define the critical habitat of these species. 16 U.S.C. §§ 1533, 1536. Section 7(a)(2) of the Act then provides, in pertinent part:

> "Each Federal agency shall, in consultation with and with the assistance of the Secretary [of the Interior], insure that any action authorized, funded, or carried out by such agency . . . is not likely to jeopardize the continued existence of any endangered species or threatened species or result in the destruction or adverse modification of habitat of such species which is determined by the Secretary, after consultation as

appropriate with affected States, to be critical." 16 U.S.C. § 1536(a)(2).

In 1978, the Fish and Wildlife Service (FWS) and the National Marine Fisheries Service (NMFS), on behalf of the Secretary of the Interior and the Secretary of Commerce respectively, promulgated a joint regulation stating that the obligations imposed by § 7(a)(2) extend to actions taken in foreign nations. 43 Fed. Reg. 874 (1978). The next year, however, the Interior Department began to reexamine its position. A revised joint regulation, reinterpreting § 7(a)(2) to require consultation only for actions taken in the United States or on the high seas, was proposed in 1983, 48 Fed. Reg. 29990, and promulgated in 1986, 51 Fed. Reg. 19926; 50 CFR 402.01 (1991).

Shortly thereafter, respondents, organizations dedicated to wildlife conservation and other environmental causes, filed this action against the Secretary of the Interior, seeking a declaratory judgment that the new regulation is in error as to the geographic scope of § 7(a)(2) and an injunction requiring the Secretary to promulgate a new regulation restoring the initial interpretation. The District Court granted the Secretary's motion to dismiss for lack of standing. The Court of Appeals for the Eighth Circuit reversed by a divided vote. On remand, the Secretary moved for summary judgment on the standing issue, and respondents moved for summary judgment on the merits. The District Court denied the Secretary's motion, on the ground that the Eighth Circuit had already determined the standing question in this case; it granted respondents' merits motion, and ordered the Secretary to publish a revised regulation. The Eighth Circuit affirmed. We granted certiorari. . . .

III

We think the Court of Appeals failed to apply the foregoing principles in denying the Secretary's motion for summary judgment. Respondents had not made the requisite demonstration of (at least) injury and redressability.

A

Respondents' claim to injury is that the lack of consultation with respect to certain funded activities abroad "increas[es] the rate of extinction of endangered and threatened species." Complaint ¶ 5, App. 13. Of course, the desire to use or observe an animal species, even for purely aesthetic purposes, is undeniably a cognizable interest for purpose of standing. See, *e.g., Sierra Club v. Morton*, 405 U.S., at 734. "But the 'injury in fact' test requires more than an injury to a cognizable interest. It requires that the party seeking review be himself among the injured." *Id.,* at 734–735. To survive the Secretary's summary judgment motion, respondents had to submit affidavits or other evidence showing, through specific facts, not only that listed species were in fact being threatened by funded activities abroad, but also that one or more of respondents' members would thereby be "directly" affected apart from their " 'special interest' in th[e] subject." *Id.*, at 735, 739. See generally *Hunt v. Washington State Apple Advertising Comm'n*, 432 U.S. 333, 343 (1977).

With respect to this aspect of the case, the Court of Appeals focused on the affidavits of two Defenders' members—Joyce Kelly and Amy Skilbred. Ms. Kelly stated that she traveled to Egypt in 1986 and "observed the traditional habitat of the endangered nile crocodile there and intend[s] to do so again, and hope[s] to observe the crocodile directly," and that she "will suffer harm in fact as the result of [the] American . . . role . . . in overseeing the rehabilitation of the Aswan High Dam on the Nile . . . and [in] develop [ing] . . . Egypt's . . . Master Water Plan." App. 101. Ms. Skilbred averred that she traveled to Sri Lanka in 1981 and "observed th[e] habitat" of "endangered species such as the Asian elephant and the leopard" at what is now the site of the Mahaweli project funded by the Agency for International Development (AID), although she "was unable to see any of the endangered species"; "this development project," she continued, "will seriously reduce endangered, threatened, and endemic species habitat including areas that I visited . . . [, which] may severely shorten the future of these species"; that threat, she concluded, harmed her because she "intend[s] to return to Sri Lanka in the future and hope[s] to be more fortunate in spotting at least the endangered elephant and leopard." *Id.*, at 145–146. When Ms. Skilbred was asked at a subsequent deposition if and when she had any plans to return to Sri Lanka, she reiterated that "I intend to go back to Sri Lanka," but confessed that she had no current plans: "I don't know [when]. There is a civil war going on right now. I don't know. Not next year, I will say. In the future." *Id.*, at 318.

We shall assume for the sake of argument that these affidavits contain facts showing that certain agency-funded projects threaten listed species—though that is questionable. They plainly contain no facts, however, showing how damage to the species will produce "imminent" injury to Mses. Kelly and Skilbred. That the women "had visited" the areas of the projects before the projects commenced proves nothing. . . . And the affiants' profession of an "inten[t]" to return to the places they had visited before—where they will presumably, this time, be deprived of the opportunity to observe animals of the endangered species—is simply not enough. Such "some day" intentions—without any description of concrete plans, or indeed even any specification of *when* the some day will be—do not support a finding of the "actual or imminent" injury that our cases require. See *supra*, at 2136.

Besides relying upon the Kelly and Skilbred affidavits, respondents propose a series of novel standing theories. The first, inelegantly styled "ecosystem nexus," proposes that any person who uses *any part* of a "contiguous ecosystem" adversely affected by a funded activity has standing even if the activity is located a great distance away. This approach, . . . is inconsistent with our opinion in *National Wildlife*

Federation, which held that a plaintiff claiming injury from environmental damage must use the area affected by the challenged activity and not an area roughly "in the vicinity" of it. 497 U.S., at 887–889; see also *Sierra Club*, 405 U.S., at 735. It makes no difference that the general-purpose section of the ESA states that the Act was intended in part "to provide a means whereby the ecosystems upon which endangered species and threatened species depend may be conserved," 16 U.S.C. § 1531(b). To say that the Act protects ecosystems is not to say that the Act creates (if it were possible) rights of action in persons who have not been injured in fact, that is, persons who use portions of an ecosystem not perceptibly affected by the unlawful action in question.

Respondents' other theories are called, alas, the "animal nexus" approach, whereby anyone who has an interest in studying or seeing the endangered animals anywhere on the globe has standing; and the "vocational nexus" approach, under which anyone with a professional interest in such animals can sue. . . . It is clear that the person who observes or works with a particular animal threatened by a federal decision is facing perceptible harm, since the very subject of his interest will no longer exist. It is even plausible—though it goes to the outermost limit of plausibility—to think that a person who observes or works with animals of a particular species in the very area of the world where that species is threatened by a federal decision is facing such harm, since some animals that might have been the subject of his interest will no longer exist, see *Japan Whaling Assn. v. American Cetacean Society*, 478 U.S. 221, 231, n. 4 (1986). It goes beyond the limit, however, and into pure speculation and fantasy, to say that anyone who observes or works with an endangered species, anywhere in the world, is appreciably harmed by a single project affecting some portion of that species with which he has no more specific connection.

B

Besides failing to show injury, respondents failed to demonstrate redressability. Instead of attacking the separate decisions to fund particular projects allegedly causing them harm, respondents chose to challenge a more generalized level of Government action (rules regarding consultation), the invalidation of which would affect all overseas projects. This programmatic approach has obvious practical advantages, but also obvious difficulties insofar as proof of causation or redressability is concerned. . . .

. . . Since the agencies funding the projects were not parties to the case, the District Court could accord relief only against the Secretary: He could be ordered to revise his regulation to require consultation for foreign projects. But this would not remedy respondents' alleged injury unless the funding agencies were bound by the Secretary's regulation, which is very much an open question. . . . [W]ith respect to consultation the initiative, and hence arguably the initial responsibility for determining statutory necessity, lies with the agencies, see § 1536(a)(2)

When the Secretary promulgated the regulation at issue here, he thought it was binding on the agencies, see 51 Fed. Reg. 19928 (1986). The Solicitor General, however, has repudiated that position here, and the agencies themselves apparently deny the Secretary's authority. (During the period when the Secretary took the view that § 7(a)(2) did apply abroad, AID and FWS engaged in a running controversy over whether consultation was required with respect to the Mahaweli project, AID insisting that consultation applied only to domestic actions.)

. . . The short of the matter is that redress of the only injury in fact respondents complain of requires action (termination of funding until consultation) by the individual funding agencies; and any relief the District Court could have provided in this suit against the Secretary was not likely to produce that action.

A further impediment to redressability is the fact that the agencies generally supply only a fraction of the funding for a foreign project. AID, for example, has provided less than 10% of the funding for the Mahaweli project. Respondents have produced nothing to indicate that the projects they have named will either be suspended, or do less harm to listed species, if that fraction is eliminated. As in *Simon*, 426 U.S., at 43–44, it is entirely conjectural whether the nonagency activity that affects respondents will be altered or affected by the agency activity they seek to achieve. There is no standing.

IV

The Court of Appeals found that respondents had standing for an additional reason: because they had suffered a "procedural injury." The so-called "citizen-suit" provision of the ESA provides, in pertinent part, that "any person may commence a civil suit on his own behalf (A) to enjoin any person, including the United States and any other governmental instrumentality or agency . . . who is alleged to be in violation of any provision of this chapter." 16 U.S.C. § 1540(g). The court held that, because § 7(a)(2) requires interagency consultation, the citizen-suit provision creates a "procedural righ[t]" to consultation in all "persons"—so that *anyone* can file suit in federal court to challenge the Secretary's (or presumably any other official's) failure to follow the assertedly correct consultative procedure, notwithstanding his or her inability to allege any discrete injury flowing from that failure. 911 F.2d, at 121–122. To understand the remarkable nature of this holding one must be clear about what it does not rest upon: This is not a case where plaintiffs are seeking to enforce a procedural requirement the disregard of which could impair a separate concrete interest of theirs (*e.g.*, the procedural requirement for a hearing prior to denial of their license application, or the procedural requirement for an environmental impact statement before a federal facility is constructed next door to them)[7]. . . .

---

[7] There is this much truth to the assertion that "procedural rights" are special: The person who has been accorded a procedural right to protect his concrete interests can assert that right without meeting all the normal standards for redressability and immediacy. Thus, under our

Rather, the court held that the injury-in-fact requirement had been satisfied by congressional conferral upon *all* persons of an abstract, self-contained, noninstrumental "right" to have the Executive observe the procedures required by law. We reject this view.

We have consistently held that a plaintiff raising only a generally available grievance about government—claiming only harm to his and every citizen's interest in proper application of the Constitution and laws, and seeking relief that no more directly and tangibly benefits him than it does the public at large—does not state an Article III case or controversy. . . .

. . . In *United States v. Richardson*, 418 U.S. 166 (1974), we dismissed for lack of standing a taxpayer suit challenging the Government's failure to disclose the expenditures of the Central Intelligence Agency, in alleged violation of the constitutional requirement, Art. I, § 9, cl. 7, that "a regular Statement and Account of the Receipts and Expenditures of all public Money shall be published from time to time." We held that such a suit rested upon an impermissible "generalized grievance," and was inconsistent with "the framework of Article III" because "the impact on [plaintiff] is plainly undifferentiated and 'common to all members of the public.'" *Richardson*, *supra*, at 171, 176–177. . . .

To be sure, our generalized-grievance cases have typically involved Government violation of procedures assertedly ordained by the Constitution rather than the Congress. But there is absolutely no basis for making the Article III inquiry turn on the source of the asserted right. Whether the courts were to act on their own, or at the invitation of Congress, in ignoring the concrete injury requirement described in our cases, they would be discarding a principle fundamental to the separate and distinct constitutional role of the Third Branch-—one of the essential elements that identifies those "Cases" and "Controversies" that are the business of the courts rather than of the political branches. "The province of the court," as Chief Justice Marshall said in *Marbury v. Madison*, 5 U.S. (1 Cranch) 137 (1803), "is, solely, to decide on the rights of individuals." Vindicating the *public* interest (including the public interest in Government observance of the Constitution and laws) is the function of Congress and the Chief Executive. The question presented here is whether the public interest in proper administration of the laws (specifically, in agencies' observance of a particular, statutorily prescribed procedure) can be converted into an individual right by a

---

case law, one living adjacent to the site for proposed construction of a federally licensed dam has standing to challenge the licensing agency's failure to prepare an environmental impact statement, even though he cannot establish with any certainty that the statement will cause the license to be withheld or altered, and even though the dam will not be completed for many years. (That is why we do not rely, in the present case, upon the Government's argument that, even if the other agencies were obliged to consult with the Secretary, they might not have followed his advice.) What respondents' "procedural rights" argument seeks, however, is quite different from this: standing for persons who have no concrete interests affected-persons who live (and propose to live) at the other end of the country from the dam.

statute that denominates it as such, and that permits all citizens (or, for that matter, a subclass of citizens who suffer no distinctive concrete harm) to sue. If the concrete injury requirement has the separation-of-powers significance we have always said, the answer must be obvious: To permit Congress to convert the undifferentiated public interest in executive officers' compliance with the law into an "individual right" vindicable in the courts is to permit Congress to transfer from the President to the courts the Chief Executive's most important constitutional duty, to "take Care that the Laws be faithfully executed," Art. II, § 3. It would enable the courts, with the permission of Congress, "to assume a position of authority over the governmental acts of another and co-equal department," *Massachusetts v. Mellon,* 262 U.S., at 489, and to become " 'virtually continuing monitors of the wisdom and soundness of Executive action.' " *Allen, supra,* 468 U.S., at 760 (quoting *Laird v. Tatum,* 408 U.S. 1, 15 (1972)). We have always rejected that vision of our role. . . .

■ JUSTICE KENNEDY, with whom JUSTICE SOUTER joins, concurring in part and concurring in the judgment:

. . . I agree with the Court's conclusion in Part III-A that, on the record before us, respondents have failed to demonstrate that they themselves are "among the injured." *Sierra Club v. Morton,* 405 U.S. 727, 735 (1972). This component of the standing inquiry is not satisfied unless

> "[p]laintiffs . . . demonstrate a 'personal stake in the outcome.' . . . Abstract injury is not enough. The plaintiff must show that he 'has sustained or is immediately in danger of sustaining some direct injury' as the result of the challenged official conduct and the injury or threat of injury must be both 'real and immediate,' not 'conjectural' or 'hypothetical.' "

Los Angeles v. Lyons, 461 U.S. 95, 101–102 (1983) (citations omitted).

While it may seem trivial to require that Mses. Kelly and Skilbred acquire airline tickets to the project sites or announce a date certain upon which they will return, see *ante,* at 2138, this is not a case where it is reasonable to assume that the affiants will be using the sites on a regular basis, see *Sierra Club v. Morton, supra,* 405 U.S., at 735, n. 8, nor do the affiants claim to have visited the sites since the projects commenced. With respect to the Court's discussion of respondents' "ecosystem nexus," "animal nexus," and "vocational nexus" theories, *ante,* at 2139–2140, I agree that on this record respondents' showing is insufficient to establish standing on any of these bases. I am not willing to foreclose the possibility, however, that in different circumstances a nexus theory similar to those proffered here might support a claim to standing. See *Japan Whaling Assn. v. American Cetacean Society,* 478 U.S. 221, 231, n. 4 (1986) ("[R]espondents . . . undoubtedly have alleged a sufficient 'injury in fact' in that the whale watching and studying of their members will be adversely affected by continued whale harvesting").

In light of the conclusion that respondents have not demonstrated a concrete injury here sufficient to support standing under our precedents, I would not reach the issue of redressability that is discussed by the plurality in Part III-B. . . .

■ JUSTICE BLACKMUN, with whom JUSTICE O'CONNOR joins, dissenting:

. . . Were the Court to apply the proper standard for summary judgment, I believe it would conclude that the sworn affidavits and deposition testimony of Joyce Kelly and Amy Skilbred advance sufficient facts to create a genuine issue for trial concerning whether one or both would be imminently harmed by the Aswan and Mahaweli projects. In the first instance, as the Court itself concedes, the affidavits contained facts making it at least "questionable" (and therefore within the province of the factfinder) that certain agency-funded projects threaten listed species. *Ante,* at 2138. The only remaining issue, then, is whether Kelly and Skilbred have shown that they personally would suffer imminent harm.

I think a reasonable finder of fact could conclude from the information in the affidavits and deposition testimony that either Kelly or Skilbred will soon return to the project sites, thereby satisfying the "actual or imminent" injury standard. The Court dismisses Kelly's and Skilbred's general statements that they intended to revisit the project sites as "simply not enough." *Ibid.* . . . [T]he fact of their past visits could demonstrate to a reasonable factfinder that Kelly and Skilbred have the requisite resources and personal interest in the preservation of the species endangered . . . to make good on their intention to return again. Cf. *Los Angeles v. Lyons,* 461 U.S. 95, 102 (1983) ("Past wrongs were evidence bearing on whether there is a real and immediate threat of repeated injury"). Similarly, Kelly's and Skilbred's professional backgrounds in wildlife preservation, see App. 100, 144, 309–310, also make it likely—at least far more likely than for the average citizen—that they would choose to visit these areas of the world where species are vanishing.

By requiring a "description of concrete plans" or "specification of *when* the some day [for a return visit] will be," *ante,* at 8, the Court, in my view, demands what is likely an empty formality. No substantial barriers prevent Kelly or Skilbred from simply purchasing plane tickets to return to the Aswan and Mahaweli projects. . . .

The Court also concludes that injury is lacking. . . . To support that conclusion, the Court mischaracterizes our decision in *Lujan v. National Wildlife Federation,* 497 U.S. 871 (1990), as establishing a general rule that "a plaintiff claiming injury from environmental damage must use the area affected by the challenged activity." *Ante,* at 2139. In *National Wildlife Federation,* the Court required specific geographical proximity because of the particular type of harm alleged in that case: harm to the plaintiff's visual enjoyment of nature from mining activities. 497 U.S., at 888. One cannot suffer from the sight of a ruined landscape without being close enough to see the sites actually being mined. Many environmental injuries, however, cause harm distant from the area immediately affected by the challenged action. . . . It cannot seriously be contended that a litigant's failure to use the precise or exact site where animals are slaughtered or where toxic waste is dumped into a river means he or she cannot show injury. . . .

A plurality of the Court suggests that respondents have not demonstrated redressability: a likelihood that a court ruling in their favor would remedy their injury. *Duke Power Co. v. Carolina Environmental Study Group, Inc.*, 438 U.S. 59, 74–75, and n. 20 (1978). The plurality identifies two obstacles. The first is that the "action agencies" (*e.g.*, AID) cannot be required to undertake consultation with petitioner Secretary. . . . Petitioner, however, officially and publicly has taken the position that his regulations regarding consultation under § 7 of the Act are binding on action agencies. 50 CFR § 402.14(a) (1991). And he has previously taken the same position in this very litigation, having stated in his answer to the complaint that petitioner "admits the Fish and Wildlife Service (FWS) was designated the lead agency for the formulation of regulations concerning section 7 of the [Endangered Species Act]." App. 246. I cannot agree with the plurality that the Secretary (or the Solicitor General) is now free, for the convenience of this appeal, to disavow his prior public and litigation positions. . . .

Emphasizing that none of the action agencies are parties to this suit (and having rejected the possibility of their being indirectly bound by petitioner's regulation), the plurality concludes that "there is no reason they should be obliged to honor an incidental legal determination the suit produced." *Ante*, at 2141. . . . Under principles of collateral estoppel, these agencies are precluded from subsequently relitigating the issues decided in this suit. . . .

The second redressability obstacle relied on by the plurality is that "the [action] agencies generally supply only a fraction of the funding for a foreign project." *Ante*, at 2142. . . . Even if the action agencies supply only a fraction of the funding for a particular foreign project, it remains at least a question for the finder of fact whether threatened withdrawal of that fraction would affect foreign government conduct sufficiently to avoid harm to listed species. . . .

The Court concludes that any "procedural injury" suffered by respondents is insufficient to confer standing. It rejects the view that the "injury-in-fact requirement [is] satisfied by congressional conferral upon *all* persons of an abstract, self-contained, noninstrumental 'right' to have the Executive observe the procedures required by law." *Ante*, at 2143. Whatever the Court might mean with that very broad language, it cannot be saying that "procedural injuries" *as a class* are necessarily insufficient for purposes of Article III standing. . . .

The consultation requirement of § 7 of the Endangered Species Act is a[n] . . . action-forcing statute. Consultation is designed as an integral check on federal agency action, ensuring that such action does not go forward without full consideration of its effects on listed species. . . . These action-forcing procedures are "designed to protect some threatened concrete interest," *ante*, at 2143, n. 8, of persons who observe and work with endangered or threatened species. That is why I am mystified by the Court's unsupported conclusion that "[t]his is not a case where plaintiffs are seeking to enforce a procedural requirement the disregard of which could impair a separate concrete interest of theirs." *Ante,* at 2142.

Congress legislates in procedural shades of gray not to aggrandize its own power but to allow maximum Executive discretion in the attainment of Congress' legislative goals. . . . Just as Congress does not violate separation of powers by structuring the procedural manner in which the Executive shall carry out the laws, surely the federal courts do not violate separation of powers when, at the very instruction and command of Congress, they enforce these procedures.

To prevent Congress from conferring standing for "procedural injuries" is another way of saying that Congress may not delegate to the courts authority deemed "executive" in nature. *Ante*, at 2145 (Congress may not "transfer from the President to the courts the Chief Executive's most important constitutional duty, to 'take Care that the Laws be faithfully executed,' Art. II, § 3"). Here Congress seeks not to delegate "executive" power but only to strengthen the procedures it has legislatively mandated. "We have long recognized that the nondelegation doctrine does not prevent Congress from seeking assistance, within proper limits, from its coordinate Branches." *Touby v. United States*, 500 U.S. 160, 165 (1991). . . .

. . . In no sense is the Court's suggestion compelled by our "common understanding of what activities are appropriate to legislatures, to executives, and to courts." *Ante*, at 2136. In my view, it reflects an unseemly solicitude for an expansion of power of the Executive Branch. . . .

In conclusion, I cannot join the Court on what amounts to a slash-and-burn expedition through the law of environmental standing. In my view, "[t]he very essence of civil liberty certainly consists in the right of every individual to claim the protection of the laws, whenever he receives an injury." *Marbury v. Madison*, 1 Cranch 137, 163 (1803).

NOTES AND QUESTIONS

1. **Injury in Fact.** In *National Wildlife Federation*, respondents challenged the federal government's actions relating to certain public lands. What areas were at stake? How would these areas be affected? How did the respondents attempt to prove standing? Why did the District Court find that National Wildlife Federation did not have standing? On what basis did the Court of Appeals disagree? Why did the majority of the *National Wildlife Federation* Court find that the respondents had not been adversely affected

or aggrieved by the government? Why did the dissenters disagree? How specific did the allegations have to be to satisfy the majority? What purpose would be served by such specificity?

2.　Injury in Fact, Continued. In *Defenders of Wildlife*, the majority stated that, in order to prove standing, the plaintiff has to demonstrate that she has suffered an "injury in fact" defined as "an invasion of a legally protected interest which is (a) concrete and particularized, and (b) actual and imminent, not 'conjectural' or 'hypothetical.'" *Lujan v. Defenders of Wildlife*, 504 U.S. 555, 560 (1992) (internal citations omitted). What injury did Defenders of Wildlife claim to have suffered? Why did the majority find that the alleged injury had not met the aforementioned requirements? Would it have made a difference if Kelly and Skilbred had bought airplane tickets to return to Aswan and Mahaweli? What if the tickets had been very cheap or refundable? On what basis did Justice Blackmun and Justice O'Connor dissent? Did you find their position compelling?

In a portion of his concurrence in the judgment, not excerpted above, Justice Stevens rejects the majority's view that the harm to the endangered species will not result in an "imminent injury" to the respondents:

> An injury to an individual's interest in studying or enjoying a species and its natural habitat occurs when someone (whether it be the Government or a private party) takes action that harms that species and habitat. In my judgment, therefore, the "imminence" of such an injury should be measured by the timing and likelihood of the threatened environmental harm, rather than—as the Court seems to suggest, *ante,* at 2138–2139, and n. 2—by the time that might elapse between the present and the time when the individuals would visit the area if no such injury should occurs. . . .
>
> [W]e have denied standing to plaintiffs whose likelihood of suffering any concrete adverse effect from the challenged action was speculative. In this case, however, the likelihood that respondents will be injured by the destruction of the endangered species is not speculative. If respondents are genuinely interested in the preservation of the endangered species and intend to study or observe these animals in the future, their injury will occur as soon as the animals are destroyed. Thus the only potential source of "speculation" in this case is whether respondents' intent to study or observe the animals is genuine. In my view, Joyce Kelly and Amy Skilbred have introduced sufficient evidence to negate petitioner's contention that their claims of injury are "speculative" or "conjectural." . . .

Defenders of Wildlife, 504 U.S. at 582–84 (internal citations omitted). When should an injury be considered too speculative to support standing?

3.　Redressability. According to the *Defenders of Wildlife* Court, in order to prove standing, a favorable decision must likely redress the injury. After concluding that the respondents had failed to show injury, in Part III-B Justice Scalia held that they also failed to demonstrate redressability. This part of his opinion was only supported by Justices Rehnquist, White, and

Thomas and therefore did not have the support of a majority. Why do you think that Justice Scalia wrote Part III-B? How did the plurality and the dissent of *Defenders of Wildlife* differ on this point? In Part III-B, the plurality of the Court sustained that "any relief the District Court could have provided in this suit against the Secretary was not likely to produce that action." *Defenders of Wildlife*, 504 U.S. at 571. Do you think that the promulgation of regulations requiring consultation for foreign projects would *likely* diminish the rate of extinction of endangered and threatened species?

4.   *Defenders of Wildlife* and *National Wildlife Federation*. The majority and dissent in *Defenders of Wildlife* focus on the impact of *National Wildlife Federation*. What are the competing positions? Which is more compelling? Given the Court's concerns about the speculative nature of Kelly and Skilbred's plans in *Defenders of Wildlife*, how could Erman and Peterson ever establish standing in *National Wildlife Federation*? What would they need to do to convince the Court that they really plan to hike through the federal lands in the future? Given the problems that Erman and Peterson had in linking their hiking with specific federal lands subject to the withdrawal program, how would Kelly and Skilbred convince the Court that the places to which they want to travel are ones at which they would see endangered species?

5.   Procedural Injuries. In evaluating Defenders of Wildlife's standing, the Court of Appeals found that the group had suffered a procedural injury. According to the Court of Appeals:

> . . . Defenders has also satisfied the standing requirement by demonstrating a procedural injury based upon the Secretary's failure to follow the required consultation procedure. . . . [W]e are persuaded that the Act is a statute imposing statutory duties which create "correlative procedural rights in a given plaintiff, the invasion of which is sufficient to satisfy the requirement of injury in fact in article III".
>
> As we observed in our earlier opinion, the Act "provides that 'any person' may commence a suit to enjoin any person who is alleged to be in violation of the ESA. *See* 16 U.S.C. § 1540(g). Environmental associations are 'persons' and may bring suit in their own name."

Defenders of Wildlife v. Lujan, 911 F.2d 117, 121–22 (8th Cir. 1990). Why did the majority reject this view? How did the dissent respond? Which position is more compelling?

Justice Scalia criticized the dissent's opinion about procedural rights on the following grounds:

> We do not hold that an individual cannot enforce procedural rights; he assuredly can, so long as the procedures in question are designed to protect some threatened concrete interest of his that is the ultimate basis of his standing. . . . If we understand this correctly, [the dissent] means that the Government's violation of a certain (undescribed) class of procedural duty satisfies the concrete-injury requirement by itself, without any showing that the procedural

violation endangers a concrete interest of the plaintiff (apart from
his interest in having the procedure observed). We cannot agree.

Defenders of Wildlife, 504 U.S. at 574 n.8 (1992). Do you find this view
convincing?

6.   Generalized Grievances and Article II. How did Justice Scalia's
opinion in *Defenders of Wildlife* convert this prudential element into a
constitutional requirement? Justice Scalia recognized that "our generalized
grievance cases have typically involved Government violation of procedures
assertedly ordained by the Constitution rather than the Congress. But there
is absolutely no basis for making the Article III inquiry turn on the source of
the asserted right." *Defenders of Wildlife*, 504 U.S. at 576. Do you find this
argument compelling? How would the constitutional authority of the
President have been harmed if the plaintiffs had prevailed in this case?

Cass Sunstein argues the *Defenders of Wildlife* Court's holding that
"Congress cannot grant standing to citizens" does not have support in the
"Court's own precedents, on the Take Care Clause, or on a particular
understanding of Article III." Cass R. Sunstein, *What's Standing After
Lujan? Of Citizen Suits, "Injuries," and Article III*, 91 MICH. L. REV. 163, 209
(1992). Regarding the Take Care Clause, Sunstein argued:

> [*Defenders of Wildlife*] seems to be built in key part on the idea that
> citizen standing—like other legislative interference with the
> President's power to execute the law—is unacceptable under
> Article II. Indeed, many of the recent standing cases might be
> thought to be Article II cases masquerading under the guise of
> Article III; we may even say that the Article II tail is wagging the
> Article III dog. But the conflation of Article II and Article III
> concerns has led to serious confusion. If a plaintiff with a plane
> ticket can sue under the ESA without offense to Article II, then it
> makes no sense to say that Article II is violated if a plaintiff lacking
> such a ticket initiates a proceeding. Beneficiary standing poses no
> Article II issue. The two articles raise quite different concerns; they
> should be analyzed separately.

Id. at 213. Assess the strength of this argument. For criticisms of Sunstein's
position, see Harold J. Kent & Ethan G. Shenkman, *Of Citizens Suits and
Citizen Sunstein*, 91 MICH. L. REV. 1793, 1796 (1993) ("We find unfortunate
Sunstein's acceptance of the private-attorney-general concept, which implies
that citizens can step into the shoes of the executive branch and assume the
sovereign's responsibility for promoting the public good in litigation."). As
discussed in Justice Stevens' dissent in *Steel Co. v. Citizens for a Better Env't*,
523 U.S. 83 (1998), *infra*, at 127–28, early in our Nation's history, private
persons regularly prosecuted criminal cases. Why was this practice not in
violation of Article II? How do you suppose Justice Scalia would respond?

7.   Zone of Interests. In *Bennett v. Spear*, 520 U.S. 154 (1997), ranch
operators and irrigation districts brought an action under the citizen-suit
provision of the ESA to challenge a biological opinion issued by the Fish and
Wildlife Service regarding the operation of the Klamath Irrigation Project,
in northern California and southern Oregon, and its impact on two varieties

of endangered fish. *See id.* at 157. The biological opinion concluded that the long-term operation of the project would likely jeopardize the continued existence of the endangered species and identified as a "reasonable and prudent alternative" the maintenance of minimum water levels on the reservoirs. *See id.* at 159. The petitioners had an interest in continuing to divert the water.

Some of the petitioners' claims were brought under the ESA's citizen suit provision, which states that "any person may commence a civil suit." *See* 16 U.S.C. § 1540(g). The Court held that this language "negates the zone-of-interests test (or, perhaps more accurately, expands the zone of interests)." *Bennett*, 520 U.S. at 164. With respect to the remaining claims, brought under the APA, the Court stated:

> In the claims that we have found not to be covered by the ESA's citizen suit provision, petitioners allege a violation of § 7 of the ESA, 16 U.S.C. § 1536 which requires . . . that each agency "use the best scientific and commercial data available," § 1536(a)(2). Petitioners contend that the available scientific and commercial data show that the continued operation of the Klamath Project will not have a detrimental impact on the endangered suckers, that the imposition of minimum lake levels is not necessary to protect the fish. . . . The obvious purpose of the requirement that each agency "use the best scientific and commercial data available" is to ensure that the ESA not be implemented haphazardly, on the basis of speculation or surmise. While this no doubt serves to advance the ESA's overall goal of species preservation, we think it readily apparent that another objective (if not indeed the primary one) is to avoid needless economic dislocation produced by agency officials zealously but unintelligently pursuing their environmental objectives. . . . Petitioners' claim that they are victims of such a mistake is plainly within the zone of interests that the provision protects.

Id. at 176. NEPA does not have a citizen suit provision. Does the zone of interest requirement deprive certain types of actors of standing to challenge the adequacy of environmental impact statements? What types of actors would these be? *See Ranchers Cattlemen Action Legal Fund United Stockgrowers v. USDA*, 415 F.3d 1078, 1103 (9th Cir. 2005) (holding that association of cattle producers' alleged economic injuries, and members' health injuries, fell outside NEPA's zone of interests); *Taubman Realty Group Ltd. v. Mineta*, 320 F.3d 475, 480–82 (4th Cir. 2003) (holding that shopping center developer's alleged traffic and pollution problems caused by construction of competing shopping center near interstate highways and asserted devaluation of developer's shopping center as commercial property was not within zone of interests intended to be protected by NEPA). *But see Nat'l Helium Corp. v. Morton*, 455 F.2d 650, 655 (10th Cir. 1971) (granting standing to a plaintiff that suffered an economic injury but also alleged environmental harm: "the plaintiffs are not primarily devoted to ecological improvement, but they are not on this account disqualified from seeking to advance such an interest"). For a general discussion of the "zone of interests" requirement see Jonathan R. Siegel, *Zone of Interests*, 92 GEO. L.J. 317 (2004).

8.   Organizational Standing. In *Sierra Club v. Morton*, 405 U.S. 727 (1972), the Sierra Club, a membership corporation with "a special interest in the conservation and sound maintenance of the national parks, game refuges, and forest of the country," brought an action seeking a declaratory judgment and an injunction to restrain federal officials from granting approval or issuing permits to a skiing development in the Sequoia National Park. *Id.* at 730. The Sierra Club alleged that the development "would destroy or otherwise adversely affect the scenery, natural and historic objects and wildlife of the park and would impair the enjoyment of the park for future generations." *Id.* at 734. The Supreme Court held:

> It is clear that an organization whose members are injured may represent those members in a proceeding for judicial review. *See, e.g., NAACP v. Button*, 371 U.S. 415, 428. But a mere "interest in a problem," no matter how longstanding the interest and no matter how qualified the organization is in evaluating the problem, is not sufficient by itself to render the organization "adversely affected" or "aggrieved" within the meaning of the APA.

Id. at 739. What should the Sierra Club have done? How hard would it have been? Before joining the majority, Justice White is said to have remarked "Why didn't the Sierra Club have one goddamn member walk through the park and then there would have been standing to sue." BOB WOODWARD & SCOTT ARMSTRONG, THE BRETHREN 164 (1979). How do national environmental groups establish standing? What kinds of incentives does this requirement generate concerning the structure of environmental groups? Under the current case law,

> [a]n association has standing to bring suit on behalf of its members when its members would otherwise have standing to sue in their own right, the interests at stake are germane to the organization's purpose, and neither the claim asserted nor the relief requested requires the participation of individual members in the lawsuit.

Friends of the Earth, Inc. v. Laidlaw Envtl. Servs., Inc., 528 U.S. 167, 169 (2000).

Who do you suppose controls the litigation when such groups sue on behalf of their members? What desirable purpose, if any, is served by the *Sierra Club v. Morton* requirement?

9.   Possible Congressional Response to *Defenders of Wildlife*. Cass Sunstein argues "the most important and novel holding in [*Defenders of Wildlife*] was that Congress cannot grant standing to citizens." *See* Sunstein, *supra*, at 209. He suggests possible congressional responses to this holding:

> I suggest that the simplest and most effective response would be the creation of a bounty for successful citizen plaintiffs. Such a bounty would build directly on the qui tam and informers' actions, and it should not raise a constitutional problem in the aftermath of Lujan.

> A more complex response would be for Congress expressly to create a property interest in the various regulatory "goods" that it wants to authorize citizens to protect. It might, for example, say that citizens generally have a beneficial interest in certain endangered species that are at risk from acts of the U.S. government. This somewhat adventurous strategy would have the advantages of building on common law notions of interest and injury and of forcing focused congressional attention on the precise nature of the rights at stake.

Sunstein, *supra*, at 223–24. Do you find this opinion compelling? Suppose that Congress modifies the ESA to include one of these approaches. How would a potential plaintiff prove standing?

10. Standing in State Courts. Absent a provision for exclusive federal jurisdiction, state courts possess the authority to decide cases involving interpretations of federal law. *See ASARCO Inc. v. Kadish*, 490 U.S. 605, 617 (1989). Unlike federal courts, state courts are not bound by the limitations of a case or controversy or other federal rules of justiciability. *Id.* Although some states have followed Article III standing requirements or enacted more restrictive doctrines, many state courts and legislatures have adopted more relaxed standards, including judge-made exceptions for cases of "great public import," taxpayer-standing laws, and environmental rights acts. *See* Christopher S. Elmendorf, *State Courts, Citizen Suits, and the Enforcement of Federal Environmental Law by Non-Article III Plaintiffs*, 110 YALE L.J. 1003, 1004 (2001). Since most environmental statutes could be interpreted as conferring concurrent jurisdiction to state courts, these courts may be able to hear the federal claims of plaintiffs that do not fulfill the federal standing requirements. *See id.* at 1014 ("all but CERCLA, and probably TSCA, accommodate state court jurisdiction"). Why do environmental groups generally bring their claims in federal courts, despite the more favorable standing rules in state courts? How would the existence of different standing requirements affect the enforcement of federal environmental law? Is uniform enforcement desirable? *See* Paul J. Katz, *Standing in Good Stead: State Courts, Federal Standing Doctrine, and the Reverse-Erie Analysis*, 99 NW. U. L. REV. 1315 (2005).

11. Standing in State Courts, Continued. In *Sierra Club v. Utah*, 148 P.3d 975 (Utah 2006), Sierra Club and Grand Canyon Trust filed a request with the Utah Air Quality Board, claiming that the proposed modification of a power plant failed to comply with the CAA. In order to prove standing, as required by the Utah Administrative Code, the environmental groups presented, among others, the affidavit of Mr. Cass:

> Mr. Cass is a videographer who has filmed and produced documentaries on the Colorado Plateau and the Escalante River. Mr. Cass also uses the Colorado Plateau for recreation. His affidavit alleges that if Intermountain Power is allowed to expand its current plant, the emissions from that plant will impair the visibility around his home in Boulder, Utah, and of the Colorado Plateau. . . . Mr. Cass' affidavit also expresses his concern that the emissions from the proposed plant will harmfully affect his health

and his family's health, negatively impact vegetation and soil around his home, decrease the value of his property, and contribute to global warming.

Id. at 978. Would this affidavit be enough to prove standing in a federal court? In reviewing the Board's decision regarding the plaintiff's standing, the Supreme Court of Utah explained:

> There are "two means by which a party can establish standing" before the courts of this state. The traditional test requires the petitioning party to establish a "distinct and palpable injury." However, if the petitioning party does not have standing under the traditional test, that party may still have standing if it can demonstrate that it is an appropriate party asserting a matter of great public importance.

Id. at 979 (citations omitted). How does the Utah standard differ from the federal standard? Which approach is more desirable?

Steel Co. v. Citizens for a Better Environment
523 U.S. 83 (1998).

■ JUSTICE SCALIA delivered the opinion of the Court:

This is a private enforcement action under the citizen-suit provision of the Emergency Planning and Community Right-To-Know Act of 1986 (EPCRA), 42 U.S.C. § 11046(a)(1). The case presents the merits question, answered in the affirmative by the United States Court of Appeals for the Seventh Circuit, whether EPCRA authorizes suits for purely past violations. It also presents the jurisdictional question whether respondent, plaintiff below, has standing to bring this action.

Respondent, an association of individuals interested in environmental protection, sued petitioner, a small manufacturing company in Chicago, for past violations of EPCRA. EPCRA establishes a framework of state, regional, and local agencies designed to inform the public about the presence of hazardous and toxic chemicals, and to provide for emergency response in the event of health-threatening release. Central to its operation are reporting requirements compelling users of specified toxic and hazardous chemicals to file annual "emergency and hazardous chemical inventory forms" and "toxic chemical release forms", which contain, *inter alia*, the name and location of the facility, the name and quantity of the chemical on hand, and, in the case of toxic chemicals, the waste-disposal method employed and the annual quantity released into each environmental medium. 42 U.S.C. §§ 11022 and 11023. The hazardous-chemical inventory forms for any given calendar year are due the following March 1st, and the toxic-chemical release forms the following July 1st. §§ 11022(a)(2) and 11023(a). . . .

In 1995 respondent sent a notice to petitioner, the Administrator, and the relevant Illinois authorities, alleging—accurately, as it turns out—that petitioner had failed since 1988, the first year of EPCRA's filing deadlines, to complete and to submit the requisite hazardous-chemical inventory and toxic-chemical release forms under §§ 11022 and 11023. Upon receiving the notice, petitioner filed all of the overdue forms with the relevant agencies. The EPA chose not to bring an action against petitioner, and when the 60-day waiting period expired, respondent filed suit in Federal District Court. Petitioner promptly filed a motion to dismiss under Federal Rules of Civil Procedure 12(b)(1) and (6), contending that, because its filings were up to date when the complaint was filed, the court had no jurisdiction to entertain a suit for a present violation; and that, because EPCRA does not allow suit for a purely historical violation, respondent's allegation of untimeliness in filing was not a claim upon which relief could be granted. . . .

The complaint asks for (1) a declaratory judgment that petitioner violated EPCRA; (2) authorization to inspect periodically petitioner's facility and records (with costs borne by petitioner); (3) an order requiring petitioner to provide respondent copies of all compliance reports submitted to the EPA; (4) an order requiring petitioner to pay civil penalties of $25,000 per day for each violation of §§ 11022 and 11023; (5) an award of all respondent's "costs, in connection with the investigation and prosecution of this matter, including reasonable attorney and expert witness fees, as authorized by Section 326(f) of [EPCRA]"; and (6) any such further relief as the court deems appropriate. App. 11. None of the specific items of relief sought, and none that we can envision as "appropriate" under the general request, would serve to reimburse respondent for losses caused by the late reporting, or to eliminate any effects of that late reporting upon respondent.

The first item, the request for a declaratory judgment that petitioner violated EPCRA, can be disposed of summarily. There being no controversy over whether petitioner failed to file reports, or over whether such a failure constitutes a violation, the declaratory judgment is not only worthless to respondent, it is seemingly worthless to all the world. See *Lewis v. Continental Bank Corp.*, 494 U.S. 472, 479 (1990).

Item (4), the civil penalties authorized by the statute, see § 11045(c), might be viewed as a sort of compensation or redress to respondent if they were payable to respondent. But they are not. These penalties—the only damages authorized by EPCRA—are payable to the United States Treasury. In requesting them, therefore, respondent seeks not remediation of its own injury—reimbursement for the costs it incurred as a result of the late filing—but vindication of the rule of law-the "undifferentiated public interest" in faithful execution of EPCRA. *Lujan v. Defenders of Wildlife, supra*, at 577; see also *Fairchild v. Hughes*, 258 U.S. 126, 129–130 (1922). This does not suffice. Justice STEVENS thinks it is enough that respondent will be gratified by seeing petitioner punished for its infractions and that the punishment will deter the risk of future harm. *Post*, at 1028–1029. If that were so, our holdings in *Linda*

R.S. v. Richard D., 410 U.S. 614 (1973), and *Simon v. Eastern Ky. Welfare Rights Organization*, 426 U.S. 26 (1976), are inexplicable. Obviously, such a principle would make the redressability requirement vanish. By the mere bringing of his suit, every plaintiff demonstrates his belief that a favorable judgment will make him happier. But although a suitor may derive great comfort and joy from the fact that the United States Treasury is not cheated, that a wrongdoer gets his just deserts, or that the Nation's laws are faithfully enforced, that psychic satisfaction is not an acceptable Article III remedy because it does not redress a cognizable Article III injury. See, *e.g.*, *Allen v. Wright*, 468 U.S. 737, 754–755 (1984); *Valley Forge Christian College v. Americans United for Separation of Church and State, Inc.*, 454 U.S. 464, 482–483 (1982). Relief that does not remedy the injury suffered cannot bootstrap a plaintiff into federal court; that is the very essence of the redressability requirement.

Item (5), the "investigation and prosecution" costs "as authorized by Section 326(f)," would assuredly benefit respondent as opposed to the citizenry at large. Obviously, however, a plaintiff cannot achieve standing to litigate a substantive issue by bringing suit for the cost of bringing suit. The litigation must give the plaintiff some other benefit besides reimbursement of costs that are a byproduct of the litigation itself. An "interest in attorney's fees is . . . insufficient to create an Article III case or controversy where none exists on the merits of the underlying claim." *Lewis v. Continental Bank Corp.*, *supra*, at 480 (citing *Diamond v. Charles*, 476 U.S. 54, 70–71 (1986)). Respondent asserts that the "investigation costs" it seeks were incurred prior to the litigation, in digging up the emissions and storage information that petitioner should have filed, and that respondent needed for its own purposes. See Brief for Respondent 37–38. The recovery of such expenses unrelated to litigation would assuredly support Article III standing, but the problem is that § 326(f), which is the entitlement to monetary relief that the complaint invokes, covers only the "costs of litigation." § 11046(f). Respondent finds itself, in other words, impaled upon the horns of a dilemma: For the expenses to be reimbursable under the statute, they must be costs of litigation; but reimbursement of the costs of litigation cannot alone support standing.

The remaining relief respondent seeks (item (2), giving respondent authority to inspect petitioner's facility and records, and item (3), compelling petitioner to provide respondent copies of EPA compliance reports) is injunctive in nature. It cannot conceivably remedy any past wrong but is aimed at deterring petitioner from violating EPCRA in the future. See Brief for Respondent 36. The latter objective can of course be "remedial" for Article III purposes, when threatened injury is one of the gravamens of the complaint. If respondent had alleged a continuing violation or the imminence of a future violation, the injunctive relief requested would remedy that alleged harm. But there is no such allegation here—and on the facts of the case, there seems no basis for it.

Nothing supports the requested injunctive relief except respondent's generalized interest in deterrence, which is insufficient for purposes of Article III. See *Los Angeles v. Lyons*, 461 U.S., at 111.

The United States, as *amicus curiae*, argues that the injunctive relief does constitute remediation because here is a presumption of [future] injury when the defendant has voluntarily ceased its illegal activity in response to litigation, even if that occurs before a complaint is filed. Brief for United States as *Amicus Curiae* 27–28, and n. 11. This makes a sword out of a shield. The "presumption" the Government refers to has been applied to refute the assertion of mootness by a defendant who, when sued in a complaint that alleges present or threatened injury, ceases the complained-of activity. See, *e.g.*, *United States v. W.T. Grant Co.*, 345 U.S. 629, 632 (1953). It is an immense and unacceptable stretch to call the presumption into service as a substitute for the allegation of present or threatened injury upon which initial standing must be based. See *Los Angeles v. Lyons*, *supra*, at 109. To accept the Government's view would be to overrule our clear precedent requiring that the allegations of future injury be particular and concrete. *O'Shea v. Littleton*, 414 U.S. 488, 496–497 (1974). "Past exposure to illegal conduct does not in itself show a present case or controversy regarding injunctive relief . . . if unaccompanied by any continuing, present adverse effects." *Id.*, at 495–496; see also *Renne v. Geary*, 501 U.S. 312, 320 (1991) ("[T]he mootness exception for disputes capable of repetition yet evading review . . . will not revive a dispute which became moot before the action commenced"). Because respondent alleges only past infractions of EPCRA, and not a continuing violation or the likelihood of a future violation, injunctive relief will not redress its injury.

Having found that none of the relief sought by respondent would likely remedy its alleged injury in fact, we must conclude that respondent lacks standing to maintain this suit, and that we and the lower courts lack jurisdiction to entertain it. However desirable prompt resolution of the merits EPCRA question may be, it is not as important as observing the constitutional limits set upon courts in our system of separated powers. EPCRA will have to await another day. . . .

■ JUSTICE STEVENS, concurring in the judgment:

The Court acknowledges that respondent would have had standing if Congress had authorized some payment to respondent. *Ante*, at 1018 ("[T]he civil penalties authorized by the statute . . . might be viewed as a sort of compensation or redress to respondent if they were payable to respondent"). Yet the Court fails to specify why payment to respondent— even if only a peppercorn—would redress respondent's injuries, while payment to the Treasury does not. Respondent clearly believes that the punishment of Steel Company, along with future deterrence of Steel Company and others, redresses its injury, and there is no basis in our previous standing holdings to suggest otherwise.

When one private party is injured by another, the injury can be redressed in at least two ways: by awarding compensatory damages or by imposing a sanction on the wrongdoer that will minimize the risk that the harm-causing conduct will be repeated. Thus, in some cases a tort is redressed by an award of punitive damages; even when such damages are payable to the sovereign, they provide a form of redress for the individual as well.

History supports the proposition that punishment or deterrence can redress an injury. In past centuries in England, in the American Colonies, and in the United States, private persons regularly prosecuted criminal cases. The interest in punishing the defendant and deterring violations of law by the defendant and others was sufficient to support the "standing" of the private prosecutor even if the only remedy was the sentencing of the defendant to jail or to the gallows. Given this history, the Framers of Article III surely would have considered such proceedings to be "Cases" that would "redress" an injury even though the party bringing suit did not receive any monetary compensation.[26]

The Court's expanded interpretation of the redressability requirement has another consequence. Under EPCRA, Congress gave enforcement power to state and local governments. 42 U.S.C. § 11046(a)(2). Under the Court's reasoning, however, state and local governments would not have standing to sue for past violations, as a payment to the Treasury would no more "redress" the injury of these governments than it would redress respondent's injury. This would be true *even if Congress explicitly granted state and local governments this power*. Such a conclusion is unprecedented. . . .

Moreover, under the Court's own reasoning, respondent would have had standing if Congress had authorized some payment to respondent. *Ante*, at 1018 ("[T]he civil penalties authorized by the statute . . . might be viewed as a sort of compensation or redress to respondent if they were payable to respondent"). This conclusion is unexceptional given that respondent has a more particularized interest than a plaintiff in a *qui tam* suit, an action that is deeply rooted in our history. *United States ex rel. Marcus v. Hess*, 317 U.S. 537, 541, n. 4 (1943) (" 'Statutes providing for actions by a common informer, who himself has no interest whatever in the controversy other than that given by statute, have been in existence for hundreds of years in England, and in this country ever since the foundation of our Government' ") (quoting *Marvin v. Trout*, 199 U.S. 212, 225 (1905)); *Adams v. Woods*, 2 Cranch 336, 341, 2 L. Ed. 297 (1805) (opinion of Marshall, C.J.) ("Almost every fine or forfeiture under a penal statute, may be recovered by an action of debt [*qui tam*] as well as by information [by a public prosecutor]"); 3 W. Blackstone, Commentaries 160 (1768); 99 Yale L.J. 341, 342, and n. 3 (1989) (describing *qui tam*

---

[26] When such a party obtains a judgment that imposes sanctions on the wrongdoer, it is proper to presume that the wrongdoer will be less likely to repeat the injurious conduct that prompted the litigation. The lessening of the risk of future harm is a concrete benefit.

actions authorized by First Congress); see also *Lujan v. Defenders of Wildlife*, 504 U.S., at 572–573.

Yet it is unclear why the separation of powers question should turn on whether the plaintiff receives monetary compensation. In either instance, a private citizen is enforcing the law. If separation-of-powers does not preclude standing when Congress creates a legal right that authorizes compensation to the plaintiff, it is unclear why separation of powers should dictate a contrary result when Congress has created a legal right but has directed that payment be made to the Federal Treasury.

Indeed, in this case (assuming for present purposes that respondent correctly reads the statute) not only has Congress authorized standing, but the Executive Branch has also endorsed its interpretation of Article III. Brief for United States as *Amicus Curiae* 7–30. It is this Court's decision, not anything that Congress or the Executive has done, that encroaches on the domain of other branches of the Federal Government.

[Nonetheless, Justice Stevens concurred in the judgment because he concluded that EPCRA did not authorize suits for wholly past violations.]

Friends of the Earth, Inc. v. Laidlaw Environmental Services

528 U.S. 167 (2000).

■ JUSTICE GINSBURG delivered the opinion of the Court:

. . . In 1986, defendant-respondent Laidlaw Environmental Services (TOC), Inc., bought a hazardous waste incinerator facility in Roebuck, South Carolina, that included a wastewater treatment plant. . . . Shortly after Laidlaw acquired the facility, the South Carolina Department of Health and Environmental Control (DHEC), acting under 33 U.S.C. § 1342(a)(1), granted Laidlaw an NPDES [National Pollutant Discharge Elimination System] permit authorizing the company to discharge treated water into the North Tyger River. . . .

Once it received its permit, Laidlaw began to discharge various pollutants into the waterway; repeatedly, Laidlaw's discharges exceeded the limits set by the permit. . . . The District Court later found that Laidlaw had violated the mercury limits on 489 occasions between 1987 and 1995. 956 F. Supp., at 613–621. . . .

On June 12, 1992, FOE [Friends of the Earth] filed this citizen suit against Laidlaw under § 505(a) of the [Clean Water] Act, alleging noncompliance with the NPDES permit and seeking declaratory and injunctive relief and an award of civil penalties. Laidlaw moved for summary judgment on the ground that FOE had failed to present evidence demonstrating injury in fact, and therefore lacked Article III standing to bring the lawsuit. In opposition to this motion, FOE submitted affidavits and deposition testimony from members of the plaintiff organizations. . . . After examining this evidence, the District Court denied Laidlaw's summary judgment motion, finding—albeit "by the very slimmest of margins"—that FOE had standing to bring the suit. . . .

On January 22, 1997, the District Court issued its judgment. 956 F. Supp. 588 (D.S.C.). It found that Laidlaw had gained a total economic benefit of $1,092,581 as a result of its extended period of noncompliance with the mercury discharge limit in its permit. *Id.*, at 603. The court concluded, however, that a civil penalty of $405,800 was adequate in light of the guiding factors listed in 33 U.S.C. § 1319(d). 956 F. Supp. at 610. In particular, the District Court stated that the lesser penalty was appropriate taking into account the judgment's "total deterrent effect." In reaching this determination, the court "considered that Laidlaw will be required to reimburse plaintiffs for a significant amount of legal fees." *Id.*, at 610–611. The court declined to grant FOE's request for injunctive relief, stating that an injunction was inappropriate because "Laidlaw has been in substantial compliance with all parameters in its NPDES permit since at least August 1992." *Id.*, at 611.

FOE appealed the District Court's civil penalty judgment, arguing that the penalty was inadequate, but did not appeal the denial of declaratory or injunctive relief. Laidlaw cross-appealed, arguing, among other things, that FOE lacked standing to bring the suit. . . .

On July 16, 1998, the Court of Appeals for the Fourth Circuit issued its judgment. 149 F.3d 303. The Court of Appeals assumed without deciding that FOE initially had standing to bring the action, *id.*, at 306, n. 3, but went on to hold that the case had become moot. The appellate court stated, first, that the elements of Article III standing—injury, causation, and redressability—must persist at every stage of review, or else the action becomes moot. *Id.*, at 306. Citing our decision in *Steel Co.*, the Court of Appeals reasoned that the case had become moot because "the only remedy currently available to [FOE]—civil penalties payable to the government—would not redress any injury [FOE has] suffered." 149 F.3d, at 306–307. The court therefore vacated the District Court's order and remanded with instructions to dismiss the action. . . .

We granted certiorari, 525 U.S. 1176 (1999), to resolve the inconsistency between the Fourth Circuit's decision in this case and the decisions of several other Courts of Appeals. . . .

Laidlaw contends first that FOE lacked standing from the outset even to seek injunctive relief, because the plaintiff organizations failed to show that any of their members had sustained or faced the threat of any "injury in fact" from Laidlaw's activities. In support of this contention Laidlaw points to the District Court's finding, made in the course of setting the penalty amount, that there had been "no demonstrated proof of harm to the environment" from Laidlaw's mercury discharge violations. 956 F. Supp. at 602; see also, *ibid.* ("[T]he NPDES permit violations at issue in this citizen suit did not result in any health risk or environmental harm.").

The relevant showing for purposes of Article III standing, however, is not injury to the environment but injury to the plaintiff. To insist upon the former rather than the latter as part of the standing inquiry (as the dissent in essence does, *post*, at 713–714) is to raise the standing hurdle higher than the necessary showing for success on the merits in an action alleging noncompliance with an NPDES permit. Focusing properly on injury to the plaintiff, the District Court found that FOE had demonstrated sufficient injury to establish standing. For example, FOE member Kenneth Lee Curtis averred in affidavits that he lived a half-mile from Laidlaw's facility; that he occasionally drove over the North Tyger River, and that it looked and smelled polluted; and that he would like to fish, camp, swim, and picnic in and near the river between 3 and 15 miles downstream from the facility, as he did when he was a teenager, but would not do so because he was concerned that the water was polluted by Laidlaw's discharges. Curtis reaffirmed these statements in extensive deposition testimony. For example, he testified that he would like to fish in the river at a specific spot he used as a boy, but that he would not do so now because of his concerns about Laidlaw's discharges. . . .

These sworn statements, as the District Court determined, adequately documented injury in fact. We have held that environmental plaintiffs adequately allege injury in fact when they aver that they use the affected area and are persons "for whom the aesthetic and recreational values of the area will be lessened" by the challenged activity. *Sierra Club v. Morton*, 405 U.S. 727, 735 (1972). See also *Defenders of Wildlife*, 504 U.S., at 562–563.

Our decision in *Lujan v. National Wildlife Federation*, 497 U.S. 871 (1990), is not to the contrary. . . .

[T]he affidavits and testimony presented by FOE in this case assert that Laidlaw's discharges, and the affiant members' reasonable concerns about the effects of those discharges, directly affected those affiants' recreational, aesthetic, and economic interests. These submissions present dispositively more than the mere "general averments" and "conclusory allegations" found inadequate in *National Wildlife Federation. Id.*, at 888. Nor can the affiants' conditional statements—that they would use the nearby North Tyger River for recreation if Laidlaw were not discharging pollutants into it—be equated with the speculative " 'some day' intentions" to visit endangered species halfway around the world that we held insufficient to show injury in fact in *Defenders of Wildlife*. 504 U.S., at 564. . . .

Laidlaw argues next that even if FOE had standing to seek injunctive relief, it lacked standing to seek civil penalties. Here the asserted defect is not injury but redressability. Civil penalties offer no redress to private plaintiffs, Laidlaw argues, because they are paid to the

Government, and therefore a citizen plaintiff can never have standing to seek them.

Laidlaw is ... wrong to maintain that citizen plaintiffs facing ongoing violations never have standing to seek civil penalties. We have recognized on numerous occasions that "all civil penalties have some deterrent effect." *Hudson v. United States*, 522 U.S. 93, 102 (1997); *see also, e.g., Department of Revenue of Mont. v. Kurth Ranch*, 511 U.S. 767, 778 (1994). More specifically, Congress has found that civil penalties in Clean Water Act cases do more than promote immediate compliance by limiting the defendant's economic incentive to delay its attainment of permit limits; they also deter future violations. ...

It can scarcely be doubted that, for a plaintiff who is injured or faces the threat of future injury due to illegal conduct ongoing at the time of suit, a sanction that effectively abates that conduct and prevents its recurrence provides a form of redress. Civil penalties can fit that description. To the extent that they encourage defendants to discontinue current violations and deter them from committing future ones, they afford redress to citizen plaintiffs who are injured or threatened with injury as a consequence of ongoing unlawful conduct.

The dissent argues that it is the *availability* rather than the *imposition* of civil penalties that deters any particular polluter from continuing to pollute. *Post*, at 718–719. This argument misses the mark in two ways. First, it overlooks the interdependence of the availability and the imposition; a threat has no deterrent value unless it is credible that it will be carried out. Second, it is reasonable for Congress to conclude that an actual award of civil penalties does in fact bring with it a significant quantum of deterrence over and above what is achieved by the mere prospect of such penalties. A would-be polluter may or may not be dissuaded by the existence of a remedy on the books, but a defendant once hit in its pocketbook will surely think twice before polluting again.

We recognize that there may be a point at which the deterrent effect of a claim for civil penalties becomes so insubstantial or so remote that it cannot support citizen standing. The fact that this vanishing point is not easy to ascertain does not detract from the deterrent power of such penalties in the ordinary case. ...

In this case we need not explore the outer limits of the principle that civil penalties provide sufficient deterrence to support redressability. Here, the civil penalties sought by FOE carried with them a deterrent effect that made it likely, as opposed to merely speculative, that the penalties would redress FOE's injuries by abating current violations and preventing future ones—as the District Court reasonably found when it assessed a penalty of $405,800. 956 F. Supp. at 610–611.

Laidlaw contends that the reasoning of our decision in *Steel Co.* directs the conclusion that citizen plaintiffs have no standing to seek civil penalties under the Act. We disagree. *Steel Co.* established that citizen suitors lack standing to seek civil penalties for violations that have abated by the time of suit. 523 U.S., at 106–107. We specifically noted in that case that there was no allegation in the complaint of any continuing or imminent violation, and that no basis for such an allegation appeared to exist. *Id.*, at 108; see also *Gwaltney*, 484 U.S., at 59, ("the harm sought to be addressed by the citizen suit lies in the present or the future, not in the past"). In short, *Steel Co.* held that private plaintiffs, unlike the Federal Government, may not sue to assess penalties for wholly past violations, but our decision in that case did not reach the issue of standing to seek penalties for violations that are ongoing at the time of the complaint and that could continue into the future if undeterred.[4] . . .

■ JUSTICE SCALIA, with whom JUSTICE THOMAS joins, dissenting:

. . . [T]he remedy petitioners seek is neither recompense for their injuries nor an injunction against future violations. Instead, the remedy is a statutorily specified "penalty" for past violations, payable entirely to the United States Treasury. Only last Term, we held that such penalties do not redress any injury a citizen plaintiff has suffered from past violations. *Steel Co. v. Citizens for a Better Environment*, 523 U.S. 83, 106–107 (1998). The Court nonetheless finds the redressability requirement satisfied here, distinguishing *Steel Co.* on the ground that in this case petitioners allege ongoing violations. . . .

That holding has no precedent in our jurisprudence, and takes this Court beyond the "cases and controversies" that Article III of the Constitution has entrusted to its resolution. Even if it were appropriate, moreover, to allow Article III's remediation requirement to be satisfied by the indirect private consequences of a public penalty, those consequences are entirely too speculative in the present case. . . .

. . . [A] generalized remedy that deters all future unlawful activity against all persons cannot satisfy the remediation requirement, even though it deters (among other things) repetition of this particular unlawful activity against these particular plaintiffs. . . .

[I]t is my view that a plaintiff's desire to benefit from the deterrent effect of a public penalty for past conduct can never suffice to establish a case or controversy of the sort known to our law. Such deterrent effect is, so to speak, "speculative as a matter of law." Even if that were not so, however, the deterrent effect in the present case would surely be speculative as a matter of fact. . . .

---

4   [T]he dissent's broader charge that citizen suits for civil penalties under the Act carry "grave implications for democratic governance," post, at 715, seems to us overdrawn. Certainly the Federal Executive Branch does not share the dissent's view that such suits dissipate its authority to enforce the law. In fact, the Department of Justice has endorsed this citizen suit from the outset, submitting amicus briefs in support of FOE in the District Court, the Court of Appeals, and this Court. *See* supra, at 702, 703. As we have already noted, supra, at 701, the Federal Government retains the power to foreclose a citizen suit by undertaking its own action. 33 U.S.C. § 1365(b)(1)(B). And if the Executive Branch opposes a particular citizen suit, the statute allows the Administrator of the EPA to "intervene as a matter of right" and bring the Government's views to the attention of the court. § 1365(c)(2).

If the Court had undertaken the necessary inquiry into whether significant deterrence of the plaintiffs' feared injury was "likely," it would have had to reason something like this: Strictly speaking, no polluter is deterred by a penalty for past pollution; he is deterred by the *fear* of a penalty for *future* pollution. That fear will be virtually nonexistent if the prospective polluter knows that all emissions violators are given a free pass; it will be substantial under an emissions program such as the federal scheme here, which is regularly and notoriously enforced; it will be even higher when a prospective polluter subject to such a regularly enforced program has, as here, been the object of public charges of pollution and a suit for injunction; and it will surely be near the top of the graph when, as here, the prospective polluter has already been subjected to *state* penalties for the past pollution. The deterrence on which the plaintiffs must rely for standing in the present case is the marginal increase in Laidlaw's fear of future penalties that will be achieved by adding federal penalties for Laidlaw's past conduct.

I cannot say for certain that this marginal increase is zero; but I can say for certain that it is entirely speculative whether it will make the difference between these plaintiffs' suffering injury in the future and these plaintiffs' going unharmed. In fact, the assertion that it will "likely" do so is entirely farfetched. . . .

Article II of the Constitution commits it to the President to "take Care that the Laws be faithfully executed," Art. II, § 3, and provides specific methods by which all persons exercising significant executive power are to be appointed, Art. II, § 2. . . . [T]he question of the conformity of this legislation with Article II has not been argued—and I, like the Court, do not address it. But Article III, no less than Article II, has consequences for the structure of our government, see *Schlesinger*, 418 U.S., at 222 and it is worth noting the changes in that structure which today's decision allows.

By permitting citizens to pursue civil penalties payable to the Federal Treasury, the Act does not provide a mechanism for individual relief in any traditional sense, but turns over to private citizens the function of enforcing the law. A Clean Water Act plaintiff pursuing civil penalties acts as a self-appointed mini-EPA. Where, as is often the case, the plaintiff is a national association, it has significant discretion in choosing enforcement targets. Once the association is aware of a reported violation, it need not look long for an injured member, at least under the theory of injury the Court applies today. See supra, at 700–702. And once the target is chosen, the suit goes forward without meaningful public control.[2] The availability of civil penalties vastly disproportionate to the

---

[2] The Court points out that the Government is allowed to intervene in a citizen suit, see ante, at 708, n. 4; 33 U.S.C. § 1365(c)(2), but this power to "bring the Government's views to the attention of the court," ante, at 708, n. 4, is meager substitute for the power to decide whether prosecution will occur. Indeed, according the Chief Executive of the United States the ability to intervene does no more than place him on a par with John Q. Public, who can intervene-whether the Government likes it or not-when the United States files suit. § 1365(b)(1)(B).

individual injury gives citizen plaintiffs massive bargaining power—which is often used to achieve settlements requiring the defendant to support environmental projects of the plaintiffs' choosing. See Greve, The Private Enforcement of Environmental Law, 65 Tulane L. Rev. 339, 355–359 (1990). Thus is a public fine diverted to a private interest.

To be sure, the EPA may foreclose the citizen suit by itself bringing suit. 33 U.S.C. § 1365(b)(1)(B). This allows public authorities to avoid private enforcement only by accepting private direction as to when enforcement should be undertaken—which is no less constitutionally bizarre. Elected officials are entirely deprived of their discretion to decide that a given violation should not be the object of suit at all, or that the enforcement decision should be postponed. See § 1365(b)(1)(A). This is the predictable and inevitable consequence of the Court's allowing the use of public remedies for private wrongs.

NOTES AND QUESTIONS

1.   **Redressability.** Why did the majority of the *Steel Co.* Court find that the requirement of redressability had not been met? What did Justice Stevens argue? Why didn't Justice Scalia take into account the historical arguments put forward by Justice Stevens?

2.   **Informational Standing.**

> In the same period in which the American economy increasingly has become based on the production and exchange of information, American government has increasingly attempted to control public and private conduct—not via command-and-control regulation, but by requiring disclosure of information. And in the same period in which informational regulation has become a hallmark of American government, informational standing has increasingly emerged as a central problem in administrative law. There is nothing constitutionally problematic about a congressional judgment that a deprivation of information counts as a legally cognizable injury. The question is whether Congress has made that judgment. In the area of informational standing, as in the law of standing generally, the relevant statutory law is the best place to start, rooting the doctrine in democratic rather than judicial judgments about the appropriate nature, and boundaries, of modern regulatory government.

Cass Sunstein, *Informational Regulation and Informational Standing: Akins and Beyond*, 147 U. PA. L. REV. 613, 674–75 (1999).

In *Federal Election Commission v. Akins*, 524 U.S. 11, 13 (1998), the plaintiffs challenged the FEC's determination that the American Israel Public Affairs Committee (AIPAC) was not a political committee under the Federal Election Campaign Act (FECA). Political committees subject to FECA are required to make public information on donations received and expenditures made. *Id.* at 14. Plaintiffs argued that the inability to access that information hindered their ability to fully exercise their rights to vote.

Id. at 16. The Supreme Court held that where information disclosure was required by law, the inability to access that information was an injury sufficient to confer standing. *Id.* at 19–26. Justice Scalia, joined by Justices O'Connor and Thomas, strenuously dissented, arguing that this type of impairment of the franchise was a generalized grievance insufficient to confer standing. *Id.* at 29–37.

Sunstein praises *Akins*, in which the injury in fact was directly related to the plaintiffs' status as voters, for reaffirming the ability of Congress to create standing for informational injury. Is *Steel Co.* distinguishable? Is the distinction compelling? Would it matter whether the plaintiff lived in the vicinity of the polluting facility?

3. *Gwaltney* Case. In *Steel Co.*, the United States, acting as amicus curiae, argued that "injunctive relief does constitute remediation because 'there is a presumption of [future] injury when the defendant has voluntarily ceased its illegal activity in response to litigation,' even if that occurs before a complaint is filed." *See Steel Co.*, 523 U.S., at 109. Could this argument have been used in *Gwaltney of Smithfield, Ltd. v. Chesapeake Bay Foundation, Inc.*, 484 U.S. 49 (1987), which is excerpted, *supra*, at Section 1.E? Would it have affected the outcome in the case?

4. Injury in Fact. In a portion of his dissent in *Laidlaw*, not excerpted above, Justice Scalia argued:

> Typically, an environmental plaintiff claiming injury due to discharges in violation of the Clean Water Act argues that the discharges harm the environment, and that the harm to the environment injures him. This route to injury is barred in the present case, however, since the District Court concluded after considering all the evidence . . . that the "permit violations at issue in this citizen suit did not result in any health risk or environmental harm," *ibid.*, . . . "the overall quality of the river exceeds levels necessary to support . . . recreation in and on the water," *id.*, at 600.
>
> The Court finds these conclusions unproblematic for standing, because "[t]he relevant showing for purposes of Article III standing . . . is not injury to the environment but injury to the plaintiff." *Ante,* at 704. . . . While it is perhaps possible that a plaintiff could be harmed even though the environment was not, such a plaintiff would have the burden of articulating and demonstrating the nature of that injury. Ongoing "concerns" about the environment are not enough, for "[i]t is the *reality* of the threat of repeated injury that is relevant to the standing inquiry, not the plaintiff's subjective apprehensions," *Los Angeles v. Lyons*, 461 U.S. 95 (1983). . . .

Laidlaw, 528 U.S. at 199. On what grounds did Friends of the Earth allege the existence of "injury in fact" in this case? Is the lack of environmental damage relevant? How did the majority and the dissent differ on this point? Is it possible to prove injury to the plaintiff without injury to the environment?

5.   "Some Day Intentions." In his dissent in *Laidlaw*, Justice Scalia noted:

> Every one of the affiants deposed by Laidlaw cast into doubt the (in any event inadequate) proposition that subjective "concerns" actually affected their conduct. Linda Moore, for example, said in her affidavit that she would use the affected waterways for recreation if it were not for her concern about pollution. Yet she testified in her deposition that she had been to the river only twice, once in 1980 (when she visited someone who lived by the river) and once after this suit was filed. Similarly, Kenneth Lee Curtis, who claimed he was injured by being deprived of recreational activity at the river, admitted that he had not been to the river since he was "a kid," and when asked whether the reason he stopped visiting the river was because of pollution, answered "no." As to Curtis's claim that the river "looke[d] and smell[ed] polluted," this condition, if present, was surely not caused by Laidlaw's discharges, which according to the District Court "did not result in any health risk or environmental harm." The other affiants cited by the Court were not deposed, but their affidavits state either that they *would* use the river if it were not polluted or harmful (as the court subsequently found it is not), or said that the river looks polluted (which is also incompatible with the court's findings). These affiants have established nothing but "subjective apprehensions."

Laidlaw, 528 U.S. at 200–01. Is this case different from the "some day intentions" that the Court found insufficient to support a finding of "actual or imminent injury" in *Lujan v. Defenders of Wildlife*, 504 U.S. 555 (1992)? On what grounds did the majority distinguish this case? Is subjective apprehension enough to meet the standard of "actual or imminent injury"?

6.   Redressability and Civil Penalties. As the Supreme Court held in *Defenders of Wildlife*, 504 U.S. at 560–61, in order to satisfy Article III's standing requirement, a plaintiff must prove that it is likely, as opposed to merely speculative, that a favorable decision will redress her injury. How was Friends of the Earth's injury redressed by the decision of the Court? Do civil penalties provide sufficient deterrence to support redressability? How did the majority and the dissent differ in this respect?

7.   Generalized Grievances and Article II. In *Defenders of Wildlife*, the Court held that "a plaintiff raising only a generally available grievance about government . . . and seeking relief that no more directly and tangibly benefits him than it does the public at large . . . does not state an Article III case or controversy." *Defenders of Wildlife*, 504 U.S. at 573–74. Are *Defenders of Wildlife* and *Laidlaw* distinguishable? Do civil penalties payable to the treasury provide individual relief to the respondents? Or are they just a "generalized remedy that deters all future unlawful activity against all persons"? *Laidlaw*, 528 U.S. at 205. How would the constitutional authority of the President be harmed in *Laidlaw* according to Justice Scalia? How did the majority respond?

8.   **Standing and Past Violations.** Justice Scalia suggests in *Gwaltney*, discussed in Section 1.E, that if a defendant was in "a state of compliance" at the time the suit was filed, the plaintiff will not suffer from any "remediable injury in fact." *Id.* at 70. He believes that past violations could meet the injury in fact and causation requirements for standing, but that the redressability requirement could not be satisfied. Why didn't the District Court grant Friends of the Earth's request for injunctive relief? When did Laidlaw come into compliance with the NPDES permit? Under what circumstances would imposing penalties on a polluter for past violations redress a harm to a plaintiff? How did the Court distinguish *Laidlaw* from its previous opinion in *Steel Co.*? What was the dissent's position on this point? Assess the strength of Justice Scalia's deterrence argument.

Massachusetts v. Environmental Protection Agency
549 U.S. 497 (2007).

[Environmental organizations petitioned EPA to regulate emissions of greenhouse gases from motor vehicles under § 202(a)(1) of the CAA. EPA denied the rule making petition. Petitioners, joined by local and state governments, sought review in the D.C. Circuit. The D.C. Circuit dismissed the petition. The substantive portion of this case was excerpted in Chapter V. This chapter focuses only on the parts of the case that discuss the plaintiffs' standing.]

■ JUSTICE STEVENS delivered the opinion of the Court:

. . . EPA maintains that because greenhouse gas emissions inflict widespread harm, the doctrine of standing presents an insuperable jurisdictional obstacle. We do not agree. . . . As Justice KENNEDY explained in his *Lujan* concurrence:

> "While it does not matter how many persons have been injured by the challenged action, the party bringing suit must show that the action injures him in a concrete and personal way. . . ." 504 U.S., at 581 (internal quotation marks omitted).

To ensure the proper adversarial presentation, *Lujan* holds that a litigant must demonstrate that it has suffered a concrete and particularized injury that is either actual or imminent, that the injury is fairly traceable to the defendant, and that it is likely that a favorable decision will redress that injury. See *id.*, at 560–561. . . . [However,] [w]hen a litigant is vested with a procedural right, that litigant has standing if there is some possibility that the requested relief will prompt the injury-causing party to reconsider the decision that allegedly harmed the litigant. *Ibid.*; see also *Sugar Cane Growers Cooperative of Fla. v. Veneman*, 289 F.3d 89, 94–95 (C.A.D.C. 2002) ("A [litigant] who alleges a deprivation of a procedural protection to which he is entitled never has to prove that if he had received the procedure the substantive result would have been altered. All that is necessary is to show that the procedural step was connected to the substantive result").

Only one of the petitioners needs to have standing to permit us to consider the petition for review. See *Rumsfeld v. Forum for Academic and Institutional Rights, Inc.*, 547 U.S. 47, 52, n. 2 (2006). We stress here, as did Judge Tatel below, the special position and interest of Massachusetts. It is of considerable relevance that the party seeking review here is a sovereign State and not, as it was in *Lujan*, a private individual.

Well before the creation of the modern administrative state, we recognized that States are not normal litigants for the purposes of invoking federal jurisdiction. As Justice Holmes explained in *Georgia v. Tennessee Copper Co.*, 206 U.S. 230, 237 (1907), a case in which Georgia sought to protect its citizens from air pollution originating outside its borders:

> "The case has been argued largely as if it were one between two private parties; but it is not. The very elements that would be relied upon in a suit between fellow-citizens as a ground for equitable relief are wanting here. The State owns very little of the territory alleged to be affected, and the damage to it capable of estimate in money, possibly, at least, is small. This is a suit by a State for an injury to it in its capacity of *quasi*-sovereign. In that capacity the State has an interest independent of and behind the titles of its citizens, in all the earth and air within its domain. It has the last word as to whether its mountains shall be stripped of their forests and its inhabitants shall breathe pure air."

Just as Georgia's "independent interest . . . in all the earth and air within its domain" supported federal jurisdiction a century ago, so too does Massachusetts' well-founded desire to preserve its sovereign territory today. *Cf. Alden v. Maine*, 527 U.S. 706, 715 (1999) (observing that in the federal system, the States "are not relegated to the role of mere provinces or political corporations, but retain the dignity, though not the full authority, of sovereignty"). That Massachusetts does in fact own a great deal of the "territory alleged to be affected" only reinforces the conclusion that its stake in the outcome of this case is sufficiently concrete to warrant the exercise of federal judicial power.

When a State enters the Union, it surrenders certain sovereign prerogatives. . . .

These sovereign prerogatives are now lodged in the Federal Government, and Congress has ordered EPA to protect Massachusetts (among others) by prescribing standards applicable to the "emission of any air pollutant from any class or classes of new motor vehicle engines, which in [the Administrator's] judgment cause, or contribute to, air pollution which may reasonably be anticipated to endanger public health or welfare." 42 U.S.C. § 7521(a)(1). Congress has moreover recognized a concomitant procedural right to challenge the rejection of its rulemaking petition as arbitrary and capricious. § 7607(b)(1). Given that procedural right and Massachusetts' stake in protecting its quasi-sovereign interests, the Commonwealth is entitled to special solicitude in our standing analysis. . . .

With that in mind, it is clear that petitioners' submissions as they pertain to Massachusetts have satisfied the most demanding standards of the adversarial process. EPA's steadfast refusal to regulate greenhouse gas emissions presents a risk of harm to Massachusetts that is both "actual" and "imminent." *Lujan*, 504 U.S., at 560 (internal quotation marks omitted). There is, moreover, a "substantial likelihood that the judicial relief requested" will prompt EPA to take steps to reduce that risk. *Duke Power Co. v. Carolina Environmental Study Group, Inc.*, 438 U.S. 59, 79 (1978).

The Injury

The harms associated with climate change are serious and well recognized. . . .

That these climate-change risks are "widely shared" does not minimize Massachusetts' interest in the outcome of this litigation. See *Federal Election Comm'n v. Akins*, 524 U.S. 11, 24 (1998) ("[W]here a harm is concrete, though widely shared, the Court has found 'injury in fact' "). According to petitioners' unchallenged affidavits, global sea levels rose somewhere between 10 and 20 centimeters over the 20th century as a result of global warming. MacCracken Decl. ¶ 5(c), Stdg. App. 208. These rising seas have already begun to swallow Massachusetts' coastal land. *Id.*, at 196 (declaration of Paul H. Kirshen ¶ 5), 216 (MacCracken Decl. ¶ 23). Because the Commonwealth "owns a substantial portion of the state's coastal property," *id.*, at 171 (declaration of Karst R. Hoogeboom ¶ 4), it has alleged a particularized injury in its capacity as a landowner. The severity of that injury will only increase over the course of the next century: If sea levels continue to rise as predicted, one Massachusetts official believes that a significant fraction of coastal property will be "either permanently lost through inundation or temporarily lost through periodic storm surge and flooding events." *Id.*, ¶ 6, at 172. Remediation costs alone, petitioners allege, could run well into the hundreds of millions of dollars. *Id.*, ¶ 7, at 172; *see also* Kirshen Decl. ¶ 12, at 198.

Causation

EPA does not dispute the existence of a causal connection between manmade greenhouse gas emissions and global warming. At a minimum, therefore, EPA's refusal to regulate such emissions "contributes" to Massachusetts' injuries.

EPA nevertheless maintains that its decision not to regulate greenhouse gas emissions from new motor vehicles contributes so insignificantly to petitioners' injuries that the agency cannot be haled into federal court to answer for them. For the same reason, EPA does not believe that any realistic possibility exists that the relief petitioners seek would mitigate global climate change and remedy their injuries. That is especially so because predicted increases in greenhouse gas emissions from developing nations, particularly China and India, are likely to offset any marginal domestic decrease.

But EPA overstates its case. Its argument rests on the erroneous assumption that a small incremental step, because it is incremental, can never be attacked in a federal judicial forum. . . . That a first step might be tentative does not by itself support the notion that federal courts lack jurisdiction to determine whether that step conforms to law.

And reducing domestic automobile emissions is hardly a tentative step. Even leaving aside the other greenhouse gases, the United States transportation sector emits an enormous quantity of carbon dioxide into the atmosphere—according to the MacCracken affidavit, more than 1.7 billion metric tons in 1999 alone. ¶ 30, Stdg. App. 219. That accounts for more than 6% of worldwide carbon dioxide emissions. *Id.*, at 232 (Oppenheimer Decl. ¶ 3); see also MacCracken Decl. ¶ 31, at 220. . . . Judged by any standard, U.S. motor-vehicle emissions make a meaningful contribution to greenhouse gas concentrations and hence, according to petitioners, to global warming.

The Remedy

While it may be true that regulating motor-vehicle emissions will not by itself *reverse* global warming, it by no means follows that we lack jurisdiction to decide whether EPA has a duty to take steps to *slow* or *reduce* it. See also *Larson v. Valente*, 456 U.S. 228, 244, n. 15 (1982) ("[A] plaintiff satisfies the redressability requirement when he shows that a favorable decision will relieve a discrete injury to himself. He need not show that a favorable decision will relieve his *every* injury"). Because of the enormity of the potential consequences associated with man-made climate change, the fact that the effectiveness of a remedy might be delayed during the (relatively short) time it takes for a new motor-vehicle fleet to replace an older one is essentially irrelevant. Nor is it dispositive that developing countries such as China and India are poised to increase greenhouse gas emissions substantially over the next century: A reduction in domestic emissions would slow the pace of global emissions increases, no matter what happens elsewhere.

We moreover attach considerable significance to EPA's "agree[ment] with the President that 'we must address the issue of global climate change,'" 68 Fed. Reg. 52929 (quoting remarks announcing Clear Skies and Global Climate Initiatives, 2002 Public Papers of George W. Bush, Vol. 1, Feb. 14, p. 227 (2004)), and to EPA's ardent support for various voluntary emission-reduction programs, 68 Fed. Reg. 52932. As Judge Tatel observed in dissent below, "EPA would presumably not bother with such efforts if it thought emissions reductions would have no discernable impact on future global warming." 415 F.3d, at 66.

In sum—at least according to petitioners' uncontested affidavits— the rise in sea levels associated with global warming has already harmed and will continue to harm Massachusetts. The risk of catastrophic harm, though remote, is nevertheless real. That risk would be reduced to some extent if petitioners received the relief they seek. We therefore hold that petitioners have standing to challenge the EPA's denial of their rulemaking petition. . . .

■ CHIEF JUSTICE ROBERTS, with whom JUSTICE SCALIA, JUSTICE THOMAS, and JUSTICE ALITO join, dissenting:

. . . Apparently dissatisfied with the pace of progress on this issue in the elected branches, petitioners have come to the courts claiming broad-ranging injury, and attempting to tie that injury to the Government's alleged failure to comply with a rather narrow statutory provision. I would reject these challenges as nonjusticiable. Such a conclusion involves no judgment on whether global warming exists, what causes it, or the extent of the problem. Nor does it render petitioners without recourse. This Court's standing jurisprudence simply recognizes that redress of grievances of the sort at issue here "is the function of Congress and the Chief Executive," not the federal courts. *Lujan v. Defenders of Wildlife*, 504 U.S. 555, 576 (1992). I would vacate the judgment below and remand for dismissal of the petitions for review. . . .

Our modern framework for addressing standing is familiar: "A plaintiff must allege personal injury fairly traceable to the defendant's allegedly unlawful conduct and likely to be redressed by the requested relief." *DaimlerChrysler*, 547 U.S., at 342 (quoting *Allen v. Wright*, 468 U.S. 737, 751 (1984) (internal quotation marks omitted)). Applying that standard here, petitioners bear the burden of alleging an injury that is fairly traceable to the Environmental Protection Agency's failure to promulgate new motor vehicle greenhouse gas emission standards, and that is likely to be redressed by the prospective issuance of such standards.

Before determining whether petitioners can meet this familiar test, however, the Court changes the rules. It asserts that "States are not normal litigants for the purposes of invoking federal jurisdiction," and that given "Massachusetts' stake in protecting its quasi-sovereign interests, the Commonwealth is entitled to *special solicitude* in our standing analysis." *Ante*, at 1454, 1455 (emphasis added).

Relaxing Article III standing requirements because asserted injuries are pressed by a State, however, has no basis in our jurisprudence, and support for any such "special solicitude" is conspicuously absent from the Court's opinion. The general judicial review provision cited by the Court, 42 U.S.C. § 7607(b)(1), affords States no special rights or status. . . .

It is not at all clear how the Court's "special solicitude" for Massachusetts plays out in the standing analysis, except as an implicit concession that petitioners cannot establish standing on traditional terms. But the status of Massachusetts as a State cannot compensate for petitioners' failure to demonstrate injury in fact, causation, and redressability.

When the Court actually applies the three-part test, it focuses, as did the dissent below, *see* 415 F.3d 50, 64 (C.A.D.C.2005) (opinion of Tatel, J.), on the State's asserted loss of coastal land as the injury in fact. If petitioners rely on loss of land as the Article III injury, however, they must ground the rest of the standing analysis in that specific injury. That alleged injury must be "concrete and particularized," *Defenders of Wildlife*, 504 U.S., at 560, and "distinct and palpable," *Allen*, 468 U.S., at 751 (internal quotation marks omitted). . . .

The very concept of global warming seems inconsistent with this particularization requirement. Global warming is a phenomenon "harmful to humanity at large," 415 F.3d, at 60 (Sentelle, J., dissenting in part and concurring in judgment), and the redress petitioners seek is focused no more on them than on the public generally—it is literally to change the atmosphere around the world.

If petitioners' particularized injury is loss of coastal land, it is also that injury that must be "actual or imminent, not conjectural or hypothetical," *Defenders of Wildlife, supra*, at 560 (internal quotation marks omitted), "real and immediate," *Los Angeles v. Lyons*, 461 U.S. 95, 102 (1983) (internal quotation marks omitted), and "certainly impending," *Whitmore v. Arkansas*, 495 U.S. 149, 158 (1990) (internal quotation marks omitted).

As to "actual" injury, the Court observes that "global sea levels rose somewhere between 10 and 20 centimeters over the 20th century as a result of global warming" and that "[t]hese rising seas have already begun to swallow Massachusetts' coastal land." *Ante*, at 1456. But none of petitioners' declarations supports that connection. . . . Thus, aside from a single conclusory statement, there is nothing in petitioners' 43 standing declarations and accompanying exhibits to support an inference of actual loss of Massachusetts coastal land from 20th century global sea level increases. It is pure conjecture.

The Court's attempts to identify "imminent" or "certainly impending" loss of Massachusetts coastal land fares no better. See ante, at 1456–1457. One of petitioners' declarants predicts global warming will cause sea level to rise by 20 to 70 centimeters *by the year 2100*. Stdg. App. 216. . . . But even placing that problem to the side, accepting a century-long time horizon and a series of compounded estimates renders requirements of imminence and immediacy utterly toothless. See *Defenders of Wildlife, supra,* at 565, n. 2, (while the concept of " 'imminence' " in standing doctrine is "somewhat elastic," it can be "stretched beyond the breaking point"). "Allegations of possible future injury do not satisfy the requirements of Art. III. A threatened injury must be *certainly impending* to constitute injury in fact." *Whitmore, supra,* at 158. (internal quotation marks omitted; emphasis added).

Petitioners' reliance on Massachusetts's loss of coastal land as their injury in fact for standing purposes creates insurmountable problems for them with respect to causation and redressability. . . .

Petitioners view the relationship between their injuries and EPA's failure to promulgate new motor vehicle greenhouse gas emission standards as simple and direct: Domestic motor vehicles emit carbon dioxide and other greenhouse gases. Worldwide emissions of greenhouse gases contribute to global warming and therefore also to petitioners' alleged injuries. Without the new vehicle standards, greenhouse gas emissions—and therefore global warming and its attendant harms—have been higher than they otherwise would have been; once EPA changes course, the trend will be reversed.

. . . First, it is important to recognize the extent of the emissions at issue here. . . . According to one of petitioners' declarations, domestic motor vehicles contribute about 6 percent of global carbon dioxide emissions and 4 percent of global greenhouse gas emissions. Stdg. App. 232. The amount of global emissions at issue here is smaller still; § 202(a)(1) of the Clean Air Act covers only *new* motor vehicles and *new* motor vehicle engines, so petitioners' desired emission standards might reduce only a fraction of 4 percent of global emissions. . . .

Petitioners are never able to trace their alleged injuries back through this complex web to the fractional amount of global emissions that might have been limited with EPA standards. In light of the bit-part domestic new motor vehicle greenhouse gas emissions have played in what petitioners describe as a 150-year global phenomenon, and the myriad additional factors bearing on petitioners' alleged injury—the loss of Massachusetts coastal land—the connection is far too speculative to establish causation.

Redressability is even more problematic. To the tenuous link between petitioners' alleged injury and the indeterminate fractional domestic emissions at issue here, add the fact that petitioners cannot meaningfully predict what will come of the 80 percent of global greenhouse gas emissions that originate outside the United States. . . . [A]ny decreases produced by petitioners' desired standards are likely to be overwhelmed many times over by emissions increases elsewhere in the world.

Petitioners offer declarations attempting to address this uncertainty, contending that "[i]f the U.S. takes steps to reduce motor vehicle emissions, other countries are very likely to take similar actions regarding their own motor vehicles using technology developed in response to the U.S. program." Stdg. App. 220; see also *id.*, at 311–312. . . . The Court previously has explained that when the existence of an element of standing "depends on the unfettered choices made by independent actors not before the courts and whose exercise of broad and legitimate discretion the courts cannot presume either to control or to predict," a party must present facts supporting an assertion that the actor will proceed in such a manner. *Defenders of Wildlife*, 504 U.S., at 562 (quoting *ASARCO Inc. v. Kadish*, 490 U.S. 605, 615 (1989) (opinion of KENNEDY, J.); internal quotation marks omitted). The declarations' conclusory (not to say fanciful) statements do not even come close.

No matter, the Court reasons, because any decrease in domestic emissions will "slow the pace of global emissions increases, no matter what happens elsewhere." *Ante*, at 1458. Every little bit helps, so Massachusetts can sue over any little bit.

The Court's sleight-of-hand is in failing to link up the different elements of the three-part standing test. What must be *likely* to be redressed is the particular injury in fact. The injury the Court looks to is the asserted loss of land. The Court contends that regulating domestic motor vehicle emissions will reduce carbon dioxide in the atmosphere, *and therefore* redress Massachusetts's injury. But even if regulation *does* reduce emissions—to some indeterminate degree, given events elsewhere in the world—the Court never explains why that makes it *likely* that the injury in fact—the loss of land—will be redressed. . . . The realities make it pure conjecture to suppose that EPA regulation of new automobile emissions will *likely* prevent the loss of Massachusetts coastal land.

NOTES AND QUESTIONS

1. **Injury in Fact.** Why is the requirement of "injury in fact" met in this case? Is the fact that climate change is a phenomenon "harmful to humanity at large" relevant? In rejecting one of the respondents' theories of standing, the majority of the *Defenders of Wildlife* Court said "they state purely speculative, nonconcrete injuries when they argue that suit can be brought by anyone with an interest in studying or seeing endangered animals anywhere on the globe and anyone with a professional interest in such animals." *Defenders of Wildlife*, 504 U.S. at 556. Is the injury sufficiently concrete in this case? How did the majority and the dissent differ on this point?

2. **Causation.** Is the injury "fairly traceable to the defendant"? What did EPA argue? Is the contribution by the United States to climate change relevant? On what grounds did the majority find that the requirement of causation is met in this case?

3. **Causation, Continued.** In *Washington Environmental Council v. Bellon*, 732 F.3d 1131 (9th Cir. 2013), the plaintiffs alleged that the failure of the Administrator of Washington State Department of Ecology to set reasonably available control technology (RACT) standards for oil refineries contributed to greenhouse gas pollution, which caused plaintiffs' members to suffer recreational, aesthetic, economic, and health injuries. Plaintiffs' members' injuries included a diminished ability to engage in snowshoeing (because of reduced snow pack), flooding of agricultural land, and the worsening of respiratory conditions. *Id.* at 1140–41. The Ninth Circuit found that these injuries were insufficiently causally connected to the defendants' failure to set RACT standards to give plaintiffs standing:

> Plaintiffs offer only vague, conclusory statements that the Agencies' failure to set RACT standards at the Oil Refineries contributes to greenhouse gas emissions, which in turn, contribute to climate-related changes that result in their purported injuries. ... While Plaintiffs need not connect each molecule to their injuries, simply saying that the Agencies have failed to curb emission of greenhouse gases, which contribute (in some undefined way and to some undefined degree) to their injuries, relies on an " 'attenuated chain of conjecture' insufficient to support standing."

Id. at 1142–43 (quoting *Salmon Spawning & Recovery All. v. Gutierrez*, 545 F.3d 1220, 1228 (9th Cir. 2008)). The court distinguished the case before it from *Massachusetts v. EPA* on the basis that whilst vehicle emissions (at issue in *Massachusetts v. EPA*) amounted to 6 percent of worldwide carbon dioxide emissions, emissions from Washington oil refineries amounted to only 5.9 percent of emissions in Washington state. *Id.* at 1143. It also noted that sovereign states have more relaxed standing requirements, and that *Massachusetts v. EPA* involved the denial of a procedural right, which permitted Massachusetts to "assert that right without meeting all the normal standards for redressability and immediacy." *Id.* at 1144. Should the proportion of emissions be determinative of causality for standing purposes? Is there any way that plaintiffs could prove the emissions from the oil refineries caused their injuries in any more specific way? Is the chain of causation between emissions and environmental changes caused by global warming more attenuated when the plaintiff is an environmental group than when it is a state? *See also Wildearth Guardians v. Salazar*, 880 F. Supp. 2d 77 (D.D.C. 2012); *cf. Wildearth Guardians v. U.S. Dep't of Agriculture*, 795 F.3d 1148 (9th Cir. 2015) (holding that plaintiffs demonstrated standing because causation was discernible).

4.   Redressability. Is it likely that a favorable decision will redress the alleged injury? What did EPA argue? What was the dissent's position? In order to prove redressability, is it enough that the requested relief will likely *reduce* the harm? Is it enough that the requested relief will likely reduce the harm in the *future*?

5.   Third Parties' Responses to the Agency's Action. In order to prove redressability, petitioners argued "[i]f the U.S. takes steps to reduce motor vehicle emissions, other countries are very likely to take similar actions regarding their own motor vehicles using technology developed in response to the U.S. program." 549 U.S. at 545. The dissent rejected this argument, relying on *Lujan v. Defenders of Wildlife*, 504 U.S. 555 (1992). Do you find this opinion compelling? Even if other countries do not respond, won't U.S. regulation reduce greenhouse gases? Should that matter?

6.   Special Solicitude of Massachusetts. On what grounds did the majority of the Court hold that states are entitled to a "special solicitude" in the standing analysis? What is the significance of the special solicitude that the Court attributed to the state of Massachusetts? What was the dissent's position on this matter? *See* Amy J. Wildermuth, *Why State Standing in* Massachusetts v. EPA *Matters*, 27 J. LAND, RESOURCES & ENVTL. L. 273 (2007). Would the standing inquiry have been different for a private plaintiff? Why? During oral argument, Justice Kennedy questioned the lawyer for the petitioners regarding the difference between the states and small and big landowners:

> JUSTICE KENNEDY: . . . Suppose there were a big landowner that owned lots of coastline. Would he have the same standing that you do or do you have some special standing as a State, and if so what is the case which would demonstrate that?

> MR. MILKEY: Well, Your Honor, first of all, we agree that a large landowner would himself or herself have—. . .

> JUSTICE KENNEDY: . . . . What about a small landowner? I asked the question about a big landowner. Suppose you have a small landowner and he owned a lot?

> MR. MILKEY: Your Honor, I think if someone is losing property because of this problem, then that person would have standing, but we're nowhere near a *de minimis* threshold here. We have shown we own property, 200 miles of coastline which we're losing, and we think the standing is straightforward.

Transcript of Oral Argument at 8–9, *Massachusetts v. EPA*, 549 U.S. 497 (2007). Do you find Mr. Milkey's position compelling?

7. Special Solicitude and Preemption. During oral argument, Justices Ginsburg and Scalia questioned the lawyer for the petitioners regarding the state's "special solicitude":

> JUSTICE GINSBURG: Mr. Milkey, does it make a difference that you're not representing a group of law students, but a number of States who are claiming that they are disarmed from regulating and that the regulatory responsibility has been given to the Federal Government and the Federal Government isn't exercising it? I thought you had a discrete claim based on the sovereignty of States and their inability to regulate dependent on the law Congress passed that gives that authority to the EPA. I thought that was—

> MR. MILKEY: Your Honor, you are correct that we are saying that provides us also an independent source of our standing.

> JUSTICE SCALIA: I don't understand that. You have standing whenever a Federal law preempts State action? You can complain about the implementation of that law because it has preempted your State action? Is that the basis of standing you're alleging?

> MR. MILKEY: In short, Your Honor—

Transcript of Oral Argument at 14–15, *Massachusetts v. EPA*, 549 U.S. 497 (2007), *cited by* Dru Stevenson, *Special Solicitude for State Standing:* Massachusetts v. EPA, 112 PENN ST. L. REV. 1, 30 (2007). Do you find Mr. Milkey's position compelling?

Dru Stevenson tries to find the origin of this "new standing rule":

> . . . The *West Virginia v. EPA* case, mentioned at oral argument, is interesting because it came from the same court that ruled against the petitioners in *Massachusetts v. EPA*. [*West Virginia v. EPA*, 362

F.3d 861 (D.C. Cir. 2004)]. . . . In the *West Virginia v. EPA* case, two states and several business and energy policy entities petitioned for review of EPA requirements compelling states to revise state implementation plans (SIPs) under the Clean Air Act, so as to reduce nitrogen oxide (NOx) emissions. The rules (which followed protracted litigation already) established emission limits for major NOx sources. The EPA contended that West Virginia and Illinois lacked standing to challenge its regulatory action. The court disagreed, holding that the states should have standing because of the way that the regulatory framework effectively tied their hands:

> Here, the states are suing as states. The NOx SIP Call directs each state to revise its SIP in accordance with EPA's NOx emissions budget for the state. The lower the emissions budget, the more difficult and onerous is the states' task of devising an adequate SIP. Thus, lower growth factors leading to lower emissions budgets causes injury to the states as states. EPA's own brief belies its argument, as it states that "under the NOx SIP Call, states have the option of participating in [a] cap and trade program or obtaining the reductions through other mechanisms." This injury is sufficient to confer standing. [*Id.*, at 868]. . . .

Id. at 31. Is *West Virginia v. EPA* distinguishable from *Massachusetts v. EPA*? On what grounds?

8.   Generalized Grievance. Given the Court's opinion in *Defenders of Wildlife*, why is the asserted harm in *Massachusetts v. EPA* not a generalized grievance? To what extent does the answer depend on the special status accorded to states by the majority?

How else might the special status accorded to Massachusetts stress traditional standing criteria? For instance, Bradford Mank argues that because states have a quasi-sovereign interest in protecting the health and safety of their citizens, including the interests of future citizens, the "actual and imminent" harm requirement may provide less of an obstacle to states when bringing suit to safeguard the interests of future generations. *See* Bradford C. Mank, *Standing and Future Generations: Does* Massachusetts v. EPA *Open Standing for Generations to Come?*, 34 COLUM. J. ENVTL. L. 1 (2009).

9.   Probabilistic Standing. In *Laidlaw*, the Supreme Court allowed the " 'reasonable fear' of pollution to form the basis of aesthetic and recreational injuries," even though no injury to the environment was detected. Robin Kundis Craig, *Removing "The Cloak of a Standing Inquiry": Pollution Regulation, Public Health, and Private Risk in the Injury-In-Fact Analysis*, 29 CARDOZO L. REV. 149, 182 (2007). Craig argues that after *Laidlaw*, federal courts "have explicitly and consciously transformed both the *Laidlaw* court's recognition of 'reasonable fear' and prior courts' reliance on *threatened* injuries into an increased risk standing jurisprudence." *See id.* at 190 (citing *Friends of the Earth, Inc. v. Gaston Copper Recycling Corp.*, 204 F.3d 149 (4th Cir. 2000) ("[threats or increased risk . . . constitutes cognizable harm], and threatened environmental injury is by nature probabilistic."); *Ecological*

Rights Found. v. Pac. Lumber Co., 230 F.3d 1141 (9th Cir. 2000) (*"Laidlaw* recognized that an increased risk of harm can itself be injury in fact sufficient for standing.")). *But see Shain v. Veneman*, 376 F.3d 815 (8th Cir. 2004) (cited by Craig, *supra*, at 194) ("If the possibility of a 100-year flood is remote in the abstract, the possibility that the flood will occur while [the plaintiffs] own or occupy the land becomes a matter of sheer speculation. Indeed, one wonders whether any of the parties . . . in this case will be alive the next time a 100-year flood occurs."), *cert. denied*, 543 U.S. 1090 (2005).

As explained by Robin Kundis Craig:

> In late 2006, the First Circuit held that RCRA's citizen suit provision "allows citizen suits when there is a reasonable prospect that a serious, near-term threat to human health or the environment exists" and that standing was no barrier to such suits. The court emphasized:
>
>> It is the threat that must be close at hand, even if the perceived harm is not. For example, if there is a reasonable prospect that a carcinogen released into the environment today may cause cancer twenty years hence, the threat is near-term even though the perceived harm will only occur in the distant future.
>
> Against the defendant's argument that the plaintiffs lacked injury-in-fact because they had failed to show that "mercury contamination in the lower Penobscot adversely affects either human health or the environment"—indeed, the plaintiffs' requested relief was a court ordered study precisely to determine whether such adverse effects were occurring—the First Circuit concluded that "probabilistic harms are legally cognizable, and the district court made a supportable finding that a sufficient probability of harm exists to satisfy the Article III standing inquiry."
>
> More specifically, the court held that, after *Laidlaw*, "the plaintiffs must show that Mallinckrodt's activities created a significantly increased risk of harm to health or the environment so as to make it objectively reasonable for the plaintiffs' members to deny themselves aesthetic and recreational use of the river," which requires the plaintiffs to "show that there is a substantial probability that harm will occur."

See Craig, *supra*, at 193 (citing *Me. People's Alliance v. Mallinckrodt, Inc.*, 471 F.3d 277 (1st Cir. 2006), cert. denied, 552 U.S. 816 (2007)). Does the *Massachusetts v. EPA* Court recognize increased risk as injury? What was the dissent's position?

The Court's opinion in *Summers v. Earth Island Institute*, 555 U.S. 488 (2009), seems to cast doubt on the ability to rely on probabilistic harms to establish standing. In *Summers*, plaintiff Sierra Club challenged the alleged illegal sale of fire-damaged timber by the U.S. Forest Service. After a settlement was reached that resolved a member's imminent injury with regard to one particular site, the Sierra Club argued that the organization still had standing based on the probability that at least one other of their 700,000 members would be harmed in the near future by the proposed government action. Writing for a 5-member majority, Justice Scalia argued that "[w]hile it is certainly possible—perhaps even likely—that one individual will meet all of these criteria, that speculation does not suffice." *Id.* at 1152. How might the threatened harm in *Summers* be distinguished from the threatened harms in *Laidlaw* and *Massachusetts v. EPA*? In what sense is probability being used in each?

B. RIPENESS AND EXCLUSIVE PRE-ENFORCEMENT REVIEW

The environmental statutes typically establish an exclusive pre-enforcement review—regulations must be challenged within a certain period following their promulgation, and cannot be challenged later, even as a defense in an enforcement proceeding. The only exception is that later challenges can be brought if they are based on grounds that arose after the expiration of the relevant statutory period. *See, e.g.*, 42 U.S.C. § 9613(a) (CERCLA) (90-days period), 42 U.S.C. § 7607(b)(1) (CAA) (60-days period), 33 U.S.C. § 1369(b) (CWA) (120-days period). These time limitations on petitions for judicial review may in some cases come into conflict with the doctrine of ripeness: Might an action filed within the prescribed period not be ripe for review?

The Supreme Court has held that the purpose of the ripeness doctrine is "to prevent the courts, through avoidance of premature adjudication, from entangling themselves in abstract disagreements over administrative policies, and also to protect the agencies from judicial interference until an administrative decision has been formalized and its effects felt in a concrete way by the challenging parties." *Abbott Labs. v. Gardner*, 387 U.S. 136, 148–49 (1967). This doctrine is based on Article III of the Constitution, which establishes that the jurisdiction of federal courts is limited to "cases" and "controversies," but also that it is drawn "from prudential reasons for refusing to exercise jurisdiction." *Nat'l Park Hospitality Ass'n v. DOI*, 538 U.S. 803, 808 (2003). Based on Article III, the Supreme Court has established that

> a federal court has neither the power to render advisory opinions nor to decide questions that cannot affect the rights of litigants in the cases before them. Its judgments must resolve a real and substantial controversy admitting of specific relief through a decree of a conclusive character, as distinguished from an opinion advising what the law would be upon an hypothetical state of facts.

Preiser v. Newkirk, 422 U.S. 395, 401 (1975). Prudential reasons are also based in concerns about contingency and uncertainty and allow the courts to consider "the need to defer to other branches of the federal government; avoidance of unnecessary constitutional decision; comity to state institutions; and statutory severability." 13B CHARLES ALAN WRIGHT ET AL., FEDERAL PRACTICE AND PROCEDURE § 3532.1 (2011).

Courts have found it difficult to determine whether constitutional or prudential requirements are at issue in a particular case:

> When the . . . balance, shifts far to the side of inappropriateness for review, a serious question arises as to the existence of the constitutionally required "case or controversy." Even when the constitutional minimum has been met, however, prudential considerations may still counsel judicial restraint. The point at which constitutional constraint fades into persuasive practicalities is difficult to discern and unnecessary to identify. . . .

Action Alliance of Senior Citizens v. Heckler, 789 F.2d 931, 940 n.12 (D.C. Cir. 1986).

In the context of judicial review of administrative actions, the D.C. Circuit has said that

> the primary focus of the ripeness doctrine as it concerns judicial review of agency action has been a prudential attempt to time review in a way that balances the petitioner's interest in prompt consideration of allegedly unlawful agency action against the agency's interest in crystallizing its policy before that policy is subjected to judicial review and the court's interests in avoiding unnecessary adjudication and in deciding issues in a concrete setting.

Eagle-Picher Indus. v. EPA, 759 F.2d 905, 915 (D.C. Cir. 1985).

In deciding whether administrative action is ripe for review, courts must evaluate (1) the fitness of the issue for judicial review and (2) the hardship to the parties of withholding court consideration. *See Whitman v. Am. Trucking Ass'ns*, 531 U.S. 457, 479 (2001); *see also Nat'l Park Hospitality Ass'n*, 538 U.S. at 808.

To determine the "fitness of the issues" for judicial review, the court should take into account the institutional capacities of, and the relationship between, courts and agencies:

> We look, for example, to see if the issue raises a purely legal question. If it does, we assume its threshold suitability for judicial determination. We also consider whether the agency or the court will benefit from deferring review until the agency's policies have crystallized and the "question arises in some more concrete and final form."

Eagle-Picher, 759 F.2d at 915.

If the court finds that either the agency or the court has a significant interest in postponing review, it will balance these interests with the hardship that the delay will cause to the plaintiff. Under the "hardship to the parties" prong, the court will consider whether immediate and practical impact on those who seek relief from the challenged action outweighs the competing institutional interest in deferring review. *Id.*

Eagle-Picher Industries, Inc. v. Environmental Protection Agency

759 F.2d 905 (D.C. Cir. 1985).

■ Before ROBINSON, CHIEF JUDGE, and EDWARDS and STARR, CIRCUIT JUDGES.

■ EDWARDS, CIRCUIT JUDGE:

In this case, the petitioners challenge the legality of the Hazardous Ranking System ("HRS"), adopted by the Environmental Protection Agency ("EPA" or the "agency") pursuant to section 105 of the Comprehensive Environmental Response, Compensation and Liability Act of 1980 ("CERCLA"). 42 U.S.C. § 9605 (1982). . . .

The HRS was promulgated on July 16, 1982, in a notice-and-comment rulemaking proceeding separate from that which produced the final NPL [National Priority List] on September 8, 1983. CERCLA's statutory review provision, section 113(a), stipulates that petitions for judicial review of regulations promulgated under CERCLA must be filed with this court within ninety days of the regulations' promulgation. The petitioners failed to seek review of the HRS during the mandated statutory period. . . .

A. Introduction

We first consider whether the petitioners' challenge is barred because it was not filed within the statutory review period. . . .

This court has repeatedly recognized that statutory time limits on petitions for review of agency action are jurisdictional in nature. These limitations serve "the important purpose of imparting finality into the administrative process, thereby conserving administrative resources." *Natural Resources Defense Council*, 666 F.2d at 602. . . . We have entertained untimely claims only in a limited number of exceptional circumstances where the petitioner lacked a meaningful opportunity to challenge the agency action during the review period due to, for example, . . . lack of ripeness during the review period. *See Geller v. FCC*, 610 F.2d 973, 977–78 (D.C.Cir.1979). . . .

The petitioners here admit that they did not seek judicial review of the HRS during the ninety day period following its promulgation. The EPA maintains that the petitioners could have challenged the HRS during the statutory review period and that consequently present review is barred. The petitioners contend that their complaint about the HRS did not become ripe for review until the NPL was promulgated and that, because they filed a petition to review the NPL within ninety days of its promulgation, their challenge to the HRS is also timely. In support of their position, the petitioners urge that our precedents, in particular *Diamond Shamrock Corporation v. Costle*, 580 F.2d 670 (D.C.Cir.1978), establish that agency rulemaking that creates a standard, such as the effluent limitation regulations in *Diamond Shamrock* and the HRS here, is never ripe for review—and thus the statutory petition period is tolled—until the agency applies the rule to the petitioner. Under this theory, the petitioners' objections to the HRS ripened only when, in order to develop the NPL, the EPA applied the HRS to sites with which the petitioners are associated. . . .

B. The Relationship Between Ripeness and Timeliness

As an initial matter, we think that the petitioners confound the obligations of the court with those of the petitioner. It is the duty of the court to make the prudential judgment whether a challenge to agency action is ripe; it is the responsibility of petitioners to file for review within the period set by Congress. While it is true that in extraordinary circumstances we have "forgiven" a petitioner's failure to file a timely petition, we have never suggested that petitioners may safely substitute their own notions of timely review for those of Congress. . . . *Diamond Shamrock*, 580 F.2d 670, so heavily relied upon by petitioners, is inapposite. In that case we simply upheld the District Court's decision that a complaint seeking review of some effluent limitation regulations issued by the EPA was not yet ripe. The court did not consider the relationship between ripeness and timeliness at all.

Considering that relationship here, we think it certainly is not the one implied by the petitioners—a rather casual means of circumventing timely filing requirements. . . .

Because the principal function of the ripeness doctrine is to aid a court in ascertaining whether it should stay its hand until agency policy has crystallized, most of the case law explicating the doctrine is forward-looking, that is, looking into the future to determine the effects of deferring review. Only rarely does case law depict the ripeness doctrine in the service of a tardy petitioner—looking backward to divine whether the court would have considered the request for review ripe had it been brought in a timely fashion. Indeed, we know of only one case from this circuit, *Geller v. FCC*, 610 F.2d 973, where we explicitly evaluated the retrospective ripeness of an untimely challenge.[43] There the petitioner solicited review of an FCC regulation nearly five years after the statutory review period had expired. We dismissed all of Geller's claims for lack of timeliness, except one which had clearly just become ripe with the passage of new legislation. 610 F.2d at 977–78.

---

[43] We are aware of only two other of our cases where the relationship between ripeness and timeliness was expressly considered. In *Investment Co. Inst.*, 551 F.2d at 1281–82, we indicated in *dictum* that an issue's lack of ripeness during the statutory period may under some circumstances excuse an untimely request for review of agency action. The ripeness of the challenge in *Investment Co. Inst.*, however, was not an issue there. In Baltimore Gas and Electric Co. v. ICC ("BG & E"), 672 F.2d 146, 149 (D.C. Cir. 1982), we stated that a "time limitation on petitions for judicial review . . . can run only against challenges ripe for review." But in *BG & E* the petitioner had filed a timely petition for review of an ICC interpretive rule, which the court determined was not yet ripe. The court merely reassured BG & E that should its claim ripen at some future date we would regard the statutory period as beginning to run then. *Id.* at 147–48. The court never considered the situation presented here, where the petitioner asks for a retrospective determination of the ripeness of an untimely claim.

We think *Geller* may suggest one of two kinds of cases where the court should perform a retrospective ripeness analysis for a petitioner who has failed to file a timely request for review. The *Geller* type can be characterized as a case in which events occur or information becomes available after the statutory review period expires that essentially create a challenge that did not previously exist.[45] The other type involves claims that, under our precedents, are without any doubt not ripe for review during the statutory period. For example, *Diamond Shamrock* held that certain effluent limitation regulations promulgated under the Federal Water Pollution Control Act ("FWPCA") 33 U.S.C. §§ 1251 *et seq.* (1982), were not ripe for review until applied in discharge permit proceedings. 580 F.2d at 672. Obviously, other would-be petitioners in the same position as those in *Diamond Shamrock*—applicants for discharge permits under the same statute—can rely on the holding in that case.

As a general proposition, however, if there is *any* doubt about the ripeness of a claim, petitioners must bring their challenge in a timely fashion or risk being barred. . . .

We do not believe that the instant case falls into either the *Geller* or clear precedent exceptions. It is not a *Geller* case because no events occurred after the statutory period that gave rise to an essentially new claim. . . . The delayed application of the rule may be relevant, however, to the clear precedent category. For example, as we noted above, other petitioners in Diamond Shamrock's position could rely on our holding that the regulations at issue in that case were not ripe until applied.

The petitioners argue that *Diamond Shamrock* also governs the ripeness issue presented by this case. We disagree. *Diamond Shamrock* involved "pre-enforcement" review by the District Court of regulations that would have been directly reviewable in this court under the review provision of the FWPCA upon the application of the regulations to the petitioner in a permit proceeding. 580 F.2d at 673. There, the court explicitly found that both the agency and the court would benefit from deferring judicial consideration until review under the organic statute was available. *Id.* at 674. By contrast, review here is sought under CERCLA's review provision, which expresses a congressional intent that review of regulations immediately follow promulgation and that it not

---

[45] In *Investment Co. Inst.* we noted the two methods by which petitioners may request review of agency regulations after the statutory period has expired. The preferred method is for the petitioners first to ask the agency to reconsider the regulation and then to request review of the agency's decision in this court. 551 F.2d at 1281. But, where not precluded by statute, the petitioners generally may challenge the rule also when it is applied to them in an agency adjudication. *Id.* at 1282, n. 13. We emphasized there, as we do here, that absent a convincing justification for failure to request review during the statutory period, the court will refuse to hear an untimely challenge. *Id.* at 1282.

The EPA argued in its brief that because the petitioners did not first ask the EPA to reconsider the HRS before challenging it in this proceeding, their challenge is barred for failure to follow the procedures outlined in *Investment Co. Inst.* We disagree. The EPA's application of the HRS to individual sites in order to decide which sites should be listed on the NPL is sufficiently analogous to the "application in agency adjudication" method to satisfy *Investment Co. Institute*'s procedural requirements.

take place at the enforcement stage. Furthermore, as we explain more fully in the succeeding section of this opinion, we find that both the EPA and the court would have benefitted from conducting the requested review of the HRS within the statutory period. Thus, *Diamond Shamrock* is in no way dispositive of the instant case.

Generally, if we determine that a petitioner's request for a retrospective ripeness evaluation does not fit into either the *Geller* or the clear precedent categories we will refuse to examine the petitioner's untimely claim to ascertain whether we would have found it ripe for adjudication had it been brought within the statutory period, unless our refusal to do so would cause a serious injustice to the petitioner. However, because we clearly articulate this policy for the first time in this case, we pause to demonstrate that the petitioners' challenge to the HRS was ripe during the review period. . . .

C. Ripeness Analysis

Applying the "fitness of the issues" prong to the instant case, we find initially that the issue presented for review—whether the HRS is arbitrary, capricious, or in excess of statutory authority—is a purely legal question and thus was "fit" in that respect for judicial resolution during the statutory period. We also find that neither the agency nor the court would have benefitted from postponing review beyond that period. Indeed, as we demonstrate below, both institutions had a significant interest in completing all review of the HRS during the statutory time frame. . . .

We need not proceed in this case to the second prong of the *Abbott Laboratories* test. As we previously explained, the purpose of the "hardship to the parties" analysis is to ascertain if the harm that deferring review will cause the petitioners outweighs the benefits it will bring the agency and the court. Because we have determined that the EPA and, to a lesser extent, the court had a *positive interest* in review during the statutory period, there are no conflicting interests to balance. . . .

We conclude that the petitioners were not justified in failing to seek review during the statutory period. . . .

NOTES AND QUESTIONS

1.   Exclusive Pre-Enforcement Review. What purpose does exclusive pre-enforcement review serve? Why is it not the norm for the judicial review of administrative actions outside of the environmental area? Why is exclusive pre-enforcement review in the environmental area often coupled with exclusive review in the D.C. Circuit? *See, e.g.*, 42 U.S.C. § 7607(b)(1) (CAA); 42 U.S.C. § 9613(a) (CERCLA); 42 U.S.C. § 6976(a)(1) (RCRA).

2.   Retrospective Ripeness Evaluation. As discussed in Chapter VII, the Hazardous Ranking System (HRS) is the system used by EPA to determine which sites will be listed on the National Priority List (NPL) pursuant to § 105 of CERCLA. In *Eagle-Picher*, petitioners challenged their inclusion on the NPL, arguing that the HRS was unlawful. *See Eagle-Picher*, 759 F.2d at 908. On what basis did the petitioner claim that its challenge was not barred? Why did the court reject this argument? Under what circumstances will the court agree to perform a retrospective ripeness evaluation? Why didn't the court consider the promulgation of the NPL to be a relevant subsequent event?

3. Pre-Enforcement and Ripeness. How do the courts determine the ripeness of "pre-enforcement" agency actions? Why did the court find that this case was ripe for review within the statutory period? What happens if the decision is not ripe for review within the statutory period? *See Atl. States Legal Found., Inc. v. EPA*, 325 F.3d 281 (D.C. Cir. 2003).

4. *Adamo Wrecking Co. v. United States.* In *Adamo Wrecking Co. v. United States*, 434 U.S. 275 (1978), the petitioner failed to comply with the National Emission Standard for Asbestos. *See id.* at 277. According to § 112(b)(1)(B) of CAA, the emission of an air pollutant in violation of an applicable emission standard is prohibited, and the knowing violation of that section subjects the violator to a fine and imprisonment under the provisions of § 113(c)(1)(C) of the CAA. *See id.* at 276–77. The Court held that the petitioner could not challenge the standard as a defense in a criminal proceeding. *See id.* at 282; *see also Yakus v. United States*, 321 U.S. 414, 431 (1944). Is this approach desirable?

5. *Sackett v. EPA.* In *Sackett v. EPA*, 566 U.S. 120 (2012), EPA issued an order under the Clean Water Act directing the Sacketts to restore a portion of wetlands on their property that the Sacketts had filled in order to construct a home. Disputing that their property was within the jurisdiction of the Clean Water Act, the Sacketts asked EPA for a hearing. EPA refused. The Sacketts then sought review of the order under the Administrative Procedures Act, which provides for judicial review of "final agency action for which there is no other adequate remedy in a court." 5 U.S.C. § 704.

EPA argued that the order was not "final agency action," but only an interim step in a process culminating in civil enforcement of the order in court, by EPA bringing suit against the Sacketts. The Supreme Court rejected EPA's argument that its order was not final, because it led to legal consequences: the Sacketts would face double penalties in any enforcement proceeding, and a higher standard before a permit to fill their property would be issued). Also, no further administrative review was available to the Sacketts.

EPA argued further that judicial review was excluded because in other parts of the CWA, express provision was made for judicial review of administrative orders. The Court held that "if the express provision of judicial review in one section of a long and complicated statute were alone enough to overcome the APA's presumption of reviewability for all final agency action, it would not be much of a presumption at all." *Id.* at 1373. What statutory language or structure would be sufficient to overcome the presumption? What would be the consequence if the Court had found that orders such as the one at issue in this case were not subject to judicial review?

6.   Preclusion of Review Under CERCLA. CERCLA provides that no federal court shall have jurisdiction to "review any challenges to removal or remedial action selected under § 9604 . . . or to review any order issued under § 9606(a)." 42 U.S.C. § 9613(h). Section 101 specifies that the terms "removal" and "remedial action" include "enforcement activities related thereto." 42 U.S.C. § 9601(20)(G)(25). There are exceptions to the preclusion provision for actions to recover response costs or damages for contribution; actions seeking reimbursement for costs incurred in a cleanup ordered under § 106; actions by the United States in exercise of authority under § 106; and certain citizens' suits. 42 U.S.C. § 9613(h)(1)–(5). The effect of the § 9604 is judicial review can only be sought after enforcement action is pursued under §§ 106 or 107; or after a cleanup (or a defined portion of a cleanup), is completed. Any person who, without "sufficient cause," fails to comply with a cleanup order, may be liable for punitive damages of three times any costs incurred as a result of the failure to comply. 42 U.S.C. § 9607(c)(3). Why do you think that CERCLA delays judicial review until enforcement actions are pursued or a cleanup completed? What are the disadvantages of the CERCLA preclusion provision? *See* Michael P. Healy, *The Effectiveness and Fairness of Superfund's Judicial Review Preclusion Provision*, 15 VA. ENVTL. L.J. 271 (1995).

7.   Trade Associations. Suppose a company started operating many years after the enactment of a regulation that affects its operations. Could the company challenge the regulation after the exclusive pre-enforcement period? Is it undesirable to preclude review under these circumstances? How do exclusive pre-enforcement review provisions create incentives for the establishment of trade associations? Are they an appropriate solution?